THE OXFORD
RUSSIAN–ENGLISH
DICTIONARY

THE OXFORD
RUSSIAN-ENGLISH
DICTIONARY

BY

MARCUS WHEELER

General Editor

B. O. UNBEGAUN

WITH THE ASSISTANCE OF

D. P. COSTELLO *and* W. F. RYAN

SECOND EDITION

OXFORD
AT THE CLARENDON PRESS

Oxford University Press, Walton Street, Oxford OX2 6DP

Oxford New York Toronto
Delhi Bombay Calcutta Madras Karachi
Petaling Jaya Singapore Hong Kong Tokyo
Nairobi Dar es Salaam Cape Town
Melbourne Auckland

and associated companies in
Berlin Ibadan

Oxford is a trade mark of Oxford University Press

Published in the United States
by Oxford University Press, New York

Hardback first edition published 1972
Hardback second edition published 1984
Reprinted 1985, 1986, 1990 (with corrections)
Flexicover edition first published 1990

British Library Cataloguing in Publication Data
Wheeler, Marcus
The Oxford Russian-English dictionary.—2nd ed.
1. Russian language—Dictionaries—English
2. English languages—Dictionaries—Russian
I. Title
491.73'21   PG2640
ISBN 0-19-864154-0
ISBN 0-19-864167-2 (Flexi)

Library of Congress Cataloging in Publication Data
Wheeler, Marcus
The Oxford Russian-English dictionary
1. Russian language—Dictionaries—English
I. Title
PG2640.W5 1984   491.73'21   83-13447
ISBN 0-19-864154-0
ISBN 0-19-864167-2 (Flexi)

Printed in Great Britain
by Richard Clay Ltd, Bungay, Suffolk

NOTE TO THE SECOND EDITION

THE success of the first edition of this Dictionary was due above all to the contribution made by the General Editor—not simply the authority of his name and his scholarship as a historian of the Russian language, but his unrivalled intuitive grasp of all registers of Russian and his scrupulous attention to the minutest detail in checking every entry. Happily, Boris Unbegaun was able to see the first edition in print; but his death, in March 1973, deprived the author of his mentor and the work of its presiding genius. The process of revision, which is not only rendered necessary by human error but is in the nature of recording living languages, has however been greatly assisted by both the generous criticisms, comments, and suggestions of a large number of professional colleagues—teachers, fellow lexicographers, and translators—and also of students, and the appearance of a number of important and helpful publications. Outstanding contributions to the preparation of the present edition have been made by Mr. S. Marder (Victoria University of Wellington, New Zealand), who submitted a comprehensive orthographic analysis of the first edition, and Mr. M. Beresford, whose suggestions combine erudition with a fine sensitivity to both Russian and English idiom. Amongst the many others whose use of the Dictionary has prompted them to aid its improvement by reporting errors or omissions, Mr. J. Bourke, Mr. R. J. Danik, Professor W. B. Edgerton, Mr. C. English, Mr. P. S. Falla (and his assistants in the preparation of the companion Oxford English–Russian Dictionary), Dr. N. J. L. Luker, Mr. J. Sullivan, and Professor R. J. Wiley deserve to be named. While recording his gratitude for all suggestions received, the author bears sole responsibility for deciding whether, and how, to use this material.

Much reliance has also been placed on published sources. In the Soviet Union, the appearance of *Novye slova i znacheniya*, edited by N. Z. Kotelova and Yu. S. Sorokin (1st edition, Moscow, 1971), initiated the publication of a continuing useful series of annotated lists of neologisms and new usage derived from analysis of a selection of the Soviet national press and literary magazines (*Novoe v russkoy leksike: Slovarnye materialy — 77*, *Slovarnye materialy — 78*, *Slovarnye materialy — 79*, and *Novye slova i znacheniya*, ed. N. Z. Kotelova, Moscow, 1980, 1981, 1982, and 1984). No less valuable, for cross-checking, has been Professor I. R. Gal'perin's Supplement (published by 'Russkiy yazyk', Moscow, 1980) to the monumental *Bol'shoy anglo-russkiy slovar'* (which first appeared in the same year as the *ORED*, 1972). Outside the U.S.S.R., the following publications have been particularly useful:

G. Gerhart, *The Russian's World: Life and Language* (Harcourt Brace Jovanovich, New York, 1974);

B. Comrie and G. Stone, *The Russian Language since the Revolution* (Clarendon Press, Oxford, 1978);

E. A. M. Wilson, *The Modern Russian Dictionary for English Speakers* (Pergamon Press, Oxford, and 'Russkiy yazyk', Moscow, 1982).

The printer's requirements necessarily limited the extent to which new entries, as opposed to corrections, could be accommodated in this revision. For reference, however, an Index is provided on pp. 928-30 of entire new entries and of the more important changes involving registration of additional—whether fresh or previously overlooked—meanings of Russian words. An Appendix of Russian Geographical Names has also been added (pp. 919-27).

The Queen's University of Belfast   MARCUS WHEELER

ACKNOWLEDGEMENTS

THE Author and Editors gratefully acknowledge the assistance of scholars in the field of Russian studies, in particular that of Mr. I. P. Foote, Mr. M. Hayward, and Mr. J. Sullivan, who read the Dictionary in proof, and of Dr. S. Utechin, who checked a substantial part of the manuscript. Valuable suggestions concerning selection of vocabulary and treatment of individual entries were made also by Mrs. B. Costello, Dr. V. Du Feu, Mrs. M. Stokes, Mr. J. S. G. Simmons and Mme. H. Unbegaun; by Professor S. Konovalov, who encouraged the project from its inception; and by members of the staff of the former Joint Services School for Linguists. A number of scholars in fields other than Russian gave help in elucidating specialist terms. Mention should also be made of the friendly interest shown in the project by professional lexicographers and others in the Soviet Union, from a number of whom the Author received generous advice. Among dictionaries used in compiling the present work, a particular debt is due to D. N. Ushakov's *Tolkovyi slovar' russkogo yazyka* (Moscow, 1935–9), to the *Slovar' russkogo yazyka* compiled under the auspices of the Russian Language Institute of the U.S.S.R. Academy of Sciences (Moscow, 1957–61), and to A. I. Smirnitsky's *Russko-angliiskii slovar'* (3rd edition, under general editorship of Professor O. S. Akhmanova, Moscow, 1958).

The Author and Editors wish to record their appreciation of the important contribution made by the late Professor D. P. Costello to the production of this Dictionary. At the time of his death, in 1964, he had worked through nearly half the manuscript draft. A large number of entries in this part of the work were improved in detail thanks to his criticisms and suggestions, and the whole Dictionary benefited by his enthusiasm and by his wide knowledge both of Russian literature and of the contemporary colloquial Russian language.

Thanks are due, finally, to the Clarendon Press for invaluable editorial and technical expertise.

LIST OF ABBREVIATIONS

a.	accusative	hist.	history
abbr.	abbreviation	hort.	horticulture
abstr.	abstract		
act.	active	i.	instrumental
adj.	adjective	imp.	imperative
adv.	adverb	impers.	impersonal
aeron.	aeronautics	impf.	imperfective
agric.	agriculture	indecl.	indeclinable
anat.	anatomy	indet.	indeterminate
anthrop.	anthropology	inf.	infinitive
approx.	approximately	inst.	instantaneous
arch.	archaic	interj.	interjection
archaeol.	archaeology	interrog.	interrogative
archit.	architecture	intrans.	intransitive
as opp. to	as opposed to	in var. senses	in various senses
astron.	astronomy	iron.	ironical
		joc.	jocular
bibl.	biblical		
biol.	biology	leg.	legal
bot.	botany	ling.	linguistics
		lit.	literature
chem.	chemistry		
coll.	colloquial	m.	masculine
collect.	collective	math.	mathematics
comm.	commercial	med.	medicine
comp.	comparative	meteor.	meteorology
concr.	concrete	mil.	military
conj.	conjunction	min.	mineral(ogy)
cul.	culinary	mus.	music
		myth.	mythology
d.	dative		
det.	determinate	n.	neuter
dial.	dialectal	n.-a.	nominative-accusative
dim.	diminutive	naut.	nautical
dipl.	diplomacy	neg.	negative
		nom.	nominative
eccl.	ecclesiastical	N.S.	New Style (of calendar)
econ.	economics	num.	numeral
electr.	electrical		
esp.	especially	obs.	obsolete
ethnol.	ethnology	onomat.	onomatopeia
euph.	euphemism	opt.	optics
exc.	except	orn.	ornithology
		o.s.	Old Style (of calendar)
f.	feminine	p.	prepositional (case)
fig.	figurative	palaeog.	palaeography
fin.	financial	part.	participle
freq.	frequentative	pass.	passive
		pejor.	pejorative
g.	genitive	pf.	perfective
geod.	geodesy	pharm.	pharmaceutical
geogr.	geography	philol.	philology
geol.	geology	philos.	philosophy
gram.	grammar	phys.	physics
		physiol.	physiology

pl.	plural	sl.	slang
poet.	poetry	superl.	superlative
polit.	politics		
p.p.p.	past participle passive	tech.	technical
pred.	predicate	text.	textiles
prep.	preposition	theatr.	theatre
pres.	present	theol.	theology
pron.	pronoun	trans.	transitive
prov.	proverb	typ.	typography
psych.	psychology		
		usu.	usually
rel.	religion		
relat.	relative (pronoun)	var.	various
rhet.	rhetorical	voc.	vocative
		vulg.	vulgar
sc.	scilicet	zool.	zoology
sing.	singular		

The Russian -н. in illustrative phraseology within entries stands for the enclitic -нибудь (in the words кто-нибудь, что-нибудь, etc.).

INTRODUCTION

THIS work is intended as a general-purpose dictionary of Russian as it is written and spoken. It is designed primarily, though not exclusively, for the use of those whose native language is English.

MODE OF PRESENTATION

A separate head-word is given for each entry, and there is a separate entry for each word. The entries include a substantial quantity of idiomatic and illustrative phraseology, but no literary quotations.

The following devices are used to economise space in the dictionary:

(i) The first letter of the head-word, followed by a full point, represents the whole head-word, thus:

това́рный ... т. соста́в (= това́рный соста́в)

(ii) The tilde sign, in conjunction with a vertical stroke, represents that part of the head-word which is to the left of the vertical stroke, thus:

роди́м|ый ... ~ое пятно́ (= роди́мое пятно́)

exceptions: the tilde is not used in indicating the genitive singular of nouns or the 1st and 2nd persons singular of the present tense of verbs with unchanged stress (for examples, see below: *Nouns* and *Verbs*); and, in cross-references from the imperfective to the perfective verbal aspect, it may, when preceded by a prefix, represent the entire head-word, thus:

ста́р|ить, ю, ишь, *impf.* (*of* со~) ... (= *of* состáрить)

Pronunciation

The Russian alphabet and orthography are to a large extent phonetically accurate and phonetic symbols have not been employed in this dictionary. Stress, however, is indicated for every word. A stress mark above the tilde, where this sign represents two or more syllables, indicates shift of stress to the syllable immediately preceding the vertical stroke dividing the head-word, thus:

запи|са́ть, шу́, ~шешь ... (= запишу́, запи́шешь)

Conversely, a stress mark above a syllable to the right of the tilde indicates shift of stress away from the syllable(s) represented by the tilde, thus:

ва́хтер, а, *pl.* ~а́ ... (= вахтера́)

Where a variant stress is permissible, both variants are shown, thus:

скобл|и́ть, ю, ~и́шь ... (= скóблишь *or* скобли́шь)

Phraseology

Idiomatic phrases are in many cases duplicated in entries for the component words. Phrases consisting of adjective and noun, however, are normally entered under the adjective component.

Meaning

Separate meanings of a Russian word are marked off by Arabic numerals, thus:

гада́тельный ... 1. pertaining to divination. 2. based on conjecture, problematical

Shades of meaning, represented by translations not considered strictly synonymous, are marked off by a semi-colon: translations considered synonymous—by a comma, thus:

га́дкий ... ugly, repulsive; vile, nasty.

Homonyms are indicated by repetition of the head-word as a separate entry, followed by a raised Arabic numeral, thus:

газ¹, а, *m.* gas.
газ², а, *m.* gauze.

It should be noted that there is no accepted all-embracing criterion for differentiating homonymy from polysemy (plurality of meanings of a single word) or 'meaning' from 'shade of meaning'.

Explanation

This dictionary presents translations, not definitions. Where necessary for the avoidance of ambiguity, however, explanatory glosses are given in brackets in italic type, thus:

интерпрета́тор, а, *m.* interpreter (*expounder*). [i.e. *not* translator]

This device is used in particular in the case of words denoting specifically Russian or Soviet concepts (e.g. да́ча, ка́ша; микрорайо́н, толка́ч). This makes it possible to use one-word transliterations rather than clumsy paraphrases as a substitute for a translation.

Indications of style or usage are given, where appropriate, in brackets, thus: (*coll.*), (*dial.*); (*fig.*), (*joc.*); (*agric.*), (*polit.*), etc.

GRAMMAR

This dictionary is not a substitute for a grammar, but users familiar with the bases of Russian grammar will, it is hoped, profit from the grammatical indications supplied.

Nouns

The genitive singular ending and gender of all nouns are shown, thus:

мо́лот, а, *m.* hammer.
мо́лни|я, и, *f.* lightning.
молок|о́, а́, *n.* milk.

Other case endings are shown where declension or stress is, in relation to generally accepted systems of classification, irregular, thus:

> **англича́н|ин, ина,** *pl.* **~е, ~,** *m.* Englishman.
> **бор|ода́, оды́,** *a.* **~оду,** *pl.* **~оды, ~бд,** *d.* **~ода́м,** *f.* beard.

(But the inserted vowel in the genitive plural ending of numerous feminine nouns with nominative singular ending -ка is not regarded as irregular, e.g. **англича́нка,** *g. pl.* англича́нок.)

Variant genitive case endings of certain *pluralia tantum* are indicated by a hyphen, thus:

> **вы́молот|ки, ~ок-ков,** *no sing.* . . . (= вы́молоток ог вы́молотков).

Nouns ending -ость derived from adjectives have not been included where an appropriate English rendering can be obtained by adding *-ness* to the corresponding adjective (e.g., **зо́ркий** . . . sharpsighted . . . **зо́ркость** . . . sharpsightedness . . .).

Adjectives

Only the masculine nominative singular of the full form of the adjective is shown. Endings of the short forms, where these are found, are shown in brackets, thus:

> **глу́п|ый (~, ~а́, ~о)** . . .

The neuter short form ending is omitted where stress is as for the feminine, thus:

> **нау́ч|ный (~ен, ~на)** . . .

Verbs

Endings are shown of the 1st and 2nd persons singular of the present tense (or of the 1st person only of verbs with infinitive ending -ать, -овать, -ять, -еть which retain stem and stress unchanged throughout the present tense), thus:

> **говор|и́ть, ю́, и́шь,** . . .
> **чита́|ть, ю,** . . .

Other endings of the present tense and endings of the past tense are shown where formation or stress are irregular, thus:

> **ид|ти́, у́, ёшь,** *past* **шёл, шла, шло** . . .
> **стере́|чь, гу́, жёшь, гу́т,** *past* **~г, ~гла́, ~гло́** . . .

Participles and gerunds, and forms of the passive voice, are not shown unless having special semantic or syntactical features.

Verbal aspects: the imperfective aspect is normally treated as the basic form of the simple verb, a cross-reference to the relevant perfective form being shown in brackets, thus:

> **чита́|ть, ю,** *impf.* (*of* про~) . . .

The corresponding entry is:

> **прочита́|ть, ю,** *pf. of* чита́ть.

In the case, however, of compound verbs formed by means of a prefix, the perfective aspect is treated as the basic form, thus:

зачит|а́ть, а́ю, *pf.* (*of* ⌐ывать) ...

Since, in a number of cases, a correspondence cannot, for semantic or other reasons, be firmly established (e.g. иска́ть–сыска́ть), the absence of a corresponding aspect is not necessarily noted.

Meanings and phraseology are shown under the basic form in each case unless peculiar to the other aspect.

Prefixes

A number of prefixes—verbal and other, and also truncated elements of words functioning as prefixes—are shown as separate entries, thus:

до- [verbal prefix]
гидро- hydro-
сов- *abbr. of* ⌐е́тский

Numerous compounded words, the meaning of which is judged sufficiently clear from a knowledge of the meaning of the prefix and root-word, have, to economise space, been excluded from the dictionary.

A

а¹, *conj.* **1.** and; while; вот ма́рки, а вот три рубля́ сда́чи here are the stamps and here is three roubles change; иди́те напра́во, пото́м нале́во, а пото́м ещё раз напра́во turn right, then left, (and) then right again; моя́ жена́ лю́бит е́здить в теа́тр, а я предпочита́ю кино́ my wife likes going to the theatre, while I prefer the cinema; а и́менно namely; to be exact. **2.** but; yet (*or not translated*); пора́ идти́ — а мы то́лько что пришли́! 'It's time to go.' 'But we've only just come!'; хотя́ ты и не хо́чешь посове́товаться с врачо́м, а на́до you may not want to see a doctor but you must; я иду́ не в кино́, а в теа́тр I am going to the theatre, not to the cinema. **3.** а то or (else), otherwise; спеши́, а то мы опозда́ем hurry up or we'll be late.

а², *interrog. particle* (*coll.*) eh?

а³, *interj.* (*expressing surprise, annoyance, pain, etc.; coll.*) ah, oh; а ну его́! oh, to hell with him!

абажу́р, а, *m.* lampshade.

аба́к|а, и, *f.* (*and* ~, ~, *m.*) (*archit.*) abacus.

абба́т, а, *m.* abbot; (Roman Catholic) priest.

аббати́с|а, ы, *f.* abbess.

аббатств|о, а, *n.* abbey.

аббревиату́р|а, ы, *f.* abbreviation.

аберра́ци|я, и, *f.* (*opt. and fig.*) aberration.

абза́ц, а, *m.* **1.** (*typ.*) indention; сде́лать а. to indent; нача́ть с но́вого ~а to begin a new line, new paragraph. **2.** paragraph.

абисси́н|ец, ца, *m.* Abyssinian, Ethiopian.

абисси́нк|а, и, *f.* Abyssinian (woman), Ethiopian (woman).

абисси́нский, *adj.* Abyssinian, Ethiopian.

абитурие́нт, а, *m.* **1.** (*obs.*) (school-)leaver. **2.** university entrant.

абляти́в, а, *m.* (*gram.*) ablative.

абонеме́нт, а, *m.* subscription; season ticket; сверх ~а beyond the terms of agreement.

абоне́нт, а, *m.* subscriber.

абони́р|овать, ую, *impf. and pf.* to subscribe (to); to take out a booking (for), reserve a seat (for) (*a season at a theatre, a series of concerts, etc.*).

абони́р|оваться, уюсь, *impf. and pf.* **1.** (на + *a.*) to subscribe (to); to take out a booking (for). **2.** *pass. of* ~овать.

аборда́ж, а, *m.* (*naut.*) boarding; взять на а. to board.

аборда́жный, *adj.* boarding; а. крюк (*naut.*) grapnel.

абориге́н, а, *m.* aboriginal.

або́рт, а, *m.* **1.** abortion, miscarriage; сде́лать себе́ а. to have an abortion. **2.** failure, cancellation.

аборти́вн|ый, *adj.* **1.** *adj. of* або́рт; ~ые сре́дства means for procuring abortion. **2.** (*biol.*) abortive.

абракада́бр|а, ы, *f.* abracadabra.

абре́к, а, *m.* abrek (*member of Caucasian mountain bands who fought the Russians in the 19th century*).

абрико́с, а, *m.* **1.** apricot. **2.** apricot-tree.

абрико́совый, *adj.* apricot.

абрикоти́н, а, *m.* apricot liqueur.

а́брис, а, *m.* contour(s); outline.

абсе́нт, а, *m.* absinthe.

абсентеи́зм, а, *m.* absenteeism (*esp. from meetings, voting, etc.*).

абсенте́ист, а, *m.* absentee (*esp. from meetings, voting, etc.*).

абси́да = апси́да.

абсолю́т, а, *m.* (*philos.*) the absolute.

абсолюти́зм, а, *m.* (*polit.*) absolutism.

абсолюти́ст, а, *m.* (*polit.*) absolutist.

абсолю́т|ный (~ен, ~на), *adj.* absolute; а. слух (*mus.*) perfect ear.

абсорби́р|овать, ую, *impf. and pf.* to absorb.

абсо́рбци|я, и, *f.* absorption.

абстраги́р|овать, ую, *impf. and pf.* to abstract.

абстра́кт|ный (~ен, ~на), *adj.* abstract.

абстракциони́зм, а, *m.* abstract art.

абстракциони́ст, а, *m.* abstract artist.

абстра́кци|я, и, *f.* abstraction.

абсу́рд, а, *m.* absurdity; довести́ до ~а to carry to the point of absurdity.

абсу́рдност|ь, и, *f.* absurdity.

абсу́рд|ный (~ен, ~на), *adj.* absurd.

абсце́сс, а, *m.* abscess.

абсци́сс|а, ы, *f.* (*math.*) abscissa.

абха́з|ец, ца, *m.* Abkhazian (*inhabitant of Abkhazia in the Caucasus*).

абха́зк|а, и, *f.* Abkhazian (woman).

абха́зский, *adj.* Abkhazian.

а́бцуг, а, *m.* (*obs.*) only in phrases с пе́рвого ~а, по пе́рвому ~у right from the start, from the first go-off.

аванга́рд, а, *m.* advance-guard, van; vanguard (*also fig.*); (*fig.*) avant-garde.

аванпо́рт, а, *m.* outer harbour.

аванпо́ст, а, *m.* (*mil.*) outpost; forward position (*also fig.*).

ава́нс, а, *m.* **1.** advance (*of money*); получи́ть а. to receive an advance (*of wages*). **2.** (*pl. only; fig.*) advances, overtures.

аванси́р|овать, ую, *impf. and pf.* to advance (*money*).

ава́нсом, *adv.* in advance, on account.

авансце́н|а, ы, *f.* (*theatr.*) proscenium.

авантя́ж|ный (∼ен, ∼на), *adj.* (*obs., coll.*) fine, showing to advantage.

авантю́р|а, ы, *f.* 1. (*pejor.*) adventure; venture, escapade; пусти́ться в ∼ы to embark on adventures. 2. (*coll.*) shady enterprise.

авантюри́зм, а, *m.* disposition to engage in adventures, ventures.

авантюри́ст, а, *m.* (*pejor.*) adventurer.

авантюр|исти́ческий, *adj.* of ∼и́зм.

авантю́р|ный (∼ен, ∼на), *adj.* adventurous; а. рома́н (*lit.*) adventure story.

ава́р, а, *m.* (*hist.*) Avar.

ава́р|ец, ца, *m.* Avar (*member of ethnic group inhabiting Caucasus*).

авари́йност|ь, и, *f.* accidents, accident rate.

авари́йн|ый, *adj.* 1. *adj.* of ава́рия; а. компле́кт survival kit; ∼ая маши́на breakdown van; (*aeron.*) ∼ая кома́нда crash crew; ∼ая поса́дка crash landing; а. сигна́л distress signal. 2. emergency, spare.

ава́ри|я, и, *f.* 1. damage; wreck, crash, accident; breakdown; (*fig., iron.*) misfortune; потерпе́ть ∼ю to crash, have an accident. 2. (*leg.*) damages, average.

ава́р|ка, ки, *f.* of ∼ and ∼ец.

ава́р|ский, *adj.* of ∼ and ∼ец.

авгу́р, а, *m.* augur; язы́к ∼ов esoteric language.

а́вгуст, а, *m.* August.

августе́йший, *adj.* (*as title of emperors*) most august.

августи́н|ец, ца, *m.* Augustinian, Austin friar.

а́вгуст|овский, *adj.* of ∼.

а́виа (= авиапо́чтой) 'by air mail'.

авиа- air-, aero-.

авиаба́з|а, ы, *f.* air base.

авиаконстру́ктор, а, *m.* aircraft designer.

авиама́тк|а, и, *f.* aircraft-carrier.

авиамодели́зм, а, *m.* model aircraft construction.

авиамодели́ст, а, *m.* model aircraft constructor, model aircraft enthusiast.

авиамоде́л|ь, и, *f.* model aircraft.

авиамоде́льный, *adj.* of ∼.

авиано́с|ец, ца, *m.* aircraft carrier.

авиапо́чт|а, ы, *f.* air mail.

авиасъёмк|а, и, *f.* air photography, aerial surveying.

авиацио́нн|ый, *adj.* of авиа́ция; ∼ая промы́шленность aircraft industry; ∼ая шко́ла flying school.

авиа́ци|я, и, *f.* 1. aviation. 2. (*collect.*) aircraft; бомбардиро́вочная а. bomber force.

авиача́ст|ь, и, *f.* air force unit.

ави́зо, *indecl., n.* 1. (*comm.*) letter of advice.

2. (*naut.*) aviso, advice-boat.

аво́сь, *adv.* (*coll.*) perhaps; на а. on the off-chance.

аво́сь|ка, и, *f.* (*coll.*) string (shopping) bag.

авра́л, а, *m.* (*naut.*) work involving all hands; (*as interj.*) all hands on deck!; (*fig.*) all hands to the pump!

авра́л|ьный, *adj.* of ∼; ∼ьная рабо́та emergency job.

авро́ра, ы, *f.* (*poet.*) aurora, dawn.

австрали́|ец, йца, *m.* Australian.

австрали́йк|а, и, *f.* Australian (woman).

австрали́йский, *adj.* Australian.

австри́|ец, йца, *m.* Austrian.

австри́йк|а, и, *f.* Austrian (woman).

австри́йский, *adj.* Austrian.

австрия́к, а, *m.* (*coll., obs.*) Austrian.

австрия́чк|а, и, *f.* (*coll., obs.*) Austrian (woman).

автарки́|я, и, *f.* (*econ., philos.*) self-sufficiency, autarky.

автенти́чный, *adj.* = аутенти́чный

авто́, *indecl., n.* (*coll.*) (motor-)car.

авто- 1. self-. 2. auto-, automatic. 3. motor-.

автоба́з|а, ы, *f.* motor-transport depot.

автобиографи́ческий, *adj.* autobiographical.

автобиографи́чност|ь, и, *f.* autobiographical nature, character.

автобиогра́фи|я, и, *f.* autobiography.

автоблокиро́вк|а, и, *f.* (*railways*) automatic block system.

авто́бус, а, *m.* (motor) 'bus, omnibus.

автоге́нный, *adj.* (*tech.*) autogenous.

авто́граф, а, *m.* (*in var. senses*) autograph.

автодро́м, а, *m.* 1. vehicle testing point. 2. motor-racing circuit.

автожи́р, а, *m.* autogyro.

автозаво́д, а, *m.* motor-car factory.

автока́р, а, *m.* motor trolley.

автокефа́льный, *adj.* (*eccl.*) autocephalous.

автокла́в, а, *m.* (*tech.*) autoclave.

автокра́т, а, *m.* autocrat.

автократи́ческий, *adj.* autocratic.

автокра́ти|я, и, *f.* autocracy.

автомагистра́л|ь, и, *f.* motorway.

автома́т, а, *m.* 1. automatic machine, slot-machine; биле́тный а. ticket machine; телефо́н-а. public telephone, call-box; (*fig.*) automaton, robot. 2. (*mil.*) (*coll.*) sub-machine-gun, tommy-gun.

автоматиза́ци|я, и, *f.* automation.

автоматизи́р|овать, ую, *impf. and pf.* 1. to render automatic. 2. to introduce automation (into); to automate.

автомати́зм, а, *m.* automatism.

автомати́ческ|ий, *adj.* 1. (*tech.*) automatic, self-acting; ∼ая винто́вка automatic (rifle); ∼ая ру́чка fountain-pen. 2. (*fig.*) automatic, involuntary.

автомати́ч|ный(∼ен,∼на), *adj.* = ∼еский 2.

автома́т|ный, *adj. of* ~ 2.

автома́тчик, а, *m.* (*mil.*) sub-machine-gunner, tommy-gunner.

автомаши́н|а, ы, *f.* motor vehicle.

автомобили́зм, а, *m.* motoring.

автомобили́ст, а, *m.* motorist.

автомоби́л|ь, я, *m.* (motor-)car, motor vehicle; управля́ть ~ем to drive a (motor-)car; а.-фургóн Dormobile.

автомоби́ль|ный, *adj. of* ~; а. завóд motor-car factory; а. спорт motoring.

автомотри́с|а, ы, *f.* (railway) diesel car.

автонóми|я, и, *f.* autonomy.

автонóм|ный (~ен, ~на), *adj.* autonomous.

автопортрéт, а, *m.* self-portrait.

áвтор, а, *m.* author; composer; а. предложéния, резолю́ции mover of resolution.

авторефера́т, а, *m.* abstract (*of dissertation, etc.*).

авториза́ци|я, и, *f.* authorization.

авториз|óванный, *p.p.p. of* ~ова́ть *and adj.* authorized.

авториз|ова́ть, у́ю, *impf. and pf.* to authorize.

авторита́р|ный (~ен, ~на), *adj.* authoritarian.

авторитéт, а, *m.* authority; пóльзоваться ~ом to enjoy authority, have prestige; счита́ться ~ом to be considered an authority.

авторитéтност|ь, и, *f.* authoritativeness; trustworthiness.

авторитéт|ный (~ен, ~на), *adj.* authoritative; trustworthy; а. истóчник an authoritative source (of information).

áвтор|ский, *adj. of* ~; а. лист (*typ.*) unit of 40,000 ens (*used in calculating author's royalties*); ~ское пра́во copyright; *as noun* ~ские, ~ских royalties.

áвторств|о, а, *n.* authorship.

авторучк|а, и, *f.* (*coll.*) fountain-pen.

автостóп, а, *m.* 1. (*railways*) automatic braking gear. 2. (*coll.*) hitch-hiking.

автостра́д|а, ы, *f.* motorway, motor highway; trunk-road.

автосцéпк|а, и, *f.* (*railways*) automatic coupling.

автоти́пи|я, и, *f.* (*typ.*) autotype.

автотра́нспорт, а, *m.* motor transport.

автохтóн, а, *m.* autochthon, aboriginal.

автохтóнный, *adj.* autochthonous.

ага́, *interj.* (expressing (i) comprehension, (ii) malicious pleasure) ah!, aha!

ага́в|а, ы, *f.* (*bot.*) agave.

агаря́н|ин, ина, *pl.* ~е, ~, *m.* (*coll., obs.*) Hagarite.

ага́т, а, *m.* (*min.*) agate.

ага́т|овый, *adj. of* ~.

агглютинати́вный, *adj.* (*ling.*) agglutinative.

агглютин|и́рующий, *adj.* = ~ати́вный.

агéнт, а, *m.* (*in var. senses*) agent.

агéнтств|о, а, *n.* agency.

агенту́р|а, ы, *f.* 1. secret service; занима́ться ~ой to be an agent. 2. (*collect.*) agents.

агиогра́фи|я, и, *f.* hagiography.

агит-, *abbr. of* ~ациóнный.

агита́тор, а, *m.* (*polit.*) agitator; canvasser.

агитациóн|ный (~ен, ~на), *adj.* (*polit.*) agitation.

агита́ци|я, и, *f.* (*polit.*) agitation; drive; вести́ ~ю to campaign, conduct a drive.

агити́р|овать, ую, *impf.* 1. (*impf. only*) (*polit.*) to agitate, carry on agitation, campaign. 2. (*pf.* с~) (*coll.*) to canvass.

аги́тк|а, и, *f.* (*polit.*) propaganda piece (*plays, posters, etc.*).

агитпрóп, а, *m.* (*abbr. of* отдéл агита́ции и пропага́нды) agitation and propaganda section (*of central and local committees of the Communist Party of the Soviet Union*).

агитпу́нкт, а, *m.* agitation centre.

áглицкий, *adj.* (*coll., obs.*) English.

áгн|ец, ца, *m.* 1. (*eccl.*) lamb (*Agnus Dei*). 2. *fig. of a meek person:* прики́нуться ~цем to feign meekness, play the innocent.

агнóстик, а, *m.* agnostic.

агностици́зм, а, *m.* agnosticism.

агности́ческий, *adj.* agnostic.

агонизи́р|овать, ую, *impf. and pf.* to be in one's death agony.

агóни|я, и, *f.* (*med.*) death agony, death-pangs; (*fig.*) last struggle.

агра́ри|й, я, *m.* (*hist.*) landowner.

агра́рный, *adj.* agrarian.

агрега́т, а, *m.* 1. (*tech.*) unit, assembly. 2. aggregate.

агресси́в|ный (~ен, ~на), *adj.* aggressive.

агрéсси|я, и, *f.* (*polit.*) aggression.

агрéссор, а, *m.* aggressor.

агрикульту́р|а, ы, *f.* agriculture.

агрикульту́рный, *adj.* agricultural.

агро- agro-, agricultural, farm.

агронóм, а, *m.* agronomist.

агронóми|я, и, *f.* agronomics; agricultural science.

ад, а, *m.* hell; (*fig.*) bedlam; душéвный а. mental torment, anguish.

ада́мов, *adj.*; ~о я́блоко Adam's apple.

ада́жио, *adv. and noun indecl., n.* (*mus.*) adagio.

адапта́ци|я, и, *f.* (*in var. senses*) adaptation.

ада́птер, а, *m.* 1. (*tech.*) adapter 2. (*mus.*) pick-up.

адвенти́ст, а, *m.* (*rel.*) (Seventh-day) Adventist.

адвока́т, а, *m.* barrister; (*fig.*) advocate.

адвокату́р|а, ы, *f.* 1. the profession of barrister. 2. (*collect.*) the Bar, the legal profession.

адеква́т|ный (~ен, ~на), *adj.* identical, coincident; adequate.

аденóид, а, *m.* (*med.*) adenoid.

адéпт, а, *m.* adherent, disciple.
аджáр|ец, ца, *m.* Adzharian.
аджáрк|а, и, *f.* Adzharian (woman).
аджáрский, *adj.* Adzharian.
администратáвн|ый, *adj.* administrative; в ~ом порядке administratively, by administrative means.
администрáтор, а, *m.* administrator; manager (*of hotel, theatre, etc.*).
администрáци|я, и, *f.* administration.
администрáр|овать, ую, *impf.* to administer; (*pejor.*) to run (an organization, *etc.*) by means of orders and decrees.
адмирáл, а, *m.* admiral.
адмиралтéй|ский, *adj. of* ~ство.
адмиралтéйств|о, а, *n.* (*obs.*) 1. naval dockyard. 2. The Admiralty.
адмирáл|ьский, *adj. of* ~; а. корáбль flagship; а. чин, ~ьское звáние flag rank; а. час (*joc., obs.*) midday drinking time.
адмирáльш|а, и, *f.* admiral's wife.
áдов, *adj.* (*rel. and fig., coll.*) *of* ад.
áдрес, а, *pl.* ~á, ~óв, *m.* (*in var. senses*) address; в а. (+*g.*) (*fig.*) aimed at, directed at; не по ~у (*fig.*) mistakenly, at the wrong door, to the wrong quarter.
адресáнт, а, *m.* sender (*of mail*).
адресáт, а, *m.* addressee; в слýчае ненахождéния ~а 'if undelivered'; за ненахождéнием ~а 'not known' (*on letters*).
áдрес-календáр|ь, я, *m.* (*obs.*) directory.
áдрес|ный, *adj. of* ~; ~ная кнáга directory; а. стол address bureau.
áдрес|овáть, ýю, *impf. and pf.* to address, direct.
áдрес|овáться, ýюсь, *impf. and pf.* (к+*dat.*) to address oneself (to).
áдски, *adv.* (*coll.*) infernally, terribly, fearfully; я а. зáнят I am terribly busy.
áдск|ий, *adj.* infernal, diabolical; (*fig.*) hellish, intolerable; ~ая скýка infernal bore; ~ая машáна infernal machine.
адсóрбци|я, и, *f.* (*chem.*) adsorption.
адъюнкт, а, *m.* 1. (*obs.*) junior scientific assistant. 2. advanced student in military academy.
адъютáнт, а, *m.* (*mil.*) aide-de-camp; стáрший а. adjutant.
адюльтéр, а, *m.* adultery.
адюльтéр|ный, *adj. of* ~.
аж, *adv. and conj.* (*coll.*) 1. (*adv.*) аж до right up to; аж на (+*a.*) right on to. 2. (*conj.*) so that, until; онá так закричáла, аж сéрдце похолодéло she cried enough to break one's heart.
áжио, *indecl., n.* (*comm.*) agio.
ажиотáж, а, *m.* 1. (*comm.*) stock-jobbing. 2. (*fig.*) stir, hullabaloo.
ажитáци|я, и, *f.* (*obs.*) agitation, excite-

ment; быть в ~и to be agitated, het up, in a state.
ажýр¹, а, *m.* open-work.
ажýр², *adv.* (*comm.*) up to date.
ажýрн|ый, *adj.* open-work; (*fig.*) delicate, fine; ~ые чулкá open-work stockings; ~ая рабóта open-work; (*archit.*) tracery.
аз, á, *m.* 1. az (*Slavonic name of the letter A*). 2. (*usu. pl.; coll.*) ABC; elements, rudiments; начинáть с ~óв to begin at the beginning; ни ~á не знать (о+*p.*) not to know the first thing (about).
азáли|я, и, *f.* (*bot.*) azalea.
азáрт, а, *m.* heat; excitement; fervour; войтá в а. to grow heated, excited.
азáрт|ный (~ен, ~на), *adj.* heated; venturesome; ~ная игрá game of chance.
азбéст, *see* асбéст.
áзбук|а, и, *f.* alphabet; the ABC (*also fig.*); а. Мóрзе Morse code.
áзбучн|ый, *adj.* alphabetical; ~ая áстина truism.
азербайджáн|ец, ца, *m.* Azerbaijani(an).
азербайджáнк|а, и, *f.* Azerbaijani(an) (woman).
азербайджáнский, *adj.* Azerbaijani.
азиáт, а, *m.* 1. Asiatic. 2. (*fig., obs.*) barbarous person.
азиáтский, *adj.* 1. Asiatic. 2. (*fig., obs.*) barbarous.
азиáтчин|а, ы, *f.* (*obs.*) barbarous manners, way of life.
áзимут, а, *m.* (*astron.*) azimuth.
азóт, а, *m.* (*chem.*) nitrogen; óкись ~а nitric oxide.
азотистокáслый, *adj.* (*chem.*) nitrite.
азóтистый, *adj.* (*chem.*) nitrous.
азотнокáслый, *adj.* (*chem.*) nitrate.
азóтн|ый, *adj.* (*chem.*) nitric; ~ая кислотá nitric acid.
áист, а, *m.* (*zool.*) stork.
ай, *interj.* (*expressing (i) fear, (ii) surprise and/or pleasure*) oh!; ай да (*expressing approval*) what а . . .!; ай да молодéц! well done!
айв|á, ы, *f.* 1. quince. 2. quince-tree.
айвóвый, *adj.* quince.
айдá, *interj.* (*coll.*) come along!, let's go!
áйсберг, а, *m.* iceberg.
айсóр, а, *m.* Aysor.
айсóрк|а, и, *f.* Aysor (woman).
академáзм, а, *m.* academic manner.
акадéмик, а, *m.* 1. academician (*member of an Academy*). 2. (*coll., obs.*) student of an academy.
академáческий, *adj.* academic(al).
академáч|ный (~ен, ~на), *adj.* academic, theoretical.
акадéми|я, и, *f.* academy.
áканье, я, *n.* akanie (*pronunciation of unstressed 'o' as 'a'*).

а́ка|ть, ю, *impf.* to pronounce unstressed 'o' as 'a' in Russian words.

ака́фист, а, *m.* (*eccl.*) acathistus (*series of doxological prayers*).

ака́ци|я, и, *f.* (*bot.*) acacia.

аквала́нг, а, *m.* aqualung.

аквалангист, а, *m.* skin-diver.

аквамари́н, а, *m.* (*min.*) aquamarine.

аквапла́н, а, *m.* surf-board.

акварелист, а, *m.* water-colour painter.

акваре́л|ь, и, *f.* water-colour; писа́ть ~ью to paint in water-colours.

акваре́льный, *adj.* water-colour.

аква́риум, а, *m.* aquarium.

аквато́ри|я, и, *f.* (*defined*) area of water.

акведу́к, а, *m.* aqueduct.

акклиматиза́ци|я, и, *f.* acclimatization.

акклиматизи́р|овать, ую, *impf. and pf.* to acclimatize.

акклиматизи́р|оваться, уюсь, *impf. and pf.* to become acclimatized.

аккомпанеме́нт, а, *m.* (*mus.*) accompaniment (*also fig.*); под а. (+*g.*) to the accompaniment of.

аккомпаниа́тор, а, *m.* (*mus.*) accompanist.

аккомпани́р|овать, ую, *impf.* (+*d.*, на+*p.*; *mus.*) to accompany; а. певцу́ на роя́ле to accompany a singer on the piano.

акко́рд, а, *m.* (*mus.*) chord; заключи́тельный а. (*fig.*) finale; взять а. to strike a chord (*on the piano*).

аккордео́н, а, *m.* accordion.

акко́рдн|ый, *adj.* ~ая пла́та payment by the job; ~ая рабо́та job paid for as a whole.

аккредити́в, а, *m.* (*fin.*) letter of credit.

аккредит|ова́ть, у́ю, *impf. and pf.* to accredit.

аккумули́р|овать, ую, *impf. and pf.* to accumulate.

аккумуля́тор, а, *m.* (*tech.*) accumulator.

аккумуля́ци|я, и, *f.* accumulation.

аккура́т, *adv.* (*coll.*) *only in phrases* в а. exactly, precisely; в ~е properly.

аккура́тност|ь, и, *f.* 1. exactness, thoroughness. 2. tidiness, neatness.

аккура́т|ный (~ен, ~на), *adj.* 1. exact, thorough. 2. tidy, neat.

акмеи́зм, а, *m.* (*lit.*) acmeism.

акмеи́ст, а, *m.* (*lit.*) acmeist.

акри́д|ы, ~, *no sing.*, *only in phrase* пита́ться ~ами и ди́ким мёдом to live on locusts and wild honey (*i.e. to live meagrely*).

акроба́т, а, *m.* acrobat.

акроба́тик|а, и, *f.* acrobatics.

акропо́л|ь, я, *m.* (*hist.*) acropolis.

акрости́х, а, *m.* acrostic.

аксельба́нт, а, *m.* aiguillette.

аксессуа́р, а, *m.* 1. accessory. 2. (*theatr.*) properties.

аксио́м|а, ы, *f.* axiom.

акт, а, *m.* 1. act. 2. (*theatr.*) act. 3. (*leg.*) deed, document; обвини́тельный а. indictment. 4. (*obs.*) speech-day (*in schools*).

актёр, а, *m.* actor (*also fig.*, *pejor.*).

актёр|ский, *adj. of* ~.

актёрств|о, а, *n.* acting; (*fig.*) affectation, posing.

акти́в[1], а, *m.* (*fin.*) assets; (*fig.*) asset.

акти́в[2], а, *m.* (*polit.*) most active members; парти́йный а. party activists.

активиза́ци|я, и, *f.* activization.

активизи́р|овать, ую, *impf. and pf.* to make more active, stir up.

активи́ст, а, *m.* (*polit.*) activist (*active member of political or social organization*).

акти́в|ный (~ен, ~на), *adj.* active, energetic.

а́ктов|ый, *adj.* ~ая бума́га (*obs.*) official paper; а. день (*official*) non-working day (*due to bad weather conditions*); а. зал assembly hall.

актри́с|а, ы, *f.* actress.

актуа́льност|ь, и, *f.* 1. (*tech.*) actuality. 2. topicality.

актуа́л|ьный (~ен, ~ьна), *adj.* 1. (*tech.*) actual. 2. topical, current; а. вопро́с pressing question, topical question.

аку́л|а, ы, *f.* (*zool.*) shark (*also fig.*).

аку́стик|а, и, *f.* acoustics.

акусти́ческий, *adj.* acoustic.

акушёр, а, *m.* obstetrician.

акуше́рк|а, и, *f.* midwife.

акуше́рский, *adj.* obstetric(al).

акуше́рств|о, а, *n.* obstetrics; midwifery.

акце́нт, а, *m.* accent.

акценти́р|овать, ую, *impf. and pf.* to accent, accentuate.

акце́пт, а, *m.* (*comm.*) acceptance.

акцепт|ова́ть, у́ю, *impf. and pf.* (*comm.*) to accept.

акци́з, а, *m.* (excise-)duty; обложи́ть ~ом to excise.

акционе́р, а, *m.* shareholder.

акционе́р|ный, *adj. of* ~; ~ное о́бщество joint-stock company.

а́кци|я[1], и, *f.* (*fin.*) share; а. на предъяви́теля ordinary share; именна́я а. nominal share; привилегиро́ванная а. preference share; (*fig.*, *coll.*; *pl. only*) stock; его́ ~и си́льно поднима́ются his stock is rising rapidly.

а́кци|я[2], и, *f.* action, démarche (*particularly in diplomacy*).

алба́н|ец, ца, *m.* Albanian.

алба́нк|а, и, *f.* Albanian (woman).

алба́нский, *adj.* Albanian.

а́лгебр|а, ы, *f.* algebra.

алгебраи́ческий, *adj.* algebraic(al).

алеба́рд|а, ы, *f.* (*hist.*) halberd.

алеба́стр, а, *m.* alabaster.

александрийский, *adj.* (*geogr.*) Alexandrian; а. лист (*med.*) senna; а. стих (*lit.*) Alexandrine (verse).

александрит, а, *m.* (*min.*) alexandrite.

алé|ть, ю, *impf.* (of за~) **1.** to redden, flush. **2.** to show red.

алжир|ец, ца, *m.* Algerian.

алжирк|а, и, *f.* Algerian (woman).

алжирский, *adj.* Algerian.

áли (*coll.*) = и́ли.

áлиби, *indecl., n.* (*leg.*) alibi; установи́ть а. to establish an alibi.

алимéнтщик, а, *m.* (*coll.*) person paying alimony.

алимéнтщиц|а, ы, *f.* (*coll.*) woman in receipt of alimony.

алимéнт|ы, ов, *no sing.* (*leg.*) alimony, maintenance.

ал|кáть, ⌣чу, ⌣чешь, *impf.* (+g.; *poet.*) to hunger (for), crave (for).

алкоголи́зм, а, *m.* alcoholism.

алкоголик, а, *m.* alcoholic; (*coll.*) drunkard.

алкоголи́ческий, *adj.* alcoholic.

алкогóл|ь, я, *m.* alcohol.

алкогóльный, *adj.* alcoholic.

Аллáх, а, *m.* Allah; A. егó вéдает God knows; одномý ~у извéстно God alone knows.

аллегори́ч|еский, *adj.* allegorical.

аллегори́ч|ный (~ен, ~на), *adj.* = ~еский.

аллегóри|я, и, *f.* allegory.

аллéгро, *adv. and noun, indecl., n.* (*mus.*) allegro.

аллé|я, и, *f.* avenue.

аллигáтор, а, *m.* alligator.

аллилýйщик, а, *m.* (*pejor.*) eulogist of the status quo.

аллилýйщин|а, ы, *f.* (*pejor.*) disposition to eulogize the status quo.

аллилýйя, *indecl., n. and as interj.* alleluia, hallelujah.

аллитерáци|я, и, *f.* alliteration.

алло, *interj.* (*on lifting telephone receiver or in course of telephone conversation*) hullo!

аллопáт, а, *m.* (*med.*) allopath(ist).

аллопáти|я, и, *f.* (*med.*) allopathy.

аллопати́ческий, *adj.* (*med.*) allopathic.

аллювиáльный, *adj.* (*geol.*) alluvial.

аллюви|й, я, *m.* (*geol.*) alluvium.

аллюр, а, *m.* pace, gait (*of horses*).

алмá-ати́нский, *adj.* (of) Alma-Ata.

алмáз, а, *m.* (uncut) diamond.

алоэ, *indecl., n.* (*bot.*) aloe; (*med.*) aloes.

алтáр|ь, я, *m.* **1.** (*eccl.*) altar; возложи́ть, принести́ на а. (+g.) to sacrifice (to). **2.** (*eccl.*) chancel; sanctuary.

алты́н, а, *m.* (*obs.*) three-kopeck piece.

алты́нник, а, *m.* (*obs., coll.*) skinflint.

алфави́т, а, *m.* alphabet.

алфави́тный, *adj.* alphabetical; а. указáтель index.

алхи́мик, а, *m.* alchemist.

алхи́ми|я, и, *f.* alchemy.

áлчност|ь, и, *f.* greed, avidity, cupidity.

áлч|ный (~ен, ~на), *adj.* greedy, grasping.

áлчущ|ий, *pres. part. of* алкáть; ~ие и жáждущие (+g.) those that hunger and thirst (after).

áл|ый (~, ~а), *adj.* scarlet.

алыч|á, и́, *f.* cherry-plum (*kind of small plum: Prunus divaricata*).

аль (*coll.*) = и́ли.

альбатрóс, а, *m.* albatross.

альбини́зм, а, *m.* (*med.*) albinism.

альбинóс, а, *m.* (*med.*) albino.

альбóм, а, *m.* album.

альвеолярный, *adj.* (*ling.*) alveolar.

альков, а, *m.* alcove.

альков|ный, *adj.* **1.** *adj. of* ~. **2.** erotic, pornographic.

альманáх, а, *m.* **1.** literary miscellany. **2.** (*obs.*) almanac.

альпакá¹, *indecl., n.* alpaca.

альпакá², *indecl., n.* (*min.*) German silver.

альпáри, *adv.* (*comm.*) at par.

альпи́йский, *adj.* alpine.

альпини́зм, а, *m.* mountaineering.

альпини́ст, а, *m.* mountain-climber.

альт, á, *pl.* ~ы́, *m.* (*mus.*) **1.** alto (*voice or singer*). **2.** viola.

альтерáци|я, и, *f.* (*mus.*) change in pitch of notes (*by a tone or semitone*); знáки ~и accidentals.

альтернати́в|а, ы, *f.* alternative.

альтернати́в|ный (~ен, ~на), *adj.* alternative.

альти́ст, а, *m.* viola-player.

альт|óвый, *adj. of* ~; ~óвая пáртия alto part.

альтруи́зм, а, *m.* altruism.

альтруи́ст, а, *m.* altruist.

альтруисти́ческий, *adj.* altruistic.

áльф|а, ы, *f.* alpha; от ~ы до омéги from A to Z.

альфóнс, а, *m.* (*pejor.*) gigolo.

алюми́ниевый, *adj.* aluminium.

алюми́ни|й, я, *m.* aluminium.

аляповáт|ый (~, ~а), *adj.* tasteless; tastelessly painted; crudely constructed.

аляфуршéт, а, *m.* fork supper.

амазóнк|а, и, f. **1.** (*myth.*) Amazon. **2.** horsewoman. **3.** riding-habit.

амальгáм|а, ы, *f.* (*chem. and fig.*) amalgam.

амальгами́р|овать, ую, *impf. and pf.* (*chem. and fig.*) to amalgamate.

аманáт, а, *m.* (*dial.*) hostage.

áмба, *interj.* (*sl.*) kaput!, it's all up!

амбáр, а, *m.* barn, granary; warehouse, storehouse.

амбáрго = эмбáрго.

амба́р|ный, *adj. of* ~.

амби́ци|я, и, *f. (obs.)* pride; arrogance; челове́к с ~ей arrogant man; вломи́ться в ~ю to take offence.

а́мбр|а, ы, *f.* amber; се́рая а. ambergris.

амбразу́р|а, ы, *f. (mil., archit.)* embrasure.

амбре́, *indecl., n.* scent, smell, fragrance *(now usu. iron.)*.

амбро́зи|я, и, *f.* ambrosia.

амбулато́ри|я, и, *f. (med.)* out-patients department *(of hospital)*; *(general practioner's)* surgery.

амбулато́р|ный, *adj. of* ~ия; а. больно́й out-patient, walking patient; а. приём out-patient reception hours; surgery hours.

амбушю́р, а, *m. (mus.)* mouthpiece.

амво́н, а, *m. (eccl.)* ambo, pulpit.

амёб|а, ы, *f. (zool.)* amoeba.

америка́н|ец, ца, *m.* American.

американи́зм, а, *m.* **1.** *(ling.)* Americanism. **2.** American methods (of work).

американи́стик|а, и, *f.* American studies.

америка́нк|а, и, *f.* **1.** American (woman). **2.** *(agric.)* amerikanka *(variety of spring wheat)*. **3.** snack bar. **4.** two-wheeled cart.

америка́нск|ий, *adj.* American; ~ие го́ры switchback *(at fairs)*; а. дя́дюшка 'rich uncle' *(character, esp. in comedies, from whom a legacy is hoped for)*; а. замо́к Yale lock; ~ая мастерска́я 'while-you-wait' shoe repair shop; а. оре́х Brazil nut.

амети́ст, а, *m. (min.)* amethyst.

амети́ст|овый, *adj. of* ~.

ампи́р|ный, *adj. of* ~.

амикошо́нств|о, а, *n. (coll.)* hail-fellow-well-met attitude.

аминокисло́т|а, ы, *f. (chem.)* aminoacid.

ами́нь, *particle (eccl.)* amen.

аммиа́к, а, *m. (chem.)* ammonia.

аммиа́чный, *adj. (chem.)* ammoniac.

аммо́ни|й, я, *m. (chem.)* ammonium.

амнисти́р|овать, ую, *impf. and pf.* to amnesty.

амни́сти|я, и, *f.* amnesty.

аморали́зм, а, *m. (philos.)* amoralism.

амора́льност|ь, и, *f.* amorality; immorality.

амора́л|ьный (~ен, ~ьна), *adj.* amoral; immoral.

амортиза́тор, а, *m. (tech.)* shock-absorber.

амортиза́ци|я, и, *f.* **1.** *(econ.)* amortization. **2.** *(tech.)* shock-absorption.

амортизи́р|овать, ую, *impf. and pf.* to amortize.

амо́рф|ный (~ен, ~на), *adj.* amorphous.

ампе́р, а, *g. pl.* а., *m. (phys.)* ampere.

ампи́р, а, *m.* Empire style *(of furniture, etc.)*.

ампи́р|ный, *adj. of* ~.

амплиту́д|а, ы, *f.* amplitude.

амплифика́ци|я, и, *f. (lit.)* amplification, inflation.

амплуа́, *indecl., n. (theatr.)* type; *(fig.)* role.

а́мпул|а, ы, *f.* ampoule.

ампута́ци|я, и, *f. (med.)* amputation.

ампути́р|овать, ую, *impf. and pf. (med.)* to amputate.

амуле́т, а, *m.* amulet.

амуни́ци|я, и, *f. (collect.)* ammunition.

Аму́р, а, *m.* **1.** *(myth.)* Cupid. **2.** аму́ры *(pl. only) (coll.)* intrigues, love affairs.

аму́р|иться, юсь, *impf.* (с+*i*; *coll.*) to flirt (with), have an affair (with).

аму́рн|ый, *adj. (coll.)* love; amorous; ~ые дела́ love affairs; ~ые пи́сьма love letters.

амфи́би|я, и, *f. (zool., bot.)* amphibian.

амфибра́хи|й, я, *m. (lit.)* amphibrach.

амфитеа́тр, а, *m. (hist.)* amphitheatre; *(theatr.)* circle.

ан, *conj. (dial.)* on the contrary; but in fact.

анабапти́зм, а, *m.* Anabaptism.

анабапти́ст, а, *m.* Anabaptist.

анабио́з, а, *m. (biol.)* anabiosis.

анагра́мм|а, ы, *f.* anagram.

анаколу́ф, а, *m. (lit.)* anacoluthon.

анакреонти́ческий, *adj. (lit.)* anacreontic.

ана́лиз, а, *m.* analysis; а. кро́ви blood test.

анализи́р|овать, ую, *impf.* to analyse.

анали́тик, а, *m.* analyst.

анали́тик|а, и, *f. (math.)* analytic geometry.

аналити́ческий, *adj.* analytic(al).

ана́лог, а, *m.* analogue.

аналоги́ческ|ий, *adj.* analogical; ~ое рассужде́ние reasoning by analogy.

аналоги́ч|ный (~ен, ~на), *adj.* analogous; ~ные слу́чаи analogous cases.

анало́ги|я, и, *f.* analogy; по ~и (с+*i*.) by analogy (with), on the analogy (of); проводи́ть ~ю to draw an analogy.

анало́|й, я, *m. (eccl.)* lectern.

ана́льный, *adj.* anal.

анана́с, а, *m.* pineapple.

анана́с|ный, *adj. of* ~.

анана́с|овый, *adj. of* ~; а. сок pineapple juice.

ана́пест, а, *m. (lit.)* anapaest.

анархи́зм, а, *m. (polit.)* anarchism.

анархи́ст, а, *m. (polit.)* anarchist.

анархи́ческий, *adj.* anarchic(al).

ана́рхи|я, и, *f.* anarchy.

ана́рхо-синдикали́зм, а, *m. (polit.)* anarcho-syndicalism.

ана́рхо-синдикали́ст, а, *m. (polit.)* anarcho-syndicalist.

ана́том, а, *m.* anatomist.

анатоми́р|овать, ую, *impf. and pf. (med.)* to dissect.

анатоми́ческий, *adj.* anatomic(al); а. теа́тр dissecting room.

анатоми́чк|а, и, *f. (coll.)* dissecting room.

анато́ми|я, и, *f.* anatomy.

ана́фем|а, ы, *f.* **1.** *(eccl.)* anathema;

excommunication; (*fig.*) преда́ть ~е to anathematize. 2. (*coll.*) accursed fellow.

анафема́тств|овать, ую, *impf.* (*eccl.*) to excommunicate.

ана́фемский, *adj.* (*coll.*) accursed.

анахоре́т, а, *m.* hermit, anchorite; (*fig.*) recluse.

анахрони́зм, а, *m.* anachronism.

анахрони́ческий, *adj.* anachronistic.

ангажеме́нт, а, *m.* (*theatr.*) engagement.

ангажи́р|овать, ую, *impf. and pf.* (*theatr.*) to engage.

анга́р, а, *m.* (*aeron.*) hangar.

а́нгел, а, *m.* angel; а.-храни́тель guardian angel; а. во плоти́ (*coll.*) (an absolute) angel; день ~а name-day.

а́нгельск|ий, *adj.* angelic (*also fig.*); ~ое терпе́ние angelic patience; а. о́браз (*obs.*) monk's habit.

ангидри́д, а, *m.* (*chem.*) anhydride.

ангидри́т, а, *m.* (*chem.*) anhydrite.

анги́н|а, ы, *f.* (*med.*) quinsy; tonsillitis.

англизи́р|овать, ую, *impf. and pf.* to anglicize.

англи́йск|ий, *adj.* 1. English; ~ая боле́знь rickets; ~ая була́вка safety-pin; а. рожо́к (*mus.*) cor anglais, alto oboe; ~ая соль Epsom salts; *as noun* а., ~ого, *m.* Baskerville (type). 2. British.

англика́нский, *adj.* (*eccl.*) Anglican.

англи́ст, а, *m.* specialist in English philology *or* English studies.

англи́стик|а, и, *f.* English philology, English studies.

англици́зм, а, *m.* (*lit.*) anglicism; (*ling.*) English loan-word.

англича́н|ин, ина, *pl.* ~е, ~, *m.* Englishman.

англича́нк|а, и, *f.* English woman.

англома́н, а, *m.* anglomane.

англоса́кс, а, *m.* Anglo-Saxon.

англосаксо́нский, *adj.* Anglo-Saxon.

англофи́л, а, *m.* anglophile.

англофи́льств|о, а, *n.* anglophilia.

англофо́б, а, *m.* anglophobe.

англофо́бств|о, а, *n.* anglophobia.

анго́рск|ий, *adj.* Angora; ~ая ко́шка Angora cat, Persian cat; ~ая шерсть Angora wool.

анда́нте, *adv.* (*mus.*) andante.

андре́евский, *adj.* а. крест St. Andrew's cross; а. флаг ensign of Imperial Russian Navy.

анекдо́т, а, *m.* 1. anecdote, story. 2. funny thing.

анекдоти́ческий, *adj.* anecdotal.

анекдоти́ч|ный (~ен, ~на), *adj.* improbable; humorous.

анеми́ческий, *adj.* anaemic.

анеми́ч|ный (~ен, ~на), *adj.* anaemic, pale.

анеми́|я, и, *f.* anaemia.

анемо́н, а, *m.* (*bot.*) anemone.

анеро́ид, а, *m.* aneroid.

анестези́р|овать, ую, *impf. and pf.* (*med.*) to anaesthetize; ~ующее сре́дство anaesthetic.

анестези́|я, и, *f.* (*med.*) anaesthesia.

анимали́ст, а, *m.* animal painter.

аними́зм, а, *m.* animism.

аними́ст, а, *m.* animist.

ани́с, а, *m.* (*bot.*) 1. anise. 2. anise apples.

ани́совк|а, и, *f.* (*coll.*) anisette.

ани́с|овый, *adj.* of ~; ~овое се́мя aniseed; ~овая во́дка anisette.

а́нкер, а, *m.* 1. (*tech.*) crutch (*in watch*). 2. (*archit.*) anchor.

анке́т|а, ы, *f.* questionnaire; poll, survey.

анна́л|ы, ов, *no sing.* annals.

аннекси́р|овать, ую, *impf. and pf.* (*polit.*) to annex.

анне́кси|я, и, *f.* (*polit.*) annexation.

аннота́ци|я, и, *f.* annotation.

анноти́р|овать, ую, *impf. and pf.* to annotate.

аннули́р|овать, ую, *impf. and pf.* to annul, nullify; to cancel; to abrogate.

аннуля́ци|я, и, *f.* annulment; cancellation; abrogation.

ано́д, а, *m.* (*phys.*) anode.

анома́ли|я, и, *f.* anomaly.

анома́л|ьный (~ен, ~ьна), *adj.* anomalous.

анони́м, а, *m.* anonymous author.

анони́мк|а, и, *f.* (*coll.*) anonymous letter.

анони́м|ный (~ен, ~на), *adj.* anonymous.

ано́нс, а, *m.* announcement, notice.

анонси́р|овать, ую, *impf. and pf.* (+a. or o+p.) to announce.

анорма́л|ьный (~ен, ~ьна), *adj.* abnormal.

анса́мбл|ь, я, *m.* 1. harmony. 2. (*mus., theatr.*) ensemble, company.

антаблеме́нт, а, *m.* (*archit.*) entablature.

антагони́зм, а, *m.* antagonism.

антагони́ст, а, *m.* antagonist.

антаркти́ческий, *adj.* antarctic.

анте́нн|а, ы, *f.* 1. (*zool.*) antenna. 2. (*tech.*) aerial; ра́мочная а. loop aerial.

анте́нн|ый, *adj.* of ~а.

анти- anti-.

антибио́тик, а, *m.* (*med.*) antibiotic.

антивещество́, а́, *n.* antimatter.

анти́к, а, *m.* (*monument, work of art, etc.*) antique.

антиква́р, а, *m.* antiquary.

антиквариа́т, а, *m.* antique-shop.

антиква́рный, *adj.* antiquarian.

антило́п|а, ы, *f.* (*zool.*) antelope.

антими́н, а, *m.* (*eccl.*) communion cloth.

антимо́ни|я[1], и, *f.* (*min.*; *obs.*) antimony.

антимо́ни|я[2], и, *f. only in phrase* разводи́ть ~и (*coll.*) to indulge in trivialities, idle chat.

антино́ми|я, и, *f.* antinomy.
антипати́ч|ный (~ен, ~на), *adj.* antipathetic.
антипа́ти|я, и, *f.* antipathy.
антиперестро́ечный, *adj.* (*polit.*) opposed to perestroika.
антипо́д, а, *m.* antipode.
антисеми́т, а, *m.* anti-Semite.
антисемити́зм, а, *m.* anti-Semitism.
антисеми́тский, *adj.* anti-Semitic.
антисе́птик|а, и, *f.* 1. antisepsis. 2. (*collect.*) antiseptics.
антисепти́ческий, *adj.* antiseptic.
антите́з|а, ы, *f.* antithesis.
антите́зис, а, *m.* (*philos.*) antithesis.
антитети́ческий, *adj.* antithetical.
антицикло́н, а, *m.* (*meteor.*) anti-cyclone.
анти́чност|ь, и, *f.* antiquity; (*hist.*) classical antiquity.
анти́чный, *adj.* ancient; classical; а. мир the ancient world; а. про́филь classical profile.
антологи́ческий, *adj.* (*lit.*) anthological.
антоло́ги|я, и, *f.* (*lit.*) anthology.
анто́нов, *adj.* (*obs.*) а. ого́нь gangrene.
анто́новк|а, и, *f.* antonovka (*kind of winter apples*).
анто́новск|ий, *adj.* ~ие я́блоки = анто́новка.
антра́кт, а, *m.* 1. (*theatr.*) interval. 2. (*mus.*) entr'acte.
антраци́т, а, *m.* (*min.*) anthracite.
антраша́, *indecl.*, *m.* entrechat; выде́лывать а. (*coll.*) to cut capers.
антреко́т, а, *m.* entrecôte, steak.
антрепренёр, а, *m.* impresario.
антрепри́з|а, ы, *f.* (*theatr.*) private theatrical concern.
антресо́л|ь, и, *f.* (*usually pl.*) 1. mezzanine. 2. shelf.
антропо́лог, а, *m.* anthropologist.
антропологи́ческий, *adj.* anthropological.
антрополо́ги|я, и, *f.* anthropology.
антропоме́три|я, и, *f.* anthropometry.
антропоморфи́зм, а, *m.* anthropomorphism.
антропоморфи́ческий, *adj.* anthropomorphic.
антропомо́рфный, *adj.* anthropoid.
антропофа́г, а, *m.* cannibal.
антропофа́ги|я, и, *f.* cannibalism.
антура́ж, а, *m.* environment; (*collect.*) entourage, associates.
анфа́с, *adv.* full face.
анфила́д|а, ы, *f.* suite (of rooms).
анча́р, а, *m.* (*bot.*) upas-tree (*Antiaris toxicaria*).
анчо́ус, а, *m.* anchovy.
аншла́г, а, *m.* notice; (*theatr.*) full house; спекта́кль идёт с ~ом the show is sold out, the house is full.
аню́тины: а. гла́зки (*bot.*) pansy.

або́рт|а, ы, *f.* (*anat.*) aorta.
апарта́мен|ты, ов, *sing.* ~, ~а, *m.* apartment.
апати́т, а, *m.* (*min.*) apatite.
апати́ч|ный (~ен, ~на), *adj.* apathetic.
апа́ти|я, и, *f.* apathy.
апа́ш, а, *m.* apache.
апелли́р|овать, ую, *impf. and pf.* to appeal.
апелля́нт, а, *m.* (*leg.*) appellant.
апелл|яцио́нный, *adj. of* ~я́ция; а. суд Court of Appeal.
апелля́ци|я, и, *f.* (*leg.*) appeal.
апельси́н, а, *m.* 1. orange. 2. orange-tree.
апельси́н|ный, *adj. of* ~.
апельси́нов|ый, *adj.* orange; ~ое варе́нье orange marmalade.
апелике́, *indecl.*, *adj.* plated.
аплоди́р|овать, ую, *impf.* (+*d.*) to applaud.
аплодисме́нт|ы, ов, *sing.* а., ~а, *m.* applause; бу́рные а. loud cheers, storm of applause.
апло́мб, а, *m.* aplomb, assurance.
апоге́|й, я, *m.* (*astron.*) apogee; (*fig.*) climax.
Апока́липсис, а, *m.* (*bibl.*) Revelation.
апокалипти́ческий, *adj.* apocalyptic.
апо́криф, а, *m.* an apocryphal work, story.
апокриф|и́ческий, *adj. of* апо́криф.
апокрифи́ч|ный (~ен, ~на), *adj.* (*coll.*) apocryphal.
аполити́зм, а, *m.* (*polit.*) political indifference; non-participation in politics.
аполити́ч|ный (~ен, ~на), *adj.* apolitical; politically indifferent.
апологе́т, а, *m.* apologist.
апологе́тик|а, и, *f.* apologetics.
аполо́ги|я, и, *f.* apologia.
апоплекси́ческий, *adj.* (*med.*) apoplectic.
апопле́кси|я, и, *f.* (*med.*) apoplexy.
апо́рт¹, а, *m.* Oporto apples.
апо́рт², *interj.* fetch! (*command to dog*).
апостерио́ри, *adv.* (*philos.*) a posteriori.
апостерио́рный, *adj.* (*philos.*) a posteriori.
апо́стол, а, *m.* 1. apostle (*also fig.*). 2. (*eccl.*, *lit.*) Books of the Apostles (*the Acts of the Apostles and the Epistles*).
апо́стольник, а, *m.* wimple.
апо́стольский, *adj.* apostolic.
апостро́ф, а, *m.* apostrophe.
апофео́з, а, *m.* apotheosis.
аппара́т, а, *m.* apparatus; instrument; organs; госуда́рственный а. machinery of State; дыха́тельный а. respiratory system; фотографи́ческий а. camera.
аппарату́р|а, ы, *f.* (*tech.*, *collect.*) apparatus, gear.
аппара́тчик, а, *m.* 1. (machine) operative. 2. (*polit.*) apparatchik (*member of party or governmental machine*).
аппе́ндикс, а, *m.* (*anat.*) appendix.
аппендици́т, а, *m.* (*med.*) appendicitis.
аппети́т, а, *m.* appetite; прия́тного ~а! bon appétit!

аппети́т|ный (~ен, ~на), *adj.* appetizing.
аппликату́р|а, ы, *f.* (*mus.*) fingering.
аппликáци|я, и, *f.* (*tech.*) appliqué work.
аппрету́р|а, ы, *f.* (*tech.*) dressing.
апрéл|ь, я, *m.* April.
апрéль|ский, *adj.* of ~.
априо́ри, *adv.* (*philos.*) a priori.
априо́р|ный (~ен, ~на), *adj.* (*philos.*) a priori.
апробáци|я, и, *f.* approbation.
апроби́р|овать, ую, *impf. and pf.* to approve.
апро́ш, а, *m.* (*typ.*) space left between words.
апси́д|а, ы, *f.* (*archit.*) apse.
аптéк|а, и, *f.* chemist's (shop); как в ~е (*coll., joc.*) just so, exactly right.
аптéкарский, *adj.* chemist's; pharmaceutical; а. магази́н non-dispensing chemist's (shop).
аптéкар|ша, ши, *f.* 1. (*coll.*) chemist's wife. 2. *f. of* ~ь.
аптéкар|ь, я, *m.* chemist.
аптéчк|а, и, *f.* first-aid set; medicine chest.
ар, а, *m.* are (*unit of land measurement*).
арáб, а, *m.* Arab, Arabian.
арабéск, а, *m.* arabesque.
арабéск|а, и, *f.* = ~.
араби́ст, а, *m.* Arabic scholar, Arabist.
арáбк|а, и, *f.* Arab (woman); Arabian (woman).
арáбск|ий, *adj.* Arab; Arabian; Arabic; а. восто́к the Arab countries (of the Near and Middle East); ~ая ло́шадь Arab (horse); ~ие ци́фры arabic numerals; а. язы́к Arabic.
арави́йский, *adj.* Arabian, of Arabia.
арáк, а, *m.* arrack (*rice or palm-sap spirit*).
аракчéевский, *adj.* 'Arakcheyevan', despotic.
аракчéевщин|а, ы, *f.* (*hist.*) the Arakcheyev regime; (*fig.*) despotism.
арамéйский, *adj.* Aramaic.
аранжи́р|овать, ую, *impf. and pf.* (*mus.*) to arrange.
аранжиро́вк|а, и, *f.* (*mus.*) arrangement.
арáп, а, *m.* 1. (*coll., obs.*) negro. 2. (*sl.*) cheat, swindler; на ~а by bluffing.
арáп|ский, *adj.* of ~; ~ские шту́чки (*coll.*) tricks.
арáпник, а, *m.* whip.
араукáри|я, и, *f.* araucaria, monkey-puzzle tree.
арб|á, ы́, *pl.* ~ы, *f.* bullock-cart.
арбалéт, а, *m.* arbalest, crossbow.
арби́тр, а, *m.* arbiter, arbitrator; umpire, referee.
арбитрáж, а, *m.* arbitration.
арбу́з, а, *m.* water-melon.
аргамáк, а, *m.* argamak (*Central Asian breed of race-horses*).

аргенти́н|ец, ца, *m.* Argentinian.
аргенти́н|ка, ки, *f.* Argentinian (woman).
аргенти́нский, *adj.* Argentine.
арго́, *indecl., n.* argot, slang.
арго́н, а, *m.* (*chem.*) argon.
арготи́ческий, *adj.* of арго́.
аргумéнт, а, *m.* argument.
аргументáци|я, и, *f.* reasoning, argumentation.
аргументи́р|овать, ую, *impf. and pf.* to argue; (*pf. only*) to prove.
Áргус, а, *m.* (*myth.*) Argus; (*fig.*) watchful guardian.
ареáл, а, *m.* (*bot. and zool.*) natural habitat; (*fig.*) region.
арéн|а, ы, *f.* arena, ring.
арéнд|а, ы, *f.* lease; сдать в ~у to rent, lease (*of owner, landlord*); взять в ~у to rent, lease (*of tenant*).
арендáтор, а, *m.* tenant, lessee.
арéнд|ный, *adj.* of ~а; ~ная плáта rent.
аренд|овáть, у́ю, *impf. and pf.* to rent, lease (*of tenant*).
арéст, а, *m.* arrest; сидéть, находи́ться под ~ом to be under arrest, in custody; а. имýщества seizure, sequestration.
арестáнт, а, *m.* (*obs.*) prisoner.
арестáнт|ский, *adj.* of ~; ~ская ро́та (*obs.*) penal battalion; *as noun* ~ская, ~ской, *f.* lock-up, cells.
арест|овáть, у́ю, *pf.* (*of* ~о́вывать) to arrest; to sequestrate.
аресто́выва|ть, ю, *impf. of* арестовáть.
ари́|ец, йца, *m.* Aryan.
ари́йский, *adj.* Aryan.
аристокрáт, а, *m.* aristocrat.
аристократ|и́ческий, *adj.,* aristocratic.
аристокрáти|я, и, *f.* aristocracy.
аритми́ч|ный (~ен, ~на), *adj.* unrhythmical.
арифмéтик|а, и, *f.* arithmetic.
арифмети́ческий, *adj.* arithmetical.
арифмо́граф, а, *m.* automatic calculating machine.
арифмо́метр, а, *m.* calculating machine.
áри|я, и, *f.* (*mus.*) aria.
áрк|а, и, *f.* arch.
аркáд|а, ы, *f.* (*archit.*) arcade.
аркáн, а, *m.* lasso.
аркáн|ить, ю, ишь, *impf.* (*pf.* за~) to lasso.
аркти́ческий, *adj.* arctic.
арлеки́н, а, *m.* harlequin.
арлекинáд|а, ы, *f.* harlequinade.
армату́р|а, ы, *f.* (*collect.*) fittings; (*tech.*) armature; steel *or* ferro-concrete reinforcement.
армату́р|ный, *adj.* of ~а.
армату́рщик, а, *m.* (*tech.*) fitter.
армé|ец, йца, *m.* 1. soldier. 2. (*obs.*) member of line regiment.

армейский, *adj. of* армия.

арми|я, и, *f.* **1.** army; A. Спасения Salvation Army; действующая a. front-line forces. **2.** (*obs.*) line regiments.

армя́к, á, *m.* armyak (*peasant's coat of heavy cloth*).

армян|и́н, и́на, *pl.* **~e, ~,** *m.* Armenian.

армя́нк|а, и, *f.* Armenian (woman).

армя́нский, *adj.* Armenian.

áрник|а, и, *f.* (*bot., med.*) arnica.

арома́т, а, *m.* scent, odour, aroma.

аромати́ч|ный (~ен, ~на), *adj.* aromatic, fragrant.

áрочный, *adj.* arched, vaulted.

арпе́дж|ио, (*mus.*) **1.** *adv.* **2.** *noun; sing. indecl., pl.* **~ии, ~ий,** *n.* arpeggio.

арсена́л, а, *m.* arsenal.

арт-, *abbr. of* артилл|е́рия, **~ери́йский.**

арта́ч|иться, усь, ишься, *impf.* (*coll.*) to jib, be restive.

артезиа́нский, *adj.* a. коло́дец artesian well.

арте́л|ь, и, *f.* artel (*co-operative association of workmen or peasants*).

арте́ль|ный, *adj. of* **~;** (*coll.*) common, collective; на **~ных** нача́лах on collective principles.

арте́льщик, а, *m.* **1.** member of an artel. **2.** collector of money(s). **3.** (*obs.*) porter.

артериа́льный, *adj.* (*anat.*) arterial.

артериосклеро́з, а, *m.* (*med.*) arteriosclerosis.

арте́ри|я, и, *f.* artery.

арти́кл|ь, я, *m.* (*gram.*) article.

арти́кул, а, *m.* во́инский a. (*hist.*) Articles of War.

артику́л, а, *m.* (*mil.; obs.*) firearms exercises; выки́дывать a. (*obs., coll.*) to play tricks.

артикули́р|овать, ую, *impf.* (*ling.*) to articulate.

артикуля́ци|я, и, *f.* (*ling.*) articulation.

артиллери́йск|ий, *adj.* (*mil.*) artillery; a. обо́з artillery-train; **~ая** подгото́вка artillery preparation, preparatory bombardment; a. склад ordnance depot.

артилле́ри|я, и, *f.* artillery.

арти́ст, а, *m.* **1.** artist(e); о́перный a. opera singer; a. бале́та ballet dancer; a. дра́мы actor; a. кино́ film actor. **2.** artist (= painter). **3.** (*fig.*) artist, expert; он — a. своего́ де́ла he is a real artist (at his job).

артисти́ческ|ий, *adj.* artistic; *as noun* **~ая, ~ой,** *f.* green-room, dressing-room.

арти́стк|а, и, *f.* **1.** artiste. **2.** (*fig.*) artist, expert (*woman*).

артишо́к, а, *m.* (*bot.*) artichoke.

артри́т, а, *m.* (*med.*) arthritis.

áрф|а, ы, *f.* harp.

арфи́ст, а, *m.* harpist.

архаи́зм, а, *m.* archaism.

архаи́ческий, *adj.* archaic.

архаи́ч|ный (~ен, ~на), *adj.* archaic.

арха́нгел, а, *m.* **1.** archangel. **2.** (*obs., iron.*) policeman.

арха́нгельский, *adj.* archangelic.

арха́ров|ец, ца, *m.* (*coll.*) ruffian.

археографи́ческий, *adj. of* археогра́фия.

археогра́фи|я, и, *f.* study (and publication) of early texts.

архео́лог, а, *m.* archaeologist.

археологи́ческий, *adj.* archaeological.

археоло́ги|я, и, *f.* archaeology.

архи- arch-.

архи́в, а, *m.* archives; сдать в a. (*coll.*) to shelve, throw out, leave out of account.

архива́риус, а, *m.* keeper of archives.

архиви́ст, а, *m.* archivist.

архи́в|ный, *adj. of* **~; ~ная** кры́са (*coll.*) employee in the archives.

архидья́кон, а, *m.* archdeacon.

архиепи́скоп, а, *m.* archbishop.

архиере́|й, я, *m.* member of higher orders of clergy (*bishop, archbishop or metropolitan*).

архимандри́т, а, *m.* (*eccl.*) archimandrite.

архимиллионе́р, а, *m.* multi-millionaire.

архипела́г, а, *m.* archipelago.

архитекто́ник|а, и, *f.* (*geol. and fig.*) architectonics.

архите́ктор, а, *m.* architect.

архитекту́р|а, ы, *f.* architecture.

архитекту́рный, *adj.* architectural.

архитра́в, а, *m.* (*archit.*) architrave.

арши́н, а, *m.* **1.** arshin (*Russian measure, equivalent to 28 inches or 71 cm*). **2.** rule one arshin in length; ме́рить на свой a. to measure by one's own bushel; как бу́дто a. проглоти́л (*coll.*) as stiff as a poker.

ары́к, а, *m.* irrigation canal (*in Central Asia*).

арьерга́рд, а, *m.* (*mil.*) rearguard.

арьерга́рдный, *adj.* (*mil.*) rearguard.

ас, а, *m.* (*air*) ace.

асе́птик|а, и, *f.* (*med.*) asepsis.

асбе́ст, а, *m.* asbestos.

асбе́стовый, *adj.* asbestos.

асепти́ческий, *adj.* (*med.*) aseptic.

асе́ссор, а, *m.* (*obs.*) assessor; колле́жский a. collegiate assessor (*8th grade in tsarist Russian civil service, equivalent to rank of major in the army*).

асимметри́ческий, *adj.* asymmetrical.

асимметри́ч|ный (~ен, ~на), *adj.* asymmetrical.

асимметри́|я, и, *f.* asymmetry.

аске́т, а, *m.* ascetic.

аскети́зм, а, *m.* asceticism.

аскети́ческий, *adj.* ascetic.

асоциа́льный, *adj.* anti-social.

аспе́кт, а, *m.* aspect, perspective.

áспид[1], а, *m.* (*zool.*) asp; (*fig.*) viper.

áспид[2], а, *m.* (*min.*) slate.

áспид|ный, *adj. of* ~²; ~ная доскá slate.

аспирáнт, а, *m.* post-graduate student.

аспирантýр|а, ы, *f.* 1. post-graduate study. 2. (*collect.*) post-graduate students.

аспирúн, а, *m.* (*med.*) aspirin; таблéтка ~а an aspirin.

ассамблé|я, и, *f.* 1. assembly. 2. (*hist.*) ball.

ассенизациóнный, *adj.* а. обóз (*collect.*) sewage-disposal men.

ассенизáци|я, и, *f.* sewage disposal.

ассигнáци|я, и, *f.* (*hist.*) assignat (*a form of paper money in use 1769–c.1840*).

ассигновáни|е, я, *n.* (*fin.*) assignation, appropriation, allocation.

ассигн|овáть, ýю, *impf. and pf.* (*fin.*) to assign, appropriate, allocate.

ассигнóвк|а, и, *f.* (*fin.*) assignment; grant (*of funds*).

ассимилúр|овать, ую, *impf. and pf.* to assimilate.

ассимиля́ци|я, и, *f.* assimilation.

ассирú|ец, йца, *m.* 1. Assyrian. 2. Aysor.

ассирú|йка, йки, *f. of* ~ец.

ассирúйский, *adj.* Assyrian.

ассирúян|ин, ина, *pl.* ~е, ~, *m.* (*obs.*) Assyrian.

ассирúян|ка, ки, *f. of* ~ин.

ассистéнт, а, *m.* 1. assistant. 2. (*in university, etc.*) junior member of teaching *or* research staff.

ассистúр|овать, ую, *impf.* (+*d.*) to assist.

ассонáнс, а, *m.* assonance.

ассортимéнт, а, *m.* assortment; range (of goods).

ассоциáци|я, и, *f.* association.

ассоциúр|овать, ую, *impf. and pf.* (с+*i.*; *philos.*) to associate (with).

астерóид, а, *m.* (*astron.*) asteroid.

астигматúзм, а, *m.* (*med.*) astigmatism.

áстм|а, ы, *f.* (*med.*) asthma.

астмáтик, а, *m.* (*med.*) asthmatic.

астматúческий, *adj.* (*med.*) asthmatic.

áстр|а, ы, *f.* (*bot.*) aster.

астрáльный, *adj.* astral.

астрóлог, а, *m.* astrologer.

астрологúческий, *adj.* astrological.

астролóги|я, и, *f.* astrology.

астроля́би|я, и, *f.* astrolabe; circumferentor.

астронóм, а, *m.* astronomer.

астрономúческий, *adj.* astronomic(al).

астронóми|я, и, *f.* astronomy.

астрофúзик|а, и, *f.* astrophysics.

асфáльт, а, *m.* asphalt.

асфальтúр|овать, ую, *impf. and pf.* (*pf. also* за~) (*tech.*) to asphalt.

асфáльтовый, *adj.* asphalt.

асфúкси|я, и, *f.* (*med.*) asphyxia.

ась, *interj.* (*coll.*) what? eh?

атавúзм, а, *m.* atavism.

атавистúческий, *adj.* atavistic.

атáк|а, и, *f.* attack.

атак|овáть, ýю, *impf. and pf.* to attack, charge, assault; а. с тыла to take in rear; а. с флáнга to take in flank.

атамáн, а, *m.* 1. (*hist.*) ataman (*Cossack chieftain*). 2. (*coll.*) (gang-)leader, (robber) chief.

атеúзм, а, *m.* atheism.

атеúст, а, *m.* atheist.

атеистúческий, *adj.* atheistic.

ательé, *indecl., n.* studio; а. мод fashion house.

áтлас, а, *m.* atlas.

атлáс, а, *m.* satin.

атлáсистый, *adj.* satiny.

атлáсный, *adj.* satin.

атлéт, а, *m.* athlete.

атлéтик|а, и, *f.* athletics.

атлетúческий, *adj.* athletic.

атмосфéр|а, ы, *f.* atmosphere.

атмосферúческий, *adj.* atmospheric.

атмосфéрн|ый, *adj.* atmospheric; ~ые осáдки atmospheric precipitation, rainfall.

атóлл, а, *m.* atoll.

áтом, а, *m.* atom.

атомистúческий, *adj.* atomistic.

áтомник, а, *m.* (*coll.*) atomic scientist.

áтомност|ь, и, *f.* (*chem.*) atomicity.

áтомн|ый, *adj.* atomic; ~ая бóмба atomic bomb; а. вес (*chem.*) atomic weight.

атомохóд, а, *m.* atomic-powered vessel.

атрибýт, а, *m.* attribute.

атропúн, а, *m.* (*med.*) atropin.

атрофúр|оваться, уюсь, *impf. and pf.* to atrophy.

атрофú|я, и, *f.* atrophy.

атташé, *indecl.*, *m.* (*dipl.*) attaché.

аттестáт, а, *m.* testimonial; certificate; pedigree; а. зрéлости school-leaving certificate; дать дурнóй а. to give a bad character.

аттестациóнн|ый, *adj.* ~ая комúссия examination board.

аттестáци|я, и, *f.* 1. attestation. 2. testimonial.

аттест|овáть, ýю, *impf. and pf.* to attest, recommend.

аттракциóн, а, *m.* (*theatr.*) attraction.

атý, *interj.* (*hunting*) tally-ho!, halloo!

аý, *interj.* 1. hi! halloo! 2. (*coll.*) it's all up!, it's done for!

аудиéнци|я, и, *f.* audience.

аудúтор, а, *m.* (*obs.*) auditor.

аудитóри|я, и, *f.* 1. auditorium; lecture-hall. 2. (*collect.*) audience.

аýка|ть, ю, *impf.* to halloo, shout 'hi'.

аýк|аться, аюсь, *impf.* (*of* ~нуться), to halloo to one another.

аýк|нуть, ну, нешь, *pf. of* ~ать.

аýк|нуться, нусь, *pf. of* ~аться; как ~нется,

так и откли́кнется serves you, *etc.*, right; do as you would be done by.

аукцио́н, а, *m.* auction; продава́ть с ~a to sell by auction.

аукцио́н|ный, *adj. of* ~; a. зал auction room.

ау́л, а, *m.* aul (*mountain village in Caucasus*).

ауспи́ци|и, й, *no sing.* auspices.

а́ут, а, *m.* (*sport*) out (*also as interj.*).

аутенти́ч|ный (~ен, ~на), *adj.* authentic.

аутодафе́, *indecl., n.* auto-da-fé.

афа́зи|я, и, *f.* (*med.*) aphasia.

афга́н|ец, ца, *m.* Afghan.

афга́нк|а, и, *f.* Afghan (woman).

афга́нский, *adj.* Afghan.

афе́р|а, ы, *f.* (*coll.*) speculation; trickery.

афери́ст, а, *m.* speculator; trickster.

афи́нск|ий, *adj.* Athenian; ~ие вечера́, ~ие но́чи orgies.

афиня́н|ин, ина, *pl.* ~е, ~, *m.* Athenian.

афи́нянк|а, и, *f.* Athenian (woman).

афи́ш|а, и, *f.* poster, placard.

афиши́р|овать, ую, *impf.* to parade, advertise.

афори́зм, а, *m.* aphorism.

афористи́ческий, *adj.* aphoristic.

афористи́ч|ный (~ен, ~на), *adj.* aphoristic.

африка́н|ец, ца, *m.* African.

африка́нк|а, и, *f.* African (woman).

африка́нск|ий, *adj.* African; ~ие стра́сти (*coll.*) unbridled passions.

афро́нт, а, *m.* (*obs.*) insult.

аффе́кт, а, *m.* (*psych., leg.*) fit of passion; temporary insanity.

аффекта́ци|я, и, *f.* affectation.

аффекти́рованный, *adj.* affected.

а́ффикс, а, *m.* (*ling.*) affix.

ах, *interj.* ah! oh!; *as noun* а́х|и, ~ов, *no sing.*, exclamations of 'ah!', 'oh!'

а́хань|е, я, *n.* (*coll.*) sighing.

а́ха|ть, ю, *impf.* (*coll.*) to sigh, to exclaim 'ah!', 'oh!'

ахилле́сов, *adj.* ~a пята́ Achilles heel; ~o сухожи́лие (*anat.*) Achilles tendon.

ахине́|я, и, *f.* (*coll.*) nonsense; нести́ ~ю to talk nonsense.

а́х|нуть, ну, нешь, *pf.* **1.** *pf. of* ~ать; он и а. не успе́л before he knew where he was. **2.** (*coll.*) to bang.

а́ховый, *adj.* (*coll.*) **1.** breath-taking; он па́рень a. he is a terrific chap. **2.** rotten.

ахромати́зм, а, *m.* achromatism.

ахромати́ческий, *adj.* achromatic.

ахтерште́в|ень, ня, *m.* (*naut.*) stern-post.

ахти́, *interj.* (*coll.*) alas!; a. мне! woe is me!; не a. как, не a. како́й not particularly, not particularly good; он был студе́нтом не a. каки́м he was not a very bright student.

ацетиле́н, а, *m.* (*chem.*) acetylene.

ацето́н, а, *m.* (*chem.*) acetone.

ацте́к, а, *m.* Aztec.

ашу́г, а, *m.* ashug (*folk poet and singer in the Caucasus*).

аэра́ри|й, я, *m.* (*med.*) aerarium.

аэро- aero-; air-, aerial.

аэровокза́л, а, *m.* airport building.

аэродина́мик|а, и, *f.* aerodynamics.

аэродро́м, а, *m.* aerodrome.

аэрозо́л|ь, я, *m.* aerosol.

аэрона́вт, а, *m.* aeronaut.

аэрона́втик|а, и, *f.* aeronautics.

аэропла́н, а, *m.* (*obs.*) aeroplane.

аэропо́рт, а, *m.* airport.

аэропо́чт|а, ы, *f.* (*obs.*) air mail.

аэроса́н|и, е́й, *no sing.* aero-sleigh.

аэросе́в, а, *m.* aerial sowing.

аэроста́т, а, *m.* balloon; a. загражде́ния barrage balloon.

аэроста́тик|а, и, *f.* aerostatics.

аэросъёмк|а, и, *f.* aerial photograph.

аэрохо́д, а, *m.* hovercraft.

Б

б, *particle* = бы (*after words ending in vowel*).

ба, *interj.* (*coll.*) hullo! well! (*expressing surprise*).

ба́б|а¹, ы, *f.* **1.** married peasant woman. **2.** (*coll. or dial.*) wife, old woman; (*pl.*) womenfolk. **3.** (*coll.*) woman; бой-б. (*coll.*) virago; ка́менная б. stone image; снежная б. snowman. **4.** (*coll.*) 'old woman' (*said of a man*).

ба́б|а², ы, *f.* (*tech.*) ram (*of pile-driver*).

ба́б|а³, ы, *f.* baba (*cylindrical cake*); ро́мовая б. rum-baba.

ба́ба-яга́, ба́бы-яги́, *f.* Baba-Yaga (*witch in Russian folk-tales*).

баба́х, *interj.* (*expressing noise of heavily falling object*) bang!

баба́хн|уть, у, ешь, *pf.* (*coll.*) to bang; ~уло (*impers.*) there was a bang.

бабби́т, а, *m.* (*tech.*) babbit.

бабёнк|а, и, *f.* (*coll.*) wench.

ба́б|ий, *adj.* (*coll.*) women's; womanish; ~ье ле́то Indian summer; ~ьи ска́зки old wives' tales.

ба́бк|а¹, и, *f.* **1.** (*coll., obs.*) grandmother. **2.** (повива́льная) б. midwife.

ба́бк|а², и, *f.* **1.** (*anat.*) pastern. **2.** knuckle-bone; ~и (*pl.*) babki (*Russian children's game*). **3.** (*tech.*) mandrel.

бáбк|а³, и, *f.* (*dial.*) shock, stook (*of corn*).

бáбник, а, *m.* (*coll.*) ladies' man.

бáбнича|ть, ю, *impf.* **1.** (*dial.*) to be a midwife. **2.** (*coll.*) to be a ladies' man.

бáбочк|а, и, *f.* butterfly; ночнáя б. moth.

бабуѝн, а, *m.* (*zool.*) baboon.

бáбушк|а, и, *f.* grandmother; (*coll.*) grandma, grannie (*as mode of address to old woman*); б. нáдвое сказáла we shall see!

бáбушкин, *adj.* grandmother's.

бабь|ё, я, *n.* (*collect.*) womenfolk.

бавáр|ец, ца, *m.* Bavarian.

бавáрк|а, и, *f.* Bavarian (woman).

бавáрский, *adj.* Bavarian.

багáж, á, *m.* luggage; сдать своѝ вéщи в б. to register one's luggage.

багáжник, а, *m.* luggage carrier, rack; boot (*of motor-car*).

багáж|ный, *adj. of* ~; б. вагóн luggage van; ~ная квитáнция luggage receipt.

баг|óр, рá, *m.* boat-hook.

багрéц, á, *m.* crimson, purple.

бáгр|ить, ю, ишь, *impf.* **1.** to gaff. **2.** (*sl.*) to steal; pilfer.

багр|ѝть, ю, ѝшь, *impf.* to paint purple, crimson; to incarnadine.

багровé|ть, ю, *impf.* (*of* по~) to turn crimson, purple.

багрóв|ый (~, ~а), *adj.* crimson, purple.

багрян|ец, ца, *m.* crimson, purple.

багряни́ц|а, ы, *f.* (*hist.*) purple (mantle).

багря́нник, а, *m.* (*bot.*) Judas-tree.

багря́н|ый (~, ~а), *adj.* (*poet.*) crimson, purple.

багу́льник, а, *m.* (*bot.*) Labrador tea, wild rosemary (*Ledum*).

бадминтóн, а, *m.* badminton.

бад|ья́, ьи́, *g. pl.* ~éй, *f.* tub.

бáз|а, ы, *f.* **1.** (*in var. senses*) base; depot; centre. **2.** basis; на ~е (+*g.*) on the basis (of); подвестѝ ~у (под+*a.*) to give good grounds (for).

базáльт, а, *m.* basalt.

базáльтовый, *adj.* basaltic.

базáр, а, *m.* market; bazaar; птѝчий б. bird-colony on sea-shore; (*fig., coll.*) row, din; что за б.! what a row!

базáр|ный, *adj. of* ~; (*coll.*) of the market-place, rough, crude; ~ная бáба noisy woman, fishwife; б. день market-day; ~ная рýгань billingsgate.

базéдов, *adj.* (*med.*) ~а болéзнь exophthalmic goitre (Basedow's disease).

базилѝк|а, и, *f.* (*archit.*) basilica.

базѝр|овать, ую, *impf.* (на+*p.*) to base (on).

базѝр|оваться, уюсь, *impf.* (на+*p.*) **1.** to be based (on), to rest (on); все егó мнéния ~уются на газéтах all his opinions are based on what he reads in the newspapers. **2.** (*mil.*) to base oneself (on), be based (on).

бáзис, а, *m.* base; basis.

бáиньки = бай-бáй.

ба|ѝ, я, *m.* bai (*rich landowner in Central Asia*).

бай-бáй, *interj.* bye-byes; порá б.! time for bye-byes!

байбáк, á, *m.* (*zool.*) steppe marmot; (*fig.*) lazybones.

байдáрк|а, и, *f.* (Aleutian) canoe.

байдáр|очный, *adj. of* ~ка; ~очная грéбля (canoe-)paddling.

бáйк|а¹, и, *f.* flannelette.

бáйк|а², и, *f.* (*dial.*) story.

бáйковый, *adj.* flannelette.

байронѝческий, *adj.* Byronic.

бак¹, а, *m.* cistern; tank.

бак², а, *m.* (*naut.*) forecastle.

бакалáвр, а, *m.* bachelor (*holder of bachelor's degree*).

бакалéйн|ый, *adj.* grocery; ~ая лáвка grocer's shop.

бакалéйщик, а, *m.* grocer.

бакалé|я, и, *f.* **1.** (*collect.*) groceries. **2.** grocer's shop.

бáкан, а, *m.* (*naut.*) buoy.

бакáут, а, *m.* (*bot.*) lignum vitae, guaiacum.

бáкен = бáкан.

бакенбáрд|ы, ~, *sing.* ~а, ~ы, *f.* side-whiskers.

бáкенщик, а, *m.* buoy-keeper.

бáкен|ы, ов, *sing.* ~, ~а, *m.* (*obs.*) side-whiskers.

бáк|и, ~, *no sing.* = бакенбáрды.

бакѝнский, *adj.* (of) Baku.

баккарá¹, *indecl., n.* (Baccarat) cut glass.

баккарá², *indecl., n.* baccarat (*card-game*).

баклáг|а, и, *f.* flask, water-bottle.

баклажáн, а, *m.* (*bot.*) aubergine, egg-plant.

баклáн, а, *m.* (*zool.*) cormorant.

баклýши, *now only in phrase* (*coll.*) бить б. to idle, fritter away one's time.

баклýшнича|ть, ю, *impf.* (*coll.*) to idle.

бáк|овый, *adj. of* ~²; bow; б. гребéц bow oarsman.

бактериáльный, *adj.* bacterial.

бактерѝйный, *adj.* bacterial.

бактерióлог, а, *m.* bacteriologist.

бактериологѝческ|ий, *adj.* bacteriological; ~ая войнá bacteriological, germ warfare.

бактериолóги|я, и, *f.* bacteriology.

бактéри|я, и, *f.* bacterium.

бакшѝш, а, *m.* bakshish; tip; bribe.

бал, а, о ~е, **на** ~ý, *pl.* ~ы́, *m.* ball, dance; кóнчен б.! it's all over, that's that.

балабóлк|а, и, *m. and f.* (*coll.*) **1.** (*f.*) pendant. **2.** (*f.*) (*child's*) rattle. **3.** (*m. and f.*) chatterbox.

балагáн, а, *m.* **1.** booth (*at fairs*). **2.** low farce; (*fig.*) farce.

балагáн|ить, ю, ишь, *impf.* (*coll.*) to play the fool.

балага́н|ный, *adj. of* ~; farcical.
балага́нщик, а, *m.* (*coll.*) **1.** showman. **2.** clown, joker.
балагу́р, а, *m.* joker, clown.
балагу́р|ить, ю, ишь, *impf.* to jest, joke.
балагу́рств|о, а, *n.* foolery, buffoonery.
бала́ка|ть, ю, *impf.* (*dial.*) to chatter, natter.
балала́ечник, а, *m.* balalaika-player.
балала́|ечный, *adj. of* ~йка.
балала́йк|а, и, *f.* balalaika.
баламу́т, а, *m.* (*coll.*) trouble-maker.
баламу́|тить, чу, тишь, *impf.* (*of* вз~) (*coll.*) to stir up, trouble (*water*); (*fig.*) to upset.
бала́нд|а, ы, *f.* (*sl.*) skilly (*in prison or camp*).
бала́нс¹, а, *m.* (*econ.*) balance; плате́жный б. balance of payment; торго́вый б. balance of trade.
бала́нс², а, *m.* pulpwood.
балансёр, а, *m.* tightrope-walker.
баланси́р, а, *m.* (*tech.*) **1.** bob, (balance) beam, equalizer; rocking beam, rocking shaft. **2.** balance-wheel (*in clock*).
баланси́р|овать, ую, *impf.* **1.** (*impf. only*) to keep one's balance, balance. **2.** (*pf.* с~) (*bookkeeping*) to balance.
балахо́н, а, *m.* loose overall; (*coll.*) shapeless garment.
балбе́с, а, *m.* (*coll.*) booby.
балбе́снича|ть, ю, *impf.* (*coll.*) to idle away one's time.
балд|а́, ы́, *f.* **1.** (*tech.*) heavy hammer, sledge-hammer. **2.** (*dial.*) knob, knur. **3.** (*m. and f.*) (*fig., coll.*) blockhead.
балдахи́н, а, *m.* canopy.
балдёж, а́, *m.* (*sl.*) 'high' (*state*).
балери́н|а, ы, *f.* ballerina.
бале́т, а, *m.* ballet.
балетме́йстер, а, *m.* ballet-master.
бале́т|ный, *adj. of* ~.
балетома́н, а, *m.* balletomane.
балетома́ни|я, и, *f.* balletomania.
ба́лк|а¹, и, *f.* beam, girder; а́нкерная б. tie-beam; попере́чная б. cross-beam; решётчатая б. lattice girder; клёпаные ~и riveted girders; прока́тные ~и rolled girders.
ба́лк|а², и, *f.* gully; dried-up river-bed.
балка́нский, *adj.* Balkan.
балка́р|ец, ца, *m.* Balkar(ian).
балко́н, а, *m.* balcony.
балл, а, *m.* **1.** (*meteor.*) number; ве́тер в пять ~ов wind force 5; о́блачность в семь ~ов 7/10ths cloud. **2.** mark (*in school*); о́бщий б. total mark(s); проходно́й б. pass mark.
балла́д|а, ы, *f.* **1.** ballad. **2.** (*mus.*) ballade.
балла́ст, а, *m.* ballast (*also fig.*).
балли́стик|а, и, *f.* ballistics.
баллисти́ческий, *adj.* ballistic.
ба́лл|овый, *adj. of* ~ 1.

балло́н, а, *m.* **1.** balloon (*vessel*); container (*of glass, metal, or rubber*); carboy; б. с кислоро́дом oxygen cylinder; кати́ть б. (на+ *a.*) to run down, knock (*fig.*). **2.** (*motor-car, etc.*) balloon tyre.
баллоти́р|овать, ую, *impf.* to ballot (for), vote (for).
баллоти́р|оваться, уюсь, *impf.* **1.** (в+*a.*, на+*a.*) to stand (for), be a candidate (for); б. на до́лжность секретаря́ па́ртии to stand for secretary of the party. **2.** (*pass. of* ~овать) to be put to the vote.
баллотиро́вк|а, и, *f.* **1.** vote, ballot, poll. **2.** voting, balloting, polling.
баллотиро́в|очный, *adj. of* ~ка; б. бюллете́нь ballot paper.
ба́лл|ьный, *adj. of* ~ 2.
бало́в|анный, *p.p.p. of* ~а́ть and *adj.* (*coll.*) spoiled.
бал|ова́ть, у́ю, *impf.* (*of* из~). **1.** to spoil, indulge; to pet, pamper. **2.** (*coll.*) to play about; to play up; мото́р ~у́ет the engine is playing up. **3.** (+*i.*; *coll.*) to play (with), amuse oneself (with), toy (with). **4.** (*coll., obs., or dial.*) to get up to monkey business (*sc.* to engage in brigandage, practise immorality, *etc.*).
бал|ова́ться, у́юсь, *impf.* **1.** to play about; to get up to monkey tricks. **2.** (+*i.*; *coll.*) to play (with), amuse oneself (with), toy (with). **3.** (*coll.*) to indulge in. **4.** = ~ова́ть 4.
ба́лов|ень, ня, *m.* **1.** spoilt child; pet, favourite; б. судьбы́ favourite of fortune. **2.** naughty child.
баловни́к, а́, *m.* (*coll.*) **1.** naughty child; mischievous person. **2.** pet; favourite. **3.** (*obs.*) one who spoils someone.
баловств|о́, а́, *n.* (*coll.*) **1.** spoiling, over-indulgence; petting, pampering. **2.** mischievousness; monkey tricks.
ба́л|очный, *adj.* (*tech.*) *of* ~ка¹.
балти́|ец, йца, *m.* sailor of the (Soviet) Baltic Fleet.
балти́йский, *adj.* Baltic.
балы́к, а́, *m.* balyk (*cured fillet of sturgeon, etc.*).
бальза́м, а, *m.* balsam; (*fig.*) balm.
бальзами́н, а, *m.* (*bot.*) balsam.
бальзами́р|овать, ую, *impf.* (*of* на~) to embalm.
бальзамиро́вк|а, и, *f.* embalming.
бальзамиро́вщик, а, *m.* embalmer.
бальзами́ческ|ий, *adj.* (*bot.*) balsam, balsamic; (*fig.*) balmy; ~ая пи́хта balsam fir; б. во́здух balmy air.
бальнео́лог, а, *m.* (*med.*) balneologist.
бальнеологи́ческий, *adj.* (*med.*) balneological.
бальнеоло́ги|я, и, *f.* (*med.*) balneology.
бальнеотерапи́|я, и, *f.* medicinal bathing.
ба́льник, а, *m.* (*school sl.*; *obs.*) report.

ба́л|ьный, *adj. of* ~; ~ьное пла́тье ball-dress.
балюстра́д|а, ы, *f.* (*archit.*) balustrade.
баля́син|а, ы, *f.* baluster.
баля́снича|ть, ю, *impf.* (*coll.*) to jest.
баля́с|ы, ~, *no sing.* banister; точи́ть б. (*fig.*, *coll.*) to jest.
бамбу́к, а, *m.* bamboo.
бамбу́ков|ый, *adj.* bamboo; ~ое положе́ние (*coll.*) awkward position.
ба́мовский, *adj.* (of the) BAM (*Baykal–Amur railway*).
бана́льност|ь, и, *f.* 1. banality. 2. banal remark; platitude.
бана́л|ьный (~ен, ~ьна), *adj.* banal, trite.
бана́н, а, *m.* banana.
бана́н|овый, *adj. of* ~.
ба́нд|а, ы, *f.* band, gang.
банда́ж, а́, *m.* 1. bandage; грыжево́й б. truss. 2. jock-strap. 3. (*tech.*) tyre, band (*of metal*).
бандеро́л|ь, и, *f.* 1. wrapper (*for dispatching newspapers, etc., by post*). 2. 'printed matter', 'book post'; отправля́ть ~ью to send as printed matter, by book post. 3. label (*certifying payment of tax, etc.*).
банди́т, а, *m.* bandit, brigand; gangster.
бандити́зм, а, *m.* brigandage; gangsterism.
банди́т|ский, *adj. of* ~.
банду́р|а, ы, *f.* (*mus.*) bandura (*Ukrainian string instrument similar to large mandoline*).
бандури́ст, а, *m.* (*mus.*) bandura-player.
банк, а, *m.* (*fin.*) bank (*also in card-games*). 2. faro (*card-game*).
ба́нк|а¹, и, *f.* (*cul.*) (glass) jar; (*med.*) cupping-glass; апте́чная б. gallipot.
ба́нк|а², и, *f.* (*naut.*) thwart; bank.
ба́нк|а³, и, *f.* bank, shoal.
банке́т¹, а, *m.* banquet.
банке́т², а, *m.* bank (*of earth or stones*), embankment.
банки́р, а, *m.* banker.
банки́р|ский, *adj. of* ~; б. дом banking-house.
банкно́т, а, *m.* (*fin.*) bank-note.
банкно́т|а, ы, *f.* = ~.
ба́нк|овский, *adj. of* ~; б. биле́т bank-note; ~овская кни́жка passbook, bank-book.
ба́нк|овый, *adj. of* ~; б. аккредити́в circular note; б. биле́т bank-note; б. слу́жащий bank clerk.
банкомёт, а, *m.* banker (*at cards*); croupier.
банкро́т, а, *m.* bankrupt; объявля́ть ~ом to declare bankrupt.
банкро́|титься, чусь, ти́шься, *impf.* (*of* о~) to become bankrupt (*also fig.*).
банкро́тств|о, а, *n.* bankruptcy.
ба́нник, а, *m.* (*mil.*) cleaning rod, rammer.
ба́н|ный, *adj. of* ~я; б. ве́ник besom used in Russian baths; (он) приста́л как б. лист (*coll.*) (he) sticks like a leech.

бант, а, *m.* bow; завяза́ть ~ом to tie in a bow.
ба́нтик, а, *m. dim. of* бант; гу́бки ~ом Cupid's bow.
ба́нщик, а, *m.* bath-house attendant.
ба́н|я, и, *f.* (*Russian*) baths; bath-house; зада́ть ~ю (+*d.*; *coll.*) to give it (someone) hot; крова́вая б. blood-bath.
бапти́зм, а, *m.* the doctrine of Baptists.
бапти́ст, а, *m.* Baptist.
бапти́стский, *adj.* Baptist.
бар¹, а, *m.* (snack-)bar.
бар², а, *m.* (*naut.*) (sand-)bar.
бар³, а, *m.* (*phys.*) bar (*unit of atmospheric pressure*).
бараба́н, а, *m.* drum (*also tech.*).
бараба́н|ить, ю, ишь, *impf.* to drum, play the drum(s); (*fig., coll.*) to patter, gabble; дождь ~ил в о́кна the rain was drumming on the windows; б. на роя́ле to drum on the piano.
бараба́н|ный, *adj. of* ~; ~ная дробь drum-roll; ~ная перепо́нка (*anat.*) ear-drum, tympanum.
бараба́нщик, а, *m.* drummer.
бара́к, а, *m.* wooden barrack; hut (*mil.; also in hospitals, esp. as infectious diseases ward*).
бара́н, а, *m.* ram; sheep; смо́трит, как б. на но́вые воро́та (*coll.*) he looks quite lost.
бара́н|ий, *adj.* 1. sheep's; согну́ть в б. рог (*coll.*) to make (someone) knuckle under. 2. sheepskin; б. полушу́бок sheepskin coat. 3. mutton; ~ья котле́та mutton chop.
бара́нин|а, ы, *f.* mutton.
бара́нк|а, и, *f.* 1. baranka (*ring-shaped roll*). 2. (*coll.*) steering-wheel.
барахл|и́ть, ю, и́шь, *impf.* (*coll.*) 1. to pink (*of an engine*). 2. to talk nonsense.
барахл|о́, а́, *n.* (*collect.; coll.*) 1. old clothes; jumble; goods and chattels, odds and ends; торго́вец ~о́м second-hand dealer. 2. trash, junk.
барахо́лк|а, и, *f.* (*coll.*) second-hand goods market, stall.
барах|о́льный, *adj. of* ~ло́.
барахо́льщик, а, *m.* (*coll.*) second-hand dealer.
бара́хта|ться, юсь, *impf.* (*coll.*) to flounder; to wallow.
бара́|чный, *adj. of* ~к.
бара́ш|ек, ка, *m.* 1. young ram; lamb; б. в бума́жке (*iron.*) bribe. 2. lambskin. 3. (*pl.*) 'white horses' (*on surface of sea, etc.*). 4. (*pl.*) fleecy clouds. 5. small curls; зави́ться~ком to have one's hair done in small curls. 6. (*tech*) wing nut, thumbscrew. 7. (*bot.*) catkin.
бара́шковый, *adj.* lambskin.
барбари́с, а, *m.* barberry.
барбо́с, а, *m.* 'Barbos' (*name given to house-dogs; fig. of* coarse, rude person).

барви́н|ок, ка, *m.* (*bot.*) periwinkle (*Vinca minor*).

бард, а, *m.* bard.

бард|а́, ы́, *f.* distillery waste.

барда́к, а́, *m.* (*coll.*) brothel; настоя́щий б. (*fig.*) complete chaos.

барелье́ф, а, *m.* bas-relief.

баре́тк|а, и, *f.* (*coll., obs.*) (woman's) shoe, slipper.

ба́рж|а, и, *f.* barge.

барж|а́, и́, *g. pl.* ~е́й = ба́ржа.

ба́ри|й, я, *m.* (*chem.*) barium.

ба́р|ин, а, *pl.* ~е and ~ы, ~, *m.* barin (*member of landowning gentry*); landowner; gentleman; master; (*as mode of address employed by peasants, servants, etc.*) sir; оде́т ~ином dressed like a gentleman; жить ~ином to live like a lord.

бари́т, а, *m.* (*min.*) barytes.

баритóн, а, *m.* baritone.

ба́рич, а, *m.* barin's son; (*coll., pejor.*) = ба́рин.

ба́рк|а, и, *f.* wooden barge.

баркаро́л|а, ы, *f.* (*mus.*) barcarole.

барка́с, а, *m.* launch; long boat.

ба́рмен, а, *m.* barman, bar-tender.

ба́рм|ы, ~, *no sing.* (*hist.*) small shoulder mantle (*worn by Moscow princes*).

барóграф, а, *m.* barograph, self-recording barometer.

барóкко, *indecl., n.* baroque.

барóметр, а, *m.* barometer.

барометри́ческий, *adj.* barometric.

барóн, а, *m.* baron.

баронéсс|а, ы, *f.* baroness.

барóнский, *adj.* baronial.

барóнств|о, а, *n.* barony.

ба́рочник, а, *m.* bargee.

ба́р|очный, *adj. of* ~ка.

барóчный, *adj.* baroque.

баррика́д|а, ы, *f.* barricade.

баррикади́р|овать, ую, *imperf.* (*of* за~) to barricade.

баррика́д|ный, *adj. of* ~a.

барс, а, *m.* (*zool.*) ounce, snow leopard (*Uncia uncia*).

ба́рск|ий, *adj. of* ба́рин; б. дом manor-house; жить на ~ую нóгу to live like a lord.

ба́рс|овый, *adj. of* ~.

ба́рственный, *adj.* lordly, grand.

ба́рств|о, а, *n.* 1. lordliness. 2. (*collect.*) gentry.

ба́рств|овать, ую, *impf.* to live in idleness and plenty.

барсу́к, á, *m.* badger.

барсу́чий, *adj.* 1. *adj. of* барсу́к. 2. badger-skin.

барха́н, а, *m.* (sand-)dune (*in steppe or desert*).

ба́рхат, а, *m.* velvet.

бархати́ст|ый (~, ~a), *adj.* velvety.

ба́рхатк|а, и, *f.* piece of velvet; velvet ribbon.

ба́рхатный, *adj.* 1. velvet; б. сезóн autumn season, autumn months. 2. (*fig.*) velvety.

ба́рхат|цы, цев, *sing.* ~ец, ~ца, *m.* (African) marigold (*Tagetes*).

бархóтк|а, и, *f.* velvet ribbon.

барч|óнок, óнка, *pl.* ~áта, ~áт, *m.* barin's son.

барчу́к, á, *m.* (*coll.*) barin's son.

ба́рщин|а, ы, *f.* (*hist.*) corvée.

ба́рын|я, и, *f.* barin's wife; lady; mistress; (*as term of address employed by peasants, servants, etc.*) madam.

бары́ш, á, *m.* profit.

бары́шник, а, *m.* 1. profiteer; speculator (*esp. in theatre tickets*). 2. horse-dealer.

бары́шнича|ть, ю, *impf.* to profiteer; (+*i.*) to speculate (in).

бары́шничеств|о, а, *n.* profiteering; speculation.

ба́рыш|ня, ни, *g. pl.* ~ень, *f.* 1. girl of gentry family; (*as term of address employed by peasants, servants, etc.*) miss. 2. (*coll.*) girl, young lady. 3. (*coll., obs.*) female assistant; телефóнная б. (*female*) telephone operator.

барье́р, а, *m.* barrier (*also fig.*); (*sport*) hurdle; взять б. to clear a hurdle; поста́вить когó-н. к ~y to make someone fight a duel.

бас, а, *pl.* ~ы́, *m.* (*mus.*) bass.

ба́с|енный, *adj. of* ~ня.

баси́ст|ый (~, ~a), *adj.* (*coll.*) bass.

ба|си́ть, шу́, си́шь, *impf.* (*coll.*) to speak (*or* sing) in a deep voice.

баск, а, *m.* Basque.

баскетбóл, а, *m.* (*sport*) basket-ball.

баскетболи́ст, а, *m.* basket-ball player.

баскóнк|а, и, *f.* Basque (woman).

ба́скский, *adj.* Basque.

басма́ч, á, *m.* (*hist.*) basmach (*member of anti-Soviet movement in Central Asia*).

басма́честв|о, а, *n.* basmachestvo (*anti-Soviet movement in Central Asia*).

баснопи́с|ец, ца, *m.* (*lit.*) writer of fables.

баснослóви|е, я, *n.* (*obs.*) 1. mythology. 2. (*collect.*) fabulous stories, fabrications.

баснослóв|ный (~ен, ~на), *adj.* 1. mythical, legendary. 2. (*fig., coll.*) fabulous.

ба́с|ня, ни, *g. pl.* ~ен, *f.* 1. fable. 2. (*fig., coll.*) fable, fabrication.

бас|óвый, *adj. of* ~; б. ключ (*mus.*) bass clef.

бас|óк, ка́, *m.* (*mus.*) bass-string.

басóн, а, *m.* braid.

бассéйн, а, *m.* 1. (*man-made*) pool; reservoir; б. для пла́вания swimming-pool. 2. (*geogr.*) basin; каменноýгольный б. coalfield.

ба́ста, *interj.* (*coll.*) that's enough! that'll do!

бастио́н, а, *m.* (*mil. and fig.*) bastion.

баст|ова́ть, у́ю, *impf.* to strike, go on strike; to be on strike.

бастр, а, *m.* brown sugar.

баст|у́ющий, *pres. part.* of ~ова́ть *and adj.* striking; *as noun* б., ~у́ющего, *m.* striker.

басурма́н, а, *m.* (*obs.*) infidel (*esp. Mohammedan*).

батале́р, а, *m.* (*naut.*) storeman; petty officer in charge of stores.

батали́ст, а, *m.* painter of battle-pieces.

бата́ли|я, и, *f.* 1. (*obs.*) battle. 2. (*coll.*) fight; row, squabble.

бата́л|ьный, *adj. of* ~ия; ~ьная карти́на battle-piece.

батальо́н, а, *m.* (*mil.*) battalion; стрелко́вый б. rifle battalion; б. свя́зи signal battalion.

батальо́н|ный, *adj. of* ~; б. команди́р battalion commander; *as noun* б., ~ного, *m.* = б. команди́р.

батаре́|ец, йца, *m.* (*mil.*; *coll.*) gunner.

батаре́йк|а, и, *f.* (*electric*) battery.

батаре́|йный, *adj. of* ~я; ~йная па́луба (*naut.*) gun deck; б. приёмник (*radio*) battery set.

батаре́|я, и, *f.* (*mil. and tech.*) battery; б. парово́го отопле́ния (central heating) radiator; б. сухи́х элеме́нтов dry battery; аккумуля́торная б. storage battery.

ба́теньк|а, и, *m.* (*coll.*) (*familiar mode of address*) old chap!

бати́ст, а, *m.* cambric, lawn.

бати́ст|овый, *adj. of* ~.

батисфе́р|а, ы, *f.* bathysphere.

ба́тник, а, *m.* shirt-waister (blouse).

бато́г, а́, *m.* (*obs. or dial.*) 1. rod, cudgel; не жале́ть ~о́в not to spare the rod. 2. walking-stick.

бато́н, а, *m.* 1. long loaf. 2. stick (*of confectionery*).

батра́к, а́, *m.* farm-labourer.

батра́|цкий, *adj. of* ~к.

батра́честв|о, а, *n.* 1. farm work. 2. (*collect.*) farm-labourers.

батра́ч|ить, у, ишь, *impf.* to work as a farm-labourer.

бату́т, а, *m.* (*sport*) trampoline.

ба́тьк|а, и, *m.* (*coll. or dial.*) = ба́тюшка 1.

ба́тюшк|а, и, *m.* 1. (*coll.*) father; как вас по ~е? what is your patronymic? 2. (*as mode of address to priests*) father. 3. (*coll.*) old chap! my dear fellow!

ба́тюшки, *interj.* б. (мой)! good gracious!

ба́т|я, и, *m.* (*dial.*) = ~юшка.

бау́л, а, *m.* trunk.

бах, *interj.* bang!

ба́ха|ть, ю, *impf. of* ба́хнуть.

ба́ха|ться, юсь, *impf. of* ба́хнуться.

бахва́л, а, *m.* (*coll.*) braggart, boaster.

бахва́л|иться, юсь, ишься, *impf.* (*coll.*; +*i.*) to brag (of).

бахва́льств|о, а, *n.* (*coll.*) bragging.

ба́хн|уть, у, ешь, *pf.* (*coll.*) 1. to bang; to bark (*of gunfire*). 2. to bang, slap; б. кого́-н. по спине́ to slap someone on the back.

ба́хн|уться, усь, ешься, *pf.* (*coll.*) to bang, bump (oneself); (+*i.*) б. голово́й о стол to bang one's head on the table.

бахром|а́, ы́, *f.* fringe.

бахро́мчатый, *adj.* fringed.

бахч|а́, и́, *f.* (water-)melon plantation; pumpkin (gourd) field.

бахчево́дств|о, а, *n.* melon-growing.

бахч|ево́й, *adj. of* ~а; ~евы́е культу́ры melons and gourds.

бац, *interj.* = бах.

ба́ца|ть, ю, *impf.* 1. *impf. of* ба́цнуть. 2. (*coll.*) to tap-dance.

баци́лл|а, ы, *f.* bacillus.

бациллоноси́тел|ь, я, *m.* (bacillus-)carrier.

ба́цн|уть, у, ешь, *pf.* (*coll.*) = ба́хнуть.

ба́шенк|а, и, *f.* turret.

ба́ш|енный, *adj. of* ~ня; ~енные часы́ tower clock.

башибузу́к, а, *m.* bashi-bazouk; Turkish irregular (soldier); (*fig.*) desperado.

башк|а́, и́, *no g. pl.*, *f.* (*coll.*) head; pate; глу́пая б. blockhead.

башки́р, а, *m.* Bashkir.

башки́р|ец, ца, *m.* (*obs.*) Bashkir.

башки́рк|а, и, *f.* Bashkir (woman).

башки́рский, *adj.* Bashkir.

башкови́т|ый (~, ~a), *adj.* (*coll.*) brainy.

башлы́к, а́, *m.* hood.

башма́к, а́, *m.* shoe (*also tech.*); (*tech.*) chock; быть под ~о́м у кого́-н. to be under someone's thumb.

башма́чник, а, *m.* shoemaker, cobbler.

башма́|чный, *adj. of* ~к.

ба́ш|ня, ни, *g. pl.* ~ен, *f.* tower; turret.

башта́н, а, *m.* = бахча́.

ба|шу́, си́шь, *see* ~си́ть.

баю́ка|ть, ю, *impf.* to sing lullabies (to).

ба́юшки-баю́, *interj.* lullaby.

баяде́р|а, ы, *f.* = ~ка.

баяде́рк|а, и, *f.* bayadère.

бая́н, а, *m.* (*mus.*) bayan (*kind of accordion*).

баяни́ст, а, *m.* (*mus.*) bayan-player.

ба́|ять, ю, ешь, *impf.* (*coll.*, *obs. or dial.*) to say, talk.

бде́ни|е, я, *n.* vigil; всено́щное б. (*eccl.*) all-night vigil.

бд|еть, *1st sing. not used*, ~ишь, *impf.* (*obs.*), to keep watch, keep vigil; б. (о+*p.*) to watch (over).

бди́тельност|ь, и, *f.* vigilance, watchfulness.

бди́тел|ьный (~ен, ~ьна), *adj.* vigilant, watchful.

бебе́, *indecl.*, *n.* (*coll.*) baby.

бебе́шк|а, и, *m.* and *f.* (*coll.*) baby; наряжа́ться ~ой to dress like a little girl.

бег, а, о ~е, на ~у́, *pl.* ~а́, ~о́в, *m.* **1.** run, running; ~о́м, на ~у́ at the double; на всём ~у́ at full speed; б. на ме́сте running on the spot; marking time (*also fig.*); б. трусцо́й (*sport*) jogging. **2.** (*sport*) race; б. на коро́ткие диста́нции sprint. **3.** (*pl.*) the races (*for horses harnessed, not ridden*); trotting races; быть на ~а́х to be at the races. **4.** быть в ~а́х to be on the run; яви́ться из ~о́в to come out of hiding.

бе́га|ть, ю, *impf.* (*indet. of* бежа́ть) **1.** to run (about); (за+*i.*; *coll.*) to run (after), chase (after). **2.** (*of someone's eyes*) to rove, roam.

бегемо́т, а, *m.* hippopotamus.

бегле́ц, а́, *m.* fugitive.

бе́глост|ь, и, *f.* fluency; dexterity.

бе́гл|ый, *adj.* **1.** (*obs.*) fugitive. **2.** fluent, quick. **3.** superficial; cursory; б. взгляд fleeting glance; ~ое замеча́ние passing remark; б. звук unstable sound; б. осмо́тр cursory inspection. **4.** б. гла́сный (*gram.*) mobile vowel. **5.** б. ого́нь (*mil.*) volley fire.

бег|ово́й, *adj.* of ~; ~ова́я доро́жка race-track, running-track; ~ова́я ло́шадь race-horse.

бего́м, *adv.* running; at the double.

бего́ни|я, и, *f.* (*bot.*) begonia.

беготн|я́, и́, *f.* (*coll.*) running about; bustle.

бе́гств|о, а, *n.* flight; escape; обрати́ть в б. to put to flight; обрати́ться в б., спаса́ться ~ом to take to flight.

бе|гу́, ~жи́шь, *see* ~жа́ть.

бегу́н, а́, *m.* runner (*also tech.*); (ме́льничные) ~ы́ runners, millstones.

бегун|о́к, ка́, *m.* **1.** (*tech.*) runner. **2.** (*pl.*) small front wheels (*of locomotive*). **3.** (*pl. only*) sulky. **4.** (*coll.*) clearance chit, loan slip.

бед|а́, ы́, *pl.* ~ы, *f.* **1.** misfortune; calamity; на ~у́ unfortunately; на свою́ ~у́ to one's cost; быть ~е́! there's trouble brewing; пришла́ б. — отворя́й воро́та (*prov.*) it never rains but it pours; семь ~ — оди́н отве́т (*prov.*) in for a penny, in for a pound. **2.** (the) trouble, the matter; (*as pred.*) it is awful!; it is a trouble; б. в том, что the trouble is (that); про́сто б.! it's simply awful!; б. мне с ним (*coll.*) he's an awful trouble; не б.! it doesn't matter; что за б.! what does it matter!, so what! **3.** (*coll.*) an awful lot. **4.** б. (как) (*as adv.*; *coll.*) awfully, terribly.

бе́декер, а, *m.* guide-book, Baedeker.

бедла́м, а, *m.* bedlam.

бедне́|ть, ю, *impf.* (*of* о~) (+*i.*) to grow poor (in).

бе́дност|ь, и, *f.* poverty (*also fig.*); indigence.

беднот|а́, ы́, *f.* **1.** (*collect.*) the poor; дереве́нская б. poor peasants. **2.** (*coll.*) poverty.

бе́д|ный (~ен, ~на́, ~но), *adj.* poor; meagre; (*fig.*) barren, jejune.

бедня́г|а, и, *m.* (*coll.*) poor fellow; poor devil.

бедня́жк|а, и, *m.* and *f.* (*coll.*) **1.** *dim. of* бедня́га. **2.** *f. of* бедня́га.

бедня́к, а́, *m.* **1.** poor man. **2.** poor peasant.

бедня́|цкий, *adj.* of ~к.

бедня́честв|о, а, *n.* (*collect.*) poor peasants.

бедня́чк|а, и, *f.* poor peasant woman.

бедо́в|ый (~, ~а), *adj.* (*coll.*) sharp, lively; mischievous; daredevil.

бедоку́р, а, *m.* (*coll.*) mischief-maker; joker.

бедоку́р|ить, ю, ишь, *impf.* (*of* на~) (*coll.*) to get up to mischief, play jokes.

бе́дренный, *adj.* (*anat.*) femoral.

бед|ро́, ра́, *pl.* ~ра, ~ер, ~рам, *n.* **1.** thigh; hip. **2.** (*joint of meat*) leg.

бе́дствен|ный (~, ~на,), *adj.* disastrous, calamitous.

бе́дстви|е, я, *n.* calamity, disaster; сигна́л ~я distress signal.

бе́дств|овать, ую, *impf.* to live in poverty.

бедуи́н, а, *m.* bedouin.

бедуи́н|ский, *adj.* of ~.

беж, *indecl.*, *adj.* beige.

бе|жа́ть, гу́, жи́шь, гу́т, *impf.* (*det. of* бе́гать) **1.** to run; (*fig.*) to run, fly; to boil over; горя́чая вода́ ~жи́т из э́того кра́на hot water runs from this tap; вре́мя ~жи́т time flies. **2.** (*impf. and pf.*) to escape.

бе́жевый, *adj.* beige.

бе́жен|ец, ца, *m.* refugee.

бе́жен|ка, ки, *f.* of ~ец.

бе́женский, *adj.* refugee.

бе́женств|о, а, *n.* **1.** flight, exodus, refuge-seeking. **2.** (*collect.*) refugees.

без, *prep.*+*g.* without; in the absence of; minus, less; не б. not without, not devoid (of); б. вас in your absence; б. пяти́ (мину́т) три five (minutes) to three; б. четверти час a quarter to one; б. ма́лого (*coll.*) almost, all but; быть б. ума́ (от) to be crazy (about); не б. того́ (*coll.*) that's about it, it can't altogether be denied.

без- in-, un-, -less.

безава́рийный, *adj.* accident-free.

безала́берност|ь, и, *f.* disorder; lack of system.

безала́бер|ный (~ен, ~на), *adj.* disorderly; slovenly.

безала́берщин|а, ы, *f.* (*coll.*) muddle; slovenliness.

безалкого́льный, *adj.* non-alcoholic; б. напи́ток non-alcoholic drink, soft drink.

безапелляцио́н|ный (~ен, ~на), *adj.* peremptory, categorical.

безбе́д|ный (~ен, ~на), *adj.* well-to-do, comfortable.

безбиле́тный, *adj.* ticketless; б. пассажи́р passenger travelling without ticket; (*on ship*) stowaway.

безбо́жи|е, я, *n.* atheism.

безбо́жник, а, *m.* atheist.

безбо́жно, *adv.* (*coll.*) shamelessly, scandalously; здесь б. деру́т they fleece you shamelessly here.

безбо́жн|ый, *adj.* 1. irreligious, anti-religious. 2. (*coll.*) shameless, scandalous; ~ые це́ны outrageous prices.

безболе́знен|ный (~, ~на), *adj.* painless.

безборо́дый, *adj.* beardless (*also fig.*).

безбоя́знен|ный (~, ~на), *adj.* fearless.

безбра́чи|е, я, *n.* celibacy.

безбра́чный, *adj.* celibate.

безбре́ж|ный (~ен, ~на), *adj.* boundless.

безбро́вый, *adj.* eyebrow-less.

безбу́р|ный (~ен, ~на), *adj.* calm, peaceful.

безве́ри|е, я, *n.* unbelief.

безве́стност|ь, и, *f.* obscurity.

безве́ст|ный (~ен, ~на), *adj.* unknown; obscure; ~ное отсу́тствие absence in place unknown.

безве́тренный, *adj.* calm.

безве́три|е, я, *n.* calm.

безви́н|ный (~ен, ~на), *adj.* guiltless.

безвку́си|е, я, *n.* lack of taste.

безвку́сиц|а, ы, *f.* lack of taste; что за б.! what bad taste!

безвку́с|ный (~ен, ~на), *adj.* tasteless (*also fig.*)

безвла́сти|е, я, *n.* anarchy.

безвла́ст|ный (~ен, ~на), *adj.* powerless.

безво́д|ный (~ен, ~на), *adj.* 1. arid; waterless. 2. (*chem.*) anhydrous.

безво́дь|е, я, *n.* aridity.

безвозвра́т|ный (~ен, ~на), *adj.* irrevocable; ~ная ссу́да permanent loan.

безвозду́шный, *adj.* airless.

безвозме́здный, *adj.* gratuitous, free of charge; б. труд unpaid work.

безво́ли|е, я, *n.* lack of will; weak will.

безволо́сый, *adj.* hairless, bald.

безво́л|ьный (~ен, ~ьна), *adj.* weak-willed.

безвре́д|ный (~ен, ~на), *adj.* harmless.

безвре́менн|ый, *adj.* untimely, premature; ~ая кончи́на untimely decease.

безвре́мень|е, я, *n.* (*obs.*) 1. hard times. 2. period of (social) stagnation.

безвы́ездно, *adv.* uninterruptedly, without a break.

безвы́ездн|ый, *adj.* uninterrupted; ~ое пребыва́ние continuous residence.

безвы́ходно, *adv.* uninterruptedly, without a break.

безвы́ход|ный (~ен, ~на), *adj.* 1. hopeless, desperate; быть в ~ном положе́нии to be in a desperate position. 2. uninterrupted.

безглаго́льный, *adj.* 1. (*gram.*) without a verb. 2. (*fig., poet.*) silent, dumb.

безгла́зый, *adj.* eyeless.

безгла́с|ный (~ен, ~на), *adj.* (*fig.*) silent, dumb.

безголо́в|ый (~, ~а), *adj.* 1. headless; (*iron.*) brainless. 2. (*fig., coll.*) forgetful, scatter-brained.

безголо́сный, *adj.* (*ling.*) unvoiced.

безголо́с|ый, *adj.* weak (*of voice*); voiceless; он стал совсе́м ~ым his voice is quite ruined.

безгра́мотност|ь, и, *f.* illiteracy.

безгра́мот|ный (~ен, ~на), *adj.* illiterate (*also fig.*); ignorant.

безграни́ч|ный (~ен, ~на), *adj.* infinite, limitless, boundless; (*fig.*) extreme, extraordinary.

безгре́шност|ь, и, *f.* innocence.

безгре́ш|ный (~ен, ~на), *adj.* innocent, sinless.

безда́рност|ь, и, *f.* 1. lack of talent. 2. person without talent.

безда́р|ный (~ен, ~на), *adj.* talentless, undistinguished.

безда́р|ь (*and* бе́здар|ь), и, *f.* (*coll.*) person without talent.

безде́йствен|ный (~, ~на), *adj.* inactive.

безде́йстви|е, я, *n.* inactivity, inertia, idleness; (*leg.*) (criminal) negligence.

безде́йств|овать, ую, *impf.* to be inactive; to lie idle; not to work (*of a machine, etc.*).

безде́лиц|а, ы, *f.* trifle, bagatelle; така́я су́мма для него́ б. for him such a sum is a trifle.

безде́лк|а, и, *f.* (*coll.*) 1. trifle, bagatelle. 2. knick-knack.

безделу́шк|а, и, *f.* knick-knack.

безде́ль|е, я, *n.* idleness.

безде́льник, а, *m.* 1. idler, loafer. 2. ne'er-do-well.

безде́льниц|а, ы, *f.* of безде́льник.

безде́льнича|ть, ю, *impf.* to idle, loaf.

безде́л|ьный (~ен, ~ьна), *adj.* (*coll.*) idle.

безде́нежный, *adj.* 1. impecunious. 2. (*econ.*) non-monetary.

безде́нежь|е, я, *n.* lack of money, impecuniousness.

безде́тност|ь, и, *f.* childlessness.

безде́т|ный (~ен, ~на), *adj.* childless.

бездефици́тный, *adj.* (*econ.*) entailing no deficit; self-supporting.

безде́ятельност|ь, и, *f.* inactivity, inertia.

безде́ятел|ьный (~ен, ~ьна), *adj.* inactive; sluggish.

бе́здн|а, ы, *f.* 1. abyss, chasm. 2. (*coll.*) a huge number; б. хлопо́т a multitude, sea of troubles; б. прему́дрости (*joc.*) a mine of information.

бездо́ждь|е, я, *n.* dry weather, drought.

бездоказа́тел|ьный (~ен, ~ьна), *adj.* unsubstantiated.

бездо́м|ный (~ен, ~на), *adj.* homeless.

бездо́нный, *adj.* bottomless; (*fig., poet.*) fathomless.

бездоро́ж|ный (~ен, ~на), *adj.* without roads.

бездоро́жь|е, я, *n.* 1. absence of roads. 2. bad condition of roads; season when roads are impassable.

бездохо́д|ный (~ен, ~на), *adj.* (*econ.*) unprofitable.

безду́м|ный, (~ен, ~на), *adj.* unthinking; feckless.

безду́ши|е, я, *n.* heartlessness, callousness.

безду́ш|ный (~ен, ~на), *adj.* 1. heartless, callous. 2. inanimate; (*fig.*) soulless.

безды́мный, *adj.* smokeless; б. по́рох (*mil.*) smokeless powder.

бездыха́н|ный (~ен, ~на), *adj.* lifeless.

безе́, *indecl.*, *n.* meringue.

безжа́лост|ный (~ен, ~на), *adj.* ruthless, pitiless.

безжи́знен|ный (~, ~на), *adj.* lifeless, inanimate; (*fig.*) spiritless.

беззабо́т|ный (~ен, ~на), *adj.* carefree, light-hearted; careless.

беззаве́т|ный (~ен, ~на), *adj.* selfless, wholehearted; ~ная хра́брость selfless courage.

беззако́ни|е, я, *n.* 1. lawlessness. 2. unlawful action.

беззако́ннича|ть, ю, *impf.* (*coll.*) to transgress, break the law.

беззако́н|ный (~ен, ~на), *adj.* 1. illegal, unlawful. 2. (*poet.*) lawless, wayward.

беззапре́тн|ый, *adj.* 1. permitted; ~ая су́мма иностра́нной валю́ты permitted amount of foreign currency. 2. unrestrained.

беззасте́нчив|ый (~, ~а), *adj.* shameless; б. лгун brazen, unblushing liar; ~ая ложь barefaced lie.

беззащи́т|ный (~ен, ~на), *adj.* defenceless, unprotected.

беззвёзд|ный (~ен, ~на), *adj.* starless.

беззву́ч|ный (~ен, ~на), *adj.* soundless, noiseless.

безземе́ль|е, я, *n.* lack of land.

безземе́льный, *adj.* landless.

беззло́би|е, я, *n.* good nature, mildness.

беззло́б|ный (~ен, ~на), *adj.* mild, good-natured.

беззу́б|ый, *adj.* 1. toothless; (*fig.*) impotent, harmless; ~ая зло́ба impotent rage. 2. (*zool.*) edentate.

безле́с|ный (~ен, ~на), *adj.* woodless; treeless.

безле́сь|е, я, *n.* 1. woodless tract. 2. absence of forest.

безли́кий, *adj.* featureless.

безли́ственный, *adj.* leafless.

безли́ч|ие, ия, *n.* = ~ность.

безли́чност|ь, и, f. lack of personality; impersonality.

безли́ч|ный (~ен, ~на), *adj.* 1. without personality, characterless, impersonal. 2. (*gram.*) impersonal.

безлоша́дный, *adj.* not possessing a horse.

безлу́н|ный (~ен, ~на), *adj.* moonless.

безлю́д|ный (~ен, ~на), *adj.* uninhabited; sparsely populated; solitary, unfrequented.

безлю́дь|е, я, *n.* 1. deficiency of population; absence of human life; в дере́вне бы́ло по́лное б. the village was completely deserted. 2. lack of suitable company, lack of the right people; на б. и Фома́ дворяни́н (*prov.*) in the land of the blind the one-eyed is king.

безме́н, а, *m.* steelyard.

безме́р|ный (~ен, ~на), *adj.* immense, excessive.

безмо́зглый, *adj.* (*coll.*) brainless.

безмо́лви|е, я, *n.* silence; цари́т б. silence reigns.

безмо́лв|ный (~ен, ~на), *adj.* silent, mute, speechless; ~ное согла́сие tacit consent.

безмо́лств|овать, ую, *impf.* to keep silence.

безмото́рный, *adj.* engineless.

безмяте́жност|ь, и, f. serenity, placidity.

безмяте́ж|ный (~ен, ~на), *adj.* serene, placid.

безнадёж|ный (~ен, ~на), *adj.* hopeless; despairing; больно́й ~ен the patient's case is hopeless.

безнадзо́рност|ь, и, f. neglect.

безнадзо́рный, *adj.* neglected.

безнака́занно, *adv.* with impunity; э́то ему́ не пройдёт б. he won't get away with this.

безнака́занност|ь, и, f. impunity.

безнака́зан|ный (~, ~на), *adj.* unpunished.

безнали́чный, *adj.* without cash transfer; б. расчёт (*fin.*) clearing.

безнача́ли|е, я, *n.* anarchy.

безнача́льный, *adj.* without beginning, from eternity.

безно́гий, *adj.* 1. legless; one-legged. 2. deprived of the use of one's legs. 3. (*zool.*) apod.

безно́сый, *adj.* noseless; б. ча́йник spoutless teapot.

безнра́вственност|ь, и, f. immorality.

безнра́вствен|ный (~, ~на), *adj.* immoral.

безо, *prep.* (*before g. of* весь *and* вся́кий) = без.

безоби́д|ный (~ен, ~на), *adj.* inoffensive.

безо́блачност|ь, и, f. cloudlessness; (*fig.*) serenity.

безо́блач|ный (~ен, ~на), *adj.* cloudless; (*fig.*) serene, unclouded.

безобра́зи|е, я, *n.* **1.** ugliness. **2.** outrage; (*pl.*) disgraceful things, shocking things. **3.** (*as pred.*; *coll.*) it is disgraceful; э́то про́сто б.! it's simply disgraceful, scandalous.

безобра́|зить, жу, зишь, *impf.* (*of* о~) **1.** to disfigure, mutilate. **2.** (*coll.*) to make a nuisance of oneself, make a disturbance.

безобра́зник, а, *m.* (*coll.*) **1.** hooligan. **2.** naughty child.

безобра́знича|ть, ю, *impf.* (*coll.*) to carry on disgracefully, outrageously; to make a nuisance of oneself; to get up to mischief.

безо́браз|ный (~ен, ~на), *adj.* **1.** unadorned; not employing images. **2.** vague.

безобра́з|ный (~ен, ~на), *adj.* **1.** ugly. **2.** disgraceful, scandalous, outrageous, shocking.

безогово́рочн|ый (~а, ~о), *adj.* unconditional, unreserved.

безопа́сность, и, *f.* safety, security; Сове́т Безопа́сности Security Council.

безопа́с|ный (~ен, ~на), *adj.* safe, secure; ~ная бри́тва safety razor.

безору́ж|ный (~ен, ~на), *adj.* unarmed.

безоснова́тельный (~ен, ~ьна), *adj.* groundless.

безостано́вочный, *adj.* unceasing; non-stop.

безотве́т|ный (~ен, ~на), *adj.* **1.** (*rare*) unanswered. **2.** meek; dumb.

безотве́тственность, и, *f.* irresponsibility.

безотве́тствен|ный (~, ~на), *adj.* irresponsible.

безотгово́рочн|ый (~а, ~о), *adj.* unquestioning, implicit.

безотка́зный, *adj.* unfailing; without hitches.

безотка́тный, *adj.* (*mil.*) non-recoil.

безотлага́тельный, *adj.* urgent.

безотлу́чно, *adv.* continually; она́ нахо́дится б. до́ма she is tied to the home, she never gets out.

безотлу́ч|ный (~ен, ~на), *adj.* ever-present; continuous.

безотноси́тельно, *adv.* (к) irrespective (of); б. к его́ пла́нам я пое́ду за́втра в Ло́ндон irrespective of his plans I shall go to London tomorrow.

безотноси́тел|ьный (~ен, ~ьна), *adj.* absolute, valid absolutely.

безотра́д|ный (~ен, ~на), *adj.* cheerless.

безотры́вн|ый, *adj.* ~ое обуче́ние workers' education (*not involving taking time off from work*).

безотчётность, и, *f.* **1.** absence of control. **2.** unaccountableness; instinctiveness.

безотчёт|ный, (~ен, ~на), *adj.* **1.** not liable to account, not subject to control. **2.** unaccountable, inexplicable; unreasoning, instinctive.

безоши́боч|ный (~ен, ~на), *adj.* correct;

faultless, infallible; ~ное предсказа́ние unerring prediction.

безрабо́тиц|а, ы, *f.* unemployment.

безрабо́тн|ый, *adj.* unemployed; *as noun* ~ые, ~ых *pl.* the unemployed.

безра́дост|ный (~ен, ~на), *adj.* joyless; dismal.

безразде́л|ьный (~ен, ~ьна), *adj.* undivided; ~ьная власть complete sway; ~ьное иму́щество indivisible property.

безразли́чи|е, я, *n.* indifference.

безразли́чно (*adv.*) indifferently; отно́ситься б. (к) to be indifferent (to); б. кто, где no matter who, where.

безразли́ч|ный (~ен, ~на), *adj.* indifferent; мне ~но it's all the same to me.

безразме́р|ный (~ен, ~на), *adj.* one-size (nylon, *etc.*); ~ные носки́ stretch socks.

безрассве́т|ный (~ен, ~на), *adj.* continuous (*of night in polar regions*).

безрассу́д|ный (~ен, ~на), *adj.* reckless; foolhardy.

безрассу́дств|о, а, *n.* recklessness; foolhardiness.

безрасчёт|ный (~ен, ~на), *adj.* uneconomical.

безрезульта́тность, и, *f.* futility; failure.

безрезульта́т|ный (~ен, ~на), *adj.* futile; unsuccessful.

безре́льсов|ый, *adj.* railless; б. тра́нспорт motor transport; ~ая доро́га road.

безрессо́рный, *adj.* unsprung.

безро́г|ий, *adj.* hornless; ~ое живо́тное pollard.

безро́д|ный (~ен, ~на), *adj.* **1.** without kith or kin. **2.** (*obs.*) of humble origin. **3.** (*fig.*) homeless, stateless.

безро́пот|ный (~ен, ~на), *adj.* uncomplaining, resigned; submissive.

безрука́вк|а, и, *f.* sleeveless jacket *or* blouse.

безру́кий, *adj.* **1.** armless. **2.** one-armed. **3.** (*fig.*) clumsy.

безры́б|е, я, *n.* absence of fish; на б. и рак ры́ба (*prov.*) in the land of the blind the one-eyed is king.

безубы́точ|ный (~ен, ~на), *adj.* (*comm.*) not entailing loss.

безуда́р|ный (~ен, ~на), *adj.* (*ling.*) unaccented, unstressed.

безуде́рж|ный (~ен, ~на), *adj.* unrestrained; impetuous.

безуе́здный, *adj.* б. го́род (*hist.*) town, not being principal town of uyezd, but possessing its own administration.

безукори́знен|ный (~, ~на), *adj.* irreproachable; impeccable.

безу́м|ец, ца, *m.* **1.** (*obs.*) madman. **2.** crazy fellow.

безу́ми|е, я, *n.* **1.** madness, insanity. **2.** (*fig.*) madness; folly; довести́ до ~я to drive crazy; люби́ть до ~я to love to distraction.

безу́мно, *adv.* madly, crazily; terribly, dreadfully; я б. за́нят I am terribly busy.

безу́м|ный (~ен, ~на), *adj.* 1. mad, insane. 2. (*fig.*) mad, crazy, senseless. 3. (*coll.*) terrible; ~ные це́ны absurd prices.

безумо́лч|ный (~ен, ~на), *adj.* incessant (*of noise*).

безу́мств|о, а, *n.* madness; foolhardiness.

безу́мств|овать, ую, *impf.* to behave like a madman; to rave.

безупре́ч|ный (~ен, ~на), *adj.* irreproachable.

безуря́диц|а, ы, *f.* disorder, confusion.

безуса́дочный, *adj.* non-shrink (*of fabrics*).

безусло́вно, *adv.* 1. unconditionally, absolutely. 2. (*coll.*) of course, it goes without saying, undoubtedly.

безусло́вност|ь, и, *f.* certainty.

безусло́в|ный (~ен, ~на), *adj.* 1. unconditional, absolute. 2. undoubted, indisputable.

безуспе́ш|ный (~ен, ~на), *adj.* unsuccessful.

безуста́нный, *adj.* tireless, indefatigable.

безу́сый, *adj.* having no moustache; (*fig.*) callow, immature, 'beardless'.

безуте́ш|ный (~ен, ~на), *adj.* inconsolable.

безу́хий, *adj.* 1. earless. 2. one-eared.

безуча́сти|е, я, *n.* apathy, unconcern, neutrality.

безуча́стност|ь, и, *f.* = безуча́стие.

безуча́ст|ный (~ен, ~на), *adj.* apathetic, unconcerned, neutral.

безъязы́кий, *adj.* dumb, without a tongue.

безъязы́ч|ный (~ен, ~на), *adj.* dumb, speechless.

безыде́йност|ь, и, *f.* lack of principle(s); lack of ideals; lack of ideological content.

безыде́|йный (~ен, ~йна), *adj.* unprincipled; lacking ideals; lacking ideological content.

безызве́стност|ь, и, *f.* 1. uncertainty. 2. obscurity.

безызве́ст|ный (~ен, ~на), *adj.* unknown, obscure.

безымя́нн|ый, *adj.* nameless; anonymous; б. па́лец third finger, ring-finger; ~ая неде́ля the third week in Lent.

безынициати́в|ный (~ен, ~на), *adj.* lacking initiative.

безынтере́с|ный (~ен, ~на), *adj.* 1. uninteresting. 2. (*obs.*) disinterested.

безыску́сствен|ный (~, ~на), *adj.* artless, ingenuous.

безысхо́д|ный (~ен, ~на), *adj.* irreparable; interminable; perpetual.

бе|й, я, *m.* bey (*Turkish title*).

бе́й(те), *imp. of* бить.

бейдеви́нд, *adv.* (*naut.*) close-hauled.

бейсбо́л, а, *m.* baseball.

бейсболи́ст, а, *m.* baseball player.

бек, а, *m.* (*sport; obs.*) back.

бека́р, а, *m.* (*also as indecl. adj.*) (*mus.*) natural; до б. С natural.

бека́с, а, *m.* (*orn.*) snipe.

бекаси́нник, а, *m.* small shot.

бекаси́ный, *adj. of* бека́с.

беке́ш|а, и, *f.* (*knee-length*) winter overcoat.

беко́н, а, *m.* bacon.

беко́нный, *adj.* bacon.

белемни́т, а, *m.* (*geol.*) belemnite.

белен|а́, ы́, *f.* (*bot.*) henbane; что ты, ~ы́ объе́лся? have you gone crazy?

беле́ни|е, я, *n.* bleaching.

белёный, *adj.* bleached.

белесова́т|ый (~, ~а), *adj.* whitish.

белёсый, *adj.* whitish.

беле́|ть, ю, *impf.* (*of* по~) 1. to grow white. 2. (*no pf.*) to show up white.

беле́|ться, юсь, *impf.* to show up white.

бел|е́ц, ьца́, *m.* (*eccl.*) novice.

бёл|и, ей, *no sing.* (*med.*) leucorrhoea.

белиберд|а́, ы́, *f.* (*coll.*) nonsense, rubbish.

белизн|а́, ы́, *f.* whiteness.

бели́л|а, ~, *no sing.* 1. whitewash; свинцо́вые б. white lead; ци́нковые б. zinc white. 2. ceruse.

бели́льный, *adj.* bleaching.

бели́л|ьня, ьни, *g. pl.* ~ен, *f.* bleaching works, bleachery.

бел|и́ть, ю́, ~и́шь, *impf.* 1. (*pf.* по~) to whitewash. 2. (*pf.* на~) to whiten (*one's face, etc.*). 3. (*pf.* вы́~) to bleach.

бел|и́ться, ю́сь, ~и́шься, *impf.* 1. *pass. of* ~и́ть. 2. (*pf.* на~) to whiten one's face.

бели́ц|а, ы, *f.* (*eccl.*) female novice.

бёл|ичий, *adj. of* ~ка[1]; б. мех squirrel (fur).

бёлк|а[1], и, *f.* squirrel; верте́ться, кружи́ться как б. в колесе́ to put in much work without visible result, run round in small circles.

бёлк|а[2], и, *f.* (*coll.*) bleaching.

белкови́н|а, ы, *f.* (*chem.*) albumen.

белко́вый, *adj.* (*chem.*) albuminous.

белладо́нн|а, ы, *f.* (*bot.*) belladonna.

беллетри́ст, а, *m.* fiction writer.

беллетри́стик|а, и, *f.* (*lit.*) fiction.

беллетристи́ческий, *adj.* (*lit.*) fictional.

бело- white-.

белобры́с|ый (~, ~а), *adj.* (*coll.*) tow-haired.

белова́т|ый (~, ~а), *adj.* whitish.

белови́к, а́, *m.* fair copy (*of MS.*).

белово́й, *adj.* clean, fair; б. экземпля́р fair copy.

белогварде́|ец, йца, *m.* (*polit.*) White Guard.

белогварде́|йский, *adj. of* ~ец.

белоголо́вый, *adj.* **1.** white-haired. **2.** fair (-haired).

бел|о́к¹, ка́, *m.* (*biol.*, *chem.*) albumen; protein.

бел|о́к², ка́, *m.* white (of egg); glair.

бел|о́к³, ка́, *m.* white (of the eye).

белока́менн|ый, *adj.* (*folk poet.*) built of white stone (*esp. as epithet of Moscow*).

белокро́ви|е, я, *n.* (*med.*) leucaemia.

белоку́р|ый (~, ~а), *adj.* blond(e), fair (-haired).

белоли́ц|ый (~, ~а), *adj.* pale, white-faced.

белоподкла́дочник, а, *m.* (*hist.*) student of aristocratic appearance and reactionary views.

белору́с, а, *m.* Byelorussian (*formerly* White Russian).

белору́ск|а, и, *f.* Byelorussian (woman).

белору́сский, *adj.* Byelorussian (*formerly* White Russian).

белору́чк|а, и, *m. and f.* (*coll.*, *pejor.*) person shirking rough *or* dirty (physical) work.

белоры́биц|а, ы, *f.* white salmon.

Белосне́жк|а, и, *f.* Snow-White.

белосне́ж|ный (~ен, ~на), *adj.* snow-white.

белоте́л|ый (~, ~а), *adj.* fair-skinned.

белошве́йк|а, и, *f.* seamstress.

белошве́йн|ый, *adj.* linen; ~ая мастерска́я seamstress's workshop.

белоэмигра́нт, а, *m.* (*polit.*) White Russian emigré.

белу́г|а, и, *f.* **1.** beluga, white sturgeon (*Huso huso*). **2.** (*dial.*) white whale; реве́ть ~ой to bellow.

белу́|жий, *adj. of* ~га.

белу́жин|а, ы, *f.* (*meat of*) white sturgeon.

белу́х|а, и, *f.* white whale (*Delphinapterus leucus*).

бе́л|ый (~, ~а́, ~о), *adj.* **1.** white; ~ая берёза silver birch; б. медве́дь polar bear; ~ая сова́ snowy owl. **2.** (*as opp. to* dark *and in var. fig. senses*) white; fair; б. биле́т (*obs.*) 'white chit' (*certificate of exemption from military service*); ~ое вино́ white wine; ~ое духове́нство secular clergy; ~ое зо́лото 'white gold' (= *cotton*); ~ое кале́ние white heat, incandescence; ~ые кровяны́е ша́рики white blood corpuscles; ~ое мя́со white meat; ~ые но́чи 'white nights', 'midnight sun'; б. у́голь 'white coal' (= *water power*); б. хлеб white bread, wheatmeal bread; на ~ом све́те in all the world; средь ~а дня in broad daylight; э́то ши́то ~ыми ни́тками it is all too obvious, it is quite transparent; *as noun* ~ые, ~ых, *pl.* white-skinned people, white men. **3.** clean; blank (= unused; *fig.* unadorned); б. лист clean sheet (of paper); ~ая страни́ца blank page (*in book*); ~ые стихи́ blank

verse. **4.** (= of superior quality, of high class, *etc.*) б. гриб (edible) boletus (*mushroom*); ~ая кость (*iron.*) blue blood; ~ая куха́рка (*obs.*) head cook. **5.** ~ая горя́чка (*med.*) delirium tremens. **6.** (*polit.*) White (*also as noun*).

бельведе́р, а, *m.* belvedere.

бельги́|ец, йца, *m.* Belgian.

бельги́йк|а, и, *f.* Belgian (woman).

бельги́йский, *adj.* Belgian.

бель|ё, я́, *n.* (*collect.*) linen; ни́жнее б. underclothes; посте́льное б. bed-linen; столо́вое б. table-linen.

бель|ево́й, *adj. of* ~ё; б. шкаф linen cupboard; ~евая прище́пка clothes-peg.

бельме́с, а, *m.* ни ~а (*coll.*) nothing; он ни ~а не понима́ет he hasn't a clue.

бельм|о́, а́, *pl.* ~а, *n.* **1.** (*med.*) cataract; как б. на глазу́ (*fig.*) a thorn in the flesh; bête noire. **2.** (*pl. only*; *also* ~ы; *coll.*) eyes.

бельэта́ж, а, *m.* **1.** first floor. **2.** (*theatr.*) dress circle.

беля́к, а́, *m.* white hare.

беля́н|а, ы, *f.* (*obs.*) barge (*of unpainted wood, used on Volga and Kama rivers*).

беля́нк|а, и, *f.* **1.** blonde woman, girl. **2.** cabbage butterfly. **3.** white mushroom.

бемо́л|ь, я, *m.* (*also as indecl. adj.*) (*mus.*) flat; ре б. D flat.

бе́мск|ий, *adj.* ~ое стекло́ Bohemian glass.

бенга́льский, *adj.* Bengal; б. ого́нь Bengal light; б. язы́к Bengali.

бенедикти́н, а, *m.* benedictine (*liqueur*).

бенедикти́н|ец, ца, *m.* (*eccl.*) member of Benedictine order.

бенедикти́нский, *adj.* (*eccl.*) Benedictine.

бенефи́с, а, *m.* (*theatr.*) benefit performance; устро́ить б. (+*d.*; *sl.*) to give someone what for.

бенефи́с|ный, *adj. of* ~; б. спекта́кль benefit performance.

бенефициа́нт, а, *m.* (*theatr.*) artist for whom benefit performance is given.

бенефи́ци|я, и, *f.* (*eccl.*) living, benefice.

бензи́н, а, *m.* benzine; petrol.

бензи́н|овый, *adj. of* ~; petrol; ~овая коло́нка petrol pump.

бензиноме́р, а, *m.* petrol gauge.

бензинопрово́д, а, *m.* petrol pipe.

бензоба́к, а, *m.* petrol tank.

бензоколо́нк|а, и, *f.* petrol pump.

бензо́л, а, *m.* (*chem.*) benzol, benzene.

бензохрани́лищ|е, а, *n.* petrol tank.

бенуа́р, а, *m.* (*theatr.*) boxes (*on level of the stalls*).

бербе́р, а, *m.* Berber.

бербе́рк|а, и, *f.* Berber (woman).

бербе́рский, *adj.* Berber.

бергамо́т, а, *m.* bergamot (*kind of pear*).

бердáнк|а, и, *f.* (*obs.*) Berdan rifle.
бёрд|о, а, *n.* (*tech.*) reed (*of loom*).
бердыш, á, *m.* (*hist.*) pole-axe.
бéрег, а, о ~е, на ~ý, *pl.* ~á, *m.* bank; shore; на ~ý мóря at the seaside; вы́броситься нá берег to run aground; вы́йти из ~óв to burst its banks; сойти́ на б. to go ashore.
бер|ёг, ~еглá, *see* берéчь.
берегов|óй, *adj.* coastal; waterside; б. вéтер offshore wind, land-wind; ~áя оборóна coastal defence; ~óе прáво (*leg.*) right of salvage; ~óе судохóдство coastal shipping; ~áя лáсточка sand-martin.
бере|гý, ~жёшь, ~гýт, *see* берéчь.
бере|ди́ть, жý, ди́шь, *impf.* (*of* раз~) (*coll.*) to irritate; б. стáрые рáны (*fig.*) to re-open old wounds.
бережён|ый, *adj.* (*coll.*) guarded, preserved; ~ая копéйка рубль бережёт (*prov.*) take care of the pennies, the pounds will take care of themselves; ~ого и Бог бережёт God helps those who help themselves.
бережли́вост|ь, и, *f.* thrift, economy.
бережли́в|ый (~, ~а), *adj.* thrifty, economical.
бéрежност|ь, и, *f.* care; caution; solicitude.
бéреж|ный (~ен, ~на), *adj.* careful; cautious; solicitous.
берёз|а, ы, *f.* birch.
берéзник, а, *no pl.*, *m.* birch grove.
березня́к, á, *no pl.*, *m.* 1. birch grove. 2. birch-wood.
берёзовик, а, *m.* brown mushroom (*Boletus scaber*).
берёз|овый, *adj. of* ~а; ~овая кáша (*coll.*) the birch; a flogging.
берéйтор, а, *m.* riding-master.
берéмене|ть, ю, ешь, *impf.* (*of* за~) (*coll.*) to become pregnant.
берéме|нная (~нна), *adj.* (+*i.*) pregnant (with).
берéменност|ь, и, *f.* pregnancy; gestation; быть на пя́том мéсяце ~и to be in the fifth month (of pregnancy).
берéм|я, ени, *n.* (*dial.*) armful; bundle.
берёст|а, ы, *no pl.*, *f.* birch-bark.
берёст|овый, *adj. of* ~а.
берестянóй, *adj.* = берёстовый.
берéт, а, *m.* beret.
бер|éчь, егý, ежёшь, егýт, *past* ~ёг, ~еглá, *impf.* 1. to take care (of), look after; to keep, guard; б. кáждую копéйку to count every penny; б. своё врéмя not to waste one's time; б. тáйну to keep a secret. 2. to spare; to spare the feelings (of).
бер|éчься, егýсь, ежёшься, егýтся, *past* ~ёгся, ~еглáсь, *impf.* 1. to be careful, take care. 2. (+*g. or* +*inf.*) to beware (of); ~еги́тесь ворóв! beware of pickpockets!;

~еги́тесь переедáть! mind you don't eat too much! 3. *pass. of* ~éчь.
бери́лл, а, *m.* (*min.*) beryl.
бери́лли|й, я, *m.* (*chem.*) beryllium, glucinium.
бéрков|ец, ца, *m.* (*obs.*) berkovets (*weight equivalent to 10 poods or 360 lb. avoirdupois*).
бéркут, а, *m.* golden eagle.
берли́нск|ий, *adj.* Berlin; ~ая лазýрь Prussian blue.
берлóг|а, и, *f.* den, lair.
бертолéтов, *adj.* ~а соль potassium chlorate (Berthollet's salt).
бер|ý, ёшь, *see* брать.
берцóв|ый, *adj.* (*anat.*) большáя ~ая кость shin-bone, tibia; мáлая ~ая кость fibula.
бес, а, *m.* demon, evil spirit; рассыпáться мéлким ~ом (перед+*i.*; *coll.*) to fawn (on), ingratiate oneself (with).
бесéд|а, ы, *f.* 1. talk, conversation. 2. discussion; провести́ ~у to give a talk; б. по прочи́танному discussion of what one has read (*in school, etc.*).
бесéдк|а, и, *f.* summer-house.
бесéд|овать, ую, *impf.* (с+*i.*) to talk, converse (with).
бесéдчик, а, *m.* (*coll.*) discussion-leader.
бесён|ок, ка, *pl.* ~я́та, ~я́т, *m.* imp, little devil (*also fig.*).
бе|си́ть, шý, ~си́шь, *impf.* (*of* вз~) (*coll.*) to enrage, madden, infuriate.
бе|си́ться, шýсь, ~си́шься, *impf.* (*of* вз~) 1. to go mad (*of animals*). 2. (*fig.*) to rage, be furious; с жи́ру б. (*coll.*) to grow fastidious, fussy; to be too well off.
бесклáссовый, *adj.* classless.
бескозы́рк|а, и, *f.* peakless cap; матрóсская б. sailor's cap.
бескозы́рный, *adj.* (*cards*) without trumps.
бесконéчно, *adv.* infinitely, endlessly; (*coll.*) extremely; я б. рад вáшему успéху I am extremely pleased about your success; б. мáлый (*math.*) infinitesimal.
бесконéчност|ь, и, *f.* endlessness; infinity; до ~и endlessly.
бесконéч|ный (~ен, ~на), *adj.* endless; infinite; interminable; ~ная дробь (*math.*) recurring decimal; б. винт (*tech.*) endless screw; б. ряд (*math.*) infinite series.
бесконтрóл|ьный (~ен, ~ьна), *adj.* uncontrolled; unchecked.
бескóрмиц|а, ы, *f.* fodder shortage.
бескорóвный, *adj.* not possessing a cow.
бескорысти|е, я, *n.* disinterestedness.
бескоры́ст|ный (~ен, ~на), *adj.* disinterested; unselfish.
бескóстный, *adj.* boneless.
бескрáйний, *adj.* boundless.
бескрóв|ный[1] (~ен, ~на), *adj.* 1. anaemic, pale. 2. bloodless; ~ная революция bloodless revolution.

бескро́вный², *adj.* (*obs.*) roofless; homeless.

бескры́лый, *adj.* wingless; (*fig.*) uninspired.

бескульту́рь|е, я, *n.* lack of culture.

беснова́ни|е, я, *n.* frenzy; raging.

беснова́тый, *adj.* possessed; raging, raving.

бесн|ова́ться, у́юсь, *impf.* to be possessed; to rage, rave.

бесо́вский, *adj.* devilish, diabolical.

беспа́лубный, *adj.* without decks.

беспа́лый, *adj.* lacking one *or* more fingers *or* toes.

беспа́мят|ный (~ен, ~на), *adj.* (*coll.*) forgetful.

беспа́мятств|о, а, *n.* **1.** unconsciousness; впасть в б. to lose consciousness. **2.** frenzy; delirium; быть в ~е to be beside oneself; to be delirious.

беспардо́нный, *adj.* shameless, brazen.

беспарти́йн|ый, *adj.* non-party; *as noun* б., ~ого, *m.*, *and* ~ая, ~ой, *f.* non-party man, woman.

беспа́спортный, *adj.* not having a passport.

беспате́нтный, *adj.* unlicensed.

беспереб о́йный, *adj.* uninterrupted; regular.

беспереса́дочный, *adj.* direct; б. по́езд through train.

бесперспекти́в|ный (~ен, ~на), *adj.* having no prospects; hopeless.

беспеча́л|ьный (~ен, ~ьна), *adj.* carefree.

беспе́чност|ь, и, *f.* carelessness, unconcern.

беспе́ч|ный (~ен, ~на), *adj.* careless, unconcerned; carefree.

беспи́сьменный, *adj.* having no written language.

беспла́новост|ь, и, *f.* absence of plan.

беспла́новый, *adj.* planless.

беспла́тно, *adv.* free of charge, gratis.

беспла́т|ный (~ен, ~на), *adj.* free, gratuitous; б. биле́т free ticket, complimentary ticket.

бесплацка́ртный, *adj.* without reserved seat(s); б. по́езд train with unreserved seats only; б. пассажи́р passenger travelling without reserving a seat.

бесплоди|е, я, *n.* sterility, barrenness.

бесплодност|ь, и, *f.* fruitlessness, futility.

бесплод|ный (~ен, ~на), *adj.* **1.** sterile, barren. **2.** (*fig.*) fruitless, futile.

бесплотный, *adj.* (*rel.*; *poet.*) incorporeal.

бесповоро́тност|ь, и, *f.* irrevocability, finality.

бесповоро́тн|ый (~а, ~о), *adj.* irrevocable, final; ~ое реше́ние final decision.

бесподо́б|ный (~ен, ~на), *adj.* matchless; incomparable; superlative; ~но! *interj.* superb!, splendid!

беспозвоно́чн|ый, *adj.* (*zool.*) invertebrate; *as noun* ~ое, ~ого, *n.* invertebrate.

беспоко́|ить, ю, ишь, *impf.* **1.** (*pf.* о~) to disturb, bother. **2.** (*pf.* по~) to disturb, worry.

беспоко́|иться, юсь, ишься, *impf.* **1.** (*pf.* о~) (о+*p.*) to worry, be worried *or* anxious (about). **2.** (*pf.* по~) (*coll.*) to worry, put oneself out; не ~йтесь! don't trouble!, don't worry!

беспоко́|йный (~ен, ~йна), *adj.* **1.** agitated; anxious; uneasy; ~йное состоя́ние a state of agitation. **2.** disturbing; restless, fidgety; б. ребёнок fidgety child.

беспоко́йств|о, а, *n.* **1.** agitation; anxiety; unrest; с ~ом anxiously. **2.** disturbance; причини́ть б. (+*d.*) to disturb.

бесполе́з|ный (~ен, ~на), *adj.* useless.

беспо́л|ый, *adj.* sexless; ~ое размноже́ние asexual reproduction.

беспоме́стный, *adj.* (*hist.*) not possessing an estate.

беспо́мощ|ный (~ен, ~на), *adj.* helpless, powerless; (*fig.*) feeble; б. ум feeble intellect.

беспоро́д|ный (~ен, ~на), *adj.* not thoroughbred, not pedigree; ~ная соба́ка mongrel.

беспоро́ч|ный (~ен, ~на), *adj.* blameless, irreproachable; immaculate; ~ное зача́тие (*rel.*) the Immaculate Conception; ~ная слу́жба irreproachable service.

беспоря́д|ок, ка, *m.* disorder, confusion; (*pl. only*; *polit.*) disturbances, riots.

беспоря́доч|ный (~ен, ~на), *adj.* disorderly; untidy.

беспоса́дочный, *adj.* б. перелёт non-stop flight.

беспо́чвен|ный (~, ~на), *adj.* groundless; unsound.

беспо́шлинн|ый, *adj.* (*econ.*) duty-free; ~ая торго́вля free trade.

беспоща́д|ный (~ен, ~на), *adj.* merciless, relentless.

бесправи|е, я, *n.* **1.** lawlessness; arbitrariness. **2.** state of possessing no rights.

бесправност|ь, и, *f.* = беспра́вие 2.

беспра́в|ный (~ен, ~на), *adj.* without rights; deprived of rights.

беспреде́л|ьный (~ен, ~ьна), *adj.* boundless; infinite.

беспредме́тник, а, *m.* supporter of abstract art.

беспредме́тн|ый, *adj.* **1.** aimless. **2.** ~ая жи́вопись abstract painting.

беспрекосло́в|ный (~ен, ~на), *adj.* unquestioning, absolute; он тре́бует ~ного повинове́ния he demands unquestioning obedience.

беспрепя́тствен|ный (~, ~на), *adj.* free, clear, unimpeded.

беспреры́вно, *adv.* continuously; uninterruptedly; дождь шёл б. в течение трёх дней it rained for three days on end.

беспрерыв|ный (~ен,~на), *adj.* continuous; uninterrupted.

беспреста́нно, *adv.* continually, incessantly.

беспреста́н|ный (~ен, ~на), *adj.* continual; incessant.

беспрецеде́нт|ный (~ен, ~на), *adj.* unprecedented.

беспри́был|ьный (~ен, ~ьна), *adj.* profitless.

беспривет|ный (~ен, ~на), *adj.* unwelcoming.

бесприд́нниц|а, ы, *f.* girl without dowry.

беспризо́рник, а, *m.* besprizornik; waif, homeless child.

беспризо́рн|ый, *adj.* **1.** neglected. **2.** stray, homeless; *as noun* б., **~ого,** *m.* waif, homeless child.

беспример|ный (~ен, ~на), *adj.* unexampled, unparalleled; ~ная хра́брость unexampled bravery.

беспри́месный, *adj.* unalloyed.

беспринци́п|ный (~ен, ~на), *adj.* unscrupulous, unprincipled.

беспристра́сти|е, я, *n.* impartiality.

беспристра́стност|ь, и, *f.* impartiality.

беспристра́ст|ный (~ен, ~на), *adj.* impartial, unbiassed.

беспричи́нн|ый, *adj.* causeless; pointless.

бесприю́т|ный (~ен, ~на), *adj.* homeless; not affording shelter; ~ная жизнь life spent in roaming.

беспробу́д|ный (~ен, ~на), *adj.* **1.** deep, heavy (*of sleep*); спать ~ным сном to be in a deep sleep. **2.** unrestrained (*of drunkenness*).

беспро́волочный, *adj.* wireless; б. телегра́ф wireless.

беспро́игрышн|ый, *adj.* safe; without risk of loss; ~ая лотере́я lottery in which no competitor loses.

беспросве́т|ный (~ен, ~на), *adj.* **1.** pitch-dark; ~ная тьма thick darkness. **2.** (*fig.*) cheerless, hopeless; ~ное го́ре unrelieved misery.

беспроце́нтный, *adj.* (*fin.*) bearing no interest.

беспу́тиц|а, ы, *f.* **1.** absence of roads. **2.** bad condition of roads. **3.** season when roads are impassable.

беспу́тник, а, *m.* (*coll.*) debauchee.

беспу́тнича|ть, ю, *impf.* (*coll.*) to lead a dissipated life, be a debauchee.

беспу́т|ный (~ен, ~на), *adj.* dissipated, dissolute.

беспу́тств|о, а, *n.* dissipation, debauchery.

бессвя́зност|ь, и, *f.* incoherence.

бессвя́з|ный (~ен, ~на), *adj.* incoherent.

бессеме́йный, *adj.* having no family.

бессе́менн|ый, *adj.* **1.** (*obs.*) seedless. **2.** (*rel.*) ~ое зача́тие the Virgin Birth (*of Christ*).

бессеменодо́льный, *adj.* (*bot.*) acotyledonous.

бессемерова́ни|е, я, *n.* (*tech.*) Bessemer process.

бессеме́ровский, *adj.* (*tech.*) Bessemer.

бессемя́нный, *adj.* seedless.

бессерде́ч|ие, ия, *n.* = ~ность.

бессерде́чност|ь, и, *f.* heartlessness; callousness.

бессерде́ч|ный (~ен, ~на), *adj.* heartless; callous.

бесси́ли|е, я, *n.* impotence; debility; (*fig.*) feebleness.

бесси́л|ьный (~ен, ~ьна), *adj.* impotent, powerless.

бессисте́мност|ь, и, *f.* unsystematic character, lack of system.

бессисте́м|ный (~ен, ~на), *adj.* unsystematic.

бессла́ви|е, я, *n.* infamy.

бессла́в|ить, лю, ишь, *impf.* (*of* о~) to defame.

бессла́в|ный (~ен, ~на), *adj.* infamous; inglorious.

бессле́дно, *adv.* without leaving a trace; completely, utterly.

бессле́дн|ый, *adj.* without leaving a trace; ~ое исчезнове́ние complete disappearance.

бессловес|ный (~ен, ~на), *adj.* dumb, speechless; (*fig.*) silent; ~ные живо́тные dumb animals; (*theatr.*) ~ная роль silent part.

бессме́н|ный (~ен, ~на), *adj.* permanent; continuous.

бессме́рти|е, я, *n.* immortality.

бессме́ртник, а, *m.* (*bot.*) immortelle.

бессме́рт|ный (~ен, ~на), *adj.* immortal; undying.

бессмы́слен|ный (~, ~на), *adj.* senseless; foolish; meaningless, nonsensical; б. посту́пок senseless act; ~ная фра́за meaningless sentence.

бессмы́слиц|а, ы, *f.* nonsense.

бессне́жный, *adj.* snowless.

бессо́вест|ный (~ен, ~на), *adj.* **1.** unscrupulous, dishonest. **2.** shameless, brazen.

бессодержа́тел|ьный (~ен, ~ьна), *adj.* empty; tame; dull.

бессозна́тел|ьный (~ен, ~ьна), *adj.* **1.** unconscious. **2.** involuntary.

бессо́нниц|а, ы, *f.* insomnia, sleeplessness.

бессо́нный, *adj.* sleepless.

бесспо́рно, *adv.* indisputably; undoubtedly.

бесспо́р|ный (~ен, ~на), *adj.* indisputable, incontrovertible.

бессре́бреник, а, *m.* disinterested person.

бессро́чн|ый, *adj.* without time-limit; б. о́тпуск indefinite leave; ~ое тюре́мное заключе́ние imprisonment for life, life term.

бесстра́ст|ный (~ен, ~на), *adj.* impassive.

бесстра́ши|е, я, *n.* fearlessness, intrepidity.

бесстра́ш|ный (~ен, ~на), *adj.* fearless, intrepid.

бессты́дник, а, *m.* shameless person.

бессты́дниц|а, ы, *f.* shameless woman, hussy.

бессты́д|ный (~ен, ~на), *adj.* shameless.

бессты́дств|о, а, *n.* shamelessness.

бессты́жий, *adj.* (*coll.*) shameless; brazen.

бессубъе́кт|ный, *adj.* ~ное предложе́ние (*gram.*) sentence not containing subject.

бессу́дный, *adj.* arbitrary, summary.

бессчётный, *adj.* innumerable.

беста́ктност|ь, и, f. 1. tactlessness. 2. tactless action.

беста́кт|ный (~ен, ~на), *adj.* tactless.

бестала́н|ный (~ен, ~на), *adj.* 1. untalented. 2. (*folk poet.*) ill-starred, luckless; ~ная голо́бушка poor devil.

бестеле́с|ный (~ен, ~на), *adj.* incorporeal.

бе́сти|я, и, f. (*coll.*) rogue; то́нкая б. sly rogue.

бестова́рь|е, я, *n.* shortage of goods.

бестолко́вщин|а, ы, f. (*coll.*) disorder, confusion.

бестолко́в|ый (~, ~а), *adj.* 1. slow-witted; muddle-headed. 2. disconnected, incoherent.

бе́столоч|ь, и, f. (*coll.*) 1. confusion. 2. muddle-headed person (*also collect.*).

бестре́пет|ный (~ен, ~на), *adj.* (*poet.*) dauntless.

бесту́жевск|ий, *adj.* ~ие ку́рсы (*hist.*) 'Bestuzhev courses' (*higher education courses for women established in St. Petersburg in 1879; named after the first director, K. N. Bestuzhev-Ryumin*).

бесту́жевк|а, и, f. (*coll.*) member of 'Bestuzhev courses'.

бесфо́рмен|ный (~, ~на), *adj.* shapeless, formless.

бесхара́ктер|ный (~ен, ~на), *adj.* lacking in character; weak-willed.

бесхво́ст|ый, *adj.* tailless; *as noun* ~ое, ~ого, *n.* (*zool.*) ecaudate.

бесхи́трост|ный (~ен, ~на), *adj.* artless; unsophisticated; ingenuous.

бесхле́биц|а, ы, f. (*coll.*) corn shortage; bread shortage.

бесхо́зн|ый, *adj.* ownerless; ~ое иму́щество property in abeyance.

бесхозя́йный, *adj.* (*obs.*) ownerless.

бесхозя́йственност|ь, и, f. thriftlessness; bad management.

бесхозя́йствен|ный (~, ~на), *adj.* thriftless; improvident.

бесхребе́т|ный (~ен, ~на), *adj.* (*fig.*) spineless, weak.

бесцве́т|ный (~ен, ~на), *adj.* colourless; (*fig.*) colourless, insipid.

бесце́л|ьный (~ен, ~ьна), *adj.* aimless; idle; ~ьная болтовня́ idle chat.

бесце́н|ный (~ен, ~на), *adj.* 1. priceless, invaluable. 2. (*obs.*) valueless.

бесце́н|ок, ка, *m.* (*coll.*) *only in phrase* за б. very cheaply; купи́ть за б. to buy for a song.

бесцеремо́н|ный (~ен, ~на), *adj.* unceremonious; familiar.

бесчелове́чност|ь, и, f. inhumanity.

бесчелове́ч|ный (~ен, ~на), *adj.* inhuman.

бесче́|стить, щу, стишь, *impf.* (*of o~*) to dishonour, disgrace.

бесче́ст|ный (~ен, ~на), *adj.* dishonourable; disgraceful.

бесче́сть|е, я, *n.* dishonour; disgrace.

бесчи́нный, *adj.* (*obs.*) unseemly, scandalous.

бесчи́нств|о, а, *n.* excess; enormity.

бесчи́нств|овать, ую, *impf.* to commit excesses.

бесчи́сленност|ь, и, f. innumerable quantity.

бесчи́слен|ный (~, ~на), *adj.* innumerable.

бесчу́вственност|ь, и, f. 1. insensibility. 2. insensitivity.

бесчу́вствен|ный (~, ~на), *adj.* 1. insensible. 2. insensitive, unfeeling.

бесчу́встви|е, я, *n.* 1. loss of consciousness; пья́ный до ~я dead drunk; бить до ~я to knock insensible. 2. insensitivity.

бесшаба́ш|ный (~ен, ~на), *adj.* (*coll.*) reckless.

бесшёрстный, *adj.* hairless, woolless.

бесшёрст|ый, *adj.* = ~ный.

бесшо́вный, *adj.* (*tech.*) seamless; jointless.

бесшу́м|ный (~ен, ~на), *adj.* noiseless.

бе́тел|ь, я, *m.* betel.

бето́н, а, *m.* (*tech.*) concrete.

бетони́ровани|е, я, *n.* (*tech.*) concreting.

бетони́р|овать, ую, *impf.* (*tech.*) to concrete.

бето́нный, *adj.* (*tech.*) concrete.

бетономеша́лк|а, и, f. (*tech.*) concrete mixer.

бето́нщик, а, *m.* concrete worker.

беф-стро́ганов, *indecl.*, *m.* (*cul.*) bœuf Stroganov.

бечев|а́, ы́, *no pl.*, *f.* tow-rope.

бечёвк|а, и, f. string, twine.

бечевни́к, а́, *m.* tow-path.

бечев|о́й, *adj. of* ~а́; ~а́я тя́га towing; *as noun* ~а́я, ~о́й, *f.* tow-path.

бешаме́л|ь, и, f. (*cul.*) Bechamel sauce.

бе́шенств|о, а, *n.* 1. (*med.*) hydrophobia; rabies. 2. fury, rage; довести́ до ~а to enrage. 3. б. ма́тки (*med.*) nymphomania.

бе́шен|ый, *adj.* **1.** rabid, mad; ~ая соба́ка mad dog. **2.** furious; violent; ~ая ско́рость furious pace; ~ые це́ны (*coll.*) exorbitant prices. **3.** ~ые де́ньги (*obs.*) easy money. **4.** б. огуре́ц 'squirting' cucumber (*Ecballium elaterium*).

бешме́т, а, *m.* beshmet (*kind of quilted coat*).

бзик, а, *m.* (*coll.*) quirk, oddity.

бибабо́, *indecl.*, *n.* glove puppet.

библе́йский, *adj.* biblical.

библио́граф, а, *m.* bibliographer.

библиографи́ческий, *adj.* bibliographical.

библиогра́фи|я, и, *f.* bibliography.

библиоте́к|а, и, *f.* (*in var. senses*) library; б. с вы́дачей книг на́ дом lending-library; б.-чита́льня reading-room.

библиоте́кар|ша, ши, *f. of* ~ь.

библиоте́кар|ь, я, *m.* librarian.

библиотекове́дени|е, я, *n.* librarianship.

библиоте́|чный, *adj. of* ~ка.

библиофи́л, а, *m.* bibliophil.

би́бли|я, и, *f.* bible; the Bible.

бива́к, а, *m.* (*mil.*) bivouac, camp; стоя́ть ~ом, на ~ах to bivouac, camp.

бива́|чный, *adj. of* ~к; б. пункт (*mil.*) bivouacking site, camping site.

би́в|ень, ня, *pl.* ~ни, ~ней, *m.* tusk.

бивуа́к, а, *m.* (*obs.*) = бива́к.

бигуд|и́, е́й, *no sing.* (*also indecl.*) (hair) curlers.

бидо́н, а, *m.* can, churn; б. для молока́ milk-can.

бие́ни|е, я, *n.* beating; throb; б. се́рдца heartbeat; б. пу́льса pulse.

биза́н|ь, и, *f.* (*naut.*) mizzen; б.-ма́чта mizzen-mast.

би́знес, а, *m.* business.

бизнесме́н, а, *m.* business man.

бизо́н, а, *m.* (*zool.*) bison.

бикарбона́т, а, *m.* (*chem.*) bicarbonate.

бикфо́рдов, *adj.* б. шнур (*tech.*) Bickford (safety) fuse.

билабиа́льный, *adj.* (*ling.*) bilabial.

биле́т, а, *m.* ticket; card; входно́й б. entrance ticket, permit; жёлтый б. (*obs.*) prostitute's passport; креди́тный б. bank-note; обра́тный б. return ticket; отпускно́й б. (*mil.*) leave-pass; партийный б. Party-membership card; почётный б. complimentary ticket; пригласи́тельный б. invitation card; экзаменацио́нный б. examination question (-paper) (*at oral examination*).

билетёр, а, *m.* ticket-collector.

билетёр|ша, ши, *f. of* ~; (*in cinema, etc.*) usherette.

биллиа́рд, а, *m.* = билья́рд.

биллио́н, а, *m.* billion (= *a 1000 millions*).

билло́н, а, *no pl.*, *m.* (*tech.*) billon (*debased silver*).

билл|ь, я, *m.* (*polit.*) bill.

би́л|о, а, *n.* **1.** (*tech.*) beater. **2.** gong.

бильбоке́, *indecl.*, *n.* cup and ball (*toy*).

бильдаппара́т, а, *m.* (*tech.*) telephote, photograph transmitter.

билья́рд, а, *m.* **1.** billiard-table. **2.** billiards; игра́ть в б. to play billiards; па́ртия в б., на ~e game of billiards.

билья́рд|ный, *adj. of* ~; б. шар billiard ball; *as noun* ~ная, ~ной, *f.* billiards room.

биметалли́зм, а, *m.* (*econ.*) bimetallism.

бимс, а, *m.* (*naut.*) beam, transom.

бино́кл|ь, я, *m.* binoculars; полево́й б. field glasses; театра́льный б. opera glasses.

бинокуля́рный, *adj.* binocular.

бино́м, а, *m.* (*math.*) binomial; б. Ньюто́на binomial theorem.

бинт, а́, *m.* bandage.

бинт|ова́ть, у́ю, *impf.* to bandage.

бинто́вк|а, и, *f.* bandaging.

био́граф, а, *m.* **1.** biographer. **2.** (*obs.*) cinematograph.

биографи́ческий, *adj.* biographical.

биогра́фи|я, и, *f.* biography; life story.

био́лог, а, *m.* biologist.

биологи́ческий, *adj.* biological.

биоло́ги|я, и, *f.* biology.

биоста́нци|я, и, *f.* biological research station.

биосфе́р|а, ы, *f.* biosphere.

биохими́ческий, *adj.* biochemical.

биохи́ми|я, и, *f.* biochemistry.

бипла́н, а, *m.* biplane.

биполя́рность, и, *f.* (*phys.*) bipolarity.

биполя́рный, *adj.* (*phys.*) bipolar.

би́рж|а, и, *f.* **1.** exchange; фо́ндовая б. stock-exchange; чёрная б. black market (*in currency*); б. труда́ labour exchange. **2.** изво́зчичья б. (*obs.*) cabstand, cab-rank.

биржеви́к, а́, *m.* **1.** stockbroker. **2.** (*obs.*) cabby.

бирж|ево́й, *adj. of* ~а; б. ма́клер stockbroker; ~ева́я сде́лка stock-exchange deal.

би́рк|а, и, *f.* **1.** (*obs.*) tally (*notched stick*). **2.** name-plate; label-tag.

бирма́н|ец, ца, *m.* Burmese, Burman.

бирма́нк|а, и, *f.* Burmese (woman).

бирма́нский, *adj.* Burmese.

бирюз|а́, ы́, *no pl.*, *f.* turquoise.

бирюзо́вый, *adj.* turquoise (**1.** *made of turquoise*. **2.** *of turquoise colour*).

бирю́к, а́, *m.* (*dial.*) lone wolf; (*fig.*) lone wolf, unsociable person; смотре́ть ~о́м (*coll.*) to look gloomy, morose.

бирю́льк|а, и, *f.* spillikin; игра́ть в ~и to play at spillikins; (*fig.*) to occupy oneself with trifles.

бирю́ч, а́, *m.* (*hist.*) crier, herald.

бис, *interj.* encore; сыгра́ть, спеть на б. to play, sing an encore.

би́сер, а, *no pl.*, *m.* beads; мета́ть б. пе́ред свиньями (*fig.*) to cast pearls before swine.

би́серин|а, ы, *f.* bead.

би́сер|ный, *adj.* of ~; (*fig.*) minute; б. по́черк minute handwriting.

биси́р|овать, ую, *impf. and pf.* to repeat, give an encore.

бискви́т, а, *m.* 1. sponge-cake. 2. (*tech.*) biscuit (*unglazed pottery*).

бискви́т|ный, *adj.* of ~; б. руле́т Swiss roll.

биссектри́с|а, ы, *f.* (*math.*) bisector.

бисульфа́т, а, *m.* (*chem.*) bisulphate.

бит|а́, ы́, *f.* (*sport*) bat.

би́тв|а, ы, *f.* battle; б. за Атланти́ческий океа́н, на Ма́рне, под Полта́вой, при Трафа́льгаре Battle of the Atlantic, of the Marne, of Poltava, of Trafalgar.

битко́м, *adv. only in phrase* б. наби́ть (*coll.*) to pack, crowd; авто́бус был б. наби́т the bus was packed, crammed.

би́тник, а, *m.* beatnik.

бит|о́к, ка́, *m.* rissole, hamburger.

биту́м, а, *m.* (*min.*) bitumen.

битуми́нозный, *adj.* (*min.*) bituminous.

би́т|ый (~, ~а), *p.p.p.* of ~ь *and adj.*; ~ая посу́да два ве́ка живёт (*prov.*) cracked pots last the longest; б. час (*coll.*) a full hour, a good hour; ~ые сли́вки whipped cream; ~ое стекло́ broken glass.

бить, бью, бьёшь, *impf.* 1. (*pf.* по~) to beat (*a person, an animal, etc.*). 2. (*pf.* по~) to beat, defeat (*in war, sports or games*); (*impf. only*) б. ка́рту (*cards*) to cover a card. 3. (уда́рить *used in place of pf.*) to strike, hit; б. кнуто́м to whip, flog; б. себя́ в грудь to thump one's chest; б. в лицо́ to strike, hit in the face (*also fig.*). 4. (*impf. only*) to strike, hit; to beat, thump, bang; б. в бараба́н to beat a drum; б. в ладо́ши to clap one's hands; б. по столу́ to bang on the table; б. за́дом to kick (*of a horse*); б. чело́м (*i*) (*hist.*) to present a petition, (*ii*) (+*d.*) to take off one's hat (to) (*fig.*). 5. (*impf. only*) to kill, slaughter (*animals*); б. гарпуно́м to harpoon; б. ры́бу острого́й to spear fish. 6. (*pf.* с~) б. ма́сло to churn butter. 7. (*impf. only*) to break, smash (*crockery, etc.*). 8. (уда́рить *used in place of pf.*) to combat, fight (against), wage war (on); to damage, injure; б. по хулига́нству to combat hooliganism; б. по чьему́-н. самолю́бию to wound someone's vanity; б. по карма́ну to cost one a pretty penny. 9. (*pf.* про~) to strike, sound; б. (в) наба́т to sound the alarm; б. отбо́й to beat a retreat (*also fig.*); часы́ бьют пять the clock is striking five; бьёт пять (*impers.*) it is striking five. 10. (*impf. only*) to spurt, gush; б. ключо́м to gush out, well up; (*fig.*) to be in full swing. 11. (*impf. only*) to shoot,

fire; (*with fire-arms*; *also fig.*) to hit; to have a range (of); б. из духово́го ружья́ to fire an air-gun; б. в цель to hit the target (*also fig.*); б. наверняка́ (*fig.*) to take no chances; б. на два киломе́тра to have a range of two kilometres. 12. (*impf. only*) на+*a.*) to strive (for, after); б. на эффе́кт to strive after effect.

бить|ё, я́, *n.* (*coll.*) beating, flogging; smashing.

би́ться, бьюсь, бьёшься, *impf.* 1. (с+*i.*) to fight (with, against); б. на поеди́нке to fight a duel. 2. (*of the heart*) to beat; се́рдце его́ переста́ло б. his heart stopped beating. 3. (о+*a.*) to knock (against), hit (against), strike; б. голово́й об сте́ну to be up against a blank wall; б., как ры́ба об лёд to struggle desperately. 4. to writhe, struggle; б. в исте́рике to writhe in hysterics. 5. (над+*i.*; *fig.*) to struggle (with), exercise oneself (over); б. над зада́чей to rack one's brains over a problem; как бы он ни би́лся however hard he tried. 6. (*of crockery, etc.*) to break, smash; легко́ б. to be very fragile. 7. б. об закла́д to bet, wager.

битю́г, а́, *m.* bityug (*Russian breed of cart-horse*); (*fig.*) strong man; он настоя́щий б. he is strong as a horse.

бифурка́ци|я, и, *f.* bifurcation.

бифште́кс, а, *m.* beefsteak.

би́цепс, а, *m.* (*anat.*) biceps.

бич, а́, *m.* whip, lash; (*fig.*) scourge.

бичева́ = бечева́.

бичева́ние, я, *n.* flogging; flagellation.

бич|ева́ть, у́ю, *impf.* to flog; (*fig.*) to lash, castigate.

бичёвка = бечёвка.

бишь, *particle* (*expressing effort to recall name, etc.*; *coll.*) now (*or not translated*); как б. его́ зову́т? what is his name?, what was the name now?; то б. that is to say.

бла́г|о¹, а, *n.* good, the good; blessing; о́бщее б. the common weal; жела́ю вам всех благ! I wish you every happiness; всех благ! (*coll.*) all the best! ни за каки́е ~а not for the world.

бла́го², *conj.* (*coll.*) since; seeing that; скажи́те ему́ сейча́с, б. он здесь tell him now since he is here.

благове́рн|ый, *now used only facetiously as noun*; б., ~ого, *m.* husband; ~ая, ~ой, *f.* wife.

благове́ст, а, *m.* ringing of church bell(s).

благове́|стить, щу, стишь, *impf.* 1. (*pf.* ~) to ring for church. 2. (*pf.* раз~) (*coll., iron.*) to publish, spread news.

**Благове́щени|е, я, *n.* (*eccl.*) the Annunciation.

благове́щен|ский, *adj.* of ~ие.

благови́д|ный (~ен, ~на), *adj.* 1. (*obs.*) comely. 2. specious, plausible; б. предло́г specious excuse.

благоволе́ни|е, я, *n.* goodwill, kindness; favour; по́льзоваться чьим-н. ~ем to be in favour with someone.

благовол|и́ть, ю́, и́шь, *impf.* (к+*d.*) to be favourably disposed (toward), favour; ~и́те (+*inf.*) have the kindness (to); ~и́те отве́тить на э́то письмо́ kindly answer this letter.

благово́ни|е, я, *n.* fragrance, aroma.

благово́нный, *adj.* fragrant.

благовоспи́танност|ь, и, *f.* good manners; good breeding.

благовоспи́тан|ный (~, ~на), *adj.* well-mannered; well brought up.

благовре́мени|е, я, *n. only in phrase* во ~и (*obs.*) opportunely.

благовре́менный, *adj.* (*obs.*) timely.

благоглу́пост|ь, и, *f.* pompous triviality.

благогове́|йный (~ен, ~йна), *adj.* reverential.

благогове́ни|е, я, *n.* reverence; veneration.

благогове́|ть, ю, *impf.* (пе́ред+*i.*) to have a reverential attitude (towards).

благодар|и́ть, ю́, и́шь, *impf.* (*of* по~) to thank; ~ю́ вас (за+*a.*) thank you (for).

благода́рност|ь, и, *f.* **1.** gratitude; не сто́ит ~и don't mention it. **2.** (*usually pl.*) thanks, acknowledgement of thanks. **3.** (*coll.*) bribe.

благода́р|ный (~ен, ~на), *adj.* **1.** grateful. **2.** rewarding; worth-while.

благода́рственн|ый, *adj.* (*obs.*) expressing thanks; б. моле́бен thanksgiving service; ~ое письмо́ letter of thanks.

благода́рств|овать, ую, *impf.* (*obs.*) *only used in forms* ~ую, ~уем, ~уй(те) thank you.

благодаря́, *prep.*+*d.* thanks to, owing to, because of; б. тому́, что owing to the fact that; б. хоро́шему кли́мату он ско́ро попра́вился thanks to the good climate he soon recovered.

благода́т|ный (~ен, ~на), *adj.* beneficial; abundant; б. край land of plenty.

благода́т|ь, и, *f.* **1.** plenty, abundance. **2.** (*rel.*) grace; Сло́во о зако́не и ~и (*hist.*) Sermon on Law and Grace.

благоде́нственный, *adj.* (*obs.*) prosperous.

благоде́нстви|е, я, *n.* (*obs.*) prosperity.

благоде́нств|овать, ую, *impf.* to prosper, flourish.

благоде́тел|ь, я, *m.* benefactor.

благоде́тельниц|а, ы, *f.* benefactress.

благоде́тел|ьный (~ен, ~ьна), *adj.* beneficial.

благоде́тельств|овать, ую, *impf.* (+*d.*) to be a benefactor (to).

благодея́ни|е, я, *n.* good deed; blessing; boon.

благоду́шеств|овать, ую, *impf.* (*coll.*) to take life easily.

благоду́ши|е, я, *n.* placidity, equability; good humour.

благоду́ш|ный (~ен, ~на), *adj.* placid, equable; good-humoured.

благожела́тел|ь, я, *m.* well-wisher.

благожела́тел|ьный (~ен, ~ьна), *adj.* well-disposed; benevolent; б. приём a friendly, cordial reception; ~ьная реце́нзия favourable review.

благожела́тельност|ь, и, *f.* goodwill; benevolence.

благозву́чи|е, я, *n.* euphony.

благозву́чност|ь, и, *f.* euphony.

благозву́ч|ный (~ен, ~на), *adj.* euphonious; melodious.

благ|о́й¹, *adj.* good; ~а́я мысль a happy thought; ~и́е наме́рения good intentions; избра́ть ~у́ю часть (*often iron.*) to choose the better part.

благ|о́й², *adj.* (*dial.*) crazy, cranky; ~и́м ма́том (*coll.*) at the top of one's voice.

благоле́пи|е, я, *n.* (*obs.*) grandeur.

благомы́слящий, *adj.* (*obs.*) right-thinking.

благонадёжност|ь, и, *f.* reliability, trustworthiness; loyalty; свиде́тельство о ~и (*obs.*) certificate of loyalty.

благонадёж|ный (~ен, ~на), *adj.* reliable, trustworthy; loyal.

благонаме́ренност|ь, и, *f.* (*obs.*) loyalty.

благонаме́рен|ный (~, ~на), *adj.* (*obs.*) loyal.

благонра́ви|е, я, *n.* good behaviour.

благонра́в|ный (~ен, ~на), *adj.* well-behaved.

благообра́зи|е, я, *n.* good looks; noble appearance.

благообра́з|ный (~ен, ~на), *adj.* good-looking; fine, fine-looking.

благополу́чи|е, я, *n.* well-being; prosperity.

благополу́чно, *adv.* well, all right; happily; safely; всё ко́нчилось б. everything turned out happily.

благополу́ч|ный (~ен, ~на), *adj.* successful; safe; б. коне́ц happy ending.

благоприобре́тени|е, я, *n.* (*obs.*) acquisition.

благоприобре́тенн|ый, *adj.* acquired; всё иму́щество у него́ ~ое, не насле́дственное his property is entirely acquired, not inherited.

благопристо́йност|ь, и, *f.* decency, decorum.

благопристо́|йный (~ен, ~йна), *adj.* (*obs.*) decent, decorous.

благоприя́т|ный (~ен, ~на), *adj.* favourable; propitious; ~ные ве́сти good news.

благоприя́тств|овать, ую, *impf.* (+*d.*) to favour; наибо́лее ~уемая держа́ва (*econ.*) most favoured nation.

благоразу́ми|е, я, *n.* prudence; sense.

благоразу́м|ный (~ен, ~на), *adj.* prudent; sensible.

благорасположе́ни|е, я, *n.* (*obs.*) favour.

благорасполо́жен|ный (~, ~на), *adj.* (*obs.*) favourably disposed.

благотворе́ни|е, я, *n.* б. возду́хов (*eccl.*; *often joc.*) healthful climate.

благоро́ди|е, я, *n.* (*obs.*) ва́ше б. (*term of address to officers of rank up to and including that of captain*) your Honour.

благоро́д|ный (~ен, ~на), *adj.* noble; б. газ noble gas; б. мета́лл precious metal; на ~ном расстоя́нии at a decent distance.

благоро́дств|о, а, *n.* nobleness; nobility.

благоскло́нност|ь, и, *f.* favour; по́льзоваться чье́й-н. ~ью to be in someone's good graces.

благоскло́н|ный (~ен, ~на), *adj.* favourable; gracious.

благослове́ни|е, я, *n.* (*eccl. and fig.*) blessing; benediction; подойти́ под б. (+*d.*) to ask a blessing (from); с ~я (+*g.*) with the blessing (of), with the consent (of).

благослове́н|ный (~, ~на), *adj.* (*eccl., poet.*) blessed, blest.

благослов|и́ть, лю, и́шь, *pf.* (*of* ~ля́ть) 1. to bless; to give one's blessing (to). 2. to be grateful to; б. свою́ судьбу́ to thank one's stars.

благослов|и́ться, лю́сь, и́шься, *pf.* (*of* ~ля́ться) (*coll.*) 1. (у+*g.*) to receive the blessing (of). 2. to cross oneself.

благослов|ля́ть(ся), ля́ю(сь), *impf. of* ~и́ть(ся).

благосостоя́ни|е, я, *n.* well-being, welfare.

благотвори́тел|ь, я, *m.* philanthropist.

благотвори́тельност|ь, и, *f.* charity, philanthropy.

благотвори́тельный, *adj.* charitable, philanthropic; б. база́р charity fête; б. спекта́кль charity performance.

благотво́р|ный (~ен, ~на), *adj.* beneficial; wholesome, salutary.

благоусмотре́ни|е, я, *n.* (*obs.*) consideration; отда́ть на чье́-н. б. to submit for someone's consideration.

благоустра́ива|ть, ю, *impf. of* благоустро́ить.

благоустро́ен|ный (~, ~на), *p.p.p. of* благоустро́ить *and adj.* well-equipped, improved; comfortable; б. дом house with all modern conveniences.

благоустро́|ить, ю, ишь, *pf.* (*of* благоустра́ивать) to equip with services and utilities; to improve.

благоустро́йств|о, а, *n.* equipping with services and utilities; improvement; отде́л ~а department of public services and utilities; б. се́льских посёлков improvement of rural settlements.

благоуха́ни|е, я, *n.* fragrance.

благоуха́нный, *adj.* fragrant, sweet-smelling.

благоуха́|ть, ю, *impf.* to be fragrant, to smell sweet.

благочести́в|ый (~, ~а), *adj.* pious, devout.

благоче́сти|е, я, *n.* piety.

благочи́ни|е, я, *n.* 1. (*sing. only*) decency, decorum. 2. (*eccl.*) deanery.

благочи́нн|ый, *adj.* 1. (*obs.*) decent, decorous. 2. (*as noun eccl.*) б., ~ого, *m.* rural dean.

блаже́н|ный (~, ~на), *adj.* 1. blessed, blissful; (*eccl.*) the Blessed; ~ной па́мяти of blessed memory; ~ное состоя́ние (state of) bliss. 2. *as noun* б., ~ного, *m.* simple person.

блаже́нств|о, а, *n.* bliss, felicity; на верху́ ~а in perfect bliss.

блаже́нств|овать, ую, *impf.* to be in a state of bliss.

блаж|и́ть, у́, и́шь, *impf.* (*coll.*) to be capricious; to indulge whims; to be eccentric.

блажно́й, *adj.* (*coll.*) capricious; eccentric.

блаж|ь, и, *f.* (*coll.*) whim, caprice.

бла́нжевый, *adj.* (*obs.*) flesh-coloured.

бланк, а, *m.* form; анке́тный б. questionnaire; фи́рменный б. letterhead; б. зака́за на кни́гу order slip for book (*in library*); запо́лнить б. to fill in a form.

бла́нк|овый, *adj. of* ~; ~овая на́дпись endorsement.

бланманже́, *indecl., n.* blancmange.

блат, а, *m.* (*sl.*) 1. crime. 2. pull, protection, influence; получи́ть по ~у to get on the quiet, come by through influence. 3. thieves' cant, thieves' Latin.

блатме́йстер, а, *m.* (*sl.*) racketeer.

блатн|о́й, *adj.* (*sl.*) criminal; ~а́я му́зыка thieves' cant, thieves' Latin.

блатня́г|а, и, *m.* (*sl.*) racketeer.

бл|ева́ть, юю, юёшь, *impf.* (*vulg.*) to puke.

блево́тин|а, ы, *f.* (*vulg.*) 1. vomit. 2. (*fig.*) filth.

бледне́|ть, ю, ешь, *impf.* (*of* по~) to grow pale; to pale.

бледноли́ц|ый, *adj.* pale; *as noun* б., ~ого, *m.* paleface.

бле́дност|ь, и, *f.* paleness, pallor.

бле́д|ный (~ен, ~на́, ~но), *adj.* pale, pallid; б. как полотно́ white as a sheet; (*fig.*) colourless, insipid; ~ная не́мочь (*med.*) chlorosis.

блёкл|ый, *adj.* faded; wan; ~ая руда́ (*min.*) tetrahedrite.

блёк|нуть, ну, нешь, *past* ~, ~ла, *impf.* (*of* по~) to fade; to wither.

блеск, а, *m.* 1. brightness, brilliance, shine; splendour, magnificence; (*as interj.*; *sl.*) б.! brilliant! super!; б. наря́да finery;

б. остроу́мия brilliance of wit; б. со́лнца brightness of the sun; во всём ~е in all (one's) glory; прида́ть б. to add lustre (to); игра́ть с ~ом на роя́ле to play the piano brilliantly. **2.** (*min.*) желе́зный б. haematite; свинцо́вый б. galena.

блесн|а́, ы́, *pl.* **~ы,** *f.* spoon-bait.

блесн|у́ть, у́, ёшь, *pf.* to flash; to shine; у меня́ ~у́ла мысль a thought flashed across my mind; у нас ~у́ла наде́жда we saw a ray of hope.

бле|сте́ть, щу́, сти́шь *and* ~ще́шь, *impf.* to shine (*also fig.*); to glitter; to sparkle; её глаза́ ~сте́ли ра́достью her eyes shone with joy; он не ~щет умо́м he is not over-blessed with intelligence, he does not shine.

блёстк|а, и, *f.* **1.** sparkle; ~и остроу́мия flashes of wit. **2.** spangle, sequin; усе́янный ~ами spangled.

блестя́щ|ий (~, ~а, ~е), *pres. part. of* блесте́ть *and adj.* shining, bright; (*fig.*) brilliant; б. ум brilliant mind.

блеф, а, *m.* bluff; его́ угро́зы оказа́лись чи́стым ~ом his threats turned out to be pure bluff.

блеф|ова́ть, у́ю, *impf.* (*coll.*) to bluff.

бле|щу́, ~ще́шь, *see* ~сте́ть.

бле́яни|е, я, *n.* bleat(ing).

бле́|ять, ю, ешь, *impf.* to bleat.

ближа́йш|ий, *superl. of* бли́зкий nearest; next; immediate; в ~ем бу́дущем in the near future; б. друг closest friend; б. нача́льник immediate superior; б. по́вод (*leg., philos.*) proximate cause, immediate cause; б. ро́дственник next of kin; при ~ем рассмотре́нии on closer examination; ~ее уча́стие personal participation.

бли́|же, *comp. of* ~зкий, ~зко nearer; (*fig.*) closer.

ближневосто́чный, *adj.* Near-Eastern.

бли́жн|ий, *adj.* **1.** near; neighbouring. **2.** (*mil.*) short range, close range, close; б. ого́нь close (range) fire. **3.** near, close (*of kinship*); *as noun* б., ~его, *m.* (*fig.*) one's neighbour; люби́ть ~его to love one's neighbour.

близ, *prep.*+*g.* near, close to, by.

бли|зиться, жусь, зишься, *impf.* to approach, draw near.

бли́з|кий (~ок, ~ка́, ~ко), *adj.* **1.** near, close; на ~ком расстоя́нии at a short distance, a short way off; at close range. **2.** (*of time*) near; imminent; ~кое бу́дущее the near future. **3.** intimate, close, near; б. ро́дственник near relation; быть ~ким с кем-н. to be on intimate terms with someone; быть ~ким (+*d.*) to be dear (to); *as noun* ~кие, ~ких one's nearest and dearest, one's people. **4.** (к) like; similar (to); close (to); б. нам по ду́ху челове́к

kindred spirit; ~кая ко́пия faithful copy; ~кая те́ма congenial topic.

бли́зко, *adv.* **1.** (от) near, close (to); close by. **2.** (*fig., coll.*) nearly, closely; б. каса́ться (+*g.*) to concern nearly; б. познако́миться (с+*i.*) to become closely acquainted (with). **3.** *as pred.* it is not far; ему́ б. ходи́ть he has not far to go.

близлежа́щий, *adj.* neighbouring, near-by.

близне́ц, а́, *m.* twin (*also* triplet, *etc.*); Близнецы́ (*astron.*) Gemini.

близору́к|ий (~, ~a), *adj.* short-sighted (*also fig.*).

близору́кост|ь, и, *f.* short-sightedness; (*med.*) myopia (*also fig.*).

бли́зост|ь, и, *f.* nearness, closeness, proximity; intimacy.

блик, а, *m.* speck, patch of light; light, highlight; со́лнечный б. patch of sunlight; ~и на карти́не lights in a picture.

блин, а́, *m.* blin (*kind of pancake*); пе́рвый б. ко́мом (*prov.*) practice makes perfect; пло́ский как б. flat as a pancake.

блинда́ж, а́, *m.* (*mil.*) dug-out.

блиндир|ова́ть, у́ю, *impf. and pf.* (*mil.*) to blind.

бли́н|чатый, *adj. of* ~; б. пиро́г pancake pie (*made with pancakes, eggs and kasha*).

бли́нчик, а, *m.* pancake; fritter.

блиста́тельност|ь, и, *f.* brilliance, splendour.

блиста́тел|ьный (~ен, ~ьна), *adj.* brilliant, splendid.

блиста́|ть ю, *impf.* to shine; б. отсу́тствием (*iron.*) to be conspicuous by one's absence.

блок¹, а, *m.* (*tech.*) block, pulley, sheave.

блок², а, *m.* (*polit.*) bloc.

блока́д|а, ы, *f.* blockade; снять ~у to raise the blockade; прорва́ть ~у to run the blockade.

блок-аппара́т, а, *m.* (*railways*) signal-box.

блок-гара́ж, а́, *m.* carport.

блокга́уз, а, *m.* (*mil.*) blockhouse.

блоки́р|овать, ую, *impf. and pf.* **1.** to blockade. **2.** (*railways*) to block.

блоки́р|оваться, уюсь, *impf. and pf.* **1.** *pass. of* ~ова́ть. **2.** (с+*i.*; *polit.*) to form a bloc with.

блокиро́вк|а, и, *f.* (*railways*) block system, signal system.

блокно́т, а, *m.* notebook, small writing-pad.

блокпо́ст, а, *m.* (*railways*) blockhouse.

блок-уча́ст|ок, ка, *m.* (*railways*) block section.

блонд|а, ы, *f.* (*usu. pl.*) white silk lace.

блонди́н, а, *m.* fair-haired man.

блонди́нист|ый (~, ~a), *adj.* (*coll.*) blonde, fair.

блонди́нк|а, и, *f.* blonde, fair woman.

блох|а́, и́, *pl.* ~и, ~а́м, *f.* flea.

бло|ши́ный, *adj. of.* ~ха́; б. уку́с flea-bite.

бло́ш|ки, ек, *f.* tiddly-winks; игра́ть в б. to play tiddly-winks.

блуд, а, *m.* lechery, fornication.

блу|ди́ть¹, жу́, ди́шь, *impf.* to lecher, fornicate.

блу|ди́ть², жу́, ~ди́шь, *impf.* (*coll.*) to wander, roam.

блудли́в|ый (~, ~а), *adj.* **1.** lascivious, lecherous. **2.** mischievous, roguish; thievish; ~ как кот, трусли́в как за́яц thievish as a cat, timid as a hare.

блу́дн|и, ей, *no sing.* (*coll.*) **1.** debauchery, lechery. **2.** getting up to mischief.

блудни́к, а́, *m.* (*obs.*) lecher, fornicator.

блудни́ц|а, ы, *f.* (*obs.*) **1.** fornicatress, loose woman. **2.** whore.

блу́д|ный, *adj. of* ~; б. сын (*eccl. and fig.*) prodigal son.

блужда́ни|е, я, *n.* wandering, roaming.

блужда́|ть, ю, *impf.* to roam, wander; to rove; б. по у́лицам to roam the streets.

блужда́|ющий, *pres. part. of* ~ть; б. взгляд vague, wandering expression; ~ющие звёзды (*obs.*) the planets; б. нерв (*anat.*) vagus (nerve); б. огонёк will-o'-the-wisp; ~ющая по́чка (*med.*) floating kidney.

блу́з|а, ы, *f.* (working) blouse; smock.

блу́зк|а, и, *f.* blouse (*worn only by women*).

блу́зник, а, *m.* (*coll., obs.*) labourer.

блу́минг = блю́минг.

блю́деч|ко, ка, *pl.* ~ки, ~ек, ~кам, *n.* saucer; small dish; б. для варе́нья jam plate.

блю́д|о, а, *n.* dish (*concr. and abstr.*); обе́д из трёх ~ three-course dinner; вку́сное б. a tasty dish; как на ~е (*of visibility of objects situated on even, open ground*) as on the palm of one's hand.

блюдоли́з, а, *m.* (*coll.*) sponger.

блю|ду́, дёшь, *see* ~сти́.

блю́д|це, ца, *g. pl.* ~ец, *n.* saucer.

блю́минг, а, *m.* (*tech.*) blooming (mill).

блю|сти́, ду́, дёшь, *past* ~л, ~ла́, *impf.* (*obs.*) to guard, watch over; to observe; б. зако́ны to abide by the law; б. поря́док to keep order.

блюсти́тел|ь, я, *m.* keeper, guardian; б. поря́дка (*coll., iron.*) arm of the law.

блю|ю́, ёшь, *see* блева́ть.

бля́д|ский, adj. of ~ь.

бляд|ь, и, *f.* (*vulg.*) whore (*especially as term of abuse, also used as interj.*).

бля́х|а, и, *f.* **1.** name plate; number plate. **2.** ме́дная б. (*as ornament on harness*) horse brass.

боа́, *indecl.* **1.** (*m.*) (*zool.*) boa, boa-constrictor. **2.** (*n.*) boa; мехово́е б. fur (boa).

боб, а́, *m.* bean; туре́цкий б. kidney bean, haricot; ~ы́ разводи́ть (*coll.*) to talk nonsense; оста́ться, сиде́ть на ~а́х (*coll.*) to get nothing for one's pains.

боб|ёр, ра́, *m.* **1.** (*sing. only*) beaver (fur). **2.** (*pl. only*) beaver collar.

бобби́н|а, ы, *f.* (*tech.*) bobbin.

бобк|и́, о́в, *no sing.* (*bot.*) bayberries.

бобко́в|ый, *adj.* bay; ~ое ма́сло bay-oil.

боб|о́вый 1. *adj. of* ~; б. стручо́к bean-pod. **2.** *as noun* ~о́вые, ~о́вых leguminous plants.

бобр, а́, *m.* beaver; уби́ть ~а́ to come off well, be in luck (*also iron.*).

бо́брик, а, *m.* (*text.*) beaver, castor; во́лосы ~ом (*coll.*) French crop; crew cut; постри́чься ~ом to have a French crop, crew cut.

бобр|о́вый, *adj. of* ~; beaver; beaver-fur; ~о́вая струя́ (*med.*) castoreum.

бобы́л|ь, я́, *m.* **1.** (*obs.*) poor, landless peasant. **2.** solitary, lonely man; жить ~ём to lead a solitary, lonely existence.

Бог, а, *vocative sing.* **Бо́же,** *m.* God; god; Бо́же мой! good God!, my God!; Б. зна́ет! Б. весть! God knows!; Б. его́ зна́ет who knows!; не дай Б.! God forbid!; ра́ди ~а! for God's sake!; с ~ом! (*obs.*) good luck!; сла́ва ~у! thank God!; как Б. на́ душу поло́жит anyhow, at random; Б. с ним let it pass; good luck to him (*iron.*); обе́дать чем Б. посла́л to take pot luck; он дава́й Б. но́ги he took to his heels.

богаде́лк|а, и, *f.* alms-woman.

богаде́л|ьня, ьни, *g. pl.* ~ен, *f.* almshouse, workhouse.

богар|а́, ы́, *f.* dry-farming (*in Central Asia*); dry-farming land.

бога́р|ный, *adj. of* ~а́.

богате́|й, я, *m.* (*coll.*) rich man.

богате́|ть, ю, ешь, *impf.* (*of* раз~) to grow rich.

бога́тств|о, а, *n.* **1.** riches, wealth; есте́ственные ~а natural resources. **2.** (*fig.*) richness, wealth.

бога́т|ый (~, ~а), *adj.* (+*i.*) rich (in), wealthy; страна́, ~ая го́рными проду́ктами a country rich in mineral products; ~ая расти́тельность luxuriant vegetation; б. переплёт a luxurious binding; б. о́пыт wide experience; чем ~ы, тем и ра́ды you are welcome to whatever we have; *as noun* б., ~ого, *m.* rich man.

богаты́р|ский, *adj. of* ~ь; heroic; (*fig.*) powerful, mighty, Herculean; б. э́пос the Russian folk-epic; ~ское сложе́ние powerful physique; б. сон profound sleep.

богаты́рств|о, а, *n.* **1.** heroic qualities. **2.** (*collect.*) bogatyrs.

богаты́р|ь, я́, *m.* **1.** bogatyr (*hero in Russian folklore*). **2.** (*fig.*) Hercules; hero.

богáч, á, *m.* rich man; ~й (*collect.*) the rich.

богдыхáн, а, *m.* (*hist.*) Chinese emperor.

богéм|а, ы, *f.* (*fig.*) Bohemia; Bohemianism.

богéм|ный, *adj.* of ~а.

богéмский, *adj.* (*geogr.*) Bohemian.

боги́н|я, и, *f.* goddess (*also fig.*).

богобóр|ец, ца, *m.* theomachist.

богобóр|ческий, *adj.* of ~ец.

богобоя́знен|ный (~, ~на), *adj.* god-fearing.

богоискáтел|ь, я, *m.* 'God-seeker'.

богомáз, а, *m.* (*coll.*) icon-dauber.

Богомáтер|ь, и, *f.* Mother of God.

богомéрзкий, *adj.* (*obs.*) 1. impious. 2. (*coll.*) hideous, repulsive.

богомóл, а, *m.* (*zool.*) praying mantis.

богомóл|ец, ьца, *m.* 1. devout person. 2. pilgrim. 3. one who prays (for someone else).

богомóл|ка, ки, *f.* 1. (*zool.*) = ~. 2. *f. of* ~ец.

богомóль|е, я, *n.* pilgrimage.

богомóл|ьный (~ен, ~ьна), *adj.* religious, devout.

богонóс|ец, ца, *m.* bearer of religious mission; нарóд-б. the Chosen People.

богоотстýпник, а, *m.* apostate.

богоотстýпничеств|о, а, *n.* apostasy.

богоподóб|ный (~ен, ~на), *adj.* god-like.

богопроти́в|ный (~ен, ~на), *adj.* 1. (*obs.*) impious. 2. (*coll.*) hideous, repulsive.

Богорóдиц|а, ы, *f.* the Virgin, Our Lady; сидéть ~ей (*coll., iron.*) to sit with arms folded.

богорóдич|ен, на, *m.* (*eccl.*) hymn in praise of the Virgin.

богослóв, а, *m.* theologian.

богослóви|е, я, *n.* theology.

богослóвский, *adj.* theological.

богослужé|бный, *adj.* of ~ние; liturgical; ~бная кни́га prayer-book.

богослужéни|е, я, *n.* divine service, worship; liturgy.

богоспасáемый, *adj.* blessed (*usu. iron.*).

боготвор|и́ть, ю́, и́шь, *impf.* 1. to worship, idolize. 2. to deify.

богоугóд|ный (~ен, ~на), *adj.* (*obs.*) pleasing to God; ~ное заведéние charitable institution.

богохýльник, а, *m.* blasphemer.

богохýльный, *adj.* blasphemous.

богохýльств|о, а, *n.* blasphemy.

богохýльств|овать, ую, *impf.* to blaspheme.

богочеловéк, а, *m.* (*theol.*) 'God-Man', God incarnate.

Богоявлéни|е, я, *n.* (*eccl.*) Epiphany.

бодá|ть, ю, *impf.* (*of* за~) to butt.

бодá|ться, юсь, *impf.* to butt (*intrans.*).

бодли́вост|ь, и, *f.* disposition to butt.

бодли́в|ый (~, ~а), *adj.* given to butting; ~ая корóва a cow that butts.

бодн|ýть, ý, ёшь, *pf.* to butt, give a butt.

бодр|и́ть, ю́, и́шь, *impf.* to stimulate, invigorate; здéшний вóздух óчень ~и́т it is very bracing here.

бодр|и́ться, ю́сь, и́шься, *impf.* to try to keep one's spirits up, try to be cheerful.

бóдрост|ь, и, *f.* cheerfulness; courage; good spirits.

бóдрствовани|е, я, *n.* keeping awake; vigilance.

бóдрств|овать, ую, *impf.* to be awake, stay awake; to keep awake, keep vigil; ей пришлóсь б. всю ночь при больнóм she had to sit up all night with the sick man.

бóдр|ый (~, ~á, ~о), *adj.* cheerful, bright; hale and hearty.

бодр|я́щий, *pres. part. of* ~и́ть *and adj.* invigorating, bracing.

бодя́г|а, и, *f.* fresh-water sponge.

боеви́к, á, *m.* 1. (*obs.*) member of revolutionary fighting group. 2. (*coll.*) hit; б. сезóна the hit of the season.

боев|óй, *adj.* 1. fighting, battle; ~ы́е дéйствия operations; б. дух fighting spirit; в б. готóвности prepared for action, cleared for action; ~óе крещéние baptism of fire; б. патрóн live cartridge; б. поря́док battle formation; ~ы́е припáсы (live) ammunition; ~áя пружи́на mainspring (*of gun*). 2. urgent; ~áя задáча urgent task. 3. (*coll.*) militant; energetic; pushing; ~áя бáба virago. 4. б. механи́зм striking mechanism (*of clock*).

боеголóвк|а, и, *f.* (*mil.*) warhead.

бо|éк, йкá, *m.* (*tech.*) firing-pin.

боеприпáс|ы, ов, *no sing.* ammunition.

боеспосóбност|ь, и, *f.* (*mil.*) fighting efficiency, fighting value.

боеспосóб|ный (~ен, ~на), *adj.* (*mil.*) efficient, battle-worthy.

бо|éц, йцá, *m.* 1. fighter; private soldier; ~йцы́ пéрвой áрмии the men of the First Army; петýх-б. fighting-cock. 2. butcher, slaughterman.

божб|á, ы́, *f.* swearing.

Бóже, *see* Бог.

бóжеск|ий, *adj.* 1. (*obs.*) divine. 2. (*coll.*) fair, just; ~ая ценá a fair price.

божéственност|ь, и, *f.* divinity; divine nature.

божéствен|ный (~, ~на), *adj.* divine (*also fig.*); б. гóлос divine voice.

божеств|ó, á, *n.* deity, divine being.

бóж|ий, ья, ье, *adj.* God's; б. человéк simple, otherworldly person; я́сно, как б. день it is as clear as noonday; ~ья корóвка (*zool.*) ladybird.

бож|и́ться, у́сь, ~ишься, *impf.* (*of* по~) to swear.

божни́ц|а, ы, *f.* 1. icon-case. 2. (*dial.*) chapel.

бож|о́к, ка́, *m.* idol (*also fig.*).

бо|й¹, я, *pl.* ~и́, ~ёв, *m.* 1. battle, fight, action, combat; ~й fighting; в ~ю́ in action; без ~я without striking a blow; взять с ~я to take by force; кула́чный б. fisticuffs; петуши́ный б. cock-fight; б. быко́в bullfight. 2. beating; бить смéртным ~ем to thrash within an inch of one's life. 3. striking, strike (*of a clock*); часы́ с ~ем striking clock; бараба́нный б. drum-beat. 4. killing, slaughtering; б. кито́в whaling; б. тюлéней sealing. 5. breakage; broken objects; в послéдней па́ртии посу́ды бы́ло мно́го ~я in the last consignment of crockery there were many breakages. 6. accuracy (*of fire-arm*); винто́вка с хоро́шим ~ем accurate rifle.

бо|й², я, *pl.* ~и, ~ев, *m.* message-boy; office-boy.

бой³-, *as indecl. adj. in compounds* lively, energetic; б.-ба́б|а, ы, *f.* virago; б.-дéвк|а, и, *f.* tomboy.

бо́|йкий (~ек, ~йка́, ~йко), *adj.* 1. bold, spry, smart; б. ум ready wit; б. язы́к glib tongue. 2. lively, animated; ~йкая торго́вля brisk trade; ~йкая у́лица busy street.

бо́йкост|ь, и, *f.* (*coll.*) 1. smartness; glibness. 2. liveliness, animation.

бойко́т, а, *m.* boycott; объяви́ть б. (+*d.*) to declare a boycott (of).

бойкоти́р|овать, ую, *impf.* to boycott.

бойни́ц|а, ы, *f.* loop-hole, embrasure.

бойн|я, и, *g. pl.* бо́ен, *f.* slaughter-house, abattoir; (*fig.*) slaughter, butchery, carnage.

бойска́ут, а. *m.* Boy Scout.

бойскаути́зм, а, *m.* scouting; the Boy Scout movement.

бойцо́вый, *adj.* fighting; б. пету́х fighting--cock.

бо́йче, *comp. of* бо́йк|ий, ~о.

бок, а, о ~е, на ~у́, *pl.* ~á, *m.* side; flank; в б. sideways; взять за ~á to put the screw on; схвати́ться за ~á (от смéха) to split one's sides (with laughter); на́ б. sideways, to the side; на ~у́ on one side; б. о́ б. side by side; пó ~у away with; пó ~у учéние! (we've done) enough studying!; пóд ~ом near by, close at hand; с ~у from the side, from the flank; с ~у на́ б. from side to side.

бока́л, а, *m.* glass, goblet; подня́ть б. (за+*a.*) to drink the health (of), raise one's glass (to).

боков|о́й, *adj.* side, flank, lateral, sidelong;

~áя ка́чка (*naut.*) rolling; ~áя ли́ния collateral line; ~áя у́лица side-street; отпра́виться на ~у́ю (*coll.*) to go to bed, turn in.

бо́ком, *adv.* 1. sideways; ходи́ть б. to sidle. 2. вы́йти б. (*coll.*) to turn out badly, give trouble.

бокс¹, а, *m.* (*sport*) boxing.

бокс², а, *m.* (*tech.*) boxcalf.

бокс³, а, *m.* boxer cut (*masculine hair-style, with hair short or shaved back and sides*).

бокс⁴, а, *m.* box (*isolation compartment in hospital*).

боксёр, а, *m.* (*sport*) boxer.

бокси́р|овать, ую, *impf.* (*sport*) to box.

бокси́т, а, *m.* (*min.*) bauxite.

бо́ксовый, *adj.* boxcalf.

болва́н, а, *m.* (*coll.*) 1. blockhead, dolt. 2. block (*esp. for shaping headgear*). 3. (*in card-games*) dummy. 4. (*obs.*) idol.

болва́нк|а, и, *f.* 1. (*tech.*) pig (*of iron, etc.*); желéзо в ~ax pig-iron. 2. block (*for shaping headgear*).

болга́р|ин, ина, *pl.* ~ы, ~, *m.* Bulgarian.

болга́рк|а, и, *f.* Bulgarian (woman).

болга́рский, *adj.* Bulgarian.

бóле (*obs.*) = бóлее.

болев|о́й, *adj.* of боль; ~óе ощущéние sensation of pain.

бóлее, *adv.* more; б. ро́бкий more timid; б. то́лстый thicker; б. и б. more and more; он всё б. и б. слабéл he was growing gradually weaker and weaker; б. и́ли мéнее more or less; не б. и не мéнее, как neither more nor less than; б. всего́ most of all; тем б., что especially as.

болéзненност|ь, и, *f.* 1. sickliness; abnormality, morbidity. 2. painfulness.

болéзнен|ный (~, ~на), *adj.* 1. sickly; unhealthy; б. румя́нец unhealthy flush; (*fig.*) abnormal, morbid; ~ное любопы́тство morbid curiosity. 2. painful.

болезнетво́рный, *adj.* (*med.*) morbific.

болéзный, *adj.* (*dial.*) piteous; мой б.! poor thing!; my dear one!

болéзн|ь, и, *f.* illness; disease; (*fig.*) abnormality; б. ро́ста growing pains.

болéльщик, а, *m.* (*coll.*) fan, supporter.

болеро́, *indecl., n.* (*Spanish dance or woman's jacket*) bolero.

болé|ть¹, ю, ешь, *impf.* 1. (+*i.*) to be ill, to be down (with); (*intrans.*) to ail; она́ с дéтства ~ет а́стмой she has suffered from asthma ever since she was a child; б. душо́й (о+*p.*) to be worried (about). 2. (за+*a.*; *coll.*) to be a fan (of), support.

болé|ть², *1st and 2nd persons not used*, ~и́т, *impf.* to ache, hurt; у меня́ зу́бы ~я́т I have toothache; у него́ ~и́т в у́хе he has ear-ache; у меня́ душа́ ~и́т (о+*p.*) my heart bleeds (for, over).

болеутоля́ющ|ий, *adj.* soothing, analgesic; ~ее сре́дство (*med.*) anodyne, analgesic.

боливи́|ец, йца, *m.* Bolivian.

боливи́йк|а, и, *f.* Bolivian (woman).

боливи́йский, *adj.* Bolivian.

болиголо́в, а, *m.* (*bot.*) hemlock.

боли́д, а, *m.* (*astron.*) fireball.

боло́нк|а, и, *f.* lap-dog.

боло́нь|я, и, *f.* plastic mackintosh.

боло́тист|ый (~, ~a), *adj.* marshy, boggy, swampy.

боло́тн|ый, *adj.* marsh; ~ая вода́ stagnant water; б. газ marsh gas; ~ая лихора́дка marsh fever, malaria.

боло́т|о, а, *n.* marsh, bog, swamp; торфяно́е б. peatbog; (*fig.*) mire, slough.

болт, а́, *m.* (*tech.*) bolt; нарезно́й б. screw-bolt; скрепля́ть ~а́ми to bolt.

болта́нк|а, и, *f.* (*aeron.*; *coll.*) bumps.

болта́|ть¹, ю, *impf.* **1.** to stir; to shake; б. ло́жкой в ча́шке ча́ю to stir one's tea with a spoon. **2.** (+*i.*) to dangle (*arms or legs*).

болта́|ть², ю, *impf.* (*coll.*) to chatter, jabber, natter; б. глу́пости to drivel; б. по-неме́цки, по-францу́зски, *etc.*, to jabber German, French, *etc.*; б. языко́м to wag one's tongue.

болта́|ться¹, юсь, *impf.* (*coll.*) **1.** to dangle, swing; to hang loosely; он так похуде́л, вся оде́жда ~ется на нём he has grown so thin that his clothes all hang on him. **2.** to hang about, loaf; чего́ вы тут весь день ~етесь? why do you hang about here all day?

болта́|ться², ется, *impf.* (*coll.*) *pass. of* ~ть²; здесь ~ется мно́го вздо́ру a lot of nonsense is being talked here.

болтли́вост|ь, и, *f.* garrulity, talkativeness.

болтли́в|ый (~, ~a), *adj.* garrulous, talkative; indiscreet.

болтн|у́ть¹, у́, ёшь, *pf.* to give a stir, give a shake.

болтн|у́ть², у́, ёшь, *pf.* to blurt out.

болтн|у́ться, ~ётся, *pf.* to work loose; to come off.

болтовн|я́, й, *f.* (*coll.*) talk; chatter; gossip; пуста́я б. idle talk.

болторе́зный, *adj.* (*tech.*) б. стано́к bolt-screwing machine.

болту́н¹, а́, *m.* (*coll.*) **1.** talker, chatterer; chatterbox. **2.** gossip.

болту́н², а́, *m.* addled egg.

болту́шк|а, и, *f.* (*coll.*) **1.** = болту́нья. **2.** scrambled eggs. **3.** swill, mash. **4.** whisk.

бол|ь, и, *f.* pain; ache; б. в боку́ stitch; зубна́я б. toothache; душе́вная б. mental anguish.

больни́ц|а, ы, *f.* hospital; лечь в ~y to go to hospital; лежа́ть в ~e to be in hospital; вы́писаться из ~ы to be discharged from hospital.

больни́|чный, *adj. of* ~ца; ~чная ка́сса hospital fund, club; б. листо́к medical certificate.

бо́льно¹, *adv.* **1.** painfully, badly; б. уши-би́ться to be badly bruised. **2.** *as pred.* it is painful (*also fig.*); мне б. дыша́ть it hurts me to breathe; б., что мы должны́ рас-ста́ться I am sorry that we have to part.

бо́льно², *adv.* (*coll.*) very, exceedingly, badly; он б. хитёр he is exceedingly wily; мне б. уж хо́чется пить I badly want a drink.

бол|ьно́й (~ен, ~ьна́), *adj.* ill, sick; diseased; sore (*also fig.*); ~ьны́е дёсны sore gums; б. зуб bad tooth; он тяжело́ ~ен he is seriously ill; б. вопро́с sore subject; ~ьно́е ме́сто sore spot; свали́ть с б. головы́ на здоро́вую, *see* голова́; *as noun* **б., ~ьно́го,** *m.;* ~ьна́я, ~ьно́й, *f.* patient, invalid; амбулато́рный б. out-patient; стациона́р-ный б. in-patient.

большáк, á, *m.* (*dial.*) **1.** head of the family. **2.** high road.

бо́льше 1. (*comp. of* большо́й *and* вели́кий) bigger, larger; greater; Ло́ндон б. Пари́жа London is larger than Paris. **2.** (*comp. of* мно́го) more; чем б... тем б. the more ... the more; б. того́ and what is more; б. не no more, no longer; он б. не живёт на той у́лице he does not live in that street any longer; б. не бу́ду! I won't do it again!; б. нет вопро́сов? any more questions? **3.** *adv.* (*coll.*) for the most part.

большевиза́ци|я, и, *f.* bolshevization.

большевизи́р|овать, ую, *impf. and pf.* to bolshevize.

большеви́зм, а, *m.* Bolshevism.

большеви́к, á, *m.* Bolshevik.

большеви́стский, *adj.* Bolshevik, Bolshe-vist.

большеголо́вый, *adj.* with a large head; macrocephalous.

бо́льш|ий, comp. of ~о́й *and* вели́кий; greater, larger; ~ей ча́стью, по ~ей ча́сти for the most part; са́мое ~ee at most; съезд бу́дет продолжа́ться са́мое ~ee три дня the congress will last at most three days.

большинств|о́, á, *n.* majority; most (of); в ~é слу́чаев in most cases; б. голосо́в a majority vote.

больш|о́й, *adj.* big, large; great; large-scale; (*coll.*) grown-up; ~áя бу́ква capital (letter); ~áя доро́га high road; ~ое знако́мство wide range of acquaintance; б. па́лец thumb; б. па́лец ноги́ big toe; на б. па́лец (*coll.*) in first-rate fashion, top-hole; ~о́й ско́ростью (*railways*) by fast goods (train); б. свет haut monde, society; когда́ я бу́ду б. when I grow up.

большу́х|а, и, *f.* (*dial.*) mistress (of the house).

большу́щий, *adj.* (*coll.*) huge.

боля́чк|а, и, *f.* sore; scab; (*fig.*) defect.

боля́щий, *pres. part. of* ~еть²; *as noun* б., ~я́щего, *m.* (*usu. joc.*) the patient.

бо́мб|а, ы, *f.* bomb.

бомбарди́р, а, *m.* 1. (*mil., hist.*) bombardier. 2. (*aeron.*) bomb-aimer. 3. (*zool.*) bombardier (*beetle*). 4. (*sport*) striker.

бомбарди́р|ова́ть, у́ю, *impf.* to bombard; to bomb; б. про́сьбами (*fig.*) to bombard with requests.

бомбардиро́вк|а, и, *f.* bombardment.

бомбардиро́вочный, *adj.* bombing.

бомбардиро́вщик, а, *m.* 1. bomber; пики́рующий б. dive-bomber; сре́дний б. medium bomber. 2. (*coll.*) bomber pilot.

бомбёжк|а, и, *f.* (*coll.*) bombing.

бомб|и́ть, лю́, и́шь, *impf.* to bomb.

бомбово́з, а, *m.* bomber.

бо́мб|овый, *adj. of* ~а; б. люк bomb-bay door (*on aircraft*); ~овая нагру́зка bomb-load; б. уда́р thud of exploding bomb.

бомбодержа́тел|ь, я, *m.* bomb-rack.

бомбомёт, а, *m.* (*mil.*) 1. (*naut.*) depth-charge gun. 2. (*obs.*) bomb-thrower.

бомбомета́ни|е, я, *n.* bomb-dropping, bomb-release.

бомбосбра́сывател|ь, я, *m.* bomb-release gear.

бомбоубе́жищ|е, а, *n.* air-raid shelter, bomb-proof shelter.

бом-бра́мсел|ь, я, *m.* (*naut.*) royal (sail).

бом-брам-сте́ньг|а, и, *f.* (*naut.*) royal mast.

бомо́нд, а, *m.* (*obs.*) beau monde, society.

бон, а, *m.* (*naut.*) boom.

бонапарти́зм, а, *m.* (*hist.*) Bonapartism.

бонапарти́ст, а, *m.* (*hist.*) Bonapartist.

бонбонье́рк|а, и, *f.* bonbonnière.

бонвива́н, а, *m.* bon vivant.

бонда́р|ить, ю, ишь, *impf.* (*dial.*) to cooper.

бонда́р|ный, *adj. of* ~ство; ~ное ремесло́ the cooper's craft.

бонда́р|ня, ни, *g. pl.* ~ен, *f.* cooperage.

бо́ндарств|о, а, *n.* coopering, cooperage.

бо́ндар|ь, я/я́, *m.* cooper.

бо́нз|а, ы, *g. pl.* ~, *m.* bonze (*Buddhist priest*); (*fig.*) superior, distant person.

бонмо́, *indecl., n.,* bon mot, witticism.

бонмоти́ст, а, *m.* wit.

бо́нн|а, ы, *f.* nursery-governess.

бонто́н, а, *m.* (*coll., obs.*) bon ton.

бо́н|ы, ~, *sing.* ~а, ~ы, *f.* 1. cheques; vouchers, tokens. 2. emergency paper money.

бор¹, а, о ~е, на ~у́, *pl.* ~ы́, ~о́в, *m.* coniferous forest; с ~у да с со́сенки, с ~у по со́сенке chosen at random; (я ви́жу), отку́да сыр б. загоре́лся (I see) how it all started.

бор², а, *m.* (*chem.*) boron.

бо́ргес, а, *m.* (*typ.*) bourgeois.

борде́л|ь, я, *m.* (*coll.*) brothel.

бордо́ 1. *indecl., n.* claret. **2.** *as adj.* claret-coloured.

бордо́вый, *adj.* claret-coloured.

бордю́р, а, *m.* border (*of fabric, wallpaper, etc.*).

боре́ни|е, я, *n.* (*rhet.*) struggle, fight.

бор|е́ц, ца́, *m.* 1. (за+а.) fighter (for). 2. (*sport*) wrestler.

боржо́м, а, *m.* (*and* ~и, *indecl., n.*) Borzhomi (*kind of mineral water*).

борз|а́я, о́й, *f.* borzoi (*dog*).

борз|о́й, *adj. of* ~а́я.

борзопи́с|ец, ца, *m.* (*iron.*) hack writer.

бо́рзый, *adj.* (*obs. or poet.*) swift, fleet.

бормаши́н|а, ы, *f.* (dentist's) drill.

бормота́ни|е, я, *n.* muttering.

бормо|та́ть, чу́, ~чешь, *impf.* to mutter.

бормоту́н, á, *m.* (*coll.*) 1. mutterer. 2. (*breed of pigeons*) drummer.

борм|очу́, о́чешь, *see* ~ота́ть.

бо́рн|ый, *adj.* (*chem.*) boric, boracic; ~ая кислота́ boric, boracic acid.

бо́ров¹, а, *m.* hog; (*fig.*) obese man.

бо́ров², а, *pl.* ~á, *m.* (*tech.*) horizontal flue.

борови́к, á, *m.* (*dial.*) (edible) boletus (*kind of mushroom*).

борови́нк|а, и, *f.* borovinka (*kind of winter apple*).

бор|ово́й, *adj. of* ~¹.

бор|ода́, оды́, *a.* ~оду, *pl.* ~оды, ~о́д, ~ода́м,** *f.* 1. beard; отпусти́ть ~оду to grow a beard; смея́ться в ~оду to laugh into one's beard. 2. wattles (*of bird*).

борода́вк|а, и, *f.* wart.

борода́вчатый, *adj.* warty.

борода́ст|ый, *adj.* (*coll.*) long-bearded, heavily bearded.

борода́т|ый (~, ~а), *adj.* bearded.

борода́ч, á, *m.* 1. (*coll.*) bearded man. 2. (*bot.*) beard grass. 3. (*orn.*) bearded vulture, lammergeyer.

боро́дк|а¹, и, *f.* small beard, tuft.

боро́дк|а², и, *f.* (*tech.*) key-bit; barb (*of hook*).

бор|озда́, озды́, *a.* ~озду́ *and* ~озду́, *pl.* ~озды, ~о́зд, ~озда́м,** *f.* furrow; (*anat.*) fissure.

бороз|ди́ть, жу́, ди́шь, *impf.* 1. (*pf.* вз~) to furrow; to leave a furrow behind one; (*fig.*) to leave a wake. 2. (*pf.* из~) to cover with furrows; морщи́ны ~ди́ли его́ лоб (*fig.*) wrinkles furrowed his brow; б. океа́ны (*poet.*) to plough, furrow the seas.

боро́здк|а, и, *f.* furrow; groove.

боро́здчатый, *adj.* furrowed; grooved.

бор|она́, оны́, *a.* ~ону, *pl.* ~оны, ~о́н, ~она́м,** *f.* (*agric.*) harrow.

борон|и́ть, ю́, и́шь, *imp.* (*of* вз~) (*agric.*) to harrow.

борон|ова́ть, у́ю, *impf.* (*of* вз~) = ~и́ть.

боронь́б|а́, ы́, f. (*agric.*) harrowing.

бор|о́ться, ю́сь, ~ешься, *impf.* (c+*i.*; за+*a.*; про́тив+*g.*) to wrestle; (*fig.*) to struggle, fight (with; for; against); б. с суеве́рием to struggle against superstition; б. со свое́й со́вестью to wrestle with one's conscience.

борт, а, о ~е, на ~у́, *pl.* **~а́, ~о́в, m.** 1. side (*of a ship*); пра́вый б. starboard side; ле́вый б. port side; на ~у́ on board (*ship or aircraft*); б.-о́-б. broadside to broadside; вы́бросить за́ б. to throw overboard (*also fig.*); челове́к за ~ом! man overboard! 2. coat-breast. 3. cushion (*billiards*).

борт|ево́й, *adj. of* ~ь.

бортмеха́ник, а, m. (*aeron.*) flight engineer.

бо́ртник, а, m. wild-honey farmer.

бо́ртничеств|о, а, n. wild-honey farming.

борт|ово́й, *adj. of* ~; б. журна́л (ship's) log--book; ~ова́я ка́чка (*naut.*) rolling.

бортпроводни́к, а́, m. air steward.

бортпроводни́ц|а, ы, f. stewardess; air hostess.

бортради́ст, а, m. radio operator (*aircraft*).

борт|ь, и, f. hive of wild bees.

борщ, а́, m. borshch (*soup made of beetroot and cabbage*).

борщ|о́к, ка́, m. (clear) beetroot soup.

борьб|а́, ы́, f. 1. (*sport*) wrestling. 2. (*fig.*) (c+*i.*; за+*a.*; про́тив+*g.*) struggle, fight (with; for; against); conflict; кла́ссовая б. the class struggle; душе́вная б. mental strife.

босико́м, *adv.* barefoot; ходи́ть б. to go barefoot.

боске́т, а, m. spinney, copse.

бос|о́й (~, ~а́, ~о), *adj.* barefooted; на ~у́ но́гу with bare feet, barefoot.

босоно́гий, *adj.* barefooted.

босоно́жк|а, и, f. 1. barefoot dancer. 2. (*pl.*) sandals; mules.

босто́н, а, m. Boston (1. *card-game.* 2. *kind of wool cloth.* 3. *name of dance*).

бося|к, а́, m. tramp; down-and-out.

бося́|цкий, *adj. of* ~к.

бот, а, m. boat.

ботанизи́рк|а, и, f. (*coll.*) plant-collecting box.

ботанизи́р|овать, ую, *impf.* to collect plants (*for study*).

бота́ник, а, m. botanist.

бота́ник|а, и, f. botany.

ботани́ческий, *adj.* botanical; б. сад botanical gardens.

ботв|а́, ы́, f. leafy tops of root vegetables (*esp. beet leaves*).

ботви́нь|я, и, f. botvinia (*cold soup of fish, pot-herbs, and kvass*).

бо́тик, а, m. (*obs.*) small boat.

бо́тик|и, ов, *sing.* ~, ~а, m. high (women's) over-shoes.

боти́н|ок, ка, g. pl. б. m. (*ankle-high*) boot.

ботфо́рт|ы, ов, *sing.* ~, ~а, m. (*obs.*) jack-boots, Hessian boots.

бо́т|ы, ов, *sing.* ~, ~а, m. high overshoes.

бо́цман, а, m. (*naut.*) boatswain.

боча́г, а́, m. (*dial.*) pool.

боча́р, а́, pl. ~ы́, m. cooper.

боча́р|ный, *adj. of* ~; coopering.

боча́р|ня, ни, g. pl. ~ен, f. (*dial.*) cooperage.

бо́чк|а, и, f. 1. barrel, cask; (*fig.*) плати́ть де́ньги на ~у to pay on the nail. 2. barrel (*liquid measure about 108 gallons*). 3. (*aeron.*) roll.

бочко́м, *adv.* sideways; пробира́ться б. to sidle.

боч|о́к, ка́, m. (*coll.*) flank.

бочо́н|ок, ка, m. small barrel, keg.

боязли́вост|ь, и, f. timidity, timorousness.

боязли́в|ый (~, ~а), *adj.* timid, timorous.

бо́язно, *adv. as pred.* (+*d.*; *coll.*) to be afraid, frightened; ей б. остава́ться одно́й по вечера́м she is frightened of being left alone in the evening.

боя́зн|ь, и, f. (+*g. or* пе́ред+*i.*) fear (of); dread of; б. темноты́ fear of the dark; б. простра́нства (*med.*) agoraphobia; из ~и for fear of, lest; он переме́ни́л фами́лию из ~и, что бу́дут смея́ться над ним he changed his name for fear of being laughed at.

боя́р|ин, ина, pl. ~е, ~, m. (*hist.*) boyar.

боя́р|ский, *adj. of* ~; ~ские де́ти (*hist.*) the lowest class of boyars.

боя́рств|о, а, n. (*collect.*; *hist.*) the boyars, the nobility.

боя́рын|я, и, f. (*hist.*) boyar's wife.

боя́рышник, а, m. (*bot.*) hawthorn.

боя́рышниц|а, ы, f. pierid butterfly (*Aporia crataegi*).

боя́рыш|ня, ни, g. pl. ~ень, f. (*hist.*) (*un-married*) daughter of a boyar.

бо|я́ться, ю́сь, и́шься, *impf.* (+*g.*) 1. to fear, be afraid (of); она́ ~и́тся темноты́ she is afraid of the dark; он ~и́тся пойти́ к врачу́ he is afraid to go to the doctor; ~ю́сь, что он (не) прие́дет I am afraid that he will (not) come; ~ю́сь, как бы (что́бы) он не прие́хал I am afraid that he may come; ~ю́сь сказа́ть I would not like to say. 2. to be afraid of, suffer from; э́ти расте́ния ~я́тся хо́лода these plants do not like the cold.

бра, *indecl., n.* sconce; lamp-bracket.

брава́д|а, ы, f. bravado.

брави́р|овать, ую, *impf.* (+*i.*) to brave, defy; б. опа́сностью to defy danger.

бра́во, *interj.* bravo!

браву́р|ный (~ен, ~на), *adj.* (*mus.*) bravura.

бра́вый, *adj.* gallant; manly.

брáг|а, и, *f.* home-brewed beer.
брадобрé|й, я, *m.* (*obs. or joc.*) barber.
брáжник, а, *m.* (*obs.*) reveller.
брáжнича|ть, ю, *impf.* (*obs.*) to revel, carouse.
бразд|á, ы́, *f.* (*poet., obs.*) furrow.
бразд|ы́, ~, *now only in phrase* б. правлéния the reins of government.
бразил|ец, ьца, *m.* Brazilian.
бразильский, *adj.* Brazilian.
бразилья́нк|а, и, *f.* Brazilian (woman).
брак¹, а, *m.* marriage; matrimony; граждáнский б. civil marriage; (*obs.*) cohabitation; свидéтельство о ~e certificate of marriage; б. по расчёту marriage of convenience; рождённый вне ~a born out of wedlock.
брак², а, *m.* waste; defective products, rejects.
бракёр, а, *m.* (*tech.*) inspector.
бракерáж, а, *m.* (*tech.*) certification, inspection.
бракóван|ный (~, ~a), *p.p.p. of* браковáть *and adj.* rejected; defective.
брак|овáть, у́ю, *impf.* (*of* за~) to reject (*manufactured articles; also fig.*).
бракóвк|а, и, *f.* rejection (*of defective articles*).
бракóвщик, а, *m.* sorter (*of manufactured articles*).
бракóвщиц|а, ы, *f. of* бракóвщик.
бракодéл, а, *m.* (*coll.*) bad workman.
браконьéр, а, *m.* poacher.
браконьéрств|о, а, *n.* poaching.
браковóдный, *adj.* divorce; б. процéсс divorce suit.
бракосочетáни|е, я, *n.* wedding, nuptials.
брам- (*naut.*) top-.
брамин, а, *m.* Brahmin.
брам-рé|й, я, *m.* (*naut.*) topgallant yard.
брáмсел|ь, я, *m.* (*naut.*) topsail.
брам-стéньг|а, и, *f.* (*naut.*) topgallant (mast).
брандахлы́ст, а, *m.* (*coll.*) 1. slops; swipes. 2. (*fig.*) worthless person.
брандвáхт|а, ы, *f.* guard-ship.
брáндер, а, *m.* 1. (*hist.*) fire-ship; запустить, подпустить б. (*fig.*) to put the cat among the pigeons. 2. block-ship.
брандмайóр, а, *m.* (*obs.*) chief of the fire brigade.
брандмáуэр, а, *m.* fire-proof wall.
брандмéйстер, а, *m.* (*obs.*) chief fireman.
брандспóйт, а, *m.* 1. fire-pump. 2. nozzle. 3. water-cannon.
бран|ить, ю́, ишь, *impf.* (*of* вы́~) to reprove; to scold; to abuse, curse (*coll.*).
бран|иться, ю́сь, ишься, *impf.* 1. (*of* по~) (*c+i*) to quarrel (with). 2. to swear, curse (*intrans.*).
брáнн|ый¹, *adj.* abusive; ~ое слóво swear-word.

брáнный², *adj.* (*obs., poet.*) martial.
бранч(л)ив|ый (~, ~a), *adj.* (*coll.*) quarrelsome.
брáный, *adj.* (*text.; obs.*) embroidered.
бран|ь¹, и, *f.* swearing; abuse; bad language.
бран|ь², и, *f.* (*obs., poet.*) пóле ~и field of battle.
брас, а, *m.* (*naut.*) brace.
браслéт, а, *m.* bracelet.
брас|овáть, у́ю, *impf.* (*naut.*) to brace.
брасс, а, *m.* (*sport*) breast stroke.
брат, а, *pl.* ~ья, ~ьев, *m.* 1. brother; молóчный б. foster-brother; свóдный б. stepbrother; единокрóвный б. half-brother (*by father*); единоутрóбный б. half-brother (*by mother*); двоюрóдный б. cousin. 2. (*fig.*) brother; comrade; ~ья-писáтели fellow-writers; наш б. (*coll.*) we, the likes of us; ваш б. (*coll.*) you, you and your sort. 3. *as familiar or patronising term of address* old man; my lad; (*pl.*) friends, lads. 4. (*eccl.*) lay brother; (*as style*) Brother, Friar; б. милосéрдия male nurse. 5. на ~a (*coll.*) a head; по два я́блока на ~a two apples a head.
братáнь|е, я, *n.* fraternization.
братá|ться, ю́сь, *impf.* (*of* по~) (*c+i*) to fraternize (with).
братв|á, ы́, *f.* (*collect.; coll.*) comrades; chaps, lads.
брáт|ец, ца, *m.* *affectionate or patronising dim. of* ~; (*as term of address*) old man, old chap; boy.
брáтин|а, ы, *f.* (*hist.*) winebowl.
братиш|ка, ки, *g. pl.* ~ек, *m.* (*coll.*) 1. little brother. 2. = брат 2.
брáти|я, и, *g. pl.* ~й, *f.* (*collect.*) brotherhood, fraternity (*also fig.*); доминикáнская б. Dominican community; актёрская б. the acting fraternity.
брáтнин, *adj.* (*coll.*) brother's, belonging to one's brother.
брáт|ок, кá, *m.* (*coll.*) = брат 2.
братоубийственный, *adj.* fratricidal (*also fig.*).
братоубийств|о, а, *n.* fratricide (*act*).
братоубийц|а, ы, *m.* fratricide (*agent*).
брáтск|ий, *adj.* brotherly, fraternal; б. привéт fraternal greetings; ~ая могила communal grave (*esp. of war dead*).
брáтств|о, а, *n.* (*abstr. and concr.*) brotherhood, fraternity.
братýш|ка, ки, *g. pl.* ~ек, *m.* *dim. of* брат; ~ки (*hist.; coll.*) 'the Little Brothers' (= *the Southern Slavs*).
бра|ть, беру́, берёшь, *past* ~л, ~лá, ~ло, *impf.* (*of* взять). 1. (*in var. senses*) to take; б. назáд, б. обрáтно to take back; б. курс (на+*a.*) to make (for), head (for); б. начáло

(в+*p*.) to originate (in); б. но́ту to sing, play a note; б. поруче́ние to undertake a commission; б. приме́р (с+*g*.) to follow the example (of); б. сло́во to take the floor; б. в ско́бки to place in brackets; б. в плен to take prisoner; б. на букси́р to take in tow; б. на пору́ки (*leg.*) to go bail (for); б. на себя́ to take upon oneself; б. под аре́ст to put under arrest; б. кого́-н. под руку to take someone's arm. **2.** to take; to get, obtain; to book; to hire; б. биле́ты to take, book tickets; б. верх to get the upper hand; б. такси́ to take a taxi; б. своё to get one's way; to make itself felt; го́ды беру́т своё age tells; б. взаймы́ to borrow; б. в аре́нду to rent; б. напрока́т to hire. **3.** (в+*n.-a.*) to take (as); б. в жёны to take to wife; б. в свиде́тели to call to witness. **4.** to seize; to grip; б. власть to seize power; его́ берёт страх he is in the grip of fear; б. за се́рдце to move deeply. **5.** to exact; to take (= to demand, require); б. штраф to exact a fine; б. сло́во с кого́-н. to get someone's word; б. вре́мя to take time. **6.** to take; to surmount; б. барье́р to clear a hurdle. **7.** (+*i.*) to succeed (by means of, by dint of); она́ берёт такти́чностью the secret of her success is tact. **8.** (*usu.*+*neg.*; *coll.*) to work, operate; to be effective; (на+*a.*; *of a fire-arm*) to have a range (of); э́ти но́жницы не беру́т these scissors don't cut; э́та винто́вка берёт на пятьсо́т ме́тров this rifle has a range of, is effective at, five hundred metres. **9.** (+*adv. of place*; *coll.*) to bear; б. вле́во to bear left. **10.** (*dial.*) to gather, collect. **11.** (*impf. only*) (*coll.*) to take bribes.

бра́|ться, беру́сь, берёшься, *past* ~лся, ~ла́сь, ~ло́сь, *impf.* (*of* взя́ться). **1.** *pass. of* ~ть. **2.** (за+*a.*) to touch, lay hands (upon); не бери́сь за то́рмоз! don't touch the brake!; б. за́ руки to link arms. **3.** (за+*a.*) to take up; to get down (to); б. за де́ло to get down to business, get down to brass tacks; б. за перо́ to take up the pen; б. за чте́ние to get down to reading. **4.** (за+*a.* *or* +*inf.*) to undertake; to take upon oneself; б. за поруче́ние to undertake a commission; б. вы́полнить рабо́ту to undertake a job; не беру́сь суди́ть I do not presume to judge. **5.** (*3rd person only*) (*coll.*) to appear, arise; не зна́ю, отку́да у них де́ньги беру́тся I don't know where they get their money from. **6.** б. за ум (*coll.*) to come to one's senses. **7.** б. нарасхва́т to sell like hot cakes.

бра́т|ья¹, *see* ~.

бра́ть|я², и, *f.* = бра́тия.

бра́унинг, а, *m.* Browning (*automatic pistol*).

брахицефа́л, а, *m.* (*anthrop.*) brachycephalous person.

брахицефа́ли|я, и, *f.* (*anthrop.*) brachycephaly.

брахма́н, а, *m.* = брами́н.

бра́чн|ый, *adj.* marriage; conjugal; ~ое свиде́тельство marriage certificate; б. наря́д (*zool.*) breeding-dress; ~ое опере́ние (*zool.*) breeding plumage.

бра́чущ|иеся, ихся, *no sing.* parties to a marriage.

бра́шпил|ь, я, *m.* (*naut.*) windlass, capstan.

бреве́нчатый, *adj.* log, made of logs.

брев|но́, на́, *pl.* ~на, ~ен, ~нам, *n.* log, beam; (*fig.*) dullard, insensitive person.

брег, а, *pl.* ~а́, *m.* (*poet.*, *arch.*) = бе́рег.

брегет, а, *m.* (*obs.*) Bréguet (watch).

бред, а, о ~е, в ~у́, *m.* delirium; ravings; (*fig.*) gibberish; быть в ~у́ to be delirious.

бре́д|ень, ня, *m.* drag-net.

бре́|дить, жу, дишь, *impf.* to be delirious, rave; (+*i.*; *fig.*) to rave about, be mad about; он ~дит джа́зом he is crazy about jazz.

бре́|диться, дится, *impf.* (*impers.*+*d.*; *coll.*) to dream (of); ему́ всё ~дилось, что он па́дает в про́пасть he was always dreaming that he was falling down a precipice.

бре́дн|и, ей, *no sing.* ravings; fantasies.

бредово́й, *adj.* **1.** delirious. **2.** (*fig.*) fantastic, nonsensical.

бре|ду́, дёшь, *see* ~сти́.

бре́|жу, дишь, *see* ~дить.

брезг|а́ть, а́ю, а́ешь, *impf.* (*of* по~) (+*i.*) to be squeamish, fastidious (about); он ~а́ет есть немы́тые фру́кты he is squeamish about eating unwashed fruit; тако́й ниче́м бы не ~а́л he is the sort of person who would balk at nothing.

брезгли́в|ец, ца, *m.* squeamish, fastidious person.

брезгли́вост|ь, и, *f.* squeamishness, fastidiousness; disgust.

брезгли́в|ый (~, ~а), *adj.* squeamish, fastidious; ~ое чу́вство feeling of disgust.

брезе́нт, а, *m.* tarpaulin.

брезе́нтовый, *adj.* tarpaulin, canvas.

бре́зж|ить(ся), ~ит(ся), *impf.* to dawn; to glimmer; ~ила заря́ dawn was breaking.

брейд-вы́мпел, а, *m.* (*naut.*) broad pennant.

брёл, а́, *see* брести́.

брело́к, а, *m.* (bracelet) charm.

бремен|и́ть, ю, и́шь, *impf.* (*obs.*) to burden.

бре́мсберг, а, *m.* (*tech.*) gravity roadway.

бре́м|я, ~ени, ~енем, ~ени, *n.* burden; load; разреши́ться от ~ени to be delivered (of a child).

бре́нн|ый (~а, ~о), *adj.* transitory; perishable; ~ые оста́нки mortal remains.

бренч|а́ть, у́, и́шь, *impf.* **1.** (+*i.*) to jingle

слы́шно бы́ло, как ~а́ли шпо́ры the jingling of spurs could be heard; он всё ~а́л моне́тами в карма́не he was always jingling coins in his pocket. 2. (*coll.*) to strum; б. на ро́яле to strum on the piano.

бр|ести́, еду́, еде́шь, *past* ~ёл, ~ела́, *impf.* 1. to shuffle; to drag oneself along. 2. to amble, stroll pensively.

брете́льк|а, и, *f.* shoulder-strap.

брете́р, а, *m.* (*obs.*) duellist, swashbuckler, bully.

брете́р|ский, *adj. of* ~.

брето́н|ец, ца, *m.* Breton.

брето́нк|а, и, *f.* Breton (woman).

брето́нский, *adj.* Breton.

бре|ха́ть, шу́, ~шешь, *impf.* (*coll.*) 1. to yelp, bark. 2. (*fig.*) to tell lies.

брехн|я́, и́, *no pl.,f.* (*coll.*) lies; nonsense.

бреху́н, а́, *m.* (*coll.*) liar.

бреху́н|ец, ца́, *m.* (*coll.*) liar; (*fig., iron.*) lawyer.

бреш|у́, ~ешь, *see* бреха́ть.

бреш|ь, и, *f.* breach; проби́ть б. (в+*p.*) to breach; (*fig.*) flaw, gap, deficit.

бре́|ю, ешь, *see* бри́ть.

бре́ющий, *pres. part. of* брить; б. полёт hedge-hopping flight.

бриг, а, *m.* brig.

брига́д|а, ы,*f.* 1. (*mil.*) brigade; (*naut.*) sub-division. 2. brigade, (work-) team; поездна́я б. train crew; уда́рная б. shock brigade.

бригади́р, а, *m.* 1. (*mil.*; *obs.*) brigadier. 2. brigade-leader; team-leader; foreman.

бригади́рш|а, и,*f.* (*obs.*) brigadier's wife.

брига́дник, а, *m.* member of a brigade, team.

брига́д|ный, *adj. of* ~а.

брига́нти́н|а, ы,*f.* brigantine.

бридж, а, *m.* bridge (*card-game*).

бри́дж|и, ей, *no sing.* breeches.

бриз, а, *m.* breeze.

бриза́нтн|ый, *adj.* high explosive; ~ые вещества́ high explosives; б. снаря́д high explosive shell.

брике́т, а, *m.* briquette.

брил|лиа́нт, а *and* ~ья́нт, а, *m.* (cut) diamond, brilliant.

бриллиа́нт|овый, *adj. of* ~.

брил|ья́нт = ~лиа́нт.

брил|ья́нтовый = ~лиа́нтовый.

брита́н|ец, ца, *m.* Briton.

брита́нк|а, и, *f.* Briton (*woman*).

брита́нский, *adj.* British; б. мета́лл Britannia metal.

бри́тв|а, ы, *f.* razor; безопа́сная б. safety razor.

бри́твенн|ый, *adj.* shaving; ~ые принадле́жности shaving things; б. реме́нь (razor-) strop.

бритт, а, *m.* (ancient) Briton.

бри́т|ый (~, ~а), *p.p.p. of* ~ь *and adj.* clean--shaven.

бр|ить, е́ю, е́ешь, *impf.* (*pf.* по~) to shave.

брить|ё, я́, *n.* shave; shaving.

бр|и́ться, е́юсь, е́ешься, *impf.* to shave, have a shave.

бри́чк|а, и, *f.* (*obs.*) britzka (*light carriage*).

бро́вк|а, и, *f.* 1. *dim. of* бровь. 2. edge (*of running track*).

бро́в|ь, и, *pl.* ~и, ~е́й, *f.* eyebrow; brow; ~и дуго́й arched eyebrows; хму́рить ~и to knit one's brows, frown; он и ~ью не повёл he did not turn a hair; попа́сть не в б., а (пря́мо) в глаз (*prov.*) to hit the nail on the head.

брод, а, *m.* ford; не зна́я ~у, не су́йся в во́ду (*prov.*) look before you leap.

броди́льн|ый, *adj.* (*tech.*) fermentative; б. чан fermenting vat; б. ферме́нт fermenting--agent.

бро|ди́ть¹, жу́, ~дишь, *impf.* to wander, roam; to amble, stroll; б. по у́лицам to roam the streets; б. в потёмках (*fig.*) to be in the dark, not to know one's way about; (*fig.*) улы́бка ~ди́ла на её лице́ a smile played about her face.

бро|ди́ть², ~дит, *impf.* to ferment.

бродя́г|а, и, *m.* tramp, vagrant; down-and--out.

бродя́жнича|ть, ю, *impf.* to be a tramp, be on the road.

бродя́жничеств|о, а, *n.* vagrancy.

бродя́ч|ий, *adj.* vagrant; wandering, roving; (*fig.*) restless; ~ие племена́ nomadic tribes; ~ая соба́ка stray dog.

броже́ни|е, я, *n.* fermentation; б. умо́в (*fig.*) intellectual ferment.

бро|жу́, ~дишь, *see* ~ди́ть.

бром, а, *m.* (*chem.*) bromine; (*med.*) bromide.

бро́мистый, *adj.* (*chem.*) bromide; б. на́трий sodium bromide.

бро́м|овый, *adj. of* ~.

броне- (*mil.*) armoured-.

бронеавтомоби́л|ь, я, *m.* armoured car.

бронебо́йк|а, и, *f.* (*coll.*) anti-tank rifle.

бронебо́йн|ый, *adj.* armour-piercing.

бронебо́йщик, а, *m.* anti-tank rifleman.

броневи́к, а́, *m.* armoured car.

бронев|о́й, *adj.* armoured; ~ые пли́ты (*mil.*) armour plating.

бронено́с|ец¹, ца, *m.* (*naut.*) battleship; ironclad.

бронено́с|ец², ца, *m.* (*zool.*) armadillo.

бронено́сный, *adj.* armoured.

бронепо́езд, а, *m.* armoured train.

бронеси́л|ы, ~, *no sing.* armoured forces.

бронета́нков|ый, *adj.* (*mil.*) armoured; ~ые ча́сти armoured units.

бронетранспортёр, а, *m.* armoured troop carrier.

бро́нз|а, ы, *f.* **1.** bronze. **2.** (*collect.*) bronzes.

бронзир|ова́ть, у́ю, *impf. and pf.* to bronze.

бронзиро́вк|а, и, *f.* bronzing.

бронзиро́вщик, а, *m.* bronzer.

бронзовщи́к, а́, *m.* worker in bronze.

бро́нзов|ый, *adj.* bronze; bronzed, tanned; ~**ая боле́знь** (*med.*) Addison's disease; **б. век** (*archeol.*) the Bronze Age; **б. зага́р** sunburn, sun-tan.

брони́рова|нный, *p.p.p.* of ~**ть** and *adj.* reserved.

брониро́в|анный, *p.p.p.* of ~**а́ть** and *adj.* armoured.

брони́р|овать, ую, *impf.* (*of* за~) to reserve, book.

бронир|ова́ть, у́ю, *impf. and pf.* to armour.

бронх, а, *m.* (*anat.*) bronchial tube.

бронхиа́льный, *adj.* (*anat.*) bronchial.

бронхи́т, а, *m.* (*med.*) bronchitis.

бро́н|я, и, *f.* reservation; commandeering; получи́ть ме́сто по ~**е** to have a seat reserved.

броня́, и́, *f.* armour; armour-plating.

броса́|ть, ю, *impf.* (*of* бро́сить). **1.** to throw, cast, fling; **б. взгляд** to dart a glance; **б. обвине́ния** to hurl accusations; **б. тень** to cast a shadow; (**на**+*a.*; *fig.*) to cast aspersions (on); **б. я́корь** to drop anchor; **б. на ве́тер** to throw away, waste; **б. запасны́е войска́ в бой** to fling reserves into the battle; (*impers.*) **его́** ~**ет то в жар, то в хо́лод** he keeps going hot and cold. **2.** to leave, abandon, desert; **б. му́жа** to desert one's husband; **б. ору́жие** to lay down one's arms; **б. рабо́ту** to give up, throw up one's work. **3.** (+*inf.*) to give up, leave off; **он всё** ~**л кури́ть** he was always trying to give up smoking.

брос|а́ться, а́юсь, *impf.* **1.** (*impf. only*) (+*i.*) to throw at one another, pelt one another (with); по пути́ в шко́лу мы ~**а́лись** снежка́ми we used to pelt one another with snowballs on the way to school. **2.** (*impf. only*) (+*i.*) to throw away; **б. деньга́ми** to throw away, squander one's money. **3.** (*pf.* ~**иться**) (**на, в**+*a.*) to throw oneself (on, upon), rush (to); **б. на еду́** to fall upon one's food; **б. на коле́ни** to fall on one's knees; **б. в объя́тия** (+*d.*) to fall into the arms (of); **б. на по́мощь** to rush to assistance; **б. на ше́ю** (+*d.*) to fall on the neck (of); кровь ~**а́лась ей в лицо́** the blood was rushing to her face. **4.** (*pf.* ~**иться**) **б. в глаза́** to be striking, arrest attention. **5.** (*pf.* ~**иться**) (+*inf.*) to begin, start.

бро́|сить, шу, сишь, *pf.* of ~**са́ть;** ~**сь(те)!** stop it!; хоть ~**сь** (*coll.*) it is no good.

бро́|ситься, шусь, сишься, *pf.* of ~**са́ться.**

бро́с|кий (~**ок,** ~**ка́,** ~**ко),** *adj.* (*coll.*) bright, loud, garish; **б. га́лстук** loud tie.

броско́м, *adv.* (*coll.*) **1.** with one throw. **2.** with a spurt.

бро́совый, *adj.* **1.** worthless; low-grade. **2. б. э́кспорт** (*econ.*) dumping.

брос|о́к, ка́, *m.* (*coll.*) **1.** throw. **2.** bound; spurt; **он пришёл пе́рвым в го́нке благодаря́ после́днему** ~**ку́** he came in first in the race by making a final spurt.

бро́шк|а, и, *f.* brooch.

бро́|шу, сишь, *see* ~**сить.**

брош|ь, и, *f.* brooch.

броши́р- (~**ова́ть,** *etc.*)=брошюр-.

брошю́р|а, ы, *f.* pamphlet, brochure.

брошюр|ова́ть, у́ю, *impf.* (*of* с~) (*tech.*) to stitch.

брошюро́вк|а, и, *f.* (*tech.*) stitching.

брошюро́вочн|ая, ой, *f.* book-stitching shop.

брошюро́вщик, а, *m.* (*tech.*) stitcher.

бру́дер, а, *m.* brooder (*for poultry*).

брудерша́фт, а, *m. only in phrase* вы́пить (на) **б.** to drink 'Bruderschaft'.

брульо́н, а, *m.* (*obs.*) rough copy.

брус, а, *pl.* ~**ья,** ~**ьев,** *m.* squared beam; паралле́льные ~**ья** (*sport*) parallel bars.

бруско́в|ый, *adj.* bar, bar-shaped; ~**ое желе́зо** bar-iron; ~**ое мы́ло** bar soap.

брусни́к|а, и, *f.* foxberry; red whortleberry (*Vaccinium vitis idaea*).

брусни́|чный, *adj. of* ~**ка.**

брус|о́к, ка́, *m.* bar; ingot; **б. мы́ла** bar of soap; точи́льный **б.** whetstone.

бру́ствер, а, *m.* (*mil.*) breastwork, parapet.

бру́тто, *indecl., adj.* gross; вес **б.** gross weight.

брыже́йк|а, и, *f.* (*anat.*) mesentery.

брыж|и, ей, *no sing.* ruff, frill.

бры́з|гать, жу, жешь, *impf.* (*of* ~**нуть**) (+*i.*) **1.** to splash, spatter; to gush, spurt; **б. гря́зью** (**на**+*a.*) to splash mud (on to), spatter with mud. **2.** (*pres.* ~**жу** or ~**гаю**) to sprinkle.

бры́зга|ться, юсь, *impf.* (*coll.*) to splash; to splash oneself, one another; соба́ки лю́бят **б. в лу́жах** the dogs enjoy splashing in the puddles; **б. духа́ми** to spray oneself with scent.

бры́зг|и, ~, *no sing.* **1.** spray, splashes (*of liquids*). **2.** fragments (*of stone, glass, etc.*).

бры́з|жу, жешь, *see* ~**гать.**

бры́з|нуть, ну, нешь, *pf. of* ~**гать;** кровь ~**нула из ра́ны** blood spurted from the wound.

брык|а́ть, а́ю, *impf.* (*of* ~**ну́ть**) to kick.

брыка́|ться, юсь, *impf.* to kick; (*fig.*) to kick, rebel.

брыкли́в|ый (~, ~**а**), *adj.* (*coll.*) inclined to kick.

брык|ну́ть, ну́, нёшь, *pf. of* ~**а́ть.**

брыку́н, а́, *m.* (*coll., dial.*) kicker.

бры́нз|а, ы, *f.* brynza (*sheep's milk cheese*).

брысь, *interj.* shoo! (*to a cat*).

брюзг|а́, и́, *m. and f.* grumbler.

брюзгли́в|ый (~, ~а), *adj.* grumbling, peevish.

брюзжа́ни|е, я, *n.* grumbling.

брюзж|а́ть, у́, и́шь, *impf.* to grumble.

брю́кв|а, ы, *f.* (*bot.*) swede.

брю́кв|енный, *adj. of* ~а.

брю́к|и, ~, *no sing.* trousers.

брюне́т, а, *m.* dark-haired man.

брюне́тк|а, и, *f.* brunette.

брю́ссельск|ий, *adj.* Brussels; ~ая капу́ста Brussels sprouts; ~ие кружева́ Brussels lace.

брюха́ст|ый (~, ~а), *adj.* (*coll.*) big-bellied.

брюха́|тить, чу, тишь, *impf.* (*vulg.*) to get with child.

брюха́т|ый, *adj.* (*coll.*) = брюха́стый; ~ая big with child.

брюх|о, а, *pl.* ~и, *n.* (*coll.*) belly; paunch; ходи́ть с ~ом (*vulg.*) to be big with child.

брюхоно́г|ие, их, (*zool.*) gasteropods.

брюши́н|а, ы, *f.* (*anat.*) peritoneum; воспале́ние ~ы (*med.*) peritonitis.

брюшк|о́, а́, *pl.* ~и́, ~о́в, *n.* 1. abdomen; (*coll.*) paunch. 2. belly-pieces [(*i*) *of fur-bearing animals*, (*ii*) *of fish as food*].

брюшно́й, *adj.* abdominal; б. тиф typhoid (fever).

бряк, *interj.* bang!, crash!

бря́кань|е, я, *n.* (*coll.*) clatter.

бря́к|ать, аю, *impf.* (*of* ~нуть) (*coll.*) 1. (+*i.*) to clatter; б. посу́дой to clatter crockery. 2. to let fall with a bang; (*fig.*) to drop a clanger. 3. to blurt out.

бря́к|аться, аюсь, *impf.* (*of* ~нуться) (*coll.*) to crash, fall heavily.

бря́к|нуть(ся), ну(сь), нешь(ся), *pf. of* ~ать(ся).

бряца́ни|е, я, *n.* 1. rattling. 2. rattle; clang; clank, clanking; б. шпор the rattle of spurs; б. ору́жием sabre-rattling.

бряца́|ть, ю, *impf.* (+*i. or* на+*p.*) to rattle; to clang; to clank; б. цимба́лами to clash cymbals; б. ору́жием (*fig.*) to rattle the sabre; кимва́л ~ющий (*iron.*) 'tinkling cymbal'.

бу́б|ен, на, *g. pl.* ~ен, *m.* tambourine.

бубен|е́ц, ца́, *m.* little bell; колпа́к с ~ца́ми cap and bells.

бубе́нчик, а, *m.* 1. *dim. of* бубене́ц. 2. (*bot.*) harebell, campanula.

бу́блик, а, *m.* boublik (*thick, ring-shaped bread roll*).

бу́б|на, ны, *g. pl.* ~ён, *f.* (*cards*) 1. (*pl.*) diamonds; ходи́ть с ~ён to lead diamonds; дво́йка ~ён the two of diamonds. 2. a diamond.

бубн|и́ть, ю́, и́шь, *impf.* (*of* про~) (*coll.*) to grumble; to mutter; to drone on (*of a speaker*).

бубно́вый, *adj.* (*cards*) diamond; б. туз ace of diamonds; (*hist.*; *fig.*) diamond-shaped patch on convict's coat.

бу́б|ны¹, ен, *see* ~ен.

бу́б|ны², ён, *see* ~на.

бубо́н, а, *m.* (*med.*) bubo.

бубо́н|ный, *adj. of* ~; ~ная чума́ (*med.*) bubonic plague.

буга́|й, я, *m.* (*dial.*) bull (*also fig.*).

бу́гел|ь, я, *m.* 1. (*naut.*) hoop. 2. (*electr.*) bow-collector.

буг|о́р, ра́, *m.* mound, knoll; bump, lump.

бугор|о́к, ка́, *m.* 1. *dim. of* ~; knob, protuberance. 2. (*med.*) tubercle.

бугорча́тк|а, и, *f.* (*med.*; *obs.*) tuberculosis.

буго́рчатый, *adj.* 1. covered with lumps. 2. (*med.*) tuberculous. 3. (*bot.*) tuberous.

бугри́ст|ый (~, ~а), *adj.* hilly; bumpy.

бугшпри́т = бушпри́т.

будди́зм, а, *m.* Buddhism.

будди́йский, *adj.* Buddhist.

будди́ст, а, *m.* Buddhist.

бу́де, *conj.* (*obs.*) if, provided that.

будёновк|а, и, *f.* (*hist.*) budyonovka (*pointed helmet worn by Red Army men during period 1918–21*).

бу́дет 1. *3rd sing. fut. of* быть; б. ему́ за э́то! he'll catch it. 2. *as pred.* (*coll.*) that's enough, that'll do; б. с вас э́того? will that do?; вы́пьем ещё одну́ буты́лку и б. we'll drink one more bottle and call it a day; уже́ за́ полночь, б. вам писа́ть it's past midnight, it's time you stopped writing.

буди́льник, а, *m.* alarmclock.

буди́р|овать, ую, *impf.* (*obs.*) to sulk.

бу|ди́ть, жу́, ~дишь, *impf.* 1. (*pf.* раз~) to wake, awaken, call. 2. (*pf.* про~) (*fig.*) to rouse, arouse; to stir up; б. мысль to set (one) thinking, give food for thought.

бу́дк|а, и, *f.* box, booth; stall; железнодоро́жная б. (railway) trackman's hut, crossing-keeper's hut; карау́льная б. sentry-box; соба́чья б. dog kennel; суфлёрская б. prompt-box; телефо́нная б. telephone booth.

бу́д|ни, ней, *sing.* (*obs. or coll.*) ~ень, ~ня, *m.* 1. weekdays; working days, workdays; по ~ням on weekdays. 2. humdrum life; colourless existence.

бу́дний, *adj.* б. день weekday.

бу́дничн|ый, *adj.* 1. б. день weekday; ~ое расписа́ние weekday timetable. 2. everyday; dull, humdrum.

бу́днишний, *adj.* = бу́дничный.

будора́ж|ить, у, ишь, *impf.* (*of* вз~) (*coll.*) to disturb; to excite.

бу́дочник, а, *m.* 1. (*obs.*) policeman on duty. 2. railway trackman; crossing-keeper.

бу́дто 1. *conj.* as if, as though; он верну́лся с таки́м ви́дом, б. его́ изби́ли he came

back looking as if he had been beaten up.
2. *conj.* that (*implying doubt as to the truth
of a reported affirmation*); он утвержда́ет, б.
говори́т свобо́дно на десяти́ языка́х he
says that he speaks, he claims to speak ten
languages fluently. **3.** (*also* б. бы, как б.)
particle (*coll.*) apparently; allegedly, ostensibly; она́ б. должна́ уха́живать за отцо́м
apparently she has to look after her father.
4. *interrog. particle* (*coll.*) really?; уж б. он
так умён? is he really all that clever?

бу́д|у, ешь, *future of* быть.

будуа́р, а, *m.* boudoir.

будуа́р|ный, *adj. of* ~.

бу́дучи, *pres. gerund of* быть being.

бу́дущ|ий, *adj.* future; next; ~ее вре́мя
(*gram.*) future tense; в ~ем году́ next year;
в б. раз next time; *as noun* ~ее, ~его, *n.*
(*i*) the future; в ближа́йшем ~ем in the
near future, (*ii*) (*gram.*) future tense.

бу́дущност|ь, и, *f.* future; ему́ предстои́т
блестя́щая б. a brilliant future lies before
him.

бу́дь(те), *imp. of* быть (*sing. also used in place
of* éсли+*main verb to form protasis of conditional sentences*) бу́дьте добры́, б. любе́зны
(+*inf. or imp.*) please; would you be good
enough (to), kind enough (to); будь, что
бу́дет come what may; не будь вас, всё
бы пропа́ло but for you all would have
been lost; будь он бога́т, будь он бе́ден,
мне всё равно́ be he rich or be he poor, it
is all one to me.

бу́|ёк, йка́, *m.* (*naut.*) anchor-buoy, life-
buoy.

бу́ер, а, *pl.* ~а́, *m.* **1.** ice-yacht, land-yacht.
2. (*obs.*) small sailing-boat.

буера́к, а, *m.* (*dial.*) gully; coombe.

буж, а́, *m.* (*med.*) probe.

бужени́н|а, ы, *f.* boiled salted pork.

бу́|жу́, ~дишь, *see* ~ди́ть.

буз|а́¹, ы́, *f.* (*dial.*) bouza (*fermented beverage
made from millet, buckwheat or barley*).

буз|а́², ы́, *f.* (*coll.*) row; подня́ть ~у́ to kick
up a row.

бузина́, ы́, *f.* (*bot.*) elder.

бузи́нник, а, *m.* (*bot.*) elder grove, elder-
bush.

бузи́н|ный, *adj. of* ~а́.

бузи́|ть (*1st person not used*), ~шь, *impf.* (*coll.*)
to kick up a row.

буз|ова́ть, у́ю, *impf.* (*coll.*) to beat.

бузотёр, а, *m.* (*coll.*) rowdy.

бузотёрств|о, а, *n.* (*coll.*) rowdyism.

бузу́н¹, а́, *m.* salt-lumps (*precipitated in salt
lakes*).

бузу́н², а́, *m.* (*coll.*) rowdy.

бу́|й, я, pl. ~й, ~ёв, *m.* buoy.

бу́йвол, а, *m.* (*zool.*) buffalo.

бу́йвол|овый, *adj. of* ~; ~овая ко́жа buff.

бу́|йный (~ен, ~йна́, ~йно), *adj.* **1.** wild;
violent, turbulent; tempestuous; ungovernable; б. сумасше́дший violent, dangerous
lunatic; б. хара́ктер ungovernable character. **2.** luxuriant, lush; б. рост luxuriant
growth.

бу́йств|о, а, *n.* unruly, riotous conduct.

бу́йств|овать, ую, *impf.* (*coll.*) to create
uproar; to behave violently.

бук, а, *m.* beech.

бу́к|а, и, *m. and f.* (*coll.*) **1.** bogy(man), bug-
bear. **2.** (*fig.*) misanthrope, unsociable person; surly person; смотре́ть ~ой to look
surly.

бука́шк|а, и, *f.* small insect.

бу́кв|а, ы, g. pl. ~, *f.* letter (of the alphabet);
б. в ~у literally; б. зако́на (*fig.*) the letter
of the law.

буква́льно, *adv.* literally; word for word.

буква́льн|ый, *adj.* literal; ~ое значе́ние
literal meaning; б. перево́д word-for-word
translation.

буква́р|ь, я́, *m.* ABC; primer.

бу́квенный, *adj.* in letters.

бу́квиц|а, ы, *f.* (*bot.*) wood betony.

буквое́д, а, *m.* pedant.

буквое́дств|о, а, *n.* pedantry.

буке́т, а, *m.* **1.** bouquet; bunch of flowers,
posy. **2.** bouquet; aroma.

букини́ст, а, *m.* second-hand bookseller.

букинисти́ческий, *adj.* б. магази́н second-
-hand bookshop.

букле́т, а, *m.* booklet.

бу́кл|я, и, *f.* curl; ringlet.

бу́ковый, *adj.* beech(en); б. жёлудь beechnut.

буко́лик|а, и, *f.* (*lit.*) bucolic literature.

буколи́ческий, *adj.* bucolic, pastoral.

букс, а, *m.* (*bot.*) box.

бу́кс|а, ы, *f.* (*tech.*) axle-box.

букси́р, а, *m.* **1.** tug, tugboat. **2.** tow-rope;
взять на б. to take in tow; (*fig.*) to give a
helping hand; тяну́ть на ~e to have in tow.

букси́р|ный, *adj. of* ~; б. парохо́д steam
tug.

букси́р|овать, ую, *impf.* to tow, have in
tow.

буксиро́вк|а, и, *f.* towing.

буксова́ни|е, я, *n.* skidding, wheel-spin.

букс|ова́ть, у́ю, *impf.* to skid (*of wheels of
locomotive, etc., to revolve on the spot without
moving forward*).

бу́кс|овый, *adj. of* ~.

булав|а́, ы́, *f.* mace.

була́вк|а, и, *f.* pin; англи́йская б. safety-
-pin; де́ньги на ~и pin-money.

була́вочник, а, *m.* **1.** pincushion, pin-box.
2. pin-maker.

була́в|очный, *adj. of* ~ка.

була́ный, *adj.* Isabel(la), dun (*colour of horse*).

була́т, а, *m.* (*hist.*) damask steel; (*fig.*) sword.

була́т|ный, *adj. of* ~; (*hist., poet.*; *conventional epithet of sword*).

булга́ч|ить, у, ишь, *impf.* (*coll.*) to stir up, excite.

бу́лин|ь, я, *m.* (*naut.*) bowline.

бу́лк|а, и, *f.* small loaf; white bread; сдо́бная б. bun.

бу́лл|а, ы, *f.* (Papal) bull.

бу́лочн|ая, ой, *f.* bakery; baker's shop.

бу́лочник, а, *m.* baker.

булты́х, *interj.* plop! (*also as pred.*) де́вочка б. в во́ду the little girl fell plop into the water.

булты́х|а́ть, а́ю, *impf.* (*of* ~ну́ть) (*coll.*) 1. to slop. 2. to drop with a plopping noise (*into liquid*).

булты́х|а́ться, а́юсь, *impf.* (*coll.*) 1. (*pf.* ~ну́ться) to fall plop. 2. (*impf. only*) to flounder (about).

булты́х|ну́ть, ну-ну́, нешь-нёшь, *pf. of* ~а́ть.

булты́х|ну́ться, нусь-ну́сь, нешься-нёшься, *pf. of* ~а́ться.

булы́жник, а, *m.* cobble-stone (*also collect.*).

бульва́р, а, *m.* avenue; boulevard.

бульва́р|ный, *adj. of* ~; ~ная пре́сса gutter press; б. рома́н cheap novel.

бульдо́г, а, *m.* bulldog.

бульдо́зер, а, *m.* bulldozer.

бу́лькань|е, я, *n.* gurgling.

бу́лька|ть, ю, *impf.* to gurgle.

бульо́н, а, *m.* broth.

бум¹, а, *m.* (*coll.*) 1. (*econ.*) boom. 2. newspaper sensation.

бум², а, *m.* (*sport*) beam.

бум³, *interj.* boom!

бума́г|а¹, и, *f.* 1. paper; газе́тная б. newsprint; б. в кле́тку squared paper. 2. document; (*pl.*) (official) papers; це́нные ~и (*fin.*) securities.

бума́г|а², и, *f.* (хлопча́тая) б. cotton; шерсть с ~ой wool and cotton.

бумагодержа́тел|ь¹, я, *m.* (*fin.*) holder of securities, bondholder.

бумагодержа́тел|ь², я, *m.* paper-clip.

бумагомара́ни|е, я, *n.* (*coll.*) scrawl.

бумагомара́тел|ь, я, *m.* (*coll.*) scribbler.

бумагопряде́ни|е, я, *n.* cotton-spinning.

бумагопряди́льн|ый, *adj.* cotton-spinning; ~ая фа́брика cotton mill.

бумагопряди́л|ьня, ьни, *g. pl.* ~ен, *f.* cotton mill.

бума́жк|а, и, *f.* 1. *dim. of* бума́га scrap of paper. 2. note; (paper) money.

бума́жник¹, а, *m.* wallet.

бума́жник², а, *m.* paper-maker.

бума́|жный¹, *adj. of* ~га¹; (*fig.*) (existing only on) paper; ~жная волоки́та red tape; ~жные де́ньги paper money; б. змей kite; ~жная фа́брика paper-mill.

бума́|жный², *adj. of* ~га²; ~жная пря́жа cotton yarn; ~жная ткань cotton fabric.

бума́жо́нк|а, и, *f.* (*coll.*) scrap of paper.

бумазе́йный, *adj.* fustian.

бумазе́|я, и, *f.* fustian.

бумера́нг, а, *m.* boomerang.

бу́нкер, а, *m.* (*tech.*) bunker.

бу́нкер|ова́ть, у́ю, *impf. and pf.* to bunker.

бу́нкер|ова́ться, у́юсь, *impf. and pf.* (*naut.*) to coal.

бункеро́вк|а, и, *f.* coaling.

бунт¹, а, *pl.* ~ы́, *m.* revolt; riot; mutiny.

бунт², а́, *m.* bale; packet; bundle.

бунта́рский, *adj.* 1. seditious; mutinous. 2. (*fig.*) rebellious; turbulent; б. дух rebellious spirit.

бунта́рств|о, а, *n.* rebelliousness.

бунта́р|ь, я́, *m.* 1. rebel (*also fig.*); insurgent; mutineer; rioter; он б. в душе́ he is a rebel at heart. 2. inciter to mutiny, rebellion.

бунт|ова́ть, у́ю, *impf.* 1. (*pf.* взбунтова́ться) to revolt, rebel; to mutiny; to riot; (*fig.*) to rage, go berserk. 2. (*pf.* вз~) to incite to revolt, mutiny.

бунт|ова́ться, у́юсь, *impf.* = ~ова́ть 1.

бунт|ово́й, *adj. of* ~².

бунто́вско́й, *adj.* rebellious, mutinous.

бунтовщи́к, а́, *m.* rebel, insurgent; mutineer; rioter.

бунчу́к, а́, *m.* (*hist.*) staff of Cossack hetman.

бур¹, а, *m.* (*tech.*) auger.

бур², а, *m.* Boer.

бур|а́, ы́, *f.* (*chem.*) borax.

бура́в, а́, *pl.* ~а́, *m.* (*tech.*) auger; gimlet.

бура́в|ить, лю, ишь, *impf.* to bore, drill.

бура́вчик, а, *m.* gimlet.

бура́к, а́, *m.* 1. (*dial.*) beetroot. 2. (*dial.*) cylindrical birch-bark box. 3. cascade (*kind of firework*).

бура́н, а, *m.* snow-storm (*in steppes*).

бурбо́н, а, *m.* (*coll., obs.*) coarse fellow; upstart.

бургоми́стр, а, *m.* burgomaster.

бурго́нское = бургу́ндское.

бургу́ндск|ий, *adj.* Burgundian; *as noun* ~ое, ~ого, *n.* burgundy (*wine*).

бурд|а́, ы́, *f.* slops.

бурдю́к, а́, *m.* wineskin, water-skin.

буреве́стник, а, *m.* stormy petrel.

бур|ево́й, *adj. of* ~я; stormy.

бурело́м, а, *m.* wind-fallen trees.

буре́ни|е, я, *n.* (*tech.*) boring, drilling; о́пытное б. test boring; уда́рное б. percussion drilling.

буре́|ть, ю, ешь, *impf.* (*of* по~) to grow brown.

буржуа́, *indecl., m.* bourgeois.

буржуази́|я, и, *f.* bourgeoisie; ме́лкая б. petty bourgeoisie.

буржуа́з|ный (~ен, ~на), *adj.* bourgeois.

буржу́|й, я, *m.* (*coll.*) bourgeois.
буржу́й|ка, ки, *f.* 1. *f. of* ~. 2. (*coll.*) small stove.
буржу́йский, *adj.* (*coll.*) bourgeois.
бури́льный, *adj.* (*tech.*) boring.
бури́льщик, а, *m.* borer; driller, drill-operator.
бур|и́ть, ю́, и́шь, *impf.* (*tech.*) to bore; to drill.
бу́рк|а¹, и, *f.* (*folk poet.*) chestnut horse.
бу́рк|а², и, *f.* felt cloak (*worn in Caucasus*).
бу́ркал|ы, ~, *no sing.* (*coll.*) eyes.
бу́рк|ать, аю, *impf.* (*of* ~нуть) (*coll.*) to mutter, growl out.
бу́рк|нуть, ну, нешь, *pf. of* ~ать.
бурла́к, а́, *m.* barge hauler.
бурла́|цкий, *adj. of* ~к.
бурла́честв|о, а, *n.* trade of barge hauler.
бурла́ч|ить, у, ишь, *impf.* to be a barge hauler.
бурли́в|ый (~, ~а), *adj.* turbulent; seething.
бурл|и́ть, ю́, и́шь, *impf.* to seethe, boil up (*also fig.*).
бурми́стр, а, *m.* (*hist.*) bailiff.
бурну́с, а, *m.* burnous.
бу́р|ный (~ен, ~на́), *adj.* 1. stormy, rough; impetuous; ~ные аплодисме́нты loud cheers, stormy applause. 2. rapid; energetic; б. рост rapid growth.
бурови́к, а́, *m.* (*tech.*) boring, drilling technician.
буров|о́й, *adj.* boring; ~а́я вы́шка derrick; ~а́я сква́жина bore, bore-hole, well.
бу́рс|а, ы, *f.* (*hist.*) seminary.
бурса́к, а́, *m.* (*hist.*) seminarist.
бурса́|цкий, *adj. of* ~к.
бу́рский, *adj.* Boer.
бу́ртик, а, *m.* (*tech., naut.*) fender.
буру́н, а́, *m.* breaker; bow-wave.
бурунду́к, а́, *m.* (*zool.*) chipmunk.
бурча́ни|е, я, *n.* (*coll.*) grumbling; (stomach-)rumbling.
бурч|а́ть, у́, и́шь, *impf.* (*of* про~) (*coll.*) 1. to mumble, mutter; to grumble. 2. (*impf. only*) to rumble; to bubble; (*impers.*) в котле́ ~и́т the cauldron is bubbling; у меня́ ~и́т в животе́ my stomach is rumbling.
бу́р|ый (~, ~а́, ~о), *adj.* brown; б. медве́дь brown bear; ~ая лиси́ца red fox.
бурья́н, а, *m.* tall weeds.
бу́р|я, и, *f.* storm (*also fig.*); б. в стака́не воды́ storm in a teacup; б. и на́тиск (*hist., lit.*) 'Sturm und Drang'.
буря́т, а, *g. pl.* ~, *m.* Buryat.
буря́тк|а, и, *f.* Buryat (woman).
буря́тский, *adj.* Buryat.
бу́син|а, ы, *f.* bead.
буссо́л|ь, и, *f.* surveying compass.
бу́с|ы, ~, *no sing.* beads.
бут, а, *m.* (*tech.*) rubble, quarry-stone.

бутафо́р, а, *m.* (*theatr.*) property-man.
бутафо́ри|я, и, *f.* (*theatr.*) properties; dummies (*in shop window*); (*fig.*) window-dressing, sham.
бутафо́р|ский, *adj. of* ~ия; (*fig.*) sham, mock-; illusory.
бутербро́д, а, *m.* slice of bread and butter; sandwich.
бути́л, а, *m.* (*chem.*) butyl.
бутиле́н, а, *m.* (*chem.*) butylene.
бу|ти́ть, чу́, ти́шь, *impf.* (*of* за~) (*tech.*) to fill with rubble.
бу́товый, *adj.* rubble.
буто́н, а, *m.* 1. bud. 2. (*coll.*) pimple.
бутонье́рк|а, и, *f.* buttonhole, posy.
бу́тс|ы, ~, *sing.* ~а, ы, *f.* football boots.
буту́з, а, *m.* (*coll.*) chubby lad.
буту́|зить, жу, зишь, *impf.* (*coll.*) to punch.
буты́лк|а, и, *f.* bottle.
буты́лочк|а, и, *f.* small bottle; vial, phial.
буты́лочник, а, *m.* glass-blower.
буты́л|очный, *adj. of* ~ка; ~очного цве́та bottle-green.
буты́л|ь, и, *f.* large bottle; carboy, drum.
бу́фер, а, *pl.* ~а́, *m.* buffer.
бу́фер|ный, *adj. of* ~; ~ное госуда́рство (*polit.*) buffer state.
буфе́т, а, *m.* 1. sideboard. 2. buffet, refreshment room; (refreshment) bar, counter.
буфе́тн|ая, ой, *f.* pantry.
буфе́т|ный, *adj. of* ~.
буфе́тчик, а, *m.* barman, bartender.
буфе́тчиц|а, ы, *f.* barmaid.
буфф, *indecl.*, *adj.* comic, buffo; о́пера-б. comic opera; теа́тр-б. comedy.
буффо́н, а, *m.* (*theatr.*) buffoon; (*fig.*) buffoon, clown.
буффона́д|а, ы, *f.* (*theatr.*) buffoonery, slapstick; (*fig.*) buffoonery.
бу́ф|ы, ~, *no sing.* gathers, puffs; б. на рукава́х puff sleeves.
бух, *interj.* (*also as pred.*) bang!; plonk!; plop!; он б. на зе́млю he fell to the ground with a thud.
буха́нк|а, и, *f.* loaf.
буха́рский, *adj.* б. ковёр Bokhara carpet.
бу́х|ать, аю, *impf.* (*of* ~нуть) 1. to thump, bang; б. кулако́м в дверь to bang on the door with one's fist. 2. to let fall with a thud. 3. to thud, thunder; слы́шно бы́ло, как вдали́ ~али пу́шки the thunder of cannon could be heard in the distance. 4. (*fig., coll.*) to blurt out.
бу́х|аться, аюсь, *impf.* (*of* ~нуться) (*coll.*) to fall heavily; to plonk oneself down.
бухга́лтер, а, *pl.* ~ы, *m.* book-keeper, accountant.
бухгалте́ри|я, и, *f.* 1. book-keeping; двойна́я б. double-entry book-keeping. 2. counting-house.

бухга́лтерск|ий, *adj.* book-keeping, account; ~ая кни́га account book.

бу́х|нуть¹, ну, нешь, *past* ~нул, *pf. of* ~ать.

бу́х|нуть², ну, нешь, *past* ~, ~ла, *impf.* to swell, expand.

бу́х|нуться, нусь, нешься, *pf. of* ~аться.

бухо́й, *adj.* (*sl.*) sozzled (= *drunk*).

бу́хт|а¹, ы, *f.* (*geogr.*) bay, bight.

бу́хт|а², ы, *f.* coil (*of rope*).

бу́хточк|а, и, *f.* creek, cove, inlet.

бу́хты-бара́хты, *only in phrase* (*coll.*) с б.-б. offhand; off the cuff; suddenly.

бу́цы = бу́тсы.

бу́ч|а, и, *f.* (*coll.*) row.

бу́чени|е, я, *n.* (*tech.*) washing in lye.

бу́ч|ить, у, ишь, *impf.* (*tech.*) to wash in lye.

бу|чу́, ти́шь, *see* ~ти́ть.

бу́ч|у, ишь, *see* ~ить.

буш|ева́ть, у́ю, *impf.* to rage; (*fig.*) to rage, storm.

бу́шел|ь, я, *m.* bushel.

бушла́т, а, *m.* (*naut.*) pea-jacket.

бушпри́т, а, *m.* (*naut.*) bowsprit.

буя́н¹, а, *m.* (*coll.*) rowdy, brawler.

буя́н², а, *m.* (*obs.*) wharf.

буя́н|ить, ю, ишь, *impf.* (*coll.*) to make a row; to brawl.

буя́нств|о, а, *n.* (*coll.*) rowdyism, brawling.

бы (*abbr.* б), *particle* **1.** *indicates hypothetical sentence* (*see also* е́сли): я мог бы об э́том догада́ться I might have guessed it; бы́ло бы о́чень прия́тно вас ви́деть it would be very nice to see you. **2.** (+ни) *forms indefinite pronouns*: кто бы ни whoever; что бы ни whatever; как бы ни however; кто бы ни пришёл whoever comes; что бы ни случи́лось whatever happens; как бы то ни́ было however that may be, be that as it may. **3.** *expresses wish*: я бы вы́пил пи́ва I should like a drink of beer. **4.** *expresses polite suggestion or exhortation*: вы бы отдохну́ли you should take a rest.

быва́|ло **1.** *see* ~ть. **2.** *particle indicating repetition of an action in past time*: моя́ мать б. ча́сто пе́ла э́ту пе́сню my mother would often sing this song.

быва́л|ый, *adj.* **1.** experienced; worldly-wise. **2.** (*coll.*) habitual, familiar; э́то де́ло ~ое this is nothing new. **3.** (*obs.*) former.

быва́|ть, ю, *impf.* **1.** to happen; to take place; заседа́ния горсове́та ~ют раз в неде́лю the town council meets once a week; ~ет, что поезда́ с се́вера опа́здывают trains from the north are apt to be late, are sometimes late; э́тому не б.! this must not occur!; I forbid it! **2.** to be; to be present; to frequent; он ~ет ка́ждый день в кабине́те с девяти́ часо́в утра́ he is in his office every day from nine a.m.; они́ ре́дко ~ют в теа́тре they seldom go to the theatre;

он ~ет у нас he comes to see us. **3.** to be inclined to be, tend to be; он ~ет раздражи́телен he is inclined to be irritable. **4.** как ни в чём не ~ло (*coll.*) as if nothing had happened; as if nothing were wrong; как не ~ло (+*g.*) to have completely disappeared; головно́й бо́ли у меня́ как не ~ло my headache has completely gone.

бы́вш|ий, *past part. of* быть *and adj.* former, ex-; ci-devant; б. президе́нт former president; ~ие лю́ди déclassés; го́род Ку́йбышев, ~ая Сама́ра Kuibyshev, formerly (called) Samara.

бы́дл|о, а, *n.* (*collect.*; *dial.*; *also fig.*) cattle.

бык¹, а́, *m.* **1.** bull; ox; рабо́чий б. draught ox; бой ~о́в bullfight; взять ~а́ за рога́ (*fig.*) to take the bull by the horns; здоро́в, как б. as strong as a horse; упере́ться, как б. to be as stubborn as an ox. **2.** male (*of certain horned animals*); оле́ний б. stag. **3.** (*pl.*) the Bovidae.

бык², а́, *m.* pier (*of a bridge*).

был|ево́й, *adj. of* ~и́на.

были́н|а, ы, *f.* (*lit.*) bylina (*Russian traditional heroic poem*).

были́нк|а, и, *f.* blade of grass.

были́н|ный, *adj. of* ~а; epic.

бы́ло, *particle* **1.** *indicates cancellation of projected or impending action*: nearly, on the point of; он пое́хал б. с ни́ми, но заболе́л he would have gone with them, but he fell ill; чуть б. не very nearly; я чуть б. не забы́л I very nearly forgot; они́ чуть б. не уби́ли его́ they all but killed him. **2.** *indicates cessation of action already, but only just, commenced*: он отпра́вился б. с ни́ми, но верну́лся he started out with them but turned back.

был|о́й, *adj.* former, past, bygone; в ~ы́е времена́ in days of old; *as noun* ~о́е, ~о́го, *n.* (*poet.*) the past, olden time; Было́е и ду́мы 'My Past and Thoughts' (*title of work by Alexander Herzen*).

быль|, и, *f.* **1.** (*obs.*) fact. **2.** true story.

быль|ё, я́, *n.* (*obs.*) grass; *now only in phrase* ~ём поросло́ long forgotten.

быстрин|а́, ы́, *pl.* ~ы, *f.* (*geogr.*) rapid(s).

быстрогла́з|ый (~, ~а), *adj.* saucy, sprightly, busybodyish.

быстроно́гий, *adj.* (*poet.*) fleet of foot.

быстрот|а́, ы́, *f.* rapidity, quickness; speed.

быстроте́кущий, *adj.* (*poet.*, *obs.*) swift-flowing.

быстроте́ч|ный (~ен, ~на), *adj.* fleeting, transient.

быстрохо́д|ный (~ен, ~на), *adj.* fast, high-speed; б. танк (*mil.*) cruiser tank.

бы́стр|ый (~, ~а́, ~о), *adj.* rapid, fast, quick; prompt.

быт, а, о ~е, в ~у́, *no pl.*, *m.* way of life;

life; домáшний б. family life; солдáтский б. army life; слýжба ⁓a consumer services.

быти|é, я, *n.* (*philos.*) being, existence, objective reality; б., по словáм Мáркса, определя́ет сознáние existence, according to Marx, determines consciousness; кни́га ⁓я́ (*bibl.*) Genesis.

бы́тност|ь, и, *f.* *only in phrase* в б. during a given period; в б. мою́ студéнтом in my student days; в б. егó в Ри́ме during his stay in Rome, in his Rome days.

быт|овáть, ýет, *impf.* to occur, be current; были́ны ещё ⁓ýют на céвере byliny still exist in the North.

бытови́к, á, *m.* (*coll.*) writer *or* artist treating themes from everyday life.

быт|овóй, *adj.* of ⁓; social; ⁓овáя жи́вопись genre painting; ⁓овáя пьéса play on theme of everyday life; ⁓овáя револю́ция social revolution; ⁓овóе явлéние everyday occurrence; комбинáт ⁓овóго обслу́живания consumer service establishment (*multiple enterprise comprising hair-dressing, dry-cleaning, household appliance repair services, etc.*).

бытописáни|е, я, *n.* (*obs.*) annals, chronicles.

бытописáтел|ь, я, *m.* **1.** (*obs.*) historian, annalist. **2.** writer on social themes.

быть, *pres. not used exc. 3rd sing.* **есть** *and* (*obs.*) *3rd pl.* **суть,** *fut.* **бýду, бýдешь,** *past* **был, былá, бы́ло (нé был, не былá, нé было),** *imp.* **бýдь(те)** (*see also* **бýдет, бýдь(те), бы́ло, есть).**

I. **1.** to be (= to exist); есть таки́е лю́ди there are such people, such people do exist. **2.** б. у (*see also* есть) to be in the possession (of); у них былá прекрáсная дáча they had a lovely dacha. **3.** to be (= to be situated, be located); (к) to come (to), be present (at); здесь был тракти́р there used to be an inn here; где вы бы́ли вчерá? where were you yesterday?; он тут был не при чём he had nothing to do with it; они́ бýдут к нам зáвтра they are coming (to see us) tomorrow; на ней былá рóзовая кóфточка she had on a pink blouse. **4.** to

be, happen, take place; э́того не мóжет б.! it cannot be!; что с ним бы́ло? what happened to him?; б. бедé there's sure to be trouble; как б.? what is to be done?; так и б. so be it, all right, very well, have it your own way; б. по семý (*obs.*) be it so enacted.

II. *as auxiliary verb* to be.

быть|é, я, *n.* (*obs.*) mode of life.

быча́ч|ий, *adj.* of бык¹; ⁓ья кóжа oxhide; ⁓ья шéя bull neck.

бы́чий, *adj.* = быча́чий.

быч|óк¹, кá, *m.* steer.

быч|óк², кá, *m.* Gobius (*small fish found in Black Sea*).

быч|óк³, кá, *m.* (*coll.*) cigarette butt.

бьеф, а, *m.* reach; вéрхний б. head water; ни́жний б. tail water.

бью, бьёшь, *see* бить.

бювáр, а, *m.* blotting-pad.

бювéт, а, *m.* pump-room.

бюджéт, а, *m.* budget.

бюджéтный, *adj.* budgetary; б. год fiscal year.

бюллетéн|ь, я, *m.* `1.` bulletin. **2.** (избирáтельный) б. voting-paper. **3.** (больни́чный) б. medical certificate; быть на ⁓е (*coll.*) to be on sick-leave, be on the sick-list.

бю́ргер, а, *m.* burgher; (*fig., iron.*) philistine.

бюрéтк|а, и, *f.* (*tech.*) burette.

бюрó, *indecl., n.* **1.** bureau, office; б. нахóдок lost-property office; спрáвочное б. inquiry office. **2.** bureau, writing-desk.

бюрокрáт, а, *m.* bureaucrat.

бюрократи́зм, а, *m.* bureaucracy; red tape.

бюрократи́ческий, *adj.* bureaucratic.

бюрокрáти|я, и, *f.* bureaucracy (*also collect.*).

бюст, а, *m.* bust; bosom.

бюстгáльтер, а, *m.* brassière.

бя́з|евый, *adj.* of ⁓ь.

бяз|ь, и, *f.* coarse calico.

бя́к|а, и, *f.* (*in children's speech*) nasty thing; nasty man.

бя́ша, *interj.* (*dial.*; *onomat.*) baa!

В

в, *prep.*

I. +*a. and p.* **1.** (+*a.*) into, to; (+*p.*) in, at; поéхать в Москвý to go to Moscow; роди́ться в Москвé to be born in Moscow; сесть в вагóн to get into the carriage; сидéть в вагóне to be in the carriage; одéться в смóкинг to put on a dinner-

-jacket; быть в смóкинге to be in a dinner--jacket; разби́ть в куски́ to smash to pieces; сáхар в кускáх sugar in lumps; привести́ в востóрг to delight, enrapture; быть в востóрге to be delighted, be in raptures. **2.** *in reference to external attributes*: рубáшка в клéтку check(ed) shirt; лицó в веснýшках freckled face. **3.** (+*n.–a. pl.* and *p. pl.*) *in reference to occupation*: пойти́ в стенографи́стки to become a shorthand-typist; служи́ть в кухáрках to be a cook. **4.** *in reference to calendar units and periods of time*: в понедéльник on Monday; в январé in January; в 1899-ом годý in 1899; в двадцáтом вéке in the twentieth century; в четы́ре часá at four o'clock; в четвёртом часý between three and four; в нáши дни in our day; в течéние (+*g.*) during, in the course (of).

II. +*a.* **1.** *in reference to objects through which vision is directed*: смотрéть в окнó to look out of the window; смотрéть в бинóкль to look through binoculars. **2.** *in attribution of resemblance*: быть в когó-н. to take after someone; онá вся в тётю she is the image of her aunt. **3.** *indicating aim or purpose*: for, as; сказáть в шýтку to say for a joke; привести́ в доказáтельство to adduce as proof. **4.** *in specification of quantitative attributes*: морóз в дéсять грáдусов ten degrees of frost; высотóй в три мéтра three metres high; вéсом в пять килогрáммов weighing five kilograms. **5.** (+раз and comp. adv.) *indicates comparison in numerical terms*: в два рáза бóльше twice as big, twice the size; в два рáза мéньше half as big, half the size. **6.** *of time*: in, within; надéюсь кóнчить черновик в мéсяц I hope to finish the rough draft in a month. **6.** *indicates game or sport played*: игрáть в кáрты, шáхматы, тéннис, футбóл to play cards, chess, tennis, football.

III. +*p.* **1.** at a distance of; в трёх киломéтрах от гóрода three kilometres from the town; они́ живýт в десяти́ минýтах ходьбы́ отсю́да they live ten minutes' walk from here. **2.** in; of (= consisting of, amounting to); пьéса в трёх дéйствиях play in three acts; рáзница в двух копéйках a difference of two kopecks.

ва-бáнк, *adv.* (*cards*) игрáть, идти́ ва-б. to stake everything; (*fig.*) to stake one's all.

вáб|ить, лю, ишь, *impf.* to lure, decoy.

вавилóнск|ий, *adj.* Babylonian; ~ое столпотворéние babel; ~ая бáшня the tower of Babel.

вавилóн|ы, ов, *no sing.* (*coll.*) **1.** (*archit.*) scrolls. **2.** flourishes (*in handwriting*), scrawl; выводи́ть, писáть в. (*fig.*) to stagger, lurch (*of a drunken person*).

вáг|а, и, *f.* (*tech.*) **1.** weighing-machine. **2.** splinter-bar; swingle-tree. **3.** lever.

вагóн, а, *m.* **1.** carriage, coach; мя́гкий, жёсткий в. soft-seated, hard-seated carriage; багáжный в. luggage van; в.-ресторáн dining-car, restaurant car; спáльный в. sleeping-car; товáрный в. goods wagon, goods truck; трамвáйный в. tram-car;

в.-цистéрна tank truck. **2.** wagon-load; (*fig., coll.*) loads, lots; игрýшек у негó в. he has loads of toys; врéмени у нас в. we have masses of time.

вагонéтк|а, и, *f.* truck; trolley.

вагонéтчик, а, *m.* truck-, trolley-operator.

вагóнник, а, *m.* carriage-building worker.

вагóн|ный, *adj.* of ~; ~ная ось carriage axle; в. парк rolling-stock.

вагоновожáт|ый, ого, *m.* tram-driver.

вагонострóени|е, я, *n.* carriage-building.

вагонострои́тельный, *adj.* carriage-building; в. завóд carriage(-building) works.

вагрáнк|а, и, *f.* (*tech.*) cupola furnace.

вáженк|а, и, *f.* (*dial.*) female reindeer.

важнéцк|ий, *adj.* (*coll.*) good, good-quality; вот у вас ~ие боти́нки that's a good pair of boots you have on.

вáжничани|е, я, *n.* airs and graces.

вáжнича|ть, ю, *impf.* (*coll.*) to give oneself airs, get a swelled head; (+*i.*) to plume oneself (on).

вáжност|ь, и, *f.* **1.** importance; significance; дéло большóй ~и a matter of great importance, of great moment; не велика́ в. (*coll.*) it's of no consequence; э́ка в.! (*coll.*) what does it matter! **2.** pomposity, pretentiousness.

вáж|ный (~ен, ~нá, ~но), *adj.* **1.** important; weighty, consequential; сáмое ~ное узнáть, откýда они́ приéхали the (important) thing is to discover where they have come from; в своéй странé он довóльно в. человéк in his own country he is a man of some consequence; ~ная ши́шка (*coll.*) bigwig, big knob. **2.** pompous, pretentious.

вáз|а, ы, *f.* vase, bowl; в. для цветóв flower vase; ночнáя в. chamber-pot.

вазели́н, а, *m.* vaseline.

вазели́н|овый, *adj.* of ~; ~овое мáсло (*med.*) liquid paraffin.

вазомотóрный, *adj.* (*med.*) vasomotor.

вазóн, а, *m.* (flower-)pot.

вáи|я, и, g. pl. ~й, *f.* **1.** (*bot.*) fern-branch. **2.** palm(-branch); недéля ~й (*eccl.*) Palm Sunday.

вáйя = вáия.

вакáнси|я, и, *f.* vacancy; бýдут две ~и в штáте в бýдущем годý there will be two vacancies on the staff next year.

вакáнт|ный (~ен, ~на), *adj.* vacant (*of posts in an institution*).

вакáци|я, и, *f.* (*obs.*) vacation.

вáкс|а, ы, *f.* (shoe) polish; blacking.

вáк|сить, шу, сишь, *impf.* (*of* на~) to black, polish.

вáкуум, а, *m.* (*tech.*) vacuum; в.-маши́на, в.-насóс vacuum pump.

вакханáли|я, и, *f.* **1.** (*usu. pl.*; *hist.*) bacchanalia. **2.** (*fig.*) orgy. **3.** (*fig.*) confusion, disorder.

вакха́нк|а, и, *f.* **1.** Bacchante, maenad. **2.** (*fig.*) bawd, hussy.

вакхи́ческий, *adj.* Bacchic.

вакци́н|а, ы, *f.* vaccine.

вакцина́ци|я, и, *f.* vaccination.

ва́к|шу, сишь, *see* ∼сить.

вал¹, а, *pl.* ∼ы́, *m.* billow, roller; девя́тый в. 'ninth wave' (*according to superstition, fatal to sailors*).

вал², а, *pl.* ∼ы́, *m.* bank, earthen wall; (*mil.*) rampart; (*geol.*) swell.

вал³, а, *pl.* ∼ы́, *m.* (*tech.*) shaft.

вал⁴, а, *m.* (*econ.*) **1.** gross output (*as indicator of industrial efficiency, by contrast with profit*). **2.** = план ∼ово́й проду́кции (*see* ∼ово́й).

вала́нда|ться, юсь, *impf.* (*coll.*) **1.** to loiter, hang about. **2.** (с+*i.*) to dawdle (over), mess about (with).

валансье́н, *indecl.*, *adj.* (*text.*) кружева́ в. Valanciennes lace.

вале́жник, а, *no pl.*, *m.* (*collect.*) windfallen trees, branches.

вал|ёк, ька́, *m.* (*tech.*) **1.** battledore. **2.** swingle-tree. **3.** (*typ.*, *etc.*) roller. **4.** (*agric.*) (threshing-)flail. **5.** (*naut.*) loom (*of an oar*).

вален|ки, ок *and* **ков,** *sing.* ∼ок, ∼ка, *m.* valenki (*felt boots*).

вале́нтност|ь, и, *f.* (*chem.*) valency.

ва́леный, *adj.* = ва́ляный.

валерья́н|а, ы, *f.* (*bot.*) valerian.

валерья́нк|а, и, *f.* (*coll.*) tincture of valerian.

валерья́нов|ый, *adj.* (*med.*) ∼ые ка́пли tincture of valerian.

вале́т, а, *m.* (*cards*) knave, jack.

ва́лик, а, *m.* **1.** (*tech.*) roller, cylinder; spindle, shaft. **2.** bolster.

вал|и́ть¹, ю́, ∼ишь, *impf.* **1.** (*pf.* по∼ *and* с∼) to throw down, bring down, send toppling; to overthrow; в. кого́-н. с ног to knock someone off his feet; в. дере́вья to fell trees; нас всех ∼и́л грипп we were all being laid low by the 'flu. **2.** (*pf.* с∼) to heap up, pile up; в. всё в одну́ ку́чу to lump everything together (*also fig.*); в. вину́ (на+*a.*) to lump the blame (on).

вал|и́ть², и́т, *impf.* (*coll.*) **1.** to flock, throng, pour; вало́м в. to throng, go en masse; лю́ди ∼и́ли на стадио́н people were flocking to the stadium; снег ∼и́т кру́пными хло́пьями the snow is coming down in large flakes; дым ∼и́л из трубы́ smoke was belching from the chimney; ему́ уж давно́ ∼и́т сча́стье he has had a long run of luck. **2.** ∼й(те)! go on!, have a go!; ∼й, беги́! be off with you!

вал|и́ться, ю́сь, ∼ишься, *impf.* (*of* по∼ *and* с∼) to fall, collapse; to topple; в. от уста́лости to drop from tiredness; у него́ всё

из рук ∼ится (*coll.*) he is all fingers and thumbs; де́ло у него́ ∼ится и́з рук his heart is not in the matter, he cannot put his mind to the matter; на бе́дного Мака́ра все ши́шки ∼ятся (*prov.*) an unfortunate man would be drowned in a tea-cup.

ва́лк|а¹, и, *f.* felling.

ва́лк|а², и, *f.* (*text.*) fulling.

ва́л|кий (∼ок, ∼ка́, ∼ко), *adj.* unsteady, shaky; (*naut.*) crank; ни ша́тко, ни ∼ко middling; neither good nor bad.

ва́лкост|ь, и, *f.* (*naut.*) crankness.

валли́|ец, йца, *m.* (*obs.*) Welshman.

валли́йк|а, и, *f.* (*obs.*) Welshwoman.

валли́йский, *adj.* (*obs.*) Welsh.

валло́н, а, *m.* Walloon.

валло́нк|а, и, *f.* Walloon (woman).

валло́нский, *adj.* Walloon.

валово́й, *adj.* **1.** (*econ.*) gross; wholesale; в. дохо́д gross revenue; в. сбор gross yield; план в. проду́кции gross output plan. **2.** general, mass (*of migration of birds*).

вало́м, *see* вали́ть².

вало́ш|ить, у, ишь, *impf.* to castrate, geld.

валто́рн|а, ы, *f.* (*mus.*) French horn.

валу́|й, я́, *m.* mushroom (*Russula foetens*).

валу́н, а́, *m.* boulder.

ва́льдшнеп, а, *m.* (*zool.*) woodcock.

вальс, а, *m.* waltz.

вальси́р|овать, ую, *impf.* to waltz.

вальц|ева́ть, у́ю, *impf.* (*tech.*) to roll.

вальцо́вк|а, и, *f.* (*tech.*) **1.** rolling. **2.** rolling press.

вальцо́вщик, а, *m.* (*tech.*) operative of rolling-mill, roller.

вальцо́в|ый, *adj.* (*tech.*); ∼ая ме́льница rolling-mill.

вальц|ы́, о́в, *no sing.* (*tech.*) rolling press.

ва́льщик, а, *m.* (*dial.*) woodcutter.

валья́жный, *adj.* (*coll.*) weighty, impressive; handsome; вид у него́ в. he has an impressive presence; в. переплёт handsome binding.

валю́т|а, ы, *f.* (*fin.*, *econ.*) **1.** currency; курс ∼ы rate of exchange. **2.** (*collect.*) foreign currency.

валю́т|ный, *adj.* of ∼a; currency.

валю́тчик, а, *m.* (*coll.*) speculator in foreign currency.

валя́льный, *adj.* fulling.

валя́л|ьня, ьни, g. pl. ∼ен, *f.* fulling-mill.

валя́льщик, а, *m.* fuller.

валя́ни|е, я, *n.* (*tech.*) fulling, milling.

ва́ляный, *adj.* felt.

валя́|ть, ю, *impf.* **1.** (*impf. only*) to drag; в. по́ полу to drag along the floor. **2.** (*pf.* вы́∼) to roll, drag; в. в грязи́ to drag in the mire. **3.** (*pf.* с∼) to knead. **4.** (*pf.* с∼) to full; to felt. **5.** (*pf.* на∼) (*coll.*) to botch, bungle; to muck about. **6.** в. дурака́ (*coll.*) to play the fool. **7.** ~й(те)! (*coll.*) go ahead!, carry on!

валя́|ться, ю́сь, *impf.* **1.** to roll. **2.** (*coll.*) to lie about, loll; весь день он ~ется в хала́те he lies about in his dressing-gown all day; её оде́жда ~лась везде́ по ко́мнате her clothes lay scattered all over the room; в. в нога́х у кого́-н. (*fig.*) to fall down at someone's feet.

вам, *d. of* вы.

ва́ми, *i. of* вы.

вампи́р, а, *m.* **1.** vampire (*also fig.*). **2.** (*zool.*) vampire-bat.

вана́ди|й, я, *m.* (*chem.*) vanadium.

ванда́л, а, *m.* (*hist. and fig.*) Vandal; vandal.

вандали́зм, а, *m.* vandalism.

ванили́н, а, *m.* vanillin.

вани́л|ь, и, *f.* vanilla.

вани́ль|ный, *adj. of* ~.

ва́нн|а, ы, *f.* bath; сидя́чая в. hip-bath; со́лнечная в. sun-bath; фотографи́ческая в. photographic bath; взять ~у, приня́ть ~у to take a bath.

ва́нночк|а, и, *f. dim. of* ва́нна; (*phot.*) developing tray; глазна́я в. eye-bath.

ва́нн|ый, *adj. of* ~а; *as noun* ~ая, ~ой, *f.* bathroom.

ва́нт|а, ы, *f.* (*naut.*) shroud.

ва́ньк|а, и, *m.* (*obs.*) cabby (*nickname of poor droshky-drivers*).

ва́нька-вста́нька, ва́ньки-вста́ньки, *m.* cork-tumbler (*doll with weight attached to its base which causes it always to recover standing position*); (*fig.*) *of person never discouraged by misfortune*).

вапориза́тор, а, *m.* (*tech.*) vaporizer.

вапориза́ци|я, и, *f.* (*tech.*) vaporization.

вар, а, *m.* **1.** pitch; cobbler's wax. **2.** (*dial.*) boiling water.

вара́кушк|а, и, *f.* (*orn.*) bluethroat.

вара́н, а, *m.* (*zool.*) giant lizard.

ва́рвар, а, *m.* barbarian.

варвари́зм, а, *m.* (*ling., lit.*) barbarism.

ва́рварский, *adj.* barbarian; (*fig.*) barbaric.

ва́рварств|о, а, *n.* barbarity; vandalism.

варга́н|ить, ю, ишь, *impf.* (*coll.*) to botch, bungle.

ва́рев|о, а, *n.* (*coll., pejor.*) broth; slop.

ва́режк|а, и, *f.* mitten (*glove with thumb but no fingers*).

варен|е́ц, ца́, *m.* fermented boiled milk.

варе́ние = ва́рка.

варе́ник, а, *m.* varenik (*curd or fruit dumpling*).

варёный, *adj.* **1.** boiled. **2.** (*coll.*) limp.

варе́нь|е, я, *n.* preserve(s) (*containing whole fruit*), jam.

вариа́нт, а, *m.* reading, variant; ver-

sion; расска́з был распространён во мно́гих ~ах many versions of the story were circulated.

вариацио́нн|ый, *adj.* variant; ~ое исчисле́ние (*math.*) calculus of variations.

вариа́ци|я, и, *f.* variation; те́ма с ~ями (*mus.*) theme and variations.

варико́зный, *adj.* (*anat.*) varicose.

вар|и́ть, ю́, ~ишь, *impf.* (*of* с~) **1.** to boil; to cook; в. карто́фель to boil potatoes; в. обе́д to cook dinner; в. глинтве́йн to mull wine; в. пи́во to brew beer. **2.** (*of the stomach*) to digest. **3.** to found (*steel*).

вар|и́ться, ю́сь, ~ишься, *impf.* (*of* с~) **1.** to boil (*intrans.*); to cook (*intrans.*); карто́фель уже́ полчаса́ ~ится the potatoes have been on for half an hour already; в. в со́бственном соку́ (*coll.*) to keep oneself to oneself. **2.** *pass. of* ~и́ть.

ва́рк|а, и, *f.* boiling; cooking; в. варе́нья preserve-making; в. желе́за iron-founding; в. пи́ва brewing.

ва́р|кий (~ок, ~ка́, ~ко), *adj.* **1.** heat-giving; ~кая печь hot stove. **2.** tender (*of meat, etc.*).

варна́к, а́, *m.* (*dial.*) (escaped) convict.

ва́рниц|а, ы, *f.* **1.** saltworks. **2.** saltpan.

варра́нт, а, *m.* (*comm.*) custom-house license; warehouse warrant.

варша́вский, *adj.* (of) Warsaw.

варьете́, *indecl.*, *n.* variety (show); теа́тр-в. music-hall.

варьи́р|овать, ую, *impf.* to vary, modify.

варя́г, а, *m.* (*hist.*) Varangian.

варя́жский, *adj.* (*hist.*) Varangian.

вас, *g., a., and p. of* вы.

васил|ёк, ька́, *m.* (*bot.*) cornflower.

васили́ск, а, *m.* basilisk.

васил|ько́вый, *adj. of* ~ёк; cornflower blue.

васса́л, а, *m.* vassal, liege(-man).

васса́льн|ый, *adj.* vassal; ~ая зави́симость vassalage.

ва́т|а, ы, *f.* cotton wool; wadding; пальто́ на ~е wadded coat.

вата́г|а, и, *f.* band, gang.

ватерклозе́т, а, *m.* water-closet.

ватерли́ни|я, и, *f.* (*naut.*) water-line; грузова́я в. load water-line.

ва́тер-маши́н|а, ы, *f.* (*text.*) water frame.

ватерпа́с, а, *m.* (*tech.*) water-level, spirit-level.

ватер-по́ло, *indecl.*, *n.* (*sport*) water polo.

вати́н, а, *m.* sheet wadding.

ва́тман, а, *m.* Whatman paper.

ва́тник, а, *m.* quilted jacket.

ва́тн|ый, *adj.* wadded, quilted; ~ое одея́ло quilt.

ватру́шк|а, и, *f.* curd tart; cheese-cake.

ватт, а, *g. pl.* в. *m.* (*electr.*) watt.

ва́ттност|ь, и, *f.* (*electr.*) wattage.

ва́фельниц|а, ы, *f.* waffle-iron.

ва́фельщик, а, *m.* waffle-maker; waffle--vendor.

ваф|ля, ли, *g. pl.* ~ель, *f.* waffle; wafer.

вахла́к, а́, *m.* (*coll.*) lout; sloven.

ва́хмистр, а, *m.* (*obs.*) cavalry sergeant-major.

ва́хт|а, ы, *f.* 1. (*naut.*) watch; стоя́ть на ~е to keep watch. 2. (*fig.*) special (collective) effort, special stint (*of Soviet workers on anniversary of October revolution, etc.*).

ва́хт|енный, *adj.* of ~а (*naut.*); в. журна́л log(-book); в. команди́р officer of the watch; *as noun* в., ~енного, *m.* watch.

ва́хтер, а, *pl.* ~а́, *m.* (*obs.*) senior watchman.

вахтёр, а, *m.* janitor, porter.

вахтпара́д, а, *m.* (*obs.*) changing of the guard.

ваш, ~его; *f.* ~а, ~ей; *n.* ~е, ~его; *pl.* ~и, ~их, *possessive pron.* your(s); э́то в. каранда́ш this is your pencil; э́тот каранда́ш в. this pencil is yours; ~его мне не ну́жно (*coll.*) I don't want anything of yours; он зна́ет бо́льше ~его (*coll.*) he knows more than you; не ~е де́ло it is none of your business; *as noun* ~и, ~их your people, your folk.

ва́шгерд, а, *m.* (*tech.*) buddle.

вая́ни|е, я, *n.* (*obs.*) sculpture.

вая́тел|ь, я, *m.* (*obs.*) sculptor.

вая́|ть, ю, *impf.* (*of* из~) (*obs.*) to sculpture; to carve, chisel.

вбега́|ть, ю, *impf.* (в+a.) to run (into).

вбе|жа́ть, гу́, жи́шь, гу́т, *pf. of* ~га́ть.

вбер|у́, ёшь, *see* вобра́ть.

вбива́|ть, ю, *impf. of* вбить.

вби́вк|а, и, *f.* knocking-in.

вбира́|ть, ю, *impf. of* вобра́ть.

вбить, вобью́, вобьёшь, *pf.* (*of* вбива́ть) to drive in, hammer in; (*sport*) в. мяч to score a goal; (*coll.*) в. в го́лову (+d.; *fig.*) to knock into someone's head; в. себе́ в го́лову to get into one's head.

вблизи́, *adv.* (от) close by; not far (from); они́ живу́т где́-то в. they live somewhere near here; в. был слы́шен водопа́д the sound of a waterfall could be heard near by; в. от библиоте́ки not far from the library; рассма́тривать в. to examine closely.

вбок, *adv.* sideways, to one side.

вбра́сывани|е, я, *n.* в. (мяча́) throw-in (*in football*).

вбра́сыва|ть, ю, *impf. of* вбро́сить.

вброд, *adv.* переходи́ть в. to wade; to ford.

вбро́|сить, шу, сишь, *pf.* (*of* вбра́сывать) to throw in(to).

вва́лива|ть, ю, *impf. of* ввали́ть.

вва́лива|ться, юсь, *impf. of* ввали́ться.

ввал|и́ть, ю́, ~ишь, *pf.* to hurl, heave into.

ввал|и́ться, ю́сь, ~ишься, *pf.* 1. (*coll.*) to tumble into, sink into. 2. (*fig., coll.*) to burst into. 3. to become hollow, sunken; с ~и́вшимися щека́ми hollow-cheeked.

введе́ни|е, я, *n.* 1. leading in(to); в. в заблужде́ние leading into temptation; В. (во храм) (*eccl.*) Feast of the Presentation of the Blessed Virgin. 2. introduction; preamble; в. в языкозна́ние introduction to philology.

вве|ду́, дёшь, *see* ~сти́.

ввез|ти́, у́, ёшь, *past* ~, ~ла́, *pf.* (*of* ввози́ть) to import.

ввек, *adv.* (*now only used before neg.*) ever; я э́того в. не забу́ду I shall not forget it as long as I live.

вверг|а́ть, а́ю, *impf. of* ~нуть.

вве́рг|нуть, ну, нешь, *past* ~, ~ла, *pf.* (*of* ~ать) (в+a.; *obs.*) to cause to fall (into); to reduce (to); в. в тюрьму́ to cast into gaol; в. в нищету́ to bring to ruin; в. в отча́яние to drive to despair.

вве́р|ить, ю, ишь, *pf.* (*of* ~я́ть) to entrust; в. та́йну кому́-н. to confide a secret in someone.

вве́р|иться, юсь, ишься, *pf.* (*of* ~я́ться) (+d.) to trust (in), put one's faith (in), put oneself in the hands of.

вверн|у́ть, у́, ёшь, *pf.* (*of* вве́ртывать) 1. to screw in, insert. 2. (*fig., coll.*) to insert, put in; в. замеча́ние to insert a comment; ему́ не удало́сь в. ни слове́чка he could not get a word in.

вверста́|ть, ю, *pf.* (*of* вве́рстывать) (*typ.*) to inset.

вве́рстыва|ть, ю, *impf. of* вверста́ть.

ввер|те́ть, чу́, ~тишь, *pf.* (*of* ~тывать) (*coll.*) to screw in.

вве́ртыва|ть, ю, *impf. of* ввернуть *and* ввертеть.

вверх, *adv.* up, upward(s); идти́ в. по ле́стнице to go upstairs; в. по тече́нию up-stream; в. дном upside down; topsy-turvy; в. нога́ми head over heels.

вверху́, *adv. and prep.* +*g.* above, overhead; в. над кры́шами домо́в above the roofs of the houses; в. страни́цы at the top of the page.

ввер|чу́, ~тишь, *see* ~те́ть.

вверя́|ть(ся), ю(сь), *impf. of* вве́рить(ся).

вве|сти́, ду́, дёшь, *past* ~л, ~ла́, *pf.* (*of* вводи́ть) to introduce, bring in; в. мо́ду to introduce a fashion; в. су́дно в га́вань to bring a ship into harbour; в. во владе́ние (*leg.*) to put in possession; в. в заблужде́ние to mislead; в. в искуше́ние to lead into temptation; в. в курс чего́-н. to acquaint with the facts of something; в. в расхо́д to put to expense; (*math.*) to interpolate.

ввечеру́, *adv.* (*obs.*) in the evening.

ввива́|ть, ю, *impf. of* ввить.

ввиду́, *prep.+g.* in view (of); в. тума́на полёт не состои́тся in view of the fog the flight will not take place; в. того́, что as; в. того́, что вы прие́хали as you have come.

ввин|ти́ть, чу́, ти́шь, *pf.* (*of* ~чивать (в+*a.*) to screw (in); в. штóпор в прóбку to insert a corkscrew into a cork.

ввинчива|ть, ю, *impf. of* ввинти́ть.

ввить, вовью́, вовьёшь, *pf.* (*of* ввива́ть) to weave in.

ввод, а, *m.* **1.** bringing in; в. в бой (*mil.*) throwing into battle; в. во владе́ние (*leg.*) putting in possession. **2.** (*electr.*) lead-in.

вво|ди́ть, жу́, ~дишь, *impf. of* ввести́.

ввóдн|ый, *adj.* introductory; (*gram.*) ~ое предложе́ние parenthetic clause; ~ое слóво parenthetic word, parenthesis; в. тон (*mus.*) leading note.

вво|жу́¹, ~дишь, *see* вводи́ть.

вво|жу́², ~зишь, *see* ввози́ть.

ввоз, а, *no pl., m.* **1.** importation. **2.** import; (*collect.*) imports.

вво|зи́ть, жу́, ~зишь, *impf. of* ввезти́.

ввóзн|ый, *adj.* imported; import; ~ые континге́нты quota of imports; ~ая пóшлина import duty.

вволáкива|ть, ю, *impf. of* вволóчь.

вволó|чь, ку́, чёшь, ку́т, *past* ~к, ~кла́, *pf.* (*coll.*) to drag in.

вво́лю, *adv.* (*coll.*) to one's heart's content, ad lib.; нае́сться в. to eat one's fill.

ввóсьмеро, *adv.* eight times; в. бóльше eight times as much.

ввосьмерóм, *adv.* eight together; они́ в. сде́лали рабóту eight of them did the job together.

ввысь, *adv.* up, upward(s).

ввя|за́ть, жу́, ~жешь, *pf.* (*of* ~зывать) to knit in; (*fig.*) to involve.

ввя|за́ться, жу́сь, ~жешься, *pf.* (в+*a.*; *coll.*) to meddle (in); to get involved (in); mixed up (in); в. в неприя́тную истóрию to get mixed up in a nasty business; в. в бой (*mil.*) to become engaged.

ввя́зыва|ть(ся), ю(сь), *impf. of* ввяза́ть(ся).

вгиб, а, *m.* bend inwards.

вгиба́|ть, ю, *impf. of* вогну́ть.

вглубь, *adv. and prep.+g.* deep down; deep into, into the depths; в. лесóв into the heart of the forest; в. страны́ far inland.

вгля|де́ться, жу́сь, ди́шься, *pf.* (*of* ~дываться) (в+*a.*) to peer (at).

вгля́дыва|ться, юсь, *impf. of* вгляде́ться.

вгоня́|ть, ю, *impf. of* вогна́ть.

вгры́з|ться, у́сь, ёшься, *pf.* (*coll.*) to get one's teeth into (*of animals*).

вда|ва́ться, ю́сь, ёшься, *impf. of* ~ться.

вдав|и́ть, лю́, ~ишь, *pf.* (*of* ~ливать) to press in.

вда́влива|ть, ю, *impf. of* вдави́ть.

вда́лблива|ть, ю, *impf. of* вдолби́ть.

вдалеке́, *adv.* in the distance; в. от a long way from.

вдали́, *adv.* in the distance, far off; в. от гóрода a long way from the city; держа́ться в. to keep aloof, keep one's distance; исчеза́ть в. to vanish into thin air.

вдаль, *adv.* afar, at a distance; гляде́ть в. to look into the distance.

вд|а́ться, а́мся, а́шься, а́стся, ади́мся, ади́тесь, аду́тся, *pf.* (*of* вдава́ться) (в+*a.*) to jut out (into); в. в подрóбности to go into details; в. в тóнкости to split hairs.

вдвига́|ть(ся), ю(сь), *impf. of* вдви́нуть(ся).

вдвижнóй, *adj.* insertable.

вдви́|нуть, ну, нешь, *pf.* (*of* ~га́ть) to push in(to).

вдви́|нуться, нусь, нешься, *pf.* (*of* ~га́ться) to push in, squeeze in.

вдвóе, *adv.* twice; double; в. бóльше twice as much, twice as big; в. ста́рше double the age; сложи́ть в. to fold double.

вдвоём, *adv.* the two together; они́ в. написа́ли статью́ the two of them together wrote the article.

вдвойне́, *adv.* twice, double; doubly (*also fig.*); плати́ть в. to pay double; он в. винова́т he is doubly to blame.

вдева́|ть, ю, *impf. of* вдеть.

вде́вятеро, *adv.* nine times.

вдевятерóм, *adv.* nine together.

вдёжк|а, и, f.* **1. threading (*of a needle*). **2.** thread.

вде́л|ать, аю, *pf.* (*of* ~ывать) (в+*a.*) to fit (into), set (into); в. ка́мень в кольцó to set a stone into a ring.

вде́лыва|ть, ю, *impf. of* вде́лать.

вде́н|у, ешь, *see* вдеть.

вдёргива|ть, ю, *impf. of* вдёрнуть.

вдёржк|а, и, f.* **1. bodkin. **2.** threading.

вдёрн|уть, у, ешь, *pf.* (*of* вдёргивать) to pull through; to thread; в. ни́тку в иглу́ to thread a needle.

вде́сятеро, *adv.* ten times; в. бóльше ten times as much.

вдесятерóм, *adv.* ten together; мы в. ten of us.

вде|ть, ~ну, ~нешь, *pf.* (*of* ~ва́ть) (в+*a.*) to put in(to); в. ни́тку в иглу́ to thread a needle.

вдоба́вок, *adv.* in addition; moreover; into the bargain.

**вдов|á, ы́, pl.* ~ы, *f.* widow; солóменная в. (*coll.*) grass widow.

вдове́|ть, ю, *impf.* (*of* о~) to be a widow(er); to be widowed.

**вдов|е́ц, ца́, m.* widower; солóменный в. grass widower.

**вдóв|ий, adj. of* ~á; ~ья часть насле́дства (*leg.*) dower, jointure.

вдови́ц|а, ы, *f.* (*obs.*) widow.

вдо́воль, *adv.* (*coll.*) **1.** in abundance; у нас вся́кого ро́да фру́ктов в. we have abundance of every kind of fruit. **2.** enough; он нае́лся в. he ate his fill.

вдовств|о́, а́, *n.* widowhood; widowerhood.

вдо́вств|овать, ую, *impf.* (*obs.*) to be a widow, a widower; ~ующая императри́ца the Dowager Empress.

вдо́в|ый (~), *adj.* widowed.

вдого́нку, *adv.* after, in pursuit of; бро́ситься вдого́нку (за+*i.*) to rush (after).

вдолб|и́ть, лю́, и́шь, *pf.* (*of* вда́лбливать) (*coll.*) в. кому́-н. в го́лову to drum, din into someone's head.

вдоль 1. *prep.* (+*g. or* по+*d.*) along; в. бе́рега along the bank; я поплы́л в. по реке́ I sailed down the river. **2.** *adv.* lengthwise, longways; разре́зать мате́рию в. to cut material lengthwise; в. и поперёк in all directions, far and wide; он изъе́здил всю Росси́ю в. и поперёк he has travelled the length and breadth of Russia; (*fig.*) minutely, in detail; он зна́ет Шекспи́ра в. и поперёк he knows Shakespeare inside out.

вдо́сталь, *adv.* **1.** (*coll.*) in plenty. **2.** (*obs.*) completely.

вдох, а, *m.* (*coll.*) breath; сде́лать глубо́кий в. to take a deep breath.

вдохнове́ни|е, я, *n.* inspiration.

вдохнове́нный, *adj.* inspired.

вдохнови́тел|ь, я, *m.* inspirer; inspiration (*of persons*); он — наш в. he is an inspiration to us.

вдохнови́тельн|ый, *adj.* (*obs.*) inspiring; ~ая речь an inspiring speech.

вдохнов|и́ть, лю́, и́шь, *pf.* (*of* ~ля́ть) (+*a. or* на+*a.*) to inspire (to); его́ слова́ ~и́ли меня́ his words inspired me; казнь бра́та ~и́ла его́ на борьбу́ his brother's execution inspired him to struggle.

вдохновля́|ть, ю, *impf. of* вдохнови́ть.

вдохн|у́ть, у́, ёшь, *pf.* (*of* вдыха́ть) (в+*a.*) **1.** to breathe in, inhale; в. све́жий во́здух в лёгкие to breathe fresh air into one's lungs. **2.** to inspire (with), instil (into); в. му́жество в кого́-н. to inspire someone with courage, instil courage into someone.

вдре́безги, *adv.* to pieces, to smithereens; разби́ть в. to smash to smithereens; в. пьян (*coll.*) dead drunk.

вдруг, *adv.* **1.** suddenly, all of a sudden; все в. all together; не говори́те все в. don't all speak at once. **2.** *as interrog. particle* (*coll.*) what if, suppose; а в. они́ узна́ют? but suppose they find out?

вдры́зг, *adv.* (*coll.*) completely; в. пьян dead drunk.

вдува́ни|е, я, *n.* inflation, blowing up; (*med.*) pneumothorax.

вдува́|ть, ю, *impf. of* вдуть.

вду́м|аться, аюсь, *pf.* (*of* ~ываться) (в+*a.*) to think over, ponder, meditate (on).

вду́мчив|ый (~, ~а), *adj.* pensive, meditative; thoughtful.

вду́мыва|ться, юсь, *impf. of* вду́маться.

вду́н|уть, у, ешь, *pf.* = вдуть.

вду|ть, ~ю, ~ешь, *pf.* (*of* ~ва́ть) to blow into; в. во́здух в ши́ну to inflate, blow up a tyre.

вдыха́ни|е, я, *n.* inhalation.

вдыха́тельный, *adj.* (*med.*) respiratory.

вдыха́|ть, ю, *impf. of* вдохну́ть.

вегетариа́н|ец, ца, *m.* vegetarian.

вегетариа́нский, *adj.* vegetarian.

вегетариа́нств|о, а, *n.* vegetarianism.

вегетати́вный, *adj.* (*biol.*) vegetative.

вегетацио́нный, *adj.* (*biol.*) vegetation; в. пери́од vegetation period.

вегета́ци|я, и, *f.* vegetation.

ве́да|ть, ю, *impf.* **1.** (*obs.*) to know. **2.** (+*i.*) to manage, be in charge of.

ве́дени|е, я, *n.* authority; быть в ~и (+*g.*) (*leg.*) to be under the jurisdiction (of); э́то вне моего́ ~я this is outside my province.

веде́ни|е, я, *n.* conducting, conduct; в. де́ла conduct of an affair, transaction.

ведёрный, *adj.* **1.** of a bucket, pail. **2.** holding a bucketful, pailful. **3.** holding one vedro (*see* ведро́ 2).

ведовств|о́, а́, *n.* (*obs.*) sorcery.

ве́дома, *only in phrases* без в., с в.; без моего́ в. unknown to me; с моего́ в. with my knowledge, with my consent.

ве́домост|ь, и, *pl.* ~и, ~е́й, *f.* **1.** list, register; платёжная в. pay-roll; в. расхо́дов expense-sheet. **2.** (*pl. only*) gazette (*as name of newspaper*); Моско́вские ~и Moscow Gazette.

ве́домственный, *adj.* departmental.

ве́домств|о, а, *n.* department; Вое́нное в. War Department.

ве́дом|ый (~, ~а), *adj.* (*obs.*) known; вам э́то ~о? did you know about it?

ведо́м|ый (~, ~а), *pres. part. pass. of* вести́ (*obs.*) driven.

ве́дренный, *adj. of* ведро́ (*obs., coll.*); в. день a fine day.

вёдр|о, а, *n.* (*obs., coll.*) fine weather.

вед|ро́, ра́, *pl.* ~ра, ~ер, *n.* **1.** bucket, pail; по́лное в. a pailful. **2.** (*liquid measure*) vedro (*approx. twenty-one pints or 12 litres*).

вед|у́, ёшь, *see* вести́.

веду́щ|ий, *pres. part. act. of* вести́ *and adj.* leading; (*tech.*) ~ее колесо́ driving-wheel; *as noun* в., ~его, *m.* (*aeron.*) leader (*of flight*).

ведь, *conj.* **1.** you see, you know (*but often requires no translation*); она́ всё покупа́ет но́вые пла́тья — в. она́ о́чень бога́та she is always buying new dresses—she is very rich, you know; но в. э́то всем изве́стно but everyone knows about this. 2. is it not?; is it?; в. э́то пра́вда? it's the truth, isn't it?

ве́дьм|а, ы, f. 1. witch. 2. (coll.) hag, harridan.

ведьм|овско́й, adj. of ~а.

ве́ер, а, pl. ~а́, m. fan (also fig.); обма́хиваться ~ом to fan oneself; рассы́паться ~ом (mil., etc.) to fan out.

веерообра́зный, adj. fan-shaped; в. свод (archit.) fan tracery.

ве́жд|ы, ~, sing. ~а, ~ы, f. (obs., poet.) eyelids.

ве́жливост|ь, и, f. politeness, courtesy, civility.

ве́жлив|ый (~, ~а), adj. polite, courteous, civil.

везде́, adv. everywhere; в. и всю́ду here, there and everywhere.

вездесу́щ|ий (~, ~а), adj. ubiquitous, omnipresent (initially as epithet of God).

вездехо́д, а, m. landrover; (mil.) cross-country vehicle.

везе́ни|е, я, n. luck.

вез|ти́, у́, ёшь, past ~, ~ла́, impf. (of по~) (det. of вози́ть) 1. to cart, convey, carry (of beasts of burden or mechanical transport). 2. (coll.) (impers.+d.), to have luck; ему́ не ~ёт в ка́рты he has no luck at cards.

везу́чий, adj. (coll.) lucky.

вей¹, imp. of вить.

вей², imp. of ве́ять.

век, а, о ~е, на ~у́, pl. ~а́ (obs. ~и), m. 1. century. 2. age; ка́менный в. Stone Age; сре́дние ~а́ the Middle Ages; испоко́н ~о́в from time immemorial; отжи́ть свой в. to have had one's day, go out of fashion; в ко́и-то ~и once in a blue moon; во ~и ~о́в for all time; на ~и ве́чные for ever; в. живи́ — в. учи́сь! (prov.) live and learn! 3. life, lifetime; на моём ~у́ in my lifetime. 4. as adv. for ages; мы с ва́ми в. не вида́лись we have not seen each other for ages.

ве́к|о, а, pl. ~и, ~, n. eyelid.

век|ова́ть, у́ю, у́ешь, impf., usu. in phrase век в. (folk poet.) to pass a lifetime.

векове́чный, adj. eternal, everlasting.

вековой, adj. ancient, age-old.

векселеда́тел|ь,я,m.(comm.) drawer(of a bill).

векселедержа́тел|ь, я, m. (comm.) payee, holder (of a bill).

ве́ксел|ь, я, pl. ~я́, m. promissory note; bill of exchange; в. на заграни́цу foreign bill; уплати́ть по ~ю to meet a bill; учи́тывать в. to discount a bill.

ве́ксель|ный, adj. of ~; в. курс rate of exchange.

ве́кш|а, и, f. (dial.) squirrel.

вёл, ~а́, see вести́.

веле́невый, adj. vellum.

веле́ни|е, я, n. (obs.) command, behest.

велеречи́в|ый (~, ~а), adj. (obs. or iron.) bombastic, magniloquent.

вел|е́ть, ю́, и́шь, impf. and pf. (+d. and inf. or чтобы) 1. to order; я ~е́л ему́ сде́лать э́то or чтобы он сде́лал э́то I ordered him to do this; де́лайте, как вам ~ено do as you are told. 2. не в. to forbid.

велика́н, а, m. giant.

велика́нский, adj. (coll.) gigantic.

велика́нш|а, и, f. (coll.) giant(ess).

вели́к|ий (~, ~а́, ~о́), adj. 1. (short form ~а, ~о) great; ~ие держа́вы the Great Powers; Екатери́на Вели́кая Catherine the Great; в. князь grand prince, grand duke; ~ая седми́ца Passion Week; В. четве́рг Maundy Thursday. 2. (short form ~а́, ~о́, pl. ~й) big, large; но́ги у неё о́чень ~й she has very big feet; от ма́ла до ~а (coll.) young and old. 3. (short form only; ~а́, ~о́, pl. ~й) (+d. or для) too big; э́ти брю́ки мне ~й these trousers are too big for me.

великова́т|ый (~, ~а), adj. (coll.) rather large, big; э́ти боти́нки мне ~ы these boots are rather big for me.

великовозра́ст|ный (~ен, ~на), adj. overgrown.

великодержа́вный, adj. great-power.

великоду́ши|е, я, n. magnanimity, generosity.

великоду́шнича|ть, ю, impf. to affect magnanimity, generosity.

великоду́ш|ный (~ен, ~на), adj. magnanimous, generous.

великокня́жеский, adj. grand-ducal.

великоле́пи|е,я,n. splendour, magnificence.

великоле́п|ный (~ен, ~на), adj. 1. splendid, magnificent; в. дворе́ц a magnificent palace. 2. excellent; э́то — ~ная иде́я that's an excellent idea; ~но! (interj.) splendid!, excellent!

великому́ченик, а, m. great martyr.

великопо́стный, adj. (eccl.) Lenten.

великоро́дный, adj. (obs.) of noble birth.

велико|ро́сс = ~ру́с.

великору́с, а, m. Great Russian.

великору́сский, adj. Great Russian.

великосве́тск|ий, adj. fashionable, society; ~ая жизнь high life.

велича́вост|ь, и, f. stateliness, majesty.

велича́в|ый (~, ~а), adj. stately, majestic.

велича́йш|ий, adj. (superl. of вели́кий) greatest, extreme, supreme; де́ло ~ей ва́жности a matter of extreme importance; с ~им удово́льствием with the greatest pleasure.

велича́ни|е, я, n. 1. glorification, extolling. 2. songs of praise (eccl.; also in honour of living persons).

величá|ть, ю, *impf.* **1.** (*coll., dial.*) to call by patronymic; как вас ~ют? what is your patronymic? **2.** (+*a. and i.*; *obs. and iron.*) to call, dignify by the name of; в. писáку гéнием to dignify a hack by the name of genius. **3.** (*folk poet.*) to honour with songs.

величá|ться, юсь, *impf.* **1.** *pass. of* ~ть. **2.** (+*i.*; *coll.*) to glory (in), plume oneself (on).

вели́чественност|ь, и, *f.* majesty, grandeur.

вели́чествен|ный (~, ~на), *adj.* majestic, grand.

вели́честв|о, а, *n.* majesty; вáше в. Your Majesty.

вели́чи|е, я, *n.* greatness; grandeur; мáния ~я megalomania.

величин|á, ы́, *pl.* ~ы, ~áм, *f.* **1.** size; дом срéдней ~ы́ a house of average size; ~óю с человéческую рýку about the size of a man's hand. **2.** (*math.*) quantity, magnitude; value; в. подъёма up gradient; в. уклóна down gradient; постоя́нная в. constant. **3.** great figure; литератýрная в. an eminent literary figure.

вело- bicycle-, cycle-.

велодрóм, а, *m.* cycle track.

велосипéд, а, *m.* bicycle; cycle.

велосипеди́ст, а, *m.* bicyclist; cyclist.

велосипéд|ный, *adj. of* ~.

вельбóт, а, *m.* whale-boat, whaler.

вельвéт, а, *m.* velveteen; в. в рýбчик corduroy.

вельвéтовый, *adj.* velveteen.

вельми́, *adv.* (*obs. or iron.*) very.

вельмóж|а, и, *m.* (*obs. or iron.*) grandee.

вельмóж|ный, *adj. of* ~а.

веля́рный, *adj.* (*ling.*) velar.

вéн|а, ы, *f.* (*anat.*) vein; воспалéние ~ phlebitis; расширéние ~ varicose veins.

венгéр|ец, ца, *m.* Hungarian.

венгéрк|а, и, *f.* **1.** Hungarian (woman). **2.** Hungarian dance. **3.** dolman (*jacket*).

венгéрск|ий, *adj.* Hungarian; *as noun* ~ое, ~ого, *n.* Hungarian wine.

венгр, а, *m.* = венгéрец.

венéрик, а, *m.* (*coll.*) venereal patient.

венéрин, *adj. of* Venus; в. волосóк (*bot.*) maidenhair; в. холм (*palmistry*) mount of Venus.

венери́ческий, *adj.* (*med.*) venereal.

венерóлог, а, *m.* specialist in venereal diseases.

венерологи|я, и, *f.* science of venereal diseases.

вéн|ец, ца, *m.* Viennese (man).

вен|éц, цá, *m.* **1.** crown; (*fig.*) completion, consummation. **2.** (*fig.*) wedding; вести́ под в. to marry, lead to the altar; под ~цóм during the wedding. **3.** (*poet.*) wreath, garland. **4.** (*astron.*) corona. **5.** (*eccl.*) halo. **6.** row of beams (*in a house*).

венециáн|ец, ца, *m.* Venetian.

венециáнк|а, и, *f.* Venetian (woman).

венециáнск|ий, *adj.* Venetian; ~ая ярь verdigris.

венéчный, *adj.* **1.** (*anat.*) coronal, coronary. **2.** *adj. of* венéц.

вéнзел|ь, я, *pl.* ~я́, ~éй, *m.* monogram; ~я́ писáть (*coll.*) to walk unsteadily (*of a drunken person*).

вéник, а, *m.* **1.** besom. **2.** birch twigs (*used in Russian baths*).

вéнич|ек, ка, *m.* (*cul.*) wire whisk.

вéн|о, а, *n.* (*anthrop.*) bride-price.

вен|óзный, *adj. of* ~а; venous.

вен|óк, кá, *m.* wreath, garland.

вéнск|ий, *adj.* Viennese; в. стул bentwood chair; ~ая и́звесть French chalk.

вентили́р|овать, ую, *impf.* (*of* про~) to ventilate (*also fig.*).

вéнтил|ь, я, *m.* (*tech.*) valve; (*mus.*) mute.

вентиля́тор, а, *m.* ventilator.

вентиля́ци|я, и, *f.* ventilation.

венценóс|ец, ца, *m.* (*epithet of monarch*; *rhet.*) wearer of crown, crowned head.

венчá|льный, *adj. of* ~ние; ~льное кольцó wedding ring; в. наря́д wedding dress.

венчáни|е, я, *n.* **1.** в. на цáрство coronation. **2.** wedding ceremony.

венчá|ть, ю, *impf.* **1.** (*pf.* в. *and* у~) to crown. **2.** (*pf.* у~) (*fig.*) to crown; конéц ~ет дéло all's well that ends well. **3.** (*pf.* об~ *and* по~) to marry (*of officiating priest*).

венчá|ться, юсь, *impf.* **1.** (*pf.* об~ *and* по~) to be married, marry. **2.** *pass. of* ~ть.

вéнчик, а, *m.* **1.** halo, nimbus. **2.** (*bot.*) corolla. **3.** edge, rim (*of vessel*). **4.** (*anat.*) crown (*of tooth*). **5.** (*tech.*) ring, bolt. **6.** (*eccl.*) paper band placed on forehead of dead person.

вепр|ь, я, *m.* wild boar.

вéр|а, ы, *f.* (в+*a.*) faith, belief (in); trust, confidence; приня́ть на ~у to take on trust; дать ~у (+*d.*) to give credence (to); си́мвол ~ы (*eccl.*) the Creed.

верáнд|а, ы, *f.* veranda.

вéрб|а, ы, *f.* **1.** willow; willow branch.

вербáльн|ый, *adj.* verbal; ~ая нóта (*dipl.*) note verbale.

вербéн|а, ы, *f.* (*bot.*) verbena.

верблю́д, а, *m.* camel; одногóрбый в. Arabian camel, dromedary; двугóрбый в. Bactrian camel.

верблюжáтник, а, *m.* camel driver.

верблю́|жий, *adj. of* ~д; ~жья шерсть camel's hair; ~жье сукнó camel-hair cloth.

верблю́жин|а, ы, *f.* camel-meat.

верблюж|óнок, óнка, *pl.* ~áта, ~áт, *m.* young of camel.

вéрб|ный, *adj. of* ~а; ~ное воскресéнье

(*eccl.*) Palm Sunday; в. базáр Palm Sunday fair.

верб|овáть, ýю, *impf.* (*of* за~ *and* на~) to recruit, enlist; (*fig.*) to win over.

вербóвк|а, и, *f.* recruiting.

вербóвщик, а, *m.* recruiter.

вéрбов|ый, *adj.* willow; osier; ~ая корзи́на wicker basket.

верди́кт, а, *m.* verdict.

верёвк|а, и, *f.* cord, rope; string; (*fig.*) noose; в. для белья́ clothes-line; свя́зывать ~ой to rope, cord, tie up.

верёв|очный, *adj. of* ~ка.

вéред, а, *m.* (*dial.*) boil, abscess.

вере|ди́ть, жý, ди́шь, *impf.* (*of* раз~) (*coll.*) to knock, irritate (*a sore place; also fig.*).

верезж|áть, ý, и́шь, *impf.* (*coll.*) to squeal.

верени́ц|а, ы, *f.* row, file, line; в. лошаде́й a string of horses; в. иде́й a series of ideas.

вéреск, а, *m.* (*bot.*) heather.

вéреск|овый, *adj. of* ~; *as pl. noun* ~овые, ~овых (*bot.*) Ericaceae.

веретéниц|а, ы, *f.* (*zool.*) slow-worm.

веретён|ный, *adj. of* ~ó; ~ное мáсло (*tech.*) axle grease; spindle oil.

веретен|ó, á, *pl.* **веретёна, веретён,** *n.* 1. spindle; shank (*of an anchor*). 2. (*tech.*) axle.

верéть|е, я, *no pl.*, *n.* (*dial.*) sacking.

верещ|áть, ý, и́шь, *impf.* (*coll.*) to squeal; to chirp (*of a cricket, etc.*).

вере|я́¹, и́, *f.* (*dial.*) gate-post.

вере|я́², и́, *f.* (*naut.*) wherry.

верзи́л|а, ы, *m. and f.* (*coll.*) lanky person.

вери́г|и, ~, *sing.* ~**а, ~и,** *f.* chains, fetters (*worn by ascetics; also fig.*).

вери́тельн|ый, *adj.* ~ая грáмота (*dipl.*) letters of credence, credentials.

вéр|ить, ю, ишь, *impf.* (*of* по~) (+*d. or* в+*a.*) to believe, have faith (in); to trust (in), rely (upon); в. в Бóга to believe in God; в. в прогрéсс to believe in progress; в. в привидéния to believe in ghosts; э́тому человéку никтó не ~ит no one believes that man; он не ~ит своéй женé he does not trust his wife; в. нá слово to take on trust; я не ~ил свои́м ушáм, свои́м глазáм I could not believe my ears, eyes.

вéр|иться, ится, *impf.* (*impers.*+*d.*) мне ~ится с трудóм I find it hard to believe; емý не ~ится, что лю́ди мóгут быть совершéнны he cannot believe in the perfectibility of man.

вермишéл|ь, и, *f.* vermicelli.

верн|éе, *adv.* (*comp. of* ~о) rather; писáтель и́ли, в., писáка a writer or, rather, a hack.

вернисáж, а, *m.* (*art*) 1. private viewing. 2. opening-day (*of an exhibition*).

вéрн|о, *adv. of* ~ый; *as particle* (*coll.*) probably, I suppose; вы, в., ужé слыхáли

нóвости you have probably already heard the news.

вернопóдданический, *adj.* (*obs. or iron.*) loyal, faithful.

вернопóдданств|о, а, *n.* (*obs. or iron.*) loyalty, allegiance.

вернопóдданн|ый, *adj.* (*obs. or iron.*) loyal, faithful; *as noun* в., ~ого, *m.* loyal subject.

вéрност|ь, и, *f.* 1. faithfulness, loyalty. 2. truth, correctness.

верн|ýть, ý, ёшь, *pf.* (*of* возвращáть) 1. to give back, return. 2. to get back, recover, retrieve; в. здорóвье to recover one's health; в. потéрянное врéмя to make up for lost time. 3. (*coll.*) to make come back.

верн|ýться, ýсь, ёшься, *pf.* (*of* возвращáться) to return, revert (*also fig.*); в. домóй to return home; в. к прéжней рабóте to return to one's old job.

вéр|ный (~ен, ~на́, ~но), *adj.* 1. faithful, loyal, true; в. свои́м убеждéниям true to one's convictions. 2. true, correct; в. слух a good ear; ~ны ли ва́ши часы́? is your watch right?; ~но ли, что вы уезжáете? is it true that you are going away? 3. sure, reliable; в. истóчник reliable source; ~ная кóпия faithful copy; в. при́знак sure sign. 4. certain, sure; ~ная смерть certain death.

вéровани|е, я, *n.* belief, creed; ~я дрéвних египтя́н the beliefs of the ancient Egyptians.

вéр|овать, ую, *impf.* (в+*a.*) to believe (in).

вероисповéдани|е, я, *n.* creed; denomination; свобóда ~я freedom of religion.

веролóм|ный (~ен, ~на), *adj.* treacherous, perfidious.

веролóмств|о, а, *n.* treachery, perfidy.

веронáл, а, *m.* (*med.*) veronal.

верони́к|а, и, *f.* (*bot.*) speedwell, veronica.

вероотстýпник, а, *m.* apostate.

вероотстýпничеств|о, а, *n.* apostasy.

веропóдóби|е, я, *n.* (*obs.*) likelihood.

веропóдóб|ный (~ен, ~на), *adj.* (*obs.*) likely.

веротерпи́мост|ь, и, *f.* (*rel.*) toleration.

веротерпи́м|ый (~, ~а), *adj.* (*rel.*) tolerant.

вероучéни|е, я, *n.* (*rel.*) dogma.

вероучи́тел|ь, я, *m.* religious teacher, apologist.

вероя́ти|е, я, *n.* probability, likelihood; по всемý ~ю, по всем ~ям in all probability; сверх вся́кого ~я beyond all expectation.

вероя́тно, *adv.* probably; он, в., бóлен probably he is ill; он, в., приéдет ночны́м пóездом he is likely to come, he will probably come by the night train.

вероя́тност|ь, и, *f.* probability; по всей ~и in all probability; теóрия ~и (*math.*) theory of probability.

вероя́т|ный (~ен, ~на), *adj.* probable, likely; э́то вполне́ ~но it is highly probable; в. насле́дник heir presumptive.

версифика́тор, а, *m.* versifier; (*also pejor.*) он не поэ́т, а в. he is not a poet but a versifier.

версифика́ци|я, и, *f.* versification.

ве́рси|я, и, *f.* version; есть ра́зные ~и э́того собы́тия there are various versions of this story.

верст|а́, ы́, *a.* ~у́ and ~у, *pl.* ~ы́, ~, *f.* verst (*3500 English feet or 1·06 km*); verst-post; за́ ~у (*coll.*) far off; ме́рить ~ы (*coll.*) to travel a long way; коло́менская в. (*coll.*) lanky person.

верста́к, а́, *m.* (*tech.*) joiner's *or* locksmith's bench.

верста́тк|а, и, *f.* (*typ.*) composing-stick.

верста́|ть[1], ю, *impf.* (*of* с~) (*typ.*) to impose, make up into pages.

верста́|ть[2], ю, *impf.* (*of* по~) (*hist.*) 1. to arrange in line; (с+*i.*; *fig.*) to rank (with), compare (with). 2. (+*a.* and *i.*) to assign (to); в. кого́-н. поме́стьем to assign an estate to someone. 3. (в+*n.-a.*) to recruit (for), conscript (for).

вёрстк|а, и, *f.* (*typ.*) 1. imposing, imposition. 2. forme; made-up matter.

верст|ово́й, *adj. of* ~а́; в. столб milestone.

ве́ртел, а, *m.* spit; skewer.

верте́п, а, *m.* 1. cave, den (*of thieves, etc.*). 2. (*theatr.*) puppet-show of the Nativity; Nativity Play.

вер|те́ть, чу́, ~тишь, *impf.* (+*a.* or *i.*) to twirl, turn round and round; в. тро́стью to twirl a cane; она́ ~тит им, как хо́чет she can twist him round her little finger; как ни ~ти́, нам придётся заплати́ть there is nothing for it, we shall have to pay.

вер|те́ться, чу́сь, ~тишься, *impf.* 1. to rotate, turn (round), revolve (*also fig.*); разгово́р у них всё ~тится о́коло войны́ conversation with them always turns on the war; его́ фами́лия весь день ~те́лась у меня́ на ко́нчике языка́ his name was on the tip of my tongue all day; в. под нога́ми, пе́ред глаза́ми (*coll.*) to be under one's feet, in the way. 2. (*coll.*) to move (among), mix (with); он бо́льшей ча́стью ~тится среди́ иностра́нцев he mixes mostly with foreigners. 3. (*coll.*) to fidget. 4. (*coll.*) to prevaricate; отве́ть на вопро́с пря́мо, не ~ти́сь answer the question directly and don't prevaricate.

вертиголо́вк|а, и, *f.* = вертише́йка.

вертика́л, а, *m.* (*astron.*) vertical.

вертика́л|ь, и, *f.* vertical line; file (*on chessboard*); down (*in crossword*).

вертика́льный, *adj.* (*math.*) vertical.

вертихво́стк|а, и, *f.* (*coll.*) flirt, coquette.

вертише́йк|а, и, *f.* (*orn.*) wryneck.

вёрт|кий (~ок, ~ка́, ~ко), *adj.* (*coll.* nimble, agile.

вертлю́г, а́, *m.* 1. (*anat.*) head of the femu 2. (*tech.*) swivel.

вертлю́|жный, *adj. of* ~г.

вертля́в|ый (~, ~а), *adj.* (*coll.*) 1. restless fidgety. 2. flighty, frivolous.

вертогра́д, а, *m.* (*obs.*) garden.

вертодро́м, а, *m.* heliport.

вертолёт, а, *m.* helicopter.

вертопра́х, а, *m.* (*coll.*) frivolous person.

вертопра́шнича|ть, ю, *impf.* (*coll.*) to behave in a frivolous way.

верту́н, а́, *m.* (*coll.*) 1. fidget; restless person. 2. tumbler-pigeon.

вертуха́|й, я, *m.* (*sl.*) screw (*prison warder*).

верту́шк|а, и, *f.* (*coll.*) 1. revolving object (*e.g. door, bookcase*). 2. whirligig, teetotum (*toy*). 3. flirt, coquette.

ве́р|ующий, *pres. part. act. of* ~овать; *as noun* в., ~ующего, *m.* believer.

верф|ь, и, *f.* dockyard; shipyard.

верх, а, *pl.* ~и́, *m.* 1. top, summit (*also fig.*); совеща́ние на ~а́х (*polit.*) summit conference; в. глу́пости the height of folly. 2. upper part, upper side; bonnet, hood (*of vehicle*); (*fig.*) ~и́ (*pl. only*) upper crust (*of society*); (*mus.*) high notes; взять, одержа́ть в. (над) to gain the upper hand (over). 3. outside, top; right side (*of material*); хвата́ть ~и́, нахвата́ться ~о́в (*fig., coll.*) to get a smattering (of), acquire a superficial knowledge (of); скользи́ть по ~а́м to touch lightly on the surface.

ве́рхн|ий, *adj.* upper; ~яя оде́жда overcoat; outer clothing; ~яя пала́та (*polit.*) upper chamber; в. реги́стр (*mus.*) highest register; ~ее тече́ние (реки́) upper reaches (of river); в. я́щик top drawer.

верхове́нств|о, а, *n.* (*obs.*) leadership.

верхо́вн|ый, *adj.* supreme; ~ое кома́ндование high command; В. Сове́т Supreme Soviet.

верхово́д, а, *m.* (*coll.*) boss, leader.

верхово́|дить, жу, дишь, *impf.* (+*i.*; *coll.*) to lord it over, boss over; он ~дит все́ми в четвёртом кла́ссе he rules the fourth form.

верх|ово́й, *adj. of* ~о́м; ~ова́я езда́ riding; ~ова́я ло́шадь saddle-horse; *as noun* в., ~ово́го, *m.* rider.

верхово́й[2], *adj.* up-river.

верхо́вь|е, я, *g. pl.* ~ев, *n.* upper reaches.

верхогля́д, а, *m.* (*coll.*) superficial person.

верхогля́днича|ть, ю, *impf.* (*coll.*) to be superficial.

верхогля́дств|о, а, *n.* (*coll.*) superficiality.

верхола́з, а, *m.* steeplejack.

ве́рхом, *adv.* 1. on high ground. 2. quite

full, brim-full; нали́ть стака́н в. to pour out a full glass.

верхо́м, *adv.* astride; on horseback; е́здить в. to ride.

верху́шк|а, и, *f.* **1.** top, summit; apex. **2.** (*fig., coll.*) bosses; профсою́зная в. trade-union bosses.

ве́рченый, *adj.* (*coll., pejor.*) flighty, frivolous.

вер|чу́, ~тишь, *see* ~те́ть.

ве́рш|а, и, *f.* fish-trap (*made of osiers*).

верши́н|а, ы, *f.* **1.** top, summit; peak; (*fig.*) peak, acme; он дости́г ~ы сла́вы he had reached the summit of his fame. **2.** (*math.*) vertex; apex.

верш|и́ть, у́, и́шь, *impf.* **1.** (+*i.*) to manage, control; в. все́ми дела́ми to run the whole show. **2.** (*dial.*) to top; в. стог to top a rick. **3.** (+*a.*) to decide.

вершко́вый, *adj.* one vershok long.

верш|о́к, ка́, *m.* vershok (*measure of length equivalent to 1¾ inches or 4·4 cm*); (*fig.*) smattering, superficial knowledge; хвата́ть ~ки́ (+*g.*) to get a smattering (of).

вес, а, *pl.* **~а́,** *m.* **1.** weight; (*fig.*) weight, authority; на в. by weight; ~ом в сто фу́нтов weighing a hundred pounds; на ~у́ balanced, hanging, suspended; держа́ться на ~у́ to be balanced; приба́вить, уба́вить в ~е to put on, lose weight; быть на в. зо́лота to be worth one's weight in gold; име́ть в. to carry weight. **2.** system of weights; апте́карский в. apothecaries' weight. **3.** уде́льный в. specific gravity.

веселе́|ть, ю, *impf.* (*of* по~) to become gay, become bright.

весел|и́ть, ю́, и́шь, *impf.* (*of* по~) to cheer, gladden; to amuse.

весел|и́ться, ю́сь, и́шься, *impf.* (*of* по~) to enjoy oneself; to amuse oneself.

ве́село, *adv.* gaily, merrily; *as pred.* (+*d.*) to enjoy oneself; нам тут о́чень в. we very much enjoy being here; мне в. бы́ло смотре́ть на вас I enjoyed seeing you.

весёлост|ь, и, *f.* **1.** gaiety; cheerfulness. **2.** (*pl. only*; *obs.*) merry-making.

весёл|ый (ве́сел, ~а́, ве́село), *adj.* gay, merry; cheerful; у него́ ~ое настрое́ние сего́дня he is in good spirits today.

весе́л|ье, ья, *g. pl.* **~ий,** *n.* **1.** gaiety, merriment. **2.** (*pl. only*; *obs.*) merry-making.

вес|е́льный, *adj.* of ~ло́; ~е́льная ло́дка rowing-boat.

весельча́к, а́, *m.* (*coll.*) convivial fellow.

вес|е́нний, *adj.* of ~на́; ~е́ннее равноде́нствие vernal equinox.

ве́|сить, шу, сишь, *impf.* **1.** to weigh (*intrans.*); ~сит три то́нны it weighs three tons. **2.** (*obs., coll.*) to weigh (*trans.*).

ве́с|кий (~ок, ~ка), *adj.* weighty.

вес|ло́, ла́, *pl.* **~ла, ~ел, ~лам,** *n.* oar; scull;

paddle; завяза́ть в. to catch a crab; подня́ть ~ла to rest on one's oars.

вес|на́, ны́, *pl.* **~ны, ~ен, ~нам,** *f.* spring (*season*).

весну́шк|и, ек, *sing.* **~ка, ~ки,** *f.* freckles.

весну́шчатый, *adj.* freckled.

весня́нк|а, и, *f.* **1.** (*zool.*) mayfly. **2.** (*ethnol.*) spring-song.

вес|ово́й, 1. *adj.* of ~. **2.** sold by weight.

весовщи́к, а́, *m.* weigher; checkweighman.

весо́мост|ь, и, *f.* (*phys.*) ponderability.

весо́м|ый (~, ~а), *adj.* (*phys.*) ponderable; (*fig.*) weighty; heavy.

вест, а, *m.* (*naut.*) **1.** west. **2.** west wind.

веста́лк|а, и, *f.* vestal (virgin).

ве|сти́, ду́, дёшь, *past* **~л, ~ла́,** *impf.* (*det. of* води́ть) **1.** (*pf.* по~) to lead; to conduct; to take; в. слепо́го to lead a blind man. **2.** (*pf.* про~) (+*i.* по +*d.*) to run (over), pass (over, across); в. смычко́м по стру́нам to run one's bow over the strings. **3.** (*pf.* про~) to conduct; to carry on; в. войну́ to wage war; в. обще́ственную рабо́ту to do social work; в. ого́нь (по+*d.*) to fire (on); в. перегово́ры to carry on negotiations; в. перепи́ску (с+*i.*) to correspond (with); в. пра́вильный о́браз жи́зни to lead a regular life; в. проце́сс to carry on a lawsuit. **4.** (*impf. only*) to drive; в. кора́бль to navigate a ship; в. самолёт to pilot an aircraft. **5.** (*impf. only*) to conduct, direct, run; в. де́ло to run a business; в. собра́ние to preside at a meeting; в. хозя́йство to keep house. **6.** (*impf. only*) to keep, conduct; в. дневни́к to keep a diary; в. кни́ги to keep books, keep accounts; в. протоко́л to keep minutes. **7.** (*impf. only*) в. себя́ to behave, conduct oneself. **8.** (*impf. only*) (к) to lead (to) (*also fig.*); куда́ ~дёт э́та доро́га? where does this road lead (to)?; э́то ни к чему́ не ~дёт this is leading nowhere. **9.** (*impf. only*) в. своё нача́ло (от) to originate (in), take rise (in); в. свой род (от) to be descended (from). **10.** и у́хом не в. (*coll.*) to pay no heed.

вестибю́л|ь, я, *m.* hall, lobby.

вести́мо, *adv.* (*dial.*) of course, certainly.

ве|сти́сь, ду́сь, дёшься, *past* **вёлся, ~ла́сь,** *impf.* (*of* по~) **1.** *pass. of* ~сти́. **2.** (*usu. impers.*; *coll.*) to be observed (*of customs, etc.*); так ~дётся уже́ три́ста лет this has been the custom for three hundred years. **3.** to multiply (*of domestic animals*).

ве́стник, а, *m.* messenger, herald; (*also in title of publications*) bulletin.

ве́стниц|а, ы, *f.* of ве́стник.

вестов|о́й, *adj.* (*obs.*) signal; ~а́я раке́та signal-rocket; *as noun* в., ~о́го, *m.* orderly.

вестовщи́к, а́, *m.* (*coll., obs.*) newsmonger, gossip.

ве́сточк|а, и, *f.* (*coll.*) news; да́йте о себе́ ∼у, как то́лько прие́дете let me hear from you as soon as you arrive.

вест|ь¹, и, *pl.* ∼и, ∼е́й, *f.* news; piece of news; пропа́сть бе́з ∼и (*mil.*) to be missing.

весть², *only in phrases* Бог в. God knows; не в. что goodness knows, heaven knows what; не (Бог) в. како́й trifling, insignificant.

вес|ы́, о́в, *no sing.* 1. scales, balance; мостовы́е в. weighbridge; пружи́нные в. spring balance; бро́сить на в. (*fig.*) to throw into the balance. 2. В. the Scales, Libra (*sign of the Zodiac*).

весь¹, вся, всё, *g.* всего́, всей, всего́, *pl.* все, всех, *pron.* all; весь день all day; вся Фра́нция the whole of France; он весь в отца́ he is the (very) image of his father; весь в лохмо́тьях all in rags; вы́йти весь to be used up; бума́га вся вы́шла the paper is all used up, there is no paper left; во в. го́лос at the top of one's voice; во всю мочь with all one's might; от всего́ се́рдца from the bottom of one's heart, with all one's heart; по всему́ го́роду all over the town; во-всю́ (*coll.*) like anything; пре́жде всего́ before all, first and foremost; при всём том for all that, moreover; вот и всё that's all; всего́ (хоро́шего)! good-bye!, all the best!; всё и вся (*coll.*) all and everything; *as noun* всё, всего́, *n.* everything; все, всех all, everyone; всем, всем, всем! attention, everyone!

вес|ь², и, *f.* (*obs.*) village.

весьма́, *adv.* very, highly; в. успе́шный о́пыт highly successful experiment.

ветви́ст|ый (∼, ∼а), *adj.* branchy, spreading.

ветв|ь, и, *pl.* ∼и, ∼е́й, *f.* branch, bough; (*fig.*) branch.

ве́т|ер, ра, *m.* 1. wind; кре́пкий в. (*naut.*) half a gale; о́чень кре́пкий в. fresh gale; ти́хий в. light air; по ∼ру before the wind, down wind; держа́ть нос по ∼ру (*fig.*) to trim one's sails to the wind; под ∼ром leeward; про́тив ∼ра close to the wind, in the teeth of the wind; в. с бе́рега off-shore wind; (*fig.*) броса́ть слова́ на в. to talk idly; у него́ в. в голове́ he is a thoughtless fellow; подби́тый ∼ром (*coll.*) (*i*) empty-headed, (*ii*) light, flimsy. 2. ∼ры (*med.*) wind, flatulence.

ветера́н, а, *m.* veteran.

ветерина́р, а, *m.* veterinary surgeon.

ветерина́ри|я, и, *f.* veterinary science; veterinary medicine.

ветерина́рный, *adj.* veterinary.

ветер|о́к, ка́, *m.* breeze.

ве́тк|а, и, *f.* branch; twig; железнодоро́жная в. branch-line.

вет|ла́, лы́, *pl.* ∼лы, ∼ел, *f.* (*bot.*) white willow.

ве́то, *indecl.*, *n.* veto; наложи́ть в. (на+*a.*) to veto.

ве́точк|а, и, *f.* twig, sprig, shoot.

ве́тошник, а, *m.* (*obs.*) old clothes dealer.

ве́тош|ь, и, *f.* old clothes, rags.

ветр = ве́тер.

ветрене́|ть, ет, *impf.* (*impers.*; *coll.*) to become windy.

ве́треник, а, *m.* (*coll.*) empty-headed, frivolous person.

ве́трени|ца¹, цы, *f. of* ∼к.

ве́трениц|а², ы, *f.* (*bot.*) anemone.

ве́треност|ь, и, *f.* empty-headedness, instability.

ве́трен|ый (∼, ∼а), *adj.* 1. windy; за́втра бу́дет ∼о it will be windy tomorrow. 2. (*fig.*) empty-headed, unstable.

ветри́л|о, а, *n.* (*poet.*) sail.

ветробо́|й, я, *no pl.*, *m.* (*dial.*, *collect.*) 1. wind-fallen wood. 2. windfalls (*fruit*).

ветрово́й, *adj. of* ве́тер.

ветрого́н, а, *m.* 1. (*tech.*) fan. 2. = ве́треник.

ветрого́нный, *adj.* (*med.*) carminative.

ветроме́р, а, *m.* (*phys.*) anemometer.

ветросилово́й, *adj.* wind-powered.

ветроуказа́тел|ь, я, *m.* (*aeron.*) drogue, wind cone, wind sock.

ветроулови́тел|ь, я, *m.* (*aeron.*) rudder air scoop.

ветрочёт, а, *m.* (*aeron.*) course and speed computer.

ветря́к, а́, *m.* 1. (*tech.*) wind turbine. 2. (*coll.*) windmill.

ветря́нк|а, и, *f.* (*coll.*) 1. windmill. 2. chicken-pox.

ветряно́й, *adj.* wind(-powered); ∼а́я ме́льница windmill.

ве́трян|ый, *adj.* ∼ая о́спа chicken-pox.

ве́тх|ий (∼, ∼а́, ∼о), *adj.* old, ancient; dilapidated, tumbledown; decrepit; В. заве́т the Old Testament.

ветхозаве́тный, *adj.* Old Testament; (*fig.*) antiquated.

ве́тхост|ь, и, *f.* decrepitude; dilapidation.

ветчин|а́, ы́, *no pl.*, *f.* ham.

ветчи́н|ный, *adj. of* ∼а́.

ветша́|ть, ю, *impf.* (*of* об∼) to decay; to become dilapidated; to become decrepit.

ве́х|а, и, *f.* landmark (*also fig.*); (*naut.*) spar-buoy; сме́на ∼ (*polit.*) volte-face; смени́ть ∼и to execute a volte-face.

ве́ч|е, а, *n.* (*hist.*) veche (*popular assembly in medieval Russian towns*).

вечево́й, *adj. of* ве́че.

ве́чер, а, *pl.* ∼а́, *m.* 1. evening; по ∼а́м in the evenings; под в., к ∼у towards evening. 2. party; evening, soirée; музыка́льный в. musical evening; вчера́ был в. у Ива́новых the Ivanovs had a party last night; в.

па́мяти Че́хова Chekhov commemoration meeting.

вечере́|ть, ет, *impf.* *(impers.)* to grow dark; **~ет** night is falling.

вечери́нк|а, и, *f.* (evening-)party.

вечерко́м, *adv.* *(coll.)* in the evening.

вече́рн|ий, *adj.* *of* ве́чер; **~яя заря́** twilight, dusk; **в. звон** vesper chimes; **~ие ку́рсы** evening classes; **~ее пла́тье** evening dress; **~яя шко́ла** night-school.

вече́рник, а, *m.* *(coll.)* night-school student.

вече́р|ня, ни, *pl. g.* **~ен,** *f.* *(eccl.)* vespers.

ве́чером, *adv.* in the evening.

ве́чер|я, и, *f.* *(obs.)* supper; **Та́йная в.** *(bibl.)* the Last Supper.

ве́чник, а, *m.* *(sl.)* lifer *(convict serving life sentence).*

ве́чно, *adv.* for ever, eternally; always; **они́ в. ссо́рятся** they are always quarrelling.

вечнозелёный, *adj.* *(bot.)* evergreen.

ве́чност|ь, и, *f.* eternity; **ка́нуть в в.** to sink into oblivion; **це́лую в.** *(coll.)* for ages, for an age; **он не приходи́л сюда́ це́лую в.** he has not been here for ages.

ве́ч|ный (~ен, ~на), *adj.* **1.** eternal, everlasting; **~ная мерзлота́** permafrost; **засну́ть ~ным сном** to take one's last sleep. **2.** endless; perpetual; **~ное владе́ние** possession in perpetuity; **~ное перо́** fountain-pen.

вечо́р, *adv.* *(coll., obs.)* yesterday evening.

вечо́рк|а, и, *f.* *(coll.)* evening paper.

ве́шалк|а, и, *f.* **1.** peg, rack, stand. **2.** tab *(on clothes for hanging on pegs).* **3.** cloak-room.

ве́ша|ть¹, ю, *impf.* *(of* пове́сить*)* to hang; **в. бельё на верёвку** to hang washing on a line; **в. уби́йцу** to hang a murderer; **в. соба́к (на+*a.* or на шéю+*d.*; coll.)** to pin accusations (upon).

ве́ша|ть², ю, *impf.* *(of* взве́сить*)* to weigh, weigh out; **в. фунт ко́фе** to weigh out a pound of coffee.

ве́ша|ться¹, юсь, *impf.* *(of* пове́ситься*)* **1.** *pass. of* ~**ть¹**; to be hung; to be hanged. **2.** to hang oneself. **3. в. на шéю кому́-н.** *(coll.)* to run after; **она́ всё ~ется молоды́м офице́рам на шéю** she is always running after young officers.

ве́ша|ться², юсь, *impf.* *(of* с~*)* *(coll.)* to weigh oneself.

веш|и́ть, у́, и́шь, *impf.* *(of* про~*)* *(geod.)* to mark out.

ве́шк|а, и, *f.* landmark; surveying rod.

ве́шний, *adj.* *(poet.)* vernal.

ве́|шу, сишь, *see* ~**сить**.

веш|у́, и́шь, *see* ~**и́ть**.

веща́ни|е, я, *n.* **1.** prophesying. **2.** *(radio)* broadcasting.

веща́|ть, ю, *impf.* **1.** *(obs.)* to prophesy.

2. *(coll.)* to pontificate, play the oracle, lay down the law. **3.** *(radio)* to broadcast.

вещ|ево́й, *adj.* *of* ~**ь**; **~ево́е дово́льствие** payment in kind; *(mil.)* clothing, kit; **в. мешо́к** hold-all; kit-bag; **в. склад** storage warehouse, store; *(mil.)* stores.

веще́ственност|ь, и, *f.* substantiality, materiality.

веще́ственн|ый, *adj.* substantial, material; **~ые доказа́тельства** material evidence.

вещество́, а́, *n.* substance; matter; **взры́вчатое в.** explosive; **отравля́ющее в.** poisongas; **се́рое в.** grey matter.

ве́щий, *adj.* *(poet.)* prophetic.

вещ|и́ца, и́цы, *f.* *dim. of* ~**ь**; little thing; bagatelle.

вещ|ный, *adj.* *of* ~**ь**; **~ное пра́во** *(leg.)* law of estate.

вещу́н, а́, *m.* *(obs.)* soothsayer.

вещ|ь, и, *pl.* ~**и, ~éй,** *f.* **1.** *(in var. senses)* thing; **пе́рвая любо́вь — чуде́сная в.** first love is a marvellous thing; **э́то в.!** *(expressing approval; coll.)* that's quite something!; **вот кака́я в.: президе́нт собира́ется посети́ть наш го́род** do you know what? the President is going to visit our town. **2.** *(pl.)* things (= (i) belongings; baggage; (ii) clothes); **ва́ши ли э́ти ~и?** are these things yours?; **тебе́ сле́дует носи́ть бо́лее тёплые ~и** you ought to be wearing warmer things; **со все́ми ~а́ми** bag and baggage. **3.** *(of artistic productions)* work; piece, thing; **его́ лу́чшие ~и ещё не переведены́** his best things have not yet been translated.

ве́ялк|а, и, *f.* *(agric.)* winnowing-fan; winnowing-machine.

ве́яни|е, я, *n.* **1.** *(agric.)* winnowing. **2.** breathing, blowing *(of wind)*. **3.** *(fig.)* current *(of opinion)*, tendency, trend; **в. вре́мени** spirit of the times.

ве́|ять, ю, ешь, *impf.* **1.** *(agric.)* to winnow. **2.** *(intrans.)* to blow *(of wind)*; **~ял прохла́дный ветеро́к** a cool breeze was blowing; *(impers., +i.)* **~ет весно́й** spring is in the air; **~ет но́выми иде́ями** new ideas are in the air. **3.** to wave, flutter; **знамёна ~яли по ве́тру** banners were fluttering in the wind.

вжива́|ться, юсь, *impf. of* вжи́ться.

вжи|ться, ву́сь, вёшься, *pf.* (в+*a.*; *coll.*) to get used (to), grow accustomed (to); **он с трудо́м ~вётся в вое́нную жизнь** he will find it hard to get used to army life.

взад, *adv.* *(coll.)* back; **в. и вперёд** backwards and forwards, to and fro; **ни в. ни вперёд** neither backwards nor forwards; **он не мог дви́нуться ни в. ни вперёд** he could not budge an inch.

взаи́мност|ь, и, *f.* reciprocity; return *(of affection)*; **отвеча́ть кому́-н. ~ью** to reciprocate someone's feelings, return someone's love; любо́вь без ~и unrequited love.

взаи́м|ный (~ен, ~на), *adj.* mutual, reciprocal; ~ная по́мощь mutual aid; в. глаго́л (*gram.*) reciprocal verb.

взаимоде́йстви|е, я, *n.* interaction; (*mil.*) co-operation, co-ordination.

взаимоде́йств|овать, ую, *impf.* to interact; (*mil.*) to co-operate.

взаимоотноше́ни|е, я, *n.* interrelation.

взаимопо́мощ|ь, и, *f.* mutual aid; ка́сса ~и mutual benefit; догово́р о ~и mutual assistance pact.

взаймы́, *adv.* взять в. to borrow; дать в. to lend, loan.

взалка́|ть, ю, *pf.* (*obs.*) to hunger (for) (+*g.* or +*inf.*; *fig.,* now *usu. iron.*).

взаме́н, *prep.*+*g.* instead (of); in return (for), in exchange (for).

взаперти́, *adv.* **1.** under lock and key; сиде́ть в. to be locked up. **2.** in seclusion.

взапра́вду, *adv.* (*coll.*) in truth, indeed.

вза́пуски, *adv.* бе́гать в. to chase one another.

взасо́с, *adv.* целова́ться в. (*coll.*) to exchange long-drawn-out kisses.

взатя́жку, *adv.* кури́ть в. (*coll.*) to inhale (*in smoking*).

вза́шей, *adv.* (*coll.*) вы́гнать в. to chuck out; to throw out (on one's neck).

взба́дрива|ть, ю, *impf.* of взбодри́ть.

взбаламу́|тить, чу, тишь, *pf.* of баламу́тить.

взба́лмошный, *adj.* (*coll.*) unbalanced, eccentric.

взба́лтывани|е, я, *n.* shaking (up).

взба́лтыва|ть, ю, *impf.* of взболта́ть.

взбега́|ть, ю, *impf.* (*of* взбежа́ть) to run up; в. на́ гору to run up a hill; в. по ле́стнице to run upstairs.

взбе|жа́ть, гу́, жи́шь, гу́т, *pf.* of ~га́ть.

взбелен|и́ться, ю́сь, и́шься, *pf.* (на+*a.*; *coll.*) to become enraged (with).

взбе|си́ть(ся), шу́(сь), ~си́шь(ся), *pf.* of беси́ть(ся).

взбива́|ть, ю, *impf.* of взбить.

взбира́|ться, юсь, *impf.* of взобра́ться.

взби́т|ый (~, ~а), *p.p.p.* of ~ь; ~ые сли́вки whipped cream.

вз|бить, обью́, обьёшь, *pf.* (*of* ~бива́ть) **1.** to beat up; в. сли́вки to whip cream; в. яи́чные белки́ to beat up white of egg. **2.** to shake up, fluff up.

взбодр|и́ть, ю́, и́шь, *pf.* (*of* взба́дривать) to cheer up; to encourage.

взболта́|ть, ю, *pf.* (*of* взба́лтывать) to shake (up) (*liquids*); пе́ред прие́мом в. миксту́ру shake the bottle before taking.

взбороз|ди́ть, жу́, ди́шь, *pf.* of борозди́ть 1.

взборон|и́ть, ю́, и́шь, *pf.* of борони́ть.

взбра́сыва|ть, ю, *impf.* of взбро́сить.

взбреда́|ть, ю, *impf.* of взбрести́.

взбре|сти́, ду́, дёшь, *past* взбрёл, ~ла́, *pf.* (*of* ~да́ть) (на+*a.*; *coll.*) to mount with difficulty; в. в го́лову, на ум to come into one's head; ему́ ~ло́ на ум, что все его́ ненави́дят he got it into his head that everyone hated him.

взбро́|сить, шу, сишь, *pf.* (*of* взбра́сывать) (*coll.*) to throw up, toss up.

взбры́згива|ть, ю, *impf.* of взбры́знуть.

взбры́з|нуть, ну, нешь, *pf.* (*of* ~гивать) (*coll.*) to sprinkle, spatter.

взбудора́жива|ть, ю, *impf.* of взбудора́жить.

взбудора́ж|ить, у, ишь, *pf.* (*coll.*) to agitate, work up.

взбунт|ова́ть(ся), у́ю(сь), *pf.* of бунтова́ть(ся).

взбуха́|ть, а́ю, *impf.* of ~нуть.

взбу́х|нуть, ну, нешь, *past* ~, ~ла, *pf.* (*of* ~а́ть) to swell out.

взбу́ч|ить, у, ишь, *pf.* (*coll.*) **1.** to thrash, beat. **2.** to reprimand.

взбу́чк|а, и, *f.* (*coll.*) **1.** thrashing, beating. **2.** reprimand; закати́ть кому́-н. ~у to give someone a ticking-off; получи́ть ~у to be hauled over the coals.

взва́лива|ть, ю, *impf.* of взвали́ть.

взвал|и́ть, ю́, ~ишь, *pf.* (*of* ~ивать) to load, lift (onto); в. мешо́к на́ спину to hoist a pack onto one's back; всю рабо́ту ~и́ли на но́вого учи́теля (*coll.*) the new teacher was loaded with all the work; всю вину́ ~и́ли на него́ he was made to shoulder all the blame.

взва́р, а, *m.* (*cul.*) stewed fruit and berries.

взве́|сить, шу, сишь, *pf.* (*of* ~шивать *and* ве́шать) to weigh; (*fig.*) to weigh, consider; в. возмо́жные после́дствия посту́пка to weigh the possible consequences of an action.

взве|сти́, ду́, дёшь, *past* ~л, ~ла́, *pf.* (*of* взводи́ть) **1.** to lead up, take up; в. куро́к (ружья́) to cock (a gun). **2.** (на+*a.*) to impute (to); на генера́ла ~ли́ обвине́ние в пораже́нии blame for the defeat was laid at the general's door.

взвес|ь, и, *f.* (*chem.*) suspension.

взве́шен|ный (~, ~а), **1.** *p.p.p.* of взве́сить. **2.** (*chem.*) suspended; ~ое состоя́ние suspension.

взве́шивани|е, я, *n.* weighing.

взве́шива|ть, ю, *impf.* of взве́сить.

взвива́|ть(ся), ю(сь), *impf.* of взви́ть(ся).

взви́|деть, жу, дишь, *pf. only in phrase* све́та не в. (*coll.*) to see stars.

взвизг, а, *m.* (*coll.*) scream; yelp (*of a dog*).

взви́згива|ть, ю, *impf. and freq.* of взви́згнуть.

взви́згн|уть, у, ешь, *pf.* to scream, cry out; to yelp (*of a dog*); соба́ка жа́лобно ~ула the dog let out a piteous yelp.

взвин|ти́ть, чу́, ти́шь, *pf.* (*of* взви́нчивать) (*coll.*) to excite, work up; **в. це́ны** to inflate prices.

взви́нчен|ный (~, ~a), *p.p.p. of* взвинти́ть *and adj.* excited, worked up; highly-strung, nervy; **не́рвы у него́ всегда́ ~ы** he is always on edge; **~ные це́ны** inflated prices.

взви́нчива|ть, ю, *impf. of* взвинти́ть.

взвить, взовью́, взовьёшь, *pf.* (*of* взвива́ть) to raise.

взви́ться, взовью́сь, взовьёшься, *pf.* (*of* взвива́ться) to rise; to fly up, soar (*of birds*); to be raised, go up (*of flags, etc.*); **за́навес взви́лся ро́вно в во́семь часо́в** the curtain went up at eight o'clock exactly.

взвод¹, а, *m.* (*mil.*) platoon.

взвод², а, *m.* (cocking) notch (*of guns*); **боево́й в., второ́й в.** full bent; **на боево́м ~e** cocked; **на пе́рвом ~e** at half-cock; **предохрани́тельный в.** safety notch; **на предохрани́тельном ~e** at safety; **быть на ~e** (*coll.*) to be in one's cups.

взво|ди́ть, жу́, ~дишь, *impf. of* взвести́.

взвод|но́й, *adj. of* ~²; **~на́я ру́чка** cocking handle.

взво́д|ный, *adj. of* ~¹; *as noun* **в., ~ного,** *m.* platoon commander.

взволно́ван|ный (~, ~a), *p.p.p. of* взволнова́ть *and adj.* agitated, disturbed; anxious, worried; **у неё в. вид** she has a worried look.

взволн|ова́ть, у́ю, *pf. of* волнова́ть.

взволн|ова́ться, у́юсь, *pf. of* волнова́ться.

взво́|ю, ешь, *see* взвыть.

взвыва́|ть, ю, *impf. of* взвыть.

взв|ыть, о́ю, о́ешь, *pf.* (*of* ~ыва́ть) to howl, set up a howl.

взгляд, а, *m.* **1.** look; glance; gaze, stare; **бро́сить в.** (**на**+*a.*) to glance (at); **на в.** to judge from appearances; **на пе́рвый в., с пе́рвого ~a** at first sight. **2.** view; opinion; **на мой в.** in my opinion, as I see it.

взгля́дыва|ть, ю, *impf. of* взгляну́ть.

взглян|у́ть, у́, ~ешь, *pf.* (**на**+*a.*) to look (at); to cast a glance (at); **в. на что-н. серьёзно** (*fig.*) to take a serious view of something.

взговор|и́ть, ю́, и́шь, *pf.* (*folk poet.*) to say.

взго́рь|е, я, *n.* (*dial.*) hillock.

взгре|ть, ю, ешь, *pf.* (*coll.*) to thrash; (*fig.*) to give it hot.

взгроможда́|ть, ю, *impf. of* взгромозди́ть.

взгроможда́|ться, юсь, *impf. of* взгромозди́ться.

взгромоз|ди́ть, жу́, ди́шь, *pf.* (*coll.*) to pile up.

взгромоз|ди́ться, жу́сь, ди́шься, *pf.* (*coll.*) to clamber up.

взгрустн|у́ть, у́, ёшь, *pf.* (*coll.*) to feel sad, depressed.

взгрустн|у́ться, ётся, *pf.* (*impers.*+*d.*; *coll.*) to feel sad, depressed; **ему́ ~у́лось** he feels depressed.

вздва́ива|ть, ю, *impf. of* вздво́ить.

вздв|о́ить, о́ю, о́ишь, *pf.* (*of* ~а́ивать) **в. ряды́** (*mil.*) to form fours.

вздёргива|ть, ю, *impf. of* вздёрнуть.

вздёрнут|ый (~, ~a), *p.p.p. of* ~ь; **в. нос** snub nose.

вздёрн|уть, у, ешь, *pf.* (*coll.*) **1.** to hitch up; to jerk up; **в. нос** to become proud. **2.** to hang.

вздор, а, *no pl.*, *m.* (*coll.*) nonsense; **городи́ть, моло́ть в.** to talk nonsense.

вздо́р|ить, ю, ишь, *impf.* (*of* по~) (*coll.*) to squabble.

вздо́р|ный (~ен, ~на), *adj.* (*coll.*) **1.** foolish, stupid. **2.** cantankerous, quarrelsome.

вздорожа́ни|е, я, *n.* rise in price.

вздорожа́|ть, ю, *pf. of* дорожа́ть.

вздох, а, *m.* sigh; deep breath; **испусти́ть после́дний в.** to breathe one's last.

вздохн|у́ть, у́, ёшь, *pf.* (*of* вздыха́ть) **1.** to sigh. **2.** (*coll.*) to take breath, have a breathing-space; **дава́йте ~ём!** let's pause for breath!

вздра́гива|ть, ю, *impf.* (*of* вздро́гнуть) to shudder, quiver.

вздремн|у́ть, у́, ёшь, *pf.* (*coll.*) to have a nap, doze.

вздремн|у́ться, ётся, *pf.* (*impers.*+*d.*; *coll.*); **как раз по́сле еды́ ему́ ~у́лось** immediately after the meal he dozed off.

вздро́гн|уть, у, ешь, *pf.* (*of* вздра́гивать) to start; to wince, flinch.

вздрю́ч|ить, у, ишь, *pf.* (*coll.*) to thrash, beat; to reprimand.

вздува́|ть, ю, *impf. of* вздуть¹.

вздума|ть, ю, *pf.* (+*inf.*; *coll.*) to take it into one's head; **она́ ~ла носи́ть чёрные ве́щи** she took it into her head to wear black; **не ~й(те)** mind you don't; **не ~йте ныря́ть здесь!** mind you don't dive in here!, don't try to dive in here!

вздума|ться, ется, *pf.* (*impers.*+*d.*; *coll.*) to take it into one's head; **ему́ ~лось пое́хать в Аме́рику** he took it into his head to go to America; **как ~ется** at one's own sweet will.

вздути|е, я, *n.* (*med.*) swelling; **в. цен** (*fig.*) inflation of prices.

вздут|ый¹ (~, ~a), *p.p.p. of* ~ь¹ *and adj.* swollen.

вздут|ый² (~, ~a), *p.p.p. of* ~ь².

взду́|ть¹, ю, ешь, *pf.* (*of* вздува́ть) **1.** to blow up, inflate. **2.** (*dial.*) to light (*a fire*).

взду́|ть², ю, ешь, *pf.* (*coll.*) to thrash, give a thrashing (to).

взду́|ться, юсь, ешься, *pf.* to swell (*intrans.*).

вздыма́|ть, ю, *impf.* to raise.

вздыма́|ться, юсь, *impf.* to rise; ∼лась мгла над о́зером mist was rising over the lake.

вздыха́ни|е, я, *n.* (*obs.*) **1.** sighing. **2.** (*pl. only*) love-sickness.

вздыха́тел|ь, я, *m.* (*coll., obs.*) admirer.

вздыха́|ть, ю, *impf.* (*of* вздохну́ть) **1.** to) breathe; to sigh. **2.** (о, по+*p.*) to pine (for; to long, sigh (for).

взима́ни|е, я, *n.* levy, collection.

взима́|ть, ю, *impf.* to levy, collect, raise (*taxes*).

взира́|ть, ю, *impf.* (на+*a.*) **1.** (*obs.*) to look (at), gaze (at). **2.** не ∼я на in spite of, notwithstanding; не ∼я на ли́ца without respect of persons.

взла́мыва|ть, ю, *impf. of* взлома́ть.

взлеза́|ть, ю, *impf. of* взлезть.

взлез|ть, у, ешь, *past* ∼, ∼ла, *pf.* (*of* ∼а́ть) to climb up.

взлеле́|ять, ю, ешь, *pf. of* леле́ять.

взлёт, а, *m.* (upward) flight (*also fig.*); (*aeron.*) take-off; в. фанта́зии flight of fancy.

взлета́|ть, ю, *impf. of* взлете́ть.

взле|те́ть, чу́, ти́шь, *pf.* (*of* ∼та́ть) to fly up; to take off; в. по ле́стнице to fly upstairs; в. на во́здух to explode, blow up (*also fig.*); в тече́ние еди́ного дня мечты́ всей жи́зни ∼те́ли на во́здух the dreams of a lifetime exploded in a day.

взлёт|ный, *adj. of* ∼; (*aeron.*) ∼ная доро́жка runway; ∼но-поса́дочная площа́дка landing strip.

взли́з|а, ы, (*coll.*) bald patch (*above the temples*).

взлом, а, *m.* breaking open, breaking in; кра́жа со ∼ом house-breaking.

взлома́|ть, ю, *pf.* (*of* взла́мывать) to break open, force; to smash; в. замо́к to force a lock; в. неприя́тельскую оборо́ну to force the enemy's defences.

взло́мщик, а, *m.* burglar, house-breaker.

взлохма́|тить, чу, тишь, *pf. of* лохма́тить *and* ∼чивать.

взлохма́|ченный (∼чен, ∼чена), *p.p.p. of* ∼тить *and adj.* tousled; dishevelled.

взлохма́чива|ть, ю, *impf.* to tousle.

взлюб|и́ть, лю́, ∼ишь, *pf., only with neg.*; не в. с пе́рвого взгля́да to take an instant dislike (to).

взман|и́ть, ю́, и́шь, *pf. of* мани́ть 2.

взмах, а, *m.* wave (*of hand*); flap, flapping (*of wings*); stroke (*of oars, etc.*); одни́м ∼ом at one stroke.

взма́хива|ть, ю, *impf. of* взмахну́ть.

взмахн|у́ть, у́, ёшь, *pf.* (+*i.*) to wave, flap; в. платко́м to wave a handkerchief.

взметн|у́ть, у́, ёшь, *pf.* (*of* взмётывать) (+*i.*) to throw up, fling up; в. рука́ми to fling up one's hands.

взметн|у́ться, у́сь, ёшься, *pf.* **1.** to leap up, fly up; и́скры ∼у́лись из-под копы́т коня́ sparks flew up from the horse's hoofs. **2.** (на+*a.* (*obs.*) to leap (upon), fly (at); соба́ки ∼у́лись на бродя́гу the dogs flew at the tramp.

взмётыва|ть, ю, *impf. of* взметну́ть.

взмётыва|ться, юсь, *impf. of* взметну́ться.

взмол|и́ться, ю́сь, ∼ишься, *pf.* (о+*p.*) to beg (for); to beseech; в. о поща́де to beg for mercy.

взмо́рь|е, я, *n.* sea-shore; seaside.

взмо|сти́ться, щу́сь, сти́шься, *pf.* (*coll.*) (на+*a.*) to perch (on).

взму|ти́ть, чу́, ти́шь, *pf. of* мути́ть.

взмыва́|ть, ю, *impf. of* взмыть.

взмы́лива|ть(ся), ю(сь), *impf. of* взмы́лить(ся).

взмы́л|ить, ю, ишь, *pf.* to cause to foam, lather.

взмы́л|иться, юсь, ишься, *pf.* to foam (*intrans.*), froth.

взм|ыть, о́ю, о́ешь, *pf.* (*of* ∼ыва́ть) to shoot upwards (*of a bird*).

взнос, а, *m.* payment; fee, dues; subscription; вступи́тельный в. entrance fee; очередно́й в. instalment; профсою́зный в. trade-union dues; чле́нский в. membership fee.

взнузда́|ть, ю, *pf.* to bridle.

взну́здыва|ть, ю, *impf. of* взнузда́ть.

взобра́|ться, взберу́сь, взберёшься, *past* ∼лся, ∼ла́сь, *pf.* (*of* взбира́ться) (на+*a.*) to climb (up), clamber (up); им пришло́сь в. на скло́н холма́ на четвере́ньках they had to clamber up the slope on all fours.

взобь|ю́, ёшь, *see* взбить.

взовь|ю́, ёшь, *see* взвить.

взо|йти́, йду́, йдёшь, *past* ∼шёл, ∼шла́, *past part.* ∼ше́дший, *pf.* (*of* всходи́ть *and* восходи́ть) (на+*a.*) **1.** to mount, ascend; to rise; в. на трибу́ну to mount the platform; со́лнце ∼шло́ в пять часо́в сего́дня the sun rose at five o'clock today; посе́вы уже́ ∼шли́ the crops are already standing; те́сто не ∼шло́ the dough would not rise. **2.** (*obs., coll.*) to enter.

взор, а, *m.* look; glance; обрати́ть на себя́ ∼ы пу́блики to come into the public eye; устреми́ть ∼ы (на+*a.*) to fasten one's eyes (on).

взорв|а́ть, у́, ёшь, *pf.* (*of* взрыва́ть) **1.** to blow up; to detonate. **2.** (*fig.*) to exasperate, madden; его́ ∼а́ло, когда́ они́ сообщи́ли о свое́й помо́лвке (*impers.*) he was exploded when they announced their engagement.

взорв|а́ться, у́сь, ёшься, *pf.* (*of* взрыва́ться) to blow up, burst, explode (*also fig.*).

взо|шёл, шла́, *see* ∼йти́.

взра|сти́ть, щу́, сти́шь, *pf.* to grow, cultivate; to bring up, nurture.

взра́щива|ть, ю, *impf. of* взрасти́ть.

взра|щу́, сти́шь, *see* ~сти́ть.

взрев|е́ть, у́, ёшь, *pf.* to let out a roar.

взре́ж|у, ешь, *see* взре́зать.

взре́|зать, жу, жешь, *pf.* to cut open.

взреза́|ть, ю, *impf. of* взре́зать.

взре́зыва|ть, ю = взреза́ть.

взро́сл|ый, *adj.* grown-up, adult; *also as noun* в., ~ого, *m.*; ~ая, ~ой, *f.*

взрыв, а, *m.* explosion; (*fig.*) burst, outburst; в. аплодисме́нтов burst of applause; в. негодова́ния outburst of indignation.

взрыва́|ть¹, ю, *impf. of* взорва́ть.

взрыва́|ть², *impf. of* взрыть.

взрыва́|ться, юсь, *impf. of* взорва́ться.

взрывн|о́й, *adj.* 1. explosive; ~а́я волна́ blast. 2. (*ling.*) plosive.

взрывча́тк|а, и, *f.* (*coll.*) explosive.

взры́вчат|ый, *adj.* explosive; ~ое вещество́ explosive.

взр|ыть, о́ю, о́ешь, *pf.* (*of* ~ыва́ть²) to plough up, turn up.

взрыхл|и́ть, ю́, и́шь, *pf.* to loosen, break up.

взрыхля́|ть, ю, *impf. of* взрыхли́ть.

взъеда́|ться, юсь, *impf. of* взъе́сться.

взъезжа́|ть, ю, *impf. of* взъе́хать.

взъерепе́н|иться, юсь, ишься, *pf. of* ерепе́ниться.

взъеро́шен|ный (~, ~а), *p.p.p. of* взъеро́шить *and adj.* tousled, dishevelled.

взъеро́шива|ть(ся), ю(сь), *impf. of* взъеро́шить(ся).

взъеро́ш|ить, у, ишь, *pf.* (*of* ~ивать) (*coll.*) to tousle, rumple.

взъеро́ш|иться, усь, ишься, *pf.* (*of* ~иваться) (*coll.*) to rumple one's hair; to become dishevelled.

взъ|е́сться, е́мся, е́шься, е́стся, еди́мся, еди́тесь, едя́тся, *past* ~е́лся, *pf.* (*of* ~еда́ться) (на+*a.*; *coll.*) to pitch into, go for (*fig.*).

взъе́|хать, ду, дешь, *pf.* (*of* ~зжа́ть) to mount, ascend (*in a vehicle or on an animal*).

взыва́|ть, ю, *impf. of* воззва́ть.

взыгра́|ть, ю, *pf.* 1. to leap (for joy); се́рдце во мне ~ло my heart leapt up. 2. to become disturbed; мо́ре ~ло the sea grew rough.

взыска́ни|е, я, *n.* 1. penalty; punishment; подве́ргнуться ~ю to incur a penalty. 2. exaction; prosecution; пода́ть на кого́-н. ко ~ю (*leg.*) to proceed against someone (*for recovery of debt, etc.*).

взыска́тел|ьный (~ен, ~ьна), *adj.* exacting; demanding; severe.

взы́|ска́ть¹, щу́, ~щешь, *pf.* (*of* ~скивать) 1. to exact; to recover; в. долг (с+*g.*) to recover a debt (from). 2. to call to account,

make answer (for); за неуда́чу в бою́ ~ска́ли с генера́лов the generals were called to account for their failure in battle; не ~щи́(те)! (*coll.*) please forgive (me)!, don't be hard on (me)!

взы́|ска́ть², щу́, ~щешь, *pf.* (*of* ~скивать) (+*i.*; *obs.*) to confer (on); to reward (with); в. ми́лостями to load with favours.

взы́скива|ть, ю, *impf. of* взыска́ть.

взыску́ющ|ий, его, *m.* (*lit.*) 'seeker'.

взы́|щу́, ~щешь, *see* ~ска́ть.

взя́ти|е, я, *n.* taking; capture.

взя́тк|а, и, *f.* 1. bribe; ~и гла́дки, *see* гла́дкий. 2. (*cards*) trick.

взя́т|ок, ка, *m.* honey-gathering.

взя́точник, а, *m.* bribe-taker.

взя́точничеств|о, а, *n.* bribery, bribe-taking, corruption.

взя́|ть, возьму́, возьмёшь, *past* ~л, ~ла́, ~ло, *pf.* (*of* брать) 1. *see* брать. 2. (*coll.*) to conclude, suppose; с чего́ вы ~ли, что он не́мец? what gave you the idea that he is a German? 3. в. да, в. и, в. да и... (*coll.*) to do something suddenly; он ~л да убежа́л he up and ran; он возьми́ да скажи́ he up and spoke; возьми́ да скажи́ speak up, speak your mind. 4. чёрт возьми́! (*coll.*) devil, deuce take it! 5. ни дать ни в. (*coll.*) exactly, neither more nor less.

взя́|ться, возьму́сь, возьмёшься, *past* ~лся, ~ла́сь, ~ло́сь, *pf.* (*of* бра́ться); отку́да ни возьми́сь (*coll.*) from nowhere, out of the blue; отку́да ни возьми́сь налете́ла саранча́ out of the blue the locusts appeared.

виаду́к, а, *m.* viaduct.

вибра́тор, а, *m.* (*electr.*) vibrator; (*radio*) oscillator.

вибрафо́н, а, *m.* (*mus.*) vibraphone, vibes.

вибра́ци|я, и, *f.* vibration.

вибри́р|овать, ую, *impf.* to vibrate; to oscillate.

виве́р, а, *m.* (*coll., obs.*) bon vivant.

виве́рр|а, ы, *f.* (*zool.*) civet.

вивисе́кци|я, и, *f.* vivisection.

виг, а, *m.* (*hist.*) whig.

вигва́м, а, *m.* wigwam.

виго́н|ь, и, *f.* vicuña; vicuña wool.

вид¹, а, *m.* 1. air, look; appearance; aspect; у вас хоро́ший в. you look well; име́ть мра́чный в. to look gloomy, have a gloomy air; приня́ть пра́здничный в. to assume a festive air; сде́лать в., бу́дто to make it appear that, pretend that; для ~у for the sake of appearances; на в., с ~у in appearance; знать по ~у to know by sight; под ~ом (+*g.*) under the guise (of); ни под каки́м ~ом on no account. 2. shape, form; condition; в любо́м ~е in any shape or form; в тре́звом ~е in a sober state; в хоро́шем ∼е in good condition, in good shape. 3. view; ко́мната с ∼ом на го́ры room with a view of the mountains; в. сбо́ку side-view; откры́тка с ∼ом picture postcard. 4. (*pl.*) prospect; ∼ы на бу́дущее prospects for the future. 5. sight; потеря́ть из ∼у to lose sight (of); упусти́ть из ∼у (*fig.*) to lose sight (of), fail to take into account; поста́вить на в. кому́-н. что-н. to reprimand someone for something; быть на ∼у́ to be in the public eye; при ∼е (+*g.*) at the sight (of); в ∼у́ (+*g.*) in sight (of); в ∼у́ того́, что as, since, seeing that; име́ть в ∼у́ (*i*) to plan, intend, (*ii*) to mean; что вы име́ли в ∼у́, говоря́ э́то? what did you mean when you said that?, (*iii*) to bear in mind; име́й(те) в ∼у́ bear in mind, don't forget; име́ться в ∼у́ (*i*) to be intended, be envisaged, (*ii*) to be meant.

вид², а, *m.* 1. (*biol.*) species. 2. kind, sort. 3. (*gram.*) aspect; соверше́нный, несоверше́нный в. perfective, imperfective aspect.

вид³, а, *m.* в. на жи́тельство residence permit; identity card.

ви́дан|ный (∼, ∼а), *p.p.p. of* вида́ть; ∼ное ли э́то де́ло? have you ever heard of such a thing?

вида́|ть, ю, *impf.* (*of* у∼) (*coll.*) to see; его́ не в. he is not to be seen; ничего́ подо́бного я не ∼л I have never seen such a thing; он ∼л ви́ды he has seen, knocked about, the world.

вида́|ться, юсь, *impf.* (*of* по∼) (с+*i.*; *coll.*) to meet; to see one another; мы с жено́й три го́да не ∼лись my wife and I had not seen one another for three years.

ви́дени|е, я, *n.* sight, vision.

виде́ни|е, я, *n.* vision, apparition.

ви́део- video-.

видеоза́пис|ь, и, *f.* videotape recording.

видеомагнитофо́н, а, *m.* videotape recorder.

ви́|деть, жу, дишь, *impf.* (*of* у∼) to see; в. кого́-н. наскво́зь to see through someone; в. во сне to dream (of); его́ то́лько и ∼дели (*coll.*) he was gone in a flash; ∼дишь (ли)?, ∼дите (ли)? (*coll.*) (do) you see?

ви́|деться, жусь, дишься, *impf.* 1. to see one another; (с+*i.*) to see. 2. (*pf.* при∼) to appear; ему́ ∼делся стра́шный сон he had a terrifying dream; Га́млету ∼делась тень отца́ на валу́ the ghost of his father appeared to Hamlet on the rampart.

ви́димо, *adv.* 1. (*obs.*) visibly. 2. evidently; он, в., чу́вствовал себя́ оскорблённым evidently he was offended.

ви́димо-неви́димо, *adv.* (*coll.*) in immense quantity; наро́ду бы́ло в.-н. there was an immense crowd.

ви́димост|ь, и, *f.* 1. visibility. 2. outward

appearance; для ∼и for show, for appearances. 3. по (всей) ∼и to all appearances.

ви́дим|ый (∼, ∼а), *p.p.p. of* ви́деть *and adj.* 1. visible. 2. apparent, evident; без ∼ой причи́ны with no apparent cause. 3. apparent, seeming.

видне́|ться, юсь, ешься, *impf.* to be visible; на горизо́нте ∼лись огни́ корабля́ a ship's lights could be seen on the horizon.

ви́дно 1. *adv.* obviously, evidently; она́, в., уста́ла obviously she is tired; *as pred.* it is obvious, it is evident, it is apparent; всем бы́ло в., что он лжёт it was obvious to everyone, everyone could see that he was lying; как в. из ска́занного as is clear from the statement. 2. *adv. as pred.* visible; in sight; берега́ ещё не́ было в. the coast was not yet visible; конца́ ещё не в. the end is not yet in sight; бы́ло хорошо́ в. visibility was good.

ви́д|ный, *adj.* 1. (∼ен, ∼на́, ∼но) visible; conspicuous. 2. distinguished, prominent. 3. (*coll.*) portly, stately; в. мужчи́на fine figure of a man.

видово́й¹, *adj. of* вид¹; в. объекти́в (*phot.*) landscape lens; в. фильм travel film, travelogue.

видово́й², *adj.* (*of* вид²) 1. (*biol.*) specific. 2. (*gram.*) aspectual.

видоизмене́ни|е, я, *n.* 1. modification, alteration. 2. modification; variety.

видоизмен|и́ть, ю́, и́шь, *pf.* (*of* ∼я́ть) to modify, alter.

видоизмен|и́ться, ю́сь, и́шься, *pf.* (*of* ∼я́ться) 1. to alter (*intrans.*). 2. *pass. of* ∼я́ть.

видоизмен|я́ть(ся), я́ю(сь), *impf. of* ∼и́ть(ся).

видообразова́ни|е, я, *n.* (*biol.*) formation of species.

ви́дыва|ть, ю, *freq. of* ви́деть (*coll.*) to see.

ви́з|а, ы, *f.* 1. visa. 2. official stamp.

визави́ 1. *adv.* opposite; они́ сиде́ли в. they sat opposite one another. 2. *indecl. noun, m. and f.* the person opposite, facing; мы с мои́м в. завяза́ли разгово́р I entered into conversation with the person facing me.

византи́|ец, йца, *m.* Byzantine.

византи́йский, *adj.* Byzantine.

византини́ст, а, *m.* Byzantinist.

визг, а, *m.* scream; squeal; yelp.

визгли́в|ый (∼, ∼а), *adj.* 1. shrill. 2. given to screaming, squealing, yelping.

визготн|я́, и́, *f.* (*coll.*) screaming; squealing; yelping.

визж|а́ть, у́, и́шь, *impf.* to scream; to squeal; to yelp.

визи́г|а, и, *no pl., f.* viziga (*foodstuff prepared from gristle of fish of sturgeon family*).

визионе́р, а, *m.* visionary, mystic.

визионе́рств|о, а, *n.* mystical propensities.

визи́р, а, *m.* 1. (*mil.*) sight; навигацио́нный в. (*aeron.*) drift sight. 2.(*phot.*) view-finder.

визи́р|овать[1], ую, *impf. and pf.* (*pf. also* за~) to visa, visé (*passport*).

визи́р|овать[2], ую, *impf. and pf.* to sight; to take a sight (on).

визи́р|ь, я, *m.* vizier.

визи́т, а, *m.* visit; call; нанести́ в. to make an (official) visit; отда́ть в. to return a visit, call; прийти́ с ~ом к кому́-н. to visit someone, pay someone a call.

визита́ци|я, и, *f.* 1. call; round (*of doctor*). 2. search (*for contraband goods*).

визитёр, а, *m.* visitor, caller.

визити́р|овать, ую, *impf.* 1. (*obs.*) to pay a visit. 2. to make a round (*of doctor*).

визи́тк|а, и, *f.* morning coat.

визи́т|ный, *adj.* of ~; ~ная ка́рточка visiting card.

ви́к|а, и, *no pl., f.* vetch, tares.

вика́ри|й, я, *m.* (*eccl.*) vicar; suffragan.

вика́рный, *adj.* (*eccl.*) suffragan.

вико́нт, а, *m.* viscount.

виктори́н|а, ы, *f.* quiz.

викто́ри|я, и, *no pl., f.* pine strawberries.

ви́лк|а, и, *f.* 1. fork. 2. (*electr.*) штёпсельная в. two-pin plug. 3. (*mil.*) bracket.

ви́лл|а, ы, *f.* villa.

ви́ллис, а, *m.* (*mil.*) jeep.

вил|о́к, ка́, *m.* (*dial.*) head of cabbage.

вилообра́з|ный (~ен, ~на), *adj.* forked.

ви́л|ы, ~, *no sing.*, pitchfork; э́то ещё ~ами на воде́ пи́сано (*fig.*) it is still in the air.

вильн|у́ть, у́, ёшь, *pf.* 1. *pf. of* виля́ть. 2. to glide away; to turn off sharply, side-track.

виля́ни|е, я, *n.* 1. wagging. 2.(*fig.*) prevarication; evasions.

виля́|ть, ю, *impf.* (*of* вильну́ть) 1. to wag; в. хвосто́м to wag one's tail; хвост у соба́ки всё вре́мя ~л the dog's tail was wagging the whole time. 2. (*fig.*) to prevaricate; to be evasive.

вин|а́, ы́, *pl.* ~ы, *f.* fault, guilt; blame; моя́ в. it is my fault; не по их ~е́ through no fault of theirs; поста́вить кому́-н. в ~у́ to accuse someone of, reproach someone with; свали́ть ~у́ (на+*a.*) to lay the blame (on).

винегре́т, а, *m.* Russian salad; (*fig.*) medley, farrago.

ви́н|и, ей, *no sing.* (*coll.*) spades (*cards*).

вини́тельный, *adj.* (*gram.*) в. паде́ж accusative case.

вин|и́ть, ю́, и́шь, *impf.* (в+*p.*) to accuse (of); (за+*a.*) (*obs., coll.*) to reproach (for).

вин|и́ться, ю́сь, и́шься, *impf.* (*of* по~) (в+*p.*; *coll.*) to confess (to).

вини́щ|е, а, *n.* (*coll.*) spirit *or* wine.

ви́нкел|ь, я, *pl.* ~я́, *m.* (*tech.*) set-square.

виннока́менн|ый, *adj.* (*chem.*) ~ая кислота́ tartaric acid.

ви́нн|ый, *adj.* wine; winy; vinous; в. ка́мень (*chem.*) tartar; ~ая кислота́ tartaric acid; в. спирт ethyl alcohol; ~ая я́года dried figs.

вин|о́, а́, *pl.* ~а, *n.* 1. wine. 2. (*sing. only;coll.*) vodka.

винова́т|ый (~, ~а), *adj.* guilty; to blame; мы все ~ы в э́том we are all to blame for this; ~! sorry!; без вины́ ~ый innocent victim.

вино́вник, а, *m.* author, initiator; culprit; в. преступле́ния perpetrator of a crime; в. побе́ды architect of victory.

вино́вност|ь, и, *f.* guilt.

вино́в|ный (~ен, ~на), *adj.* (в+*p.*) guilty (of); объявля́ть ~ным to bring in a verdict of guilty; призна́ть себя́ ~ным to plead guilty.

виногра́д, а (у), *m.* 1. vine. 2. (*collect.*) grapes; зе́лен в.! sour grapes!

виногра́дарств|о, а, *n.* viticulture; wine-growing.

виногра́дар|ь, я, *m.* wine-grower.

виногра́дин|а, ы, *f.* (*coll.*) grape.

виногра́дник, а, *m.* vineyard.

виногра́д|ный, *adj.* of ~; ~ная лоза́ vine; в. сезо́н vintage; ~ное су́сло must.

виноде́л, а, *m.* wine-grower.

виноде́ли|е, я, *n.* wine-making.

виноку́р, а, *m.* distiller.

виноку́рени|е, я, *n.* distillation.

виноку́р|енный, *adj.* of ~ние; в. заво́д distillery.

виноку́р|ня, ни, *g. pl.* ~ен, *f.* (*obs.*) distillery.

виноторго́в|ец, ца, *m.* wine-merchant.

виноторго́вл|я, и, *f.* 1. wine-trade. 2. wine-shop.

виночерпи|й, я, *m.* (*hist.*) cup-bearer.

винт[1], а́, *m.* 1. screw; подъёмный в. jack-screw; упо́рный в. stop screw; устано́вочный в. adjusting set screw. 2. screw, propeller; дать ~а́ (*sl.*) to take to one's heels, scarper. 3. spiral; ле́стница ~о́м spiral staircase.

винт[2], а́, *m.* vint (*card-game*).

винт[3], а́, *m.* (*sl.*) rifle.

ви́нт|ик, а, *m.* 1. *dim. of* ~[1]; у него́ ~а не хвата́ет (*coll.*) he has a screw loose somewhere. 2. (*fig., coll., of a person*) cog.

вин|ти́ть[1], чу́, ти́шь, *impf.* to screw up.

вин|ти́ть[2], чу́, ти́шь, *impf.* (*coll.*) to play vint.

винто́вк|а, и, *f.* rifle.

винт|ово́й, *adj.* of ~[1]; spiral; ~ова́я ле́стница spiral staircase; ~ова́я наре́зка thread (*of screw*); в. парохо́д screw steamer; ~ова́я переда́ча (*tech.*) helical gear.

винтообра́з|**ный** (~ен, ~на), *adj.* spiral.

винторе́зный, *adj.* (*tech.*) screw-cutting.

вин|**чу́, ти́шь**, *see* ~ти́ть.

виньётк|**а, и,** *f.* vignette.

вио́л|**а, ы,** *f.* viol; viola.

виолончели́ст, а, *m.* (violon)cellist.

виолонче́л|**ь, и,** *f.* (violon)cello.

ви́ра[1], *interj.* (*dockers' sl.*) lift!

ви́р|**а**[2], **ы,** *f.* (*hist.*) wergeld.

вира́ж[1], **а,** *m.* (*phot.*) intensifier; в.-фикса́ж tone-fixing bath.

вира́ж[2], **а́,** *m.* **1.** turn; круто́й в. steep turn. **2.** bend, curve (*of road, racing-track, etc.*).

вири́р|**овать, ую,** *impf. and pf.* (*phot.*) to intensify.

виртуа́л|**ьный** (~ен, ~ьна), *adj.* virtual.

виртуо́з, а, *m.* virtuoso.

виртуо́зност|**ь, и,** *f.* virtuosity.

виртуо́з|**ный** (~ен, ~на), *adj.* masterly.

вируле́нт|**ный** (~ен, ~на), *adj.* (*med.*) virulent.

ви́рус, а, *m.* (*med.*) virus.

ви́рус|**ный**, *adj.* of ~.

ви́рш|**и, ей,** *no sing.* **1.** (*lit.*) (syllabic) verses (*based on Polish form*). **2.** (*coll.*) doggerel.

вис, а, *m.* (*sport*) hanging (on the pole).

ви́селиц|**а, ы,** *f.* gallows, gibbet.

ви́сельник, а, *m.* **1.** hanged man. **2.** (*coll.*) gallows-bird.

ви|**се́ть, шу́, си́шь,** *impf.* to hang; to be hanging, be suspended; в. на волоске́ to hang by a thread; в. в во́здухе (*i*) to be in the air, (*ii*) to be unfounded.

ви́ски, *indecl., n.* whisky.

виско́з|**а, ы,** *f.* **1.** (*tech.*) viscose. **2.** (*coll.*) rayon.

вислоу́х|**ий** (~, ~а), *adj.* lop-eared.

ви́смут, а, *m.* (*chem.*) bismuth.

ви́сн|**уть, у, ешь,** *impf.* (на+*p.*) to hang (on); to droop; в. у кого́-н. на ше́е (*fig., coll.*) to hang on someone's neck.

вис|**о́к, ка́,** *m.* (*anat.*) temple.

высоко́сный, *adj.* в. год leap-year.

висо́чный, *adj.* (*anat.*) temporal.

вист, а, *m.* whist (*card-game*).

висю́льк|**а, и,** *f.* (*coll.*) pendant.

вися́чий, *adj.* hanging, pendent; в. замо́к padlock; в. мост suspension bridge.

витали́зм, а, *m.* (*philos.*) vitalism.

витали́ст, а, *m.* (*philos.*) vitalist.

витами́н, а, *m.* vitamin.

витами́нный, *adj.* vitaminous.

витамин|**о́зный** = ~ный.

вита́|**ть, ю,** *impf.* (*lit.*) to be; to wander (*of thoughts*); to hover; он ~ет в ми́ре фанта́зий he inhabits a world of fantasy; он всё ещё говори́л, но мы́сли у него́ ~ли далеко́ he went on speaking but his thoughts were far away; в. в облака́х to be up in the clouds; смерть ~ла над ней death was hovering over her.

витиева́т|**ый** (~, ~а), *adj.* flowery, ornate, rhetorical.

вити́йств|**о, а,** *n.* (*obs.*) oratory, rhetoric.

вити́йств|**овать, ую,** *impf.* (*obs.*) to orate.

вити́|**я, и,** *m.* (*coll., iron.*) orator.

вит|**о́й**, *adj.* twisted; spiral; ~а́я ле́стница spiral staircase.

вит|**о́к, ка́,** *m.* **1.** (*tech.*) spire. **2.** circuit (*of planet by space vehicle*). **3.** (*fig.*) round.

витра́ж, а, *m.* stained-glass window.

витри́н|**а, ы,** *f.* **1.** (shop-)window. **2.** show-case.

ви|**ть, вью, вьёшь,** *past* ~л, ~ла́, ~ло, *impf.* (*of* с~) to twist, wind; в. венки́ to weave garlands; в. гнездо́ to build a nest; в. верёвки из кого́-н. (*coll.*) to twist round one's little finger.

ви|**ться, вьюсь, вьёшься,** *past* ~лся, ~ла́сь, ~ло́сь, *impf.* (*of* с~) **1.** to wind, twine. **2.** to curl, wave (*of hair*). **3.** to hover, circle (*of birds*). **4.** to writhe, twist (*of reptiles*).

витю́т|**ень, ня,** *m.* wood-pigeon.

ви́тяз|**ь, я,** *m.* (*poet., arch.*) knight; hero.

вихля́|**ть, ю,** *imp.* (*coll.*) to reel.

вихля́|**ться, юсь,** *impf.* (*coll.*) to wobble.

вих|**о́р, ра́,** *m.* forelock.

вихра́ст|**ый** (~, ~а), *adj.* (*coll.*) shaggy; shock-headed.

вихрево́й, *adj.* (*phys.*) vortical.

вихр|**ь, я,** *m.* **1.** whirlwind; сне́жный в. blizzard. **2.** (*fig.*) vortex.

ви́це- vice-.

вице-адмира́л, а, *m.* vice-admiral.

вице-коро́л|**ь, я́,** *m.* viceroy.

вицмунди́р, а, *m.* uniform (*of civil servants*).

виши́, *indecl., n.* Vichy (water).

вишнёвк|**а, и,** *f.* cherry brandy.

вишнёвый, *adj.* **1.** cherry; в. сад cherry orchard. **2.** cherry-coloured.

ви́ш|**ня, ни,** *g. pl.* ~ен, *f.* **1.** cherry-tree. **2.** cherry; (*collect.*) cherries.

вишь (*contraction of* ви́дишь; *coll.*) look!, just look!; в. что сде́лал! look what he's done!

вка́лыва|**ть, ю,** *impf.* **1.** *impf. of* вколо́ть. **2.** *impf. only* (*sl.*) to work hard.

вка́п|**ать, аю,** *pf.* (*of* ~ывать[1]) (*coll.*) to pour in.

вка́пыва|**ть**[1]**, ю,** *impf. of* вка́пать.

вка́пыва|**ть**[2]**, ю,** *impf. of* вкопа́ть.

вка|**ти́ть, чу́, ~тишь,** *pf.* (*of* ~тывать) **1.** to roll into, onto; to wheel in, into; в. бо́чку в подва́л to roll a barrel into a cellar. **2.** (*fig., coll.*) to administer; to put in, on; в. пощёчину (+*d.*) to slap in the face; в. в спи́сок to place in a list.

вка|**ти́ться, чу́сь, ~тишься,** *pf.* (*of* ~тываться) to roll in (*intrans.*); (*coll.*) to run in.

вка́тыва|ть(ся), ю(сь), *impf. of* вкати́ть-(ся).

вклад, а, *m.* 1. (*fin.*) deposit; investment. 2. endowment; (*fig.*) contribution; внести́ ва́жный в. в нау́ку to make an important contribution to learning.

вкла́дк|а, и, *f.* supplementary sheet.

вклад|но́й 1. *adj. of* ~. 2. supplementary, inserted; в. лист loose leaf.

вкла́дчик, а, *m.* depositor; investor.

вкла́дыва|ть, ю, *impf. of* вложи́ть.

вкла́д|ыш, а, *m.* 1. = ~ка. 2. (*tech.*) bush, bearing brass.

вкле́ива|ть, ю, *impf. of* вкле́ить.

вкле́|ить, ю, ~ишь, *pf.* (*of* ~ивать) to stick in; в. сло́во в разгово́р (*fig.*, *coll.*) to put in a word.

вкле́йк|а, и, *f.* 1. sticking in. 2. inset (*in a book*).

вклеп|а́ть, а́ю, *pf.* (*of* ~ывать) 1. to rivet in. 2. (*fig.*, *coll.*) to mix up (in), involve (in).

вклеп|а́ться, а́юсь, *pf.* (*of* ~ываться) 1. to be riveted in. 2. (*fig.*, *coll.*) to be mixed up in.

вклёпыв|ать(ся), аю(сь), *impf. of* вклепа́ть-(ся).

вкли́нива|ть(ся), ю(сь), *impf. of* вклини́ть-(ся).

вклин|и́ть, ю, ~ишь, *pf.* to wedge in; в. сло́во (*fig.*, *coll.*) to put a word in.

вклин|и́ться, ю́сь, ~и́шься, *pf.* 1. *pass. of* ~и́ть. 2. (в+*a.*) to edge one's way into; (*mil.*) to drive a wedge (into).

включа́тел|ь, я, *m.* switch.

включ|а́ть(ся), а́ю(сь), *impf. of* ~и́ть(ся).

включа́|я, *pres. gerund of* ~ть; *as prep.*+*a.* including, inclusive; вы́ставка откры́та ка́ждый день, в. воскресе́нье the exhibition is open every day including Sundays.

включе́ни|е, я, *n.* 1. inclusion, insertion; со ~ем (+*g.*) including. 2. (*tech.*) switching on, turning on.

включи́тельно, *adv.* inclusive; с пя́того по девя́тое в. from the 5th to the 9th inclusive.

включ|и́ть, у́, и́шь, *pf.* (*of* ~а́ть) 1. (в+*a.*) to include (in); to insert (in); в. в себя́ to include, comprise, take in; в. в пове́стку дня to enter on the agenda; в. в спи́сок to enter on a list. 2. (*tech.*) to switch on, turn on; to plug in; в. ра́дио to put the wireless on; в. ско́рость to engage a gear; в. сцеп-ле́ние to let in the clutch.

включ|и́ться, у́сь, и́шься, *pf.* (*of* ~а́ться) 1. (в+*a.*) to join (in), enter (into); в. в за́говор to enter into a conspiracy. 2. *pass. of* ~и́ть.

вкола́чива|ть, ю, *impf. of* вколоти́ть.

вкол|оти́ть, очу́, ~о́тишь, *pf.* (*of* ~а́чи-вать) to knock in, hammer in (*also fig.*); в. в го́лову (+*d.*; *coll.*) to knock into some-

one's head; в. себе́ в го́лову to get it into one's head.

вкол|о́ть, ю́, ~ешь, *pf.* (*of* вка́лывать) (в+*a.*) to stick (in, into).

вконе́ц, *adv.* (*coll.*) completely, absolutely.

вко́пан|ный (~, ~а), *p.p.p. of* вкопа́ть; как в. rooted to the ground.

вкопа́|ть, ю, *pf.* to dig in.

вкорен|и́ть, ю, и́шь, *pf.* (*of* ~я́ть) to incul-cate.

вкорен|и́ться, ю́сь, и́шься, *pf.* (*of* ~я́ться) to be inculcated; to take root.

вкореня́|ть(ся), ю(сь), *impf. of* вкорени́ть(ся).

вко́ротке́, *adv.* (*coll.*, *obs.*). 1. shortly. 2. in brief.

вкось, *adv.* obliquely; slantwise; вкривь и в., *see* вкривь.

вкрад|у́сь, ёшься, *see* вкра́сться.

вкра́дчив|ый (~, ~а), *adj.* insinuating, in-gratiating.

вкра́дыва|ться, юсь, *impf. of* вкра́сться.

вкра́п|ить, лю, ишь, *pf.* (*of* ~ливать) to sprinkle (with); (*fig.*) to intersperse (with); он ~ил в речь цита́ты he interspersed his speech with quotations.

вкра́пленник, а, *m.* (*geol.*) phenocryst, por-phyritic crystal.

вкра́плива|ть, ю, *impf. of* вкра́пить.

вкрапл|я́ть, я́ю, *impf.* = ~ивать.

вкра́|сться, ду́сь, дёшься, *past* ~лся, *pf.* (*of* ~дываться) to steal in, creep in; в текст ~лось мно́го оши́бок many mistakes have crept into the text; в. в дове́рие к кому́-н. to worm oneself, insinuate oneself into someone's confidence.

вкра́тце, *adv.* briefly; succinctly.

вкривь, *adv.* aslant; (*fig.*) wrongly, per-versely; всё, что́ говорю́, он понима́ет в. he misinterprets everything I say; в. и вкось all over the place; (*fig.*, *coll.*) indis-criminately.

вкруг = вокру́г.

вкругову́ю, *adv.* (*coll.*) round; пусти́ть ча́шу в. to send the cup round (*at banquets*).

вкру|ти́ть, чу́, ~тишь, *pf.* (*of* ~чивать) to twist in.

вкруту́ю, *adv.* (*coll.*) яйцо́ в. hard-boiled egg; свари́ть яйцо́ в. to hard-boil an egg.

вкру́чива|ть, ю, *impf. of* вкрути́ть.

вкру|чу́, ~тишь, *see* ~ти́ть.

вку́пе, *adv.* (*obs.*) together.

вкус, а, *m.* 1. taste (*also fig.*); про́бовать на в. to taste; войти́ во в. (+*g.*) to begin to en-joy, develop a taste (for); на в. и цвет това́рища нет (*prov.*) tastes differ; э́то де́ло ~а it is a matter of taste; челове́к со ~ом a man of taste. 2. manner, style; во ~е Ренеса́нса in the Renaissance style.

вку|си́ть, шу́, ~сишь, *pf.* (*of* ~ша́ть) 1.

(*obs.*) to taste, partake (of). **2.** (*fig., poet.*) to taste, savour, experience.

вкус|ный (~ен, ~на́, ~но), *adj.* good, nice (*to taste*); appetizing, tasty.

вкусов|о́й, *adj.* gustatory; ~ы́е вещества́ flavouring substances; ~ы́е о́рганы organs of taste.

вкуша́|ть, ю, *impf. of* вкуси́ть.

вку|шу́, ~сишь, *see* ~си́ть.

влаг|а, и, *no pl., f.* moisture, liquid.

влага́лищ|е, а, *n.* (*anat., bot.*) vagina.

влага́|ть, ю, *impf. of* вложи́ть.

влагоме́р, а, *m.* hygrometer.

владе́л|ец, ьца, *m.* owner; proprietor.

владе́ни|е, я, *n.* **1.** ownership; possession; вступи́ть во в. иму́ществом to take possession of property. **2.** property, possession; domain, estate; колониа́льные ~я colonial possessions.

владе́тел|ь, я, *m.* possessor; sovereign.

владе́тельный, *adj.* sovereign.

владе́|ть, ю, ешь, *impf.* (+*i.*) **1.** to own, possess. **2.** to control; to be in possession (of); в. собо́й to control oneself; им ~ют стра́сти he is at the mercy of his passions. **3.** (*fig.*) to have (a) command (of); to have the use (of); в. перо́м to wield a skilful pen; она́ ~ет шестью́ языка́ми she has a command of six languages; он не ~ет пра́вой руко́й he has no use of his right arm.

Влади́мирк|а, и, *f.* (*coll.*) the Vladimir road (*the road to Siberia*); идти́ по ~е to be exiled, be going into exile.

влады́к|а, и, *m.* **1.** master, sovereign. **2.** member of higher orders of clergy (*bishop, archbishop, or metropolitan*).

влады́честв|о, а, *n.* dominion, sway.

влады́честв|овать, ую, *impf.* (над+*i.*) to hold sway, exercise dominion (over).

влады́чиц|а, ы, *f.* **1.** mistress, sovereign. **2.** В. (*eccl.*) Our Lady.

влажне́|ть, ю, ешь, *impf.* (*of* по~) to become damp, humid.

вла́жност|ь, и, *f.* humidity, dampness.

вла́ж|ный (~ен, ~на́, ~но), *adj.* humid, damp; moist.

вла́мыва|ться, юсь, *impf. of* вломи́ться.

вла́ств|овать, ую, *impf.* (над+*i.*) to rule, hold sway (over).

властели́н, а, *m.* (*usu. fig.*) ruler; lord, master.

власти́тел|ь, я, *m.* sovereign, potentate; в. дум dominant influence.

вла́ст|ный (~ен, ~на), *adj.* **1.** imperious, commanding; masterful. **2.** (в+*p.*; *leg.*) authoritative, competent; я не ~ен в э́том де́ле I have no competence to deal with this matter.

властолюби́в|ый (~, ~а), *adj.* power-loving; power-seeking.

властолюби|е, я, *n.* love of power; lust for power.

власт|ь, и, *pl.* ~и, ~е́й, *f.* **1.** power; во ~и (+*g.*) at the mercy (of), in the power (of); прийти́ к ~и to come to power; у ~и in power. **2.** power, authority; (*pl.*) authorities; ме́стная в., в. на места́х local authority; сове́тская в. the Soviet régime; в. предержа́щая the powers that be. **3.** ва́ша в. (*coll.*) as you like, please yourself.

власяни́ц|а, ы, *f.* hair shirt.

влач|и́ть, у́, и́шь, *impf.* (*obs., poet.*) to drag; в. жа́лкое существова́ние to drag out a miserable existence.

влач|и́ться, у́сь, и́шься, *impf.* (*obs., poet.*) to drag oneself along.

вле́во, *adv.* to the left (*also fig., polit.*).

влеза́|ть, ю, *impf. of* влезть.

влез|ть, у, ешь, *past* ~, ~ла, *pf.* (*of* ~а́ть) **1.** to climb in, into, up; to get in, into; в. на де́рево to climb up a tree; ей пришло́сь в. в окно́ she had to get in by the window; в. в долги́ (*fig.*) to get into debt; в. в ду́шу (+*g.*) to worm oneself into someone's confidence; to worm confidences out of someone. **2.** (*coll.*) to get on, board; в. в авто́бус to get on the bus. **3.** (*coll.*) to fit in, go in, go on; все э́ти ве́щи не ~ут в мою́ су́мку these things will not all go into my bag; сапоги́ мне не ~ли my boots would not go on; ско́лько ~ет (*i*) as much as possible, (*ii*) as much as you like.

влеп|и́ть, лю́, ~ишь, *pf.* to stick in, fasten in; (*coll.*) в. пощёчину кому́-н. to slap someone's face; в. пу́лю в лоб кому́-н. to put a bullet in someone's brain.

влепля́|ть, ю, *impf. of* влепи́ть.

влет|а́ть, а́ю, *impf. of* ~е́ть.

вле|те́ть, чу́, ти́шь, *pf.* (*of* ~та́ть) to fly in, into; (*fig., coll.*) to rush in, into; в. в исто́рию to get into trouble; (*impers.*) ему́ опя́ть ~те́ло he is in trouble again.

влече́ни|е, я, *n.* (к) attraction (to); bent (for); он чу́вствует си́льное в. к Восто́ку he is strongly drawn to the East; сле́довать своему́ ~ю to follow one's bent.

вле|чь, ку́, чёшь, ку́т, *past* влёк, ~кла́, *impf.* to draw, drag; to attract; в. за собо́й to involve, entail.

вле|чься, ку́сь, чёшься, ку́тся, *past* ~кся, ~кла́сь, *impf.* **1.** (к) to be drawn (to); to be attracted (by). **2.** *pass. of* ~чь.

влива́ни|е, я, *n.* infusion; (*med.*) внутриве́нное в. intravenous administration.

влива́|ть, ю, *impf. of* влить.

влипа́|ть, ю, *impf. of* влипнуть.

влип|нуть, ну, нешь, *past* ~, ~ла, *pf.* (*coll.*) to get into a mess; to put one's foot in it; to get caught.

вли|ть, волью́, волье́шь, *past* ~л, ~ла́, ~ло, *pf.* (*of* ~ва́ть) 1. to pour in; в. по ка́пле to instil, administer drops; (*med.*) to infuse; (*fig.*) to instil; в. наде́жду в кого́-н. to instil hope into someone. 2. (*mil.*) to bring in; в. пополне́ния в часть to reinforce a unit.

влия́ни|е, я, *n.* influence; по́льзоваться ~ем to have influence, be influential.

влия́тел|ьный (~ен, ~ьна), *adj.* influential.

влия́|ть, ю, *impf.* (*of* по~) (на+*a.*) to influence, have an influence on, affect.

вложе́ни|е, я, *n.* 1. enclosure; со ~ем 'enclosure' (*on letters*). 2. (*fin.*) investment.

влож|и́ть, у́, ~ишь, *pf.* (*of* вкла́дывать *and* влага́ть) 1. to put in, insert; to enclose (*with a letter*); он ~и́л всю свою́ ду́шу в рабо́ту (*fig.*) he put his whole soul into his work; в. в уста́ кому́-н. to put into someone's mouth. 2. (*fin.*) to invest.

влом|и́ться, лю́сь, ~ишься, *pf.* (*of* вла́мываться) to break in, into; в. в амби́цию (*coll.*) to take offence.

влопа|ться, юсь, *pf.* (*coll.*) 1. to get into an awkward situation. 2. to fall in love.

влюб|и́ть, лю́, ~ишь, *pf.* (*of* ~ля́ть) (в+*a.*) to make fall in love (with).

влюб|и́ться, лю́сь, ~ишься, *pf.* (*of* ~ля́ться) (в+*a.*) to fall in love (with).

влюблённост|ь, и, *f.* love; being in love.

влюблён|ный (~, ~а́), *p.p.p. of* влюби́ть *and adj.* 1. (*p.p.p.*) in love; в. по́ уши head over ears in love. 2. (*adj.*) loving; tender.

влюбля́|ть, ю, *impf. of* влюби́ть.

влюбля́|ться, юсь, *impf. of* влюби́ться.

влю́бчив|ый (~, ~а), *adj.* (*coll.*) amorous, susceptible.

вляпа|ться, юсь, *pf.* (*coll.*) to plunge into; (*fig.*) в. в исто́рию to get into a mess.

вма́|зать, жу, жешь, *pf.* to cement, putty in.

вма́зыва|ть, ю, *impf. of* вма́зать.

вмен|и́ть, ю́, йшь, *pf.* (*of* ~я́ть) (*d.*+в+*a.*) 1. to regard (as); в. в вину́ to lay to the charge of; в. в заслу́гу to regard as a merit; в. в обя́занность to impose as a duty; он ~и́л себе́ в обя́занность чте́ние всех газе́т he imposed on himself the duty of reading all the newspapers. 2. to impute.

вменя́емост|ь, и, *f.* (*leg.*) responsibility; liability.

вменя́ем|ый (~, ~а), *adj.* (*leg.*) responsible, liable; of sound mind.

вменя́|ть, ю, *impf. of* вмени́ть.

вме|си́ть, шу́, ~сишь, *pf.* (*of* ~шива́ть[2]) to knead in.

вме́сте, *adv.* together; at the same time; в. с тем at the same time, also.

вмести́лищ|е, а, *n.* receptacle.

вмести́мост|ь, и, *f.* capacity.

вмести́тел|ьный (~ен, ~ьна), *adj.* capacious; spacious, roomy.

вме|сти́ть, щу́, сти́шь, *pf. of* ~ща́ть.

вме́сто, *prep.*+*g.* instead of; in place of.

вмеша́тельств|о, а, *n.* interference; intervention; хирурги́ческое в. surgical operation.

вмеша́|ть, ю, *pf.* (*of* вме́шивать[1]) (в+*a.*) 1. to mix in. 2. (*coll., fig.*) to mix up (in), implicate (in).

вмеш|а́ться, а́юсь, *pf.* (*of* ~иваться) (в+*a.*) to interfere (in), meddle (with); to intervene (in); в. в чужу́ю жизнь to meddle with other people's lives; полице́йский ~а́лся в дра́ку a policeman intervened in the fight.

вме́шива|ть[1], ю, *impf. of* вмеша́ть.

вме́шива|ть[2], ю, *impf. of* вмеси́ть.

вме́шива|ться, юсь, *impf. of* вмеша́ться.

вмеща́|ть, ю, *impf.* (*of* вмести́ть) 1. to contain; to hold; to accommodate; э́та бо́чка ~ет пятьдеся́т ли́тров this barrel holds fifty litres; зал ~ет пятьсо́т челове́к the hall can seat five hundred. 2. (в+*a.*) to put, place (in, into).

вмеща́|ться, юсь, *impf.* (*of* вмести́ться) 1. to go in; ва́ши башмаки́ не ~ются в мой чемода́н your shoes will not go into my case. 2. *pass. of* ~ть 2.

вмиг, *adv.* in an instant; in a flash.

вмина́|ть, ю, *impf. of* вмять.

вмя́тин|а, ы, *f.* dent.

вмять, вомну́, вомнёшь, *pf.* (*of* вмина́ть) to press in.

внаём, внайми́, *adv.* отда́ть в. to let, hire out, rent; взять в. to hire, rent; сдаётся в. 'to let'.

внаки́дку, *adv.* (*coll.*) носи́ть в. to wear thrown over the shoulders.

внакла́де, *adv.* (*coll.*) оста́ться в. to be the loser, come off loser; не оста́ться в. (от+*g.*) to be none the worse off (for).

внакла́дку, *adv.* пить чай в. to drink tea with sugar in (*as opp. to* вприку́ску).

внача́ле, *adv.* at first, in the beginning.

вне, *prep.*+*g.* outside; out of; в. зако́на without the law; объяви́ть в. зако́на to outlaw; в. ко́нкурса hors concours; в. о́череди out of turn; в. пла́на over and above the plan; в. себя́ beside oneself; в. вся́ких сомне́ний beyond any doubt.

вне- extra-.

внебра́чный, *adj.* extra-marital; в. ребёнок illegitimate child.

вневойскови́к, а́, *m.* civilian receiving military training.

вневойсков|о́й, *adj.* ~а́я подгото́вка military training for civilians.

вневре́менный, *adj.* timeless.

внедрени|е, я, *n.* **1.** introduction; inculcation; indoctrination. **2.** (*geol.*) intrusion.

внедр|ить, ю, ишь, *pf.* (*of* ~ять) **1.** to inculcate, instil; **в. в молодых привычку к чистоте** to inculcate habits of cleanliness into the young. **2.** to introduce; **в. новые методы** to introduce new methods.

внедр|иться, юсь, ишься, *pf.* (*of* ~яться) to take root.

внедря|ть(ся), ю(сь), *impf. of* внедрить(ся).

внезапно, *adv.* suddenly, all of a sudden.

внезапност|ь, и, *f.* **1.** suddenness. **2.** (*obs.*) unexpected event.

внезапный, *adj.* sudden.

внеклассн|ый, *adj.* out of school (hours); extra-curricular; ~ые занятия out of school activities.

внеклассовый, *adj.* (*polit.*) non-class.

внематочный, *adj.* (*med.*) extra-uterine.

внемл|ю, ешь, *see* внимать.

внеочередн|ой, *adj.* **1.** out of turn; задать в. вопрос to ask a question out of order. **2.** extraordinary; extra; в. съезд extraordinary congress; ~ая смена extra shift.

внепартийный, *adj.* (*polit.*) non-party.

внеплановый, *adj.* (*econ.*) not provided for by the plan; extraordinary.

внесени|е, я, *n.* **1.** bringing in, carrying in. **2.** paying in, deposit (*of money*). **3.** entry, insertion (*into an agreement, etc.*). **4.** moving, submission (*of a resolution*).

внеслужебный, *adj.* leisure-time.

внес|ти, у, ёшь, *past* ~, ~ла, *pf.* (*of* вносить) **1.** to bring in, carry in; в. раненых to bring in the wounded. **2.** (*fig.*) to introduce, put in; в. ясность в дело to clarify a matter; в. свой вклад в дело to do one's bit. **3.** to pay in, deposit. **4.** to bring in, move, table; в. законопроект to bring in a bill; в. предложение to move, table a resolution. **5.** to insert, enter; в. поправки в текст речи to emend the text of a speech; в. в список to enter on a list. **6.** to bring about, cause; в. раздоры to cause bad feeling.

внестудийный, *adj.* (*of radio or television transmission*) outside.

внешкольник, а, *m.* adult education specialist.

внешкольн|ый, *adj.* ~ое образование adult education.

внешне, *adv.* outwardly.

внешн|ий, *adj.* **1.** outer, exterior; outward; external; outside; в. вид outward appearance; в. угол (*math.*) external angle; в. лоск surface polish. **2.** foreign; ~яя политика foreign policy; ~яя торговля foreign trade.

внешност|ь, и, *f.* exterior; surface; appearance; судить по ~и to judge by appearances.

внештатный, *adj.* not on permanent staff; not established.

вниз, *adv.* down, downwards; в. головой head first; идти в. по лестнице to go downstairs; в. по течению downstream; в. по Волге down the Volga.

внизу, *adv.* below; downstairs; *prep.*+*g.* в. страницы at the foot of the page.

вник|ать, аю, *impf. of* ~нуть.

вник|нуть, ну, нешь, *past* ~, ~ла, *pf.* (*of* ~ать) (в+*a.*) to go carefully (into), investigate thoroughly; в. в обстоятельства убийства to investigate the circumstances of a murder.

внимани|е, я, *n.* **1.** attention; heed; notice, note; обращать в. (на+*a.*) (i) to pay attention, give heed (to), take note (of) (ii) to draw attention (to); он весь в. he is all ears; принимая во в. taking into account. **2.** attention(s); kindness, consideration; оказать в. to do a kindness; пользоваться ~ем to be the object of attentions. **3.** (*interj.*) в.! look out! mind out!; в. на старт! (*sport*) get set!

внимательност|ь, и, *f.* **1.** attentiveness. **2.** thoughtfulness, consideration.

внимател|ьный (~ен, ~ьна), *adj.* **1.** attentive. **2.** (к+*d.*) thoughtful, considerate (towards).

внима|ть, ю *and* **внемлю,** *impf.* (*of* внять) (+*d.*; *poet., obs.*) to hear (*fig.*); to heed; в. молитве to hear prayer.

вничью, *adv.* (*sport*) drawn; партия окончилась в. the game ended in a draw; наша хоккейная команда сыграла сегодня в. our hockey team drew today.

внове, *adv. as pred.* new, strange; всё во французском быту ей было в. everything about life in France was new to her.

вновь, *adv.* **1.** afresh, anew; again. **2.** newly; в. прибывший newcomer.

вно|сить, шу, ~сишь, *impf. of* внести.

внук, а, *m.* grandson; grandchild (*also fig.*).

внучк|а, и, *f.* (*obs.*) granddaughter.

внутренн|ий, *adj.* **1.** inner, interior; internal; intrinsic; ~ие болезни internal diseases; в. мир inner life, private world; ~ие причины intrinsic causes; ~ее сгорание internal combustion; в. смысл inner meaning. **2.** home, inland; ~ие доходы inland revenue; Министерство ~их дел Ministry of Internal Affairs.

внутренност|ь, и, *f.* **1.** interior. **2.** (*pl. only*) entrails, intestines; internal organs; (*anat.*) viscera.

внутри, *adv. and prep.*+*g.* inside, within; в. дома inside the house.

внутри- intra-.

внутривенный, *adj.* (*med.*) intravenous.

внутриматочный, *adj.* intra-uterine.

внутрипарти́йный, *adj.* within the Party, inner-Party.

внутрь, *adv. and prep.+g.* within, inside; inwards; открыва́ться в. to open inwards; войти́ в. до́ма to go inside the house.

внуча́т|а, ~, *no sing.* grandchildren.

внуча́тный, *adj.* в. брат second cousin; в. племя́нник great-nephew.

внуча́т|ый = ~ный.

вну́чк|а, и, *f.* granddaughter.

внуша́емост|ь, и, *f.* suggestibility.

внуше́ни|е, я, *n.* **1.** (*psych.*) suggestion. **2.** reproof, reprimand.

внуши́тел|ьный (~ен, ~ьна), *adj.* inspiring, impressive; (*coll.*) imposing, striking; ~ьное зда́ние imposing edifice; ~ьное зре́лище inspiring sight.

внуш|и́ть, у́, и́шь, *pf.* (*of* ~а́ть) (+*a. and d.*) to inspire (with); to instil; to suggest; его́ вид ~и́л мне страх the sight of him inspired me with fear; в. уве́ренность в себе́ to instil self-confidence; он уме́л в. слу́шателям, что он всегда́ прав he had the power of suggesting to his audience that he was always right.

внюха|ться, юсь, *pf.* (в+*a.*; *coll.*) to take a sniff (at) (*also fig.*).

внюхива|ться, юсь, *impf. of* внюхаться.

вня́т|ный (~ен, ~на), *adj.* **1.** distinct. **2.** (*obs.*) intelligible.

вня|ть, *future not used, past* ~л, ~ла́, ~ло, *imp.* вонми́(те), *pf. of* внима́ть.

во[1], *prep.* = в.

во[2], *interj.* (*coll.*) = вот.

во́бл|а, ы, *f.* vobla (*Caspian roach*).

вобр|а́ть, вберу́, вберёшь, *past* ~а́л, ~ала́, ~а́ло, *pf.* (*of* вбира́ть) to absorb, suck in; to inhale.

вове́к(и), *adv.* (*obs.*) for ever; в. веко́в for ever and ever.

вовлека́|ть, ю, *impf. of* вовле́чь.

вовл|е́чь, еку́, ечёшь, еку́т, *past* ~ёк, ~екла́, *pf.* to draw in, involve; to inveigle.

вовне́, *adv.* outside.

вовну́трь, *adv. and prep.+g.* (*coll.*) inside.

во́-время, *adv.* at the proper time, at the normal time; in time; говори́ть не в. to speak out of turn.

во́все, *adv.* (+*neg.*; *coll.*) at all; он в. не бога́тый челове́к he is not at all a rich man; вы в. не по́няли, в чём де́ло you have completely failed to grasp the point.

вовсю́, *adv.* to its (one's) utmost; with might and main; бежа́ть в. to run as fast as one's legs will carry one.

во-вторы́х, *adv.* secondly, in the second place.

вогна́|ть, вгоню́, вго́нишь, *past* ~л, ~ла́, ~ло, *pf.* (*of* вгоня́ть) to drive in; в. гвоздь в сте́ну to drive a nail into the wall; в. в гроб to be the death of; в. в кра́ску to put to the blush; в. кого́-н. в пот to make someone go hot and cold.

во́гнут|ый (~, ~а), *p.p.p. of* ~ь *and adj.* concave.

вогн|у́ть, у́, ёшь, *pf.* (*of* вгиба́ть) to bend, curve inwards.

вод|а́, ы́, *a.* ~у, *pl.* ~ы, ~ам (*obs.* ~а́м), *f.* **1.** water; е́хать ~о́й, по ~е́ to go by water; жёлтая в. (*med.*; *coll.*) glaucoma; тёмная в. (*med.*) amaurosis; ~о́й не разольёшь as thick as thieves; выводи́ть на чи́стую ~у to show up, unmask; и концы́ в во́ду none will be the wiser; как две ка́пли ~ы́ похо́жи as like as two peas; как с гу́ся в. like water off a duck's back; мно́го ~ы́ утекло́ much water has flowed under the bridge; он ~ы́ не замути́т he could not hurt a fly; как в ~у опу́щенный downcast, dejected; чи́стой, чисте́йшей ~ы́ (*tech. and fig.*) of the first water. **2.** (*pl.*) the waters; watering-place, spa. **3.** (*coll.*) 'padding' (*in lecture, etc.*).

водворе́ни|е, я, *n.* settlement; establishment.

водвор|и́ть, ю́, и́шь, *pf.* **1.** to settle, install, house. **2.** to establish; в. мир и споко́йствие to introduce peace and quiet.

водворя́|ть, ю, *impf. of* водвори́ть.

водеви́л|ь, я, *m.* (*theatr.*) **1.** vaudeville (*one-act comic piece with songs*). **2.** musical comedy.

води́тел|ь, я, *m.* **1.** driver. **2.** (*obs.*) leader.

води́тельств|о, а, *n.* (*obs.*) leadership.

во|ди́ть, жу́, ~дишь, *impf.* (*indet. of* вести́) **1.** (*see also* вести́) to lead; to conduct; to drive. **2.** (*see also* вести́) в. дру́жбу (c+*i.*) to be friends (with); в. знако́мство (c+*i.*) to keep up an acquaintance (with). **3.** (+*i.*, по+*d.*; *see also* вести́) to pass (over, across); в. глаза́ми (по+*d.*) to cast one's eye (over) (*only* в. *used in this phrase*). **4.** (*coll.*) to keep (*animals, birds, etc.*); в. пчёл to keep bees.

во|ди́ться, жу́сь, ~дишься, *impf.* **1.** (c+*i.*) to associate (with); to play (with); он с на́ми бо́льше не ~дится he will not play with us any more. **2.** to be, be found; в э́той реке́ ~дятся лосо́си salmon abounds in this river; львы́ не ~дятся в Евро́пе lions are not found in Europe; (*fig.*) у него́ де́нег никогда́ не ~дится he never has any money. **3.** to be the custom; to happen; так у нас ~дится it is the custom here; э́то за ни́ми ~дится (*pejor.*) they are always doing this.

води́ц|а, ы, *f. dim. of* вода́.

во́дк|а, и, *f.* vodka; дать на ~у to tip; кре́пкая в. (*chem.*) aqua fortis; ца́рская в. (*chem.*) aqua regis.

во́дник, а, *m.* water-transport worker.

воднолы́жник, а, *m.* water-skier.

во́дн|ый, *adj.* **1.** water; watery; ~ые лы́жи (*i*) water-skiing, (*ii*) water-skis; ~ое по́ло water polo; в. путь waterway; в. спорт aquatic sports. **2.** (*chem.*) aqueous; ~ое соедине́ние hydrate.

водобоя́зн|ь, и, *f.* (*med.*) hydrophobia.

водовмести́лищ|е, а, *n.* reservoir.

водово́з, а, *m.* water-carrier.

водоворо́т, а, *m.* whirlpool; maelstrom (*also fig.*).

водогре́йк|а, и, *f.* water-heater.

водоём, а, *m.* reservoir (*natural or artificial*).

водоизмеще́ни|е, я, *n.* (*naut.*) displacement; су́дно ~ем в шесть ты́сяч тонн a vessel of six thousand tons displacement.

водока́чк|а, и, *f.* water-tower.

водола́з¹, а, *m.* diver.

водола́з², а, *m.* Newfoundland (dog).

водола́зк|а, и, *f.* polo-necked sweater.

водола́з|ный, *adj.* of ~¹; в. костю́м diving-suit.

водоле́|й, я, *m.* **1.** (water-)bailer. **2.** (*coll.*) spouter. **3.** В. (*astron.*) Aquarius.

водолече́бниц|а, ы, *f.* hydropathic establishment.

водолече́бный, *adj.* hydropathic.

водолече́ни|е, я, *n.* hydropathic treatment; water-cure.

водоли́в, а, *m.* **1.** (water-)bailer, water-pumper. **2.** chief bargee.

водоме́р, а, *m* . (*tech.*) water-gauge.

водоме́р|ный, *adj.* of ~; в. кран gauge-cock; ~ное стекло́ gauge-glass; ~ная тру́бка gauge-tube.

водомёт, а, *m.* (*poet., obs.*) fountain.

водомо́ин|а, ы, *f.* gully, ravine (*formed by running water*).

водонапо́рн|ый, *adj.* only in phrase ~ая ба́шня water-tower.

водонепроница́ем|ый (~, ~а), *adj.* water-tight; waterproof; ~ая перебо́рка (*naut.*) watertight bulkhead.

водоно́с, а, *m.* **1.** water-carrier. **2.** (*dial.*) yoke (*for carrying water-buckets*).

водоотво́д, а, *m.* drainage system.

водоотво́дн|ый, *adj.* drainage; ~ая кана́ва draining ditch; ~ая тру́бка waste-pipe.

водоотли́вн|ый, *adj.* discharge; в. насо́с hydrant; ~ая систе́ма (*naut.*) bilge system.

водоочисти́тельный, *adj.* water-purifying.

водопа́д, а, *m.* waterfall.

водоплава́ющ|ий, *adj.* ~ие пти́цы water-fowl; ~ая маши́на amphibious vehicle.

водопо́|й, я, *m.* **1.** watering-place; water-trough; pond. **2.** watering (*of animals*).

водопрово́д, а, *m.* **1.** water-pipe; (the) plumbing. **2.** water-supply; дом с ~ом house with running water.

водопрово́д|ный, *adj.* of ~; ~ная маги-страль water-main; ~ная сеть water-supply; ~ная ста́нция waterworks.

водопрово́дчик, а, *m.* plumber.

водопроница́ем|ый (~, ~а), *adj.* permeable to water.

водоразде́л, а, *m.* (*geogr.; fig.*) watershed.

водораспредели́тел|ь, я, *m.* water-distributor.

водоре́з, а, *m.* (*naut.*) cutwater.

водоро́д, а, *m.* (*chem.*) hydrogen.

водоро́дистый, *adj.* (*chem.*) hydrogen; hydride (of).

водоро́дн|ый, *adj.* hydrogen; ~ая бо́мба hydrogen bomb.

во́доросл|ь, и, *f.* (*bot.*) alga; морска́я в. seaweed.

водосбо́р, а, *m.* **1.** (*natural or artificial*) reservoir (*used for water-supply, irrigation, etc.*). **2.** (*tech.*) (*water-collecting*) header.

водосбо́рн|ый, *adj.* **1.** ~ая пло́щадь (*geogr.*) basin. **2.** (*tech.*) water-collecting.

водосли́в, а, *m.* (*tech.*) waste-gate; sluice.

водоснабже́ни|е, я, *n.* water-supply.

водоспу́ск, а, *m.* floodgate.

водосто́к, а, *m.* drain; gutter.

водосто́|чный, *adj.* of ~к; ~чная труба́ drain-pipe.

водотру́бный, *adj.* в. котёл (*tech.*) water-tube boiler.

водоупо́р|ный (~ен, ~на), *adj.* water-proof.

водохо́дн|ый, *adj.* amphibious; ~ая авто-маши́на (*mil.*) amphibious vehicle, DUKW.

водохрани́лищ|е, а, *n.* reservoir; cistern, tank.

водочерпа́лк|а, и, *f.* water-engine.

водочерпа́тельный, *adj.* (*tech.*) water-lifting.

во́дочк|а, и, *f.* (*coll.*) dim. of во́дка.

во́д|очный, *adj.* of ~ка.

водружа́|ть, ю, *impf. of* водрузи́ть.

водру|зи́ть, жу́, зи́шь, *pf.* (*of* ~жа́ть) to hoist, erect.

водяне́|ть, ю, *impf.* to grow watery.

водяни́к, а́, *m.* (*dial.*) water-sprite.

водяни́ст|ый (~, ~а), *adj.* watery; (*fig., coll.*) wishy-washy.

водя́нк|а, и, *f.* (*med.*) dropsy.

водян|о́й¹, *adj.* **1.** adj. of вода́. **2.** water, aquatic; ~ые пти́цы waterfowl; ~ые расте́ния aquatic plants. **3.** water-driven, water-operated; ~а́я ме́льница water-mill; ~о́е отопле́ние hot-water heating. **4.** в. знак watermark.

водян|о́й², о́го, *m.* water-sprite.

водян|о́чный, *adj.* of ~ка.

во|ева́ть, юю, юешь, *impf.* (с+*i.*) **1.** to wage war (with), make war (upon); to be at war. **2.** (*coll.*) to quarrel (with).

воевод|а, ы, *m.* **1.** (*hist.*) voivode (*commander of an army in medieval Russia; also, in Muscovite period, governor of a town or province*). **2.** governor of province (*in Poland*).

воевóдств|о, а, *n.* **1.** (*hist.*) office of voivode. **2.** province (*in Poland*).

воедúно, *adv.* together; собрáть в. to bring together.

воен- military.

военачáльник, а, *m.* commander; leader in war.

военизáци|я, и, *f.* militarization.

военизúр|овать, ую, *impf. and pf.* to militarize; to place on a war footing.

военкóм, а, *m.* (*abbr. of* воéнный комиссáр) military commissar.

военкомáт, а, *m.* (*abbr. of* воéнный комиссариáт) military registration and enlistment office.

военкóр, а, *m.* (*abbr. of* воéнный корреспондéнт) war correspondent.

воéнно- military.

воéнно-воздýшн|ый, *adj.* ~ые сúлы Air Force(s).

воéнно-морскóй, *adj.* naval; в. флот the Navy.

военнообя́занн|ый, ого, *m.* man liable for call-up (*including reservists*).

военноплéнн|ый, ого, *m.* prisoner of war.

воéнно-полевóй, *adj.* (*mil.*) field; в. суд court-martial.

военнослýжащ|ий, его, *m.* serviceman.

воéнно-учéбный, *adj.* military training.

воéнн|ый, *adj.* military; war; army; в. врач (army) medical officer; ~ое врéмя wartime; в. завóд munitions factory; в. коммунúзм (*hist.*) War Communism; в. минúстр Minister of War; В~ое министéрство War Ministry, War Office; на ~ую нóгу on a war footing; в. óкруг Command, military district; ~ое положéние martial law; ~ое учúлище military college; *as noun* в., ~ого, *m.* soldier, serviceman; ~ые (*collect.*) the military.

военрýк, а, *m.* (*abbr. of* воéнный руководúтель) military instructor.

воéнщин|а, ы, *f.* (*coll., pejor.*) **1.** (*collect.; obs.*) soldiery. **2.** militarists, military clique. **3.** military outlook.

вожáк, á, *m.* **1.** guide; в. медвéдя, в. с медвéдем bearleader; в. слепóго blind man's guide. **2.** leader. **3.** leader (*of herd, flock*).

вожáт|ый, ого, *m.* **1.** guide. **2.** leader (*of youth organization*). **3.** (*coll.*) tram-driver. **4.** (*agric.*) leader (*of herd*).

вожделéни|е, я, *n.* desire, lust (*also fig.*).

вожделéнн|ый, *adj.* (*poet., obs.*) desired, longed-for; ~ое здрáвие perfect health.

вожделé|ть, ю, ешь, *impf.* (к+*d.*) **1.** to long (for). **2.** (*obs.*) to lust (after).

вождéни|е, я, *n.* leading; driving; в. кораблá navigation; в. самолёта flying, piloting.

вожд|ь, я́, *m.* leader; chief.

вожжá|ться, юсь, *impf.* (с+*i.*; *coll.*) to bother oneself (with), trouble oneself (over).

вóжж|и, ей, *sing.* ~á, ~й, *f.* reins; отпустúть в. to give a horse the reins; (*fig.*) to slacken the reins; емý ~á под хвост попáла (*coll.*) he has taken to acting capriciously.

во|жý¹, ~дишь, *see* ~дúть.

во|жý², ~зишь, *see* ~зúть.

воз, а, о ~е, на ~ý, *pl.* ~ы́, *m.* **1.** cart, waggon; что с ~а упáло, то пропáло (*prov.*) is no use crying over spilt milk. **2.** cartload. **3.** (*fig., coll.*) load(s), heap(s); в. врéмени loads of time.

возблагодар|úть, ю́, úшь, *pf.* (*obs.*) to give thanks to.

возбран|úть, ю́, úшь, *pf.* to prohibit, forbid; в. вход подрóсткам не достúгшим восемнáдцати лет to prohibit entry to young people under the age of eighteen.

возбран|я́ть, я́ю, *impf. of* ~úть.

возбраня́|ться, ется, *impf.* to be prohibited, be forbidden; купáться тут не ~ется swimming is permitted here.

возбудúмост|ь, и, *f.* excitability.

возбудúм|ый (~, ~а), *adj.* excitable.

возбудúтел|ь, я, *m.* **1.** agent; stimulus; (*fig.*) instigator; дрóжжи — в. брожéния yeast is an agent of fermentation. **2.** (*med.*) в. болéзни pathogenic organism. **3.** (*tech.*) exciter.

возбу|дúть, жý, дúшь, *pf.* (*of* ~ждáть) **1.** to excite, rouse, arouse; в. аппетúт to whet the appetite; в. любопы́тство to excite, stimulate curiosity. **2.** (прóтив+*g.*) to stir up (against), incite (against), instigate (against). **3.** (*leg.*) to institute; в. дéло (прóтив+*g.*) to institute proceedings (against), bring an action (against); в. иск (прóтив+*g.*) to bring a suit (against); в. ходáтайство (о+*p.*) to submit a petition (for).

возбуждáемост|ь, и, *f.* excitability.

возбуждá|ть, ю, *impf. of* возбудúть.

возбуждá|ющий, *pres. part. act. of* ~ть; ~ющее срéдство (*med.*) stimulant.

возбу|жý, дúшь, *see* ~дúть.

возбуждéни|е, я, *n.* excitement; в состоя́нии крáйнего ~я in a state of extreme excitement.

возбу|ждённый, *p.p.p. of* ~дúть *and adj.* excited.

возведéни|е, я, *n.* **1.** raising; erection. **2.** в. во вторýю, в трéтью стéпень (*math.*) rais-

ing to the second, third power. **3.** в. обви-
не́ния bringing of an accusation.

возвед|у́, ёшь, *see* возвести́.

возвели́чива|ть, ю, *impf. of* возвели́чить.

возвели́ч|ить, у, ишь, *pf.* (*of* ~ивать) (*obs.*)
to extol.

возве|сти́, ду́, дёшь, *past* ~л, ~ла́, *pf.* (*of*
возводи́ть) **1.** to elevate; в. в сан патриа́р-
ха to elect to the patriarchate; в. на
престо́л to elevate to the throne. **2.** to
raise, erect, put up; в. высо́тный дом to
erect a skyscraper. **3.** (*math.*) to raise; в.
во втору́ю сте́пень to raise to the second
power; в. в куб to cube. **4.** to bring, advance, level (*a charge, an accusation, etc.*); в.
клевету́ на кого́-н. to cast aspersions on
someone. **5.** (к+*d.*) to trace (to), derive
(from); в. происхожде́ние к норма́ннам
to trace one's ancestry to the Northmen.

возве|сти́ть, щу́, сти́шь, *pf.* (*of* ~ща́ть) to
proclaim, announce; в. побе́ду to pro-
claim a victory.

возвеща́|ть, ю, *impf. of* возвести́ть.

возве|щу́, сти́шь, *see* ~сти́ть.

возво|ди́ть, жу́, ~дишь, *impf. of* возвести́.

возво|жу́, ~дишь, *see* ~ди́ть.

возвра́т, а, m. return; repayment, reim-
bursement; в. боле́зни relapse; в. со́лнца
(*astron.*) solstice.

возвра|ти́ть, щу́, ти́шь *pf.* (*of* ~ща́ть) **1.** to
return, give back; to pay back; в. иму́-
щество to restore property. **2.** to recover,
retrieve; в. де́ньги, о́тданные взаймы́ to
recover a loan. **3.** to make return.

возвра|ти́ться, щу́сь, ти́шься, *pf.* (*of*
~ща́ться) to return; (*fig.*) to revert; в. ко
всем ста́рым привы́чкам to revert to all
one's old habits.

возвра́т|ный, adj. 1. *adj. of* ~; на ~ном
пути́ on the way back. **2.** (*med.*) recurring.
3. (*gram.*) reflexive. **4.** ~ная по́шлина
drawback (duty).

возвраща́|ть(ся), ю(сь), *impf. of* возвра-
ти́ть(ся) *and* верну́ть(ся).

возвраще́ни|е, я, n. return; его́ в. бы́ло
отло́жено без сро́ка his return was post-
poned indefinitely; он настоя́л на немéд-
ленном ~и кольца́ he insisted on immediate
return of the ring.

возвы́|сить, шу, сишь, *pf.* (*of* ~ша́ть) **1.** to
raise, elevate; в. в обще́ственном мне́нии
to raise in public opinion. **2.** в. го́лос to
raise one's voice.

возвы́|ситься, шусь, сишься, *pf.* (*of*
~ша́ться) (*in var. senses*) to raise, go up;
они́ ~сились в на́шем мне́нии they have
risen in our estimation.

возвыша́|ть, ю, *impf.* **1.** *impf. of* возвы́сить.
2. (*impf. only*) to elevate, ennoble.

возвыша́|ться, юсь, *impf.* **1.** *impf. of* воз-
вы́ситься. **2.** (*impf. only*) (над+*i.*) to tower
(above) (*also fig.*); за́мок ~ется над го́ро-
дом the castle towers above the city; он
~ется умо́м над това́рищами he towers
above his fellows in intellect.

возвыше́ни|е, я, n. 1. rise; raising; в.
Моско́вской Ру́си the rise of Muscovite
Russia. **2.** eminence; raised place.

возвы́шенност|ь, и, f. 1. (*geogr.*) height;
eminence. **2.** loftiness, sublimity.

возвы́шен|ный, p.p.p. of возвы́сить *and adj.*
1. high; elevated. **2.** lofty, sublime, elevated; ~ные идеа́лы lofty ideals; в. стиль
elevated style.

возвы́|шу, сишь, *see* ~сить.

возгла́в|ить, лю, ишь, *pf.* (*of* ~ля́ть) to
head, be at the head of.

возглавля́|ть, ю, *impf. of* возгла́вить.

во́зглас, а, m. 1. cry, exclamation; в.
удивле́ния cry of astonishment; в. с ме́ста
exclamation from the audience. **2.** (*eccl.*)
concluding words of prayer (*pronounced in
a loud voice*).

возгла|си́ть, шу́, си́шь, *pf.* (*of* ~ша́ть) to
proclaim.

возглаша́|ть, ю, *impf. of* возгласи́ть.

возглаше́ни|е, я, n. 1. proclamation. **2.** ex-
clamation. **3.** = во́зглас 2.

возгна́|ть, возгоню́, возго́нишь, *past* ~л,
~ла́, ~ло, *pf. of* возгоня́ть.

возго́нк|а, и, f. (*chem.*) sublimation.

возгон|ю́, ~ишь, *see* возгна́ть.

возгоня́|ть, ю, *impf.* (*chem.*) to subli-
mate.

возгора́емост|ь, и, f. inflammability.

возгора́емый, adj. inflammable.

возгора́ни|е, я, n. (*tech.*) inflammation, ig-
nition; то́чка ~я flash-point.

возгора́|ться, юсь, *impf. of* возгоре́ться.

возгор|ди́ться, жу́сь, ди́шься, *pf.* to be-
come proud; (+*i.*) to begin to pride oneself (on).

возгор|е́ться, ю́сь, и́шься, *pf.* **1.** to flare
up (*also fig.*); внеза́пно ~е́лась ссо́ра
ме́жду ни́ми suddenly there flared up a
quarrel between them. **2.** (+*i.*) to be in-
flamed (with); она́ ~е́лась стра́стью к
кино́ she was seized with a passion for the
cinema.

возда|ва́ть, ю́, ёшь, *impf. of* возда́ть.

возда́|м, шь, ст, *see* ~ть.

возда́|ть, м, шь, ст, ди́м, ди́те, ду́т, *past* ~л,
~ла́, ~ло, *pf.* (*of* ~ва́ть) to render; в.
кому́-н. до́лжное to give someone his due;
в. кому́-н. по заслу́гам to reward someone
according to his deserts.

воздая́ни|е, я, n. (*obs.*) recompense; retri-
bution.

воздвига́|ть, ю, *impf.* to raise, erect; в.

гоне́ние (на+*a.*; *obs.*) to raise a hue-and--cry (after).

воздвига́|ться, юсь, *impf.* **1.** *pass. of* ~ть. **2.** to rear (up) (*intrans.*).

воздви́г|нуть, ну, нешь, *past* ~, ~ла, *pf. of* ~а́ть.

воздви́г|нуться, нусь, нешься, *past* ~ся, ~лась, *pf. of* ~а́ться.

Воздви́жени|е, я, *n.* (*eccl.*) Exaltation of the Cross (*Christian festival celebrated on 14 September*).

воздева́|ть, ю, *impf. of* возде́ть.

возде́йстви|е, я, *n.* influence; оказа́ть мора́льное в. (на+*a.*) to bring moral pressure to bear (upon); он э́то сде́лал под физи́ческим ~ем he did it under coercion.

возде́йств|овать, ую, *impf. and pf.* (на+*a.*) to influence, affect; to exert influence, bring influence to bear (upon); to bring pressure to bear (upon); в. на кого́-н. си́лой приме́ра to influence someone by one's example; страсть к приключе́ниям ~овала на его́ реше́ние сде́латься моряко́м love of adventure influenced his decision to become a sailor.

возде́л|ать, аю, *pf.* (*of* ~ывать) to cultivate, till.

возде́лыва|ть, ю, *impf. of* возде́лать.

воздержа́вш|ийся, *past part. of* воздержа́ться; *as noun* **в., ~егося,** *m.* abstainer; предложе́ние бы́ло при́нято при трёх ~ихся the motion was carried with three abstentions.

воздержа́ни|е, я, *n.* **1.** abstinence. **2.** abstention.

возде́ржанност|ь, и, *f.* abstemiousness; temperance.

возде́ржан|ный (~, ~на), *adj.* abstemious; temperate.

воздерж|а́ться, у́сь, *pf.* (*of* ~иваться) (от +*g.*) **1.** to restrain oneself, keep oneself (from); to abstain (from); to refrain (from); в. от мя́са to abstain from meat; я до́лее не мог в. от гне́ва I could no longer contain my rage. **2.** to abstain (*from voting*). **3.** to withhold acceptance (of).

возде́ржива|ться, юсь, *impf. of* воздержа́ться.

возде́ржност|ь, и, *f.* = возде́ржанность.

возде́рж|ный (~ен, ~на), *adj.* = ~анный.

возде́|ть, ну, нешь, *pf.* (*of* ~ва́ть) *only in phrase* в. ру́ки (*obs.*) to lift up one's hands.

во́здух¹, а, *no pl., m.* air; на (откры́том) ~е out of doors; вы́йти на в. to go out of doors; в ~е (*fig.*) in the air; в ~е носи́лось чу́вство предстоя́щей беды́ a sense of impending disaster was in the air; *as interj.* в.! (enemy) aircraft approaching!

во́здух², а, *pl.* ~и, *m.* (*eccl.*) paten.

воздуходу́вк|а, и, *f.* (*tech.*) blast-engine; blower.

воздуходу́вный, *adj.* (*tech.*) blast.

воздухоме́р, а, *m.* (*phys.*) aerometer.

воздухоохлажда́емый, *adj.* air-cooled.

воздухопла́вани|е, я, *n.* aeronautics.

воздухопла́вател|ь, я, *m.* **1.** aeronaut. **2.** balloonist.

воздухопла́вательный, *adj.* **1.** aeronautic. **2.** (*mil.*) balloon.

возду́ш|ный, *adj.* **1.** air, aerial; ~ная желе́зная доро́га overhead railway; ~ные за́мки castles in the air; в. змей kite; ~ная ли́ния airline; посла́ть ~ные поцелу́и to blow kisses; ~ная прово́дка overhead cable; ~ное сообще́ние aerial communication; ~ная трево́га air-raid warning; в. шар balloon; ~ная я́ма air-pocket. **2.** air--driven, air-operated; в. насо́с air-pump. **3.** (~ен, ~на), airy, light; flimsy; в. пиро́г soufflé; ~ное пла́тье flimsy dress.

воздыха́ни|е, я, *n.* (*obs.*) lamentation; complaint.

воздыха́|ть, ю, *impf.* (*obs.*) = вздыха́ть.

воз|жгу́, жжёшь, жгут, *see* ~же́чь.

воз|же́чь, жгу́, жжёшь, жгут, *past* ~жёг, ~жгла́, *pf.* (*of* ~жига́ть) (*obs.*) to light, kindle (*also fig.*).

возжига́|ть, ю, *impf. of* возже́чь.

воззва́ни|е, я, *n.* appeal; в. к шахтёрам appeal to miners.

воз|ва́ть, ову́, овёшь, *past* ~ва́л, ~вала́, ~ва́ло, *pf* (*of* взыва́ть) (к+*d.*, о+*p.*) to appeal (to), call (for); он ~ва́л к избира́телям о подде́ржке he appealed to the electors for their support.

возз|ову́, овёшь, *see* ~ва́ть.

воззре́ни|е, я, *n.* view, opinion, outlook.

воззр|е́ть, ю́, и́шь, *pf. of* взира́ть.

воззр|и́ться, ю́сь, и́шься, *pf.* (на+*a.*; *coll.*) to stare (at).

во|зи́ть, жу́, ~зишь, *impf.* (*indet. of* везти́) **1.** to cart, convey; to carry; to draw (*of beasts of burden or mechanical transport*); э́тот парово́з ~зит до тридцати́ ваго́нов this engine draws up to thirty coaches. **2.** (+*i.*, по+*d.*; *coll.*) to pass (over), run (over). **3.** (*coll.*) to beat, flog.

во|зи́ться, жу́сь, ~зишься, *impf.* **1.** to play noisily, romp (*of children*). **2.** (с +*i*, над +*i.*) to take trouble (over), spend time (on), busy oneself (with); (*coll.*) to potter; to tinker (with), fiddle about (with); он мно́го ~зится над ле́кциями he takes much trouble over the preparation of his lectures; он лю́бит в. в саду́ he likes pottering about in the garden.

во́зк|а, и, *f.* (*coll.*) carting, carriage.

возлага́|ть, ю, *impf. of* возложи́ть.

во́зле, *adv. and prep.*+*g.* by, near; past; он

стоя́л в. he was standing near-by; ка́ждый день он хо́дит в. моего́ до́ма he walks up and down past my house every day.

возлеж|а́ть, у́, и́шь, *impf.* (*of* возле́чь) (*obs.*) to recline.

возл|е́чь, я́гу, я́жешь, я́гут, *imp.* ~я́г, *past* ~ёг, ~егла́, *pf. of* ~ежа́ть.

возлик|ова́ть, у́ю, *pf.* to rejoice.

возлия́ни|е, я, *n.* 1. libation. 2. (*coll.*) drinking-bout.

возлож|и́ть, у́, ~ишь, *pf.* (*of* возлага́ть) to lay on (*also fig.*); в. вено́к на моги́лу to lay a wreath on a grave; наро́д ~и́л все наде́жды на но́вого президе́нта the people had placed all their hopes on the new president.

возлюб|и́ть, лю́, ~ишь, *pf.* (*obs.*) to love.

возлю́бленн|ый, *adj.* beloved; *as noun* (i) в., ~ого, *m.* 1. boy-friend. 2. lover. (ii) ~ая, ~ой, *f.* 1. girl-friend, sweetheart. 2. mistress.

возля́|гу, жешь, гут, *see* возле́чь.

возме́зди|е, я, *n.* retribution; requital.

возме|сти́ть, щу́, сти́шь, *pf.* (*of* ~ща́ть) to compensate, make up (for); to replace; в. поте́рянное вре́мя to make up for lost time; в. расхо́ды to refund expenses.

возмечта́|ть, ю, *pf.* 1. to dream, start dreaming. 2. в. о себе́ (*coll.*) to form a high opinion of oneself, become conceited.

возмеща́|ть, ю, *impf. of* возмести́ть.

возмеще́ни|е, я, n. 1. compensation, indemnity; (*leg.*) damages; получи́ть в. убы́тков по суду́ to be awarded damages. 2. replacement; refund, reimbursement.

возме|щу́, сти́шь, *see* ~сти́ть.

возмо́жно, *adv.* 1. possibly; (+*comp.*) as . . . as possible; в. лу́чше as well as possible; иди́те в. скоре́е go as soon as possible. 2. *as pred.* it is possible; в., что мы за́втра уе́дем we may possibly go away tomorrow.

возмо́жность|ь, и, f. 1. possibility; по (ме́ре) ~и as far as possible; до после́дней ~и to the uttermost. 2. opportunity; ему́ да́ли в. пое́хать в Росси́ю he has been given an opportunity of going to Russia; при пе́рвой ~и at the first opportunity, at one's earliest convenience. 3. (*pl.*) means, resources; у него́ больши́е ~и he has great potentialities.

возмо́ж|ный (~ен, ~на), *adj.* 1. possible; врач сде́лал для неё всё ~ное the doctor did all in his power for her. 2. the greatest possible; с ~ной то́чностью with the greatest possible accuracy, as accurately as possible.

возмо́|чь, гу́, жешь, гут, *past* ~г, ~гла́, *pf.* (*obs.*) to be able.

возмужа́лост|ь, и, f. maturity; manhood.

возмужа́лый, *adj.* mature; grown up.

возмужа́|ть, ю, *pf.* 1. to grow up. 2. to gain in strength, become stronger.

возмути́тел|ьный (~ен, ~ьна), *adj.* 1. disgraceful, scandalous. 2. (*obs.*) seditious, subversive.

возму|ти́ть, щу́, ти́шь, *pf.* 1. (*obs.*) to disturb, trouble. 2. (*fig., obs.*) to stir up, incite. 3. to anger, rouse the indignation (of).

возму|ти́ться, щу́сь, ти́шься, *pf.* 1. to be indignant (at); to be exasperated (by); все ~ти́лись его́ заявле́нием all were filled with indignation by his announcement. 2. (*obs.*) to rebel, rise in revolt.

возмуща́|ть, ю, *impf. of* возмути́ть.

возмуща́|ться, юсь, *impf. of* возмути́ться.

возмуще́ни|е, я, n. 1. indignation. 2. (*obs.*) revolt, rebellion. 3. (*astron.*) perturbation. 4. магни́тное в. (*phys.*) magnetic disturbance.

возмущён|ный (~, ~а́), *p.p.p. of* возмути́ть *and adj.* (+*i.*) indignant (at).

возму|щу́, ти́шь, *see* ~ти́ть.

вознагра|ди́ть, жу́, ди́шь, *pf.* to reward; to recompense; to compensate, make up (for); его́ ~ди́ли за заслу́ги золоты́ми часа́ми he was rewarded for his services with a gold watch.

вознагражда́|ть, ю, *impf. of* вознагради́ть.

вознагражде́ни|е, я, n. 1. reward, recompense; compensation. 2. fee, remuneration.

вознаме́рива|ться, юсь, *impf. of* вознаме́риться.

вознаме́р|иться, юсь, ишься, *pf.* (+*inf.*) to conceive a design, idea; она́ ~илась сде́латься актри́сой she conceived the idea of going on the stage.

вознегод|ова́ть, у́ю, *pf.* to become indignant.

возненави́|деть, жу, дишь, *pf.* to conceive hatred (for), come to hate.

вознесе́ни|е, я, n. ascent; В. (*eccl.*) Ascension (Day).

вознес|ти́, у́, ёшь, *past* ~, ~ла́, *pf.* (*of* возноси́ть) (*poet.*) to raise, lift up; в. моли́тву to offer up a prayer.

вознес|ти́сь, у́сь, ёшься, *past* ~ся, ~ла́сь, *pf.* (*of* возноси́ться) 1. (*poet.*) to rise; to ascend. 2. (*coll.*) to become conceited.

возник|а́ть, а́ю, *impf.* (*of* ~нуть) to arise, spring up; на на́ших глаза́х ~а́л но́вый го́род a new town was springing up before our eyes; у меня́ ~а́ет мысль the thought occurs to me.

возникнове́ни|е, я, n. rise, beginning, origin.

возни́к|нуть, ну, нешь, *past* ~, ~ла, *pf. of* ~а́ть.

возни́ц|а, ы, m. coachman, driver.

возни́ч|ий, его, m. 1. (*obs.*) coachman, driver. 2. В. (*astron.*) Auriga.

возно|си́ть, шу́, ~сишь, *impf. of* вознести́.

возно|си́ться, шу́сь, ~си́шься, *impf. of* вознести́сь.

возноше́ни|е, я, *n.* (*obs.*) raising, elevation; в. даро́в (*eccl.*) elevation (of the host).

возно|шу́, ~си́шь, *see* ~си́ть.

возн|я́, и́, *no pl., f.* (*coll.*) **1.** row, noise; мыши́ная в. (*fig.*) petty intrigues. **2.** bother, trouble; у него́ мно́го ~и́ с автомоби́лем he has a lot of trouble with his car.

возоблада́|ть, ю, *pf.* (над+*i.*) to prevail (over).

возобнов|и́ть, лю́, и́шь, *pf.* (*of* ~ля́ть) **1.** to renew, resume. **2.** to restore.

возобновле́ни|е, я, *n.* renewal, resumption; revival (*of a play*).

возобновля́|ть, ю, *impf. of* возобнови́ть.

воз|о́к, ка́, *m.* closed sleigh.

возомн|и́ть, ю́, и́шь, *pf.* в. о себе́ (*iron.*) to get a false idea of one's own importance; в. себя́ авторите́том to consider oneself (*falsely*) an authority.

возоп|и́ть, лю́, и́шь, *pf.* (*obs.*) to cry out.

возра́д|оваться, уюсь, *pf.* (+*d.*; *obs.*) to be delighted (at).

возража́|ть, ю, *impf. of* возрази́ть; не ~ю I have no objection; вы не ~ете? have you any objection(s)?, do you mind?

возраже́ни|е, я, *n.* **1.** objection; retort; без ~й! don't argue! **2.** (*leg.*) answer.

возра|зи́ть, жу́, зи́шь, *pf.* (*of* ~жа́ть) (про́тив+*g. or* на+*a.*) **1.** to object, raise an objection (to); to take exception (to); to retort; про́тив э́того не́чего в. nothing can be said against it. **2.** to say.

во́зраст, а, *m.* age; одного́ ~а of the same age; о́троческий в. boyhood; преде́льный в. age-limit; быть на ~е to be of age; вы́йти из ~а to pass the age, exceed the age-limit; он вы́шел из ~а для вое́нной слу́жбы he is over the age for military service; прекло́нный в. declining years.

возраста́ни|е, я, *n.* growth, increase; increment.

возраст|а́ть, а́ю, *impf. of* ~и́; ~а́ющая ско́рость (*phys.*) accelerated velocity.

возраст|и́, у́, ёшь, *past* возро́с, возросла́, *pf.* (*of* ~а́ть) to grow, increase.

возраст|но́й, *adj. of* во́зраст; ~на́я гру́ппа age group.

возро|ди́ть, жу́, ди́шь, *pf.* (*of* ~жда́ть) to regenerate; to revive; его́ слова́ ~ди́ли в ней во́лю к жи́зни his words revived in her the will to live.

возро|ди́ться, жу́сь, ди́шься, *pf.* (*of* ~жда́ться) to revive (*intrans.*).

возрожда́|ть, ю, *impf. of* возроди́ть.

возрожда́|ться, юсь, *impf. of* возроди́ться.

возрожде́ни|е, я, *n.* rebirth; revival; эпо́ха Возрожде́ния Renaissance.

возроп|та́ть, щу́, ~щешь, *pf.* (*obs.*) to cry out (*in protest*).

во́зчик, а, *m.* carter, carrier.

возыме́|ть, ю, ешь, *pf.* to conceive (*wish intention, etc.*); больно́й ~л жела́ние пое́сть фру́ктов the invalid conceived a desire for fruit; в. де́йствие to take effect; ва́ши предупрежде́ния наконе́ц ~ли де́йствие your warnings have at last taken effect; в. си́лу to come into force.

возьм|у́(сь), ёшь(ся), *see* взя́ть(ся).

во́ин, а, *m.* warrior; fighter.

во́инск|ий, *adj.* **1.** military; ~ая пови́нность liability for military service; в. по́езд troop-train. **2.** martial, warlike.

во́инствен|ный (~, ~на), *adj.* warlike; bellicose.

во́инств|о, а, *n.* (*collect.*; *obs.*) host, army.

во́инствующ|ий, *adj.* militant; ~ая це́рковь the church militant; Сою́з ~их безбо́жников (*hist.*) League of Militant Atheists.

вои́стину, *adv.* (*obs.*) indeed; verily; (Христо́с) в. воскре́с! (*response at Orthodox Easter service*) He (Christ) is risen indeed!

вои́тел|ь, я, *m.* **1.** (*poet.*) warrior. **2.** (*coll.*) rowdy.

вои́тельниц|а, ы, *f.* **1.** (*poet.*) female warrior, Amazon. **2.** (*coll.*) shrew, termagant.

во|й, я, *no pl., m.* howl, howling; wail, wailing.

вой|ду́, дёшь, *see* ~ти́.

во́йлок, а, *m.* felt; strip of felt.

во́йлочный, *adj.* felt.

войн|а́, ы́, *pl.* ~ы, *f.* war; warfare; вести́ ~у́ to wage war; объяви́ть ~у́ to declare war.

войск|а́, ~, *sing.* ~о, ~а, *n.* **1.** troops; forces; наёмные в. mercenaries. **2.** (*sing.*) army; (*hist.*) host (*of Cossacks*); запоро́жское ~о the Zaporozhian host. **3.** (*sing.; fig.*) host, multitude.

войсков|о́й, *adj.* **1.** military. **2.** (*hist.*) of the host; в. круг Cossack assembly; в. старшина́ Lieutenant-Colonel (*of Cossack troops*).

во|йти́, йду́, йдёшь, *past* ~шёл, ~шла́, *pf.* (*of* входи́ть) (в.+*a.*) to enter; to go in(to); to come in(to); в. в аза́рт to grow heated; в. в дове́рие к кому́-н. to be taken into someone's confidence; в. в исто́рию to go down to history; в. в колею́ to carry on as normal; в. в лета́ to get on (in years); в. в мо́ду to become fashionable; в. в погово́рку to pass into a proverb; в. в роль to (begin to) feel one's feet.

вока́бул|ы, ~, *no sing.* (*obs.*) foreign words (*as object of study*).

вокали́з, а, *m. and* вокали́з|а, ы, (*obs.*) *f.* exercise in vocalization.

вокализа́ци|я, и, *f.* (*ling., mus.*) vocalization.

вокали́зм, а, *m.* (*ling.*) vowel-system.

вокали́ст, а, *m.* (*mus.*) teacher of singing.

вока́льный, *adj.* vocal; в. ве́чер sing-song.

вокза́л, а, *m.* (large) station; station building; железнодоро́жный в. railway (*esp. main or terminus*) station; морско́й в. port arrival and departure building; речно́й в. river-boat station.

вокза́л|ьный, *adj. of* ~ station.

вокру́г, *adv. and prep.*+*g.* round, around, about; путеше́ствие в. све́та voyage round the world; верте́ться в. да о́коло (*coll.*) to beat about the bush.

ВОКС, а, *m.* (*abbr. of* Всесою́зное о́бщество культу́рной свя́зи с заграни́цей) (*hist.*) All-Union Society for Cultural Relations with Foreign Countries.

вол, а́, *m.* ox, bullock.

вола́н, а, *m.* 1. flounce (*on woman's skirt*). 2. shuttlecock; игра́ в в. badminton; battledore and shuttlecock.

Волапю́к, а, *m.* Volapuk (*artificial international language*).

волга́р|ь, я́, *m.* (*coll.*) native of Volga region.

волды́р|ь, я́, *m.* blister; bump.

волево́й, *adj.* 1.(*psych.*) volitional. 2. strong-willed; tough.

волеизъявле́ни|е, я, *n.* will, pleasure; command; по короле́вскому ~ю at the king's pleasure, by royal command.

волейбо́л, а, *m.* (*sport*) volley-ball.

волейболи́ст, а, *m.* volley-ball player.

во́лей-нево́лей, *adv.* (*coll.*) willy-nilly.

волжа́н|ин, ина, *pl.* ~е, ~, *m.* native of Volga region.

волжа́н|ка, ки, *f. of* ~ин.

во́лжский, *adj.* Volga, of the Volga.

волк, а, *pl.* ~и, ~о́в, *m.* wolf; морско́й в. (*coll.*) old salt; смотре́ть ~ом (*fig.*) to scowl; в. в ове́чьей шку́ре wolf in sheep's clothing; хоть ~ом вы́ть (*coll.*) it's enough to make you despair; с ~а́ми жить, по-во́лчьи выть (*prov.*) when in Rome do as the Romans do; сде́лать так, чтоб и в. был сыт и о́вцы це́лы (*prov.*) to run with the hare and hunt with the hounds.

волк-маши́н|а, ы, *f.* (*text.*) willow, willy.

волкода́в, а, *m.* wolf-hound.

волн|а́¹, ы́, *pl.* ~ы, ~а́м, *f.* (in var. senses) wave; breaker.

волн|а́², ы́, *f.* (*dial.*) wool.

волне́ни|е, я, *n.* 1. choppiness (*of water*). 2. (*fig.*) agitation, disturbance; emotion; прийти́ в в. to become agitated, excited. 3. (*usu. pl.; polit.*) disturbance(s); unrest.

волни́ст|ый (~, ~а), *adj.* wavy; watered (*of stuffs*); ~ое желе́зо corrugated iron; ~ая ме́стность undulating ground.

волн|ова́ть, у́ю, *impf.* (*of* вз~) to disturb, agitate (*also fig.*); to excite; to worry; его́ всё ~у́ет he is easily excited; не ну́жно в. больно́го the patient must not be disturbed.

волн|ова́ться, у́юсь, *impf.* 1. (*of water, etc.*) to be agitated, choppy; to ripple, wave. 2. to be disturbed, agitated; to worry, be nervous; to be excited; она́ ~у́ется о де́тях she worries about her children; он всегда́ ~у́ется пе́ред экза́меном he is always nervous before an examination. 3. (*polit.; obs.*) to be in a state of ferment, of unrest; наро́д всё бо́лее ~ова́лся popular unrest was increasing.

волново́д, а, *m.* (*electr.*) wave-guide.

волнов|о́й, *adj.* wave, undulatory; ~а́я тео́рия (*phys.*) wave theory.

волноло́м, а, *m.* breakwater.

волноме́р, а, *m.* (*tech.*) wave-meter.

волнообра́з|ный (~ен, ~на), *adj.* undulatory; wavy, undulating.

волноре́з, а, *m.* breakwater.

волноуказа́тел|ь, я, *m.* (*radio*) wave detector.

волну́шк|а, и, *f.* coral milky cap (*mushroom*).

волн|у́ющий, *pres. part. act. of* ~ова́ть *and adj.* disturbing, worrying; exciting, thrilling, stirring; ~у́ющие изве́стия disturbing, exciting news; ~у́ющая по́весть thrilling, exciting story.

вол|о́вий, *adj. of* ~; (*fig.*) very strong; ~о́вья шку́ра oxhide; у него́ ~о́вья си́ла he is as strong as an ox.

во́лок, а, *m.* portage; перепра́вить ~ом to portage.

воло́к(ся), ла́(сь), *see* волочь(ся).

волоки́т|а¹, ы, *f.* (*coll.*) red tape.

волоки́т|а², ы, *m.* (*coll.*) ladies' man; philanderer.

волоки́тств|о, а, *n.* (*coll.*) philandering.

волоки́тчик, а, *m.* (*coll.*) red-tape merchant, red-tape monger.

волокни́ст|ый (~, ~а), *adj.* fibrous; stringy.

волок|но́, на́, *pl.* ~на, ~он, ~нам, *n.* fibre, filament.

волонтёр, а, *m.* (*obs.*) volunteer.

волоо́кий, *adj.* (*poet.*) ox-eyed.

во́лос, а, *pl.* ~ы (*and coll.* ~а́), воло́с, ~а́м, *m.* 1. hair; (*pl.*) hair (*of the head*); рвать на себе́ ~ы to tear one's hair; схвати́ть за́ ~ы to take by the hair; при ви́де тру́па ~ы у меня́ ста́ли ды́бом the sight of the corpse made my hair stand on end; э́то притя́нуто за́ волосы it is far fetched; ни на́ волос not a bit; у него́ ни на́ волос ума́ he has not a grain of sense. 2. hair (*as material*); подкла́дка из ко́нского ~а horsehair lining.

волоса́тик, а, *m.* (*zool.*) hair-worm.

волоса́т|ый (~, ~а), *adj.* hairy; hirsute; pilose.

волоси́стый, *adj.* (*min.*) fibrous.

волосн|о́й, *adj.* (*phys.*) capillary; ~ы́е сосу́ды (*anat.*) capillaries.

волос|о́к, ка́, *m.* **1.** *dim. of* во́лос; на в. (от +*g.*) within a hairbreadth (of); висе́ть, держа́ться на ~ке́ to hang by a thread; я не тро́нул ~ка́ у неё I did not touch a hair of her head. **2.** hair-spring. **3.** (*electr.*) filament.

волосте́л|ь, я, *m.* (*hist.*) volost head.

волостно́й, *adj.* volost.

во́лост|ь, и, *pl.* ~и, ~е́й, *f.* (*hist.*) volost (*smallest administrative division of tsarist Russia*).

волосяно́й, *adj.* hair, of hair; в. покро́в (*anat.*) scalp.

волоче́ни|е, я, *n.* dragging; (*tech.*) в. про́волоки wire-drawing.

волочи́льн|ый, *adj.* (*tech.*) wire-drawing; ~ая доска́ draw-plate.

волочи́льщик, а, *m.* (*tech.*) wire-drawer.

волоч|и́ть, у́, ~ишь, *impf.* **1.** to drag; в. но́гу to drag one's foot; в. но́ги to shuffle one's feet; е́ле но́ги в. to be hardly able to drag one's legs along; в. де́ло to drag out an affair. **2.** (*tech.*) to draw.

волоч|и́ться, у́сь, ~ишься, *impf.* **1.** *pass. of* ~и́ть. **2.** to drag (*intrans.*), trail. **3.** (за+*i.*; *coll.*) to run after; три ме́сяца он уже́ ~ится за ней he has been running after her for three months.

вол|о́чь, оку́, очёшь, оку́т, *past* ~о́к, ~окла́, *impf.* (*coll.*) to drag.

вол|о́чься, оку́сь, очёшься, оку́тся, *past* ~о́кся, ~окла́сь, *impf.* (*coll.*) **1.** to drag (*intrans.*), trail. **2.** to drag (oneself) along; to shuffle.

воло́шский, *adj.* (*hist.*) Wallachian; в. оре́х (*obs.*) walnut.

волхв, а́, *m.* magician, sorcerer; soothsayer; три ~а́ the Three Wise Men, the Magi.

волхв|ова́ть, у́ю, *impf.* to practise magic, sorcery.

волча́нк|а, и, *f.* (*med.*) lupus.

волч|е́ц, ца́, *m.* (*bot.*) thistle.

во́лч|ий, *adj. of* волк; wolf, lupine; в. аппети́т (*coll.*) voracious appetite; в. биле́т, па́спорт (*hist., coll.*) passport (*in tsarist Russia*) with note of political unreliability of holder; у него́ в. па́спорт he is a marked man; ~ья пасть cleft palate; ~ья я́года (*bot.*) spurge-flax; ~ья я́ма (*mil.*) trou-de-loup.

волчи́х|а, и, *f.* (*coll.*) she-wolf.

волчи́ц|а, ы, *f.* she-wolf.

волч|о́к¹, ка́, *m.* **1.** top (*toy*); верте́ться ~ко́м to spin like a top. **2.** (*tech.*) gyroscope.

волч|о́к², ка́, *m.* judas (*in door of prison cell*).

волч|о́нок, о́нка, *pl.* ~а́та, ~а́т, *m.* wolf-cub.

волше́бник, а, *m.* magician; wizard.

волше́бниц|а, ы, *f.* enchantress.

волше́б|ный (~ен, ~на), *adj.* **1.** magical; в. жезл, ~ная па́лочка magic wand; ~ное ца́рство fairyland; в. фона́рь magic lantern. **2.** (*fig.*) bewitching, enchanting.

волшебств|о́, а́, *n.* magic; (*fig.*) magic, enchantment.

волы́н|ить, ю, ишь, *impf.* (*coll.*) to dawdle, delay, be dilatory, slack.

волы́нк|а¹, и, *f.* bagpipes.

волы́нк|а², и, *f.* dawdling, delay, dilatoriness, slacking; hold-up; тяну́ть ~у to dawdle, delay, be dilatory.

волы́нщик¹, а, *m.* piper.

волы́нщик², а, *m.* (*coll.*) dawdler, slacker.

вольго́тный, *adj.* (*coll.*) free, free-and-easy.

во́льн|ая, ой, *f.* (*hist.*) letter of enfranchisement (*given to freed serf*); дать кому́-н. ~ую to give someone his freedom.

во́льниц|а, ы, *m. and f.* **1.** (*f.*; collect.; *hist.*) freemen; outlaws (*runaway serfs, Cossacks, etc., in Muscovite Russia*). **2.** (*m. and f.*; *coll.*) self-willed person, child.

во́льнича|ть, ю, *impf.* (*pejor.*) to take liberties, make free.

во́льн|о, *adv. of* ~ый; (*as mil. command*) в.! stand at ease!

вольно́, *as pred.+d. and inf.* (*coll.*; *addressed to person complaining of misfortune*) в. тебе́ it's of your own choosing; ты простуди́лась? в. ж тебе́ бы́ло вы́йти без пальто́ have you caught cold? well, you *would* go out without a coat.

вольноду́м|ец, ца, *m.* (*hist.*) free-thinker.

вольноду́м|ный (~ен, ~на), *adj.* (*hist.*) free-thinking.

вольноду́мств|о, а, *n.* (*hist.*) free-thinking.

вольнолюби́в|ый (~, ~а), *adj.* freedom-loving.

вольнонаёмн|ый, *adj.* **1.** civilian (*employed in or for military establishment*); в э́том ла́гере нет ~ого соста́ва in this camp there are no civilian staff. **2.** (*obs.*) hired; free-lance.

вольноопределя́ющ|ийся, егося, *m.* (*hist.*) 'volunteer' (*person with secondary education serving term in tsarist Russian army on privileged conditions*).

вольноотпу́щенник, а, *m.* (*hist.*) freedman; emancipated serf.

вольноотпу́щенн|ый, *adj.* (*hist.*) freed, emancipated; *as noun* в., ~ого, *m.* = ~ик.

вольнопрактику́ющий, *adj.* conducting a private practice (*of doctors, etc.*).

вольнослу́шател|ь, я, *m.* occasional student (*permitted to attend university, etc., lecture courses without having the formal status of student*).

во́льност|ь, и, *f.* **1.** freedom, liberty; поэти́ческая в. poetic license; позволя́ть себе́ ~и to take liberties. **2.** (*usu. pl.*; *hist.*) liberties, rights.

во́л|ьный, *adj.* **1.** free; в. го́род free city; в. каза́к, ~ьная пти́ца one's own master. **2.** (*econ.*) free, unrestricted; в. ры́нок free market; ~ьная прода́жа unrestricted sale. **3.** (*obs.*) private; жить на ~ьной кварти́ре (*mil.*) to live out (*as opp. to* in barracks); служи́ть по ~ьному на́йму to work by private agreement; перейти́ на ~ьные хлеба́ to turn free-lance. **4.** (*of clothing*) free, loose. **5.** в. перево́д (*lit.*) free translation; ~ьные стихи́ vers libre. **6.** (*sport*) free, free-style; ~ьная борьба́ free-style wrestling; в. стиль (*in swimming*) free-style; в. уда́р free kick; ~ьные упражне́ния free exercises. **7.** поста́вить на в. дух, на в. жар, на в. пар (*cul.*) to leave to cook (*after source of heat has been removed or switched off*). **8.** в. ка́менщик Freemason. **9.** (~ен, ~ьна́), free, familiar (*in behaviour*). **10.** (~ен, ~ьна́, *pl.* ~ьны́), (*full form not used*) free, at liberty; ты ~ен де́лать, что хо́чешь you are a free agent, you are at liberty to do as you wish.

вольт¹, а, *g. pl.* ~, *m.* (*electr.*) volt.

вольт², а, о ~е, на ~у́, *m.* **1.** (*sport*) vault. **2.** volte (*in fencing*). **3.** (*sl.*) cheating (*at cards*); вы́кинуть в. (*fig.*, *coll.*) to play a trick.

вольта́ж, а, *m.* (*electr.*) voltage.

вольтерья́н|ец, ца, *m.* (*hist.*) Voltairian, free-thinker.

вольтерья́нств|о, а, *n.* (*hist.*) Voltairianism, free-thinking.

вольтижёр, а, *m.* (*sport*) trick-rider, equestrian acrobat.

вольтижи́р|овать, ую, *impf.* (*sport*) to do acrobatics on horseback.

вольтижиро́вк|а, и, *f.* (*sport*) acrobatics on horseback.

вольтме́тр, а, *m.* (*electr.*) voltmetre.

во́льтов, *adj.* (*electr.*) voltaic.

вольфра́м, а, *m.* (*chem.*) tungsten.

вольфрами́т, а, *m.* (*min.*) wolframite.

вольфра́м|овый, *adj. of* ~; ~овая ла́мпочка tungsten lamp; ~овая руда́ wolfram.

воль|ю́, ёшь, *see* влить.

волюнтари́зм, а, *m.* (*philos.*) libertarianism.

волюнтари́ст, а, *m.* (*philos.*) libertarian.

волю́т|а, ы, *f.* (*archit.*) volute, scroll.

во́л|я, и, *no pl.*, *f.* **1.** (*in var. senses*) will; volition; wish(es); после́дняя в. last will; свобо́дная в. free will; в. к жи́зни will to live; си́ла ~и will-power; челове́к с си́льной ~ей strong-willed person; ~ею суде́б as the fates decree; счита́ться с ~ей избира́телей to take into account the wishes of the voters; в. ва́ша (*coll.*) (*i*) as you please, as you like, (*ii*) say what you like; в свое́й ~е in one's power; по до́брой ~е freely, of one's own free will; не по свое́й ~е against one's will. **2.** freedom, liberty; вы́пустить, отпусти́ть на ~ю to set at liberty; на ~е at liberty; at large; с ~и (*prison sl.*) from outside; дать ~ю (+*d.*) to give free play (to), give free rein (to), give vent (to); дать ~ю рука́м (*coll.*) to be free with one's hands, fists.

вон¹, *adv.* out; off, away; вы́йти в. to go away; в. отсю́да! get out!; в. его́! out with him!; из рук в. пло́хо wretchedly; пье́са была́ сы́грана из рук в. пло́хо the play was wretchedly played; из ря́да в. выходя́щий outstanding; у меня́ э́то из ума́ в. (*coll.*) it went right out of my mind.

вон², *particle* there, over there; в. он идёт there he goes; куда́ вы положи́ли газе́ту? — на стол, в. там where have you put the paper? — over there, on the table; в. он кто! so that's who he is!; в. оно́ что (*coll.*) so that's it!

во́на, *particle* (*coll.*, *dial.*) **1.** = вон². **2.** *as interj.* в. so that's it!

вон|жу́, зи́шь, *see* ~зи́ть.

вонза́|ть, ю, *impf. of* вонзи́ть.

вонза́|ться, юсь, **1.** *impf. of* ~ться. **2.** *pass. of* ~ть.

вон|зи́ть, жу́, зи́шь, *pf.* (*of* ~за́ть) **1.** (в+*a.*) to plunge, thrust (into). **2.** (*sl.*) to drink.

вон|зи́ться, жу́сь, зи́шься, *pf.* (*of* ~за́ться) **1.** to pierce, penetrate; стрела́ ~зи́лась ему́ в се́рдце the arrow pierced his heart. **2.** *pass. of* ~зи́ть.

вони́щ|а, и, *f.* (*coll.*) stink, stench.

вонми́, *see* внять.

вон|ь, и, *no pl.*, *f.* stink, stench.

воню́ч|ий (~, ~а), *adj.* stinking, fetid.

воню́чк|а, и, *f.* (*coll.*) stinker; (*zool.*) skunk.

воня́|ть, ю, *impf.* **1.** (+*i.*) to stink, reek (of); весь дом ~ет чесноко́м the whole house reeks of garlic. **2.** (*pf.* на~) (*vulg.*) to fart.

вообража́|емый, *pres. part. pass. of* ~ть *and adj.* imaginary; fictitious.

вообража́|ть, ю, *impf.* (*of* вообрази́ть) **1.** to imagine, fancy; в. жизнь в ка́менном ве́ке to imagine life in the Stone Age; он ~ет, что слы́шит го́лос своего́ уме́ршего отца́ he imagines that he can hear the voice of his dead father; ~ю, как вы чу́вствуете себя́ I can imagine how you feel. **2.** (*coll.*) в. о себе́ to fancy oneself; он сли́шком ~ет о себе́ he thinks too much of himself.

вообража́|ться, юсь, *impf.* **1.** (+*i.*; *obs.*) to imagine oneself; ему́ ~ется, бу́дто он вели́кий учёный (*impers.*) he imagines that he is a great scholar. **2.** *pass. of* ~ть.

воображе́ни|е, я, *n.* imagination; fancy; у неё живо́е в. she has a lively imagination; э́то одно́ твоё в. it's just your imagination.

вообрази́м|ый (~, ~а), *pres. part. pass. of* вообрази́ть *and adj.* imaginable.

вообра|зи́ть, жу́, зи́шь, *pf. of* ~жа́ть; ~зи́(те)! fancy!, (just) imagine!

вообра|зи́ться, жу́сь, зи́шься, *pf. of* ~жа́ться.

вообще́, *adv.* 1. in general; on the whole; в. говоря́, я не люблю́ рабо́тать по ноча́м generally speaking I do not like working at night; он сейча́с за́нят, но в. он лени́вый челове́к he is busy at the moment but on the whole he is a lazy man. 2. always; altogether; она́ вы́глядит бле́дной в., а не то́лько сего́дня she always looks pale, not just today.

воодушев|и́ть, лю́, и́шь, *pf. (of* ~ля́ть) to inspire, rouse; to inspirit, hearten; его́ речь ~и́ла всю страну́ his speech was an inspiration to the whole nation.

воодушевле́ни|е, я, *n.* 1. rousing; inspiriting. 2. animation; enthusiasm, fervour; говори́ть с больши́м ~ем to speak with great fervour.

воодушевлён|ный (~, ~á), *p.p.p. of* воодушеви́ть *and adj.* animated; enthusiastic, fervent.

воодушевля́|ть, ю, *impf. of* воодушеви́ть.

вооруж|а́ть(ся), а́ю(сь), *impf. of* ~и́ть(ся).

вооруже́ни|е, я, *n.* 1. arming. 2. arms, armament; в., состоя́щее из пу́шек и пулемётов an armament consisting of cannon and machine-guns. 3. equipment; па́русное в. (*naut.*) rig.

вооружён|ный (~, ~á), *p.p.p. of* вооружи́ть *and adj.* armed; в. до зубо́в armed to the teeth; в. но́выми све́дениями armed with fresh information; ~ные си́лы armed forces.

вооруж|и́ть, у́, и́шь, *pf. (of* ~а́ть) 1. (+*i.*) to arm; to equip (with) (*also fig.*); в. кора́бль (*obs.*) to fit out a ship. 2. (про́тив+*g.*) to set (against), instigate (against).

вооруж|и́ться, у́сь, и́шься, *pf. (of* ~а́ться) 1. to arm oneself, take up arms; (*fig.*) to equip oneself, provide oneself; в. ули́ками to provide oneself with evidence; в. терпе́нием to arm oneself with patience. 2. *pass. of* ~и́ть.

воо́чию, *adv.* 1. with one's own eyes, for oneself; я в. убеди́лся в том, что он небре́жно пра́вил маши́ной I could see for myself that he was driving carelessly. 2. clearly, plainly; показа́ть в. to show clearly.

во-пе́рвых, *adv.* first, first of all, in the first place.

воп|и́ть, лю́, и́шь, *impf. (coll.)* to cry out; to howl; to wail.

вопи|ю́щий, *pres. part. act. of* ~я́ть *and adj.* scandalous; crying; ~ю́щее безобра́зие crying shame; ~ю́щее противоре́чие glar-

ing contradiction; глас ~ю́щего в пусты́не, *see* глас.

вопи|я́ть, ю́, е́шь, *impf. (obs.)* to cry out, clamour; в. об отмще́нии to cry out for vengeance.

во́плениц|а, ы, *f. (dial.)* (professional) mourner.

вопло|ти́ть, щу́, ти́шь, *pf. (of* ~ща́ть) to embody, incarnate; в. в себе́ to be the embodiment (of), incarnation (of); Ле́вин, в «А́нне Каре́нине» Толсто́го, ~ти́л в себе́ тип «ка́ющегося дворяни́на» Levin, in Tolstoy's *Anna Karenina*, embodied the type of the 'repentant nobleman'.

воплоща́|ть, ю, *impf. of* воплоти́ть.

воплоще́ни|е, я, *n.* embodiment, incarnation; он — в. здоро́вья he is the picture of health; в. Христа́ the Incarnation.

воплощён|ный (~, ~á), *p.p.p. of* воплоти́ть *and adj.* incarnate; personified; он — ~ная добросо́вестность he is conscientiousness personified.

вопл|ь, я, *m.* cry, wail; wailing, howling.

вопреки́, *prep.*+*d.* despite, in spite of; against, contrary to, in the teeth of; он вы́шел в. предписа́нию врача́ he went out against doctor's orders; в. предупрежде́ниям regardless of warnings; в. сове́ту contrary to advice.

вопро́с, а, *m.* 1. question; зада́ть в. to put, pose a question; ко́свенный в. (*gram.*) indirect question. 2. question, problem; matter; подня́ть, поста́вить в. (о+*p.*) raise the question (of); поста́вить под в. to call in question; возмо́жность сверхзвуково́го полёта бо́льше не под ~ом the possibility of supersonic flight is no longer in question; в. жи́зни и сме́рти matter of life and death; спо́рный в. moot point; что за в.! what a question!, of course!; (*sometimes does not require translation*) како́е ва́ше мне́ние по вопро́су национализа́ции земли́? what is your opinion about nationalization of the land?

вопроси́тельный, *adj.* interrogative; interrogatory; в. знак question-mark; в. взгляд inquiring look.

вопро|си́ть, шу́, си́шь, *pf. (of* ~ша́ть) (*obs.*) to question, inquire (of).

вопро́сник, а, *m.* questionnaire.

вопро́сный, *adj.* containing questions; в. лист question-paper; form.

вопроша́|ть, ю, *impf. of* вопроси́ть; ~ющий взгляд inquiring look.

вопр|у́, ёшь, *see* впере́ть.

вопь|ю́, ёшь, *see* впить.

вор, а, *pl.* ~ы, ~о́в, *m.* 1. thief; карма́нный в. pickpocket; магази́нный в. shoplifter. 2. (*hist.*) criminal (*esp. one guilty of high treason*); ту́шинский в. (*hist.*) 'the impostor of Tushino' (*the second pseudo- -Dmitri*).

вóрван|ь, и, *f.* train-oil; blubber.

ворв|áться, у́сь, ёшься, *past* ~áлся, ~алáсь, *pf.* (*of* врывáться²) to burst (into); он ~áлся ко мне в кóмнату he burst into my room.

вори́шк|а, и, *m.* petty thief.

ворк|овáть, у́ю, *impf.* (*of pigeons*) to coo; (*fig.*) to bill and coo.

воркотн|я́, и́, *f.* (*coll.*) grumbling.

вороб|éй, ья́, *m.* sparrow; стáрый в., стрé-ляный в. (*fig.*) old hand; стáрого ~ья́ на мяки́не не проведёшь (*prov.*) an old bird is not caught with chaff.

вороб|ьи́ный, *adj. of* ~éй; ~ьи́ная ночь 1. short summer night. 2. night of con-tinuous thunder and/or summer-lighting.

ворóванный, *adj.* stolen.

воровáт|ый (~, ~а), *adj.* thievish; furtive; в. взгляд furtive glance.

вор|овáть, у́ю, *impf.* 1. (*pf.* c~) to steal; в. дéньги у когó-н. to steal money from some-one. 2. *impf. only* to be a thief; с сáмых рáнних лет он ~у́ет he has been a thief from his earliest years.

воровк|а, и, *f. of* вор.

воровски́, *adv.* (*coll.*) furtively.

воровск|óй, *adj.* 1. of thieves; в. язы́к, ~óе аргó thieves' Latin, thieves' cant. 2. (*hist.*) illegal; ~и́е дéньги counterfeit money.

воровств|ó, á, *n.* stealing; theft; литерату́рное в. plagiarism.

вóрог, а, *m.* (*folk poet.*) 1.foe. 2.fiend.

ворожб|á, ы́, *no pl.*, *f.* sorcery; fortune- -telling.

вороже|я́, и́, *f.* sorceress; fortune-teller.

ворож|и́ть, у́, и́шь, *impf.* (*of* по~) to prac-tise sorcery; to tell fortunes; емý бáбушка ~и́т (*coll.*) (*i*) he holds good cards, (*ii*) he has a friend at court.

вóрон, а, *m.* raven.

ворóн|а, ы, *f.* 1. crow; бéлая в. rara avis (*of someone outstanding*); в. в павли́ньих пéрьях daw in peacock's feathers; ни пáва, ни в. neither one thing nor another; пу́ганая в. кустá бои́тся (*prov.*) a burnt child dreads the fire. 2. (*fig.*) gaper, loafer, Johnny- -head-in-air; ~ считáть (*coll.*) to be a gaper, loafer, Johnny-head-in-air.

воронён|ый, *adj.* (*tech.*) blued; ~ая сталь blue steel, burnished steel.

ворóн|ий, *adj. of* ~a.

ворон|и́ть, ю́, и́шь, *impf.* (*tech.*) to blue, burnish.

ворóнк|а, и, *f.* 1. funnel (*for pouring liquids*). 2. (*mil.*) crater.

вóрон|ов, *adj. of* ~; *only in phrase* цвет ~ова крылá raven (*of hair, etc.*).

ворон|óй, *adj.* black (*of horses*); прокати́ть на ~ы́х (*coll.*) to blackball.

воронь|ё, я́, *n.* (*collect.*) carrion-crows (*also fig.*).

вóрот¹, а, *pl.* ~ы, *m.* collar (*of garment*); neckband; схвати́ть зá в. to seize by the collar, collar.

вóрот², а, *m.* (*tech.*) winch; windlass.

ворóт|а (*coll.* ~á), ~, *no sing.* 1. gate, gates; gateway; шлюзные в. lock-gate; въéхать в в. to enter the gates; стоя́ть в ~ах to stand in the gateway; пришлá бедá, отворя́й ~á (*prov.*) misfortunes never come singly. 2. (*sport*) goal, goal-posts.

вороти́л|а, ы, *m.* (*coll.*) bigwig, big noise.

воро|ти́ть¹, чу́, ~ти́шь, *pf.* (*coll.*) 1. to bring back; to get back; to call back; сдéланного не ~ти́шь what's done can't be undone. 2. to turn aside, back.

воро|ти́ть², чу́, ~ти́шь, *impf.* (*coll.*) (+*i.*) to be in charge (of), run; он тут всем ~ти́т he runs the whole show here. 2. нос, ры́ло в. (от) (*coll.*) to turn up one's nose (at); (*impers.*) (с души́) меня́ ~ти́т от э́того дéла this business makes me sick.

воро|ти́ться, чу́сь, ~ти́шься, *pf.* (*coll.*) to return.

воротни́к, á, *m.* collar; отложнóй в. turn- -down collar; стоя́чий в. stand-up collar.

воротнич|óк, кá, *m.* collar.

ворóт|ный, *adj. of* ~a; в. створ gate-post; (*med.*) ~ная вéна portal vein.

вóрох, а, *pl.* ~á, *m.* heap, pile; (*fig., coll.*) heaps, masses, lots; мне нáдо в. пи́сем написáть I have lots of letters to write; в. новостéй lots of news.

ворóча|ть, ю, *impf.* (*coll.*) 1. to turn, move; в. глазáми to roll one's eyes. 2. (+*i.*; *fig.*) to have control (of); в. ты́сячами, в. мил-лиóнами to be rolling (*in money*).

ворóча|ться, юсь, *impf.* to turn, move (*intrans.*); в. с бóку нá бок to toss and turn; ~йтесь! (*coll.*) get a move on!

воро|чу́(сь), ~ти́шь(ся), *see* ~ти́ть(ся).

ворош|и́ть, у́, и́шь, *impf.* (*of* раз~) 1. в. сéно to turn, ted hay. 2. (*fig., coll.*) to stir up.

ворош|и́ться, у́сь, и́шься, *impf.* (*coll.*) to move about, stir.

ворс, а, *no pl.*, *m.* pile; nap; по ~у with the pile, nap.

ворси́льн|ый, *adj.* (*text.*) ~ая маши́на teaser; ~ая ши́шка teasel.

ворси́нк|а, и, *f.* 1. (*text.*) hair. 2. (*physiol., bot.*) fibre.

ворси́ст|ый (~, ~а), *adj.* 1. (*text.*) fleecy, with thick pile. 2. (*bot.*) lanate.

ворсовáльн|ый, *adj.* ~ая маши́на (*text.*) teaser.

ворс|овáть, у́ю, *impf.* (*of* на~) (*text.*) to tease.

ворся́нк|а, и, *f.* (*bot.*) teasel.

ворча́нь|е, я, *n.* grumbling; growling.

ворч|а́ть, у́, и́шь, *impf.* (на+*a.*) to grumble (at); to growl (at); в. себѣ́ подъ носъ to mutter (into one's beard); э́ти соба́ки ~а́т на всѣхъ чужи́хъ людей these dogs always growl at strangers.

ворчли́в|ый (~, ~а), *adj.* querulous.

ворчу́н, а́, *m.* (*coll.*) grumbler.

восвоя́си, *adv.* (for) home; онъ ужé отпра́вился в. he has already set out for home.

восемна́дцатый *adj.* eighteenth.

восемна́дцат|ь, и, *num.* eighteen.

во́с|емь, ьми́, ьмью́, *and* **емью́,** *num.* eight.

во́с|емьдесят, ьми́десяти, *num.* eighty.

вос|емьсо́т, ьмисо́т, емьюста́ми (*coll.* **ьмиста́ми**)**,** *num.* eight hundred.

во́семью, *adv.* eight times (*in multiplication*).

воск, а, *m.* wax, beeswax; го́рный в. (*min.*) ozocerite.

воскли́кн|уть, у, ешь, *pf.* to exclaim.

восклица́ни|е, я, *n.* exclamation.

восклица́тельный, *adj.* exclamatory; в. знакъ exclamation mark.

восклица́|ть, ю, *impf.* (*of* воскликнуть) to exclaim.

воско́вк|а, и, *f.* wax-paper; stencil (*for use in duplicating machine, etc.*).

воско́в|о́й, *adj.* wax, waxen; ~а́я свѣча́ wax candle; ~а́я бума́га greaseproof paper; ~о́е лицо́ waxen complexion.

воскрес|а́ть, а́ю, *impf.* (*of* ~нуть) to rise again, rise from the dead; (*fig.*) to revive.

воскресе́ни|е, я, *n.* resurrection.

воскресе́нь|е, я, *n.* Sunday.

воскре|си́ть, шу́, си́шь, *pf.* (*of* ~ша́ть) to raise from the dead, resurrect; (*fig.*) to resurrect, revive; о́тдыхъ ~си́лъ его́ си́лы the rest revived his energies; в. ста́рый обы́чай to resurrect an old custom.

воскре́сник, а, *m.* voluntary Sunday work.

воскре́с|нуть, ну, нешь, *past* ~, ~ла, *pf. of* ~а́ть.

воскре́сн|ый, *adj.* Sunday.

воскреша́|ть, ю, *impf. of* воскреси́ть.

воскреше́ни|е, я, *n.* raising from the dead, resurrection; (*fig.*) revival.

воскур|и́ть, ю́, ~ишь, *pf.* (*of* ~я́ть) (*obs.*) to burn (*incense*); в. фимиа́мъ кому́-н. to sing one's praises.

воскур|я́ть, я́ю, *impf. of* ~и́ть.

вослѣ́д = вслѣд.

воспалѣ́ни|е, я, *n.* (*med.*) inflammation; в. брюши́ны peritonitis; в. кишо́къ enteritis; в. лёгкихъ pneumonia; в. по́чекъ nephritis; ро́жистое в. erysipelas.

воспалён|ный (~, ~а́), *p.p.p. of* воспали́ть *and adj.* sore; inflamed (*also fig.*); ~ное воображе́ние fevered imagination.

воспали́тельный, *adj.* (*med.*) inflammatory; в. процéссъ inflammation.

воспал|и́ть, ю́, и́шь, *pf.* (*of* ~я́ть) to inflame.

воспал|и́ться, ю́сь, и́шься, *pf.* (*of* ~я́ться) to become inflamed; (+*i.*; *obs.*) to become inflamed (with), be on fire (with); в. гнѣ́вомъ to flare up with rage.

воспал|я́ть(ся), я́ю(сь), *impf. of* ~и́ть(ся).

воспар|и́ть, ю́, и́шь, *pf.* (*of* ~я́ть) (*poet.*) to soar; в. ду́хомъ (*iron.*) to be carried away.

воспар|я́ть, я́ю, *impf. of* воспари́ть.

воспева́|ть, ю, *impf. of* воспѣ́ть.

восп|ѣ́ть, ою́, оёшь, *pf.* (*of* ~ева́ть) (*poet.*) to sing (of), hymn; в. по́двиги наро́дныхъ геро́евъ to sing of the deeds of national heroes.

воспита́ни|е, я, *n.* 1. education; upbringing. 2. (good) breeding.

воспи́танник, а, *m.* 1. pupil; в. сре́дней шко́лы secondary schoolboy. 2. ward (*a minor*).

воспи́танност|ь, и, *f.* (good) breeding.

воспи́танный, *p.p.p. of* воспита́ть *and adj.* well brought up.

воспита́тел|ь, я, *m.* tutor, educator.

воспита́тельниц|а, ы, *f.* governess.

воспита́тельный, *adj.* educational; в. домъ foundling hospital.

воспит|а́ть, а́ю, *pf.* (*of* ~ывать) 1. to educate, bring up. 2. to cultivate, foster; в. са́мые хоро́шие накло́нности въ комъ-н. to bring out the best in someone. 3. (из+*g.*) to make (of); в. солда́тъ изъ сбро́да to make an army of a rabble.

воспи́тыва|ть, ю, *impf. of* воспита́ть.

воспламенѣ́ни|е, я, *n.* ignition.

воспламен|и́ть, ю́, и́шь, *pf.* (*of* ~я́ть) to kindle, ignite; (*fig.*) to fire, inflame; егó слова́ ~и́ли воображе́ние his words fired the imagination of the audience.

воспламен|и́ться, ю́сь, и́шься, *pf.* (*of* ~я́ться) to catch fire, ignite; (*fig.*) to take fire, flare up.

воспламеня́емост|ь, и, *f.* inflammability.

воспламеня́емый, *adj.* inflammable.

воспламеня́|ть(ся), ю(сь), *impf. of* воспламени́ть(ся).

воспо́лн|ить, ю, ишь, *pf.* to fill in; в. пробѣ́лы свои́хъ зна́ний to fill in the gaps in one's knowledge.

восполня́|ть, ю, *impf. of* воспо́лнить.

воспо́льз|оваться, уюсь, *pf. of* по́льзоваться.

воспомина́ни|е, я, *n.* 1. recollection, memory; жить ~ями to live on memories; отъ егó иму́щества оста́лось одно́ в. of his possessions nothing is left. 2. *pl.* (*lit.*) memoirs; reminiscences.

воспослѣ́д|овать, ую, *pf.* (*obs.*) to follow, ensue; ~овалъ цѣ́лый рядъ несча́стныхъ слу́чаев a whole chapter of accidents ensued.

восп|ою́, оёшь, *see* ~ёть.

воспрепя́тств|овать, ую, *pf. of* препя́тствовать.

воспрети́тельный, *adj.* prohibitive.

воспре|ти́ть, щу́, ти́шь, *pf.* (*of* ~ща́ть) (+*a. or inf.*) to forbid, prohibit; в. вход to prohibit entry; в. разгова́ривать за столо́м to forbid talking at meals.

воспреща́|ть, ю, *impf. of* воспрети́ть.

воспреща́|ться, юсь, *impf.* to be prohibited; кури́ть ~ется no smoking; посторо́нним вход ~ется unauthorized persons not admitted.

воспреще́ни|е, я, *n.* prohibition.

восприе́мник, а, *m.* godfather.

восприе́мниц|а, ы, *f.* godmother.

восприи́мчив|ый (~, ~а), *adj.* **1.** receptive; impressionable. **2.** susceptible; он о́чень ~ к на́сморку he is very susceptible to colds.

восприм|у́, ~ешь, *see* восприня́ть.

воспринима́ем|ый (~, ~а), *adj.* perceptible.

воспринима́|ть, ю, *impf. of* восприня́ть.

воспри|ня́ть, му́, ~мешь, *past* ~ня́л, ~няла́, ~няло, *pf.* (*of* ~нима́ть) **1.** to perceive, apprehend; to grasp, take in. **2.** to take (for), interpret; в. молча́ние как знак согла́сия to take silence as a mark of consent. **3.** в. от купе́ли (*eccl.*) to stand godfather, godmother (to).

восприя́ти|е, я, *n.* (*philos., psych.*) perception.

воспроизведе́ни|е, я, *n.* reproduction; в. челове́ческого ро́да reproduction of the human species; ве́рное в. карти́ны Ру́бенса faithful reproduction of a painting by Rubens.

воспроизве|сти́, ду́, дёшь, *past* ~л, ~ла́, *pf.* (*of* воспроизводи́ть) (*in var. senses*) to reproduce; в. в па́мяти to recall; в. по́длинный докуме́нт to reproduce an original document; он то́лько ~л утвержде́ния профе́ссора he merely echoed the professor's statements.

воспроизводи́тельный, *adj.* reproductive.

воспроизво|ди́ть, жу́, ~дишь, *impf. of* воспроизвести́.

воспроизво́дств|о, а, *n.* (*econ.*) reproduction.

воспроти́в|иться, люсь, ишься, *pf. of* проти́виться.

воспря́н|уть, у, ешь, *pf.* **1.** (*obs.*) to leap up. **2.** (*coll.*) to cheer up; в. ду́хом to take heart.

воспыла́|ть, ю, *pf.* (+*i.*) to be inflamed (with); to blaze (with); в. гне́вом to blaze with anger; в. любо́вью (к+*d.*) to be smitten with love (for).

воссе́да|ть, ю, *impf. of* воссе́сть.

восс|е́сть, я́ду, я́дешь, *past* ~е́л, *pf.* to sit

(*in state, formally*); в. на престо́л to mount the throne.

восслáв|ить, лю, ишь, *pf.* (*of* ~ля́ть) (*obs.*) to hymn, praise.

восславля́|ть, ю, *impf. of* восслáвить.

воссоедине́ни|е, я, *n.* reunion, reunification.

воссоедин|и́ть, ю́, и́шь, *pf.* (*of* ~я́ть) to reunite.

воссоединя́|ть, ю, *impf. of* воссоедини́ть.

воссозда|ва́ть, ю́, ёшь, *impf. of* ~ть.

воссозда́ни|е, я, *n.* reconstruction.

воссоз|да́ть, да́м, да́шь, да́ст, дади́м, дади́те, даду́т, *past* ~да́л, ~дала́, ~да́ло, *pf.* (*of* ~дава́ть) to reconstruct, reconstitute; он ~да́л в кни́ге собы́тия Троя́нской войны́ in his book he has reconstructed the events of the Trojan War.

восста|ва́ть, ю́, ёшь, *impf. of* ~ть.

восстáв|ить, лю, ишь, *pf.* (*obs.*) to set up, erect; в. перпендикуля́р (*math.*) to raise a perpendicular.

восставля́|ть, ю, *impf. of* восстáвить.

восстанáвлива|ть, ю, *impf. of* восстанови́ть.

восстáни|е, я, *n.* rising, insurrection.

восстанови́тел|ь, я, *m.* **1.** renovator, restorer. **2.** restorative (*for hair*).

восстанови́тельный, *adj.* of restoration, reconstruction.

восстанов|и́ть, лю́, ~ишь, *pf.* (*of* восстанáвливать) **1.** to restore, renew; to rehabilitate; в. мир to restore peace; в. хозя́йство страны́ to restore the economy of a country; в. в па́мяти to recall, recollect; в. кого́-н. в права́х to restore someone's rights, rehabilitate; его́ ~и́ли в до́лжности заве́дующего he has been reinstated as manager. **2.** (про́тив+*g.*) to set (against); они́ ~и́ли сосе́дей про́тив себя́ свое́й гру́бостью they have set their neighbours against them by their rudeness. **3.** (*chem.*) to reduce.

восстановле́ни|е, я, *n.* **1.** restoration, renewal; rehabilitation; в. в права́х restoration of rights, rehabilitation; в. в до́лжности reinstatement. **2.** (*chem.*) reduction.

восстановля́|ть, ю, *impf.* **1.** of восстанови́ть. **2.** (*chem.*) to reduce.

восстá|ть, ну, нешь, *imp.* ~нь, *pf.* (*of* ~ва́ть) **1.** (*obs.*) to rise (up). **2.** (на+*a.*, про́тив +*g.*) to rise (against); (*fig.*) to be up in arms (against), fly in the face (of); всё дереве́нское населе́ние ~ло на врага́ the whole countryside rose against the enemy; вы ~ли про́тив здра́вого смы́сла you are flying in the face of the dictates of common sense.

воссыла́|ть, ю, *impf.* (*obs.*) to offer up, send up.

восто́к, а, *m.* **1.** east; на в., с ~а to, from the east. **2.** В. the East; Бли́жний В. the

Near East; Сре́дний В. the Middle East; Да́льний В. the Far East.

востокове́д, а, *m.* orientalist.

востокове́дени|е, я, *n.* oriental studies.

востокове́дный, *adj.* of oriental studies.

востокове́д|ческий, *adj.* = ~ный.

восто́рг, а, *m.* delight; rapture; быть в ~е (от+*g.*) to be delighted (with); приходи́ть в в. (от+*g.*) to go into raptures (over).

восторга́|ть, ю, *impf.* to delight, enrapture.

восторга́|ться, юсь, *impf.* (+*i.*) to be delighted (with); to go into, be in raptures (over); она́ ~ется бале́том she goes into raptures over the ballet.

восто́рженност|ь, и, *f.* 1. enthusiasm. 2. proneness to enthusiasm.

восто́ржен|ный (~, ~на), *adj.* enthusiastic, full of lofty enthusiasm; ~ная голова́ exalté; в. приём enthusiastic reception; его́ нове́йшая пье́са получи́ла ~ные о́тзывы his latest play has received enthusiastic comment.

восторжеств|ова́ть, у́ю, *pf. of* торжествова́ть.

восто́чник, а, *m.* (*coll.*) orientalist.

восто́чн|ый, *adj.* east, eastern; oriental; ~ая це́рковь the Eastern Church.

востре́бовани|е, я, *n.* claiming, demand; до ~я to be called for, on demand; посла́ть паке́т до ~я to send a parcel to be called for, send a parcel poste restante.

востре́б|овать, ую, *pf.* to claim, call for (*from post-office, etc.*).

вострепе|та́ть, щу́, ~щешь, *pf.* (*obs.*) to begin to tremble.

востро́, *adv.* (*coll.*) держа́ть у́хо в. to keep a sharp look-out.

вострогла́зый, *adj.* (*coll.*) sharp-eyed; bright-eyed.

востроно́сый, *adj.* (*coll.*) sharp-nosed.

во́ст|рый (~ёр, ~ра́, ~ро), *adj.* (*dial.*) sharp.

восхвале́ни|е, я, *n.* eulogy.

восхвал|и́ть, ю́, ~ишь, *pf.* (*of* ~я́ть) to laud, extol, eulogize.

восхваля́|ть, ю, *impf. of* восхвали́ть.

восхити́тел|ьный (~ен, ~ьна), *adj.* entrancing, ravishing; delightful; delicious; ~ьная пе́сня an entrancing song; из рестора́на нёсся в. за́пах a delicious smell came from the restaurant.

восхи|ти́ть, щу, тишь, *pf.* (*poet., obs.*) to carry away.

восхи|ти́ть, щу́, ти́шь, *pf.* (*fig.*) to carry away, delight, enrapture; красота́ италья́нских озёр его́ ~ти́ла he was carried away by the beauty of the Italian lakes.

восхи|ти́ться, щу́сь, ти́шься, *pf.* (+*i.*) to be carried away (by); to admire; все

~ти́лись его́ хра́бростью his courage was the admiration of all.

восхища́|ть(ся, ю(сь), *impf. of* восхити́ть(ся).

восхище́ни|е, я, *n.* delight, rapture; admiration.

восхищён|ный (~, ~á), *p.p.p. of* восхити́ть *and adj.* rapt; admiring; в. взгляд rapt gaze.

восхи́|щу, тишь, *see* ~ти́ть.

восхи|щу́(сь), ти́шь(ся), *see* ~ти́ть(ся).

восхо́д, а, *m.* 1. rising; в. со́лнца sunrise. 2. (*obs.*) the east.

восхо|ди́ть, жу́, ~дишь, *impf.* 1. *impf. of* взойти́. 2. (*impf. only*) (к) to go back (to), date (from); в. к дре́вности to go back to antiquity.

восход|я́щий, *pres. part. of* ~и́ть *and adj.* ~я́щая звезда́, ~я́щее свети́ло (*fig.*) rising star; ~я́щее поколе́ние rising generation; ~я́щая интона́ция (*ling.*), ~я́щее ударе́ние (*mus.*) rising intonation.

восхожде́ни|е, я, *n.* ascent; в. на Монбла́н the ascent of Mont Blanc.

восчу́вств|овать, ую, *pf.* (*obs. or iron.*) to feel.

восше́стви|е, я, *n.* (на престо́л) accession (to the throne).

восьм|а́я, *see* ~о́й.

восьмери́чн|ый, *adj.* eightfold; и ~ое name of letter 'и' in old Russian orthography.

восьмёрк|а, и, *f.* 1. (*coll.*) eight; number eight (*of 'buses, etc.*). 2. (*cards*) eight; в. черве́й eight of hearts. 3. eight (*boat*). 4. figure of eight.

во́сьмер|о, ы́х, *num.* 1. eight; нас бы́ло в. there were eight of us; в. сане́й eight sledges. 2. eight pairs; в. перча́ток eight pairs of gloves.

восьми́- eight-, octo-.

восьмивесе́льный, *adj.* eight-oared.

восьмигра́нник, а, *m.* (*math.*) octahedron.

восьмидесятиле́тний, *adj.* 1. of eighty years; в. юбиле́й eightieth anniversary. 2. eighty-year-old.

восьмидеся́тник, а, *m.* 'man of the eighties' (*of nineteenth century*).

восьмидеся́тый, *adj.* eightieth.

восьмикла́ссник, а, *m.* pupil of eighth form.

восьмикла́ссниц|а, ы, *f. of* восьмикла́ссник.

восьмикра́тный, *adj.* eightfold; octuple.

восьмиле́тний, *adj.* 1. eight-year. 2. eight--year-old.

восьмино́г, а, *m.* (*zool.*) octopus.

восьмисо́тый, *adj.* eight-hundredth.

восьмисти́ши|е, я, *n.* (*lit.*) octave, octet.

восьмисто́пный, *adj.* (*lit.*) eight-foot, octonarian.

восьмиуго́льник, а, *m.* (*math.*) octagon.

восьмиуго́льный, *adj.* octagonal.

восьмичасово́й, *adj.* eight-hour; в. рабо́чий день eight-hour (working-)day.

восьм|о́й, *adj.* eighth; *as noun* ~а́я, ~о́й, *f.* (*in var. senses*) an eighth.

восьму́шк|а, и, *f.* 1. (*coll.*) eighth of a pound (*in weight*). 2. octavo; писа́ть на ~е to write on octavo.

вот, *particle* 1. here (is), there (is); this is; в. мой дом here is my house, this is my house; в. авто́бус here's, there's the 'bus; в. авто́бус идёт here comes the 'bus; в. и я here I am; в. мы пришли́ here we are; в. где я живу́ this is where I live. 2. (*emphasizing pronouns*; *unstressed*) в. э́ти ту́фли ей нра́вились *these* are the shoes she liked; в. ему́ я бы э́того не поруча́л I would not trust *him* with this. 3. (*in exclamations*; *always stressed*) here's a . . ., there's a . . . (for you); в́. тип! there's a character (for you)!; в́. так исто́рия! here's a pretty kettle of fish!; (*expressing surprise*) в́. как!, в́. что! really? you don't mean to say so!; слы́шали ли вы но́вость? коро́ль у́мер. В. как! have you heard the news? the king is dead. No! (not) really?; в. так та́к!, в. тебе́ на́! well!; well, I never!; говоря́т, что Пётр обручи́лся с Ли́зой. В. так та́к! they say Peter and Elizabeth are engaged. Well!; (*surprise and disapproval*) в́. ещё! indeed!; what(ever) next!; good heavens!; не дашь ли мне пять фу́нтов взаймы́? ну, в. ещё! will you lend me five pounds? well, what next!; (*approval and/or encouragement*) в. та́к!, в.-в.! that's right!; that's it!; (*accompanying blows*) в́. тебе́! take that!; в́. тебе́, в́. тебе́! take that, and that!; (*expressing disagreeable surprise at unwelcome turn of events or at non--occurrence of expected event*) вот тебе́ и... so much for . . .; вот тебе́ и пое́здка в Пари́ж! so much for the trip to Paris!, we've (you've, *etc.*) had the trip to Paris!

вот-во́т, *adv.* just, on the point of; вода́ в.-в. закипи́т the water is just boiling, is on the boil; по́езд в.-в. придёт the train is just coming.

воти́р|овать, ую, *impf. and pf.* to vote (for); в. увеличе́ние дота́ций студе́нтам to vote an increase of students' grants.

вотиро́вк|а, и, *f.* voting.

вотк|а́ть, у́, ёшь, *past* ~а́л, ~ала́, ~а́ло, *pf.* to interweave.

воткн|у́ть, у́, ёшь, *pf.* (*of* втыка́ть) (в+*a.*) to stick (into), drive (into); в. кол в зе́млю to drive a stake into the ground; она́ ~у́ла ему́ гвозди́ку в петли́цу she stuck a carnation in his buttonhole.

вотр|у́, ёшь, *see* втере́ть.

во́тский, *adj.* Votyak.

во́тум, а, *no pl.*, *m.* vote; в. (не)дове́рия (+*d.*) vote of (no) confidence (in).

во́тчин|а, ы, *f.* (*hist.*) inherited estate, lands; allodium, patrimony (*in Muscovite Russia as opp. to* поме́стье).

во́тчинник, а, *m.* (*hist.*) great landowner (*in Muscovite Russia*).

во́тчинный, *adj.* (*hist.*) allodial, patrimonial.

вотще́, *adv.* (*obs.*) in vain, to no purpose.

вотя́к, а́, *m.* Votyak (*former name of Udmurt*).

вотя́цкий, *adj.* = во́тский.

вотя́чк|а, и, *f.* Votyak (woman).

воцаре́ни|е, я, *n.* accession (to the throne).

воцар|и́ться, ю́сь, и́шься, *pf.* (*of* ~я́ться) 1. to come to the throne. 2. (*fig.*) to set in; в лесу́ ~и́лась тишина́ in the forest silence fell.

воцаря́|ться, ю́сь, *impf. of* воцари́ться.

вочелове́чени|е, я, *n.* (*theol.*) incarnation.

вочелове́ч|иться, усь, ишься, *pf.* (*theol.*) to become man, be incarnate.

вош|ёл, ла́, *see* войти́.

во́шк|а, и, *f.* (*coll.*) louse.

вошь, вши, *i.* ~ю, *pl.* вши, вшей, *f.* louse.

вощанк|а, и, *f.* 1. wax-paper; waxed cloth. 2. cobbler's wax. 3. stencil.

вощано́й, *adj.* wax.

вощёный, *adj.* waxed.

вощи́н|а, ы, *f.* 1. (*collect.*) empty honeycomb. 2. unrefined beeswax.

вощ|и́ть, у́, и́шь, *impf.* (*of* на~) to wax; to polish with wax.

во́|ю, ешь, *see* выть.

вою́|ю, ешь, *see* воева́ть.

воя́ж, а, *m.* (*obs. or iron.*) journey, travels.

вояжёр, а, *m.* 1. (*obs. or iron.*) traveller. 2. commercial traveller.

воя́к|а, и, *m.* (*coll., iron.*) warrior; fire-eater.

впада́|ть, ю, *impf.* 1. *impf. of* впасть. 2. *impf. only* (*of rivers*) to fall (into), flow (into); Ока́ ~ет в Во́лгу the Oka flows into the Volga. 3. *impf. only* (в+*a.*) to verge (on), approximate (to).

впаде́ни|е, я, *n.* confluence; mouth (*of rivers*).

впа́дин|а, ы, *f.* cavity, hollow; глазна́я в. eye-socket.

впад|у́, ёшь, *see* впасть.

впа́ива|ть, ю, *impf. of* впая́ть.

впа́йк|а, и, *f.* 1. soldering-in. 2. soldered-in piece.

впа́л|ый, *adj.* hollow, sunken; ~ые щёки hollow cheeks.

впа|сть, ду́, дёшь, *pf.* (*of* ~да́ть) 1. (в+*a.*) to fall (into), lapse (into), sink (into); в. в бе́дность to fall into penury; в. в грех to lapse into sin: в. в де́тство to sink into dotage; в. в неми́лость to fall into disgrace. 2. (*of eyes, cheeks*) to fall in, sink.

впа|я́ть, я́ю, *pf.* (*of* ~ивать) to solder in.

впервИ́нку, *adv.* (*coll.*) for the first time;

ему́ не в. éхать в Росси́ю it is not the first time he has been to Russia.

впер|о́й, *adv.* (*coll.*) = ~ы́е.

впервы́е, *adv.* for the first time, first; семи́десяти лет он в. полетéл на самолёте at the age of seventy he went in an aeroplane for the first time; когдá в. я приéхал в Ло́ндон when I first came to London.

вперевáлку, *adv.* (*coll.*) ходи́ть в. to waddle.

вперегóнки, *adv.* (*coll.*) бéгать в. to run races.

вперёд, *adv.* **1.** forward(s), ahead; (*of clocks and watches*) fast; взад и в. back and forth; большо́й шаг в. (*fig.*) a big step forward; рáзве вáши часы́ не иду́т в.? surely your watch is fast?; в.! (*mil. command*) forward! **2.** in future, henceforward; в. будь осторо́жнее be more careful in future. **3.** in advance; заплати́ть в. to pay in advance; дать очки́ в. (*sport*) to give points; дав мне пять очко́в в., он всё-таки вы́играл he gave me five points and still won.

впереди́ 1. *adv.* in front, ahead. **2.** *adv.* in (the) future; ahead. **3.** *prep.*+*g.* in front of, before; лейтенáнт марширо́вал в. взвóда the lieutenant marched at the head of the platoon.

вперемéжку, *adv.* (*coll.*) alternately; на парáде солдáты и моряки́ шли в. soldiers and sailors alternated in the parade.

вперемéшку, *adv.* (*coll.*) pell-mell, higgledy--piggledy; in confusion; все его́ вéщи лежáли в. на полу́ ко́мнаты all his things lay in confusion on the floor of the room.

впер|éть, вопру́, вопрёшь, *past* ~, ~лá, *pf.* (*of* впирáть) (*coll.*) **1.** to barge in; он про́сто ~ в дом, не дождáвшись приглашéния he simply barged into the house without waiting to be invited. **2.** to shove in, thrust in.

впер|éться, вопру́сь, вопрёшься, *past* ~ся, ~лась, *pf.* (*of* впирáться) (*coll.*) to barge in.

впер|и́ть, ю́, и́шь, *pf.* (*of* ~я́ть) (в+*a.*) to direct (upon); в. взор to fasten one's gaze (upon).

впер|и́ться, ю́сь, и́шься, *pf.* (*of* ~я́ться) (*coll.*) to stare (at), fasten one's eyes (upon).

вперя́|ть(ся), ю(сь), *impf. of* впери́ть(ся).

впечатлéни|е, я, *n.* impression; ~я дéтства childhood impressions; произвести́ в. (на +*a.*) to make an impression (upon); его́ речь произвелá в. на всех his speech made an impression on all; у меня́ создáлось в., что онá недово́льна I formed the impression that she was dissatisfied.

впечатли́тельност|ь, и, *f.* impression-ability.

впечатли́тел|ьный (~ен, ~ьна), *adj.* impressionable.

впечатля́|ющий, *adj.* impressive.

впивá|ть, ю, *impf.* **1.** *impf. of* впить. **2.** *impf. only* to drink in, enjoy (*esp. olfactory sensations*).

впивá|ться¹, юсь, *impf. of* впи́ться¹.

впивá|ться², юсь, *impf. of* впи́ться².

впирá|ть(ся), ю(сь), *impf. of* вперéть(ся).

впи́санный, *p.p.p. of* вписáть *and adj.* (*math.*) inscribed.

впи|сáть, шу́, ~шешь, *pf.* (*of* ~сывать) **1.** to enter; to insert; в. своё и́мя в спи́сок to enter one's name on a list; в. фрáзу в ру́копись статьи́ to insert a sentence into the manuscript of an article. **2.** (*math.*) to inscribe.

впи|сáться, шу́сь, ~шешься, *pf.* (*of* ~сываться) (*coll.*) to be enrolled, join.

впи́ск|а, и, *f.* (*coll.*) **1.** entry. **2.** insertion; страни́ца былá полнá впи́сок the page was full of insertions.

впи́сыва|ть(ся), ю(сь), *impf. of* вписáть(ся).

впит|áть, áю, *pf.* (*of* ~ывать) to absorb; (*fig.*) to absorb, take in; за удиви́тельно коро́ткий срок он ~áл в себя́ всю филосо́фию Кáнта in an amazingly short time he had absorbed the whole of Kant's philosophy.

впит|áться, áюсь, *pf.* (*of* ~ывáться) (в+*a.*) to soak (into).

впи́тыва|ть(ся), ю(сь), *impf. of* впитáть(ся).

впи|ть, вопью́, вопьёшь, *past* ~л, ~лá, ~ло, *pf.* (*of* ~вáть) to imbibe, absorb.

впи|ться¹, вопью́сь, вопьёшься, *past* ~лся, ~лась, *pf.* (*of* ~вáться) (в+*a.*) **1.** to stick (into); to bite; to sting; ко́шка ~лась в неё когтя́ми the cat stuck its claws into her; вáша собáка ~лась мне в но́гу your dog has bitten me in the leg; гвоздь ~лся мне в но́гу a nail stuck into my foot. **2.** в. взо́ром, глазáми to fix, fasten one's eyes (upon).

впи|ться², вопью́сь, вопьёшься, *past* ~лся, ~лась, *pf.* (*coll.*) to become hardened to drink.

впих|áть, áю, *pf.* (*coll.*) = ~ну́ть.

впи́хива|ть, ю, *impf. of* впихáть *and* впихну́ть.

впих|ну́ть, ну́, нёшь, *pf.* (*of* ~ивать) to stuff in, cram in; to shove; в. кого́-н. в ко́мнату to shove someone into a room.

вплавь, *adv.* swimming; каки́м о́бразом перепрáвился он чéрез рéку? в. how did he get across the river? he swam it.

вплé|сти, ту́, тёшь, *past* ~л, ~лá, *pf.* (*of* ~тáть) (в+*a.*) to plait (into), intertwine; (*fig., coll.*) to involve (in); вы ~ли меня́ в хоро́шенькое дéло you have got me into a fine mess.

вплетá|ть, ю, *impf. of* вплести́.

вплé|ту́, тёшь, *see* ~сти́.

вплотну́ю, *adv.* close; (*fig.*) in (real) earnest;

поста́вить стол в. к стене́ to put the table right against the wall; приня́ться за де́ло в. to get to grips with the matter, tackle the matter in real earnest.

вплоть, *adv.* 1. в. до (right) up to; он шути́л в. до моме́нта ка́зни he was joking right up to the moment of his execution; мы танцева́ли в. до утра́ we danced till morning; всё живо́е исче́зло, в. до крыс every living thing had vanished, even the rats. 2. в. (к+*d.*) right against, right up to; толпа́ подошла́ в. к воро́там the crowd came right up to the gates.

вплыва́|ть, ю, *impf. of* вплыть.

вплы|ть, ву́, вёшь, *past* ~л, ~ла́, ~ло, *pf.* (*of* ~ва́ть) to swim in; to sail in, steam in.

впова́лку, *adv.* (*coll.*) side by side (*in prone position; only of human beings*).

вполгла́за, *adv.* (*coll.*) спать в. to sleep with one eye open.

вполго́лоса, *adv.* in an undertone, under one's breath.

вполз|а́ть, а́ю, *impf. of* ~ти́.

вполз|ти́, у́, ёшь, *past* ~, ~ла́, *pf.* (*of* ~а́ть) to creep in, crawl in; to creep up, crawl up.

вполне́, *adv.* fully, entirely; quite; э́то в. доста́точно that is quite enough; он в. знако́м с пра́вилами игры́ he is perfectly familiar with the rules of the game; он в. понима́ет, в како́й он опа́сности he is quite aware of his danger.

вполоборо́та, *adv.* half-turned; (*of a portrait, etc.*) half-face.

вполови́ну, *adv.* (*coll.*) by half; за две неде́ли коли́чество прису́тствующих уменьши́лось в. after two weeks the attendance had dropped by half.

вполпьяна́, *adv.* (*coll.*) half seas over.

впопа́д, *adv.* (*coll.*) to the point; opportunely; вы спроси́ли о́чень в. your question was very much to the point.

впопыха́х, *adv.* (*coll.*) 1. in a hurry, hastily. 2. in one's haste; в. я оста́вил мой зо́нтик в по́езде in my haste I left my umbrella on the train.

впо́ру, *adv.* (*coll.*) 1. at the right time, opportunely; его́ прие́зд был о́чень в. his arrival was very opportune. 2. just right, exactly; быть, прийти́сь в. to fit; э́тот костю́м мне соверше́нно в. this suit fits me perfectly; бе́дному да во́ру вся́кое пла́тье в. (*prov.*) beggars cannot be choosers. 3. *as pred.* it is possible; так поступа́ть в. лишь дураку́ only a fool would behave like that; тут в. двоим спра́виться there is enough work here for two.

впорхн|у́ть, у́, ёшь, *pf.* (*of birds or butterflies*) to flit in(to), flutter in(to); (*fig.*) to fly (into).

впосле́дствии, *adv.* subsequently; afterwards.

впотьма́х, *adv.* (*coll.*) in the dark; (*fig.*) броди́ть в. to be in the dark.

впра́вду, *adv.* (*coll.*) really, in reality.

впра́ве, *as pred.* быть в. (+*inf.*) to have a right (to); он был в. серди́ться на вас he had a right to be angry with you.

впра́в|ить, лю, ишь, *pf.* (*of* ~ля́ть) 1. (*med.*) to set, reduce (*fractured or dislocated bone*). 2. to tuck in (*shirt, trousers*).

впра́вк|а, и, f. (*med.*) setting, reduction.

вправля́|ть, ю, *impf. of* впра́вить.

впра́во, *adv.* (от+*g.*) to the right (of).

впредь, *adv.* in future, henceforward; в. до until; в. до конца́ ме́сяца until the end of the month; в. до распоряже́ния until further notice.

впригля́дку, *adv.* (*coll., joc.*) *only in phrase* пить чай в. to have tea without sugar.

вприку́ску, *adv.* (*coll.*) *only in phrase* пить чай в. to drink unsweetened tea while holding a piece of loaf sugar in the mouth (*as opp. to* внакла́дку).

вприпры́жку, *adv.* (*coll.*) skipping; hopping.

вприся́дку, *adv.* пляса́ть в. to dance squatting.

впро́голодь, *adv.* half-starving.

впрок, *adv.* 1. for future use; заготови́ть в. to lay in, store; to preserve, put by; заготови́ть я́йца в. to put down eggs. 2. to advantage; э́то не пойдёт ему́ в. it will not profit him, he will do no good by it; ху́до на́житое в. не идёт (*prov.*) ill-gotten wealth never thrives.

впроса́к, *adv.* (*coll.*); попа́сть в. to put one's foot into it.

впросо́нках, *adv.* (*coll.*) half asleep.

впро́чем, *conj.* 1. however, but; он у́мный челове́к, в. он ча́сто ошиба́ется he is a clever man, but he often makes mistakes. 2. (*expressing indecisiveness, revision of opinion*) or rather; приезжа́йте за́втра, в. лу́чше бы́ло бы послеза́втра come tomorrow, or rather, the day after would be better.

впры́гива|ть, ю, *impf. of* впры́гнуть.

впры́г|нуть, ну, нешь, *pf.* (*of* ~ивать) (в, на+*a.*) to jump (into, on).

впры́скивани|е, я, n. injection.

впры́скива|ть, ю, *impf. of* впры́снуть.

впры́сн|уть, у, ешь, *pf.* (*of* впры́скивать) to inject.

впряга́|ть(ся), ю(сь), *impf. of* впрячь(ся).

впрямь, *adv.* (*coll.*) really, indeed.

впря|чь, гу́, жёшь, гу́т, *past* впряг, ~гла́, ~гло, *pf.* (*of* ~га́ть) (в+*a.*) to harness (to), put (to).

впря́|чься, гу́сь, жёшься, гу́тся, *past* впря́гся, ~гла́сь, *pf.* (*of* ~га́ться) 1. (в+*a.*) to harness oneself (to). 2. *pass. of* ~чь.

впуск, а, m. admission, admittance.

впуска́|ть, ю, *impf. of* впусти́ть.

впускн|óй, *adj.* admittance; inlet; ~áя трубá inlet pipe.

впýсте, *adv.* (*obs.*) fallow; лежáть в. to lie fallow.

впу|стить, щý, ~стишь, *pf.* (*of* ~скáть) to admit, let in.

впустýю, *adv.* (*coll.*) for nothing, to no purpose.

впýт|ать, аю, *pf.* (*of* ~ывать) to twist in; (*fig.*) to entangle, involve, implicate.

впýт|аться, аюсь, *pf.* (*of* ~ываться) *pass. of* ~ать; (*fig.*) to get mixed up (in).

впýтыва|ть(ся), ю(сь), *impf. of* впýтать(ся).

впу|щý, ~стишь, *see* ~стить.

впя́теро, *adv.* five times; в. бóльше five times as much.

впятерóм, *adv.* five (together); в э́ту игрý мóжно игрáть в. five can play this game.

враг, á, *m.* 1. enemy; (*collect.*) the enemy. 2. (*obs.*) the Fiend, the Devil.

вражд|á, ы́, *f.* enmity, hostility.

враждéб|ный (~ен, ~на), *adj.* hostile.

вражд|овáть, ýю, *impf.* (с+*i.* and мéжду собóю) to be at enmity, at odds (with).

врáжеский, *adj.* (*mil.*) enemy.

врáж|ий, *adj.* (*folk poet.*) enemy; hostile; ~ья сила (*obs.*) Satan, the Devil.

враз, *adv.* (*coll.*) all together, simultaneously.

вразбивку, *adv.* (*coll.*) at random.

вразбрóд, *adv.* (*coll.*) separately; in disunity.

вразбрóс, *adv.* (*coll.*) separately; сéять в. (*agric.*) to sow broadcast.

вразвáлку, *adv.* (*coll.*) ходить в. to waddle.

вразнóс, *adv.* (*coll.*) торговáть в. to peddle.

вразрéз, *adv.*, *only in phrase* идти в. (с+*i.*) to go against; э́то идёт в. с мои́ми интерéсами it goes against my own interests.

вразря́дку, *adv.* (*typ.*) набрáть в. to space.

вразуми́тел|ьный (~ен, ~ьна), *adj.* 1. intelligible; perspicuous. 2. instructive.

вразум|и́ть, лю́, и́шь, *pf.* (*of* ~ля́ть) to teach, make understand; ничéм их не ~и́шь they will never learn.

вразумля́|ть, ю, *impf. of* вразуми́ть.

врáк|и, ~, *no sing.* (*coll.*) nonsense, rubbish.

врал|ь, я́, *m.* (*coll.*) liar; chatterbox.

врань|ё, я́, *n.* (*coll.*) lies; nonsense.

врасплóх, *adv.* unexpectedly, unaware; застáть, захвати́ть, засти́гнуть в. to take unawares.

врассыпнýю, *adv.* in all directions; helter-skelter.

врастáни|е, я, *n.* growing in.

враст|áть, áю, *impf.* (*of* ~и́) to grow in(to); ~áющий нóготь ingrowing nail.

враст|и́, ý, ёшь, *past* врос, врослá, *pf. of* ~áть.

врастя́жку, *adv.* (*coll.*) 1. at full length; упáсть в. to fall flat. 2. говори́ть в. to drawl.

врат|á, ~, *no sing.* (*poet.*, *obs.*) = ворóта.

вратáр|ь, я́, *m.* 1. (*sport*) goalkeeper. 2. (*obs.*) gate-keeper.

вр|ать, у, ёшь, *past* ~ал, ~алá, ~áло, *impf.* (*of* на~ *and* со~) (*coll.*) 1. to lie, tell lies. 2. to talk nonsense.

врач, á, *m.* doctor, physician; зубнóй в. dentist.

врачéбный, *adj.* medical.

врач|евáть, ýю, *impf.* (*of* у~) (*obs.*) to doctor, treat; (*fig.*) to heal.

вращáтельный, *adj.* rotary.

вращá|ть, ю, *impf.* to revolve, rotate; в. глазáми to roll one's eyes.

вращá|ться, юсь, *impf.* to revolve, rotate (*intrans.*); он ~ется в худóжественных кругáх he moves in artistic circles.

вращéни|е, я, *n.* rotation; revolution.

вред, á, *no pl.*, *m.* harm, hurt, injury; damage; без ~á (для+*g.*) without detriment (to).

вреди́тел|ь, я, *m.* 1. (*agric.*) pest; vermin. 2. (*polit.*) wrecker, saboteur.

вреди́тель|ский, *adj. of* ~ 2.

вреди́тельств|о, а, *n.* 1. wrecking, sabotage. 2. act of sabotage.

вре|ди́ть, жý, ди́шь, *impf.* (*of* по~) (+*d.*) to injure, harm, hurt; в. здорóвью to be injurious to health.

врéдно, *adv. as pred.* it is harmful, it is injurious; в. для торгóвли it is bad for trade.

врéд|ный (~ен, ~нá, ~но), *adj.* harmful, injurious; unhealthy.

врé|жу(сь), жешь(ся), *see* ~зать(ся).

вре|жý, ди́шь, *see* ~ди́ть.

врé|зать, жу, жешь, *pf.* (*of* ~зáть) to cut in; to set in, socket.

врез|áть, áю, *impf. of* ~áть.

врé|заться, жусь, жешься, *pf.* (*of* ~зáться) (в+*a.*) 1. to cut (into); to force one's way (into); в. в зéмлю to dig into the ground; в. в толпý to run into a crowd. 2. to be engraved (on); черты́ её лицá ~зались в егó пáмять her features were engraved on his memory. 3. (*pf. only*) (*coll.*) to fall in love (with).

врез|áться, áюсь, *impf. of* ~áться.

врéзыва|ть(ся), ю(сь), *impf.* = врезáть(ся).

временáми, *adv.* at times, now and then, now and again.

временни́к, á, *m.* chronicle, annals.

временнóй, *adj.* 1. (*philos.*) temporal. 2. (*gram.*) tense. 3. (*tech.*) time.

врéменн|ый, *adj.* temporary; provisional; В~ое прави́тельство (*hist.*) the Provisional Government (*of Russia, March–November 1917*).

временщи́к, á, *m.* (*hist.*) favourite (*enjoying position of trust or power*).

врéм|я, ени, енем, ени, *pl.* ~енá, ~ён,

~ена́м, *n.* **1.** time; times; во в. о́но (*arch. or joc.*) in the old days; в да́нное в. at present, at the present moment; в ми́рное в. in peace-time; (в) пе́рвое в. at first; (в) после́днее в. lately, of late; в своё в. (*i*) (*in ref. to past*) in one's time, once, at one time; (*ii*) (*in ref. to future*) in due course; in one's own time; в ско́ром ~ени in the near future, shortly, before long; в то же (са́мое) в. at the same time, on the other hand; до поры́ до ~ени for the time being; за после́днее в. lately, of late; на в. for a while; на пе́рвое в. for the initial period, initially; по средне-европе́йскому ~ени by Central European time; с незапа́мятных ~ён from time immemorial, time out of mind; с тече́нием ~ени in the course of time; всё в. all the time, continually; ра́ньше ~ени prematurely; са́мое в. (+*inf. or* +*d.*) (*coll.*) just the time (to, for); the (right) time (to, for); апре́ль — са́мое в. побыва́ть в Пари́же April is the (right) time to be in Paris; ско́лько ~ени? what is the time?; тем ~енем meanwhile. **2.** в. го́да season. **3.** (*gram.*) tense. **4.** в то в. как while, whereas. **5.** во в. (+*g.*) during, in.

времяисчисле́ни|е, я, *n.* calendar (*system of reckoning time*).

время́нк|а, и, *f.* **1.** small stove. **2.** step-ladder. **3.** temporary structure *or* fitting.

времяпрепровожде́ние, я, *n.* way of spending one's time.

вре́тищ|е, а, *n.* (*obs.*) sackcloth.

врид, а, *m.* (*abbr. of* вре́менно исполня́ющий до́лжность) acting (*director, manager, etc.*).

вро́вень, *adv.* (с+*i.*) level (with); в. с края́ми to the brim.

вро́де **1.** *prep.* +*g.* like; у него́ есть га́лстук в. моего́ he has a tie like mine; не́что в. (*coll.*) a sort of, a kind of; оркестр на́чал игра́ть не́что в. фокстро́та the band began to play some sort of foxtrot. **2.** *particle* such as, like; весь его́ разгово́р состои́т из односло́жных слов в. «да» и «нет» his entire conversation consists of monosyllables such as 'yes' and 'no'.

врождён|ный (~, ~á), *adj.* innate; congenital.

врознь, *adv.* (*obs.*) = врозь.

врозь, *adv.* separately, apart.

вро́|ю(сь), ~ешь(ся), *see* врыть(ся).

вруб, а, *m.* (*mining*) cut.

вруб|а́ть(ся), а́ю(сь), *impf. of* ~и́ть(ся).

вруб|и́ть, лю́, ~ишь, *pf.* (*of* ~а́ть) to cut in(to).

вруб|и́ться, лю́сь, ~ишься, *pf.* (*of* ~а́ться) (в+*a.*) to cut one's way (into), hack one's way (through).

вру́бов|ый, *adj.* ~ая маши́на coal-cutter.

врукопа́шную, *adv.* hand to hand; схвати́ться в. to come to grips.

врун, á, *m.* (*coll.*) liar.

вру́нь|я, и, *f. of* врун.

вруч|а́ть, а́ю, *impf. of* ~и́ть.

вруче́ни|е, я, *n.* handing, delivery; в. солда́ту меда́ли investiture of a soldier with a medal; (*leg.*) service (*of summons, etc.*).

вруч|и́ть, у́, и́шь, *pf.* (*of* ~а́ть) to hand, deliver; to entrust; в. суде́бную пове́стку to serve a subpoena.

вручи́тел|ь, я, *m.* bearer (*of message, writ, etc.*).

вручну́ю, *adv.* by hand.

врыва́|ть, ю, *impf. of* врыть.

врыва́|ться¹, юсь, *impf. of* врыться.

врыва́|ться², юсь, *impf. of* ворва́ться.

вр|ыть, о́ю, о́ешь, *pf.* (*of* ~ыва́ть) to dig in(to), bury (in).

вр|ы́ться, о́юсь, о́ешься, *pf.* (*of* ~ыва́ться¹) to dig oneself (into), bury oneself (in).

вряд (ли), *adv.* (*coll.*) hardly, scarcely (*expressing doubt*); в. ли стои́т it is hardly worth it; в. ли они́ уже́ приду́т they will scarcely come now.

вса|ди́ть, жу́, ~дишь, *pf.* (*of* ~живать) **1.** to thrust, plunge (into); в. нож в спи́ну (+*d.*) to stab in the back (*also fig.*); в. пу́лю в лоб кому́-н. to put a bullet in someone's brains. **2.** (*coll.*) to put, sink (into); он ~ди́л весь свой капита́л в одно́ риско́ванное предприя́тие he has sunk all his capital in one doubtful venture.

вса́дник, а, *m.* **1.** rider, horseman. **2.** (*hist.*) knight.

вса́дниц|а, ы, *f.* horsewoman.

вса́жива|ть, ю, *impf. of* всади́ть.

вса|жу́, ~дишь, *see* ~ди́ть.

вса́сывани|е, я, *n.* suction; absorption.

вса́сыва|ть(ся), ю(сь), *impf. of* всоса́ть(ся).

все- all-, omni-, pan-.

всё **1.** *pron., see* весь. **2.** *adv.* always; all the time; он в. отвеча́ет одно́ и то же he always gives the same answer; он в. руга́ется he swears all the time. **3.** в. (ещё) still; дождь в. (ещё) идёт it is still raining; дождь в. (ещё) шёл it kept on raining. **4.** (*coll.*) only, all; он провали́лся на экза́мене,— в. из-за тебя́! he has failed his examination—all because of you! **5.** *as conj.* however, nevertheless; как ни стара́юсь, в. не разбира́ю, что он говори́т however hard I try, I cannot make out what he says. **6.** *as particle* (*strengthening comparative*) в. бо́лее и бо́лее more and more; он в. толсте́ет he is becoming fatter and fatter.

всеве́дени|е, я, *n.* omniscience.

всеве́дущий, *adj.* omniscient.

всеви́дящий, *adj.* all-seeing.

всевла́сти|е, я, *n.* absolute power.

всевла́стный, *adj.* all-powerful.

всевобу́ч, а, *m.* (*abbr. of* всео́бщее вое́нное обуче́ние) universal military training.

всевозмо́жный, *adj.* various; all kinds of; every possible; в. това́р goods of all kinds.

всево́лновый, *adj.* (*radio*) all-wave.

всевы́шний, *adj.* (*rel.*) the Most High (*also as noun*).

всегда́, *adv.* always; как в. as ever.

всегда́шний, *adj.* usual, customary, wonted.

всего́, *adv.* **1.** in all, all told; в. упла́чено две ты́сячи рубле́й in all two thousand roubles has been paid. **2.** only; в.-на́всего all in all; нас бы́ло в. пя́теро there were only five of us; в. ничего́ (*coll.*) practically nothing; то́лько и в. (*coll.*) that's all.

вседержи́тел|ь, я, *m.* (*rel.*) the Almighty.

вседне́вный, *adj.* (*obs.*) daily, everyday.

всезна́йк|а, и, *m. and f.* (*coll., iron.*) know-all.

всезна́йств|о, а, *n.* (*coll., iron.*) knowingness; behaviour of a know-all.

вселе́ни|е, я, *n.* installation, quartering; moving in.

вселе́нн|ая, ой, *no pl., f.* universe.

вселе́нский, *adj.* universal; (*eccl.*) ecumenical; в. собо́р ecumenical council.

всел|и́ть, ю́, и́шь, *pf.* (*of* ~я́ть) **1.** to install, quarter (in). **2.** (*fig., rhet.*) to inspire (in); в. страх (в+*a.*) to strike fear (into).

всел|и́ться, ю́сь, и́шься, *pf.* (*of* ~я́ться) (в+*a.*) **1.** to move in(to). **2.** (*fig.*) to be implanted (in); to seize.

вселя́|ть(ся), ю(сь), *impf. of* всели́ть(ся).

всеме́рный, *adj.* utmost, with all the means at one's disposal.

все́меро, *adv.* seven times.

всемеро́м, *adv.* seven (together).

всеми́лостиве́йший, *adj.* (*hist.*) most gracious.

всеми́рный, *adj.* world; world-wide.

всемогу́ществ|о, а, *n.* omnipotence.

всемогу́щ|ий (~, ~а), *adj.* omnipotent, all--powerful; (*of God*) Almighty.

всенаро́дн|ый, *adj.* national; nation-wide; ~ая пе́репись general census.

всенаро́дно, *adv.* **1.** throughout the nation. **2.** publicly.

всенижа́йший, *adj.* most humble.

всено́щн|ая, ой, *f.* (*eccl.*) night service (*vespers and matins*).

всеобу́ч, а, *m.* (*abbr. of* всео́бщее обуче́ние) universal education.

всео́бщ|ий, *adj.* general; universal; ~ая во́инская пови́нность universal military service; ~ая забасто́вка general strike.

всеобъе́млющ|ий (~, ~а), *adj.* all-embracing, comprehensive.

всеору́жи|е, я, *n. only in phrase* во ~и fully armed; во ~и све́дений in full possession of the facts.

всепоглоща́ющий, *adj.* all-consuming (*also fig.*).

всеподда́ннейш|ий, *adj.* (*obs.*) loyal, humble; ~ее проше́ние humble petition.

всепожира́ющий, *adj.* all-consuming.

всеросси́йский, *adj.* All-Russian.

всерьёз, *adv.* seriously, in earnest.

всеси́л|ьный (~ен, ~ьна), *adj.* all-powerful.

всеславя́нский, *adj.* pan-Slav(ic).

всесожже́ни|е, я, *n.* holocaust.

всесосло́вный, *adj.* of all classes.

всесою́зный, *adj.* All-Union (*esp. in designations of institutions, associations, etc., as opp. to those of individual republics of the Soviet Union*).

всесторо́нний, *adj.* all-round; thorough, detailed.

всё-таки, *conj. and particle* for all that, still, all the same.

всеуслы́шани|е, я, *n. only in phrase* во в. publicly, for all to hear; объяви́ть во в. to announce publicly.

всеце́ло, *adv.* completely; exclusively.

всеча́сный, *adj.* (*obs.*) hourly.

всея́дный, *adj.* omnivorous.

вска́кива|ть, ю, *impf. of* вскочи́ть.

вска́пыва|ть, ю, *impf. of* вскопа́ть.

вскараб́к|аться, аюсь, *pf.* (*of* кара́бкаться *and* ~иваться) (на+*a.*; *coll.*) to scramble (up, on to), clamber (up, on to).

вскара́бкива|ться, юсь, *impf. of* вскара́бкаться.

вска́рмлива|ть, ю, *impf. of* вскорми́ть.

вскачь, *adv.* at a gallop.

вски́дыва|ть(ся), ю(сь), *impf. of* вски́нуть(ся).

вски́|нуть, ну, нешь, *pf.* (*of* ~дывать) to throw up; в. на пле́чи to shoulder; в. глаза́ми to look up suddenly.

вски́|нуться, нусь, нешься, *pf.* (*of* ~дываться) (на+*a.*; *coll.*) **1.** to leap up (on to). **2.** (*fig.*) to turn (on), go (for).

вскипа́|ть, ю, *impf. of* вскипе́ть.

вскип|е́ть, лю́, и́шь, *pf.* (*of* ~а́ть) **1.** to boil up. **2.** (*fig.*) to flare up, fly into a rage; в. негодова́нием to flare with indignation.

вскипя|ти́ть, чу́, ти́шь, *pf. of* кипяти́ть.

вскипя|ти́ться, чу́сь, ти́шься, *pf.* **1.** *pass. of* вскипяти́ть **2.** (*coll.*) to flare up, fly into a rage.

всклоко́чен|ный (~, ~а), *p.p.p. of* всклоко́чить *and adj.* (*coll.*) dishevelled, tousled.

всклоко́чива|ть, ю, *impf. of* всклоко́чить.

всклоко́ч|ить, у, ишь, *pf.* (*of* ~ивать) (*coll.*) to dishevel, tousle.

вскло́чива|ть, ю, *impf. of* всклочи́ть.

всклоч|и́ть, у́, и́шь, *pf.* (*of* ~ивать) (*coll.*) to dishevel, tousle.

всколыхн|у́ть, у́, ёшь, *pf.* to stir; to rock; (*fig.*) to stir up.

вско́лыхн|у́ться, у́сь, ёшься, *pf.* to rock (*intrans.*); (*fig.*) to be roused.

вскользь, *adv.* slightly; in passing; упомяну́ть в. to mention in passing.

вскопа́|ть, ю, *pf.* (*of* вска́пывать) to dig up.

вско́ре, *adv.* soon, shortly after.

вскорм|и́ть, лю́, ~ишь, *pf.* (*of* вска́рмливать) to rear.

вскоч|и́ть, у́, ~ишь, *pf.* (*of* вска́кивать) 1. (в, на+*a.*, с+*g.*) to leap up (into, on to; from). 2. (*coll.*) to come up (*of bumps, boils, etc.*). 3. в. (в копе́ечку) (+*d.*; *coll.*) to cost dear.

вскри́кива|ть, ю, *impf. of* вскри́кнуть.

вскри́к|нуть, ну, нешь, *pf.* (*of* ~ивать) to cry out.

вскрич|а́ть, у́, и́шь, *pf.* to exclaim.

вскро́|ю, ешь, *see* вскры́ть.

вскруж|и́ть, у́, ~и́шь, *pf. only in phrase* в. го́лову кому́-н. to turn someone's head.

вскрыва́|ть(ся), ю(сь), *impf. of* вскры́ть(ся).

вскры́ти|е, я, *n.* 1. opening, unsealing. 2. (*fig.*) revelation, disclosure. 3. (*geogr.*) opening (*of rivers after break-up of ice*). 4. (*med.*) lancing. 5. (*med.*) dissection; post-mortem (examination).

вскр|ы́ть, о́ю, о́ешь, *pf.* (*of* ~ыва́ть) 1. to open, unseal. 2. (*fig.*) to reveal, disclose; в. ко́зыря (*cards*) to turn up a trump. 3. (*med.*) to lance, open. 4. (*med.*) to dissect.

вскр|ы́ться, о́юсь, о́ешься, *pf.* (*of* ~ыва́ться) 1. to come to light, be revealed. 2. (*geogr.*) to become clear (of ice; *of rivers*); become open. 3. (*med.*) to break, burst.

всласть, *adv.* (*coll.*) to one's heart's content.

вслед 1. *adv.* (за+*i.*) after; посла́ть письмо́ в. to forward a letter. 2. *prep.*+*d.* after; смотре́ть в. to follow with one's eyes.

всле́дствие, *prep.*+*g.* in consequence of, owing to; в. дождя́ па́ртия в те́ннис не состоя́лась owing to the rain the game of tennis did not take place.

вслепу́ю, *adv.* 1. blindly. 2. blindfold.

вслух, *adv.* aloud.

вслу́ш|аться, аюсь, *pf.* (*of* ~иваться) (в+*a.*) to listen attentively (to).

вслу́шива|ться, юсь, *impf. of* вслу́шаться.

всма́трива|ться, юсь, *impf. of* всмотре́ться.

всмотр|е́ться, ю́сь, ~ишься, *pf.* (*of* всма́триваться) (в+*a.*) to peer (at); to scrutinize.

всмя́тку, *adv.* яйцо́ в. soft-boiled, lightly-boiled egg; сапоги́ в. (*coll.*) nonsense; все его́ мы́сли — про́сто сапоги́ в. all his ideas are quite half-baked.

вс|ова́ть, у́ю, у́ёшь, *pf.* (*of* ~о́вывать) (*coll.*) to put in, stick in; to slip in.

всо́выва|ть, ю, *impf. of* всова́ть *and* всу́нуть.

всос|а́ть, у́, ёшь, *pf.* (*of* вса́сывать) to suck in; (*fig.*) to absorb, imbibe; в. с молоко́м ма́тери to imbibe with one's mother's milk.

всос|а́ться, у́сь, ёшься, *pf.* (*of* вса́сываться) (в+*a.*) 1. to fasten upon (*with mouth, lips, etc.*). 2. to soak through (into).

вспа́ива|ть, ю, *impf. of* вспои́ть.

вспа́рива|ть, ю, *impf. of* вспа́рить.

вспа́р|ить, ю, ишь, *pf.* (*of* ~ивать) 1. (*dial.*) to steam. 2. (*coll.*) to put into a sweat. 3. (*coll.*) to thrash.

вспа́рхива|ть, ю, *impf. of* вспорхну́ть.

вспа́рыва|ть, ю, *impf. of* вспоро́ть.

вспа|сть, ду́, дёшь, *past* ~л, *pf.* (*obs.*) *only in phrases* в. на ум, на мысль (+*d.*) to occur to one.

вспа|ха́ть, шу́, ~шешь, *pf.* (*of* ~хивать) to plough up.

вспа́хива|ть, ю, *impf. of* вспаха́ть.

вспа́шк|а, и, *f.* ploughing.

вспаш|у́, ~ешь, *see* вспаха́ть.

вспе́нива|ть(ся), ю(сь), *impf. of* вспе́нить(ся).

вспе́н|ить, ю, ишь, *pf.* (*of* ~ивать) to make foam, make froth, make lather; в. коня́ to get one's horse into a lather.

вспе́н|иться, юсь, ишься, *pf.* (*of* ~иваться) to froth; to lather (*intrans.*).

вспетуш|и́ться, у́сь, и́шься, *pf. of* петуши́ться.

всплакн|у́ть, у́, ёшь, *pf.* to shed a few tears, have a little cry.

всплеск, а, *m.* splash.

всплёскива|ть, ю, *impf. of* всплесну́ть.

всплес|ну́ть, ну́, нёшь, *pf.* (*of* ~кивать) to splash; в. рука́ми to clasp one's hands (*under stress of emotion*).

всплыва́|ть, ю, *impf. of* всплыть.

всплы|ть, ву́, вёшь, *past* ~л, ~ла́, ~ло, *pf.* (*of* ~ва́ть) to rise to the surface, surface; (*fig.*) to come to light, be revealed; ~ли но́вые све́дения об обстоя́тельствах уби́йства new evidence has come to light about the circumstances of the murder; э́тот вопро́с ~вёт вероя́тно на сле́дующем собра́нии this question will probably come up at the next meeting.

вспо|и́ть, ю́, и́шь, *pf.* (*of* вспа́ивать) to nurse; to rear в.-вскорми́ть (*fig., coll.*) to bring up.

вспола́скива|ть, ю, *impf. of* вcполосну́ть.

всполосн|у́ть, у́, ёшь, *pf.* (*of* вспола́скивать) to rinse.

вспо́лох, а, *m.* (*obs.*) alarm.

вспо́лох|и, ов, *no sing.* 1. (flashes of) summer lightning; (*collect.*) flashes, glow (*from fire, explosion, etc.*). 2. (*dial.*) Northern lights.

всполош|и́ть, у́, и́шь, *pf.* (*of* полоши́ть) (*coll.*) to rouse; to alarm.

всполош|и́ться, у́сь, и́шься, *pf.* (*of* полоши́ться) (*coll.*) to take alarm.

вспоминá|ть(ся), ю(сь), *impf. of* вспóмнить(ся).

вспóм|нить, ню, нишь, *pf.* (*of* ~инáть) to remember, recall, recollect.

вспóм|ниться[1], нюсь, нишься, *pf.* (*of* ~инáться) (*impers.*+*d.*) мне, *etc.*, ~нилось I, *etc.*, remembered.

вспóмн|иться[2], юсь, ишься, *pf.* (*obs.*) to collect oneself.

вспомогáтельный, *adj.* auxiliary; subsidiary, branch; в. глагóл (*gram.*) auxiliary verb.

вспомоществовáни|е, я, *n.* (*obs.*) relief, assistance.

вспомян|ýть, ý, ~ешь, *pf.* (+*a.* or о+*p.*; *coll.*) to remember.

вспор|óть, ю, ~ешь, *pf.* (*of* вспáрывать) (*coll.*) to rip open.

вспорхн|ýть, ý, ёшь, *pf.* to take wing.

вспоте́|ть, ю, *pf.* (*of* потéть) to come out in a sweat; to mist over (*of spectacles, etc.*).

вспры́гива|ть, ю, *impf. of* вспры́гнуть.

вспры́г|нуть, ну, нешь, *pf.* (*of* ~ивать) (на+*a.*) to jump up (on to), spring up (on to).

вспры́скивани|е, я, *n.* (*med.*) injection.

вспры́скива|ть, ю, *impf. of* вспры́снуть.

вспры́с|нуть, ну, нешь, *pf.* (*of* ~кивать) **1.** to sprinkle; (*fig., coll.*) to celebrate; в. сдéлку to wet a bargain. **2.** (*med.*) to inject.

вспýгива|ть, ю, *impf. of* вспугнýть.

вспуг|нýть, нý, нёшь, *pf.* (*of* ~ивать) to scare away; to put up (*birds*).

вспух|áть, áю, *impf. of* ~нуть.

вспýх|нуть, ну, нешь, *pf.* (*of* ~áть) to swell up.

вспýчива|ть, ю, *impf. of* вспýчить.

вспýч|ить, у, ишь, *pf.* (*of* ~ивать) (*usu. impers.*) to distend; у негó живóт ~ило his abdomen is distended.

вспыл|и́ть, ю́, и́шь, *pf.* to flare up; в. (на+*a.*) to fly into a rage (with).

вспы́льчив|ый (~, ~a), *adj.* hot-tempered; irascible.

вспы́хива|ть, ю, *impf. of* вспы́хнуть.

вспы́х|нуть, ну, нешь, *pf.* (*of* ~ивать) **1.** to burst into flame, blaze up; to flash out; (*fig.*) to flare up; to break out; на грани́це ~нули бои́ fighting flared up on the frontier. **2.** to blush.

вспы́шк|а, и, *f.* flash; (*astron.*) flare; (*fig.*) outburst, burst; outbreak (*of epidemic, etc.*).

вспять, *adv.* (*obs.*) back(wards).

вставáни|е, я, *n.* rising; почти́ть ~ем to stand in honour (of).

встава́|ть, ю́, ёшь, *impf. of* ~ть.

встáв|ить, лю, ишь, *pf.* (*of* ~ля́ть) to put in, insert; в. в рáму to frame; в. себé зýбы to have a set of (false) teeth made; в. шпóны

(*typ.*) to interline; в. перó (+*d.*; *obs., vulg.*) to give the sack, give the boot.

встáвк|а, и, *f.* **1.** fixing, insertion; framing, mounting. **2.** inset. **3.** interpolation.

вставля́|ть, ю, *impf. of* встáвить.

вставн|óй, *adj.* inserted; ~ы́е зýбы false teeth; ~ы́е рáмы double window-frames.

встарь, *adv.* of old, in olden time(s).

встáскива|ть, ю, *impf. of* встащи́ть.

встá|ть, ну, нешь, *pf.* (*of* ~вáть) **1.** to get up, rise; to stand up; он рáно ~л сегóдня ýтром he got up early this morning; он вчерá ~л впервы́е со дня несчáстного слýчая he got up yesterday for the first time since his accident; в. с лéвой ноги́ to get out of bed on the wrong side; в. из-за столá to rise from table; (*fig.*) в. на свои́ нóги to stand on one's own feet; в. грýдью за (+*a.*) to stand up for. **2.** to stand; в. на рабóту to start work. **3.** (в+*a.*) to go (into), fit (into); большóй шкаф не ~нет в эту кóмнату the large cupboard will not go into this room. **4.** (*fig.*) to arise, come up; тот же сáмый вопрóс ~л на прóшлом собрáнии the same question arose at the last meeting. **5.** (*coll.*) to get out, get off (*means of conveyance*).

встащ|и́ть, ý, ~ишь, *pf.* (*of* встáскивать) (*coll.*) to pull up.

встревá|ть, ю, *impf. of* встрять.

встревóжен|ный (~, ~на), *p.p.p. of* встревóжить *and adj.* anxious.

встревóж|ить, у, ишь, *pf. of* тревóжить.

встрёпанный, *p.p.p. and adj.* (*coll.*) dishevelled; как в. full of beans.

встреп|áть, лю́, ~лешь, *pf.* (*of* ~ывать) (*coll.*) to dishevel.

встрепен|ýться, ýсь, ёшься, *pf.* **1.** to rouse oneself, start (up). **2.** to begin to beat faster (*of heart*).

встрёпк|а, и, *f.* (*coll.*) **1.** scolding. **2.** shock.

встрёпыва|ть, ю, *impf. of* встрепáть.

встрé|тить, чу, тишь, *pf.* (*of* ~чáть) **1.** to meet (with), encounter; в. сопротивлéние to encounter resistance. **2.** to greet, receive; в. аплодисмéнтами to greet with cheers; в. Нóвый год to see the New Year in.

встрé|титься, чусь, тишься, *pf.* (*of* ~чáться) (c+*i.*) **1.** to meet (with), encounter, come across; в. с затруднéниями to encounter difficulties. **2.** to be found, occur.

встрéч|а, и, *f.* **1.** meeting, encounter; reception; в. Нóвого гóда New Year's Eve party. **2.** (*sport*) match, meeting.

встречá|ть, ю, *impf. of* встрéтить.

встречá|ться, юсь, *impf.* **1.** *impf. of* встрéтиться. **2.** *impf.* only to be found, be met with; в Шотлáндии ещё ~ются ди́кие кóшки wild cats are still to be found in Scotland.

встре́чн|ый, *adj.* **1.** proceeding from opposite direction; в. ве́тер head wind; *as noun* пе́рвый в. the first person you meet, anyone; (ка́ждый) в. и попере́чный every Tom, Dick, and Harry. **2.** counter; в. иск (*leg.*) counter-claim; в. план counter-plan; в. бой (*mil.*) encounter battle; (*naut.*) action on opposite courses.

встрихн|у́ть, у́, ёшь, *pf.* (*coll.*) to be alarmed.

встря́ск|а, и, *f.* (*coll.*) **1.** shaking; он получи́л си́льную ~у he has been badly shaken up, he has received a severe shock. **2.** real telling off.

встря́|ть, ну, нешь, *pf.* (*of* встрева́ть) (в+*a.*; *coll.*) to get mixed up (in).

встря́хива|ть(ся), ю(сь), *impf. of* встряхну́ть(ся).

встря́х|ивать, ну́, нёшь, *pf.* (*of* ~ивать) to shake; (*fig.*) to shake up, rouse.

встрях|ну́ться, ну́сь, нёшься, *pf.* (*of* ~иваться) **1.** to shake oneself. **2.** (*fig.*) to rouse oneself; to cheer up; ~ни́тесь! pull yourself together! **3.** (*coll.*) to have a fling.

вступа́|ть(ся), ю(сь), *impf. of* вступи́ть(ся).

вступи́тельн|ый, *adj.* introductory; в. взнос entrance fee; ~ая ле́кция inaugural lecture.

вступ|и́ть, лю́, ~ишь, *pf.* (*of* ~а́ть) **1.** (в+*a.*) to enter (into), join (in); в. в бой to join battle; в. в де́йствие to come into force; в. в брак to marry; в. в свои́ права́ to come into one's own. **2.** (на+*a.*) to mount, go up; в. на престо́л to ascend the throne.

вступ|и́ться, лю́сь, ~ишься, *pf.* (*of* ~а́ться) **1.** (за+*a.*) to stand up (for), take (some-one's) part. **2.** (*coll.*) to intervene.

вступле́ни|е, я, *n.* **1.** entry, joining. **2.** prelude, opening, introduction, preamble.

всу́е, *adv.* (*obs.*) in vain; призва́ть в. и́мя Бо́жье to take the name of God in vain.

всу́н|уть, у, ешь, *pf.* (*of* всо́вывать) to stick in; to slip in.

всухомя́тку, *adv.* (*coll.*) есть в. to live on, eat cold food without liquids.

всу́чива|ть, ю, *impf. of* всучи́ть.

всу́ч|ить, жу́, ~дишь, *pf.* (*of* ~ивать) **1.** to entwine. **2.** (+*d.*; *fig.*, *coll.*, *pejor.*) to foist (on), palm off (on).

всхли́п|нуть, ну, нешь, *pf.* (*of* ~ывать) to sob.

всхли́пыванье, я, *n.* sobbing; sobs.

всхли́пыва|ть, ю, *impf. of* всхли́пнуть.

всхо|ди́ть, жу́, ~дишь, *impf. of* взойти́.

всхо́д|ы, ов, *no sing.* (corn-)shoots.

всхо́жест|ь, и, *f.* (*agric.*) germinating capacity.

всхо́жий, *adj.* (*agric.*) capable of germinating.

всхрап|ну́ть, ну́, нёшь, *pf.* **1.** *pf. of* ~ывать. **2.** (*coll.*) to have a nap.

всхра́пыва|ть, ю, *impf.* (*of* всхрапну́ть) to snore; to snort (*of a horse*).

всы́п|ать, лю, лешь, *pf.* (*of* ~а́ть) **1.** (в+*a.*) to pour (into). **2.** (+*d.*; *coll.*) to swear at; to beat; в. по пе́рвое число́ to knock into the middle of next week.

всыпа́|ть, ю, *impf. of* всы́пать.

всы́пк|а, и, *f.* rating; beating, drubbing.

всю́ду, *adv.* everywhere.

вся, *see* весь[1].

вся́к, *short form* (*obs.*) *of* ~ий; *as pron.* (*obs.*) everyone.

вся́к|ий, *adj.* **1.** any; без ~ого сомне́ния beyond any doubt; во ~ом слу́чае in any case, at any rate; *as pron.* anyone. **2.** all sorts of; every; на в. слу́чай against every eventuality; to be on the safe side; тут мно́го ~их моше́нников here are all sorts of rogues.

вся́чески, *adv.* (*coll.*) in every way possible; в. стара́ться to try one's hardest, try all ways.

вся́ческ|ий, *adj.* (*coll.*) all kinds of; все и ~ие уло́вки every sort and kind of trick.

вся́чин|а, ы, *f.* (*coll.*) вся́кая в. all kinds of things; odds and ends.

вся́чинк|а, и, *f.* (*coll.*) жить со ~ой to have one's ups and downs.

вта́йне, *adv.* secretly, in secret.

вта́лкива|ть, ю, *impf. of* втолкну́ть.

вта́птыва|ть, ю, *impf. of* втопта́ть.

вта́скива|ть(ся), ю(сь), *impf. of* втащи́ть-(ся).

втач|а́ть, а́ю, *pf.* (*of* ~ивать) (в+*a.*) to stitch in(to).

вта́чива|ть, ю, *impf. of* втача́ть.

вта́чк|а, и, *f.* **1.** stitching in. **2.** patch.

втащ|и́ть, у́, ~ишь, *pf.* (*of* вта́скивать) (в+*a.*, на+*a.*) to drag (into, on to).

втащ|и́ться, у́сь, ~ишься, *pf.* (*of* вта́скиваться) (*coll.*) to drag oneself.

втека́|ть, ю, *impf. of* втечь.

втёмную, *adv.* without seeing one's cards; (*fig.*) blindly, in the dark; де́йствовать в. to take a leap in the dark.

втемя́ш|ить, у, ишь, *pf.* (+*d.*; *coll.*) to impress (upon); в. что-н. кому́-н. в башку́ to get something into someone's skull.

втемя́ш|иться, усь, ишься, *pf.* (+*d.*; *coll.*) to get into one's head.

втер|е́ть, вотру́, вотрёшь, *past* ~, ~ла, *pf.* (*of* втира́ть) (в+*a.*) to rub in(to); в. очки́ кому́-н. (*fig.*, *coll.*) to bluff, pull the wool over someone's eyes.

втер|е́ться, вотру́сь, вотрёшься, *past* ~ся, ~лась, *pf.* (*of* втира́ться) **1.** (в+*a.*; *coll.*) to insinuate oneself, worm oneself into; ему́ удало́сь в. в дове́рие к премье́р--мини́стру he succeeded in worming his way into the confidence of the Prime Minister. **2.** to sink in(to), soak in(to).

вте|са́ться, шу́сь, ~шешься, pf. (of ~сыва́ться) (в+a.; coll.) to insinuate oneself in(to), brazen one's way in(to).

втёсыва|ться, юсь, impf. of втеса́ться.

вте|чь, ку́, чёшь, ку́т, past ~к, ~кла́, pf. (of ~ка́ть) to flow in(to).

втира́ни|е, я, n. 1. rubbing in. 2. embrocation, liniment.

втира́|ть(ся), ю(сь), impf. of втере́ть(ся).

вти́скива|ть(ся), ю(сь), impf. of вти́снуть(ся).

вти́с|нуть, ну, нешь, pf. (of ~кивать) (в+a.) to squeeze in(to).

вти́с|нуться, нусь, нешься, pf. (of ~киваться) (coll.) to squeeze (oneself) in(to).

втихомо́лку, adv. (coll.) surreptitiously; on the quiet, on the sly.

втих|у́ю, adv. (coll.) = ~омо́лку.

втолкн|у́ть, у́, ёшь, pf. (of вта́лкивать) (в+a.) to push in(to), shove in(to).

втолк|ова́ть, у́ю, pf. (of ~о́вывать) (+d.; coll.) to din (into), ram (into).

втолко́выва|ть, ю, impf. of втолкова́ть.

втоп|та́ть, чу́, ~чешь, pf. (of вта́птывать) to trample in; в. в грязь (fig.) to drag in the mire.

втор|а́, ы́, f. (mus.) second voice; second violin.

вторáчива|ть, ю, impf. of второчи́ть.

вторг|а́ться, а́юсь, impf. of ~ну́ться.

вто́рг|нуться, нусь, нешься, past ~ся, ~лась, pf. (of ~а́ться) (в+a.) to invade; to encroach (upon), trespass (on), intrude (in); (also fig.).

вторже́ни|е, я, n. invasion; intrusion.

вто́р|ить, ю, ишь, impf. (+d.) 1. (mus.) to play, sing second part (to). 2. (fig., pejor.) to echo, repeat; он про́сто ~ит отцо́вским мне́ниям he simply echoes his father's opinions.

втори́чн|ый, adj. 1. second; ~ое предупрежде́ние second warning. 2. secondary; ~ые половы́е при́знаки secondary sexual characteristics.

вто́рник, а, m. Tuesday.

вто́рни|чный, adj. of ~к.

второбра́чный, adj. (obs.) (born) of second marriage.

второго́дник, а, m. pupil remaining in same form for second year.

Второзако́ни|е, я, n. (bibl.) Deuteronomy.

втор|о́й, adj. 1. second; ~а́я мо́лодость second youth; ~а́я скри́пка second violin; (fig.) second fiddle; в. час (it is) past one; из ~ы́х рук (at) second hand. 2. as noun ~о́е, ~о́го, n. main course (of meal). 3. as particle ~о́е (coll.) in the second place.

второкла́ссник, а, m. second-form boy.

второкла́ссниц|а, ы, f. second-form girl.

второкла́ссный, adj. second-class; (pejor.) second-rate.

второку́рсник, а, m. second-year student.

второочередно́й, adj. secondary.

второпя́х, adv. 1. hurriedly, in haste. 2. in one's hurry.

второразря́дный, adj. second-rate.

второсо́ртный, adj. second-quality; inferior.

второстепе́нный, adj. secondary; minor.

второчи́ть, у́, и́шь, pf. (of втора́чивать) to strap to one's saddle.

втрав|и́ть, лю́, ~ишь, pf. (of ~ливать) (в+a.) to inveigle (into).

втра́влива|ть, ю, impf. of втрави́ть.

втре́ска|ться, юсь, pf. (в+a.; coll.) to fall (for), fall in love (with).

в-тре́тьих, adv. thirdly, in the third place.

втри́дешева, adv. (coll.) three times as cheap; excessively cheaply; прода́ть в. to sell for a song.

втри́дорога, adv. (coll.) triple the price; extremely dear(ly); плати́ть в. to pay through the nose.

втро́е, adv. three times; treble.

втроём, adv. three (together); мы пое́хали в Ло́ндон в. the three of us went to London.

втройне́, adv. three times as much, treble.

втуз, а, m. (abbr. of вы́сшее техни́ческое уче́бное заведе́ние) technical college.

вту́лк|а, и, f. 1. (tech.) bush. 2. plug; bung.

вту́не, adv. (obs.) in vain.

втыка́|ть, ю, impf. of воткну́ть.

вты́чк|а, и, f. (coll.) 1. sticking in. 2. plug, bung.

втюр|и́ться, юсь, ишься, pf. (в+a.; coll.) to fall in love (with).

втя́гива|ть(ся), ю(сь), impf. of втяну́ть(ся).

втяжно́й, adj. (tech.) suction.

втя|ну́ть, ну́, ~нешь, pf. (of ~гивать) 1. to draw (in, into, up); pull (in, into, up); to absorb, take in; в. живо́т to pull in one's stomach; в. жи́дкость to take in a liquid. 2. (fig.) to draw (into), involve (in); в. в спор to draw into an argument.

втя|ну́ться, ну́сь, ~нешься, pf. (of ~гива́ться) (в+a.) 1. to draw (into), enter; коло́нна ~ну́лась в уще́лье the column entered the defile. 2. (of cheeks) to sag, fall in. 3. (coll.) to get accustomed (to), used (to); вы ско́ро ~нетесь в рабо́ту you will soon get used to the work. 4. to become keen (on); он о́чень ~ну́лся в игру́ в те́ннис he has become very keen on tennis.

втя́па|ться, юсь, pf. (в+a.; coll.) to get involved (in); to get into a mess.

вуалётк|а, и, f. veil.

вуали́р|овать, ую, impf. (of за~) to veil, draw a veil (over).

вуа́л|ь, и, f. veil.

вуз, а, *m.* (*abbr. of* вы́сшее уче́бное заведе́ние) institution of higher education.

ву́зов|ец, ца, *m.* student (*at any institution of higher education*).

ву́зов|ка, ки, *f. of* ~ец.

ву́з|овский, *adj. of* ~.

вулка́н, а, *m.* volcano; де́йствующий, поту́хший в. active, extinct volcano; жить (как) на ~е (*fig.*) to be living on the edge of a volcano.

вулканиза́ци|я, и, *f.* (*tech.*) vulcanization.

вулканизи́р|овать, ую, *impf. and pf.* (*tech.*) to vulcanize.

вулкани́зм, а, *m.* (*geol.*) vulcanism.

вулканиз|ова́ть, у́ю = ~и́ровать.

вулкани́ческий, *adj.* volcanic (*also fig.*).

вульгариза́тор, а, *m.* vulgarizer.

вульгариза́ци|я, и, *f.* vulgarization.

вульгаризи́р|овать, ую, *impf. and pf.* to vulgarize.

вульгари́зм, а, *m.* (*ling.*) vulgarism.

вульга́рност|ь, и, *f.* vulgarity.

вульга́р|ный (~ен, ~на), *adj.* (*in var. senses*) vulgar; в. маркси́зм vulgar Marxism.

вундерки́нд, а, *m.* infant prodigy.

вурдала́к, а, *m.* werewolf; vampire.

вход, а, *m.* 1. entry. 2. entrance.

вхо|ди́ть, жу́, ~дишь, *impf. of* войти́.

вход|но́й, *adj. of* ~; ~на́я пла́та entrance fee.

вход|я́щий, *pres. part. of* ~и́ть *and adj.* incoming; в. журна́л book of entries; в. у́гол (*math.*) re-entrant angle; *as noun* ~я́щая, ~я́щей, *f.* incoming paper.

вхожде́ни|е, я, *n.* entry.

вхо́ж|ий (~, ~а), *adj.* (*coll.*) быть ~им (в+*a.*, к) to be (well) received (at); to be well in (with).

вхолосту́ю, *adv.* (*tech.*) рабо́тать в. to run idle.

вцеп|и́ться, лю́сь, ~ишься, *impf.* (*of* ~ля́ться) (в+*a.*) to seize hold of (by).

вцепля́|ться, юсь, *impf. of* вцепи́ться.

вчера́, *adv.* yesterday; (*in past-tense narration*) the day before.

вчера́|шний, *adj. of* ~; есть у вас ~шняя «Пра́вда»? have you yesterday's *Pravda*?; иска́ть ~шнего дня to waste time on a hopeless quest.

вчерне́, *adv.* in rough; я написа́л свою́ ле́кцию в. I have made a rough draft of my lecture.

вчер|ти́ть, чу́, ~тишь, *pf.* (*of* ~чивать) (*math.*) to inscribe.

вче́рчива|ть, ю, *impf. of* вчерти́ть.

вче́тверо, *adv.* four times; four times as much; сложи́ть в. to fold in four.

вчетверо́м, *adv.* four (together).

в-четвёртых, *adv.* fourthly, in the fourth place.

вчин|и́ть, ю́, и́шь, *pf.* (*of* ~я́ть) (*leg.*; *obs.*) в. иск to bring an action.

вчиня́|ть, ю, *impf. of* вчини́ть.

вчисту́ю, *adv.* (*coll.*, *obs.*) 1. finally, definitively; он был уво́лен в. he was pensioned off. 2. completely.

вчит|а́ться, а́юсь, *pf.* (*of* ~ываться) (в+*a.*) to get a grasp (of) (*a text*).

вчи́тыва|ться, юсь, *impf.* 1. *impf. of* вчита́ться. 2. *impf. only* to try to grasp the meaning (of).

вчу́же, *adv.* disinterestedly, vicariously; я в. любова́лся его́ успе́хом his success gave me vicarious pleasure.

вше́стеро, *adv.* six times; six times as much.

вшестеро́м, *adv.* six (together).

вшива́|ть, ю, *impf. of* вшить.

вшиве|ть, ю, *impf.* (*of* за~ *and* обо~) to become lice-ridden.

вши́вк|а, и, *f.* (*coll.*) 1. sewing in. 2. patch.

вшивно́й, *adj.* sewn in.

вши́в|ый (~, ~а), *adj.* lousy, lice-ridden.

вширь, *adv.* in breadth.

вшить, вошью́, вошьёшь, *pf.* (*of* вшива́ть) (в+*a.*) to sew in(to).

въеда́|ться, юсь, *impf. of* въе́сться.

въе́длив|ый (~, ~а), *adj.* (*coll.*) corrosive; (*fig.*) acid; ~ое замеча́ние acid remark; в. челове́к caustic person.

въе́дчив|ый (~, ~а), *adj.* = въе́дливый.

въезд, а, *m.* 1. entry. 2. entrance.

въезд|но́й, *adj. of* ~; ~на́я ви́за entry visa.

въезжа́|ть, ю, *impf. of* въе́хать.

въе́|сться, мся, стся, ди́мся, ди́тесь, дя́тся, *past* ~лся, *pf.* (*of* ~да́ться) (в+*a.*) to eat (into).

въе́|хать, ду, дешь, *pf.* (*of* ~зжа́ть) (в+*a.*) to enter, ride in(to), drive in(to); to ride, drive up; в. в мо́рду, в ры́ло (+*d.*; *vulg.*) to slap in the face.

въя́в|е, *adv.* = ~ь.

въявь, *adv.* (*obs.*) 1. openly; ви́деть в. to see with one's own eyes. 2. in reality; и в. случи́лось так, как я сказа́л it really did happen as I said.

вы, вас, вам, ва́ми, вас, *pron.* (*pl. and formal mode of address to one person*) you; быть на в. (с+*i.*) to be on formal terms (with).

вы- *prefix indicating* 1. motion outwards. 2. action directed outwards. 3. acquisition (*as outcome of a series of actions*). 4. completion of a process.

выба́лтыва|ть, ю, *impf. of* вы́болтать.

выбега́|ть, ю, *impf. of* вы́бежать.

выбега́|ться, юсь, *pf.* 1. (*coll.*) to wear oneself out with running. 2. to become sterile (*of livestock*).

вы́бе|жать, гу, жишь, гут, *pf.* (*of* ~га́ть) to run out.

вы́бел|ить, ю, ишь, *pf. of* бели́ть 3.

вы́белк|а, и, *f.* bleaching; whitening.

вы́бер|у, ешь, *see* вы́брать.

выбива́|ть(ся), ю(сь), *impf. of* вы́бить(ся).

выбира́|ть(ся), ю(сь), *impf. of* вы́брать(ся).

вы́б|ить, ью, ьешь, *pf.* (*of* ~ива́ть) **1.** to knock out; to dislodge; в. из седла́ to unseat, unhorse; в. из коле́й (*fig.*) to unsettle, upset; в. дурь из кого́-н. to knock the nonsense out of someone. **2.** to beat (clean); в. ковёр to beat a carpet. **3.** to beat; to stamp; to print (*fabrics*); в. медь to beat copper; в. меда́ль to strike a medal. **4.** to beat down; град ~ил посе́вы the hail had beaten down the crops. **5.** to beat out; to drum; в. бараба́нную дробь to beat a tattoo.

вы́б|иться, ьюсь, ьешься, *pf.* (*of* ~ива́ться) **1.** to get out; to break loose (from); в. из коле́й to go off the rails; в. в лю́ди to make one's way in the world; в. из сил to strain oneself to breaking point, wear oneself out. **2.** to come out, show (*intrans.*; *usually of hair, from under hat*).

вы́боин|а, ы, *f.* **1.** rut, pot-hole. **2.** dent; groove.

вы́бойк|а, и, *f.* **1.** beating (*of metals*). **2.** (*text.*) print.

вы́бойчатый, *adj.* (*text.*) printed.

вы́болта|ть, ю, *pf.* (*of* выба́лтывать) (*coll.*) to let out, blurt out.

вы́болта|ться, юсь, *pf.* (*coll.*) **1.** to talk oneself to a standstill. **2.** to talk (*to let out secrets*).

вы́бор, а, *m.* **1.** choice; option. **2.** selection; assortment; в э́том магази́не име́ется большо́й в. конфе́т this shop has a large selection of sweets. **3.** (*pl. only*) election(s); дополни́тельные в. by-election.

вы́борк|а, и, *f.* **1.** selection. **2.** (*coll.*) excerpt.

вы́борност|ь, и, *f.* appointment by election.

вы́борн|ый, *adj.* **1.** elective. **2.** electoral; в. бюллете́нь ballot-paper. **3.** elected; *as noun* в., ~ого, *m.* delegate.

вы́борочный, *adj.* selective.

вы́борщик, а, *m.* **1.** elector (*in indirect elections*). **2.** selector.

вы́бор|ы, ов, *see* ~.

вы́бран|ить, ю, ишь, *pf. of* брани́ть.

вы́бра́сывател|ь, я, *m.* ejector (*in firearms*).

вы́бра́сыва|ть(ся), ю(сь), *impf. of* вы́бросить(ся).

вы́б|рать, еру, ерешь, *pf.* (*of* ~ира́ть) **1.** to choose, select; pick out. **2.** to elect. **3.** в. пате́нт (*leg.*) to take out a patent. **4.** to take (everything) out. **5.** (*naut.*) to haul in.

вы́б|раться, ерусь, ерешься, *pf.* (*of* ~ира́ться) **1.** to get out; в. из затрудне́ний to get out of a difficulty. **2.** to move (house). **3.** (*coll.*) to (manage to) get to; несмотря́

на боле́знь, мать всё-таки ~ра́лась в це́рковь in spite of being ill mother managed to get to church.

выбрива́|ть(ся), ю(сь), *impf. of* вы́брить(ся).

вы́бр|ить, ею, еешь, *pf.* (*of* ~ива́ть) to shave.

вы́бр|иться, еюсь, еешься, *pf.* (*of* ~ива́ться) to shave, have a shave.

вы́бро|сить, шу, сишь, *pf.* (*of* выбра́сывать) **1.** to throw out; в. за́ борт to throw overboard (*also fig.*); в. на у́лицу to throw on to the street. **2.** to reject, discard, throw away; в. зря to waste; в. из головы́ to put out of one's head, dismiss. **3.** (*in var. senses*) to put out; в. флаг to hoist a flag; в. ло́зунг to put out, launch a slogan.

вы́бро|ситься, шусь, сишься, *pf.* (*of* выбра́сываться) to throw oneself out, leap out; (*naut.*) в. на мель, на́ берег to run aground; в. с парашю́том из самолёта to bale out of an aircraft.

выбыва́ни|е, я, *n.* knock-out (*sports competition*).

выбыва́|ть, ю, *impf. of* вы́быть.

вы́быти|е, я, *n.* departure; за ва́шим ~ем письмо́ бы́ло возвращено́ отправи́телю in view of your having gone away the letter was returned to the sender.

вы́б|ыть, уду, удешь, *pf.* (*of* ~ыва́ть) (из) to leave, quit; в. из стро́я (*mil.*) (*i*) to leave the ranks (*ii*) to become a casualty.

выва́лива|ть(ся), ю(сь), *impf. of* вы́валить(ся).

вы́вал|ить, ю, ишь, *pf.* (*of* ~ивать) **1.** to throw out. **2.** (*coll.*) to pour out (*intrans.*; *a crowd*).

вы́вал|иться, юсь, ишься, *pf.* (*of* ~иваться) to fall out, tumble out.

вы́валя|ть, ю, *pf.* (*of* валя́ть 2) to drag (in, through) (*mud, snow, etc.*).

вы́валя|ться, юсь, *pf.* (в+*p.*) to get covered (*in mud, snow, etc.*).

выва́рива|ть, ю, *impf. of* вы́варить.

вы́вар|ить, ю, ишь, *pf.* (*of* ~ивать) **1.** to boil down; to extract by boiling; в. соль из морско́й воды́ to extract salt from sea water. **2.** to boil thoroughly. **3.** to remove (*stains, etc.*) by boiling.

вы́варк|а, и, *f.* decoction, extraction.

вы́вед|ать, аю, *pf.* (*of* ~ывать) to find out; в. секре́т у кого́-н. to worm a secret out of someone.

вы́веде́ни|е, я, *n.* **1.** leading out, bringing out. **2.** deduction, conclusion. **3.** hatching (out); growing (*of plants*); breeding, raising. **4.** putting up, erection. **5.** getting out, removal (*of stains*); extermination (*of pests*).

вы́ведр|ить, ит, *pf.* (*impers.*; *dial.*) to become fine, clear up (*of weather*).

вывéдыва|ть, ю, *impf.* **1.** *impf. of* вы́ведать.

2. *impf. only* to investigate, try to find out; в. чьи-н. наме́рения to sound out some-one's intentions.

вы́вез|ти, у, ешь, *past* ~, ~ла, *pf.* (*of* выво-зи́ть) 1. to take out, remove; to bring out. 2. (*econ.*) to export. 3. (*coll.*) to save, rescue; счастли́вый слу́чай ~ меня́ a lucky chance saved me. 4. в. в свет to bring out (into society).

вы́вер|ить, ю, ишь, *pf.* (*of* ~я́ть) to adjust; to regulate (*clocks and watches*).

вы́верк|а, и, f. adjustment; regulation (*of clocks and watches*).

вы́вер|нуть, ну, нешь, *pf.* (*of* ~тывать) 1. to unscrew; to pull out. 2. (*coll.*) to twist, wrench. 3. (*coll.*) to dislocate. 4. to turn (inside) out.

вы́вер|нуться, нусь, нешься, *pf.* (*of* ~ты-ваться) 1. to come unscrewed. 2. (*coll.*) to slip out. 3. (*coll.*) to get out (of), extricate oneself (from). 4. (*coll.*) to appear, emerge (*from behind something, from round a corner*). 5. (*coll.*) to be dislocated.

вы́верт, а, m. (*coll.*) 1. caper; танцева́ть с ~ами to caper. 2. mannerism; affectation; челове́к с ~ом eccentric.

вы́вер|теть, чу, тишь, *pf.* (*coll.*) to unscrew.

вывёртыва|ть(ся), ю(сь), *impf. of* вы́вер-нуть(ся).

вывёрчива|ть, ю, *impf. of* вы́вертеть.

выверя́|ть, ю, *impf. of* вы́верить.

вы́ве|сить¹, шу, сишь, *pf.* (*of* ~шивать) 1. to put up; to post up. 2. to hang out (*linen, flags, etc.*).

вы́ве|сить², шу, сишь, *pf.* (*of* ~шивать) to weigh.

вы́веск|а, и, f. 1. sign, signboard. 2. (*fig.*) screen, pretext; он обману́л её под ~ой любе́зности he deceived her under the mask of kindness. 3. (*sl.*) mug (= *face*).

вы́ве|сти, ду, дешь, *past* ~л, ~ла, *pf.* (*of* выводи́ть) 1. to lead out, bring out; в. самолёт из што́пора to pull an aeroplane out of a spin; в. кого́-н. в лю́ди to help someone on in life; в. из заблужде́ния to undeceive; в. кого́-н. из себя́ to drive someone out of his wits; в. из стро́я to disable, put out of action (*also fig.*); в. из терпе́ния to exasperate; в. кого́-н. на доро́гу (*fig.*) to set someone on the right path; в. на чи́стую во́ду to expose, show up. 2. to turn out, force out; в. из соста́ва прези́диума to remove from the presidium. 3. to remove (*stains*); to exterminate (*pests*). 4. to deduce, conclude. 5. to hatch (out); to grow (*plants*); to breed, raise. 6. to put up, erect. 7. to depict, portray (*in a lit. work*). 8. to write, draw, trace out pains-takingly. 9. в. балл, в. отме́тку to give a mark.

вы́ве|стись, дусь, дешься, *pf.* (*of* выво-ди́ться) 1. to go out of use; to lapse. 2. to disappear; to come out (*of stains*); to be-come extinct. 3. to hatch out (*intrans.*).

выве́тривани|е, я, n. 1. airing. 2. (*geol.*) weathering.

выве́трива|ть(ся), ю(сь), *impf. of* вы́вет-рить(ся).

вы́ветр|ить, ю, ишь, *pf.* (*of* ~ивать) 1. to air; to ventilate; to remove (by ventilation); в. дурно́й за́пах to remove a bad smell. 2. (*fig.*) to remove. 3. (*impers.*; *geol.*) to weather.

вы́ветр|иться, юсь, ишься, *pf.* (*of* ~иваться) 1. (*geol.*) to weather. 2. to disappear (*by action of wind or fresh air; also fig.*); в. из па́мяти to be effaced from memory.

вывёшива|ть, ю, *impf. of* вы́весить.

вы́вин|тить, чу, тишь, *pf.* (*of* ~чивать) to unscrew.

вы́вин|титься, чусь, тишься, *pf.* (*of* ~чи-ваться) to come unscrewed.

выви́нчива|ть(ся), ю(сь), *impf. of* вы́вин-тить(ся).

вы́вих, а, m. 1. dislocation; dislocated part. 2. (*fig., coll.*) kink; oddity, quirk.

выви́хива|ть, ю, *impf. of* вы́вихнуть.

вы́вих|нуть, ну, нешь, *pf.* (*of* ~ивать) to dislocate, put out (of joint); он ~нул себе́ но́гу he has dislocated his foot.

вы́вод, а, m. 1. deduction, conclusion. 2. (*electr.*) outlet; leading-out wire. 3. lead-ing out, bringing out. 4. hatching (out); growing (*of plants*); breeding, raising.

выво|ди́ть(ся), жу́(сь), ~дишь(ся), *impf. of* вы́вести(сь).

вы́водк|а, и, f. 1. removal (*of stains*). 2. exercising (*of horses*).

выводно́й, adj. 1. (*tech.*) discharge. 2. (*anat.*) excretory.

вы́вод|ок, ка, m. brood (*also fig.*); hatch; litter.

выво|жу́¹, ~дишь, *see* ~ди́ть.

выво|жу́², ~зишь, *see* ~зи́ть.

вы́воз, а, m. 1. export. 2. removal.

вы́во|зить, жу, зишь, *pf.* (в+*p.*; *coll.*) to cover (*in mud, snow, etc.*).

выво|зи́ть, жу́, ~зишь, *impf. of* вы́везти.

вы́возк|а, и, f. (*coll.*) carting out.

вывозно́й, adj. export.

вывола́кива|ть, ю, *impf. of* вы́волочь.

вы́волочк|а, и, f. (*coll.*) 1. dragging out. 2. beating. 3. dressing-down.

вы́воло|чь, ку, чешь, кут, *past* ~к, ~кла *pf.* (*of* вывола́кивать) (*coll.*) to drag out.

выворо́чива|ть, ю, *impf. of* вы́воротить.

вы́воро|тить, чу, тишь, *pf.* (*of* вывора́чи-вать) (*coll.*) 1. to pull out, shake loose. 2. to twist, wrench. 3. to turn (inside) out. 4. to overturn.

вы́гад|ать, аю, *pf.* (*of* ~ывать) to gain; to save, economize; что вы ~али на э́том? what did you gain by it?

вы́га́дыва|ть, ю, *impf. of* вы́гадать.

вы́гарк|и, ов, *no sing.* slag.

вы́гиб, а, *m.* curve; curvature.

вы́гиба́|ть(ся), ю(сь), *impf. of* вы́гнуть(ся).

вы́гла|дить, жу, дишь, *pf. of* гла́дить 1.

вы́гля|деть¹, жу, дишь, *pf.* (*coll.*) to discover; to spy out.

вы́гля|деть², жу, дишь, *impf.* to look (like); он ~дит о́чень молоды́м he looks very young; он ~дит грузи́ном he looks like a Georgian; она́ пло́хо ~дит she does not look well.

вы́гля́дыва|ть, ю, *impf. of* вы́глянуть.

вы́гля|нуть, ну, нешь, *pf.* (*of* ~дывать) **1.** to look out. **2.** to peep out, emerge, become visible; из-за туч ~нуло со́лнце the sun peeped out from behind the clouds.

вы́г|нать, оню, онишь, *pf.* (*of* ~оня́ть) **1.** to drive out; to expel; в. со слу́жбы (*coll.*) to sack. **2.** to distil. **3.** (*coll.*) to make (*a sum of money, etc.*).

вы́гнива́|ть, ю, *impf. of* вы́гнить.

вы́гни|ть, ю, ешь, *pf.* (*of* ~ва́ть) to rot away; to rot at the core.

вы́гнут|ый (~, ~а), *p.p.p. of* ~ь *and adj.* curved; convex.

вы́гн|уть, у, ешь, *pf.* (*of* выгиба́ть) to bend; в. спи́ну to arch the back.

вы́гн|уться, усь, ешься, *pf.* (*of* выгиба́ться) to bend (*intrans.*).

выгова́рива|ть, ю, *impf.* **1.** *impf. of* вы́говорить. **2.** *impf. only* (+ *d.*; *coll.*) to reprimand, tell off.

вы́говор, а, *m.* **1.** accent; pronunciation. **2.** reprimand; rebuke; dressing-down, ticking-off.

вы́говор|ить, ю, ишь, *pf.* (*of* выгова́ривать) **1.** to articulate, speak. **2.** (*leg.*) to reserve; to stipulate; в. себе́ пра́во расторже́ния контра́кта to reserve the right of annulment of contract.

вы́говор|иться, юсь, ишься, *pf.* (*coll.*) to speak out.

вы́год|а, ы, *f.* advantage, benefit; profit, gain; interest.

вы́годно, *adv.* **1.** advantageously. **2.** *as pred.* it is profitable, it pays.

вы́год|ный (~ен, ~на), *adj.* advantageous, beneficial; profitable.

вы́гон, а, *m.* pasture; common.

вы́гонк|а, и, *f.* distillation.

выгоня́|ть, ю, *impf. of* вы́гнать.

выгора́жива|ть, ю, *impf. of* вы́городить.

выгора́|ть, ет, *impf. of* вы́гореть.

вы́гор|еть¹, ит, *pf.* (*of* ~а́ть) **1.** to burn down, burn out (*intrans.*). **2.** to fade.

вы́гор|еть², ит, *pf.* (*of* ~а́ть) (*3rd person only or impers.*; *coll.*) to succeed, come off.

вы́горо|дить, жу, дишь, *pf.* (*of* выгора́живать) **1.** to fence off. **2.** (*fig., coll.*) to shield, screen.

вы́гравир|овать, ую, *pf. of* гравирова́ть.

выгра́нива|ть, ю, *impf. of* вы́гранить.

вы́гран|ить, ю, ишь, *pf.* (*of* ~ивать) (*tech.*) to cut (*crystal, glass*).

вы́греб¹, а, *m.* **1.** raking out; clearing away. **2.** cesspool.

вы́гре|б², see ~сти.

выгреба́|ть, ю, *impf. of* вы́грести.

выгребн|о́й, *adj.* refuse; ~а́я я́ма cesspool.

вы́гре|сти¹, бу, бешь, *past* ~б, ~бла, *pf.* (*of* ~ба́ть) to rake out; to clear away.

вы́гре|сти², бу, бешь, *past* ~б, ~бла, *pf.* (*of* ~ба́ть) to row (out), pull (out).

выгружа́|ть(ся), ю(сь), *impf. of* вы́грузить(ся).

вы́гру|зить, жу, зишь, *pf.* (*of* ~жа́ть) to unload, unlade; to disembark.

вы́гру|зиться, жусь, зишься, *pf.* (*of* ~жа́ться) to disembark; (*mil.*) to detrain, debus.

вы́грузк|а, и, *f.* unloading; disembarkation.

вы́грузчик, а, *m.* unloader; stevedore.

выгрыза́|ть, ю, *impf. of* вы́грызть.

вы́грыза́|ть, у, ешь, *past* ~, ~ла, *pf.* (*of* ~а́ть) to gnaw out.

выда|ва́ть(ся), ю(сь), ёшь(ся), *impf. of* вы́дать(ся).

вы́дав|ить, лю, ишь, *pf.* (*of* ~ливать) **1.** to press out, squeeze out (*also fig.*; в. улыбку to force a smile. **2.** to break, knock out.

выда́влива|ть, ю, *impf. of* вы́давить.

выда́ива|ть, ю, *impf. of* вы́доить.

выда́лблива|ть, ю, *impf. of* вы́долбить.

вы́дань|е, я, *n. only in phrase* (*coll., obs.*) на в. marriageable.

вы́да|ть, м, шь, ст, дим, дите, дут, *pf.* (*of* ~ва́ть) **1.** to give (out), issue, produce; в. ве́ксель to draw a bill; в. зарпла́ту to pay out wages; в. про́пуск to issue a pass; в. кого́-н. за́муж (за + *a.*) to give someone in marriage (to); в. на-гора́ (*tech.*) to hoist, wind (to the surface); в. у́голь на-гора́ to produce coal. **2.** to give away, betray; to deliver up, extradite; в. голово́й to betray. **3.** (за + *a.*) to pass off (as), give out to be; (себя́) to pose (as); в. себя́ за свяще́нника to pose as a clergyman.

вы́да|ться, мся, шься, стся, димся, дитесь, дутся, *pf.* (*of* ~ва́ться) **1.** to protrude, project, jut out; (*fig.*) to stand out, be conspicuous. **2.** (*coll.*) to happen; как то́лько ~лся хоро́ший денёк, мы пое́хали в дере́вню on the first fine day that came along we went into the country.

вы́дач|а, и, *f.* **1.** issuing. **2.** issue; payment. **3.** extradition.

выдаю́щийся, *pres. part. of* выдава́ться *and adj.* prominent, salient; (*fig.*) eminent, outstanding; prominent.

выдвига́|ть(ся), ю(сь), *impf. of* вы́двинуть(ся).

выдвиже́н|ец, ца, *m.* worker promoted to an administrative post.

выдвиже́ни|е, я, *n.* **1.** nomination. **2.** promotion, advancement.

выдвиже́н|ка, ки, *f. of* ~ец.

выдвиже́нчеств|о, а, *n.* system of promotion of workers to positions of responsibility and authority.

выдвижно́й, *adj.* sliding; (*tech.*) telescopic.

вы́дви|нуть, ну, нешь, *pf.* (*of* ~га́ть) **1.** to move out, pull out. **2.** (*fig.*) to bring forward, advance; в. обвине́ние to bring an accusation. **3.** to promote; в. на до́лжность секретаря́ to promote to the post of secretary. **4.** to nominate, propose; в. чью-н. кандидату́ру, кого́-н. в кандида́ты to propose someone as candidate.

вы́дви|нуться, нусь, нешься, *pf.* (*of* ~га́ться) **1.** to move forward, move out; to slide in and out (*of a drawer, etc.*). **2.** to rise, get on (in the world). **3.** *pass. of* ~нуть.

вы́двор|ить, ю, ишь, *pf.* (*of* ~я́ть) (*coll. and leg.; obs.*) to evict; (*fig.*) to throw out.

выдворя́|ть, ю, ишь, *impf. of* вы́дворить.

вы́дел, а, *m.* apportionment.

вы́дел|ать, аю, *pf.* (*of* ~ывать) **1.** to manufacture; to process. **2.** to dress, curry (*leather*).

выделе́ни|е, я, *n.* **1.** (*physiol.*) secretion; excretion. **2.** (*chem.*) isolation. **3.** apportionment.

выдели́тельный, *adj.* (*physiol.*) secretory; excretory.

вы́дел|ить, ю, ишь, *pf.* (*of* ~я́ть) **1.** to pick out, single out; (*mil.*) to detach, detail; (*typ.*) в. курси́вом to italicize. **2.** to assign, earmark; to allot. **3.** (*physiol.*) to secrete; to excrete. **4.** (*chem.*) to isolate. **5.** to emit.

вы́дел|иться, юсь, ишься, *pf.* (*of* ~я́ться) **1.** to take one's share (*of a legacy*). **2.** (+*i.*) to stand out (for); to make a mark (by); он ~ился остроу́мием he was noted for his wit. **3.** to ooze out, exude. **4.** *pass. of* ~ить.

вы́делк|а, и, *f.* **1.** manufacture. **2.** workmanship. **3.** dressing, currying.

выде́лыва|ть, ю, *impf. of* вы́делать; что ты тепе́рь ~ешь? (*coll.*) what are you up to now?

выделя́|ть(ся), ю(сь), *impf. of* вы́делить(ся).

выдёргива|ть, ю, *impf. of* вы́дернуть.

выдержанност|ь, и, *f.* **1.** consistency. **2.** self-possession; firmness.

вы́держа|нный (~н, ~на), *p.p.p. of* ~ть *and adj.* **1.** consistent; ~нная поли́тика consistent policy. **2.** self-possessed; firm. **3.** mature; seasoned (*of wine, cheese, wood, etc.*).

вы́держ|ать, у, ишь, *pf.* (*of* ~ивать) **1.** to bear, hold; лёд вас не ~ит the ice will not hold you. **2.** (*fig.*) to bear, stand (up to), endure; to contain oneself; не в. to give in, break down; я не мог э́того бо́льше в. I could stand it no longer; ва́ши мне́ния не ~ат кри́тики your opinions will not stand up to criticism; выраже́ние лица́ у него́ бы́ло тако́е коми́чное, что я не ~ал his expression was so funny that I could not contain myself. **3.** в. экза́мен to pass an examination. **4.** в. не́сколько изда́ний to run into several editions. **5.** to keep, lay up; to mature; to season. **6.** в. под аре́стом to keep in custody. **7.** to maintain, sustain; в. роль to keep up a part, sustain an act; в. хара́ктер to stand firm; в. па́узу to pause.

выде́ржива|ть, ю, *impf. of* вы́держать.

вы́держк|а[1], и, *f.* **1.** endurance; self-possession. **2.** (*phot.*) exposure.

вы́держк|а[2], и, *f.* excerpt, quotation.

вы́дер|нуть, ну, нешь, *pf.* (*of* ~гивать) to pull out.

выдира́|ть, ю, *impf. of* вы́драть[1].

выдира́|ться, юсь, *impf. of* вы́драться.

вы́до|ить, ю, ишь, *pf.* (*of* выда́ивать) **1.** to milk (dry). **2.** to obtain (by milking).

вы́долб|ить, лю, ишь, *pf.* (*of* выда́лбливать) **1.** to hollow out, gouge out. **2.** (*coll.*) to learn by rote.

вы́дох, а, *m.* exhalation

вы́дохн|уть, у, ешь, *pf.* (*of* выдыха́ть) to breathe out.

вы́дохн|уться, усь, ешься, *pf.* (*of* выдыха́ться) to have lost fragrance, smell; (*of wines, etc.*) to be flat; (*fig.*) to be past one's best, be played out.

вы́др|а, ы, *f.* otter (*also fig., coll., of a thin, unattractive woman*).

вы́д|рать[1], еру, ерешь, *pf.* (*of* ~ира́ть) to tear out.

вы́д|рать[2], еру, ерешь, *pf.* (*of* драть 4) (*coll.*) to thrash, flog.

вы́д|раться, ерусь, ерешься, *pf.* (*of* ~ира́ться) (*coll.*) to extricate oneself.

вы́дрессир|овать, ую, *pf. of* дрессирова́ть.

вы́дуб|ить, лю, ишь, *pf. of* дуби́ть.

выдува́льщик, а, *m.* glass-blower.

выдува́|ть, ю, *impf. of* вы́дуть.

вы́дувк|а, и, *f.* (*tech.*) (glass-)blowing.

выдувно́й, *adj.* blown (*of glass*).

вы́думан|ный (~, ~а), *p.p.p. of* вы́думать *and adj.* made-up, fabricated; ~ная исто́рия fabrication, fiction.

вы́дум|ать, аю, *pf.* (*of* ~ывать) to invent; to

make up, fabricate; он по́роха не ~ает he will not set the Thames on fire; не вы́думай напи́ться! mind you don't get drunk!

вы́думк|а, и, *f.* **1.** invention; idea (*discovery, device*); голь на ~и хитра́ (*prov.*) necessity is the mother of invention. **2.** (*coll.*) inventiveness. **3.** (*coll.*) invention, fabrication (*lie*).

вы́думщик, а, *m.* (*coll.*) **1.** inventor. **2.** fabricator (*liar*).

выду́мыва|ть, ю, *impf. of* вы́думать; не ~й (*coll.*) don't argue; де́лай то, что тебе́ ве́лено, а не ~й do what you are told and don't argue.

вы́ду|ть, ю, ешь, *pf.* (*of* ~ва́ть) **1.** to blow out. **2.** (*impf.* дуть) (*tech.*) to blow. **3.** в ого́нь (*coll.*) to blow up a fire. **4.** (*impf.* дуть) (*coll.*) to drain, toss off (*drink*).

выдыха́ни|е, я, *n.* exhalation.

выдыха́|ть(ся), ю(сь), *impf. of* вы́дохнуть-(ся).

выеда́|ть, ю, *impf. of* вы́есть.

вы́еденн|ый, *p.p.p. of* вы́есть; не сто́ит ~ого яйца́ it is not worth a brass farthing.

вы́езд, а, *m.* **1.** departure. **2.** exit (*concr.*). **3.** (*obs.*) turn-out, equipage. **4.** (*obs.*) going out (*to balls, theatres, etc.*).

вы́ез|дить, жу, дишь, *pf.* (*of* ~жа́ть) to break(-in); to train (*horses*).

вы́ездк|а, и, *f.* breaking-in; training (*of horses*).

вы́езд|но́й, *adj. of* вы́езд; ~на́я се́ссия суда́ assizes; в. матч (*sport*) away match; в. лаке́й (*obs.*) footman; ~но́е пла́тье (*obs.*) evening dress; party dress.

выезжа́|ть, ю, *impf. of* вы́ездить *and* вы́ехать.

вы́емк|а, и, *f.* **1.** taking out; collection (*of letters from letter-box*); в. докуме́нтов seizure of documents. **2.** excavation. **3.** hollow; groove; (*archit.*) fluting. **4.** (*railways*) cutting. **5.** (*tailoring*) cut, cutting.

вы́е|сть, м, шь, ст, дим, дите, дят, *pf.* (*of* ~да́ть) to eat away; (*coll.*) to corrode.

вы́е|хать, ду, дешь, *pf.* (*of* ~зжа́ть) **1.** to go out, depart (*in or on a vehicle or on an animal*); to drive out; to ride out. **2.** to leave, move (*from dwelling-place*). **3.** (на+ *p.*) (*fig., coll.*) to make use (of), exploit, take advantage (of).

выжа́рива|ть, ю, *impf. of* вы́жарить.

вы́жар|ить, ю, ишь, *pf.* (*of* ~ивать) (*coll.*) **1.** to heat up. **2.** to roast to a turn; to fry up.

вы́ж|ать¹, му, мешь, *pf.* (*of* ~има́ть) **1.** to press out, wring (out); to squeeze out; в. после́дние си́лы из кого́-н. to squeeze the last ounce of effort out of someone; ~атый лимо́н (*fig.*) a has-been. **2.** (*sport*) to lift (*weights*).

вы́ж|ать², ну, нешь, *pf.* (*of* ~ина́ть) to reap clean.

вы́жд|ать, у, ешь, *pf.* (*of* выжида́ть) (+*g.*) to wait (for); to bide one's time.

вы́ж|ечь, гу, жешь, *pf.* (*of* ~ига́ть) **1.** to burn down; to burn out; to scorch. **2.** (*med.*) to cauterize. **3.** to make a mark, *etc.*, by burning; в. клеймо́ (на+*p.*) to brand.

вы́жжен|ный, *p.p.p. of* вы́жечь *and adj.* ~ная земля́ scorched earth.

выжива́ни|е, я, *n.* survival; в. наибо́лее приспосо́бленных (*biol.*) survival of the fittest.

выжива́|ть, ю, *impf. of* вы́жить.

вы́жиг|а, и, *m. and f.* (*coll.*) cunning rogue; skinflint.

выжига́ни|е, я, *n.* **1.** scorching; в. по де́реву poker-work. **2.** (*med.*) cauterization.

выжига́|ть, ю, *impf. of* вы́жечь; в. по де́реву to do poker-work.

выжида́ни|е, я, *n.* waiting; temporizing.

выжида́тельн|ый, *adj.* waiting; temporizing; занима́ть ~ую пози́цию to temporize, play a waiting game.

выжида́|ть, ю, *impf. of* вы́ждать.

вы́жим, а, *m.* (*sport*) press-up.

выжима́л|а, ы, *m. and f.* (*sl.*) exploiter.

выжима́ни|е, я, *n.* **1.** squeezing; wringing. **2.** (*sport*) (weight-)lifting.

выжима́|ть, ю, *impf. of* вы́жать¹.

вы́жимк|и, ов, *no sing.* husks, marc; льняны́е в. linseed-cake.

выжина́|ть, ю, *impf. of* вы́жать².

вы́жи|ть, ву, вешь, *pf.* (*of* ~ва́ть) **1.** to survive; to live through. **2.** (*coll.*) to live on in spite of something, hold out, stick it out; они́ три ме́сяца ~ли на плаву́чей льди́не they stuck it out for three months on an ice-floe. **3.** в. из ума́ to lose possession of one's faculties. **4.** (*coll.*) to drive out, hound out; to get rid of.

вы́жлец, а, *m.* (*hunting*) hound.

выжля́тник, а, *m.* (*hunting*) whipper-in.

вызва́нива|ть, ю, *impf. of* вы́звонить.

вы́з|вать, ову, овешь, *pf.* (*of* ~ыва́ть) **1.** to call (out); to send for; в. актёра to call for an actor; в. врача́ to call a doctor, send for a doctor; в. ученика́ to call out a pupil; в. по телефо́ну to ring up; в. в суд (*leg.*) to summon(s), subpoena. **2.** to challenge; в. на дуэ́ль to challenge to a duel, call out; в. на открове́нность to draw out. **3.** to call forth, provoke; to cause; to stimulate, rouse; в. любопы́тство to provoke curiosity; в. пожа́р to cause a fire.

вы́з|ваться, овусь, овешься, *pf.* (*of* ~ыва́ться) (+*inf. or* в+*a.*) to volunteer; to offer; в. помо́чь to offer to help; в. в экспеди́цию to volunteer for an expedition.

вы́звезд|ить, ит, *pf. impers.* ~ит, ~ило, the stars are (were) out, it is (was) a starlit night.

вы́звол|ить, ю, ишь, *pf.* (*of* ~я́ть) (*coll.*) to help out; в. из беды́ to get out of trouble.

вызволя́|ть, ю, *impf. of* вы́зволить.

вы́звон|ить, ю, ишь, *pf.* (*of* вызва́нивать) **1.** to ring (out) (*of bells*). **2.** (*fig.*) to ring, jingle.

выздора́влива|ть, ю, *impf. of* вы́здороветь.

вы́здорове|ть, ю, ешь, *pf.* (*of* выздора́вливать) to recover, get better.

выздоровле́ни|е, я, *n.* recovery; convalescence.

вы́зов, а, *m.* **1.** call; в. по телефо́ну telephone call. **2.** summons. **3.** challenge; бро́сить в. to throw down a challenge.

вы́золо|тить, чу, тишь, *pf. of* золоти́ть.

вы́золочен|ный (~, ~а), *p.p.p. of* вы́золотить *and adj.* gilt.

вызрева́|ть, ю, *impf. of* вы́зреть.

вы́зре|ть, ю, ешь, *pf.* (*of* ~ва́ть) to ripen.

вы́зубр|ить, ю, ишь, *pf.* (*of* зубри́ть²) (*coll.*) to learn by heart.

вызыва́|ть(ся), ю(сь), *impf. of* вы́звать(ся).

вызыва́|ющий, *pres. part. act. of* ~ть *and adj.* defiant; provocative.

вы́игр|ать, аю, *pf.* (*of* ~ывать) to win; to gain; в. вре́мя to gain time; он ~ал в моём мне́нии he has gone up in my estimation.

выи́грыва|ть, ю, *impf. of* вы́играть.

вы́игрыш, а, *m.* **1.** win; winning. **2.** gain, winnings; prize; быть в ~е to be winner; (*fig.*) to be the gainer, stand to gain.

вы́игрышн|ый, *adj.* **1.** winning; в. ход winning move; в. заём premium bonds (issue); в. биле́т lottery ticket. **2.** advantageous; effective; ~ое положе́ние advantageous position; ~ая нару́жность winsome appearance.

вы́и|скать, щу, щешь, *pf.* to light upon, track down, run to earth.

вы́и|скаться, щусь, щешься, *pf.* (*coll., iron.*) to turn up, put in an appearance.

выи́скива|ть, ю, *impf.* to seek out, try to trace.

вы́|йти, йду, йдешь, *past* ~шел, ~шла, *pf.* (*of* ~ходи́ть) **1.** to go out; to come out; она́ вчера́ ~шла в пе́рвый раз по́сле боле́зни she went out yesterday for the first time since her illness; в. в лю́ди to get on in the world; в. в отста́вку to retire; в. в офице́ры to be commissioned, get a commission; в. в тира́ж (*of a bond, etc.; fin.*) to be drawn; (*fig.*) to take a back seat; в. в фина́л (*sport*) to reach the final; в. из берего́в to overflow its banks; в. из бо́я (*mil.*) to disengage; в. из ваго́на to alight from a carriage; в. из во́зраста to pass the age limit; в. из головы́, из па́мяти, из ума́ (*coll.*) to go out of one's head; в. из грани́ц (+*g.*), из

преде́лов (+*g.*) (*fig.*) to exceed the bounds (of); в. из долго́в to get out of debt; в. из игры́ to go out of a game; в. из положе́ния to get out of a (tight) spot; в. из себя́ to lose one's temper; в. из терпе́ния to lose patience; в. на вы́зовы (*theatr.*) to take a call; в. на прогу́лку to go out for a walk; в. на сце́ну to come on to the stage. **2.** (в свет) (*of publications*) to come out, appear. **3.** (*of photographs or persons photographed*) to come out; вы хорошо́ ~шли на э́том сни́мке you have come out well in this photo. **4.** в., в. за́муж (за+*a.*) (*of a woman*) to marry. **5.** to come (out); to turn out (*also impers.*); to ensue; не в. (+*i. of noun*; *coll.*) to be lacking (in); в. победи́телем to come out victor; из него́ ~шел бы хоро́ший лётчик he would have made a good pilot; из э́того куска́ мате́рии ~шла хоро́шенькая блу́за that piece of material has made a pretty blouse; из э́того ничего́ не ~йдет nothing will come of it; ~шло, (что) он ни одного́ сло́ва не по́нял it turned out that he did not understand a single word; как бы чего́ не ~шло (*coll.*) it will come to no good; ро́стом не ~шел (*coll.*) he has not grown much; умо́м не ~шел (*coll.*) he is not too bright. **6.** to be by origin; она́ ~шла из крестья́н she is of peasant origin, comes of peasant stock. **7.** to be used up; (*of a period of time*) to have expired; горчи́ца вся ~шла the mustard is used up; срок уже́ ~шел time is up. **8.** го́да ~шли (+*d. or g.*; *coll.*) (*i*) to be of age, (*ii*) to be over the age (for).

вы́ка|зать, жу, жешь, *pf.* (*of* ~зывать) (*coll.*) to manifest, display (*abstract qualities*).

выка́зыва|ть, ю, *impf. of* вы́казать.

выка́лива|ть, ю, *impf. of* вы́калить.

вы́кал|ить, ю, ишь, *pf.* (*of* ~ивать) (*tech.*) to fire.

выка́лыва|ть, ю, *impf. of* вы́колоть.

выка́пчива|ть, ю, *impf. of* вы́коптить.

выка́пыва|ть(ся), ю(сь), *impf. of* вы́копать(ся).

вы́карабк|аться, аюсь, *pf.* (*of* ~иваться) to scramble out; (*fig., coll.*) to get (oneself) out; в. из боле́зни to get over an illness.

выкара́бкива|ться, юсь, *impf. of* вы́карабкаться.

выка́рмлива|ть, ю, *impf. of* вы́кормить.

вы́кат|ать, аю, *pf.* (*of* ~ывать¹) **1.** to roll out. **2.** (*impf.* ката́ть) to smooth out; to mangle (*linen*). **3.** (*coll.*) to roll (in).

вы́кат|аться, аюсь, *pf.* (*of* ~ываться¹) (*coll.*) **1.** *pass. of* ~ать. **2.** to roll (*intrans.*).

вы́ка|тить, чу, тишь, *pf.* (*of* ~тывать²) **1.** to roll out; to wheel out. **2.** (*coll.*) to come rolling out, come bowling out; (*fig.*) to hare out. **3.** в. глаза́ (*coll.*) to open one's eyes wide, star~

вы́ка|титься, чусь, тишься, *pf.* (*of* ⌣ты-
ваться²) to roll out (*intrans.*).

вы́катк|а¹, и, *f.* mangling.

вы́катк|а², и, *f.* rolling out.

вы́ка́тыва|ть(ся)¹, ю(сь), *impf. of* вы́ка-
тать(ся).

вы́ка́тыва|ть(ся)², ю(сь), *impf. of* вы́ка-
тить(ся); ∼йся (*coll.*) be off! get out!

вы́ка|ть, ю, *impf.* (*coll.*) to address formally,
address as 'вы'.

вы́кач|ать, аю, *pf.* (*of* ⌣ивать) to pump out;
(*fig.*, *coll.*) to extort.

вы́кача|ть, ю, *impf. of* вы́качать.

вы́качк|а, и, *f.* pumping out; (*fig.*, *coll.*)
extortion.

вы́кашива|ть, ю, *impf. of* вы́косить.

вы́кашлива|ть(ся), ю(сь), *impf. of* вы́ка-
шлять(ся).

вы́кашл|ять, яю, *pf.* (*of* ⌣ивать) to cough
up.

вы́кашл|яться, яюсь, *pf.* (*of* ⌣иваться) to
clear one's throat.

вы́ки́дыва|ть, ю, *impf. of* вы́кинуть.

вы́кидыш, а, *m.* (*med.*) 1. miscarriage; abortion. 2. foetus (*after miscarriage or abortion*).

вы́ки|нуть, ну, нешь, *pf.* (*of* ⌣дывать) 1. to
throw out, reject. 2. to put out; в. флаг to
hoist a flag. 3. (*med.*) to have a miscarriage;
to have an abortion. 4. (*coll.*) в. но́мер,
шту́ку, фо́кус to play a trick.

вы́кипа́|ть, ет, *impf. of* вы́кипеть.

вы́кип|еть, ит, *pf.* (*of* ∼а́ть) to boil away.

вы́кипя|тить, чу, тишь, *pf.* to boil out, boil
through.

вы́кладк|а, и, *f.* 1. laying-out; lay-out.
2. (*tech.*) facing; в. кирпичо́м bricking.
3. (*mil.*) kit; в по́лной ∼е in full marching
order. 4. (*math.*) computation.

вы́кла́дыва|ть, ю, *impf. of* вы́ложить.

вы́кл|евать, юю, юешь, *pf.* (*of* ∼ёвывать)
1. to peck out. 2. to peck up.

вы́кл|еваться, ююсь, юешься, *pf.* (*of*
∼ёвываться) to hatch out (*of birds*).

вы́клёвыва|ть(ся), ю(сь), *impf. of* вы́кле-
вать(ся); пока́ что ничего́ не ∼ется (*coll.*)
at the moment nothing is happening, there
are no bites.

вы́кле́ива|ть, ю, *impf. of* вы́клеить.

вы́кле|ить, ю, ишь, *pf.* (*of* ⌣ивать) (*coll.*)
to paste up; в. обо́ями to paper.

вы́клика́|ть, ю, *impf. of* вы́кликнуть.

вы́клик|нуть, ну, нешь, *pf.* (*of* ∼а́ть) to call
out; в. по спи́ску to call over the roll.

вы́ключа́тел|ь, я, *m.* switch.

вы́ключа́|ть, ю, *impf. of* вы́ключить.

вы́ключ|ить, у, ишь, *pf.* (*of* ∼а́ть) 1. to
turn off, switch off. 2. to remove, exclude;
в. кого́-н. из спи́ска to take someone's
name off a list. 3. (*typ.*) to justify.

выкля́нчива|ть, ю, *impf.* 1. *impf. of* выклян-
чить. 2. *impf. only* в. что́-н. у кого́-н. to try
to get something out of someone.

вы́клянч|ить, у, ишь, *pf.* (*of* ∼ивать) (у +
g.; *coll.*) to cadge (from, off), get (out of).

вы́к|овать, ую, уешь, *pf.* (*of* ∼о́вывать) to
forge (*also fig.*).

вы́ко́выва|ть, ю, *impf. of* вы́ковать.

вы́ковы́рива|ть, ю, *impf. of* вы́ковырять.

вы́ковыр|ять, яю, *pf.* (*of* ⌣ивать) to pluck
out, pick out; (*coll.*) to hunt out.

вы́кола́чива|ть, ю, *impf. of* вы́колотить.

вы́коло|тить, чу, тишь, *pf.* (*of* вы́кола́чи-
вать) 1. to knock out, beat out. 2. to beat
(*a carpet, etc.*). 3. (*coll.*) to extort, wring out.
4. (*coll.*) to make (*money*).

вы́кол|оть, ю, ешь, *pf.* (*of* выка́лывать) 1. to
thrust out; в. глаза́ кому́-н. to put out
someone's eyes; хоть глаз ∼и, *see* глаз. 2. to
tattoo.

вы́колуп|ать, аю, *pf.* (*of* ⌣ывать) (*coll.*) to
pick out.

вы́колу́пыва|ть, ю, *impf. of* вы́колупать.

вы́копа|ть, ю, *pf.* (*of* выка́пывать) 1. to dig;
в. я́му to dig a hole. 2. (*impf. also* копа́ть)
to dig up, dig out; to exhume; (*fig.*, *coll.*)
to unearth.

вы́копа|ться, юсь, *pf.* (*of* выка́пываться)
(*coll.*) to dig oneself out.

вы́коп|тить, чу, тишь, *pf.* (*of* выка́пчи-
вать) to smoke (*trans.*).

вы́корм|ить, лю, ишь, *pf.* (*of* выка́рмли-
вать) to rear, bring up.

вы́корм|ок, ка, *m.* (*coll.*) fosterling; (*fig.*)
protégé; (*pejor.*) creature.

вы́кормыш, а, *m.* = вы́кормок.

вы́корч|евать, ую, *pf.* (*of* ∼ёвывать) to up-
root; (*fig.*) to root out, extirpate.

вы́корчёвыва|ть, ю, *impf. of* вы́корчевать.

вы́ко|сить, шу, сишь, *pf.* (*of* выка́шивать)
to mow clean.

вы́кра́дыва|ть(ся), ю(сь), *impf. of* вы́-
красть(ся).

вы́кра́ива|ть, ю, *impf. of* вы́кроить.

вы́кра|сить, шу, сишь, *pf.* (*of* ⌣шивать) to
paint; to dye.

вы́кра|сть, ду, дешь, *past* ∼л, *pf.* (*of* ⌣ды-
вать) to steal; (*fig.*) to plagiarize.

вы́кра|сться, дусь, дешься, *past* ∼лся, *pf.*
(*of* ⌣дываться) (*coll.*) to steal away, steal
out.

вы́кра́шива|ть, ю, *impf. of* вы́красить.

вы́крест, а, *m.* (*coll.*) convert (*to Christianity*,
esp. of Jews).

вы́кре|стить, щу, стишь, *pf.* (*coll.*) to con-
vert (*to Christianity*).

вы́крик, а, *m.* cry, shout; yell.

вы́кри́кива|ть, ю, *impf. of* вы́крикнуть.

вы́крик|нуть, ну, нешь, *pf.* (*of* ⌣ивать) to
cry out; to yell.

вы́кристаллиз|оваться, уюсь, *pf.* (*of* ~о́вы-ваться) to crystallize (*also fig.*).

вы́кристаллизо́выва|ться, юсь, *impf. of* вы́кристаллизоваться.

вы́кро|ить, ю, ишь, *pf.* (*of* выкра́ивать) 1. (*tailoring*) to cut out. 2. (*fig.*) to find; в. вре́мя to make, find time.

вы́кройк|а, и, *f.* pattern; снять ~y to cut out a pattern.

выкрута́с|ы, ов, *no sing.* (*coll.*) intricate movements, figures; flourishes (*in handwriting*); (*fig.*) peculiarities, idiosyncrasies; говори́ть с ~ами to speak affectedly; челове́к с ~ами eccentric.

вы́кру|тить, чу, тишь, *pf.* (*of* ~чивать) 1. to unscrew. 2. (*tech.*) to twist; в. верёвку to twist a rope; (*coll.*) ему́ ~тили ру́ку they twisted his arm.

вы́кру|титься, чусь, тишься, *pf.* (*of* ~чиваться) 1. to come unscrewed. 2. (*fig., coll.*) to extricate oneself, get oneself out (of); ему́ удало́сь в. из беды́ he has managed to get himself out of the mess.

выкру́чива|ть(ся), ю(сь), *impf. of* вы́крутить(ся).

выкувы́ркива|ть, ю, *impf. of* вы́кувырнуть.

вы́кувыр|нуть, ну, нешь, *pf.* (*of* ~кивать) (*coll.*) to overturn.

вы́куп, а, *m.* 1. (*leg.*) redemption. 2. ransom; redemption-fee, redemption-dues.

вы́купа|ть(ся), ю(сь), *pf. of* купа́ть(ся).

выкупа́|ть, а́ю, *impf. of* вы́купить.

вы́куп|ить, лю, ишь, *pf.* (*of* ~а́ть) 1. to ransom. 2. to redeem; в. из-под зало́га to get out of pawn.

выкупно́й, *adj.* redemption.

выку́рива|ть, ю, *impf. of* вы́курить.

вы́кур|ить, ю, ишь, *pf.* (*of* ~ивать) 1. to smoke; to finish smoking; пойдёмте, — но, пре́жде всего́, ~ите ва́шу папиро́су! let's go, but first of all finish your cigarette. 2. to smoke out; (*fig., coll.*) to drive out. 3. to distil.

вы́ку|сить, шу, сишь, *pf.* (*of* ~сывать) to bite through; на́кось, ~си! (*coll.*) you'll get nothing out of me!; you shan't have it!

вы́ку́сыва|ть, ю, *impf. of* вы́кусить.

вы́куша|ть, ю, *pf.* (*obs.*) to drink.

вы́ку|шу, сишь, *see* ~сить.

вы́ку|ю, ешь, *see* вы́ковать.

выла́влива|ть, ю, *impf. of* вы́ловить.

вы́лаз, а, *m.* (*coll.*) opening (*in animal's burrow, etc.*).

вы́ла|зить, жу, зишь, *pf.* (*coll.*) to climb all over.

выла́|зить, жу, зишь, *impf.* (*dial.*) to fall out, come out.

вы́лазк|а, и, *f.* 1. (*mil.*) sally, sortie (*also fig.*). 2. ramble, excursion, outing.

вы́лака|ть, ю, *pf.* (*of* лака́ть) to lap up.

вы́ла́мыва|ть, ю, *impf. of* вы́ломать *and* вы́ломить.

выла́щива|ть, ю, *impf. of* вы́лощить.

вы́леж|ать, у, ишь, *pf.* (*of* ~ивать) (*coll.*) to remain lying down; to stay in bed, keep one's bed.

вы́леж|аться, усь, ишься, *pf.* (*of* ~иваться) (*coll.*) 1. to have a thorough rest. 2. to ripen; to mature (*of tobacco, etc.*).

вылёжива|ть(ся), ю(сь), *impf. of* вы́лежать(ся).

вылеза́|ть, ю, *impf. of* вы́лезть.

вы́лезт|и = ~ь.

вы́лез|ть, у, ешь, *past* ~, ~ла, *pf.* (*of* ~а́ть) 1. to crawl out; to climb out; (*coll.*) to get out, alight. 2. to fall out, come out; по́сле боле́зни у него́ ~ли почти́ все во́лосы almost all his hair fell out after his illness. 3. (с+*i.*; *coll., pejor.*) to come out with; он, должно́ быть, ~ет с каки́м-н. глу́пым замеча́нием he is sure to come out with some fatuous remark.

вы́леп|ить, лю, ишь, *pf. of* лепи́ть.

вы́лет, а, *m.* flight (*of birds*); (*aeron.*) take-off, commencement of flight; sortie.

вылета́|ть, ю, *impf. of* вы́лететь.

вы́ле|теть, чу, тишь, *pf.* (*of* ~та́ть) 1. to fly out; (*aeron.*) to take off; (*fig., coll.*) to rush out, dash out; в. пу́лей to go like a shot from a gun; не дожда́вшись отве́та, он ~тел из ко́мнаты without waiting for an answer he rushed from the room; в. из головы́ to escape one; его́ сообще́ние ~тело у меня́ из головы́ I clean forgot his message; в. в трубу́ (*coll.*) to become bankrupt, go broke. 2. в. со слу́жбы (*fig., coll.*) to be given the sack.

выле́чива|ть(ся), ю(сь), *impf. of* вы́лечить(ся).

вы́леч|ить, у, ишь, *pf.* (*of* ~ивать) (от) to cure (of) (*also fig.*).

вы́леч|иться, усь, ишься, *pf.* (*of* ~иваться) (от) to recover (from), be cured (of); to get over (*also fig.*); он ~ился от наркома́нии he has been cured of his drug-addiction.

вы́леч|у¹, ишь, *see* ~ить.

вы́ле|чу², тишь, *see* ~теть.

вылива́|ть(ся), ю(сь), *impf. of* вы́лить(ся).

вы́ли|зать, жу, жешь, *pf.* (*of* ~зывать) to lick clean, lick up.

вы́ли́зыва|ть, ю, *impf. of* вы́лизать.

вы́линя|ть, ю, *pf. of* линя́ть.

вы́лит|ый (~, ~а), *p.p.p. of* ~ь; (*fig., coll.; long form only*) он — в. оте́ц he is the (spit and) image of his father, the very spit of his father.

вы́л|ить, ью, ьешь, *pf.* (*of* ~ива́ть) 1. to pour out; to empty (out). 2. (*tech.*) to cast, found; to mould.

вы́л|иться, ьюсь, ьешься, *pf.* (*of* ~ива́ться)
1. to run out, flow out; (*fig.*) to flow (from),
spring (from); её жа́лобы ~ились пря́мо
из се́рдца her complaints came straight
from the heart. **2.** (в+*a. or* в фо́рму +*g.*)
to take the form (of); to be expressed,
express itself (in); никто́ не знал, во что
~ьется его́ восто́рг no one knew how his
feeling of delight would express itself.

вы́лов|ить, лю, ишь, *pf.* (*of* выла́вливать)
1. to fish out; уто́пленника наконе́ц ~или
из реки́ the drowned man has at last been
fished out of the river. **2.** to draw out (*catch
all the fish in a stream, etc.*); в. всю ры́бу в
пруду́ to draw out a pond.

вы́лож|ить, у, ишь, *pf.* (*of* выкла́дывать)
1. to lay out, spread out; (*fig., coll.*) to tell;
to reveal, make an exposé (of). **2.** (+*i.*) to
cover, lay (with); в. дёрном to turf; в.
ка́мнем to face with masonry, revet;
(*tailoring*) to decorate, embellish (with).
3. (*dial.*) to geld.

вы́лом, а, *m.* **1.** breaking open; breaking
off. **2.** breach.

вы́лома|ть, ю, *pf.* (*of* выла́мывать) to break
open; to break off.

вы́лом|ить, лю, ишь, *pf.* (*coll.*) = вы́ло-
мать.

вы́ломк|а, и, *f.* breaking off.

вы́лощен|ный (~, ~а), *p.p.p. of* вы́лощить
and adj. **1.** glossy. **2.** (*coll., fig.*) polished,
smooth.

вы́лощ|ить, у, ишь, *pf.* (*of* выла́щивать) to
polish; (*fig., coll.*) to make polished, sophis-
ticated.

вы́лу|дить, жу, дишь, *pf.* (*of* ~живать) to
tin(-plate).

вылу́жива|ть, ю, *impf. of* вы́лудить.

вы́лу|жу, дишь, *see* ~дить.

вы́луп|ить, лю, ишь, *pf.* (*of* ~ля́ть) (*coll.*)
to peel; to shell; в. глаза́ to goggle.

вы́луп|иться, люсь, ишься, *pf.* (*of* ~ля́ться)
to hatch (out); не счита́й утя́т, пока́ не
~ились (*prov.*) don't count your chickens
before they are hatched.

вылупля́|ть(ся), ю(сь), *impf. of* вы́лупить(ся).

вылу́щива|ть, ю, *impf. of* вы́лущить.

вы́лущ|ить, у, ишь, *pf.* (*of* ~ивать) **1.** to
shell (*peas*). **2.** (*med.*) to remove (*by surgical
operation*).

вы́л|ью, ьешь, *see* ~ить.

вы́ма|зать, жу, жешь, *pf.* (*of* ма́зать 2 *and*
~зывать) (+*i.*) to smear (with), daub
(with); (*coll.*) to dirty; в. свои́ па́льцы в
черни́лах to make one's fingers inky.

вы́ма|заться, жусь, жешься, *pf.* (*of* ма́зать-
ся 1 *and* ~зываться) (*coll.*) to get dirty, make
oneself dirty.

выма́зыва|ть(ся), ю(сь), *impf. of* вы́ма-
зать(ся).

выма́лива|ть, ю, *impf.* **1.** *impf. of* вы́молить.
2. *impf. only* to beg for.

выма́лыва|ть, ю, *impf. of* вы́молоть.

выма́нива|ть, ю, *impf. of* вы́манить.

вы́ман|ить, ю, ишь, *pf.* (*of* ~ивать) **1.** (у+
g.) to cheat, swindle (out of); to wheedle
(out of); у него́ ~или поже́ртвование they
wheedled a contribution out of him. **2.**
(из+*g.*) to entice (from), lure (out of, from).

вы́мар|ать, аю, *pf.* (*of* ~ывать) (*coll.*) **1.** to
soil, dirty. **2.** to strike out, cross out.

выма́рива|ть, ю, *impf. of* вы́морить.

вы́марк|а, и, *f.* striking out, crossing out,
deletion.

выма́рыва|ть, ю, *impf. of* вы́марать.

выма́тыва|ть, ю, *impf. of* вы́мотать.

вы́махн|уть, у, ешь, *pf.* (*coll.*) to fly out; to
leap out.

выма́чива|ть, ю, *impf. of* вы́мочить.

выма́щива|ть, ю, *impf. of* вы́мостить.

вы́межева|ть, ю, *pf.* (*of* вымежёвывать)
(*agric.*) to measure out (*strips of land*).

вымежёвыва|ть, ю, *impf. of* вы́межевать.

вы́м|ени, енем, *see* ~я.

выме́нива|ть, ю, *impf. of* вы́менять.

вы́мен|ять, яю, *pf.* (*of* ~ивать) (на+*a.*) to
receive in exchange, barter (for); в. про-
ду́кты на оде́жду to barter produce for
clothing.

вы́м|ереть, ру, решь, *past* ~ер, ~ерла, *pf.*
(*of* ~ира́ть) **1.** to die out, become extinct.
2. to become desolate, deserted.

вымерз|а́ть, а́ю, *impf. of* вы́мерзнуть.

вы́мерз|нуть, ну, нешь, *past* ~, ~ла, *pf.* (*of*
~а́ть) **1.** to be killed by frost. **2.** to freeze
(right through).

выме́рива|ть, ю, *impf. of* вы́мерить.

вы́мер|ить, ю, ишь, *pf.* (*of* ~ивать) to
measure.

вы́мер|ший, *past part. of* ~еть *and adj.* ex-
tinct.

вы́меря|ть, ю = вы́мерить.

вымеря́|ть, ю = выме́ривать.

вы́ме|сти, ту, тешь, *past* ~л, *pf.* (*of* ~та́ть)
1. to sweep out; to sweep clean; в. сор to
sweep out refuse; в. ко́мнату to sweep a
room clean. **2.** (*coll.*) to throw out, chuck
out.

вы́ме|стить, щу, стишь, *pf.* (*of* ~ща́ть)
1. (+*d.*; *obs.*) to retaliate, take reprisals
(against). **2.** (на+*p.*) to vent; в. зло́бу на
ком-н. to vent one's anger on someone.

вы́мет|ать¹, аю, *pf.* (*of* ~ывать) **1.** to put
out, cast out (*a net, etc.*). **2.** в. икру́ to
spawn.

вы́мет|ать², аю, *pf.* (*of* ~ывать) в. пе́тли to
make buttonholes.

вымета́|ть, ю, *impf. of* вы́мести.

вымета́|ться, юсь, *impf.* (*coll.*) to clear out,
clear off (*intrans.*).

вымётыва|ть, ю, *impf. of* выметать.

вымеща|ть, ю, *impf. of* выместить.

вы́ме|щу, стишь, *see* ~стить.

вымина́|ть, ю, *impf. of* вымять.

вымира́|ть, ю, *impf. of* вымереть.

вы́м|ну, нешь, *see* ~ять.

вымога́тел|ь, я, *m.* extortioner.

вымога́тельский, *adj.* extortionate.

вымога́тельств|о, а, *n.* extortion.

вымога́|ть, ю, *impf.* to extort; to wring (out); угро́зами он нере́дко ~л у неё обеща́ния he frequently wrung promises out of her by means of threats.

вы́моин|а, ы, *f.* (*dial.*) gully.

вымока́|ть, ю, *impf. of* вымокнуть.

вы́мок|нуть, ну, нешь, *past* ~, ~ла, *pf* (*of* ~а́ть) 1. (*of crops, foodstuffs, etc.*) to rot, ret; to become soggy. 2. to be drenched, be soaked; мы ~ли до ни́тки we are soaked to the skin.

вымола́чива|ть, ю, *impf. of* вымолотить.

вы́молв|ить, лю, ишь, *pf.* to say, utter (*usually with neg.*); за весь ве́чер он сло́ва не ~ил he did not say a word all evening.

вы́мол|ить, ю, ишь, *pf.* (*of* выма́ливать) to obtain by asking, by entreaties; to beg (for) and obtain; (у Бо́га) to obtain by prayer.

вы́молот, а, *m.* 1. threshing. 2. grain (obtained by threshing).

вы́моло|тить, чу, тишь, *pf.* (*of* вымола́чивать) to thresh (out).

вы́молот|ки, ок-ков, *no sing.* (*dial.*) chaff.

вы́м|олоть, елю, елешь, *pf.* (*of* выма́лывать) (*coll.*) to obtain by grinding.

вымора́жива|ть, ю, *impf. of* выморозить.

вы́мор|ить, ю, ишь, *pf.* (*of* мори́ть[1] *and* выма́ривать) to exterminate; го́лодом в. to starve out.

вы́моро|зить, жу, зишь, *pf.* (*of* вымора́живать) 1. to cool; to air, give an airing (to). 2. to freeze out; freeze to death (*trans.*).

вы́морочн|ый, *adj.* (*leg.*) escheated; ~ое иму́щество escheat.

вы́мо|стить, щу, стишь, *pf.* (*of* мости́ть *and* выма́щивать) to pave.

вы́мота|ть, ю, *pf.* (*of* выма́тывать) (*coll.*) 1. to wind (*wool*). 2. to wind off, use up (*wool*); (*fig.*) to use up; to exhaust; в. ду́шу to annoy, wear out; они́ ~ли не́рвы друг дру́гу they got on one another's nerves.

вы́мота|ться, юсь, *pf.* (*of* выма́тываться) (*coll.*) 1. *pass. of* ~ть. 2. to be worn out.

вы́моч|ить, у, ишь, *pf.* (*of* выма́чивать) 1. to soak, drench. 2. to ret (*flax, hemp*); to steep, macerate.

вы́мо|щу, стишь, *see* ~стить.

вы́м|ою, оешь, *see* ~ыть.

вы́мпел, а, *m.* 1. pendant, pennant. 2. (*naut.*) unit; эска́дра в соста́ве двадцати́ ~ов a squadron consisting of twenty units.

3. (*aeron.*) message bag (*used for messages dropped by air*).

вы́мр|у, ешь, *see* вымереть.

вы́мучен|ный (~, ~а), *p.p.p. of* вымучить *and adj.* forced; (*lit.*) laboured.

вы́мучива|ть, ю, *impf. of* вымучить.

вы́муч|ить, у, ишь, *pf.* (*of* ~ивать) (из+*g.*) to extort (from), force (out of); он наконе́ц ~ил согла́сие у отца́ at last he extorted his father's consent.

вы́муштр|овать, ую, *pf. of* муштрова́ть.

вымыва́|ть(ся), ю(сь), *impf. of* вымыть-(ся).

вы́мыс|ел, ла, *m.* 1. invention, fabrication. 2. fantasy, flight of imagination.

вы́мы|слить, слю, слишь, *pf.* (*of* ~шля́ть) (*obs.*) to think up, invent; to imagine.

вы́м|ыть, ою, оешь, *pf.* (*of* мыть *and* ~ыва́ть) 1. to wash; to wash out, off; в. го́лову кому́-н. to give someone a dressing-down. 2. to wash away.

вы́м|ыться, оюсь, оешься, *pf.* (*of* мы́ться *and* ~ыва́ться) to wash oneself.

вы́мышлен|ный (~, ~а), *p.p.p. of* вымыслить *and adj.* fictitious, imaginary.

вымышля́|ть, ю, *impf. of* вымыслить.

вы́м|я, ени, ени, енем, ени, *pl.* ~ена́, ~ён, ~ена́м, *n.* udder.

вы́м|ять, ну, нешь, *pf.* (*of* ~ина́ть) 1. to knead, work (*clay*). 2. (*dial.*) to trample down.

вына́шива|ть, ю, *impf. of* выносить.

вынесе́ни|е, я, *n.* в. пригово́ра (*leg.*) pronouncement of sentence.

вы́нес|ти, у, ешь, *pf.* (*of* выноси́ть) 1. to carry out, take out; to take away; (*of sea or river current, etc.*) to carry away; в. поко́йника to carry out a body for burial; в. на бе́рег to wash ashore; в. ле́вую но́гу to step off with the left foot; в. на поля́ to enter in the margin (*of a book*); в. под строку́ to make a footnote; в. сор из избы́ to wash one's dirty linen in public. 2. (*fig.*) to take away, carry away, derive; в. прия́тное впечатле́ние to be favourably impressed. 3. в. вопро́с (на собра́ние, на обсужде́ние) to put, submit a question (to a meeting, for discussion). 4. в. на свои́х плеча́х (*fig.*) to shoulder, take the full weight (of), bear the full brunt (of). 5. to bear, stand, endure; не в. to be unable to stand, be unable to take, be allergic (to) (*diet, treatment, etc.*). 6. в. благода́рность to express gratitude, return thanks; в. пригово́р (+*d.*) to pass sentence (on); в. реше́ние to decide; (*leg.*) to pronounce judgement.

вы́нес|тись, усь, ешься, *past* ~ся, ~лась, *pf.* (*of* выноси́ться) (*coll.*) to fly out, rush out.

вы́ни|зать, жу, жешь, *pf.* (*of* ~зыва́ть) (*obs.*) to decorate, adorn (*with string of beads, pearls, etc.*).

выни́зыва|ть, ю, *impf. of* вы́низать.

вынима́|ть, ю, *impf. of* вы́нуть.

вынима́|ться, ется, *impf.* (*of* вы́нуться) (*coll.*) to come out; э́тот я́щик не ~ется this drawer does not come out.

вы́нос, а, *m.* 1. (из це́ркви) bearing-out, carrying-out (*of bier, at funerals*). 2. trace; ло́шадь под ~ом trace-horse.

выно|си́ть, шу, сишь, *pf.* (*of* вына́шивать) to bear, bring forth (*a child at full term*); в. мысль (*fig.*) to give birth to an idea.

выно|си́ть, шу́, ~сишь, *impf.* 1. *impf. of* вы́нести. 2. *impf. only* (+*neg.*) to be unable to bear, be unable to stand; я его́ не ~шу́ I can't stand him. 3. хоть святы́х ~си́ (*coll.*) it is intolerable.

вы́носк|а, и, *f.* 1. taking out, carrying out. 2. marginal note; footnote.

вынósливост|ь, и, *f.* (powers of) endurance; staying-power.

вынósлив|ый (~, ~а), *adj.* hardy (*also hort.*).

вынoснó|й, *adj.* 1. inserted in footnote. 2. ~а́я ло́шадь trace-horse.

вы́ношен|ный (~, ~а), *p.p.p. of* выноси́ть *and adj.*; в. ребёнок child born at full term; в. прое́кт (*fig.*) mature project.

вы́но|шу, сишь, *see* ~си́ть.

выно|шу́, ~сишь, *see* ~си́ть.

вы́ну|дить, жу, дишь, *pf.* (*of* ~жда́ть) 1. (+*inf.*) to force, compel; его́ ~дили уе́хать из страны́ he was forced to leave the country. 2. (у+*g.*) to extort, force (from, out of); они́ ~дили у него́ призна́ние в свое́й вине́ they have extorted an admission of guilt from him.

вынужда́|ть, ю, *impf. of* вы́нудить.

вы́нужден|ный (~, ~а), *p.p.p. of* вы́нудить *and adj.* forced, compulsory; ~ная поса́дка (*aeron.*) forced landing.

вы́н|уть, у, ешь, *pf.* (*of* ~има́ть) 1. to take out; to pull out, extract; to draw out (*money from bank, etc.*). 2. ~ь да поло́жь (*coll.*) here and now, on the spot; there and then; он тре́бует шампа́нского — ~ь да поло́жь he demands champagne here and now.

вы́ны́рива|ть, ю, *impf. of* вы́нырнуть.

вы́ныр|нуть, ну, нешь, *pf.* (*of* ~ивать) to come up, come to the surface (*of diver*); (*fig., coll.*) to turn up; как для него́ хара́ктерно — он опя́ть ~ул без гроша́ how like him to turn up without a farthing again!

вы́нюх|ать, аю, *pf.* (*of* ~ивать) (*coll.*) to sniff up; (*fig.*) to nose out, sniff out; в формулиро́вке предложе́ния он ~ал что́-то недо́брое he smelled a rat in the wording of the offer.

выню́хива|ть, ю, *impf. of* вы́нюхать.

выня́нчива|ть, ю, *impf. of* вы́нянчить.

вы́нянч|ить, у, ишь, *pf.* (*of* ~ивать) (*coll.*) to bring up, nurse.

вы́пад, а, *m.* 1. (*fig.*) attack. 2. (*sport*) lunge, thrust.

выпада́|ть, ю, *impf. of* вы́пасть.

выпаде́ни|е, я, *n.* 1. falling out. 2. (*med.*) prolapsus.

выпа́ива|ть, ю, *impf. of* вы́поить.

выпа́лива|ть, ю, *impf. of* вы́палить.

вы́пал|ить, ю, ишь, *pf.* (*of* ~ивать) (*coll.*) 1. (в+*a.*) to shoot, fire (at). 2. (*fig.*) to blurt out. 3. (*dial.*) to fire (*trans.*), burn up.

выпа́лыва|ть, ю, *impf. of* вы́полоть.

выпа́рива|ть, ю, *impf. of* вы́парить.

вы́пар|ить, ю, ишь, *pf.* (*of* ~ивать) 1. to steam; to clean, disinfect (by steaming). 2. (*chem.*) to evaporate. 3. to clean (*in a steam-bath*).

вы́парк|а, и, *f.* (*coll.*) 1. steaming. 2. evaporation.

выпарнó|й, *adj.* (*tech.*) evaporation.

выпа́рхива|ть, ю, *impf. of* вы́порхнуть.

выпа́рыва|ть, ю, *impf. of* вы́пороть¹.

вы́пас, а, *m.* pasture.

вы́па|сть, ду, дешь, *past* ~л, *pf.* (*of* ~да́ть) 1. to fall out. 2. to fall (*of rain, snow, etc.*); но́чью ~ло мно́го сне́гу there was a heavy fall of snow in the night. 3. to befall, fall (to); им ~ло тяжёлое испыта́ние a severe test has befallen them; ему́ ~л жре́бий стоя́ть на карау́ле в день Рождества́ it fell to his lot to be on guard on Christmas Day. 4. to occur, turn out; ночь ~ла звёздная it turned out a starry night. 5. (*sport*) to lunge, thrust.

вы́па|хать, шу, шешь, *pf.* (*of* ~хивать) 1. to exhaust (*soil*). 2. to turn up with the plough.

выпа́хива|ть, ю, *impf. of* вы́пахать.

вы́пачка|ть, ю, *pf.* to soil, dirty; to stain.

вы́пачка|ться, юсь, *pf.* to make oneself dirty.

вы́па|шу, шешь, *see* ~хать.

вы́пе|к, *see* ~чь.

выпека́|ть, ю, *impf. of* вы́печь.

вы́п|ереть, ру, решь, *past* ~ер, ~ерла, *pf.* (*of* ~ира́ть) 1. to push out, shove out. 2. to stick out, bulge out, protrude. 3. (*sl.*) to throw out, kick out, sling out.

вы́пест|овать, ую, *pf. of* пе́стовать.

вы́печк|а, и, *f.* 1. baking. 2. batch (*of loaves, etc.*).

вы́пе|чь, ку, чешь, кут, *past* ~к, ~кла, *pf.* (*of* ~ка́ть) to bake.

выпива́л|а, ы, *m. and f.* (*coll.*) tippler.

выпива́|ть, ю, *impf.* 1. *impf. of* вы́пить. 2. (*impf. only; coll.*) to be fond of the bottle.

вы́пивк|а, и, *f.* (*coll.*) 1. drinking-bout. 2. (*collect.*) drinks.

выпивóх|а, и, *m. and f.* (*sl.*) tippler; boozer.

вы́пи|вши, *past gerund of* ~ть; (*coll.*) drunk (*also used as predicative adjective*).

вы́пилива|ть, ю, *impf. of* вы́пилить.

вы́пил|ить, ю, ишь, *pf.* (*of* ~ивать) to saw, saw up, saw off; в. рáмку лóбзиком to make a fretwork frame.

вы́пилк|а, и, *f.* 1. sawing. 2. sawn-up, sawn-off object.

выпирá|ть, ю, *impf. of* вы́переть.

вы́пи|сать, шу, шешь, *pf.* (*of* ~сывать) 1. to copy out; to excerpt. 2. to delineate scrupulously; to trace out. 3. to write out; в. квитáнцию to write out a receipt. 4. to order; to subscribe (to); to send for (*in writing*); в. кни́гу to order a book; éсли ей стáнет хýже, вам придётся в. её сы́на if she gets worse you will have to send for her son. 5. to strike off the list; в. из больни́цы to discharge from hospital.

вы́пи|саться, шусь, шешься, *pf.* (*of* ~сываться) 1. to leave (*on discharge*); to be discharged; он ужé ~сался из больни́цы he is already out of hospital. 2. (*obs.*) to write oneself out.

вы́писк|а, и, *f.* 1. copying, excerpting. 2. writing out. 3. extract, excerpt; ~и из газéт newspaper extracts. 4. ordering; subscription. 5. discharge.

вы́писыва|ть(ся), ю(сь), *impf. of* вы́писать(ся).

вы́пис|ь, и, *f.* extract, copy; метри́ческая в. birth certificate.

вы́п|ить, ью, ьешь, *pf.* (*of* выпивáть *and* пить) to drink; to drink up, off.

вы́пихива|ть, ю, *impf. of* вы́пихнуть.

вы́пих|нуть, ну, нешь, *pf.* (*of* ~ивать) (*coll.*) to shove out, bundle out.

вы́пи|шу, шешь, *see* ~сать.

вы́плав|ить, лю, ишь, *pf.* (*of* ~лять) to smelt.

вы́плавк|а, и, *f.* 1. smelting. 2. smelted metal.

выплавля́|ть, ю, *impf. of* вы́плавить.

вы́пла|кать, чу, чешь, *pf.* 1. (*coll., folk poet.*) to sob out. 2. (*coll.*) to obtain by weeping, by tearful entreaties. 3. (*coll., folk poet.*) в. (все) глазá to cry one's eyes out.

вы́пла|каться, чусь, чешься, *pf.* (*coll.*) to have a good cry, have one's cry out.

вы́плат|а, ы, *f.* 1. payment. 2. (*coll.*) payment by instalments; купи́ть на ~у to purchase by instalments.

вы́пла|тить, чу, тишь, *pf.* (*of* ~чивать) 1. to pay (out). 2. to pay off (*debts*).

выплáчива|ть, ю, *impf. of* вы́платить.

вы́пла|чу¹, тишь, *see* ~тить.

вы́пла|чу², чешь, *see* ~кать.

выплёвыва|ть, ю, *impf. of* вы́плюнуть.

вы́пле|скать, щу, щешь, *pf.* (*of* ~скивать) to splash out.

выплёскива|ть, ю, *impf. of* выплескáть *and* вы́плеснуть.

вы́плес|нуть, ну, нешь, *pf.* (*of* ~кивать) to splash out; в. с водóй и ребёнка (*fig.*) to throw out the baby with the (bath-)water.

вы́пле|сти, ту, тешь, *pf.* (*of* ~тáть) 1. to undo, untie. 2. to weave.

выплетá|ть, ю, *impf. of* вы́плести.

выплывá|ть, ю, *impf. of* вы́плыть.

вы́плы|ть, ву, вешь, *pf.* (*of* ~вáть) 1. to swim out; (*fig.*) онá ~ла из кóмнаты she sailed out of the room. 2. to come to the surface, come up; (*fig., coll.*) to emerge; to appear; to crop up; прéжнее недоразумéние снóва ~ло the old misunderstanding has cropped up again.

вы́плюн|уть, у, ешь, *pf.* (*of* выплёвывать) to spit out.

вы́по|ить, ю, ишь, *pf.* (*of* выпáивать) to feed (*livestock*).

выполáскива|ть, ю, *impf. of* вы́полоскать.

выползá|ть, ю, *impf. of* вы́ползти.

вы́ползо|к, ка, *m.* (*dial.*) 1. slough. 2. worm.

вы́полз|ти, у, ешь, *past* ~, ~ла, *pf.* (*of* ~áть) (из+*g.*) to crawl out, creep out (from).

вы́полир|овать, ую, *pf.* (*coll.*) to polish (up).

выполнéни|е, я, *n.* execution, carrying-out; fulfilment.

выполни́м|ый (~, ~a), *pres. part. pass. of* вы́полнить *and adj.* practicable, feasible.

вы́полн|ить, ю, ишь, *pf.* (*of* ~я́ть) to execute, carry out; to fulfil; в. свои́ обя́занности to discharge one's obligations, do one's duty; в. приказáние to carry out an order.

выполня́|ть, ю, *impf. of* вы́полнить.

вы́поло|скать, щу, щешь, *pf.* (*of* выполáскивать) to rinse out.

вы́пол|оть, ю, ешь, *pf.* (*of* выпáлывать) to weed out.

вы́порот|ок, ка, *m.* unborn animal (*removed from female for fur*).

вы́пор|оть, ю, ешь, *pf.* (*of* выпáрывать) (*coll.*) to rip out, rip up.

вы́пор|оть², ю, ешь, *pf. of* порóть².

вы́порхн|уть, у, ешь, *pf.* (*of* выпáрхивать) to flit out (*of birds*); (*fig., coll.*) to dart out.

вы́поте|ть, ю, ешь, *pf.* (*coll.*) to sweat out.

вы́потрош|ить, у, ишь, *pf. of* потроши́ть.

вы́прав|ить, лю, ишь, *pf.* (*of* ~ля́ть) 1. to straighten (out). 2. to correct; to improve. 3. (*coll.*) to get, obtain (*documents*); в. пáспорт to get a passport.

вы́прав|иться, люсь, ишься, *pf.* (*of* ~ля́ться) 1. to become straight. 2. to improve (*intrans.*).

вы́правк|а, и, *f.* 1. bearing. 2. (*typ.*) correction.

выправля́|ть(ся), ю(сь), *impf. of* вы́пра-
вить(ся).

выпра́стыва|ть(ся), ю(сь), *impf. of* вы́-
простать(ся).

выпра́шива|ть, ю, *impf.* 1. *impf. of* вы́про-
сить. 2. *impf. only* to solicit, try to get;
он всё ~ет разреше́ние на вы́езд he is
always trying to get permission to go
abroad.

выпрева́|ть, ю, *impf. of* вы́преть.

вы́пре|ть, ю, ешь, *pf.* (*of* ~ва́ть) (*coll., dial.*)
to rot (*of crops*).

выпрова́жива|ть, ю, *impf. of* вы́проводить.

вы́прово|дить, жу, дишь, *pf.* (*of* выпрова́-
живать) (*coll.*) to send packing; to show
the door (to).

вы́про|сить, шу, сишь, *pf.* (*of* выпра́ши-
вать) (y + g.) to get (out of), obtain, elicit
(by begging); наконе́ц он ~сил разреше́-
ние на вы́езд at last he elicited permission
to go abroad.

вы́проста|ть, ю, *pf.* (*of* выпра́стывать)
(*coll.*) 1. to free, work loose. 2. to empty.

вы́проста|ться, юсь, *pf.* (*of* выпра́сты-
ваться) (*coll.*) 1. to free oneself, work (oneself) free. 2. to defecate.

вы́про|шу, сишь, *see* ~сить.

вы́п|ру, решь, *see* ~ереть.

выпры́гива|ть, ю, *impf. of* вы́прыгнуть.

вы́прыг|нуть, ну, нешь, *pf.* (*of* ~ивать) to
jump out, spring out.

выпряга́|ть, ю, *impf. of* вы́прячь.

выпрями́тел|ь, я, m. (*electr.*) rectifier.

вы́прям|ить, лю, ишь, *pf.* (*of* ~ля́ть) 1. to
straighten (out). 2. (*electr.*) to rectify.

вы́прям|иться, люсь, ишься, *pf.* (*of* ~ля́ть-
ся) to become straight; в. во весь рост to
draw oneself up to one's full height.

выпрямля́|ть(ся), ю(сь), *impf. of* вы́пря-
мить(ся).

вы́пря|чь, гу, жешь, гут, *past* ~г, ~гла, *pf.*
(*of* ~га́ть) to unharness.

выпу́гива|ть, ю, *impf. of* вы́пугнуть.

вы́пуг|нуть, ну, нешь, *pf.* (*of* ~ивать) to
scare off; to start (*game*).

вы́пукло-во́гнутый, *adj.* (*phys.*) convexo-
-concave.

вы́пуклост|ь, и, f. 1. protuberance; pro-
minence, bulge. 2. (*phys.*) convexity. 3. relief (*in sculpture, etc.*). 4. (*sing. only*; *fig.*)
clarity, distinctness.

вы́пуклый, *adj.* 1. protuberant; prominent,
bulging. 2. (*phys.*) convex. 3. in relief.
4. (*fig.*) clear, distinct.

вы́пуск, а, m. 1. output; issue; discharge
(*of steam, gases, etc.*); в. из печа́ти publication. 2. part, number, instalment (*of serial
publication*). 3. leavers; graduates (*those
who complete studies at the same time*); он —
са́мый блестя́щий из прошлого́днего ~а

по хи́мии he is the most brilliant of those
who graduated in chemistry last year. 4.
cut, omission. 5. (*obs.*) edging, piping. 6.
брю́ки на в. *see* навы́пуск.

выпуска́|ть, ю, *impf. of* вы́пустить.

выпуска́|ющий, *pres. part. act. of* ~ть; *as
noun* в., ~ющего, m. person responsible for
seeing newspaper *or* journal through press.

выпускни́к, а́, m. 1. graduate. 2. final-year
student.

выпуск|но́й, *adj. of* вы́пуск; в. кла́пан (*tech.*)
exhaust valve; в. кран (*tech.*) discharge
cock; ~на́я труба́ (*tech.*) exhaust pipe;
~на́я цена́ (*econ.*) market price; в. экза́мен
final examination, finals; *as noun* в., ~но́го,
m., ~на́я, ~но́й, f. final-year student.

вы́пу|стить, щу, стишь, *pf.* (*of* ~ска́ть)
1. to let out; to release; в. во́ду из ва́нны
to let the water out of a bath; в. из тюрьмы́
to release from prison; в. (пулемётную)
о́чередь (*mil.*) to fire a burst. 2. to put out,
issue; to turn out, produce; в. в прода́жу
to put on the market; в. заём to float a
loan; в. офице́ров to turn out officers; в.
кинокарти́ну to release a film. 3. to cut
(out), omit. 4. (*tailoring*) to let out, let down.
5. to show; в. свои́ ко́гти to show one's
claws. 6. (*typ.*) to see through the press.

вы́пут|ать, аю, *pf.* (*of* ~ывать) to disen-
tangle.

вы́пут|аться, аюсь, *pf.* (*of* ~ываться) to
disentangle oneself, extricate oneself (*also
fig.*).

вы́пу́тыва|ть(ся), ю(сь), *impf. of* вы́пу-
тать(ся).

вы́пуч|енный, p.p.p. of ~ить *and adj.*; (*coll.*)
с ~енными глаза́ми wide-eyed, goggle-
-eyed.

выпу́чива|ть, ю, *impf. of* вы́пучить.

вы́пуч|ить, у, ишь, *pf.* (*of* ~ивать) в. глаза́
(*coll.*) to open one's eyes wide.

вы́пушк|а, и, f. edging, braid, piping.

вы́пыт|ать, аю, *pf.* (*of* ~ывать) (y + g.) to
elicit, extort (*information, secrets, etc., from*).

выпы́тыва|ть, ю, *impf.* 1. *impf. of* вы́пы-
тать. 2. *impf. only* to try to discover (*by
interrogation*); в. секре́т у кого́-н. to try to
get a secret out of someone.

вы́п|ь, и, f. bittern (*bird*).

вы́пя́лива|ть, ю, *impf. of* вы́пялить.

вы́пял|ить, ю, ишь, *pf.* (*of* ~ивать) (*coll.*)
to stick out; в. глаза́ to open one's eyes
wide, stare.

вы́пя|тить, чу, тишь, *pf.* (*of* ~чивать)
(*coll.*) 1. to stick out; в. грудь to stick out
one's chest. 2. (*fig.*) to over-emphasize.

вы́пя|титься, чусь, тишься, *pf.* (*of* ~чи-
ваться) (*coll.*) to stick out (*intrans.*), protrude.

выпя́чива|ть(ся), ю(сь), *impf. of* вы́пя-
тить(ся).

выраба́тыва|ть, ю, *impf. of* вы́работать.

вы́работа|ть, ю, *pf. (of* выраба́тывать**) 1.** to manufacture; to produce, make. **2.** to work out, draw up; в. пове́стку дня для заседа́ния to draw up an agenda for a meeting; в. хоро́ший стиль to work up a good style; в. си́лу хара́ктера to develop, acquire strength of character. **3.** (*coll.*) to earn, make. **4.** (*tech.*) to work out (*a mine*).

вы́работк|а, и, *f.* **1.** manufacture; production, making. **2.** working-out, drawing-up. **3.** output, yield. **4.** (*coll.*) make; хоро́шей ~и well-made. **5.** (*tech.*) (mine-)working.

выра́внивани|е, я, *n.* smoothing-out, levelling; equalization; alignment.

выра́внива|ть(ся), ю(сь), *impf. of* вы́ровнять(ся).

выража́|ть, ю, *impf. of* вы́разить.

выража́|ться, юсь, *impf.* **1.** *impf. of* вы́разиться; мя́гко ~ясь to put it mildly. **2.** (*coll.*) to swear, use swear-words.

выраже́ни|е, я, *n.* (*in var. senses*) expression.

вы́ражен|ный (~, ~а), *p.p.p. of* вы́разить *and adj.* pronounced, marked; он говори́т по-англи́йски, но с ре́зко ~ным неме́цким акце́нтом he speaks English, but with a very pronounced German accent.

вырази́тел|ь, я, *m.* one who expresses; exponent, spokesman; он был еди́нственным в исто́рии страны́ ~ем стремле́ний всего́ наро́да he was the only man in the country's history who had expressed the aspirations of the entire people.

вырази́тел|ьный (~ен, ~ьна), *adj.* expressive; significant; ~ьное чте́ние elocution.

вы́ра|зить, жу, зишь, *pf. (of* ~жа́ть**)** to express; to convey; to voice; его́ докла́д ~зил взгля́ды прису́тствующих на ми́тинге his report conveyed the views of the meeting.

вы́ра|зиться, жусь, зишься, *pf. (of* ~жа́ться**) 1.** to express oneself. **2.** (в+*p.*) to manifest itself (in). **3.** (в+*p.*) to amount to, come to; изде́ржки ~зились в шести́ рубля́х the costs came to six roubles.

вы́разуме|ть, ю, *pf.* (*obs.*) to understand.

выраста́|ть, ю, *impf. of* вы́расти.

вы́р|асти, асту, астешь, *past* ~ос, ~осла, *pf. (of* ~аста́ть**) 1.** to grow (up). **2.** (в+*a.*) to grow (into), develop (into), become; их дру́жба ~осла в любо́вь their friendship grew into love. **3.** (из+*g.*) to grow (out of) (*clothing*). **4.** to increase; населе́ние за пять лет ~осло на два́дцать проце́нтов in five years the population had increased by twenty per cent. **5.** to appear, rise up; пе́ред на́шими глаза́ми ~ос Арара́т Mount Ararat rose up before our eyes. **6.** в. в чьих-н. глаза́х to rise in someone's estimation.

выра|стить, щу, стишь, *pf. (of* ~щивать**)** to bring up (*children*); to rear, breed (*livestock*); to grow, cultivate (*plants*).

выра́щива|ть, ю, *impf. of* вы́растить.

вы́рв|ать¹, у, ешь, *pf. (of* вырыва́ть¹**) 1.** to pull out, tear out; в. зуб to pull out a tooth; в. себе́ зуб (у врача́) to have a tooth out; он ~ал кни́гу у меня́ из рук he snatched the book out of my hands. **2.** (*fig.*) to extort, wring; в. призна́ние у кого́-н. to wring a confession out of someone.

вы́рв|ать², у, ешь, *pf. of* рвать².

вы́рв|аться, усь, ешься, *pf. (of* вырыва́ться**) 1.** (из+*g.*) to tear oneself away (from); to break out (from), break loose (from), break free (from); to get away (from); в. из чьих-н. объя́тий to tear oneself away from someone's embrace; в. из чьих-н. рук to break loose from someone's grip; едва́ ли мне уда́стся до ле́та в. из Москвы́ I shall hardly manage to get away from Moscow before the summer. **2.** to come loose, come out; не́сколько страни́ц ~алось из э́той кни́ги several pages have come out of this book. **3.** (*of a sound, a remark, etc.*) (из, у+*g.*) to break (from), burst (from), escape; из груди́ старика́ ~ался стон a groan broke from the old man. **4.** to shoot up, shoot out; пла́мя ~алось из трубы́ a flame shot up from the chimney; четвёртая маши́на вдруг ~алась вперёд на пе́рвое ме́сто the fourth car suddenly shot ahead into first place.

вы́рез, а, *m.* cut; notch; пла́тье с больши́м ~ом low-necked dress; покупа́ть (арбу́з) на в. (*coll.*) to buy (a water-melon) on trial.

вы́ре|зать, жу, жешь, *pf. (of* ~за́ть**) 1.** to cut out; to excise. **2.** to cut, carve; to engrave. **3.** (*fig.*) to slaughter, butcher.

выреза́|ть, ю, *impf. of* вы́резать.

вы́резк|а, и, *f.* **1.** cutting-out, excision; carving; engraving. **2.** газе́тная в. press-cutting. **3.** fillet steak.

вырезно́й, *adj.* **1.** cut; carved. **2.** low--necked, décolleté.

вырезывани|е, я, *n.* cutting-out; excision; carving; engraving.

вырезыва|ть, ю, *impf.* = выреза́ть.

вы́реш|ить, у, ишь, *pf.* (*coll.*) to decide finally.

вы́рис|овать, ую, *pf. (of* ~о́вывать**)** to draw carefully, draw in detail.

вы́рис|оваться, уется, ся, *pf. (of* ~о́вываться**)** to appear (in outline); to stand out; на горизо́нте ~ова́лась го́рная цепь a mountain chain stood out against the horizon.

вырисо́выва|ть(ся), ю(сь), *impf. of* вы́рисовать(ся).

вы́ровня|ть, ю, *pf. (of* выра́внивать**) 1.** to smooth (out), level; в. доро́гу to level a road; в. шаг to regulate one's pace. **2.** to equalize; to align. **3.** (*mil.*) to draw up in line; в. ряды́ to dress ranks. **4.** в. самолёт to straighten out an aeroplane.

вы́ровня|ться, юсь, *pf.* (*of* выра́вниваться) **1.** to become level; to become even; (*mil.*) to form up; to dress, take up dressing; (*sport*) to equalize. **2.** (*fig.*) to catch up, draw level; несмотря́ на боле́знь ему́ удало́сь в. с други́ми ученика́ми кла́сса despite his illness he has managed to catch up with the rest of the class. **3.** (*fig.*) to improve, get better; (*coll.*) to become more equable.

вы́род|иться, ится, *pf.* (*of* вырожда́ться) to degenerate.

вы́род|ок, ка, *m.* (*coll.*) degenerate; он — в. в на́шей семье́ he is the black sheep of our family.

вырожда́|ться, юсь, *impf. of* вы́родиться.

вырожде́н|ец, ца, *m.* degenerate.

вырожде́ни|е, я, *n.* degeneration.

вы́рон|ить, ю, ишь, *pf.* to drop.

вы́рост, а, *no pl.*, *m.* **1.** growth, excrescence; offshoot. **2.** шить на в. to make (*clothes*) with room for growth.

вы́ростковый, *adj.* calf(-leather).

вы́рост|ок, ка, *m.* year-old calf; calf-leather.

вы́р|ою, оешь, *see* ~ыть.

выруба́|ть(ся), ю(сь), *impf. of* вы́рубить(ся).

вы́руб|ить, лю, ишь, *pf.* (*of* ~а́ть) **1.** to cut down, fell; to hew out. **2.** to cut out; в. дыру́ to make a hole. **3.** to carve (out).

вы́руб|иться, люсь, ишься, *pf.* (*of* ~а́ться) to cut one's way out.

вы́рубк|а, и, *f.* **1.** cutting down, felling; hewing out. **2.** (*dial.*) clearing (*in forest*).

вы́руга|ть(ся), ю(сь), *pf. of* руга́ть(ся).

выру́лива|ть, ю, *impf. of* вы́рулить.

вы́рул|ить, ю, ишь, *pf.* (*of* ~ивать) (*aeron.*) to taxi.

выруча́|ть, ю, *impf. of* вы́ручить.

вы́руч|ить, у, ишь, *pf.* (*of* ~а́ть) **1.** to rescue; to come to the help, aid (of). **2.** to gain; to make (*coll.*); он ~ил мно́го де́нег от прода́жи свои́х карти́н he has made a lot of money from the sale of his pictures; в. затра́ченное to recover one's expenses.

вы́ручк|а, и, *f.* **1.** rescue, assistance; прийти́ на ~у to come to the rescue. **2.** gain; proceeds, receipts; earnings.

вырыва́ни|е[1], я, *n.* **1.** pulling out; extraction (*of teeth, etc.*). **2.** uprooting.

вырыва́ни|е[2], я, *n.* digging (up).

вырыва́|ть[1], ю, *impf. of* вы́рвать[1].

вырыва́|ть[2], ю, *impf. of* вы́рыть.

вырыва́|ться, юсь, *impf. of* вы́рваться.

вы́р|ыть, ою, оешь, *pf.* (*of* ~ыва́ть[2]) to dig up, dig out, unearth; в. труп to exhume

а corpse; где вы ~ыли э́ту ру́копись? (*fig.*, *coll.*) where did you dig up this manuscript?

вы́ря|дить, жу, дишь, *pf.* (*coll.*) to dress up (*trans.*).

вы́ря|диться, жусь, дишься, *pf.* (*coll.*) to dress up (*intrans.*).

выряжа́|ть(ся), ю(сь), *impf. of* вы́рядить(ся).

вы́са|дить, жу, дишь, *pf.* (*of* ~живать) **1.** to set down; to help down; to make alight; в. на бе́рег to put ashore; в. деса́нт (*mil.*) to make a landing; пья́ницу ~дили из авто́буса the drunken man was made to get off the 'bus. **2.** (*hort.*) to transplant. **3.** (*coll.*) to smash; to break in.

вы́са|диться, жусь, дишься, *pf.* (*of* ~живаться) (из, с+*g.*) to alight (from), get off; в. (с су́дна) to land, disembark; в. (с самолёта) to land.

вы́садк|а, и, *f.* **1.** debarkation, disembarkation; landing. **2.** (*hort.*) transplanting.

выса́жива|ть(ся), ю(сь), *impf. of* вы́садить(ся).

вы́са|жу, дишь, *see* ~дить.

выса́сыва|ть, ю, *impf. of* вы́сосать.

высва́та|ть, ю, *pf.* (*coll., obs.*) to make a match, arrange a marriage (with).

высва́тыва|ть, ю, *impf.* **1.** *impf. of* вы́сватать. **2.** *impf. only* to try to make a match, arrange a marriage (with); to seek in marriage.

высве́рлива|ть, ю, *impf. of* вы́сверлить.

вы́сверл|ить, ю, ишь, *pf.* to drill, bore.

вы́сви|стать, щу, щешь, *pf.* (*of* ~стывать) (*coll.*) **1.** to whistle; в. мело́дию to whistle a tune. **2.** to whistle for, whistle up.

вы́сви|стеть, щу, стишь, *pf.* = ~стать.

высви́стыва|ть, ю, *impf. of* вы́свистать.

высвобо|дить, жу, дишь, *pf.* **1.** to free, liberate; to disentangle, disengage. **2.** (*coll.*) to help (to) escape; не́которые ме́стные жи́тели ~дили заключённых some of the local inhabitants helped the prisoners escape.

высвобожда́|ть, ю, *impf. of* вы́свободить.

вы́сев|ки, ок, *no sing.* bran, siftings.

высева́|ть, ю, *impf. of* вы́сеять.

высека́|ть, ю, *impf. of* вы́сечь[2].

вы́се|ку, чешь, *see* ~чь.

выселе́н|ец, ца, *m.* evacuee.

выселе́ни|е, я, *n.* eviction.

вы́сел|ить, ю, ишь, *pf.* (*of* ~я́ть) **1.** to evict. **2.** to evacuate, move.

вы́сел|иться, юсь, ишься, *pf.* (*of* ~я́ться) to move (*from one dwelling-place to another*).

вы́сел|ок, ка, *m.* settlement.

выселя́|ть(ся), ю(сь), *impf. of* вы́селить(ся).

вы́семен|иться, ится, *pf.* (*agric.*) to go to seed.

вы́сечк|а, и, *f.* carving; hewing.

вы́се|чь¹, ку, чешь, кут, *past* ∼к, ∼кла, *pf.* (*of* сечь¹) to beat, flog.

вы́се|чь², ку, чешь, кут, *past* ∼к, ∼кла, *pf.* (*of* ∼кать) to cut (out); to carve, sculpture; to hew; в. огóнь to strike fire (*from a flint*).

вы́се|ять, ю, *pf.* (*of* ∼ивать) (*agric.*) to sow.

вы́си|деть, жу, дишь, *pf.* (*of* ∼живать) 1. to hatch (out) (*of birds; also fig.*). 2. to stay; to sit out (*trans.*); мы ∼дели до концá лéкции we sat the lecture out.

вы́сидк|а, и, *f.* (*coll.*) 1. incubation. 2. imprisonment.

вы́си|жива|ть, ю, *impf.* of вы́сидеть.

вы́|ситься, шусь, сишься, *impf.* to tower (up), rise.

выска́блива|ть, ю, *impf.* of вы́скоблить.

вы́ска|зать, жу, жешь, *pf.* (*of* ∼зывать) to express; to state; в. мнéние to advance an opinion; в. предположéние to suggest, come out with a suggestion.

вы́ска|заться, жусь, жешься, *pf.* (*of* ∼зываться) 1. to speak out; to speak one's mind; to have one's say. 2. to speak (for *or* against); никтó не ∼зался прóтив законопроéкта no one spoke against the bill.

выска́зывани|е, я, *n.* 1. utterance. 2. pronouncement; opinion.

выска́зыва|ть(ся), ю(сь), *impf.* of вы́сказать(ся).

выска́кива|ть, ю, *impf.* of вы́скочить.

выска́льзыва|ть, ю, *impf.* of вы́скользнуть.

вы́скобл|ить, ю, ишь, *pf.* (*of* выска́бливать) to scrape out; to erase; (*med.*) to remove.

вы́скользн|уть, у, ешь, *pf.* (*of* выска́льзывать) to slip out (*also fig.*); арестáнт ∼ул из рук охрáны (*coll.*) the prisoner slipped through his escort's fingers.

вы́скоч|ить, у, ишь, *pf.* (*of* выска́кивать) 1. to jump out; to leap out, spring out; (*fig., coll.*) to butt in, come out (with); он ∼ил с крáйне неумéстным замечáнием he came out with an extremely uncalled-for remark. 2. (*of a boil, etc.*) (*coll.*) to come up. 3. (*coll.*) to drop out, fall out. 4. в. в лю́ди (*fig., coll.*) to fall on one's feet.

вы́скочк|а, и, *m. and f.* (*coll.*) upstart, parvenu.

выскреба́|ть, ю, *impf.* of вы́скрести.

вы́скре|сти, бу, бешь, *past* ∼б, ∼бла, *pf.* 1. to scrape out, scrape off. 2. to rake out.

вы́слан|ный (∼, ∼а), *p.p.p.* of вы́слать; *as noun* в., ∼ного, *m.*, ∼ная, ∼ной, *f.* exile, deportee.

вы́|слать, шлю, шлешь, *pf.* (*of* ∼сылáть) 1. to send, send out, dispatch. 2. (*polit.*) to exile; to deport.

вы́сле|дить, жу, дишь, *pf.* to trace; to track down.

выслéжива|ть, ю, *impf.* 1. *impf.* of вы́следить. 2. *impf. only* to be on the track of; to shadow.

вы́сле|жу, дишь, *see* ∼дить.

вы́слуг|а, и, *f.* period of service; за ∼у лет for long service, for meritorious service; за ∼ой двадцати́ лет on the expiry of twenty years' service.

вы́слу́жива|ть(ся), ю(сь), *impf.* of вы́служить(ся).

вы́служ|ить, у, ишь, *pf.* 1. to qualify for, obtain (*as result of service*); он ∼ил повышéние he has qualified for promotion. 2. to serve (out); он ∼ил двáдцать пять лет на Дáльнем Востóке he has completed twenty-five years' service in the Far East.

вы́служ|иться, усь, ишься, *pf.* 1. to gain promotion, be promoted. 2. (*coll., pejor.*) to gain favour (with), get in (with); он ∼ился пéред бригади́ром he is well in with the foreman.

вы́слуша|ть, ю, *pf.* (*of* выслу́шивать) 1. to hear out. 2. (*med.*) to sound; to listen to.

выслу́шивани|е, я, *n.* (*med.*) auscultation.

выслу́шива|ть, ю, *impf.* of вы́слушать.

высма́трива|ть, ю, *impf.* of вы́смотреть.

высме́ива|ть, ю, *impf.* of вы́смеять.

вы́сме|ять, ю, ешь, *pf.* (*of* ∼ивать) to deride, ridicule.

вы́смол|ить, ю, ишь, *pf.* of смоли́ть.

вы́сморка|ть(ся), ю(сь), *pf.* of сморкáть(ся).

вы́смотр|еть, ю, ишь, *pf.* (*of* высмáтривать) 1. to scrutinize, look through. 2. to spy out; to locate (*by eye*). 3. (*coll.*) в. глазá to tire one's eyes out.

высóвыва|ть(ся), ю(сь), *impf.* of вы́сунуть(ся).

высóк|ий (∼, ∼á, ∼ó), *adj.* (*in var. senses*) high; tall; lofty; elevated, sublime; (*mus.*) high, high-pitched; ∼ая водá high water, high tide; в. стиль elevated style; я о нём ∼огó мнéния I have a high opinion of him; в ∼ой стéпени highly; ∼ие договáривающиеся стóроны, *see* договáриваться.

высóко, *adv.* 1. high (up); лежáть в. над у́ровнем мóря to be high above sea level. 2. *as pred.* it is high (up); it is a long way up; окнó бы́ло в. от земли́ the window was high up off the ground.

высóко- high-, highly-; (*meteor.*) alto-.

высокоблагорóди|е, я, *n.* (вáше) в. (your) Honour, (your) Worship (*title, in tsarist Russia, of civil servants of the eighth to the sixth classes and of officers from the rank of major to that of colonel*).

высокогóрный, *adj.* Alpine, mountain.

высококáчественный, *adj.* high-quality.

высококвалифици́рованный, *adj.* highly qualified; в. рабóтник (highly) skilled workman.

высокомéри|е, я, *n.* haughtiness, arrogance.

высокомéрнича|ть, ю, *impf.* (*coll.*) to behave haughtily, arrogantly.

высокоме́р|ный (~ен, ~на), *adj.* haughty, arrogant.

высокомолекуля́рный, *adj.* (*phys.*) high--molecular.

высокопа́р|ный (~ен, ~на), *adj.* (*lit.*) high--flown, stilted; bombastic, turgid.

высокопоста́вленный, *adj.* of high rank.

высокопревосходи́тельств|о, а, *n.* (ва́ше) в. (your) Excellency (*title, in tsarist Russia, of officers and civil servants of the first and second class*).

высокопреосвяще́нств|о, а, *n.* (ва́ше) в. (your) Eminence, (your) Grace (*title of archbishops and metropolitans of the Orthodox Church*).

высокопреподо́би|е, я, *n.* (ва́ше) в. (your) Reverence (*title of archimandrites, abbots, and archpriests of the Orthodox Church*).

высокопро́б|ный (~ен, ~на), *adj.* sterling, standard; (*fig.*) sterling, of high quality.

высокоро́ди|е, я, *n.* (ва́ше) в. (your) Honour, (your) Worship (*title, in tsarist Russia, of civil servants of the fifth class*).

высокосо́ртный, *adj.* high-grade.

высокоторже́ственный, *adj.* solemn.

высокоуважа́емый, *adj.* (*obs.*; *mode of address in letters*) honoured (*Sir*), respected (*Sir*).

высокоу́м|ный (~ен, ~на), *adj.* (*iron.*) clever, brainy.

высокочасто́тный, *adj.* (*electr.*) high-frequency.

высокочти́мый, *adj.* (*obs.*) highly esteemed.

вы́сол|ить, ю, ишь, *pf.* (*coll.*) to salt well.

вы́сос|ать, у, ешь, *pf.* (*of* выса́сывать) **1.** to suck out, suck dry. **2.** (*fig., coll.*) to get out (of), extort (from); в. все со́ки из to exhaust, wear out; в. из па́льца to invent, fabricate; всё э́то из па́льца ~ано it is an entire fabrication.

высот|а́, ы́, *pl.* ~ы, ~, *f.* **1.** height, altitude; (*mus.*) pitch; го́род нахо́дится на ~е́ ты́сячи фу́тов над у́ровнем мо́ря the town is a thousand feet above sea level; набра́ть ~у́ (*aeron.*) to gain altitude. **2.** height, eminence (*concr.*); кома́ндные ~ы commanding heights (*also fig.*). **3.** high level; high quality. **4.** (*fig.*) на до́лжной ~е́ up to the mark; быть, оказа́ться на ~е́ положе́ния to rise to the occasion; быть на ~е́ зада́чи to be equal to a task. **5.** (*math.*) в. треуго́льника altitude of a triangle.

высо́тник, а, *m.* **1.** workman employed on construction of skyscrapers. **2.** high-altitude flier. **3.** (*coll.*) high-jumper.

высо́тн|ый, *adj.* **1.** high-altitude. **2.** ~ое зда́ние high-rise building, tower block.

высотоме́р, а, *m.* **1.** (*aeron.*) altimeter. **2.** (*mil.*) height-finder.

вы́сох|нуть, ну, нешь, *past* ~, ~ла, *pf.* (*of*

высыха́ть) 1. to dry (out); to dry up (*o, rivers, etc.*). **2.** to wither, fade; (*fig.*) to waste away, fade away.

вы́сох|ший, *past part. act. of* ~нуть *and adj.* dried-up; shrivelled; wizened.

высоча́йш|ий, *adj.* **1.** *superl. of* высо́кий. **2.** (*epithet of tsar or emperor*) imperial, royal; проше́ние на ~ее и́мя petition to His Imperial Majesty.

высоче́нный, *adj.* (*coll.*) very high, very tall.

высо́честв|о, а, *n.* (ва́ше) в. (your) Highness.

вы́сп|аться, люсь, ишься, *pf.* (*of* высыпа́ться²) (*coll.*) to have a good sleep; to have one's sleep out.

выспева́|ть, ю, *impf. of* вы́спеть.

вы́спе|ть, ю, *pf.* (*coll.*) to ripen.

выспра́шива|ть, ю, *impf. of* вы́спросить.

вы́спренний, *adj.* high-flown; bombastic.

вы́спро|сить, шу, сишь, *pf.* (*of* выспра́шивать) (*coll.*) **1.** to inquire. **2.** to inquire of, interrogate; to pump посла́ ~сили о поли́тике прави́тельства его́ страны́ the ambassador was pumped about his government's policy; ~сили у посла́ наме́рения его́ прави́тельства the ambassador was pumped about his government's intentions.

вы́став|ить, лю, ишь, *pf.* (*of* ~ля́ть) **1.** to bring out, bring forward; to display, exhibit; в. на прода́жу to display for sale; в. на свет to expose to the light; в. напока́з to show off, parade. **2.** (*mil.*) to post (*guard, etc.*). **3.** (+*i.*) to represent (as), make out (as); в. в плохо́м све́те to represent in an unfavourable light; в. в смешно́м ви́де to make a laughing-stock (of); его́ ~или тру́сом he was made out to be a coward. **4.** to put forward; to adduce; в. свою́ кандидату́ру to come forward as a candidate; в. до́воды to adduce arguments. **5.** to put down, set down (*in writing*); в. отме́тки to put down marks; в. число́ на письме́ to date a letter. **6.** to take out, remove; в. око́нную ра́му to take out a window frame. **7.** (*coll.*) to send out, turn out, throw out; to give the brush-off (to); в. из ко́мнаты to send out of the room; в. со слу́жбы to sack.

вы́став|иться, люсь, ишься, *pf.* (*of* ~ля́ться) **1.** (*coll.*) to lean out; to thrust oneself forward; (*fig.; pejor.*) to show off. **2.** to exhibit (*intrans.; of an artist*).

вы́ставк|а, и, *f.* **1.** exhibition, show; display. **2.** (show-)window, (shop-)window.

выставля́|ть, ю, *impf. of* вы́ставить.

выставля́|ться, юсь, *impf. of* вы́ставиться.

выставно́й, *adj.* removable.

вы́став|очный, *adj. of* ~ка; в. комите́т exhibition committee.

вы́стáива|ть(ся), ю(сь), *impf. of* вы́стоять(ся).

вы́стега|ть¹, ю, *pf. of* стегáть².

вы́стега|ть², ю, *pf.* (*coll.*) to thrash, flog.

вы́стёгива|ть, ю, *impf. of* вы́стегнуть.

вы́стегн|уть, у, ешь, *pf.* (*coll.*) to flick out.

вы́стел|ить, ю, ешь, *pf.* = вы́стлать.

вы́ст|елю, елешь, *see* ~лать.

вы́стилá|ть, ю, *impf. of* вы́стлать *and* вы́стелить.

вы́стирá|ть, ю, *pf. of* стирáть².

вы́ст|лать, елю, елешь, *pf.* to cover; to pave; они́ ~лали лино́леумом пол во всех ко́мнатах they have covered all their floors with linoleum.

вы́сто|ять, ю, ишь, *pf.* (*of* вы́стáивать) 1. to stand; нам пришло́сь в. весь путь we had to stand the whole way. 2. to stand one's ground.

вы́сто|яться, юсь, ишься, *pf.* (of вы́стáиваться) 1. to mature, ripen. 2. to become stale, flat. 3. to rest (*of horses*).

вы́стрáгива|ть, ю, *impf. of* вы́строгать.

вы́страда|ть, ю, *pf.* 1. to suffer; to go through. 2. to gain, achieve through suffering.

вы́стрáива|ть(ся), ю(сь), *impf. of* вы́строить(ся).

вы́стрáчива|ть, ю, *impf. of* вы́строчить.

вы́стрел, а, *m.* shot; report; произвести́ в. to fire a shot; разда́лся в. a shot rang out; на в. (от+*g.*) (*coll.*) within gunshot (of).

вы́стрéлива|ть, ю, *impf. of* вы́стрелять.

вы́стрел|ить, ю, ишь, *pf.* to shoot, fire; я ~ил в него́ три рáза I fired three shots at him.

вы́стреля|ть, ю, *pf.* (*of* вы́стрéливать) (*coll.*) 1. to use up in shooting; мы ~ли все патро́ны we had used up all our cartridges. 2. to kill off (*by shooting*).

вы́стри|г, гу, жешь, *see* ~чь.

вы́стригá|ть, ю, *impf. of* вы́стричь.

вы́стри|чь, гу, жешь, гут, *past* ~г, ~гла, *pf.* to cut, clip out; to shear.

вы́строга|ть, ю, *pf.* (*of* строгáть *and* вы́стрáгивать) (*tech.*) to plane, shave.

вы́стро|ить, ю, ишь, *pf.* (*of* вы́стрáивать) 1. to build. 2. to draw up, order, arrange; (*mil.*) to form up.

вы́стро|иться, юсь, ишься, *pf.* (*of* вы́стрáиваться) 1. (*mil.*) to form up (*intrans.*). 2. *pass. of* ~ить.

вы́строч|ить, у, ишь, *pf.* (*of* вы́стрáчивать) to hemstitch.

вы́струга|ть, ю, *pf.* = вы́строгать.

вы́сту|дить, жу, дишь, *pf.* (*coll.*) to cool; дом ~дило (*impers.*) the house had grown cold.

вы́стýжива|ть, ю, *impf. of* вы́студить.

вы́сту|жу, дишь, *see* ~дить.

вы́стука|ть, ю, *pf.* (*of* вы́стýкивать) (*coll.*) 1. (*med.*) to tap. 2. to tap out; в. мело́дию to tap out a tune; в. сообщéние to tap out a message (*prison sl.*); to type out.

вы́стýкивани|е, я, *n.* percussion; tapping.

вы́стýкива|ть, ю, *impf. of* вы́стукать.

вы́ступ, а, *m.* 1. protuberance, projection, ledge; в. фро́нта (*mil.*) salient. 2. (*tech.*) lug.

выступá|ть, ю, *impf.* 1. *impf. of* вы́ступить. 2. (*impf. only*) to project, jut out, stick out. 3. (*impf. only*) to strut, pace.

вы́ступ|ить, лю, ишь, *pf.* 1. to come forward; to come out; героиня ~ила из-за кули́с the heroine came forward from the wings; в. в похо́д (*mil.*) to take the field; сыпь ~ила у неё на рукáх a rash has come out on her arms. 2. (из+*g.*) to go beyond; в. из берего́в to overflow its banks. 3. to appear (*publicly*); to come out (with, as); в. в печáти to appear in print; в. за предложéние to come out in favour of a proposal; в. защи́тником (*leg.*) to appear for the defence; в. с рéчью to make a speech; в. по рáдио с доклáдом to give a broadcast talk, give a talk on the radio.

выступлéни|е, я, *n.* 1. appearance (*in public*); speech. 2. setting out.

вы́стывá|ть, ю, *impf. of* вы́стыть.

вы́сты|ть, ну, нешь, *pf.* (*coll.*) to cool off, become cold.

вы́су|дить, жу, дишь, *pf.* (*coll.*) to obtain by court decision.

вы́сýжива|ть, ю, *impf. of* вы́судить.

вы́сý|жу, дишь, *see* ~дить.

вы́сун|уть, у, ешь, *pf.* (*of* высо́вывать) to put out, thrust out; в. язы́к to put one's tongue out; бежáть ~я язы́к (*coll.*) to run without pausing for breath; нельзя́ но́су в. (из дому) (*coll.*) one can't show one's face (outside).

вы́сун|уться, усь, ешься, *pf.* (*of* высо́вываться) to show oneself, thrust oneself forward; в. в окно́ to lean out of the window.

вы́сýшива|ть, ю, *impf. of* вы́сушить.

вы́суш|ить, у, ишь, *pf.* 1. to dry (out). 2. (*coll.*) to emaciate. 3. (*coll., fig.*) to make callous, make hard.

вы́счита|ть, ю, *pf.* 1. to calculate, compute; to reckon out. 2. (*coll.*) to deduct.

вы́счи́тыва|ть, ю, *impf. of* вы́считать.

вы́с|ший, *adj.* (*comp. and superl. of* высо́кий) highest; supreme; high; higher; ~шего кáчества of the highest quality; ~шая мéра наказáния supreme penalty; (*leg.*) capital punishment; суд ~шей инстáнции High Court; ~шее образовáние higher education; ~шее о́бщество (high) society; ~шее учéбное заведéние higher education establishment; ~шая шко́ла university; в ~шей стéпени in the highest degree.

высыла́|ть, ю, *impf. of* вы́слать.

вы́сылк|а, и, *f.* **1.** sending, dispatching. **2.** expulsion; exile.

вы́сып|ать, лю, лешь, *pf.* **1.** to pour out; to empty (out); to spill; (*fig.*, *coll.*) to pour out, tell; в. все свои́ забо́ты to pour out all one's troubles; ну, ~айте всё! come on, spill the beans! **2.** (*coll.*) to pour out (*intrans.*) **3.** to break out (*of a rash, etc.*); (*impers.*) у него́ ~ало на всем те́ле he has come out in a rash all over.

высыпа́|ть, ю, *impf. of* вы́сыпать.

высып|а́ться, люсь, лешься (*coll.* ~ешься), *pf.* **1.** *pass. of* ~ать. **2.** to pour out; to spill (*intrans.*).

высыпа́|ться[1], юсь, *impf. of* высыпаться.

высыпа́|ться[2], юсь, *impf. of* вы́спаться.

вы́сыпк|а, и, *f.* **1.** (*coll.*) pouring out, spilling. **2.** (*hunting*) descent (*of birds, etc.*).

высыха́|ть, ю, *impf. of* вы́сохнуть.

выс|ь, и, *f.* height; (*usu. pl.*) summit; (*fig.*) the world of fantasy; он всё вита́ет в заобла́чной ~и he lives in the clouds.

выта́лкива|ть, ю, *impf. of* вы́толкать *and* вы́толкнуть.

вытанц|ева́ть(ся), у́ет(ся), *pf. of* вытанцо́вывать(ся).

вытанцо́выва|ть, ю, *impf.* (*coll.*) to execute assiduously (*steps of a dance*).

вытанцо́выва|ться, ется, *impf.* (*coll.*) to succeed, come off; де́ло не ~ется it is not coming off.

выта́плива|ть, ю, *impf. of* вы́топить.

выта́птыва|ть, ю, *impf. of* вы́топтать.

вытара́щива|ть, ю, *impf. of* вы́таращить.

вы́тараш|ить, у, ишь, *pf.* (*coll.*) в. глаза́ to open one's eyes wide.

вы́таска|ть, ю, *pf.* (*coll.*) to drag out, fish out.

выта́скива|ть, ю, *impf. of* вы́таскать *and* вы́тащить.

вы́тача|ть, ю, *pf. of* тача́ть.

выта́чива|ть, ю, *impf. of* вы́точить.

вы́тачк|а, и, *f.* tuck, dart.

вы́тащ|ить, у, ишь, *pf.* (*of* выта́скивать) **1.** to drag out; to pull out, extract; (*coll.*) в. кого́-н. to drag someone out, drag someone off; они́ ~или его́ в кино́ they have dragged him off to the cinema; в. кого́-н. из беды́ to help someone out of trouble. **2.** (*coll.*) to steal, pinch; у меня́ ~или бума́жник I have had my wallet stolen.

вы́твер|дить, жу, дишь, *pf.* (*coll.*) to get by heart.

вытве́ржива|ть, ю, *impf. of* вы́твердить.

вытворя́|ть, ю, *impf.* (*coll.*) to get up to, be up to; что ты тепе́рь ~ешь? what are you up to now?

вытека́|ть, ю, *impf.* **1.** *impf. of* вы́течь. **2.** (*impf. only*) to flow (from, out of) (*of a river*). **3.** (*impf. only*) (*fig.*) to result, follow (from);

отсю́да ~ет, что вы оши́блись from this it follows that you are mistaken.

вы́те|ку, чешь, кут, *see* ~чь.

вы́т|ереть, ру, решь, *past* ~ер, ~ерла, *pf.* (*of* ~ира́ть) **1.** to wipe (up); to dry, rub dry; в. но́ги to wipe one's feet; в. посу́ду to dry the crockery; в. пыль со стола́ to dust the table. **2.** (*coll.*) to wear out, wear threadbare.

вы́терп|еть, лю, ишь, *pf.* to bear, endure; to suffer; я е́ле ~ел, когда́ он сказа́л э́то I could hardly stand it when he said that.

вы́терт|ый (~, ~а), *p.p.p. of* вы́тереть *and adj.* threadbare.

вы́те|сать, шу, шешь, *pf.* to square off.

вытесне́ни|е, я, *n.* **1.** ousting; supplanting. **2.** (*phys.*) displacement.

вы́тесн|ить, ю, ишь, *pf.* **1.** to crowd out; to force out; (*fig.*) to oust; to supplant. **2.** (*phys.*) to displace.

вытесня́|ть, ю, *impf. of* вы́теснить.

вытёсыва|ть, ю, *impf. of* вы́тесать.

вы́те|чь, ку, чешь, кут, *past* ~к, ~кла, *pf.* (*of* ~ка́ть) to flow out, run out; у него́ глаз ~к he has lost an eye.

вы́те|шу, шешь, *see* ~сать.

вытира́|ть, ю, *impf. of* вы́тереть.

вы́тисн|ить, ю, ишь, *pf.* to stamp, imprint, impress.

вы́тисн|уть, у, ешь, *pf.* = ~ить.

вытисня́|ть, ю, *impf. of* вы́тиснить.

вы́тк|ать, у, ешь, *pf.* **1.** to weave, finish weaving; в. ковёр to weave a carpet; в. цветы́ на ковре́ to weave a flower pattern on a carpet.

вы́толка|ть, ю, *pf.* (*of* выта́лкивать) (*coll.*) to throw out; его́ ~ли в ше́ю (*sl.*) he was thrown out on his neck.

вы́толкн|уть, у, ешь, *pf.* (*of* выта́лкивать) **1.** to throw out. **2.** (*coll.*) to push out, force out.

вы́топ|ить, лю, ишь, *pf.* (*of* выта́пливать) **1.** (*coll.*) to heat. **2.** to melt (down).

вы́топ|тать, чу, чешь, *pf.* (*of* выта́птывать) to trample down.

вытора́чива|ть, ю, *impf. of* вы́точить.

вы́торг|овать, ую, *pf.* **1.** to gain, obtain (*by bargaining, haggling*); to get a reduction (of); он ~овал де́сять рубле́й из цены́ э́тих сапо́г he got a reduction of ten roubles on the price of these boots, he got these boots reduced by ten roubles; (*fig.*, *coll.*) to manage to get; он ~овал отсро́чку для оконча́ния диссерта́ции he has managed to get an extension of time to finish his dissertation. **2.** (*coll.*) to make (a profit of); to net, clear.

выторго́выва|ть, ю, *impf.* **1.** *impf. of* вы́торговать. **2.** to try to get (*by bargaining*); to haggle over.

вы́тороч|ить, у, ишь, *pf.* (*of* вытора́чивать) to unstrap from the saddle.

вы́точен|ный (~, ~а), *p.p.p. of* вы́точить *and adj.* сло́вно в. chiselled (*of facial features*); perfect, perfectly-formed (*of bodies*).

вы́точ|ить, у, ишь, *pf.* (*of* выта́чивать) 1. to turn (*tech.*) 2. (*coll.*) to sharpen. 3. (*coll.*) to gnaw through.

вы́трав|ить, лю, ишь, *pf.* (*of* трави́ть¹ *and* ~ля́ть) 1. to exterminate, destroy. 2. to remove, get out (*by chemical action*); в. пятно́ to remove a stain. 3. to etch. 4. (*of cattle, etc.*) to trample down (*crops, etc.*).

вытра́влива|ть, ю, *impf.* (*coll.*) = вытравля́ть.

вытравля́|ть, ю, *impf. of* вы́травить.

вытравно́й, *adj.* corrosive, erosive.

вытра́ива|ть, ю, *impf. of* вы́троить.

вытра́лива|ть, ю, *impf. of* вы́тралить.

вы́трал|ить, ю, ишь, *pf.* (*mil.*) to sweep (*mines*).

вы́треб|овать, ую, *pf.* 1. to obtain on demand. 2. to send for, summon(s); в. кого́-н. в суд пове́сткой to summons somebody.

вытрезви́тел|ь, я, *m.* 'sobering-up' station (*in U.S.S.R.*)

вы́трезв|ить, лю, ишь, *pf.* to sober.

вы́трезв|иться, люсь, ишься, *pf.* (*coll.*) to sober up (*intrans.*).

вытрезвля́|ть(ся), ю(сь), *impf. of* вы́трезвить(ся).

вы́тро|ить, ю, ишь, *pf.* (*of* вытра́ивать) (*dial., tech.*) 1. to distil three times. 2. to plough up three times.

вы́т|ру, решь, *see* ~ереть.

вы́тру|сить, шу, сишь, *pf.* (*coll.*) to drop, let fall; to spill.

вытряса́|ть, ю, *impf. of* вы́трясти.

вы́тряс|ти, у, ешь, *past* ~, ~ла, *pf.* 1. to shake out. 2. to clean by shaking out; в. ковёр to shake out a carpet.

вытряха́|ть, ю, *impf.* (*dial., coll.*) = вытря́хивать.

вытря́хива|ть, ю, *impf. of* вы́тряхнуть.

вы́тряхн|уть, у, ешь, *pf.* to drop, let fall; to shake out.

выту́рива|ть, ю, *impf. of* вы́турить.

вы́тур|ить, ю, ишь, *pf.* (*coll.*) to throw out, chuck out.

выть, во́ю, во́ешь, *impf.* to howl (*of animals, the wind, etc.*); (*fig., coll.*) to howl, wail.

выть|ё, я́, *no pl., n.* (*coll.*) howling; wailing.

вы́тяга|ть, ю, *pf.* (*obs.*) to win (by a lawsuit).

вытя́гива|ть(ся), ю(сь), *impf. of* вы́тянуть(ся).

вы́тяжени|е, я, *n.* stretching.

вы́тяжк|а, и, *f.* 1. drawing out, extraction. 2. (*chem., med.*) extract. 3. stretching, ex-

tension; на ~у, *see* навы́тяжку.

вытяжн|о́й, *adj.* for extracting, for drawing out; в. пла́стырь drawing plaster; ~а́я труба́ ventilating pipe; в. шкаф fume cupboard.

вы́тянут|ый (~, ~а), *p.p.p. of* ~ь *and adj.* stretched; ~ое лицо́ (*fig.*) a long face.

вы́тян|уть, у, ешь, *pf.* (*of* вытя́гивать) 1. to stretch (out); to extend. 2. to draw out, extract (*also fig.*); (*impers.*) газ ~уло в окно́ the gas had escaped through the window; (*fig., coll.*) в. всю ду́шу (+d. or у+g.) to wear (someone) out; в. все жи́лы (у, из+g.) to exhaust. 3. (*coll.*) to endure, stand, stick; он до́лго не ~ет при тако́м кли́мате he won't stick it for long in a climate like that. 3. (*coll.*) to weigh. 5. (*coll.*) to flog.

вы́тян|уться, усь, ешься, *pf.* (*of* вытя́гиваться) 1. to stretch (*intrans.*); to stretch oneself (out); он засну́л ~увшись на полу́ he fell asleep stretched out on the floor; лицо́ у неё ~улось (*coll.*) her face lengthened, her face fell. 2. (*coll.*) to grow, shoot up. 3. to stand erect; в. в стру́нку, в. во фронт (*mil.*) to stand at attention.

вы́у|дить, жу, дишь, *pf.* 1. to catch. 2. (*fig., pejor.*) to extract, dig up.

выу́жива|ть, ю, *impf. of* вы́удить.

вы́утюж|ить, у, ишь, *pf. of* утю́жить.

вы́учен|ик, а, *m.* pupil (*of a craftsman*); disciple, follower.

вы́уч|ить, у, ишь, *pf.* (*of* учи́ть *and* ≤ивать) 1. to learn. 2. (+a. *and* d. or +inf.) to teach; он ~ил нас испа́нскому языку́ he taught us Spanish; он ~ил её пра́вить маши́ной he has taught her to drive (a car).

вы́уч|иться, усь, ишься, *pf.* (*of* учи́ться) (+d. or inf.) to learn.

вы́учк|а, и, *f.* teaching, training; отда́ть на ~у (+d.) to apprentice (to); он прошёл хоро́шую ~у he has had a sound schooling; боева́я в. (*mil.*) battle training.

выха́жива|ть, ю, *impf. of* вы́ходить.

вы́харка|ть, ю, *pf.* (*coll.*) to hawk (up).

выха́ркива|ть, ю, *impf. of* вы́харкать.

вы́харк|нуть, ну, нешь, *pf.* = ~ать.

выхва́лива|ть, ю, *impf. of* вы́хвалить.

вы́хвал|ить, ю, ишь, *pf.* to praise.

выхваля́|ть, ю, *impf.* = выхва́ливать.

выхваля́|ться, юсь, *impf.* 1. (*coll.*) to sing one's own praises, blow one's own trumpet. 2. *pass. of* ~ть.

вы́хва|тить, чу, тишь, *pf.* 1. to snatch out, snatch away from; он про́сто ~тил газе́ту из-под моего́ но́са he simply snatched up the newspaper from under my nose. 2. to pull out, draw; в. нож to draw a knife. 3. to pull out, take out, pick up (*at random*); он ~тил кни́гу из ку́чи и на́чал чита́ть he picked up a book from the pile and began to read; в. цита́ту (*fig.*) to quote at random.

выхва́тыва|ть, ю, *impf. of* вы́хватить.

вы́хвачен|ный (~, ~а), *p.p.p. of* вы́хватить; ~ из жи́зни true to life, taken from the life.

выхва|чу, тишь, *see* ~тить.

вы́хлеба|ть, ю, *pf.* (*coll.*) to eat up.

вы́хлеб|нуть, ну, нешь, *pf.* = ~ать.

вы́хлёбыва|ть, ю, *impf. of* вы́хлебать.

вы́хлеста|ть, ю, *pf.* (*coll.*) **1.** to flog, lash. **2.** to flick out. **3.** (*sl.*) to drink off, drain.

вы́хлестн|уть, у, ешь, *pf.* (*coll.*) **1.** to flick out. **2.** to splash out.

вы́хлёстыва|ть, ю, *impf. of* вы́хлестнуть.

вы́хлоп, а, *m.* (*tech.*) exhaust.

выхлопа́тыва|ть, ю, *impf. of* вы́хлопотать.

выхлопно́й, *adj.* (*tech.*) exhaust.

вы́хлопо|тать, чу, чешь, *pf.* (*of* выхлопа́тывать) to obtain (after much trouble).

вы́ход, а, *m.* **1.** going out; leaving, departure; в. за́муж marriage (*of woman*); в. в отста́вку retirement. **2.** way out, exit; outlet; из э́того положе́ния ~а не́ было (*fig.*) there was no way out of this situation; дать в. (+*d.*) to give vent (to); знать все хо́ды и ~ы (*coll.*) to know all the ins and outs. **3.** appearance (*of a publication*); (*theatr.*) entrance. **4.** (*econ.*) output; yield. **5.** (*geol.*) outcrop. **6.** (*eccl.*) вели́кий, ма́лый в. great, little entrance. **7.** быть на ~ах (*theatr.*) to play a supernumerary part.

вы́ход|ец, ца, *m.* **1.** emigrant; immigrant; он роди́лся в США, а роди́тели бы́ли ~цами из Гре́ции he was born in the United States but his parents were emigrants from Greece; в. с того́ све́та apparition, ghost. **2.** person springing from different social group; он — в. из крестья́н he is of peasant origin.

вы́хо|дить¹, жу, дишь, *pf.* (*of* выха́живать) (*coll.*) **1.** to tend, nurse. **2.** to rear, bring up; to grow (*plants*).

вы́хо|дить², жу, дишь, *pf.* (*of* выха́живать) (*coll.*) to pass (through); go all over.

выхо|ди́ть, жу́, ~дишь, *impf.* **1.** *impf. of* вы́йти. **2.** (*impf. only*) to look out (on), give (on), face; его́ ко́мната ~дит о́кнами на у́лицу his room looks onto the street. **3.** не в. из головы́, из ума́ to be unforgettable, stick in one's mind. **4.** *as pred.* ~дит (*coll.*) it turns out.

вы́ходк|а, и, *f.* **1.** (*pejor.*) trick; escapade. **2.** outburst. **3.** (*coll.*) initial step of a dance.

выходни́к, а́, *m.* (*coll.*) person working on day off.

выходн|о́й, *adj.* **1.** exit; ~а́я дверь street door. **2.** в. день day off, free day, rest-day; ~а́я оде́жда 'best' clothes, walking-out clothes; ~о́е пла́тье party dress; *as noun* (*i*) в., ~о́го, *m.* = в. день, (*ii*) в., ~о́го, *m.*,

~а́я, ~о́й, *f.* person having day off; он сего́дня в. it is his day off today. **3.** ~о́е посо́бие (*also as noun* ~ы́е, ~ы́х) gratuity on discharge. **4.** (*theatr.*) ~а́я роль supernumerary part. **5.** (*typ.*) в. лист title-page; ~ы́е све́дения imprint.

вы́ход|я́щий, *pres. part. of* ~и́ть; из ря́да вон ~я́щий outstanding; *as noun* в., ~я́щего, *m.* (*chess, cards*) extra player, bye; в пе́рвом ту́ре он был ~я́щим he had a bye in the first round.

вы́хо|жу, дишь, *see* ~дить.

выхо|жу́, ~дишь, *see* ~ди́ть.

выхола́жива|ть, ю, *impf. of* вы́холодить.

выхола́щива|ть, ю, *impf. of* вы́холостить.

вы́хол|енный, *p.p.p. of* ~ить *and adj.* well-cared-for; well-groomed.

вы́хол|ить, ю, ишь, *pf.* to care for, tend.

вы́холо|дить, жу, дишь, *pf.* (*of* выхола́живать) to cool.

вы́холо|стить, щу, стишь, *pf.* (*of* выхола́щивать) to castrate, geld; (*fig.*) to emasculate.

вы́холо|щенный, *p.p.p. of* ~стить *and adj.* castrated, gelded; (*fig.*) emasculated; ~щенная ло́шадь gelding.

вы́хухолевый, *adj.* musquash.

вы́хухол|ь, я, *m.* **1.** desman, musk-rat. **2.** (*fur*) musquash.

вы́цапа|ть, ю, *pf.* (у+*g.*; *coll.*) to seize, grasp.

вы́царапа|ть, ю, *pf.* (*coll.*) **1.** to scratch; (+*a. and d.*) to scratch out; они́ почти́ ~ли друг дру́гу глаза́ they almost scratched each other's eyes out. **2.** (*fig.*) to extract, get (out of); он ~л у отца́ ещё де́сять рубле́й he has got another ten roubles out of his father.

вы́цара́пыва|ть, ю, *impf. of* вы́царапать.

вы́цве|сти (*coll.* ~сть), ту, тешь, *past* ~л, *pf.* to fade.

выцвета́|ть, ю, *impf. of* вы́цвести.

вы́цве|тший, *past part. of* ~сти *and adj.* faded.

вы́це|дить, жу, дишь, *pf.* **1.** to filter, rack (off); to decant. **2.** (*fig., coll.*) to drink off, drain.

выце́жива|ть, ю, *impf. of* вы́цедить.

вы́чали|ть, ю, *impf. of* вы́чалить.

вы́чал|ить, ю, ишь, *pf.* to haul up, beach (*a boat*).

вычека́нива|ть, ю, *impf. of* вы́чеканить.

вы́чекан|ить, ю, ишь, *pf.* to mint; to strike; в. меда́ль to strike a medal.

вы́ч|ел, ла, *see* ~есть.

вы́чёркива|ть, ю, *impf. of* вы́черкнуть.

вы́черкн|уть, у, ешь, *pf.* to cross out, strike out; to expunge, erase; в. кого́-н. из спи́ска живы́х to give up as dead.

вы́черпа|ть, ю, *pf.* (из+*g.*) to take out (*fluids*); to bail (out); в. во́ду из ло́дки to bail out a boat.

вычёрпыва|ть, ю, *impf. of* вы́черпать.

вы́чер|тить, чу, тишь, *pf.* to draw; to trace.

вы́черчен|ный (~, ~а), *p.p.p. of* вы́чертить *and adj.* finely-drawn; ~ные бро́ви pencilled eyebrows.

вычёрчива|ть, ю, *impf. of* вы́чертить.

вы́чер|чу, тишь, *see* ~тить.

вы́че|сать, шу, шешь, *pf.* (*of* ~сывать) to comb out.

вы́ческ|а, и, *no pl., f.* combing out.

вы́чес|ки, ок, *no sing.* (*text.*) combings.

вы́ч|есть, ту, тешь, *past* ~ел, ~ла, *pres. gerund* ~тя, *pf.* (*of* ~ита́ть) 1. (*math.*) to subtract. 2. to deduct, keep back; пять проце́нтов из ва́шего жа́лованья ~ли на страхова́ние five per cent. of your salary has been kept back for insurance.

вычёсыва|ть, ю, *impf. of* вы́чесать.

вы́чет, а, *m.* deduction; за ~ом (+*g.*) except; less, minus, allowing for; он зараба́тывает две́сти рубле́й в ме́сяц за ~ом нало́гов he earns two hundred roubles a month less taxes.

вы́че|шу, шешь, *see* ~сать.

вычисле́ни|е, я, *n.* calculation.

вычисли́тел|ь, я, *m.* 1. calculator. 2. (*mil.*) plotter. 3. calculating-machine.

вычисли́тельн|ый, *adj.* calculating, computing; ~ая маши́на computer.

вы́числ|ить, ю, ишь, *pf.* to calculate, compute.

вычисля́|ть, ю, *impf. of* вы́числить.

вы́чи|стить, щу, стишь, *pf.* (*of* чи́стить *and* ~ща́ть) 1. to clean (up, out). 2. (*fig.*) to purge; to expel; его́ ~стили из па́ртии he has been expelled from the party.

вычита́ем|ое, ого, *n.* (*math.*) subtrahend.

вычита́ни|е, я, *n.* (*math.*) subtraction.

вы́чита|ть, ю, *pf.* (*of* вычи́тывать) 1. (*coll.*) to find (*by reading, perusing*); я ~л сообще́ние о его́ сме́рти в одно́й из вчера́шних газе́т I found a report of his death in one of yesterday's newspapers. 2. (*typ.*) to read (*manuscripts, proofs*).

вычита́|ть, ю, *impf. of* вы́честь.

вы́читк|а, и, *f.* (*typ.*) reading.

вычи́тыва|ть¹, ю, *impf.* = вычита́ть.

вычи́тыва|ть², ю, *impf.* 1. *impf. of* вы́читать. 2. *impf. only* to reprimand, tell off.

вычища́|ть, ю, *impf. of* вы́чистить.

вы́чи|щу, стишь, *see* ~стить.

вы́ч|ту, тешь, *see* ~есть.

вы́чур|ы, ~, *sing.* ~а, ~ы, *f.* 1. fancy; mannerism; (*lit.; obs.*) conceit. 2. (*obs.*) intricate pattern (*on fabrics*).

вы́чур|ный (~ен, ~на), *adj.* fanciful; mannered; precious.

вы́шага|ть, ю, *pf.* (*coll.*) to pace out.

вы́ша́рива|ть, ю, *impf. of* вы́шарить.

вы́шар|ить, ю, ишь, *pf.* (*coll.*) to rummage out, ferret out.

вышвы́рива|ть, ю, *impf. of* вы́швырнуть *and* вышвыря́ть.

вы́швырн|уть, у, ешь, *pf.* to throw out, hurl out; (*fig., coll.*) to chuck out.

вышвыря́|ть, ю, *pf.* (*coll.*) to throw out.

вы́ше 1. *comp. of* высо́кий *and* высо́ко; higher, taller. 2. *prep.*+*g.* above, beyond; over; э́то в. моего́ понима́ния it is beyond my comprehension, it passes my understanding; в. свои́х сил beyond one's powers, beyond one; зада́ча оказа́лась в. его́ сил the task proved to be beyond him; быть в. (+*g.*) to rise superior (to); в по́лдень температу́ра подняла́сь в. восьми́десяти гра́дусов by midday the temperature had risen to over eighty degrees; дере́вня на Во́лге, в. Сара́това a village on the Volga, above Saratov. 3. *adv.* (*lit.*) above; смотри́ в. *vide supra.*

вы́ше- above-, afore-.

вышеизло́женный, *adj.* foregoing.

вы́|шел, шла, *see* ~йти.

вышелу́шива|ть, ю, *impf. of* вы́шелушить.

вы́шелуш|ить, у, ишь, *pf.* to peel; to shell.

вышена́званный, *adj.* afore-named.

вышеозна́ченный, *adj.* aforesaid, above--mentioned.

вышеприведённый, *adj.* above-cited; в. приме́р the above-cited example, the example above.

вышере́ченный, *adj.* (*obs., now iron.*) afore--mentioned.

вышеска́занный, *adj.* aforesaid.

вышестоя́щ|ий, *adj.* higher; (*polit.*) ~ие о́рганы вла́сти the higher organs of power.

вышеука́занный, *adj.* foregoing.

вышеупомя́нутый, *adj.* afore-mentioned.

вышиба́л|а, ы, *m.* 1. (*sl.*) chucker-out. 2. (*coll.*) rude fellow.

вышиба́|ть, ю, *impf. of* вы́шибить.

вы́шиб|ить, у, ешь, *past* ~, ~ла, *pf.* (*coll.*) 1. to knock out; в. ду́шу, в. дух (из+*g.*) to bump off, beat to death. 2. to chuck out.

вышива́льный, *adj.* embroidery.

вышива́льщиц|а, ы, *f.* needle-woman.

вышива́ни|е, я, *n.* embroidery, needle--work.

вышива́|ть, ю, *impf. of* вы́шить.

вы́шивк|а, и, *f.* embroidery, needle-work.

вы́шиваный, *adj.* embroidered.

вышин|а́, ы́, *pl.* ~ы, *f.* height; в ~е́ aloft, high up; ~о́й в ты́сячу ме́тров a thousand metres high, up.

вы́ш|ить, ью, ьешь, *imp.* ~ей, *pf.* (*of* ~ива́ть) to embroider (on; with); в. узо́р на пла́тье to embroider a pattern on a dress; в. узо́р гла́дью to embroider a pattern in satin-stitch.

вы́шк|а, и, f. 1. turret. 2. (watch-)tower; диспе́тчерская в. (aeron.) control tower; сторожева́я в. watch-tower; бурова́я в. derrick.

вы́школ|ить, ю, ишь, pf. of шко́лить.

вы́шлиф|овать, ую, pf. 1. (tech.) to polish. 2. (fig., coll.) to polish, give a polish to; to smarten up.

вышлифо́выва|ть, ю, impf. of вы́шлифовать.

вы́|шлю, шлешь, see ~слать.

вышмы́гива|ть, ю, impf. of вышмыгнуть.

вы́шмыгн|уть, у, ешь, (coll.) to slip out.

вы́шн|ий, adj. heavenly, divine; ~яя си́ла the power of the Most High.

вышны́рива|ть, ю, impf. of вы́шнырнуть and вы́шнырять.

вы́шнырн|уть, у, ешь, (coll.) to jump out.

вы́шныря|ть, ю, pf. (coll.) 1. to rush all round. 2. to smell out, scent out (information).

вышпа́рива|ть, ю, impf. of вы́шпарить.

вы́шпар|ить, ю, ишь, pf. (coll.) to smoke out; to scald out (insects, etc.).

выштукату́рива|ть, ю, impf. of вы́штукатурить.

вы́штукатур|ить, ю, ишь, pf. to stucco.

вы́шу|тить, чу, тишь, pf. to laugh at, make fun of; to poke fun at.

вышу́чива|ть, ю, impf. of вы́шутить.

выщела́чива|ть, ю, impf. of вы́щелочить.

вы́щёлкива|ть, ю, impf. (coll.) (of nightingales, etc.) to warble forth; (fig.; of horses' hoofs) to clatter.

вы́щелоч|ить, у, ишь, pf. (of выщела́чивать) 1. (chem.) to leach, lixiviate. 2. to steep, soak (linen) in lye.

вы́щерб|ить, лю, ишь, pf. (coll.) to dent; to jag.

выщербля́|ть, ю, impf. of вы́щербить.

вы́щип|ать, лю, лешь, pf. to pull out, pull up; в. пе́рья у ку́рицы to pluck a hen.

вы́щипн|уть, у, ешь, pf. to pull out; to pluck out.

выщи́пыва|ть, ю, impf. of вы́щипать and вы́щипнуть.

вы́щупа|ть, ю, pf. 1. (med.) to find (by probing). 2. (coll.) to run one's hands over; to ransack.

выщу́пыва|ть, ю, impf. of вы́щупать.

вы́|я, и, f. (obs. or rhet.) neck.

вы́яв|ить, лю, ишь, pf. (of ~ля́ть) 1. to display, reveal. 2. to bring out; to make known. 3. (pejor.) to show up, expose.

вы́яв|иться, люсь, ишься, pf. (of ~ля́ться) to appear, come to light, be revealed.

выявле́ни|е, я, n. revelation; showing up, exposure.

выявля́|ть(ся), ю(сь), impf. of вы́явить(ся).

выясне́ни|е, я, n. elucidation; explanation.

вы́ясн|ить[1], ю, ишь, pf. to elucidate; to clear up, explain.

вы́ясн|ить[2], ит, pf. (impers.; dial.) to clear up (of weather).

вы́ясн|иться, ится, pf. to become clear; to turn out, prove (intrans.); как ~илось, он лгал всё вре́мя he was lying all the time as it turned out.

выясн|я́ть(ся), я́ю(сь), impf. of вы́яснить(ся).

вью, вьёшь, see вить.

вью́г|а, и, f. snow-storm, blizzard.

вью́|жный, adj. of ~га.

вьюк, а, m. pack; load.

вьюн, а́, m. 1. loach (fish). 2. (fig., coll.) restless, mobile person; верте́ться ~о́м, ви́ться ~о́м о́коло кого́-н. to be all over someone, try to get round someone.

вьюн|о́к, ка́, m. (bot.) bindweed, convolvulus.

вьюр|о́к, ка́, m. (orn.) mountain finch, brambling.

вью́ч|ить, у, ишь, impf. (of на~) to load (up).

вью́чн|ый, adj. pack; ~ое живо́тное beast of burden; ~ое седло́ pack-saddle.

вью́шк|а, и, f. damper.

вью́щ|ийся, pres. part. of ви́ться and adj.; ~иеся во́лосы curly hair; ~ееся расте́ние (bot.) creeper, climber; в. плющ tree ivy.

вя́|жу, ~жешь, see ~за́ть.

вя́жущий, pres. part. act. of вяза́ть and adj. 1. astringent. 2. (tech.) binding, cementing.

вяз, а, m. elm(-tree).

вяза́льн|ый, adj. knitting; в. крючо́к crochet hook; ~ая спи́ца knitting-needle.

вяза́льщик, а, m. 1. knitter. 2. binder.

вяза́ни|е, я, n. 1. knitting. 2. binding, tying.

вяза́нк|а, и, f. (coll.) knitted garment (jumper, jacket, etc.).

вяза́нк|а, и, f. bundle; truss.

вя́заный, adj. knitted.

вяза́нь|е, я, n. knitting (object in process of being knitted).

вя|за́ть, жу́, ~жешь, impf. 1. (pf. с~) to tie, bind; (tech.) to tie, clamp; в. кому́-н. ру́ки to tie someone's hands. 2. (pf. с~) to knit. 3. (impf. only) to be astringent; (impers.) у меня́ ~жет во рту my mouth feels constricted.

вя|за́ться, жу́сь, ~жешься, impf. (с+i.) to accord, agree (with); to fit in, be in keeping (with), tally; ва́ше предположе́ние о причи́не ава́рии не ~жется с э́тими све́дениями your theory as to the cause of the crash does not fit in with this evidence; его́ вычисле́ния никогда́ не ~за́лись с мои́ми his calculations never tallied with mine; де́ло не ~за́лось, пока́ вы не прие́хали the business was making no progress until you came.

вязи́га = визи́га.

вя́зк|а, и, *f.* **1.** tying, binding. **2.** knitting. **3.** bunch, string; **в. ключе́й** bunch of keys.

вя́з|кий (~ок, ~ка́, ~ко), adj. 1. viscous, sticky; boggy. **2.** (*tech.*) ductile, malleable; tough. **3.** (*coll.*) astringent.

вя́зкост|ь, и, *f.* **1.** viscosity, stickiness; bogginess. **2.** (*tech.*) ductility, malleability; toughness.

вя́зн|уть, у, ешь, *impf.* (в+*p.*) to stick, get stuck (in); to sink (into); **в. в грязи́** to stick in the mud.

вя́зовый, *adj.* elm.

вя́з|че, *comp. of* ~кий *and* ~ко.

вя́зчик, а, *m.* binder.

вяз|ь, и, *no pl., f.* **1.** (*palaeog.*) ornamental ligatured script. **2.** interwoven ornament (*in pattern*).

вя́ка|ть, ю, *impf.* (*coll., dial.*) to speak in-

distinctly; to talk nonsense, blather.

вя́лени|е, я, *n.* (*of meat, fish, etc.*) drying; dry-curing, jerking.

вя́леный, *adj.* dried.

вя́л|ить, ю, ишь, *impf.* (*of* про~) to dry (*in the sun*); to dry-cure, jerk (*meat, fish, etc.*).

вя́лост|ь, и, *f.* flabbiness; limpness; (*fig.*) sluggishness; inertia; slackness; **в. кише́чника** looseness of bowels.

вя́л|ый, *adj.* **1.** faded. **2.** (~, ~á, ~о) flabby, flaccid; limp; (*fig.*) sluggish; inert; slack; ~ое настрое́ние sluggish disposition; **в. ры́нок** (*econ.*) slack market.

вя́н|уть, у, ешь, *past* ~ул, ~ула *and* вял, вя́ла, *impf.* (*of* за~) to fade, wither; (*fig.*) to droop, flag; **у́ши ~ут от тако́го разгово́ра** it makes one sick to listen to such talk.

вя́хир|ь, я, *m.* wood-pigeon.

вя́щ|ий, *adj.* (*obs. or joc.*) greater; **к ~ему несча́стью** to crown the misfortune; **для ~ей предосторо́жности** to make assurance doubly sure.

Г

га, *indecl., n., abbr. of* гекта́р.

габарди́н, а, *m.* gaberdine.

габари́т, а, *m.* (*tech.*) **1.** (*railways*) clearance. **2.** size, dimension (*of a machine*).

габари́т|ный, *adj. of* ~; ~ные воро́та (*railways*) clearance gauge; ~ная высота́ overall height; overhead clearance.

гава́нн|а, ы, *f.* (*coll.*) Havana (*tobacco or cigar*).

га́ван|ский, *adj. of* ~ь.

га́ван|ь, и, *f.* harbour.

га́вка|ть, ю, *impf.* (*coll.*) to bark.

га́врик, а, *m.* (*sl.*) **1.** petty crook. **2.** mate.

га́г|а, и, *f.* eider-duck.

гага́ка|ть, ет, *impf.* (*dial. or coll.; onomat., of geese*) to cackle.

гага́р|а, ы, *f.* (*orn.*) loon, diver.

гага́рк|а, и, *f.* (*orn.*) razorbill.

гага́т, а, *m.* (*min.*) jet.

гага́чий, *adj. of* га́ра; **г. пух** eiderdown.

гад, а, *m.* **1.** (*obs.*) amphibian, reptile. **2.** (*fig., coll.*) repulsive person; (*pl.*) vermin.

гада́лк|а, и, *f.* fortune-teller.

гада́ни|е, я, *n.* **1.** divination, fortune-telling; **г. на ка́ртах** card-reading, cartomancy; **г. по руке́** palmistry. **2.** guess-work.

гада́тел|ьный (~ен, ~ьна), *adj.* problematic, conjectural, hypothetical; ~ьная кни́га fortune-telling book.

гада́|ть, ю, *impf.* **1.** (*pf.* по~) (на+*p.* or по+*d.*) to tell fortunes (by); **г. на кофе́йной**

гу́ще to make wild guesses. **2.** *impf. only* (о+*p.*) to guess, conjecture, surmise.

га́дин|а, ы, *f.* (*fig.*) reptile; (*coll.*) repulsive person; (*pl.*) vermin.

га́|дить, жу, дишь, *impf.* (*of* на~) **1.** (*of animals*) to defecate. **2.** (на+*a.* or *p.*, в+*p.*) to foul, defile. **3.** (+*d.; coll.*) to play dirty tricks (on).

га́д|кий (~ок, ~ка́, ~ко), *adj.* nasty, vile, repulsive; **г. утёнок** ugly duckling.

га́дк|о¹, а, *adv. of* ~ий.

га́дко², *as pred.* **мне, etc., г. I, etc.,** loathe (it); **I, etc.,** am repelled.

гадли́вост|ь, и, *f.* aversion, disgust.

гадли́в|ый (~, ~а), *adj.* ~ое чу́вство (feeling of) disgust.

га́дост|ный (~ен, ~на), *adj.* disgusting; (*coll.*) poor, bad.

га́дост|ь, и, f. 1. (*coll.*) filth, muck. **2.** dirty trick; **он спосо́бен на вся́кую г.** he is capable of the lowest trick; **говори́ть ~и** to say foul things.

гадю́к|а, и, *f.* **1.** adder, viper. **2.** (*coll.*) repulsive person.

га́ер, а, *m.* (*obs.*) buffoon, clown.

га́ерств|о, а, *n.* (*obs.*) buffoonery, tomfoolery.

га́ерств|овать, ую, *impf.* (*obs., pejor.*) to play the buffoon; to clown.

га́ечный, *adj. of* га́йка; **г. ключ** spanner, wrench.

гáже, *comp. of* гáдкий.

газ[1], **а**, *m.* **1.** gas. **2.** (*coll.*) на пóлном ∼е (∼ý) at top speed; дать г. to step on the gas, step on it; сбáвить г. to reduce speed. **3.** (*pl.*; *med.*) wind; скоплéние ∼ов flatulence, wind.

газ[2], **а**, *no pl., m.* gauze.

газан|**ýть**, **ý, ёшь**, *pf.* (*sl.*) **1.** to step on it (*in a car*). **2.** to scram.

газáци|**я, и,** *f.* aeration.

газгóльдер, а, *m.* gasholder.

газéл|**ь**[1]**, и,** *f.* (*zool.*) gazelle.

газéл|**ь**[2]**, и,** *f.* (*lit.*) ghazal (*Arabic verse form*).

газéт|**а, ы,** *f.* newspaper.

газéт|**ный,** *adj. of* ∼а; ∼ная бумáга news-print; г. стиль journalese.

газéтчик, а, *m.* **1.** newspaper-seller; newspaper-boy. **2.** (*coll.*) journalist.

гáзик, а, *m.* 'Gazik' (*small lorry produced by Gorky motor-vehicle works*).

газирóванный, *adj.* aerated.

газир|**овáть, ую,** *impf.* to aerate.

газирóвк|**а, и,** *f.* **1.** aeration. **2.** (*coll.*) aerated water.

газификáци|**я, и,** *f.* **1.** supplying with gas. **2.** gasification.

газифицир|**овать, ую,** *impf. and pf.* **1.** to supply with gas; to install gas (in). **2.** (*tech.*) to extract gas (from).

газобаллóн, а, *m.* gas cylinder.

газовщи́к, á, *m.* gas-works employee; gas-man.

гáзов|**ый**[1]**,** *adj. of* газ[1]; ∼ая колóнка geyser; ∼ая плитá gas cooker, gas-stove; г. рожóк gas-burner; gas bracket; ∼ая свáрка oxy-acetylene welding; г. счётчик gas-meter; ∼ая атáка (*mil.*) gas attack; ∼ая кáмера gas chamber.

гáзовый[2]**,** *adj. of* газ[2].

газогенерáтор, а, *m.* (*tech.*) gas generator, gas producer.

газокали́льн|**ый,** *adj.* г. колпачóк gas mantle; ∼ая лáмпа incandescent gas-lamp.

газоли́н, а, *m.* gasolene.

газомéр, а, *m.* gas-meter.

газомёт, а, *m.* (*mil.*) gas projector.

газомотóр, а, *m.* (*tech.*) gas-engine.

газóн, а, *m.* grass-plot, lawn; по ∼ам ходи́ть воспрещáется keep off the grass.

газонепроницáемый, *adj.* gas-proof, gas-tight.

газонокоси́лка, и, *f.* lawn-mower.

газообрáз|**ный** (∼ен, ∼на), *adj.* (*phys.*) gaseous, gasiform.

газопровóд, а, *m.* gas pipeline; gas-main.

газопровóд|**ный,** *adj. of* ∼.

газоубéжищ|**е, а,** *n.* gas-proof shelter.

газохрани́лищ|**е, а,** *n.* gas-holder; gasometer.

гайст, а, *m.* (*coll.*) traffic-cop.

гайдамáк, а, *m.* (*hist.*) haydamak (*Ukrainian Cossack; also member of anti-Bolshevik Ukrainian cavalry detachment in 1918*).

гайдамá|**цкий,** *adj. of* ∼к.

гайдýк, á, *m.* (*hist.*) heyduck (**1.** *rebel against Turkish domination in Balkans.* **2.** *footman in house of wealthy landowner*).

гáйк|**а, и,** *f.* nut, female screw; у негó в головé не хватáет ∼и (*coll.*) he's got a screw loose.

гаймори́т, а, *m.* (*med.*) antritis.

гáйморов, *adj.* ∼а пóлость (*anat.*) antrum of Highmore.

гак[1]**, а,** *m.* (*naut.*) hook.

гак[2]**, а,** *m.* (*coll.*) superfluity; часá три с ∼ом about three hours or more.

галá, *indecl. adj.* gala; г.-представлéние gala performance.

галáктик|**а, и,** *f.* (*astron.*) galaxy.

галантерéйност|**ь, и,** *f.* (*obs., coll.*) urbanity, gallantry.

галантерé|**йный,** *adj.* **1.** *adj. of* ∼я; г. магази́н haberdashery, fancy-goods shop. **2.** (*obs., coll.*) urbane, gallant.

галантерé|**я, и,** *f.* haberdashery, fancy goods.

галанти́р, а, *m.* galantine.

галáнтност|**ь, и,** *f.* gallantry (= *courtliness*).

галáнт|**ный** (∼ен, ∼на, ∼но), *adj.* gallant (= *courtly*).

гал|**дёж, á,** *m.* (*coll.*) din, racket.

галд|**éть,** *1st pers. not used,* **и́шь,** *impf.* (*coll.*) to make a din, racket.

галéр|**а, ы,** *f.* galley.

галерé|**я, и,** *f.* (*in var. senses*) gallery.

галёрк|**а, и,** *f.* (*theatr.*; *coll.*) **1.** gallery, 'the gods'. **2.** 'the gods' (= *those occupying gallery seats*).

галéр|**ный,** *adj. of* ∼а.

галéт|**а, ы,** *f.* (ship's) biscuit.

гáлечник, а, *m.* (*collect.*) pebbles, shingle.

гáлечный, *adj.* pebble, shingle; pebbly, shingly.

галимáть|**я, и́,** *f.* (*coll.*) rubbish, nonsense.

галифé, *indecl., n.* riding-breeches, jodhpurs.

галици́йский, *adj.* Galician.

гáлк|**а, и,** *f.* daw, jackdaw; считáть гáлок (*i*) to stand gaping, gawp (*ii*) to loaf.

галл, а, *m.* Gaul.

гáлли|**й, я,** *m.* (*chem.*) gallium.

галлици́зм, а, *m.* Gallicism.

галломáни|**я, и,** *f.* gallomania.

галлóн, а, *m.* gallon.

галлофóби|**я, и,** *f.* gallophobia.

гáлльский, *adj.* Gallic.

галлюцинáци|**я, и,** *f.* hallucination.

галлюцини́р|**овать, ую,** *impf.* to have hallucinations.

галогéн, а, *m.* (*chem.*) halogen.

галóид, а, *m.* (*chem.*) haloid.

галóп, а, *m.* 1. gallop; ∼ом at a gallop; лёгкий г. canter; скакáть ∼ом to gallop; поднять в г. to put into a gallop. 2. galop (*dance*).

галопи́р|овать, ую, *impf.* to gallop.

гáл|очий, *adj.* of ∼ка.

галóш|а, и, *f.* galosh; сесть в ∼у (*coll.*) to get into a fix, into a spot.

галс, а, *m.* (*naut.*) tack; прáвым (лéвым) ∼ом on the starboard (port) tack.

гáлстук, а, *m.* (neck)tie, cravat; заложи́ть, зали́ть за г. (*coll.*) to booze; г.-бáбочка bow-tie.

галу́н, á, *m.* lace, galloon.

галу́шк|а, и, *f.* (*cul.*) dumpling.

гальванизáци|я, и, *f.* (*phys.*) galvanization.

гальванизи́р|овать, ую, *impf. and pf.* (*phys.*) to galvanize.

гальвани́ческий, *adj.* (*phys.*) galvanic.

гальвáно, *indecl.*, *n.* (*typ.*) electrotype.

гальванóметр, а, *m.* (*phys.*) galvanometer.

гальваноплáстик|а, и, *f.* electroplating.

гáл|ька, ьки, *f.* 1. (*g. pl.* ∼ек) pebble. 2. (*collect.*) pebble, shingle.

гальйóн, а, *m.* (*naut.*) (the) heads.

гам, а, *m.* (*coll.*) din, uproar.

гамадри́л, а, *m.* (*zool.*) hamadryad (*baboon*).

гамáк, á, *m.* hammock.

гамáш|а, и, *f.* gaiter, legging.

гáмм|а[1], ы, *f.* (*mus.*) scale; gamut (*also fig.*).

гáмм|а[2], ы, *f.* gamma (*letter of Greek alphabet*); г.-лучи́ (*phys.*) gamma-rays.

гáнгли|й, я, *m.* (*anat.*) ganglion.

гангрéн|а, ы, *f.* gangrene.

гангренóзный, *adj.* gangrenous.

гáнгстер, а, *m.* (*sport*) gangster.

гандикáп, а, *m.* (*sport*) handicap.

ганзéйский, *adj.* (*hist.*) Hanseatic.

гантéл|ь, и, *f.* (*sport*) dumb-bell.

гарáж, á, *m.* garage.

гарáнт, а, *m.* (*leg.*) guarantor.

гаранти́йный, *adj.* guarantee.

гаранти́р|овать, ую, *impf. and pf.* 1. to guarantee, vouch for. 2. (от+*g.*) to guarantee (against).

гарáнти|я, и, *f.* guarantee.

гардемари́н, а, *m.* (*hist.*) 1. naval cadet. 2. (корабéльный) г. midshipman.

гардерóб, а, *m.* 1. wardrobe (*article of furniture*). 2. cloakroom. 3. (*collect.*) wardrobe (*clothes belonging to one person*).

гардерóбн|ая, ой, *f.* cloakroom.

гардерóбщик, а, *m.* cloakroom attendant.

гардерóбщи|ца, цы, *f.* of ∼к.

гарди́н|а, ы, *f.* curtain.

гар|евóй, *adj.* of ∼ь; ∼евáя дорóжка cinder path.

гарéм, а, *m.* harem.

гáрк|ать, аю, *impf. of* ∼нуть.

гáрк|нуть, ну, нешь, *pf.* (*of* ∼ать) (*coll.*) to bark (out), bawl (out); г. на когó-н. to bark at someone.

гармонизáци|я, и, *f.* (*mus.*) harmonization.

гармонизи́р|овать, ую, *impf. and pf.* (*mus.*) to harmonize (*trans.*).

гармóник|а, и, *f.* 1. accordion, concertina; губнáя г. mouth organ. 2. ∼ой, в ∼у as *adv.* pleated; concertina'ed.

гармони́р|овать, ую, *impf.* (с+*i.*) to harmonize (*intrans.*) (with), go (with); to tone (with).

гармони́ст[1], а, *m.* accordion player, concertina player.

гармони́ст[2], а, *m.* (*mus.*) specialist in harmony.

гармони́ческий, *adj.* (1. (*mus.*) harmonic. 2. harmonious. 3. (*tech.*) rhythmic.

гармони́ч|ный (∼ен, ∼на, ∼но), *adj.* harmonious.

гармóни|я[1], и, *f.* 1. (*mus.*) harmony. 2. (*fig.*) harmony, concord.

гармóни|я[2], и, *f.* (*coll.*) accordion, concertina.

гармóн|ь, и, *f.* (*coll.*) accordion, concertina.

гармóшк|а, и, *f.* = гармóнь.

гáрн|ец, ца, *m.* (*obs.*) garnets (*Russian dry measure* = 3·28 *litres*).

гарнизóн, а, *m.* garrison.

гарнизóн|ный, *adj.* of ∼; ∼ная слу́жба garrison duty.

гарни́р, а, *m.* (*cul.*) trimmings, garnish.

гарниту́р, а, *m.* set; suite.

гáрн|ый, *adj.* (*obs.*); ∼ое мáсло lamp oil.

гáрпи|я, и, *f.* harpy.

гарпу́н, á, *m.* harpoon.

гарпу́н|ный, *adj.* of ∼; ∼ная пу́шка harpoon-gun.

гарт, а, *m.* type-metal; printer's pie.

гáрус, а, *m.* worsted (yarn); вышивка ∼ом worsted work.

гарц|евáть, у́ю, *impf.* to caracole, prance.

гар|ь, и, *f.* 1. burning; пáхнет ∼ю there's a smell of burning. 2. cinders, ashes.

гаси́льник, а, *m.* (*obs.*) extinguisher.

гаси́тел|ь, я, *m.* extinguisher; (*fig.*) suppressor; г. просвещéния obscurantist.

га|си́ть, шу́, ∼сишь, *impf.* (*of* по∼) 1. (*pf. also* за∼) to put out, extinguish; г. свет to put out the light. 2. г. и́звесть to slake lime. 3. (*fig.*) to suppress, stifle. 4. to cancel; г. долг to liquidate a debt; г. почтóвую мáрку to frank a postage stamp.

гáс|нуть, ну, нешь, *past* ∼, ∼ла, *impf.* (*of* по∼) to be extinguished, go out; to grow feeble; он ∼нет не по дням, а по часáм he is sinking hourly.

гастри́т, а, *m.* gastritis.

гастри́ческий, *adj.* gastric.

гастролёр, а, *m.* **1.** artiste on tour. **2.** (*coll.*) casual worker.

гастроли́р|овать, ую, *impf.* to tour, be on tour (*of an artiste*).

гастро́л|ь, и, *f.* tour; temporary engagement (*of artiste*).

гастро́льный, *adj.* touring (*of artistes*).

гастроно́м¹, а, *m.* gastronome, gourmet.

гастрон|о́м², а, *m.* = ~оми́ческий магази́н.

гастрономи́ческий, *adj.* **1.** gastronomical. **2.** г. магази́н grocer's (shop), provision shop.

гастроно́ми|я, и, *f.* **1.** connoisseur's taste in food. **2.** provisions, delicatessen.

га|ти́ть, чу́, ти́шь, *impf.* to make a road (of brushwood) across (*marshy ground*).

гат|ь, и, *f.* road of brushwood; бреве́нчатая г. corduroy road.

га́убиц|а, ы, *f.* (*mil.*) howitzer.

га́уб|ичный, *adj. of* ~ица.

гауптва́хт|а, ы, *f.* (*mil.*) **1.** (*obs.*) guardhouse, guardroom. **2.** detention cell.

га́ч|и, ей (*sing.* ~а, ~и), *f.* (*dial.*) **1.** trousers. **2.** haunches (*of an animal*).

гаше́ни|е, я, *n.* extinguishing; slaking.

гашён|ый, *p.p.p. of* гаси́ть *and adj.*; ~ая и́звесть slaked lime.

гаше́тк|а, и, *f.* trigger.

гаши́ш, а, *m.* hashish.

гвалт, а, *m.* (*coll.*) row, uproar, rumpus.

гварде́|ец, йца, *m.* (*mil.*) guardsman.

гварде́йский, *adj.* (*mil.*) Guards'; г. миноме́т multi-rail rocket launcher.

гва́рди|я, и, *f.* (*mil.*) Guards; ~и (*preceding* капита́н, *etc., in titles of rank*) Guards.

гво́здик, а, *m.* tack (*small nail*).

гвозди́к|а¹, и, *f.* (*bot.*) pink(s); пе́ристая г. carnation(s); туре́цкая г., борода́тая г. sweet-william.

гвозди́к|а², и, *f.* (*collect.*) cloves.

гвозди́льный, *adj.* nail, nail-making.

гвоз|ди́ть, жу́, ди́шь, *impf.* (*coll.*) **1.** to bang, bash; to bang away. **2.** to repeat, keep on.

гвозди́|чный¹, *adj. of* ~ка¹.

гвозди́|чный², *adj. of* ~ка²; ~чное ма́сло oil of cloves.

гвозд|ь, я, *pl.* ~и, ~е́й, *m.* **1.** nail; tack; peg; пове́сить шля́пу на г. to hang one's hat on a peg; ~ём засе́сть (*fig.*) to become firmly fixed. **2.** (+*g.*; *fig., coll.*) the crux (of); the pièce de résistance (of); highlight (of); г. вопро́са the crux of the matter; г. ве́чера the highlight of the evening; г. сезо́на the hit of the season. **3.** (и) ника́ких ~е́й! (*coll.*) and that's that!, and that's the end of it!

где, *adv.* **1.** (*interrog. and relat. adv.*) where; г. бы ни wherever; г. бы то ни́ было по matter where. **2.** (*coll.*) somewhere; any-

where. **3.** г....., г.... (*coll.*) in one place ..., in another .... **4.** г. (уж) (+*d. and inf.*)(*coll.*) how should one, how is one to; г. мне знать? how should I know?

где́-либо, *adv.* anywhere.

где́-нибудь, *adv.* somewhere; anywhere.

где́-то, *adv.* somewhere.

гебра́ист, а, *m.* Hebraist.

гегелья́н|ец, ца, *m.* Hegelian.

гегелья́нств|о, а, *n.* Hegelianism.

гегемо́н, а, *m.* leader.

гегемони́зм, а, *m.* (*polit.*) 'hegemonism'.

гегемо́ни|я, и, *f.* hegemony, supremacy.

гедони́зм, а, *m.* hedonism.

гедони́ст, а, *m.* hedonist.

гедонисти́ческий, *adj.* hedonistic.

гей, *interj.* hi!

ге́йзер, а, *m.* geyser.

река́томб|а, ы, *f.* hecatomb.

гекза́метр, а, *m.* hexameter.

гекса́эдр, а, *m.* (*math.*) hexahedron.

гекта́р, а, *m.* hectare.

гекто- hecto-.

ге́ли|й, я, *m.* (*chem.*) helium.

геликопте́р, а, *m.* (*obs.*) = вертолёт.

гелио́граф, а, *m.* heliograph.

гелиотро́п, а, *m.* (*bot. and min.*) heliotrope.

гелиоцентри́ческий, *adj.* heliocentric.

гельминтоло́ги|я, и, *f.* helminthology.

ге́мм|а, ы, *f.* stone with engraved design.

гемоглоби́н, а, *m.* (*physiol.*) haemoglobin.

геморроида́льн|ый, *adj.* (*med.*) haemorrhoidal; ~ая ши́шка pile.

геморро́|й, я, *m.* (*med.*) haemorrhoids, piles.

гемофили|я, и, *f.* (*med.*) haemophilia.

ген- (*abbr. of* генера́льный) general.

ген, а, *m.* (*physiol.*) gene.

генеалоги́ческий, *adj.* genealogical.

генеало́ги|я, и, *f.* genealogy.

ге́незис, а, *m.* origin, source, genesis.

генера́л, а, *m.* general (*mil.*; *also, hist., denotes status of member of first four grades of tsarist Russian civil service*); г.-майо́р major-general; г.-лейтена́нт lieutenant-general; г.-полко́вник colonel-general; г.-губерна́тор governor-general.

генера́л-ба́с, а, *m.* (*mus.*) figured bass.

генерали́ссимус, а, *m.* generalissimo.

генералите́т, а, *m.* (*collect.*) the generals; the top brass.

генера́льн|ый, *adj.* (*in var. senses*) general; г. констру́ктор chief designer; ~ая ли́ния па́ртии (*polit.*) Party general line; ~ая репети́ция dress rehearsal; ~ое сраже́ние decisive battle; г. штаб general staff.

генера́льский, *adj.* general's; г. чин rank of general.

генера́льш|а, и, *f.* (*coll.*) general's wife.

генера́тор, а, *m.* (*tech.*) generator; г. колеба́ний oscillator; г. то́ка current generator.

генера́тор|ный, *adj. of* ~; г. газ producer gas.
гене́тик|а, и, *f.* genetics.
генети́ческий, *adj.* genetic.
гениа́льност|ь, и, *f.* genius; greatness.
гениа́л|ьный (ен, ьна), *adj.* of genius, great; brilliant; ~ьная иде́я a stroke of genius.
ге́ни|й, я, *m.* genius; a genius; злой г. evil genius.
ге́н|ный, *adj. of* ~; ~ная инжене́рия genetic engineering.
геншта́б, а, *m.* general staff.
генштаби́ст, *m.* (*coll.*) general staff officer.
гео- geo-.
гео́граф, а, *m.* geographer.
географи́ческий, *adj.* geographical.
геогра́фи|я, и, *f.* geography.
геодези́ст, а, *m.* land-surveyor.
геодези́ческий, *adj.* geodesic, geodetic.
геоде́зи|я, и, *f.* geodesy, (land-)surveying.
гео́лог, а, *m.* geologist.
геологи́ческий, *adj.* geological.
геоло́ги|я, и, *f.* geology.
гео́метр, а, *m.* geometrician.
геометри́ческий, *adj.* geometric(al).
геоме́три|я, и, *f.* geometry.
георги́н, а, *m.* (*bot.*) dahlia.
георги́н|а, ы, *f.* = ~.
геофи́зик|а, и, *f.* geophysics.
геофизи́ческий, *adj.* geophysical.
гепа́рд, а, *m.* cheetah.
гера́льдик|а, и, *f.* heraldry.
геральди́ческий, *adj.* heraldic.
гера́н|ь, и, *f.* geranium.
герб, а́, *m.* arms, coat of arms.
герба́ри|й, я, *m.* herbarium.
гербици́д, а, *m.* herbicide, weed-killer.
гербо́вник, а, *m.* armorial.
ге́рбов|ый, *adj.* 1. heraldic. 2. bearing a coat of arms; ~ая бума́га stamped paper; ~ая ма́рка duty stamp. 3. г. сбор stamp-duty.
геркуле́с, а, *m.* 1. (a) Hercules (*strong man*). 2. (*sing. only*) rolled oats; porridge.
геркуле́совский, *adj.* Herculean.
герма́н|ец, ца, *m.* 1. Teuton; ancient German; ~цы the Germanic, Nordic peoples. 2. (*coll.*) German.
германиза́ци|я, и, *f.* Germanization.
германизи́р|овать, ую, *impf. and pf.* to Germanize.
германи́зм, а, *m.* Germanism.
герма́ни|й, я, *m.* (*chem.*) germanium.
германи́ст, а, *m.* specialist in Germanic studies.
германи́стик|а, и, *f.* Germanic studies.
герма́нск|ий, *adj.* 1. Germanic; Teutonic; ~ие языки́ Germanic languages. 2. (*coll.*) German.
гермафроди́т, а, *m.* hermaphrodite.

ермети́чески, *adv.* г. закры́тый hermetically sealed.
гермети́ческ|ий, *adj.* 1. hermetic, sealed; air-tight, water-tight; ~ая каби́на (*aeron.*) pressurized cabin. 2. hermetic, secret.
геро́изм, а, *m.* heroism.
геро́ик|а, и, *f.* heroics; heroic spirit; heroic style.
геро́ин|я, и, *f.* heroine.
герои́ческ|ий, *adj.* heroic; ~ие ме́ры heroic measures.
геро́|й, я, *m.* hero; (*lit.*) character.
геро́йский, *adj.* heroic.
геро́йств|о, а, *n.* heroism.
геро́льд, а, *m.* (*hist.*) herald.
геру́нди́в, а, *m.* (*gram.*) gerundive.
геру́нди|й, я, *m.* (*gram.*) gerund.
герц, а, *g. pl.* г. *m.* (*phys.*) hertz, cycle per second.
ге́рцог, а, *m.* duke.
герцоги́н|я, и, *f.* duchess.
ге́рцогский, *adj.* ducal.
ге́рцогств|о, а, *n.* duchy.
геста́по, *indecl., n.* Gestapo.
гетероге́нный, *adj.* heterogeneous.
ге́тман, а, *m.* (*hist.*) hetman.
ге́тр|ы, гетр, *sing.* ~а, ~ы, *f.* 1. gaiters. 2. (*sport, coll.*) football socks. 3. leg-warmers.
ге́тто, *indecl., n.* ghetto.
геше́фт, а, *m.* (*coll.*) deal, speculation.
гиаци́нт, а, *m.* 1. (*bot.*) hyacinth. 2. (*min.*) jacinth.
ги́бел|ь, и, *f.* 1. death; destruction, ruin; loss; wreck; downfall. 2. (+*g.*; *coll.*) masses (of), swarms (of), hosts (of).
ги́бел|ьный (~ен, ~ьна), *adj.* disastrous, fatal.
ги́б|кий (~ок, ~ка́, ~ко), *adj.* 1. flexible, pliant; lithe, lissom; г. стан slender build. 2. adaptable, versatile. 3. tractable.
ги́бкост|ь, и, *f.* 1. flexibility, pliancy. 2. versatility, resourcefulness.
ги́бл|ый, *adj.* (*coll.*) bad, rotten, good-for-nothing; ~ое де́ло a bad job.
ги́б|нуть, ну, нешь, *past* ~, ~ла, *impf.* (*of* по~) to perish.
гибри́д, а, *m.* hybrid, mongrel.
гибридиза́ци|я, и, *f.* hybridization.
гига́нт, а, *m.* giant.
гига́нтский, *adj.* gigantic.
гигие́н|а, ы, *f.* hygiene, hygienics.
гигиени́ческ|ий, *adj.* hygienic, sanitary; ~ая повя́зка sanitary towel; ~ая бума́га toilet paper.
гигро́метр, а, *m.* hygrometer.
гигроско́п, а, *m.* hygroscope.
гигроскопи́ческий, *adj.* hygroscopic.
гид, а, *m.* guide.
гида́льго, *indecl., m.* hidalgo.
ги́др|а, ы, *f.* (*myth., zool.*; *fig.*) hydra.

гидра́влик|а, и, *f.* hydraulics.
гидравли́ческий, *adj.* hydraulic.
гидра́т, а, *m.* (*chem.*) hydrate.
гидро- hydro-.
гидро́граф, а, *m.* 1. hydrograph. 2. hydrographer.
гидрографи́ческий, *adj.* hydrographic.
гидрогра́фи|я, и, *f.* hydrography.
гидродина́мик|а, и, *f.* hydrodynamics.
гидро́лиз, а, *m.* (*chem.*) hydrolysis.
гидроло́ги|я, и, *f.* hydrology.
гидроме́три|я, и, *f.* hydrometry.
гидрооки́с|ь, и, *f.* hydroxide.
гидропа́ти|я, и. *f.* hydropathy.
гидропу́льт, а, *m.* 1. stirrup pump. 2. water-cannon.
гидросамолёт, а, *m.* seaplane.
гидроста́нци|я, и, *f.* hydro-electric (power-) station.
гидроста́тик|а, и, *f.* hydrostatics.
гидросульфи́т, а, *m.* (*chem.*) hydrosulphite.
гидротерапи́|я, и, *f.* hydrotherapy.
гидроте́хник, а, *m.* hydraulic engineer.
гидроте́хник|а, и, *f.* hydraulic engineering.
гидроустано́вк|а, и, *f.* (*tech.*) hydro-electric power-plant.
гидрофо́н, а, *m.* (*naut.*) hydrophone.
гидроэлектри́ческий, *adj.* hydro-electric.
гидроэлектроста́нци|я, и, *f.* hydro-electric power-station.
гие́н|а, ы, *f.* hyena.
гик, а, *m.* (*coll.*) whoop.
ги́к|ать, аю, *impf.* (*of* ~нуть) (*coll.*) to whoop.
ги́к|нуть, ну, нешь, *pf.* (*of* ~ать) to whoop.
гил|ь, и, *f.* (*obs., coll.*) nonsense.
гильде́йский, *adj. of* ги́льдия.
ги́льди|я, и, *f.* (*hist.*) guild; class, order (*of merchants in tsarist Russia*).
ги́льз|а, ы, *f.* case, empty; патро́нная г. cartridge-case; папиро́сная г. cigarette-wrapper; г. цили́ндра (*tech.*) cylinder sleeve.
гильоти́н|а, ы, *f.* guillotine.
гильотини́р|овать, ую, *impf. and pf.* to guillotine.
гимн, а, *m.* hymn; госуда́рственный г. national anthem.
гимнази́ст, а, *m.* grammar-school boy.
гимнази́стк|а, и, *f.* grammar-school girl.
гимна́зи|я, и, *f.* grammar school, high school.
гимна́ст, а, *m.* gymnast.
гимнастёрк|а, и, *f.* soldier's blouse.
гимна́стик|а, и, *f.* gymnastics.
гимнасти́ческ|ий, *adj.* gymnastic; г. зал gymnasium; ~ие снаря́ды gymnastic apparatus.
гинеко́лог, а, *m.* gynaecologist.

гинекологи́ческий, *adj.* gynaecological.
гинеколо́ги|я, и, *f.* gynaecology.
гине́|я, и, *f.* guinea.
гипе́рбол|а, ы, *f.* 1. hyperbole. 2. (*math.*) hyperbola.
гиперболи́ческий, *adj.* 1. hyperbolical. 2. (*math.*) hyperbolic.
гиперболи́ч|ный (~ен, ~на), *adj.* exaggerated.
гипертони́|я, и, *f.* (*med.*) hypertonia, high blood-pressure.
гипертрофи́рованный, *adj.* (*biol.*) hypertrophied.
гипертрофи́|я, и, *f.* (*biol.*) hypertrophy.
гипно́з, а, *m.* hypnosis.
гипнотизёр, а, *m.* hypnotist.
гипнотизи́р|овать, ую, *impf.* (*of* за~) to hypnotize.
гипноти́зм, а, *m.* hypnotism.
гипноти́ческий, *adj.* hypnotic.
гипосульфи́т, а, *m.* (*chem.*) hyposulphite.
гипо́тез|а, ы, *f.* hypothesis.
гипотену́з|а, ы, *f.* (*math.*) hypotenuse.
гипотети́ческий, *adj.* hypothetical.
гиппопота́м, а, *m.* hippopotamus.
гипс, а, *m.* 1. (*min.*) gypsum, plaster of Paris. 2. plaster cast. 3. (*med.*) plaster.
гипс|ова́ть, у́ю, *impf.* (*of* за~) to plaster; to gypsum.
ги́псовый, *adj.* 1. gypseous. 2. plaster; г. сле́пок plaster-cast.
гиреви́к, а́, *m.* (*sport*) weight-lifter.
гир|ево́й, *adj. of* ~я́.
гирля́нд|а, ы, *f.* garland, wreath.
гироко́мпас, а, *m.* gyrocompass.
гироско́п, а, *m.* gyroscope.
гироскопи́ческий, *adj.* gyroscopic.
ги́р|я, и, *f.* weight; г. для гимна́стики dumb-bells.
гисто́лог, а, *m.* histologist.
гистологи́ческий, *adj.* histological.
гистоло́ги|я, и, *f.* histology.
гита́р|а, ы, *f.* guitar.
гитари́ст, а, *m.* guitarist.
гитлери́зм, а, *m.* Hitlerism; Naz(i)ism.
ги́тлеров|ец, ца, *m.* Hitlerite, Nazi; German soldier (*in Second World War*).
ги́тлеровский, *adj.* Hitlerite, Nazi.
ги́чк|а, и, *f.* (*naut.*) gig.
глав- (*abbr. of* гла́вный) chief, main.
глав|а́[1], ы́, *pl.* ~ы, *f.* 1. (*obs. or rhet.*) head. 2. (*m. and f.*) head, chief; г. делега́ции head of a delegation; быть во ~е́ (+*g.*) to be at the head (of), lead; во ~е́ (с+*i.*) under the leadership (of), led (by). 3. поста́вить во ~у́ угла́ to regard as of paramount importance. 4. (*archit.*) cupola (*of a church*).
глав|а́[2], ы́, *pl.* ~ы, *f.* chapter (*of a book*).
глава́р|ь, я́, *m.* leader; ringleader.
главе́нств|о, а, *n.* supremacy.

главе́нств|овать, ую, *impf.* (в+*p.*, над+*i.*) to have command (over), hold sway (over).

главк, а, *m.* (*abbr. of* гла́вный комите́т) central directorate (*department of Ministry controlling either branch of industry falling within competence of Ministry or establishments in a particular area*).

главнокома́ндующ|ий, его, *m.* commander-in-chief; верхо́вный г. supreme commander.

гла́вн|ый, *adj.* chief, main, principal; head, senior; г. врач head physician; г. инжене́р chief engineer; ~ая кварти́ра (*mil.*; *obs.*) headquarters; ~ая кни́га ledger; ~ое предложе́ние main clause; ~ое управле́ние main directorate, central directorate; ~ым о́бразом chiefly, mainly, for the most part; *as noun* ~ое, ~ого, *n.* the chief thing, the main thing, the essentials.

глаго́л, а, *m.* 1. (*gram.*) verb. 2. (*arch.*) word.

глаго́лиц|а, ы, *f.* (*ling.*) the Glagolitic alphabet.

глаголи́ческий, *adj.* (*ling.*) Glagolitic.

глаго́льный, *adj.* verbal.

гладиа́тор, а, *m.* gladiator.

гладиа́торский, *adj.* gladiatorial.

глади́льн|ый, *adj.* ironing; ~ая доска́ ironing-board.

гла́|дить, жу, дишь, *impf.* (*of* по~¹) 1. (*pf. also* вы~) to iron, press. 2. to stroke; г. по голо́вке (*coll.*) to pat on the back; г. про́тив ше́рсти to rub the wrong way.

гла́д|кий (~ок, ~ка́, ~ко), *adj.* 1. smooth; (*of hair*) straight; (*of fabrics*) plain, unfigured; с него́ взя́тки ~ки (*coll.*) you'll get nothing out of him. 2. fluent, facile. 3. (*coll.*) sleek, well-nourished.

гла́д|ко, *adv. of* ~кий; smoothly, swimmingly; де́ло сошло́ г. the affair went off smoothly; г. вы́бритый clean-shaven.

гладкоство́льный, *adj.* (*of firearms*) smooth-bore.

глад|ь¹, и, *f.* smooth surface (*of water*); тишь да г. (*coll.*) peace and quiet.

глад|ь², и, *f.* satin-stitch; вышива́ть ~ью to satin-stitch.

гла́же, *comp. of* гла́дкий, гла́дко.

гла́жень|е, я, *n.* ironing.

глаз, а, о ~е, в ~у́, *pl.* ~а́, ~, ~а́м, *m.* eye; eyesight; дурно́й г. evil eye; невооружён-ный г. naked eye; не в бровь, а в г. (*coll.*) to hit the mark, strike home; в ~а́ to one's face; я его́ в ~а́ не вида́л I have never seen him; в ~а́х (+*g.*) in the eyes (of); он был геро́ем в ~а́х ма́тери he was a hero in his mother's eyes; ни в одно́м ~у́ (*coll.*) not at all drunk; за ~а́ (*i*) in absence; руга́ть кого́-н. за ~а́ to abuse someone behind his back, (*ii*) (*coll.*) enough, more than enough; на ~а́, на ~а́х before one's eyes; не попа-

да́йся мне на ~а́! keep out of my sight!; дитя́ вы́росло на роди́тельских ~а́х the child grew before its parents' eyes; на-г. approximately, by eye; с ~у на́ г. tête-à-tête, cheek-by-jowl; с г. доло́й out of sight; убира́йся с г. доло́й! get out of my sight!; с г. доло́й — из се́рдца вон out of sight, out of mind; не спуска́ть с г., г. с+*g.* not to let out of one's sight; с пья́ных г. in a drunken condition, drunk; смотре́ть во все ~а́ to be all eyes; хоть г. вы́коли it's pitch dark; закрыва́ть ~а́ (на+*a.*) to close one's eyes (to), connive (at); открыва́ть кому́-н. ~а́ (на+*a.*) to open someone's eyes (to); премье́р-мини́стр откры́л нам ~а́ на неизбе́жность войны́ the Prime Minister opened our eyes to the fact that war was inevitable; идти́ куда́ ~а́ гляди́т to follow one's nose.

глаза́ст|ый (~, ~а), *adj.* (*coll.*) big-eyed; quick-sighted.

глазена́п|ы, ов, *no sing.* (*coll.*, *joc.*) eyes.

глазе́т, а, *m.* brocade.

глазе́|ть, ю, *impf.* (*of* по~) (на+*a.*; *coll.*) to stare (at), gawk (at).

глази́р|ованный, *p.p.p. of* ~ова́ть *and adj.* glazed; glossy; (*cul.*) iced, glacé.

глази́р|ова́ть, у́ю, *impf. and pf.* to glaze; (*cul.*) to ice.

глазиро́вк|а, и, *f.* glazing; icing; торт с ~ой iced cake.

глазни́к, а́, *m.* (*coll.*) oculist.

глазни́ц|а, ы, *f.* eye-socket.

глазн|о́й, *adj. of* глаз; г. врач oculist; г. нерв optic nerve; ~о́е я́блоко eyeball.

глаз|о́к, ка́, *pl.* ~ки, ~ок *and* ~ки́, ~ко́в, *m.* 1. (*pl.* ~ки) *dim. of* ~; одни́м ~ко́м with half an eye; де́лать, стро́ить ~ки кому́-н. to make eyes at someone; аню́тины ~ки (*bot.*) pansy. 2. (*pl.* ~ки) pigmented spot (*on some birds and insects*). 3. (*pl.* ~ки) (*coll.*) peephole; inspection hole; glory hole (*of furnace*); head (*of periscope*). 4. (*pl.* ~ки) bud; eye (*of potato*). 5. (*pl.* ~ки) (*tech.*) eye, eyelet.

глазоме́р, а, *m.* 1. measurement by eye. 2. ability to judge by eye; хоро́ший г. good eye.

глазоме́р|ный, *adj. of* ~; ~ное определе́ние estimation by eye.

глазу́н|ья, ьи, *g. pl.* ~ий, *f.* fried eggs.

глазу́р|ь, и, *f.* 1. glaze (*on pottery*). 2. (*cul.*) icing.

гла́нд|а, ы, *f.* (*anat.*) tonsil; удали́ть ~ы to take out tonsils.

глас, а, *m.* 1. (*obs.*) voice; г. вопию́щего в пусты́не the voice of one crying in the wilderness. 2. (*eccl.*) tune.

гла|си́ть, шу́, си́шь, *impf.* 1. (*obs.*) to announce. 2. to say, run; докуме́нт ~си́т сле́дующее the paper runs as follows; как ~си́т погово́рка as the saying goes.

гла́сно[1], *adv.* openly, publicly.

гла́сно[2], *as pred.* (*obs.*) it is well known.

гла́сност|ь, и, *f.* **1.** publicity; преда́ть ~и to give publicity (to), make known, publish. **2.** *glasnost*, openness.

гла́сный[1], *adj.* open, public; г. суд public trial.

гла́сн|ый[2], *adj.* vowel, vocalic; *as noun* г., ~ого, *m.* vowel.

гла́сн|ый[3], **ого,** *m.* (*hist.*) (*town, province, etc.*) councillor.

глаша́та|й, я, *m.* **1.** (*hist.*) town crier, public crier. **2.** (*fig., rhet.*) herald.

гле́тчер, а, *m.* glacier.

гли́н|а, ы, *f.* clay; валя́льная г. fuller's earth; жи́рная г. loam; огнеупо́рная г. fire-clay; фарфо́ровая г. china clay, porcelain clay; ма́зать ~ой to clay.

гли́нист|ый, *adj.* clayey, argillaceous; ~ая по́чва loam.

глинобитный, *adj.* pisé (*of clay, mixed with straw, gravel, etc.*).

глинозём, а, *m.* (*chem.*) alumina.

глинтве́йн, а, *m.* mulled wine; де́лать г. to mull wine.

гли́нян|ый, *adj.* **1.** clay; earthenware; ~ая посу́да earthenware crockery. **2.** clayey.

глиссер, а, *m.* (*naut.*) speed-boat.

глист, а́, *m.* (intestinal) worm.

глистого́нный, *adj.* (*med.*) vermifuge.

глицери́н, а, *m.* glycerine.

гло́бус, а, *m.* globe.

гло|да́ть, жу́, ~жешь, *impf.* to gnaw (*also fig.*)

глота́|ть, ю, *impf.* to swallow

гло́тк|а, и, *f.* **1.** (*anat.*) gullet. **2.** (*coll.*) throat.

глот|о́к, ка́, *m.* gulp, mouthful; drink.

гло́х|нуть, ну, нешь, *past* ~, ~ла, *impf.* **1.** (*pf.* о~) to become deaf. **2.** (*pf.* за~) to die away, subside (*of noise*). **3.** (*pf.* за~) to become wild, go to seed.

глуб|же, *comp.* of ~о́кий *and* ~око́.

глубин|а́, ы́, *pl.* ~ы, *f.* **1.** depth. **2.** (*pl.*) (the) depths, deep places. **3.** heart, interior (*also fig.*); в ~е́ ле́са in the heart of the forest; в ~е́ веко́в in ancient times; в ~е́ души́ at heart, in one's heart of hearts; от ~ы́ души́ with all one's heart. **4.** (*fig.*) depth, profundity; intensity.

глуби́нн|ый, *adj.* **1.** deep; deep-laid; deep-sea; ~ая бо́мба depth charge; г. лов ры́бы deep-sea fishing. **2.** remote, out-of-the-way.

глубо́к|ий (~, ~а́, ~о́), *adj.* **1.** (*in var. senses*) deep; ~ая вспа́шка deep ploughing; г. сон deep sleep; ~ая таре́лка soup-plate; ~ая оборо́на defence in depth; в ~ом тылу́ (*mil.*) deep in the rear; г. вира́ж (*aeron.*) steep turn. **2.** profound; thorough,

thoroughgoing; considerable, serious; ~ие зна́ния thorough knowledge; ~ая оши́бка serious error. **3.** (*of time, age, seasons*) late; advanced; extreme; до ~ой но́чи (until) far into the night; ~ая дре́вность extreme antiquity; ~ая ста́рость extreme old age; ~ая стару́ха a very old woman; наступи́ла ~ая зима́ it was mid-winter. **4.** (*fig.; of feelings, etc.*) deep, profound, intense; с ~им приско́рбием (*in obituary formula*) with deep regret.

глубоко́[1], *adv.* deep; (*fig.*) deeply, profoundly; г. сиде́ть в воде́ (*of a vessel*) to draw much water.

глубоко́[2], *as pred.* it is deep.

глубоково́д|ный (~ен, ~на), *adj.* **1.** deep-water. **2.** deep-sea.

глубокомы́сленный, *adj.* thoughtful; serious.

глубокомы́сли|е, я, *n.* profundity; perspicacity.

глубокоуважа́емый, *adj.* much-esteemed; (*in formal letters*) dear.

глубоме́р, а, *m.* depth gauge.

глубоча́йший, *superl.* of глубо́кий.

глуб|ь, и, *f.* depth; г. реки́ the river-bottom.

глум|и́ться, лю́сь, и́шься, *impf.* (над+*i.*) to mock (at); to desecrate.

глумле́ни|е, я, *n.* mockery; gibe; desecration.

глумли́вый, *adj.* (*coll.*) mocking; gibing.

глупе́|ть, ю, *impf.* (*of* по~) to grow stupid.

глуп|е́ц, ца́, *m.* fool, blockhead.

глуп|и́ть, лю́, и́шь, *impf.* (*of* с~) to make a fool of oneself; to do something foolish.

глупова́т|ый (~, ~а), *adj.* silly; rather stupid.

глу́пост|ь, и, *f.* **1.** foolishness, stupidity. **2.** foolish, stupid action; foolish, stupid thing. **3.** (*usu. pl.*) nonsense; ~и! (stuff and) nonsense!

глу́п|ый (~, ~а́, ~о), *adj.* foolish, stupid; silly; (*coll.*) она́ ещё ~а́ she is still young and innocent.

глупы́ш[1]**, а́,** *m.* (*coll.*) silly; silly little thing.

глупы́ш[2]**, а́,** *m.* (*orn.*) fulmar.

глуха́р|ь, я́, *m.* **1.** (*orn.*) capercailzie, wood-grouse. **2.** (*coll.*) deaf person. **3.** (*tech.*) propeller (*with hexahedral or square head*).

глу́хо[1]**,** *adv.* of глухо́й; (*coll.*) = на́глухо.

глу́хо[2]**,** *as pred.* **1.** it is lonely, deserted. **2.** (*coll.*) it is no good.

глухова́т|ый (~, ~а), *adj.* somewhat deaf, hard of hearing.

глух|о́й (~, ~а́, ~о), *adj.* **1.** deaf (*also fig.*); он был ~ к на́шим мольба́м he was deaf to our entreaties; *as noun* г., ~о́го, *m.* deaf man; ~а́я, ~о́й, *f.* deaf woman. **2.** (*of sound*) muffled, confused, indistinct. **3.** in-

distinct, obscure; ~а́я молва́ vague rumours. 4. (*ling.*) voiceless. 5. thick, dense;
wild; г. лес dense forest. 6. remote, out-
-of-the-way; god-forsaken; в ~о́й прови́н-
ции in the depths of the country; ~а́я
у́лица lonely street. 7. sealed; blank,
blind; ~а́я стена́ blind wall. 8. (*of clothing*)
buttoned-up, done up; not open. 9. г. ряд
(*mil.*) blank file. 10. (*of times or seasons*)
dead; late; ~а́я ночь dead of night; ~а́я
пора́ slack period; г. сезо́н dead season.

глухома́н|ь, и, *f.* (*coll.*) out-of-the-way
place, backwoods.

глухоне|мо́й, *adj.* deaf and dumb; *as noun*
г., ~о́го, *m.* deaf mute.

глухот|а́, ы́, *f.* deafness.

глу́|ше, *comp. of* ~хо́й *and* ~хо.

глуши́тел|ь, я, *m.* 1. (*tech.*) silencer,
muffler. 2. (*fig.*) suppressor.

глуш|и́ть, у́, ~и́шь, *impf.* 1. (*pf.* о~) to
stun, stupefy; г. ры́бу to stun fish (*by means
of explosives*). 2. (*pf.* за~) to muffle (*sounds*);
г. боль to dull pain; г. мото́р to stop the
engine; г. радиопереда́чи to jam broad-
casts. 3. (*pf.* за~) (*coll.*) to put out (*a fire,
etc.*). 4. (*pf.* за~) to choke, stifle (*growth*). 5.
(*pf.* за~) (*fig.*) to suppress, stifle; г. кри́тику
to suppress criticism. 6. (*impf. only*) (*sl.*) to
soak up (= to drink in large quantities).

глуш|ь, и́, *f.* overgrown part (*of forest or
garden*); backwoods (*also fig.*).

глы́б|а, ы, *f.* clod; lump, block.

глюко́з|а, ы, *f.* glucose, grape sugar, dex-
trose.

гля|де́ть, жу́, ди́шь, *impf.* (*of* по~) 1.
(на+*a.*) to look (at); to peer (at); to gaze
(upon); г. ко́со (на+*a.*) to take a poor view
(of); г. в о́ба to be on one's guard; г. в гроб
to have one foot in the grave; г. сквозь
па́льцы (на+*a.*) to wink (at), shut one's
eyes (to), turn a blind eye (to); идти́ куда́
глаза́ ~дя́т to follow one's nose. 2. (на+*a.*;
coll.) to look to (= to take as an example).
3. (на+*a.*) to heed, mark; не́чего на них
г. don't take any notice of them. 4. (*coll.*) to
look for, seek (*with one's eyes*). 5. (*impf. only*)
to show, appear. 6. (*impf. only*) (на+*a.*) to
look (on to), face, give (on to). 7. (*impf.
only*) (+*i. or adv.*; *coll.*) to look, look like,
appear; она́ ~ди́т плакса́й she looks a cry-
-baby. 8. (за+*i.*; *coll.*) to look after, see to.
9. ~ди́(те) (*expressing warning or threat*) mind
(out); ~ди́ не (+*imp.*) mind you don't . . .
10. того́ и ~ди́ (*coll.*) it looks as if; I'm
afraid; того́ и ~ди́ бу́дет бу́ря I'm afraid
there's going to be a storm. 11. ~дя́
(по+*d.*, *coll.*) depending (on).

гля|де́ться, жу́сь, ди́шься, *impf.* (*of* по~)
(в+*a.*) to look at oneself (in).

глядь, *interj.* lo and behold!, hey presto!

гля́н|ец, ца, *m.* gloss, lustre.

гля́|нуть, ну, нешь, *pf.* (на+*a.*) glance (at).

глянцеви́т|ый (~, ~а), *adj.* glossy, lustrous.

гм, *interj.* hm!

гна|ть, гоню́, го́нишь, *past* ~л, ~ла́, ~ло,
impf. 1. (*det. of* гоня́ть) to drive. 2. to urge
(on); to whip up (*an animal*); (*coll.*) to drive
(*a vehicle*) hard. 3. (*coll.*) to dash, tear. 4. to
hunt, chase; (*fig.*) to persecute. 5. to turn
out, turf out. 6. to distil. 7. (*usu. imp.*; *coll.*)
to give. 8. (*dial.*) to raft (*timber*).

гна́|ться, гоню́сь, го́нишься, *past* ~лся,
~ла́сь, ~ло́сь, *impf.* (*indet. of* гоня́ться)
(за+*i.*) to pursue; to strive (for, after);
(*fig.*) to keep up with.

гнев, а, *m.* anger, rage, wrath; не во гнев
будь ска́зано if you don't mind me saying
so.

гне́ва|ться, юсь, *impf.* (*of* раз~) (на+*a.*;
obs.) to be angry (with).

гнев|и́ть, лю́, и́шь, *impf.* (*of* про~) (*obs.*) to
anger, enrage.

гневли́в|ый (~, ~а), *adj.* (*obs.*) irascible.

гне́в|ный (~ен, ~на́, ~но), *adj.* angry, irate.

гнедо́й, *adj.* bay (*colour of horse*).

гнез|ди́ться, жу́сь, ди́шься, *impf.* 1. to
nest, build one's nest; to roost. 2. (*fig.*) to
have its seat; to be lodged.

гнезд|о́, а́, *pl.* гнёзда, *n.* 1. nest; eyrie.
2. den, lair (*also fig.*); г. сопротивле́ния
(*mil.*) pocket of resistance. 3. brood (*also
fig.*). 4. (*bot., med.*) nidus; cluster. 5. (*tech.*)
socket; seat; housing. 6. (*ling.*) 'nest' (*group
of words of same root*).

гнездова́ни|е, я, *n.* nesting; пора́ ~я nesting
season.

гнездово́й, *adj. of* гнездо́.

гнейс, а, *m.* (*min.*) gneiss.

гне|сти́, ту́, тёшь, *impf.* to oppress, weigh
down; to press; его́ ~тут забо́ты he is
weighed down by cares.

гнёт, а, *m.* 1. (*obs.*) press; weight. 2. op-
pression, yoke (*fig.*).

гнету́щий, *pres. part. act. of* гнести́ *and adj.*
oppressive.

гни́д|а, ы, *f.* nit.

гние́ни|е, я, *n.* decay, putrefaction, rot.

гнил|о́й (~, ~а́, ~о), *adj.* 1. rotten (*also fig.*);
decayed; putrid; corrupt. 2. (*of weather*)
damp, muggy.

гнилокро́ви|е, я, *n.* (*med.*) septicaemia.

гни́лостный, *adj.* 1. putrefactive. 2. putrid.

гни́лост|ь, и, *f.* rottenness (*also fig.*);
putridity.

гнилу́шк|а, и, *f.* piece of rotten wood;
(*coll.*) rotten stump (*of tooth*).

гнил|ь, и, *f.* 1. rotten stuff. 2. mould.

гни́ль|ё, я́, *n.* (*collect.*) rotten stuff.

гнильц|а́, ы́, *f.* (*coll.*) rottenness; с ~о́й
slightly rotten.

гни|ть, ю, ёшь, *impf.* (*of* с~) to rot, decay; to decompose.

гноекро́ви|е, я, *n.* (*med.*) pyaemia.

гное́ни|е, я, *n.* suppuration.

гноетече́ни|е, я, *n.* suppuration.

гно|и́ть, ю́, и́шь, *impf.* (*of* с~) to let rot, allow to decay; г. наво́з to ferment manure; г. в тюрьме́ to leave to rot in prison.

гно|и́ться, ю́сь, и́шься, *impf.* to suppurate, discharge matter.

гно́ищ|е, а, *n.* (*obs.*) garbage dump.

гно|й, я, в ~е *or* в ~ю́, *m.* pus, matter.

гнойни́к, а́, *m.* abscess; ulcer.

гно́йный, *adj.* purulent.

гном, а, *m.* gnome.

гно́м|а, ы, *f.* maxim, aphorism.

гноми́ческий, *adj.* gnomic.

гно́мон, а, *m.* gnomon, sun-dial.

гносеоло́ги|я, и, *f.* (*philos.*) gnosiology; theory of knowledge.

гно́стик, а, *m.* gnostic.

гностици́зм, а, *m.* gnosticism.

гнус, а, *m.* (*collect.*) midges.

гнуса́в|ить, лю, ишь, *impf.* to speak through one's nose.

гнуса́вост|ь, и, *f.* twang; nasal intonation.

гнуса́в|ый (~, ~а), *adj.* nasal.

гну́сност|ь, и, *f.* 1. vileness, foulness. 2. vile, foul action.

гну́с|ный (~ен, ~на́, ~но), *adj.* vile, foul.

гну́т|ый, *p.p.p. of* гнуть *and adj.* bent; ~ая ме́бель bent-wood furniture.

гнуть, гну, гнёшь, *impf.* (*of* со~) 1. to bend, bow (*trans.*); г. спи́ну, ше́ю (пе́ред+*i.*) (*coll.*) to cringe (before), kow-tow (to); г. свою́ ли́нию to have it one's own way. 2. (*coll.*) to drive at; aim at; я не понима́ю, куда́ ты гнёшь I don't know what you are driving at.

гнуть|ё, я́, *n.* bending.

гну́ться, гнусь, гнёшься, *impf.* (*of* со~) 1. to bend (*intrans.*), be bowed; to stoop. 2. (*impf. only*) to bend (*intrans.*), be flexible.

гнуш|а́ться, а́юсь, *impf.* (*of* по~) 1. (+*g. or i.*) to abhor, have an aversion (to). 2. (+*inf.*) to disdain (to).

гобеле́н, а, *m.* gobelin, tapestry.

гобои́ст, а, *m.* (*mus.*) oboist.

гобо́|й, я, *m.* oboe.

гова́рива|ть (*pres. tense not used*), *impf.* (*freq. of* говори́ть; *coll.*); он ~л he often used to say, he would often say.

говень|е, я, *n.* fasting (*as preparation for Communion*).

гов|е́ть, е́ю, е́ешь, *impf.* (*eccl.*) to prepare for Communion (*by fasting*); (*coll.*) to fast, go without food.

говн|о́, а́, *n.* (*vulg.*) shit.

го́вор, а, *m.* 1. sound of voices (*usu. human*,

but also *fig.*); г. волн the murmur of the waves. 2. (*coll.*) talk, rumour. 3. mode of speech, accent. 4. dialect.

говори́л|ьня, ьни, *g. pl.* ~ен, *f.* (*coll., pejor.*) talking-shop.

говор|и́ть, ю́, и́шь, *impf.* 1. (*impf. only*) to (be able to) speak, talk; он ещё не ~и́т he can't speak yet; г. по-францу́зски to speak French. 2. (*pf.* сказа́ть) to say; to tell; to speak, talk; г. пра́вду to tell the truth; г. де́ло to talk sense; ~я́т they say, it is said; ~я́т тебе́! (*emphasizing command*) do you hear?; что вы ~и́те? (*expressing incredulity*) you don't mean to say so!; ~и́т Москва́! (*introducing radio programme*) this is Radio Moscow!; не́чего (и) г. it goes without saying, needless to say; что и г. (*coll.*) it cannot be denied; что ни ~и́ say what you like; и не ~и́! certainly!, of course!; ина́че ~я́ in other words; со́бственно ~я́ strictly speaking; не ~я́ уже́ (о+*p.*) not to mention. 3. (*pf.* по~) (о+*p.*) to talk (about), discuss. 4. (*impf. only*) to mean, convey, signify; э́ти карти́ны мне ничего́ не ~я́т these pictures convey nothing to me. 5. (*impf. only*) (о+*p.*) to point (to), indicate, betoken, testify (to); всё ~и́т о том, что он ко́нчил самоуби́йством everything points to his having committed suicide. 6. (*impf. only*) г. в по́льзу (+*g.*) to tell in favour (of); to support, back.

говор|и́ться, и́тся, *impf. pass. of* ~и́ть; как ~и́тся as they say, as the saying goes.

говорли́вост|ь, и, *f.* garrulity, talkativeness.

говорли́в|ый (~, ~а), *adj.* garrulous, talkative.

говор|о́к, ка́, *m.* (*coll.*) 1. sound of voices, hum of conversation. 2. accent, speech.

говору́н, а́, *m.* (*coll.*) talker, chatterer.

говору́н|ья, ьи, *g. pl.* ~ий, *f. of* ~.

говя́дин|а, ы, *f.* beef.

говя́жий, *adj.* beef.

го́гол|ь, я, *m.* (*orn.*) golden-eye (*Clangula bucephala*); ходи́ть ~ем to strut.

го́голь-мо́гол|ь *and* го́гель-мо́гел|ь, я, *m.* egg-flip.

го́гот, а, *m.* cackle (*of geese*); (*coll.*) loud laughter.

гоготань|е, я, *n.* cackling.

гого|та́ть, чу́, ~чешь, *impf.* 1. to cackle (*of geese*). 2. (*coll.*) to cackle, roar with laughter.

год, а, в ~у́, о ~е, *pl.* ~ы *and* ~а́, *g.* ~о́в *an* лет, *m.* 1. (*g. pl.* лет) year; високо́сный г. leap-year; кру́глый г. (*as adv.*) the whole year round; в бу́дущем, про́шлом ~у́ next, last year; в теку́щем ~у́ during the current year; в г. a year, per annum; из ~а в г year in, year out; г. от ~у every year; спуст три ~́а three years later; че́рез три ~́а in three years' time; бе́з ~у неде́ля (*coll.*) only a few days; мы ~́ы не вида́лись we have not met for years; встреча́ть Но́вый г. to see the New Year in; ей пошёл пятна́дцатый г. she is in her fifteenth year. **2.** двадца́тые, тридца́тые, *etc.*, ~́ы (*g.* ~о́в) the twenties, the thirties, *etc.* **3.** **~á** *and* **~́ы, ~о́в** (*pl. only*) years, age, time; шко́льные ~á school-days; в ~́ы (+*g.*) in the days (of), during; в те ~́ы in those days; в ~áх advanced in years; не по ~áм beyond one's years, precocious(ly).

года́ми, *adv.* for years (*on end*).

годи́н|а, ы, *f.* **1.** (*rhet.*) time, period; г. войны́ war-time; тяжёлая г. hard times. **2.** (*arch.*) year.

го|ди́ть, жу́, ди́шь, *impf.* (*coll.*) to wait, loiter.

го|ди́ться, жу́сь, ди́шься, *impf.* **1.** (на+*a.*, для+*g.*, *or* +*d.*) to be fit (for), be suited (for), do (for), serve (for); э́та мате́рия ни на что, никуда́ не ~ди́тся this material is no good (for anything); не ~ди́тся it's no good, it won't do. **2.** (в+*n.–a.*) to serve (as), be suited to be; он не ~ди́тся в офице́ры he is not cut out to be an officer. **3.** (в+*n.–a.*) to be old enough to be; она́ ~ди́тся тебе́ в ма́тери she is old enough to be your mother. **4.** не ~ди́тся (+*inf.*) it does not do (to), one should not.

годи́чн|ый, *adj.* **1.** lasting a year; ~ое путеше́ствие a year's journey. **2.** annual, yearly; г. съезд annual conference; ~ые ко́льца (*bot.*) annual rings.

го́дност|ь, и, *f.* fitness, suitability; validity.

го́д|ный (~ен, ~на́, ~но), *adj.* fit, suitable, valid; г. к вое́нной слу́жбе fit for military service; г. к пла́ванию seaworthy; биле́т го́ден три ме́сяца the ticket is valid for three months.

годова́лый, *adj.* one year old, yearling.

годови́к, á, *m.* (*dial.*) yearling (*animal*).

годово́й, *adj.* annual, yearly; г. дохо́д annual revenue.

годовщи́н|а, ы, *f.* anniversary.

гой¹, *interj.* (*folk poet.*) hail!

го|й², я, *m.* goy, gentile.

гол, а, *m.* (*sport*) goal; заби́ть г. to score a goal.

гола́вл|ь, я, *m.* chub (*fish*).

го́лб|ец, ца, *m.* (*dial.*) store-room, cellar.

голго́ф|а, ы, *f.* Calvary (*also fig.*)

голена́стый, *adj.* **1.** (*coll.*) long-legged. **2.** *as pl. noun* (*zool.*) waders, Grallatores.

голени́щ|е, а, *n.* top (*of a boot*).

го́лен|ь, и, *f.* shin.

гол|е́ц, ьца́, *m.* loach (*fish*).

голизн|á, ы́, *f.* nakedness.

голи́к, á, *m.* **1.** (*dial.*) besom. **2.** (*naut.*) sea-mark.

голки́пер, а, *m.* (*sport*) goalkeeper.

голла́нд|ец, ца, *m.* Dutchman; лету́чий г. Flying Dutchman.

голла́ндк|а¹, и, *f.* Dutchwoman.

голла́ндк|а², и, *f.* **1.** tiled stove. **2.** animal (*cow, hen, etc.*) of Dutch breed. **3.** (*naut.*) jumper.

голла́ндск|ий, *adj.* Dutch; ~ая печь tiled stove; ~ое полотно́ holland (*cloth*); г. сыр Dutch cheese.

голов|á, ы́, *a.* **го́лову,** *pl.* **го́ловы, голо́в, ~áм,** *f.* **1.** head (*also fig.*); г. в го́лову (*mil.*) shoulder to shoulder; на све́жую го́лову while one is fresh; быть ~о́й, на́ голову вы́ше кого́-н. (*fig.*) to be head and shoulders above someone; с ~ы́ до ног from head to foot; с ~о́й погрузи́ться, окуну́ться, уйти́ (во что-н.) (*fig.*) to throw oneself (into something), plunge (into something), get up to one's neck (in something); свали́ть с больно́й ~ы́ на здоро́вую to lay the blame on someone else; че́рез чью-н. го́лову (*fig.*) behind someone's back; у неё г. шла кру́гом her head was going round and round; у меня́ г. кру́жится I feel giddy; у них г. кру́жится от успе́хов they are giddy with success; вы́дать ~о́й (*obs.*) to give away, betray; вы́мыть, намы́лить кому́-н. го́лову to give someone a dressing-down; го́лову пове́сить to hang one's head. **2.** head (*of cattle*). **3.** (*fig.*) head (*as unit of calculation*); с ~ы́ per head. **4.** (*fig.*) head; brain, mind; wits; он па́рень **с ~о́й** he's a bright lad; лома́ть го́лову to rack one's brains; не теря́ть ~ы́ to keep one's head; ей пришла́ в го́лову мысль it occurred to her, it struck her, the thought crossed her mind. **5.** (*fig.*) head (= *person*); горя́чая г. hothead; сме́лая г. bold spirit. **6.** (*fig.*) head, life; на свою́ го́лову to one's cost, to one's misfortune; заплати́ть, поплати́ться за что-н. ~о́й to pay for something with one's life; отвеча́ть, руча́ться ~о́й за что-н. to stake one's life on something. **7.** (*m. and f.*) (*fig.*) head; person in charge; городско́й г. (*obs.*) mayor; сам себе́ г. one's own master. **8.** (*fig.*) head, van; в ~áх at the head of the bed. **9.** г. са́хару sugar-loaf; г. сы́ру a cheese; г. капу́сты head of cabbage. **10.** в пе́рвую го́лову in the first place, first and foremost.

головáстик, а, *m.* tadpole.

голове́шк|а, и, *f.* brand, smouldering piece of wood.

голови́зн|а, ы, *f.* jowl (*of sturgeon*).

голо́вк|а, и, *f.* **1.** *dim. of* головá. **2.** head, cap, nose; tip; г. по́ршня piston head; г. лу́ка an onion, onion bulb; спи́чечная г. match-head. **3.** (*collect.*; *coll.*) heads, big shots. **4.** (*pl.*) vamp (*of boot*). **5.** (*obs.*)

head-scarf (*worn by married peasant or merchant-class women*).

головн|о́й, *adj.* 1. *adj. of* голова́; ~а́я боль headache; г. плато́к head-scarf; г. убо́р headgear, head-dress. 2. (*anat.*) encephalic; г. мозг brain, cerebrum. 3. (*obs.*) brain, cerebral; ~а́я рабо́та brain work. 4. г. го́лос (*mus.*) head-voice, falsetto. 5. (*fig.*) head, leading; ~а́я железнодоро́жная ста́нция railhead; г. отря́д (*mil.*) vanguard, leading detachment; ~а́я похо́дная заста́ва (*mil.*) advance party.

головн|я́[1], й, *g. pl.* ~е́й, *f.* charred log.

головн|я́[2], й, *g. pl.* ~е́й, *f.* blight, smut, rust (*disease of crops*).

головокруже́ни|е, я, *n.* giddiness, dizziness (*also fig.*); vertigo.

головокружи́тельн|ый, *adj.* dizzy, giddy (*also fig.*); ~ая высота́ dizzy height; ~ые перспекти́вы breath-taking prospects.

головоло́мк|а, и, *f.* puzzle, conundrum.

головоло́мный, *adj.* puzzling.

головомо́йк|а, и, *f.* (*coll.*) reprimand, dressing-down.

головоно́г|ие, их, *sing.* ~ое, ~ого, *n.* (*zool.*) cephalopoda.

головоре́з, а, *m.* (*coll.*) 1. cutthroat; bandit. 2. blackguard, rascal.

головотя́п, а, *m.* (*coll.*) bungler, muddler.

головотя́пств|о, а, *n.* (*coll.*) bungling.

голбву́шк|а, и, *f.* 1. *affect. dim. of* голова́; пропа́ла моя́ г. it's all up with me, I've had it. 2. (*folk poet.*; *coll.*) fellow, chap; бе́дная г. poor wretch.

го́лод, а (у), *m.* 1. hunger; starvation; во́лчий г. ravenous appetite; умира́ть с ~у to die of starvation; мори́ть ~ом to starve (*trans.*). 2. famine. 3. dearth, acute shortage; шерстяно́й г. wool shortage.

голода́ни|е, я, *n.* 1. starvation. 2. fasting.

голод|а́ть, а́ю, *impf.* 1. to hunger, starve. 2. to fast, go without food.

голода́|ющий, *pres. part. act. of* ~ть *and adj.* starving, hungry, famished; *as noun* г., ~ющего, *m.*; ~ющая, ~ющей, *f.* starving person.

голо́д|ный (го́лоден, ~а́, ~но), *adj.* 1. hungry; г. как соба́ка, как волк hungry as a hunter. 2. (*caused by*) hunger, starvation; ~ные бо́ли hunger-pangs; г. похо́д hunger-march; ~ная смерть starvation. 3. (*of food, food supplies, etc.*) meagre, scanty, poor; г. год lean year; г. край barren country; г. паёк starvation rations.

голодо́вк|а, и, *f.* 1. starvation. 2. hunger-strike; объяви́ть ~у to go on hunger-strike.

голодра́|нец, нца, *m.* (*coll.*) beggar.

голоду́х|а, и, *f.* (*coll.*) hunger.

гололе́диц|а, ы, *f.* ice-covered ground, icy condition of roads

голоно́гий, *adj.* bare-legged; bare-foot.

го́лос, а, *pl.* ~а́, *m.* 1. voice; во весь г. at the top of one's voice; быть в ~е to be in good voice; с ~а by ear. 2. (*mus.*) voice, part; фу́га на четы́ре ~а four-part fugue. 3. (*fig.*) voice, word, opinion; в оди́н г. with one accord, unanimously; име́ть свой г. to have one's say. 4. vote; пра́во ~а the vote, suffrage, franchise; пода́ть г. (за + a.) to vote (for), cast one's vote (for); победи́ть большинство́м ~о́в to outvote.

голосемя́нный, *adj.* (*bot.*) gymnospermous.

голоси́ст|ый (~, ~а), *adj.* loud-voiced; vociferous; loud.

голо|си́ть, шу́, си́шь, *impf.* 1. (*coll.*) to sing loudly; to cry. 2. (*obs.*) to wail; to keen; г. по поко́йнику to keen a dead person.

голосло́вно, *adv.* without adducing any proof.

голосло́в|ный (~ен, ~на), *adj.* unsubstantiated, unfounded; unsupported by evidence.

голосова́ни|е, я, *n.* voting; poll; всео́бщее г. universal suffrage; поста́вить на г. to put to the vote.

голос|ова́ть, у́ю, *impf.* (*of* про~) 1. (за + a.; про́тив + g.) to vote (for; against). 2. to put to the vote, vote on. 3. (*sl.*) to (try to) hitch a lift.

голосоведе́ни|е, я, *n.* (*mus.*) harmonisation of themes.

голосов|о́й, *adj.* vocal; (*anat.*) ~ы́е свя́зки vocal chords; ~а́я щель glottis.

голоу́сый, *adj.* (*coll.*) clean-shaven; (*fig.*) young, immature.

голошта́нник, а, *m.* (*coll.*) ragamuffin.

голубево́дств|о, а, *n.* pigeon breeding.

голубегра́мм|а, ы, *f.* (*mil.*) pigeon(-carried) message.

голубеста́нци|я, и, *f.* (postal-)pigeon loft.

голубе́|ть, ю, *impf.* (*of* по~) to show blue; to turn blue.

голуб|е́ц[1], ца́, *m.* (*min.*) mountain-blue, azurite.

голуб|е́ц[2], ца́, *m.* (*usually pl.*) golubets (*rissole rolled in cabbage-leaves*).

голубизн|а́, ы́, *f.* blueness.

голуби́к|а, и, *f.* great bilberry, bog whortleberry (*Vaccinium uliginosum*).

голуби́н|ый, *adj.* 1. *adj. of* го́лубь; ~ая по́чта pigeon post. 2. (*fig.*) dove-like.

голу́|бить, блю, бишь, *impf.* (*of* при~) (*folk poet.*) to caress, fondle.

голуби́ц|а[1], ы, *f.* = голуби́ка.

голуби́ц|а[2], ы, *f.* 1. female pigeon, dove. 2. (*fig.*; *of a girl*) innocent creature.

голу́бк|а, и, *f.* 1. female pigeon, dove. 2. (*fig.*; *as term of endearment*) (my) dear, (my) darling.

голубогла́з|ый (~, ~a), *adj.* blue-eyed.

голуб|о́й, *adj.* pale blue, sky-blue; ~а́я кровь (*fig.*) blue blood; г. песе́ц blue fox; ~о́е то́пливо 'blue fuel' (= natural gas).

голуб|о́к, ка́, *m.* 1. *dim. of* го́лубь; *fig.* = голу́бчик. 2. (*bot.*) columbine, aquilegia.

**голу́бушк|а, и, *f.* 1. (*coll.*; *as mode of address*) (my) dear. 2. *affect. dim. of* голу́бка 1.

голу́бчик, а, *m.* (*coll.*; *as mode of address*) 1. my dear; dear friend; dear (so and so). 2. (*iron.*) my friend.

го́луб|ь, я, *g. pl.* ~е́й, *m.* 1. pigeon, dove; г. свя́зи (*mil.*) carrier-pigeon. 2. (*fig.*; *as mode of address to man*) = голу́бчик.

голубя́тник, а, *m.* 1. pigeon-fancier. 2. pigeon-hawk.

голубя́т|ня, ни, *g. pl.* ~ен, *f.* dovecot(e), pigeon loft.

го́л|ый (~, ~а́, ~о), *adj.* 1. naked, bare (*also fig.*); ~ая голова́ (*i*) bare head, (*ii*) bald head; г. про́вод naked wire; ~ыми рука́ми with one's bare hands; (*fig.*) without a hand's turn. 2. (*coll.*) poor; ~ как со́кол poor as a church mouse. 3. (*coll.*) unmixed, pure, neat; г. спирт pure spirit. 4. (*fig.*, *coll.*) bare, pure, unadorned; ~ые ци́фры bare figures.

голытьб|а́, ы́, *f.* (*collect.*; *coll.*) the poor.

голы́ш, а́, *m.* 1. (*coll.*) naked child; naked person. 2. (*obs.*) pauper. 3. round flat stone.

гол|ь, и, *no pl.*, *f.* 1. (*collect.*) the poor; г. перека́тная the down-and-outs, the utterly destitute; г. на вы́думки хитра́ necessity is the mother of invention. 2. (*obs.*) bare place, barren place.

голь|ё, я́, *n.* 1. (*cul.*) tripe. 2. raw hide.

гольём, *adv.* (*coll.*) 1. bare, clean. 2. neat, unmixed.

гольф, а, *m.* 1. golf; игро́к в г. golfer. 2. ~ы (*coll.*) plus-fours; knee-length stockings.

голя́к, а́, *m.* (*coll.*) beggar, tramp.

гомеопа́т, а, *m.* homoeopath(ist).

гомеопати́ческий, *adj.* 1. homoeopathic. 2. (*fig.*) minute, very small.

гомеопа́ти|я, и, *f.* homoeopathy.

гомери́ческий, *adj.* Homeric (= *on heroic scale*); г. смех Homeric laughter.

гоме́ровский, *adj.* Homeric (= *pertaining to Homer*); г. вопро́с the Homeric question.

гоминда́н, а, *m.* (*polit.*) Kuomintang.

гоминда́нов|ец, ца, *m.* member, supporter of Kuomintang.

гоминда́новский, *adj.* Kuomintang.

гомоге́нный, *adj.* homogeneous.

го́мон, а, *m.* (*coll.*) hubbub.

гомон|и́ть, ю́, и́шь, *impf.* (*coll.*) to talk noisily, shout (*of large number of people*).

гомосексуали́зм, а, *m.* homosexuality.

гомосексуали́ст, а, *m.* homosexual.

гомосексуа́льный, *adj.* homosexual.

гон, а, *m.* 1. dash, rush. 2. hunt, chase, pursuit. 3. (*area of*) hunt. 4. (*of animals*) heat; во вре́мя ~a (when) on heat. 5. (*agric.*) row.

гондо́л|а, ы, *f.* 1. gondola. 2. (*aeron.*) car (*of balloon*); (*tech.*) nacelle. 3. (*railways*) gondola.

гондолье́р, а, *m.* gondolier.

гоне́ни|е, я, *n.* persecution.

гон|е́ц, ца́, *m.* courier; (*fig.*) herald, harbinger.

гонио́метр, а, *m.* (*phys.*) goniometer.

гони́тел|ь, я, *m.* persecutor.

го́нк|а, и, *f.* 1. dashing, rushing. 2. (*coll.*) haste, hurry. 3. (*sport*) race; гребны́е ~и boat race; г. вооруже́ний arms race. 4. (*coll.*, *obs.*) scolding, dressing-down. 5. (*dial.*) floatage, raftage.

го́н|кий (~ок, ~ка́, ~ко), *adj.* 1. fast; ~кая соба́ка hound. 2. (*of trees*) fast-growing.

гоноко́кк, а, *m.* (*med.*) gonococcus.

го́нор, а, *m.* (*coll.*) arrogance, conceit.

гонора́р, а, *m.* fee, honorarium; а́вторский г. royalties.

гоноре́|я, и, *f.* gonorrhoea.

го́ночный, *adj. of* го́нка; г. автомоби́ль racing car.

гонт, а, *m.* (*collect.*; *tech.*) shingles.

гонто́в|ой, *adj. of* гонт; ~а́я кры́ша shingle roof.

гонча́р, а́, *m.* potter.

гонча́рн|ый, *adj.* potter's; ~ые изде́лия pottery; г. круг potter's wheel.

го́нч|ая, ей, *f.* hound.

го́нщик, а, *m.* 1. racer; велосипеди́ст-г. racing cyclist. 2. drover. 3. rafter.

гоню́(сь), го́нишь(ся), *see* гна́ть(ся).

гоня́|ть, ю, *impf.* 1. (*indet. of* гнать) to drive. 2. (*coll.*) to make run errands. 3. (по+*d.*; *coll.*) to make run over, grill (on) (*something learnt, read, etc.*). 4. г. голубе́й to race pigeons. 5. г. ло́дыря, соба́к (*coll.*) to idle, kick one's heels.

гоня́|ться, юсь, *impf.* 1. (*indet. of* гна́ться) (за+*i.*) to chase, pursue, hunt. 2. (с+*i.*; *obs.*) to race.

гоп, *interj.* hup!, jump!

гопа́к, а́, *m.* hopak (*Ukrainian dance*).

гопля́, *interj.* hup!, jump!

гор- *abbr. of* 1. городско́й; горко́м = городско́й комите́т. 2. го́рный; горпромы́шленность = го́рная промы́шленность.

гор|а́, ы́, *a.* ~у, *pl.* ~ы, *a.* ~а́м, *f.* 1. mountain; hill; г. с плеч a load off one's mind; ката́ться с ~ы́ to toboggan; в ~у uphill; идти́ в ~у to go uphill; (*fig.*) to go up in the world; не за ~а́ми (*fig.*) not far off; под ~у downhill (*also fig.*); пир ~о́й lavish, riotous feast; надéяться на когó-н. как на кáменную ~у to place implicit faith in someone; стоя́ть за когó-н. ~óй to be solidly behind someone. **2.** (*fig.*) heap, pile, mass.

горáзд (~а, ~о), *pred. adj.* (+*inf. or* на+*a.*; *coll.*) good (at), clever (at); он на всё г. he's a Jack of all trades; кто во что г. each in his own way; он г. вы́пить he is no mean drinker.

горáздо, *adv.* (+*comp. adjs. and advs.*) much, far, by far; г. лу́чше far better.

горб, á, о ~é, на ~у́, *m.* **1.** hump; (*dial.*) back; свои́м ~óм by the sweat of one's brow; испытáть на своём ~у́ to learn by bitter experience. **2.** protuberance, bulge; ~óм (*as adv.*) sticking out.

горбáт|ый (~, ~а), *adj.* humpbacked, hunchbacked, gibbous; г. мост humpback bridge; г. нос hooked nose; ~ого моги́ла испрáвит (*prov.*) can the leopard change his spots?

горби́нк|а, и, *f.* small protuberance; нос с ~ой aquiline nose.

гóрб|ить, лю, ишь, *impf.* (*of* с~) to arch, hunch; г. спи́ну to arch one's back.

гóрб|иться, люсь, ишься, *impf.* (*of* с~) to stoop, become bent.

горбонóс|ый (~, ~а), *adj.* hook-nosed.

горбу́н, á, *m.* hunchback.

горбу́ш|а¹, и, *f.* hunchback salmon.

горбу́ш|а², и, *f.* sickle.

горбу́шк|а, и, *f.* crust (*of loaf*).

горбы́л|ь, я́, *m.* (*tech.*) slab.

гордел́вост|ь, и, *f.* haughtiness, pride.

гордел́в|ый (~, ~а), *adj.* haughty, proud.

гордéц, á, *m.* arrogant man.

гóрдиев, *adj.*; г. у́зел Gordian knot.

гор|ди́ться, жу́сь, ди́шься, *impf.* **1.** (+*i.*) to be proud (of), pride oneself (on). **2.** to put on airs, be haughty.

гóрдост|ь, и, *f.* (*in var. senses*) pride.

гóрд|ый (~, ~á, ~о, ~ы́), *adj.* (*in var. senses*) proud.

горды́н|я, и, *f.* arrogance; aloofness.

гордя́чк|а, и, *f.* arrogant woman.

гóр|е, я, n. **1.** grief, sorrow, woe; на своё г. to one's sorrow. **2.** misfortune, trouble; г. в том, что... the trouble is that... **3.** (*as pred.*, +*d.*; *coll.*) woe (unto), woe betide.

гóре- (*in compounds*) sorry, woeful; apology for a...; г.-поэ́т poetaster; г.-войскá a Fred Karno's army.

горé, *adv.* (*arch.*) on high; upwards; г. сердцá (*eccl.*) sursum corda.

гор|евáть, ю́ю, ю́ешь, *impf.* **1.** (о+*p.*) to grieve (for). **2.** (*coll. or dial.*) to be in need, be penurious.

горевóй, *adj.* (*coll. or dial.*) piteous, unhappy.

горéлк|а¹, и, *f.* burner; г. Бу́нзена Bunsen burner; при́мусная г. Primus stove.

горéлк|а², и, *f.* (*dial.*) vodka.

горéл|ки, ок, *no sing.* (*game of*) catch.

горéл|ый, *adj.* **1.** burnt; пáхло ~ым there was a smell of burning. **2.** rotten, decomposed (*of skins*).

горельéф, а, *m.* (*art*) high relief.

горемы́к|а, и, *m. and f.* (*coll.*) unlucky individual, victim of misfortune.

горемы́ч|ный (~ен, ~на), *adj.* hapless, ill-starred; down on one's luck.

горéни|е, я, n. burning, combustion; (*fig.*) enthusiasm.

гóрест|ный (~ен, ~на), *adj.* sad, sorrowful pitiful, mournful.

гóрест|ь, и, *f.* **1.** sorrow, grief. **2.** (*pl.*) afflictions, misfortunes, troubles.

гор|éть, ю́, и́шь, *impf.* **1.** to burn, be on fire 2. to burn, be alight; в ку́хне у них ~é. свет the lights were burning in thei kitchen; ~и́т ли пéчка? is the stove alight? дéло ~и́т things are going like a house o: fire; земля́ ~éла у негó под ногáми (*i*) h went like greased lightning, (*ii*) the plac was getting too hot for him, (*iii*) he wa impatient to be off. **3.** (+*i.*; *fig.*) to bur (with); г. желáнием (+*inf.*) to burn wit the desire (to), be impatient (to). **4.** glitter, shine. **5.** to rot, ferment.

гóр|ец, ца, *m.* mountain-dweller, high lander.

гóреч|ь, и, *f.* **1.** bitter taste. **2.** bitter stuf 3. bitterness.

гóрж|а, и, *f.* (*mil.*) gorge.

горжéтк|а, и, *f.* boa, throat-wrap.

горизóнт, а, *m.* **1.** horizon (*also fig.*), skylin **2.** г. воды́ (*tech.*) water-level.

горизонтáл|ь, и, *f.* **1.** horizontal; по ~и (*crossword*) across. **2.** (*geogr.*) contour line.

горизонтáл|ьный (~ен, ~ьна), *adj.* ho! zontal; г. полёт (*aeron.*) horizontal fligh level flight.

гори́лк|а, и, *f.* = горéлка².

гори́лл|а, ы, *f.* gorilla.

гори́ст|ый (~, ~а), *adj.* mountainous, hill

горихвóстк|а, и, *f.* redstart (*bird*).

горицвéт, а, *m.* (*bot.*) lychnis; ragged rob

гóрк|а, и, *f.* **1.** hillock. **2.** cabinet, stan 3. (*aeron.*) steep climb. **4.** крáсная г. (*co* the week following Easter week.

гóркн|уть, у, ешь, *impf.* (*of* про~) to tu rancid.

горкóм, а, *m.* (*abbr. of* городскóй коми́те town, city committee.

горлáн, а, *m.* (*coll.*) bawler.

горлáн|ить, ю, ишь, *impf.* (*coll.*) to bawl.

горлáст|ый (~, ~а), *adj.* (*coll.*) noisy, lou mouthed.

гóрлинк|а, и, *f.* = гóрлица.

гóрлиц|а, ы, *f.* **1.** turtle-dove. **2.** (*obs.*) голу́бка.

гóрл|о, а, *n.* **1.** throat; дыха́тельное г. windpipe; драть г. to bawl; во всё г. at the top of one's voice; по г. up to the neck (*also fig.*); сыт по г. full up; (*fig.*) fed up; приста́ть с ножóм к ~у (+*d.*) to press, importune; приста́вить нож к чьему́-н. ~у to hold a knife to one's throat; промочи́ть г. (*coll.*) to wet one's whistle; словá застря́ли у меня́ в ~е the words stuck in my throat; схвати́ть за г. to catch, take by the throat. **2.** neck (*of a vessel*). **3.** narrow entrance to a gulf, bay.

горлови́н|а, ы, *f.* mouth, orifice; manhole hatch; г. вулка́на crater.

горлово́й, *adj.* **1.** *adj. of* гóрло; throat; guttural. **2.** raucous.

горлодёр, а, *m.* (*coll.*) **1.** bawler. **2.** табак-г. rough shag.

гóрлыш|ко, ка, *g. pl.* ~ек, *n.* **1.** *dim. of* гóрло. **2.** neck (*of a bottle*).

гормóн, а, *m.* (*physiol.*) hormone.

гормона́льный, *adj.* hormone(-containing).

горн¹, а, *m.* furnace, forge.

горн², а, *m.* bugle.

гóрн|ий, *adj.* **1.** (*arch., poet.*) heavenly, celestial; lofty. **2.** ~ее ме́сто (*eccl.*) east end (*of church, area behind altar*).

горни́л|о, а, *n.* **1.** (*obs.*) hearth, furnace. **2.** (*fig.*) crucible.

горни́ст, а, *m.* bugler.

гóрниц|а, ы, *f.* **1.** (*obs.*) chamber. **2.** (*dial.*) clean part of peasant's hut.

гóрничн|ая, ой, *f.* (house)maid; stewardess (*on ship*).

горнов|óй, *adj. of* горн¹; *as noun* г., ~óго, *m.* furnace-worker.

горновосходи́тел|ь, я, *m.* mountaineer, mountain-climber.

горнозавóдский, *adj.* mining and metallurgical.

горнозавóдчик, а, *m.* owner of a mine *or* foundry.

горнопромы́шленност|ь, и, *f.* mining industry.

горнопромы́шленный, *adj.* mining.

горнорабóч|ий, его, *m.* miner.

горноста́евый, *adj.* ermine.

горноста́|й, я, *m.* **1.** (*zool.*) ermine; stoat. **2.** ermine (*fur*).

гóрн|ый, *adj.* **1.** *adj. of* горá; mountain; mountainous; ~ая болéзнь mountain sickness; ~ая цепь mountain range; ~ая артилле́рия (*mil.*) mountain artillery. **2.** mineral; г. лён asbestos; ~ая порóда rock; г. хруста́ль rock crystal. **3.** mining; ~ое дéло mining; г. институ́т College of Mines. **4.** ~ое сóлнце artificial sunlight.

горня́к, á, *m.* (*coll.*) **1.** miner. **2.** mining engineer; mining student.

горня́|цкий, *adj. of* ~к 1.

гóрод, а, *pl.* ~á, *m.* **1.** town; city; вы́ехать за г. to go out of town; жить за ~ом to live out of town, in the suburbs; ни к селу́, ни к ~у (*coll.*) for no reason at all, inappropriate(ly). **2.** (*sports and games*) base; home.

горо|ди́ть, ожу́, óди́шь, *impf.* to enclose, fence; огорóд г. to make unnecessary fuss; г. чепуху́, чушь to talk nonsense.

городи́ш|ко, ка, *g. pl.* ~ек, *m.* small town.

городи́щ|е, а, *n.* **1.** very large town. **2.** (*archaeol.*) site of ancient settlement.

город|ки́, кóв, *sing.* ~óк, ~ка́, *m.* gorodki (*game similar to skittles*).

городни́ч|ий, его, *m.* (*hist.*) governor of a town.

городов|óй¹, *adj.* (*obs.*) *of* гóрод; ~óе положéние municipal statutes.

городов|óй², óго, *m.* (*hist.*) policeman.

городóк, ка́, *m.* **1.** small town; воéнный г. cantonment; университéтский г. campus. **2.** block of wood (*in game* городки́).

городск|óй, *adj.* urban; city; municipal; (*coll.*) *as noun* г., ~óго, *m.* city-dweller, town-dweller.

городьб|á, ы́, *f.* **1.** fencing, enclosure. **2.** fence, hedge.

горожа́н|ин, ина, *pl.* ~е, ~, *m.* city-dweller, town-dweller; townsman.

горожа́н|ка, ки, *g. pl. of* ~ин; townswoman.

гороскóп, а, *m.* horoscope.

горóх, а (у), *no pl.*, *m.* **1.** pea. **2.** (*collect.*) peas; как об стéну, в стéну, от стены́ г. (*coll.*) like being up against a brick wall; при царé Горóхе in days of yore.

горóхов|ый, *adj.* **1.** pea. **2.** greenish-khaki; ~ое пальтó (*hist.*; *coll.*) agent of secret police; чу́чело ~ое scarecrow; шут г. buffoon, laughing-stock.

горóш|ек, ка, *m.* **1.** *dim. of* горóх; души́стый г. (*bot.*) sweet peas; мéлким ~ком рассыпа́ться (пéред+*i.*) to cringe (before). **2.** (*collect.*) spots, spotted design (*on material*).

горóшин|а, ы, *f.* a pea.

гóрский, *adj. of* гóрец; mountain, highland.

горсовéт, а, *m.* (*abbr. of* городскóй совéт) town, city soviet.

гóрсточк|а, и, *f.* handful.

горст|ь, и, *g. pl.* ~éй, *f.* **1.** cupped hand; держа́ть ру́ку ~ью to cup one's hand. **2.** handful (*also fig.*).

горта́нный, *adj.* **1.** (*anat.*) laryngeal. **2.** (*ling.*) guttural.

горта́н|ь, и, *f.* larynx; у негó язы́к прили́п к ~и he was struck dumb; he was tongue-tied.

горте́нзи|я, и, *f.* hydrangea.

гóрче, *comp. of* гóрький.

горч|и́ть, и́т, *impf.* (*impers.*) to have a bitter taste.

горчи́ц|а, ы, *f.* mustard.

горчи́чник, а, *m.* mustard-poultice.

горчи́чниц|а, ы, *f.* mustard-pot.

горчи́чн|ый, *adj. of* горчи́ца; г. газ mustard gas; ∼ое се́мя mustard seed.

го́рше, *comp. of* го́рький.

горше́чник, а, *m.* potter.

горше́чный, *adj.* pottery; г. това́р pottery, earthenware.

го́рший (*obs.*) *comp. of* го́рький; more bitter (*fig.*).

горш|о́к, ка́, *m.* pot; jug; vase; ночно́й г. chamber-pot.

го́рьк|ая, ой, *f.* vodka; пить ∼ую (*coll.*) to hit the bottle.

го́р|ький (∼ек, ∼ька́, ∼ько), *adj.* 1 (*comp.* ∼че) bitter; ∼ькое ма́сло rancid butter. 2. (*comp.* ∼ше, ∼ший) (*fig.*) bitter; hard; ∼ькие слёзы bitter tears; ∼ьким о́пытом узна́ть to learn by bitter experience. 3. (*coll.*) hapless, wretched. 4. г. пья́ница (*coll.*) inveterate drunkard.

го́рько¹, *adv.* bitterly.

го́рько², *as pred.* 1. мне г. во рту I have a bitter taste in my mouth. 2. it is bitter; мне г. I am sorry, I am grieved.

горю́н, а́, *m.* (*coll.*) unfortunate.

горю́н|ья, ьи, *g. pl.* ∼ий, *f. of* ∼.

горю́ч|ее, его, *n.* fuel.

горю́чест|ь, и, *f.* combustibility; inflammability.

горю́ч|ий, *adj.* 1. combustible, inflammable. 2. (*folk poet.*) burning; ∼ие слёзы bitter tears.

го́рюшк|о, а, *n.* (*coll.*) grief, affliction; а ему́ и ∼а ма́ло he does not care a jot.

горячело́мкий, *adj.* (*tech.*) hot-short.

горя́ч|ечный, *adj. of* ∼ка; feverous; г. бред delirium; ∼ечная руба́шка strait-jacket.

горя́ч|ий (∼, ∼а́, ∼о́), *adj.* 1. hot (*also fig.*); по ∼им следа́м (*i*) (+*g.*) hot on the heels (of), (*ii*) (*fig.*) forthwith; под ∼ую ру́ку in the heat of the moment. 2. passionate; ardent, fervent. 3. hot-tempered; mettlesome; ∼ая голова́ hothead. 4. heated; impassioned; г. спор heated argument. 5. busy; ∼ее вре́мя busy season. 6. (*tech.*) high-temperature; ∼ая обрабо́тка heat treatment.

горячи́тельн|ый, *adj.* (*obs.*) hot, warming; ∼ые напи́тки strong drink.

горяч|и́ть, у́, и́шь, *impf.* (*of* раз∼) to excite, irritate.

горяч|и́ться, у́сь, и́шься, *impf.* (*of* раз∼) to get excited, become impassioned.

горя́чк|а, и, *f.* 1. fever (*also fig.*). 2. feverish activity; feverish haste; поро́ть ∼у (*coll.*) to act impetuously, in the heat of the moment. 3. (*m. and f.*; *coll.*) hothead; firebrand.

горя́чност|ь, и, *f.* zeal, fervour, enthusiasm; impulsiveness.

горячо́¹, *adv.* hot.

горячо́², *as pred.* it is hot.

гос- (*abbr. of* госуда́рственный) State; Госи: да́т State Publishing House; Госпла́н Sta Planning Commission; Госстра́х Nation Insurance.

госпитализа́ци|я, и, *f.* hospitalization.

го́спитал|ь, я, *m.* hospital (*esp. military*).

госпита́льный, *adj. of* го́спиталь.

госпо́д|ень, ня, не, *adj.* (*eccl.*) the Lord' моли́тва ∼ня the Lord's Prayer.

го́споди, *interj.* good heavens!, good Lord good gracious!;

господ|и́н, и́на, *pl.* ∼а́, ∼, ∼а́м, *m.* 1. ma ter; сам себе́ г. one's own master; г. своег сло́ва a man of one's word. 2. gentlema э́ти ∼а́ (*often iron.*) these gentlemen. 3. (*style*) Mr.; ∼а́ (*as form of address*) (*i*) gentle men, (*ii*) ladies and gentlemen; (*as styl* Messrs.

госпо́дский, *adj.* seigniorial, manorial; дом manor-house.

госпо́дств|о, а, *n.* 1. supremacy, dominio mastery. 2. predominance.

госпо́дств|овать, ую, *impf.* 1. to hold sway exercise dominion. 2. to predominate, pre vail. 3. (над+*i.*) to command, dominate to tower (above).

госпо́дств|ующий, *pres. part. act. of* ∼ова and *adj.* 1. ruling; г. класс ruling class. : predominant, prevailing. 3. (*of physic* *features*) commanding.

Госпо́дь, Го́спода, *voc.* Го́споди, *m.* Go the Lord; г. его́ зна́ет! (the) Lord knows

госпож|а́, и́, *f.* 1. mistress. 2. lady. 3. (*style*) Mrs.; Miss.

госпожи́н|ки, ок, *no sing.* (*dial.*) fast befor the feast of the Assumption.

гостево́й, *adj.* guest, guests'.

гостеприи́м|ный (∼ен, ∼на), *adj.* hosp table.

гостеприи́мств|о, а, *n.* hospitality.

гости́н|ая, ой, *f.* 1. drawing-room, sittin -room. 2. drawing-room suite.

гости́н|ец, ца, *m.* (*coll.*) present.

гости́ниц|а, ы, *f.* hotel, inn.

гости́н|ичный, *adj. of* ∼ица.

гостинодво́|рец, рца, *m.* (*obs.*) shopkeepe (*in a bazaar*).

гости́ный, *adj.*; г. двор arcade, bazaar.

гости́ть, гощу́, гости́шь, *impf.* (у) to sta (with), be on a visit (to).

гост|ь, я, *g. pl.* ∼е́й, *m.* guest, visitor; пойт в ∼и (к+*d.*) to visit; быть в гостя́х (y to be a guest (at, of), be visiting; в гостя́ хорошо́, а до́ма лу́чше there's no plac like home.

го́ст|ья, ьи, *g. pl.* ∼ий, *f. of* ∼ь.

госуда́рственност|ь, и, *f.* State system.

госуда́рственн|ый, *adj.* State, public;

переворо́т coup d'état; ~ая изме́на high treason; ~ое пра́во public law; ~ая слу́жба public service; г. слу́жащий civil servant; Г. сове́т (*hist.*) State Council; ~ые экза́мены final examinations (*in higher education institutions*).

госуда́рств|о, а, *n.* State.

госуда́рын|я, и, *f.* 1. sovereign; Г. (*as form of address*) Your Majesty. 2. (*obs.*) mistress; ми́лостивая г. (*as form of address*) madam.

госуда́р|ь, я, *m.* 1. sovereign; Г. (*as form of address*) Your Majesty, Sire. 2. (*obs.*) master; ми́лостивый г. (*as form of address*) sir.

гот, а, *m.* (*hist.*) Goth.

го́тик|а, и, *f.* (*archit.*) Gothic style.

готи́ческий, *adj.* (*art*) Gothic; г. шрифт Gothic script, black-letter.

готова́л|ьня, ьни, *g. pl.* ~ен, *f.* case of drawing instruments.

гото́в|ить, лю, ишь, *impf.* 1. to prepare, make ready; to train. 2. to cook. 3. to lay in, store. 4. (+*d.*; *fig.*) to have in store (for).

гото́в|иться, люсь, ишься, *impf.* 1. (к+*d.* or +*inf.*) to get ready (for, to); to prepare oneself (for), make preparations (for). 2. (*impf. only*) to be at hand, in the offing, impending, imminent; ~ятся кру́пные собы́тия great events are in the offing.

гото́вност|ь, и, *f.* 1. readiness, preparedness; в боево́й ~и ready for action; (*naut.*) cleared for action. 2. readiness, willingness.

гото́во, *as pred.*; и г. (*coll.*) and that's that.

гото́в|ый (~, ~a), *adj.* 1. (к+*d.*) ready (for), prepared (for); г. к де́йствию ready for action; я не ~ I'm not ready; г. к услу́гам (*epistolary formula*) yours faithfully. 2. (на+ *a.* or +*inf.*) ready (for, to), prepared (for, to); willing (to); мы ~ы на всё we are prepared for anything; она́ .не ~а идти́ she is not willing to go. 3. (+*inf.*) on the point (of), on the verge (of), ready (to); он ~ был ка́ждую мину́ту расхохота́ться he was on the verge of bursting out laughing. 4. ready-made, finished; ~ое пла́тье ready--made clothes; ~ые изде́лия finished articles. 5. на всём ~ом with all found; на ~ых харча́х with full board and lodging. 6. (*short form only*; *coll.*) (*i*) finished (= *dead*), (*ii*) tight, plastered (= *drunk*).

го́тский, *adj.* Gothic (*of the Goths and Gothic language*).

гофма́ршал, а, *m.* (*hist.*) Marshal of the (Imperial) Court.

гофме́йстер, а, *m.* (*hist.*) steward of the household.

гофриро́ванн|ый, *p.p.p.* of гофрирова́ть and *adj.*; ~ое желе́зо corrugated iron; ~ые во́лосы waved hair; ~ая ю́бка pleated

skirt; ~ый воротни́к goffered collar.

гофрир|ова́ть, у́ю, *impf. and pf.* 1. to corrugate; to wave; to crimp. 2. to goffer.

гофриро́вк|а, и, *no pl.*, *f.* 1. corrugation; goffering; waving. 2. waves (*of hair*).

граб, а, *m.* (*bot.*) hornbeam.

гра́бар|ь, я, *m.* (*dial.*) navvy.

грабёж, а́, *m.* robbery (*also fig.*, *coll.*).

граби́тел|ь, я, *m.* robber.

граби́тельский, *adj.* 1. predatory. 2. extortionate, exorbitant (*of prices*).

граби́тельств|о, а, *n.* (*obs.*) robbery.

гра́б|ить¹, лю, ишь, *impf.* (*of* о~) to rob, pillage; (*fig.*) to rob.

гра́б|ить², лю, ишь, *impf.* to rake.

гра́блени|е, я, *n.* raking.

гра́блены|й, *adj.* stolen.

гра́б|ли, лей *or* ~ель, *no sing.* rake.

гра́б|овый, *adj.* of ~.

гравёр, а, *m.* engraver.

гравёр|ный, *adj.* of ~; ~ное иску́сство engraving.

гра́ви|й, я, *m.* gravel.

грави́йн|ый, *adj.* of гра́вий; ~ые карье́ры gravel pits.

гравирова́льн|ый, *adj.* engraving; ~ая доска́ steel plate, copper plate; ~ая игла́ etching needle.

гравир|ова́ть, у́ю, у́ешь, *impf.* (*of* вы́~) to engrave.

гравиро́вк|а, и, *f.* engraving.

гравиро́вщик, а, *m.* engraver.

гравитацио́нный, *adj.* gravitation(al).

гравита́ци|я, и, *f.* (*phys.*) gravitation.

гравю́р|а, ы, *f.* engraving, print; etching; г. на де́реве woodcut; г. на лино́леуме linocut; г. на ме́ди copper-plate engraving.

град¹, а, *m.* 1. hail. 2. (*fig.*) hail, shower, torrent; volley.

град², а, *m.* (*arch. or poet.*) city, town.

града́ци|я, и, *f.* gradation, scale.

градие́нт, а, *m.* gradient.

гра́дин|а, ы, *f.* (*coll.*) hailstone.

гради́р|ня, ни, *g. pl.* ~ен, *f.* 1. salt-pan. 2. (water-)cooling tower.

гради́р|овать, ую, *impf. and pf.* to evaporate, graduate (*salt*).

градоби́ти|е, я, *n.* damage done by hail.

градово́й, *adj.* of град¹.

гра́дом, *adv.* thick and fast; уда́ры посы́пались г. blows showered down, rained down.

градонача́льник, а, *m.* (*hist.*) town governor (*of a town independent administratively of its province*).

градонача́льств|о, а, *n.* (*hist.*) 1. town, borough (*independent administratively of province*). 2. town governor's office.

градострои́тел|ь, я, *m.* town-planner.

градострои́тельный, *adj.* town-planning.

градострои́тельств|о, а, *n.* town-planning.

градуи́р|овать, ую, *impf. and pf.* **1.** to graduate (*to mark with lines to indicate degrees, etc.*). **2.** to grade.

гра́дус, а, *m.* **1.** degree (*unit of measurement*); у́гол в 40 ~ов angle of 40 degrees; сего́дня 20 ~ов тепла́, моро́за it is twenty degrees above, below zero today. **2.** (*fig.*) degree, pitch; stage; в после́днем ~е in the final stage (*of an illness*). **3.** под ~ом (*coll.*) under the weather, one over the eight.

гра́дусник, а, *m.* thermometer.

гра́дус|ный, *adj.* of ~; ~ная се́тка (*geogr.*) grid.

граждани́н, а, *pl.* гра́ждане, гра́ждан, *m.* **1.** citizen; пото́мственный почётный г. (*hist.*) hereditary honorary citizen (*title conferred in tsarist Russia on persons not of gentle birth for services*). **2.** person.

гражда́нк|а¹, и, *f.* citizeness.

гражда́нк|а², и, *f.* (*coll.*) **1.** = гражда́нская а́збука. **2.** the Civil War (*in Russia 1917–1921*).

гражда́нск|ий, *adj.* **1.** (*leg., etc.*) civil; citizen's; civic; г. иск civil suit; предъяви́ть г. иск (к+*d.*) to bring a civil suit (against); г. ко́декс civil code; ~ое пра́во civil law; ~ая смерть deprivation of civil rights. **2.** civil, secular (*as opp. to ecclesiastical*); г. брак (*i*) civil marriage, (*ii*) (*coll., obs.*) cohabitation, free union; ~ая панихи́да civil funeral rite. **3.** civilian (*as opp. to military*); ~ое пла́тье civilian clothes, civvies, mufti. **4.** civic, befitting a citizen; ~ие доброде́тели civic virtues. **5.** (*of poetry, etc.*) civic, having social content. **6.** ~ая война́ civil war. **7.** ~ая а́збука, ~ая печа́ть Russian type (*introduced by Peter the Great in place of Church Slavonic*).

гражда́нственност|ь, и, *f.* **1.** civilization; civil society. **2.** civic spirit.

гражда́нств|о, а, *n.* **1.** citizenship, nationality; права́ ~а civic rights; получи́ть права́ ~а to be granted civic rights; (*fig.*) to achieve general recognition. **2.** (*collect.*; *obs.*) citizenry.

грамза́пис|ь, и, *f.* gramophone recording.

грамм, а, *m.* gramme, gram.

грамма́тик, а, *m.* grammarian.

грамма́тик|а, и, *f.* **1.** grammar. **2.** grammar(-book).

граммати́ческий, *adj.* grammatical.

граммофо́н, а, *m.* gramophone (*with loudspeaker horn*).

граммофо́н|ный, *adj.* of ~; ~ная пласти́нка gramophone record.

гра́мот|а, ы, *f.* **1.** reading and writing, ability to read and write. **2.** official document; deed.

грамоте́|й, я, *m.* (*coll.*) **1.** one who can rea and write. **2.** scholar.

гра́мотк|а, и, *f.* (*coll.*) letter, note.

гра́мотность|ь, и, *f.* **1.** literacy (*also fig.* **2.** grammatical correctness. **3.** competenc

гра́мот|ный (~ен, ~на), *adj.* **1.** literat able to read and write. **2.** grammaticall correct. **3.** competent. **4.** полити́чески politically aware.

грампласти́нк|а, и, *f.* gramophone recor

гран, а, *m.* grain (*unit of weight*); в э́том н ни ~а и́стины there is not a grain of trut in it.

грана́т¹, а, *m.* **1.** pomegranate. **2.** pom granate tree.

грана́т², а, *m.* (*min.*) garnet.

грана́т|а, ы, *f.* (*mil.*) shell, grenade; ручна́ г. hand-grenade.

грана́тник, а, *m.* pomegranate tree.

грана́т|ный, *adj.* of ~а; г. ого́нь shell-fire

грана́товый¹, *adj.* pomegranate.

грана́т|овый², **1.** *adj.* of ~². **2.** rich red.

гранатомёт, а, *m.* (*mil.*) grenade cup di charger, grenade thrower.

гранатомётчик, а, *m.* grenade-throwe grenadier.

гранд, а, *m.* grandee (*Spanish nobleman*).

грандио́зност|ь, и, *f.* grandeur; imme sity.

грандио́з|ный (~ен, ~на), *adj.* grandios mighty; vast.

гране́ни|е, я, *n.* cutting (*of precious stone glass*).

гранён|ый, *adj.* **1.** cut, faceted; ~ое стекл cut glass. **2.** cut-glass.

грани́льный, *adj.* lapidary; diamond-cu ting.

грани́л|ьня, ьни, *g. pl.* ен, *f.* lapidary wor shop; г. алма́зов diamond-cutting shop.

грани́льщик, а, *m.* lapidary; г. алма́зо diamond-cutter.

грани́т, а, *m.* granite.

грани́тный, *adj.* granite.

гран|и́ть, ю, и́шь, *impf.* to cut, facet; (*col* г. мостову́ю to loaf, saunter, promenade.

грани́ц|а, ы, *f.* **1.** frontier, border; за ~ abroad; е́хать за ~у to go abroad. **2.** (*fig* boundary, limit; вы́йти из ~ to overste the limits, overstep the mark; перейт все ~ы to pass all bounds; в ~ах прили́чи within the bounds of decency.

грани́ч|ить, у, ишь, *impf.* (с+*i.*) **1.** t border (upon), be contiguous (with). (*fig.*) to border (on), verge (on); э́то ~ит изме́ной it borders on treason.

гра́нк|а, и, *f.* (*typ.*) slip, galley-proof.

грануди́р|овать, ую, *impf. and pf.* to gran late.

грануля́ци|я, и, *f.* (*tech., astron., med.*) gran lation.

грань|ь, и, *f.* 1. border, verge; на ~и сумасшéствия on the verge of insanity; «полѝтика на ~и войнь́» brinkmanship. 2. side, facet; edge. 3. (*math.*) period.

грассѝр|овать, ую, *impf.* to pronounce one's r's in the French manner.

грат, а, *m.* (*tech.*) barb, burr.

граф, а, *m.* count.

граф|á, ы́, *f.* (*book-keeping, etc.*) column (*of a table or page*).

грáфик¹, а, *m.* 1. graph; chart. 2. schedule; тóчно по ~у according to schedule.

грáфик², а, *m.* draughtsman.

грáфик|а, и, *f.* 1. (*art*) drawing. 2. script.

графѝн, а, *m.* carafe; decanter.

графѝн|я, и, *f.* countess.

графѝт, а, *m.* 1. (*min.*) graphite, black-lead. 2. pencil-lead.

графѝт|ный, *adj.* = ~овый.

графѝтовый, *adj.* graphite.

граф|ѝть, лю́, ѝшь, *impf.* (*of* раз~) to rule (*paper*).

графѝческий, *adj.* graphic.

графлёный, *adj.* (vertically) ruled.

графóлог, а, *m.* graphologist.

графолóги|я, и, *f.* graphology.

графомáн, а, *m.* graphomaniac; (*fig.*) pulp-writer, hack.

графомáни|я, и, *f.* graphomania.

грáфский, *adj.* of граф.

грáфств|о, а, *n.* 1. title of count. 2. county.

грациóз|ный (~ен, ~на), *adj.* graceful.

грáци|я, и, *f.* 1. gracefulness. 2. Г. (*myth.*) Grace; (*fig.*) beauty.

грач, á, *m.* (*orn.*) rook.

грач|ѝный, *adj.* of ~.

грач|óнок, óнка, *pl.* ~áта, ~áт, *m.* (*orn.*) young rook.

гребёнк|а, и, *f.* 1. comb; стричь под ~у to crop close; стричь всех под однý ~у to treat all alike, reduce all to the same level. 2. (*tech.*) rack; (*text.*) hackle.

гребéнчатый, *adj.* 1. (*zool.*) cristate; pectinate. 2. comb-shaped; г. подшѝпник (*tech.*) collar thrust bearing.

грéб|ень, ня, *m.* 1. comb. 2. (*tech.*) comb; (*text.*) hackle. 3. (*of bird*) comb, crest; петушѝный г. cock's comb. 4. crest (*of hill or wave*). 5. (*archit.*) ridge-piece, roof-tree. 6. (*agric.*) ridge.

греб|éц, ца́, *m.* rower, oarsman.

гребеш|óк, ка́, *m.* = грéбень.

грéбл|я¹, и, *f.* 1. rowing. 2. (*dial.*) raking.

грéбл|я², и, *f.* (*dial.*) dyke.

гребневѝд|ный (~ен, ~на), *adj.* comb-shaped, pectinate.

гребнечесáльн|ый, *adj.*; ~ая машѝна (*text.*) hackling machine, comber.

гребнѝст|ый (~, ~а), *adj.* (high-)crested.

гребн|óй, *adj.* 1. rowing; г. спорт rowing.

2. г. вал propeller shaft; г. винт propeller screw; ~óе колесó paddle wheel.

греб|óк, ка́, *m.* 1. stroke (*in rowing*). 2. blade (*of a mill-wheel or paddle-wheel*).

грегориáнский, *adj.*, = григориáнский.

грёз|а, ы, *f.* day-dream, reverie.

грé|жу, *see* ~зить.

грé|зить, жу, зишь, *impf.* to dream; г. наявý to day-dream.

грé|зиться, жусь, зишься, *impf.* (*of* при~) (*impers.*, + *d.*) to dream; мне ~зилось, что... I used to dream that . . .

грéйдер, а, *m.* (*tech.*) 1. grader. 2. (*coll.*) earth road (*levelled but unmetalled*).

грéйдер|ный, *adj.* of ~; ~ная дорóга grader road.

грéйпфрут, а, *m.* grapefruit.

грек, а, *m.* Greek.

грéлк|а, и, *f.* hot-water bottle; электрѝческая г. electric blanket.

грем|éть, лю́, ѝшь, *impf.* to thunder, roar; peal; rattle; (*fig.*) to resound, ring out; ѝмя егó ~éло по всей Еврóпе his name resounded throughout Europe.

грему́ч|ий, *adj.* roaring; г. газ detonating-gas; ~ая змея́ rattlesnake; ~ая ртуть (*chem.*) fulminate of mercury; г. стýдень nitrogelatine, blasting gelatine.

грему́шк|а, и, *f.* 1. rattle (*child's toy*). 2. sleigh-bell.

грéн|а, ы, *f.* (*collect.*) silkworm eggs.

гренадéр, а, *m.* grenadier.

гренадéр|ский, *adj.* of ~; г. полк Grenadiers.

грен|óк, ка́, *m.* (finger of) toast; (*cul.*) croûton.

гре|стѝ, бу́, бёшь, *past* ~б, ~блá, *impf.* 1. to row. 2. to rake; г. лопáтой дéньги (*coll.*) to rake in the shekels.

греть, грéю, грéешь, *impf.* 1. (*intrans.*) to give out warmth. 2. (*trans.*) to warm, heat; г. (себé) рýки to warm one's hands; (*fig.*, *coll.*, *pejor.*) to be on to a good thing.

грé|ться, юсь, ешься, *impf.* 1. to warm oneself. 2. *pass.* of греть.

грех, á, *m.* 1. (*rel. or fig.*) sin; приня́ть на себя́ г. to take the blame upon oneself; нéчего ~á тайть it must be owned; такóй г. I own it; подáльше от ~á get out of harm's way; как на г. as ill-luck would have it. 2. (*as pred.* + *inf.*; *coll.*) it is a sin, it is sinful; не г. (+*inf.*) it does not, would not hurt (to); there is no harm (in); не г. вы́пить рю́мочку-две there is no harm in (drinking) a glass or two. 3. с ~óм пополáм (only) just; мы с ~óм пополáм расшифровáли твой пóчерк we just managed to decipher your handwriting.

грехóв|ный (~ен, ~на), *adj.* sinful.

греховóдник, а, *m.* (*coll.*, *obs.*) sinner; (*of a child*) naughty boy.

греховóдниц|а, ы, *f. of* греховóдник.

греховóднича|ть, ю, *impf. (coll., obs.)* to be a sinner.

грехопадéни|е, я, *n. (bibl.)* the Fall; *(fig.)* fall.

грéцкий, *adj.;* г. орéх walnut.

грéч|а, и, *f. (coll.)* buckwheat.

гречáнк|а, и, *f.* Greek woman.

грéческий, *adj.* Greek; Grecian.

гречúх|а, и, *f.* buckwheat.

грéчнев|ый, *adj.* buckwheat; ~ая кáша buckwheat porridge.

греш|úть, ý, úшь, *impf.* 1. *(pf.* со~) to sin. 2. *(pf.* по~) (прóтив+*g.*; *fig.*) to sin (against).

грéшник, а, *m.* sinner.

грéшниц|а, ы, *f. of* грéшник.

грéш|ный (~ен, ~нá), *adj.* sinful; culpable; г. человéк *(parenth.)* I am ashamed to say; ~ным дéлом *(parenth.)* much as I regret it, I am ashamed to say.

греш|óк, кá, *m.* peccadillo.

гриб, á, *m.* fungus, mushroom; съедóбный г. mushroom, edible fungus; несъедóбный г. toadstool; учéние о ~áх *(bot.)* mycology; г. съесть *(obs.)* to be unsuccessful, meet with failure; растú как ~ы́ to spring up like mushrooms.

грибкóвый, *adj.* fungoid.

грибнúц|а, ы, *f.* 1. mushroom spawn. 2. *(coll.)* mushroom soup.

грибн|óй, *adj. of* гриб; fungoid; mushroom; г. дождь rain during sunshine; ~áя похлёбка mushroom soup.

гриб|óк, кá, *m.* 1. *dim. of* гриб. 2. *(biol.)* fungus, microorganism. 3. mushroom *(for darning stockings).*

грúв|а, ы, *f.* 1. mane. 2. wooded ridge. 3. *(dial.)* shoal.

гривáст|ый (~, ~а), *adj.* with a long mane.

грúвенник, а, *m. (coll.)* ten-kopeck piece.

грúвн|а, ы, *f.* 1. *(hist.)* grivna *(unit of currency in medieval Russia).* 2. *(obs.)* ten kopecks. 3. *(hist.)* pendant.

гривуáз|ный (~ен, ~на), *adj.* obscene, indecent.

григориáнск|ий, *adj.* Gregorian; г. календáрь, ~ое летосчислéние Gregorian Calendar.

грúдниц|а, ы, *f. (hist.)* quarters of body-guard.

грид|ь, и, *f. (collect.; hist.) (prince's)* body-guard.

грим, а, *m.* make-up *(theatr. only)*; grease-paint.

гримáс|а, ы, *f.* grimace; дéлать ~ы to make, pull faces.

гримáсник, а, *m.* grimacer.

гримáснича|ть, ю, *impf.* to grimace; to make, pull faces.

гримёр, а, *m. (theatr.)* make-up man.

гримир|овáть, ýю, *impf.* 1. *(theatr.) (pf.* на~) to make up. 2. *(pf.* за~) (+*i.*) to make up (as); (+*i. or* под+*a.*; *fig.*) to make to appear, make out (as); г. Наполéона герóем, под герóя to paint Napoleon as a hero.

гримир|овáться, ýюсь, *impf. (of* за~) *(theatr.)* to make up *(intrans.)*; (+*i. or* под +*a.*; *fig.*) to make oneself out, seek to appear; г. патриóтом, под патриóта to make oneself out a patriot.

гримирóвк|а, и, *f. (theatr.)* making-up.

грипп, а, *m.* influenza.

гриппóзный, *adj.* influenzal.

гриф¹, а, *m.* 1. *(myth.)* gryphon. 2. *(zool.)* vulture.

гриф², а, *m. (mus.)* finger-board *(of stringed instruments).*

гриф³, а, *m.* seal, stamp.

гриф⁴, а, *m. (sport)* grip *(in wrestling).*

грúфел|ь, я, *m.* slate-pencil.

грúфельн|ый, *adj.* slate; ~ая доскá slate; г. слáнец *(geol.)* grapholite.

грифóн, а, *m.* 1. *(myth., archit.)* gryphon. 2. griffon *(dog).*

гроб, а, о ᷉е, в ~ý, *pl.* ~ы́ *and* ~á, *m.* 1. coffin; идтú за ᷉ом to follow the coffin. 2. *(obs.)* grave, burial-place. 3. *(fig.)* the grave (= *death*); вогнáть в г. to drive to the grave; до ᷉а, по г. жúзни *(coll.)* until death, as long as one shall live; стоя́ть однóй ногóй в ~ý to have one foot in the grave.

гроб|úть, лю, ишь, *impf. (sl.)* to destroy; to ruin.

гробнúц|а, ы, *f.* tomb, sepulchre.

гробов|óй, *adj.* 1. *adj. of* гроб; ~áя доскá *(fig.)* the grave; вéрный до ~óй доскú faithful unto death. 2. sepulchral, deathly; г. гóлос sepulchral voice; ~óе молчáние deathly silence.

гробовщúк, á, *m.* coffin-maker; undertaker.

гробокопáтел|ь, я, *m. (obs.)* gravedigger *(iron. = dry-as-dust historian, etc.).*

грог, а, *m.* grog.

гроз|á, ы́, *pl.* ᷉ы, *f.* 1. (thunder)storm. 2. calamity, disaster. 3. *(fig.; of a person or thing)* terror. 4. *(obs.)* threats.

грозд|ь, и, *pl.* ᷉и, ~éй, *f. and* ᷉ья, ᷉ьев, *m.* cluster, bunch *(of fruit or flowers).*

гро|зúть, жý, зúшь, *impf.* 1. *(pf.* при~) (+*d. and i. or* + *inf.*) to threaten; он ~зúл мне револьвéром he was threatening me with a revolver; г. убúть когó-н. to threaten to kill someone. 2. *(pf.* по~) (+*i.*) to make threatening gestures; г. кулакóм комý-н. to shake one's fist at someone. 3. *(no pf.)* to threaten; емý ~зúт банкрóтство he is threatened with bankruptcy; дом ~зúт падéнием the house threatens to collapse.

гро|зи́ться, жу́сь, зи́шься, *impf.* (*of* по~) (*coll.*) **1.** (+*inf.*) to threaten. **2.** to make threatening gestures.

гро́з|ный (~ен, ~на́, ~но), *adj.* **1.** menacing, threatening. **2.** dread, terrible; formidable; ~ная опа́сность terrible danger. **3.** (*coll.*) stern, severe.

гроз|ово́й, *adj. of* ~а́; ~ова́я ту́ча storm-cloud, thundercloud.

гром, а, *pl.* ~ы, ~о́в, *m.* thunder (*also fig.*); уда́р ~а a thunderclap; г. среди́ я́сного не́ба a bolt from the blue; мета́ть ~ы и мо́лнии (*fig.*) to fulminate.

грома́д|а¹, ы, *f.* mass, bulk, pile; (+*g.*) a mass (of), heaps (of).

грома́д|а², ы, *f.* (*hist.*) gromada (*rural commune or assembly in Ukraine and Byelorussia*).

грома́дин|а, ы, *f.* (*coll.*) vast object.

грома́д|ный (~ен, ~на), *adj.* huge, vast, enormous, colossal.

громи́л|а, ы, *m.* (*coll.*) **1.** burglar. **2.** thug.

гром|и́ть, лю́, и́шь, *impf.* (*of* раз~) **1.** to destroy; (*mil.*) to smash, rout. **2.** (*fig.*) to thunder against, fulminate against.

гро́м|кий (~ок, ~ка́, ~ко), *adj.* **1.** loud. **2.** famous; notorious; ~кое поведе́ние infamous conduct. **3.** fine-sounding, specious; ~кие слова́ (*iron.*) big words.

гро́мко, *adv.* loud(ly); aloud.

громкоговори́тел|ь, я, *m.* loud-speaker.

громоголо́сый, *adj.* loud-voiced.

громове́рж|ец, ца, *m.* the thunderer (*epithet of Zeus; myth. and fig.*).

громов|о́й, *adj.* **1.** *adj. of* гром; ~ы́е раска́ты peals of thunder. **2.** thunderous, deafening; ~ы́е рукоплеска́ния thunderous applause. **3.** crushing, smashing.

громогла́сно, *adv.* **1.** loudly. **2.** out loud, publicly.

громогла́с|ный (~ен, ~на), *adj.* **1.** loud; loud-voiced. **2.** public, open.

громозву́ч|ный (~ен, ~на), *adj.* (*obs.*) **1.** loud. **2.** (*fig.*) triumphal; highflown.

громоз|ди́ть, жу́, ди́шь, *impf.* (*of* на~) to pile up, heap up.

громоз|ди́ться, жу́сь, ди́шься, *impf.* **1.** to tower. **2.** (*coll.*) to clamber up.

громо́зд|кий (~ок, ~ка), *adj.* cumbersome, unwieldly.

громоотво́д, а, *m.* lightning-conductor (*also fig.*).

громоподо́б|ный (~ен, ~на), *adj.* thunderous.

гро́м|че, *comp. of* ~кий *and* ~ко.

громыха́|ть, ю, *impf.* (*coll.*) to rumble.

гросс, а, *m.* gross.

гро́ссбух, а, *m.* ledger.

гроссме́йстер, а, *m.* **1.** grand master (*at chess*). **2.** (*hist.*) Grand Master (*of order of knights in Middle Ages*).

грот¹, а, *m.* grotto.

грот², а, *m.* mainsail.

грот- (*naut.*) main-.

гроте́ск, а, *m.* (*art*) grotesque.

гроте́скный, *adj.* grotesque.

гро́х|ать(ся), аю(сь), *impf. of* ~нуть(ся).

гро́хн|уть, у, ешь, *pf.* (*coll.*) **1.** to crash, bang. **2.** (*trans.*) to drop with a crash, bang down.

гро́хн|уться, усь, ешься, *pf.* (*coll.*) to fall with a crash.

гро́хот¹, а, *m.* crash, din; thunder.

гро́хот², а, *m.* (*tech., agric.*) riddle, screen, sifter.

грохота́нь|е, я, *n.* crashing; rumbling.

грох|ота́ть, очу́, о́чешь, *impf.* **1.** to crash; roll, rumble; roar. **2.** (*coll.*) to roar (with laughter).

грохо|ти́ть, чу́, ти́шь, *impf.* (*of* про~) (*tech., agric.*) to riddle, sift, screen.

грош, а́, *m.* **1.** half-kopeck piece. **2.** grosz (*Polish unit of currency*). **3.** *pl.* ~и́, ~е́й (*fig., coll.*) penny, farthing; э́тому г. ме́дный, ло́маный цена́; э́то ~а́ ме́дного, ло́маного не сто́ит it's not worth a brass farthing; и в г. не ста́вить not to give a brass farthing (for); купи́ть за ~и́ to buy for a song. **4.** *pl.* ~и́, ~е́й (*sl.*) brass (= *money*).

грошо́вый, *adj.* (*coll.*) **1.** dirt-cheap; (*fig.*) cheap, shoddy. **2.** insignificant, trifling.

грубе́|ть, ю, ешь, *impf.* (*of* о~) to grow coarse, rude.

груб|и́ть, лю́, и́шь, *impf.* (*of* на~) (+*d.*) to be rude (to).

грубия́н, а, *m.* (*coll.*) boor.

грубия́н|ить, ю, ишь, *impf.* (*of* на~) (+*d.*; *coll.*) to be rude (to); to behave boorishly.

гру́бо, *adv.* **1.** coarsely, roughly. **2.** crudely. **3.** rudely. **4.** roughly (= *approximately*); г. говоря́ roughly speaking.

грубова́т|ый (~, ~а), *adj.* rather coarse, rude.

гру́бост|ь, и, *f.* **1.** rudeness; coarseness; grossness. **2.** rude remark; coarse action; говори́ть ~и to be rude.

грубошёрстный, *adj.* (*of cloth, etc.*) coarse.

гру́б|ый (~, ~а́, ~о), *adj.* **1.** coarse, rough; ~ое сукно́ coarse fabric; г. го́лос gruff voice. **2.** (*of workmanship, etc.*) crude, rude. **3.** gross, flagrant; г. обма́н gross deception. **4.** rude; coarse, crude; ~ое сло́во rude, coarse word. **5.** rough (= *approximate*); в ~ых черта́х in rough outline.

гру́д|а, ы, *f.* heap, pile.

груда́ст|ый (~, ~а), *adj.* broad-chested; big-breasted, big-bosomed.

груди́н|а, ы, *f.* (*anat.*) breastbone.

груди́нк|а, и, *f.* brisket; breast (*of lamb, etc.*).

грудни́ц|а, ы, *f.* (*med.*) mastitis.

грудн|о́й, *adj.* **1.** breast; chest; г. го́лос chest-voice; ~а́я жа́ба (*med.*) angina pectoris; ~а́я железа́ (*anat.*) mammary gland; ~а́я кле́тка (*anat.*) thorax. **2.** at the breast; г. ребёнок infant in arms. **3.** г. мох (*bot.*) Iceland moss.

грудобрю́шн|ый, *adj.*; ~ая прегра́да (*anat.*) diaphragm.

груд|ь, и, о ~и, в (на) ~и́. *pl.* ~и. ~е́й, *f.* 1. breast, chest; стоя́ть ~ью (за+a.) to stand up (for), champion; г. с ~ью, г. на́ г. би́ться to fight hand to hand. **2.** (*female*) breast; bosom, bust; корми́ть ~ью to breast-feed; отня́ть от ~и to wean. **3.** (shirt-)front.

гружёный, *adj.* loaded, laden.

груз, а, *m.* 1. weight; load, cargo, freight. **2.** (*fig.*) weight, burden. **3.** (*pendulum*) bob.

**груздь|ь, я́, *pl.* ~и, ~е́й, *m.* milk-agaric (*mushroom*).

**грузи́л|о, а, *n.* sinker.

**грузи́н, а, *g. pl.* г. *m.* Georgian.

**грузи́нк|а, и, *f.* Georgian (woman).

**грузи́нский, *adj.* Georgian.

гру|зи́ть, жу́, ~зи́шь, *impf.* 1. (*pf.* за~ *and* на~) to load; to lade, freight; г. су́дно to lade a ship. **2.** (*pf.* по~) (в, на+a.) to load; г. това́р на су́дно to put a cargo aboard a ship.

**гру|зи́ться, жу́сь, ~зи́шься, *impf.* (*of* по~) to load (*intrans.*), take on cargo.

**гру́зк|а, и, *f.* lading.

**грузне́|ть, ю, ешь, *impf.* (*of* по~) to grow heavy, corpulent.

**гру́зност|ь, и, *f.* weightiness, bulkiness; unwieldiness; corpulence.

**гру́зн|уть, у, ешь, *impf.* to go down, sink.

**гру́з|ный (~ен, ~на́, ~но), *adj.* weighty, bulky; unwieldy; corpulent.

**грузови́к, а́, *m.* lorry.

**грузовладе́л|ец, ьца, *m.* owner of freight.

**грузов|о́й, *adj.* goods, cargo, freight; ~о́е движе́ние goods traffic; ~о́е су́дно cargo boat, freighter.

**грузооборо́т, а, *m.* turnover of goods.

**грузоотправи́тел|ь, я, *m.* consignor of goods.

**грузоподъёмность|ь, и, *f.* payload capacity; freight-carrying capacity.

**грузоподъёмный, *adj.*; г. кран (loading) crane.

**грузополуча́тел|ь, я, *m.* consignee.

**грузопото́к, а, *m.* goods traffic.

**грузотакси́, *indecl.*, *n.* 'taxi-lorry' (*lorry operated for hire from taxi-station*).

**гру́зчик, а, *m.* docker, stevedore.

**грум, а, *m.* groom.

грунт, а, *m.* 1. soil, earth; bottom; переса-ди́ть в г. to plant out. **2.** priming, prime coating (*of a picture*).

**грунт|ова́ть, у́ю, *impf.* (*of* за~) (*art*) to prime.

**грунто́вк|а, и, *f.* priming, first coat (*of paint*).

**грунтов|о́й, *adj.* of грунт; ~ые во́ды subsoil waters; ~а́я доро́га dirt road, earth road.

**гру́пп|а, ы, *f.* (*in var. senses*) group; г. кро́ви (*med.*) blood group.

**группи́р|ова́ть, у́ю, *impf.* (*of* с~) to group; to classify.

**группи́р|ова́ться, у́ется, *impf.* (*of* с~) to group, form groups.

группиро́вк|а, и, *f.* 1. grouping, classifica-tion; г. сил (*mil.*) distribution of forces **2.** group, grouping.

**группово́д, а, *m.* group leader.

**группов|о́й, *adj.* group; ~ые заня́тия group study, group work; ~ые и́гры team games г. полёт formation flying; г. сни́мок group photograph.

**группо́вщин|а, ы, *f.* clique-formation cliquishness.

**гру|сти́ть, ″ щу́, сти́шь, *impf.* to grieve mourn; (по+d.) to pine (for).

**гру́стно[1], *adv.* sadly, sorrowfully.

**гру́стно[2], *as pred.* it is sad; ей г. she feel sad; нам г. узна́ть, что we are sorry to hea that...

гру́ст|ный (~ен, ~на́, ~но), *adj.* 1. sad melancholy. **2.** sad(-making); (*coll.*) griev ous, distressing.

**грусть|ь, и, *f.* sadness, melancholy.

гру́ш|а, и, *f.* 1. pear. **2.** pear-tree. **3.** зем ляна́я г. Jerusalem artichoke. **4.** pear -shaped object.

**грушеви́д|ный (~ен, ~на), *adj.* pear -shaped.

**гру́шевый, *adj.* pear; г. компо́т stewe pears.

грушо́вк|а, и, *f.* 1. pear liqueur. **2.** gru shovka (*kind of apple-tree*).

**гры́ж|а, и, *f.* (*med.*) hernia, rupture.

**грыжево́й *and* гры́жевый, *adj.* hernial; банда́ж truss.

**гры́зл|о, а, *n.* bit (*of bridle*).

грызн|я́, и́, *f.* (*coll.*) 1. fight (*of animals*). squabble.

грыз|ть, у́, ёшь, *past* ~, ~ла, *impf.* 1. gnaw; to nibble; г. но́гти to bite on nails. **2.** (*coll.*) to nag (at). **3.** (*fig.*) devour, consume; нас ~ло любопы́тст we were consumed with curiosity.

гры́з|ться, у́сь, ёшься, *past* ~ся, ~лас *impf.* 1. to fight (*of animals*). **2.** (*coll.*) squabble, bicker.

**грызу́н, а́, *m.* rodent.

**гры́мз|а, ы, *m. and f.* (*coll.*) grumbler.

**грю́ндер, а, *m.* company promoter.

**грю́ндерств|о, а, *n.* company promotion.

гряд|а́, ы́, *pl.* ~ы, ~, ~а́м, *f.* 1. ridge. **2.** b (*in garden*). **3.** row, series.

гряди́л|ь, я, *m.* plough-beam.

гря́дк|а¹, и, *f.* *dim. of* гряда́.

гря́дк|а², и, *f.* edge (*of cart or sledge*).

гря́дков|ый, *adj.* of гря́дка¹; ~ая культу́ра (*hort.*) growing in beds.

грядово́й, *adj.* (*hort.*) growing, grown in beds.

гряду́щ|ий *pres. part. act. of* грясти́ (*obs.*) and *adj.* (*rhet.*) coming, future; ~ие дни days to come; на сон г. (*coll.*) at bedtime, before going to bed; *as noun* ~ее, ~его, *n.* the future.

грязев|о́й, *adj.* mud; ~а́я ва́нна mud-bath.

грязелече́бниц|а, ы, *f.* institution for mud--cures, therapeutic mud-baths.

грязелече́ни|е, я, *n.* mud-cure.

грязне́|ть, ю, *impf.* to get covered in mud, become dirty.

грязн|и́ть, ю́, и́шь, *impf.* (*of* на~) 1. to make dirty, soil; (*fig.*) to sully, besmirch. 2. to litter.

грязн|и́ться, ю́сь, и́шься, *impf.* to become dirty.

гря́зн|о¹, *adv. of* ~ый.

гря́зно², *as pred.* it is dirty.

грязну́л|я, и, *m. and f.* (*coll.*) guttersnipe; slut.

грязн|у́ть, у, ешь, *impf.* to sink in the mire (*also fig.*).

гря́з|ный (~ен, ~на́, ~но), adj. 1. muddy, mud-stained. **2.** dirty; ~ное бельё dirty washing (*also fig.*). **3.** untidy; slovenly; ~ная тетра́дь untidy copy-book. **4.** (*fig.*) dirty, filthy; ~ное де́ло dirty business. **5.** mud-grey. **6.** refuse, garbage; ~ное ведро́ refuse-pail, garbage-pail, slop-pail.

гряз|ь, и, о ~и, в ~й, f. 1. mud (*also fig.*); меси́ть г. (*coll.*) to wade through mud; заброса́ть ~ью, смеша́ть с ~ью; втопта́ть, затопта́ть в г. (*fig.*) to sling mud (at). **2.** (*pl.*) (*therapeutic*) mud; mud-baths; mud-cure. **3.** dirt, filth (*also fig.*).

гря́н|уть, у, ешь, *pf.* **1.** (*of sounds and fig.*) to burst out, crash out; ~ул гром there was a clap of thunder; ~ул вы́стрел a shot rang out. **2.** to strike up (*a song, etc.*).

гря́н|уться, усь, ешься, *pf.* to crash.

гря|сти́, ду́, дёшь, *impf.* (*obs.*) to approach.

гуа́но, *indecl., n.* guano.

гуа́ш|ь, и, *f.* (*art*) gouache; gouache painting.

губ|а́¹, ы́, pl. ~ы, ~а́м, f. 1. lip; наду́ть ~ы to pout; по ~а́м кому́-н. пома́зать (*coll.*) to raise false hopes in someone; у него́ губа́ не ду́ра (*coll.*) he knows which side his bread is buttered; молоко́ на ~а́х не обсо́хло he is still green. **2.** (*pl.*) pincers.

губ|а́², ы́, pl. ~ы, ~а́м, f. bay, inlet, firth (*in N. Russia*).

губ|а́³, ы́, pl. ~ы, ~а́м, f. tree-fungus.

губ|а́⁴, ы́, pl. ~ы, ~а́м, f. (*hist.*) guba (*judicial division of Muscovite Russia*).

губа́ст|ый (~, ~а), adj. (*coll.*) thick-lipped.

губерна́тор, а, *m.* governor.

губерна́торск|ий, adj. of a governor; (*joc.*) положе́ние ху́же ~ого a critical situation, a tight spot.

губерна́торств|о, а, *n.* governorship.

губерна́торш|а, и, f. (*coll.*) governor's wife.

губе́рни|я, и, f. (*hist.*) guberniya, province; пошла́ писа́ть г. (*joc.*) everything is in commotion.

губе́рн|ский, adj. of ~ия; г. го́род principal town of province.

губи́тел|ь, я, *m.* destroyer.

губи́тел|ьный (~ен, ~ьна), adj. destructive, ruinous; baneful, pernicious.

губ|и́ть, лю́, ~ишь, *impf.* (*of* по~) to destroy; to be the undoing (of); to ruin, spoil.

губ|и́ться, ~ится, *impf.* (*of* по~) to be destroyed; to be wasted.

гу́б|ка¹, ки, f. *dim. of* губа́¹.

гу́бк|а², и, f. sponge; мыть ~ой to sponge.

губн|о́й¹, adj. 1. lip; ~а́я пома́да lipstick. **2.** (*ling.*) labial.

губ|но́й², adj. of ~а́⁴.

губошлёп, а, m. (*coll.*) **1.** mumbler. **2.** lout.

гу́бчат|ый, adj. porous, spongy; ~ое желе́зо sponge iron, porous iron; г. каучу́к foam rubber.

гуверна́нтк|а, и, f. governess.

гуверн|ёр, а, *m.* tutor.

гугено́т, а, *m.* (*hist.*) Huguenot.

гугни́в|ый (~, ~а), adj. (*coll.*) speaking through the nose.

гу-гу́ *only used in phrase* ни г.! not a word!; об э́том ни г.! don't let it go any further!

гуд, а, *m.* (*coll.*) buzzing; drone; hum.

гуде́ни|е, я, *n.* buzzing; drone; hum; honk (*of a motor-car horn, etc.*).

гу|де́ть, жу́, ди́шь, *impf.* **1.** to buzz; to drone; to hum; у меня́ ~де́ло в уша́х (*impers.*) there was a buzzing in my ears. **2.** (*of a factory whistle, steamer's siren, etc.*) to hoot; to honk. **3.** (*coll.*) to ache.

гуд|о́к, ка́, m. 1. hooter, siren, horn, whistle. **2.** hoot(ing); honk; toot; по ~ку́ when the whistle blows. **3.** (*hist.*) rebeck (*three--stringed viol*).

гудро́н, а, *m.* tar.

гудрони́р|овать, ую, *impf. and pf.* to tar.

гудро́н|ный, adj. of ~; ~ное шоссе́ tarred highroad.

гуж, а́, m. 1. tug (*part of harness*); взя́лся за г., не говори́, что не дюж (*prov.*) in for a penny in for a pound. **2.** cartage.

гужев|о́й, adj. 1. adj. of гуж. **2.** cart; ~а́я доро́га cart-track; г. тра́нспорт cartage, animal-drawn transport.

гужо́м, *adv.* **1.** by cartage; возѝть г. to cart. **2.** (*dial.*) in file.

гу́зк|**а, и,** *f.* rump (*of a bird*).

гу́зн|**о, а,** *n.* (*vulg.*) arse, buttocks.

гул, а, *m.* rumble; hum; boom.

гу́л|**кий, (∼ок, ∼ка́, ∼ко), adj. 1.** resonant; echoing. **2.** booming, rumbling.

гулли́в|**ый (∼, ∼а),** *adj.* (*coll.*) gadabout.

гульб|**а́, ы́,** *f.* (*coll.*) idling; revelry.

гу́льбищ|**е, а,** *n.* **1.** (*obs.*) promenade. **2.** (*coll.*) revels, carousal.

гу́льден, а, *m.* **1.** (*hist.*) gulden (*coin*). **2.** guilder (*Dutch unit of currency*).

гульн|**у́ть, у́, ёшь,** *pf.* (*coll.*) to make merry.

гу́л|**я, и,** *m. and f.* (*coll.*) dove, pigeon.

гуля́к|**а, и,** *m. and f.* (*coll.*) idler; flâneur; playboy.

гуля́нк|**а, и,** *f.* (*coll.*) **1.** fête; outdoor party. **2.** feast.

гуля́н|**ье, ья,** *g. pl.* ∼**ий,** *n.* **1.** walking; (going for a) walk. **2.** fête; outdoor party. **3.** (*obs. or dial.*) pleasure-ground.

гуля́|**ть, ю,** *impf.* (*of* по∼) **1.** to walk, stroll; to take a walk, go for a walk; г. по рука́м to pass from hand to hand. **2.** (*impf. only*) (*coll.*) not to be working; (*of land*) to be untilled; мы сего́дня ∼ем we have got the day off today. **3.** (*coll.*) to make merry, have a good time; to carouse, go on the spree. **4.** (c+*i.*; *coll.*) to go (with) (= *have a sexual relationship with*). **5.** (*of a baby*; *coll.*) to lie awake.

гуля́ш, а, *m.* (*cul.*) goulash.

гуля́щ|**ий,** *adj.* (*coll.*) idle; *as noun* ∼**ая, ∼ей,** *f.* streetwalker.

гумани́зм, а, *m.* **1.** humanism. **2.** (*hist.*) the revival of learning.

гумани́ст, а, *m.* humanist.

гуманисти́ческий, *adj.* humanist.

гуманита́рн|**ый,** *adj.* **1.** pertaining to the humanities; ∼ые нау́ки the humanities, the Arts (*as opp. to natural sciences*). **2.** humane.

гума́нность, и, *f.* humanity, humaneness.

гума́н|**ный (∼ен, ∼на),** *adj.* humane.

гуме́нный, *adj.* of гумно́.

гуме́нц|**е, а,** *n.* **1.** *dim. of* гумно́. **2.** (*eccl.*) tonsure.

гу́мка|**ть, ю,** *impf.* (*coll.*) to repeat frequently 'hm!'.

гу́мм|**а, ы,** *f.* (*med.*) gumma (*kind of tumour*).

гу́мми, *indecl.*, *n.* gum.

гуммиара́бик, а, *m.* gum arabic.

гуммигу́т, а, *m.* gamboge.

гуммила́стик, а, *m.* india-rubber.

гумми́р|**овать, ую,** *impf. and pf.* to (stick with) gum.

гуммо́зный, *adj.* (*med.*) gummatous.

гум|**но́, на́,** *pl.* ∼**на, ∼ен** *and* ∼**ён, ∼нам,** *n.* **1.** threshing-floor. **2.** barn.

гу́мус, а, *m.* (*agric.*) humus.

гундо́|**сить, шу, сишь,** *impf.* (*coll.*) to speak through one's nose.

гунн, а, *m.* (*hist.*) Hun.

гу́нтер, а, *m.* hunter (*horse*).

гу́н|**я, и,** *f.* (*obs. or dial.*) old rags.

гури́|**ец, йца,** *m.* Gurian (*inhabitant of western districts of Georgia*).

гури́йк|**а, и,** *f.* Gurian (woman).

гури́йский, *adj.* Gurian.

гу́ри|**я, и,** *f.* houri.

гурма́н, а, *m.* gourmet, epicure.

гурма́нств|**о, а,** *n.* connoisseurship (*of food and drink*).

гурт[1]**, а,** *m.* herd, drove; flock.

гурт[2]**, а,** *m.* **1.** milling (*of a coin*). **2.** frieze.

гуртовщи́к, а́, *m.* **1.** herdsman; drover. **2.** (*obs.*) cattle-dealer.

гурто́м, *adv.* (*coll.*) **1.** wholesale; in bulk. **2.** together; in a body, en masse.

гурьб|**а́, ы́,** *f.* crowd, gang.

гуса́к, а́, *m.* gander.

гуса́р, а, *m.* hussar.

гуса́рский, *adj.* hussar.

гус|**ёк, ька́,** *m.* goose.

гу́с|**ельный,** *adj.* of ∼ли.

гу́сениц|**а, ы,** *f.* **1.** (*zool.*) caterpillar. **2.** (caterpillar) track.

гу́сеничн|**ый,** *adj.* (*zool., tech.*) caterpillar; ∼ая ле́нта (*tech.*) caterpillar track; г. тра́ктор caterpillar tractor; г. ход caterpillar drive.

гус|**ёнок, ёнка,** *pl.* ∼**я́та,** *m.* gosling.

гуси́н|**ый,** *adj.* goose; ∼ая ко́жа goose-flesh; ∼ые ла́пки crow's feet; ∼ое перо́ goose-quill.

гуси́т, а, *m.* (*hist.*) Hussite.

гу́сл|**и, ей,** *no sing.* (*mus.*) psaltery, gusli.

гусля́р, а́-а, *m.* psaltery player.

густе́|**ть, ет,** *impf.* (*of* по∼) to thicken, get thicker, get denser.

гу́|**стить, щу́, сти́шь,** *impf.* to thicken (*trans.*).

гу́сто[1]**,** *adv.* thickly, densely.

гу́сто[2]**,** *as pred.* (*coll.*) there is much, there is plenty; у меня́ де́нег не г. I'm a bit hard up, a bit pushed.

густоволо́сый, *adj.*, thick-haired, shaggy.

густ|**о́й (∼, ∼а́, ∼о), adj. 1.** (*in var. senses*) thick, dense; ∼а́я листва́ thick foliage; г. тума́н dense fog; ∼о́е населе́ние dense population; ∼ые бро́ви bushy eyebrows. **2.** (*of sound or colour*) deep, rich.

густоли́ственный, *adj.* with thick foliage, leafy.

густонаселённый, *adj.* densely populated.

густопсо́вый, *adj.* **1.** a breed of borzoi. **2.** (*fig.*) out-and-out.

густот|**а́, ы́,** *f.* **1.** thickness, density. **2.** (*of sound or colour*) deepness, richness.

гусы́н|**я, и,** *f.* goose.

гусь|ь, я, *pl.* ~и, ~е́й, *m.* goose; как с ~я вода́ like water off a duck's back; хоро́ш гусь! (*iron.*) a fine fellow indeed!

гусько́м, *adv.* in (single) file, in crocodile.

гуся́тин|а, ы, *f.* goose(-meat).

гуся́тник, а, *m.* 1. goose-pen, goose-run. 2. goshawk.

гу́т|а, ы, *f.* (*obs.*) glass-foundry.

гутали́н, а, *m.* shoe-polish.

гути́р|овать, ую, *impf.* (*obs.*) to savour.

гуто́р|ить, ю, ишь, *impf.* (*dial.*) to natter.

гуттапе́рч|а, и, *f.* gutta percha.

гуттапе́рч|евый, *adj. of* ~а.

гуцу́л, а, *m.* Huzul (*Ukrainian inhabitant of Carpathian region*).

гуцу́лк|а, и, *f.* Huzul (woman).

гуцу́льский, *adj.* Huzul.

гу́щ|а, и, *f.* 1. dregs, lees, grounds, sediment; кофе́йная г. coffee grounds. 2. thicket; (*fig.*) thick, centre, heart; в са́мой ~е собы́тий in the thick of things.

гу́ще, *comp. of* густо́й, гу́сто.

гущин|а́, ы́, *f.* (*coll.*) 1. thickness. 2. thicket.

гэ́льский, *adj.* Gaelic.

гю́йс, а, *m.* (*naut.*) jack.

гяу́р, а, *m.* giaour.

Д

да¹, *particle* 1. yes. 2. (*interrog.*) yes?, is that so?, really?, indeed?; он мно́го лет прожива́л в Пари́же. — Да? а я и не знал he lived in Paris for many years. Really? I didn't know. 3. (*emphatic*) why; well; да не мо́жет быть! why, that's impossible!; да в чём де́ло? well, what's it all about? 4. *emphasizes predicate:* когда́-н. да ко́нчится it must end some time; э́то что́-н. да зна́чит there's something behind this. 5. (вот) э́то да! (*coll.*) splendid!, super!

да², *particle* (+*3rd person pres. or fut. of verb*) may, let; да здра́вствует..! long live . . .!

да³, *conj.* 1. (*mainly in conventional phrases*) and; день да ночь day and night; ко́жа да ко́сти skin and bone. 2. (да и, да ещё) and (besides); and what is more; бы́ло за́ по́лночь, да и снег шёл it was past midnight and (what is more) it was snowing; принеси́те мне во́дки, да поскоре́е! bring me some vodka, and quick about it!; он занима́лся, занима́лся, да и провали́лся на экза́мене he studied and studied and then he (went and) failed his exam. 3. да и то́лько and that's all, and no more; она́ ворчи́т, да и то́лько she does nothing but grouse. 4. but; я охо́тно проводи́л бы тебя́, да вре́мени не́ту I would gladly come with you but I haven't the time.

дабы́, *conj.* (*obs.*) in order (to, that).

дава́й(те), *as particle* 1. (+*inf. or 1st plur. of fut. tense*) let's; дава́йте приостано́вимся мину́точку-две let's pause for a minute or two; дава́йте заку́рим let's light up. 2. (+*imp.; coll.*) come on; дава́й, расскажи́ что-н. come on, tell us a story. 3. (+*inf.; coll.*) *expresses inception of action:* а он дава́й бежа́ть he just took to his heels.

да|ва́ть, ю́, ёшь, *impf. of* дать.

да|ва́ться, ю́сь, ёшься, *impf.* (*of* ~ться) 1. *pass. of* дава́ть. 2. to let oneself be caught;

не д. (+*d.*) to dodge, evade. 3. легко́ д. to come easily, naturally; ру́сский язы́к ему́ легко́ даётся Russian comes easily to him.

да́веча, *adv.* (*coll.*) lately, recently.

да́вешний, *adj.* (*coll.*) recent; late.

дави́л|о, а, *n.* press.

дави́льный, *adj.*; д. пресс winepress.

дави́л|ьня, ьни, *g. pl.* ~ен, *f.* winepress.

дави́льщик, а, *m.* presser, treader.

дав|и́ть, лю́, ~ишь, *impf.* 1. (*also* на+*a.*) to press (upon); (*fig.*) to oppress, weigh (upon), lie heavy (on); се́рдце ~ит (*impers.*) (my) heart is heavy. 2. to crush; to trample. 3. to squeeze (*juice out of fruit, etc.*).

дав|и́ться, лю́сь, ~ишься, *impf.* (*of* по~) 1. (+*i. or* от) to choke (with); д. от ка́шля to choke with coughing. 2. (*pf.* у~) (*coll.*) to hang oneself. 3. *pass. of* ~и́ть.

да́вка, и, *f.* (*coll.*) 1. crushing, squeezing. 2. throng, crush.

давле́ни|е, я, *n.* pressure (*also fig.*); под ~ем (+*g.*) under pressure (of); through stress (of).

да́вленый, *adj.* pressed, crushed.

давне́нько, *adv.* (*coll.*) for quite a long time.

да́вн|ий, *adj.* 1. ancient. 2. of long standing; с ~их пор, времён of old, for a long time.

давни́шний, *adj.* (*coll.*) = да́вний.

давно́, *adv.* 1. long ago; он д. у́мер he died long ago; д. бы так (*expressing approval of someone's action*) not before (it was) time. 2. for a long time (*up to and including the present moment*); long since; мы д. живём в дере́вне we have been living in the country for a long time.

давнопроше́дш|ий, *adj.* remote (*in time*); ~ее вре́мя (*gram.*) pluperfect tense.

да́вност|ь, и, *f.* 1. antiquity; remoteness. 2. long standing. 3. (*leg.*) prescription.

давны́м-давно́, *adv.* (*coll.*) very long ago, ages (and ages) ago.

дагерроти́п, а, *m.* daguerrotype.

дагерроти́пный, *adj.* daguerrotype.

дагеста́н|ец, ца, *m.* Dagestani.

дагеста́нк|а, и, *f.* Dagestani (woman).

дагеста́нский, *adj.* Dagestani.

да́же, *particle* even; е́сли д. even if; о́чень д. пло́хо extremely bad.

да́к|ать, аю, *impf.* (*coll.*) to keep saying 'yes'.

дактили́ческий, *adj.* (*lit.*) dactylic.

дактилоло́ги|я, и, *f.* finger-speech.

дактилоско́пи|я, и, *f.* identification by means of finger-prints; taking of finger--prints.

да́ктил|ь, я, *m.* (*lit.*) dactyl.

дала́й-ла́м|а, ы, *m.* Dalai Lama.

да́лее, *adv.* further; не д., как вчера́, он был здесь he was here only yesterday; и так д. (*abbr.* и т. д.) and so on, etcetera.

далёк|ий (~, ~а́, ~о́, *and* ~о), *adj.* 1. (*in var. senses*) distant, remote; far(away); д. путь long journey; ~ое про́шлое distant past; д. от и́стины wide of the mark; я ~ от того́, что́бы жела́ть I am far from wishing. 2. (*only with neg.*; *coll.*) clever, bright; она́ не о́чень ~а́ she is not awfully bright.

далеко́ *and* далёко¹, *adv.* 1. far, far off; (от) far (from); д. зайти́ (*fig.*) to go too far, burn one's boats; д. пойти́ (*fig.*) to go far (= *to be a success*). 2. far, by a long way, by much; д. за (*of time*) long after; д. не far from; она́ д. не краса́вица she is far from beautiful.

далеко́ *and* далёко², *as pred.* it is far, it is a long way; (+*d.* до; *fig.*) to be far (from), be much inferior (to); ему́ д. до соверше́нства he is far from perfect.

да́лече, *adv.* (*obs. or dial.*) = далеко́.

дал|ь, и, о ~и, в ~й, *f.* 1. distance; distant prospect. 2. (*coll.*) distant spot. 3. така́я д.! (*coll.*) it is so far, such a long way!

дальневосто́чный, *adj.* Far Eastern.

дальне́йш|ий, *adj.* further, furthest; в ~ем (*i*) in future, henceforth, (*ii*) below, herein--after.

да́льн|ий, *adj.* 1. distant, remote; Д. Восто́к the (Soviet) Far East; ~ее пла́вание long voyage; ~его де́йствия long-range; ~его сле́дования (*of a train*) long-distance. 2. (*of kinship*) distant. 3. без ~их слов without more ado.

дальнобо́йност|ь, и, *f.* (*mil.*) long range.

дальнобо́йный, *adj.* (*mil.*) long-range.

дальнови́дени|е, я, *n.* (*obs.*) television.

дальнови́дност|ь, и, *f.* foresight.

дальнови́д|ный (~ен, ~на), *adj.* far--sighted.

дальнозо́р|кий (~ок, ~ка), *adj.* long--sighted.

дальнозо́ркост|ь, и, *f.* long sight.

дальноме́р, а, *m.* range-finder.

дальноме́рщик, а, *m.* range-finder operator.

да́льност|ь, и, *f.* distance; range; д. полёта снаря́да range of a missile.

дальтони́зм, а, *m.* colour-blindness, Daltonism.

дальто́ник, а, *m.* colour-blind person.

да́льше, *adj. and adv.* 1. *comp. of* далёкий. 2. (*adv.*) farther; ти́ше е́дешь, д. бу́дешь (*prov.*) more haste, less speed; д. не́куда (*coll.*) that's the limit. 3. (*adv.*) further; расска́зывать д. to go on (telling a story); д.! go on! 4. (*adv.*) then, next; они́ не зна́ли, что д. де́лать they did not know what to do next. 5. (*adv.*) longer; ждать д. нельзя́ бы́ло it was impossible to wait any longer.

да́м|а, ы, *f.* 1. lady. 2. partner (*in dancing*). 3. (*cards*) queen.

дама́сск|ий, *adj.*; ~ая сталь Damascus steel.

да́мб|а, ы, *f.* dike.

да́мк|а, и, *f.* king (*at draughts*).

да́м|ский, *adj. of* ~а; ~ская су́мка ladies' handbag; д. кавале́р, д. уго́дник ladies' man.

да́нник, а, *m.* (*hist.*) tributary.

да́нн|ые, ых 1. data; facts, information. 2. qualities, gifts, potentialities. 3. grounds.

да́нн|ый, *p.p.p. of* дать *and adj.* given; present; in question; в д. моме́нт at the present moment, at present; в ~ом слу́чае in this case, in the case in question; ~ая (величина́) (*math.*) datum.

данти́ст, а, *m.* dentist.

дан|ь, и, *f.* 1. (*hist.*) tribute; обложи́ть ~ью to lay under tribute. 2. (*fig.*) tribute; debt; отда́ть д. (+*d.*) to appreciate, recognize.

дар, а, *pl.* ~ы́, *m.* 1. gift, donation; grant. 2. (+*g.*) gift (of); д. сло́ва (*i*) the gift of the gab, (*ii*) speech, ability to speak. 3. (*pl.*) (*eccl.*) the sacraments (*of bread and wine*).

дарвини́зм, а, *m.* Darwinism.

дарвини́ст, а, *m.* Darwinist.

даре́ни|е, я, *n.* donation.

дарён|ый, *adj.* received as a present; ~ому коню́ в зу́бы не смо́трят (*prov.*) one should not look a gift horse in the mouth.

дари́тел|ь, я, *m.* donor.

дар|и́ть, ю́, ~ишь, *impf.* (*of* по~) 1. (+*d.* of person) to give, make a present. 2. (+*a.* of person and *i.*) to favour (with), bestow (upon); д. кого́-н. улы́бкой to bestow a smile upon someone.

дармое́д, а, *m.* (*coll.*) parasite, sponger, scrounger.

дармое́днича|ть, ю, *impf.* (*coll.*) to sponge, scrounge.

дармое́дств|о, а, *n.* (*coll.*) parasitism, sponging, scrounging.

дарова́ни|е, я, *n.* (1. *obs.*) donation, giving. 2. gift, talent.

дар|ова́ть, у́ю, *impf. and pf.* to grant, confer.

даровитост|ь, и, *f.* giftedness.

дарови́т|ый (∼, ∼а), *adj.* gifted, talented.

дарово́й, *adj.* free (of charge), gratuitous.

даровщи́нк|а, и, *f.*; на ∼у (*coll.*) for nothing, for free.

да́ром, *adv.* 1. free (of charge), gratis; э́то вам д. не пройдёт you'll pay for this. 2. in vain, to no purpose; пропа́сть д. to be wasted. 3. *as conj.*; д. что (*coll.*) although.

дароно́сиц|а, ы, *f.* (*eccl.*) pyx.

дарохрани́тельниц|а, ы, *f.* (*eccl.*) tabernacle.

да́рственн|ый, *adj.* 1. (*obs.*) received as a present. 2. confirming a gift; ∼ая на́дпись dedicatory inscription; ∼ая за́пись (*leg.*) settlement, deed.

да́т|а, ы, *f.* date.

да́тельный, *adj.* (*gram.*) dative.

дати́р|овать, ую, *impf. and pf.* to date (= (*i*) *affix a date to*, (*ii*) *establish the date of*).

да́тский, *adj.* Danish.

датча́н|ин, ина, *pl.* ∼e, ∼, *m.* Dane.

датча́нк|а, и, *f.* Danish woman.

дать, дам, дашь, даст, дади́м, дади́те, даду́т, *past* дал, дала́, да́ло, да́ли, *pf.* (*of* дава́ть) 1. to give; д. взаймы́ to lend (*money*); д. на во́дку, на чай to tip; д. обе́д to give a dinner; д. уро́ки to give lessons; д. показа́ния to testify, depose. 2. to give, administer; д. лека́рство to give medicine; д. кому́-н. пощёчину (*coll.*) to box someone's ears. 3. (по+*d.*, в+*a.*; *coll.*) to give (it); to hit; д. кому́-н. по́ уху to clip someone on the ear-hole; я те дам! (*coll.*; *expressing vague threat*) I'll give you what-for!, I'll teach you! 4. (*fig.*) to give; д. кля́тву to take an oath; д. нача́ло (+*d.*) to give rise (to); д. сло́во to pledge one's word; д. себе́ труд (+*inf.*) to put oneself to the trouble (of). 5. (*fig.*) to give, grant; д. во́лю (+*d.*) to give (free) rein (to), give vent (to); д. газ (*coll.*) to open the throttle; д. доро́гу (+*d.*) to make way (for); д. но́гу (*aeron.*) to give (it) rudder; не д. поко́я (+*d.*) to give no peace; д. кому́-н. сло́во to give someone the floor (*at a meeting*); д. ход (+*d.*) to set in motion, get going; д. ход кому́-н. (*coll.*) to help someone on, give someone a leg-up. 6. +*certain nouns expresses action related to meaning of noun*: д. залп to fire a volley; д. звоно́к to ring (*a bell*); д. отбо́й to ring off (*on telephone*); д. отпо́р (+*d.*) to repulse; д. течь to spring a leak; д. тре́щину to crack. 7. (+*inf.*) to let; д. поня́ть to give to understand; д. себя́ знать, д. себя́ почу́вствовать to make oneself (itself) felt; да́йте ему́ говори́ть let

him speak. 8. дай+*1st person of fut. tense expresses decision to take some action*: дай вы́купаюсь I think I'll take a bath. 9. ни д. ни взять (*i*) exactly the same, neither more nor less, (*ii*) as like as two peas.

да́ться, да́мся, да́шься, *etc.*, *past* да́лся, дала́сь, *pf.* 1. *pf. of* дава́ться. 2. (+*d.*) to have become an obsession (with).

да́ч|а¹, и, *f.* 1. giving. 2. helping, portion.

да́ч|а², и, *f.* 1. dacha (*holiday cottage in the country in environs of city or large town*). 2. быть на ∼e to be in the country; пое́хать на ∼у to go to the country.

да́ч|а³, и, *f.* (*forestry*) (piece of) woodland.

дачевладе́л|ец, ьца, *m.* owner of a dacha.

дачевладе́л|ица, ицы, *f. of* ∼ец.

да́чник, а, *m.* (holiday) visitor (in the country).

да́ч|ный, *adj.* о, ∼а²; д. о́тдых country holiday; д. по́езд suburban train.

дашна́к, а, *m.* (*hist.*) Dashnak (*member of Armenian nationalist movement*).

дая́ни|е, я, *n.* (*rhet.*; *obs. or iron.*) donation, contribution.

два (*f.* две), двух, двум, двумя́, о двух, *num.* two; два-три, две-три two or three, a couple; ни д. ни полтора́ (*coll.*) neither one thing nor another; в двух слова́х briefly, in short; в д. счёта in no time, in two ticks; в двух шага́х a short step away; ка́ждые д. дня every other day, on alternate days.

двадцати- twenty-.

двадцатигра́нник, а, *m.* (*math.*) icosahedron.

двадцатиле́ти|е, я, *n.* 1. period of twenty years. 2. twentieth anniversary.

двадцатиле́тний, *adj.* 1. twenty-year, of twenty years. 2. twenty-year-old.

двадцатипятиле́ти|е, я, *n.* 1. period of twenty-five years. 2. twenty-fifth anniversary.

двадца́т|ый, *adj.* twentieth; одна́ ∼ая a twentieth; ∼ое января́ the twentieth of January; ∼ые го́ды the twenties.

два́дцат|ь, и, *i.* ью, *num.* twenty; д. оди́н, *etc.*, twenty-one, *etc.*; д. одно́ (*card-game*) vingt-et-un.

два́дцатью, *adv.* twenty times.

два́жды, *adv.* twice; я́сно как д. два четы́ре as plain as a pikestaff.

дванадеся́тый и двунадеся́тый, *adj.*; д. пра́здник (*eccl.*) major festival (*each of the twelve major festivals of the Orthodox Church*).

двенадцатипе́рстн|ый, *adj.*; ∼ая кишка́ (*anat.*) duodenum.

двенадцатисло́жный, *adj.* dodecasyllabic.

двена́дцатый, *adj.* twelfth.

двена́дцат|ь, и, *adj.* twelve.

двер|но́й, *adj.* of ∼ь; д. проём doorway; ∼на́я ру́чка door-handle.

две́р|ца, ы, *g. pl.* **~ец,** *f.* door (*of car, cupboard, etc.*).

двер|ь, и, о ~и, в ~й, *pl.* **~и, ~ей,** *i.* **~я́ми** *and* **~ьми́,** *f.* door; **в ~я́х** in the doorway; **у ~е́й** close at hand; **при закры́тых ~я́х** behind closed doors, in camera.

две́сти, двухсо́т, двумста́м, двумяста́ми, о двухста́х, *num.* two hundred.

дви́гател|ь, я, *m.* motor, engine; (*fig.*) mover, motive force.

дви́гательн|ый, *adj.* **1.** motive; **~ая си́ла** moving force, impetus. **2.** (*anat.*) motor.

дви́га|ть, ю *and* **дви́жу,** *impf.* (*of* **дви́нуть**) **1.** (**~ю**) to move. **2.** (**~ю**) (**+** *i.*) to move (*part of the body*); to make a movement (*of*). **3.** (**дви́жу**) to set in motion, get going (*also fig.*); **д. вперёд** (*fig.*) to advance, further.

дви́га|ться, юсь *and* **дви́жусь** *impf.* (*of* **дви́нуться**) **1.** to move (*intrans.*); **д. вперёд** to advance (*also fig.*). **2.** to start, get going. **3.** *pass. of* **~ть.**

движе́ни|е, я, *n.* **1.** (*in var. senses*) movement; motion; **д. вперёд** forward movement, advance; **привести́ в д.** to set in motion. **2.** (*physical*) movement, exercise. **3.** traffic; **д. в одно́м направле́нии** one-way traffic; **пра́вила у́личного ~я** traffic regulations. **4. д. по слу́жбе** promotion, advancement. **5.** impulse.

дви́жимост|ь, и, *f.* movables, chattels; personal property.

дви́жим|ый, *pres. part. pass. of* **дви́гать** *and adj.* **1.** (*part.*) moved, prompted, actuated. **2.** (*adj.*) movable; **~ое иму́щество** movable, personal property.

движ|о́к, ка́, *m.* **1.** (*tech.*) slide, runner. **2.** (wooden) shovel. **3.** (*coll.*) (small) engine, motor.

дви́жущ|ий, *pres. part. act. of* **дви́гать** *and adj.;* **~ие си́лы** driving force.

дви́|нуть, ну, нешь, *pf.* **1.** *pf. of* **~гать.** **2.** (*coll.*) to hit, cosh.

дви́|нуться, нусь, нешься, *pf. of* **~гаться.**

дво́е, двои́х, *num.* **1.** (**+** *m. nouns denoting persons, personal pronouns in pl. or nouns used only in pl.*) two; **д. сынове́й** two sons; **нас бы́ло д.** there were two of us; **д. сане́й** two sledges; **д. су́ток** forty-eight hours. **2.** (**+** *nouns denoting objects usually found in pairs*) two pairs; **д. глаз** two pairs of eyes; **д. чуло́к** two pairs of stockings; **на свои́х (на) двои́х** on Shanks's pony.

двебо́рь|е, я, *n.* (*sport*) biathlon.

двебра́чи|е, я, *n.* bigamy.

двевла́сти|е, я, *n.* diarchy.

дведу́ши|е, я, *n.* duplicity.

дведу́ш|ный (~ен, ~на), *adj.* two-faced.

двеже́н|ец, ца, *m.* bigamist (*of a man*).

двежёнств|о, а, *n.* bigamy (*of man*).

двему́жи|е, я, *n.* bigamy (*of woman*).

двему́жниц|а, ы, *f.* bigamist (*of a woman*).

двоето́чи|е, я, *n.* (*gram.*) colon.

дво|и́ть, ю́, и́шь, *impf.* **1.** to double. **2.** to divide in two. **3.** (*chem.*) to rectify, distil. **4.** to plough a second time.

дво|и́ться, ю́сь, и́шься, *impf.* **1.** to divide in two (*intrans.*). **2.** to appear double; **у него́ ~и́лось в глаза́х** he saw (objects) double.

двои́чн|ый, *adj.* (*math.*) binary; **~ая автомати́ческая вычисли́тельная маши́на** binary computer; **~ая ци́фра** binary digit, bit.

дво́йк|а, и, *f.* **1.** (*figure*) two. **2.** (*coll.*) No. 2 (*bus, tram, etc.*). **3.** 'two' (*out of five, according to marking system used in Russian educational establishments*). **4.** (*cards*) two; **д. треф** two of clubs. **5.** pair-oar (*boat*).

двойни́к, а́, *m.* **1.** (a person's) double. **2.** (*coll.*) twin.

двойн|о́й, *adj.* double, twofold, binary; **д. подборо́док** double chin; **~а́я бухгалте́рия** double-entry book-keeping; **вести́ ~у́ю игру́** to play a double game.

дво́|йня, йни, *g. pl.* **~ен,** *f.* twins.

двойня́шк|а, и, *f.* **1.** (*coll.*) twin. **2.** twin, double (*e.g. two trees growing together*).

дво́йственност|ь, и, *f.* **1.** duality. **2.** duplicity.

дво́йствен|ный (~, ~на), *adj.* **1.** dual; **~ное число́** (*gram.*) dual number. **2.** two-faced. **3.** bipartite.

двойча́тк|а, и, *f.* twin kernel, philippine.

двор, а́, *m.* **1.** yard, court, courtyard. **2.** (peasant) homestead. **3. ско́тный д.** farmyard; **пти́чий д.** poultry-yard. **4. на ~е́** out of doors, outside; **по ~а́м, ко ~а́м** (*obs.*) to one's home, home(wards); **со ~а́** (*obs.*) from home. **5.** (royal) court; **при ~е́** at court. **6. быть ко ~у́** to be (found) suitable; **быть не ко ~у́** not to be wanted.

двор|е́ц, ца́, *m.* palace; **Д. бракосочета́ния** Wedding Palace.

дворе́цк|ий, ого, *m.* butler, major-domo.

дво́рник, а, *m.* **1.** dvornik; caretaker, janitor. **2.** (*coll.*) windscreen-wiper.

дво́рницк|ий, *adj. of* **дво́рник** 1; *as noun* **~ая, ~ой,** *f.* dvornik's lodge.

дво́рничих|а, и, *f.* (*coll.*) **1.** wife of dvornik. **2.** yardwoman.

дво́рн|я, и, *f.* (*collect.*) servants, menials (*before 1861*).

дворня́г|а, и, *f.* (*coll.*) mongrel (dog).

дворня́жк|а, и, *f.* = **дворня́га.**

дворо́в|ый, *adj.* **1.** *adj. of* **двор** 1, 2; **~ые постро́йки** outbuildings, farm buildings; **~ая соба́ка** watch-dog. **2. ~ые лю́ди** house-serfs; *as noun* **д., ~ого,** *m.;* **~ая, ~ой,** *f.* house-serf.

дворцо́вый, *adj. of* **дворе́ц; д. переворо́т** palace revolution.

дворян|и́н, и́на, *pl.* ~е, ~, *m.* nobleman, member of the gentry.

дворя́н|ка, ки, *f. of* дворяни́н.

дворя́нск|ий, *adj.* of the nobility; of the gentry; ~ое зва́ние the rank of gentleman.

дворя́нств|о, a, n. (*collect.*) nobility, gentry.

двою́родный, *adj.* related through grand-parent; д. брат (first) cousin (*male*); д. дя́дя (first) cousin once removed.

двоя́кий, *adj.* double, two-fold.

двоя́ко, *adv.* in two ways.

двояково́гнутый, *adj.* (*phys.*) concavo-con-cave.

двояковы́пуклый, *adj.* (*phys.*) convexo-con-vex.

дву-, двух- bi-, di-, two-, double-.

двубо́ртный, *adj.* double-breasted.

двугла́в|ый, *adj.* two-headed; ~ая мы́шца (*anat.*) biceps; д. орёл double-headed eagle.

двугла́сн|ый, ого, m. (*gram.*) diphthong.

двуго́рбый, *adj.* having two humps.

двугра́нный, *adj.* two-sided; dihedral.

двугри́венн|ый, ого, m. (*coll.*) twenty-kopeck piece.

двудо́льный, *adj.* 1. two-part. 2. (*bot.*) dicotyledonous.

двудо́мный, *adj.* (*bot.*) diclinous.

двужи́льный, *adj.* 1. (*coll.*) strong; hardy, tough. 2. (*tech.*) twin-core.

двузна́чный, *adj.* two-digit.

двузу́бый, *adj.* two-prong, two-tine.

двуко́лк|а, и, f. two-wheeled cart.

двуко́нный, *adj.* two-horse.

двукопы́тный, *adj.* cloven-footed.

двукра́тный, *adj.* twofold, double; reiter-ated.

двукры́л|ый, *adj.* dipterous; *as noun* ~ые, ~ых (*zool.*) Diptera.

двули́к|ий (~, ~a), *adj.* two-faced (*also fig.*).

двули́чи|е, я, n. double-dealing, duplicity.

двули́чност|ь, и, f. duplicity.

двули́ч|ный (~ен, ~на), *adj.* (*fig.*) two-faced; hypocritical.

двунадеся́тый = двана́деся́тый.

двуно́гий, *adj.* two-legged, biped.

двуо́кис|ь, и, f. (*chem.*) dioxide.

двупе́рсти|е, я, n. (*eccl.*) making the sign of the cross with two fingers (*as done by the Old Believers*).

двупе́рст(н)ый, *adj.* (*eccl.*) two-fingered; with two fingers (*of making the sign of the cross*).

двупла́нный, *adj.* two-dimensional.

двупо́лый, *adj.* bisexual.

двупо́ль|е, я, n. (*agric.*) two-field rotation of crops.

двуро́г|ий, *adj.* two-horned; ~ая луна́ crescent moon.

двуру́чный, *adj.* two-handed; two-handled.

двуру́шник, a, m. double-dealer.

двуру́шнича|ть, ю, *impf.* to play a double game.

двуру́шничеств|о, a, n. double dealing.

двусве́тный, *adj.* with two tiers of windows.

двуска́тн|ый, *adj.* with two sloping sur-faces; ~ая кры́ша gable roof.

двусло́жный, *adj.* disyllabic.

двусме́нный, *adj.* in two shifts, two-shift.

двусмы́сленност|ь, и, f. 1. ambiguity. 2. ambiguous expression, double entendre.

двусмы́слен|ный (~, ~на), *adj.* ambiguous.

двуспа́льный, *adj.* double (*of beds*).

двуство́лк|а, и, f. double-barrelled gun.

двуство́льный, *adj.* double-barrelled.

двуство́рчат|ый, *adj.* bivalve; ~ые две́ри folding doors.

двусти́ши|е, я, n. (*lit.*) distich, couplet.

двусто́пный, *adj.* (*lit.*) of two feet (*verse*).

двусторо́нн|ий, *adj.* 1. double-sided; ~ее воспале́ние лёгких double pneumonia. 2. two-way. 3. bilateral; ~ее соглаше́ние bilateral agreement.

двутавро́в|ый, *adj.*; ~ая ба́лка I-beam.

двууглеки́сл|ый, *adj.* (*chem.*) bicarbonate; д. натр, ~ая со́да sodium bicarbonate.

двуутро́бк|а, и, f. (*zool.*) marsupial.

двуха́томный, *adj.* diatomic.

двухвёрстк|а, и, f. (*coll.*) map on scale of two versts to the inch.

двухвёрстный, *adj.* 1. two versts in length. 2. in proportion of two versts to the inch.

двухвесе́льный, *adj.* pair-oar.

двухгоди́чный, *adj.* of two years' duration.

двухгодова́лый, *adj.* two-year-old.

двухдне́вный, *adj.* of two days.

двухдюймо́вый, *adj.* two-inch.

двухкварти́рный, *adj.* containing two flats.

двухколе́йный, *adj.* (*railways*) double-track.

двухколёсный, *adj.* two-wheeled.

двухкра́сочный, *adj.* two-tone.

двухлеме́шный, *adj.*; д. плуг two-share plough.

двухле́тний, *adj.* 1. of two years' duration. 2. two-year-old. 3. (*bot.*) biennial.

двухле́тник, a, m. (*bot.*) biennial.

двухма́чтовый, *adj.* two-masted.

двухме́стн|ый, *adj.* two-seater; ~ая каю́та two-berth cabin.

двухме́сячный, *adj.* 1. of two months' dura-tion. 2. two-month-old. 3. (*of periodicals, etc.*) appearing every two months.

двухмото́рный, *adj.* twin-engined.

двухнеде́льник, a, m. (*coll.*) fortnightly (*magazine, etc.*).

двухнеде́льный, *adj.* 1. of two weeks' dura-tion. 2. two-week-old. 3. (*of publications*) fortnightly.

двухпала́тный, *adj.* (*polit.*) bicameral, two-chamber.

двухпа́лубный, *adj.* (*naut.*) having two decks.

двухпарти́|йный, *adj.* (*polit.*) two-party.

двухря́дный, *adj.* double-row.

двухсо́тенный, *adj.* (*coll.*) costing two hundred roubles.

двухсотле́ти|е, я, *n.* bicentenary.

двухсотле́тний, *adj.* 1. of two hundred years' duration. 2. bicentenary.

двухсо́тый, *adj.* two-hundredth.

двухстепе́нн|ый, *adj.*; ~ые вы́боры indirect elections.

двухсу́точный, *adj.* forty-eight-hour.

двухта́ктный, *adj.* (*tech.*) two-stroke.

двухто́мник, а, *m.* (*coll.*) two-volume book, work.

двухты́сячный, *adj.* 1. two-thousandth. 2. costing two thousand roubles.

двухцве́тный, *adj.* two-coloured.

двухчасово́й, *adj.* 1. two-hour. 2. (*coll.*) two o'clock.

двухъя́русный, *adj.* two-tier(ed).

двухэта́жный, *adj.* two-storeyed; double--deck.

двучле́н, а, *m.* (*math.*) binomial.

двучле́нный, *adj.* (*math.*) binomial.

двуязы́чи|е, я, *n.* bilingualism.

двуязы́ч|ный (~ен, ~на), *adj.* bilingual.

де (*coll.*) *enclitic particle indicating attribution of utterance to another speaker*: они́-де не мо́гут прийти́ (they say) they can't come.

дебаркаде́р, а, *m.* 1. landing-stage. 2. (*obs.*) platform (*on railway station*).

дебати́р|овать, ую, *impf.* to debate.

деба́т|ы, ов, *no sing.* debate.

дебе́л|ый (~, а), *adj.* (*coll.*) plump, corpulent.

де́бет, а, *m.* debit.

дебет|ова́ть, у́ю, *impf. and pf.* to debit.

деби́т, а, *m.* (*tech.*) yield, output (*of oil, etc.*).

дебито́р, а, *m.* debtor.

деблоки́р|овать, ую, *impf. and pf.* (*mil.*) to relieve, raise the blockade (of).

дебо́ш, а, *m.* (*coll.*) riot; uproar, shindy.

дебоши́р, а, *m.* (*coll.*) rowdy, brawler.

дебоши́р|ить, ю, ишь, *impf.* (*coll.*) to kick up a row, create a shindy.

дебоши́рств|о, а, *n.* (*coll.*) rowdyism.

де́бр|и, ей, *no sing.* 1. jungle; thickets. 2. the wilds. 3. (*fig.*) maze, labyrinth; запу́таться в ~ях (+*g.*) to get bogged down in.

дебю́т, а, *m.* 1. début. 2. (*chess*) opening.

дебюта́нт, а, *m.* débutant.

дебюта́нтк|а, и, *f.* débutante.

дебюти́р|овать, ую, *impf. and pf.* to make one's début.

дебю́т|ный, *adj.* of ~; д. спекта́кль (*theatr.*) début, first performance; д. ход (*chess*) opening move.

де́в|а, ы, *f.* 1. (*obs.*) girl, maiden; unmarried girl; ста́рая д. (*coll.*) old maid. 2. Д. (*rel.*) the Virgin. 3. Д. (*astron.*) Virgo.

девалориза́ци|я, и, *f.* debunking.

девальва́ци|я, и, *f.* (*econ.*) devaluation.

дева́|ть, ю 1. *impf. of* деть. 2. (*in past tense* = деть) to put, do (with); куда́ ты ~л письмо́? what have you done with the letter?

дева́|ться, юсь 1. *impf. of* де́ться; она́ не зна́ла, куда́ д. от смуще́ния she did not know where to put herself for embarrassment. 2. (*in past tense* = де́ться) to get to, disappear; куда́ ~лись мои́ часы́? where has my watch got to?

де́вер|ь, я, *pl.* ~ья́, ~е́й *and* ~ьёв (*coll.*) brother-in-law (*husband's brother*).

девиа́ци|я, и, *f.* (*tech.*) deviation.

деви́з, а, *m.* motto; device (*in heraldry*).

деви́з|а, ы, *f.* bill of exchange (*cheque, etc.*) payable in foreign currency.

деви́ц|а, ы, *f.* (*obs.*) unmarried woman, spinster; girl; в ~ах unmarried, before marriage.

деви́ческий = де́вичий.

деви́честв|о, а, *n.* girlhood; spinsterhood.

де́вич|ий, *adj.* girlish; maidenly; ~ья фами́лия maiden name; ~ья па́мять (*joc.*) memory like a sieve; ~ья ко́жа (*pharm.*) althea paste.

деви́чник, а, *m.* (*ethnol.*) party for girls given by a bride on the eve of her wedding.

деви́ч|я, ей, *f.* (*obs.*) maids' room.

де́вк|а, и, *f.* 1. (*coll. and dial.*) girl, wench, lass; засиде́ться в ~ах to remain a long time unmarried; оста́ться в ~ах to become an old maid. 2. (*coll.*) tart, whore.

Девома́тер|ь, и, *f.* (*rel.*) the Virgin Mother.

дево́н, а, *m.* (*geol.*) Devonian period.

дево́нский, *adj.* (*geol.*) Devonian.

де́вочк|а, и, *f.* (*little*) girl.

де́вственник, а, *m.* virgin.

де́вственниц|а, ы, *f.* virgin.

де́вственност|ь, и, *f.* virginity; chastity; обе́т ~и vow of chastity.

де́вствен|ный (~, ~на), *adj.* 1. virgin; ~ная плева́ (*anat.*) hymen. 2. virginal, innocent. 3. (*fig.*) virgin; д. лес virgin forest.

де́вств|о, а, *n.* spinsterhood.

де́вушк|а, и, *f.* 1. (*unmarried*) girl. 2. (*obs.*) maid. 3. (*coll.*; *as mode of address to shopassistant, etc.*) miss.

девча́т|а, ~, *no sing.* (*coll.*) girls.

девчо́нк|а, и, *f.* (*coll.*) 1. slut. 2. kid; slip of a girl.

девчу́рк|а, и, *f.* (*coll.*) little girl.

девчу́шк|а, и, *f.* (*coll.*) little girl.

девяно́ст|о, *g., d., i. and p.* а, *num.* ninety.

девяно́стый, *adj.* ninetieth.

девятерно́й, *adj.* ninefold.

де́вятер|о, ы́х, *num.* 1. (+*m. nouns denoting*

persons, *personal pronouns in pl. or nouns used only in pl.*) nine. **2.** (+*nouns denoting objects usually found in pairs*) nine pairs.

девятидеся́тый (*obs.*) = девяно́стый.

девятикра́тный, *adj.* ninefold.

девятиле́тний, *adj.* **1.** nine-year; of nine years' duration. **2.** nine-year-old.

девятисо́тый, *adj.* nine-hundredth.

девя́тк|а, и, *f.* **1.** (*figure*) nine. **2.** (*coll.*) No. 9 (*bus, tram, etc.*). **3.** (*coll.*) group of nine objects. **4.** (*cards*) nine.

девятна́дцатый, *adj.* nineteenth.

девятна́дцат|ь, и, *num.* nineteen.

девя́тый, *adj.* ninth; д. вал 'the ninth wave' (*symbol of impending danger*).

де́вят|ь, и́, *i.* ью́, *num.* nine.

девятьсо́т, девятисо́т, девятиста́м, девятьюста́ми, о девятиста́х, *num.* nine hundred.

де́вятью, *adv.* nine times.

дегаза́тор, а, *m.* decontaminator.

дегазацио́нн|ый, *adj.* of дегаза́ция; ~ая часть decontamination unit.

дегаза́ци|я, и, *f.* decontamination.

дегази́р|овать, ую, *impf. and pf.* to decontaminate.

дегенера́т, а, *m.* degenerate.

дегенерати́вност|ь, и, *f.* degeneracy.

дегенерати́в|ный (~ен, ~на), *adj.* degenerate.

дегенера́ци|я, и, *f.* degeneration.

дегенери́р|овать, ую, *impf. and pf.* to degenerate.

дёг|оть, тя, *no pl., m.* tar; ло́жка ~тя в бо́чке мёда a fly in the ointment.

деграда́ци|я, и, *f.* degradation.

дегради́р|овать, ую, *impf. and pf.* to become degraded.

дегтя́рн|ый, *adj.* tar; ~ая вода́ (*pharm.*) tar water; ~ое мы́ло coal-tar soap.

дегуста́тор, а, *m.* taster.

дегуста́ци|я, и, *f.* tasting; д. вин wine-tasting.

дегусти́р|овать, ую, *impf. and pf.* to carry out a tasting (of).

дед, а, *m.* **1.** grandfather; (*pl.; fig.*) grandfathers, forefathers. **2.** (*coll.; as mode of address to an old man*) grand-dad, grandpa. **3.** д.-моро́з Father Christmas, Santa Claus.

де́довый, *adj.* **1.** grandfather's. **2.** old-world; old-fashioned.

дедукти́вный, *adj.* deductive.

деду́кци|я, и, *f.* deduction.

дедуци́р|овать, ую, *impf. and pf.* to deduce.

де́душк|а, и, *m.* grandfather.

дееприча́сти|е, я, *n.* (*gram.*) gerund (*e.g.* чита́я, чита́вши).

деепри́част|ный, *adj. of* ~ие.

дееспосо́бност|ь, и, *f.* **1.** energy, activity. **2.** (*leg.*) capability.

дееспосо́б|ный (~ен, ~на), *adj.* **1.** energetic, active. **2.** (*leg.*) capable.

деж|а́, и́, *pl.* ~и, ~е́й, *f.* (*dial.*) vat.

дежу́р|ить, ю, ишь, *impf.* **1.** to be on duty. **2.** to be in constant attendance, not to leave one's post.

дежу́рк|а, и, *f.* **1.** duty room. **2.** pilot flame.

дежу́рн|ый, *adj.* **1.** duty; on duty; д. офице́р (*mil.*) orderly officer; д. пункт (*mil.*) guard-room; ~ая апте́ка chemist's shop open after normal closing hour *or* on holiday. **2.** ~ое блю́до plat du jour. **3.** *as noun* д., ~ого, *m.,* ~ая, ~ой, *f.* man, woman on duty; кто д.? who is on duty?; д. по шко́ле teacher on duty; д. по полётам (*aeron.*) duty pilot. **4.** *as noun* ~ая, ~ой, *f.* duty room.

дежу́рств|о, а, *n.* (being on) duty; расписа́ние ~а rota, (*mil.*) roster; смени́ться с ~а to come off duty, be relieved.

дезабилье́, *indecl., n.* déshabillé.

дезавуи́р|овать, ую, *impf. and pf.* to repudiate, disavow.

дезерти́р, а, *m.* deserter.

дезерти́р|овать, ую, *impf. and pf.* to desert.

дезерти́рств|о, а, *n.* desertion.

дезинсекцио́нн|ый, *adj. of* дезинсе́кция; ~ые сре́дства insecticides.

дезинсе́кци|я, и, *f.* insecticide.

дезинфекцио́нный, *adj. of* дезинфе́кция.

дезинфе́кци|я, и, *f.* disinfection; (*coll.*) disinfectant.

дезинфици́р|овать, ую, *impf. and pf.* to disinfect.

дезинформа́ци|я, и, *f.* misinformation.

дезинформи́р|овать, ую, *impf. and pf.* to misinform.

дезодора́тор, а, *m.* deodorant.

дезодора́ци|я, и, *f.* deodorization.

дезорганиза́ци|я, и, *f.* disorganization.

дезорганиз|ова́ть, у́ю, *impf. and pf.* to disorganize.

дезориента́ци|я, и, *f.* disorientation.

дезориенти́р|овать, ую, *impf. and pf.* to disorient; to cause to lose one's bearings, confuse.

дезориенти́р|оваться, уюсь, *impf. and pf.* to lose one's bearings.

дей́зм, а, *m.* deism.

дей́ст, а, *m.* deist.

действенност|ь, и, *f.* efficacy; effectiveness.

действен|ный (~, ~на), *adj.* efficacious; effective.

действи|е, я, *n.* **1.** action, operation; activity; ввести́ в д. to bring into operation, bring into force. **2.** functioning (*of a machine etc.*). **3.** effect; action; под ~ем (+*g.*) under the influence (of); не ока́зывать никако́го ~я to have no effect.

4. action (*of a story, etc.*); д. происхо́дит во вре́мя пе́рвой мирово́й войны́ the action takes place during the First World War. 5. act (*of a play*). 6. (*math.*) operation.

действи́тельно, *adv.* really; indeed.

действи́тельност|ь, и, *f.* 1. reality. 2. realities; conditions, life; совреме́нная кита́йская д. present-day conditions in China; в ~и in reality, in fact. 3. validity (*of a document*). 4. efficacy (*of a medicine, etc.*).

действи́тел|ьный (~ен, ~ьна), *adj.* 1. real, actual; true, authentic; ~ьное положе́ние веще́й the true state of affairs; э́то бы́ли его́ ~ьные слова́ these were his actual words; ~ьная слу́жба (*mil.*) active service; ~ьное число́ (*math.*) real number; д. член Акаде́мии нау́к (full) member of the Academy of Sciences. 2. valid; удостове-ре́ние ~ьно на шесть ме́сяцев the licence is valid for six months. 3. efficacious (*of a medicine, etc.*). 4. (*tech.*) effective. 5. д. зало́г (*gram.*) active voice.

действ|овать, ую, *impf.* 1. (*impf. only*) to act; to work, function; to operate; телефо́н не ~ует the telephone is not working, is out of order; ~ует ли у больно́го кише́чник? are the patient's bowels open? 2. (*pf.* по~) (на+*a.*) to affect, have an effect (upon), act (upon); лека́рство ~ует the medicine is taking effect; д. кому́-н. на не́рвы to get on someone's nerves. 3. (*impf. only*) (+*i.*; *coll.*) to work, operate; to use; д. локтя́ми to use one's elbows.

де́йствующ|ий, *pres. part. act.* of де́йствовать and *adj.*; ~ая а́рмия army in the field; д. вулка́н active volcano; ~ее лицо́ (*i*) (*theatr., lit.*) character, (*ii*) active participant; ~ие ли́ца (*theatr.*) dramatis personae.

дека~ deca~.

де́к|а, и, *f.* (*mus.*) sounding-board.

декабри́ст, а, *m.* (*hist.*) Decembrist.

декабри́ст|ский, *adj.* of ~.

дека́бр|ь, я́, *m.* December.

дека́брь|ский, *adj.* of ~.

дека́д|а, ы, *f.* 1. ten-day period. 2. (ten--day) festival; д. молда́вской литерату́ры и иску́сства (Ten-day) Festival of Moldavian Literature and Art.

декада́нс, а, *m.* decadence.

декаде́нт, а, *m.* decadent.

декаде́нтский, *adj.* decadent.

декаде́нтств|о, а, *n.* decadence.

дека́дник, а, *m.* (*polit.*) ten-day campaign.

дека́д|ный, *adj.* of ~а.

декали́тр, а, *m.* decalitre.

декальки́р|овать, ую, *impf. and pf.* (*art*) to transfer.

декалькома́ни|я, и, *f.* transfer-making; transfer (*of a design on to glass, pottery, etc.*).

декаме́тр, а, *m.* decametre.

дека́н, а, *m.* dean (*of university*).

декана́т, а, *m.* 1. office of dean (*of university*). 2. dean's office (*building*).

дека́нств|о, а, *n.* (*of university*) duties of dean, deanship.

декатир|ова́ть, у́ю, *impf. and pf.* (*text.*) to sponge (*woollen cloth, to prevent shrinking*).

дека́эдр, а, *m.* (*math.*) decahedron.

деквалифика́ци|я, и, *f.* loss of professional skill.

де́кел|ь, я, *m.* (*typ.*) tympan.

деклама́тор, а, *m.* reciter, declaimer.

деклама́ци|я, и, *f.* recitation, declamation.

деклами́р|овать, ую, *impf.* (*of* про~) 1. to recite, declaim. 2. (*pejor.*) to rant.

деклара́тивност|ь, и, *f.* (*pejor.*) tendency to make pronouncements for effect, pretentiousness.

деклара́ти́в|ный (~ен, ~на), *adj.* 1. declaratory; solemn. 2. (*pejor.*) made for effect, pretentious.

деклара́ци|я, и, *f.* declaration.

деклари́р|овать, ую, *impf. and pf.* to declare, proclaim.

декласси́рованный, *adj.* déclassé.

декови́льк|а, и, *f.* (*tech.*) tub (*on colliery rail-way, etc.*).

деко́кт, а, *m.* (*med.*; *obs.*) decoction.

декольте́, *indecl.*, *n.* décolleté (*also as adj.*); décolletage.

декольтиро́ванный, *adj.* 1. décolleté. 2. bare(d).

декорати́в|ный (~ен, ~на), *adj.* decorative, ornamental.

декора́тор, а, *m.* decorator; scene-painter.

декора́ци|я, и, *f.* 1. scenery, décor. 2. (*fig.*) window-dressing.

декори́р|овать, ую, *impf. and pf.* to decorate.

деко́рум, а, *m.* decorum.

декре́т, а, *m.* decree.

декрети́р|овать, ую, *impf. and pf.* to decree.

декре́т|ный, *adj.* of ~; д. о́тпуск maternity leave.

декстри́н, а, *m.* (*chem.*) dextrine.

де́ланност|ь, и, *f.* artificiality; affectation.

де́ланный, *p.p.p.* of де́лать and *adj.* artificial, forced, affected.

де́ла|ть, ю, *impf.* (*of* с~) 1. to make (= to construct, produce). 2. to make (= to cause to become); д. кого́-н. несча́стным to make someone unhappy; д. из кого́-н. посме́шище to make a laughing-stock of someone. 3. to do; д. не́чего there is nothing for it, it can't be helped; от не́чего д. for want of anything better to do; д. под себя́ to foul *or* wet one's bed. 4. (+*var. nouns*) to make, do, give; д. вид to pretend, feign; д. вы́воды to draw conclusions; д. вы́говор (+*d.*) to reprimand; д. гла́зки

(+*d*.; *coll.*) to make eyes (at); д. докла́д to give a report; д. комплиме́нт (+*d*.) to pay a compliment; д. предложе́ние (+*d*.) to propose (*marriage*) (to); д. уси́лия to make an effort; д. честь (+*d*.) (*i*) to honour, (*ii*) to do credit. **5.** (*of distance covered*) to do, make; д. два́дцать узло́в (*naut.*) to make twenty knots.

де́ла|ться, юсь, *impf.* (*of* с~) **1.** to become, get, grow. **2.** to happen; что там ~ется? what is going on?; что с ней ~ется? what is the matter with her? **3.** (*coll.*) to break out, appear.

делега́т, а, *m.* delegate.

делега́т|ский, *adj. of* ~.

делега́ци|я, и, *f.* delegation; group.

делеги́р|овать, ую, *impf. and pf.* to delegate.

делёж, а́, *m.* sharing, division; partition.

делёж|ка, ки, *f.* (*coll.*) = ~.

деле́ни|е, я, *n.* **1.** (*in var. senses*) division; д. кле́ток (*biol.*) cell-fission; знак ~я (*math.*) division sign. **2.** (*on graduated scale*) point, degree, unit.

дел|е́ц, ьца́, *m.* (*pejor.*) smart operator, person on the make.

деликате́с, а, *m.* dainty; delicacy.

деликатнича|ть, ю, *impf.* (*coll.*) to be over-nice; (с+*i*.) to treat unnecessarily softly, be too soft with someone.

деликатност|ь, и, *f.* (*in var. senses*) delicacy.

деликат|ный (~ен, ~на), *adj.* (*in var. senses*) delicate.

дели́м|ое, ого, *n.* (*math.*) dividend.

дели́мост|ь, и, *f.* divisibility.

дели́тел|ь, я, *m.* divisor.

дел|и́ть, ю́, ~ишь, *impf.* **1.** (*pf.* раз~) to divide; д. по́ровну to divide into equal parts; д. шесть на́ три to divide six by three. **2.** (*pf.* по~) (с+*i*.) to share (with); д. с кем-н. го́ре и ра́дость to share someone's sorrows and joys.

дел|и́ться, ю́сь, ~ишься, *impf.* **1.** (*pf.* раз~) (на+*a*.) to divide (into). **2.** (*impf. only*) (на+*a*.) to be divisible (by). **3.** (*pf.* по~) (+*i*., с+*i*.) to share (with); to communicate (to), impart (to); д. куско́м хле́ба с кем-н. to share a crust of bread with someone; д. ве́стью с кем-н. to impart news to someone; д. впечатле́ниями с кем-н. to compare notes with someone.

дел|о, а, *pl.* ~а́, ~, ~а́м, *n.* **1.** business, affair(s); ме́жду ~ом (*coll.*) at odd moments, between times; по ~у, по ~а́м on business; э́то моё д. that is my affair; име́ть д. (с+*i*.) to have to do (with), deal (with); не вме́шивайтесь не в своё д. mind your own business; как (ва́ши) ~а́? how are things going (with you)?, how are you getting on?; за чем д. ста́ло? what's holding things up?; привести́ свои́ ~а́ в поря́-

док to put one's affairs in order; без ~а не входи́ть no entry except on business; таки́е-то ~а́! (*coll.*) so that's how it is!; д. в шля́пе (*coll.*) it's in the bag; говори́ть д. to talk sense; вот э́то д.! (*coll.*) now you're talking!; д. за ва́ми it's up to you; како́е мне до э́того д.? what has this to do with me?; что тебе́ за д.? what does it matter to you?; пе́рвым ~ом in the first instance, first of all. **2.** cause; д. ми́ра the cause of peace; э́то д. его́ жи́зни it's his life's work. **3.** (+*adj*.) occupation; (*obs.*) business, concern; вое́нное д. soldiering; military science; го́рное д. mining. **4.** matter; point; д. вку́са matter of taste; д. привы́чки matter of habit; д. че́сти point of honour; д. в том, что... the point is that...; в то́м-то и д. that's (just) the point; не в э́том д. that's not the point; совсе́м друго́е д. quite another matter; д. идёт о (+*p*.) it is a matter of . . . **5.** fact, deed; thing; на са́мом ~е in actual fact, as a matter of fact; и на слова́х и на ~е in word and deed; на слова́х..., на ~е же in theory, nominally . . . but actually; в са́мом ~е really, indeed. **6.** (*leg.*) case; cause; вести́ д. to plead a cause; возбуди́ть д. (про́тив) to bring an action (against), institute proceedings (against). **7.** file, dossier; ли́чное д. personal file; приложи́ть к ~у to file. **8.** battle, fighting. **9.** *idiomatic phrases*: то и д. continually, time and again; то ли д. (*coll.*) what a difference (*how much better*).

делови́тост|ь, и, *f.* business-like character, efficiency.

делови́т|ый (~, ~а), *adj.* business-like, efficient.

делов|о́й, *adj.* **1.** business; work; ~о́е письмо́ business letter; ~а́я пое́здка business trip; ~о́е вре́мя working time. **2.** business-like.

делопроизводи́тел|ь, я, *m.* chief clerk; д. шко́лы school secretary.

делопроизво́дств|о, а, *n.* office work, clerical work; record keeping.

де́льн|ый, *adj.* **1.** business-like, efficient. **2.** sensible, practical; ~ое предложе́ние sensible suggestion.

де́льт|а, ы, *f.* delta.

дельтапла́н, а, *m.* hang-glider.

дельтапланери́зм, а, *m.* hang-gliding.

дельтови́дн|ый, *adj.* delta-shaped; д. самолёт delta-wing aircraft; ~ая мы́шца (*anat.*) deltoid muscle.

дельфи́н, а, *m.* dolphin.

деля́г|а, и, *m.* **1.** (*coll.*) person pursuing his own interests. **2.** (*obs.*) good worker.

деля́нк|а, и, *f.* plot (of land); piece (of woodland).

деля́ческий, *adj.* narrow-minded, narrowly pragmatic (*not related to moral or philosophical principle*).

деля́честв|о, а, *n.* narrow-mindedness, narrowly pragmatic attitude.

демаго́г, а, *m.* demagogue.

демагоги́ческий, *adj.* demagogic.

демаго́ги|я, и, *f.* demagogy.

демаркацио́нн|ый, *adj.*; ~ая ли́ния line of demarcation.

демарка́ци|я, и, *f.* demarcation.

демаски́р|овать, ую, *impf. and pf.* (*mil.*) to unmask.

демикото́н, а, *m.* (*text.*) jean.

демилитариза́ци|я, и, *f.* demilitarization.

демилитаризи́р|овать, ую, *impf. and pf.* to demilitarize.

демисезо́нн|ый, *adj.*; ~ое пальто́ light overcoat (*for spring and autumn wear*).

демиу́рг, а, *m.* demiurge, creator.

демобилизацио́нный, *adj.* demobilization.

демобилиза́ци|я, и, *f.* demobilization.

демобилиз|ова́ть, у́ю, *impf. and pf.* to demobilize.

демограф|и́ческий, *adj.* of ~ия; д. взрыв population explosion.

демогра́фи|я, и, *f.* demography.

демокра́т, а, *m.* 1. democrat. 2. plebeian.

демократиза́ци|я, и, *f.* democratization.

демократизи́р|овать, ую, *impf. and pf.* to democratize.

демократи́ческий, *adj.* 1. democratic. 2. plebeian.

демокра́ти|я, и, *f.* democracy; стра́ны наро́дной ~и the People's Democracies. 2. the common people, lower classes.

де́мон, а, *m.* demon.

демони́ческий, *adj.* demonic, demoniacal.

демонстра́нт, а, *m.* (*polit.*) demonstrator.

демонстрати́в|ный (~ен, ~на), *adj.* 1. demonstrative, done for effect. 2. demonstration; ~ная ле́кция demonstration lecture. 3. (*mil.*) feint, decoy.

демонстра́тор, а, *m.* demonstrator.

демонстра́ци|я, и, *f.* 1. (*in var. senses*) demonstration. 2. (public) showing (*of a film*, *etc.*). 3. (*mil.*) feint, manœuvre.

демонстри́р|овать, ую, *impf. and pf.* 1. to demonstrate, make a demonstration. 2. (*pf. also* про~) to show, display; to give a demonstration (of); д. но́вый кинофи́льм to show a new film.

демонта́ж, а, *m.* (*tech.*) dismantling.

демонти́р|овать, ую, *impf. and pf.* (*tech.*) to dismantle.

демрализа́ци|я, и, *f.* demoralization.

деморализ|ова́ть, у́ю, *impf. and pf.* to demoralize.

де́мос, а, *m.* (*hist.*) the people, plebs.

де́мпинг, а, *m.* (*econ.*) dumping.

де́мпфер, а, *m.* (*tech.*) damper; shock absorber.

денатурализа́ци|я и, *f.* (*leg.*) denaturalization.

денатурализ|ова́ть, у́ю, *impf. and pf.* (*leg.*) to denaturalize.

денатура́т, а, *m.* methylated spirits.

денатури́р|овать, ую, *impf. and pf.* (*chem.*) to denature.

денационализа́ци|я, и, *f.* 1. (*polit.*) denationalization. 2. loss *or* suppression of national characteristics.

денационализи́р|овать, ую, *impf. and pf.* (*polit.*) to denationalize.

денацифика́ци|я, и, *f.* denazification.

денацифици́р|овать, ую, *impf. and pf.* to denazify.

де́нди, *indecl.*, *m.* dandy.

дендри́т, а, *m.* (*anat.*, *min.*) dendrite.

дендроло́ги|я, и, *f.* dendrology.

де́нежк|а, и, *f.* 1. (*obs.*) half-kopeck coin. 2. *usu. pl.* (*coll.*) money; пла́кали на́ши ~и that's our money down the drain.

де́нежный, *adj.* 1. monetary; money; д. автома́т cash dispenser; д. знак bank-note; д. перево́д money order; д. ры́нок money-market; д. штраф fine; д. я́щик strong-box. 2. (*coll.*) moneyed; д. челове́к a man of means.

ден|ёк, ька́, *m.*, *dim. of* день.

денни́к, а́, *m.* (*dial.*) loose box.

денни́ц|а, ы, *f.* (*poet.*) 1. dawn. 2. morning star.

де́нно, *adv.*; д. и но́щно day and night.

денно́й, *adj.* (*obs.*) day, daylight.

деномина́ци|я, и, *f.* (*econ.*) denomination.

денонса́ци|я, и, *f.* (*dipl.*) denouncement.

денонси́р|овать, ую, *impf. and pf.* (*dipl.*) to denounce.

денщи́к, а́, *m.* (*mil.*, *obs.*) batman.

день, дня, *m.* 1. day; afternoon; в 4 ч. дня at 4 p.m.; днём in the afternoon; д.-деньско́й all day long; д. рожде́ния birthday; д. откры́тых двере́й open day; д. в д. to the day; д. ото дня with every passing day, day by day; в оди́н прекра́сный д. one fine day; во дни о́ны in those days; изо дня в д. day after day; на друго́й, сле́дующий д. next day; на дню (*obs.*) in the course of the day; на днях (*i*) the other day, (*ii*) one of these days, any day now; не по дням, а по часа́м hourly, fast, rapidly; со дня на́ д. daily, from day to day; че́рез д. every other day, on alternate days. 2. (*pl.*) days (= (*i*) time, period, (*ii*) life); его́ дни сочтены́ his days are numbered.

де́н|ьги, ег, ьгам *or* ьга́м, *sing.* (*coll.*) ~ьга́, ~ьги́, *f.* money; ме́лкие д. small change; нали́чные д. cash, ready money; при ~ьга́х in funds; не при ~ьга́х hard up.

деньжа́т|а, ~, *no sing.* (*coll.*) money, cash.

деньжо́н|ки, ок, *no sing.* (*coll.*) money, cash.

деонтоло́ги|я, и, *f.* medical ethics.

департа́мент, а, *m.* department.

депе́ш|а, и, *f.* **1.** dispatch. **2.** (*obs.*) telegram.

депо́, *indecl.*, *n.* (*railways*) depot; shed, roundhouse; пожа́рное д. fire-station.

депо́в|ец, ца, *m.* engine-shed worker.

депо́вский, *adj.* of депо́.

депози́т, а, *m.* (*fin.*) deposit.

депози́тор, а, *m.* (*fin.*) depositor.

депоне́нт, а, *m.* (*fin.*) depositor.

депони́р|овать, ую, *impf. and pf.* (*fin.*, *leg.*) to deposit.

депресси́вн|ый, *adj.* of депре́ссия; д. пери́од (*econ.*) depression, slump; ~ое состоя́ние (*econ. and psych.*) depression.

депре́сси|я, и, *f.* **1.** (*econ.*) depression, slump. **2.** (*psych.*) depression.

депута́т, а, *m.* deputy; delegate; пала́та ~ов Chamber of Deputies.

депута́ци|я, и, *f.* deputation.

дёр, у, *m.* (за)да́ть ~у (*coll.*) to take to one's heels.

дератиза́ци|я, и, *f.* rodent control.

де́рвиш, а, *m.* dervish.

дёрга|ть, ю, *impf.* (*of* дёрнуть) **1.** to pull, tug; д. кого́-н. за рука́в to tug at someone's sleeve, pluck by the sleeve. **2.** to pull out; д. зу́бы (*i*) to pull out teeth, (*ii*) to have teeth out (*at the dentist's*); д. лён to pull flax. **3.** (*impf. only*) to harass, pester. **4.** (*impf. only*) (*coll.*) to cause to twitch; (*impers.*) to twitch; его́ всего́ ~ло he was twitching all over. **5.** (*impf. only*) (+*i.*; *coll.*) to move sharply, jerk; д. плеча́ми to shrug one's shoulders.

дёрга|ться, юсь, *impf.* (*of* дёрнуться) **1.** *pass. of* ~ть. **2.** to twitch; рот у него́ непреста́нно ~ется his mouth twitches incessantly.

дерга́ч¹, а́, *m.* (*orn.*) landrail, corncrake.

дерга́ч², а́, *m.* (*tech.*) nail extractor.

деревене́|ть, ю, *impf.* (*of* о~) to grow stiff, numb.

дереве́нский, *adj.* **1.** village. **2.** rural, country.

дереве́нщик, а, *m.* (*lit.*) member of 'village prose' school.

дереве́нщин|а, ы, *m. and f.* (*coll.*) (country) bumpkin.

дере́в|ня, ни, *g. pl.* ~е́нь, *f.* **1.** village. **2.** (the) country (*as opp. to the town*).

дере́в|о, а, *pl.* ~ья, ~ьев, *n.* **1.** tree; за ~ьями ле́са не ви́деть not to see the wood for the trees. **2.** (*sing. only*) wood (*as material*).

дерево-земляно́й, *adj.* (*mil.*) earth-and-timber.

деревообде́лочник, а, *m.* woodworker.

деревообде́лочный, *adj.* wood-working.

деревообрабо́тк|а, и, *f.* woodworking.

дереву́шк|а, и, *f.* hamlet.

де́ревц|е, а *and* деревц|о́, а́, *n.* sapling.

деревяни́ст|ый (~, ~а), *adj.* **1.** ligneous. **2.** hard (*of fruit, etc.*).

деревя́нн|ый, *adj.* **1.** wood; wooden. **2.** (*fig.*) wooden; expressionless, dead; dull; ~ое выраже́ние лица́ wooden expression; д. го́лос expressionless voice. **3.** ~ое ма́сло lamp-oil (*low-grade olive oil*).

деревя́шк|а, и, *f.* **1.** piece of wood. **2.** (*coll.*) wooden leg.

держа́в|а, ы, *f.* **1.** (*polit.*) power; вели́кие ~ы the Great Powers. **2.** (*hist.*) orb (*as emblem of monarchy*).

держа́вный, *adj.* **1.** holding supreme power, sovereign. **2.** powerful.

держа́лк|а, и, *f.* **1.** (*coll.*) handle. **2.** umbrella stand. **3.** base (*of standard lamp*).

де́ржаный, *adj.* (*coll.*) used, worn, second-hand.

держа́тел|ь, я, *m.* **1.** (*fin.*) holder. **2.** bracket; socket; holder.

держ|а́ть, у́, ~ишь, *impf.* **1.** to hold; to hold on to; ~и́те во́ра! stop thief! **2.** to hold up, support. **3.** (*in var. senses*) to keep, hold; д. в посте́ли to keep in bed; д. банк (*card-games*) to be banker; д. курс (на+*a.*) to hold course (for), head (for); (*fig.*) to be working (for); д. путь (к, на+*a.*) to head (for), make (for); д. пари́ to bet; д. чью-н. сто́рону to take someone's side; д. язы́к за зуба́ми to hold one's tongue; д. в ку́рсе to keep posted; д. в неве́дении to keep in the dark; д. в плену́ to hold prisoner. **4.** to keep (= *to own, possess*); д. лошаде́й to keep horses. **5.** д. себя́ to behave. **6.** +*certain nouns* = to carry out: д. корректу́ру to read proofs; д. речь to make a speech; д. экза́мен to sit, take an examination.

держ|а́ться, у́сь, ~ишься, *impf.* **1.** (за+*a.*) to hold (on to); ~и́тесь за пери́ла hold on to the banister. **2.** (на+*p.*) to be held up (by), be supported (by); д. на ни́точке to hang by a thread (*also fig.*). **3.** to keep, stay, be; д. вме́сте to stick together; д. в стороне́ to hold aloof. **4.** to hold oneself; (*fig.*) to behave. **5.** to last; to hold together; у неё всё ещё ~ится америка́нский акце́нт she still retains her American accent; э́тот стол у вас е́ле ~ится this table of yours is on its last legs. **6.** to hold out, stand firm; to hold one's ground. **7.** (+*g.*) to keep (to); д. ле́вой стороны́ to keep to the left; д. бе́рега to hug the shore. **8.** (+*g.*) to adhere (to), stick (to); д. те́мы to stick to the subject; д. убежде́ний to have the courage of one's convictions. **9.** то́лько ~и́сь! (*interj.*) and how!

дерза́ни|е, я, *n*. daring.

дерз|а́ть, а́ю, *impf*. (*of* ~ну́ть) to dare.

дерз|и́ть, (у́), и́шь, *impf*. (*of* на~) (+*d.*; *coll.*) to be impertinent (to), cheek.

де́рз|кий (~ок, ~ка́, ~ко), *adj*. 1. impertinent, cheeky. 2. daring, audacious.

дерзнове́ни|е, я, *n*. (*obs.*) audacity.

дерзнове́н|ный (~ен, ~на), *adj*. 1. (*obs.*) impertinent, insolent. 2. daring, audacious.

дерзн|у́ть, у́, ёшь, *pf. of* дерза́ть.

де́рзост|ный (~ен, ~на), *adj*. (*obs.*) = де́рзкий.

де́рзост|ь, и, *f*. 1. impertinence; cheek; rudeness; говори́ть ~и to be impertinent, cheeky, rude. 2. daring, audacity.

дерива́т, а, *m*. (*tech.*) derivative.

дерива́ци|я, и, *f*. 1. (*mil.*) drift. 2. (*math.*) derivation. 3. canalization.

дермати́н, а, *m*. leatherette.

дермати́т, а, *m*. dermatitis.

дермато́лог, а, *m*. dermatologist.

дерматоло́ги|я, и, *f*. dermatology.

дёрн, а, *m*. turf.

дерни́н|а, ы, *f*. (a) turf, sod.

дерни́ст|ый (~, ~а), *adj*. turfy.

дерн|ова́ть, у́ю, *impf*. to cover with turf; to make a turf edging round.

дерно́вый, *adj. of* дёрн.

дёрн|уть, у, ешь, *pf*. 1. *pf. of* дёргать; чёрт ~ет (~ул); нелёгкая ~ет (~ула) *or* (*impers.*) ~ет (~уло) кого́-н. (+*inf.*; *coll.*) to be possessed (to do something); чёрт меня́ ~ул дать сло́во I don't know what possessed me to promise. 2. to get going, get cracking. 3. (*coll.*) to go off. 4. (*coll.*) to drink up; to take a swig. 5. (*coll.*) to start vigorously to do something; д. плясову́ю to strike up a (dance) tune.

дёрн|уться, усь, ешься, *pf*. (*of* дёргаться) to start up (with a jerk), to dart.

дер|у́, ёшь, *see* драть.

дерьм|о́, а́, *n*. (*vulg.*) dung, muck (*also fig.*).

дерю́г|а, и, *f*. sackcloth, sacking.

дерю́жный, *adj*. sackcloth.

деря́бн|уть, у, ешь, *pf*. (*sl.*) 1. to make (= *to acquire by sharp practice*). 2. to drink up.

деса́нт, а, *m*. (*mil.*) 1. (*airborne or amphibious*) landing; д. с бо́ем opposed landing. 2. landing force.

деса́нтный, *adj*. (*mil.*) landing.

дёсенный, *adj*. (*anat.*) gingival.

десе́рт, а, *m*. dessert.

десе́рт|ный, *adj. of* ~; ~ная ло́жка dessert spoon; ~ное вино́ sweet wine.

де́скать, *particle indicating reported speech* (*coll.*): она́, д., ничего́ подо́бного не хоте́ла сказа́ть she said she had not meant anything of the kind.

десн|а́, ы́, *pl*. ~ы, дёсен, *f*. (*anat.*) gum.

десни́ц|а, ы, *f*. (*obs. or poet.*) right hand.

де́спот, а, *m*. despot.

деспоти́зм, а, *m*. despotism.

деспоти́ческий, *adj*. despotic.

деспоти́ч|ный (~ен, ~на), *adj*. despotic.

деспоти́|я, и, *f*. despotism.

дестабилизи́р|овать, ую, *impf. and pf*. (*polit.*) to destabilize.

дест|ь, и, *g. pl*. ~е́й, *f*. quire (*of paper*) (ру́сская д. = 24 sheets; метри́ческая д. = 50 sheets).

десятери́к, а́, *m*. measure *or* object containing ten units.

десятери́чн|ый, *adj*. (*obs.*) tenfold; и ~ое name of letter 'i' in old Russian orthography.

десятерно́й, *adj*. tenfold.

де́сятер|о, ы́х, *num*. 1. (+*m*. nouns denoting persons, personal pronouns in pl. or nouns used only in pl.) ten. 2. (+nouns denoting objects usually found in pairs) ten pairs.

десятибо́рь|е, я, *n*. (*sport*) decathlon.

десятигра́нник, а, *m*. decahedron.

десятизу́б|ый, *adj.*; ~ые ко́шки (*mountaineering*) crampons.

десятикра́тный, *adj*. tenfold.

десятиле́ти|е, я, *n*. 1. decade. 2. tenth anniversary.

десятиле́тк|а, и, *f*. ten-year (secondary) school.

десятиле́тний, *adj*. 1. ten-year, decennial. 2. ten-year-old.

десяти́н|а, ы, *f*. 1. desyatina (*land measure equivalent to 2·7 acres*). 2. tithe.

десятирублёвк|а, и, *f*. (*coll.*) ten-rouble note.

десятисло́жный, *adj*. (*lit.*) decasyllabic.

десятиуго́льник, а, *m*. (*math.*) decagon.

десяти́чн|ый, *adj*. decimal; ~ая дробь decimal fraction.

деся́тка, и, *f*. 1. (*figure*) ten. 2. (*coll.*) No. 10 (*bus, tram, etc.*). 3. (*coll.*) group of ten objects. 4. (*cards*) ten. 5. (*coll.*) ten-rouble note. 6. ten-oared boat.

деся́тник, а, *m*. (*obs.*) foreman.

деся́т|ок, ка, *m*. 1. ten. 2. ten years, decade (*of life*). 3. (*pl.*) (*math.*) tens. 4. (*pl.*) tens. 5. неро́бкого ~ка no coward.

деся́тск|ий, ого, *m*. (*hist.*) peasant policeman.

деся́т|ый, *num*. tenth; расска́зывать из пя́того в ~ое, с пя́того на ~ое to relate inconsequentially; э́то де́ло ~ое (*coll.*) it is of no consequence.

деся́т|ь, и, ью́, *num*. ten.

де́сятью, *adv*. ten times (*in multiplication*).

дет- *abbr. of* де́тский.

детализа́ци|я, и, *f*. working out in detail.

детализи́р|овать, ую *and* детализ|ова́ть, у́ю, *impf. and pf*. to work out in detail.

дета́л|ь, и, *f.* 1. detail. 2. part, component (*of a machine, etc.*).

дета́л|ьный (~ен, ~ьна), *adj.* detailed; minute.

детвор|а́, ы́, *no pl., f.* (*collect.; coll.*) children.

детдо́м, а, *m.* (*abbr. of* де́тский дом) children's home.

детекти́в, а, *m.* 1. detective. 2. detective story.

детекти́вный, *adj.*; д. рома́н detective story.

дете́ктор, а, *m.* (*tech.*) detector; spark indicator.

детёныш, а, *m.* young (*of animals*; whelp, cub, calf, *etc.*).

детермини́зм, а, *m.* determinism.

детермини́ст, а, *m.* determinist.

де́т|и, ~е́й, ~ям, ~ьми́, о ~ях, *sing.* дитя́, children; д. боя́рские, *see* боя́рский.

дети́н|а, ы, *m.* (*coll.*) big fellow, hefty chap.

дети́н|ец, ца, *m.* (*hist.*) citadel.

де́тищ|е, а, *g. pl.* ~, *n.* child, offspring; (*fig.*) child, creation.

де́тный, *adj.* (*coll.*) having children.

детона́тор, а, *m.* (*tech.*) detonator.

детона́ци|я, и, *f.* (*tech.*) detonation.

детони́р|овать¹, ую, *impf.* (*tech.*) to detonate.

детони́р|овать², ую, *impf.* to sing, play out of tune.

детородный, *adj.* genital.

деторожде́ни|е, я, *n.* procreation.

детоуби́йств|о, а, *n.* infanticide (*action*).

детоуби́йц|а, ы, *m. and f.* infanticide (*agent*).

детри́т, а, *m.* 1. (*physiol.*) detritus. 2. vaccine.

детса́д, а, *m.* (*abbr. of* де́тский сад) kindergarten, nursery school.

де́тск|ая, ой, *f.* nursery.

де́тск|ий, *adj.* 1. child's, children's; д. дом children's home; д. сад kindergarten, nursery school; ~ая сме́ртность infantile mortality; ~ая ко́мната (*i*) = ~ая, (*ii*) room for mothers and children (*at railway station, etc.*), (*iii*) juvenile delinquents' room (*at police station*); ~ая коло́ния reformatory (school). 2. childish. 3. ~ое ме́сто (*anat.*) placenta.

де́тскост|ь, и, *f.* childishness.

де́тств|о, а, *n.* childhood; с ~а from childhood, from a child; впада́ть в д. to lapse into dotage.

деть, де́ну, де́нешь, *pf.* (*of* дева́ть) to put, do (with); куда́ ты дел моё перо́? what have you done with my pen?; не знать, куда́ глаза́ д. not to know where to look; э́того никуда́ не де́нешь there's no getting away from it, there's no disputing it.

де́|ться, нусь, нешься, *pf.* (*of* дева́ться) to get to, disappear.

де-фа́кто, *adv.* de facto.

дефе́кт, а, *m.* defect.

дефекти́в|ный (~ен, ~на), *adj.* defective; handicapped; д. ребёнок (mentally) defective *or* (physically) handicapped child.

дефе́ктный, *adj.* imperfect, faulty.

дефекто́лог, а, *m.* specialist on mental defects and physical handicaps (*in children*).

дефектол|оги́ческий, *adj. of* ~о́гия.

дефектоло́ги|я, и, *f.* study of mental defects and physical handicaps (*in connexion with education of blind, spastic, etc., children*).

дефектоско́п, а, *m.* (*tech.*) fault detector.

дефектоскопи́|я, и, *f.* (*tech.*) fault detection.

дефиле́, *indecl., n.* (*mil.*) defile.

дефили́р|овать, ую, *impf.* (*of* про~) to march past, go in procession.

дефини́ци|я, и, *f.* definition.

дефи́с, а, *m.* hyphen.

дефици́т, а, *m.* 1. (*econ.*) deficit. 2. shortage, deficiency; д. в то́пливе fuel shortage.

дефици́т|ный (~ен, ~на), *adj.* 1. (*econ.*) showing a loss. 2. in short supply; scarce.

дефля́ци|я, и, *f.* 1. (*econ.*) deflation. 2. (*geol.*) deflation, wind erosion.

деформа́ци|я, и, *f.* deformation.

деформи́р|овать, ую, *impf. and pf.* to deform; to transform.

деформи́р|оваться, уюсь, *impf. and pf.* to change one's shape; to become deformed.

дехка́н|ин, ина, *pl.* ~е, ~, *m.* peasant (*in Uzbekistan and Tadzhikistan*).

дехка́н|ский, *adj. of* ~ин.

децентрализа́ци|я, и, *f.* decentralization.

децентрализ|ова́ть, у́ю, *impf. and pf.* to decentralize.

деци- deci-.

децили́тр, а, *m.* decilitre.

децима́льный, *adj.* decimal.

дециме́тр, а, *m.* decimetre.

дешеве́|ть, ю, *impf.* (*of* по~) to fall in price, become cheaper.

дешеви́зн|а, ы, *f.* cheapness; low price.

дешев|и́ть, лю́, и́шь, *impf.* (*coll.*) to under-price.

дешёвк|а, и, *f.* 1. low price; купи́ть по ~е to buy cheap. 2. sale at reduced prices; купи́ть на ~е (*coll.*) to buy at a sale. 3. (*fig.*) cheap stuff; worthless object.

деше́вле, *comp. of* дешёвый *or* дёшево; д. па́реной ре́пы dirt-cheap.

дёшево, *adv.* cheap, cheaply; (*fig.*) cheaply, lightly; д. да гни́ло cheap and nasty; д. и серди́то cheap but good; д. отде́латься to get off lightly; э́то вам д. не пройдёт this will cost you dear; д. остри́ть to make cheap jokes; д. сто́ить to be of no account.

дешёв|ый (дёшев, дешева́, дёшево), *adj.* 1. cheap. 2. (*fig.*) cheap; empty, worthless; ~ая острота́ cheap witticism.

дешифри́р|овать, ую, *impf. and pf.* to decipher, decode.

дешифро́вк|а, и, *f.* decipherment, de-ciphering, decoding.

де-ю́ре, *adv.* de jure.

дея́ни|е, я, *n.* (*obs. or rhet.*) act; action; Дея́ния апо́столов the Acts of the Apostles.

де́ятел|ь, я, *m.* agent; госуда́рственный д. statesman; обще́ственный д. public figure; заслу́женный д. иску́сства, нау́ки Honoured Artist, Scientist (*honorific title in U.S.S.R.*).

де́ятельност|ь, и, *f.* **1.** activity, activities; work; обще́ственная д. public work; педагоги́ческая д. educational work, teaching. **2.** (*physiol., psych., etc.*) activity, operation; д. се́рдца operation of the heart.

де́ятел|ьный (~ен, ~ьна), *adj.* active, energetic.

де́|яться, ется, *impf.* (*coll.*) to happen; что там ~ется? what's going on?

джаз, а, *m.* **1.** jazz band. **2.** jazz music.

джаз-ба́нд, а, *m.* jazz band.

джа́зовый, *adj.* jazz.

джем, а, *m.* jam.

дже́мпер, а, *m.* jumper.

джентльме́н, а, *m.* gentleman.

джентльме́нск|ий, *adj.* gentlemanly; ~ое соглаше́ние gentlemen's agreement.

джентльме́нств|о, а, *n.* gentlemanliness.

джерсе́ and джéрси, *indecl., adj.* jersey (*material*).

джиги́т, а, *m.* Dzhigit (*Caucasian horseman*).

джигит|ова́ть, у́ю, *impf.* to engage in trick riding.

джигито́вк|а, и, *f.* trick riding (*originally by Caucasian horsemen*).

джин[1], а, *m.* gin (*liquor*).

джин[2], а, *m.* (*tech.*) (cotton-)gin.

джи́нс|ы, ов, *no sing.* jeans.

джи́у-джи́тсу, *indecl., n.* ju-jutsu.

джо́нк|а, и, *f.* junk (*Chinese sailing vessel*).

джо́ул|ь, я, *g. pl.* ~ей, *m.* (*phys.*) joule.

джу́нгл|и, ей, *no sing., f.* jungle.

джут, а, *m.* jute.

джу́т|овый, *adj. of* ~.

дзот, а, *m.* (*abbr. of* де́рево-земляна́я огнева́я то́чка) (*mil.*) earth-and-timber pill-box.

диабе́т, а, *m.* diabetes.

диабе́тик, а, *n.* diabetic.

диа́гноз, а, *n.* diagnosis.

диагно́ст, а, *m.* diagnostician.

диагно́стик|а, и, *f.* diagnostics.

диагности́р|овать, ую, *impf. and pf.* to diagnose.

диагона́л|ь, и, *f.* diagonal; по ~и diagonally.

диагона́л|ьный (~ен, ~ьна), *adj.* diagonal.

диагра́мм|а, ы, *f.* diagram.

диаде́м|а, ы, *f.* diadem.

диа́кон, а, *m.* = дья́кон.

диакони́сс|а, ы, *f.* deaconess.

диакрити́ческий, *adj.*; д. знак (*ling.*) diacritical mark.

диале́кт, а, *m.* dialect.

диалекта́льный, *adj.* dialectal.

диалекти́зм, а, *m.* dialect word, expression.

диале́ктик, а, *m.* (*philos.*) dialectician.

диале́ктик|а, и, *f.* (*philos.*) dialectics.

диалекти́ческий[1], *adj.* (*philos.*) dialectical.

диалекти́ческий[2], *adj.* (*ling.*) dialectal.

диале́ктный, *adj.* (*ling.*) dialectal.

диалектологи́ческий, *adj.* (*ling.*) dialectological.

диалектоло́ги|я, и, *f.* (*ling.*) dialectology.

диало́г, а, *m.* dialogue.

диалоги́ческий, *adj.* having dialogue form.

диама́нт, а, *m.* (*obs.*) diamond.

диама́т, а, *m.* (*abbr. of* диалекти́ческий материали́зм) dialectical materialism.

диа́метр, а, *m.* diameter.

диаметра́льно, *adv.*; д. противополо́жный diametrically opposite.

диаметра́льный, *adj.* **1.** diametral. **2.** diametrical.

диапазо́н, а, *m.* **1.** (*mus.*) diapason, range. **2.** (*fig.*) range, compass; у него́ о́чень большо́й д. интере́сов he has a very wide range of interests. **3.** (*tech.; fig.*) range; д. волн (*radio*) wave band; д. скоросте́й (*aeron.*) air speed bracket.

диапозити́в, а, *m.* (*phot.*) slide, transparency.

диатри́б|а, ы, *f.* diatribe.

диафи́льм, а, *m.* slide film.

диафра́гм|а, ы, *f.* **1.** diaphragm. **2.** (*phys.*) stop; (*phot.*) aperture.

ди́в|а, ы, *f.* (*obs.*) diva, prima donna.

дива́н[1], а, *m.* divan (*couch*); sofa.

дива́н[2], а, *m.* **1.** (*hist.*) divan (*Turkish Council of State*). **2.** (*lit.*) divan (*Persian name for collection of lyric poetry*).

дива́н|ный, *adj. of* ~[1]; (*obs.*) as noun ~ная, ~ной, *f.* divan-room.

диверса́нт, а, *m.* saboteur.

диве́рси|я, и, *f.* **1.** (*mil.*) diversion. **2.** sabotage.

дивертисме́нт, а, *m.* (*theatr.*) variety show, music-hall entertainment; divertissement (*ballet programme*).

дивиде́нд, а, *m.* dividend.

дивизио́н, а, *m.* (*mil.*) **1.** battalion (*of artillery or cavalry*). **2.** division (*of small warships*).

дивизио́н|ный, *adj.* **1.** *adj. of* диви́зия; д. кома́ндный пункт division command post. **2.** *adj. of* ~.

диви́зи|я, и, *f.* (*mil.*) division.

див|и́ть, лю́, и́шь, *impf.* (*coll.*) to amaze.

див|и́ться, лю́сь, и́шься, *impf.* (*of* по~) (+*d.*) to be surprised, wonder, marvel (at); (на+*a.*) to look upon with wonder.

ди́в|ный (~ен, ~на), *adj.* **1.** amazing; что тут ~ного? what's extraordinary about that? **2.** marvellous, wonderful.

ди́в|о, а, *n.* wonder, marvel; ~у да́ться to wonder, marvel; что за д.! how extraordinary!; на д. marvellously. **2.** *as pred.* it is amazing; не д. it is no wonder.

дидакти́ческий, *adj.* didactic.

дие́з, а, *m.* (*and as indecl. adj.*) (*mus.*) sharp; ре-д. D sharp.

дие́т|а, ы, *f.* diet; посади́ть на ~у to place on a diet; соблюда́ть ~у to keep to a diet.

диете́тик|а, и, *f.* dietetics.

диети́ческий, *adj.* dietetic; д. магази́н health food shop; д. проду́кт dietetic foodstuff.

дизайн, а, *m.* design.

диза́йнер, а, *m.* designer.

ди́зел|ь, я, *m.* diesel engine.

ди́зельный, *adj.* diesel.

дизентери́|я, и, *f.* dysentery.

дика́р|ский, *adj. of* ~ь.

дика́рств|о, а, *n.* shyness.

дика́р|ь, я́, *m.* **1.** savage; (*fig.*) barbarian. **2.** (*fig., coll.*) shy, unsociable person. **3.** (*coll.*) non-official holiday-maker.

ди́к|ий (~, ~а́, ~о), *adj.* **1.** wild (*as opp. to tame, cultivated*); ~ая ко́шка wild cat; ~ое по́ле (*hist.*) steppe frontier region; ~ое я́блоко crab-apple. **2.** savage (= *pertaining to primitive society*); *also as noun* д., ~ого, *m.*). **3.** wild (= *unrestrained*); ~ие кри́ки wild cries; д. восто́рг wild delight. **4.** queer, absurd; fantastic, preposterous, ridiculous; ~ое предложе́ние fantastic suggestion. **5.** shy; unsociable. **6.** (*obs.*) dark-grey. **7.** ~ое мя́со (*med.*) proud flesh. **8.** not officially organized.

ди́к|о¹, *adv.* **1.** *adv. of* ~ий; д. расти́ to grow wild. **2.** in fright; startled; д. озира́ться to look around wildly.

ди́ко², *as pred.* it is absurd, it is ridiculous; д. задава́ть таки́е вопро́сы it is ridiculous to ask such questions.

дикобра́з, а, *m.* porcupine.

дико́вин|а, ы *and* ~ка, ~ки, *f.* (*coll.*) marvel, wonder; э́то мне не в ~(к)у I see nothing remarkable about it.

дико́винный, *adj.* strange, unusual, remarkable.

дикорасту́щий, *adj.* wild.

ди́кост|ь, и, *f.* **1.** wildness; savagery. **2.** shyness; unsociableness. **3.** absurdity, queerness; э́то соверше́нная д. it is quite absurd.

дикта́нт, а, *m.* dictation.

дикта́т, а, *m.* (*polit.*) diktat.

дикта́тор, а, *m.* dictator.

дикта́торский, *adj.* dictatorial.

дикта́торств|о, а, *n.* **1.** dictatorship. **2.** (*coll.*) dictatorial attitude.

диктату́р|а, ы, *f.* dictatorship; д. пролетариа́та dictatorship of the proletariat.

дикт|ова́ть, у́ю, у́ешь, *impf.* (*of* про~) to dictate.

дикто́вк|а, и, *f.* dictation; под чью-н. ~у to someone's dictation; (*fig.*) at someone's bidding.

ди́ктор, а, *m.* (radio-)announcer.

диктофо́н, а, *m.* dictophone.

ди́кци|я, и, *f.* diction; enunciation.

диле́мм|а, ы, *f.* dilemma.

дилета́нт, а, *m.* dilettante, dabbler.

дилета́нтств|о, а, *n.* dilettantism.

дилижа́нс, а, *m.* stage-coach.

динами́зм, а, *m.* dynamism.

дина́мик, а, *m.* loudspeaker; (*audio equipment*) ба́совый д. woofer; высокочасто́тный д. tweeter.

дина́мик|а, и, *f.* **1.** dynamics. **2.** (*fig.*) dynamics; movement, action; в пье́се ма́ло ~и there is little action in the play.

динами́т, а, *m.* dynamite.

динами́тчик, а, *m.* **1.** dynamiter. **2.** (*coll.*) terrorist.

динами́ческий, *adj.* dynamic.

дина́мо, *indecl., n., and* дина́мо-маши́н|а, ы, *f.* dynamo.

дина́р, а, *m.* dinar (*unit of currency in Iraq, Tunisia, and Yugoslavia*).

династи́ческий, *adj.* dynastic.

дина́сти|я, и, *f.* dynasty.

ди́нго, *indecl., m.* (*zool.*) dingo.

диноза́вр, а, *m.* dinosaur.

диора́м|а, ы, *f.* diorama.

дипкурье́р, а, *m.* (*abbr. of* дипломати́ческий курье́р) diplomatic courier.

дипло́м, а, *m.* **1.** diploma; degree (*certificate*). **2.** (*coll.*) degree work, research. **3.** pedigree.

диплома́т, а, *m.* diplomat, diplomatist.

диплома́тик|а, и, *f.* (*palaeog.*) diplomatic(s).

дипломати́ческий, *adj.* diplomatic; д. ко́рпус corps diplomatique; д. курье́р diplomatic courier; Queen's Messenger.

дипломати́ч|ный (~ен, ~на), *adj.* (*fig.*) diplomatic.

диплома́ти|я, и, *f.* diplomacy.

дипломи́рованный, *adj.* graduate; professionally qualified, certificated.

дипло́мник, а, *m.* student engaged on degree thesis.

дипло́м|ный, *adj. of* ~; ~ная рабо́та degree work, degree thesis.

директи́в|а, ы, *f.* directive; instruction.

дире́ктор, а, *pl.* ~а́, *m.* director, manager; д. шко́лы head (master, mistress); principal.

директри́с|а¹, ы, *f.* (*obs.*) head mistress.

директри́с|а², ы, *f.* **1.** (*math.*) directrix. **2.** (*mil.*) д. стрельбы́ base line.

дире́кци|я, и, *f.* management; board (of directors).

дирижа́бл|ь, я, *m.* airship, dirigible.

дирижёр, a, *m.* conductor (*of band or orchestra*).

дирижёр|ский, *adj. of* ~; ~ская па́лочка conductor's baton.

дирижи́р|овать, у́ю, *impf.* (+*i.*; *mus.*) to conduct.

дисгармони́р|овать, ую, *impf.* 1. (*mus.*) to be out of tune. 2. (*fig.*) to clash, jar; to be out of keeping.

дисгармо́ни|я, и, *f.* (*mus. and fig.*) disharmony; discord.

диск, a, *m.* 1. disk; д. номеронабира́теля telephone dial. 2. (*sport*) discus. 3. (cartridge-)drum (*of automatic weapon*).

ди́скант, a, *m.* (*mus.*) treble.

дисквалифика́ци|я, и, *f.* disqualification.

дисквалифици́р|овать, ую, *impf. and pf.* to disqualify.

дискобо́л, a, *m.* discus-thrower.

диск|ова́ть, у́ю, *impf.* (*agric.*) to disc-harrow.

дисковéчер, a, *m.* disco(thèque) (*event*).

ди́сков|ый, *adj.* disc-shaped; ~ая борона́ disc-harrow.

диско́нт, a, *m.* (*fin.*) discount.

дисконти́р|овать, ую, *impf. and pf.* (*fin.*) to discount.

ди́скос, a, *m.* (*eccl.*) paten.

дискотéк|а, и, *f.* disco(thèque) (*place*).

дискотé|чный, *adj. of* ~ка.

дискредити́р|овать, ую, *impf. and pf.* to discredit.

дискримина́ци|я, и, *f.* discrimination.

дискримини́р|овать, ую, *impf. and pf.* to discriminate against; to deprive of equality of rights; д. национа́льные меньшинства́ to discriminate against national minorities.

дискуссио́нн|ый, *adj.* 1. *adj. of* дискуссия; в ~ом поря́дке as a basis for discussion. 2. debatable, open to question.

диску́сси|я, и, *f.* discussion.

дискути́р|овать, ую, *impf. and pf.* (+*a. or* o+*p.*) to discuss.

дислока́ци|я, и, *f.* 1. (*mil.*) stationing, distribution (*of troops*). 2. (*geol.*) displacement. 3. (*med.*) dislocation.

дислоци́р|овать, ую, *impf. and pf.* (*mil.*) to station (*troops*).

диспансéр, a, *m.* (*med.*) clinic, (health) centre (*for treatment and prevention of disease*).

диспансериза́ци|я, и, *f.* clinic system, health centre system.

диспепси|я, и, *f.* dyspepsia.

диспéтчер, a, *m.* controller (*of movement of transport, etc.*); (*aeron.*) flying control officer.

диспéтчер|ский, *adj. of* ~; (*aeron.*) ~ская вы́шка control tower; ~ская слу́жба flying control organization; *as noun* ~ская, ~ской, *f.* controller's office; (*aeron.*) control tower.

ди́спут, a, *m.* disputation, debate; public

defence of dissertation.

диссерта́нт, a, *m.* author of dissertation.

диссерта́ци|я, и, *f.* dissertation, thesis.

диссидéнт, a, *m.* (*rel.*) nonconformist.

диссимиля́ци|я, и, *f.* dissimilation.

диссона́нс, a, *m.* (*mus. and fig.*) dissonance, discord.

диссони́р|овать, ую, *impf.* to strike a discordant note, be discordant.

дистанцио́нн|ый, *adj.*; д. взрыва́тель, ~ая тру́бка time fuse; ~ое управлéние remote control.

диста́нци|я, и, *f.* 1. distance; на большо́й, ма́лой ~и at a great, short distance. 2. (*sport*) distance; сойти́ с ~и to withdraw, scratch. 3. (*mil.*) range. 4. (*railways*) division, region.

дистилли́р|овать, ую, *impf. and pf.* to distil.

дистилля́ци|я, и, *f.* distillation.

дистрофи́|я, и, *f.* (*med.*) dystrophia.

дисципли́н|а, ы, *f.* (*in var. senses*) discipline.

дисциплина́рный, *adj.* disciplinary; д. батальо́н penal battalion.

дисциплини́рова|нный, *p.p.p. of* ~ть *and adj.* disciplined.

дисциплини́р|овать, ую, *impf. and pf.* to discipline.

дитя́, *g. and d.* ~ти, *i.* ~тею, *p.* о ~ти, *pl.* дéти, *n.* child; baby.

дифира́мб, a, *m.* 1. dithyramb. 2. (*fig.*) eulogy; петь ~ы (+*d.*) to sing the praises (of), extol, eulogize.

дифтер|и́йный, *adj. of* ~и́я; diphtheritic.

дифтер|и́т, a, *m.* = ~и́я.

дифтер|и́тный, *adj.* = ~и́йный.

дифтери́|я, и, *f.* diphtheria.

дифто́нг, a, *m.* diphthong.

диффама́ци|я, и, *f.* (*leg.*) defamation, libel.

дифференциа́л, a, *m.* 1. (*math.*) differential. 2. (*tech.*) differential gear.

дифференциа́льн|ый, *adj.* differential; ~ое исчислéние (*math.*) differential calculus.

дифференци́р|овать, ую, *impf. and pf.* to differentiate.

дича́|ть, ю, *impf.* (*of o*~) to run wild, become wild; (*fig.*) to become unsociable.

дичи́н|а, ы, *f.* (*coll.*) game.

дич|и́ться, у́сь, и́шься, *impf.* (+*g.*; *coll.*) to be shy (of); to avoid.

дич|о́к, ка́, *m.* 1. wilding (*wild fruit-bearing plant*). 2. (*fig.*) shy person.

дич|ь, и, *f.* 1. (*collect.*) game; wildfowl. 2. wilderness, wilds. 3. (*coll.*) nonsense; поро́ть д. to talk nonsense.

диэлéктрик, a, *m.* (*phys.*) dielectric, non-conductor.

длан|ь, и, *f.* (*arch. or poet.*) palm (*of hand*).

длин|а́, ы́, *f.* length; в ~у́ longwise, lengthwise: во всю ~у́ at full length; мéры ~ы́ long measures; ∼о́й в шесть ме́тров six metres long.

дли́нно- long-.

длиннов́олновый, *adj.* (*radio*) long-wave.

длиннот|а́, ы́, *pl.* ∼**ы,** *f.* **1.** (*obs. or coll.*) length. **2.** (*pl.*) longueurs, prolixities.

длинну́щий, *adj.* (*coll.*) (terribly) long.

дли́н|ный (∼ен, ∼на́, ∼но), *adj.* long; lengthy; д. рубль (*coll.*) easy money, quick money; у него́ д. язы́к he has a long tongue.

дли́тельност|ь, и, *f.* duration.

дли́тел|ьный (∼ен, ∼ьна), *adj.* long, protracted, long-drawn-out; ∼ьная боле́знь lingering illness.

дл|и́ться, и́тся, *impf.* (*of* про∼) to last.

для, *prep.*+*g.* **1.** for (the sake of); э́то д. тебя́ this is for you. **2.** (*expressing purpose*) for; маши́на д. выка́чивания воды́ machine for pumping out water; я э́то сде́лал то́лько д. ви́ду I only did it for appearances' sake; д. того́, что́бы... in order to . . . **3.** for, to (= *in relation to, in respect of*); д. нас не сто́ит for us it is not worth while; вре́дно д. дете́й bad for children; непроница́емый д. воды́ waterproof. **4.** for, of (= *in relation to a stated norm*); он о́чень высо́к д. свои́х лет he is very tall for his age; э́то поведе́ние типи́чно д. них such behaviour is typical of them.

днева́л|ить, ю, ишь, *impf.* (*coll.*) to be on duty.

дневальн|ый, ого, *m.* (*mil.*) orderly, fatigue man.

днева́ть, дню́ю, дню́ешь, *impf.* to spend the day; д. и ночева́ть to spend all one's time.

дневк|а, и, *f.* day's rest.

дневни́к, а́, *m.* diary, journal; вести́ д. to keep a diary.

дневн|о́й, *adj.* **1.** day; в ∼о́е вре́мя during daylight hours; д. свет daylight; ∼а́я сме́на day shift; д. спекта́кль matinée. **2.** day's, daily; ∼а́я зарпла́та day's pay.

днём, *adv.* **1.** in the day-time, by day. **2.** in the afternoon; сего́дня д. this afternoon.

дни́щ|е, а, *n.* bottom (*of vessel or barrel*).

дно, дна, *pl.* **до́нья, до́ньев,** *n.* **1.** bottom (*of sea, river, etc.*); идти́ ко дну to go to the bottom, sink; золото́е 'д. (*fig.*) gold-mine **2.** bottom (*of vessel*); вверх дном upside down; пить до дна to drink to the dregs; ни дна ему́ ни покры́шки! (*coll.*) bad luck to him!

дноуглуби́тел|ь, я, *m.* dredger.

до, *prep.*+*g.* **1.** (*of place or indicating length, etc.*) to, up to; as far as; от Ленингра́да до Москвы́ from Leningrad to Moscow; дое́хать до Кали́нина to go as far as Kalinin; ю́бка до коле́н knee-length skirt. **2.** (*of time*) to, up to; until, till; до шести́ часо́в till six o'clock; рабо́тать от

девяти́ (часо́в) до шести́ to work from nine (o'clock) to six; до сих пор up to now, till now, hitherto; до тех пор till then, before; до тех пор, пока́ until; до свида́ния! good--bye!, au revoir! **3.** before; до войны́ before the war; до на́шей э́ры (до н. э.) before Christ (B.C.); до того́, как before. **4.** (*expressing degree or limiting point*) to, up to, to the point of; до бо́ли until it hurt(s); до того́..., что to the point where; мы до того́ уста́ли, что и засну́ть не удало́сь we were too tired even to be able to sleep. **5.** under, up to (= *not over, not more than*); де́ти до пяти́ лет children under five, under--fives; зараба́тывать до ты́сячи рубле́й to earn up to a thousand roubles. **6.** about, approximately; у нас в больни́це до двух ты́сяч ко́ек in our hospital there are about two thousand beds. **7.** with regard to, concerning; что до меня́ as far as I am concerned; у меня́ до тебя́ де́ло (*coll.*) I want (to see) you, I want a word with you; не быть охо́тник до not to be keen on, not to like; мне, *etc.*, не до (*coll.*) I, *etc.*, don't feel like, am not in the mood for; мне не до разгово́ра I am not in a mood for talk.

до- *prefix* I. (*of verbs*) **1.** *expresses completion of action*: дочита́ть кни́гу to finish (reading) a book. **2.** *indicates that action is carried to a certain point*: дочита́ть до страни́цы 270 to read as far as page 270. **3.** *expresses supplementary action*: докупи́ть to buy in addition. **4.** (+*reflexive vbs.*) *expresses eventual attainment of object*: дозвони́ться to ring until one gets an answer. **5.** (+*reflexive vbs.*) *expresses continuation of action with injurious consequences*: доигра́ться до беды́ (*coll.*) to carry on until one gets into a mess. II. (*of adjectives*) *indicates priority in chronological sequence* (pre-): довое́нный pre-war; де́ти дошко́льного во́зраста children under school age.

доба́в|ить, лю, ишь, *pf.* (*of* ∼ля́ть) (+*a. or g.*) to add.

доба́вк|а, и, *f.* **1.** addition. **2.** second helping.

добавле́ни|е, я, *n.* addition; appendix, addendum; extra.

добавля́|ть, ю, *impf. of* доба́вить.

доба́вочн|ый, *adj.* additional, supplementary; accessory; ∼ое вре́мя (*sport*) extra time; д. нало́г surtax; ∼ая труба́ (*tech.*) extension pipe.

добега́|ть, ю, *impf. of* добежа́ть.

добега́|ться, юсь, *pf.* (до+*g.*) to run oneself (to the point of); д. до уста́лости to tire oneself out running.

добе|жа́ть, гу́, жи́шь, гу́т, *pf.* (*of* ∼га́ть) (до+*g.*) to run (to, as far as); to reach (*also fig.*).

добела́, *adv.* **1.** to white heat; раскалённый

д. white-hot. **2.** clean, white; чёрного кобеля́ не отмо́ешь д. (*prov.*) the leopard can't change his spots.

добива́|ть, ю, *impf. of* доби́ть.

добива́|ться, юсь, *impf.* **1.** *impf. of* доби́ться. **2.** (+*g.*) to try to get, strive (for), aim (at).

добира́|ть, ю, *impf. of* добра́ть.

добира́|ться, юсь, *impf. of* добра́ться.

до|би́ть, бью́, бьёшь, *pf.* (*of* ~бива́ть) to finish off, do for, deal the final blow (*also in var. senses corresponding to meanings of prefix and simple verb*).

до|би́ться, бью́сь, бьёшься, *pf.* (*of* добива́ться)' (+*g.*) to get, obtain, secure; д. своего́ to get one's way; не д. то́лку от кого́-н. to be unable to get any sense out of someone.

до́блест|ный (~ен, ~на), *adj.* valiant, valorous.

до́блест|ь, и, *f.* valour, prowess; за трудову́ю д. (*honour conferred in U.S.S.R.*) 'For Labour Prowess'.

до|бра́ть, беру́, берёшь, *past* ~бра́л, ~брала́, ~бра́ло, *pf.* (*of* ~бира́ть) **1.** to finish gathering. **2.** (*typ.*) to finish setting up.

до|бра́ться, беру́сь, берёшься, *past* ~бра́лся, ~брала́сь, ~брало́сь, *pf.* (*of* ~бира́ться) **1.** (до+*g.*) to get (to), reach. **2.** (*coll.*) to get, deal with; я до тебя́ ~беру́сь! I'll get you!

добра́чн|ый, *adj.* pre-marital; ~ая фами́лия maiden name.

добре́|сти, ду́, дёшь, *past* ~л, ~ла́, *pf.* (до+ *g.*) to get (to), reach (*slowly or with difficulty*).

добре́|ть¹, ю, ешь, *impf.* (*of* по~) to become kinder.

добре́|ть², ю, ешь, *impf.* (*of* раз~)(*coll.*) to become corpulent, put on weight.

добр|о́¹, а́, *n.* **1.** good; good deed; жела́ю вам ~а́ I wish you well; от ~а́ ~а́ не и́щут let well alone; нет ху́да без ~а́ every cloud has a silver lining; э́то не к ~у́ it is a bad omen, it bodes ill; помина́ть ~о́м to speak well (of), remember kindly. **2.** (*collect.; coll.*) goods, property.

добро́², *particle* (*coll.*) good; all right.

добро́³; д. пожа́ловать! welcome!

добро́⁴, *as conj.* (+бы) it would be a different matter if, there would be some excuse if.

доброво́л|ец, ьца, *m.* volunteer.

доброво́льно, *adv.* voluntarily, of one's own free will.

доброво́л|ьный (~ен, ~ьна), *adj.* voluntary.

доброво́льческий, *adj.* volunteer.

доброде́тел|ь, и, *f.* virtue.

доброде́тел|ьный (~ен, ~ьна), *adj.* virtuous.

добродуши|е, я, *n.* good-nature.

добродуш|ный (~ен, ~на), *adj.* good--natured; genial.

доброжела́тел|ь, я, *m.* well-wisher.

доброжела́тел|ьный (~ен, ~ьна), *adj.* benevolent.

доброка́чествен|ный (~, ~на), *adj.* **1.** of good quality. **2.** (*med.*) benign.

добро́м, *adv.* (*coll.*) of one's own free will, voluntarily.

добронра́в|ный (~ен, ~на), *adj.* (*obs.*) well-behaved.

добропоря́доч|ный (~ен, ~на), *adj.* respectable.

добросерде́ч|ный (~ен, ~на), *adj.* good--hearted.

добросо́вест|ный (~ен, ~на), *adj.* conscientious.

добрососе́дский, *adj.* neighbourly; friendly.

доброт|а́, ы́, *f.* goodness, kindness.

добро́тность|ь, и, *f.* (good) quality; д. сукна́ quality of cloth.

добро́т|ный (~ен, ~на), *adj.* of good, high quality; durable.

доброхо́т, а, *m.* (*obs.*) well-wisher.

доброхо́т|ный (~ен, ~на), *adj.* (*obs.*) **1.** benevolent. **2.** voluntary.

добр|ый (~, ~а́, ~о, ~ы́), *adj.* **1.** (*in var. senses*) good; ~ое и́мя good name; д. конь good horse; д. знако́мый good friend; д. ма́лый decent chap; ~ое у́тро! good morning!; всего́ ~ого! good-bye!, all the best!; д. час! good luck!; по ~у́ по здоро́ву while the going is (was) good. **2.** kind, good; бу́дьте ~ы́ (+*imper.*) please, would you be so kind as to. **3.** (*coll.*) a good (= *fully, no less than*); оста́лось нам идти́ ~ых пяти́ км we had still a good five kilometres to go. **4.** по ~ой во́ле of one's own free will. **5.** чего́ ~ого (*introducing expression of anticipation of unpleasant eventuality*) who knows it may be.

добря́к, а́, *m.* (*coll.*) good-natured person.

добу|ди́ться, жу́сь, ~дишься, *pf.* (*coll.*) to wake, succeed in waking.

добыва́|ть, ю, *impf. of* добы́ть.

добы́тчик, а, *m.* (*coll.*) **1.** getter (*of minerals etc.*). **2.** bread-winner.

до|бы́ть, бу́ду, бу́дешь, *past* ~бы́л, ~была́ ~бы́ло, *pf.* (*of* ~быва́ть) **1.** to get, obtain procure. **2.** to extract, mine, quarry.

добы́ч|а, и, *f.* **1.** extraction (*of minerals*) mining, quarrying. **2.** booty, spoils, loo **3.** (*hunting*) bag; catch (*of fish*). **4.** minera products; output.

дова́рив|ать, аю, *impf. of* довари́ть.

довар|и́ть, ю́, ~ишь, *pf.* (*of* ~ивать) **1.** finish cooking; to do to a turn. **2.** to coo a little longer.

дове́да|ться, юсь, *pf.* (*obs. or coll.*) to fin out by inquiry.

довез|ти́, у́, ёшь, *past* ~, ~ла́, *pf.* (*of* довозить¹) to take (to).

дове́ренност|ь, и, *f.* **1.** warrant, power of attorney; получи́ть де́ньги по ~и to obtain money by proxy. **2.** (*obs.*) trust.

дове́р|енный, *p.p.p. of* ~ить *and adj.* trusted; ~енное лицо́; *also as noun* д., ~енного, *m.* agent, proxy; person empowered to act for someone.

дове́ри|е, я, *n.* trust, confidence; по́льзоваться чьим-н. ~ем to enjoy someone's confidence; поста́вить вопро́с о ~и to call for a vote of confidence.

довери́тел|ь, я, *m.* principal (*person empowering another to act for him*).

довери́тельный, *adj.* **1.** confiding. **2.** (*obs.*) confidential (= *classified; of documents*). **3.** (*obs.*) empowering to act for one.

дове́р|ить, ю, ишь, *pf.* (*of* ~я́ть) (+*d.*) to entrust (to).

дове́р|иться, юсь, ишься, *pf.* (*of* ~я́ться) (+*d.*) to trust (in), confide (in).

до́верху, *adv.* to the top; to the brim.

дове́рчивост|ь, и, *f.* trustfulness, credulity.

дове́рчив|ый (~, ~a), *adj.* trustful, credulous.

доверш|а́ть, а́ю, *impf. of* ~и́ть.

доверше́ни|е, я, *n.* completion, consummation; в д. всего́ to crown all, on top of it all.

доверш|и́ть, у́, и́шь, *pf.* (*of* ~а́ть) to complete.

довер|я́ть, я́ю, *impf.* **1.** *impf. of* ~ить. **2.** (*impf. only*) (+*d.*) to trust, confide (in).

довер|я́ться, я́юсь, *impf. of* ~иться.

дове́с|ок, ка, *m.* makeweight.

дове|сти́, ду́, дёшь, *past* ~л, ~ла́, *pf.* (*of* доводи́ть) **1.** (до+*g.*) to lead (to), take (to), accompany (to). **2.** (до+*g.*) to bring (to); to drive (to), reduce (to); д. до соверше́нства to perfect; д. до сумасше́ствия to drive mad; д. до слёз to reduce to tears; д. до све́дения (+*g.*) to inform, let know, bring to the notice (of).

дове|сти́сь, дётся, *past* ~ло́сь, *pf.* (*of* доводи́ться) (*impers.*+*d.*; *coll.*) to have occasion (to); to manage (to); to happen (to); нам ~ло́сь заста́ть его́ до́ма we happened to catch him in.

довин|ти́ть, чу́, ти́шь, *pf.* (*of* ~чивать) to screw up.

дови́нчива|ть, ю, *impf. of* довинти́ть.

довле́|ть, ет, *impf.* **1.** (*obs.*) to suffice; д. себе́ to be self-sufficient; ~ет дне́ви зло́ба ero sufficient unto the day is the evil thereof. **2.** (над+*i.*; *vulg.*) to dominate, prevail over).

до́вод, а, *m.* argument.

дово|ди́ть, жу́, ~дишь, *impf. of* довести́.

дово|ди́ться, жу́сь, ~дишься, *impf.* **1.** *impf. of* довести́сь. **2.** (+*d. and i.*) to be

related (to as); он ~дится ей племя́нником he is her nephew.

дово́дк|а, и, *f.* (*tech.*) finishing; lapping.

довое́нный, *adj.* pre-war.

дово|зи́ть, жу́, ~зишь, *impf. of* довезти́.

дово|зи́ть², жу́, ~зишь, *pf.* (*coll.*) to finish carrying.

дово́льно¹, *adv.* **1.** enough; *as pred.* it is enough; с нас э́того д. we've had enough of this; д. спо́рить stop arguing. **2.** quite, fairly; rather, pretty; д. хоро́ший фильм quite a good film; д. глу́пый челове́к rather a stupid person.

дово́льно², *adv.* contentedly.

дово́л|ьный (~ен, ~ьна), *adj.* **1.** contented, satisfied; д. вид contented expression. **2.** (+*i.*) content (with), satisfied (with), pleased (with); д. собо́й pleased with oneself, self-satisfied; он не осо́бенно ~ен но́вой рабо́той he does not like his new job very much. **3.** (*obs.*) considerable.

дово́льстви|е, я, *n.* (*mil.*) allowance (*of money, food or clothing*).

дово́льств|о, а, *n.* **1.** content, contentment. **2.** (*coll.*) ease, prosperity.

дово́льств|овать, ую, *impf.* **1.** (*obs.*) to satisfy, make content. **2.** (*mil.*) to supply, maintain.

дово́льств|оваться, уюсь, *impf.* (*of* у~) **1.** (+*i.*) to be content (with), be satisfied (with). **2.** *pass. of* ~овать.

довре́менный, *adj.* (*obs.*) premature.

довы́бор|ы, ов, *no sing.* by-election.

дог, а, *m.* Great Dane.

догад|а́ться, а́юсь, *pf.* (*of* ~ываться) to guess; to have the sense to.

дога́дк|а, и, *f.* **1.** surmise, conjecture; теря́ться в ~ах to be lost in conjecture. **2.** (*coll.*) imagination; прояви́ть ~у to be on the spot.

дога́длив|ый (~, ~a), *adj.* quick-witted, shrewd.

дога́дыва|ться, юсь, *impf.* **1.** *impf. of* догада́ться. **2.** (*impf. only*) to suspect.

догля|де́ть, жу́, ди́шь, *pf.* (*coll.*) **1.** to watch to the end, see through. **2.** to keep an eye out; (за+*i.*) to keep an eye (on).

до́гм|а, ы, *f.* **1.** dogma, dogmatic assertion. **2.** (*pl.*) foundations, bases (*of a theory, intellectual discipline, etc.*).

до́гмат, а, *m.* **1.** (*rel.*) doctrine, dogma; д. непогреши́мости па́пы the doctrine of the infallibility of the Pope. **2.** tenet, foundation; одни́м из ~ов ло́гики явля́ется зако́н тожде́ственности the law of identity is one of the foundations of logic.

догмати́зм, а, *m.* dogmatism (*in general, also in Marxist polit. jargon, as a deviation opp. to revisionism*).

догма́тик, а, *m.* **1.** dogmatic person. **2.**

'dogmatist' (*in Marxist polit. jargon, as opp. to revisionist*).

догмати́ческий, *adj.* dogmatic.

до|гна́ть, гоню́, го́нишь, *past* ~гна́л, ~гна-ла́, ~гна́ло, *pf.* (*of* ~гоня́ть) 1. to catch up (with) (*also fig.*); д. и перегна́ть За́пад (*polit. slogan*) to catch up with and pass the West. 2. (до+*g.*) to drive (to); (*fig., coll.*) to raise (to).

догова́рива|ть, ю, *impf. of* договори́ть.

догова́рива|ться, юсь, *impf.* 1. *impf. of* договори́ться. 2. (*impf. only*) (о+*p.*) to negotiate (about), treat (for); Высо́кие ~ющиеся сто́роны (*dipl.*) the High Contracting Parties.

догово́р, а *and* (*coll.*) до́говор, *pl.* ~а́, *m.* agreement; (*polit.*) treaty, pact; заключи́ть ми́рный д. to conclude a peace treaty.

договорённост|ь, и, *f.* agreement, understanding.

договор|и́ть, ю́, и́шь, *pf.* (*of* догова́ривать) to finish saying; to finish telling.

договор|и́ться, ю́сь, и́шься, *pf.* (*of* догова́риваться) 1. (о+*p.*) to come to an agreement, understanding (about); to arrange. 2. (до+*g.*) to come (to); to talk (to the point of).

догово́рник, а, *m.* (*coll.*) worker under contract for a particular job.

догово́рн|ый, *adj.* 1. agreed; contractual; ~ая цена́ agreed price. 2. fixed by treaty.

догола́, *adv.* stark naked; разде́ться д. to strip to the skin.

догоня́л|ки, ок, *no sing.* (*children's game*) 'he'.

догоня́|ть, ю, *impf. of* догна́ть.

догор|а́ть, а́ю, *impf. of* ~е́ть.

догор|е́ть, ю́, и́шь, *pf.* (*of* ~а́ть) to burn down, burn out.

догружа́|ть, ю, *impf. of* догрузи́ть.

догру|зи́ть, жу́, ~зи́шь, *pf.*(*of* ~жа́ть) 1. to finish loading. 2. to load in addition.

догу́лива|ть, ю, *impf. of* догуля́ть.

догуля́|ть, ю, *pf.* (*of* догу́ливать) (*coll.*) to spend in pleasure (the remainder of); дава́йте ~ем о́тпуск let's make the most of what's left of the holidays.

дода|ва́ть, ю́, ёшь, *impf. of* ~ть.

дода́|ть, м, шь, ст, ди́м, ди́те, ду́т, *past* до́дал, ~ла́, до́дало, *pf.* (*of* ~ва́ть) to make up (the rest of); to pay up.

доде́л|ать, аю, *pf.* (*of* ~ывать) to finish.

доде́лыва|ть, ю, *impf. of* доде́лать.

доду́м|аться, аюсь, *pf.* (*of* ~ываться) (до+ *g.*) to hit (upon) (*afterthought*).

доду́мыва|ться, юсь, *impf. of* доду́маться.

доеда́|ть, ю, *impf. of* дое́сть.

доезжа́|ть, ю, *impf. of* дое́хать.

доезжа́ч|ий, его, *m.* whipper-in.

дое́ни|е, я, *n.* milking.

до|е́сть, е́м, е́шь, е́ст, еди́м, еди́те, едя́ *pf.* (*of* ~еда́ть) to eat up, finish eating.

до|е́хать, е́ду, е́дешь, *pf.* (*of* ~езжа́ть) (до+*g.*) to reach, arrive (at). 2. (*fig., coll.*) to wear out.

дож, а, *m.* (*hist.*) doge.

дожа́рива|ть, ю, *impf. of* дожа́рить.

дожа́р|ить, ю, ишь, *pf.* (*of* ~ивать) to finis roasting, frying; to roast, fry to a turn.

дожд|а́ться, у́сь, ёшься, *past* ~а́лся, ~ала́с ~ало́сь, *pf.* 1. (+*g.*) to wait (for); конца́ спекта́кля to wait until the en of the show. 2. д. того́, что to end u (by); он ~а́лся того́, что ему́ показа́л дверь he ended up by being shown the doo.

дождева́льный, *adj.*; д. аппара́т (*agric.* water-sprinkler.

дождева́ни|е, я, *n.* (*agric.*) irrigation b sprinkling.

дождеви́к, а́, *m.* 1. (*coll.*) raincoat. 2. puf -ball (*Lycoperdon giganteum*).

дождев|о́й, *adj. of* дождь; ~а́я ка́пля rair -drop; ~о́е о́блако rain-cloud, nimbus; ~о пла́тье oilskins.

дождеме́р, а, *m.* rain-gauge.

до́ждик, а, *m.* shower.

дожди́нк|а, и, *f.* (*coll.*) rain-drop.

дожд|и́ть, и́т, *impf.* (*impers.; coll.*) to rain, b raining.

дождли́в|ый (~, ~а), *adj.* rainy.

дожд|ь, я́, *m.* 1. rain (*also fig.*); под ~ём i the rain; ме́лкий д. drizzle; проливно́й д downpour; д. идёт it is raining; д. лье как из ведра́ it is raining cats and dog 2. (*fig.*) rain, hail, cascade; д. искр cascad of sparks; д. руга́тельств torrent of abuse сы́паться ~ём to rain down, cascade.

дожива́|ть, ю, *impf.* 1. *impf. of* дожи́т 2. (*impf. only*) to live out; д. свой век to liv out one's days.

дожида́|ться, юсь, *impf.* (*of* дожда́ться (+*g.*) to wait (for).

дожи́нк|и, ок, *no sing.* (*dial.*) harvest festiva

до|жи́ть, живу́, живёшь, *past* ~жил, ~жил ~жило, *pf.* (*of* ~жива́ть) 1. (до+*g.*) to liv (till); to attain the age (of); она́ ~жила́ д конца́ войны́ she lived to see the end of th war. 2. (до+*g.*) to come (to), be reduce (to); до чего́ мы ~жили! what have w come to! 3. (*coll.*) to stay, spend (the res of); я доживу́ ле́то в Пари́же I shall spen the rest of the summer in Paris.

до́з|а, ы, *f.* dose.

доза́тор, а, *m.* measure, measuring hoppe

до|зва́ться, зову́сь, зовёшься, *past* ~зва́л ся, ~звала́сь, ~зва́ло́сь, *pf.* (*coll.*) to ca until one gets an answer, его́ не ~зовёшьс he never comes when he is called.

дозволе́ни|е, я, *n.* (*obs.*) permission.

дозво́л|енный, *p.p.p. of* ~ить *and adj.* permitted

дозво́л|ить, ю, ишь, *pf.* (*of* ~я́ть) (*obs. or coll.*) to permit, allow.

дозвол|я́ть, я́ю, *impf. of* ~и́ть.

дозвон|и́ться, ю́сь, и́шься, *pf.* (*coll.*) (до+ *g.,* к+*d.*) to ring (*at doorbell, on telephone*) until one gets an answer; to get through (*on telephone*); я не мог к тебе́ д. I rang you but could get no reply, could not get through.

дозву́ковый, *adj.* subsonic.

дози́р|овать, ую, *impf. and pf.* to measure out (in doses).

дозиро́вк|а, и, *f.* dosage.

дозна|ва́ться, ю́сь, ёшься, *impf.* 1. *impf. of* ~ться. 2. (*impf. only*) (о+*p.*) to inquire (about).

дозна́ни|е, я, *n.* (*leg.*) inquiry; inquest.

дозн|а́ться, а́юсь, *pf.* (*of* ~ава́ться) to find out, ascertain.

дозо́р, а, *m.* patrol.

дозо́р|ный, *adj. of* ~; ~ная шлю́пка patrol boat; *as noun* д., ~ного, *m.* (*mil.*) scout.

дозрева́|ть, ю, *impf. of* дозре́ть.

дозре́лый, *adj.* fully ripe.

дозр|е́ть, е́ю, *pf.* (*of* ~ева́ть) to ripen.

доигр|а́ть, а́ю, *pf.* (*of* ~ывать) to finish (playing).

доигр|а́ться, а́юсь, *pf.* (*of* ~ываться) (до+ *g.*) to play (until); (*fig.*) to get oneself (into), land oneself (in); вот и ~а́лся! now you've (he's, *etc.*) done it!

доигрыва|ть(ся), ю(сь), *impf. of* доигра́ть(ся).

дои́льн|ый, *adj.*; ~ая маши́на milking machine.

дои́льщица, ы, *f.* = доя́рка.

до|иска́ться, ищу́сь, и́щешься, *pf.* (*of* ~и́скиваться) (*coll.*) 1. (+*g.*) to find, discover. 2. to find out, ascertain.

дои́скива|ться, юсь, *impf.* 1. *impf. of* доиска́ться. 2. (*impf. only*) to try to find out.

доистори́ческий, *adj.* prehistoric.

до|и́ть, ю, ~ишь, *impf.* (*of* по~) to milk; (*fig.*) to milk (*of money*).

до|и́ться, ~и́тся, *impf.* 1. to give milk; хорошо́ д. to be a good milker. 2. *pass. of* ~и́ть.

до́йк|а, и, *f.* milking.

до́йн|ый, *adj.* milch; ~ая коро́ва milch cow (*also fig.*).

до|йти́, йду́, йдёшь, *past* ~шёл, ~шла́, *pf.* (*of* ~ходи́ть) 1. (до+*g.*) (*in var. senses*) to reach; письмо́ ~шло́ до меня́ то́лько сего́дня the letter only reached me today; слух ~шёл до нас a rumour reached us; д. до све́дения (+*g.*) to come to the notice (of), come to the ears (of); д. до того́, что...; to reach a point where...; ру́ки не ~шли́ (до+*g.*) I, *etc.*, had no time (for). 2. (*coll.*) (до+*g.*) to make an impression (upon), get through (to), penetrate (to), touch; его́

про́поведь про́сто не ~шла́ до слу́шателей his homily left his audience quite unmoved. 3. (*impers.*; *also* де́ло ~йдёт, ~шло́ до+*g.*) to come (to), be a matter (of); де́ло ~шло́ до проце́сса it came to a court case. 4. (*coll.*) to be done (= *to be cooked*); to be ripe.

док, а, *m.* dock.

до́к|а, и, *m. and f.* (*coll.*) expert, authority.

доказа́тел|ьный (~ен, ~ьна), *adj.* demonstrative, conclusive.

доказа́тельств|о, а, *n.* 1. proof, evidence. 2. (*math.*) demonstration.

док|аза́ть, ажу́, а́жешь, *pf.* (*of* ~а́зывать) 1. to demonstrate, prove; счита́ть ~а́занным to take for granted; что и тре́бовалось д. (*math.*) quod erat demonstrandum (Q.E.D.). 2. (*coll.*) д. на кого́-н. to inform on someone.

доказу́ем|ый (~, ~а), *adj.* demonstrable.

дока́зыва|ть, ю, *impf.* 1. *impf. of* доказа́ть. 2. (*impf. only*) to argue, try to prove.

дока́нчива|ть, ю, *impf. of* доко́нчить.

дока́пыва|ться, юсь, *impf. of* докопа́ться.

док|ати́ться, ачу́сь, а́тишься, *pf.* (*of* ~а́тываться) 1. (до+*g.*) to roll (to). 2. (*of sounds*) to roll, thunder, boom. 3. (*fig., coll.*) (до+*g.*) to sink (into), come (to); д. до преступле́ния to sink into crime.

дока́тыва|ться, юсь, *impf. of* докати́ться.

до́кер, а, *m.* docker.

докла́д, а, *m.* 1. report; lecture; paper; talk, address; чита́ть д. to give a report, read a paper. 2. announcement (*of arrival of guest, etc.*); войти́ без ~а to enter unannounced.

докладн|о́й, *adj.*; ~а́я запи́ска report, memorandum; *as noun* ~а́я, ~о́й, *f.* = ~а́я запи́ска.

докла́дчик, а, *m.* speaker, lecturer; reader of a report.

докла́дыва|ть(ся), ю(сь), *impf. of* доложи́ть(ся).

доко́ле (and доко́ль), *adv.* (*obs.*) 1. (*interrog.*) how long. 2. (*relat.*) as long as; until.

докона́|ть, ю, *pf.* (*coll.*) to finish off, be the end (of).

доко́нч|ить, у, ишь, *pf.* (*of* дока́нчивать) to finish, complete.

докопа́|ться, юсь, *pf.* (*of* дока́пываться) (до+*g.*) 1. to dig down (to). 2. (*fig.*) to get to the bottom (of); to find out, discover.

до́красна́, *adv.* to redness; to red heat; раскалённый д. red-hot.

докрич|а́ться, у́сь, и́шься, *pf.* 1. to shout until one is heard. 2. д. до хрипоты́, to shout oneself hoarse.

до́ктор, а, *pl.* **а́,** *m.* doctor.

доктора́льный, *adj.* didactic.

доктора́нт, а, *m.* person working for degree of doctor.

до́ктор|ский, *adj.* of ~; ~ская диссерта́ция thesis for degree of doctor.

до́кторш|а, и, *f.* (*coll.*) 1. doctor's wife. 2. woman-doctor.

доктри́н|а, ы, *f.* doctrine.

доктринёр, а, *m.* doctrinaire.

доктринёрский, *adj.* doctrinaire.

доктринёрств|о, а, *n.* doctrinaire attitude.

доку́да, *adv.* (*coll.*) 1. (*interrog.*) how far. 2. (*relat.*) as far as.

доку́к|а, и, *f.* (*obs. or coll.*) tiresome request.

докуме́нт, а, *m.* 1. document, paper; предъяви́ть ~ы to produce one's papers. 2. (*leg.*) deed; instrument.

документа́льный, *adj.* documentary; д. фильм documentary (film).

документа́ци|я, и, *f.* 1. documentation. 2. (*collect.*) documents, papers.

документи́р|овать, ую, *impf. and pf.* to document.

докуп|а́ть¹, а́ю, *impf. of* ~и́ть.

докупа́|ть², ю, *pf.* to finish bathing (*trans.*).

докуп|и́ть, лю́, ~ишь, *pf.* (*of* ~а́ть¹) to buy in addition.

докуча́|ть, ю, *impf.* (+*d. and i.*; *coll.*) to bother (with), pester (with), plague (with).

доку́члив|ый (~, ~а), *adj.* (*coll.*) tiresome; importunate.

доку́ч|ный (~ен, ~на), *adj.* (*coll.*) tiresome, boring.

дол, а, *m.* (*poet.*) dale, vale; за гора́ми, за ~а́ми far and wide; по гора́м, по ~а́м up hill and down dale.

долбёжк|а, и, *f.* (*sl.*) swotting; учи́ться в ~у to learn by rote.

долб|и́ть, лю́, и́шь, *impf.* 1. to hollow; to chisel, gouge. 2. (*coll.*) to repeat, say over and over. 3. (*sl.*) to swot (up); to learn by rote.

долг, а, о ~е, в ~у́, *pl.* ~и́, *m.* 1. duty; по ~у слу́жбы in the performance of one's duty. 2. debt; в д. on credit; войти́, влезть в ~и́ to get into debt; быть у кого́-н. в ~у́ to be indebted to someone; отда́ть после́дний д. to pay the last honours; д. платежо́м кра́сен one good turn deserves another.

дол|гий (~ог, ~га́, ~го), *adj.* long, of long duration; ~гая пе́сня (*fig.*) a long story; отложи́ть в д. я́щик to shelve, put off.

до́лго, *adv.* 1. long, a long time. 2. д. ли (+*inf. or* до+*g.*) one may easily, it can easily happen that; д. ли до беды́ accidents will happen.

долгове́ч|ный (~ен, ~на), *adj.* lasting; long-lived.

долгов|о́й, *adj.* of долг 2; ~о́е обяза́тельство promissory note; ~о́е отделе́ние (*hist.*) debtor's prison.

долговре́менн|ый, *adj.* of long duration ~ая огнева́я то́чка, ~ое огнево́е соору же́ние (*mil.*) pillbox (*of reinforced concrete*)

долговя́з|ый (~, ~а), *adj.* (*coll.*) lanky.

долгоде́нстви|е, я, *n.* (*obs.*) long life.

долгоигра́ющ|ий, *adj.*; ~ая пласти́нк long-playing (gramophone) record.

долголе́ти|е, я, *n.* longevity.

долголе́тний, *adj.* of many years; of man years' standing, long-standing.

долгоно́сик, а, *m.* weevil.

долгосро́чный, *adj.* long-term; of long dura tion.

долгот|а́, ы́, *pl.* ~ы, *f.* 1. (*sing. only*) dura tion. 2. longitude.

долготерпели́в|ый (~, ~а), *adj.* long-suffer ing.

долготерпе́ни|е, я, *n.* long-suffering.

долгун|е́ц, ца́, *m.* (лён-)д. long-stalked fla (*commercial brand*).

долево́й¹, *adj.* lengthwise.

долев|о́й², *adj.* of до́ля; ~о́е отчисле́ни royalty.

до́лее, *comp. of* до́лго.

долет|а́ть, а́ю, *impf. of* ~е́ть.

доле|те́ть, чу́, ти́шь, *pf.* (*of* ~та́ть) (до+g 1. to fly (to, as far as). 2. to reach (*also fig.* to be wafted (to).

долж|а́ть, а́ю, *impf.* (*of* за~) (*obs.*) 1. (у+g to borrow (from). 2. (+*d.*) to owe.

до́лж|ен (~на́, ~но́), *pred. adj.* 1. owing; д. мне три рубля́ he owes me three rouble 2. (+*inf.*) expresses obligation: я д. идти́ must go, I have to go; он д. был отказа́ть he had to refuse. 3. (+*inf.*) expresses prob bility or expectation; она́ ~на́ ско́ро прий she should be here soon; ~но́ быть pr bably; вы с ним, ~но́ быть, уже́ знако́м you must have met him; you probably m him.

долженств|ова́ть, у́ю, *impf.* (+*inf.*; *obs.*) be obliged (to); to be intended (to).

должни́к, а́, *m.* debtor.

до́лжно, *pred.* (+*inf.*) one should, ought (t

должностн|о́й, *adj.* official; ~о́е лицо́ o cial, functionary, public servant; ~о́е п ступле́ние malfeasance in office.

до́лжност|ь, и, *g. pl.* ~е́й, *f.* post, appoi ment, office; duties.

до́лжн|ый, *adj.* due, fitting, proper; ~ о́бразом properly; *as noun* ~ое, ~ого due, воздава́ть д. (+*d.*) to do justice.

долива́|ть, ю, *impf. of* доли́ть.

доли́вк|а, и, *f.* refilling, replenishment; fuelling.

доли́н|а, ы, *f.* valley.

доли́н|ный, *adj.* of ~a.

дол|и́ть, ью́, ьёшь, *past* ~и́л, ~ила́, ~и́ *pf.* (*of* ~ива́ть) 1. to add; to pour in ad tion. 2. to fill (up); to refill.

дóллар, а, *m.* dollar.

долож|úть¹, ý, ~ишь, *pf.* (*of* доклáдывать) **1.** (+*a. or* о+*p.*) to report; to give a report (on). **2.** (о+*p.*) to announce (*a guest, etc.*).

долож|úть², ý, ~ишь, *pf.* (*of* доклáдывать) to add.

долож|úться, ýсь, ~ишься, *pf.* (*of* доклáдываться) to announce one's arrival.

долóй, *adv.* (+*a.*; *coll.*) down (with), away (with); д. измéнников! down with the traitors!; уйдú с глаз д.! out of my sight! **2.** off (with); шáпки д.! hats off!

долот|ó, á, *pl.* **~á, ~,** *n.* chisel.

дóлу, *adv.* (*poet.*) down, downwards.

дóльк|а, и, *f.* segment, clove.

дóльний, *adj.* (*poet.*) **1.** *adj. of* дол. **2.** earthly, terrestrial.

дóльше, *adv.* longer.

дол|я, и, *g. pl.* **~éй,** *f.* **1.** part, portion; share; quota, allotment; войтú в ~ю (с+*i.*) to go shares (with); в егó словáх нé было и ~и úстины there was not a grain of truth in his words; кнúга в четвёртую, восьмýю ~ю листá quarto, octavo. **2.** (*anat., bot.*) lobe. **3.** lot, fate; вы́пасть на чью-н. ~ю to fall to someone's lot. **4.** (*obs.*) *unit of weight equivalent to 44 mg.*

дом, а (у), *pl.* **~á,** *m.* **1.** (*in var. senses*) building, house; block (of flats); Д. культýры Palace of Culture; д. óтдыха rest home, holiday home; Д. Совéтской Áрмии Soviet Army Club; д. терпúмости brothel. **2.** home; house, household; вестú д. to keep house, run the house; хлопотáть по ~у to busy oneself with housework, with domestic chores; на ~ý at home; брать рабóту нá д. to take work home; тоскá по ~у homesickness. **3.** house (= *dynasty*), lineage; д. Ромáновых the House of Romanov.

дóма, *adv.* at home, in; быть как д. to feel at home; бýдьте как д. make yourself at home; у негó не все д. he's not all there.

домаркси́стский, *adj.* pre-Marxist.

домахá|ть, ю, *pf.* (*coll.*) (до+*g.*) to get (to).

домáшн|ий, *adj.* **1.** house; home; domestic; д. áдрес home address; ~ие забóты household chores; ~ее плáтье house dress; ~яя рабóтница domestic servant; ~яя хозя́йка housewife; под ~им арéстом under house arrest. **2.** home-made; homespun; home--brewed. **3.** tame (*as opp. to* wild); domestic; ~ие живóтные domestic animals; ~ие птúцы poultry. **4.** *as noun* ~ие, ~их one's people, one's family.

домáшност|ь, и, *f.* (*coll. or dial.*) **1.** housekeeping. **2.** household equipment.

домéн, а, *m.* (*hist.*) domain, state lands.

домéнн|ый, *adj. of* дóмна; ~ая печь blast furnace.

дóменщик, а, *m.* blast-furnace operator.

дóмик, а, *m. dim. of* дом.

доминáнт|а, ы, *f.* **1.** (*mus.*) dominant. **2.** (*fig.*) leitmotiv.

доминикáн|ец, ца, *m.* Dominican (monk).

доминиóн, а, *m.* dominion (*member of British Commonwealth*).

доминúр|овать, ую, *impf.* **1.** to dominate, prevail (*fig.*). **2.** (*geogr.*) (над+*i.*) to dominate, command.

доминó, *indecl., n.* **1.** dominoes (*game*). **2.** domino (*costume*).

домúш|ко, ка, *pl.* **~ки, ~ек, ~кам,** *m.* (*coll.*) small, wretched house; hovel.

домкрáт, а, *m.* (*tech.*) jack.

дóмн|а, ы, *f.* blast furnace.

домовúн|а, ы, *f.* (*dial.*) coffin.

домовúт|ый (~, ~а), *adj.* thrifty, economical; ~ая хозя́йка good housewife.

домовладéл|ец, ьца, *m.* house-owner; landlord.

домовнúц|а, ы, *f.* (*coll. or dial.*) housekeeper.

домовнúча|ть, ю, *impf.* (*coll. or dial.*) to keep house.

домовóдств|о, а, *n.* (art of) housekeeping; household management.

домов|óй, óго, *m.* (*folklore*) house-spirit.

домóв|ый, *adj.* **1.** house; household; ~ая кнúга house register, register of tenants; ~ая контóра house-manager's office; д. паýк house-spider. **2.** housing; д. трест housing trust.

домогáтельств|о, а, *n.* **1.** solicitation, importunity. **2.** demand, bid; д. госпóдства bid for power.

домогá|ться, юсь, *impf.* (+*g.*) to seek (after), solicit, covet.

домодéльный, *adj.* home-made.

домóй, *adv.* home, homewards; нам порá д. it's time for us to go home.

домоправúтел|ь, я, *m.* (*obs.*) steward.

домоправлéни|е, я, *n.* (*obs.*) household management.

доморóщенный, *adj.* **1.** home-bred. **2.** (*fig.*) crude; primitive; homespun.

домосéд, а, *m.* stay-at-home.

домостроéни|е, я, *n.* house-building.

домострои́тельный, *adj.* house-building.

домоткáный, *adj.* home-spun.

домоуправлéни|е, я, *n.* house management (committee).

домохозя́|ин, ина, *pl.* **~ева, ~ев,** *m.* householder. **2.** (*obs.*) head of peasant household.

домохозя́йк|а, и, *f.* housewife.

домочáд|ец, ца, *m.* (*obs.*) member of household.

дóмр|а, ы, *f.* (*mus.*) domra (*Russian stringed instrument similar to mandoline*).

домрабóтниц|а, ы, *f.* domestic servant, maid.

домрачé|й, я, *m.* (*obs.*) = домрúст.

домрúст, а, *m.* domra-player.

дому́шник, а, *m.* (*sl.*) burglar, house-breaker.

домч|а́ть, у́, и́шь, *pf.* (*coll.*) to bring quickly (*in a vehicle, etc.*).

домч|а́ться, у́сь, и́шься, *pf.* (*coll.*) to reach quickly (*at a run or gallop*).

до́мыс|ел, ла, *m.* conjecture.

дон, *interj.* (*onomat.*) ding-dong.

донага́, *adv.* stark naked.

дона́шива|ть, ю, *impf. of* доноси́ть[1].

доне́льзя, *adv.* to the utmost; in the extreme; он д. упря́м he is obstinate in the extreme.

донесе́ни|е, я, *n.* dispatch, report, message; д. о боевы́х поте́рях casualty report.

донес|ти́[1], у́, ёшь, *past* ~, ~ла́, *pf.* (*of* доноси́ть[2]) (до+*g.*) to carry (to, as far as); to carry, bear (*a sound or smell*).

донес|ти́[2], у́, ёшь, *past* ~, ~ла́, *pf.* (*of* доноси́ть[3]) 1. to report, announce; (+*d.*) to inform. 2. (на+*a.*) to inform (on, against), denounce.

донес|ти́сь, у́сь, ёшься, *past* ~ся, ~ла́сь, *pf.* (*of* доноси́ться[2]) 1. (*of sounds or smells, also of news, etc.*) to reach; до нас уже́ ~ся слух a rumour had already reached us. 2. (*coll.*) to reach quickly.

дон|е́ц, ца́, *m.* Don Cossack.

донжуа́н, а, *m.* Don Juan, philanderer.

донжуа́нств|о, а, *n.* philandering.

до́низу, *adv.* to the bottom.

донима́|ть, ю, *impf. of* доня́ть.

донкихо́тский, *adj.* quixotic.

донкихо́тств|о, а, *n.* quixotry.

до́нник, а, *m.* (*bot.*) melilot, sweet clover.

до́нный, *adj. of* дно; д. лёд ground ice; д. заря́д (*mil.*) base charge.

до́нор, а, *m.* (blood-)donor.

до́нор|ский, *adj. of* ~; д. пункт blood donation centre.

доно́с, а, *m.* denunciation, information, delation.

дон|оси́ть[1], ошу́, ~о́сишь, *pf.* (*of* дона́шивать) 1. to finish carrying. 2. to wear out. 3. д. ребёнка to bear at full term.

дон|оси́ть[2, 3], ошу́, ~о́сишь, *impf. of* донести́[1, 2].

дон|оси́ться[1], ~о́сится, *pf.* to wear out, be worn out.

дон|оси́ться[2], ~о́сится, *impf. of* донести́сь.

доно́счик, а, *m.* informer.

донско́й, *adj.* (of the river) Don; д. каза́к Don Cossack.

до́нц|е, а, *n.* *dim. of* дно.

доны́не, *adv.* (*rhet.*) hitherto.

до|ня́ть, йму́, ймёшь, *past* ~ня́л, ~няла́, ~ня́ло, *pf.* (*of* ~нима́ть) (*coll.*) to weary, tire out, exasperate.

дообе́денный, *adj.* pre-prandial.

дооктя́брьский, *adj.* pre-October (*before the Russian Revolution of October 1917*).

допека́|ть, ю, *impf. of* допе́чь.

допетро́вский, *adj.* pre-Petrine, before Pete the Great.

допе́|чь, ку́, чёшь, ку́т, *past* ~к, ~кла́, *p̧* (*of* ~ка́ть) 1. to bake until done; to finis. baking. 2. (*fig., coll.*) to wear out, plague pester.

допива́|ть, ю, *impf. of* допи́ть.

допи|са́ть, шу́, ~шешь, *pf.* (*of* ~сыва́ть) 1. to finish writing. 2. to add.

допи́сыва|ть, ю, *impf. of* дописа́ть.

доп|и́ть, ью́, ьёшь, *past* ~и́л, ~ила́, ~и́ло, *pf.* (*of* ~ива́ть) to drink (up).

допла́т|а, ы, *f.* additional payment; exces fare.

допл|ати́ть, ачу́, ~а́тишь, *pf.* (*of* ~а́чивать) to pay in addition, in excess.

допла́чива|ть, ю, *impf. of* доплати́ть.

доплыва́|ть, ю, *impf. of* доплы́ть.

доплы́|ть, ву́, вёшь, *past* ~л, ~ла́, ~ло, *pf.* (*of* ~ва́ть) (до+*g.*) to swim (to, as far as) to sail (to, as far as); (*fig.*) to reach.

допо́длинно, *adv.* (*coll.*) for certain.

допо́длинный, *adj.* (*coll.*) authentic, genuine

**дополне́ни|е, я, n.* 1. supplement, addition addendum. 2. (*gram.*) object; прямо́е д. direct object; ко́свенное д. indirect object

дополни́тельно, *adv.* in addition.

дополни́тельн|ый, *adj.* supplementary, ad ditional, extra; ~ое вре́мя (*sport*) extr time; д. окла́д extra pay; д. у́гол (*math.* supplement; ~ые цвета́ complementar colours.

допо́лн|ить, ю, ишь, *pf.* (*of* ~я́ть) to supple ment, add to; (*fig.*) to embellish (*a story* etc.); д. друг дру́га to complement on another.

допо́лн|я́ть, я́ю, *impf. of* ~ить.

допото́пный, *adj.* antediluvian.

допра́шива|ть, ю, *impf. of* допроси́ть.

допризы́вник, а, *m.* youth undergoing pre -conscription military training.

допризы́вный, *adj.* pre-conscription.

допро́с, а, *m.* (*leg.*) interrogation, examina tion; перекрёстный д. cross-examination

допр|оси́ть, ошу́, о́сишь, *pf.* (*of* ~а́ши вать) (*leg.*) to interrogate, question, exa mine.

допр|оси́ться, ошу́сь, ~о́сишься, *pf.* (*coll.* 1. to obtain, find out by asking; у неѓ ничего́ не ~о́сишься one cannot get any thing out of him. 2. (+*g. or inf.*) to make get (*to do something*).

до́пуск, а, *m.* 1. right of entry, admittance 2. (*tech.*) tolerance.

допуска́|ть, ю, *impf. of* допусти́ть.

допусти́м|ый (~, ~а), *adj.* permissible, ad missible; ~ая нагру́зка permissible load.

допу|сти́ть, щу́, ~стишь, *pf.* (*of* ~ска́ть) 1. (до+*g.*, к+*d.*) to admit (to); д. к ко́н курсу to allow to compete. 2. to allow permit; to tolerate. **3.** to grant, assume; ~стим let us suppose, let us assume. **4.** to commit.

допущéни|е, я, *n.* assumption.

допыт|áться, áюсь, *pf.* (*of* ~ываться) to find out.

допытыва|ться, юсь, *impf. of* допытáться; (*impf. only*) to try to find out, try to elicit.

дóпьянá, *adv.* (*coll.*) dead drunk; напоить д. to make dead drunk.

дораст|áть, áю, *impf. of* ~й.

дораст|и, ý, ёшь, *past* дорóс, доросла́, *pf.* (*of* дорастáть) **1.** (до+g.) to grow (to); (*fig.*) to attain (to), come up (to). **2.** не д. чтобы (+*inf.*) not to be old enough (to); она́ ещё не доросла́, чтобы éздить на велоси- пéде she is not old enough yet to ride a bicycle.

дорв|áться, ýсь, ёшься, *past* ~áлся, ~ала́сь, ~ало́сь, *pf.* (до; *coll.*) to fall upon, seize upon.

дореволюциóнный, *adj.* pre-revolutionary.

дорефóрменный, *adj.* before the reform(s) (*esp. with reference to the emancipation of serfs and other reforms in Russia in the 1860s*).

дори́ческий, *adj.* (*ling., archit.*) Doric, Dorian.

дорóг|а, и, f. **1.** road, way (*also fig.*); желéз- ная д. railway(s); д. пéрвого кла́сса first- -class road; д. госуда́рственного значéния national highway; вы́йти на ~y to get on, succeed; дать, уступи́ть кому́-н. ~y to let someone pass, make way for someone (*also fig.*); идти́ своéй ~ой to go one's own way; перебежáть, переби́ть кому́-н. ~y to steal a march on someone; пойти́ по плохóй ~e to be on the down- ward path; стать кому́-н. ~y to stand in someone's way; туда́ ему́ и д. (*coll.*) it serves him right; ска́тертью д.! good riddance! **2.** journey; отпра́виться в ~y to set out; запасти́ прови́зии на ~y to lay in supplies for the journey; в ~e on the journey, en route; с ~и after the jour- ney, from the road. **3.** (the) way, route; показáть ~y to show the way, direct; сби́ться с ~и to lose one's way; нам с ни́ми бы́ло по ~e we went the same way; нам с ни́м да́льше нé было по ~e our ways parted (*also fig.*).

дóрого, *adv.* dear, dearly; д. обойти́сь (+*d.*) to cost one dear; д. бы я дал, чтобы... (*coll.*) I would give anything to . . .

дороговизн|а, ы, f. dearness, expensiveness.

дорóгой, *adv.* on the way, en route.

дорог|óй (дóрог, дорогá, дóрого), *adj.* **1.** dear, expensive; costly; по ~óй ценé at a high price; ~áя побéда dearly-bought vic- tory. **2.** dear; precious; *as noun* д., ~óго, *m.*, ~áя, ~óй, *f.* (my) dear.

дорóд|ный (~ен, ~на), *adj.* portly, burly.

дорóдств|о, а, *n.* **1.** portliness, burliness. **2.** (*obs.*) courage, prowess.

дорожá|ть, ет, *impf.* (*of* вз~ *and* по~) to rise (in price), go up.

доро́же, *comp. of* дорогóй *and* дóрого.

дорож|и́ть, ý, и́шь, *impf.* (+*i.*) to value; to prize, set store (by).

дорож|и́ться, ýсь, и́шься, *impf.* (*coll.*) to ask too high a price, overcharge.

дорóжк|а, и, f. **1.** path, walk. **2.** (*sport*) track; lane. **3.** (*aeron.*) runway. **4.** strip (*of carpet, linoleum or fabric*); runner. **5.** (*of tape recorder*) track.

доро́жник, а, m. road-worker.

дорóжн|ый, *adj.* **1.** *adj. of* дорóга; д. знак road sign; д. отдéл highways department; ~ое строи́тельство road-building. **2.** travel, travelling; ~ые расхóды travelling expenses. **3.** *as noun* д., ~ого, *m.* (*obs.* traveller.

дорса́льный, *adj.* dorsal.

дортуа́р, а, m. (*obs.*) dormitory.

досáд|а, ы, f. vexation, disappointment, spite; кака́я д.! what a nuisance!

доса|ди́ть[1], жý, ди́шь, *pf.* (*of* ~жда́ть) (+*d.*) to annoy, vex.

доса|ди́ть[2], жý, ~дишь, *pf.* to finish planting.

доса́длив|ый (~, ~а), *adj.* expressing vexa- tion, irritation, disappointment; д. жест a gesture of vexation.

доса́дно, *as pred.* it is vexing, annoying; it is a nuisance.

досáд|ный (~ен, ~на), *adj.* vexing, annoy- ing; disappointing.

досáд|овать, ую, *impf.* (на+*a.*) to be annoyed (with), be vexed (with).

досажда́|ть, ю, *impf. of* досади́ть[1].

досéле, *adv.* (*obs.*) up to now.

доси|дéть, жý, ди́шь, *pf.* (*of* ~жива́ть) (до +*g.*) to sit (until), stay (until).

досижива|ть, ю, *impf. of* досидéть.

доск|á, и́, а. ~ý, *pl.* ~и, *g.* досóк, *d.* ~áм, *f.* **1.** board, plank; д. для объявлéний notice-board; д. почёта board of honour (*with photographs and names of outstanding workers*); как д. (худóй) thin as a rake; прочéсть от ~и́ до ~и́ to read from cover to cover; ста́вить на одну́ ~ý (с+*i.*) to put on a level (with); пьян в ~ý (*sl.*) dead drunk. **2.** slab; plaque, plate.

доскона́л|ьный (~ен, ~ьна), *adj.* thorough.

до|сла́ть, шлю, шлёшь, *pf.* (*of* ~сыла́ть) **1.** to send in addition; to send the re- mainder. **2.** (*mil.*) to seat, chamber (*a car- tridge, etc.*).

дослéдовани|е, я, *n.* (*leg.*) supplementary examination, further inquiry; напра́вить дéло на д. to remit a case for further in- quiry.

досле́д|овать, ую, *impf. and pf.* (*leg.*) to submit to supplementary examination, further inquiry.

досло́вно, *adv.* verbatim, word for word.

досло́вный, *adj.* literal, verbatim; д. перево́д literal translation.

дослу́жива|ть(ся), ю(сь), *impf. of* дослужи́ть(ся).

дослуж|и́ть, у́, ~ишь, *pf.* (*of* ~ивать) (до+ g.) to serve (until); to finish a period of service.

дослуж|и́ться, у́сь, ~ишься, *pf.* (*of* ~иваться) to obtain as a result of service; д. до чи́на майо́ра to rise to the rank of major; д. до пе́нсии to qualify for a pension.

досма́трива|ть, ю, *impf. of* досмотре́ть.

досмо́тр, а, *m.* examination (*at Customs, etc.*).

досмотр|е́ть, ю́, ~ишь, *pf.* (*of* досма́тривать) 1. (до+g.) to watch, look at (to, as far as); мы ~е́ли пье́су до тре́тьего а́кта we saw the play as far as the third act. 2. не д. to overlook, to allow to escape one's notice.

досмо́трщик, а, *m.* inspector, examiner.

досове́тский, *adj.* pre-Soviet.

доспева́|ть, ю, *impf. of* доспе́ть.

доспе́|ть, ю, ешь, *pf.* (*of* ~ва́ть) to ripen, mature; вре́мя ~ло (*obs.*) the time has come.

доспе́х|и, ов, *sing.* ~, ~а, *m.*, armour.

досро́чный, *adj.* ahead of schedule, early.

доста|ва́ть(ся), ю́(сь), ёшь(ся), *impf. of* ~ть(ся).

доста́в|ить, лю, ишь, *pf.* (*of* ~ля́ть) 1. to deliver, convey; to supply, furnish. 2. to give, cause; д. слу́чай to afford an opportunity; д. удово́льствие to give pleasure.

доста́вк|а, и, *f.* delivery, conveyance (*of goods, etc.*).

доставля́|ть, ю, *impf. of* доста́вить.

доста́вщик, а, *m.* delivery man, roundsman.

доста́ива|ть, ю, *impf. of* достоя́ть.

доста́т|ок, ка, *m.* 1. sufficiency. 2. prosperity; жить в ~ке to be comfortably off. 3. (*pl. only*) income.

доста́точно[1], *adv.* sufficiently, enough.

доста́точно[2], *as pred.* it is enough; д. сказа́ть suffice it to say; д. бы́ло одного́ взгля́да one glance was enough.

доста́точност|ь, и, *f.* 1. sufficiency. 2. (*obs.*) easy circumstances.

доста́точ|ный (~ен, ~на), *adj.* 1. sufficient. 2. (*coll.*) prosperous, well-to-do.

доста́|ть, ну, нешь, *pf.* (*of* ~ва́ть) 1. to fetch; to take out; д. плато́к из карма́на to take a handkerchief out of one's pocket. 2. (+g. *or* до+g.) to touch; to reach; д. руко́й до потолка́ to touch the ceiling. 3. to get, obtain. 4. (*impers.*+g.; *coll.*) to suffice.

доста́|ться, нусь, нешься *pf.* (*of* ~ва́ться)
(+d.) 1. to pass (to) (by inheritance); ему́ ~лось большо́е име́ние he came into a large estate. 2. to fall to one's lot. 3. (*impers.*; *coll.*) ему́, *etc.*, ~нется he, *etc.*, will catch it.

достига́|ть, ю, *impf. of* дости́гнуть *and* дости́чь.

дости́г|нуть, ну, нешь, *past* ~, ~ла, *pf.* (*of* ~а́ть) 1. (+g. *or* до+g.) to reach; д. га́вани to reach harbour; д. ста́рости to reach old age; слух ~ до на́ших уше́й a rumour had come to our ears. 2. (+g.) to attain, achieve.

достиже́ни|е, я, *n.* achievement, attainment.

достижи́м|ый (~, ~а), *adj.* accessible; attainable.

дости́чь = дости́гнуть.

достове́рност|ь, и, *f.* authenticity; trustworthiness.

достове́р|ный (~ен, ~на), *adj.* authentic; trustworthy.

достодо́лжный, *adj.* (*obs.*) due, just.

достое́вщин|а, ы, *f.* 1. mental imbalance (*as exemplified especially by characters in the novels of Dostoevsky*). 2. analysis of character in the manner of Dostoevsky.

досто́инств|о, а, *n.* 1. merit, virtue. 2. (*sing. only*) dignity; чу́вство со́бственного ~а self-respect. 3. (*econ.*) value; моне́ты ма́лого ~а coins of small denomination. 4. (*obs.*) rank, title.

досто́йно, *adv.* 1. suitably, fittingly, adequately, properly. 2. (*obs.*) with dignity.

досто́|йный (~ин, ~йна), *adj.* 1. (+g.) worthy (of), deserving; д. внима́ния worthy of note; д. похвалы́ praiseworthy. 2. deserved; fitting, adequate; ~йная награ́да deserved reward. 3. suitable, fit. 4. worthy.

достопа́мят|ный (~ен, ~на), *adj.* memorable.

достопочте́нный, *adj.* (*obs.*) venerable; (*iron.*) worthy.

достопримеча́тельност|ь, и, *f.* sight; place, object of note; осма́тривать ~и to go sight-seeing, see the sights.

достопримеча́тел|ьный (~ен, ~ьна), *adj.* remarkable, notable.

достоя́ни|е, я, *n.* property.

досто|я́ть, ю́, и́шь, *pf.* (*of* доста́ивать) to wait standing (until).

досту́ка|ться, юсь, *pf.* (*coll.*) to get what one had been asking for, get the punishment one deserves.

до́ступ, а, *m.* 1. entrance. 2. access, admission, admittance.

досту́п|ный (~ен, ~на), *adj.* 1. accessible; easy of access. 2. (для+g.) open (to); available (to). 3. simple; easily understood;

intelligible. **4.** (*of prices*) moderate, reasonable. **5.** affable, approachable. **6.** ∼ная же́нщина (*obs.*) loose woman, woman of easy virtue.

достуЧ|а́ться, у́сь, и́шься, *pf.* (*coll.*) to knock until one is heard.

досу́г, а, *m.* **1.** leisure, leisure-time; на ∼е at leisure, in one's spare time. **2.** (*as pred.*; +*d. and inf.*; *coll.*) to have time (to, for); где мне д. чита́ть? what time have I for reading?

досу́ж|ий, *adj.* (*coll.*) **1.** leisure; ∼ее вре́мя leisure-time, spare time. **2.** idle; ∼ие разгово́ры idle talk.

до́суха, *adv.* (until) dry; вы́тереть д. to rub dry.

досчита́|ть, ю, *pf.* (*of* досчи́тывать) **1.** to finish counting. **2.** (до+*g.*) to count (up to); д. до ста to count up to a hundred.

досчи́тыва|ть, ю, *impf. of* досчита́ть.

досыла́|ть, ю, *impf. of* досла́ть.

досы́п|ать, лю, лешь, *pf.* (*of* ∼а́ть) to pour in, fill up.

досып|а́ть, а́ю, *impf. of* ∼ать.

до́сыта, *adv.* (*coll.*) to satiety.

досье́, *indecl., n.* dossier, file.

досю́да, *adv.* (*coll.*) as far as here, up to here.

досяга́емост|ь, и, *f.* reach; (*mil.*) range; вне преде́лов ∼и beyond reach.

досяга́ем|ый (∼, ∼а), *adj.* attainable, accessible.

дот, а, *m.* (*abbr. of* долговре́менная огнева́я то́чка) (*mil.*) (*reinforced concrete*) pill-box.

дота́скива|ть(ся), ю(сь), *impf. of* дотащи́ть(ся).

дота́ци|я, и, *f.* (State) grant, subsidy.

дотащ|и́ть, у́, ∼ишь, *pf.* (*of* дота́скивать) (*coll.*) (до+*g.*) to carry, drag (to).

дотащ|и́ться, у́сь, ∼ишься, *pf.* (*of* дота́скиваться) (*coll.*) to drag oneself; ра́неный едва́ ∼и́лся до свои́х пози́ций the wounded man hardly managed to drag himself to his lines.

дотемна́, *adv.* until it gets (got) dark.

дотла́, *adv.* utterly, completely; разорён д. razed to the ground; сгоре́ть д. to burn to the ground.

дото́ле, *adv.* (*obs.*) until then, hitherto.

дото́шный, *adj.* (*coll.*) meticulous.

дотра́гива|ться, юсь, *impf. of* дотро́нуться.

дотро́н|уться, усь, ешься, *pf.* (*of* дотра́гиваться) (до+*g.*) to touch.

дотя́гива|ть(ся), ю(сь), ешь(ся), *impf. of* дотяну́ть(ся).

дотян|у́ть, у́, ∼ешь, *pf.* (*of* дотя́гивать) (до+*g.*) **1.** to draw, drag, haul (to, as far as). **2.** (*coll.*) to reach, make. **3.** to stretch out (to, as far as). **4.** (*coll.*) to hold out (till); to live (till); он до утра́ не ∼ет he won't last till morning. **5.** (*coll.*) to put off (till).

дотян|у́ться, у́сь, ∼ешься, *pf.* (*of* дотя́гиваться) (до+*g.*) **1.** to reach; to touch. **2.** (*coll.*) to stretch (to), reach; о́чередь ∼у́лась до конца́ у́лицы the queue stretched to the end of the street. **3.** (*coll.*; *of time*) to drag by (until).

доу́чива|ть(ся), ю(сь), *impf. of* доучи́ть(ся).

доуч|и́ть, у́, ∼ишь, *pf.* (*of* ∼ивать) **1.** to finish teaching; (до+*g.*) to teach (up to). **2.** to finish learning; (до+*g.*) to learn (up to, as far as).

доуч|и́ться, у́сь, ∼ишься, *pf.* (*of* ∼иваться) **1.** to complete one's studies, finish one's education. **2.** (до+*g.*) to study (up to, till).

дох|а́, и́, *pl.* ∼и, *f.* fur-coat (*with fur on both sides*).

до́хлый, *adj.* **1.** dead (*of animals*). **2.** (*coll.*) sickly; weakly (*of human beings*).

дохля́тин|а, ы (*coll.*) **1.** *f.* carcase; (*collect.*) carrion. **2.** *m. and f.* feeble, sickly person.

до́х|нуть, ну, нешь, *past* ∼, ∼ла, *impf.* (*of* по∼) to die (*of animals*).

дохн|у́ть, у́, ёшь, *pf.* **1.** to breathe (*of a single breath*); тут д. не́где there is no room to breathe here. **2.** to blow.

дохо́д, а, *m.* income; receipts; revenue.

дохо|ди́ть, жу́, ∼дишь, *impf. of* дойти́.

дохо́дност|ь, и, *f.* profitableness; income.

дохо́д|ный (∼ен, ∼на), *adj.* **1.** profitable, lucrative, paying. **2.** *adj. of* ∼.

дохо́дчив|ый (∼, ∼а), *adj.* intelligible, easy to understand.

дохристиа́нский, *adj.* pre-Christian.

доце́нт, а, *m.* senior lecturer, (university) reader.

доценту́р|а, ы, *f.* post of senior lecturer, (university) reader. **2.** (*collect.*) = доце́нты.

до́чери, до́черью, *see* дочь.

до́черин = дочéрнин.

дочéрн|ий, *adj.* **1.** daughter's. **2.** daughter; branch; ∼ее предприя́тие (*comm.*) branch (establishment).

дочéрнин, *adj.* (*coll.*) daughter's.

до́чиста, *adv.* **1.** clean; вы́мыть д. to wash clean. **2.** (*fig., coll.*) clean, completely; еró обыгра́ли д. they cleaned him out (*at cards*).

дочит|а́ть, а́ю, *pf.* (*of* ∼ывать) **1.** to finish reading. **2.** (до+*g.*) to read (to, as far as).

дочит|а́ться, а́юсь, *pf.* (*of* ∼ываться) (*coll.*) (до+*g.*) to read (to the point of).

дочи́тыва|ть(ся), ю(сь), *impf. of* дочита́ть(ся).

до́чк|а, и, *f.* (*coll.*) = дочь.

дочу́рк|а, и, *f.* (*coll.*) *dim. of* дочь.

доч|ь, ∼ери, *i.* ∼ерью, *pl.* ∼ери, ∼ерéй, ∼еря́м, ∼ерьми́, о ∼еря́х, *f.* daughter.

дошко́льник, а, *m.* **1.** child under school age. **2.** specialist on training of pre-school-age children.

дошко́льный, *adj.* pre-school.

до́шлый, *adj.* (*coll.*) cunning, shrewd.

доща́ник, а, *m.* flat-bottomed boat.

доща́тый, *adj.* made of planks, boards; д. насти́л duckboards.

доще́чк|а, и, *f.* 1. *dim. of* доска́. 2. door--plate, name-plate.

доя́рк|а, и, *f.* milkmaid.

дра́г|а, и, *f.* (*tech.*) drag, dredge.

драги́р|овать, ую, *impf. and pf.* (*tech.*) to drag, dredge.

драго́й, *adj.* (*obs. or poet.*) dear, precious.

драгома́н, а, *m.* dragoman.

драгоце́нност|ь, и, *f.* 1. jewel; gem; precious stone; (*pl.*) jewelry. 2. object of great value; (*pl.*) valuables.

драгоце́н|ный (~ен, ~на), *adj.* precious (*also fig.*); ~ные ка́мни precious stones.

драгу́н, а, *g. pl.* ~, *m.* dragoon.

дража́йш|ий, *superl. of* дорого́й; ~ая полови́на 'better half'.

драже́, *indecl.*, *n.* dragée; шокола́дное д. chocolate drop.

дразн|и́ть, ю́, ~ишь, *impf.* 1. to tease; его́ ~и́ли тру́сом they used to mock him by calling him a coward. 2. to excite; to tantalize.

дра́|ить, ю, ишь, *impf.* (*naut.*) to polish; to swab.

драйв, а, *m.* drive (*in tennis*).

дра́к|а, и, *f.* fight; у них дошло́ до ~и they came to blows.

драко́н, а, *m.* 1. dragon. 2. (*heraldry*) wyvern.

драко́новский, *adj.* Draconian.

дра́ла, *as pred.* (*coll.*) (he) ran off, made off; встал да и д. he got up and made off; дать д. to take to one's heels.

дра́м|а, ы, *f.* 1. drama. 2. (*fig.*) tragedy, calamity.

драматиза́ци|я, и, *f.* dramatization.

драматизи́р|овать, ую, *impf. and pf.* to dramatize.

драмати́зм, а, *m.* 1. (*theatr.*) dramatic effect. 2. (*fig.*) dramatic character, quality; tension.

драмати́ческ|ий, *adj.* 1. dramatic; drama, theatre; ~ое иску́сство dramatic art, art of the theatre; д. теа́тр theatre (*as opp. to* cinema, ballet, opera). 2. dramatic, theatrical; ~им то́ном in a dramatic tone. 3. (*fig.*) dramatic; tense. 4. (*mus.*) strong (*of a voice*).

драмати́ч|ный (~ен, ~на), *adj.* (*fig.*) dramatic.

драмату́рг, а, *m.* playwright, dramatist.

драматурги́|я, и, *f.* 1. dramatic art. 2. (*collect.*) plays, drama; д. Че́хова the plays of Chekhov. 3. dramatic theory, drama.

драмкруж|о́к, ка́, *m.* dramatic circle.

драндуле́т, а, *m.* (*coll., joc.*) old, dilapidated conveyance; jalopy.

драни́ц|а, ы, *f.* (*dial.*)= дра́нка.

дра́нк|а, и, *f.* (*tech.*) 1. lathing, shingle. 2. lath.

дра́ночный, *adj. of* дра́нка.

дра́ный, *adj.* (*coll.*) tattered, ragged.

дран|ь, и, *f.* (*collect.*; *tech.*) lathing, shingle.

драп, а, *m.* thick woollen cloth.

драпан|у́ть, у́, ёшь, *pf. of* драпа́ть.

драпа́|ть, ю, *impf.* (*of* ~ну́ть) (*sl.*) to clear out, scarper.

драпир|ова́ть, у́ю, *impf.* to drape.

драпир|ова́ться, у́юсь, *impf.* 1. (в+*a. or* +*i.*) to drape oneself (in); (*fig.*) to affect, make a parade (of). 2. *pass. of* ~ова́ть.

драпиро́вк|а, и, *f.* 1. draping. 2. curtain; hangings.

драпиро́вщик, а, *m.* upholsterer.

дра́п|овый, *adj. of* ~.

драпри́, *indecl.*, *n.* 1. draperies. 2. hangings, curtains.

дра́тв|а, ы, *f.* waxed thread.

дра|ть, деру́, дерёшь, *past* ~л, ~ла́, ~ло, *impf.* 1. (*impf. only*) to tear (up, to pieces); д. го́рло (*coll.*) to bawl; д. нос (*coll.*) to turn up one's nose, put on airs; д. на себе́ во́лосы (*fig.*) to tear one's hair. 2. (*pf.* co~) to tear off; д. лы́ко (с лип) to bark (lime--trees); д. шку́ру to flay. 3. (*pf.* за~) to kill (*of wild animals*). 4. (*pf.* вы́~) (*coll.*) to beat, flog, thrash; to tear out; д. зу́бы to pull out teeth. 5. (*pf.* co~) (с+*g.*; *fig.*, *coll.*) to fleece; to sting; д. с живо́го и мёртвого to fleece unmercifully. 6. (*pf.* по~) чёрт его́ (по)дери́! damn him! 7. (*impf. only*) (*coll.*) to sting, irritate; д. у́ши (+*d.*) to jar (on); у меня́ в го́рле дерёт (*impers.*) I have a sore throat. 8. (*impf. only*) (*coll.*) to run away, make off; д. во все лопа́тки, со всех ног to run as fast as one's legs can carry one.

дра́|ться, деру́сь, дерёшься, *past* ~лся, ~ла́сь, ~ло́сь, *impf.* 1. (с+*i.*) to fight (with); д. на дуэ́ли to fight a duel. 2. (*fig.*) (за+*a.*) to fight, struggle (for). 3. (*pf.* по~) to hit, to give a hiding.

дра́хм|а, ы, *f.* 1. drachma (*Greek unit of currency*). 2. dram (*apothecaries' weight*).

драце́н|а, ы, *f.* (*bot.*) club palm, cabbage--tree (*Cordyline australis*).

драч¹, а́, *m.* (*tech.*) plane.

драч², а́, *m.* (*coll.*) flayer, knacker.

драчли́вост|ь, и, *f.* pugnacity.

драчли́в|ый (~, ~а), *adj.* pugnacious.

драчу́н, а́, *m.* (*coll.*) pugnacious, quarrelsome fellow.

драчу́н|ья, и, *g. pl.* ~ий, (*coll.*) *f. of* ~.

дребеде́н|ь, и, *f.* (*coll.*) nonsense; сплошна́я д. absolute rubbish.

дре́безг, а, *m.* (*coll.*) **1.** tinkling sound (*as of breaking glass, etc.*). **2.** (*pl. only*) разби́ть(ся) в (ме́лкие) ~и to smash to smithereens.

дребезж|а́ть, и́т, *impf.* to jingle, tinkle.

древеси́н|а, ы, *f.* **1.** wood (*substance*); wood-pulp. **2.** timber.

древе́сниц|а, ы, *f.* (*zool.*) **1.** tree-frog. **2.** leopard moth.

древе́сн|ый, *adj.* of де́рево; ~ая ма́сса wood-pulp; д. са́хар wood sugar, xylose; д. спирт wood alcohol; д. у́голь charcoal; д. у́ксус (*chem.*) wood vinegar, pyroligneous acid.

дре́вк|о, а, *pl.* ~и, ~ов, *n.* pole, staff; shaft (*of spear, etc.*); д. зна́мени flagstaff.

древлехрани́лищ|е, а, *n.* (*obs.*) archive.

древнегре́ческий, *adj.* ancient, classical Greek.

древнееевре́йский, *adj.* ancient, classical Hebrew.

древнеру́сский, *adj.* Old Russian.

древнецерко́внославя́нский, *adj.* (*ling.*) Old Church Slavonic.

дре́в|ний (~ен, ~ня), *adj.* **1.** ancient; ~няя исто́рия ancient history; ~ние языки́ classical languages; *as noun* ~ние, ~них, the ancients. **2.** very old, aged.

дре́вност|ь, и, *f.* **1.** (*sing. only*) antiquity. **2.** (*pl.*; *archaeol.*) antiquities.

дре́в|о, а, *pl.* ~еса́, ~е́с, ~еса́м, *n.* (*poet.*) tree; д. позна́ния добра́ и зла the tree of the knowledge of good and evil.

древови́д|ный (~ен, ~на), tree-like; д. па́поротник tree-fern.

древонасажде́ни|е, я, *n.* **1.** tree-plantation. **2.** planting of trees.

дрези́н|а, ы, *f.* (*railways*) trolley, hand car.

дрейф, а, *m.* (*naut.*) drift, leeway; лечь в д. to heave to; лежа́ть в ~е to lie to.

дре́йф|ить, лю, ишь, *impf.* (*of* c~) (*coll.*) to be a coward, funk.

дрейф|ова́ть, у́ю, *impf.* (*naut.*) to drift; ~у́ющий лёд drift ice; нау́чная ~у́ющая ста́нция drift-ice research unit.

дрек, а, *m.* (*naut.*) grapnel.

дреко́лье, я, *n.* (*collect.*) staves (*as weapon*).

дрел|ь, и, *f.* (*tech.*) (hand-)drill.

дрем|а́, ы́ (*and* дрём|а, ы), *f.* (*poet.*) drowsiness, sleepiness.

дрем|а́ть, лю́, ~лешь, *impf.* to doze; to slumber; не д. (*also fig.*) to be watchful; to be wide awake.

дрем|а́ться, ~лется, *impf.* (*impers.* +*d.*) to feel sleepy, drowsy.

дремо́т|а, ы, *f.* drowsiness, sleepiness, somnolence.

дремо́тный, *adj.* drowsy, sleepy, somnolent.

дрему́ч|ий (~, ~а), *adj.* (*poet.*) thick, dense (*of a forest*).

дрена́ж, а, *m.* **1.** (*tech. and med.*) drainage. **2.** (*med.*) drainage-tube.

дренажи́р|овать, ую, *impf. and pf.* (*med.*) to drain.

дрена́ж|ный, *adj.* of ~; ~ная труба́ drain-pipe.

дрени́р|овать, ую, *impf. and pf.* to drain.

дресв|а́, ы́, *f.* gravel.

дрессиро́ванн|ый, *p.p.p.* of дрессирова́ть *and adj.*; ~ые живо́тные performing animals.

дрессир|ова́ть, у́ю, *impf.* (*of* вы́~) to train (*animals*); (*fig.*) to school.

дрессиро́вк|а, и, *f.* training.

дрессиро́вщик, а, *m.* trainer.

дриа́д|а, ы, *f.* (*myth.*) dryad.

дроби́лк|а, и, *f.* (*tech.*) crusher.

дроби́льн|ый, *adj.* (*tech.*) crushing; ~ая маши́на crusher.

дроби́н|а, ы, *f.* pellet.

дроб|и́ть, лю́, и́шь, *impf.* (*of* раз~) **1.** to break up, crush, smash (to pieces). **2.** (*fig.*) to subdivide, split up.

дроб|и́ться, и́тся, *impf.* (*of* раз~) **1.** to break to pieces, smash, smash to pieces. **2.** to divide, split up.

дробле́ни|е, я, *n.* **1.** crushing, breaking up. **2.** (*fig.*) subdivision, splitting up. **2.** (*biol.*) cell-division.

дроблёный, *adj.* splintered, crushed, ground.

дробни́ц|а, ы, *f.* ammunition-pouch.

дро́б|ный (~ен, ~на), *adj.* **1.** separate; subdivided, split up; minute. **2.** staccato, abrupt; д. стук staccato knocking; д. дождь fine rain. **3.** (*math.*) fractional.

дробови́к, а́, *m.* shot-gun.

дроб|ь, и, *pl.* ~и, ~е́й, *f.* **1.** (*collect.*) small shot. **2.** drumming; tapping; trilling. **3.** (*math.*) fraction. **4.** oblique stroke.

дров|а́, ~, ~а́м, *no sing.* firewood; наколо́ть д. to chop firewood; кто в лес, кто по дрова́ (*fig.*) at sixes and sevens, inharmoniously.

дро́вн|и, ~е́й, *no sing.* (*peasant*) wood-sledge.

дровоко́л, а, *m.* (*obs.*) woodcutter.

дровосе́к, а, *m.* **1.** woodcutter. **2.** (*pl.*) (*zool.*) Cerambycidae.

дровяни́к, а́, *m.* **1.** (*obs.*) firewood merchant. **2.** (*coll.*) woodshed.

дров|яно́й, *adj.* of ~а́; д. сара́й woodshed; д. склад wood pile, wood store.

дрог|а́, и́, *a.* ~у, *pl.* ~и, *f.* centre pole (*of cart*).

дро́г|и, ~, *no sing.* **1.** dray cart. **2.** hearse.

дро́г|нуть[1], ну, нешь, *past* ~, ~ла, *impf.* to be chilled, freeze.

дро́гн|уть[2], у, ешь, *past* ~ул, ~ула, *pf.* **1.** to shake, move; to quaver; to flicker. **2.** to waver, falter; у меня́ рука́ не ~ет (+*inf.*) I shall not hesitate to . . .

дрожа́ни|е, я, *n.* trembling, vibration.

дрожа́тельный, *adj.* tremulous, shivery; **д. парали́ч** (*med.*) shaking palsy, Parkinson's disease.

дрож|а́ть, у́, и́шь, *impf.* 1. to tremble; to shiver, shake; to quiver; to vibrate; to quaver; to flicker; **д. от хо́лода, испу́га** to shiver with cold, with fright. 2. (**за**+*a.* or **пе́ред**+*i.*; *fig.*) to tremble (for; before). 3. (**над**+*i.*) to grudge; **д. над ка́ждой копе́йкой** to count every penny.

дрожж|ево́й, *adj. of* ~и; ~евы́е грибки́ (*bot.*) Ascomycetes.

дро́жж|и, е́й, *no sing.* yeast, leaven; **ста́вить на** ~а́х to leaven; **пивны́е д.** barm, brewer's yeast.

дро́ж|ки, ~ек, ~кам, *no sing.* droshky.

дрож|ь, и, f. 1. shivering, trembling; tremor, quaver. 2. (varied) tints.

дрозд, а́, m. thrush; **пе́вчий д.** song-thrush; **чёрный д.** blackbird.

дрок, а, m. (*bot.*) gorse.

дромаде́р, а, m. (*zool.*) dromedary.

дро́ссел|ь, я, m. (*tech.*) throttle, choke.

дро́тик, а, m. javelin.

дрочён|а, ы, f. (*cul.*) batter.

друг¹, а, *pl.* **друзья́, друзе́й, m.** friend; **д. до́ма** friend of the family.

друг² (*short form of* ~о́й) **д.** ~а each other, one another; **д. за** ~ом one after another; **д. с** ~ом with each other.

друг|о́й, *adj.* 1. other, another; different; **и тот и д.** both; **ни тот ни д.** neither; **никто́ д.** none other; **э́то** ~о́е де́ло that is another matter; ~и́ми слова́ми in other words; **с** ~о́й стороны́ on the other hand; **на д. день** the next day; *as noun* ~и́е, ~и́х others. 2. second. 3. (*coll.*) the odd.

дру́жб|а, ы, f. friendship; **не в слу́жбу, а в** ~у out of friendship.

дружелю́би|е, я, *n.* friendliness.

дружелю́б|ный (~ен, ~на), *adj.* friendly, amicable.

дру́жеск|ий, *adj.* friendly; **быть на** ~ой ноге́ (**с**+*i.*) to be on friendly terms (with).

дру́жественн|ый, *adj.* friendly, amicable; ~ая держа́ва friendly power.

дру́жеств|о, а, *n.* (*obs.*) friendship.

дружи́н|а, ы, f. 1. (*hist.*) (prince's) armed force. 2. militia unit, detachment (*in tsarist Russia*); **боева́я д.** (*hist.*) armed workers' detachment. 3. squad, team; **доброво́льная наро́дная д.** voluntary people's (militia) patrol (*as organized in U.S.S.R. since 1958 to assist police in maintaining public order, combatting hooliganism, etc.*).

дружи́нник, а, m. 1. (*hist.*) member of (prince's) armed force. 2. (*hist.*) member of militia detachment; member of armed band. 3. member of voluntary people's

(militia) patrol, vigilante; **д.** противовозду́шной оборо́ны air-raid warden.

друж|и́ть, у́, ~и́шь, *impf.* 1. (**с**+*i.*) to be friends (with), on friendly terms (with). 2. (*obs.*) to make friends, unite.

друж|и́ться, у́сь, ~и́шься, *impf.* (*of* по~) (**с**+*i.*) to make friends (with).

дружи́щ|е, а, m. (*coll.*) old chap (*as mode of address*).

дру́жк|а¹, и, m. (*ethnol.*) best man (*at wedding*).

дру́жк|а²: друг ~у, *etc.* (*coll.*) = друг дру́га, *etc.*

дру́жно, *adv.* 1. harmoniously, in concord. 2. simultaneously, in concert; раз, два, ~! heave-ho!, all together! 3. rapidly, smoothly (*of coming of spring, thawing of snow, etc.*).

дру́жный (~ен, ~на́, ~но), *adj.* 1. amicable; harmonious. 2. simultaneous, concerted; ~ые уси́лия concerted efforts. 3. ~ная весна́ spring with rapid, uninterrupted thawing of snow.

друж|о́к, ка́, m. (*coll.*) pal; (*as mode of address*) my dear.

друзья́, *see* друг.

друммо́ндов, *adj.*; **д. свет** (*theatr.*) limelight.

дры́г|ать, аю, *impf.* (*of* ~нуть) (+*i.*; *coll.*) to jerk, twitch.

дры́г|нуть, ну, нешь, *pf. of* ~ать.

дры́х|нуть, ну, нешь, *past* ~ *and* ~нул, ~ла, *impf.* (*coll.*) to sleep.

дря́бл|ый (~, ~а́, ~о), *adj.* flabby (*also fig.*); flaccid; sluggish.

дря́бн|уть, у, ешь, *impf.* (*coll.*) to become flabby.

дря́гил|ь, я, m. (*obs.*) carrier, porter.

дрязг, а (у), m. (*collect.; obs. or dial.*) refuse, rubbish.

дря́зг|и, ~, *no sing.* (*coll.*) squabbles; annoyances, unpleasantnesses.

дрян|но́й (~ен, ~на́, ~но), *adj.* (*coll.*) worthless, rotten; good-for-nothing.

дрян|ь, и, f. (*coll.*) 1. trash, rubbish. 2. *as pred.* it is rotten, it is no good; **пого́да — д.** the weather is awful. 3. (*of a person*) a bad lot, a good-for-nothing.

дряхле́|ть, ю, *impf.* (*of* о~) to grow decrepit.

дря́хлост|ь, и, f. decrepitude, senile infirmity.

дря́хл|ый (~, ~а́, ~о), *adj.* decrepit, senile.

дуали́зм, а, m. (*philos.*) dualism.

дуб, а, *pl.* ~ы́, **m.** 1. oak. 2. (*coll.*) blockhead, numskull.

дуба́|сить, шу, сишь, *impf.* (*coll.*) 1. to cudgel. 2. (**по**+*d.*, **в**+*a.*) to bang (on).

дуби́льн|ый, *adj.* tanning, tannic; ~ое вещество́ tannin; ~ая кислота́ tannic acid.

дуби́л|ьня, ьни, *g. pl.* ~ен, **f.** tannery.

дуби́льщик, а, m. tanner.

дуби́н|а, ы, f. 1. club, cudgel. 2. (*coll.*) blockhead, numskull.

дуби́нк|а, и, *f.* truncheon, baton.

дуб|и́ть, лю́, и́шь, *impf.* (*of* вы́~) to tan.

дублёный, *adj.* tanned (*also fig.* = weather-beaten).

дублёр, а, *m.* (*theatr.*) understudy; (*cinema*) actor dubbing a part.

дублёт, а, *m.* duplicate.

дублика́т, а, *m.* duplicate.

дубли́р|овать, ую, *impf.* **1.** to duplicate; д. ро́ль (*theatr.*) to understudy a part. **2.** (*cinema*) to dub. **3.** д. че́рез копи́рку to make a carbon copy (of).

дубня́к, а́, *m.* wood of oak-trees.

дубова́т|ый (~, ~а), *adj.* (*coll.*) coarse; stupid, thick.

дубо́в|ый, *adj.* **1.** oak; д. лист oak-leaf; д. гроб oak coffin. **2.** (*fig., coll.*) coarse; thick; ~ая голова́ blockhead, numskull. **3.** (*fig., coll.*) hard (= inedible).

дуб|о́к, ка́, *m.* oakling.

дубра́в|а, ы, *f.* **1.** oak forest. **2.** (*poet.*) leafy grove.

дубь|ё, я́, *no pl., n.* (*collect.; coll.*) **1.** cudgels. **2.** fools, blockheads.

дуг|а́, й, *pl.* ~и, *f.* **1.** shaft-bow (*part of harness*). **2.** arc, arch; бро́ви ~о́й arched brows; согну́ть в ~у́, в три ~и́ (*coll.*) to bring under, compel to submit.

дуг|ово́й, *adj. of* ~а́; ~ова́я ла́мпа arc-lamp; ~ова́я сва́рка arc welding.

дугообра́з|ный (~ен, ~на), *adj.* arched, bow-shaped.

дуд|е́ть, *1st person not used,* и́шь, *impf.* (*coll.*) to play the pipe, fife.

ду́дк|а, и, *f.* pipe, fife; пляса́ть под чью-н. ~у (*fig.*) to dance to someone's tune.

**ду́дки, *interj.* (*coll.*) not if I know it!, not on your life!

ду́жк|а, и, *f.* **1.** *dim. of* дуга́. **2.** hoop (*at croquet*). **3.** handle.

дука́т, а, *m.* ducat.

дул|о, а, *n.* muzzle, barrel (*of firearms*); д. без наре́зки smooth bore.

ду́л|ьный, *adj. of* ~о; ~ьная ско́рость muzzle velocity.

ду́л|ьце, ьца, *g. pl.* ~ец, *n.* **1.** *dim. of* ~о. **2.** (*mus.*) mouthpiece (*of wind instruments*).

ду́м|а, ы, *f.* **1.** thought, meditation; (*folk poet.*) ду́мать ~у to meditate, brood. **2.** duma (*Ukrainian folk ballad*). **3.** (*hist.*) duma, council, representative assembly; Госуда́рственная Д. the State Duma.

ду́ма|ть, ю, *impf.* (*of* по~) **1.** (о+*p. or* над+*i.*) to think (about); to be concerned (about); мно́го о себе́ д. to have a high opinion of oneself. **2.** (*impf. only*) д. что... to think, suppose that...; я ~ю! of course!, I should think so! **3.** (+*inf.*) to think of, intend; он ~ет пое́хать в Ло́ндон he is thinking of going to London; и не ~ю (+*inf.*) I would

not dream (of); и д. не смей (+*inf.*) don't dare (to). **4.** (+*indirect question*) to wonder.

ду́ма|ться, ется, *impf.* (*impers.*+*d.*) to seem; мне ~ется I think, I fancy; ~ется it seems.

ду́м|ец, ца, *m.* (*hist.*) member of duma; councillor.

ду́мк|а, и, *f.* **1.** *dim. of* ду́ма 1. **2.** (*coll.*) small pillow. **3.** dumka (*Ukrainian folk-lyric*).

ду́мный, *adj.* (*hist.*) of the Boyars' Council.

ду́м|ский, *adj. of* ~а 3; ~ские де́ньги credit notes (*issued by the Provisional Government in 1917*).

дунове́ни|е, я, *n.* puff, breath (*of wind*).

ду́н|уть, у, ешь, *pf.* to blow.

ду́пел|ь, я, *pl.* ~я́, *m.* (*orn.*) great snipe.

дупле́т, а, *m.* doublet (*at billiards*).

дупли́ст|ый (~, ~а), *adj.* hollow.

дупл|о́, а́, *pl.* ~а, ду́пел, *n.* **1.** hollow (*in tree-trunk*). **2.** cavity (*in a tooth*).

-дур, *indecl. adj.,* (*mus.*) major.

ду́р|а, ы, *f. of* дура́к.

дура́к, а́, *m.* **1.** (*hist.*) jester, fool. **2.** fool, ass; д. ~о́м an utter fool; не д. (+*inf.*) (to be) expert (at); оста́вить в ~ах to make a fool of; оста́ться в ~ах to be fooled, make a fool of oneself; валя́ть, лома́ть ~а́ to play the fool; to make a fool of oneself; на ~а́ for fun, for a joke; ~а́м зако́н не пи́сан (*prov.*) fools rush in where angels fear to tread; нашёл ~а́! not likely!, no thanks!

дурале́|й, я, *m.* = дура́к 2.

дура́цкий, *adj.* (*coll.*) stupid, foolish, idiotic; д. колпа́к dunce's cap.

дура́честв|о, а, *n.* folly, absurdity; foolish trick.

дура́ч|ить, у, ишь, *impf.* (*of* о~) to fool, dupe.

дура́ч|иться, усь, ишься, *impf.* to play the fool.

дура́ч|о́к, ка́, *m.* **1.** *affectionate dim. of* дура́к. **2.** (*coll.*) idiot, imbecile.

дура́шлив|ый (~, ~а), *adj.* (*coll.*) stupid.

ду́р|ень, ня, *m.* (*coll.*) fool, simpleton.

дуре́|ть, ю, *impf.* (*of* о~) to become stupid.

дур|и́ть, ю́, и́шь, *impf.* (*coll.*) **1.** to be naughty (*of children*); to play tricks. **2.** to be obstinate (*esp. of horses*).

дурма́н, а, *m.* **1.** (*bot.*) thorn-apple (*Datura stramonium*). **2.** (*coll.*) drug, narcotic; intoxicant.

дурма́н|ить, ю, ишь, *impf.* (*of* о~) to stupefy.

дурне́|ть, ю, *impf.* (*of* по~) to grow ugly.

ду́рно, *adv. of* дурно́й.

ду́рно, *as pred.* (*impers.*+*d.*) мне, *etc.*, д. I, *etc.*, feel faint, bad, queer.

дур|но́й (~ен, ~на́, ~но), *adj.* **1.** (*in var. senses*) bad, evil; nasty; д. вкус nasty taste; д. глаз the evil eye; ~ы́е мы́сли evil thoughts; ~ы́е привы́чки bad habits; д.

сон bad dream. **2.** (собо́ю) ugly. **3.** (*coll.*) foolish, stupid. **4.** ~на́я боле́знь (*coll.*) venereal disease.

дурнот|а́, ы́, *f.* (*coll.*) faintness; nausea; чу́вствовать ~у́ to feel faint, sick.

дурну́шк|а, и, *f.* (*coll.*) plain girl, plain Jane.

ду́рост|ь, и, *f.* (*coll.*) folly, stupidity.

дуршла́г, а, *m.* (*cul.*) colander.

дур|ь, и, *f.* (*coll.*) foolishness, stupidity; вы́бить, вы́колотить д. (из) to knock the nonsense (out of).

ду́с|я, и, *f.* (*coll., affect. mode of address*) darling.

ду́т|ый, *p.p.p.* of ~ь and adj. **1.** hollow. **2.** inflated; ~ые ши́ны pneumatic tyres. **3.** (*fig.*) inflated, exaggerated; ~ые ци́фры exaggerated figures.

дуть, ду́ю, ду́ешь, *impf.* **1.** (*pf.* по~) to blow; сего́дня ду́ет ве́тер с за́пада there is a west wind today; от окна́ ду́ет there is a draught from the window; в ус не ду́ет (*coll.*) he does not give a damn. **2.** (*pf.* вы́~) to blow (*glassware*). **3.** (*pf.* от~) (*coll.*) to thrash; д. и в хвост и в гри́ву to urge on, drive relentlessly. **4.** (*pf.* вы́~) (*coll.*) to drink deep. **5.** (*coll.*) to rush. **6.** (*coll.*) to do something (*e.g.*, to play a musical instrument) with abandon, energetically.

дутьё|ё, я́, *n.* **1.** (*tech.*) blowing, blast; про́ба че́рез д. bubble test. **2.** (glass-)blowing.

ду́|ться, юсь, ешься, *impf.* (*coll.*) **1.** (на+*a.*) to grumble (at), pout (at). **2.** (в+*a.*) to play with abandon.

дух, а, *m.* **1.** (*rel., philos., and fig.*) spirit; свято́й д. the Holy Spirit, the Holy Ghost; д. ве́ка Zeitgeist (*spirit of the age*). **2.** spirit(s); heart; mind; настрое́ние ~а, расположе́ние ~а mood, temper, humour; быть в ~е to be in good (high) spirits; не в ~е in low spirits; па́дать ~ом to lose heart, become despondent; собра́ться с ~ом to take heart, pluck up one's courage; прису́тствие ~а presence of mind; хва́тит ~у (на+*a.*) to have the strength (for); у меня́ ~у не хвата́ет (+*inf.*) I have not the heart (to); э́то не в моём ~е it is not to my taste; что́-то в э́том ~е something of the sort. **3.** breath; (*coll.*) air; перевести́ д. to take breath; испусти́ть д. (*fig.*) to give up the ghost; во весь д. (*coll.*) at full speed, flat out; одни́м ~ом in one breath; (*fig.*) at one go, at a stretch; о нём ни слу́ху ни ~у nothing is heard of him. **4.** spectre, ghost. **5.** (*coll.*) smell.

духа́н, а, *m.* dukhan (*inn in Caucasus*).

дух|и́, о́в, *no sing.*, perfume, scent.

духобо́р, а, *m.* Dukhobor.

духобо́рств|о, а, *n.* the Dukhobor religious sect.

ду́хов, *adj.*; Д. день (*eccl.*) Whit Monday.

духове́нств|о, а, *n.* (*collect.*) clergy, priesthood.

духови́д|ец, ца, *m.* clairvoyant; medium.

духови́т|ый (~, ~а), *adj.* (*coll., dial.*) aromatic.

духо́вк|а, и, *f.* oven.

духо́вн|ая, ой, *f.* testament, will.

духовни́к, а́, *m.* (*eccl.*) confessor.

духо́вност|ь, и, *f.* spirituality.

духо́вн|ый, *adj.* **1.** spiritual; inner, inward; ~ые запро́сы spiritual demands; д. мир inner world; д. о́блик spiritual make-up. **2.** ecclesiastical, church; religious; ~ое лицо́ ecclesiastic; ~ая му́зыка church music, sacred music; д. оте́ц confessor, spiritual director; д. сан holy orders. **3.** ~ое завеща́ние (last) will, testament. **4.** ~ое о́ко (the) mind's eye.

духов|о́й, *adj.* **1.** (*mus.*) wind; д. инструме́нт wind instrument; д. орке́стр brass band. **2.** (hot-)air; ~о́е отопле́ние hot-air heating; ~а́я печь oven; ~о́е ружьё air-gun; д. утю́г steam iron. **3.** (*cul.*) steamed.

духот|а́, ы́, *f.* stuffiness, closeness; stuffy heat.

душ, а, *m.* shower-bath; приня́ть д. to take a shower(-bath).

душ|а́, и́, а. ~у, *pl.* ~и, *f.* **1.** soul; (*fig.*) heart; без ~и́ (от; *obs.*) beside oneself (with); д. в ~у at one, in harmony; в ~е́ (*i*) inwardly, secretly, (*ii*) at heart; для ~и́ for one's private satisfaction; за ~о́й to one's name; у него́ за ~о́й ни гроша́ he hasn't a penny to his name; от ~и́ from the heart; от всей ~и́ with all one's heart; по ~е́ (+*d.*) to one's liking; по ~а́м говори́ть (с+*i.*) to have a heart-to-heart talk (with); вложи́ть ~у (в+*a.*) to put one's heart (into); изли́ть, отвести́ ~у to pour out one's heart; ~и́ не ча́ять (в+*p.*) to worship, adore; ско́лько ~е́ уго́дно to one's heart's content; ~о́й и те́лом heart and soul; ни ~о́й, ни те́лом in no wise, in no respect. **2.** feeling, spirit; говори́ть с ~о́й to speak with feeling. **3.** (*fig.*) (the) soul; moving spirit; inspiration; д. о́бщества the life and soul of the party. **4.** (*fig.*) spirit (= person); сме́лая д. a bold spirit. **5.** (*fig.*) soul (= person); на ~у per head; ни (живо́й) ~и́ not a (living) soul. **6.** (моя́) (*coll.*; *affectionate mode of address*) my dear, darling.

душев|а́я, о́й, *f.* shower-room.

душевнобольн|о́й, *adj.* insane; suffering from mental illness; *as noun* д., ~о́го, *m.* ~а́я, ~о́й, *f.* insane person; mental patient.

душе́вн|ый, *adj.* **1.** mental, psychical; ~ая боле́знь mental illness; ~ое потрясе́ние nervous shock. **2.** sincere, cordial, heartfelt; ~ая бесéда friendly chat; д. человéк understanding person.

душев|óй¹, adj. per head; ~ое потреблéние consumption per head.

душевóй², adj. of душ.

душегрéйк|а, и, f. (woman's) sleeveless jacket (usu. wadded or fur-lined).

душегýб, а, m. (coll.) murderer.

душегýб|ка, ки, f. 1. f. of ~. 2. dugout (canoe). 3. (hist.) mobile gas-chamber.

душегýбств|о, а, n. (coll.) murder.

дýшеньк|а, и, m. and f. (obs., coll.) darling (affectionate mode of address).

душеполéз|ный (~ен, ~на), adj. (obs.) edifying.

душеприкáзчик, а, m. (leg.; obs.) executor.

душеприкáзчиц|а, ы, f. (leg.; obs.) executrix.

душераздирáющий, adj. heart-rending.

душеспаси́тел|ьный (~ен, ~ьна), adj. (eccl. or iron.) salutary, edifying.

дýшечк|а, и, m. and f. = дýшенька.

души́ст|ый (~, ~а), adj. fragrant, sweet--scented.

души́тел|ь, я, m. strangler, suffocator; (fig.) suppressor.

душ||и́ть¹, ý, ~ишь, impf. (of за~) 1. to strangle; to stifle, smother, suffocate; (fig.) to stifle, suppress; д. поцелýями to smother with kisses. 2. (impf. only) to choke; егó ~и́л кáшель, гнев he choked with coughing, with rage.

душ||и́ть², ý, ~ишь, impf. (of на~) to scent, perfume.

душ||и́ться¹, ýсь, ~ишься, impf., pass. of ~и́ть¹.

душ||и́ться², ýсь, ~ишься, impf. (of на~) (+i.) to perfume oneself (with); онá всегдá ~ится францýзскими духáми she always uses French perfume.

дýшк|а, и, m. and f. (coll.) dear (person); он такóй д., онá такáя д. he, she is such a dear.

душни́к, á, m. vent (in stove).

дýшно, as pred. it is stuffy; it is stifling, suffocating; мне стáло д. I felt suffocated.

дýш|ный (~ен, ~нá, ~но), adj. stuffy, close, sultry; stifling.

душ|óк, кá, m. (coll.) 1. smell (esp. of decaying matter); с ~кóм high, tainted. 2. (fig.) smack, taint; tinge; газéта с либерáльным ~кóм (pejor.) newspaper with a liberal tinge.

дуэли́ст, а, m. duellist.

дуэл|ь, и, f. duel; вы́звать на д. to challenge; дрáться на ~и to fight a duel.

дуэля́нт, а, m. = дуэли́ст.

дуэ́н|ья, ьи, g. pl. ~ий, f. duenna.

дуэ́т, а, m. duet.

ды́б|а, ы, f. (hist.) rack (instrument of torture).

ды́б|иться, ится, impf. 1. to stand on end. 2. (of a horse) to rear, prance.

ды́бом, adv. on end; вóлосы у негó встáли д. his hair stood on end.

дыбы́; на д. on to the hind legs; становиться на д. to rear, prance; (fig.) to kick, resist.

ды́лд|а, ы, m. and f. (coll.) lanky fellow, girl.

дым, а (у), о ~е, в ~ý, pl. ~ы́, m. 1. smoke; в д. (coll.) completely; там д. коромы́слом (coll.) it's a bedlam there. 2. (hist.) household, hearth (as unit for taxation).

дым||и́ть, лю́, и́шь, impf. (of на~) to smoke (intrans.), emit smoke.

дым||и́ться, и́тся, impf. to smoke (intrans.); (of fog) to billow.

ды́мк|а, и, f. 1. haze (also fig.). 2. (obs.) gauze.

ды́мный, adj. smoky; д. пóрох black powder, gunpowder.

дымов|óй, adj. of дым; ~áя завéса (mil.) smoke-screen; ~áя мáска (anti-)smoke mask; д. снаря́д (mil.) smoke-shell; ~áя трубá flue, chimney; funnel, smoke-stack.

дымогáр|ный, adj.; д. котёл fire-tube boiler; ~ая трубá flue, fire tube.

дым|óк, кá, m. puff of smoke.

дымомёт, а, m. (mil.) smoke projector.

дымохóд, а, m. flue.

ды́мчат|ый (~, ~а), adj. smoke-coloured.

ды́нный, adj. of ды́ня.

ды́н|я, и, f. melon.

дыр|á, ы́, pl. ~ы, f. 1. hole; заткнýть ~ý (fig.) to stop a gap. 2. (fig., coll.) hole (= remote place). 3. (pl. only) gaps, shortcomings.

дырокóл, а, m. hole-puncher, punch.

дыря́в||ить, лю, ишь, impf. (coll.) to make a hole (in).

дыря́в|ый (~, ~а), adj. full of holes, holey.

дыхáни|е, я, n. breathing; breath; вторóе д. (fig.) second wind; искýсственное д. artificial respiration.

дыхáтельн|ый, adj. respiratory; ~ое гóрло (anat.) windpipe; ~ые пути́ respiratory tract.

дыш||áть, ý, ~ишь, impf. (+i.) to breathe; д. мéстью to breathe vengeance; éле д. to be at one's last gasp; (fig.) to be on one's last legs.

ды́шл|о, а, n. shaft, pole, beam (attached to front axle of cart, etc., drawn by two horses).

дья́вол, а, m. devil; какóго ~а?, за каки́м ~ом?, на кой ~? (coll.) why the devil?, why the deuce?

дья́вол|ёнок, ёнка, pl. ~я́та, ~я́т, m. (coll.) imp.

дья́вольский, adj. devilish, diabolical; (coll.) damnable.

дья́вольщина, ы, f. (coll.) devilment; что за д.! what the hell's going on?

дьяк, á, m. (hist.) 1. (prince's) scribe. 2. clerk, secretary.

дья́кон, а, pl. ~á, ~óв, m. (eccl.) deacon.

дья́кониц|а, ы, *f.* (*coll.*) deacon's wife.
дья́конств|о, а, *n.* (*eccl.*) diaconate.
дьяч|о́к, ка́, *m.* (*eccl.*) sacristan, sexton; reader.
дю́же, *adv.* (*coll. or dial.*) terribly, awfully.
дю́ж|ий, (~, ~а́, ~е), *adj.* (*coll.*) sturdy, hefty, robust.
дю́жин|а, ы, *f.* dozen; чёртова д. baker's dozen.
дю́жинный, *adj.* ordinary, commonplace.
дюйм, а, *m.* inch.
дюймо́вк|а, и, *f.* (*coll.*) 1. inch(-thick) plank. 2. one-inch nail.
дюймо́вый, *adj.* one-inch.
дю́н|а, ы, *f.* dune.

дюра́л|ь, я, *m.* = ~юми́ний.
дюралюми́ни|й, я, *m.* (*tech.*) duralumin.
дюшéс, а, *m.* Duchess pear.
дя́гил|ь, я, *m.* (*bot.*) angelica.
дя́деньк|а, и, *m.* *affectionate form of* дя́дя.
дя́дин, *adj.* uncle's.
дя́дьк|а, и, *m.* 1. *pejor. form of* дя́дя. 2. (*coll.*) = дя́дя 2. 3. (*obs.*) tutor (*in noble families*); usher (*in boys' private schools*).
дя́дюшк|а, и, *m.* (*coll.*) *affectionate form of* дя́дя.
дя́д|я, и, *pl.* ~и, ~ей, *and* ~ья́, ~ьёв, *m.* 1. uncle. 2. (*coll.*) mister (*as term of address by children to any male of mature age*).
дя́т|ел, ла, *m.* woodpecker.

Е

еб|а́ть, у́, ёшь, *impf.* (*of* уéть) (*vulg.*) to fuck.
ев- (*in words derived from Greek*) eu-.
Ева́нгели|е, я, *n.* (*collect.*) the Gospels; e. gospel (*also fig.*).
евангéлик, а, *m.* (an) evangelical.
евангели́ст, а, *m.* 1. Evangelist. 2. (an) evangelical.
евангели́ческ|ий, *adj.* evangelical; ~ая це́рковь Evangelical Church
ева́нгельский, *adj.* gospel.
евгéник|а, и, *f.* eugenics.
евкали́пт(овый), = эвкали́пт(овый).
éвнух, а, *m.* eunuch.
евразийский, *adj.* (*geogr.*) Eurasian.
евразийств|о, а, *n.* Eurasianism (*theory asserting special character of Russian and related Eastern cultures*).
еврé|й, я, *m.* Jew; Hebrew.
еврéйк|а, и, *f.* Jewess.
еврéйский, *adj.* Jewish.
еврéйств|о, а, *n.* 1. (*collect.*) Jewry, the Jews. 2. Jewishness.
европé|ец, йца, *m.* European.
европеиза́ци|я, и, *f.* Europeanization.
европеизи́р|овать, ую, *impf. and pf.* to europeanize.
европéйск|ий, *adj.* European; Western.
евста́хиев, *adj.*; ~а труба́ (*anat.*) Eustachian tube.
евфеми́зм, а, *m.* euphemism.
евхаристи́ческий, *adj.* (*eccl.*) eucharistal.
евхари́сти|я, и, *f.* (*eccl.*) Eucharist.
егермéйстер, а, *m.* (*obs.*) master of the hunt.
éгер|ский, *adj. of* ~ь; e. полк regiment of chasseurs.
éгер|ь, я, *pl.* ~и, ~ей *and* ~я́, ~éй, *m.* 1. huntsman. 2. (*mil.*) chasseur.
еги́петск|ий, *adj.* Egyptian; (*fig.*) severe,

hard; ~ая тьма pitch darkness; ~ая синь Egyptian blue (*a copper pigment*).
египто́лог, а, *m.* Egyptologist.
египтоло́ги|я, и, *f.* Egyptology.
египтя́н|ин, ина, *pl.* ~е, ~, *m.* Egyptian.
египтя́н|ка, ки, *f. of* ~ин.
егó 1. *g. and a. sing. of* он; *g. sing. of* онó. 2. (*possessive adj.*) his; its.
егоз|а́, ы́, *m. and f.* (*coll.*) fidget.
его|зи́ть, жу́, зи́шь, *impf.* (*coll.*) 1. to fidget. 2. (пéред+*i.*) to fawn (upon).
егозли́в|ый (~, ~а), *adj.* (*coll.*) fidgety.
ед|а́, ы́, *f.* 1. food. 2. meal; во врéмя ~ы́ at meal-times, during a meal, while eating.
еда́|ть, *no pres., past* ~л, ~ла, (*coll.*) *freq. of* есть[1].
едва́, *adv. and conj.* 1. (*adv.*) hardly, barely, only just (= *with difficulty*); мы е. попа́ли на пóезд we only just caught the train. 2. (*adv.*) hardly, scarcely, barely, only just (= *only slightly*); печь е. гори́т the fire is barely alight. 3. едва́-едва́ *emphatic variant of* e. 1, 2. 4. e. ли (*adv.*) hardly, scarcely (*in judgements of probability*); e. ли он отка́жется от тако́го соблазни́тельного предложéния he will hardly refuse such a tempting offer. 5. e. (ли) не (*adv.*) nearly, almost, all but; я е. не пóмер сó смеху I nearly died laughing; э́та оши́бка e. ли не грубéйшая из замéченных мнóю that is perhaps (= I am inclined to think) the worst howler I have ever seen. 6. (*conj.*) hardly, scarcely, barely; e...., как scarcely ... when,; no sooner ... than; e. самолёт взлетéл, как оди́н из мото́ров заéло no sooner had the plane taken off than one of the engines seized up.
ед|и́м, и́те, я́т, *see* есть[1].
единéни|е, я, *n.* unity.

едини|ть, ю, ишь, *impf.* (*obs.*) to unite.

единиц|а, ы, *f.* **1.** one; figure 1; (*math.*) unity. **2.** (*in var. senses*) unit; e. мóщности unit of power; ~ы воéнно-морскóго флóта naval units. **3.** 'one' (*lowest mark in Russian university and school marking system*). **4.** individual; (тóлько) ~ы only a few, only a handful.

единичност|ь, и, *f.* singleness; single occurrence.

единичн|ый, *adj.* **1.** single, unitary; e. слýчай solitary instance; ~ые слýчаи isolated cases. **2.** individual; ~ое сéльское хозя́йство farming on an individual basis.

единобóжи|е, я, *n.* monotheism.

единобóрств|о, а, *n.* (*rhet.*) single combat.

единобрáчи|е, я, *n.* monogamy.

единобрáчный, *adj.* monogamous; (*bot.*) monogamian, monogynous.

единовéр|ец, ца, *m.* **1.** co-religionist. **2.** member of Edinoverie (*see* ~ие).

единовéри|е, я, *n.* **1.** community of religion. **2.** Edinoverie (*an Old Believer sect which reached an organizational compromise with the official Orthodox Church*).

единовéр|ный (~ен, ~на), *adj.* (+*d.* or с+*i.*) of the same faith (as).

единовéр|ческий, *adj.* of ~ие 2.

единовлáсти|е, я, *n.* autocracy, absolute rule.

единовлáст|ный (~ен, ~на), *adj.* autocratic; dictatorial; e. прави́тель absolute ruler.

единоврéменно, *adv.* **1.** but once, once only. **2.** simultaneously.

единоврéменн|ый, *adj.* **1.** extraordinary, unique; ~ое пособие extraordinary grant. **2.** (+*d.* or с+*i.*) simultaneous (with).

единоглáси|е, я, *n.* unanimity.

единоглáсно, *adv.* unanimously; при́нято e. carried unanimously.

единоглáсный, *adj.* unanimous.

единодержáви|е, я, *n.* (*obs.*) monarchy, autocracy.

единодержáв|ный (~ен, ~на), *adj.* (*obs.*) having autocratic powers, unlimited powers.

единодýши|е, я, *n.* unanimity.

единодýш|ный (~ен, ~на), *adj.* unanimous.

единóжды, *adv.* (*obs.*) once; e. три — три three ones are three.

единокрóв|ный (~ен, ~на), *adj.* **1.** (*obs.*) consanguineous; e. брат half-brother. **2.** of the same stock.

единоли́чник, а, *m.* individual peasant-farmer (*working his own holding*).

единоли́чн|ый, *adj.* individual; personal; ~ое решéние individual decision; ~ое хозя́йство individual peasant holding.

единомы́сли|е, я, *n.* agreement of opinion; like-mindedness.

единомы́шленник, а, *m.* **1.** person who holds the same views; like-minded person; мы с ним ~и по вопрóсам внéшней поли́тики we agree, we think the same way on matters of foreign policy. **2.** confederate, accomplice.

единонаслéди|е, я, *n.* (*leg.*) primogeniture.

единоначáли|е, я, *n.* one-man management; unified management; combined (military and political) command.

единоначáльник, а, *m.* **1.** combined (military and political) commander. **2.** sole director.

единообрáзи|е, я, *n.* uniformity.

единообрáз|ный (~ен, ~на), *adj.* uniform.

единоплемéнник, а, *m.* member of the same tribe; fellow-countryman.

единоплемéнный, *adj.* of the same tribe; of the same nationality.

единорóг, а, *m.* **1.** (*myth.*) unicorn. **2.** (*hist.*) 'unicorn' (*name of kind of cannon*). **3.** (*zool.*) narwhal.

единорóдный, *adj.* (*obs.*) only-begotten; e. сын only son.

единосýщный, *adj.* (*theol.*) (+*d.*) consubstantial (with).

единоутрóб|ный (~ен, ~на), *adj.* (*obs.*) uterine; e. брат half-brother, uterine brother.

еди́нственно, *adv.* only, solely; e. возмóжный ход the only possible move; онá присýтствовала e. из любопы́тства she came solely from curiosity.

еди́нственн|ый, *adj.* **1.** only, sole; one and only; e. сын only son; он e. пережи́л кораблекрушéние he was the sole survivor of the shipwreck; e. в своём рóде the only one of its kind, unique specimen; ~ое число́ (*gram.*) singular (number). **2.** (*obs.*) unique, unequalled.

еди́нств|о, а, *n.* (*in var. senses*) unity.

еди́н|ый (~, ~а), *adj.* **1.** one; single; sole; не́ было там ни ~ой души́ there was not a soul there; всё ~о (*coll.*) it's all one; все до ~ого to a man. **2.** united, unified; e. и недели́мый one and indivisible; ~ая срéдняя шкóла comprehensive school. **3.** common, single; ~ая вóля single will, purpose.

éд|кий (~ок, ~кá, ~ко), *adj.* **1.** caustic; acrid, pungent; e. натр (*chem.*) caustic soda; e. зáпах pungent smell. **2.** (*fig.*) caustic, sarcastic.

éдкост|ь, и, *f.* **1.** causticity; pungency; (*fig.*) sarcasm. **2.** sarcasm, sarcastic remark.

едóк, á, *m.* **1.** mouth; head; у негó в семьé дéсять ~óв he has ten mouths to feed; на ~á per head. **2.** (*coll.*) (big) eater; плохóй e. a poor eater.

éд|у, ешь, *see* éхать.

едýн, á, *m.* (*coll.*) mouth (= едóк 2).

éдучи, *pres. gerund* (*coll.*) *of* éхать.

éд|че, *comp. of* ~кий.

её **1.** *g. and a. of* онá. **2.** (*possessive adj.*) her.

ёж, ежá, *m.* hedgehog (*also mil.* = *obstruction of barbed wire entangled with stakes or iron bars*).

ёж|а, и, *f.* (*agric.*) orchard grass (*Dactylis*).

ежеви́к|а, и, *f.* **1.** (*collect.*) blackberries. **2.** bramble, blackberry bush.

ежеви́|чный, *adj. of* ~ка; ~чное варéнье bramble preserves.

ежегóдник, а, *m.* annual, year-book.

ежегóдный, *adj.* annual, yearly.

ежеднéвн|ый, *adj.* daily; everyday; ~ая лихорáдка quotidian fever.

éжели, *conj.* (*obs. or coll.*) if.

ежемéсячник, а, *m.* monthly (magazine).

ежемéсячный, *adj.* monthly.

ежеминýтный, *adj.* **1.** occurring every minute, at intervals of a minute; у нас есть е. автóбусный рейс в гóрод we have a one-minute bus service to town. **2.** incessant, continual.

еженедéльник, а, *m.* weekly (newspaper, magazine).

еженедéльный, *adj.* weekly.

еженóщный, *adj.* nightly.

ежесекýндный, *adj.* **1.** occurring every second. **2.** (*coll.*) incessant, continual.

ежесýточный, *adj.* daily (= *occurring every 24 hours*).

ежечáсный, *adj.* hourly.

ёжик, а, *m.* **1.** *dim. of* ёж. **2.** стри́чься ~ом to have a crew cut. **3.** brush (*for cleaning Primus stove, etc.*); steel wool.

ёж|иться, усь, ишься, *impf.* (*of* съ~) **1.** to shiver, huddle oneself up (*from cold, fever, etc.*). **2.** (*fig., coll.*) to shrink (*from fear, shyness, etc.*).

ежи́х|а, и, *f.* female hedgehog.

ежóв|ый, *adj. of* ёж; держáть в ~ых рукави́цах (*coll.*) to rule with a rod of iron.

езд|á, ы́, *f.* **1.** ride, riding; drive, driving; going; е. на велосипéде bicycling. **2.** *in phrases indicating distance from one point to another:* journey; отсю́да до óзера — дóбрых три часá ~ы́ from here to the lake is a good three hours' journey.

éз|дить, жу, дишь, *impf.* **1.** (*indet. of* éхать) to go (*in or on a vehicle or on an animal*); to ride, drive; е. верхóм to ride (on horseback). **2.** to (be able to) ride, drive. **3.** (к) to visit (*habitually*). **4.** (*coll.*) to slip.

езд|овóй, *adj. of* ~á; ~овы́е собáки draught-dogs; *as noun* е., ~овóго, *m.* (*mil.*) driver.

ездóк, á, *m.* **1.** rider; horseman. **2.** тудá я бóльше не е. I am not going there again.

езжá|ть, *no pres., past* ~л, ~ла, (*coll.*), *freq. of* éздить; ~й(те) (*as imper. of* éхать) go!, get going!

éзжен|ый, *adj.*; ~ая дорóга beaten track; (*coll.*) ~ая лóшадь broken-in horse.

езóп, ~овский, *see* эзóп.

ей, *d. and i. of* онá.

ей-Бóгу, *interj.* (*coll.*) truly!, really and truly!

ей-éй, *interj.* (*coll.*) truly!, in very truth!

ёк|ать, аю, *impf.* (*of* ~нуть) (+сéрдце) (*coll.*) to miss a beat; to go pit-a-pat.

ёкн|уть, у, ешь, *pf. of* ёкать.

ектен|ья́, ьи́, *g. pl.* ~и́й, *f.* (*eccl.*) ektenia (*part of Orthodox liturgy consisting of versicles and responses*).

ел, éла, *see* есть¹.

éле, *adv.* **1.** hardly, barely, only just (= *with difficulty*); егó речь былá е. слышнá his speech was hardly audible. **2.** hardly, scarcely, barely, only just (= *only slightly*); пóезд е. дви́гался the train was scarcely moving. **3.** éле-éле *emphatic variant of* е.; он е.-е. спáсся he had a very narrow escape.

élевый, *adj.* (*bot.*) fir, spruce.

елé|й, я, *m.* (*eccl.*) anointing oil; unction; (*fig.*) unction; balm.

елéй|ный, *adj.* **1.** (*eccl.*) *adj. of* ~. **2.** unctuous.

елеосвящéни|е, я, *n.* (*eccl.*) extreme unction.

ел|éц, ьцá, *m.* dace (*fish*).

ели́ко, *adv.* (*obs.*) as far as, as much as; е. возмóжно as far as possible.

ёлк|а, и, *f.* fir(-tree), spruce; рождéственская е. Christmas-tree; зажéчь ~y to light up the Christmas-tree; быть на ~e (*coll.*) to be at a Christmas, New Year's party.

ел|óвый, *adj. of* ~ь; ~óвые ши́шки fir-cones; головá ~óвая (*coll.*) blockhead, numskull.

ело|зить, жу, зишь, *impf.* (*coll.*) to crawl.

ёлочк|а, и, *f.* **1.** *dim. of* ёлка. **2.** herring-bone (pattern); он нóсит зелёный пиджáк ~ой, в ~y he wears a green herring-bone jacket.

ёлочн|ый, *adj. of* ёлка; ~ые украшéния Christmas-tree decorations.

ел|ь, и, *f.* spruce (*Picea*); fir(-tree); (*comm.*) white wood; обыкновéнная е. Norway spruce, common spruce (*Picea abies*).

éльник, а, *m.* **1.** fir-grove, fir-plantation. **2.** (*collect.*) fir-wood; fir-twigs.

ем, ешь, ест, *see* есть¹.

ём|кий (~ок, ~кá), *adj.* capacious.

ёмкост|ь, и, *f.* capacity, cubic content; ё. цистéрны tankage; мéры ~и measures of capacity; ё. ры́нка (*econ.*) market capacity.

éмл|ю, ешь, *see* имáть.

ему́, *d. of* он, онó.

ендов|á, ы́, *f.* (*hist.*) flagon (*large copper or earthenware vessel with spout formerly used in Russia for pouring out wine, beer, mead, etc.*).

енóт, а, *m.* **1.** (*zool.*) raccoon. **2.** raccoon (fur).

енóт|овый, *adj.* of ~; ~овая шýба raccoon coat, coonskin coat.

епанч|á, и́, *g. pl.* ~éй, *f.* (*hist.*) cloak, mantle.

епархиáлк|а, и, f. (*hist.*; *coll.*) church secondary schoolgirl.

епархиáльн|ый, *adj.* (*eccl.*) diocesan; ~ое учи́лище (*obs.*) church secondary school for girls (*mainly for children of the Orthodox clergy*).

епáрхи|я, и, f. (*eccl.*) diocese, see; bishopric; eparchy (*in Orthodox Church*).

епи́скоп, а, *m.* bishop.

епископáл|ьный, *adj.* (*eccl.*) episcopalian.

епи́скопский, *adj.* episcopal.

епи́скопств|о, а, *n.* episcopate.

епитим|ья́, ьи́, *g. pl.* ~и́й, *f.* (*eccl.*) penance.

епитрахи́л|ь, и, f. (*eccl.*) stole.

ер, а, *m.* (hard) yer (*name of Russian letter* 'ъ').

ералáш, а, *m.* **1.** (*coll.*) jumble, confusion; у негó в головé пóлный е. his thoughts are in complete confusion. **2.** mixture of preserved fruits. **3.** eralash (*card-game*).

ерепéн|иться, юсь, ишься, *impf.* (*of* взъ~) (*coll.*) to bristle (*fig.*).

éрес|ь, и, *pl.* ~и, ~ей, *f.* **1.** heresy. **2.** (*coll.*) городи́ть е. to talk nonsense.

ерети́к, á, *m.* heretic.

ерети́ческий, *adj.* heretical.

ёрза|ть, ю, *impf.* (*coll.*) to fidget.

ермóлк|а, и, f. skull-cap.

ерóш|ить, у, ишь, *impf.* (*coll.*) to rumple, ruffle; to dishevel.

ерóш|иться, ится, *impf.* (*coll.*) to bristle, stick up.

ерунд|á, ы́, f. (*coll.*) **1.** nonsense, rubbish; говори́ть ~ý to talk nonsense. **2.** trifle, trifling matter; child's play.

ерунди́стик|а, и, f. (*coll.*) nonsense.

ерунд|и́ть, *1st sing. not used,* ~и́шь, *impf.* (*coll.*) to talk nonsense; to play the fool.

ерундóв|ский, *adj.* = ~ый.

ерундóвый, *adj.* (*coll.*) **1.** foolish. **2.** trifling.

ёрш[1], ершá, *m.* **1.** (*fish*) ruff. **2.** (lamp-chimney) brush. **3.** notched nail *or* spike. **4.** hair sticking up; ~óм (*as adv.*) sticking up, on end.

ёрш[2], ершá, *m.* (*coll.*) mixture of beer and vodka.

ерши́ст|ый (~, ~а), *adj.* (*coll.*) **1.** bristling; sticking up. **2.** (*fig.*) obstinate; unyielding.

ерш|и́ться, у́сь, и́шься, *impf.* (*coll.*) **1.** to stick up. **2.** to grow heated, fly into a rage.

ершóвый, *adj.* of ёрш[1] 1.

еры́, *indecl., n.* yery (*name of Russian letter* 'ы').

ер|ь, я, *m.* (soft) yer (*name of Russian letter* 'ь').

есаýл, а, *m.* (*hist.*) esaul (*Cossack captain*).

éсли, *conj.* if; е. не unless; е. тóлько provided; е. бы не but for, if it were not for;

е. бы не ты, он мог бы кóнчить самоуби́йством but for you he might have committed suicide; (o,) е. бы (*in exclamations*) if only; что е...? what if...?; (a) что, е. бы (*introducing suggestion of course of action*) what about, how about; е. бы да кáбы if ifs and ans were pots and pans.

ессентук|и́, óв, *no sing.* Essentuki (*kind of mineral water*).

ест, *see* есть[1].

естéственник, а, *m.* **1.** scientist. **2.** science student.

естéственно[1], *adv.* **1.** naturally. **2.** *as particle* naturally, of course.

естéственно[2], *as pred.* it is natural.

естéствен|ный (~, ~на), *adj.* (*in var. senses*) natural; ~ные богáтства natural resources; ~ное закры́тие (*mil.*) natural cover; ~ная нáдобность, ~ная потрéбность (*euph.*) needs of nature; ~ные наýки natural sciences; е. отбóр (*biol.*) natural selection.

естеств|ó, á, *n.* **1.** nature; essence; е. вопрóса the nature of the question. **2.** (*obs.*) Nature.

естествовéд, а, *m.* (*obs.*) (natural) scientist.

естествовéдени|е, я, *n.* (*obs.*) natural history, (natural) science.

естествознáни|е, я, *n.* (natural) science.

естествоиспытáтел|ь, я, *m.* (natural) scientist.

есть[1], ем, ешь, ест, еди́м, еди́те, едя́т, *past* **ел, éла,** *imper.* **ешь,** *impf.* (*of* съ~) **1.** to eat; е. глазáми to devour with one's eyes. **2.** (*impf. only*) to corrode, eat away. **3.** (*impf. only*) to sting, cause to smart. **4.** (*impf. only*) (*coll.*) to torment; to nag.

есть[2] 1. *3rd sing.* (*also, rarely, substituted for all persons*) *pres. of* быть; и е. (*coll.*) yes, indeed; как е. (*coll.*) entirely, completely. **2.** there is, there are; у меня́, егó, *etc.*, е. I have, he has, *etc.*; е. такóе дéло (*coll.*) all right, O.K.

есть[3], *interj.* (*mil.*; *in acknowledgement of a superior's order*) yes, sir; (*naut.*) aye-aye, very good.

еть (and ети́), ебý, ебёшь, *past* **ёб, ебли́,** *impf.* = ебáть.

ефрéйтор, а, *m.* (*mil.*) lance-corporal.

éхать, éду, éдешь, *impf.* (*of* по~) (*det. of* éздить) to go (*in or on a vehicle or on an animal*); to ride, drive; е. вéрхом to ride (on horseback); е. пóездом, на пóезде to go by train; е. на парохóде to go by boat; е. в Ри́гу (*vulg.*) to puke, spew; дáльше е. нéкуда (*coll.*) that's the end, last straw.

ехи́дн|а, ы, f. **1.** (*zool.*) echidna. **2.** Australian viper. **3.** (*fig., coll.*) viper, snake.

ехи́днича|ть, ю, *impf.* (*of* съ~) (*coll.*) to employ malicious innuendo; to be malicious.

ехи́д|ный (~ен, ~на), *adj.* (*coll.*) malicious, spiteful; snide; venomous (*fig.*).

ехи́дств|о, а, *n.* (*coll.*) malice, spite; innuendo.

ехи́дств|овать, ую, *impf.* (*coll.*) = ехи́дничать.

ешь, *see* есть[1].

ещё, *adv.* **1.** still; yet; е. не, нет е. not yet; всё е. still; пока́ е. for the present, for the time being; э́то е. ничего́! that's nothing! **2.** some more; any more; yet, further; again; мо́жно нали́ть е. (вина́, *etc.*)? may I pour you some more (wine, *etc.*)?; есть ли е. хлеб? is there any more bread?; е. оди́н one more, yet another; е. раз (*i*) once more, again, (*ii*) *as interj.* encore!; наде́юсь, е. приду́ I hope I shall come again. **3.** already; as long ago as, as far back as; е. в 1900-ом году́ in 1900 already, as long ago as 1900; что тут но́вого? е. Маркс э́то дока́зывал what is new in this? (Why,) Marx argued thus. **4.** (+*comp.*) still, yet, even; е. гро́мче even louder; е. и е. more and more. **5.** (+*pronouns and adverbs*) *as emphatic particle*: кого́ е. мы не спра́шивали? whomever did we not ask? ты ви́дел инду́са? — како́го е. инду́са? have you seen the Indian? — What Indian, for heaven's sake? **6.** е. бы (*i*) yes, rather!, and how!, I'll say!, (*ii*) it would be surprising if...; е. бы вы с ни́ми не сошли́сь it would be surprising if you and they didn't get on. **7.** а е. *expresses reproach or sarcastic criticism*: тепе́рь ворчи́шь, а е. сам предложи́л you grumble now, but it was you who suggested it.

е́ю, *i.* of она́.

ея́, *g.* of она́ *in pre-1918 orthography.*

Ж

ж = же.

жа́б|а[1], ы, *f.* (*zool.*) toad.

жа́б|а[2], ы, *f.* (*med.*) quinsy; грудна́я ж. angina pectoris.

жа́берный, *adj.* (*zool.*) branchiate.

жа́б|ий, adj. of ~а[1].

жабо́, *indecl., n.* jabot.

жа́бр|ы, ~, sing. ~а, ~ы, *f.* (*zool.*) gills; branchia; взять за ж. (*fig., coll.*) to bring pressure to bear upon.

жа́велев, adj.; ~а вода́ liquid bleach.

жаве́л|ь, я, m. = ~ева вода́.

жа́ворон|ок, ка, m. (*orn.*) lark; лесно́й ж. wood lark; хохла́тый ж. crested lark.

жа́дин|а, ы, *m. and f.* (*coll.*) greedy person.

жадне́|ть, ю, *impf.* (*coll.*) to become greedy.

жа́днича|ть, ю, *impf.* (*coll.*) to be greedy; to be mean.

жа́дност|ь, и, *f.* **1.** greed; greediness; avidity. **2.** avarice, meanness.

жа́д|ный (~ен, ~на́, ~но), adj. 1. (к+*d.*) greedy (for); avid (for); он всегда́ был ~ным к но́вым ощуще́ниям he was always greedy for new sensations. **2.** avaricious, mean.

жа́жд|а, ы, *no pl., f.* thirst; (+*g.*; *fig.*) thirst, craving (for); ж. зна́ний thirst for knowledge.

жа́жд|ать, у, *impf.* (*obs.*) to be thirsty; (+*g. or inf.*; *fig.*) to thirst (for, after); а́лчущие и ~ущие, *see* а́лчущий.

жаке́т, а, m. 1. (*obs.*) morning coat. **2.** (*ladies'*) jacket.

жаке́тк|а, и, *f.* (*coll.*) jacket.

жакт, а, m. (*abbr. of* жили́щно-аре́ндное кооперати́вное това́рищество) housing lease co-operative society (*up to 1937*).

жа́кт|овский, adj. of ~.

жале́йк|а, и, *f.* (*mus.*; *dial.*) zhaleyka (*kind of pipe played by peasants, made from cow's horn or birchbark*).

жале́|ть, ю, *impf.* (*of* по~) **1.** to pity, feel sorry (for). **2.** (о+*p. or* +*g.*; что) to regret, be sorry (for, about); ~ю об утра́ченном вре́мени I regret the waste of time; ~ю, что не оста́лся до конца́ ма́тча I am sorry I did not stay till the end of the match. **3.** (+*a. or g.*) to spare; to grudge; не ~я сил not sparing oneself, unsparingly.

жа́л|ить, ю, ишь, *impf.* (*of* у~) to sting; to bite.

жа́л|иться[1], юсь, ишься, *impf.* (*coll.*) to sting; to bite.

жа́л|иться[2], юсь, ишься, *impf.* (*dial.*) to complain.

жа́л|кий (~ок, ~ка́, ~ко), adj. pitiful, pitiable, pathetic, wretched (= (*i*) *arousing pity*, (*ii*) *arousing contempt*); име́ть ж. вид to be a sorry sight.

жа́лко[1], adv. of ~ий.

жа́лко[2], as pred. (impers.) 1. (+*d. and g.*) to pity, feel sorry (for); ей ж. бы́ло себя́ she felt sorry for herself. **2.** (it is) a pity, a shame; (+*d. and g. or a.*) it grieves (me, *etc.*); to regret, feel sorry; мне ста́ло ж. да́нного обеща́ния I began to regret giving a promise. **3.** (+*g. or* +*inf.*) to grudge.

жа́л|о, а, *n.* **1.** sting (*also fig.*). **2.** point (*of pin, needle, etc.*).

жа́лоб|а, ы, *f.* complaint; пода́ть ~у (на+ *a.*) to make, lodge a complaint (about).

жа́лоб|ный (~ен, ~на), *adj.* **1.** plaintive; doleful, mournful. **2.** *adj. of* ~a; ~ная кни́га complaints book.

жа́лобщик, а, *m.* **1.** person lodging complaint. **2.** (*leg.*) plaintiff.

жа́лова|нный, *p.p.p. of* ~ть *and adj.* (*hist.*) granted, received as grant; ~нная гра́мота letters patent, charter.

жа́лованье, я, *n.* **1.** salary. **2.** (*obs.*) reward; donation.

жа́л|овать, ую, *impf.* (*of* по~) **1.** (+*a. and i. or* +*d. and a.*) to grant (to); to bestow, confer (on); to reward (with); ж. сторо́нников землёй, ж. сторо́нникам зе́млю to grant land to one's supporters, reward one's supporters with (grants of) land. **2.** (*coll.*) to favour, regard with favour. **3.** (к; *obs.*) to visit, come to see.

жа́л|оваться, уюсь, *impf.* (*of* по~) (на+*a.*) to complain (of, about); он всё ~уется офице́рам на харчи́ he is always complaining to officers about the food; ж. в суд to go to law.

жалоно́сный, *adj.* (*zool.*) stinging, possessing a sting.

жа́лостлив|ый (~, ~а), *adj.* (*coll.*) **1.** compassionate, sympathetic. **2.** pitiful.

жа́лост|ный (~ен, ~на), *adj.* (*coll.*) **1.** piteous; doleful, mournful. **2.** compassionate, sympathetic.

жа́лост|ь, и, *f.* pity, compassion; из ~и (к) out of pity (for); кака́я ж.! what a pity!

жаль, *as pred.* (*impers.*) **1.** (+*d. and a. or g.*) to pity, feel sorry (for); мне ж. тебя́ I pity you. **2.** (it is) a pity; (+*d.*) it grieves (me, *etc.*); to regret, feel sorry; ж., что вас там не бу́дет it is a pity that you will not be there; нам ж. бы́ло расстава́ться it grieved us to part. **3.** (+*g. or* +*inf.*) to grudge. **4.** *as adv.* unfortunately.

жа́л|ьче, (*coll.*) *comp. of* ~ко.

жалюзи́, *indecl., n.* Venetian blind, jalousie.

жанда́рм, а, *m.* gendarme.

жандарме́ри|я, и, *f.* (*collect.*) gendarmerie.

жанда́рм|ский, *adj. of* ~.

жанр, а, *m.* **1.** genre. **2.** genre-painting.

жанри́ст, а, *m.* genre-painter.

жа́нр|овый, *adj. of* ~.

жанти́льнича|ть, ю, *impf.* (*coll.*) to behave in an affected way, put on airs.

жанти́л|ьный (~ен, ~ьна), *adj.* (*coll.*) affected.

жар, а (у), о ~е, в ~у́, *no pl. m.* **1.** heat; heat of the day; hot place; в ~у́ (+*g.*) in the heat (of). **2.** (*coll.*) embers; как ж. горе́ть to gleam, glitter; чужи́ми рука́ми ж. загреба́ть to use others to pull one's chestnuts out of the fire. **3.** fever; (high) temperature. **4.** (*fig.*) heat, ardour;

с ~ом приня́ться за что-н. to set about something with a will.

жар|а́, ы́, *f.* heat; hot weather.

жарго́н, а, *m.* **1.** jargon; slang, cant (*of a particular social or occupational group*). **2.** (*obs.*) Yiddish (language).

жарго́н|ный, *adj. of* ~.

жардинье́рк|а, и, *f.* flower-stand, jardinière.

жа́рев|о, а, *n.* (*collect.*; *coll.*) roast or fried food.

жа́рен|ое, ого, *n.* (*coll.*) roast meat.

жа́реный, *adj.* roast, broiled; fried; grilled.

жа́р|ить, ю, ишь, *impf.* **1.** (*pf.* за~ *or* из~) (на огне́) to roast, broil; (на сковороде́) to fry; (на решётке) to grill. **2.** (*of the sun*) to burn, scorch. **3.** (*coll.*) *used as substitute for other verbs to emphasize speed of action or vigour of performance*: ~ь за по́мощью! run for help as fast as you can!; ж. на гармо́шке to bash out a tune on the accordion.

жа́р|иться, юсь, ишься, *impf.* **1.** (*pf.* за~ *or* из~) to roast, fry (*intrans.*). **2.** ж. на со́лнце (*coll.*) to roast, grill (oneself), bask in the sun. **3.** *pass. of* ~ить.

жа́р|кий (~ок, ~ка́, ~ко), *adj.* **1.** hot; torrid; tropical; ж. по́яс (*geogr.*) torrid zone. **2.** (*fig.*) hot, heated; ardent; passionate; ж. спор heated argument.

жа́р|ко¹, *adv. of* ~кий.

жа́рко², *as pred.* it is hot; мне, *etc.*, ж. I am, *etc.*, hot.

жарк|о́е, о́го, *n.* roast (meat).

жаро́в|ня, ни, *g. pl.* ~ен, *f.* brazier.

жаровой, *adj.* **1.** *adj. of* жар 1. **2.** caused by heat; ж. уда́р heat-stroke.

жар|о́к, ка́, *m.* (*coll.*) fever; (slight) temperature.

жаропонижа́ющ|ий, *adj.* (*med.*) febrifugal; *as noun* ~ее, ~его, *n.* febrifuge.

жаросто́йкий, *adj.* (*tech.*) heat-resisting, heatproof.

жаротру́бный, *adj.*; ж. котёл (*tech.*) fire-tube boiler, flue boiler.

жароупо́рный = жаросто́йкий.

Жар-пти́ц|а, ы, *f.* (*folklore*) the Fire-bird.

жа́р|че, *comp. of* ~кий *and* ~ко.

жары́н|ь, и, *f.* (*coll.*) intense heat (*of atmosphere*); very hot weather.

жасми́н, а, *m.* jasmin(e), jessamin(e).

жа́тв|а, ы, *no pl., f.* reaping, harvesting; harvest (*also fig.*).

жа́тв|енный, *adj. of* ~a; ~енная маши́на binder, harvester, reaping-machine.

жа́тк|а, и, *f.* binder, harvester, reaping-machine.

жать¹, жму, жмёшь, *impf.* (*no pf.*) **1.** to press, squeeze; ж. ру́ку to shake (someone) by the hand. **2.** to press out, squeeze out. **3.** to pinch, be tight (*of shoes or clothing*); в плеча́х жмёт (*impers.*) it is tight on the shoulders. **4.** (*fig., coll.*) to oppress.

жать², жну, жнёшь, *impf. (of* с~) to reap, cut, mow.

жа́ться, жму́сь, жмёшься, *impf.* **1.** to huddle up; ж. в у́гол to skulk in a corner. **2.** (к) to press close (to), draw closer (to). **3.** (*coll.*) to hesitate, vacillate. **4.** (*coll.*) to stint oneself; to be stingy.

жбан, а, *m.* (wooden) jug.

жва́чк|а, и, *f.* chewing, rumination. **2.** cud; жева́ть ~у to chew the cud, ruminate; (*fig.*) to repeat something monotonously. **3.** (*coll.*) chewing-gum.

жва́чн|ый, *adj.* (*zool.*) ruminant; *as noun* ~ое, ~ого, *n.* ruminant.

жгу, жжёшь, жгут, *see* жечь.

жгут, а́, *m.* **1.** plait; braid; wisp. **2.** (*med.*) tourniquet.

жгу́тик, а, *m.* (*zool.*) flagellum.

жгу́чест|ь, и, *f.* burning heat.

жгу́ч|ий (~, ~а, ~е), *adj.* burning hot (*also fig.*); ~ая боль smart, smarting pain; ж. брюне́т person with jet-black hair and eyes; ж. вопро́с burning question.

ждать, жду, ждёшь, *past* ждал, ждала́, жда́ло, *impf.* **1.** (+*g.*) to wait (for); to await; заста́вить ж. to keep waiting; не заста́вить себя́ ж. to come quickly; ж. не дожда́ться (*coll.*) to wait impatiently, be on tenterhooks; что нас ждёт? what is in store for us?; того́ и жди (*coll.*) any time now, any minute. **2.** (+*g.*) to expect (= to hope for). **3.** (+что) to expect; мы жда́ли, что вы поя́витесь на ми́тинге we expected you to come to the meeting.

же¹, *conj.* **1.** but; иди́, е́сли тебе́ охо́та, я же оста́нусь здесь you go, if you feel like it, but I shall stay here. **2.** (*introducing clause elucidating or modifying preceding clause*) and; с тех пор как я его́ зна́ю, зна́ю же я его́ два́дцать лет, я всегда́ ве́рил ему́ ever since I have known him, and I have known him for twenty years, I have always trusted him; Ока́ впада́ет в Во́лгу, Во́лга же в Каспи́йское мо́ре the Oka flows into the Volga, and the Volga flows into the Caspian Sea. **3.** after all; расскажи́ ей — она́ же твоя́ мать tell her—she's your mother, after all.

же², *emphatic particle*: когда́ же они́ прие́дут? whenever will they come?; что же ты де́лаешь? whatever are you doing, what *are* you doing?; сего́дня же он собира́лся прие́хать it was today that he intended to come.

же³, *particle expressing identity*: тот же, тако́й же the same, idem; тогда́ же at the same time; там же in the same place, ibidem; Петрося́н, он же Петро́в Petrosyan, alias Petrov.

жева́ни|е, я, *n.* mastication; rumination.

жёваный *adj.* (*coll.*) chewed up; crumpled.

жева́тельн|ый, *adj.* masticatory, manducatory; ~ая рези́нка chewing gum.

жева́ть, жую́, жуёшь, *impf.* to chew, masticate; to ruminate; ж. губа́ми to munch; (*fig.*) ж. жва́чку, *see* жва́чка; ж. вопро́с to chew over a question.

жёг, жгла, *see* жечь.

жезл, а́, *m.* **1.** rod; staff (of office); baton; (*eccl.*) crozier; (*hist.*) warder. **2.** staff (*token of authority to proceed on single-line railways*). **3.** Jacob's staff (*used by surveyors*).

жезлов|о́й, *adj.*; ~а́я систе́ма staff system (*on single-line railways*).

жела́ни|е, я, *n.* **1.** (+*g.*) wish (for), desire (for); бу́дет по ва́шему ~ю it shall be as you wish; я всегда́ стара́юсь счита́ться с ва́шими ~ями I always try to consult your wishes; при всём ~и with the best will in the world. **2.** desire, lust.

жела́|нный, *p.p.p. of* ~ть *and adj.* wished for, longed for, desired, beloved; ж. гость welcome visitor.

жела́тельно¹, *adv.* preferably.

жела́тельно², *as pred.* it is desirable; it is advisable, preferable; ж., что́бы вы прису́тствовали it is desirable that you should be present, your presence is desirable.

жела́тел|ьный (~ен, ~ьна), *adj.* **1.** desirable; advisable, preferable. **2.** ~ьное наклоне́ние (*gram.*) optative mood.

желати́н, а, *no pl.*, *m.* gelatin(e).

желати́новый, *adj.* gelatinous.

жела́|ть, ю, *impf. (of* по~) **1.** (+*g.*) to wish (for), desire. **2.** (что́бы *or* +*inf.*) to wish, want; я ~ю, что́бы вы при́няли уча́стие в игре́ I want you to join in the game; ~ете ли вы познако́миться с ним? do you wish to meet him? **3.** (+*d. and g. or inf.*) to wish (*someone something*); ~ю вам вся́ких благ (*coll.*) I wish you every happiness; ~ю вам успе́ха good luck!; э́то оставля́ет ж. лу́чшего, мно́гого it leaves much to be desired.

жела́|ющий, *pres. part. act. of* ~ть; ~ющие persons interested, those who so desire.

желва́к, а́, *m.* (*med.*) tumour; (*fig.*) moving knot of muscle.

желе́, *indecl.*, *n.* jelly.

желе́з|а, ы́, *pl.* же́лезы, ~, ~а́м, *f.* (*anat.*) gland *pl.*; (*coll.*) tonsils; же́лезы вну́тренней секре́ции endocrine glands.

желе́зистый¹, *adj.* (*anat.*) glandular.

желе́зист|ый² (~, ~а), *adj.* ferriferous; (*chem.*) ferrocyanide (of); ferruginous; chalybeate (*of water*); ж. препара́т iron preparation.

желе́зк|а, и, *f.* (*coll.*) **1.** piece of iron. **2.** (*obs.*) railway. **3.** chemin-de-fer (*card-game*).

железк|а, и, *f.* (*anat.*) glandule.

железнéни|е, я, *n.* (*tech.*) iron plating.

железнодорóжник, а, *m.* railwayman.

железнодорóжн|ый, *adj.* rail, railway; ~ая вéтка branch line; ~ая перевóзка rail transport; ~ое полотнó permanent way; ж. путь (railway) track; ж. ýзел (railway) junction.

желéзн|ый, *adj.* 1. iron (*also fig.*); (*chem.*) ferric, ferrous; ж. блеск (*min.*); ж. век the Iron Age; ~ое дéрево (*bot.*) lignum vitae (*Guaiacum officinale*); ж. зáнавес the 'Iron Curtain'; ~ая кислотá ferric acid; ж. колчедáн (*min.*) iron pyrites; ~ая кóмната strong-room; ж. купорóс (*min.*) green vitriol; ж. лом scrap iron; ~ые опúлки iron filings; за ~ой решёткой (*coll.*) behind bars; ~ая рудá iron-stone, iron-ore; ~ые товáры ironmongery, hardware; ~ая травá (*bot.*) vervain. 2. ~ая дорóга railway(s); по ~ой дорóге by rail; ~ая дорóга мéстного значéния local line. 3. (*sl.*) reliable, dependable.

железня́к, á, *m.* (*min.*) iron-stone, iron clay.

желéз|о, а, *pl.* (*obs. or poet.*) ~ы, *n.* 1. iron; ж. в болвáнках pig-iron; óкись ~а (*chem.*) ferric oxide. 2. (*collect.*) iron; hardware. 3. (*pl.*) (*obs.*) fetters, irons.

желéзо- iron-, ferro-.

железобетóн, а, *m.* (*tech.*) reinforced concrete, ferro-concrete.

железобетóн|ный, *adj. of* ~.

железоплавúльный, *adj.*; ж. завóд (*tech.*) iron foundry.

железопрокáтный, *adj.*; ж. завóд (*tech.*) rolling mill.

жёлоб, а, *pl.* ~á, ~óв, *m.* gutter; trough; chute.

желоб|óк, кá, *m.* (*tech.*) groove, channel, flute.

желóбчатый, *adj.* (*tech.*) channelled, fluted.

желóнк|а, и, *f.* (*tech.*) sludge pump, sand pump.

желтé|ть, ю, *impf.* 1. (*pf.* по~) to turn yellow. 2. (*impf. only*) to be yellow, show up yellow.

желтé|ться, ется, *impf.* to be yellow, show up yellow.

желтизн|á, ы́, *f.* yellowness; yellow spot; sallow complexion.

желтúнк|а, и, *f.* (*coll.*) yellow spots; yellow shade.

жел|тúть, чý, тúшь, *impf.* to colour yellow.

желтовáт|ый (~, ~а), *adj.* yellowish; sallow.

желт|óк, кá, *m.* yolk.

желтокóжий, *adj.* yellow-skinned.

желтолúц|ый (~, ~а), *adj.* sallow.

желторóт|ый (~, ~а), *adj.* 1. yellow-beaked. 2. (*fig.*) inexperienced, green.

желтофиóл|ь, и, *f.* (*bot.*) wallflower.

желтоцвéт, а, *m.* (*bot.*) golden rod.

желт|óчный, *adj. of* ~óк.

желтýх|а, и, *f.* (*med.*) jaundice.

желтý|шный, *adj. of* ~ха; jaundiced.

жёлт|ый (~, ~á, ~о *and* ~ó), *adj.* yellow; ж. билéт (*hist., coll.*) 'yellow ticket' (*prostitute's passport in tsarist Russia*); ~ая водá (*med.*) glaucoma; ж. дом (*coll., obs.*) lunatic asylum; ~ая лихорáдка yellow fever; ~ая прéсса the yellow press.

желт|ь, и, *f.* yellow (paint).

желудёвый, *adj. of* жёлудь; ж. кóфе acorn coffee.

желýд|ок, ка, *m.* stomach; несварéние ~ка indigestion.

желýдоч|ек, ка, *m.* (*anat.*) ventricle.

желýдочный, *adj.* stomach; stomachic, gastric; ж. зонд stomach pump; ж. сок gastric juice.

жёлуд|ь, я, *g. pl.* ~éй, *m.* acorn.

жёлч|ный (~ен, ~на), *adj.* 1. bilious; ж. кáмень gall-stone; ж. пузы́рь gall-bladder. 2. (*fig.*) peevish, irritable; atrabilious.

жёлч|ь (*coll.* желчь), и, *no pl.*, *f.* bile, gall also *fig.*); разлúтие ~и (*med.*) jaundice.

жемáн|иться, юсь, ишься, *impf.* (*coll.*) to attitudinize, behave with false modesty.

жемáнниц|а, ы, *f.* (*coll.*) affected creature.

жемáннича|ть, ю, *impf.* (*coll.*) to behave affectedly.

жемáн|ный (~ен, ~на), *adj.* affected.

жемáнств|о, а, *n.* affectedness.

жéмчуг, а, *pl.* ~á, *m.* pearl(s); мéлкий ж. seed-pearls.

жемчýжин|а, ы, *f.* pearl (*also fig.*).

жемчýжниц|а, ы, *f.* 1. pearl-oyster. 2. pearl disease.

жемчýжн|ый, *adj. of* жéмчуг; (*fig.*) pearly (-white); ~ая болéзнь pearl disease; ~ое ожерéлье pearl necklace.

жен- *abbr. of* жéнский.

жен|á, ы́, *pl.* ~ы, ~, ~áм, *f.* 1. wife; быть у ~ы́ под башмакóм to be henpecked. 2. (*poet., obs.*) woman.

женáт|ый (~), *adj.* married; ж. (на+*p.*) married (to; *of man*).

жéнин, *adj.* (*obs.*) wife's.

жен|úть, ю́, ~ишь, *impf. and pf.* (*pf. also* по~) to marry (off); без меня́ меня́ ~úли (*fig., coll.*) I was roped in without being consulted.

женúтьб|а, ы, *no pl.*, *f.* marriage.

жен|úться, ю́сь, ~ишься, *impf. and pf.* (на+*p.*) (*of man*) to marry, get married (to).

женúх, á, *m.* 1. fiancé; смотрéть ~óм (*coll.*) to look happy. 2. bridegroom. 3. suitor. 4. eligible bachelor.

жениха́|ться, юсь, *impf.* (*coll. or dial.*) to be engaged; to be courting.

женихо́вский, *adj.* (*coll.*) *of* жени́х.

женихо́вств|о, а, *n.* (*coll.*) engagement; courting(-days).

жёнк|а, и, *f.* (*coll.*) **1.** *affect. form of* жена́. **2.** (*obs. or dial.*) woman.

женолю́б, а, *m.* ladies' man.

женолюби́в|ый (~), adj.; ж. челове́к ladies' man.

женолюби́|е, я, *n.* fondness for women.

женонави́стник, а, *m.* misogynist.

женонави́стнический, *adj.* misogynous.

женонави́стничеств|о, а, *n.* misogyny.

женоподо́б|ный (~ен, ~на), adj. effeminate.

женотде́л, а, *m.* (*hist.*) women's section (*section of Communist party committees dealing with political work among women*).

жен-премье́р, а, *m.* (*theatr.*) jeune premier.

же́нск|ий, adj. 1. woman's; female; feminine; ~ое зва́ние, ~ая на́ция, ~ое сосло́вие (*obs.*) the female sex; ж. вопро́с the question of women's rights; ~ое ца́рство petticoat government. **2.** (*gram.*) feminine. **3.** *as noun* ~ое, ~ого, *n.* (*coll.*) menstruation.

же́нственност|ь, и, *f.* femininity; (*pejor.*) effeminacy.

же́нствен|ный (~, ~на), adj. feminine, womanly; (*pejor.*) womanish, effeminate.

же́нщин|а, ы, *f.* woman.

женьше́н|ь, я, *m.* (*bot., med.*) ginseng.

жёрдочк|а, и, *f.* (*coll.*) pole; perch (*in bird-cage*).

жерд|ь, и, *pl.* **~и, ~е́й,** *f.* pole; stake; худо́й, как ж. (*coll.*) thin as a lath.

жереб́|ая (~а), adj. in foal.

жереб|ёнок, ёнка, *pl.* **~я́та, ~я́т,** *m.* foal, colt.

жереб́|е́ц, ца́, *m.* stallion.

жереб|и́ться, и́тся, *impf.* (*of* o~) to foal.

жере́бчик, а, *m. dim. of* жеребе́ц; мыши́ный ж. (*obs.*) old lecher.

жеребьёвк|а, и, *f.* casting of lots, sortition; (*sport*) draw (*for play-off*).

жереб|я́чий, adj. of ~ёнок; ж. смех (*coll.*) horse-laugh.

же́рех, а, *m.* chub (*fish*).

жерли́ц|а, ы, *f.* kind of fishing tackle (*for catching pike, etc.*).

жерл|о́, а́, *pl.* **~а, ~,** *n.* mouth, orifice; muzzle (*of gun*); ж. вулка́на crater.

жёрнов, а, *pl.* **~а́, ~о́в,** *m.* millstone.

же́ртв|а, ы, *f.* **1.** sacrifice (*also fig.*); принести́ ~у (+*d.*) to make a sacrifice (to); принести́ в ~у to sacrifice. **2.** victim; пасть ~ой (+*g.*) to fall victim (to).

же́ртвенник, а, *m.* **1.** sacrificial altar. **2.** (*eccl.*) credence table.

же́ртвенный, adj. sacrificial.

же́ртвовател|ь, я, *m.* donor.

же́ртв|овать, ую, *impf.* (*of* по~) **1.** to make

a donation (of), present. **2.** (+*i.*) to sacrifice, give up.

жертвоприноше́ни|е, я, *n.* sacrifice; oblation.

жест, а, *m.* gesture (*also fig.*).

жестикули́р|овать, ую, *impf.* to gesticulate.

жестикуля́ци|я, и, *f.* gesticulation.

жёст|кий (~ок, ~а́, ~ко), adj. hard; tough; (*fig.*) rigid, strict; ж. ваго́н hard-seated carriage, 'hard' carriage; ~кая вода́ hard water; ~кие во́лосы wiry hair.

жёст|ко¹, adv. of ~кий.

жёстко², *as pred.* it is hard.

жесткокры́л|ые, ых, *sing.* ~ое, ~ого, *n.* (*zool.*) Coleoptera.

жесто́к|ий (~, ~а́, ~о), adj. cruel; brutal; (*fig.*) severe, sharp.

жестокосе́рд|ный (~ен, ~на), adj. hard-hearted.

жестокосе́рд|ый = ~ный.

жесто́кост|ь, и, *f.* cruelty, brutality.

жесто|ча́йший, *superl. of* ~кий.

жёст|че, *comp. of* ~кий *and* ~ко.

жест|ь, и, *f.* tin-plate.

жестя́ник, а, *m.* tinman, tin-smith.

жестя́нк|а, и, *f.* **1.** tin, can; ж. из-под сарди́нок sardine tin. **2.** (*coll.*) piece of tin.

жест|яно́й, adj. of ~ь; ~яна́я посу́да tinware.

жестя́нщик, а, *m.* tinman, tin-smith.

жето́н, а, *m.* **1.** medal. **2.** counter.

жечь, жгу, жжёшь, жгут, *past* жёг, жгла, *impf.* **1.** (*pf.* с~) to burn (up, down); ж. му́сор to burn up refuse. **2.** (*impf. only*) to burn, sting; от э́того ликёра жжёт го́рло (*impers.*) this liqueur burns one's throat.

же́чься, жгусь, жжёшься, жгу́тся, *past* жёгся, жгла́сь, *impf.* **1.** to burn, sting (*intrans.*). **2.** (*coll.*) to burn oneself.

жже́ни|е, я, *n.* **1.** burning. **2.** burning pain; heartburn.

жжёнк|а, и, *f.* hot punch.

жжёный, adj. burnt, scorched; ж. ко́фе roasted coffee.

жжёшь, *see* жечь.

жива́ть, *no pres.* (*coll.*) *freq. of* жить.

жив|ей, *see* ~o 5.

живе́те, *indecl., n.,* old name of letter ж.

жив|е́ц¹, ца́, *m.* live bait, sprat.

жив|е́ц², ца́, *m.* (*obs., coll.*) member of Living Church.

живи́тел|ьный (~ен, ~ьна), adj. life-giving; bracing; ~ьная вла́га (*coll.*) intoxicating liquor.

жив|и́ть, лю, и́шь, *impf.* to give life to, animate; to brace.

жив|и́ться, лю́сь, и́шься, *impf.* (+*i.; obs.*) to live (on), make a living (by).

живи́ц|а, ы, *f.* soft resin.

жи́вност|ь, и, *no pl.*, *f.* (*collect.*; *coll.*) poultry, fowl.

жи́в|о, *adv.* **1.** vividly. **2.** with animation. **3.** keenly; extremely, exceedingly; он ж. чу́вствовал оскорбле́ние he felt deeply insulted. **4.** (*coll.*) quickly, promptly. **5.** ж.!, ~е́й! (*coll.*) make haste!, look lively!

живодёр, а, *m.* knacker; (*fig.*) fleecer, flay-flint; profiteer.

живодёр|ня, ни, *g. pl.* ~ен, *f.* (*coll.*) knacker's yard.

живоде́рств|о, а, *n.* (*coll.*) cruelty.

жив|о́й (~, ~а́, ~о), *adj.* **1.** living, live, alive; он ещё в ~ы́х he is still alive; оста́ться в ~ы́х to survive, escape with one's life; ~ (и) здоро́в (*coll.*) safe and sound; ни ~ ни мёртв (*coll.*) petrified (*with fright, astonishment*); ж. вес live weight; ~а́я вода́ (*folklore*) water of life; ~а́я и́згородь (quickset) hedge; ж. инвента́рь livestock; ~ые карти́ны tableaux (vivants); шить на ~у́ю ни́тку to tack; на ~у́ю ни́тку (*coll.*) hastily, anyhow; стоя́ть в ~о́й о́череди to queue in person; ж. портре́т (+*g.*) the living image (of); ~а́я ра́на open wound; ~а́я си́ла (*mil.*) men and beasts (*as opp. to* matériel); ~ым сло́вом рассказа́ть to tell by word of mouth; ж. уголо́к nature corner (*in schools*); ~ые цветы́ natural flowers; не́ было ви́дно ни (одно́й) ~о́й души́ there was not a living soul to be seen; на нём не́ было ~о́го ме́ста he was all battered and bruised; забра́ть, заде́ть за ~о́е to touch, sting to the quick. **2.** lively; keen; brisk; animated; ж. ум lively mind; проявля́ть ж. интере́с (к) to take a keen interest (in); принима́ть ~ое уча́стие (в+*p.*) to take an active part (in); to feel keen sympathy with. **3.** lively, vivacious; bright; ~ые глаза́ bright eyes. **4.** keen, poignant. **5.** (*short form only*; +*i.*) expresses *raison d'être*: он ~ одни́ми ша́хматами he lives for chess alone; чем она́ ~а́? what makes her tick?

жи́вокост|ь, и, *f.* (*bot.*) larkspur.

живопис|а́ть, у́ю, *impf. and pf.* (*obs.*) to describe vividly, paint a vivid picture (of).

живопи́с|ец, ца, *m.* painter; ж. вы́весок sign-painter.

живопи́с|ный (~ен, ~на), *adj.* **1.** pictorial. **2.** picturesque (*also fig.*).

живопи́с|ь, и, *f.* **1.** painting. **2.** (*collect.*) paintings; италья́нская ж. paintings of the Italian school; стенна́я ж. murals.

живородя́щий, *adj.* (*zool.*) viviparous.

живорожде́ни|е, я, *n.* (*zool.*) viviparity.

живоры́бный, *adj.*; ж. садо́к fishpond.

жи́вост|ь, и, *f.* liveliness, vivacity; animation.

живо́т, а́, *m.* **1.** abdomen, belly; stomach; (*coll.*) у него́ ж. подво́дит he feels hungry; же́нщина с ~о́м (*coll.*) pregnant woman. **2.** (*arch.*) life; не на ж., а на сме́рть to the death; не щадя́ ~а́ своего́ not counting the cost. **3.** (*obs. or dial.*) animals, beasts; (*pl.*) goods and chattels.

животвор|и́ть, ю́, и́шь, *impf.* (*of* о~) to revive.

животво́р|ный (~ен, ~на), *adj.* life-giving.

животво́р|ящий, *pres. part. act. of* ~и́ть *and adj.* (*obs. or poet.*) life-giving; ж. крест (*theol.*) the life-giving cross.

живо́тик, а, *m.* (*coll.*) tummy.

животи́н|а, ы, *f.* (*coll.*) domestic animal; (*fig.*) beast.

животново́д, а, *m.* cattle-breeder.

животново́дств|о, а, *n.* stock-raising, animal husbandry.

животново́дческий, *adj.* cattle-breeding, stock-raising.

живо́тно|е, го, *n.* animal; (*fig.*, *pejor.*) beast, brute.

живо́тный, *adj.* **1.** animal; ж. жир animal fat; ж. у́голь animal charcoal; ж. эпос (*lit.*) bestiary. **2.** bestial, brute.

животрепе́щущий, *adj.* **1.** topical; stirring, exciting. **2.** lively, full of life. **3.** (*joc.*) unsound, unstable.

живу́чест|ь, и, *f.* **1.** vitality, tenacity of life. **2.** (*fig.*) firmness, stability.

живу́ч|ий (~, ~а), *adj.* **1.** tenacious of life; (*bot.*) hardy; он ~ как ко́шка he has nine lives like a cat. **2.** (*fig.*) firm, stable.

жи́вчик, а, *m.* **1.** (*coll.*) lively person. **2.** (*biol.*) spermatozoon. **3.** (*coll.*) perceptible pulsing of artery on temple *or* twitching of eyelid.

живь|ё, я́, *n.* (*collect.*; *dial.*) live things.

живьём, *adv.* **1.** (*coll.*) alive; постара́йтесь схвати́ть его́ ж. try to catch him alive. **2.** (*dial.*) anyhow; in rough and ready fashion.

жига́н|уть, у́, ёшь, *pf.* (*coll.*) to lash.

жид, а́, *m.* (*obs. or pejor.*) **1.** (*obs.*) Jew. **2.** (*pejor. and vulg.*) Yid.

жи́д|кий (~ок, ~ка́, ~ко), *adj.* **1.** liquid; fluid; ~кое то́пливо liquid fuel, fuel oil. **2.** watery; (*of liquids*) weak, thin; ж. чай weak tea. **3.** sparse, scanty; ~кая борода́ straggly beard. **4.** (*coll.*; *of voice or sound*) weak, thin. **5.** (*fig.*) weak, feeble.

жи́дкостный, *adj.* (*tech.*) liquid; fluid.

жи́дкост|ь, и, *f.* **1.** liquid; fluid. **2.** wateriness; weakness, thinness (*also fig.*).

жидо́вк|а, и, *f.* (*obs. or pejor.*) Jewess.

жидо́вск|ий, *adj.* (*obs. or pejor.*) Jewish; ~ая смола́ (*min.*) Jew's pitch.

жи́ж|а, и, *no pl.*, *f.* liquid; swill; slush.

жи́|же, *comp. of* ~дкий.

жи́жиц|а, ы, *f.* (*coll.*) *dim. of* жи́жа.

жизнедея́тельност|ь, и, *f.* **1.** (*biol.*) vital activity. **2.** (*obs.*) life's work.

жизнедея́тел|ьный (~ен, ~ьна), *adj.* **1.** (*biol.*) active. **2.** lively; energetic.

жи́зненност|ь, и, *f.* **1.** vitality. **2.** closeness to life; (*art*) lifelikeness.

жи́знен|ный (~, ~на), *adj.* **1.** life; (*biol.*) vital; ~ные отправле́ния vital functions; ж. путь life; ~ные си́лы vitality, sap; ж. у́ровень standard of living. **2.** close to life; lifelike. **3.** (*fig.*) vital, vitally important; ж. вопро́с question of vital importance; ~ные це́нтры страны́ nerve-centres of a country.

жизнеописа́ни|е, я, *n.* biography.

жизнера́достност|ь, и, *f.* joie de vivre; cheerfulness.

жизнера́дост|ный (~ен, ~на), *adj.* full of joie de vivre; cheerful.

жизнеспосо́бност|ь, и, *f.* (*biol.*) viability; (*fig.*) vitality.

жизнеспосо́б|ный (~ен, ~на), *adj.* capable of living; (*biol.*) viable; (*fig.*) vigorous, flourishing.

жизнесто́|йкий (~ек, ~йка), *adj.* tenacious of life; tough, durable.

жизн|ь, и, *f.* life; existence; ж. моя́! my dear!; зарабо́тать на ж. to earn one's living; как ж.? (*coll.*) how are you?; лиши́ть себя́ ~и to take one's life; не на ж., а на смерть to the death; ни в ж. never, not for anything; о́браз ~и way of life; вести́ широ́кий о́браз ~и to live in style; по ж. for life; провести́ что-н. в ж. to put something into practice; проже́чь ж. to dissipate one's life, fritter away one's life; ~и не рад (*coll.*) upset, distressed, miserable; из-за э́того он и ~и не рад he is very vexed about it.

жиклёр, а, *m.* (*tech.*) (carburettor) jet.

жил- *abbr. of* ~и́щный, ~о́й.

жи́л|а¹, ы, *f.* **1.** vein; tendon, sinew; тяну́ть ~ы (из; *coll.*) to torment, rack. **2.** (*min.*) vein, lode. **3.** filament, strand (*of cable*).

жи́л|а², ы, *m. and f.* (*coll., pejor.*) skinflint.

жиле́т, а, *m.* waistcoat.

жиле́тк|а, и, *f.* (*coll.*) waistcoat; пла́кать в ~у (+*d.*) to cry on someone's shoulder.

жиле́т|ный, *adj. of* ~; ж. карма́н waistcoat pocket, vest-pocket.

жил|е́ц, ьца́, *m.* **1.** lodger; tenant. **2.** (*obs.*) inhabitant; он не ж. (на бе́лом све́те) (*coll.*) he is not long for this world.

жи́лист|ый (~, ~а), *adj.* **1.** having prominent veins. **2.** sinewy; (*fig.*) wiry; ~oe мя́со stringy meat.

жи́л|ить, ю, ишь, *impf.* (у; *coll.*) to swindle.

жи́л|иться¹, юсь, ишься, *impf.* (*coll.*) to heave, strain.

жи́л|иться², юсь, ишься, *impf.* (*pejor., coll.*) to stint; to be miserly.

жили́ц|а, ы, *f. of* жиле́ц.

жили́чк|а, и, *f.* (*coll.*) = жили́ца.

жили́щ|е, а, *n.* **1.** dwelling, abode; habitation. **2.** lodging; (living) quarters.

жили́щ|ный, *adj. of* ~e; ~ные усло́вия housing conditions; ~но-бытовы́е усло́вия living conditions.

жи́лк|а, и, *f.* **1.** (*anat., geol.*) vein; (*zool., bot.*) fibre, rib (*of insect's wing or of leaf*). **2.** (*fig.*) vein, streak; bent; артисти́ческая ж. artistic streak; попа́сть в ~y (*obs.*) to do something opportunely.

жилкова́ни|е, я, *n.* (*zool., bot.*) nervation.

жи́л|о, а, *n.* (*obs. or dial.*) habitation.

жилова́т|ый (~, ~а), *adj.* (*coll.*) with prominent veins.

жил|о́й, *adj.* **1.** dwelling; residential; inhabited; ж. дом dwelling house, block of flats (*as opp. to* office block, *etc.*); ж. кварта́л residential area; ~ые ко́мнаты rooms lived in; ~а́я пло́щадь (*i*) floor space, (*ii*) housing, accommodation (= *available dwelling space*). **2.** habitable, fit to live in.

жилотде́л, а, *m.* (*abbr. of* жили́щный отде́л) housing department (*of local Soviet*).

жилпло́щад|ь, и, *f.* (*abbr. of* жила́я пло́щадь) *see* жило́й.

жилстройтельств|о, а, *n.* (*abbr. of* жили́щное строи́тельство) house building.

жилфо́нд, а, *m.* (*abbr. of* жили́щный фонд) housing, accommodation.

жиль|ё, я́, *n.* **1.** habitation; dwelling; мы не нашли́ никако́го при́знака ~я́ we could find no sign of life. **2.** lodging; (living) accommodation. **3.** (*obs.*) storey, floor.

жи́ль|ный, *adj.* venous; ~ая поро́да (*geol.*) veinstone, matrix, gangue.

жим, а, *m.* (*sport*) press (*in weight-lifting*).

жи́молост|ь, и, *f.* (*bot.*) honeysuckle.

жи́нк|а, и, *f.* (*dial.*) = жёнка.

жир, а (у), о ~e, в ~ý, *pl.* ~ы́, *m.* fat; grease.

жира́ф, а, *m.* giraffe.

жира́ф|а, ы, *f.* = ~.

жире́|ть, ю, *impf.* (*of* о~ *and* раз~) to grow fat, stout, plump.

жирномоло́чный, *adj.* (*agric.*) giving milk with high fat content.

жи́р|ный (~ен, ~на́, ~но), *adj.* **1.** fatty; (*chem.*) aliphatic; rich (*of food*); greasy; ~ная кислота́ fatty acid, aliphatic acid; ~ное пятно́ grease stain. **2.** fat, plump. **3.** rich (*of soil*); lush (*of vegetation*); ~ная земля́ loam. **4.** (*typ.*) bold, heavy; ж. шрифт bold (-face) type. **5.** (*coll.*) ж. кусо́к fat sum (*of money*); ~но бу́дет! that's too much!

жи́ро, *indecl., n.* (*fin.*) endorsement.

жир|ова́ть¹, у́ю, *impf.* to lubricate, oil, grease.

жир|ова́ть², у́ет, *impf.* to fatten (*intrans.*).

жирови́к, а́, *m.* 1. (*med.*) fatty tumour. 2. (*min.*) steatite, soapstone.

жиров|о́й, *adj.* 1. fatty, aliphatic; (*anat.*) adipose; ~а́я ткань adipose tissue; ~о́е перерожде́ние (*med.*) fatty degeneration. 2. ~а́я промы́шленность fat-products industry. 3. ~о́е яйцо́ wind-egg.

жирово́ск, а, *m.* (*physiol.*) adipocere.

жиропо́т, а, *m.* (*tech.*) suint, yolk (*of wool*).

жироприка́з, а, *m.* (*fin.*) (banking) order.

жироско́п, а, *m.* (*phys.*) gyroscope.

жите́йск|ий, *adj.* 1. worldly; of life, of the world; ~ая му́дрость worldly wisdom; ~ое мо́ре the ups and downs of life. 2. everyday; де́ло ~ое (*coll.*) there's nothing extraordinary in that.

жи́тел|ь, я, *m.* inhabitant; dweller.

жи́тельств|о, а, *n.* residence; вид на ж. residence permit; ме́сто ~а residence, domicile; ме́сто постоя́нного ~а permanent address.

жи́тельств|овать, ую, *impf.* (*obs.*) to reside, dwell.

жити|е́, я́, *n.* 1. life, biography; ~я́ святы́х Lives of the Saints. 2. (*obs.*) life, existence.

жити́йн|ый, *adj.* of житие́; ~ая литерату́ра hagiology, hagiography.'

жи́тниц|а, ы, *f.* granary (*also fig.*).

жи́тный, *adj.* cereal; ж. двор (*obs.*) granary.

жи́т|о, а, *no pl.*, *n.* (*unground*) corn (*denotes rye in Ukraine, barley in N. Russia, spring-sown cereals in general in E. Russia*).

жить, живу́, живёшь, *past* жил, жила́, жи́ло (не́ жил, не жила́, не́ жило), *impf.* 1. to live; ж. в Москве́ to live in Moscow; ж. ве́село to have a good time; ж. припева́ючи to be in clover; ж. на широ́кую но́гу to live in style; ж. со дня на́ день to live from hand to mouth; ж. да ж. бы ему́ (*of a person untimely dead*) he should have lived to see another day; жил-был once upon a time there lived . . . (*formula for opening of fairy-tale*). 2. (+*i.* or на+*a.*) to live (on); (+*i.*; *fig.*) to live (in, for); нам не́чем ж. we have nothing to live on; ж. на свои́ сре́дства to support oneself, live on one's own means; ж. наде́ждами to live in hopes; ж. иску́сством to live for art. 3. (в+*p.*; *of domestic servants*) to work (as); ж. в прислу́гах (у) to be a maid (at), work as a maid (for).

жить|ё, я́, *n.* (*coll.*) 1. life; existence; ~я́ тут нет от мух the flies make life here impossible. 2. habitation, residence; кварти́ра гото́ва для ~я́ the flat is ready for habitation.

житьё-бытьё, житья́-бытья́, *n.* (*coll.*) life; existence.

жи́ться, живётся, *past* жило́сь, *impf.* (*impers.*+*d.*; *coll.*) to live, get on; ей ве́село

живётся she leads a gay life; как вам жило́сь в Аме́рике? how did you get on in America?

жмот, а, *m.* (*coll.*) miser.

жму, жмёшь, *see* жать¹.

жму́р|ить, ю, ишь, *impf.* (*of* за~) ж. глаза́ to screw up one's eyes, narrow one's eyes.

жму́р|иться, юсь, ишься, *impf.* (*of* за~) to screw up one's eyes, narrow one's eyes.

жму́р|ки, ок, *no sing.* blind man's buff.

жмых|и́, о́в, *sing.* ~, ~а́, *m.* (*agric.*) oil-cake.

жне́йк|а, и, *f.* (*agric.*) binder, harvester reaping-machine.

жнец, а́, *m.* reaper.

жне|я́, и́, *f.* (*obs. or dial.*) 1. *f. of* ~ц. 2. reaping-machine.

жни́в|о, а, *n.* (*dial.*) = ~ьё.

жнивь|ё, я́, *pl.* ~я, *n.* 1. stubble-field. 2. (*sing. only*) stubble. 3. (*sing. only*) (*dial.*) harvest, harvest-time.

жнитв|о́, а́, *n.* (*dial.*) 1. stubble. 2. harvest, harvest-time.

жни́ц|а, ы, *f. of* жнец.

жну, жнёшь, *see* жать².

жоке́|й, я, *m.* jockey.

жоке́йк|а, и, *f.* (*coll.*) jockey cap.

жоке́й|ский, *adj. of* ~.

жо́лоб = жёлоб.

жо́лудь = жёлудь.

жом, а, *m.* 1. (*tech.*) press. 2. (*sing.* (*collect.*) husks, marc.

жонглёр, а, *m.* juggler.

жонглёрств|о, а, *n.* sleight-of-hand; juggling (*also fig.*).

жонгли́р|овать, ую, *impf.* (+*i.*) to juggle (with) (*also fig.*); он лю́бит ж. ци́фрами he likes juggling with figures.

жо́п|а, ы, *f.* (*vulg.*) arse; arsehole.

жо́рнов = жёрнов.

жох, а, *m.* (*coll.*) rogue.

жрань|ё, я́, *n.* (*vulg.*) guzzling, hogging.

жратв|а́, ы́, *f.* (*vulg.*) 1. guzzling, hogging. 2. (*sl.*) grub.

жр|ать, у́, ёшь, *past* ~ал, ~ала́, ~а́ло, *impf.* (*of* со~) 1. (*of animals*) to eat. 2. (*vulg.*) to guzzle, gobble.

жре́би|й, я, *m.* 1. lot; броса́ть, мета́ть ж. to cast lots; вы́нуть, тяну́ть ж. to draw lots. 2. (*fig.*) lot, fate, destiny; ж. бро́шен the die is cast.

жрец, а́, *m.* priest (*of heathen religious cult*); (*fig.*) devotee.

жре́ческий, *adj.* priestly.

жре́честв|о, а, *n.* priesthood.

жри́ц|а, ы, *f.* priestess; ж. любви́ woman of easy virtue.

жу́желиц|а, ы, *f.* (*zool.*) ground beetle.

жужжа́ни|е, я, *n.* hum, buzz, drone; humming, buzzing, droning.

жужж|а́ть, у́, и́шь, *impf.* to hum, buzz, drone; to whizz (*of projectiles*).

жуи́р, а, *m.* playboy.

жуи́р|овать, ую, *impf.* to lead a gay life, life of pleasure.

жук, а́, *m.* **1.** beetle; ма́йский ж. may-bug, cockchafer. **2.** (*coll.*) rogue.

жу́лик, а, *m.* petty thief; cheat, swindler; (card-)sharper.

жуликова́т|ый (∼, ∼а), *adj.* (*coll.*) roguish.

жуль|ё, я́, *n.* (*collect.*; *coll.*) rogues.

жу́льнича|ть, ю, *impf.* (*of* с∼) (*coll.*) to cheat; to swindle.

жу́льнический, *adj.* (*coll.*) roguish; under-hand, dishonest.

жу́льничеств|о, а, *n.* (*coll.*) **1.** cheating (*at games*). **2.** underhand, dishonest action; sharp practice.

жупа́н, а, *m.* (*hist.*) zhupan (*kind of jerkin worn by Poles and Ukrainians*).

жу́пел, а, *m.* **1.** bugbear, bogy. **2.** (*rel.*) brimstone.

журавл|и́ный, *adj. of* ∼ь; ∼и́ные но́ги spindle shanks.

жура́вл|ь, я́, *m.* **1.** (*orn.*) crane; не сули́ ∼я́ в не́бе, а дай сини́цу в ру́ки (*prov.*) a bird in the hand is worth two in the bush. **2.** (*well*) sweep, shadoof.

жур|и́ть, ю́, и́шь, *impf.* (*coll.*) to reprove, take to task.

журна́л, а, *m.* **1.** magazine; periodical; journal. **2.** journal, diary; register; ж. заседа́ний minutes, minute-book.

журнали́ст, а, *m.* **1.** journalist. **2.** ledger--clerk.

журнали́стик|а, и, *f.* **1.** journalism. **2.** (*collect.*) periodical press.

журнали́стский, *adj.* journalistic.

журна́л|ьный, *adj. of* ∼; ∼ьная статья́ magazine article.

журфи́кс, а, *m.* (*obs.*) at-home.

журча́ни|е, я, *n.* purling, babbling, murmur.

журч|а́ть, у́, и́шь, *impf.* to purl, babble, murmur (*of water; also fig., poet.*).

жу́т|кий (∼ок, ∼ка́, ∼ко), *adj.* terrible, terrifying; awe-inspiring, eerie.

жу́тко¹, *adv.* terrifyingly; (*coll.*) terribly, awfully.

жу́тко², *as pred.* (*impers.*+*d.*) мне, *etc.*, ж. I, *etc.*, am terrified, feel awestruck.

жут|ь, и, *f.* **1.** terror; awe; воспомина́ния о де́тстве для него́ — пря́мо ж. memories of childhood simply terrify him. **2.** *as pred.* = ∼ко².

жу́хл|ый (∼, ∼а), *adj.* withered, dried-up; hardened; tarnished.

жу́х|нуть, нет, *past* ∼, ∼ла, *impf.* to dry up; to become hard; to become tarnished.

жу́ч|ить, у, ишь, *impf.* (*coll.*) to scold.

жу́чк|а, и, *f.* (*coll.*) house-dog (*from name 'Zhuchka', very frequently given to mongrel dogs*).

жуч|о́к, ка́, *m.* **1.** *dim. of* жук. **2.** (*coll.*) wood--engraver (*insect*).

жу́|ю, ёшь, *see* жева́ть.

жюри́, *indecl.* **1.** *n.* (*collect.*) judges (*of competition, etc.*). **2.** *m.* (*obs.*) umpire, referee.

З

за, *prep.* I. +*a. and i.* (+*a.*: *indicates motion or action*; +*i.*: *indicates rest or state*). **1.** behind; за крова́ть, за крова́тью behind the bed. **2.** beyond; across, the other side of; за боло́то, за боло́том beyond the marsh; за́ борт, за бо́ртом overboard; за́ угол, за угло́м round the corner; за́ городом out of town; за рубежо́м abroad. **3.** at; сесть за роя́ль to sit down at the piano; сиде́ть за роя́лем to be at the piano. **4.** (*denoting occupation*) at, to (*or translated by participle*); приня́ться за рабо́ту to set to work, get down to work; заста́ть кого́-н. за рабо́той to find someone at work, working; сесть за кни́гу to sit down with a book, get down to reading; проводи́ть всё своё вре́мя за чте́нием to spend all one's time reading. **5.** вы́йти за́муж за (+*a.*) (*of a woman*) to marry; (быть) за́мужем за (+*i.*) (to be) married (to).

II. +*a.* **1.** after (*of time*); over (*of age*); далеко́ за́ полночь long after midnight; ему́ уже́ за́ сорок he is already over forty. **2.** *expresses distance in space or time*: самолёт разби́лся за ми́лю от дере́вни the aeroplane crashed a mile from the village; за два дня до его́ сме́рти two days before his death; за час an hour before, an hour early. **3.** during, in the space of; за́ ночь during the night, overnight; за су́тки in the space of twenty-four hours; за после́днее вре́мя recently, lately, of late. **4.** (+*verbs having sense of* to take hold of, *etc.*) by; вести́ за́ руку to lead by the hand. **5.** (*in var. senses*) for; плати́ть за биле́т to pay for a ticket; подписа́ть за дире́ктора to sign for the

director; боя́ться, ра́доваться за кого́-н. to fear, be glad for someone; слыть за знатока́ to pass for an expert; есть за трои́х to eat (enough) for three; за ва́ше здоро́вье! your health!, cheers!
III. +*i*. **1.** after; друг за дру́гом one after another; год за го́дом year after year; сле́довать за кем-н. to follow someone. **2.** (*fig.*) after; следи́ть за детьми́ to look after children; уха́живать за больны́м to look after a sick person; волочи́ться за же́нщиной (*coll.*) to run after a woman. **3.** for (= in order to fetch, obtain); идти́ за молоко́м to go for milk; посла́ть за до́ктором to send for a doctor; зайти́ за кем-н. to call for someone. **4.** at, during; за за́втраком at breakfast. **5.** for, on account of, because of; за неиме́нием, недоста́тком (+*g*.) for want of; за темното́й for the darkness, on account of the darkness; за чем де́ло ста́ло? what's up? **6.** (+*pronouns*) (*i*) *ascribes habits, qualities,* (*ii*) *imputes responsibility*: за ним во́дятся стра́нности he has his peculiarities; за тобо́й пять рубле́й you are owing five roubles; о́чередь за ва́ми it is your turn. **7.** *indicates provenance of a document, etc.*: письмо́ за по́дписью гла́вного реда́ктора a letter signed by the editor-in-chief.
за- *prefix* I. (*of verbs*) **1.** *indicates commencement of action*: зала́ять to start barking. **2.** *indicates direction of action beyond given point*: заверну́ть за́ угол to turn a corner. **3.** *indicates continuation of action to excess*: закорми́ть to overfeed. **4.** *forms perfective aspect of some verbs.* II. (*of nouns and adjs.*) trans-; Закавка́зье Transcaucasia; заатланти́ческий transatlantic.
заадрес|ова́ть, у́ю, *pf.* (*coll.*) to address, write the address (on).
заале́|ть, ет, *pf. of* але́ть.
заале́|ться, ется = ~ть.
зааплоди́р|овать, ую, *pf.* to break out into applause, start clapping.
зааренд|ова́ть, у́ю, *pf.* (*of* ~о́вывать) to rent, lease.
зарендо́выва|ть, ю, *impf. of* зарендова́ть.
зааркан|ить, ю, ишь, *pf. of* аркани́ть.
заарта́ч|иться, усь, ишься, *pf.* (*coll.*) to become restive, stubborn.
заасфальти́р|овать, ую, *pf. of* асфальти́ровать.
заатланти́ческий, *adj.* transatlantic.
заа́ха|ть, ю, *pf.* (*coll.*) to begin to sigh, begin to groan.
заба́в|а, ы, *f.* **1.** game; pastime. **2.** amusement, fun; он э́то сде́лал для ~ы he did it for fun.
забавля́|ть, ю, *impf.* to amuse, entertain, divert.

забавля́|ться, юсь, *impf.* to amuse oneself.
заба́вник, а, *m.* (*coll.*) amusing chap, entertaining person; humorist.
заба́вн|о¹, *adv. of* ~ый.
заба́вно², *as pred.* it is amusing, funny; мне з. I find it amusing, funny; з.! how funny!
заба́в|ный (~ен, ~на), *adj.* amusing; funny.
забаллоти́р|овать, ую, *pf.* to blackball, reject, fail to elect.
заба́лтыва|ть, ю, *impf. of* заболта́ть¹ 2.
забараба́н|ить, ю, ишь, *pf.* to begin to drum.
забаррикади́р|овать, ую, *pf. of* баррикади́ровать.
забаст|ова́ть, у́ю, *pf.* to go, come out on strike.
забасто́вк|а, и, *f.* strike; всео́бщая з. general strike; италья́нская з. sit-down strike, go-slow.
забасто́в|очный, *adj. of* ~ка.
забасто́вщик, а, *m.* striker.
забве́ни|е, я, *n.* **1.** oblivion; преда́ть ~ю to consign to oblivion. **2.** (*obs.*) unconsciousness; drowsiness.
забве́нный, *adj.* (*obs.*) forgotten.
забе́г, а, *m.* (*sport*) heat, race.
забега́ловк|а, и, *f.* (*coll.*) snack bar.
забега́|ть, ю, *pf.* **1.** to start running. **2.** to assume a shifty expression.
забега́|ть, ю, *impf. of* забежа́ть.
забега́|ться, юсь, *pf.* (*coll.*) to run oneself to a standstill.
забе|жа́ть, гу́, жи́шь, гу́т, *pf.* (*of* ~га́ть) **1.** to run up. **2.** (к; *coll.*) to drop in (to see). **3.** to run off; to stray. **4.** з. вперёд to run ahead; (*fig., coll.*) to anticipate.
забеле́|ть, ет, *pf.* to begin to turn white.
забел|и́ть, ю́, ~и́шь, *pf.* **1.** to whiten, paint white. **2.** (*coll.*) to add milk, cream (to); з. чай молоко́м to put milk in tea.
забе́лк|а, и, *f.* (*coll.*) **1.** whitening. **2.** milk or cream added to tea, *etc.*
забере́мене|ть, ю, *pf.* (*of* бере́менеть) to become pregnant.
забеспоко́|иться, юсь, ишься, *pf.* to begin to worry.
забива́ни|е, я, *n.* (*coll.*) jamming (*of radio transmissions*).
забива́|ть(ся), ю(сь), *impf. of* заби́ть(ся)¹.
заби́вк|а, и, *f.* (*coll.*) driving in; blocking up, stopping up.
забинт|ова́ть, у́ю, *pf.* (*of* ~о́вывать) to bandage.
забинт|ова́ться, у́юсь, *pf.* (*of* ~о́вываться) to bandage oneself.
забинто́выва|ть(ся), аю(сь), *impf. of* забинтова́ть(ся).
забира́|ть(ся), ю(сь), *impf. of* забра́ть(ся).

заби́т|ый (~, ~а), *p.p.p.* of ~ь and *adj.* cowed, downtrodden.

заб|и́ть¹, ью́, ьёшь, *pf.* (*of* ~ива́ть) **1.** to drive in, hammer in, ram in; з. себе́ в го́лову to get (it) firmly fixed in one's head. **2.** (*sport*) to score; з. мяч to kick the ball into the goal; з. гол to score a goal. **3.** to seal, stop up, block up; з. ще́ли па́клей to caulk up cracks with oakum. **4.** to obstruct; (*of plants*) to choke; (*coll.*) to jam (*radio transmissions*). **5.** (+*i.*; *coll.*) to cram, stuff (with). **6.** to beat up, knock senseless; (*fig.*) to render defenceless. **7.** (*coll.*) to beat (*at something*); to outdo, surpass. **8.** to slaughter (*cattle*).

заб|и́ть², ью́, ьёшь, *pf.* (*in var. senses*; *trans. and intrans.*) to begin to beat (*in some cases forms perfective aspect of* бить); з. трево́гу to sound the alarm; у нас из сква́жины ~и́ла нефть we have struck oil.

заб|и́ться¹, ью́сь, ьёшься, *pf.* (*of* ~ива́ться) **1.** (в+*a.*) to hide (in), take refuge (in). **2.** (в+*a.*) to get (into), penetrate. **3.** (+*i.*) to become cluttered (with), clogged (with).

заб|и́ться², ью́сь, ьёшься, *pf.* to begin to beat (*intrans.*).

забия́к|а, и, *m. and f.* (*coll.*) squabbler; trouble-maker; bully.

заблаговре́менно, *adv.* in good time; well in advance; з. предупреди́ть to warn in advance.

заблаговре́менный, *adj.* timely, done in good time.

заблагорассу́|дить, жу, дишь, *pf.* (*obs.*) to think fit.

заблагорассу́|диться, ится, *pf.* (*impers.*) to like, think fit; to come into one's head; он придёт, когда́ ему́ ~ится he will come when he thinks fit, when he feels so disposed.

забле|сте́ть, щу́, сти́шь *and* ~щешь, *pf.* to begin to shine, glitter, glow.

забле́|ять, ю, ешь, *pf.* to begin to bleat.

заблу|ди́ться, жу́сь, ~дишься, *pf.* to lose one's way, get lost; з. в трёх со́снах to lose one's way in broad daylight.

заблу́дш|ий, *adj.* (*obs.*) lost, stray; ~ая овца́ a lost sheep.

заблужда́|ться, юсь, *impf.* to be mistaken.

заблужде́ни|е, я, *n.* error; delusion; ввести́ в з. to delude, mislead; впасть в з. to be deluded.

забода́|ть, ю, *pf.* of бода́ть.

забо́|й¹, я, *m.* (*mining*) (pit-)face.

забо́|й², я, *m.* slaughtering.

забо́йник, а, *m.* (*tech.*) beetle, rammer.

забо́йщик, а, *m.* face-worker, (coal-)hewer, getter (*in mine*).

забола́чива|ть(ся), ет(ся), *impf.* of заболо́тить(ся).

заболева́емост|ь, и, *f.* sickness rate; number of cases; з. полиомиели́том утро́илась за про́шлую неде́лю the number of cases of infantile paralysis has tripled during the last week.

заболева́ни|е, я, *n.* **1.** sickness, illness. **2.** falling sick, falling ill.

заболева́|ть¹, ю, *impf.* of заболе́ть¹.

заболева́|ть², ет, *impf.* of заболе́ть².

заболе́|ть¹, ю, ешь, *pf.* (*of* ~ва́ть¹) to fall ill, fall sick; (+*i.*) to be taken ill (with), go down (with).

забол|е́ть², и́т, *pf.* (*of* ~ева́ть²) to (begin to) ache, hurt; у меня́ ~е́л зуб I have toothache.

за́болон|ь, и, *f.* (*bot.*) alburnum, sap-wood.

заболо́|тить, чу, тишь, *pf.* (*of* забола́чивать) to swamp, turn into swamp. (*intrans.*)

заболо́|титься, тится, *pf.* (*of* забола́чиваться) to turn into swamp. (*intrams.*)

заболта́|ть¹, ю, *pf.* **1.** (+*i.*) to begin to swing. **2.** (*impf.* забалтывать) to mix (in).

заболта́|ть², ю, *pf.* (*coll.*) to start chattering, nattering.

заболта́|ться¹, юсь, *pf.* (*coll.*) to begin to swing.

заболта́|ться², юсь, *pf.* (*coll.*) to become engrossed in conversation.

забо́р¹, а, *m.* fence.

забо́р², а, *m.* **1.** taking away. **2.** obtaining on credit.

забо́рист|ый (~, ~а), *adj.* (*coll.*) **1.** strong (*of liquor, tobacco, etc.*). **2.** (*fig.*) з. анекдо́т risqué story; з. моти́в racy tune.

забо́р|ный¹, *adj.* **1.** *adj.* of ~¹. **2.** coarse, indecent; risqué; ~ная литерату́ра pornography.

забо́р|ный², *adj.* of ~²; ~ная кни́жка (*i*) ration book, (*ii*) account (*book in which purchases obtained on credit are entered*).

забо́ртный, *adj.* (*naut.*) outboard; з. дви́гатель outboard engine; з. кла́пан (*tech.*) seacock; з. трап companion ladder.

забо́т|а, ы, *f.* **1.** cares, trouble(s); без ~ carefree; (*coll.*) вот не́ было ~ы! there was trouble enough already; ему́ ма́ло ~ы what does he care? **2.** care, attention(s); concern; з. о челове́ке concern for people's welfare.

забо́|тить, чу, тишь, *impf.* to trouble, worry, cause anxiety.

забо́|титься, чусь, тишься, *impf.* (*of* по~) (о+*p.*) **1.** to worry, be troubled (about) **2.** to take care (of); to take trouble (about); to care (about); она́ всё ~тится о де́тях she is always thinking of the children; он ни о чём не ~тится he does not care about anything.

забо́тливост|ь, и, *f.* solicitude, care, thoughtfulness.

забо́тлив|ый (~, ~a), *adj.* solicitous, thoughtful.

забрако́в|анный, *p.p.p. of* ~а́ть; з. това́р rejects.

забрак|ова́ть, у́ю, *pf. of* бракова́ть.

забра́л|о, а, *n.* visor; с откры́тым ~ом openly, frankly.

забра́сыва|ть, ю, *impf. of* заброса́ть *and* забро́сить.

забра́|ть¹, заберу́, заберёшь, *past* ~л, ~ла́, ~ло, *pf.* (*of* забира́ть) 1. to take (*in one's hands*); to take (with one); з. во́жжи to take the reins; з. с собо́й ве́щи to take one's things with one; з. себе́ в го́лову to take it into one's head; з. за живо́е to touch to the quick. 2. to take away; to seize, appropriate. 3. (*of emotions; coll.*) to come over, seize; его́ ~ла́ охо́та пое́хать в Аме́рику he was seized with a desire to go to America. 4. to take in (*part of a garment, etc.*). 5. to turn off, aside. 6. (*tech.*) to catch; (*of an anchor*) to bite.

забра́|ть², заберу́, заберёшь, *past* ~л, ~ла́, ~ло, *pf.* (*of* забира́ть) to stop up, block up.

забра́|ться, заберу́сь, заберёшься, *past* ~лся, ~ла́сь, ~ло́сь, *pf.* (*of* забира́ться) 1. (в+*a.*) to get (into); (в, на+*a.*) to climb (into, on to); з. в чужо́й дом to get into someone else's house. 2. to get to; to hide out, go into hiding; куда́ они́ ~ли́сь? where have they got to?

забре́|дить, жу, дишь, *pf.* to become delirious.

забре́зж|ить, ит, *pf.* to begin to dawn; to begin to appear; чуть ~ил свет it was barely light; ~ило (*impers.*) it is just beginning to get light.

забре|сти́, ду́, дёшь, *past* ~л, ~ла́, *pf.* (*coll.*) 1. to drop in. 2. to go astray, wander off.

забр|и́ть, е́ю, е́ешь, *pf.* (*obs.*) to call up (into the army); з. лоб (+*d.*) = з.

заброни́р|овать, ую, *pf.* (*of* брони́ровать) to reserve.

забронир|ова́ть, у́ю, *pf.* (*of* бронирова́ть) to armour.

забро́с, а, *m.*; в ~е (*coll.*) in a state of neglect.

заброса́|ть, ю, *pf.* (*of* забра́сывать) (+*i.*) 1. to fill (up) (with); з. я́му золо́й to fill up a hole with ashes. 2. to shower (with), bespatter (with); з. кого́-н. гря́зью to sling mud at someone (*also fig.*); з. кого́-н. бла́нками to deluge someone with forms.

забро́|сить, шу, сишь, *pf.* (*of* забра́сывать) 1. to throw (*with force* or *to a distance*); to cast (*also fig.*); кто ~сил мя́чик в окно́? who threw a ball through the window?; вое́нная слу́жба ~сила его́ на Да́льний Восто́к military service took him to the Far East. 2. to throw (*a part of the body, etc.*); з. го́лову наза́д to throw one's head back. 3. (*pf.*

only) to mislay. 4. to throw up, give up, abandon; to neglect, let go; з. иссле́дования to throw up one's research; з. дете́й to neglect children. 5. to take, bring (*to a certain place*). 6. to leave behind (*somewhere*).

забро́шенност|ь, и, *f.* 1. neglect. 2. desertion.

забро́|шенный, *p.p.p. of* ~сить *and adj.* 1. neglected. 2. deserted, desolate.

забры́зг|ать¹, аю, *pf.* (*of* ~ивать) (+*i.*) to splash; to bespatter (with).

забры́з|гать², жет, *pf.* to begin to play (*of a fountain*).

забры́згива|ть, ю, *impf. of* забры́згать¹.

забубённ|ый, *adj.* (*coll.*) reckless; wild; ~ая голо́вушка desperate fellow, reprobate.

заб|у́ду, у́дешь, *see* ~ы́ть.

забукси́р|овать, ую, *pf.* to take in tow.

забулды́г|а, и, *m.* (*coll.*) debauchee, profligate.

забу|ти́ть, чу́, ти́шь, *pf.* (*of* бути́ть) to fill with rubble; (+*i.*) to fill in (with).

забуха́|ть, ет, *impf. of* забу́хнуть.

забу́х|нуть, нет, *past* ~, ~ла, *pf.* to swell; to become stuck.

забуя́н|ить, ю, ишь, *pf.* to become unruly, get out of hand.

забыва́|ть(ся), ю(сь), *impf. of* забы́ть(ся).

забы́вчив|ый (~, ~a), *adj.* forgetful; absent--minded.

заб|ы́ть, у́ду, у́дешь, *pf.* (*of* ~ыва́ть) 1. (+*a.*, о+*p.* or *inf.*) to forget; и ду́мать ~у́дь! (*coll.*) get it out of your head!; себя́ не з. to take care of oneself. 2. to leave behind, forget (to bring); вы опя́ть ~ы́ли биле́ты you have forgotten the tickets again.

забыть|ё, я́, в ~и́, *n.* 1. drowsy state. 2. half-conscious state, oblivion. 3. (state of) distraction; в ~и́ distractedly.

заб|ы́ться, у́дусь, у́дешься, *pf.* (*of* ~ыва́ться) 1. to doze off, drop off. 2. to become unconscious, lose consciousness. 3. to sink into a reverie. 4. to forget oneself. 5. *pass. of* ~ы́ть.

зав, а, *m.* (*abbr. of* ~е́дующий) (*coll.*) manager; chief, head.

зав, *abbr. of* 1. заве́дующий. 2. заво́дский.

зава́л, а, *m.* obstruction, blockage.

зава́лива|ть(ся), ю(сь), *impf. of* завали́ть-(ся).

зава́линк|а, и, *f.* zavalinka (*mound of earth round a Russian peasant hut serving as protection from the weather and often used for sitting out*).

завал|и́ть, ю́, ~ишь, *pf.* (*of* ~ивать) 1. to block up, obstruct; to fill (*so as to block up*); з. вход мешка́ми с песко́м to block up the entrance with sandbags. 2. (+*i.*; *coll.*) to pile (with); to fill cram-full (with); (*fig.*) to overload (with); прила́вок ~ен коро́бками the stall is piled high with boxes; реда́кция ~ена рабо́той the editors are snowed under with work. **3.** (*coll.*) to throw back; to tip up, cant. **4.** (*coll.*) to knock down, demolish. **5.** (*fig.*, *coll.*) to make a mess (of), muck up. **6.** (*impers.*; *coll.*) to block up, stuff up; у меня́ у́хо ~и́ло my ear feels blocked up.

завал|и́ться, ю́сь, ~ишься, *pf.* (*of* ~ива́ться) **1.** to fall; to collapse; нож ~и́лся за шкаф the knife has fallen behind the cupboard. **2.** (*coll.*) to lie down; з. спать to fall into bed. **3.** (*coll.*) to overturn, tip up. **4.** (*fig.*, *coll.*) to miscarry, come to grief; (*of a person*) to slip up.

зава́лк|а, и, *f.* **1.** filling up. **2.** (*tech.*) (furnace) charge.

за́вал|ь, и, *f.* (*collect.*; *coll.*) shop-soiled goods; trash.

заваля́|ться, ется, *pf.* (*coll.*) **1.** to be still on hand; э́тот това́р ~ется these goods will not sell. **2.** to remain without attention; to be shelved.

заваля́щий, *adj.* (*coll.*) long unsold, shop-soiled; worthless, useless.

зава́рива|ть(ся), ет(ся), *impf. of* завари́ть(ся).

завар|и́ть, ю́, ~ишь, *pf.* (*of* ~ива́ть) **1.** to make (*drinks, etc., by pouring on boiling water*); з. чай to brew tea; з. ка́шу (*fig.*) to start trouble; ну и ~и́л ка́шу! now the fat's in the fire! **2.** to scald. **3.** (*tech.*) to weld. **4.** (*coll.*) to start, initiate.

завар|и́ться, ~ится, *pf.* (*of* ~ива́ться) **1.** (*of drinks*) to have brewed. **2.** (*coll.*) to start; ~и́лось большо́е де́ло there's big trouble brewing.

зава́рк|а, и, *f.* **1.** brewing (*of tea, etc.*). **2.** scalding. **3.** (*tech.*) welding. **4.** (*coll.*) enough tea for one brew.

заварно́й, *adj.* (*cul.*) boiled.

завару́х|а, и, *f.* (*coll.*) commotion, stir.

заведе́ни|е, я, *n.* **1.** establishment, institution. **2.** (*obs.*) custom, habit; здесь уж тако́е з. it is the custom here.

заве́д|овать, ую, *impf.* (+*i.*) to manage, superintend; to be in charge (of).

заве́домо, *adv.* wittingly; (+*adj.*) known to be; з. зна́я being fully aware; переда́ть з. необосно́ванный слух to pass on a rumour known to be unfounded.

заве́домый, *adj.* notorious; undoubted.

заве|ду́, дёшь, *see* ~сти́.

заве́дующ|ий, его, *m.* (+*i.*) manager; head; person in charge (of); з. уче́бной ча́стью director of studies; з. отде́лом head of a department.

завез|ти́, у́, ёшь, *past* ~, ~ла́, *pf.* (*of* заво-зи́ть) **1.** to convey, deliver; з. запи́ску по доро́ге домо́й to deliver a note on the way

home. **2.** to take (to a distance *or* out of one's way).

заверб|ова́ть, у́ю, *pf. of* вербова́ть.

завере́ни|е, я, *n.* assurance; protestation.

завери́тел|ь, я, *m.* witness (*to a signature, etc.*).

заве́р|ить, ю, ишь, *pf.* (*of* ~я́ть) **1.** (в+*p.*) to assure (of). **2.** to certify; з. по́дпись to witness a signature.

заве́рк|а, и, *f.* certification.

заверн|у́ть, у́, ёшь, *pf.* (*of* завёртывать) **1.** (в+*a.*) to wrap (in); ~и́те его́ в одея́ло wrap him in a blanket. **2.** to tuck up, roll up (*sleeve, etc.*). **3.** to turn (*intrans.*); з. напра́во to turn to the right. **4.** (*coll.*) to drop in, call in. **5.** to screw tight; to turn off (*by screwing*); з. га́йку to screw a nut tight; з. кран to turn off a tap; з. во́ду to turn the water off. **6.** (*of weather conditions*; *coll.*) to come on, come down.

заверн|у́ться, у́сь, ёшься, *pf.* (*of* завёрты-ваться) **1.** (в+*a.*) to wrap oneself up (in), muffle oneself (in). **2.** *pass. of* ~у́ть.

завер|те́ть, чу́, ~тишь, *pf.* **1.** to begin to twirl. **2.** з. кого́-н. (*fig.*, *coll.*) to turn someone's head.

завер|те́ться, чу́сь, ~тишься, *pf.* **1.** to begin to turn, begin to spin. **2.** (*coll.*) to become flustered; to lose one's head.

завёртк|а, и, *f.* **1.** wrapping up. **2.** (*coll.*) package.

завёртыва|ть(ся), ю(сь), *impf. of* заверну́ть(ся).

заверш|а́ть, а́ю, *impf. of* ~и́ть.

завершéни|е, я, *n.* completion; end; в з. in conclusion.

заверш|и́ть, у́, и́шь, *pf.* (*of* ~а́ть) to complete, conclude, crown.

завер|я́ть, я́ю, *impf. of* ~ить.

заве́с|а, ы, *f.* (*obs.*) curtain; дымова́я з. (*mil.*) smoke-screen; (*fig.*) veil, screen; при-подня́ть ~у to lift the veil.

заве́|сить, шу, сишь, *pf.* (*of* ~шивать) to curtain (off).

заве|сти́, ду́, дёшь, *past* ~л, ~ла́, *pf.* (*of* заводи́ть[1]) **1.** to take, bring (*to a place*); to leave, drop off (*at a place*). **2.** to take (to a distance *or* out of one's way). **3.** to set up; to start; з. де́ло (*coll.*) to set up in business; з. птицефе́рму to start a poultry farm; з. перепи́ску с кем-н. to start up a correspondence with someone. **4.** to acquire. **5.** to institute, introduce (*a custom*); з. привы́чку (+*inf.*) to get into the habit (of); у нас так ~дено́ this is our custom. **6.** to wind (up), start (*a mechanism*); з. часы́ to wind up a clock; з. мото́р to crank an engine; как ~дённый (*coll.*) like a machine.

заве|сти́сь, ду́сь, дёшься, *past* ~лся, ~ла́сь,

pf. (*of* заводи́ться) 1. to be; to appear; в по́гребе ~ли́сь кры́сы there are rats in the cellar. 2. to be established, be set up; ~ло́сь обыкнове́ние it has become a habit. 3. (+*i.*; *coll.*) to acquire; з. свои́м до́мом to acquire a home of one's own. 4. (*of a mechanism*) to start (*intrans.*).

завѐт, а, *m.* 1. (*rhet.*) behest, bidding, ordinance. 2. Ве́тхий, Но́вый з. the Old, the New Testament.

завѐтн|ый, *adj.* cherished; intimate; secret, hidden; стать кинозвездо́й — её ~ая мечта́ her secret dream is to become a film--star.

завѐтренный, *adj.* leeward.

завѐш|ать, аю, *pf.* (*of* ~ивать) (+*a. and i.*) to hang (all over); он ~ал сте́ны своего́ кабине́та фотогра́фиями he has hung the walls of his study with photographs.

заве́шива|ть, ю, *impf. of* заве́сить *and* заве́шать.

завеща́ни|е, я, *n.* will, testament.

завеща́тел|ь, я, *m.* (*leg.*) testator.

завеща́тельниц|а, ы, *f.* (*leg.*) testatrix.

завеща́|ть, ю, *impf. and pf.* (+*a. and d.*) to leave (to), bequeath (to); (*leg.*) to devise (to).

завѐ|ять, ет, *pf.* 1. to begin to blow (*of the wind*). 2. (*of blizzard, etc.*) to cover.

завзя́тый, *adj.* (*coll.*) inveterate, out-and--out, downright; incorrigible.

завива́|ть(ся), ю(сь), *impf. of* зави́ть(ся).

зави́вк|а, и, *f.* 1. waving; curling; сде́лать себе́ ~у to have one's hair waved. 2. (hair-) wave.

зави́|деть, жу, дишь, *pf.* (*coll.*) to catch sight of.

зави́д|ки, ок, *no sing.* (*coll.*); меня́, *etc.*, беру́т з. I, *etc.*, feel envious.

зави́дно, *as pred.* (*impers.*+*d.*) to feel envious.

зави́д|ный (~ен, ~на), *adj.* enviable.

зави́д|овать, ую, *impf.* (*of* по~) (+*d.*) to envy.

завиду́щий, *adj.* (*coll.*) envious, covetous.

завизж|а́ть, у́, и́шь, *pf.* to begin to scream, squeal.

завизи́р|овать, ую, *pf. of* визи́ровать.¹

завин|ти́ть, чу́, ти́шь, *pf.* (*of* ~чивать) to screw up.

завин|ти́ться, чу́сь, ти́шься, *pf.* (*of* ~чиваться) to screw up (*intrans.*).

зави́нчива|ть(ся), ю(сь), *impf. of* завинти́ть(ся).

завира́льный, *adj.* (*coll.*) false; nonsensical.

завира́|ться, юсь, *impf. of* завра́ться.

завиру́х|а, и, *f.* (*dial.*) 1. snow-storm. 2. (*coll.*) bother, fuss.

зависа́|ть, ю, *impf.* (*aeron.*) to hover.

зави́|сеть, шу, сишь, *impf.* (от) 1. to de-

pend (on). 2. to lie in the power (of); я помогу́ тебе́, наско́лько от меня́ ~сит I will help you as far as in me lies.

зави́симост|ь, и, *f.* dependence; в ~и (от) depending (on), subject (to).

зави́сим|ый (~, ~а), *adj.* (от) dependent (on).

зави́стлив|ый (~, ~а), *adj.* envious.

зави́стник, а, *m.* envious person.

за́вист|ь, и, *f.* envy.

завит|о́й *and* ~ый **(зави́т, ~а́, зави́то),** *adj.* curled; waved.

завит|о́к, ка́, *m.* 1. curl, lock. 2. flourish (*in handwriting*). 3. (*archit.*) volute, scroll. 4. (*bot.*) tendril. 5. (*anat.*) helix.

зав|и́ть, ью́, ьёшь, *past* ~и́л, ~ила́, ~и́ло, *pf.* (*of* ~ива́ть) to curl; to wave; to twist, wind; з. го́ре верёвочкой (*coll.*) to pack up one's troubles.

зав|и́ться, ью́сь, ьёшься, *past* ~и́лся, ~ила́сь, *pf.* (*of* ~ива́ться) 1. to curl, wave, twine (*intrans.*). 2. to curl, wave one's hair; to have one's hair curled, waved.

завко́м, а, *m.* (*abbr. of* заводско́й комите́т) factory committee.

завладева́|ть, ю, *impf. of* завладе́ть.

завладе́|ть, ю, *pf.* (*of* ~ва́ть) (+*i.*) to take possession (of); to seize, capture (*also fig.*); свои́м красноре́чием он ~л внима́нием слу́шателей he gripped the audience with his eloquence.

завлека́|тельный (~ен, ~ьна), *adj.* (*coll.*) alluring; fascinating, captivating.

завлека́|ть, ю, *impf. of* завле́чь.

завле́|чь, ку́, чёшь, ку́т, *past* ~к, ~кла́, *pf.* (*of* ~ка́ть) 1. to lure, entice. 2. to fascinate, captivate.

заво́д¹, а, *m.* 1. factory, mill; works. 2. (ко́нский) з. stud(-farm).

заво́д², а, *m.* 1. winding up. 2. winding mechanism; игру́шка с ~ом clockwork toy. 3. period of running (*of clock, etc.*); часы́ с су́точным ~ом twenty-four-hour clock.

заво́д³, а, *m. only in phrase* э́того (и) в ~е нет (*coll.*) it has never been the custom.

заводи́л|а, ы, *m. and f.* (*coll.*) instigator; live--wire.

заво|ди́ть¹, жу́, ~дишь, *impf. of* завести́.

заво|ди́ть², жу́, ~дишь, *pf.* (*coll.*) to walk off one's feet.

завод|и́ться, ~ится, *impf. of* завести́сь.

заво́дк|а, и, *f.* winding up; starting.

заводн|о́й, *adj.* 1. clockwork. 2. (*tech.*) winding, starting; ~а́я рукоя́тка, ру́чка starting crank.

заводоуправле́ни|е, я, *n.* works management.

заво́д|ский, *adj. of* ~¹; ~ская ло́шадь stud--horse; *as noun* з., ~ского, *m.* factory worker.

заво́д|ско́й = ~ский; з. треуго́льник (*coll.*) 'factory triangle' (= *leadership comprising factory manager, Party secretary, and trade union secretary*).

заво́дчик[1], а, *m.* 1. factory-owner, mill-owner.

заво́дчик[2], а, *m.* (*coll., obs.*) instigator, author.

за́вод|ь, и, *f.* creek, backwater.

завоева́ни|е, я, *n.* 1. winning. 2. conquest; (*fig.*) achievement, gain, attainment; но-ве́йшие ~я те́хники the latest achievements of technology.

завоева́тел|ь, я, *m.* conqueror.

завоева́тельн|ый, *adj.* aggressive; ~ая война́ war of conquest.

заво|ева́ть, ю́ю, ю́ешь, *pf.* (*of* ~ёвывать) to conquer; (*fig.*) to win, gain; з. о́бщие симпа́тии to gain general sympathy.

завоёвыва|ть, ю, *impf. of* завоева́ть; to try to get.

заво́з, а, *m.* delivery; carriage.

заво|зи́ть[1], жу́, ~зишь, *impf. of* завезти́.

заво|зи́ть[2], жу́, ~зишь, *pf.* (*coll.*) to dirty, soil.

заво|зи́ться[1], жу́сь, ~зишься, *impf., pass. of* ~зи́ть[1].

заво|зи́ться[2], жу́сь, ~зишься, *pf.* (*coll.*) to begin to play about.

заво́зный, *adj.* brought in; imported.

заво́лакива|ть(ся), ю(сь), *impf. of* заво-ло́чь(ся).

заво́лжск|ий, *adj.* (situated, living) on the left bank of the Volga; ~ие ста́рцы (*hist.*) trans-Volga monks (*adherents of 'non-possessor' doctrine of Nil Sorsky*).

заволн|ова́ться, у́юсь, *pf.* to become agitated.

заволо́|чь, ку́, чёшь, ку́т, *past* ~к, ~кла́, *pf.* (*of* заволáкивать) to cloud; to obscure; тума́н ~к со́лнце the sun was obscured by fog; её глаза́ ~кло́ слеза́ми her eyes were clouded with tears.

заволо́|чься, чётся, ку́тся, *past* ~кся, ~кла́сь, *pf.* (*of* заволáкиваться) to cloud over, become clouded.

завоп|и́ть, лю́, и́шь, *pf.* (*coll.*) to cry out, yell; to give a cry.

завора́жива|ть, ю, *impf. of* заворожи́ть.

завора́чива|ть[1], ю, *impf.* = завёртывать.

завора́чива|ть[2], ю, *impf.* 1. *impf. of* заворо-ти́ть. 2. (*impf. only*) (+*i.*; *coll.*) to be boss (of).

заворож|и́ть, у́, и́шь, *pf.* (*of* заворáживать) to cast a spell (over), bewitch; (*fig.*) to fascinate.

заворо́т, а, *m.* (*coll.*) 1. turn, turning. 2. bend (*in road, river, etc.*).

завор|оти́ть, очу́, о́тишь, *pf.* (*of* заворáчи-вать[2]) 1. to turn. 2. to turn in; to drop in. 3. to roll up; to tuck up.

заворо́шк|а, и, *f.* (*coll.*) complication(s).

завр|а́ться, у́сь, ёшься, *past* ~а́лся, ~ала́сь *pf.* (*of* завира́ться) (*coll.*) to become en tangled in lies; to become an inveterate liar

завсегда́, *adv.* (*coll.*) always.

завсегда́та|й, я, *m.* habitué.

за́втра, *adv.* tomorrow; (*in past-tense narra tion*) the next day; до з.! see you to morrow!; не ны́нче-з. (*coll.*) any day now

за́втрак, а, *m.*; breakfast; lunch(eon); кор-ми́ть ~ами (*coll.*) to feed with empty hopes.

за́втрака|ть, ю, *impf.* (*of* по~) to (have) breakfast; to (have) lunch.

за́втрашн|ий, *adj.* tomorrow's; з. ден тomorrow; забо́титься о ~ем дне to take thought for the morrow.

завуали́ров|анный, *p.p.p. of* ~ать *and adj.* (*phot.*) fogged.

завуали́р|овать, ую, *pf. of* вуали́ровать.

за́вуч, а, *m.* (*abbr. of* заве́дующий уче́бной ча́стью) director of studies.

завхо́з, а, *m.* (*abbr. of* заве́дующий хозя́й-ством) bursar, steward.

завши́ве|ть, ю, *pf. of* вши́веть.

завши́вленный, *adj.* (*coll.*) lice-ridden.

завыва́|ть, ю, *impf.* to howl; to sough.

завы́|сить, шу, сишь, *pf.* (*of* ~ша́ть) to raise too high; з. отме́тку на экза́мене to give too high a mark in an examination.

зав|ы́ть, о́ю, о́ешь, *pf.* to begin to howl.

завыша́|ть, ю, *impf. of* завы́сить.

завя|за́ть[1], жу́, ~жешь, *pf.* (*of* ~зывать) 1. to tie (up); to knot; з. шнурки́ боти́нок to tie up one's shoe-laces. 2. to bind (up). 3. (*fig.*) to start; з. бой to join battle; з. перепи́ску to start a correspondence.

завяза́|ть[2], ю, *impf. of* завя́знуть.

завя|за́ться, ~жется, *pf.* (*of* ~зываться) 1. *pass. of* ~за́ть. 2. to start; to arise. 3. (*bot.*) to set.

завязи́|ть, ть, *no 1st person*, шь, *pf.* (*coll.*) to get stuck (*trans.*).

завя́зк|а, и, *f.* 1. string, lace, band. 2. be-ginning, start; opening (*of novel, etc.*).

завя́з|нуть, ну, нешь, *past* ~, ~ла, *pf.* (*of* ~а́ть[2]) to stick, get stuck; з. в долга́х to be over head and ears in debt.

завя́зыва|ть(ся), ет(ся), *impf. of* завяза́ть (-ся).

завя́з|ь, и, *f.* (*bot.*) ovary.

завя́лый, *adj.* (*obs.*) withered, faded.

завя́|нуть, ну, нешь, *past* ~л, *pf. of* вя́нуть.

загад|а́ть, а́ю, *pf.* (*of* ~ывать) 1. з. зага́дки to ask riddles. 2. to guess one's fortune; to decide, settle (*by tossing a coin, etc.*). 3. to think of (= to select arbitrarily, at ran-dom); ~а́йте число́ think of a number. 4. to plan ahead, look ahead. 5. (*coll.*) give orders.

загá|дить, жу, дишь, *pf.* (*of* ~жива́ть) (*coll.*) to soil, dirty, befoul.

загáдк|а, и, *f.* riddle; enigma; mystery.

загáдоч|ный (~ен, ~на), *adj.* enigmatic; mysterious.

загáдыва|ть, ю, *impf. of* загадáть.

загáжива|ть, ю, *impf. of* загáдить.

загáр, а, *m.* sunburn, (sun-)tan.

загасá|ть, ет, *impf. of* загáснуть.

зага|си́ть, шу́, ~си́шь, *pf. of* гаси́ть 1.

загáс|нуть, нет, *past* ~, ~ла, *pf.* (*of* ~áть) (*coll.*) to go out.

загвоз|ди́ть, жу́, ди́шь, *pf.* 1. (*obs.*) to spike (*a gun*). 2. (*coll.*) to pose, set (*a problem, etc.*).

загвóздк|а, и, *f.* (*coll.*) snag, obstacle; вот в чём з.! there's the rub!

заги́б, а, *m.* 1. fold; bend. 2. (*coll.*) exaggeration; (*polit.*) deviation.

загибá|ть(ся), ю(сь), *impf. of* загну́ть(ся).

заги́бщик, а, *m.* (*polit.; coll.*) deviationist.

загипнотизи́р|овать, ую, *pf. of* гипнотизи́ровать.

загипс|овáть, у́ю, *pf. of* гипсовáть.

заглáви|е, я, *n.* title; heading; под ~ем entitled, headed.

заглáв|ный, *adj. of* ~ие; з. лист title-page; ~ная бу́ква capital letter; ~ные бу́квы initials; ~ная роль (*theatr.*) title-role, name--part.

заглá|дить, жу, дишь, *pf.* (*of* ~жива́ть) 1. to iron (out), press. 2. (*fig.*) to make up (for), make amends (for); з. грехи́ to expiate one's sins.

заглá|диться, дится, *pf.* (*of* ~жива́ться) 1. to iron out (*intrans.*); to become smooth. 2. (*fig.*) to fade.

заглáжива|ть, ю, *impf. of* заглáдить.

заглáжива|ться, ется, *impf. of* заглáдиться.

заглáзно, *adv.* (*coll.*) behind someone's back.

заглáзн|ый, *adj.* (*coll.*) done, said in someone's absence, behind someone's back; ~ое реше́ние (*leg.*) judgment by default; ~ая клеветá scandal uttered about someone behind his back.

заглáтыва|ть, ю, *impf. of* заглотáть.

заглотá|ть, ю, *pf.* (*of* заглáтывать) to swallow.

заглóхн|уть, у, ешь, *pf. of* глóхнуть 2, 3.

заглуш|áть, áю, *impf. of* ~и́ть.

заглуш|и́ть, у́, и́шь, *pf.* (*of* глуши́ть *and* ~áть) 1. to drown, deaden, muffle (*sound*). 2. to jam (*radio transmissions*). 3. (*of plants*) to choke. 4. (*fig.*) to suppress, stifle. 5. to alleviate, soothe.

заглу́шк|а, и, *f.* 1. (*tech.*) choke, plug, stopper. 2. lid (*for central tube of samovar*).

заглядéнь|е, я, *n.* (*coll.*) lovely sight; э́то прóсто з.! isn't that lovely?, what a beautiful sight!

загля|дéться, жу́сь, ди́шься, *pf.* (*of* ~ды-ваться) (на+*a.*; *coll.*) to stare (at); to be unable to take one's eyes off; to be lost in admiration (of).

заглядыва|ть, ю, *impf. of* заглянуть.

заглядыва|ться, юсь, *impf. of* загляде́ться.

заглян|у́ть, у́, ~ешь, *pf.* (*of* загля́дывать) 1. to peep; to glance; она́ ~у́ла в окнó и уви́дела, что де́ти засну́ли she peeped in at the window and saw that the children had gone to sleep; з. в газе́ты to glance at the newspapers. 2. (*coll.*) to look in, drop in; ~и́те к нам, пожáлуйста! please look in (to see us)!

загнáива|ть(ся), ю(сь), *impf. of* загнои́ть-(ся).

зáгнанный, *p.p.p. of* загнáть *and adj.* 1. tired out, exhausted; (*of a horse*) winded; как з. зверь at the end of one's tether. 2. downtrodden, cowed.

загнá|ть, загоню́, загóнишь, *past* ~л, ~лá, ~ло, *pf.* (*of* загоня́ть¹) 1. to drive in; з. корóв в хлев to drive the cows into the shed, get the cows in; з. мяч в ворóта (*sport*) to score, shoot a goal. 2. to drive (off). 3. to tire out, exhaust; to override (*a horse*). 4. (*coll.*) to drive home; з. свáи в зе́млю to drive piles into the ground. 5. (*sl.*) to flog (= to sell). 6. з. копе́йку (*sl.*) to make (some) money.

загнивáни|е, я, *n.* rotting, putrescence; (*fig.*) decay; (*med.*) suppuration.

загнивá|ть, ю, *impf. of* загни́ть.

загни́|ть, ю́, ёшь, *past* ~л, ~лá, ~ло, *pf.* (*of* ~вáть) to begin to rot; to rot, decay (*also fig.*); (*med.*) to fester.

загно|и́ть, ю́, и́шь, *pf.* (*of* загнáивать) (*coll.*) 1. to allow to fester. 2. to allow to rot, allow to decay.

загно|и́ться, и́тся, *pf.* (*of* загнáиваться) to fester.

загн|у́ть, у́, ёшь, *pf.* (*of* загибáть) 1. to turn up, turn down; to bend, fold; to crease; з. страни́цу to dog-ear a page. 2. to turn (*intrans.*); з. зá угол to turn a corner. 3. (*coll.*) to utter (*a swear-word or vulgarism*); ну и словéчко ~у́л! (*iron.*) what language! 4. (*coll.*) to ask (*an exorbitant price*).

загн|у́ться, у́сь, ёшься, *pf.* (*of* загибáться) 1. to turn up, stick up; to turn down. 2. (*sl.*) to turn up one's toes (= to die).

заговáрива|ть, ю, *impf. of* заговори́ть¹.

заговáрива|ться, юсь, *impf.* (*of* заговори́ться) 1. to be carried away by a conversation. 2. (*impf. only*) to rave; to ramble (*in speech*); говори́, да не ~йся! talk sense!

зáговень|е, я, *n.* (*eccl.*) last day before fast.

заговé|ться, юсь, *pf.* (*eccl.*) to eat meat for the last time (*before a fast*).

зáговор, а, *m.* 1. plot, conspiracy. 2. charm, spell.

загово́р|и́ть[1], ю, и́шь, *pf.* (*of* загова́ривать) **1.** (*coll.*) to talk someone's head off; to tire out with much talk. **2.** to cast a spell (over); (от) to put on a spell (against); to exorcize; з. зу́бы кому́-н. (*coll.*) to distract someone with smooth talk.

загово́р|и́ть[2], ю, и́шь, *pf.* **1.** to begin to speak. **2.** to (be able to) speak; to learn to speak.

загово́р|и́ться, ю́сь, и́шься, *pf. of* загова́риваться.

загово́рщик, а, *m.* conspirator, plotter.

загово́рщицкий, *adj.* (*coll.*) conspiratorial.

загог|ота́ть, очу́, о́чешь, *pf.* to begin to cackle; (*coll.*) to begin to guffaw.

загогу́лин|а, ы, *f.* (*coll.*) flourish.

за́годя, *adv.* (*coll.*) in good time.

загол|и́ть, ю́, и́шь, *pf.* (*of* ~я́ть) to bare.

заголо́в|ок, ка, *m.* **1.** title; heading. **2.** headline.

заголя́|ть, ю, *impf. of* загол́ить.

заго́н, а, *m.* **1.** driving in; rounding-up. **2.** enclosure (*for cattle*); pen. **3.** strip (*of ploughed land*). **4.** быть в ~е (*fig.*) to be kept down; у кого́-н. в ~е under someone's thumb. **5.** в ~е (*sl.*) to one's credit, 'chalked up'; у него́ в ~е три дня he has three days' (work) to his credit.

заго́нщик, а, *m.* (*hunting*) beater.

за|гоню́, го́нишь, *see* ~гна́ть.

загоня́|ть[1], ю, *impf. of* загна́ть.

загоня́|ть[2], ю, *pf.* (*coll.*) **1.** to tire out; to work to death. **2.** (*sl.*) to grill (*with questions*).

загора́жива|ть(ся), ю(сь), *impf. of* загоро-ди́ть(ся).

загора́|ть(ся), ю(сь), *impf. of* загоре́ть(ся).

заго́рб|ок, ка, *m.* (*coll.*) upper part of the back (*between shoulder-blades*).

загор|ди́ться, жу́сь, ди́шься, *pf.* (*coll.*) to become proud, become stuck-up.

загоре́лый, *adj.* sunburnt; brown, bronzed.

загор|е́ть, ю́, и́шь, *pf.* (*of* ~а́ть) to become sunburnt, become brown; to acquire a tan.

загор|е́ться, ю́сь, и́шься, *pf.* (*of* ~а́ться) **1.** to catch fire; to begin to burn; в библио-те́ке ~е́лось (*impers.*) a fire broke out in the library. **2.** (+*i.*; от) to blaze (with), burn (with) (*fig.*); его́ глаза́ ~е́лись от гне́ва his eyes blazed with anger; она́ ~е́лась от смуще́ния she went red with embarrassment. **3.** (*impers.*+*d.*; *coll.*) to want very much; to have a burning desire; ей ~е́лось ви́деть Рим she had a burning desire to see Rome. **4.** (*fig.*) to break out, start; ~е́лась дра́ка a fight broke out.

загоро|ди́ть, жу́, ~ди́шь, *pf.* (*of* загора́жи-вать) **1.** to enclose, fence in. **2.** to barri-cade; to obstruct; з. кому́-н. свет to stand in someone's light.

загоро|ди́ться, жу́сь, ~ди́шься, *pf.* (*of* загора́живаться) **1.** to barricade oneself; з. ши́рмой to screen oneself off. **2.** *pass. of* ~ди́ть.

загоро́дк|а, и, *f.* (*coll.*) **1.** fence. **2.** enclo-sure.

за́городн|ый, *adj.* out-of-town; country; ~ая экску́рсия excursion into the country.

заго|сти́ться, щу́сь, сти́шься, *pf.* (*coll.*) to outstay one's welcome.

заготови́тел|ь, я, *m.* official in charge of (State) procurements.

загото́в|и́тельный, *adj. of* ~ка; з. аппара́т official organization in charge of (State) procurements; з. пункт storage place; ~и́тельная цена́ (*econ.*) fixed price (*for purchases by State*).

загото́в|ить, лю, ишь, *pf.* (*of* ~ля́ть) **1.** to lay in; to make a stock (of), stockpile, store. **2.** to prepare.

загото́вк|а, и, *f.* **1.** (State) procurement (*of agricultural products, timber, etc.*). **2.** laying in; stocking up, stockpiling. **3.** half-finished product; (*tech.*) blank, billet.

заготовля́|ть, ю, *impf. of* загото́вить.

загото́вщик, а, *m.* = заготови́тель.

заграба́ст|ать, аю, *pf.* (*of* ~ывать) (*coll., pejor.*) to seize; to make off with.

заграба́стыва|ть, ю, *impf. of* заграба́стать.

заграб|ить, лю, ишь, *pf.* (*coll.*) to seize; to plunder.

загради́тел|ь, я, *m.* (*naut.*) minelayer.

загради́тельный, *adj.* (*mil.*) barrage; (*naut.*) mine-laying; з. аэроста́т barrage balloon; з. ого́нь defensive fire.

загра|ди́ть, жу́, ди́шь, *pf.* (*of* ~жда́ть) to block, obstruct; з. путь to bar the way.

загражда́|ть, ю, *impf. of* загради́ть.

загражде́ни|е, я, *n.* **1.** blocking, obstruc-tion. **2.** obstacle, barrier, obstruction.

заграни́ц|а, ы, *f.* (*coll.*) foreign countries (*see also* грани́ца).

заграни́чный, *adj.* foreign (**1.** = of foreign make, *etc.* **2.** = for foreign travel, *etc.*; з. па́спорт foreign passport).

загреба́|ть, ю, *impf. of* загрести́[1]; чужи́ми рука́ми жар з., *see* жар.

загрёбистый, *adj.* (*coll.*) greedy.

загребн|о́й, *adj.*; ~о́е весло́ stroke oar; *as noun* з., ~о́го, *m.* stroke (*rower*).

загребу́щий, *adj.* (*coll.*) greedy.

загрем|е́ть[1], лю́, и́шь, *pf.* (*coll.*) to crash down.

загрем|е́ть[2], лю́, и́шь, *pf.* to begin to thunder.

загре|сти́[1], бу́, бёшь, *past* ~б, ~бла́, *pf.* (*of* ~ба́ть) (*coll.*) to rake up, gather; (*fig.*) to rake in; з. жар to bank up the fire; з. де́ньги to rake in the shekels.

загре|сти́[2], бу́, бёшь, *past* ~б, ~бла́, *pf.* to begin to row.

загри́в|ок, ка, *m.* 1. withers (*of horse*). 2. (*coll.*) nape (of the neck).

загримир|ова́ть(ся), у́ю(сь), *pf. of* гримирова́ть(ся).

загрипп|ова́ть, у́ю, *pf.* (*coll.*) to catch flu, go down with flu.

загро́бн|ый, *adj.* 1. beyond the grave; ~ая жизнь the future life. 2. sepulchral (*of voice*).

загроможда́|ть, ю, *impf. of* загромозди́ть.

загромоз|ди́ть, жу́, ди́шь, *pf.* (*of* загромозжда́ть) to block up, encumber; (*fig.*) to pack, cram; з. расска́з подро́бностями to cram a story with detail.

загрох|ота́ть, очу́, о́чешь, *pf.* to begin to rumble, begin to rattle.

загрубе́л|ый, *adj.* coarsened, callous.

загрубе́|ть, ю, *pf.* to become coarsened; to become callous (*also fig.*).

загружа́|ть, ю, *impf. of* загрузи́ть 2, 3.

загру́женност|ь (*and* загружённост|ь), и, *f.* 1. utilised capacity (*of transport services, etc.*). 2. programme (*of work*), commitment.

загр|узи́ть, ужу́, у́зи́шь, *pf.* 1. (*impf.* грузи́ть) to load. 2. (*impf.* ~ужа́ть) (*tech.*) to feed, charge, prime; з. то́пливо в печь to stoke a furnace. 3. (*impf.* ~ужа́ть) (*coll.*) to keep fully occupied, provide with a full--time job; to fill out (a period of time) with occupations.

загру|зи́ться, жу́сь, зи́шься, *pf.* (*of* ~жа́ться) 1. (+*i.*) to load up (with), take on. 2. (*coll.*) to take on a job, a commitment.

загру́зк|а, и, *f.* 1. loading. 2. (*tech.*) feeding, charging, priming. 3. capacity (*of work*), load; заво́д рабо́тает при по́лной ~е the factory is working at full capacity.

загру́з|очный, *adj. of* ~ка; з. ковш, я́щик hopper; з. лото́к feed chute, loading chute.

загрунт|ова́ть, у́ю, *pf. of* грунтова́ть.

загру|сти́ть, щу́, сти́шь, *pf.* to grow sad.

загрыза́|ть, ю, *impf. of* загры́зть.

загры́з|ть, у́, ёшь, *past* ~, ~ла, *pf.* (*of* ~а́ть) 1. to bite to death; (*fig.*) to worry the life out of, worry to death. 2. to tear to pieces.

загрязне́ни|е, я, *n.* soiling; pollution; contamination.

загрязн|и́ть, ю́, и́шь, *pf.* (*of* ~я́ть) to soil, make dirty; to pollute.

загрязн|и́ться, ю́сь, и́шься, *pf.* (*of* ~я́ться) to make oneself dirty, become dirty.

загрязня́|ть(ся), ю(сь), *impf. of* загрязни́ть(ся).

загс, а, *m.* (*abbr. of* отде́л за́писи а́ктов гражда́нского состоя́ния) registry office.

загси́р|оваться, уюсь, *impf. and pf.* (*coll.*) to be married (in a registry office).

загуб|и́ть, лю́, ~ишь, *pf.* 1. to ruin; з. чей-н. век, з. чью-н. жизнь to make someone's life a misery. 2. (*coll.*) to squander.

загу́л, а, *m.* (*coll.*) drinking(-bout).

загуля́|ть, ю, *pf.* (*coll.*) to take to drink, start drinking.

зад, а, о ~е, на ~у́, *pl.* ~ы́, *m.* 1. back; ~о́м наперёд back to front. 2. hind quarters; buttocks; croup, rump; бить ~о́м to kick (*of animal*). 3. (*pl.*) = задво́рки 1. 4. повтори́ть ~ы́ (*coll.*) to repeat what one has learned before; to pass on stale news.

зада́брива|ть, ю, *impf. of* задо́брить.

зада|ва́ть, ю́, ёшь, *impf. of* ~ть.

зада|ва́ться[1], ю́сь, ёшься, *impf. of* ~ться.

зада|ва́ться[2], ю́сь, ёшься, *impf.* (*coll.*) to give oneself airs, put on airs.

задав|и́ть, лю́, ~ишь, *pf.* to crush; to run over, knock down.

зада́ни|е, я, *n.* task, job.

зада́рива|ть, ю, *impf. of* задари́ть.

задар|и́ть, ю́, ~ишь, *pf.* (*of* ~ива́ть) 1. to load with presents. 2. to bribe.

зада́ром, *adv.* (*coll.*) 1. for nothing: very cheaply; купи́ть з. to buy for a song. 2. in vain, to no purpose.

зада́тк|и, ов, *no sing.* instincts, inclinations.

зада́т|ок, ка, *m.* deposit, advance.

за|да́ть, да́м, да́шь, *past* ~да́л, ~дала́, ~да́ло, *pf.* (*of* ~дава́ть) to set; to give; з. уро́к to set a lesson; з. вопро́с to put a question; з. бал to give a dance; з. корм коро́вам to feed the cows; з. тон to set the tone; з. тя́гу to take to one's heels; з. стра́ху (+*d.*) to strike terror (into); я ему́ ~да́м! (*coll.*) I'll give him what-for!

за|да́ться, да́мся, да́шься, *past* ~да́лся, ~дала́сь, *pf.* (*of* ~дава́ться[1]) 1. з. це́лью, мы́слью (+*inf.*) to set oneself (to), make up one's mind (to); з. вопро́сом to ask oneself the question. 2. (*coll.*) to turn out (well); to work out, succeed; пое́здка не ~дала́сь the trip was not a success.

зада́ч|а, и, *f.* 1. (*math., etc.*) problem. 2. task; mission.

зада́чник, а, *m.* book of (mathematical) problems.

задвига́|ть, ю, *pf.* to begin to move.

задвига́|ть, ю, *impf. of* задви́нуть.

задвига́|ться, юсь, *impf.* 1. *impf. of* задви́нуться. 2. (*impf. only*) to be drawable, be slidable.

задви́жк|а, и, *f.* bolt; catch, fastening; (*tech.*) slide-valve.

задвижно́й, *adj.* sliding.

задви́н|уть, у, ешь, *pf.* (*of* задвига́ть) 1. to push; з. задви́жку to shoot a bolt. 2. to bolt; to bar; to close; з. за́навес to draw a curtain (across).

задви́н|уться, усь, ешься, *pf.* (*of* задвига́ться) to shut; to slide (*intrans.*).

задво́р|ки, ок, *no sing.* 1. backyard; (*fig.*) out--of-the-way place, backwoods. 2. быть на ~ках (*fig.*) to take a back seat.

задева́|ть¹, ю, *impf. of* заде́ть.

задева́|ть², ю, *pf.* (*coll.*) to mislay; куда́ ~л мои́ очки́? where did I put my spectacles?

задева́|ться¹, юсь, *impf., pass. of* ~ть¹.

задева́|ться², юсь, *pf.* (*coll.*) to disappear; куда́ ты ~лся? where did you get to?

заде́л, а, *m.* (*coll.*) **1.** undertaking (*begun but not completed*). **2.** (*tech.*) surplus (*of goods or products*). **3.** amount (*of work done, etc.*) in hand.

заде́л|ать, аю, *pf.* (*of* ~ывать) to do up; to block up, close up; з. посы́лку to do up a parcel; (*naut.*) з. течь to stop a leak.

заде́ла|ться¹, юсь, *impf., pass. of* ~ть.

заде́л|аться², аюсь, *pf.* (*of* ~ываться) (*coll.*) to become; to turn; он ~алоя литературове́дом he has turned literary critic.

заде́лк|а, и, *f.* doing up; blocking up, stopping up.

заде́лыва|ть(ся), ю(сь), *impf. of* заде́лать(ся).

задёрга|ть¹, ю, *pf.* (+*a. or i.*) to begin to tug.

задёрга|ть², ю, *pf.* to wear out (by tugging on the reins); (*fig., coll.*) to break the spirit of (by nagging, *etc.*).

задёргива|ть, ю, *impf. of* задёрнуть.

задеревене́лый, *adj.* numb(ed), stiff.

задеревене́|ть, ю, *pf.* (*coll.*) to become numb, become stiff.

задержа́ни|е, я, *n.* **1.** detention; arrest. **2.** (*med.*) з. мочи́ retention of urine. **3.** (*mus.*) suspension.

задерж|а́ть, у́, ~ишь, *pf.* (*of* ~ивать) **1.** to detain; to delay; до́ждик ~а́л нача́ло ма́тча the start of the match was delayed by a shower. **2.** to withhold, keep back; to retard; з. зарпла́ту to stop wages; з. дыха́ние to hold one's breath. **3.** to detain, arrest.

задерж|а́ться, у́сь, ~ишься, *pf.* (*of* ~иваться) **1.** to stay too long; to linger. **2.** *pass. of* ~а́ть.

заде́ржива|ть(ся), ю(сь), *impf. of* задержа́ть(ся).

заде́ржк|а, и, *f.* delay; hold-up.

задёрн|уть, у, ешь, *pf.* (*of* задёргивать) **1.** to pull; to draw; з. за́навески to draw the curtains. **2.** to cover; to curtain off.

заде́т|ый (~, ~а), *p.p.p. of* ~ь; **1.** з. насме́шками stung by taunts. **2.** (*med.*; *coll.*) affected; пра́вое лёгкое у него́ ~о he has a spot on his right lung.

заде́|ть, ну, нешь, *pf.* (*of* ~ва́ть¹) **1.** to touch, brush (against), graze; (*fig.*) to offend, wound; его́ ~ло за живо́е he was stung to the quick. **2.** to catch (on, against).

за́дешево, *adv.* (*coll.*) very cheaply.

зади́р|а, ы, *m. and f.* (*coll.*) bully; trouble-maker.

задира́|ть(ся)¹, ю(сь), *impf. of* задра́ть(ся).

задира́|ться², юсь, *impf.* (*coll.*) to pick a quarrel.

задненёбный, *adj.* (*ling.*) velar.

заднепрохо́дный, *adj.* (*anat.*) anal.

заднеязы́чный, *adj.* (*ling.*) velar, back.

за́дн|ий, *adj.* back, rear; hind; ~яя мысль ulterior motive; з. план background; з. прохо́д (*anat.*) anus; ~им умо́м кре́пок (*coll.*) wise after the event; з. ход (*tech.*) backward movement; (*naut.*) stern-board; дать з. ход to back; ~им число́м later, with hindsight; поме́тить ~им число́м to antedate; быть без ~их ног (*coll.*) to be falling off one's feet; ходи́ть на ~их ла́пках (пе́ред) (*coll.*) to dance attendance on).

за́дник, а, *m.* **1.** back, counter (*of shoe*). **2.** (*theatr.*) back drop.

за́дниц|а, ы, *f.* (*vulg.*) arse, buttocks.

задо́бр|ить, ю, ишь, *pf.* (*of* задабривать) to cajole; to coax; to win over (*by bribes, etc.*).

зад|о́к, ка́, *m.* back (*of conveyance or furniture*).

задолб|и́ть, лю́, и́шь, *pf.* **1.** to begin to peck. **2.** (*coll.*) to learn off by rote.

задо́лго, *adv.* long before; он ко́нчил рабо́ту з. до ве́чера he finished the work long before evening.

задолжа́|ть, ю, *pf. of* должа́ть.

задолжа́|ться, юсь, *pf.* (*coll.*) to run into debt.

задо́лженност|ь, и, *f.* debts; погаси́ть з. to pay off one's debts.

за́дом, *adv.* backwards.

задо́р, а, *m.* fervour, ardour; passion.

задо́ринк|а, и, *f.* unevenness, roughness; (*fig., coll.*) без сучка́, без ~и *or* ни сучка́, ни ~и without a hitch.

задо́р|иться, юсь, ишься, *impf.* (*coll.*) to become provocative.

задо́р|ный (~ен, ~на), *adj.* **1.** fervent, ardent; impassioned. **2.** provocative; quick-tempered.

задох|ну́ться, ну́сь, нёшься, *past* ~ся, ~лась *and* ~ну́лся, ~ну́лась, *pf.* (*of* задыха́ться) **1.** to suffocate; to choke; (*fig.*) з. от гне́ва to choke with anger. **2.** to pant; to gasp for breath.

задра́знива|ть, ю, *impf. of* задразни́ть.

задразн|и́ть, ю́, ~ишь, *pf.* (*coll.*) to tease unmercifully.

задра́ива|ть, ю, *impf. of* задра́ить.

задра́|ить, ю, ишь, *pf.* (*naut.*) to batten down.

задрапир|ова́ть, у́ю, *pf.* (+*a. and i.*) to drape (with).

задрапир|ова́ться, у́юсь, *pf.* (+*i. or* в+*a.*) to drape oneself (with), wrap oneself up (in).

задрапиро́выва|ть(ся), ю(сь), *impf. of* задрапирова́ть(ся).

зад|ра́ть, еру́, ерёшь, *past* ~ра́л, ~рала́, ~ра́ло, *pf.* (*of* ~ира́ть) **1.** to tear to pieces; to kill (*of wolves, etc.*). **2.** (*coll.*) to lift up; to pull up; з. го́лову to crane one's neck; з. нос (*fig.*) to cock one's nose. **3.** to break (*finger-nail, etc.*); з. ко́жу на па́льце to split a finger. **4.** (*coll.*) to insult; to provoke.

зад|ра́ться, ерётся, *past* ~ра́лся, ~рала́сь, ~ра́лось, *pf.* (*of* ~ира́ться) **1.** to break (*intrans.*; *finger-nail, etc.*); to split (*intrans.*). **2.** (*coll.*) to ride up (*of clothing*). **3.** *pass. of* ~ра́ть.

задрем|а́ть, лю́, ~лешь, *pf.* to doze off, begin to nod.

задри́пан|ный (~, ~а), adj. (*coll.*) bedraggled.

задрож|а́ть, у́, и́шь, *pf.* to begin to tremble; to begin to shiver.

за́друг|а, и, f. (*ethnol.*) zadruga (*patriarchal commune among the Southern Slav peoples*).

задры́га|ть, ю, pf. (*coll.*) to begin to jerk, begin to twitch.

задува́|ть, ю, *impf. of* заду́ть.

заду́ма|ть, ю, pf. (*of* заду́мывать) **1.** (+a. *or inf.*) to plan; to intend; to conceive the idea (of). **2.** з. число́ to think of a number.

заду́ма|ться, юсь, pf. to become thoughtful, pensive; to fall to thinking; о чём вы ~лись? what are you thinking about?

заду́мчивост|ь, и, f. thoughtfulness, pensiveness; reverie.

заду́мчив|ый (~, ~а), adj. thoughtful, pensive.

заду́мыва|ть, ю, *impf. of* заду́мать.

заду́мыва|ться, юсь, *impf.* to be thoughtful, be pensive; to meditate; to ponder; не ~ясь, он согласи́лся he agreed without a moment's thought.

задур|и́ть, ю́, и́шь, pf. (*coll.*) to start playing the fool; он мне едва́ не ~и́л го́лову he nearly drove me crazy.

заду́|ть, ю, ешь, pf. (*of* ~ва́ть) **1.** to blow out. **2.** (*tech.*) з. до́мну to blow in a blast--furnace. **3.** to begin to blow.

задуше́в|ный (~ен, ~на), adj. sincere; cordial; intimate.

задуш|и́ть, у́, ~ишь, pf. *of* души́ть[1].

зад|ы́[1], see ~.

зад|ы́[2] = ~во́рки.

задым|и́ть, лю́, и́шь, pf. 1. to begin to (emit) smoke. **2.** to blacken with smoke. **3.** (*mil.*) to lay a smoke-screen.

задым|и́ться, и́тся, pf. 1. to begin to (emit) smoke. **2.** to be blackened with smoke.

задымля́|ть, ю, *impf. of* задыми́ть 2, 3.

задыха́|ться, юсь, *impf. of* задохну́ться.

задыш|а́ть, у́, ~ишь, pf. to begin to breathe.

заеда́ни|е, я, n. (*tech.*) jamming.

заеда́|ть(ся), ю(сь), *impf. of* зае́сть(ся).

зае́зд, а, m. 1. calling in (*en route*). **2.** (*sport*) lap, round, heat.

заез|ди́ть, жу, дишь, pf. to override (*a horse*); (*fig.*) to wear out; to work too hard.

заезжа́|ть, ю, *impf. of* зае́хать.

зае́зженный, adj. (*coll.*) **1.** hackneyed, trite. **2.** worn out.

зае́зж|ий, adj. visiting; ~ая тру́ппа touring company; он здесь з. челове́к he is a stranger, he is passing through; з. двор (*obs.*) wayside inn.

заём, за́йма, m. loan.

заёмн|ый, adj. loan; ~ое письмо́ (*leg.*) acknowledgement of debt.

заёмщик, а, m. borrower, debtor.

заёрза|ть, ю, pf. (*coll.*) **1.** to begin to fidget. **2.** to dirty, wear out as a result of fidgeting.

зае́|сть[1], м, шь, ст, ди́м, ди́те, дя́т, pf. (*of* ~да́ть) **1.** to bite to death; (*fig.*) to torment, oppress; его́ ~ла тоска́ he fell a prey to melancholy. **2.** (*impers.*; *tech.*) to jam; (*naut.*) to foul; кана́т ~ло the cable has fouled. **3.** (*dial.*) to seize, appropriate.

зае́|сть[2], м, шь, ст, ди́м, ди́те, дя́т, *past* ~л, *pf.* (*of* ~да́ть) (+a. *and i.*) to take (with); он ~л пилю́лю са́харом he took the pill with sugar.

зае́|сться, мся, шься, стся, ди́мся, ди́тесь, дя́тся, *past* ~лся, *pf.* (*of* ~да́ться) (*coll.*) to become fastidious, become fussy.

зае́|хать, ду, дешь, pf. (*of* ~зжа́ть) **1.** (к) to call in (at); (в+a.) to enter, ride into, drive into; (за+a.) to go beyond, past; (за+i.) to call for; to fetch. **2.** to go too far (*also fig.*); он ~хал в кана́ву he landed in the ditch; ведь куда́ он ~хал со свои́м хвастовство́м! look where he got himself with his boasting! **3.** (+d. в+a.; *coll.*) to strike; я ~хал ему́ в мо́рду I gave him a sock on the jaw.

зажа́р|ить(ся), ю(сь), ишь(ся), pf. *of* жа́рить(ся).

зажа́|ть, му́, мёшь, pf. (*of* ~има́ть) to squeeze; to press; to clutch; з. в руке́ to grip; з. рот кому́-н. (*fig.*) to stop someone's mouth; з. кри́тику to suppress criticism.

заж|гу́, жёшь, гу́т, *see* ~е́чь.

зажд|а́ться, у́сь, ёшься, *past* ~а́лся, ~ала́сь, ~а́лось, *pf.* (*coll.*) to be tired of waiting (for).

зажелте́|ть, ю, ешь, pf. 1. to turn yellow. **2.** to begin to appear, begin to show up yellow.

зажел|ти́ть, чу́, ти́шь, pf. (*coll.*) to paint yellow; to stain yellow.

заж|е́чь, гу́, жёшь, гу́т, *past* ~ёг, ~гла́, *pf.* (*of* ~ига́ть) to set fire to; to kindle, light; з. спи́чку to strike a match; (*fig., rhet.*) to kindle; to inflame.

заж|е́чься, гу́сь, жёшься, гу́тся, *past*

зажёгся, зажгла́сь, *pf.* (*of* ~игаться) to catch fire; to light up; (*fig.*) to flame up.

зажива́|ть(ся), ю(сь), *impf. of* зажи́ть(ся).

зажив|и́ть, лю́, и́шь, *pf.* to heal.

заживля́|ть, ю, *impf. of* заживи́ть.

за́живо, *adv.* alive; з. погребённый buried alive.

зажига́лк|а, и, f. 1. (cigarette) lighter. 2. (*coll.*) incendiary (bomb).

зажига́тел|ьный (~ен, ~ьна), *adj.* inflammatory (*also fig.*); incendiary; ~ьная бо́мба incendiary (bomb); ~ьная речь inflammatory speech.

зажига́|ть(ся), ю(сь), *impf. of* заже́чь(ся).

зажи́л|ить, ю, ишь, *pf.* (*coll.*) to fail to return (*something borrowed*).

зажи́лива|ть, ю, *impf. of* зажи́лить.

зажи́м, а, m. 1. (*tech.*) clamp; clutch; clip. 2. (*electr.*) terminal. 3. (*fig.*) suppression; clamping down.

зажима́|ть, ю, *impf. of* зажа́ть.

зажи́мист|ый (~, ~а), *adj.* (*coll.*) 1. strong, powerful; у него́ ~ая рука́ he has a strong grip. 2. tight-fisted, stingy.

зажимно́й, *adj.* (*coll.*) tight-fisted.

зажи́мный, *adj.* (*tech.*) clamping; з. винт clamping screw.

зажи́мщик, а, m. (*coll.*) suppressor.

зажире́лый, *adj.* (*dial.*) excessively stout, overweight.

зажире́|ть, ю, *pf.* (*coll.*) to put on weight to excess.

зажит|о́й, p.p.p. of ~ь **and** *adj.* earned; *as noun* ~о́е, ~о́го, *n.* (*coll.*) earned income.

зажи́точност|ь, и, f. prosperity; easy circumstances.

зажи́точ|ный (~ен, ~на), *adj.* well-to-do; prosperous.

за́жит|ый = ~о́й.

зажи́|ть, ву́, вёшь, *past* за́жил, ~ла́, за́жило, *pf.* (*of* ~ва́ть) 1. to heal (*intrans.*); to close up (*of wound*). 2. to begin to live; з. по-но́вому to begin a new life; з. семе́йной жи́знью to settle down; з. трудово́й жи́знью to begin to earn one's own living.

зажи́|ться, ву́сь, вёшься, *past* ~лся, ~ла́сь, *pf.* (*of* ~ва́ться) (*coll.*) to live to a great age; to exceed one's allotted span.

зажму́р|ить(ся), ю(сь), ишь(ся), *pf. of* жму́рить(ся).

зажужж|а́ть, у́, и́шь, *pf.* to begin to buzz; to begin to drone.

зажу́лива|ть, ю, *impf. of* зажу́лить.

зажу́л|ить, ю, ишь, *pf.* (*coll.*) to obtain by fraud.

зажу́хлый, *adj.* (*coll.*) tarnished, dull; dry, stiff (*of leather, etc.*).

заз|ва́ть, ову́, овёшь, *past* ~ва́л, ~вала́, ~ва́ло, *pf.* (*of* ~ыва́ть) (*coll.*) to press (to come); to press an invitation on.

зазвен|е́ть, и́т, *pf.* to begin to ring.

зазво́нист|ый (~, ~а), *adj.* (*coll.*) loud.

зазвон|и́ть, ю́, и́шь, *pf.* to begin to ring.

зазвуч|а́ть, у́, и́шь, *pf.* to begin to sound; to begin to resound.

здра́вный, *adj.* to the health (of), in honour (of); они́ вы́пили з. тост за посла́ they drank the ambassador's health.

зазева́|ться, юсь, *pf.* (на+*a.*; *coll.*) to stand gaping (at); to gape (at).

зазелене́|ть, ю, *pf.* to turn green.

зазелен|и́ть, ю́, и́шь, *pf.* (*coll.*) to paint green; to colour green.

заземле́ни|е, я, n. (*electr.*) 1. earthing. 2. earth.

заземл|и́ть, ю́, и́шь, *pf.* (*electr.*) to earth.

заземл|я́ть, я́ю, *impf. of* ~и́ть.

зазим|ова́ть, у́ю, *pf.* to winter; to pass the winter.

зази́м|ок, ка, m. (*dial.*) 1. first snow. 2. first frost(s). 3. fresh sledge track.

зазна|ва́ться, ю́сь, ёшься, *impf. of* ~ться.

зазна́йств|о, а, n. (*coll.*) conceit.

зазна́|ться, ю́сь, *pf.* (*of* ~ва́ться) (*coll.*) to give oneself airs, become conceited.

зазно́б|а, ы, f. 1. (*folk poet.*) passion. 2. (*coll.*) sweetheart.

зазноб|и́ть, лю́, и́шь, *pf.* (*coll.*) 1. to be frozen; to get shivery. 2. (*impers.*) его́ ~и́ло he is beginning to be feverish.

зазно́бушк|а, и, f. (*folk poet.*) sweetheart.

заз|ову́, овёшь, *see* ~ва́ть.

зазо́р¹, а, m. (*coll.*) shame, disgrace.

зазо́р², а, m. gap; (*tech.*) clearance; (*mil.*) windage.

зазо́р|ный (~ен, ~на), *adj.* (*coll.*) shameful, disgraceful.

зазре́ни|е, я, n.; без ~я (со́вести) (*coll.*) without a twinge of conscience.

за́зр|ить, ит, *pf.,* only in phrase со́весть ~ит, ~и́ла (*coll.*) conscience forbids, forbade (it).

зазу́брен|ный (~, ~а), p.p.p. of зазубри́ть¹ **and** *adj.* notched, jagged, serrated.

зазу́брива|ть, ю, *impf. of* зазубри́ть.

зазу́брин|а, ы, f. notch, jag.

зазубр|и́ть¹, ю́, и́шь, *pf.* (*of* зубри́ть **and** ~ивать) to notch, serrate.

зазубр|и́ть², ю́, ~и́шь, *pf.* (*of* зубри́ть **and** ~ивать) (*sl.*) 1. to learn by rote. 2. to start cramming.

зазы́в, а, m. (*coll.*) pressing invitation.

зазыва́|ть, ю, *impf. of* зазва́ть.

зазя́б|нуть, ну, нешь, *past* ~, ~ла, *pf.* (*coll.*) 1. to become frozen. 2. (*hort.*) to die of frost.

заигра́|ть, ю, *pf.* 1. to begin to play; з. весёлый моти́в to strike up a lively tune. 2. to begin to sparkle. 3. to wear out (*cards, etc.*); з. пье́су to stage a play so often that it becomes stale.

зайгрыва|ть¹, ю, *impf. of* заигра́ть.

зайгрыва|ть², ю, *impf.* (с+*i.*; *coll.*) to flirt (with); to make advances (to) (*also fig.*).

зайк|а, и, *m. and f.* stammerer, stutterer.

заика́ни|е, я, *n.* stammer(ing), stutter(ing).

заика́|ться, юсь, *impf.* **1.** to stammer, stutter; to falter (*in speech*). **2.** (о+*p.*; *coll.*) to hint (at), to mention in passing; он никогда́ не ~ется о свое́й про́шлой жи́зни he never breathes a word about his past life.

заикн|у́ться, у́сь, ёшься, *pf. of* заика́ться 2.

зай́мк|а, и, *f.* (*hist.*) **1.** squatting (*on land*). **2.** squatter's holding. **3.** isolated arable field.

'заимода́в|ец, ца, *m.* creditor, lender.

заимообра́зно, *adv.* on credit, on loan.

заимообра́з|ный (~ен, ~на), *adj.* **1.** borrowed, taken on credit. **2.** lent, loaned.

заимствовани|е, я, *n.* borrowing.

заимствован|ный (~, ~а), *p.p.p. of* займствовать; ~ное сло́во (*ling.*) loan-word.

зай́мств|овать, ую, *impf.* (*of* по~) to borrow.

зайндеве|ть, ет, *pf.* (*of* и́ндеветь) (*coll.*) to be covered with hoar-frost.

заинтересо́ван|ный (~, ~а), *p.p.p. of* заинтересова́ть *and adj.* (в+*p.*) interested (in); он ~ в возмо́жности торго́вых сноше́ний с Да́льним Восто́ком he is interested in the possibility of trade relations with the Far East; ~ная сторона́ interested party.

заинтерес|ова́ть, у́ю, *pf.* to interest; to excite the curiosity (of).

заинтерес|ова́ться, у́юсь, *pf.* (+*i.*) to become interested; to take an interest (in).

заинтриг|ова́ть, у́ю, *pf. of* интригова́ть 2.

зайскива|ть, ю, *impf.* (у *or* пе́ред) to try to ingratiate oneself (with).

зайскива|ющий, *pres. part. act. of* ~ть *and adj.* ingratiating.

зайскр|и́ться, ю́сь, ишься, *pf.* to begin to sparkle.

зай|ду́, дёшь, *see* ~ти́.

зай́мищ|е, а, *n.* (*dial.*) water-meadow.

займодержа́тел|ь, я, *m.* loan-holder.

займ|у́, ёшь, *see* заня́ть.

за|йти́, йду́, йдёшь, *past* ~шёл, ~шла́, *pf.* (*of* ~ходи́ть¹) **1.** (к, в+*a.*) to call (on); to look in (at); по пути́ домо́й я ~шёл к Ивано́вым I dropped in at the Ivanovs on the way home; не забу́дьте з. в апте́ку don't forget to look in at the chemist's. **2.** (за+*i.*) to call for, fetch. **3.** (в+*a.*) to get (*to a place*); to find oneself (*in a place*); мы ~шли́ в во́ду по го́рло we got up to our necks in water; разгово́р ~шёл о выступле́нии президе́нта по ра́дио the conversation turned on the President's broadcast; з. на цель (*aeron.*) to be over the target; з. в тыл врага́ (*mil.*) to take the enemy

in the rear. **4.** (за+*a.*) to go behind; to turn; to go on, continue (after); to set (*of sun, etc.*); (*fig., obs.*) to wane; з. за́ угол to turn a corner; з. плечо́м (*mil.*) to wheel; заседа́ние ~шло́ далеко́ за́ по́лночь the meeting went on until long after midnight; з. сли́шком далеко́ (*fig.*) to go too far.

зай́чик, а, *m.* (*coll.*) **1.** *affect. dim. of* за́яц. **2.** reflection of a sunray. **3.** catkin.

зайчи́х|а, и, *f.* doe-hare.

зайч|о́нок, о́нка, *pl.* ~а́та, ~а́т, *m.* leveret.

закабал|и́ть, ю́, и́шь, *pf.* to enslave.

закабал|и́ться, ю́сь, и́шься, *pf.* **1.** (+*d.*) to tie oneself in slavery (to). **2.** *pass. of* ~и́ть.

закабал|я́ть(ся), я́ю(сь), *impf. of* ~и́ть(ся).

закавка́зский, *adj.* Trans-Caucasian.

закавы́ч|ить, у, ишь, *pf.* (*coll.*) to place in inverted commas.

закавы́чк|а, и, *f.* (*coll.*) **1.** obstacle, hitch. **2.** innuendo.

зака́дровый, *adj.* з. го́лос (*TV, cinema*) voice-over.

закады́чный, *adj.* з. друг (*coll.*) bosom friend.

зака́з¹, а, *m.* order; ваш з. ещё не гото́в your order is not ready yet; на з. to order; мне де́лают костю́м на з. I am having a suit made to measure; социа́льный з. (*polit.*) demand formulated by a social class.

зака́з², а, *m.* (*obs.*) prohibition.

зака|за́ть¹, жу́, ~жешь, *pf.* (*of* ~зывать) to order; to reserve.

зака|за́ть², жу́, ~жешь, *pf.* (+*inf. or a.*; *obs. or coll.*) to forbid.

зака́зник, а, *m.* (game) reserve.

заказн|о́й, *adj.* **1.** made to order; made to measure. **2.** ~о́е письмо́ registered letter; посла́ть письмо́ ~ы́м to send a letter registered; *as noun* ~о́е, ~о́го, *n.* registered postal packet.

зака́зчик, а, *m.* customer, client.

зака́зыва|ть, ю, *impf. of* заказа́ть.¹

зака́ива|ться, юсь, *impf. of* зака́яться.

зака́л, а, *m.* **1.** (*tech.*) temper; (*fig.*) stamp, cast; он челове́к ста́рого ~а he is one of the old school. **2.** (*fig.*) strength of character; guts, backbone.

закалён|ный (~, ~а́), *p.p.p. of* закали́ть *and adj.* hardened, hard; з. в боя́х battle-hardened.

зака́лива|ть, ю, *impf. of* закали́ть.

закал|и́ть, ю́, и́шь, *pf.* (*of* ~ивать *and* ~я́ть) (*tech.*) to temper; to case-harden; (*fig.*) to temper, harden; to make hard, hardy.

зака́лк|а, и, *f.* tempering; hardening.

зака́лыва|ть, ю, *impf. of* заколо́ть.

закал|я́ть, ю, *impf. of* закали́ть.

закамене́лый, *adj.* (*coll.*) hard as stone.

закамене́|ть, ю, *pf.* (*coll.*) to turn to stone, become petrified.

зака́нчива|ть, ю, *impf. of* зако́нчить.

зака́п|ать, аю (*obs.* ∼лю, ∼лешь), *pf.*
1. to begin to drip; дождь ∼ал it began to
spot with rain. **2.** (*impf.* ∼ывать) to spot;
вот ты ∼ала себе пла́тье черни́лами look,
you have spotted your dress with ink.

зака́пыва|ть(ся), ю(сь), *impf. of* зако-
па́ть(ся) *and* зака́пать 2.

зака́рмлива|ть, ю, *impf. of* закорми́ть.

закаспи́йский, *adj.* Trans-Caspian.

зака́т, а, *m.* setting; з. (со́лнца) sunset; он
пришёл на ∼е he came at sunset; (*fig.*) decline; на ∼е дней in one's declining years.

заката́|ть, ю, *pf.* (*of* зака́тывать) **1.** to
begin to roll. **2.** (в+*a.*) to roll up (in). **3.**
to roll out. **4.** з. в тюрьму́ (*sl.*) to throw
into prison.

зака́тист|ый (∼, ∼а), *adj.* (*coll.*) rolling;
з. смех peals of laughter.

зака|ти́ть, чу́, ∼тишь, *pf.* (*of* ∼тывать)
(*coll.*) to roll; з. глаза́ to screw up one's eyes
(*in pain*); она́ ∼ти́ла ему́ пощёчину she
slapped his face; з. исте́рику to go off into
hysterics; з. сце́ну to make a scene.

зака|ти́ться, чу́сь, ∼тишься, *pf.* (*of* ∼ты-
ваться) **1.** to roll (*intrans.*); ма́льчик пла́кал,
потому́ что мяч ∼ти́лся под стол the
little boy was crying because the ball
had rolled under the table. **2.** to set (*of
heavenly bodies*); (*fig.*) to wane; to vanish,
disappear; его́ сла́ва давно́ ∼ти́лась his
fame had long since waned; моя́ звезда́
∼ти́лась my luck is out. **3.** (*coll.*) to go off;
он ∼ти́лся на неде́лю в Ло́ндон he went
off to London for a week; з. сме́хом to go
off into peals of laughter.

зака́тный, *adj.* sunset.

зака́тыва|ть, ю, *impf. of* заката́ть *and* за-
кати́ть.

зака́тыва|ться, юсь, *impf. of* закати́ться.

закача́|ть, ю, *pf.* **1.** to begin to shake, begin
to swing; он ∼л голово́й he began shaking
his head. **2.** to rock (to sleep). **3.** (*impers.*) to
make feel sick by rocking; я собира́юсь в
каю́ту: меня́ ∼ло I am going to my cabin;
I feel sick.

закача́|ться, юсь, *pf.* to begin to rock
(*intrans.*), begin to sway.

зака́шива|ть, ю, *impf. of* закоси́ть.

зака́шля|ться, юсь, *pf.* to have a fit of
coughing.

зака́|яться, юсь, ешься, *pf.* (*of* ∼иваться)
(+*inf.*; *coll.*) to forswear; to swear to give
up; он ∼я́лся кури́ть he has sworn that he
will give up smoking.

заква́|сить, шу, сишь, *pf.* (*of* ∼шивать) to
ferment; to leaven.

заква́ск|а, и, *f.* ferment; leaven; (*fig., coll.*)
у него́ хоро́шая з. he promises well, he has
received a good start in life.

заква́шива|ть, ю, *impf. of* заква́сить.

закида́|ть, ю, *pf.* (*coll.*) **1.** (+*a. and i.*) to be-
spatter (with); to shower (with); з. камня́-
ми to stone; кандида́тов ∼ли вопро́сами
the candidates were plied with questions;
з. гря́зью (*fig.*) to sling mud (at). **2.** to fill
up (with); to cover (with).

заки́дыва|ть, ю, *impf. of* закида́ть *and* заки́-
нуть.

заки́дыва|ться, юсь, *impf. of* заки́нуться.

заки́н|уть, у, ешь, *pf.* to throw (out, away);
to cast, toss; з. но́гу на́ ногу to cross one's
legs; з. винто́вку за́ спину to sling a rifle on
one's back; з. у́дочку (*fig., coll.*) to put out
a feeler; з. слове́чко (о+*p.*) (*coll.*) to throw
out a hint (about); ∼ьте слове́чко за меня́
put in a word for me.

заки́н|уться, усь, ешься, *pf.* **1.** to fall back.
2. to jib, shy (*of a horse*).

закипа́|ть, ю, *impf. of* закипе́ть.

закип|е́ть, лю́, и́шь, *pf.* to begin to boil; to
be on the boil; (*fig.*) to be in full swing.

закиса́|ть, ю, *impf. of* заки́снуть.

заки́с|нуть, ну, нешь, *past* ∼, ∼ла, *pf.* **1.** to
turn sour. **2.** (*fig., coll.*) to become apathe-
tic.

за́кис|ь, и, *f.* (*chem.*) protoxide; з. азо́та
nitrous oxide; з. желе́за ferrous oxide.

закла́д, а, *m.* (*obs.*) **1.** pawning; mortgaging;
мои́ часы́ в ∼е my watch is in pawn. **2.**
bet, wager; би́ться об з. to bet, wager.

закла́дк|а¹, и, *f.* laying (*of bricks, etc.*).

закла́дк|а², и, *f.* bookmark.

закладн|а́я, о́й, *f.* (*leg., obs.*) mortgage
(-deed).

заклад|но́й¹, *adj. of* ∼ка¹; ∼на́я ра́ма fixed
frame.

заклад|но́й², *adj. of* ∼; ∼на́я квита́нция
pawn-ticket.

закла́дчик, а, *m.* (*obs*) pawner; mortgagor.

закла́дыва|ть, ю, *impf. of* закла́сть *and*
заложи́ть.

закла́ни|е, я, *n.* immolation, sacrifice;
идти́ (как) на з. to go to the slaughter.

закла́|сть, ду́, дёшь, *past* ∼л, ∼ла́, ∼ло, *pf.*
(*coll.*) to fill up; to block up; to pile.

зак|ла́ть, олю́, о́лешь, *past* ∼ла́л, *pf.* (*obs.*)
to sacrifice, immolate.

закл|ева́ть, юю́, юёшь, *pf.* **1.** to begin to
peck; to begin to bite (*of fish*). **2.** to peck to
death; (*fig., coll.*) to go for.

заклёвыва|ть, ю, *impf. of* заклева́ть.

закле́ива|ть(ся), ю(сь), *impf. of* закле́ить-
(ся).

закле́|ить, ю, ишь, *pf.* to glue up; to stick
up; з. конве́рт to seal an envelope.

закле́|иться, ится, *pf.* to stick (*intrans.*).

заклейм|и́ть, лю́, и́шь, *pf. of* клейми́ть.

заклепа́|ть, ю, *pf.* (*of* заклёпывать) (*tech.*) to
rivet.

заклёпк|а, и, *f.* (*tech.*) 1. riveting. 2. rivet.

заклёпник, а, *m.* (*tech.*) riveting hammer.

заклёпыва|ть, ю, *impf. of* заклепа́ть.

заклина́ни|е, я, *n.* 1. incantation; spell. 2. exorcism.

заклина́тел|ь, я, *m.* exorcist; з. змей snake--charmer.

заклина́|ть, ю, *impf.* (*of* закля́сть) 1. to conjure; to invoke. 2. to exorcize (*by means of incantation*). 3. to enchant, endow with magical powers. 4. to conjure, adjure; to entreat.

закли́нива|ть, ю, *impf. of* заклини́ть.

заклин|и́ть, ю́, и́шь, *pf.* 1. to wedge ,fasten with a wedge. 2. to jam.

заключа́|ть, ю, *impf. of* заключи́ть.

заключа́|ться, а́юсь, *impf.* (*of* ~и́ться) 1. *pass. of* ~а́ть. 2. (*impf. only*) (в+*p.*) to consist of); to lie (in); гла́вное затрудне́ние ~а́ется в недоста́тке де́нежных средств the principal difficulty consists in the lack of funds. 3. з. в монасты́рь to enter a monastery.

заключе́ни|е, я, *n.* 1. conclusion, end; в з. in conclusion. 2. conclusion, inference. 3. з. догово́ра conclusion of a treaty. 4. (*leg.*) resolution, decision; переда́ть на з. to submit for a decision. 5. confinement, detention; тюре́мное з. imprisonment.

заключён|ный (~, ~а́, ~о́), *p.p.p. of* заключи́ть; *as noun* з., ~ного, *m. and* ~ная, ~ной, *f.* (*leg.*) prisoner, convict.

заключи́тельн|ый, *adj.* final, concluding; з. акко́рд (*mus.*) finale; ~ое сло́во concluding remarks.

заключ|и́ть, у́, и́шь, *pf.* (*of* ~а́ть) 1. (+*i.*) to conclude, end (with). 2. to conclude, infer. 3. to conclude, enter into; з. брак to contract marriage; з. догово́р to conclude a treaty; з. сде́лку to strike a bargain. 4. з. в себе́ to contain, enclose; to comprise; з. в ско́бки to enclose in brackets. 5. to confine; з. в тюрьму́ to imprison; з. под стра́жу to take into custody.

заключ|и́ться, у́сь, и́шься, *pf. of* ~а́ться.

закля́|сть, ну́, нёшь, *past* ~л, ~ла́, ~ло, *pf. of* заклина́ть.

закля́|сться, ну́сь, нёшься, *past* ~лся, ~ла́сь, ~лось, *pf.* (*obs.*) to swear to give up.

закля́ти|е, я, *n.* (*obs.*) 1. incantation. 2. oath, pledge.

закля́тый, *adj.* 1. (*coll.*) passionate; inveterate; з. враг sworn enemy. 2. enchanted, bewitched; з. дом haunted house.

зак|ова́ть, ую́, уёшь, *pf.* 1. to chain; з. в кандалы́ to shackle, put in irons; (*fig., obs.*) to chain, bind, hold down; (*poet.*) моро́з ~ова́л зе́млю the land was in the grip of frost. 2. to begin to forge. 3. to injure in shoeing (*a horse*).

зако́выва|ть, ю, *impf. of* закова́ть.

заковыля́|ть, ю, *pf.* (*coll.*) to begin to hobble.

заковы́рист|ый (~, ~а), *adj.* (*coll.*) subtle, complicated; odd.

заковы́чк|а, и, *f.* = закавы́чка.

зако́л, а, *m.* weir.

закола́чива|ть, ю, *impf. of* заколоти́ть.

заколдо́ван|ный (~, ~а), *p.p.p. of* заколдова́ть *and adj.* bewitched, enchanted; spellbound; (*fig.*) з. круг vicious circle.

заколд|ова́ть, у́ю, *pf.* to bewitch, enchant; to lay a spell (on).

заколдо́outyва|ть, ю, *impf. of* заколдова́ть.

заколеб|а́ться, ~лю́сь, ~ле́шься, *pf.* to begin to shake; (*fig.*) to begin to waver, begin to vacillate.

зако́лк|а, и, *f.* 1. stabbing. 2. pinning. 3. hairpin.

заколо́д|ить, ит, *pf.* (*impers.+d.*; *dial.*) to stand in the way (of), impede; почему́ он не прие́хал? ~ило ему́, что ли? why hasn't he come? has he been held up?

заколо|ти́ть, чу́, ~ти́шь, *pf.* (*of* закола́чивать) (*coll.*) 1. to board up; to nail up. 2. to knock in, drive in. 3. to beat the life out of; to knock insensible. 4. to begin to knock; в дверь ~ти́ли there was a knocking on the door.

заколо|ти́ться, чу́сь, ~ти́шься, *pf.* (*coll.*) 1. *pass. of* ~ти́ть. 2. to begin to beat; се́рдце у неё ~ти́лось her heart began to thump.

закол|о́ть, ю́, ~ешь, *pf.* (*of* зака́лывать *and* коло́ть²) 1. to stab (to death), spear, stick. 2. to pin (up). 3. to begin to chop. 4. (*impers.*) у меня́, *etc.*, ~о́ло в боку́ I, *etc.*, have a stitch in my side.

закол|о́ться, ю́сь, ~ешься, *pf.* to stab oneself.

заколы́х|а́ться, ~шется, *pf.* to begin to sway; to begin to wave, begin to flutter.

закольц|ева́ть, у́ю, у́ешь, *pf. of* кольцева́ть.

зако́н, а, *m.* law; свод ~ов code, statute book; объяви́ть вне ~а to outlaw; з. Бо́жий (*as school subject, etc.*) scripture, divinity.

зако́нник, а, *m.* (*coll.*) 1. one versed in law, lawyer. 2. one who keeps to letter of the law.

законнорождённый, *adj.* legitimate (*child*).

зако́нност|ь, и, *f.* lawfulness, legality.

зако́н|ный (~ен, ~на, ~но), *adj.* lawful, legal; legitimate, rightful; з. брак lawful wedlock; з. владе́лец rightful owner.

законове́д, а, *m.* 1. jurist. 2. tutor in law.

законове́дени|е, я, *n.* jurisprudence, law.

законода́тел|ь, я, *m.* legislator; lawgiver.

законода́тельный, *adj.* legislative.

законода́тельств|о, а, *n.* legislation.

закономе́рност|ь, и, *f.* regularity; conformity with a law; normality.

закономе́р|ный (~ен, ~на), *adj.* **1.** regular, natural. **2.** *as pred.* ~но it is in order.

законопа́|тить, чу, тишь, *pf.* **1.** to caulk up; з. у́ши (*fig., coll.*) to block up one's ears. **2.** (*fig., coll.*) to coop up; pack off (to).

законопа́|титься, чусь, тишься, *pf.* (*coll.*) to box oneself up, shut oneself up.

законопа́чива|ть(ся), ю(сь), *impf. of* законопа́тить(ся).

законоположе́ни|е, я, n. (*leg.*) statute.

законопослу́шный, *adj.* (*obs.*) law-abiding.

законопрое́кт, а, m. (*polit., leg.*) bill.

законосовеща́тельн|ый, *adj.* (*polit., leg.*) concerned with discussion and/or preparation of bills; ~ая коми́ссия consultative commission.

законоуче́ни|е, я, n. (*obs.*) religious instruction.

законоучи́тел|ь, я, m. (*obs.*) religious teacher.

законсерви́р|овать, ую, *pf. of* консерви́ровать.

законспири́р|овать, ую, *pf.* (*of* конспири́ровать) to keep secret, keep dark.

законтракт|ова́ть, у́ю, *pf.* (*of* контрактова́ть) to contract (for), enter into a contract (for).

законтракт|ова́ться, у́юсь, *pf.* (*of* контрактова́ться) to contract to work (for); to hire oneself out (to).

законфу́|зиться, жусь, зишься, *pf.* to show embarrassment.

зако́нченност|ь, и, f. finish; completeness.

зако́нчен|ный (~, ~а), *p.p.p. of* зако́нчить *and adj.* finished; complete; (*coll.*) consummate; он явля́ется ~ным проза́иком he is a finished prose-writer; з. лгун a consummate liar.

зако́нч|ить, у, ишь, *pf.* (*of* зака́нчивать) to end, finish.

зако́нч|иться, усь, ишься, *pf.* (*of* зака́нчиваться) to end, finish (*intrans.*).

закопа́|ть, ю, *pf.* (*of* зака́пывать) **1.** to begin to dig. **2.** to bury.

закопа́|ться, юсь, *pf.* (*of* зака́пываться) (*coll.*) **1.** to begin to rummage. **2.** to bury oneself. **3.** (*mil.*) to dig in.

закопёрщик, а, m. 1. foreman pile-driver. **2.** (*fig., coll.*) ringleader.

закопте́лый, *adj.* (*coll.*) sooty; smutty.

закопт|е́ть, и́т, *pf.* (*of* копте́ть¹) to become covered with soot.

закоп|ти́ть, чу́, ти́шь, *pf.* (*of* копти́ть) **1.** to smoke. **2.** to blacken with smoke.

закоп|ти́ться, чу́сь, ти́шься, *pf.* **1.** to be smoked. **2.** to become covered with soot.

закоренелый, *adj.* deep-rooted; ingrained; inveterate.

закорене́|ть, ю, ешь, *pf.* **1.** (*fig.*) to take root. **2.** (в+*p.*) to become steeped (in); он ~л в греха́х he became an inveterate sinner.

закор|ки, ок, *no sing.* (*coll.*) back, shoulders; он перенёс де́вочку че́рез ре́ку на ~ках carried the little girl across the river on his shoulders.

закорм|и́ть, лю́, ~ишь, *pf.* (*of* зака́рмливать) to overfeed; to stuff.

закорю́чк|а, и, f. (*coll.*) **1.** hook; flourish (*in handwriting*). **2.** (*fig., dial.*) hitch, snag.

зако|си́ть, шу́, ~сишь, *pf.* (*of* зака́шивать) (*agric.*) **1.** to begin to mow, begin to scythe. **2.** to mow up, scythe up.

закосне́лый, *adj.* incorrigible, inveterate.

закосне́|ть, ю, *pf. of* косне́ть.

закостене́лый, *adj.* ossified; stiff.

закостене́|ть, ю, *pf.* to ossify; (*fig.*) он ~л от хо́лода he became stiff with cold.

закостыля́|ть, ю, *pf.* (*coll.*) to hobble, limp.

закоу́л|ок, ка, m. 1. back street, (dark) alley. **2.** (*coll.*) secluded corner; обыска́ть все углы́ и ~ки to search in every nook and cranny; знать все ~ки (*fig.*) to know all the ins and outs.

закочене́лый, *adj.* numb with cold.

закочене́|ть, ю, ешь, *pf. of* кочене́ть.

закра́дыва|ться, юсь, *impf. of* закра́сться.

закра́ива|ть, ю, *impf. of* закрои́ть.

закра́ин|а, ы, f. 1. (*geogr.*) zakraina (*water at edge of frozen river, lake, etc.*). **2.** (*tech.*) flange.

закра́па|ть, ю, *pf.* **1.** to begin to fall (*of raindrops*). **2.** to spot.

закра́пыва|ть, ю, *impf. of* закра́пать 2.

закра́|сить, шу, сишь, *pf.* (*of* ~шивать) **1.** to paint over, paint out. **2.** to begin to paint.

закрасне́|ть, ю, ешь, *pf.* to begin to show red.

закрасне́|ться, юсь, ешься, *pf.* **1.** to begin to show red. **2.** to blush.

закра́|сться, ду́сь, дёшься, *past* ~лся, *pf.* (*of* ~дываться) to steal in, creep in; (*fig.*) у меня́ ~лось подозре́ние a suspicion creeped into my mind.

закра́шива|ть, ю, *impf. of* закра́сить.

закре́п|а, ы, f. catch; fastener.

закрепи́тел|ь, я, m. (*chem., phot.*) fixing agent, fixer.

закрепи́тельный, *adj.*; з. тало́н voucher.

закреп|и́ть, лю́, и́шь, *pf.* **1.** to fasten, secure; (*naut.*) to make fast; (*phot.*) to fix. **2.** (*fig.*) to consolidate; мы ~и́ли прошлого́дние успе́хи we have consolidated last year's successes. **3.** (+*a.* за+*i.*) to allot, assign (to); to appoint, attach (to); з. за собо́й to secure; за на́ми ~и́ли одну́ из но́вых кварти́р we have been assigned one of the new flats; он ~и́л за собо́й места́ на за́втрашнее представле́ние в Большо́м теа́тре he has secured seats for tomorrow's performance at the Bolshoi Theatre. **4.** (*impers.*; *coll.*) его́, *etc.*, ~и́ло he, *etc.*, has got over his diarrhoea.

закреп|и́ться, лю́сь, и́шься, *pf.* **1.** *pass. of* ~**и́ть. 2.** (на + *a.*) to consolidate one's hold (on).

закрепля́|ть(ся), ю(сь), *impf. of* закрепи́ть(ся).

закрепо|сти́ть, щу́, сти́шь, *pf.* to enserf.

закрепоща́|ть, ю, *impf. of* закрепости́ть.

закрепоще́ни|е, я, *n.* **1.** enserfment. **2.** slavery; serfdom.

закрив|и́ть, лю́, и́шь, *pf.* **1.** to bend; to fold. **2.** (*coll.*) to begin to bend.

закрив|и́ться, лю́сь, и́шься, *pf.* **1.** to become crooked. **2.** (*coll.*) to begin to bend (*intrans.*).

закривля́|ть(ся), ю(сь), *impf. of* закриви́ть(ся).

закристаллиз|ова́ться, у́юсь, *pf. of* кристаллизова́ться.

закрич|а́ть, у́, и́шь, *pf.* **1.** to cry out. **2.** to begin to shout; to give a shout.

закро|и́ть, ю́, и́шь, *pf.* (*of* закра́ивать) **1.** to cut out. **2.** (*tech.*) to groove.

закро́|й, я, *m.* **1.** cutting out. **2.** cut; style (*of dress*). **3.** (*tech.*) groove.

закро́йны|й, *adj.* for cutting clothes; ~е но́жницы cutting-out scissors.

закро́йщик, а, *m.* cutter.

за́кром, а, *pl.* ~а́, *m.* corn-bin; (*fig., rhet.*) granary.

закругле́ни|е, я, *n.* **1.** rounding, curving. **2.** curve; curvature. **3.** (*lit.*) well-rounded period.

закруглён|ный (~, ~а́), *p.p.p. of* закругли́ть *and adj.* rounded; (*lit.*) well-rounded.

закругл|и́ть, ю́, и́шь, *pf.* to make round; з. фра́зу to round off a sentence.

закругл|и́ться, ю́сь, и́шься, *pf.* to become round.

закругля́|ть(ся), ю(сь), *impf. of* закругли́ть(ся).

закруж|и́ть, у́, ~и́шь, *pf.* **1.** to begin to whirl (*trans. and intrans.*); з. кому́-н. го́лову (*fig., coll.*) to turn someone's head. **2.** to make giddy, make dizzy; она́ его́ совсе́м ~и́ла (*fig., coll.*) she has swept him off his feet. **3.** (*dial.*) to lead astray.

закруж|и́ться, у́сь, ~и́шься, *pf.* **1.** to begin to whirl, begin to go round; у меня́ голова́ ~и́лась my head began to swim. *pf. of* кружи́ться.

закрута́с|ы, ов, *no sing.* (*coll., obs.*) flourishes.

закру|ти́ть, чу́, ~тишь, *pf.* **1.** to twist; to twirl; to wind round; они́ ~ти́ли ему́ ру́ки за́ спину they twisted his arms behind his back. **2.** to turn; to screw in; (*fig.*) з. слове́чко to make a caustic remark. **3.** (*fig., coll.*) to turn someone's head. **4.** (*coll., dial.*) to go drinking.

закру|ти́ться, чу́сь, ~тишься, *pf.* **1.** to

twist; to twirl; to wind round (*intrans.*). **2.** to begin to whirl.

закру́чива|ть(ся), ю(сь), *impf. of* закрути́ть(ся).

закрыва́|ть(ся), ю(сь), *impf. of* закры́ть(ся).

закры́ти|е, я, *n.* **1.** closing; shutting. **2.** (*mil.*) cover.

закры́т|ый (~, ~а), *p.p.p. of* ~ь *and adj.* closed, shut; private; с ~ыми глаза́ми (*fig.*) blindly; ~ое голосова́ние secret ballot; при ~ых дверя́х behind closed doors, in private; ~ое заседа́ние private meeting; з. ко́нкурс closed competition; ~ое мо́ре inland sea; ~ое пла́тье high-necked dress; в ~ом помеще́нии indoors; з. просмо́тр private view; з. распредели́тель store closed to non-members; ~ое уче́бное заведе́ние (private) boarding-school.

закр|ы́ть, о́ю, о́ешь, *pf.* (*of* ~ыва́ть) **1.** to close, shut; з. глаза́ to pass away; я ему́ ~ы́л глаза́ I attended him on his deathbed; з. глаза́ (на + *a.*) to shut one's eyes (to); з. ско́бки to close brackets; з. счёт to close an account. **2.** to shut off, turn off. **3.** to close down, shut down. **4.** to cover.

закр|ы́ться, о́юсь, о́ешься, *pf.* (*of* ~ыва́ться) **1.** to close, shut; to end; to close down; (*intrans.*). **2.** to cover oneself; to take cover; они́ ~лись от дождя́ зонто́м they took cover from the rain beneath the awning. **3.** *pass. of* ~ы́ть.

закули́сный, *adj.* (occurring) behind the scenes; (*fig.*) secret; underhand, undercover.

за́куп, а, *m.* (*hist.*) zakup (*peasant in Kievan Russia repaying loan by means of labour*).

закупа́|ть, ю, *impf. of* закупи́ть.

закупа́|ться¹, юсь, *impf., pass. of* ~ть.

закупа́|ться², юсь, *pf.* (*coll.*) to bathe excessively.

закуп|и́ть, лю́, ~ишь, *pf.* (*of* ~а́ть) **1.** to buy up (wholesale). **2.** to lay in; to stock up with. **3.** (*obs.*) to bribe.

заку́пк|а, и, *f.* purchase.

закупно́й, *adj.* bought, purchased.

заку́порива|ть, ю, *impf. of* заку́порить.

заку́пор|ить, ю, ишь, *pf.* **1.** to cork; to stop up. **2.** (*fig., coll.*) to shut up; coop up.

заку́порк|а, и, *f.* **1.** corking. **2.** (*med.*) embolism, thrombosis.

заку́п|очный, *adj. of* ~ка; ~очная цена́ purchase price.

заку́пщик, а, *m.* purchaser; buyer.

заку́рива|ть(ся), ю(сь), *impf. of* закури́ть(ся).

закур|и́ть, ю́, ~ишь, *pf.* **1.** to light up (*cigarette, pipe, etc.*). **2.** to begin to smoke; ещё не ко́нчив шко́лу он ~и́л he began to smoke before he had left school. **3.** (*dial.*) to begin to distil.

закур|и́ться, ю́сь, ~ишься, *pf.* 1. to begin to smoke (*intrans.*). 2. (*coll.*) to smoke excessively; to make oneself ill by excessive smoking.

заку|си́ть[1], шу́, ~сишь, *pf.* (*of* ~сывать) to bite; (*fig.*) з. удила́ to take the bit between the teeth; з. язы́к to hold one's tongue; to shut up.

заку|си́ть[2], шу́, ~сишь, *pf.* (*of* ~сывать) 1. to have a snack, have a bite; з. на́скоро to snatch a hasty bite. 2. (+*a. and i.*) to take (with); з. во́дку ры́бкой to drink vodka with fish hors-d'œuvres.

заку́ск|а, и, *f.* (*usu. pl.*) hors-d'œuvre; snack; на ~y for a titbit; (*fig., coll.*) as a special treat.

заку́с|очный, *adj. of* ~ка; *as noun* ~очная, ~очной, *f.* snack bar.

заку́сыва|ть, ю, *impf. of* закуси́ть.

заку́т, а, *m.* (*dial.*) 1. storeroom. 2. kennel; (pig-)sty.

заку́та|ть, ю, *pf.* (*of* заку́тывать) to wrap up, muffle; з. в одея́ло to tuck up (in bed).

заку́та|ться, юсь, *pf.* (*of* заку́тываться) to wrap oneself up, muffle oneself.

заку|ти́ть, чу́, ~ти́шь, *pf.* to begin to drink; to go drinking.

заку|ти́ться, чу́сь, ~ти́шься, *pf.* (*coll.*) to spend (all) one's time drinking.

заку́тк|а, и, *f.* (*dial.*) 1. *dim. of* заку́т. 2. chimney-corner (*in peasant's hut*).

заку́тыва|ть(ся), ю(сь), *impf. of* заку́тать(ся).

зал, а, *m.* hall; з. ожида́ния waiting-room.

за́л|а, ы, *f.* (*obs. or coll.*) = ~.

зала́в|ок, ка, *m.* (*dial.*) chest, locker.

зала́|дить, жу, дишь, *pf.* (*coll.*) 1. (+*inf.*) to take to; он ~дил заходи́ть к нам по вечера́м he has taken to calling in on us in the evening. 2. з. одно́ и то́ же to harp on the same string.

залакир|ова́ть, у́ю, *pf.* to varnish over; (*fig.*) to make shiny.

зала́мыва|ть, ю, *impf. of* заломи́ть.

залата́|ть, ю, *pf. of* лата́ть.

зал|га́ться, гу́сь, жёшься, гу́тся, *past* ~га́лся, ~гала́сь, ~га́ло́сь, *pf.* (*coll.*) to become an inveterate liar.

залега́ни|е, я, *n.* (*geol.*) 1. bedding. 2. bed, seam.

залега́|ть, ю, *impf. of* зале́чь.

заледене́лый, *adj.* 1. covered with ice; ice-bound. 2. ice-cold, icy.

заледене́|ть, ю, *pf.* (*of* ледене́ть) (*coll.*) 1. to be covered with ice; to freeze up, ice up. 2. to become cold as ice; to become numb.

залежа́лый, *adj.* (*coll.*) 1. stale. 2. long unused.

залеж|а́ться, у́сь, и́шься, *pf.* 1. to lie too long; to lie idle a long time. 2. (*econ.*) to find no market 3. become stale.

залёжива|ться, юсь, *impf. of* залежа́ться.

за́леж|ь, и, *f.* 1. (*geol.*) deposit, bed, seam; 2. (*agric.*) fallow land. 3. (*sing. only; collect.*; *coll.*) stale goods.

залеза́|ть, ю, *impf. of* зале́зть.

зале́з|ть, у, ешь, *past* ~, ~ла, *pf.* 1. (на+*a.*) to climb (up, on to). 2. (в+*a.*; *coll.*) to get (into); to creep (into); з. кому́-н. в карма́н to pick someone's pocket; з. в во́ду по го́рло to get up to one's neck in water; он ~ в отцо́вские сапоги́ he got into his father's boots; з. в долги́ to run into debt.

зален|и́ться, ю́сь, ~ишься, *pf.* (*coll.*) to grow lazy.

залепе|та́ть, чу́, ~чешь, *pf.* (*coll.*) to begin to babble.

залеп|и́ть, лю́, ~ишь, *pf.* (+*a. and i.*) to paste up, paste over; to glue up; всю сте́ну ~и́ли афи́шами the whole wall had been pasted over with bills; глаза́ у него́ ~и́ло сне́гом his eyes were stuck up with snow; з. кому́-н. пощёчину (*vulg.*) to slap someone's face.

залепля́|ть, ю, *impf. of* залепи́ть.

залета́|ть[1], ю, *pf.* (*coll.*) to begin to fly.

залета́|ть[2], ю, *impf. of* залете́ть.

зале|те́ть, чу́, ти́шь, *pf.* 1. (в+*a.*) to fly (into); (за+*a.*) to fly (over, beyond); пти́ца ~те́ла в ко́мнату a bird flew into the room; мы ~те́ли за Се́верный по́люс we flew over the North Pole. 2. (в+*a.*) to fly (into), land (*on the way*); нам пришло́сь з. в Стокго́льм за горю́чим we had to land at Stockholm to refuel. 3. (*fig., coll.*) з. высоко́, з. далеко́ to go up in the world.

залётн|ый, *adj.* (*coll.*) ~ая пти́ца bird of passage (*also fig.*); з. гость unexpected visitor.

залечива|ть, ю, *impf. of* залечи́ть.

залеч|и́ть, у́, ~ишь, *pf.* 1. to heal; to remedy. 2. (*coll.*) з. до́ смерти to doctor to death; to murder (*by unskilful treatment*).

залеч|и́ться, и́тся, *pf.* (*coll.*) to heal (up).

зал|е́чь, я́гу, я́жешь, я́гут, *past* ~ёг, ~егла́, *pf. of* ~ега́ть) 1. to lie down; to lie low; to lie in wait. 2. (*geol.*) to lie, be deposited; здесь руда́ ~егла́ на глубине́ ста ме́тров there is a deposit of ore here at a depth of a hundred metres. 3. (*fig.*) to take root; to become ingrained. 4. (*med.*) to become blocked; нос у него́ ~ёг, у него́ в носу́ ~егло́ his nose is blocked.

зали́в, а, *m.* bay; gulf; creek, cove.

залива́|ть[1], ю, *impf.* (*coll.*) to lie, tell lies.

залива́|ть[2](ся), ю(сь), *impf. of* зали́ть(ся).

зали́вист|ый (~, ~а), *adj.* (*of sound*) modulating.

зали́вк|а, и, *f.* mending; stopping up, filling in (*with liquid substance*).

заливн|о́е, о́го, *n.* fish *or* meat in aspic.

заливн|о́й, *adj.* **1.** з. луг water-meadow. **2.** for pouring; ∼а́я труба́ funnel. **3.** (*folk poet.*) trilling. **4.** jellied; ∼а́я ры́ба fish in aspic.

зали|за́ть, жу́, ∼жешь, *pf.* **1.** to lick clean. **2.** з. у себя́ во́лосы to sleek down one's hair.

зали́зыва|ть, ю, *impf. of* зализа́ть.

зал|и́ть, ью́, ьёшь, *past* ∼и́л, ∼ила́, ∼и́ло, *pf.* (*of* ∼ива́ть) **1.** to flood, inundate; (*fig.*) ко́мнату ∼и́ло све́том the room was flooded with light; толпа́ ∼ила́ у́лицы the crowd filled the streets to overflowing. **2.** (+*a. and i.*) to pour (over); to spill (on); кто ∼и́л но́вую ска́терть черни́лами? who has spilled ink on the new table-cloth?; з. кра́ской to give a wash of paint; з. ту́шью to ink in. **3.** to quench, extinguish (*with water*); з. пожа́р to put out a fire; з. го́ре (вино́м) to drown one's sorrows. **4.** to stop up (*with liquid substance, as putty, rubber solution, etc.*); з. гало́ши to mend galoshes. **5.** to begin to pour (*intrans.*).

зал|и́ться, ью́сь, ьёшься, *past* ∼и́лся, ∼ила́сь, *pf.* (*of* ∼ива́ться) **1.** to be flooded, inundated. **2.** to pour; to spill (*intrans.*); вода́ ∼ила́сь мне за воротни́к water has gone down my neck. **3.** to spill on oneself; ты весь'∼и́лся су́пом you have spilled soup all over yourself. **4.** (+*i.*) to break into, burst into; соба́ка ∼ила́сь ла́ем the dog began to bark furiously; з. пе́сней to break into a song; з. слеза́ми to burst into tears, dissolve in tears. **5.** to set (*of jellies*).

залихва́тск|ий, *adj.* (*coll.*) devil-may-care; ∼ая пе́сня rollicking song.

зало́г¹, а, m. **1.** deposit; pledge; security; под з. (+ *g.*) on the security of; отда́ть в з. to pawn; to mortgage; вы́купить из ∼а to redeem; to pay off mortgage (on). **2.** (*fig.*) pledge, token.

зало́г², а, m. (*gram.*) voice.

зало́г|овый, *adj. of* ∼; ∼овое свиде́тельство mortgage-deed.

залогода́тел|ь, я, m. depositor; mortgagor.

залогодержа́тел|ь, я, m. pawnee.

залож|и́ть, у́, ∼ишь, *pf.* (*of* закла́дывать) **1.** to put (behind); он ∼и́л ру́ки за́ спину he put his hands behind his back. **2.** to lay (the foundation of). **3.** (*coll.*) to mislay. **4.** (+*i.*) to pile up, heap up (with); to block up (with); (*impers.* +*d.*) мне нос ∼и́ло my nose is blocked, is stuffed up. **5.** to mark, put a marker in; я ∼и́л страни́цу девяно́сто I have put a marker in at page ninety. **6.** to pawn; to mortgage. **7.** to harness. **8.** to lay in, store, put by.

зало́жник, а, m. hostage.

залом|и́ть, лю́, ∼ишь, *pf.* (*of* зала́мывать) **1.** to break off. **2.** (*coll.*) з. це́ну to ask an exorbitant price; з. ша́пку to cock one's hat.

залосн|и́ться, и́тся, *pf.* (*coll.*) to become shiny.

залп, а, m. volley; salvo; вы́стрелить ∼ом to fire a volley, salvo; ∼ом (*fig., coll.*) without pausing for breath; вы́пить ∼ом to drain at one draught.

залуп|и́ть, лю́, ∼ишь, *pf.* (*coll.*) **1.** to peel off; to tear off. **2.** to ask an exorbitant price for. **3.** to begin to beat. **4.** to beat up.

залуп|и́ться, ∼ится, *pf.* (*coll.*) to peel off, flake off.

залупля́|ть(ся), ет(ся), *impf. of* залупи́ть-(ся).

залуча́|ть, ю, *impf. of* залучи́ть.

залуч|и́ть, у́, и́шь, *pf.* (*coll.*) to entice, lure.

заль|сти́ть, щу́, сти́шь, *pf.* (*coll.*) **1.** (+*d.*) to begin to flatter. **2.** (*dial.*) to win over by flattery.

залюб|ова́ться, у́юсь, *pf.* (+*i.*) to be lost in admiration (of).

заля́па|ть, ю, *pf.* (*coll.*) to make dirty.

зам, а, m. *abbr. of* ∼ести́тель.

зам-, *prefix* = ∼ести́тель.

зама́|зать, жу, жешь, *pf.* (*of* ма́зать *and* ∼зывать) **1.** to paint over; to efface; (*fig.*) to slur over. **2.** to putty; to lute. **3.** to daub, smear; to soil.

зама́|заться, жусь, жешься, *pf.* (*of* ма́зать-ся *and* ∼зываться) to smear oneself; to get dirty.

зама́зк|а, и, f. **1.** putty. **2.** closing up with putty, luting.

зама́зыва|ть(ся), ю(сь), *impf. of* зама́-зать(ся).

зама́й, *only in phrase* не з. (*dial.*) don't touch, leave alone.

зама́лива|ть, ю, *impf. of* замоли́ть.

зама́лчива|ть, ю, *impf. of* замолча́ть.

зама́нива|ть, ю, *impf. of* замани́ть.

заман|и́ть, ю́, ∼ишь, *pf.* to entice, lure; to decoy.

зама́нчив|ый (∼, ∼а), *adj.* tempting, alluring.

замара́|ть, ю, pf. (*of* мара́ть 1) **1.** to soil, dirty; (*fig.*) to disgrace; з. свою́ репута́цию to sully one's reputation. **2.** to blot out, efface.

замара́|ться, юсь, *pf. of* мара́ться 1.

замара́шк|а, и, m. and f. (*coll.*) slut, sloven; grubby child.

зама́рива|ть, ю, *impf. of* замори́ть.

замарин|ова́ть, у́ю, *pf. of* маринова́ть.

замаскир|ова́ть, у́ю, *pf.* to mask; to disguise; to camouflage; з. свои́ чу́вства (*fig.*) to conceal one's feelings.

замаскир|ова́ться, у́юсь, *pf.* to disguise oneself.

замаскиро́выва|ть(ся), ю(сь), *impf. of* за-маскирова́ть(ся).

зама́слива|ть(ся), ю(сь), *impf. of* зама́с-лить(ся).

замáсл|ить, ю, ишь, *pf.* **1.** to oil, grease. **2.** to make oily, make greasy. **3.** (*fig.*, *sl.*) to butter up.

замáсл|иться, юсь, ишься, *pf.* to become oily, become greasy.

заматерéлый, *adj.* hardened, inveterate.

заматерé|ть, ю, *pf.* to become hardened.

замат|орéлый = ~ерéлый.

замáтыва|ть(ся), ю(сь), *impf. of* замотáть(ся).

замáх, а, *m.* threatening gesture.

зама|хáть, шý, ~шешь, *pf.* to begin to wave.

замáхива|ться, юсь, *impf. of* замахнýться.

замахн|ýться, ýсь, ёшься, *pf.* (+*i.*) to raise threateningly; он дáже ~ýлся рукóй на беззащи́тную старýху he even lifted up his hand against a defenceless old woman.

замáчива|ть, ю, *impf. of* замочи́ть.

замáшк|а, и, *f.* (*coll.*, *pejor.*) way, manner.

замáщива|ть, ю, *impf. of* замости́ть.

замá|ять, ю, ешь, *pf.* (*coll.*) to tire out, wear out.

замá|яться, юсь, ешься, *pf.* (*coll.*) to be tired out, exhausted.

замая́ч|ить, у, ишь, *pf.* to loom; вдали́ ~или огни́ гáвани the lights of the harbour loomed up in the distance.

замедлéни|е, я, *n.* **1.** slowing down, deceleration; (*mus.*) ritardando. **2.** delay; без ~я without delay, at once.

замéдленн|ый, *p.p.p. of* замéдлить *and adj.* retarded; delayed; бóмба ~ого дéйствия delayed-action bomb.

замéдл|ить, ю, ишь, *pf.* **1.** to slow down, retard; з. шаг to slacken one's pace; з. ход to reduce speed. **2.** (+*inf.* or +*i.* or с+*i.*) to delay (in); to be long (in); отвéт не ~ил прийти́ the answer was not long in coming; з. (с) отвéтом to delay in answering.

замéдл|иться, ится, *pf.* **1.** to slow down; to slacken, become slower. **2.** *pass of* ~ить.

замедля́|ть(ся), ет(ся), *impf. of* замéдлить(ся).

замел|и́ть, ю, и́шь, *pf.* (*coll.*) to chalk over.

замéн|а, ы, *f.* **1.** substitution; replacement; з. смéртной кáзни тюрéмным заключéнием commutation of death sentence to imprisonment. **2.** substitute.

замени́|мый, *pres. part. pass. of* ~ть *and adj.* replaceable.

замени́тел|ь, я, *m.* (+*g.*) substitute; з. кóжи leather substitute.

замен|и́ть, ю́, ~ишь, *pf.* **1.** (+*a. and i.*) to replace (by), substitute (for); мы ~и́ли кероси́н электри́чеством we have replaced oil by electricity; з. мáсло маргари́ном to use margarine instead of butter. **2.** to take the place of; онá ~и́ла ребёнку мать she was (like) a mother to the child; трýдно

бýдет з. егó it will be hard to replace him.

заменя́|ть, я́ю, *impf. of* ~и́ть.

зам|ерéть, рý, рёшь, *past* ~ер ~ерлá, ~ерлó, *pf.* (*of* ~ирáть) **1.** to stand still; to freeze, be rooted to the spot; to die (*fig.*); сéрдце моё ~ерло, когдá дверь откры́лась my heart stopped beating when the door opened. **2.** to die down, die away; к полýночи стрельбá ~ерлá towards midnight firing died down.

замерзáни|е, я, *n.* freezing; тóчка ~я freezing point; на тóчке ~я (*fig.*) at a standstill.

замерзá|ть, ю, *impf. of* замёрзнуть.

замёрз|нуть, ну, нешь, *past* ~, ~ла, *pf.* (*of* ~áть) to freeze (up); to freeze to death; to be killed by frost.

зáмертво, *adv.* **1.** like one dead; онá упáла з. she collapsed in a dead faint. **2.** (*coll.*) dead drunk.

заме|си́ть, шý, ~сишь, *pf.* (*of* ~шивать) to mix; з. тéсто to knead dough.

заме|сти́, тý, тёшь, *past* ~л, ~лá, *pf.* (*of* ~тáть) **1.** to sweep up. **2.** to cover (up); (*impers.*) дорóгу ~лó снéгом the road is covered with snow; (*fig.*) з. следы́ to cover up one's traces.

замести́тел|ь, я, *m.* substitute; deputy; з. дирéктора deputy director; з. президéнта vice-president; быть ~ем (+*g.*) to stand proxy (for), substitute (for).

замести́тельств|о, а, *n.* position of deputy; acting tenure of office; по ~у by proxy.

заме|сти́ть, щý, сти́шь, *pf.* (*of* ~щáть) **1.** (+*a. and i.*) to replace (by); to substitute (for). **2.** (+*a. and i.*) to appoint (to); они́ ~сти́ли кáфедру психолóгии нéмцем they have appointed a German to the chair of psychology. **3.** to deputize for, act for; to serve in place of.

заметá|ть¹, ю, *impf. of* замести́.

заметá|ть², ю, *pf.* (*of* замётывать) to tack, baste; *p.p.p. as pred.* (*coll.*) замётано! all right!, agreed!

заме|тáться, чýсь, ~чешься, *pf.* to begin to rush about; to begin to toss.

замé|тить, чу, тишь, *pf.* (*of* ~чáть) **1.** to notice, remark; ~тили ли вы, что он чáсто повторя́ется? have you noticed that he often repeats himself?; я ~тил за ним склóнность повторя́ться I have noticed that he has a tendency to repeat himself. **2.** to take notice (of); to make a note (of). **3.** to remark, observe; «совершéнно вéрно» — ~тил он 'perfectly true', he remarked.

замéтк|а, и, *f.* **1.** mark. **2.** note; ~и на поля́х marginal notes; взять на ~у (*coll.*) to make a note (of). **3.** notice; paragraph; ни однá газéта не удостóила вы́ставки ~ой not a single newspaper gave the exhibition a notice.

заме́т|ный (~ен, ~на), *adj.* 1. noticeable; appreciable; ме́жду ни́ми есть ~ная ра́зница в во́зрасте there is an appreciable difference in age between them; ~но (*as pred.*) it is noticeable; ~но, как он не лю́бит говори́ть о де́тстве it is noticeable that he does not like talking about his childhood. 2. outstanding.

заме́тыва|ть, ю, *impf. of* замета́ть².

замеча́ни|е, я, *n.* 1. remark, observation. 2. reprimand; reproof; он у меня́ на ~и (*obs.*) he is in my bad books.

замеча́тел|ьный (~ен, ~ьна), *adj.* remarkable; splendid, wonderful.

замеча́|ть, ю, *impf. of* заме́тить.

замече́н|ный (~, ~а), *p.p.p. of* заме́тить; з. (в+*p.*) discovered, noticed, detected (in); он был неоднокра́тно ~ во взя́точничестве he was several times discovered taking bribes.

замечта́|ться, юсь, *pf.* to give oneself up to day-dreaming; to fall into a reverie; он опя́ть ~лся he is day-dreaming again.

замеша́тельств|о, а, *n.* confusion; embarrassment; привести́ в з. to throw into confusion; прийти́ в з. to be confused, be embarrassed.

замеша́|ть, ю, *pf.* (в+*a.*) to mix up, entangle (in).

замеша́|ться, юсь, *pf.* (в+*a.*) 1. to become mixed up, entangled (in). 2. to mix (with), mingle (in, with); з. в толпу́ to mingle with the crowd.

заме́шива|ть(ся), ю(сь), *impf. of* замеси́ть *and* замеша́ть(ся).

заме́шк|а, и, *f.* (*coll.*) delay.

заме́шка|ться, юсь, *pf.* (*coll.*) to linger, tarry.

замеща́|ть, ю, *impf. of* замести́ть.

замеще́ни|е, я, *n.* 1. substitution. 2. appointment; бу́дет ко́нкурс на з. вака́нтной до́лжности there will be a competition to fill the vacancy.

замина́|ть, ю, *impf. of* замя́ть.

зами́нк|а, и, *f.* (*coll.*) 1. hitch. 2. hesitation (*in speech*).

замира́ни|е, я, *n.* dying out, dying down; он ждал с ~ем се́рдца he waited with a sinking heart.

замира́|ть, ю, *impf. of* замере́ть.

замире́ни|е, я, *n.* peace-making.

замир|и́ть, ю́, и́шь, *pf.* (*obs.*) to pacify; to reconcile.

замир|и́ться, ю́сь, и́шься, *pf.* (с+*i.*; *obs.*) to make peace (with).

замиря́|ть(ся), ю(сь), *impf. of* замири́ть(ся).

за́мкнут|ый (~, ~а), *adj.* 1. exclusive. 2. reserved; адмира́л — о́чень з. челове́к the admiral is a very reserved person; вести́ ~ую жизнь to lead an unsociable life.

замкн|у́ть, у́, ёшь, *pf.* (*of* замыка́ть) to lock; to close; з. ше́ствие, з. коло́нну to bring up the rear; з. цепь (*electr.*) to close the circuit.

замкн|у́ться, у́сь, ёшься, *pf.* (*of* замыка́ться) 1. *pass. of* ~у́ть. 2. to shut oneself up; з. в круг to form a circle; (*fig.*) з. в себя́ to become reserved, retire into oneself.

замле́|ть, ю, *pf.* (*coll.*) to become numb; to go to sleep (*of a limb*).

зам|ну́, нёшь, *see* ~я́ть.

замоги́льный, *adj.* sepulchral (*of voice*).

за́м|ок, ка, *m.* castle; возду́шные ~ки castles in the air.

зам|о́к, ка́, *m.* 1. lock; америка́нский з. Yale lock; вися́чий з. padlock; под ~ко́м under lock and key; за семью́ ~ка́ми well and truly hidden. 2. (*archit.*) keystone. 3. bolt (*of fire-arm*). 4. clasp (*of necklace, etc.*); clip (*of ear-ring*).

замока́|ть, ет, *impf. of* замо́кнуть.

замо́кн|уть, ет, *pf.* to become drenched, become soaked.

замо́лв|ить, лю, ишь, *pf.* (*coll.*); з. слове́чко за (+*a.*) to put in a word (for); прошу́ вас з. слове́чко за меня́ у нача́льства will you, please, put in a word for me with the authorities.

замол|и́ть, ю́, ~ишь, *pf.* (*of* зама́ливать); з. грехи́ to atone for one's sins by prayer.

замолка́|ть, ю, *impf. of* замо́лкнуть.

замо́лк|нуть, ну, нешь, *past* ~, ~ла, *pf.* to fall silent; to stop, cease (*speaking, etc.*); внеза́пно пе́ние ~ло suddenly the singing ceased.

замолч|а́ть¹, у́, и́шь, *pf.* to fall silent; (*fig.*), to cease corresponding.

замолч|а́ть², у́, и́шь, *pf.* (*of* зама́лчивать) (*coll.*) to keep silent about; to hush up.

замора́живани|е, я, *n.* freezing; з. зарпла́ты wage-freezing.

замора́жива|ть, ю, *impf. of* заморо́зить.

заморд|ова́ть, у́ю, *pf.* (*coll.*) to torment.

замор|и́ть, ю́, и́шь, *pf.* (*of* зама́ривать) (*coll.*) 1. to overwork; з. ло́шадь to founder a horse. 2. to underfeed; з. червячка́ to have a bite, have a snack.

заморо́|женный, *p.p.p. of* ~зить *and adj.* frozen; iced; ~женное мя́со frozen meat; ~женное шампа́нское iced champagne.

заморо́|зить, жу, зишь, *pf.* (*of* замора́живать) to freeze; to ice.

за́морозк|и, ов, *no sing.* (light) frosts.

замо́рский, *adj.* oversea(s).

замо́рыш, а, *m.* (*coll.*) weakling; runt.

замо|сти́ть, щу́, сти́шь, *pf.* (*of* мости́ть *and* зама́щивать) to pave.

замота́|ть, ю, *pf.* (*of* зама́тывать) 1. to wind, twist; to roll up. 2. (*fig.*) to tire out. 3. (*sl.*) to pinch, whip. 4. (+*i.*) to begin to shake; з. голово́й to begin to shake one's head; з. хвосто́м to begin to wag its tail.

замота́|ться, юсь, *pf.* (*of* зама́тываться) (*coll.*) 1. to wind round. 2. to be tired out, be fagged out. 3. to begin to shake; to begin to swing (*intrans.*).

замоч|и́ть, у́, ~ишь, *pf.* (*of* зама́чивать) 1. to wet; to soak; з. лён to ret (rate, rait) flax. 2. (*fig.*, *coll.*) to celebrate.

замо́чник, а, *m.* locksmith.

замо́чн|ый, *adj.* *of* замо́к; ~ая сква́жина keyhole.

за́муж, *adv.*; вы́йти з. за кого́-н. to marry someone (*of woman*); вы́дать кого́-н. з. (за +*a.*) to give someone in marriage (to); она́ вы́шла з. за моряка́, несмотря́ на то, что её оте́ц всё мечта́л вы́дать её за врача́ she has married a sailor despite the fact that her father always dreamed of marrying her to a doctor.

за́мужем, *adv.*; быть з. (за+*i.*) to be married (to) (*of woman*).

заму́жеств|о, а, *n.* marriage (*of woman*); у неё о́чень счастли́вое з. she is very happily married.

заму́жняя, *adj.* married (*of woman*).

замундшту́чива|ть, ю, *impf.* *of* замундшту́-чить.

замундшту́ч|ить, у, ишь, *pf.* to bit.

замур|ова́ть, у́ю, *pf.* to brick up; to immure.

замуро́выва|ть, ю, *impf.* *of* замурова́ть.

заму́сл|ить, ю, ишь = замусо́лить.

замусо́лива|ть, ю, *impf.* *of* замусо́лить.

замусо́л|ить, ю, ишь, *pf.* to beslobber.

заму|ти́ть, чу́, ~ти́шь, *pf.* *of* мути́ть; он воды́ не ~ти́т he won't cause any trouble.

замухры́шк|а, и, *m. and f.* (*coll.*, *pejor.*) poor specimen.

заму́чива|ть, ю, *impf.* *of* заму́чить.

заму́ч|ить, у, ишь, *pf.* (*of* му́чить *and* ~ивать) to torment; to wear out; to plague the life out of; to bore to tears.

заму́ч|иться, усь, ишься, *pf.* (*of* му́читься) to be worn out, worried to death.

за́мш|а, и, *f.* chamois (leather); suede.

за́мш|евый, *adj.* *of* ~а.

замше́лый, *adj.* mossy, moss-covered.

замше́|ть, ет, *pf.* to be overgrown with moss.

замыва́|ть, ю, *impf.* *of* замы́ть.

замыка́ни|е, я, *n.* locking; коро́ткое з. (*electr.*) short circuit.

замыка́|ться, юсь, *pf.* (*coll.*) to be tired out.

замыка́|ть(ся), ю(сь), *impf.* *of* замкну́ть(ся).

за́мыс|ел, ла, *m.* project, plan; design, scheme; idea; его́ но́вая пье́са осно́вана на о́чень оригина́льном ~ле his new play is based on a very original idea; злы́е ~лы evil designs.

замы́сл|ить, ю, ишь, *pf.* (*of* замышля́ть)

(+*a.* *or* *inf.*) to plan; to contemplate, meditate; он ~ил самоуби́йство he contemplated suicide; они́ ~или убежа́ть под покро́вом темноты́ had planned to escape under cover of darkness.

замыслова́т|ый (~, ~а), *adj.* intricate, complicated.

зам|ы́ть, о́ю, о́ешь, *pf.* (*of* ~ыва́ть) to wash off, wash out.

замышля́|ть, ю, *impf.* *of* замы́слить.

зам|я́ть, ну́, нёшь, *pf.* (*of* ~ина́ть) (*coll.*) to put a stop to; з. разгово́р to change the subject.

зам|я́ться, ну́сь, нёшься, *pf.* (*coll.*) to stumble; to stop short (*in speech*).

за́навес, а, *m.* curtain; под з. (*theatr.*) near the end of an act.

занаве́|сить, шу, сишь, *pf.* (*of* ~шивать) to curtain; to cover.

занаве́с|ка, ки, *f.* curtain (*of light material*).

занаве́шива|ть, ю, *impf.* *of* занаве́сить.

занаво́|зить, жу, зишь, *pf.* 1. (*dial.*) to manure. 2. (*coll.*) to befoul.

зана́шива|ть, ю, *impf.* *of* заноси́ть[2].

зане́, *conj.* (*arch.*) since, because.

занеме́|ть, ю, *pf.* (*coll.*) to grow numb.

занемога́|ть, ю, *impf.* *of* занемо́чь.

занемо́|чь, гу́, жешь, гут, *past* ~г, ~гла́, *pf.* to fall ill, be taken ill.

занес|ти́, у́, ёшь, *past* ~, ~ла́, *pf.* (*of* заноси́ть[1]) 1. to bring import. 2. to raise, lift; з. но́гу в стре́мя to raise one's foot into the stirrup. 3. to note down; з. в протоко́л to enter in the minutes. 4. (*coll.*) to carry (away); куда́ его́ нелёгкая ~ла́? where the devil has he got to?; (*impers.*) каки́м ве́тром вас сюда́ ~ло́? what wind blows you here? 5. (*impers.*) з. сне́гом to cover with snow; доро́гу ~ло́ сне́гом the road is snowed up.

занес|ти́сь, усь, ёшься, *past* ~ся, ~ла́сь, *pf.* (*of* заноси́ться[1]) (*coll.*, *pejor.*) to be carried away (*fig.*).

занима́тел|ьный (~ен, ~ьна), *adj.* entertaining, diverting; absorbing.

занима́|ть[1], ю, *impf.* (*of* заня́ть) 1. to occupy; з. го́род to occupy a city; з. кварти́ру to occupy a flat; крова́ть ~ет мно́го ме́ста the bed takes up a lot of room; он ~ет высо́кое положе́ние (*fig.*) he occupies a high post. 2. to occupy; to interest; она́ ни-ка́к не могла́ з. дете́й she simply could not keep the children occupied; его́ ~ют бо́льше всего́ вопро́сы филосо́фии his chief interest is in philosophy. 3. to take (*of time*); э́то ~ет мно́го вре́мени this takes a lot of time. 4. (*impers.*; *coll.*) дух ~ет it takes your breath away!

занима́|ть[2], ю, *impf.* (*of* заня́ть) to borrow.

занима́|ться[1], юсь, *impf.* (*of* заня́ться) (+*i.*) 1. to be occupied (with), be engaged (in);

to work (at, on); to study; чем вы ~лись вчера? what were you doing yesterday?; он ~ется подготовкой новой экспедиции he is engaged in preparations for a new expedition; до замужества она ~лась музыкой before her marriage she was studying music. 2. to busy oneself (with); to devote oneself (to); з. собой to devote attention to one's appearance. 3. (c+i.) to assist; to attend to.

занима|ться², *impf.* (*of* заняться) to catch fire; ~лась заря day was breaking.

заново, *adv.* anew.

заноз|а, ы, *f.* 1. splinter. 2. *m. and f.* (*fig.*, *coll.*) thorn in the flesh; nagger.

занозист|ый (~, ~a), *adj.* (*coll.*) splintery; (*fig.*) nagging.

зано|зить, жу, зишь, *pf.* to get a splinter into.

занос¹, а, *m.* snow-drift.

занос², а, *m.* 1. bringing, importing, import. 2. raising, lifting.

зано|сить¹, шу, ~сишь, *impf. of* занести.

зано|сить², шу, ~сишь, *pf.* (*of* занашивать) to wear out.

зано|ситься¹, шусь, ~сишься, *impf. of* занестись.

зано|ситься², ~сится, *pf.* to be worn out; to wear out (*intrans.*).

заносный, *adj.* alien, imported.

заносчив|ый (~, ~a), *adj.* arrogant, haughty.

заноч|евать, ую, *pf.* (*coll.*) to stay for the night.

зануд|а, ы, *m. and f.* (*coll.*) tiresome person, pain in the neck.

занумер|овать, ую, *pf.* (*of* нумеровать) to number.

занятие, я, *n.* 1. occupation; pursuit. 2. (*pl.*) studies; work; часы ~й working hours.

занят|ный (~ен, ~на), *adj.* (*coll.*) entertaining, amusing.

занятой, *adj.* busy.

занятост|ь, и, *f.* being busy; у нас в эту неделю большая з. we are very busy this week; (*econ.*) полная з. full employment.

занят|ый (~, ~а, ~о), *p.p.p. of* ~ь *and adj.* 1. occupied; здесь ~о this place is taken; ~о engaged (*of telephone number*); на этом заводе ~о свыше тысячи рабочих over a thousand people are employed in this factory; быть ~ым собой to be self-centred. 2. busy.

зан|ять(ся), займу(сь), займёшь(ся), *past* ~ял(ся), ~яла(сь), ~яло(сь), *pf. of* занимать(ся); у кого-н. дух ~яло (*impers.*; *coll.*) to be out of breath; (*fig.*) to be breathless.

заоблачн|ый, *adj.* (*poet.*, *fig.*) beyond the clouds; ~ая высь, *see* высь.

заодно, *adv.* 1. in concert, at one; действо-

вать з. to act in concert; насчёт этого мужчины — з. с женщинами on this the men are in agreement with the women. 2. (*coll.*) at the same time; купите з. и апельсинов buy some oranges at the same time.

заозёрный, *adj.* situated on the other side of the lake.

заокеанский, *adj.* transoceanic.

заор|ать, у, ёшь, *pf.* (*coll.*) to begin to bawl, begin to yell.

заострённост|ь, и, *f.* pointedness, sharpness.

заострённый, *p.p.p. of* заострить *and adj.* pointed, sharp.

заостр|ить, ю, ишь, *pf.* to sharpen; (*fig.*) to stress, emphasize; з. внимание (на+*a.*) to stimulate an interest (in).

заостр|иться, ится, *pf.* to become sharp; to become pointed.

заостр|ять(ся), яет(ся), *impf. of* ~ить(ся).

заочник, а, *m.* student taking correspondence course; external student.

заочно, *adv.* 1. in one's absence. 2. by correspondence course, externally.

заочн|ый, *adj.* 1. (*leg.*) з. приговор judgment by default. 2. з. курс correspondence course; ~ое обучение postal tuition.

запад, а, *m.* 1. west. 2. the West; the Occident.

запада|ть, ю, *impf. of* запасть.

западник, а, *m.* Westernizer, Westernist.

западничеств|о, а, *n.* Westernism.

западный, *adj.* west, western; westerly.

западн|я, и, *g. pl.* ~ей, *f.* trap, snare; попасть в ~ю to fall into a trap (*also fig.*).

запаздывани|е, я, *n.* 1. lateness, being late. 2. (*tech.*) lag.

запаздыва|ть, ю, *impf. of* запоздать; (*impf. only*; *tech.*) to lag.

запаива|ть, ю, *impf. of* запаять.

запайк|а, и, *f.* soldering.

запак|овать, ую, *pf.* to pack (up); to wrap up, do up.

запаковыва|ть, ю, *impf. of* запаковать.

запако|стить, щу, стишь, *pf. of* пакостить 1.

запал¹, а, *m.* fuse; touchhole.

запал², а, *m.* heaves; broken wind.

запалива|ть, ю, *impf. of* запалить.¹

запал|ить¹, ю, ишь, *pf.* (*coll.*) to set fire to, kindle; to light.

запал|ить², ю, ишь, *pf.* (*dial.*) 1. to water (*a horse*) when overheated. 2. to override (*a horse*).

запал|ить³, ю, ишь, *pf.* (*coll.*) 1. to open fire. 2. (+*i.*) to hurl.

запал|ьный, *adj. of* ~¹; ~ьная свеча sparking plug.

запальчивост|ь, и, *f.* (quick) temper.

запальчив|ый, (~a), *adj.* quick-tempered.

запа́мят|овать, ую, *pf.* (*obs.*, *coll.*) to forget.

запанибра́та, *adv.*; (*coll.*) быть з. с кем-н. to be hail-fellow-well-met with someone.

запанибра́тский, *adj.* (*coll.*) hail-fellow-well-met.

запанибра́тств|о, а, *n.* (*coll.*, *obs.*) hail-fellow-well-met terms.

запа́рива|ть(ся), ю(сь), *impf. of* запа́рить(ся).

запа́р|ить, ю, ишь, *pf.* 1. (*coll.*) to put into a sweat. 2. to stew; to bake.

запа́р|иться, юсь, ишься, *pf.* 1. (*coll.*) to get into a sweat. 2. to be worn out.

запарши́ве|ть, ю, *pf. of* парши́веть.

запа́рыва|ть, ю, *impf. of* запоро́ть.

запа́с, а, *m.* 1. supply, stock; reserve; з. това́ров stock-in-trade; прове́рить з. to take stock; про з. for emergency; отложи́ть про з. to put by; истощи́ть з. терпе́ния (*fig.*) to exhaust one's reserves of patience; приобрести́ большо́й з. слов to acquire a large vocabulary. 2. (*mil.*) reserve; его́ уво́лили в з. he has been transferred to the reserve. 3. hem; вы́пустить з. to let out.

запаса́|ть(ся), ю(сь), *impf. of* запасти́(сь).

запа́слив|ый (~, ~а), *adj.* thrifty; provident.

запа́сник, а, *m.* (*coll.*) reservist.

запасн|о́й, *adj.* 1. spare; reserve; з. вы́ход emergency exit; з. путь siding; з. батальо́н (*mil.*) depot battalion; з. сте́ржень re-fill (*for pen*); ~а́я часть spare part; з. я́корь (*naut.*) sheet anchor, spare bower anchor. 2. *as noun* з., ~о́го, *m.* reservist.

запа́сн|ый, *adj.* = ~о́й.

запас|ти́, у́, ёшь, *past* ~, ~ла́, *pf.* (*of* ~а́ть) (+*a. or g.*) to stock, store; to lay in a stock of.

запас|ти́сь, у́сь, ёшься, *past* ~ся, ~ла́сь, *pf.* (*of* ~а́ться) (+*i.*) to provide oneself (with); to stock up (with); з. терпе́нием (*fig.*) to arm oneself with patience.

запа́|сть, ду́, дёшь, *past* ~л, *pf.* (*of* ~да́ть) to fall (behind); to sink down; слова́ его́ ~ли мне в ду́шу (*fig*). his words are imprinted in my mind.

запат|ова́ть, у́ю, *pf. of* патова́ть.

за́пах, а, *m.* smell.

запа|ха́ть, шу́, ~шешь, *pf.* (*agric.*) 1. to plough in. 2. to begin to plough.

запа́хива|ть¹(ся), ю(сь), *impf. of* запахну́ть(ся).

запа́хива|ть², ю, *impf. of* запаха́ть.

запа́хн|уть, у, ешь, *pf.* to begin to emit a smell.

запахн|у́ть, у́, ёшь, *pf.* (*of* запа́хивать¹) 1. to wrap over (*folds of a garment*). 2. (*coll.*) з. за́навеску to draw the curtain.

запахн|у́ться, у́сь, ёшься, *pf.* (в+*a.*) to wrap oneself tighter (into).

запа́чка|ть, ю, *pf. of* па́чкать 1.

запа́шк|а, и, *f.* 1. ploughing up. 2. plough-land, arable land.

запа́ш|о́к, ка́, *m.* (*coll.*) faint smell.

запая́|ть, ю, *pf.* (*of* запа́ивать) 1. to solder. 2. (*coll.*) з. кому́-н. в у́хо to box someone's ears.

запе́в, а, *m.* introduction (*to song*); solo part.

запева́л|а, ы, *m.* leader (of choir); precentor; (*fig.*, *coll.*) leader, instigator.

запева́|ть, ю, *impf.* (*of* запе́ть) to lead the singing, set the tune.

запека́нк|а, и, *f.* 1. baked pudding. 2. spiced brandy.

запека́|ть(ся), ю(сь), *impf. of* запе́чь(ся).

запелена́|ть, ю, *pf. of* пелена́ть.

запе́н|ить, ю, ишь, *pf.* to froth up.

запе́н|иться, юсь, ишься, *pf.* to begin to froth up, begin to foam (*intrans.*).

зап|ере́ть, ру́, рёшь, *past* ~ер, ~ерла́, ~ерло, *pf.* (*of* ~ира́ть) 1. to lock; з. на засо́в to bolt. 2. to lock in; to shut up. 3. to bar; to block up.

зап|ере́ться, ру́сь, рёшься, *past* ~ерся́, ~ерла́сь, ~ерло́сь, *pf.* (*of* ~ира́ться) 1. to lock oneself in. 2. (в+*p.*; *coll.*) to refuse to admit; to refuse to speak (about); to shut up (*intrans.*).

зап|е́ть, ою́, оёшь, *pf.* 1. *pf. of* ~ева́ть. 2. to begin to sing; з. пе́сню to break into a song; з. друго́е (*fig.*) to change one's tune. 3. (*coll.*) з. пе́сню to plug a song.

запеча́т|ать, аю, *pf.* (*of* ~ывать) to seal.

запечатлева́|ть(ся), ю(сь), *impf. of* запеча́тле́ть(ся).

запечатле́|ть, ю, *pf.* to imprint, impress, engrave; з. что-н. в па́мяти (*fig.*) to imprint something on one's memory.

запечатле́|ться, юсь, *pf.* (*fig.*) to imprint itself, stamp itself, impress itself; черты́ его́ лица́ ~лись у де́вочки в па́мяти his features stamped themselves in the little girl's memory.

запеча́тыва|ть, ю, *impf. of* запеча́тать.

запе́|чь, ку́, чёшь, ку́т, *past* ~к, ~кла́, *pf.* (*of* ~ка́ть) to bake.

запе́|чься, чётся, ку́тся, *past* ~кся, ~кла́сь, *pf.* (*of* ~ка́ться) 1. to bake (*intrans.*). 2. to clot, coagulate. 3. to become parched.

запива́|ть, ю, *impf. of* запи́ть.

запина́|ться, юсь, *impf.* (*of* запну́ться) to hesitate; to stumble, halt (*in speech*); to stammer; з. ного́й to trip up; з. о ка́мень to strike against a stone.

запи́нк|а, и, *f.* hesitation (*in speech*).

запира́тельств|о, а, *n.* (*pejor.*) denial, disavowal.

запира́|ть(ся), ю(сь), *impf. of* запере́ть(ся).

запи|са́ть, шу́, ~шешь, *pf.* (*of* ~сывать) 1.

to note, make a note (of); to take down (in writing); to record (*with sound-recording apparatus*); з. ле́кцию to take notes of a lecture. **2.** to enter, register, enrol; ~ши́те меня́ пожа́луйста на приём к врачу́ please, make an appointment with the doctor for me. **3.** (+ *a.* на+*a.*; *leg.*) to make over (to); он ~са́л всю со́бственность на свою́ племя́нницу he made over all his property to his niece. **4.** (*coll.*) to begin to write, begin to correspond.

запи|са́ться, шу́сь, ~ше́шься, *pf.* (*of* ~сы́ваться) **1.** to register, enter one's name, enrol; з. в клуб to join a club; з. к врачу́ to make an appointment with the doctor. **2.** to forget the time in writing. **3.** *pass. of* ~са́ть.

запи́ск|а, и, *f.* **1.** note; дипломати́ческая з., делова́я з. memorandum, minute. **2.** ~и (*pl.*) notes; memoirs; (*as title of learned journals*) transactions.

записн|о́й¹, *adj.*; ~а́я кни́жка notebook.

записно́й², *adj.* (*coll.*) inveterate; regular.

запи́сыва|ть(ся), ю(сь), *impf. of* записа́ть(ся).

за́пис|ь, и, *f.* **1.** writing down; recording. **2.** entry; record; (*leg.*) deed; метри́ческая з. registration of vital statistics.

зап|и́ть, ью́, ьёшь, *past* ~и́л, ~ила́, ~и́ло, *pf.* (*of* ~ива́ть) **1.** (*coll.*; *past* ~и́л) to take to drink; to go on a blind. **2.** (*past* ~и́л; + *a.* and *i.*) to wash down (with); to take (with, after); з. пилю́лю водо́й to take a pill with water.

запиха́|ть, ю, *pf.* (*coll.*) to cram into.

запи́хива|ть, ю, *impf. of* запиха́ть.

запих|ну́ть, ну́, нёшь, *pf.* (*coll.*) = ~а́ть.

запи́чка|ть, ю, *pf.* (*coll.*) to stuff, cram.

запи|шу́, ~ше́шь, *see* ~са́ть.

запла́кан|ный (~, ~а), *adj.* tear-stained; in tears.

запла́|кать, чу, чешь, *pf.* to begin to cry.

заплани́р|овать, ую, *pf. of* плани́ровать¹.

запла́т|а, ы, *f.* patch (*in garments*); наложи́ть ~у (на+*a.*) to patch.

заплата́|ть, ю, *pf.* (*of* плата́ть) (*coll.*) to patch.

запла|ти́ть, чу́, ~тишь, *pf. of* плати́ть.

заплачк|а, и, *f.* (*anthrop.*; *dial.*) lamentation (*of bride, in course of wedding rite; at funerals*).

запла́|чу, чешь, *see* ~кать.

запла|чу́, ~тишь, *see* ~ти́ть.

заплёван|ный (~, ~а), *p.p.p. of* заплева́ть and *adj.* bespattered (with spittle); dirty.

запл|ева́ть, юю́, юёшь, *pf.* (*coll.*) to spit on; to spit at; (*fig.*) to rain curses on.

заплёвыва|ть, ю, *impf. of* заплева́ть.

запле|ска́ть, ска́ю, and ~щу́, ~щешь, *pf.* **1.** to splash. **2.** to begin to splash.

заплёскива|ть, ю, *impf. of* заплеска́ть and заплесну́ть.

заплёсневелый, *adj.* mouldy, mildewed.

заплёсневе|ть, ю, *pf. of* плёсневеть.

заплесн|у́ть, у́, ёшь, *pf.* (*of* заплёскивать) (*coll.*) to splash into; to swamp.

запле|сти́, ту́, тёшь, *past* ~л, ~ла́, *pf.* to braid, plait.

запле|сти́сь, ту́сь, тёшься, *past* ~лся, ~ла́сь, *pf.* **1.** (*coll.*) to stumble, be unsteady on one's legs; to falter (*in speech*). **2.** (*dial.*) to wind (*intrans.*). **3.** *pass. of* ~сти́.

заплета́|ть(ся), ю(сь), *impf. of* заплести́(сь).

заплёчный, *adj.* over the shoulders; з. мешо́к rucksack; з. ма́стер (*obs.*) executioner.

заплёч|ье, ья, g. pl. ~ий and ~ьев, *n.* shoulder-blade.

запломбир|ова́ть, у́ю, *pf.* (*of* пломбирова́ть and ~о́вывать) **1.** з. зуб to stop, fill a tooth. **2.** to seal.

запломбиро́выва|ть, ю, *impf. of* запломбирова́ть.

заплута́|ться, юсь, *pf.* (*coll.*) to lose one's way, stray.

запл|ы́в, а, *m.* round, heat (*of water sports*).

заплыва́|ть, ю, *impf. of* заплы́ть.

заплы́|ть¹, ву́, вёшь, *past* ~л, ~ла́, ~ло, *pf.* to swim far out; to sail away.

заплы́|ть², ву́, вёшь, *past* ~л, ~ла́, ~ло, *pf.* to be swollen; to be bloated; ~вшие жи́ром глаза́ bloated eyes.

запн|у́ться, у́сь, ёшься, *pf. of* запина́ться.

запове́да|ть, ю, *pf.* (*of* запове́дывать) (*rhet.*) to command.

запове́дник, а, *m.* reserve; preserve; госуда́рственный з. national park.

запове́дн|ый, *adj.* **1.** prohibited; з. лес forest reserve; ~ое име́ние entailed estate. **2.** (*poet.*) precious.

запове́дыва|ть, ю, *impf. of* запове́дать.

за́повед|ь, и, *f.* precept; (*rel. and fig.*) commandment; де́сять ~ей the Ten Commandments.

заподо́зрива|ть, ю, *impf. of* заподо́зрить.

заподо́зр|ить, ю, ишь, *pf.* **1.** (+ *a.* в+*p.*) to suspect (of); его́ ~или в прича́стности к за́говору he was suspected of complicity in the plot. **2.** (*obs.*) to suspect, be suspicious of; з. чьи-н. наме́рения to suspect someone's intentions.

запо́ем, *adv.*; пить з. to be a heavy drinker; (*fig., coll.*) heavily, unrestrainedly; чита́ть з. to read avidly; кури́ть з. to smoke like a chimney.

запозда́лый, *adj.* belated.

запозда́|ть, ю, *pf.* (*of* запа́здывать) (с+*i.*) to be late (with); он ~л с упла́той аре́нды he is late in paying his rent.

запо|и́ть, ю́, и́шь, *pf.* (*coll., dial.*) to give too much to drink (to).

запо́|й, я, *m.* (addiction to periodical) hard drinking; пить ~ем, *see* ~ем; страда́ть ~ем to have a weakness for the bottle.

запо́й|ный, *adj. of* ~; з. пери́од drunken bout; з. пья́ница chronic drunkard.

запола́скива|ть, ю, *impf. of* заполоска́ть *and* заполосну́ть.

запо́лза|ть, ю, *pf.* to begin to crawl.

заполза́|ть, ю, *impf. of* заползти́.

заполз|ти́, у́, ёшь, *past* ~, ~ла́, *pf.* (в, под+*a.*) to creep, crawl (into, under).

запо́лн|ить, ю, ишь, *pf.* (*of* ~я́ть) to fill in, fill up; чем вы ~или вре́мя? how did you fill in the time?; з. бланк to fill in a form; з. пробе́л to fill a gap.

заполня́|ть, ю, *impf. of* запо́лнить.

заполон|и́ть, ю́, и́шь, *pf.* (*of* ~я́ть) (*folk poet. and arch.*) to take captive; (*fig.*) to captivate, enthrall.

заполон|я́ть, я́ю, *impf. of* ~и́ть.

заполо|ска́ть, щу́, ~щешь, *pf.* (*of* заполаскивать) (*coll.*) 1. to begin to rinse. 2. to rinse out.

заполо|ска́ться, щу́сь, ~щешься, *pf.* (*coll.*) 1. to begin to paddle. 2. to enjoy paddling.

заполосн|у́ть, у́, ёшь, *pf.* (*of* заполаскивать) (*coll.* to rinse out.

заполуч|а́ть, а́ю, *impf. of* ~и́ть.

заполуч|и́ть, у́, ~ишь, *pf.* (*of* ~а́ть) (*coll.*) to get hold of, pick up; я мог бы з. биле́ты на представле́ние в суббо́ту I could get tickets for Saturday's performance; з. на́сморк to pick up a cold.

заполя́рный, *adj.* (*geogr.*) 1. polar (*situated within one or other of the polar circles*). 2. trans-polar; з. возду́шный путь trans-polar air route.

заполя́рь|е, я, *n.* (*geogr.*) polar regions.

запомина́|ть(ся), ю(сь), *impf. of* запо́мнить(ся); ~ющее устро́йство computer memory.

запо́мн|ить, ю, ишь, *pf.* (*of* запомина́ть) 1. to memorize. 2. (*pf. only*) (+*neg.*; *coll.*) to remember; никто́ не ~ит тако́й жары́ no one remembers such heat.

запо́мн|иться, юсь, ишься, *pf.* (*of* запомина́ться) to be retained, stick in one's memory; ему́ ~ился день землетрясе́ния the day of the earthquake is stuck in his memory.

за́понк|а, и, *f.* cuff-link; stud.

запо́р¹, а, *m.* 1. bolt; lock; на ~(е) locked; bolted (and barred). 2. (*coll.*) closing; locking; bolting.

запо́р², а, *m.* constipation.

запора́шива|ть, ет, *impf. of* запороши́ть.

запоро́ж|ец, ца, *m.* (*hist.*) Zaporozhian Cossack.

запоро́жский, *adj.* (*hist.*) Zaporozhian.

запор|о́ть, ю́, ~ешь, *pf.* (*of* запа́рывать)

(*coll.*) 1. to flog to death. 2. to begin to talk (nonsense).

запорош|и́ть, и́т, *pf.* (*of* запора́шивать) 1. (+*i.*) to powder (with); (*impers.*) доро́гу ~и́ло сне́гом the road was powdered with snow; глаза́ мои́ ~и́ло пы́лью there is dust in my eyes. 2. to begin to powder.

запорхн|у́ть, у́, ёшь, *pf.* (*coll.*) to flutter (away, in).

запо|сти́ться, щу́сь, сти́шься, *pf.* (*coll.*) 1. to begin to fast. 2. to make oneself weak by fasting.

запотева́|ть, ю, *impf. of* запоте́ть.

запоте́лый, *adj.* misted; dim; (*from perspiration*).

запоте́|ть, ю, *pf.* (*of* поте́ть *and* ~ва́ть) to mist over.

започива́|ть, ю, *pf.* (*obs.*) to retire (*for the night*).

зап|ою́, оёшь, *see* ~е́ть.

запра́вдашный (*coll., dial.*) true, authentic.

заправи́л|а, ы, *m.* (*coll.*) boss.

заправ|ить, лю, ишь, *pf.* (*of* ~ля́ть) 1. to insert; з. брю́ки в сапоги́ to tuck one's trousers into one's boots. 2. to prepare; to adjust; з. ла́мпу to trim a lamp; з. автомоби́ль бензи́ном to fill a car up with petrol. 3. (+*i.*) to mix in; to season (with); з. со́ус муко́й to thicken a sauce with flour.

заправ|иться, люсь, ишься, *pf.* (*of* ~ля́ться) 1. (*coll.*) to satisfy hunger; to eat one's fill. 2. з. (горю́чим) to refuel (*intrans.*).

запра́вк|а, и, *f.* 1. seasoning. 2. refuelling.

заправля́|ть(ся), ю(сь), *impf. of* запра́вить(ся).

запра́вочн|ый, *adj.* з. пункт, ~ая ста́нция (petrol) filling station.

запра́вский, *adj.* (*coll.*) real, true; thorough; он — з. моря́к he is a real sailor.

запра́шива|ть, ю, *impf. of* запроси́ть.

запреде́льный, *adj.* (*obs.*) 1. lying beyond the bounds (of). 2. fantastic; other-worldly.

запресто́льн|ый, *adj.* (*eccl.*) situated behind the altar; з. о́браз altar-piece; ~ое украше́ние reredos.

запре́т, а, *m.* prohibition, ban; наложи́ть з. (на+*a.*) to place a ban (on).

запрети́тельн|ый, *adj.* prohibitive; prohibitory; (*econ.*) ~ая по́шлина prohibitive duty.

запре|ти́ть, щу́, ти́шь, *pf.* (*of* ~ща́ть) to prohibit, forbid, ban; врач ~ти́л мне кури́ть, врач ~ти́л мне куре́ние the doctor has forbidden me to smoke; з. пье́су to ban a play.

запре́тн|ый, *adj.* forbidden; ~ая зо́на (*mil.*) restricted area.

запреща́|ть, ю, *impf. of* запрети́ть.

запреща́|ться, ется, *impf.* to be forbidden, to be prohibited; (*in official notices, etc.*) вход ~ется no entry; кури́ть ~ется no smoking.

запреще́ни|е, я, *n.* prohibition; (*leg.*) з. на
иму́щество distraint, arrest on property;
суде́бное з. injunction.

заприме́|тить, чу, тишь, *pf.* (*coll.*) 1. to
notice, perceive. 2. to recognize, spot; я
~тил его́ в толпе́ по кра́сной руба́шке I
spotted him in the crowd by his red shirt.

заприхо́д|овать, ую, *pf. of* приходовать.

запрограмми́р|овать, ую, *pf. of* программи́ровать.

запрода|ва́ть, ю́, ёшь, *impf. of* ~ть.

запрода́ж|а, и, *f.* (*comm.*) forward contract,
provisional sale.

запрода́ж|ный, *adj. of* ~а; ~ная за́пись
document concerning sale.

запрода́|ть, а́м, а́шь, а́ст, адим, адите,
аду́т, *past* ~ал, ~ала́, ~ало, *pf.* (*of* ~ава́ть)
(*comm.*) to conclude a forward contract (on),
sell on part-payment; to agree to sell.

запроекти́р|овать, ую, *pf. of* проекти́ровать[1] 1.

запроки́дыва|ть, ю, *impf. of* запроки́нуть.

запроки́н|уть, у, ешь, *pf.* (*coll.*) to throw
back; он захохота́л ~ув го́лову he threw
back his head and guffawed.

запроки́н|уться, усь, ешься, *pf.* (*coll.*) to
lean back, slump back.

запропада́|ть, ю, *impf. of* запропа́сть.

запропа|сти́ть, щу́, сти́шь, *pf.* (*coll.*) to
mislay.

запропа|сти́ться, щу́сь, сти́шься, *pf.* (*coll.*)
to get lost, disappear; куда́ ты ~сти́лся?
where on earth did you get to?

запропа́|сть, ду́, дёшь, *past* ~л, *pf.* (*of*
~да́ть) (*coll.*) to get lost, disappear.

запро́с, а, *m.* 1. inquiry; (*polit.*) question.
2. overcharging; це́ны без ~а fixed prices.
3. (*pl. only*) spiritual needs.

запро|си́ть, шу́, ~сишь, *pf.* (*of* запра́шивать) 1. (о+*p.*) to inquire (about); (+*a.*)
to inquire (of), question; мини́стра ~си́ли
о его́ расхо́дах the Minister was questioned
about his expenditure. 2. з. сли́шком высо́кую це́ну to ask an exorbitant price.

за́просто, *adv.* (*coll.*) without ceremony,
without formality.

запротоколи́р|овать, ую, *pf.* to enter in the
minutes.

запротоко́л|ить, ю, ишь, *pf.* (*coll.*) = ~и́ровать.

запро|шу́, ~сишь, *see* ~си́ть.

зап|ру́, рёшь, *see* ~ере́ть.

запру́д|а, ы, *f.* 1. dam, weir 2. mill-pond.

запру|ди́ть, жу́, ~ди́шь, *pf.* 1. (~ди́шь) to
dam. 2. (~ди́шь) (*fig., coll.*) to block (up);
to fill to overflowing.

запружа́|ть, ю, *impf. of* запруди́ть.

запру́жива|ть, ю, *impf.*, = запружа́ть.

запры́га|ть, ю, *pf.* to begin to jump; (*coll.*)
се́рдце у неё ~ло her heart began to

thump.

запры́гива|ть, ю, *impf. of* запры́гнуть.

запры́гн|уть, у, ешь, *pf.* (за+*a.*; *coll.*) to
leap (over).

запры́ска|ть, ю, *pf.* (*coll.*) 1. to begin to
sprinkle. 2. to besprinkle.

запры́скива|ть, ю, *impf. of* запры́скать.

запряга́|ть, ю, *impf. of* запря́чь.

запря́жк|а, и, *f.* 1. harnessing. 1. equipage.

запря́|тать, чу, чешь, *pf.* (*coll.*) to hide.

запря́|таться, чусь, чешься, *pf.* (*coll.*) to
hide oneself.

запря́тыва|ть(ся), ю(сь), *impf. of* запря́тать(ся).

запря́|чь, гу́, жёшь, гу́т, *past* ~г, ~гла́, *pf.*
(*of* ~га́ть) to harness (*also fig.*); з. воло́в to
yoke oxen.

запря́|чься, гу́сь, жёшься, гу́тся, *past* ~гся,
~гла́сь, *pf.* 1. *pass. of* ~чь. 2. (*fig., coll.*) to
harness oneself; to buckle to, get down to.

запу́ганный *p.p.p. of* запуга́ть *and adj.*
broken-spirited.

запуга́|ть, ю, *pf.* to intimidate, cow.

запу́гива|ть, ю, *impf. of* запуга́ть.

запу́дрива|ть, ю, *impf. of* запу́дрить.

запу́др|ить, ю, ишь, *pf.* to powder.

запузы́рива|ть, ю, *impf.* (*sl.*) to do something vigorously; з. на фортепья́но to
knock out a tune on the piano.

запул|и́ть, ю́, и́шь, *pf.* (+*a. or i.*; *coll., dial.*)
to sling, chuck; з. ка́мнем в окно́ to sling a
stone at a window.

запу́с|кать, ка́ю, *impf. of* ~ти́ть.

запусте́лый, *adj.* neglected; desolate.

запустени|е, я, *n.* neglect; desolation.

запусте́|ть, ет, *pf.* to fall into neglect; to
become desolate.

запу|сти́ть[1], щу́, ~сти́шь, *pf.* (*of* ~ска́ть)
1. (+*i.* в+*a.*; *coll.*) to throw (at), fling (at);
он ~сти́л кирпичо́м в окно́ he flung a brick
at the window. 2. (в+*a.*) to thrust (*hands,
etc.*, into); ко́шка ~сти́ла ко́гти в мышь the
cat dug its claws into the mouse; з. ко́гти,
ла́пы, ру́ки (в+*a.*; *fig.*) to get one's hands
on; з. глаза́ (*pejor.*) to let one's eyes roam.
3. to start (up) (*mechanism*); з. мото́р to
start up the engine; з. раке́ту to launch
a rocket. 4. (в+*a.*) (*coll.*) to put (into), let
loose (in); з. коро́в в луг to let cows loose
in a meadow.

запу|сти́ть[2], щу́, ~сти́шь, *pf.* (*of* ~ска́ть)
1. to neglect, allow to fall into neglect; з.
дела́ to neglect one's affairs. 2. to allow to
neglect a garden. 2. to allow to develop
unchecked; он ~сти́л на́сморк и тепе́рь
заболе́л бронхи́том he neglected his cold
and now he is ill with bronchitis.

запу́тан|ный, *p.p.p. of* запу́тать *and adj.*
tangled; (*fig.*) intricate, involved; з. вопро́с
knotty question.

запу́та|ть, ю, *pf.* **1.** to tangle (up). **2.** (*fig.*) to confuse; to complicate; to muddle; еró сообще́ние ~ло де́ло his statement has complicated matters; тако́го ро́да вопро́сы то́лько ~ют кандида́тов questions of this kind will only confuse the candidates. **3.** (в+*a.*; *fig.*) to involve (in).

запу́та|ться, юсь, *pf.* **1.** to become entangled; to foul (*intrans.*); (в+*p.*; *fig.*) to entangle oneself (in), be caught (in). **2.** (в+*p.*; *fig.*) to become entangled (in), become involved (in); to become complicated; з. в долга́х to become involved in debts; докла́дчик ~лся в слова́х the lecturer became tied up in knots.

запу́тыва|ть(ся), ю(сь), *impf. of* запу́тать(ся).

запуш|и́ть, и́т *pf.* to cover lightly (*of snow or frost*).

запу́щен|ный, *p.p.p. of* запусти́ть² *and adj.* neglected.

запча́ст|ь, и, *f.* spare part.

запыла́|ть, ю, *pf.* to blaze up, flare up.

запыл|и́ть, ю́, и́шь, *pf.* (*of* пыли́ть) to cover with dust, make dusty.

запыл|и́ться, ю́сь, и́шься, *pf.* (*of* пыли́ться) to become dusty.

запыха́|ться, юсь, *impf.* (*coll.*) to puff, pant.

запы́ха|ться, юсь, *pf.* (*coll.*) to be out of breath.

запьяне́|ть, ю, *pf.* (*coll.*) to get drunk.

запья́нств|овать, ую, *pf.* to take to drink.

запя́сть|е, я, *n.* **1.** wrist; (*anat.*) carpus. **2.** (*poet.*) bracelet.

запят|а́я, о́й, *f.* **1.** comma. **2.** (*coll.*) difficulty, snag.

запя́т|ки, ок, *no sing.* footboard (*at back of carriage*).

запятна́|ть, ю, *pf. of* пятна́ть.

зарабаты́ва|ть(ся), ю(сь), *impf. of* зарабо́тать(ся).

зарабо́та|ть, ю, *pf.* **1.** to earn. **2.** to begin to work; to start (up).

зарабо́та|ться, юсь, *pf.* (*coll.*) **1.** to overwork, tire oneself out with work. **2.** to work late; он вчера́ ~лся далеко́ за́ по́лночь he went on working long after midnight last night.

за́работн|ый, *adj.*; ~ая пла́та wages, pay, salary.

за́работ|ок, ка, *m.* **1.** earnings; лёгкий з. easy money. **2.** (*pl. only*) (seasonal) labour, work.

зара́внива|ть, ю, *impf. of* заровня́ть.

заража́емост|ь, и, *f.* susceptibility to infection.

заража́|ть(ся), ю(сь), *impf. of* зарази́ть(ся).

зараже́ни|е, я, *n.* infection.

зара|жу́, зи́шь, *see* ~зи́ть.

зара́з, *adv.* (*coll.*) at once; at a sitting; at one fell swoop.

зара́з|а, ы, *f.* **1.** infection, contagion. **2.** (*fig., coll.*) pest, plague (*of person*).

зарази́тел|ьный (~ен, ~ьна), *adj.* infectious; catching; (*fig.*) з. смех infectious laughter.

зара|зи́ть, жу́, зи́шь, *pf.* (*of* ~жа́ть) (+*i.*) to infect (with); (*also fig.*) з. свои́м приме́ром to infect with one's example.

зара|зи́ться, жу́сь, зи́шься, *pf.* (*of* ~жа́ться) (+*i.*) to be infected (with); catch (*also fig.*).

зара́з|ный (~ен, ~на), *adj.* **1.** infectious; contagious. **2.** of *or* for infectious diseases; з. бара́к infectious diseases ward; з. больно́й patient suffering from infectious disease, infectious case; *as noun* з., ~ного, *m.*, ~ная, ~ной, *f.* infectious case.

зара́не, *adv.* (*obs.*) = ~е.

зара́нее, *adv.* beforehand; in good time; заплати́ть з. to pay in advance; преступле́ние с з. обду́манным наме́рением premeditated crime; ра́доваться з. (+*d.*) to look forward (to).

зарапо́рт|ова́ться, у́юсь, *pf.* (*coll.*) to let one's tongue run away with one.

зараста́|ть, ю, *impf. of* зарасти́.

зараст|и́, у́, ёшь, *past* заро́с, заросла́, *pf.* **1.** (+*i.*) to be overgrown (with). **2.** (*of a wound*) to heal, skin over.

зарв|а́ться, у́сь, ёшься, *past* ~а́лся, ~ала́сь, ~ало́сь, *pf.* (*of* зарыва́ться) (*coll.*) to go too far; to overstep the mark.

зарде́|ть, ю, *pf.* (*poet.*) = ~ться I.

зарде́|ться, юсь, *pf.* (*poet.*) **1.** to redden, grow red. **2.** to blush.

за́рев|о, а, *n.* glow; з. (от) пожа́ра the glow of a fire.

зар|ево́й, *adj. of* ~ево.

зарегистри́р|овать, ую, *pf.* (*of* регистри́ровать) to register.

зарегистри́р|оваться, уюсь, *pf.* (*of* регистри́роваться) **1.** to register oneself. **2.** (*coll.*) to register one's marriage. **3.** *pass. of* ~овать.

зарегистр|ова́ть(ся), у́ю(сь), pf., = ~и́ровать(ся).

заре́з, а, m. 1. (*coll.*) disaster; до ~у extremely, badly, urgently; мне до ~у нужны́ пять рубле́й I badly need five roubles. **2.** (*dial.*) killing, slaughtering.

заре́|зать, жу, жешь, *pf.* **1.** to murder; to knife; з. свинью́ to stick a pig; (*of a wolf*) to devour, kill; хоть заре́жь (*coll.*) extremely, urgently; come what may. **2.** (*fig.*) to undo, be the undoing of; to do for; без ножа́ з. to do for; to make mincemeat of.

зареза́|ть(ся), ю(сь), *impf. of* заре́зать(ся).

заре́|заться, жусь, жешься, *pf.* (*coll.*) to cut one's throat.

зарезыва|ть(ся), ю(сь), *impf.,* = заре́-
за́ть(ся).

зарека́|ться, ю́сь, *impf.* of заре́чься.

зарекоменд|ова́ть, у́ю, *pf. only in phrase* з.
себя́ (+*i.*) to prove oneself, show oneself
(to be); хорошо́ з. себя́ to show to advantage.

зарекомендо́выва|ть, ю, *impf.* of зареко-
мендова́ть.

заре|ку́сь, чёшься, ку́тся, *see* ∼чься.

заре́чный, *adj.* situated on the other side of
the river.

заре́чь|е, я, *n.* part of town, etc., on the
other side of a river.

заре́|чься, ку́сь, чёшься, ку́тся, *past* ∼кся,
∼кла́сь, *pf.* (of ∼ка́ться) (+*inf.*; *coll.*) to
renounce; to promise to give up, vow to
give up; он ∼кся кури́ть he has promised
to give up smoking.

заржа́ве|ть, ет, *pf.* (of ржа́веть) to rust; to
have grown rusty.

заржа́влен|ный (∼, ∼а), *adj.* rusty.

зарис|ова́ть, у́ю, *pf.* (of ∼о́вывать) to sketch.

зарис|ова́ться, у́юсь, *pf.* (of ∼о́вываться)
(*coll.*) to spend too much time in drawing.

зарисо́вк|а, и, *f.* **1.** sketching. **2.** sketch.

зарисо́выва|ть(ся), ю(сь), *impf.* of зарисо-
ва́ть(ся).

за́р|иться, юсь, ишься, *impf.* (of по∼)
(на+*a.*; *coll.*) to hanker (after).

зарни́ц|а, ы, *f.* summer lightning.

заровня́|ть, ю, *pf.* (of зара́внивать) to level,
even up; з. я́му to fill up a hole.

заро|ди́ть, жу́, ди́шь, *pf.* (of ∼жда́ть) to
generate, engender (*also fig.*).

заро|ди́ться, жу́сь, ди́шься, *pf. pass.* of
∼ди́ть; (*fig.*) to arise; у него́ ∼ди́лось сом-
не́ние a doubt arose in his mind.

заро́дыш, а, *m.* (*biol.*) foetus; (*bot.*) bud;
(*fig.*) embryo, germ; подави́ть в ∼е to nip
in the bud.

заро́дышевый, *adj.* embryonic.

зарожда́|ть(ся), ю(сь), *impf.*/of зароди́ть(ся).

зарожде́ни|е, я, *n.* conception; (*fig.*) origin.

заро|жу́, ди́шь, *see* ∼ди́ть.

зарок, а, *m.* **1.** (solemn) promise, vow,
pledge, undertaking; дать з. to pledge oneself, give an undertaking. **2.** (*dial.*) charm,
incantation.

зарон|и́ть, ю́, ∼ишь, *pf.* **1.** (*coll.*) to drop
(behind); to let fall. **2.** (*fig.*) to excite,
arouse; з. сомне́ния to give rise to doubts.

зарон|и́ться, ю́сь, ∼ишься, *pf.* (в+*a.*; *obs.*)
to sink in, make an impression (on).

зароня́|ть, ю, *impf.* of зарони́ть.

за́росл|ь, и, *f.* brake; thicket.

зар|о́ю, о́ешь, *see* ∼ы́ть.

зарпла́т|а, ы, *f.* (*abbr.* of за́работная пла́та)
wages, pay, salary.

заруба́|ть, ю, *impf.* of заруби́ть.

зарубе́жный, *adj.* foreign.

заруб|и́ть, лю́, ∼ишь, *pf.* (of ∼а́ть) **1.** to kill
(*with sabre, axe, etc.*). **2.** to notch, make an
incision (on); ∼и́ э́то себе́ на носу́, на лбу,
на стене́ (*coll.*) put that in your pipe and
smoke it. **3.** (*tech.*) to hew.

зару́бк|а, и, *f.* **1.** notch; incision. **2.** (*tech.*)
hewing.

зарубц|ева́ться, у́ется, *pf.* (of рубцева́ться
and ∼о́вываться) to cicatrize.

зарубцо́выва|ться, ется, *impf.* of зарубце-
ва́ться.

зару́бщик, а, *m.* (coal-)hewer.

заруга́|ть, ю, *pf.* (*coll.*) to abuse, scold.

заруми́нива|ть(ся), ю(сь), *impf.* of зару-
мя́нить(ся).

зарумя́н|ить, ю, ишь, *pf.* to redden.

зарумя́н|иться, юсь, ишься, *pf.* **1.** to
redden (*intrans.*); to blush, colour. **2.** (*coll.*)
to brown, bake brown.

заруч|а́ться, а́юсь, *impf.* of ∼и́ться.

заруч|и́ться, у́сь, и́шься, *pf.* **1.** (+*i.*) to
secure; з. подде́ржкой to enlist support;
з. согла́сием to obtain consent. **2.** (*sl.*) to
secure oneself (*in a suit at cards*).

зару́чк|а, и, *f.* (*coll.*) pull, protection.

зарыва́|ть, ю, *impf.* of зары́ть.

зарыва́|ться¹, юсь, *impf.* of зары́ться.

зарыва́|ться², юсь, *impf.* of зарва́ться.

зарыда́|ть, ю, *pf.* to begin to sob.

зар|ы́ть, о́ю, о́ешь, *pf.* (of ∼ыва́ть) to bury;
з. тала́нт в зе́млю (*fig.*) to bury one's talent,
hide one's light under a bushel.

зар|ы́ться, о́юсь, о́ешься, *pf.* (of ∼ыва́ться)
1. to bury oneself; з. лицо́м в поду́шку to
bury one's head in the pillow; з. в дере́вне
(*fig., coll.*) to bury oneself in the country;
з. в кни́ги to bury oneself in one's books.
2. (*mil.*) to dig in. **3.** (*dial.*) to become fussy.

зар|я́, и́, а. ∼ю́ and (*rare*) зо́рю, *pl.* зо́ри,
зо́рь, ∼я́м, and зо́рям, *f.* **1.** (*a.* ∼ю́) dawn,
daybreak; на ∼е́ at dawn, at daybreak;
встать с ∼ёй to rise at crack of dawn; что
ты встал ни свет ни з. ? what made you get
up at this unearthly hour ? **2.** (*a.* ∼ю́) (ве-
че́рняя) з. sunset, evening glow; от ∼й до
∼й from night to morning, all night long.
3. (*a.* ∼ю́) (*fig.*) start, outset; dawn, threshold. **4.** (*a.* зо́рю, *d. pl.* зо́рям) (*mil.*)
reveille; retreat; бить зо́рю to beat retreat.

заря́д, а, *m.* **1.** charge (*also electr.*), cartridge;
холосто́й з. blank cartridge; (*fig., coll.*)
round (*of drinks*). **2.** (*fig.*) fund, supply.

заря|ди́ть¹, жу́, ∼ди́шь, *pf.* (of ∼жа́ть) **1.**
to load (*fire-arm*). **2.** (*electr.*) to charge.

заря|ди́ть², жу́, ди́шь, *pf.* (*coll.*) to keep
on, persist in; с утра́ ∼ди́л дождь it has
kept on raining since the morning; он
∼ди́л одно́ и то же he keeps saying the
same thing over and over again.

заря|диться, жусь, ~дишься, *pf.* (*of* ~жаться) 1. to be loaded; (*electr.*) to be charged. 2. (*fig., coll.*) to cheer oneself up, revive oneself.

заря́дк|а, и, *f.* 1. loading (*of fire-arms*); (*electr.*) charging. 2. exercises; drill.

заря́д|ный, *adj. of* ~; з. я́щик ammunition wagon.

заряжа́|ть(ся), ю(сь), *impf. of* заряди́ть(ся).

заряжа́|ющий, *pres. part. act. of* ~ть; *as noun* з., ~ющего, *m.* (*mil.*) loader.

заря́|жу́, ~ди́шь, *see* ~ди́ть.

заса́д|а, ы, *f.* ambush.

заса|ди́ть, жу́, ~дишь, *pf.* (*of* ~живать) 1. (+ *a. and i.*) to plant (with); з. сад плодо́выми дере́вьями to plant a garden with fruit-trees. 2. (+ *a.* в + *a.*; *coll.*) to plant (into), plunge (into), drive (into). 3. (*coll.*) to shut in, confine; to keep in; з. (в тюрьму́) to put in prison, lock up; боле́знь на це́лый ме́сяц ~ди́ла меня́ в го́спиталь illness kept me in hospital for a whole month. 4. (+ *a.* за + *a.*; *coll.*) to set (to); его́ ~ди́ли за изуче́ние ру́сского языка́ he was set to learn Russian. 5. (в + *a.*) get (*a knife, axe, etc.*) stuck (in).

заса́дк|а, и, *f.* planting.

заса́жива|ть, ю, *impf. of* засади́ть.

заса́жива|ться, юсь, *impf.* 1. *impf. of* засе́сть. 2. *pass. of* ~ть.

заса|жу́, ~дишь, *see* ~ди́ть.

заса́лива|ть¹, ю, *impf. of* засали́ть.

заса́лива|ть², ю, *impf. of* засоли́ть.

заса́л|ить, ю, ишь, *pf.* (*of* ~ивать¹) to soil, make greasy.

заса́рива|ть, ю, *impf. of* засори́ть.

заса́сыва|ть, ю, *impf. of* засоса́ть.

заса́харен|ный, *p.p.p. of* заса́харить *and adj.* candied; ~ные фру́кты crystallized fruits, candied fruits.

заса́харива|ть, ю, *impf. of* заса́харить.

заса́хар|ить, ю, ишь, *pf.* (*of* ~ивать) to candy.

засверка́|ть, ю, *pf.* to begin to sparkle, begin to twinkle.

засве|ти́ть, чу́, ~ти́шь, *pf.* 1. to light. 2. (+ *d.* в + *a.*; *coll.*) to strike, hit; з. кому́-н. в физионо́мию кулако́м to stick one's fist in someone's face.

засве|ти́ться, ~ти́тся, *pf.* to light up (*also fig.*).

засветле́|ть, ю, *pf.* to show up.

за́светло, *adv.* (*coll.*) before nightfall, before dark.

засве|чу́, ~тишь, *see* ~ти́ть.

засвиде́тельств|овать, ую, *pf. of* свиде́тельствовать 2.

засви|ста́ть, щу́, ~щешь = ~сте́ть.

засви|сте́ть, щу́, сти́шь, *pf.* 1. to begin to whistle.

засда|ва́ться, юсь, ёшься, *impf. of* ~ться.

засда́|ться, мся, шься, стся, ди́мся, ди́тесь, ду́тся, *past* ~лся, ~ла́сь, *pf.* (*sl.*) to misdeal.

засе́в, а, *m.* 1. sowing. 2. seed, seed-corn. 3. sown area.

засева́|ть, ю, *impf. of* засе́ять.

заседа́ни|е, я, *n.* meeting; conference; session, sitting.

заседа́тел|ь, я, *m.* assessor; прися́жный з. juryman.

заседа́|ть, ю, *impf.* to sit; to meet.

засе́ива|ть, ю, *impf. of* засе́ять.

засе́|к, кла, *see* ~чь.

за́сек|а, и, *f.* abat(t)is.

засека́|ть(ся), ет(ся), *impf. of* засе́чь(ся).

засекре́|тить, чу, тишь, *pf.* 1. to place on secret list; to classify as secret, restrict. 2. to give access to secret documents; to admit to secret work.

засекре́ченный, *p.p.p. of* засекре́тить *and adj.* hush-hush, secret.

засекре́чива|ть, ю, *impf. of* засекре́тить.

засе|ку́, чёшь, ку́т, *see* ~чь.

засе́|л, ла, *see* ~сть.

заселе́ни|е, я, *n.* settlement; colonization.

заселённый, *p.p.p. of* засели́ть *and adj.* populated; inhabited; ре́дко з. sparsely populated.

засел|и́ть, ю, и́шь, *pf.* (*of* ~я́ть) to settle; to colonize; to populate; з. но́вый дом to occupy a new house.

засел|я́ть, я́ю, *impf. of* ~и́ть.

засемен|и́ть, ю́, и́шь, *pf.* to begin to mince (*of gait*).

зас|е́сть, я́ду, я́дешь, *past* ~е́л, *pf.* (*o,* ~а́живаться) (*coll.*) 1. to sit down (to). 2. to sit firm, sit tight; to ensconce onself; з. в тюрьму́ to go to prison. 3. (в + *p.*) to lodge (in), stick (in); пу́ля ~е́ла у него́ в боку́ a bullet had lodged in his side; моти́в ~е́л у меня́ в голове́ (*fig.*) the tune has stuck in my head.

засе́чк|а, и, *f.* 1. notch, mark. 2. (*geogr.*) intersection. 3. (*med.*) canker.

засе́|чь, ку́, чёшь, ку́т, *past* ~к, ~кла, *pf.* (*of* ~ка́ть) 1. to flog to death. 2. to notch. 3. (*geogr.*) to determine by intersection.

засе́|чься, чётся, ку́тся, *past* ~кся, ~кла́сь, *pf.* (*of* ~ка́ться) to overreach itself, cut, hitch (*of horse*).

засе́|ять, ю, ешь, *pf.* (*of* ~ва́ть *and* ~ивать) to sow.

заси|де́ть, ди́т, *pf.* (*of* ~живать) (*coll.*) to fly-spot.

заси|де́ться, жу́сь, ди́шься, *pf.* (*of* ~живаться) (*coll.*) to sit too long, stay too long; to sit up late; to stay late; з. за рабо́той to sit up late working; з. в де́вках, *see* де́вка.

засиженный, *p.p.p.* of засидеть and *adj.* (*coll.*) з. (мухами) fly-blown.

засижива|ть(ся), **ю(сь)**, *impf.* of засидеть(ся).

засиль|е, **я**, *no pl.*, *n.* (*pejor.*) domination, sway.

засим, *adv.* (*obs.*) hereafter, after this.

засине|ть(ся), **ю(сь)**, *pf.* to become blue; to appear blue (in the distance).

засинива|ть, **ю**, *impf.* of засинить.

засин|ить, **ю**, **ишь**, *pf.* (*of* ~ивать) 1. to over-blue (*in laundering*). 2. to cover with blue paint.

засин|ять, **яю**, = ~ивать.

засия|ть, **ю**, *pf.* 1. to begin to shine, begin to beam. 2. to appear, come out; месяц ~л из-за туч the moon appeared from behind the clouds.

заска|кать, **чу**, ~чешь, *pf.* 1. to begin to jump; to break into a gallop. 2. (*impf.* ~кивать) (в+*a.*) to gallop (away to, up to).

заска|каться, **чусь**, ~чешься, *pf.* (*coll.*) to gallop until exhausted.

заскакива|ть, **ю**, *impf.* of заскакать 2 and заскочить.

заскво|зить, **зит**, *pf.* to begin to show light through.

заскирд|овать, **ую**, *pf.* of скирдовать.

заскоб|ить, **лю**, **ишь**, *pf.* (*coll.*) to place in brackets.

заскок, **а**, *m.* (*coll.*) 1. leap, jump. 2. crazy idea; это у тебя з.? have you gone crazy?, are you out of your mind?

заскорузлый, *adj.* 1. hardened, calloused. 2. (*fig.*) coarsened, callous. 3. (*fig.*) backward, retarded.

заскоруз|нуть, **ну**, **нешь**, *past* ~, ~ла, *pf.* 1. to harden, coarsen, become callous; (*also fig.*). 2. (*fig.*) to stagnate; to become retarded.

заскоч|ить, **у**, ~ишь, *pf.* (*of* заскакивать) 1. (за+*a.*, на+*a.*) to jump, spring (behind, onto). 2. (в+*a.*; *fig.*) to drop in (to, at).

засла|стить, **щу**, **стишь**, *pf.* (*of* ~щивать) 1. to take (*medicine, etc.*) with something sweet. 2. to sweeten, put sugar into.

за|слать, **шлю**, **шлёшь**, *pf.* (*of* ~сылать) to send, despatch; з. не по адресу to send to the wrong address; з. шпиона to send out a spy.

заслащива|ть, **ю**, *impf.* of засластить.

засле|дить, **жу**, **дишь**, *pf.* (*of* ~живать) (*coll.*) to leave dirty foot-marks on.

заслёжива|ть, **ю**, *impf.* of заследить.

засле|зиться, **зится**, *pf.* to begin to water.

заслеп|ить, **лю**, **ишь**, *pf.* (*of* ~лять) (*coll.*) to blind.

заслепля|ть, **ю**, *impf.* of заслепить.

заслон, **а**, *m.* 1. screen, barrier. 2. (*mil.*) covering force.

заслон|ить, **ю**, **ишь** and (*coll.*) ~ишь, *pf. and* (*of* ~ять) 1. to hide, cover; to shield, screen. 2. (*fig.*) to push into the background.

заслон|иться, **юсь**, **ишься** and (*coll.*) ~ишься, *pf.* (*of* ~яться) 1. (от) to shield oneself, screen oneself (from). 2. *pass.* of ~ить.

заслонк|а, **и**, *f.* oven-door; stove-door.

заслон|ять(ся)[1], **яю(сь)**, *impf.* of ~ить(ся).

заслоня|ться[2], **юсь**, *pf.* (*coll.*) to begin to pace up and down.

заслуг|а, **и**, *f.* merit, desert; service; contribution; их наказали по ~ам they have been punished according to their deserts; у него большие ~и перед родным городом he has rendered great services to his home town.

заслуженно, *adv.* deservedly; according to (one's) deserts.

заслужен|ный (and ~ный), *p.p.p.* of заслужить *adj.* 1. deserved, merited. 2. meritorious, of merit; (*as honorific in U.S.S.R.*) Honoured. 3. ~ный профессор professor emeritus. 4. (*fig., joc.*) time-honoured; good old.

заслужива|ть, **ю**, *impf.* (*of* заслужить) (+*g.*) to deserve, merit.

заслужива|ться, **юсь**, *impf.* 1. *impf.* of заслужиться. 2. *pass.* of ~ть.

заслуж|ить, **у**, ~ишь, *pf.* (*of* ~ивать) (+*a.*) 1. to deserve, merit; win, earn. 2. (*coll., obs.*) to repay, pay back. 3. (*dial.*) to atone for, make up for.

заслуж|иться, **усь**, ~ишься, *pf.* (*of* ~иваться) (*coll.*) to serve for too long.

заслуш|ать, **аю**, *pf.* (*of* ~ивать) to hear, listen to (*a public or official pronouncement*).

заслуш|аться, **аюсь**, *pf.* (*of* ~иваться) (+*g.*) to listen spellbound (to).

заслушива|ть(ся), **ю(сь)**, *impf.* of заслушать(ся).

заслыш|ать, **у**, **ишь**, *pf.* 1. to hear, catch. 2. (*coll.*) to smell; з. запах to detect a smell.

заслыш|аться, **ится**, *pf.* (*coll.*) to begin to be audible; to be able to be heard.

заслюн|ить, **ю**, *impf.* of заслюнить.

заслюн|ить, **ю**, **ишь**, *pf.* of слюнить and ~ивать) (*coll.*) to slobber over.

засмалива|ть, **ю**, *impf.* of засмолить.

засмаркива|ть, **ю**, *impf.* of засморкать.

засматрива|ть, **ю**, *impf.* (в+*a.*; *coll.*) to look (into); to peep (into); з. в окно к кому-н. to look in at someone's window.

засматрива|ться, **юсь**, *impf.* of засмотреться.

засмеива|ть, **ю**, *impf.* of засмеять.

засме|ять, **ю**, **ёшь**, *pf.* (*coll.*) to ridicule.

засме|яться, **юсь**, **ёшься**, *pf.* to begin to laugh.

засмол|ить, **ю**, **ишь**, *pf.* to tar; to caulk.

засмо́рканный, *p.p.p. of* засморка́ть *and adj.* (*coll.*) snotty.

засморка́|ть, ю, *pf.* (*coll.*) to make snotty.

засмотр|е́ться, ю́сь, ~ишься, *pf.* (*of* засма́триваться) (на+*a.*) to be lost in contemplation (of), be carried away (by the sight of).

заснежённый, *adj.* snow-covered.

заснима́|ть, ю, *impf. of* засня́ть.

засн|иму́, и́мешь, *see* ~я́ть.

засн|у́ть, у́, ёшь, *pf.* (*of* засыпа́ть[1]) to go to sleep, fall asleep; (*fig.*) to die down; (*rhet.*) з. ве́чным сном to go to one's eternal rest.

засн|я́ть, иму́, и́мешь, *past* ~я́л, ~яла́, ~я́ло, *pf.* (*of* ~има́ть) to photograph, snap (*coll.*); (*cinema sl.*) to shoot.

засо́в, а, *m.* bolt, bar.

засо́ве|ститься, щусь, стишься, *pf.* (+*inf.*; *coll.*) to feel ashamed (to).

засо́выва|ть, ю, *impf. of* засу́нуть.

засо́л, а, *m.* salting; pickling.

засол|и́ть, ю́, ~и́шь, *pf.* (*of* заса́ливать[2]) to salt; to pickle.

засо́льщик, а, *m.* salter, pickler.

засоре́ни|е, я, *n.* littering, obstruction, clogging up.

засор|и́ть, ю́, и́шь, *pf.* (*of* заса́ривать *and* ~я́ть) 1. to clog, block up, stop. 2. to litter; to get dirt into; (*fig.*) з. чью-н. ду́шу to poison someone's mind.

засор|и́ться, ю́сь, и́шься, *pf.* (*of* заса́риваться *and* ~я́ться) to become obstructed, blocked up.

засоря́|ть(ся), ю(сь), *impf. of* засори́ть(ся).

засо́с, а, *m.* sucking in.

засос|а́ть, у́, ёшь, *pf.* (*of* заса́сывать) 1. to suck in, engulf, swallow up (*also fig.*) 2. (*coll.*) to exhaust by sucking. 3. to begin to suck.

засо́х|нуть, ну, нешь, *past* ~, ~ла, *pf.* (*of* засыха́ть) 1. to dry (up). 2. to wither.

за́спанный, *p.p.p. of* заспа́ть *and adj.* (*coll.*) sleepy.

засп|а́ть, лю́, и́шь, *past* ~а́л, ~ала́, ~а́ло, *pf.* (*of* засыпа́ть[2]) (*dial.*) to smother (a baby) in one's sleep, overlie.

засп|а́ться, лю́сь, и́шься, *past* ~а́лся, ~ала́сь, ~ а́лось, *pf.* (*of* засыпа́ться[1]) (*coll.*) to oversleep.

заспирт|ова́ть, у́ю, *pf.* (*of* ~о́вывать) to preserve in alcohol.

заспирто́выва|ть, ю, *impf. of* заспиртова́ть.

засп|лю́, и́шь, *see* ~а́ть.

заспо́р|ить, ю, ишь, *pf.* to begin to argue.

заспо́р|иться, юсь, ишься, *pf.* (*coll.*) to get carried away by argument.

заспор|и́ться, ю́сь, и́шься, *pf.* (*coll.*) to go well; to be a success.

засра́м|ить, лю́, и́шь, *pf.* (*coll.*) to put to shame.

заста́в|а, ы, *f.* 1. gate (*of town*). 2. (*hist.*; *mil.*) barrier. 3. (*mil.*) picket; outpost.

застава́|ть, ю́, ёшь, *impf. of* ~ть.

заста́в|ить[1], лю, ишь, *pf.* (*of* ~ля́ть[1]) 1. to cram, fill; з. ко́мнату ме́белью to cram a room with furniture. 2. to block up, obstruct. 3. (*library sl.*) з. кни́гу to put a book in the wrong place.

заста́в|ить[2], лю, ишь, *pf.* (*of* ~ля́ть[2]) (+*a. and inf.*) to compel, force, make; он ~ил нас жда́ть себя́ два часа́ he kept us waiting for two hours; они́ не ~или до́лго проси́ть себя́ they agreed with alacrity.

заста́вк|а, и, *f.* illumination (*in book or MS*)

заставля́|ть[1, 2], ю, *impf. of* заста́вить[1, 2].

заста́в|очный, *adj. of* ~ка.

заста́ива|ться, юсь, *impf. of* застоя́ться.

заста́|ну, нешь, *see* ~ть.

застарева́|ть, ю, *impf. of* застаре́ть.

застаре́лый, *adj.* inveterate; chronic.

застаре́|ть, ю, *pf.* (*of* ~ва́ть) (*coll.*) to become inveterate; to become chronic.

заста́|ть, ну, нешь, *pf.* (*of* ~ва́ть) to find; ~ли ли вы его́ до́ма? did you find him in?; я ~л его́ ещё спя́щим I found him still asleep; з. враспло́х to catch napping; з. на ме́сте преступле́ния to catch red-handed.

заста́|ю, ёшь, *see* ~ва́ть.

застега́|ть, ю, *pf.* (*coll.*) 1. to begin to flog. 2. з. до́ смерти to flog to death.

застёгива|ть, ю, *impf. of* застегну́ть.

застёгива|ться, юсь, *impf.* 1. *impf. of* застегну́ться. 2. *pass. of* ~ть. 3. to fasten, do up (*intrans.*); во́рот ~ется на пу́говицу the collar does up with a button.

застег|ну́ть, ну́, нёшь, *pf.* (*of* ~ивать) to fasten, do up; з. (на пу́говицы) to button up.

застег|ну́ться, ну́сь, нёшься, *pf.* (*of* ~иваться) to button oneself up; з. на все пу́говицы to do up all one's buttons.

застёжк|а, и, *f.* fastening; clasp, buckle, hasp; з.-мо́лния zip fastener.

застекл|и́ть, ю́, и́шь, *pf.* (*of* ~я́ть) to glaze, fit with glass; з. портре́т to frame a portrait.

застекл|я́ть, я́ю, *impf. of* ~и́ть.

застел|и́ть, ю́, ~ешь, *pf.*, = застла́ть 1.

застен|о́к, ка, *m.* torture-chamber.

засте́нчив|ый (~, ~а), *adj.* shy; bashful.

засти́|г, гла, *see* ~чь.

засти|га́ть, га́ю, *impf. of* ~гнуть *and* ~чь.

засти́|гнуть = ~чь.

застила́|ть, ю, *impf. of* застла́ть.

засти́лк|а, и, *f.* 1. covering. 2. floor-covering.

застир|а́ть, а́ю, *pf.* (*of* ~ывать) (*coll.*) 1. to wash off. 2. to ruin by washing. 3. (*rare*) to begin to wash.

засти́рыва|ть, ю, *impf. of* застира́ть.

за́|стить, щу, стишь, *impf.* (*coll.*) з. свет to stand in the light.

засти|чь, гну, гнешь, *past* ~г, ~гла, *pf.* (*of* ~гать) to catch; to take unawares; нас ~гла гроза́ we were caught by the storm.

заст|ла́ть, елю́, е́лешь, *pf.* (*of* ~ила́ть) 1. (+*i.*) to cover (with); з. ковро́м to carpet, lay a carpet (over). 2. (*fig.*) to hide from view; to cloud; облака́ ~ла́ли со́лнце clouds obscured the sun; слёзы ~ла́ли её глаза́ tears dimmed her eyes.

засто́|й, я, *m.* stagnation (*fig.*); в ~e at a standstill; (*polit.*, *pejor.*) 'the period of stagnation' (c. 1965–82); (*econ.*) depression; з. кро́ви (*med.*) haemostasia.

засто́й|ный, *adj.* stagnant (*fig.*); ~ные го́ды (*polit.*, *pejor.*) = ~; (*econ.*) unwanted, idle as a result of depression.

засто́льн|ый, *adj.* table-, occurring at table; ~ая бесе́да table-talk; ~ая пе́сня drinking-song; ~ая речь after-dinner speech.

застопорива|ть(ся), ю(сь), *impf. of* застопорить(ся).

застопор|ить, ю, ишь, *pf.* (*of* ~ивать) (*tech.*) to stop; (*fig.*, *coll.*) to bring to a standstill.

застопор|иться, юсь, ишься, *pf.* (*of* ~иваться) (*tech.*) to stop (*of a machine*); (*fig.*, *coll.*) to come to a standstill.

засто|я́ться, ю́сь, и́шься, *pf.* (*of* заста́иваться) 1. to stand too long. 2. to stagnate. 3. (*coll.*) to linger.

застра́гива|ть, ю, *impf. of* застрога́ть 2.

застра́ива|ть, ю, *impf. of* застро́ить.

застрахо́ван|ный, *p.p.p. of* застрахова́ть *and adj.* insured; *as noun* з., ~ного, *m.* insured person.

застрах|ова́ть, у́ю, *pf.* (*of* страхова́ть *and* ~о́вывать) (от) to insure (against).

застрах|ова́ться, у́юсь, *pf.* (*of* страхова́ться *and* ~о́вываться) to insure oneself.

застрахо́выва|ть(ся), ю(сь), *impf. of* застрахова́ть(ся).

застра́чива|ть, ю, *impf. of* застрочи́ть.

застраща́|ть, ю, *pf.* (*coll.*) to frighten, intimidate.

застра́щива|ть, ю, *impf. of* застраща́ть.

застрева́|ть, ю, *impf. of* застря́ть.

застре́лива|ть(ся), ю(сь), *impf. of* застрели́ть(ся).

застрел|и́ть, ю́, ~ишь, *pf.* (*of* ~ивать) to shoot (dead).

застрел|и́ться, ю́сь, ~ишься, *pf.* (*of* ~иваться) to shoot oneself; to blow one's brains out.

застре́льщик, а, *m.* 1. (*mil.*) skirmisher, tirailleur. 2. (*fig.*) pioneer, leader.

застреля́|ть, ю, *pf.* (*coll.*) to begin to shoot, begin to fire.

застре́х|а, и, *f.* (*dial.*) eaves.

застрига́|ть, ю, *impf. of* застри́чь 2.

застри́|чь, гу́, жёшь, гу́т, *past* ~г, ~гла, *pf.* (*coll.*) 1. to begin to cut. 2. (*impf.* ~га́ть) to cut (nails) too short.

застрога́|ть, ю, *pf.* 1. to begin to plane. 2. (*pf. of* застра́гивать) to plane (down).

застро́|ить, ю, ишь, *pf.* (*of* застра́ивать) 1. to build (over, on, up). 2. to begin to build.

застро́йк|а, и, *f.* building; пра́во ~и building permit.

застро́йщик, а, *m.* person building (or having built for him) his own house.

застроч|и́ть, у́, ~ишь, *pf.* 1. (*impf.* застра́чивать) to sew up, stitch up. 2. (*coll.*) to begin to scribble, dash off (*a letter, etc.*). 3. (*coll.*) to rattle away (*of or with automatic weapons*).

заструга́|ть, ю, *pf.* = застрога́ть.

застру́гива|ть, ю, *impf. of* заструга́ть.

застря́|ну, нешь, *see* ~ть.

застря́па|ться, юсь, *pf.* (*coll.*) to devote too much time to cooking.

застря́|ть, ну, нешь, *pf.* (*of* застрева́ть) 1. to stick; з. в грязи́ to get stuck in the mud; слова́ ~ли у него́ в го́рле the words stuck in his throat. 2. (*fig.*, *coll.*) to be held up; to become bogged down.

засту|ди́ть, жу́, ~дишь, *pf.* (*of* ~жива́ть) (*coll.*) to expose to cold; to aggravate by exposure to cold.

засту|ди́ться, жу́сь, ~дишься, *pf.* (*of* ~жива́ться) (*coll.*) to catch cold, catch a chill.

засту́жива|ть(ся), ю(сь), *impf. of* засту-ди́ть(ся).

засту|жу́, ~дишь, *see* ~ди́ть.

за́ступ, а, *m.* spade.

заступа́|ть(ся), ю(сь), *impf. of* заступи́ть-(ся).

заступ|и́ть, лю́, ~ишь, *pf.* (*of* ~а́ть) 1. to take the place of; з. отца́ сироте́ to become a father to an orphan. 2. (на пост) to take up (a post).

заступ|и́ться, лю́сь, ~ишься, *pf.* (за+*a.*) to stand up for; to take someone's part; to plead (for).

засту́пник, а, *m.* defender, protector.

засту́пничеств|о, а, *n.* protection.

застыва́|ть, ю, *impf. of* засты́ть.

засты|ди́ть, жу́, ди́шь, *pf.* (*coll.*) to shame, cause to feel shame.

засты|ди́ться, жу́сь, ди́шься, *pf.* (*coll.*) feel shame; to become confused.

засты|жу́, ди́шь, *see* ~ди́ть.

засты́лый, *adj.* (*coll.*) congealed; stiff.

засты́|ну, нешь, *see* ~ть.

засты́|нуть = ~ть.

засты́|ть *and* ~нуть, ну, нешь, *pf.* (*of* ~ва́ть) 1. to thicken, set; to harden; to congeal, coagulate. 2. (*coll.*) to become stiff; (*fig.*) з. от у́жаса to be paralyzed with fright. 3. (*coll.*) to freeze (*also fig.*).

засу|ди́ть, жу́, ∠дишь, *pf.* (*of* ∠живать) (*coll.*) to condemn.

засуе|ти́ться, чу́сь, ти́шься, *pf.* 1. to begin to bustle about, begin to fuss. 2. to wear oneself out with fussing.

засу́жива|ть, ю, *impf. of* засуди́ть.

засу|жу́, ∠дишь, *see* ∠ди́ть.

засу́н|уть, у, ешь, *pf.* (*of* засо́вывать) to shove in, thrust in; to tuck in; з. ру́ки в карма́н to thrust one's hands into one's pockets.

засу́сл|ить, ю, ишь, *pf. of* су́слить.

засусо́л|ить, ю, ишь, *pf. of* сусо́лить.

за́сух|а, и, *f.* drought.

засухоусто́йчив|ый (∼, ∼а), *adj.* (*agric.*) drought-resisting.

засу́чива|ть, ю, *impf. of* засучи́ть.

засуч|и́ть, у́, ∠ишь, *pf.* (*of* ∠ивать) (рукава́, *etc.*) to roll up (*sleeves, etc.*).

засу́шива|ть(ся), ю(сь), *impf. of* засу́шить(ся).

засуш|и́ть, у́, ∠ишь, *pf.* (*of* ∠ивать) to dry up (*plants; also fig.*).

засуш|и́ться, у́сь, ∠ишься, *pf.* (*of* ∠иваться) to dry up (*intrans.*), shrivel.

засу́шлив|ый (∼, ∼а), *adj.* droughty, dry.

засчит|а́ть, а́ю, *pf.* (*of* ∼ывать) to take into consideration; з. в упла́ту до́лга to reckon towards payment of a debt.

засчи́тыва|ть, ю, *impf. of* засчита́ть.

засыла́|ть, ю, *impf. of* засла́ть.

засы́лк|а, и, *f.* sending, despatching.

засы́п|ать¹, лю, лешь, *pf.* (*of* ∼а́ть³) 1. to fill up. 2. (+*i.*) to cover (with), strew (with); за одну́ ночь доро́жка была́ ∼ана опа́вшими ли́стьями in a single night the path was strewn with fallen leaves. 3. (+*i.*; *fig., coll.*) з. вопро́сами to bombard with questions; з. поздравле́ниями to shower congratulations (on). 4. (+*a. or g.* в+*a.*; *coll.*) to put (into), add (to); з. овса́ в я́сли to pour oats into the manger.

засы́п|ать², лю, лешь, *pf.* (*of* ∼а́ть⁴) (*sl.*) to give away, betray.

засыпа́|ть¹, ю, *impf. of* засну́ть.

засыпа́|ть², ю, *impf. of* заспа́ть.

засыпа́|ть³, ⁴, ю, *impf. of* засы́пать¹, ².

засы́п|аться¹, люсь, лешься, *pf.* (*of* ∼а́ться²) 1. to get into; песо́к ∼ался мне в башмаки́ I have got sand into my shoes. 2. (+*i.*) *pass. of* ∼ать¹.

засы́п|аться², люсь, лешься, *pf.* (*of* ∼а́ться³) (*coll.*) 1. to be caught; (*sl.*) to be nabbed. 2. to come to grief, slip up.

засыпа́|ться¹, юсь, *impf. of* заспа́ться.

засыпа́|ться², ³, юсь, *impf. of* засы́паться¹, ².

засы́пк|а, и, *f.* 1. filling up; covering, strewing. 2. pouring in, putting in.

засыха́|ть, ю, *impf. of* засо́хнуть.

зас|я́ду, я́дешь, *see* ∼е́сть.

затавр|и́ть, ю́, и́шь, *pf.* (*of* таври́ть) to brand (*cattle, etc.*).

затаён|ный, *p.p.p. of* затаи́ть *and adj.* secret; suppressed; ∼ная мечта́ secret dream.

затаива|ть(ся), ю(сь), *impf. of* затаи́ть(ся).

зата|и́ть, ю́, и́шь, *pf.* (*of* ∼ивать) 1. to conceal; to suppress; з. дыха́ние to hold one's breath. 2. to harbour, cherish; з. оби́ду (на+*a.*) to nurse a grievance (against).

зата|и́ться, ю́сь, и́шься, *pf.* (*of* ∼иваться) (*coll.*) to hide (*intrans.*); з. в себе́ (*fig.*) to become reserved, retire into oneself.

зата́лкива|ть, ю, *impf. of* затолка́ть *and* затолкну́ть.

затанц|ева́ться, у́юсь, *pf.* (*coll.*) to dance until exhausted.

зата́плива|ть¹, ², ю, *impf. of* затопи́ть¹, ².

зата́птыва|ть, ю, *impf. of* затопта́ть.

зата́сканный, *p.p.p. of* затаска́ть *and adj.* worn; threadbare; (*fig.*) hackneyed, trite.

затаск|а́ть, а́ю, *pf.* (*of* ∼ивать¹) (*coll.*) 1. to wear out; to make dirty (with wear); (*fig.*) to make hackneyed, make trite. 2. to drag about; з. по суда́м to drag through the courts. 3. to begin to drag.

затаск|а́ться, а́юсь, *pf.* (*of* ∼иваться) (*coll.*) to wear out, become worn out; to become dirty (with wear).

зата́скива|ть¹, ю, *impf. of* затаска́ть.

зата́скива|ть², ю, *impf. of* затащи́ть.

зата́скива|ться, юсь, *impf. of* затаска́ться.

зата́чива|ть, ю, *impf. of* заточи́ть¹.

затащ|и́ть, у́, ∠ишь, *pf.* (*of* зата́скивать²) (*coll.*) to drag off, drag away; (*fig.*) они́ ∼и́ли его́ в теа́тр they have dragged him off to the theatre.

затвердева́|ть, ю, *impf. of* затверде́ть.

затверде́лост|ь, и, *f.* = затверде́ние.

затверде́лый, *adj.* hardened.

затверде́ни|е, я, *n.* 1. hardening. 2. (*med.*) induration, callosity. 3. (*med.*) callus.

затверде́|ть, ю, *pf.* (*of* ∼ва́ть) to harden, become hard; to set.

затвер|ди́ть, жу́, ди́шь, *pf.* (*of* ∠живать) (*coll.*) 1. to learn by rote. 2. з. одно́ и то же to harp on one string.

затве́ржива|ть, ю, *impf. of* затверди́ть.

затво́р, а, *m.* 1. shutting; bolting. 2. bolt, bar; breech-block (*of fire-arm*); water-gate, flood-gate; (*phot.*) shutter. 3. (*eccl.*) cell; seclusion, solitude.

затвор|и́ть, ю́, ∠ишь, *pf.* (*of* ∼я́ть) to shut, close.

затвор|и́ться, ю́сь, ∠ишься, *pf.* (*of* ∼я́ться) 1. to shut, close (*intrans.*). 2. to shut oneself in, lock oneself in. 3. (*eccl.*) to become a recluse; з. в монасты́рь, в монастыре́ to go into a monastery, become a monk.

затво́рник, а, *m.* hermit, anchorite, recluse;

он живёт совершённым ~ом (*fig.*) he is a complete recluse.

затворни|ческий, *adj. of* ~к, solitary; ~ческая жизнь the life of a recluse.

затворничеств|о, а, *n.* (*eccl.*) seclusion, solitary life.

затвор|я́ть(ся), я́ю(сь), *impf. of* ~и́ть(ся).

затева́|ть, ю, *impf. of* затея́ть.

затейлив|ый (~, ~а), *adj.* **1.** intricate, involved; ~ая речь involved discourse; ~ое украше́ние intricate ornament. **2.** ingenious, original; inventive; ~ая игру́шка ingenious toy.

затейник, а, *m.* **1.** practical joker; humorist. **2.** entertainer; organizer (of entertainments).

зате́|йный (~ен, ~йна), *adj.* (*coll.*) = ~йливый.

затейщик, а, *m.* (*coll.*) instigator.

затёк, ла́, *see* зате́чь.

затека́|ть, ю, *impf. of* зате́чь.

зате|ку́, чёшь, ку́т, *see* ~чь.

затем, *adv.* **1.** after that, thereupon, then, next. **2.** for that reason; з. что because, since, as; заче́м ты прие́хала? з., что слыха́ла, что ты заболе́л why have you come? because I heard that you had been taken ill; з. что́бы in order that; она́ прие́хала з., что́бы уха́живать за тобо́й she has come (in order) to look after you.

затемне́ни|е, я, *n.* **1.** darkening; obscuring (*also fig.*). **2.** (*med.*) dark patch. **3.** (*mil.*) black-out. **4.** (*psych.*) black-out.

затемн|и́ть, ю́, и́шь, *pf.* (*of* ~я́ть) **1.** to darken; to obscure (*also fig.*). **2.** (*mil.*) to black-out.

затемн|и́ться, ю́сь, и́шься, *pf.* (*of* ~я́ться) to become dark; to become obscure; (*fig.*) to become obscured, become clouded.

за́темно, *adv.* (*coll.*) before daybreak.

затемн|я́ть(ся), я́ю(сь), *impf. of* ~и́ть(ся).

затен|и́ть, ю́, и́шь, *pf.* (*of* ~я́ть) to shade.

затен|я́ть, я́ю, *impf. of* ~и́ть.

зате́плива|ть(ся), ю(сь), *impf. of* зате́плить(ся).

зате́пл|ить, ю, ишь, *pf.* (*of* ~ивать) (*obs., folk poet.*) to light (*candle, etc.*).

зате́пл|иться, юсь, ишься, *pf.* (*of* ~иваться) (*obs., folk poet.*) to begin to gleam.

зат|ере́ть, ру́, рёшь, *past* ~ёр, ~ёрла, *pf.* (*of* ~ира́ть) **1.** to rub out. **2.** to block, jam; (*impers.*) су́дно ~ёрло льда́ми the ship was ice-bound; (*fig., coll.*) з. кого́-н. to keep someone down, impede someone's career. **3.** (*coll.*) to make dirty, soil.

зат|ере́ться, ру́сь, рёшься, *past* ~ёрся, ~ёрлась, *pf.* (*of* ~ира́ться) (*coll.*) **1.** (в+а.) to get (into), worm one's way (into). **2.** to begin to rub oneself.

зате́рива|ть(ся), ю(сь), *impf. of* затеря́ть(ся).

затерпн|уть, ет, *pf. of* те́рпнуть.

зате́рянный, *p.p.p. of* затеря́ть *and adj.* forgotten, forsaken.

затер|я́ть, я́ю, *pf.* (*of* ~ивать) (*coll.*) to lose, mislay.

затер|я́ться, я́юсь, *pf.* (*of* ~иваться) to be lost, be mislaid; (*fig.*) to become forgotten; моё перо́ ~я́лось (*coll.*) my pen has vanished; з. в толпе́ to be lost in a crowd.

зате|са́ть, шу́, ~шешь, *pf.* (*of* ~сывать) to rough-hew; to sharpen (*stake, etc.*).

зате|са́ться, шу́сь, ~шешься, *pf.* (*o,* ~сываться) (*coll.*) to worm one's way in, intrude.

затесн|и́ть, ю́, и́шь, *pf.* (*of* ~я́ть) (*coll.*) **1.** to jostle, press. **2.** (*fig.*) to oppress, persecute.

затесн|и́ться, ю́сь, и́шься, *pf.* (*of* ~я́ться) (*coll.*) to begin to crowd.

затесн|я́ть(ся), я́ю(сь), *impf. of* ~и́ть(ся).

затёсыва|ть(ся), ю(сь), *impf. of* затеса́ть(ся).

зате́|чь, ку́, чёшь, ку́т, *past* ~к, ~кла́, *pf.* (*of* ~ка́ть) **1.** (в+а.; за+а.) to pour, flow, leak (into; behind). **2.** to swell up. **3.** to become numb; у меня́ нога́ ~кла́ I have pins and needles in my foot.

зате́|я, и, f. **1.** undertaking, enterprise, venture. **2.** (*usually pl.*) piece of fun; escapade; practical joke. **3.** (*pl., obs.*) embellishment, ornament; (*lit.*) conceit; жить без ~й to live simply, unpretentiously.

зате́|ять, ю, *pf.* (*of* ~вать) (*coll.*) to undertake, venture; to organize; з. дра́ку to start a fight.

затира́|ть(ся), ю(сь), *impf. of* затере́ть(ся).

зати́ск|ать, аю, *pf.* (*of* ~ивать) (*coll.*) to smother with caresses.

зати́скива|ть(ся), ю(сь), *impf. of* зати́скать *and* зати́снуть(ся).

зати́с|нуть, ну, нешь, *pf.* (*of* ~кивать) (*coll.*) to squeeze in.

зати́с|нуться, нусь, нешься, *pf.* (*of* ~киваться) (*coll.*) to squeeze (oneself) in.

затих|а́ть, а́ю, *impf. of* ~нуть.

зати́х|нуть, ну, нешь, *past* ~, ~ла, *pf.* (*of* ~а́ть) to die down, abate; to die away, fade (*of noise*).

зати́шь|е, я, *n.* calm; lull.

затк|а́ть, у́, ёшь, *past* ~а́л, ~ала́, ~а́ло, *pf.* (+*a. and i.*) to cover all over with a woven pattern.

заткн|у́ть, у́, ёшь, *pf.* (*of* затыка́ть) **1.** (+*a. and i.*) to stop up; to plug; з. буты́лку про́бкой to cork a bottle; з. рот, гло́тку кому́-н. (*coll.*) to shut someone up; ~й гло́тку! shut your mouth! **2.** to stick, thrust; з. кого́-н. за по́яс (*fig., coll.*) to outdo someone.

заткн|у́ться, у́сь, ёшься, *pf.* (*coll.*) to shut
up; ~и́сь! shut up!

затмева́|ть, ю, *impf. of* затми́ть.

затме́ни|е, я, *n.* 1. (*astron.*) eclipse. 2. (*fig.*,
coll.) black-out, mental derangement.

затм|и́ть, и́шь, *pf.* (*of* ~ева́ть) 1. to
darken. 2. (*fig.*) to eclipse; to overshadow.

зато́, *conj.* (*coll.*) but then, but on the other
hand; but to make up for it; до́рого, з.
хоро́шая вещь it is expensive, but then it
is good.

затова́ренност|ь, и, *f.* (*econ.*) glut.

затова́ренный, *p.p.p. of* затова́рить *and adj.*
(*econ.*) surplus.

затова́ривани|е, я, *n.* glutting; overstock-
ing.

затова́рива|ть(ся), ю(сь), *impf. of* затова́-
рить(ся).

затова́р|ить, ю, ишь, *pf.* (*of* ~ивать) (*econ.*)
to accumulate (excess stock of), overstock.

затова́р|иться, юсь, ишься, *pf.* (*of* ~иваться)
(*econ.*) 1. to be over-stocked. 2. (*coll.*)
to have a surplus.

затолка́|ть, ю, *pf.* (*of* зата́лкивать) to jostle
(*to the point of discomfort*).

затолкн|у́ть, у́, ёшь, *pf.* (*of* зата́лкивать)
(*coll.*) to shove in.

зато́н, а, *m.* 1. backwater. 2. (river-)boat
yard. 3. dam, weir.

затон|у́ть, у́, ~ешь, *pf.* to sink (*intrans.*).

затоп|и́ть¹, лю́, ~ишь, *pf.* (*of* зата́пливать)
to light (*a stove*); to turn on the heating.

затоп|и́ть², лю́, ~ишь, *pf.* (*of* ~ля́ть) 1. to
flood; to submerge. 2. to sink; з. кора́бль
to scuttle a ship.

зато́пк|а, и, *f.* 1. fire-lighting. 2. kindling
(-wood).

затопля́|ть, ю, *impf. of* затопи́ть².

затоп|та́ть, чу́, ~чешь, *pf.* (*of* зата́пты-
вать) to trample (down, in); to trample
underfoot.

затоп|чу́, ~чешь, *see* ~та́ть.

зато́р¹, а, *m.* blocking, obstruction; з. у́-
личного движе́ния traffic-jam, congestion.

зато́р², а, *m.* mash (*in brewing and distilling*).

затормо|зи́ть, жу́, зи́шь, *pf. of* тормози́ть.

затормош|и́ть, и́шь, *pf.* (*coll.*) to pester.

зато́р|ный, *adj. of* ~².

заточ|а́ть, а́ю, *impf. of* ~и́ть².

заточе́ни|е, я, *n.* confinement; incarcera-
tion, captivity.

заточ|и́ть¹, у́, ~ишь, *pf.* (*of* зата́чивать) to
sharpen.

заточ|и́ть², у́, ~и́шь, *pf.* (*of* ~а́ть) to confine,
shut up; to incarcerate.

затравене́|ть, ет, *pf. of* травене́ть.

затрав|и́ть, лю́, ~ишь, *pf.* (*of* трави́ть¹ *and*
~ливать) to hunt down, bring to bay;
(*fig., coll.*) to persecute; to badger; to worry
the life out of.

затра́вк|а, и, *f.* 1. (*tech.*) priming-tube.
2. touchhole.

затра́влива|ть, ю, *impf. of* затрави́ть.

затра́вник, а, *m.* (*tech.*) priming-tube.

затра́гива|ть, ю, *impf. of* затро́нуть.

затрапе́з|ный¹, *adj.* taking place in the
refectory, at table; ~ная бесе́да table-talk.

затрапе́зный², *adj.* (*obs.*) working-, every-
day- (*of dress*).

затра́т|а, ы, *f.* expense; outlay.

затра́|тить, чу, тишь, *pf.* (*of* ~чивать) to
expend, spend.

затра́чива|ть, ю, *impf. of* затра́тить.

затре́б|овать, ую, *pf.* to request, require;
to ask for.

затреп|а́ть, лю́, ~лешь, *pf.* (*of* ~ывать)
1. to wear out; to make dirty (with wear).
2. (*fig.*) to wear out; з. чьё-н. и́мя to give
someone a bad name. 3. to begin to scutch.

затреп|а́ться, лю́сь, ~лешься, *pf.* (*of* ~ы-
ваться) 1. to wear out (*intrans.*), be worn
out. 2. (*fig.*) я совсе́м ~а́лся (*coll.*) I have
stayed gossiping too long. 3. to begin to
flutter.

затрёпыва|ть(ся), ю(сь), *impf. of* затре-
па́ть(ся).

затре́щин|а, ы, *f.* (*coll.*) box on the ears.

затро́н|уть, у, ешь, *pf.* (*of* затра́гивать)
1. to affect; to touch, graze. 2. (*fig.*) to
touch (on); з. вопро́с to broach a question;
з. чьё-н. самолю́бие to wound someone's
self-esteem.

затрудне́ни|е, я, *n.* difficulty.

затруднённый, *p.p.p. of* затрудни́ть *and adj.*
laboured.

затрудни́тельност|ь, и, *f.* difficulty; straits.

затрудни́тел|ьный (~ен, ~ьна), *adj.* diffi-
cult; embarrassing.

затрудн|и́ть, ю́, и́шь, *pf.* (*of* ~я́ть) 1. to
trouble; to cause trouble (to); to embarrass.
2. to make difficult; to hamper.

затрудн|и́ться, ю́сь, и́шься, *pf.* (*of* ~я́ться)
(+*inf. or i.*) to find difficulty (in); з. отве́-
том to find difficulty in replying; он ~и́лся
испо́лнить мою́ про́сьбу he found difficulty
in complying with my request.

затрудн|я́ть(ся), я́ю(сь), *impf. of* ~и́ть(ся)

затума́н|ивать(ся), иваю(сь), иваешь-
(ся), *impf. of* ~ить(ся).

затума́н|ить, ю, ишь, *pf.* (*of* ~ивать) 1. to
befog; to cloud, dim; (*impers.*) ~ило гори-
зо́нт the horizon was obscured by fog;
слёзы ~или её глаза́ tears dimmed her
eyes. 2. (*fig.*) to obscure.

затума́н|иться, юсь, ишься, *pf.* (*of* ~ивать-
ся) 1. to grow foggy, become clouded
(with). 2. (*fig.*) to grow sad. 3. (*fig.*) to become obscure.

затуп|и́ть, лю́, ~ишь, *pf.* (*of* ~ля́ть) to
blunt; to dull.

затуп|и́ться, лю́сь, ⌣ишься, *pf.* (*of* ⌣ля́ть-
ся) to become blunt(ed).

затупля́|ть(ся), ю(сь), *impf. of* затупи́ть-
(ся).

зату́рка|ть, ю, *pf.* (*coll.*) to nag.

затуха́ни|е, я, *n.* extinction; (*tech.*) damp-
ing; fading.

затух|а́ть, а́ет, *impf. of* ⌣нуть.

зату́х|нуть, нет, *past* ~, ~ла, *pf.* (*of* ~а́ть)
1. to go out, be extinguished. 2. (*fig.*, *coll.*)
to die away (*of sounds*); (*tech.*) to damp; to
fade.

зату́ш|ева́ть, у́ю, *pf.* (*of* ⌣ёвывать) 1. to
shade. 2. (*fig.*, *coll.*) to conceal; to draw a
veil over.

затушёвыва|ть, ю, *impf. of* затушева́ть.

затуш|и́ть, у́, ⌣ишь, *pf.* to put out, extin-
guish; (*fig.*) to suppress.

за́тхлый, *adj.* mouldy, musty; stuffy; (*fig.*)
stagnant.

затыка́|ть, ю, *impf. of* заткну́ть.

заты́л|ок, ка, *m.* 1. back of the head; (*anat.*)
occiput; scrag (*cut of meat*). 2. станови́ться
в з. to form up in file.

заты́лочный, *adj.* (*anat.*) occipital.

заты́чк|а, и, *f.* (*coll.*) 1. stopping up; plug-
ging.2. stopper; plug; spigot;(*fig.*) stopgap.

затя́гива|ть(ся), ю(сь), *impf. of* затяну́ть-
(ся).

затяжеле́|ть, ю, *pf.* (*coll.*, *dial.*) to become
pregnant.

затя́жк|а, и, *f.* 1. inhaling (*in smoking*).
2. prolongation; (*coll.*) dragging out. 3. de-
laying, putting off. 4. (*tech.*) tie-beam.

затяжн|о́й, *adj.* long drawn-out, pro-
tracted; ⌣а́я боле́знь lingering illness.

затя́нут|ый, *p.p.p. of* ⌣ь *and adj.* tightly but-
toned, corseted.

затя́|нуть, ну́, ⌣нешь, *pf.* (*of* ⌣гивать) 1. to
tighten; (*naut.*) to haul taut. 2. to cover;
to close; (*impers.*) не́бо ~ну́ло ту́чами it has
clouded over; ра́ну ~ну́ло the wound has
closed. 3. (*coll.*) to drag down, drag in;
(*fig.*) to inveigle. 4. (*coll.*) to drag out, spin
out. 5. з. пе́сню (*coll.*) to strike up a song.

затя́|ну́ться, ну́сь, ⌣нешься, *pf.* (*of* ⌣ги-
ва́ться) 1. to lace oneself up; з. по́ясом to
tighten one's belt. 2. to be covered; to close
(*intrans.*), skin over (*of a wound*). 3. (*coll.*) to
be delayed; to linger; to be dragged out,
drag on (*intrans.*); вечери́нка ~ну́лась до
по́лночи the party dragged on till midnight.
4. to inhale (*in smoking*).

зау́л|ок, ка, *m.* (*coll.*) back street.

зау́мн|ый, *adj.* unintelligible; з. язы́к a
kind of futuristic language (*based on arbitrary
usage and invented words having no objective
reference*).

за́ум|ь, и, *no pl.*, *f.* = ⌣ный язы́к.

зауны́в|ный (~ен, ~на), *adj.* doleful.

заупоко́йн|ый, *adj.* for the repose of the
soul (*of the dead*); ~ая слу́жба requiem.

заупря́м|иться, люсь, ишься, *pf.* to begin
to be obstinate, turn obstinate.

зауря́д, а, *m.* (*obs.*) 1. acting rank, brevet
rank. 2. (*fig.*, *coll.*) mediocrity.

зауря́д|ный (~ен, ~на), *adj.* ordinary,
commonplace; mediocre.

заусе́ниц|а, ы, *f.* 1. agnail, hangnail. 2.
(*tech.*) wire-edge.

за́утра, *adv.* (*poet.*, *obs.*) on the morrow.

за́утрен|я, и, *f.* (*eccl.*) prime.

заутю́жива|ть, ю, *impf. of* заутю́жить.

заутю́ж|ить, у, ишь, *pf.* to iron (out).

зау́ченный, *p.p.p. of* заучи́ть *and adj.*
studied.

зау́чива|ть(ся), ю(сь), *impf. of* заучи́ть(ся).

зау́|чи́ть, чу́, ⌣чишь, *pf.* (*of* ⌣чивать) 1. to
learn by heart. 2. (*coll.*) to din learning into.

зауч|и́ться, у́сь, ⌣ишься, *pf.* (*of* ⌣иваться)
(*coll.*) to overstudy.

зауша́тельский, *adj.* disparaging, abusive.

зауша́тельств|о, а, *n.* disparagement,
abuse.

зауш|а́ть, а́ю, *impf. of* ⌣и́ть.

зауше́ни|е, я, *n.* box on the ears; (*fig.*) slap
in the face, insult.

зауш|и́ть, у́, и́шь, *pf.* (*of* ~а́ть) (*obs.*) to box
on the ears; (*fig.*) to insult.

заушни́ц|а, ы, *f.* (*med.*) mumps.

зау́шный, *adj.* behind the ears; (*med.*) parotid.

зафарширова́ть|ова́ть, у́ю, *pf. of* фарширова́ть.

зафикси́р|овать, ую, *pf. of* фикси́ровать.

зафрахт|ова́ть, у́ю, *pf.* (*of* фрахтова́ть *and*
~о́вывать) to charter, freight.

зафрахто́выва|ть, ю, *impf. of* зафрахтова́ть.

заха́жива|ть, ю, *freq. of* заходи́ть[1]; он
часте́нько к нам ~л he often used to drop
in (*to see us*).

заха́п|ать, аю, *pf.* (*of* ~ывать) (*coll.*) to
grab, lay hold of.

заха́пыва|ть, ю, *impf. of* заха́пать.

захва́лива|ть, ю, *impf. of* захвали́ть.

захвал|и́ть, ю́, ⌣ишь, *pf.* (*coll.*) to praise to
excess; to spoil by flattery.

захва́т, а, *m.* 1. seizure, capture; usurpa-
tion. 2. (*tech.*) claw.

захва́танный *p.p.p. of* захвата́ть *and adj.*
soiled by handling, thumbed; (*fig.*, *coll.*)
trite, hackneyed.

захват|а́ть, а́ю, *pf.* (*of* ⌣ывать[2]) (*coll.*) to
make dirty by handling; to thumb.

захва|ти́ть, чу́, ⌣тишь, *pf.* (*of* ⌣тывать[1])
1. to take; з. горсть ви́шен to take a hand-
ful of cherries; они́ ~ти́ли с собо́й дете́й
they have taken the children with them.
2. to seize; to capture; з. власть to seize
power; мы ~ти́ли три́ста пле́нных we took
three hundred prisoners. 3. (*fig.*) to carry

away; to thrill, excite; кни́га меня́ ∼ти́ла I was thrilled by the book. **4.** (*coll.*) to catch; з. после́дний по́езд to catch the last train; я успе́л з. его́ в кабине́те I managed to catch him in his office; ∼ти́ла ли тебя́ гроза́? were you caught by the storm? **5.** to stop (*an illness, etc.*) in time. **6.** (*impers.*) от э́того у меня́ дух ∼ти́ло it took my breath away.

захва́тнический, *adj.* (*pejor.*) aggressive.

захва́тчик, а, *m.* invader; aggressor.

захва́тыва|ть¹, ю, *impf. of* захвати́ть.

захва́тыва|ть², ю, *impf. of* захвата́ть.

захва́тыва|ющий, *pres. part. act. of* ∼ть¹ *and adj.* (*fig.*) gripping; слу́шать но́вости с ∼ющим интере́сом to listen to news with keen interest.

захвора́|ть, ю, *pf.* (*coll.*) to be taken ill.

захиле́|ть, ю, *pf. of* хиле́ть.

захире́лый, *adj.* faded; ailing.

захире́|ть, ю, *pf. of* хире́ть.

захлеб|ну́ть, ну́, нёшь, *pf.* (*of* ∼ывать) (*coll.*) **1.** to swallow, take a mouthful of. **2.** (+*a. and i.*) to take (with), wash down (with).

захлеб|ну́ться, ну́сь, нёшься, *pf.* (*of* ∼ываться) **1.** to choke (*intrans.*); to swallow the wrong way. **2.** (*fig., coll.*) з. от восто́рга to be transported with delight; ата́ка ∼ну́лась (*mil.*) the attack misfired.

захлёбыва|ть, ю, *impf. of* захлебну́ть.

захлёбыва|ться, юсь, *impf.* (*of* захлебну́ться) to choke (*intrans.*); (*fig.*) з. от сме́ха to choke with laughter; говори́ть ∼ющимся го́лосом to speak in a voice choked with emotion.

захлест|а́ть, а́ю, *pf.* (*of* ∼ывать²) (*coll.*) **1.** to flog to death. **2.** to begin to pour (*of rain*).

захлест|ну́ть, ну́, нёшь, *pf.* (*of* ∼ывать¹) **1.** to fasten, secure. **2.** to flow over, swamp, overwhelm; (*fig.*) её ∼ну́ла волна́ сча́стья a wave of happiness flowed over her.

захлёстыва|ть¹, ю, *impf. of* захлеста́ть.

захлёстыва|ть², ю, *impf. of* захлестну́ть.

захло́п|нуть, ну, нешь, *pf.* (*of* ∼ывать) **1.** to slam. **2.** to shut in.

захло́п|нуться, нусь, нешься, *pf.* (*of* ∼ываться) to slam to; to close with a bang.

захлопо|та́ться, чу́сь, ∼че́шься, *pf.* (*coll.*) to be worn out (with bustling about).

захло́пыва|ть(ся), ю(сь), *impf. of* захло́пнуть(ся).

захлороформи́р|овать, ую, *pf. of* хлороформи́ровать.

захмеле́|ть, ю, *pf. of* хмеле́ть.

захо́д, а, *m.* **1.** (со́лнца) sunset. **2.** stopping (at), calling (at), putting in (at); э́тот парохо́д пришёл из Аме́рики без ∼а в Шербу́р this ship has arrived from America without calling at Cherbourg.

захо|ди́ть¹, жу́, ∼дишь, *impf. of* зайти́.

захо|ди́ть², жу́, ∼дишь, *pf.* to begin to walk; он ∼ди́л по ко́мнате he began to pace up and down the room.

захо|ди́ться, жу́сь, ∼дишься, *pf.* (*coll.*) to tire oneself out with walking, walk oneself off one's feet.

захо́жий, *adj.* (*coll.*) newly-arrived; он — з. челове́к he is a stranger.

захо|жу́, ∼дишь, *see* ∼ди́ть.

захолоде́|ть, ю, *pf.* (*coll.*) to become cold; (*impers.*) to turn cold.

захолу́стный, *adj.* remote; з. быт (*fig.*) provincial life.

захолу́ст|ье, ья, *g. pl.* ∼ий (*coll.* ∼ьев), *n.* out-of-the-way place.

захороне́ни|е, я, *n.* burial.

захорон|и́ть, ю́, ∼ишь, *pf.* (*of* хорони́ть) **1.** to bury. **2.** (*dial.*) to hide.

захо|те́ть(ся), чу́(сь), ∼чешь(ся), ти́м(ся), ти́те(сь), тя́т(ся), *pf. of* хоте́ть(ся).

захребе́тник, а, *m.* (*dial.*) parasite.

захуда́лый, *adj.* impoverished, decayed.

заца́п|ать, аю, *pf.* (*of* ∼ывать) (*coll.*) to grab; to lay hold of.

заца́пыва|ть, ю, *impf. of* заца́пать.

зацве|сти́, ту́, тёшь, *past* ∼л, ∼ла́, *pf.* (*of* ∼та́ть) to break into blossom.

зацвета́|ть, ю, *impf. of* зацвести́.

зацве|ту́, тёшь, *see* ∼сти́.

зацел|ова́ть, у́ю, *pf.* (*coll.*) to smother with kisses, rain kisses on.

зацеп|и́ть, лю́, ∼ишь, *pf.* (*of* ∼ля́ть) **1.** to hook. **2.** (за+*a.*) to catch (on); з. ного́й за ка́мень to catch one's foot on a stone; (*tech.*) to engage (*gears*); (*fig.*) to sting.

зацеп|и́ться, лю́сь, ∼ишься, *pf.* (*of* ∼ля́ться) (за+*a.*) **1.** to catch (on); чуло́к у неё ∼и́лся за гвоздь her stocking caught on a nail. **2.** to catch hold (of).

заце́пк|а, и, *f.* (*coll.*) **1.** peg, hook. **2.** hooking. **3.** (*fig.*) pull, protection. **4.** hitch, catch (*fig.*).

зацепля́|ть(ся), ю(сь), *impf. of* зацепи́ть(ся).

зачаро́ванный, *p.p.p. of* зачарова́ть *and adj.* spell-bound.

зачар|ова́ть, у́ю, *pf.* (*of* ∼о́вывать) to bewitch, enchant, captivate.

зачаро́выва|ть, ю, *impf. of* зачарова́ть.

зача|сти́ть, щу́, сти́шь, *pf.* (*coll.*) **1.** (+*inf.*) to take (to); он ∼сти́л игра́ть в те́ннис по вечера́м he has taken to playing tennis in the evening; они́ ∼сти́ли к нам в го́сти they have taken to visiting us, they have become regular visitors at our house. **2.** to begin to go fast; докла́дчик ∼сти́л так, что переводи́ть его́ слова́ ста́ло невозмо́жно the lecturer began to go so fast that it was impossible to translate; дождь ∼сти́л it began to rain cats and dogs.

зачасту́ю, *adv.* (*coll.*) often, frequently.

зача́ти|е, я, *n.* (*physiol.*) conception.

зача́т|ок, ка, *m.* **1.** embryo. **2.** rudiment (*biol.*). **3.** (*usually pl.*; *fig.*) beginning, germ.

зача́точн|ый, *adj.* rudimentary; в ∼ом состоя́нии in embryo.

зач|а́ть, ну́, нёшь, *past* ∼а́л, ∼ала́, ∼а́ло, *pf.* (*of* ∼ина́ть) **1.** to conceive (*trans. and intrans.*). **2.** (+*a. or inf.*) (*coll.*) to begin.

зача́х|нуть, ну, нешь, *past* ∼нул *and* ∼, ∼ла, *pf. of* ча́хнуть.

зача|щу́, сти́шь, *see* ∼сти́ть.

зач|ёл, ла́, *see* ∼е́сть.

заче́м, *interrog. and relat. adv.* why; what for; з. ты пришла́? why did you come?; вот з. пришла́ that's why I came.

заче́м-то, *adv.* for some reason or other.

зачёркива|ть, ю, *impf. of* зачеркну́ть.

зачерк|ну́ть, ну́, нёшь, *pf.* (*of* ∼ивать) to cross out, strike out.

зачерне́|ть, ю, *pf.* to show black.

зачерне́|ться, юсь, *pf.* to turn black.

зачерни́|ть, ю́, и́шь, *pf.* (*of* черни́ть I *and* ∼я́ть) to blacken, paint black.

зачерн|я́ть, я́ю, *impf. of* ∼и́ть.

зачерп|а́ть, аю, *pf.* to begin to ladle.

зачерп|ну́ть, ну́, нёшь, *pf.* (*of* ∼ывать) to draw up, scoop; to ladle.

заче́рпыва|ть, ю, *impf. of* зачерпну́ть.

зачерстве́лый, *adj.* stale; (*fig.*) hard--hearted.

зачерстве́|ть, ю, *pf. of* черстве́ть I.

зачер|ти́ть, чу́, ∼тишь, *pf.* (*of* ∼чивать) **1.** to cover with pencil-strokes. **2.** to sketch.

заче́рчива|ть, ю, *impf. of* зачерти́ть.

зачер|чу́, ∼тишь, *see* ∼ти́ть.

заче|са́ть, шу́, ∼шешь, *pf.* **1.** to begin to scratch. **2.** (*impf.* ∼сывать) to comb back.

заче|са́ться, шу́сь, ∼шешься, *pf.* (*coll.*) **1.** to begin to scratch oneself. **2.** to begin to itch.

зач|е́сть, ту́, тёшь, *past* ∼ёл, ∼ла́, *pf.* (*of* ∼и́тывать[1]) **1.** to take into account, reckon as, credit; з. де́сять рубле́й в упла́ту до́лга to account ten roubles towards payment of a debt; з. проведённый на вое́нной слу́жбе год за два го́да to reckon a year spent on war service as two years. **2.** (+*d. and a.*) to pass (*trans.*); мы ∼ли́ ему́ перево́д с францу́зского we passed him in French translation.

зачёсыва|ть, ю, *impf. of* зачеса́ть.

зачёт, а, *m.* **1.** reckoning; в з. пла́ты in payment. **2.** test (*in school, etc.*); получи́ть з., сдать з. (по+*d.*) to pass a test (in); поста́вить (+*d.*) з. (по+*d.*) to pass (in); поста́вили мне з. по исто́рии they have passed me in history.

зачёт|ный, *adj. of* ∼. **1.** ∼ная квита́нция receipt. **2.** ∼ная кни́жка (student's) record

book; ∼ная се́ссия test period; ∼ная стрельба́ classification shoot.

зачехл|и́ть, ю́, и́шь, *pf. of* чехли́ть.

зач|ешу́, ∼е́шешь, *see* ∼еса́ть.

зачи́н, а, *m.* (*lit.*) beginning; introduction (*of folk-tale, etc.*).

зачина́тел|ь, я, *m.* (*rhet.*) author, founder.

зачина́|ть, ю, *impf. of* зача́ть.

зачи́нива|ть, ю, *impf. of* зачини́ть.

зачин|и́ть, ю́, ∼ишь, *pf.* (*of* ∼ивать) (*coll.*) to mend; to patch; to sharpen (*a pencil*).

зачи́нщик, а, *m.* (*pejor.*) instigator, ring--leader.

зачи́сл|ить, ю, ишь, *pf.* (*of* ∼я́ть) **1.** to include; з. в счёт to enter in an account. **2.** to enrol, enlist; з. в штат to take on the staff, on the strength.

зачи́сл|иться, юсь, ишься, *pf.* (*of* ∼я́ться) (в+*a.*) **1.** to join, enter. **2.** *pass. of* ∼ить.

зачисл|я́ть(ся), я́ю(сь), *impf. of* ∼и́ть(ся).

зачи́|стить, щу, стишь, *pf.* (*of* ∼ща́ть) **1.** to smooth out. **2.** to clean up, clean out.

зачит|а́ть, а́ю, *pf.* (*of* ∼ывать[2]) (*coll.*) **1.** to read out. **2.** to borrow and fail to return to its owner, take and keep (*a book*). **3.** to exhaust (*by continual reading aloud*). **4.** (*university sl.*) to exceed one's allotted time (*in lecturing*). **5.** (*no impf.*) to begin to read.

зачит|а́ться, а́юсь, *pf.* (*of* ∼ываться) **1.** to become engrossed in reading; to go on reading; вчера́ я ∼а́лся далеко́ за́ полночь last night I went on reading until long after midnight. **2.** (*coll.*) to make oneself stale by excessive reading.

зачи́тыва|ть[1], ю, *impf. of* заче́сть.

зачи́тыва|ть[2], ю, *impf. of* зачита́ть.

зачи́тыва|ться, юсь, *impf.* **1.** *impf. of* зачита́ться. **2.** *pass. of* ∼ть[2].

зачища́|ть, ю, *impf. of* зачи́стить.

зачи́|щу, стишь, *see* ∼стить.

зач|ну́, нёшь, *see* ∼а́ть.

зачтён|ный (∼, ∼а́), *p.p.p. of* заче́сть.

зач|ту́, тёшь, *see* ∼е́сть.

зачумлённый, *adj.* infected with plague.

зачу́|ять, ю, ешь, *pf.* (*coll.*) to scent, smell.

заша́рка|ть, ю, *pf.* (*coll.*) **1.** (*impf.* заша́ркивать) to scratch (*with one's feet*). **2.** to begin to scrape (one's feet).

заша́ркива|ть, ю, *impf. of* заша́ркать I.

зашва́рт|ова́ть, у́ю, *pf.* (*of* ∼о́вывать) (*naut.*) to moor, tie up.

зашва́рт|ова́ться, у́юсь, *pf.* (*of* ∼о́вываться (*naut.*) to moor, tie up (*intrans.*).

зашварто́выва|ть(ся), ю(сь), *impf. of* зашвартова́ть(ся).

зашвы́рива|ть, ю, *impf. of* зашвырну́ть *and* зашвыря́ть.

зашвыр|ну́ть, ну́, нёшь, *pf.* (*of* ∼ивать) (*coll.*) to throw, fling (away).

зашвыр|я́ть, я́ю, *pf.* (*of* ~ива́ть) (+*a. and i.*; *coll.*) to shower (with); з. кого́-н. ка́мнями to stone someone, throw stones at someone.

зашелохн|у́ть, у́, ёшь, *pf.* (*obs.*) to ripple.

зашиб|а́ть, а́ю, *impf.* (*coll.*) **1.** *impf. of* ~и́ть. **2.** to drink (*intrans.*).

зашиб|а́ться, а́юсь, *impf. of* ~и́ться.

зашиб|и́ть, у́, ёшь, *past* ~, ~ла, *pf.* (*of* ~а́ть) (*coll.*) **1.** to bruise, knock, hurt; он ~ себе́ коле́но he has bruised his knee. **2.** з. деньгу́ (*sl.*) to coin money.

зашиб|и́ться, у́сь, ёшься, *past* ~ся, ~лась, *pf.* (*of* ~а́ться) (*coll.*) to bruise oneself, knock oneself.

зашива́ть, ю, *impf. of* заши́ть.

заш|и́ть, ью, ьёшь, *pf.* (*of* ~ива́ть) **1.** to mend. **2.** to sew up; з. посы́лку в холст to sew up a parcel in sacking. **3.** (*med.*) to put (a) stitch(es) in.

зашифр|ова́ть, у́ю, *pf.* (*of* шифрова́ть *and* ~о́вывать) to encipher, put into code.

зашифро́выва|ть, ю, *impf. of* зашифрова́ть.

за|шлю́, шлёшь, *see* ~сла́ть.

зашнур|ова́ть, у́ю, *pf.* (*of* шнурова́ть *and* ~о́вывать) to lace up.

зашнуро́выва|ть, ю, *impf. of* зашнурова́ть.

зашпакл|ева́ть, юю, *pf.* (*of* шпаклева́ть *and* ~ёвывать) to putty (*woodwork, etc., before painting*).

зашпаклёвыва|ть, ю, *impf. of* зашпаклева́ть.

зашпи́л|ить, ю, ишь, *pf.* (*of* ~ивать) to pin up, fasten with a pin.

зашпи́лива|ть, ю, *impf. of* зашпи́лить.

зашта́тный, *adj.* (*obs.*) supernumerary, extra; з. чино́вник official not on permanent staff; з. го́род unimportant town (*not being, or having ceased to be, the administrative centre of an uyezd*).

заштемпелева́|ть, ю, *pf.* (*of* штемпелева́ть) to stamp, postmark.

заштопа|ть, ю, *pf.* (*of* што́пать) to darn.

заштрих|ова́ть, у́ю, *pf. of* штрихова́ть.

заштукату́рива|ть, ю, *impf. of* заштукату́рить.

заштукату́р|ить, ю, ишь, *pf.* (*of* ~ивать) to plaster.

защеко|та́ть, чу́, ~чешь, *pf.* (*coll.*) **1.** to torment by tickling. **2.** to begin to tickle.

защёлк|а, и, *f.* click, latch (*of lock*); catch, pawl.

защёлкива|ть, ю, *impf. of* защёлкнуть.

защёлк|нуть, ну, нешь, *pf.* (*of* ~ивать) (*coll.*) to latch.

защем|и́ть, лю́, и́шь, *pf.* (*of* ~ля́ть) **1.** to pinch, jam, nip; з. па́лец to pinch one's finger. **2.** (*impers.*; *coll.*) у неё ~и́ло се́рдце her heart aches.

защемля́|ть, ю, *impf. of* защеми́ть.

защип|ну́ть, ну́, нёшь, *pf.* (*of* ~ывать)

to take (*with pincers, tongs, etc.*); to ni tweak; to curl (*hair*); to punch (*tickets*).

защи́пыва|ть, ю, *impf. of* защипну́ть.

защи́т|а, ы, *no pl., f.* defence; protectio (*collect.*) the defence (*leg. and sport*); в ~ (+*g.*) in defence (of); под ~ой (+*g.*) und the protection (of); свиде́тели ~ы witness for the defence.

защи|ти́ть(ся), щу́(сь), ти́шь(ся), *pf.* ~ща́ть(ся).

защи́тник, а, *m.* **1.** defender, protecto (*leg.*) counsel for the defence; колле́гия ~с the Bar. **2.** (*sport*) (full-)back; ле́вы пра́вый з. left, right back.

защи́тн|ый, *adj.* protective; ~ая окра́ск (*zool.*) protective coloration; ~ые очк goggles; з. цвет khaki.

защища́|ть, ю, *impf.* **1.** (*impf. of* защити́т to defend, protect. **2.** (*no pf.*) to defen (*leg.*); to stand up for; з. диссерта́цию to defend a thesis (*before examiners*).

защища́|ться, юсь, *impf.* (*of* защити́тьс **1.** to defend oneself, protect oneself. **2.** *pas of* ~ть.

за́|щу, сти́шь, *see* ~стить.

заяви́тел|ь, я, *m.* (*leg.*) declarant, d ponent.

заяв|и́ть, лю́, ~ишь, *pf.* (*of* ~ля́ть) **1.** (+*a* о+*p. or* что) to announce, declare; з. сво права́ (на+*a.*) to claim one's rights (to); об ухо́де со слу́жбы to announce one's r tirement. **2.** (*obs.*) to certify, attest.

заяв|и́ться, лю́сь, ~ишься, *pf.* (*coll.*) to a pear, turn up.

заяв|к|а, и, *f.* (на+*a.*) claim (for); deman (for).

заявле́ни|е, я, *n.* **1.** statement, declaratio **2.** application; пода́ть з. to put in an app cation.

заявля́|ть, ю, *impf. of* заяви́ть.

зая́длый, *adj.* (*coll.*) inveterate.

за́|яц, йца, *m.* **1.** hare; (*prov.*) одни́ уда́ром уби́ть двух ~йцев to kill two bir with one stone. **2.** (*coll.*) stowaway; ga ·crasher; е́хать ~йцем to travel witho paying for a ticket.

зая́|чий, *adj. of* ~ц; ~чья губа́ (*med.*) har lip; (*bot.*) ~чья ла́пка hare's foot; з. щаве́ wood sorrel.

збру́|я, и = сбру́я.

зва́ни|е, я, *n.* **1.** (*obs.*) profession, callin **2.** rank; title.

зва́ный, *adj.* **1.** invited. **2.** with invite guests; з. ве́чер guest-night; з. обе́д ba quet.

зва́тельный, *adj.* (*gram.*) з. паде́ж vocati case.

зва|ть, зову́, зовёшь, *past* ~л, ~ла́, ~л *impf.* (*of* по~) **1.** to call; з. на по́мощь call for help. **2.** to ask, invite. **3.** (*imp* *only*) to call; как вас зову́т? what is your name? меня́ зову́т Влади́мир my name is Vladimir, I am called Vladimir.

зва́|ться, зову́сь, зовёшься, *past* ∼лся́, ∼ла́сь, ∼ло́сь, *impf.* (+*i.*; *coll.*) to be called; её сестра́ ∼ла́сь Татья́ной her sister was called Tatyana.

звезд|а́, ы́, *pl.* ∼ы, ∼, ∼а́м, *f.* 1. star; (*fig.*) з. экра́на film star; ве́рить в свою́ ∼у́ to believe in one's lucky star; роди́ться под счастли́вой ∼о́й to be born under a lucky star; он ∼ с не́ба не хвата́ет (*coll., iron.*) he won't set the Thames on fire. 2. (*zool.*) морска́я з. starfish.

звёзд|ный, *adj. of* ∼а́; ∼ная ка́рта celestial map; ∼ная ночь starlit night.

звездообра́з|ный (∼ен, ∼на), *adj.* star-shaped; з. дви́гатель (*tech.*) radial engine.

звездочёт, а, *m.* (*obs.*) astrologer.

звёздочк|а, и, *f.* 1. *dim. of* звезда́. 2. asterisk.

звен|е́ть, ю́, и́шь, *impf.* 1. to ring; у неё ∼е́ло в уша́х there was a ringing in her ears. 2. (+*i.*) з. моне́тами to jingle coins; з. стака́нами to clink glasses.

звен|о́, а́, *pl.* ∼ья, ∼ьев, *n.* 1. link (*of a chain; also fig.*). 2. (*fig.*) team, section (*in agriculture, etc.*); (*aeron.*) flight. 3. row (*of logs*).

звен|ьево́й, *adj. of* ∼о́; *as noun* з., ∼ьево́го, *m.* team leader; section leader (*of Pioneers*).

звер|ёк, ька́, *m. dim. of* ∼ь.

зверёныш, а, *m.* (*coll.*) young of wild animal.

звере́|ть, ю, ешь, *impf.* (*of* о∼) to become brutalized.

звери́н|ец, ца, *m.* menagerie.

звер|и́ный, *adj. of* ∼ь; of wild animals; ∼и́ное число́ (*bibl.*) number of the Beast.

зверобо́|й¹, я, *m.* hunter, trapper.

зверобо́|й², я, *m.* (*bot.*) St. John's wort.

зверово́дств|о, а, *n.* breeding of animals for furs.

зверово́дческий, *adj.* fur-breeding.

звероло́в, а, *m.* hunter, trapper.

звероло́в|ный, *adj. of* ∼; з. про́мысел hunting, trapping.

звероподо́б|ный (∼ен, ∼на), *adj.* beast-like; bestial.

зве́рски, *adv.* 1. brutally, bestially. 2. (*coll.*) terribly, awfully; я з. уста́л I am terribly tired.

зве́рский, *adj.* 1. brutal, bestial. 2. (*coll.*) terrific, tremendous; у него́ з. аппети́т he has a tremendous appetite.

зве́рств|о, а, *n.* brutality; atrocity; ∼а atrocities (*in war, etc.*).

зве́рств|овать, ую, *impf.* to behave with brutality; to commit atrocities.

звер|ь, я, *pl.* ∼и, ∼е́й, *m.* 1. wild animal, wild beast; пушно́й з. fur-bearing animal. 2. (*fig.*) brute, beast; смотре́ть ∼ем to look (very) savage, look (very) fierce.

зверь|ё, я́, *no pl.*, *n.* (*collect.*) wild animals, wild beasts; (*fig.*) brutes, beasts.

звон, а, *m.* 1. (ringing) sound, peal; з. моне́т chinking of coins; з. стака́нов clinking of glasses; слы́шал з., да не зна́ет, где он he does not know what he is talking about. 2. (*fig., coll.*) rumour; gossip.

звона́р|ь, я́, *m.* 1. bell-ringer. 2. (*fig., coll.*) rumour-monger; gossip.

звон|и́ть, ю́, и́шь, *impf.* 1. (*pf. of* по∼) (в+*a.*) to ring; з. кому́-н. (по телефо́ну) to telephone someone, ring someone up; вы не туда́ ∼и́те you've got the wrong number; ∼я́т someone is ringing; з. во все колокола́ (*fig.*) to set all the bells a-ringing. 2. (о+*p.*) to gossip (about).

звон|и́ться, ю́сь, и́шься, *impf.* (*of* по∼) to ring (*a doorbell*).

зво́н|кий (∼ок, ∼ка́, ∼ко), *adj.* 1. ringing, clear; ∼кая моне́та hard cash, coin. 2. (*ling.*) voiced.

звон|ко́вый, *adj. of* ∼о́к.

зво́нниц|а, ы, *f.* belfry (*of old Russian churches*).

звон|о́к, ка́, *m.* bell; дать з. to ring; з. по телефо́ну telephone call; встава́ть по ∼ку́ to get up when the bell goes.

зво́н|че and (*coll.*) ∼чее, *comp. of* ∼кий and ∼ко.

звук, а, *m.* sound; пусто́й звук (*fig.*) (mere) name, empty phrase; я звал её, а она́ ни ∼а I kept calling her but she never uttered a sound; (*ling.*) гла́сный з. vowel; согла́сный з. consonant.

звукови́к, а́, *m.* (*mil., coll.*) member of sound-locating *or* sound-ranging unit.

звук|ово́й, *adj. of* ∼; з. барье́р sound barrier; ∼ова́я волна́ sound wave; ∼ово́е измене́ние (*ling.*) sound change; ∼ово́е кино́, з. фильм sound-film(s), talkie(s).

звукоза́пис|ь, и, *f.* sound recording.

звуконепроница́емый, *adj.* sound-proof.

звукоопера́тор, а, *m.* sound producer (*in film industry*).

звукоподража́ни|е, я, *n.* onomatopoeia.

звукоподража́тельный, *adj.* onomatopoeic.

звукопрово́дный, *adj.* (*phys.*) sound-conducting.

звукоря́д, а, *m.* (*mus.*) scale.

звукоснима́тел|ь, я, *m.* (*radio*) pick-up.

звукоула́вливател|ь, я, *m.* (*mil.*) sound-locator.

звукоулови́тел|ь, я, *m.* = звукоула́вливатель.

звуча́ни|е, я, *n.* 1. (*ling.*) phonation. 2. sound(s).

звуч|а́ть, у́, и́шь, *impf.* (*of* про∼) 1. to be heard; to sound; вдали́ ∼а́ли голоса́ voices could be heard in the distance;

э́тот пасса́ж ~и́т прекра́сно (*mus.*) this passage sounds splendid. **2.** (+*adv. or i.*; *fig.*) to sound; to express, convey; з. трево́гой to sound a note of alarm; з. и́скренно to ring true.

звуч|ный (~ен, ~на́, ~но), *adj.* sonorous.

звя́кань|е, я, *n.* jingling; tinkling.

звя́к|ать, аю, *impf. of* ~нуть.

звя́к|нуть, ну, нешь, *pf.* (*of* ~ать) **1.** (+*i.*) to jingle; to tinkle. **2.** (+*d.*) з. по телефо́ну (*coll.*) to ring up.

зга, *only in phrase* ни зги не ви́дно it is pitch dark.

зда́ни|е, я, *n.* building, edifice.

здесь, *adv.* **1.** (*of place*) here; (*on letters*) local. **2.** (*coll.*) here, at this point (*of time*); in this; з. мы засмея́лись here we burst out laughing; з. нет ничего́ смешно́го there is nothing funny in this.

зде́шний, *adj.* local; of this place; вы з. жи́тель? нет, я не з. are you a resident of this place? no, I am a stranger here.

здоро́ва|ться, юсь, *impf.* (*of* по~) (с+*i.*) to greet; to pass the time of day (with); з. за́ руку to shake hands (*in greeting*).

здорове́нн|ый, *adj.* (*coll.*) robust, muscular; big, strong; ~ая ба́ба muscular woman; з. го́лос powerful voice.

здорове́|ть, ю, ешь, *impf.* (*of* по~) (*coll.*) to become stronger.

здо́рово (*coll.*) **1.** (*adv.*) splendidly, magnificently; ты з. порабо́тал you have worked splendidly. **2.** (*adv.*) very, very much; вчера́ они́ з. вы́пили they had a great deal to drink yesterday. **3.** (*interj.*) well done!

здоро́во¹, *interj.* (*coll.*) hullo.

здоро́в|о², *adv. of* ~ый¹; healthily, soundly; (за) з. живёшь for nothing, without rhyme or reason.

здоро́в|ый¹ (~, ~а), *adj.* **1.** healthy; бу́дь(те) ~(ы)! (*on parting*) good luck!; (*to someone sneezing*) (God) bless you! **2.** health--giving, wholesome; (*fig.*) sound, healthy; з. кли́мат healthy climate; ~ая иде́я sound idea.

здоро́в|ый² (~, ~а́, ~о́), *adj.* (*coll.*) **1.** robust, sturdy. **2.** strong, powerful; sound; з. моро́з sharp frost; ~ая трёпка sound thrashing. **3.** (*short form* +*inf.*) clever (at), good (at), expert; он ~ льстить же́нщинам he is expert at flattering women.

здоро́вь|е, я, *no pl.*, *n.* health; пить за чье-н. з. to drink someone's health; за ва́ше з.! your health!; как ва́ше з.? how are you?; на з. to your heart's content, as you please.

здорови́к, а́, *m.* (*coll.*) person in the pink of health.

здрав- (*abbr. of* ~оохране́ние) health(-).

здра́ви|е, я, *n.* (*obs.*) health; ~я жела́ю! *soldiers' reply to senior officer's greeting.*

здра́виц|а, ы, *f.* toast; провозгласи́ть ~у за (+*a.*) to propose a toast to.

здра́вниц|а, ы, *f.* sanatorium.

здравомы́слящий, *adj.* sensible, judicious.

здравоохране́ни|е, я, *n.* (care of) public health; Министе́рство ~я Ministry of Health; о́рганы ~я (public) health services.

здравоохрани́тельный, *adj.* public health.

здравотде́л, а, *m.* health department (*of local authority*).

здра́вств|овать, ую, *impf.* to be healthy; to thrive, prosper; ~уй(те)! how do you do; how are you; да ~ует! long live!

здра́в|ый (~, ~а), *adj.* **1.** sensible; з. смысл common sense. **2.** (*obs.*) healthy; ~ и невреди́м safe and sound; быть в ~ом уме́ to be in one's right mind.

зе́бр|а, ы, *f.* (*zool.*) zebra.

зе́бр|овый, *adj. of* ~а.

зев, а, *m.* **1.** (*anat.*) pharynx; воспале́ние ~а (*med.*) pharyngitis. **2.** (*obs.*) jaws.

зева́к|а, и, *m. and f.* idler, gaper.

зев|а́ть, а́ю, *impf.* **1.** (*pf.* ~ну́ть) to yawn. **2.** (*no pf.*) (*coll.*) to gape, stand gaping; не ~а́й! keep your wits about you! **3.** (*pf.* про~) (*coll.*) to miss opportunities, let chances slip through one's fingers. **4.** (*no pf.*) (*dial.*) to shout, bawl.

зева́|ться, ется, *impf.* (*impers.*+*d.*) (*coll.*) to have an urge to yawn; мне сего́дня ~ется I can't stop yawning today.

зев|ну́ть, ну́, нёшь, *pf. of* ~а́ть 1.

зев|о́к, ка́, *m.* yawn.

зево́т|а, ы, *f.* (fit of) yawning.

зелёненьк|ая, ой, *f.* (*coll.*, *obs.*) three-rouble note.

зелене́|ть, ю, *impf.* **1.** (*pf.* по~) to turn green, come out green. **2.** to show green.

зелен|и́ть, ю́, и́шь, *impf.* (*of* по~) to make green, paint green.

зеленн|о́й, *adj.*; ~а́я ла́вка greengrocer's (shop).

зеленова́т|ый (~, ~а), *adj.* greenish.

зеленогла́з|ый (~, ~а), *adj.* green-eyed.

зеленщи́к, а́, *m.* greengrocer.

зелён|ый (зе́лен, ~ а́, зе́лено), *adj.* green (о colour; *of vegetation*; unripe; *also fig.*); ~о вино́ (*folk poet. or coll.*) vodka; з. горо́шек green peas; ~ые насажде́ния (plantation of) trees and shrubs; ~ая ску́ка intolerabl boredom; ~ое я́блоко green apple; з. юне greenhorn; ~ая у́лица 'go' (*of traffic sig nals*); дать ~ую у́лицу (*fig.*) to give the g -ahead, green light (to); прогна́ть по ~о у́лице (*hist.*) to make to run the gauntlet.

зе́лен|ь, и, *no pl.*, *f.* **1.** green colour. **2.** (*co lect.*) verdure. **3.** (*collect.*) greens (*gree vegetables*).

зело́, *adv.* (*arch.*) very.

зе́л|ье, ья, *g. pl.* ~ий, *n.* **1.** potion; приворо́тное з. philtre. **2.** (*fig.*) poison; з. замо́рское (*obs.*) tobacco. **3.** (*fig., coll.*) venomous person; pest (*sl.*).

земе́льн|ый, *adj.* land; з. банк (*hist.*) Land Bank; з. наде́л allotment; ~ая ре́нта ground-rent; ~ая со́бственность (property in) land.

зе́м|ец, ца, *m.* member of zemstvo.

землеве́дени|е, я, *n.* physical geography.

землевладе́л|ец, ьца, *m.* landowner.

землевладе́л|ьческий, *adj.* of ~ец.

землевладе́ни|е, я, *n.* land-ownership.

земледе́л|ец, ьца, *m.* (peasant) farmer.

земледе́ли|е, я, *n.* agriculture, farming.

земледе́льческий, *adj.* agricultural.

землеко́п, а, *m.* navvy.

землеме́р, а, *m.* land-surveyor.

землеме́ри|е, я, *n.* land-surveying, geodesy.

землеме́рный, *adj.* geodetic; з. шест Jacob's staff.

землепа́шеств|о, а, *n.* (*obs.*) tillage.

землепа́ш|ец, ца, *m.* (*obs.*) tiller.

землепо́льзовани|е, я, *n.* land-tenure.

землепрохо́д|ец, ца, *m.* (*obs.*) explorer.

землеро́йк|а, и, *f.* (*zool.*) shrew.

землетрясе́ни|е, я, *n.* earthquake.

землеустро́йств|о, а, *n.* land-tenure regulations.

землечерпа́лк|а, и, *f.* (*tech.*) dredger, excavator.

землечерпа́ни|е, я, *n.* (*tech.*) dredging.

земли́ст|ый (~, ~а), *adj.* earthy; sallow (*of complexion*).

зем|ля́, ли́, *a.* ~лю, *pl.* ~ли, ~е́ль, ~ля́м, *f.* **1.** earth; (dry) land; уви́деть ~лю to sight land; упа́сть на ~лю to fall to the ground. **2.** land; soil (*fig.*); поме́щичья з. (*collect.*) landed estates; на чужо́й ~ле́ on foreign soil. **3.** earth, soil.

земля́к, а́, *m.* fellow-countryman, person from same district.

земляни́к|а, и, *no pl., f.* (*collect.*) wild strawberries.

земля́н|ин, ина, *pl.* ~е, ~, *m.* **1.** (*hist.*) landholder. **2.** earth-dweller.

земляни́|чный, *adj.* of ~ка.

земля́нк|а, и, *f.* dug-out; adobe cottage.

земля́н|о́й, *adj.* **1.** earthen, of earth; ~ы́е рабо́ты excavations. **2.** earth-; ~а́я гру́ша Jerusalem artichoke; з. оре́х peanut; з. червь earth-worm.

земля́честв|о, а, *n.* **1.** friendly society of persons coming from same district. **2.** national group (*of foreign students at Soviet universities*).

земля́чк|а, и, *f.* of земля́к.

зе́мно, *adv.*, *only in phrase* з. кла́няться (*obs.*) to bow to the ground.

земново́дн|ый, *adj.* amphibious; *as noun* (*zool.*) ~ые, ~ых, amphibia; *sing.* ~ое, ~ого, *n.* amphibian.

земн|о́й, *adj.* **1.** earthly; terrestrial; ~а́я кора́ (earth-)crust; з. шар the globe; ~ы́е вое́нные си́лы land forces; з. покло́н bow to the ground. **2.** (*fig.*) mundane.

земноро́дный, *adj.* (*poet., rhet.*) earth-born, mortal.

зе́м|ский, *adj.* **1.** of ~ля́ 2; (*hist.*) з. нача́льник land captain (*holder of office established in 1889*); ~ское ополче́ние militia; З. собо́р Assembly of the Land (*in Muscovite Russia*). **2.** of ~ство.

зе́мств|о, а, *n.* **1.** zemstvo (*elective district council in Russia, 1864–1917*). **2.** zemstvo system (*of local administration*).

зе́мщин|а, ы, *f.* (*hist.*) **1.** populace. **2.** zemshchina (*boyar domains, as opp. to oprichnina, under Tsar Ivan IV*).

зени́т, а, *m.* zenith (*also fig.*).

зени́тк|а, и, *f.* (*mil.; coll.*) anti-aircraft gun.

зени́тн|ый, *adj.* **1.** (*astron.*) zenithal; ~ое расстоя́ние zenith-distance. **2.** (*mil.*) anti-aircraft.

зени́тчик, а, *m.* (*mil.*) anti-aircraft gunner.

зени́ц|а, ы, *f.* (*arch.*) pupil (*of the eye*); бере́чь как ~у о́ка to keep as the apple of one's eye.

зе́ркал|о, а, *pl.* ~а́, зерка́л, ~а́м, *n.* looking-glass; mirror (*also fig.*); криво́е з. distorting mirror.

зерка́льн|ый, *adj.* of зе́ркало; (*fig.*) smooth; ~ое стекло́ plate glass; ~ое окно́ plate-glass window; ~ое изображе́ние looking-glass reflection; ~ая пове́рхность smooth surface; з. карп (*zool.*) mirror carp.

зерни́ст|ый (~, ~а), *adj.* granular; ~ая икра́ unpressed caviar(e).

зер|но́, на́, *pl.* ~на, ~ен, ~нам, *n.* **1.** grain; seed; (*fig.*) grain; kernel, core; горчи́чное з. mustard seed; жемчу́жное з. pearl; ко́фе в ~нах coffee beans; з. и́стины grain of truth. **2.** (*collect., sing. only*) grain, corn.

зернови́д|ный (~ен, ~на), *adj.* granular.

зернво́з, а, *m.* grain carrier (*ship*).

зернов|о́й, *adj.* grain, corn; ~ы́е зла́ки cereals; ~а́я торго́вля grain trade.

зернодроби́лк|а, и, *f.* (*agric.*) corn-crusher.

зерносовхо́з, а, *m.* State grain farm.

зерносуши́лк|а, и, *f.* (*agric.*) grain dryer.

зернохрани́лищ|е, а, *n.* granary.

зерца́л|о, а, *n.* **1.** (*arch.*) looking-glass. **2.** (*pl. only; hist.*) breastplate.

зефи́р, а, *m.* **1.** З. (*poet.*) Zephyr. **2.** zephyr (*material*).

зигза́г, а, *m.* zigzag.

зижди́тел|ь, я, *m.* (*obs. or rhet.*) founder, author; (*rel.*) the Creator.

зижди́тельный, *adj.* (*obs.*) creative.

зи́жд|иться, ется, *impf.* (на+*p.*; *obs. or rhet.*) to be founded (on), based (on).

зил, а, *m.* Zil (*motor-vehicle produced by Likhachev factory*).

зим, а, *m.* Zim (*motor-vehicle produced by former Molotov factory*).

зим|а́, ы́, *a.* ~у, *pl.* ~ы, *d.* ~ам, *f.* winter; на́ ~у for the winter; всю ~у all winter; ско́лько лет, ско́лько ~, *see* ле́то.

зимбабви́|ец, йца, *m.* Zimbabwean (man).

зимбабви́йк|а, и, *f.* Zimbabwean (woman).

зимбабви́йский, *adj.* Zimbabwean.

зи́м|ний, *adj. of* ~á; winter; wintry.

зим|ова́ть, у́ю, *impf.* (*of* пере~ *and* про~) to winter, pass the winter; to hibernate; знать, где ра́ки ~у́ют, *see* рак.

зимо́вк|а, и, *f.* 1. wintering, hibernation; оста́ться на ~у to stay for the winter. 2. polar station.

зимо́вщик, а, *m.* winterer.

зимо́вь|е, я, *n.* winter quarters, winter hut.

зимо́й, *adv.* in winter.

зиморо́д|ок, ка, *m.* (*orn.*) kingfisher.

зипу́н, а́, *m.* homespun coat.

зис, а, *m.* Zis (*motor-vehicle produced by former Stalin factory*).

зия́ни|е, я, я, *n.* 1. gaping, yawning. 2. (*ling.*) hiatus.

зия́|ть, ю, *impf.* to gape, yawn; ~ющая бе́здна yawning abyss.

злак, а, *m.* (*bot.*) grass; хле́бные ~и cereals.

зла́т|о, а, *n.* (*arch.; poet.*) gold.

златове́рхий, *adj.* (*folk poet.*) with roof(s) of gold.

златогла́вый, *adj.* gold-domed; with gold cupolas.

златоку́дрый, *adj.* (*poet.*) golden-haired.

зла́чн|ый, *adj.* (*obs.*) lush; (*coll.*) ~ое ме́сто haunt of vice.

зле́йший, *superl. of* злой.

зл|ить, ю, ишь, *impf.* (*of* обо~ *and* разо~) to anger; to vex; to irritate.

зл|и́ться, юсь, и́шься, *impf.* (*of* обо~ *and* разо~) 1. (на+*a.*) to be in a bad temper; to be angry (with). 2. (*fig., poet.*) to rage (*of a storm*).

зло¹, зла, *no pl. except g.* зол, *n.* 1. evil; harm; отплати́ть ~м за добро́ to repay good with evil. 2. evil, misfortune, disaster; из двух зол вы́брать ме́ньшее to choose the lesser of two evils; жела́ть кому́-н. зла to bear someone malice. 3. (*sing. only*) malice, spite; vexation; он э́то сде́лал то́лько со зла he did it purely from malice, out of spite; меня́ з. берёт it vexes me, it annoys me, I feel vexed, annoyed.

зло², *adv. of* ~й.

злоб|а, ы, *f.* malice; spite; anger; по ~е out of spite; со ~ой maliciously; з. дня topic of the day, latest news; довле́ет

дне́ви з. его́ (*arch.*) sufficient unto the day is the evil thereof.

злоб|иться, люсь, ишься, *impf.* (на+*a.*; *coll.*) to feel malice (towards); to be in a bad temper (with).

злоб|ный (~ен, ~на), *adj.* malicious, spiteful; bad-tempered.

злободне́вност|ь, и, *f.* topical interest, topical character.

злободне́вн|ый, *adj.* topical; ~ые вопро́сы burning topics of the day.

злоб|ствовать, ую, *impf.* to bear malice; (на+*a.*) to have it in (for).

злове́щ|ий (~, ~а), *adj.* ominous, ill-omened; sinister.

зловони|е, я, *n.* stink, stench.

зловон|ный (~ен, ~на), *adj.* fetid, stinking.

зловре́д|ный (~ен, ~на), *adj.* pernicious; noxious.

злоде́|й, я, *m.* 1. villain, scoundrel (*also joc.*) 2. (*theatr.; obs.*) villain.

злоде́йский, *adj.* villainous.

злоде́йств|о, а, *n.* 1. villainy. 2. crime, evil deed.

злоде́йств|овать, ую, *impf.* to act villainously.

злодея́ни|е, я, *n.* crime, evil deed.

зложела́тельный, *adj.* (*obs.*) malevolent.

злой (зол, зла, зло), *adj.* 1. evil; bad; з. ге́ний evil genius. 2. wicked; malicious; malevolent; vicious; зла́я улы́бка malevolent smile; со злым у́мыслом with malicious intent; (*leg.*) of malice prepense. 3. (*short form only*) angry; быть злым (на+*a.*) to be angry (with). 4. (*of animals*) fierce, savage; «зла́я соба́ка» 'beware of the dog!' 5. dangerous; severe; з. моро́з severe frost. 6. (*coll.*) bad, nasty; з. ка́шель bad cough. 7. (*sl.*) terrible (= keen, enthusiastic).

злока́чественн|ый, *adj.* (*med.*) malignant; ~ая о́пухоль malignant tumour; ~ое малокро́вие pernicious anaemia.

злоключе́ни|е, я, *n.* mishap, misadventure.

злоко́зненный, *adj.* (*obs.*) crafty, wily; perfidious.

злонаме́рен|ный (~, ~на), *adj.* ill-intentioned.

злонра́ви|е, я, *n.* (*obs.*) bad character; depravity.

злонра́в|ный (~ен, ~на), *adj.* (*obs.*) having a bad character; depraved.

злопа́мятност|ь, и, f. = злопа́мятство.

злопа́мят|ный (~ен, ~на), *adj.* rancorous.

злопа́мятств|о, а, *n.* rancour.

злополу́ч|ный (~ен, ~на), *adj.* unlucky, ill-starred.

злопыха́тел|ь, я, *m.* (*coll.*) disingenuous, spiteful critic.

злопыха́тельский, *adj.* (*coll.*) disingenuously spiteful, malevolent; ranting.

злопыхáтельств|о, а, *n.* (*coll.*) malevolence; ranting.

злорáдный, *adj.* gloating, maliciously rejoicing at others' misfortune.

злорáдств|о, а, *n.* Schadenfreude (*malicious delight in others' misfortunes*).

злорáдств|овать, ую, *impf.* to rejoice at, gloat over, others' misfortune.

злослóви|е, я, *n.* scandal, backbiting.

злослóв|ить, лю, ишь, *impf.* to say spiteful things.

злóст|ный (~ен, ~на), *adj.* 1. malicious. 2. conscious, intentional; ~ное банкрóтство fraudulent bankruptcy; з. неплатéльщик persistent defaulter (*in payment of debt*). 3. inveterate, hardened.

злост|ь, и, *f.* malicious anger, fury; их з. берёт на негó they are furious with him.

злосчáст|ный (~ен, ~на), *adj.* ill-fated, ill-starred.

злóт|ый, ого, *m.* zloty (*Polish currency*).

злоумы́шленник,а,*m.*(*obs.*); plotter; criminal.

злоумы́шленный, *adj.* (*obs.*) with criminal intent.

злоумышля́|ть, ю, *impf.* (*obs.*) to plot.

злоупотреб|и́ть, лю́, и́шь, *pf.* (*of* ~ля́ть) (+*i.*) to abuse; to indulge in to excess; to overdo; з. влáстью to abuse power; з. чьим-н. внимáнием to take up too much of someone's time.

злоупотреблéни|е, я, *n.* (+*i.*) abuse (of); з. довéрием breach of confidence.

злоупотреб|ля́ть, ля́ю, *impf. of* ~и́ть.

злоязы́чи|е, я, *n.* (*obs.*) slander, back-biting.

злоязы́чн|ый (~ен, ~на), *adj.* (*obs.*) slanderous.

злы́д|ень, ня, *m.* (*dial.*) 1. (*obs.*) rogue, rascal. 2. wicked person; wicked creature.

злю́к|а, и, *m. and f.* (*coll.*) bad-tempered person; (*f.*) shrew.

злю́чк|а, и, *m. and f.* = злю́ка.

злю́щий, *adj.* (*coll.*) furious.

змееви́д|ный (~ен, ~на), *adj.* serpentine; sinuous, snaky.

змееви́к, á, *m.* 1. (*tech.*) coil(-pipe). 2. (*min.*) serpentine, ophite.

змеёныш, а, *m.* young snake.

зме|и́ный, *adj.* 1. *adj. of* ~я́; ~и́ная кóжа snake-skin. 2. cunning, crafty; wicked.

змеи́ст|ый (~, ~а), *adj.* serpentine, sinuous.

зме|и́ться, и́тся, *impf.* to wind, coil; (*fig.*, *poet.*, *pejor.*) to glide; по её лицý ~и́лась улы́бка a smile stole across her face.

змей, змея, *m.* 1. (*obs. or coll.*) = змея́. 2. dragon. 3. (бумáжный) з. kite; запусти́ть змéя to fly a kite.

змéйк|а, и, *f.* 1. *dim. of* змея́; бежáть ~ой to glide. 2. (*mil.*) broken file.

змéйковый, *adj.*; з. аэростáт kite balloon.

зме|я́, й, *pl.* ~и, ~й, *f.* snake (*also fig.*);

отогрéть, пригрéть ~ю́ на своéй грудú to cherish a snake in one's bosom.

змий|й, я, *m.* (*arch.*) serpent, dragon; the Serpent (*Old Testament representation of the Devil*); напи́ться до зелёного ~я (*coll.*) to drink oneself into delirium tremens.

знавáть, *pres. not used, impf.* (*coll.*) *freq. of* знать.

знак, а, *m.* 1. (*in var. senses*) sign; mark; token, symbol; ~и препинáния stops, punctuation marks; ~и отли́чия decorations (and medals); ~и разли́чия (*mil.*) badges of rank, insignia; в з. (+*g.*) as a mark (of), as a token (of), to show. 2. omen. 3. signal; подáть з. to give a signal.

знакóм|ить, лю, ишь, *impf.* (*of* по~) (+*a.* с+*i.*) to acquaint (with); to introduce (to).

знакóм|иться, люсь, ишься, *impf.* (*of* по~) (с+*i.*) 1. to meet, make the acquaintance (*of a person*). 2. to introduce oneself; ~ьтесь! (*informal mode of introduction*) may I introduce you? 3. to become acquainted (with), familiarize oneself (with); to study, investigate; з. с мéстностью to get to know a locality; з. с теóрией относи́тельности to go into the theory of relativity.

знакóмств|о, а, *n.* 1. (с+*i.*) acquaintance (with). 2. acquaintances; (*collect.*) acquaintance; у негó большóе з. he has a wide circle of acquaintances; по ~у by exploiting one's personal connexions, by pulling strings. 3. (с+*i.*) knowledge (of).

знакóм|ый (~, ~а), *adj.* 1. familiar; егó лицó мне ~о his face is familiar. 2. (с+*i.*) familiar (with); быть ~ым (с+*i.*) to be acquainted (with), know; я с ней ~ с дéтства I have known her since childhood. 3. *as noun* з., ~ого, *m.*; ~ая, ~ой, *f.* acquaintance, friend.

знаменáтел|ь, я, *m.* (*math.*) denominator; óбщий з. common denominator; привести́ к одномý ~ю (*fig.*) to reduce to a common denominator.

знаменáтел|ьный (~ен, ~ьна), *adj.* 1. significant, important. 2. (*gram.*) principal (*as opp. to* subordinate).

знáм|ени, енем, *etc., see* ~я.

знáмени|е, я, *n.* sign; ~я врéмени signs of the times.

знамени́тост|ь, и, *f.* celebrity.

знамени́т|ый (~, ~а), *adj.* 1. celebrated, famous, renowned. 2. (*coll.*) outstanding, superlative.

знамен|овáть, ýю, *impf.* to signify, mark.

знаменóс|ец, ца, *m.* standard-bearer (*also fig.*).

знамёнщик, а, *m.* (*mil.*) colour bearer.

знáмо, *as pred.* (*coll. or dial.*) it is well known.

знáм|я, *g.*, *d.*, *and p.* ~ени, *i.* ~енем, *pl.* ~ёна, ~ён, *n.* banner; standard; под ~енем (+*g.*; *fig.*, *rhet.*) in the name of;

высóко держáть з. свобóды to keep the flag of freedom flying.

знáни|е, я, *n.* **1.** knowledge; теóрия ~я (*philos.*) theory of knowledge; у негó хорóшее з. сцéны he has a good knowledge of the stage; со ~ем дéла capably, competently. **2.** (*pl. only*) learning; accomplishments.

знáт|ный (~ен, ~нá, ~но), *adj.* **1.** (*adj. of* ~ь²) in an exalted station. **2.** outstanding, distinguished; ~ные лю́ди celebrities, leading figures. **3.** (*coll.*) splendid; ~ные блúнчики splendid pancakes; ~ная сýмма a splendid sum (*of money*).

знатóк, á, *m.* expert; connoisseur.

зна|ть¹, ю, *impf.* to know, have a knowledge of; ~ете ли вы Алексáндрова? do you know Alexandrov?; з. в лицó to know by sight; з. своё дéло to know one's job; з. своё мéсто to know one's place; з. мéру to know when to stop; не з. покóя to know no peace; з. толк (в+*p.*) to be knowledgeable (about); з. урóк to know a lesson; он хорошó ~ет Пýшкина he has a good knowledge of Pushkin; з. себé цéну to know one's own value; онú не ~ли о нáших намéрениях they were unaware of our intentions; дать комý-н. з. to let someone know; дáйте мне з. о вас let me hear from you; дать себя́ з. to make itself felt; он з. не хóчет he won't listen; ~й (себé) unconcerned; онá ~й себé пéла she was singing away quite unconcerned; то и ~й (*coll.*) continually; как з., почём з.? who can tell?, how should I know?; кто егó ~ет, Бог егó ~ет, чёрт егó ~ет (*coll.*) goodness knows!, God knows!, the devil (only) knows!; ~ешь (ли), ~ете (ли) (*coll.*) you know, do you know what.

знат|ь², и, *no pl.,f.* (*collect.*) the nobility, the aristocracy.

знать³, *as pred.* (*coll.*) evidently, it seems.

знá|ться, юсь, *impf.* (с+*i.*; *coll.*) to associate (with).

знáхар|ка, ки, *f. of* ~ь.

знáхар|ь, я, *m.* sorcerer, witch-doctor; quack(-doctor).

знáч|ащий, *pres. part. act. of* ~ить *and adj.* significant, meaningful.

значéни|е, я, *n.* **1.** meaning, significance. **2.** importance, significance; придáть большóе з. (+*d.*) to attach great importance (to); э́то не имéет ~я it is of no importance. **3.** (*math.*) value.

знáчимост|ь, и, *f.* significance.

знáчимый, *adj.* significant.

знáчит (*coll.*) so, then; well then; он ýмер до войны́? з., вы нé были с ним знакóмы he died before the war? then you didn't know him.

значúтел|ьный (~ен, ~ьна), *adj.* **1.** considerable, sizeable; в ~ьной стéпени to a considerable extent. **2.** important, great; игрáть ~ьную роль to play an important part. **3.** significant, meaningful.

знáч|ить, у, ишь, *impf.* **1.** to mean, signify. **2.** to mean, have significance, be of importance; ничегó не ~ит it is of no importance; получúть приглашéние на бал óчень мнóго ~ит для неё to be invited to a dance means a great deal to her.

знáч|иться, усь, ишься, *impf.* to be; to be mentioned, appear; з. в отпускý to be on leave; з. в спúске to appear on a list.

знач|óк, кá, *m.* **1.** badge. **2.** mark (*in margin of book, etc.*).

знá|ющий, *pres. part. act. of* ~ть *and adj.* expert; learned, erudite.

зноб|úть, úт, *impf.* **1.** (*coll.*) to chill. **2.** (*impers.*) меня́, *etc.*, ~úт I, *etc.*, feel shivery, feverish.

зноб|кий (~ок, ~кá, ~ко), *adj.* (*dial.*) **1.** sensitive to cold. **2.** chilly.

зно|й, я, *m.* intense heat; sultriness.

знó|йный (~ен, ~йна), *adj.* hot, sultry; burning (*also fig.*).

зоб, а, *pl.* ~ы́, ~óв, *m.* **1.** crop, craw (*of birds*). **2.** (*med.*) goitre.

зобáст|ый (~, ~а), *adj.* (*coll.*) **1.** with a large crop (*of birds*). **2.** goitrous.

зов, а, *m.* **1.** call, summons. **2.** (*coll.*) invitation.

зов|ý, ёшь, *see* звать.

зодиáк, а, *m.* (*astron.*) zodiac; знáки ~а signs of the zodiac.

зодиакáльный, *adj.* (*astron.*) zodiacal, of the zodiac.

зóдчес|кий, *adj. of* ~тво.

зóдчеств|о, а, *n.* architecture.

зóдч|ий, его, *m.* (*obs.*) architect.

зол¹, *see* злой.

зол², *g. pl. of* зло¹.

зол|á, ы́, *no pl.,f.* ashes, cinders.

золóвк|а, и, *f.* sister-in-law (*husband's sister*).

золотáрник, а, *m.* (*bot.*) golden rod.

золотúльщик, а, *m.* gilder.

золотúст|ый (~, ~а), *adj.* golden (*of colour*).

золо|тúть, чý, тúшь, *impf.* (*of* вы́~ *and* по~) to gild.

золо|тúться, тúтся, *impf.* **1.** to become golden. **2.** to shine (*of something golden*).

золотнúк¹, á, *m.* zolotnik (*old Russian measure of weight, equivalent to $\frac{1}{96}$ of Russian pound*); мал з., да дóрог (*coll.*) small but precious.

золотнúк², á, *m.* (*tech.*) slide valve; цилиндрúческий з. piston valve.

золотникóвый, *adj. of* золотнúк²; з. двúгатель pusher-type engine; з. привóд eccentric drive.

зо́лот|о, а, *no pl.*, *n.* gold; (*collect.*) gold
(*coins*, *ware*); плати́ть ~ом to pay in gold;
есть на ~е to eat off gold plate. **2.** (*fig.*)
она́ настоя́щее з. she is pure gold, a treasure; не всё то з., что блести́т (*prov.*) all is
not gold that glitters; на вес ~а worth its
weight in gold.

золотоволо́сый, *adj.* golden-haired.

золотоиска́тел|ь, я, *m.* gold-prospector;
gold-digger.

золот|о́й, *adj.* **1.** gold; golden (*also fig.*);
~ых дел ма́стер goldsmith; з. песо́к gold-
-dust; з. запа́с (*econ.*) gold reserves; ~а́я
ры́бка goldfish; ~о́е руно́ (*myth.*) golden
fleece; з. век the Golden Age; ~о́е дно
(*fig.*) gold-mine; ~а́я молодёжь jeunesse
dorée, gilded youth; ~ы́е ру́ки skilful
fingers; ~а́я середи́на golden mean; ~о́е
сече́ние (*math.*) golden section. **2.** (*coll.*) invaluable, precious; мой з.! my precious!,
my darling! **3.** *as noun* з., ~о́го *m.* gold
coin; ten-rouble piece.

золото́сный, *adj.* gold-bearing; з. райо́н
gold-field.

золотопромы́шленник, а, *m.* owner of
gold-mines.

золотопромы́шленност|ь, и, *f.* gold-min-
ing.

золоторо́т|ец, ца, *m.* (*obs.*, *coll.*) tramp,
down-and-out.

золототы́сячник, а, *m.* (*bot.*) centaury.

золотошве́йный, *adj.* of gold embroidery.

золоту́х|а, и, *f.* (*med.*) scrofula.

золоту́шный, *adj.* (*med.*) scrofulous.

золоче́ни|е, я, *n.* gilding.

золочёный, *adj.* gilded, gilt.

Зо́лушк|а, и, *f.* Cinderella.

зо́льник, а, *m.* (*tech.*) ashpit.

зо́н|а, ы, *f.* **1.** zone; area, belt; з. де́йствий
(*mil.*) zone of operations; з. досяга́емости
(*mil.*) field of fire; з. пораже́ния (*mil.*) area
under fire. **2.** (*geol.*) stratum, layer.

зона́льный, *adj.* zone; regional.

зонд, а, *m.* **1.** (*med.*) probe. **2.** (*geol.*) bore.
3. weather-balloon, sonde.

зонди́р|овать, ую, *impf.* (*med. and fig.*) to
sound, probe; з. по́чву (*fig.*) to explore the
ground.

зо́н|ный, *adj.* of ~а; (*railways*) regional.

зонт, а́, *m.* **1.** umbrella. **2.** awning. **3.**
(chimney) cowl.

зо́нтик, а, *m.* **1.** umbrella; sunshade,
parasol. **2.** (*bot.*) umbel.

зо́нти|чный, *adj.* of ~к; (*bot.*) umbellate,
umbelliferous.

зоо́лог, а, *m.* zoologist.

зоологи́ческий, *adj.* **1.** zoological; з. парк,
з. сад zoological garden(s). **2.** (*fig.*) brutish, bestial.

зооло́ги|я, и, *f.* zoology.

зоопа́рк, а, *m.* zoological gardens, zoo.

зооте́хник, а, *m.* livestock specialist.

зо́ри, *see* заря́.

зо́р|кий (~ок, ~ка́, ~ко), *adj.* **1.** sharp-
-sighted. **2.** (*fig.*) perspicacious, penetrat-
ing; vigilant.

зо́рьк|а, и, (*folk poet.*) *affect. form of* заря́.

зо́рю, *see* заря́.

зра́з|ы, ~, *sing.* (*rare*) ~а, ~ы, *f.* (*cul.*) zrazy
(*meat cutlets stuffed with rice, buckwheat kasha,
etc.*).

зрач|о́к, ка́, *m.* pupil (*of the eye*).

зре́лищ|е, а, *n.* **1.** sight. **2.** spectacle; show;
pageant.

зре́лищ|ный, *adj.* of ~е; ~ные предприя́тия
places of entertainment.

зре́лост|ь, и, *f.* ripeness; maturity (*also fig.*);
полова́я з. puberty; аттеста́т ~и school-
-leaving certificate.

зре́л|ый (~, ~а́, ~о), *adj.* ripe; mature (*also
fig.*); дости́гнуть ~ого во́зраста to reach
maturity; з. ум a mature mind; по ~ом
размышле́нии on reflection, on second
thoughts.

зре́ни|е, я, *n.* (eye)sight; по́ле ~я (*phys.*)
field of vision; обма́н ~я optical illusion;
то́чка ~я point of view; под э́тим угло́м
~я from this standpoint.

зре|ть¹, ю, ешь, *impf.* (*of* со~) to ripen; to
mature (*also fig.*); у нас ~ет план our plans
are maturing.

зреть², зрю, зришь, *impf.* (*of* у~) (*obs.*) **1.** to
behold. **2.** (на+*a.*) to gaze (upon).

зри́м|ый (~, ~а), *p.p.p. of* зреть² *and adj.*
visible.

зри́тел|ь, я, *m.* spectator, observer; быть
~ем to look on.

зри́тельн|ый, *adj.* **1.** visual; optic; з. нерв
optic nerve; ~ая па́мять visual memory;
~ая труба́ telescope. **2.** з. зал hall, audi-
torium.

зря, *adv.* (*coll.*) to no purpose, for nothing;
болта́ть з. to chatter idly; рабо́тать з. to
plough the sand.

зря́чий, *adj.* sighted (*as opp. to* blind).

зуа́в, а, *m.* zouave.

зуб, а, *m.* **1.** (*pl.* ~ы, ~о́в) tooth; з. му́д-
рости wisdom tooth; вооружённый до
~о́в armed to the teeth; име́ть з. (про́тив),
точи́ть ~ы (на+*a.*; *coll.*) to have it in for
someone; положи́ть ~ы на по́лку (*coll.*) to
tighten one's belt; он по-неме́цки ни в з.
толкну́ть (*coll.*) he does not know a word
of German; не по ~а́м beyond one's
capacity; (*coll.*) э́та пробле́ма мне не по
~а́м I cannot get my teeth into this problem; э́то у меня́ в ~а́х навя́зло (*coll.*)
it sticks in my gullet, I am sick and tired
of it; у тебя́ з. на́ з. не попада́ет your

teeth are chattering; хоть вѝдит óко, да з.
неймёт (*coll.*) there's many a slip 'twixt
the cup and lip; ⌒ы заговорѝть, *see* заго-
ворѝть¹; держáть язы́к за ⌒áми to hold
one's tongue. **2.** (*pl.* ⌒ья, ⌒ьев) tooth, cog.
зубáст|ый (⌒, ⌒а), *adj.* (*coll.*) large-toothed;
(*fig.*) sharp-tongued.
зуб|éц, цá, *m.* **1.** tooth, cog; з. вѝлки prong.
2. merlon (*of wall*). **3.** (*radar*) blip.
зубѝл|о, а, *n.* (*tech.*) point-tool, chisel.
зýбно-губнóй, *adj.* (*ling.*) labio-dental.
зубн|óй, *adj.* **1.** dental; з. боль tooth-
-ache; з. врач dentist; ⌒áя пáста tooth-
-paste; з. порошóк tooth-powder; ⌒áя
щётка tooth-brush. **2.** (*ling.*) dental.
зубóвн|ый, *adj.*, *only in phrases* скрéжет з.
gnashing of teeth; дéлать что-н. со
скрéжетом ⌒ым to do something with extreme unwillingness.
зубоврачéбн|ый, *adj.* *of* зубнóй врач; з.
кабинéт dental surgery; ⌒ая шкóла dental
school.
зубоврачевáни|е, я, *n.* dentistry.
зуб|óк, кá, *pl.* ⌒кѝ, *m.* **1.** (*g. pl.* ⌒óк) *dim. of*
⌒; подарѝть на з. (*coll.*) to bring a present
for a (new-born) baby; вы́учить на з. (*coll.*)
to learn by rote; попáсть на з. кому́-н.
(*coll., fig.*) to be torn to pieces by someone.
2. (*g. pl.* ⌒кóв) bit (*of coal-cutting machine*).
зуболечéбниц|а, ы, *f.* dental surgery.
зубоскáл|ить, ю, ишь, *impf.* (*coll.*) to scoff,
mock.
зубоскáльств|о, а, *n.* (*coll.*) scoffing, mock-
ing.
зуботы́чин|а, ы, *f.* (*vulg.*) sock on the jaw.
зубочѝстк|а, и, *f.* toothpick.
зубр, а, *m.* **1.** (*zool.*) (European) bison.
2. (*fig.*) die-hard.
зубрёжк|а, и, *f.* (*coll.*) cramming.
зубрѝл|а, ы, *m. and f.* (*coll.*) crammer.
зубр|ѝть¹, ю́, ⌒ѝшь, *impf.* (*of* за⌒) to notch,
serrate.
зубр|ѝть², ю́, ⌒ ѝшь, *impf.* (*of* вы́⌒ *and* за⌒)
(*coll.*) to cram.
зубрóвк|а, и, *f.* **1.** sweet grass, holy grass.
2. zubrovka (*sweet-grass vodka*).
зубчáтк|а, и, *f.* (*tech.*) rack-wheel.
зубчáт|ый, *adj.* **1.** (*tech.*) toothed, cogged;

⌒ая желéзная дорóга rack-railway; ⌒ое
колесó rack-wheel, cogwheel, pinion; з.
насóс gear pump; ⌒ая рéйка rack. **2.**
jagged, indented.
зуд, а, *m.* itch; (*fig.*) itch, urge; писáтель-
ский з. the urge to write, to be a writer.
зуд|á, ы́, *m. and f.* (*coll.*) bore (*person*).
зуд|éть, ѝт, *impf.* **1.** (*coll.*) to itch (*intrans.*).
2. (*fig.*) to itch, feel an itch (*to do something*).
зу|дѝть, жу́, дѝшь, *impf.* (*coll.*) **1.** to nag at.
2. to cram.
зу|ёк, йкá, *m.* (*orn.*) plover.
зулу́с, а, *m.* Zulu.
зулу́сский, *adj.* Zulu.
зу́ммер, а, *m.* (*tech.*) buzzer.
зурн|á, ы́, *f.* (*mus.*) zurna (*kind of clarinet*).
зыб|иться, лется (*past and 1st and 2nd persons
of pres. not used*) *impf.* (*obs.*) to be ruffled (*of
the sea*); to toss (*intrans.*).
зы́бк|а, и, *f.* (*dial.*) cradle.
зы́б|кий (⌒ок, ⌒кá, ⌒ко), *adj.* unsteady,
shaky; (*fig.*) vacillating.
зыбу́н, á, *m.* marshy ground; bog.
зыбу́ч|ий, *adj.* unsteady, unstable; ⌒ие
пескѝ quicksands.
зыб|ь, и, *pl.* ⌒и, ⌒éй, *f.* (*on water*) ripple;
мёртвая з. swell; (*poet.*) lop.
зык, а, *m.* (*coll.*) loud voice; loud cry.
зы́к|ать, аю, *impf. of* ⌒нуть.
зы́к|нуть, ну, нешь, *pf.* (*of* ⌒ать) **1.** to
shout, cry out. **2.** to whistle, whizz.
зы́ч|ный (⌒ен, ⌒на), *adj.* (*coll.*) loud, shrill.
зюйд, а, *m.* (*naut.*) **1.** south. **2.** southerly
wind.
зюйдвéстк|а, и, *f.* sou'wester (*hat*).
зэк, а, *m.* (*sl.*) prisoner, convict.
зя́б|кий (⌒ок, ⌒кá, ⌒ко), *adj.* chilly, sensi-
tive to cold.
зя́б|левый, *adj.* *of* ⌒ь; ⌒левая вспáшка
autumn ploughing.
зя́блик, а, *m.* chaffinch.
зяб|нуть, ну, нешь, *past* ⌒, ⌒ла, *impf.* to
suffer from cold, feel the cold.
зяб|ь, и, *f.* (*agric.*) land ploughed in autumn
for spring sowing.
зят|ь, я, *pl.* ⌒ья́, ⌒ьёв, *m.* **1.** son-in-law.
2. brother-in-law (*sister's husband or husband's sister's husband*).

И

и¹, *conj.* **1.** and; добрó и зло good and evil;
indicating temporal sequence: я встал и вы́мыл-
ся и побрѝлся I got up and washed and
shaved; *introducing narrative*: и настáло
ýтро and then came the morning; *emphasizing questions*: и рáзве э́то не прáвда? and

is it not the truth?; *adversative*: мужчѝна,
и плáчет! a man, and crying!; и так дáлее,
и прóчее (*abbr.* и т. д., и пр.) etcetera, and
so on, and so forth. **2.** и ...и both ... and;
и тот и другóй both. **3.** too; (*with negation*)
either; онá сказáла, что и муж придёт she

said that her husband would come too; и он не знал he did not know either. **4.** even; и знато́к ошиба́ется even an expert may be mistaken; я не мог бы и поду́мать об э́том I would not (even) think of it. **5.** (*emphatic*) в то́м-то и де́ло that is the whole point. **6.** и... да (*concessive*): я и пое́хал бы, да не́когда (*coll.*) I should like to go, but I have not time; и рад э́то сде́лать, но не могу́ much as I should like to, I can't.

и², *interj.* (*expressing disagreement; coll.*) oh!; и, по́лно! that's quite enough!; (*iron.*) you don't say (so)!

ибери́йский, *adj.* Iberian.

и́бис, а, *m.* (*orn.*) ibis.

и́бо, *conj.* for.

и́в|а, ы, *f.* willow; корзи́ночная и. osier; плаку́чая и. weeping willow.

Ива́н, а, *m.* John; И. Купа́л|а, ы (*and ~о, ~а*), *no pl.*, St. John Baptist's Day (*24 June O.S.*); ночь на Ива́на Купа́лу Midsummer Night.

ива́н-да-ма́рья, **ива́н-да-ма́рьи**, *no pl., f.* (*bot.*) **1.** cow-wheat (*Melampyrum nemorosum*). **2.** heart's ease (*Viola tricolor*).

Ива́нов, *adj.*; И. день St. John's Day, Midsummer Day (*24 June O.S.*).

ива́новск|ий¹, *adj.* only in phrase во всю ~ую (*coll.*) with all one's might; extremely loudly; крича́ть во всю ~ую to shout at the top of one's voice; скака́ть во всю ~ую to go hell-for-leather.

ива́новский², *adj.*; и. червя́к (*dial.*) glow-worm.

ива́н-чай, **ива́н-ча́я**, *no pl., m.* (*bot.*) rose-bay, willow-herb.

иваси́, *indecl., f.* iwashi (*kind of sardine fished in Far Eastern waters*).

ивня́к, а́, *no pl., m.* **1.** osier-bed. **2.** (*collect.*) osier(s).

и́в|овый, *adj.* of ~а.

и́волг|а, и, *f.* (*orn.*) oriole.

иври́т, а, *m.* (modern) Hebrew.

игл|а́, ы́, *pl.* ~ы, ~, *f.* **1.** needle. **2.** (*bot.*) needle; thorn, prickle; ело́вая и. fir-needle. **3.** quill, spine (*of porcupine, etc.*).

игли́ст|ый (~, ~а), *adj.* prickly; covered with quills; и. скат thornback (*fish*).

иглови́дный (~ен, ~на), *adj.* needle-shaped.

иглодержа́тел|ь, я, *m.* needle-holder.

иглоко́ж|ие, их, *sing.* ~ее, ~его, *n.* (*zool.*) Echinodermata.

иглообра́з|ный (~ен, ~на), *adj.* needle-shaped.

игнори́р|овать, ую, *impf. and pf.* to ignore; to disregard.

и́г|о, а, *n.* yoke (*fig.*); тата́рское и. the Tatar yoke.

иго́лк|а, и, *f.* needle; сиде́ть как на ~ах to be on thorns, on tenterhooks; каблуки́ на ~ах stiletto heels.

иго́лочк|а, и, *f.* dim. of иго́лка; (*coll.*) оде́тый с ~и spick and span; костю́м с ~и brand-new suit.

иго́льник, а, *m.* needle-case.

иго́льн|ый, *adj.* of игла́; ~ое у́шко eye of a needle.

иго́льчат|ый, *adj.* **1.** needle-shaped; ~ые каблуки́ stiletto heels. **2.** (*min.*) needle (-shaped), acicular; ~ые криста́ллы acicular crystals; ~ая руда́ needle ore. **3.** (*tech.*) needle; и. кла́пан needle valve.

иго́рный, *adj.* playing, gaming; и. дом gaming-house; и. прито́н gambling-den; и. стол gaming-table.

игр|а́, ы́, *pl.* ~ы, *f.* **1.** play (*action*), playing; у скрипа́чки была́ блестя́щая и. the violinist's performance was brilliant; и. све́та на стене́ the play of light on the wall; и. слов play upon words; биржева́я и. stock exchange speculation; и. приро́ды freak, sport of nature. **2.** game; аза́ртная и. game of chance; ко́мнатные ~ы indoor games, party games; олимпи́йские ~ы Olympic games; (*fig.*) опа́сная и. dangerous game; и. не сто́ит свеч the game is not worth the candle; игра́ть, вести́ большу́ю, кру́пную ~у́ to play for high stakes; раскры́ть чью-н. ~у́ to uncover someone's game. **3.** (*sport, cards*) game (*part of set, match, etc.*); взять ~у́ при свое́й пода́че to win one's service. **4.** (*cards*) hand; сдать хоро́шую ~у́ to deal a good hand. **5.** turn (to play); сейча́с твоя́ и. it is your turn now.

игра́лищ|е, а, *n.* (*obs., rhet.*) plaything.

игра́льн|ый, *adj.* playing; ~ые ка́рты playing cards; ~ые ко́сти dice.

и́граный, *adj.* (*coll.*) (already) used.

игра́|ть, ю, *impf.* (*of* сыгра́ть) **1.** to play; и. пье́су to put on a play; и. роль to play a part; и. Ле́ди Ма́кбет to play, take the part of, Lady Macbeth; э́то не ~ет ро́ли it is of no importance, it does not signify; и. коме́дию to act (*fig.*); и. симфо́нию to play a symphony; и. пе́рвую, втору́ю скри́пку (*fig.*) to play first, second fiddle; и. кому́-н. в ру́ку (*fig.*) to play into someone's hand; и. глаза́ми to flash one's eyes; и. слова́ми to play upon words; и. ферзём to move the queen (*at chess*); и. в ка́рты, те́ннис, футбо́л, ша́хматы, *etc.*, to play cards, tennis, football, chess, *etc.*; и. в зага́дки to talk in riddles; и. в пря́тки to play hide-and-seek; (*fig.*) to be secretive; и. в скро́мность to feign modesty; и. на роя́ле, скри́пке, *etc.*, to play the piano, the violin, *etc.*; и. на билья́рде to play billiards;

и. на би́рже to speculate on the Stock Exchange; и. на (+р.) to play on (fig.); и. на чу́вствах толпы́ to play on the emotions of a crowd. 2. (impf. only) (+i. or c+i.) to play with, toy with, trifle with (also fig.); и. чьи́ми-н. чу́вствами to trifle with someone; и. с огнём (fig.) to play with fire. 3. (impf. only) to play; to sparkle (of wine, jewellery, etc.); улы́бка ~ла на её лице́ a smile played on her face.

игра́|ющий, pres. part. act. of ~ть; as noun и., ~ющего, m. player.

и́грек, а, m. (the letter) y; (math.) y (second unknown quantity).

игре́невый, adj. skewbald.

игре́ц, а́, m. 1. (obs.) musician, strolling player. 2. (coll.) player; швец и жнец, и в ду́ду и. jack-of-all-trades.

игри́в|ый (~, ~а), adj. playful; skittish (of a woman); (coll.) naughty, ribald.

игри́ст|ый (~, ~а), adj. sparkling (of wine).

игр|ово́й, adj. of ~á; и. автома́т fruit machine.

игро́к, а́, m. 1. (в+a., на+р.) player (of); и. в футбо́л football-player; хоро́ший и. на балала́йке a good balalaika player. 2. gambler.

игроте́к|а, и, f. compendium of children's games; games store.

игру́шечный, adj. 1. toy; и. магази́н toy-shop; и. парово́з toy engine. 2. (coll.) tiny.

игру́шк|а, и, f. (fig.) plaything.

и́гр|ывать, pres. not used; freq. of ~áть (coll.).

игуа́н|а, ы, f. (zool.) iguana.

игу́мен, а, m. (eccl.) Father Superior (of monastery).

игу́мен|ья, ьи, g. pl. ~ий, f. (eccl.) Mother Superior (of a convent).

идеа́л, а, m. ideal.

идеализи́р|овать, ую, impf. and pf. to idealize.

идеали́зм, а, m. (in var. senses) idealism.

идеали́ст, а, m. (in var. senses) idealist.

идеалисти́ческий, adj. (philos.) idealist(ic).

идеалисти́ч|ный (~ен, ~на), adj. idealistic.

идеа́л|ьный (~ен, ~ьна), adj. 1. (philos.) ideal. 2. (coll.) ideal, perfect.

иде́йк|а, и, f. (pejor.) dim. of иде́я.

иде́йност|ь, и, f. 1. ideological content. 2. 'progressive' character (of work of art, etc.—from Marxist point of view). 3. principle, integrity (from Marxist point of view).

иде́|йный (~ен, ~йна), adj. 1. ideological. 2. expressing an idea or ideas; committed, engagé; ~йная пье́са play of ideas. 3. 'progressive' (from Marxist point of view); ~йное иску́сство 'progressive' art. 4. high-principled, acting on principle (from Marxist point of view).

идентифика́ци|я, и, f. identification.

идентифици́р|овать, ую, impf. and pf. to identify.

иденти́ч|ный (~ен, ~на), adj. identical.

идеогра́мм|а, ы, f. (ling.) ideogram.

идеогра́фи|я, и, f. (ling.) ideography.

идео́лог, а, m. ideologist; (coll.) idea-monger.

идеологи́ческий, adj. ideological.

идеоло́ги|я, и, f. ideology.

идёт (3rd sing. pres. of идти́) as interj. (coll.) (all) right!

иде́|я, и, f. 1. idea (also coll.); notion, concept; (philos.) Idea; боро́ться за ~ю to fight for an idea; пода́ть ~ю to suggest, make a suggestion; навя́зчивая и. obsession, idée fixe; счастли́вая и. happy thought. 2. point, purport (of a work of art, of fiction, etc.).

идилли́ческий, adj. idyllic.

иди́лли|я, и, f. idyll (lit. and fig.).

идио́м|а, ы, f. (and ~, ~а, m.) idiom.

идиомати́зм, а, m. idiom.

идиома́тик|а, и, f. (ling.) 1. study of idiom(s). 2. (collect.) idiom, idiomatic expressions.

идиомати́ческий, adj. idiomatic.

идиосинкрази|я, и, f. 1. idiosyncrasy. 2. (med.) allergy.

идио́т, а, m. idiot, imbecile (med. and coll.).

идиоти́зм¹, а, m. idiocy, imbecility (med. and coll.).

идиоти́зм², а, m. (ling.) idiom.

идио́тический, adj. idiotic, imbecile.

идио́тский, adj. idiotic, imbecile.

и́дйш, indecl., m. Yiddish (language).

и́дол, а, m. 1. idol (also fig.); стоя́ть, сиде́ть ~ом to stand, sit like a stone image. 2. (coll., pejor.) callous or obtuse person.

идолопокло́нник, а, m. idolater.

идолопокло́ннический, adj. idolatrous.

идолопокло́нств|о, а, n. idolatry.

ид|ти́ (итти́), у́, ёшь, past шёл, шла, impf. (of пойти́; det. of ходи́ть) 1. to go; (impf. only) to come; и. в го́ру to go uphill; авто́бус ~ёт the bus is coming; кто ~ёт? who goes there?; и. гуля́ть to go for a walk; и. в прода́жу to go for sale, be up for sale; и. в но́гу to keep in step (also fig.); и. на охо́ту to go hunting; и. на сме́ну (+d.) to take the place (of), succeed. 2. (на+a.) to enter; (в+n.-a.) to become; и. на госуда́рственную слу́жбу to enter Government service; и. в лётчики to become an airman. 3. (в+a.) to be used (for); (на+a.) to go to make; и. в корм to be used for fodder; и. в лом to go for scrap; и. на ю́бку to go to make a skirt. 4. (из, от) to come (from), proceed (from); из трубы́ шёл чёрный дым black smoke was coming from the chimney. 5. (of news, etc.) to go round; шла мо́лва, что... word went round that . . ., rumour had it that . . . 6. (coll.) to sell, be sold; хорошо́ и. to be selling well;

за бесцéнок to go for a song. **7.** (*of machines, machinery, etc.*) to go, run, work. **8.** (*of rain, etc.*) to fall; дождь, снег ~ёт it is raining, snowing. **9.** (*of time*) to pass; шли гóды years passed; ей ~ёт тридцáтый год she is in her thirtieth year. **10.** to go on, be in progress; (*of entertainments*) to be on, be showing; переговóры ~ýт negotiations are in progress; сегóдня ~ёт «Ревизóр» 'The Government Inspector' is on tonight. **11.** (+*d. or* к) to suit, become; э́та шля́па ей не ~ёт this hat does not become her. **12.** (в, на+*a.*; *coll.*) to go (in, on). **13.** (+*i. or* с+*g.*) to play, lead, move (*at chess, cards, etc.*); и. ферзём to move one's queen; и. с червéй to lead a heart. **14.** (о+*p.*; *of a discussion, etc.*) to be (about); дéло ~ёт, речь ~ёт о том, что... the point is that . . ., it is a matter of . . .

йд|ы, ~, *no sing.* (*hist.*) Ides.

иегови́ст, а, *m.* (*rel.*) Jehovah's witness.

иезуи́т, а, *m.* (*eccl.*) Jesuit.

иезуи́тский, *adj.* (*eccl.*) Jesuit; (*fig.*) jesuitical.

иéн|а, ы, *f.* yen (*Japanese currency*).

иерархи́ческий, *adj.* hierarchic(al).

иерáрхи|я, и, *f.* hierarchy.

иерати́ческ|ий, *adj.* hieratic; ~ое письмó (*ling.*) hieratic script.

иерé|й, я, *m.* priest.

иерéйский, *adj.* priestly.

иеремиáд|а, ы, *f.* jeremiad.

иерóглиф, а, *m.* hieroglyph.

иероглифи́ческий, *adj.* hieroglyphic.

иеромонáх, а, *m.* (*eccl.*) father (*priest in monastic order, as opp. to lay brother*).

иждивéн|ец, ца, *m.* dependant.

иждивéни|е, я, *n.* **1.** maintenance; на чьём-н. ~и at someone's expense; жить на своём ~и to maintain oneself, keep oneself. **2.** (*obs.*) means, funds.

иждивéнчеств|о, а, *n.* dependence.

и́же, *relat. pron.* (*arch.*) who, which; *now only used in phrase* и и́же с ним(и) (and others) of that ilk, and company.

и́жиц|а, ы, *f.* 'v' (*last letter of Church Slavonic and pre-1918 Russian alphabet*); от азá до ~ы (*fig.*) from A to Z; прописáть ~у (+*d.*) (*obs. or joc.*) to lecture, bring to book; to give a lesson (to); с ногáми ~ей (*coll.*) knock-kneed.

из (изо), *prep.*+*g.* from, out of; of. **1.** *indicates place of origin of action, source, etc.*: приéхать из Лóндона to come from London; пить из чáшки to drink out of a cup; узнáть из газéт to learn from the newspapers; из достовéрных истóчников from reliable sources, on good authority; вы́йти из себя́ to be beside oneself; вы́йти из употреблéния to pass out of use, become obsolete; он из крестья́н he is of peasant

origin. **2.** *with numeral or in partitive sense*: оди́н из её поклóнников one of her admirers; ни оди́н из ста not one in a hundred; млáдший из всех the youngest of all; главнéйшие собы́тия из истóрии Росси́и the principal events in the history of Russia; трус из трýсов a craven. **3.** *indicates material*: из чегó э́то сдéлано? what is it made of?; варéнье из абрикóсов apricot jam; обéд из трёх блюд a three-course dinner; лóжки из серебрá silver spoons; букéт из крáсных гвозди́к bouquet of carnations; (*fig.*; *of human potential*) из негó вы́йдет хорóший трубáч he will make a good trumpet-player. **4.** *indicates agency*: изо всех сил with all one's might; из послéдних срéдств with one's last penny. **5.** *indicates cause, motive*: из благодáрности in gratitude; из ли́чных вы́год for private gain; из рéвности from jealousy; мнóго шýму из ничегó a lot of fuss about nothing.

из- (*also* **изо-, изъ-,** *and* **ис-**) *verbal prefix indicating*: **1.** motion outwards. **2.** action over entire surface of object, in all directions. **3.** expenditure of instrument *or* object in course of action; continuation *or* repetition of action to extreme point; exhaustiveness of action.

изб|á, ы́, *a.* ~ý, *pl.* ~ы, *f.* **1.** izba (*peasant's hut or cottage*); и.-читáльня, ~ы-читáльни, *f.* village reading-room. **2.** (*hist.*) government office (*in Muscovite Russia*).

избáб|иться, люсь, ишься, *pf.* (*coll.*) to become womanish, effeminate.

избави́тел|ь, я, *m.* deliverer.

избáв|ить, лю, ишь, *pf.* (*of* ~ля́ть) (от) to save, deliver (from); ~ьте меня́ от вáших замечáний spare me your remarks; ~ьте меня́! leave me alone!; ~и Бог! God forbid!

избáв|иться, люсь, ишься, *pf.* (*of* ~ля́ться) (от) to be saved (from), escape; to get out (of); to get rid (of); и. от привы́чки to get out of a habit.

избавлéни|е, я, *n.* deliverance.

избавля́|ть(ся), ю(сь), *impf. of* избáвить(ся).

избалóванный, *p.p.p. of* избаловáть *and* *adj.* spoilt.

избал|овáть, ýю, *pf.* (*of* баловáть *and* ~óвывать) to spoil (*a child, etc.*).

избал|овáться, ýюсь, *pf.* (*of* ~óвываться) to become spoilt.

избалóвыва|ть(ся), ю(сь), *impf. of* избаловáть(ся).

избáч, á, *m.* village librarian.

избéга|ть, ю, *pf.* (*coll.*) to run about, run all over.

избег|áть, áю, *impf.* (*of* ~нуть *and* избежáть) (+*g. or inf.*) to avoid; (*impf. only*) to shun; to escape, evade; и. встреча́ться с кем-н. to avoid meeting someone; и. штра́фа to evade a penalty.

избега́|ться, юсь, *pf.* (*coll.*) 1. to exhaust oneself by running (about). 2. to get out of hand (*of an undisciplined child*).

избе́г|нуть, ну, нешь, *past* ~нул *and* ~, ~ла, *pf. of* ~а́ть.

избежа́ни|е, я, *n.*; во и. (+*g.*) in order to avoid.

избе́|жа́ть, гу́, жи́шь, гу́т, *pf. of* ~га́ть.

избива́|ть(ся), ю(сь), *impf. of* изби́ть(ся).

избие́ни|е, я, *n.* 1. slaughter, massacre; и. младе́нцев (*bibl.*; *also fig. of persecutions*) Massacre of the Innocents. 2. (*leg.*) assault and battery.

избира́тел|ь, я, *m.* elector, voter.

избира́тельност|ь, и, *f.* (*radio*) selectivity.

избира́тельн|ый, *adj.* 1. electoral; и. бюлле́тень voting-paper; ~ая кампа́ния election campaign; и. о́круг electoral district; ~ое пра́во suffrage; franchise; и. спи́сок electoral roll, register of voters; ~ая у́рна ballot-box; и. уча́сток polling station; и. ценз voting qualification. 2. (*tech.*) selective.

избира́|ть, ю, *impf. of* избра́ть.

изби́т|ый, *p.p.p. of* ~ь *and adj.*; (*fig.*) hackneyed, trite.

из|би́ть, обью́, обьёшь, *pf.* (*of* ~бива́ть) 1. to beat unmercifully, beat up. 2. to slaughter, massacre. 3. (*coll.*) to wear down, ruin.

из|би́ться, обью́сь, обьёшься, *pf.* (*of* ~бива́ться) (*coll.*) 1. to bruise oneself. 2. to be worn out, be ruined.

избл|ева́ть, юю, юёшь, *pf.* (*of* ~ёвывать) 1. (*obs.*) to bring up, throw up; (*fig.*) to bring out (*coarse or vituperative language*). 2. (*coll.*) to vomit over.

изблёвыва|ть, ю, *impf. of* изблева́ть.

изб|но́й, *adj. of* ~а́.

избо́ин|а, ы, *no pl.*, *f.* (*agric.*) oilcake.

изболе́|ть(ся), ю(сь), *pf.* (*coll.*) to be in torment.

избо́рник, а, *m.* (*hist.*, *lit.*) miscellany, anthology.

избороз|ди́ть, жу́, ди́шь, *pf. of* борозди́ть 2.

избоче́н|иваться, ива́юсь, *impf. of* ~иться.

избоче́н|иться, юсь, ишься, *pf.* (*of* ~ивать ся) (*coll.*) to stand in a challenging pose (with one hip forward and one hand on it).

избра́ни|е, я, *n.* election.

избра́нник, а, *m.* (*rhet.*) elect, chosen one; favoured one, darling.

избра́нн|ица, ицы, *f. of* ~ик.

и́збран|ный, *p.p.p. of* избра́ть *and adj.* 1. selected; ~ные сочине́ния Пу́шкина selected works of Pushkin. 2. select; *as noun* ~ные, ~ных, *no sing.*, élite.

из|бра́ть, беру́, берёшь, *past* ~бра́л, ~брала́, ~бра́ло, *pf.* (*of* ~бира́ть) (+*a. and i.*) to elect (as, for); to choose; его́ ~бра́ли чле́ном парла́мента, he has been elected a Member of Parliament.

и́збура- brownish-; и.-жёлтый brownish--yellow.

избу́шк|а, и, *f. dim. of* изба́.

избыва́|ть, ю, *impf. of* избы́ть.

избы́т|ок, ка, *m.* surplus, excess; abundance, plenty; в ~ке in plenty; от ~ка се́рдца, от ~ка чувств out of the fullness of the heart.

избы́точ|ный (~ен, ~на), *adj.* 1. surplus. 2. abundant, plentiful.

из|бы́ть, бу́ду, бу́дешь, *past* ~бы́л, ~была́, ~бы́ло, *pf.* (*of* ~быва́ть) (*obs.*) to rid oneself of.

изб|яно́й, *adj. of* ~а́.

извая́ни|е, я, *n.* statue, sculpture; graven image.

извая́|ть, ю, *pf. of* вая́ть.

изве́д|ать, аю, *pf.* (*of* ~ывать) to come to know, learn the meaning of; и. го́ре to taste, have the taste of, grief.

изве́дыва|ть, ю, *impf. of* изве́дать.

изве́ка, *adv.* (*obs.*) of old.

и́зверг, а, *m.* monster, cruel person; и. ро́да челове́ческого scum of the earth.

изверг|а́ть, а́ю, *impf.* (*of* ~нуть) to throw out, disgorge; (*physiol.*) to excrete; (*fig.*) to eject, expel.

изверг|а́ться, а́юсь, *impf.* (*of* ~нуться) 1. to erupt (*of volcanoes*). 2. *pass. of* ~а́ть.

изве́рг|нуть(ся), ну(сь), нешь(ся), *past* ~(ся) *and* ~нул(ся), ~ла(сь), *pf. of* ~а́ть(ся).

изверже́ни|е, я, *n.* 1. eruption (*of volcano*). 2. ejection, expulsion; (*physiol.*) excretion. 3. (*pl. only*; *obs.*) excreta, ordure.

изве́рженный, *p.p.p. of* изве́ргнуть *and adj.* (*geol.*) igneous, eruptive, volcanic.

изве́рива|ться, юсь, *impf. of* изве́риться.

изве́р|иться, юсь, ишься, *pf.* (*of* ~иваться) (в+*a. or p.*) to lose faith (in), lose confidence (in); и. в люде́й, и. в лю́дях to lose faith in people.

извер|ну́ться, ну́сь, нёшься, *pf.* (*of* ~тываться[1] *and* извора́чиваться) (*coll.*) to dodge, take evasive action (*also fig.*); и. при отве́те to give an evasive answer.

извер|те́ться, чу́сь, ~ти́шься, *pf.* (*of* ~тываться[2]) (*coll.*) 1. to wear out (*intrans.*) as a result of turning (*of propeller, etc.*). 2. (*no impf.*; *fig.*) to become flighty; to go to the bad.

извёртыва|ться[1], юсь, *impf. of* изверну́ться.

извёртыва|ться[2], юсь, *impf. of* изверте́ться.

изве|сти́, ду́, дёшь, *past* ~л, ~ла́, *pf.* (*of*

изводи́ть) (*coll.*) **1.** to spend, use up; to waste. **2.** to destroy, exterminate. **3.** to vex, exasperate; to torment.

изве́сти|е, я, *n.* **1.** (о+*p.*) news (of); intelligence; information; после́дние ~я the latest news. **2.** (*pl. only*; *as title of periodicals*) proceedings, transactions; ~я Акаде́мии нау́к Proceedings of the Academy of Sciences.

изве|сти́сь, ду́сь, дёшься, *past* ~лся, ~ла́сь, *pf.* (*of* изводи́ться) (*coll.*) **1.** to consume oneself, eat one's heart out; to exhaust oneself, wear oneself out; и. от за́висти to consume oneself with envy. **2.** to perish, disappear. **3.** *pass. of* ~сти́.

изве|сти́ть, щу́, сти́шь, *pf.* (*of* ~ща́ть) to inform, notify.

изве́стк|а, и, *f.* (slaked) lime.

известк|ова́ть, у́ю, *impf. and pf.* (*agric.*) to lime.

известко́вый, *adj. of* и́звесть.

изве́стно **1.** *as pred.* it is (well) known; как и. as is well known; наско́лько мне и. as far as I know. **2.** (*as particle; coll.*) of course, certainly.

изве́стност|ь, и, *f.* **1.** fame, reputation; repute; notoriety; приноси́ть и. (+*d.*) to bring fame (to); по́льзоваться гро́мкой ~ью to be far-famed. **2.** publicity; привести́ в и. to make known, make public; поста́вить кого́-н. в и. to inform, notify. **3.** (*coll.*) notability, prominent figure.

изве́ст|ный (~ен, ~на), *adj.* **1.** (+*d.*) well-known (to); (+*i.*) (well-)known (for); (за+ *a.*) (well-)known (as); он ~ен свое́й бо́дростью he is well known for his cheerfulness; челове́к, и. как пья́ница a well-known drunkard. **2.** notorious. **3.** (a) certain; ~ным о́бразом in a certain way; в ~ных слу́чаях in certain cases; до ~ной сте́пени, в ~ной ме́ре to a certain extent. **4.** *as noun* ~ное, ~ного, *n.* (*math.*) the known.

известня́к, а́, *m.* limestone.

известняко́вый, *adj.* limestone.

и́звест|ь, и, *f.* lime; гашёная и. slaked lime; негашёная и. quicklime; хло́рная и. chloride of lime; раство́р ~и mortar, grout; whitewash; преврати́ть в и. to calcify.

изве́т, а, *m.* (*obs.*) denunciation, delation.

изве́тчик, а, *m.* (*obs.*) informer, delator.

изветша́лый, *adj.* (*obs.*) dilapidated.

изветша́|ть, ет, *pf.* (*obs.*) to become completely dilapidated.

извеща́|ть, ю, *impf. of* извести́ть.

извеще́ни|е, я, *n.* notification, notice; (*comm.*) advice; ~я морепла́вателям Instructions to Mariners.

изви́в, а, *m.* winding, bend.

извива́|ть, ю, *impf. of* изви́ть.

извива́|ться, юсь, *impf.* (*of* изви́ться) **1.** to

coil (*intrans.*); to wriggle. **2.** (*impf. only*) to twist, wind (*intrans.*); to meander.

изви́лин|а, ы, *f.* bend, twist; ~ы мо́зга (*anat.*) convolutions of the brain.

изви́лист|ый (~, ~а), *adj.* winding; tortuous; sinuous; (*of river*) meandering.

извине́ни|е, я, *n.* **1.** excuse. **2.** apology; приня́ть ~я to accept an apology. **3.** pardon; прошу́ ~я I beg your pardon, I apologize.

извини́тел|ьный (~ен, ~ьна), *adj.* **1.** excusable, pardonable. **2.** apologetic.

извин|и́ть, ю́, и́шь, *pf.* (*of* ~я́ть) **1.** to excuse (= *to pardon*); ~и́те (меня́)! I beg your pardon, excuse me!, (I'm) sorry!; ~и́те, что я опозда́л sorry I'm late; прошу́ и. меня́ за беста́ктное замеча́ние I apologize for my tactless remark; ~и́те за выраже́ние (*coll.*) if you will excuse the expression; уж ~и́(те)! (*coll.*; *expresses disagreement*) excuse me! **2.** to excuse (= *to justify*); э́то ниче́м нельзя́ и. this is inexcusable.

извин|и́ться, ю́сь, и́шься, *pf.* (*of* ~я́ться) **1.** (пе́ред) to apologize (to); ~и́тесь за меня́ present my apologies, make my excuses. **2.** (+*i.*) to excuse oneself (on account of, on the ground of); to make excuses.

извин|я́ть, я́ю, *impf. of* ~и́ть.

извин|я́ться, я́юсь, *impf. of* ~и́ться; ~я́юсь (*coll.*) I apologize, (I'm) sorry!

извиня́|ющийся, *pres. part. of* ~ться *and adj.* apologetic.

из|ви́ть, овью́, овьёшь, *past* ~ви́л, ~вила́, ~ви́ло, *pf.* (*of* ~вива́ть) to coil, twist, wind (*trans.*).

из|ви́ться, овью́сь, овьёшься, *past* ~ви́лся, ~вила́сь, *pf.* (*of* ~вива́ть).

извлека́|ть(ся), ю(сь), *impf. of* извле́чь(ся).

извлече́ни|е, я, *n.* **1.** extraction; (*math.*) и. ко́рня extraction of root, evolution. **2.** extract, excerpt.

извле́|чь, ку́, чёшь, ку́т, *past* ~к, ~кла́, *pf.* (*of* ~ка́ть) to extract; (*fig.*) to extricate; to derive, elicit; и. уро́к (из) to learn a lesson (from); и. дохо́д, по́льзу, удово́льствие (из) to derive profit, benefit, pleasure (from); и. ко́рень (*math.*) to find the root.

извле́|чься, ку́сь, чёшься, ку́тся, *past* ~кся, ~кла́сь, *pf.* (*of* ~ка́ться) to come out (*to be extracted*).

извне́, *adv.* from without.

изво́д[1], а, *m.* (*coll.*) **1.** waste. **2.** vexation.

изво́д[2], а, *m.* (*lit.*) recension, text (*of a manuscript document*).

изво|ди́ть(ся), жу́(сь), ~дишь(ся), *impf. of* извести́(сь).

изво́з, а, *m.* (*hist.*) carrying (*on horse-drawn carts*); промышля́ть ~ом to be a carrier (*by trade*).

изво|зи́ть, жу́, ~зишь, *pf.*; и. в грязи́ (*coll.*) to drag through the mud.

извóзнича|ть, ю, *impf.* to be a carrier.

извóз|ный, *adj. of* ~; и. прóмысел carrier's trade.

извóзчик, а, *m.* **1.** carrier; (легковóй) и. cabman, cabby; (ломовóй) и. carter, drayman. **2.** (*coll.*) cab; éхать на ~е to go in a cab.

извóзчи|чий, *adj. of* ~к; ~чья би́ржа cabstand, cab-rank.

изволéни|е, я, *n.* (*obs.*) will, pleasure; по ~ю Бóжию Deo volente.

извóл|ить, ю, ишь, *impf.* **1.** (+*inf. or g.*; *obs. or iron. except in imp.*) to wish, desire; чегó ~ите? what can I do for you?; ~ь(те) (*coll.*) if you wish, all right; with pleasure; ~ь, я остáнусь all right, I will stay; дáйте мне папирóсу. —~ьте give me a cigarette. —with pleasure! **2.** (+*inf.*; *expresses respectful attention* (*obs.*) *or ironical disapproval*) to deign, be pleased (*often equivalent to polite form of indicative of following verb*); бáрин ~ит спать the master is asleep; а как вы ~ите поживáть? and, pray, how are you?; ~ь(те) kindly, please be good enough; ~ьте молчáть! kindly be quiet!

извóльнича|ться, юсь, *pf.* (*coll.*) to become wayward, get out of hand.

изворáчива|ться, юсь, *impf. of* извернýться.

изворóт, а, *m.* **1.** bend, twist. **2.** (*pl.*; *fig.*) tricks, wiles.

изворóтист|ый (~, ~а), *adj.* (*coll.*) = изворóтливый.

изворóтлив|ый (~, ~а), *adj.* versatile, resourceful; wily, shrewd.

извра|ти́ть, щу́, ти́шь, *pf.* (*of* ~щáть) **1.** to pervert. **2.** to misinterpret, misconstrue; и. и́стину to distort the truth; и. чью-н. мысль to misinterpret someone.

извращá|ть, ю, *impf. of* изврат́ить.

извращéни|е, я, *n.* **1.** perversion. **2.** misinterpretation, distortion (*fig.*).

извращённый, *p.p.p. of* изврат́ить *and adj.* perverted; unnatural.

изгá|дить, жу, дишь, *pf.* (*of* ~живать) (*coll.*) **1.** to befoul, soil. **2.** (*fig.*) to make a mess of.

изгá|диться, жусь, дишься, *pf.* (*of* ~живаться) (*coll.*) to turn nasty (*of weather*); to go to the bad.

изгáжива|ть(ся), ю(сь), *impf. of* изгáдить(ся).

изги́б, а, *m.* **1.** bend, twist; winding. **2.** inflexion (*of voice*); nuance.

изгибá|ть(ся), ю(сь), *impf. of* изогнýть(ся).

изглá|дить, жу, дишь, *pf.* (*of* ~живать) to efface, wipe out (*also fig.*); и. из пáмяти to blot out of one's memory.

изглáжива|ть, ю, *impf. of* изглáдить.

изгнáни|е, я, *n.* **1.** banishment; expulsion. **2.** exile.

изгнáнник, а, *m.* exile (*person*).

из|гнáть, гоню́, гóнишь, *past* ~гнáл, ~гналá, ~гнáло, *pf.* (*of* ~гоня́ть) to banish, expel; to exile; и. из употреблéния to prohibit the use of, ban; и. плод (*med.*) to procure an abortion.

изгó|й, я, *m.* (*hist.*) izgoy (*person in Kievan Russian society with changed status; e.g. illiterate son of priest, ruined merchant, freed slave*); (*fig.*) social odd man out.

изголóвь|е, я, *n.* head of the bed; сидéть у ~я to sit at the bedside; служи́ть ~ем to serve as a pillow.

изголодá|ться, юсь, *pf.* **1.** to be famished, starve. **2.** (по+*d.*) to yearn (for).

из|гоню́, гóнишь, *see* ~гнáть.

изгоня́|ть, ю, *impf. of* изгнáть.

изгóрб|иться, люсь, ишься, *pf.* (*coll.*) **1.** to arch the back (*of cat, etc.*). **2.** to warp (*intrans.*).

и́згород|ь, и, *f.* fence; живáя и. hedge.

изготáвлива|ть, ю, *impf.* = изготовля́ть.

изготóв|ить, лю, ишь, *pf.* (*of* ~ля́ть) **1.** to manufacture. **2.** (*obs.*) to prepare; и. ружьё (*mil.*) to come to the ready. **3.** (*obs.*) to cook.

изготóв|иться, люсь, ишься, *pf.* (*of* ~ля́ться) **1.** to get ready, place oneself in readiness. **2.** *pass. of* ~ить.

изготóв|ка, ки, *f.* = ~лéние; взять ружьё на ~ку (*mil.*) to come to the ready.

изготовлéни|е, я, *n.* **1.** manufacture. **2.** (*mil.*) preparation; 'ready' position.

изготовля́|ть(ся), ю(сь), *impf. of* изготóвить(ся).

изгрыз|áть, áю, *impf. of* ~ть.

изгры́з|ть, у́, ёшь, *past* ~, ~ла, *pf.* (*of* ~áть) to gnaw to shreds.

издавá|ть, ю́, ёшь, *impf. of* ~ть.

издавá|ться, ётся, *impf. of* ~ться.

и́здавна, *adv.* for a long time; from time immemorial.

издал|екá (*more rarely* ~ёка), *adv.* from afar; from a distance; гóрод ви́ден и. the town is visible from afar; приéхать и. to come from a distance; говори́ть и. (*coll.*) to speak in a roundabout way.

и́здал|и, *adv.* = ~екá.

издáни|е, я, *n.* **1.** publication; promulgation (*of law*). **2.** edition; пéрвое и. first edition; испрáвленное и. revised edition.

издáтел|ь, я, *m.* publisher.

издáтель|ский, *adj. of* ~ *and* ~ство; ~ское дéло publishing; ~ская фи́рма publishing house.

издáтельств|о, а, *n.* publishing house.

издá|ть, м, шь, ст, ди́м, ди́те, ду́т, *past* ~л, ~лá, ~ло, *pf.* (*of* ~вáть) **1.** to publish; и.

закон to promulgate a law; и. ука́з to issue an edict. 2. to produce, emit (*a smell*); to let out (*a sound*); и. крик to let out a cry.

изда́|ться, стся, *past* ~лся, ~ла́сь, ~ло́сь, *pf.* to be published.

издева́тельский, *adj.* mocking.

издева́тельств|о, а, *n.* 1. mocking, scoffing. 2. mockery; taunt, insult.

издева́|ться, юсь, *impf.* (над) to mock (at), scoff (at).

издёвк|а, и, *f.* (*coll.*) taunt, insult.

изде́ли|е, я, *n.* 1. (*sing. only*) make; куста́рного ~я hand-made; фабри́чного ~я factory-made. 2. (manufactured) article; (*pl.*) wares.

издёрган|ный, *p.p.p.* of издёргать *and adj.* harassed; overstrained; ~ные не́рвы shattered nerves.

издёрг|ать, аю, *pf.* (*of* ~ивать) (*coll.*) 1. to pull to pieces. 2. to harass; to overstrain.

издёрг|аться, аюсь, *pf.* (*of* ~иваться) (*coll.*) 1. *pass. of* ~ать. 2. to become overwrought, become unhinged.

издёргива|ть(ся), ю(сь), *impf.* of издёргать(ся).

издерж|а́ть, у́, ~ишь, *pf.* (*of* ~ивать) to spend; to expend.

издерж|а́ться, у́сь, ~ишься, *pf.* (*of* ~иваться) (*coll.*) 1. to have spent all one has, be spent up. 2. *pass. of* ~а́ть.

издёржива|ть(ся), ю(сь), *impf.* of издержа́ть(ся).

издёрж|ки, ек, *sing.* ~ка, ~ки, *f.* expenses; суде́бные и. (*leg.*) costs; и. произво́дства production costs.

издира́|ть, ю, *impf.* of изодра́ть.

издо́льщин|а, ы, *f.* (*hist.*, *econ.*) share--cropping.

издо́х|нуть, ну, нешь, *past* ~, ~ла, *pf.* (*of* издыха́ть) to die (*of animals*); (*sl.*; *of human beings*) to peg out, kick the bucket.

издре́вле, *adv.* (*obs.*) from the earliest times.

издроб|и́ть, лю́, и́шь, *pf.* to pulverize, granulate.

издыха́ни|е, я, *n.* (one's) last breath; до после́днего ~я to one's last breath; при после́днем ~и at one's last gasp.

издыха́|ть, ю, *impf.* of издо́хнуть.

изжа́р|ить(ся), ю(сь), ишь(ся), *pf. of* жа́рить(ся) 1, 2.

изжёванный, *p.p.p.* of изжева́ть *and adj.* (*coll.*) 1. crumpled. 2. (*fig.*) hackneyed.

изж|ева́ть, ую́, уёшь, *pf.* (*of* ~ёвывать) (*coll.*) to chew up.

изжёвыва|ть, ю, *impf.* of изжева́ть.

из|же́чь, ожгу́, ожжёшь, ожгу́т, *past* ~жёг, ~ожгла́, *pf.* (*of* ~жига́ть) (*coll.*) 1. to burn all over; to burn holes in; она́ ~ожгла́ ру́ки

утюго́м she has burned her hands all over on the iron. 2. to use up (*fuel, by burning*).

из|же́чься, ожгу́сь, ожжёшься, ожгу́тся, *past* ~жёгся, ~ожгла́сь, *pf.* (*of* ~жига́ться) (*coll.*) 1. to burn oneself all over; to be covered with burns; но́ги у неё ~ожгли́сь от кислоты́ her legs were all covered with burns from the acid. 2. to be burned up, be used up (*of fuel*).

изжива́|ть, ю, *impf.* of изжи́ть.

изжига́|ть(ся), ю(сь), *impf.* of изже́чь(ся).

изжи́ти|е, я, *n.* elimination.

изжи́|ть, ву́, вёшь, *past* ~л, ~ла́, ~ло, *pf.* (*of* ~ва́ть) 1. to eliminate. 2. (*obs.*) to overcome (gradually); и. разочарова́ние to get over a disappointment. 3. и. себя́ to become obsolete.

изжо́г|а, и, *f.* heartburn.

из-за, *prep.*+*g.* 1. from behind; из-за две́ри from behind the door; встать из-за стола́ to rise from the table; прие́хать из-за мо́ря to come from oversea(s); (*fig.*) спле́тничать о ком-н. из-за угла́ to gossip about someone behind his back. 2. because of, through; не засыпа́ть из-за шу́ма to be unable to get to sleep because of the noise; ссо́риться из-за пустяко́в to fall out over trifles; то́лько из-за тебя́ мы опозда́ли it was all because of you that we were late. 3. for; жени́ться из-за де́нег to marry for money.

и́ззелена- greenish-.

иззя́б|нуть, ну, нешь, *past* ~, ~ла, *pf.* (*coll.*) to feel frozen, feel chilled to the marrow.

излага́|ть, ю, *impf.* of изложи́ть.

изла́мыва|ть(ся), ю(сь), *impf.* of излома́ть(ся).

изле́нива|ться, юсь, *impf.* of излени́ться.

излен|и́ться, ю́сь, ~ишься, *pf.* (*of* ~ива́ться) (*coll.*) to grow incorrigibly lazy, become a lazybones.

излёт, а, *m.* (*tech.*) end of trajectory; пу́ля на ~е spent bullet.

излече́ни|е, я, *n.* 1. medical treatment; он был на ~и в Москве́ he was undergoing medical treatment in Moscow; отпра́вить в го́спиталь на и. to send to hospital for treatment. 2. recovery.

излечи́ва|ть(ся), ю(сь), *impf.* of излечи́ть(ся).

излечи́м|ый (~, ~а), *adj.* curable.

излеч|и́ть, у́, ~ишь, *pf.* (*of* ~ивать) to cure.

излеч|и́ться, у́сь, ~ишься, *pf.* (*of* ~ива́ться) (от) to make a complete recovery (from); (*fig.*) to rid oneself (of), shake off.

излива́|ть(ся), ю(сь), *impf.* of изли́ть(ся).

из|ли́ть, олью́, ольёшь, *past* ~ли́л, ~лила́, ~ли́ло, *pf.* (*of* ~лива́ть) 1. (*obs.*) to pour out, shed. 2. (*fig.*) to pour out, give vent to; и. свой гнев на (+a.) to vent one's anger (on); и. ду́шу to unbosom oneself.

изли́|ться, олью́сь, олье́шься, *past* ~ли́лся, ~лила́сь, ~ли́ло́сь, *pf.* (*of* ~лива́ться) 1. (*obs. or poet.*) to stream, pour out (*intrans.*); ~лили́сь слёзы tears welled up. 2. (в+*p.*) to find expression (in). 3. (в+*p.*) to give vent to one's feelings (in); (на+*a.*) to vent itself (on); его́ гнев ~ли́лся на всех окружа́ющих his anger vented itself on all about him.

изли́ш|ек, ка, *m.* 1. surplus; remainder. 2. excess; нам э́того хва́тит с ~ком we have more than enough, enough and to spare; и. осторо́жности excessive caution.

изли́шеств|о, а, *n.* excess; over-indulgence.

изли́шеств|овать, ую, *impf.* to go to excess, over-indulge oneself.

изли́шн|е, *adv.* excessively; unnecessarily, superfluously.

изли́ш|ний (~ен, ~ня, ~не), *adj.* excessive; unnecessary, superfluous.

излия́ни|е, я, *n.* outpouring, effusion (*fig.*).

излов|и́ть, лю́, ~ишь, *pf.* (*coll.*) to catch.

изловч|и́ться, у́сь, и́шься, *pf.* (*coll.*) to contrive, manage; он ~и́лся и вы́бил ору́жие из руки́ проти́вника he contrived to knock his opponent's weapon out of his hand; он ~и́лся попа́сть в цель he managed to hit the target.

изложе́ни|е, я, *n.* exposition, account.

излож|и́ть, у́, ~ишь, *pf.* (*of* излага́ть) to expound, state; to set forth; to word, draft; и. на бума́ге to commit to paper.

изло́жниц|а, ы, *f.* (*tech.*) mould.

изло́м, а, *m.* 1. break, fracture; sharp bend. 2. душе́вный и. mental unbalance.

изло́ман|ный, *p.p.p. of* изло́ма́ть *and adj.* 1. broken. 2. winding, tortuous. 3. (*fig.*) unbalanced, unhinged; warped.

излома́|ть, ю, *pf.* (*of* изла́мывать) 1. to break, smash. 2. (*coll.*) to break (*in health*); (*impers.*) to have (crippling) rheumatism; всю спи́ну у неё ~ло she is crippled with rheumatism in her back. 3. (*fig., coll.*) to warp, corrupt.

излома́|ться, юсь, *pf.* (*of* изла́мываться) 1. to be broken, be smashed. 2. (*fig., coll.*) to be affected; to resort to hypocrisy.

излуч|а́ть, а́ю, *impf.* (*of* ~и́ть) to radiate (*also fig.*); её глаза́ ~а́ли не́жность her eyes radiated tenderness.

излуч|а́ться, а́ется *impf.* (*of* ~и́ться) 1. (из) to emanate (from). 2. *pass. of* ~а́ть.

излуче́ни|е, я, *n.* radiation; emanation.

излу́чин|а, ы, *f.* bend, wind.

излу́чист|ый (~, ~а), *adj.* winding, meandering.

излуч|и́ть(ся), у́(сь), и́шь(ся), *pf. of* ~а́ть(ся).

излю́бленный, *adj.* favourite.

изма́|зать, жу, жешь, *pf.* (*of* ма́зать 3 *and* ~зывать) (*coll.*) 1. to make dirty, smear; и. пальто́ кра́ской to get paint all over one's coat. 2. to use up (*paint, grease, etc.*).

изма́|заться, жусь, жешься, *pf.* (*of* ма́заться 1 *and* ~зываться) (*coll.*) 1. to get dirty; он ~за́лся в кра́ске he has got paint all over himself. 2. *pass of* ~зать.

изма́зыва|ть(ся), ю(сь), *impf. of* изма́зать(ся).

измар|а́ть, а́ю, *pf.* (*of* ~ывать) to make dirty, soil.

изма́рыва|ть, ю, *impf. of* измара́ть.

изма́тыва|ть(ся), ю(сь), *impf. of* измота́ть(ся).

изма́чива|ть(ся), ю(сь), *impf. of* измочи́ть(ся).

изма́|ять, ю, *pf.* (*coll.*) to exhaust, tire out.

изма́|яться, юсь, *pf.* (*coll.*) to be exhausted, tired out.

измельча́ни|е, я, *n.* growing small; growing shallow; (*fig.*) becoming shallow, becoming superficial.

измельча́|ть, ю, *pf. of* мельча́ть.

измельч|и́ть, у́, и́шь, *pf. of* мельчи́ть.

изме́н|а, ы, *f.* betrayal; treachery; госуда́рственная и. high treason; супру́жеская и. unfaithfulness, (conjugal) infidelity.

измене́ни|е, я, *n.* change, alteration; (*gram.*) inflexion.

измен|и́ть¹, ю́, ~ишь, *pf.* (*of* ~я́ть) to change, alter; (*polit.*) и. законопрое́кт to amend a bill.

измен|и́ть², ю́, ~ишь, *pf.* (*of* ~я́ть) (+*d.*) to betray; to be unfaithful (to); (*fig.*) зре́ние ~и́ло ему́ his eyesight had failed him; сча́стье нам ~и́ло our luck is out.

измен|и́ться, ю́сь, ~ишься, *pf.* (*of* ~я́ться) 1. to change, alter (*intrans.*); to vary (*intrans.*); и. к лу́чшему, к ху́дшему to change for the better, for the worse; и. в лице́ to change countenance.

изме́нник, а, *m.* traitor.

изме́ннический, *adj.* treacherous, traitorous.

изме́нчивост|ь, и, *f.* 1. changeableness; mutability; inconstancy, fickleness. 2. (*biol.*) variability.

изме́нчив|ый (~, ~а), *adj.* changeable; inconstant, fickle; ~ая пого́да changeable weather.

изменя́ем|ый, *pres. part. pass. of* изменя́ть *and adj.* variable; ~ые величи́ны (*math.*) variables.

измен|я́ть(ся), я́ю(сь), *impf. of* ~и́ть(ся).

измере́ни|е, я, *n.* 1. measurement, measuring; sounding, fathoming (*of sea bottom*); taking (*of temperature*). 2. (*math.*) dimension; двух, трёх ~й two-, three-dimensional.

измери́м|ый (~, ~a), *adj.* measurable.

измери́тел|ь, я, *m.* **1.** measuring instrument, gauge. **2.** (*econ.*) index.

измери́тельный, *adj.* (for) measuring.

изме́р|ить, ю, ишь, *pf.* (*of* ~я́ть) to measure; и. кому́-н. температу́ру to take someone's temperature.

измер|я́ть, я́ю, *impf. of* ~ить.

измождён|ный (~, ~á), *adj.* emaciated; worn out.

измок|а́ть, а́ю, *impf. of* ~нуть.

измо́к|нуть, ну, нешь, *past* ~, ~ла, *pf.* (*of* ~а́ть) (*coll.*) to get soaked, get drenched.

измо́р, a, *no pl., m.*; взять ~ом to reduce by starvation, starve out; (*fig., coll.*) взять кого́-н. ~ом to nag, worry someone into doing something.

измор|и́ть, ю́, и́шь, *pf.* (*coll.*) to wear out, exhaust.

и́змороз|ь, и, *f.* hoar-frost; rime.

и́зморос|ь, и, *f.* drizzle.

измота́|ть, ю, *pf.* (*of* изма́тывать) (*coll.*) to exhaust, wear out.

измота́|ться, юсь, *pf.* (*of* изма́тываться) (*coll.*) to be exhausted, worn out.

измоча́лива|ть(ся), ю(сь), *impf. of* измоча́лить(ся).

измоча́л|ить, ю, ишь, *pf.* (*of* ~ивать) to shred; to reduce to shreds (*also fig., coll.*).

измоча́л|иться, юсь, ишься, *pf.* (*of* ~иваться) to become frayed, be in shreds; (*fig., coll.*) to be worn to a shred, go to pieces.

измоч|и́ть, у́, ~ишь, *pf.* (*of* изма́чивать) (*coll.*) to soak through.

измоч|и́ться, у́сь, ~ишься, *pf.* (*of* изма́чиваться) (*coll.*) to be soaked through.

изму́ч|ать, аю, *pf.* = ~ить.

изму́ч|аться, аюсь, *pf.* = ~иться.

изму́ченный, *p.p.p. of* изму́чить *and adj.* worn out, tired out; у вас и. вид you look worn out.

изму́чива|ть(ся), ю(сь), *impf. of* изму́чить(ся).

изму́ч|ить, у, ишь, *pf.* **1.** (*pf. of* ~ивать) to torment; to tire out, exhaust. **2.** *pf. of* му́чить.

изму́ч|иться, усь, ишься, *pf.* **1.** (*pf. of* ~иваться) to be tired out, be exhausted. **2.** *pf. of* му́читься.

измыва́тельств|о, а, *n.* (*coll.*) mocking, scoffing.

измыва́|ться, юсь, *impf.* (над; *coll.*) to mock (at), scoff (at).

измы́зг|ать, аю, *pf.* (*of* ~ивать) (*coll.*) **1.** to make dirty all over. **2.** to wear threadbare.

измы́зг|аться, аюсь, *pf.* (*of* ~иваться) (*coll.*) **1.** to get dirty all over. **2.** to become threadbare.

измы́згива|ть(ся), ю(сь), *impf. of* измы́згать(ся).

измы́лива|ть, ю, *impf. of* измы́лить.

измы́л|ить, ю, ишь, *pf.* (*of* ~ивать) to use up (*soap*).

измы́сл|ить, ю, ишь, *pf.* (*of* измышля́ть) **1.** to fabricate, invent. **2.** to contrive.

измыта́р|ить, ю, ишь, *pf.* (*coll.*) to wear out; to try.

измыта́р|иться, юсь, ишься, *pf.* (*coll.*) to be worn out; to be sorely tried.

измышле́ни|е, я, *n.* fabrication, invention (*action and product*).

измышля́|ть, ю, *impf. of* измы́слить.

измя́т|ый, *p.p.p. of* ~ь *and adj.* **1.** crumpled, creased. **2.** (*fig.*) haggard, jaded.

из|мя́ть(ся), омну́, омнёт(ся), *pf. of* мять-(ся)[1].

изна́нк|а, и, *f.* the wrong side (*of material, clothing*); с ~и on the inner side; вы́вернуть на ~y to turn inside out; и. жи́зни the seamy side of life.

изнаси́ловани|е, я, *n.* rape, assault, violation.

изнаси́л|овать, ую, *pf.* (*of* наси́ловать 2) to rape, assault, violate.

изнача́льный, *adj.* primordial.

изна́шивани|е, я, *n.* wear; wear and tear.

изна́шива|ть(ся), ю(сь), *impf. of* износи́ть-(ся).

изне́женност|ь, и, *f.* delicacy; softness; effeminacy.

изне́женный, *p.p.p. of* изне́жить *and adj.* **1.** pampered; delicate. **2.** soft, effete; effeminate.

изне́жива|ть(ся), ю(сь), *impf. of* изне́жить(ся).

изне́ж|ить, у, ишь, *pf.* (*of* ~ивать) to pamper, coddle; to render effeminate.

изне́ж|иться, усь, ишься, *pf.* (*of* ~иваться) to go soft, become effete; to become effeminate.

изнемога́|ть, ю, *impf. of* изнемо́чь.

изнеможе́ни|е, я, *n.* exhaustion; быть в ~и to be utterly exhausted; рабо́тать до ~я to work to the point of exhaustion.

изнеможён|ный (~, ~á), *adj.* exhausted.

изнемо́|чь, гу́, ~жешь, ~гут, *past* ~г, ~гла́, *pf.* (*of* ~га́ть) (от) to be exhausted (from), grow faint (from).

изне́рвнича|ться, юсь, *pf.* (*coll.*) to get into a state of nerves.

изничтож|а́ть, а́ю, *impf. of* ~и́ть.

изничто́ж|ить, у, ишь, *pf.* (*of* ~а́ть) (*coll.*) to destroy, wipe out.

изно́с, a (у), *m.* (*coll.*) wear; wear and tear, deterioration; не знать ~у (a) to wear well; носи́ть что́-н. до ~у (a) to wear something until quite worn out; (+d.) э́тим боти́нкам нет ~у (a) these boots will stand any amount of hard wear.

изно|си́ть, шу́, ~сишь, *pf.* (*of* изна́шивать) to wear out.

изно|си́ться, шу́сь, ᴖси́шься, *pf.* (*of* изна́-
шиваться) to wear out (*intrans.*); (*fig., coll.*)
to be used up, be played out; to age
(prematurely).

изно́шенный, *p.p.p. of* износи́ть *and adj.*
worn out; и. костю́м threadbare suit; (*fig.,
coll.*) worn; (prematurely) aged.

изнуре́ни|е, я, *n.* (*physical*) exhaustion.

изнурённый, *p.p.p. of* изнури́ть *and adj.*
(*physically*) exhausted, worn out; jaded; у
него́ был и. вид he looked worn out; и.
го́лодом faint with hunger.

изнури́тел|ьный (ᴖен, ᴖьна), *adj.* ex-
hausting; ᴖьная боле́знь wasting disease.

изнур|и́ть, ю́, и́шь, *pf.* (*of* ᴖя́ть) to exhaust,
wear out.

изнур|я́ть, я́ю, *impf. of* ᴖи́ть.

изнутри́, *adv.* from within; дверь запи-
ра́ется и. the door fastens on the inside.

изныва́|ть, ю, *impf. of* изны́ть.

изн|ы́ть, о́ю, о́ешь, *pf.* (*of* ᴖыва́ть) to lan-
guish, be exhausted; и. от жа́жды to be
tormented by thirst; и. от тоски́ (по+*d.*;
poet.) to pine (for).

изо, *prep.* = из.

изо-¹, *prefix* = из-.

изо-², iso-.

изоба́р|а, ы, *f.* (*meteor.*) isobar.

изоба́т|а, ы, *f.* (*geogr.*) isobath, depth curve,
submarine contour.

изоби́|деть, жу, дишь, *pf.* (*coll.*) to hurt,
insult.

изоби́ли|е, я, *n.* abundance, plenty, pro-
fusion; рог ᴖя cornucopia.

изоби́л|овать, ую, *impf.* (+*i.*) to abound
(in), be rich (in).

изоби́л|ьный (ᴖен, ᴖьна), *adj.* 1. abun-
dant. 2. (+*i.*) abounding in.

изоблич|а́ть, а́ю, *impf.* 1. *impf. of* ᴖи́ть.
2. (*no pf.*) (+*a.* в+*p.*) to show (to be), point
to (as being); все его́ посту́пки ᴖа́ли в нём
моше́нника his every action pointed to his
being a swindler; его́ похо́дка ᴖа́ет в нём
моряка́ one can tell by his gait that he is a
sailor.

изобличе́ни|е, я, *n.* exposure; conviction.

изоблич́ительный, *adj.* damning.

изоблич|и́ть, у́, и́шь, *pf.* (*of* ᴖа́ть) (+*a.*
в+*p.*) to expose (as), convict (of); to unmask; его́ ᴖи́ли во лжи he stands con-
victed as a liar.

изобража́|ть(ся), ю(сь), *impf. of* изобра-
зи́ть(ся).

изображе́ни|е, я, *n.* 1. (*artistic*) representa-
tion. 2. representation, portrayal; image;
imprint; и. в зе́ркале reflection.

изобрази́тельн|ый, *adj.* graphic; decora-
tive; ᴖые иску́сства fine arts.

изобра|зи́ть, жу́, зи́шь, *pf.* (*of* ᴖжа́ть)
1. (+*i.*) to depict, portray, represent (as);

и. из себя́ (+*a.*; *coll.*) to make oneself
out (to be), represent oneself (as); и. Га́м-
лета сла́бым челове́ком to portray Hamlet
as a weak character (*of actor or producer*); и.
из себя́ хоро́шего певца́ to make oneself
out a good singer. 2. to imitate, take off.

изобра|зи́ться, зи́тся, *pf.* (*of* ᴖжа́ться) 1.
to appear, show itself. 2. *pass. of* ᴖжа́ться.

изобре|сти́, ту́, тёшь, *past* ᴖл, ᴖла́, *pf.* (*of*
ᴖта́ть) to invent; to devise, contrive.

изобрета́тел|ь, я, *m.* inventor.

изобрета́тельност|ь, и, *f.* inventiveness.

изобрета́тел|ьный (ᴖен, ᴖьна), *adj.* inven-
tive; resourceful.

изобрета́тель|ский, *adj. of* ᴖ.

изобрета́тель|ство, ства, *n.* = ᴖ ность.

изобрета́|ть, ю, *impf. of* изобрести́.

изобрете́ни|е, я, *n.* invention (*process and
product*).

изо́гнутый, *p.p.p. of* ᴖь *and adj.* bent,
curved, winding.

изогн|у́ть, у́, ёшь, *pf.* (*of* изгиба́ть) to bend,
curve.

изогн|у́ться, у́сь, ёшься, *pf.* (*of* изги-
ба́ться) to bend, curve (*intrans.*).

изогра́ф, а, *m.* (*obs.*) icon-painter.

изогра́фи|я, и, *f.* (*obs.*) icon-painting.

изо́дранный, *p.p.p. of* изодра́ть *and adj.*
tattered.

изо|дра́ть, деру́, дерёшь, *past* ᴖдра́л,
ᴖдрала́, ᴖдра́ло, *pf.* (*of* ᴖдира́ть) (*coll.*)
1. to tear to pieces; to tear in several places.
2. to scratch all over.

изо|йти́, йду́, йдёшь, *past* ᴖшёл, ᴖшла́, *pf.
of* исходи́ть².

изол|га́ться, гу́сь, жёшься, гу́тся, *past*
ᴖга́лся, ᴖгала́сь, ᴖга́лось, *pf.* to become
an inveterate, hardened liar.

изоли́рованный, *p.p.p. of* изоли́ровать *and
adj.* 1. isolated; separate. 2. (*tech.*) insu-
lated.

изоли́р|овать, ую, *impf. and pf.* 1. to isolate;
to quarantine. 2. (*tech.*) to insulate.

изолиро́вк|а, и, *f.* (*tech.*) 1. insulation. 2.
(*coll.*) insulating tape.

изолиро́вочный, *adj.* (*tech.*) insulating.

изоля́тор¹, а, *m.* (*tech.*) insulator.

изоля́тор², а, *m.* 1. (*med.*) isolation ward.
2. solitary confinement cell. 3. (*polit.* 'isola-
tor' (*special prison in U.S.S.R. for political
detainees and espionage suspects*).

изоляциони́зм, а, *m.* (*polit.*) isolationism.

изоляциони́ст, а, *m.* (*polit.*) isolationist.

изоля|цио́нный, *adj. of* ᴖ ция; ᴖ цио́нная
ле́нта (*tech.*) insulating tape.

изоля́ци|я, и, *f.* 1. isolation; (*med.*) quaran-
tine. 2. (*tech.*) insulation.

изома́слян|ый, *adj.* ᴖ ая кислота́ (*chem.*) iso-
butyric acid.

изомéрный, *adj.* (*chem.*) isomeric.

изомóрфный, *adj.* (*min.*) isomorphous.

изóрванный, *p.p.p.* of изорвáть and *adj.* tattered, torn.

изорв|áть, ý, ёшь, *past* ∼áл, ∼алá, ∼áло, *pf.* (*of* изрывáть¹) to tear (to pieces).

изорв|áться, ётся, *past* ∼áлся, ∼алáсь, ∼áлось, *pf.* (*coll.*) to be in tatters.

изотéрм|а, ы, *f.* (*geogr.*) isotherm.

изотермический, *adj.* 1. (*phys.*) isothermal. 2. having regulated temperature.

изотóп, а, *m.* (*chem.*) isotope.

изохрóнный, *adj.* isochronous.

изошýтк|а, и, *f.* (*coll.*) cartoon, humorous drawing.

изощрéни|е, я, *n.* sharpening (*fig.*); refinement.

изощрённый, *p.p.p.* of изощрить and *adj.* refined; keen.

изощр|ить, ю, ишь, *pf.* (*of* ∼я́ть) to sharpen (*fig.*); to cultivate, refine; и. слух to train one's ear; и. ум to cultivate one's mind.

изощр|иться, юсь, ишься, *pf.* (*of* ∼я́ться) 1. to acquire refinement. 2. (в+*p.*) to excel (in); и. в придýмывании каламбýров to excel in punning.

изощр|я́ть(ся), я́ю(сь), *impf.* of ∼ить(ся).

из-под, *prep.+g.* 1. from under; сдéлать что-н. из-под пáлки to do something under the lash; у негó укрáли бумáжник из-под нóсу he had his wallet stolen from under his nose; из-под полы́ on the sly; under the counter. 2. from near; мы приéхали из-под Москвы́ we have come from near Moscow 3. (for) (*indicates purpose of object*); бáнка из-под варéнья jam-jar.

израз|éц, цá, *m.* tile.

израз|цóвый, *adj.* of ∼éц.

изрáильский, *adj.* 1. (*hist.*) Israelitish. 2. Israeli.

израильтя́н|ин, ина, *pl.* ∼е, ∼, *m.* 1. (*hist.*) Israelite. 2. Israeli.

израильтя́н|ка, ки, *f.* of ∼ин.

изрáн|ить, ю, ишь, *pf.* to cover with wounds.

израсхóд|овать(ся), ую(сь), *pf.* of расхóдовать(ся).

и́зредка, *adv.* now and then; from time to time.

изрéзанный, *p.p.p.* of изрéзать and *adj.*; и. бéрег indented coastline.

изрé|зать, жу, жешь, *pf.* (*of* ∼зывать and ∼зáть) 1. to cut to pieces; to cut up. 2. (*geogr.*) to indent.

изрез|áть, áю, *impf.* (*coll.*) of ∼áть.

изрéзыва|ть, ю, *impf.* of изрéзать.

изрекá|ть, ю, *impf.* of изрéчь.

изречéни|е, я, *n.* apophthegm, dictum, saying.

изрé|чь, кý, чёшь, кýт, *past* ∼к, ∼клá, *pf.*

(*of* ∼кáть) (*obs.* or *iron.*) to speak (solemnly); to utter; так ∼к thus he spake; и. мýдрое слóво to utter a word of wisdom.

изреше|тить, чý, тишь, *pf.* (*of* ∼чивать) to pierce with holes; и. пýлями to riddle with bullets.

изрешéчива|ть, ю, *impf.* of изрешетить.

изрис|овáть, ýю, *pf.* (*of* ∼óвывать) 1. to cover with drawings. 2. (*coll.*) to use up (*pencil, paper, etc.*).

изрисóвыва|ть, ю, *impf.* of изрисовáть.

изруб|áть, áю, *impf.* of ∼ить.

изруб|ить, лю́, ∼ишь, *pf.* (*of* ∼áть) to chop up; to hack to pieces; to mince (*meat*).

изругá|ть, ю, *pf.* to abuse, curse violently.

изрывá|ть¹, ю, *impf.* of изорвáть.

изрывá|ть², ю, *impf.* of изры́ть.

изры́г|ать, áю, *impf.* (*of* ∼нýть) to vomit, throw up; пýшки ∼áли дым и плáмень the cannon were belching forth smoke and flames; (*fig.*) и. ругáтельства to let forth a stream of oaths.

изры́г|нуть, нý, нёшь, *pf.* of ∼áть.

изры́т|ый, *p.p.p.* of ∼ь pitted; и. óспой pock-marked.

изр|ы́ть, óю, óешь, *pf.* (*of* ∼ывáть²) to dig up; to dig through.

изря́дно, *adv.* (*coll.*) fairly, pretty; tolerably; я и. устáл I am pretty tired; они́ вчерá вéчером и. вы́пили they had a fair amount to drink last night.

изря́д|ный (∼ен, ∼на), *adj.* (*coll.*) fair, handsome; fairly large, tolerable; ∼ое коли́чество a fair amount; и. пья́ница a pretty heavy drinker.

изувéр, а, *m.* bigot, fanatic.

изувéрский, *adj.* bigoted, fanatical.

изувéрств|о, а, *n.* bigotry, fanaticism; (fanatical) cruelty.

изувéчива|ть, ю, *impf.* of изувéчить.

изувéч|ить, у, ишь, *pf.* (*of* ∼ивать) to maim, mutilate.

изувéч|иться, усь, ишься, *pf.* (*coll.*) 1. to maim oneself, mutilate oneself. 2. *pass.* of ∼ить.

изукрá|сить, шу, сишь, *pf.* (*of* ∼шивать) to decorate (lavishly); и. дом флáгами to bedeck a house with flags; (*coll., iron.*) и. синякáми to 'adorn' with bruises.

изукрáшива|ть, ю, *impf.* of изукрáсить.

изуми́тел|ьный (∼ен, ∼ьна), *adj.* amazing, astounding.

изум|и́ть, лю́, и́шь, *pf.* (*of* ∼ля́ть) to amaze, astound.

изум|и́ться, лю́сь, и́шься, *pf.* (*of* ∼ля́ться) to be amazed, astounded.

изумлéни|е, я, *n.* amazement.

изумлённый, *p.p.p.* of изуми́ть and *adj.* amazed, astounded; dumbfounded.

изумля|ть(ся), ю(сь), *impf. of* изуми́ть(ся).
изумру́д, а, *m.* emerald.
изумру́дный, *adj.* 1. emerald. 2. emerald (-green).
изуро́дованный, *p.p.p. of* изуро́довать *and adj.* maimed, mutilated; disfigured.
изуро́д|овать, ую, *pf. of* уро́довать.
изу́стно, *adv.* (*obs.*) orally, by word of mouth.
изуч|а́ть, а́ю, *impf.* (*of* ~и́ть) to learn; (*impf. only*) to study; он два го́да ~а́ет гре́ческий язы́к he has been studying Greek for two years.
изуче́ни|е, я, *n.* study, studying.
изуч|и́ть, у́, ~ишь, *pf.* (*of* ~а́ть) 1. to learn; за шесть ме́сяцев она ~и́ла и испа́нский и италья́нский языки́ in six months she had learned both Spanish and Italian. 2. to come to know (very well), come to understand; он кра́йне за́мкнут, но я всё-таки ~и́л его́ he is extremely reserved, but I came to understand him in the end.
изъеда́|ть, ю, *impf. of* изъе́сть.
изъе́денный, *p.p.p. of* изъе́сть *and adj.*; и. мо́лью moth-eaten.
изъе́з|дить, жу, дишь, *pf.* (*of* ~жива́ть) 1. to travel all over, traverse; мы ~дили весь свет we have been all round the world. 2. (*coll.*) to wear out (*vehicle or road surface*).
изъе́зженный, *p.p.p. of* изъе́здить *and adj.* well-worn, rutted.
изъе́зжива|ть, ю, *impf. of* изъе́здить.
изъе́|сть, ст, дя́т, *past* ~л, ~ла, *pf.* (*of* ~да́ть) 1. to eat away. 2. to corrode.
изъяви́тельн|ый, *adj., only used in phrase* ~ое наклоне́ние (*gram.*) indicative mood.
изъяв|и́ть, лю́, ~ишь, *pf.* (*of* ~ля́ть) to indicate, express; и. своё согла́сие to give one's consent.
изъявле́ни|е, я, *n.* expression.
изъявля́|ть, ю, *impf. of* изъяви́ть.
изъязв|и́ть, лю́, и́шь, *pf.* (*of* ~ля́ть) (*med.*) to ulcerate.
изъязвле́ни|е, я, *n.* (*med.*) ulceration.
изъязвлённый, *p.p.p. of* изъязви́ть *and adj.* ulcered, ulcerous.
изъязвля́|ть, ю, *impf. of* изъязви́ть.
изъя́н, а, *m.* 1. defect, flaw; това́р с ~ом defective goods; у него́ мно́го ~ов he has many defects. 2. damage, loss.
изъясне́ни|е, я, *n.* (*obs.*) explanation; declaration.
изъясни́тельный, *adj.* (*obs.*) explanatory.
изъясн|и́ть, ю́, и́шь, *pf.* (*of* ~я́ть) (*obs.*) to explain, expound.
изъясн|и́ться, ю́сь, и́шься, *pf.* (*of* ~я́ться) (*obs.*) to express oneself; и. в любви́ to declare one's love.
изъясн|я́ть(ся), я́ю(сь), *impf. of* ~и́ть(ся).
изъя́ти|е, я, *n.* 1. withdrawal; removal; и.

из обраще́ния (моне́ты) (*fin.*) immobilization (of currency). 2. exception; без вся́кого ~я without exception; в и. из пра́вил as an exception to the rule.
из|ъя́ть, ыму́, ы́мешь, *pf.* (*of* ~ыма́ть) to withdraw; to remove; и. из обраще́ния to withdraw from circulation; to immobilize (*currency*); и. в по́льзу госуда́рства to confiscate.
изыма́|ть, ю, *impf. of* изъя́ть.
из|ыму́, ы́мешь, *see* ~ъя́ть.
изыска́ни|е, я, *n.* (*usually pl.*) investigation, research; prospecting; survey.
изы́сканност|ь, и, *f.* refinement.
изы́скан|ный 1. (~, ~а), *p.p.p. of* изыска́ть. 2. (~, ~на), *adj.* refined; recherché.
изыска́тел|ь, я, *m.* prospector.
изыска́тельский, *adj.* prospecting.
изы|ска́ть, щу́, ~щешь, *pf.* (*of* ~скивать) to find (*after search or investigation*); to search out; и. сре́дства на постро́йку домо́в to find funds for house-building.
изы́скива|ть, ю, *impf.* (*of* изыска́ть) to search out; to try to find.
изю́бр, а, *m.* (*zool.*) Manchurian deer.
изю́м, а (у), *no pl., m.* raisins; sultanas; э́то не фунт ~у! (*joc.*) it is no light matter, it is no joke.
изю́мин|а, ы, *f.* raisin.
изю́мин|ка, ки, *f., dim. of* ~а; (*fig.*) pep, go, spirit; с ~кой spirited; в ней нет ~ки she has no go in her.
изя́ществ|о, а, *n.* elegance, grace.
изя́щ|ный (~ен, ~на), *adj.* elegant, graceful; (*obs.*) ~ные иску́сства fine arts; ~ная литерату́ра belles-lettres.
икани|е, я, *n.* hiccupping.
ик|а́ть, а́ю, *impf.* (*of* ~ну́ть) to hiccup.
ик|ну́ть, ну́, нёшь, *pf. of* ~а́ть.
ико́н|а, ы, *f.* icon.
ико́н|ный, *adj. of* ~а.
иконобо́р|ец, ца, *m.* (*hist.*) iconoclast.
иконобо́рческий, *adj.* (*hist.*) iconoclastic.
иконобо́рчеств|о, а, *n.* (*hist.*) iconoclasm.
иконогра́фи|я, и, *f.* 1. iconography. 2. (*collect.*) portraits.
иконопи́с|ец, ца, *m.* icon-painter.
иконопи́сный, *adj.* 1. *adj. of* и́конопись. 2. (*fig.*) icon-like (*severe, severely beautiful*).
и́конопис|ь, и, *f.* icon-painting.
иконоста́с, а, *m.* (*eccl.*) iconostasis.
ико́рный, *adj. of* икра́[1].
ико́т|а, ы, *f.* hiccups.
икр|а́[1], ы́, *no pl. f.* 1. (hard) roe; spawn; мета́ть ~у́ to spawn; (*fig., coll.*) to rage. 2. caviar(e); pâté; зерни́стая и. soft caviar(e); па́юсная и. pressed caviar(e); баклажа́нная и. aubergine pâté.
икр|а́[2], ы́, *pl.* ~ы, *f.* (*anat.*) calf.
икри́нк|а, и, *f.* (*coll.*) grain of roe.

икри́ст|ый (~, ~а), *adj.* containing much roe.

икр|и́ться, ю́сь, и́шься, *impf.* to spawn.

икрометáни|е, я, *n.* spawning.

икрянóй, *adj.* 1. hard-roed. 2. (made from) roe.

икс, а, *m.* (*the letter*) x; (*math.*) x (*unknown quantity*).

икс-лучⷶ|й, éй, *no sing.* (*obs.*) X-rays.

ил, а, *m.* silt.

и́ли, *conj.* or; и.... и. either . . . or; и. вы меня́ не понимáете? don't you understand me?

и́лист|ый (~, ~а), *adj.* covered with silt; containing silt.

иллю́зи|я, и, *f.* illusion.

иллюзóр|ный (~ен, ~на), *adj.* illusory.

иллюминáтор, а, *m.* (*naut.*) porthole.

иллюминáци|я, и, *f.* illumination.

иллюмини́р|овать, ую, *impf. and pf.* to illuminate (*in var. senses*).

иллюстрати́в|ный (~ен, ~на), *adj.* illustrative; и. материáл illustration(s).

иллюстрáтор, а, *m.* illustrator.

иллюстрáци|я, и, *f.* illustration (*in various senses*).

иллюстри́р|ованный, *p.p.p. of* ~овать *and adj.* illustrated.

иллюстри́р|овать, ую, *impf. and pf.* (*pf. also* про~) to illustrate (*also fig.*).

илóт, а, *m.* (*hist. or fig.*) helot.

и́л|овый, *adj.* = ~и́стый.

иль = и́ли.

и́льк|а, и, *f.* (*zool.*) 1. (North American) mink. 2. mink (*fur*).

и́льк|овый, *adj. of* ~а.

ильм, а, *m.* (*bot.*) elm (*Ulmus scabra*).

и́льм|овый, *adj. of* ~.

им 1. *i. of pron.* он, онó. 2. *d. of pron.* они́.

имажини́зм, а, *m.* (*lit.*) imagism.

имажини́ст, а, *m.* (*lit.*) imagist.

имáм, а, *m.* imam (*Mohammedan priest or leader*).

имáть (*inf. and past not used*), éмлю, éмлешь, *impf.* (*arch., now only iron.*) to take.

имби́р|ный, *adj. of* ~ь.

имби́р|ь, я́, *m.* ginger.

и́м|ени, енем, *see* ~я.

имéни|е, я, *n.* 1. estate, landed property. 2. (*sing. only*) *obs.*) property, possessions.

имени́нник, а, *m.* one whose name-day it is; сидéть, смотрéть ~ом (*joc.*) to look cheery, look on top of the world.

имени́н|ный, *adj. of* ~ы; и. пирóг name-day cake.

имени́н|ы, ~, *no sing.* 1. name-day (*day of saint after whom person is named*); спрáвить и. to celebrate one's name-day. 2. name-day celebration; пойти́ на и. к комý-н. to go to someone's name-day party.

имени́тельный, *adj.* (*gram.*) nominative.

имени́т|ый (~, ~а), *adj.* (*obs.*) distinguished.

и́менно, *adv.* 1. (a) и. namely; to wit, videlicet (viz.); нас там бы́ло трóе, а и.: Петрóв, Иванóв и я there were three of us there, namely Petrov, Ivanov, and myself. 2. just, exactly; to be exact; где и. онá живёт? where exactly does she live?; в то врéмя я был в Росси́и, а и. в Одéссе I was in Russia then, in Odessa to be exact; вот и. э́то я и говори́л that's just what I was saying; вот и.! exactly!, precisely!

именн|óй, *adj.* 1. nominal; ~ы́е áкции (*fin.*) inscribed stock; ~óе кольцó ring engraved with owner's name; и. спи́сок nominal roll; и. укáз edict signed by tsar; и. чек cheque payable to person named; и. экземпля́р autographed copy. 2. *adj. of* и́мя з.

именóван|ный, *p.p.p. of* именовáть *and adj.*; (*math.*) ~ное числó concrete number.

имен|овáть, у́ю, *impf.* (*of* на~) to name.

имен|овáться, у́юсь, *impf.* 1. (+*i.*) to be called; to be termed. 2. *pass. of* ~овáть.

именослóв, а, *m.* 1. (*arch.*) list of names, roll. 2. (*eccl.*) litany (*of saints*).

именýемый, *pres. part. pass. of* именовáть; царь Ивáн, и. Грóзным Tsar Ivan, called the Terrible.

имé|ть, ю, ешь, *impf.* 1. to have (*of abstract possession*); и. возмóжность (+*inf.*) to have an opportunity (to), be in a position (to); и. дéло (с+*i.*) to have dealings (with), have to do (with); и. значéние (для) to matter (to), be important (to); и. мéсто to take place; и. нáглость, несчáстье, *etc.* (+*inf.*) to have the effrontery, the misfortune, *etc.* (to); и. стыд to be ashamed; и. в виду́ to bear in mind, think of, mean; ничегó не и. прóтив (+*g.*) to have no objection(s) (to); и. сто мéтров в высоту́ to be 100 metres high. 2. (+*inf. forms future tense in formal utterance*; *obs.*) зáвтра ~ет быть банкéт there is to be a banquet tomorrow.

имé|ться, ется, *impf.* to be; to be present, be available (~ется у, ~ются у *are equivalent to* есть у); в нáшем гóроде ~ется два кинó there are two cinemas in our town, we have two cinemas in our town; банáнов у нас не ~ется we have no bananas, bananas are not to be had here; и. налицó to be available, be on hand.

имé|ющийся, *pres. part. of* ~ться *and adj.* available; present.

и́ми, *i. of pron.* они́.

имитáтор, а, *m.* mimic.

имитáци|я, и, *f.* 1. mimicry; mimicking. 2. imitation (*artefact*); и. жéмчуга imitation pearl. 3. (*mus.*) imitation.

имити́р|овать, ую, *impf.* 1. to mimic. 2. to make imitation goods. 3. (*mus.*) to imitate.

имманёнт|ный (~ен, ~на), *adj.* (*philos.*, *theol.*) immanent.

иммигра́нт, а, *m.* immigrant.

иммигра|цио́нный, *adj. of* ~ция; ~цио́нные зако́ны immigration laws.

иммигра́ци|я, и, *f.* 1. immigration. 2. (*collect.*) immigrants.

иммигри́р|овать, ую, *impf. and pf.* to immigrate.

иммора́л|ьный (~ен, ~ьна), *adj.* immoral.

иммуниза́ци|я, и, *f.* (*med.*) immunization.

иммунизи́р|овать, ую, *impf. and pf.* (*med.*) to immunize.

иммунитёт, а, *m.* (*med.*, *leg.*) immunity.

имму́н|ный (~ен, ~на), *adj.* (к) immune (to).

императи́в, а, *m.* (*philos.*, *gram.*) imperative.

императи́в|ный (~ен, ~на), *adj.* imperative.

импера́тор, а, *m.* emperor.

импера́торский, *adj.* imperial.

императри́ц|а, ы, *f.* empress.

империа́л[1], а, *m.* (*obs.*) imperial (*Russian gold coin of 10 or, after 1897, 15 roubles*).

империа́л[2], а, *m.* (*obs.*) imperial, outside (*of omnibus or tram*).

империали́зм, а, *m.* imperialism.

империали́ст, а, *m.* imperialist.

империалисти́ческий, *adj.* imperialist(ic).

импёри|я, и, *f.* empire.

импёрский, *adj.* imperial.

импоза́нт|ный (~ен, ~на), *adj.* imposing, striking.

импони́р|овать, ую, *impf.* (+*d.*) to impress, strike (*fig.*); его́ зна́ния ~овали всем знако́мым everyone he knew was impressed by his learning.

и́мпорт, а, *m.* import.

импортёр, а, *m.* importer.

импорти́р|овать, ую, *impf. and pf.* (*econ.*) to import.

и́мпорт|ный, *adj. of* ~; ~ные по́шлины import duties.

импотёнт, а, *m.* impotent man.

импотёнт|ный (~ен, ~на), *adj.* (*med.*) impotent.

импотёнци|я, и, *f.* (*med.*) impotence.

импреса́рио, *indecl.*, *m.* impresario.

импрессиони́зм, а, *m.* (*art*) impressionism.

импрессиони́ст, а, *m.* (*art*) impressionist.

импрессионисти́ческий, *adj.* (*art*) impressionistic.

импрессиони́ст|ский, *adj.* = ~и́ческий.

импровиза́тор, а, *m.* improvisator.

импровиза́торский, *adj.* improvisatory.

импровиза́ци|я, и, *f.* improvisation.

импровизи́рова|нный, *p.p.p. of* ~ть *and adj.* improvised; impromptu, extempore.

импровизи́р|овать, ую, *impf.* (*of* сымпровизи́ровать) to improvize; to extemporize.

и́мпульс, а, *m.* impulse, impetus.

импульси́в|ный (~ен, ~на), *adj.* impulsive.

и́мут, *3rd pl. of arch. verb* я́ти: мёртвые сра́му не и. (*rhet.*) 'de mortuis nil nisi bonum'.

иму́ществ|енный, *adj. of* ~о; и. ценз property qualification; и. иск (*leg.*) real action.

иму́ществ|о, а, *n.* property, belongings; stock; дви́жимое и. (*leg.*) personalty, personal estate; недви́жимое и. realty, real estate.

иму́щий, *adj.* propertied; well-off; власть иму́щие the powers that be.

и́м|я, *g.*, *d.*, *and p.* ~ени, *i.* ~енем, *pl.* ~ена́, ~ён, ~ена́м, *n.* 1. first, Christian name; name; по ~ени О́льга Olga by name; во и. (+*g.*) in the name of; посла́ть на и. (+*g.*) to address to; запиши́те счёт на моё и. put it down to my account; от ~ени (+*g.*) on behalf of; то́лько по ~ени only in name, only nominally; он тепе́рь изве́стен под други́м ~енем he now goes by, under another name; ~енем зако́на in the name of the law; ~ени (+*g.*) named in honour of (*usually not translated*); Теа́тр ~ени Го́рького the Gorki Theatre; Вое́нная акаде́мия ~ени Фру́нзе the Frunze Military Academy; называ́ть ве́щи свои́ми ~ена́ми to call a spade a spade. 2. (*fig.*) name, reputation; челове́к с больши́м ~енем a man with a great name; у него́ европе́йское и. he has a European reputation; приобрести́ и. to acquire, make a name; замара́ть своё и. to ruin one's good name; кру́пные ~ена́ в о́бласти фи́зики great names in the field of physics. 3. (*gram.*) noun, nomen (*any part of speech declined as opp. to conjugated*); и. прилага́тельное (noun) adjective; и. существи́тельное noun (substantive); и. числи́тельное numeral.

имяре́к, а, *m.* 1. (*obs. or joc.*) so-and-so. 2. (*in official forms, etc.*) indicates space for signatory's name.

ин- (*abbr. of* иностра́нный) foreign.

инакомы́слящ|ий, *adj.* differently minded; heterodox; *as noun* и., ~его, *m.* dissident.

ина́че 1. (*adv.*) differently, otherwise; так и́ли и. in either event, at all events; не ина́че (как) (*coll.*) precisely, of course; не ина́че как полко́вник none other than the colonel. 2. (*conj.*) otherwise, or (else); спеши́те, и. вы опозда́ете hurry up, or you will be late.

инвали́д, а, *m.* invalid; и. войны́ disabled soldier; и. труда́ industrial invalid.

инвали́дност|ь, и, *f.* disablement; посо́бие по ~и disablement relief; перейти́ на и. to be registered as a disabled person; по ~и перейти́ на пе́нсию (*mil.*) to be invalided out on pension; уво́литься по ~и (*mil.*) to be invalided out.

инвали́д|ный, *adj. of* ~; и. дом home for invalids.

инвекти́в|а, ы, *f.* invective.

инвентариза́ци|я, и, *f.* inventory making, inventorying, stock-taking.

инвентариз|ова́ть, у́ю, *impf. and pf.* to inventory.

инвента́р|ный, *adj. of* ~ь; ~ная о́пись inventory.

инвента́р|ь, я́, *m.* **1.** stock; equipment, appliances; живо́й и. live stock; сельскохозя́йственный и. agricultural implements; торго́вый и. stock-in-trade. **2.** inventory.

инве́рси|я, и, *f.* (*lit.*) inversion.

инвести́р|овать, ую, *impf. and pf.* to invest.

инвести́тор, а, *m.* investor.

инвеститу́р|а, ы, *f.* investiture.

инвести́ци|я, и, *f.* investment.

инволю́ци|я, и, *f.* (*physiol.*) involution.

ингаля́|тор, а, *m.* (*med.*) inhaler.

ингаля|цио́нный, *adj. of* ~ция.

ингаля́ци|я, и, *f.* (*med.*) inhaling.

ингредие́нт, а, *m.* ingredient.

ингу́ш, á, *g. pl.* ~е́й, *m.* Ingush.

ингу́ш|ка, ки, *f. of* ~.

ингу́шский, *adj.* Ingush.

и́ндеве|ть, ет, *impf.* (*of* за~) to become covered with hoar-frost.

инде́|ец, йца, *pl.* ~йцы, ~йцев, *m.* (American) Indian.

инде́йк|а, и, *f.* turkey(-hen).

инде́|йский, *adj. of* ~ец; и. пету́х turkey-cock.

и́ндекс, а, *m.* index; и. цен (*econ.*) price index; почто́вый и. post-code, Zip code.

индиа́нк|а, и, *f.* (*of* индє́ец *and* инди́ец) Indian (woman).

индиви́д, а, *m.* individual.

индивидуализа́ци|я, и, *f.* individualization.

индивидуализи́р|овать, ую, *impf. and pf.* to individualize.

индивидуали́зм, а, *m.* individualism.

индивидуали́ст, а, *m.* individualist.

индивидуалисти́ческий, *adj.* individualistic.

индивидуалисти́ч|ный (~ен, ~на), *adj.* individualistic.

индивидуа́льност|ь, и, *f.* individuality.

индивидуа́л|ьный (~ен, ~ьна), *adj.* individual; ~ьные осо́бенности individual peculiarities; ~ьное хозя́йство individual holding; в ~ьном поря́дке individually; и. слу́чай individual case, single case.

индиви́дуум, а, *m.* individual.

инди́го, *indecl., n.* **1.** indigo (*colour*). **2.** (*bot.*) indigo plant.

инди́|ец, йца, *pl.* ~йцы, ~йцев, *m.* Indian.

и́нди|й, я, *m.* (*chem.*) indium.

инди́йский, *adj.* Indian.

индикати́в, а, *m.* (*gram.*) indicative.

индика́тор, а, *m.* **1.** (*tech.*) indicator. **2.** (*chem.*) reagent.

индика́тор|ный, *adj. of* ~; ~ная диагра́мма indicator diagram; ~ная мо́щность indicated horse-power (*abbr.* I.H.P.).

инди́кт, а, *m.* (*hist.*) indiction (*period of 15 years*).

индиффере́нтност|ь, и, *f.* indifference.

индиффере́нт|ный (~ен, ~на), *adj.* (к) indifferent (to).

индоевропе́йский, *adj.* Indo-European.

индокита́йский, *adj.* Indo-Chinese.

индонези́|ец, йца, *pl.* ~йцы, ~йцев, *m.* Indonesian.

индонези́|йка, йки, *f. of* ~ец.

индонези́йский, *adj.* Indonesian.

индоссаме́нт, а, *m.* (*fin.*) endorsement, indorsation.

индосса́нт, а, *m.* (*fin.*) endorser.

индосса́т, а, *m.* (*fin.*) endorsee.

индосси́р|овать, ую, *impf. and pf.* (*fin.*) to endorse.

индуи́зм, а, *m.* Hinduism.

индукти́вный, *adj.* (*philos., phys.*) inductive.

инду́ктор, а, *m.* (*electr.*) inductor, field magnet.

инду́ктор|ный, *adj. of* ~; и. вы́зов induction call; и. телефо́нный аппара́т magneto telephone, sound power telephone.

индукци|о́нный, *adj. of* ~я; ~о́нная кату́шка induction coil.

инду́кци|я, и, *f.* (*philos., phys.*) induction.

индульге́нци|я, и, *f.* (*eccl.*) indulgence.

инду́с, а, *m.* Hindu; (*obs.*) Indian.

инду́с|ка, ки, *f. of* ~.

инду́сский, *adj.* Hindu; (*obs.*) Indian.

индустриализа́ци|я, и, *f.* industrialization.

индустриализи́р|овать, ую, *impf. and pf.* to industrialize.

индустриа́льный, *adj.* industrial.

инду́стри|я, и, *f.* industry.

индю́к, á, *m.* turkey(-cock); наду́лся как и. (*coll.*) he got on his high horse.

индю́ш|а́чий, *adj.* = ~ечий.

индю́ш|ечий, *adj. of* ~ка.

индю́шк|а, и, *f.* turkey(-hen).

индю́ш|о́нок, о́нка, *pl.* ~а́та, ~а́т, *m.* turkey-poult.

и́не|й, я, *no pl., m.* hoar-frost, rime.

ине́ртност|ь, и, *f.* inertness, sluggishness, inaction.

ине́рт|ный (~ен, ~на), *adj.* inert (*phys. and fig.*); sluggish, inactive.

ине́рци|я, и, *f.* (*phys. and fig.*) inertia; momentum; дви́гаться по ~и to move under its own momentum; (*fig.*) де́лать что́-н. по ~и to do something from force of inertia, mechanically.

инженéр, а, *m.* person with higher technical education; engineer; граждáнский и., и. путéй сообщéния, и.-стрóитель civil engineer.

инженéри|я, и, *f.* (*obs.*) engineering.

инженéрн|ый, *adj.* engineering; ~ые войскá (*mil.*) Engineers; ~ое дéло engineering.

инженю, *indecl., f.* (*theatr.*) ingénue.

инжи́р, а, *m.* fig.

инжи́рный, *adj.* fig.

и́нист|ый (~, ~а), *adj.* rimy, covered with hoar-frost.

инициáл|ы, ов, *sing.* ~, ~а, *m.* initials.

инициати́в|а, ы, *f.* initiative; по сóбственной ~е on one's own initiative.

инициати́в|ный, *adj.* 1. initiating, originating; ~ная грýппа organizing body, action committee. 2. (~ен, ~на) full of initiative, enterprising.

инкассáтор, а, *m.* (*fin.*) collector, receiver (*of bill, cheque, etc.*).

инкассáци|я, и, *f.* encashment, collection, receipt (*of money or bills*).

инкасси́р|овать, ую, *impf. and pf.* (*fin.*) to encash, collect, receive (*money, bill*).

инкáссо, *indecl., n.* (*fin.*) encashment.

ин-квáрто, *adv.* (*also as adj. and noun, indecl.*) (*typ.*) quarto.

инквизи́тор, а, *m.* inquisitor.

инквизи́торский, *adj.* inquisitorial.

инквизи́ци|я, и, *f.* inquisition.

инкóгнито, *adv.* (*also as indecl. noun, m. and n.*) incognito.

инкорпорáци|я, и, *f.* incorporation.

инкорпори́р|овать, ую, *impf. and pf.* to incorporate.

инкримини́р|овать, ую, *impf. and pf.* (+*a. and d.*) to charge (with); емý ~ýют поджóг he is being charged with arson.

инкрустáци|я, и, *f.* inlaid work, inlay.

инкрусти́р|овать, ую, *impf. and pf.* to inlay.

инкубáтор, а, *m.* incubator.

инкубациóнный, *adj.* incubative, incubatory; и. перíод (*med.*) incubation.

инкубáци|я, и, *f.* incubation (*of chickens and med.*).

инкунáбул|ы, ~, *sing.* ~а, ~ы, *f.* (*lit.*) incunabula.

иновéр|ец, ца, *m.* (*rel.*) adherent of different faith, creed.

иновéри|е, я, n. (*rel.*) adherence to different faith, creed.

иновéрный, *adj.* (*rel.*) belonging to different faith, creed.

иногдá, *adv.* sometimes.

иногорóдн|ий, *adj.* 1. of, from another town; ~яя пóчта mail for, from other towns. 2. *as noun* и., ~его, *m.* (*hist.*) non--Cossack peasant living in Cossack community.

инозéм|ец, ца, *m.* (*obs.*) foreigner.

инозéмный, *adj.* (*obs.*) foreign.

ин|óй, *adj.* 1. different; other; ~ыми словáми in other words; не кто и., как; не что ~óе, как none other than; тот и́ли и. one or other, this or that. 2. some; и. раз sometimes; и. (человéк) мог и согласи́ться some might agree.

и́нок, а, *m.* monk.

и́нокин|я, и, *f.* nun.

ин-октáво, *adv.* (*also as adj. and noun, indecl.*) (*typ.*) octavo.

инокули́р|овать, ую, *impf. and pf.* to inoculate.

инокуля́ци|я, и, *f.* inoculation.

иномы́сли|е, я, n. (*obs.*) dissent, difference of opinion.

иноплемéнник, а, *m.* (*obs.*) member of different tribe, nationality.

иноплемéнный, *adj.* (*obs.*) of another tribe, nationality; foreign.

инорóд|ец, ца, *m.* (*hist.*) non-Russian (*member of national minority in tsarist Russia*).

инорóдн|ый, *adj.* heterogeneous; ~ое тéло (*med. or fig.*) foreign body.

инорóд|ческий, *adj.* of ~ец.

иносказáни|е, я, n. allegory.

иносказáтель|ный (~ен, ~ьна), *adj.* allegorical.

инослáвный, *adj.* (*rel.*) non-Orthodox.

инострáн|ец, ца, *m.* foreigner.

инострáнный, *adj.* foreign.

инотдéл, а, *m.* foreign department (*of Soviet institutions*).

инохóд|ец, ца, *m.* ambler (*horse*).

и́ноход|ь, и, *f.* amble.

и́ноческий, *adj.* monastic.

и́ночеств|о, а, n. monasticism; monastic life.

иноязы́чн|ый, *adj.* 1. speaking another language. 2. belonging to another language; ~ое слóво loan-word.

инсинуáци|я, и, *f.* insinuation.

инсинуи́р|овать, ую, *impf. and pf.* to insinuate.

инсоля́ци|я, и, *f.* (*phys., med.*) insolation.

инспекти́р|овать, ую, *impf.* to inspect.

инспéктор, а, *pl.* ~á, ~óв, *m.* inspector; (*mil.*) inspecting officer.

инспéктор|ский, *adj.* of ~.

инспéкци|я, и, *f.* 1. inspection. 2. inspectorate.

инспирáтор, а, *m.* inciter.

инспири́р|овать, ую, *impf. and pf.* to incite; to inspire; кто ~овáл э́ту статью́? who inspired this article?; и. слýхи to start rumours.

инстáнци|я, и, *f.* (*leg.*) instance; (*polit.*) level of authority; суд пéрвой ~и court of first instance; по ~ям from instance to instance, through all stages; (*mil.*) кома́ндная и. chain of command.

инсти́нкт, а, *m.* instinct.

инстинкти́в|ный (~ен, ~на), *adj.* instinctive.

институ́т, а, *m.* 1. institution; и. бра́ка, и. ча́стной со́бственности the institution of marriage, of private property. 2. (*educational or scientific*) institute, institution; педагоги́ческий и. teacher training college. 3. girls' private boarding school (*in tsarist Russia*).

институ́тк|а, и, *f.* boarding schoolgirl (*in tsarist Russia*); (*fig.*, *coll.*) innocent, unsophisticated girl.

институ́т|ский, *adj.* of ~ 2, 3.

инструкта́ж, а, *m.* instructing; (*mil.*, *aeron.*) briefing.

инструкти́в|ный (~ен, ~на), *adj.* instructional.

инструкти́р|овать, ую, *impf. and pf.* (*pf. also* про~) to instruct, give instructions to.

инстру́ктор, а, *m.* instructor.

инстру́ктор|ский, *adj.* of ~.

инстру́кци|я, и, *f.* instructions, directions.

инструме́нт, а, *m.* instrument; tool, implement; (*sing.*; *collect.*) tools.

инструментали́ст, а, *m.* (*mus.*) instrumentalist.

инструмента́льн|ая, ой, *f.* tool-shop.

инструмента́льн|ый, *adj.* 1. (*mus.*) instrumental. 2. (*tech.*) tool-making; ~ая сталь tool steel.

инструмента́льщик, а, *m.* tool-maker, instrument-maker.

инструмента́ри|й, я, *m.* (*collect.*) instruments, tools.

инструмент|ова́ть, у́ю, *impf. and pf.* (*mus.*) to arrange for instruments.

инструменто́вк|а, и, *f.* (*mus.*) instrumentation.

инсули́н, а, *m.* (*med.*) insulin.

инсу́льт, а, *m.* (*med.*) cerebral thrombosis; (apoplectic) stroke.

инсурге́нт, а, *m.* (*obs.*) insurgent.

инсуррекци|я, и, *f.* (*obs.*) insurrection.

инсцени́р|овать, ую, *impf. and pf.* 1. to dramatize, adapt for stage *or* screen (*a novel*, *etc.*). 2. (*fig.*) to feign, stage; и. о́бморок to stage a faint.

инсцениро́вк|а, и, *f.* 1. dramatization, adaptation for stage *or* screen. 2. (*fig.*) pretence; act.

интегра́л, а, *m.* (*math.*) integral.

интегра́льн|ый, *adj.* (*math.*) integral; ~ое исчисле́ние integral calculus.

интегра́ци|я, и, *f.* (*math.*) integration.

интегри́р|овать, ую, *impf. and pf.* (*math.*) to integrate.

интелле́кт, а, *m.* intellect.

интеллектуа́л|ьный (~ен, ~ьна), *adj.* intellectual.

интеллиге́нт, а, *m.* member of the intelligentsia, intellectual.

интеллиге́нт|ный (~ен, ~на), *adj.* cultured, educated.

интеллиге́нт|ский, *adj.* (*pejor.*) of ~; dilettante.

интеллиге́нци|я, и, *f.* 1. (*hist.*) intelligentsia. 2. (*collect.*) professional class(es).

интенда́нт, а, *m.* (*mil.*) quartermaster.

интенда́нтств|о, а, *n.* (*mil.*) quartermaster service, commissariat.

интенси́в|ный (~ен, ~на), *adj.* intensive.

интенсифици́р|овать, ую, *impf. and pf.* to intensify.

интерва́л, а, *m.* (*in var. senses*) interval.

интерве́нт, а, *m.* (*polit.*) interventionist.

интерве́нци|я, и, *f.* (*polit.*) intervention.

интервью́, *indecl.*, *n.* (press) interview.

интервью́е́р, а, *m.* (press) interviewer.

интервьюи́р|овать, ую, *impf. and pf.* to interview.

интере́с, а, *m.* interest 1. (*attention*) предста́вить и. to be of interest; прояви́ть и. (к) to show interest (in). 2. (*advantage*); (*pl.*) interests; како́й мне и.? how do I stand to gain?; в ва́ших ~ах пое́хать it is in your interest to go; игра́ть на и. (*coll.*, *obs.*) to play for money.

интере́снича|ть, ю, *impf.* (*coll.*) to show off.

интере́сно, *as pred.* it is, would be interesting; и. знать, кто э́тот высо́кий иностра́нец it would be interesting to know who the tall foreigner is; и., что из него́ вы́йдет I wonder how he will turn out.

интере́с|ный (~ен, ~на), *adj.* 1. interesting; в ~ном положе́нии (*euph.*) in an interesting condition. 2. striking, attractive.

интерес|ова́ть, у́ю, *impf.* to interest.

интерес|ова́ться, у́юсь, *impf.* (+*i.*) to be interested (in).

интерлю́ди|я, и, *f.* (*mus.*) interlude.

интерме́ди|я, и, *f.* (*theatr.*) interlude.

интерме́ццо, *indecl.*, *n.* (*mus.*) intermezzo.

интерна́т, а, *m.* 1. boarding school. 2. boarding house (*at private school*).

интернациона́л, а, *m.* 1. international (organization); Пе́рвый И. (*hist.*) the First International. 2. И. the 'Internationale'.

интернационализа́ци|я, и, *f.* internationalization.

интернационализи́р|овать, ую, *impf. and pf.* to internationalize.

интернационали́зм, а, *m.* internationalism.

интернационали́ст, а, *m.* internationalist.

интернациона́льный, *adj.* international.

интерни́рова|нный, *p.p.p.* of ~ть; *as noun* и., ~нного, *m.* internee.

интерни́р|овать, ую, *impf. and pf.* to intern.

интерпелли́р|овать, ую, *impf. and pf.* (*polit.*) to interpellate.

интерпелля́ци|я, и, *f.* (*polit.*) interpellation; question in Parliament.

интерполи́р|овать, ую, *impf. and pf.* to interpolate.

интерполя́ци|я, и, *f.* interpolation.

интерпрета́тор, а, *m.* interpreter (*expounder*).

интерпрета́ци|я, и, *f.* interpretation; но́вая и. ро́ли Га́млета a new interpretation of the part of Hamlet.

интерпрети́р|овать, ую, *impf. and pf.* to interpret (*expound*).

интерфере́нци|я, и, *f.* (*phys.*) interference.

интерье́р, а, *m.* (*art*) interior.

инти́мност|ь, и, *f.* intimacy.

инти́м|ный (~ен, ~на), *adj.* intimate.

интоксика́ци|я, и, *f.* (*med.*) intoxication; алкого́льная и. alcoholic poisoning.

интона́ци|я, и, *f.* intonation.

интони́р|овать, ую, *impf.* to intone.

интри́г|а, и, *f.* 1. intrigue. 2. (*obs.*) (love-) affair. 3. plot of story *or* play.

интрига́н, а, *m.* intriguer, schemer.

интриг|ова́ть, у́ю, *impf.* 1. (*no pf.*) to intrigue, carry on an intrigue. 2. (*pf.* за~) to intrigue (*excite curiosity of*).

интроду́кци|я, и, *f.* (*mus.*) introduction.

интроспе́кци|я, и, *f.* introspection.

интуитиви́зм, а, *m.* (*philos.*) intuitionism.

интуити́в|ный (~ен, ~на), *adj.* intuitive.

интуи́ци|я, и, *f.* intuition.

инфанте́ри|я, и, *f.* (*obs.*) infantry.

инфантили́зм, а, *m.* infantilism.

инфанти́льный, *adj.* infantile.

инфа́ркт, а, *m.* (*med.*) infarct; infarction; coronary thrombosis; heart attack.

инфекцио́нн|ый, *adj.* infectious; ~ая больни́ца isolation hospital.

инфе́кци|я, и, *f.* infection.

инферна́льный, *adj.* infernal, of hell.

инфильтра́ци|я, и, *f.* infiltration.

инфинити́в, а, *m.* (*gram.*) infinitive.

инфици́р|овать, ую, *impf. and pf.* to infect.

инфлюэ́нц|а, ы, *f.* influenza.

инфля́ци|я, и, *f.* (*econ.*) inflation.

ин-фо́лио, *adv.* (*also as adj. and noun, indecl.*) (*typ.*) folio.

информа́тор, а, *m.* informant; полити́ческий и. political information officer.

информ|ацио́нный, *adj. of* ~а́ция.

информа́ци|я, и, *f.* information.

информи́р|овать, ую, *impf. and pf.* to inform.

инфракра́сный, *adj.* infra-red.

инфузо́ри|я, и, *f.* (*zool.*) infusoria.

инциде́нт, а, *m.* incident (*quarrel, clash*); пограни́чный и. frontier incident.

инъе́кци|я, и, *f.* injection.

ио́д, ~истый, ~ный, ~офо́рм, *see* йод, *etc.*

ио́н, а, *m.* (*phys.*) ion.

иониза́ци|я, и, *f.* (*phys., med.*) ionization.

иони́ческ|ий, *adj.* Ionian, Ionic; ~ая коло́нна Ionic column.

ио́нный, *adj.* (*phys.*) ionic.

ио́та = йо́та.

иподья́кон, а, *m.* (*eccl.*) subdeacon.

ипоме́|я, и, *f.* (*bot.*) morning glory.

ипоста́с|ь, и, *f.* (*theol.*) hypostasis.

ипоте́к|а, и, *f.* mortgage.

ипоте́|чный, *adj. of* ~ка.·

ипохо́ндрик, а, *m.* hypochondriac.

ипохо́ндри|я, и, *f.* hypochondria.

ипподро́м, а, *m.* hippodrome; racecourse.

ипри́т, а, *m.* mustard gas, yperite.

ира́к|ец, ца, *m.* Iraqi.

ира́кский, *adj.* Iraqi.

ира́н|ец, ца, *m.* Iranian.

ира́н|ка, ки, *f. of* ~ец.

ира́нский, *adj.* Iranian.

ира́чк|а, и, *f.* Iraqi (woman).

и́рбис, а, *m.* (*zool.*) ounce.

ири́ди|й, я, *m.* (*chem.*) iridium.

и́рис, а, *m.* (*bot.*) iris.

ири́с, а, *m.* toffee.

ири́ск|а, и, (*coll.*) *f.* (a) toffee.

ирла́нд|ец, ца, *m.* Irishman.

ирла́нд|ка, ки, *f. of* ~ец.

ирла́ндский, *adj.* Irish.

ирмо́с, а, *m.* (*eccl. mus.*) introduction (*to hymn or canon*).

и́род, а, *m.* (*coll.*) tyrant, monster.

иронизи́р|овать, ую, *impf.* (над) to speak ironically (about).

ирони́ческий, *adj.* ironic(al).

ирони́ч|ный (~ен, ~на), *adj.* = ~еский.

иро́ни|я, и, *f.* irony.

иррациона́л|ьный (~ен, ~ьна), *adj.* irrational; ~ьное число́ (*math.*) irrational number, surd.

иррегуля́рн|ый, *adj.* irregular; ~ые войска́ (*mil.*) irregulars.

иррига́ци|я, и, *f.* (*agric. and med.*) irrigation.

иск, а, *m.* (*leg.*) suit, action; предъяви́ть и. (к) кому́-н. to sue, prosecute someone, bring an action against someone; отказа́ть в ~е to reject a suit; и. за клевету́ libel action; и. за оскорбле́ние де́йствием action for assault and battery.

искажа́|ть, ю, *impf. of* исказить.

искаже́ни|е, я, *n.* distortion, perversion; ~я в те́ксте corruptions of a text.

искажённый, *p.p.p. of* исказить *and adj.* distorted, perverted.

иска|зи́ть, жу́, зи́шь, *pf.* (*of* ~жа́ть) to distort, pervert, twist; to misrepresent; боль ~зи́ла черты́ её лица́ pain has distorted her features; и. чьи-н. слова́ to twist someone's words; и. фáкты to misrepresent the facts.

искалéч|енный, *p.p.p. of* ~ить *and adj.* crippled, maimed.

искалéчива|ть, ю, *impf. of* искалéчить.

искалéч|ить, у, ишь, *pf. (of* ~ивать *and* калéчить) 1. to cripple, maim. 2. (*coll.*) to break.

искáлыва|ть, ю, *impf. of* исколóть.

искáни|е, я, *n.* 1. (+*g.*) search (for), quest (of). 2. (*pl.*) strivings.

искáп|ать, аю, *pf. (of* ~ывать[1]) (*coll.*) to sprinkle all over, spill all over; и. свой брюки чернúлами to spill ink all over one's trousers.

искáпыва|ть[1], ю, *impf. of* искáпать.

искáпыва|ть[2], ю, *impf. of* ископáть.

искáтел|ь, я, m. 1. seeker, searcher; и. жéмчуга pearl-diver. 2. (*tech.*) (view-)finder.

искáтел|ьный (~ен, ~ьна), *adj.* ingratiating.

искáтельств|о, а, *n.* ingratiating oneself.

искáть, ищý, úщешь, *impf.* 1. (+*a.*) to look for, search for; to seek (*something concr.*); и. игóлку, квартúру to be looking for a needle, for a flat. 2. (+*g.*) to seek, look for (*something abstr.*); и. мéста to look for a job; и. слýчая, совéта to seek an opportunity, seek advice. 3. (c+*g. or* на+*p.*; *leg.*) to claim (from). 4. (+*inf.*; *obs.*) to seek (to).

исключáть, áю, *impf. of* ~úть.

исключá|я, *pres. gerund of* ~ть *and prep.*+*g.* excepting, with the exception of; и. присýтствующих the present company excepted.

исключéни|е, я, *n.* 1. exception; за ~ем (+*g.*) with the exception (of). 2. exclusion; expulsion; по мéтоду ~я by process of elimination.

исключúтельно, *adv.* 1. exceptionally. 2. exclusively, solely. 3. exclusive; до странúцы семь и. to page seven exclusive.

исключúтел|ьный (~ен, ~ьна), *adj.* 1. exceptional; и. слýчай exceptional case; ~ьной вáжности of exceptional importance. 2. exclusive; ~ьное прáво exclusive right, sole right. 3. (*coll.*) excellent.

исключ|úть, ý, úшь, *pf. (of* ~áть) 1. to exclude; to eliminate; и. из спúска to strike off a list. 2. to expel; to dismiss. 3. to rule out; не ~енó, что нáши проигрáют the possibility of our side losing cannot be ruled out.

исковéрка|нный, *p.p.p. of* ~ть *and adj.* (*coll.*) corrupt(ed); ~нное слóво corrupted word, corruption.

исковéрка|ть, ю, *pf. of* ковéркать.

иск|овóй, *adj. of* ~; ~овóе заявлéние (*leg.*) statement of claim.

исколáчива|ть, ю, *impf. of* исколотúть.

исколе|сúть, шý, сúшь, *pf. (coll.)* to travel all over.

исколо|тúть, чý, ~тишь, *pf. (of* исколáчивать) (*coll.*) 1. to beat; и. когó-н. до полусмéрти to beat someone within an inch of his life. 2. to spoil, damage by knocking in nails, *etc.*

искол|óть, ю, ~ешь, *pf. (of* искáлывать) to prick all over, cover with pricks.

искóмка|ть, ю, *pf. of* кóмкать.

искóм|ый, *adj.* sought for; *as noun* ~ое, ~ого, *n.* (*math.*) unknown quantity.

исконú, *adv.* (*rhet.*) from time immemorial.

искóнный, *adj.* primordial; immemorial.

ископáем|ое, ого, *n.* 1. mineral. 2. fossil (*also fig., iron.*).

ископáемый, *adj.* fossilized.

ископá|ть, ю, *pf. (of* искáпывать[2]) to dig up.

искорёж|ить(ся), у(сь), ишь(ся), *pf. of* корёжить(ся).

искоренéни|е, я, *n.* eradication.

искорен|úть, ю, úшь, *pf. (of* ~ять) to eradicate.

искорен|ять, яю, *impf. of* ~úть.

úскорк|а, и, f. *dim. of* úскра.

úскоса, *adv.* (*coll.*) aslant, sideways; взгляд и. sidelong glance.

úскр|а, ы, f. spark; (*fig.*) flash; промелькнýть, как и. to flash by; и. надéжды glimmer of hope; у меня ~ы из глаз посыпались (*coll.*) I saw stars.

искрéни|е, я, *n.* (*tech.*) sparking.

úскренн|е = ~о.

úскрен|ний (~ен, ~на), *adj.* sincere, candid.

úскренно, *adv.* sincerely, candidly; и. ваш, и. прéданный вам (*epistolary formula*) Yours sincerely; Yours faithfully.

úскренност|ь, и, f. sincerity, candour.

искрив|úть, лю, úшь, *pf. (of* ~лять) to bend; (*fig.*) to distort.

искривлéни|е, я, *n.* bend; (*fig.*) distortion; и. позвонóчника curvature of the spine.

искривл|ять, яю, *impf. of* искривúть.

искрúст|ый (~, ~а), *adj.* sparkling.

искр|úть, úт, *impf.* (*tech.*) to spark.

úскр|úться, ~úтся, *impf.* to sparkle; to scintillate (*also fig.*).

искровл|ённый, *p.p.p. of* ~úть *and adj.* blood-stained.

искровен|úть, ю, úшь, *pf.* (*coll.*) 1. to wound so as to draw blood. 2. to stain with blood.

искр|овóй, *adj. of* ~á; и. зазóр, и. промежýток (*electr.*) spark-gap; и. разрядник (*radio*) spark discharger; и. телегрáф (*obs.*) wireless telegraph.

искрогасúтел|ь, я, m. (*tech.*) spark-extinguisher.

искромётный, *adj.* sparkling; (*fig.*) и. взгляд flashing glance.

искромса́|ть, ю, *pf. of* кромса́ть.

искроудержа́тел|ь, я, m. (*tech.*) spark-arrester.

искрош|и́ть, у́, ~ишь, *pf.* (*of* кроши́ть) to crumble; to mince; (*fig.*) to cut to pieces (*with sabres*).

искрош|и́ться, ~ится, *pf.* (*of* кроши́ться) to crumble (*intrans.*).

искупа́|ть¹, ю, *pf.* (*coll.*) to bath.

искуп|а́ть², а́ю, *impf. of* ~и́ть.

искупа́|ться¹, юсь, *pf.* (*coll.*) to bathe; to take a bath.

искупа́|ться², юсь, *impf., pass. of* ~ть².

искупи́тел|ь, я, m. (*theol.*) redeemer.

искупи́тел|ьный (~ен, ~ьна), *adj.* expiatory, redemptive; ~ьная же́ртва sin offering.

искуп|и́ть, лю, ~ишь, *pf.* (*of* ~а́ть²) **1.** (*theol. and fig.*) to redeem; to expiate, atone for. **2.** to make up for, compensate for.

искупле́ни|е, я, n. redemption, expiation, atonement.

иску́с, а, m. novitiate, probation (*in religious orders*); test, ordeal.

искус|а́ть, а́ю, *pf.* (*of* ~ывать) to bite badly, all over; to sting badly, all over.

искуси́тел|ь, я, m. tempter.

иску|си́ть, шу́, си́шь, *pf. of* ~ша́ть.

иску|си́ться, шу́сь, си́шься, *pf.* **1.** (в+*p.*) to become expert (at), become a past master (in, of). **2.** *pass. of* ~си́ть.

иску́сник, а, m. (*coll.*) expert, past master.

иску́с|ный (~ен, ~на), *adj.* skilful; expert.

иску́сственност|ь, и, f. artificiality.

иску́сствен|ный, *adj.* **1.** artificial, synthetic; ~ное пита́ние (младе́нца) bottle feeding; ~ная цепь (*tech.*) phantom circuit. **2.** (~, ~на) (*fig.*) artificial, feigned.

иску́сств|о, а, n. **1.** art; изобрази́тельные, изя́щные ~a fine arts. **2.** craftsmanship, skill; и. верховой езды́ horsemanship; де́лать что-н. из любви́ к ~y to do something for its own sake.

искусствове́д, а, m. art critic.

искусствове́дени|е, я, n. art criticism.

иску́сыва|ть, ю, *impf. of* искуса́ть.

искуша́|ть, ю, *impf.* (*of* искуси́ть) to tempt; to seduce; и. судьбу́ to tempt fate, tempt Providence.

искуше́ни|е, я, n. temptation; seduction; ввести́ в и. to lead into temptation; подда́ться ~ю, впасть в и. to yield to temptation.

искуше́нный, *p.p.p. of* искуси́ть *and adj.* experienced; tested.

исла́м, а, m. Islam.

исла́нд|ец, ца, m. Icelander.

исла́нд|ка, ки, f. of ~ец.

исла́ндский, *adj.* Icelandic.

испа́ко|стить, щу, стишь, *pf. of* па́костить.

испа́н|ец, ца, m. Spaniard.

испа́нк|а¹, и, f. Spanish woman.

испа́нк|а², и, f. (*coll.*) Spanish 'flu.

испа́нский, *adj.* Spanish.

испаре́ни|е, я, n. **1.** evaporation. **2.** exhalation; fumes.

испа́рин|а, ы, f. perspiration.

испар|и́ть, ю́, и́шь, *pf.* (*of* ~я́ть) to evaporate (*trans.*); to exhale.

испар|и́ться, ю́сь, и́шься, *pf.* (*of* ~я́ться) to evaporate; (*fig., joc.*) to vanish into thin air.

испар|я́ть(ся), я́ю(сь), *impf. of* ~и́ть(ся).

испа|ха́ть, шу́, ~шешь, *pf.* (*of* ~хивать) (*coll.*) to plough all over.

испа́хива|ть, ю, *impf. of* испаха́ть.

испа́чка|ть, ю, *pf. of* па́чкать.

испепел|и́ть, ю́, и́шь, *pf.* (*of* ~я́ть) to reduce to ashes, incinerate.

испепел|я́ть, я́ю, *impf. of* ~и́ть.

испестр|ённый, *p.p.p.* of ~и́ть *and adj.* speckled, mottled; variegated.

испестр|и́ть, ю́, и́шь, *pf.* (*of* ~я́ть) to speckle; to mottle; to make variegated.

испестр|я́ть, я́ю, *impf. of* ~и́ть.

испечённый, *p.p.p.* of испе́чь; вновь и. (*coll.*) new-fledged.

испе́|чь, ку́, чёшь, ку́т, *past* ~к, ~кла́, *pf. of* печь.

испещр|и́ть, ю́, и́шь, *pf.* (*of* ~я́ть) (+*a.* and *i.*) to spot (with); to mark all over (with); и. сте́ну на́дписями to cover a wall with inscriptions.

испещр|я́ть, я́ю, *impf. of* ~и́ть.

испи|са́ть, шу́, ~шешь, *pf.* (*of* ~сывать) **1.** to cover with writing; он уже́ ~са́л два́дцать тетра́дей he has already filled up twenty exercise books. **2.** to use up (in writing) (*pencil, paper, etc.*).

испи|са́ться, шу́сь, ~шешься, *pf.* (*of* ~сываться) (*coll.*) **1.** to be used up (*of writing instrument*). **2.** to write oneself out; to be used up (*of a writer*).

испи́сыва|ть(ся), ю(сь), *impf. of* исписа́ть(ся).

испито́й, *adj.* (*coll.*) haggard, gaunt; hollow-cheeked.

испи́|ть, изопью́, изопьёшь, *past* ~л, ~ла́, ~ло, *pf.* **1.** (*dial.*) to have a drink of, sup. **2.** (*fig., rhet.*) to drain.

испове́да́л|ьня, ьни, g. pl. ~ен, *f.* (*eccl.*) confessional.

испове́дани|е, я, n. creed, confession (*of faith*).

испове́д|ать, аю, *pf.* (*coll.*) = ~овать¹.

испове́д|аться, аюсь, *pf.* (*coll.*) = ~ова́ться¹.

испове́д|овать¹, ую, *impf. and pf.* **1.** (*eccl.*)

to confess (*trans.*), hear confession (of). **2.** (*coll.*) to draw out. **3.** to confess.

исповед|овать², ую, *impf.* to profess (a *faith*).

исповед|оваться¹, уюсь, *impf. and pf.* **1.** (+*d. or* y; *eccl.*) to confess, make one's confession (to). **2.** (+*d. or* перед; *fig., coll.*) to confess; to unburden oneself of, acknowledge; он мне ~овался в свои́х сомне́ниях he confessed his doubts to me.

исповед|оваться², уюсь, *impf. and pf., pass. of* ~овать².

испове́дыва|ть(ся), ю(сь), *impf.* (*obs.*) = испове́довать(ся).

и́сповед|ь, и, f. (*eccl.*) confession; быть на ~и to be at confession.

испога́нива|ть, ю, *impf. of* испога́нить.

испога́н|ить, ю, ишь, *pf.* (*of* ~ивать) (*coll.*) to foul, defile.

испо́д, а, m. (*dial.*) underside, bottom; wrong side (*of garment*).

и́сподволь, *adv.* (*coll.*) in leisurely fashion; by degrees.

исподло́бья, *adv.* from under the brows (*distrustfully, sullenly*).

исподни́зу, *adv.* (*coll.*) from underneath.

испо́дн|ий, *adj.* (*obs.*) under; *as noun* ~ee, ~его, *n.* undergarment.

исподтишка́, *adv.* (*coll., pejor.*) in an underhand way; on the quiet, on the sly; смея́ться и. to laugh in one's sleeve.

испоко́н, *adv.*; *only in phrases* и. ве́ку, и. веко́в from time immemorial.

испола́ть, *interj.* (*rhet.*) hail!

испо́лза|ть, ю, *pf.* (*coll.*) to crawl all over.

исполи́н, а, m. giant.

исполи́нский, *adj.* gigantic.

исполко́м, а, m. (*abbr. of* исполни́тельный комите́т) executive committee.

исполне́ни|е, я, n. **1.** fulfilment (*of wish*); execution (*of order*); discharge (*of duties*); привести́ в и. to carry out, execute. **2.** performance (*of play, etc.*); execution (*of music*); (*theatr., mus.*) в ~и (+*g.*) (as) played (by), (as) performed (by).

испо́лненный, *p.p.p. of* испо́лнить *and adj.* (+*g.*) full (of).

исполни́м|ый (~, ~а), *adj.* feasible, practicable, realizable.

исполни́тел|ь, я, m. **1.** executor; суде́бный и. bailiff. **2.** (*theatr., mus., etc.*) performer; соста́в ~ей cast.

исполни́тельност|ь, и, f. assiduity; expedition.

исполни́тел|ьный, *adj.* **1.** executive; и. лист (*leg.*) writ, court order. **2.** (~ен, ~ьна) efficient and dependable.

исполн|и́ть¹, ю, ишь, *pf.* (*of* ~я́ть) **1.** to carry out, execute (*orders, etc.*); to fulfil (a *wish*); и. обеща́ние to keep a promise; и.

про́сьбу to grant a request. **2.** to perform; и. роль (+*g.*) to take the part (of).

исполн|и́ть², ю, ишь, *pf.* (*of* ~я́ть) (+*a. and i. or g.*; *obs.*) to fill (with); сообще́ние о побе́де ~ило всех ра́достью (ра́дости) the report of the victory delighted everyone.

исполн|и́ться, юсь, ишься, *pf.* (*of* ~я́ться) **1.** to be fulfilled. **2.** (+*i. or g.*; *obs.*) to become filled (with). **3.** (*impers.* +*d. expresses passage of time*) ему́ ~илось семь лет he is seven, he was seven last birthday; ~илось пять лет с тех пор, как он уе́хал в Аме́рику five years have passed (it is five years) since he went to America.

исполн|я́ть(ся), я́ю(сь), *impf. of* ~и́ть(ся); ~я́ющий обя́занности (+*g.*) acting.

исполос|ова́ть, у́ю, *pf. of* полосова́ть.

и́сполу, *adv.* half and half; де́лать что-н. и. to go halves; обрабо́тать зе́млю и. to farm land on the métayage system.

использовани|е, я, n. utilization.

использ|овать, ую, *impf. and pf.* to make (good) use of, utilize; to turn to account.

испо́льщик, а, m. métayer; sharecropper (*under half-and-half system*).

испо́льщин|а, ы, f. métayage, sharecropping.

испо́р|тить(ся), чу(сь), тишь(ся), *pf. of* по́ртить(ся).

испо́рченност|ь, и, f. depravity.

испо́рчен|ный, *p.p.p. of* испо́ртить *and adj.* **1.** depraved; corrupted. **2.** (*of perishable goods, etc.*) spoiled; bad, rotten; ~ные зу́бы rotten teeth; ~ное мя́со tainted meat. **3.** (*coll.*) spoiled (*child*).

испохаб|ить, лю, ишь, *pf.* (*coll.*) to corrupt.

испошл|ить, ю, ишь, *pf.* (*coll.*) to vulgarize.

исправи́лк|а, и, f. (*coll.*) reformatory.

исправи́м|ый (~, ~а), *adj.* corrigible.

исправи́тельно-трудово́й, *adj.* corrective labour; и.-т. ко́декс corrective labour code.

исправи́тельный, *adj.* correctional; corrective; и. дом reformatory.

испра́в|ить, лю, ишь, *pf.* (*of* ~ля́ть) **1.** to rectify, correct, emend. **2.** to repair, mend. **3.** to reform, improve, amend.

испра́в|иться, люсь, ишься, *pf.* (*of* ~ля́ться) **1.** to improve (*intrans.*); to reform (*intrans.*), turn over a new leaf. **2.** *pass. of* ~ить.

исправле́ни|е, я, n. **1.** correcting; repairing. **2.** improvement; correction; и. те́кста emendation of a text.

испра́влен|ный, *p.p.p. of* испра́вить *and adj.* improved, corrected; ~ное изда́ние revised edition; и. хара́ктер reformed character.

исправля́|ть, ю, *impf.* **1.** *impf. of* испра́вить. **2.** (*obs.*) и. обя́занности (+*g.*) to carry out the duties (of), act as.

исправля́|ться, юсь, *impf. of* испра́виться.

испра́вник, а, *m.* (*hist.*) police chief (*head of uyezd constabulary in tsarist Russia*).

испра́вност|ь, и, *f.* 1. good condition; в (по́лной) ∼и in good working order, in good repair. 2. punctuality; preciseness; meticulousness.

испра́в|ный (∼ен, ∼на), *adj.* 1. in good order. 2. punctual; precise; meticulous.

испражне́ни|е, я, *n.* 1. defecation. 2. faeces.

испражн|и́ться, ю́сь, и́шься, *pf. of* ∼я́ться.

испражн|я́ться, я́юсь, *impf.* (*of* ∼и́ться) to defecate.

испра́шива|ть, ю, *impf.* (*of* испроси́ть) to beg, solicit; и. ми́лость to ask a favour.

испро́б|овать, ую, *pf.* 1. to test. 2. to make trial of, try out; и. все возмо́жности to try everything, leave no stone unturned.

испро|си́ть, шу́, ∼сишь, *pf.* (*of* испра́шивать) to obtain (by asking).

испрям|и́ть, лю́, и́шь, *pf.* (*of* ∼ля́ть) (*coll.*) to straighten (out).

испрямля́|ть, ю, *impf. of* испрями́ть.

испу́г, а (у), *m.* fright; alarm; с ∼у from fright.

испу́ганный, *p.p.p. of* испуга́ть *and adj.* frightened, scared, startled.

испуга́|ть(ся), ю(сь), *pf. of* пуга́ть(ся).

испуска́|ть, ю, *impf. of* испусти́ть.

испу|сти́ть, щу́, ∼стишь, *pf.* (*of* ∼ска́ть) to emit, let out; и. вздох to heave a sigh; и. дух to breathe one's last; и. крик to utter a cry.

испыта́ни|е, я, *n.* 1. test, trial; (*fig.*) ordeal; быть на ∼и to be on trial, be on probation. 2. examination; вступи́тельные ∼я, приёмные ∼я entrance examination.

испы́т|анный, *p.p.p. of* ∼а́ть *and adj.* tried, well-tried.

испыта́тел|ь, я, *m.* tester; лётчик-и. test pilot.

испыта́тельн|ый, *adj.* test, trial; probationary; ∼ая коми́ссия examining board; и. полёт test-flight; и. полиго́н (*mil.*) testing ground; и. пробе́г trial run; и. срок, и. стаж period of probation; ∼ая ста́нция experimental station.

испыт|а́ть, а́ю, *pf.* (*of* ∼ывать) 1. to test, put to the test; и. чьё-н. терпе́ние to try someone's patience. 2. to feel, experience.

испыту́ющий, *adj.*; и. взгляд searching look.

испы́тыва|ть, ю, *impf. of* испыта́ть.

иссека́|ть, ю, *impf. of* иссе́чь.

и́ссера-, *adv.* grey-; и.-голубо́й grey-blue.

иссече́ни|е, я, *n.* (*med.*) excision, removal (*by means of operation*).

иссе́|чь¹, ку́, чёшь, ку́т, *past* ∼к, ∼кла́, *pf.* (*of* ∼ка́ть) 1. (*obs.*) to carve (*in stone, etc.*). 2. (*med.*) to excise, remove (*by means of operation*).

иссе́|чь², ку́, чёшь, ку́т, *past* ∼к, ∼кла, *pf.* (*of* ∼ка́ть) 1. to cut up, cleave. 2. (*obs.*) to cut (*with a whip, etc.*), lash, cover with lashes.

и́ссиня-, *adv.* bluish-.

иссле́|ди́ть, жу́, ди́шь, *pf.* (*of* ∼жива́ть) (*coll.*) to cover with dirty footprints.

иссле́довани|е, я, *n.* 1. investigation; research; exploration; и. больно́го examination of a patient; и. кро́ви blood analysis, test; он занима́ется ∼ями по ру́сской исто́рии he is engaged in research on Russian history. 2. (*scientific*) paper; study.

иссле́довател|ь, я, *m.* researcher; investigator; explorer.

иссле́довательский, *adj.* research.

иссле́д|овать, ую, *impf. and pf.* to investigate, examine; to research into; to explore; to analyse.

иссле́жива|ть, ю, *impf. of* исследи́ть.

иссо́х|нуть, ну, нешь, *past* ∼, ∼ла, *pf.* (*of* иссыха́ть) 1. to dry up. 2. to wither; (*fig., coll.*) to decline, fade away.

и́сстари, *adv.* from of old, of yore; так и. ведётся it is an old custom.

исстрада́|ться, юсь, *pf.* to become worn out, wretched (*with suffering*).

исстре́лива|ть, ю, *impf. of* исстреля́ть.

исстрел|я́ть, я́ю, *pf.* (*of* ∼ивать) 1. to use up (*ammunition*). 2. (*coll.*) to riddle (*with shot*).

исступле́ни|е, я, *n.* frenzy; и. восто́рга ecstasy, transport; гне́вное и. rage.

исступлённост|ь, и, *f.* state of frenzy.

исступлённый, *adj.* frenzied; ecstatic.

иссуш|а́ть, а́ю, *impf. of* ∼и́ть.

иссуш|и́ть, у́, ∼ишь, *pf.* (*of* ∼а́ть) to dry up; (*fig.*) to consume, waste.

иссыха́|ть, ю, *impf. of* иссо́хнуть.

иссяк|а́ть, а́ю, *impf. of* ∼нуть.

исся́к|нуть, ну, нешь, *past* ∼, ∼ла, *pf.* (*o* ∼а́ть) to run dry, dry up; (*fig.*) to run low, fail.

иста́плива|ть, ю, *impf. of* истопи́ть.

иста́ск|анный, *p.p.p. of* ∼а́ть *and adj.* 1. worn out; threadbare. 2. (*fig., coll.*) worn; haggard.

истаск|а́ть, а́ю, *pf.* (*of* ∼ивать) to wear out.

истаск|а́ться, а́юсь, *pf.* (*of* ∼иваться) to wear out (*intrans.*); (*fig., coll.*) to be worn out.

иста́скива|ть(ся), ю(сь), *impf. of* истаска́ть(ся).

иста́чива|ть, ю, *impf. of* источи́ть¹.

иста́|ять, ю, ешь, *pf.* to melt (completely); и. от тоски́ to pine, languish.

истека́|ть, ю, *impf. of* исте́чь.

исте́|кший, *past part. of* ∼чь *and adj.* past, preceding; в тече́ние ∼кшего го́да during the past year; 15-го числа́ ∼кшего ме́сяца on the 15th ult(imo).

истер|е́ть, изотру́, изотрёшь, *past* ⌐, ⌐ла, *pf. (of* истира́ть) **1.** to grate. **2.** to wear out, use up (*by rubbing*); и. в порошо́к to reduce to powder.

истер|е́ться, изотрётся, *past* ⌐ся, ⌐лась, *pf. (of* истира́ться) to wear out (*intrans.*), be worn out (*by rubbing*).

истёрз|анный, *p.p.p. of* ⌐а́ть *and adj.* tattered, lacerated; (*fig.*) tormented.

истерза́|ть, ю, *pf.* **1.** to tear in pieces; to mutilate. **2.** to torment, worry the life out of.

исте́рик, а, *m.* hysterical subject.

исте́рик|а, и, *f.* hysterics.

истери́ческий, *adj.* hysterical; и. припа́док fit of hysterics.

истери́чк|а, и, *f.* hysterical woman.

истери́ч|ный (~ен, ~на), *adj.* hysterical.

истери́|я, и, *f.* (*med.*) hysteria; (*fig.*) вое́нная и. war hysteria.

истёртый, *p.p.p. of* истере́ть *and adj.* worn, old.

ист|е́ц, ца́, *m.* (*leg.*) plaintiff; petitioner (*in divorce case*).

истече́ни|е, я, *n.* **1.** outflow; и. кро́ви haemorrhage. **2.** expiry, expiration; по ~и сро́ка каранти́на on the expiry of the quarantine period.

исте́|чь, ку́, чёшь, ку́т, *past* ⌐к, ⌐кла́, *pf. (of* ~ка́ть) **1.** (*obs.*) to flow out. **2.** и. кро́вью to bleed profusely; (*fig., rhet.*) to pour out one's life-blood. **3.** to expire, elapse; вре́мя ~кло́ time is up.

и́стин|а, ы, *f.* truth; изби́тая и. truism; свята́я и. God's truth, gospel truth; во ~у (*obs.*) in truth, verily.

и́стин|ный (~ен, ~на), *adj.* true, veritable; ~ная высота́ true altitude; ~ное со́лнечное вре́мя apparent solar time.

истира́ни|е, я, *n.* abrasion.

истира́|ть(ся), ю(сь), *impf. of* истере́ть(ся).

истле|ва́ть, ва́ю, *impf. of* ~ть.

истле́|ть, ю, *pf. (of* ~ва́ть) **1.** to rot, decay. **2.** to smoulder to ashes.

истма́т, а, *m.* (*abbr. of* истори́ческий материали́зм) historical materialism.

и́стово, *adv.* (*obs.*) properly, religiously, devoutly; assiduously, punctiliously; и. крести́ться to cross oneself religiously.

и́стов|ый (~, ~а), *adj.* (*obs.*) proper; devout; assiduous, punctilious.

исто́к, а, *m.* source.

истолкова́ни|е, я, *n.* interpretation, commentary.

истолкова́тел|ь, я, *m.* interpreter, commentator, expounder.

истолк|ова́ть, у́ю, *pf. (of* ~о́вывать) to interpret, expound; to comment upon; и. замеча́ние в дурну́ю сто́рону to put a nasty construction on a remark.

истолко́выва|ть, ю, *impf. of* истолкова́ть.

истол|о́чь, ку́, чёшь, ку́т, *past* ~о́к, ~кла́, *pf.* to pound, crush.

исто́м|а, ы, *f.* lassitude; (*pleasurable*) languor.

истом|и́ть, лю́, и́шь, *pf. (of* томи́ть *and* ~ля́ть) to exhaust, weary.

истом|и́ться, лю́сь, и́шься, *pf. (of* ~ля́ться) (от) to be exhausted, worn out (with, from); to be weary (of); и. от жа́жды to be faint with thirst.

истом|лённый, *p.p.p. of* ~и́ть *and adj.* exhausted, worn out.

истомля́|ть(ся), ю(сь), *impf. of* истоми́ть(ся).

истоп|и́ть, лю́, ~ишь, *pf. (of* иста́пливать) **1.** to heat up. **2.** (*coll.*) to spend, use up (*fuel*). **3.** to melt down.

истопни́к, а́, *m.* stoker, boiler-man.

истоп|та́ть, чу́, ~чешь, *pf.* **1.** to trample (down, over). **2.** (*coll.*) to wear out (*footwear*).

исторг|а́ть, а́ю, *impf. of* ~нуть.

исторг|нуть, ну, нешь, *past* ~, ~ла, *pf. (of* ~а́ть) **1.** (*rhet.*) to throw out, expel; и. из свое́й среды́ to ostracize. **2.** (у *or* из; *obs.*) to wrest, wrench (from); (*fig.*) to force (from), extort; и. обеща́ние to extort a promise.

истори́зм, а, *m.* historical method.

исто́рийк|а, и, *f.* (*coll.*) **1.** anecdote, story **2.** episode, incident.

исто́рик, а, *m.* historian.

историо́граф, а, *m.* historiographer.

историогра́фи|я, и, *f.* historiography.

истори́ческий, *adj.* **1.** historical. **2.** historic.

истори́чност|ь, и, *f.* historicity.

истори́ч|ный (~ен, ~на), *adj.* historical.

исто́ри|я, и, *f.* **1.** history; войти́ в ~ю to go down in history. **2.** (*coll.*) story. **3.** (*coll.*) incident, event; scene, row; вчера́ случи́лась со мно́й заба́вная и. a funny thing happened to me yesterday; вот так и.! here's a pretty kettle of fish!; ве́чная (*or* обы́чная) и.! the (same) old story!

истоск|ова́ться, у́юсь, *pf.* (по+*d.*) to yearn (for); to be wearied with longing (for).

источ|а́ть, а́ю, *impf. (of* ~и́ть²) (*obs.*) to shed; to give off, impart.

источ|и́ть¹, у́, ~ишь, *pf. (of* иста́чивать) **1.** to grind down. **2.** to eat away, gnaw through.

источ|и́ть², у́, ~ишь, *pf. of* ~а́ть.

исто́чник, а, *m.* **1.** spring. **2.** (*fig.*) source; и. информа́ции source of information; ве́рный и. reliable source; и. све́та source of light; и. боле́зни (*med.*) nidus; служи́ть ~ом (+*g.*) to be a source (of).

источникове́дени|е, я, *n.* source study.

истóшный, *adj.* (*coll.*) heart-rending.

истощ|áть(ся), áю(сь), *impf. of* ~и́ть(ся).

истощéни|е, я, *n.* emaciation; exhaustion; война́ на и. war of attrition.

истощ|ённый, *p.p.p. of* ~и́ть *and adj.* emaciated; exhausted.

истощ|и́ть, ý, и́шь, *pf.* (*of* ~а́ть) to emaciate; to exhaust; to drain, sap; и. кóпи to work out mines.

истощ|и́ться, ýсь, и́шься, *pf.* (*of* ~а́ться) to become emaciated; to become exhausted (*also fig.*); все на́ши запа́сы ~и́лись all our supplies had run out.

истра́|тить, чу, тишь, *pf. of* тра́тить.

истра́|титься, чусь, тишься, *pf.* 1. *pass of* ~тить. 2. (*coll.*) to overspend.

истреби́тел|ь, я, *m.* 1. destroyer. 2. fighter (*aircraft*).

истреби́тель|ный, *adj.* 1. destructive. 2. *adj. of* ~ 2; ~ная авиа́ция fighters (*collect.*), Fighter Command.

истреб|и́ть, лю́, и́шь, *pf.* (*of* ~ля́ть) to destroy; to exterminate, extirpate.

истреблéни|е, я, *n.* destruction; extermination, extirpation.

истребля́|ть, ю, *impf. of* истреби́ть.

истрéбовани|е, я, *n.* demand, order.

истрéб|овать, ую, *pf.* to obtain on demand.

истрёп|анный, *p.p.p. of* ~а́ть *and adj.* torn, frayed; worn.

истреп|а́ть, лю́, ~лешь, *pf.* (*of* ~ывать) to tear, fray; to wear to rags; и. нéрвы (*coll.*) to fray one's nerves.

истрёпыва|ть, ю, *impf. of* истрепа́ть.

истрéска|ться, ется, *pf.* (*coll.*) to crack, become cracked.

истука́н, а, *m.* idol, statue (*fig., coll.*; *of a person devoid of feeling or understanding*).

и́стый, *adj.* true, genuine; keen; и. учёный a true scholar; и. люби́тель живóтных a genuine animal-lover.

исты́к|ать, аю, *pf.* (*of* ~ивать) (*coll.*) to riddle, pierce all over.

исты́кива|ть, ю, *impf. of* исты́кать.

истяза́ни|е, я, *n.* torture.

истяза́тел|ь, я, *m.* torturer.

истяза́|ть, ю, *impf.* to torture.

исхле|ста́ть, щý, ~щешь, *pf.* (*of* ~сты́вать) (*coll.*) 1. to lash, flog. 2. to wear out (*a whip*).

исхлёстыва|ть, ю, *impf. of* исхлеста́ть.

исхлопа́тыва|ть, ю, *impf. of* исхлопота́ть.

исхлопо|та́ть, чý, ~чешь, *pf.* (*of* исхлопа́тывать) (*coll.*) to obtain (*by dint of application in the right quarters*).

исхóд, а, *m.* 1. outcome, issue; end; быть на ~е to be nearing the end, be coming to an end; на ~е дня towards evening; день был на ~е the day was drawing to a close. 2. (*eccl.*) И. (the Book of) Exodus.

исхода́тайств|овать, ую, *pf.* to obtain (*by petition, after official application*).

исхо|ди́ть[1], жý, ~дишь, *pf.* (*coll.*) to go, walk all over.

исхо|ди́ть[2], жý, ~дишь, *impf.* (*of* изойти́) 1. (*impf. only*) (из) to issue (from), come (from); to emanate (from); откýда ~ди́л э́тот слух? where did this rumour come from? 2. (*impf. only*) (из) to proceed (from), base oneself (on); и. из необоснóванных предположéний to proceed from unfounded assumptions. 3. и. крóвью to become weak through loss of blood; и. слеза́ми to cry one's heart out.

исхóдн|ый, *adj.* initial; ~ая тóчка, ~ое положéние point of departure; и. пункт маршрýта (*aeron.*) flight departure point; ~ая ста́дия initial phase.

исходя́щ|ая, ей, f. outgoing paper.

исхуда́лый, *adj.* emaciated, wasted.

исхуда́ни|е, я, *n.* emaciation.

исхуда́|ть, ю, *pf.* to become emaciated, become wasted.

исцара́п|ать, аю, *pf.* (*of* ~ывать) to scratch badly; to scratch all over.

исцара́пыва|ть, ю, *impf. of* исцара́пать.

исцелéни|е, я, *n.* 1. healing, cure. 2. recovery.

исцел|и́мый, *pres. part. pass. of* ~и́ть *and adj.* curable.

исцели́тел|ь, я, *m.* healer.

исцел|и́ть, ю́, и́шь, *pf.* (*of* ~я́ть) to heal, cure.

исцел|я́ть, я́ю, *impf. of* ~и́ть.

исча́ди|е, я, *n.* (*rhet.*) offspring, progeny; *esp. in phrase* и. а́да fiend, devil incarnate.

исча́х|нуть, ну, нешь, *past* ~, ~ла, *pf.* to waste away.

исчез|а́ть, а́ю, *impf.* (*of* ~нуть) to disappear, vanish.

исчезновéни|е, я, *n.* disappearance.

исчéз|нуть, ну, нешь, *past* ~, ~ла, *pf. of* ~а́ть.

исчёрк|ать, аю (*and* ~а́ть, ~а́ю), *pf.* 1. to cover with crossings-out. 2. to scribble all over.

и́счерна- blackish-.

исчéрп|ать, аю, *pf.* (*of* ~ывать) 1. to exhaust, drain; и. все свои́ срéдства to exhaust all one's resources; (*fig.*) и. терпéние to exhaust someone's patience. 2. to settle, conclude; и. вопрóс to settle a question; и. повéстку дня to conclude the agenda.

исчéрпыва|ть, ю, *impf. of* исчéрпать.

исчéрпыва|ющий, *pres. part. act. of* ~ть *and adj.* exhaustive.

исчер|ти́ть, чý, ~тишь, *pf.* (*of* ~чивать) 1. to cover with lines. 2. to use up (*pencil, chalk, etc.*).

исчёрчива|ть, ю, *impf. of* исчертить.

исчирка|ть, ю, *pf.* (*coll.*) to use up (*matches*).

исчислени|е, я, *n.* calculation; (*math.*) calculus.

исчисл|ить, ю, ишь, *pf.* (*of* ∼ять) to calculate, compute; to estimate.

исчисл|ять, яю, *impf. of* ∼ить.

исчисля|ться, ется, *impf.* (+*i. or* в+*a.*) to amount to, come to; to be estimated (at); убытки ∼лись в сто рублей the damages came to one hundred roubles; потери ∼ются тысячами the casualties are estimated at thousands.

итак, *conj.* thus; so then.

итальян|ец, ца, *n.* Italian.

итальян|ка, ки, *f. of* ∼ец.

итальянск|ий, *adj.* Italian; ∼ая забастовка sit-down strike, working to rule.

и т. д. (*abbr. of* и так далее) et cetera; and so on, and so forth.

итеративный, *adj.* (*ling.*) iterative.

итог, а, *m.* **1.** sum, total; общий и. grand total. **2.** (*fig.*) result; подвести и. to sum up; в ∼e as a result, in the upshot; в конечном ∼e in the end.

итого, *adv.* in all, altogether.

итоговый, *adj.* total, final.

итож|ить, у, ишь, *impf.* to sum up, add up.

и т. п. (*abbr. of* и тому подобное) and the like; et cetera.

иттерби|й, я, *m.* (*chem.*) ytterbium.

итти = идти.

иттри|й, я, *m.* (*chem.*) yttrium.

иудаизм, а, *m.* Judaism.

иуде|й, я, *m.* Jew (*by religion*).

иудей|ка, ки, *f. of* ∼.

иудейский, *adj.* (*hist. and rel.*) Judaic.

их¹, *a. and g. of* они.

их², *possessive adj.* **1.** their(s); их машина меньше, чем наша their car is smaller than ours. **2.** (*obs.; in formal speech*) his; her; это их пальто this is her coat.

ихневмон, а, *m.* (*zool.*) ichneumon.

ихний, *possessive adj.* (*coll.*) their(s).

ихтиозавр, а, *m.* ichthyosaurus.

ихтиол, а, *m.* (*med.*) ichthyol.

ихтиолог, а, *m.* ichthyologist.

ихтиологический, *adj.* ichthyological.

ихтиологи|я, и, *f.* ichthyology.

ишак, á, *m.* **1.** donkey, ass (*also fig.*). **2.** hinny.

иша|чий, *adj. of* ∼к.

ишиас, а, *m.* (*med.*) sciatica.

ишь, *interj.* (*coll.*) expressing surprise or disgust: look!; и. ты! = и.! or expresses disagreement or objection.

ищейк|а, и, *f.* bloodhound, sleuth-hound (*also fig., pejor.*).

ищущий, *pres. part. act. of* искать *and adj.*; и. взгляд searching, wistful look.

июл|ь, я, *m.* July.

июль|ский, *adj. of* ∼.

июн|ь, я, *m.* June.

июнь|ский, *adj. of* ∼.

Й

йог, а, *m.* yogi.

йод, а, *m.* iodine.

йодист|ый, *adj.* (*chem.*) containing iodine; й. калий potassium iodide; ∼ая соль iodized salt.

йод|ный, *adj. of* ∼; и. раствор tincture of iodine.

йодоформ, а, *m.* iodoform.

йот, а, *m.* (*ling.*) letter J; yod (*name of sound* [j]).

йот|а, ы, *f.* iota; ни на ∼y not a jot, not an iota.

йотаци|я, и, *f.* (*ling.*) appearance of yod before vowel; vowel softening.

йотир|овать, ую, *impf. and pf.* (*ling.*) to pronounce (vowels) with yod; to give soft pronunciation.

К

к, ко, *prep.*+*d.* **1.** (*of space and fig.*) to, towards; мы приближались к Берлину we were nearing Berlin; прислоните его к стене place it against the wall; лицом к лицу face to face; к лучшему for the better; молитва к Богу prayer to God; любовь к детям love of children; к общему удивле-нию to everyone's surprise; к (не)счастью (un)fortunately; к чёрту его! to hell with him!; шляпа ей к лицу her hat becomes her; к вашим услугам at your service; (*in addition to*) прибавить три к пяти to add three and five; к тому же besides, moreover. **2.** (*of time*) to, towards; by; зима подходи́ла к концу́ winter was drawing to a close; к утру́ towards morning, by morning; к пе́рвому января́ by the first of January; я приду́ к восьми́ (часа́м) I will be there by eight (o'clock); к тому́ вре́мени by then, by that time; к сро́ку on time. **3.** for; к чему́? what for?; э́то ни к чему́ it is no good, no use; к обе́ду, к у́жину, *etc*., for dinner, for supper, *etc*. **4.** (*in titles of pamphlets, articles in newspapers and periodicals, etc.*) on; on the occasion of; к столе́тию со дня рожде́ния Льва Толсто́го (on the occasion of) the centenary of the birth of Lev Tolstoy; к вопро́су о... *often requires no translation.*

-ка, *particle* (*coll.*) **1.** *modifying force of imp.*: скажи́-ка мне do tell me; да́й-ка мне посмотре́ть just let me see; ну́-ка well; ну́-ка, спо́йте что́-н.! come on, sing us something! **2.** *with 1st sing. of future tense, expressing decision or intention*: напишу́-ка ей письмо́ I think I'll write to her; куплю́-ка тот га́лстук perhaps I'll buy that tie, how would it be to buy that tie.

каба́к, á, *m.* (*obs.*) tavern, low bar; (*coll. fig.*) pigsty.

кабал|á, ы́, *f.* **1.** (*hist.*) kabala (*agreement exacting obligation of labour for creditor in case of non-payment of debt*). **2.** (*hist.*) debt-slavery kabala slavery. **3.** (*fig.*) servitude, bondage.

кабал|и́ть, ю́, и́шь, *impf.* to enslave.

каба́л|ьный (~ен, ~ьна), *adj.* **1.** relating to, bound by kabala; к. холо́п kabala serf. **2.** (*fig.*) imposing bondage, enslaving; ~ьные усло́вия crushing terms. **3.** (*fig.*) in bondage.

каба́н¹, á, *m.* **1.** wild boar. **2.** boar (*male domestic pig*).

каба́н², á, *m.* block (*of unprocessed mineral ore, etc.*).

каба́н|ий, *adj. of* ~¹.

кабар|rá, ги́, *g. pl.* ~о́г, *f.* (*zool.*) musk-deer.

кабарди́н|ец, ца, *m.* Kabarda (man).

кабаре́, *indecl., n.* cabaret.

каба́тчик, а, *m.* (*obs.*) publican, tavern-keeper.

каба́|цкий, *adj.* **1.** *adj. of* ~к. **2.** (*fig., coll.*) coarse, vulgar; ~цкие нра́вы public bar manners; голь ~цкая (*folk poet.*) tavern riff-raff.

кабач|о́к¹, ка́, *m.* **1.** *dim. of* каба́к. **2.** (*coll.*) small restaurant.

кабач|о́к², ка́, *m.* vegetable marrow.

каббал|á, ы́, *f.* (*rel. and fig.*) cab(b)ala.

каббали́стик|а, и, *f.* (*rel. and fig.*) cab(b)alism.

каббалисти́ческий, *adj.* (*rel. and fig.*) cab(b)alistic.

ка́бел|ь, я, *m.* (*electr. and naut.*) cable; воз-

ду́шный к. overhead cable; к. абоне́нта service cable.

ка́бель|ный, *adj. of* ~; к. кана́т cable-laid rope; ~ное телеви́дение cable television.

ка́бельтов, а, *pl.* ~ы, ~ых, ~ым, ~ыми, *m.* (*naut.*) **1.** cable('s length) (*measure = 185·2 metres*). **2.** cable, hawser.

ка́бельтовый, *adj.* (*naut.*) of one cable's length.

кабеста́н, а, *m.* (*tech.*) capstan.

каби́н|а, ы, *f.* cabin; cockpit; cab (*of a lorry*); (для купа́льщиков) bathing-hut.

кабине́т¹, а, *m.* **1.** study; consulting-room, surgery; физи́ческий к. physics laboratory; отде́льный к. private room (*in restaurant*); к. заду́мчивости (*euph., joc.*) lavatory; к. красоты́ beauty parlour. **2.** suite (*of furniture*).

кабине́т², а, *m.* (*polit.*) cabinet.

кабине́т|ный, *adj.* **1.** *adj. of* ~¹. **2.** к. портре́т cabinet photograph. **3.** (*fig.*) theoretical; к. учёный, страте́г armchair scientist, strategist.

каби́н|ка, ки, *f. dim. of* ~a.

каблогра́мм|а, ы, *f.* cable(gram).

каблу́к, á, *m.* heel (*of footwear*); ту́фли на рези́новых ~áх rubber-heeled shoes; быть под ~о́м у кого́-н. (*fig., coll.*) to be under someone's thumb.

каблуч|о́к, ка́, *m.* **1.** *dim. of* каблу́к. **2.** (*archit.*) ogee.

кабота́ж, а, *m.* **1.** cabotage; coasting-trade. **2.** coastal shipping.

кабота́жник, а, *m.* coaster, coasting vessel.

кабота́жнича|ть, ю, *impf.* to coast; to ply coastwise.

кабота́ж|ный, *adj. of* ~; ~ное пла́вание coastwise navigation.

кабриоле́т, а, *m.* cabriolet.

кабы, *conj.* (*coll. and folk poet.*) if; е́сли бы да к., *see* е́сли.

кавале́р¹, а, *m.* **1.** partner (*at dances*); (*in mixed company on social occasions*) (gentle-)man; была́ весёлая вечери́нка, но ~ов не хвата́ло it was a gay party but there were not enough men. **2.** (*coll.*) admirer, cavalier; да́мский к. carpet-knight.

кавале́р², а, *m.* (о́рдена) knight, holder (of an order); гео́ргиевский к. holder of the St. George Cross.

кавалерга́рд, а, *m.* horse-guardsman.

кавалерга́рд|ский, *adj. of* ~.

кавалер|и́йский, *adj.* **1.** *adj. of* ~и́я. **2.** of a cavalryman, of a horseman.

кавалери́ст, а, *m.* **1.** cavalryman. **2.** (*coll.*) horseman.

кавале́ри|я, и, *f.* cavalry; лёгкая к. light horse.

кавале́рственн|ый, *adj., only in phrase* ~ая да́ма Dame of the Order of St. Catherine.

кавалька́д|а, ы, *f.* cavalcade.

кавардак, а́, *m.* (*coll.*) mess, muddle.

ка́верз|а, ы, *f.* (*coll.*) 1. chicanery. 2. mean trick, dirty trick; устро́ить ~у кому́-н. to play someone a mean trick.

ка́вер|зить, жу, зишь, *impf.* (*of* на~) (*coll.*, *pejor.*) to play mean, dirty tricks.

ка́верзник, а, *m.* (*coll.*) one who plays (enjoys playing) mean, dirty tricks.

ка́верзный, *adj.* (*coll.*) 1. (*pejor.*) given to playing mean, dirty tricks. 2. tricky, ticklish.

каве́рн|а, ы, *f.* (*med. and geol.*) cavity.

кавка́з|ец, ца, *m.* Caucasian.

кавка́зк|а, и, *f.* Caucasian (woman).

кавка́зский, *adj.* Caucasian.

каву́н, а́, *m.* (*dial.*) water-melon.

кавы́ч|ки, ек, *no sing.* inverted commas, quotation marks; откры́ть к. to quote; закры́ть к. to unquote; в ~ках in inverted commas, in quotes; (*fig.*, *coll.*) so-called, would-be; демокра́тия в ~ках a so-called 'democracy'; знато́к в ~ках would-be expert.

кага́л, а, *m.* 1. (*hist.*) kahal (*assembly of elders of Jewish communes*). 2. (*fig.*, *coll.*) bedlam, uproar.

када́стр, а, *m.* (*leg.*) land-survey.

када́стровый, *adj.* (*leg.*) cadastral.

каде́нци|я, и, *f.* 1. (*mus. and lit.*) cadence. 2. (*mus.*) cadenza.

каде́т[1], а, *m.* cadet.

каде́т[2], а, *m.* (*abbr. of* конституцио́нный демокра́т) (*polit.*, *hist.*) Constitutional Democrat (Cadet).

каде́т|ский[1], *adj. of* ~[1]; к. ко́рпус (*hist.*) military school.

каде́т|ский[2], *adj. of* ~[2].

кади́л|о, а, *n.* (*eccl.*) thurible, censer.

кади́л|ьный, *adj.* 1. *adj. of* ~о. 2. of incense; к. за́пах smell of incense.

ка|ди́ть, жу́, ди́шь, *impf.* (*eccl.*) to burn incense; (+*d.*; *fig.*, *coll.*) to burn incense to, flatter.

ка́дк|а, и, *f.* tub, vat.

ка́дми|й, я, *m.* (*chem.*) cadmium.

ка́дочник, а, *m.* cooper.

ка́д|очный, *adj. of* ~ка.

кадр[1], а, *m.* 1. (*mil.*) cadre; (*pl.*; *collect.*) (regular, peace-time) establishment; он слу́жит в ~ах he is a regular (soldier). 2. (*pl. only*) personnel; отде́л ~ов personnel department (*of institution, factory, etc.*). 3. (*pl. only*) specialists; skilled workers (*esp. of trained functionaries of a political party*); руково́дящие ~ы парти́йной организа́ции моско́вской о́бласти the leadership of the Party organization in Moscow oblast.

кадр[2], а, *m.* (*cinema*) 1. frame, still. 2. close-up.

кадри́л|ь, и, *f.* quadrille (*dance*).

кадрови́к, а́, *m.* 1. (*mil.*) regular (soldier). 2. member of permanent staff; experienced, skilled man.

ка́дровый, *adj.* 1. (*mil.*) regular. 2. experienced, skilled; trained.

кады́к, а́, *m.* (*coll.*) Adam's apple.

каёмк|а, и, *f.* (*coll.*) *dim. of* кайма́.

каёмчатый, *adj.* with edge(s), with border(s).

кажде́ни|е, я, *n.* (*eccl.*) censing.

каждого́дный, *adj.* (*obs.*) annual.

каждодне́вный, *adj.* daily; diurnal.

ка́жд|ый, *adj.* 1. every, each; к. день every day; ~ые два дня every two days; ~ую весну́ every spring; к. из них получи́л по пять фу́нтов they received five pounds each; на ~ом шагу́ at every step. 2. *as noun* everyone; всех и ~ого (*coll.*) all and everyone, all and sundry.

кажи́сь (*coll.*, *dial.*) it seems, it would seem.

ка|жу́[1], ди́шь, *see* ~ди́ть.

ка|жу́[2], ~жешь, *see* ~за́ть.

каза́к, а́, *pl.* ~и́, *m.* Cossack.

казаки́н, а, *m.* kazakin (*man's knee-length coat with pleated skirt*).

каза́н, а́, *m.* (*dial.*) copper (*vessel*).

каза́рм|а, ы, *f.* barracks (*also fig.*; *coll. of ugly, clumsy buildings*).

каза́рм|енный, *adj. of* ~а; (*fig.*, *pejor.*) к. вид barrack-like appearance; ~енная острота́ barrack-room humour.

ка|за́ть, жу́, ~жешь, *impf.* (*coll.*) to show; не к. глаз, но́су not to show up.

ка|за́ться, жу́сь, ~жешься, *impf.* (*of* показа́ться) 1. to seem, appear; он ~жется у́мным he appears clever; она́ ~жется ста́рше свои́х лет she looks older than she is. 2. (*impers.*) (мне, *etc.*) ~жется, ~за́лось it seems, seemed (to me, *etc.*); apparently; мне ~жется, что он был прав I think he was right; всё, ~за́лось, шло хорошо́ everything seemed to be going well; за́втра, ~жется, начина́ются его́ кани́кулы apparently his holidays begin tomorrow; вы, ~жется, из Москвы́? you are from Moscow, I believe?; ~за́лось бы it would seem, one would think.

каза́х, а, *m.* Kazakh.

каза́хский, *adj.* Kazakh.

каза́цкий, *adj.* Cossack.

каза́честв|о, а, *n.* (*collect.*) the Cossacks.

каза́чий, *adj.* Cossack.

каза́чк|а, и, *f.* Cossack (woman).

каза́ч|о́к[1], ка́, *m.* 1. (*coll.*) *affect. dim. of* каза́к. 2. (*hist.*) page, boy-servant.

каза́ч|о́к[2], ка́, *m.* kazachok (*Ukrainian dance*).

каза́шк|а, и, *f.* Kazakh (woman).

казеи́н, а, *m.* (*chem.*) casein.

казейн|овый, *adj. of* ~.

каземáт, а, *m.* casemate.

казёнк|а, и, *f.* (*coll., obs.*) 1. state liquor store, wine-shop. 2. (state-retailed) vodka.

казéнник, а, *m.* breech ring (*of fire-arm*).

казённокóштный, *adj.* (*obs.*); к. студéнт state-aided student, student receiving education and maintenance at state expense.

казённ|ый, *adj.* 1. (*hist.*) fiscal; of State, of Treasury; ~ое имýщество State property; на к. счёт at public cost; (*joc., coll.*) free, gratis; ~ое винó (*obs.*) vodka (*sold under State monopoly*); ~ая палáта (provincial) revenue department. 2. (*fig.*) bureaucratic, formal; к. язы́к language of officialdom, official jargon. 3. (*fig.*) banal, undistinguished, conventional. 4. ~ая часть (*mil.*) breech, breech end.

казёнщин|а, ы, *f.* (*coll.*) 1. conventionalism. 2. red tape.

казимúр, а, *m.* (*text.*) kerseymere.

казимúр|овый, *adj. of* ~.

казинó, *indecl., n.* casino.

казн|á, ы́, *no pl., f.* 1. (*hist.*) Exchequer, Treasury; public purse, public coffers. 2. the State (*as a legal person*); перейтú из чáстных рук в ~ý to pass from private ownership to the State. 3. (*folk poet.*) money; property. 4. (= казённая часть) breech, breech end.

казначé|й, я, *m.* 1. treasurer, bursar. 2. (*mil.*) paymaster; (*naut.*) purser.

казначéй|ский, *adj.* 1. *of* ~. 2. *of* ~ство; к. билéт treasury note.

казначéйств|о, а, *n.* Treasury, Exchequer.

казначéйш|а, и, *f.* (*obs., coll.*) wife of treasurer.

казначé|я, и, *f.* (*eccl.*) treasurer.

казн|úть, ю́, úшь, *impf. and pf.* 1. to execute, put to death. 2. (*impf. only; fig.*) to punish, chastise; to castigate.

казн|úться, ю́сь, úшься, *impf.* 1. *pass. of* ~úть. 2. (*coll.*) to blame oneself; to torment oneself (*with remorse*).

казнокрáд, а, *m.* embezzler of public funds.

казнокрáдств|о, а, *n.* embezzlement of public funds.

казн|ь, и, *f.* execution, capital punishment; смéртная к. death penalty; (*fig.*) torture, punishment.

кáзов|ый, *adj.* (*obs.*) for show; к. товáр shop-window goods; ~ая сторонá дéла the bright side of the affair.

казуáльный, *adj.* random; accidental.

казуáр, а, *m.* (*orn.*) cassowary.

казуúст, а, *m.* casuist (*also fig.*).

казуúстик|а, и, *f.* casuistry (*also fig.*).

казуистúческий, *adj.* casuistic(al).

кáзус, а, *m.* 1. (*leg.*) exceptional case, special case; (*med.*) isolated case. 2. (*coll.*) extra-

ordinary occurrence; вот так к.! here's an amazing thing, here's a rum start! 3. к. бéлли casus belli.

кáзусный, *adj.* (*obs.*) involved.

Кáин, а, *m.* (*coll.*) Cain (*fratricide, murderer*).

кáин|ов, *adj. of* ~; ~ова печáть the mark of Cain.

кайл|á, ы́, *f.* (miner's) hack.

кайл|ó, á, *n.* = ~á.

ка|ймá, ймы́, *pl.* ~ймы́, ~ём, ~ймáм, *f.* edging, border; hem, selvedge.

каймáн, а, *m.* (*zool.*) cayman.

кайнозóйский, *adj.* (*geol.*) cainozoic.

кáйр|а, ы, *f.* (*orn.*) guillemot.

кайф, а, *m.* (*sl.*) kicks, 'high'; ловúть к. to get a kick.

как[1], *adv. and particle* 1. how; к. вам нрáвится Москвá? how do you like Moscow?; к. чýдно! how wonderful!; к. вы поживáете? how do you do?; к. (вáши) делá? how are you getting on?; забы́л, к. э́то дéлается I have forgotten how to do this; к. вам не сты́дно! you ought to be ashamed!; к. его́ фамúлия, к. его́ зовýт? what is his name?, what is he called?; к. называ́ется э́тот цветóк? what is this flower called?; к. вы дýмаете? what do you think?; к. его́ женá отнóсится к э́тому вопрóсу? what does his wife think about the question?; *expressing surprise and/or displeasure*: к.! ты опя́ть здесь what! are you here again?; к. же так? how is that?; (*coll.*) к. знать? who knows?; (*coll.*) к. сказáть it all depends; кýпишь ли э́то для меня́? ну, э́то ещё к. сказáть will you buy it for me? well, that all depends; (*coll.*) к. есть completely, utterly; он к. есть дурáк he is a complete fool; (*coll.*) расскажú нам к. и что tell us all about it, tell us how it's going; (*coll.*) к.-никáк nevertheless, for all that; к.-никáк, но мы попáли вó время nevertheless, we managed to arrive in time; к. же (*coll. or iron.*) naturally, of course. 2. *with fut. tense of pf. verbs expresses suddenness of action*: (*coll.*) мы спокóйно слýшали рáдио, а — он к. вскóчит! we were listening quietly to the wireless when all of a sudden he jumped up; онá к. закричúт! she suddenly cried out. 3. к. ни, к. ... ни however; к. ни пóздно ho*w*ever late it is; к. он ни умён clever as he is; к. ни старáйтесь however hard you may try, try as you may. 4. (*following* бедá, прéлесть, страх, ужáсно, *etc., in elliptical construction; coll.*) terribly, awfully, wonderfully, *etc.*; мне страх к. хóчется пить! I have a terrible thirst!; онá прéлесть к. одéта she is beautifully dressed.

как[2], *conj.* 1. as; like; бéлый к. снег white as snow; совéтую тебé э́то к. друг I give you this advice as a friend; он говорúт по-ру́сски к. настоя́щий ру́сский he speaks Russian like a native; бу́дьте к. до́ма make yourself at home; к. наприме́р as, for instance; к. наро́чно as luck would have it; к. попа́ло anyhow, at sixes and sevens; (*with comp.*) к. мо́жно, к. нельзя́ as . . . as possible; к. мо́жно, скоре́е as soon as possible; к. нельзя́ лу́чше as well as possible. **2.** к...., так и both . . . and; к. ма́льчики, так и де́вочки both the boys and the girls. **3.** *following verbs of perceiving not translated*: я ви́дел, к. она́ ушла́ I saw her go out; ты слы́шал, к. часы́ би́ли по́лночь? did you hear the clock strike midnight? **4.** (*coll.*) when; since; к. пойдёшь, зайди́ за мной when you go, call for me; прошло́ два го́да, к. мы встре́тились it is two years since we met; к. ско́ро (*obs.*), к. то́лько as soon as, when; к. вдруг when suddenly. **5.** (+*neg.*) but, except, than; что ему́ остава́лось де́лать, к. не созна́ться? what could he do but confess? **6.** в то вре́мя к.; до того́ к.; ме́жду тем к.; тогда́ к., *see* вре́мя, до, ме́жду, тогда́. **7.** к. бу́дто, к. бы, к.-ли́бо, к.-нибу́дь, к. ра́з, к.-то, *see separate entries.*

какаду́, *indecl., m.* (*orn.*) cockatoo.
кака́о, *indecl., n.* **1.** cocoa. **2.** cacao(-tree).
кака́о|вый, *adj. of* ~; ~вые бобы́ cocoa-beans.
как бу́дто 1. *conj.* as if, as though; она́ побледне́ла, к. б. уви́дела при́зрак she turned pale as if she had seen a ghost; к. б. вы не зна́ете! as if you didn't know! **2.** *particle* (*coll.*) apparently, it would seem; они́ к. б. за́втра прие́дут apparently they are coming tomorrow.
как бы 1. (+*inf.*) how; к. б. э́то сде́лать? how is it to be done, I wonder. **2.** к. б. ни however; к. б. то ни́ было however that may be, be that as it may. **3.** as if, as though; к. б. в шу́тку as if in jest. **4.** к. б. не (*expressing anxious expectation*) what if, supposing; (*following verb*) (that, lest); к. б. он не был в дурно́м настрое́нии! I am afraid that he may be in a bad temper; бою́сь, к. б. он не был в дурно́м настрое́нии I am afraid (that) he may be in a bad temper. **5.** (*coll.*) к. б. не так! not likely, certainly not.
ка́к-ли́бо, *adv.* somehow.
ка́к-нибу́дь, *adv.* **1.** somehow (or other). **2.** (*coll.*) anyhow; он всё де́лает к.-н. he does things all anyhow. **3.** (*coll.*) some time; загляни́те к.-н. look in some time.
как-ника́к, *adv.* (*coll.*) nevertheless, for all that.
каков́ (~а́, ~о́, ~ы́), *pron.* (*interrog., and in exclamations expressing strong feeling*) what; of what sort; к. результа́т? what is the result?; к. он? what is he like?; к. он собо́й? what does he look like?; а пого́да-

-то ~а́! what (splendid, filthy) weather!; вот он к.! (*coll.*) what a chap!
каково́, *adv.* (*coll.*) how; к. ему́ живётся? how is he getting on?; к. мне э́то слы́шать! I am extremely sorry to hear it.
каково́й, *relat. pron.* (*obs.*) which.
как|о́й, *pron.* **1.** (*interrog. and relat.; and in exclamations*) what; ~и́е у вас впечатле́ния о Ло́ндоне? what are your impressions of London?; ~о́е сего́дня число́? what is today's date?; ~и́м о́бразом? how?; не зна́ю, ~у́ю кни́гу ему́ дать I don't know what book to give him; ~а́я беда́! what a misfortune, how unfortunate!; ~а́я на́глость! what impudence!; ~а́я хоро́шенькая де́вушка! what a pretty girl! **2.** (тако́й) к. such as; он (тако́й) плут, ~и́х никогда́ не быва́ло he is a rogue such as never was, there has never been such a rogue; гнев, ~о́го он никогда́ не испы́тывал anger such as he had never felt. **3.** к. ни whatever, whichever; к. есть, к. ни на есть (*coll.*) whatever you please, any you please; дай мне ~у́ю ни на есть кни́гу give me any book you please. **4.** *expressing negation*: (*in rhet. questions*) к. он учёный? what kind of scholar is that?, how can you call him a scholar?; (*coll.*) понра́вился ли тебе́ э́тот фильм? ~о́е! я не вы́терпел и получа́са! did you like the film? what! I stuck it less than half an hour!; ~о́е там nothing of the kind, quite the contrary; ты хорошо́ спал? ~о́е там! did you sleep well? I most certainly did not! **5.** к. тако́й? which (exactly)?; пришёл Ивано́в. — К. тако́й Ивано́в? Ivanov is here. Which Ivanov? **6.** (*coll.*) any; нет ли у вас ~о́го вопро́са? have you any questions?; ни в ~у́ю in no circumstances, not for anything.
како́й-ли́бо, *pron.* = како́й-нибу́дь 1.
как|о́й-нибу́дь, *pron.* **1.** some; any; мы э́то сде́лаем ~и́м-н. спо́собом we shall do it somehow; да́йте мне кни́гу хоть ~у́ю-н. give me a book, any one at all. **2.** (*with numerals*) some (*and not more*), only; за́мок нахо́дится в ~и́х-н. трёх киломе́трах отсю́да the castle is some three kilometres from here; ~и́е-н. пять рубле́й some five roubles.
как|о́й-то, *pron.* **1.** some, a. **2.** a kind of; э́то ~а́я-то боле́знь it is a kind of disease.
какофони́ческий, *adj.* cacophonous.
какофо́ни|я, и, *f.* cacophony.
как ра́з, *adv.* just, exactly; к. р. то, что мне ну́жно just what I need; к. р. вас я иска́л you are the very person I was looking for; *as ·pred.* э́ти ту́фли мне к. р. these shoes are just right.
ка́к-то, *adv.* **1.** somehow; он к.-то ухитри́лся сде́лать э́то he managed to do it

somehow; в э́том до́ме к.-то всегда́ хо́лодно somehow it is always cold in this house. **2.** how; посмотрю́, к.-то он вы́вернется из э́того положе́ния I wonder how he will get himself out of this situation. **3.** (*coll.*) к.-то (раз) once. **4.** namely, as for example.

ка́ктус, а, *m.* (*bot.*) cactus.

кал, а, *m.* faeces, excrement.

каламбу́р, а, *m.* pun.

каламбури́ст, а, *m.* punster.

каламбу́р|ить, ю, ишь, *impf.* (*of* c~) to pun.

каламбу́рный, *adj.* punning.

каламя́нк|а, и, *f.* (*text.*) stout linen cloth; calamanco.

каланч|а́, и́, *g. pl.* ~е́й, *f.* watch-tower; пожа́рная к. fire observation tower; (*fig., coll.*) bean-pole.

кала́ч, а́, *m.* kalach (*kind of white, wheatmeal loaf*); меня́ ~о́м туда́ не зама́нишь (*coll.*) nothing will induce me to go there; (*fig., coll.*) тёртый к. person who has knocked about the world.

кала́чиком, *adv.* (*coll.*) in the shape of a kalach; лежа́ть к. to lie curled up.

кала́ч|ный, *adj. of* ~.

калейдоско́п, а, *m.* kaleidoscope.

калейдоскопи́ческий, *adj.* kaleidoscopic.

кале́к|а, и, *m. and f.* cripple.

календа́р|ный, *adj. of* ~ь; к. ме́сяц calendar month; ~ное и́мя name derived from that of a saint.

календа́р|ь, я́, *m.* calendar; (*sport*) fixture list.

кале́нд|ы, ~, *no sing.* (*hist.*) calends.

кале́ни|е, я, *n.* incandescence; бе́лое к. white heat; довести́ до бе́лого ~я (*fig., coll.*) to rouse to fury.

кале́н|ый, *adj.* **1.** red-hot. **2.** ~ые оре́хи roasted nuts.

кале́ч|ить, у, ишь, *impf.* (*of* искале́чить) to cripple, maim, mutilate; (*fig.*) to twist, pervert.

кале́ч|иться, усь, ишься, *impf.* (*of* искале́читься) **1.** to become a cripple. **2.** *pass. of* ~ить.

ка́ли, *indecl.*, *n.* (*chem.*; *obs.*) potash; *only used now in phrase* е́дкое к. caustic potash.

кали́бр, а, *m.* **1.** calibre. **2.** (*tech.*) gauge.

калибр|ова́ть, у́ю, *impf.* (*tech.*) to calibrate.

калибро́вк|а, и, *f.* (*tech.*) calibration.

ка́лиевый, *adj.* (*chem.*) potassic, potassium.

ка́ли|й, я, *m.* (*chem.*) potassium.

кали́йн|ый, *adj.* (*chem.*) potassium; ~ое удобре́ние potash fertilizer.

кали́к|а, и, *m.* **1.** (*hist.*) pilgrim. **2.** (*folk poet.*) ~и перехо́жие wandering minstrels.

кали́льн|ый, *adj.* (*tech.*) к. жар temperature of incandescence; ~ая печь temper furnace; ~ая се́тка (incandescent) mantle.

кали́н|а, ы, *no pl.*, *f.* (*bot.*) guelder rose, snowball-tree.

кали́н|овый, *adj. of* ~а.

кали́тк|а, и, *f.* (wicket-)gate.

кал|и́ть, ю, и́шь, *impf.* **1.** (*tech.*) to heat. **2.** to roast (*chestnuts, etc.*).

кали́ф, а, *m.* caliph; к. на час (*iron.*) king for a day.

каллиграфи́ческий, *adj.* calligraphic.

каллигра́фи|я, и, *f.* calligraphy.

калмы́к, а́, *m.* Kalmuck, Kalmyk.

калмы́цкий, *adj.* Kalmuck, Kalmyk.

калмы́чк|а, и, *f.* Kalmuck, Kalmyk (woman).

ка́л|овый, *adj. of* ~.

ка́ломел|ь, и, *f.* calomel.

калори́йност|ь, и, *f.* calorie content.

калори́метр, а, *m.* (*phys.*) calorimeter.

калориме́три|я, и, *f.* (*phys.*) calorimetry.

калори́фер, а, *m.* (*tech.*) heater, radiator.

кало́ри|я, и, *f.* calorie; больша́я к. large (kilogram-)calorie; ма́лая к. small (gram-)calorie; брита́нская к. British thermal unit.

кало́ш|а, и, *f.* = гало́ша.

калу́жниц|а, ы, *f.* (*bot.*) king-cup, marsh marigold.

калы́м, а, *no pl.*, *m.* (*ethnol.*) bride-money.

кальвини́зм, а, *m.* Calvinism.

кальвини́ст, а, *m.* Calvinist.

кальвинисти́ческий, *adj.* Calvinistic(al).

ка́л|ька, ьки, *g. pl.* ~ек, *f.* **1.** tracing-paper. **2.** (tracing-paper) copy. **3.** (*ling.*) loan translation, calque.

кальки́р|овать, ую, *impf.* (*of* c~) **1.** to trace. **2.** (*ling.*) to make a loan translation of.

калькули́р|овать, ую, *impf.* (*of* c~) (*comm.*) to calculate.

калькуля́тор, а, *m.* (*comm.*) calculator.

калькуля|цио́нный, *adj. of* ~ция; ~цио́нная ве́домость cost sheet; cost record.

калькуля́ци|я, и, *f.* (*comm.*) calculation.

кальсо́н|ы, ~, *no sing.* pants, drawers.

ка́льциевый, *adj.* (*chem.*) calcium, calcic.

ка́льци|й, я, *m.* (*chem.*) calcium.

кальцина́ци|я, и, *f.* (*chem.*) calcination.

кальци́т, а, *m.* (*min.*) calcite.

калья́н, а, *m.* hookah.

каля́ка|ть, ю, *impf.* (*of* по~) (*coll.*) to chat.

кама́зский, *adj.* KamAZ (*of the Kama motor-vehicle factory*).

камари́ль|я, и, *f.* camarilla, clique.

кама́ринск|ая, ой, *f.* Kamarinskaya (*Russian folk-dance*).

ка́мбал|а, ы, *f.* **1.** flat-fish (*generic term*). **2.** plaice; flounder.

ка́мби|й, я, *m.* (*bot.*) cambium.

ка́мбуз, а, *m.* (*naut.*) galley, caboose.

камво́льный, *adj.* (*text.*) worsted.

каме́дистый, *adj.* gummy.

каме́д|ь, и, *f.* gum.

камел|ёк, ька́, *m.* fire-place.

каме́ли|я, и, *f.* (*bot.*) camellia.

камене́|ть, ю, *impf.* (*of* o~) to become petrified, turn to stone; (*fig.*) to harden (*intrans.*).

камени́ст|ый (~, ~a), *adj.* stony.

ка́менк|а¹, и, *f.* stove (*in bath-house in rural Russia*).

ка́менк|а², и, *f.* (*orn.*) wheat-ear.

каменноуго́льн|ый, *adj.* coal; к. бассе́йн coal-field; ~ые ко́пи coal-mine.

ка́менн|ый, *adj.* 1. stone-; stony; к. век the Stone Age; ~ая кла́дка masonry, stone--work; ~ая соль rock-salt; к. у́голь coal; ~ая боле́знь (*med.*) gravel; к. мешо́к (*hist.*; *rhet.*) prison cell; к. о́кунь bass (*fish*). 2. (*fig.*) stony; hard, immovable; ~ое се́рдце stony heart.

каменоло́м|ня, ни, *g. pl.* ~ен, *f.* quarry.

каменотёс, а, *m.* (stone)mason.

ка́менщик, а, *m.* (stone)mason, bricklayer; (*hist.*) во́льные ~и Freemasons.

ка́м|ень, ня, *pl.* ~ни, ~не́й *and* (*coll.*) ~е́нья, ~е́ньев, *m.* stone; па́дать ~нем to fall like a stone; ~ня на ~не не оста́вить to raze to the ground; (*fig.*) броса́ть ~нем (в+*a.*) to cast stones (at); у него́ к. на се́рдце лежи́т a weight sits heavy on his heart; держа́ть к. за па́зухой (на+*a.*, про́тив) to harbour a grudge (against); к. с души́ мое́й свали́лся a load has been taken off my mind.

ка́мер|а, ы, *f.* 1. chamber (*in var. senses*); тюре́мная к. prison cell; к. хране́ния (багажа́) cloak-room. 2. (фотографи́ческая) к. camera. 3. inner tube (*of tire*); bladder (*of football*).

камерге́р, а, *m.* chamberlain.

камерди́нер, а, *m.* valet.

камери́стк|а, и, *f.* lady's maid.

ка́мер|ный¹, *adj. of* ~a.

ка́мерн|ый², *adj.* (*mus.*) к. конце́рт chamber concert; ~ая му́зыка chamber music.

камерто́н, а, *m.* tuning-fork.

ка́мер-ю́нкер, а, *m.* gentleman of the bed-chamber.

ка́меш|ек, ка, *m.* *dim. of* ка́мень; pebble; (*fig.*, *coll.*) бро́сить к. в чей-н. огоро́д to make digs at someone.

каме́|я, и, *f.* cameo.

камзо́л, а, *m.* camisole.

камила́вк|а, и, *f.* (*eccl.*) kamelaukion (*Orthodox priest's headgear*).

ками́н, а, *m.* fire-place; (open) fire.

ками́н|ный, *adj. of* ~; ~ная по́лка mantelpiece; ~ная решётка fender, fireguard.

камк|а́, и́, *f.* (*text.*) damask.

камло́т, а, *m.* (*text.*) camlet.

камло́т|овый, *adj. of* ~.

камнедроби́лк|а, и, *f.* stone-breaker, stone--crusher.

камнело́мк|а, и, *f.* (*bot.*) saxifrage.

камо́рк|а, и, *f.* (*coll.*) closet, very small room; box room.

кампане́йск|ий, *adj.* (*pejor.*) ~ая рабо́та work done by spurts.

кампане́йщин|а, ы, *f.* (*pejor.*) system of working by spurts (*as opp. to* working according to plan, methodically).

кампа́ни|я, и, *f.* 1. (*mil. and fig.*) campaign. 2. (*naut.*) cruise.

кампе́шев|ый, *adj.* (*bot.*) ~ое де́рево campeachy wood, logwood.

камуфле́т, а, *m.* (*mil.*) camouflet; (*fig.*, *coll.*, *joc.*) dirty trick.

камуфля́ж, а, *no pl.*, *m.* camouflage.

камфар|а́, ы́, *f.* camphor.

камфа́р|ный, *adj. of* ~а́.

камф|ора́ = ~ара́.

камфо́рк|а, и, *f.* = конфо́рка.

камча́тк|а, и, *f.* (*text.*) damask linen.

камча́т(н)ый, *adj.* 1. (*folk poet.*) damask. 2. damasked, figured (*of linen*).

камы́ш, а́, *m.* reed, rush (*also collect.*).

камы́ш|евый, *adj. of* ~.

камыш|о́вый, *adj. of* ~; ~о́вое кре́сло cane chair; ~о́вая жа́ба natterjack.

кана́в|а, ы, *f.* ditch; сто́чная к. gutter.

канавокопа́тел|ь, я, *m.* (*tech.*) trench digger, trench excavator.

кана́д|ец, ца, *g. pl.* ~цев, *m.* Canadian.

кана́дк|а, и, *f.* Canadian (woman).

кана́дск|ий, *adj.* Canadian; ~ая пи́хта balsam fir.

кана́л, а, *m.* 1. canal. 2. (*in var. senses*) channel; дипломати́ческие ~ы diplomatic channels. 3. (*anat.*) duct, canal; мочеиспуска́тельный к. urethra. 4. bore (*of barrel of gun*).

канализа|цио́нный, *adj. of* ~ция; ~цио́нная труба́ sewer(-pipe).

канализа́ци|я, и, *f.* 1. sewerage. 2. sewer (system).

канализи́р|овать, ую, *impf. and pf.* to provide with sewerage-system.

кана́льский, *adj.* (*coll.*, *obs.*) rascally, roguish.

кана́льств|о, а, *n.* (*coll.*, *obs.*) trickery, knavery.

кана́л|ья, ьи, *g. pl.* ~ий, *m. and f.* (*coll.*) rascal, scoundrel.

канаре́|ечный, *adj.* 1. *adj. of* ~йка. 2. canary(-coloured).

канаре́йк|а, и, *f.* canary.

кана́т, а, *m.* rope; cable, hawser.

кана́т|ный, *adj. of* ~; к. заво́д rope-yard; ~ная желе́зная доро́га funicular railway; к. плясу́н rope-dancer.

канатохо́д|ец, ца, *m.* rope-walker.

канв|а́, ы́, *no pl.*, *f.* canvas; (*fig.*) groundwork; outline, design; к. рома́на the outline of a novel.

канв|óвый, *adj. of* ~á.

кандал|ы́, óв, *no sing.* shackles, fetters; ручны́е к. manacles, handcuffs; закова́ть в к. to put into irons.

кандáл|ьный, *adj. of* ~ы́.

канделя́бр, а, *m.* candelabrum.

кандидáт, а, *m.* 1. candidate; к. в члéны коммунисти́ческой пáртии candidate--member of the Communist Party. 2. kandididat (*holder of first higher degree, awarded on dissertation, in Soviet Union*).

кандидáт|ский, *adj. of* ~; к. ми́нимум qualifying examinations for admission to the course leading to the degree of kandidat; к. стаж (*polit.*) probation period (*period as candidate-member of the Soviet Communist Party*).

кандидатýр|а, ы, *f.* candidature; вы́ставить чью-н. ~у to nominate someone for election.

кани́кул|ы, ~, *no sing.* (*school*) holidays; (*university, etc.*) vacation.

кани|куля́рный, *adj. of* ~кулы.

кани́стр|а, ы, *f.* jerrican.

канитéл|ить, ю, ишь, *impf.* (*of* про~) (*coll., pejor.*) to drag out; к. когó-н. to waste someone's time.

канитéл|иться, юсь, ишься, *impf.* (*of* про~) (*coll., pejor.*) to waste time; to mess about; to maunder.

канитéл|ь, и, *f.* 1. gold thread, silver thread; wire-ribbon. 2. (*fig., coll.*) long--drawn-out proceedings; тяну́ть, разводи́ть к. to spin out, drag out proceedings, procrastinate; довóльно ~и! this has gone on, dragged on long enough!

канитéл|ьный (~ен, ~ьна), *adj.* (*coll.*) 1. long-drawn-out; tedious. 2. к. человéк procrastinating person. 3. *adj. of* ~ь 1.

канитéльщик, а, *m.* 1. wire-ribbon spinner. 2. (*fig., coll.*) time-waster.

канифáс, а, *m.* (*obs.*) 1. sail-cloth. 2. dimity.

канифóл|ить, ю, ишь, *impf.* (*of* на~) to rosin.

канифóл|ь, и, *f.* rosin, colophony.

канкáн, а, *m.* cancan.

канкани́р|овать, ую, *impf.* (*coll.*) to dance the cancan.

каннелю́р|а, ы, *f.* (*archit.*) flute.

каннибáл, а, *m.* cannibal.

каннибали́зм, а, *m.* cannibalism.

канóн, а, *m.* (*in var. senses*) canon.

канонáд|а, ы, *f.* cannonade.

канонéрк|а, и, *f.* gunboat.

канонéрск|ий, *adj.*; ~ая лóдка gunboat.

канонизáци|я, и, *f.* (*eccl.*) canonization.

канонизи́р|овать, ую, *impf. and pf.* (*eccl. and fig.*) to canonize.

канониз|овáть, у́ю, *impf. and pf.* = ~и́ровать.

канóник, а, *m.* (*eccl.*) canon.

канони́р, а, *m.* gunner.

канони́ческ|ий, *adj.* 1. (*eccl.*) canonical; (*lit.*) definitive. 2. (*eccl.*) ~ое прáво canon law.

канони́чность, и, *f.* (*eccl. and lit.*) canonicity.

кант, а, *m.* 1. edging, piping. 2. mount (*for picture, etc.*).

кантáт|а, ы, *f.* (*mus.*) cantata.

кантиáн|ец, ца, *m.* (*philos.*) Kantian.

кантиáнский, *adj.* (*philos.*) Kantian.

кантилéн|а, ы, *f.* (*mus.*) cantilena.

кант|овáть[1], у́ю, *impf.* (*of* о~) to border; to mount (*picture, etc.*).

кант|овáть[2], у́ю, *impf.* (*tech.*) to cant.

кантóн, а, *m.* (*administrative unit*) canton.

кантонáльный, *adj.* cantonal.

кантони́ст, а, *m.* (*hist.*) soldier's son.

канýн, а, *m.* eve; (*eccl.*) vigil; к. Нóвого гóда New Year's eve.

кáн|уть, у, ешь, *pf.* (*obs.*) to drop, sink; к. в вéчность, к. в Лéту (*fig.*) to sink into oblivion; как в вóду к. to disappear without a trace, vanish into thin air.

канцеляри́ст, а, *m.* clerk.

канцеля́ри|я, и, *f.* office.

канцеля́р|ский, *adj. of* ~; ~ские принадлéжности stationery; ~ская рабóта clerical work; к. стол office desk; ~ская кры́са (*fig., pejor.*) office drudge; к. пóчерк clerkly hand; к. слог officialese.

канцеля́рщин|а, ы, *f.* (*coll.*) red tape.

кáнцлер, а, *m.* chancellor.

канцóн|а, ы, *f.* (*mus.*) canzonet.

каньóн, а, *m.* (*geogr.*) canyon.

каню́к, á, *m.* 1. (*orn.*) buzzard. 2. (*fig., dial.*) moaner, grumbler.

каню́ч|ить, у, ишь, *impf.* (*coll., pejor.*) to moan, grumble; to pester.

каоли́н, а, *m.* china clay, kaolin.

кап- *abbr. of* капиталисти́ческий.

кáп|ать, лю, лешь, (*coll.* ~аю, ~аешь), *impf.* (*of* ~нуть) 1. (*3rd person only*) to drip, drop; to trickle; to dribble; to fall (in drops); из глаз у неё ~али слёзы tear--drops were falling from her eyes; дождь ~лет it is spotting with rain; с потолкá ~ало there was a drip from the ceiling; над нáми не ~лет (*fig., coll.*) we can take our time, there is no hurry. 2. to pour out (*in drops*); к. лекáрство в рю́мку to pour medicine into a glass. 3. (+*i.*; *coll.*) to spill; ты ~лешь водóй на скáтерть you are spilling water on the cloth.

капéлл|а, ы, *f.* 1. choir. 2. chapel; к. Богомáтери Lady chapel.

капеллáн, а, *m.* chaplain.

капéл|ь, и, *f.* 1. drip (*of thawing snow*). 2. thaw.

капельдúнер, а, *m.* (*obs.*) usher, box-keeper (*in theatre*).

ка́пельк|а, и, *f.* 1. small drop; к. росы́ dew-drop; вы́пить всё до ~и to drink to the last drop. 2. (*sing. only*; *fig.*) grain, minute quantity; в нём нет ни ~и здра́вого смы́сла he has not a grain of common sense; она́ ни ~и не смути́лась she was not a whit put out; *as adv.* ~y (*coll.*) a little; подожди́ ~y! wait a moment!

капельме́йстер, а, *m.* (*mus.*) conductor, bandmaster.

капельме́йстер|ский, *adj.* of ~; ~ская па́лочка conductor's baton.

ка́пельниц|а, ы, *f.* (medicine) dropper.

ка́пельный, *adj.* (*coll.*) tiny.

ка́пер, а, *m.* (*naut.*) privateer.

ка́перс, а, *m.* 1. (*bot.*) caper. 2. (*pl. only*; *cul.*) capers.

ка́перств|о, а, *n.* (*naut.*) privateering.

капилля́р, а, *m.* (*phys., anat.*) capillary.

капилля́рный, *adj.* (*phys., anat.*) capillary.

капита́л, а, *m.* (*fin.*) capital; к. и проце́нты, к. с проце́нтами principal and interest.

капита́л|ец, ьца, *m. dim. of* ~; *coll.* a tidy sum.

капитализа́ци|я, и, *f.* (*fin.*) capitalization.

капитализи́р|овать, ую, *impf. and pf.* (*fin.*) to capitalize.

капитали́зм, а, *m.* capitalism.

капитали́ст, а, *m.* capitalist.

капиталисти́ческий, *adj.* capitalist(ic).

капиталовложе́ни|е, я, *n.* capital investment.

капита́льн|ый, *adj.* capital; main, fundamental; most important; к. вопро́с fundamental question; к. ремо́нт major repairs; ~ая стена́ main wall.

капита́н, а, *m.* captain.

капита́н|ский, *adj.* of ~; к. мо́стик captain's bridge.

капите́л|ь, и, *f.* 1. (*archit.*) capital. 2. (*typ.*) small capitals.

капи́тул, а, *m.* (*eccl., hist.*) chapter (*of canons or of members of an order*).

капитули́р|овать, ую, *impf. and pf.* (пе́ред) to capitulate (to).

капитуля́нт, а, *m.* (*pejor.*) faint-heart; truckler.

капитуля́нтств|о, а, *n.* truckling.

капитуля́ци|я, и, *f.* capitulation.

ка́пищ|е, а, *n.* (*heathen*) temple.

капка́н, а, *m.* trap; попа́сться в к. to fall into a trap (*also fig.*).

капка́н|ный, *adj.* of ~; к. про́мысел trapping.

каплиц|а, ы, *f.* (*Roman Catholic*) chapel.

каплу́н, á, *m.* capon.

ка́п|ля, ли, *g. pl.* ~ель, *f.* 1. drop; по ~ле, к. за ~лей drop by drop; до ~ли to the last drop; похо́жи как две ~ли воды́ as like as two peas; ~ли в рот не беру́ (*euph.*) I never touch a drop (*sc. of alcoholic liquor*);

(*fig.*) к. в мо́ре a drop in the ocean; после́дняя к. the last straw; би́ться до после́дней ~ли кро́ви to fight to the last. 2. (*pl.*; *med.*) drops. 3. (*fig., coll.*) drop, bit; у него́ (нет) ни ~ли благоразу́мия he hasn't a drop of sense; ни ~ли (*as adv.*) not a bit, not a whit.

ка́п|нуть, ну, нешь, *pf.* (*of* ~ать) to drop, let fall a drop.

кап|о́к, ка́, *no pl.*, *m.* (*text.*) kapok.

ка́пор, а, *m.* hood; bonnet.

капо́т, а, *m.* 1. house-coat (*woman's informal indoor attire*). 2. capote (*French soldier's*) greatcoat. 3. (*tech.*) hood, bonnet, cowl; к. мото́ра (*aeron.*) engine cowling.

капра́л, а, *m.* (*mil.*) corporal.

капра́л|ьский, *adj.* of ~.

капра́льств|о, а, *n.* (*mil.*) rank of corporal.

капри́з, а, *m.* caprice, whim; vagary.

капри́зник, а, *m.* capricious person, capricious child.

капри́знича|ть, ю, *impf.* to behave capriciously; (*of a child*) to play up.

капри́з|ный (~ен, ~на), *adj.* 1. capricious; (*of a child*) wilful. 2. freakish.

капризу́л|я, и, *m. and f.* (*coll.*) capricious, self-willed child.

каприфо́л|ь, и, *f.* (*bot.*) honeysuckle.

капри́ччио, *indecl.*, *n.* (*mus.*) capriccio.

капро́н, а, *m.* kapron (*artificial fibre, similar to nylon, produced in Soviet Union*).

капро́н|овый, *adj.* of ~.

ка́псул|а, ы, *f.* capsule.

ка́псюл|ь, я, *m.* (percussion) cap (*in explosives*).

ка́псюль|ный, *adj.* of ~; ~ное ружьё percussion musket.

каптена́рмус, а, *m.* (*mil.*) quartermaster-sergeant.

капу́ст|а, ы, *f.* cabbage.

капу́стник, а, *m.* 1. cabbage field. 2. cabbage worm. 3. actors', artists', *or* students' party.

капу́стниц|а, ы, *f.* cabbage butterfly.

капу́ст|ный, *adj.* of ~a.

капу́т, *indecl.*, *n.* (*coll.*) end, destruction; *used as adj. or adv.* done for, kaput; тут ему́ и к. he's done for, it's all up with him.

капуци́н, а, *m.* 1. Capuchin (friar). 2. (*zool.*) Capuchin monkey. 3. (*bot.*) nasturtium.

капюшо́н, а, *m.* hood, cowl.

ка́р|а, ы, *f.* (*rhet.*) punishment, retribution.

караби́н, а, *m.* carbine.

карабине́р, а, *m.* car(a)bineer.

кара́бка|ться, юсь, *impf.* (*of* вс~) (*coll.*) to clamber.

карава́|й, я, *m.* cottage loaf.

карава́н, а, *m.* 1. caravan. 2. convoy (*of ships, etc.*).

карава́н-сара́|й, я, *m.* caravanserai.

карага́ч, а, *m.* (*bot.*) elm.

кара́емый, *adj.* (*leg.*) punishable.

кара́им, а, *m.* Karaite (*member of Jewish sect who reject the Talmud*).

каракалпа́к, а, *m.* (*ethnol.*) Karakalpak.

карака́тиц|а, ы, *f.* **1.** (*zool.*) cuttlefish. **2.** (*fig., joc.*) short-legged, clumsy person.

кара́ковый, *adj.* dark-bay.

кара́кул|евый, *adj. of* ~ь.

кара́кул|ь, я, *no pl., m.* astrakhan (fur).

каракульч|а́, и́, *f.* astrakhan (fur).

кара́кул|я, и, *f.* scrawl, scribble.

карамбо́л|ь, я, *m.* (*in billiards*) cannon.

караме́л|ь, и, *no pl., f.* **1.** (*collect.*) caramels. **2.** caramel.

караме́льк|а, и, *f.* (*coll.*) caramel.

караме́ль|ный, *adj. of* ~.

каранда́ш, а́, *m.* pencil.

каранда́ш|ный, *adj. of* ~; к. рису́нок pencil drawing.

каранти́н, а, *m.* **1.** quarantine; сня́тие ~а (*naut.*) pratique; подве́ргнуть ~y to place in quarantine. **2.** quarantine station.

каранти́н|ный, *adj. of* ~; ~ное свиде́тель-ство (*naut.*) bill of health.

карапу́з, а, *m.* (*coll.*) chubby lad.

кара́с|ь, я, *m.* (*fish*) crucian; сере́бряный к. Prussian carp.

кара́т, а, *m.* carat.

кара́тел|ь, я, *m.* **1.** (*obs.*) punisher, chas-tiser. **2.** member of punitive expedition.

кара́тельный, *adj.* punitive.

кара́|ть, ю, *impf.* (*of* по~) to punish, chastise.

карау́л, а, *m.* **1.** guard; watch; вступи́ть в к. to mount guard; нести́ к., стоя́ть в ~е to be on guard; смени́ть к. to relieve the guard. **2.** *word of command*: на к.! present arms!; взять на к. to present arms. **3.** *as interj.* help!; крича́ть к. to shout for help.

карау́л|ить, ю, ишь, *impf.* **1.** to guard. **2.** (*coll.*) to lie in wait for, watch out for.

карау́лк|а, и, *f.* (*coll.*) guardroom.

карау́л|ьный, *adj. of* ~; ~ьная бу́дка sentry-box; *as noun* к., ~ьного, *m.* sentry, sentinel, guard.

карау́л|ьня, ьни, *g. pl.* ~ен, *f.* guardroom.

карау́льщик, а, *m.* (*coll.*) sentry, guard.

кара́ч|ки, ек, *no sing.* (*coll.*); на к., на ~ках on all fours; стать на к. to get on all fours.

карби́д, а, *m.* (*chem.*) carbide.

карбо́ван|ец, ца, *m.* **1.** karbovanets (*Ukrainian name of the Russian rouble*). **2.** (*pl.*) money.

карбо́лк|а, и, *f.* (*coll.*) carbolic acid.

карбо́ловый, *adj.* (*chem.*) carbolic.

карбона́т, а, *m.* (*chem.*) carbonate.

карбору́нд, а, *m.* carborundum.

карбу́нкул, а, *m.* (*min., med.*) carbuncle.

карбюра́тор, а, *m.* (*tech., chem.*) carburet-tor.

карбюри́р|овать, ую, *impf. and pf.* (*chem.*) to carburettor.

карг|а́, и́, *pl.* ~и́, ~, ~а́м, *f.* **1.** (*dial.*) crow. **2.** (*coll.*) ста́рая к. hag, harridan, crone.

ка́рд|а, ы, *f.* (*tech.*) card.

кардамо́н, а, *m.* (*bot.*) cardamom.

кардина́л, а, *m.* (*eccl.*) cardinal.

кардина́льный, *adj.* cardinal.

кардина́л|ьский, *adj. of* ~.

кардиогра́мм|а, ы, *f.* cardiogram.

каре́, *indecl., n.* (*mil.*) square.

каре́л, а, *m.* Karelian.

каре́лк|а, и, *f.* Karelian (woman).

каре́льск|ий, *adj.* Karelian; ~ая берёза Karelian birch.

каре́т|а, ы, *f.* carriage, coach; к. запряжён-ная па́рой, четвёркой carriage and pair, coach and four; почто́вая к. stage-coach; к. ско́рой по́мощи (*obs.*) ambulance.

каре́тк|а, и, *f.* (*tech.*) carriage, frame.

каре́тник, а, *m.* **1.** coach-house. **2.** coach--builder.

кариати́д|а, ы, *f.* (*archit.*) caryatid.

ка́рий, *adj.* (*of colour of eyes*) brown, hazel; (*of colour of horses*) chestnut, dark-chest-nut.

карикату́р|а, ы, *f.* **1.** caricature. **2.** car-toon.

карикатури́ст, а, *m.* **1.** caricaturist. **2.** car-toonist.

карикату́р|ить, ю, ишь, *impf.* (*coll., obs.*) to caricature.

карикату́р|ный, *adj. of* ~а; ~ная фигу́ра ludicrous figure.

карио́з, а, *m.* (*med.*) caries, decay.

карио́зный, *adj.* (*med.*) carious.

карка́с, а, *m.* (*tech.*) frame; (*fig.*) framework.

карка́с|ный, *adj. of* ~; к. дом framehouse.

ка́рк|ать, аю, *impf.* (*of* ~нуть) **1.** to caw, croak. **2.** (*fig.*) to croak, prophesy ill.

ка́рк|нуть, ну, нешь, *pf. of* ~ать 1.

ка́рлик, а, *m.* dwarf; pygmy.

ка́рликов|ый, *adj.* (*anthrop., bot., and fig.*) dwarf; pygmean; ~ые племена́ the Pyg-mies.

ка́рли|ца, цы, *f. of* ~к.

кармази́н, а, *m.* (*obs.*) cramoisy, crimson (*cloth*).

кармази́н|ный, *adj. of* ~; к. цвет crimson.

карма́н, а, *m.* pocket; (*fig., coll.*) э́то мне не по ~y I can't afford it; бить по ~y to cost a pretty penny; наби́ть себе́ к. to fill one's pockets; то́щий к. empty pocket; держи́ к. ши́ре ! you've got a hope ! ; не лезть за сло́вом в к. to have a ready tongue.

карма́нник, а, *m.* pickpocket.

карма́н|ный, *adj. of* ~; к. вор pickpocket; ~ные де́ньги pocket money.

карми́н, а, *m.* carmine.

карми́нный, *adj.* carmine.

карнава́л, а, *m.* carnival.

карни́з, а, *m.* (*archit.*) 1. cornice. 2. ledge.

кароте́л|ь, и, *f.* carrot (*variety having short roots*).

карп, а, *m.* (*fish*) carp.

карт, а, *m.* (*sport*) go-cart.

ка́рт|а, ы, *f.* 1. (*geogr.*) map. 2. (playing-) card; игра́ть в ~ы to play cards; име́ть хоро́шие ~ы to have a good hand; его́ ка́рта би́та (*fig.*) his game is up; поста́вить на ~у to stake, risk; на ~е at stake; раскры́ть свои́ ~ы to show one's hand.

карта́в|ить, лю, ишь, *impf.* to burr.

карта́вост|ь, и, *f.* (*ling.*) burr.

карта́вый, *adj.* 1. pronounced gutturally. 2. having a burr.

картве́л, а, *m.* (*ethnol.*) Georgian.

картёж, а́, *no pl.*, *m.* (*coll.*) card-playing; gambling school.

картёжник, а, *m.* (*coll.*) card-player; gambler (*at cards*).

картёжный, *adj.* (*coll.*) card-playing; gambling.

картезиа́нский, *adj.* (*philos.*) Cartesian.

карте́л|ь, я, *m.* (*fin.*) cartel.

ка́ртер, а, *m.* (*tech.*) crank case.

карте́ч|ный, *adj. of* ~ь.

карте́ч|ь, и, *f.* 1. (*mil.*) case-shot; grape-shot. 2. buck-shot.

карти́н|а, ы, *f.* 1. (*in var. senses*) picture. 2. (*theatr.*) scene.

ка́ртинг, а, *m.* (*sport*) go-carting.

карти́нк|а, и, *f.* picture; illustration; лубо́чные ~и crude, coloured woodcuts; (*pejor.*) crude pictures; мо́дная к. fashion-plate; переводны́е ~и transfers.

карти́н|ный (~ен, ~на), *adj.* 1. *adj. of* ~а; ~ная галере́я art gallery, picture-gallery. 2. picturesque.

карто́граф, а, *m.* cartographer.

картографи́р|овать, ую, *impf.* to map, draw a map of.

картографи́ческий, *adj.* cartographic.

картогра́фи|я, и, *f.* cartography.

карто́н, а, *m.* 1. cardboard, pasteboard. 2. (*artists' sl.*) sketch, cartoon.

картона́ж, а, *m.* cardboard article; cardboard box.

картона́ж|ный, *adj. of* ~; ~ная фа́брика cardboard box factory.

карто́нк|а, и, *f.* cardboard box; к. для шля́пы hat-box, bandbox.

карто́н|ный, *adj. of* ~; (*fig.*) к. до́мик house of cards.

картоте́к|а, и, *f.* card-index.

картофелекопа́лк|а, и, *f.* (*agric.*) potato-digger.

карто́фелин|а, ы, *f.* (*coll.*) potato.

карто́фел|ь, я, *no pl.*, *m.* 1. (*collect.*) potatoes;

к. в мунди́ре potatoes boiled in their jackets; жа́реный к. fried potatoes; молодо́й к. new potatoes. 2. potato plant.

карто́фель|ный, *adj. of* ~; ~ное пюре́ mashed potatoes.

ка́рточк|а, и, *f.* 1. card; визи́тная к. visiting card; к. вин wine-list; ката́ложная к. index card; к. куша́ний bill of fare; продово́льственная к. food-card, ration card. 2. season ticket. 3. (*coll.*) photo.

ка́рточ|ный, *adj.* 1. *adj. of* ка́рта; к. долг gambling-debt; к. стол card-table; (*coll.*) к. до́мик house of cards (*also fig.*); к. фо́кус card trick. 2. *adj. of* ~ка; к. катало́г card index; ~ная систе́ма rationing system.

карто́шк|а, и, *f.* (*coll.*) 1. (*collect.*) potatoes. 2. potato; нос ~ой bulbous nose.

карту́з, а́, *m.* 1. (peaked) cap. 2. (*mil.*) powder bag. 3. (*obs.*) paper-bag.

карусе́л|ь, и, *f.* roundabout, merry-go-round.

карусе́ль|ный, *adj. of* ~; (*tech.*) к. стано́к vertical lathe.

ка́рцер, а, *m.* cell, lock-up.

карье́р[1], а, *m.* career, full gallop; во весь к. at full speed, in full career; пусти́ть ло́шадь в к., ~ом to put a horse into full gallop; (*fig.*, *coll.*) с ме́ста в к. straight away, without more ado.

карье́р[2], а, *m.* quarry; sand-pit.

карье́р|а, ы, *f.* career; сде́лать ~у to make good, get on.

карьери́зм, а, *m.* careerism.

карьери́ст, а, *m.* careerist.

карье́р|ный, *adj. of* 1. ~[1,2]. 2. ~а.

каса́ни|е, я, *n.* contact; (*math.*) то́чка ~я point of contact.

каса́тельн|ая, ой, *f.* (*math.*) tangent.

каса́тельно, *prep.* +*g.* touching, concerning.

каса́тельств|о, а, *n.* (к) connexion (with); я не име́л никако́го ~а к э́тому заявле́нию I had nothing to do with this statement.

каса́тик, а, *m.* (*folk poet.*) darling.

каса́т|ка, ки, *f.* 1. (*orn.*) swallow. 2. (*zool.*) killer whale. 3. (*folk poet.*) *f. of* ~ик.

каса́|ться, юсь, *impf.* (*of* косну́ться) 1. (+*g.*) to touch (+*g.*; +*g.*) to touch (on, upon); к. больно́го вопро́са to touch on a sore subject. 3. (+*g. or* до; *fig.*) to concern, relate (to); э́то тебя́ не ~ется it is no concern of yours; что ~ется as to, as regards, with regard to.

ка́ск|а, и, *f.* helmet.

каска́д, а, *m.* 1. cascade; к. красноре́чия (*fig.*) flood of eloquence. 2. leaping from horseback (*as circus turn*).

каскадёр, а, *m.* stunt man.

каска́д|ный, *adj.* 1. *adj. of* ~. 2. (*theatr.*) music-hall.

каспи́йский, *adj.* (*geogr.*) Caspian.

ка́сс|а, ы, ƒ. 1. till; cash-box; несгора́емая к. safe. **2.** cash. **3.** booking-office; box--office; к. взаимопо́мощи benefit fund, mutual aid fund; сберега́тельная к. savings bank. **4.** (*typ.*) case.

касса|цио́нный, *adj. of* ~ция; ~цио́нная жа́лоба appeal; к. суд Court of Appeal, Court of Cassation.

кассаци|я, и, ƒ. (*leg.*) **1.** cassation. **2.** (*coll.*) пода́ть ~ю to appeal.

кассе́т|а, ы, ƒ. (*mus. and phot.*) cassette; plate-holder.

кассе́т|ный, *adj. of* ~а; к. магнитофо́н cassette recorder.

касси́р, а, m. cashier.

касси́р|овать, ую, *impf. and pf.* (*leg.*) to annul, quash.

касси́р|ша, ши, ƒ. of ~.

ка́сс|овый, *adj. of* ~а; ~овая кни́га cash--book; к. счёт cash-account.

ка́ст|а, ы, ƒ. caste.

кастанье́т|ы, ~, *sing.* ~а, ~ы, ƒ. castanets.

кастеля́нш|а, и, ƒ. linen-keeper (*in institution*).

касте́т, а, m. knuckleduster.

касто́рк|а, и, ƒ. (*coll.*) castor oil.

касто́ров|ый[1], *adj.*; ~ое ма́сло castor oil.

касто́р|овый[2], *adj. of* ~; ~овая шля́па beaver (hat).

кастра́т, а, m. eunuch.

кастра́ци|я, и, ƒ. castration.

кастри́р|овать, ую, *impf. and pf.* to castrate; to geld.

кастрю́л|я, и, ƒ. saucepan.

кат[1], а, m. (*dial. or obs.*) executioner.

кат[2], а, m. (*naut.*) cat; к.-ба́лка cathead.

катава́си|я, и, ƒ. (*coll.*) confusion, muddle.

катакли́зм, а, m. cataclysm.

катако́мб|а, ы, ƒ. catacomb.

катала́жк|а, и, ƒ. (*coll.*) lock-up.

ката́лиз, а, m. (*chem.*) catalysis.

катализа́тор, а, m. (*chem.*) catalyst.

катало́г, а, m. catalogue.

каталогиза́тор, а, m. cataloguer.

каталогизи́р|овать, ую, *impf. and pf.* to catalogue.

катало́жн|ая, ой, ƒ. catalogue room.

катало́|жный, *adj. of* ~г.

ка́тал|ь, я, m. porter, barrow man.

катамара́н, а, m. catamaran.

ката́ни|е, я, n. 1. rolling. **2.** к. в экипа́же driving; к. верхо́м riding; к. на ло́дке boating; к. на конька́х skating; фигу́рное к. figure skating; к. с гор tobogganing.

ка́тань|е, я, n., *only in phrase* не мытьём, так ~ем (*coll.*) by hook or by crook.

катапу́льт|а, ы, ƒ. (*hist. and aeron.*) catapult.

ката́р, а, m. catarrh.

катара́кт, а, m. (*geogr.*) cataract.

катара́кт|а, ы, ƒ. (*med.*) cataract.

катара́льный, *adj.* catarrhal.

катастро́ф|а, ы, ƒ. catastrophe, disaster; accident.

катастрофи́ческий, *adj.* catastrophic.

катастрофи́ч|ный (~ен, ~на), *adj.* catastrophic.

кат|а́ть, а́ю, *impf.* **1.** (*indet. of* ~и́ть) to roll; to wheel, trundle. **2.** to drive, take for a drive. **3.** to roll (*from clay, dough, etc.*). **4.** (*pf.* вы́~) к. бельё to mangle linen.

кат|а́ться, а́юсь, *impf.* **1.** (*indet. of* ~и́ться) to roll (*intrans.*); (*coll.*) к. от бо́ли to roll in pain; к. со́ смеху to split one's sides with laughter. **2.** to go for a drive; к. верхо́м to ride, go riding; к. на велосипе́де to cycle, go cycling; к. на конька́х to skate, go skating; к. на ло́дке to go boating.

катафа́лк, а, m. 1. catafalque. **2.** hearse.

катафо́т, а, m. cat's eye (*on road*).

категори́чески, *adv.* categorically; к. отказа́ться to refuse flatly.

категори́ческий, *adj.* categorical.

категори́ч|ный (~ен, ~на), *adj.* categorical.

катего́ри|я, и, ƒ. category.

ка́тер, а, *pl.* ~а́, m. (*naut.*) cutter; мото́рный к. motor-launch; сторожево́й к. patrol boat; торпе́дный к. motor torpedo-boat.

ка́тер|ный, *adj. of* ~.

кате́тер, а, m. (*med.*) catheter.

катехи́зис, а, m. catechism.

ка|ти́ть, чу́, ~тишь, *impf.* (*of* по~) **1.** *det. of* ~та́ть. **2.** (*coll.*) to bowl along, rip, tear.

ка|ти́ться, чу́сь, ~тишься, *impf.* (*of* по~) **1.** *det. of* ~та́ться; к. с горы́ to slide downhill; к. под гору (*fig.*) to go downhill. **2.** (*coll.*) to rush, tear. **3.** to flow, stream; (*fig.*) to roll; слёзы ~ти́лись по её щека́м tears were rolling down her cheeks; день ~ти́тся за днём day after day rolls by. **4.** (*coll.*) ~ти́сь, ~ти́тесь отсю́да! get out!

ка́т|кий (~ок, ~ка́), *adj.* (*coll.*) **1.** that can be rolled easily. **2.** slippery.

като́д, а, m. (*phys.*) cathode.

като́дн|ый, *adj.* (*phys.*) cathodic; ~ые лучи́ cathode rays; ~ая тру́бка cathode-ray tube.

кат|о́к[1], ка́, m. skating-rink.

кат|о́к[2], ка́, m. 1. (*in var. senses*) roller. **2.** к. (для белья́) mangle.

като́лик, а, m. (Roman) Catholic.

католико́с, а, m. Catholicos (*head of the Armenian Church*).

католици́зм, а, m. (Roman) Catholicism.

католи́ческий, *adj.* (Roman) Catholic.

католи́честв|о, а, n. (Roman) Catholicism.

католи́чк|а, и, ƒ. of като́лик.

ка́торг|а, и, *no pl.*, *ƒ.* penal servitude, hard labour (*in a place of exile*).

каторжа́н|ин, ина, *pl.* ~е, ~, *m.* convict; ex-convict.

ка́торжник, а, *m.* convict.

ка́тор|жный, *adj. of* ~га; ~жные рабо́ты hard labour; (*fig.*) drudgery; ~жная тюрьма́ convict prison.

кату́шк|а, и, *f.* 1. reel, bobbin; (*text.*) spool. 2. (*electr.*) coil, bobbin.

ка́тыш, а, *m.* 1. pellet, ball. 2. block of wood.

ка́тыш|ек, ка, *m.* (*coll.*) pellet.

катю́ш|а, и, *f.* (*mil.*; *coll.*) Katyusha (*lorry-mounted multiple rocket launcher*).

каузáльный, *adj.* (*philos.*) causal.

кау́рый, *adj.* (*of colour of horses*) light-chestnut.

каусти́ческий, *adj.* (*chem.*) caustic.

каучу́к, а, *m.* (india-)rubber, caoutchouc.

каучу́к|овый, *adj. of* ~; rubber.

каучуконо́с, а, *m.* (*bot.*) rubber-bearing plant.

кафе́, *indecl.*, *n.* café.

ка́федр|а, ы, *f.* 1. pulpit; rostrum, platform; говори́ть с ~ы to speak from the platform. 2. (*fig.*; *at a university*) chair; получи́ть ~у to obtain a chair. 3. (*fig.*; *at a university*) department, sub-faculty; заседа́ние ~ы sub-faculty meeting.

кафедра́льный, *adj.*; к. собо́р cathedral.

ка́фел|ь, я, *m.* Dutch tile.

ка́фель|ный, *adj. of* ~; ~ная печь tiled stove.

кафете́ри|й, я, *m.* cafeteria.

кафешанта́н, а, *m.* café chantant.

кафоли́ческий, *adj.* (*epithet of the Orthodox Church*) ecumenical, universal.

кафта́н, а, *m.* caftan.

каца́п, а, *m.* 'butcher' (*term of abuse used by Ukrainians of Russians*).

кача́лк|а, и, *f.* rocking-chair; конь-к. rocking-horse.

кача́ни|е, я, *n.* 1. rocking, swinging; к. ма́ятника swing of pendulum. 2. pumping.

кач|а́ть, а́ю, *impf.* (*of* ~ну́ть) 1. (+*a.* or *i.*) to rock, swing; to shake; к. колыбе́ль to rock a cradle; к. голово́й to nod, shake one's head; (*impers.*) его́ ~а́ло из стороны́ в сто́рону he was reeling; ло́дку ~а́ет the boat is rolling. 2. to lift up, chair (*as mark of esteem or congratulation*). 3. to pump.

кач|а́ться, а́юсь, *impf.* (*of* ~ну́ться) 1. to rock, swing (*intrans.*); (*of vessel*) to roll, pitch. 2. to reel, stagger.

каче́л|и, ей, *no sing.* (*child's*) swing.

ка́чественный, *adj.* 1. qualitative. 2. high-quality.

ка́честв|о, а, *n.* 1. quality; ни́зкого ~a of inferior quality; в ~е (+*g.*) in the character (of), in the capacity (of); в ~е преподава́тельницы она́ отли́чна (in her capacity) as a teacher she is excellent. 2. (*chess*)

вы́играть, проигра́ть к. to gain, lose an exchange.

ка́чк|а, и, *f.* rocking; tossing; (*naut.*) бортова́я к. rolling; килева́я к. pitching.

ка́чкий, *adj.* (*coll.*) unstable, wobbly.

кач|ну́ть(ся), ну́(сь), нёшь(ся), *pf. of* ~а́ть(ся).

ка|чу́, ~ти́шь, *see* ~ти́ть.

качу́рк|а, и, *f.* (*orn.*) petrel.

ка́ш|а, и, *f.* 1. kasha (*dish of cooked grain or groats*); ма́нная к. semolina; ри́совая к. boiled rice. 2. (*fig.*, *coll.*) берёзовая к. the birch; с ним ~и не сва́ришь one can't get on with him; у него́ к. во рту he mumbles; ма́ло ~и ел (*of someone young and/or inexperienced*); сапоги́ у тебя́ ~и про́сят your boots are agape; завари́ть ~у to start something, stir up trouble; расхлеба́ть ~у to put things right.

кашало́т, а, *m.* (*zool.*) cachalot, sperm-whale.

кашева́р, а, *m.* (*obs.*) cook (*in mil. unit or workmen's canteen*).

ка́ш|ель, ля, *m.* cough.

кашеми́р, а, *m.* (*text.*) cashmere.

ка́шиц|а, ы, *f.* (*coll.*) thin gruel; бума́жная к. paper pulp.

ка́шк|а¹, ки, *f.* *dim. of* ~a; pap.

ка́шк|а², и, *f.* (*bot.*; *coll.*) clover.

ка́шлян|уть, у, ешь, *pf.* to give a cough.

ка́шля|ть, ю, *impf.* 1. to cough. 2. to have a cough.

кашне́, *indecl.*, *n.* scarf, muffler.

кашта́н, а, *m.* 1. chestnut; таска́ть ~ы из огня́ (*fig.*) to pull the chestnuts out of the fire. 2. chestnut-tree; ко́нский к. horse-chestnut.

кашта́н|овый, *adj.* 1. *adj. of* ~. 2. chestnut (-coloured).

каю́к¹, а, *m.* caique.

каю́к² (*coll.*) *only in phrase* к. (пришёл) (+*d.*) it's the end (of); тут ему́ и к. that's the end of him, he's done for.

каю́р, а, *m.* dog-team (*or reindeer-team*) driver.

каю́т|а, ы, *f.* cabin, stateroom.

каю́т-компа́ни|я, и, *f.* 1. (*on warships*) wardroom. 2. (*on passenger vessels*) passengers' lounge.

ка́|ющийся, *pres. part. of* ~яться *and adj.* repentant, contrite, penitent.

ка́|яться, юсь, ешься, *impf.* 1. (*pf.* рас~) (в+*p.*) to repent (of); он сам тепе́рь ~ется he is sorry himself now. 2. (*pf.* по~) (в+*p.*) to confess. 3. (*coll.*) ~юсь I am sorry to say, I (must) confess; я, ~юсь, совсе́м об э́том забы́л I am sorry to say I had forgotten all about it.

квадра́нт, а, *m.* 1. (*math.*) quadrant. 2. (*mil.*) quadrant, gunner's clinometer.

квадра́т, а, *m.* (*math.*) square; возвести́ в к. to square; в ~e squared; (*fig., joc.*) дура́к в ~e doubly a fool.

квадра́тн|ый, *adj.* square; (*anat.*) ~ая мы́шца quadrate muscle; (*math.*) к. ко́рень square root; ~ое уравне́ние quadratic equation.

квадрату́р|а, ы, *f.* (*math.*) quadrature; (*fig.*) к. кру́га squaring the circle.

квадрильо́н, а, *m.* (*math.*) quadrillion.

ква́зи- quasi-.

квазизвезд|а́, ы́, *f.* (*astron.*) quasar.

ква́канье|е, я, *n.* croaking.

ква́ка|ть, ю, *impf.* to croak.

квакн|уть, у, ешь, *pf.* to give a croak.

ква́кушк|а, и, *f.* (*coll.*) frog.

квалификац|ио́нный, *adj.* of ~ия; ~ио́нная коми́ссия board of experts.

квалифика́ци|я, и, *f.* qualification.

квалифици́рова|нный (~н, ~на), *p.p.p.* of ~ть *and adj.* 1. qualified, skilled. 2. к. труд skilled work, specialist work.

квалифици́р|овать, ую, *impf. and pf.* 1. to check, test. 2. to qualify (as); как к. тако́е поведе́ние? how should one qualify such conduct?

квант, а, *m. and* ~а, ~ы, *f.* (*phys.*) quantum.

ква́нт|овый, *adj.* of ~; ~овая тео́рия quantum theory.

ква́рт|а, ы, *f.* 1. (*liquid measure*) quart. 2. (*mus.*) fourth. 3.(*fencing and cards*) quart.

кварта́л, а, *m.* 1. block (*of buildings*); (*obs.*) quarter, ward. 2. quarter (*of year*).

кварта́льн|ый, *adj.* 1. quarterly; к. отчёт quarterly account. 2. of quarter of city; (*as noun*) к., ~ого, *m.* (*hist.*; *coll.*) non-commissioned police officer.

кварте́т, а, *m.* (*mus.*) quartet(te).

кварти́р|а, ы, *f.* 1. flat; lodging; apartment(s); к. и стол board and lodging; сдаётся к. flat, apartment(s) to let; гла́вная к. (*mil.*) general headquarters. 2. *pl.* (*mil.*) quarters, billets; зи́мние ~ы winter quarters.

квартира́нт, а, *m.* lodger, tenant.

квартира́нт|ка, ки, *f.* of ~.

квартирме́йстер, а, *m.* (*mil. and naut.*) quartermaster.

кварти́рник, а, *m.* (*obs.*) craftsman working at home.

кварти́р|ный, *adj.* of ~a; ~ная пла́та rent; ~ное расположе́ние (*mil.*) billeting.

квартир|ова́ть, у́ю, *impf.* 1. (*coll.*) to lodge. 2. (*mil.*) to be billeted, be quartered.

квартиронанима́тел|ь, я, *m.* tenant.

квартирохозя́ин, а, *m.* landlord.

квартирохозя́йк|а, и, *f.* landlady.

квартпла́т|а, ы, *f.* (*abbr. of* кварти́рная пла́та) rent.

кварц, а, *m.* (*min.*) quartz.

кварц|евый, *adj.* of ~.

кварци́т, а, *m.* (*min.*) quartzite.

квас, а, *pl.* ~ы́, *m.* kvass.

ква́|сить, шу, сишь, *impf.* to pickle; to make sour.

квас|но́й, *adj.* of ~; к. патриоти́зм (*fig.*) jingoism.

квас|о́к, ка́, *m.* 1. *dim. of* ~. 2. (*coll.*) sour tang.

квасцо́вый, *adj.* (*chem.*) aluminous.

квасц|ы́, о́в, *no sing.* (*chem.*) alum.

квашени́н|а, ы, *f.* 1. (*coll.*) sauerkraut. 2. (*agric.*) fermented vegetable leaves.

ква́шен|ый, *adj.* sour, fermented; ~ая капу́ста sauerkraut.

квашн|я́, и́, *g. pl.* ~е́й, *f.* 1. kneading trough. 2. (*dial.*) leavened dough.

квёл|ый (~, ~а́, ~о), *adj.* (*dial. or fig.*) weakly, poorly.

кве́рху, *adv.* up, upwards.

кви́нт|а, ы, *f.* (*mus.*) fifth; (*coll.*) пове́сить нос на ~у to look dejected.

квинте́т, а, *m.* (*mus.*) quintet(te).

квинтэссе́нци|я, и, *f.* quintessence.

квит, ~ы, *as pred.* (*coll.*) quits; мы с тобо́й ~ы we are quits.

квитанц|ио́нный, *adj. of* ~ия.

квита́нци|я, и, *f.* receipt; бага́жная к. luggage-ticket.

квит|о́к, ка́, *m.* (*coll.*) ticket, check.

кво́рум, а, *m.* quorum.

кво́т|а, ы, *f.* quota.

ке́гель = кегль.

кегельба́н, а, *m.* skittle-alley.

ке́гл|и, ей, *sing.* ~я, ~и, *f.* skittles.

кегл|ь, я, *m.* (*typ.*) point; к. 8 8 point.

кедр, а, *m.* cedar; гимала́йский к. deodar; лива́нский к. cedar of Lebanon; сиби́рский к. Siberian pine; европе́йский к. Cembran (Arolla) pine.

кедро́вк|а, и, *f.* (*orn.*) nutcracker.

кедр|о́вый, *adj.* of ~; к. стла́ник dwarf Siberian pine (*Pinus pumila*).

ке́д|ы, ов *or* ~, *no sing.* baseball boots, tennis shoes.

кейф, а, *m.* (*coll., obs.*) (taking one's) ease, putting one's feet up.

кекс, а, *m.* fruit-cake.

ке́лар|ь, я, *m.* (*eccl.*) cellarer.

келе́йник, а, *m.* (*eccl.*) lay brother.

келе́йно, *adv.* in secret, privately; они́ к. реши́ли де́ло they decided the matter in camera.

келе́йный, *adj.* 1. *adj. of* ке́лья. 2. (*fig., pejor.*) secret, private.

кельт, а, *m.* Celt.

ке́льтский, *adj.* Celtic.

ке́л|ья, ьи, *g. pl.* ~ий, *f.* (*eccl.*) cell.

кем, *i. of* кто.

ке́мпинг, а, *m.* camping-site.

кенгуру́, *indecl.*, *m.* kangaroo.

кента́вр, а, *m.* (*myth.*) centaur.

ке́пк|а, и, *f.* (*coll.*) cloth cap.

кера́мик|а, и, *f.* ceramics.

керами́ческий, *adj.* ceramic.

ке́рвел|ь, я, *m.* (*bot.*) chervil; ди́кий к. cow-parsley.

керога́з, а, *m.* paraffin stove.

кероси́н, а, *m.* paraffin, kerosene.

кероси́нк|а, и, *f.* (*coll.*) paraffin stove.

кероси́н|овый, *adj.* of ~; ~овая ла́мпа oil lamp.

ке́сарев, *adj.* (*med.*) ~о сече́ние Caesarean section.

ке́сар|ь, я, *m.* monarch, lord.

кессо́н, а, *m.* (*tech.*) caisson, coffer-dam.

кессо́н|ный, *adj.* of ~; ~ная боле́знь caisson disease.

ке́т|а, ы, *f.* Siberian salmon.

кетме́н|ь, я, *m.* (*agric.*) ketmen (*kind of hoe used in Central Asia*).

ке́т|овый, *adj.* of ~а.

кефа́л|ь, и, *f.* grey mullet.

кефи́р, а, *m.* kefir.

киберне́тик|а, и, *f.* cybernetics.

кибернети́ческий, *adj.* cybernetic.

киби́тк|а, и, *f.* 1. kibitka, covered wagon. 2. nomad tent.

кив|а́ть, а́ю, *impf.* (*of* ~ну́ть) 1. (голово́й) to nod (one's head); to nod assent. 2. (на + *a.*) to motion (to); (*fig.*) refer (to), put the blame (on to).

ки́вер, а, *pl.* ~а́, *m.* shako.

кив|ну́ть, ну́, нёшь, *pf. of* ~а́ть.

кив|о́к, ка́, *m.* nod.

ки|да́ть, да́ю, *impf.* (*of* ~ну́ть) to throw, fling, cast (*usage as for* броса́ть).

ки|да́ться, да́юсь, *impf.* (*of* ~ну́ться) 1. to throw oneself, fling oneself; to rush. 2. (+ *i.*) to throw, fling, shy. 3. *pass. of* ~да́ть.

кизи́л, а, *m.* (*bot.*) cornel.

кизя́к, а́, *m.* pressed dung (*used as fuel*).

ки|й, я, *pl.* ~и́, ~ёв, *m.* (billiard) cue.

кикимор|а, ы, *f.* 1. (*folklore*) kikimora (*hobgoblin in female form*). 2. (*fig., coll.*) вы́глядеть ~ой to look a fright.

кикс, а, *m.* (*sl.*) miss (*at billiards*).

кил|а́, ы́, *f.* (*dial.*) rupture, hernia.

килева́ни|е, я, *n.* (*naut.*) careening, careenage.

кил|ева́ть, у́ю, *impf.* (*naut.*) to careen.

кил|ево́й, *adj.* of ~ь; ~ева́я ка́чка pitching.

кило́, *indecl.*, *n.* kilogram(me).

килова́тт, а, *m.* (*electr.*) kilowatt.

килогра́мм, а, *m.* kilogram(me).

килокало́ри|я, и, *f.* large calorie.

киломе́тр, а, *m.* kilometre.

кил|ь, я, *m.* 1. (*naut.*) keel. 2. (*aeron.*) fin.

кильва́тер, а, *m.* (*naut.*) wake; идти́ в к.

(+ *d.*) to follow in the wake (of).

кильва́тер|ный, *adj.* of ~; ~ная коло́нна line ahead.

ки́льк|а, и, *f.* sprat.

кимва́л, а, *m.* cymbal.

кимоно́, *indecl.*, *n.* kimono.

кингсто́н, а, *m.* (*naut.*) Kingston valve; откры́ть ~ы to scuttle (a ship).

кинемато́граф, а, *m.* (*obs.*) cinematograph.

кинематографи́ческий, *adj.* cinematographic.

кинематогра́фи|я, и, *f.* cinematography.

кинеско́п, а, *m.* television tube.

кине́тик|а, и, *f.* (*phys.*) kinetics.

кинети́ческий, *adj.* (*phys.*) kinetic.

кинжа́л, а, *m.* dagger.

кинжа́л|ьный, *adj.* 1. *adj.* of ~. 2. (*mil.*) close-range, hand-to-hand.

кино́, *indecl.*, *n.* (*abstr. and concr.*) cinema.

кино- film-, cine-.

киноаппара́т, а, *m.* cinecamera.

киноаппарату́р|а, ы, *f.* cinematographic equipment.

киноарти́ст, а, *m.* film actor.

киноарти́стк|а, и, *f.* film actress.

киноателье́, *indecl.*, *n.* film studio.

ки́новар|ь, и, *f.* cinnabar, vermilion.

кинове́дени|е, я, *n.* study of the film (*as an art*)

кинокарти́н|а, ы, *f.* (*non-documentary*) film.

кироле́нт|а, ы, *f.* reel (of film).

киномеха́ник, а, *m.* cinema operator.

кинооперáтор, а, *m.* camera-man.

кинопередви́жк|а, и, *f.* portable (motion picture) projector.

киноплёнк|а, и, *f.* (ciné) film.

кинорежиссёр, а, *m.* film director.

киносеа́нс, а, *m.* (cinema) performance, showing.

киносту́ди|я, и, *f.* film studio.

киносъёмк|а, и, *f.* filming, shooting.

кинотеа́тр, а, *m.* cinema.

киноустано́вк|а, и, *f.* projecting machine.

кинофика́ци|я, и, *f.* 1. inclusion in cinema circuit. 2. adaptation for the cinema, for the screen.

кинофици́р|овать, ую, *impf. and pf.* 1. to include in cinema circuit, bring cinema to. 2. to adapt for the cinema, for the screen.

кинохро́ник|а, и, *f.* news-reel.

ки́|нуть(ся), ну(сь), нешь(ся), *pf. of* ~да́ть(ся).

кио́ск, а, *m.* kiosk, stall; газе́тный к. news-stand.

киоскёр, а, *m.* stall-holder.

кио́т, а, *m.* icon-case.

ки́п|а, ы, *f.* 1. pile, stack. 2. (*measure*) pack, bale; к. хло́пка bale of cotton.

кипари́с, а, *m.* (*bot.*) cypress.

кипе́ни|е, я, *n.* boiling; то́чка ~я boiling point.

кип|е́ть, лю́, и́шь, *impf.* (*of* вс~) to boil, seethe; к. ключо́м to gush up; к. негодова́нием (*fig.*) to seethe with indignation; рабо́та ~е́ла work was in full swing; как в котле́ к. to be hard pressed.

кипре́|й, я, *m.* (*bot.*) willow-herb.

кипу́чест|ь, и, *f.* ebullience, turbulence.

кипу́ч|ий (~, ~а), *adj.* 1. boiling, seething. 2. (*fig.*) ebullient, turbulent; ~ая де́ятельность feverish activity.

кипяти́льник, а, *m.* kettle, boiler, boiling--tank.

кипяти́льный, *adj.* boiling; к. бак copper.

кипя|ти́ть, чу́, ти́шь, *impf.* (*of* вс~) to boil.

кипя|ти́ться, чу́сь, ти́шься, *impf.* 1. to boil (*intrans.*) 2. (*fig., coll.*) to get excited. 3. *pass. of* ~ти́ть.

кипят|о́к, ка́, *m.* 1. boiling water. 2. (*fig., coll.*) testy person, irritable person.

кипячёный, *adj.* boiled.

кира́с|а, ы, *f.* (*mil., hist.*) cuirass.

кираси́р, а, *m.* (*mil., hist.*) cuirassier.

кирги́з, а, *m.* Kirghiz.

кирги́зк|а, и, *f.* Kirghiz (woman).

кирги́зский, *adj.* Kirghiz.

кири́ллиц|а, ы, *f.* Cyrillic alphabet.

ки́рк|а, и, *f.* (Protestant) church.

кирк|а́, и́, *f.* pick(axe).

кирк|о́вый, *adj. of* ~а́.

киркомоты́г|а, и, *f.* pickaxe.

кирпи́ч, а́, *m.* 1. brick. 2. (*collect.*) bricks; необожжённый, сама́нный к. adobe. 3. (*coll.*) no-entry sign.

кирпи́ч|ик, а, *m.* 1. *dim. of* ~. 2. (*pl.*) bricks (*as child's plaything*).

кирпи́ч|ный, *adj. of* ~; к. заво́д brickworks; к. чай brick-tea.

киря́|ть, ю, *impf.* (*sl.*) to booze.

ки́с|а, ы, *f.* = ~ка.

кисе́|йный, *adj. of* ~я; (*coll., obs.*) ~йная ба́рышня prim young lady.

кисе́л|ь, я́, *m.* kissel (*kind of blancmange*); (*fig., coll.*) деся́тая (*or* седьма́я) вода́ на ~е́ distant connexion, distant relative; за семь вёрст ~я́ хлеба́ть to go a long way for nothing, to go on a fool's errand.

кисе́ль|ный, *adj. of* ~; моло́чные ре́ки, ~ные берега́ land flowing with milk and honey.

кисе́т, а, *m.* tobacco pouch.

кисе́|я, и́, *f.* muslin.

ки́ск|а, и, *f.* (*coll.*) puss, pussy-cat.

кис-ки́с, *interj.* puss-puss! (*when calling cat*).

ки́сленький, *adj.* (*coll.*) slightly sour.

кисле́|ть, ю, *impf.* (*coll.*) to become sour.

кисли́нк|а, *f.*, *only in phrase* с ~ой (*coll.*) slightly sour, sourish.

кислова́т|ый (~, ~а), *adj.* sourish; acidulous.

кислоро́д, а, *m.* oxygen.

кислоро́дно-ацетиле́новый, *adj.* oxy-acety-lene.

кислоро́дный, *adj.* (*chem.*) oxygen.

ки́сло-сла́дкий, *adj.* sour-sweet.

кислот|а́, ы́, *pl.* ~ы, *f.* 1. sourness; acidity. 2. (*chem.*) acid.

кисло́тност|ь, и, *f.* (*chem.*) acidity.

кисло́тный, *adj.* (*chem.*) acid.

кислотоупо́рный, *adj.* (*tech.*) acid-proof; acid resistant.

ки́с|лый (~ел, ~ла́, ~ло), *adj.* 1. sour; (*fig.*) ~лое настрое́ние sour mood; ~лая улы́бка sour smile. 2. fermented; ~лая капу́ста sauerkraut; ~лые щи sauerkraut soup. 3. (*chem.*) acid.

кисля́тин|а, ы, *f.* (*coll.*) 1. sour(-tasting) stuff. 2. (*fig., pejor.*) sour puss, misery.

ки́с|нуть, ну, нешь, *past* ~, ~ла, *impf.* 1. to turn sour. 2. (*fig., coll.*) to mope; to look sour.

кист|а́, ы́, *f.* (*med.*) cyst.

кистеви́дный, *adj.* (*bot.*) racemose.

кисте́н|ь, я́, *m.* bludgeon, flail.

ки́сточк|а, и, *f.* 1. brush; к. для бритья́ shaving-brush. 2. tassel.

кист|ь¹, и, *pl.* ~и, ~е́й, *f.* 1. (*bot.*) cluster, bunch; к. виногра́да bunch of grapes. 2. brush; маля́рная к. paintbrush. 3. tassel.

кист|ь², и, *pl.* ~и, ~е́й, *f.* hand.

кит, а́, *m.* whale.

китаеве́д, а, *m.* sinologist, sinologue.

китаеве́дени|е, я, *n.* sinology.

кита́|ец, йца, *pl.* ~йцы, ~йцев, *m.* Chinese, Chinaman.

китаизи́р|овать, ую, *impf.* to sinify, adapt to Chinese conditions.

кита́ист, а, *m.* sinologist, sinologue.

кита́йк|а, и, *f.* (*text.*) nankeen.

кита́йск|ий, *adj.* Chinese; ~ая гра́мота double-dutch; к. и́дол joss; к. храм joss-house; ~ая тушь India(n) ink.

китайч|о́нок, о́нка, *pl.* ~а́та, ~а́т, *m.* Chinese child.

китая́нк|а, и, *f.* Chinese woman.

ки́тел|ь, я, *pl.* ~я́, ~е́й, *m.* (*single-breasted, military or naval*) jacket with high collar.

китобо́|й, я, *m.* whaler, whaling ship.

китобо́йн|ый, *adj.* whaling; к. про́мысел whaling; ~ое су́дно whaler.

кит|о́вый, *adj. of* ~; к. жир blubber; к. ус whalebone, baleen.

китоло́в, а, *m.* whaleman.

кито|ло́вный, *adj.* = ~бо́йный.

китообра́зный, *adj.* (*zool.*) cetacean.

кич|и́ться, у́сь, и́шься, *impf.* (+*i.*) to plume oneself (on); to strut.

ки́чк|а, и, *f.* (*dial.*) 1. kichka (*married woman's head-dress*). 2. (*fig.*) front (*of boat*).

кичли́вост|ь, и, *f.* conceit; arrogance.

кичли́в|ый (~, ~а), *adj.* conceited, arrogant, haughty, strutting.

киш|éть, ý, и́шь, *impf.* (+*i.*) to swarm (with), teem (with).

кишéчник, а, *m.* (*anat.*) bowels, intestines; очи́стить к. to open the bowels.

киш|éчный, *adj. of* ~éчник *and* ~кá; intestinal.

киш|кá, ки́, *g. pl.* ~óк, *f.* **1.** (*anat.*) gut, intestine; двенадцатипéрстная к. duodenum; прямáя к. rectum; слепáя к. caecum; тóнкая, тóлстая к. small, large intestine; (*fig., coll.*) к. тонкá! he, *etc.*, isn't up to that!; вы́пустить ~ки́ to disembowel; лезть из ~óк to put one's guts into; надорвáть ~ки́ (сó смеху) to laugh oneself sick; тянýться ~кóй to go in file. **2.** hose; поли́ть ~кóй to hose.

кишлáк, á, *m.* kishlak (*village in Central Asia*).

кишлá|чный, *adj. of* ~к.

кишми́ш, á, *no pl., m.* raisins, sultanas.

кишмя́, *adv., only in phrase* к. кишéть to swarm.

клавеси́н, а, *m.* (*mus.*) harpsichord.

клавиатýр|а, ы, *f.* keyboard.

клавикóрд|ы, ов, *no sing.* (*mus.*) clavichord.

клáвиш|а, и, *m.* key (*of piano, typewriter, etc.*).

клáвиш|а, и, *f.* = ~.

клáвиш|ный, *adj. of* ~; ~ные инструмéнты keyboard instruments.

клад, а, *m.* treasure; (*fig., coll.*) treasure (-house); моя́ секретáрша — настоя́щий к. my secretary is a real treasure.

клáдбищ|е, а, *n.* cemetery, graveyard; churchyard.

кладби́щенский, *adj. of* клáдбище; к. стóрож sexton.

клáдез|ь, я, *m., arch., now only in joc. phrase* к. премýдрости mine of information.

клáд|ка, и, *f.* laying; кáменная к. masonry; кирпи́чная к. brickwork.

кладов|áя, óй, *f.* pantry, larder; storeroom.

кладóвк|а, и, *f.* (*coll.*) pantry, larder.

кладовщи́к, á, *m.* storeman.

кла|дý, дёшь, *see* ~сть.

клáдчик, а, *m.* bricklayer.

клад|ь, и, *f.* **1.** (*sing. only*) load; ручнáя к. hand luggage. **2.** haycock.

клáк|а, и, *no pl., f.* (*collect.*) claque.

клакёр, а, *m.* (*theatr.*) claqueur.

клан, а, *m.* clan.

кля́ня|ться, юсь, *impf.* (*of* поклони́ться) **1.** (+*d. or* с+*i.*) to bow (to); to greet; к. в пóяс to bow from the waist; (*fig.*) мы с ним не ~емся I am not on speaking terms with him; честь имéю к. *obs. leave-taking formula.* **2.** to send, convey greetings; ~йтесь емý от меня́ give him my regards. **3.** (+*d. or* пéред; *coll.*) to cringe (before); to humiliate oneself (before). **4.** (+*d. and i.; obs.*) lay before, offer; к. комý-н. хлéбом-сóлью to offer someone hospitality.

клáпан, а, *m.* **1.** (*tech.*) valve; предохрани́тельный к. safety valve. **2.** (*mus.*) vent. **3.** (*anat.*) сердéчный к. mitral valve. **4.** (*on clothing, etc.*) flap.

кларнéт, а, *m.* clarinet.

кларнети́ст, а, *m.* clarinettist.

класс, а, *m.* **1.** (*in various senses*) class; роспóдствующий, прáвящий к. ruling class; к. млекопитáющих (class of) mammalia; игрá высóкого ~a high class play. **2.** class-room.

клáссик, а, *m.* **1.** (*in various senses* (classic; classic(al) author. **2.** classical scholar.

клáссик|а, и, *f.* the classics.

классификáтор, а, *m.* classifier.

классификáци|я, и, *f.* classification.

классифици́р|овать, ую, *impf. and pf.* to classify.

классици́зм, а, *m.* **1.** (*lit., art*) classicism. **2.** classical education.

класси́ческий, *adj.* (*in var. senses*) classic(al).

клáсс|ный, *adj.* (*of* ~) **1.** ~ная доскá blackboard; ~ная кóмната classroom; ~ная рабóта class work. **2.** к. вагóн passenger coach. **3.** (*sport*) first-class. **4.** (*sl.*) classy.

клáссовост|ь, и, *f.* class character.

клáссов|ый, *adj.* (*polit.*) class; ~ая борьбá class struggle; к. враг class enemy; ~ые разли́чия class distinctions; ~ое сознáние class-consciousness.

клáсс|ы, ов (*children's game*) hopscotch.

кла|сть, дý, past ~л, ~ла, *impf.* (*of* положи́ть) **1.** to lay; to put (*into prone position or fig.*); to place; к. больнóго на носи́лки to lay a patient on a stretcher; к. сáхар в чай to put sugar in one's tea; к. на мéсто to replace; к. не на мéсто to mislay; к. на мýзыку to set to music; к. в лýзу, к. шарá (*billiards*) to pocket a ball; к. я́йца to lay eggs (*of birds and insects*); к. руль (*naut.*) to put the wheel over; к. начáло, к. конéц чемý-н. to start something, put an end to something; (*fig.*) к. под сукнó to shelve. **2.** (*pf.* сложи́ть) to build. **3.** to assign, set aside (*time, money*); мы ~дём пятьдеся́т рублéй на э́ту поéздку we are setting aside fifty roubles for this trip.

клáузул|а, ы, *f.* (*leg.*) clause, proviso, stipulation.

клёв, а, *m.* biting, bite; сегóдня хорóший к. the fish are biting well today.

кл|евáть, юю, юёшь, *impf.* (*of* ~юнуть) **1.** to peck. **2.** (*of fish*) to bite; вчерá ры́ба не ~евáла the fish were not biting yesterday. **3.** (*coll.*) к. нóсом to nod (*from drowsiness*). **4.** (*fig., impers., coll.*) ~юёт things are going well, better.

кл|евáться, ~юётся, *impf.* (*of birds*) to peck (one another).

клёвер, а, *m.* (*bot.*) clover.
клёвер|ный, *adj. of ~*.
клевет|а́, ы́, *f.* slander; calumny, aspersion; libel; возвести́ на кого́-н. ~у́ to slander someone, cast aspersions on someone.
клеве|та́ть, щу́, ~щешь, *impf.* (*of* на~) (на+*a.*) to slander, calumniate; to libel.
клеветни́к, а́, *m.* slanderer.
клеветн|и́ца, и́цы, *f. of ~и́к.*
клеветни́ческий, *adj.* slanderous; libellous, defamatory.
клеве|щу́, ~щешь, *see ~та́ть.*
клев|о́к, ка́, *m.* (*coll.*) 1. peck. 2. (*mil.*) burst (of shrapnel) on impact.
клевре́т, а, *m.* (*obs.*) minion, creature.
клёвый, *adj.* (*sl.*) nice; attractive.
кле|ево́й, *adj. of ~й;* ~ева́я кра́ска size paint.
клеёнк|а, и, *f.* oil-cloth.
клеёнчатый, *adj.* oilskin.
клеёный, *adj.* gummed, glued.
кле́|ить, ю, ишь, *impf.* 1. (*pf.* с~) to glue; to gum; to paste. 2. (*pf.* под~) к. де́вушку (*sl.*) to pick up a girl.
кле́|иться, ится, *impf.* (*coll.*) 1. to become sticky. 2. (*fig.; usually with neg.*) to get on, go well; моя́ рабо́та что́-то пло́хо ~ится my work is not going too well somehow; разгово́р не ~и́лся the conversation was sticky. 3. *pass. of ~ить.*
кле|й, я, о ~е, на ~ю́, *m.* glue; мучно́й к. paste; пти́чий к. bird-lime; ры́бий к. isinglass; fish-glue; к. и но́жницы (*iron.*) scissors and paste.
кле́йк|а, и, *f.* glueing.
кле́йк|ий, *adj.* sticky; ~ая бума́га (для мух) fly-paper.
клейкови́н|а, ы, *f.* gluten.
кле́йкост|ь, и, *f.* stickiness.
клеймёный, *adj.* branded.
клейм|и́ть, лю́, и́шь, *impf.* (*of* за~) to brand, stamp; (*fig.*) to brand, stigmatize; к. позо́ром to hold up to shame.
клеймле́ни|е, я, *n.* branding, stamping.
клейм|о́, а́, *pl.* ~а, *n.* brand, stamp; пробирное к. hall-mark, mark of assay; фабри́чное к. trade-mark; к. позо́ра (*fig.*) stigma.
кле́йстер, а, *m.* paste.
клёкот, а, *m.* (*of birds*) scream.
клеко|та́ть, чу́, ~чешь, *impf.* (*of birds*) to scream.
клёмм|а, ы, *f.* (*electr.*) terminal.
клён, а, *m.* maple.
клёновый, *adj. of* клён.
клепа́л|о, а, *n.* (*tech.; obs.*) riveting hammer.
клепа́льн|ый, *adj.* riveting; ~ая маши́на riveter, riveting machine.
клепа́льщик, а, *m.* riveter (*operator*).
клёпаный, *adj.* (*tech.*) riveted.
клепа́|ть¹, ю, *impf.* (*tech.*) to rivet.

клеп|а́ть², лю́, ~лешь, *impf.* (*of* наклепа́ть) (на+*a.; coll.*) to slander, cast aspersions (on).
клёпк|а¹, и, *f.* riveting.
клёпк|а², и, *f.* stave, lag; (*fig., coll.*) у него́ како́й-то ~и не хвата́ет he has got a screw loose.
клептома́н, а, *m.* kleptomaniac.
клептома́ни|я, и, *f.* kleptomania.
клерикали́зм, а, *m.* (*polit.*) clericalism.
клер|ова́ть, у́ю, *impf.* (*tech.*) to refine, clarify.
клёст, а́, *m.* (*orn.*) crossbill.
клётк|а, и, *f.* 1. cage; coop; hutch. 2. (*on paper*) square; (*on material*) check. 3. (*anat.*) грудна́я к. thorax. 4. (*biol.*) cell.
клетн|ева́ть, юю, юешь, *impf.* (*naut.*) to serve (*a rope*).
клету́шк|а, и, *f.* (*coll.*) closet, tiny room.
клетча́тк|а, и, *f.* 1. (*bot., tech.*) cellulose. 2. (*anat.*) cellular tissue.
клётчатый, *adj.* 1. checked; к. плато́к checked head-scarf. 2. (*biol.*) cellular.
клет|ь, и, *pl.* ~и, ~е́й, *f.* 1. (*dial.*) store-room; shed. 2. (*in mines*) cage.
клёцк|а, и, *f.* (*cul.*) dumpling.
клёш, а, *m.* (*and indecl. adj.*) flare; ~и, брю́ки-к. flared trousers, bell-bottomed trousers; ю́бка-к. flared skirt.
клешн|я́, и́, *g. pl.* ~е́й, *f.* claw (*of a crustacean*).
клещ, а́, *m.* (*zool.*) tick.
клещеви́н|а, ы, *f.* (*bot.*) Palma Christi (*castor-oil plant*).
клещ|и́, е́й, *no sing.* 1. pincers, tongs; (*fig. coll.*) э́того из меня́ ~а́ми не вы́тянешь wild horses shall not drag it from me. 2. (*mil.; fig.*) pincers, pincer-movement.
кли́вер, а, *m.* (*naut.*) jib.
клие́нт, а, *m.* client.
клиенту́р|а, ы, *f.* (*collect.*) clientèle.
кли́зм|а, ы, *f.* (*med.*) enema, cluster; ста́вить ~у (+*d.*) to give an enema.
клик, а, *m.* (*poet.*) cry, call.
кли́к|а, и, *f.* clique.
кли́к|ать, чу, чешь, *impf.* (*of* ~нуть) 1. (*coll.*) to call, hail. 2. (+*a. and i.; dial.*) to call (*name*); его́ ~чут Ива́ном he is called Ivan. 3. (*of geese and swans*) to honk.
кли́к|нуть, ну, нешь, *pf. of* ~ать.
кликуш|а, и, *f.* hysterical woman.
кликушеский, *adj.* hysterical.
кликушеств|о, а, *n.* hysterics.
кли́макс, а, *m.* = климакте́рий.
климакте́ри|й, я, *m.* (*physiol.*) climacteric.
климакте́рический, *adj.* (*physiol.*) climacteric.
кли́мат, а, *m.* climate.
климати́ческий, *adj.* climatic.
клин, а, *pl.* ~ья, ~ьев, *m.* 1. wedge; загна́ть к. (в+*a.*) to drive a wedge (into); борода́

~ом wedge-shaped beard; (*fig.*) вбить к. (между) to drive a wedge (between); к. ~ом вышибается (*prov.*) like cures like; свет не ~ом сошёлся there are plenty more fish in the sea. **2.** (*archit.*) quoin. **3.** gore (*in skirt*); gusset (*in underwear*). **4.** (*agric.*) field; озимый к. winter field; посевной к. sown area.

кли́ник|а, и, *f.* clinic.

клиници́ст, а, *m.* clinical physician, clinical surgeon.

клини́ческий, *adj.* clinical.

клинови́дный, *adj.* wedge-shaped.

клин|ово́й, *adj. of* ~; к. затво́р (*mil.*) breech mechanism.

клин|о́к, ка́, *m.* blade.

клинообра́з|ный (~ен, ~на), *adj.* wedge-shaped; ~ные письмена́ cuneiform characters.

клинопи́сный, *adj.* cuneiform.

кли́нопис|ь, и, *f.* cuneiform (characters, text).

кли́пер, а, *m.* (*naut.*) clipper.

кли́пс|ы, ~, *sing.* ~а, ~ы, *f.* ear-rings (*for unpierced ears*).

клир, а, *m.* (*collect.*; *eccl.*) the clergy (*of a parish*).

кли́ринг, а, *m.* (*fin.*) clearing, clearance.

кли́ринг|овый, *adj. of* ~.

кли́рос, а, *m.* choir (*part of church*).

клисти́р, а, *m.* (*med.*; *obs.*) enema, clyster.

кли́тор, а, *m.* (*anat.*) clitoris.

клич, а, *m.* (*rhet.*) call; боево́й к. war-cry; кли́кнуть к. to issue a call.

кличк|а, и, *f.* **1.** name (*of domestic animal, pet*). **2.** nickname. **3.** conspiratorial name.

клише́, *indecl.*, *n.* (*typ. and fig.*) cliché.

клоа́к|а, и, *f.* **1.** cesspit, sink, sewer (*also fig., concr. and abstr.*). **2.** (*zool.*) cloaca.

клобу́к, а́, *m.* (*eccl.*) klobúk (*headgear of Orthodox monk*).

клозе́т, а, *m.* (*coll.*, *obs.*) water closet, W.C.

клозе́т|ный, *adj. of* ~; ~ная бума́га toilet paper.

клок, а́, *pl.* кло́чья, кло́чьев *and* ~й, ~о́в, *m.* **1.** rag, shred; разорва́ть в кло́чья to tear to shreds, tatters. **2.** tuft; к. се́на wisp of hay; к. ше́рсти flock.

клоко́т, а, *no pl.*, *m.* bubbling; gurgling.

клоко|та́ть, чу́, ~чешь, *impf.* to bubble; to gurgle; to boil up (*also fig.*); в нём всё ~та́ло от гне́ва he was seething with rage.

клон, а, *m.* (*biol.*) clone.

клон|и́ть, ю́, ~ишь, *impf.* **1.** to bend; to incline; (*impers.*) ло́дку ~и́ло на́ бок the boat was heeling; старика́ уже́ ~и́ло ко сну́ the old man was already nodding. **2.** (*fig., coll.*) to lead (*conversation*); куда́ ты ~ишь? what are you driving at?

клон|и́ться, ю́сь, ~ишься, *impf.* **1.** to bow, bend (*intrans.*). **2.** (к; *fig.*) to be nearing;

to be leading up (to), be heading (for); день ~и́лся к ве́черу the day was declining; де́ло ~ится к развя́зке the affair is coming to a head; к чему́ э́то ~ится? what is it leading up to?

клоп, а́, *m.* **1.** bug. **2.** (*fig.*, *coll.*; *in addressing a child*) kid.

клопо́вник, а, *m.* (*coll.*) bug-infested place.

клоп|о́вый, *adj. of* ~.

клопомо́р, а, *m.* insecticide.

кло́ун, а, *m.* clown.

клоуна́д|а, ы, *f.* clownery, clowning.

кло́ун|ский, *adj. of* ~; к. колпа́к fool's cap.

клох|та́ть, чу́, ~чешь, *impf.* (*coll.*) to cluck.

клочкова́т|ый (~, ~а), *adj.* **1.** tufted, shaggy. **2.** patchy, scrappy.

клоч|о́к, ка́, *m.* *dim. of* клок; разорва́ть в ~ки́ to tear to shreds, tatters; к. бума́ги scrap of paper; к. земли́ plot of land; к. лазу́ри среди́ облако́в a patch of blue sky between the clouds.

клуб¹, а, *m.* **1.** club. **2.** club-house; офице́рский к. officers' mess.

клуб², а, *pl.* ~ы́, ~о́в, *m.* puff; ~ы́ пы́ли clouds of dust.

клу́б|ень, ня, *m.* (*bot.*) tuber.

клуб|и́ть, и́т, *impf.* to blow up, puff out; к. пыль to raise clouds of dust.

клуб|и́ться, и́тся, *impf.* to swirl; to curl, wreathe.

клубнево́й, *adj.* (*bot.*) tuberose.

клубнепло́д|ы, ов, *sing.* ~, ~а, *m.* (*bot., agric.*) root crops, tuber crops.

клубни́к|а, и, *f.* **1.** (cultivated) strawberry. **2.** (*collect.*) (cultivated) strawberries.

клубни́|чный, *adj. of* ~ка; ~чное варе́нье strawberry preserve.

клу́б|ный, *adj. of* ~¹.

клуб|о́к, ка́, *m.* **1.** ball; сверну́ться ~ко́м, в к. to roll oneself up into a ball. **2.** (*fig.*) tangle, mass; к. интри́г network of intrigue; к. противоре́чий mass of contradictions. **3.** (*fig.*) lump (in the throat); слёзы у неё подступи́ли ~ко́м к го́рлу a lump rose in her throat.

клу́мб|а, ы, *f.* (flower-)bed.

клупп, а, *m.* (*tech.*) die-stock, screw-stock.

клу́ш|а, и, *f.* **1.** (*dial.*) broody hen. **2.** lesser black-backed gull.

клык, а́, *m.* **1.** canine (tooth). **2.** fang; tusk.

клюв, а, *m.* beak; bill.

клюз, а, *m.* (*naut.*) hawse-hole.

клю́к|а́, и́, *f.* walking-stick.

клю́к|ать, аю, *impf. of* ~нуть.

клю́кв|а, ы, *f.* cranberry (*Oxycoccus palustris*); (*coll.*) вот так к.! here's a pretty kettle of fish!; развеси́стая к. myth, fable (*of credulous travellers' fabrications*).

клю́кв|енный, *adj. of* ~а; к. кисе́ль cranberry jelly; к. морс cranberry water.

клю́к|нуть, ну, нешь, *pf.* (*of* ~ать) (*coll.*) to take a drop.

клю́н|уть, у, ешь, *pf. of* клева́ть.

ключ[^1], а́, *m.* 1. (*in var. senses*) key; clue; запере́ть на к. to lock; га́ечный к. spanner, wrench; францу́зский к. monkey-wrench; к. к ши́фру key to a cipher; (*mil.*) к. ме́стности key point. 2. (*archit.*) keystone. 3. (*mus.*) key, clef; басо́вый к. bass clef; скрипи́чный к. treble clef.

ключ[^2], а́, *m.* spring; source; кипе́ть ~о́м to bubble over; бить ~о́м to spout, jet; (*fig.*) to be in full swing.

ключа́р|ь, я́, *m.* (*eccl.*) sacrist.

ключ|ево́й[^1], *adj. of* ~[^1]; ~евы́е о́трасли промы́шленности key industries; (*mil.*) ~евы́е пози́ции key positions; (*mus.*) к. знак clef.

ключ|ево́й[^2], *adj. of* ~[^2]; ~ева́я вода́ spring water.

ключи́ц|а, ы, *f.* (*anat.*) clavicle, collar-bone.

клю́чник, а, *m.* (*obs.*) steward.

клю́чниц|а, ы, *f.* (*obs.*) housekeeper.

клю́шк|а, и, *f.* (*sport*) (golf-)club; (hockey) stick; (*coll.*) walking-stick.

кл|юю́, юёшь, *see* ~ева́ть.

кля́кс|а, ы, *f.* blot, smudge.

кля́нч|у, нёшь, *see* ~сть.

кля́нч|ить, у, ишь, *impf.* (у) (*coll.*) to beg (of).

кляп, а, *m.* gag; засу́нуть к. в рот (+*d.*) to gag.

кля|сть, ну́, нёшь, *past* ~л, ~ла́, ~ло, *impf.* to curse.

кля|сться, ну́сь, нёшься, *past* ~лся, ~ла́сь, *impf.* (*of* по~) (в+*p.*, +*inf. or* +что) to swear, vow; к. в ве́рности to vow fidelity; к. отомсти́ть to vow vengeance; к. че́стью to swear on one's honour.

кля́тв|а, ы, *f.* oath, vow; ло́жная к. perjury; дать ~у to take an oath.

кля́тв|енный, *adj. of* ~а; дать ~енное обеща́ние to promise on oath.

клятвопреступле́ни|е, я, *n.* perjury.

клятвопресту́пник, а, *m.* perjurer.

кля́уз|а, ы, *f.* 1. (*coll.*) slander, scandal; tale-bearing. 2. (*leg.*; *obs.*) barratry; затева́ть ~у to institute vexatious litigation.

кля́узник, а, *m.* (*coll.*) scandalmonger; tale-bearer.

кля́узнича|ть, ю, *impf.* (*of* на~) (*coll.*) to spread slander; to bear tales.

кля́узн|ый, *adj.* (*coll.*) captious, pettifogging; случи́лось ~ое де́ло a tiresome thing happened.

кля́ч|а, и, *f.* (*pejor.*; *of horse*) jade.

кнел|ь, и, *f.* (*collect.*; *cul.*) quenelles.

кнехт, а, *m.* (*naut.*) bollard, bitts.

кни́г|а, и, *f.* 1. book; тебе́ и ~и в ру́ки (*coll.*) you know best. 2. number (*of a journal, magazine*).

книгове́дени|е, я, *n.* bibliography.

книговеде́ни|е, я, *n.* book-keeping.

книгое́д, а, *m.* (*zool. and fig.*) bookworm.

книгоизда́тел|ь, я, *m.* publisher.

книгоизда́тельский, *adj.* publishing.

книгоизда́тельств|о, а, *n.* 1. publishing-house. 2. publishing.

книголю́б, а, *m.* bibliophile.

книгоно́ш|а, и, *m. and f.* book-pedlar, colporteur.

книгопеча́тани|е, я, *n.* (book-)printing.

книгопеча́т|ный, *adj. of* ~ание; к. стано́к printing-press.

книготорго́в|ец, ца, *m.* bookseller.

книготорго́вл|я, и, *f.* 1. book trade. 2. bookshop.

книгохрани́лищ|е, а, *n.* 1. library. 2. book-stack.

кни́жечк|а, и, *f.* booklet.

кни́жк|а[^1], и, *f.* 1. *dim. of* кни́га; записна́я к. notebook. 2. (*document*) book, card; забо́рная к. ration book; расчётная к. pay-book; чcóковая к. cheque-book. 3. (сберега́тельная) к. savings-bank book; положи́ть де́ньги на ~у to deposit money at a savings-bank; на кни́жку on credit.

кни́жк|а[^2], и, *f.* (*zool.*) third stomach (*of ruminants*).

кни́жник, а, *m.* 1. (*bibl.*) scribe. 2. bibliophile. 3. bookseller.

кни́жн|ый, *adj.* 1. *adj. of* кни́га; к. знак book-plate; ~ая по́лка bookshelf; к. шкаф bookcase. 2. bookish, abstract; pedantic; к. стиль pedantic style; ~ая учёность book-learning; к. червь bookworm.

кни́зу, *adv.* downwards.

кни́ксен, а, *m.* curts(e)y.

кни́ц|а, ы, *f.* (*tech.*, *naut.*) knee, gusset.

кно́пк|а, и, *f.* 1. drawing-pin; прикрепи́ть ~ой to pin. 2. press-button (*fastener*). 3. (*electr.*) button; knob; нажа́ть все ~и (*fig.*, *coll.*) to pull wires, do all in one's power.

кно́п|очный, *adj. of* ~ка.

кнут, а́, *m.* whip; (*hist.*) knout; щёлкать ~о́м to crack a whip.

кнутови́щ|е, а, *n.* whip-handle.

княги́н|я, и, *f.* princess (*wife of prince*).

княже́ни|е, я, *n.* (*hist.*) reign.

кня́жеств|о, а, *n.* principality.

кня́ж|ить, у, ишь, *impf.* (*hist.*) to reign.

кня́жич, а, *m.* prince (*prince's unmarried son*).

княж|на́, ны́, *g. pl.* ~о́н, *f.* princess (*prince's unmarried daughter*).

князёк, ька́, *m.* 1. (*coll.*) princeling. 2. (*tech.*) roof-ridge.

кня́з|ь, я, *pl.* ~ья́, ~е́й, *m.* prince; вели́кий к. (*in medieval Russia*) grand prince; (*in tsarist Russia*) grand duke.

ко, *see* к.

коагуля́ци|я, и, *f.* coagulation.
коалиц|ио́нный, *adj. of* ~ия.
коали́ци|я, и, *f.* (*polit.*) coalition.
ко́бальт, а, *m.* (*chem.*) cobalt.
ко́бальт|овый, *adj. of* ~; ~овая кра́ска
cobalt; ~овое стекло́ smalt.
кобе́л|ь, я, *m.* (male) dog.
кобе́н|иться, юсь, ишься, *impf.* (*coll.*) to be
capricious; to make faces.
ко́бз|а́, ~ы́, *f.* kobza (*Ukrainian mus. instru-
ment similar to guitar*).
кобза́р|ь, я́, *m.* kobza-player.
ко́бр|а, ы, *f.* cobra.
кобу́р|а́, ы́, *f.* holster.
ко́бчик, а, *m.* (*orn.*) merlin.
кобы́л|а¹, ы, *f.* mare.
кобы́л|а², ы, *f.* 1. (*hist.*) punishment-bench.
2. vaulting-horse.
кобы́л|ий, *adj. of* ~а¹.
кобы́лк|а¹, и, *f.* filly.
кобы́лк|а², и, *f.* bridge (*of stringed instru-
ments*).
ко́ваный, *adj.* 1. forged; hammered. 2.
(*fig.*) terse.
кова́р|ный (~ен, ~на), *adj.* insidious,
crafty; perfidious.
кова́рств|о, а, *n.* insidiousness, craftiness;
perfidy.
кова́ть, кую́, куёшь, *impf.* 1. (*pf.* вы́~) to
forge (*also fig.*); to hammer (*iron*); к. побе́ду
to forge victory; куй желе́зо, пока́ горячо́
(*prov.*) strike while the iron is hot. 2. (*pf.*
под~) to shoe (*horses*).
ковбо́|й, я, *m.* cowboy.
ковбо́йк|а, и, *f.* (*coll.*) 1. cowboy hat. 2.
cowboy shirt.
ков|ёр, ра́, *m.* carpet; rug; к.-самолёт the
magic carpet.
кове́рка|ть, ю, *impf.* (*of* ис~) 1. to spoil,
ruin (*concr. and abstr.*). 2. (*fig.*) to distort;
to mangle, mispronounce; к. чужу́ю мысль
to distort someone else's ideas; к. слова́ to
mangle words; он ~ет францу́зский язы́к
he murders the French language.
коверко́т, а, *m.* covert coat.
ко́вк|а, и, *f.* 1. forging. 2. shoeing.
ко́в|кий (~ок, ~ка́, ~ко), *adj.* malleable,
ductile.
ко́вкост|ь, и, *f.* malleability, ductility.
коври́г|а, и, *f.* loaf.
коври́жк|а, и, *f.* gingerbread; ни за каки́е
~и (*coll.*) not for the world.
ко́врик, а, *m.* rug.
ковче́г, а, *m.* 1. ark; Но́ев к. Noah's ark.
2. (*eccl.*) shrine.
ковш, а́, *m.* 1. scoop, ladle, dipper. 2. (*tech.*)
bucket.
ко́в|ы, ~, *no sing.* (*obs.*) snare, trap; toils;
стро́ить к. кому́-н. to lay a trap for someone.
ковы́л|ь, я́, *m.* (*bot.*) feather-grass.

ковыля́|ть, ю, *impf.* (*coll.*) to hobble; to
stump; (*of child*) to toddle.
ковыр|ну́ть, ну́, нёшь, *pf. of* ~я́ть.
ковыр|я́ть, я́ю, *impf.* (*of* ~ну́ть) (*coll.*) 1. to
dig into; (в+*p.*) to pick (at); к. в зуба́х to
pick one's teeth. 2. to tinker (up), potter.
ковыря́|ться, юсь, *impf.* (*coll.*) 1. (в+*p.*) to
rummage (in). 2. to tinker.
когда́¹, *adv.* 1. (*interrog. and relat.*) when;
(*coll.*) есть к.! there's no time for it!; есть к.
мне болта́ть! I've no time for talk! 2. к.
(бы) ни whenever; к. бы вы ни пришли́, к.
(вы) ни придёте whenever you come. 3.
(*coll.*) к...., к. sometimes . . ., sometimes; я
занима́юсь к. у́тром, к. ве́чером sometimes
I work in the morning, sometimes in the
evening. 4. (*coll.*) к. как it depends. 5.
(*coll.*) = к.-н.
когда́², *conj.* 1. when; while, as; я её встре́-
тил, к. шёл домо́й I met her as I was going
home. 2. (*coll.*) if; к. так, согла́сен с тобо́й
if that is the case, I agree.
когда́-либо, *adv.* = когда́-нибудь.
когда́-нибудь, *adv.* 1. (*in future*) some time,
some day. 2. ever; вы бы́ли к.-н. в Кита́е?
have you ever been in China?
когда́-то, *adv.* 1. (*in past*) once; some time;
formerly. 2. (*in future*) some day (*indefinitely
distant*); к.-то ещё бу́дет тако́й прия́тный
ве́чер it will be a long time before we have
such a pleasant evening again.
кого́, *a. and g. of* кто.
когó́рт|а, ы, *f.* cohort.
ко́г|оть, тя, *pl.* ~ти, ~те́й, *m.* claw; talon;
показа́ть свои́ ~ти (*fig.*) to show one's
teeth; попа́сть в ~ти (к кому́-н.) to fall
into the clutches (of someone).
когти́ст|ый (~, ~а), *adj.* sharp-clawed.
когти́т|ь, ~, *impf.* (*dial.*) to claw to pieces,
tear with claws.
код, а, *m.* code; телегра́фный к. cable code;
по ~у in code.
ко́д|а, ы, *f.* (*mus.*) coda.
кодеи́н, а, *m.* (*pharm.*) codeine.
ко́декс, а, *m.* 1. (*leg. and fig.*) code; мора́ль-
ный к. moral code; уголо́вный к. criminal
code. 2. (*lit.*) codex.
кодифика́ци|я, и, *f.* codification.
кодифици́р|овать, ую, *impf. and pf.* (*leg.*) to
codify.
ко́е-где́ (*and* кой-где́), *adv.* here and there,
in places.
ко́е-ка́к (*and* кой-ка́к), *adv.* (*coll.*) 1. anyhow
(*badly, carelessly*). 2. somehow (or other),
just (*with great difficulty*); к.-к. мы доплы́ли
до того́ бе́рега somehow we managed to
swim to the other side.
ко́е-како́й (*and* кой-како́й), *pron.* some.
ко́е-кто́ (*and* кой-кто́), ко́е-кого́, *pron.* somebody; some people.

ко́ечный, *adj. of* ко́йка; к. больно́й in--patient.

ко́е-что́ (*and* кой-что́), ко́е-чего́, *pron.* some-thing; a little.

ко́ж|а, и, *f.* **1.** skin; hide; (*anat.*) cutis; гуси́-ная к. goose-flesh; (*fig., coll.*) из ∼и (вон) лезть to go all out, do one's utmost; к. да ко́сти skin and bone. **2.** leather; свина́я к. pig-skin; теля́чья к. calf. **3.** peel, rind; (*bot.*) epidermis.

кожа́н[1], **а́,** *m.* (*obs.*) leather coat.

кожа́н[2], **а́,** *m.* large bat.

ко́жанк|а, и, *f.* (*coll.*) leather jacket, jerkin.

ко́жаный, *adj.* leather(n).

коже́венный, *adj.* leather; leather-dressing, tanning; к. заво́д tannery; к. това́р leather goods.

коже́вник, а, *m.* currier, leather-dresser, tanner.

кожими́т, а, *m.* imitation leather, leatherette.

ко́жиц|а, ы, *f.* **1.** thin skin, film, pellicle; к. колбасы́ sausage-skin. **2.** peel, skin (*of fruit*).

ко́жник, а, *m.* (*coll.*) dermatologist.

ко́жный, *adj.* skin; (*med.*) cutaneous.

кожур|а́, ы́, *f.* rind, peel, skin (*of fruit*).

кожу́х, а́, *m.* **1.** leather jacket, sheepskin jacket. **2.** (*tech.*) housing, casing, jacket; к. гребно́го колеса́ paddle-box.

коз|а́, ы́, *pl.* ∼ы, *f.* **1.** goat. **2.** she-goat. **3.** (*coll.*) tomboy.

коз|ёл, ла́, *m.* he-goat; к. отпуще́ния scapegoat; от него́ как от ∼ла́ молока́ he is good for nothing.

козеро́г, а, *m.* **1.** (*zool.*) wild (mountain) goat, ibex. **2.** К. (*astron.*) Capricorn

козе́тк|а, и, *f.* (*coll.*) settee.

ко́з|ий, *adj. of* ∼а́; к. пасту́х goatherd; ∼ья но́жка (*med.*) molar forceps; (*coll.*) *denotes home-made cigarette.*

козл|ёнок, ёнка, *pl.* ∼я́та, ∼я́т, *m.* kid.

коз|ли́ный, *adj. of* ∼ёл; ∼ли́ная боро́дка goatee; к. го́лос reedy voice.

козло́вый, *adj.* goatskin.

ко́з|лы, ел, лам, *no sing.* **1.** (coach-)box. **2.** trestle(s); saw-horse. **3.** (*mil.*) соста́вить винто́вки в к. to pile arms.

козл|я́та, я́т, *pl. of* ∼ёнок.

козля́т|ки, ок, *no sing., affect. dim. of* ∼а.

ко́зн|и, ей, *sing.* (*rare*) ∼ь, ∼и, *f.* (*obs.*) machinations, intrigues; snare.

козово́д, а, *m.* goat breeder.

козово́дств|о, а, *n.* goat-breeding.

козодо́|й, я, *m.* (*orn.*) nightjar, goatsucker.

козу́л|я, и, *f.* roe(buck).

козыр|ёк, ька́, *m.* **1.** (cap) peak; взять под к. (+*d.*) to salute. **2.** (*mil.*) head cover (*in trenches*).

козыр|но́й, *adj. of* ко́зырь.

козыр|ну́ть, ну́, нёшь, *pf. of* ∼я́ть.

ко́зыр|ь, я, *pl.* ∼и, ∼е́й, *m.* **1.** (*cards and fig.*) trump; объяви́ть ∼я to call one's hand; откры́ть свои́ ∼и (*fig.*) to lay one's cards on the table; покры́ть ∼ем to trump; ходи́ть с ∼я to lead trumps; (*fig.*) to play a trump card; гла́вный к. (one's) trump card. **2.** (*coll.*) card, swell; ходи́ть ∼ем to swagger.

козыр|я́ть[1], **я́ю,** *impf.* (*of* ∼ну́ть) (*coll.*) **1.** (*cards*) to lead trumps, play a trump; (*fig.*) to play one's trump card. **2.** (+*i.*) to show off.

козыр|я́ть[2], **я́ю,** *impf.* (*of* ∼ну́ть) (+*d.*; *coll.*) to salute.

козя́вк|а, и, *f.* (*coll.*) small insect.

кой, *interrog. and relat. pron.* (*obs.*) which; до ко́их пор? how long?; ни в ко́ем слу́чае on no account; (*coll.*) на к. чорт? why in the world, what the devil for?

ко́йк|а, и, *f.* **1.** berth, bunk (*on board ship*). **2.** bed (*in hospital*).

кок, а, *m.* **1.** (ship's) cook. **2.** quiff.

ко́к|а, и, *f.* (*bot.*) coca.

кока́н, а, *m.* cocaine.

кокаини́зм, а, *m.* cocainism.

кокаини́ст, а, *m.* cocaine addict.

кока́рд|а, ы, *f.* cockade.

ко́к|ать, аю, *impf.* (*of* ∼нуть) (*coll.*) to crack, break.

коке́тк|а, и, *f.* coquette.

коке́тлив|ый (∼, ∼а), *adj.* coquettish.

коке́тнича|ть, ю, *impf.* **1.** (с+*i.*) to coquet(te), flirt (with). **2.** (+*i.*) to show off, flaunt.

коке́тств|о, а, *n.* coquetry.

коки́л|ь, я, *m.* (*tech.*) chill mould.

коки́льн|ый, *adj.*; ∼ое литьё (*tech.*) chill casting.

кокк, а, *m.* (*med.*) coccus.

коклю́ш, а, *m.* whooping-cough.

коклю́шк|а, и, *f.* bobbin.

ко́к|нуть, ну, нешь, *pf. of* ∼ать.

ко́кон, а, *m.* cocoon.

коко́с, а, *m.* **1.** coco(-tree). **2.** coco-nut.

коко́с|овый, *adj. of* ∼; ∼овое волокно́ coir; ∼овое ма́сло coco-nut oil; к. оре́х coco--nut; ∼овая па́льма coco(-tree), coco-nut tree.

коко́тк|а, и, *f.* courtesan, cocotte.

коко́шник, а, *m.* kokoshnik (*Russian peasant woman's head-dress*).

кокс, а, *m.* coke; вы́жиг ∼а (*tech.*) coke firing.

коксова́льн|ый, *adj.* (*tech.*) coking; ∼ая печь coke oven.

кокс|ова́ть, у́ю, *impf.* (*tech.*) to coke.

кокс|ова́ться, у́юсь, *impf.* (*tech.*) to coke (*intrans.*).

ко́кс|овый, *adj. of* ∼; ∼овая печь coke oven; ∼овое число́ coking value.

коكс|у́ющийся, *pres. part. act. of* ~ова́ться *and adj.*; к. у́голь coking coal.

кокте́йл|ь, я, *m.* cocktail; cocktail party.

кол, á, *m.* **1.** (*pl.* ~ья́, ~ьев) stake, picket; посади́ть на́ к. to impale; (*coll.*) стоя́ть ~о́м в го́рле to stick in one's throat; ему́ хоть к. на голове́ теши́ he is very pig--headed; у него́ нет ни ~а́ ни двора́ he has neither house nor home. **2.** (*pl.* ~ы́, ~о́в) (*lowest mark in school*) one.

ко́лб|а, ы, *f.* (*chem.*) retort.

колбас|а́, ы́, *pl.* ~ы, *f.* sausage.

колба́сник, а, *m.* sausage-maker; pork butcher.

колба́с|ный, *adj. of* ~á; к. яд ptomaine.

колго́т|ки, ок, *no sing.* tights.

колдо́бин|а, ы, *f.* (*dial.*) **1.** rut, pothole (*in road*). **2.** deep place (*in lake, river, etc.*).

колд|ова́ть, у́ю, *impf.* to practise witch-craft.

колдовско́й, *adj.* magical; (*fig.*) magical, bewitching.

колдовств|о́, á, *n.* witchcraft, sorcery, magic.

колдо́говор, а, *m.* (*abbr. of* коллекти́вный догово́р) collective agreement.

колду́н, á, *m.* sorcerer, magician, wizard.

колду́н|ья, ьи, *g. pl.* ~ий, *f.* witch, sorceress.

колеба́ни|е, я, *n.* **1.** (*phys.*) oscillation, vibration; к. ма́ятника swing of the pendulum. **2.** fluctuation, variation; к. ку́рса (*fin.*) stock exchange fluctuations, fluctuations in the rate of exchange. **3.** (*fig.*) hesitation; wavering, vacillation.

колеба́тельный, *adj.* (*tech.*) oscillatory, vibratory.

колеб|а́ть, ~лю, ~лешь, *impf.* (*of* по~) to shake; (*fig.*) к. обще́ственные усто́и to shake the foundations of society.

колеб|а́ться, ~люсь, ~лешься, *impf.* (*of* по~) **1.** to shake to and fro, sway; (*phys.*) to oscillate. **2.** to fluctuate, vary. **3.** (*fig.*) to hesitate; to waver, vacillate.

коле́нк|а, и, *f.* (*coll.*) knee.

коленко́р, а, *m.* (*text.*) calico; (*coll.*) э́то совсе́м друго́й к. that's quite another matter.

коленко́р|овый, *adj. of* ~.

коле́н|ный, *adj. of* ~o; (*anat.*) к. суста́в knee-joint; ~ная ча́шка patella, knee-cap.

коле́н|о, а, *n.* **1.** (*pl.* ~и, ~ей, ~ям) knee; преклони́ть ~и to genuflect; стать на ~и (пе́ред) to kneel (to); стоя́ть на ~ях to be kneeling, be on one's knees; по к., по ~и knee-deep, up to one's knees; (*coll.*) ему́ мо́ре по к. he doesn't care a damn for anything; поста́вить кого́-н. на ~и to bring someone to his knees. **2.** (*pl. only*; ~и, ~ей, ~ям) lap; сиде́ть у кого́-н. на ~ях to sit

on someone's lap. **3.** (*pl.* ~ья, ~ьев) (*tech.*) knee, joint; (*bot.*) joint, node; к. трубы́ knee pipe, elbow pipe. **4.** (*pl.* ~а, ~, ~ам) bend (*of river, etc.*). **5.** (*pl.* ~а, ~, ~ам) (*obs.*) generation; ро́дственники до пя́того ~а cousins five times removed; двена́дцать ~ изра́илевых the twelve tribes of Israel. **6.** (*pl.* ~а, ~, ~ам) (*coll.*) figure (*in dance, song, etc.*); выде́лывать к. to execute a figure; (*pejor.*) вы́кинуть к. to play a trick.

коленопреклоне́ни|е, я, *n.* genuflection.

коле́н|це, ца, *g. pl.* ~ец, *n.* (*coll.*) вы́кинуть к. to play a trick.

коле́нчат|ый, *adj.* (*tech.*) elbow-shaped, cranked; к. вал crankshaft; к. рыча́г toggle lever, bell crank; ~ая труба́ knee pipe.

ко́лер¹, а, *m.* (*art*) colour, shade.

ко́лер², а, *m.* staggers (*disease of horses*).

коле́сик|о, а, *n.* **1.** *dim. of* колесо́. **2.** castor.

коле|си́ть, шу́, си́шь, *impf.* (*coll.*) **1.** to go in a roundabout way. **2.** to go all over, travel about.

коле́сник, а, *m.* wheelwright.

колесни́ц|а, ы, *f.* chariot; погреба́льная к. hearse; триумфа́льная к. triumphal car.

колёс|ный, *adj.* **1.** *adj. of* ~о́. **2.** wheeled, on wheels.

колес|о́, á, *pl.* ~а, *n.* wheel; гребно́е к. paddle-wheel; запасно́е к. spare wheel; зубча́тое к. cog-wheel; махово́е к. fly--wheel; рулево́е к. driving wheel; цепно́е к. sprocket; грудь ~о́м (*fig.*) well-developed chest; *as adv.* with chest well out; вста́вить кому́-н. па́лки в ~а to put a spoke in some-one's wheel; кружи́ться, как бе́лка в ~é to run round in small circles; но́ги ~о́м bandy legs; ходи́ть ~о́м to turn somer-saults.

колесова́ни|е, я, *n.* breaking on the wheel.

колес|ова́ть, у́ю, *impf. and pf.* to break on the wheel.

коле́ч|ко, ка, *pl.* ~ки, ~ек, ~кам, *n.* (*coll.*) ringlet.

коле|я́, и́, *f.* **1.** rut; (*fig.*) войти́ в ~ю́ to settle down (again); вы́битый из ~й un-settled. **2.** (*railways*) track; gauge.

ко́ли (*and* **коль**) (*obs. or dial.*) if; (*coll.*) к. на то пошло́ while we are about it; коль ско́ро if, as soon as.

коли́бри, *indecl., m. and f.* (*orn.*) humming-bird.

ко́лик|и, ~, *no sing.* (*med.*) colic; смея́ться до ~ (*coll.*) to make oneself ill with laughing.

колир|ова́ть, у́ю, *impf.* (*hort.*) to graft.

колиро́вк|а, и, *f.* (*hort.*) grafting.

коли́т, а, *m.* (*med.*) colitis.

коли́чественн|ый, *adj.* quantitative; ~ое числи́тельное cardinal number.

коли́честв|о, а, *n.* quantity, amount; num-ber.

ко́лк|а, и, *f.* chopping.

ко́л|кий¹ (~ок, ~ка́, ~ко), *adj.* easily split.

ко́л|кий² (~ок, ~ка́, ~ко), *adj.* prickly; (*fig.*) sharp, biting, caustic.

ко́лкост|ь, и, *f.* **1.** (*fig.*) sharpness. **2.** sharp, caustic remark; говори́ть ~и to make sharp remarks.

коллаборациони́ст, а, *m.* (*polit.*; *pejor.*) colborator.

коллаборациони́ст|ский, *adj. of* ~.

колле́г|а, и, *m.* colleague.

коллегиа́л|ьный (~ен, ~ьна), *adj.* joint, collective; corporate; ~ьное реше́ние collective decision.

колле́ги|я, и, *f.* **1.** board, collegium. **2.** college; к. адвока́тов, к. правозасту́пников the Bar.

колле́дж, а, *m.* college.

колле́жский, *adj.* (*in titles of officials in tsarist Russia*) collegiate; к. сове́тник collegiate counsellor.

коллекти́в, а, *m.* group, body; (*in many phrases does not require separate translation*) к. машини́стов engine-drivers; нау́чный к. (the) scientists; парти́йный к. Party members.

коллективиза́ци|я, и, *f.* collectivization.

коллективизи́р|овать, ую, *impf. and pf.* to collectivize.

коллективи́зм, а, *m.* collectivism.

коллективи́ст, а, *m.* collectivist.

коллекти́вн|ый, *adj.* collective; joint; ~ое владе́ние joint ownership; ~ое хозя́йство collective farm; ~ое руково́дство (*polit.*) collective leadership (*as opp. to one-man rule*).

колле́ктор, а, *m.* **1.** (*electr.*) commutator. **2.** (*in sewage system*) manifold. **3.** библиоте́чный к. central library.

коллекционе́р, а, *m.* collector.

коллекциони́р|овать, ую, *impf.* to collect.

колле́кци|я, и, *f.* collection.

колли́зи|я, и, *f.* clash, conflict.

колло́ди|й, я, *m.* (*chem.*) collodion.

колло́ид, а, *m.* (*chem.*) colloid.

коллоида́льный, *adj.* (*chem.*) colloidal.

колло́идный, *adj.* (*chem.*) colloidal.

колло́квиум, а, *m.* oral examination.

колоб|о́к, ка́, *m.* small round loaf.

колобро́|дить, жу, дишь, *impf.* (*coll.*) **1.** to roam, wander; to loaf. **2.** to make a noise; to get up to mischief.

коловоро́т, а, *m.* (*tech.*) brace.

коловра́тност|ь, и, *f.* (*obs.*) mutability, inconstancy.

коловра́т|ный (~ен, ~на), *adj.* **1.** rotary. **2.** (*fig., obs.*) inconstant, changeable.

коловраще́ни|е, я, *n.* (*obs.*) rotation.

коло́д|а¹, ы, *f.* **1.** block, log. **2.** (water-)trough.

коло́д|а², ы, *f.* pack (*of cards*).

коло́де|зный, *adj. of* ~ц.

коло́де|зь, зя, *m.* (*obs.*) = ~ц.

коло́д|ец, ца, *m.* **1.** well. **2.** (*tech.*) shaft.

коло́дк|а, и, *f.* **1.** boot-tree; last. **2.** (*tech.*) shoe. **3.** (*pl.*; *hist.*) stocks; наби́ть ~и на́ ноги кому́-н. to put someone in stocks.

коло́дник, а, *m.* convict (*in stocks*).

кол|о́к, ка́, *m.* (*mus.*) peg.

ко́локол, а, *pl.* ~á, ~о́в, *m.* bell.

колоко́льный, *adj. of* ко́локол; к. звон peal, chime.

колоко́ль|ня, ьни, g. pl. ~ен, *f.* steeple, bell-tower, church-tower; (*coll.*) смотре́ть со свое́й ~ьни на что-н. to take a narrow, parochial view of something.

колоко́льчик, а, *m.* **1.** small bell; handbell. **2.** (*bot.*) bluebell.

коло́маз|ь, и, *f.* wheel grease.

колониа́льный, *adj.* colonial; к. магази́н (*obs.*) grocer's shop.

колониза́тор, а, *m.* colonizer.

колониза́ци|я, и, *f.* colonization.

колониз|ова́ть, у́ю, *impf. and pf.* to colonize.

колони́ст, а, *m.* colonist.

коло́ни|я, и, *f.* (*in various senses*) colony; settlement.

коло́нк|а, и, *f.* **1.** geyser. **2.** (*street*) water fountain. **3.** бензи́новая к. petrol pump. **4.** (*typ.*) column; газе́тная полоса́ в шесть коло́нок newspaper page with six columns.

коло́нн|а, ы, *f.* column; к. цифр column of figures; (*mil.*) та́нковая к. tank column; похо́дная к. column of route; со́мкнутая к. close column; к. по три column of threes.

колонна́д|а, ы, *f.* colonnade.

коло́нный, *adj.* columned.

колон|о́к, ка́, *m.* (*zool.*) Siberian polecat.

колонти́тул, а, *m.* (*typ.*) running title.

колонци́фр|а, ы, *f.* (*typ.*) page number.

колора́дский, *adj.*; к. жук Colorado beetle.

колорату́р|а, ы, *f.* (*mus.*) coloratura.

колорату́р|ный, *adj. of* ~а.

колори́ст, а, *m.* (*art*) colourist.

колори́т, а, *m.* colouring, colour; (*fig.*) ме́стный к. local colour; он прида́л расска́зу о встре́че я́ркий к. he painted a glowing picture of the encounter.

колори́т|ный (~ен, ~на), *adj.* colourful, picturesque, graphic (*also fig.*); язы́к у него́ о́чень к. his language is highly coloured.

ко́лос, а, *pl.* ~ья, ~ьев, *m.* (*agric.*) ear, spike.

колоси́ст|ый (~, ~а), *adj.* (*agric.*) full of ears.

коло|си́ться, си́тся, *impf.* (*agric.*) to form ears.

колосни́к, á, *m.* **1.** furnace-bar, grate-bar; (*pl.*) fire-bars. **2.** (*pl.*; *theatr.*) flies; grid-iron.

коло́сс, а, *m.* colossus.

колосса́льный, *adj.* colossal.

коло|ти́ть, чу́, ～ти́шь, *impf.* (*of* поколоти́ть) **1.** (по+*d.*, в+*a.*) to strike (on); to batter (on), pound (on); к. в дверь to bang on the door. **2.** (*coll.*) to thrash, drub. **3.** (*impf. only*) к. лён to scutch flax. **4.** (*impf. only*) (*coll.*) to break, smash. **5.** (*impf. only*) (*coll.*) to shake; (*impers.*) его́ ～ти́ла лихора́дка he was shaking with fever.

коло|ти́ться, чу́сь, ～ти́шься, *impf.* (*of* поколоти́ться) **1.** (о+*a.*) to beat (against); to strike (against); к. голово́й об сте́ну to beat one's head against a wall. **2.** (*impf. only*) (*coll.*) to pound; to shake; се́рдце у неё ～ти́лось her heart was pounding. **3.** *pass. of* ～ти́ть.

колоту́шк|а, и, *f.* **1.** (*coll.*) punch. **2.** beetle (*tech.*) **3.** (*wooden*) rattle (*used by night watchman*).

ко́лот|ый¹ (～, ～а), *p.p.p. of* ～ь¹ *and adj.* к. са́хар chipped sugar.

ко́лот|ый² (～, ～а), *p.p.p. of* ～ь² *and adj.* ～ая ра́на stab.

кол|о́ть¹, ю́, ～ешь, *impf.* (*of* расколо́ть) to break, chop, split; к. дрова́ to chop wood; к. оре́хи to crack nuts.

кол|о́ть², ю́, ～ешь, *impf.* (*of* заколо́ть) **1.** to prick; (*impers.*) у меня́ ～ет в боку́ I have a stitch in my side. **2.** to stab. **3.** to slaughter (*cattle*). **4.** (*fig.*) to sting, taunt; к. глаза́ кому́-н. (+*i.*) to cast a thing in someone's teeth; пра́вда глаза́ ～ет (*prov.*) home truths are unpalatable.

ко́лоть|е, я (*and* коло́ть|ё, я́), *n.* (*coll.*) stitch.

кол|о́ться¹, ю́сь, ～ешься, *impf.*, *pass. of* ～о́ть¹.

кол|о́ться², ю́сь, ～ешься, *impf.* to prick (*intrans.*).

коло́ш|а, и, *f.* (*tech.*) blast furnace charge.

колошма́|тить, чу, тишь, *impf.* (*of* отколошма́тить) (*coll.*) to beat, thrash.

коло́шник, а́, *m.* (*tech.*) furnace throat.

колошнико́|вый, *adj. of* ～; к. газ blast furnace gas.

колпа́к, а́, *m.* **1.** cap; ночно́й к. nightcap; шутовско́й к. fool's cap. **2.** lamp-shade; (*tech.*) cowl; броневой к. armoured hood; стекля́нный к. bell-glass; (*fig., coll.*) жить под стекля́нным ～о́м to live in the public view, have no privacy; держа́ть под стекля́нным ～о́м to keep in cotton-wool (= *to treat as a child*). **3.** (*fig., coll.*) simpleton.

колпач|о́к, ка́, *m.* **1.** *dim. of* колпа́к. **2.** (gas) mantle.

колту́н, а́, *m.* (*med.*) plica (polonica).

колумба́ри|й, я, *m.* columbarium.

колу́н, а́, *m.* (wood-)chopper, hatchet.

колупа́|ть, ю, *impf.* (*coll.*) to pick, scratch.

колхо́з, а, *m.* (*abbr. of* колле́ктивное хозя́йство) collective farm.

колхо́зник, а, *m.* member of collective farm.

колхо́зн|ица, ицы, *f. of* ～ик.

колхо́з|ный, *adj. of* ～; ～ное строи́тельство organization of collective farms; к. строй collective farm system.

колча́н, а, *m.* quiver.

колчеда́н, а, *m.* (*min.*) pyrites.

колчено́гий, *adj.* (*coll.*) **1.** lame. **2.** rickety, wobbly (*of furniture*).

колыбе́л|ь, и, *f.* cradle; (*fig.*) к. нау́ки the cradle of learning; с ～и from the cradle; от ～и до моги́лы from the cradle to the grave.

колыбе́ль|ный, *adj. of* ～; ～ная пе́сня lullaby.

колыма́г|а, и, *f.* (*obs.*) heavy, unwieldy carriage; (*iron.*) wagon, 'bus.

колы|ха́ть, ～шу, ～шешь, *impf.* (*of* ～хну́ть) to sway, rock.

колы|ха́ться, ～шется, *impf.* (*of* ～хну́ться) to sway, heave; to flutter; to flicker.

колых|ну́ть(ся), ну́(сь), нёшь(ся), *pf. of* ～а́ть(ся).

ко́лыш|ек, ка, *m.* peg.

коль, *see* ко́ли.

колье́, *indecl.*, *n.* necklace.

коль|ну́ть, ну́, нёшь, *inst. pf. of* ～о́ть².

кольра́би, *indecl.*, *f.* (*bot.*) kohlrabi.

кольт, а, *m.* colt (*pistol*).

кольц|ева́ть, у́ю, *impf.* **1.** (*of* закольцева́ть) to girdle, ring-bark (*a tree*). **2.** (*of* окольцева́ть) to ring (*bird's leg., etc.*).

кольцев|о́й, *adj.* annular; circular; ～а́я доро́га ring road; ～а́я развя́зка roundabout.

кольцеобра́з|ный (～ен, ～на), *adj.* ring-shaped.

кол|ьцо́, ьца́, *pl.* ～ьца, ～е́ц, ～ьцам, *n.* **1.** ring; сверну́ться ～ьцо́м to coil up; годи́чное к. (*bot.*) ring; обруча́льное к. wedding ring; трамва́йное к. circle, terminus (on tram-route). **2.** (*tech.*) ring; collar; hoop.

ко́льчат|ый, *adj.* annulate(d); ～ые че́рви (*zool.*) Annelida.

кольчу́г|а, и, *f.* shirt of mail, hauberk.

колю́ч|ий (～, ～а), *adj.* prickly; thorny; (*fig.*) sharp, biting; ～ая и́згородь prickly hedge; ～ая про́волока barbed wire; к. язы́к sharp tongue.

колю́чк|а, и, *f.* (*coll.*) **1.** prickle; thorn; quill (*of porcupine*). **2.** burr.

ко́люшк|а, и, *f.* (*fish*) stickleback.

ко́л|ющий, *pres. part. act. of* ～о́ть² *and adj.* ～ющая боль shooting pain.

коляд|а́, ы́, *f.* kolyada (*custom of house-to-house Christmas carol-singing*).

коляд|ова́ть, у́ю, *impf.* to go round carol-singing.

коля́ск|а, и, *f.* **1.** carriage, barouche. **2.** perambulator. **3.** (motor-cycle) side-car.

ком¹, а, *pl.* ～ья, ～ ьев, *m.* lump; ball; clod; сне́жный к. snow-ball; (*fig.*) к. в го́рле lump in the throat; пéрвый блин ᴗом (*prov.*) practice makes perfect.

ком², *p. of* кто.

ком-, *abbr. of* 1. коммунист́ический. 2. команд́ир. 3. комáндный.

-ком, *abbr. of* 1. комитéт. 2. комиссáр. 3. комиссариáт.

кóм|а, ы, *f.* (*med.*) coma.

комáнд|а, ы, *f.* 1. (word of) command, order; подáть ᴗу to give a command. 2. command; принять ᴗу (над) to take command (of). 3. (*mil.*) party, detachment, crew; (*naut.*) crew, ship's company; пожáрная к. fire-brigade. 4. (*sport*) team.

команд́ир, а, *m.* (*mil.*) commander, commanding officer; (*naut.*) captain.

командир|овáть, ýю, *impf. and pf.* to post; to dispatch, send on a mission.

командирóвк|а, и, *f.* 1. posting, dispatching (*on official business*). 2. mission; (official business) trip; éхать в ᴗу to go on a mission; он в ᴗе he is away on business, on a commission; я получил ᴗу в Казахстáн I have been given a commission to execute in Kazakhstan; нау́чная к. scientific mission. 3. (*coll.*) warrant, authority (*for travelling on official business, on commission*).

командирóв|очный, *adj. of* ᴗка; ᴗочные дéньги travelling allowance; ᴗочное удостоверéние warrant, authority (*for travelling on official business, on commission*); *as noun* ᴗочные, ᴗочных, travelling allowance, travelling expenses.

команд́итн|ый, *adj.* (*comm.*) ᴗое товáрищество sleeping partnership.

комáнд|ный, *adj.* 1. *adj. of* ᴗа; ᴗная дóлжность duties of a commander; к. пункт command post; к. состáв the officers (*of a military unit*). 2. (*fig.*) commanding; ᴗные высóты commanding heights, key points.

комáндовани|е, я, *n.* 1. commanding, command; принять к. (над) to take command (of, over). 2. (*collect.*) command.

комáнд|овать, ую, *impf.* (*of* с~) 1. to give orders. 2. (+*i.*) to command, be in command (of). 3. (*fig., coll.*) (+*i or* над) to order about. 4. (*fig.*) (над) to command (*terrain*).

командóр, а, *m.* (*hist.*) knight commander. 2. commodore (*of yacht club*).

комáндующ|ий, его, *m.* commander.

комáр, á, *m.* gnat, mosquito; (*coll.*) к. нóса не подтóчит not a thing can be said against it.

комар|и́ный, *adj. of* ᴗ; к. укýс mosquito bite; (*fig., coll.*) minute, midget.

коматóзный, *adj.* (*med.*) comatose.

комбáйн, а, *m.* (*tech.*) combine, multi-purpose machine; зерновóй к. combine harvester.

комбáйнер, а, *m.* (*agric.*) combine operator.

комбáт, а, *m.* (*abbr. of* команд́ир батальóна) battalion commander.

комбикóрм, а, *pl.* ᴗá, *m.* (*agric.*) mixed fodder.

комбикóрм|овый, *adj. of* ᴗ.

комбинáт, а, *m.* 1. industrial complex; combine; к. бытовóго обслýживания, *see* бытовóй. 2. comprehensive school.

комбинáтор, а, *m.* (*pejor.*) schemer, contriver.

комбинатóрный, *adj.* (*math.*) combinative.

комбинац|иóнный, *adj. of* ᴗия.

комбинáци|я¹, и, *f.* 1. combination;-(*econ.*) merger. 2. (*fig.*) scheme, system; (*polit., sport*) manœuvre.

комбинáци|я², и, *f.* (*underwear*) 1. slip. 2. combinations.

комбинезóн, а, *m.* 1. overalls. 2. jump-suit.

комбини́рованный, *adj.* combined.

комбини́р|овать, ую, *impf.* (*of* скомбини́ровать) 1. to combine, arrange. 2. (*coll.*) *pejor.*) to scheme, contrive; to devise a scheme, a system.

комди́в, а, *m.* (*abbr. of* команд́ир диви́зии) divisional commander.

комедиáнт, а, *m.* 1. (*obs.*) actor. 2. (*pejor.*) play-actor; hypocrite.

комеди́йный, *adj.* (*lit., theatr.*) comic; comedy; к. актёр comedy actor.

комéди|я, и, *f.* comedy. 2. (*fig., pejor.*) play-acting; farce; ломáть ᴗю, разы́грывать ᴗю to put on an act, enact a farce.

кóм|ель, ля, *m.* butt, butt-end (*of tree, etc.*).

комендáнт, а, *m.* 1. (*mil.*) commandant; к. гóрода town major; к. (стáнции) R.T.O. 2. manager; warden; к. теáтра theatre manager; к. общежи́тия warden of a hostel.

комендáнт|ский, *adj. of* ᴗ; к. час (*mil.*) curfew.

комендатýр|а, ы, *f.* commandant's office.

комендóр, а, *m.* (*naut.*) seaman gunner.

комéт|а, ы, *f.* comet.

коми́зм, а, *m.* 1. comedy, the comic element; к. положéния the funny side of a situation. 2. comicality; с ᴗом передразни́ть когó-н. to give a comical imitation of someone.

кóмик, а, *m.* 1. comic actor. 2. (*fig.*) comedian, comical fellow.

Коминтéрн, а, *m.* (*hist.*) (*abbr. of* Коммуни́стический Интернационáл) Comintern.

коминтéрн|овский, *adj. of* ᴗ.

комиссáр, а, *m.* commissar, commissioner; верхóвный к. high commissioner.

комиссариáт, а, *m.* commissariat.

комиссáр|ский, *adj. of* ᴗ.

комиссионéр, а, *m.* (commission-)agent, factor, broker.

комисс|иóнный, *adj. of* ᴗия 2; к. магази́н

commission shop (*where second-hand goods are sold on commission*); *as noun* ~ио́нные, ~ио́нных, (*comm.*) commission; получи́ть ~ио́нные to receive a commission.

коми́сси|я, и, *f.* **1.** commission, committee; к. по разоруже́нию disarmament commission; сле́дственная к. committee of investigation. **2.** (*comm.*) commission; брать на ~ю to take on commission.

комите́т, а, *m.* committee.

коми́ческ|ий, *adj.* **1.** comic; ~ая о́пера comic opera. **2.** comical, funny.

коми́ч|ный (~ен, ~на), *adj.* comical, funny.

ко́мка|ть, ю, *impf.* (*of* скомкать) **1.** (*pf. also* искомкать) to crumple. **2.** (*fig., coll.*) to make a hash of, muff.

коммента́ри|й, я, *m.* **1.** commentary. **2.** (*pl.*) comment; ~и изли́шни comment is superfluous.

коммента́тор, а, *m.* commentator.

коммента́р|овать, ую, *impf. and pf.* to comment (upon).

коммерса́нт, а, *m.* merchant; business man.

комме́рци|я, и, *f.* commerce, trade.

комме́рческ|ий, *adj.* **1.** commercial, mercantile; к. флот mercantile marine. **2.** of trade off the ration, on free market; к. магази́н shop retailing goods officially controlled at prices above those fixed; ~ие це́ны free market prices.

коммивояжёр, а, *m.* commercial traveller.

комму́н|а, ы, *f.* (*in var. senses*) commune.

коммуна́льник, а, *m.* municipal employee.

коммуна́льн|ый, *adj.* **1.** communal; municipal; ~ая кварти́ра 'communal' flat (*in which kitchen and toilet facilities are shared by a number of tenants*); ~ые услу́ги public utilities; ~ое хозя́йство municipal economy. **2.** *adj. of* комму́на.

коммуни́зм, а, *m.* communism.

коммуникацио́нн|ый, *adj.* ~ая ли́ния line of communication.

коммуника́ци|я, и, *f.* (*in var. senses*) communication; (*mil.*) line of communication.

коммуни́ст, а, *m.* communist.

коммунисти́ческ|ий, *adj.* communist; ~ое строи́тельство the building of communism.

коммута́тор, а, *m.* (*electr.*) **1.** commutator. **2.** switchboard.

коммюнике́, *indecl., n.* communiqué.

ко́мнат|а, ы, *f.* room.

ко́мнатн|ый, *adj.* **1.** of a room. **2.** indoor; ~ые и́гры indoor games; ~ые расте́ния indoor plants; ~ая соба́чка lap-dog; ~ая температу́ра room temperature.

комо́д, а, *m.* chest of drawers.

ком|о́к, ка́, *m. dim. of* ~; сверну́ться в к. to roll oneself up into a ball; (*fig.*) к. в го́рле lump in the throat; к. не́рвов bundle of nerves.

комо́лый, *adj.* (*dial.*) polled.

компа́кт|ный (~ен, ~на), *adj.* compact, solid.

компане́йск|ий, *adj.* (*coll.*) **1.** sociable, companionable. **2.** equally shared; расхо́ды на ~их нача́лах expenses equally shared; устро́ить ве́чер на к. счёт to go shares in giving a party.

компа́ни|я, и, *f.* (*in var. senses*) company; води́ть ~ю с кем-н. (*coll.*) to associate with someone; расстро́ить ~ю to break up a party; соста́вить кому́-н. ~ю to keep someone company; я провёл ве́чер в ~и с Воло́дей I spent the evening in Volodya's company; он тебе́ не к. he is no company for you; пойти́ це́лой ~ей to go all together; гуля́ть ~ей to go about in a group; (*coll.*) за ~ю for company; ну, ещё стака́нчик с тобо́й за ~ю! well, just one more to keep you company!

компаньо́н, а, *m.* **1.** (*comm.*) partner. **2.** companion.

компаньо́н|ка, ки, *f.* **1.** *f. of* ~. **2.** (lady's) companion.

компа́рти|я, и, *f.* (*abbr. of* Коммунисти́ческая па́ртия) Communist Party.

ко́мпас, а, *m.* compass; гла́вный к. standard compass; морско́й к. mariner's compass.

ко́мпас|ный, *adj. of* ~; ~ная стре́лка compass needle; к. я́щик binnacle.

компатрио́т, а, *m.* compatriot.

компа́унд, а, *m.* (*tech.*) compound.

компе́ндиум, а, *m.* compendium, digest.

компенсацио́нный, *adj.* compensatory, compensating; (*tech.*) к. ма́ятник compensation-pendulum.

компенса́ци|я, и, *f.* compensation.

компенси́р|овать, ую, *impf. and pf.* **1.** to compensate, indemnify (for). **2.** (*tech.*) to compensate, equilibrate.

компете́нт|ный (~ен, ~на), *adj.* competent.

компете́нци|я, и, *f.* competence; э́то не в мое́й ~и it is outside my competence, it is beyond my scope.

компили́р|овать, ую, *impf.* (*of* скомпили́ровать) (*pejor.*) to compile.

компиляти́в|ный (~ен, ~на), *adj. of* компиля́ция; к. труд compilation.

компиля́тор, а, *m.* (*pejor.*) compiler.

компиля́ци|я, и, *f.* (*pejor.*) compilation.

ко́мплекс, а, *m.* (*in var. senses*) complex; set; к. неполноце́нности inferiority complex.

ко́мплексн|ый, *adj.* **1.** (*math.*) complex; ~ое число́ complex number. **2.** over-all, all-embracing, all-in; к. обе́д table d'hôte dinner.

компле́кт, а, *m.* **1.** complete set; к. белья́

bedding, bed-clothes; к. вы́пусков «Коммуни́ста» за 1955 г. a complete set of 'Communist' for 1955. 2. complement; specified number; сверх ~a above the specified number; у нас ещё не хвата́ет двух челове́к до по́лного ~a we are still two short of the full complement.

компле́ктный, adj. complete.

комплект|ова́ть, у́ю, impf. (of у~) 1. to complete; to replenish; к. журна́л to acquire a complete set of a periodical. 2. (mil.) to bring up to strength; to (re)man.

компле́кци|я, и, f. build; (bodily) constitution.

комплеме́нт, а, m. complement.

комплиме́нт, а, m. compliment; сде́лать к. (+d.) to pay a compliment (to).

компло́т, а, m. (obs.) plot, conspiracy.

компози́тор, а, m. (mus.) composer.

компози́ци|я, и, f. (in various senses) composition; класс ~и (mus.) composition class.

компоне́нт, а, m. component.

компон|ова́ть, у́ю, impf. (of скомпонова́ть) to put together, arrange; to group; к. статью́ to put together an article.

компоно́вк|а, и, f. putting together, arrangement; grouping.

компо́ст, а, m. (hort.) compost.

компо́стер, а, m. punch (for 'bus tickets, etc.).

компости́р|овать, ую, impf. (of прокомпости́ровать) to punch ('bus tickets, etc.).

компо́ст|ный, adj. of ~; ~ная я́ма compost pit.

компо́т, а, m. compote, stewed fruit.

компре́сс, а, m. (med.) compress; согрева́ющий к. hot compress; поста́вить к. to apply a compress.

компре́ссор, а, m. (tech., med.) compressor.

компромети́р|овать, ую, impf. (of скомпромети́ровать) to compromise.

компроми́сс, а, m. compromise; идти́ на к. to make a compromise, meet half-way.

компроми́сс|ный, adj. of ~; ~ное реше́ние compromise settlement.

комсомо́л, а, m. (abbr. of Коммунисти́ческий Сою́з Молодёжи) Komsomol (Young Communist League).

комсомо́л|ец, ьца, m. member of Komsomol.

комсомо́л|ка, ки, f. of ~ец.

комсомо́л|ьский, adj. of ~.

комсо́рг, а, m. (abbr. of комсомо́льский организа́тор) Komsomol organizer.

кому́, d. of кто.

комфо́рт, а, m. comfort.

комфорта́бельный, adj. comfortable.

кон, а, о ~е, на ~у́, m. 1. (in games of chance) kitty; поста́вить де́ньги на́ к. to place one's stake, put one's money in (the kitty); быть,

стоя́ть на ~у́ (fig.) to be at stake. 2. (games) game; round.

кона́|ться, юсь, impf. (dial.) to draw lots (for first turn at a game).

конве́йер, а, m. (tech.) conveyor (belt); сбо́рочный к., к. сбо́рки assembly line.

конве́йер|ный, adj. of ~; ~ная систе́ма conveyor (belt) system.

конве́кци|я, и, f. (phys.) convection.

конве́нт, а, m. (polit.) convention.

конвенциона́льный, adj. conventional.

конвенц|ио́нный, adj. of ~ия; к. тари́ф agreed tariff.

конве́нци|я, и, f. (leg.) convention, agreement.

конверге́нци|я, и, f. convergence.

конве́рси|я, и, f. (econ.) conversion.

конве́рт, а, m. 1. envelope. 2. (gramophone record) sleeve. 3. sleeping bag (for infants).

конверти́р|овать, ую, impf. and pf. (econ.) to convert.

конве́ртор, а, m. (tech.) converter.

конво́й|р, а, m. escort.

конвои́р|овать, ую, impf. to escort, convoy.

конво́|й, я, m. escort, convoy; вести́ под ~ем to convoy, conduct under escort.

конво́й|ный, adj. of ~; ~ное су́дно escort vessel; as noun к., ~ного, m. escort.

конвульси́в|ный (~ен, ~на), adj. (med.) convulsive.

конву́льси|я, и, f. (med.) convulsion.

конгениа́л|ьный (~ен, ~ьна), adj. congenial; (+d.) well suited (to), in harmony (with); перево́д, к. оригина́лу a translation in the spirit of the original.

конгломера́т, а, m. 1. conglomeration. 2. (geol.) conglomerate.

конгре́сс, а, m. congress.

кондач|о́к, only in coll. phrase с ~ка́ off-hand, perfunctorily.

конденса́тор, а, m. condenser.

конденсацио́нн|ый, adj. condensing, obtained by condensation; ~ая вода́ condensation water; к. горшо́к condensing vessel.

конденса́ци|я, и, f. condensation.

конденси́р|овать, ую, impf. and pf. to condense.

конди́тер, а, m. confectioner, pastry-cook.

конди́терск|ая, ой, f. confectioner's, sweet-shop; pastry-cook's.

конди́терск|ий, adj. ~ие изде́лия confectionery; к. магази́н = ~ая.

кондициони́рование|е, я, n. conditioning; к. во́здуха air conditioning.

кондициони́р|овать, ую, impf. to condition.

конди́ци|я, и, f. 1. (comm.) standard. 2. (hist.) жить на ~ях to be a resident tutor.

ко́ндо́вый, adj. 1. having solid, close-grained timber (also fig. as epithet of old Russia). 2. (fig.) of the good old-fashioned sort.

кóндор, a, m. (orn.) condor.

кондотьéр, a, m. (hist.) condottiere; soldier of fortune.

кондуит, a, m. conduct-book.

кондуктор¹, a, pl. ~á, ~óв, m. ('bus, tram) conductor; (railway) guard.

кондуктор², a, pl. ~ы, ~ов, m. (electr.) conductor.

кондукторш|а, и, f. (coll.) conductress.

коневóд, a, m. horse-breeder.

коневóдств|о, a, n. horse-breeding.

коневóд|ческий, adj. of ~ство.

кон|ёк, ькá, m. 1. dim. of ~ь; морскóй к. (zool.) hippocampus, sea-horse. 2. ornament on peak of gable. 3. (fig., coll.) hobby-horse; hobby; сесть на своегó ~ькá to mount one's hobby-horse. 4. (orn.) pipit. 5. see ~ький.

кон|éц, цá, m. 1. (in var. senses) end; óстрый к. point; тóлстый к. butt(-end); тóнкий к. tip; в к. (coll.) completely; в ~цé ~цóв in the end, after all; и дéло с ~цóм and there's an end to it; из ~цá в к. from end to end, all over; ~цы́ с ~цáми своди́ть (coll.) to make both ends meet; на э́тот (тот) к. to this (that) end; на худóй к. (coll.) at the worst, if the worst comes to the worst; один к. (coll.) it comes to the same thing in the end; со всех ~цóв from all quarters; хорони́ть ~цы́ (coll.) to bury, remove traces; и ~цы́ в вóду and none will be the wiser; пришёл ему́ к. that's the end of him. 2. (coll.) distance, way (from one place to another); в один к. one way; в óба ~цá there and back. 3. (naut.) rope's end.

конéчно, adv. of course, certainly; no doubt; он, к., прав no doubt he is right; к. да! rather!; к. нет! certainly not!

конéчност|ь¹, и, f. finiteness.

конéчност|ь², и, f. (anat.) extremity.

конéч|ный (~ен, ~на), adj. 1. final, last; ultimate; ~ная стáнция terminus; ~ная цель ultimate aim; в ~ном итóге, счёте ultimately, in the last analysis. 2. finite.

конин|а, ы, no pl., f. horse-flesh.

кони́ческ|ий, adj. conic(al); ~ое сечéние conic section.

кóнк|а, и, f. horse-tramway; horse-drawn tram.

конклáв, a, m. conclave.

конкордáт, a, m. concordat.

конкретизи́р|овать, ую, impf. and pf. to render concrete, give concrete expression to.

конкрéт|ный (~ен, ~на), adj. concrete; specific.

конкубинáт, a, m. concubinage.

конкурéнт, a, m. competitor; rival.

конкурéнци|я, и, f. competition; вне ~и hors-concours.

конкури́р|овать, ую, impf. (c+i.) to compete (with).

кóнкурс, a, m. 1. competition; объяви́ть к. (на+a.) to announce a vacancy (for); вне ~a hors-concours; (fig.) in a class by itself.

кóнкурс|ный, adj. of ~; к. экзáмен competitive examination.

кóнник, a, m. cavalryman.

кóнниц|а, ы, f. cavalry; horse (collect.; mil.).

конногвардé|ец, йца, m. (mil.) 1. horse-guardsman. 2. (in tsarist Russian army) life-guard.

коннозавóдств|о, a, n. 1. horse-breeding. 2. stud(-farm).

коннозавóдчик, a, m. owner of stud(-farm).

кóн|ный, adj. of ~ь; horse; mounted; equestrian; ~ная áрмия cavalry army; ~ная артиллéрия horse artillery; к. двор stables; к. привóд horse-drive; ~ная стáтуя equestrian statue; на ~ной тя́ге horse-drawn; ~ная я́рмарка horse-market.

коновáл, a, m. 1. horse-doctor, farrier. 2. (coll.) quack(-doctor).

коновóд¹, a, m. (mil.) horse-holder.

коновóд², a, m. (coll.) ringleader.

коновó|дить, жу, дишь, impf. (+i.; coll.) to be ringleader (of).

кóновязь|ь, и, f. tether; tethering-post.

конокрáд, a, m. horse-thief.

конокрáдств|о, a, n. horse-stealing.

конопá|тить, чу, тишь, impf. (of законопáтить) to caulk.

конопáтк|а, и, f. 1. caulking. 2. caulking-iron.

конопáтчик, a, m. caulker.

конопáтый, adj. (dial.) freckled; pock-marked.

конопá|чу, тишь, see ~тить.

конопл|я́, и́, f. (bot.) hemp.

конопля́ник, a, m. hemp-field.

конопля́нк|а, и, f. (orn.) linnet.

конопля́|ный, adj. of ~; ~ное мáсло hemp-seed oil.

коносамéнт, a, m. (comm.) bill of lading.

консервати́в|ный (~ен, ~на), adj. conservative.

консервати́зм, a, m. conservatism.

консервáтор, a, m. (esp. polit.) conservative.

консервáтори|я, и, f. conservatoire, academy of music.

консервáторский, adj. conservative.

консервáтор|ский, adj. of ~ия.

консервáци|я, и, f. 1. conservation. 2. temporary closing-down.

консерви́рован|ный (~, ~a), p.p.p. of консерви́ровать and adj.; ~ные фрýкты bottled fruit, tinned fruit.

консерви́р|овать, ую, impf. and pf. (pf. also законсерви́ровать) 1. to preserve (to tin, *bottle, etc.*). **2.** к. предприя́тие to close down an enterprise temporarily.

консе́рв|ный, *adj. of* ~ы; ~ная ба́нка tin; к. нож tin-opener; ~ная фа́брика cannery.

консе́рв|ы, ов, *no sing.* **1.** tinned goods. **2.** goggles.

конси́лиум, а, *m.* (*med.*) consultation.

консисте́нци|я, и, *f.* (*phys., med.*) consistence.

консисто́ри|я, и, *f.* (*eccl.*) consistory.

ко́н|ский, *adj. of* ~ь; ~ские бобы́ broad beans; к. во́лос horse-hair; к. заво́д stud(-farm); ~ские состяза́ния horse-races; к. хвост 'pony-tail' (*hair style*).

консолида́ци|я, и, *f.* consolidation.

консолиди́р|овать, ую, *impf. and pf.* **1.** to consolidate. **2.** (*fin.*) to fund.

консо́л|ь, и, *f.* (*archit.*) **1.** console, cantilever. **2.** pedestal.

консоме́, *indecl., n.* (*cul.*) consommé.

консона́нс, а, *m.* (*mus.*) consonance.

консонанти́зм, а, *m.* (*ling.*) system of consonants.

консо́рциум, а, *m.* (*fin.*) consortium.

конспе́кт, а, *m.* **1.** synopsis, summary, abstract. **2.** notes (*for a lecture*).

конспекти́в|ный (~ен, ~на), *adj.* concise, summary.

конспекти́р|овать, ую, *impf.* (*of* за~ *and* проконспекти́ровать) to make an abstract of.

конспирати́в|ный (~ен, ~на), *adj.* secret, clandestine.

конспира́тор, а, *m.* conspirator.

конспира́ци|я, и, *f.* security, secrecy (*of an illegal organization*).

конспири́р|овать, ую, *impf.* (*of* законспири́ровать) to observe the rules of security (*in an illegal organization*).

конста́нт|а, ы, *f.* (*math., phys.*) constant.

констата́ци|я, и, *f.* ascertaining; verification, establishment.

констати́р|овать, ую, *impf. and pf.* to ascertain; to verify, establish; к. смерть to certify death; к. факт to establish a fact.

констелля́ци|я, и, *f.* (*astron.*) constellation.

конститу́и́р|овать, ую, *impf. and pf.* to constitute, set up.

конституционали́зм, а, *m.* (*polit.*) constitutionalism.

конституциона́льный, *adj.* (*med., physiol.*) constitutional.

конституцио́нный, *adj.* (*polit.*) constitutional.

конститу́ци|я, и, *f.* (*polit., med.*) constitution.

констру́и́р|овать, ую, *impf. and pf.* (*pf. also* сконструи́ровать) **1.** to construct; to design. **2.** to form (*a government, etc.*).

конструктиви́зм, а, *m.* (*art*) constructivism.

констру́ктивный, *adj* **1.** structural; constructional; к. фа́ктор (*tech.*) efficiency factor, construction factor. **2.** constructive.

констру́ктор, а, *m.* designer, constructor.

констру́ктор|ский, *adj. of* ~; ~ское бюро́ design office.

констру́кци|я, и, *f.* **1.** construction, structure; design. **2.** (*gram.*) construction.

ко́нсул, а, *m.* consul.

ко́нсульский, *adj.* consular.

ко́нсульств|о, а, *n.* consulate.

консульта́нт, а, *m.* consultant, adviser; tutor (*in higher education institution*).

консультати́вный, *adj.* consultative, advisory.

консультац|ио́нный, *adj. of* ~ия; ~ио́нное бюро́ advice bureau; ~ио́нная пла́та consultation fee.

консульта́ци|я, и, *f.* **1.** consultation; specialist advice. **2.** advice bureau; де́тская к. children's clinic; же́нская к. ante-natal clinic; юриди́ческая к. legal advice office. **3.** tutorial; supervision (*in higher education institution*).

консульти́р|овать, ую, *impf.* **1.** (с+*i.*) to consult. **2.** (*pf.* проконсульти́ровать) to advise; to act as tutor (to).

консульти́р|оваться, уюсь, *impf.* (*of* проконсульти́роваться) **1.** (с+*i.*) to consult. **2.** to have a consultation; to obtain advice; to be a pupil of.

конта́кт, а, *m.* **1.** contact; вступи́ть в к. с кем-н. to come into contact, get in touch with someone; быть в ~е (с+*i.*) to be in touch (with). **2.** (*electr.*) к. приёмный socket; к. штыково́й plug.

конта́ктн|ый, *adj.* (*tech.*) contact; к. рельс contact rail, live rail; ~ая сва́рка point welding; ~ые ли́нзы (*med.*) contact lenses.

контамина́ци|я, и, *f.* (*ling.*) contamination.

конте́кст, а, *m.* context.

континге́нт, а, *m.* **1.** (*econ.*) quota. **2.** contingent; batch; к. новобра́нцев batch, squad of recruits.

контине́нт, а, *m.* continent.

континента́льный, *adj.* continental.

контокорре́нт, а, *m.* account current (a/c).

конто́р|а, ы, *f.* office, bureau; почто́вая к. post office.

конто́рк|а, и, *f.* (writing-)desk, bureau.

конто́р|ский, *adj. of* ~а; ~ская кни́га (account-)book; ledger.

конто́рщик, а, *m.* clerk.

ко́нтр|а¹, ы, *f.* (*coll.*) (*pl.*) disagreement, dispute; быть в ~ах (с+*i.*) to be at odds (with); у них вы́шли ~ы they have fallen out.

ко́нтр|а², ы, *m. and f.* (*sl.*) counter-revolutionary.

контраба́нд|а, ы, *f.* **1.** contraband, smuggling; занима́ться ~ой to smuggle. **2.** contraband (*goods*).

контрабанди́ст, а, *m.* smuggler, contrabandist.

контраба́ндный, *adj.* contraband.

контраба́с, а, *m.* (*mus.*) double-bass.

контраге́нт, а, *m.* contractor.

контр-адмира́л, а, *m.* rear-admiral.

контра́кт, а, *m.* contract.

контракта́ци|я, и, *f.* contracting (for).

контракт|ова́ть, у́ю, *impf.* (*of* законтрактова́ть) to contract for (*supply of, performance of work by*); к. рабо́тников to engage workmen.

контракт|ова́ться, у́юсь, *impf.* (*of* законтрактова́ться) **1.** to contract, undertake (*to supply goods, perform work*). **2.** *pass of* ~ова́ть.

контра́кт|овый, *adj. of* ~; ~овая я́рмарка trade fair, industrial fair.

контра́льто, *indecl., n.* (*mus.*) contralto.

контра́льто|вый, *adj. of* ~.

контрама́рк|а, и, *f.* complimentary ticket.

контрапу́нкт, а, *m.* (*mus.*) counterpoint.

контрапункти́ческий, *adj.* (*mus.*) contrapuntal.

контрапу́нкт|ный, *adj.* = ~и́ческий.

контрассигна́ци|я, и, *f.* countersign.

контрассигни́р|овать, ую, *impf. and pf.* to countersign.

контрассигно́вк|а, и, *f.* countersign.

контра́ст, а, *m.* contrast; по ~у (с+*i.*) by contrast (with).

контрасти́р|овать, ую, *impf.* (с+*i.*) to contrast (with).

контра́стный, *adj.* contrasting.

контратак|а, и, *f.* (*mil.*) counter-attack.

контратак|ова́ть, у́ю, *impf. and pf.* to counter-attack.

контргайк|а, и, *f.* (*tech.*) lock-nut, check-nut.

контрибу́ци|я, и, *f.* (war) indemnity; contribution; наложи́ть ~ю (на+*a.*) to impose an indemnity (on); to lay under contribution.

ко́нтрик, а, *m.* (*sl.*) = ко́нтра.²

контр-манёвр, а, *m.* (*mil.*) counter-manœuvre.

контрма́рш, а, *m.* (*mil.*) countermarch.

контрнаступле́ни|е, я, *n.* counter-offensive.

контрове́рз|а, ы, *f.* controversy.

контроле́р, а, *m.* inspector; ticket-collector.

контроли́р|овать, ую, *impf.* (*of* про~) to check; к. биле́ты to inspect tickets.·

контро́ллер, а, *m.* (*electr.*) controller.

контро́л|ь, я, *m.* **1.** control. **2.** check(ing); inspection; (*tech.*) monitoring; предста́вить ци́фры ~ю to check one's figures. **3.** (*collect.*) inspectors.

контро́ль|ный, *adj. of* ~; ~ная вы́шка (*naut.*) conning tower; ~ная коми́ссия control commission; ~ная систе́ма (*radio*) monitor-

ing system; ~ные ци́фры (*econ.*) scheduled figures; к. пле́нный (*mil.*) prisoner for identification.

контрпа́р, а, *m.* (*tech.*) counter-steam, back-steam.

контрпрете́нзи|я, и, *f.* counter-claim.

контрприка́з, а, *m.* countermand.

контрразве́дк|а, и, *f.* counter-espionage.

контрразве́дчик, а, *m.* member of counter-espionage.

контрреволюционе́р, а, *m.* counter-revolutionary.

контрреволюцио́нный, *adj.* counter-revolutionary.

контрреволю́ци|я, и, *f.* counter-revolution.

контруда́р, а, *m.* (*mil.*) counter-blow.

контрфо́рс, а, *m.* (*archit.*) buttress, counter-fort.

контрэска́рп, а, *m.* (*mil.*) counterscarp.

конту́жен|ный (~, ~а), *p.p.p. of* конту́зить *and adj.;* ~ные (*mil.*) shell-shock cases.

конту́|зить, жу, зишь, *pf.* to contuse; to shell-shock.

конту́зи|я, и, *f.* contusion, bruising; shell-shock.

ко́нтур, а, *m.* **1.** contour. **2.** (*electr.*) circuit.

ко́нтур|ный, *adj. of* ~; ~ная ка́рта contour map.

кону́р|а́, ы́, *f.* kennel (*also fig., coll.*).

ко́нус, а, *m.* cone.

конусообра́з|ный (~ен, ~на), *adj.* conical.

конфедера́т, а, *m.* (*hist.*) confederate.

конфедерати́вный, *adj.* confederative.

конфедера́тк|а, и, *f.* (*hist.*) konfederatka (*Polish national or military headgear—rectangular cap with no peak*).

конфедера́ци|я, и, *f.* confederation.

конфекцио́н, а, *m.* ready-made clothes shop.

конфера́нс, а, *m.* (*theatr.*) compèring.

конферансье́, *indecl., m.* (*theatr.*) compère, master of ceremonies.

конфере́нц-за́л, а, *m.* conference chamber.

конфере́нци|я, и, *f.* conference.

конфе́т|а, ы, *f.* sweet.

конфе́т|ный, *adj.* **1.** *adj. of* ~a; ~ная бума́жка sweet wrapper. **2.** (*coll., pejor.*) sugary, treacly.

конфетти́, *indecl., n.* confetti.

конфигура́ци|я, и, *f.* configuration, conformation.

конфиденциа́л|ьный (~ен, ~ьна), *adj.* confidential.

конфирма́нт, а, *m.* (*eccl.*) confirmation candidate.

конфирма́ци|я, и, *f.* **1.** (*eccl.*) confirmation. **2.** (*obs.*) ratification.

конфирм|ова́ть, у́ю, *impf. and pf.* **1.** (*eccl.*) to confirm. **2.** (*obs.*) to ratify.

конфиска́ци|я, и, *f.* confiscation, seizure.

конфиск|овáть, ýю, *impf. and pf.* to confiscate.

конфлúкт, а, *m.* 1. clash, conflict. 2. (*polit.*) dispute.

конфлúкт|ный, *adj. of* ~; ~ная комúссия arbitration tribunal.

конфликт|овáть, ýю, *impf.* (с+*i.*) (*coll.*) to to clash (with), come up (against).

конфóрк|а, и, *f.* ring (*on cooking stove*); crown, top ring (*on samovar*).

конфýз, а, *m.* discomfiture, embarrassment; какóй к. (получúлся)! how awkward, how embarrassing!; привестú в к. to place in an embarrassing position.

конфý|зить, жу, зишь, *impf.* (*of* с~) to confuse, embarrass; to place in an embarrassing position.

конфý|зиться, жусь, зишься, *impf.* (*of* с~) 1. to feel embarrassed; to be shy. 2. (+*g.*) to feel ashamed (of); to be shy (in front of).

конфýзлив|ый (~, ~а), *adj.* bashful; shy.

конфýзный, *adj.* (*coll.*) awkward, embarrassing.

концев|óй, *adj.* final; ~áя строкá end-line.

концентрáт, а, *m.* 1. concentrated product. 2. (*geol.*) concentrate.

концентрациóнный, *adj.* к. лáгерь concentration camp.

концентрáци|я, и, *f.* (*in var. senses*) concentration.

концентрúрова|нный, *p.p.p. of* ~ть *and adj.* concentrated.

концентрúр|овать, ую, *impf.* (*of* с~) (*in var. senses*) to concentrate; (*mil.*) to mass; (*fig.*) к. внимáние на вопрóсе to concentrate one's attention on a question.

концентрúр|оваться, уюсь, *impf.* (*of* с~) 1. to mass, collect (*intrans.*). 2.(*fig.*; на+*p.*) to concentrate.

концентрúческий, *adj.* concentric.

концентрúчност|ь, и, *f.* concentricity.

концéнтр|ы, ов, *sing.* ~, ~а, *m.* concentric circles.

концéпт, а, *m.* (*philos.*) concept.

концептуалúзм, а, *m.* (*philos.*) conceptualism.

концéпци|я, и, *f.* conception, idea.

концéрн, а, *m.* (*econ.*) concern.

концéрт, а, *m.* (*mus.*) 1. concert; recital; симфонúческий к. symphony concert; быть на ~е to be at a concert; (*coll.*) кошáчий к. caterwauling; (*fig.*) hooting, barracking. 2. concerto.

концертáнт, а, *m.* performer (*in a concert*).

концертúр|овать, ую, *impf.* to give concerts.

концертмéйстер, а, *m.* (*mus.*) 1. leader (*of orchestra*). 2. solo performer.

концéрт|ный, *adj. of* ~; к. роя́ль concert grand (piano).

концессионéр, а, *m.* concessionaire.

концéсси|я, и, *f.* (*econ.*) concession.

концлáгер|ь, я, *m.* (*abbr. of* концентрациóнный лáгерь) concentration camp.

концóвк|а, и, *f.* 1. (*typ.*) tail-piece; colophon. 2. (*fig.*) ending (*of lit. work*).

конч|áть(ся), áю(сь), *impf. of* ~úть(ся).

конч|енный, *p.p.p. of* ~úть; *as interj.* ~ено! enough!; всё ~ено! it's all over!; с ним всё ~ено it's all up with him.

кóнчен|ый, *adj.* (*coll.*) decided, settled; э́то дéло ~ое the matter is settled; к. человéк (*coll.*) goner.

кóнчик, а, *m.* tip; point; на ~е языкá on the tip of one's tongue.

кончúн|а, ы, *f.* (*rhet.*) decease, demise; end.

конч|úть, у, ишь, *pf.* (*of* ~áть) 1. to finish, end; к. речь выражéнием благодáрности to end a speech with thanks; на э́том он ~ил here he stopped; я ~ил that is all (I have to say); к. шкóлу to finish school course; к. университéт to graduate, go down (*from university*); к. самоубúйством to commit suicide; к. плóхо, дýрно, сквéрно to come to a bad end. 2. (с+*i.*) to be finished (with), give up. 3. (+*inf.*) to stop.

конч|úться, усь, ишься, *pf.* (*of* ~áться) 1. (+*i.*) to end (in), finish (by); to come to an end; э́тим дéло не ~илось that was not the end of it; дéло ~илось ничéм it came to nothing. 2. (*obs.*) to die, expire.

конъектýр|а, ы, *f.* (*philol.*) conjecture.

конъектýрный, *adj.* (*philol.*) conjectural.

конъюнктивúт, а, *m.* (*med.*) conjunctivitis.

конъюнктýр|а, ы, *f.* 1. state of affairs, juncture; междунарóдная к. international situation. 2. (*econ.*) state of the market.

конъюнктýр|ный, *adj. of* ~а 2; ~ные цéны (free) market prices.

конъюнктýрщик, а, *m.* (*coll., pejor.*) opportunist, time-server.

кон|ь, я́, *pl.* ~и, ~éй, *m.* 1. horse; боевóй к. war-horse, charger; нá к., по ~ям! (*mil. command*) mount!; (*prov.*) дарёному ~ю в зýбы не смóтрят never look a gift horse in the mouth; не в ~я́ корм pearls before swine. 2. (vaulting-)horse. 3. (*chess*) knight.

кон|ьки́, ько́в, *sing.* ~ёк, ~ька́, *m.* skates; к. на рóликах roller skates; катáться на ~ька́х to skate.

конькобéж|ец, ца, *m.* skater.

конькобéжный, *adj.* skating.

конья́к, á (ý), *m.* brandy.

конья́|чный, *adj. of* ~к.

кóнюх, а, *m.* groom, stable-man.

конЮш|ня, ни, *g. pl.* ~ен, *f.* stable; Áвгиевы ~ни (*myth. or fig.*) Augean stables.

кооперати́в, а, *m.* **1.** co-operative society. **2.** (*coll.*) co-operative store.

кооперати́вн|ый, *adj.* co-operative; ~ое движе́ние (*econ., polit.*) the co-operative movement; ~ое това́рищество co-operative society.

коопера́тор, а, *m.* co-operator, member of co-operative society.

коопера́ци|я, и, *f.* **1.** co-operation. **2.** (*collect.*) co-operative societies; потреби́тельская, сельскохозя́йственная к. consumers', agricultural co-operative societies.

коопери́р|овать, ую, *impf. and pf.* (*econ.*) **1.** to organize on co-operative lines. **2.** to recruit to a co-operative organization.

коопери́р|оваться, уюсь, *impf. and pf.* (*econ.*) **1.** to co-operate. **2.** *pass. of* ~овать.

коопта́ци|я, и, *f.* co-optation.

коопти́р|овать, ую, *impf. and pf.* to co-opt.

координа́т|а, ы, *f.* (*math.*) co-ordinate.

координа́тный, *adj.* (*math.*) co-ordinate.

координа́тор, а, *m.* co-ordinator.

координа́ци|я, и, *f.* co-ordination.

координи́р|овать, ую, *impf. and pf.* to co-ordinate.

копа́л, а, *m.* copal.

копа́ни|е, я, *n.* digging.

коп|а́ть, а́ю, *impf.* **1.** (*pf.* ~ну́ть) to dig. **2.** (*pf.* вы́~) to dig up, dig out.

копа́|ться, юсь, *impf.* **1.** (в+*p.*) to rummage (in); to root (in); (*fig.*) к. в душе́ to be given to soul-searching. **2.** (*coll.*; c+*i.*) to dawdle (over). **3.** *pass. of* ~ть.

копе́ечк|а, и, *f. dim. of* копе́йка; (*coll.*) э́то влети́т тебе́ в ~у it will cost you a pretty penny.

копе́ечн|ый, *adj.* '**1.** one-kopeck; worth one kopeck. **2.** (*in price*) minute, insignificant; ~ые расхо́ды trifling expenses. **3.** (*fig., coll.*) petty; twopenny-halfpenny.

копе́йк|а, и, *g. pl.* **копе́ек,** *f.* kopeck; к. в ~у exactly; до после́дней ~и to the last farthing; зашиби́ть, сколоти́ть ~у to turn an honest penny; к. рубль бережёт (*prov.*) take care of the pence, the pounds will take care of themselves.

коп|ёр, ра́, *m.* (*tech.*) **1.** pile-driver. **2.** mine headframe.

ко́п|и, ей, *sing.* ~ь, ~и, *f.* mines.

копи́лк|а, и, *f.* money-box.

копи́рк|а, и, *f.* (*coll.*) carbon paper, copying paper; писа́ть под ~у to make a carbon copy.

копирова́льн|ый, *adj.* copying; ~ая бума́га carbon paper.

копи́р|овать, ую, *impf.* (*of* с~) to copy; to imitate, mimic.

копиро́вк|а, и, *f.* copying.

копиро́вщик, а, *m.* copyist.

коп|и́ть, лю́, ~ишь, *impf.* (*of* на~) to accu-

mulate, amass; to store up; к. де́ньги to save up; (*fig.*) к. си́лы to save one's strength.

коп|и́ться, лю́сь, ~ишься, *impf.* (*of* на~) to accumulate (*intrans.*).

ко́пи|я, и, *f.* copy; duplicate; replica; заве́ренная к. (*leg.*) attested copy; снять ~ю (c+*g.*) to copy, make a copy (of); (*fig.*) он то́чная к. своего́ отца́ he is the very image of his father.

коп|на́, ны́, *pl.* ~ны, ~ён, ~на́м, *f.* shock, stook (*of corn*); к. се́на haycock; (*fig., coll.*) heap, pile; к. воло́с shock of hair.

копн|и́ть, ю́, и́шь, *impf.* (*of* с~) (*agric.*) to shock, stook; to cock (*hay*).

коп|ну́ть, ну́, нёшь, *pf. of* ~а́ть.

копотли́в|ый (~, ~а), *adj.* (*coll.*) slow, sluggish; ~ое де́ло slow, sticky job.

копотн|я́, и́, *f.* (*coll.*) dawdling.

копоту́н, а́, *m.* (*coll.*) dawdler.

ко́пот|ь, и, *f.* soot; lamp-black.

копош|и́ться, у́сь, и́шься, *impf.* **1.** to swarm. **2.** (*fig., coll.*) to stir, creep in; у меня́ в голове́ ~и́лось сомне́ние a doubt was beginning to stir in my head. **3.** (*coll.*) to potter about.

ко́пр|а, ы, *f.* copra.

коп|ро́вый, *adj. of* ~ёр.

копт|е́ть[1], и́т, *impf.* (*of* за~) (*coll.*) to be blackened (*from smoke, with soot*).

коп|те́ть[2], чу́, ти́шь, *impf.* (над) (*coll.*) **1.** to swot (at), plug away (at). **2.** to vegetate, rot away (*fig.*).

копти́лк|а, и, *f.* (*coll.*) oil-lamp (*of primitive design*).

копти́льный, *adj.* for smoking.

копти́л|ьня, ьни, *g. pl.* ~ен, *f.* smoking-shed.

коп|ти́ть, чу́, ти́шь, *impf.* **1.** (*pf.* за~) to smoke, cure in smoke. **2.** (*pf.* за~) to blacken (*with smoke*); к. стекло́ to smoke glass; к. не́бо (*coll.*) to idle one's life away. **3.** (*pf.* на~) to smoke (*intrans.*).

копу́н, а́, *m.* (*coll.*) dawdler.

копче́ни|е, я, *n.* **1.** smoking, curing in smoke. **2.** (*collect.*) smoked products.

копчён|ый, *adj.* smoked, smoke-dried; ~ая селёдка bloater.

ко́пчик, а, *m.* (*anat.*) coccyx.

коп|чу́[1], ти́шь, *see* ~те́ть[2].

коп|чу́[2], ти́шь, *see* ~ти́ть.

копы́тн|ый, *adj.* **1.** hoof. **2.** (*zool.*) hoofed, ungulate; *as noun* ~ые, ~ых, ungulate animals.

копы́т|о, а, *n.* hoof.

коп|ь, *see* ~и.

коп|ьё, ья́, *pl.* ~ья, ~ий, ~ьям, *n.* spear, lance; мета́ние ~ья́ (*sport*) javelin throwing; би́ться на ~ьях to tilt, joust; (*fig., iron.*) ~ья лома́ть (из-за) to break a lance (over).

копь|ё², я́, *n.* у меня́ ни ~я́ нет (*coll.*) I haven't a penny.

копьеви́д|ный (~ен, ~на), *adj.* (*bot.*) lanceolate.

кор|а́, ы́, *f.* **1.** (*bot.*) cortex; bark, rind. **2.** (*anat.*) к. головно́го мо́зга cerebral cortex. **3.** crust; земна́я к. (earth-)crust; (*fig.*) под ~о́й его́ суро́вости бы́ло до́брое се́рдце he had a kind heart beneath his hard exterior.

кораб|е́льный, *adj. of* ~ль; ~е́льная авиа́ция shipborne aircraft; к. лес ship timber; к. инжене́р naval architect; к. ма́стер shipwright.

корабе́льщик, а, *m.* **1.** (*obs.*) sea-captain. **2.** (*coll.*) shipwright.

кораблевожде́ни|е, я, *n.* navigation.

кораблекруше́ни|е, я, *n.* ship-wreck; потерпе́ть к. to be ship-wrecked.

кораблестрое́ни|е, я, *n.* ship-building.

кораблестрои́тел|ь, я, *m.* ship-builder, naval architect.

кора́бл|ик, а, *m.* **1.** *dim. of* ~ь. **2.** toy boat. **3.** (*zool.*) nautilus; argonaut.

кора́бл|ь, я́, *m.* **1.** ship, vessel; лине́йный к. battleship; флагма́нский к. flagship; сади́ться на к. to go on board (ship); сжечь свои́ ~и́ (*fig.*) to burn one's boats; большо́му ~ю́ большо́е пла́ванье (*prov.*) a great ship asks deep waters. **2.** (*archit.*) nave.

кора́лл, а, *m.* coral.

кора́ллов|ый, *adj.* **1.** coral. **2.** coralline; coral-red; ~ые уста́ coral lips.

Кора́н, а, *m.* the Koran.

корве́т, а, *m.* (*naut.*) corvette.

ко́рд|а, ы, *f.* lunge (longe); гоня́ть ло́шадь на ~е to lunge a horse.

кордебале́т, а, *m.* corps de ballet.

корди́т, а, *m.* cordite.

кордо́н, а, *m.* cordon.

кор|ево́й, *adj. of* ~ь.

коре́|ец, йца, *m.* Korean.

корёж|ить, у, ишь, *impf.* (*of* ис~) (*coll.*) **1.** to bend, warp; (*impers.*) его́ ~ило от бо́ли he was writhing with pain. **2.** (*fig.*) to make indignant.

корёж|иться, усь, ишься, *impf.* (*of* ис~) (*coll.*) **1.** to bend, warp (*intrans.*) **2.** к. от бо́ли to writhe with pain.

коре́йк|а, и, *f.* brisket (*of pork or veal*).

коре́йский, *adj.* Korean.

корена́ст|ый (~, ~а), *adj.* **1.** thickset, stocky. **2.** with strong roots.

корениза́ци|я, и, *f.* (*polit.*) indigenisation.

корени́зр|овать, ую, *impf. and pf.* (*polit.*) to place under local (indigenous) authority.

корени́т|ься, ся, *impf.* (в+*p.*) to be rooted (in).

коренни́к, а́, *m.* shaft-horse, thill-horse, wheeler.

коренн|о́й, *adj.* radical, fundamental; к. зуб molar (tooth); к. жи́тель native; ~о́е населе́ние indigenous population; ~а́я ло́шадь = ~и́к.

ко́р|ень, ня, *pl.* ~ни, ~не́й, *m.* **1.** (*in var. senses*) root; в ~не radically; в ~ню́ between the shafts; вы́рвать с ~нем to uproot, tear up by the roots (*also fig.*); красне́ть до ~не́й воло́с to blush to the roots of one's hair; пусти́ть ~ни to take root (*also fig.*); смотре́ть в к. чего́-н. to get at the root of something; хлеб на ~ню́ standing crop. **2.** (*math.*) root; radical; знак ~ня radical sign; куби́ческий к. cube root; показа́тель ~ня root index.

ко́рень|я, ев, *no sing.* roots (*of vegetables, herbs, etc., for culinary and medicinal purposes*).

ко́реш, а, *m.* (*sl.*) pal, mate.

кореш|о́к, ка́, *m.* **1.** spine (*of book*). **2.** counterfoil. **3.** *dim. of* ко́рень. **4.** (*sl.*) pal, mate.

корея́нк|а, и, *f.* Korean (woman).

корзи́н|а, ы, *f.* basket.

корзи́нк|а, и, *f.* small basket, punnet; рабо́чая к. work-basket; (*bot.*) calathide.

корзи́н|ный, *adj. of* ~a; ~ное произво́дство basket-making.

корзи́нщик, а, *m.* basket-maker.

коридо́р, а, *m.* corridor, passage.

коридо́р|ный, *adj. of* ~; *as noun* к., ~ного, *m.* boots (*in hotel*).

кори́нк|а, и, *no pl.*, *f.* currants.

кори́нфский, *adj.* (*archit.*) Corinthian.

кор|и́ть, ю́, и́шь, *impf.* (+*a.* за) to upbraid (for); (+*a. and i.*) to reproach (with), cast in someone's teeth.

корифе́|й, я, *m.* (*rhet.*) coryphaeus (*fig.*), leading light.

кори́ц|а, ы, *f.* cinnamon.

кори́чневый, *adj.* brown.

ко́рк|а, и, *f.* **1.** crust. **2.** peel, rind. **3.** scab. **4.** (*fig.*) прочита́ть от ~и до ~и to read from cover to cover; руга́ть, брани́ть кого́-н. на все ~и (*coll.*) to give it someone hot, tear someone off a strip.

корм, а, о ~е, на ~е *and* на ~у́, *pl.* ~á, ~о́в, *m.* **1.** fodder; forage; на подно́жном ~у́ at grass. **2.** feeding.

корм|á, ы́, *f.* (*naut.*) stern, poop.

корме́жк|а, и, *f.* (*coll.*) feeding.

корми́л|ец, ьца, *m.* **1.** bread-winner. **2.** (*obs.*) benefactor. **3.** (*dial. mode of address to man*) old man.

корми́лиц|а, ы, *f.* **1.** wet-nurse. **2.** (*obs.*) benefactress.

корми́л|о, а, *n.* (*naut. and fig.*) helm; (*fig., rhet.*) быть у ~а правле́ния to be at the helm.

корм|и́ть, лю́, ~ишь, *impf.* **1.** (*pf.* на~ *and* по~) to feed; к. с ло́жки to spoon-feed; к.

грудью to nurse, (breast-)feed; не ~я (ехать) (obs.) (to ride) non-stop; (coll.) eró хлебом не ~й, только дай смотреть футбол he is mad about watching football. 2. (pf. про~ keep, maintain.

кормиться, люсь, ~ишься, impf. 1. (pf. по~) to eat, feed (intrans.). 2. (pf. про~) (+ i.) to live (on); к. уроками to make a living by giving tuition.

кормление, я, n. 1. feeding. 2. (hist.) 'feeding' (in Muscovite Russia, system by which boyars responsible for local administration retained revenues for their own use).

кормовой¹, adj. of ~á; ~овóе веслó scull; к. флаг ensign; ~овая часть after-part, stern-part; ~овая рубка roundhouse.

кормовой², adj. of ~; fodder, forage; ~овые культуры, растения fodder crops; ~овая свёкла mangel-wurzel.

кормушка, и, f. (agric.) (feeding-)trough, (feeding-)rack, manger.

кормчий, его, m. (arch. or fig., rhet.) helmsman, pilot; ~ая книга (hist., lit.) Nomocanon.

корнать, ю, impf. (of o~ and об~) (coll.) to crop, cut short.

корневище, а, n. (bot.) rhizome.

корневой, adj. of ~ень; ~невые языки (ling.) isolating languages.

корнеплод, а, m. root plant.

корнер, а, pl. ~ы or ~á, m. (sport) corner; забить гол с ~а to score a goal from, off a corner.

корнерезка, и, f. (agric.) root-cutting machine.

корнет, а, m. (mil. and mus.) cornet.

корнет-а-пистон, а, m. (mus.) cornet-à-piston(s).

корнетист, а, m. (mus.) cornet-player, cornetist.

корнишон, а, m. (cul.) gherkin.

корноухий (~, ~а), adj. (coll.) crop-eared.

короб, а, pl. ~á, m. 1. box, basket (of bast). 2. (tech.) box, chest. 3. (mil.) body (of machine-gun). 4. body (of a carriage). 5. (fig., coll.) целый к. новостей heaps of news; наговорить с три ~а to spin a long yarn.

коробейник, а, m. (obs.) pedlar.

коробить, лю, ишь, impf. (of по~) 1. to warp. 2. (fig.) to jar upon, grate upon; (impers.) меня ~ит от eró акцента his accent jars upon me.

коробиться, люсь, ишься, impf. (of по~ and c~) to warp, buckle.

коробка, и, f. box, case, canister; дверная к. door-frame; к. скоростей (tech.) gear-box; черепная к. (anat.) cranium.

коробóк, ка, m. small box.

коробочка, и, f. 1. dim. of коробка. 2. (bot.) boll.

коробчатый, adj. box shaped; (tech.) ~ое железо channel iron.

корова, ы, f. cow; морская к. sea-cow manatee.

коровай, я, m. = каравай.

коровий, adj. of ~a; ~ье масло butter.

коровка, ки, f. affect. dim. of ~a; божья к. lady-bird.

коровник¹, а, m. cow-shed.

коровник², а, m. cow-man.

коровница, ы, f. dairy-maid.

королева, ы, f. queen.

королевич, а, m. king's son.

королевна, ны, g. pl. ~ен, f. king's daughter.

королевский, adj. royal; king's; regal, kingly; (chess) к. слон king's bishop.

королевство, а, n. kingdom.

королёк, ька, m. 1. (orn.) желтоголовый к. goldcrest; красноголовый к. firecrest. 2. blood-orange. 3. (min.) regulus.

король, я, m. king; (fig.) нефтяной к. oil king.

коромысло, а, n. 1. yoke (for carrying buckets); beam (of scales). 2. (tech.) rocking shaft, rocker arm. 3. (coll.) там шёл дым ~ом all hell was let loose.

корона, ы, f. 1. crown (also fig.); coronet. 2. (astron.) corona.

коронационный, adj. of ~ция.

коронация, и, f. coronation.

коронка, и, f. crown (of tooth).

коронный, adj. crown, of state; (theatr.) ~ая роль best part.

короновать, ую, impf. and pf. to crown.

короста, ы, f. scab.

коростель, я, m. (orn.) corncrake, landrail.

коротать, ю, impf. (of c~) (coll.) to pass, while away (time).

короткий (короток, ~á, коротко, pl. ~ки), adj. 1. short; brief; это пальто тебе ~кó this coat is too short for you; рассказать в ~ких словах to tell in a few words; ~кая расправа short shrift; к. удар short and sharp blow; (coll.) руки коротки! just try! you couldn't if you tried!; ум ~ок limited intelligence. 2. (fig.) close, intimate; (coll.) быть на ~кой ноге с кем-н. to be on intimate terms with someone.

короткó¹, see ~ий.

короткó², adv. 1. briefly; к. говоря in short. 2. intimately.

коротковолновый, adj. (radio) short-wave.

короткость, и, f. (coll.) intimacy, familiarity.

коротышка, и, m. and f. (coll.) dumpy, tubby person; squab.

короче, comp. of ~откий and ~отко shorter; к. говоря in short, to cut a long story short.

корочка, и, f. dim. of корка.

корп|éть, лю́, и́шь, *impf.* (над, за+*i.*) (*coll.*) to pore (over), sweat (over).

ко́рпи|я, и, *f.* (*obs.*) lint.

корпорати́вный, *adj.* corporative.

корпора́ци|я, и, *f.* corporation.

ко́рпус¹, а, *pl.* ∼ы, *m.* **1.** body; trunk, torso. **2.** length (*of animal, as unit of measurement*); на́ша ло́шадь опереди́ла други́х на три ∼а our horse won by three lengths. **3.** hull; (*tech.*) frame, body, case. **4.** (*typ.*) long primer.

ко́рпус², а, *pl.* ∼á, ∼о́в, *m.* **1.** (*mil.*) corps; каде́тский, морско́й к. military school, naval college; дипломати́ческий к. diplomatic corps. **2.** building; block.

корректи́в, а, *m.* amendment, correction.

корректи́р|овать, ую, *impf.* (*of* про∼) to correct.

корректиро́вщик, а, *m.* (*mil.*) **1.** spotter. **2.** spotter (aircraft).

корре́кт|ный (∼ен, ∼на), *adj.* correct, proper.

корре́ктор, а, *m.* proof-reader, corrector.

корректу́р|а, ы, *f.* **1.** proof-reading, correction. **2.** proof(-sheet); держа́ть ∼y to read, correct proofs; к. в гра́нках galley proof(s); к. в листа́х page proof(s). **3.** (*mil.*) correction, adjustment (*of fire*).

корректу́р|ный, *adj. of* ∼а; ∼ные зна́ки proof symbols; к. о́ттиск proof(-sheet).

корре́кци|я, и, *f.* (*med.*) correction.

корреля́т, а, *m.* correlate.

коррелят́и́вный, *adj.* correlative.

корреля́ци|я, и, *f.* correlation.

корреспонде́нт, а, *m.* correspondent.

корреспонде́нци|я, и, *f.* **1.** correspondence; заказна́я, проста́я к. registered, non-registered mail. **2.** newspaper contribution from a correspondent.

корреспонди́р|овать, ую, *impf.* (*in var. senses*) to correspond.

корро́зи|я, и, *f.* (*chem.*) corrosion.

корру́пци|я, и, *f.* (*polit.*) corruption.

корса́ж, а, *m.* bodice, corsage.

корса́р, а, *m.* corsair.

корсе́т, а, *m.* corset.

корсе́тниц|а, ы, *f.* corsetière.

корт, а, *m.* (tennis-)court.

корте́ж, а, *m.* cortège; motorcade.

ко́ртик, а, *m.* dagger, dirk.

ко́рточ|ки, ек, *no sing.* сиде́ть на ∼ках, сесть на к. to squat.

кору́нд, а, *m.* (*min.*) corundum.

корча́г|а, и, *f.* (*dial.*) earthenware pot, ewer.

корч|ева́ть, у́ю, *impf.* to stub, grub up, root out.

корчёвк|а, и, *f.* stubbing, grubbing up, rooting out.

корче́мств|о, а, *n.* (*obs.*) bootlegging.

ко́рч|и, ей, *sing.* ∼а, ∼и, *f.* (*coll.*) convulsions,

spasm; му́читься в ∼ах to writhe with pain; зла́я ∼а (*med.*) ergotism.

ко́рч|ить, у, ишь, *impf.* (*of* с∼) **1.** to contort; (*coll.*) к. грима́сы, ро́жи to make, pull faces. **2.** (*impf. only*) (*coll.*) к. из себя́ to pose (as); к. дурака́ to play the fool.

корчм|а́, мы́, *g. pl.* ∼ём, *f.* (*obs.*) inn, tavern (*in Ukraine and Byelorussia*).

корчма́р|ь, я́, *m.* (*obs.*) innkeeper.

ко́ршун, а, *m.* (*orn.*) kite; (*fig.*) налете́ть, набро́ситься ∼ом (на+*a.*) to pounce (on), swoop (onto).

коры́ст|ный (∼ен, ∼на), *adj.* mercenary, mercenary-minded.

корыстолюб|ец, ца, *m.* profit-seeker, mercenary-minded person.

корыстолюби́в|ый (∼, ∼а), *adj.* self-interested, mercenary-minded.

корыстолюби|е, я, *n.* self-interest, cupidity.

коры́ст|ь, и, *f.* (*coll.*) **1.** profit, gain; кака́я тебе́ в э́том к.? what are you getting out of it? **2.** cupidity.

коры́т|о, а, *n.* wash-tub; trough; оста́ться у разби́того ∼а to be no better off than before, be back where one started.

кор|ь, и, *f.* measles.

кор|ьё, я́, *n.* (*collect., dial.*) bark (*stripped from the tree*).

корю́шк|а, и, *f.* smelt (*fish*).

коря́в|ый (∼, ∼а), *adj.* (*coll.*) **1.** rough, uneven; gnarled. **2.** (*fig.*) clumsy, uncouth. **3.** (*dial.*) pock-marked.

коря́г|а, и, *f.* snag (*tree or boughs impeding navigation*).

кос|а́¹, ы́, *a.* ∼у́, *pl.* ∼ы, *f.* plait, pigtail, braid.

кос|а́², ы́, *a.* ∼у́, *pl.* ∼ы, *f.* scythe; нашла́ к. на ка́мень he (has) met his match, he ran (has run) into a brick wall.

кос|а́³, ы́, *a.* ∼у́, *pl.* ∼ы, *f.* (*geogr.*) **1.** spit. **2.** (*dial.*) belt (*of trees*).

коса́р|ь¹, я́, *m.* mower (*agent*).

коса́р|ь², я́, *m.* chopper (*tool*).

ко́свенн|ый, *adj.* indirect, oblique; ∼ые ули́ки circumstantial evidence; (*gram.*) к. паде́ж oblique case; ∼ая речь indirect speech.

косе́канс, а, *m.* (*math.*) cosecant.

коси́лк|а, и, *f.* mowing-machine, mower.

ко́синус, а, *m.* (*math.*) cosine.

ко|си́ть¹, шу́, ∼си́шь, *impf.* (*of* с∼) to mow; to cut; (*fig.*) to mow down; ∼си́ ∼са́ пока́ роса́ (*prov.*) make hay while the sun shines.

ко|си́ть², шу́, си́шь, *impf.* (*of* с∼) **1.** to squint; к. на о́ба гла́за to have a squint in both eyes. **2.** (+*a. or i.*) to twist, slant (*mouth, eyes*). **3.** to be crooked.

ко|си́ться, шу́сь, си́шься, *impf.* (*of* по∼) **1.** to slant. **2.** (*coll.*) (на+*a.*) to cast a sidelong look (at); (*fig.*) to look askance (at).

коси́ц|а, ы, *f.* 1. lock (*of hair*). 2. (*dim. of* коса́¹) pigtail.

космá|тить, чу, тишь, *impf.* (*coll.*) to tousle.

космáт|ый (~, ~а), *adj.* shaggy.

космéтик|а, и, *f.* cosmetics.

космети́ческий, *adj.* cosmetic; к. кабинéт beauty parlour; к. ремóнт redecoration (*papering, painting of interior of house*).

кóсмик, а, *m.* (*coll.*) 1. cosmic ray specialist. 2. being from outer space.

косми́ческий, *adj.* cosmic, outer space; к. корáбль space vehicle, space ship.

космогóни|я, и, *f.* cosmogony.

космогрáфи|я, и, *f.* cosmography.

космодрóм, а, *m.* space-vehicle launching site.

космонáвт, а, *m.* astronaut, cosmonaut, space man.

космонáвтик|а, и, *f.* astronautics, (outer) space exploration.

космополи́т, а, *m.* cosmopolite.

космополити́зм, а, *m.* cosmopolitanism.

космополити́ческий, *adj.* cosmopolitan.

кóсмос, а, *m.* cosmos; outer space.

кóсм|ы, ~, *no sing.* (*coll.*) locks, mane.

коснé|ть, ю, *impf.* (*of* за~) 1. (в+*p.*) to stagnate (in). 2. to stick.

косноязы́чи|е, я, *n.* confused articulation.

косноязы́ч|ный (~ен, ~на), *adj.* speaking thickly.

косн|у́ться, у́сь, ёшься, *pf. of* касáться.

кóс|ный (~ен, ~на), *adj.* inert, sluggish; stagnant.

кóсо, *adv.* slantwise, askew; obliquely; смотрéть к. to look askance, scowl.

кособóк|ий (~, ~а), *adj.* (*coll.*) crooked, lop-sided.

косоворóтк|а, и, *f.* (Russian) shirt, blouse (*with collar fastening at side*).

косоглáзи|е, я, *n.* squint, cast in the eye.

косоглáз|ый (~, ~а), *adj.* cross-eyed, squint-eyed.

косогóр, а, *m.* slope, hill-side.

кос|óй¹ (~, ~á, ~о), *adj.* 1. slanting; oblique; к. пóчерк sloping handwriting; к. у́гол (*math.*) oblique angle; ~áя чертá oblique stroke; ~áя сáжень в плечáх (*coll.*) broad shoulders. 2. squinting; cross-eyed. 3. к. взгляд (*fig.*) sidelong glance.

кос|óй², óго, *m.* (*folk poet.*) hare.

косолáп|ый (~, ~а), *adj.* pigeon-toed; (*fig.*) clumsy.

косоугóльный, *adj.* (*math.*) oblique-angled.

костёл, а, *m.* (Roman Catholic) church.

костенé|ть, ю, *impf.* (*of* о~) to grow stiff; to grow numb.

кост|ёр, рá, *m.* bonfire; camp-fire.

кости́ст|ый (~, ~а), *adj.* bony.

ко|сти́ть, щу́, сти́шь, *impf.* (*coll.*) to abuse.

костля́в|ый (~, ~а), *adj.* bony.

кóстный, *adj.* osseous; (*anat.*) к. мозг marrow.

костоéд|а, ы, *f.* (*med.*) caries.

костопрáв, а, *m.* bone-setter.

кóсточк|а, и, *f.* 1. *dim. of* кость; (*coll.*) воéнная к. old soldier, military man; перемывáть ~и (+*d.*) to gossip about, pull to pieces; разбирáть по ~ам to go through (a thing, matter) with a fine comb. 2. stone (*of fruit*). 3. ball (*of abacus*). 4. bone (*of corset, etc.*).

кострéц, á, *m.* leg of meat.

косты́л|ь, я́, *m.* 1. crutch; ходи́ть на ~я́х to walk on crutches. 2. (*tech.*) spike, drive. 3. (*aeron.*) tail skid.

костыля́|ть, ю, *impf.* (*coll.*) 1. to cudgel. 2. to hobble.

кост|ь, и, *pl.* **~и, ~éй,** *f.* 1. bone; слонóвая к. ivory; (*fig., coll.*) бéлая к. blue blood; язы́к без ~éй loose tongue; лечь ~ьми́ (*rhet.*) to fall in battle; пересчитáть комý-н. ~и to give someone a drubbing. 2. die; игрáть в ~и to dice.

костю́м, а, *m.* 1. dress, clothes; в ~е Адáма, Éвы (*joc.*) in one's birthday suit; маскарáдный к. fancy-dress. 2. suit; costume; англи́йский к. tailor-made coat and skirt; вечéрний к. dress suit; парáдный к. full dress.

костюмéр, а, *m.* (*theatr.*) costumier.

костюмéр|ный, *adj.* of ~; *as noun* ~ная, ~ной, *f.* (*theatr.*) wardrobe.

костюмирóва|нный, *p.p.p. of* ~ть *and adj.* 1. in costume; in fancy-dress. 2. к. бал, вéчер fancy-dress ball.

костюми́р|овать, ую, *impf. and pf.* (*theatr.*) to dress.

костюми́р|оваться, уюсь, *impf. and pf.* to put on costume; to put on fancy-dress.

костю́м|ный, *adj.* of ~; ~ная пьéса period play.

костя́к, á, *m.* skeleton; (*fig.*) backbone.

костян|óй, *adj.* (made of) bone; ~áя мукá bone-meal; к. нóжик ivory knife.

костя́шк|а, и, *f.* 1. *dim. of* кость. 2. knuckle. 3. ball (*of abacus*).

косу́л|я, и, *f.* roe deer.

косу́шк|а, и, *f.* (*obs.*) half-bottle of vodka.

косы́нк|а, и, *f.* (triangular) kerchief, scarf.

косьб|á, ы́, *f.* mowing.

костя́к¹, á, *m.* 1. (door-)post; jamb; cheek. 2. slope; sloping object.

кося́к², á, *m.* 1. herd (*of mares with only one stallion*). 2. shoal, school; flock.

кот, á, *m.* 1. tom-cat; морскóй к. (*zool.*) sea-bear; (*coll.*) к. наплáкал nothing to speak of, practically nothing; купи́ть ~á в мешкé to buy a pig in a poke; (*prov.*) не всё ~у́ мáсленица, придёт и вели́кий пост after dinner comes the reckoning. 2. (*sl.*) pimp.

котáнгенс, а, *m.* (*math.*) cotangent.
кот|ёл, лá, *m.* 1. copper, cauldron; (*fig.*) óбщий к. common stock. 2. (*tech.*) boiler. 3. (*pl.*) hopscotch.
котел|óк, кá, *m.* 1. pot. 2. mess-tin. 3. bowler (hat).
котéльн|ая, ой, *f.* boiler-house.
котéл|ьный, *adj. of* ∼ 2; ∼ьное желéзо boiler plate.
котéльщик, а, *m.* boiler-maker.
кот|ёнок, ёнка, *pl.* ∼я́та, ∼я́т, *m.* kitten.
кóтик, а, *m.* 1. fur-seal. 2. sealskin. 3. *affect. dim. of* кот. 4. (*affect. mode of address*) darling. 5. (*pl.*) *dim. of* коты́.
кóтик|овый, *adj. of* ∼ 1, 2; к. прóмысел sealing; sealskin trade; ∼овая шáпка sealskin cap.
котильóн, а, *m.* cotillion.
коти́р|овать, ую, *impf. and pf.* (*fin.*) to quote.
коти́р|оваться, уюсь, *impf. and pf.* 1. (*fin.*) (в+*a.*) to be quoted (at). 2. (*fig.*) to be rated.
котирóвк|а, и, *f.* (*fin.*) quotation.
ко|ти́ться, чýсь, ти́шься, *impf.* (*of* о∼) to kitten, have kittens; to have young.
котлéт|а, ы, *f.* cutlet; отбивнáя к. chop.
котловáн, а, *m.* (*tech.*) foundation ditch, trench.
котлови́н|а, ы, *f.* (*geogr.*) hollow, basin.
кот|овáть, ýю, *impf.* (*sl.*) to be courting.
котóмк|а, и, *f.* wallet; knapsack.
котóр|ый, *pron.* 1. *interrog. and relat.* which; к. час? what time is it?; в ∼ом часý он зашёл? what time did he call?; к. раз? how many times?; (*coll.*) к. раз я тебé э́то говорю́? how many times have I told you! 2. *relat.* who. 3. (*coll.*) к.... к. some ... some (others); ∼ые бы́ли в чулкáх, ∼ые с гóлыми ногáми some were wearing stockings and some were bare-legged.
котóрый-либо, *pron.* = к.-нибудь.
котóрый-нибудь, *pron.* some; one or other.
коттéдж, а, *m.* small (detached) house.
коту́рн, а, *m.* (*theatr., hist.*) buskin; станови́ться на ∼ы (*fig.*) to assume a tragic tone.
кот|ы́, óв, *no sing.* (*dial.*) (*woman's*) fur slippers.
кот|я́та, я́т, *see* ∼ёнок.
кóуш, а, *m.* (*naut.*) thimble.
кóфе, *indecl., m.* coffee; к. в зёрнах coffee beans.
кофеи́н, а, *m.* caffeine.
кóфе|й, я, *m.* (*coll., obs.*) coffee.
кофéйник, а, *m.* coffee-pot.
кофéйниц|а, ы, *f.* 1. coffee-grinder. 2. coffee tin.
коф|éйный, *adj. of* ∼е.
кофé|йня, йни, *g. pl.* ∼ен, *f.* (*obs.*) coffee-house.

кóфт|а, ы, *f.* 1. (*woman's*) jacket. 2. (*coll.*) (*woman's*) short, warm overcoat.
кóфточк|а, и, *f.* blouse.
кочáн, á (*and dial.* кочнá), *m.* к. капýсты head of cabbage.
коч|евáть, ýю, *impf.* 1. to be a nomad, to roam from place to place, wander. 2. (*of birds and animals*) to migrate.
кочéвк|а, и, *f.* (*coll.*) 1. nomad camp. 2. wandering; nomadic existence.
кочéвник, а, *m.* nomad.
кочевóй, *adj.* 1. nomadic. 2. (*of birds and animals*) migratory.
кочевря́ж|иться, усь, *impf.* (*coll.*) 1. to be obstinate. 2. to pose, put on airs.
кочéв|ье, ья, *g. pl.* ∼ий, *n.* 1. nomad encampment. 2. nomad territory.
кочегáр, а, *m.* stoker, fireman.
кочегáрк|а, и, *f.* stoke-hole, stoke-hold.
кочене́|ть, ю, *impf.* (*of* за∼ *and* о∼) to become numb; to stiffen.
кочер|гá, ги́, *g. pl.* ∼ёг, *f.* poker.
кочеры́жк|а, и, *f.* cabbage-stalk, cabbage-stump.
кóчет, а, *m.* (*dial.*) cock.
кóчк|а, и, *f.* hummock; tussock.
кочковáт|ый (∼, ∼а), *adj.* hummocky, tussocky.
ко|чýсь, ти́шься, *see* ∼ти́ться.
кош, а, *m.* 1. (nomads') tent. 2. (*hist.*) camp (*of Zaporozhian Cossacks*).
кошáтник, а, *m.* 1. dealer in (stolen) cats. 2. (*coll.*) cat-lover.
кош|áчий, *adj. of* ∼кá; feline; к. глаз (*min.*) cat's eye; к. концéрт caterwauling; (*fig.*) hooting, barracking; ∼áчьи ухвáтки cat-like (cattish) ways; *as noun* (*zool.*) ∼áчьи, ∼áчьих, Felidae.
кош|евóй, *adj. of* ∼; к. атамáн commander of Cossack camp.
кошел|ёк, ькá, *m.* purse; (*fig.*) тугóй к. tight-filled purse.
кошéл|ь, я́, *m.* 1. (*obs.*) purse. 2. (*dial.*) bag.
кошени́л|евый, *adj. of* ∼ь.
кошени́л|ь, и, *f.* cochineal.
кóшк|а, и, *f.* 1. cat; (*fig., coll.*) игрáть в ∼и-мы́шки to play cat-and-mouse; жить как к. с собáкой to lead a cat-and-dog life; чёрная к. пробежáла мéжду ни́ми they have fallen out; нóчью все ∼и сéры when candles are out all cats are grey; у негó ∼и скребýт на сéрдце he is heavy-hearted. 2. (*tech., naut.*) grapnel, drag. 3. mountaineering boot. 4. (*pl.*) cat-o'-nine-tails.
кошм|á, ы́, *pl.* ∼ы, ∼, *f.* large piece of felt.
кошмáр, а, *m.* nightmare (*also fig.*).
кошмáр|ный (∼ен, ∼на), *adj.* nightmarish; (*fig.*) horrible, awful.
кошт, а, *m.* (*obs.*) expense; на казённом ∼е at Government expense.

ко|шу́, си́шь, see ~си́ть.

коще́|й, я, *m.* **1.** Koshchei (*an evil being in Russian folk-lore*); *fig. of a tall, thin old man.* **2.** (*fig., coll.*) miser.

кощу́нствен|ный (~, ~на), *adj.*blasphemous.

кощу́нств|о, а, *n.* blasphemy.

кощу́нств|овать, ую, *impf.* to blaspheme.

коэффицие́нт, а, *m.* (*math.*) coefficient, factor; (*tech.*) к. мо́щности power factor; к. поле́зного де́йствия efficiency; к. поте́рь loss factor.

краб, а, *m.* (*zool.*) crab.

кра́вч|ий, его, *m.* royal carver (*in Muscovite Russia*).

кра́г|и, ~, *sing.* ~а, ~и, *f.* **1.** leggings. **2.** cuffs (*of gloves*).

кра́ден|ый, *adj.* stolen; ~ое (*collect.*) stolen goods.

кра|ду́, дёшь, see ~сть.

кра́дучись, *adv.* stealthily; идти́ к. to creep, slink.

краеве́д, а, *m.* student of local lore, history and economy.

краеве́дени|е, я, *n.* study of local lore, history and economy.

краеве́д|ческий, *adj. of* ~ение; к. музе́й museum of local lore, history, and economy.

краево́й, *adj. of* край 4.

краеуго́льный, *adj.* (*rhet.*) basic; к. ка́мень corner-stone.

кра́ж|а, и, *f.* theft; larceny; к. со взло́мом burglary; квалифици́рованная к. (*leg.*) aggravated theft.

кра|й, я, о ~е, в ~ю́, *pl.* ~я́, ~ёв, *m.* **1.** edge; brim; brink (*also fig.*); пере́дний к. (*mil.*) first line, forward positions; быть на ~ю́ моги́лы to have one foot in the grave; конца́-~ю нет there is no end to it; ~ем у́ха слу́шать to overhear; на ~ю́ све́та at the world's end; че́рез к. overmuch, beyond measure; хлебну́ть че́рез к. (*coll.*) to have a drop too much. **2.** side (*of meat*); то́лстый к. rib-steak; то́нкий к. chine (*of beef*), upper cut. **3.** land, country; в на́ших ~я́х in our part of the world; в чужи́х ~я́х in foreign parts. **4.** (*administrative division of U.S.S.R.*) krai.

край- *abbr. of* краево́й.

кра́йне, *adv.* extremely.

кра́йн|ий, *adj.* **1.** (*in var. senses*) extreme; last; uttermost; в ~ем слу́чае in the last resort; по ~ей ме́ре at least; ~яя плоть (*anat.*) foreskin, prepuce. **2.** (*sport*) outside, wing; к. напада́ющий outside forward, wing forward.

кра́йност|ь, и, *f.* **1.** extreme; в ~и in the last resort; до ~и in the extreme, extremely. **2.** extremity; быть в ~и to be reduced to extremity.

краковя́к, а, *m.* (*dance*) Cracovienne.

крал, а, *see* красть.

кра́л|я, и, *f.* (*coll.*) beauty; (*cards*) queen.

крамо́л|а, ы, *f.* (*obs.*) sedition.

крамо́льник, а, *m.* (*obs.*) maker of, participant in sedition; plotter.

крамо́льный, *adj.* (*obs.*) seditious.

кран[1], а, *m.* tap, cock.

кран[2], а, *m.* crane; к.-двуно́га (*naut.*) sheer-legs.

кра́н|ец, ца, *m.* (*naut.*) fender.

краниоло́ги|я, и, *f.* craniology.

крановщи́к, а́, *m.* crane operator.

кра́н|овый, *adj. of* ~[1], [2].

крап, а, *no pl., m.* **1.** specks. **2.** pattern on the backs of playing cards.

кра́п|ать, ает *and* лет *impf.* to spatter; дождь ~лет it is spitting with rain.

крапи́в|а, ы, *f.* (stinging-)nettle; (*collect.*) nettles; глуха́я к. dead nettle.

крапи́вник, а, *m.* (*orn.*) wren.

крапи́вниц|а, ы, *f.* nettle-rash.

крапи́в|ный, *adj. of* ~а; ~ная лихора́дка nettle-rash; ~ное се́мя (*obs., joc., of civil servants*) tribe of quill-drivers, pen-pushers.

кра́пин|а, ы, *f.* speck; spot.

кра́пин|ка, ки, *f.* = ~а.

краплёный, *adj.* (*of cards*) marked.

крас|а́, ы́, *f.* **1.** (*obs.*) beauty; (*iron.*) во всей свое́й ~е́ in all one's glory. **2.** (*rhet.*) ornament.

краса́в|ец, ца, *m.* handsome man; Adonis.

краса́виц|а, ы, *f.* beauty (*beautiful woman*).

краса́вчик, а, *m.* (*coll.*) **1.** = краса́вец. **2.** (*iron.*) dandy.

краси́вост|ь, и, *f.* (mere) prettiness.

краси́в|ый (~, ~а), *adj.* beautiful; handsome; fine.

краси́льный, *adj.* appertaining to dyes.

краси́л|ьня, ьни, *g. pl.* ~ен, *f.* dye-house, dye-works.

краси́льщик, а, *m.* dyer.

краси́тел|ь, я, *m.* dye(-stuff).

кра́|сить, шу, сишь, *impf.* (*of* по~) **1.** to paint; to colour; он кра́сит ло́дку в бе́лое с голубы́м he is painting the boat white and blue. **2.** to dye; to stain (*wood, glass*). **3.** (*impf. only*) to adorn.

кра́|ситься, шусь, сишься, *impf.* **1.** (*pf.* на~) to make up. **2.** (*of newly dyed or newly-painted objects*) to stain. **3.** *pass. of* ~ситься.

кра́ск|а, и, *f.* **1.** painting; colouring; dyeing. **2.** paint; dye; акваре́льная к. water-colour; ма́сляная к. oil-colour; типогра́фская к. printer's ink; писа́ть ~ами to paint. **3.** (*pl., fig.*) colours; сгуща́ть ~и (*coll.*) to lay it on thick. **4.** blush; вогна́ть кого́-н. в ~у (*coll.*) to make someone blush.

красне́|ть, ю, *impf.* (*of* по~) **1.** to redden, become red. **2.** to blush, colour; (*fig.*) к. за+*a.* to blush for. **3.** (*impf. only*) to show red.

краснé|ться, юсь, *impf.* to show red.

красноармé|ец, йца, *m.* Red Army man.

красноармé|йский, *adj. of* ~ец *and* Крáсная Áрмия.

краснобá|й, я, *m.* (*coll.*) phrase-monger, rhetorician.

краснобáйств|о, а, *n.* (*coll.*) eloquence, fair--sounding speech.

краснобýрый, *adj.* reddish-brown.

красновáт|ый (~, ~а), *adj.* reddish.

красногвардé|ец, йца, *m.* (*hist.*) Red Guard.

красногвардé|йский, *adj. of* ~ец.

краснодерéв|ец, ца, *m.* cabinet-maker.

краснодерéв|щик, щика, *m.* = ~ец.

краснозвёздный, *adj.* having the red star (*emblem of the Soviet Army*).

краснознамённый, *adj.* holding the order of the Red Banner.

краснокóж|ий (~, ~а), *adj.* red-skinned; *as noun* к., ~его, *m.* red-skin.

краснолéсь|е, я, *n.* pine forest.

краснолúцый, *adj.* red-faced, rubicund.

красноречúв|ый (~, ~а), *adj.* eloquent; expressive; (*fig.*) telltale, significant.

красноречи|е, я, *n.* eloquence; oratory.

краснот|á, ы́, *f.* 1. redness. 2. red spot.

краснофлóт|ец, ца, *m.* Red Navy man.

краснофлóт|ский, *adj. of* ~ец *and* Крáсный Флóт.

краснощёкий, *adj.* red-checked.

краснýх|а, и, *f.* (*med.*) German measles.

крáс|ный (~ен, ~нá, ~но), *adj.* 1. red (*also fig., polit.*); ~ное дéрево mahogany; ~ная шáпочка Little Red Riding Hood; к. уголóк 'Red Corner' (*room in factories, etc., providing recreational and educational facilities*); (*fig.*) ~ная строкá (first line of) new paragraph; сказáть для ~ного словцá to say as a joke, for effect; ~ная цена́ (*coll.*) outside figure, the most which one is willing to pay; проходúть ~ной ни́тью to stand out, run through (*of theme, motif*); пустúть ~ного петухá (*coll.*) to set fire, commit act of arson; попáсть под ~ную шáпку (*coll., obs.*) to become a soldier. 2. (*obs., folk poet. or coll.*) beautiful; (*fig.*) fine; ~ная дéвица bonny lass; лéто ~ное glorious summer; (*prov.*) долг платежóм ~ен one good turn deserves another; к. ýгол place of honour (*in peasant hut*). 3. *signifies that object qualified is of high quality or value:* ~ная рыба cartilaginous fish; (*obs.*) к. товáр textiles; к. зверь superior types of game (*such as bear, elk*); к. лес conifer forest.

крас|овáться, ýюсь, *impf.* 1. to impress by one's beauty, stand out vividly. 2. (+*i.*) (*coll.*) to flaunt, show off.

красот|á, ы́, *pl.* ~ы, *f.* beauty; (*coll.*) к.! splendid!

красóтк|а, и, *f.* (*coll.*) 1. good-looking girl. 2. (*obs.*) sweetheart.

крáс|очный, *adj.* 1. *adj. of* ~ка. 2. (~очен, ~очна) colourful, highly coloured.

кра|сть, дý, дёшь, *past* ~л, ~ла, *impf.* (*of* у~) to steal.

крá|сться, дýсь, дёшься, *past* ~лся, ~лась, *impf.* to steal, creep, sneak.

крат, *only in phrase* вó сто к. a hundredfold.

крáтер, а, *m.* crater.

крáт|кий (~ок, ~ká, ~ко), *adj.* short; brief; concise; в ~ких словáх in short, briefly; *as noun* ~кая, ~кой, *f. only in* и с ~кой old name of Russian letter й (*now* и ~кое).

крáтко, *adv.* briefly.

кратковрéменный, *adj.* of short duration, brief; transitory.

краткосрóч|ный (~ен, ~на), *adj.* short--term.

крáтн|ое, ого, *n.* (*math.*) multiple; óбщее наимéньшее к. least common multiple.

крáт|ный (~ен, ~на), *adj.* (+*d.*) divisible without remainder (by); дéвять — числó ~ное трём nine is a multiple of three.

крат|чáйший, *superl. of* ~кий.

крáт|че, *comp. of* ~кий *and* ~ко.

крах, а, *m.* (*fin. and fig.*) crash; failure.

крахмáл, а, *m.* starch.

крахмáлист|ый (~, ~а), *adj.* containing starch.

крахмáл|ить, ю, ишь, *impf.* (*of* на~) to starch.

крахмáл|ьный, *adj. of* ~; starched; к. воротничóк stiff collar.

крáше (*coll.*) *comp. of* красúв|ый *and* ~о; к. в гроб клáдут pale as a ghost.

крáшени|е, я, *n.* dyeing.

крашенúн|а, ы, *f.* (*obs.*) coarse, thick linen.

крáшеный, *adj.* 1. painted; coloured. 2. dyed. 3. made-up, wearing make-up; (*pejor.*) painted.

краюх|а, и, *f.* (*coll.*) thick slice of bread.

креатýр|а, ы, *f.* creature, minion.

кревéтк|а, и, *f.* (*zool.*) shrimp.

крéдит, а, *m.* (*book-keeping*) credit.

кредúт, а, *m.* credit; открыть, предостáвить к. to give credit; отпустúть в к. to supply on credit; (*fig.*) пóльзоваться ~ом (у) to have credit (with).

кредúтк|а, и, *f.* (*obs.*) bank-note.

кредúт|ный, *adj. of* ~; к. билéт (*obs.*) bank--note.

кредит|овáть, ýю, *impf. and pf.* (*fin.*) to credit, give credit (to).

кредит|овáться, ýюсь, *impf. and pf.* (*fin.*) 1. to obtain funds on credit. 2. *pass. of* ~овáть.

кредитóр, а, *m.* creditor; к. по закладнóй mortgagee.

кредитоспосóбност|ь, и, *f.* solvency.

кредитоспосо́б|ный (~ен, ~на), *adj.* solvent.

кре́до, *indecl.*, *n.* credo.

крез, а, *m.* Crœsus.

кре́йсер, а, *pl.* ~ы *and* ~а́, *m.* (*naut.*) cruiser; лине́йный к. battle cruiser.

кре́йсер|ский, *adj.* of ~; кре́йсерская ско́рость cruising speed.

кре́йсерств|о, а, *n.* (*naut.*) cruise, cruising.

кре́йси́р|овать, ую, *impf.* (*naut.*) to cruise.

кре́кинг, а, *m.* (*tech.*) 1. cracking (*oil refining*). 2. oil refinery.

кре́кинг-проце́сс, а, *m.* (*tech.*) cracking (*oil refining*).

креки́р|овать, ую, *impf. and pf.* (*tech.*) to crack.

крем, а, *m.* (*in var. senses*) cream; (сапо́жный) к. shoe-polish.

кремальёр|а, ы, *f.* (*tech.*) rack and pinion gear.

кремато́ри|й, я, *m.* crematorium.

кремац|ио́нный, *adj.* of ~ия; ~ио́нная печь incinerator.

крема́ци|я, и, *f.* cremation.

крем|ень, ня́, *m.* flint; (*fig.*) hard-hearted person; skinflint.

кремеш|о́к, ка́, *m.* piece of flint.

кремл|ёвский, *adj.* of ~ь.

кремленоло́ги|я, и, *f.* Kremlinology.

кремл|ь, я́, *m.* citadel; (моско́вский) к. the Kremlin.

кремнёв|ый, *adj.* made of flint; ~ое ружьё flint-lock.

кремнезём, а, *m.* (*min.*, *chem.*) silica.

кремнеки́слый, *adj.* (*chem.*) silicic; к. на́трий sodium silicate.

кре́мниевый, *adj.* (*chem.*) silicic.

кре́мни|й, я, *m.* (*chem.*) silicon.

кремни́стый, *adj.* 1. (*min.*) siliceous. 2. (*obs.*) stony.

крем|овый, *adj.* 1. *adj.* of ~. 2. cream (-coloured).

крен, а, *m.* (*naut.*) list, heel; (*aeron.*) bank; дать к. (*naut.*) to list, heel (over); (*aeron.*) to bank.

кре́ндел|ь, я, *pl.* ~и *and* ~я́, ~е́й, *m.* (*cul.*) pretzel; ни за каки́е ~я́ (*coll.*) not for anything; выпи́сывать ~я́ to stagger, lurch; сверну́ться ~ем to curl up.

крен|и́ть, ю́, и́шь, *impf.* (*of* на~) to cause to heel, list.

крен|и́ться, ю́сь, и́шься, *impf.* (*of* на~) (*naut.*) to list, heel (over); (*aeron.*) to bank.

крео́л, а, *m.* creole.

крео́л|ьский, *adj.* of ~.

креп, а, *m.* crêpe; тра́урный к. mourning crape.

крепдеши́н, а, *m.* crêpe de chine.

крепёжный, *adj.* к. лес pit-props.

крепи́льщик, а, *m.* (*tech.*) timberer (*in mines*).

крепи́тельный, *adj.* 1. (*tech.*) strengthening. 2. (*med.*) astringent.

креп|и́ть, лю́, и́шь, *impf.* 1. (*tech. and fig.*) to strengthen; (*mining*) to timber. 2. (*naut.*) to make fast, hitch, lash; к. паруса́ to furl sails. 3. (*med.*) to constipate, render costive.

креп|и́ться, лю́сь, и́шься, *impf.* 1. to hold out. 2. *pass. of* ~и́ть.

креп|кий (~ок, ~ка́, ~ко), *adj.* 1. strong; sound; sturdy, robust; (*fig.*) firm; к. моро́з hard frost; ~кие напи́тки spirits; ~кое словцо́ (*coll.*) swear-word, strong language; к. сон sound sleep; к. чай strong tea; ~ок на́ ухо hard of hearing. 2. (*coll.*) well-off.

кре́пко, *adv.* strongly; firmly; soundly; (*coll.*) к.-на́крепко very firmly; к.-на́крепко завяза́ть to tie really tight.

крепкоголо́в|ый (~, ~а), *adj.* (*coll.*) pig--headed.

крепколо́б|ый (~, ~а), *adj.* (*coll.*) pig--headed.

крепле́ни|е, я, *n.* 1. strengthening; fastening. 2. (*mining*) timbering. 3. (*naut.*) lashing; furling. 4. (ski) binding.

креплёный, *adj.* (*of wines*) fortified.

кре́пн|уть, у, ешь, *impf.* (*of* о~) to get stronger.

крепостни́к, а́, *m.* advocate of serfdom.

крепостни́|ческий, *adj.* of ~к *and* ~чество.

крепостни́честв|о, а, *n.* serfdom.

крепостн|о́й[1], *adj.* serf; к. крестья́нин (*peasant*) serf; ~о́е пра́во serfdom; *as noun* к., ~о́го, *m.* serf.

крепостн|о́й,[2] *adj.* of кре́пость[2].

кре́пост|ь[1], и, *f.* (*in var. senses*) strength.

кре́пост|ь[2], и, *f.* fortress.

кре́пост|ь[3], и, *f.* (*hist.*, *leg.*) ку́пчая к. deed of purchase.

крепча́|ть, ет, *impf.* to grow stronger, get up (*of wind*); to get harder (*of frost*).

креп|че, *comp. of* ~кий *and* ~ко.

крепы́ш, а́, *m.* (*coll.*) brawny fellow; sturdy child.

креп|ь, и, *f.* (*mining*) timbering.

кре́с|ло, ла, *g. pl.* ~ел, *n.* arm-chair, easy--chair; (*theatr.*) stall.

кресс-сала́т, а, *m.* cress, watercress.

крест, а́, *m.* 1. cross; поста́вить к. (на+*p.*) to give up for lost; целова́ть к. (+*d.*) (*obs.*) to take an oath (to). 2. the sign of the cross; осени́ть себя́ ~о́м to cross oneself, make the sign of the cross.

крест|е́ц, ца́, *m.* (*anat.*) sacrum.

крести́льный, *adj.* baptismal.

крести́н|ы, ~, (*no sing.*) 1. christening. 2. christening-party.

кре|сти́ть, щу́, ~стишь, *impf.* 1. (*pf.* к. *or* о~) to baptize, christen. 2. (*no pf.*) (+*a.* у) to be godfather, godmother (*to the child of*); (*obs.*, *coll.*) не дете́й к. мне с ни́ми I have no connection with them. 3. (*of* пере~) to make the sign of the cross over.

кре|сти́ться, щу́сь, ⌣сти́шься, *impf.* 1. (*pf.* к. *or* o⌣) to be baptized, be christened. 2. (*pf.* пере⌣) to cross oneself.

крест-на́крест, *adv.* crosswise.

кре́стник, a, *m.* god-son, god-child.

кре́стниц|а, ы, *f.* god-daughter, god-child.

кре́ст|ный, *adj. of* ⌣; ⌣ное зна́мение sign of the cross; к. ход (religious) procession; ⌣ное целова́ние oath-taking; (*coll.*) с на́ми ⌣ная си́ла! good heavens!

крёстн|ый, *adj.* к. отец (*also as noun* к., ⌣ого, *m.*) god-father; ⌣ая мать (*also as noun* ⌣ая, ⌣ой, *f.*) god-mother; ⌣ые де́ти god-children.

крестови́к, á, *m.* garden-spider.

крестови́н|а, ы, *f.* (*railways*) frog.

кресто́вник, a, *m.* (*bot.*) ragwort, groundsel.

крест|о́вый, *adj. of* ⌣; к. похо́д crusade.

крестоно́с|ец, ца, *m.* crusader.

крестообра́з|ный (⌣ен, ⌣на), *adj.* cruciform; (*bot., zool.*) cruciate.

крестоцве́тн|ые, ых (*bot.*) cruciferae.

крестцо́вый, *adj.* (*anat.*) sacral.

крестья́н|ин, ина, *pl.* ⌣e, ⌣, *m.* peasant.

крестья́нк|а, и, *f.* peasant woman.

крестья́нский, *adj.* peasant.

крестья́нств|о, a, *n.* 1. (*collect.*) the peasants, peasantry. 2. (*obs.*) the life of a peasant, farm-labouring.

крестья́нств|овать, ую, *impf.* (*obs.*) to till the soil.

крети́н, a, *m.* cretin; (*fig., coll.*) idiot, imbecile.

кретини́зм, a, *m.* cretinism; (*fig., coll.*) idiocy, imbecility.

крето́н, a, *m.* (*text.*) cretonne.

кре́чет, a, *m.* (*orn.*) gerfalcon.

креще́ндо, *adv.* (*mus.*) crescendo.

креще́ни|е, я, *n.* 1. baptism, christening; боево́е к. baptism of fire. 2. Epiphany.

креще́н|ский, *adj. of* ⌣ие 2; к. моро́з, хо́лод *of severe frost, cold*; (*fig., coll.*) coldness, severity.

крещён|ый, *adj.* baptized; *as noun* к., ⌣ого, *m.* (*coll.*) Christian.

кре|щу́, ⌣сти́шь, *see* ⌣сти́ть.

крив|а́я, о́й, *f.* (*math., econ., etc.*) curve; (*coll.*) к. вы́везет something will turn up; его́ на ⌣о́й не объе́дешь you won't catch him napping.

кри́вд|а, ы, *f.* (*arch. and folk poet.*) falsehood; injustice.

криве́|ть, ю, *impf.* (*of* o⌣) to lose one eye.

кривизн|а́, ы́, *f.* crookedness; curvature.

крив|и́ть, лю́, и́шь, *impf.* (*of* c⌣) to bend, distort; (*coll.*) к. гу́бы, рот to twist one's mouth, curl one's lip; к. (*pf.* по⌣) душо́й to act against one's conscience.

крив|и́ться, лю́сь, и́шься, *impf.* 1. (*pf.* по⌣) to become crooked, bent. 2. (*pf.* c⌣) (*coll.*) to make a wry face.

кривля́к|а, и, *m. and f.* (*coll.*) poseur; affected person.

кривля́нь|е, я, *n.* affectation.

кривля́|ться, юсь, *impf.* (*coll.*) to be affected, behave in an affected manner.

кривобо́к|ий (⌣, ⌣a), *adj.* lop-sided.

кривогла́з|ый (⌣, ⌣a), *adj.* blind in one eye.

криводу́ши|е, я, *n.* (*obs.*) duplicity, crookedness.

криводу́ш|ный (⌣ен, ⌣на), *adj.* (*obs.*) dishonest, crooked.

крив|о́й (⌣, ⌣á, ⌣o), *adj.* 1. crooked; ⌣о́е зе́ркало distorting mirror; ⌣а́я улы́бка wry smile; (*fig.*) ⌣ы́е пути́ crooked ways. 2. (*coll.*) one-eyed.

криволине́йный, *adj.* (*math.*) curvilinear; (*tech.*) к. паз cam slot, cam groove.

кривоно́г|ий (⌣, ⌣a), *adj.* bandy-legged, bow-legged.

кривото́лк|и, ов, *no sing.* false interpretations.

кривоши́п, a, *m.* (*tech.*) crank; crankshaft.

кри́зис, a, *m.* crisis.

крик, a, *m.* cry, shout; ⌣и clamour, outcry; после́дний к. мо́ды the last word in fashion.

крикли́в|ый (⌣, ⌣a), *adj.* 1. clamorous, bawling. 2. loud, penetrating. 3. (*fig., coll.*) loud; blatant.

кри́кн|уть, у, ешь, *inst. pf. of* крича́ть.

крику́н, á, *m.* (*coll.*) 1. shouter, bawler. 2. babbler.

кримина́л, a, *m.* (*coll.*) 1. foul play. 2. crime.

криминали́ст, a, *m.* (*leg.*) specialist in crime detection.

криминали́стик|а, и, *f.* (science of) crime detection.

кримина́льный, *adj.* criminal.

кримино́лог, a, *m.* criminologist.

кримино́логи|я, и, *f.* criminology.

кри́нка = кры́нка.

криноли́н, a, *m.* crinoline.

криптогра́мм|а, ы, *f.* cryptogram.

криптогра́фи|я, и, *f.* cryptography.

криста́лл, a, *m.* crystal.

кристаллиза́ци|я, и, *f.* crystallization.

кристаллиз|ова́ть, у́ю, *impf. and pf.* (*pf. also* за⌣) to crystallize (*trans.*).

кристаллиз|ова́ться, у́юсь, *impf. and pf.* (*pf. also* за⌣) to crystallize (*intrans.; also fig.*).

кристаллографи́ческий, *adj.* crystallographic.

кристаллогра́фи|я, и, *f.* crystallography.

криста́л|ьный, *adj.* 1. crystalline. 2. (⌣ен, ⌣ьна) (*fig.*) crystal-clear.

крите́ри|й, я, *m.* criterion.

кри́тик, a, *m.* critic.

кри́тик|а, и, *f.* 1. criticism. 2. critique.

критика́н, a, *m.* (*coll., pejor.*) fault-finder, carper.

критика́нств|овать, ую, *impf.* (*coll.*, *pejor.*) to engage in fault-finding; to carp.

критик|ова́ть, у́ю, *impf.* to criticize.

критици́зм, а, *m.* 1. critical attitude. 2. (*philos.*) criticism.

крити́ческий, *adj.* (*in var. senses*) critical; к. моме́нт (*fig.*) crucial moment.

кри́ц|а, ы, *f.* (*tech.*) bloom.

кри|ча́ть, чу́, чи́шь, *impf.* (*of* ~кнуть) 1. to cry, shout; to yell, scream; к. (на+*a.*) to shout (at); к. о по́мощи to call for help. 2. (о+*p.*) (*coll.*, *pejor.*) to make a song (about), cry out (against).

крича́|щий, *pres. part. act. of* ~ть *and adj.* (*fig.*, *coll.*) loud; blatant.

кри́|чный, *adj. of* ~ца (*tech.*); к. горн finery, bloomery; ~чное произво́дство finery process.

кроа́т, а, *m.* = хорва́т.

кроа́тский, *adj.* = хорва́тский.

кров, а, *m.* roof; shelter; оста́ться без ~а to be left without a roof over one's head.

крова́в|ый, *adj.* 1. bloody; (*fig.*) ~ая ба́ня blood-bath. 2. blood-stained.

крова́т|ь, и, *f.* bed; bedstead.

кро́в|ельный, *adj. of* ~ля.

кро́вельщик, а, *m.* roof-maker.

кровено́сн|ый, *adj.* appertaining to the circulation of the blood; ~ая систе́ма circulatory system; к. сосу́д blood-vessel.

крови́нк|а, и, *f.* (*coll.*) drop of blood; у него́ ни ~и в лице́ he is deathly pale.

кро́в|ля, ли, *g. pl.* ~ель, *f.* roof.

кро́вн|ый, *adj.* 1. blood; ~ое родство́ blood relationship, consanguinity; ~ая месть blood feud. 2. (*of animals*) thorough-bred. 3. (*fig.*) vital, deep, intimate; моё ~ое де́ло an affair which concerns me closely; ~ые интере́сы vital interests; ~ые де́ньги money earned by the sweat of one's brow. 4. (*fig.*) deadly; ~ая оби́да deadly insult.

кровожа́д|ный (~ен, ~на), *adj.* bloodthirsty.

кровоизлия́ни|е, я, *n.* (*med.*) haemorrhage.

кровообраще́ни|е, я, *n.* circulation of the blood.

кровооста́навливающ|ий, *adj.* ~ее сре́дство styptic.

кровопи́йц|а, ы, *g. pl.* ~, *m. and f.* (*fig.*, *rhet.*) blood-sucker.

кровоподте́к, а, *m.* bruise.

кровопроли́ти|е, я, *n.* bloodshed.

кровопроли́тный, *adj.* bloody; sanguinary.

кровопуска́ни|е, я, *n.* (*med.*) blood-letting, phlebotomy.

кровосмеше́ни|е, я, *n.* incest.

кровосо́с, а, *m.* 1. vampire bat. 2. (*dial.*) vampire. 3. (*coll.*) blood-sucker.

кровосо́сн|ый, *adj.* ~ая ба́нка cupping-glass.

кровотече́ни|е, я, *n.* haemorrhage; bleeding.

кровоточи́вост|ь, и, *f.* (*med.*) haemophilia.

кровоточи́в|ый (~, ~а), *adj.* 1. bleeding. 2. (*med.*; *obs.*) haemophiliac.

кровоточи́т|ь, ~, *impf.* to bleed.

кровоха́ркани|е, я, *n.* blood-spitting; (*med.*) haemoptysis.

кров|ь, и, о ~и, **в** ~й, *g. pl.* ~е́й, *f.* blood (*also fig.*); в к., до ~и till it bleeds, till blood flows; изби́ть, разби́ть в к. to draw blood; пусти́ть к. (+*d.*) to bleed (*trans.*); (*fig.*) по ~и by birth; к. с молоко́м (*coll.*) the very picture of health, blooming; у него́ к. кипи́т his blood is up; страсть к игре́ у него́ в ~й gambling is in his blood; войти́ в плоть и к. to become ingrained; по́ртить кому́-н. к. to put someone out, annoy someone; се́рдце у меня́ облива́ется ~ью my heart bleeds; пить чью-н. к. (*rhet.*) to suck someone's blood, batten on someone.

кровяни́ст|ый (~, ~а), *adj.* containing some blood.

кров|яно́й, *adj. of* ~ь.

кро|и́ть, ю́, и́шь, *impf.* (*of* с~) to cut (out).

кро́йк|а, и, *f.* cutting (out).

кроке́т, а, *m.* croquet.

кроке́т|ный, *adj. of* ~.

кроки́, *indecl.*, *n.* sketch-map; rough sketch.

кроки́р|овать, ую, *impf.* to sketch.

крокир|ова́ть, у́ю, *impf. and pf.* (at croquet) to roquet.

крокоди́л, а, *m.* crocodile.

крокоди́л|ов *and* ~овый, *adj. of* ~.

кро́лик, а, *m.* rabbit.

кроликово́д, а, *m.* rabbit-breeder.

кроликово́дств|о, а, *n.* rabbit-breeding.

кро́ли|ковый *and* ~чий, *adj. of* ~к; ~чий мех rabbit-skin.

кро́л|ь, я, *m.* (*sport*) crawl (stroke).

крольча́тник, а, *m.* rabbit-hutch.

крольчи́х|а, и, *f.* doe-rabbit.

кро́ме, *prep.*+*g.* 1. except. 2. besides, in addition to; к. того́ besides, moreover, furthermore; (*coll.*) к. шу́ток joking apart.

кроме́шн|ый, *adj.* ад к. inferno; тьма ~ая (*New Testament*) outer darkness; (*fig.*) pitch darkness.

кро́мк|а, и, *f.* edge; (*of material*) selvage; пере́дняя, за́дняя к. leading (*aeron.*) edge, trailing edge; к. на ~у with edges overlapping, (*naut.*) clinker-built; к. тротуа́ра kerb.

кромса́|ть, ю, *impf.* (*of* ис~) (*coll.*) to cut up carelessly.

крон, а, *m.* chrome yellow.

кро́н|а[1], ы, *f.* crown (*of a tree*).

кро́н|а[2], ы, *f.* (*unit of currency*) crown.

кронци́ркул|ь, я, *m.* (*tech.*) calipers.

кро́ншнеп, а, *m.* (*orn.*) curlew.

кронште́йн, а, *m.* (*tech.*) bracket; corbel.

кропа́|ть, ю, *impf.* (*coll.*) **1.** (*obs.*) to mend, patch. **2.** to potter away at. **3.** to scribble.

кропи́л|о, а, *n.* (*eccl.*) aspergillum.

кроп|и́ть, лю́, и́шь, *impf.* (*of* о~) **1.** to besprinkle; to asperse. **2.** (*intrans.*; *of rain*) to trickle, spot.

кропотли́в|ый (~, ~а), *adj.* **1.** laborious; ~ая рабо́та minute, laborious work. **2.** painstaking, precise; minute.

кросс, а, *m.* (*sport*) cross-country (race).

кроссво́рд, а, *m.* crossword.

кроссо́в|ки, ок, *sing.* ~ка, ~ки, *f.* track shoes.

крот, а́, *m.* **1.** mole. **2.** moleskin.

кро́т|кий (~ок, ~ка́, ~ко), *adj.* gentle; mild, meek.

крото́вин|а, ы, *f.* mole-hill.

крот|о́вый, *adj.* **1.** *of* ~; ~о́вая нора́ mole-hill. **2.** moleskin.

кро́тост|ь, и, *f.* gentleness; mildness; meekness.

крох|а́, и́, *a.* ~у, *pl.* ~и, ~а́м, *f.* crumb (*pl. also fig.*).

крохобо́р, а, *m.* (*coll.*) narrow pedant.

крохобо́рств|о, а, *n.* (*coll.*) narrow pedantry.

крохобо́рств|овать, ую, *impf.* (*coll.*) to behave pedantically.

кро́хотный, *adj.* (*coll.*) tiny, minute.

кро́шев|о, а, *n.* (*coll.*) **1.** (*cш.*) hash. **2.** medley.

кро́шечк|а, и, *f.* *dim. of* кро́шка.

кро́шечный, *adj.* (*coll.*) tiny, minute.

крош|и́ть, у́, ~ишь, *impf.* **1.** (*pf.* ис~, на~ *or* рас~) to crumb, crumble; to chop, hack; (*fig.*) to hack to pieces. **2.** (*pf.* на~) (+*i.*) to drop, spill crumbs (of); к. хле́бом на́ пол to drop crumbs on to the floor.

крош|и́ться, ~ится, *impf.* (*of* ис~ *and* рас~) to crumble, break into small pieces.

кро́шк|а, и, *f.* **1.** crumb. **2.** (*fig.*) a tiny bit; ни ~и not a bit. **3.** (*coll., affect. of a child*) little one.

круг, а, *pl.* ~и́, *m.* **1.** (*p. sing.* в, на ~у́ = *circular area*; в, на ~е = *circumference*) circle; движе́ние по ~у movement in a circle; на к. on average, taking it all round; к. сы́ра a cheese; ~и́ (на воде́) ripples (on water); стать в к. to form a circle. **2.** (*sport*; *p. sing.*, на ~у́) бегово́й к. race-course, ring; к. почёта lap of honour. **3.** (*fig.*; *p. sing.* в ~у́) sphere, range; compass; вне ~а свои́х обя́занностей outside one's province. **4.** (*fig.*; *p. sing.* в ~у́) circle (*of persons*); официа́льные ~и́ official quarters; в семе́йном ~у́ in the family circle.

кру́гленьк|ий, *adj.* (*coll.*) **1.** *dim. of* кру́глый; ~ая су́мма a round sum. **2.** rotund, portly.

кругле́|ть, ю, *impf.* (*of* по~) to become round.

круглова́т|ый (~, ~а), *adj.* roundish.

круглогодово́й, *adj.* all-the-year-round.

круглогу́бц|ы, ев, *no sing.* (*tech.*) round pliers.

круглоли́ц|ый (~, ~а), *adj.* round-faced, chubby.

круглоро́т|ые, ых (*zool.*) Cyclostomata.

круглосу́точный, *adj.* round-the-clock, twenty-four-hour.

кру́гл|ый (~, ~а́, ~о), *adj.* **1.** (*in var. senses*) round; к. год all the year round; ~ые су́тки day and night; к. по́черк round hand; ~ая су́мма round sum; в ~ых ци́фрах, для ~ого счёта in round figures. **2.** (*coll.*) complete, utter, perfect; к. дура́к perfect fool; ~ое неве́жество crass ignorance; к., ~ая сирота́ orphan (having *neither* father *nor* mother).

кругля́ш, а́, *m.* (*dial.*) rounded stone.

кругов|о́й, *adj.* circular; ~а́я пору́ка mutual responsibility, guarantee; ~а́я ча́ша loving-cup; ~а́я доро́га roundabout route; ~а́я оборо́на all-round defence.

кругово́рот, а, *m.* rotation, circulation.

кругозо́р, а, *m.* **1.** prospect. **1.** (*fig.*) horizon, range of interests.

круго́м¹, *adv.* **1.** round, around; он обошёл маши́ну к. he walked around the car. **2.** (all) around, round about; к. всё бы́ло ти́хо all around was still. **3.** (*coll.*) completely, entirely; он был к. в долга́х he was head over heels in debt; вы к. винова́ты you are entirely to blame, you haven't a leg to stand on.

круго́м², *prep.*+*g.* round, around.

кругооборо́т, а, *m.* circuit, circulation.

кругообра́з|ный (~ен, ~на), *adj.* circular.

кругосве́тный, *adj.* round-the-world.

кружа́л|о¹, а, *n.* (*archit.*) bow member, curve piece.

кружа́л|о², а, *n.* (*hist.*) tavern, pothouse.

круж|ева́, ~е́в, ~ева́м = ~ево.

кружевни́ц|а, ы, *f.* lace-maker.

кружев|но́й, *adj. of* ~а́ *and* кру́жево.

кру́жев|о, а, *n.* lace.

круж|и́ть, у́, ~ишь, *impf.* **1.** to whirl, spin round; (*fig.*) к. кому́-н. го́лову to turn someone's head. **2.** to circle. **3.** (*coll.*) to wander.

круж|и́ться, у́сь, ~ишься, *impf.* (*of* за~) to whirl, spin round; to circle; у меня́ ~ится голова́ my head is going round, I feel giddy.

кру́жк|а, и, *f.* **1.** mug; tankard; (*measure*) к. пи́ва glass of beer. **2.** collecting-box. **3.** (*med.*) douche.

кружковщи́н|а, ы, *f.* clannishness, cliquishness.

круж|ко́вый, *adj. of* ~о́к 2.

кру́жный, *adj.* roundabout, circuitous.

круж|о́к, ка́, *m.* **1.** *dim. of* круг; стри́чься в к. to have one's hair bobbed. **2.** (*lit., polit., etc.*) circle, study group.

круи́з, а, *m.* cruise.

круп¹, а, *m.* (*med.*) croup.

круп², а, *m.* croup, crupper (*of horse*).

круп|а́, ы́, *pl.* ~ы, *f.* **1.** (*collect.*) groats; гре́чневая к. buckwheat; ма́нная к. semolina; овся́ная к. oatmeal; перло́вая к. pearl-barley. **2.** (*fig.*) sleet.

крупени́к, а́, *m.* buckwheat pudding with curd.

крупи́нк|а, и, *f.* grain.

крупи́ц|а, ы, *f.* grain, fragment, atom; у него́ нет ни ~ы здра́вого смы́сла he hasn't a grain of common sense.

крупне́|ть, ю, *impf.* (*of* по~) to grow larger.

кру́пн|о, *adv. of* ~ый; к. наре́зать to cut into large pieces; к. писа́ть to write large; к. поспо́рить (с+*i.*) to have high words (with), have a slanging-match (with).

крупнозерни́стый, *adj.* coarse-grained, large-grained.

крупнокали́берный, *adj.* large-calibre.

кру́п|ный (~ен, ~на́, ~но), *adj.* **1.** large, big; large-scale; (*fig.*) prominent, outstanding; ~ные де́ньги money in large denominations; ~ные поме́щики big landowners; ~ная промы́шленность large-scale industry; к. рога́тый скот (horned) cattle; ~ным ша́гом at a round pace; засня́ть ~ным пла́ном (*cinema*) to take a close-up (*of*). **2.** coarse; к. песо́к coarse sand; к. шаг (*tech., aeron.*) coarse pitch. **3.** important; serious; ~ная неприя́тность serious trouble; к. разгово́р (*fig.*) high words.

круп|о́зный, *adj. of* ~¹; ~о́зное воспале́ние лёгких lobar pneumonia.

крупору́шк|а, и, *f.* (*agric.*) hulling mill, peeling mill.

крупча́тк|а, и, *f.* finest wheaten flour.

крупча́тый, *adj.* granular.

крупье́, *indecl., m.* croupier.

крутизн|а́, ы́, *f.* **1.** steepness. **2.** steep slope.

крути́льн|ый, *adj.* (*tech.*) torsion(al); (*text.*) doubling; ~ая маши́на twisting machine, (*text.*) twiner.

кру|ти́ть, чу́, ~тишь, *impf.* (*of* за~ *and* с~) **1.** to twist; to twirl; к. верёвку to twist a rope; к. папиро́су to roll a cigarette; к. усы́ to twirl one's moustache; к. шёлк to twist, throw silk; (*coll.*; +*i.*) она́ ~тит им, как хо́чет she twists him round her little finger. **2.** to turn, wind (*tap, handle, etc.*). **3.** to whirl (*trans.*). **4.** (*coll.*; с+*i*) to go out (with), have an affair (with).

кру|ти́ться, чу́сь, ~тишься, *impf.* **1.** to turn, spin, revolve. **2.** to whirl. **3.** (*fig., coll.*) to be in a whirl.

кру́то, *adv.* **1.** steeply. **2.** suddenly; abruptly;

sharply; к. поверну́ть to turn round sharply. **3.** (*coll.*) sternly, severely; drastically; к. распра́виться с кем-н. to give someone short shrift. **4.** thoroughly; к. замеси́ть те́сто to make a thick dough; к. отжа́ть to squeeze dry, wring out thoroughly; к. посоли́ть to put (too) much salt (into).

крут|о́й (~, ~а́, ~о), *adj.* **1.** steep; к. вира́ж (*aeron.*) steep turn. **2.** sudden; abrupt, sharp. **3.** (*coll.*) stern, severe; drastic; к. нрав stern temper; ~ы́е ме́ры drastic measures. **4.** (*cul.*) thick; well-done; к. кипято́к fiercely boiling water; ~о́е яйцо́ hard-boiled egg.

кру́ч|а, и, *f.* steep slope, cliff.

кру́|че, *comp. of* ~то́й *and* ~то.

круче́ни|е, я, *n.* **1.** (*text.*) twisting, spinning. **2.** (*tech.*) torsion.

кручён|ый, *adj.* **1.** twisted; ~ые ни́тки lisle thread. **2.** (*sport*) spinning, turning; with spin on.

кручи́н|а, ы, *f.* (*folk poet.*) sorrow, woe.

кручи́н|иться, юсь, ишься, *impf.* (*folk poet.*) to sorrow, grieve.

кру|чу́, ~тишь, *see* ~ти́ть.

круше́ни|е, я, *n.* **1.** wreck; ruin; к. по́езда derailment. **2.** (*fig.*) ruin; collapse; downfall.

круши́н|а, ы, *f.* (*bot.*) buckthorn.

круш|и́ть, у́, и́шь, *impf.* to shatter, destroy (*also fig.*).

круш|и́ться, у́сь, и́шься, *impf.* (*obs. or poet.*) to sorrow, be afflicted.

крыжо́венный, *adj.* gooseberry.

крыжо́вник, а, *m.* **1.** gooseberry bush(es). **2.** (*collect.*) gooseberries.

крыла́тк|а¹, и, *f.* **1.** (*obs.*) (man's) loose cloak with cape. **2.** (*bot.*) ash-key.

крыла́тк|а², и, *f.* (*tech.*) wing nut; vane.

крыла́т|ый, *adj.* winged (*also fig.*); ~ые слова́ pithy saying(s); (*tech.*) к. болт butterfly bolt; ~ая га́йка wing nut.

крыл|е́чко, е́чка, *n. dim. of* ~ьцо́.

крыл|о́, а́, *pl.* ~ья, ~ьев, *n.* (*in var. senses*) wing; sail, vane (*of windmill*); splash-board, mud-guard, wing (*of car, carriage*).

крылоно́г|ие, их, (*zool.*) Pteropoda.

кры́лыш|ко, ка, *pl.* ~ки, ~ек, ~кам, *n. dim. of* крыло́; (*fig.*) под ~ком under the wing (of).

крыл|ьцо́, ьца́, *pl.* ~ьца, ~е́ц, ~ьца́м, *n.* porch; perron; front (*or* back) steps.

кры́мский, *adj.* Crimean.

крымча́к, а́, *m.* inhabitant of the Crimea.

кры́нк|а, и, *f.* earthenware pot, pitcher.

кры́с|а, ы, *f.* rat; су́мчатая к. opossum; канцеля́рская к. (*fig., coll.*) quill-driver.

крыс|ёнок, ёнка, *pl.* ~я́та, ~я́т, *m.* young rat.

кры́с|иный, *adj. of* ~а; к. яд rat poison.

крысоло́в, а, *m.* rat-catcher.

крысоло́вк|а, и, *f.* 1. rat-trap. 2. (*dog*) rat-catcher.

кры́т|ый, *p.p.p.* of ~ь and *adj.* covered; sheltered, with an awning; к. ры́нок covered market.

крыть, кро́ю, кро́ешь, *impf.* (*of* по~) 1. to cover; to roof; to coat (*with paint*); (*cards*) to cover, trump. 2. (*coll.*) to swear (at); ему́ не́чем к. he hasn't a leg to stand on.

кры́ться, кро́юсь, кро́ешься, *impf.* 1. (в+*p.*) to be, lie (in). 2. to be concealed.

кры́ш|а, и, *f.* roof.

кры́шк|а, и, *f.* 1. lid; cover. 2. (*sl.*) death, end; ему́ к. he's done for, he's finished.

крю́|к, ка́, *m.* 1. (*pl.* ~ки́, ~ко́в) hook; (*pl.* ~чья, ~чьев) hook (*for supporting load*). 2. detour; (*coll.*) дать ~ку, сде́лать к. to make a detour. 3. (*mus.*) (*pl.* ~ки́, ~ко́в) kryuk (*old Russian neum*).

крю́ч|ить, ит, *impf.* (*of* с~) (*impers.*, *coll.*) его́ ~ит (от бо́ли) he is writhing (in pain).

крючкова́т|ый (~, ~а), *adj.* hooked.

крючкотво́р, а, *m.* (*obs.*, *coll.*) pettifogger.

крючкотво́рств|о, а, *n.* (*obs.*, *coll.*) chicanery.

крю́чник, а, *m.* carrier, stevedore.

крюч|о́к, ка́, *m.* 1. hook; спусково́й к. trigger. 2. (*fig.*; *obs.*, *pejor.*) hitch, catch. 3. (*fig.*, *obs.*) pettifogger.

крюшо́н, а, *m.* cup (*beverage*).

кря́ду, *adv.* (*coll.*) running; три дня к. она́ опа́здывала на слу́жбу three days running she was late for work.

кряж, а, *m.* 1. (mountain-)ridge. 2. block, log.

кря́жист|ый (~, ~а), *adj.* thick; (*fig.*) thick-set.

кря́к|ать, аю, *impf.* (*of* ~нуть) 1. to quack. 2. (*coll.*) to wheeze.

кря́кв|а, ы, *f.* wild duck, mallard.

кря́к|нуть, ну, нешь, *inst. pf.* of ~ать.

кряхте́|ть, чу́, ти́шь, *impf.* to groan; to wheeze, grunt.

ксёндз, а́, *m.* Roman Catholic (*esp. Polish*) priest.

ксилогра́фи|я, и, *f.* 1. wood-engraving. 2. woodcut.

ксилофо́н, а, *m.* (*mus.*) xylophone.

кста́ти, *adv.* 1. to the point, apropos. 2. opportunely; вы пришли́ как раз к. you came just at the right moment; э́тот пода́рок оказа́лся о́чень к. the present has proved most welcome. 3. (*coll.*) at the same time, incidentally; к. зайди́те пожа́луйста в апте́ку will you please call at the chemist's at the same time. 4. к. (сказа́ть) by the way; к., где вы купи́ли э́тот га́лстук? by the way, where did you buy that tie?

кти́тор, а, *m.* churchwarden.

кто, кого́, кому́, кем, ком, *pron.* 1. (*interrog.*) who; к. э́то тако́й? who is that?; к. из вас э́то сде́лал? which of you did it?; к. идёт? (*mil.*) who goes there?; к. кого́ (*sc.* побьёт)? who will win? 2. (*relat.*) who (*normally after pronoun antecedent*); тот, к. he who; те, к. those who; блаже́н, к.... blessed is he who . . .; спаса́йся к. мо́жет! every man for himself! 3. (*indef.*) к. (бы) ни who(so)ever; к. ни придёт whoever comes; к. бы то ни́ был whoever it may be. 4. (*indef.*) some . . . others; к. что лю́бит, кому́ что нра́вится tastes differ; разбежа́лись к. куда́ they scattered in all directions; к. в лес, к. по дрова́ (*coll.*) to be (*etc.*) at sixes and sevens. 5. (*coll.*; *indef.*) anyone; е́сли к. позвони́т, дай мне знать if anyone rings, let me know. 6. к.-к., а... (кого́-кого́, а...) кому́-кому́, а...) *contrasts action, attitude, etc., of one or more members of a group with that of remainder* (*coll.*): кого́-кого́, а меня́ э́то вполне́ устра́ивает I don't know about anyone else, but it suits me fine.

кто́-либо, кого́-либо, *pron.* = кто́-нибудь.

кто́-нибудь, кого́-нибудь, *pron.* anyone, anybody; someone, somebody.

кто́-то, кого́-то, *pron.* someone, somebody.

куафёр, а, *m.* (*obs.*) coiffeur.

куафю́р|а, ы, *f.* (*obs.*) coiffure.

куб¹, а, *pl.* ~ы́, *m.* 1. (*math.*) cube; два в ~е two cubed. 2. (*coll.*) cubic metre.

куб², а, *pl.* ~ы́, *m.* boiler, water-heater, (tea-)urn; still.

куба́н|ец, ца, *m.* Kuban Cossack.

куба́нк|а, и, *f.* flat, round fur hat.

куба́нский, *adj.* (*geogr.*) (of the) Kuban.

ку́барем, *adv.* (*coll.*) head over heels, headlong; скати́ться к. to roll head over heels.

куба́р|ь, я́, *m.* peg-top.

кубату́р|а, ы, *f.* cubic content.

куби́зм, а, *m.* (*art*) cubism.

ку́бик, а, *m.* 1. *dim.* of куб. 2. (*pl.*) blocks, bricks (*as children's toy*). 3. (*coll.*) cubic centimetre.

куби́н|ец, ца, *m.* Cuban.

куби́н|ка, ки, *f.* of ~ец.

куби́нский, *adj.* Cuban.

куби́ческий, *adj.* cubic; к. ко́рень (*math.*) cube root.

кубови́д|ный (~ен, ~на), *adj.* cube-shaped, cuboid.

куб|ово́й, *adj.* of ~².

ку́бовый, *adj.* indigo.

ку́б|ок, ка, *m.* goblet, bowl, beaker; переходя́щий к. (*sport, etc.*) cup; встре́ча на к. cup-tie.

кубоме́тр, а, *m.* cubic metre.

ку́брик, а, *m.* (*naut.*) crew's quarters; orlop (-deck).

кубы́шк|а и, *f.* (*coll.*) 1. (*obs.*) money-box.

2. (*joc.*) dumpy woman. **3.** yellow water-lily.

кувáлд|а, ы, *f.* sledge-hammer (*also fig.*, *coll.*, *of a clumsy woman*).

кувéрт, а, *m.* (*obs.*) place (*at table*); стол на двáдцать ~ов table laid for twenty persons.

кувши́н, а, *m.* jug; pitcher.

кувши́нк|а, и, *f.* (*bot.*) water-lily.

кувырк|áться, áюсь, *impf.* (*of* ~нýться) to turn somersaults, go head over heels.

кувырк|нýться, нýсь, нёшься, *inst. pf. of* ~áться.

кувыркóм, *adv.* (*coll.*) head over heels; topsy-turvy; полетéть к. to go head over heels; всё пошлó к. everything went haywire.

кугуáр, а, *m.* (*zool.*) puma, cougar.

кудá, *adv.* **1.** (*interrog. and relat.*) where (*expressing motion*), whither; к. ты идёшь? where are you going?; к. он положи́л мою кни́гу? where did he put my book? **2.** к. (бы) ни wherever; к. бы то ни́ бы́ло anywhere; (*coll.*) к. ни кинь wherever one looks, on all sides; к. ни шло come what may. **3.** (*coll.*) what for; к. вам стóлько багажá? what do you want so much luggage for? **4.** (+*comp.*; *coll.*) much, far; сегóдня мне к. лýчше I am much better today. **5.** (*coll.*) хоть к. fine, excellent. **6.** (*expressing doubt, indredulity*; *coll.*) how (could that be; could you, he, etc.); к чáсу я намéрен дочитáть до страни́цы 200 — к. тебé! I intend to reach page 200 by one o'clock—you'll never do it!; узнáли ли тебя́ они́? к. им дид they recognize you? how could they? **7.** (*coll., iron.*) к. как very; к. как прия́тно слýшать егó гóлос it is *so* nice to listen to his voice.

кудá-либо, *adv.* = кудá-нибудь.

кудá-нибудь, *adv.* anywhere; somewhere.

кудá-то, *adv.* somewhere.

кудáхтань|е, я, *n.* cackling, clucking.

кудáх|тать, чу, чешь, *impf.* to cackle, cluck.

кудéл|ь, и, *f.* (*text.*) tow.

кудéсник, а, *m.* magician, sorcerer.

кудлáтый, *adj.* (*coll.*) shaggy.

кудревáт|ый (~, ~а), *adj.* rather curly; (*fig.*) florid, ornate.

кýдр|и, éй, *no sing.* curls.

кудря́в|иться, люсь, ишься, *impf.* to curl.

кудря́в|ый (~, ~а), *adj.* **1.** curly; curly-headed. **2.** leafy, bushy; ~ая капýста curly kale. **3.** (*fig.*) florid, ornate.

кудря́ш|ки, ек, *no sing.* (*coll.*) ringlets.

кузéн, а, *m.* cousin.

кузи́н|а, ы, *f.* cousin.

кузнéц, á, *m.* (black)smith; farrier.

кузнéчик, а, *m.* grasshopper.

кузнéчный, *adj.* blacksmith's; к. мех bellows.

кузни́ц|а, ы, *f.* forge, smithy.

кýзов, а, *pl.* ~ы and ~á, *m.* **1.** basket. **2.** body (*of carriage, etc.*).

кукарéка|ть, ю, *impf.* to crow.

кукарекý cock-a-doodle-doo.

кýкиш, а, *m.* (*coll.*) fig (*gesture of derision or contempt, generally accompanying refusal to comply with a request, and consisting of extending clenched fist with thumb placed between index and middle fingers*); показáть комý-н. к. to make this gesture (*cf.* to cock a snook, give the V-sign); к. в кармáне *of defiance expressed in the absence of the person defied*; получи́ть к. с мáслом to come away empty-handed, receive a snub.

кýк|ла, лы, *g. pl.* ~ол, *f.* doll; теáтр ~ол puppet-theatre.

кук|овáть, ýю, *impf.* to (cry) cuckoo.

кýколк|а, и, *f.* **1.** (*affect. dim. of* кýкла) dolly. **2.** (*zool.*) chrysalis, pupa.

кýкол|ь¹, я, *m.* (*bot.*) cockle.

кýкол|ь², я, *m.* (*eccl.*) cowl.

кýкольник, а, *m.* (*coll.*) puppeteer.

кýкольн|ый, *adj.* **1.** doll's; к. теáтр puppet-theatre; ~ая комéдия (*fig., coll.*) farce; play-acting. **2.** doll-like.

кýк|ситься, шусь, сишься, *impf.* (*coll.*) to sulk; to be in the dumps.

кукурýз|а, ы, *f.* maize, Indian corn.

кукурýз|ный, *adj. of* ~а.

кукýшк|а¹, и, *f.* cuckoo; часы́ с ~ой cuckoo-clock.

кукýшк|а², и, *f.* small steam locomotive.

кулáк¹, á, *m.* **1.** fist; бронирóванный к. the mailed fist; дойти́ до ~óв to come to blows; смея́ться в ~ to laugh in one's sleeve. **2.** (*mil.*) striking force.

кулáк², á, *m.* kulak.

кулáк³, á, *m.* (*tech.*) cam.

кулá|цкий, *adj. of* ~к².

кулáчеств|о, а, *n.* (*collect.*) the kulaks.

кулáчк|а, и, *f. of* кулáк².

кулáчк|и, *only in phrases* идти́ на к. to come to blows; би́ться на ~ах to engage in fisticuffs.

кулач|кóвый, *adj. of* ~óк²; к. вал camshaft.

кулá|чный, *adj. of* ~к¹, ³; к. бой fisticuffs; ~чное прáво fist-law.

кула|чóк¹, чкá, *m. dim. of* ~к¹.

кулач|óк², кá, *m.* (*tech.*) cam.

кулебя́к|а, и, *f.* kulebyaka (*pie containing meat, fish, or vegetables, etc.*).

кул|ёк, ькá, *m.* bag (*made from bast or paper*); из ~ькá в рогóжку (*coll.*) out of the frying-pan into the fire.

кулéш, á, *m.* (*coll.*) thin gruel.

кýли, *indecl.*, *m.* coolie.

кули́к, á, *m.* (*orn.*) stint; sandpiper (*Calidris*).

кулинáр, а, *m.* cookery specialist.

кулинáри|я, и, *f.* cookery.

кулина́рный, *adj.* culinary.

кули́с|а, ы, *f.* (*tech.*) link.

кули́с|ный, *adj. of* ~а; к. ка́мень sliding block, link block, guiding shoe; ~ное распределе́ние link gear, link motion, slide block mechanism.

кули́с|ы, ~, *sing.* ~а, ~ы, *f.* (*theatr.*) wings, side-scenes, slips; за ~ами behind the scenes (*also fig.*).

кули́ч, а́, *m.* Easter cake.

кули́чк|и, *only in phrases.* (*coll.*) у чёрта на ~ах, к чёрту на к. at (to) the world's end.

куло́н¹, а, *m.* pendant.

куло́н², а, *m.* (*electr.*) coulomb.

кулуа́р|ный, *adj. of* ~ы.

кулуа́р|ы, ов, *sing. not used,* lobby (*in Parliament; also fig.*).

кул|ь, я́, *m.* sack (*formerly also dry measure* = *325 lb. approx.*).

кульминацио́нный, *adj.* к. пункт culmination (point).

кульмина́ци|я, и, *f.* culmination.

кульмини́р|овать, ую, *impf. and pf.* to culminate.

культ, а, *m.* (*in var. senses*) cult; служи́тели ~a ministers of religion: к. ли́чности (*hist.*) cult of personality (*esp. of J. Stalin*).

культ- (*abbr. of* ~у́рный) cultural, educational, recreational.

культива́тор, а, *m.* (*agric.*) cultivator (*machine*).

культива́ци|я, и, *f.* (*agric.*) treatment of the ground with a cultivator (*machine*).

культиви́ровани|е, я, *n.* cultivation (*also fig.*).

культиви́р|овать, ую, *impf.* to cultivate (*also fig.*).

культма́ссов|ый, *adj.* ~ая рабо́та education of the masses.

ку́льт|овый, *adj. of* ~; ~овая му́зыка religious music.

культпохо́д, а, *m.* 1. cultural crusade. 2. cultural outing (*visit by group to museum, theatre, etc.*).

культрабо́тник, а, *m.* 'culture secretary', 'culture officer' (*person in charge of cultural, and/or educational activities in an organization or establishment*).

культтова́р|ы, ов, *no sing.* 'cultural supplies' (*office equipment, musical instruments, etc., used in the organization of cultural and/or educational activities*).

культу́р|а, ы, *f.* 1. (*in var. senses*) culture. 2. standard, level; к. ре́чи standard of speech; повы́сить ~у земледе́лия to raise the standard of farming. 3. (*agric.*) зерновы́е ~ы cereals; кормовы́е ~ы forage crops. 4. (*agric.*) cultivation, growing; к. карто́феля potato-growing.

культу́рничеств|о, а, *n.* (*pejor.*) culture-mongering (*promotion of cultural and/or educational activities to exclusion of political questions*).

культу́рно, *adv.* in a civilized manner.

культу́рно-бытов|о́й, *adj.* ~ое обслу́живание culture and welfare service.

культу́рно-просвети́тельный, *adj.* cultural and educational.

культу́рност|ь, и, *f.* (level of) culture; cultivation; (*fig.*) он отлича́лся ~ью he was exceptionally cultivated.

культу́р|ный (~ен, ~на), *adj.* 1. cultured, cultivated. 2. (*in var. senses*) cultural. 3. (*agric., hort.*) cultured; cultivated.

культуртре́гер, а, *m.* (*iron.*) 'Kulturträger', person with civilizing mission.

культ|я́, и́, *f.* stump (*of maimed or amputated limb*).

культя́|пка, пки, *f.* (*coll.*) = ~.

кум, а, *pl.* ~овья́, ~овьёв, *m.* god-father of one's child; fellow-sponsor; father of one's god-child; gossip (*in arch. sense*).

кум|а́, ы́, *f.* 1. god-mother of one's child; fellow-sponsor; mother of one's god-child; gossip (*in arch. sense*), cummer (*dial.*). 2. *in folklore, conventional epithet of fox.*

кума́н|ёк, ька́, *m.* (*coll.*) *affect. of* кум; *as form of address* my friend.

кума́ч, а́, *m.* red calico.

куми́р, а, *m.* idol (*also fig.*).

куми́р|ня, ни, *g. pl.* ~ен, *f.* heathen temple.

кум|и́ться, лю́сь, и́шься, *impf.* (*of* по~) (с+*i.*; *coll.*) to become god-parent to someone's child; (*fig.*) to become acquainted (with).

кумовств|о́, а́, *n.* 1. relationship of god-parent to parent, *or* of god-parents. 2. (*fig.*) favouritism, nepotism.

кумуляти́вн|ый, *adj.* cumulative; (*mil.*) к. заря́д hollow charge; снаря́д ~ого де́йствия hollow-charge projectile.

ку́мушк|а, и, *f.* 1. *affect. of* кума́; *as form of address* my good woman. 2. (*coll.*) gossip, scandal-monger.

кумы́с, а, *m.* koumiss (*fermented mare's milk*).

кумысолече́бниц|а, ы, *f.* koumiss-cure institution.

кумысолече́ни|е, я, *n.* koumiss cure, treatment.

куна́к, а́, *m.* friend (*among the mountain-dwellers of the Caucasus*).

кунжу́т, а, *m.* (*bot.*) sesame.

кунжу́т|ный, *adj. of* ~.

ку́н|ий, *adj. of* ~ица.

куни́ц|а, ы, *f.* (*zool.*) marten.

кунстка́мер|а, ы, *f.* cabinet of curiosities.

кунту́ш, а́, *m.* (*hist.*) kuntush (*kind of coat worn by Polish noblemen*).

кунштю́к, а, *m.* (*coll.*) trick, dodge.

ку́п|а, ы, *f.* group, clump (*of trees*).

купа́ла, *see* Ива́н.

купа́льник, а, *m.* bathing costume.

купа́льный, *adj.* bathing, swimming; к. костю́м swimming costume.

купа́л|ьня, ьни, *g. pl.* ~ен, *f.* (enclosed) bathing-place; dressing-shed.

купа́льщик, а, *m.* bather.

купа́|ть, ю, *impf.* (*of* вы́~) to bathe; to bath.

купа́|ться, юсь, *impf.* (*of* вы́~) to bathe; to have, take a bath; (*coll.*) к. в зо́лоте to roll in money.

купе́, *indecl., n.* compartment (*of railway carriage*).

купе́л|ь, и, *f.* (*eccl.*) font.

куп|е́ц, ца́, *m.* merchant.

купе́ческ|ий, *adj.* merchant, mercantile; ~ое сосло́вие the merchant class.

купе́честв|о, а, *n.* (*collect.*) the merchants.

купин|а́, ы́, *f.* (*arch.*) bush; неопали́мая к. (*bibl.*) the burning bush.

куп|и́ть, лю́, ~ишь, *pf.* (*of* покупа́ть) to buy, purchase.

купле́т, а, *m.* **1.** stanza, strophe. **2.** (*pl.*) satirical ballad(s), song(s) (*containing topical allusions*).

куплети́ст, а, *m.* singer of satirical songs, ballads.

ку́пл|я, и, *f.* buying, purchase.

ку́пол, а, *pl.* ~а́, *m.* cupola, dome.

куполообра́з|ный (~ен, ~на), *adj.* dome-shaped.

ку́пол|ьный, *adj. of* ~.

купо́н, а, *m.* **1.** coupon; (*theatr.*) ticket. **2.** suit-length.

купоро́с, а, *m.* (*chem.*) vitriol.

ку́пч|ая, ей, *f.* (*also* к. кре́пость) (*hist., leg.*) deed of purchase.

купчи́х|а, и, *f.* **1.** *f. of* купе́ц. **2.** merchant's wife.

купю́р|а, ы, *f.* **1.** cut (*in lit., mus., etc., work*). **2.** (*fin.*) denomination (*of paper money, bonds, etc.*).

кур, а, *m.* (*arch.*) cock; *now only in phrase* (*coll.*) как к. во́ щи (попа́сть) (to get oneself) into the soup.

ку́р|а, ы, *f.* (*obs.*) = ~ица.

кураг|а́, и́, *f.* (*collect.*) dried apricots.

кура́ж, а́, *m.* (*obs.*) boldness, spirit; вы́пить для ~а to summon up Dutch courage; быть в ~е to be lit up.

кура́ж|иться, усь, ишься, *impf.* (*coll.*) to swagger, boast; (над) to bully.

кура́нт|ы, ов, *no sing.* **1.** chiming clock.; chimes. **2.** (*hist.*) gazette.

кура́тор, а, *m.* (*obs.*) curator.

куре́т, а, *m.* (*sport and fig.*) curvet.

ку́рв|а, ы, *f.* (*vulg.*) whore, tart.

кургáн, а, *m.* barrow, burial mound; tumulus.

кургу́з|ый (~, ~a), *adj.* (*coll.*) **1.** too short and/or tight. **2.** bob-tailed. **3.** short, stumpy.

курд, а, *m.* Kurd.

ку́рдский, *adj.* Kurd.

курдю́к, а́, *m.* fat(ty) tail (*of certain breeds of sheep*).

курдя́нк|а, и, *f.* Kurdish woman.

ку́рев|о, а, *n.* (*coll.*) tobacco, baccy; something to smoke; у меня́ нет ~a I haven't got a smoke.

куре́ни|е, я, *n.* **1.** smoking. **2.** incense.

кур|ёнок, ёнка, *pl.* ~я́та, ~я́т, *m.* (*dial.*) chicken.

куре́н|ь, я́, *m.* **1.** (*dial.*) hut, shanty. **2.** (*hist.*) kuren (*unit of Zaporozhian Cossack troop*).

курза́л, а, *m.* kursaal.

куриа́льный, *adj.* (*leg., eccl.*) curial.

кури́лк|а¹, и, *f.* (*coll.*) smoking-room.

кури́лка², *only in phrase* жив к.! there's life in the old dog yet.

кури́льниц|а, ы, *f.* (*obs.*) censer; incense-burner.

кури́л|ьня, ьни, *g. pl.* ~ен, *f.* к. о́пиума opium-den.

кури́льщик, а, *m.* smoker.

кури́н|ые, ых (*orn.*) Gallinaceae.

кури́н|ый, *adj.* hen's; chicken's; ~ая грудь pigeon-chest; ~ая слепота́ (*med.*) night-blindness; (*bot.*) buttercup.

кури́тельн|ый, *adj.* smoking; ~ая бума́га cigarette paper; ~ая (ко́мната) smoking-room.

кур|и́ть, ю́, ~ишь, *impf.* (*of* по~) **1.** to smoke; к. тру́бку to smoke a pipe. **2.** (+*a.* *or i.*) to burn; to fumigate (with); к. ла́даном to burn incense; к. фимиа́м кому́-н. (*fig.*) to burn incense to someone. **3.** to distil.

кур|и́ться, ~ится, *impf.* **1.** to smoke (*intrans.*). **2.** (+*i.*) to emit (smoke, steam). **3.** *pass. of* ~и́ть.

ку́р|ица, ицы, *pl.* ~ы, ~, *f.* hen; (*fig., coll.*) мо́края к. milksop, wet hen; ~ам на́ смех it would make a cat laugh; де́нег у него́ ~ы не клюю́т he is rolling in money.

куркý́м|а, ы, *f.* curry.

курн|о́й, *adj.* ~а́я изба́ hut having stove but without chimney.

курно́с|ый (~, ~a) (*coll.*) snub-nosed.

курово́дств|о, а, *n.* poultry-breeding.

кур|о́к, ка́, *m.* cocking-piece; взвести́ к. to cock; спусти́ть к. to pull the trigger.

куроле́|сить, шу, сишь, *impf.* (*of* на~) (*coll.*) to play tricks, get up to mischief.

куропа́тк|а, и, *f.* (*orn.*) (се́рая) partridge; бе́лая к. willow grouse; тундряна́я к. ptarmigan.

куро́рт, а, *m.* health resort.

куро́ртник, а, *m.* health resort visitor.

куро́рт|ный, *adj. of* ~; ~ное лече́ние spa treatment.

куросле́п, а, *m.* (*bot.*) buttercup.

ку́рочк|а, и, *f.* 1. pullet. 2. moor-hen.

курс, а, *m.* 1. (*in var. senses*) course; но́вый к. (*polit.*) new policy; быть на тре́тьем ~е to be in the third year (*of course of studies*); держа́ть к. (на+*a.*) to head (for); быть в ~е де́ла to be au courant, be in the know. 2. (*fin.*) rate (of exchange).

курса́нт, а, *m.* 1. member of a course. 2. student (*of mil. school or academy*).

курси́в, а, *m.* italic type, italics; ~ом in italics.

курси́вный, *adj.* (*typ.*) italic.

курси́р|овать, ую, *impf.* (ме́жду) to ply, run (between).

курси́стк|а, и, *f.* (*obs.*) girl-student.

курсо́вк|а, и, *f.* board and treatment authorization (*at health resort*).

курта́ж, а, *m.* (*comm.*) brokerage.

куртиза́нк|а, и, *f.* courtesan.

курти́н|а, ы, *f.* 1. (*mil.*; *obs.*) curtain. 2. flower-bed.

ку́ртк|а, и, *f.* (*man's*) jacket.

курфю́рст, а, *m.* (*hist.*) elector.

курча́в|иться, ится, *impf.* to curl.

курча́в|ый (~, ~а), *adj.* (*coll.*) curly; curly-headed.

курч|о́нок, о́нка, *pl.* ~а́та, ~а́т, *m.* (*coll.*) chicken.

ку́р|ы[1], *see* ~ица.

ку́р|ы[2], *only in phrase* стро́ить к. (+*d.*) (*joc.*) to flirt (with), pay court (to).

курьёз, а, *m.* curious, amusing incident; для, ра́ди ~а for fun.

курьёз|ный (~ен, ~на), *adj.* curious, funny.

курье́р, а, *m.* messenger; courier.

курье́р|ский, *adj.* 1. *adj. of* ~. 2. fast; к. по́езд express; на ~ских (*coll.*) post-haste.

кур|я́та, *see* ~ёнок.

куря́тин|а, ы, *f.* chicken, fowl (*as meat*).

куря́тник, а, *m.* hen-house, hen-coop.

кус, а, *pl.* ~ы́, *m.* (*coll.*) morsel.

куса́|ть, ю, *impf.* to bite; to sting; к. себе́ ло́кти (*fig.*) to be whipping the cat.

куса́|ться, юсь, *impf.* 1. to bite (= *to be given to biting*). 2. to bite one another. 3. (*coll.*) to be exorbitant; э́то — хоро́шая вещь, но ~ется it's good, but they sting you for it.

куса́ч|ки, ек, *no sing.* pliers; wire-cutters.

кусково́й, *adj.* broken in lumps; к. са́хар lump sugar.

кус|о́к, ка́, *m.* lump; piece, bit; slice; cake (*of soap*); зарабо́тать к. хле́ба to earn one's bread and butter.

куст[1], а́, *m.* bush, shrub; спря́таться в ~ы́ (*fig.*) to rat, make oneself scarce.

куст[2], а́, *m.* (*econ.*) group.

куста́рник, а, *m.* (*collect.*) bush(es), shrub(s); shrubbery.

куста́рник|овый, *adj. of* ~; ~овое расте́ние shrub.

куста́рнича|ть, ю, *impf.* 1. to be a handicraftsman; to exercise a craft at home. 2. (*coll.*, *pejor.*) to use primitive methods; to work in an amateurish manner.

куста́рничеств|о, а, *n.* (*pejor.*) work done by primitive methods; amateurish, inefficient work.

куста́рн|ый, *adj.* 1. handicraft; ~ые изде́лия hand-made goods; ~ая промы́шленность cottage industry. 2. (*fig.*, *pejor.*) amateurish, primitive.

куста́рщин|а, ы, *f.* = куста́рничество.

куста́р|ь, я́, *m.* handicraftsman.

кусти́ст|ый (~, ~а), *adj.* bushy.

куст|и́ться, и́тся, *impf.* to put out side-shoots.

кустова́ни|е, я, *n.* (*electr.*) interconnexion.

кустов|о́й, *adj. of* куст[2]; ~о́е совеща́ние group conference.

ку́та|ть, ю, *impf.* (*of* за~) (в+*a.*) to muffle up (in).

ку́та|ться, юсь, *impf.* (*of* за~) (в+*a.*) to muffle oneself up (in).

куте́ж, а́, *m.* drinking-bout; riot, binge.

кутерьм|а́, ы́, *f.* (*coll.*) commotion, stir, bustle, hubbub.

кути́л|а, ы, *m.* fast liver; hard drinker.

ку|ти́ть, чу́, ~тишь, *impf.* (*of* ~тну́ть) to booze; to go on the booze.

кут|ну́ть, ну́, нёшь, *inst. pf.* (*of* ~и́ть) to go on the booze, go on a binge.

куту́зк|а, и, *f.* (*coll.*) jail, lock-up.

куха́рк|а, и, *f.* cook.

кухми́стерск|ая, ой, *f.* (*obs.*) eating-house, cook-shop.

ку́х|ня, ни, *g. pl.* ~онь, *f.* 1. kitchen; cook-house. 2. cooking, cuisine. 3. (*fig.*, *coll.*; *sing. only*) intrigues, machinations.

ку́хонн|ый, *adj.* kitchen; ~ая плита́ kitchen-range; к. шкаф dresser; (*joc.*) ~ая латы́нь low Latin.

ку́ц|ый (~, ~а), *adj.* 1. tailless; bob-tailed. 2. (*of clothing*) short; (*fig.*) limited, abbreviated.

ку́ч|а, и, *f.* 1. heap, pile; (*coll.*) вали́ть всё в одну́ ~у to lump everything together. 2. (*coll.*; +*g.*) heaps (of), piles (of); у него́ к. де́нег he has heaps of money; ку́ча мала́ sacks on the mill (*children's game*).

кучево́й, *adj.* (*meteor.*) cumulus.

ку́чер, а, *pl.* ~а́, ~о́в, *m.* coachman, driver.

кучерско́й, *adj.* coachman's.

кучеря́в|ый (~, ~а), *adj.* (*dial.*) curly; curly-haired.

ку́ч|ка, ки, *f,* *dim. of* ~а; к. люде́й small group of people.

ку́чный, *adj.* (*of shots*) closely-grouped.

ку|чу́, ~тишь, *see* ~ти́ть.

куш¹, а, *m.* (*coll.*) large sum (*of money*).

куш², *interj.* (*coll.*; *to a dog*) lie down!

кушáк, á, *m.* sash, girdle.

ку́шань|е, я, *n.* food; dish.

ку́ша|ть, ю, *impf.* (*of* по~ *and* с~) (*in polite invitation to eat*) to eat, have, take.

кушéтк|а, и, *f.* couch.

ку́щ|а, и, *g. pl.* ~ *and* ~ей, *f.* **1.** (*obs., poet.*) tent, hut; пра́здник ~ей (Jewish) Feast of Tabernacles. **2.** foliage; crest (*of tree*).

ку|ю́, ёшь, *see* кова́ть.

кэб, а, *m.* cab.

кювéт, а, *m.* **1.** (*mil.*) cuvette, cunette. **2.** ditch (*at side of road*).

кювéтк|а, и, *f.* (*phot.*) cuvette, bath.

кюрасó, *indecl., n.* curaçao (*liqueur*).

кюрé, *indecl., m.* (*eccl.*) curé.

Л

лабáз, а, *m.* (*obs.*) corn-chandler's shop, ware-house; grain merchant's shop, ware-house.

лабáзник, а, *m.* (*obs.*) corn-chandler, grain merchant.

лабиализáци|я, и, *f.* (*ling.*) labialization.

лабиализ|овáть, у́ю, *impf. and pf.* (*ling.*) to labialize.

лабиáльный, *adj.* (*ling.*) labial.

лабио-дентáльный, *adj.* (*ling.*) labio-dental.

лабири́нт, а, *m.* (*in var. senses*) labyrinth, maze.

лаборáнт, а, *m.* laboratory assistant.

лаборатóри|я, и, *f.* laboratory.

лаборатóр|ный, *adj. of* ~ия.

лабрадóр, а, *m.* (*min.*) labradorite.

лáв|а¹, ы, *f.* lava.

лáв|а², ы, *f.* (*mining*) drift.

лáв|а³, ы, *f.* (Cossack) cavalry charge.

лавáнд|а, ы, *f.* (*bot.*) lavender.

лави́н|а, ы, *f.* avalanche (*also fig.*).

лави́р|овать, ую, *impf.* **1.** (*naut.*) to tack; л. про́тив вéтра to beat up against the wind. **2.** (*fig.*) to manœuvre, avoid taking sides.

лáвк|а¹, и, *f.* bench.

лáвк|а², и, *f.* shop; store.

лáвочк|а¹, и, *f.* *dim. of* лáвка¹.

лáвочк|а², и, *f.* *dim. of* лáвка²; (*fig., coll.*) shady concern; gang; нáдо закры́ть э́ту лáвочку a stop must be put to this business.

лáвочник, а, *m.* shop-keeper, retailer.

лавр, а, *m.* **1.** (*bot.*) laurel; bay(-tree). **2.** (*pl.; fig.*) laurels; пожинáть ~ы to win laurels; почи́ть на ~ах to rest on one's laurels.

лáвр|а, ы, *f.* monastery (*of highest rank*).

лаврови́шн|евый, *adj. of* ~я; ~евые кáпли laurel water.

лаврови́шн|я, и, *f.* (*bot.*) cherry-laurel.

лáвр|овый, *adj. of* ~; ~óвый венóк laurel wreath, (*fig.*) laurels; ~óвый лист bay leaf; ~óвая рóща laurel grove; *as noun* ~óвые, ~óвых (*bot.*) Lauraceae.

лáвр|ский, *adj. of* ~а.

лавсáн, а, *m.* lavsan (*synthetic fibre similar to terylene*).

лаг, а, *m.* (*naut.*) **1.** log. **2.** broadside; пали́ть всем ~ом to fire a broadside.

лáгерник, а, *m.* (*coll.*) inmate of camp.

лáгер|ный, *adj. of* ~ь; ~ная жизнь nomad existence; л. сбор (*mil.*) annual camp; ~ная тéма (*lit.*) 'the (concentration) camp theme' (*as genre of anti-Stalinist Soviet writing*).

лáгер|ь, я, *m.* **1.** (*pl.* ~я́, ~éй) camp; жить в ~я́х to camp out; (*mil.*) располагáться, стоя́ть ~ем to camp, be encamped; снять л. to break up, strike camp. **2.** (*pl.* ~и, ~ей) (*fig.*) camp; дéйствовать на два ~я to have a foot in both camps.

лагли́н|ь, я, *m.* (*naut.*) log-line.

лагу́н|а, ы, *f.* lagoon.

лад, а, о ~е, в ~у́, *pl.* ~ы́, ~óв, *m.* **1.** (*mus. and fig.*) harmony, concord; петь в л., не в л. to sing in, out of tune; запéть на другóй л. (*fig.*) to sing a different tune; жить в ~у́ (с+*i.*) to live in harmony (with); быть не в ~áх (с+*i.*) to be at odds (with), at variance (with); (*coll.*) идти́, пойти́ на л. to go well, be successful; дéло не идёт на л. things are not going well. **2.** manner, way; на рáзные ~ы́ in various ways; на свой л. in one's own way, after one's own fashion; на стáрый л. in the old style. **3.** (*mus.*) stop; fret (*of stringed instrument*).

лáд|а, ы, *m. and f.* (*folk poet.*) beloved.

лáдан, а, *m.* incense, frankincense; л. рóсный (*pharm.*) benzoin; дышáть на л. (*fig., coll.*) to have one foot in the grave.

лáданк|а, и, *f.* amulet.

лá|дить, жу, дишь, *impf.* **1.** (с+*i.*) to get on (with), be on good terms (with); они́ не ~дят they don't get on. **2.** (*coll.*) to prepare, make ready; to tune (*mus. instrument*). **3.** (*coll.*) л. однó и то же to harp on the same string.

лáд|иться, ится, *impf.* (*coll.*) to go well, succeed.

лáдно, *adv.* (*coll.*) **1.** harmoniously. **2.** well;

all right; всё ко́нчилось л. everything ended happily. **3.** *particle* л.! all right!, very well!

ла́д|ный (~ен, ~на́, ~но), *adj.* (*coll.*) **1.** fine, excellent. **2.** harmonious.

ладо́нный, *adj.* (*anat.*) palmar.

ладо́н|ь, и, f. palm (*of hand*); быть (ви́дным) как на ~и to be clearly visible.

ладо́ши, *only in phrases* бить, ударя́ть, хло́пать в л. to clap one's hands.

лад|ья́, ьи́, g. pl. ~е́й, f. **1.** (*poet.*) boat. **2.** (*chess*) castle, rook.

лаж, а, m. (*comm.*) agio.

ла́|жу¹, дишь, *see* ~дить.

ла́|жу², зишь, *see* ~зить.

лаз, а, m. **1.** (*tech.*) manhole. **2.** (*hunting*) track; стать на л. (+*g.*) to get on the track (of).

лазаре́т, а, m. **1.** (*mil.*) field hospital; sick quarters; (*naut.*) sick-bay. **2.** (*obs.*) infirmary.

лазе́йк|а, и, f. hole, gap; (*fig., coll.*) loophole; оста́вить себе́ ~у to leave oneself a loophole.

ла́зер, а, m. (*phys., tech.*) laser.

ла́|зить, жу, зишь, *impf.* (*indet. of* ле́зть) **1.** (на+*a.*, по+*d.*) to climb, clamber (on to, up); л. на сте́ну to climb a wall; л. по дере́вьям to climb trees; л. по кана́ту to swarm up a rope. **2.** (в+*a.*) to climb (into), get (into); л. в окно́ to get in through the window.

лазо́ревк|а, и, f. (*orn.*) blue tit.

лазо́ревый, *adj.* (*poet.*) sky-blue, azure; л. ка́мень (*min.*) lapis lazuli.

лазу́ревый, *adj.* = лазо́ревый, лазу́рный.

лазу́р|ный (~ен, ~на), *adj.* sky-blue, azure.

лазу́р|ь, и, f. azure; берли́нская л. Prussian blue.

лазу́тчик, а, m. (*mil., obs.*) spy, scout.

ла|й, я, m. bark(ing).

ла́йб|а, ы, f. (*one- or two-masted*) sailing boat (*used formerly in Baltic Sea and on rivers Dnieper and Dniester*).

ла́йк|а¹, и, f. Eskimo dog.

ла́йк|а², и, f. kid-skin.

ла́йк|овый, *adj. of* ~а²; ~овые перча́тки kid gloves.

ла́йнер, а, m. (*naut., aeron.*) liner.

лак, а, m. varnish, lacquer; япо́нский л. black japan.

лака́|ть, ю, *impf.* (*of* вы́~) to lap (up).

лаке́|й, я, m. footman, man-servant; lackey, flunkey (*also fig., pejor.*).

лаке́й|ский, *adj. of* ~; (*fig.*) servile.

лаке́йств|о, а, n. servility; dancing attendance.

лаке́йств|овать, ую, *impf.* (пе́ред) to dance attendance (on), kow-tow (to).

лакиро́в|анный, p.p.p. of ~а́ть **and** *adj.* var-

nished, lacquered; ~анная ко́жа patent leather; ~анные ту́фли patent-leather shoes.

лакир|ова́ть, у́ю, *impf.* (*of* от~) to varnish, lacquer; (*fig., pejor.*) to varnish.

лакиро́вк|а, и, f. **1.** varnishing, lacquering (*also fig., pejor.*). **2.** varnish. **3.** (*fig.*) gloss, polish.

лакиро́вщик, а, m. varnisher (*also fig., pejor.*).

ла́кмус, а, m. (*chem.*) litmus.

ла́кмус|овый, *adj. of* ~; ~овая бума́га litmus paper.

ла́ков|ый, *adj.* varnished, lacquered; ~ые ту́фли patent-leather shoes; (*bot.*) ~ое де́рево varnish-tree.

ла́ком|ить, лю, ишь, *impf.* (*of* по~) (*coll.*) to regale (with), treat (to).

ла́ком|иться, люсь, ишься, *impf.* (*of* по~) (+*i.*) to treat oneself (to).

лакомк|а, и, m. and f. gourmand; быть ~ой to have a sweet tooth.

ла́комств|о, а, n. dainty, delicacy.

ла́ком|ый (~, ~а), *adj.* **1.** dainty, tasty; л. кусо́к titbit, tasty morsel (*also fig.*). **2.** (*coll.*) (до) fond (of), partial (to).

лакони́зм, а, m. laconic brevity.

лакони́ческий, *adj.* laconic.

лакони́ч|ный (~ен, ~на), *adj.* = ~еский.

лакрима́тор, а, m. tear gas.

лакри́ц|а, ы, f. (*bot.*) liquorice.

лакта́ци|я, и, f. lactation.

лактобацилли́н, а, m. yoghurt.

лакто́з|а, ы, f. (*chem.*) lactose.

ла́м|а¹, ы, f. (*zool.*) llama.

ла́м|а², ы, m. (*rel.*) lama.

лама́изм, а, m. (*rel.*) lamaism.

ламбреке́н, а, m. pelmet.

ла́мп|а, ы, f. **1.** lamp; предохрани́тельная л. safety-lamp; рудни́чная л. Davy lamp; л. дневно́го све́та fluorescent lamp. **2.** (*radio*) valve; tube; односе́точная л. one-grid valve; двухсе́точная л. space charge tetrode; смеси́тельная л. frequency changer valve.

лампа́д|а, ы, f. icon-lamp.

лампа́дн|ый, *adj.* ~ое ма́сло lamp-oil.

лампа́с, а, m. stripe (*on side of trousers*).

ла́мп|овый, *adj. of* ~а; ~овое стекло́ lamp-chimney; (*tech.*) л. выпрями́тель tube rectifier; л. генера́тор valve oscillator, vacuum tube generator.

ла́мпочк|а, и, f. **1.** *dim. of* ла́мпа. **2.** (electric light) bulb; (*tech.*) л. нака́ливания incandescent lamp. **3.** до ~и (*sl.*) to hell (with it).

лангу́ст, а, m. (*also* лангу́ст|а, ~ы, f.) spiny lobster; rock lobster.

ландо́, indecl., n. landau.

ландскне́хт, а, m. **1.** (*hist.*) lansquenet, landsknecht. **2.** (*card game*) lansquenet.

ландша́фт, a, m. landscape.

ла́ндыш, a, m. lily of the valley.

лани́т|а, ы, f. (arch.) cheek.

ланоли́н, a, m. (pharm.) lanolin.

ланце́т, a, m. (med.) lancet; вскрыть ∼ом to lance.

ланце́т|ный, adj. 1. adj. of ∼. 2. (bot.) lanceolate.

ланцетови́д|ный (∼ен, ∼на), adj. (bot.) lanceolate.

лан|ь, и, f. fallow deer; doe (of fallow deer).

ла́п|а, ы, f. 1. paw; pad (joc. of human hand); (fig., coll.) попа́сть в ∼ы к кому́-н. to fall into someone's clutches; в ∼ах у кого́-н. in someone's clutches. 2. (tech.) tenon, dovetail. 3. (naut.) fluke (of anchor). 4. (fig.) bough (of coniferous tree).

лапида́р|ный (∼ен, ∼на), adj. lapidary, terse.

ла́п|ка, ки, f. dim. of ∼a; (fig., coll.) стоя́ть, ходи́ть на за́дних ∼ках (перед) to dance attendance (upon).

лапла́нд|ец, ца, m. Lapp, Laplander.

лапла́нд|ка, ки, f. of ∼ец.

лапла́ндский, adj. Lappish.

ла́потник, a, m. 1. bast-shoe maker. 2. (obs., coll.) peasant.

ла́пот|ный, adj. of ∼ь; ∼ная Росси́я (rhet.) the old (as opp. to post-1917) Russia.

ла́п|оть, тя, pl. ∼ти, ∼те́й, m. bast shoe, bast sandal; ходи́ть в ∼тя́х to wear bast shoes, sandals.

лапсерда́к, a, m. lapserdak (long overcoat worn by Jews).

лапт|а́, ы́, f. 1. (Russian ball game) lapta. 2. lapta bat.

ла́пчатый, adj. 1. (bot.) palmate. 2. web-footed; гусь л. (fig., coll.) cunning fellow, sly one.

лапш|а́, и́, f. 1. noodles. 2. noodle soup.

лар|ёк, ька́, m. stall.

лар|е́ц, ца́, m. casket, small chest.

ларёчник, a, m. (coll.) stall-holder.

ларинги́т, a, m. laryngitis.

ларингоско́п, a, m. laryngoscope.

ларинготоми́|я, и, f. laryngotomy.

ла́рчик, a, m. small box; (coll.) а л. про́сто открыва́лся the explanation was quite simple.

ла́р|ы, ов, sing. ∼, ∼a, m. л. и пена́ты lares and penates.

лар|ь, я́, m. 1. chest, coffer; bin; л. с муко́й bin containing flour. 2. stall.

ла́ск|а¹, и, f. 1. caress, endearment. 2. kindness.

ла́с|ка², ки, g. pl. ∼ок, f. (zool.) weasel.

ласка́тельн|ый, adj. 1. caressing; ∼ое и́мя pet name. 2. (obs.) cajoling, unctuous. 3. (gram.) affectionate, expressing endearment.

ласка́|ть, ю, impf. 1. to caress, fondle, pet. 2. (obs.) to comfort, console.

ласка́|ться, юсь, impf. 1. (к) to make up to; to snuggle up to; to coax; (of a dog) to fawn (upon). 2. (coll.) to exchange caresses.

ла́сковый, adj. affectionate, tender; (fig.) gentle; л. ве́тер soft wind.

лассо́, indecl., n. lasso.

ласт, a, m. flipper.

ла́стик¹, a, m. (material) lasting.

ла́стик², a, m. (coll.) india-rubber.

ла́|ститься, щусь, сти́шься, impf. (к, о́коло) (coll.) to make up (to), fawn (upon).

ла́стовиц|а, ы, f. gusset (in shirt).

ластоно́г|ое, ого, n. (zool.) Pinniped.

ла́сточк|а, и, f. swallow; берегова́я л. sand-martin; городска́я л. (house) martin; прыжо́к в во́ду ∼ой swallow-dive; пе́рвая л. (fig.) the first signs; одна́ л. весны́ не де́лает (prov.) one swallow does not make a summer.

ла́т|анный, p.p.p. of ∼а́ть and adj. worn, patched.

лататы́, only in coll. phrase зада́ть л. to take to one's heels.

лата́|ть, ю, impf. (of за∼) (coll.) to patch.

латви́|ец, йца, m. Latvian.

латви́|йка, йки, f. of ∼ец.

латви́йский, adj. Latvian.

латиниза́ци|я, и, f. latinization.

латинизи́р|овать, ую, impf. and pf. to latinize.

латини́зм, a, m. 1. Latin construction (borrowed by another language). 2. Latin loan-word.

латини́ст, a, m. Latin scholar.

лати́ниц|а, ы, f. Roman alphabet, Roman letters.

лати́нский, adj. Latin.

лати́нств|о, a, n. (obs.) 1. the Roman Catholic faith. 2. (collect.) Roman Catholics.

лати́нщин|а, ы, f. Latin culture; Latinity.

лати́нян|ин, ина, pl. ∼е, ∼, m. 1. (hist.) inhabitant of Latium. 2. (obs.) Roman Catholic.

латифу́нди|и, й, sing. ∼я, ∼и, f. latifundia.

латифунди́ст, a, m. 1. 'latifundista' (large land-owner in South America). 2. pejor. = feudal-type, exploiting land-owner.

ла́тк|а, и, f. (coll.) patch.

ла́тник, a, m. armour-clad warrior.

лату́к, a, m. (bot.) lettuce.

лату́нный, adj. brass.

лату́н|ь, и, f. brass.

ла́т|ы, ∼, no sing. (hist.) armour.

латы́н|ь, и, f. (coll.) Latin.

латы́ш, á, pl. ∼и́, ∼е́й, m. Lett.

латы́ш|ка, ки, f. of ∼.

латы́шский, adj. Lettish, Latvian.

лауреа́т, a, m. prize-winner.

лафа́, *as pred.*; *impers.* (*coll.*) тебе́, ему́, *etc.* л. you are, he is, *etc.*, in clover, having a wonderful time.

лафе́т, а, *m.* (*mil.*) gun-carriage.

ла́цкан, а, *pl.* ~ы, ~ов, *m.* lapel.

лачу́г|а, и, *f.* hovel, shack.

ла́|ять, ю, ешь, *impf.* to bark; to bay.

ла́|яться, юсь, ешься, *impf.* (*coll.*) (на+*a.*) to rail, snarl (at).

лба, лбу, *etc.*, *see* лоб.

лгать, лгу, лжёшь, лгут, *past* лгал, лгала́, лга́ло, *impf.* 1. (*pf.* со~) to lie; to tell lies. 2. (*pf.* на~) (на+*a.*) to slander.

лгун, а́, *m.* liar.

лгуни́шк|а, и, *m.* (*coll.*) paltry liar.

лебед|а́, ы́, *f.* (*bot.*) goose-foot, orach.

лебед|ёнок, ёнка, *pl.* ~я́та, ~я́т, *m.* cygnet.

лебеди́н|ый, *adj.* of ле́бедь; ~ая по́ступь graceful gait; (*fig.*) ~ая пе́сня swan-song; ~ая ше́я swan-neck; (*tech.*) S-bend pipe.

лебёдк|а[1], и, *f.* (female) swan, pen(-swan.)

лебёдк|а[2], и, *f.* (*tech.*) winch, windlass.

ле́бед|ь, я, *pl.* ~и, ~е́й, *m.* swan, cob(-swan).

лебе|зи́ть, жу́, зи́шь, *impf.* (*coll.*) (пе́ред) to fawn (upon), cringe (to).

леб|я́жий, *adj.* of ~едь; л. пух swan's down.

лев[1], льва, *m.* lion; морско́й л. sea-lion; муравьи́ный л. ant-lion.

лев[2], а, *m.* (*Bulgarian monetary unit*) lev.

лева́д|а, ы, *f.* (*dial.*) 1. meadow. 2. riparian woodlands (*flooded at season of thaw; in S. Russia*).

лева́к, а́, *m.* 1. (*polit.*) leftist. 2. (*coll.*) moonlighter; black marketeer.

лева́цкий, *adj.* (*polit.*; *pejor.*) ultra-left.

лева́честв|о, а, *n.* 1. (*polit.*) leftism. 2. (*coll.*) moonlighting; black marketeering.

леве́|ть, ю, *impf.* (*of* по~) (*polit.*) to become more left, move to the left.

левиафа́н, а, *m.* leviathan.

левизн|а́, ы́, *f.* (*polit.*) leftishness.

левко́|й, я, *m.* (*bot.*) stock, gilly-flower.

ле́во, *adv.* (*naut.*) to port; л. руля́! port helm!; л. на борт! hard-a-port!

левобере́жный, *adj.* left-bank.

левре́тк|а, и, *f.* Italian greyhound.

левш|а́, и́, *i.* ~о́й, *g. pl.* ~е́й, *m. and f.* left-hander.

ле́в|ый, *adj.* 1. left; left-hand; (*naut.*) port; л. борт port side, port hand; ~ая сторона́ left-hand side, (*of horse, carriage, etc.*) near side; (*of material*) wrong side; (*fig.*) встать с ~ой ноги to get out of bed on the wrong side. 2. (*pl.*) left-wing; *as noun* л., ~ого, *m.* left-winger; (*pl.*; *collect.*) the left.

лега́в|ая, ой, *f.* (*длинношёрстая*) setter; (*короткошёрстая*) pointer.

лега́в|ый, ого, *m.* (*coll.*) police spy, informer.

легализа́ци|я, и, *f.* legalization.

легализ|и́ровать(ся), и́рую(сь), = ~ова́ть(ся).

легализ|ова́ть, у́ю, *impf. and pf.* to legalize.

легализ|ова́ться, у́юсь, *impf. and pf.* to become legalized.

лега́л|ьный (~ен, ~ьна), *adj.* legal.

лега́т, а, *m.* legate.

лега́то, *mus.* 1. *adv.* legato. 2. *indecl. noun* slur.

леге́нд|а, ы, *f.* legend.

легенда́р|ный (~ен, ~на), *adj.* legendary (*also fig.*).

легио́н, а, *m.* (*in var. senses*) legion; иностра́нный л. the Foreign Legion; о́рден почётного ~а Legion of Honour; и́мя им л. their name is legion.

легионе́р, а, *m.* legionary.

леги́рова|нный, *p.p.p.* of ~ть and adj. alloy(ed).

леги́р|овать, ую, *impf.* to alloy.

легислату́р|а, ы, *f.* term of office.

лёг|кий (~ок, ~ка́, ~ко́, *pl.* ~ки́ *or* ~ки́), *adj.* 1. light (*in weight*). 2. easy; л. слог simple style; у него́ л. хара́ктер he is easy to get on with; ~ко́ сказа́ть! easier said than done! 3. (*in var. senses*) light; slight; ~кая атле́тика (*sport*) field and track athletics; ~кая простуда slight cold; л. слу́чай (*заболева́ния*) mild case; ~кие фигу́ры (*chess*) minor pieces; ~кое чте́ние light reading(-matter); (*coll.*) ~ок на поми́не, вы ~ки́ на поми́не! talk of the devil!; (*coll.*) у него́ ~кая рука́ he is lucky, he has luck; с ва́шей ~ой руки́ once you start(ed) the ball rolling; же́нщина лёгкого поведе́ния woman of easy virtue.

легко́, *adv.* easily, lightly, slightly; э́то ему́ л. даётся it comes easily to him; л. косну́ться to touch lightly.

легкоатле́т, а, *m.* (field and track) athlete.

легкове́ри|е, я, *n.* credulity, gullibility.

легкове́р|ный (~ен, ~на), *adj.* credulous, gullible.

легкове́с, а, *m.* (*sport*) light-weight.

легкове́с|ный (~ен, ~на), *adj.* 1. light-weight; light. 2. (*fig.*, *pejor.*) superficial.

легководола́з, а, *m.* frogman.

легково́й, *adj.* passenger (*conveyance*); л. автомоби́ль (motor) car; л. изво́зчик cab, cabman.

лёгк|ое, ого, *n.* 1. (*anat.*) lung; воспале́ние одного́ ~ого, обо́их ~их single, double pneumonia. 2. (*sing. only*) (*cul.*) lights.

легкомы́слен|ный (~, ~на), *adj.* light(-minded), thoughtless; flippant, frivolous, superficial; л. посту́пок thoughtless action.

легкомы́сли|е, я, *n.* light-mindedness, thoughtlessness; flippancy, levity.

легкопла́в|кий (~ок, ~ка), *adj.* fusible, easily melted.

лёгкост|ь, и, *f.* 1. lightness. 2. easiness.

легóнько, *adv.* (*coll.*) **1.** slightly. **2.** gently.

лёгочный, *adj.* (*med.*) pulmonary.

легчá|ть, ет, *impf.* (*of* по~) **1.** to lessen, abate. **2.** (*impers.* +*d.*); to get better; to feel better.

лёг|че, *comp. of* ~кий *and* ~кó; больнóму л. the invalid is feeling better; мне от э́того не л. I am none the better for it; (*coll.*) час óт часу не л. worse and worse; л. на поворóтах! mind what you say!

лёд, льда, о льдé, на льдý, *m.* ice; л. разбит, л. слóман (*fig.*) the ice is broken.

ледáщий, *adj.* (*coll.*) puny; feeble.

леденé|ть, ю, *impf.* (*of* за~ *and* о~) (*intrans.*) **1.** to freeze. **2.** to become numb with cold; (*fig.*) кровь ~ет (one's) blood runs cold.

леден|éц, цá, *m.* fruit-drop.

ледени́ст|ый (~, ~а), *adj.* frozen; icy.

леден|и́ть, и́т, *impf.* (*of* о~) (*trans.*) to freeze; (*fig.*) to chill.

леден|я́щий, *pres. part. of* ~и́ть *and adj.* chilling, icy.

лéди, *indecl.*, *f.* lady.

лéдник, а, *m.* **1.** ice-house. **2.** ice-box; вагóн-л. refrigerator van.

ледни́к, á, *m.* glacier.

леднико́вый, *adj.* glacial; л. перио́д ice age.

ледови́тый, *adj.* Сéверный Л. океáн the Arctic Ocean.

ледóв|ый, *adj.* ice; ~ые плáвания Arctic voyages; ~ое побóище the Battle on the Ice (*fought on 5 April 1242 between the army of Alexander Nevsky and the Teutonic Knights*).

ледокóл, а, *m.* ice-breaker.

ледокóл|ьный, *adj. of* ~.

ледорéз, а, *m.* **1.** (*naut.*) ice-cutter. **2.** (*tech.*) starling.

ледорýб, а, *m.* ice-axe.

ледостáв, а, *m.* freezing-over (*of river*).

ледохóд, а, *m.* drifting of ice, floating of ice (*at time of freeze-up and thaw*).

ледышк|а, и, *f.* (*coll.*) **1.** piece of ice. **2.** (*fig.*, *joc.*) iceberg.

лед|яной, *adj.* **1.** *adj. of* ~; ~янáя горá ice slope (*for tobogganing*); iceberg. **2.** icy (*also fig.*); ice-cold. **3.** ~яно́е стеклó frosted glass.

лéер, а, *m.* (*naut.*) taut rope, yard.

лёжа, *adv.* lying down, in lying position.

лежáк, á, *m.* chaise-longue, deck chair.

лежáлый, *adj.* stale, old.

лежáнк|а, и, *f.* stove-bench (*a shelf on which it is possible to sleep, running along the side of a Russian stove*).

леж|áть, ý, и́шь, *impf.* (*in var. senses*) to lie; to be (situated); л. в больни́це to be in hospital; л. больны́м to be laid up; врач велéл мне л. the doctor told me to stay in bed; л. на боку́, на печи́ (*fig.*, *coll.*) to idle away one's time; л. у когó-н. на душé to be on one's mind; э́то ~и́т у меня́ на сóвести it

lies heavy on my conscience; э́то ~и́т на вáшей отвéтственности this is your responsibility; у меня́ душá не ~и́т (к) I have a distaste (for), an aversion (to, from, for).

леж|áться, и́тся, *impf.* (+*d.*) ему́ не ~áлось в постéли he would, could not stay in bed.

лежáч|ий, *adj.* lying, recumbent; л. больнóй bed-patient; ~его не бьют never hit a man when he is down.

лéжбищ|е, а, *n.* breeding-ground (*of certain aquatic mammals*); л. тюлéней seal-rookery.

лежебóк|а, и, *m. and f.* (*coll.*) lazy-bones, lie-abed.

лéж|ень, ня, *m.* (*tech.*) **1.** ledger; foundation beam; mud sill. **2.** (*railways*) sleeper.

лёжк|а, и, *f.* **1.** (*coll.*) lying. **2.** (*coll.*) lying position; лежáть в ~y to be on one's back (*of sick person*); напи́ться в ~y to become dead drunk. **3.** lair (*of wild animal*).

лежмя́, *adv.* (*coll.*) лежáть л. to lie without getting up; to lie helpless.

лéзви|е, я, *n.* **1.** edge (*of cutting instrument*). **2.** safety-razor blade.

лезги́нк|а, и, *f.* lezghinka (*Caucasian dance*).

лез|ть, у, ешь, *past* ~, ~ла, *impf.* (*of* по~) **1.** (на+*a.*, по+*d.*) to climb (up, on to). **2.** (в+*a.*, под+*a.*) to clamber, crawl (through, into, under). **3.** to make one's way stealthily; кудá ~ешь? (*coll.*) where do you think you're going? **4.** (в+*a.*) to thrust the hand (into). **5.** (в+*a.*) to fit (into). **6.** to stick out (*intrans.*). **7.** to slip out of position. **8.** to come on (*in spite of obstacles*). **9.** (в+*a.*) to try to climb (*into a higher station in life*). **10.** to fall out (*of hair, fur*). **11.** to come to pieces (*of fabrics, leather, etc.*); л. нá стену (*fig.*, *coll.*) to climb up the wall; не л. в кармáн за слóвом not to be at a loss for a word; л. в пéтлю (*coll.*) to stick one's neck out.

ле|й, я, *m.* lei (*Romanian monetary unit*).

лейб-гвáрди|я, и, *f.* (*hist.*) Life-Guards.

лейб-мéдик, а, *m.* (*hist.*) physician in ordinary.

лейбори́ст, а, *m.* (*polit.*) Labourite.

лейбори́стск|ий, *adj.* (*polit.*) Labour; ~ая пáртия Labour Party.

лéйденск|ий, *adj.* ~ая бáнка (*phys.*) Leyden jar.

лéйк|а¹, и, *f.* **1.** watering-can. **2.** (*naut.*) bail. **3.** funnel (*for pouring liquids*).

лéйк|а², и, *f.* Leica (*camera*).

лейкеми́|я, и, *f.* (*med.*) leucaemia.

лейкóм|а, ы, *f.* (*med.*) leucoma.

лейкоци́т, а, *m.* (*physiol.*) leucocyte.

лейтенáнт, а, *m.* lieutenant; млáдший л. second lieutenant (*but there are three ranks in the Soviet Army, viz.* млáдший л., л., *and* стáрший л., *corresponding to the two ranks of* second lieutenant *and* lieutenant *in the British Army*).

лейтмоти́в, а, *m.* (*mus. and fig.*) leit-motiv.

лека́л|о, а, *n.* **1.** (*tech.*) template, gauge, pattern. **2.** instrument for drawing curves.

лека́рственный, *adj.* medicinal; officinal.

лека́рств|о, а, *n.* medicine; drug.

ле́кар|ь, я, *pl.* ~и, ~е́й, *m.* (*obs. or pejor.*) physician.

ле́ксик|а, и, *f.* vocabulary.

лексико́граф, а, *m.* lexicographer.

лексикографи́ческий, *adj.* lexicographical.

лексикогра́фи|я, и, *f.* lexicography.

лексико́лог, а, *m.* lexicologist.

лексиколо́ги|я, и, *f.* lexicology.

лекси́ческий, *adj.* lexical.

ле́ктор, а, *m.* lecturer.

лектори́|й, я, *m.* **1.** centre organizing public lectures. **2.** lecture-hall.

лектори́|я, и, *f.* (*obs.*) reading-room (*in university library*).

ле́ктор|ский, *adj. of* ~; *as noun* ~ская, ~ской, *f.* lecturers' common room.

ле́кторств|о, а, *n.* lecturing; lectureship.

лектри́с|а, ы, *f.* lecturer, lectrice.

лекцио́нный, *adj. of* ле́кция; л. зал lecture-room; л. ме́тод преподава́ния teaching method based on lectures.

ле́кци|я, и, *f.* lecture; чита́ть ~ю to lecture, deliver a lecture; (*fig., coll.*) to read a lecture.

леле́|ять, ю, *impf.* **1.** to coddle, pamper. **2.** (*fig.*) to cherish, foster; л. мечту́ to cherish a hope.

ле́мех, а (*and* леме́х, а́), *m.* ploughshare.

леме́|шный, *adj. of* ~ех.

ле́мм|а, ы, *f.* (*math.*; *lit.*) lemma.

ле́мминг, а, *m.* (*zool.*) lemming.

лему́р, а, *m.* (*zool.*) lemur.

лен, а, *m.* (*hist.*) fief, fee; отда́ть в л. to give in fee.

лён, льна, *m.* (*bot.*) flax; л.-долгуне́ц long-fibred flax; го́рный л. (*min.*) asbestos.

лендло́рд, а, *m.* landlord, land-owner (*in Great Britain and Ireland*).

лени́в|ец, ца, *m.* **1.** lazy-bones; sluggard. **2.** (*zool.*) sloth. **3.** (*tech.*) idler, idling sprocket.

лени́в|ый (~, ~а), *adj.* **1.** lazy, idle; sluggish. **2.** (*cul.*) prepared in accordance with a hasty recipe.

ле́нин|ец, ца, *m.* Leninist.

лениниа́н|а, ы, *f.* (*collect.*) Leniniana (*works of lit. and art devoted to V. I. Lenin*).

ленини́зм, а, *m.* Leninism.

ле́нинский, *adj. of* Lenin; Leninist; л. призы́в (*hist.*) 'The Lenin enrolment' (*mass enrolment of new members of Communist Party following Lenin's death*).

лени́|ться, ю́сь, ~ишься, *impf.* **1.** to be lazy, idle. **2.** (+*inf.*) to be too lazy (to); он призна́лся, что он ~и́лся им писа́ть he

admitted that he had been too lazy to write to them.

ле́нник, а, *m.* (*hist.*) vassal, feudatory.

ле́нный, *adj.* (*hist.*) feudatory; feudal.

ле́ност|ь, и, *f.* laziness, idleness; sloth.

ле́нт|а, ы, *f.* ribbon, band; tape; а́ннинская л. ribbon of Order of St. Anne; гу́сеничная л. caterpillar track; изоляцио́нная л. insulating tape; кинематографи́ческая л. (reel of) film; патро́нная л. cartridge belt; ви́ться ~ой to twist, meander.

ле́нт|очный, *adj. of* ~а; л. глист, л. червь tape-worm; ~очная пила́ band-saw; л. то́рмоз band brake; л. транспортёр conveyor belt; ~очная застро́йка (*fig.*) ribbon development.

лентя́|й, я, *m.* lazy-bones; sluggard.

лентя́йнича|ть, ю, *impf.* (*coll.*) to be lazy, idle; to loaf.

ленц|а́, ы́, *f.* (*coll.*) disposition to laziness; он с ~о́й he is inclined to be lazy.

ле́нчик, а, *m.* saddle-tree.

лен|ь, и, *f.* **1.** laziness, idleness; indolence. **2.** (*as pred.*+*d. and inf.*; *coll.*) to feel too lazy (to), not to feel like; ему́ бы́ло л. вы́ключить ра́дио he was too lazy to turn the wireless off; на́до бы пойти́, да л. I ought to go, but I don't feel like it; все, кому́ не л. anyone who feels like it.

леопа́рд, а, *m.* leopard.

лепестко́вый, *adj.* (*bot.*) petalled.

лепест|о́к, ка́, *m.* petal.

ле́пет, а, *m.* babble (*also fig.*); prattle.

лепе|та́ть, чу́, ~чешь, *impf.* to babble; to prattle.

лепёшк|а, и, *f.* **1.** flat cake; (*fig., coll.*) разби́ться, расшиби́ться в ~у to strain every nerve, go through fire and water. **2.** (*medicinal*) tablet, pastille.

леп|и́ть, лю́, ~ишь, *impf.* **1.** (*pf.* вы́~ *and* с~) to model, fashion; to mould; л. гнездо́ to build a nest. **2.** (*pf.* на~) (*coll.*) to stick (on). **3.** (*sl.*) to lie, tell lies.

леп|и́ться, лю́сь, ~ишься, *impf.* **1.** (по+*d.*) to cling (to) (*of things adhering to a steep or precipitous surface*). **2.** (*coll.*) to crawl.

ле́пк|а, и, *f.* modelling.

лепн|о́й, *adj.* modelled, moulded; ~о́е украше́ние stucco moulding.

лепрозо́ри|й, я, *m.* leper hospital.

ле́пт|а, ы, *f.* mite; внести́ свою́ ~у to contribute one's mite.

ле́пщик, а, *m.* modeller, sculptor.

лес, а(у), *pl.* ~а́, *m.* **1.** (в ~у́) forest, wood(s); вы́йти из ~а (и́з ~у) to come out of the wood; купи́ть л. to buy woodlands; кра́сный, чёрный л. coniferous, deciduous forest; быть как в ~у́ (*fig., coll.*) to be all at sea; л. ру́бят — ще́пки летя́т (*prov.*) you can't make omelettes without breaking eggs; кто в л., к. по дрова́ (to be, *etc.*) at sixes and sevens. **2.** (в ~е) (*sing. only*; *collect.*) timber; л. на корню́ standing timber.

лес|а́[1], *pl. of* ~.

лес|а́[2], **о́в** scaffolding.

леса́[3], **лёсы**, *pl.* **лёсы, лёс,** *f.* fishing-line.

лесби́йск|ий, *adj.* of Lesbos; ~ая любо́вь Lesbianism.

лесбия́нк|а, и, *f.* Lesbian (*female homosexual*).

ле́сенк|а, и, *f.* (*coll.*) *dim. of* ле́стница; short flight of stairs; short ladder.

лесни́н|а, ы, *f.* (*dial.*) trunk (*of a timber tree*).

леси́ст|ый (~, ~а), *adj.* wooded, woody.

лесни́к, а́, *m.* forester.

лесни́честв|о, а, *n.* forest area.

лесни́ч|ий, его, *m.* forestry officer; forest warden.

лес|но́й, *adj.* of ~; л. двор, склад timber-yard; ~но́е де́ло timber industry; л. институ́т forestry institute, school of forestry; ~ные насажде́ния afforestation; л. пито́мник nursery forest.

лесово́д, а, *m.* forestry specialist; graduate of forestry institute.

лесово́дств|о, а, *n.* forestry.

лесово́з, а, *m.* timber ship; timber lorry.

лесозаво́д, а, *m.* timber mill.

лесозагото́вк|а, и, *f.* **1.** timber cutting. **2.** logging; wooding. **3.** (*pl.*) (State) timber purchasing.

лес|о́к, ка́, *m.* small wood, copse, grove.

лесоматериа́л, а, *m.* timber.

лесонасажде́ни|е, я, *n.* **1.** afforestation. **2.** (forest) plantation.

лесоохране́ни|е, я, *n.* forest preservation.

лесопа́рк, а, *m.* forest park.

лесопи́лк|а, и, *f.* saw-mill.

лесопи́льн|ый, *adj.* sawing; л. заво́д saw-mill; ~ая ра́ма log frame; gang saw.

лесопи́л|ьня, ьни, *g. pl.* ~ен, *f.* = ~ка.

лесополос|а́, ы́, *f.* woodland belt, forest belt.

лесопоса́д|ки, ок forest plantations.

лесопромы́шленник, а, *m.* timber merchant.

лесопромы́шленност|ь, и, *f.* timber industry.

лесору́б, а, *m.* lumber-man.

лесосе́к|а, и, *f.* (wood-)cutting area.

лесоспла́в, а, *m.* timber rafting.

лесосте́п|ь, и, *f.* (*geogr.*) forest-steppe.

лесота́ск|а, и, *f.* (*tech.*) log conveyer.

лесоту́ндр|а, ы, *f.* (*geogr.*) forest-tundra.

леспромхо́з, а, *m.* (*abbr. of* лесно́е промышленное хозя́йство) (State) timber industry enterprise.

лёсс, а, *m.* (*geol.*) loess.

ле́стниц|а, ы, *f.* stairs, staircase; ladder; верёвочная л. rope-ladder; пара́дная л.

front staircase; пожа́рная л. fire-escape; складна́я л. steps, step-ladder; чёрная л. backstairs.

ле́стни|чный, *adj. of* ~ца; ~чная кле́тка well (*of stairs*).

лест|ный (~ен, ~на), *adj.* **1.** complimentary. **2.** flattering; ему́ бы́ло ~но, что... he felt flattered that . . . .

лест|ь, и, *f.* flattery; adulation.

лёт, а, на ~у́, о ~е, *m.* flight, flying; стреля́ть в пти́цу в л. to shoot at a bird in flight; на ~у́ in the air, on the wing; (*fig.*, *coll.*) hurriedly, in passing; хвата́ть на ~у́ to be quick to grasp (*an idea, etc.*); to be quick on the uptake.

Ле́т|а, ы, *f.* (*myth.*) Lethe; ка́нуть в ~у to sink into oblivion.

лет|а́, ~, *pl.* 1. years; age; ско́лько вам ~? how old are you?; ему́ бо́льше, ме́ньше сорока́ ~ he is over, under forty; с де́тских лет from childhood; мы одни́х лет we are of the same age; сре́дних лет middle-aged; быть в ~а́х to be elderly, getting on (in years); на ста́рости ~ in one's old age. **2.** *g. pl.* (*as g. pl. of* год) years; прошло́ мно́го ~ many years (have) passed, elapsed.

лета́льный, *adj.* lethal, fatal.

летарги́ческий, *adj.* lethargic.

летарги́|я, и, *f.* lethargy.

лета́тельн|ый, *adj.* flying; л. аппара́т aircraft; (*zool.*) ~ая перепо́нка wing membrane (*in bats*).

лет|а́ть, а́ю, *indet. of* ~е́ть.

лета́|ющий, *pres. part. of* ~ть *and adj.*; ~ющая лягу́шка (*zool.*) tree-frog.

ле|те́ть, чу́, ти́шь, *impf.* (*of* по~) **1.** to fly. **2.** (*fig.*) (*in var. senses*) to fly; to rush, tear; л. на всех пара́х to run at full tilt; л. стрело́й to go like an arrow. **3.** (*fig.*, *coll.*) to fall, drop (*intrans.*); ли́стья ~тя́т the leaves are falling; а́кции ~тя́т вниз shares are dropping (sharply).

лётк|а, и, *f.* (*tech.*) tap hole; slag notch.

ле́тний, *adj.* summer; л. сад pleasure garden(s).

ле́тник, а, *m.* (*bot.*) annual.

лётн|ый, *adj.* (suitable for, appertaining to) flying; ~ое де́ло flying; ~ое по́ле airfield; л. соста́в aircrew.

лет|о, а, *pl.* ~а́, *n.* summer; ба́бье л. Indian summer; (*coll.*) ско́лько ~, ско́лько зим it's ages since we met!

лет|о́к, ка́, *m.* (*bee-keeping*) entrance (*in hive*).

ле́том, *adv.* in summer.

летопи́с|ец, ца, *m.* chronicler, annalist.

летопи́сный, *adj.* annalistic.

ле́топис|ь, и, *f.* chronicle, annals.

летосчисле́ни|е, я, *n.* chronology.

лету́н, а́, *m.* **1.** flyer, flier. **2.** (*fig.*, *coll.*) rolling-stone, drifter.

летуче́ст|ь, и, *f.* (*chem.*) volatility.
лету́ч|ий, *adj.* 1. flying; ~ая мышь bat; ~ая ры́ба flying-fish. 2. (*fig.*) passing, ephemeral; brief; л. листо́к leaflet; л. ми́тинг emergency, extraordinary meeting. 3. (*med.*) shifting. 4. (*chem.*) volatile.
лету́чк|а, и, *f.* (*coll.*) 1. leaflet. 2. emergency meeting, extraordinary meeting. 3. mobile detachment; (*med.*) mobile dressing station; ремо́нтная л. emergency repairs team; хирурги́ческая л. mobile surgical unit.
лётчик, а, *m.* pilot; aviator, flyer; л.-испыта́тель test-pilot; л.-истреби́тель fighter pilot.
лече́бник, а, *m.* book of home cures.
лече́бниц|а, ы, *f.* clinic.
лече́бный, *adj.* 1. medical. 2. medicinal.
лече́ни|е, я, *n.* (medical) treatment; амбулато́рное л. out-patient treatment.
леч|и́ть, у́, ~ишь, *impf.* to treat (*medically*); его́ ~ат от шо́ка he is being treated for shock.
леч|и́ться, у́сь, ~ишься, *impf.* 1. (от) to receive, undergo (medical) treatment (for); л. впры́скиваниями to take a course of injections. 2. *pass. of* ~и́ть.
ле|чу́[1], ти́шь, *see* ~те́ть.
леч|у́[2], ~ишь, *see* ~и́ть.
лечь, ля́гу, ля́жешь, ля́гут, *past* лёг, легла́, *imp.* ляг, ля́гте, *pf.* (*of* ложи́ться) 1. to lie (down); л. в больни́цу to go (in) to hospital; л. в посте́ль, л. спать to go to bed; (*coll.*) неуже́ли де́ти ещё не легли́? aren't the children in bed yet?; л. в осно́ву (+*g.*) to underlie; (*naut.*) л. в дрейф to lie to, heave to. 2. (на+*a.*) to fall (on); (*rhet.*) л. костьми́ to fall in battle; (*fig.*) отве́тственность ля́жет на вас it will be your duty, it will be incumbent upon you; подозре́ние легло́ на иностра́нцев suspicion fell upon the foreigners; л. на со́весть to weigh on one's conscience.
ле́ш|ий, его, *m.* (*in Russ. myth.*) wood-goblin; к ~ему! (*coll. expletive*) go to the devil!; како́го ~его... what the devil, why the devil. . . .
лещ, а́, *m.* (*fish*) bream.
лещи́н|а, ы, *f.* (*bot.*) hazel.
лже- pseudo-, false-, mock-.
лжеприся́г|а, и, *f.* (*leg.*) perjury.
лжесвиде́тел|ь, я, *m.* false witness.
лжесвиде́тельств|о, а, *n.* false evidence.
лжесвиде́тельств|овать, ую, *impf.* to give false evidence.
лжеуче́ни|е, я, *n.* false doctrine.
лжец, а́, *m.* liar.
лжёшь, *see* лгать.
лжи́вост|ь, и, *f.* falsity, mendacity.
лжи́в|ый (~, ~а), *adj.* 1. lying; mendacious. 2. false, deceitful.

ли (ль) 1. *interrog. particle* возмо́жно ли? is it possible?; придёт ли он? is he coming? 2. *conj.* whether, if; не зна́ю, придёт ли он I don't know whether he is coming; посмотри́, идёт ли по́езд go and see if the train is coming. 3. ли... ли whether ... or; сего́дня ли, за́втра ли whether today or tomorrow; ра́но ли, по́здно ли, но приду́ I shall come sooner or later.
лиа́н|а, ы, *f.* (*bot.*) liana.
либера́л, а, *m.* liberal.
либерали́зм, а, *m.* 1. liberalism. 2. (*pejor.*) tolerance.
либера́льнича|ть, ю, *impf.* (*of* с~) (с+*i.*; *coll., pejor.*) to act the liberal; to show (excessive) tolerance (towards).
либера́л|ьный (~ен, ~ьна), *adj.* 1. liberal. 2. (excessively) tolerant.
ли́бо, *conj.* or; л.... л. (either) . . . or; л. пан, л. пропа́л all or nothing.
либретти́ст, а, *m.* librettist.
либре́тто, *indecl., n.* libretto.
ли́в|ень, ня, *m.* heavy shower, downpour; cloud-burst; (*fig.*) л. свинца́ hail of bullets.
ли́вер[1], а, *m.* (*cul.*) pluck.
ли́вер[2], а, *m.* (*tech.*) pipette.
ли́вер|ный, *adj. of* ~[1]; ~ная колбаса́ liver sausage.
ливмя́, *adv.* (*coll.*) л. лить (*of rain*) to pour, come down in torrents.
ли́в|невый, *adj. of* ~ень; (*meteor.*) cumulo-nimbus.
ливре́|йный, *adj. of* ~я; л. слуга́ livery servant.
ливре́|я, и, *f.* livery.
ли́г|а, и, *f.* league; Л. на́ций (*hist.*) League of Nations.
лигату́р|а[1], ы, *f.* (*chem.*) base metal (*added to precious metals to harden them*).
лигату́р|а[2], ы, *f.* (*ling. and med.*) ligature.
лигни́н, а, *m.* (*chem.*) lignin(e).
лигни́т, а, *m.* (*min.*) lignite.
ли́дер, а, *m.* 1. leader (*of political party or organisation*). 2. (*sport*) leader (*in tournament, etc.*). 3. (*naut.*) flotilla leader.
ли́дерств|о, а, *n.* 1. leadership (*of political party or public organization*). 2. (*sport*) first place, lead; занима́ть л. to be in the lead.
лиди́р|овать, ую, *impf.* (*sport*) to take first place, be in the lead.
ли|за́ть, жу́, ~жешь, *impf.* (*of* ~зну́ть) to lick; (*fig., coll.*) л. ру́ки (но́ги, пя́тки) кому́-н. to lick someone's boots.
ли|за́ться, жу́сь, ~жешься, *impf.* (*coll.*) to neck, smooch.
ли́зис, а, *m.* (*med.*) lysis.
лиз|ну́ть, ну́, нёшь, *inst. pf. of* ~а́ть.
лизоблю́д, а, *m.* (*coll., pejor.*) lickspittle.
лизо́л, а, *m.* (*chem.*) lysol.
лик[1], а, *m.* 1. (*obs.*) face. 2. representation

of face (*on icon*). 3. л. луны́ face of the moon.

лик², а, *m.* (*eccl.*, *arch.*) assembly; причис-
ли́ть к ~у святы́х to canonize.

ликбе́з, а, *m.* (*abbr. of* ликвида́ция безгра́-
мотности) campaign against illiteracy.

ликвида́тор, а, *m.* (*comm.*, *etc.*) liquidator.

ликвида́ци|я, и, *f.* 1. (*comm.*) liquidation;
л. долго́в settlement of debts. 2.(*polit.*, *etc.*)
liquidation; elimination, abolition.

ликвиди́р|овать, ую, *impf. and pf.* 1.(*comm.*)
to liquidate, wind up. 2. to liquidate; to
eliminate, abolish.

ликвиди́р|оваться, уюсь, *impf. and pf.* 1. to
wind up (one's activities). 2. *pass. of*
~овать.

ликви́дн|ый, *adj.* (*fin.*) liquid; ~ые сред-
ства ready money.

ликёр, а, *m.* liqueur.

ликова́ни|е, я, *n.* rejoicing, exultation.

лик|ова́ть, у́ю, *impf.* to rejoice, exult.

лик-трос, а, *m.* (*naut.*) bolt-rope.

лик|у́ющий, *pres. part. of* ~ова́ть *and adj.*
exultant, triumphant.

лиле́йный, *adj.* 1. (*poet.*) lily-white. 2. (*bot.*)
liliaceous.

лилипу́т, а, *m.* Lilliputian.

ли́ли|я, и, *f.* lily.

лилове́|ть, ю, *impf.* (*of* по~) to turn violet.

лило́вый, *adj.* lilac, violet.

лима́н, а, *m.* 1. estuary. 2. flood plain.

лима́нный, *adj. of* ~.

лими́т, а, *m.* quota; limit.

лимити́р|овать, ую, *impf. and pf.* to estab-
lish a quota (or maximum) in respect of.

лимитро́ф, а, *m.* border state (*esp. of the
Baltic states in relation to the U.S.S.R.*).

лимитро́ф|ный, *adj. of* ~.

лимо́н, а, *m.* lemon; вы́жатый л. (*fig.*, *coll.*)
has-been.

лимона́д, а, *m.* 1. lemonade; lemon squash.
2. squash (*of fruit or berries, not necessarily
lemon, as beverage*).

лимо́н|ить, ю, ишь, *impf.* (*of* с~) (*thieves' sl.*)
to knock off, pinch.

лимоннокислый, *adj.* (*chem.*) citric acid.

лимо́нн|ый, *adj.* lemon; ~ая кислота́
(*chem.*) citric acid.

лимузи́н, а, *m.* limousine.

ли́мф|а, ы, *f.* (*physiol.*) lymph.

лимфати́ческий, *adj.* (*physiol.*) lymphatic
(*also fig.*, *obs.*).

лингафо́нный, *adj.* л. кабине́т language
laboratory.

лингви́ст, а, *m.* linguist.

лингви́стик|а, и, *f.* linguistics.

лингвисти́ческий, *adj.* linguistic.

лингвострановеде́ни|е, я, *n.* language
learning through study of a country's
customs and institutions.

линейк|а¹, и, *f.* 1. line (*on paper, blackboard,
etc.*); писа́ть по ~ам to write on the lines;
но́тные ~и (*mus.*) staves. 2. ruler; логариф-
ми́ческая л. slide-rule. 3. (*typ.*) набо́рная
л. setting-rule. 4. ла́герная л. camp line(s).

линейк|а², и, *f.* (*obs.*) break, wagonette.

лине́йн|ый, *adj.* 1. (*math.*) linear; ~ые
ме́ры long measures. 2. (*mil.*, *naut.*) of the
line; л. кора́бль battleship.

лин|ёк, ька́, *m.* (*naut.*) rope's end, colt.

ли́нз|а, ы, *f.* lens.

ли́ни|я, и, *f.* (*in var. senses*) line; (*fig.*) л.
поведе́ния line of conduct, policy; про-
вести́ ~ю в поли́тике to pursue a policy;
вести́ (*coll. also* гнуть) свою́ ~ю to have
one's own way; вести́ ~ю на что-н. to
direct one's efforts towards something; по
~и наиме́ньшего сопротивле́ния on the
line of least resistance.

линко́р, а, *m.* (*abbr. of* лине́йный кора́бль)
battleship.

лино-бати́ст, а, *m.* lawn, cambric.

линова́ный, *adj.* lined, ruled.

лин|ова́ть, у́ю, *impf.* (*of* на~) to rule.

лино́леум, а, *m.* linoleum.

линч, а, *m.* зако́н ~а, суд ~а lynch law.

линч|ева́ть, у́ю, *impf. and pf.* to lynch.

лин|ь¹, я́, *m.* (*fish*) tench.

лин|ь², я́, *m.* (*naut.*) line.

ли́ньк|а, и, *f.* moult(ing).

линю́ч|ий (~, ~а), *adj.* (*coll.*) liable to fade.

линя́лый, *adj.* (*coll.*) 1. faded, discoloured.,
2. having moulted.

линя́|ть, ет, *impf.* 1. (*pf.* по~) to fade, lose
colour; (*of paint*) to run. 2. (*pf.* вы́~) (*of
animals*) to shed hair; to cast the coat; (*of
birds*) to moult, shed feathers; (*of snakes*) to
slough.

ли́п|а¹, ы, *f.* lime(-tree).

ли́п|а², ы, *f.* (*sl.*) forgery.

ли́п|ка, ки, *f.* dim. of ~а¹; (*coll.*) ободра́ть
как ~ку to fleece.

ли́п|кий (~ок, ~ка́, ~ко), *adj.* sticky, adhe-
sive; л. пла́стырь sticking plaster.

ли́п|нуть, ну, нешь; *past* ~, ~ла, *impf.* (к)
to stick to), adhere (to).

липня́к, á, *m.* (*coll.*) lime-grove.

ли́п|овый¹, *adj. of* ~а¹; л. мёд white honey;
л. цвет lime-blossom; л. чай limeleaf tea.

ли́повый², *adj.* (*sl.*) sham, fake, forged.

ли́р|а¹, ы, *f.* lyre.

ли́р|а², ы, *f.* (*monetary unit*) lira.

лири́зм, а, *m.* lyricism.

ли́рик, а, *m.* lyric poet.

ли́рик|а, и, *f.* 1. lyric poetry; lyrics. 2. (*fig.*,
pejor.) lyricism.

лири́ческ|ий, *adj.* 1. lyric; (*lit.*) л. беспоря́-
док poetic disorder; ~ое отступле́ние
lyrical digression. 2. (*of disposition, etc.*)
lyrical.

лири́ч|ный (~ен, ~на), *adj.* lyrical.

ли́р|ный, *adj.* (*obs. or poet.*) of ~a[1].

лирохво́ст, а, *m.* lyre-bird.

лис, а, *m.* (*obs.*) (dog-)fox.

лис|а́, ы́, *pl.* ~ы, *f.* fox; чернобу́рая л. silver fox; Л. Патрике́евна (*in Russ. folk-tales*) Reynard; прики́дываться ~о́й (*fig.*, *coll.*) to fawn, toady.

ли́сел|ь, я, *pl.* ~я́, *m.* (*naut.*) studding-sail.

лис|ёнок, ёнка, *pl.* ~я́та, ~я́т, *m.* fox-cub.

ли́с|ий, *adj.* of ~а́; л. мех fox fur; л. хвост (fox-)brush.

лис|и́ть, и́шь, *impf.* (*coll.*) to fawn, flatter.

лиси́ц|а, ы, *f.* fox; vixen.

лиси́чк|а, и, *f.* 1. *dim.* of лиси́ца. 2. (*mushroom*) chanterelle. 3. paper-chase.

лист[1], а́, *pl.* ~ья, ~ьев, *m.* leaf (*of plant*); blade (*of cereal*).

лист[2], а́, *pl.* ~ы́, ~о́в, *m.* 1. leaf, sheet (*of paper, etc.*); (*metal*) plate; в л. in folio; корректу́ра в ~а́х page-proofs; печа́тный л. printer's sheet, quire; игра́ть с ~а́ (*mus.*) to play at sight. 2. исполни́тельный л. (*leg.*) writ of execution; опро́сный л. questionnaire; охра́нный л. safe-conduct; похва́льный л. (*obs.*) certificate of progress and good conduct (*in schools*).

листа́ж, а́, *m.* number of sheets (*in a book*).

листа́|ть, ю, *impf.* (*coll.*) to turn over the pages of.

листв|а́, ы́, *f.* (*collect.*) leaves, foliage.

ли́ственниц|а, ы, *f.* (*bot.*) larch.

ли́ственный, *adj.* (*bot.*) deciduous.

листо́вк|а, и, *f.* leaflet.

лист|ово́й, *adj.* of ~; ~ово́е желе́зо sheet iron; ~ова́я рессо́ра laminated spring.

лист|о́к, ка́, *m.* 1. *dim.* of ~[1]. 2. leaflet. 3. form, pro-forma. 4. (*sl.*) rag (*newspaper*.)

листопа́д, а, *m.* (autumn) fall of the leaves.

лит- *abbr.* of литерату́рный.

лита́врщик, а, *m.* (kettle)drummer.

лита́вр|ы, ~, *sing.* ~a, ~ы, *f.* kettledrum.

литви́н, а, *m.* (*obs.*) Lithuanian.

литви́нк|а, и, *f.* (*obs.*) Lithuanian (woman).

лите́йн|ая, ой, *f.* foundry, smelting-house.

лите́йный, *adj.* founding, casting.

лите́йщик, а, *m.* founder, caster, smelter.

ли́тер, а, *m.* (*coll.*) travel warrant.

ли́тер|а, ы, *f.* 1. (*typ.*) type. 2. (*obs.*) letter (*of the alphabet*).

литера́тор, а, *m.* literary man, man of letters.

литерату́р|а, ы, *f.* literature; худо́жественная л. belles-lettres, literature.

литерату́р|ный (~ен, ~на), *adj.* literary; ~ная со́бственность copyright.

литературове́д, а, *m.* specialist in study of literature; literary critic.

литературове́дени|е, я, *n.* study of literature; literary criticism.

литерату́рщин|а, ы, *f.* (*coll.*) striving after literary effect; selfconscious writing.

ли́терный, *adj.* 1. marked with a letter. 2. (*sl.*) hush-hush (*of factories, etc., designated only by a letter of the alphabet for security reasons*).

литер|ова́ть, у́ю, *impf. and pf.* to rate by system of letters.

ли́ти|й, я, *m.* (*chem.*) lithium.

ли́тник, а, *m.* (*tech.*) pouring gate, pouring channel, flow gate.

литобрабо́тник, а, *m.* ghost-writer.

лито́в|ец, ца, *m.* Lithuanian.

лито́вк|а, и, *f.* Lithuanian (woman).

лито́вский, *adj.* Lithuanian.

лито́граф, а, *m.* lithographer.

литографи́р|овать, ую, *impf. and pf.* to lithograph.

литогра́фи|я, и, *f.* 1. lithograph. 2. lithography.

литогра́фск|ий, *adj.* lithographic; ~ая печа́ть lithograph.

лит|о́й, *adj.* cast; ~а́я сталь cast steel, ingot steel.

литр, а, *m.* litre.

литра́ж, а́, *m.* capacity (*in litres*).

литро́вый, *adj.* litre (*of one litre capacity*).

литурги́ческий, *adj.* liturgical.

литурги́|я, и, *f.* liturgy.

лить, лью, льёшь, *past* лил, лила́, ли́ло, *imp.* лей, *impf.* 1. to pour (*trans. and intrans.*); to shed, spill; л. слёзы to shed tears; дождь льёт как из ведра́ it is raining cats and dogs; л. во́ду на чью-н. ме́льницу to play into someone's hands. 2. (*tech.*) to found, cast, mould.

лить|ё, я́, *no pl., n.* (*tech.*) 1. founding, casting, moulding. 2. (*collect.*) castings, mouldings.

ли́|ться, льётся, *past* ~лся, ~ла́сь, ~ло́сь, *impf.* 1. to flow; to stream, pour. 2. *pass.* of ~ть.

лиф, а, *m.* bodice.

лифт, а, *m.* lift, elevator.

лифтёр, а, *m.* lift operator, lift-boy.

ли́фчик, а, *m.* 1. brassière. 2. (child's) bodice.

лиха́ч, а́, *m.* 1. (*obs.*) driver of smart cab. 2. (*pejor.*) road-hog. 3. dare-devil.

лиха́честв|о, а, *n.* foolhardiness.

лихв|а́, ы́, *f.* interest; отплати́ть с ~о́й to. repay with interest.

лих|о[1], а, *n.* (*poet.*) evil, ill; не помина́йте ~ом (*coll.*) remember me (us) kindly; узна́ть, почём фунт ~а (*coll.*) to fall on hard times, plumb the depths of misfortune.

ли́х|о[2], *adv.* of ~о́й[2]; л. заломи́ть ша́пку to cock one's hat at a jaunty angle.

лиходе́|й, я, *m.* (*obs.*) evil-doer.

лиходейств|о, а, *n.* (*obs.*) evil-doing.
лихоим|ец, ца, *m.* (*obs.*) usurer; extortioner.
лихоимств|о, а, *n.* (*obs.*) extortion; bribe-
-taking; bribery and corruption.
лих|ой¹ (~, ~á, ~о), *adj.* (*dial. and folk poet.*)
evil; ~á бедá начáло (*or* начáть) (*coll.*) the
first step is the hardest.
лих|ой² (~, ~á, ~о), *adj.* (*coll.*) dashing,
spirited; jaunty.
лихорá|дить, жу, дишь, *impf.* 1. to be in a
fever. 2. *impers.* меня ~дит I feel feverish.
лихорáдк|а, и, *f.* 1. fever (*also fig.*); пере-
межáющаяся (болóтная) л. malaria. 2.
rash.
лихорáдоч|ный (~ен, ~на), *adj.* feverish
(*also fig.*).
лихост|ь, и, *f.* (*coll.*) spirit, mettle; swagger.
лихтер, а, *m.* (*naut.*) lighter.
лиц|евáть, ýю, *impf.* (*of* пере~) to turn
(*clothing*).
лицев|ой, *adj.* 1. (*anat.*) facial. 2. exterior;
~áя сторонá (*of building*) façade, front; (*of
material*) right side; (*of coin, etc.*) obverse.
3. ~áя рýкопись illuminated manuscript.
4. (*book-keeping*) л. счёт personal account.
лицедé|й, я, *m.* (*obs.*) 1. actor. 2. (*fig.*) hypo-
crite, dissembler.
лицедéйств|о, а, *n.* (*obs.*) 1. acting. 2.
theatrical performance. 3. (*fig.*) play-act-
ing, dissembling.
лицезр|éть, ю, йшь, *impf.* (*obs. and iron.*) to
behold with one's own eyes.
лицейст, а, *m.* pupil of Lyceum, lycée.
лицé|й, я, *m.* 1. Lyceum (*high school or law
school in pre-revolutionary Russia*). 2. lycée (*in
France*).
лицéй|ский, *adj.* of ~.
лицемéр, а, *m.* hypocrite, dissembler.
лицемéри|е, я, *n.* hypocrisy, dissimulation.
лицемéр|ить, ю, ишь, *impf.* to play the
hypocrite, dissemble.
лицемéр|ный (~ен, ~на), *adj.* hypocritical.
лицéнзи|я, и, *f.* (*econ.*) licence.
лицеприяти|е, я, *n.* (*obs.*) partiality.
лицеприят|ный (~ен, ~на), *adj.* (*obs.*) par-
tial, based on partiality.
лицеприятств|овать, ую, *impf.* (*obs.*) to be
partial; to show bias.
лиц|ó, á, *pl.* ~а, *n.* 1. face; чертú ~á
features; измениться, перемениться ~óм,
в ~é to change countenance; сказáть в л.
комý-н. to say to someone's face; знать
когó-н. в л. to know someone by sight; на
нём ~á нет he looks awful; ~óм в грязь не
удáрить not to disgrace oneself; быть к
~ý (+*d.*) to suit, become; (*fig.*) to become,
befit; нам не к ~ý такúе постýпки such
actions do not become us; ~óм к ~ý face
to face; постáвить ~óм к ~ý to confront;
онú на однó л. (*coll.*) they are as like as two

peas; рáдость былá напúсана у неё на ~é
joy was written all over her face; показáть
своё (настоящее) л. to show one's true
worth; пéред (пред) ~óм (+*g.*) in the face
(of); с ~á некрасúв (*coll.*) ugly; (исчéзнуть)
с ~á землú (to vanish) from the face of the
earth. 2. exterior; (*of material*) right side;
(*fig.*) показáть товáр ~óм to show something to advantage; to make the best of
something. 3. person; дéйствующее л.
(*theatr., lit.*) character; дéйствующие ~а
dramatis personae; должностнóе л. official, functionary; перемещённые ~а displaced persons; подставнóе л. dummy,
man of straw; физúческое л. (*leg.*) natural
person; юридúческое л. (*leg.*) juridical
person; в ~é (+*g.*) in the person (of);
невзирáя на ~а without respect of persons;
от ~á (+*g.*) in the name (of), on behalf
(of). 4. identity.
личин|а¹, ы, *f.* mask; (*fig.*) guise; под ~ой
(+*g.*) in the guise (of), under cover (of);
сорвáть ~у с когó-н. to unmask someone.
личин|а², ы, *f.* (*tech.*) scutcheon, key-plate.
личинк|а¹, и, *f.* larva, grub; maggot.
личинк|а², и, *f.* (*mil.*) боевáя л. bolt head
(*of rifle*); elevator (*in machine-gun*).
лично, *adv.* personally, in person.
личн|ой, *adj.* 1. face; ~ой крем face cream.
2. (*anat.*) facial.
личност|ь, и, *f.* 1. personality. 2. person,
individual; тёмная л. shady character;
удостоверéние ~и identity card; устано-
вúть чью-н. л. to establish someone's identity. 3. (*pl.*) personal remarks, personali-
ties; переходúть на ~и to become personal.
личн|ый, *adj.* personal, individual; private;
~ое местоимéние (*gram.*) personal pronoun; ~ая охрáна body-guard; л. сек-
ретáрь private secretary; ~ая собствен-
ность personal property; л. состáв staff.
лишá|й, я, *m.* 1. (*bot.*) lichen. 2. (*med.*)
herpes; опоясывающий л. shingles; стри-
гýщий л. ringworm; чешýйчатый л. psoria-
sis.
лишáйник, а, *m.* (*bot.*) lichen.
лиш|áть(ся), áю(сь), *impf. of* ~úть(ся).
лиш|ек, ка, *m.* (*coll.*) surplus; с ~ком odd,
and more, just over; дéсять миль с ~ком
ten odd miles, ten miles and a bit.
лишéн|ец, ца, *m.* disfranchised person (*in
U.S.S.R. up to 1936*).
лишéни|е, я, *n.* 1. deprivation; л. граж-
дáнских прав (*leg.*) disfranchisement. 2.
privation, hardship.
лишён|ный (~, ~á, ~ó), *p.p.p. of* лишúть
and adj. (+*g.*) lacking (in), devoid (of); он
не лишён острoýмия he is not without
wit.

лиши́|ть, у́, и́шь, *pf.* (*of* ~а́ть) (+*g.*) to deprive (of); л. кого́-н. насле́дства to disinherit someone; л. себя́ жи́зни to take one's life.

лиши́|ться, у́сь, и́шься. *pf.* (*of* ~а́ться) (+*g.*) to lose, be deprived (of); л. зре́ния to lose one's sight; л. чувств to faint away.

ли́шн|ий, *adj.* **1.** superfluous; unnecessary; бы́ло бы не ~е (+*inf.*) it would not be out of place; он здесь л. he is one too many here. **2.** left over; spare, odd; л. раз once more; с ~им (*coll.*) and more, odd; со́рок фу́нтов с ~им forty pounds odd.

лишь, *adv. and conj.* only; не хвата́ет л. одного́ one thing only is lacking; л. вошёл, собáка залáяла no sooner had he entered than the dog began to bark; л. то́лько as soon as; л. бы if only, provided that; л. бы он мог прие́хать provided that he can come.

лоб, лба, о лбé, во (на) лбу́; *pl.* лбы, лбов, *m.* forehead, brow; покáтый л. receding forehead; стреля́ть в л. to fire point-blank; атáка в л. frontal attack; пусти́ть себе́ пу́лю в л. to blow out one's brains; (*coll.*) на лбу напи́сано writ large on one's face; что в л., что по лбу it is all one, it comes to the same thing; будь он семи́ пяде́й во лбу be he a Solomon.

лобáст|ый (~, ~а), *adj.* having a large forehead.

лобби́ст, а, *m.* (*polit.*) lobbyist.

лобзáни|е, я, *n.* (*obs.*) kiss.

лобзá|ть, ю, *impf.* (*obs.*) to kiss.

лóбзик, а, *m.* fret-saw.

лобкóв|ый, *adj.* ~ая кость (*anat.*) pubis.

лóбн|ый, *adj.* (*anat.*) frontal; ~ое мéсто (*hist.*) place of execution.

лобов|óй, *adj.* frontal, front; ~áя атáка (*mil.*) frontal attack; л. фонáрь headlight; ~óе сопротивлéние (*aeron.*) drag.

лобогре́йк|а, и, *f.* (*agric.*) harvester, reaping machine (*of simple design*).

лоб|óк, кá, *m.* (*anat.*) pubis.

лоботря́с, а, *m.* (*coll.*) lazy-bones, idler.

лобызá|ть, ю, *impf.* (*obs.*) to kiss.

лов, а, *m.* **1.** = ~ля. **2.** = улóв.

ловелáс, а, *m.* (*coll.*) Lovelace, lady-killer.

лов|éц, цá, *m.* fisherman; hunter.

лов|и́ть, лю́, ~ишь, *impf.* (*of* поймáть) to (try to) catch; (*fig.*) л. ры́бу в му́тной водé to fish in troubled waters; л. чей-н. взгляд to try to catch someone's eye; л. (удóбный) момéнт, слýчай to seize an opportunity; л. кáждое слóво to devour every word; л. себя́ на чём-н. to catch oneself at something; л. кого́-н. на слóве to take someone at his word; л. стáнцию (*radio*) to try to pick up a station.

ловкáч, á, *m.* (*coll.*) dodger.

лóв|кий (~ок, ~кá, ~ко), *adj.* **1.** adroit, dexterous, deft; л. ход master stroke. **2.** cunning, smart. **3.** (*coll.*) comfortable.

**лóвк|о, *adv. of* ~ий; л. ли вам здесь сидéть? (*coll.*) are you comfortable sitting here?

лóвкост|ь, и, *f.* **1.** adroitness, dexterity, deftness; л. рук sleight of hand. **2.** cunning, smartness.

лóв|ля, ли, *g. pl.* ~ель, *f.* **1.** catching, hunting; ры́бная л. fishing; л. силкáми snaring. **2.** fishing-ground.

ловýшк|а, и, *f.* snare, trap (*also fig.*); поймáть в ~у to ensnare, entrap.

лóв|че (and ~чée), *comp. of* ~кий *and* ~ко.

лóвчий[1], *adj.* **1. hunting. **2.** serving as snare, trap.

лóвч|ий[2], его, *m.* (*hist.*) huntsman, master of hounds.

лог, а, в ~е *or* **в ~ý,** *pl.* ~á, ~óв, *m.* broad gully.

логари́фм, а, *m.* (*math.*) logarithm.

логарифми́р|овать, ую, *impf. and pf.* (*math.*) to find the logarithm of.

логарифми́ческ|ий, *adj.* (*math.*) logarithmic; ~ая линéйка slide-rule.

лóгик|а, и, *f.* logic.

**логи́ческий, adj.* logical.

логи́чност|ь, и, *f.* logicality.

логи́ч|ный (~ен, ~на), *adj.* = ~еский.

лóговищ|е, а, *n.* den, lair.

лóгов|о, а, *n.* = ~ище.

логопáти|я, и, *f.* speech defect.

логопéд, а, *m.* speech therapist.

логопеди́|ческий, *adj. of* ~ия.

логопéди|я, и, *f.* speech therapy.

лóдк|а, и, *f.* boat; двухвесéльная л. pair-oar; гóночная л. gig, yawl; подвóдная л. submarine; спасáтельная л. life-boat; летáющая л. flying-boat; катáться на ~e to go boating.

лóдочк|а, и, *f.* dim. of лóдка.

лóдочник, а, *m.* boatman.

лóд|очный, *adj. of* ~ка.

лоды́жк|а, и, *f.* **1.** (*anat.*) ankle-bone. **2.** (*mil.*) tumbler (*part of the lock of a machine-gun*).

лóдырнича|ть, ю, *impf.* (*coll.*) to loaf, idle.

лóдыр|ь, я, *m.* (*coll.*) loafer, idler; гоня́ть ~я to loaf, idle.

лóж|а[1], и, *f.* **1.** (*theatr.*) box. **2.** (*masonic*) lodge.

лóж|а[2], и, *f.* (gun-)stock.

ложби́н|а, ы, *f.* (*geogr.*) narrow, shallow gully; л. бю́ста (*fig., coll.*) cleavage.

лóж|е, а, *n.* **1.** (*obs.*) bed, couch. **2.** bed, channel (*of river*). **3.** gun-stock.

лóжечк|а[1], и, *f.* dim. of лóжка.

лóжечк|а[2], и, *f.* под ~ой in the pit of the stomach.

лож|и́ться, у́сь, и́шься, *impf. of* лечь.

ло́жк|а, и, f. 1. spoon; десе́ртная л. dessert-spoon; столо́вая л. table-spoon; ча́йная л. tea-spoon; че́рез час по ча́йной ~е (fig., coll.) in minute doses. 2. spoonful; л. дёгтя в бо́чке мёда a fly in the ointment.

ло́жно- pseudo-.

ло́жност|ь, и, f. falsity, error.

ло́ж|ный (~ен, ~на), adj. false, erroneous; sham, dummy; ~ная скро́мность false modesty; ~ная трево́га false alarm.

ложь, лжи, f. lie, falsehood.

лоз|а́, ы́, pl. ~ы, f. 1. rod. 2. withe. 3. vine.

лозня́к, а́, m. willow-bush.

ло́зунг, а, m. 1. slogan, catchword; watch-word. 2. (mil.; obs.) pass-word.

лойя́льн|ость, ~ый = лоя́льн|ость, ~ый.

локализа́ци|я, и, f. localization.

локализ|ова́ть, у́ю, impf. and pf. to localize.

лока́льный, adj. local.

лока́ут, а, m. (polit.) lock-out.

локаути́р|овать, ую, impf. and pf. (polit.) to lock-out.

локомоби́л|ь, я, m. traction-engine, portable engine.

локомоти́в, а, m. locomotive.

локо́н, а, m. lock, curl, ringlet.

локотни́к, а́, m. arm (of a chair); elbow-rest.

ло́к|оть, тя, pl. ~ти, ~те́й, m. 1. elbow; с про́дранными ~тя́ми out at elbow(s); рабо́тать ~тя́ми (coll.) to elbow one's way; чу́вство ~тя (fig.) feeling of comradeship; бли́зок л., да не уку́сишь (prov.) so near and yet so far. 2. (measure) (obs.) cubit, ell.

локтев|о́й, adj. (anat.) ~а́я кость ulna; funny-bone.

лом, а, pl. ~ы́, ~о́в, m. 1. crow-bar. 2. (sing. only; collect.) scrap, waste; желе́зный л. scrap-iron.

лома́к|а, и, m. and f. (coll.) poseur, affected person.

ло́ман|ый, adj. broken; л. англи́йский язы́к broken English; ~ого гроша́ не сто́ит (coll.) it is not worth a brass farthing.

лома́нь|е, я, n. (coll.) affectation; mincing, simpering.

лома́|ть, ю, impf. (of с~) 1. to break; to fracture. 2. (no pf.) (fig.) л. себе́ го́лову (над) to rack one's brains (over); л. дурака́ to play the fool; л. ру́ки to wring one's hands; л. ша́пку (пе́ред) to bow obsequiously (to). 3. (no pf.) л. ка́мень to quarry stone. 4. (no pf.; of pain, sickness) (coll.) to rack; to cause to ache; (impers.) меня́ всего́ ~ло I was aching all over.

лома́|ться, юсь, impf. 1. (pf. с~) to break (intrans.). 2. (no pf.) (of voice) to crack, break. 3. (pf. по~) (coll.) to pose, put on airs. 4. (pf. по~) (coll.) to make difficulties, be obstinate.

ломба́рд, а, m. pawn-shop; заложи́ть в л. to pawn.

ломба́рд|ный, adj. of ~; ~ная квита́нция pawn ticket.

ло́мберный, adj. л. стол card-table.

лом|и́ть, лю́, ~ишь, impf. (coll.) 1. to break. 2. to break through, rush. 3. (impers.) to cause to ache; у меня́ ~ит спи́ну my back aches. 4. (coll.) л. це́ну to demand an extortionate price.

лом|и́ться, люсь, ~ишься, impf. 1. to be (near to) breaking; (от) to burst (with), be crammed (with); ве́тви ~ятся от плодо́в the boughs are groaning with fruit. 2. (coll.) to force one's way; л. в откры́тую дверь (fig.) to force an open door.

ло́мк|а, и, f. 1. breaking (also fig.). 2. (usually pl., obs.) quarry.

ло́м|кий (~ок, ~ка́, ~ко), adj. fragile, brittle.

ломови́к, а́, m. = ломово́й изво́зчик.

ломов|о́й, adj. dray, draught; л. изво́зчик drayman, carter; ~а́я ло́шадь cart-horse, draught-horse; ~а́я подво́да dray; as noun л., ~о́го, m. = л. изво́зчик.

ломоно́с, а, m. (bot.) clematis.

ломо́т|а, ы, f. (coll.) rheumatic pain, ache.

ломо́т|ный, adj. of ~а.

лом|о́ть, тя́, pl. ~ти́, ~те́й, m. large flat slice; round (of bread); отре́занный л. fig., of person no longer dependent, standing on his own feet.

ло́мтик, а, m. slice; ре́зать ~ами to slice.

лонжеро́н, а, m. (tech.) longeron; (aeron.) (wing) spar.

ло́н|о, а, no pl., n. (obs.) bosom, lap; л. семьи́ the bosom of the family; на ~е приро́ды in the open air.

лопа́р|ка, ки, f. of ~ь¹.

лопа́рский, adj. Lapp(ish).

лопа́р|ь¹, я, m. Lapp, Laplander.

лопа́р|ь², я́, m. (naut.) fall.

ло́паст|ный, adj. of ~ь; (bot.) laciniate.

ло́паст|ь, и, pl. ~и, ~е́й, f. 1. blade; fan, vane (of propeller, etc.); (wheel) paddle; л. о́си axle tree. 2. (bot.) lamina.

лопа́т|а, ы, f. spade, shovel; грести́ де́ньги ~ой (fig., coll.) to rake it (sc. money) in.

лопа́тк|а, и, f. 1. shovel; trowel, scoop; (cul.) spatula; blade (of turbine). 2. (anat.) shoulder-blade, scapula; (part of joint of meat) shoulder; положи́ть на о́бе лопа́тки to throw (in wrestling); бежа́ть во все ~и (coll.) to run as fast as one's legs can carry one.

ло́па|ть, ю, impf. (of с~) (coll.) to gobble up.

ло́па|ться, аюсь, impf. of ~нуть.

ло́п|нуть, ну, нешь, pf. (of ~аться) 1. to break, burst; to split, crack; чуть не л. от сме́ха to split one's sides with laughter, burst with laughter; (*fig.*) у меня терпéние ~нуло my patience is exhausted. **2.** (*fig.*, *coll.*) to fail, be a failure; (*fin.*) to go bankrupt, crash.

лопо|тáть, чý, ~чешь, *impf.* (*coll.*) to mutter, mumble.

лопоýх|ий (~, ~а), *adj.* lop-eared.

лопýх, á, *m.* **1.** (*bot.*) burdock. **2.** (*sl.*) fool.

лорд, а, *m.* lord; палáта ~ов House of Lords.

лорд-кáнцлер, а, *m.* Lord Chancellor.

лорд-мэ́р, а, *m.* Lord Mayor.

лорéтк|а, и, *f.* (*obs.*) courtesan, cocotte.

лорнéт, а, *m.* lorgnette.

лорнир|овать, ую, *impf. and pf.* to quiz(z).

лосин|а, ы, *f.* **1.** elk-skin, chamois leather. **2.** (*pl.; hist.*) buckskin breeches. **3.** (*meat*) elk.

лос|иный, *adj. of* ~ь.

лоск, а, *m.* lustre, gloss, shine (*also fig.*); в л. (*coll.*) completely, entirely; пья́ный в л. blind drunk.

лóскут, а, *no pl., m.* (*collect.*) rags, pieces.

лоскýт, á, *pl.* ~ы́, ~óв *and* ~ья́, ~ьéв, *m.* rag, shred, scrap.

лоскýтник, а, *m.* rag merchant, rag dealer.

лоскýтн|ый, *adj.* **1.** scrappy. **2.** made of scraps; ~ая монáрхия *iron. of Austro--Hungarian Empire.*

лосн|и́ться, ю́сь, и́шься, *impf.* to be glossy, shine.

лососи́н|а, ы, *f.* salmon (flesh).

лосóс|ь, я, *pl.* лосóси, лосóсей, *m.* salmon; каспи́йский л. Caspian sea-trout.

лос|ь, я, *pl.* ~и, ~éй, *m.* elk.

лосьóн, а, *m.* lotion.

лот[1], а, *m.* (*naut.*) (sounding-)lead, plummet.

лот[2], а, *m.* (*obs.*) lot (*unit of measurement equivalent to half an ounce or 12·8 gr.*).

лотерé|йный, *adj. of* ~я; л. билéт lottery--ticket.

лотерé|я, и, *f.* lottery, raffle; разы́грывать в ~ю to raffle, dispose of by lottery.

лóтлин|ь, я, *m.* (*naut.*) leadline.

лотó, *indecl., n.* lotto.

лот|óк, ка́, *m.* **1.** hawker's stand; hawker's tray. **2.** chute; gutter; (*tech.*) trough; мéльничный л. mill-race.

лóтос, а, *m.* (*bot.*) lotus.

лотóчник, а, *m.* hawker.

лотóшник, а, *m.* (*coll.*) lotto player, bingo player.

лохáнк|а, и, *f.* (wash-)tub; пóчечная л. (*anat.*) calix (of the kidney).

лохáн|ь, и, *f.* (wash-)tub.

лохмá|тить, чу, тишь, *impf.* (*coll.*) to tousle.

лохмá|титься, чусь, тишься, *impf.* (*coll.*) to become tousled, dishevelled.

лохмáт|ый (~, ~а), *adj.* **1.** shaggy(-haired). **2.** dishevelled, tousled.

лохмóть|я, ев, *no sing.* rags; в ~ях in rags ragged.

лóци|я, и, *f.* (*naut.*) sailing directions.

лóцман, а, *m.* **1.** (*naut.*) pilot. **2.** pilot-fish

лошадёнк|а, и, *f.* (*pejor.*) jade.

лошади́н|ый, *adj.* of horses; ~а дóза (*joc.*) very large dose; ~ая си́ла horse-power.

лошáдк|а, и, *f.* **1.** *dim. of* лóшадь; (*in child' speech*) gee-gee. **2.** hobby-horse; rocking-horse.

лошáдник, а, *m.* (*coll.*) horse-lover.

лóшад|ь, и, *pl.* ~и, ~éй, ~я́м, ~ьми́, ~я́х, horse; беговáя, скаковáя л. race-horse верховáя л. saddle-horse; вью́чная pack-horse; заводнáя л. (*mil.*) led horse завóдская л. stud-horse; кавалери́йская troop-horse, cavalry horse; кореннáя shaft-horse; ломовáя л. dray-horse; при стяжнáя л. outrunner; упряжнáя л. draugh horse; чистокрóвная л. thoroughbred сади́ться на л. to mount; ходи́ть за ~ы to groom a horse.

лошáк, á, *m.* hinny.

лощён|ый, *adj.* glossy, polished; ~ая пря́ж glazed yarn; (*fig.*) ~ые манéры polishe manners; л. молодóй человéк (*coll.*) swell masher.

лощи́н|а, ы, *f.* (*geogr.*) hollow, depressio

лощ|и́ть, у́, и́шь, *impf.* (*of* на~) **1.** to polish **2.** to gloss, glaze.

лоя́льност|ь, и, *f.* fairness; honesty; loyalty

лоя́л|ьный (~ен, ~ьна), *adj.* fair; honest loyal (*to State authorities*).

луб, а, *pl.* ~ья́, ~ьев, *m.* (*bot.*) (lime) bas

луб|óк[1], ка́, *m.* **1.** (*med.*) splint. **2.** strip bast.

луб|óк[2], ка́, *m.* **1.** cheap popular prin **2.** (*fig.*) popular literature.

лубóчный[1], *adj. of* ~óк[1].

лубóчный[2], *adj. of* ~óк[2]; ~óчная карти́нк cheap popular print.

луб|яно́й, *adj. of* ~.

луг, а, о ~е, на ~у́, *pl.* ~á, ~óв, *m.* meadow заливнóй л. water-meadow.

луговóдств|о, а, *n.* grass farming, meadoŵ cultivation.

луг|овóй, *adj. of* ~; л. бéрег lower ban (= *right bank of most rivers in European Russia*) ~овáя собáчка (*zool.*) prairie-dog.

луди́льщик, а, *m.* tinsmith, tinman.

лу|ди́ть, жу́, ~дишь, *impf.* (*of* вы́~ *and* по~ (*tech.*) to tin.

лýж|а, и, *f.* puddle, pool; сесть в ~у (*fig. coll.*) to get into a mess; to slip up.

лужáйк|а, и, *f.* grass-plot, (forest)glade.

лужéни|е, я, *n.* (*tech.*) tinning.

лужён|ый, *adj.* tinned, tin-plate; ~а глóтка (*fig., coll.*) throat of cast iron, iro palate.

луж|о́к, ка́, *m. dim. of* луг.

лу́з|а, ы, *f.* (billiard-)pocket.

лук¹, а, *m.* (*collect.*) onions; зелёный л. spring onions; л.-поре́й leek; голо́вка ⌣а onion.

лук², а, *m.* bow; натяну́ть л. to bend, draw a bow.

лук|а́, и́, *pl.* ⌣и, *f.* **1.** bend (*of river, road, etc.*). **2.** pommel (*of saddle*); за́дняя л. rear arch; пере́дняя л. front arch.

лука́в|ец, ца, *m.* (*coll.*) crafty, sly person; (*joc.*) slyboots.

лука́в|ить, лю, ишь, *impf.* (*of* с⌣) to be cunning.

лука́вств|о, а, *n.* craftiness, slyness.

лука́в|ый (⌣, ⌣а), *adj.* **1.** crafty, sly, cunning; *as noun* л., ⌣ого, *m.* the Evil One. **2.** arch.

лу́ковиц|а, ы, *f.* **1.** an onion. **2.** (*bot., anat.*) bulb. **3.** 'onion' cupola (*of Russian churches*). **4.** (*coll.*) 'turnip' watch.

лу́кови|чный, *adj. of* ⌣ца; bulbous.

лукомо́рь|е, я, *n.* (*poet.*) cove, creek.

луко́ш|ко, ка, *pl.* ⌣ки, ⌣ек, *n.* bast basket; punnet.

лун|а́, ы́, *pl.* ⌣ы, *f.* moon; the Moon.

лунати́зм, а, *m.* sleep-walking, somnambulism.

луна́тик, а, *m.* sleep-walker, somnambulist.

лунати́ческий, *adj.* somnambulistic.

лу́нк|а, и, *f.* hole; (*anat.*) alveolus, socket.

лу́нник¹, а, *m.* (*bot.*) honesty.

лу́нник², а, *m.* lunik, Moon rocket.

лу́н|ный, *adj. of* ⌣а; (*astron.*) lunar; л. год lunar year; ⌣ное затме́ние lunar eclipse; ⌣ная ночь moonlit night; л. свет moonlight; л. ка́мень (*min.*) moonstone.

лунохо́д, а, *m.* Moon research vehicle.

лун|ь, я́, *m.* (*orn.*) harrier; полево́й л. hen-harrier; седо́й, бе́лый, как л. white as snow (*of hair*).

лу́п|а, ы, *f.* magnifying glass.

лупи́н, а, *m.* (*bot.*) lupin(e).

луп|и́ть¹, лю, ⌣ишь, *impf.* **1.** (*pf.* об⌣) to peel; to bark. **2.** (*pf.* с⌣) (*coll.*) to fleece; л. с кого́-н. втри́дорога to make someone pay through the nose.

луп|и́ть², лю, ⌣ишь, *impf.* (*of* от⌣) (*coll.*) to thrash, flog.

луп|и́ться, ⌣ится, *impf.* (*of* об⌣) to peel (off), scale; (*coll.*) to come off, chip (*of paint, plaster, etc.*).

лупогла́зый, *adj.* (*coll.*) pop-eyed, goggle-eyed.

лупц|ева́ть, у́ю, *impf.* (*of* от⌣) (*coll.*) to beat, flog.

луч, а́, *m.* ray; beam; рентге́новские, рентге́новы ⌣й X-rays; л. наде́жды (*fig.*) ray, gleam of hope.

луч|ево́й, *adj.* **1.** *adj. of* ⌣. **2.** radial. **3.** (*anat.*) ⌣ева́я кость radius. **4.** (*med.*) ⌣ева́я боле́знь radiation sickness.

лучеза́р|ный (⌣ен, ⌣на), *adj.* (*poet.*) radiant, resplendent.

лучи́н|а, ы, *f.* **1.** splinter, chip (*of kindling wood; also collect.*). **2.** torch (*for lighting peasant hut*).

лучи́ст|ый (⌣, ⌣а), *adj.* **1.** radiant (*also fig. and phys.*); л. грибо́к (*med.*) Actinomyces. **2.** radial.

луч|и́ть, у́, и́шь, *impf.* л. ры́бу to spear fish (*at night, with the aid of torch-light*).

луч|и́ться, и́тся, *impf.* (*poet.*) to shine brightly, sparkle.

лучко́в|ый, *adj.* bow-shaped; ⌣ая пила́ frame-saw.

лу́чник, а, *m.* (*hist.*) archer.

лу́чше, *adj. and adv.* **1.** (*comp. of* хоро́ший *and* хорошо́) better; тем л. so much the better; л. всего́, л. всех best of all; как мо́жно л. as well as possible, to the best of one's abilities; (*pred.*) it is better; л. ли вам сего́дня? are you better today?; л. не спра́шивай better not ask; нам л. верну́ться we had better go back. **2.** *as particle* rather, instead; ты им говори́ или, л., я позвоню́ you talk to them, or, rather, I'll give them a ring; дава́йте л. поговори́м об э́том let's talk it over instead.

лу́чш|ий, *adj.* (*comp. and superl. of* хоро́ший) better; best; к ⌣ему for the better; в ⌣ем слу́чае at best; всего́ ⌣его! all the best!

лущ|и́ть, у́, и́шь, *impf.* **1.** (*pf.* об⌣) to shell, hull, pod (*peas, etc.*); to crack (*nuts*). **2.** (*pf.* вз⌣) to remove stubble (from).

лы́ж|а, и, *f.* ski; snow-shoe; бе́гать, ходи́ть на ⌣ах to ski; навостри́ть ⌣и (*fig.*) to take to one's heels, show a clean pair of heels; напра́вить ⌣и (*fig.*) to head (for).

лы́жник, а, *m.* skier.

лы́ж|ный, *adj. of* ⌣а; л. спуск ski-run.

лыжн|я́, и́, *f.* ski-track.

лы́к|о, а, *pl.* ⌣и, *n.* bast; драть л. to bark lime-trees; не вся́кое л. в стро́ку one must make allowances; я не ⌣ом шит I was not born yesterday; ⌣а не вя́жет (*of the incoherent speech of a drunk person*).

лысе́|ть, ю, *impf.* (*of* об ⌣ *and* по⌣) to grow bald.

лы́син|а, ы, *f.* bald spot, bald patch; star (*on horse's forehead*).

лысу́х|а, и, *f.* (*orn.*) coot.

лы́с|ый (⌣, ⌣а́, ⌣о), *adj.* bald.

ль = ли.

льв|ёнок, ёнка, *pl.* ⌣я́та, ⌣я́т, *m.* young lion, lion cub.

льви́н|ый, *adj. of* лев¹; ⌣ая до́ля (*fig.*) the lion's share; (*bot.*) л. зев, ⌣ая пасть snap-dragon; л. зуб dandelion.

льви́ц|а, ы, *f.* lioness.

льв|я́та, *pl. of* ~ёнок.

льго́т|а, ы, *f.* privilege; advantage,

льго́тник, а, *m.* (*coll.*) privileged person.

льго́тн|ый, *adj.* privileged; favourable; л. биле́т privilege ticket, free ticket; ~ые дни (*comm.*) days of grace; на ~ых усло́виях on preferential terms.

льда́, *g. sing. of* лёд.

льди́н|а, ы, *f.* block of ice, ice-floe.

льди́нк|а, и, *f.* piece of ice.

льди́стый, *adj.* icy; ice-covered.

льна, льну, *see* лён.

льново́д, а, *m.* flax grower.

льново́дств|о, а, *n.* flax growing.

льнопряде́ни|е, я, *n.* flax spinning.

льнопряди́льн|ый, *adj.* flax-spinning; ~ая фа́брика flax-mill.

льнопряди́л|ьня, ьни, *g. pl.* ~ен, *f.* flax--mill.

льнотереби́лк|а, и, *f.* (*agric.*) flax puller.

льнотрепа́лк|а, и, *f.* (*agric.*) scutching--sword; swingling machine.

льнуть, льну, льнёшь, *impf.* (*of* при~) (к) 1. to cling (to), stick (to). 2. (*fig., coll.*) to have a weakness (for). 3. (*fig., coll.*) to make up (to), (*sl.*) try to get in (with).

льня́н|о́й, *adj.* 1. of flax; ~о́е ма́сло linseed--oil; ~о́е се́мя linseed, flax-seed; ~о́го цве́та flaxen. 2. linen; ~а́я промы́шленность linen industry.

льсте́ц, а́, *m.* flatterer.

льсти́в|ый (~, ~а), *adj.* flattering; (*of a person*) smooth-tongued.

льстить, льщу, льстишь, *impf.* (*of* по~) 1. (+*dat.*) to flatter; to gratify; э́то льстит его́ самолю́бию it flatters his self-esteem; 2. (+*a.,* *with reflexive pron. only*) to delude; л. себя́ наде́ждой to flatter oneself with the hope.

льсти́ться, льщусь, льсти́шься, *impf.* (*of* по~) (на+*a., obs.*+*i.*) to be tempted (by).

лью, льёшь, *see* лить.

люб, ~а́, ~о, *adj.* (*pred. only; coll.*) dear; pleasant; ~о (+*inf.*) it is pleasant (to); ~о-до́рого it is a real pleasure.

любвеоби́л|ьный (~ен, ~ьна), *adj.* loving; full of love.

любе́знича|ть, ю, *impf.* (с+*i.*) (*coll.*) 1. to pay compliments (to); to pay court (to). 2. to stand on ceremony (with).

любе́зность|ь, и, *f.* 1. courtesy; politeness, civility. 2. kindness; оказа́ть, сде́лать кому́-н. л. to do someone a kindness. 3. compliment; говори́ть ~и кому́-н. to pay someone compliments.

любе́з|ный (~ен, ~на), *adj.* 1. courteous; polite; obliging. 2. kind, amiable; л. чита́тель gentle reader; бу́дьте ~ны... (*polite form of request*) be so kind as .... 3. (*obs.*) dear; (*as mode of address to inferior*)

my (good) man. 4. *as noun* л., ~ного, *m.,* ~ная, ~ной, *f.* (*coll. and folk poet.*) beloved.

люби́м|ец, ца, *m.* pet, favourite.

люби́мчик, а, *m.* (*coll., pejor.*) favourite.

люби́м|ый (~, ~а), *adj.* 1. beloved, loved. 2. favourite.

люби́тел|ь, я, *m.* 1. (+*g. or* +*inf.*) lover; л. му́зыки music-lover; л. соба́к dog--fancier; он л. спле́тничать he loves gossiping. 2. amateur.

люби́тельский, *adj.* 1. amateur; л. спекта́кль amateur performance. 2. amateurish. 3. choice.

люби́тельств|о, а, *n.* amateurishness.

люб|и́ть, лю, ~ишь, *impf.* 1. to love. 2. to like, be fond (of). 3. (*of plants, etc.*) (*coll.*) to need, require, like; фиа́лки ~ят тень violets like shade.

люб|ова́ться, у́юсь, *impf.* (*of* по~) (+*i.* на+*a.*) to admire; to feast one's eyes (upon); л. на себя́ в зе́ркало to admire oneself in the looking-glass.

любо́вник, а, *m.* 1. lover. 2. (*theatr.*) jeune premier.

любо́вниц|а, ы, *f.* mistress.

любо́вн|ый, *adj.* 1. love-; ~ая исто́рия love-affair; л. напи́ток love-potion; ~ое письмо́ love-letter. 2. loving.

люб|о́вь, ви́, *i.* ~о́вью, *f.* (к) love (for, of); де́лать что-н. с ~о́вью to do something with enthusiasm, con amore.

любозна́тел|ьный (~ен, ~ьна), *adj.* inquisitive.

любо́й 1. *adj.* any; either (*of two*); л. цено́й at any price. 2. *as noun* anyone.

любопы́т|ный (~ен, ~на), *adj.* (*in var. senses*) curious; interesting; *as noun* л., ~ного, *m.* curious, inquisitive person; (*impers.;* +*d. and inf.*) ~но знать, что с ним ста́ло it would be interesting to know what happened to him; мне ~но слу́шать, о чём они́ спо́рят I am curious to hear what they are arguing about; ~но, придёт ли она́ I wonder if she will come.

любопы́тств|о, а, *n.* curiosity; пра́здное л. idle curiosity.

любопы́тств|овать, ую, *impf.* (*of* по~) to be curious.

любостяжа́ни|е, я, *n.* (*obs.*) cupidity.

люб|я́щий, *pres. part. act. of* ~и́ть *and adj.* loving, affectionate; л. вас (*in letters*) yours affectionately.

лю́гер, а, *m.* (*naut.*) lugger.

люд, а, *m.* (*collect.; coll.*) people; рабо́чий л. working-people.

люд|и, е́й, ~ям, ~ьми, о ~ях, *no sing.* 1. (*pl. of* челове́к) people; вы́биться, вы́йти в л. to rise in the world, get on in life; вы́вести кого́-н. в л. to put someone on his feet, set someone up; уйти́ в л. to go away from home (*to work*); на ∼я́х in the presence of others, in company; на ∼я́х и смерть красна́ (*prov.*) two in distress make sorrow less. **2.** (*mil.*) men. **3.** (*obs.*) servants.

лю́д|ный (∼ен, ∼на), *adj.* **1.** populous, thickly-populated. **2.** crowded.

людое́д, а, *m.* **1.** cannibal. **2.** ogre.

людое́дств|о, а, *n.* cannibalism.

людск|а́я, о́й, *f.* (*obs.*) servants' hall.

людск|о́й, *adj.* **1.** human; ∼и́е пересу́ды talk of the town. **2.** (*mil.*) л. соста́в personnel, effectives. **3.** (*obs.*) servants'.

люизи́т, а, *m.* (*chem.*) lewisite.

люк, а, *m.* **1.** (*naut.*) hatch hatchway. **2.** (*theatr.*) trap. **3.** световóй л. sky-light.

люкс¹, а, *m.* (*phys.*) lux (*unit of light*).

люкс², *indecl. adj.* de luxe, luxury.

лю́льк|а¹, и, *f.* cradle.

лю́льк|а², и, *f.* (*dial.*) pipe.

люмба́го, *indecl.*, *n.* lumbago.

люмина́л, а, *m.* (*pharm.*) luminal.

люминесце́нтн|ый, *adj.* luminescent; ∼ые ла́мпы fluorescent lighting.

люминесце́нци|я, и, *f.* (*phys.*) luminescence.

лю́мпен-пролетариа́т, а, *m.* Lumpenproletariat.

люне́т, а, *m.* **1.** (*mil.*) lunette. **2.** (*tech.*) rest, support, collar plate.

лю́рик, а, *m.* (*orn.*) little auk.

лю́стр|а, ы, *f.* chandelier.

люстри́н, а, *m.* lustrine, lutestring.

люстри́н|овый, *adj. of* ∼.

лютера́н|ин, ина, *pl.* ∼е, ∼, *m.* (*rel.*) Lutheran.

лютера́нский, *adj.* (*rel.*) Lutheran.

лютера́нств|о, а, *n.* (*rel.*) Lutheranism.

лю́тик, а, *m.* (*bot.*) buttercup.

лю́тиков|ые, ых, (*bot.*) ranunculi.

лю́тн|евый, *adj. of* ∼я.

лю́тн|я, ни, *g. pl.* ∼ен, *f.* (*mus.*) lute.

лю́т|ый (∼, ∼а́, ∼о), *adj.* ferocious, fierce, cruel (*also fig.*).

люф|а́, ы́, *f.* (*bot.*) loofah.

люце́рн|а, ы, *f.* (*bot.*) lucerne.

лю́эс, а, *m.* (*med.*) syphilis.

люэти́ческий, *adj.* (*med.*) syphilitic.

ля, *indecl.*, *n.* (*mus.*) A; ля дие́з A sharp; ля бемо́ль A flat.

ляг(те), *imp. of* лечь.

ляга́вая = лега́вая.

ляг|а́ть, а́ю, *impf.* (*of* ∼ну́ть) to kick.

ляга́|ться, юсь, *impf.* to kick (*intrans.*); to kick one another.

ляг|ну́ть, ну́, нёшь, *inst. pf. of* ∼а́ть.

ля́|гу, жешь, гут, *see* лечь.

лягуш|а́чий (*and* ∼ечий), *adj. of* ∼ка.

лягу́шк|а, и, *f.* frog.

лягуш|о́нок, о́нка, *pl.* ∼а́та, ∼а́т, *m.* young frog.

ляд, а, *m.* (*coll.*) на кой л.? what the devil, why the devil?; ну его́ к ∼у! to hell with him!

ляду́нк|а, и, *f.* cartridge-pouch.

ля́жк|а, и, *f.* thigh, haunch.

лязг, а, *no pl.*, *m.* clank, clang; clack (*of teeth*).

ля́зга|ть, ю, *impf.* (+*i.*) to clank, clang; он ∼л зуба́ми his teeth were chattering; л. це́пью to rattle a chain.

ля́мз|ить, ю, ишь, *impf.* (*of* с∼) (*sl.*) to pinch (= to steal).

ля́мк|а, и, *f.* strap; тяну́ть ∼ами, на ∼ах to tow, take in tow; тяну́ть ∼у (*fig.*, *coll.*) to toil, sweat, be engaged in drudgery.

ля́п|ать, аю, *impf.* (*coll.*) **1.** (*pf.* на∼) to make hastily *or* any old how. **2.** *impf. of* ∼нуть.

ля́пис, а, *m.* (*chem.*) lunar caustic, silver nitrate.

ля́пис-лазу́р|ь, и, *f.* lapis lazuli.

ля́п|нуть, ну, нешь, *pf.* (*of* ∼ать) (*coll.*) **1.** to blurt out, blunder out. **2.** to strike, slap; л. кого́-н. по́ уху to box someone's ears.

ля́псус, а, *m.* blunder, lapsus; slip (of tongue, pen).

ля́сы, *only in phrase* (*coll.*) точи́ть л. to chatter, talk idly.

лях, а, *m.* (*hist.*) Pole.

M

мавзоле́|й, я, *m.* mausoleum.

мавр, а, *m.* Moor.

маврита́нский, *adj.* **1.** Moorish; (*archit.*, *etc.*) Moresque. **2.** Mauritanian.

ма́врский, *adj.* (*obs.*) Moorish.

маг, а, *m.* **1.** (*hist.*) magus; Magian. **2.** magician, wizard.

магази́н, а, *m.* **1.** shop; универса́льный м. department store. **2.** (*obs.*) store, depot; (*mil.*) magazine. **3.** (*in fire-arm*) magazine.

магази́н|ный, *adj. of* ∼; ∼ная коро́бка magazine (*of fire-arm*)

магази́нщик, а, *m.* **1.** (*coll.*, *obs.*) shop-keeper. **2.** (*sl.*) shop-lifter.

магара́дж|а, и, *m.* Maharaja(h).

магары́ч, а́, *m.* (*coll.*) entertainment (*provided by person on . making a good bargain*); wetting a bargain; поста́вить м. to stand a round (of drinks); с вас м.! you owe us a drink!

маги́ст|ерский, *adj. of* ~р 3.
магист|е́рский, *adj. of* ~р 1, 2.
маги́стр, а, *m.* 1. holder of a master's degree. 2. master's degree. 3. head of a knightly *or* monastic order.
магистра́л|ь, и, *f.* main; main line; га́зовая м. gas main; доро́жная м. arterial road; железнодоро́жная м. main railway line.
магистра́ль|ный, *adj. of* ~; м. локомоти́в long-haul locomotive.
магистра́т, а, *m.* city, town council.
магистрату́р|а, ы, *f.* magistracy.
маги́ческий, *adj.* magic(al).
ма́ги|я, и, *f.* magic.
магна́т, а, *m.* 1. (*hist.*) member of Upper House of Diet in Poland *or* Hungary. 2. magnate.
магнези́т, а, *m.* (*min.*) magnesite.
магне́зи|я, и, *f.* (*chem.*) magnesia.
магнетизёр, а, *m.* (*obs.*) mesmerist.
магнетизи́р|овать, ую, *impf.* (*obs.*) to mesmerize.
магнети́зм, а, *m.* 1. magnetism. 2. (*phys.*) magnetics. 3. (*obs.*) hypnotism.
магнети́т, а, *m.* (*min.*) magnetite.
магнети́ческий, *adj.* magnetic.
магне́то, *indecl., n.* (*tech.*) magneto.
магнетро́н, а, *m.* (*radio*) magnetron.
ма́гниевый, *adj.* magnesium.
ма́гни|й, я, *m.* (*chem.*) magnesium.
магни́т, а, *m.* magnet.
магни́тный, *adj.* magnetic; м. железня́к magnetite, loadstone.
магнитофо́н, а, *m.* tape-recorder, tape-recording machine.
магнитофо́н|ный, *adj. of* ~; ~ная за́пись tape-recording.
магни́то-электри́ческий, *adj.* electro-magnetic.
магно́ли|я, и, *f.* (*bot.*) magnolia.
магомета́н|ин, ина, *pl.* ~е, ~, *m.* Mohammedan.
магомета́нств|о, а, *n.* Mohammedanism.
мада́м, *indecl., f.* 1. madam(e). 2. (*obs., coll.*) governess. 3. (*obs.*) dressmaker.
мадемуазе́л|ь, и, *f.* 1. mademoiselle. 2. (*obs., coll.*) governess.
маде́р|а, ы, *f.* Madeira (*wine*).
мадо́нн|а, ы, *f.* madonna.
мадрига́л, а, *m.* madrigal.
madья́р, а, *pl.* ~ы, ~, *m.* Magyar.
мадья́рский, *adj.* Magyar.
маёвк|а, и, *f.* 1. May-Day meeting (*workers' gathering on 1 May, illegal before the 1917 Russian revolution*). 2. spring-time outing, picnic.
мает|а́, ы́, *f.* (*coll.*) trouble, bother.
мажо́р, а, *m.* 1. (*mus.*) major key. 2. (*fig.*) a cheerful mood; быть в ~е to be in high spirits.
мажордо́м, а, *m.* major-domo.

мажо́рный, *adj.* 1. (*mus.*) major. 2. (*fig.*) cheerful.
ма́занк|а, и, *f.* (*dial.*) cottage of daubed brick or wood (*esp. in S. Russia*).
ма́заный, *adj.* 1. (*coll.*) dirty, stained, soiled. 2. adobe.
ма́|зать, жу, жешь, *impf.* 1. (*pf.* на~, по~) to oil, grease, lubricate. 2. (*pf.* вы́~, на~, по~) to smear (with), anoint (with); м. хлеб ма́слом to spread butter on bread, butter bread; м. по губа́м (*fig., coll.*) to excite false expectations. 3. (*pf.* за~, из~; *coll.*) to soil, stain. 4. (*pf.* на~; *coll.*) to daub. 5. (*pf.* про~²; *coll.*) to miss (*in shooting, football, etc.*).
ма́|заться, жусь, жешься, *impf.* 1. (*pf.* вы́~, за~, из~) to soil oneself, stain oneself. 2. (*coll.*) to soil, stain (*of objects; intrans.*). 3. (*pf.* на~, по~) to make up; она́ си́льно ~жется (*coll.*) she makes up heavily.
мази́лк|а¹, и, *f.* paint-brush.
мази́лк|а², и, *m. and f.* (*coll., pejor.*) dauber.
ма́з|кий (~ок, ~ка́, ~ко), *adj.* (*coll.*) liable to stain, soil (*of newly-painted wall, etc.*).
мазн|у́ть, у́, ёшь, *pf.* 1. to dab. 2. (*coll.*) to hit.
мазн|я́, и́, *f.* (*coll.*) 1. daub. 2. poor play.
маз|о́к, ка́, *m.* 1. dab; stroke (*of paint-brush*); класть после́дние ~ки́ (*fig.*) to put the finishing touches. 2. (*med.*) smear (*for microscopic examination*). 3. (*coll.*) miss (*in shooting, football, etc.*).
мазохи́зм, а, *m.* (*med.*) masochism.
мазохи́ст, а, *m.* masochist.
мазу́рик, а, *m.* (*sl.*) rogue, swindler.
мазу́рк|а, и, *f.* mazurka.
мазу́т, а, *m.* (*tech.*) fuel oil.
маз|ь, и, *f.* 1. ointment. 2. grease; де́ло на ~и́ (*fig., coll.*) things are going swimmingly.
маи́с, а, *m.* maize.
маи́с|овый, *adj. of* ~; ~овая ка́ша polenta.
ма́|й, я, *m.* May.
майда́н, а, *m.* 1. public square. 2. (*sl.*) gambling-den (*in bazaar or prison*).
ма́йк|а, и, *f.* T-shirt, sports-jersey; vest.
ма́йна, *interj.* (*naut.*) heave ho!
майо́лик|а, и, *f.* majolica.
майоне́з, а, *m.* (*cul.*) mayonnaise.
майо́р, а, *m.* major (*mil. rank*).
майора́н, а, *m.* (*bot.*) marjoram.
майора́т, а, *m.* (*leg.*) 1. (right of) primogeniture. 2. entailed estate.
майо́р|ский, *adj. of* ~.
ма́й|ский, *adj. of* ~; м. жук may-bug, cockchafer.
мак, а, *m.* 1. poppy. 2. (*collect.*) poppy-seed.
мака́к|а, и, *f.* (*zool.*) macaque.
мака́о, *indecl.* 1. *m.* (*orn.*) macaw. 2. *n.* macao (*gambling game*).
макарони́зм, а, *m.* (*lit.*) macaronism.
макарони́ческий, *adj.* (*lit.*) macaronic.

макаро́нник, а, *m.* baked macaroni pudding.

макаро́н|ный, *adj. of* ~ы.

макаро́н|ы, ~, *sing.* ~а, ~ы, *f.* macaroni.

мак|а́ть, а́ю, *impf. (of* ~ну́ть) to dip.

македо́н|ец, ца, *m.* Macedonian.

македо́нский, *adj.* Macedonian; Алекса́ндр ~ Alexander the Great.

маке́т, а, *m.* 1. model. 2. (*mil.*) dummy.

макиавелли́зм, а, *m.* Machiavellianism.

макиавеллисти́ческий, *adj.* Machiavellian.

макинто́ш, а, *m.* mackintosh.

макла́к, а́, *m.* (*obs.*) 1. second-hand dealer. 2. jobber, middleman.

макла́честв|о, а, *n.* (*obs.*) 1. second-hand dealing. 2. jobbing.

ма́клер, а, *m.* (*comm.*) broker.

ма́клерств|о, а, *n.* (*comm.*) brokerage.

мак|ну́ть, ну́, нёшь, *pf. of* ~а́ть.

ма́ковк|а, и, *f.* 1. poppy-head. 2. (*coll.*) crown (*of head*). 3. (*coll.*) cupola.

ма́к|овый, *adj. of* ~; *as noun* ~о́вые, ~о́вых (*bot.*) Papaveraceae; (*fig., coll.*) как ~ов цвет blooming, ruddy (*of complexion*).

макре́л|ь, и, *f.* mackerel.

макроко́см, а, *m.* macrocosm.

макроскопи́ческий, *adj.* macroscopic.

макроцефа́ли|я, и, *f.* (*anthrop.*) macrocephalism.

макси́м, а, *m.* Maxim gun.

ма́ксим|а, ы, *f.* maxim.

максимали́зм, а, *m.* (*hist.*) maximalism.

максимали́ст, а, *m.* (*hist.*) maximalist.

максима́льный, *adj.* maximum.

макси́мк|а, и, *f.* (*coll.*) slow train.

ма́ксимум, а, *m.* 1. maximum. 2. *as adv.* at most; м. сто рубле́й a hundred roubles at most.

макулату́р|а, ы, *f.* 1. (*typ.*) spoiled sheet(s), spoilage. 2. (*fig.*) pulp literature.

маку́шк|а, и, *f.* 1. top, summit. 2. crown (*of head*); у нас у́шки на ~е (*fig.*) we are on the qui vive, on our guard.

мала́г|а, и, *f.* Malaga (wine).

мала́|ец, йца, *m.* Malay.

мала́йский, *adj.* Malay, Malayan.

малаха́|й, я, *m.* (*dial.*) malakhai (= 1. *fur cap with large ear-flaps.* 2. *beltless caftan*).

малахи́т, а, *m.* (*min.*) malachite.

мал|ева́ть, юю, юешь, *impf. (of* на~) 1. (*coll.*) to paint; не так стра́шен чёрт, как его́ ~ю́ют (*prov.*) the devil is not so black as he is painted.

мале́йший, *adj.* (*superl. of* ма́лый) least, slightest.

мал|ёк, ька́, *m.* young fish; (*collect.*) fry.

ма́леньк|ий, *adj.* 1. little, small; ~ие лю́ди humble folk. 2. slight; diminutive; игра́ть по ~ой to play for small stakes. 3. young; *as noun* м., ~ого, *m.*; ~ая, ~ой, *f.* the baby, the child; ~ие the young.

мале́нько, *adv.* (*coll.*) a little, a bit.

ма́л|ец, ьца-ьца́, *m.* (*coll.*) lad, boy.

мали́н|а, ы, *no pl., f.* 1. (*collect.*) raspberries. 2. raspberry-bush; raspberry-cane. 3. raspberry juice. 4. *fig., coll. of something pleasurable* (*cf.* a piece of cake); у нас житьё — м. we are in clover.

мали́нник, а, *no pl., m.* raspberry-canes.

мали́н|ный, *adj. of* ~а.

мали́новк|а¹, и, *f.* (*orn.*) robin (redbreast).

мали́новк|а², и, *f.* (*coll.*) raspberry-flavoured vodka.

мали́новый¹, *adj.* 1. raspberry. 2. crimson.

мали́новый², *adj. only in phrase* м. звон mellow chime.

ма́лк|а, и, *f.* (*tech.*) bevel.

ма́ло, *adv.* little, few; not enough; у нас м. вре́мени we have little time; э́того ма́ло this is not enough; об э́том м. кто зна́ет few (people) know about it; я м. где быва́л I have been in few places; м. ли что! what does it matter!; м. ли что мо́жет случи́ться who knows what may happen, anything may happen; м. того́ moreover; м. того́, что... not only...., it is not enough that... ; м. того́, что он сам прие́хал, он привёз всех това́рищей it was not enough that he came himself, but he had to bring all his friends.

малоазиа́тский, *adj.* of Asia Minor.

малоблагоприя́т|ный (~ен, ~на), *adj.* unfavourable.

малова́ж|ный (~ен, ~на), *adj.* of little importance, insignificant.

малова́т (~а, ~о), *adj.* (*coll.*) on the small side; м. ро́стом undersized.

малова́то, *adv.* (*coll.*) not quite enough; not very much.

малове́р, а, *m.* sceptic.

малове́ри|е, я, *n.* lack of faith, scepticism.

малове́р|ный (~ен, ~на), *adj.* lacking faith, lacking conviction, sceptical.

маловеро́ят|ный (~ен, ~на), *adj.* unlikely, improbable.

малове́с|ный (~ен, ~на), *adj.* light-weight; (*comm.*) light, short-weight.

маловодный, *adj.* containing little water; shallow; dry (*of land*).

маловодь|е, я, *n.* 1. shortage of water. 2. low water-level, shallowness.

малов́ыгод|ный (~ен, ~на), *adj.* unprofitable, unrewarding.

малоговоря́щий, *adj.* not enlightening, not illuminating.

малогра́мот|ный (~ен, ~на), *adj.* 1. semi-literate. 2. crude, ignorant.

малодействи́тел|ьный (~ен, ~ьна), *adj.* ineffective.

малодоказа́тел|ьный (~ен, ~ьна), *adj.* not persuasive, unconvincing.

малодостове́р|ный (~ен, ~на), *adj.* improbable; not well-founded.

малодохо́д|ный (~ен, ~на), *adj.* unprofitable.

малоду́шеств|овать, ую, *impf.* to lose heart; to be faint-hearted.

малоду́ши|е, я, *n.* faint-heartedness, pusillanimity.

малоду́ш|ный (~ен, ~на), *adj.* faint-hearted, pusillanimous.

малое́зжен(н)ый, *adj.* 1. (*of horse, etc.*) little ridden; (*of carriage*) little used. 2. (*of road*) little used, unfrequented.

малое́зж|ий, *adj.* = ~ен(н)ый 2.

малозаме́т|ный (~ен, ~на), *adj.* 1. barely visible, barely noticeable. 2. ordinary, undistinguished.

малоземе́ль|е, я, *n.* shortage of (arable) land.

малоземе́льный, *adj.* having insufficient (arable) land.

малознако́м|ый (~, ~а), *adj.* little known, unfamiliar.

малозначи́тел|ьный (~ен, ~ьна), *adj.* of little significance, of little importance.

малоиму́щ|ий (~, ~а), *adj.* needy, indigent.

малокали́берный, *adj.* small-calibre; (*of fire-arm*) small-bore.

малокро́ви|е, я, *n.* anaemia.

малокро́в|ный (~ен, ~на), *adj.* anaemic.

малоле́т|ний, *adj.* 1. young; juvenile. 2. *as noun* м., ~его, *m.* infant; juvenile, minor.

малоле́тств|о, а, *n.* infancy; nonage, minority.

малолитра́жк|а, и, *f.* (*coll.*) car with small cylinder capacity, mini-car.

малолитра́жный, *adj.* of small (cylinder) capacity.

малолю́дность|ь, и, *f.* scarcity of people; poor attendance (*at meeting, etc.*).

малолю́д|ный (~ен, ~на), *adj.* 1. not crowded, unfrequented; ~ное собра́ние poorly attended meeting. 2. thinly populated.

малолю́д|ье, ья, *n.* = ~ность.

ма́ло-ма́льски, *adv.* (*coll.*) in the slightest degree, at all.

малома́льский, *adj.* (*coll.*) slightest, most insignificant.

маломо́ч|ный (~ен, ~на), *adj.* (*econ.*) having small resources; ~ные крестья́не poor peasants.

маломо́щ|ный (~ен, ~на), *adj.* lacking power; ~ное предприя́тие small concern.

малонадёжный, *adj.* unreliable, undependable.

малонаселённый, *adj.* thinly, sparsely populated.

малообщи́тел|ьный (~ен, ~ьна), *adj.* unsociable, uncommunicative.

малооснова́тел|ьный (~ен, ~ьна), *adj.* 1. unfounded. 2. (*of person*) undependable.

малоподви́ж|ный (~ен, ~на), *adj.* not mobile, slow-moving.

малоподе́ржанный, *adj.* little used, almost unused.

ма́ло-пома́лу, *adv.* (*coll.*) little by little, bit by bit.

малопоня́тлив|ый (~, ~а), *adj.* (*coll.*) not very bright, slow in the uptake.

малопоня́т|ный (~ен, ~на), *adj.* hard to understand; obscure.

малоприбы́л|ьный (~ен, ~ьна), *adj.* bringing little profit, of little profit.

малоприго́д|ный (~ен, ~на), *adj.* of little use.

малоразви́т|ый (~, ~а), *adj.* 1. undeveloped. 2. underdeveloped. 3. uneducated.

малоразгово́рчив|ый (~, ~а), *adj.* taciturn.

малоро́сл|ый (~, ~а), *adj.* undersized, stunted.

малоро́сс, а, *m.* (*obs.*) Little Russian (*Ukrainian*).

малоросси́йский, *adj.* (*obs.*) Little Russian (*Ukrainian*).

малоросси́я́н|ин, ина, *pl.* ~е, *m.* = малоро́сс.

мало|ру́сский, *adj.* = ~росси́йский.

малосве́дущ|ий (~, ~а), *adj.* ill-informed.

малосеме́йный, *adj.* having a small family.

малоси́л|ьный (~ен, ~ьна), *adj.* 1. weak, feeble. 2. (*tech.*) low-powered.

малосодержа́тел|ьный (~ен, ~ьна), *adj.* uninteresting; (*fig.*) empty, shallow.

малосо́л|ьный (~ен, ~ьна), *adj.* slightly, inadequately salted.

малосостоя́тел|ьный[1] (~ен, ~ьна), *adj.* poor, poorer.

малосостоя́тел|ьный[2] (~ен, ~ьна), *adj.* unconvincing.

ма́лост|ь, и, *f.* (*coll.*) 1. a bit; trifle, bagatelle. 2. *as adv.* a little, a bit; м. поспа́ть to take a nap.

малосуще́ствен|ный (~, ~на), *adj.* of small importance, immaterial.

малотира́жный, *adj.* of small circulation, published in a small number of copies.

малоубеди́тел|ьный (~ен, ~ьна), *adj.* unconvincing.

малоупотреби́тел|ьный (~ен, ~ьна), *adj.* infrequent, rarely used.

малоуспе́ш|ный (~ен, ~на), *adj.* unsuccessful.

малоце́н|ный (~ен, ~на), *adj.* of little value.

малочи́сленност|ь, и, *f.* small number; paucity.

малочи́слен|ный (~, ~на), *adj.* small (in numbers); scanty.

мáл|ый[1] (∼, ∼á, ∼ó), *adj.* little, (too) small; м. рóстом short, of small stature; м. ход! (*naut.*) slow speed (ahead)!; эти сапоги мне ∼ы́ these boots are too small for me; ∼ ∼á мéньше (*coll.*) *of children of one family, viewed in descending order of size*; от ∼а до велика young and old (*i.e. all, regardless of age*); по ∼ой мéре at least; с ∼ых лет from childhood; *as noun* ∼ое, ∼ого, *n.* little; сáмое ∼ое (*coll.*) at the least; без ∼ого almost, all but; за ∼ым дéло стáло (*frequently iron.*) one small thing is lacking.

мáл|ый[2], **ого**, *m.* (*coll.*) fellow, chap; lad, boy.

малы́ш, **á**, *m.* (*coll.*) child, kid; little boy.

мáльв|а, **ы**, *f.* (*bot.*) mallow, hollyhock.

мальв|á, **ы́**, *f.* (*collect., coll.*) children, kids.

мальвáзи|я, **и**, *f.* malmsey (*wine*).

мальти́|ец, **йца**, *m.* Maltese.

мальти́йский, *adj.* Maltese.

мальтузиáнский, *adj.* Malthusian.

мальтузиáнств|о, **а**, *n.* Malthusianism.

мáльчик, **а**, *m.* 1. boy, lad; (male) child; м. с пáльчик Tom Thumb. 2. (*obs.*) apprentice.

мальчикóвый, *adj.* boy's, boys'.

мальчи́шеский, *adj.* 1. boyish. 2. (*pejor.*) childish, puerile.

мальчи́шеств|о, **а**, *n.* boyishness; (*pejor.*) childishness.

мальчи́шк|а, **и**, *m.* (*coll.*) urchin, boy; в сравнéнии с однокла́ссниками он м. by comparison with his class-mates he is a child.

мальчи́шник, **а**, *m.* stag-party.

мальчугáн, **а**, *m.* (*coll., affect.*) little boy.

малюсенький, *adj.* (*coll.*) tiny, wee.

малю́тк|а, **и**, *m. and f.* baby, little one.

маля́р, **á**, *m.* (house-)painter, decorator.

маляри́йный, *adj.* malarial.

маляри́|я, **и**, *f.* (*med.*) malaria.

маля́р|ный, *adj. of* ∼.

мáм|а, **ы**, *f.* mummy, mamma.

мамалы́г|а, **и**, *f.* (*dial.*) polenta.

мамáш|а, **и**, *f.* (*coll.*) mummy, mamma.

мамелю́к, **а**, *m.* (*hist.*) Mameluke.

мáменькин, *adj.* mother's; м. сынóк (*coll., iron.*) mother's darling.

мáмин, *adj.* mother's.

мáмк|а, **и**, *f.* (*obs.*) (wet-)nurse.

мамóн|а, **ы**, *f.* mammon.

мáмонт, **а**, *m.* mammoth.

мáмонт|овый, *adj. of* ∼; ∼овое дéрево (*bot.*) sequoia, Wellingtonia.

мáмочк|а, **и**, *f.* (*coll.*) mummy.

манáт|ки, **ок**, *no sing.* (*sl.*) possessions, goods and chattels.

манáт|ья, **ьи́**, *g. pl.* ∼éй, *f.* monk's habit.

мангани́т, **а**, *m.* (*min.*) manganite.

мáнго, *indecl., n.* (*bot.*) mango.

мáнго|вый, *adj. of* ∼.

мáнгровый, *adj.* (*bot.*) mangrove.

мангýст|а, **ы**, *f.* (*zool.*) mongoose.

мандари́н[1], **а**, *m.* mandarin (*Chinese official*).

мандари́н[2], **а**, *m.* mandarin(e), tangerine.

мандари́н|ный, *adj. of* ∼[2].

мандари́н|овый, *adj.* = ∼ный.

мандари́н|ский, *adj. of* ∼[1].

мандáт, **а**, *m.* 1. warrant. 2. (*polit.*) mandate; credentials.

мандáт|ный, *adj. of* ∼; ∼ная коми́ссия credentials committee; ∼ная систéма голосовáния card vote system; ∼ная терри́тория mandated territory.

мандоли́н|а, **ы**, *f.* (*mus.*) mandolin(e).

мандолини́ст, **а**, *m.* mandolin(e)-player.

мандрагóр|а, **ы**, *f.* (*bot.*) mandragora.

мандри́л, **а**, *m.* (*zool.*) mandrill.

манёвр, **а**, *m.* 1. (*in var. senses*) manœuvre; (*pl.; mil.*) manœuvres. 2. (*pl.*) shunting.

манёвренность, **и**, *f.* manœuvrability.

манёвр|енный, *adj. of* ∼; ∼енная войнá war of movement; ∼енный самолёт manœuvrable aircraft; м. паровóз shunting engine.

маневри́р|овать, **ую**, *impf.* (*of* с∼) 1. to manœuvre. 2. (+*i.*) to make good use (of), use to advantage. 3. (*railways*) to shunt.

маневрóвый, *adj.* (*railways*) shunting.

манéж, **а**, *m.* riding-school, manège.

манéжик, **а**, *m.* play-pen.

манéж|ить, **у**, **ишь**, *impf.* 1. to break in (*a horse*). 2. (*fig., coll.*) to tire out (*with waiting*).

манекéн, **а**, *m.* lay figure, dummy.

манекéнщиц|а, **ы**, *f.* mannequin.

манéр, **а**, *m.* (*coll.*) manner; таки́м ∼ом in this manner, in this way; на англи́йский м. in the English manner.

манéр|а, **ы**, *f.* 1. manner, style; м. вести́ себя́ way of behaving; м. держáть себя́ bearing, carriage; у негó неприя́тная м. опáздывать на свидáния he has an unpleasant way of being late for appointments; петь в ∼е Карýзо to sing in the style of Caruso. 2. (*pl.*) manners; у негó плохи́е ∼ы he has no manners.

манéрк|а, **и**, *f.* (*mil.*) mess tin.

манéрнича|ть, **ю**, *impf.* (*coll.*) to behave affectedly.

манéрность, **и**, *f.* affectation; preciosity.

манéр|ный (∼ен, ∼на), *adj.* affected; precious.

манжéт|а, **ы**, *f.* cuff.

маниакáльный, *adj.* maniacal.

мáни|е, **я**, *n.* (*arch.*) *now only in phrases* ∼ем, по ∼ю (руки́, жезлá, *etc.*) with a motion (of the hand, the baton, *etc.*); (*fig.*) по ∼ю (богóв, царя́, *etc.*) by the will (of the gods, the Tsar, *etc.*).

маникю́р, **а**, *m.* manicure.

маникюрш|а, и, *f.* manicurist.

манипули́р|овать, ую, *impf.* to manipulate.

манипуляци|я, и, *f.* 1. manipulation. 2. (*fig.*) machination, intrigue.

ман|и́ть, ю́, ~и́шь, *impf.* 1. (*pf.* по~) to beckon. 2. (*pf.* вз~) (*fig.*) to attract; to lure, allure.

манифе́ст, а, *m.* manifesto; proclamation.

манифеста́нт, а, *m.* (*polit.*, *etc.*) demonstrator.

манифеста́ци|я, и, *f.* (street) demonstration.

манифести́р|овать, ую, *impf. and pf.* to demonstrate, take part in a demonstration.

мани́шк|а, и, *f.* (false) shirt-front, dicky.

ма́ни|я, и, *f.* 1. mania; м. вели́чия megalomania. 2. (*fig.*) passion, craze; у неё м. противоре́чить she has a passion for contradicting.

манки́р|овать, ую, *impf. and pf.* 1. (+*i.*) to neglect. 2. to be absent; (+*a.*; *obs.*) to miss, be absent from. 3. (+*d.*; *obs.*) to be impolite to.

ма́нн|а, ы, *f.* manna; ждать (+*g.*) как ~ы небе́сной to await with impatience; пита́ться ~ой небе́сной (*joc.*) to be half-starved.

ма́нн|ый, *adj.* ~ая крупа́ semolina.

мановéни|е, я, *n.* (*obs.*) beck, nod; ~ем руки́ with a wave of one's hand.

маноме́тр, а, *m.* (*tech.*) pressure-gauge, manometer.

манометри́ческий, *adj.* (*tech.*) manometric.

манса́рд|а, ы, *f.* attic, garret.

манти́ль|я, и, *f.* mantilla.

манти́сс|а, ы, *f.* (*math.*) mantissa.

ма́нти|я, и, *f.* cloak, mantle; robe, gown.

манто́, *indecl.*, *n.* (lady's) coat.

манускри́пт, а, *m.* manuscript.

мануфакту́р|а, ы, *f.* 1. manufactory. 2. (*obs.*) textile mill. 3. (*sing. only*; *collect.*) cotton textiles.

мануфакту́р|ный, *adj. of* ~а.

манче́стер, а, *m.* (*text.*) velveteen.

маньчжу́р, а, *m.* Manchurian.

маньчжу́рский, *adj.* Manchurian.

манья́к, а, *m.* maniac, person in the grip of an obsession.

марабу́, *indecl.*, *n.* (*orn.*) marabou.

мара́зм, а, *m.* (*med.*) marasmus; ста́рческий м. senility, dotage; (*fig.*) decay.

мара́к|овать, ую, *impf.* (*coll.*) to have some notion (about), be not completely at sea.

мара́л, а, *m.* (*zool.*) Siberian deer.

мараски́н, а, *m.* maraschino (*liqueur*).

мара́тел|ь, я, *m.* (*coll.*) dauber; scribbler.

мара́|ть, ю, *impf.* (*coll.*) 1. (*pf.* за~) to soil, dirty; (*fig.*) to sully, stain; м. ру́ки (о+*a.*) to soil one's hands (on). 2. (*pf.* на~) to

daub; to scribble. 3. (*pf.* вы́~) to cross out, strike out.

мара́|ться, юсь, *impf.* (*coll.*) 1. (*pf.* за~) to soil oneself, get dirty. 2. (*no pf.*) to be dirty; to stain (*intrans.*). 3. (*no pf.*; *pf.*) to soil one's hands. 4. (*of infants*; *euph.*) to soil oneself, make a mess. 5. *pass. of* ~ть.

марафо́нский, *adj.* м. бег (*sport*) Marathon race.

мара́шк|а, и, *f.* (*typ.*) turn.

ма́рган|ец, ца, *m.* (*chem.*) manganese.

ма́рган|цевый, *adj. of* ~ец.

марганцо́вистый, *adj.* (*chem.*) manganous, manganic.

марганцо́вый, *adj.* = ма́рганцевый.

маргари́н, а, *m.* margarine.

маргари́н|овый, *adj. of* ~; (*fig.*) bogus, ersatz.

маргари́тк|а, и, *f.* (*bot.*) daisy.

маргина́ли|и, ев *and* ий, *no sing.* marginalia.

маре́в|о, а, *n.* 1. mirage. 2. heat haze.

маре́н|а, ы, *f.* (*bot.*) madder.

маре́нго, *indecl. adj.* black flecked with grey.

ма́ри, *indecl.* (*collect.*) the Mari (*inhabitants of Mari Autonomous Republic in U.S.S.R.*, *formerly the Cheremis*).

мари́|ец, йца, *m.* Mari.

мари́йский, *adj.* Mari.

мари́н|а, ы, *f.* (*art*) sea-scape.

марина́д, а, *m.* marinade; pickles.

марини́ст, а, *m.* painter of sea-scapes.

марино́в|анный, *p.p.p. of* ~а́ть *and adj.* (*cul.*) pickled.

марин|ова́ть, у́ю, *impf.* 1. (*pf.* за~) to pickle 2. (*pf.* про~) (*fig.*, *coll.*) to put off, shelve

марионе́т|ка, ки, *f.* marionette; puppe (*also fig.*); теа́тр ~ок puppet-theatre.

марионе́т|очный, *adj. of* ~ка; ~очное госуда́рство puppet state.

ма́рк|а[1], и, *f.* 1. (postage-)stamp. 2. (*monetary unit in Germany and Finland*) mark 3. mark; brand; фабри́чная м. trade-mark како́й ма́рки? what make?. 4. counter 5. grade, sort, brand; това́р вы́сшей ~ goods of the highest grade. 6. (*fig.*) name reputation; держа́ть ~у to maintain one' reputation.

ма́рк|а[2], и, *f.* (*hist.*) mark (*medieval Germa territorial unit or rural commune*).

маркгра́ф, а, *m.* (*hist.*) margrave.

марке́р, а, *m.* (*in var. senses*) marker.

маркетри́, *indecl.*, *n. and adj.* marquetry.

марки́з, а, *m.* marquis, marquess.

марки́з|а[1], ы, *f.* marchioness.

марки́з|а[2], ы, *f.* sun-blind; awning; mar quee.

маркизе́т, а, *m.* (*text.*) voile.

маркизе́т|овый, *adj. of* ~.

ма́рк|ий (~ок, ~ка), *adj.* easily soiled.

маркир|ов́ать, ́ую, *impf. and pf. (in var. senses)* to mark.

маркит́ант, а, *m. (hist.)* sutler.

маркси́зм, а, *m.* Marxism.

маркси́зм-ленини́зм, а-а, *m.* Marxism-Leninism.

маркси́ст, а, *m.* Marxist.

маркси́стский, *adj.* Marxist, Marxian.

маркси́стско-ле́нинский, *adj.* Marxist-Leninist.

маркше́йдер, а, *m.* mine-surveyor.

маркше́йдер|ский, *adj. of* ~; ~ская съёмка mine surveying.

м́арл|евый, *adj. of* ~я; м. бинт gauze bandage.

м́арл|я, и, *f.* gauze; cheesecloth.

мармел́ад, а, *m.* fruit jelly *(sweets).*

мармори́р|овать, ую, *impf. and pf. (tech.)* to marble.

марод́ёр, а, *m.* marauder, pillager.

мародёрск|ий, *adj.* marauding; ~ие це́ны *(fig., coll.)* exorbitant prices.

мародёрств|о, а, *n.* pillage, looting.

мародёрств|овать, ую, *impf.* to maraud, pillage, loot.

мароќен, а, *m.* 1. morocco(-leather). 2. *(text.)* marocain.

мароќен|овый, *adj. of* ~.

м́ар|очный, *adj. of* ~ка¹; ~очное вин́о fine wine.

марс¹, а, *m. (naut.)* top.

Марс², а, *m. (astron., myth.)* Mars *(in myth. sense, a.* ~а).

марсал́а, ́ы, *f.* Marsala (wine).

м́арсел|ь, я, *m. (naut.)* topsail.

марсель́ез|а, ы, *f.* Marseillaise.

марсиа́н|ин, ина, *pl.* ~е, ~, *m.* Martian.

м́арс|овый, *adj. of* ~¹.

март, а, *m.* March.

март́ен, а, *m. (tech.)* 1. open-hearth furnace. 2. open-hearth steel.

март́еновский, *adj. (tech.)* open-hearth.

мартенси́т, а, *m. (tech.)* martensite.

мартинѓал, а, *m.* martingale.

мартирол́ог, а, *m.* martyrology.

м́арт|овский, *adj. of* ~.

март́ышк|а, и, *f.* marmoset; *(fig., coll.)* monkey.

марцип́ан, а, *m.* marzipan.

марш¹, а, *m. (in var. senses)* march.

марш², *interj. (as word of command)* forward!; ш́агом м.! quick march!; *(coll.)* off you go!

марш³, а, *m.* flight of stairs.

м́аршал, а, *m.* marshal.

м́аршал|ьский, *adj. of* ~.

м́аршальств|о, а, *n.* rank of marshal.

м́арш|евый, *adj. of* ~¹; м. пор́ядок marching order; ~евые ч́асти drafts, reinforcements.

маршир|ов́ать, ́ую, *impf.* to march; м. на м́есте to mark time.

маршир́овк|а, и, *f.* marching.

марш-марш, а, *m.* quick march.

маршр́ут, а, *m.* 1. route, itinerary. 2. through goods-train.

маршрутиз́аци|я, и, *f.* conveyance by through goods-train.

маршр́ут|ный, *adj. of* ~; м. п́оезд through goods-train; ~ное такси́ fixed-route taxi.

маседу́ан, а, *m. (cul.)* macedoine.

м́аск|а, и, *f.* mask; противоѓазовая м. gas--mask; *(fig.)* сбр́осить с себ́я ~у to throw off the mask.

маскар́ад, а, *m.* masked ball, masquerade.

маскар́ад|ный, *adj. of* ~; м. кост́юм fancy dress.

маскир|ов́ать, ́ую, *impf. (of* за~) to mask, disguise; *(mil.)* to camouflage; м. сво́и нам́ерения *(fig.)* to disguise one's intentions.

маскир́овк|а, и, *f.* masking, disguise; *(mil.)* camouflage.

м́аслениц|а, ы, *f.* Shrove-tide; carnival; не всё ќоту м., *see* кот.

м́аслени|чный, *adj. of* ~ца.

масл́ёнк|а, и, *f.* 1. butter-dish. 2. oil-can.

масл|ёнок, ёнка, *pl.* ~я́та, ~я́т, *m. Boletus lutens (edible mushroom).*

м́аслен|ый, *adj.* 1. buttered; oiled, oily; ~ая неде́ля = ~ица; ~ые кра́ски = м́асло 3. 2. *(fig., coll.)* oily, unctuous. 3. *(fig., coll.)* voluptuous, sensual.

масли́н|а, ы, *f.* 1. olive-tree. 2. olive.

м́асл|ить, ю, ишь, *impf. (of* на~ *and* по~) 1. to butter. 2. to oil; to grease.

м́асл|иться, ится, *impf.* 1. to leave greasy marks. 2. *(coll.)* to shine; to glisten. 3. *pass. of* ~ить.

м́асличный, *adj. (of plants)* oil-yielding.

масли́|чный, *adj. of* ~на; ~чная гор́а Mount of Olives.

м́ас|ло, ла, *pl.* ~л́а, ~ел, ~л́ам, *n.* 1. *(сли́воч-ное)* butter. 2. oil; как по ~лу *(fig., coll.)* swimmingly. 3. oil (paints); писа́ть ~лом to paint in oils.

маслоб́ойк|а, и, *f.* 1. churn. 2. oil press.

маслоб́ойн|ый, *adj.* м. заво́д = ~я.

маслоб́о|йня, йни, *g. pl.* ~ен, *f.* 1. creamery. 2. oil-mill.

маслод́ел, а, *m.* 1. butter manufacturer. 2. oil manufacturer.

маслодели|е, я, *n.* 1. butter manufacturing. 2. oil manufacturing.

маслозав́од, а, *m.* 1. creamery, butter--dairy. 2. oil-mill.

маслом́ер, а, *m.* oil gauge; dipstick.

маслопров́од, а, *m.* oil pipe, oil pipe--line.

маслор́одный, *adj.* м. газ *(chem.)* ethylene.

маслосист́ем|а, ы, *f.* lubrication system.

масляни́ст|ый (~, ~а), *adj.* fatty; м. сыр full-fat cheese.

ма́сл|яный, *adj. of* ∼o; ∼яная кислота́ (*chem.*) butyric acid; ∼яные кра́ски oil paints.

масо́н, **а**, *m.* freemason, mason.

масо́нский, *adj. n.* masonic.

масо́нств|о, **а**, *n.* freemasonry.

ма́сс|а, **ы**, *f.* **1.** (*in var. senses*) mass; ∼ы (*polit.*) the masses; в ∼е on the whole, in the mass. **2.** (*ceramics*) paste. **3.** древе́сная м. wood-pulp. **4.** (*coll.*) a lot, lots.

масса́ж, **а**, *m.* massage.

массажи́ст, **а**, *m.* masseur.

массажи́стк|а, **и**, *f.* masseuse.

масси́в, **а**, *m.* (*geogr.*) massif, mountain--mass; (*fig.*) expanse; жили́щным м. housing unit; лесно́й м. forest tract.

масси́в|ный (∼ен, ∼на), *adj.* massive.

масси́ровани|е, **я**, *n.* massing, concentration.

масси́рова|нный, *p.p.p. of* ∼ты[1] *and adj.* (*mil.*) massed, concentrated.

масси́р|овать[1], **ую**, *impf. and pf.* (*mil.*) to mass, concentrate.

масси́р|овать[2], **ую**, *impf. and pf.* to massage.

массови́к, **а́**, *m.* organizer of popular cultural and recreational activities.

массо́вк|а, **и**, *f.* (*coll.*) **1.** mass meeting. **2.** group excursion. **3.** crowd scene (*in play, film*).

ма́ссов|ый, *adj.* (*in var. senses*) mass; popular; ∼ые аре́сты mass arrests; ∼ое произво́дство mass production.

маста́к, **а́**, *m.* (*coll.*) expert, past master.

ма́стер, **а**, *pl.* ∼а́, *m.* **1.** foreman. **2.** master craftsman, skilled workman; золоты́х дел м. goldsmith. **3.** (на+*a.*, *or* +*inf.*) expert, master (at, of); м. на все ру́ки all-round expert; быть ∼ом своего́ де́ла to be an expert at one's job; он м. танцева́ть вальс he is an expert at the waltz.

мастер|и́ть, **ю́**, **и́шь**, *impf.* (*of* с∼) (*coll.*) to make, build; мы ∼и́м себе́ са́ни we are making ourselves a sledge.

мастеров|о́й, **о́го**, *m.* (*obs.*) workman, (factory-)hand.

мастерск|а́я, **о́й**, *f.* workshop; studio; (*in factory*) shop.

мастерски́, *adv.* skilfully; in masterly fashion.

мастерско́й, *adj.* masterly.

мастерств|о́, **а́**, *n.* **1.** trade, craft. **2.** skill, craftsmanship.

масти́к|а, **и**, *f.* **1.** mastic. **2.** putty. **3.** floor--polish.

масти́к|овый, *adj. of* ∼а; ∼овое де́рево mastic (tree).

масти́т, **а**, *m.* (*med.*) mastitis.

масти́т|ый (∼, ∼а), *adj.* venerable; м. учёный old and eminent scholar.

мастодо́нт, **а**, *m.* mastodon.

мастурби́р|овать, **ую**, *impf.* to masturbate.

маст|ь, **и**, *pl.* ∼и, ∼е́й, *f.* **1.** colour (*of animal's hair or coat*). **2.** (*cards*) suit; ходи́ть в м. to follow suit.

масшта́б, **а**, *m.* scale; м. — две ми́ли в дю́йме the scale is two miles to the inch; (*fig.*) в большо́м, ма́леньком ∼е on a large, small scale; конфли́кт большо́го ∼а large-scale conflict.

масшта́бност|ь, **и**, *f.* (*fig.*) (large) scale, range, dimensions.

мат[1], **а**, *m.* (*chess*) checkmate, mate; объяви́ть м. (+*d.*) to mate.

мат[2], **а**, *m.* (floor-, door-)mat.

мат[3], **а**, *m.* mat (*roughened or frosted groundwork*); нанести́ м. (на+*a.*) to mat, frost.

мат[4], **а**, *m.* (*coll.*) *only in phrase* благи́м ∼ом at the top of one's voice.

мат[5], **а**, *m.* foul language, abuse; руга́ться ∼ом to use foul language.

матема́тик, **а**, *m.* mathematician.

матема́тик|а, **и**, *f.* mathematics.

математи́ческ|ий, *adj.* mathematical; ∼ое обеспе́чение (*computer*) software.

матере́|ть, **ю**, *impf.* (*coll.*) **1.** to grow to full size. **2.** (*fig.*) to become hardened.

матереуби́йств|о, **а**, *n.* matricide (*act*).

матереуби́йц|а, **ы**, *m. and f.* matricide (*agent*).

материа́л, **а**, *m.* (*in var. senses*) material; stuff.

материали́зм, **а**, *m.* materialism.

материализ|ова́ть(ся), **у́ю(сь)**, *impf. and pf.* to materialize (*trans. and intrans.*).

материали́ст, **а**, *m.* materialist.

материалисти́ческий, *adj.* (*philos.*) materialist.

материалисти́ч|ный (∼ен, ∼на), *adj.* (*pejor.*) materialistic.

материа́льност|ь, **и**, *f.* materiality.

материа́л|ьный (∼ен, ∼ьна), *adj.* (*in var. senses*) material; ∼ьная заинтересо́ванность material incentive(s); ∼ьные затрудне́ния financial difficulties; ∼ьное положе́ние economic conditions; ∼ьная часть (*tech., mil.*) equipment, matériel.

матери́к, **а́**, *m.* **1.** continent, mainland. **2.** subsoil.

материко́вый, *adj.* continental.

матери́нский, *adj.* maternal, motherly.

матери́нств|о, **а**, *n.* maternity, motherhood.

матер|и́ться, **ю́сь**, **и́шься**, *impf.* (*coll.*) to use foul language.

мате́ри|я[1], **и**, *f.* **1.** (*philos.*) matter. **2.** (*med.*) matter, pus. **3.** (*fig., coll.*) subject, topic (of conversation).

мате́ри|я[2], **и**, *f.* (*text.*) material, cloth.

ма́терный, *adj.* (*coll.*) obscene, abusive.

матеро́й, *adj.* (*coll.*) full-grown, grown-up; м. волк (*fig.*) an old hand.

матéрчатый, *adj.* (*coll.*) made of cloth.
матерщи́н|а, ы, *f.* (*coll.*) foul language.
матёрый, *adj.* (*coll.*) **1.** experienced, practised. **2.** inveterate, out-and-out.
матинé, *indecl., n.* **1.** matinée coat. **2.** (*obs.*) matinée.
мáтиц|а, ы, *f.* (*tech.*) tie-beam, joist.
мáтк|а, и, *f.* **1.** (*anat.*) uterus, womb. **2.** female (*of animals*); queen (bee). **3.** (*coll.*) mother. **4.** (*naut.*) (submarine) tender.
мáтов|ый, *adj.* mat(t); dull; suffused (*of light*); ~ое стекло́ frosted glass.
мáточник, а, *m.* **1.** queen bee's cell. **2.** (*bot.*) style, ovary.
мáточн|ый, *adj.* **1.** (*anat.*) uterine. **2.** (*min.*) ~ая поро́да matrix.
матрáс, а, *m.* mattress.
матрá|ц = ~с.
матрёшк|а, и, *f.* matryoshka (*Russian wooden doll containing progressively smaller dolls*).
матриархáльный, *adj.* matriarchal.
матриархáт, а, *m.* matriarchy.
матри́кул, а, *m.* student's record card.
мáтриц|а, ы, *f.* **1.** (*typ.*) matrix. **2.** (*tech.*) die, mould.
матрици́р|овать, ую, *impf. and pf.* (*typ.*) to make matrix-moulds (of).
матро́с, а, *m.* sailor, seaman.
матро́ск|а[1], и, *f.* sailor's jacket.
матро́ск|а[2], и, *f.* (*coll.*) sailor's wife.
мáтушк|а, и, *f.* (*coll.*) **1.** mother; ~и (мой)! *exclamation of surprise or fright.* **2.** priest's wife. **3.** *familiar term of address to a woman.*
матч, а, *m.* (*sport*) match.
мат|ь, g., d., p. ~ери, ~ерью, *pl.* ~ери, ~ерéй, *f.* **1.** mother. **2.** (*coll.*) *term of address to a woman.*
мáть-и-мáчех|а, и, *f.* (*bot.*) coltsfoot.
мáузер, а, *m.* Mauser (*automatic pistol or rifle*).
мах, а (у), *m.* swing, stroke; (*coll.*) дать ~у to let a chance slip; to make a blunder; одни́м ~ом, с одного́ ~у at one stroke, in a trice; с ~у rashly, without thinking.
махáльн|ый, ого, *m.* (*mil., sport*) signaller.
ма|хáть, шý, ~шешь, *impf.* (*of* ~хнýть) (+*i.*) to wave; to brandish; to wag; to flap.
махи́н|а, ы, *f.* (*coll.*) bulky and cumbersome object.
махинáци|я, и, *f.* machination, intrigue.
мах|нýть, нý, нёшь, *pf.* **1.** *pf. of* ~áть; м. рукой (на+*a.*) (*fig., coll.*) to give up as a bad job. **2.** (*coll.*) to go, travel. **3.** (*coll.*) to rush; to leap.
маховóк, á, *m.* fly-wheel.
махов|óй, *adj.* **1.** (*tech.*) ~óе колесо́ fly--wheel. **2.** (*orn.*) ~ьíе пéрья wing-feathers.
мáхонький, *adj.* (*coll.*) wee.

махóрк|а, и, *f.* makhorka (*inferior kind of tobacco*).
махрóвый, *adj.* **1.** (*bot.*) double. **2.** (*fig., coll.*) double-dyed, arrant. **3.** (*text.*) terry.
мац|á, ы́, no pl., *f.* matzoth (*Jewish biscuits of unleavened wheatmeal*).
мáчех|а, и, *f.* stepmother.
мáчт|а, ы, *f.* mast.
мáчт|овый, *adj. of* ~a.
маши́н|а, ы, *f.* **1.** machine, mechanism (*also fig.*). **2.** car. **3.** (*obs., coll.*) train.
машинáл|ьный (~ен, ~ьна**),** *adj.* mechanical (*fig.*); м. отвéт an automatic response.
машинизáци|я, и, *f.* mechanization.
машинизи́р|овать, ую, *impf. and pf.* to mechanize.
машини́ст, а, *m.* **1.** machinist, engineer (*workman in charge of machinery*). **2.** (*railways*) engine-driver. **3.** (*theatr.*) scene-shifter.
машини́стк|а, и, *f.* (girl-)typist.
маши́н|ка, ки, *f. dim. of* ~a; (пи́шущая) м. typewriter.
маши́нно-трáкторн|ый, *adj.* ~ая стáнция (*hist.*) machine and tractor station.
маши́н|ный, *adj. of* ~a.
машинопи́сный, *adj.* typewritten; м. текст typescript.
машинопи́с|ь, и, *f.* **1.** typewriting. **2.** typescript.
машиностроéни|е, я, *n.* mechanical engineering, machinery construction.
машиностро|и́тельный, *adj. of* ~éние.
маэ́стро, *indecl., m.* maestro; master.
маяќ, á, *m.* **1.** lighthouse; beacon (*also fig.*). **2.** (*fig.*) leading light.
мáятник, а, *m.* pendulum.
мá|яться, юсь, ешься, *impf.* (*coll.*) **1.** (с+*i.*) to toil (with, over). **2.** to pine, suffer.
маяч|ить, у, ишь, *impf.* (*coll.*) **1.** to loom (up), appear indistinctly. **2.** to lead a wretched life.
мая́чник, а, *m.* lighthouse-keeper.
мгл|а, ы, *f.* **1.** haze; mist. **2.** gloom, darkness.
мгли́ст|ый (~, ~a**),** *adj.* hazy.
мгновéни|е, я, *n.* instant, moment; в м. óка in the twinkling of an eye.
мгновéн|ный (~ен, ~на**),** *adj.* instantaneous.
мéбел|ь, и, *f.* furniture; (*fig.*) для ~и a figurehead, fifth wheel (*said of a useless person*).
мéбельщик, а, *m.* upholsterer; furniture--dealer.
меблирó|ванный, p.p.p. of ~вáть and *adj.* furnished.
меблир|овáть, ýю, *impf. and pf.* to furnish.
меблирóвк|а, и, *f.* **1.** furnishing. **2.** furniture, furnishings.
мегагéрц, а, *m.* (*radio*) megahertz.

мегаломáни|я, и, *f.* megalomania.

мегафóн, а, *m.* megaphone.

мегéр|а, ы, *f.* (*coll.*) shrew, termagant.

мегóм, а, *m.* (*electr.*) megohm.

мёд, а, о ~е, в ~ý, *pl.* ~ы́, ~óв, *m.* 1. honey. 2. mead.

мед- *abbr. of* медицинский.

медали́ст, а, *m.* medallist; medal winner.

медáл|ь, и, *f.* medal.

медальóн, а, *m.* medallion, locket.

медбрáт, а, *m.* male nurse.

медвéдиц|а, ы, *f.* she-bear; (*astron.*) Большáя М. the Great Bear (Ursa Major); Мáлая М. the Little Bear (Ursa Minor).

медвéдк|а, и, *f.* 1. (*zool.*) mole-cricket. 2. handcart. 3. (*tech.*) punch press.

медвéд|ь, я, *m.* 1. bear (*also fig.*); бéлый м. polar bear. 2. (*obs., coll.*) bearskin.

медвеж|áта, *pl. of* ~óнок.

медвежáтин|а, ы, *f.* bear's flesh.

медвежáтник, а, *m.* 1. bear-leader. 2. bear--hunter. 3. bear-pit, bear-garden.

медвé|жий, *adj. of* ~дь; м. ýгол (*coll.*) god--forsaken place; ~жья услýга well-meant action having opposite effect; ~жья болéзнь (*euph.*) diarrhoea induced by fear.

медвеж|óнок, óнка, *pl.* ~áта, ~áт, *m.* bear--cub.

медвя́н|ый, *adj.* 1. (*poet.*) honeyed. 2. smelling of honey. 3. ~ая росá honey-dew.

меделя́нск|ий, *adj.* ~ая собáка mastiff.

медеплави́льный, *adj.* copper-smelting.

меджли́с, а, *m.* Majlis (*Persian parliament*).

медиáн|а, ы, *f.* (*math.*) median.

мéдик, а, *m.* 1. physician, doctor. 2. medical student.

медикамéнт, а, *m.* medicine.

медици́н|а, ы, *f.* medicine.

медици́нский, *adj.* medical.

меди́чк|а, и, *f.* (*coll.*) (woman) medical student.

мéдленно, *adv.* slowly.

мéдлен|ный (~, ~на), *adj.* slow.

медли́тел|ьный (~ен, ~ьна), *adj.* sluggish; slow, tardy.

мéдл|ить, ю, ишь, *impf.* to linger; to tarry; (c+*i.*) to be slow (in); он ~ит с отвéтом he is a long time replying.

мéдник, а, *m.* copper-smith; tinker.

мéдно-крáсный, *adj.* copper-coloured.

меднолитéйный, *adj.* copper-smelting.

мéдн|ый, *adj.* 1. copper; brazen (*also fig.*); м. лоб (*fig., coll.*) blockhead; учи́ться на ~ые грошú, на ~ые дéньги to receive a poor boy's schooling. 2. (*chem.*) cupric, cuprous; м. колчедáн copper pyrites; м. купорóс copper sulphate, bluestone.

медóвый, *adj. of* мёд; м. мéсяц honeymoon.

мед|óк¹, кá, *m. dim. of* мёд.

медóк², а, *m.* Médoc (*wine*).

медонóсный, *adj.* melliferous, nectariferous.

медосмóтр, а, *m.* (*abbr. of* медицинский осмóтр) medical examination.

медоточи́в|ый (~, ~а), *adj.* (*obs.*) mellifluous, honeyed.

медпýнкт, а, *m.* (*abbr. of* медицинский пункт) first aid post.

медсестр|á, ы́, *f.* (*abbr. of* медицинская сестрá) (hospital) nurse.

медýз|а, ы, *f.* 1. (*zool.*) jellyfish, medusa. 2. М. (*myth.*) Medusa.

медуни́ц|а, ы, *f.* (*bot.*) lungwort.

мед|ь, и, *f.* copper; жёлтая м. brass.

медя́к, á, *m.* (*coll.*) copper (coin).

медяни́ц|а, ы, *f.* slow-worm, blind-worm.

медя́нк|а¹, и, *f.* grass-snake.

медя́нк|а², и, *f.* (*chem.*) verdigris.

меж = мéжду.

меж- *inter-.*

меж|á, и́, *pl.* ~и, ~, ~áм, *f.* boundary; boundary-strip.

междомéти|е, я, *n.* (*gram.*) interjection.

междоусóби|е, я, *n.* civil strife; intestine strife (*especially in mediaeval Russia*).

междоусóб|ица, ицы, *f.* (*obs.*) = ~ие.

междоусóбный, *adj.* intestine.

мéжду, *prep.+i.* (+*g. pl., obs.*) 1. between; м. дéлом at odd moments; м. нáми (говоря́) between ourselves; between you and me; м. прóчим incidentally; м. тем meanwhile; м. тем, как while, whereas; м. двух огнéй between two fires. 2. among, amongst.

междувéдомственный, *adj.* inter-departmental.

междугорóдный, *adj.* inter-town, inter-urban.

междунарóдник, а, *m.* specialist on international law *or* affairs.

междунарóдный, *adj.* international.

междупýт|ье, я, *n.* (*railways*) track spacing.

междуря́дь|е, я, *n.* (*agric.*) space between rows.

междуцáрстви|е, я, *n.* interregnum.

межевáни|е, я, *n.* land surveying, survey.

меж|евáть, ýю, *impf.* to survey; to establish the boundaries (of).

межеви́к, á, *m.* surveyor.

меж|евóй, *adj. of* ~á; м. знак landmark, boundary-mark.

межéн|ь, и, *f.* 1. lowest water-level (*in river or lake*). 2. (*dial.*) midsummer.

межеýм|ок, ка, *m.* (*coll.*) 1. person of limited intelligence; a mediocrity. 2. person *or* thing lacking definite qualities.

межеýмочный, *adj.* (*coll.*) mediocre; ill--defined; neither one thing nor another.

межзýбный, *adj.* (*ling.*) interdental.

межклéточный, *adj.* (*biol.*) intercellular.

межконтинентáльный, *adj.* inter-conti-

nental; м. баллисти́ческий снаря́д inter-
continental ballistic missile.

межплане́тн|ый, *adj.* interplanetary; ~ая
автомати́ческая ста́нция 'interplanetary
automatic station' (*unmanned space research
vehicle*).

межрёберный, *adj.* (*anat.*) intercostal.

мездр|а́, ы́, *f.* inner side (*of hide*).

мезозо́йский, *adj.* (*geol.*) mesozoic.

мезолити́ческий, *adj.* (*archaeol.*) meso-
lithic.

мезони́н, а, *m.* 1. attic story. 2. mezzanine
(floor).

мексика́н|ец, ца, *m.* Mexican.

мексика́нк|а, и, *f.* Mexican (woman)

мексика́нский, *adj.* Mexican.

мел, а, о ~е, в ~у́, *m.* chalk; whiting; white-
wash.

мела́нжев|ый, *adj.* (*text.*) ~ая ни́тка blended
yarn; ~ое произво́дство blended yarn
fabric production.

меланхо́лик, а, *m.* melancholic (person).

меланхоли́ческий, *adj.* melancholy.

меланхоли́ч|ный (~ен, ~на), *adj.* =
~еский.

меланхо́ли|я, и, *f.* melancholy; (*med.*)
melancholia.

мела́сс|а, ы, *f.* molasses.

меле́|ть, ет, *impf.* (*of* об~) to grow shallow.

мелиор|ати́вный, *adj. of* ~а́ция.

мелиора́тор, а, *m.* (*agric.*) specialist in
melioration, land improvement.

мелиора́ци|я, и, *f.* (*agric.*) melioration, land
improvement (*either by drainage or by irrigation*).

мел|и́ть, ю́, и́шь, *impf.* (*of* на~) to chalk;
to polish with whiting.

ме́л|кий (~ок, ~ка́, ~ко), *adj.* 1. small,
petty. 2. shallow; shallow-draught. 3. (*of
rain, sand, etc.*) fine; м. шаг (*tech.*) fine pitch.
4. (*fig.*) petty, small-minded; ~кая душо́н-
ка petty person; ~кая со́шка small fry.

ме́лко, *adv.* 1. fine, into small particles.
2. not deep; м. пла́вать (*fig., coll.*) to lack
depth.

мелкобуржуа́з|ный (~ен, ~на), *adj.* petty-
-bourgeois.

мелково́д|ный (~ен, ~на), *adj.* shallow.

мелково́дь|е, я, *n.* shallow water.

мелкозерни́ст|ый (~, ~а), *adj.* fine-grained,
small-grained.

мелколе́сь|е, я, *n.* young forest.

мелкопоме́стный, *adj.* (*hist.*) small (*of land-
owners*).

мелкосо́бственнический, *adj.* relating to
small property holders.

мелкот|а́, ы́, *f.* 1. smallness; (*fig.*) pettiness,
meanness. 2. (*collect.; coll.*) small fry.

мелкотова́рный, *adj.* (*econ.*) small-scale.

мелово́й, *adj.* 1. consisting of chalk. 2. white

as chalk. 3. cretaceous.

мелодеклама́ци|я, и, *f.* recitation of poetry
to musical accompaniment.

мело́дик|а, и, *f.* melodics.

мелоди́ческий, *adj.* melodious, tuneful.

мелоди́ч|ный (~ен, ~на), *adj.* = ~еский.

мело́ди|я, и, *f.* melody, tune.

мелодра́м|а, ы, *f.* melodrama.

мелодрамати́ческий, *adj.* melodramatic.

мел|о́к, ка́, *m.* piece of chalk; игра́ть на м.
(*cards, billiards, etc.*) to play on credit.

мелома́н, а, *m.* music-lover.

мело́чной[1], *adj.* (*obs.*) retail.

мело́чной[2] = ме́лочный.

ме́лочност|ь, и, *f.* pettiness, small-minded-
ness, meanness.

ме́лоч|ный (~ен, ~на), *adj.* 1. petty, trifling.
2. (*pejor.*) petty, paltry, small-minded.

ме́лоч|ь, и, *pl.* ~и, ~е́й, *f.* 1. (*collect.*) small
items; small fry; кру́пные я́блоки мы
съе́ли, оста́лась м. we had eaten the big
apples, only the small ones were left.
2. (*collect.*) small coin; (small) change.
3. (*pl.*) trifles, trivialities; разме́ниваться
на ~и, по ~а́м to fritter away one's energies.

мел|ь, и, о ~и, на ~й, *f.* shoal; bank;
песча́ная м. sandbank; на ~й aground;
(*fig.*) on the rocks, in low water; сесть на
м. to run aground; сиде́ть (как рак) на ~й
(*fig., coll.*) to be on the rocks, be in low water.

мельк|а́ть, а́ю, *impf.* (*of* ~ну́ть) to be
glimpsed fleetingly.

мельк|ну́ть, ну́, нёшь, *inst. pf. of* ~а́ть; у
меня́ ~ну́ла мысль I had a sudden idea.

ме́льком, *adv.* in passing, cursorily.

ме́льник, а, *m.* miller.

ме́льниц|а, ы, *f.* mill; э́то вода́ на на́шу
~у (*fig., coll.*) it affords support to our
cause.

ме́льничих|а, и, *f.* (*coll.*) miller's wife.

ме́льни|чный, *adj. of* ~ца.

мельхио́р, а, *m.* cupro-nickel, German silver.

мельхио́р|овый, *adj. of* ~.

мельча́йший, *superl. of* ме́лкий.

мельча́|ть, ю, *impf.* (*of* из~) 1. to grow
shallow. 2. to become small; to grow
smaller. 3. (*fig.*) to become petty.

ме́л|ьче, *comp. of* ~кий *and* ~ко.

мельч|и́ть, у́, и́шь, *impf.* (*of* из~ *and* раз~)
1. to crush, crumble. 2. to reduce in size.
3. to reduce the significance of.

мелю́, ме́лешь, *see* моло́ть.

мелюзг|а́, и́, *f.* (*collect.; coll.*) small fry.

мембра́н|а, ы, *f.* (*phys.*) membrane; (*tech.*)
diaphragm.

мемора́ндум, а, *m.* (*dipl.*) memorandum.

мемориа́л, а, *m.* 1. (*comm.*) day-book.
2. (*obs.*) note-book.

мемориа́льный, *adj.* memorial.

мемуари́ст, а, *m.* author of memoirs.

мемуа́р|ы, ов, *no sing.* memoirs.

ме́н|а, ы, *f.* exchange, barter.

менаже́р, а, *m.* (*sport*) manager.

менажи́р|овать, ую, *impf.* (*sport*) to manage, be manager (of).

ме́нее, *adv.* (*comp. of* ма́ло) less; тем не м. none the less.

менестре́л|ь, я, *m.* (*hist.*) minstrel.

ме́нзул|а, ы, *f.* (*tech.*) plane-table.

мензу́рк|а, и, *f.* (*pharm.*) measuring-glass.

менинги́т, а, *m.* (*med.*) meningitis.

мени́ск, а, *m.* (*math., phys.*) meniscus.

менов|о́й, *adj.* (*econ.*) exchange; ~а́я торго́вля barter.

менструа́льный, *adj.* (*physiol.*) menstrual.

менструа́ци|я, и, *f.* (*physiol.*) menstruation.

менструи́р|овать, ую, *impf.* (*physiol.*) to menstruate.

ме́нтик, а, *m.* (*obs.*) hussar's pelisse.

менто́л, а, *m.* (*chem.*) menthol.

ме́нтор, а, *m.* (*obs.*) mentor.

менуэ́т, а, *m.* minuet.

ме́ньше, *comp. of* ма́ленький *and* ма́ло, smaller, less.

меньшеви́зм, а, *m.* (*polit.*) Menshevism.

меньшеви́к, а́, *m.* (*polit.*) Menshevik.

меньшеви́стский, *adj.* (*polit.*) Menshevist.

ме́ньш|ий, *adj.* (*comp. of* ма́ленький, ма́лый) lesser, smaller; younger; по ~ей ме́ре at least; са́мое ~ee at the least.

меньшинств|о́, а́, *n.* minority.

меньшо́й, *adj.* (*coll.*) youngest.

меню́, *indecl., n.* menu, bill of fare.

меня́, *a. and g. of* я.

меня́л|а, ы, *m.* (*coll.*) money-changer.

меня́льный, *adj.* (*comm.*) money-changing.

меня́|ть, ю, *impf.* **1.** (*no pf.*) to change. **2.** (+*a.* на+*a.*; *pf.* об~, по~) to exchange (for).

меня́|ться, юсь, *impf.* **1.** (*no pf.*) to change; м. в лице́ to change countenance. **2.** (+*i.*; *pf.* об~, по~) to exchange; м. с кем-н. ко́мнатами to exchange rooms with someone.

ме́р|а, ы, *f.* (*in var. senses*) measure; вы́сшая м. наказа́ния capital punishment; в ~у (+*g.*) to the extent (of); по ~е возмо́жности, по ~е сил as far as possible; по ~е того́, как as, (in proportion) as; по кра́йней, ма́лой, ме́ньшей ~е at least; в ~у fairly; сверх ~ы, чрез ~у, не в ~у excessively, immoderately; знать ~у, *see* знать¹.

ме́ргел|ь, я, *m.* (*geol.*) marl.

мере́жк|а, и, *f.* hem-stitch, open work.

мере́нг|а, и, *f.* meringue.

мере́ть, мру, мрёшь, *past* мёр, мёрла, *impf.* (*coll.*) **1.** to die (*in large numbers*); мрут, как му́хи they are dying like flies. **2.** (*of the heart*) to stop beating.

мере́щ|иться, усь, ишься, *impf.* (*of* по~) (*coll.*; +*d.*) **1.** to seem (to), appear (to); она́ мне ~ится her image haunts me; э́то тебе́ ~ится you only imagine you see it. **2.** (*obs.*) to appear dimly.

мерза́в|ец, ца, *m.* (*coll.*) blackguard, scoundrel.

ме́рз|кий (~ок, ~ка́, ~ко), *adj.* disgusting, loathsome; abominable, foul.

мерзлот|а́, ы́, *f.* frozen condition of ground; ве́чная м. permafrost.

мерзлотове́дени|е, я, *n.* study of frozen soil conditions.

мёрзлый, *adj.* frozen, congealed.

мёрз|нуть, ну, нешь, *past* ~, ~ла, *impf.* (*of* за~) to freeze.

ме́рзост|ь, и, *f.* **1.** vileness, loathsomeness. **2.** loathsome thing, nasty thing; abomination; м. запусте́ния (*bibl. or iron.*) abomination of desolation.

меридиа́н, а, *m.* meridian.

мери́л|о, а, *n.* standard, criterion.

мери́льный, *adj.* measuring.

ме́рин, а, *m.* gelding; врёт как си́вый м. (*coll.*) he's an out-and-out liar.

мерино́с, а, *m.* **1.** merino (sheep). **2.** merino (wool).

мерино́совый, *adj.* merino.

ме́р|ить, ю, ишь, *impf.* **1.** (*pf.* с~) to measure; м. взгля́дом to look up and down. **2.** (*pf.* по~, при~) to try on (*clothing, footwear*).

ме́р|иться, юсь, ишься, *impf.* (*of* по~) (+*i.*) to measure (against); м. ро́стом с кем-н. to compare heights with someone.

ме́рк|а, и, *f.* measure; подходи́ть ко всему́ с одно́й ~ой (*fig.*) to apply the same standard to all alike.

меркантили́зм, а, *m.* **1.** (*econ.*) mercantilism. **2.** (*fig.*) mercenary spirit.

мерканти́л|ьный, *adj.* **1.** mercantile. **2.** (~ен, ~ьна) (*fig., pejor.*) mercenary.

ме́рк|нуть, нет, *past* ~нул *and* ~, ~ла, *impf.* (*of* по~) to grow dark, grow dim; (*fig.*) to fade.

Мерку́ри|й, я, *m.* (*myth., astron.*) Mercury.

мерла́н, а, *m.* (*fish*) whiting.

мерлу́шк|а, и, *f.* lambskin.

ме́рный, *adj.* **1.** measured; rhythmical. **2.** (*tech.*) measuring.

мероприя́ти|е, я, *n.* measure.

мерсериза́ци|я, и, *f.* (*tech.*) mercerization.

мерсеризо́в|анный, *p.p.p. of* ~а́ть *and adj.* (*tech.*) mercerized.

мерсериз|ова́ть, у́ю, *impf. and pf.* (*tech.*) to mercerize.

ме́ртвенный, *adj.* deathly, ghastly.

мертве́|ть, ю, *impf.* **1.** (*pf.* о~) to grow numb; (*med.*) to mortify. **2.** (*pf.* по~) to be benumbed (*with fright, grief, etc.*).

мертве́ц, а́, *m.* corpse, dead man.

мертве́цк|ая, ой, *f.* (*coll.*) mortuary, morgue.

мертве́цки, *adv.* (*coll.*) *only in phrases* м. пьян dead drunk; напи́ться м. to become dead drunk.

мертвечи́н|а, ы, *f.* 1. (*collect.*) carrion. 2. (*fig., coll.*) deadness, (a) dead thing.

мертв|и́ть, лю́, и́шь, *impf.* to deaden.

мертворождённый, *adj.* still-born.

мёртв|ый (~, ~á, ~о, *pl.* ~ы; *in fig. senses* ~б, ~ы́), *adj.* dead; ни жив ни ~ more dead than alive; ~ая зыбь (*naut.*) swell; м. инвента́рь (*agric.*) dead stock; м. капита́л (*fin.*) dead stock, unemployed capital; ~ая пе́тля (*aeron.*) loop; пить ~ую (*coll.*) to drink hard; ~ое простра́нство (*geogr., mil.*) dead ground; спать ~ым сном (*coll.*) to sleep like the dead; быть на ~ой то́чке to be at a standstill; ~ая хва́тка mortal grip; м. час quiet time (*in sanatoria, etc.*).

мерца́|ть, ю, *impf.* to twinkle, glimmer, flicker.

ме́сив|о, а, *n.* 1. mash. 2. (*fig., coll.*) medley; jumble.

ме|си́ть, шу́, ~сишь, *impf.* (*of* с~) to knead; м. грязь (*coll., joc.*) to wade through mud.

месмери́зм, а, *m.* mesmerism.

месс|а, ы, *f.* (*rel., mus.*) mass.

мессиа́нский, *adj.* Messianic.

мессиа́нств|о, а, *n.* Messianism.

месси́|я, и, *m.* Messiah.

места́ми, *adv.* (*coll.*) here and there, in places.

месте́ч|ко¹, ка, *pl.* ~ки, ~ек, ~кам, *n.* small town (*in Ukraine and Byelorussia*).

месте́ч|ко², ка, *pl.* ~ки, ~ек, ~кам, *n. dim.* of ме́сто; тёплое м. (*coll.*) cushy job.

ме|сти́, ту́, тёшь, *past* мёл, ~ла́, *impf.* 1. to sweep. 2, to whirl; *impers.* ~тёт there is a snow-storm.

местко́м, а, *m.* (*abbr. of* ме́стный комите́т) local (trade union) committee.

ме́стничес|кий, *adj. of* ~тво.

ме́стничеств|о, а, *n.* 1. (*hist.*) order of precedence (*based on birth and service*). 2. (*pejor.*) regionalism, giving priority to local interests.

ме́стност|ь, и, *f.* 1. locality, district; area. 2. (*mil.*) ground, country, terrain.

ме́стный, *adj.* (*in var. senses*) local; м. коло-ри́т local colour. 2. (*gram.*) locative.

-ме́стный -seated, -seater.

ме́ст|о, а, *pl.* ~а́, ~, ~а́м, *n.* 1. place; site; больно́е м. (*fig.*) tender spot, sensitive point; де́тское м. (*anat.*) after-birth, placenta; о́бщее м. platitude; отхо́жее м. latrine; пусто́е м. blank (space), (*fig.*) a nobody, a nonentity; сла́бое м. (*fig.*) weakness, weak spot; у́зкое м. bottleneck; м. де́йст-

вия, м. происше́ствия scene (of action); на ~е преступле́ния in the act, red-handed; знать своё м. (*fig.*) to know one's place; име́ть м. to take place; поста́вить на своё м., указа́ть кому́-н. его́ м. (*fig.*) to put someone in his place; не находи́ть себе́ ~а (*fig.*) to fret, worry; не к ~у (*fig.*) out of place; по ~а́м! to your places!; ни с ~а! don't move!, stay put!; честь и м.! (*obs., now joc.*) kindly be seated! 2. (*in theatre, etc.*) seat; (*on ship or train*) berth, seat. 3. space; room; нет ~а there is no room. 4. post, situation; job; быть без ~а to be out of work. 5. passage (*of book or mus. work*). 6. piece (*of luggage*). 7. (*pl.*) the provinces, the country; на ~а́х in the provinces; делега́ты с ~ provincial delegates.

местоблюсти́тел|ь, я, *m.* (*eccl.*) locum tenens.

местожи́тельств|о, а, *n.* (place of) residence; без определённого ~а of no fixed abode.

местоиме́ни|е, я, *n.* (*gram.*) pronoun.

местоиме́нный, *adj.* (*gram.*) pronominal.

местонахожде́ни|е, я, *n.* location, the whereabouts.

местоположе́ни|е, я, *n.* site, situation, position.

местопребыва́ни|е, я, *n.* abode, residence.

месторожде́ни|е, я, *n.* 1. (*geol.*) deposit; layer. 2. (*obs*). birth-place.

мест|ь, и, *f.* vengeance, revenge.

ме́сяц, а, *m.* 1. month; медо́вый м. honeymoon. 2. moon; молодо́й м. new moon.

месяцесло́в, а, *m.* (*obs.*) calendar.

ме́сячник, а, *m.* month (*marked by special observances or devoted to some special cause*).

ме́сячн|ый, *adj.* monthly; *as noun* ~ые, ~ых, *no sing.* (*coll.*) (menstrual) period.

мета́лл, а, *m.* metal; презре́нный м. filthy lucre.

металлиза́ци|я, и, *f.* (*tech.*) metallization.

металлизи́р|овать, ую, *impf. and pf.* to metallize.

металли́ст, а, *m.* metal-worker.

металли́ческ|ий, *adj.* metal; metallic (*also fig.*); ~ая болва́нка pig-metal; ~ая отли́вка cast metal.

металлоно́с|ный (~ен, ~на), *adj.* metalliferous.

металлообраба́тывающий, *adj.* metal-working.

металлоплави́льный, *adj.* smelting.

металлопрока́тный, *adj.* (*tech.*) rolling.

металлопромы́шленност|ь, и, *f.* metal industry.

металлоре́жущий, *adj.* metal-cutting.

металлу́рг, а, *m.* metallurgist.

металлурги́ческий, *adj.* metallurgical; м. заво́д metal works, iron and steel works.

металлу́рги|я, и, *f.* **1.** metallurgy. **2.** metallurgical science.

метаморфо́з, а, *m.* = ~а.

метаморфо́з|а, ы, *f.* metamorphosis.

мета́н, а, *m.* (*chem.*) methane, marsh gas.

мета́ни|е, я, *n.* **1.** throwing, casting, flinging. **2.** м. икры́ spawning.

метано́л, а, *m.* (*chem.*) methanol, methyl alcohol.

метате́з|а, ы, *f.* (*ling.*) metathesis.

мета́тел|ь, я, *m.* (*sport*) thrower; м. ди́ска discus thrower.

мета́тельный, *adj.* missile; м. снаря́д projectile.

ме|та́ть[1], чу́, ~чешь, *impf.* (*of* ~тну́ть) **1.** to throw, cast, fling; м. гром и мо́лнии (*fig.*, *coll.*) to rage, fulminate; рвать и м. (*coll.*) to be in a rage; м. жре́бий to cast lots; м. се́но to stack hay. **2.** м. икру́ to spawn. **3.** (*cards*) м. банк to keep the bank.

мета́|ть[2], ю, *impf.* (*of* на~, с~) to baste, tack; м. пе́тли to edge buttonholes.

ме|та́ться, чу́сь, ~чешься, *impf.* to rush about; to toss (*in bed*).

метафи́зик, а, *m.* metaphysician.

метафи́зик|а, и, *f.* metaphysics.

метафизи́ческий, *adj.* metaphysical.

мета́фор|а, ы, *f.* metaphor.

метафори́ческий, *adj.* metaphorical.

мете́л|ица, ицы, *f.* (*poet.*) = ~ь.

метёлк|а, и, *f.* **1.** *dim. of* метла́; под ~у (*fig.*, *coll.*) entirely, to the last particle. **2.** (*bot.*) panicle.

мете́л|ь, и, *f.* snow-storm; blizzard.

мете́льчатый, *adj.* (*bot.*) panicular, paniculate.

мете́льщик, а, *m.* sweeper.

метеопрогнози́ровани|е, я, *n.* weather forecasting.

метео́р, а, *m.* meteor.

метеори́зм, а, *m.* (*med.*) flatulence.

метеори́т, а, *m.* (*astron.*) meteorite.

метеори́ческий, *adj.* meteoric.

метео́р|ный, *adj. of* ~.

метеоро́лог, а, *m.* meteorologist.

метеорологи́ческий, *adj.* meteorological.

метеороло́ги|я, и, *f.* meteorology.

метеосво́дк|а, и, *f.* (*abbr. of* метеорологи́ческая сво́дка) weather report.

метеоста́нци|я, и, *f.* (*abbr. of* метеорологи́ческая ста́нция) meteorological station.

метиза́ци|я, и, *f.* (*biol.*) cross-breeding.

мети́зный, *adj.* metal-ware, hardware.

мети́з|ы, ов, *no sing.* (*abbr. of* металли́ческие изде́лия) metal wares, hardware.

мети́л, а, *m.* (*chem.*) methyl.

мети́с, а, *m.* **1.** (*biol.*) mongrel, half-breed. **2.** (*anthrop.*) metis, mestizo.

ме́|тить[1], чу, тишь, *impf.* (*of* на~ *and* по~) to mark.

ме́|тить[2], чу, тишь, `impf.` (*of* на~) **1.** (в+*a.*) to aim (at); (*fig.*, *coll.*; в+*n.-a. pl.*) to aim (at), aspire (to); он всегда́ ~тил в профессора́ it had always been his aim (ambition) to become a professor. **2.** (*fig.*; в+*a.*, на+*a.*) to drive (at), mean.

ме́тк|а, и, *f.* **1.** marking. **2.** mark.

ме́т|кий (~ок, ~ка́, ~ко), *adj.* well-aimed, accurate; м. стрело́к a good shot; (*fig.*) ~кое замеча́ние apt remark; ~ко вырази́ться to be very much to the point.

ме́ткост|ь, и, *f.* marksmanship; accuracy; (*fig.*) neatness, pointedness.

мет|ла́, лы́, *pl.* ~лы, ~ел, ~лам, *f.* broom.

мет|ну́ть, ну́, нёшь, *inst. pf. of* ~а́ть[1].

ме́тод, а, *m.* method.

мето́д|а, ы, *f.* (*obs.*) method.

методи́зм, а, *m.* (*rel.*) Methodism.

мето́дик|а, и, *f.* **1.** method(s), system; principles; м. ру́сского языка́ methods of teaching Russian; м. пожа́рного де́ла principles of fire-fighting. **2.** methodology.

методи́ст[1], а, *m.* methodologist; specialist (*on principles of, methods of teaching, etc.*).

методи́ст[2], а, *m.* (*rel.*) Methodist.

методи́ст|ский, *adj. of* ~[2].

метод|и́ческий, *adj.* **1.** methodical, systematic. **2.** *adj. of* ~ика; м. приём a procedure; ~и́ческое совеща́ние conference on (*teaching, etc.*) methods.

методи́ч|ный (~ен, ~на), *adj.* methodical, orderly.

методо́лог, а, *m.* methodologist.

методологи́ческий, *adj.* methodological.

методоло́ги|я, и, *f.* methodology.

метони́ми|я, и, *f.* (*lit.*) metonymy.

мето́п, а, *m.* (*archit.*) metope.

метр[1], а, *m.* (*unit of measurement and lit.*) metre.

метр[2], а, *m.* (*obs. or joc.*) master.

метра́ж, а, *m.* **1.** metric area. **2.** length in metres.

метранпа́ж, а, *m.* (*typ.*) maker-up.

метрдоте́л|ь, я, *m.* head waiter.

ме́трик|а[1], и, *f.* (*lit.*) metrics.

ме́трик|а[2], и, *f.* birth-certificate.

метри́ческий[1], *adj.* metric.

метри́ческ|ий[2], *adj.* (*lit.*) metrical; ~ое ударе́ние ictus, metrical stress.

метри́ческ|ий[3], *adj.* ~ая кни́га register of births; ~ое свиде́тельство birth-certificate.

метро́, *indecl.*, *n.*, *abbr. of* ~полите́н.

метрологи́ческий, *adj.* metrological.

метроло́ги|я, и, *f.* metrology.

метроно́м, а, *m.* (*phys., mus.*) metronome.

метрополите́н, а, *m.* underground (railway), metro(politan railway).

метрополи|я, и, *f.* mother country, centre (*of empire*).

ме|ту́, тёшь, *see* ~сти́.

мёт|че, *comp. of* ~кий *and* ~ко.

ме́тчик, а, *m.* (*tech.*) 1. punch, stamp. 2. marker.

метчи́к, а́, *m.* (*tech.*) tap-borer, screw-tap.

мех¹, а, о ~е, в ~у́ (~е), на ~у́, *pl.* ~а́, ~о́в, *m.* fur; на ~у́ fur-lined.

мех², а, *pl.* ~и́, ~о́в, *m.* 1. (*pl.*) bellows. 2. wine-skin, water-skin.

механиза́тор, а, *m.* 1. specialist on mechanization. 2. (*agric.*) machine operator, machine servicer.

механиза́ци|я, и, *f.* mechanization.

механизи́рова|нный, *p.p.p. of* ~ть *and adj.* mechanized.

механизи́р|овать, ую, *impf. and pf.* to mechanize.

механи́зм, а, *m.* mechanism, gear(ing); (*pl., collect.*) machinery (*also fig.*).

меха́ник, а, *m.* 1. mechanic. 2. student of, specialist in mechanics.

меха́ник|а, и, *f.* 1. mechanics. 2. (*fig., coll.*) trick; knack; подвести́ (подстро́ить) ~у кому́-н. to play a trick on someone.

механи́ст, а, *m.* (*philos.*) mechanist.

механисти́ческий, *adj.* (*philos.*) mechanistic.

механи́ческий, *adj.* 1. (*in var. senses*) mechanical; power-driven; м. моме́нт momentum; м. пресс power press; м. тка́цкий стано́к power loom; м. цех machine shop. 2. of mechanics. 3. (*philos.*) mechanistic.

механи́ч|ный (~ен, ~на), *adj.* (*fig.*) mechanical, automatic.

мехово́й, *adj. of* мех¹.

меховщи́к, а́, *m.* furrier.

мецена́т, а, *m.* Maecenas, patron.

мецена́тств|о, а, *n.* patronage of literature, of arts.

ме́ццо-сопра́но, *indecl., f. and n.* (*mus.*) mezzo-soprano.

ме́ццо-ти́нто, *indecl., n.* (*art*) mezzotint.

меч, а́, *m.* sword; дамо́клов м. sword of Damocles; преда́ть огню́ и ~у́ to put to the sword; скрести́ть ~и́ (*fig., rhet.*) to cross swords.

мечено́с|ец, ца, *m.* 1. sword-bearer. 2. (*hist.*) member of German Order of Knights of the Sword.

ме́чен|ый, *adj.* marked; ~ые а́томы (*phys.*) labelled, tagged atoms.

мече́т|ь, и, *f.* mosque.

меч-ры́б|а, ы, *f.* sword-fish.

мечт|а́, ы́ (*g. pl. not used*) *f.* dream, day-dream.

мечта́ни|е, я, *n.* day-dreaming, reverie.

мечта́тел|ь, я, *m.* dreamer; day-dreamer.

мечта́тел|ьный (~ен, ~ьна), *adj.* dreamy.

мечта́|ть, ю, *impf.* (о+*p.*) to dream (of, about); м. мно́го, высоко́, *etc.*, о себе́ (*coll.*) to think much of oneself.

ме́|чу, тишь, *see* ~тить.

ме|чу́, ~чешь, *see* ~та́ть¹.

меша́лк|а, и, *f.* (*coll.*) mixer, stirrer; agitator (*in washing machine*).

мешани́н|а, ы, *f.* (*coll.*) medley, jumble.

меша́|ть¹, ю, *impf.* (*of* по~) 1. (+*d.*+*inf.*) to prevent (from); to hinder, impede, hamper; что ~ет вам прие́хать в Москву́? what prevents you from coming to Moscow? 2. (+*d.*) to disturb; вам не ~ет, что я игра́ю на пиани́но? does it disturb you when I play the piano? не ~ло бы (+*inf.*) (*coll.*) it would not be a bad thing (to).

меша́|ть², ю, *impf.* 1. (*pf.* по~) to stir, agitate; м. у́голь в пе́чке to poke the fire; м. в котле́ to stir the cauldron. 2. (*pf.* с~) (с+*i.*) to mix (with), blend (with). 3. (*pf.* с~) to confuse, mix up.

меша́|ться, юсь, *impf.* 1. (*coll.*; в+*a.*) to interfere (in), meddle (with); не ~йтесь не в своё де́ло! mind your own business! 2. (*pf.* с~) *pass. of* ~ть².

ме́шка|ть, ю, *impf.* (*coll.*; с+*i.*) to linger, tarry (over); to loiter.

мешкова́т|ый (~, ~а), *adj.* 1. (*of clothing*) baggy. 2. awkward, clumsy.

мешкови́н|а, ы, *f.* sacking, hessian.

ме́шкот|ный (~ен, ~на), *adj.* (*coll.*) 1. sluggish, slow. 2. long (*of a job*).

меш|о́к, ка́, *m.* 1. bag; sack; вещево́й м. haversack, knapsack; kit-bag; ка́менный м. (*hist.; rhet.*) prison cell; огнево́й м. (*mil.*) fire pocket; ~ки́ под глаза́ми bags under the eyes. 2. (*dry measure*) bag (= 3 *poods*). 3. (*fig., coll.*) clumsy fellow.

мешо́ч|ек, ка, *m. dim. of* мешо́к; sac, follicle, utricle.

мещан|и́н, и́на, *pl.* ~е, ~, *m.* 1. (*hist.*) petty bourgeois (*member of urban lower middle class comprising small traders, craftsmen, junior officials, etc.*). 2. (*fig.*) Philistine.

меща́н|ский, *adj. of* ~и́н; (*fig.*) Philistine; bourgeois, vulgar, narrow-minded.

меща́нств|о, а, *n.* 1. (*collect.*) petty bourgeoisie, lower middle class. 2. (*fig.*) philistinism, vulgarity, narrow-mindedness.

мзд|а, ы, *no pl., f.* (*arch., now joc.*) recompense, payment (*iron.* = bribe).

мздои́м|ец, ца, *m.* (*obs.*) bribe-taker.

мздои́мств|о, а, *n.* (*obs.*) bribery.

ми, *indecl., n.* (*mus.*) mi; E.

миг¹, а, *m.* moment, instant.

миг², а, *m.* (*abbr. of* Микоя́н и Гуре́вич, *designers' names*) Mig (*Soviet fighter aircraft*).

мига́тель|ный, *adj.* ~ая перепо́нка nict(i-t)ating membrane.

мига́ни|е, я, *n.* 1. winking; twinkling. 2. blinking.

миг|а́ть, а́ю, *impf.* (*of* ~ну́ть) 1. to blink. 2. (+*d.*) to wink (at); (*fig.*) to wink, twinkle.

миг|ну́ть, ну́, нёшь, *inst. pf. of* ~а́ть.
ми́гом, *adv.* (*coll.*) in a flash; in a jiffy.
миграцио́нный, *adj. of* мигра́ция.
мигра́ци|я, и, *f.* migration.
мигре́н|ь, и, *f.* migraine.
мигри́р|овать, ую, *impf.* to migrate.
мид, а, *m.* (*abbr. of* Министе́рство иностра́нных дел) Ministry of Foreign Affairs, Foreign Office.
ми́дел|ь, я, *m.* (*naut.*) midship section.
мизансце́н|а, ы, *f.* (*theatr.*) mise en scène.
мизантро́п, а, *m.* misanthrope.
мизантропи́ческий, *adj.* misanthropic.
мизантро́пи|я, и, *f.* misanthropy.
мизги́р|ь, я́, *m.* (*dial.*) spider.
мизере́ре, *indecl., n.* (*eccl.*) miserere.
мизе́р|ный (~ен, ~на), *adj.* scanty, wretched.
мизи́н|ец, ца, *m.* little finger; little toe; он не сто́ит ва́шего ~ца (*fig.*) he is not a patch on you.
мизи́н|цевый, *adj. of* ~ец.
миколо́ги|я, и, *f.* mycology.
микроавто́бус, а, *m.* minibus.
микроампе́р, а, *m.* (*electr.*) microampere.
микро́б, а, *m.* microbe.
микробио́лог, а, *m.* microbiologist.
микробиоло́ги|я, и, *f.* microbiology.
микрока́рт|а, ы, *f.* microfiche.
микроко́кк, а, *m.* (*biol., med.*) micrococcus.
микроко́см, а, *m.* microcosm.
микрометри́ческий, *adj.* micrometrical.
микроме́три|я, и, *f.* micrometry.
микро́н, а, *m.* (*phys.*) micron.
микрооргани́зм, а, *m.* (*biol.*) micro-organism.
микроплёнк|а, и, *f.* microfilm.
микропроце́ссор, а, *m.* microprocessor.
микрорайо́н, а, *m.* **1.** mikroraion (*administrative subdivision of urban* raion *in U.S.S.R.*). **2.** (*town planning*) neighbourhood unit; м. шко́лы school catchment area.
микроско́п, а, *m.* microscope.
микроскопи́ческий, *adj.* microscopic.
микроскопи́ч|ный (~ен, ~на), *adj.* = ~еский.
микроскопи́|я, и, *f.* microscopy.
микрострукту́р|а, ы, *f.* microstructure.
микрофо́н, а, *m.* microphone; mouthpiece (*of telephone*).
микроцефа́л, а, *m.* (*med.*) microcephalic.
микроцефа́ли|я, и, *f.* (*med.*) microcephaly.
миксту́р|а, ы, *f.* (liquid) medicine, mixture.
мила́ш|а, и, *f.* (*coll.*) darling.
мила́шк|а, и, *f.* **1.** (*coll.*) pretty girl; nice girl. **2.** (*vulg.*) sweetheart, tart.
ми́ленький, *adj.* **1.** pretty; nice; sweet; dear. **2.** (*as form of address*) darling.
милитариза́ци|я, и, *f.* militarization.
милитари́зм, а, *m.* militarism.
милитариз|ова́ть, у́ю, *impf. and pf.* to militarize.

милитари́ст, а, *m.* militarist.
милитаристи́ческий, *adj.* militaristic.
милиц|е́йский, *adj. of* ~ия.
милиционе́р, а, *m.* **1.** militia-man. **2.** policeman (*in the U.S.S.R.*).
мили́ци|я, и, *f.* militia (*in U.S.S.R., civil police force*).
миллиа́рд, а, *m.* milliard; (*in U.S. usage*) billion.
миллиарде́р, а, *m.* multi-millionaire.
миллиа́рдный, *adj.* **1.** milliardth; (*in U.S. usage*) billionth. **2.** worth a milliard.
миллиба́р, а, *m.* (*meteor.*) millibar.
милливо́льт, а, *m.* (*electr.*) millivolt.
миллигра́мм, а, *m.* milligramme.
миллиме́тр, а, *m.* millimetre.
миллио́н, а, *m.* million.
миллионе́р, а, *m.* **1.** millionaire. **2.** (*fig.*) one who has accomplished something which can be estimated in millions of units; лётчик-м. pilot who has flown over a million kilometres.
миллио́нный, *adj.* **1.** millionth. **2.** worth millions. **3.** million strong.
ми́л|овать, ую, *impf.* (*of* по~) (*obs.*) to pardon, spare.
мил|ова́ть, у́ю, *impf.* (*folk poet.*) to caress, fondle.
мил|ова́ться, у́юсь, *impf.* (*folk poet.*) to exchange caresses.
милови́д|ный (~ен, ~на), *adj.* pretty, nice-looking.
мило́рд, а, *m.* (mi)lord.
милосе́рди|е, я, *n.* mercy, charity; сестра́ ~я (*obs.*) nurse.
милосе́рд|ный (~ен, ~на), *adj.* merciful, charitable.
ми́лостив|ый (~, ~а), *adj.* (*obs.*) gracious, kind; м. госуда́рь (*form of address*) sir; (*in letters*) (Dear) Sir; ~ая госуда́рыня madam; (*in letters*) (Dear) Madam.
ми́лостын|я, и, *no pl., f.* alms.
ми́лост|ь, и, *f.* **1.** favour, grace; *pl.* favours; ~и про́сим! (*coll.*) welcome!; you are always welcome!; сде́лай(те) м. (*obs.*) be so kind, be so good; скажи́(те) на м.! (*coll., iron.*) you don't say (so)! **2.** mercy; charity; сда́ться на м. победи́теля to surrender at discretion; из ~и out of charity. **3.** (*form of address to superior*) ва́ша м. your worship.
ми́лочк|а, и, *f.* (*coll.*) dear, darling.
ми́л|ый (~, ~а́, ~о), *adj.* **1.** nice, sweet; lovable; э́то о́чень ~о с ва́шей стороны́ it is very nice of you. **2.** dear; *as noun* м., ~ого, *m.*; ~ая, ~ой, *f.* dear, darling.
мильто́н, а, *m.* (*sl.*) cop, fuzz.
ми́л|я, и, *f.* mile.
мим, а, *m.* (*theatr.*) mime.
мимео́граф, а, *m.* duplicating machine.
ми́мик|а, и, *f.* mimicry.

мимикри́|я, и, *f.* (*biol.*) mimicry, mimesis.
мими́ст, а, *m.* mimic.
мими́ческий, *adj.* mimic.
ми́мо, *adv. and prep.+g.* by, past; пройти́, прое́хать м. to pass by, go past; м.! miss(ed)!;
мимое́здом, *adv.* (*coll.*) in passing.
мимо́з|а, ы, *f.* (*bot.*) mimosa.
мимолёт|ный (~ен, ~на), *adj.* fleeting, transient.
мимохо́дом, *adv.* in passing; м. упомяну́ть (*fig., coll.*) to mention in passing.
ми́н|а¹, ы, *f.* **1.** (*mil., naut.*) mine. **2.** (*mil.*) mortar shell, bomb.
ми́н|а², ы, *f.* mien, expression; сде́лать весёлую (хоро́шую) ~у при плохо́й игре́ to put a brave face on a sorry business.
минаре́т, а, *m.* minaret.
миндалеви́дн|ый, *adj.* almond-shaped; ~ая железа́ (*anat.*) tonsil.
минда́лин|а, ы, *f.* **1.** almond. **2.** (*anat.*) tonsil.
минда́л|ь, я́, *m.* **1.** almond-tree. **2.** (*collect.*) almonds.
минда́льнича|ть, ю, *impf.* (с+*i.*; *coll.*) to sentimentalize (over), be excessively soft (towards).
минда́ль|ный, *adj. of* ~.
минёр, а, *m.* (*mil.*) mine-layer.
минера́л, а, *m.* mineral.
минералоги́ческий, *adj.* mineralogical.
минерало́ги|я, и, *f.* mineralogy.
минера́льный, *adj.* mineral.
минздра́в, а, *m.* (*abbr. of* Министе́рство здравоохране́ния) Ministry of Health.
миниатю́р|а, ы, *f.* (*art*) miniature.
миниатюри́ст, а, *m.* miniature-painter, miniaturist.
миниатю́р|ный (~ен, ~на), *adj.* **1.** *adj. of* ~а. **2.** (*fig.*) diminutive, tiny, dainty.
минима́л|ьный (~ен, ~ьна), *adj.* minimum.
ми́нимум, а, *m.* **1.** minimum; м. за́работной пла́ты minimum wage; прожи́точный м. living wage; техни́ческий м. essential technical qualifications. **2.** (*as adv.*) at the least, at the minimum.
мини́р|овать, ую, *impf. and pf.* (*mil., naut.*) to mine.
министе́рский, *adj.* ministerial.
министе́рств|о, а, *n.* (*polit.*) ministry.
мини́стр, а, *m.* (*polit.*) minister; м.-президе́нт, премье́р-м. Prime Minister, premier.
ми́ни-ю́бк|а (*and* миниюбк|а), и, *f.* miniskirt.
ми́нн|ый, *adj.* (*mil.*) mine; ~ое заграж-де́ние minefield.
мин|ова́ть, у́ю, *impf. and pf.* **1.** to pass (by); ~у́я подро́бности omitting details. **2.** (*pf. only*) to be over, be past; опа́сность ~ова́ла the danger is past. **3.** (*only with* не+*g.*) to

escape; не м. тебе́ тюрьмы́ you cannot escape being sent to prison.
мино́г|а, и, *f.* (*zool.*) lamprey.
миноиска́тел|ь¹, я, *m.* (*mil.*) mine-detector (*apparatus*).
миноиска́тел|ь², я, *m.* (*mil.*) sapper.
миномёт, а, *m.* (*mil.*) mortar; гварде́йский м. multi-rail rocket launcher.
миномёт|ный, *adj. of* ~.
миномётчик, а, *m.* (*mil.*) mortar man.
минонос|ец, ца, *m.* (*naut.*) torpedo-boat; эска́дренный м. destroyer.
мино́р, а, *m.* **1.** (*mus.*) minor key. **2.** (*fig.*) blues; быть в ~е to have the blues, be in the dumps.
мино́рн|ый, *adj.* **1.** (*mus.*) minor. **2.** (*fig.*) gloomy, depressed; быть в ~ом настрое́нии to have the blues, be in the dumps.
мину́вш|ий, *adj.* past; *as noun* ~ее, ~его, *n.* the past.
ми́нус, а, *m.* **1.** (*math.*) minus. **2.** (*fig., coll.*) defect, shortcoming.
ми́нусовый, *adj.* (*electr.*) negative.
мину́т|а, ы, *f.* (*in var. senses*) minute.
мину́т|ный, *adj.* **1.** *adj. of* ~а; ~ная стре́лка minute-hand. **2.** momentary; transient, ephemeral; ~ная встре́ча brief encounter.
мин|у́ть, ~ешь, *pf.* **1.** (*past* ~у́л, ~у́ла) = минова́ть. **2.** (*past* ~у́л, ~у́ла) (+*d.*) to pass (*only in expressions of age*); ему́ ~у́ло два́дцать лет he has turned twenty.
миньо́н, а, *m.* (*typ.*) minion (*7-point type*).
миокарди́т, а, *m.* (*med.*) myocarditis.
мио́лог, а, *m.* myologist.
миоло́ги|я, и, *f.* myology.
мио́пи|я, и, *f.* (*med.*) myopia.
миоце́н, а, *m.* miocene.
мир¹, а, *m.* peace; почётный м. peace with honour; заключи́ть м. to make peace; м. вам! peace be with you!; иди́те с ~ом go in peace.
мир², а, *pl.* ~ы́, *m.* world (*also fig.*); universe; не от ~а сего́ (*coll.*) other-worldly, not of this world; в ~у́ in the world (*as opp. to in a monastery*); ходи́ть по́ ~у to beg, live by begging; пусти́ть по́ ~у to ruin utterly; на ~у́ и смерть красна́ (*prov.*) company in distress makes trouble less.
мир³, а, *m.* (*hist.*) mir (*Russian village community*); всем ~ом all together; с ~у по ни́тке го́лому руба́шка (*prov.*) every little helps.
мирабе́л|ь, и, *f.* mirabelle plum.
мира́ж, а, *m.* mirage (*also fig.*); optical illusion.
мира́кл|ь, я, *m.* (*lit., theatr.*) miracle-play.
мирво́л|ить, ю, ишь, *impf.* (+*d.*; *coll.*) to connive (at); to be over-indulgent (towards).
мир|и́ть, ю́, и́шь, *impf.* **1.** (*pf.* по~) to reconcile. **2.** (*pf.* при~) (с+*i.*) to reconcile

(to); больша́я зарпла́та ~и́ла его́ с не-
прия́тными усло́виями рабо́ты high wages
reconciled him to unpleasant working conditions.

мир|и́ться, ю́сь, и́шься, *impf.* (c+*i*.) **1.** (*pf.*
по~) to be reconciled (with), make it up
(with). **2.** (*pf.* при~) to reconcile oneself
(to); м. со свои́м положе́нием to accept
the situation.

ми́р|ный (~ен, ~на), *adj.* **1.** *adj. of* ~¹;
2. peaceful; peaceable; ~ное сосущество-
ва́ние (*polit.*) peaceful co-existence.

ми́р|о, а, *n.* (*eccl.*) chrism; одни́м ~ом
ма́заны (*fig., joc.*) tarred with the same
brush.

миров|а́я, о́й, *f.* peaceful settlement; amic-
able agreement.

мировоззре́ни|е, я, *n.* (world-)outlook,
Weltanschauung; (one's) philosophy.

мир|ово́й¹, *adj. of* ~²; ~ова́я война́ world
war; ~ова́я скорбь Weltschmerz; (*coll.,*
joc.) first-rate, first-class.

мирово́й², *adj.* (*obs.*) conciliatory; (*hist.*) м.
посре́дник arbitrator; м. судья́ Justice of
the Peace.

мирое́д, а, *m.* (*obs., coll.*) extortioner, blood-
sucker (*among peasants*).

мирозда́ни|е, я, *n.* the universe.

миролюби́вост|ь, и, *f.* peaceable disposi-
tion.

миролюби́в|ый (~, ~а), *adj.* peaceable,
pacific.

миролюби|е, я, *n.* peaceableness.

мироощуще́ни|е, я, *n.* attitude, disposition.

миропома́зани|е, я, *n.* (*eccl.*) anointing.

миросозерца́ни|е, я, *n.* = мировоззре́ние.

миротво́р|ец, ца, *m.* peace-maker.

ми́рр|а, ы, *f.* (*bot.*) myrrh.

мирско́й¹, *adj.* secular, lay; mundane,
worldly.

мир|ско́й², *adj. of* ~³; ~ская схо́дка peasants'
meeting.

мирт, а, *m.* (*bot.*) myrtle.

ми́рт|овый, *adj. of* ~.

миря́н|ин, ина, *pl.* ~e, ~, *m.* (*obs.*) layman
(*as opp. to clergy*).

ми́ск|а, и, *f.* basin, bowl.

мисс, *indecl., f.* Miss.

миссионе́р, а, *m.* missionary.

миссионе́р|ский, *adj. of* ~.

миссионе́рств|о, а, *n.* missionary work.

ми́ссис, *indecl., n.* missis, Mrs.

ми́сси|я, и, *f.* **1.** (*in var. senses*) mission. **2.**
legation.

ми́стер, а, *m.* mister, Mr.

мисте́ри|я, и, *f.* **1.** (*rel.*) mystery; элевси́н-
ские ~и the Eleusinian mysteries. **2.** (*hist.,*
theatr.) mystery, miracle-play.

ми́стик, а, *m.* mystic.

ми́стик|а, и, *f.* mysticism.

мистифика́тор, а, *m.* hoaxer.

мистифика́ци|я, и, *f.* hoax, leg-pull.

мистифици́р|овать, ую, *impf. and pf.* to
hoax, mystify.

мистици́зм, а, *m.* mysticism.

мисти́ческий, *adj.* mystic(al).

мистра́л|ь, я, *m.* mistral (*wind*).

мите́н|ки, ок, *sing.* ~ка, ~ки, *f.* mittens.

ми́тинг, а, *m.* (political) mass-meeting.

митинг|ова́ть, у́ю, *impf.* (*coll.*) **1.** to hold a
mass-meeting (about). **2.** (*pejor.*) to discuss
endlessly.

митинго́вый, *adj. of* ми́тинг.

митка́л|евый, *adj. of* ~ь.

митка́л|ь, я́, *m.* (*text.*) calico.

ми́тр|а, ы, *f.* (*eccl.*) mitre.

митрополи́т, а, *m.* (*eccl.*) metropolitan.

митрополи́|чий, *adj. of* ~т.

митропо́ли|я, и, *f.* (*eccl.*) metropolitan see.

ми́ттел|ь, я, *m.* (*typ.*) English (*14-point*
type).

миф, а, *m.* myth (*also fig.*).

мифи́ческий, *adj.* mythic(al).

мифологи́ческий, *adj.* mythological.

мифоло́ги|я, и, *f.* mythology.

мифотво́рчеств|о, а, *n.* myth-making.

мице́ли|й, я, *m.* (*bot.*) mycelium.

ми́чман, а, *pl.* (*in naval usage*) ~а́, ~о́в, *m.*
(*naut.*) **1.** (*in Soviet Navy*) warrant officer.
2. (*in Imperial Russian Navy*) midshipman.

ми́чман|ский, *adj. of* ~.

мише́н|ь, и, *f.* target (*also fig.*).

ми́шк|а, и, *m.* (*dim. of* Михаи́л) **1.** (*pet-*
-name for) bear. **2.** Teddy bear.

мишур|а́, ы́, *f.* **1.** tinsel. **2.** (*fig.*) trumpery.

мишу́рный, *adj.* tinsel, trumpery, tawdry;
(*also fig.*).

миэли́т, а, *m.* (*med.*) myelitis.

младе́н|ец, ца, *m.* baby, infant.

младе́нческий, *adj.* infantile.

младе́нчеств|о, а, *n.* infancy, babyhood.

млад|о́й (~, ~а́, ~о), *adj.* (*arch. or poet.*)
young; стар и ~ one and all (*without*
respect of age).

младопи́сьменный, *adj.* м. язы́к language
having newly acquired a written form.

мла́дост|ь, и, *f.* (*arch. or poet.*) youth.

мла́дший, *adj.* (*comp. and superl. of* молодо́й)
1. younger. **2.** the youngest. **3.** junior;
м. кома́ндный соста́в non-commissioned
officers; м. офице́рский соста́в junior officers, subaltern officers; м. лейтена́нт second
lieutenant (*see also* лейтена́нт).

млекопита́юще|ее, его, *n.* (*zool.*) mammal.

мле|ть, ю, *impf.* **1.** (*obs.*) to grow numb.
2. (от) to be overcome (*with delight, with*
fright, etc.).

мле́чный, *adj.* milk; lactic; м. сок (*bot.*)
latex; (*physiol.*) chyle; М. путь (*astron.*) the
Milky Way, the Galaxy.

мне, *d. and p. of* я.

мнемони́ческий, *adj.* mnemonic.

мне́ни|е, я, *n.* opinion.

мнимоуме́рший, *adj.* apparently dead.

мни́м|ый, *adj.* **1.** imaginary (*also math.*); ~ая величина́ imaginary quantity. **2.** sham, pretended; м. больно́й hypochondriac.

мни́тельност|ь, и, *f.* **1.** hypochondria. **2.** mistrustfulness, suspiciousness.

мни́тел|ьный (~ен, ~ьна), *adj.* **1.** hypochondriac; valetudinarian. **2.** mistrustful, suspicious.

мн|ить, ю, ишь, *impf.* **1.** (*obs.*) to think, imagine. **2.** м. мно́го о себе́ to think much of oneself.

мни́т|ься, ~ся, *impf.* (*impers.*; *obs. or poet.*) ~ся it seems, methinks.

мно́г|ие, их, *adj. and noun* many; во ~их отноше́ниях in many respects.

мно́го, *adv.* (+*g.*) much; many; a lot (of); м. вре́мени much time; м. лет many years; о́чень м. знать to know a great deal; м. лу́чше much better; ни м., ни ма́ло (*coll.*) neither more nor less.

мно́го- many-, poly-, multi-.

многоа́томный, *adj.* (*phys.*) polyatomic.

многобо́жи|е, я, *n.* polytheism.

многобра́чи|е, я, *n.* polygamy.

многобра́ч|ный (~ен, ~на), *adj.* polygamous.

многова́то, *adv.* (*coll.*) a bit too much, rather much (many).

многовеково́й, *adj.* centuries-old.

многовла́сти|е, я, *n.* = многонача́лие.

многово́д|ный (~ен, ~на), *adj.* (*of rivers, etc.*) full, having high water-level.

многово́дь|е, я, *n.* **1.** fulness, high water--level. **2.** time of high water-levels.

многоговоря́щий, *adj.* revealing, suggestive.

многогра́нник, а, *m.* (*math.*) polyhedron.

многогра́нный, *adj.* (*math.*) polyhedral; (*fig.*) many-sided.

многоде́тност|ь, и, *f.* possession of many children.

многоде́т|ный (~ен, ~на), *adj.* having many children.

мно́г|ое, ого, *n.* much, a great deal; во ~ом in many respects.

многожён|ец, ца, *m.* polygamist.

многожёнств|о, а, *n.* polygamy.

многожи́льный, *adj.* (*tech.*) multiple.

многоземе́л|ьный (~ен, ~ьна), *adj.* possessing, owning much land; ~ьное хозя́йство large-scale cultivation.

многозначи́тельност|ь, и, *f.* significance.

многозначи́тел|ьный (~ен, ~ьна), *adj.* significant.

многозна́ч|ный (~ен, ~на), *adj.* **1.** (*math.*)

expressed by several figures. **2.** (*ling.*) polysemantic; ~ное сло́во polyseme.

многокаска́дный, *adj.* (*radio*) multistage.

многокле́точный, *adj.* (*biol.*) multi-cellular.

многокра́сочный, *adj.* polychromatic, many-coloured.

многокра́тный, *adj.* **1.** repeated, re-iterated; multiple. **2.** (*gram.*) frequentative, iterative.

многола́мповый, *adj.* multi-valve.

многоле́ти|е, я, *n.* expression of wishes for long life.

многоле́тний, *adj.* **1.** lasting *or* living many years; of many years' standing. **2.** (*bot.*) perennial.

многоле́тник, а, *m.* (*bot.*) perennial.

многоли́кий, *adj.* many-sided.

многолю́дност|ь, и, *f.* populousness; size (*of meeting, etc.*).

многолю́д|ный (~ен, ~на), *adj.* populous; crowded.

многолю́дств|о, а, *n.* throng.

многомиллио́нн|ый, *adj.* of many millions.

многому́жи|е, я, *n.* polyandry.

многонациона́л|ьный (~ен, ~ьна), *adj.* multi-national.

многонача́ли|е, я, *n.* multiple authority (*absence of clearly-defined spheres of authority*).

многоно́жк|а, и, *f.* (*zool.*) myriapod.

многообеща́ющий, *adj.* **1.** promising, hopeful. **2.** significant.

многообра́зи|е, я, *n.* variety, diversity.

многообра́з|ный (~ен, ~на), *adj.* varied, diverse.

многопо́ль|е, я, *n.* (*agric.*) crop-rotation system involving seven or eight fields.

многопо́ль|ный, *adj.* of ~е.

многоречи́в|ый (~, ~а), *adj.* loquacious, verbose, prolix.

многосеме́|йный (~ен, ~йна), *adj.* having a large family.

многосло́в|ный (~ен, ~на), *adj.* verbose, prolix.

многосло́жный, *adj.* **1.** complex, complicated. **2.** polysyllabic.

многосло́йн|ый, *adj.* multi-layer; multi--ply; ~ая фане́ра plywood.

многостано́чник, а, *m.* workman operating a number of machines simultaneously.

многостепе́нн|ый, *adj.* many-stage; ~ые вы́боры election by several stages.

многосторо́н|ний (~ен, ~ня), *adj.* **1.** (*math.*) polygonal; multilateral (*also fig.*). **2.** (*fig.*) many-sided, versatile.

многострада́л|ьный (~ен, ~ьна), *adj.* suffering, unfortunate.

многоступе́нчатый, *adj.* (*tech.*) multi-stage.

многотира́жк|а, и, *f.* (*coll.*) factory newspaper; house organ.

многотира́жный, *adj.* published in large editions.

многотóмный, *adj.* in many volumes.
многотóчи|е, я, *n.* dots (...); (*typ.*) marks of omission; omission points.
многоуважа́емый, *adj.* respected; (*in letters*) dear.
многоуго́льник, а, *m.* (*math.*) polygon.
многоуго́льный, *adj.* (*math.*) polygonal.
многофа́зный, *adj.* (*electr.*) polyphase.
многоцве́тный, *adj.* **1.** many-coloured, multi-coloured. **2.** (*typ.*) polychromatic. **3.** (*bot.*) multiflorous.
многочи́слен|ный (~, ~на), *adj.* numerous.
многочле́н, а, *m.* (*math.*) multinomial.
мно́жественност|ь, и, *f.* plurality.
мно́жественн|ый, *adj.* plural; ~ое число́ (*gram.*) plural (number).
мно́жеств|о, а, *n.* a great number, a quantity; multitude; (*math.*) set.
мно́жим|ое, ого, *n.* (*math.*) multiplicand.
мно́жител|ь, я, *m.* multiplier, factor.
мно́ж|ить, у, ишь, *impf.* **1.** (*pf.* по~, у~) (*math.*) to multiply. **2.** (*pf.* у~) to increase, augment.
мно́ж|иться, усь, ишься, *impf.* (*of* у~) **1.** to multiply, increase (*intrans.*). **2.** *pass. of* ~ить.
мной, мно́ю, *i. of* я.
мобилиза|цио́нный, *adj. of* ~ция.
мобилиза́ци|я, и, *f.* mobilization.
мобилизо́ванност|ь, и, *f.* complete readiness for action.
мобилизо́в|анный, *p.p.p. of* ~а́ть; *as noun* mobilized soldier.
мобилиз|ова́ть, у́ю, *impf. and pf.* (на+*a.*) to mobilize (for).
моби́льный *adj.* mobile.
могика́н|е, ~, *pl. only*, the Mohicans; после́дний из ~ the last of the Mohicans.
моги́л|а, ы, *f.* grave; свести́ в ~у to bring to one's grave.
моги́льник, а, *m.* (*archaeol.*) burial ground.
моги́льный, *adj.* **1.** *adj. of* моги́ла. **2.** sepulchral.
моги́льщик, а, *m.* grave-digger.
мо|гу́, ~гут, *see* мочь.
могу́ч|ий (~, ~а), *adj.* mighty, powerful.
могу́ществен|ный (~, ~на), *adj.* powerful; potent.
могу́ществ|о, а, *n.* power, might.
мо́д|а, ы, *f.* fashion, vogue; выходи́ть из ~ы to go out of fashion; по после́дней ~е in the latest fashion.
мода́льност|ь, и, *f.* (*philos.*) modality.
мода́льный, *adj.* modal.
модели́зм, а, *m.* modelling.
модели́р|овать, ую, *impf. and pf.* (*pf. also* с~) to model, fashion.
моде́л|ь, и, *f.* (*in var. senses*) model, pattern.
модельé́р, а, *m.* modeller.
моде́ль|ный, *adj.* **1.** *adj. of* ~. **2.** fashionable.

моде́льщик, а, *m.* (*tech.*) modeller, pattern maker.
модера́тор, а, *m.* (*tech.*) governor.
моде́рн, а, *m.* modernist style (*in art, furnishing, etc.*); *as indecl. adj.* modern.
модерниза́ци|я, и, *f.* modernization.
модернизи́р|овать, ую, *impf. and pf.* to modernize.
модерни́зм, а, *m.* (*art*) modernism.
модерниз|ова́ть, у́ю, *impf. and pf.* = ~и́ровать.
модерни́ст, а, *m.* (*art*) modernist.
моди́стк|а, и, *f.* milliner, modiste.
модифика́ци|я, и, *f.* modification.
модифици́р|овать, ую, *impf. and pf.* to modify.
мо́дник, а, *m.* (*coll.*) dandy.
мо́днича|ть, ю, *impf.* (*coll.*) **1.** to dress in the latest fashion, follow the fashion. **2.** (*coll.*) to behave affectedly.
мо́д|ный (~ен, ~на́, ~но), *adj.* **1.** fashionable, stylish. **2.** *adj. of* ~а; м. журна́л fashion magazine.
модули́р|овать, ую, *impf.* (*mus. and tech.*) to modulate.
мо́дул|ь, я, *m.* (*math.*) modulus.
модуля́ци|я, и, *f.* (*mus. and tech.*) modulation.
мо́дус, а, *m.* modus.
мо́жет, *see* мочь.
можжеве́ловый, *adj.* juniper.
можжеве́льник, а, *m.* (*bot.*) juniper.
мо́жно, *pred.* (*impers.*+*inf.*) **1.** it is possible; м. бы́ло э́то предви́деть it was possible to foresee it, it could have been foreseen; как м.+*comp.* as . . . as possible; как м. скоре́е as soon as possible. **2.** it is permissible; м. идти́? may I (we) go?; м.! (*sc.* войти́) come in!
моза́ик|а, и, *f.* mosaic; inlay.
моза́ичный, *adj.* inlaid, mosaic, tesselated.
мозг, а, в ~у́, *pl.* ~и́, ~о́в, *m.* **1.** brain (*also fig.*), nerve tissue; головно́й м. brain, cerebrum; спинно́й м. spinal cord; шевели́ть ~а́ми (*coll.*) to use one's head. **2.** (*anat.*) marrow; до ~а косте́й (*fig., coll.*) to the core.
мо́зглый, *adj.* dank.
мозгля́вый, *adj.* (*coll.*) weakly, puny.
мозгови́т|ый (~, ~а), *adj.* (*coll.*) brainy.
мозгово́й, *adj.* (*anat.*) cerebral; (*fig.*) brain.
мозжеч|о́к, ка́, *m.* (*anat.*) cerebellum.
мозж|и́ть, и́т, *impf.* (*coll.*) to ache; мозжи́т нога́ my leg is aching; (*impers.*) мозжи́т но́гу my leg is aching; мозжи́т в ноге́ I've an ache in my leg.
мозо́лист|ый (~, ~а), *adj.* callous(ed); (*fig.*) toil-hardened; ~ые ру́ки horny hands.
мозо́л|ить, ю, ишь, *impf.* (*of* на~) to make callous; м. глаза́ (+*d.*; *fig., coll.*) to plague (with one's presence).

мозо́ль|ь, и, *f.* corn; callus, callosity; ру́ки в ∼ях callus(ed) hands; наступи́ть кому́-н. на люби́мую м. (*fig.*, *coll.*) to tread on someone's pet corn.

мозо́ль|ный, *adj. of* ∼; м. пла́стырь corn-plaster.

мой, *possessive adj.* my; mine; ты зна́ешь лу́чше моего́ (*coll.*) you know better than I; *as noun* **мой, мои́х** my people; по-мо́ему in my opinion; as I think right.

мо́йк|а, и, *f.* **1.** washing. **2.** (*tech.*) washer.

мо́кко, *indecl.*, *m.* mocha (*coffee*).

мо́к|нуть, ну, нешь, *past* ∼, ∼ла, *impf.* **1.** (*pf.* вы́∼) to become wet, become soaked. **2.** to soak (*intrans.*).

мокри́ц|а, ы, *f.* wood-louse.

мокрова́тый, *adj.* moist, damp.

мокро́т|а, ы, *f.* (*med.*) phlegm.

мокрот|а́, ы́, *f.* humidity, moistness.

мо́кр|ый (∼, ∼а́, ∼о) *adj.* wet, damp; soggy; ∼о (*impers.*, *pred.*) it is wet; ∼ая ку́рица (*coll.*) milksop; у неё глаза́ на ∼ом ме́сте (*coll.*) she is easily moved to tears.

мол[1], а, *m.* mole, pier.

мол[2], (*contraction of* мо́лвил) he says (said), they say (said), *etc.* (*indicating reported speech*); он, м., никогда́ там не́ был he said he had never been there.

молв|а́, ы́, *f.* (*obs.*) rumour, talk; идёт м. it is rumoured, rumour has it; дурна́я м. ill repute.

мо́лв|ить, лю, ишь, *pf.* (*obs.*) to say.

молдава́н|ин, ина, *pl.* ∼е, ∼, *m.* Moldavian.

молдава́нк|а, и, *f.* Moldavian (woman).

молдав|а́нский = ∼ский.

молда́вский, *adj.* Moldavian.

моле́б|ен, на, *m.* (*eccl.*) service; public prayer.

моле́бстви|е, я, *n.* = моле́бен.

моле́кул|а, ы, *f.* (*phys.*) molecule.

молекуля́рный, *adj.* molecular.

моле́л|ьня, ьни, *g. pl.* ∼ен, *f.* chapel, meeting-house (*of rel. sects*).

моле́ни|е, я, *n.* **1.** praying. **2.** entreaty, supplication.

молески́н, а, *m.* (*text.*) moleskin.

молибде́н, а, *m.* (*chem.*) molybdenum.

молибде́н|овый, *adj. of* ∼.

моли́тв|а, ы, *f.* prayer.

моли́твенник, а, *m.* prayer-book.

моли́тв|енный, *adj. of* ∼а.

мол|и́ть, ю́, ∼ишь, *impf.* (*a. and* о+*p.*) to pray (for), entreat (for), supplicate (for), beseech; ∼ю́ вас о по́мощи I beg you to help me.

мол|и́ться, ю́сь, ∼ишься, *impf.* **1.** (*pf.* по∼; о+*p.*) to pray (for), offer prayers (for); он ∼ится Бо́гу he is saying his prayers. **2.** (*fig.*; на+*a.*) to idolize.

мо́лкн|уть, у, ешь, *impf.* (*poet.*) to fall silent.

моллю́ск, а, *m.* mollusc; shell-fish.

молниено́сно, *adv.* with lightning speed, like lightning.

молниено́с|ный (∼ен, ∼на), *adj.* (quick as) lightning; ∼ная война́ blitzkrieg.

молниеотво́д, а, *m.* lightning-conductor.

молни́р|овать, ую, *impf. and pf.* to inform by express telegram.

мо́лни|я, и, *f.* **1.** lightning. **2.** (телегра́мма-)м. express telegram. **3.** (застёжка-)м. zip-fastener.

молодёж|ный, *adj. of* ∼ь.

молодёж|ь, и, *f.* (*collect.*) youth; young people.

молоде́|ть, ю, ешь, *impf.* (*of* по∼) to grow young again.

молод|е́ц, ца́, *m.* fine fellow; вести́ себя́ ∼цо́м (*coll.*) to put up a good show; *as interj.* м.! (*coll.*) well done!

молоде́цкий, *adj.* (*coll.*) dashing, spirited.

молоде́честв|о, а, *n.* spirit, mettle, dash.

моло|ди́ть, жу́, ди́шь, *impf.* to make look younger.

моло|ди́ться, жу́сь, ди́шься, *impf.* to try to look younger than one's age.

молоди́ц|а, ы, *f.* (*dial.*) young married (peasant) woman.

моло́д|ка, ки, *f.* **1.** = ∼и́ца. **2.** pullet.

молодня́к, а́, *m.* (*collect.*) **1.** saplings. **2.** young animals; cubs. **3.** (*coll.*) the younger generation.

молодожён|ы, ов, *sing.* ∼, ∼а, *m.* **1.** newly-married couple, newly-weds. **2.** (*sing.*) newly-married man.

молод|о́й (мо́лод, ∼а́, мо́лодо), *adj.* **1.** young; youthful (*also of inanimate objects*); м. задо́р youthful hotheadedness; м. карто́фель new potatoes; м. ме́сяц new moon; мо́лодо-зе́лено! (*iron.*, *of young or inexperienced person*) he has a lot to learn! **2.** *as noun* (*coll.*) м., ∼о́го, *m.* bridegroom; ∼а́я, ∼о́й, *f.* bride; ∼ые, ∼ы́х newly-married couple, newly-weds.

мо́лодост|ь, и, *f.* youth; youthfulness.

молоду́х|а, и, *f.* (*dial.*) = молоди́ца.

молодцева́т|ый (∼, ∼а), *adj.* dashing, sprightly.

моло́дчик, а, *m.* (*coll.*) **1.** rogue, rascal. **2.** (*pejor.*) lackey, myrmidon.

молодчи́н|а, ы, *m.* (*coll.*) fine fellow; *as interj.* м.! well done!

моложа́вост|ь, и, *f.* youthful appearance (*for one's years*).

моложа́в|ый (∼, ∼а), *adj.* young-looking; име́ть м. вид to look young for one's age.

моло́|же, *comp. of* ∼до́й.

моло́зив|о, а, *no pl.*, *n.* colostrum; (*of cow*) beestings.

молок|и́, ∼, *no sing.* soft roe, milt.

молок|о́, а́, *no pl.*, *n.* milk.

молокосо́с, а, *m.* (*coll.*) greenhorn, raw youth.

мо́лот, а, *m.* hammer; кузне́чный м. sledge--hammer.

молоти́лк|а, и, *f.* threshing-machine.

молоти́л|о, а, *n.* (*agric.*) swingle.

молоти́льщик, а, *m.* thresher.

моло|ти́ть, чу́, ~ти́шь, *impf.* (*of* с~) to thresh.

молотобо́|ец, йца, *m.* (*tech.*) hammerer; blacksmith's striker.

молот|о́к, ка́, *m.* hammer; прода́ть с ~ка́ to sell by auction.

молото́ч|ек, ка, *m.* **1.** *dim. of* молото́к. **2.** (*anat.*) malleus.

мо́лот-ры́б|а, ы, *f.* (*zool.*) hammer-head shark.

мо́лот|ый (~, ~а), *p.p.p. of* моло́ть *and adj.* ground.

моло́ть, мелю́, ме́лешь, *impf.* (*of* с~) to grind, mill; м. вздор (*fig., coll.*) to talk non-sense, talk rot.

молотьб|а́, ы́, *f.* threshing.

молоча́|й, я, *m.* (*bot.*) spurge, euphorbia.

моло́чн|ая, ой, *f.* dairy; creamery.

моло́чник¹, а, *m.* milk-jug; milk-can.

моло́чник², а, *m.* milkman.

моло́чниц|а¹, ы, *f.* milk-seller; dairy-maid.

моло́чниц|а², ы, *f.* (*med.*) thrush.

моло́чност|ь, и, *f.* (*agric.*) yield (*of cow*).

моло́чн|ый, *adj.* **1.** *adj. of* молоко́; м. брат foster-brother; ~ое стекло́ frosted glass; opal glass; ~ое хозя́йство dairy-farm(ing). **2.** milky; lactic; ~ая кислота́ (*chem.*) lactic acid.

мо́лча, *adv.* silently, in silence.

молчали́в|ый (~, ~а), *adj.* **1.** taciturn, silent. **2.** tacit, unspoken.

молча́льник, а, *m.* (*eccl.*) one who has taken a vow of silence.

молча́ни|е, я, *n.* silence.

молч|а́ть, у́, и́шь, *impf.* to be silent, keep silence.

молч|ко́м, *adv.* (*coll.*) = ~а.

молчо́к, indecl., m. (*coll.*) silence; об э́том — м.! not a word of (about) this!

мол|ь¹, и, *f.* (clothes-)moth.

мол|ь², и, *f.* (*chem.*) mole (*gram molecule*).

мольб|а́, ы́, *f.* entreaty, supplication.

мольбе́рт, а, *m.* easel.

моме́нт, а, *m.* **1.** moment; instant. **2.** fea-ture, element, factor (*of process, situation, etc.*). **3.** (*phys.*) moment; м. ине́рции mo-ment of inertia.

момента́льно, *adv.* in a moment, instantly.

момента́льный, *adj.* instantaneous; м. сни́мок snapshot.

моме́нтами, *adv.* (*coll.*) now and then.

мона́д|а ы, *f.* (*philos.*) monad.

мона́рх, а, *m.* monarch.

монархи́зм, а, *m.* monarchism.

монархи́ст, а, *m.* monarchist.

монархи́ческ|ий, *adj.* monarchic(al).

мона́рхи|я, и, *f.* monarchy.

мона́рший, *adj. of* мона́рх.

монасты́рский, *adj.* monastic, conventual.

монасты́р|ь, я́, *m.* monastery; (же́нский) convent; в чужо́й м. со свои́м уста́вом не су́йся (*prov.*) when in Rome do as the Romans do.

мона́х, а, *m.* monk; friar; постри́чься в ~и to take the monastic vows; жить ~ом (*fig., iron.*) to have a monkish existence.

мона́хин|я, и, *f.* nun; постри́чься в ~и to take the veil.

мона́шенк|а, и, *f.* **1.** (*coll.*) nun. **2.** (*zool.*) praying mantis.

мона́шеский, *adj.* monastic; (*fig., joc.*) monkish.

мона́шеств|о, а, *n.* **1.** monasticism. **2.** (*collect.*) monks, regular clergy.

монго́л, а, *m.* Mongol, Mongolian.

монголове́дени|е, я, *n.* Mongolian studies.

монго́льский, *adj.* Mongolian.

моне́т|а, ы, *f.* coin; зво́нкая м. specie, hard cash; разме́нная м. change; ходя́чая м. currency; плати́ть кому́-н. той же ~ой (*fig.*) to pay someone in his own coin; приня́ть за чи́стую ~у (*fig., coll.*) to take at face value, take in good faith.

моне́тный, *adj.* monetary; м. двор mint.

монетоприёмник, а, *m.* coin-box (*of auto-matic machine*).

моне́тчик, а, *m.* coiner.

мони́зм, а, *m.* (*philos.*) monism.

мони́ст|о, а, *n.* necklace.

монито́р, а, *m.* (*naut.*) monitor.

монога́ми|я, и, *f.* monogamy.

моногра́мм|а, ы, *f.* monogram.

монографи|я, и, *f.* monograph.

моно́кл|ь, я, *m.* (*single*) eye-glass, monocle.

моноко́к, а, *m.* (*aeron.*) monocoque.

монокульту́р|а, ы, *f.* (*agric.*) one-crop sys-tem, monoculture.

моноли́т, а, *m.* monolith.

моноли́тност|ь, и, *f.* monolithic character, solidity.

моноли́т|ный (~ен, ~на), *adj.* monolithic (*also fig.; polit.*); (*fig.*) solid.

моноло́г, а, *m.* monologue, soliloquy.

моно́м, а, *m.* (*math.*) monomial.

мономан, а, *m.* (*med.*) monomaniac.

мономани|я, и, *f.* (*med.*) monomania.

монометалли́зм, а, *m.* (*econ.*) monometal-lism.

монопла́н, а, *m.* monoplane.

монополиза́ци|я, и, *f.* monopolization.

монополизи́р|овать, ую, *impf. and pf.* to monopolize.

монополи́ст, а, *m.* monopolist.

монополисти́ческий, *adj.* monopolistic.

монопо́ли|я, и, *f.* (*econ. and fig.*) monopoly.

монопо́л|ьный, *adj.* of ~ия; ~ьное пра́во exclusive rights.

моноре́льсовый, *adj.* monorail.

монотеи́зм, а, *m.* monotheism.

монотеисти́ческий, *adj.* monotheistic.

моноти́п, а, *m.* (*typ.*) monotype.

моното́нный, *adj.* monotonous.

монофто́нг, а, *m.* (*ling.*) monophthong.

монохо́рд, а, *m.* (*mus.*) monochord.

монпансье́, *indecl.,* *n.* fruit drops.

монстр, а, *m.* monster.

монта́ж, а, *m.* **1.** (*tech.*) assembling, mounting, installation. **2.** (*cinema*) montage; (*art, mus., lit.*) arrangement; м. о́перы по ра́дио arrangement of an opera for radio.

монтажёр, а, *m.* (*cinema, phot.*) montage specialist.

монта́жник, а, *m.* rigger, erector, fitter.

монта́ж|ный, *adj.* of ~; *as noun* ~ная, ~ной, *f.* (*tech.*) assembly shop; (*cinema*) clipping room.

монтёр, а, *m.* **1.** fitter. **2.** electrician.

монти́р|овать, ую, *impf.* (*of* с~) **1.** (*tech.*) to assemble, mount, fit. **2.** (*art, cinema, etc.*) to mount; to arrange.

монуме́нт, а, *m.* monument.

монумента́льный, *adj.* monumental (*also fig.*).

мопс, а, *m.* pug(-dog).

мор, а, *m.* (*obs. and coll.*) wholesale deaths, high mortality.

морализи́р|овать, ую, *impf.* to moralize.

морали́ст, а, *m.* moralist.

мора́л|ь, и, *f.* **1.** (code of) morals, ethics. **2.** (*coll.*) moralizing; чита́ть м. to moralize. **3.** moral (*of a story, etc.*).

мора́льный, *adj.* (*in var. senses*) moral; ethical.

морато́ри|й, я, *m.* (*leg., comm.*) moratorium.

морг¹, а, *m.* morgue, mortuary.

морг², а, *m.* (*obs.*) *land measure* = *approx.* 1¼ *acres* (*in Poland and Lithuania*).

морганати́ческий, *adj.* morganatic.

морг|а́ть, а́ю, *impf.* (*of* ~ну́ть) to blink; to wink.

морг|ну́ть, ну́, нёшь, *pf.* of ~а́ть; гла́зом не ~ну́в (*coll.*) without batting an eyelid.

мо́рд|а, ы, *f.* **1.** snout, muzzle. **2.** (*coll.*; *of human face*) mug.

морда́ст|ый (~, ~а), *adj.* (*coll.*) **1.** with a large muzzle. **2.** (*of people*) with a big, fat face.

мордв|а́, ы́, *f.* (*collect.*) the Mordva, the Mordvinians.

мордви́н, а, *m.* Mordvinian.

мордви́н|ка, ки, *f.* of ~.

мордо́вский, *adj.* Mordvinian.

мо́р|е, я, *pl.* ~я́, ~е́й, *n.* sea; за́ ~ем oversea(s); из-за ~я from overseas; на́ м. at sea; у ~я by the sea; ему́ м. по коле́но (*coll.*) he

doesn't care a damn.

море́н|а, ы, *f.* (*geol.*) moraine.

море́н|ный, *adj.* of ~a.

морёный, *adj.* (*of wood*) water-seasoned.

морепла́вани|е, я, *n.* navigation, seafaring.

морепла́вател|ь, я, *m.* navigator, seafarer.

морепла́вательный, *adj.* nautical, navigational.

морехо́д, а, *m.* sea-farer.

морехо́дност|ь, и, *f.* seaworthiness.

морехо́дный, *adj.* nautical.

морехо́дств|о, а, *n.* (*obs.*) navigation.

морж, а́, *m.* walrus.

моржи́х|а, и, *f.* of морж.

морж|о́вый, *adj.* of ~.

Мо́рзе, *indecl.* morse; а́збука М. Morse code.

морзи́ст, а, *m.* Morse code signaller.

морзя́нк|а, и, *f.* (*coll.*) Morse code.

мори́лк|а, и, *f.* (*tech.*) mordant.

мор|и́ть¹, ю́, и́шь, *impf.* **1.** (*pf.* вы́~ *and* по~) to exterminate. **2.** (*pf.* у~) to exhaust wear out; м. го́лодом to starve. **3.** (*dial.*) to quench.

мор|и́ть², ю́, и́шь, *impf.* to stain (*wood*); м. дуб to fume oak.

морко́вк|а, и, *f.* (*coll.*) a carrot.

морко́в|ный, *adj.* of ~ь.

морко́в|ь, и, *f.* carrots.

мормо́н, а, *m.* (*rel.*) Mormon.

моров|о́й, *adj.* ~о́е пове́трие, ~а́я я́зва plague, pestilence.

моро́жен|ое, ого, *n.* ice(-cream).

моро́женщик, а, *m.* ice-cream vendor.

моро́женщи|ца, ы, *f.* of ~к.

моро́жен|ый, *adj.* frozen, chilled; ~ое мя́со chilled meat.

моро́з, а, *m.* **1.** frost; у меня́ м. по ко́же подира́ет (пошёл) it makes (made) my flesh creep. **2.** (*usually in pl.*) intensely cold weather.

морози́льник, а, *m.* deep-freezer.

морози́льщик, а, *m.* (*coll.*) refrigerator ship.

моро́|зить, жу, зишь, *impf.* (*of* по~) **1.** to freeze, congeal. **2.** *impers.* ~зит it is freezing.

моро́зн|ый, *adj.* frosty; ~о (*impers., pred.*) it is freezing.

морозосто́йкий, *adj.* (*bot.*) frost-resisting.

морозоусто́йчив|ый (~, ~а), *adj.* = морозосто́йкий.

морок|а́, и́, *f.* (*coll., fig.*) darkness, confusion; с ним одна́ м. you can get no sense out of him.

морос|и́ть, и́т, *impf.* to drizzle.

моро́ч|ить, у, ишь, *impf.* (*of* об~) (*coll.*) to fool, pull the wool over the eyes of; м. го́лову кому́-н. to take someone in.

моро́шк|а, и, *f.* cloudberry (*Rubus chamaimorus*).

морс, а, *m.* fruit drink.

морск|о́й, *adj.* **1.** sea; maritime; marine, nautical; м. волк (*coll.*) old salt, sea-dog; ~а́я звезда́ starfish; м. ёж (*zool.*) sea-urchin, echinus; ~а́я игла́ needle-fish, pipe-fish; ~а́я капу́ста (*bot.*) sea-kale; м. конёк (*zool.*) sea-horse, hippocamp; ~а́я пе́нка (*min.*) meerschaum; м. разбо́йник pirate; ~а́я сви́нка guinea-pig; ~а́я свинья́ porpoise. **2.** naval; ~а́я пехо́та marines; м. флот navy, fleet.

морти́р|а, ы, *f.* (*mil.*) mortar.

морти́р|ный, *adj. of* ~а.

морфе́м|а, ы, *f.* (*ling.*) morpheme.

мо́рфи|й, я, *m.* (*pharm.*) morphia, morphine.

морфини́зм, а, *m.* addiction to morphine.

морфини́ст, а, *m.* morphine addict.

морфологи́ческий, *adj.* morphological.

морфоло́ги|я, и, *f.* morphology.

морщи́н|а, ы, *f.* wrinkle; crease.

морщи́нист|ый (~, ~a), *adj.* wrinkled, lined; creased.

мо́рщ|ить, у, ишь, *impf.* **1.** (*pf.* на~) м. лоб to knit one's brow. **2.** (*pf.* с~) to wrinkle, pucker; м. гу́бы to purse one's lips.

морщ|и́ть, и́т, *impf.* to crease, ruck up (*intrans.*).

мо́рщ|иться, усь, ишься, *impf.* **1.** (*pf.* на~) to knit one's brow. **2.** (*pf.* по~ *and* с~) to make a wry face, wince. **3.** (*pf.* с~) to crease, wrinkle.

моря́к, а́, *m.* sailor.

моска́л|ь, я́, *m.* (*obs., pejor.*) Muscovite.

москате́л|ь, и, *f.* (*collect.*) dry-salter's wares (*paints, oil, gum, etc.*).

москате́ль|ный, *adj. of* ~; ~ная торго́вля dry-saltery.

москате́льщик, а, *m.* dry-salter.

москвитя́н|ин, ина, *pl.* ~е, *m.* (*obs.*) Muscovite.

москви́ч, а́, *m.* **1.** Muscovite, inhabitant of Moscow. **2.** Moskvich (*trade name of a Soviet-made motor-car*).

моски́т, а, *m.* mosquito.

моски́т|ный, *adj. of* ~; ~ная се́тка mosquito net.

моско́вк|а, и, *f.* (*orn.*) coal tit.

моско́вск|ий, *adj.* (of) Moscow; ~ая Русь (*hist.*) Muscovy.

мост, ~á, о ~е, на ~у́, *pl.* ~ы́, *m.* **1.** bridge. **2.** (*tech.*) shaft.

мо́стик, а, *m.* **1.** *dim. of* мост. **2.** капита́нский м. (*naut.*) (*captain's*) bridge.

мости́льщик, а, *m.* paviour.

мо|сти́ть, щу́, сти́шь, *impf.* **1.** (*pf.* вы́~, за~) to pave. **2.** (*pf.* на~) to lay (*a floor*).

мостк|и́, о́в, *no sing.* **1.** planked footway. **2.** wooden platform (*at edge of stream, on scaffolding*).

мостов|а́я, о́й, *f.* road(way), carriage way.

мост|ово́й, *adj. of* ~.

мо́ськ|а, и, *f.* (*coll.*) pug-dog.

мот, а, *m.* prodigal, spendthrift.

мота́льный, *adj.* (*tech.*) winding.

мот|а́ть[1], а́ю, *impf.* **1.**(*pf.* за~, на~) to wind, reel; м. себе́ что-н. на ус (*fig., coll.*) to make a mental note of something. **2.** (*pf.* ~ну́ть) (+*i.*; *coll.*) to shake (*head, etc.*).

мота́|ть[2], ю, *impf.* (*of* про~) (*coll.*) to squander.

мота́|ться[1], ется, *impf.* (*coll.*) to dangle.

мота́|ться[2], юсь, *impf.* (*coll.*) to rush about; м. по́ свету to knock about the world.

моте́л|ь, я, *m.* motel.

моти́в[1], а, *m.* **1.** motive. **2.** reason; привести́ ~ы в по́льзу предложе́ния to adduce reasons in support of an assertion.

моти́в[2], а, *m.* **1.** (*mus.*) tune. **2.** (*mus. and fig.*) motif.

мотиви́р|овать, ую, *impf. and pf.* to give reasons (for), justify.

мотивиро́вк|а, и, *f.* reason(s), justification.

мот|ну́ть, ну́, нёшь, *pf. of* ~а́ть[1].

мото- **1.** (*abbr. of* мото́рный) motor-. **2.** (*abbr. of* моторизо́ванный) motorized. **3.** (*abbr. of* мотоци́кл) motor-cycle.

мотобо́т, а, *m.* motor-boat.

мотови́л|о, а, *n.* (*tech.*) reel.

мото́вк|а, и, *f.* (*coll.*) *f. of* мот.

мотово́з, а, *m.* petrol engine (*on railways for shunting, etc.*).

мотовско́й, *adj.* wasteful, extravagant.

мотовств|о́, а́, *n.* wastefulness, extravagance, prodigality.

мотого́н|ки, ок, *no sing.* motor-cycle races.

мотодрези́н|а, ы, *f.* motor trolley (*on rails*).

мотодро́м, а, *m.* motor-cycle racing track.

мот|о́к, ка́, *m.* skein, hank.

мотоколя́ск|а, и, *f.* motorized wheel-chair.

мотокро́сс, а, *m.* motocross, scramble.

мотомеханизи́рованный, *adj.* (*mil.*) mechanized.

мотопе́д, а, *m.* moped.

мотопехо́т|а, ы, *f.* motorized infantry.

мото́р, а, *m.* motor, engine; подвесно́й м. outboard engine.

моторесу́рс, а, *m.* (*tech.*) life (*of an engine, etc.*).

моториза́ци|я, и, *f.* motorization.

моторизо́в|анный, *p.p.p. of* ~а́ть *and adj.* (*mil.*) motorized.

моториз|ова́ть, у́ю, *impf. and pf.* to motorize.

мотори́ст, а, *m.* motor-mechanic.

мото́рк|а, и, *f.* (*coll.*) motor-boat.

мото́р|ный[1], *adj. of* ~; м. ваго́н front car (*of set, on electric railway or tramway, and containing power unit*); ~ная устано́вка power plant, power unit.

мото́рный[2], *adj.* (*physiol., psych.*) motor.

моторо́ллер, а, *m.* (motor-)scooter.
мотоци́кл, а, *m.* motor-cycle.
мотоцикле́т, а, *m.* = мотоци́кл.
мотоцикли́ст, а, *m.* motor-cyclist.
мотошле́м, а, *m.* crash helmet.
моты́г|а, и, *f.* hoe, mattock.
моты́ж|ить, у, ишь, *impf.* to hoe.
моты́л|ёк, ька́, *m.* butterfly, moth.
моты́л|ь¹, я́, *m.* mosquito grub (*used to feed fish in aquaria*).
моты́л|ь², я́, *m.* (*tech.*) crank.
мотылько́в|ые, ых (*bot.*) Papilionaceae.
мох, мха *and* **мо́ха, о мхе** *and* **о мо́хе, во (на) мху́,** *pl.* **мхи, мхов,** *m.* moss.
мохна́т|ый (∼, ∼а), *adj.* hairy, shaggy; ∼ое полоте́нце Turkish towel.
моцио́н, а, *m.* exercise; constitutional; де́лать, соверша́ть м. to take exercise.
моч|а́, и́, *f.* urine, water.
моча́л|ить, ю, ишь, *impf.* **1.** to strip into fibres. **2.** (*coll.*) to torment, vex.
моча́лк|а, и, *f.* loofah; washing-up mop.
моча́л|о, а, *n.* bast.
мочеви́н|а, ы, *f.* (*chem.*) urea.
мочево́й, *adj.* urinary, uric; м. пузы́рь (*anat.*) bladder.
мочего́нный, *adj.* (*med.*) diuretic.
мочеиспуска́ни|е, я, *n.* urination.
мочеиспуска́тельный, *adj.* м. кана́л (*anat.*) urethra.
мочёный, *adj.* soaked.
мочеотделе́ни|е, я, *n.* urination.
мочеполово́й, *adj.* (*anat.*) urino-genital.
мочето́чник, а, *m.* (*anat.*) ureter.
моч|и́ть, у́, ∼ишь, *impf.* (*of* на∼) **1.** to wet, moisten. **2.** to soak; to steep, macerate; м. селёдку to souse herring.
моч|и́ться, у́сь, ∼ишься, *impf.* (*of* по∼) (*coll.*) to urinate, make water.
мо́чк|а¹, и, *f.* soaking, macerating; retting.
мо́чк|а², и, *f.* **1.** (*anat.*) lobe of the ear. **2.** (*bot.*) fibril.
мочь¹, могу́, мо́жешь, мо́гут, *past* **мог, могла́,** *impf.* (*of* с∼) to be able; мо́жет быть, быть мо́жет perhaps, maybe; мо́жет (*coll.*) = мо́жет быть; не мо́жет быть! impossible!; как живёте-мо́жете? (*coll.*) how are you? how are things with you?; не могу́ знать (*obs.*) I don't know.
моч|ь², и, *f.* (*coll.*) power, might; во всю м., изо всей ∼и,́ что есть ∼и with all one's might, with might and main; ∼и нет (как) it is unendurable, unbearable; ∼и нет, как хо́лодно it's so cold, I can stand it no longer.
моше́нник, а, *m.* rogue, scoundrel; swindler.
моше́ннича|ть, ю, *impf.* (*of* с∼) to play the swindler.
моше́ннический, *adj.* rascally, swindling.
моше́нничеств|о, а, *n.* swindling; cheating (*at games*).

мо́шк|а, и, *f.* midge.
мошкар|а́, ы́, *f.* (*collect.*) (swarm of) midges.
мош|на́, ны́, *pl.* ∼ны́, ∼о́н, *f.* purse, pouch; больша́я, туга́я м. (*fig., coll.*) well-filled purse; наби́ть ∼ну́ (*fig., coll.*) to fill one's purse.
мошо́нк|а, и, *f.* (*anat.*) scrotum.
мошо́ночный, *adj.* scrotal.
моще́ни|е, я, *n.* paving.
мощённый, *p.p.p.* of мости́ть.
мощёный, *adj.* paved.
мо́щ|и, е́й, *no sing.* (*rel.*) relics; живы́е м. (*coll., joc., of a very thin person*) walking skeleton.
мо́щность, и, *f.* power; (*tech.*) capacity, rating; output; номина́льная м. rated power, rated capacity; дви́гатель ∼ью в сто лошади́ных сил a hundred horsepower engine.
мо́щ|ный (∼ен, ∼на́, ∼но), *adj.* powerful, mighty; vigorous.
мо|щу́, сти́шь, *see* ∼сти́ть.
мощ|ь, и, *f.* power, might.
мо́|ю, ешь, *see* мыть.
мо́ющ|ий, *pres. part. act.* of мыть *and adj.* detergent; ∼ие сре́дства detergents.
мраз|ь, и, *no pl., f.* (*coll.*) rubbish; (*pejor., of human beings*) dregs, scum.
мрак, а, *m.* darkness, gloom (*also fig., rhet.*); покры́то ∼ом неизве́стности shrouded in mystery; у него́ м. на душе́ he is in the dumps, in a black mood.
мракобе́с, а, *m.* obscurantist.
мракобе́си|е, я, *n.* obscurantism.
мра́мор, а, *m.* marble.
мра́морный, *adj.* marble; (*fig.*) (white as) marble; marmoreal.
мра́морщик, а, *m.* marble-cutter.
мрачне́|ть, ю, *impf.* (*of* по∼) to grow dark; to grow gloomy.
мра́ч|ный (∼ен, ∼на́, ∼но), *adj.* **1.** dark, sombre. **2.** (*fig.*) gloomy, dismal.
мре́|ть, ешь, *impf.* (*coll.*) to be dimly visible.
мсти́тел|ь, я, *m.* avenger.
мсти́тел|ьный (∼ен, ∼ьна), *adj.* vindictive.
мстить, мщу, мсти́шь, *impf.* (*of* ото∼) (+*d.* за+*a.*) to take vengeance (on for), revenge oneself (upon for); (за+*a.*) to avenge; м. врагу́ to take vengeance on one's enemy; м. за дру́га to avenge one's friend.
муа́р, а, *m.* moire, watered silk.
муа́ровый, *adj.* moiré.
мудрен|е́е, *comp.* of ∼ый, only in phrase (*coll.*) у́тро ве́чера м. sleep on it.
мудрён|ый (∼, ∼а́), *adj.* (*coll.*) **1.** strange, queer, odd; не ∼о́, что... it is no wonder that... **2.** difficult, abstruse, complicated.
мудре́ц, а́, *m.* (*rhet.*) sage, wise man; на вся́кого ∼а́ дово́льно простоты́ (*prov.*) Homer sometimes nods.
мудр|и́ть, ю́, и́шь, *impf.* (*of* на∼) (*coll.*) to

subtilize; to complicate matters unnecessarily; не ~и́те! don't try to be clever!

му́дрост|ь, и, *f.* wisdom; в э́том нет никако́й ~и (*coll.*) there is nothing mysterious about it.

му́дрств|овать, ую, *impf.* (*obs., coll.*) to philosophize; to bandy sophistries.

му́др|ый (~, ~а́, ~о), *adj.* wise, sage.

муж, а, *m.* 1. (*pl.* ~ья́, ~е́й, ~ья́м) husband. 2. (*pl.* ~и́, ~е́й, ~а́м) (*obs. or rhet.*) man; госуда́рственный м. statesman; м. нау́ки man of science.

мужа́|ть, ю, *impf.* (*obs.*) to grow up, reach manhood.

мужа́|ться, юсь, *impf.* to take heart, take courage; ~йтесь! courage!

мужело́ж|ец, ца, *m.* bugger, sodomite.

мужело́жств|о, а, *n.* buggery, sodomy.

мужен|ёк, ька́, *m.* (*coll.*) hubby.

мужеподо́б|ный (~ен, ~на), *adj.* mannish; masculine.

му́ж|еский, *adj.* (*obs.*) = ~ско́й; м. род (*gram.*) masculine gender.

му́жествен|ный (~, ~на), *adj.* manly, steadfast.

му́жеств|о, а, *n.* courage, fortitude.

мужи́к, а́, *m.* 1. muzhik, moujik (*Russian peasant*). 2. (*fig.*) lout, clod, bumpkin. 3. (*coll.*) man, fellow. 4. (*dial.*) husband.

мужикова́т|ый (~, ~а), *adj.* (*coll.*) loutish, boorish.

мужи́цкий, *adj. of* мужи́к 1.

му́жний, *adj.* (*coll.*) husband's.

му́жн|ин, *adj.* = ~ий.

мужск|о́й, *adj.* masculine; male; м. портно́й gentlemen's tailor; м. род (*gram.*) masculine gender; ~а́я шко́ла boys' school.

мужчи́н|а, ы, *m.* man.

му́з|а, ы, *f.* muse.

музееве́дени|е, я, *n.* museum management studies.

музе́|й, я, *m.* museum.

музе́й|ный, *adj. of* ~.

му́зык|а, и, *f.* 1. music. 2. instrumental music. 3. (*coll.*) band; вое́нная м. military band. 4. (*fig., coll.*) (*complicated, protracted*) business, affair; он испо́ртил всю ~у he upset the apple-cart.

музыка́льность|ь, и, *f.* 1. melodiousness. 2. musical talent.

музыка́л|ьный (~ен, ~ьна), *adj.* (*in var. senses*) musical; м. комба́йн music centre.

музыка́нт, а, *m.* musician.

музыкове́д, а, *m.* musicologist.

музыкове́дени|е, я, *n.* musicology.

му́к|а, и, *f.* torment; (*pl.*) pangs, throes; родовы́е ~и birth-pangs; хожде́ние по ~ам (*rel.*) Purgatory; (*fig.*) (*series of*) trials and tribulations, purgatory.

мук|а́, и́, *f.* meal; flour; перемéлется —

м. бу́дет (*coll.*) it will all come right in the end.

мукомо́л, а, *m.* miller.

мукомо́льный, *adj.* flour-grinding.

мул, а, *m.* mule.

мула́т, а, *m.* mulatto.

мулл|а́, ы́, *m.* mullah.

му́льд|а, ы, *f.* 1. (*geol.*) flexure. 2. (*tech.*) charging box, charging trough.

мультиплика́тор, а, *m.* (*in var. tech. senses*) multiplier.

мультиплика́ци|я, и, *f.* (animated) cartoon (*film*).

мультфи́льм, а, *m.* = мультиплика́ция.

муля́ж, а́, *m.* (*art*) plaster cast.

мумифика́ци|я, и, *f.* mummification.

мумифици́р|оваться, уется, *impf. and pf.* to be (become) mummified.

му́ми|я[1], и, *f.* mummy (*embalmed corpse*).

му́ми|я[2], и, *f.* mummy (*brown pigment*).

мунди́р, а, *m.* full-dress uniform; полково́й м. regimentals; карто́фель в ~е potatoes cooked in their jackets.

мундшту́к, а́, *m.* 1. mouth-piece (*of Russian cigarette*); cigarette-holder. 2. mouth-piece (*of musical instrument, pipe*). 3. curb, curb-bit.

муниципализи́р|овать, ую, *impf. and pf.* to municipalize.

муниципалите́т, а, *m.* municipality.

муниципа́льный, *adj.* municipal.

мур|а́, ы́, *f.* (*coll.*) mess; nonsense.

мурав|а́[1], ы́, *f.* (*poet.*) grass, sward.

мурав|а́[2], ы́, *f.* (*tech.*) glaze.

мурав|е́й, ья́, *m.* ant.

мураве́йник, а, *m.* 1. ant-hill. 2. ant-bear.

мура́в|ить, лю, ишь, *impf.* to glaze (*pottery*).

мура́вленый, *adj.* (*tech.*) glazed.

муравье́д, а, *m.* (*zool.*) ant-eater.

мурав|ьи́ный, *adj.* 1. *adj. of* ~е́й. 2. (*chem.*) formic.

мура́ш, а́, *m.* = ~ка.

мура́шк|а, и, *f.* 1. (*dial.*) small ant. 2. (*coll.*) small insect; ~и по спине́ бе́гают it gives one the creeps.

мурл|о́, а́, *n.* (*coll.*) (ugly) mug.

мурлы́|кать, чу, чешь, *impf.* 1. to purr. 2. (*coll.*) to hum.

муска́т, а, *m.* 1. nutmeg. 2. (*kind of grape*) muscadine, muscat. 3. muscatel, muscat (*wine*).

муска́т|ный, *adj. of* ~; м. оре́х nutmeg; м. цвет mace.

му́скул, а, *m.* muscle; у него́ ни оди́н м. не дро́гнул (*fig.*) he didn't move a muscle.

мускулату́р|а, ы, *f.* (*collect.*) muscular system.

му́скулист|ый (~, ~а), *adj.* muscular, sinewy, brawny.

му́скульный, *adj.* muscular.

мýскус, а, *m.* musk.

мýскусн|ый, *adj.* musky; м. бык musk-ox; ~ая кры́са musk-rat, musquash; ~ая у́тка musk-duck, Muscovy duck.

муслѝн, а, *m.* muslin.

муслѝн|овый, *adj. of* ~.

мýсл|ить, ю, ишь, *impf. (of* на~*) (coll.)* **1.** to wet moisten (*with saliva*); м. ни́тку to moisten a thread (*when threading a needle*). **2.** to beslobber; to soil (*with wet or sticky hands*); м. кни́гу to dog-ear, soil a book.

мýсл|иться, юсь, ишься, *impf. (of* на~*)* to slobber over oneself; to dirty oneself.

мусóл|ить, ю, ишь, *impf. (of* за~, на~*)* **1.** = мýслить. **2.** (*fig.*) to spend much time (over); м. вопрóс to drag out a question.

мýсор, а, *m.* **1.** sweepings, dust; rubbish, refuse, garbage. **2.** débris.

мýсор|ить, ю, ишь, *impf. (of* на~*) (coll.)* to litter, leave litter about.

мýсор|ный, *adj. of* ~; ~ная повóзка dust cart; м. ящик dustbin.

мусоропровóд, а, *m.* refuse chute.

мусоросжигáтельн|ый, *adj.* ~ая печь incinerator.

мусороубóрочный, *adj.* refuse collection.

мýсорщик, а, *m.* **1.** dustman. **2.** scavenger.

мусс, а, *m.* (*cul.*) mousse.

муссѝр|овать, ую, *impf.* **1.** to whip up, make to foam. **2.** (*fig.*) to puff up (*reports*), inflate (*significance of something*).

муссóн, а, *m.* (*geogr.*) monsoon.

муст, а, *n.* must.

мустáнг, а, *m.* (*zool.*) mustang.

мусульмáн|ин, ина, *pl.* ~е, ~, *m.* Moslem.

мусульмáнский, *adj.* Moslem.

мусульмáнств|о, а, *n.* Mohammedanism, Islam.

мутáци|я, и, *f.* (*biol.*) mutation.

му|тѝть, чý, тѝшь, *impf.* **1.** (*pf.* вз~, за~) (*pres. also* ~тишь, *etc.*) to trouble, make muddy (*liquids*). **2.** (*pf.* по~) (*fig.*) to stir up, upset. **3.** (*pf.* по~) (*fig.*) to dull, make dull. **4.** (*impers.*) меня́, *etc.*, ~ти́т I *etc.*, feel sick.

му|тѝться, чýсь, тѝшься, *impf.* **1.** (*pf.* за~) (*pres. also* ~тишься, *etc.*) to grow turbid (*of liquids*). **2.** (*pf.* по~) (*fig.*) to grow dull, dim. **3.** (*impers.; coll.*) у меня́ ~ти́тся в головé my head is going round.

мутнé|ть, ет, *impf. (of* по~*)* to grow turbid, grow muddy; (*fig.*) to grow dull.

мýтност|ь, и, *f.* **1.** turbidity. **2.** dullness.

мýт|ный (~ен, ~ná, ~но), *adj.* **1.** turbid; в ~ной водé ры́бу ловѝть (*fig.*) to fish in troubled waters. **2.** (*fig.*) dull(ed); confused; ~ные глазá lacklustre eyes; ~ное сознáние dulled consciousness.

мутóвк|а¹, и, *f.* whisk.

мутóвк|а², и, *f.* (*bot.*) whorl.

мýтор|ный (~ен, ~на), *adj.* (*coll.*) disagree-

able; dreary, sombre; емý бы́ло ~но на душé he was in a sombre mood.

мут|ь, и, *f.* **1.** lees, sediment. **2.** murk.

мýфел|ь, я, *m.* (*tech.*) muffle.

муфлóн, а, *m.* (*zool.*) moufflon.

мýфт|а, ы, *f.* **1.** muff. **2.** (*tech.*) sleeve joint, coupling; соединѝтельная м. coupling sleeve, clutch sleeve; (*electr.*) connecting box; м. сцеплéния clutch.

мýфти|й, я, *m.* (*rel.*) mufti.

мýх|а, и, *f.* fly; какáя м. егó укусѝла? (*fig., coll.*) what's bitten him?; дéлать из ~и слонá (*fig.*) to make a mountain out of a mole-hill; быть под ~ой, с ~ой (*coll.*) to be three sheets in the wind; зашибѝть ~у to hit the bottle.

мухолóвк|а, и, *f.* **1.** fly-paper. **2.** (*bot.*) Venus's fly-trap, sundew. **3.** (*orn.*) fly-catcher.

мухомóр, а, *m.* **1.** fly-agaric (*mushroom*). **2.** (*coll.*) decrepit old person.

мухóртый, *adj.* (*colour of horse*) bay with yellowish markings.

мучéни|е, я, *n.* torment, torture.

мýченик, а, *m.* martyr.

мýчени|ца, цы, *f. of* ~к.

мýчени|ческий, *adj. of* ~к; мýка ~ческая (*coll.*) excruciating torment.

мýченичеств|о, а, *n.* martyrdom.

мýченск|ий, *adj. only in phrase* мýка ~ая (*coll.*) excruciating torment.

мучѝтел|ь, я, *m.* torturer; tormentor.

мучѝтел|ьный (~ен, ~ьна), *adj.* excruciating; agonizing.

мýч|ить, у, ишь, *impf. (of* за~, из~*)* to torment; to worry, harass.

мýч|иться, усь, ишься, *impf. (of* за~, из~*)* **1.** (+*i.*, от) *pass. of* ~ить; м. от бóли to be racked with pain. **2.** (из-за) to worry (about), feel unhappy (about). **3.** (над) to torment oneself (over, about).

мучнѝк, á, *m.* dealer in flour and meal.

мучнѝст|ый (~, ~а), *adj.* farinaceous.

мучнѝ|бе, бго, *n.* farinaceous foods.

мучнóй, *adj. of* мукá.

мýшк|а¹, и, *f.* **1.** *dim. of* мýха; шпáнская м. (*med.*) Spanish fly, cantharides. **2.** (*artificial*) beauty-spot (*on face*).

мýшк|а², и, *f.* foresight (*of fire-arm*); взять на ~y to take aim (at).

мушкéт, а, *m.* musket.

мушкетёр, а, *m.* musketeer.

муштáбел|ь, я, *m.* maulstick.

муштр|á, ы́, *f.* **1.** drill. **2.** regimentation.

муштр|овáть, ýю, *impf. (of* вы́~*)* to drill.

муэдзѝн, а, *m.* muezzin.

мха, мху, *see* мох.

мчать, мчу, мчишь, *impf.* to rush, whirl along (*trans.*; *coll. also intrans.*).

мч|áться, усь, ѝшься, *impf.* to rush, race,

tear along; м. во весь опо́р to go at full speed; вре́мя ~и́тся time flies.

мши́ст|ый (~, ~а), *adj.* mossy.

мще́ни|е, я, *n.* vengeance, revenge.

мы, *a., g., p.* нас, *d.* нам, *i.* на́ми, *pron.* we; мы с ва́ми you and I.

мы́з|а, ы, *f.* farm-stead, country house (*in Estonia and other regions bordering on Gulf of Finland*).

мы́зга|ть, ю, *impf.* (*coll.*) to soil, crumple.

мы́ка|ть, ю, *impf.* (*tech.*) to ripple, hackle (*flax*); го́ре м. (*fig., coll.*) to lead a dog's life.

мы́ка|ться, юсь, *impf.* (*coll.*) to roam, wander.

мы́л|ить, ю, ишь, *impf.* (*of* на~) to soap; to lather; м. кому́-н. го́лову (*fig., coll.*) to give someone a dressing down.

мы́л|иться, юсь, ишься, *impf.* (*of* на~) 1. to soap oneself. 2. to lather, form a lather.

мы́л|кий (~ок, ~ка́, ~ко), *adj.* freely lathering.

мы́л|о, а, *pl.* ~а́, ~, ~а́м, *n.* 1. soap. 2. (*of horse*) foam, lather.

мылова́р, а, *m.* soap-boiler.

мылова́рени|е, я, *n.* soap-boiling.

мылова́р|енный, *adj. of* ~е́ние; м. заво́д soap works, soap factory.

мы́льниц|а, ы, *f.* soap-dish; soap-box.

мы́л|ьный, *adj. of* ~о; м. ка́мень soapstone, steatite; ~ьные хло́пья soap-flakes.

мыс, а, *m.* (*geog.*) cape, promontory.

мы́сик, а, *m.* 1. (*coll.*) protuberance; jutting out part. 2. widow's peak.

мы́сленн|ый, *adj.* mental; м. о́браз mental image; ~ое пожела́ние unspoken wish.

мы́слим|ый (~, ~а), *adj.* conceivable, thinkable.

мысли́тел|ь, я, *m.* thinker.

мысли́тельный, *adj.* intellectual, of thought; м. проце́сс thought process.

мы́сл|ить, ю, ишь, *impf.* 1. to think; to reason. 2. to conceive.

мысл|ь, и, *f.* (o+*p.*) thought (of, about); idea; за́дняя м. ulterior motive, arrière pensée; о́браз ~ей way of thinking, views; у него́ э́того и в ~ях не́ было it never even crossed his mind; быть с кем-н. одни́х ~ей to be of the same opinion as someone; пода́ть м. to suggest an idea; собира́ться с ~ями to collect one's thoughts.

мыта́р|ить, ю, ишь, *impf.* (*of* за~) (*coll.*) to harass, torment, try.

мыта́р|иться, юсь, ишься, *impf.* (*of* за~) (*coll.*) to be harassed; to suffer afflictions, undergo trials.

мыта́рств|о, а, *n.* ordeal, affliction, hardship.

мы́тар|ь, я, *m.* 1. (*in Bible*) publican. 2. (*hist.*) collector of transit dues.

мыть, мо́ю, мо́ешь, *impf.* (*of* вы́~, по~) to wash.

мыть|ё, я́, *n.* wash, washing; не ~ём, так ка́таньем by hook or by crook.

мыть|ся, мо́юсь, мо́ешься, *impf.* (*of* вы́~, по~) 1. to wash (oneself). 2. *pass. of* ~.

мыч|а́ть, у́, и́шь, *impf.* 1. to low, moo; to bellow. 2. (*fig., coll.*) to mumble.

мыша́ст|ый (~, ~а), *adj.* mouse-coloured, mousey.

мышело́вк|а, и, *f.* mouse-trap.

мы́шечный, *adj.* muscular.

мыш|и́ный, *adj. of* ~ь; ~и́ная возня́ (суета́) pointless fussing over trifles; м. жере́бчик (*obs.*) old lecher.

мы́шк|а[1], и, *f. dim. of* мышь.

мы́шк|а[2], и, *f.* oxter; под ~у, под ~и, под ~ой, под ~ами under one's arm; in one's armpit(s); взять под ~у to put under one's arm; нести́ под ~ой to carry under one's arm.

мышле́ни|е, я, *n.* thinking, thought.

мыш|о́нок, о́нка, *pl.* ~а́та, ~а́т, *m.* young mouse.

мы́шц|а, ы, *f.* muscle.

мыш|ь, и, *pl.* ~и, ~е́й, *f.* 1. mouse. 2. лету́чая м. bat.

мышья́к, а́, *m.* (*chem., pharm.*) arsenic.

мышьяко́вистый, *adj.* (*chem.*) arsenious.

мышьяко́вый, *adj.* (*chem.*) arsenic.

мэр, а, *m.* mayor.

мю́зик-хо́лл, а, *m.* music-hall.

мя́г|кий (~ок, ~ка́, ~ко), *adj.* soft; (*fig.*) mild, gentle; м. ваго́н (*railways*) soft-(seated) carriage, sleeping car; м. знак (*ling.*) soft sign (*name of Russian letter* 'ь'); ~кое кре́сло easy chair; ~кая поса́дка soft landing (*of space vehicle*); м. хлеб new bread.

мя́гко, *adv.* softly; (*fig.*) mildly, gently; м. выража́ясь (*iron.*) to put it mildly, to say the least.

мягкосерде́чи|е, я, *n.* soft-heartedness.

мягкосерде́ч|ный (~ен, ~на), *adj.* soft--hearted.

мягкоте́лый, *adj.* soft; (*fig.*) spineless.

мягкошёрстный, *adj.* soft-haired.

мя́г|че, *comp. of* ~кий *and* ~ко.

мягчи́тельный, *adj.* (*med.*) emollient.

мягч|и́ть, у́, и́шь, *impf.* (*of* с~) to soften.

мяки́н|а, ы, *f.* chaff; ста́рого воробья́ на ~е не проведёшь (*prov.*) an old bird is not caught with chaff.

мя́киш, а, *m.* inside, soft part (*of loaf*).

мя́к|нуть, ну, нешь, *past* ~, ~ла, *impf.* (*of* раз~) to soften; to become soft (*also fig.*).

мя́кот|ь, и, *f.* 1. fleshy part of body. 2. pulp (*of fruit*).

мя́лк|а, и, *f.* (*tech.*) brake (*for flax or hemp*).

мя́мл|ить, ю, ишь, *impf.* (*coll.*) 1. (*pf.* про~)

to mumble. **2.** (*no pf.*) to vacillate; to procrastinate.

мя́мл|я, и, *g. pl.* ~**ей,** *m. and f.* (*coll.*) **1.** mumbler. **2.** irresolute person.

мяси́ст|ый (~, ~**a**), *adj.* fleshy; meaty; pulpy.

мясн|а́я, о́й, *f.* butcher's (shop).

мясни́к, а́, *m.* butcher.

мяс|но́й, *adj. of* ~о; ~**ны́е** консе́рвы tinned meat.

мя́с|о, а, *n.* **1.** flesh; сла́дкое м. (*anat.*) sweetbread; вы́рвать пу́говицу с ~ом to rip out a button with a bit of cloth. **2.** meat; пу́шечное м. (*fig.*) cannon fodder. **3.** (*coll.*) beef.

мясое́д, а, *m.* (*eccl.*) season during which it is allowed to eat meat (*esp. from Christmas to Shrovetide*).

мясокомбина́т, а, *m.* meat processing and packing factory.

мясопу́ст, а, *m.* (*eccl.*) **1.** season during which it is forbidden to eat meat. **2.** Shrovetide.

мясору́бк|а, и, *f.* mincing-machine.

мясохладобо́|йня, йни, *g. pl.* ~**ен,** *f.* combined slaughter-house and meat store.

мя|сти́сь, ту́сь, те́шься, *impf.* (*obs.*) to be disturbed.

мя́т|а, ы, *f.* (*bot.*) mint; пе́речная м. peppermint.

мяте́ж, а́, *m.* mutiny, revolt.

мяте́жник, а, *m.* mutineer, rebel.

мяте́жный, *adj.* **1.** rebellious, mutinous. **2.** (*fig.*) restless; stormy.

мя́тн|ый, *adj.* mint; ~**ые** леденцы́ peppermints.

мя́т|ый, *p.p.p. of* ~**ь** *and adj.*; м. пар (*tech.*) waste steam, exhaust steam.

мять, мну, мнёшь, *impf.* **1.** (*pf.* раз~) to work up, knead; м. гли́ну to pug clay; м. лён to brake flax. **2.** (*pf.* из~, с~) to crumple; to rumple (*a dress, etc.*); м. траву́ to trample grass.

мя́ться¹, мнётся, *impf.* (*of* из~, по~, *and* с~) to become crumpled; to rumple easily.

мя́ться², мнусь, мнёшься, *impf.* (*coll.*) to vacillate, hum and ha.

мя́ука|ть, ю, *impf.* to mew, miaow.

мяч, а́, *m.* ball.

мя́чик, а, *m. dim. of* мяч.

Н

на¹, *interj.* (*coll.*) here; here you are; here, take it; на́ кни́гу! here, take the book!; вот тебе́ на́! well, I never! well, how d'you like that?

на², *prep.* **I.** +*a.* **1.** on (to); to; into; over, through; положи́те кни́гу на стол put the book on the table; сесть на авто́бус, по́езд to board a 'bus, a train; сесть на парохо́д to go on board; на Украи́ну to the Ukraine; на Се́вер to the North; на се́вер от (to) north of; на заво́д to the factory; на конце́рт to a concert; слепо́й на оди́н глаз blind in one eye; перевести́ на англи́йский to translate into English; положи́ть на му́зыку to set to music; сла́ва его́ греме́ла на весь мир his fame resounded throughout the world. **2.** (*of time*) at; on; until, to (*or untranslated*); на друго́й день, на сле́дующий день (the) next day; на Но́вый год on New Year's day; на Рождество́ at Christmas; на Па́сху at Easter; отложи́ть на бу́дущую неде́лю to put off until the following week. **3.** for; на два дня for two days; на́ зиму for the winter; на э́тот раз this time, for this once; на чёрный день (*fig.*) for a rainy day; собра́ние назна́чено на понеде́льник the meeting is fixed for Monday; на что э́то тебе́ ну́жно? what do you want it for?; ко́мната на двои́х a room for two; уро́к на за́втра the lesson for tomorrow; лес

на постро́йку building timber; учи́ться на инжене́ра (*coll.*) to study engineering; на беду́ unfortunately. **4.** by (*or untranslated*); коро́че на дюйм shorter by an inch; купи́ть на вес to buy by weight; опозда́ть на час to be an hour late; четы́ре ме́тра (в длину́) на два (в ширину́) four metres (long) by two (broad); помно́жить пять на три to multiply five by three; дели́ть на два to divide into two. **5.** worth (*of something*); на рубль ма́рок a rouble's worth of stamps.

II. +*p.* **1.** on, upon; in; at; на столе́ on the table; на бума́ге on paper (*also fig.*); на Украи́не in the Ukraine; на Се́вере in the North; на заво́де at the factory; на конце́рте at a concert; на со́лнце in the sun; на чи́стом, во́льном во́здухе in the open air; на дворе́, на у́лице out of doors; на рабо́те at work; на излече́нии undergoing medical treatment; на вёслах under oars; на мо́ре за sea; идти́ на паруса́х to go sailing; игра́ть на роя́ле to play the piano; висе́ть на потолке́ to hang from the ceiling; жа́рить на ма́сле to fry; на свои́х глаза́х before one's eyes; на его́ па́мяти within his recollection; писа́ть на неме́цком языке́ to write in German; оши́бка на оши́бке blunder upon blunder. **2.** (*of time*) in (*or untranslated*); during; на э́той неде́ле this week; на лету́ in flight, during (the) flight; на кани́кулах during the holidays. **3.**

(*made, prepared with, of*); on (= *operated by means of*); на ва́те padded; матра́ц на рессо́рах sprung mattress; э́тот дви́гатель рабо́тает на не́фти this engine runs on oil.

на- *as verbal prefix* I. *forms pf. aspect.*

II. *indicates* 1. action continued to sufficiency, to point of satisfaction or exhaustion. 2. action relating to determinate quantity or number of objects.

наба́в|ить, лю, ишь, *pf.* (*of* ~ля́ть) to add (to), increase; н. ша́гу to quicken one's pace.

наба́вк|а, и, *f.* addition, increase; extra charge; н. к зарпла́те rise (in wages).

набавля́|ть, ю, *impf. of* наба́вить.

наба́вочный, *adj.* (*coll.*) extra, additional.

набаламу́|тить, чу, тишь, *pf.* (*coll.*) to make trouble; to upset.

набалда́шник, а, *m.* knob; walking-stick handle.

набало́в|анный, *p.p.p. of* ~а́ть *and adj.* spoiled.

набал|ова́ть, у́ю, *pf.* (*coll.*) 1. to spoil. 2. to get up to mischief.

набальзами́р|овать, ую, *pf. of* бальзами́ровать.

наба́т, а, *m.* alarm bell, tocsin; бить (ударя́ть) (в) н. to sound the alarm (*also fig.*).

наба́т|ный, *adj. of* ~.

набе́г, а, *m.* raid; foray, inroad, incursion.

набе́га|ть, ю, *pf.* (*coll.*) to cause oneself (*heart trouble, etc.*) by running.

набега́|ть, ю, *impf.* 1. *impf. of* набежа́ть. 2. *impers.* (*coll.*) to ruck up.

набе́га|ться, юсь, *pf.* to be tired out with running about; to have one's fill of running.

набе|гу́, жи́шь, гу́т, *see* ~жа́ть.

набе|жа́ть, гу́, жи́шь, гу́т, *pf.* (*of* ~га́ть) 1. (на+*a.*) to run against, run into. 2. (*coll.*) to come running (together). 3. (*of liquids*) to run into; to fill up; (*fig.*; *of money, etc.*) to accumulate. 4. (*of wind*) to spring up.

набекре́нь, *adv.* (*coll.*) (*of hats*) aslant, tilted; с шля́пой н. with one's hat on one side; у него́ мозги́ н. (*joc.*) he is crack-brained.

набел|и́ть(ся), ю́(сь), ~и́шь(ся), *pf. of* бели́ть(ся) 2.

на́бело, *adv.* clean, without corrections and erasures; переписа́ть н. to make a fair copy of.

на́бережн|ая, ой, *f.* embankment, quay.

набива́|ть(ся), ю(сь), *impf. of* наби́ть(ся).

наби́вк|а, и, *f.* 1. (*action and substance*) stuffing, padding, packing. 2. (*text.*) printing.

набивно́й, *adj.* (*text.*) printed.

набира́|ть(ся), ю(сь), *impf. of* набра́ть(ся).

наби́т|ый (~, ~а), *p.p.p. of* ~ь *and adj.* packed, crowded; зал ~ битко́м the hall is crowded out; н. дура́к arrant fool.

наб|и́ть¹, ью, ьёшь, *pf.* (*of* ~ива́ть) 1. (+*a. and i.*) to stuff (with), pack (with), fill (with); н. тру́бку to fill one's pipe; н. це́ны to knock up the prices; to bid up; н. оско́мину to set one's teeth on edge (*also fig.*); н. ру́ку на чём-н. (*fig., coll.*) to become a practised hand at something, become a dab hand. 2. (*text.*) to print.

наб|и́ть², ью, ьёшь, *pf.* н. гвозде́й в сте́ну to drive (*a number of*) nails into a wall; н. у́ток to bag (*a number of*) duck; н. посу́ды to smash (*a lot of*) crockery.

наб|и́ться, ью́сь, ьёшься, *pf.* (*of* ~ива́ться) 1. to crowd (*into a place*); битко́м н. to be crowded out. 2. (*coll*; +*d.*) to impose oneself (upon), inflict oneself (upon); н. к кому́-н. в го́сти to invite oneself to someone's house (*etc.*).

наблюда́тел|ь, я, *m.* observer, spectator.

наблюда́тельност|ь, и, *f.* power of observation, observation.

наблюда́тел|ьный, *adj.* 1. (~ен, ~ьна) observant. 2. observation; н. пункт (*mil.*) observation post.

наблюда́|ть, ю, *impf.* 1. to observe; to watch. 2. (за+*i.*) to take care (of), look after. 3. (за *and*, *obs.*, над+*i.*) to supervise, superintend; н. за у́личным движе́нием to control traffic; н. за поря́дком to be responsible for keeping order.

наблюде́ни|е, я, *n.* 1. observation. 2. supervision, superintendence.

наблю|сти́, ду́, дёшь, *past* ~л, ~ла́, *pf.* (*obs.*) to make an observation.

набо́б, а, *m.* nabob.

на́божност|ь, и, *f.* piety.

на́бож|ный (~ен, ~на), *adj.* devout, pious.

набо́йк|а, и, *f.* 1. (*text.*) printed cloth. 2. printed pattern on cloth. 3. heel (*of foot-wear*).

набо́йщик, а, *m.* 1. (*text.*) (linen-)printer. 2. filler, stuffer.

на́бок, *adv.* on one side, awry.

наболе́|вший, *past part. of* ~ть *and adj.* sore, painful (*also fig.*).

набол|е́ть, е́ет, *pf.* to become painful.

наболта́|ть¹, ю, *pf.* (*coll.*) to mix in (*a quantity of*).

наболта́|ть², ю, *pf.* (*coll.*) 1. (+*a. or g.*) to talk a lot (*of nonsense, etc.*). 2. (на+*a.*) to gossip (about), talk (about); на неё ~ли they told a lot of lies about her.

на́больш|ий, его, *m.* (*dial.*) 1. boss. 2. head of family.

набо́р, а, *m.* 1. recruitment. 2. levy. 3. (*typ.*) composition, type-setting. 4. (*typ.*)

composed matter. **5.** set, collection; н. слов mere verbiage. **6.** decorative plate (on harness, belt, etc.).

набóрн|ая, ой, f. type-setting office.

набóрн|ый,| adj. type-setting; ~ая доскá galley.

набóрщик, а, m. compositor, type-setter.

набрáсыва|ть(ся), ю(сь), impf. of набросáть(ся) and набрóсить(ся).

набрá|ть, наберý, наберёшь, past ~л, ~лá, ~ло, pf. (of набирáть) **1.** (+g. or a.) to gather; to collect, assemble; н. ýгля to take on coal; н. нóмер to dial a (telephone) number; н. скóрость to pick up, gather speed; н. высотý (aeron.) to climb; н. водý в рот (fig.) to keep mum. **2.** to recruit, enrol, engage. **3.** (typ.) to compose, set up.

набрá|ться, наберýсь, наберёшься, past ~лся, ~лáсь, ~лóсь, pf. (of набирáться) **1.** (usually impers.) to assemble, collect; to accumulate; ~лóсь мнóго нарóду a large crowd collected. **2.** (+g.; coll.) to find, collect; to acquire; (pejor.) to pick up; н. хрáбрости to take courage; н. блох to pick up fleas.

набре|стú, дý, дёшь, past ~л, ~лá, pf. **1.** (на+a.) to come across; to happen upon; я ~л на интерéсную мысль I have hit on an interesting idea. **2.** to collect, gather; ~лó мнóго нарóду a large crowd gathered.

набросá|ть¹, ю, pf. (of набрáсывать) **1.** to sketch, outline, adumbrate; н. план to outline a plan. **2.** to jot down.

набросá|ть², ю, pf. to throw about; to throw (in successive instalments).

набрó|сить, шу, сишь, pf. (of набрáсывать) to throw (on, over); н. шаль на плéчи to throw a shawl over one's shoulders.

набрó|ситься, шусь, сишься, pf. (of набрáсываться) (in var. senses) to fall upon; to go for; собáка ~силась на меня the dog went for me; н. на когó-н. с вопрóсами to deluge someone with questions.

набрóс|ок, ка, m. sketch, draft.

набрызга|ть, ю, pf. (+i. or g.) to splash.

набрюшник, а, m. abdominal band.

набрюшный, adj. abdominal.

набух|áть, áю, impf. of ~нуть.

набýх|нуть, ну, нешь, past ~, ~ла, pf. (of ~áть) to swell.

наб|ью, ьёшь, see ~úть.

навáг|а, и, f. (zool.) navaga (a small fish of the cod family).

наваждéни|е, я, n. delusion; hallucination.

навáк|сить, шу, сишь, pf. of вáксить.

навáлива|ть(ся), ю(сь), impf. of навалúть(ся).

навал|úть, ю, ~ишь, pf. (of ~ивать) to heap, pile; to load (also fig.); impers. снéгу

~úло по колéно the snow had piled up knee deep.

навал|úться, юсь, ~ишься, pf. (of ~иваться) (на+a.) **1.** (coll.) to fall (upon). **2.** to lean (on, upon); to bring all one's weight to bear (on).

навáлк|а, и, f. loading, lading; в ~у loose, unpacked.

навáлом, adv. piled up.

наваля|ть¹, ю, pf. of валять 5.

наваля|ть², ю, pf. н. вóйлока, вáленок to make (a quantity of) felt, felt boots.

навáр, а, m. grease (on the surface of soup).

навáрива|ть, ю, impf. of наварúть¹.

навáрист|ый (~, ~a), adj. with large fat content (of soup).

навар|úть¹, ю, ~ишь, pf. (of ~ивать) to weld on.

навар|úть², ю, ~ишь, pf. to cook, boil (a quantity of).

навевá|ть, ю, impf. of навéять.

навéд|аться, аюсь, pf. (of ~ываться) (к; coll.) to call (on).

наведéни|е, я, n. **1.** laying; placing. **2.** (philos.; obs.) induction.

наве|дý, дёшь, see ~стú.

навéдыва|ться, юсь, impf. of навéдаться.

навез|тú¹, ý, ёшь, past ~, ~лá, pf. (of навозúть¹) (на+a.; coll.) to drive (on, against).

навез|тú², ý, ёшь, past ~, ~лá, pf. (of навозúть²) to bring (a quantity of).

навéк, adv. for ever.

навéк|и = ~.

навéл|ь, я, m. navel orange.

наверб|овáть, ýю, pf. of вербовáть.

навéрно, adv. **1.** probably, most likely. **2.** (obs.) for sure; certainly, exactly.

навéрно|е, adv. = ~ 1.

наверн|ýть, ý, ёшь, pf. (of навёртывать) **1.** to screw (on). **2.** to wind (round). **3.** (sl.) to scoff up (= eat).

наверн|ýться, ýсь, ёшься, pf. (of навёртываться) **1.** (coll.) to turn up; (of tears) to well up. **2.** pass. of ~ýть.

навернякá, adv. (coll.) **1.** for sure, certainly. **2.** safely, without taking risks; бить н. to take no chances; держáть парú н. to bet on a certainty.

наверстá|ть, ю, pf. (of навёрстывать) to make up (for), catch up (with); н. потéрянное врéмя to make up for lost time; н. упýщенное to repair an omission.

навёрстыва|ть, ю, impf. of наверстáть.

навер|тéть¹, чý, ~тишь, pf. (of ~тывать) to wind (round), twist (round).

навер|тéть², чý, ~тишь, pf. (of ~чивать) to drill (a number of) (holes, etc.).

навёртыва|ть, ю, impf. of навернýть and навертéть¹.

навёртыва|ться, юсь, impf. of навернýться.

наве́рх, *adv.* up, upward; upstairs; to the top.

наверху́, *adv.* above; upstairs.

наве́рчива|ть, ю, *impf. of* навертѣ́ть².

наве́с, а, *m.* 1. penthouse; awning. 2. overhang, jutting-out part. 3. (*sport*) lob.

навеселе́, *adv.* (*coll.*) tipsy.

наве́|сить, шу, сишь, *pf.* (*of* ~шивать¹) 1. (+*a. or g.*) to hang (up), suspend; н. карти́н to hang (*a number of*) pictures. 2. (*sport*) to lob.

наве́ск|а¹, и, *f.* hinge-plate.

наве́ск|а², и, *f.* (*chem.*) dose by weight.

навесн|о́й, *adj.* ~а́я дверь door on hinges; ~а́я пе́тля hinge.

наве́сный, *adj.* (*mil.*) н. ого́нь plunging fire.

наве|сти́¹, ду́, дёшь, *past* ~л, ~ла́, *pf.* (*of* наводи́ть) (на+*a.*) 1. to direct (at); to aim (at); н. кого́-н. на мысль to suggest an idea to someone; н. на след to put on the track. 2. to cover (with); н. лоск, гля́нец to polish, gloss, glaze. 3. to lay, put, make; н. поря́док to introduce order, establish order; н. спра́вку to make an inquiry; н. ску́ку to bore; н. страх to inspire fear.

наве|сти́², ду́, дёшь, *past* ~л, ~ла́, *pf.* (*of* наводи́ть) to bring (*a quantity of*).

наве|сти́ть, щу́, сти́шь, *pf.* (*of* ~ща́ть) to visit, call on.

наве́т, а, *m.* (*obs.*) slander, calumny.

наве́тренный, *adj.* windward.

наве́тчик, а, *m.* (*obs.*) slanderer.

наве́чно, *adv.* for ever; in perpetuity.

наве́ш|ать¹, аю, *pf.* (*of* ~ивать¹) (+*a. or g.*) to hang (up), suspend.

наве́ш|ать², аю, *pf.* (*of* ~ивать²) to weigh out (*a quantity of*).

наве́шива|ть¹, ю, *impf. of* наве́сить *and* наве́шать¹.

наве́шива|ть², ю, *impf. of* наве́шать².

навеща́|ть, ю, *impf. of* навести́ть.

наве́|ять¹, ю, ешь, *pf.* (*of* ~ва́ть) to blow; (*fig.*;+ *a.* на+*a.*) to cast (on, over), plunge (into); его́ расска́з ~ял грусть на слу́шателей his story cast a gloom over the audience, plunged the audience into gloom.

наве́|ять², ю, ешь, *pf.* (*of* ~ва́ть) to winnow (*a quantity of*).

на́взничь, *adv.* backwards, on one's back.

навзры́д, *adv.* пла́кать н. to sob.

навива́|ть, ю, *impf. of* нави́ть.

навига́тор, а, *m.* navigator.

навигац|ио́нный, *adj. of* ~ия.

навига́ци|я, и, *f.* (*in var. senses*) navigation.

навин|ти́ть, чу́, ти́шь, *pf.* (*of* ~чивать) (на+*a.*) to screw (on).

навинчива|ть, ю, *impf. of* навинти́ть.

навис|а́ть, а́ю, *impf.* (*of* ~нуть) (на+*a.*, над) to hang (over), overhang; (*of cliffs,*

etc.) to beetle; (*fig.*) to impend, threaten; над на́ми ~а́ет опа́сность danger threatens us, is imminent; н. над фла́нгами врага́ to hang on the enemy's flanks.

нави́слый, *adj.* (*coll.*) overhanging, beetling.

нави́с|нуть, ну, нешь, *past* ~, ~ла, *pf. of* ~а́ть.

нави́с|ший, *past part. act. of* ~нуть *and adj.* ~шие бро́ви beetling brows.

нави́ть, ью́, ьёшь, *past* ~и́л, ~ила́, ~и́ло, *pf.* (*of* ~ива́ть) (+*a. or g.*) 1. to wind (on). 2. to load, stack (*straw, hay*).

навлека́|ть, ю, *impf. of* навле́чь.

навле|ку́, чёшь, ку́т, *see* ~чь.

навле́|чь, ку́, чёшь, ку́т, *past* ~к, ~кла́, *pf.* (*of* ~ка́ть) (на+*a.*) to bring (on); to draw (on); н. на себя́ гнев to incur anger.

наво|ди́ть, жу́, ~дишь, *impf. of* навести́; наводя́щие вопро́сы leading questions; наводя́щий, наводи́вший 'he' (*in children's games*).

наво́дк|а, и, *f.* (*mil.*) laying, training; прямо́й ~ой over open sights.

наводне́ни|е, я, *n.* flood, inundation.

наводн|и́ть, ю́, и́шь, *pf.* (*of* ~я́ть) (+*a. and i.*) to flood (with), inundate (with), deluge (with); (*fig.*) н. ры́нок дешёвыми това́рами to flood the market with cheap goods.

наводн|я́ть, я́ю, *impf. of* ~и́ть.

наво́дчик, а, *m.* 1. gun-layer. 2. (*sl.*) tipper-off (*thieves' informant*).

наво́|жу, зишь, *see* ~зить.

наво|жу́¹, ~дишь, *see* ~ди́ть.

наво|жу́², ~зишь, *see* ~зить.

наво́з, а, *m.* manure, dung.

наво́|зить, жу, зишь, *impf.* (*of* у~) to manure.

наво|зи́ть¹, ², жу́, ~зишь, *impf. of* навезти́¹, ².

наво|зи́ть³, жу́, ~зишь, *pf.* (*coll.*) to get in (*a supply of*).

наво́зник, а, *m.* dung-beetle.

наво́з|ный, *adj. of* ~; н. жук dung-beetle; гром не из ту́чи, а из ~ной ку́чи (*coll.*) his bark is worse than his bite.

наво́|й, я, *m.* (*text.*) weaver's beam.

на́волок|а, и, *f.* pillow-case, pillow-slip.

на́воло|чка, а, *f.* = ~ка.

навоня́|ть, ю, *pf.* (*coll.*; +*i.*) to stink (of).

навора́жива|ть, ю, *impf. of* наворожи́ть.

навора́чива|ть, ю, *impf. of* навороти́ть.

навор|ова́ть, у́ю, *pf.* (*coll.*) to steal (*a quantity of*).

наворож|и́ть, у́, и́шь, *pf.* (*of* навора́живать) (*coll.*) 1. to foretell, prophesy; она́ ~и́ла мне до́лгий век she prophesied me a long life. 2. to make, earn by fortune-telling. 3. to endow with magical properties.

наворо|ти́ть, чу́, ⌣ти́шь, *pf.* (*of* навора́чи-вать) (*coll.*; +*a. or g.*) to heap up, pile up.

наворо|чу́, ⌣ти́шь, *see* ⌣ти́ть.

наворс|ова́ть, у́ю, *pf. of* ворсова́ть.

наворч|а́ть, у́, и́шь, *pf.* (*coll.*; на+*a.*) to grumble (at).

навостр|и́ть, ю́, и́шь, *pf.* (*coll.*) to sharpen; н. у́ши to prick up one's ears; н. лы́жи to take to one's heels.

навостр|и́ться, ю́сь, и́шься, *pf.* (в+*p.* or +*inf.*; *coll.*) to become good (at), become adept (at); он ⌣и́лся пляса́ть he has become a good dancer.

навощ|и́ть, у́, и́шь, *pf. of* вощи́ть.

навр|а́ть¹, у́, ёшь, *past* ⌣а́л, ⌣ала́, ⌣а́ло, *pf.* (*coll.*) 1. (*pf. of* врать) to romance, tell yarns. 2. (в+*p.*) to make mistakes (in); н. в расска́зе to get the story wrong. 3. (на+*a.*) to slander.

навр|а́ть², у́, ёшь, *pf.* (*coll.*; +*a. or g.*) to tell (*a lot of*) (*sc.* lies); н. вся́ких небыли́ц to tell all manner of tales.

навре|ди́ть, жу́, ди́шь, *pf.* (+*d.*) to do much harm (to).

навря́д (ли), *adv.* scarcely, hardly.

навсегда́, *adv.* for ever, for good; раз н. once (and) for all.

навстре́чу, *adv.* to meet; towards; пойти́ н. кому́-н. to go to meet someone; (*fig.*) to meet someone half-way.

навы́ворот, *adv.* (*coll.*) 1. inside out, wrong side out. 2. (*fig.*) wrong way round.

на́вык, а, *m.* experience, skill (*in practical or manual work*).

навы́кат(е), *adv.* глаза́ н. bulging eyes.

навык|а́ть, а́ю, *impf. of* ⌣нуть.

навы́к|нуть, ну, нешь, *past* ⌣, ⌣ла, *pf.* (*of* ⌣а́ть) (*coll.*; к *or* +*inf.*) to acquire the habit (of), skill (in).

навы́лет, *adv.* (right) through; он был ра́нен н. в ру́ку he was wounded by a bullet passing right through his arm.

навы́нос, *adv.* for consumption off the premises.

навы́пуск, *adv.* worn outside; брю́ки н. trousers worn over boots; руба́ха н. shirt worn outside trousers.

навы́рез, *adv.* купи́ть арбу́з н. to buy a water-melon with the right to sample a section.

навы́тяжку, *adv.* стоя́ть н. to stand at attention.

нав|ь, и, *f.* (*in Russian myth.*) ghost, spirit.

нав|ью́, ьёшь, *see* ⌣и́ть.

навью́чива|ть, ю, *impf. of* навью́чить.

навью́ч|ить, у, ишь, *pf.* (*of* вью́чить *and* ⌣ивать) to load (up).

навя|за́ть¹, жу́, ⌣жешь, *pf.* (*of* ⌣зывать) 1. (на+*a.*) to tie on (to), fasten (to). 2. (*fig.*; +*d. and a.*) to thrust (on); to foist

(on); н. кому́-н. сове́т to thrust advice on someone.

навя|за́ть², жу́, ⌣жешь, *pf.* (*of* ⌣зывать) (+*a. or g.*) to knit (*a number of*).

навяз|а́ть³, а́ет, *impf. of* ⌣нуть.

навя|за́ться, жу́сь, ⌣жешься, *pf.* (*of* ⌣зы-ваться) (*coll.*; +*d.*) 1. to thrust oneself (upon), intrude oneself (upon). 2. *pass. of* ⌣за́ть¹.

навя́з|нуть, нет, *past* ⌣, ⌣ла, *pf.* (*of* ⌣а́ть) to stick; э́то ⌣ло у нас в зуба́х (*fig.*) we are sick and tired of it.

навя́зчив|ый (⌣, ⌣а), *adj.* 1. importunate; obtrusive. 2. persistent; ⌣ая иде́я idée fixe, obsession.

навя́зыва|ть(ся), ю(сь), *impf. of* навяза́ть-(ся).

нагада́|ть, ю, *pf.* (*coll.*; +*a. or g.*) to foretell, predict.

нага́|дить, жу, дишь, *pf. of* га́дить.

нага́йк|а, и, *f.* whip.

нага́н, а, *m.* revolver.

нага́р, а, *m.* deposit formed as result of combustion; (candle-)snuff.

на́гел|ь, я, *m.* (*tech.*) wooden pin.

нагиба́|ть(ся), ю(сь), *impf. of* нагну́ть(ся).

нагишо́м, *adv.* (*coll.*) stark naked.

нагла́|дить¹, жу, дишь, *pf.* (*of* ⌣живать) to smooth (out).

нагла́|дить², жу, дишь, *pf.* (*of* ⌣живать) to iron (*a quantity of*).

нагла́жива|ть, ю, *impf. of* нагла́дить.

нагла́зник, а, *m.* 1. eye-shade. 2. blinker.

нагле́|ть, ю, *impf.* (*of* об⌣) to become impudent, become insolent.

наглец́, а́, *m.* impudent fellow, insolent fellow.

на́глост|ь, и, *f.* impudence, insolence, effrontery, impertinence.

наглота́|ться, юсь, *pf.* (+*g.*) to swallow (*a large quantity of*).

на́глухо, *adv.* tightly, hermetically; застег-ну́ться н. to do up all one's buttons.

на́гл|ый (⌣, ⌣а́, ⌣о), *adj.* impudent, insolent, impertinent.

нагля|де́ться, жу́сь, ди́шься, *pf.* (на+*a.*) to see enough (of); на э́тот вид гляжу́ — не ⌣жу́сь I never tire of looking at this view.

нагля́дно, *adv.* clearly, graphically; by visual demonstration.

нагля́дност|ь, и, *f.* 1. clearness. 2. use of visual methods, use of visual aids.

нагля́д|ный (⌣ен, ⌣на), *adj.* 1. clear; graphic, obvious; ⌣ное доказа́тельство ocular demonstration. 2. visual; ⌣ные посо́бия visual aids; н. уро́к object--lesson.

наг|на́ть¹, оню́, о́нишь, *past* ⌣на́л, ⌣нала́, ⌣на́ло, *pf.* (*of* ⌣оня́ть) 1. to overtake, catch up (with). **2.** to make up (for). **3.** (*fig.*, *coll.*) to inspire, arouse, occasion.

наг|на́ть², оню́, о́нишь, *pf.* (+*a. or g.*) **1.** to herd together (*a number of*). **2.** to distil (*a quantity of*).

нагне|сти́, ту́, тёшь, *pf.* (*of* ~та́ть) to compress, force; (*tech.*) to supercharge.

нагнета́тел|ь, я, *m.* (*tech.*) supercharger.

нагнета́тельн|ый, *adj.* (*tech.*) н. кла́пан pressure valve; ~ая труба́ force pipe.

нагнета́|ть, ю, *impf. of* нагнести́.

нагне|ту́, тёшь, *see* ~сти́.

нагное́ни|е, я, *n.* (*med.*) **1.** fester. **2.** suppuration.

нагнойт|ься, и́тся, *pf.* (*med.*) to fester, suppurate.

нагн|у́ть, у́, ёшь, *pf.* (*of* нагиба́ть) to bend.

нагн|у́ться, у́сь, ёшься, *pf.* (*of* нагиба́ться) to bend (down), stoop.

нагова́рива|ть, ю, *impf. of* наговори́ть¹.

наговор, а, *m.* **1.** slander, calumny. **2.** incantation.

наговор|и́ть¹, ю́, и́шь, *pf.* (*of* нагова́ривать) **1.** (*coll.*; на+*a.*) to slander, calumniate. **2.** н. пласти́нку to have a recording made (of one's voice), record (one's voice). **3.** to pronounce incantations over.

наговор|и́ть², ю́, и́шь, *pf.* (+*a. or g.*) to talk, say a lot (of); н. чепухи́ to talk a lot of nonsense.

наговор|и́ться, ю́сь, и́шься, *pf.* to talk oneself out; они́ не мо́гут н. they cannot talk enough.

наг|о́й (~, ~á, ~o), *adj.* naked, nude, bare.

наголе́нный, *adj.* worn, *etc.*, on shin(s); н. щито́к shin-pad.

на́голо, *adv.* bare; остри́чь на́голо to cut close to the skin, crop close; с ша́шками наголо́ with drawn swords.

на́голову, *adv.* разби́ть н. to rout, smash.

наголода́|ться, юсь, *pf.* to be half-starved.

наго́льный, *adj.* н. тулу́п uncovered sheepskin coat.

нагоня́|й, я, *m.* (*coll.*) scolding, rating.

нагоня́|ть, ю, *impf. of* нагна́ть.

на-гора́, *adv.* (*mining*) to the surface, to the top.

нагора́жива|ть, ю, *impf. of* нагороди́ть.

нагор|а́ть, а́ю, *impf. of* ~е́ть.

нагор|е́ть¹, и́т, *pf.* (*of* ~а́ть) **1.** to need snuffing (*of a candle*). **2.** (+*g.*) to be used up (*of fuel*).

нагор|е́ть², и́т, *pf.* (*of* ~а́ть) (*impers.*; +*d.*) (*coll.*) тебе́ за э́то ~и́т you'll get it hot for this.

нагóрн|ый, *adj.* **1.** mountainous, hilly. **2.** (*of river bank*) high. **3.** ~ая про́поведь (*bibl.*) Sermon on the Mount.

нагоро|ди́ть, жу́, ~ди́шь, *pf.* (*of* нагора́жи-

вать) **1.** to build, erect (*in large quantity*). **2.** (*coll.*) to pile up, heap up. **3.** (*fig.*) to talk, write (*a lot of nonsense*); н. вздо́ра, чепухи́ to talk a lot of nonsense.

нагóрь|е, я, *n.* table-land, plateau.

нагот|á, ы́, *f.* nakedness, nudity.

нагото́ве, *adv.* in readiness; ready to hand; быть н. to hold oneself in readiness, be on call.

нагото́в|ить, лю, ишь, *pf.* (+*a. or g.*) **1.** to lay in (*a supply of*). **2.** to cook (*a large quantity of*).

нагото́в|иться, люсь, ишься, *pf.* (*coll.*; +*g.* на+*a.*) to have enough (for), provide enough (for); на них не ~ишься еды́ one cannot provide enough food for them; он так бы́стро растёт, на него́ не ~ишься оде́жды he is growing so fast, it is impossible to keep him in clothes.

награ́б|ить, лю, ишь, *pf.* (+*a. or g.*) to amass by robbery.

награ́д|а, ы, *f.* **1.** reward, recompense. **2.** award; decoration; (*in schools*) prize.

награ|ди́ть, жу́, ди́шь, *pf.* (*of* ~жда́ть) (+*a. and i.*) **1.** to reward (with). **2.** to decorate (with); to award, confer; (*fig.*) to endow (with); н. кого́-н. о́рденом to confer a decoration upon someone, award someone a decoration; приро́да ~ди́ла его́ вели́кими тала́нтами nature has endowed him with great talents.

наград|но́й, *adj. of* ~а.

наградн|ы́е, ы́х, *pl. only* bonus.

награжда́|ть, ю, *impf. of* награди́ть.

награждённ|ый, *p.p.p. of* награди́ть; *as noun* н., ~о́го, *m.* recipient (of an award).

нагре́в, а, *m.* (*tech.*) heat, heating; пове́рхность ~а heating surface.

нагрева́тел|ь, я, *m.* (*tech.*) heater.

нагрева́тельный, *adj.* (*tech.*) heating.

нагрева́|ть(ся), ю(сь), *impf. of* нагре́ть(ся).

нагре́|ть, ю, *pf.* (*of* ~ва́ть) **1.** to warm, heat; н. ру́ки (*fig.*) to feather one's nest. **2.** (*coll.*) to swindle; они́ ~ли меня́ на пять рубле́й they swindled me out of five roubles.

нагре́|ться¹, юсь, *pf.* (*of* нагрева́ться) to become warm, become hot; to warm up, heat up.

нагре́|ться², юсь, *pf.* (*of* ~ва́ться) (*coll.*) to be swindled.

нагримир|ова́ть, у́ю, *pf. of* гримирова́ть.

нагромождá|ть, ю, *impf. of* нагромозди́ть.

нагромоз|ди́ть, жу́, ди́шь, *pf.* (*of* громозди́ть *and* нагроможда́ть) to pile up, heap up.

нагруб|и́ть, лю́, и́шь, *pf. of* груби́ть.

нагрубия́н|ить, ю, ишь, *pf. of* грубия́нить.

нагру́дник, а, *m.* **1.** bib. **2.** breastplate.

нагру́дный, *adj.* breast.

нагружа́|ть(ся), ю(сь), *impf. of* нагрузи́ть(ся).

нагру|зи́ть, жу́, ‿зи́шь, *pf.* (*of* грузи́ть *and* ~жа́ть) (+*a. and i.*) **1.** to load (with). **2.** (*fig.*) to burden (with).

нагру|зи́ться, жу́сь, ‿зи́шься, *pf.* (*of* ~жа́ться) (+*i.*) to load oneself (with), burden oneself (with).

нагру́зк|а, и, *f.* **1.** loading. **2.** load; поле́зная н. (*tech.*) payload, working load. **3.** (*fig.*) work; commitments, obligation(s); парти́йная н. party work, party obligations; преподава́тельская н. teaching load.

нагрязн|и́ть, ю́, и́шь, *pf. of* грязни́ть.

нагря́н|уть, у, ешь, *pf.* (*coll.*) to appear unexpectedly; (на+*a.*) to descend (on).

нагу́л, а, *m.* (*agric.*) fattening.

нагу́лива|ть, ю, *impf. of* нагуля́ть.

нагул|я́ть, я́ю, *pf.* (*of* ‿ивать) to acquire, develop (*as result of feeding, exercise, etc.*); н. жи́ру (*agric.*) to fatten, put on weight; н. брюшко́ (*fig., joc.*) to develop a paunch; н. аппети́т to work up an appetite.

нагуля́|ться, юсь, *pf.* to have had a long walk.

над, *prep.*+*i.* **1.** over, above. **2.** on; at; рабо́тать над диссерта́цией to be working on a dissertation; смея́ться над to laugh at.

над- super-, over-.

нада|ва́ть, ю́, ёшь, *pf.* (*coll.*; +*d. and a. or g.*) to give (*a large quantity of*).

надав|и́ть[1], лю́, ‿ишь, *pf.* (*of* ‿ливать) (на+*a.*) to press (on).

надав|и́ть[2], лю́, ‿ишь, *pf.* (+*a. or g.*) **1.** to press, squeeze (*a number of*). **2.** (*coll.*) to swat (*a quantity of*).

нада́влива|ть, ю, *impf. of* надави́ть[1].

нада́ива|ть, ю, *impf. of* надои́ть.

нада́рива|ть, ю, *impf. of* надари́ть.

надар|и́ть, ю́, и́шь, *pf.* (*of* ‿ивать) (*coll.*; +*a. or g. and d.*) to present (*a large quantity of*).

надба́в|ить, лю, ишь, *pf.* = наба́вить.

надба́вк|а, и, *f.* = наба́вка.

надбавля́|ть, ю, *impf. of* надба́вить.

надбива́|ть, ю, *impf. of* надби́ть.

надби́т|ый, *p.p.p. of* ~ь *and adj.* cracked; chipped.

над|би́ть, обью́, обьёшь, *pf.* (*of* ~бива́ть) to crack; to chip.

надбро́вный, *adj.* (*anat.*) superciliary.

надвига́|ть(ся), ю(сь), *impf. of* надви́нуть(ся).

надви́н|уть, у, ешь, *pf.* (*of* надвига́ть) to move, pull (up to, over).

надви́н|уться, усь, ешься, *pf.* (*of* надвига́ться) to approach, draw near.

надво́дный, *adj.* above-water; н. борт free-board; н. кора́бль surface ship.

на́двое, *adv.* **1.** in two. **2.** ambiguously; ба́бушка н. сказа́ла (*coll.*) I wouldn't be too sure about that.

надво́рный, *adj.* situated in the yard; н.

сове́тник (*obs.*) court counsellor (*civil servant of seventh class, equivalent in rank to lieutenant-colonel*).

надвя|за́ть, жу́, ‿жешь, *pf.* (*of* ‿зывать) to add (*in knitting*); to add a length (*of string, thread, etc.*).

надвя́зыва|ть, ю, *impf. of* надвяза́ть.

надгорта́нник, а, *m.* (*anat.*) epiglottis.

надгро́би|е, я, *n.* **1.** (*obs.*) epitaph. **2.** gravestone.

надгро́бн|ый, *adj.* (placed on, over, a) grave; funeral, graveside; ~ое сло́во graveside oration.

надгрыз|а́ть, а́ю, *impf. of* ~ть.

надгры́з|ть, у́, ёшь, *past* ~, ~ла, *pf.* (*of* ~а́ть) to nibble (at).

надда|ва́ть, ю́, ёшь, *impf. of* ~ть.

надда́|ть, м, шь, ст, ди́м, ди́те, ду́т, *past* ~л, ~ла́, ~ло, *pf.* (*of* ~ва́ть) (*coll.*; +*a. or g.*) to add, increase, enhance; н. хо́ду to increase the pace; ~й! get a move on!

наддув, а, *m.* (*tech., aeron.*) supercharge.

надёв|анный, *p.p.p. of* ~а́ть *and adj.* worn, used (*of clothing*).

надева́|ть, ю, *impf. of* наде́ть.

наде́жд|а, ы, *f.* hope, prospect; подава́ть ~y to hold out hope; подава́ть ~ы to promise well, shape well.

надёж|ный (~ен, ~на), *adj.* reliable, trustworthy; safe.

наде́л, а, *m.* allotment; land holding (*esp. after the emancipation of the serfs in 1861*).

наде́ла|ть, ю, *pf.* (+*a. or g.*) **1.** to make (*a quantity of*). **2.** (*coll.*; +*g.*) to cause (*a lot of*), make (*a lot of*). **3.** (*coll.*) to do (*something wrong*); что ты ~л? what have you done?

надел|ённый, *p.p.p. of* ~и́ть; он ~ён больши́ми спосо́бностями he is richly talented.

надел|и́ть, ю́, и́шь, *pf.* (*of* ~я́ть) (+*a. and i.*) to invest (with), to provide (with); (*fig.*) to endow (with).

наде́|ну, нешь, *see* ~ть.

надёрг|ать, аю, *pf.* (*of* ~ивать) (+*a. or g.*) to pull, pluck (*a quantity of*).

надёргива|ть, ю, *impf. of* надёргать *and* надёрнуть.

надёр|нуть, ну, нешь, *pf.* (*of* ~гивать) (на+*a.*) to pull (on, over).

над|еру́, ерёшь, *see* ~ра́ть.

наде́|ть, ну, нешь, *pf.* (*of* ~ва́ть) to put on (*clothes, etc.*).

наде́|яться, юсь, ешься, *impf.* (*of* по~) **1.** (на+*a.*) to hope (for). **2.** (на+*a.*) to rely (on). **3.** to expect.

надзе́мный, *adj.* overground.

надзира́тел|ь, я, *m.* overseer, supervisor; кла́ссный н. (*obs.*) form-master.

надзира́|ть, ю, *impf.* (за+*i.*) to oversee, supervise.

надзо́р, а, *m.* **1.** supervision, surveillance. **2.** (*collect.*) inspectorate; прокуро́рский н. Directorate of Public Prosecutions.

надив|и́ться, лю́сь, и́шься, *pf.* (*coll.*; +*d.* *or* на+*a.*) to admire sufficiently; не мо́жешь н. на его́ му́жество one cannot sufficiently admire his courage.

надира́|ть, ю, *impf. of* надра́ть.

надира́|ться, юсь, *impf. of* надра́ться.

надка́лыва|ть, ю, *impf. of* надколо́ть.

надкла́ссовый, *adj.* (*polit.*) transcending class.

надко́жиц|а, ы, *f.* (*bot.*) cuticle.

надколе́нн|ый, *adj.* ~ая ча́шка knee-cap; (*anat.*) patella.

надкол|о́ть, ю́, ~ешь, *pf.* (*of* надка́лывать) **1.** to crack. **2.** to score.

надко́стниц|а, ы, *f.* (*anat.*) periosteum; воспале́ние ~ы (*med.*) periostitis.

надкры́ль|е, я, *n.* (*zool.*) shard, elytron; wing-case.

надку|си́ть, шу́, ~сишь, *pf.* (*of* ~сывать) to take a bite (of).

надку́сыва|ть, ю, *impf. of* надкуси́ть.

надла́мыва|ть(ся), ю(сь), *impf. of* надломи́ть(ся).

надлежа́щий, *adj.* fitting, proper; appropriate.

надлеж|и́т, *past* ~а́ло, (*impers.*; +*d. and inf.*) it is necessary, it is required; н. вам яви́ться в де́сять часо́в you are required to present yourself at ten o'clock.

надло́м, а, *m.* **1.** crack. **2.** (*fig.*) sharp deterioration of psychological state; crack-up. **3.** violent expression of emotion.

надлом|и́ть, лю́, ~ишь, *pf.* (*of* надла́мывать) to break partly; to crack; (*fig.*) to overtax, break down.

надлом|и́ться, лю́сь, ~ишься, *pf.* (*of* надла́мываться) **1.** to crack (*also fig.*); здоро́вье у него́ ~и́лось he has had a breakdown. **2.** *pass. of* ~и́ть.

надло́м|ленный, *p.p.p. of* ~и́ть *and adj.* broken (*also fig.*).

надме́нност|ь, и, *f.* haughtiness, arrogance.

надме́н|ный (~ен, ~на), *adj.* haughty, arrogant.

надня́х, *adv.* **1.** in a few days' time; one of these days. **2.** the other day.

на́до¹ = над.

на́до², +*d. and inf.* it is necessary; one must, one ought; (+*a. or g.*) there is need of; не н. (*i*) one need not, (*ii*) one must not; мне н. идти́ I must go, I ought to go; мне н. вина́ I need some wine; так ему́ и н. serves him right!; н. быть (*coll.*) probably; что н. (*as pred.*; *coll.*) the best there is.

на́до|бно (*obs.*) = ~.

на́добност|ь, и, *f.* necessity, need; име́ть н. в чём-н. to require something.

на́доб|ный (~ен, ~на), *adj.* (*obs.*) necessary, needful.

надоеда́|ть, ю, *impf. of* надое́сть.

надое́длив|ый (~, ~а), *adj.* boring, tiresome.

надое́|сть, м, шь, ст, ди́м, ди́те, дя́т, *pf.* (*of* ~да́ть) **1.** (+*d. and i.*) to get on the nerves (of), to pester (with), plague (with); to bore (with); он мне до чёртиков ~л I'm sick to death of him. **2.** (*impers.*; +*d. and inf.*) мне, *etc.*, ~ло I, *etc.*, am tired (of), sick (of); нам ~ло игра́ть в чехарду́ we are tired of playing leapfrog.

надо|и́ть, ю́, и́шь, *pf.* (*of* надаи́вать) (+*a. or g.*) to obtain (*a quantity of* milk).

надо́|й, я, *m.* (*agric.*) yield (of milk).

на́долб|а, ы, *f.* stake; противота́нковые ~ы anti-tank obstacles.

надо́лго, *adv.* for a long time.

надо́мник, а, *m.* craftsman working at home.

надорв|а́ть, у́, ёшь, *past* ~а́л, ~ала́, ~а́ло, *pf.* (*of* надрыва́ть) to tear slightly; (*fig.*) to (over)strain, overtax; н. живо́тики (со́ смеху) (*coll.*) to split one's sides (with laughter).

надорв|а́ться, у́сь, ёшься, *past* ~а́лся, ~ала́сь, ~а́лось, *pf.* (*of* надрыва́ться) **1.** to tear slightly (*intrans.*); to (over)strain oneself. **2.** to let oneself go, let rip.

надоу́м|ить, лю, ишь, *pf.* (*of* ~ливать) (*coll.*) to advise, to give the (*required*) idea.

надоу́млива|ть, ю, *impf. of* надоу́мить.

надпа́рыва|ть, ю, *impf. of* надпоро́ть.

надпи́лива|ть, ю, *impf. of* надпили́ть.

надпил|и́ть, ю́, ~ишь, *pf.* (*of* ~ивать) to make an incision in (*by sawing*).

надпи|са́ть, шу́, ~шешь, *pf.* (*of* ~сывать) **1.** to inscribe; to superscribe. **2.** (*obs.*) to address (*an envelope, etc.*).

надпи́сыва|ть, ю, *impf. of* надписа́ть.

на́дпис|ь, и, *f.* inscription; superscription; (*on medal, coin, etc.*) legend; переда́точная н. (*comm.*) endorsement.

надпор|о́ть, ю́, ~ешь, *pf.* (*of* надпа́рывать) (*coll.*) to unstitch, unpick (*a few stitches*).

надпо́чечный, *adj.* (*anat.*) adrenal.

над|ра́ть, еру́, ерёшь, *past* ~ра́л, ~рала́, ~ра́ло, *pf.* (*of* ~ира́ть) (+*a. or g.*) to tear off, strip (*a quantity of*); н. у́ши кому́-н. to pull someone's ears.

над|ра́ться, еру́сь, ерёшься, *past* ~ра́лся, ~рала́сь, ~ра́лось, *pf.* (*of* ~ира́ться) (*coll.*) to become sozzled.

надре́з, а, *m.* cut, incision; notch.

надре́|зать, жу, жешь, *pf.* (*of* ~за́ть *and* ~зывать) to make an incision (in).

надрез|а́ть, а́ю, *impf. of* ~ать.

надре́зыва|ть, ю, *impf.* = надреза́ть.

надруга́тельств|о, а, *n.* (над) outrage (upon).

надруга́|ться, юсь, *pf.* (над) to outrage, do violence to.

надры́в, а, *m.* 1. slight tear, rent. 2. strain. 3. (*fig.*) sharp deterioration of psychological state; crack-up. 4. violent expression of emotion.

надрыва́|ть(ся), ю(сь), *impf. of* надорва́ть(ся).

надры́в|ный (~ен, ~на), *adj.* 1. hysterical. 2. heart-rending.

надса́д|а, ы, *f.* (*coll.*) strain; effort.

надса|ди́ть, жу́, ~дишь, *pf.* (*of* ~жива́ть) (*coll.*) 1. to (over)strain. 2. (+*d.*) to vex, distress.

надса|ди́ться, жу́сь, ~дишься, *pf.* (*of* ~жива́ться) (*coll.*) to (over)strain oneself.

надса́д|ный (~ен, ~на), *adj.* (*coll.*) back-breaking; heavy; н. ка́шель hacking cough.

надса́жива|ть(ся), ю(сь), *impf. of* надсади́ть(ся).

надсма́трива|ть, ю, *impf.* (за+*i.* or над) to oversee, supervise; to inspect.

надсмо́тр, а, *m.* supervision; surveillance.

надсмо́трщик, а, *m.* overseer, supervisor; jailer.

надста́в|ить, лю, ишь, *pf.* (*of* ~ля́ть) to lengthen (*garment or part of garment*).

надста́вк|а, и, *f.* added piece, extension.

надставля́|ть, ю, *impf. of* надста́вить.

надставно́й, *adj.* put on.

надстра́ива|ть, ю, *impf. of* надстро́ить.

надстро́|ить, ю, ишь, *pf.* (*of* надстра́ивать) 1. to build on. 2. to raise the height (of).

надстро́йк|а, и, *f.* 1. building on; raising. 2. superstructure (*also philos.*).

надстро́чн|ый, *adj.* superlinear.

надтре́снут|ый (~, ~а), *adj.* cracked (*also fig.*).

надува́л|а, ы, *m. and f.* (*coll.*) swindler, cheat.

надува́тельский, *adj.* (*coll.*) swindling, underhand.

надува́тельств|о, а, *n.* (*coll.*) swindling, cheating.

надува́|ть(ся), ю(сь), *impf. of* наду́ть(ся).

надувн|о́й, *adj.* pneumatic; ~а́я рези́новая ло́дка inflatable rubber dinghy.

наду́манный, *adj.* far-fetched, forced.

наду́м|ать, аю, *pf.* (*coll.*) 1. (+*inf.*) to decide (to). 2. (*impf.* ~ывать) to think up, make up.

наду́мыва|ть, ю, *impf. of* наду́мать.

наду́т|ый (~, ~а), *p.p.p. of* ~ь *and adj.* (*coll.*) 1. swollen. 2. haughty; puffed up. 3. sulky. 4. (*lit.*) inflated, turgid.

наду́|ть, ю, ешь, *pf.* (*of* ~ва́ть) 1. to inflate, blow up; to puff out; н. велосипе́дную ка́меру to inflate, blow up a bicycle tire; *impers.* (*pf. only*) ве́тром ~ло пы́ли the wind

blew the dust up; мне ~ло в у́хо I have ear-ache from the draught; н. гу́бы (*coll.*) to pout one's lips. 2. (*coll.*) to dupe; to swindle.

наду́|ться[1], юсь, ешься, *pf.* (*of* ~ва́ться) 1. to fill out, swell out; паруса́ ~лись the sails filled out. 2. (*fig., coll.*) to be puffed up. 3. (*fig., coll.*) to pout; to sulk.

наду́|ться[2], юсь, ешься, *pf.* (*coll.*; +*g.*) to swig (*a quantity of*).

наду́ш|енный, *p.p.p. of* ~и́ть *and adj.* scented, perfumed.

надуш|и́ть(ся), у́(сь), ~ишь(ся), *pf. of* души́ть(ся)[2].

надшива́|ть, ю, *impf. of* надши́ть.

над|ши́ть, ошью́, ошьёшь, *pf.* (*of* ~шива́ть) 1. to lengthen (*a garment*). 2. to stitch on (to).

надым|и́ть, лю́, и́шь, *pf. of* дыми́ть.

надыш|а́ть, у́, ~ишь, *pf.* 1. to make the air (*in a room, etc.*) warm with one's breathing. 2. (*coll.*; на+*a.*) to breathe (on).

надыш|а́ться, у́сь, ~ишься, *pf.* 1. (+*i.*) to breathe in, inhale. 2. не н. (на+*a.*) to dote (on, upon).

наеда́|ться, юсь, *impf. of* нае́сться.

наедине́, *adv.* privately, in private; н. с (+*i.*) alone (with).

нае́|ду, дешь, *see* ~хать.

нае́зд, а, *m.* 1. flying visit; быва́ть ~ом to pay short, infrequent visits. 2. (*cavalry*) raid.

нае́з|дить, жу, дишь, *pf.* (*of* ~жива́ть) 1. to cover (*driving or riding*); мы ~дили сто миль за два часа́ we covered a hundred miles in two hours. 2. (*coll.*) to make (= gain, acquire) (*by conveying*); н. де́сять рубле́й to make ten roubles. 3. (доро́гу, *etc.*) to use (a road, *etc.*) a good deal. 4. to break in (*a horse*).

нае́здник, а, *m.* 1. horseman, rider; jockey; (*mil.*; *obs.*) raider. 2. (*zool.*) ichneumon-fly.

нае́здничеств|о, а, *n.* 1. horsemanship. 2. (*obs.*) (cavalry) raiding.

наезжа́|ть, ю, *impf.* 1. (*coll.*) to pay occasional visits. 2. *impf. of* нае́хать.

нае́з|женный, *p.p.p. of* ~дить *and adj.* well-trodden, beaten.

нае́зжива|ть, ю, *impf. of* нае́здить.

нае́зж|ий, *adj.* (*coll.*) newly-arrived; ~ие лю́ди new-comers.

нае́з|жу, *see* ~дить.

на|ём, ~йма, *m.* hire; renting; взять в н. to rent; сдать в н. to let.

наёмник, а, *m.* 1. (*hist.*) mercenary. 2. hireling (*also fig.*).

наёмный, *adj.* hired; rented.

наёмщик, а, *m.* tenant, lessee.

нае́|сться, мся, шься, стся, ди́мся, ди́тесь, дя́тся, *past* ~лся, ~лась, *pf.* (*of* ~да́ться)

1. to eat one's fill. **2.** (+*g. or i.*) to eat (a large quantity of), stuff oneself (with).

наé|хать, ду, дешь, *pf.* (*of* ~зжáть) **1.** (на+*a.*) to run (into, over), collide (with); на нас ~хал автóбус a 'bus ran into us (over us). **2.** (*coll.*) to come, arrive (*unexpectedly or in numbers*).

нажáл|оваться, уюсь, *pf.* (*coll.*; на+*a.*) to complain (of).

нажáрива|ть(ся), ю(сь), *impf. of* нажáрить-(ся).

нажáр|ить¹, ю, ишь, *pf.* (*of* ~ивать) (*coll.*) to overheat.

нажáр|ить², ю, ишь, *pf.* to roast, fry (*a quantity of*).

нажáр|иться, юсь, ишься, *pf.* (*of* ~иваться) (*coll.*) to bask, warm oneself (*for a long time*).

наж|áть¹, мý, мёшь, *pf.* (*of* ~имáть) **1.** (+*a. or* на+*a.*) to press (on); н. (на) кнóпку to press the button. **2.** (*fig., coll.*; на+*a.*) to put pressure (upon). **3.** (*fig., coll.*) to press on, press ahead; ~мём и вы́полним э́ту рабóту! let us press on and finish this job!

наж|áть², нý, нёшь, *pf.* (*of* ~инáть) (+*a. or g.*) to reap, harvest (*a quantity of*).

наждáк, á, *m.* emery.

наждá|чный, *adj. of* ~к; ~чная бумáга emery paper.

наж|éчь, гý, жёшь, гýт, *past* ~ёг, ~глá, *pf.* (*of* ~игáть) (+*a. or g.*) to burn (*a quantity of*).

нажúв|а¹, ы, *f.* gain, profit.

нажúв|а², ы, *f.* = ~ка.

наживá|ть(ся), ю(сь), *impf. of* нажúть(ся).

нажив|úть, лю́, и́шь, *pf.* (*of* ~ля́ть) to bait.

нажúвк|а, и, *f.* bait.

наживля́|ть, ю, *impf. of* наживúть.

наживн|óй¹, *adj., only in phrase* э́то дéло ~óе (*coll.*) it'll come (with time).

наживнóй², *adj.* usable as bait.

нажи|вý, вёшь, *see* ~ть.

нажигá|ть, ю, *impf. of* нажéчь.

нажúм, а, *m.* **1.** pressure (*also fig.*). **2.** (*tech.*) clamp.

нажимá|ть, ю, *impf. of* нажáть¹.

нажúмист|ый (~, ~а), *adj.* (*coll.*) exacting; stubborn, insistent.

нажимн|óй, *adj.* (*tech.*) pressure; н. винт stop screw; ~óе приспособлéние pressure mechanism.

нажина́|ть, ю, *impf. of* нажáть².

нажира́|ться, юсь, *impf. of* нажрáться.

наж|úть, ивý, ивёшь, *past* ~úл, ~илá, ~úло, *pf.* (*of* ~ивáть) to acquire, gain; (*fig.*) to contract (*disease*), incur.

наж|úться, ивусь, ивёшься, *past* ~úлся, ~илáсь, *pf.* (*of* ~ивáться) to become rich, make a fortune.

нажи́|ться², вýсь, вёшься, *pf.* (*coll.*) to live (*somewhere*) long enough.

наж|мý, мёшь, *see* ~áть¹.

наж|нý, нёшь, *see* ~áть².

нажр|áться, усь, ёшься, *pf.* (*of* нажирáть-ся) (*coll.*; +*g. or i.*) to gorge oneself (with).

назáвтра, *adv.* (*coll.*) on *or* for the next day.

назáд, *adv.* **1.** back, backwards; н.! back!, stand back! **2.** (тому́) н. ago.

назади́, *adv.* (*coll.*) behind.

назализáци|я, и, *f.* (*ling.*) nasalization.

назализи́р|овать, ую, *impf. and pf.* (*ling.*) to nasalize.

назáльный, *adj.* (*ling.*) nasal.

назвáнива|ть, ю, *impf.* (*coll.*) to keep ringing (*on telephone, etc.*).

назвáни|е, я, *n.* name, appellation; title (*book*).

назвáный, *adj.* sworn; adopted; (*fig.*) он мой н. брат he is my sworn brother.

наз|вáть¹, овý, овёшь, *past* ~вáл, ~валá, ~вáло, *pf.* (*of* ~ывáть) (+*i.*) to call; to name, designate; они́ ~вáли дочь Татья́ной they have called their daughter Tatyana; он ~вáл себя́ Никола́ем he gave his name as Nicholas.

наз|вáть², овý, овёшь, *past* ~вáл, ~валá, ~вáло, *pf.* (*coll.*; +*g.*) to invite (*a number of*).

наз|вáться¹, овýсь, овёшься, *past* ~вáлся, ~валáсь, *pf.* (*of* ~ывáться) to call oneself.

наз|вáться², овýсь, овёшься, *past* ~вáлся, ~валáсь, *pf.* (*coll.*) to invite oneself.

наздрáвств|оваться, уюсь, *pf.* на вся́кое чиха́нье не ~уешься (*coll.*) one cannot please everyone.

назём, а, *m.* (*dial.*) manure, dung.

назёмн|ый, *adj.* ground, surface; terrestrial; ~ые войскá (*mil.*) ground troops; ~ая (пóчта) surface mail.

нáземь, *adv.* (down) to the ground.

назидáни|е, я, *n.* (*obs., now iron.*) edification; сказáть что-н. в н. кому́-н. to say something for someone's edification.

назидáтел|ьный (ен, ~ьна), *adj.* edifying.

нáзло́ 1. *adv.* out of spite. **2.** *prep.* (+*d.*) to spite.

назнач|áть, áю, *impf. of* ~úть.

назначéни|е, я, *n.* **1.** fixing, setting. **2.** appointment. **3.** (*med.*) prescription. **4.** purpose. **5.** destination.

назнáч|ить, у, ишь, *pf.* (*of* ~áть) **1.** to fix, set, appoint; н. день встрéчи to fix, appoint a day for a meeting; н. опла́ту to fix a rate of pay. **2.** (+*i.*) to appoint, nominate; егó ~или команди́ром рóты he has been appointed company commander. **3.** (*med.*) to prescribe.

назóйливост|ь, и, *f.* importunity.

назóйлив|ый (~, ~а), *adj.* importunate.

назревá|ть, ю, *impf.* (*of* назрéть) **1.** to ripen, mature; to gather head. **2.** (*fig.*) to become imminent; кри́зис ~л a crisis was brewing.

назре́|ть, ю, ешь, *pf. of* ~ва́ть.

назубо́к, *adv.* (*coll.*) знать н. to know by heart.

называ́|емый, *pres. part. pass. of* ~ть; так н. so-called.

называ́|ть, ю, *impf. of* назва́ть[1].

называ́|ться[1], юсь, *impf.* (*of* назва́ться[1]) (+*i.*) 1. to call oneself. 2. to be called; как ~ется э́то село́? what is this village called? what is the name of this village?; что ~ется (*coll.*) as they say. 3. (*obs.*) to give one's name.

наибо́лее, *adv.* (the) most.

наибо́льший, *adj.* the greatest; the largest; о́бщий н. дели́тель (*math.*) highest common factor.

наивнича́|ть, ю, *impf.* (*coll.*) to affect naïveté.

наи́вност|ь, и, *f.* naïveté (naivety).

наи́в|ный (~ен, ~на), *adj.* naïve.

наивы́сш|ий, *adj.* the highest; в ~ей сте́пени to the utmost.

наигра́нн|ый 1. *p.p.p. of* наигра́ть. **2.** *adj.* (*fig.*) put on, assumed; forced; ~ая весё́лость assumed gaiety.

наигра́|ть, ю, *pf.* (*of* наи́грывать) 1. (*coll.*) to make, acquire (*by playing*). 2. (*coll.*) to strum. 3. н. пласти́нку to make a recording.

наигра́|ться, юсь, *pf.* (*coll.*) to play for a long time, for long enough.

наи́грыва|ть, ю, *impf. of* наигра́ть.

наи́грыш, а, *m.* 1. folk-tune. 2. (*theatr. sl.*) artificiality.

наизна́нку, *adv.* inside out; вы́вернуть н. to turn inside out.

наизу́сть, *adv.* by heart; from memory.

наилу́чший, *adj.* (the) best.

наиме́нее, *adv.* (the) least.

наименова́ни|е, я, *n.* appellation, designation.

наимен|ова́ть, у́ю, *pf. of* именова́ть.

наиме́ньш|ий, *adj.* (the) least; о́бщее ~ee кра́тное (*math.*) lowest common multiple.

наипа́че, *adv.* (*obs.*) still more; in particular.

наискосо́к, *adv.* = на́искось.

на́искось, *adv.* obliquely, slantwise.

наи́ти|е, я, *n.* inspiration; по ~ю instinctively, intuitively.

наихудший, *adj.* (the) worst.

найдё́ныш, а, *m.* foundling.

найми́т, а, *m.* hireling.

на|йти́[1], йду́, йдёшь, *past* ~шё́л, ~шла́, *pf.* (*of* ~ходи́ть) (*in var. senses*) to find; to discover; н. себе́ моги́лу, смерть (*rhet.*) to meet one's death.

на|йти́[2], йду́, йдёшь, *past* ~шё́л, ~шла́, *pf.* (*of* ~ходи́ть) 1. (на+*a.*) to come (across, over, upon); to come (up against); что э́то на неё ~шло́? what has come over her?

2. (*impers.*; *coll.*) to gather, collect; ~шло́ мно́го наро́ду a large crowd collected.

на|йти́сь, йду́сь, йдёшься, *past* ~шё́лся, ~шла́сь, *pf.* (*of* ~ходи́ться[1]) 1. to be found; to turn up. 2. not to be at a loss; я не ~шё́лся, что сказа́ть I was at a loss for what to say.

найто́в, а, *m.* (*naut.*) lashing, seizing.

найто́в|ить, лю, ишь, *impf.* (*of* об~) (*naut.*) to lash, seize.

нака́вер|зить, жу, зишь, *pf. of* ка́верзить.

нака́з, а, *m.* 1. (*obs.*) order; instructions. 2. mandate (*in Soviet governmental system, list of desiderata presented by electors to deputy*).

наказа́ни|е, я, *n.* 1. punishment. 2. (*fig.*, *coll.*) nuisance; мне с ним (су́щее, пря́мо, про́сто) н. he is a (perfect) nuisance to me.

нака|за́ть[1], жу́, ~жешь, *pf.* (*of* ~зывать) to punish.

нака|за́ть[2], жу́, ~жешь, *pf.* (*of* ~зывать) (*obs. or dial.*; +*d.*) to instruct, bid.

наказу́емый, *adj.* (*leg.*) punishable.

нака́л, а, *m.* 1. incandescence. 2. (*radio*) heating.

накал|ё́нный, *p.p.p. of* ~и́ть *and adj.* 1. incandescent; white-hot. 2. (*fig.*) strained, tense; ~ё́нная междунаро́дная обстано́вка tense international situation.

нака́лива|ни|е, я, *n.* (*tech.*) incandescing.

нака́лива|ть(ся), ю(сь), *impf. of* накали́ть(ся).

накал|и́ть, ю́, и́шь, *pf.* (*of* ~ивать) to heat, incandesce.

накал|и́ться, ю́сь, и́шься, *pf.* (*of* ~иваться) to glow, incandesce.

нака́лыва|ть(ся), ю(сь), *impf. of* наколо́ть(ся).

наканифо́л|ить, ю, ишь, *pf. of* канифо́лить.

накану́не 1. (*adv.*) the day before. **2.** (*prep.*+*g.*) on the eve (of); н. Рождества́ Христо́ва on Christmas Eve.

нака́п|ать, аю, *pf.* (*of* ~ывать[1]) 1. (+*a.* or *g.*) to pour by drops; н. лека́рства to pour out some medicine. 2. (+*g.* or *i.*) to spill; он ~ал на столе́ черни́лами (черни́л) he has spilled ink on the table.

нака́пливать(ся) = накопля́ть(ся).

нака́пыва|ть[1], ю, *impf. of* нака́пать.

нака́пыва|ть[2], ю, *impf. of* накопа́ть.

нака́рка|ть, ю, *pf.* (*coll.*) to bring down (evil) by one's own prophecies.

нака́т, а, *m.* layer (*of beams or planks*).

накат|а́ть[1], аю, *pf.* (*of* ~ывать) 1. to roll out; to roll smooth. 2. (*coll.*) to write hurriedly; н. письмо́ to dash off a letter.

накат|а́ть[2], аю, *pf.* (*of* ~ывать) (+*a.* or *g.*) to roll (*a quantity of*).

наката́|ться, юсь, *pf.* (*coll.*) to have had enough (*of driving, riding*).

нака|ти́ть, чу́, ~тишь, *pf.* (*of* ~тывать)

(на+*a*.) to roll up (onto); (*impers*.; *coll*.) на него ~тúло he is out of his senses, he has taken leave of his senses.

накáтыва|ть, ю, *impf. of* накатáть *and* накатúть.

накач|áть[1], áю, *pf.* (*of* ~ивать) to pump up, pump full.

накачá|ть[2], ю, *pf.* to pump (*a quantity of*).

накачáться, áюсь, *pf.* (*of* ~иваться) 1. (*coll*.) to become sozzled. 2. *pass. of* ~áть.

накáчива|ть(ся), ю(сь), *impf. of* накачáть(ся).

накид|áть, áю, *pf.* (*of* ~ывать) = набросáть[2].

накúдк|а, и, *f.* 1. cloak, mantle; wrap. 2. pillow-cover. 3. increase; extra charge.

накúдыва|ть(ся), ю(сь), *impf. of* накидáть *and* накúнуть(ся).

накú|нуть, ну, нешь, *pf.* (*of* ~дывать) 1. to throw on, throw over. 2. (на+*a*.) to add (*to the price of*).

накú|нуться, нусь, нешься, *pf.* (*of* ~дываться) (на+*a*.) to fall (on, upon).

накип|áть, áет, *impf. of* ~éть.

накип|éть, úт, *pf.* (*of* ~áть) to form a scum; to form a scale; (*fig*.; *impers*.) to swell, boil; в нём ~éла злоба he is boiling with resentment.

нáкип|ь, и, *f.* 1. scum. 2. scale, fur, coating, deposit.

наклáд, а, *m.* быть, остáться в ~e (*coll*.) to be down, come off loser.

наклáдк|а, и, *f.* 1. (*tech*.) bracket. 2. false hair, hair-piece.

накладн|áя, óй, *f.* invoice, way-bill.

наклáдно, *adv.* (*coll*.) to one's disadvantage, to one's cost.

накладн|óй, *adj.* 1. laid on, super-imposed; ~óе зóлото rolled gold; ~ые расхóды overhead expenses, overheads. 2. false; ~áя бородá false beard.

наклáдыва|ть, ю, *impf. of* наложúть.

наклеве|тáть, щý, ~щешь, *pf. of* клеветáть.

наклёвыва|ться, юсь, *impf. of* наклюнуться.

наклéива|ть, ю, *impf. of* наклéить.

наклé|ить, ю, ешь, *pf.* (*of* ~ивать) to stick on, paste on.

наклéйк|а, и, *f.* 1. sticking on, pasting on. 2. label.

наклепá|ть[1], ю, *pf.* (*of* наклёпывать) to rivet.

наклеп|áть[2], лю, ~лешь, *pf. of* клепáть[2].

наклёпыва|ть, ю, *impf. of* наклепáть[1].

наклик|áть, áю, *impf. of* ~áть.

наклú|кать, чу, чешь, *pf.* (*of* ~кáть) н. на себя to bring upon oneself; н. бедý (на+*a*.) to bring disaster (upon).

наклóн, а, *m.* slope, incline; declivity.

наклонéни|е[1], я, *n.* inclination.

наклонéни|е[2], я, *n.* (*gram*.) mood.

наклон|úть, ю, ~ишь, *pf.* (*of* ~я́ть) to incline, bend; to bow.

наклон|úться, ю́сь, ~ишься, *pf.* (*of* ~я́ться) to stoop, bend.

наклóнност|ь, и, *f.* 1. (к) leaning (towards), penchant (for). 2. inclination, propensity, proclivity; дурны́е ~и evil propensities.

наклóнн|ый, *adj.* inclined, sloping; ~ая плóскость inclined plane; катúться по ~ой плóскости (*fig*.) to go downhill, go to the dogs (*morally*).

наклон|я́ть(ся), я́ю(сь), *impf. of* ~úть(ся).

наклю́н|уться, усь, ешься, *pf.* (*of* наклёвываться) 1. to peck its way out of the shell. 2. (*coll*.) to turn up; слýчай ~ется an occasion will present itself.

накля́узнича|ть, ю, *pf. of* кля́узничать.

наковáл|ьня, ьни, *g. pl.* ~ен, *f.* 1. anvil. 2. (*anat*.) incus.

накóжный, *adj.* (*med*.) cutaneous.

наколáчива|ть, ю, *impf. of* наколотúть[1, 2].

наколéнник, а, *m.* knee-guard.

наколéнный, *adj.* worn on the knee.

наколк|а, и, *f.* 1. head-dress (*fastened with pins*). 2. (*sl*.) tip-off.

наколо|тúть[1], чý, ~тишь, *pf.* (*of* наколáчивать) (*coll*.) 1. to knock on. 2. to knock up (*money*).

наколо|тúть[2], чý, ~тишь, *pf.* (*of* наколáчивать) (+*a. or g*.) н. гвоздéй to drive in (*a number of*) nails; н. посýды to smash (*a quantity of*) crockery.

накол|óть[1], ю, ~ешь, *pf.* (*of* накáлывать) (+*a. or g*.) to split (*a quantity of*); н. дров to chop (*a quantity of*) wood.

накол|óть[2], ю, ~ешь, *pf.* (*of* накáлывать) 1. to prick; н. узóр to prick out a pattern. 2. to pin down; н. бáбочку на булáвку to pin down a butterfly. 3. to slaughter, stick (*a number of*).

накол|óться, ю́сь, ~ешься, *pf.* (*of* накáлываться) to prick oneself.

наконéц, *adv.* 1. at last; finally, in the end; н.-то! at last!, about time too! 2. after all.

наконéчник, а, *m.* tip, point; ferrule; н. стрелы́ arrow-head.

наконéчн|ый, *adj.* final; ~ое ударéние (*gram*.) end-stress.

накопá|ть, ю, *pf.* (*of* накáпывать) (+*a. or g*.) to dig up (*a number of*).

накопúтел|ь, я, *m.* (computer) storage.

накоп|úть, лю́, ~ишь, *pf.* (*of* копúть; ~ля́ть *and* накáпливать) (+*a. or g*.) to accumulate, amass.

накоп|úться, лю́сь, ~ишься, *pf.* (*of* ~ля́ться *and* накáпливаться) to accumulate.

накоплéни|е, я, *n.* accumulation.

накопля́|ть(ся), ю(сь), *impf. of* накопúть(ся).

накоп|ти́ть[1], чу́, ти́шь, *pf. of* копти́ть 3.

накоп|ти́ть[2], чу́, ти́шь, *pf.* (+*a. or g.*) to smoke (= cure) (*a quantity of*).

накорм|и́ть, лю́, ⌐ишь, *pf. of* корми́ть.

накоротке́, *adv.* произвести́ ата́ку н. to carry out a rapid attack at close range.

нако|си́ть, шу́, ⌐сишь, *pf.* (+*a. or g.*) to mow (down) (*a quantity of*).

нако́стн|ый, *adj.* (situated on) bone; ⌐ая о́пухоль bone tumour.

накра́пыва|ть, ет, *impf.* (*impers. or* +дождь) to trickle, drizzle; ста́ло н. it began to spit (*with rain*).

накра́|сить, шу, сишь, *pf.* (*of* ⌐шивать) 1. to paint. 2. to make up.

накра́|сится, шусь, сишься, *pf. of* кра́сить-ся.

накра́|сть, ду́, дёшь, *past* ⌐л, *pf.* (*of* ⌐дывать) (+*a. or g.*)to steal (*a number of*).

накрахма́л|ить, ю, ишь, *pf. of* крахма́лить.

накра́шива|ть, ю, *impf. of* накра́сить.

накрен|и́ть, ю́, и́шь, *pf.* 1. *pf. of* крени́ть. 2. (*impf.* ⌐я́ть) to tilt to one side, tilt.

накрен|и́ться, ю́сь, и́шься, *pf.* 1. *pf. of* крени́ться. 2. (*impf.* ⌐я́ться) to tilt, list.

накрен|я́ть(ся), я́ю(сь), *impf. of* ⌐и́ть(ся).

на́крепко, *adv.* 1. fast, tight; закры́ть н. to shut fast. 2. (*coll.*) categorically; strictly; приказа́ть н. to give a strict injunction.

на́крест, *adv.* crosswise; сложи́ть ру́ки крест-н. to cross one's arms.

накрич|а́ть, у́, и́шь, *pf.* (на+*a.*) to shout (at).

накрич|а́ться, у́сь, и́шься, *pf.* (*coll.*) to have shouted to one's heart's content.

накро|и́ть, ю́, и́шь, *pf.* (+*a. or g.*) to cut out (*a quantity of*).

накрош|и́ть, у́, ⌐ишь, *pf.* (*of* кроши́ть) 1. to crumble, shred (*a quantity of*). 2. to spill crumbs.

накр|о́ю, о́ешь, *see* ⌐ы́ть.

накро|ю́, и́шь, *see* ⌐и́ть.

накру|ти́ть[1], чу́, ⌐тишь, *pf.* (*of* ⌐чивать) to wind, turn.

накру|ти́ть[2], чу́, ⌐тишь, *pf.* 1. to twist (*a quantity of*). 2. (*coll.*) to do, say (*something complicated or unusual*).

накру́чива|ть, ю, *impf. of* накрути́ть[1].

накрыва́|ть(ся), ю(сь), *impf. of* накры́ть(ся).

накр|ы́ть, о́ю, о́ешь, *pf.* (*of* ⌐ыва́ть) 1. to cover; н. (на) стол to lay the table; н. к у́жину to lay supper. 2.(*fig., coll.*) to catch; н. на ме́сте преступле́ния to catch red-handed.

накр|ы́ться, о́юсь, о́ешься, *pf.* (*of* ⌐ыва́ть-ся) (+*i.*) to cover oneself (with).

нактбу́з, а, *m.* (*naut.*) binnacle.

накуп|а́ть, а́ю, *impf. of* ⌐и́ть.

накуп|и́ть, лю́, ⌐ишь, *pf.* (*of* ⌐а́ть) (+*a. or g.*) to buy up (*a number or quantity of*).

наку́р|енный, *p.p.p. of* ⌐и́ть *and adj.* smoky,

smoke-filled; в ко́мнате ⌐ено the room is full of (tobacco) smoke.

чакур|и́ть[1], ю́, ⌐ишь, *pf.* (+*i.*) to fill with smoke, with fumes.

накур|и́ть[2], ю́, ⌐ишь, *pf.* (+*a. or g.*) to distil (*a quantity of*).

накур|и́ться, ю́сь, ⌐ишься, *pf.* (*coll.*) to smoke to one's heart's content.

чакуроле́|сить, шу, сишь, *pf. of* куроле́сить.

наку́т|ать, аю, *pf.* (*of* ⌐ывать) (+*a. or g.* на+*a.*) to put on (*clothing, etc.*); мно́го ⌐али на ребёнка the child was well wrapped up.

наку́тыва|ть, ю, *impf. of* наку́тать.

нала́влива|ть, ю, *impf. of* налови́ть.

налага́|ть, ю, *impf. of* наложи́ть.

нала́|дить, жу, дишь, *pf.* (*of* ⌐живать) 1. to regulate, adjust; to repair, put right. 2. to set going, arrange; н. дела́ to get things going.

нала́|диться, жусь, дишься, *pf.* (*of* ⌐жи-ваться) 1. to go right; рабо́та ⌐дилась the work is well in hand. 2. *pass. of* ⌐дить.

нала́дчик, а, *m.* (*tech.*) adjuster.

нала́жива|ть(ся), ю(сь), *impf. of* нала́-дить(ся).

налака́|ться, юсь, *pf.* 1. н. молока́ to lap up one's fill of milk. 2. (*coll.*) to get drunk.

налако́м|иться, люсь, ишься, *pf.* (*coll.*; +*i.*) to have one's fill (of dainties).

на|лга́ть, лгу́, лжёшь, лгу́т, *past* ⌐лга́л, ⌐лгала́, ⌐лга́ло, *pf.* 1. to lie, tell lies. 2. (*impf.* лгать 2) (на+*a.*) to slander.

нале́во, *adv.* 1. (от) to the left (of); н.! (*mil.*) left turn! 2. (*coll.*) on the side (= *illicitly*)

налега́|ть, ю, *impf. of* нале́чь.

налегке́, *adv.* (*coll.*) 1. without luggage; путеше́ствовать н. to travel light. 2. lightly clad.

належ|а́ть, у́, и́шь, *pf.* (*coll.*) to acquire as result of lying a long time; н. про́лежни to develop bed-sores.

налез|а́ть[1, 2], а́ю, *impf. of* ⌐ть[1, 2].

нале́з|ть[1], у, ешь, *past* ⌐, ⌐ла, *pf.* (*of* ⌐а́ть[1]) to get in, get on (*in large numbers, in quantities*).

нале́з|ть[2], ет, *pf.* (*of* ⌐а́ть[2]) (*of clothing or footwear*) (на+*a.*) to fit, go on.

налеп|и́ть[1], лю́, ⌐ишь, *pf.* (*of* лепи́ть 2 *and* ⌐ля́ть) to stick on.

налеп|и́ть[2], лю́, ⌐ишь, *pf.* (+*a. or g.*) to model (*a number of*).

налеп|ля́ть, ля́ю, *impf. of* ⌐и́ть.

налёт[1], а, *m.* (*in var. senses*) raid; кавалери́й-ский н. cavalry raid; возду́шный н. air--raid; с ⌐а(*fig.*) suddenly, without warning, without preparation; бить с ⌐а to swoop down on; он ду́мает, что он смо́жет по-би́ть реко́рд с ⌐а he thinks he will be able to beat the record just like that.

налёт², a, *m.* deposit; thin coating; (*on bronze*) patina; (*fig.*) touch, soupçon; н. в го́рле (*med.*) patch, spot; с ~ом иро́нии with a touch of irony.

налет|а́ть¹, а́ю, *impf. of* ~е́ть.

налет|а́ть², а́ю, *pf.* to have flown (so many hours *or* miles).

нале|те́ть¹, чу́, ти́шь, *pf.* (*of* ~та́ть¹) 1. (на+a.) to fall (upon); to swoop down (on); to fly (upon, against); to run (into) (*of vehicles*). 2.(*of wind, storm*) to spring up.

нале|те́ть², чу́, ти́шь, *pf.* (*of* ~та́ть¹) to fly in, drift in (*in quantities, in large numbers*).

налётчик, a, *m.* burglar, robber; raider.

на|ле́чь, ля́гу, ля́жешь, ля́гут, *imp.* ~ля́г, *past* ~лёг, ~легла́, *pf.* (*of* ~легла́ть) (на+a.) 1. to lean (on); to weigh down (on); to lie (upon); н. плечо́м на дверь to try to force the door with one's shoulder; н. на подчинённых (*fig.*) to come down upon one's subordinates. 2. to apply oneself (to), throw oneself (into); н. на вёсла to ply one's oars.

нали́в, a, *m.* 1. pouring in. 2. swelling, ripening; «бе́лый н.» name of kind of apple.

налива́|ть(ся), ю(сь), *impf. of* нали́ть(ся).

нали́вк|а, и, *f.* fruit liqueur; вишнёвая н. cherry brandy.

наливн|о́й, *adj.* 1. (*tech.*) worked by water; for conveying liquids; ~о́е колесо́ overshot wheel; ~о́е су́дно (*naut.*) tanker. 2. ripe, juicy.

нали́м, a, *m.* (*fish*) burbot, eel-pout.

налин|ова́ть, у́ю, *pf. of* линова́ть.

налип|а́ть, а́ет, *impf. of* ~нуть.

налип|нуть, нет, *past* ~, ~ла, *pf.* (*of* ~а́ть) (на+a.) to stick (to).

налито́й, *adj.* 1. juicy, ripe. 2. fleshy, well-fleshed.

нал|и́ть, ью́, ьёшь, *past* ~и́л, ~ила́, ~и́ло, *pf.* (*of* ~ива́ть) to pour out; (+i.) to fill (with); н. бо́чку водо́й to fill a barrel with water.

нал|и́ться, ью́сь, ьёшься, *past* ~и́лся, ~ила́сь, ~и́ло́сь, *pf.* (*of* ~ива́ться) 1. (+i.) to fill (with); н. кро́вью to become bloodshot. 2. to ripen, become juicy. 3. *pass. of* ~и́ть.

налицо́, *adv.* present, available, on hand.

нали́честв|овать, ую, *impf.* to be present, be on hand.

нали́чи|е, я, *n.* presence; быть, оказа́ться в ~и to be present, be available; при ~и (+g.) in the presence (of), given.

нали́чник, a, *m.* 1. casing, jambs and lintel of a door *or* window. 2. lock-plate.

нали́чност|ь, и, *f.* 1. amount on hand; cash-in-hand; н. това́ров в магази́не stock-in-trade. 2. = нали́чие.

нали́чн|ый, *adj.* on hand, available; ~ые (де́ньги) ready money, cash; плати́ть ~ыми to pay in cash, pay down; за н. расчёт for cash; н. соста́в (*mil.*) available personnel, effectives.

нало́бник, a, *m.* (*part of harness*) frontlet.

налов|и́ть, лю́, ~ишь, *pf.* (+a. *or* g.) to catch (*a number of*).

наловч|и́ться, у́сь, и́шься, *pf.* (+inf.) to become proficient (in), become good (at).

нало́г, a, *m.* tax.

нало́г|овый, *adj. of* ~.

налогоплате́льщик, a, *m.* tax-payer.

наложе́ни|е, я, *n.* 1. imposition; н. аре́ста (*leg.*) seizure; н. швов (*med.*) suture, stitching. 2. (*math.*) superposition.

налож|енный, *p.p.p. of* ~и́ть; ~енным платежо́м cash on delivery (C.O.D.).

налож|и́ть¹, у́, ~ишь, *pf.* 1. (*impf.* накла́дывать) to lay in, on; to put in, on; to superimpose; to apply; н. повя́зку to apply a bandage; н. на себя́ ру́ки to lay hands on oneself. 2. (*impf.* накла́дывать) to load, pack; н. корзи́ну бельём, н. белья́ в корзи́ну to load a basket with linen. 3. (*impf.* налага́ть) (на+a.) to lay (on), impose; н. на себя́ бре́мя to undertake a burden; н. штраф to impose a fine; н. аре́ст на чье́-н. иму́щество (*leg.*) to seize someone's property.

налож|и́ть², у́, ~ишь, *pf.* (*of* накла́дывать) to put, lay (*a quantity of*).

нало́жниц|а, ы, *f.* (*obs.*) concubine.

нало́|й, я, *m.* = анало́й.

налома́|ть, ю, *pf.* (+a. *or* g.) to break (*a quantity of*); н. бока́ кому́-н. (*coll.*) to give someone a sound thrashing; н. дров (*coll., joc.*) to commit follies.

налопа́|ться, юсь, *pf.* (*coll.*) to gorge oneself.

налощ|и́ть, у́, и́шь, *pf. of* лощи́ть.

нал|ью́, ьёшь, *see* ~и́ть.

налюб|ова́ться, у́юсь, *pf.* (+i. *or* на+a.) to gaze to one's heart's content (at) (*usually with neg.*).

нал|я́гу, я́жешь, я́гут, *see* ~е́чь.

наля́па|ть, ю, *pf. of* ля́пать.

нам, *d. of* мы.

намагни́|тить, чу, тишь, *pf.* (*of* ~чивать) to magnetize.

намагни́чива|ть, ю, *impf. of* намагни́тить.

нама́з, a, *m.* (Mohammedan) prayer.

нама́|зать, жу, жешь, *pf. of* ма́зать *and* ~зывать.

нама́|заться, жусь, жешься, *pf.* 1. (*impf.* ~зываться) (+i.) to rub oneself (with). 2. *pf. of* ма́заться.

нама́зыва|ть(ся), ю(сь), *impf. of* нама́зать(ся).

намал|ева́ть, ю́ю, ю́ешь, *pf. of* малева́ть.

намара́|ть, ю, *pf. of* мара́ть 2.

намарин|овать, у́ю, *pf.* (+*a. or g.*) to pickle (*a quantity of*).

намаслива|ть, ю, *impf.* = **маслить.**

намасл|ить, ю, ишь, *pf. of* **~ивать** *and* **маслить.**

наматывани|е, я, *n.* winding, reeling.

наматыва|ть, ю, *impf. of* **намотать².**

намачива|ть, ю, *impf. of* **намочить.**

нама́|яться, юсь, ешься, *pf.* (*coll.*) **1.** to be tired out. **2.** to have had a lot of trouble.

намедни, *adv.* (*dial.*) the other day, lately.

намёк, а, *m.* **1.** hint, allusion; **то́нкий н.** gentle hint; **сде́лать н.** to drop a hint; **с ~ом** (на+*a.*) with a suggestion (of). **2.** (*fig.*) faint resemblance.

намек|а́ть, а́ю, *impf.* (*of* **~ну́ть**) (на+*a.,* о+*p.*) to hint (at), allude (to).

намек|ну́ть, ну́, нёшь, *pf. of* **~а́ть.**

намел|и́ть, ю́, и́шь, *pf. of* **мели́ть.**

наменя́|ть, ю, *pf.* (+*a. or g.*) to obtain (*a quantity of*) by exchange.

намерева́|ться, юсь, *impf.* (+*inf.*) to intend (to), mean (to).

намерен (~а, ~о), *adj.* used as pred. **быть н.** (+*inf.*) to intend; **я н. за́втра е́хать** I intend to go tomorrow; **что вы ~ы сде́лать?** what do you intend to do?

намерени|е, я, *n.* intention; purpose.

наме́ренный, *adj.* intentional, deliberate.

намерз|а́ть, а́ю, *impf. of* **~нуть.**

намёрз|нуть, ну, нешь, *past* **~, ~ла,** *pf.* (*of* **~а́ть**) to freeze (on); **на ступе́ньках ~ло мно́го льда** a lot of ice had formed on the steps.

намёрз|нуться, нусь, нешься, *past* **~ся, ~лась,** *pf.* (*coll.*) to get frozen.

намер|ить, ю, ишь, *pf.* **1.** (+*a. or g.*) to measure out (*a quantity of*). **2.** to measure (*a certain quantity* or *distance*)'.

на́мертво, *adv.* tightly, fast.

наме|си́ть, шу́, ~сишь, *pf.* (+*a. or g.*) to knead (*a quantity of*).

наме|сти́, ту́, тёшь, *past* **~л, ~ла́,** *pf.* (*of* **~та́ть¹**) (+*a. or g.*) **1.** to sweep together (*a quantity of*). **2.** to cause to drift; **~ло́ мно́го сне́гу** big snow-drifts have formed.

наме́стник, а, *m.* **1.** deputy. **2.** (*hist.*) governor-general.

наме́стни|ческий, *adj. of* **~к.**

наме́стничеств|о, а, *n.* (*hist.*) region ruled by governor-general.

намёт¹, а, *m.* casting-net.

намёт², а, *m.* (*dial.*) gallop.

намета́|ть¹, ю, *impf. of* **намести́.**

намета́|ть², ю, *pf. of* **мета́ть².**

наме|та́ть³, чу́, ~чешь, *pf.* (+*a. or g.*) to throw together (*a quantity of*).

наме|та́ть⁴, чу́, ~чешь, *pf.* (*of* **~тывать**) (*coll.*) to train; **н. глаз** to acquire a (good)

---

eye; **н. ру́ку** (на+*a.*) to become proficient (in).

наме́|тить¹, чу, тишь, *pf. of* **ме́тить¹** *and* **~ча́ть¹.**

наме́|тить², чу, тишь, *pf.* **1.** (*impf.* **~ча́ть²**) to plan, project; to have in view; **н. пое́здку в Росси́ю** to plan a visit to Russia. **2.** (*impf.* **~ча́ть²**) to nominate; to select; **его́ ~тили кандида́том в председа́тели** he has been nominated for chairman; **н. зда́ние к разруше́нию** to designate a building for demolition. **3.** *pf. of* **ме́тить².**

наме́|титься, чусь, тишься, *pf.* (*of* **~ча́ться**) to be outlined; to take shape.

намётк|а¹, и, *f.* **1.** basting, tacking. **2.** basting thread, tacking thread.

намётк|а², и, *f.* rough draft, preliminary outline.

намётыва|ть, ю, *impf. of* **намета́ть⁴.**

намеча́|ть¹, ю, *impf.* = **ме́тить.**

намеча́|ть², ю, *impf. of* **наме́тить².**

намеча́|ться¹, юсь, *impf. of* **наме́титься.**

наме́|чу, тишь, *see* **~тить.**

наме́|чу, чешь, *see* **~та́ть.**

намеш|а́ть, а́ю, *pf.* (*of* **~ивать**) (+*a. or g.* в+*a.*) to add (to), mix in(to).

намёшива|ть, ю, *impf. of* **намеша́ть.**

на́ми, *i. of* **мы.**

намина́|ть, ю, *impf. of* **намя́ть.**

намно́го, *adv.* much, far (*with comparatives*); **н. лу́чше** much better.

нам|ну́, нёшь, *see* **~я́ть.**

намозо́л|ить, ю, ишь, *pf. of* **мозо́лить.**

намок|а́ть, а́ю, *impf.* (*of* **~нуть**) to become wet, get wet.

намо́к|нуть, ну, нешь, *past* **~, ~ла,** *pf. of* **~а́ть.**

намоло|ти́ть, чу́, ~тишь, *pf.* (+*a. or g.*) to thresh (*a quantity of*).

нам|оло́ть, елю́, е́лешь, *pf.* (+*a. or g.*) to grind, mill (*a quantity of*); **н. вздо́ру, чепухи́** (*coll.*) to talk a lot of nonsense.

намо́рдник, а, *m.* muzzle.

намо́рщ|ить(ся), у(сь), ишь(ся), *pf. of* **мо́рщить(ся).**

намо|сти́ть, щу́, сти́шь, *pf. of* **мости́ть 2.**

намота́|ть¹, ю, *pf. of* **мота́ть¹.**

намота́|ть², ю, *pf.* (*of* **нама́тывать**) (+*a. or g.*) to wind (*a quantity of*).

намоч|и́ть, у́, ~ишь, *pf.* (*of* **нама́чивать**) **1.** to wet, moisten. **2.** to soak, steep. **3.** (*intrans.; coll.*) to spill water (on the floor, *etc.*).

намудр|и́ть, ю́, и́шь, *pf. of* **мудри́ть.**

наму́сл|ить, ю, ишь, *pf. of* **му́слить.**

наму́с|олить = **~лить.**

наму́сор|ить, ю, ишь, *pf. of* **му́сорить.**

наму|ти́ть, чу́, ~ти́шь, *pf.* **1.** to stir up mud; to make muddy. **2.** (*intrans.; fig., coll.*) to make a mess; to create chaos.

намуч|иться, усь, ишься, *pf.* (*coll.*) to be worn out; to have had a hard time.
намы́в, а, *m.* (*geol.*) alluvium.
намывно́й, *adj.* (*geol.*) alluvial.
намы́ливать(ся) = мы́лить(ся).
намы́л|ить(ся), ю(сь), ишь(ся), *pf. of* ~ивать(ся) *and* мы́лить(ся).
нам|ы́ть, о́ю, о́ешь, *pf.* (+*a. or g.*) 1. to wash (*a quantity of*). 2. (*of a river*) to deposit.
нам|я́ть¹, ну́, нёшь, *pf.* (*of* ~ина́ть) to hurt (*by pressure or friction*); to crush; н. кому́-н. бока́, шею to give someone a sound thrashing.
нам|я́ть², ну́, нёшь, *pf.* (+*a. or g.*) 1. to mash (*a quantity of*). 2. to trample down (*a certain area of*).
нанесе́ни|е, я, *n.* 1. drawing, plotting (*on a map*). 2. infliction; н. уда́ров assault and battery.
нанес|ти́¹, у́, ёшь, *past* ~, ~ла́, *pf.* (*of* наноси́ть) 1. (на ка́рту) to draw, plot (on a map). 2. to cause; to inflict; н. оскорбле́ние to insult; н. визи́т to pay a visit. 3. (+*a.* на+*a.*) to dash (against); (*impers.*) ло́дку ~ло́ на мель the boat struck a shoal.
нанес|ти́², у́, ёшь, *past* ~, ~ла́, *pf.* (+*a. or g.*) 1. to bring (*a quantity of*). 2. to pile up (*a quantity of*); (*of sand, snow, etc.*) to drift.
нанес|ти́³, ёт, *past* ~ла́, *pf.* н. яи́ц to lay (*a number of*) eggs.
нани|за́ть, жу́, ~жешь, *pf. of* низа́ть *and* ~зывать.
нани́зыва|ть, ю, *impf.* = низа́ть.
нанима́тел|ь, я, *m.* 1. tenant. 2. (*obs.*) employer.
нанима́|ть(ся), ю(сь), *impf. of* наня́ть(ся).
на́нк|а, и, *f.* (*text.*) nankeen.
на́нк|овый, *adj. of* ~а.
на́ново, *adv.* (*coll.*) anew, afresh.
нано́с, а, *m.* (*geol.*) alluvium; drift.
нано|си́ть¹, шу́, ~сишь, *impf. of* нанести́.
нано|си́ть², шу́, ~сишь, *pf.* (+*a. or g.*) to bring (*a quantity of*).
нано́сный, *adj.* 1. (*geol.*) alluvial. 2. (*fig., coll.*) alien; borrowed. 3. (*obs.*) slanderous.
на́нсук, а, *m.* (*text.*) nainsook.
наню́х|аться, аюсь, *pf.* (*of* ~иваться) (+*g.*) 1. to smell to one's heart's content; to take snuff to one's heart's content. 2. to be intoxicated (with).
наню́хива|ться, юсь, *impf. of* наню́хаться.
на́н|ятый, *p.p.p. of* ~я́ть.
на|ня́ть, найму́, наймёшь, *past* ~ня́л, ~няла́, ~няло, *pf.* (*of* ~нима́ть) to rent; to hire; н. на рабо́ту to engage, take on.
на|ня́ться, найму́сь, наймёшься, *past* ~ня́лся, ~няла́сь, *pf.* (*of* ~нима́ться) (*coll.*) to become employed, get a job.
наобеща́|ть, ю, *pf.* (+*a. or g.*) to promise

(much); н. с три ко́роба to promise the world.
наоборо́т, *adv.* 1. back to front; проче́сть сло́во н. to read a word backwards. 2. the other way round; the wrong way (round); он всё понима́ет н. he takes everything the wrong way. 3. on the contrary; как раз н. quite the contrary; и н. and vice versa; я не сержу́сь, а, н., рад был, что вы пришли́ I am not angry; on the contrary, I was glad that you came.
наобу́м, *adv.* without thinking; at random.
наор|а́ть, у́, ёшь, *pf.* (на+*a.*; *coll.*) to shout (at).
на́отмашь, *adv.* 1. with the back of the hand; уда́рить н. to strike a swinging blow. 2. out from the body.
наотре́з, *adv.* flatly, point-blank.
напа́да|ть, ет, *pf.* to fall (*in a certain quantity*); в тече́ние но́чи ~ло мно́го сне́га there was a heavy fall of snow during the night.
напада́|ть, ю, *impf. of* напа́сть.
напада́ющ|ий, его, *m.* (*sport*) forward.
нападе́ни|е, я, *n.* 1. attack, assault. 2. (*sport*) forwards, forward-line.
напа́|дки, ок, кам, *no sing.* attacks.
напа|ду́, дёшь, *see* ~сть.
напа́ива|ть¹, ю, *impf. of* напои́ть.
напа́ива|ть², ю, *impf. of* напая́ть.
напа́ко|стить, щу, стишь, *pf. of* па́костить.
напа́лм, а, *m.* (*chem.*; *mil.*) napalm.
напа́лм|овый, *adj. of* ~.
напа́р|ить, ю, ишь, *pf.* (+*a. or g.*) to steam (*a quantity of*).
напа́рник, а, *m.* fellow worker, mate.
напа́рыва|ть(ся), ю(сь), *impf. of* напоро́ть(ся).
напас|ти́сь, у́сь, ёшься, *past* ~ся, ~ла́сь, *pf.* (*coll.*; *usually* +*neg.*) to lay in, save up enough.
напа́|сть¹, ду́, дёшь, *past* ~л, *pf.* (*of* ~да́ть) (на+*a.*) 1. to attack; to descend (on). 2. to come (over); to grip, seize; на нас всех ~л страх fear seized us all. 3. to come (upon, across); я ~л на мысль the thought occurred to me.
напа́ст|ь², и, *f.* (*coll.*) misfortune, disaster.
напа́чка|ть, ю, *pf. of* па́чкать.
напая́|ть, ю, ешь, *pf.* (*of* напа́ивать²) to solder (onto).
напе́в, а, *m.* tune, melody.
напева́|ть, ю, *impf.* 1. *impf. of* напе́ть. 2. to hum; to croon.
напе́в|ный (~ен, ~на), *adj.* melodious.
напека́|ть, ю, *impf. of* напе́чь¹.
на́перво, *adv.* (*coll.*) at first.
наперебо́й, *adv.* vying with one another.
напереве́с, *adv.* in a horizontal position.
наперего́нки, *adv.* racing one another; бе́гать н. to race (with) one another.

напере́д, *adv.* (*coll.*) **1.** in front. **2.** in advance.

напереко́р, *adv. and prep.* (+*d.*) in defiance (of), counter (to).

наперере́з, *adv.* (*and prep.*+*d.*) so as to cross one's path; бежа́ть кому́-н. н. to run to head someone off.

наперерыв, *adv.* = наперебо́й.

на|пере́ть, пру́, прёшь, *past* ~пёр, ~пёрла, *pf.* (*of* ~пира́ть) (*coll.*; на+*a.*) to press; to put pressure (upon).

напере|хва́т, *adv.* (*dial.*) **1.** = ~ре́з. **2.** = ~бо́й.

наперечёт, *adv.* **1.** through and through; every single one. **2.** (*pred. only*) very few, not many.

напе́рсник, а, *m.* (*obs.*) confidant.

напе́рсниц|а, ы, *f.* (*obs.*) **1.** confidante. **2.** mistress.

напе́рсный, *adj.* (*eccl.*) pectoral.

напёрст|ок, ка, *m.* thimble.

наперстя́нк|а, и, *f.* (*bot.*) foxglove.

напе́рч|ить, у, ишь, *pf. of* пе́рчить.

нап|е́ть, ою́, оёшь, *pf.* (*of* ~ева́ть) **1.** to sing (*air, melody*). **2.** н. пласти́нку to make a recording of one's voice. **3.** (*coll.*; +*d.* or в у́ши +*d.*) to give someone a piece of one's mind.

напеча́та|ть(ся), ю(сь), *pf. of* печа́тать(ся).

напе́|чь[1], чёт, *past* ~кло́, *pf.* (*of* ~ка́ть) (*impers.*; *coll.*) to burn, scorch (*with the sun*); го́лову у меня́ ~кло́ my head got scorched.

напе́|чь[2], ку́, чёшь, ку́т, *past* ~к, ~кла́, *pf.* (+*a. or g.*) to bake (*a number of*); н. расска́зов (*fig., coll.*) to concoct stories.

напива́|ться, юсь, *impf. of* напи́ться.

напи́лива|ть, ю, *impf. of* напили́ть.

напил|и́ть, ю́, ~ишь, *pf.* (*of* ~ива́ть) (+*a. or g.*) to saw (*a quantity of*).

напи́л|ок, ка, *m.* (*coll.*) = ~ьник.

напи́льник, а, *m.* (*tech.*) file.

напира́|ть, ю, *impf.* (*coll.*; на+*a.*) **1.** *impf. of* напере́ть. **2.** to emphasize, stress.

написа́ни|е, я, *n.* **1.** way of writing (*a letter of the alphabet*). **2.** spelling.

напи|са́ть, шу́, ~шешь, *pf. of* писа́ть.

напит|а́ть, а́ю, *pf.* **1.** (*impf.* пита́ть) to sate, satiate. **2.** (*impf.* ~ывать) (+*i.*) to impregnate (with).

напит|а́ться, а́юсь, *pf.* **1.** (*coll.*) to sate oneself; to take one's fill. **2.** (*impf.* ~ываться) (+*i.*) to be impregnated (with).

напи́т|ок, ка, *m.* drink, beverage; прохлади́тельные ~ки soft drinks.

напи́тыва|ть(ся), ю(сь), *impf. of* напита́ть(ся).

нап|и́ться, ью́сь, ьёшься, *past* ~и́лся, ~ила́сь, ~и́ло́сь, *pf.* (*of* ~ива́ться) **1.** (+*g.*) to slake one's thirst (with, on); to have a drink (of). **2.** to get drunk.

напих|а́ть, а́ю, *pf.* (*of* ~ивать) (в+*a.*) to cram (into), stuff (into).

напи́хива|ть, ю, *impf. of* напиха́ть.

напи́чка|ть, ю, *pf. of* пи́чкать.

напи|шу́, ~шешь, *see* ~са́ть.

напла́в|ить, лю, ишь, *pf.* (+*a. or g.*) to melt, smelt (*a quantity of*).

напла́канный, *adj.* tear-stained, red (with crying).

напла́|каться, чусь, чешься, *pf.* **1.** to have one's cry out, have a good cry. **2.** (*coll.*) to have trouble; он ещё ~чется there is trouble in store for him yet.

напла́ст|анный, *p.p.p. of* ~а́ть *and adj.* sliced.

напласта́|ть, ю, *pf.* (*coll.*; +*g.*) to slice, cut in slices.

напластова́ни|е, я, *n.* (*geol.*) bedding, stratification.

напла́|чу, чешь, *see* ~кать.

наплева́тельский, *adj.* (*coll.*) devil-may-care.

напл|ева́ть, юю́, юёшь, *pf.* **1.** (+*g.*) to spit (out). **2.** (*fig., coll.*; на+*a.*) to wash one's hands (of); н.! to hell with it! who cares!; н. на него́! damn him! to hell with him!; мне н.! I don't give a damn!

напле|сти́[1], ту́, тёшь, *past* ~л, ~ла́, *pf.* (+*a. or g.*) to make by weaving (*a number of*); н. вздо́ру (*fig., coll.*) to talk a lot of nonsense.

напле|сти́[2], ту́, тёшь, *past* ~л, ~ла́, *pf.* (на+*a.*; *coll.*) to slander.

наплечник, а, *m.* shoulder strap.

наплечный, *adj.* (worn on the) shoulder.

напло|ди́ть, жу́, ди́шь, *pf.* (*coll.*) to bring forth, produce (*in great numbers*); (*joc.*) to breed.

напло|ди́ться, жу́сь, ди́шься, *pf.* (*coll.*) to multiply.

напло|и́ть, ю́, и́шь, *pf. of* плои́ть.

наплы́в, а, *m.* **1.** influx (*of people, etc.*). **2.** (*med., bot.*) canker; excrescence.

наплыва́|ть, ю, *impf. of* наплы́ть.

наплы́|ть, ву́, вёшь, *past* ~л, ~ла́, ~ло, *pf.* (*of* ~ва́ть) **1.** (на+*a.*) to run (against), dash (against). **2.** (*of incrustation, etc.*) to form.

наповал, *adv.* outright, on the spot.

наподо́бие, *prep.* (+*g.*) like, resembling, in the likeness of.

напо́|енный, *p.p.p. of* ~и́ть 1, 2.

напо|ённый, *p.p.p. of* ~и́ть 3.

напо|и́ть, ю́, и́шь, *pf.* (*of* пои́ть *and* напа́ивать[1]) **1.** to give to drink; to water (*an animal*). **2.** to make drunk. **3.** (*poet.*) to impregnate; to fill.

напока́з, *adv.* for show; вы́ставить н. to show off (*also fig.*).

наполз|а́ть, а́ю, *impf. of* ~ти́.

наполз|ти́[1], у́, ёшь, *past* ~, ~ла́, *pf.* (*of* ~а́ть) (на+*a.*) to crawl (over, against).

наполз|ти́², у́, ёшь, *past* ⌣, ⌣ла́, *pf.* to crawl in (*in great numbers*).

наполне́ни|е, я, *n.* filling; пульс хоро́шего ⌣я (*med.*) normal pulse.

наполни́тел|ь, я, *m.* (*tech.*) filler.

наполн|и́ть, ю, ишь, *pf.* (*of* ⌣я́ть) to fill.

наполн|и́ться, ю́сь, ишься, *pf.* (*of* ⌣я́ться) (+*i.*) to fill (with) (*intrans.*).

наполн|я́ть(ся), я́ю(сь), *impf. of* ⌣и́ть(ся).

наполови́ну, *adv.* half; зал ещё н. пуст the hall is still half empty; де́лать де́ло н. to do a thing by halves.

напома́|дить, жу, дишь, *pf. of* пома́дить.

напомина́ни|е, я, *n.* 1. reminding. 2. reminder.

напомина́|ть, ю, *impf. of* напо́мнить.

напо́мн|ить, ю, ишь, *pf.* (*of* напомина́ть) 1. (+*d. o+p. or* +*d. and a.*) to remind (of); портре́т ⌣ил мне о про́шлом *or* ⌣ил мне про́шлое the portrait reminded me of the past. 2. to remind (of), recall (= *to resemble*); он ⌣ил мне моего́ де́да he reminded me of my grandfather.

напо́р, а, *m.* pressure (*also fig.*); (*of water, steam, etc.*) head; он поддéрживал меня́ с ⌣ом (*coll.*) he supported me vigorously.

напо́ристост|ь, и, *f.* (*coll.*) energy; push, go.

напо́рист|ый (⌣, ⌣а), *adj.* (*coll.*) energetic; pushing.

напо́р|ный, *adj. of* ⌣ (*tech.*); н. бак pressure tank; н. кла́пан pressure valve; н. насо́с force pump; ⌣ная труба́ rising pipe, rising main.

напор|о́ть¹, ю́, ⌣ешь, *pf.* (*of* напа́рывать) (*coll.*) to tear, cut; н. ру́ку на гвоздь to cut one's hand on a nail.

напор|о́ть², ю́, ⌣ешь, *pf.* to rip (*a quantity of*); (*coll.*) н. вздо́ру, чепухи́ to talk a lot of nonsense.

напор|о́ться, ю́сь, ⌣ешься, *pf.* (*of* напа́рываться) (на+*a.*) 1. to cut oneself (on). 2. to run (upon, against); (*fig.*) to run (into, up against).

напор|о́ть¹, чу, тишь, *pf.* (+*a. or g.*) to spoil (*a quantity of*).

напор|о́ть², чу, тишь, *pf.* (+*d.*) to injure, harm.

напосле́док, *adv.* (*coll.*) in the end, finally, after all.

нап|ою́¹, оёшь, *see* ⌣е́ть.

нап|о́ю², и́шь, *see* ⌣и́ть.

напра́в|ить, лю, ишь, *pf.* (*of* ⌣ля́ть) 1. (на+*a.*) to direct (to, at); н. внима́ние to direct one's attention (to); н. свой путь to bend one's steps (towards); н. уда́р to aim a blow (at). 2. to send; н. заявле́ние to send in an application. 3. to sharpen; н. бри́тву to set a razor. 4. (*coll.*) н. рабо́ту to organize work.

напра́в|иться, люсь, ишься, *pf.* (*of* ⌣ля́ть-

ся) 1. (к, в+*a.*, на+*a.*) to make (for). 2. (*coll.*) to get going, get under way (*fig.*). 3. *pass. of* ⌣ить.

напра́вк|а, и, *f.* setting (*of razor, etc.*).

направле́ни|е, я, *n.* 1. (*in var. senses*) direction; по ⌣ю (к) in the direction (of), towards; взять н. на се́вер to make for, head for the north. 2. (*mil.*) sector. 3. (*fig.*) trend, tendency; н. ума́ turn of mind; либера́льное н. liberal tendency. 4. (*official*) order, warrant; directive; н. в санато́рий warrant for stay at, certificate approving treatment at a sanatorium. 5. (*official*) action; effect; дать н. де́лу to take action on a matter.

напра́вленност|ь, и, *f.* 1. direction, tendency, trend. 2. purposefulness.

напра́в|ленный, *p.p.p. of* ⌣ить *and adj.* 1. (*radio*) directional. 2. purposeful; unswerving.

направля́|ть, ю, *impf. of* напра́вить.

направля́|ться, юсь, *impf. of* напра́виться; ⌣емся в Му́рманск we are bound for Murmansk.

направля́ющ|ая, ей, *f.* (*tech.*) guide.

направля́|ющий, *pres. part. act. of* ⌣ть *and adj.* (*tech.*) guiding, guide; leading; н. ва́лик, н. ро́лик guide roller; ⌣ющая лине́йка, н. шабло́н former bar; н. сте́ржень, н. штифт guide pin, guide bolt.

напра́во, *adv.* to the right; on the right.

направти́к|ова́ться, у́юсь, *pf.* (в+*p.*; *coll.*) to acquire skill (in).

напра́слин|а, ы, *f.* (*coll.*) wrongful accusation, slander.

напра́сно, *adv.* 1. vainly, in vain; to no purpose. 2. wrong, unjustly, mistakenly; н. вы пришли́ без де́нег it was a mistake for you to come without money.

напра́с|ный (⌣ен, ⌣на), *adj.* 1. vain, idle; ⌣ная наде́жда vain hope. 2. unfounded, wrongful.

напра́шива|ться, юсь, *impf. of* напроси́ться; (*impf. only*) to arise, suggest itself; ⌣ется вопро́с the question inevitably arises.

наприме́р for example, for instance.

напрока́|зить, жу, зишь, *pf. of* прока́зить.

напрока́знича|ть, ю, *pf. of* прока́зничать.

напрока́т, *adv.* for hire, on hire; взять н. to hire; дать, отда́ть н. to hire out, let.

напролёт, *adv.* (*coll.*) through, without a break; рабо́тать всю ночь н. to work the whole night through.

напроло́м, *adv.* straight, regardless of obstacles (*also fig.*).

напропалу́ю, *adv.* (*coll.*) regardless of the consequences; all out.

напроро́ч|ить, у, ишь, *pf. of* проро́чить.

напро|си́ться, шу́сь, ⌣сишься, *pf.* (*of* напра́шиваться) (*coll.*) to thrust oneself upon;

н. на комплиме́нты to fish for compliments.

напро́тив, *adv. and prep.*+*g.* **1.** opposite; он живёт н. (на́шего до́ма) he lives opposite (our house). **2.** (+*d.*) in defiance (of); to contradict; она́ всё де́лает мне н. she does everything to spite me. **3.** on the contrary.

на́прочь, *adv.* (*coll.*) completely.

нап|ру́, рёшь, *see* ~ере́ть.

напру́жива|ть(ся), ю(сь), *impf. of* напру́житься.

напру́ж|ить, у, ишь, *pf.* (*of* ~ивать) (*coll.*) to strain; to tense, tauten.

напру́ж|иться, усь, ишься, *pf.* (*of* ~иваться) (*coll.*) to become tense, become taut.

напряга́|ть(ся), ю(сь), *impf. of* напря́чь(ся).

напря|гу́, жёшь, *see* ~чь.

напряже́ни|е, я, *n.* **1.** tension; effort, exertion. **2.** (*phys., tech.*) strain; stress; (*electr.*) tension; voltage; н. на зажи́мах terminal voltage, electrode potential; н. смеще́ния grid bias.

напряжённост|ь, и, *f.* tenseness; intensity; tension.

напряжён|ный (~, ~на), *adj.* tense, strained; intense; intensive; ~ные отноше́ния strained relations; ~ная рабо́та intensive work.

напрями́к, *adv.* (*coll.*) **1.** straight. **2.** (*fig.*) straight out, bluntly.

напря́|чь, гу́, жёшь, гу́т, *past* ~г, ~гла́, *pf.* (*of* ~га́ть) to tense, strain (*also fig.*); н. все си́лы to strain every nerve.

напря́|чься, гу́сь, жёшься, гу́тся, *past* ~гся, ~гла́сь, *pf.* **1.** to become tense. **2.** to exert oneself, strain oneself.

напу́др|ить(ся), ю(сь), ишь(ся), *pf. of* пу́дрить(ся).

напу́льсник, а, *m.* wrist-band.

на́пуск, а, *m.* **1.** letting in. **2.** (*hunting*) letting loose, slipping (*from leash*). **3.** (*in dress, blouse, etc.*) full front. **4.** (*tech.*) lap joint.

напуска́|ть(ся), ю(сь), *impf. of* напусти́ть(ся).

напускно́й, *adj.* assumed, put on.

напу́|сти́ть, щу́, ~стишь, *pf.* (*of* ~ска́ть) **1.** (+*g.*) to let in; н. воды́ в ва́нну to fill a bath. **2.** to let loose, slip, set on (*hounds, etc.*). **3.** (на себя́+*a.*) to affect, put on; н. на себя́ ва́жность to assume an air of importance. **4.** н. стра́ху на кого́-н. (*coll.*) to strike fear into someone.

напу́|сти́ться, щу́сь, ~стишься, *pf.* (*of* ~ска́ться) (*coll.*; на+*a.*) to fly at, go for.

напу́та|ть, ю, *pf.* (*coll.*; в+*p.*) to make a mess (of), make a hash (of); to confuse, get wrong; вы ~ли в а́дресе you got the address wrong.

напу́тственн|ый, *adj.* parting, farewell;

~ое сло́во parting words.

напу́тстви|е, я, *n.* parting words, farewell speech.

напу́тств|овать, ую, *impf. and pf.* to address, counsel (at parting); н. до́брыми пожела́ниями to bid farewell, wish bon voyage.

напух|а́ть, а́ет, *impf. of* ~нуть.

напух|нуть, нет, *past* ~, ~ла, *pf.* (*of* ~а́ть) to swell.

напу́|щу́, ~стишь, *see* ~сти́ть.

напы́ж|иться, усь, ишься, *pf. of* пы́житься.

напыл|и́ть, ю́, и́шь, *pf. of* пыли́ть.

напы́щенност|ь, и, *f.* **1.** pomposity. **2.** bombast.

напы́щен|ный (~, ~на), *adj.* **1.** pompous. **2.** bombastic, high-flown.

напя́лива|ть, ю, *impf. of* напя́лить.

напя́л|ить, ю, ишь, *pf.* (*of* ~ивать) **1.** to stretch on. **2.** (*coll.*) to pull on, struggle into (*a tight garment*).

нар- (*abbr. of* наро́дный) people's; national; нарсу́д 'People's Court' (*in U.S.S.R.*).

нараба́тыва|ть, ю, *impf. of* нарабо́тать².

нарабо́та|ть¹, ю, *pf.* (+*a. or g.*) to make, turn out (*a quantity of*).

нарабо́та|ть², ю, *pf.* (*of* нараба́тывать) to make, earn.

нарабо́та|ться, юсь, *pf.* (*coll.*) to have worked enough; to have tired oneself with work.

наравне́, *adv.* (с+*i.*) **1.** on a level (with); ма́льчик шёл н. с солда́тами the small boy kept pace with the soldiers. **2.** equally (with); on an equal footing (with).

нара́д|оваться, уюсь, *pf.* (+*d. or* на+*a.*; *usually*+*neg.*) to rejoice, delight sufficiently (in); она́ на сы́на не ~уется she dotes on her son.

нараспа́шку, *adv.* (*coll.*) unbuttoned; у него́ душа́ н. (*fig.*) he wears his heart upon his sleeve.

нараспе́в, *adv.* in a sing-song voice; drawlingly.

нараста́ни|е, я, *n.* growth, accumulation.

нараст|а́ть, а́ю, *impf. of* ~и́.

нарас|ти́, ту́, тёшь, *past* наро́с, наросла́, *pf.* (*of* ~та́ть) **1.** (на+*p.*) to grow (on), form (on); мох наро́с на камня́х moss has grown on the stones. **2.** to increase; (*of sound*) to swell. **3.** to accumulate.

нара|сти́ть, щу́, сти́шь, *pf.* (*of* ~щивать) **1.** to graft (on). **2.** to lengthen; (*fig.*) to increase, augment.

нарасхва́т, *adv.* продава́ться н. to sell like hot cakes; э́ту кни́гу покупа́ют н. there is a great demand for this book.

нара́щива|ть, ю, *impf. of* нарасти́ть.

нарва́л, а, *m.* (*zool.*) narwhal.

нарв|а́ть¹, у́, ёшь, *past* ~а́л, ~ала́, ~а́ло

pf. (+*a. or g.*) **1.** to pick (*a quantity of*). **2.** to tear (*a quantity of*).

нарв|а́ть², ёт, *past* ~а́л, ~ала́, ~а́ло, *pf.* (*of* нарыва́ть) to gather, come to a head (*of a boil or abscess*); у меня́ па́лец ~а́л *or* (*impers.*) па́лец ~а́ло I have a gathering on my finger.

нарв|а́ться, у́сь, ёшься, *past* ~а́лся, ~ала́сь, ~а́лось, *pf.* (*of* нарыва́ться) (*coll.*; на+*a.*) to run into, run up (against).

нард, а, *m.* spikenard, nard.

наре́|жу, жешь, *see* ~за́ть.

наре́з, а, *m.* **1.** (*tech.*) thread; groove (*in rifling*). **2.** (*hist., econ.*) lot, plot (*of land*).

наре́|зать¹, жу, жешь, *pf.* (*of* ~за́ть) **1.** to cut into pieces; to slice; to carve. **2.** (*tech.*) to thread; to rifle. **3.** (*hist., econ.*) to allot, parcel out (*land*).

наре́|зать², жу, жешь, *pf.* (+*a. or g.*) to cut, slice (*a quantity of*).

нарез|а́ть, а́ю, *impf. of* ~а́ть¹.

наре́|заться, жусь, жешься, *pf.* (*of* ~за́ться) **1.** (*coll.*) to get drunk. **2.** *pass. of* ~зать¹.

нарез|а́ться, а́юсь, *impf. of* ~а́ться.

наре́зк|а, и, *f.* **1.** cutting (into pieces), slicing. **2.** (*tech.*) thread; rifling.

нарезно́й, *adj.* (*tech.*) threaded; rifled.

нарека́ни|е, я, *n.* censure; reprimand.

нарека́|ть, ю, *impf. of* наре́чь.

**нареч|ённый, *p.p.p. of* ~ь and *adj.* (*obs.*) betrothed; *as noun* н., ~ённого, *m.* fiancé; ~ённая, ~ённой, *f.* fiancée.

наречи|е¹, я, *n.* dialect.

наречи|е², я, *n.* adverb.

наре́чный, *adj.* adverbial.

наре́|чь, ку́, чёшь, ку́т, *past* ~к, ~кла́, *pf.* (*of* ~ка́ть) (*obs.*) (+*a. and i. or d. and a.*) to name; ма́льчика ~кли́ Серге́ем, ма́льчику ~кли́ и́мя Серге́й they named the boy Sergei.

нарза́н, а, *m.* Narzan (*kind of mineral water*).

нарза́н|ный, *adj. of* ~.

нарис|ова́ть, у́ю, *pf. of* рисова́ть.

нарица́тельн|ый, *adj.* **1.** (*econ.*) nominal; ~ая сто́имость nominal cost. **2.** (*gram.*) и́мя ~ое common noun.

нарко́з, а, *m.* **1.** narcosis, anaesthesia. **2.** anaesthetic, drug; ме́стный н. local anaesthetic.

нарко́м, а, *m.* (*abbr. of* наро́дный комисса́р) (*hist.*) people's commissar.

наркома́н, а, *m.* drug addict.

наркома́ни|я, и, *f.* drug addiction.

наркома́т, а, *m.* (*abbr. of* наро́дный комиссариа́т) (*hist.*) people's commissariat.

наркотизи́р|овать, ую, *impf. and pf.* (*med.*) to narcotize, anaesthetize.

нарко́тик, а, *m.* narcotic.

наркоти́ческ|ий, *adj.* narcotic; ~ие сре́дства narcotics, drugs.

наро́д, а (у), *m.* (*in var. senses*) people; англи́йский н. the English people, the people of England; челове́к из ~а a man of the people; ма́ло бы́ло ~у на ми́тинге there were not many people at the meeting; вы — упря́мый н. (*coll.*) you are a stubborn lot.

наро́д|ец, ца, *m. dim.* (*affect. or pejor.*) *of* ~.

наро|ди́ть, жу́, ди́шь, *pf.* (+*a. or g.*) to give birth to (*a number of*).

наро|ди́ться, жу́сь, ди́шься, *pf.* (*of* ~жда́ться) **1.** (*coll.*) to be born. **2.** (*fig.*) to come into being, arise.

наро́дник, а, *m.* (*hist.*) narodnik, populist.

наро́дничес|кий, *adj. of* ~тво.

наро́дничеств|о, а, *n.* (*hist.*) narodnik movement, populism.

наро́дност|ь, и, *f.* **1.** nationality. **2.** (*sing. only*) national character; national traits.

народнохозя́йственный, *adj.* pertaining to the national economy.

наро́дн|ый, *adj.* **1.** national; ~ое хозя́йство national economy; н. поэ́т national poet; н. арти́ст СССР (*designation of recipient of official honour*) national artist of the U.S.S.R. **2.** folk; ~ое иску́сство folk art. **3.** (*polit.*) of the (*sc. common, working*) people, popular; ~ая во́ля (*hist.*) Narodnaya volya ('The People's Will'); Н. фронт Popular Front. **4.** *forms part of the official designation of certain Communist states, also of certain organs of power and offices in the U.S.S.R.*; страны́ ~ой демокра́тии 'the People's Democracies'; Венге́рская ~ая Респу́блика the Hungarian People's Republic; н. заседа́тель assessor (*in courts*); н. сле́дователь examining magistrate; н. суд 'People's Court' (*court of first instance*); н. судья́ judge in 'People's Court' (*elected presiding magistrate*).

народовла́сти|е, я, *n.* democracy, sovereignty of the people.

народово́л|ец, ьца, *m.* (*hist.*) member of 'Narodnaya volya'.

народово́л|ьческий, *adj. of* ~ец.

народонаселе́ни|е, я, *n.* population.

нарожда́|ться, юсь, *impf. of* народи́ться.

нарожде́ни|е, я, *n.* birth, springing up; н. ме́сяца appearance of new moon.

наро́ст, а, *m.* **1.** outgrowth, excrescence; burr, tumour (*in animals and plants*). **2.** (*tech.*) incrustation, scale.

нарочи́то, *adv.* deliberately, intentionally.

нарочи́т|ый (~, ~а), *adj.* deliberate, intentional.

наро́чно, *adv.* **1.** on purpose, purposely. **2.** for fun, pretending.

**на́рочн|ый (*obs.* наро́чный), ого, *m.* courier; express messenger, special messenger.

наро́ч|ный, *adj.* = ~и́тый.

на́рт|енный, *adj. of* ~ы.

на́рт|ы, ~, *sing.* ~а, ~ы, *f.* sledge (*drawn by reindeer or dogs*).

наруб|и́ть, лю́, ⌐ишь, *pf.* (+*a. or g.*) to chop (*a quantity of*); to cut (*a quantity of*).

нару́бк|а, и, *f.* notch.

нару́жно, *adv.* outwardly.

нару́жност|ь, и, *f.* exterior; (outward) appearance; н. обма́нчива appearances are deceptive.

нару́жн|ый, *adj.* (*in var. senses*) external, exterior, outward; (*tech.*) male (*of screw thread*); ~ое (лека́рство) medicine for outward application, 'not to be taken'; ~ое споко́йствие outward calm.

нару́жу, *adv.* outside, on the outside; вы́йти н. to come out; (*fig.*) to come to light, transpire.

нарука́вник, а, *m.* oversleeve; armlet.

нарука́вн|ый, *adj.* (worn on the) sleeve; ~ая повя́зка arm-band, brassard.

нарумя́н|ить(ся), ю(сь), ишь(ся), *pf. of* румя́нить(ся).

нару́чник, а, *m.* handcuff, manacle.

нару́чн|ый, *adj.* worn on the arm; ~ые часы́ wrist-watch.

наруш|а́ть, а́ю, *impf. of* ⌐ить.

наруше́ни|е, я, *n.* breach; infringement, violation; offence (*against the law*).

наруши́тел|ь, я, *m.* transgressor, infringer.

наруш|и́ть, у, ишь, *pf.* (*of* ⌐а́ть) **1.** to break, disturb (*sleep, quiet, etc.*). **2.** to break, infringe (upon), violate, transgress.

нарци́сс, а, *m.* narcissus, daffodil.

на́р|ы, ~, *no sing.* plank-bed; bunk.

нары́в, а, *m.* abscess; boil.

нарыва́|ть(ся), ю(сь), *impf. of* нарва́ть[2](ся).

нарывно́й, *adj.* vesicatory; н. пла́стырь poultice.

нар|ы́ть, о́ю, о́ешь, *pf.* (+*a. or g.*) to dig (*a quantity of*).

наря́д[1], а, *m.* attire, apparel, costume.

наря́д[2], а, *m.* **1.** order, warrant. **2.** (*mil.*) detail (*group of soldiers*). **3.** (*mil.*) duty; расписа́ние ~ов roster; duty detail, orders.

наря|ди́ть[1], жу́, ⌐ди́шь, *pf.* (*of* ~жа́ть) **1.** (в+*a.*) to dress (in), array (in). **2.** (+*i.*) to dress up (as).

наря|ди́ть[2], жу́, ⌐ди́шь, *pf.* (*of* ~жа́ть) to detail, appoint; н. в карау́л to put on guard; н. сле́дствие to set up, order an inquiry.

наря|ди́ться[1], жу́сь, ⌐ди́шься, *pf.* (*of* ~жа́ться) **1.** (в+*a.*) to array oneself (in). **2.** to dress up. **3.** *pass. of* ~ди́ть[1].

наря|ди́ться[2], жу́сь, ⌐ди́шься, *pf.* (*of* ~жа́ться) *pass. of* ~ди́ть[2].

наря́дност|ь, и, *f.* elegance, smartness.

наря́д|ный[1] (~ен, ~на), *adj.* well-dressed; elegant; smart (*also of items of dress*).

наря́д|ный[2], *adj. of* ~[2]; *as noun* ~ная, ~ной, *f.* (*coll.*) office (*where work is assigned*).

наряду́, *adv.* (с+*i.*) side by side (with), equally (with); де́ти н. со взро́слыми grown-ups and children alike; н. с э́тим at the same time.

наряжа́|ть(ся), ю(сь), *impf. of* наряди́ть(ся).

нас, *a., g., and p. of* мы.

наса|ди́ть[1], жу́, ⌐ди́шь, *pf.* (*of* ⌐жива́ть) (+*a. or g.*) **1.** to plant (*a quantity of*). **2.** to sit (*a number of*).

наса|ди́ть[2], жу́, ⌐ди́шь, *pf.* (*of* ⌐жива́ть) to stick, pin; to haft; н. на ве́ртел to spit; н. червяка́ на крючо́к to fix a worm on to a hook.

наса|ди́ть[3], жу́, ⌐ди́шь, *pf.* (*of* ~жда́ть) (*fig.*) to implant, inculcate; to propagate.

наса́дк|а, и, *f.* **1.** setting, fixing, putting on. **2.** (*tech.*) nozzle, mouthpiece. **3.** bait.

насажа́|ть, ю, *pf.* = насади́ть[1].

насажда́|ть, ю, *impf. of* насади́ть[3].

насажде́ни|е, я, *n.* **1.** planting, plantation; (*fig.*) spreading, propagation, dissemination. **2.** (*forest*) stand; wood.

наса|жде́нный, *p.p.p. of* ~ди́ть[3].

наса́|женный, *p.p.p. of* ~ди́ть[1, 2].

наса́жива|ть, ю, *impf. of* насади́ть[1, 2].

наса́жива|ться, юсь, *impf. of* насе́сть[1].

наса́лива|ть, ю, *impf. of* насоли́ть.

наса́харива|ть, ю, *impf. of* наса́харить.

наса́хар|ить, ю, ишь, *pf.* (*of* ~ивать) to sugar, sweeten (*with sugar*).

насви́стыва|ть, ю, *impf.* (*coll.*) to whistle (*a tune*); (*of birds*) to pipe, twitter.

наседа́|ть, ю, *impf.* (*of* насе́сть[2]) (на+*a.*) **1.** to press (*of mil. forces, crowds, etc.*). **2.** (*of dust, etc.*) to settle, collect.

насе́дк|а, и, *f.* brood-hen, sitting hen.

насека́|ть, ю, *impf. of* насе́чь.

насеко́м|ое, ого, *n.* insect.

насекомоя́дный, *adj.* insectivorous.

населе́ни|е, я, n.* **1. population; inhabitants. **2.** peopling, settling.

населённост|ь, и, *f.* density of population.

насел|ённый, *p.p.p. of* ~и́ть *and adj.* **1.** populated; н. пункт (*official designation*) locality, place; built-up area. **2.** populous, densely populated.

насел|и́ть, ю́, и́шь, *pf.* (*of* ~я́ть) to people, settle.

насе́льник, а, *m.* inhabitant.

насел|я́ть, я́ю, *impf.* **1.** to inhabit. **2.** *impf. of* ~и́ть.

насе́ст, а, *m.* roost, perch.

нас|е́сть[1], я́дет, *past* ~е́л, *pf.* (*of* ~а́живать-ся) to sit down (*in numbers*).

нас|е́сть[2], я́ду, я́дешь, *past* ~е́л, *pf. of* ~еда́ть.

насе́чк|а, и, *f.* **1.** notching; making incisions; embossing; (*med.*) scarification. **2.** cut, incision; notch. **3.** inlay.

насе́|чь, ку́, че́шь, ку́т, *past* ~к, ~кла́, *pf.* (*of* ~ка́ть) 1. to make incisions (in, on); to notch. 2. to emboss; to damascene.

насе́|ять, ю, ешь, *pf.* (+*a. or g.*) to sow (*a quantity of*).

наси|де́ть, жу́, ди́шь, *pf.* (*of* ~жива́ть) 1. to hatch. 2. to warm (*by sitting*).

наси|де́ться, жу́сь, ди́шься, *pf.* (*coll.*) to sit long enough.

наси́|женный, p.p.p. *of* ~де́ть; ~женное яйцо́ fertilized egg; ~женное ме́сто (*fig.*) familiar spot, old haunt.

наси́жива|ть, ю, *impf. of* насиде́ть.

наси|жу́, ди́шь, *see* ~де́ть.

наси́ли|е, я, n. violence, force.

наси́л|овать, ую, *impf.* 1. to coerce, constrain. 2. (*pf.* из~) to rape, violate.

наси́лу, adv. (*coll.*) with difficulty, hardly.

наси́льник, а, m. 1. user of force; aggressor. 2. violator.

наси́льнича|ть, ю, *impf.* (*coll.*) 1. to commit acts of violence. 2. to rape.

наси́льнический, adj. forcible, violent.

наси́льно, adv. by force, forcibly; н. мил не бу́дешь (*prov.*) love cannot be compelled.

наси́льственный, adj. violent; forcible.

наска|за́ть, жу́, ~жешь, pf. (*coll.*; +*a. or g.*) to say, talk a lot (of); н. новосте́й to have a lot of news to tell.

наска|ка́ть, чу́, ~чешь, pf. (*of* ~кивать) 1. (на+*a.*) to ride (into); to run (against), collide (with). 2. to ride up, gallop up.

наска́кива|ть, ю, *impf. of* наскака́ть *and* наскочи́ть.

наскандал|ить, ю, ишь, pf. *of* скандалить.

насквозь, adv. through (and through); throughout; промо́кнуть н. to get wet through; ви́деть (знать) кого́-н. н. (*fig.*) to see through someone.

наско́к, а, m. 1. swoop; sudden attack, descent; де́йствовать ~ом to act on impulse; с ~а (*fig.*, *coll.*) hurriedly, just like that. 2. (*fig.*, *coll.*) attack.

наско́лько, adv. 1. (*interrog.*) how much?; how far? 2. (*relat.*) as far as, so far as; н. мне изве́стно as far as I know, to the best of my knowledge.

на́скоро, adv. (*coll.*) hastily, hurriedly.

наскоч|и́ть, у́, ~ишь, pf. (*of* наска́кивать) 1. to run (against), collide (with); н. на неприя́тность (*fig.*) to get into trouble. 2. (*fig.*, *coll.*) to fly (at).

наскреба́|ть, ю, *impf. of* наскрести́.

наскре|сти́, бу́, бёшь, *past* ~б, ~бла́, *pf.* (*of* ~ба́ть) to scrape up, scrape together; (*fig.*) н. де́нег на пое́здку to scrape up some money for an outing.

наску́ч|ить, у, ишь, pf. (*coll.*) 1. (+*d.*) to bore; мне э́то ~ило I am sick of it. 2. (*obs.*; +*i.*) to be bored (by), grow tired (of).

насла|ди́ть, жу́, ди́шь, pf. (*of* ~жда́ть) to delight, please.

насла|ди́ться, жу́сь, ди́шься, pf. (*of* ~жда́ться) (+*i.*) to enjoy; to take pleasure (in), delight (in).

наслажда́|ть(ся), ю(сь), *impf. of* наслади́ть(ся).

наслажде́ни|е, я, n. enjoyment, delight.

насла́ива|ться, юсь, *impf. of* наслои́ться.

насла|сти́ть, щу́, сти́шь, pf. (*coll.*) to make very (too) sweet.

на|сла́ть¹, шлю́, шлёшь, pf. (*of* ~ сыла́ть) (*obs.*) to send down (*calamities, etc.*).

на|сла́ть², шлю́, шлёшь, pf. (+*a. or g.*) to send (*a quantity of*).

насле́ди|е, я, n. legacy; heritage.

насле|ди́ть, жу́, ди́шь, pf. (*of* следи́ть²) to leave (dirty) marks, traces.

насле́дник, а, m. heir; legatee; (*fig.*) successor.

насле́дниц|а, ы, f. heiress.

насле́дный, adj. first in the line of succession; н. принц Crown prince.

насле́довани|е, я, n. inheritance.

насле́д|овать, ую, *impf. and pf.* 1. (*pf. also* у~) to inherit. 2. (+*d.*) to succeed (to).

насле́дственност|ь, и, f. heredity.

насле́дственный, adj. hereditary, inherited.

насле́дств|о, а, n. 1. inheritance, legacy; получи́ть в н., по ~у to inherit. 2. (*fig.*) heritage.

наслое́ни|е, я, n. 1. (*geol.*) stratification. 2. layer, deposit. 3. (*fig.*) later development, extraneous feature (*of culture or individual personality*).

насло|и́ться, ю́сь, и́шься, pf. (*of* насла́иваться) (на+*a.*) to be deposited (on), accumulate (on).

наслуж|и́ться, у́сь, ~ишься, pf. (*coll.*) to have served for long enough.

наслу́ша|ться, юсь, pf. (+*g.*) 1. to hear (a lot of). 2. to hear enough, listen to long enough; я не ~юсь э́тих пе́сен I cannot hear enough of these songs.

наслы́шан, *adj.* used as pred. (*obs.*; о+*p.*) familiar (with) by hearsay; мы о вас мно́го ~ы we have heard a lot about you.

наслы́ш|аться, усь, ишься, pf. (о+*p.*) to have heard a lot (about).

наслы́шк|а, и, f. по ~е (*coll.*) by hearsay.

насма́рку, adv. (*coll.*) пойти́ н. to come to nothing.

на́смерть, adv. to death; стоя́ть н. to fight to the last ditch; испуга́ть н. to frighten to death.

насмеха́тельств|о, а, n. (*obs.*) mockery.

насмеха́|ться, юсь, *impf.* (над) to jeer (at), gibe (at), ridicule.

насмеш|и́ть, у́, и́шь, pf. (*of* смеши́ть) (кого́-н.) to make (someone) laugh.

насмешк|а, и, *f.* mockery, ridicule; gibe.

насмешлив|ый (~, ~а), *adj.* **1.** mocking, derisive. **2.** sarcastic.

насмешник, а, *m.* (*coll.*) scoffer.

насме|яться, юсь, ёшься, *pf.* **1.** (*coll.*) to have a good laugh. **2.** (над) to laugh (at); н. над чьйми-н. чувствами to insult someone's feelings.

насморк, а, *m.* cold (in the head); схватить, получить н. to catch a cold; у меня сделался насморк I have caught a cold.

насмотр|еться, юсь, ~ишься, *pf.* **1.** (+*g.*) to see a lot (of). **2.** (на+*a.*) to have looked enough (at), to see enough (of); не н. not to tire of looking (at).

насобач|иться, усь, ишься, *pf.* (*coll.*; +*inf.*) to become adept (at), become a good hand (at).

нас|овать, ую, уёшь, *pf.* (*of* ~о́вывать) (*coll.*; +*g. or a.*) to shove in, stuff in (*a quantity of*); н. конфет в карманы to stuff sweets into one's pockets.

насовыва|ть, ю, *impf. of* насовать.

насол|и́ть[1], ю, ~йшь, *pf.* (*of* насаливать) **1.** to salt; to put much salt (into). **2.** (*fig.*; +*d.*) to spite, injure; to do a bad turn (to).

насол|и́ть[2], ю, ~йшь, *pf.* (+*a. or g.*) to salt, pickle (*a quantity of*).

насоло|ди́ть, жу́, ди́шь, *pf. of* солоди́ть.

насор|и́ть, ю, йшь, *pf. of* сори́ть.

насос[1], а, *m.* pump.

насос[2], а, *m.* (*disease of horses*) lampas.

насос|а́ть, у́, ёшь, *pf.* (+*a. or g.*) **1.** to suck (*a quantity of*). **2.** to pump.

насос|а́ться, у́сь, ёшься, *pf.* **1.** (+*g.*) to have sucked one's fill. **2.** (*coll.*) to get drunk.

насос|ный, *adj. of* ~[1]; н. агрегат pumping unit; ~ная станция pumping station.

насочин|и́ть, ю, йшь, *pf.* (*coll.*) (+*a. or g.*) to talk a lot of nonsense; to make up (a lot of falsehoods).

наспех, *adv.* hastily; carelessly.

насплётнича|ть, ю, *pf. of* сплётничать.

наст, а, *m.* thin crust of ice over snow.

наста|ва́ть, ю, ёшь, *impf. of* ~ть.

настави́тел|ьный (~ен, ~на), *adj.* edifying, instructive; н. тон didactic tone.

настав|ить[1], лю, ишь, *pf.* (*of* ~ля́ть) **1.** to lengthen; to put on, add on; н. нос кому-н. to fool, dupe someone; н. рога кому-н. to cuckold someone. **2.** (на+*a.*) to aim (at), point (at); н. револьвер на кого-н. to point a revolver at someone.

настав|ить[2], лю, ишь, *pf.* (*of* ~ля́ть) to edify; to exhort, admonish; н. на путь истинный to set on the right path.

настав|ить[3], лю, ишь, *pf.* (+*a. or g.*) to set up, place (*a quantity of*).

наставк|а, и, *f.* addition.

наставлёни|е, я, *n.* **1.** exhortation, admoni-

tion. **2.** directions, instructions; (*mil.*) manual.

наставля́|ть, ю, *impf. of* наста́вить.

наста́вник, а, *m.* **1.** (*obs.*) mentor, preceptor; классный н. form-master. **2.** instructor (*of apprentices*).

наста́вни|ческий, *adj. of* ~к; н. тон edifying tone.

наста́вничеств|о, а, *n.* (*obs.*) tutorship.

наставно́й, *adj.* lengthened; added.

наста́ива|ть[1, 2], ю, *impf. of* настоя́ть[1, 2]

наста́ива|ться, юсь, *impf. of* настоя́ться[2].

наста́|ть, ну, нешь, *pf.* (*of* ~ва́ть) (*of times or seasons*) to come, begin.

наста|ю́, ёшь, *see* ~ва́ть.

на́стежь, *adv.* wide open; открыть н. to open wide.

настели́ть = настла́ть.

наст|елю́, е́лешь, *see* ~ла́ть.

настённый, *adj.* wall.

настиг|а́ть, а́ю, *impf. of* ~нуть *and* насти́чь.

настигн|уть, у, ешь, *pf.* = насти́чь.

насти́л, а, *m.* flooring; planking.

настила́|ть, ю, *impf. of* настла́ть.

насти́лк|а, и, *f.* **1.** laying, spreading. **2.** = насти́л.

насти́льн|ый, *adj.* (*mil.*) grazing; н. огонь grazing fire; ~ая бомба anti-personnel bomb.

настира́|ть, ю, *pf.* (+*a. or g.*) to wash, launder (*a quantity of*).

насти́|чь, гну, гнешь, *past* ~г, ~гла, *pf.* (*of* ~га́ть) to overtake (*also fig.*).

наст|ла́ть, елю́, ~е́лешь, *pf.* (*of* ~ила́ть) to lay, spread; н. пол to lay a floor; н. солому to spread straw.

насто́|й, я, *m.* infusion.

насто́йк|а, и, *f.* **1.** liqueur (*prepared by maceration, not distilled*). **2.** (*pharm.*) tincture.

насто́йчив|ый (~, ~а), *adj.* **1.** persistent. **2.** urgent, insistent.

насто́лько, *adv.* so; so much; н., наско́лько as much as.

насто́льн|ый, *adj.* **1.** table, desk; н. те́ннис table tennis. **2.** (*fig.*) for constant reference, in constant use; ~ая кни́га, ~ое руково́дство reference book; handbook, manual.

настора́жива|ть(ся), ю(сь), *impf. of* насторожи́ть(ся).

насторо|же́, *adv.* быть н. to be on one's guard; to be on the qui vive.

насторо|же́нный (and ~же́нный), *p.p.p. of* ~жи́ть *and adj.* guarded, suspicious.

насторож|и́ть, у́, и́шь, *pf.* (*of* настора́живать) to put on one's guard; н. слух, у́ши (н. внима́ние *fig. only*) to prick up one's ears (*also fig.*).

насторож|и́ться, у́сь, и́шься, *pf.* (*of* настора́живаться) to prick up one's ears.

настоя́ни|е, я, *n.* insistence.

настоя́тел|ь, я, *m.* (*eccl.*) 1. prior, superior. 2. senior priest (*of a church*).

настоя́тельниц|а, ы, *f.* (*eccl.*) prioress, mother superior.

настоя́тел|ьный (~ен, ~ьна), *adj.* 1. persistent; insistent. 2. urgent, pressing.

насто|я́ть¹, ю́, и́шь, *pf.* (*of* наста́ивать) (на + *p.*) to insist (on); н. на своём to insist on having it one's own way; он ~я́л на том, чтобы пойти́ самому́ he insisted on going himself.

насто|я́ть², ю́, и́шь, *pf.* (*of* наста́ивать) to draw, infuse; н. чай to let tea draw; н. во́дку на ви́шнях to prepare a liqueur from cherries.

насто|я́ться¹, ю́сь, и́шься, *pf.* (*coll.*) to stand a long time.

насто|я́ться², ю́сь, и́шься, *pf.* (*of* наста́иваться) 1. to draw, brew (*of tea, etc.*). 2. *pass. of* ~я́ть².

настоя́щ|ий, *adj.* 1. present; this; в ~ее вре́мя at present, now; ~ее вре́мя (*gram.*) the present tense; *as noun* ~ее, ~его, *n.* the present (time). 2. real, genuine; ~ая цена́ fair price. 3. (*coll., pejor.*) complete, utter, absolute; он н. дура́к he is an absolute fool.

настрада́|ться, ю́сь, *pf.* to suffer much.

настра́ива|ть(ся), ю(сь), *impf. of* настро́ить(ся).

настра́чива|ть, ю, *impf. of* настрочи́ть².

настреля́|ть, ю, *pf.* (+ *a. or g.*) to shoot (*a quantity of*).

настри́г, а, *m.* (*agric.*) 1. shearing, clipping. 2. clip.

настри́|чь, гу́, жёшь, гу́т, *past* ~г, ~гла, *pf.* (+ *a. or g.*) (*agric.*) to shear, clip (*a number of*).

на́строго, *adv.* (*coll.*) strictly.

настрое́ни|е, я, *n.* 1. (*also* н. ду́ха) mood, temper, humour; челове́к ~я a man of moods; быть в плохо́м, *etc.*, ~и to be in a bad, *etc.*, mood; н. умо́в state of opinion, public mood. 2. (+ *inf.*) mood (for); у меня́ нет ~я танцева́ть, я не в ~и танцева́ть I am not in a mood for dancing, I don't feel like dancing.

настро́енност|ь, и, *f.* mood, humour.

настро́|ить¹, ю, ишь, *pf.* (*of* настра́ивать) 1. (*mus.*) to tune; to tune up, attune; н. приёмник на сре́днюю волну́ to tune in to medium wave. 2. (*fig.*; на + *a.*) to dispose (to), incline (to); to incite; н. кого́-н. на весёлый лад to make someone happy, cheer someone up; н. кого́-н. (про́тив) to incite someone (against).

настро́|ить², ю, ишь, *pf.* (+ *a. or g.*) to build (*a quantity of*).

настро́|иться, юсь, ишься, *pf.* (*of* настра́иваться) 1. (на + *a.*) to dispose oneself (to);

(+ *inf.*) to make up one's mind (to); он ~и́лся на мра́чный лад he has made himself gloomy, he has got into a gloomy mood; я ~и́лся е́хать в Москву́ I made up my mind to go to Moscow. 2. *pass. of* ~ить¹.

настро́йк|а, и, *f.* 1. (*mus., radio*) tuning. 2. (*radio, aeron.*) tuning call. 3. (*tech.*) н. станка́ tooling.

настро́йщик, а, *m.* tuner.

настропал|и́ть, ю́, и́шь, *pf.* (*coll.*) to incite, set on.

настроч|и́ть¹, у́, и́шь, *pf. of* строчи́ть.

настроч|и́ть², у́, и́шь, *pf.* (*of* настра́чивать) (*coll.*) to incite, set on.

настря́па|ть, ю, *pf.* 1. (+ *a. or g.*) to cook (*a quantity of*). 2. (*fig., coll.*) to cook up.

насту|ди́ть, жу́, ~ди́шь, *pf.* (*of* ~жива́ть) (*coll.*) to cool, make cold.

настуж|а́ть = ~ива́ть.

настужива|ть, ю, *impf. of* настуди́ть.

насту́к|ать, аю, *pf.* (*of* ~ивать) (*coll.*) 1. to discover by tapping. 2. to knock out, bash out (*on typewriter*).

насту́кива|ть, ю, *impf. of* насту́кать.

наступа́тельный, *adj.* (*mil.*) offensive; (*fig.*) aggressive.

наступа́|ть¹, а́ю, *impf. of* ~и́ть.

наступа́|ть², ю, *impf.* (*mil.*) to advance, be on the offensive.

наступа́|ющий¹, *pres. part. act. of* ~ть¹ and *adj.* coming.

наступа́|ющий², *pres. part. act. of* ~ть² and *noun* н., ~ющего, *m.* attacker.

наступ|и́ть¹, лю́, ~ишь, *pf.* (*of* ~а́ть¹) (на + *a.*) to tread (on); медве́дь (*or* слон) наступи́л ему́ на у́хо he has absolutely no ear for music.

наступ|и́ть², ~ит, *pf.* (*of* ~а́ть¹) (*of times or seasons*) to come, begin; to ensue; to set in (*also fig.*); ~ит вре́мя, когда́... there will come a time, when . . . .

наступле́ни|е¹, я, *n.* (*mil.*) offensive; attack; перейти́ в н. to assume the offensive.

наступле́ни|е², я, *n.* coming, approach.

насту́рци|я, и, *f.* (*bot.*) nasturtium.

настыва́|ть, ю, *impf. of* насты́ть.

насты́|ть, ну, нешь, *pf.* (*of* ~ва́ть) (*coll.*) to become cold.

насул|и́ть, ю́, и́шь, *pf.* (+ *a. or g.*) (*coll.*) to promise (much).

насу́п|ить(ся), лю(сь), ишь(ся), *pf. of* су́пить(ся) *and* ~ливать(ся).

насу́пливать(ся) = су́пить(ся).

насупроти́в, *adv. and prep.* + *g.* (*dial.*) opposite.

насурьм|и́ть(ся), лю́(сь), и́шь(ся), *pf. of* сурьми́ть(ся).

на́сухо, *adv.* dry; вы́тереть н. to wipe dry.

насуш|и́ть, у́, ~ишь, *pf.* (+ *a. or g.*) to dry (*a quantity of*).

насущност|ь, и, *f.* urgency.

насущ|**ный** (**ен**, **~на**), *adj.* vital, urgent; хлеб н. daily bread (*also fig.*).

нас|**ую́**, **уёшь**, *see* ~**ова́ть**.

насчёт, *prep.*+*g.* about; as regards, concerning.

насчита́ть, **а́ю**, *pf.* (*of* ~**ывать**) to count, number.

насчи́тыва|**ть**, **ю**, *impf.* 1. *impf. of* насчита́ть. 2. (*no pf.*) to number (= *to contain*); э́тот го́род ~ет свы́ше ста ты́сяч жи́телей this city has over one hundred thousand inhabitants.

насчи́тыва|**ться**, **ется**, *impf.* (*impers.*) to number (= *to be, be contained*); в на́шем селе́ ~ется не бо́лее двухсо́т жи́телей the population of our village numbers no more than two hundred.

насыла́|**ть**, **ю**, *impf. of* насла́ть[1].

насы́п|**ать**, **лю**, **лешь**, *pf.* (*of* ~**а́ть**) 1. (+*a. or g.*) to pour (in, into); to fill (with); н. муки́ в мешо́к to pour flour into a bag; н. мешо́к муко́й to fill up a bag with flour. 2. (+*a. or g.* на+*a.*) to spread (on); н. песку́ на доро́жку to spread sand on the path. 3. to raise (*a heap or pile of sand, etc.*).

насып|**а́ть**, **а́ю**, *impf. of* ~**ать**.

насы́пк|**а**, **и**, *f.* pouring (in), filling.

насыпно́й, *adj.* poured; piled (up); н. холм artificial mound.

на́сып|**ь**, **и**, *f.* embankment (*of railway or road*).

насы́|**тить**, **щу**, **тишь**, *pf.* (*of* ~**ща́ть**) 1. to sate, satiate. 2. (*chem.*) to saturate, impregnate.

насы́|**титься**, **щусь**, **тишься**, *pf.* (*of* ~**ща́ть**ся) 1. to be full; to be sated. 2. (*chem.*) to become saturated.

насыща́|**ть(ся)**, **ю(сь)**, *impf. of* насы́тить(ся).

насыще́ни|**е**, **я**, *n.* 1. satiety, satiation. 2. (*chem.*) saturation.

насы́щенност|**ь**, **и**, *f.* 1. saturation. 2. (*fig.*) richness.

насы́|**щенный**, *p.p.p. of* ~**тить** *and adj.* 1. saturated. 2. (*fig.*) rich.

ната́лкива|**ть(ся)**, **ю(сь)**, *impf. of* натолкну́ть(ся).

ната́плива|**ть**, **ю**, *impf. of* натопи́ть[1].

ната́птыва|**ть**, **ю**, *impf. of* натопта́ть.

ната́ск|**анный**, *p.p.p. of* ~**а́ть**.

ната́ск|**а́ть**[1], **а́ю**, *pf.* (*of* ~**ивать**) to train (*hounds*); (*fig., coll.*) to coach, cram.

ната́ск|**а́ть**[2], **а́ю**, *pf.* (+*a. or g.*) 1. to bring, lay (*a quantity of*). 2. (*coll.*) to fish out, hook (*a quantity of*); н. из устаре́вших сочине́ний (*fig., pejor.*) to fish up outdated authorities.

ната́скива|**ть**, **ю**, *impf. of* натаска́ть[1] *and* натащи́ть[1].

ната́счик, **а**, *m.* trainer (of hounds).

натащ|**и́ть**[1], **у́**, **~ишь**, *pf.* (*of* ната́скивать) to pull (on, over).

натащ|**и́ть**[2], **у́**, **~ишь**, *pf.* (+*a. or g.*) to bring (*a quantity of*); to pile up (*a quantity of*).

ната́|**ять**, **ю**, **ешь**, *pf.* (+*a. or g.*) to melt (*a quantity of snow or ice*) (*also intrans.*).

натвор|**и́ть**, **ю́**, **и́шь**, *pf.* (+*g.*; *coll.*, *pejor.*) to do, get up to; н. вся́ких глу́постей to get up to every sort of stupid trick; что ты ~и́л! what ever have you done?

на́те, *interj.* (*coll.*, *addressed to more than one person or, politely, to one*) here (you are)!, there (you are)! (= *take it!*); тепе́рь н. вам and now see what's happened.

натёк, **а**, *m.* 1. (*geol.*) deposit. 2. (*coll.*) pool (*of some liquid*).

натека́|**ть**, **ет**, *impf. of* нате́чь.

нате́льн|**ый**, *adj.* worn next the skin; ~ое бельё (*collect.*) underclothes, body linen; ~ая фуфа́йка vest.

на|**тере́ть**[1], **тру́**, **трёшь**, *past* ~**тёр**, ~**тёрла**, *pf.* (*of* ~**тира́ть**) 1. to rub (in, on); н. ру́ки вазели́ном to rub vaseline into one's hands. 2. to polish (*floors, etc.*). 3. to rub sore; to chafe; н. себе́ мозо́ль to get a corn.

на|**тере́ть**[2], **тру́**, **трёшь**, *past* ~**тёр**, ~**тёрла**, *pf.* (+*a. or g.*) to grate, rasp (*a quantity of*).

на|**тере́ться**, **тру́сь**, **трёшься**, *past* ~**тёрся**, ~**тёрлась**, *pf.* (*of* ~**тира́ться**) 1. (+*i.*) to rub oneself (with). 2. *pass. of* ~тере́ть.

натерп|**е́ться**, **лю́сь**, ~**ишься**, *pf.* (+*g.*; *coll.*) to have endured much; to have gone through much.

натёр|**тый**, *p.p.p. of* ~**е́ть**.

нате́|**чь**, **чёт**, **кут́**, *past* ~**к**, ~**кла́**, *pf.* (*of* ~**ка́ть**) (*of liquids*) to accumulate.

нате́ш|**иться**, **усь**, **ишься**, *pf.* (*coll.*) 1. to enjoy oneself, have a good time. 2. (над) to have a good laugh (at).

натира́ни|**е**, **я**, *n.* 1. rubbing in. 2. polishing (*of floors, etc.*). 3. (*coll.*) embrocation, ointment.

натира́|**ть(ся)**, **ю(сь)**, *impf. of* натере́ть(ся).

на́тиск, **а**, *m.* 1. onslaught, charge, onset. 2. pressure. 3. (*typ.*) impress.

нати́ска|**ть**, **ю**, *pf.* (+*a. or g.*) 1. (*coll.*) to cram in, stuff in (*a quantity of*). 2. (*coll.*) to shove (someone) about. 3. (*typ.*) to impress (*a quantity of*).

на́-тка = на́те (*but addressed familiarly to one person*).

натк|**а́ть**, **у́**, **ёшь**, *past* ~**а́л**, ~**ала́**, ~**а́ло**, *pf.* (+*a. or g.*) to weave (*a quantity of*).

наткн|**у́ть**, **у́**, **ёшь**, *pf.* (*of* натыка́ть) 1. to stick, pin. 2. to stick, pin (*a quantity of*).

наткн|**у́ться**, **у́сь**, **ёшься**, *pf.* (*of* натыка́ться) (на+*a.*) 1. to run (against), strike; to stumble (upon); н. на гвоздь to run against a nail; н. на неожи́данное сопротивле́ние (*fig.*) to meet with unexpected resistance. **2.** (*fig.*) to stumble (upon, across), come (across); н. на интере́сную мысль to stumble across an interesting idea.

натолкн|у́ть, у́, ёшь, *pf.* (*of* ната́лкивать) (+*a.* на+*a.*) **1.** to push (against), shove (against). **2.** (*fig.*) to direct, lead (into, onto); он меня́ ∼у́л на мысль he suggested the idea to me; н. на грех to lead into sin.

натолкн|у́ться, у́сь, ёшься, *pf.* (*of* ната́лкиваться) (на+*a.*) to run (against); (*fig.*) to run across.

натол|о́чь, ку́, чёшь, ку́т, *past* ∼о́к, ∼кла́, *pf.* (+*a. or g.*) to pound, crush (*a quantity of*).

натоп|и́ть[1], лю́, ∼ишь, *pf.* (*of* ната́пливать) to heat well, heat up.

натоп|и́ть[2], лю́, ∼ишь, *pf.* (+*a. or g.*) **1.** to melt (*a quantity of*). **2.** to heat (*a quantity of*).

натоп|та́ть, чу́, ∼чешь, *pf.* (*of* ната́птывать) (*coll.*; в, на+*p.*) to make dirty footmarks (in, on).

наторг|ова́ть, у́ю, *pf.* (*coll.*) **1.** (+*a. or g.*) to make, gain (*by commerce*). **2.** (на+*a.*) to sell (for).

наторе́лый, *adj.* (*coll.*) skilled, expert.

наторе́|ть, ю, *pf.* (в+*p.*; *coll.*) to become skilled (at, in), become expert (at, in).

наточ|и́ть, у́, ∼ишь, *pf. of* точи́ть[1].

натоща́к, *adv.* on an empty stomach.

натр, а, *m.* (*chem.*) natron; е́дкий н. caustic soda.

натрав|и́ть[1], лю́, ∼ишь, *pf.* (*of* ∼ливать) (на+*a.*) to set (*dog*) (on); (*fig.*) to stir up (against).

натрав|и́ть[2], лю́, ∼ишь, (*of* ∼ливать) to etch.

натрав|и́ть[3], лю́, ∼ишь, *pf.* (+*a. or g.*) to exterminate (*a quantity of*).

натра́влива|ть, ю, *impf. of* натрави́ть[1, 2].

натравл|я́ть = ∼ивать.

натрениро́ванный, *adj.* trained.

натренир|ова́ть(ся), у́ю(сь), *pf. of* трениров́ать(ся).

на́три|евый, *adj. of* ∼й.

на́три|й, я, *m.* (*chem.*) sodium.

на́трое, *adv.* in three.

натро́нн|ый, *adj.* (*chem.*) sodium; ∼ая и́звесть sodium carbonate.

нат|ру́, рёшь, *see* ∼ере́ть.

натруб|и́ть, лю́, и́шь, *pf.* (*coll.*) to trumpet a good deal; н. в у́ши кому́-н. to din into someone's ears.

натру|ди́ть, жу́, ∼ди́шь, *pf.* (*of* ∼жива́ть) to tire out, overwork.

натру|ди́ться, жу́сь, ∼ди́шься, *pf.* (*coll.*) **1.** to become tired out. **2.** to have worked long enough; to have overworked.

натру́жива|ть, ю, *impf. of* натруди́ть.

натряс|ти́, у́, ёшь, *past* ∼, ∼ла́, *pf.* (+*a. or g.*) to scatter, let fall (*a quantity of*).

натряс|ти́сь, у́сь, ёшься, *past* ∼ся, ∼ла́сь, *pf.* (*coll.*) **1.** to be shaken much; (*fig.*) to shake, quake much. **2.** to be scattered; to spill.

нату́г|а, и, *f.* effort, strain.

на́туго, *adv.* (*coll.*) tightly; ту́го-на́туго very tightly.

нату́жива|ть(ся), ю(сь), *impf. of* нату́жить(ся).

нату́ж|ить, у, ишь, *pf.* (*of* ∼ивать) (*coll.*) to tense, tighten.

нату́ж|иться, усь, ишься, *pf.* (*of* ∼иваться) (*coll.*) to exert all one's strength; to strain.

нату́жный, *adj.* (*coll.*) strained, forced.

нату́р|а, ы, *f.* **1.** (*in var. senses*) nature. **2.** (artist's) model, sitter; рисова́ть с ∼ы to paint from life. **3.** (*econ.*) kind; плати́ть ∼ой to pay in kind. **4.** на ∼e (*coll.*) on the spot, (cinema) on location.

натурализа́ци|я, и, *f.* naturalization.

натурали́зм, а, *m.* naturalism.

натурализ|ова́ть, у́ю, *impf. and pf.* to naturalize.

натурали́ст, а, *m.* (*in var. senses*) naturalist.

натуралисти́ческий, *adj.* naturalistic.

нату́рально, *adv.* (*obs.*) naturally, of course.

нату́ральност|ь, и, *f.* genuineness; naturalness.

натура́л|ьный (∼ен, ∼ьна), *adj.* **1.** (*in var. senses*) natural; в ∼ьную величину́ life-size. **2.** real; genuine; н. смех unforced laughter. **3.** (*econ.*) in kind; н. обме́н barter.

нату́рн|ый, *adj.* (*art*) from life; н. класс life class; ∼ая съёмка (cinema) shooting on location, take made on location.

натуропла́т|а, ы, *f.* payment in kind.

нату́рщик, а, *m.* (artist's) model, sitter.

нату́рщи|ца, цы, *f. of* ∼к.

наты́кать = наткну́ть.

натыка́|ть(ся), ю(сь), *impf. of* наткну́ть(ся).

натюрмо́рт, а, *m.* (*art*) still life.

натюрмо́рт|ный, *adj. of* ∼.

натя́гива|ть(ся), ю(сь), *impf. of* натяну́ть(ся).

натяже́ни|е, я, *n.* pull, tension.

натя́жк|а, и, *f.* (*coll.*) **1.** strained interpretation; допусти́ть ∼у to stretch a point; ∼ой (*fig.*) at a stretch. **2.** = натяже́ние.

натяжн|о́й, *adj.* (*tech.*) tension; ∼о́е при способле́ние tension device, stretcher; н. ро́лик tension pulley; н. рыча́г tension lever.

натя́нутост|ь, и, *f.* tension (*also fig.*).

натя́н|утый, *p.p.p. of* ∼у́ть *and adj.* **1.** tight. **2.** (*fig.*) strained; forced; ∼утые отноше́ния strained relations; ∼утое сравне́ние far-fetched simile.

натя|ну́ть, ну́, ~нешь, *pf.* (*of* ~гива́ть) **1.** to stretch; to draw (tight); **н. лук** to draw a bow; **н. верёвку** (*naut.*) to haul a rope taut. **2.** to pull on; **н. ша́пку на́ уши** to pull a cap over one's ears.

натя|ну́ться, ну́сь, ~нешься, *pf.* (*of* ~ги́ваться) to stretch (*intrans.*).

науга́д, *adv.* at random, by guess-work.

науго́льник, а, *m.* (*tech.*) (try-)square, back square; bevel, bevel square.

наудалу́ю, *adv.* (*coll.*) at a venture.

науда́чу, *adv.* at random; by guesswork.

нау|ди́ть, жу́, ~дишь, *pf.* (+*a* or *g.*) to hook (*a number of*).

нау́к|а, и, *f.* **1.** science; learning; study; scholarship; **обще́ственные ~и** social sciences, social studies; **прикладны́е ~и** applied science; **то́чные ~и** exact science. **2.** (*coll.*) lesson; **э́то тебе́ н.!** let this be a lesson to you!

нау|сти́ть, щу́, сти́шь, *pf.* (*of* ~ща́ть) (*obs.*) to incite, egg on.

нау́ськ|ать, аю, *pf.* (*of* ~ивать) (на+*a.*) to set (*dogs on*).

нау́ськива|ть, ю, *impf. of* нау́ськать.

наутёк, *adv.* **пусти́ться н.** (*coll.*) to take to one's heels.

нау́тро, *adv.* next morning.

науч|и́ть, у́, ~ишь, *pf.* (*of* учи́ть) (+*a.* and *d.* or +*inf.*) to teach; **н. кого́-н. ру́сскому языку́** to teach someone Russian; **н. кого́-н. пра́вить маши́ной** to teach someone to drive (a car).

науч|и́ться, у́сь, ~ишься, *pf.* (*of* учи́ться) (+*d.* or *inf.*) to learn.

нау́чно-иссле́довательск|ий, *adj.* scientific research; **~ая рабо́та** (scientific) research work.

нау́чно-фантасти́ческий, *adj.* science fiction.

нау́ч|ный (~ен, ~на), *adj.* scientific; **н. рабо́тник** member of staff of scientific or other learned body; **~ная фанта́стика** science fiction.

нау́шник¹, а, *m.* **1.** ear-flap; ear-muff. **2.** ear-phone, head-phone.

нау́шник², а, *m.* (*pejor.*) informer, slanderer.

нау́шнича|ть, ю, *impf.* (+*d.* на+*a.*) to tell tales (about), inform (on, about).

нау́шничеств|о, а, *n.* tale-bearing, informing.

наущá|ть, ю, *impf. of* наусти́ть.

нау|щу́, сти́шь, *see* ~сти́ть.

нафаб|рить, ю, ишь, *pf. of* фа́брить.

нафтали́н, а, *m.* (*chem.*) naphthalene, naphthaline.

нафтали́н|ный, *adj. of* ~.

нафтали́н|овый = ~ный; **н. ша́рик** camphor ball, moth-ball.

наха́л, а, *m.* impudent, insolent fellow, cheeky fellow; smart aleck.

наха́лк|а, и, *f.* impudent, insolent woman.

наха́льнича|ть, ю, *impf.* to be impudent, insolent.

наха́л|ьный (~ен, ~ьна), *adj.* impudent, impertinent; cheeky, brazen.

наха́льств|о, а, *n.* impudence, impertinence, effrontery; **име́ть н.** (+*inf.*) to have the cheek (to), have the face (to).

нахам|и́ть, лю́, и́шь, *pf.* (*coll.*; +*d.*) to play someone a caddish trick, to speak offensively.

нахва́лива|ть, ю, *impf. of* нахвали́ть.

нахвал|и́ть, ю́, ~ишь, *pf.* (*of* ~ивать) (*coll.*) to praise (highly).

нахвал|и́ться, ю́сь, ~ишься, *pf.* (*coll.*) **1.** to boast much. **2.** (+*i.*; *usually* +*neg.*) to praise sufficiently; **я не могу́ им н.** I cannot speak too highly of him.

нахват|а́ть, а́ю, *pf.* (*of* ~ывать) (*coll.*; +*a.* or *g.*) to pick up, get hold (of), come by.

нахват|а́ться, а́юсь, *pf.* (*of* ~ываться) (*coll.*, *fig.*; +*g.*) to pick up, come by; **в солда́тах он нахвата́лся ара́бских слов** in the army he picked up a few words of Arabic.

нахле́бник, а, *m.* **1.** (*obs.*) boarder, paying guest. **2.** parasite, hanger-on.

нахле|ста́ть, щу́, ~щешь, *pf.* (*of* ~стывать) (*coll.*) to whip.

нахле|ста́ться, ~щу́сь, ~щешься, *pf.* (*of* ~стываться) (*sl.*) to get sloshed (*drunk*).

нахлёстыва|ть(ся), ю(сь), *impf. of* нахлеста́ть(ся).

нахлобу́чива|ть, ю, *impf. of* нахлобу́чить.

нахлобу́ч|ить, у, ишь, *pf.* (*of* ~ивать) (*coll.*) **1.** to pull down (over one's head *or* eyes). **2.** **н. кому́-н.** (*fig.*) to rate someone, give someone a dressing down.

нахлобу́чк|а, и, *f.* **1.** (*coll.*) rating, dressing down. **2.** (*obs.*) blow on the head.

нахлы́н|уть, ет, *pf.* (на+*a.*) to flow, gush (over, into); (*fig.*) to surge, crowd; **~ули слёзы** tears welled (in my, her, *etc.*, eyes); **на меня́ ~ули мы́сли** thoughts crowded into my mind.

нахму́р|енный, *p.p.p. of* ~ить *and adj.* frowning, scowling.

нахму́р|ить(ся), ю(сь), ишь(ся), *pf. of* хму́рить(ся).

нахо|ди́ть, жу́, ~дишь, *impf. of* найти́.

нахо|ди́ться¹, жу́сь, ~дишься, *impf. of* найти́сь.

нахо|ди́ться², жу́сь, ~дишься, *impf.* to be (situated); **где ~дится ста́нция?** where is the station?

нахо|ди́ться³, жу́сь, ~дишься, *pf.* (*coll.*) to tire oneself by walking; to have walked long enough.

нахо́дк|а, и, *f.* **1.** find. **2.** (*fig., coll.*) godsend.

нахо́дчивост|ь, и, f. 1. resource, resourcefulness. 2. readiness, quick-wittedness.

нахо́дчив|ый (~, ~а), adj. 1. resourceful. 2. ready, quick-witted.

нахожде́ни|е, я, n. 1. finding. 2. ме́сто ~я the whereabouts.

нахоло|ди́ть, жу́, ди́шь, pf. of холоди́ть 1.

нахо́хл|иться, юсь, ишься, pf. (of хо́хлиться) (fig., coll.) to bristle (up).

нахохо|та́ться, чу́сь, ~че́шься, pf. (coll.) to have had a good laugh.

нахра́пист|ый (~, ~а), adj. (coll., pejor.) high-handed.

нахра́пом, adv. (coll.) unceremoniously, insolently, with a high hand.

нацара́п|ать, аю, pf. (of ~ывать) 1. to scratch. 2. (fig., coll.) to scrawl, scribble.

нацара́пыва|ть, ю, impf. of нацара́пать.

наце|ди́ть, жу́, ~ди́шь, pf. (+a. or g.) 1. to fill (a vessel) through a strainer. 2. to pour through a strainer (a quantity of).

наце́лива|ть(ся), ю(сь), impf. of наце́лить(ся).

наце́л|ить, ю, ишь, pf. 1. (impf. це́лить and ~ивать) to aim, level. 2. (impf. ~ивать) (fig.) to aim, direct.

наце́л|иться, юсь, ишься, pf. (of ~иваться) 1. (в+a.) to aim (at), take aim (at). 2. (fig., coll.; на+a.) to aim (at, for).

на́цело, adv. (coll.) entirely, without remainder.

наце́нива|ть, ю, impf. of нацени́ть.

нацен|и́ть, ю́, ~ишь, pf. (of ~ивать) (comm.) to raise the price of.

наце́нк|а, и, f. addition (to price).

нацеп|и́ть, лю́, ~ишь, pf. (of ~ля́ть) to fasten on; to attach (by means of hook or pin).

нацеп|ля́ть, ля́ю, impf. of ~и́ть.

наци́зм, а, m. Nazism.

национализа́ци|я, и, f. nationalization.

национализи́р|овать, ую, impf. and pf. to nationalize.

национали́зм, а, m. nationalism.

национали́ст, а, m. nationalist.

националисти́ческий, adj. nationalist(ic).

национа́льност|ь, и, f. 1. nationality (in var. senses: the words н. and национа́льный in Soviet parlance refer not to the State but to the particular national groups which compose it; e.g. гражда́нство — сове́тское, национа́льность — ру́сская (or евре́йская, армя́нская, etc.) citizenship—Soviet, nationality Russian (or Jewish, Armenian, etc.)); ethnic group. 2. national character, national idiosyncrasy.

национа́льн|ый, adj. national (see also ~ость); ~ые словари́ dictionaries of languages of peoples of the Soviet Union.

наци́ст, а, m. Nazi.

наци́стский, adj. Nazi.

на́ци|я, и, f. nation.

нацме́н, а, m. (coll.) member of a national minority.

нацме́н|ка, ки, f. of ~.

нача|ди́ть, жу́, ди́шь, pf. of чади́ть.

нача́л|о, а, n. beginning; commencement; в ~е четвёртого soon after three (o'clock); для ~a to start with, for a start; по ~у at first; положи́ть н. (+d.) to begin, commence. 2. origin, source; вести́ н. (от), взять н. (в+p.) to originate (from, in). 3. principle, basis; рабо́тать на но́вых ~ах to work on a new basis; ~a матема́тики the elements of mathematics. 4. (obs.) command, authority; быть под ~ом у кого́-н. to be under someone; отда́ть под н., под ~a (+d.) to put under, place in the charge (of).

нача́льник, а, m. head, chief; superior; н. свя́зи chief signal officer; н. отде́ла head of a department.

нача́льнический, adj. overbearing, imperious.

нача́льн|ый, adj. 1. initial, first; ~ая ско́рость initial speed; (artillery) muzzle velocity. 2. elementary; ~ая шко́ла primary school.

нача́льственный, adj. overbearing, domineering.

нача́льств|о, а, n. 1. (collect.) (the) authorities. 2. command, direction. 3. (coll.) head, boss.

нача́льствовани|е, я, n. command.

нача́льств|овать, ую, impf. (над) to command, be in command (of).

нача́тк|и, ов, no sing. rudiments, elements.

нач|а́ть, ну́, нёшь, past ~а́л, ~ала́, ~а́ло, pf. (of ~ина́ть) to begin, start, commence; н. с ~а́ла to begin at the beginning; н. всё снача́ла to start all over again, start afresh; н. с того́, что он ни одного́ сло́ва не по́нял to begin with, he did not understand a single word; он на́чал моли́твой (or с моли́твы) he began with a prayer.

нач|а́ться, ну́сь, нёшься, past ~алcя, ~ала́сь, pf. (of ~ина́ться) to begin, start; to break out.

начека́н|ить, ю, ишь, pf. (+a. or g.) to mint (a quantity of).

начеку́, adv. on the alert, on the qui vive.

начерн|и́ть, ю́, и́шь, pf. of черни́ть 1.

на́черно, adv. roughly; написа́ть н. to make a rough copy.

наче́рпа|ть, ю, pf. (+a. or g.) to scoop up (a quantity of).

начерта́ни|е, я, n. tracing; outline.

начерта́тельн|ый, adj. only in phrase ~ая геоме́трия descriptive geometry.

начерта́|ть, ю, *pf.* to trace (*also fig.*); to inscribe.

начер|ти́ть, чу́, ⌐чишь, *pf. of* черти́ть¹.

начёс, а, *m.* **1.** nap (*of material*). **2.** (hair dressed in) fringe.

наче|са́ть¹, шу́, ⌐шешь, *pf.* (+*a. or g.*) to comb, card (*a quantity of*).

наче|са́ть², шу́, ⌐шешь, *pf.* (*of* ⌐сывать) (*coll.*) to injure by scratching.

нач|е́сть, ту́, тёшь, *pf.* (*of* ~и́тывать) (*bookkeeping*) to recover.

начёсыва|ть, ю, *impf. of* начеса́ть².

начёт, а, *m.* (*book-keeping*) recovery of unauthorized expenditure; recovery of deficit in account; сде́лать н. на кого́-н. to recover unauthorized expenditure from someone.

начётист|ый (~, ~а), *adj.* (*coll.*) disadvantageous, unprofitable.

начётничеств|о, а, *n.* (*pejor.*) dogmatism (*based on uncritical, mechanical reading*).

начётчик, а, *m.* **1.** person well-read in Scriptures. **2.** (*fig., pejor.*) dogmatist (*person basing opinions uncritically on wide but mechanical reading*).

начина́ни|е, я, *n.* undertaking.

начина́тел|ь, я, *m.* originator, initiator.

начина́тельный, *adj.* (*gram.*) н. глаго́л inceptive verb.

начина́|ть(ся), ю(сь), *impf. of* нача́ть(ся).

начина́|ющий, *pres. part. act. of* ~ть; *as noun* н., ~ющего, *m.* beginner.

начина́я, *as prep.* (с+*g.*) as (from), starting (with).

начин|и́ть¹, ю́, и́шь, *pf.* (*of* ~я́ть) (+*i.*) to fill (with), stuff (with).

начин|и́ть², ю́, ⌐ишь, *pf.* (+*a. or g.*) **1.** to mend (*a quantity of*). **2.** н. карандаше́й to sharpen (*a number of*) pencils.

начи́нк|а, и, *f.* (*cul.*) stuffing, filling.

начин|я́ть, я́ю, *impf. of* ~и́ть¹.

начисле́ни|е, я, *n.* additional sum; extra.

начи́сл|ить, ю, ишь, *pf.* (*of* ~я́ть) (*bookkeeping*) to add (to someone's account); to charge extra.

начисл|я́ть, я́ю, *impf. of* ~ить.

начи́|стить¹, щу, стишь, *pf.* (*of* ~ща́ть) to polish, shine (*trans.*).

начи́|стить², щу, стишь, *pf.* (+*a. or g.*) to peel (*a quantity of*); to clean (*a quantity of*) (*vegetables, etc.*).

на́чисто, *adv.* **1.** clean, fair; переписа́ть н. to make a fair copy (of). **2.** (*coll.*) completely, thoroughly; н. отказа́ться to refuse flatly. **3.** (*coll.*) openly, without equivocation.

начистоту́, *adv.* openly, without equivocation.

начист|у́ю, *adv.* (*coll.*) **1.** = ~оту́. **2.** utterly, altogether.

начи́танност|ь, и, *f.* (wide) reading; erudition.

начи́тан|ный (~, ~на), *adj.* well-read, widely-read.

начита́|ть, ю, *pf.* (+*a. or g.*) to read (*a number of*).

начита́|ться, юсь, *pf.* **1.** (+*g.*) to have read (*much of*). **2.** to have read one's fill.

начи́тыва|ть, ю, *impf. of* наче́сть.

начища́|ть, ю, *impf. of* начи́стить.

нач|ну́, нёшь, *see* ~а́ть.

начу|ди́ть, жу́, ди́шь, *pf.* (*coll.*) to behave oddly; что ты там начуди́л? what have you been up to?

наш, ~его, *f.* ~а, ~ей; *n.* ~е, ~его; *pl.* ~и, ~их, *possessive pronoun* our(s); ~его (*after comp.*) we; у них де́нег бо́льше ~его they have more money than we; ~а взяла́! (*coll.*) we've won!; знай ~их! (*coll.*) that's the sort we are! we'll show you!; ~е вам! (*coll.*) hello there! (служи́ть) и ~им и ва́шим (*coll.*) to run with the hare and hunt with the hounds; *as noun* ~и, ~их, our people, people on our side; его́ счита́ют одни́м из ~их they regard him as one of us.

нашал|и́тъ, ю́, и́шь, *pf.* to be naughty.

нашаты́р|ный, *adj. of* ~ь; н. спирт liquid ammonia.

нашаты́р|ь, я́, *m.* (*chem.*) sal ammoniac, ammonium chloride.

нашеп|та́ть, чу́, ~чешь, *pf.* (*of* ~тывать) **1.** (+*a. or g.*) to whisper (*a number of*) (*also fig.*). **2.** (на+*a.*) to put a spell (upon).

нашёптыва|ть, ю, *impf. of* нашепта́ть.

наше́стви|е, я, *n.* invasion, descent.

на́шивать, *freq. of* носи́ть.

нашива́|ть, ю, *impf. of* наши́ть¹.

наши́вк|а, и, *f.* (*mil.*) stripe, chevron (*on sleeve*); tab.

нашивно́й, *adj.* sewed (sewn) on.

наш|и́ть¹, ью́, ьёшь, *pf.* (*of* ~ива́ть) to sew on.

наш|и́ть², ью́, ьёшь, *pf.* (+*a. or g.*) to sew (*a quantity of*).

нашлёпа|ть, ю, *pf.* (*coll.*) to slap; to spank.

на|шлю́, шлёшь, *see* ~сла́ть.

нашпиг|ова́ть, у́ю, *pf. of* шпигова́ть.

нашпи́лива|ть, ю, *impf. of* нашпи́лить.

нашпи́л|ить, ю, ишь, *pf.* (*of* ~ивать) (*coll.*) to pin on.

нашум|е́ть, лю́, и́шь, *pf.* to make much noise; (*fig.*) to cause a sensation.

нащёлка|ть, ю, *pf.* (+*a. or g.*) to crack (*a quantity of*) (*nuts, etc.*).

нащип|а́ть, лю́, ~лешь, *pf.* (+*a. or g.*) to pluck, pick (*a quantity of*).

нащу́п|ать, аю, *pf.* (*of* ~ывать) to find, discover (*by groping*).

нащу́пыва|ть, ю, *impf.* (*of* нащу́пать) to grope (for, after); to fumble (for, after); to feel about (for) (*also fig.*); н. по́чву (*fig.*) to feel one's way, see how the land lies.

наэлектриз|ова́ть, у́ю, *pf.* (*of* ~о́вывать) to electrify (*also fig.*).

наэлектризо́выва|ть, ю, *impf. of* наэлектризова́ть.

найбеднича|ть, ю, *pf. of* я́бедничать.

наяву́, *adv.* waking; in reality; гре́зить н. to day-dream.

найд|а, ы, *f.* (*myth.*) naiad.

ная́рива|ть, ю, *impf.* (*coll.*) to bash out (*a tune, etc., on a mus. instrument*).

не¹, not; не..., he neither . . . nor.

не², *separable component of pronouns* не́кого *and* не́чего; мне не́ с кем разгова́ривать I have no one to talk to; не́ о чем бы́ло говори́ть there was nothing to talk about.

не- un-, in-, non-, mis-, dis-.

неаккура́тност|ь, и, *f.* **1.** carelessness; inaccuracy. **2.** unpunctuality. **3.** untidiness.

неаккура́т|ный (~ен, ~на), *adj.* **1.** careless; inaccurate. **2.** unpunctual. **3.** untidy.

неандерта́л|ец, ьца, *m.* (*anthrop.*) Neanderthal man.

неандерта́льский, *adj.* (*anthrop.*) Neanderthal.

неаполита́н|ец, ца, *m.* Neapolitan.

неаполита́нский, *adj.* Neapolitan.

неаппети́т|ный (~ен, ~на), *adj.* unappetizing (*also fig.*).

небезопа́с|ный (~ен, ~на), *adj.* unsafe, insecure.

небезоснова́тел|ьный (~ен, ~ьна), *adj.* not unfounded.

небезразли́ч|ный (~ен, ~на), *adj.* not indifferent.

небезрезульта́т|ный (~ен, ~на), *adj.* not fruitless, not futile.

небезупре́ч|ный (~ен, ~на), *adj.* not irreproachable.

небезуспе́ш|ный (~ен, ~на), *adj.* not unsuccessful.

небезызве́ст|ный (~ен, ~на), *adj.* not unknown; ~но, что... it is no secret that....

небезынтере́с|ный (~ен, ~на), *adj.* not without interest.

небелёный, *adj.* unbleached.

небережли́в|ый (~, ~а), *adj.* thriftless, improvident.

неб|еса́, *pl. of* ~о.

небескоры́ст|ный (~ен, ~на), *adj.* not disinterested.

небе́сн|ый, *adj.* heavenly, celestial; ~ая импе́рия (*hist.*) the Celestial Empire (*China*); ~ая меха́ника (*astron.*) celestial mechanics; ~ые свети́ла heavenly bodies; н. свод firmament; Ца́рство ~ое the Kingdom of Heaven; ~ого цве́та sky-blue.

небесполе́з|ный (~ен, ~на), *adj.* of some use.

небеспристра́ст|ный (~ен, ~на), *adj.* not impartial.

неблагови́д|ный (~ен, ~на), *adj.* **1.** unseemly, improper. **2.** (*obs.*) unsightly.

неблагода́рност|ь, и, *f.* ingratitude.

неблагода́р|ный (~ен, ~на), *adj.* **1.** ungrateful. **2.** thankless.

неблагожела́тел|ьный (~ен, ~ьна), *adj.* malevolent, ill-disposed.

неблагозву́чи|е, я, *n.* disharmony, dissonance.

неблагозву́ч|ный (~ен, ~на), *adj.* inharmonious, disharmonious.

неблагонадёж|ный (~ен, ~на), *adj.* (*hist.*) unreliable (*esp. politically*).

неблагополу́чи|е, я, *n.* trouble.

неблагополу́чно, *adv.* not successfully, not favourably; дела́ у них обстоя́т н. their affairs are in a bad way, things are not turning out happily for them.

неблагополу́ч|ный (~ен, ~на), *adj.* unfavourable, bad; де́ло име́ло н. исхо́д the affair had a bad ending; (*impers.*) у нас ~но things are going badly, we are in a bad way.

неблагопристо́йност|ь, и, *f.* obscenity, indecency, impropriety.

неблагопристо́|йный (~ен, ~йна), *adj.* obscene, indecent, improper.

неблагоприя́т|ный (~ен, ~на), *adj.* unfavourable, inauspicious.

неблагоразу́м|ный (~ен, ~на), *adj.* imprudent, ill-advised, unwise.

неблагоро́д|ный (~ен, ~на), *adj.* ignoble, base; н. мета́лл base metal.

неблагоро́дств|о, а, *n.* baseness.

неблагоскло́н|ный (~ен, ~на), *adj.* unfavourable; (к) ill-disposed (towards).

неблагоустро́ен|ный (~, ~на), *adj.* uncomfortable; badly planned.

нёбн|ый, *adj.* **1.** (*anat.*) palatine; ~ая занаве́ска uvula. **2.** (*ling.*) palatal.

нёб|о, а, *pl.* ~еса́, ~ес, ~еса́м, *n.* sky; heaven; попа́сть па́льцем в н. (*coll.*) to miss the point, be wide of the mark; как н. от земли́ (as far removed) as heaven from earth, worlds apart; жить ме́жду ~ом и землёй not to have a roof above one's head; под откры́тым ~ом in the open (air); с ~а свали́ться (*fig., coll.*) to fall from the moon; упа́сть с ~а на зе́млю (*fig.*) to come down to earth; нам н. с овчи́нку показа́лось (*coll.*) we were frightened out of our wits.

нёб|о, а, *n.* (*anat.*) palate.

небога́т|ый (~, ~а), *adj.* **1.** of modest means. **2.** (*fig.*) modest.

небожи́тел|ь, я, *m.* (*myth.*) celestial being, god.

небольш|о́й, *adj.* small; not great; о́чень ~ое расстоя́ние a very short distance; ты́сяча с ~и́м a thousand odd; де́ло ста́ло за ~и́м one small thing is lacking.

небосво́д, а, *m.* firmament; the vault of heaven.

небоскло́н, а, *m.* horizon (*strictly*, sky immediately over horizon).

небоскрёб, а, *m.* (*obs.*) skyscraper.

небо́сь, *adv.* (*coll.*) 1. probably, most likely, I dare say; ты, н., мно́го книг чита́л I suppose you've read lots of books. 2. (*obs.*) don't be afraid (= не бо́йся).

небре́жнича|ть, ю, *impf.* (*coll.*) to be careless.

небре́жност|ь, и, *f.* carelessness, negligence.

небре́ж|ный (~ен, ~на), *adj.* careless, negligent; slipshod; offhand.

небри́т|ый (~, ~а), *adj.* unshaven.

небыва́лый, *adj.* 1. unprecedented. 2. fantastic, imaginary. 3. (*coll.*) inexperienced.

небыва́льщин|а, ы, *f.* 1. (*obs.*) fable. 2. fantastic story.

небыли́ц|а, ы, *f.* fable; cock-and-bull story.

небыти́|е́, я́, *n.* non-existence.

небью́щийся, *adj.* unbreakable.

неважне́цкий, *adj.* (*coll.*) indifferent, so-so.

нева́жно, *adv.* not too well, indifferently; дела́ иду́т н. things are not going too well.

нева́ж|ный (~ен, ~на́, ~но), *adj.* 1. unimportant, insignificant. 2. poor, indifferent.

невдалеке́, *adv.* not far away, not far off.

невдо|гра́д (*dial.*) = ~мёк.

невдомёк, *adv.* (+*d.*) (*coll.*) мне бы́ло н. it never occurred to me, I never thought of it.

неве́дени|е, я, *n.* ignorance; пребыва́ть в блаже́нном ~и (*iron.*) to be in a state of blissful ignorance.

неве́домо, *adv.* (*coll.*; +что, как, когда́, куда́, *etc.*) God knows, no one knows; он так и появи́лся, н. отку́да he just turned up, God knows where from.

неве́дом|ый (~, ~а), *adj.* 1. unknown. 2. (*fig.*) mysterious.

неве́ж|а, и, *m. and f.* boor, lout.

неве́жд|а, ы, *m. and f.* ignoramus.

неве́жествен|ный (~, ~на), *adj.* ignorant.

неве́жеств|о, а, *n.* 1. ignorance. 2. (*coll.*) rudeness, bad manners.

неве́жливост|ь, и, *f.* rudeness, impoliteness, bad manners.

неве́жлив|ый (~, ~а), *adj.* rude, impolite.

невезе́ни|е, я, *n.* (*coll.*) bad luck.

невели́к|ий (~, ~а́, ~о́), *adj.* 1. small, short. 2. slight, insignificant.

неве́ри|е, я, *n.* unbelief; lack of faith.

неве́рност|ь, и, *f.* 1. incorrectness. 2. disloyalty; infidelity, unfaithfulness.

неве́р|ный (~ен, ~на́, ~но), *adj.* 1. incorrect; ~ная но́та false note. 2. unsteady,

uncertain; ~ная похо́дка unsteady gait; н. слух (*mus.*) unsure ear; Фома́ н. (*coll.*) a doubting Thomas. 3. faithless, disloyal; unfaithful; н. друг false friend. 4. dim, flickering (*of light*). 5. *as noun* н., ~ного, *m.* (*rel.*) infidel.

невероя́ти|е, я, *n.* *now only in phrase* до ~я incredibly.

невероя́тно, *adv.* incredibly, unbelievably.

невероя́тност|ь, и, *f.* 1. improbability. 2. incredibility; до ~и incredibly, to an unbelievable extent.

невероя́т|ный (~ен, ~на), *adj.* 1. improbable, unlikely. 2. incredible, unbelievable (*also fig.*); ~но (*impers.*, *as pred.*) it is incredible, it is unbelievable, it is beyond belief.

неве́рующ|ий, *adj.* (*rel.*) unbelieving; *as noun* н., ~его, *m.*; ~ая, ~ей, *f.* unbeliever.

невес|ёлый (~ел, ~ела́, ~ело), *adj.* joyless, mirthless; melancholy, sombre.

невесо́мост|ь, и, *f.* weightlessness.

невесо́мый, *adj.* 1. (*phys.*) imponderable. 2. weightless (*also fig.*).

невест|а, ы, *f.* 1. fiancée; bride. 2. (*coll.*) marriageable girl.

неве́стк|а, и, *f.* 1. daughter-in-law (*son's wife*). 2. sister-in-law (*brother's wife*).

неве́сть, *adv.* (*coll.*; +кто, что, ско́лько, *etc.*) God knows, goodness knows, heaven knows.

невеще́ственный, *adj.* immaterial.

невзачёт, *adv.* (*coll.*) э́то н. it does not count.

невзго́д|а, ы, *f.* adversity, misfortune.

невзира́я, *prep.* (на+*a.*) in spite of, regardless of; н. на ли́ца without respect of persons.

невзнача́й, *adv.* (*coll.*) by chance; unexpectedly.

невзно́с, а, *m.* non-payment (*of fees, etc.*).

невзра́ч|ный (~ен, ~на), *adj.* unprepossessing, unattractive; plain.

невзыска́тел|ьный (~ен, ~ьна), *adj.* modest, undemanding.

не́видал|ь, и, *f.* (*coll.*) wonder, prodigy; вот н.!, э́ка(я) н.! (*iron.*) that's nothing.

невида́н|ный (~, ~а), *adj.* unprecedented.

невиди́мк|а, и 1. *m. and f.* invisible being; сде́латься ~ой to become invisible; челове́к-н. invisible man; ша́пка-н. cap of darkness. 2. invisible hairpin.

невиди́мост|ь, и, *f.* invisibility.

невиди́м|ый (~, ~а), *adj.* invisible.

невид|ный (~ен, ~на), *adj.* 1. invisible. 2. (*coll.*) insignificant.

невидя́щ|ий, *adj.* unseeing; смотре́ть ~им взгля́дом to look vacantly.

неви́нност|ь, и, *f.* (*in var. senses*) innocence.

неви́н|ный (~ен, ~на), *adj.* (*in var. senses*)

innocent; ~ная же́ртва innocent victim; ~ные удово́льствия innocent pleasures.

невино́в|ный (~ен, ~на), *adj.* (в+*p.*) innocent (of); (*leg.*) not guilty; призна́ть ~ным to acquit.

невку́с|ный (~ен, ~на), *adj.* unpalatable.

невменя́емост|ь, и, *f.* (*leg.*) irresponsibility.

невменя́ем|ый (~, ~а), *adj.* 1. (*leg.*) irresponsible. 2. (*coll.*) beside oneself.

невмеша́тельств|о, а, *n.* (*polit.*) non-intervention, non-interference.

невмого́ту, *adv.* (*coll.*; +*d.*) unbearable (to, for), unendurable (to, for); э́то мне н. I can't stand it, this is more than I can stand; ста́ло н. it became unbearable, it became too much.

невмо́чь = невмого́ту.

невнима́ни|е, я, *n.* 1. inattention; carelessness. 2. (к) lack of consideration (for).

невнима́тельност|ь, и, *f.* inattention, thoughtlessness.

невнима́тел|ьный (~ен, ~ьна), *adj.* (*in var. senses*) inattentive, thoughtless.

невня́т|ный (~ен, ~на), *adj.* indistinct, incomprehensible.

не́вод, а, *pl.* ~а́, ~о́в, *m.* seine, sweep-net.

невозбра́н|ный (~ен, ~на), *adj.* (*obs.*) free, unrestricted.

невозвра́т|ный (~ен, ~на), *adj.* irrevocable, irretrievable.

невозвраще́н|ец, ца, *m.* (*polit.*) defector.

невозвраще́ни|е, я, *n.* failure to return.

невозде́ланн|ый, *adj.* uncultivated, untilled; ~ая земля́ waste land.

невозде́ржанност|ь, и, *f.* intemperance; incontinence; (*fig.*) lack of self-control, lack of self-restraint.

невозде́ржан|ный (~, ~на), *adj.* intemperate; incontinent; (*fig.*) uncontrolled, unrestrained; он ~ на язы́к he has a loose tongue.

невозде́ржност|ь, и, *f.* = невозде́ржанность.

невозде́рж|ный (~ен, ~на), *adj.* = невозде́ржанный.

невозмо́жност|ь, и, *f.* impossibility; до ~и (*coll.*) to the last degree; за ~ью (+*g. or inf.*) owing to the impossibility (of).

невозмо́ж|ный (~ен, ~на), *adj.* 1. impossible; ~но (*impers., as pred.*) it is impossible; *as noun* ~ное, ~ного, *n.* the impossible. 2. insufferable.

невозмути́м|ый (~, ~а), *adj.* 1. imperturbable. 2. calm, unruffled.

невознагради́м|ый (~, ~а), *adj.* 1. irreparable. 2. that can never be repaid.

нево́лей, *adv.* (*obs.*) against one's will, forcibly.

невол|и́ть, ю, ишь, *impf.* (*of* при~) (*coll.*) to force, compel.

нево́льник, а, *m.* (*obs.*) slave.

нево́льн|ица, ицы, *f. of* ~ик.

нево́льничеств|о, а, *n.* (*obs.*) slavery.

нево́льн|ичий, *adj. of* ~ик; н. ры́нок slave market; н. труд slave labour.

нево́льно, *adv.* involuntarily; unintentionally, unwittingly.

нево́льн|ый, *adj.* 1. involuntary; unintentional. 2. forced; ~ая поса́дка forced landing.

нево́л|я, и, *f.* 1. bondage; captivity. 2. (*coll.*) necessity.

невообрази́м|ый (~, ~а), *adj.* unimaginable, inconceivable; н. шум (*fig.*) unimaginable din.

невооружённ|ый, *adj.* unarmed; ~ым гла́зом with the naked eye.

невоспи́танност|ь, и, *f.* ill breeding; bad manners.

невоспи́танный, *adj.* ill-bred.

невоспламеня́ем|ый (~, ~а), *adj.* uninflammable, non-inflammable.

невосполни́м|ый (~, ~а), *adj.* irreplaceable.

невосприи́мчивост|ь, и, *f.* 1. lack of receptivity. 2. (*med.*) immunity.

невосприи́мчив|ый (~, ~а), *adj.* 1. unreceptive. 2. (*med.*) (к) immune (to).

невостре́бованный, *adj.* not called for, unclaimed.

невпопа́д, *adv.* (*coll.*) out of place, inopportunely; отвеча́ть н. to answer irrelevantly.

невпроворо́т, *adv.* (*coll.*) 1. a lot, a great deal. 2. too much; э́то нам н. it's too hard for us.

невразуми́тел|ьный (~ен, ~ьна), *adj.* unintelligible, incomprehensible.

невралги́ческий, *adj.* neuralgic.

невралги́|я, и, *f.* neuralgia; н. седа́лищного не́рва sciatica.

неврасте́ник, а, *m.* neurasthenic.

неврастени́|ческий, *adj. of* ~я.

неврастени́ч|ный (~ен, ~на), *adj.* neurasthenic (*of person*).

неврастени́|я, и, *f.* neurasthenia.

невреди́м|ый (~, ~а), *adj.* unharmed, intact; цел и ~ safe and sound.

неври́т, а, *m.* neuritis.

невро́з, а, *m.* neurosis.

неврологи́ческий, *adj.* neurological.

невроло́ги|я, и, *f.* neurology.

невропато́лог, а, *m.* neuro-pathologist.

невропатоло́ги|я, и, *f.* neuro-pathology.

невроти́ческий, *adj.* neurotic.

невруче́ни|е, я, *n.* non-delivery.

невтерпёж, *adv.* (+*d.*; *coll.*) unbearable; мне, *etc.*, ста́ло н. I, *etc.*, cannot stand it any longer.

невы́год|а, ы, *f.* 1. disadvantage. 2. loss.

невы́год|ный (~ен, ~на), *adj.* 1. disadvantageous, unfavourable; показа́ть себя́ с ~ной стороны́ to place oneself in an unfavourable light, show oneself at a disadvantage; ста́вить в ~ное положе́ние to place at a disadvantage. **2.** unprofitable, unremunerative; ~но (*impers.*, *pred.*) it does not pay.

невы́держанност|ь, и, *f.* **1.** lack of self-control. **2.** inconsistency.

невы́держанный, *adj.* **1.** lacking self-control. **2.** inconsistent; н. стиль uneven style. **3.** (*of cheese, wine, etc.*) unmatured.

невы́езд, а, *m.* constant residence in one place; дать подпи́ску о ~е to give a written undertaking not to leave a place.

невыла́з|ный (~ен, ~на), *adj.* such that one cannot emerge from it; ~ная грязь a veritable quagmire; быть в ~ных долга́х (*fig.*) to be up to the eyes in debt.

невыноси́м|ый (~, ~а), *adj.* unbearable, insufferable, intolerable.

невыполне́ни|е, я, *n.* non-fulfilment; (+*g.*) failure to carry out.

невыполни́м|ый (~, ~а), *adj.* impracticable; unrealizable.

невырази́м|ый (~, ~а), *adj.* inexpressible, beyond expression; *as noun* ~ые, ~ых (*joc.*, *euph.*) inexpressibles (= pants).

невырази́тел|ьный (~ен, ~ьна), *adj.* inexpressive, expressionless.

невы́сказанный, *adj.* unexpressed, unsaid.

невысо́к|ий (~, ~а́, ~о), *adj.* rather low; rather short; ~ого ка́чества of poor quality; быть ~ого мне́ния (о+*p.*) to have a low opinion (of).

невы́ход, а, *m.* failure to appear; н. на рабо́ту absence (from work).

невя́зк|а, и, *f.* (*coll.*) discrepancy.

не́г|а, и, *f.* **1.** comfort; abundance. **2.** voluptuousness, languor.

негаси́м|ый (~, ~а), *adj.* (*rhet.*) ever-burning, eternal (*of flame, etc.*); unquenchable (*also fig.*).

негати́в, а, *m.* (*phot.*) negative.

негати́вный, *adj.* (*in var. senses*) negative.

негашён|ый, *adj.* ~ая и́звесть quick-lime.

не́где, *adv.* (+*inf.*) there is nowhere; н. доста́ть э́ту кни́гу this book is nowhere to be had; я́блоку н. упа́сть there's not an inch of room.

неги́бкий, *adj.* inflexible.

негла́сный, *adj.* secret.

неглиже́, *indecl.*, *n.* négligé.

неглижи́р|овать, ую, *impf.* (*coll.*, *obs.*; +*i.*) to neglect, disregard.

неглубо́кий, *adj.* rather shallow; (*fig.*) superficial.

неглу́п|ый (~, ~а́, ~о), *adj.* quite intelligent; он о́чень ~ he is no fool.

него́, *a. and g. of* он *when governed by preps.*

него́дник, а, *m.* reprobate, scoundrel; ne'er-do-well.

него́дност|ь, и, *f.* worthlessness; привести́ в н. to put out of commission.

него́д|ный (~ен, ~на), *adj.* **1.** unfit, unsuitable. **2.** worthless, good-for-nothing; н. чек dud cheque.

негодова́ни|е, я, *n.* indignation.

негод|ова́ть, у́ю, *impf.* (на+*a.*, про́тив) to be indignant (with).

негод|у́ющий, *pres. part. act. of* ~ова́ть *and adj.* indignant.

негодя́|й, я, *m.* scoundrel, rascal.

негостеприи́мный, *adj.* inhospitable.

негоциа́нт, а, *m.* (*obs.*) merchant.

чегр, а, *m.* black (man), Negro.

негра́мотност|ь, и, *f.* illiteracy (*also fig.*).

негра́мот|ный (~ен, ~на), *adj.* **1.** illiterate (*also fig.*); *as noun* н., ~ного, *m.*; ~ная, ~ной, *f.* illiterate person. **2.** (*fig.*) crude, inexpert.

негрит|ёнок, ёнка, *pl.* ~я́та, ~я́т, *m.* black child, Negro child, piccaninny.

негрито́с, а, *m.* negrito.

негритя́нк|а, и, *f.* black woman, Negress.

негритя́нский, *adj.* Negro.

негро́мкий, *adj.* low.

не́гр|ский = ~итя́нский.

не́гус, а, *m.* Negus.

неда́вний, *adj.* recent.

неда́вно, *adv.* recently.

недалёк|ий (~, ~а́, ~о *or* ~о́), *adj.* **1.** not far off, near; short; на ~ом расстоя́нии at a short distance. **2.** (*fig.*) not bright, dull-witted.

недалеко́ (*and* недалёко), *adv.* not far, near; за приме́ром идти́ н. one does not have to search far for an example.

недальнови́дност|ь, и, *f.* lack of foresight, short-sightedness (*fig.*).

недальнови́д|ный (~ен, ~на), *adj.* short-sighted (*fig.*).

неда́ром, *adv.* not for nothing, not without reason; not without purpose.

недви́жимост|ь, и, *f.* (*leg.*) immovable property, real estate.

недви́жим|ый[1], *adj.* immovable; ~ое иму́щество = ~ость.

недви́жим|ый[2], (~, ~а), *adj.* motionless.

недвусмы́сленный, *adj.* unequivocal, unambiguous.

недееспосо́б|ный (~ен, ~на), *adj.* **1.** (*leg.*) incapable. **2.** unable to function.

недействи́тельност|ь, и, *f.* **1.** ineffectiveness; inefficacity. **2.** (*leg.*) invalidity; nullity.

недействи́тел|ьный (~ен, ~ьна), *adj.* **1.** (*obs.*) ineffective, ineffectual. **2.** (*leg.*) invalid; null, null and void.

неделика́т|ный (~ен, ~на), *adj.* **1.** indelicate, indiscreet. **2.** rude, coarse.

недели́мост|ь, и, *f.* indivisibility.

недели́м|ый (~, ~a), *adj.* indivisible; **н. фонд** (*fig., leg.*) indivisible fund (*of a collective farm*).

неде́льный, *adj.* of a week's duration; **я вы́полню э́ту рабо́ту в н. срок** I will finish this work in a week's time; **н. о́тпуск** a week's leave.

неде́л|я, и, *f.* week; **~ями** for weeks (at a time); **на э́той ~e** this week.

недержа́ни|е, я, *n.* only in phrase **н. мочи́** (*med.*) irretention of urine.

неде́шево, *adv.* (*coll.*) at a considerable price, rather dear (*also fig.*).

недисциплини́рованност|ь, и, *f.* indiscipline.

недисциплини́рованный, *adj.* undisciplined.

недобо́р, а, *m.* arrears; shortage.

недоброжела́тел|ь, я, *m.* ill-wisher.

недоброжела́тельност|ь, и, *f.* malevolence, ill-will.

недоброжела́тел|ьный (~ен, ~ьна), *adj.* malevolent, ill-disposed.

недоброжела́тель|ство = **~ность.**

недоброка́чественност|ь, и, *f.* poor quality, bad quality.

недоброка́чествен|ный (~, ~на), *adj.* of poor quality, low-grade, bad.

недобросо́вестност|ь, и, *f.* **1.** bad faith; unscrupulousness, lack of scruple. **2.** carelessness.

недобросо́вест|ный (~ен, ~на), *adj.* **1.** unscrupulous. **2.** lacking in conscientiousness; careless.

недо́бр|ый, *adj.* **1.** unkind; unfriendly. **2.** bad, evil; **~ая весть** bad news; **~ые лю́ди** (*obs.*) wicked men (*euph.* = brigands).

недове́ри|е, я, *n.* distrust; mistrust; **во́тум ~я** vote of no confidence.

недове́рчив|ый (~, ~a), *adj.* distrustful; mistrustful.

недове́с, а, *m.* short weight.

недове́|сить, шу, сишь, *pf.* (*of* **~шивать**) **1.** (+*g.*) to give short weight (of). **2.** to prove to be short-weight.

недове́шива|ть, ю, *impf. of* **недове́сить.**

недово́л|ьный (~ен, ~ьна), *adj.* (+*i.*) dissatisfied, discontented, displeased (with); *as noun* **н., ~ьного,** *m.* malcontent.

недово́льств|о, а, *n.* dissatisfaction, discontent, displeasure.

недовы́работк|а, и, *f.* underproduction.

недога́длив|ый (~, ~a), *adj.* slow(-witted).

недогля|де́ть, жу́, ди́шь, *pf.* **1.** (+*g.*) to overlook, miss. **2.** (за+*i.*) not to take sufficient care (of), not to look after properly.

недоговорённост|ь, и, *f.* **1.** reticence. **2.** lack of agreement.

недогру́зк|а, и, *f.* underloading; (*fig.*) short time (*in factory or works*).

недода|ва́ть, ю́, ёшь, *impf. of* **~ть.**

недо|да́ть, да́м, да́шь, да́ст, дади́м, дади́те даду́т, *past* **~да́л, ~дала́, ~да́ло,** *pf.* (*o* **~дава́ть**) to give short; to deliver short **он мне ~да́л три рубля́** he gave me three roubles short.

недода́ч|а, и, *f.* deficiency in payment o supply.

недоде́ланный, *adj.* unfinished.

недоде́лк|а, и, *f.* incompleteness.

недодерж|а́ть, у́, ~ишь, *pf.* **1.** (*phot.*) t under-expose; to under-develop. **2.** to keep for too short a time in the necessary place

недоде́ржк|а, и, *f.* **1.** (*phot.*) under-exposure under-development. **2.** keeping for to short a time in the necessary place.

недоеда́ни|е, я, *n.* under-nourishment, ma nutrition.

недоеда́|ть, ю, *impf.* to be undernourished be underfed.

недозво́лен|ный (~, ~a), *adj.* illicit, unlaw ful.

недозре́лый, *adj.* unripe, immature (*als fig.*).

недоймк|а, и, *f.* arrears.

недои́м|очный, *adj. of* **~ка.**

недои́мщик, а, *m.* person in arrears (i paying taxes, *etc.*).

недока́зан|ный (~, ~a), *adj.* not proved not proven.

недоказа́тельный, *adj.* unconvincing, in adequate.

недоказу́емый, *adj.* indemonstrable.

недоко́нчен|ный (~, ~a), *adj.* unfinished incomplete.

недолга́, *only in phrase* **(вот) и вся н.** (*coll.* and that is all there is to it.

недо́л|гий (~ог, ~га́, ~го), *adj.* short, brie

недо́лго, *adv.* **1.** not long; **н.** ду́мая withou hesitation. **2.** (*coll.*) **н. и** (+*inf.*) one ca easily; it is easy (to), it is a simple matte (to); **тут и потону́ть н.** one could easil drown here; **недо́лго и до греха́** seriou trouble could easily happen.

недолгове́ч|ный (~ен, ~на), *adj.* short -lived, ephemeral.

недолёт, а, *m.* (*mil.*) falling short (*of bullet* *shells*).

недолю́блива|ть, ю, *impf.* (+*a.* or *g.*; *coll.* not to be overfond of; **они́ ~ли дру друга** there was no love lost between them

недоме́рива|ть, ю, *impf. of* **недоме́рить.**

недоме́р|ить, ю, ишь, *pf.* (*of* **~ивать**) t give short measure.

недоме́р|ок, ка, *m.* undersize object.

недомога́ни|е, я, *n.* indisposition.

недомога́|ть, ю, *impf.* to be indisposed, b unwell.

недомо́лвк|а, и, *f.* innuendo; reservatio omission.

недомы́сли|е, я, *n.* thoughtlessness, inability to think things out.

недонесе́ни|е, я, *n.* failure to give information (*concerning crime committed or meditated*); н. о преступле́нии (*leg.*) misprision of felony.

недоно́с|ок, ка, *m.* **1.** prematurely born child. **2.**(*fig.*, *coll.*, *pejor.*) retarded person, immature person.

недоно́шен|ный (~, ~а), *adj.* prematurely born.

недооце́нива|ть, ю, *impf. of* недооцени́ть.

недооцен|и́ть, ю́, ~ишь, *pf.* (*of* ~ивать) to underestimate, underrate.

недооце́нк|а, и, *f.* underestimation, underestimate.

недопечённый, *adj.* half-baked.

недополуч|а́ть, а́ю, *impf. of* ~и́ть.

недополуч|и́ть, у́, ~ишь, *pf.* (*of* ~а́ть) to receive less (than one's due).

недопусти́м|ый (~, ~а), *adj.* inadmissible, intolerable.

недора́звитост|ь, и, *f.* under-development, backwardness.

недора́звит|ый, *adj.* under-developed, backward; ~ые стра́ны (*polit.*, *econ.*) under-developed countries.

недоразуме́ни|е, я, *n.* misunderstanding.

недо́рого, *adv.* not dear, cheaply.

недор|ого́й (~ог, ~ога́, ~ого), *adj.* inexpensive; reasonable (*of price*).

недоро́д, а, *m.* harvest failure.

не́доросл|ь, я, *m.* **1.** (*hist.*) minor. **2.** (*fig.*, *coll.*) young ignoramus, young oaf.

недоска́занност|ь, и, *f.* understatement.

недослы́ш|ать, у, ишь, *pf.* **1.** (+*a.* or *g.*) to fail to hear all of. **2.** (*intrans.*; *coll.*) to be hard of hearing.

недосмо́тр, а, *m.* oversight.

недосмотр|е́ть, ю́, ~ишь, *pf.* **1.** (+*g.*) to overlook, miss. **2.** (за+*i.*) not to take sufficient care (of), not to look after properly.

недосо́л, а, *m.* insufficient salting; н. на столе́, *see* пересо́л.

недос|па́ть, плю́, пи́шь, *pf.* (*of* ~ыпа́ть) not to have one's sleep out.

недоста|ва́ть, ёт, *impf.* (*of* ~ть) (*impers.*; +*g.*) to be missing, be lacking, be wanting; ему́ ~ёт о́пыта he lacks experience; мне о́чень ~ва́ло вас I missed you very much; э́того ещё ~ва́ло! that would be (*or* is) the limit!, that would be (*or* is) the last straw!

недоста́т|ок, ка, *m.* **1.** (+*g.* or в+*p.*) shortage (of), lack (of), deficiency (in); за ~ком (+*g.*) for want (of); име́ть н. в рабо́чей си́ле to be short-handed. **2.** shortcoming, imperfection; defect; н. зре́ния defective eyesight.

недоста́точно, *adv.* **1.** insufficiently. **2.** not enough.

недоста́точност|ь, и, *f.* insufficiency; inadequacy.

недоста́точ|ный (~ен, ~на), *adj.* insufficient; inadequate; н. глаго́л (*gram.*) defective verb.

недоста́|ть, нет, *pf. of* ~ва́ть.

недоста́ч|а, и, *f.* (*coll.*) lack, shortage.

недостаю́щий, *adj.* missing.

недостижи́м|ый (~, ~а), *adj.* unattainable.

недостове́р|ный (~ен, ~на), *adj.* not authentic, apocryphal.

недосто́|йный (~ин, ~йна), *adj.* unworthy.

недосту́пност|ь, и, *f.* inaccessibility.

недосту́п|ный (~ен, ~на), *adj.* inaccessible (*also fig.*); э́то ~но моему́ понима́нию it is beyond my comprehension.

недосу́г, а, *m.* (*coll.*) lack of time, lack of leisure; придёт он на конце́рт? нет, ему́, мол, н. is he coming to the concert? No, he says he is busy.

недосчит|а́ться, а́юсь, *pf.* (*of* ~ываться) (+*g.*) to find missing, miss; to be out (in one's accounts); он ~а́лся десяти́ рубле́й he found he was ten roubles short; по́сле налёта мы ~а́лись трёх бомбардиро́вщиков after the raid we found three of our bombers were missing.

недосчи́тыва|ться, юсь, *impf. of* недосчита́ться.

недосыпа́|ть, ю, *impf. of* недоспа́ть.

недосяга́ем|ый (~, ~а), *adj.* unattainable.

недотёп|а, ы, *m. and f.* (*coll.*) duffer.

недотро́г|а, и, *m. and f.* (*coll.*) touchy person.

недоумева́|ть, ю, *impf.* to be perplexed, be at a loss; to wonder.

недоуме́ни|е, я, *n.* perplexity, bewilderment; быть в ~и to be in a quandary.

недоуме́нный, *adj.* puzzled, perplexed.

недоу́чк|а, и, *m. and f.* (*coll.*) half-educated person.

недохва́тк|а, и, *f.* (*coll.*) shortage.

недочёт, а, *m.* **1.** deficit; shortage. **2.** defect, shortcoming.

не́др|а, ~, *no sing.* **1.** depths (*of the earth*); н. земли́ bowels of the earth; разве́дка ~ prospecting of mineral wealth. **2.** (*fig.*) depths, heart.

недрема́нн|ый, *adj.* (*obs.*) unwinking, unslumbering; ~ое о́ко (*fig.*, *iron.*) the unwinking eye (*sc.* of authority).

недре́млющий, *adj.* unwinking, unslumbering; vigilant, watchful.

не́друг, а, *m.* enemy, foe.

недружелю́б|ный (~ен, ~на), *adj.* unfriendly.

недру́жный, *adj.* disunited; disjointed.

неду́г, а, *m.* ailment, disease.

недужи́т|ься, ~ся, *impf.* (*impers.*; +*d.*; *coll.*) to be unwell, be poorly.

недýрно, *adv.* not badly, well enough; н.! not bad!

недур|нóй (∼ён, ∼нá, ∼но), *adj.* 1. not bad. 2. (собóй) not bad-looking.

недюжинный, *adj.* out of the ordinary, outstanding, exceptional.

неё, *a. and g.* of онá *when governed by preps.*

неестéствен|ный (∼, ∼на), *adj.* (*in var. senses*) unnatural.

неждáнно, *adv.* (*coll.*) unexpectedly; н.--негáданно quite unexpectedly.

неждáнный, *adj.* (*coll.*) unexpected.

нежелáни|е, я, *n.* unwillingness, disinclination.

нежелáтел|ьный (∼ен, ∼ьна), *adj.* 1. undesirable. 2. unwanted; (+*d.*) contrary to the wishes (of); н. посетńтель unwanted visitor; э́то бы́ло мне ∼ьно it was not what I wanted.

нéжели, *conj.* (*obs.*) than.

нéженк|а, и, *m. and f.* (*coll.*) molly-coddle.

нежив|óй, *adj.* 1. lifeless; родńться ∼ы́м to be still-born. 2. inanimate, inorganic. 3. (*fig.*) dull, lifeless.

нежńзнен|ный (∼, ∼на), *adj.* 1. impracticable; inapplicable. 2. weird.

нежилóй, *adj.* 1. uninhabited. 2. not fit for habitation; uninhabitable.

нéжит|ь¹, и, *f.* (*collect.*) (*in Russian folklore*) the spirits (*gnomes, goblins, etc.*).

нéж|ить², у, ишь, *impf.* to pamper, coddle; caress.

нéж|иться, усь, ишься, *impf.* to luxuriate; н. на сóлнце to bask in the sun.

нéжнича|ть, ю, *impf.* (*coll.*) 1. to bill and coo, canoodle. 2. (*fig.*) to be over-indulgent.

нéжност|ь, и, *f.* 1. tenderness. 2. delicacy. 3. (*pl. only*) display of affection, endearments; compliments, flattery.

нéж|ный (∼ен, ∼нá, ∼но), *adj.* 1. tender; affectionate; ∼ные взгля́ды tender glances. 2. delicate (= soft, fine, *of colours, taste, skin, etc.*). 3. tender, delicate; н. пол the weaker sex.

незабвéн|ный (∼, ∼на), *adj.* unforgettable.

незабýдк|а, и, *f.* (*bot.*) forget-me-not.

незабывáем|ый (∼, ∼а), *adj.* unforgettable.

незавéренный, *adj.* uncertified.

незавńд|ный (∼ен, ∼на), *adj.* unenviable; poor.

незавńсимо, *adv.* independently; н. от irrespective of.

незавńсимост|ь, и, *f.* independence.

незавńсим|ый (∼, ∼а), *adj.* independent.

незавńсящ|ий, *only in phrase* по ∼им от нас, *etc.*, обстоя́тельствам (*or* причńнам) owing to circumstances beyond our, *etc.*, control.

незадáч|а, и, *f.* (*coll.*) ill-luck.

незадáчлив|ый (∼, ∼а), *adj.* (*coll.*) unlucky, luckless.

незадóлго, *adv.* (до, пéред) shortly (before), not long (before).

незаконнорождённост|ь, и, ***f.* illegitimacy.

незаконнорождённый, *adj.* illegitimate.

незакóнност|ь, и, ***f.* illegality, unlawfulness.

незакóнный, *adj.* illegal, illicit, unlawful; illegitimate.

незакономéрност|ь, и, ***f.* exceptionality, exceptional character.

незакономéр|ный (∼ен, ∼на), *adj.* exceptional.

незакóнченност|ь, и, ***f.* incompleteness unfinished state.

незакóнчен|ный (∼, ∼а), *adj.* incomplete, unfinished.

незамедлńтельно, *adv.* without delay.

незамедлńтел|ьный (∼ен, ∼ьна), *adj.* immediate.

незаменńм|ый (∼, ∼а), *adj.* 1. irreplaceable. 2. indispensable.

незамерзáющий, *adj.* non-freezing; ice-free; (*tech.*) anti-freeze.

незамéтно, *adv.* imperceptibly, insensibly.

незамéт|ный (∼ен, ∼на), *adj.* 1. imperceptible. 2. inconspicuous, insignificant.

незамýжняя, *adj.* unmarried, single, maiden.

незамыслoвáт|ый (∼, ∼а), *adj.* simple, uncomplicated.

незапáмятн|ый, *adj.* immemorial; с ∼ых времён from time immemorial.

незапя́тнанный, *adj.* unsullied, stainless.

незарабóтанный, *adj.* unearned.

незаразный, *adj.* non-contagious.

незаслýжен|ный (∼, ∼на), *adj.* undeserved, unmerited.

незастрóенный, *adj.* undeveloped, not built over.

незатéйлив|ый (∼, ∼а), *adj.* simple, plain; modest.

незатухáющий, *adj.* (*radio*) undamped; continuous.

незаурń́д|ный (∼ен, ∼на), *adj.* outstanding, exceptional.

нéзачем, *adv.* (+*inf.*) there is no point (in), it is pointless; there is no need (to); it is no use, it is useless; н. бóльше ждать there is no point in waiting any longer.

незашифрóванный, *adj.* not in cipher, not in code; en clair.

незвáный, *adj.* uninvited.

нездéшний, *adj.* 1. (*coll.*) not of these parts; я н. I am a stranger here. 2. unearthly, supernatural, mysterious; н. мир the other world.

нездорóвит|ься, ∼ся, *impf.* (*impers.*; +*d.*) to feel unwell.

нездорóв|ый (∼, ∼а), *adj.* 1. unhealthy, morbid (*also fig.*); sickly; unwholesome;

~ая обстано́вка unhealthy environment.
2. (*pred.*) unwell, poorly.
нездоро́вь|е, я, *n.* indisposition; ill-health.
неземно́й, *adj.* **1.** (*obs.*) supernatural, un-earthly. **2.** not belonging *or* pertaining to the earth.
незло́бив|ый (~, ~а), *adj.* mild, forgiving.
незлопа́мят|ный (~ен, ~на), *adj.* forgiving.
незнако́м|ец, ца, *m.* stranger.
незнако́м|ка, ки, *f. of* ~ец.
незнако́м|ый (~, ~а), *adj.* **1.** unknown, unfamiliar. **2.** (с+*i.*) unacquainted (with).
незна́ни|е, я, *n.* ignorance.
незна́чащий, *adj.* insignificant, of no signi-ficance.
незначи́тел|ьный (~ен, ~ьна), *adj.* insig-nificant, negligible; unimportant.
незна́ющ|ий, *adj.* (+*g.*) ignorant (of); н. уста́ли indefatigable; ~ая грани́ц любо́вь love that knows no bounds.
незре́лост|ь, и, *f.* unripeness; (*fig.*) imma-turity.
незре́л|ый (~, ~а), *adj.* unripe (*also fig.*); (*fig.*) immature.
незри́м|ый (~, ~а), *adj.* invisible.
незы́блем|ый (~, ~а), *adj.* unshakeable, stable.
неизбе́жност|ь, и, *f.* inevitability.
неизбе́ж|ный (~ен, ~на), *adj.* inevitable, unavoidable; inescapable.
неизбы́в|ный (~ен, ~на), *adj.* unescapable, permanent.
неизве́дан|ный (~, ~на), *adj.* unexplored, unknown; not experienced before.
неизве́стност|ь, и, *f.* **1.** uncertainty; быть в ~и (о+*p.*) to be uncertain (about), be in the dark (about). **2.** obscurity; жить в ~и to live in obscurity.
неизве́ст|ный (~ен, ~на), *adj.* (*in var. senses*) unknown; uncertain; ~но где, когда, *etc.*, no one knows where, when, *etc.* (= somewhere, at some time, *etc.*); *as noun* н., ~ного, *m.*, ~ная, ~ной, *f.* unknown person; ~ное, ~ного, *n.* (*math.*) unknown (quantity).
неизвини́тел|ьный (~ен, ~ьна), *adj.* inex-cusable, unpardonable.
неизглади́м|ый (~, ~а), *adj.* indelible, in-effaceable.
неи́зданный, *adj.* unpublished.
неизлечи́м|ый (~, ~а), *adj.* incurable.
неизме́н|ный (~ен, ~на), *adj.* **1.** invariable, immutable. **2.** (*rhet.*) devoted, true.
неизменя́ем|ый (~, ~а), *adj.* unalterable.
неизмери́мо, *adv.* immeasurably.
неизмери́мост|ь, и, *f.* immeasurability; immensity.
неизмери́м|ый (~, ~а), *adj.* immeasurable; immense.
неизрече́нный, *adj.* (*obs.*) ineffable.

неизъясни́м|ый (~, ~а), *adj.* inexplicable; ineffable, indescribable.
неиме́ни|е, я, *n.* absence; lack, want; за ~ем лу́чшего for want of something better.
неимове́р|ный (~ен, ~на), *adj.* incredible, unbelievable.
неиму́щий, *adj.* indigent, poor.
неискорени́м|ый (~, ~а), *adj.* ineradicable.
неи́скрен|ний (~ен, ~на), *adj.* insincere.
неи́скренност|ь, и, *f.* insincerity.
неиску́с|ный (~ен, ~на), *adj.* unskilful, in-expert.
неискушённост|ь, и, *f.* inexperience, inno-cence.
неискушён|ный (~, ~а́), *adj.* inexperi-enced, innocent, unsophisticated.
неисповеди́м|ый (~, ~а), *adj.* inscrutable.
неисполне́ни|е, я, *n.* non-execution, non--performance; н. зако́на failure to observe a law.
неисполни́м|ый (~, ~а), *adj.* impractic-able; unrealizable.
неиспо́рчен|ный (~, ~а), *adj.* (*fig.*) un-spoiled, innocent.
неиспо́рченност|ь, и, *f.* (*fig.*) innocence.
неисправи́м|ый (~, ~а), *adj.* **1.** incorri-gible. **2.** irremediable, irreparable.
неиспра́вност|ь, и, *f.* **1.** disrepair. **2.** care-lessness.
неиспра́в|ный (~ен, ~на), *adj.* **1.** out of order; faulty, defective. **2.** careless.
неиспы́танный, *adj.* untried, untested.
неиссяка́ем|ый (~, ~а), *adj.* inexhaustible.
неи́стовств|о, а, *n.* **1.** fury, frenzy. **2.** bru-tality, savagery.
неи́стовств|овать, ую, *impf.* **1.** to rage, rave. **2.** to commit brutalities.
неи́стов|ый (~, ~а), *adj.* furious, frenzied; ~ые апло́дисме́нты tempestuous applause.
неистощи́м|ый (~, ~а), *adj.* inexhaustible.
неистреби́м|ый (~, ~а), *adj.* ineradicable; undying.
неисчерпа́ем|ый (~, ~а), *adj.* inexhaustible.
неисчисли́м|ый (~, ~а), *adj.* innumerable; incalculable.
ней, *d.*, *i.*, *and p. of* она́ when governed by *preps.*
нейзи́льбер, а, *m.* German silver.
нейло́н, а, *m.* nylon.
нейло́новый, *adj.* nylon, made of nylon.
неймёт (*no other form in use*), *impf.*, *only in prov.* (хоть) ви́дит о́ко, да зуб н. there's many a slip 'twixt cup and lip.
неймётся, *impf.* (*impers.*; +*d.*; *coll.*) ему́ н. he is set on it, there is no holding him; ей н. she will not sit still.
нейро́н, а, *m.* (*physiol.*) neuron.
нейтрализа́ци|я, и, *f.* (*in var. senses*) neutral-ization.
нейтрали́зм, а, *m.* (*polit.*) neutralism.

нейтрализ|ова́ть, у́ю, *impf. and pf.* (*in var. senses*) to neutralize.

нейтралите́т, а, *m.* (*polit.*) neutrality.

нейтра́льност|ь, и, *f.* (*in var. senses*) neutrality.

нейтра́л|ьный (~ен, ~ьна), *adj.* (*in var. senses*) neutral.

нейтро́н, а, *m.* (*phys.*) neutron.

неказ́ист|ый (~, ~а), *adj.* (*coll.*) not much to look at; unprepossessing.

неквалифиц́ированный, *adj.* unqualified; **н.** рабо́чий unskilled labourer.

не́кий, *pron.* a certain; a kind of; вас спра́шивал н. господ́ин Па́влов a (certain) Mr. Pavlov was asking for you.

некле́точный, *adj.* (*biol.*) non-cellular.

не́когда¹, *adv.* once, formerly; in the old days.

не́когда², *adv.* there is no time; мне сего́дня н. разгова́ривать с ва́ми I have no time to chat today.

не́кого, не́кому, не́кем, не́ о ком, *pron.* (+*inf.*) there is nobody (to); н. вин́ить nobody is to blame; ей не́ с кем пойт́и she has nobody to go with (her).

неколеб́имый = непоколеб́имый.

некомпете́нт|ный (~ен, ~на), *adj.* not competent, unqualified.

некомпле́кт|ный (~ен, ~на), *adj.* incomplete; not up to strength.

некороно́ванный, *adj.* uncrowned.

некорре́ктност|ь, и, *f.* discourtesy, impoliteness.

некорре́кт|ный (~ен, ~на), *adj.* discourteous, impolite.

не́котор|ый, *pron.* some; он ~ое вре́мя не дв́игался с ме́ста for a time he did not budge; мы с ~ых пор живём здесь we have been living here for some time; ~ым о́бразом somehow, in some way; в, до ~ой сте́пени to some extent, to a certain extent; *as noun* ~ые, ~ых, some; some people.

некрас́ив|ый (~, ~а), *adj.* 1. ugly, not good-looking; unsightly. 2. (*coll.*; *of conduct, actions, etc.*) ugly, dirty.

некредитоспосо́бност|ь, и, *f.* insolvency.

некредитоспосо́б|ный (~ен, ~на), *adj.* insolvent.

некре́п|кий (~ок, ~ка́), *adj.* rather weak.

некро́з, а, *m.* (*med.*) necrosis.

некроло́г, а, *m.* obituary (notice).

некрома́нти|я, и, *f.* necromancy.

некро́пол|ь, я, *m.* necropolis.

некру́п|ный (~ен, ~на́, ~но), *adj.* medium-sized, not large.

некры́т|ый (~, ~а), *adj.* roofless.

некста́ти, *adv.* inopportunely; mal à propos. вот н.! what a nuisance!

некта́р, а, *m.* nectar.

не́кто, *pron.* someone; н. Петро́в one Petrov, a certain Petrov.

не́куда, *adv.* (+*inf.*) there is nowhere (to); мне н. пойт́и I have nowhere to go.

некульту́рност|ь, и, f. 1. low level of civilization; uncivilized ways. 2. bad manners, boorishness.

некульту́р|ный (~ен, ~на), *adj.* 1. uncivilized; backward. 2. rough(-mannered), boorish. 3. (*bot.*) uncultivated.

некуря́щ|ий, *adj.* non-smoking; *as noun* **н., ~его,** *m.* non-smoker; ваго́н для ~их non-smoking carriage.

нела́д|ный (~ен, ~на), *adj.* (*coll.*) wrong, bad; у него́ ~но с гру́дью there is something the matter with his chest; будь он ~ен! blast him!

нела́д|ы, о́в, *no sing.* (*coll.*) 1. discord, disagreement; у них н. they don't hit it off. 2. trouble, something wrong.

нела́сковый, *adj.* reserved, unfriendly.

нелега́льност|ь, и, f. illegality.

нелега́л|ьный (~ен, ~ьна), *adj.* illegal; перейт́и на ~ьное положе́ние (*of resistance movements, etc.*) to go underground.

нелега́льщин|а, ы, f. (*coll.*) illegal activities; illegal literature.

нелёгкая (*coll.*) н. его́ сюда́ несёт! what the deuce brings him here?; куда́ их н. понесла́? where the deuce have they gone?

нелёг|кий (~ок, ~ка́), *adj.* 1. difficult, not easy. 2. heavy, not light (*also fig.*).

неле́пост|ь, и, f. absurdity, nonsense.

неле́п|ый (~, ~а), *adj.* absurd, ridiculous.

неле́ст|ный (~ен, ~на), *adj.* unflattering, uncomplimentary.

нелету́чий, *adj.* (*chem.*) non-volatile.

нелицеприя́т|ный (~ен, ~на), *adj.* (*obs.*) impartial.

нел́ишний, *adj.* not superfluous; not out of place.

нело́в|кий (~ок, ~ка́, ~ко), *adj.* 1. awkward; gauche; clumsy. 2. uncomfortable. 3. (*fig.*) awkward; embarrassing; ~кое молча́ние awkward silence; ~ко при нём ссыла́ться на э́то it is awkward to refer to it in his presence; ему́ ~ко приглаша́ть бал незнако́мую да́му he feels awkward about inviting a lady he does not know to the dance.

нело́вко, *adv.* awkwardly; uncomfortably; чу́вствовать себя́ н. to feel ill at ease, feel awkward, feel uncomfortable.

нело́вкост|ь, и, f. 1. awkwardness, gaucherie, clumsiness (*also fig.*); чу́вствовать н. to feel awkward, feel uncomfortable. 2. blunder, gaffe.

нелоѓичност|ь, и, f. illogicality.

нелоѓич|ный (~ен, ~на), *adj.* illogical.

нельзя́, *adv.* (+*inf.*) 1. it is impossible; н

не призна́ть it is impossible not to admit, one cannot but admit. **2.** it is not allowed; здесь н. кури́ть smoking is not allowed here. **3.** one ought not, one should not; н. ложи́ться (спать) так по́здно you ought not to go to bed so late. **4.** как н. (+*comp. adv.*) as . . . as possible; как н. лу́чше in the best possible way.

не́льм|а, ы, *f.* white salmon.

нелюбе́зност|ь, и, *f.* ungraciousness; discourtesy.

нелюбе́з|ный (~ен, ~на), *adj.* ungracious, unobliging; discourteous.

нелюби́м|ый (~, ~а), *adj.* unloved.

нелюб|о́вь, ви́, *f.* (к) dislike (for).

нелюбопы́т|ный (~ен, ~на), *adj.* **1.** incurious. **2.** uninteresting.

нелюди́м, а, *m.* unsociable person.

нелюди́м|ый (~, ~а), *adj.* unsociable.

нём, *p. of* он, оно́.

нема́ло, *adv.* **1.** not a little; not a few. **2.** a good deal; considerably.

немалова́ж|ный (~ен, ~на), *adj.* of no small importance.

нема́лый, *adj.* no small; considerable.

неме́дленно, *adv.* immediately, forthwith.

неме́дленный, *adj.* immediate.

неме́ркнущий, *adj.* (*fig., rhet.*) unfading.

неме́тчин|а, ы, *f.* (*obs.*) **1.** Germany; foreign parts. **2.** (*pejor.*) German (or foreign) way of life.

неме́|ть, ю, *impf.* (*of* о~) **1.** to become dumb, grow dumb. **2.** (*pf. also* за~) to become numb, grow numb.

не́м|ец, ца, *m.* **1.** German. **2.** (*obs.*) foreigner.

неме́цк|ий, *adj.* **1.** German; ~ая овча́рка Alsatian (dog). **2.** (*obs.*) foreign.

немига́ющий, *adj.* unwinking.

немилосе́рд|ный (~ен, ~на), *adj.* merciless, unmerciful (*also fig.*).

неми́лостив|ый (~, ~а), *adj.* ungracious; harsh.

неми́лост|ь, и, *f.* disgrace, disfavour; впасть в н. to fall into disgrace.

неми́л|ый (~, ~а́, ~о), *adj.* (*folk poet.*) unloved; hated.

немину́ем|ый (~, ~а), *adj.* inevitable, unavoidable.

не́мк|а, и, *f.* German (woman).

немно́г|ие, *adj.* few, a few; *as noun* н., ~их few.

немно́го, *adv.* **1.** (+*g.*) a little, some, not much; a few, not many; вре́мени оста́лось н. little time is left, time is short. **2.** a little, somewhat, slightly; я н. уста́л I am a little tired; н. спустя́ not long after.

немно́г|ое, ого, *n.* few things, little.

немногосло́в|ный (~ен, ~на), *adj.* laconic, brief, terse.

немно́жко, *adv.* (*coll.*) a little; a trifle, a bit.

немну́щийся, *adj.* (*text.*) non-creasing crease-resistant; 'non-iron'.

немо́жется, *impers.*; +*d.* (*coll.*) мне, *etc.* н. I, *etc.*, am unwell, poorly.

нем|о́й (~, ~а́, ~о), *adj.* **1.** dumb; ~а́я а́збука deaf-and-dumb alphabet; *as noun* н., ~о́го, *m.* dumb man, mute; ~ы́е (*collect.*) the dumb. **2.** (*fig.*) dead, silent; ~а́я тишина́ deathly hush. **3.** (*fig.*) mute; н. согла́сный (*ling.*) mute consonant; н. фильм silent film.

немо́лчный, *adj.* (*poet.*) incessant, unceasing.

немот|а́, ы́, *f.* dumbness; muteness.

не́моч|ь, и, *f.* (*coll.*) illness, sickness; бле́дная н. (*med.*) chlorosis, green sickness; чёрная н. (*coll., obs.*) falling sickness (*epilepsy*).

не́мощ|ный (~ен, ~на), *adj.* sick; feeble, sickly.

не́мощ|ь, и, *f.* (*coll.*) sickness; feebleness.

нему́, *d. of* он, оно́ *after preps.*

немудрён|ый (~, ~а́), *adj.* (*coll.*) simple, easy; э́то де́ло ~ое it is a simple matter; ~о́ (*impers.*; *as pred.*) it is no wonder.

немы́слим|ый (~, ~а), *adj.* (*coll.*) unthinkable, inconceivable.

ненави́|деть, жу, дишь, *impf.* to hate, detest, loathe.

ненави́стник, а, *m.* hater.

ненави́ст|ный (~ен, ~на), *adj.* hated; hateful.

не́навист|ь, и, *f.* hatred, detestation.

ненагля́дный, *adj.* (*coll.*) **1.** beloved. **2.** (*folk poet.*) wondrously beautiful.

ненадёванный, *adj.* (*coll.*) new, not yet worn.

ненадёж|ный (~ен, ~на), *adj.* unreliable, untrustworthy; insecure.

ненадобност|ь, и, *f.* uselessness; за ~ью as not wanted.

ненадо́лго, *adv.* for a short while, not for long.

ненаме́ренно, *adv.* unintentionally, unwittingly, accidentally.

ненаме́рен|ный (~, ~а), *adj.* unintentional, accidental.

ненападе́ни|е, я, *n.* non-aggression; пакт о ~и non-aggression pact.

ненаро́ком, *adv.* (*coll.*) unintentionally, accidentally.

ненаруши́м|ый (~, ~а), *adj.* inviolable.

ненаст|ный (~ен, ~на), *adj.* (*of weather*) bad, foul.

ненастоя́щий, *adj.* artificial; counterfeit.

ненасть|е, я, *n.* bad, foul weather.

ненасы́т|ный (~ен, ~на), *adj.* insatiable (*also fig.*).

ненатура́л|ьный (~ен, ~ьна), *adj.* **1.** affected; not natural. **2.** ~artificial, imitation.

ненау́ч|ный (~ен, ~на), *adj.* unscientific.

ненорма́льност|ь, и, *f.* abnormality.

ненорма́л|ьный (~ен, ~ьна), *adj.* **1.** (*in var. senses*) abnormal. **2.** mad.

нену́ж|ный (~ен, ~на́, ~но), *adj.* unnecessary; superfluous.

необду́ман|ный (~, ~на), *adj.* thoughtless, precipitate.

необеспе́ченн|ый, *adj.* **1.** without means; unprovided for; ~ая жизнь precarious existence. **2.** (+*i.*) not provided (with).

необита́ем|ый (~, ~а), *adj.* uninhabited; н. о́стров desert island.

необозри́м|ый (~, ~а), *adj.* boundless, immense.

необосно́ванност|ь, и, *f.* groundlessness.

необосно́ван|ный (~, ~на), *adj.* unfounded, groundless.

необрабо́тан|ный (~, ~а), *adj.* **1.** (*of land*) uncultivated, untilled. **2.** (*of materials*) raw, crude. **3.** (*fig.*) unpolished; untrained.

необразо́ванност|ь, и, *f.* lack of education.

необразо́ван|ный (~, ~на), *adj.* uneducated.

необрати́м|ый (~, ~а), *adj.* irreversible.

необу́здан|ный (~, ~на), *adj.* unbridled; ungovernable.

необходи́мост|ь, и, *f.* necessity; по ~и perforce, necessarily.

необходи́м|ый (~, ~а), *adj.* necessary, essential; ~о (*impers.*; *as pred.*) it is necessary, it is imperative.

необщи́тел|ьный (~ен, ~ьна), *adj.* unsociable.

необъясни́м|ый (~, ~а), *adj.* inexplicable, unaccountable.

необъя́т|ный (~ен, ~на), *adj.* immense, unbounded.

необыкнове́н|ный (~ен, ~на), *adj.* unusual, uncommon.

необыча́|йный (~ен, ~йна), *adj.* extraordinary, exceptional.

необы́ч|ный (~ен, ~на), *adj.* unusual.

необяза́тел|ьный (~ен, ~ьна), *adj.* **1.** not obligatory, optional. **2.** unobliging.

неограни́чен|ный (~, ~на), *adj.* unlimited, unbounded; ~ная мона́рхия absolute monarchy; ~ные полномо́чия plenary powers.

неоднокра́тно, *adv.* repeatedly.

неоднокра́тный, *adj.* repeated.

неодноро́дност|ь, и, *f.* heterogeneity; н. строе́ния (*tech.*) non-uniformity of structure.

неодноро́д|ный (~ен, ~на), *adj.* heterogeneous; dissimilar, not uniform.

неодобре́ни|е, я, *n.* disapproval, disapprobation.

неодобри́тел|ьный (~ен, ~ьна), *adj.* disapproving.

неодоли́м|ый (~, ~а), *adj.* invincible, insuperable.

неодушевлён|ный (~, ~на), *adj.* inanimate.

неожи́данност|ь, и, *f.* **1.** unexpectedness, suddenness. **2.** surprise.

неожи́дан|ный (~, ~на), *adj.* unexpected, sudden.

неозо́йский, *adj.* (*geol.*) neozoic.

неоклассици́зм, а, *m.* neo-classicism.

неоконча́тел|ьный (~ен, ~ьна), *adj.* inconclusive.

неоко́нченный, *adj.* unfinished.

неоли́т, а, *m.* (*archaeol.*) New Stone Age.

неолити́ческий, *adj.* (*archaeol.*) neolithic.

неологи́зм, а, *m.* neologism.

нео́н, а, *m.* (*chem.*) neon.

нео́н|овый, *adj.* of ~; ~овая ла́мпа neon lamp.

неопа́с|ный (~ен, ~на), *adj.* harmless, not dangerous.

неопера́бельный, *adj.* (*med.*) inoperable.

неопери́вшийся, *adj.* unfledged; (*fig.*) callow.

неописуе́м|ый (~, ~а), *adj.* indescribable.

неопла́тн|ый, *adj.* that cannot be repaid; н. должни́к insolvent debtor; я у вас в ~ом долгу́ (*fig.*) I am eternally indebted to you.

неопо́знан|ный (~, ~на), *adj.* unidentified.

неопра́вданный, *adj.* unjustified, unwarranted.

неопределённост|ь, и, *f.* vagueness, uncertainty.

неопределён|ный (~ен, ~на), *adj.* **1.** indefinite; ~ное наклоне́ние, ~ная фо́рма глаго́ла (*gram.*) infinitive; н. член (*gram.*) indefinite article. **2.** indeterminate; vague, uncertain; ~ное уравне́ние (*math.*) indeterminate equation.

неопредели́м|ый (~, ~а), *adj.* indefinable.

неопровержи́м|ый (~, ~а), *adj.* irrefutable.

неопря́тност|ь, и, *f.* slovenliness; untidiness, sloppiness.

неопря́т|ный (~ен, ~на), *adj.* slovenly; untidy, sloppy; dirty.

нео́пытност|ь, и, *f.* inexperience.

нео́пыт|ный (~ен, ~на), *adj.* inexperienced.

неорганизо́ванност|ь, и, *f.* lack of organization; disorganization.

неорганизо́ван|ный (~, ~на), *adj.* unorganized; disorganized.

неоргани́ческий, *adj.* inorganic.

неосведомлённый, *adj.* ill-informed.

неосе́длый, *adj.* nomadic.

неосла́б|ный (~ен, ~на), *adj.* unremitting, unabated.

неосмотри́тельност|ь, и, *f.* imprudence; indiscretion.

неосмотри́тел|ьный (~ен, ~ьна), *adj.* imprudent, incautious; indiscreet.

неоснова́тел|ьный (~ен, ~ьна), *adj.* **1.** un-founded, lacking foundation. **2.** (*coll.*) frivolous.

неоспори́мост|ь, и, *f.* incontestability, indisputability.

неоспори́м|ый (~, ~a), *adj.* unquestionable, incontestable, indisputable.

неосторо́жност|ь, и, *f.* carelessness; imprudence.

неосторо́ж|ный (~ен, ~на), *adj.* careless; imprudent, indiscreet, incautious.

неосуществи́м|ый (~, ~a), *adj.* impracticable, unrealizable.

неосяза́ем|ый (~, ~a), *adj.* impalpable, intangible.

неотврати́мост|ь, и, *f.* inevitability.

неотврати́м|ый (~, ~a), *adj.* inevitable.

неотвя́з|ный (~ен, ~на), *adj.* importunate; obsessive.

неотвя́зчив|ый (~, ~a), *adj.* importunate; obsessive.

неотдели́м|ый (~, ~a), *adj.* inseparable.

неотёсан|ный (~, ~на), *adj.* **1.** unpolished. **2.** (*fig.*) uncouth.

нéоткуда, *adv.* there is nowhere; мне н. э́то получи́ть there is nowhere I can get it from.

неотло́жк|а, и, *f.* (*coll.*) emergency medical service.

неотло́жност|ь, и, *f.* urgency.

неотло́ж|ный (~ен, ~на), *adj.* urgent, pressing; ~ная по́мощь first aid.

неотлу́чно, *adv.* constantly, permanently.

неотлу́ч|ный (~ен, ~на), *adj.* ever-present; permanent.

неотрази́м|ый (~, ~a), *adj.* irresistible (*also* *fig.*); ~ые до́воды incontrovertible arguments.

неотсту́пност|ь, и, *f.* persistence; importunity.

неотсту́п|ный (~ен, ~на), *adj.* persistent; importunate.

неотчётлив|ый (~, ~a), *adj.* vague, indistinct.

неотчужда́емост|ь, и, *f.* (*leg.*) inalienability.

неотчужда́ем|ый (~, ~a), *adj.* (*leg.*) inalienable.

неотъе́млем|ый (~, ~a), *adj.* inalienable; ~ое пра́во inalienable right, imprescriptible right; ~ая часть integral part.

неофициа́л|ьный (~ен, ~ьна), *adj.* unofficial.

неохо́т|а, ы, *f.* **1.** reluctance. **2.** (+*d.,* as *pred.*) мне, *etc.,* н. идти́ I, *etc.,* have no wish to go, am not keen to go.

неохо́тно, *adv.* reluctantly; unwillingly.

неоцени́м|ый (~, ~a), *adj.* inestimable, priceless, invaluable.

неощути́м|ый (~, ~a), *adj.* imperceptible.

неощути́тел|ьный (~ен, ~ьна), *adj.* imperceptible, insensible.

непа́рный, *adj.* odd (*not forming a pair*).

непарти́йный, *adj.* **1.** non-Party; н. большеви́к non-Party Bolshevik (*one, not a member of the Soviet Communist Party, but acting in its spirit*). **2.** unbefitting a member of the Communist Party.

непереводи́м|ый (~, ~a), *adj.* untranslatable.

непередава́ем|ый (~, ~a), *adj.* inexpressible, indescribable.

непереходный, *adj.* (*gram.*) intransitive.

непеча́тный, *adj.* (*coll.*) unprintable.

непи́сан|ый, *adj.* unwritten; ~ые пра́вила unwritten rules.

неплатёж, á, *m.* non-payment.

неплатёжеспосо́бност|ь, и, *f.* (*fin.*) insolvency.

неплатёжеспосо́б|ный (~ен, ~на), *adj.* (*fin.*) insolvent.

непла́тельщик, а, *m.* defaulter; person in arrears with payment (*of taxes, etc.*).

неплодоро́д|ный (~ен, ~на), *adj.* barren, sterile; infertile.

неплодотво́р|ный (~ен, ~на), *adj.* unproductive.

непло́хо, *adv.* not badly, quite well.

неплох|о́й (~, ~á, ~o), *adj.* not bad, quite good.

непобеди́м|ый (~, ~a), *adj.* invincible.

непова́дно, as *pred.* (*impers.;* +*d. and inf.*) (*coll.*) чтобы н. бы́ло to teach (someone) not (to do something again); мальчи́шку вы́пороли, чтобы ему́ н. бы́ло кра́сть я́блоки they gave the boy a thrashing to teach him not to steal apples again.

непови́н|ный (~ен, ~на), *adj.* innocent.

неповинове́ни|е, я, *n.* insubordination, disobedience.

неповоро́тлив|ый (~, ~a), *adj.* clumsy, awkward; sluggish, slow.

неповтори́м|ый (~, ~a), *adj.* unique.

непого́д|а, ы, *f.* bad weather.

непогреши́мост|ь, и, *f.* infallibility.

непогреши́м|ый (~, ~a), *adj.* infallible.

неподалёку, *adv.* not far off.

непода́тлив|ый (~, ~a), *adj.* stubborn, intractable; unyielding, tenacious.

непода́тный, *adj.* exempt from capitation.

неподве́домствен|ный (~, ~на), *adj.* (+*d.*) not subject to the authority (of), beyond the jurisdiction (of).

неподви́жност|ь, и, *f.* immobility.

неподви́ж|ный (~ен, ~на), *adj.* motionless, immobile, immovable (*also* *fig.*); fixed, stationary; ~ное лицо́ immobile countenance; н. загради́тельный ого́нь (*mil.*) standing barrage.

неподгора́ющ|ий, *adj.* ~ая кастрю́ля non--stick saucepan.

неподде́льност|ь, и, *f.* genuineness; sincerity.

неподде́л|ьный (~ен, ~ьна), adj. genuine; unfeigned, sincere.

неподку́пност|ь, и, f. incorruptibility, integrity.

неподку́п|ный (~ен, ~на), adj. incorruptible.

неподоба́ющий, adj. unseemly, improper.

неподража́ем|ый (~, ~а), adj. inimitable.

неподсу́д|ный (~ен, ~на), adj. (+d.) not under the jurisdiction (of).

неподходя́щий, adj. unsuitable, inappropriate.

неподчине́ни|е, я, n. insubordination; н. суде́бному постановле́нию (leg.) contempt of court.

непозволи́тел|ьный (~ен, ~ьна), adj. inadmissible, impermissible.

непознава́ем|ый (~, ~а), adj. (philos.) unknowable.

непокла́дист|ый (~, ~а), adj. 1. obstinate, uncompromising. 2. (coll., obs.) clumsy.

непоко́|йный (~ен, ~йна), adj. (coll.) troubled; restless, disturbed.

непоколеби́м|ый (~, ~а), adj. steadfast, unshakeable, inflexible.

непоко́рност|ь, и, f. recalcitrance; unruliness.

непоко́р|ный (~ен, ~на), adj. refractory, recalcitrant; unruly.

непокры́т|ый (~, ~а), adj. uncovered, bare.

непола́дк|а, и, f. 1. defect, fault. 2. (in pl.) disagreement, quarrel.

неполноправ́ный, adj. not possessing full rights.

неполнот|а́, ы́, f. incompleteness.

неполноце́нност|ь, и, f. ко́мплекс ~и inferiority complex.

непо́л|ный (~он, ~на́, ~но), adj. not fully; incomplete; defective; с тех пор прошло́ непо́лных два́дцать лет since then not quite twenty years had passed; ~ная семья́ single-parent family; ~ное сре́днее образова́ние incomplete secondary education (comprising seven years' schooling).

непоме́р|ный (~ен, ~на), adj. excessive, inordinate.

непонима́ни|е, я, n. incomprehension.

непоня́тливост|ь, и, f. slowness, dulness.

непоня́тлив|ый (~, ~а), adj. slow-witted, stupid, dull.

непоня́т|ный (~ен, ~на), adj. unintelligible, incomprehensible; ~но (impers., as pred.) it is incomprehensible; мне ~но, как он мог э́то сде́лать I cannot understand how he could do it.

непопада́ни|е, я, n. miss (in shooting).

непоправи́м|ый (~, ~а), adj. irreparable, irremediable; irretrievable.

непоро́ч|ный (~ен, ~на), adj. pure, chaste;

~ное зача́тие (rel.) the Immaculate Conception (of the Virgin).

непоря́д|ок, ка, m. disorder; violation of order.

непоря́доч|ный (~ен, ~на), adj. dishonourable.

непосвящён|ный (~, ~а́), adj. uninitiated.

непосе́д|а, ы, m. and f. (coll.) fidget; rolling stone.

непосе́дливост|ь, и, f. restlessness.

непосе́длив|ый (~, ~а), adj. fidgety, restless.

непосеще́ни|е, я, n. (+g.) non-attendance (at).

непоси́л|ьный (~ен, ~ьна), adj. beyond one's strength, excessive.

непосле́довательност|ь, и, f. inconsistency; inconsequence.

непосле́довател|ьный (~ен, ~ьна), adj. inconsistent; inconsequent.

непослуша́ни|е, я, n. disobedience.

непослу́ш|ный (~ен, ~на), adj. disobedient, naughty.

непосре́дственност|ь, и, f. spontaneity; ingenuousness.

непосре́дствен|ный (~, ~на), adj. 1. immediate, direct. 2. (fig.) direct; spontaneous, ingenuous.

непостижи́м|ый (~, ~а), adj. incomprehensible, inscrutable; уму́ ~о it passes understanding.

непостоя́н|ный (~ен, ~на), adj. inconstant, changeable.

непостоя́нств|о, а, n. inconstancy.

непоти́зм, а, m. nepotism.

непотопля́ем|ый (~, ~а), adj. unsinkable.

непотре́б|ный (~ен, ~на), adj. (obs.) obscene, indecent; ~ные слова́ obscenities.

непотре́бств|о, а, n. (obs.) obscenity; indecent conduct.

непоча́тый, adj. (coll.) untouched, not begun, entire; н. край (or у́гол) (+g.) a wealth (of), a whole host (of).

непочте́ни|е, я, n. disrespect.

непочти́тел|ьный (~ен, ~ьна), adj. disrespectful.

непра́вд|а, ы, f. untruth, falsehood, lie; все́ми пра́вдами и ~ами by fair means or foul; by hook or by crook.

неправдоподо́би|е, я, n. improbability, unlikelihood.

неправдоподо́б|ный (~ен, ~на), adj. improbable, unlikely; implausible.

непра́вед|ный (~ен, ~на), adj. (obs.) iniquitous, unjust.

непра́вильно, adv. 1. irregularly. 2. incorrectly, erroneously; in conjunction with verbs frequently = mis-; e.g., н. истолкова́ть to misinterpret.

неправильност|ь, и, *f.* **1.** irregularity; anomaly. **2.** incorrectness.

неправил|ьный (~ен, ~ьна), *adj.* **1.** irregular; anomalous; н. глагол irregular verb; ~ьная дробь (*math.*) improper fraction; ~ьные черты лица irregular features. **2.** incorrect, erroneous, wrong, mistaken; н. подход (к делу) wrong approach, wrong attitude.

неправомерност|ь, и, *f.* illegality.

неправомер|ный (~ен, ~на), *adj.* illegal.

неправомочност|ь, и, *f.* (*leg.*) incompetence.

неправомоч|ный (~ен, ~на), *adj.* (*leg.*) not competent; not entitled.

неправоспособност|ь, и, *f.* (*leg.*) disability, disqualification; incapacity.

неправоспособ|ный (~ен, ~на), *adj.* (*leg.*) disqualified.

неправот|а, ы, *f.* **1.** error. **2.** wrongness; injustice.

неправ|ый (~, ~а, ~о), *adj.* **1.** wrong, mistaken. **2.** unjust.

непревзойдённый, *adj.* unsurpassed; matchless.

непредвиденный, *adj.* unforeseen.

непреднамерен|ный (~, ~на), *adj.* unpremeditated.

непредубеждённый, *adj.* unprejudiced, unbiased.

непредумышленный, *adj.* unpremeditated.

непредусмотрительност|ь, и, *f.* improvidence, short-sightedness

непредусмотрител|ьный (~ен, ~ьна), *adj.* improvident, short-sighted.

непреклонност|ь, и, *f.* inflexibility; inexorability.

непреклон|ный (~ен, ~на), *adj.* inflexible, unbending; inexorable, adamant.

непрелож|ный•(~ен, ~на), *adj.* **1.** immutable, unalterable. **2.** indisputable.

непременно, *adv.* **1.** without fail; certainly; они н. придут завтра they are sure to come tomorrow. **2.** absolutely; мне н. нужно поговорить с ним it is absolutely essential that I speak to him.

непремен|ный (~ен, ~на), *adj.* indispensable; н. секретарь permanent secretary.

непреобори|мый (~, ~а), *adj.* insuperable; irresistible.

непреодоли|мый (~, ~а), *adj.* insuperable, insurmountable; irresistible; ~ая сила (*leg.*) force majeure.

непререкаем|ый (~, ~а), *adj.* unquestionable, indisputable; н. тон peremptory tone.

непрерывно, *adv.* uninterruptedly, continuously.

непрерывност|ь, и, *f.* continuity.

непрерыв|ный (~ен, ~на), *adj.* uninterrupted, unbroken; continuous; ~ная дробь (*math.*) continued fraction; н. лист through plate (*in ship-building*); ~ная палуба (*naut.*) flush deck; н. сварной шов (*tech.*) line welding, continuous weld.

непрестанно, *adv.* incessantly, continually.

непрестан|ный (~ен, ~на), *adj.* incessant, continual.

неприветлив|ый (~, ~а), *adj.* unfriendly, ungracious; bleak.

непривычк|а, и, *f.* want of habit; с ~и он быстро захмелел being unaccustomed to strong drink, he quickly became drunk.

непривыч|ный (~ен, ~на), *adj.* unaccustomed, unwonted; unusual.

непригляд|ный (~ен, ~на), *adj.* unattractive, unsightly.

непригод|ный (~ен, ~на), *adj.* unfit, useless; unserviceable; ineligible.

неприемлем|ый (~, ~а), *adj.* unacceptable.

непризнанный, *adj.* unrecognized, unacknowledged.

неприкаянный, *adj.* (*coll.*) restless, unable to find anything to do; ходить, бродить, *etc.*, как н. to go about, wander about, *etc.*, like a lost soul.

неприкосновенност|ь, и, *f.* inviolability; дипломатическая н. diplomatic immunity.

неприкосновен|ный (~ен, ~на), *adj.* inviolable; н. запас (*mil.*) emergency ration, iron ration; н. капитал reserve capital.

неприкрашенный, *adj.* plain, unvarnished.

неприкрыт|ый, *adj.* undisguised; ~ая ложь barefaced lie.

неприличи|е, я, *n.* indecency, impropriety, unseemliness.

неприлич|ный (~ен, ~на), *adj.* indecent, improper; unseemly, unbecoming.

непримени|мый (~, ~а), *adj.* inapplicable.

неприметный|ный (~ен, ~на), *adj.* **1.** imperceptible. **2.** (*fig.*) unremarkable, undistinguished.

непримиримост|ь, и, *f.* irreconcilability; intransigence.

непримири|мый (~, ~а), *adj.* irreconcilable; intransigent, uncompromising.

непринуждённост|ь, и, *f.* unconstraint; naturalness, ease.

непринуждён|ный (~, ~на), *adj.* unconstrained; natural, relaxed, easy; spontaneous.

неприспособлен|ный (~, ~на), *adj.* (к) unadapted (to); maladjusted.

непристойност|ь, и, *f.* obscenity; indecency.

непристо|йный (~ен, ~йна), *adj.* obscene; indecent.

неприступ|ный (~ен, ~на), *adj.* **1.** inaccessible; unassailable, impregnable. **2.** (*fig.*) inaccessible, unapproachable.

неприсутственный, *adj.* (*obs.*) н. день public holiday.

непритво́р|ный (~ен, ~на), *adj.* unfeigned, genuine.

неприхотли́вост|ь, и, *f.* **1.** unpretentiousness; modesty. **2.** simplicity, plainness.

неприхотли́в|ый (~, ~а), *adj.* **1.** unpretentious; modest, undemanding. **2.** simple, plain; ~ая пи́ща frugal meal.

непричáст|ный (~ен, ~на), *adj.* (к) not implicated (in), not privy (to).

неприя́знен|ный (~, ~на), *adj.* hostile, inimical.

неприя́зн|ь, и, *f.* hostility, enmity.

неприя́тел|ь, я, *m.* enemy; (*mil.*) the enemy.

неприя́тельский, *adj.* hostile; (*mil.*) enemy.

неприя́тност|ь, и, *f.* unpleasantness; nuisance, annoyance, trouble.

неприя́т|ный (~ен, ~на), *adj.* unpleasant, disagreeable; annoying, troublesome.

непробу́дный, *adj.* from which there is no waking; н. сон deep sleep; н. пья́ница inveterate drunkard.

непроводни́к, á, *m.* (*phys.*) non-conductor, dielectric.

непрогля́д|ный (~ен, ~на), *adj.* (*of darkness, fog, etc.*) impenetrable; pitch-dark.

непродолжи́тел|ьный (~ен, ~ьна), *adj.* of short duration, short-lived; в ~ьном вре́мени shortly, in a short time.

непродукти́в|ный (~ен, ~на), *adj.* unproductive.

непрое́зжий, *adj.* impassable.

непрозра́чност|ь, и, *f.* opacity.

непрозра́ч|ный (~ен, ~на), *adj.* opaque.

непроизводи́тел|ьный (~ен, ~ьна), *adj.* unproductive; wasteful.

непроизво́л|ьный (~ен, ~ьна), *adj.* involuntary.

непрола́з|ный (~ен, ~на), *adj.* (*coll.*) impassable.

непромока́ем|ый (~, ~а), *adj.* waterproof; н. плащ mackintosh, waterproof (coat), raincoat.

непроница́емост|ь, и, *f.* impenetrability; impermeability.

непроница́ем|ый (~, ~а), *adj.* **1.** impenetrable, impermeable; (для) impervious (to); н. для зву́ка sound-proof. **2.** inscrutable, impassive.

непропорциона́льност|ь, и, *f.* disproportion.

непропорциона́л|ьный (~ен, ~ьна), *adj.* disproportionate.

непрости́тел|ьный (~ен, ~ьна), *adj.* unforgivable, unpardonable, inexcusable.

непротивле́ни|е, я, *n.* non-resistance.

непроходи́мо, *adv.* (*coll.*) utterly, hopelessly.

непроходи́м|ый (~, ~а), *adj.* **1.** impassable. **2.** (*fig., coll.*) complete, utter; н. дура́к utter fool.

непро́ч|ный (~ен, ~на), *adj.* fragile, flimsy; (*fig.*) precarious, unstable.

непро́шеный, *adj.* (*coll.*) unbidden, uninvited; непро́шеное одолже́ние an un-solicited service.

непрям|о́й (~, ~á, ~о), *adj.* **1.** indirect; circuitous. **2.** (*fig., coll.*) evasive.

непутёвый, *adj.* (*coll.*) good-for-nothing, useless.

непутём, *adv.* (*coll.*) badly; де́лать всё н. to make a mess of everything.

непью́щий, *adj.* non-drinking; temperate, abstemious (*in relation to alcoholic liquor*).

неработоспосо́б|ный (~ен, ~на), *adj.* unable to work, disabled.

нерабо́ч|ий, *adj.* non-working; ~ее вре́мя time off, free time.

нера́венств|о, а, *n.* inequality, disparity.

неравно́, *particle expressing anticipation of disagreeable eventuality* (*coll.*); н. опозда́ем suppose we are late; н. он зайдёт, а нас до́ма не бу́дет what if he comes while we are out.

неравноду́ш|ный (~ен, ~на), *adj.* (к) not indifferent (to).

неравноме́р|ный (~ен, ~на), *adj.* uneven, irregular.

неравнопра́в|ный (~ен, ~на), *adj.* not enjoying equal rights.

нера́в|ный (~ен, ~на́, ~но), *adj.* unequal.

нераде́ни|е, я, *n.* (*obs.*) = неради́вость.

неради́вост|ь, и, *f.* negligence, carelessness, remissness.

неради́в|ый (~, ~а), *adj.* negligent, careless, remiss.

неразбери́х|а, и, *f.* (*coll.*) muddle, confusion.

неразбо́рчив|ый (~, ~а), *adj.* **1.** illegible, indecipherable. **2.** (*fig.*) undiscriminating; not fastidious; н. в сре́дствах unscrupulous.

неразви́т|ой (нера́звит, ~á, ~о), *adj.* undeveloped; (intellectually) backward.

нера́звитост|ь, и, *f.* lack of development; у́мственная н. backwardness.

неразга́данн|ый, *adj.* unsolved; ~ая та́йна unresolved mystery.

неразгово́рчив|ый (~, ~а), *adj.* taciturn, not talkative.

нераздели́м|ый (~, ~а), *adj.* indivisible, inseparable.

неразде́л|ьный (~ен, ~ьна), *adj.* indivisible, inseparable; ~ьное иму́щество (*leg.*) common estate.

неразличи́м|ый (~, ~а), *adj.* indistinguishable; indiscernible.

неразлу́ч|ный (~ен, ~на), *adj.* inseparable.

неразрешённый, *adj.* **1.** unsolved. **2.** prohibited, banned.

неразреши́м|ый (~, ~а), *adj.* insoluble.

неразры́в|ный (~ен, ~на), *adj.* indissoluble.

неразу́ми|е, я, *n.* (*obs.*) folly, foolishness.

неразу́м|ный (~ен, ~на), *adj.* unreasonable; unwise; foolish.

нераска́янный, *adj.* unrepentant.

нерасположе́ни|е, я, *n.* (к) dislike (for), disinclination (for, to).

нерасполо́женный, *adj.* (к) ill-disposed (towards); unwilling (to), disinclined (to).

нераспоряди́тел|ьный (~ен, ~ьна), *adj.* inefficient, unauthoritative.

нераспростране́ни|е, я, *n.* non-proliferation (*esp. of nuclear weapons*).

нерассуди́тельност|ь, и, f. lack of common sense, want of sense.

нерассуди́тел|ьный (~ен, ~ьна), *adj.* unreasoning; lacking common sense.

нераствори́м|ый (~, ~а), *adj.* insoluble.

нерасторжи́м|ый (~, ~а), *adj.* indissoluble.

нерастороп|ный (~ен, ~на), *adj.* sluggish, slow.

нерасчётливост|ь, и, f. 1. extravagance, wastefulness. 2. improvidence.

нерасчётлив|ый (~, ~а), *adj.* 1. extravagant, wasteful. 2. improvident.

нерациона́л|ьный (~ен, ~ьна), *adj.* irrational.

нерв, а, *m.* (*anat. and fig.*) nerve; гла́вный н. (*fig.*) nerve-centre; де́йствовать кому́-н. на ~ы to get on someone's nerves.

нерва́ци|я, и, f. (*bot.*) nervation.

нерви́р|овать, ую, *impf.* to get on someone's nerves, irritate.

нерви́ческий, *adj.* (*obs.*) nervous.

не́рвнича|ть, ю, *impf.* to be *or* become fidgety, fret, be *or* become irritable.

нервнобольн|о́й, о́го, *m.* nervous patient, person suffering from nervous disorder.

не́рвност|ь, и, f. irritability, edginess.

не́рв|ный (~ен, ~на́, ~но), *adj.* 1. (*in var. senses*) nervous; neural; ~ное волокно́ nerve-fibre; н. припа́док fit of nerves; ~ная систе́ма the nervous system; н. у́зел (*anat.*) ganglion; н. центр nerve-centre. 2. irritable, highly strung.

нерво́з|ный (~ен, ~на), *adj.* nervy, irritable.

нервю́р|а, ы, f. (*aeron.*) rib; н. крыла́ wing-rib.

нереа́л|ьный (~ен, ~ьна), *adj.* 1. unreal. 2. impracticable.

нерегуля́р|ный (~ен, ~на), *adj.* irregular (*also mil.*).

нере́д|кий (~ок, ~ка́, ~ко), *adj.* not infrequent; not uncommon.

нере́дко, *adv.* not infrequently, quite often.

не́рест, а, *m.* (*zool.*) spawning.

нерести́лищ|е, а, *n.* spawning-ground.

нереши́мост|ь, и, f. indecision.

нереши́тельност|ь, и, f. indecision; indecisiveness; быть в ~и to be undecided.

нереши́тел|ьный (~ен, ~ьна), *adj.* indecisive, irresolute.

нержаве́йк|а, и, f. (*coll.*) stainless steel.

нержаве́ющ|ий, *adj.* non-rusting; ~ая сталь stainless steel.

неро́б|кий (~ок, ~ка́, ~ко), *adj.* not timid; он челове́к ~кого деся́тка he is no coward.

неро́вност|ь, и, f. 1. unevenness, roughness. 2. inequality; irregularity.

неро́в|ный (~ен, ~на́, но), *adj.* 1. uneven, rough; н. грунт rough country. 2. unequal; irregular; н. пульс irregular pulse; ~ён час (*coll., obs.,* now = не ро́вен час) who knows what may happen; one never knows.

неро́вн|я, и, (*and* неровн|я́, й), *m. and f.* (*coll.*) он ей н. he is not her equal.

не́рп|а, ы, f. (*zool.*) nerpa (*species of freshwater seal*).

неру́дный, *adj.* (*tech.*) non-metallic.

нерукотво́рный, *adj.* (*rel. and poet.*) not made by hands.

неруши́м|ый (~, ~а), *adj.* inviolable, indissoluble.

неря́х|а, и, *m. and f.* sloven; (*f.*) slattern, slut.

неря́шеств|о, а, *n.* = неря́шливость.

неря́шливост|ь, и, f. slovenliness, slatternliness; untidiness.

неря́шлив|ый (~, ~а), *adj.* 1. slovenly, untidy. 2. careless, slipshod.

несваре́ни|е, я, *n.* only in phrase н. желу́дка indigestion.

несве́дущ|ий (~, ~а), *adj.* (в+*p.*) ignorant (about), not well-informed (about).

несве́ж|ий (~, ~а́, ~е), *adj.* 1. not fresh, stale; tainted. 2. (*fig.*) weary, wan.

несвобо́дн|ый, *adj.* ~ое сочета́ние (*ling.*) set phrase.

несвоевре́мен|ный (~ен, ~на), *adj.* inopportune, untimely, unseasonable.

несво́йствен|ный (~ен, ~на), *adj.* not characteristic; э́то ему́ ~но it is not like him.

несвя́з|ный (~ен, ~на), *adj.* disconnected, incoherent.

несгиба́емый, *adj.* unbending, inflexible.

несгово́рчив|ый (~, ~а), *adj.* intractable.

несгора́емый, *adj.* fire-proof, incombustible; н. шкаф safe.

несде́ржанный, *adj.* unrestrained.

несе́ни|е, я, *n.* performance, execution.

несесе́р, а, *m.* toilet-case.

несжима́ем|ый (~, ~а), *adj.* incompressible.

несказа́нный, *adj.* unspeakable, ineffable.

нескла́диц|а, ы, f. (*coll.*) nonsense.

нескла́д|ный (~ен, ~на), *adj.* 1. incoherent. 2. ungainly, awkward. 3. absurd.

несклоня́ем|ый (~, ~а), *adj.* (*gram.*) indeclinable.

не́скольк|о[1], **их**, *num.* some, several; a few; в ~их слова́х in a few words; н. челове́к several people.

не́сколько[2], *adv.* somewhat, rather, slightly; они ста́ли н. разочаро́ванными they have become rather disillusioned.

нескончаем|ый (~, ~а), *adj.* interminable, never-ending.

нескро́мност|ь, и, *f.* 1. immodesty, lack of modesty. 2. indelicacy; indiscretion. 3. indiscreetness.

нескро́м|ный (~ен, ~на́, ~но), *adj.* 1. immodest; vain. 2. indiscreet.

несло́ж|ный (~ен, ~на́, ~но), *adj.* simple, not complicated.

неслы́хан|ный (~, ~на), *adj.* unheard of, unprecedented.

неслы́ш|ный (~ен, ~на), *adj.* inaudible.

несменя́емост|ь, и, *f.* irremovability (from office).

несменя́ем|ый (~, ~а), *adj.* irremovable.

несме́т|ный (~ен, ~на), *adj.* countless, incalculable, innumerable.

несмолка́ем|ый (~, ~а), *adj.* ceaseless, unremitting, never-abating.

несмотря́, *prep.* (на+*a.*) in spite of, despite; notwithstanding; н. ни на что in spite of everything.

несмыва́ем|ый (~, ~а), *adj.* indelible, ineffaceable.

несно́с|ный (~ен, ~на), *adj.* intolerable, insupportable.

несоблюде́ни|е, я, *n.* non-observance.

несовершеннолети|е, я, *n.* minority.

несовершенноле́тн|ий, *adj.* under age; *as noun* н., ~его, *m.* minor.

несоверше́н|ный (~ен, ~на), *adj.* 1. imperfect, incomplete. 2. (*gram.*) imperfective.

несовмести́м|ый (~, ~а), *adj.* incompatible.

несогла́си|е, я, *n.* 1. disagreement; н. в мне́ниях difference of opinion; н. ме́жду двумя́ ве́рсиями discrepancy between two versions. 2. discord, variance. 3. (*sing. only*) refusal.

несогла́с|ный (~ен, ~на), *adj.* 1. (с+*i.*) not agreeing (with). 2. (с+*i.*) inconsistent (with), incompatible (with). 3. (на+*a.* or +*inf.*) not consenting (to), not agreeing (to); я на это ~ен I cannot agree to this. 4. discordant.

несогласова́ни|е, я, *n.* (*gram.*) non-agreement.

несогласо́ванност|ь, и, *f.* lack of co-ordination, non-coordination.

несогласо́ванный, *adj.* uncoordinated, not concerted.

несозву́ч|ный (~ен, ~на), *adj.* (+*d.*) dissonant; inconsonant (with).

несозна́тельност|ь, и, *f.* thoughtlessness; irresponsibility; (*political*) backwardness.

несозна́тел|ьный (~ен, ~ьна), *adj.* 1. irresponsible. 2. unconscious of social obligations.

несоизмери́мост|ь, и, *f.* incommensurability.

несоизмери́м|ый (~, ~а), *adj.* incommensurable, incommensurate.

несократи́мый, *adj.* (*math.*) irreducible.

несокруши́м|ый (~, ~а), *adj.* indestructible; unconquerable.

несоли́д|ный (~ен, ~на), *adj.* not impressive, unimpressive, light-weight.

несо́лоно, *adv.* (*coll.*) *only in phrase* уйти́ н. хлеба́вши to get nothing for one's pains, go away empty-handed.

несомне́нно, *adv.* undoubtedly, doubtless.

несомне́н|ный (~ен, ~на), *adj.* undoubted, indubitable, unquestionable.

несообрази́тел|ьный (~ен, ~ьна), *adj.* slow(-witted).

несообра́зност|ь, и, *f.* 1. incongruity, incompatibility. 2. absurdity.

несообра́з|ный (~ен, ~на), *adj.* 1. (с+*i.*) incongruous (with), incompatible (with). 2. absurd.

несоотве́тствен|ный (~, ~на), *adj.* (+*d.*) incongruous (with), not corresponding (to).

несоотве́тстви|е, я, *n.* lack of correspondence, disparity.

несоразме́рност|ь, и, *f.* disproportion.

несоразме́р|ный (~ен, ~на), *adj.* disproportionate.

несосве́тимый, *adj.* = несусве́тный.

несостоя́тельност|ь, и, *f.* 1. insolvency, bankruptcy. 2. modest means. 3. groundlessness.

несостоя́тел|ьный (~ен, ~ьна), *adj.* 1. insolvent, bankrupt. 2. not wealthy, of modest means. 3. groundless, unsupported.

неспе́л|ый (~, ~а́, ~о), *adj.* unripe.

неспе́ш|ный (~ен, ~на), *adj.* unhurried.

несподру́ч|ный (~ен, ~на), *adj.* (*coll.*) inconvenient, awkward.

неспоко́|йный (~ен, ~йна), *adj.* restless; uneasy.

неспосо́бност|ь, и, *f.* incapacity, inability.

неспосо́б|ный (~ен, ~на), *adj.* dull, not able; (к+*d.*, на+*a.*) incapable (of); она́ ~на к му́зыке she has no aptitude for music; н. на ложь incapable of a lie.

несправедли́вост|ь, и, *f.* injustice, unfairness.

несправедли́в|ый (~, ~а), *adj.* 1. unjust, unfair. 2. incorrect, unfounded.

неспровоци́рованный, *adj.* unprovoked.

непроста́, *adv.* (*coll.*) not without purpose; with an ulterior motive.

несравне́нно, *adv.* 1. incomparably, matchlessly. 2. far, by far; н. лу́чше far better.

несравне́н|ный (~ен, ~на), adj. incomparable, matchless.

несравни́м|ый (~, ~а), adj. 1. incomparable; unmatched. 2. not comparable.

нестерпи́м|ый (~, ~а), adj. unbearable, unendurable.

нес|ти́[1], у́, ёшь, past ~, ~ла́, impf. (of по~), det. 1. to carry. 2. to bear; to support. 3. (fig.) to bear; to suffer; to incur; н. убы́тки (fin.) to incur losses. 4. to perform; н. дежу́рство to be on duty. 5. (fig.) to bear, bring; н. ги́бель to bring destruction. 6. (impers.; coll.) куда́ вас ~ёт? wherever are you going? 7. (impers.; coll.; +i.) to stink (of), reek (of); от него́ ~ёт чесноко́м he reeks of garlic. 8. (impers.; coll.) его́, etc., ~ёт he has, etc., diarrhoea. 9. (coll.) (вздор, чепуху́, etc.) to talk (nonsense).

нес|ти́[2], ёт, past ~, ~ла́, impf. (of с~) to lay (eggs).

нес|ти́сь[1], у́сь, ёшься, past ~ся, ~ла́сь, impf. (of по~), det. 1. to rush, tear, fly; (on water, in the air) to float, drift; (по+d., вдоль; над) to skim (along; over). 2. (of sounds, smells, etc.) to spread, be diffused.

нес|ти́сь[2], ётся, past ~ся, ~ла́сь, impf. (of с~) to lay (eggs) (intrans.).

нестойкий, adj. (chem.) unstable, non-persistent.

нестоя́щий, adj. (coll.) worthless, good-for-nothing.

нестроеви́к, а́, m. (mil.) non-combatant.

нестроево́й[1], adj. unfit for building purposes.

нестроево́й[2], adj. (mil.) non-combatant, administrative.

нестро́|йный (~ен, ~йна́, ~йно), adj. 1. clumsily built. 2. discordant, dissonant. 3. disorderly.

несть (obs.) there is not.

несура́зност|ь, и, f. 1. absurdity, senselessness. 2. awkwardness.

несура́з|ный (~ен, ~на), adj. 1. absurd, senseless. 2. awkward.

несусве́т|ный (~ен, ~на), adj. (coll.) extreme; utter; unimaginable; ~ная чепуха́ utter nonsense.

несу́шк|а, и, f. (coll.) laying hen, hen in lay.

несуще́ствен|ный (~, ~на), adj. inessential, immaterial.

несу́щ|ий, pres. part. act. of нести́ and adj. (tech.) carrying; supporting; н. винт rotor (of helicopter); ~ая пове́рхность lifting surface; (aeron.) airfoil.

несхо́д|ный (~ен, ~на), adj. 1. unlike, dissimilar. 2. (coll.; of price) unreasonable.

несчастли́в|ец, ца, m. unlucky person, an unfortunate.

несчастли́в|ый (~, ~а), adj. 1. unfortunate, luckless. 2. unhappy.

несча́ст|ный (~ен, ~на), adj. 1. unhappy; unfortunate, unlucky; н. слу́чай accident. 2. as noun н., ~ного, m. wretch; an unfortunate.

несча́сть|е, я, n. 1. misfortune; к ~ю unfortunately. 2. accident.

несчёт|ный (~ен, ~на), adj. innumerable, countless.

несъедо́бный, adj. 1. uneatable. 2. inedible; н. гриб toadstool.

нет[1] 1. no; not; вы его́ ви́дели? н. you saw him?—No; вы не ви́дели его́? н., ви́дел you didn't see him? Yes, I did; н. да н., н. как н. (coll.; emphatic) absolutely not, absolutely nothing; н.-н. да и взгля́нет на меня́ he glanced at me from time to time. 2. nothing, naught; свести́ на н. to bring to naught; свести́сь (сойти́) на н. to come to naught; as noun н., ~а, m.; на н. и суда́ н. (prov.) what cannot be cured must be endured; пироги́ с ~ом (joc.) pie without filling; быть в ~ях (в ~ex) (obs. or joc.) to be missing, be adrift.

нет[2], (+g.) (there) is not, (there) are not; здесь н. собо́ра there is not a cathedral here; у меня́ н. вре́мени I have no time.

нета́ктич|ный (~ен, ~на), adj. tactless.

нетвёрдо, adv. 1. unsteadily, not firmly. 2. not definitely; знать н. to have a shaky knowledge of; я н. уве́рен I am not quite sure.

нетвёрд|ый (~, ~а́, ~о), adj. unsteady; shaky (also fig.).

нетерпёж, а́, m. (coll.) impatience.

нетерпели́в|ый (~, ~а), adj. impatient.

нетерпе́ни|е, я, n. impatience.

нетерпи́мост|ь, и, f. intolerance.

нетерпи́м|ый (~, ~а), adj. 1. intolerable. 2. intolerant.

нетле́н|ный (~ен, ~на), adj. imperishable.

нетопы́р|ь, я́, m. (zool.) bat.

неторопли́в|ый (~, ~а), adj. leisurely, unhurried.

нето́чност|ь, и, f. 1. inaccuracy, inexactitude. 2. error, slip.

нето́ч|ный (~ен, ~на́, ~но), adj. inaccurate, inexact.

нетре́бовател|ьный (~ен, ~ьна), adj. not exacting, undemanding; unpretentious.

нетре́зв|ый (~, ~а́, ~о), adj. not sober, drunk; в ~ом ви́де in a state of intoxication.

нетро́нут|ый (~, ~а), adj. untouched; (fig.) chaste, virginal.

нетрудово́й, adj. 1. not derived from labour; н. дохо́д unearned income. 2. not engaged in labour.

нетрудоспосо́бност|ь, и, f. disablement, disability; incapacity for work.

нетрудоспосо́б|ный (~ен, ~на), adj. disabled; invalid.

нéтто, *indecl. adj.* (*comm.*) net.

нéту (*coll.*) = нет².

нéтях, *see* нет¹.

неубедител|ьный (~ен, ~ьна), *adj.* unconvincing.

неýбранный, *adj.* 1. untidy. 2. unharvested.

неуважéни|е, я, *n.* disrespect, lack of respect.

неуважител|ьный (~ен, ~ьна), *adj.* 1. (*of cause, ground, etc.*) inadequate; not acceptable. 2. (*obs.*) disrespectful.

неувéренност|ь, и, *f.* uncertainty; н. в себé diffidence.

неувéрен|ный, *adj.* 1. (~, ~а) uncertain; н. в себé diffident. 2. (~, ~на) hesitating; vacillating.

неувяда́|емый (~ем, ~ема), *adj.* = ~ющий.

неувяда́ющий, *adj.* (*rhet.*) unfading, everlasting.

неувя́зк|а, и, *f.* (*coll.*) lack of co-ordination; misunderstanding.

неугаси́м|ый (~, ~а), *adj.* inextinguishable, unquenchable (*also fig.*).

неугомóн|ный (~ен, ~на), *adj.* (*coll.*) indefatigable, irrepressible.

неуда́ч|а, и, *f.* failure.

неуда́члив|ый (~, ~а), *adj.* unlucky.

неуда́чник, а, *m.* unlucky person, failure.

неуда́ч|ный (~ен, ~на), *adj.* unsuccessful; unfortunate; ~ное выражéние unfortunate expression; ~ное нача́ло bad start.

неудержи́м|ый (~, ~а), *adj.* irrepressible.

неудóб|ный (~ен, ~на), *adj.* 1. uncomfortable. 2. (*fig.*) inconvenient; awkward; embarrassing.

неудобовари́м|ый (~, ~а), *adj.* indigestible (*also fig.*).

неудобопоня́т|ный (~ен, ~на), *adj.* unintelligible, obscure.

неудобопроизноси́м|ый (~, ~а), *adj.* 1. unpronounceable. 2. (*joc.*) unrepeatable (= obscene), risqué.

неудобочита́емый, *adj.* difficult to read, obscure.

неудóбств|о, а, *n.* 1. discomfort; inconvenience. 2. embarrassment.

неудóбь, *adv. now only in joc. phrase* н. сказýемый risqué.

неудовлетворéни|е, я, n. 1. non-compliance; н. жа́лобы rejection of a complaint, failure to act on a complaint. 2. dissatisfaction.

неудовлетворённост|ь, и, f. dissatisfaction, discontent.

неудовлетворён|ный, *adj.* 1. (~, ~на) dissatisfied, discontented. 2. (~, ~а́) unsatisfied.

неудовлетвори́тел|ьный (~ен, ~ьна), *adj.* unsatisfactory.

неудовóльстви|е, я, *n.* displeasure.

неуём|ный (~ен, ~на), *adj.* (*coll.*) irrepressible; ~ная печа́ль uncontrollable grief.

неужéли, *interrog. particle* really? is it possible?; н. он так дýмает? does he really think that?; н. ты не знал, что мы здесь? did you really not know that we were here? surely you knew that we were here?

неужи́вчивост|ь, и, *f.* unaccommodating nature; quarrelsome disposition.

неужи́вчив|ый (~, ~а), *adj.* unaccommodating, difficult (to get on with); quarrelsome.

неýжто, *interrog. particle* (*coll.*) = неужéли.

неузнава́емост|ь, и, *f.* unrecognizability; он похудéл до ~и he has become so thin that you would not recognize him.

неузнава́ем|ый (~, ~а), *adj.* unrecognizable.

неуклóн|ный (~ен, ~на), *adj.* steady, steadfast; undeviating.

неуклю́жест|ь, и, *f.* clumsiness, awkwardness.

неуклю́ж|ий (~, ~а, ~е), *adj.* clumsy; awkward.

неукосни́тел|ьный (~ен, ~ьна), *adj.* strict, rigorous.

неукроти́м|ый (~, ~а), *adj.* indomitable.

неулови́м|ый (~, ~а), *adj.* 1. elusive, difficult to catch. 2. (*fig.*) imperceptible.

неумéл|ый (~, ~а), *adj.* clumsy; unskilful.

неумéни|е, я, *n.* inability; lack of skill.

неумéренност|ь, и, *f.* 1. immoderation. 2. intemperance.

неумéрен|ный (~, ~на), *adj.* 1. immoderate; excessive. 2. intemperate.

неумéст|ный (~ен, ~на), *adj.* 1. inappropriate; misplaced, out of place. 2. irrelevant.

неýм|ный (~ён, ~на́, ~нó), *adj.* foolish, silly.

неумоли́м|ый (~, ~а), *adj.* implacable; inexorable.

неумолка́ем|ый (~, ~а), *adj.* (*of sounds*) incessant, unceasing.

неумóл|чный (~чен, ~чна), *adj.* = ~ка́емый.

неумы́шлен|ный (~, ~на), *adj.* unpremeditated; unintentional, inadvertent.

неупла́т|а, ы, *f.* non-payment.

неупотреби́тел|ьный (~ен, ~ьна), *adj.* not in use, not current.

неуравновéшен|ный (~, ~на), *adj.* (*psych.*) unbalanced.

неурожá|й, я, *m.* bad harvest, failure of crops.

неурожа́й|ный, *adj. of* ~; н. год lean year, bad harvest year.

неурóчный, *adj.* untimely.

неуря́диц|а, ы, *f.* (*coll.*) 1. disorder, mess. 2. (*pl.*) squabbling.

неуси́дчив|ый (~, ~a), *adj.* restless, not persevering.

неуспева́емост|ь, и, *f.* poor progress (*in studies*).

неуспева́ющий, *adj.* backward, not making satisfactory progress.

неуста́н|ный (~ен, ~на), *adj.* tireless, unwearying.

неусто́йк|а, и, *f.* 1. (*leg.*) forfeit (*for breach of contract*). 2. (*coll.*) failure.

неусто́йчивост|ь, и, *f.* instability, unsteadiness.

неусто́йчив|ый (~, ~a), *adj.* unstable, unsteady; ~ое равнове́сие unstable equilibrium.

неустрани́м|ый (~, ~a), *adj.* unremovable; ~ое препя́тствие insurmountable obstacle.

неустраши́м|ый (~, ~a), *adj.* fearless, intrepid, undaunted.

неустро́ен|ный (~, ~на), *adj.* unsettled, not put in order, badly organized.

неустро́йств|о, a, *n.* disorder.

неусту́пчив|ый (~, ~a), *adj.* unyielding, uncompromising.

неусы́п|ный (~ен, ~на), *adj.* vigilant; indefatigable.

неутеши́тел|ьный (~ен, ~ьна), *adj.* not comforting, depressing; ~ьные ве́сти distressing news.

неуте́ш|ный (~ен, ~на), *adj.* inconsolable; disconsolate.

неутоли́м|ый (~, ~a), *adj.* unquenchable; unappeasable; (*fig.*) insatiable.

неутоми́м|ый (~, ~a), *adj.* tireless, indefatigable.

не́уч, a, *m.* (*coll.*) ignoramus.

неучти́вост|ь, и, *f.* discourtesy, impoliteness, incivility.

неучти́в|ый (~, ~a), *adj.* discourteous, impolite, uncivil.

неую́т|ный (~ен, ~на), *adj.* bleak, comfortless.

неуязви́м|ый (~, ~a), *adj.* 1. invulnerable. 2. unassailable.

неф, a, *m.* (*archit.*) nave.

нефри́т¹, a, *m.* (*med.*) nephritis.

нефри́т², a, *m.* (*min.*) nephrite, jade.

нефте- oil-.

нефтеналивн|о́й, *adj.* equipped for carrying oil in bulk; ~о́е су́дно oil-tanker.

нефтено́с|ный (~ен, ~на), *adj.* oil-bearing.

нефтеперего́нный, *adj.* oil-refining; н. заво́д oil refinery.

нефтеперераба́тывающий, *adj.* oil-refining.

нефтепрово́д, a, *m.* oil pipe-line.

нефтехрани́лищ|e, a, *n.* oil-tank, oil reservoir.

нефт|ь, и, *f.* oil, petroleum; н.-сыре́ц crude oil.

нефтя́|ник, a, *m.* oil(-industry) worker.

нефтя́нк|а, и, *f.* (*coll.*) 1. oil-engine. 2. oil-barge.

нефтян|о́й, *adj.* oil; ~а́я вы́шка derrick; н. фонта́н oil-gusher.

нехва́тк|а, и, *f.* (*coll.*) shortage.

нехи́т|рый (~ёр, ~ра́, ~ро́), *adj.* 1. artless, guileless. 2. (*coll.*) simple; uncomplicated.

нехоро́ш|ий (~, ~а́, ~о́), *adj.* bad.

нехорошо́, *adv.* badly; чу́вствовать себя́ н. to feel unwell.

не́хотя, *adv.* 1. reluctantly, unwillingly. 2. inadvertently, unintentionally.

не́христ|ь, я, *m.* 1. (*obs.*) unbeliever. 2. (*coll.*) brute, hard-hearted person.

нецелесообра́з|ный (~ен, ~на), *adj.* inexpedient; pointless.

нецензу́р|ный (~ен, ~на), *adj.* unprintable.

неча́янность|ь, и, *f.* 1. unexpectedness. 2. surprise. 3. unexpected event.

неча́янный, *adj.* 1. unexpected. 2. accidental; unintentional.

не́чего, не́чему, не́чем, не́ о чем 1. *pron.* (+*inf.*) there is nothing (to); мне н. чита́ть I have nothing to read; не́ о чем бы́ло говори́ть there was nothing to talk about; от н. де́лать for want of something better to do, to while away the time; н. сказа́ть! (*coll., iron.*) indeed!; well, I declare! 2. *as pred.* (*impers.*; +*inf.*) it's no good, it's no use; there is no need; н. жа́ловаться it's no use complaining; н. и говори́ть, что... it goes without saying that....

нечелове́ческий, *adj.* 1. superhuman. 2. inhuman.

нечести́в|ый (~, ~a), *adj.* impious, profane.

нече́стност|ь, и, *f.* dishonesty.

нече́ст|ный (~ен, ~на́), *adj.* 1. dishonest. 2. dishonourable.

не́чет, a, *m.* (*coll.*) odd number.

нечёт|кий (~ок, ~ка́), *adj.* illegible; indistinct; inaccurate, slipshod.

нечётный, *adj.* odd.

нечистопло́т|ный (~ен, ~на), *adj.* 1. dirty; untidy, slovenly. 2. (*fig.*) unscrupulous.

нечистот|а́, ы́, *pl.* ~ы, ~, *f.* 1. dirtiness. 2. *pl. only* sewage, garbage.

нечи́ст|ый (~, ~а́, ~о), *adj.* 1. unclean, dirty (*also fig.*); ~ое де́ло suspicious affair; ~ая пи́ща (*rel.*) unclean food. 2. impure, adulterated; ~ая поро́да impure breed; ~ое произноше́ние defective pronunciation. 3. careless, inaccurate. 4. dishonourable; dishonest; быть ~ым на́ руку to be light-fingered. 5. ~ая си́ла; *also as noun* н., ~ого, *m.* the Evil one, the Evil Spirit.

не́чист|ь, и, *f.* (*collect.*; *coll.*) 1. evil spirits. 2. (*fig., pejor.*) scum, vermin.

нечленоразде́л|ьный (~ен, ~ьна), *adj.* inarticulate.

не́что, *pron.* (*nom. and a. cases only*) something.

нечувстви́тел|ьный (~ен, ~ьна), *adj.* **1.** (к) insensitive (to). **2.** imperceptible.

нешу́точ|ный (~ен, ~на), *adj.* grave, serious; де́ло ~ное it is no joke, it is no laughing matter.

нещад|ный (~ен, ~на), *adj.* merciless.

неэвкли́дов, *adj.* ~а геоме́трия non-Euclidean geometry.

нея́вк|а, и, *f.* non-appearance, failure to appear.

неядови́тый, *adj.* non-poisonous; (*chem.*) non-toxic.

нея́сность, и, *f.* vagueness, obscurity.

нея́с|ный (~ен, ~на́, ~но), *adj.* vague, obscure.

нея́сыт|ь, и, *f.* tawny owl.

ни 1. *correlative conj.* ни… ни neither … nor; ни тот ни друго́й neither (the one nor the other); ни то ни сё neither one thing nor the other; ни ры́ба, ни мя́со neither fish, flesh nor good red herring; ни с того́, ни с сего́ all of a sudden; for no apparent reason; ни за что, ни про что for no reason at all. **2.** *particle* not a; ни оди́н, ни одна́, ни одно́ not a, not one, not a single; на у́лице не́ было ни (одно́й) души́ there was not a soul about; ни ша́гу да́льше! not a step further!; ни гу-гу́! (*coll.*) not a word! mum's the word! **3.** *separable component of prons.* никако́й, никто́, ничто́, *following preps.*; ни в како́м (ни в ко́ем) слу́чае on no account; ни за что на све́те! not for the world! **4.** (*particle, in combination with* как, кто, куда́, *etc.*) = -ever; как бы мы ни стара́лись however hard we tried; что бы он ни говори́л whatever he might say.

ни́в|а, ы, *f.* (corn-)field; на ~е просвеще́ния (*fig.*) in the field of education.

нивели́р, а, *m.* (*tech.*) level.

нивели́р|овать, ую, *impf. and pf.* (*tech. and fig.*) **1.** to level. **2.** to survey, contour.

нивели́ровк|а, и, *f.* **1.** levelling. **2.** surveying, contouring.

нивели́ровщик, а, *m.* **1.** leveller. **2.** surveyor.

нигде́, *adv.* nowhere.

нигили́зм, а, *m.* nihilism.

нигили́ст, а, *m.* nihilist.

нигилисти́ческий, *adj.* nihilistic.

нидерла́нд|ец, ца, *m.* Dutchman.

нидерла́ндский, *adj.* Netherlands.

нижа́йший, *superl. of* ни́зкий; ваш н. слуга́ your very humble servant.

ни́же, 1. *comp. of* ни́зкий *and* ни́зко. **2.** *prep.* (+g.) *and adv.* below, beneath.

нижеподписа́вшийся, *adj.* (the) undersigned.

нижесле́дующий, *adj.* following.

нижеупомя́нутый, *adj.* undermentioned.

ни́жн|ий, *adj.* (*in var. senses*) lower; ~ее бельё underclothes, underwear; ~яя пала́та Lower Chamber, Lower House; н. чин (*mil., obs.*) other rank, ranker; ~яя ю́бка slip; н. эта́ж ground floor.

ни|жу́, ~жешь, *see* ~за́ть.

низ, а, *pl.* ~ы́, *m.* **1.** bottom; ground floor. **2.** (*pl.*) lower classes. **3.** (*pl.; mus.*) low notes.

ни|за́ть, жу́, ~жешь, *impf.* (*of* на~) to string, thread; н. слова́ to speak very smoothly.

ни за что, *adv.* in no circumstances.

низведе́ни|е, я, *n.* bringing down.

низверг|а́ть, а́ю, *impf.* (*of* ~нуть) to precipitate; (*fig.*) to overthrow.

низверг|а́ться, а́юсь, *impf.* (*of* ~нуться) **1.** to crash down. **2.** *pass. of* ~а́ть.

низве́рг|нуть(ся), ну(сь), нешь(ся), *past* ~(ся), ~ла(сь), *pf. of* ~а́ть(ся).

низверже́ни|е, я, *n.* overthrow.

низве|сти́, ду́, дёшь, *past* ~л, ~ла́, *pf.* (*of* низводи́ть) to bring down; (*fig.*) to bring low; to reduce.

низво|ди́ть, жу́, ~дишь, *impf. of* низвести́.

низи́н|а, ы, *f.* low place, depression.

ни́з|кий (~ок, ~ка́, ~ко), *adj.* **1.** (*in var. senses*); low; ~кого происхожде́ния of humble origin. **2.** base, mean; н. посту́пок shabby act.

низколо́б|ый (~, ~а), *adj.* with a low forehead.

низкоопла́чиваемый, *adj.* poorly-paid.

низкопокло́нник, а, *m.* toady, crawler.

низкопокло́нннича|ть, ю, *impf.* (пе́ред) to cringe (to), grovel (before).

низкопокло́нств|о, а, *n.* cringing, servility.

низкопро́б|ный (~ен, ~на), *adj.* **1.** base, low-grade (*of precious metals*). **2.** (*fig.*) base; inferior.

низкоро́сл|ый (~, ~а), *adj.* undersized, stunted.

низкосо́рт|ный (~ен, ~на), *adj.* low-grade; of inferior quality.

низлага́|ть, ю, *impf. of* низложи́ть.

низложе́ни|е, я, *n.* deposition, dethronement.

низлож|и́ть, у́, ~ишь, *pf.* (*of* низлага́ть) to depose, dethrone.

ни́зменность, и, *f.* **1.** (*geogr.*) lowland (*not exceeding 600 ft. above sea-level*). **2.** baseness.

ни́змен|ный (~, ~на), *adj.* **1.** low-lying. **2.** low; base, vile.

низово́й¹, *adj.* (*geogr.*) lower; situated down stream; н. ве́тер wind blowing from downstream (*esp. from mouth of Volga*).

низово́й², *adj.* local; (*polit.*) grass-roots; н. аппара́т basic organization; н. рабо́тник worker in basic organization.

низо́в|ье, ья, *g. pl.* **~ьев,** *n.* the lower reaches (*of a river*).

низо|йти́, йду́, йдёшь, *past* **нисшёл, ~шла́,** *pf.* (*of* нисходи́ть) (*obs.*) to descend.

ни́зом, *adv.* (*coll.*) along the bottom; е́хать **н.** to take the lower road.

ни́зост|ь, и, f. lowness; baseness, meanness.

низри́н|уть, у, ешь, *pf.* (*rhet.*) to throw down, overthrow.

низри́н|уться, усь, ешься, *pf.* (*rhet.*) to crash down.

ни́зш|ий, *superl.* of **ни́зкий,** lowest; **~ее образова́ние** primary education; **~ие слу́жащие** the most junior employees.

никак¹, *adv.* by no means, in no way, nowise; **он н. не мог узна́ть её а́дрес** in no way could he discover her address; **н. нельзя́** it is quite impossible; **н. нет** *respectful reply in negative to question.*

никак², *adv.* (*coll.*) it seems, it would appear; **они́, н., уже́ пришли́** they are here already, it seems.

никак|о́й, *pron.* no; **не... ~о́го, ~о́й, ~и́х** no . . . whatever; **я не име́ю ~о́го представле́ния (поня́тия)** I have no idea, no conception; **~и́х возраже́ний!** no objections!; **учёный он н.** (*coll.*) he is no scholar; **и ~и́х (гвозде́й)!** (*coll.*) and that's all there is to it, and that's that.

ни́келевый, *adj.* nickel.

никелиро́в|анный, *p.p.p.* of **~а́ть** and *adj.* nickel-plated.

никелир|ова́ть, у́ю, *impf. and pf.* to plate with nickel, nickel.

никелиро́вк|а, и, f. nickel-plating.

ни́кел|ь, я, m. nickel.

ни́к|нуть, ну, нешь, *past.* **~, ~ла,** *impf.* (*of* по~ *and* с~) to droop, flag (*also fig.*).

никогда́, *adv.* never; **как н.** as never before.

нико́|й, *pron.* (*obs.*) no; *now only in phrases* **~им о́бразом** by no means, in no way; **ни в ко́ем слу́чае** on no account, in no circumstances.

никоти́н, а, m. nicotine.

никоти́н|ный, *adj.* of **~.**

никоти́н|овый, *adj.* = **~ный.**

никто́, никого́, никому́, нике́м, ни о ком, *pron.* nobody, no one; **там никого́ не́ было** there was nobody there; **н. друго́й** nobody else; **ни у кого́ нет э́того** no one has it.

никуда́, *adv.* nowhere; **э́то н. не годи́тся** (*fig.*) this won't do, it is no good at all; **н. не го́дный** good-for-nothing, worthless, useless.

никуд|ы́шный, *adj.* (*coll.*) = **~а́ не го́дный.**

никчёмный, *adj.* (*coll.*) useless, good-for-nothing; needless.

ним, *i.* of **он, оно́;** *d.* of **они́** *after preps.*

нима́ло, *adv.* not in the least, not at all.

нимб, а, m. halo, nimbus.

ни́ми, *i.* of **они́** *after preps.*

ни́мф|а, ы, f. 1. nymph. 2. (*pl., anat.*) labia minora. 3. (*zool.*) pupa.

нимфома́ни|я, и, f. nymphomania.

нимфома́нк|а, и, f. nymphomaniac.

нио́би|й, я, m. (*chem.*) niobium.

ниотку́да, *adv.* from nowhere; **н. не сле́дует, что...** it in no way follows that . . .

нипочём, *adv.* (*coll.*) 1. (+*d.*) it is nothing (to); **э́то ему́ н.** it is child's play to him; **ему́ н. провести́ це́лую ночь на заня́тиях** he thinks nothing of spending a whole night working. 2. for nothing, dirt-cheap; **прода́ть н.** to sell for a song. 3. never, in no circumstances.

ни́ппел|ь, я, pl. ~я́, ~е́й, m. (*tech.*) nipple.

нирва́н|а, ы, f. nirvana.

ниско́лько 1. *adv.* not at all, not in the least; no whit; **ей от э́того бы́ло н. не лу́чше** she was none the better for it. 2. *pron.* (*coll.*) none at all; **ско́лько вам э́то сто́ило? — н.** how much did it cost you? It cost me nothing.

ниспада́|ть, ет, *impf.* of **ниспа́сть.**

ниспа́|сть, сть, ду́, дёшь, *past* **~л, ~ла,** *pf.* (*of* **~да́ть**) (*obs.*) to fall, drop.

ниспо|сла́ть, шлю́, шлёшь, *pf.* (*of* **~сыла́ть**) (*rel.*) to send down (*sc. from heaven*).

ниспосыла́|ть, ю, *impf.* of **ниспосла́ть.**

ниспроверг|а́ть, а́ю, *impf.* (*of* **~нуть**) to overthrow, overturn (*also fig.*).

ниспрове́рг|нуть, ну, нешь, *past* **~, ~ла,** *pf.* of **~а́ть.**

ниспроверже́ни|е, я, n. overthrow.

ниста́гм, а, m. (*med.*) nystagmus.

нисхо|ди́ть, жу́, ~дишь, *impf.* of **низойти́.**

нисход|я́щий, *pres. part. act.* of **~и́ть** and *adj.* 1. descending; **по ~я́щей ли́нии** in the line of descent, in a descending line. 2. (*ling.*) falling.

нисше́стви|е, я, n. descending, descent.

нитеви́д|ный (~ен, ~на), *adj.* thread-like, filiform; **н. пульс** (*med.*) thready pulse.

нитево́д, а, m. (*text.*) thread guide; **ро́лик ~a** yarn tension bowl.

ните́ло́вк|а, и, f. (*text*) thread picker.

нитере́зк|а, и, f. (*text.*) thread cutter.

ни́тк|а, и, f. thread; **н. же́мчуга** string of pearls; **на живу́ю ~y** (*fig., coll.*) hastily, anyhow; **ши́то бе́лыми ~ами** (*fig., coll.*) transparent, patent, obvious; **до (после́дней) ~и обобра́ть** (*fig., coll.*) to fleece, leave without a shirt to one's back; **промо́кнуть до ~и** (*fig.*) to get soaked to the skin; **вы́тянуться в ~y** (*fig., coll.*) (*i*) to stand in line, (*ii*) to become worn to a shadow.

нито́н, а, m. (*chem.*) niton.

ни́точк|а, и, f. *dim.* of **ни́тка;** **по ~е разобра́ть** (*fig.*) to analyse minutely, subject to minute scrutiny; ходи́ть по ~е (*fig.*) to toe the line, sing small.

ни́т|очный, *adj. of* ~ка; ~очное произво́дство spinning.

нитра́т, а, *m.* (*chem.*) nitrate.

нитри́р|овать, ую, *impf. and pf.* (*chem.*) 1. to nitride. 2. to nitrate.

нитри́т, а, *m.* (*chem.*) nitrite.

нитрифика́ци|я, и, *f.* (*chem.*) nitrification.

нитрифици́р|овать, ую, *impf. and pf.* (*chem., bot.*) to nitrify.

нитробензо́л, а, *m.* (*chem.*) nitrobenzene.

нитрова́ни|е, я, *n.* (*chem.*) nitration.

нитроглицери́н, а, *m.* (*chem.*) nitroglycerine.

нитроипри́т, а, *m.* (*chem., mil.*) nitrogen mustard (gas).

нитроклетча́тк|а, и, *f.* (*chem.*) nitrocellulose.

нитросоедине́ни|е, я, *n.* nitro-compound.

нитча́тк|а, и, *f.* 1. tape-worm. 2. (*bot.*) hair-weed, crow-silk.

ни́тчатый, *adj.* filiform.

нит|ь, и, *f.* 1. (*in var. senses*) thread; путево́дная н. clue; ~и дру́жбы bonds of friendship; проходи́ть кра́сной ~ью (*fig.*) to stand out, run through (*of theme, motif*). 2. (*bot., electr.*) filament; н. нака́ла (*electr.*) glow-lamp filament; (*radio*) heated filament. 3. (*med.*) suture.

ни́тянк|а, и, *f.* (*coll.*) knitted cotton glove.

ни́тяный, *adj.* cotton.

них, *a. and g. of* они́ *when governed by preps.*

ниц, *adv.* (*obs.*) face downwards; пасть н. to prostrate oneself, kiss the ground.

ничего́[1], *g. of* ничто́.

ничего́[2], *adv.* 1. (*also* н. себе́) so-so; passably, not (too) badly; all right; ко́рмят здесь н. the food here is not too bad; как вы чу́вствуете себя́? — н. how do you feel? all right. 2. *as indecl. adj.* not (too) bad, passable, tolerable; на́ша кварти́ра н. our flat is not too bad; па́рень он н. he is not a bad chap.

нич|е́й (~ья́, ~ье́), *pron.* nobody's, no one's; ~ья́ земля́ no man's land; *as noun* ~ья́, ~ье́й, *f.* (*sport*) draw, drawn game; сыгра́ть в ~ью́ to play a drawn game, draw.

ниче́йный, *adj.* (*coll.*) 1. no man's. 2. (*sport*) drawn.

ничко́м, *adv.* prone, face downwards.

ничто́, ничего́, ничему́, ниче́м, ни о чём, *pron.* 1. nothing; э́то ничего́ не зна́чит it means nothing; ниче́м не ко́нчилось it came to nothing; ничего́ подо́бного! nothing of the kind!; э́то ничего́! it's nothing! it doesn't matter!; ничего́! (*coll.*) that's all right! never mind! 2. nought; nil.

ничто́же, *pron.* н. сумня́ся, н. сумня́шеся (*iron.*) without a second's hesitation.

ничто́жеств|о, а, *n.* 1. nothingness. 2. a nonentity, a nobody.

ничто́жност|ь, и, *f.* 1. insignificance. 2. a nonentity, a nobody.

ничто́ж|ный (~ен, ~на), *adj.* insignificant; paltry, worthless.

ничу́ть, *adv.* (*coll.*) not at all, not in the least, not a bit; н. не быва́ло not at all.

ничь|я́, е́й, *f. see* ниче́й.

ни́ш|а, и, *f.* niche, recess; (*archit.*) bay.

нища́|ть, ю, *impf.* (*of* об~) to grow poor, be reduced to beggary.

ни́щенк|а, и, *f.* beggar-woman.

ни́щенский, *adj.* beggarly.

ни́щенств|о, а, *n.* 1. begging. 2. beggary.

ни́щенств|овать, ую, *impf.* 1. to beg, go begging. 2. to be destitute.

нищет|а́, ы́, *f.* 1. destitution; indigence, poverty (*also fig.*). 2. (*collect.*) beggars; the poor.

ни́щ|ий, *adj.* 1. destitute; indigent, poverty-stricken; ~ая бра́тия (*folk poet.*) the poor; н. ду́хом poor in spirit. 2. *as noun* н., ~его, *m.* beggar, mendicant; pauper.

но[1], *conj.* 1. but; *after concessive clause not translated or* still, nevertheless; хотя́ он и бо́лен, но наме́рен прийти́ although he is ill, he (still) intends to come. 2. (*coll.*) *as noun* a 'but'; snag, difficulty; тут есть одно́ «но» there is just one snag in it.

но[2], *interj.* gee up!

нова́тор, а, *m.* innovator.

нова́тор|ский, *adj. of* ~ *and* ~ство.

нова́торств|о, а, *n.* innovation.

нове́йший, *superl. of* но́вый; newest; latest.

нове́лл|а, ы, *f.* 1. short story. 2. (*in Roman law*) novel.

новелли́ст, а, *m.* short story-writer.

но́веньк|ий, *adj.* 1. brand-new. 2. *as noun* н., ~ого, *m.* new boy; ~ая, ~ой, *f.* new girl.

новизн|а́, ы́, *f.* novelty; newness.

нови́к, а́, *m.* 1. (*hist.*) young courtier. 2. (*obs.*) novice.

новин|а́, ы́, *f.* (*dial.*) 1. virgin soil. 2. freshly-reaped corn. 3. piece of unbleached linen.

нови́нк|а, и, *f.* novelty; мне в ~у е́хать самолётом it is a new experience for me to travel by 'plane.

нович|о́к, ка́, *m.* 1. (в+*p.*) novice (at), beginner (at), tiro; (*sport*) colt. 2. (*in school*) new boy; new girl.

новобра́н|ец, ца, *m.* recruit.

новобра́чн|ая, ой, *f.* bride.

новобра́чн|ые, ых, *pl.* newly-married couple, newly-weds.

новобра́чн|ый, ого, *m.* bridegroom.

нововведе́ни|е, я, *n.* innovation.

нового́дний, *adj.* new year's.

новогре́ческий, *adj.* н. язы́к modern Greek.

новозаве́тный, *adj.* of the New Testament.

новозела́нд|ец, ца, *m.* New Zealander.

новозела́нд|ка, ки, *f. of* ~ец.

новозела́ндский, *adj.* New Zealand.

новоиспечённый, *adj.* (*coll.*, *joc.*) newly made; newly fledged.

новока́ин, а, *m.* (*pharm.*) novocaine.

новолу́ни|е, я, *n.* new moon.

новомо́д|ный (~ен, ~на), *adj.* in the latest fashion, up-to-date; (*fig.*, *pejor.*) new-fangled.

новообразова́ни|е, я, *n.* new growth; new formation; (*med.*) neoplasm.

новообращённый, *adj.* (*rel. and fig.*) newly converted.

новопреста́вленный, *adj.* (*rel.*) the late, the late-lamented.

новоприбы́вш|ий, *adj.* newly-arrived; *as noun* н., ~его, *m.* new-comer.

новорождённ|ый, *adj.* **1.** new-born; *as noun* н., ~ого, *m.* the baby. **2.** *as noun* one celebrating his birthday; поздра́вить ~ого to wish many happy returns (of a birthday).

новосёл, а, *m.* new settler.

новосе́ль|е, я, *n.* **1.** new home; new abode. **2.** house-warming; справля́ть н. to give a house-warming party.

новостро́йк|а, и, *f.* 1. erection of new buildings. **2.** newly-erected building; шко́ла-н. new school.

но́вост|ь, и, *g. pl.* ~éй, *f.* **1.** news; tidings; э́то что ещё за ~и!, вот ещё ~и! (*coll.*) Well, I like that! did you ever! **2.** novelty.

новоте́льный, *adj.* newly-calved.

новоя́вленный, *adj.* (*rel. or iron.*) newly brought to light.

но́вшеств|о, а, *n.* innovation, novelty.

но́в|ый (~, ~á, ~о), *adj.* **1.** new; novel; fresh; Н. год new year's day; Н. заве́т the ⸰New Testament; Н. свет the New World; что ~ого? what's the news?, what's new? **2.** modern; recent; ~ая исто́рия modern history; ~ые языки́ modern languages.

нов|ь, и, *f.* virgin soil.

ног|á, и́, *a.* ~у, *pl.* ~и, ног, ~áм, *f.* foot; leg; вверх ~а́ми head over heels; без (за́дних) ног (*coll.*) dead-beat; в ~а́х посте́ли at the foot of the bed; валя́ться в ~а́х у кого́-н. to prostrate oneself before someone; идти́ в ~у (с+*i.*) to keep step (with), keep pace (with) (*also fig.*); идти́ н. за́ ~у (*coll.*) to plod along; к ~é! (*mil.*) order arms!; положи́ть ~у на́ ~у to cross one's legs; сиде́ть н. на́ ~у to sit with legs crossed; он не стоя́л на ~а́х he could barely stand upright (*sc. from weakness, intoxication, etc.*); поста́вить кого́-н. на́ ~и (*fig.*) to set someone on his feet; стать на́ ~и (*fig.*) to stand on one's own feet; под-ня́ть кого́-н. на́ ~и to goad someone into

action; жить на широ́кую (большу́ю, ба́рскую) ~у to live in (grand) style, live like a lord; быть на коро́ткой ~é (с+*i.*) to be on a good footing (with), be intimate (with); хрома́ть на о́бе ~й to be lame in both legs; (*fig.*, *coll.*) to go badly, creak; верте́ться у кого́-н. под ~а́ми to get under someone's feet; сбить с ног to knock down; сби́ться с ~й to lose the step, get out of step; дать ~у to keep in step, get in step; встать с ле́вой ~й to get out of bed on the wrong side; со всех ног (*coll.*) as fast as one's legs will carry one; е́ле ~и унести́ to escape by the skin of one's teeth; он дава́й Бог ~и (*coll.*) he took to his heels; ног под собо́й не слы́шать (от ра́дости) (*coll.*) to be beside oneself (with joy); ног под собо́й не чу́вствовать (от уста́лости, *etc.*) to be barely able to stand (from tiredness, *etc.*); мое́й ~й у вас не бу́дет (*coll.*) I shall not set foot in your house again; мы — ни ~о́й туда́ (*coll.*) we never go near the place; стоя́ть одно́й ~о́й в моги́ле to have one foot in the grave; протяну́ть ~и (*coll.*) to turn up one's toes.

ноготк|и́, о́в (*bot.*) marigold.

ногот|о́к, ка́, *m. dim. of* но́готь; мужичо́к с н. Tom Thumb.

ног|оть, тя, *pl.* ~ти, ~те́й, *m.* (finger-, toe-) nail.

ног|тево́й, *adj. of* ~оть.

ногтое́д|а, ы, *f.* (*med.*) whitlow.

нож, á, *m.* knife; перочи́нный н. penknife; разрезно́й н. paper-knife; н.-пила́ bread-knife; садо́вый н. pruning-knife; н. в спи́ну (*fig.*) stab in the back; э́то мне н. о́стрый (*fig.*) for me this is sheer hell; без ~á заре́зать to do for; быть на ~а́х (с+*i.*) to be at daggers drawn (with); под ~о́м under the knife (= *during a surgical operation*); приставать к кому́-н. с ~о́м к го́рлу to pester someone, importune someone.

нож|ево́й, *adj. of* ~; н. ма́стер cutler; ~евы́е това́ры cutlery.

но́жик, а, *m.* knife.

но́жк|а, и, *f.* 1. *dim. of* нога́; подста́вить ~у (+*d.*) to trip up. **2.** leg (*of furniture, utensils, etc.*); stem (*of wine-glass*). **3.** (*bot.*) stalk; stem (*of mushroom*).

но́жниц|ы, ~, *pl.* **1.** scissors, pair of scissors; shears. **2.** (*econ.*) discrepancy.

ножн|о́й, *adj. of* нога́; н. приво́д foot drive, pedal operation, treadle drive; н. то́рмоз foot brake, pedal brake; ~а́я шве́йная маши́на treadle sewing-machine.

но́ж|ны, ~ен, ~нам (*and* **нож|ны́, ~о́н, ~на́м**) sheath; scabbard.

ножо́вк|а, и, *f.* hacksaw.

ножо́вщик, а, *m.* cutler.

ножо́вый, *adj.* = ножево́й.

ноздрева́тост|ь, и, *f.* porosity, sponginess.

ноздрева́т|ый (~, ~а), *adj.* porous, spongy.

ноздр|я́, и́, *pl.* ~и, ~е́й, *f.* nostril.

нока́ут, а, *m.* (*sport*) knock-out.

нокаути́р|овать, ую, *impf. and pf.* (*sport*) to knock out.

нокда́ун, а, *m.* (*sport*) knock-down.

ноктю́рн, а, *m.* (*mus.*) nocturne.

нолево́й, *adj.* = нулево́й.

нол|ь, я́, *m.* = нуль; ноль-ноль *indicates timing of event at the hour exactly;* экспре́сс в Берли́н отхо́дит в пять н.-н., в двена́дцать н.-н., в семна́дцать н.-н. the express for Berlin departs at five o'clock (0500), at twelve noon (1200), at seventeen hundred (1700).

нома́д, а, *m.* nomad.

номенклату́р|а, ы, *f.* 1. nomenclature. 2. list, schedule, catalogue. 3. nomenklatura (*system by which in the U.S.S.R. appointments to specified posts in government or economic administration are made by organs of the Communist Party*).

номенклату́р|ный, *adj. of* ~а.

но́мер, а, *pl.* ~а́, *m.* 1. number; number, issue (*of newspaper, magazine, etc.*). 2. size; како́й н. боти́нок вы но́сите? what size do you take in shoes? 3. room (*in hotel*). 4. item on the programme, number, turn; со́льный н. solo (number); эстра́дный н. music-hall turn. 5. (*coll.*) trick; вы́кинуть н. to play a trick; вот так н.! (*coll.*) what a funny thing! 6. (*mil.*) н. оруди́йного расчёта member of a gun crew, gun number.

номерн|о́й 1. *adj. of* но́мер; numbered. 2. *as noun* н,. ~о́го, *m.* boots (*in a hotel*).

номер|о́к, ка́, *m.* 1. tally; label, ticket (*in cloakroom, etc.*). 2. small room (*in a hotel*).

номина́л, а, *m.* (*econ.*) face-value; по ~у at face-value.

номина́льн|ый, *adj.* 1. nominal; ~ая цена́ face value. 2. (*tech.*) rated, indicated, nominal.

номогра́мм|а, ы, *f.* (*math.*) nomogram, nomograph.

но́н|а, ы, *f.* (*mus.*) ninth.

но́не, *adv.* (*dial.*) = ны́не.

нонпаре́л|ь, и, *f.* (*typ.*) nonpareil.

но́нче, *adv.* (*dial.*) = ны́нче.

но́н|ы, ~ (*in Roman calendar*) nones.

нор|а́, ы́, *pl.* ~ы, ~, ~а́м, *f.* burrow, hole; lair; (*of hare*) form.

норве́ж|ец, ца, *m.* Norwegian.

норве́жк|а, и, *f.* Norwegian (woman).

норве́жский, *adj.* Norwegian.

норд, а, *m.* (*naut.*) 1. north. 2. north wind.

норд-ве́ст, а, *m.* (*naut.*) 1. north-west. 2. north-wester(-ly wind).

норд-о́ст, а, *m.* (*naut.*) 1. north-east. 2. north-easter(-ly wind).

но́ри|я, и, *f.* (*tech.*) noria, bucket chain.

но́рк|а¹, и, *f.* *dim. of* нора́.

но́рк|а², и, *f.* (америка́нская) н. mink (*mustela vison*); (европе́йская) н. marsh-otter (*mustela lutreola*).

но́рк|овый, *adj. of* ~а².

но́рм|а, ы, *f.* 1. standard, norm. 2. rate; н. вы́работки rate of output; сверх ~ы in excess of planned rate.

нормализа́ци|я, и, *f.* standardization.

нормализ|ова́ть, у́ю, *impf. and pf.* to standardize.

норма́л|ь, и, *f.* (*math., phys.*) normal.

норма́льно, *as pred.* (*coll.*) it is all right, O.K.

норма́льност|ь, и, *f.* normality.

норма́л|ьный (~ен, ~ьна), *adj.* (*in var. senses*) normal; н. уста́в model regulations; ~ьная колея́ (*railways*) standard gauge.

норма́нд|ец, ца, *m.* Norman (*inhabitant of Normandy*).

норма́ндски|й, *adj.* Norman; ~е острова́ Channel Islands.

норма́нн, а, *m.* (*hist.*) Northman, Norseman.

норма́нский, *adj.* (*hist.*) Norse.

НОРМАТИ́В, а, *m.* (*econ.*) norm.

нормати́в|ный (~ен, ~на), *adj.* 1. *adj. of* ~; corresponding to norm. 2. normative.

нормирова́ни|е, я, *n.* 1. regulation, normalization; н. труда́ norm-fixing, norm-setting (*in production*). 2. rationing.

нормиро́в|анный, *p.p.p. of* ~а́ть; н. рабо́чий день fixed working hours; ~анное снабже́ние rationing.

нормир|ова́ть, у́ю, *impf. and pf.* 1. to regulate, normalize; н. за́работную пла́ту to fix wages. 2. to ration, place on the ration.

нормиро́в|ка, ки, *f.* (*coll.*) = ~а́ние.

нормиро́вщик, а, *m.* regulator; н. труда́ norm-setter.

но́ров, а, *m.* 1. (*obs.*) custom. 2. (*coll.*) obstinacy, capriciousness; челове́к с ~ом difficult person. 3. (*of horses*) restiveness.

норови́ст|ый (~, ~а), *adj.* (*coll.*) restive; jibbing.

норов|и́ть, лю, и́шь, *impf.* (*coll.*) 1. (+*inf.*) to strive (to), aim (at). 2. (в+n.-a.) to strive to become; он ~и́т в писа́тели he has literary aspirations.

нос, а, о ~е, на ~у́, *pl.* ~ы́, *m.* 1. nose; у меня́ идёт кровь ~ом (из ~у) my nose is bleeding; говори́ть в н. to speak through one's nose; ~ом к ~у (*coll.*) face to face; на ~у́ (*coll.*) near at hand, imminent; заруби́ э́то себе́ на ~у́! put that in your pipe and smoke it!; э́то мне не по ~у (*coll.*) it's not to my liking; оста́вить с ~ом (*coll.*) to dupe, make a fool of; оста́ться с ~ом (*coll.*) to be duped, be left looking a fool; задра́ть н., подня́ть н. (*coll.*) to cock one's nose, put on airs; клева́ть ~ом (*coll.*) to nod; натяну́ть н. кому́-н. (*coll.*) to make a fool of someone; н. вороти́ть (от) (*coll.*) to turn up one's nose (at); пове́сить ~ом (на кви́нту) (*coll.*) to be crestfallen, be discouraged; показа́ть н. (*coll.*) to cock a snook; сова́ть н. не в своё де́ло (*coll.*) to poke one's nose into other people's affairs; ткнуть кого́-н. ~ом во что-н. (*coll.*) to thrust something under someone's nose; уткну́ться ~ом во что-н. (*coll.*) to bury one's face (oneself) in something. 2. beak. 3. (*naut.*) bow, head; prow.

носа́ст|ый (~, ~а), *adj.* big-nosed.

носа́т|ый (~, ~а), *adj.* = носа́стый.

но́сик, а, *m.* 1. *dim. of* нос. 2. toe (*of a shoe*). 3. spout.

носи́л|ки, ок, *no sing.* 1. stretcher. 2. sedan(-chair); litter. 3. (hand-)barrow.

носи́льн|ый, *adj.* for personal wear; ~ое бельё personal linen.

носи́льщик, а, *m.* porter.

носи́тел|ь, я, *m.* 1. (*fig.*) bearer; repository. 2. н. зара́зы (*biol., med.*) carrier. 3. (*chem.*) vehicle.

но|си́ть, шу́, ~сишь, *impf.* 1. *indet. of* нести́. 2. (*indet. only*) to carry; to bear (*also fig.*); н. свою́ де́вичью фами́лию to use one's maiden name; н. кого́-н. на рука́х (*indet. only*) to make a fuss of someone, make much of someone. 3. (*indet. only*) to wear; to carry.

но|си́ться, шу́сь, ~сишься, *impf.* 1. *indet. of* нести́сь; э́то ~сится в во́здухе (*fig.*) it is in the air, it is rumoured. 2. (c+*i.*) to fuss (over), make much (of); н. с мы́слью to nurse an idea, be obsessed with an idea. 3. (*intr.*) to wear; э́та мате́рия хорошо́ ~сится this stuff wears well.

но́ск|а¹, и, f. 1. carrying; bearing. 2. wearing.

но́ск|а², и, f. laying.

но́ск|ий¹ (~ок, ~ка), *adj.* (*of clothing, foot-wear, etc.*) hard-wearing, durable.

но́ск|ий², *adj.* ~ая ку́рица a good layer.

носов|о́й, *adj.* 1. *adj. of* нос; н. плато́к (pocket) handkerchief. 2. (*ling.*) nasal. 3. (*naut.*) bow, fore; ~а́я часть (су́дна) ship's bows, fore part; ~а́я ча́шка (*aeron.*) bow cap.

носогло́тк|а, и, f. (*anat.*) nasopharynx.

носогло́точный, *adj.* (*anat.*) nasopharyngeal.

носогре́йк|а, и, f. (*coll.*) nose-warmer (*short pipe*).

нос|о́к¹, ка́, m. 1. toe (*of boot or stocking*). 2. *dim of* ~.

нос|о́к², ка́, pl. ~ки́, ~ко́в, m. sock.

носоло́ги|я, и, f. (*med.*) nosology.

носоро́г, а, *m.* rhinoceros.

носо́|чный, *adj. of* ~к².

ностальги́|я, и, f. homesickness.

носу́х|а, и, f. (*zool.*) coati.

но́счик, а, *m.* carrier, porter.

но́т|а¹, ы, f. 1. (*mus.*) note. 2. (*pl.*) (sheet) music; игра́ть по ~ам (без нот) to play from music (without music); как по ~ам (*fig.*) without a hitch, according to plan.

но́т|а², ы, f. (diplomatic) note.

нотабе́н|а, ы, f. *and* **нотабе́н|е** *indecl.* nota bene (N.B.); поста́вить ~у to mark.

нотариа́льный, *adj.* notarial.

нота́риус, а, *m.* notary.

нота́ци|я¹, и, f. (*coll.*) lecture, reprimand; прочита́ть кому́-н. ~ю to read someone a lecture.

нота́ци|я², и, f. notation.

нотифика́ци|я, и, f. notification.

нотифици́р|овать, ую, *impf. and pf.* to notify, inform officially.

но́т|ка, ки, f. *dim. of* ~а¹.

но́тный, *adj. of* но́ты.

ноу́мен, а, *m.* (*philos.*) noumenon.

ноумена́льный, *adj.* (*philos.*) noumenal.

ноч|ева́ть, у́ю, *impf.* (*of* пере~) to pass the night.

ночёвк|а, и, f. spending the night, passing the night.

ноч|ка, ки, f. (*coll.*) *dim. of* ~ь.

ночле́г, а, *m.* 1. lodging for the night. 2. = ночёвка.

ночле́жк|а, и, f. (*coll.*) doss-house.

ночле́жник, а, *m.* 1. (*coll.*) (overnight) visitor, guest. 2. dosser.

ночле́|жный, *adj. of* ~г; н. дом doss-house.

ночни́к¹, а́, *m.* night-light.

ночни́к², а́, *m.* (*coll.*) night-driver; night-flier, night-flying ace.

ночн|о́е, о́го, *n.* pasturing of horses for the night.

ночн|о́й, *adj.* night; nocturnal; ~а́я ба́бочка moth; н. горшо́к chamber-pot; н. сто́лик bedside table; ~ы́е ту́фли bedroom slippers; ~а́я фиа́лка wild orchid.

ноч|ь, и, о ~и, в ~и́, pl. ~и, ~е́й, f. night; глуха́я н. the dead of night; споко́йной ~и! good-night!; по ~а́м (*of recurring events*) by night, at night.

но́чью, *adv.* by night.

но́ш|а, и, f. burden.

ноше́ни|е, я, n. 1. carrying. 2. wearing.

но́шеный, *adj.* worn; second-hand.

но́щно, *adv. only in phrase.* де́нно и н. (*coll.*) day and night.

но́|ю, ешь, *see* ныть.

но́ющ|ий, *pres. part. act. of* ныть; ~ая боль ache.

ноя́бр|ь, я́, *m.* November.

ноя́брь|ский, *adj. of* ~.

нрав, а, *m.* 1. disposition, temper; быть (+*d.*) по ~у to please. 2. (*pl.*) manners, customs, ways.

нра́в|иться, люсь, ишься, *impf.* (*of* по~) (+*d.*) to please; мне, ему́, *etc.*, ~ится I like, he likes, *etc.*; мне óчень ~ится э́та пье́са I like this play very much; онá мне кáк-то ~ится I rather like her; мы стара́емся н. вам we try to please you; (*impers.*) ей не ~ится ката́ться на лóдке she does not like going in boats.

нра́в|ный (~ен, ~на), *adj.* (*coll.*) testy, peppery.

нравоописа́тельный, *adj.* descriptive of manners; н. ромáн novel of manners.

нравоуче́ни|е, я, *n.* **1.** moralizing; moral admonition. **2.** (*lit.*) moral.

нравоучи́тельный, *adj.* moralistic, edifying.

нра́вственност|ь, и, *f.* morality; morals.

нра́вствен|ный (~, ~на), *adj.* moral.

ну, *interj. and particle* **1.** well!; well . . . then!; come on!; ну, ну! come, come!, come now! **2.** (да) ну? not really?, you don't mean to say so! **3.** *expressing surprise and pleasure or displeasure* well; what; why; ну и... what (a) . . .!, here's . . . (for you)!, there's . . . (for you)!; ну вот и...! there you are, you see . . .!; ну, неуже́ли?! what! really?; no? really?; ну, прáво!, ну, однáко же! well, to be sure!; ну и денёк! what a day!; ну и молодéц! (*also iron.*) there's a good boy!, there's a clever chap! **4.** *indicating resumption of talk; expressing concession, resignation, relief, qualified recognition of point* well; ну вот (*in narration*) well, well then; ну что ж, нý так well then; ну хорошó all right then, very well then; ведь вы сказáли, что вы их уви́дели, не прáвда ли? — ну да, но тóлько сзáди but you did say you saw them, didn't you? Yes, I know, but only from behind. **5.** нý как (+*fut.*) suppose, what if; нý как они́ не приду́т вó-время? suppose they don't come in time? **6.** (*as pred.*; +*inf.*) to start; он ну кричáть he started yelling. **6.** а нý (+*g.*) to hell (with)!, to the deuce (with)!; а ну тебя́! to hell with you!

нуби́йский, *adj.* Nubian.

нуди́зм, а, *m.* nudism, naturism.

нуди́ст, а, *m.* nudist, naturist.

ну́|дить, жу, дишь, *impf.* (*obs.*) **1.** to force, compel. **2.** to wear out.

ну|ди́ть, жу́, ди́шь, *impf.* (*coll.*) to wear out (*with complaints, questions, etc.*).

ну́дност|ь, и, *f.* tediousness.

ну́д|ный (~ен, ~на), *adj.* (*coll.*) tedious, boring.

нужд|á, ы́, *pl.* ~ы, *f.* **1.** want, straits; indigence. **2.** need; necessity; в слу́чае ~ы́ if necessary, if need be; н. всему́ нау́чит necessity is the mother of invention; ~ы́ нет, нет ~ы́ (*coll.*) no matter!, never mind; ~ы́ нет, что здесь те́сно, затó нам вéсело

it doesn't matter if it's a bit crowded here so long as we enjoy ourselves. **3.** (*coll., euph.*) call of nature.

нужда́емост|ь, и, *no pl.*, *f.* (в+*p.*) needs (in), requirements (in).

нужда́|ться, юсь, *impf.* **1.** to be in want; to be needy, hard-up. **2.** (в+*p.*) to need, require; to be in need (of).

ну́жник, а, *m.* (*coll.*) latrine.

ну́жно (+*d.*) **1.** (*impers.*; +*inf. or* +чтóбы) it is necessary; (one) ought, (one) should, (one) must, (one) need(s); н. бы́ло (бы) взять такси́ you should have taken a taxi; н., чтóбы онá реши́лась she ought to make up her mind. **2.** (*impers.*, +*a. or g.*; *coll.*) I, *etc.*, need; мне н. пять рубле́й I need five roubles. **3.** *see* ну́жный.

ну́ж|ный (~ен, ~нá, ~но, ~ны́), *adj.* necessary; requisite; (*predic. forms* +*d.*) I, *etc.*, need; что вам ~но? what do you need? what do you want? óчень (мне) ~но! (*coll.*, *iron.*) won't that be nice! a fat lot of good that is!

ну́-ка, *interj.* now!, now then!; come!, come on!

ну́ка|ть, ю, *impf.* (*coll.*) to urge; to say 'come on'.

нул|евóй, *adj. of* ~ь; (*math.*) zero.

нул|ь, я́, *m.* **1.** nought; zero; nil; cipher; своди́ться к ~ю́ (*fig.*) to come to nothing, come to nought. **2.** (*fig.*) nonentity, cipher.

нумера́тор, а, *m.* **1.** numerator. **2.** (*electr.*) annunciator.

нумера́ци|я, и, *f.* **1.** numeration. **2.** numbering.

нумер|овáть, у́ю, *impf.* (*of* за~ *and* пере~) to number; н. страни́цы to paginate.

нумизмáт, а, *m.* numismatist.

нумизмáтик|а, и, *f.* numismatics.

нумизмати́ческий, *adj.* numismatic.

ну́нци|й, я, *m.* nuncio.

ну́те(-ка), *interj.* well then!, come on!

ну́три|я, и, *f.* (*zool.*) coypu; (*fur of coypu*) nutria.

нутромéр, а, *m.* (*tech.*) internal calipers.

нутр|ó, á, *n.* (*coll.*) **1.** inside, interior. **2.** (*fig.*) core, kernel. **3.** (*fig.*) instinct(s), intuition; ~óм понимáть to understand intuitively; всем ~óм with one's whole being; э́то мне не по ~у́ it goes against the grain with me; игрáть ~óм (*theatr. sl.*) to live the part.

нутряно́й, *adj.* internal.

ны́не, *adv.* (*obs.*) **1.** now. **2.** today.

ны́нешн|ий, *adj.* present; present-day; в ~ие временá nowadays.

ны́нче, *adv.* (*coll.*) **1.** today; не н.-зáвтра any day now. **2.** now.

ныр|нýть, нý, нёшь, *pf. of* ~я́ть.

нырóк, кá, *m.* (*coll.*) **1.** dive. **2.** diver.

ныр|о́к², ка́, *m.* (*orn.*) pochard.

ныря́л|о, а, *n.* (*tech.*) plunger, plunger pis-ton.

ныр|я́ть, я́ю, *impf.* (*of* ~ну́ть) to dive.

ны́тик, а, *m.* (*coll.*) grumbler, moaner, whiner.

ныть, но́ю, но́ешь, *impf.* 1. to ache. 2. (*coll., pejor.*) to moan, whine; to make a fuss.

ныть|ё, я́, *n.* (*coll., pejor.*) moaning, whining.

нэп, а, *m.* (*abbr. of* но́вая экономи́ческая поли́тика) (*polit., econ., hist.*) NEP (New Economic Policy).

нэ́пман, а, *m.* (*pejor.*) 'Nepman', profiteer (*during period of New Economic Policy*).

нэ́п|овский, *adj. of* ~.

нюа́нс, а, *m.* nuance, shade.

нюанси́р|овать ую, *impf. and pf.* (*mus.*) to bring out fine shades of feeling, observe nuances.

нюни, *only in phrase* распусти́ть н. (*coll.*) to snivel, whimper.

ню́н|я, и, *m. and f.* (*coll.*) sniveller, cry-baby.

нюх, а, *m.* scent; (*fig.*) flair.

нюха́льщик, а, *m.* (*coll.*) snuff-taker.

ню́хательный, *adj.* н. табáк snuff.

нюха|ть, ю, *impf.* (*of* по~) to smell (at); н. табáк to take snuff; не ~л (+*g.*) to have no experience (of); пóроха не ~л (*fig.*) he's still wet behind the ears; он матемáтики и не ~л he doesn't know the first thing about mathematics.

нюхн|у́ть, у́, ёшь, *inst. pf.* (*coll.*) to take a sniff of.

ня́нч|ить, у, ишь, *impf.* to nurse.

ня́нч|иться, усь, ишься, *impf.* (с+*i.*) 1. to (dry-)nurse. 2. (*fig.*) to fuss (over).

ня́ньк|а, и, *f.* (*coll.*) = ня́ня; у семи́ ня́нек дитя́ без гла́зу (*prov.*) too many cooks spoil the broth (*lit.* where there are seven nurses the child is without supervision).

ня́н|я, и, *f.* 1. (dry-) nurse. 2. (*coll.*) (hos-pital) nurse.

O

о¹ (об, обо), *prep.* 1. (+*p.*) of, about, con-cerning; on; о чём вы ду́маете? what are you thinking about?; ле́кция бу́дет о Пу́шкине the lecture will be on Pushkin. 2. (+*p.*) with, having; стол о трёх нóжках a table with three legs, three-legged table; пáлка о двух концáх a two-edged weapon. 3. (+*a.*) against; on, upon; опере́ться о сте́ну to lean against the wall; споткну́ться о кáмень to stumble against a stone; бок ó бок side by side; рукá óб руку hand in hand. 4. (+*a. or p.*) (*obs. or coll.*) (*of time*) on, at, about; об э́ту пóру about this time; о Рождестве́ about Christmas-time.

о², *interj.* oh!

о- (об-, обо-, объ-) *verbal prefix indicating* 1. transformation; process of becoming something. 2. action applied to entire sur-face of object *or* to series of objects.

оáзис, а, *m.* oasis (*also fig.*).

об, *prep. see* о¹.

об- (обо-, объ-) *verbal prefix* 1. = о-. 2. in-dicating action *or* motion about an ob-ject.

óба, обо́их, *m. and n.*; óбе, обе́их, *f. num.* both; гляде́ть в о., смотре́ть в о. (*coll.*) to keep one's eyes open, be on one's guard; обе́ими рукáми with both hands (*fig., coll.*); very willingly, readily.

обáб|иться, люсь, ишься, *pf.* 1. (*of a man*) to become effeminate. 2. (*of a woman*) to become sluttish; to become coarse.

обагр|и́ть, ю́, и́шь, *pf.* (*of* ~я́ть) to crimson,

incarnadine; о. кро́вью to stain with blood; о. ру́ки в крови́ (кро́вью) to steep one's hands in blood.

обагр|и́ться, ю́сь, и́шься, *pf.* (*of* ~я́ться) to be crimsoned; о. (кро́вью) to be stained with blood.

обагр|я́ть(ся), я́ю(сь), *impf. of* ~и́ть(ся).

обалдева́|ть, ю, *impf. of* обалде́ть.

обалде́лый, *adj.* (*coll.*) crazed; stunned.

обалде́|ть, ю, *pf.* (*of* ~вáть) (*coll.*) to become dulled, become crazed; to be stunned (*by surprise, etc.*).

обанкро́|титься, чусь, тишься, *pf. of* банкро́титься.

обая́ни|е, я, *n.* fascination, charm.

обая́тел|ьный (~ен, ~ьна), *adj.* fascinat-ing, charming.

обва́л, а, *m.* 1. fall(ing), crumbling; col-lapse; caving-in. 2. landslip; снéжный о. snow-slip, avalanche.

обва́лива|ть¹(ся), ю(сь), *impf. of* обвали́ть-(ся).

обва́лива|ть², ю, *impf. of* обваля́ть.

обва́лист|ый (~, ~а), *adj.* (*coll.*) liable to fall, liable to cave in.

обвал|и́ть, ю́, ~ишь, *pf.* (*of* ~ивать¹) 1. to cause to fall, cause to collapse; to crumble (*trans.*). 2. to heap round; о. избу́ камня́ми to heap stones round a hut.

обвал|и́ться, ю́сь, ~ишься, *pf.* (*of* ~ивать-ся) to fall, collapse, cave in; to crumble.

обвал|я́ть, я́ю, *pf.* (*of* ~ивать²) (+*a.*, в+*p.*) to roll (in).

обва́рива|ть(ся), ю(сь), *impf. of* обвари́ть-(ся).

обвар|и́ть, ю́, ~ишь, *pf. (of* ~ивать) **1.** to pour boiling water over. **2.** to scald.

обвар|и́ться, ю́сь, ~ишься, *pf. (of* ~ива́ться) **1.** to scald oneself. **2.** *pass. of* ~и́ть.

обвева́|ть, ю, *impf. of* обве́ять.

обве|ду́, дёшь, *see* ~сти́.

обвез|ти́, у́, ёшь, *past* ~, ~ла́, *pf. (of* обво-зи́ть) **1.** to convey round. **2.** (*coll.*) to go the round of.

обвенча́|ть(ся), ю(сь), *pf. of* венча́ть(ся)[1].

обверн|у́ть, у́, ёшь, *pf. (of* обвёртывать) (+*i.*) to wrap up (in).

обвер|те́ть, чу́, ~тишь, *pf. (of* ~тывать) (+*i.*) to wrap up (in); о. ше́ю ша́рфом to wrap a scarf about one's neck.

обвёртыва|ть, ю, *impf. of* обверну́ть *and* обверте́ть.

обве́с[1]**, а,** *m.* false weight, short weight.

обве́с[2]**, а,** *m.* о. мо́стика (*naut.*) bridge cloth, dodger.

обве́|сить, шу, сишь, *pf. (of* ~шивать[1]) to give short weight to; to cheat (*in weighing goods*).

обве|сти́, ду́, дёшь, *past* ~л, ~ла́, *pf. (of* обводи́ть) **1.** to lead round, take round; о. вокру́г па́льца (*fig., coll.*) to twist round one's little finger. **2.** (+*i.*) to encircle (with); to surround (with); о. рвом to surround with a ditch; о. взо́ром, глаза́ми to look round (at), take in (with one's eyes). **3.** to outline; о. чертёж ту́шью to outline a sketch in ink. **4.** (*sport*) to dodge; to get past.

обве́тр|енный, *p.p.p. of* ~ить *and adj.* weather-beaten; chapped.

обве́тре|ть, ет, *pf.* to become weather--beaten.

обве́трива|ть(ся), ю(сь), *impf. of* обве́трить-(ся).

обве́тр|ить, ю, ишь, *pf. (of* ~ивать) to expose to the wind; (*impers.*) мне ~ило гу́бы my lips are chapped.

обве́тр|иться, юсь, ишься, *pf. (of* ~иваться) to become weather-beaten.

обветша́лый, *adj.* decrepit, decayed; dilapidated.

обветша́|ть, ю, *pf. of* ветша́ть.

обве́ш|ать, аю, *pf. (of* ~ивать[2]) (*coll.;* +*i.*) to hang round (with), cover (with).

обве́шива|ть[1]**, ю,** *impf. of* обве́сить.

обве́шива|ть[2]**, ю,** *impf. of* обве́шать.

обве́|ять, ю, ешь, *pf. (of* ~вать) **1.** (+*i.*) to fan (with). **2.** (*agric.*) to winnow.

обвива́|ть(ся), ю(сь), *impf. of* обви́ть(ся).

обвине́ни|е, я, *n.* **1.** charge, accusation; пу́нкты ~я (*leg.*) counts of an indictment; по ~ю (в+*p.*) on a charge (of); возвести́ на кого́-н. о. (в+*p.*) to charge someone

(with); вы́нести о. to find guilty. **2.** (*leg.*) the prosecution (*as party in lawsuit*).

обвини́тел|ь, я, *m.* accuser; (*leg.*) prosecutor; госуда́рственный о. public prosecutor.

обвини́тельн|ый, *adj.* accusatory; о. акт (bill of) indictment; о. пригово́р verdict of 'guilty'; ~ая речь speech for the prosecution, indictment.

обвин|и́ть, ю́, и́шь, *pf. (of* ~я́ть) **1.** (в+*p.*) to accuse (of), charge (with). **2.** (*leg.*) to prosecute, indict.

обвиня́ем|ый, ого, *m.* (*leg.*) the accused; defendant.

обвин|я́ть, я́ю, *impf. of* ~и́ть.

обвис|а́ть, а́ет, *impf. (of* ~нуть) to hang, droop; to sag; to grow flabby.

обви́сл|ый, *adj.* (*coll.*) flabby; hanging; ~ые усы́ drooping moustache.

обви́с|нуть, нет, *past* ~, ~ла, *pf. of* ~а́ть.

обви́|ть, обовью́, обовьёшь, *past* ~л, ~ла, ~ло, *pf. (of* ~ва́ть) to wind (round), entwine; о. ше́ю рука́ми to throw one's arms round someone's neck.

обви́|ться, обовью́сь, обовьёшься, *past* ~лся, ~ла́сь, *pf. (of* ~ва́ться) to wind round, twine oneself round.

обво́д, а, *m.* **1.** enclosing, surrounding. **2.** outlining; о. су́дна (*naut., tech.*) line.

обводне́ни|е, я, *n.* **1.** irrigation. **2.** filling up (with water).

обводни́тельный, *adj.* irrigation.

обводн|и́ть, ю́, и́шь, *pf. (of* ~я́ть) **1.** to irrigate. **2.** to fill up (with water).

обво́дный, *adj.* о. кана́л (*tech.*) by-pass.

обводн|я́ть, я́ю, *impf. of* ~и́ть.

обвола́кива|ть(ся), ю(сь), *impf. of* обволо́чь(ся).

обволо́|чь, ку́, чёшь, ку́т, *past* ~к, ~кла́, *pf. (of* обвола́кивать) to cover; to envelope (*also fig.*).

обволо́|чься, ку́сь, чёшься, ку́тся, *past* ~кся, ~кла́сь, *pf. (of* обвола́киваться) (+*i.; coll.*) to become covered (with), enveloped (by, in).

обвора́жива|ть, ю, *impf. of* обворожи́ть.

обвор|ова́ть, у́ю, *pf. (of* ~о́вывать) (*coll.*) to rob.

обворо́выва|ть, ю, *impf. of* обворова́ть.

обворожи́тел|ьный (~ен, ~ьна), *adj.* fascinating, charming, enchanting.

обворож|и́ть, у́, и́шь, *pf. (of* обвора́живать) to fascinate, charm, enchant.

обвя|за́ть[1]**, жу́, ~жешь,** *pf. (of* ~зывать) to tie round; о. верёвкой to cord, rope; о. го́лову платко́м to tie a head-scarf round one's head.

обвя|за́ть[2]**, жу́, ~жешь,** *pf. (of* ~зывать) to edge in chain-stitch.

обвя|за́ться, жу́сь, ~жешься, *pf. (of*

⌣зыва́ться) 1. (+i.) to tie round oneself; о. верёвкой to tie a rope round oneself. 2. *pass. of* ~за́ть.

обвя́зыва|ть(ся), ю(сь), *impf. of* обвяза́ть(ся).

обга́|дить, жу, дишь, *pf.* (*of* ~жива́ть) (*vulg.*) to shit on, shit up.

обга́жива|ть, ю, *impf. of* обга́дить.

обгла́дыва|ть, ю, *impf. of* обглода́ть.

обгло́д|анный, *p.p.p. of* ~а́ть; ~анная кость picked bone, bare bone.

обгло|да́ть, жу́, ~жешь, *pf.* (*of* обгла́дывать) to pick, gnaw round.

обгло́д|ок, ка, *m.* (*coll.*) bare bone.

обго́н, а, *m.* passing.

обгон|ю́, ~ишь, *see* обогна́ть.

обгоня́|ть, ю, *impf. of* обогна́ть.

обгор|а́ть, а́ю, *impf. of* ~е́ть.

обгоре́лый, *adj.* burnt; charred; scorched.

обгор|е́ть, ю́, и́шь, *pf.* to be scorched; to be burnt on the surface, receive surface burns.

обгрыз|а́ть, а́ю, *impf. of* ~ть.

обгры́з|ть, у́, ёшь, *past* ~, ~ла, *pf.* (*of* ~а́ть) to gnaw round.

обда|ва́ть(ся), ю́(сь), ёшь(ся), *impf. of* обда́ть(ся).

обд|а́ть, а́м, а́шь, а́ст, ади́м, ади́те, аду́т, *past* ~а́л, ~ала́, ~а́ло, *pf.* (*of* ~ава́ть) (+i.) 1. to pour over; о. кого́-н. кипятко́м to pour boiling water over someone. 2. (*fig.*) to seize, cover; о. взгля́дом презре́ния to fix with a look of scorn; меня́ ~а́ло хо́лодом (*impers.*) I came over cold.

обд|а́ться, а́мся, а́шься, а́стся, ади́мся, ади́тесь, аду́тся, *past* ~а́лся, ~ала́сь, *pf.* (*of* ~ава́ться) (+i.) to pour over oneself; о. кипятко́м to scald oneself.

обде́л|ать, аю, *pf.* (*of* ~ывать) 1. to finish; to dress (*leather, stone, etc.*); о. драгоце́нные ка́мни to set precious stones. 2. (*fig.*) to manage, arrange; о. те́му (*coll.*) to treat, handle a subject; о. свои́ дели́шки (*coll.*) to manage one's affairs with profit; он ма́стер о. свои́ дели́шки he is expert at taking care of number one. 3. *euph.* = обга́дить.

обдел|и́ть, ю́, ~ишь, *pf.* (*of* ~я́ть) (+a. and i.) to do out of one's (fair) share (of); он ~и́л сестёр насле́дством he did his sisters out of their share of the legacy.

обде́лыва|ть, ю, *impf. of* обде́лать.

обдел|я́ть, я́ю, *impf. of* ~и́ть.

обдёрга|нный, *p.p.p. of* ~ть *and adj.* (*coll.*) shabby; ragged, in rags.

обдёрг|ать, аю, *pf.* (*of* ~ивать) (*coll.*) to tear down, pull down; to trim, even up.

обдёргива|ть, ю, *impf. of* обдёргать *and* обдёрнуть.

обдёргива|ться, юсь, *impf. of* обдёрнуться.

обдерн|и́ть, ю́, и́шь, *pf.* (*of* ~я́ть) to turf.

обдёр|нуть, ну, нешь, *pf.* (*of* ~гивать) to adjust, pull down (*dress, skirt, etc.*).

обдёр|нуться, нусь, нешься, *pf.* (*of* ~гиваться) (*coll.*) 1. to adjust one's dress. 2. (*cards*) to pull out the wrong card.

обдерн|я́ть, я́ю, *impf. of* ~и́ть.

обдер|у́, ёшь, *see* ободра́ть.

обдира́л|а, ы, *m.* (*coll.*) fleecer.

обдира́|ть, ю, *impf. of* ободра́ть.

обди́рк|а, и, *f.* 1. peeling; hulling; skinning, flaying. 2. (*dial.*) groats.

обди́рный, *adj.* peeled; hulled.

обдува́л|а, ы, *m.* (*coll.*) cheat, trickster.

обдува́|ть, ю, *impf. of* обду́ть.

обду́манно, *adv.* after careful consideration; deliberately (= after deliberation).

обду́манност|ь, и, *f.* deliberation; deliberateness; careful planning.

обду́ман|ный 1. (~, ~а), *p.p.p. of* обду́мать. 2. (~, ~на), *adj.* well-considered, well-weighed, carefully thought out; с зара́нее ~ным наме́рением deliberately; (*leg.*) of malice prepense.

обду́м|ать, аю, *pf.* (*of* ~ывать) to consider, think over, weigh.

обду́мыва|ть, ю, *impf. of* обду́мать.

обду́|ть¹, ю, ешь, *pf.* (*of* ~ва́ть) to blow (on, round).

обду́|ть², ю, ешь, *pf.* (*of* ~ва́ть) (*coll.*) to cheat; to fool, dupe.

о́бе, *see* о́ба.

обе́га|ть, ю, *pf.* (*of* обега́ть) 1. to run (all over, all round). 2. to run round (to see); за неде́лю до отъе́зда нам удало́сь о. всех знако́мых in the week before our departure we managed to look in on all our acquaintances.

обега́|ть, ю, *impf. of* обе́гать *and* обежа́ть.

обе́д, а, *m.* 1. dinner; зва́ный о. dinnerparty; сесть за о. to sit down to dinner; звать к ~у to ask to dinner. 2. dinner-time (= mid-day); пе́ред ~ом before dinner; in the morning; по́сле ~а after dinner; in the afternoon.

обе́да|ть, ю, *impf.* (*of* по~) to have dinner, dine.

обе́д|енный¹, *adj. of* ~; ~енное вре́мя dinner time; о. переры́в lunch hour, lunch break; о. стол dinner table.

обе́д|енный², *adj. of* ~ня.

обедне́|вший, *past part. act. of* ~ть *and adj.* impoverished.

обедне́|лый, *adj.* (*coll.*) = ~вший.

обедне́ни|е, я, *n.* impoverishment.

обедне́|ть, ю, *pf. of* бедне́ть.

обедн|и́ть, ю́, и́шь, *pf.* (*of* ~я́ть) to impoverish.

обе́д|ня, ни, *g. pl.* ~ен, *f.* (*eccl.*) mass; испо́ртить ~ню кому́-н. (*fig., coll.*) to spoil someone's game, put a spoke in someone's wheel.

обедн|я́ть, я́ю, *impf. of* ~и́ть.

обе|жа́ть, гу́, жи́шь, гу́т, *pf.* (*of* ~га́ть) 1. to run (over, round). 2. to run (past). 3. (*sport*) to outrun, pass.

обезбо́ливани|е, я, *n.* anaesthetization.

обезбо́лива|ть, ю, *impf. of* обезбо́лить.

обезбо́лива|ющий, *pres. part. act. of* ~ть; ~ющее сре́дство anaesthetic.

обезбо́л|ить, ю, ишь, *pf.* (*of* ~ивать) to anaesthetize.

обезво́|дить, жу, дишь, *pf.* (*of* ~живать) to dehydrate.

обезво́|женный, *p.p.p. of* ~дить *and adj.* dehydrated.

обезво́жива|ть, ю, *impf. of* обезво́дить.

обезвре́|дить, жу, дишь, *pf.* (*of* ~живать) to render harmless; to neutralize.

обезвре́жива|ть, ю, *impf. of* обезвре́дить.

обезгла́в|ить, лю, ишь, *pf.* (*of* ~ливать) 1. to behead, decapitate. 2. (*fig.*) to deprive of a head, of a leader.

обезгла́влива|ть, ю, *impf. of* обезгла́вить.

обезде́неже|ть, ю, *pf.* (*coll.*) to run short of money.

обездо́л|енный, *p.p.p. of* ~ить *and adj.* unfortunate, hapless.

обездо́лива|ть, ю, *impf. of* обездо́лить.

обездо́л|ить, ю, ишь, *pf.* (*of* ~ивать) to deprive of one's share.

обезжи́р|енный, *p.p.p. of* ~ить *and adj.* fatless; skimmed.

обезжи́р|ить, ю, *impf. of* обезжи́рить.

обезжи́р|ить, ю, ишь, *pf.* (*of* ~ивать) to deprive of fat, remove fat (from); to skim.

обеззара́жива|ть, ю, *impf. of* обеззара́зить.

обеззара́жива|ющий, *p.p.p. of* ~ть *and adj.* disinfectant.

обеззара́|зить, жу, зишь, *pf.* (*of* ~живать) to disinfect.

обеззе́мел|енный, *p.p.p. of* ~ить *and adj.* landless, deprived of land.

обезземе́лива|ть, ю, *impf. of* обезземе́лить.

обезземе́л|ить, ю, ишь, *pf.* (*of* ~ивать) to dispossess of land.

обеззу́бе|ть, ю, *pf.* (*coll.*) to lose one's teeth.

обезле́си|ть, шь, *pf.* to deforest.

обезли́чени|е, я, *n.* 1. depersonalization. 2. depriving of personal responsibility; removal of personal responsibility (from).

обезли́ч|енный, *p.p.p. of* ~ить *and adj.* 1. pooled (*of workshop tools, etc.: assigned to and made the responsibility of no one individual user*). 2. impersonal, multiple, group (*in which no one individual bears responsibility*); ~енное руково́дство group management. 3. (*econ., fin.*) not owned by a specified person; ~енная облига́ция (*fin.*) bearer bond.

обезли́чива|ть, ю, *impf. of* обезли́чить.

обезли́ч|ить, у, ишь, *pf.* (*of* ~ивать) 1. to deprive of individuality, depersonalize. 2. to deprive of personal responsibility; to do away with personal responsibility (for). 3. (*econ., fin.*) to remove from ownership by a specified person; to make available to bearer unspecified.

обезли́чк|а, и, *f.* lack of personal responsibility; (*railways*) multiple manning.

обезлюде́|ть, ю, *pf.* to become depopulated.

обезобра́жива|ть, ю, *impf. of* обезобра́зить.

обезобра́|зить, жу, зишь, *pf.* (*of* ~живать *and* безобра́зить) to disfigure.

обезопа́|сить, шу, сишь, *pf.* (от) to secure (against).

обезопа́|ситься, шусь, сишься, *pf.* (от) to secure oneself, make oneself secure (against).

обезору́жива|ть, ю, *impf. of* обезору́жить.

обезору́ж|ить, у, ишь, *pf.* (*of* ~ивать) to disarm (*also fig.*).

обезу́ме|ть, ю, *pf.* to lose one's senses, lose one's head; о. от испу́га to become panic-stricken.

обезья́н|а, ы, *f.* monkey; ape.

обезья́н|ий, *adj. of* ~а; (*zool.*) simian; (*fig.*) ape-like.

обезья́нник, а, *m.* monkey-house.

обезья́ннича|нье, я, *n.* (*coll.*) aping.

обезья́ннича|ть, ю, *impf.* (*of* с~) (*coll.*) to ape.

обел|и́ть, ю́, и́шь, *pf.* (*of* ~я́ть) (*fig.*) to whitewash; to vindicate; to prove the innocence (of).

обел|и́ться, ю́сь, и́шься, *pf.* (*of* ~я́ться) to vindicate oneself, obtain recognition of one's innocence.

обел|я́ть(ся), я́ю(сь), *impf. of* ~и́ть(ся).

обер- 1. (*in designations of holders of rank or office*) chief-. 2. (*coll., pejor.*) arch-.

оберега́|ть(ся), ю(сь), *impf. of* обере́чь(ся).

обере́|чь, гу́, жёшь, гу́т, *past* ~г, ~гла́, *pf.* (*of* ~га́ть) (от) to guard (against), protect (from).

обере́|чься, гу́сь, жёшься, гу́тся, *past* ~гся, ~гла́сь, *pf.* (*of* ~га́ться) 1. (от) to guard oneself (from, against), protect oneself (from). 2. *pass. of* ~чь.

обер-конду́ктор, а, *m.* chief guard (*of a train*).

оберн|у́ть, у́, ёшь, *pf.* (*of* обора́чивать) 1. (*impf. also* обёртывать) to wind (round), twist (round); о. вокру́г па́льца (*coll.*) to twist round one's little finger. 2. (*impf. also* обёртывать) to wrap up. 3. (*impf. also* обёртывать) to turn; о. лицо́ (к) to turn one's face (towards); о. в свою́ по́льзу (*fig.*) to turn to account, turn to advantage. 4. (*coll.*) to overturn, upturn. 5. (*comm.*) to turn over. 6. (*coll.*) to work through, go through.

оберн|у́ться, у́сь, ёшься, *pf. (of* обора́чиваться*)* **1.** (*impf. also* обёртываться) to turn; о. лицо́м to turn one's head. **2.** (*impf. also* обёртываться) to turn out; собы́тия ~у́лись и́наче, чем мы ожида́ли events turned out otherwise than we expected. **3.** (*coll.*) to (go and) come back; я ~у́сь за два часа́ I shall be back in two hours. **4.** (*coll.*) to manage, get by. **5.** (*impf. also* обёртываться) (+*i. or* в+*a.*) to turn into, become (*also fig.*); о. вампи́ром to turn into a vampire.

обер-прокуро́р, а, *m.* (*hist.*) chief procurator (*title of official in charge of Holy Synod set up in 1721*).

обёртк|а, и, *f.* wrapper; envelope; (*of book*) (*obs.*) dust-jacket, cover.

оберто́н, а, *m.* (*mus.*) overtone.

обёрт|очный, *adj.* of ~ка; ~очная бума́га wrapping paper.

обёртыва|ть(ся), ю(сь), *impf. of* оберну́ть(ся).

обескро́в|ить, лю, ишь, *pf. (of* ~ливать) to drain of blood; to bleed white; (*fig.*) to render lifeless.

обескро́в|ленный, *p.p.p. of* ~ить *and adj.* bloodless; (*fig.*) anaemic, lifeless.

обескро́влива|ть, ю, *impf. of* обескро́вить.

обескура́жива|ть, ю, *impf. of* обескура́жить.

обескура́ж|ить, у, ишь, *pf.* (*coll.*) to discourage, dishearten; to dismay.

обеспа́мяте|ть, ю, *pf.* **1.** to lose one's memory. **2.** to lose consciousness, become unconscious, faint.

обеспе́чени|е, я, *n.* **1.** securing, guaranteeing; ensuring. **2.** (+*i.*) providing (with), provision (of, with). **3.** guarantee; security (= pledge). **4.** security (= material maintenance); safeguard(s); социа́льное о. social security. **5.** (*mil.*) security; protection.

обеспе́ченност|ь, и, *f.* **1.** (+*i.*) being provided (with), provision (of, with); о. школ уче́бниками the provision of schools with text-books. **2.** (material) security.

обеспе́ч|енный, *p.p.p. of* ~ить *and adj.* well--to-do; well provided for.

обеспе́чива|ть, ю, *impf. of* обеспе́чить.

обеспе́ч|ить, у, ишь, *pf. (of* ~ивать) **1.** to provide for. **2.** (+*i.*) to provide (with), guarantee supply (of); о. экспеди́цию обору́дованием to provide an expedition with equipment. **3.** to secure, guarantee; to ensure, assure. **4.** (от) to safeguard (from), protect (from).

обеспло́|дить, жу, дишь, *pf. (of* ~живать) to sterilize; to render barren.

обеспло́жива|ть, ю, *impf. of* обеспло́дить.

обеспоко́|ить(ся), ю(сь), *pf. of* беспоко́ить(ся) 1.

обесси́ле|ть, ю, *pf.* to grow weak, lose one's

strength; to collapse, break down.

обесси́лива|ть, ю, *impf. of* обесси́лить.

обесси́л|ить, ю, ишь, *pf. (of* ~ивать) to weaken.

обессла́в|ить, лю, ишь, *pf. (of* бессла́вить) to defame.

обессме́р|тить, чу, тишь, *pf.* to immortalize.

обессу́д|ить, *pf. now only used in imp.* не ~ь(те) (please) don't take it amiss, (please) don't be angry.

обесто́чива|ть, ю, *impf. of* обесто́чить.

обесто́ч|ить, у ишь, *pf. (of* ~ивать) (*electr.*) to de-energise.

обесцве́|тить, чу, тишь, *pf. (of* ~чивать) to decolo(u)rize, deprive of colour; (*fig.*) to render colourless, tone down.

обесцве́|титься, чусь, тишься, *pf. (of* ~чиваться) to become colourless (*also fig.*).

обесцве́чива|ть(ся), ю(сь), *impf. of* обесцве́тить(ся).

обесце́нени|е, я, *n.* depreciation; loss of value.

обесце́н|енный, *p.p.p. of* ~ить *and adj.* depreciated.

обесце́нива|ть(ся), ю(сь), *impf. of* обесце́нить(ся).

обесце́н|ить, ю, ишь, *pf. (of* ~ивать) to depreciate, cheapen.

обесце́н|иться, юсь, ишься, *pf. (of* ~ивать ся) **1.** (*intrans.*) to depreciate, cheapen. **2** *pass.* of ~ить.

обесче́|стить, щу, стишь, *pf. of* бесче́стить.

обе́т, а, *m.* (*rhet.*) vow, promise.

обетова́нн|ый, *adj.* ~ая земля́, о. край the Promised Land.

обеща́ни|е, я, *n.* promise; дать, сдержа́ть о. to give, keep a promise (one's word).

обеща́|ть, ю, *impf. and pf.* to promise.

обеща́|ться, юсь, *impf. and pf.* (*coll.*) **1.** to promise. **2.** to give (exchange) a promise (*sc.* to marry).

обжа́ловани|е, я, *n.* appeal; о. пригово́ра (*leg.*) appealing against a sentence.

обжа́л|овать, ую, *pf.* (*leg.*) to lodge a complaint (against); to appeal (against).

обжа́рива|ть, ю, *impf. of* обжа́рить.

обжа́р|ить, ю, ишь, *pf. (of* ~ивать) (*cul.*) to fry on both sides, all over.

обжа́ть¹, обожму́, обожмёшь, *pf. of* (обжима́ть) to press out; to wring out.

обжа́ть², обожну́, обожнёшь, *pf. (of* обжина́ть) (*dial.*) to reap (*the whole of*).

обже́чь, обожгу́, обожжёшь, обожгу́т, *past* **обжёг, обожгла́,** *pf. (of* обжига́ть) **1.** to burn, scorch; о. себе́ па́льцы to burn one's fingers (*also fig.*). **2.** to bake (*bricks, etc.*); to calcine (*lime*).

обже́чься, обожгу́сь, обожжёшься, обожгу́тся, *past* **обжёгся, обожгла́сь,** *pf.* **1.** (+*i. or* на+*p.*) to burn oneself (on, with); о.

горя́чим ча́ем to scald oneself with hot tea; о. крапи́вой to be stung by a nettle; обжёгшись на молоке́, ста́нешь дуть и на́ воду (*prov.*) a burnt child dreads the fire. **2.** (*fig.*, *coll.*) to burn one's fingers.

обжива́|ть(ся), ю(сь), *impf. of* обжи́ть(ся).

обжи́г, а, *m.* (*tech.*) kilning, glazing; (*of clay*) baking; (*of ores*) roasting; (*of lime*) calcining.

обжига́л|а, ы, *m.* (*tech.*) kiln-worker.

обжига́тельн|ый, *adj.* (*tech.*) glazing; baking; roasting; ~ая печь kiln.

обжига́|ть(ся), ю(сь), *impf. of* обже́чь(ся).

обжи́м, а, *m.* (*tech.*) **1.** pressing out. **2.** cap tool, snap tool, riveting set.

обжима́|ть, ю, *impf. of* обжа́ть¹.

обжи́м|ка, ки, *f.* (*tech.*) = ~; пла́тье в ~ку (*coll.*) tight-fitting dress.

обжи́мный, *adj.* (*tech.*) pressing, blooming; о. стан blooming mill, roughing mill.

обжина́|ть, ю, *impf. of* обжа́ть².

обжира́|ться, юсь, *impf. of* обожра́ться.

обжи́т|о́й (*and* ~ый), *p.p.p. of* ~ь.

обж|и́ть, иву́, иве́шь, *past* ~и́л, ~ила́, ~и́ло, *pf.* (*of* ~ива́ть) (*coll.*) to render habitable.

обж|и́ться, иву́сь, иве́шься, *past* ~и́лся, ~ила́сь, *pf.* (*of* ~ива́ться) (*coll.*) to make oneself at home, feel at home.

обжо́р|а, ы, *m. and f.* (*coll.*) glutton, gormandizer.

обжо́рлив|ый (~, ~а), *adj.* gluttonous.

обжо́рный, *adj.* о. ряд (*obs.*) refreshment stall (*in market*).

обжо́рств|о, а, *n.* gluttony.

обжу́лива|ть, ю, *impf. of* обжу́лить.

обжу́л|ить, ю, ишь, *pf.* (*coll.*) to cheat, swindle.

обзаведе́ни|е, я, *n.* **1.** (+*i.*) providing (with), fitting out. **2.** (*coll.*) establishment; (*collect.*) fittings, appointments, paraphernalia.

обзаве|сти́сь, ду́сь, дёшься, *past* ~лся, ~ла́сь, *pf.* (*of* обзаводи́ться) (+*i.*; *coll.*) to provide oneself (with); to set up; о. семьёй to settle down to married life; о. хозя́йством to set up house.

обзаво|ди́ться, жу́сь, ~дишься, *impf. of* обзавести́сь.

обзо́р, а, *m.* **1.** survey, review. **2.** (*mil.*) field of view.

обзо́р|ный, *adj. of* ~; ~ная ле́кция, ~ная статья́ survey.

обзыва́|ть, ю, *impf. of* обозва́ть.

обива́|ть, ю, *impf. of* оби́ть; о. (все) поро́ги (*fig.*) to leave no stone unturned.

оби́вк|а, и, *f.* **1.** upholstering. **2.** upholstery.

обивно́й, *adj.* for upholstery.

оби́д|а, ы, *f.* **1.** offence, injury, insult; (sense of) grievance, resentment; быть на кого́-н. в оби́де to bear a grudge against

someone; затаи́ть ~у to bear a grudge, nurse a grievance; проглоти́ть ~у to swallow an insult; не дава́ть себя́ в ~у to (be able to) stick up for oneself; не в ~у будь ска́зано no offence meant. **2.** (*coll.*) annoying thing, nuisance; кака́я о.! what a nuisance!

оби́|деть, жу, дишь, *pf.* (*of* ~жа́ть) **1.** to offend; to hurt (the feelings of), wound. **2.** to hurt; to do damage (to); му́хи не ~дит (*fig.*) he would not harm a fly. **3.** (+*i.*; *following* Бог, приро́да, *etc.*) to stint, begrudge; приро́да не ~дела его́ тала́нтом he has plenty of natural ability.

оби́|деться, жусь, дишься, *pf.* (*of* ~жа́ться) (на+*a.*) to take offence (at), take umbrage (at); to feel hurt (by), resent.

оби́д|ный (~ен, ~на), *adj.* **1.** offensive; мне ~но I feel hurt, it pains me. **2.** (*coll.*) annoying, tiresome; ~но (*impers.*) it is a pity, it is a nuisance; ~но, что мы опозда́ли it is a pity that we were late.

оби́дчивост|ь, и, *f.* touchiness, susceptibility (*to offence*), sensitivity.

оби́дчив|ый (~, ~а), *adj.* touchy, susceptible (*to offence*), sensitive.

оби́дчик, а, *m.* (*coll.*) offender.

обижа́|ть, ю, *impf. of* оби́деть.

обижа́|ться, юсь, *impf. of* оби́деться; не ~йтесь don't be offended.

оби́|женный, *p.p.p. of* ~деть *and adj.* offended, hurt, aggrieved; быть ~жен (на+*a.*) to have a grudge (against); у него́ был о. вид he had an aggrieved air, he looked offended; о. Бо́гом, о. приро́дой (*joc.*) not over-blessed (with talents); ill-starred.

оби́ли|е, я, *n.* abundance, plenty; жить в ~и to live in comfort.

оби́л|овать, ую, *impf.* (+*i.*; *obs.*) to abound (in).

оби́л|ьный (~ен, ~ьна), *adj.* abundant, plentiful; (+*i.*) rich (in); ~ьное угоще́ние lavish entertainment; о. урожа́й bumper crop; день, о. происше́ствиями an eventful day.

обину́ясь, *only in phrase* не о. without a moment's hesitation.

обиня́к, а́, *m. only in phrases* говори́ть ~о́м, ~а́ми to beat about the bush; говори́ть без ~о́в to speak plainly, speak in plain terms.

обира́|ть, ю, *impf. of* обобра́ть.

обита́ем|ый (~, ~а), *adj.* inhabited.

обита́тел|ь, я, *m.* inhabitant; resident; (*of a house*) inmate.

обита́|ть, ю, *impf.* (в+*p.*) to live (in), dwell (in), reside (in).

оби́тел|ь, и, *f.* **1.** cloister. **2.** (*fig.*; *obs.*) abode, dwelling-place.

обѝтель|ский, *adj. of* ~.

обѝ|ть, обобью́, обобьёшь, *pf.* (*of* ~ва́ть)
1. (c+*g.*) to knock (off, down from); о.
плоды́ с я́блони to knock down fruit from
an apple-tree. **2.** (+*i.*) to upholster (with),
cover (with); о. гвоздя́ми to stud; о. желе́-
зом to bind with iron. **3.** to wear out (*the
surface of, at the edges*); о. подо́л ю́бки to
wear the hem of a skirt; о. штукату́рку to
chip off plaster.

обихо́д, а, *m.* **1.** custom, use, practice;
повседне́вный о. everyday practice; пред-
ме́ты дома́шнего ~а household articles;
пусти́ть в о. to bring into (general) use;
вы́йти из ~а to be no longer in use, fall
into disuse. **2.** (*eccl.*) ordinary; rules of
church singing.

обихо́д|ный (~ен, ~на), *adj.* everyday;
~ное выраже́ние colloquial expression.

обка́лыва|ть, ю, *impf. of* обколо́ть.

обка́п|ать, аю, *pf.* (*of* ~ывать¹) (+*i.*) to let
drops (of) fall on; to cover with drops (of).

обка́пыва|ть¹, ю, *impf. of* обка́пать.

обка́пыва|ть², ю, *impf. of* обкопа́ть.

обка́рмлива|ть, ю, *impf. of* обкорми́ть.

обкат|а́ть, а́ю, *pf.* (*of* ~ывать) **1.** to roll.
2. to roll smooth (*a road surface, etc.*). **3.**
(*tech.*) to run in (*a new vehicle, etc.*).

обка́тк|а, и, *f.* (*tech.*) running in.

обка́тыва|ть, ю, *impf. of* обката́ть.

обкла́дк|а, и, *f.* (*in var. senses*) facing; о.
дёрном turfing.

обкла́дыва|ть, ю, *impf. of* обложи́ть.

обкол|о́ть, ю́, ~ешь, *pf.* (*of* обка́лывать)
1. to cut away (*ice, etc.*). **2.** to prick all
over.

обко́м, а, *m.* (*abbr. of* областно́й комите́т)
oblast committee.

обкопа́|ть, ю, *pf.* (*of* обка́пывать²) (*coll.*)
to dig round.

обкорм|и́ть, лю́, ~ишь, *pf.* (*of* обка́рмли-
вать) to overfeed.

обкорна́|ть, ю, *pf. of* корна́ть.

обкра́дыва|ть, ю, *impf. of* обокра́сть.

обку́р|енный, *p.p.p. of* ~и́ть *and adj.* ~енная
тру́бка seasoned pipe; ~енные па́льцы
tobacco-stained fingers.

обку́рива|ть, ю, *impf. of* обкури́ть.

обкур|и́ть, ю́, ~ишь, *pf.* (*of* ~ивать) **1.** о.
тру́бку to season a pipe. **2.** to fumigate.
3. (*coll.*) to envelope with (tobacco) smoke;
to stain with tobacco.

обкус|а́ть, а́ю, *pf.* (*of* ~ывать) to bite
round; to nibble.

обку́сыва|ть, ю, *impf. of* обкуса́ть.

обла́в|а, ы, *f.* **1.** (*hunting*) battue; beating
up. **2.** (*fig.*) (*police*) raid, swoop; cordon;
cordoning off; round-up.

облага́емый, *adj.* taxable.

облага́|ть, ю, *impf. of* обложи́ть.

облага́|ться, юсь, *impf.* (*of* обложи́ться) о.
нало́гом to be liable to tax, be taxable.

облагоде́тельств|овать, ую, *pf.* (*obs. or
iron.*) to do a great favour.

облагора́жива|ть, ю, *impf. of* облагоро́дить.

облагоро́|дить, жу, дишь, *pf.* (*of* облаго-
ра́живать) to ennoble.

облада́ни|е, я, *n.* possession.

облада́тел|ь, я, *m.* possessor.

облада́|ть, ю, *impf.* (+*i.*) to possess, be
possessed (of); о. хоро́шим здоро́вьем to
enjoy good health; о. пра́вом to have the
right; о. больши́м тала́нтом to have great
talents, be very talented.

обла́|зить, жу, зишь, *pf.* (*coll.*) to climb
round, climb all over.

о́блак|о, а, *pl.* ~а́, ~о́в, *n.* cloud; кучевы́е
~а́ cumuli; пе́ристые ~а́ cirri; сло́истые
~а́ strati; быть, носи́ться в ~а́х (*fig.*) to
live in the clouds; свали́ться с ~о́в (*fig.*) to
appear from nowhere.

обла́мыва|ть(ся), ю(сь), *impf. of* облома́ть-
(ся).

обла́п|ить, лю, ишь, *pf.* (*of* ~ливать) (*coll.*)
to hug.

облапли́ва|ть, ю, *impf. of* обла́пить.

облапо́шива|ть, ю, *impf. of* облапо́шить.

облапо́ш|ить, у, ишь, *pf.* (*of* ~ивать) (*coll.*)
to cheat, swindle.

обласка́|ть, ю, *pf.* to treat with affection,
display much kindness towards.

областно́й, *adj.* **1.** oblast; provincial;
regional. **2.** (*ling.*) dialectal; regional.

о́бласт|ь, и, *g. pl.* ~е́й, *f.* **1.** (*designation of
administrative division of U.S.S.R.*) oblast;
province; прие́хать из ~и to come from
oblast (*fig., coll.* = from administrative
centre of oblast). **2.** region, district; belt;
о. вечнозелёных расте́ний evergreen belt;
озёрная о. lake district. **3.** (*anat., med.*)
tract; region. **4.** (*fig.*) province, field,
sphere, realm, domain; о. микробиоло́гии
the field of microbiology; о. мифоло́гии
the realm of mythology.

обла́тк|а, и, *f.* **1.** (*eccl.*) wafer, host. **2.**
(*pharm.*) capsule. **3.** paper seal.

обла́т|очный, *adj. of* ~ка.

облач|а́ть(ся), а́ю(сь), *impf. of* ~и́ть(ся).

облаче́ни|е, я, *n.* **1.** (в+*a.*) robing (in).
2. (*eccl.*) vestments, robes.

облач|и́ть, у́, и́шь, *pf.* (*of* ~а́ть) (в+*a.*)
1. (*eccl.*) to robe (in). **2.** (*rhet. or coll., joc.*)
to array (in), get up (in).

облач|и́ться, у́сь, и́шься, *pf.* (*of* ~а́ться)
1. (*eccl.*) to robe, put on robes. **2.** (*rhet. or
coll., joc.*) to array oneself.

о́блачк|о, а, *pl.* ~а́, ~о́в, *n. dim. of* о́блако.

о́блачност|ь, и, *f.* **1.** cloudiness. **2.** (*meteor.*)
cloud conditions; о. в де́сять ба́ллов ten
tenths cloud.

облач|ный (~ен, ~на), *adj.* cloudy.

облега|ть, ю, *impf.* **1.** *impf. of* **облечь¹. 2.** (*of clothes*) to fit tightly; о. фигу́ру to outline the figure.

облега|ющий, *pres. part. act. of* ~ть *and adj.* tight-fitting.

облегч|а́ть(ся), а́ю(сь), *impf. of* ~и́ть(ся).

облегче́ни|е, я, n. **1.** facilitation. **2.** relief; вздохну́ть с ~ем to heave a sigh of relief.

облегч|и́ть, у́, и́шь, *pf.* (*of* ~а́ть) **1.** to facilitate. **2.** to lighten. **3.** to relieve; to alleviate; to mitigate; (*leg.*) to commute; о. ду́шу to relieve one's mind.

облегч|и́ться, у́сь, и́шься, *pf.* (*of* ~а́ться) **1.** to be relieved, find relief. **2.** to become easier; to become lighter. **3.** (*coll., euph.*) to relieve oneself.

обледене́лый, *adj.* ice-covered.

обледене́ни|е, я, n. icing(-over); пери́од ~я Ice Age.

обледене́|ть, ю, *pf.* to ice over, become covered with ice.

облеза́|ть, а́ет, *impf. of* ~ть.

обле́зл|ый, *adj.* (*coll.*) shabby, bare; ~ая ко́шка mangy cat.

обле́з|ть, ет, *past* ~, ~ла, (*of* ~а́ть) (*coll.*) **1.** (*of fur, etc.*) to come out, come off. **2.** to grow bare (*of fur, feathers, etc.*); to grow mangy. **3.** (*of paintwork, etc.*) to peel off.

облека́|ть(ся), ю(сь), *impf. of* облечь²(ся).

облени́ва|ться, юсь, *impf. of* облени́ться.

облен|и́ться, ю́сь, ~ишься, *pf.* (*of* ~ива́ться) to grow lazy.

облеп|и́ть, лю́, ~ишь, *pf.* (*of* ~ля́ть) **1.** to stick (to); (*fig.*) to cling (to); to surround, throng; нас ~и́ла ку́ча мальчи́шек we were surrounded by a swarm of small boys. **2.** (+*a. and i.*) to paste all over (with), plaster (with); о. сте́ну объявле́ниями to plaster a wall with notices.

облепи́х|а, и, f. (*bot.*) sea buckthorn (*Hippophae rhamnoides*).

облепля́|ть, ю, *impf. of* облепи́ть.

облесе́ни|е, я, n. afforestation.

обле|си́ть, шу́, си́шь, *pf.* to afforest.

облёт, а, m. buzzing (*by aircraft*).

облет|а́ть¹, а́ю, *impf. of* ~е́ть.

облет|а́ть², а́ю, *pf.* (*of* ~ывать) **1.** to fly (all round, all over); мы ~а́ли всю Евро́пу we have flown all over Europe; она́ ~а́ла всех подру́г (*fig., coll.*) she flew round to all her girl-friends. **2.** to test (*an aircraft*).

обле|те́ть, чу́, ти́шь, *pf.* (*of* ~та́ть¹) **1.** (+*a. or* вокру́г) to fly (round). **2.** (*of news, rumours, etc.*) to spread (round, all over); за полчаса́ весть о побе́де ~те́ла го́род in half an hour the news of the victory had spread round the town. **3.** (*of leaves*) to fall.

облётыва|ть, ю, *impf. of* облета́ть².

облеч|ённый, *p.p.p. of* ~ь² *and adj.* **1.** о.

вла́стью invested with power. **2.** (*ling.*) ~ённое ударе́ние circumflex accent (*as mark of perispomenon or properispomenon stress in ancient Greek*).

обл|е́чь¹, я́гу, я́жешь, я́гут, *past* ~ёг, ~егла́, *pf.* (*of* ~ега́ть) to cover, surround, envelop (*also fig.*); ту́чи ~егли́ го́ру rain-clouds enveloped the mountain.

обле́|чь², ку́, чёшь, ку́т, *past* ~к, ~кла́, *pf.* (*of* ~ка́ть) (+*a.* в+*a. or* +*a. and i.*) to clothe (in); to invest (with), vest (in); (*fig.*) to wrap (in), shroud (in); о. полномо́чиями to invest with authority, commission; о. та́йной to shroud in mystery; о. свою́ мысль непоня́тными слова́ми to wrap one's idea in unintelligible words; о. кого́-н. дове́рием to express confidence in someone.

обле́|чься, ку́сь, чёшься, ку́тся, *past* ~кся, ~кла́сь, *pf.* (*of* ~ка́ться) (в+*a.*) to clothe oneself (in), dress oneself (in); (*fig.*) to take the form (of), assume the shape (of).

облива́ни|е, я, n. **1.** spilling (over), pouring (over). **2.** shower-bath; sponge-down.

облива́|ть, ю, *impf. of* обли́ть.

облива́|ться, юсь, *impf. of* обли́ться; се́рдце у меня́ кро́вью ~ется my heart bleeds.

обли́вк|а, и, f. **1.** glazing. **2.** glaze.

обливно́й, *adj.* glazed.

облигац|ио́нный, *adj. of* ~ия.

облига́ци|я, и, f. (*fin.*) bond, debenture.

обли́з|анный, *p.p.p. of* ~а́ть *and adj.* (*fig.*) smooth.

обли|за́ть, жу́, ~жешь, *pf.* (*of* ~зывать) to lick (all over); to lick clean; па́льчики ~жешь (*fig., coll.*) (*sc.* it is, it will be) a real treat.

обли|за́ться, жу́сь, ~жешься, *pf.* (*of* ~зываться) **1.** to smack one's lips (*also fig.*). **2.** (*of an animal*) to lick itself.

обли́зыва|ть, ю, *impf. of* облиза́ть; о. гу́бы (*fig., coll.*) to smack one's lips.

обли́зыва|ться, юсь, *impf. of* облиза́ться.

о́блик, а, m. **1.** look, aspect, appearance. **2.** (*fig.*) cast of mind, temper.

облиня́|ть, ю, *pf.* (*coll.*) **1.** to fade, lose colour (*also fig.*). **2.** to moult, lose hair *or* feathers.

облип|а́ть, а́ю, *impf. of* ~нуть.

обли́п|нуть, ну, нешь, *past* ~, ~ла, *pf.* (*of* ~а́ть) (+*i.*) to become stuck (in, with).

облисполко́м, а, m. (*abbr. of* областно́й исполни́тельный комите́т) oblast executive committee.

о́блит|ый (~, ~а́, ~о), *and* обли́тый (~, ~а́, ~о), *p.p.p. of* обли́ть; (*fig.*; +*i.*) covered (by), enveloped (in); о. све́том луны́ bathed in moonlight.

обл|и́ть, оболью́, обольёшь, *past* ~и́л, ~ила́, ~и́ло *and* ~и́л, ~ила́, ~и́ло, *pf.* (*of* ~ива́ть) **1.** (*p.p.p.* ~и́тый) to pour (over), sluice (over); to spill (over); о. скáтерть винóм to spill wine over the table-cloth; о. презрéнием (*fig.*) to pour contempt (on); о. грязью, о. помóями (*fig., coll.*) to fling mud (at). **2.** (*p.p.p.* ~**и́тый**) to glaze.

обли́|ться, оболью́сь, обольёшься, *past* ~**лся**, ~**лáсь**, ~**лóсь** *and* ~**лось**, *pf.* (*of* ~**вáться**) **1.** to have a shower-bath, douche oneself; о. гóлодной водóй to have a cold shower. **2.** to pour over oneself, spill over oneself; о. пóтом to be bathed in sweat; о. слезáми to melt into tears. **3.** *pass. of* ~ть.

облиц|евáть, у́ю, у́ешь, *pf.* (*of* ~**óвывать**) (+*a. and i.*) to face (with), revet (with).

облицóвк|а, и, *f.* facing, revetment; lining, coating.

облицóв|очный, *adj. of* ~**ка**; о. кирпи́ч facing brick, decorative tile.

облицóвыва|ть, ю, *impf. of* облицевáть.

облич|áть, áю, *impf.* (*of* ~**и́ть**) **1.** to expose, unmask, denounce. **2.** (*impf. only*) to reveal, display, manifest; to point (to).

обличéни|е, я, *n.* exposure, unmasking, denunciation.

обличи́тел|ь, я, *m.* exposer, unmasker, denouncer.

обличи́тельн|ый, *adj.* denunciatory; ~**ая** речь, ~**ая** статья́ diatribe, tirade.

облич|и́ть, у́, и́шь, *pf. of* ~**áть**.

обли́чь|е, я, *n.* **1.** (*coll.*) face; **2.** aspect, appearance (*also fig.*).

облобызá|ть, ю, *pf.* (*obs., joc.*) to kiss.

обложéни|е, я, *n.* **1.** taxation; assessment, rating. **2.** (*mil.; obs.*) investment.

облóж|енный, *p.p.p. of* ~**и́ть**; о. язы́к (*med.*) furred tongue.

облож|и́ть, у́, ~**ишь**, *pf.* **1.** (*impf.* обклáдывать) to put (round); to edge; о. больнóго подýшками to surround a patient with pillows; о. стéну мрáмором to face a wall with marble. **2.** (*impf.* обклáдывать) to cover; (*impers.*) кругóм ~**и́ло** (нéбо) the sky is completely overcast; гóрло у негó ~**и́ло** (*med.*) his throat is furred. **3.** (*impf.* обклáдывать) to surround; о. крéпость (*mil.; obs.*) to invest a fortress; (*hunting*) to close round, corner. **4.** (*impf.* облагáть) to assess; о. налóгом to tax; о. мéстным налóгом to rate. **5.** (*impf.* обклáдывать) (*coll.*) to swear (at), berate.

облож|и́ться, ýсь, ~**ишься**, *pf.* **1.** (*impf.* обклáдываться) (+*i.*) to put round oneself, surround oneself (with). **2.** *pass. of* ~**и́ть**.

облóжк|а, и, *f.* (dust-)cover; folder.

обложнóй, *adj.* о. дождь (*coll.*) incessant rain.

облокáчива|ться, юсь, *impf. of* облокоти́ться.

облоко|ти́ться, чýсь, ~**ти́шься**, *pf.* (*of*

облокáчиваться) (на+*a.*) to lean one's elbow(s) (on, against).

облóм, а, *m.* **1.** breaking off. **2.** break. **3.** (*archit.*) profile. **4.** (*coll.*) clodhopper, bumpkin.

обломá|ть, ю, *pf.* (*of* облáмывать) **1.** to break off; о. зýбы (обо что-н.) (*coll.*) to come a cropper. **2.** to break (*horses*). **3.** (*fig., coll.*) to talk into, cajole.

обломá|ться, юсь, *pf.* (*of* облáмываться) to break off, snap.

облом|и́ть, лю́, ~**ишь**, *pf.* to break off.

облом|и́ться, лю́сь, ~**ишься**, *pf.* = ~**áться**.

облóмовщин|а, ы, *f.* 'oblomovism' (*sluggishness and indecision, as typified by the hero of Goncharov's novel 'Oblomov'*).

облóм|ок, ка, *m.* **1.** fragment. **2.** (*pl.*) débris, wreckage.

обломó|чный, *adj. of* ~**к**; ~**чные** гóрные порóды (*geol.*) disintegrated rock formations; detritus.

облон|ó, *n. indecl.* (*abbr. of* областнóй отдéл нарóдного образовáния) oblast education department.

облуп|и́ть, лю́, ~**ишь**, *pf. of* лупи́ть[1] **1** *and* ~**ливать**.

облуп|и́ться, лю́сь, ~**ишься**, *pf. of* лупи́ться *and* ~**ливаться**.

облýп|ленный, *p.p.p. of* ~**и́ть** *and adj.* chipped; знать как ~**ленного** (*coll.*) to know inside out.

облýплива|ть, ю, *impf.* (*of* облупи́ть) **1.** to peel; to shell (*eggs*). **2.** (*fig., coll.*) to fleece.

облýплива|ться, юсь, *impf.* (*of* облупи́ться) to peel (off), scale; to come off, chip (*of paint, plaster, etc.*).

облупл|я́ть(ся), я́ю(сь), *impf.* = ~**ивать**(ся).

облуч|áть, áю, *impf. of* ~**и́ть**.

облучéни|е, я, *n.* (*med.*) irradiation.

облуч|и́ть, у́, и́шь, *pf.* (*of* ~**áть**) to irradiate.

облуч|óк, кá, *m.* coachman's seat.

облущ|и́ть, у́, и́шь, *pf. of* лущи́ть.

облы́ж|ный (~**ен**, ~**на**), *adj.* (*coll.*) false.

облысé|ть, ю, ешь, *pf. of* лысéть.

облюб|овáть, у́ю, *pf.* (*of* ~**óвывать**) to pick, choose, select.

облюбóвыва|ть, ю, *impf. of* облюбовáть.

обл|я́гу, я́жешь, я́гут, *see* ~**éчь**[1].

обмá|зать, жу, жешь, *pf.* (*of* ~**зывать**) **1.** to coat (with); to putty (with). **2.** to soil (with), besmear (with); о. себé рýки мáслом to cover one's hands with oil.

обмá|заться, жусь, жешься, *pf.* (*of* ~**зываться**) **1.** (+*i.*) to besmear oneself (with), get oneself covered (with). **2.** *pass. of* ~**зать**.

обмáзк|а, и, *f.* **1.** coating; puttying.

обмáзыва|ть(ся), ю(сь), *impf. of* обмá-зать(ся).

обмáкива|ть, ю, *impf. of* обмакнýть.

обма́к|ну́ть, ну́, нёшь, *past* ~ну́л, *pf.* (*of* ~ивать) to dip; о. блин в смета́ну to dip a pancake into sour cream.

обма́н, а, *m.* fraud, deception; о. зре́ния optical illusion; ввести́ в о. to deceive; не да́ться кому́-н. в о. not to be taken in by someone.

обма́нк|а, и, *f.* (*min.*) blende; рогова́я о. hornblende; смоляна́я о. pitchblende.

обма́нны|й, *adj.* fraudulent; ~м путём fraudulently, by fraud.

обман|у́ть, у́, ~ешь, *pf.* (*of* ~ывать) to deceive; to cheat, swindle; о. чьё-н. дове́рие to betray someone's trust; о. чьи-н. наде́жды to disappoint someone's hopes.

обман|у́ться, у́сь, ~ешься, *pf.* (*of* ~ываться) to be deceived; о. в свои́х ожида́ниях to be disappointed in one's expectations.

обма́нчив|ый (~, ~а), *adj.* deceptive, delusive; нару́жность ~а appearances are deceptive.

обма́нщик, а, *m.* deceiver; cheat, fraud.

обма́нllыва|ть(ся), ю(сь), *impf. of* обману́ть(ся).

обмар|а́ть, а́ю, *pf.* (*of* ~ывать) (*coll.*) to soil, dirty.

обма́рыва|ть, ю, *impf. of* обмара́ть.

обма́тыва|ть(ся), ю(сь), *impf. of* обмота́ть(ся).

обма́хива|ть(ся), ю(сь), *impf. of* обмахну́ть(ся).

обмах|ну́ть, ну́, нёшь, *pf.* (*of* ~ивать) 1. to fan. 2. to dust (off); to brush (off); о. сор со ска́терти to brush crumbs off the cloth.

обмах|ну́ться, ну́сь, нёшься, *pf.* (*of* ~иваться) 1. to fan oneself. 2. *pass. of* ~ну́ть.

обма́чива|ть(ся), ю(сь), *impf. of* обмочи́ть(ся).

обмеле́ни|е, я, *n.* shallowing, shoaling.

обмеле́|ть, ет, *pf.* (*of* меле́ть) 1. to become shallow. 2. (*naut.*) to run aground.

обме́н, а, *m.* (+*i.*) exchange (of), interchange (of); barter; о. мне́ниями exchange of opinions; о. веще́ств (*biol.*) metabolism; в о. (за+*a.*) in exchange (for).

обме́нива|ть(ся), ю(сь), *impf. of* обмени́ть(ся) *and* обменя́ть(ся).

обмен|и́ть, ю́, ~ишь, *pf.* (*of* ~ивать) (*coll.*) to exchange (*accidentally*); to barter; to swop.

обмен|и́ться, ю́сь, ~ишься, *pf.* (*of* ~иваться) (+*i.*) (*coll.*) to exchange (*accidentally*).

обме́н|ный, *adj. of* ~.

обмен|я́ть, я́ю, *pf.* (*of* меня́ть 2 *and* ~ивать) (+*a.* на+*a.*) to exchange (for).

обмен|я́ться, я́юсь, *pf.* (*of* меня́ться 2 *and* ~иваться) (+*i.*) to exchange; to swop; о. взгля́дами to exchange looks; о. впечатле́ниями to compare notes.

обме́р[1], а, *m.* measurement.

обме́р[2], а, *m.* false measure.

об|мере́ть, омру́, омрёшь, *past* ~мер, ~мерла́, ~мерло, *pf.* (*of* ~мира́ть) (*coll.*) to faint; о. от у́жаса to be horror-struck; я ~мер my heart stood still.

обме́рива|ть(ся), ю(сь), *impf. of* обме́рить(ся).

обме́р|ить[1], ю, ишь, *pf.* (*of* ~ивать) to measure.

обме́р|ить[2], ю, ишь, *pf.* (*of* ~ивать) to cheat in measuring; to give short measure (to).

обме́р|иться, юсь, ишься, *pf.* (*of* ~иваться) (*coll.*) to make a mistake in measuring.

обме|сти́, ту́, тёшь, *past* ~л, ~ла́, *pf.* (*of* ~та́ть[1]) to sweep off; to dust.

обмета́|ть[1], ю, *impf. of* обмести́.

обме|та́ть[2], чу́, ~чешь, *pf.* (*of* ~тывать) 1. to overstitch, oversew; to whipstitch; to hem. 2. (*impers.*; *coll.*) у меня́ ~та́ло гу́бы my lips are cracked (with cold sores).

обмётыва|ть, ю, *impf. of* обмета́ть[2].

обмина́|ть, ю, *impf. of* обмя́ть.

обмира́|ть, ю, *impf. of* обмере́ть.

обмозг|ова́ть, у́ю, *pf.* (*of* ~о́вывать) (*coll.* to think over, turn over (in one's mind).

обмозго́выва|ть, ю, *impf. of* обмозгова́ть.

обмок|а́ть, а́ю, *impf. of* ~ну́ть.

обмо́к|нуть, ну, нешь, *past* ~, ~ла, *pf.* (*of* ~а́ть) (*coll.*) to get wet all over.

обмола́чива|ть, ю, *impf. of* обмолоти́ть.

обмо́лв|иться, люсь, ишься, *pf.* (*coll.*) 1. to make a slip in speaking. 2. (+*i.*) to say; to utter; не о. ни сло́вом (o+*p.*) to say not a word (about).

обмо́лвк|а, и, *f.* slip of the tongue.

обмоло́т, а, *m.* (*agric.*) threshing.

обмоло|ти́ть, чу́, ~тишь, *pf.* (*of* обмола́чивать) (*agric.*) to thresh.

обмора́жива|ть(ся), ю(сь), *impf. of* обморо́зить(ся).

обморо́жени|е, я, *n.* frost-bite.

обморо́|женный, *p.p.p. of* ~зить *and adj.* frost-bitten.

обморо́|зить, жу, зишь, *pf.* (*of* обмора́живать); я ~зил себе́ нос, ру́ки, *etc.* my nose is, hands, *etc.*, are frost-bitten.

обморо́|зиться, жусь, зишься, *pf.* (*of* обмора́живаться) to suffer frost-bite, be frostbitten.

о́бморок, а, *m.* fainting-fit; swoon; (*med.*) syncope; в глубо́ком ~е in a dead faint; упа́сть в о. to faint (away); to swoon.

обморо́ч|ить, у, ишь, *pf. of* моро́чить.

о́бморо́|чный, *adj. of* ~к; ~чное состоя́ние (*med.*) syncope.

обмота́|ть, ю, *pf.* (*of* обма́тывать) (+*a.* ано *i. or a.* вокру́г) to wind (round); о. ше́ю шарфом, о. шарф вокру́г ше́и to wind a scarf round one's neck.

обмота́|ться, юсь, *pf.* (*of* обма́тываться)
1. (+*i.*) to wrap oneself (in). **2.** *pass. of* ~ть.

обмо́тк|а, и, *f.* (*electr.*) winding.

обмо́т|ки, ок, *no sing.* puttees, leg-wrap-
pings.

обмо́т|очный, *adj. of* **1.** ~ка. **2.** ~ки.

обмоч|и́ть, у́, ~ишь, *pf.* (*of* обма́чивать) to
wet; о. посте́ль (*coll.*) to wet the bed.

обмоч|и́ться, у́сь, ~ишься, *pf.* (*of* обма́чи-
ваться) to wet oneself (*also coll.*).

обм|о́ю, о́ешь, *see* ~ы́ть.

обмундирова́ни|е, я, *n.* **1.** fitting out (with
uniform). **2.** uniform.

обмундир|ова́ть, у́ю, *pf.* (*of* ~о́вывать) to
fit out (with uniform).

обмундир|ова́ться, у́юсь, *pf.* (*of* ~о́вывать-
ся) to fit oneself out (with uniform); to
draw uniform.

обмундиро́в|ка, ки, *f.* = ~а́ние.

обмундиро́в|очный, *adj. of* ~ка; ~очные
де́ньги uniform allowance.

обмундиро́выва|ть(ся), ю(сь), *impf. of*
обмундирова́ть(ся).

обмуро́вк|а, и, *f.* brick-work.

обмыва́ни|е, я, *n.* bathing, washing.

обмыва́|ть(ся), ю(сь), *impf. of* обмы́ть(ся).

обмы́л|ок, ка, *m.* (*coll.*) remnant of a cake
of soap.

обм|ы́ть, о́ю, о́ешь, *pf.* (*of* ~ыва́ть) to bathe,
wash; о. ра́ну to bathe a wound.

обм|ы́ться, о́юсь, о́ешься, *pf.* (*of* ~ыва́ться)
1. to bathe, wash. **2.** *pass. of* ~ы́ть.

обмяк|а́ть, а́ю, *impf.* (*of* ~нуть) (*coll.*) to
become soft; (*fig.*) to become flabby.

обмя́к|нуть, ну, нешь, *past* ~, ~ла, *pf. of*
~а́ть.

об|мя́ть, омну́, омнёшь, *pf.* (*of* ~мина́ть)
to press down; to trample down.

обнагле́|ть, ю, ешь, *pf. of* нагле́ть.

обнадёжива|ть, ю, *impf. of* обнадёжить.

обнадёж|ить, у, ишь, *pf.* (*of* ~ивать) to
give hope (to), reassure.

обнаж|а́ть(ся), а́ю(сь), *impf. of* ~и́ть(ся).

обнаже́ни|е, я, *n.* **1.** baring, uncovering.
2. (*fig.*) revealing. **3.** (*geol.*) о. го́рной
поро́ды outcrop.

обнаж|ённый, *p.p.p. of* ~и́ть *and adj.* naked,
bare; nude.

обнаж|и́ть, у́, и́шь, *pf.* (*of* ~а́ть) **1.** to bare,
uncover; о. го́лову to bare one's head; о.
шпа́гу to draw the sword. **2.** (*fig.*) to lay
bare, reveal.

обнаж|и́ться, у́сь, и́шься, *pf.* (*of* ~а́ться)
1. to bare oneself, uncover oneself. **2.** *pass.
of* ~и́ть.

обнайто́в|ить, лю, ишь, *pf. of* найто́вить.

обнаро́довани|е, я, *n.* publication, promul-
gation.

обнаро́д|овать, ую, *pf. and impf.* (*lit.*) to
publish, promulgate.

обнару́жени|е, я, *n.* **1.** disclosure; display-
ing, revealing. **2.** discovery; detection.

обнару́жива|ть(ся), ю(сь), *impf. of* обнару́-
жить(ся).

обнару́ж|ить, у, ишь, *pf.* (*of* ~ивать) **1.** to
disclose; to display, reveal; о. свою ра́дость
to betray one's joy. **2.** to discover, bring
to light; to detect.

обнару́ж|иться, усь, ишься, *pf.* (*of* ~ивать-
ся) **1.** to be revealed; to come to light.
2. *pass. of* ~иваться.

обна́шива|ть, ю, *impf. of* обноси́ть[1].

обнес|ти́[1], у́, ёшь, *past* ~, ~ла́, *pf.* (*of* об-
носи́ть[2]) (+*i.*) to enclose (with); о. изго-
ро́дью to fence (in); о. пери́лами to rail in,
off.

обнес|ти́[2], у́, ёшь, *past* ~, ~ла́, *pf.* (*of*
обноси́ть[3]) (+*i.*) to serve round; ~ли́ ли
вы всех госте́й шампа́нским? have you
passed round the champagne to all the
guests? have all the guests had champagne?

обнес|ти́[3], у́, ёшь, *past* ~, ~ла́, *pf.* (*of* об-
носи́ть[4]) (+*a. and i.*) to pass over, leave
out (*in serving something*); меня́ ~ли́ вино́м
I have not had (been offered) wine.

обнима́|ть(ся), ю(сь), *impf. of* обня́ть(ся).

обни́мк|а, и, *f. only in phrase* в ~у (*coll.*) in an
embrace, embracing one another.

обнища́лый, *adj.* impoverished; beggarly.

обнища́ни|е, я, *n.* impoverishment, pauper-
ization.

обнища́|ть, ю, *pf. of* нища́ть.

обнов|и́ть, лю́, и́шь, *pf.* (*of* ~ля́ть) **1.** to
renovate; to renew; to reform. **2.** to repair,
restore; о. свои́ зна́ния (*fig.*) to refresh one's
knowledge; о. свои́ си́лы (*fig.*) to recruit
(one's forces). **3.** (*coll.*) to use for the first
time, inaugurate; to wear for the first
time.

обнов|и́ться, лю́сь, и́шься, *pf.* (*of* ~ля́ться)
1. to revive, be restored. **2.** *pass. of* ~и́ть.

обно́вк|а, и, *f.* (*coll.*) new acquisition, 'new
toy'; new dress.

обновле́н|ец, ца, *m.* (*hist.*) 'Renovationist'
(*member of 'Renovation' church in 1920s*).

обновле́ни|е, я, *n.* renovation, renewal.

обновля́|ть(ся), ю(сь), *impf. of* обнови́ть-
(ся).

обно|си́ть[1], шу́, ~сишь, *pf.* (*of* обна́ши-
вать) (*coll.*) to wear in (*new clothing or footwear*).

обно|си́ть[2, 3, 4], шу́, ~сишь, *impf. of* об-
нести́[1, 2, 3].

обно|си́ться, шу́сь, ~сишься, *pf.* (*coll.*)
1. to have worn out all one's clothes; to be
out at elbow. **2.** to become worn in, become comfortable (*of new clothes*).

обно́с|ки, ков, *sing.* ~ок, ~ка, *m.* (*coll.*) old
clothes.

обню́х|ать, аю, *pf.* (*of* ~ивать) to sniff (around).

обню́хива|ть, ю, *impf. of* обню́хать.

обн|я́ть, иму́, и́мешь, *past* ~я́л, ~яла́, ~я́ло, *pf.* (*of* ~има́ть) (*in var. senses*) to embrace; to clasp in one's arms; (*fig.*) to envelop; он шёл, ~я́в её за та́лию he was walking with his arm round her waist; о. взгля́дом to survey; о. умо́м (*fig.*) to comprehend, take in.

обн|я́ться, иму́сь, и́мешься, *past* ~я́лся, ~яла́сь, ~яло́сь, *pf.* (*of* ~има́ться) to embrace; to hug one another.

обо, *prep.* = о.

обобра́|ть, оберу́, оберёшь, *past* ~л, ~ла́, ~ло, *pf.* (*of* обира́ть) (*coll.*) 1. to pick, gather; о. кусты́ мали́ны to pick raspberries. 2. to rob; (*sl.*) to clean out.

обобра́ться, оберу́сь, оберёшься, *pf.* (*coll.*; +*g.*) не оберёшься beyond count, innumerable.

обобщ|а́ть, а́ю, *impf. of* ~и́ть.

обобще́ни|е, я, *n.* generalization.

обобществ|и́ть, лю́, и́шь, *pf.* (*of* ~ля́ть) to socialize; to collectivize.

обобществле́ни|е, я, *n.* socialization; collectivization.

обобществля́|ть, ю, *impf. of* обобществи́ть.

обобщ|и́ть, у́, и́шь, *pf.* (*of* ~а́ть) to generalize.

обобь|ю́, ёшь, *see* оби́ть.

обовши́ве|ть, ю, ешь, *pf. of* вши́веть.

обогати́тел|ь, я, *m.* (*mining tech.*) 1. concentrator; enriching agent. 2. ore concentration specialist.

обогати́тельный, *adj.* (*mining tech.*) concentrating; о. аппара́т ore separator.

обога|ти́ть, щу́, ти́шь, *pf.* (*of* ~ща́ть) 1. (*in var. senses*) to enrich. 2. (*mining tech.*) to concentrate; о. руду́ to concentrate ore, dress ore.

обога|ти́ться, щу́сь, ти́шься, *pf.* (*of* ~ща́ть-ся) 1. to become rich; (+*i.*) to enrich oneself (with). 2. *pass. of* ~ти́ть.

обогаща́|ть(ся), ю(сь), *impf. of* обогати́ть-(ся).

обогаще́ни|е, я, *n.* 1. (*in var. senses*) enrichment. 2. (*mining tech.*) concentration; о. руды́ ore concentration, ore dressing.

обогна́|ть, обгоню́, обго́нишь, *past* ~л, ~ла́, ~ло, *pf.* (*of* обгоня́ть) to pass, leave behind; to outstrip, outdistance (*also fig.*).

обогн|у́ть, у́, ёшь, *pf.* (*of* огиба́ть) 1. to round; to skirt; (*naut.*) to double. 2. to bend round; о. о́бруч вокру́г бо́чки to hoop a barrel.

обоготворе́ни|е, я, *n.* deification, idolization.

обоготвор|и́ть, ю́, и́шь, *pf.* (*of* ~я́ть) to deify, idolize.

обоготвор|я́ть, я́ю, *impf. of* ~и́ть.

обогре́в, а, *m.* (*tech.*) heating.

обогрева́ни|е, я, *n.* heating, warming.

обогрева́тел|ь, я, *m.* (*tech.*) heater.

обогрева́|ть(ся), ю(сь), *impf. of* обогре́ть-(ся).

обогре́|ть, ю, ешь, *pf.* (*of* ~ва́ть) to heat, warm.

обогре́|ться, юсь, ешься, *pf.* (*of* ~ва́ться) 1. to warm oneself; to warm up. 2. *pass. of* ~ть.

о́бод, а, *pl.* ~ья, ~ьев, *m.* rim; felloe.

обод|о́к, ка́, *m.* thin rim, thin border, fillet.

ободо́|чный, *adj. of* ~к; ~чная кишка́ (*anat.*) colon.

ободра́н|ец, ца, *m.* (*coll.*) ragamuffin, ragged fellow.

обо́др|анный, *p.p.p. of* ~а́ть *and adj.* ragged.

ободра́ть, обдеру́, обдерёшь, *pf.* (*of* обдира́ть) 1. to strip; to skin, flay; to peel; о. кору́ с де́рева to bark a tree. 2. (*fig., coll.*) to fleece.

ободре́ни|е, я, *n.* encouragement, reassurance.

ободри́тел|ьный (~ен, ~ьна), *adj.* encouraging, reassuring.

ободр|и́ть, ю́, и́шь, *pf.* (*of* ~я́ть) to cheer up; to encourage, reassure.

ободр|и́ться, ю́сь, и́шься, *pf.* (*of* ~я́ться) 1. to cheer up, take heart. 2. *pass. of* ~и́ть.

ободр|я́ть(ся), я́ю(сь), *impf. of* ~и́ть(ся).

обо́его, обо́ему (*no nom. or a.*), *m. and n. num.* both; обо́его по́ла of both sexes.

обоепо́л|ый (~, ~а), *adj.* (*biol.*) bisexual; (*bot.*) monoecious.

обожа́ни|е, я, *n.* adoration.

обожа́тел|ь, я, *m.* (*coll.*) admirer.

обожа́|ть, ю, *impf.* to adore, worship.

обож|гу́, жёшь, гу́т, *see* обже́чь.

обожд|а́ть, у́, ёшь, *past* ~а́л, ~ала́, ~а́ло, *pf.* (*coll.*) to wait (for a while).

обожеств|и́ть, лю́, и́шь, *pf.* (*of* ~ля́ть) to deify, worship.

обожествле́ни|е, я, *n.* deification, worshipping.

обожествля́|ть, ю, *impf. of* обожестви́ть.

обожжённый, *p.p.p. of* обже́чь.

обожм|у́, ёшь, *see* обжа́ть¹.

обожн|у́, ёшь, *see* обжа́ть².

обожр|а́ться, у́сь, ёшься, *past* ~а́лся, ~ала́сь, *pf.* (*of* обжира́ться) (*coll.*) to guzzle, stuff oneself.

обо́з, а, *m.* 1. string of carts; string of sledges; пожа́рный о. (*collect.*) fire-fighting vehicles, fire brigade. 2. (*mil.*) (*unit*) transport; быть в ~е (*fig.*) to bring up the rear, be left behind.

обозва́|ть, обзову́, обзовёшь, *past* ~л, ~ла́, ~ло, *pf.* (*of* обзыва́ть) (+*a. and i.*) to call; о. кого́-н. дурако́м to call someone a fool.

обозл|ённый, *p.p.p. of* ~и́ть *and adj.* embittered.

обозл|и́ть, ю́, и́шь, *pf.* 1. *pf. of* зли́ть. 2. to embitter.

обозл|и́ться, ю́сь, и́шься, *pf. of* зли́ться.

обознава́|ться, ю́сь, ёшься, *impf. of* ~ться.

обозна́|ться, ю́сь, ешься, *pf. (of* ~ва́ться*)* (*coll.*) to take someone for someone else; to be mistaken.

обознач|а́ть, а́ю, *impf.* 1. (*no pf.*) to mean. 2. (*pf.* ~ить) to mark, designate; о. на ка́рте грани́цу to mark a frontier on a map. 3. (*pf.* ~ить) to reveal; to emphasize.

обознач|а́ться, а́юсь, *impf. (of* ~иться*)* 1. to appear; to reveal oneself. 2. *pass. of* ~а́ть 2, 3.

обозначе́ни|е, я, *n.* 1. marking, designation. 2. sign, symbol; усло́вные ~я conventional signs (*on maps, etc.*).

обозна́ч|ить, у, ишь, *pf. of* ~а́ть 2, 3.

обозна́ч|иться, усь, ишься, *pf. of* ~а́ться.

обо́зник, а, *m.* driver.

обо́з|ный, *adj. of* ~; *as noun* о., ~ного, *m.* (*mil.*) driver.

обозрева́тел|ь, я, *m.* author of survey, author of review; columnist (*see* обозре́ние 2); полити́ческий о. political correspondent (*of newspaper*).

обозрева́|ть, ю, *impf. of* обозре́ть.

обозре́ни|е, я, *n.* 1. surveying, viewing; looking round. 2. survey; review (*exposé,* not *critical notice*). 3. review (*periodical journal*). 4. (*theatr.*) revue.

обозр|е́ть, ю́, и́шь, *pf. (of* ~ева́ть*)* 1. to survey, view; to look round. 2. (*fig.*) to survey, (pass in) review (*in print*).

обозри́м|ый (~, ~а), *adj.* visible.

обо́|и, ев, *no sing.* wall-paper; окле́ить ~ями to paper.

обой|дённый, *p.p.p. of* ~ти́.

обо́йм|а, ы, *g. pl.* ~, *f.* 1. (*mil.*) cartridge clip, charger. 2. (*tech.*) iron ring; о. шарикоподши́пника ball race.

обо́|йный, *adj. of* ~и.

обо|йти́, йду́, йдёшь, *past* ~шёл, ~шла́, *pf.* (*of* обходи́ть[1]) 1. to go round, pass; о. фланг проти́вника (*mil.*) to turn the enemy's flank. 2. to make the round (of), go (all) round; (*of doctor, sentry, etc.*) to make (go) one's round(s); слух ~шёл весь го́род the rumour spread all over the town. 3. to avoid; to leave out; to pass over; о. молча́нием to pass over in silence; о. зако́н to get round (evade) a law; о. затрудне́ние to get round a difficulty. 4. (*coll., pejor.*) to take in, get round.

обо|йти́сь, йду́сь, йдёшься, *past* ~шёлся, ~шла́сь, *pf. (of* обходи́ться*)* 1. (с+*i.*) to treat; пло́хо о. с кем-н. to treat someone badly. 2. (*coll.*) to cost, come to; во ско́лько

~шёлся ваш костю́м? how much did your suit come to? 3. (+*i.*) to manage (with, on), make do (with, on); о. ста рубля́ми to make do with one hundred roubles; без ва́шей по́мощи мы бы не ~шли́сь without your aid we could not have managed. 4. to turn out, end; всё ~шло́сь благополу́чно everything turned out all right; как-н. ~йдётся! things will turn out all right somehow! things will sort themselves out!

обо́йщик, а, *m.* paper-hanger; interior decorator, upholsterer.

о́бок, *adv. and prep.* +*g. or d.* (*coll.*) close by; near.

обокра́|сть, обокраду́, обокрадёшь, *past* ~л, ~ла, *pf. (of* обкра́дывать*)* to rob.

оболва́нива|ть, ю, *impf. of* оболва́нить.

оболва́н|ить, ю, ишь, *pf. (of* ~ивать*)* (*coll.*) 1. to rough-hew. 2. (*fig.*) to make a fool of.

обо|лга́ть, лгу́, лжёшь, *past* ~лга́л, ~лгала́, ~лга́ло, *pf.* to slander, calumniate.

оболо́чк|а, и, *f.* 1. cover, envelope, jacket; shell; (*tech.*) casing. 2. (*anat.*) membrane; ра́дужная о. iris; рогова́я о. cornea; сли́зистая о. mucous membrane. 3. (*bot.*) coat.

обо́лтус, а, *m.* (*coll.*) blockhead, booby.

обольсти́тел|ь, я, *m.* (*obs.*) seducer.

обольсти́тел|ьный (~ен, ~ьна), *adj.* seductive, captivating.

оболь|сти́ть, щу́, сти́шь, *pf. (of* ~ща́ть*)* 1. to captivate. 2. to seduce.

оболь|сти́ться, щу́сь, сти́шься, *pf. (of* ~ща́ться*)* to be (labour) under a delusion; (+*i.*) to flatter oneself (with).

обольща́|ть(ся), ю(сь), *impf. of* обольсти́ть(ся).

обольще́ни|е, я, *n.* 1. seduction. 2. delusion.

обо́ль|ю, ёшь, *see* обли́ть.

обомле́|ть, ю, ешь, *pf.* (*coll.*) to be stupefied.

обомн|у́, ёшь, *see* обмя́ть.

обомр|у́, ёшь, *see* обмере́ть.

обомше́лый, *adj.* moss-grown.

обоня́ни|е, я, *n.* (sense of) smell; име́ть то́нкое о. to have a fine sense of smell.

обоня́тельный, *adj.* (*anat.*) olfactory.

обоня́|ть, ю, *impf.* to smell.

обора́чиваемост|ь, и, *f.* (*fin., econ.*) turnover.

обора́чива|ть(ся), ю(сь), *impf. of* оберну́ть(ся) *and* оборо́ти́ть(ся).

оборва́н|ец, ца, *m.* ragamuffin, ragged fellow.

обо́рв|анный, *p.p.p. of* ~а́ть *and adj.* torn, ragged.

оборв|а́ть, у́, ёшь, *past* ~а́л, ~ала́, ~а́ло, *pf. (of* обрыва́ть*)* 1. to tear off, pluck

(*petals, etc.*); to strip (*a shrub of blossom, etc.*).
2. to break; to snap. 3. (*fig.*) to cut short,
interrupt; (*coll.*) to snub.

оборв|а́ться, у́сь, ёшься, *past* ~а́лся,
~ала́сь, ~а́ло́сь, *pf.* (*of* обрыва́ться) 1. to
break; to snap. 2. to (*lose one's hold of something and*) fall; (*of objects*) to come away. 3.
to stop suddenly, stop short, come abruptly
to an end.

обо́рвыш, а, *m.* (*coll.*) ragamuffin.

обо́рк|а, и, *f.* frill, flounce.

оборо́н|а, ы, *no pl., f.* 1. defence. 2. (*mil.*)
defences, defensive positions.

оборони́тельный, *adj.* defensive.

оборон|и́ть, ю́, и́шь, *pf.* (*of* ~я́ть) to de-
fend; ~и́ Бог (~и́ Бо́же, ~и́ Го́споди)!
(*obs.*) God forbid!

оборон|и́ться, ю́сь, и́шься, *pf.* (*of* ~я́ться)
(от) to defend oneself (from).

оборо́н|ный, *adj. of* ~а; ~ная промы́шлен-
ность war industry.

обороноспосо́бност|ь, и, *f.* defence ca-
pacity.

обороноспосо́б|ный (~ен, ~на), *adj.* pre-
pared for defence.

оборон|я́ть(ся), я́ю(сь), *impf. of* ~и́ть(ся).

оборо́т, а, *m.* 1. turn; (*tech.*) revolution,
rotation; приня́ть дурно́й о. (*fig.*) to take
a bad turn. 2. circulation; (*fin., comm., railways*) turnover; ввести́, пусти́ть в о. to put
into circulation. 3. back (= *reverse side*);
смотри́ на ~е please turn over; взять
кого́-н. в о. (*fig., coll.*) to get at someone.
4. turn (of speech); о. ре́чи phrase, locution.
5. (*tech.*) knee, bend (*in a pipe*).

обо́рот|ень, ня, *m.* werewolf.

оборо́тист|ый (~, ~а), *adj.* (*coll.*) resource-
ful.

оборо́|ти́ть, чу́, ~тишь, *pf.* (*of* обора́чивать)
(*coll.*) to turn.

оборо́|ти́ться, чу́сь, ~тишься, *pf.* (*of* обо-
ра́чиваться) (*coll.*) 1. to turn (round).
2. (в+*a. or* +*i.*) to turn (into).

оборо́тлив|ый (~, ~а), *adj.* (*coll.*) resource-
ful.

оборо́т|ный, *adj. of* ~; о. капита́л (*fin.,
comm.*) working capital; ~ная сторона́
verso; reverse side (*also fig.*); э ~ное *name
of letter* 'э'.

обору́довани|е, я, *n.* 1. equipping. 2. equip-
ment.

обору́д|овать, ую, *impf. and pf.* to equip,
fit out; (*fig., coll.*) to manage, arrange.

обо́рыш, а, *m.* (*coll.*) left-over, remnant.

обоснова́ни|е, я, *n.* 1. basing. 2. basis,
ground.

обосно́в|анный, *p.p.p. of* ~а́ть *and adj.* well-
-founded, well-grounded.

обосн|ова́ть, у́ю, у́ешь, *pf.* (*of* ~о́вывать)
to ground, base; to substantiate.

обосн|ова́ться, у́юсь, у́ешься, *pf.* (*of* ~о́вы-
ваться) 1. to settle down. 2. *pass. of*
~ова́ть.

обосно́выва|ть(ся), ю(сь), *impf. of* обосно-
ва́ть(ся).

обосо́б|ить, лю, ишь, *pf.* (*of* ~ля́ть) to iso-
late.

обосо́б|иться, люсь, ишься, *pf.* (*of* ~ля́ться)
to stand apart, keep aloof.

обособле́ни|е, я, *n.* isolation.

обосо́бленно, *adv.* apart; aloof; жить о. to
live by oneself.

обосо́б|ленный, *p.p.p. of* ~ить *and adj.* iso-
lated, solitary.

обособля́|ть(ся), ю(сь), *impf. of* обосо́бить-
(ся).

обостре́ни|е, я, *n.* aggravation, exacerba-
tion; о. боле́зни (*med.*) acute condition.

обостр|ённый, *p.p.p. of* ~и́ть *and adj.* 1.
sharp, pointed. 2. of heightened sensitivity;
о. слух a keen ear. 3. strained, tense.

обостр|и́ть, ю́, и́шь, *pf.* (*of* ~я́ть) 1. to
sharpen, intensify. 2. to strain; to aggra-
vate, exacerbate.

обостр|и́ться, ю́сь, и́шься, *pf.* (*of* ~я́ться)
1. to become sharp, become pointed. 2. (*of
the senses, etc.*) to become more sensitive,
become keener. 3. to become strained; to
become aggravated, become exacerbated;
боле́знь ~и́лась (*med.*) the condition has
become acute. 4. *pass. of* ~и́ть.

обостр|я́ть(ся), я́ю(сь), *impf. of* ~и́ть(ся).

оботр|у́, ёшь, *see* обтере́ть.

обо́чин|а, ы, *f.* edge; side (*of road, etc.*).

обою́дност|ь, и, *f.* mutuality, reciprocity.

обою́д|ный (~ен, ~на), *adj.* mutual, reci-
procal; по ~ному согла́сию by mutual
consent.

обоюдоо́стрый, *adj.* double-edged, two-
-edged (*also fig.*).

обраба́тыва|ть, ю, *impf. of* обрабо́тать.

обраба́тыва|ющий, *pres. part. act. of* ~ть *and
adj.* ~ющая промы́шленность manufac-
turing industry.

обрабо́та|ть, ю, *pf.* (*of* обраба́тывать) 1.
to work (up); to treat, process; (*tech.*) to
machine; о. зе́млю to work the land; о.
ра́ну to dress a wound. 2. to polish, perfect
(*a lit. production, etc.*). 3. (*fig., coll.*) to work
upon, win round.

обрабо́тк|а, и, *f.* working (up); treatment,
processing; (*tech.*) machining; о. земли́ cul-
tivation of the land.

обра́д|овать(ся), ую(сь), *pf. of* ра́довать(ся).

о́браз[1], а, *m.* 1. shape, form; appearance;
по ~у своему́ и подо́бию (*rhet. or joc.*) in
one's own image. 2. (*lit.*) image; мы́слить
~ами to think in images. 3. (*lit.*) type;
figure; о. Га́млета the Hamlet type. 4.
mode, manner; way; о. де́йствий line of

action, policy; о. жи́зни way of life, mode of life; о. правле́ния form of government; по ~у пе́шего хожде́ния (*joc.*) on foot, on Shank's mare; обстоя́тельство ~а де́йствия (*gram.*) adverbial modifier of manner; каки́м ~ом? how?; таки́м ~ом thus: гла́вным ~ом mainly, chiefly, largely; ра́вным ~ом equally.

о́браз², **а**, *pl.* ~**á**, *m.* icon.

образ|е́ц, **ца́**, *m.* **1.** model, pattern (*also fig.*); ста́вить в о. to set up as a model. **2.** specimen, sample; (*of material*) pattern.

образи́н|а, **ы**, *f.* (*coll., pejor.*) ugly mug; (*as term of abuse*) scum.

образн|о́й, *adj.* of о́браз²; *as noun* ~**а́я**, ~**о́й**, *f.* **1.** icon-room. **2.** icon-maker's workshop.

о́бразност|ь, **и**, *f.* picturesqueness; (*lit.*) figurativeness; imagery.

о́браз|ный (~**ен**, ~**на**), *adj.* picturesque, graphic; (*lit.*) figurative; employing images.

образова́ни|е¹, **я**, *n.* formation; о. слов word-formation; о. па́ра (*tech.*) production of steam.

образова́ни|е², **я**, *n.* education.

образо́ванност|ь, **и**, *f.* education (= *educated state*).

образо́в|анный, *p.p.p.* of ~**а́ть** and *adj.*; о. челове́к an educated person.

образова́тел|ьный (~**ен**, ~**ьна**), *adj.* educational; о. ценз educational qualification.

образ|ова́ть¹, **у́ю**, *impf.* (*in pres. tense*) *and pf.* (*of* ~**о́вывать**) to form; to make up.

образ|ова́ть², **у́ю**, *pf.* (*of* ~**о́вывать**) (*obs.*) to educate.

образ|ова́ться, **у́ется**, *pf.* (*of* ~**о́вываться**) **1.** to form; to arise. **2.** (*coll.*) to turn out well; не беспоко́йтесь, всё ~у́ется! don't worry, everything will be all right! **3.** *pass.* *of* ~**ова́ть**.

образовыва|ть(ся), **ю(сь)**, *impf.* of образова́ть(ся).

образу́м|ить, **лю**, **ишь**, *pf.* (*coll.*) to bring to reason, make listen to reason.

образу́м|иться, **люсь**, **ишься**, *pf.* (*coll.*) to come to one's senses, see reason.

образу́ющ|ая, **ей**, *f.* (*math.*) generatrix.

образцо́в|ый, *adj.* model; exemplary; ~ое поведе́ние exemplary conduct; ~ое произведе́ние masterpiece; ~ое хозя́йство model farm.

обра́зчик, **а**, *m.* specimen, sample; (*of material*) pattern.

обра́м|ить, **лю**, **ишь**, *pf.* (*of* ~**ля́ть**) to frame.

обрамле́ни|е, **я**, *n.* **1.** framing. **2.** frame; (*fig.*) setting.

обрамля́|ть, **ю**, *impf.* of обра́мить.

обраста́ни|е, **я**, *n.* **1.** overgrowing. **2.** (*fig.*) accumulation, acquisition.

обраст|а́ть, **а́ю**, *impf.* of ~**й**.

обраст|и́, **у́**, **ёшь**, *past* обро́с, обросла́, *pf.*

(*of* ~**а́ть**) (+*i.*) **1.** to become (be) overgrown (with); о. гря́зью (*coll.*) to be coated with mud. **2.** (*fig.*) to become (be) surrounded (by), become (be) cluttered (with); to acquire, accumulate; он обро́с нену́жной ме́белью he has surrounded himself with superfluous items of furniture.

обра́т, **а**, *m.* skim milk.

обрати́мост|ь, **и**, *f.* reversibility.

обрати́м|ый (~, ~**а**), *adj.* reversible.

обра|ти́ть, **щу́**, **ти́шь**, *pf.* (*of* ~**ща́ть**) (*in var. senses*) to turn; (в+*a.*) to turn (into); о. внима́ние (на+*a.*) to pay attention (to), take notice (of); notice; о. чьё-н. внима́ние (на+*a.*) to call, draw someone's attention (to); о. на себя́ внима́ние to attract attention (to oneself); о. иму́щество в капита́л to realize property; о. в бе́гство to put to flight; о. в свою́ ве́ру to convert (to one's faith); о. в шу́тку to turn into a joke.

обра|ти́ться, **щу́сь**, **ти́шься**, *pf.* (*of* ~**ща́ться**) **1.** to turn; to revert; о. лицо́м к стене́ to turn (one's face) towards the wall; о. в бе́гство to take to flight. **2.** (к) to turn (to), appeal (to); to apply (to); to accost; она́ не зна́ла, к кому́ о. за по́мощью she did not know to whom to turn for help; о. с призы́вом к кому́-н. to appeal to someone; о. к юри́сту to take legal advice; о. к славянове́дению to take up Slavonic studies. **3.** (в+*a.*) to turn (into), become; о. в ци́ника to become a cynic; о. в слух (*fig.*) to be all ears; to prick up one's ears. **4.** (в+*a.*) to be converted (to).

обра́тно, *adv.* **1.** back; backwards; туда́ и о. there and back; пое́здка туда́ и о. round trip; взять о. to take back; идти́ о., е́хать о. to go back; to return, retrace one's steps. **2.** conversely; inversely; о. пропорциона́льный inversely proportional. **3.** (*vulg.*) again.

обра́тн|ый, *adj.* **1.** reverse; о. а́дрес sender's address; о. биле́т return ticket; ~**ая** вспы́шка back-firing; о. кла́пан (*tech.*) return valve; о. путь return journey; ~**ые** растя́жки (*aeron.*) landing wires; име́ющий ~**ую** си́лу (*leg.*) retroactive, retrospective; о. уда́р backfire; о. ход (*tech.*) reverse motion, back stroke; ~**ая** связь (*electr.*) feed-back. **2.** opposite; в ~**ую** сто́рону in the opposite direction. **3.** (*math.*) inverse; ~**ое** отноше́ние inverse ratio.

обраща́|ть, **ю**, *impf.* of обрати́ть.

обраща́|ться, **юсь**, *impf.* **1.** *impf.* of обрати́ться. **2.** (*physiol., econ., etc.*) to circulate. **3.** (с+*i.*) to treat; пло́хо о. с кем-н. to treat someone badly, maltreat someone. **4.** (с+*i.*) to handle, manage (*an inanimate object*); он, по-ви́димому, не уме́ет о. с автома́том apparently he does not know how to handle a sub-machine-gun.

обраще́ни|е, я, *n.* **1.** (к) appeal (to), address (to). **2.** (в+*a.*) conversion (to, into); о. в ве́ру conversion to faith. **3.** circulation; изъя́ть из ~я to withdraw from circulation; пусти́ть в о. to put in circulation. **4.** (с+*i.*) treatment (of); плохо́е о. ill-treatment. **5.** (с+*i.*) handling (of), use (of). **6.** manner.

обревиз|ова́ть, у́ю, *pf. of* ревизова́ть.

обре́з¹, а, *m.* edge; в о. (*coll.*; +*g.*) only just enough; де́нег у меня́ в о. I have not a penny to spare.

обре́з², а, *m.* sawn-off gun.

обре́зани|е, я, *n.* circumcision.

обреза́ни|е, я, *n.* **1.** cutting. **2.** trimming; paring; pruning; bevelling.

обре́|зать, жу, жешь, *pf.* (*of* ~зыва́ть *and* ~за́ть) **1.** to clip, trim; to pare; to prune; to bevel; о. кому́-н. кры́лья (*fig.*) to clip someone's wings. **2.** to cut; о. себе́ па́лец to cut one's finger. **3.** to circumcise. **4.** (*coll.*) to cut short; to snub.

обреза́|ть, а́ю, *impf. of* ~ать.

обре́|заться, жусь, жешься, *pf.* (*of* ~за́ться *and* ~зыва́ться) **1.** to cut oneself. **2.** *pass. of* ~зать.

обреза́|ться, а́юсь, *impf. of* ~аться.

обрезно́й, *adj.* (*tech.*) trimming.

обре́з|ок, ка, *m.* scrap; (*pl.*) ends; clippings.

обре́зыва|ть(ся), ю(сь), *impf. of* обре́зать-(ся).

обрека́|ть, ю, *impf. of* обре́чь.

обре|ку́, чёшь, ку́т, *see* ~чь.

обремени́тел|ьный (~ен, ~ьна), *adj.* burdensome, onerous.

обремен|и́ть, ю́, и́шь, *pf.* (*of* ~я́ть) to burden.

обремен|я́ть, я́ю, *impf. of* ~и́ть.

обреми́|зиться, жусь, зи́шься, *pf.* (*obs.*, *coll.*) to get into a mess, into difficulties.

обре|сти́, ту́, тёшь (*arch.* обря́щу, обря́-щешь), *past* ~л, ~ла́, *pf.* (*of* ~та́ть) (*rhet.*) to find; ищи́те да обря́щете seek and ye shall find.

обре|сти́сь, ту́сь, тёшься, *past* ~лся, ~ла́сь, *pf.* (*obs.*) to be found; to turn up.

обрета́|ть, ю, *impf. of* обрести́.

обрета́|ться, юсь, *impf.* (*obs. or coll.*) to be; to pass one's time.

обрече́ни|е, я, *n.* doom.

обречённост|ь, и, *f.* being doomed; чу́вство ~и feeling of doom.

обреч|ённый, *p.p.p. of* ~ь and *adj.* doomed.

обре́|чь, ку́, чёшь, ку́т, *past* ~к, ~кла́, *pf.* (*of* ~ка́ть) to condemn, doom.

обреше́|тить, чу, тишь, *pf.* (*of* ~чивать) to lath.

обрешёчива|ть, ю, *impf. of* обреше́тить.

обрис|ова́ть, у́ю, *pf.* (*of* ~о́вывать) to outline, delineate, depict (*also fig.*).

обрис|ова́ться, у́юсь, *pf.* (*of* ~о́вываться)

1. to appear (in outline); to take shape. **2.** *pass of* ~ова́ть.

обрисо́вк|а, и, *f.* outlining, delineation, depicting.

обрисо́выва|ть(ся), ю(сь), *impf. of* обрисо-ва́ть(ся).

обри́т|ый, *p.p.p. of* ~ь and *adj.* shaven.

обр|и́ть, е́ю, е́ешь, *pf.* to shave (off).

обр|и́ться, е́юсь, е́ешься, *pf.* to shave one's head.

обро́к, а, *m.* (*hist.*) quit-rent; быть на ~е, ходи́ть по ~у to be liable for quit-rent.

оброн|и́ть, ю́, ~ишь, *pf.* **1.** to drop (*sc. and lose*). **2.** to let drop, let fall (*a remark, etc.*).

обро́|чный, *adj. of* ~к; о. крестья́нин peasant on quit-rent.

обруб|а́ть, а́ю, *impf. of* ~и́ть.

обруб|и́ть¹, лю́, ~ишь, *pf.* (*of* ~а́ть) to chop off; to lop off; to dock.

обруб|и́ть², лю́, ~ишь, *pf.* (*of* ~а́ть) to hem.

обру́б|ок, ка, *m.* stump.

обруга́|ть, ю, *pf.* to curse; to call names; (*coll.; of book reviews, etc.*) to tear to pieces.

обрусе́лый, *adj.* russified, russianized.

обрусе́ни|е, я, *n.* russification, russianization.

обрусе́|ть, ю, *pf.* to become russified, become russianized.

обруси́|ть, шь, *pf.* to russify, russianize.

о́бруч, а, *pl.* ~и, ~е́й, *m.* hoop.

обруча́льн|ый, *adj.* ~ое кольцо́ wedding ring; о. обря́д betrothal.

обруч|а́ть(ся), а́ю(сь), *impf. of* ~и́ть(ся).

обруче́ни|е, я, *n.* betrothal.

обруч|и́ть, у́, и́шь, *pf.* (*of* ~а́ть) to betrothe.

обруч|и́ться, у́сь, и́шься, *pf.* (*of* ~а́ться) (с+*i.*) to become engaged (to).

обру́шива|ть(ся), ю(сь), *impf. of* обру́-шить(ся).

обру́ш|ить, у, ишь, *pf.* (*of* ~ивать) to bring down, rain down.

обру́ш|иться, усь, ишься, *pf.* (*of* ~иваться) **1.** to come down, collapse, cave in. **2.** (*fig.*) to come down (upon), fall (upon).

обры́в, а, *m.* **1.** precipice. **2.** (*tech.*) break, rupture.

обрыва́|ть(ся), ю(сь), *impf. of* оборва́ть(ся).

обры́вист|ый (~, ~а), *adj.* steep, precipitous; (*fig.*) abrupt.

обры́в|ок, ка, *m.* scrap; snatch (*of tune, song, etc.*); ~ки мы́слей desultory thoughts; ~ки разгово́ра scraps of conversation.

обры́зг|ать, аю, *pf.* (*of* ~ивать) (+*i.*) to besprinkle (with); to splash; to bespatter (with).

обры́згива|ть, ю, *impf. of* обры́згать.

обры́ска|ть, ю, *pf.* (*coll.*) to go through, hunt through.

обрю́зглый, *adj.* flabby, flaccid.

обрю́зг|нуть, ну, нешь, *past* ~, ~ла, *pf.* to become flabby, become flaccid.

обрю́зг|ший = ~лый.

обря́д, а, *m.* rite, ceremony.

обря|ди́ть, жу́, ~ди́шь, *pf.* (*of* ~жа́ть) (*coll., joc.*) (+*i.*) to get up (in), trick out (in).

обря|ди́ться, жу́сь, ~ди́шься, *pf.* (*of* ~жа́ться) (*coll., joc.*) (+*i.*) to get oneself up (in).

обря́дност|ь, и, *f.* (*collect.*) rites, ritual, ceremonial.

обря́довый, *adj.* ritual, ceremonial.

обряжа́|ть(ся), ю(сь), *impf. of* обряди́ть(ся).

обса|ди́ть, жу́, ~дишь, *pf.* (*of* ~живать) to plant round; о. кла́дбище ти́сами to surround a cemetery with yew-trees.

обса́жива|ть, ю, *impf. of* обсади́ть.

обса́лива|ть, ю, *impf. of* обса́лить *and* обсоли́ть.

обса́л|ить, ю, ишь, *pf.* (*of* ~ивать) (*coll.*) to smear with grease, spill grease on.

обса́сыва|ть, ю, *impf. of* обсоса́ть.

обса́харива|ть, ю, *impf. of* обса́харить.

обса́хар|ить, ю, ишь, *pf.* (*of* ~ивать) (*coll.*) to sugar.

обсемене́ни|е, я, *n.* 1. (*agric.*) sowing. 2. (*bot.*) going to seed.

обсемен|и́ть, ю, и́шь, *pf.* (*of* ~я́ть) (*agric.*) to sow (*a field*).

обсемен|и́ться, ю́сь, и́шься, *pf.* (*of* ~я́ться) 1. (*bot.*) to go to seed. 2. *pass. of* ~и́ть.

обсемен|я́ть(ся), я́ю(сь), *impf. of* ~и́ть(ся).

обсервато́ри|я, и, *f.* observatory.

обсерва|цио́нный, *adj. of* ~ция.

обсерва́ци|я, и, *f.* observation.

обсидиа́н, а, *m.* (*min.*) obsidian.

обска|ка́ть, чу́, ~чешь, *pf.* (*of* ~кивать) 1. to gallop round. 2. (*pf. only*) to outgallop.

обска́кива|ть, ю, *impf. of* обскака́ть 1.

обскура́нт, а, *m.* obscurant, obscurantist.

обскуранти́зм, а, *m.* obscurantism.

обскуранти́стский, *adj.* obscurantist.

обсле́довани|е, я, *n.* (+*g.*) inspection (of), inquiry (into); investigation (of); observation, tests (*in hospital*).

обсле́довател|ь, я, *m.* inspector, investigator.

обсле́д|овать, ую, *impf. and pf.* to inspect; to investigate; о. больно́го to examine a patient.

обслу́живани|е, я, *n.* service; (*tech.*) servicing, maintenance; бытово́е о. consumer service (*including such facilities as hairdressing, dry-cleaning, domestic utensil repairs, etc.*) медици́нское о. health service.

обслу́жива|ть, ю, *impf. of* обслужи́ть; о. стано́к to mind a machine; (*naut.*) о. ору́дия to man the guns; ~ющий персона́л (serving) staff; (*collect.*) assistants, attendants.

обслуж|и́ть, у́, ~ишь, *pf.* (*of* ~ивать) to attend (to), serve; (*tech.*) to service; to mind, operate; о. потреби́теля to serve a customer.

обслюн|и́ть, ю́, и́шь, *pf.* (*coll.*) to slobber all over.

обсол|и́ть, ю́, *pf.* (*of* обса́ливать) to salt all over.

обсос|а́ть, у́, ёшь, *pf.* (*of* обса́сывать) 1. to suck round (*a sweet, etc.*). 2. (*fig., coll.*) to chew over.

обсо́х|нуть, ну, нешь, *past* ~, ~ла, *pf.* (*o* обсыха́ть) to dry, become dry; у него́ молоко́ на губа́х не ~ло (*fig.*) he is still green.

обста́в|ить, лю, ишь, *pf.* (*of* ~ля́ть) 1. (+*i.*) to surround (with), encircle (with). 2. (+*i.*) to furnish (with). 3. (*fig.*) to arrange; to organize. 4. (*coll.*) to get the better (of); to get round, cheat.

обста́в|иться, люсь, ишься, *pf.* (*of* ~ля́ться) 1. (+*i.*) to surround oneself (with). 2. to establish oneself, set oneself up (*in lodgings, etc.*). 3. *pass. of* ~ить.

обставля́|ть(ся), ю(сь), *impf. of* обста́вить(ся).

обстано́вк|а, и, *f.* 1. furniture; décor (*also theatr.*). 2. situation, conditions; environment; set-up; боева́я о. (*mil.*) tactical situation.

обстано́в|очный, *adj. of* ~ка; ~очная пье́са (*theatr.*) spectacular.

обстир|а́ть, а́ю, *pf.* (*of* ~ывать) (*coll.*) to do the washing (*for a number of*).

обсти́рыва|ть, ю, *impf. of* обстира́ть.

обстоя́тел|ьный (~ен, ~ьна), *adj.* 1. circumstantial, detailed. 2. (*coll.; of a person*) thorough, reliable.

обстоя́тельственный, *adj.* (*gram.*) adverbial.

обстоя́тельств|о[1], а, *n.* circumstance; смягча́ющие ~а ̃extenuating circumstances; по незави́сящим от меня́ ~ам for reasons beyond my control; по семе́йным ~ам due to family circumstances; ни при каки́х ~ах in no circumstances; смотря́ по ~ам depending on circumstances.

обстоя́тельств|о[2], а, *n.* (*gram.*) adverbial modifier.

обсто|я́ть, и́т, *impf.* to be; to get on; как ~и́т де́ло? how is it going? how are things going?; как ~я́т ва́ши дела́? how are you getting on?; всё ~и́т благополу́чно all is well, everything is going all right; вот как ~и́т де́ло that is the way it is, that's how matters stand.

обстра́гива|ть, ю, *impf. of* обстрога́ть.

обстра́ива|ть(ся), ю(сь), *impf. of* обстро́ить(ся).

обстрека́|ть, ю, *pf. of* стрека́ть.

обстре́л, а, *m.* firing, fire; артиллери́йский о. bombardment, shelling; быть под ~ом to be under fire; попа́сть под о. to come under fire.

обстре́лива|ть(ся), ю(сь), *impf. of* обстреля́ть(ся).

обстре́л|янный, *p.p.p. of* ~я́ть *and adj.* seasoned, experienced (of *soldiers, also fig.*); ~янная пти́ца (*coll.*) old hand, person who has knocked around.

обстрел|я́ть, я́ю, *pf.* (*of* ~ивать) to fire (at, on); to bombard.

обстрел|я́ться, я́юсь, *pf.* (*of* ~ива́ться) (*coll.*) to become seasoned (by being in battle); to receive a baptism of fire.

обстрога́|ть, ю, *pf.* (*of* обстра́гивать) to plane; to whittle.

обстро́|ить, ю, ишь, *pf.* (*of* обстра́ивать) to build (up).

обстро́|иться, юсь, ишься, *pf.* (*of* обстра́иваться) 1. to be built (up); (*coll.*) to spring up. 2. to build for oneself.

обструга́|ть, ю, *pf.* = обстрога́ть.

обструкциони́зм, а, *m.* (*polit.*) obstructionism.

обструкциони́ст, а, *m.* (*polit.*) obstructionist.

обстру́кци|я, и, *f.* (*polit.*) obstruction; filibustering.

обступ|а́ть, а́ю, *impf. of* ~и́ть.

обступ|и́ть, лю́, ~ишь, *pf.* (*of* ~а́ть) to surround; to cluster (round).

обсу|ди́ть, жу́, ~дишь, *pf.* (*of* ~жда́ть) to discuss; to consider.

обсужда́|ть, ю, *impf. of* обсуди́ть.

обсужде́ни|е, я, *n.* discussion.

обсу́шива|ть(ся), ю(сь), *impf. of* обсуши́ть(ся).

обсуш|и́ть, у́, ~ишь, *pf.* (*of* ~ивать) to dry (out).

обсуш|и́ться, у́сь, ~ишься, *pf.* (*of* ~иваться) to dry oneself, get dry.

обсчит|а́ть, а́ю, *pf.* (*of* ~ывать) to cheat (*in counting out money*).

обсчит|а́ться, а́юсь, *pf.* (*of* ~ываться) to make a mistake (*in counting*); вы ~а́лись на шесть копе́ек you were six kopecks out.

обсчи́тыва|ть(ся), ю(сь), *impf. of* обсчита́ть(ся).

обсы́п|ать, лю, лешь, *pf.* (*of* ~а́ть) (+*i.*) to strew; to sprinkle.

обсып|а́ть, а́ю, *impf. of* ~ать.

обсы́п|аться, люсь, лешься, *pf.* = осы́паться.

обсыха́|ть, ю, *impf. of* обсо́хнуть.

обта́ива|ть, ю, *impf. of* обта́ять.

обта́чива|ть, ю, *impf. of* обточи́ть.

обта́|ять, ю, *pf.* (*of* ~ивать) 1. to melt away (around). 2. to become clear (*of ice*).

обтека́ем|ый, *adj.* (*tech.*) streamlined; ~ая фо́рма streamline form.

обтека́тел|ь, я, *m.* (*aeron. tech.*) fairing.

обтека́|ть, ю, *impf. of* обтёчь.

обтер|е́ть, оботру́, оботрёшь, *past* ~, ~ла, *pf.* (*of* обтира́ть) 1. to wipe; wipe dry. 2. (+*i.*) to rub (with).

обтер|е́ться, оботру́сь, оботрёшься, *past* ~ся, ~лась, *pf.* (*of* обтира́ться) 1. to wipe oneself dry, dry oneself. 2. to sponge down. 3. (*coll.*) to wear thin, rub (*as result of friction*). 4. (*fig., coll.*) to adapt oneself, become acclimatized.

обтерп|е́ться, лю́сь, ~ишься, *pf.* (*coll.*) to become acclimatized, become accustomed.

обтёс|анный, *p.p.p. of* ~а́ть; гру́бо о. rough-finished.

обте|са́ть, шу́, ~шешь, *pf.* (*of* ~сывать) 1. to square; to rough-hew; to dress, trim. 2. (*fig., coll.*) to teach manners (to), lick into shape.

обте|са́ться, шу́сь, ~шешься, *pf.* (*of* ~сываться) (*coll.*) to acquire (*polite*) manners, acquire polish.

обтёсыва|ть(ся), *impf. of* обтеса́ть(ся).

обтё|чь, ку́, чёшь, ку́т, *past* ~к, ~кла́, *pf.* (*of* ~ка́ть) 1. to flow round. 2. (*mil.*) to by-pass.

обтира́ни|е, я, *n.* 1. sponge-down. 2. (*coll.*) lotion.

обтира́|ть(ся), ю(сь), *impf. of* обтере́ть(ся).

обточ|и́ть, у́, ~ишь, *pf.* (*of* обта́чивать) to grind; (*tech.*) to turn, machine, round off.

обто́чк|а, и, *f.* (*tech.*) turning, machining, rounding off.

обтрёп|анный, *p.p.p. of* ~а́ть *and adj.* 1. frayed. 2. shabby.

обтреп|а́ть, лю́, ~лешь, *pf.* to fray.

обтреп|а́ться, лю́сь, ~лешься, *pf.* 1. to become frayed, fray. 2. to become shabby.

обтюра́тор, а, *m.* 1. (*anat. and tech.*) obturator. 2. (*phot.*) shutter. 3. (*mil.*) gas-check (*in breech of gun*).

обтюра́ци|я, и, *f.* (*tech.*) obturation; stopping-up.

обтя́гива|ть, ю, *impf. of* обтяну́ть.

обтя́жк|а, и, *f.* 1. cover (*for furniture*). 2. (*aeron.*) skin. 3. пла́тье в ~у close-fitting dress.

обтя|ну́ть, ну́, ~нешь, *pf.* (*of* ~гивать) 1. (+*i.*) to cover (*furniture*) (with). 2. to fit close (to).

обува́|ть(ся), ю(сь), *impf. of* обу́ть(ся).

обу́вк|а, и, *f.* (*coll.*) boots.

обувн|о́й, *adj. of* о́бувь; о. магази́н shoe shop; ~а́я промы́шленность boot and shoe industry.

обувщи́к, а́, *m.* boot and shoe operative.

о́був|ь, и, *no pl., f.* footwear; boots, shoes.

обу́гливани|е, я, *n.* carbonization.

обу́глива|ть(ся), ю(сь), *impf. of* обу́глить(ся).

обу́гл|ить, ю, ишь, *pf.* (*of* ~ивать) to char; to carbonize.

обу́гл|иться, юсь, ишься, *pf.* (*of* ~иваться) to become charred, char.

обужива|ть, ю, *impf. of* обузить.

обу́з|а, ы, *f.* burden; быть ~ой для кого-н. to be a burden to someone.

обузд|а́ть, а́ю, *pf.* (*of* ~ывать) to bridle, curb (*also fig.*); (*fig.*) to restrain, control; о. свой хара́ктер to restrain oneself; о. свои́ стра́сти to curb one's passions.

обу́зд|ить, жу, зишь, *pf.* (*of* ~живать) to make too tight.

обурева́|ть, ет, *impf.* to shake; to grip; его́ ~ют сомне́ния he is a prey to doubts.

обуржуа́зивани|е, я, *n.* embourgeoisement.

обуржуа́|зиться, жусь, зишься, *pf.* to become bourgeois, undergo embourgeoisement.

обусло́в|ить, лю, ишь, *pf.* (*of* ~ливать) 1. to condition; (+*i.*) to make conditional (upon), stipulate (for); он ~ил своё согла́сие предоставле́нием маши́ны he made his consent conditional upon the provision of a car. 2. to cause, bring about; to be the condition of.

обусло́в|иться, люсь, ишься, *pf. of* ~ливаться.

обусло́влива|ть, ю, *impf. of* обусло́вить.

обусло́влива|ться, юсь, *impf.* (*of* обусло́виться) (+*i.*) to be conditioned (by), be conditional (upon); to depend (on); разме́р ~ется тре́бованиями the size is conditioned by the requirements.

обу́т|ый, *p.p.p. of* ~ь; оде́тый и о. clothed and shod.

обу́|ть, ю, ешь, *pf.* (*of* ~ва́ть) 1. о. кого́-н. to put on someone's boots (shoes) for him. 2. to provide with boots, shoes.

обу́|ться, юсь, ешься, *pf.* (*of* ~ва́ться) 1. to put on one's boots, shoes. 2. to provide oneself with boots, shoes.

о́бух, а (*and* обу́х, а́), *m.* butt, back; head (*of an axe*); (*naut.*) eye-bolt; меня́ то́чно ~ом по голове́ (*coll.*) you could have knocked me down with a feather; плетью ~а не перешибёшь (*prov.*) the weakest goes to the wall.

обуч|а́ть(ся), а́ю(сь), *impf. of* ~и́ть(ся).

обуче́ни|е, я, *n.* teaching; instruction, training; совме́стное о. (лиц обо́его по́ла) co-education.

обуч|и́ть, у́, ~ишь, *pf.* (*of* учи́ть *and* ~а́ть) (кого́-н. чему́-н.) to teach (someone something); to instruct, train (in).

обуч|и́ться, у́сь, ~ишься, *pf.* (*of* учи́ться *and* ~а́ться) (+*d. or* +*inf.*) to learn.

обу́шный, *adj. of* о́бух.

обуш|о́к, ка́, *m.* pick (with detachable point); (*naut.*) eye-bolt.

обуя́|ть, ет, *pf.* (*obs.*) to seize; to grip; его́ ~л страх fear had seized him.

обха́жива|ть, ю, *impf.* (*coll.*) to cajole, try to get round.

обхва́т, а, *m.* (*measurement of circumference*) girth; в ~е in circumference; ме́рить в ~е to girth.

обхва|ти́ть, чу́, ~тишь, *pf.* (*of* ~тывать) to encompass (with outstretched arms); to clasp.

обхва́тыва|ть, ю, *impf. of* обхвати́ть.

обхо́д, а, *m.* 1. (*doctor's, postman's, etc.*) round; (*guard's, policeman's*) beat; пойти́ в о. to go round, make (go) one's round(s). 2. roundabout way; by-pass. 3. (*mil.*) turning movement, wide enveloping movement. 4. evasion, circumvention (*of law, etc.*).

обходи́тел|ьный (~ен, ~ьна), *adj.* pleasant; courteous; well-mannered.

обхо|ди́ть¹, жу́, ~дишь, *impf. of* обойти́.

обхо|ди́ть², жу́, ~дишь, *pf.* to go all round.

обхо|ди́ться, жу́сь, ~дишься, *impf. of* обойти́сь.

обхо́дн|ый, *adj.* roundabout, circuitous; о. путь detour; ~ым путём in a roundabout way; ~ое движе́ние (*mil.*) turning movement.

обхо́дчик, а, *m.* (*railway*) trackman.

обхожде́ни|е, я, *n.* manners; (с+*i.*) treatment (of), behaviour (towards).

обче́сться, обочту́сь, обочтёшься, *past* обчёлся, обочла́сь, *pf.* (*coll.*) = обсчита́ться; (их) раз, два и обчёлся (they) can be counted on the fingers of one hand.

обчи́|стить, щу, стишь, *pf.* (*of* ~ща́ть) 1. to clean; to brush. 2. (*fig., coll.*) to clean out (= to rob).

обчи́|ститься, щусь, стишься, *pf.* (*of* ~ща́ться) 1. to clean oneself; to brush oneself. 2. *pass. of* ~стить.

обчища́|ть(ся), ю(сь), *impf. of* обчи́стить(ся).

обша́рива|ть, ю, *impf. of* обша́рить.

обша́р|ить, ю, ишь, *pf.* (*of* ~ивать) to rummage; to ransack.

обша́рка|ть, ю, *pf.* (*coll.*) to wear out (*by much walking*).

обша́рпа|нный, *p.p.p. of* ~ть; ~нное зда́ние dilapidated building.

обша́рпа|ть, ю, *pf.* (*coll.*) to wear (away).

обшива́|ть, ю, *impf. of* обши́ть¹, ².

обши́вк|а, и, *f.* 1. edging, bordering. 2. trimming, facing. 3. boarding, panelling; о. фане́рой veneering; (*tech.*) sheathing; (*naut.*) planking; стальна́я о. plating; нару́жная о. skin-plating.

обши́в|очный, *adj. of* ~ка.

обши́р|ный (~ен, ~на), *adj.* extensive (*also*

fig.); spacious; vast; у него́ ~ное знако́мство he has a very wide circle of acquaintance.

об|ши́ть[1], ошью́, ошьёшь, *pf.* (*of* ~шива́ть) **1.** to edge, border. **2.** to trim, face. **3.** to sew round (*a package*). **4.** to plank; to revet; (*tech.*) to sheathe.

об|ши́ть[2], ошью́, ошьёшь, *pf.* (*of* ~шива́ть) to sew for; to make clothes for; она́ сама́ ~ши́ла всю семью́ she has made all the family's clothes herself.

обшла́г, á, *pl.* ~á, *m.* cuff.

обща́|ться, ю́сь, *impf.* (с+*i.*) to associate (with), mix (with).

общевойсково́|й, *adj.* (*mil.*) common to all arms; ~е кома́ндование combined command.

общедосту́п|ный (~ен, ~на), *adj.* **1.** of moderate price. **2.** (*of book, etc.*) popular.

общежите́йский, *adj.* everyday, ordinary.

общежи́ти|е, я, *n.* **1.** hostel. **2.** society, community; communal life.

общеизве́ст|ный (~ен, ~на), *adj.* well-known, generally known; notorious.

общенаро́дный, *adj.* common to whole people; national, public; о. пра́здник public holiday.

обще́ни|е, я, *n.* intercourse; relations, links; ли́чное о. personal contact.

общеобразова́тельны|й, *adj.* of general education; ~е предме́ты general subjects.

общепоня́т|ный (~ен, ~на), *adj.* comprehensible to all, within the grasp of all.

общепри́знан|ный (~, ~а), *adj.* universally recognized.

общепри́нят|ый (~, ~а), *adj.* generally accepted.

общераспространённый, *adj.* in general use, generally used, generally found.

общесою́зн|ый, *adj.* All-Union (*common to or valid for the entire U.S.S.R.*); ~ого значе́ния of importance for the entire U.S.S.R.

обще́ственник, а, *m.* social activist; person actively engaging in public life.

обще́ственност|ь, и, *f.* **1.** (*collect.*) (the) public, the community; public opinion; англи́йская о. the English public. **2.** (*collect.*) community; communal organizations; о. заво́да factory organizations; нау́чная о. the scientific community, scientific circles. **3.** disposition to public work, disposition to serve the community; дух ~и public spirit; public-spiritedness.

обще́ственн|ый, *adj.* **1.** social, public; ~ая жизнь public life; ~ое мне́ние public opinion; ~ые нау́ки social sciences; ~ое пита́ние public catering; ~ое порица́ние public censure; ~ая рабо́та public work, social work; ~ые рабо́ты public works; ~ая со́бственность public property, public

ownership. **2.** voluntary, unpaid, amateur; на ~ых нача́лах on a voluntary basis; ~ые организа́ции voluntary organizations.

о́бществ|о, а, *n.* **1.** (*in var. senses*) society; association; первобы́тное о. primitive society; нау́ка об ~е social science; быва́ть в ~е to frequent society, be a socialite. **2.** (*econ.*) company; акционе́рное о. joint-stock company. **3.** company, society; в ~е кого́-н. in someone's company; попа́сть в дурно́е о. to fall into bad company.

обществове́дени|е, я, *n.* social science, civics.

обществове́д|ческий, *adj. of* ~ение.

общеупотреби́тел|ьный (~ен, ~ьна), *adj.* in general use.

общечелове́ческий, *adj.* common to all mankind.

о́бщ|ий, *adj.* general; common; о. враг common enemy; ~ее де́ло common cause; о. знако́мый mutual acquaintance; ~ее ме́сто commonplace; ~ее собра́ние general meeting; ~ее согла́сие common consent; ~ая су́мма sum total; о. наибо́льший дели́тель (*math.*) the greatest common divisor; ~ее наиме́ньшее кра́тное (*math.*) the least common multiple; в ~ем on the whole, in general, in sum; в ~их черта́х in general outline; не име́ть ничего́ ~его (с+*i.*) to have nothing in common (with).

о́бщин|а, ы, *f.* community; commune.

о́бщин|ный, *adj.* communal; ~ая земля́ common (land).

общип|а́ть, лю́, ~лешь, *pf.* (*of* щипа́ть 4 *and* ~ывать) to pluck.

общи́пыва|ть, ю, *impf. of* общипа́ть.

общи́тельност|ь, и, *f.* sociability.

общи́тел|ьный (~ен, ~ьна), *adj.* sociable.

о́бщност|ь, и, *f.* community; о. интере́сов community of interests.

общо́, *adv.* (*coll.*) generally; он изложи́л свои́ взгля́ды сли́шком о. he expounded his views in too general terms.

объего́рива|ть, ю, *impf. of* объего́рить.

объего́р|ить, ю, ишь, *pf.* (*of* ~ивать) (*coll.*) to cheat, swindle.

объеда́|ть(ся), ю(сь), *impf. of* объе́сть(ся).

объедине́ни|е, я, *n.* **1.** unification. **2.** union, association.

объедин|ённый, *p.p.p. of* ~и́ть *and adj.* united; Организа́ция Объединённых На́ций United Nations Organization.

объедини́тельный, *adj.* unifying, uniting.

объедин|и́ть, ю́, и́шь, *pf.* (*of* ~я́ть) to unite; to join; о. ресу́рсы to pool resources; о. уси́лия to combine efforts.

объедин|и́ться, ю́сь, и́шься, *pf.* (*of* ~я́ться) (с+*i.*) to unite (with).

объедин|я́ть(ся), я́ю(сь), *impf. of* ~и́ть(ся).

объёд|ки, ков, *sing.* ~ок, ~ка, *m.* (*coll.*) leavings (*of food*), leftovers, scraps.

объёзд, а, *m.* 1. riding round, going round. 2. circuit, detour. 3. (*obs.*) mounted posse.

объёз|дить¹, жу, дишь, *pf.* (*of* ~жа́ть¹) to travel over.

объёз|дить², жу, дишь, *pf.* (*of* ~жа́ть²) to break in (*horses*).

объёздк|а, и, *f.* breaking in (*of horses*).

объёздчик¹, а, *m.* mounted patrol; лесно́й о. forest warden.

объёздчик², а, *m.* horse-breaker.

объезжа́|ть¹, ю, *impf.* of объёздить¹ *and* объёхать.

объезжа́|ть², ю, *impf.* of объёздить².

объёзжий, *adj.* roundabout, circuitous; о. путь detour.

объёкт, а, *m.* 1. (*in var. senses*) object. 2. (*mil.*) objective. 3. establishment; works; строи́тельный о. building site.

объекти́в, а, *m.* (*opt.*) objective, object-glass, lens.

объектива́ци|я, и, *f.* = объективиза́ция.

объективиза́ци|я, и, *f.* objectification.

объективи́зм, а, *m.* 1. (*term of Marxist philosophy*) objectivism. 2. objectivity.

объективи́р|овать, ую, *impf. and pf.* to objectify.

объекти́вност|ь, и, *f.* objectivity.

объекти́в|ный (~ен, ~на), *adj.* 1. objective. 2. unbiassed.

объёкт|ный, *adj.* of ~ 1.

объёкт|овый, *adj.* of ~ 3.

объём, а, *m.* volume (*also fig.*); bulk, size, capacity.

объёмист|ый (~, ~а), *adj.* (*coll.*) voluminous, bulky.

объёмн|ый, *adj.* by volume, volumetric; о. вес weight by volume; о. заря́д space charge; ~ое отноше́ние volume ratio.

объё|сть, м, шь, ст, ди́м, ди́те, дя́т, *past* ~л, *pf.* (*of* ~да́ть) 1. to eat round; to nibble. 2. (*coll.*) о. кого́-н. to eat someone out of house and home.

объё|сться, мся, шься, стся, ди́мся, ди́тесь, дя́тся, *past* ~лся, *pf.* (*of* ~да́ться) to overeat.

объё|хать, ду, дешь, *pf.* (*of* ~зжа́ть¹) 1. to go round, skirt. 2. to overtake, pass. 3. to travel over.

объяв|и́ть, лю́, ~ишь, *pf.* (*of* ~ля́ть) to declare, announce; to publish, proclaim; to advertise; о. войну́ to declare war; о. ко́нкурс to announce a competition; о. собра́ние откры́тым to declare a meeting open; о. вне зако́на to outlaw.

объяв|и́ться, лю́сь, ~ишься, *pf.* (*of* ~ля́ться) 1. (*coll.*) to turn up, appear. 2. (+*i.*) to announce oneself (to be), declare oneself (to be). 3. *pass.* of ~и́ть.

объявле́ни|е, я, *n.* 1. declaration, announcement; notice; о. войны́ declaration of war. 2. advertisement; дать о. в газе́ту, помести́ть о. в газе́те to put an advertisement in a paper.

объявля́|ть(ся), ю(сь), *impf.* of объяви́ть(ся).

объяде́ни|е, я, *n.* 1. (*obs.*) overeating. 2. (*as pred.*; *coll.*) something delicious; то́рты э́ти — пря́мо о. these cakes are simply delicious.

объясне́ни|е, я, *n.* (*in var. senses*) explanation; о. в любви́ declaration of love.

объясни́м|ый (~, ~а), *adj.* explicable, explainable.

объясни́тельный, *adj.* explanatory.

объясн|и́ть, ю́, и́шь, *pf.* (*of* ~я́ть) to explain.

объясн|и́ться, ю́сь, и́шься, *pf.* (*of* ~я́ться) 1. to explain oneself; (с+*i.*) to have a talk (with); to have it out (with); о. в любви́ (+*d.*) to make a declaration of love (to). 2. to become clear, be explained; тепе́рь всё ~и́лось everything is now clear.

объясн|я́ть, я́ю, *impf.* of ~и́ть.

объясн|я́ться, я́юсь, *impf.* 1. *impf.* of ~и́ться. 2. to speak; to make oneself understood; уме́ете ли вы о. по-францу́зски? can you make yourself understood in French?; о. же́стами и зна́ками to use sign language. 3. (+*i.*) to be accounted for (by); э́тим ~я́ется его́ стра́нное поведе́ние that accounts for his strange behaviour.

объя́ти|е, я, *n.* embrace; с распростёртыми ~ями with open arms; бро́ситься кому́-н. в ~я to fall into someone's arms; заключи́ть в ~я to embrace, fold in one's arms.

объя́т|ый, *p.p.p.* of ~ь; о. пла́менем enveloped in flames; о. стра́хом terror-stricken; о. ду́мой wrapped in thought.

объя́|ть, обойму́, обоймёшь (*and coll.* обыму́, обы́мешь), *pf.* (*obs.*) 1. to comprehend, grasp. 2. to seize, grip, come over; у́жас ~л его́ terror seized him.

обыва́тел|ь, я, *m.* 1. (*obs.*) inhabitant, resident. 2. (*fig.*) philistine.

обыва́тельский, *adj.* 1. (*obs.*) belonging to the local inhabitants. 2. (*fig.*) philistine; narrow-minded.

обыва́тельщин|а, ы, *f.* philistinism; narrow-mindedness.

обыгр|а́ть, а́ю, *pf.* (*of* ~ывать) 1. to beat (*at a game*); to win; о. кого́-н. на что́-н. to win something of someone. 2. (*theatr.*) to use with (good) effect, play up; (*fig.*) to turn to advantage, turn to account. 3. (*mus.*) to mellow (*an instrument by playing*).

обы́грыва|ть, ю, *impf.* of обыгра́ть.

обыдёнкой, *adv.* (*dial.*) in one day.

обы́денност|ь, и, *f.* **1.** ordinariness. **2.** everyday occurrence.

обы́денн|ый, *adj.* ordinary; commonplace, everyday; ~ое происше́ствие everyday occurrence.

обыдёнщин|а, ы, *f.* uneventfulness; commonplaceness.

обыкнове́ни|е, я, *n.* habit, wont; по ~ю as usual; име́ть о. (+*inf.*) to be in the habit (of).

обыкнове́нно, *adv.* usually, as a rule.

обыкнове́н|ный (~ен, ~на), *adj.* usual; ordinary; commonplace; ~ная исто́рия everyday occurrence; бо́льше ~ного more than usual.

о́быск, а, *m.* search; о́рдер на пра́во ~а search warrant.

обы|ска́ть, щу́, ~щешь, *pf.* (*of* ~скивать) to search.

обы|ска́ться, щу́сь, ~щешься, *pf.* (*coll.*) to carry out a search (in vain).

обы́скива|ть, ю, *impf. of* обыска́ть.

обы́ча|й, я, *m.* custom; (*leg.*) usage; по ~ю in accordance with custom; э́то у нас в ~е it is our custom.

обы́чно, *adv.* usually; as a rule.

обы́чн|ый, *adj.* usual; ordinary; ~ое пра́во (*leg.*) customary law.

обюрокра́|тить, чу, тишь, *pf.* (*of* ~чивать) (*coll.*) to make bureaucratic.

обюрокра́|титься, чусь, тишься, *pf.* (*of* ~чиваться) (*coll.*) to become a bureaucrat, become bureaucratic.

обюрокра́чива|ть(ся), ю(сь), *impf. of* обюрокра́тить(ся).

обя́занност|ь, и, *f.* duty; responsibility; во́инская о. military service; по ~и as in duty bound; in the line of duty; исполня́ть ~и дире́ктора to act as director; исполня́ющий ~и дире́ктора acting director.

обя́зан|ный (~, ~а), *adj.* **1.** (+*inf.*) obliged, bound; он ~ верну́ться he is obliged to go back, it is his duty to go back. **2.** (+*d.*) obliged, indebted (to); я вам о́чень ~ I am very much obliged to you; она́ вам ~а свое́й жи́знью she owes you her life; мы э́тим ~ы Петро́ву we have Petrov to thank for this.

обяза́тельно, *adv.* without fail; я о. приду́ I shall come without fail; он о. там бу́дет he is sure to be there, he is bound to be there.

обяза́тельност|ь, и, *f.* **1.** obligatoriness; binding force. **2.** (*obs.*) obligingness.

обяза́тел|ьный (~ен, ~ьна), *adj.* **1.** obligatory; compulsory; binding; ~ьное обуче́ние compulsory education; ~ьное постановле́ние binding decree. **2.** (*obs.*) obliging.

обяза́тельственн|ый, *adj.* (*leg.*) ~ое пра́во liability law.

обяза́тельств|о, а, *n.* **1.** obligation; engagement; долгово́е о. promissory note; взять на себя́ о. (+*inf.*) to pledge oneself (to), undertake (to). **2.** (*pl.*; *leg.*) liabilities.

обя|за́ть, жу́, ~жешь, *pf.* (*of* ~зывать) **1.** to bind, oblige, commit; о. кого́-н. яви́ться в определённое вре́мя to bind someone to appear at a stated time. **2.** to oblige; вы меня́ о́чень ~жете you will oblige me greatly, you will do me a great favour, I shall be greatly indebted to you.

обя|за́ться, жу́сь, ~жешься, *pf.* (*of* ~зываться) to bind oneself, pledge oneself, undertake.

обя́зыва|ть, ю, *impf. of* обяза́ть; ни к чему́ не ~ющий non-committal.

обя́зыва|ться, юсь, *impf. of* обяза́ться; не хочу́ ни пе́ред ке́м о. I wish to be beholden to no one.

ова́л, а, *m.* oval.

ова́льный, *adj.* oval.

ова́ци|я, и, *f.* ovation.

овдове́|вший, *past part. of* ~ть *and adj.* widowed.

овдове́|ть, ю, *pf.* to become a widow(er).

овева́|ть, ю, *impf. of* ове́ять.

ов|éн, на́, *m.* **1.** (*obs.*) ram. **2.** (*astron.*) Aries, the Ram (*first sign on the Zodiac*).

ов|ёс, са́, *m.* oats.

ов|е́чий, *adj. of* ~ца́; волк в ~е́чьей шку́ре a wolf in sheep's clothing.

ове́чк|а, и, *f. dim. of* овца́; (*fig.*) harmless creature.

овещ|естви́ть, лю́, и́шь, *pf.* (*of* ~ля́ть) to substantiate.

овеществля́|ть, ю, *impf. of* овеществи́ть.

ове́я|нный, *p.p.p. of* ~ть; о. сла́вой covered with glory.

ове́|ять, ю, ешь, *pf.* (*of* ~ва́ть) (+*i.*) **1.** to fan. **2.** (*fig.*) to surround (with), cover (with).

ови́н, а, *m.* barn (*for drying crops*).

овладева́|ть, ю, *impf. of* овладе́ть.

овладе́ни|е, я, *n.* (+*i.*) mastery; mastering.

овладе́|ть, ю, *pf.* (*of* ~ва́ть) (+*i.*) **1.** to seize; to take possession (of); о. собо́й to get control of oneself, regain self-control; мно́ю ~ла ра́дость I was overcome with joy. **2.** (*fig.*) to master.

о́вод, а, *pl.* ~ы, ~ов (*and* ~а́, ~о́в), gadfly.

овощево́дств|о, а, *n.* vegetable-growing.

овощехрани́лищ|е, а, *n.* vegetable store.

о́вощ|и, е́й, *sing.* ~, ~а, *m.* vegetables; вся́кому ~у своё вре́мя (*prov.*) there is a time for everything, everything in good season.

овощно́й, *adj.* vegetable; о. магази́н greengrocery, greengrocer's (shop); о. стол vegetarian cooking.

овра́г, а, *m.* ravine, gully.

овра́ж|**ек**[1], ка, *m. dim. of* овра́г.

овра́ж|**ек**[2], ка, *m. (zool.)* gopher.

овра́жист|**ый** (~, ~а), *adj.* abounding in ravines.

овра́|**жный**, *adj. of* ~г; о. песо́к pit sand.

овсе́ц, а́, *no pl., m. (coll.) dim. of* овёс; да́ть ло́шади ~а́ to give a horse his oats.

овсю́г, а́, *m. (bot.)* wild oats.

овся́ниц|**а**, ы, *f. (bot.)* fescue.

овся́нк|**а**[1], и, *f.* 1. oatmeal. 2. oatmeal porridge.

овся́нк|**а**[2], и, *f. (orn.)* (yellow) bunting, yellow-hammer.

овся́н|**о́й**, *adj. of* овёс; о. ко́лос ear of oats; ~о́е по́ле field of oats.

овся́н|**ый**, *adj.* made of oats; oatmeal; ~ая ка́ша oatmeal porridge; ~ая крупа́ oatmeal.

овуля́ци|**я**, и, *f. (biol.)* ovulation.

овц|**а́**, ы́, *pl.* ~ы, ове́ц, ~а́м, *f.* sheep; ewe; заблу́дшая о. *(fig.)* lost sheep.

овцебы́к, а, *m.* musk-ox.

овцево́д, а, *m.* sheep-breeder.

овцево́дств|**о**, а, *n.* sheep-breeding.

овча́р, а́, *m.* shepherd.

овча́рк|**а**, и, *f.* sheep-dog; неме́цкая о. Alsatian (dog).

овча́р|**ня**, ни, *g. pl.* ~ен, *f.* sheep-fold.

овчи́н|**а**, ы, *f.* sheepskin.

овчи́н|**ка**, ки, *f. dim. of* ~а; ей не́бо с ~ку показа́лось she was frightened out of her wits; о. вы́делки не сто́ит *(fig.)* the game is not worth the candle.

овчи́нный, *adj.* sheepskin.

ога́р|**ок**, ка, *m.* candle-end; *pl.* cinders; *(tech.)* skimmings, scoria.

огиба́|**ть**, ю, *impf. of* обогну́ть.

оглавле́ни|**е**, я, *n.* table of contents.

огла|**си́ть**, шу́, си́шь, *pf. (of* ~ша́ть) 1. to proclaim, announce; о. резолю́цию to read out a resolution; о. жениха́ и неве́сту to publish banns of marriage. 2. to divulge, make public. 3. to fill *(with loud cries, etc.)*.

огла|**си́ться**, шу́сь, си́шься, *pf. (of* ~ша́ться) 1.(+*i.*) to resound (with). 2. *pass. of* ~си́ть.

огла́ск|**а**, и, *f.* publicity; избега́ть ~и to shun publicity; получи́ть ~у to be made known, receive publicity; преда́ть ~е to make public, make known.

огла́ша|**ть(ся)**, ю(сь), *impf. of* огласи́ть(ся).

оглаше́ни|**е**, я, *n.* proclaiming, publication; не подлежи́т ~ю confidential *(classification of document)*; *(eccl.)* (publication of) banns.

оглашённый, *adj.* как о. *(coll.)* like one possessed.

оглоб|**ля**, ли, *g. pl.* ~ель, *f.* shaft; поверну́ть ~ли *(fig., coll.)* to turn back, retrace one's steps.

огло́х|**нуть**, ну, нешь, *past* ~, ~ла, *pf. of* гло́хнуть 1.

оглуп|**и́ть**, лю́, ~и́шь, *pf. (of* ~ля́ть) 1. to fool, make a fool of; to deceive. 2. to distort; to misrepresent.

оглупля́|**ть**, ю, *impf.* 1. *impf. of* оглупи́ть. 2. to try to fool, try to deceive.

оглуш|**а́ть**, а́ю, *impf. of* ~и́ть.

оглуши́тел|**ьный** (~ен, ~ьна), *adj.* deafening.

оглуш|**и́ть**, у́, и́шь, *pf.* 1. *pf. of* глуши́ть 1. 2. *(impf.* ~а́ть) to deafen; to stun *(also fig.)*.

огля|**де́ть**, жу́, ди́шь, *pf. (of* ~дывать) to look round; to examine, inspect.

огля|**де́ться**, жу́сь, ди́шься, *pf. (of* ~дываться) 1. to look round. 2. to get used to things around one; *(fig.)* to adapt oneself, become acclimatized; о. в темноте́ to become accustomed to the darkness.

огля́дк|**а**, и, *f.* 1. looking back; бежа́ть без ~и to run without turning one's head. 2. care, caution; без ~и carelessly; де́йствовать с ~ой to act circumspectly.

огля́дыва|**ть(ся)**, ю(сь), *impf. of* огляде́ть(ся) *and* огляну́ть(ся).

огля|**ну́ть**, ну́, ~нешь, *inst. pf. (of* ~дывать) to take a look over.

огля|**ну́ться**, ну́сь, ~нешься, *pf. (of* ~дываться) to turn (back) to look at something; to glance back.

огневи́дный, *adj. (geol.)* igneous, plutonic.

огневи́к, а́, *m.* 1. fire-stone. 2. *(med.)* anthrax. 3. *(coll.)* gunner.

огневи́ц|**а**, ы, *f. (dial.)* fever.

огнев|**о́й**, *adj. of* ого́нь; *(fig.)* fiery; *(geol.)* igneous, pyrogenous; о. бой *(mil.)* firing; о. вал *(mil.)* barrage; ~ая коро́бка fire-box; ~о́е окаймле́ние box barrage; ~ы́е сре́дства weapons; ~ая то́чка *(mil.)* weapon emplacement.

огнегаси́тельный, *adj.* fire-extinguishing; о. прибо́р fire-extinguisher.

огнеды́шащ|**ий**, *adj.* fire-spitting; ~ая гора́ *(obs.)* volcano.

огнемёт, а, *m. (mil.)* flame-thrower.

о́гненный, *adj.* fiery *(also fig.)*.

огнеопа́с|**ный** (~ен, ~на), *adj.* inflammable.

огнепокло́нник, а, *m.* fire-worshipper.

огнепокло́нни|**ческий**, *adj. of* ~к.

огнепокло́нничеств|**о**, а, *n.* fire-worship.

огнеприпа́с|**ы**, ов, *no sing.* ammunition.

огнесто́|**йкий** (~ек, ~йка), *adj.* fire-proof, fire-resistant.

огнестре́льн|**ый**, *adj.* ~ое ору́жие fire-arm(s); ~ая ра́на bullet wound.

огнетуши́тел|**ь**, я, *m.* fire-extinguisher.

огнеупо́р|**ный** (~ен, ~на), *adj.* fire-resistant, fire-proof; refractory; ~ная гли́на fire-clay; о. кирпи́ч fire-brick.

огнеупо́ры, ов, *no sing.* (*tech.*) refractory materials.

огни́в|о, а, *n.* steel (*used formerly for striking fire from a flint*).

ого́, *interj.* oho!

огова́рива|ть(ся), ю(сь), *impf. of* оговори́ть(ся).

огово́р, а, *m.* slander.

оговор|и́ть[1], ю́, и́шь, *pf.* (*of* огова́ривать) to slander.

оговор|и́ть[2], ю́, и́шь, *pf.* (*of* огова́ривать) 1. to stipulate (for); to fix, agree (on); мы ~и́ли усло́вия рабо́ты we have fixed the conditions of work. 2. to make a reservation, make a proviso (concerning); to specify; он ~и́л своё несогла́сие he specified his disagreement.

оговор|и́ться, ю́сь, и́шься, *pf.* (*of* огова́риваться) 1. to make a reservation, make a proviso. 2. to make a slip in speaking. 3. *pass. of* ~и́ть.

огово́р|ка, ки, *f.* 1. reservation, proviso; без ~ок without reserve; он согласи́лся, но с не́которыми ~ками he agreed but made certain reservations. 2. slip of the tongue.

огово́рщик, а, *m.* (*coll.*) slanderer.

оголе́ни|е, я, *n.* denudation.

огол|ённый, *p.p.p. of* ~и́ть *and adj.* bare, nude; uncovered, exposed.

огол|е́ц, ьца́, *m.* (*coll.*) lad, (young) fellow.

огол|и́ть, ю́, и́шь, *pf.* (*of* ~я́ть) to bare; to strip, uncover; о. фланг (*mil.*) to expose one's flank.

огол|и́ться, ю́сь, и́шься, *pf.* (*of* ~я́ться) 1. to strip (oneself). 2. to become exposed. 3. *pass. of* ~и́ть.

оголте́лый, *adj.* (*coll.*) unbridled; frenzied.

огол|я́ть(ся), я́ю(сь), *impf. of* ~и́ть(ся).

огон|ёк, ька́, *m.* 1. (small) light; блужда́ющий о. will o' the wisp; весёлый о. merry twinkle; зайти́ к кому́-н. на о. (*coll.*) to drop in on someone (*seeing a light in the window*). 2. (*fig.*) zest, spirit.

ог|о́нь, ня́, *m.* 1. fire (*also fig.*); говори́ть с ~нём to speak with fervour; анто́нов о. gangrene; ~нём и мечо́м with fire and sword; меж двух ~не́й between two fires, between the devil and the deep blue sea; пройти́ о. и во́ду to go through fire and water; из ~ня́ да в по́лымя (*fig.*) out of the frying-pan into the fire. 2. (*mil.*) fire; firing; управле́ние ~нём fire control; закреплённый о. в то́чку fire on fixed lines; отвеча́ть ~нём to fire back. 3. light; хвостово́й о. (*aeron.*) tail light; опознава́тельный о. recognition lights; тако́го челове́ка днём с ~нём не найдёшь (*coll.*) you will not find another such in a month of Sundays.

огора́жива|ть(ся), ю(сь), *impf. of* огороди́ть(ся).

огоро́д, а, *m.* kitchen-garden; бро́сить ка́мешек в чей-н. о. (*fig.*, *coll.*) to throw stones at someone; to make hints about someone.

огоро|ди́ть, жу́, ~ди́шь, *pf.* (*of* огора́живать) to fence in, enclose.

огоро|ди́ться, жу́сь, ~ди́шься, *pf.* (*of* огора́живаться) 1. to fence oneself in. 2. *pass. of* ~ди́ть.

огоро́дник, а, *m.* market-gardener.

огоро́днича|ть, ю, *impf.* (*coll.*) to go in for market-gardening, be a market-gardener.

огоро́дничеств|о, а, *n.* market-gardening.

огоро́д|ный, *adj. of* ~; ~ное хозя́йство market-gardening, market-garden.

огоро́ш|ить, у, ишь, *pf.* (*coll.*) to take aback, disconcert.

огорч|а́ть(ся), а́ю(сь), *impf. of* ~и́ть(ся).

огорче́ни|е, я, *n.* grief, affliction; chagrin; быть в ~и to be in distress.

огорчи́тел|ьный (~ен, ~ьна), *adj.* distressing.

огорч|и́ть, у́, и́шь, *pf.* (*of* ~а́ть) to grieve, distress, pain.

огорч|и́ться, у́сь, и́шься, *pf.* (*of* ~а́ться) to grieve; to be distressed, be pained; не ~а́йтесь! cheer up!

огра́б|ить, лю, ишь, *pf. of* гра́бить[1].

ограбле́ни|е, я, *n.* robbery; burglary.

огра́д|а, ы, *f.* fence.

огра|ди́ть, жу́, ди́шь, *pf.* (*of* ~жда́ть) 1. (*obs.*) to enclose, fence in. 2. (от) to guard (against, from), protect (against).

огра|ди́ться, жу́сь, ди́шься, *pf.* (*of* ~жда́ться) (от) to defend oneself (against); to protect oneself (against), guard oneself (against, from).

огражда́|ть(ся), ю(сь), *impf. of* огради́ть(ся).

ограниче́ни|е, я, *n.* limitation, restriction.

ограни́ченност|ь, и, *f.* limitedness, scantiness; (*fig.*) narrowness, narrow-mindedness.

ограни́ч|енный, *p.p.p. of* ~ить *and adj.* limited; о. челове́к (*fig.*) narrow(-minded) person, hidebound person.

ограни́чива|ть(ся), ю(сь), *impf. of* ограни́чить(ся).

ограничи́тел|ь, я, *m.* (*tech.*) о. хо́да catch, stop, stop piece, arresting device.

ограничи́тельный, *adj.* restrictive, limiting.

ограни́ч|ить, у, ишь, *pf.* (*of* ~ивать) to limit, restrict, cut down; о. себя́ в расхо́дах to cut down one's expenditure; о. ора́тора вре́менем to set a speaker a time limit.

ограни́ч|иться, усь, ишься, *pf.* (*of* ~ивать-ся) (+*i.*) 1. to limit oneself (to), confine oneself (to); он ~ился кра́ткой ре́чью he confined himself to a short speech. 2. to be limited (to), be confined (to).

огребá|ть, ю, *impf. of* огрестú; о. дéньги (*coll.*) to rake in money.

огре|стú, бý, бёшь, *past* ∼б, ∼блá, *pf.* (*of* ∼бáть) to rake round.

огрé|ть, ю, *pf.* (*coll.*) to catch a blow, fetch a blow.

огрéх, а, *m.* 1. (*agric.*) gap (*in sowing, ploughing, etc.*). 2. (*coll.*) fault, imperfection (*in work*).

огрóм|ный (∼ен, ∼на), *adj.* huge; vast; enormous.

огрубéлый, *adj.* coarse, hardened.

огрубé|ть, ю, *pf. of* грубéть.

огрýз|нуть, ну, нешь, *past* ∼, ∼ла, *pf.* (*coll.*) to grow stout.

огрыз|áться, áюсь, *impf.* (*of* ∼нýться) (на+*a.*) to snap (at) (*of a dog; also fig.*).

огрыз|нýться, нýсь, нёшься, *pf. of* ∼áться.

огрыз|ок, ка, *m.* bit, end; о. карандашá (*coll.*) pencil stub, stump.

огýз|ок, ка, *m.* rump.

огýлом, *adv.* (*coll.*) wholesale, indiscriminately.

огýльно, *adv.* without grounds; о. обвинять to make a groundless accusation.

огýл|ьный (∼ен, ∼ьна), *adj.* 1. wholesale, indiscriminate; ∼ьное охáивание wholesale disparagement. 2. unfounded, groundless. 3. (*obs.*) wholesale (*comm.*).

огур|éц, цá, *m.* cucumber.

огурé|чный, *adj. of* ∼ц; ∼чная травá (*bot.*) borage.

огýрчик, а, *m. affect. dim. of* огурéц; как о. (*coll.*) *of person of ruddy, healthy appearance.*

óд|а, ы, *f.* ode.

одáлжива|ть, ю, *impf. of* одолжúть.

одалúск|а, и, *f.* odalisque.

одарённост|ь, и, *f.* endowments, (natural) gifts, talent.

одар|ённый, *p.p.p. of* ∼úть *and adj.* gifted, talented.

одáрива|ть, ю, *impf. of* одарúть.

одар|úть, ю, úшь, *pf.* 1. (*impf.* ∼úвать) to give presents (to); онá ∼úла всех детéй игрýшками she has given all the children toys. 2. (*impf.* ∼ять) (+*i.*) to endow (with); прирóда ∼úла егó разнообрáзными спосóбностями nature has endowed him with a variety of talents.

одар|ять, яю, *impf. of* ∼úть.

одевá|ть(ся), ю(сь), *impf. of* одéть(ся).

одéж|а, и, *f.* (*coll.*) clothes.

одéжд|а, ы, *f.* 1. clothes; garments; clothing; вéрхняя о. outer clothing, overcoat; произвóдственная о. industrial clothing, overalls; фóрменная о. uniform. 2. (*tech.*) surfacing, top dressing (*of road*).

одёжк|а, и, *f. dim. of* одéжда; по ∼е протягивай нóжки (*prov.*) cut your coat according to the cloth.

одеколóн, а, *m.* eau-de-Cologne; цветóчный о. flower-scented eau-de-Cologne.

одеколóн|ный, *adj. of* ∼.

одел|úть, ю, úшь, *pf.* (*of* ∼ять) (+*i.*) 1. to present (with). 2. (*obs.*) to endow (with).

одел|ять, яю, *impf. of* ∼úть.

од|ёр, рá, *m.* (*coll.*) old hack (*horse*).

одёргива|ть, ю, *impf. of* одёрнуть.

одеревенéлый, *adj.* numb; (*fig.*) lifeless.

одеревенé|ть, ю, *pf. of* деревенéть.

одерж|áть, ý, ∼ишь, *pf.* (*of* ∼ивать) to gain; о. верх (над) to gain the upper hand (over), prevail (over); о. побéду to gain a (the) victory, carry the day.

одéржива|ть, ю, *impf. of* одержáть.

одержúм|ый (∼, ∼а), *adj.* 1. (+*i.*) possessed (by); afflicted (by); о. стрáхом ridden by fear; о. навязчивой идéей obsessed by an idée fixe. 2. *as noun* о., ∼ого, *m.* one possessed, madman.

одёр|нуть, ну, нешь, *pf.* (*of* ∼гивать) 1. to pull down, straighten (*article of clothing*). 2. (*fig., coll.*) to call to order; to silence; to snub.

одеснýю, *adv.* (*obs.*) to the right; on the right hand.

одессúт, а, *m.* inhabitant of Odessa.

одéт|ый, *p.p.p. of* ∼ь *and adj.* (+*i. or* в+*a.*) dressed (in), clothed (in); with one's clothes on; о. снéгом snow-clad; хорошó о. well--dressed.

одé|ть, ну, нешь, *pf.* (*of* ∼вáть) (+*i. or* в+*a.*) to dress (in), clothe (in).

одé|ться, нусь, нешься, *pf.* (*of* ∼вáться) 1. to dress (oneself); to clothe oneself; о. в вечéрнее плáтье to put on an evening dress. 2. *pass. of* ∼ть.

одеял|о, а, *n.* blanket; coverlet; стёганое о. counterpane, quilt; лоскýтное о. patchwork quilt.

одеяни|е, я, *n.* garb, attire.

одúн, одногó, *m.*; однá, однóй, *f.*; однó, одногó, *n.*; *pl.* однú, однúх, *num. and pron.* 1. one; о. стол one table; однú нóжницы one pair of scissors; однó one thing; однó дéло..., другóе дéло... it is one thing . . ., another thing . . .; за другúм one after the other; однú... другúе some . . . others; с однóй стороны... с другóй (стороны) on the one hand . . . on the other hand; однó врéмя at one time; о. раз once; однúм рóсчерком перá with a stroke of the pen; однúм слóвом in a word; о.-двá one or two; о.-едúнственный one and only; о. из тысячи one in a thousand; в о. гóлос with one voice, with one accord; в о. прекрáсный день one fine day, once upon a time; все до одногó all to a man; однó к одномý (*coll.*) moreover; one way and another; все, как о. one and all; о. на о.

in private, tête-à-tête; face to face; по
одному́ one by one, one at a time; in single
file. **2.** a, an; a certain; я встре́тил одного́
моего́ бы́вшего колле́гу I met an old colleague of mine. **3.** alone; by oneself; да́йте
ей сде́лать э́то одно́й let her do it by herself; я живу́ о. I live alone; о.-одинёхонек,
о.-одинёшенек all by oneself. **4.** only;
alone; nothing but; он о. зна́ет доро́гу he
alone knows the way; она́ чита́ет одни́
детекти́вные рома́ны she reads nothing
but detective stories. **5.** о., о. и тот же the
same, one and the same; мы с ней одного́
во́зраста she and I are the same age; э́то
одно́ и то же it is the same thing; мне э́то
всё одно́ it is all one to me.

одина́кий, *adj.* (*obs. or coll.*) identical.

одина́ково, *adv.* equally, alike.

одина́ковост|ь, и, *f.* identity (*of views, etc.*).

одина́ков|ый (~, ~а), *adj.* (c+*i.*) identical
(with), the same (as).

одина́рный, *adj.* single.

одинё|хонек, ~шенек, *see* оди́н 3.

одиннадцатиле́тний, *adj.* eleven-year-old.

оди́ннадцат|ь, и, *num.* eleven.

оди́ннадцатый, *adj.* eleventh.

одино́к|ий (~, ~а), *adj.* **1.** solitary; lonely;
lone. **2.** *as noun* о., ~ого, *m.* single man,
bachelor; ~ая, ~ой, *f.* single woman.

одино́ко, *adv.* lonely; чу́вствовать себя́ о.
to feel lonely.

одино́честв|о, а, *n.* solitude; loneliness.

одино́чк|а, и 1. *m. and f.* lone person;
куста́рь-о. craftsman working alone; мать-
-о. unmarried mother; жить ~ой to live
alone; в ~у alone, on one's own; по ~е one
by one. **2.** (*coll.*) one-man cell, solitary
confinement. **3.** single-oar (*rowing-boat*).

одино́чн|ый, *adj.* **1.** individual; one-man;
~ое заключе́ние solitary confinement. **2.**
single; о. вы́стрел single shot; о. ого́нь
(*mil.*) single-round firing.

одио́з|ный (~ен, ~на), *adj.* odious, offensive.

одиссе́|я, и, *f.* (*fig.*) Odyssey.

одича́лый, *adj.* (having gone) wild.

одича́ни|е, я, *n.* running wild.

одича́|ть, ю, *pf. of* дича́ть.

одна́жды, *adv.* once; one day; о. у́тром
(ве́чером, но́чью) one morning (evening,
night).

одна́ко 1. *adv. and conj.* however; but;
though. **2.** *interj.* you don't say so!; not
really!

одноа́ктный, *adj.* (*theatr.*) one-act.

одноато́мный, *adj.* monoatomic.

однобо́к|ий (~, ~а), *adj.* one-sided (*also
fig.*).

однобо́ртный, *adj.* single-breasted.

одновале́нтный, *adj.* (*chem.*) univalent,
monovalent.

одновесе́льный, *adj.* one-oared.

одновреме́нно, *adv.* simultaneously, at the
same time.

одновреме́нност|ь, и, *f.* simultaneity; syn-
chronism.

одновреме́нный, *adj.* simultaneous; synchronous.

одногла́зк|а, и, *f.* (*zool.*) cyclops.

одногла́зый, *adj.* one-eyed.

одногоди́чный, *adj.* one-year, of one year's
duration.

одного́д|ок, ка, *m.* (c+*i.*; *coll.*) of the same
age (as).

одного́рбый, *adj.* о. верблю́д dromedary,
Arabian camel.

однодво́р|ец, ца, *m.* (*hist.*) odnodvorets
(*member of special group of smallholders in
18th-century Russia, descendants of lowest
category of service class*).

однодне́вный, *adj.* one-day.

однодо́льный, *adj.* (*bot.*) monocotyledonous.

однодо́мный, *adj.* (*bot.*) monoecious.

однооду́м, а, *m.* person with idée fixe, obses-
sional.

одножи́льный, *adj.* (*electr.*) single-core.

однозву́чный, *adj.* monotonous.

однозна́чащий, *adj.* **1.** synonymous. **2.**
monosemantic.

однозна́ч|ный (~ен, ~на), *adj.* **1.** synony-
mous. **2.** (*ling.*) monosemantic. **3.** (*math.*)
simple; ~ное число́ simple number, digit.

одноимён|ный (~ен, ~на), *adj.* of the same
name.

однокали́берный, *adj.* of the same calibre.

однока́мерный, *adj.* (*zool.*) monothalamous.

однока́шник, а, *m.* (*obs., coll.*) school-fellow.

однокла́ссник, а, *m.* classmate.

однокле́точный, *adj.* (*biol.*) unicellular.

одноклу́бник, а, *m.* (*coll.*) fellow-member of
club.

одноколе́йный, *adj.* single-track.

одноколе́нчатый, *adj.* (*tech.*) single-jointed.

одноко́лк|а, и, *f.* (*coll.*) gig.

одноко́нный, *adj.* one-horse.

однокопы́тный, *adj.* (*zool.*) solidungular,
solid-hoofed.

одноко́нтурный, *adj.* (*electr.*) single-circuit.

однокорпу́сный, *adj.* (*naut.*) single-hull.

однокра́тный, *adj.* single; о. глаго́л (*gram.*)
instantaneous verb.

однокурсник, а, *m.* fellow-member of
course.

однола́мповый, *adj.* (*radio*) single-valve.

однолетний, *adj.* **1.** one-year. **2.** (*bot.*)
annual.

однолетник, а, *m.* (*bot.*) annual.

однолет|ок, ка, *m.* (c+*i.*) (*coll.*) of the same
age (as).

одноима́стный, *adj.* of one colour.

одно́мачтовый, *adj.* single-masted.

одноме́стный, *adj.* single-seated, single--seater.

одномото́рный, *adj.* single-engine.

одноно́гий, *adj.* one-legged.

однообра́зи|е, я, *n.* monotony.

однообра́зност|ь, и, *f.* = однообра́зие.

однообра́з|ный (~ен, ~на), *adj.* monotonous.

одноо́кис|ь, и, *f.* (*chem.*) monoxide.

одноо́сный, *adj.* uniaxial, monoaxial.

однопала́тный, *adj.* (*polit.*) unicameral, single-chamber.

однопа́лубный, *adj.* one-decked.

одноплеме́нный, *adj.* of the same tribe.

однополча́н|ин, ина, *pl.* ~е, ~, *m.* comrade--in-arms (*one serving in the same regiment*).

однопо́лый, *adj.* (*bot.*) unisexual.

однопо́люсный, *adj.* (*phys.*) unipolar.

однопу́тк|а, и, *f.* (*coll.*) single-track railway.

однопу́тный, *adj.* one-way.

одноро́гий, *adj.* one-horned, unicornous.

одноро́дност|ь, и, *f.* homogeneity, uniformity.

одноро́д|ный (~ен, ~на), *adj.* **1.** homogeneous, uniform. **2.** similar.

однору́кий, *adj.* one-handed, one-armed.

одноря́дк|а, и, *f.* (*hist.*) single-breasted caftan.

односельча́н|ин, ина, *pl.* ~е, ~, *m.* fellow--villager.

односло́жно, *adv.* говори́ть о. to speak in monosyllables.

односло́жност|ь, и, *f.* **1.** monosyllabism. **2.** (*fig.*) terseness, abruptness.

односло́ж|ный, *adj.* **1.** monosyllabic. **2.** (~ен, ~на) (*fig.*) terse, abrupt.

односло́йный, *adj.* single-layer; one-ply, single-ply.

односпа́льн|ый, *adj.* ~ая крова́ть single bed.

одноство́льн|ый, *adj.* ~ое ружьё single--barrelled gun.

одноство́рчат|ый, *adj.* **1.** (*zool.*) univalve. **2.** ~ая дверь single door.

односторо́нн|ий, *adj.* **1.** one-sided (*also fig.*); unilateral. **2.** one-way; ~ее движе́ние one-way traffic; о. ум (*fig.*) one-track mind.

однота́ктный, *adj.* (*tech.*) one-stroke, single--cycle.

одноте́с, а, *m.* plank nail.

одноти́п|ный (~ен, ~на), *adj.* of the same type, of the same kind; о. кора́бль sister--ship.

одното́мник, а, *m.* one-volume edition, omnibus volume.

однато́мный, *adj.* one-volume.

однофа́зный, *adj.* (*electr.*) single-phase, monophase.

однофами́л|ец, ьца, *m.* (с+*i.*) person bearing the same surname (as), namesake.

одноцве́тный, *adj.* one-colour; (*typ.*) monochrome.

одноцили́ндровый, *adj.* one-cylinder.

одночле́н, а, *m.* (*math.*) monomial.

одночле́нный, *adj.* (*math.*) monomial.

одноше́рстный, *adj.* (*of animals*) of one colour.

одноэта́жный, *adj.* **1.** single-stage. **2.** one--storeyed.

однои́дерный, *adj.* mononuclear.

однои́русный, *adj.* single-stage.

одобре́ни|е, я, *n.* approval.

одобри́тел|ьный (~ен, ~ьна), *adj.* approving.

одо́бр|ить, ю, ишь, *pf.* (*of* ~я́ть) to approve (of); не о. to disapprove (of).

одобр|я́ть, я́ю, *impf. of* ~ить.

одолева́|ть, ю, *impf. of* одоле́ть.

одоле́|ть, ю, *pf.* (*of* ~ва́ть) **1.** to overcome, conquer; его́ ~л сон he was overcome by sleepiness; нас ~ло злово́ние the stench overpowered us. **2.** (*fig.*) to master; to cope (with); to get through; о. всю прему́дрость to master all the ins and outs.

одолж|а́ть, а́ю, *impf. of* ~и́ть.

одолжа́|ться, юсь, *impf.* (+*d. or* у) to be obliged (to), be beholden (to); ~йтесь! (*obs., coll.*) have some!

одолже́ни|е, я, *n.* favour, service; сде́лайте мне о. do me a favour; я сочту́ э́то за о. I shall esteem it, regard it as a favour.

одолж|и́ть, у́, и́шь, *pf.* (*of* ода́лживать *and* ~а́ть) **1.** (+*d.*) to lend. **2.** (*coll.*; у) to borrow (from).

одома́шнени|е, я, *n.* domestication, taming.

одома́шн|енный, *p.p.p. of* ~ить *and adj.* domesticated.

одома́шнива|ть, ю, *impf. of* одома́шнить.

одома́шн|ить, ю, ишь, *pf.* (*of* ~ивать) to domesticate, tame.

одонто́лог, а, *m.* odontologist.

одонтоло́ги|я, и, *f.* (*med.*) odontology.

одр, а́, *m.* (*arch.*; *now only in certain phrases*) bed, couch; на сме́ртном ~е́ on one's death-bed.

одревесне́ни|е, я, *n.* lignification.

одряхле́|ть, ю, *pf. of* дряхле́ть.

одува́нчик, а, *m.* (*bot.*) dandelion.

оду́м|аться, аюсь, *pf.* (*of* ~ываться) to change one's mind; to think better of it; to bethink oneself.

оду́мыва|ться, юсь, *impf. of* одума́ться.

одура́чива|ть, ю, *impf. of* одура́чить.

одура́ч|ить, у, ишь, *pf.* (*of* дура́чить *and* ~ивать) (*coll.*) to make a fool (of), fool.

одуре́лый, *adj.* (*coll.*) dulled, besotted.

одуре́ни|е, я, *n.* stupefaction, torpor.

одуре́|ть, ю, *pf. of* дуре́ть.

одурма́нива|ть, ю, *impf. of* одурма́нить.

одурма́н|ить, ю, ишь, *pf.* (*of* дурма́нить *and* ~ивать) to stupefy.

о́дур|ь, и, *f.* (*coll.*) stupefaction, torpor; со́нная о. (*bot.*) deadly nightshade.

одуря́|ть, ю, *impf.* (*coll.*) to stupefy; ~ющий за́пах heavy scent.

одутлова́т|ый (~, ~а), *adj.* puffy.

одухотворённост|ь, и, *f.* spirituality.

одухотворённый, *p.p.p.* *of* одухотвори́ть *and adj.* inspired.

одухотвор|и́ть, ю́, и́шь, *pf.* (*of* ~я́ть) 1. to inspire; to animate. 2. to attribute soul (to) (*natural phenomena, animals, etc.*).

одухотвор|я́ть, я́ю, *impf.* *of* ~и́ть.

одушев|и́ть, лю́, и́шь, *pf.* (*of* ~ля́ть) to animate.

одушев|и́ться, лю́сь, и́шься, *pf.* (*of* ~ля́ться) to be animated.

одушевле́ни|е, я, *n.* animation.

одушевлённый, *p.p.p.* *of* одушеви́ть *and adj.* animated.

одушевля́|ть(ся), ю(сь), *impf.* *of* одушеви́ть(ся).

оды́шк|а, и, *f.* short breath; страда́ть ~ой to be short-winded.

ожереб|и́ться, лю́сь, и́шься, *pf.* *of* жереби́ться.

ожере́л|ье, я, *n.* necklace.

ожесточ|а́ть(ся), а́ю(сь), *impf.* *of* ~и́ть(ся).

ожесточе́ни|е, я, *n.* bitterness.

ожесточённост|ь, и, *f.* = ожесточе́ние.

ожесточённый, *p.p.p.* *of* ожесточи́ть *and adj.* bitter; embittered; hardened.

ожесточ|и́ть, у́, и́шь, *pf.* (*of* ~а́ть) to embitter; to harden.

ожесточ|и́ться, у́сь, и́шься, *pf.* (*of* ~а́ться) to become embittered; to become hardened.

оже́чь(ся) = обже́чь(ся).

огива́льный, *adj.* (*archit.*) ogival.

ожива́|ть, ю, *impf.* *of* ожи́ть.

ожив|и́ть, лю́, и́шь, *pf.* (*of* ~ля́ть) 1. to revive. 2. (*fig.*) to enliven, vivify, animate.

ожив|и́ться, лю́сь, и́шься, *pf.* (*of* ~ля́ться) 1. to become animated, liven (up). 2. *pass.* *of* ~и́ть.

оживле́ни|е, я, *n.* 1. animation, gusto. 2. reviving; enlivening.

оживлённый, *p.p.p.* *of* оживи́ть *and adj.* animated; lively.

оживля́|ть(ся), ю(сь), *impf.* *of* оживи́ть(ся).

оживотвор|и́ть, ю́, и́шь, *pf.* *of* животвори́ть.

ожида́ни|е, я, *n.* expectation; waiting; обману́ть ~я to disappoint; в ~и (+*g.*) pending; быть в ~и (*of a woman; euph.*) to be expecting; сверх ~я beyond expectation.

ожида́|ть, ю, *impf.* (+*g.*) to wait (for); to expect, anticipate; о. ребёнка (*of a woman*)

to be expecting a baby; мы э́того не ~ли we were not expecting that; как я и ~л just as I expected.

ожижа́тел|ь, я, *m.* (*tech.*) liquefier.

ожижа́|ть, ю, *impf.* (*tech.*) to liquefy.

ожиже́ни|е, я, *n.* (*chem.*) liquefaction (*of* gas); (*meteor.*) thinning; liquation.

ожире́ни|е, я, *n.* obesity; о. се́рдца adipose heart.

ожире́|ть, ю, *pf.* *of* жире́ть.

ож|и́ть, иву́, иве́шь, *past* ~и́л, ~ила́, ~и́ло, *pf.* (*of* ~ива́ть) to come to life, revive (*also fig.*).

ожо́г, а, *m.* burn; scald.

озабо́|тить, чу, тишь, *pf.* (*of* ~чивать) to trouble, worry, cause anxiety.

озабо́|титься, чусь, тишься, *pf.* (*of* ~чиваться) (+*i.*) to attend (to); о. загото́вкой то́плива to see to the laying in of fuel.

озабо́ченност|ь, и, *f.* preoccupation; anxiety.

озабо́|ченный, *p.p.p.* *of* ~тить *and adj.* preoccupied; anxious, worried.

озабо́чива|ть(ся), ю(сь), *impf.* *of* озабо́тить(ся).

озагла́в|ить, лю, ишь, *pf.* (*of* ~ливать) to entitle; to head (*a chapter, etc.*).

озагла́влива|ть, ю, *impf.* *of* озагла́вить.

озада́ченност|ь, и, *f.* perplexity, puzzlement.

озада́ч|енный, *p.p.p.* *of* ~ить *and adj.* perplexed, puzzled.

озада́чива|ть, ю, *impf.* *of* озада́чить.

озада́ч|ить, у, ишь, *pf.* (*of* ~ивать) to perplex, puzzle, take aback.

озар|и́ть, ю́, и́шь, *pf.* (*of* ~я́ть) to light up, illuminate, illumine; улы́бка ~и́ла её лицо́ a smile lit up her face; их ~и́ло (*fig.*) it dawned upon them.

озар|и́ться, ю́сь, и́шься, *pf.* (*of* ~я́ться) 1. (+*i.*) to light up (with); её лицо́ ~и́лось ра́достью her face lit up with joy. 2. *pass.* *of* ~и́ть.

озар|я́ть(ся), я́ю(сь), *impf.* *of* ~и́ть(ся).

озвере́лый, *adj.* brutal; brutalized.

озвере́|ть, ю, *pf.* *of* звере́ть.

озву́ч|енный, *p.p.p.* *of* ~ить; о. фильм sound film.

озву́чива|ть, ю, *impf.* *of* озву́чить.

озву́ч|ить, у, ишь, *pf.* (*of* ~ивать) (*cinema*) to wire for sound.

оздорови́тел|ьный (~ен, ~ьна), *adj.* sanitary.

оздоров|и́ть, лю́, и́шь, *pf.* (*of* ~ля́ть) to render (more) healthy, bring into a healthy state (*also fig.*); о. ме́стность to improve the sanitary conditions of a locality.

оздоровля́|ть, ю, *impf.* *of* оздорови́ть.

озелене́ни|е, я, *n.* planting with trees and gardens.

озелен|и́ть, ю́, и́шь, *pf.* (*of* ~я́ть) to plant with trees and gardens.

озелен|я́ть, я́ю, *impf. of* ~и́ть.

о́земь, *adv.* (*coll.*) to the ground, down.

озерк|о́, а́, *pl.* ~и́, ~о́в, *n. dim. of* о́зеро.

озёрный, *adj. of* о́зеро; о. райо́н lake district.

о́зер|о, а, *pl.* озёра, озёр, *n.* lake.

ози́м|ый, *adj.* winter; ~ая культу́ра winter crop; ~ое по́ле winter-field; *as noun* ~ые, ~ых winter crops.

о́зим|ь, и, *f.* winter crop.

озира́|ть, ю, *impf.* (*obs.*) to view.

озира́|ться, юсь, *impf.* to look round; to look back.

озло́б|ить, лю, ишь, *pf.* (*of* ~ля́ть) to embitter.

озло́б|иться, лю́сь, ишься, *pf.* (*of* ~ля́ться) to become embittered.

озлобле́ни|е, я, *n.* bitterness, animosity.

озло́б|ленный, *p.p.p. of* ~ить *and adj.* embittered.

озлобля́|ть(ся), ю(сь), *impf. of* озло́бить(ся).

ознако́м|ить, лю, ишь, *pf.* (*of* ~ля́ть) (с+*i.*) to acquaint (with).

ознако́м|иться, люсь, ишься, *pf.* (*of* ~ля́ться) (с+*i.*) to familiarize oneself with.

ознакомля́|ть(ся), ю(сь), *impf. of* ознако́мить(ся).

ознаменова́ни|е, я, *n.* marking, commemoration; в о. (+*g.*) to mark, to commemorate, in commemoration (of).

ознамен|ова́ть, у́ю, *pf.* (*of* ~о́вывать) to mark, commemorate; to celebrate.

означа́|ть, ю, *impf.* to mean, signify, stand for; что ~ют э́ти бу́квы? what do these letters stand for?

озна́ченный, *adj.* (*obs.*) the aforesaid.

озно́б, а, *m.* shivering; chill; почу́вствовать о. to feel shivery.

озноб|и́ть, лю́, и́шь, *pf.* (*of* ~ля́ть) (*coll.*) я ~и́л себе́ у́ши, *etc.*, my ears, *etc.*, are frozen.

озноб|ля́|ть, ю, *impf. of* ознобить.

озокери́т, а, *m.* (*min.*) ozocerite.

озоло|ти́ть, чу́, ти́шь, *pf.* 1. to gild. 2. (*coll.*) to load with money.

озо́н, а, *m.* ozone.

озона́тор, а, *m.* (*phys.*) ozonizer.

озони́ровани|е, я, *n.* ozonization.

озони́рова|нный, *p.p.p. of* ~ть *and adj.* ozonized.

озони́р|овать, ую, *impf. and pf.* to ozonize.

озорни́к, а́, *m.* (*coll.*) 1. naughty child, mischievous child. 2. mischief-maker.

озорнича́|ть, ю, *impf.* (*of* с~) (*coll.*) 1. (*of a child*) to be naughty, get up to mischief. 2. (*of an adult*) to make mischief, play dirty tricks.

озорно́й, *adj.* (*coll.*) mischievous, naughty.

озорств|о́, а́, *n.* (*coll.*) mischief, naughtiness.

озя́б|нуть, ну, нешь, *past* ~, ~ла, *pf.* to be cold, be chilly; я ~ ! I am frozen!

ой (*or* **ой-ой-ой**), *interj.* expressing surprise, fright or pain o; oh.

ой-ли, *interj.* (*coll.*) expressing doubt really?; is it possible?

ока|за́ть, жу́, ~жешь, *pf.* (*of* ~зывать) to render, show; о. влия́ние (на+*a.*) to influence, exert influence (upon); о. внима́ние (+*d.*) to pay attention (to); о. давле́ние (на+*a.*) to exert pressure (upon), bring pressure to bear (upon); о. де́йствие (на+*a.*) to have an effect (upon); to take effect; о. му́жество (*obs.*) to display bravery; о. по́мощь (+*d.*) to help, give help; о. предпочте́ние (+*d.*) to show preference (for), prefer; о. соде́йствие (+*d.*) to render assistance; о. сопротивле́ние (+*d.*) to offer, put up resistance (to); о. услу́гу (+*d.*) to do, render a service; to do a good turn; о. честь (+*d.*) to do an honour.

ока|за́ться, жу́сь, ~жешься, *pf.* (*of* ~зываться) 1. to turn out (to be), prove (to be); to be found (to be); он ~за́лся отли́чным расска́зчиком he proved to be a first-rate story-teller; ~за́лось, что она́ всё вре́мя лгала́ it turned out that she had been telling lies all the time. 2. to find oneself; to be found; я ~за́лся в больни́це I found myself in hospital; трёх экземпля́ров не ~за́лось three copies were missing.

ока́зи|я, и, *f.* 1. opportunity; посла́ть письмо́ с ~ей to profit by an opportunity to send a letter. 2. unexpected happening; что за о.! what an odd thing! how odd!

ока́зыва|ть(ся), ю(сь), *impf. of* оказа́ть(ся).

окайм|и́ть, лю́, и́шь, *pf.* (*of* ~ля́ть) (+*i.*) to border (with), edge (with).

окаймля́|ть, ю, *impf. of* окайми́ть.

ока́лин|а, ы, *f.* cinder; (*tech.*) scale; slag, dross.

окамене́лост|ь, и, *f.* fossil.

окамене́лый, *adj.* fossilized; petrified.

окамене́|ть, ю, *pf. of* камене́ть.

окант|ова́ть, у́ю, *pf. of* кантова́ть[1].

оканто́вк|а, и, *f.* mount (*for picture, etc.*).

ока́нчива|ть(ся), ю(сь), *impf. of* око́нчить(ся).

о́кань|е, я, *n.* okanie (*pronunciation of unstressed 'o' as 'o'*).

ока́пыва|ть(ся), ю(сь), *impf. of* окопа́ть(ся).

ока́рмлива|ть, ю, *impf. of* окорми́ть.

ока|ти́ть, чу́, ~тишь, *pf.* (*of* ~чивать) to pour (over); о. холо́дной водо́й to pour cold water (over) (*also fig.*).

ока|ти́ться, чу́сь, ~тишься, *pf.* (*of* ~чиваться) to pour over oneself.

о́ка|ть, ю, *impf.* to pronounce unstressed 'o' as 'o' in Russian words.

окáчива|ть(ся), ю(сь), *impf. of* окатúть(ся).

окая́нный, *adj.* damned, cursed.

окая́нств|о, а, *n.* (*eccl.*) sinfulness.

окая́нств|овать, ую, *pf.* (*eccl.*) to live a life of sin.

океáн, а, *m.* ocean.

океáнографи|я, и, *f.* oceanography.

океанографи́ческий, *adj.* oceanographic.

океáнский, *adj.* ocean; oceanic; о. парохóд ocean(-going) liner.

оки́дыва|ть, ю, *impf. of* оки́нуть.

оки́|нуть, ну, нешь, *pf.* (*of* ~дывать) to cast round; о. взгля́дом, о. взóром to take in at a glance; to glance over.

óкис|ел, ла, *m.* (*chem.*) oxide.

окислéни|е, я, *n.* (*chem.*) oxidation.

окисли́тел|ь, я, *m.* (*chem.*) oxidizer, acidifier.

окисли́тельный, *adj.* (*chem.*) oxidizing.

окисл|и́ть, ю, и́шь, *pf.* (*of* ~я́ть) (*chem.*) to oxidize.

окисл|и́ться, ю́сь, и́шься, *pf.* (*of* ~я́ться) (*chem.*) 1. to oxidize. 2. *pass. of* ~и́ть.

окисл|я́ть(ся), я́ю(сь), *impf. of* ~и́ть(ся).

óкис|ь, и, *f.* (*chem.*) oxide; безвóдная о. anhydride; водна́я о. hydroxide; о. желéза ferric oxide; о. мéди cupric oxide; о. углерóда carbon monoxide.

окклюди́р|овать, ую, *impf. and pf.* (*chem.*) to occlude.

окклюзи|я, и, *f.* (*chem.*) occlusion.

оккульти́зм, а, *m.* occultism.

оккýльтный, *adj.* occult.

оккупáнт, а, *m.* invader, occupier.

оккупа́ционный, *adj. of* ~ция; ~циóнная áрмия army of occupation.

оккупáци|я, и, *f.* (*mil.*) occupation.

оккупи́р|овать, ую, *impf. and pf.* (*mil.*) to occupy.

оклáд¹, а, *m.* 1. salary scale; salary; основнóй о. (*mil.*) basic pay. 2. tax, assessment.

оклáд², а, *m.* setting, framework (*of icon*).

оклáдист|ый (~, ~а), *adj.* (*of beard*) broad and thick.

окладнóй, *adj. of* оклáд¹; о. лист tax sheet.

оклеве|тáть, щý, ~щешь, *pf.* to slander, calumniate, defame.

оклéива|ть, ю, *impf. of* оклéить.

оклé|ить, ю, ишь, *pf.* (*of* ~ивать) (+*i.*) to cover (with); to glue over (with), paste over (with); о. кóмнату обóями to paper a room.

оклéйк|а, и, *f.* glueing, pasting; о. обóями papering.

óклик, а, *m.* hail, call.

оклик|áть, áю, *impf. of* ~нуть.

окли́к|нуть, ну, нешь, *pf.* (*of* ~áть) to hail, call (to).

окн|ó, á, *pl.* ~а, óкон, ~ам, *n.* 1. window; опускнóе о. sash window; слуховóе о. dormer-window; кóмната в три ~á room with three windows; о. вы́дачи serving-

hatch. 2. (*fig.*) gap; aperture. 3. (*school sl.*) free period.

óк|о, а, *pl.* óчи, очéй, *n.* (*arch. or poet.*) eye; в мгновéние ~а in the twinkling of an eye; о. за о. an eye for an eye.

ок|овáть, ую́, уёшь, *pf.* (*of* ~óвывать) to bind (*with metal*); (*fig.*) to fetter, shackle.

окóвк|а, и, *f.* binding (*with metal*); nailing (*of boots*).

окóв|ы, ~, *no sing.* fetters (*also fig.*); сбрóсить с себя́ о. to cast off one's chains.

окóвыва|ть, ю, *impf. of* оковáть.

окола́чива|ться, юсь, *impf.* (*coll.*) to lounge about, kick one's heels.

околд|овáть, ýю, *pf.* (*of* ~óвывать) to bewitch, entrance, enchant (*also fig.*).

околдóвыва|ть, ю, *impf. of* околдовáть.

околевá|ть, ю, *impf. of* околéть.

околéлый, *adj.* (*coll.*; *of animals*) dead.

околéсиц|а, ы, *f.* nonsense, rubbish; нести́ ~у to talk stuff and nonsense.

околéс|ная, ной, *f.* = ~ица.

околé|ть, ю, *pf.* (*of* ~вáть) (*of animals and pejor. of persons*) to die.

околиц|а, ы, *f.* 1. outskirts (of a village); вы́ехать за ~у to leave the confines of a village; на ~е on the outskirts. 2. (*dial.*) neighbourhood. 3. (*dial.*) roundabout route.

околи́чност|ь, и, *f.* (*obs.*) circumlocution; innuendo; говори́ть без ~ей to speak plainly.

óколо, *prep.+g. and adv.* 1. by; close (to); near; around, about; он сидéл о. меня́ he was sitting by me; никогó нет о. there is nobody about; гдé-н. о. (э́того мéста) hereabouts, somewhere here; (чтó-н.) о. э́того, о. тогó thereabouts. 2. about; о. полýночи about midnight; о. шести́ мéтров about six metres.

околодо|к, ~чный = околóток, околóточ-ный.

околоплóдник, а, *m.* (*bot.*) pericarp, seed vessel.

околосердéчн|ый, *adj.* ~ая сýмка (*anat.*) pericardium.

околóт|ок, ка, *m.* 1. neighbourhood. 2. (*obs.*) ward, town district, precinct; area, sector (*of public transport*). 3. (*obs.*) police--station. 4. (*mil.*; *obs.*) aid post, dressing--station.

околóто|чный, *adj. of* ~к; о. надзирáтель *or as noun* о., ~чного, *m.* (*obs.*) police--officer.

околоýшный, *adj.* (*anat.*) parotid.

околоцвéтник, а, *m.* (*bot.*) perianth.

околпáчива|ть, ю, *impf. of* околпáчить.

околпáч|ить, у, ишь, *pf.* (*of* ~ивать) (*coll.*) to fool, dupe.

окóлыш, а, *m.* cap-band.

окóльнич|ий, его, *m.* (*hist.*) okolnichy (*in Muscovite period, member of social group with status second to that of boyars*).

окóльны|й, *adj.* roundabout; ~е пути́ devious ways; вы́ведать ~м путём (*fig.*) to find out in a roundabout way.

е콜ьц|ева́ть, у́ю, *pf. of* кольцева́ть 2.

оконéчност|ь, и, *f.* extremity.

окóнн|ый, *adj. of* окно́; ~ая ра́ма window--frame, sash; ~ое стекло́ window-pane; window-glass.

оконфу́|зить, жу, зишь, *pf.* (*coll.*) to embarrass, confuse.

оконча́ни|е, я, *n.* 1. end; conclusion, termination; о. сро́ка expiration; по ~и университе́та on graduating; о. сле́дует (*note to serial article, story, etc.*) to be concluded. 2. (*gram.*) ending.

оконча́тельно, *adv.* finally, definitively; completely.

оконча́тельный, *adj.* final, definitive.

окóнч|ить, у, ишь, *pf.* (*of* ока́нчивать) to finish, end; о. шко́лу to leave school; о. университе́т to graduate, go down (from university).

окóнч|иться, ится, *pf.* (*of* ока́нчиваться) 1. to finish, end, terminate; to be over. 2. *pass. of* ~ить.

окóп, а, *m.* (*mil.*) trench; entrenchment.

окопа́|ть, ю, *pf.* (*of* ока́пывать) to dig round.

окопа́|ться, юсь, *pf.* (*of* ока́пываться) 1. (*mil.*) to entrench (oneself), dig in. 2. (*fig., iron.*) to find oneself a soft spot, comfortable hide-out. 3. *pass. of* ~ть.

окóп|ный, *adj. of* ~; ~ная война́ trench warfare.

окора́чива|ть, ю, *impf. of* окороти́ть.

окóрк|а, и, *f.* barking, bark stripping.

окóрм|ить, лю́, ~ишь, *pf.* (*of* ока́рмливать) 1. to overfeed, cram (stuff) with food. 2. to poison with bad food.

окорна́|ть, ю, *pf. of* корна́ть.

óкоро|к, ка, *pl.* ~ка́, *m.* ham, gammon; (*of mutton, veal*) leg.

окоро|ти́ть, чу́, ти́шь, *pf.* (*of* окора́чивать) (*coll.*) to make too short; to crop.

окостенева́|ть, ю, *impf. of* окостене́ть.

окостене́лый, *adj.* ossified (*also fig.*).

окостене́|ть, ю, *pf.* (*of* костене́ть *and* ~ва́ть) to ossify (*also fig.*).

окóт, а, *m.* (time of) having kittens (*also of time of bringing forth young of certain other animals*).

око|ти́ться, чу́сь, ти́шься, *pf. of* коти́ться.

окочене́лый, *adj.* stiff with cold.

окочене́|ть, ю, *pf. of* кочене́ть.

окóш|ко, ка, *pl.* ~ки, ~ек, ~кам, *n. dim. of* окно́.

окра́ин|а, ы, *f.* 1. outskirts; outlying districts. 2. (*obs.*) ~ы borders, marches (*of a country*).

окра́|сить, шу, сишь, *pf.* (*of* ~шивать) to paint, colour; to dye; to stain; слегка́ о. to tinge, tint.

окра́ск|а, и, *f.* 1. painting, colouring; dyeing; staining. 2. colouring, coloration; colour; защи́тная о. (*zool.*) protective coloration. 3. (*fig.*) tinge, tint; (*polit.*) slant; ирони́ческая о. ironic tinge, touch of irony; стилисти́ческая о. stylistic nuance; прида́ть чему-н. другу́ю ~у to put a different complexion on something.

окра́шива|ть, ю, *impf. of* окра́сить.

окре́п|нуть, ну, нешь, *past* ~, ~ла, *pf. of* кре́пнуть.

окре́ст, *prep.*+*g. and adv.* (*obs.*) around, about.

окре|сти́ть, щу́, ~сти́шь, *pf.* 1. (*impf.* крести́ть) to baptize, christen. 2. (*coll.*; +*a. and i.*) to nickname; его́ ~сти́ли медве́дем he was nicknamed 'the bear'.

окре|сти́ться, щу́сь, ~сти́шься, *pf. of* крести́ться 1.

окре́стност|ь, и, *f.* 1. environs. 2. neighbourhood, vicinity.

окре́стный, *adj.* 1. neighbouring. 2. surrounding.

окриве́|ть, ю, *pf. of* криве́ть.

óкрик, а, *m.* hail; shout, cry; гру́бый о. harsh bellow.

окри́кива|ть, ю, *impf. of* окри́кнуть.

окри́к|нуть, ну, нешь, *pf.* (*of* ~ивать) to hail, shout (to).

окрова́в|ить, лю, ишь, *pf.* (*of* ~ливать) to stain with blood.

окрова́в|иться, люсь, ишься, *pf.* (*of* ~ливаться) to spill blood on oneself.

окрова́в|ленный, *p.p.p. of* ~ить *and adj.* blood-stained; bloody.

окрова́влива|ть(ся), ю(сь), *impf. of* окрова́вить(ся).

окровене́|ть, ю, *pf.* (*coll.*) to become covered with blood; to become soaked in blood.

окровен|и́ть, ю́, и́шь, *pf.* (*coll.*) to stain with blood.

окроп|и́ть, лю́, и́шь, *pf.* (*of* кропи́ть *and* ~ля́ть) to (be)sprinkle.

окропля́|ть, ю, *impf. of* окропи́ть.

окро́шк|а, и, *f.* 1. okroshka (*cold kvass soup with chopped vegetables and meat or fish*). 2. (*fig., coll.*) hodge-podge, jumble.

óкруг, а, *pl.* ~а́, *m.* (*territorial division of U.S.S.R. for administrative, legal, military, etc., purposes*) okrug; region, district; circuit; вое́нный о. military district, command; избира́тельный о. electoral district.

окру́г|а, и, *f.* (*coll.*) neighbourhood.

округл|ённый, *p.p.p. of* ~и́ть *and adj.* rounded (*also fig.*).

округлѣ́|ть, ю, *pf. of* круглѣ́ть.

округл|и́ть, ю́, и́шь, *pf.* (*of* ~я́ть) **1.** to round (off) (*also fig.*). **2.** to express in round numbers.

округл|и́ться, ю́сь, и́шься, *pf.* (*of* ~я́ться) **1.** to become rounded. **2.** to be expressed in round numbers.

окру́глост|ь, и, *f.* **1.** roundedness. **2.** protuberance, bulge.

округл|ый (~, ~а), *adj.* rounded, roundish.

округл|я́ть(ся), я́ю(сь), *impf. of* ~и́ть(ся).

окруж|а́ть, а́ю, *impf. of* ~и́ть.

окружа́|ющий, *pres. part. act. of* ~ть and *adj.* surrounding; ~ющая обстано́вка surroundings; *as noun* ~ющее, ~ющего, *n.* environment; ~ющие, ~ющих one's associates; entourage.

окруже́ни|е, я, *n.* **1.** encirclement; попа́сть в о. (*mil.*) to be encircled, be surrounded. **2.** surroundings; environment; milieu; в ~и (+*g.*) accompanied (by); surrounded (by), in the midst (of); он появи́лся в ~и боле́льщиков he appeared surrounded by fans.

окруж|и́ть, у́, и́шь, *pf.* (*of* ~а́ть) (*in var. senses*) to surround; to encircle; о. кого́-н. забо́тами to lavish attentions on someone.

окружко́м, а, *m.* (*abbr.* of окружно́й комите́т), *see* окружно́й.

окружн|о́й, *adj.* **1.** *adj. of* о́круг; о. комите́т district committee; о. суд circuit court. **2.** operating (situated) about a circle; ~а́я желе́зная доро́га circle line; ~а́я ско́рость (*tech.*) peripheral speed.

окру́жност|ь, и, *f.* **1.** circumference; circle; име́ть де́сять ме́тров в ~и to be ten metres in circumference; на три ми́ли в ~и within a radius of three miles, for three miles round. **2.** (*obs.*) neighbourhood.

окру́жн|ый, *adj.* (*obs.*) **1.** = ~о́й. **2.** neighbouring.

окру|ти́ть, чу́, ~тишь, *pf.* (*of* ~чивать) **1.** (+*i.*) to wind round. **2.** (*coll.*) to marry (*see* ~ти́ться).

окру|ти́ться, чу́сь, ~тишься, *pf.* (*of* ~чиваться) **1.** (+*i.*) to wind round oneself. **2.** (*coll.*) to get spliced (= to get married).

окру́чива|ть(ся), ю(сь), *impf. of* окрути́ть(ся).

окрыл|и́ть, ю́, и́шь, *pf.* (*of* ~я́ть) to inspire, encourage.

окрыл|я́ть, я́ю, *impf. of* ~и́ть.

окры́с|иться, ишься, *pf.* (на+*a.*; *coll.*) to snap (at).

оксиацетиле́нов|ый, *adj.* ~ая сва́рка oxy-acetylene welding.

оксиди́р|овать, ую, *impf. and pf.* (*chem.*) to oxidize.

оксидиро́вк|а, и, *f.* (*chem.*) oxidation.

оксю́морон, а, *m.* (*lit.*) oxymoron.

окта́в|а, ы, *f.* **1.** (*mus. and lit.*) octave. **2.** (*mus.*) low bass.

окта́н, а, *m.* (*chem.*) octane.

окта́нов|ый, *adj.* (*chem.*) octane; ~ое то́пливо (high-)octane fuel; ~ое число́ octane number, octane rating.

окта́эдр, а, *m.* (*math.*) octahedron.

окте́т, а, *m.* (*mus.*) octet.

октрои́р|овать, ую, *impf. and pf.* to grant; to concede.

октябр|ёнок, ёнка, *pl.* ~я́та, ~я́т, *m.* oktyabryonok ('pre-Pioneer': *Soviet child of seven years or upward preparing for entry into Pioneers*).

октя́бр|ь, я́, *m.* October (*fig.* = *Russian revolution of October 1917*).

октя́брь|ский, *adj. of* ~.

оку́кливани|е, я, *n.* (*zool.*) pupation.

оку́клива|ться, ется, *impf. of* окуклиться.

оку́кл|иться, ится, *pf.* (~иваться) (*zool.*) to pupate.

окули́р|овать, ую, *impf. and pf.* (*hort.*) to inoculate, engraft.

окулиро́вк|а, и, *f.* (*hort.*) inoculation, grafting.

окули́ст, а, *m.* oculist.

окуля́р, а, *m.* eye-piece, ocular.

окун|а́ть(ся), а́ю(сь), *impf. of* ~у́ть(ся).

о́кун|евый, *adj. of* ~ь.

окун|у́ть, у́, ёшь, *pf.* (*of* ~а́ть) to dip; о. ло́жку в па́току to dip a spoon into the treacle.

окун|у́ться, у́сь, ёшься, *pf.* (*of* ~а́ться) **1.** to dip (oneself). **2.** (*fig.*; в+*a.*) to plunge (into), become (utterly) absorbed (in), engrossed (in); о. в спор to plunge into an argument; он ~у́лся в сочине́ния Плато́на he has become utterly absorbed in the works of Plato.

о́кун|ь, я, *pl.* ~и, ~е́й, *m.* perch (*fish*).

окуп|а́ть(ся), а́ю(сь), *impf. of* ~и́ть(ся).

окуп|и́ть, лю́, ~ишь, *pf.* (*of* ~а́ть) to compensate, repay, make up (for); о. расхо́ды to cover one's outlay.

окуп|и́ться, лю́сь, ~ишься, *pf.* (*of* ~а́ться) to be compensated, be repaid; (*fig.*) to pay; to be justified, be requited, be rewarded; затра́ченные на́ми уси́лия ~и́лись our efforts were rewarded.

окургу́|зить, жу, зишь, *pf.* (*coll.*) to cut too short.

оку́ривани|е, я, *n.* fumigation.

оку́рива|ть, ю, *impf. of* окури́ть.

окур|и́ть, ю́, ~ишь, *pf.* (*of* ~ивать) to fumigate; о. се́рой to sulphurate.

оку́р|ок, ка, *m.* cigarette-end, cigarette stub; cigar-butt.

оку́т|ать, аю, *pf.* (*of* ~ывать) **1.** (+*i.*) to wrap up (in). **2.** (*fig.*) to shroud, cloak; о. та́йной to shroud in mystery.

окут|а́ться, а́юсь, *pf.* (*of* ~ываться) 1. (+*i.*) wrap up (in). 2. (*fig.*) to shroud, cloak; о. та́йной to shroud in mystery.

оку́тыва|ть(ся), ю(сь), *impf. of* оку́тать(ся).

оку́чива|ть, ю, *impf. of* оку́чить.

оку́ч|ить, у, ишь, *pf.* (*of* ~ивать) (*agric.*) to earth up.

ола́д|ья, ьи, *g. pl.* ~ий, *f.* fritter; карто́-фельная о. potato cake.

олеа́ндр, а, *m.* oleander.

оледене́лый, *adj.* frozen.

оледене́|ть, ю, *pf. of* ледене́ть.

оледен|и́ть, ю́, и́шь, *pf. of* ледени́ть.

олеи́н, а, *m.* (*chem.*) olein.

олеи́нов|ый, *adj.* (*chem.*) olein, oleic; ~ая кислота́ oleic acid.

оленево́д, а, *m.* reindeer-breeder.

оленево́дств|о, а, *n.* reindeer-breeding.

оле́н|ий, *adj. of* ~ь; ~ьи porа́ antlers; о. лиша́й, о мох (*bot.*) reindeer moss; о. por (*chem.*) hartshorn; о. язы́к (*bot.*) hart's tongue.

оле́нин|а, ы, *f.* venison.

оле́н|ь, я, *m.* deer; безро́гий о. pollard; благоро́дный о. stag, red deer; се́верный о. reindeer; кана́дский о. wapiti.

олеогра́фи|я, и, *f.* oleograph(y).

оли́в|а, ы, *f.* olive; olive-tree.

оливи́н, а, *m.* (*min.*) olivine, chrysolite.

оли́вк|а, и, *f.* olive; olive-tree.

оли́вков|ый, *adj.* 1. olive; ~ая ветвь olive branch (*fig.*; *as symbol of peace*); ~ое ма́сло olive oil. 2. olive-coloured.

олига́рх, а, *m.* oligarch.

олигархи́ческий, *adj.* oligarchical.

олига́рхи|я, и, *f.* oligarchy.

олигоце́н, а, *m.* (*geol.*) oligocene (epoch).

олимпиа́д|а, ы, *f.* olympiad, competition.

олимпи́|ец, йца, *m.* (*myth. and fig.*) Olympian.

олимпи́йски|й[1], *adj.* Olympic; ~е и́гры Olympic games, Olympics.

олимпи́йск|ий[2], *adj.* of Olympus; ~ое споко́йствие (*fig.*) Olympian calm.

оли́ф|а, ы, *f.* drying oil.

олицетворе́ни|е, я, *n.* personification; em-bodiment.

олицетвор|ённый, *p.p.p. of* ~и́ть; он — ~ённая хи́трость he is cunning personified.

олицетвор|и́ть, ю́, и́шь, *pf.* (*of* ~я́ть) to personify; to embody.

олицетвор|я́ть, я́ю, *impf. of* ~и́ть.

о́лов|о, а, *n.* tin; за́кись ~а stannous oxide; о́кись ~а stannic oxide.

оловоно́сный, *adj.* tin-bearing, stanniferous.

оловя́нистый, *adj.* stannous.

оловя́нн|ый, *adj.* tin; stannic; о. ка́мень (*min.*) tin spar, tin ore, cassiterite; ~ая кис-лота́ stannic acid; о. колчеда́н (*min.*) tin pyrites, stannite; ~ое ма́сло (*chem.*) stannic

chloride; ~ая посу́да tinware; pewter; ~ая соль stannic salt; ~ая фо́льга tin foil.

о́лух, а, *m.* (*coll.*) blockhead, dolt, oaf; о. царя́ небе́сного perfect fool, complete idiot.

олу́ш|а, и, *f.* се́верная о. (*orn.*) gannet.

ольх|а́, и́, *pl.* ~и, *f.* alder(-tree).

ольх|о́вый, *adj. of* ~а́.

ольша́ник, а, *m.* alder thicket.

оля́пк|а, и, *f.* (*orn.*) dipper.

ом, а, *m.* (*electr.*) ohm.

ома́р, а, *m.* lobster.

оме́г|а, и, *f.* omega; от а́льфы до ~и (*fig.*) from A to Z, from beginning to end.

оме́л|а, ы, *f.* mistletoe.

омерзе́ни|е, я, *n.* loathing; внуши́ть о. (+*d.*) to inspire loathing (in).

омерзе́|ть, ю, *pf.* to become loathsome; мне э́тот пейза́ж ~л I have come to loathe this view.

омерзи́тел|ьный (~ен, ~ьна), *adj.* loath-some, sickening; быть в ~ьном настрое́-нии (*coll.*) to be in a foul mood.

омертве́лост|ь, и, *f.* stiffness, numbness; (*med.*) necrosis, mortification.

омертве́л|ый, *adj.* stiff, numb; (*med.*) necro-tic; ~ая ткань dead tissue.

омертве́ни|е, я, *n.* = омертве́лость.

омертве́|ть, ю, *pf. of* мертве́ть 1.

омертв|и́ть, лю́, и́шь, *pf.* (*of* ~ля́ть) 1. to deaden. 2. (*econ.*) to withdraw from circu-lation.

омёт, а, *m.* stack (of straw).

омеща́нива|ться, юсь, *impf. of* омеща́-ниться.

омеща́н|иться, юсь, ишься, *pf.* (*of* ~и-ваться) (*coll., pejor.*) to become a philistine.

оми́ческий, *adj.* (*electr.*) ohmic.

омле́т, а, *m.* omelette.

омме́тр, а, *m.* (*electr.*) ohmmeter.

о́мнибус, а, *m.* (horse-drawn) omnibus.

омове́ни|е, я, *n.* ablution(s); (*eccl.*) lavabo.

омола́жива|ть(ся), ю(сь), *impf. of* омоло-ди́ть(ся).

омоло|ди́ть, жу́, ди́шь, *pf.* (*of* омола́жи-вать) to rejuvenate.

омоло|ди́ться, жу́сь, ди́шься, *pf.* (*of* омола́-жива́ться) to rejuvenate, rejuvenesce.

омоложе́ни|е, я, *n.* rejuvenation.

омо́ним, а, *m.* (*ling.*) homonym.

омони́мик|а, и, *f.* 1. study of homonyms. 2. (*collect.*) homonyms.

омоними́ческий, *adj.* (*ling.*) homonymous.

омони́ми|я, и, *f.* (*ling.*) homonymy.

омоч|и́ть, у́, ~ишь, *pf.* (*obs.*) to wet; to moisten.

омоч|и́ться, у́сь, ~ишься, *pf.* (*obs.*) to become wet; to become moist.

омрач|а́ть(ся), а́ю(сь), *impf. of* ~и́ть(ся).

омрач|и́ть, у́, и́шь, *pf.* (*of* ~а́ть) to darken, cloud.

омрач|и́ться, у́сь, и́шься, *pf.* (*of* ~а́ться) to become darkened, become clouded (*also fig.*).

омулёвый, *adj. of* о́муль.

о́мул|ь, я, *g. pl.* ~ей, *m.* omul (*sea fish of salmon family, found also in Lake Baikal*).

о́мут, а, *m.* 1. whirlpool; (*fig.*) whirl, maelstrom. 2. deep place (*in river or lake*); в ти́хом ~е че́рти во́дятся (*prov.*) still waters run deep.

омша́ник, а, *m.* heated structure (*for housing bees in winter, etc.*).

омыва́|ть, ю, 1. *impf. of* омы́ть. 2. *impf.* (*geogr.*) to wash (*of seas*).

омыва́|ться, юсь, *impf.* (*geogr.*) to be washed; за́падный бе́рег Ирла́ндии ~ется Атланти́ческим океа́ном the west coast of Ireland is washed by the Atlantic.

омыле́ни|е, я, *n.* (*chem.*) saponification.

ом|ы́ть, о́ю, о́ешь, *pf.* (*of* ~ыва́ть) (*rhet., obs.*) to wash, lave; о. кро́вью to steep in blood.

он, его́, ему́, им, о нём, *pron.* he.

она́, её, ей, ей (е́ю), о ней, *pron.* she.

она́гр, а, *m.* (*zool.*) onager.

онани́зм, а, *m.* onanism, masturbation.

онани́р|овать, ую, *impf.* to masturbate.

онани́ст, а, *m.* masturbator.

онда́тр|а, ы, *f.* (*animal*) musk-rat, musquash; (*fur*) musquash.

онда́тр|овый, *adj. of* ~а.

ондуля́тор, а, *m.* (*electr.*) undulator.

онемéлый, *adj.* 1. dumb. 2. numb.

онемé|ть, ю, *pf. of* немéть.

онемéчива|ть, ю, *impf. of* онемéчить.

онемéч|ить, у, ишь, *pf.* (*of* ~ивать) to Germanize.

онёр, а, *m.* (*cards*) honour; со всеми́ ~ами (*fig., joc.*) with everything it takes, with everything one could want.

они́, их, им, и́ми, о них, *pron.* they.

о́никс, а, *m.* onyx.

онколо́ги|я, и, *f.* (*med.*) oncology.

онко́л|ь, я, *m.* (*fin., comm.*) call-account.

оно́, его́, ему́, им, о нём, *pron.* 1. it. 2. (= э́то) this, that; о. и ви́дно that is evident. 2. *as emphatic particle* о. коне́чно well, of course; вот о. что! oh, I see!

ономáстик|а, и, *f.* (*ling.*) onomastics.

онтогене́з, а, *m.* (*biol.*) ontogenesis.

онтологи́ческий, *adj.* (*philos.*) ontological.

онтоло́ги|я, и, *f.* (*philos.*) ontology.

ону́ч|а, и, *f.* onucha (*sock or cloth puttee worn in boot or bast-shoe*).

о́ный, *pron.* (*obs.*) that; the above-mentioned; во вре́мя о́но in those days; (*joc.*) in days of old.

ооли́т, а, *m.* (*min.*) oolite.

опада́|ть, ю, *impf. of* опа́сть.

опада́|ющий, *pres. part. act. of* ~ть *and adj.* (*bot.*) deciduous.

опа́здыва|ть, ю, *impf.* 1. *impf. of* опозда́ть. 2. (*impf. only*) (*coll.*) to be slow (*of clocks and watches*).

опа́ива|ть, ю, *impf. of* опои́ть.

опа́л, а, *m.* opal.

опа́л|а, ы, *f.* disgrace, disfavour; быть в ~е to be in disgrace, be out of favour.

опалесце́нци|я, и, *f.* (*phys.*) opalescence.

опалеси́р|овать, ую, *impf. and pf.* (*phys.*) to opalesce.

опа́лива|ть(ся), ю(сь), *impf. of* опали́ть(ся).

опал|и́ть, ю́, и́шь, *pf.* (*of* пали́ть[1] *and* ~ивать) to singe.

опал|и́ться, ю́сь, и́шься, *pf.* (*of* ~ива́ться) to singe oneself.

опа́ловый, *adj.* opal; opaline.

опа́луб|ить, лю, ишь, *pf.* (*tech.*) to case, sheathe, tub.

опа́лубк|а, и, *f.* (*tech.*) 1. casing, lining, sheathing, tubbing; о. кры́ши roof-boarding. 2. concrete mould, form.

опа́лый, *adj.* (*coll.*) sunken; emaciated.

опа́льный[1], *adj.* disgraced; in disgrace, out of favour.

опа́льн|ый[2], *adj.* ~ая маши́на (*tech.*) cloth singeing machine.

опа́мят|оваться, уюсь, *pf.* (*obs.*) to come to one's senses, collect oneself.

опа́р|а, ы, *f.* 1. leavened dough. 2. leaven.

опарши́ве|ть, ю, *pf. of* парши́веть.

опаса́|ться, юсь, *impf.* 1. (+*g.*) to fear, be afraid (of). 2. (+*g. or inf.*) to beware (of); to avoid, keep off; он ~ется алкого́ля he does not touch alcohol; о. сли́шком мно́го пить to beware of drinking to excess.

опасе́ни|е, я, *n.* fear; apprehension; misgiving(s).

опа́ск|а, и, *f.* с ~ой (*coll.*) with caution, cautiously; warily.

опа́слив|ый (~, ~а), *adj.* (*coll.*) cautious; wary.

опа́сност|ь, и, *f.* danger; peril; вне ~и out of danger; смотре́ть ~и в глаза́ to look dangers in the face.

опа́с|ный (~ен, ~на), *adj.* dangerous, perilous.

опа́|сть, ду́, дёшь, *pf.* (*of* ~да́ть) 1. (*of leaves*) to fall (off). 2. to subside; (*of a swelling, etc.*) to go down.

опаха́л|о, а, *n.* fan.

опа|ха́ть, шу́, ~шешь, *pf.* (*of* ~хива́ть[1]) to plough round.

опа́хива|ть[1], ю, *impf. of* опаха́ть.

опа́хива|ть[2], ю, *impf. of* опахну́ть.

опах|ну́ть, ну́, нёшь, *pf.* (*of* ~ива́ть[2]) to fan.

опе́к|а, и, *f.* 1. guardianship, wardship, tutelage (*also fig.*); trusteeship; быть под ~ой кого́-н. to be under someone's guardianship; взять под ~y to take as ward; (*fig.*) to take charge (of), take under one's wing; учреди́ть ~y над кем-н. to place someone in ward. **2.** (*collect.*) guardians, board of guardians; Междунаро́дная о. International Trusteeship. **3.** (*fig.*) care; surveillance; вы́йти из-под ~и to become one's own master.

опека́|емый, *pres. part. pass. of* ~ть; *as noun* **о.**, ~емого, *m.* ward.

опека́|ть, ю, *impf.* **1.** to be guardian (to), have the wardship (of). **2.** (*fig.*) to take care (of), watch (over).

опеку́н, á. *m.* (*leg.*) guardian, tutor; trustee.

опеку́н|ский, *adj. of* ~; О. сове́т (*obs.*) board of guardians.

опеку́нств|о, а, *n.* guardianship, tutorship.

опён|ок, ка, *pl.* ~ки, ~ков, *m.* honey agaric (*mushroom*).

о́пер|а, ы, *f.* opera; из друго́й ~ы, не из той ~ы (*coll.*) quite a different matter.

опера́бельный, *adj.* (*med.*) operable.

операти́вност|ь, и, *f.* drive; energy (*in getting things done*).

операти́в|ный, *adj.* **1.** (~ен, ~на) energetic; efficient; ~ное руково́дство efficient and flexible leadership. **2.** executive. **3.** (*med.*) operative; surgical; ~ное вмеша́тельство surgical interference. **4.** (*mil.*) operation(s), operational; strategical; ~ное иску́сство campaign tactics; ~ная сво́дка summary of operations.

опера́тор, а, *m.* operator; (*med.*) surgeon.

опера|цио́нный, *adj. of* ~ция; ~цио́нное отделе́ние (*in hospital*) surgical wing; о. стол operating-table; *as noun* ~цио́нная, ~цио́нной, *f.* theatre, operating-room.

опера́ци|я, и, *f.* (*med., mil., etc.*) operation; перенести́ ~ю to have, undergo an operation; to be operated (upon); сде́лать ~ю to perform an operation.

опере|ди́ть, жу́, ди́шь, *pf.* (*of* ~жа́ть) **1.** to outstrip, leave behind. **2.** to forestall.

опережа́|ть, ю, *impf. of* опереди́ть.

опере́ни|е, я, *n.* feathering, plumage; хвостово́е о. (*aeron.*) tail unit.

опере́нный, *adj.* feathered.

опере́т|ка, ки, *f.* = ~та.

опере́т|очный, *adj. of* ~ка *and* ~та.

оперетт|а, ы, *f.* musical comedy, operetta.

опере́ть, обопру́, обопрёшь, *past* опёр, оперла́, *pf.* (*of* опира́ть) (о+*a.*) to lean (against).

опере́ться, обопру́сь, обопрёшься, *past* опёрся, оперла́сь, *pf.* (*of* опира́ться) (на+*a.*; о+*a.*) to lean (on; against); о. о подоко́нник to lean against the window-sill; о. на подде́ржку жены́ (*fig.*) to lean for support on one's wife.

опери́р|овать, ую, *impf. and pf.* **1.** (*med.*) to

operate (upon). **2.** (*mil.*) to operate, act. **3.** (+*i.*; *fin., etc.*) to operate (with), execute operations (with); (*fig.*) to use, handle; о. недоста́точными да́нными to operate with inadequate data.

опер|и́ть, ю́, и́шь, *pf.* (*of* ~я́ть) to feather (*an arrow*); to adorn with feathers.

опер|и́ться, ю́сь, и́шься, *pf.* (*of* ~я́ться) **1.** (*of birds*) to be fledged. **2.** (*fig.*) to stand on one's own feet.

о́перн|ый, *adj.* opera; operatic; о. певе́ц, ~ая певи́ца opera singer; о. теа́тр opera-house.

опёрт|ый (~, ~á, ~о), *p.p.p. of* опере́ть.

опер|ши́сь, *past gerund of* ~е́ться; о. (на+*a.*) leaning (on).

опер|я́ть(ся), я́ю(сь), *impf. of* ~и́ть(ся).

опеча́л|ить(ся), ю(сь), ишь(ся), *pf. of* печа́лить(ся).

опеча́т|ать, аю, *pf.* (*of* ~ывать) to seal up.

опеча́т|ка, ки, *f.* misprint; спи́сок ~ок (list of) errata.

опе́ш|ить, у, ишь, *pf.* (*coll.*) to be taken aback.

опива́|ться, юсь, *impf. of* опи́ться.

опи́вк|и, ов, *no sing.* (*coll.*) dregs.

о́пи|й, я, *m.* opium.

о́пий|ный, *adj. of* ~.

опи́лива|ть, ю, *impf. of* опили́ть.

опил|и́ть, ю́, ~ишь, *pf.* (*of* ~ивать) to saw; to file.

опи́л|ки, ок, *no sing.* sawdust; (*metal*) filings.

опира́|ть(ся), ю(сь), *impf. of* опере́ть(ся).

описа́ни|е, я, *n.* description; account; э́то не поддаётся ~ю it is beyond description, it beggars description.

опи́с|анный, *p.p.p. of* ~а́ть *and adj.* (*math.*) circumscribed.

описа́тельный, *adj.* descriptive.

описа́тельств|о, а, *n.* (*pejor.*) (bare) description.

опи|са́ть, шу́, ~шешь, *pf.* (*of* ~сывать) **1.** to describe. **2.** to iist, inventory; о. иму́щество (*leg.*) to distrain property. **3.** (*math.*) to describe, circumscribe.

опи|са́ться, шу́сь, ~шешься, *pf.* to make a slip of the pen.

опи́ск|а, и, *f.* slip of the pen.

опи́сыва|ть, ю, *impf. of* описа́ть.

о́пис|ь, и, *f.* list, schedule; inventory; о. иму́щества (*leg.*) distraint.

опи́|ться, обопью́сь, обопьёшься, *past* ~лся, ~ла́сь, ~ло́сь, *pf.* (*of* ~ва́ться) (*coll.*) to drink to excess, drink oneself stupid.

о́пиум, а, *m.* opium.

о́пиум|ный, *adj. of* ~.

опла́|кать, чу, чешь, *pf.* (*of* ~кивать) to mourn (over); to bewail, bemoan.

опла́кива|ть, ю, *impf. of* опла́кать.

опла́т|а, ы, *f.* pay, payment; remuneration;

поча́сная о. payment by the hour; сде́льная о. piece work payment.

опла|ти́ть, чу́, ~ти́шь, *pf.* to pay (for); о. расхо́ды to meet the expenses, foot the bill; о. счёт to settle the account, pay the bill; о. убы́тки to pay damages.

опла́|ченный, *p.p.p.* of ~ти́ть; с ~ченным отве́том reply-paid.

опла́чива|ть, ю, *impf.* of оплати́ть.

опла́|чу, чешь, *see* ~кать.

опла|чу́, ~ти́шь, *see* ~ти́ть.

оплёв|анный, *p.p.p.* of ~а́ть; как о. as if in disgrace.

опл|ева́ть, юю́, юёшь, *pf.* (*of* ~ёвывать) **1.** (*coll.*) to cover with spittle. **2.** (*fig.*) to spit upon, humiliate. **3.** (*fig.*) to spurn.

оплёвыва|ть, ю, *impf.* of оплева́ть.

опле|сти́, ту́, тёшь, *past* ~л, ~ла́, *pf.* (*of* ~та́ть) **1.** to twine (round); to braid; о. буты́ль соло́мой to wicker a bottle. **2.** (*fig., coll.*) to twist, get round.

оплета́|ть, ю, *impf.* of оплести́.

оплеу́х|а, и, *f.* (*coll.*) slap in the face.

опле́ч|ье, ья, *g. pl.* ~ий, *n.* (*obs.*) shoulder(s) (*of garment*).

оплеши́ве|ть, ю, *pf.* of плеши́веть.

оплодотворе́ни|е, я, *n.* impregnation, fecundation; fertilization.

оплодотвори́тел|ь, я, *m.* (*bot.*) fertilizer.

оплодотвор|и́ть, ю́, и́шь, *pf.* (*of* ~я́ть) to impregnate (*also fig.*), fecundate; to fertilize.

оплодотвор|я́ть, я́ю, *impf.* of ~и́ть.

опломбир|ова́ть, у́ю, *pf.* of пломбирова́ть.

опло́т, а, *m.* (*rhet.*) stronghold, bulwark.

оплоша́|ть, ю, *pf.* (*coll.*) to take a false step, blunder.

опло́шност|ь, и, *f.* false step, blunder.

опло́ш|ный (~ен, ~на), *adj.* (*obs.*) **1.** mistaken; о. посту́пок false step. **2.** blundering.

оплыва́|ть, ю, *impf.* of оплы́ть.

оплы́|ть[1], ву́, вёшь, *pf.* (*of* ~ва́ть) **1.** to become swollen, swell up. **2.** (*of a candle*) to gutter. **3.** to fall (*as result of a landslide*).

оплы́|ть[2], ву́, вёшь, *pf.* (*of* ~ва́ть) to sail round; to swim round; о. о́стров to sail round an island; о. о́зеро to sail round the edge of) a lake.

опове|сти́ть, щу́, сти́шь, *pf.* (*of* ~ща́ть) to notify, inform.

оповеща́|ть, ю, *impf.* of оповести́ть.

оповеще́ни|е, я, *n.* notification; радиосе́тка ~я (*mil.*) (early) warning system.

опога́н|ить, ю, ишь, *pf.* of пога́нить.

оподельдо́к, а, *m.* (*med., hist.*) opodeldoc.

оподле́|ть, ю, *pf.* of подле́ть.

опо́|ек, йка, *m.* calf(-leather).

опо́ечный, *adj.* calf(-skin).

опозда́|вший, *past part. act.* of ~ть; *as noun* о., ~вшего, *m.* late-comer.

опозда́ни|е, я, *n.* being late; lateness; delay; по́езд при́был без ~я the train arrived on time; с ~ем на де́сять мину́т ten minutes late.

опозда́|ть, ю, *pf.* (*of* опа́здывать) to be late; to be overdue; о. на ле́кцию to be late for the lecture; о. на полчаса́ to be half an hour late; о. с упла́той нало́гов to be late in paying taxes.

опознава́ни|е, я, *n.* identification; о. самолётов aircraft recognition.

опознава́тельный, *adj.* distinguishing; о. знак landmark, (*naut.*) beacon; (*on wings of aircraft*) marking.

опозна|ва́ть, ю́, ёшь, *impf.* of ~ть.

опозна́ни|е, я, *n.* (*leg.*) identification.

опозна́|ть, ю, *pf.* (*of* ~ва́ть) to identify.

опозо́рени|е, я, *n.* (*leg.*) defamation.

опозо́р|ить(ся), ю(сь), ишь(ся), *pf.* of позо́рить(ся).

опо|и́ть, ю́, и́шь, *pf.* (*of* опа́ивать) **1.** to injure by giving too much to drink. **2.** (*obs.*) to poison (*by means of a potion*).

опо́йковый, *adj.* calf(-skin).

опо́к|а[1], и, *f.* (*tech.*) flask, mould box, casting box, box form; литьё в ~ах flask casting.

опо́к|а[2], и, *f.* (*geol.*) silica clay.

опола́скива|ть, ю, *impf.* of ополоска́ть and ополосну́ть.

ополза́|ть, а́ю, *impf.* of ~ти́[1, 2].

опо́лз|ень, ня, *m.* landslide, landslip.

о́полз|невый, *adj.* of ~ень.

ополз|ти́[1], у́, ёшь, *past* ~, ~ла́, *pf.* (*of* ~а́ть) to crawl round.

ополз|ти́[2], ёт, *past* ~, ~ла́, *pf.* (*of* ~а́ть) to slip.

ополо|ска́ть, щу́, ~щешь, *pf.* (*of* опола́скивать) = ~сну́ть.

ополосн|у́ть, у́, ёшь, *pf.* (*of* опола́скивать) to rinse; to swill.

ополоу́ме|ть, ю, *pf.* (*coll.*) to go crazy, be beside oneself.

ополч|а́ть(ся), а́ю(сь), *impf.* of ~и́ть(ся).

ополче́н|ец, ца, *m.* militiaman; home guard.

ополче́ни|е, я, *n.* **1.** militia; home guard. **2.** (*collect.; hist.*) irregulars; levies.

ополче́н|ский, *adj.* of ~ец and ~ие.

ополч|и́ть, у́, и́шь, *pf.* (*of* ~а́ть) (на+*a.* or про́тив; *obs.*) to arm (against); (*fig.*) to enlist the support of (against).

ополч|и́ться, у́сь, и́шься, *pf.* (*of* ~а́ться) (на+*a.* or про́тив) to take up arms (against); (*fig.*) to be up in arms (against); to turn (against).

ополя́ч|ить, у, ишь, *pf.* to polonize.

опо́мн|иться, юсь, ишься, *pf.* to come to one's senses, collect oneself.

опо́р, а, *m. only in phrase* во весь о. at full speed, at top speed, full tilt.

опо́р|а, ы, *f.* support (*also fig.*); (*tech.*) bearing; pier (*of a bridge*); (*fig.*) buttress; то́чка

~ы (*phys., tech.*) fulcrum, bearing, point of rest.

опора́жнива|ть, ю, *impf. of* опоро́жнить.

опо́р|ки, ков, *sing.* ~ок, ~ка, *m.* down-at-heel shoes.

опо́р|ный, *adj. of* ~a; (*tech.*) bearing, supporting; о. ка́мень abutment stone; ~ная при́зма fulcrum; о. пункт (*mil.*) strong point; ~ная сва́я bridge pile; о. столб chock (block).

опоро́жн|ить, ю, ишь, *pf.* (*of* опора́жнивать) to empty; to drain (at a draught); о. кише́чник to evacuate one's bowels.

опорожня́|ть, ю, *impf.* = опора́жнивать.

опоро́с, а, *m.* farrow (*of sow*).

опороси́|ться, шься, *pf. of* пороси́ться.

опоро́ч|ить, у, ишь, *pf. of* поро́чить.

опосля́, *adv.* (*coll. or dial.*) afterwards.

опосре́дств|овать, ую, *impf. and pf.* (*philos.*) to mediate.

опо́ссум, а, *m.* (*zool.*) opossum.

опосты́ле|ть, ю, *pf.* (*coll.*; +*d.*) to grow hateful (to), grow wearisome (to).

опохмел|и́ться, ю́сь, и́шься, *pf.* (*of* ~я́ться) (*coll.*) to take a hair of the dog that bit you.

опохмел|я́ться, я́юсь, *impf. of* ~и́ться.

опочива́л|ьня, ьни, *g. pl.* ~ен, *f.* (*obs.*) bed-chamber.

опочива́|ть, ю, *impf. of* опочи́ть.

опочи́|ть, ю, ешь, *pf.* (*of* ~ва́ть) (*obs.*) 1. to go to sleep. 2. (*fig., poet.*) to pass to one's rest.

опошле́|ть, ю, *pf. of* пошле́ть.

опошл|ить, ю, ишь, *pf.* (*of* ~я́ть) to vulgarize, debase.

опоя́|сать, шу, шешь, *pf.* (*of* ~сывать) 1. to gird, engird(le). 2. (*fig.*) to girdle.

опоя́|саться, шусь, шешься, *pf.* (*of* ~сываться) 1. (+*i.*) to gird oneself (with), gird on. 2. *pass. of* ~сать.

опоя́сыва|ть(ся), ю(сь), *impf. of* опоя́сать(ся).

оппозиционе́р, а, *m.* member of the opposition.

оппози|цио́нный, *adj. of* ~ция.

оппози́ци|я, и, *f.* opposition.

оппоне́нт, а, *m.* opponent; официа́льный о. official opponent (*at defence of dissertation, etc.*).

оппони́р|овать, ую, *impf.* (+*d.*) to oppose, act as opponent (to).

оппортуни́зм, а, *m.* opportunism.

оппортуни́ст, а, *m.* opportunist.

оппортунисти́ческий, *adj.* opportunist.

оппортунисти́ч|ный (~ен, ~на), *adj.* = ~еский.

оппортуни́ст|ский, *adj. of* ~.

опра́в|а, ы, *f.* setting, mounting; case; очки́ без ~ы rimless spectacles.

оправда́ни|е, я, *n.* 1. justification. 2. excuse. 3. (*leg.*) acquittal, discharge.

оправда́тельный, *adj.* о. пригово́р verdict of 'not guilty'; о. докуме́нт voucher.

оправд|а́ть, а́ю, *pf.* (*of* ~ывать) 1. to justify, warrant; to vindicate; to authorize; о. ожида́ния to come up to expectations; о. себя́ to justify oneself; о. расхо́ды to authorize expenses. 2. to excuse; о. посту́пок боле́знью to excuse an action by reason of sickness. 3. (*leg.*) to acquit, discharge.

оправд|а́ться, а́юсь, *pf.* (*of* ~ываться) 1. to justify oneself; to vindicate oneself; о. незна́нием (*leg.*) to plead ignorance. 2. to be justified; моё предсказа́ние ~а́лось my prediction has come true; расхо́ды ~а́лись the expense was worth it.

опра́вдыва|ть, ю, *impf. of* оправда́ть.

опра́вдыва|ться, юсь, *impf.* 1. *impf. of* оправда́ться. 2. to try to justify oneself, try to vindicate oneself.

опра́в|ить, лю, ишь, *pf.* (*of* ~ля́ть) 1. to put in order, set right, adjust (*dress, coiffure, etc.*). 2. to set, mount.

опра́в|иться, люсь, ишься, *pf.* (*of* ~ля́ться) 1. to put (one's dress, *etc.*) in order. 2. (от) to recover (from). 3. (*coll.*) to urinate.

опра́вк|а, и, *f.* 1. (*tech.*) mandrel, chuck; (riveting) drift. 2. setting, mounting.

оправля́|ть(ся), ю(сь), *impf. of* опра́вить(ся).

опра́стыва|ть(ся), ю(сь), *impf. of* опроста́ть(ся).

опра́шива|ть, ю, *impf. of* опроси́ть.

определе́ни|е, я, *n.* 1. definition; (*chem., phys., etc.*) determination. 2. (*leg.*) decision. 3. (*gram.*) attribute.

определё́н|ный (~ен, ~на), *adj.* 1. definite; determinate; fixed; о. за́работок fixed wage; о. член (*gram.*) definite article. 2. certain; в ~ных слу́чаях in certain cases.

определи́м|ый (~, ~а), *adj.* definable.

определи́тел|ь, я, *m.* (*math.*) determinant.

определ|и́ть, ю́, и́шь, *pf.* (*of* ~я́ть) 1. to define; to determine; to fix, appoint; о. боле́знь to diagnose a disease; о. ме́ру наказа́ния to fix a punishment; о. расстоя́ние to judge a distance. 2. (*obs.*) to appoint; to allot, assign; о. на слу́жбу to appoint to a post; о. пай to assign a share.

определ|и́ться, ю́сь, и́шься, *pf.* (*of* ~я́ться) 1. to be formed; to take shape; to be determined. 2. (*obs.*) to find a place; о. на слу́жбу to take service. 3. (*aeron.*) to obtain a fix, find one's position. 4. *pass. of* ~и́ть.

определ|я́ть(ся), я́ю(сь), *impf. of* ~и́ть(ся).

опресне́ни|е, я, *n.* desalination.

опресн|ённый, *p.p.p. of* ~и́ть; ~ённая вода́ distilled water.

опресни́тел|ь, я, *m.* (water-)distiller.

опресн|и́ть, ю́, и́шь, *pf.* (*of* ~я́ть) to distil (*salt water*); to desalinate.

опре́снок|и, ов, *sing.* ~, ~а, *m.* unleavened bread.

опресн|я́ть, я́ю, *impf. of* ~и́ть.

опри́чник, а, *m.* (*hist.*) oprichnik (*member of oprichnina*).

опри́чнин|а, ы, *f.* (*hist.*) oprichnina (*special administrative élite established in Russia by Ivan IV, also the territory assigned to this élite*).

опри́чн|ый, *adj. of* ~ина.

опри́чь, *prep.+g.* (*obs.*) except, save.

опро́б|овать, ую, *pf.* 1. (*tech.*) to test. 2. to sample, try.

опроверг|а́ть, а́ю, *impf. of* ~нуть.

опрове́рг|нуть, ну, нешь, *past* ~, ~ла, *pf.* (*of* ~а́ть) to refute, disprove.

опроверже́ни|е, я, *n.* refutation; disproof; denial.

опрокидн|о́й, *adj.* грузови́к с ~ым я́щиком tip-up lorry.

опроки́дыватель|ь, я, *m.* (*tech.*) tipper, tipple, dumper.

опроки́дыва|ть(ся), ю(сь), *impf. of* опроки́нуть(ся).

опроки́|нуть, ну, нешь, *pf.* (*of* ~дывать) 1. to overturn; to topple over. 2. (*mil.*) to overthrow; to overrun. 3. (*sl.*) to knock back (= *drink off*). 4. (*fig.*) to upset; to refute.

опроки́|нуться, нусь, нешься, *pf.* (*of* ~дываться) 1. to overturn; to topple over, tip over; to capsize. 2. *pass. of* ~нуть.

опроме́тчив|ый (~, ~а), *adj.* precipitate, rash, hasty, unconsidered.

о́прометью, *adv.* headlong.

опро́с, а, *m.* (*mil., etc.*) interrogation; (*leg., etc.*) (cross-)examination; referendum.

опро|си́ть, шу́, ~сишь, *pf.* (*of* опра́шивать) to interrogate; to (cross-)examine.

опро́с|ный, *adj. of* ~; о. лист questionnaire; (*leg.*) interrogatory.

опроста́|ть, ю, *pf.* (*of* опра́стывать) (*coll.*) to empty; to remove the contents (of).

опроста́|ться, юсь, *pf.* (*of* опра́стываться) (*coll.*) 1. to become empty. 2. *pass. of* ~ть. 3. to defecate.

опро|сти́ться, щу́сь, сти́шься, *pf.* (*of* ~ща́ться) to adopt the 'simple life'.

опростоволо́|ситься, шусь, сишься, *pf.* (*coll.*) to make a gaffe, blunder.

опротест|ова́ть, у́ю, *pf.* (*of* ~о́вывать) 1. о. ве́ксель (*fin.*) to protest a bill. 2. (*leg.*) to appeal (against).

опротесто́выва|ть, ю, *impf. of* опротестова́ть.

опроти́ве|ть, ю, *pf.* to become loathsome, become repulsive.

опроща́|ться, юсь, *impf. of* опрости́ться.

опроще́ни|е, я, *n.* adoption of the 'simple life'.

опры́ск|ать, аю, *pf.* (*of* ~ивать) to sprinkle; to spray.

опры́ск|аться, аюсь, *pf.* (*of* ~иваться) 1. to sprinkle oneself; to spray oneself. 2. *pass. of* ~ать.

опры́скиватель|ь, я, *m.* (*agric.*) sprinkler; sprayer.

опры́скива|ть(ся), ю(сь), *impf. of* опры́скать(ся).

опрыща́ве|ть, ю, *pf. of* прыща́веть.

опря́тность|ь, и, *f.* neatness, tidiness.

опря́т|ный (~ен, ~на), *adj.* neat, tidy.

опта́нт, а, *m.* (*leg.*) person having right of option (*of citizenship*).

оптати́вный, *adj.* (*gram.*) optative.

опта́ци|я, и, *f.* (*leg.*) option (*of citizenship*); пра́во ~и right of option (*of citizenship of one or other of two states*).

о́птик, а, *m.* optician.

о́птик|а, и, *f.* 1. optics. 2. (*collect.*) optical instruments.

оптима́льный, *adj.* optimum, optimal.

оптими́зм, а, *m.* optimism.

оптими́ст, а, *m.* optimist.

оптимисти́ческий, *adj.* optimistic.

о́птимум, а, *m.* (*biol., etc.*) optimum.

опти́р|овать, ую, *impf. and pf.* (*leg.*) to opt (for).

опти́ческ|ий, *adj.* optic, optical; о. обма́н optical illusion; ~ая ось optic axis; ~ое стекло́ optical glass, lens.

оптови́к, а́, *m.* wholesale dealer, wholesaler.

опто́вый, *adj.* wholesale.

о́птом, *adv.* wholesale; о. и в ро́зницу wholesale and retail.

опубликова́ни|е, я, *n.* publication; о. зако́на promulgation of a law.

опублик|ова́ть, у́ю, *pf.* (*of* публикова́ть *and* ~о́вывать) to publish; о. зако́н to promulgate a law.

опублико́выва|ть, ю, *impf. of* опубликова́ть.

о́пус, а, *m.* (*mus.*) opus.

опуска́|ть(ся), ю(сь), *impf. of* опусти́ть(ся).

опускн|о́й, *adj.* movable; ~а́я дверь trapdoor.

опусте́лый, *adj.* deserted.

опусте́|ть, ю, *pf. of* пусте́ть.

опу|сти́ть, щу́, ~стишь, *pf.* (*of* ~ска́ть) 1. to lower; to let down; о. што́ры to draw the blinds; о. глаза́ to look down; о. го́лову (*fig.*) to hang one's head; о. ру́ки (*fig.*) to lose heart. 2. to turn down (*collar, etc.*). 3. to omit.

опу|сти́ться, щу́сь, ~стишься, *pf.* (*of* ~ска́ться) 1. to lower oneself. 2. to sink; to fall; to go down; о. в кре́сло to sink into a chair; о. на коле́ни to go down on one's knees; у него́ ру́ки ~сти́лись (*fig.*) he has lost heart. 3. (*fig.*) to sink; to let oneself go, go to pieces.

опустош|а́ть, а́ю, *impf. of* ~и́ть.

опустоше́ни|е, я, *n.* devastation, ruin.

опустоши́тел|ьный (~ен, ~ьна), *adj.* devastating.

опустош|и́ть, у́, и́шь, *pf.* (*of* ~а́ть) to devastate, lay waste, ravage.

опу́т|ать, аю, *pf.* (*of* ~ывать) to enmesh, entangle (*also fig.*); (*fig.*) to ensnare.

опу́тыва|ть, ю, *impf. of* опутать.

опух|а́ть, а́ю, *impf. of* ~нуть.

опу́хлый, *adj.* (*coll.*) swollen.

опу́х|нуть, ну, нешь, *past* ~, ~ла, *pf.* (*of* ~а́ть) to swell (up).

о́пухол|ь, и, *f.* swelling; (*med.*) tumour.

опуш|а́ть, а́ю, *impf. of* ~и́ть.

опуш|и́ть, у́, и́шь, *pf.* (*of* ~а́ть) 1. (ме́хом) to edge, trim (with fur). 2. (*of hoar-frost or snow*) to powder; to cover; бо́роду у него́ ~и́ло сне́гом his beard was powdered with snow.

опу́шк|а¹, и, *f.* edging, trimming.

опу́шк|а², и, *f.* edge (*of a forest, of a wood*).

опуще́ни|е, я, *n.* 1. lowering; letting down; о. ма́тки (*med.*) prolapsus (prolapse) of the uterus. 2. omission.

опу́|щенный, *p.p.p. of* ~сти́ть; как в во́ду о. (*fig.*) crestfallen, downcast.

опыле́ни|е, я, *n.* (*bot.*) pollination; перекре́стное о. cross-pollination.

опы́ливател|ь, я, *m.* (*agric.*) insecticide dust sprayer.

опы́лива|ть, ю, *impf. of* опыли́ть 2.

опыли́тел|ь, я, *m.* 1. (*bot.*) pollinator. 2. (*agric.*) = опы́ливатель.

опыл|и́ть, ю́, и́шь, *pf.* 1. (*impf.* ~я́ть) (*bot.*) to pollinate. 2. (*impf.* ~ивать) (*agric.*) to spray with insecticide dust.

опыл|я́ть, я́ю, *impf. of* ~и́ть 1.

о́пыт, а, *m.* 1. experience; на ~е, по ~у by experience. 2. experiment; test, trial; attempt.

о́пытник, а, *m.* experimenter.

о́пытност|ь, и, *f.* experience.

о́пыт|ный, *adj.* 1. (~ен, ~на) experienced. 2. experimental; узна́ть ~ным путём to learn by means of experiment; ~ная ста́нция experimental station.

опьяне́лый, *adj.* intoxicated.

опьяне́ни|е, я, *n.* intoxication.

опьяне́|ть, ю, *pf. of* пьяне́ть.

опьян|и́ть, ю́, и́шь, *pf.* (*of* пьяни́ть and ~я́ть) to intoxicate, make drunk; успе́х ~и́л его́ success has gone to his head.

опьян|я́ть, я́ю, *impf. of* ~и́ть.

опьяня́|ющий, *pres. part. act. of* ~ть and *adj.* intoxicating.

опя́ть, *adv.* again.

опя́ть-таки, *adv.* (*coll.*) 1. (and) what is more; он холостя́к, о.-т. бога́тый челове́к he is a bachelor, and what is more he is a rich man. 2. but again; however; я посту-

ча́л ещё раз, о.-т. ничего́ не послы́шалось I knocked again, but again there was nothing to be heard.

ора́в|а, ы, *f.* (*coll.*) crowd, horde.

ора́кул, а, *m.* oracle.

ора́л|о, а, *n.* (*obs. and dial.*) plough.

ора́нжевый, *adj.* orange (*colour*).

оранжере́|йный, *adj. of* ~я; ~йное расте́ние hothouse plant (*also fig.*).

оранжере́|я, и, *f.* hothouse, greenhouse, conservatory.

ора́р|ь, я́, *m.* (*eccl.*) stole.

ора́тор, а, *m.* orator, (public) speaker.

орато́ри|я, и, *f.* 1. (*mus.*) oratorio. 2. (*eccl.*) oratory.

ора́тор|ский, *adj. of* ~; oratorical; ~ское иску́сство oratory.

ора́торств|овать, ую, *impf.* to orate, harangue, speechify.

ор|а́ть¹, у́, ёшь, *impf.* (*coll.*) to bawl, yell.

ор|а́ть², у́, ёшь and ю́, ~ешь, *impf.* (*dial.*) to plough.

орби́т|а, ы, *f.* 1. (*astron. and fig.*) orbit; вы́вести на ~у to put into orbit; о. влия́ния sphere of influence. 2. (*anat.*) eye-socket; глаза́ у него́ вы́шли из ~ (*fig.*) his eyes leaped from their sockets.

орг-, *abbr. of* организацио́нный.

орга́зм, а, *m.* (*physiol.*) orgasm.

о́рган, а, *m.* (*biol., polit., etc.*) organ; исполни́тельный о. agency; ~ы вла́сти organs of government; ~ы (*sc.* госбезопа́сности) (*coll., iron.*) 'the organs' (*of State security*); ~ы печа́ти organs of the press; ~ы ре́чи speech organs.

орга́н, а, *m.* (*mus.*) organ.

организа́тор, а, *m.* organizer.

организа́тор|ский, *adj. of* ~; о. тала́нт talent for organization.

организа́|цио́нный, *adj. of* ~ция.

организа́ци|я, и, *f.* (*in var. senses*) organization; О. Объединённых На́ций United Nations Organization.

органи́зм, а, *m.* organism.

организо́ванност|ь, и, *f.* (good) organization; orderliness.

организо́ванный, *p.p.p. of* организова́ть and *adj.* organized; orderly, disciplined.

организ|ова́ть, у́ю, *impf. and pf.* (*pf. also* с~) to organize.

организ|ова́ться, у́юсь, *impf. and pf.* 1. to be organized. 2. to organize (*intrans.*).

орга́ник|а, и, *f.* (*coll.*) organic chemistry.

органи́ст, а, *m.* organist.

органи́ческ|ий, *adj.* organic; ~ая хи́мия organic chemistry; ~ое це́лое integral whole.

органи́ч|ный (~ен, ~на), *adj.* organic.

орга́н|ный, *adj. of* ~; о. конце́рт concerto for organ.

органогра́фи|я, и, *f.* (*biol.*) organography.

органотерапи́|я, и, *f.* organotherapy.

орга́нчик, а, *m.* **1.** *dim. of* орга́н. **2.** musical--box.

о́рги|я, и, *f.* orgy.

орд|а́, ы́, *pl.* ~ы, ~, ~ам, *f.* (*hist. and fig.*) horde; Золота́я о. the Golden Horde.

орда́ли|я, и, *f.* (*hist.*) ordeal.

о́рден¹, а, *pl.* ~а́, ~о́в, *m.* order; decoration; о. Подвя́зки Order of the Garter; о. Почётного Легио́на Legion of Honour; о. Трудово́го Кра́сного Зна́мени Order of the Red Banner of Labour.

о́рден², а, *pl.* ~ы, ~ов, *m.* **1.** order; иезуи́тский о. Society of Jesus; о. тамплие́ров Order of Knights Templars. **2.** = о́рдер².

орденоно́с|ец, ца, *m.* holder of an order *or* decoration.

орденоно́сный, *adj.* decorated with an order.

о́рден|ский, *adj. of* ~; ~ская ле́нта ribbon.

о́рдер¹, а, *pl.* ~а́, ~о́в, *m.* order, warrant; (*leg.*) writ; о. на о́быск search warrant; о. на поку́пку coupon; о. на кварти́ру authorization to an apartment.

о́рдер², а, *pl.* ~ы, ~ов, *m.* (*archit.*) order; кори́нфский о. Corinthian order.

ордина́р, а, *m.* normal level (*of water in reservoir, etc.*).

ордина́р|ец, ца, *m.* (*mil.*) orderly; batman.

ордина́р|ный (~ен, ~на), *adj.* **1.** ordinary. **2.** (*obs.*) on the staff, permanent.

ордина́т|а, ы, *f.* (*math.*) ordinate.

ордина́тор, а, *m.* house-surgeon.

ординату́р|а, ы, *f.* **1.** appointment as house--surgeon; permanent appointment (*of professor*). **2.** clinical studies (*in medical school*).

орд|ы́нский, *adj. of* ~а́.

ор|ёл, ла́, *m.* eagle; о. и́ли ре́шка heads or tails.

орео́л, а, *m.* halo, aureole.

оре́х, а, *m.* **1.** nut; америка́нский о. Brazil nut; гре́цкий о. walnut; коко́совый о. coco-nut; лесно́й о., обыкнове́нный о. hazel-nut; муска́тный о. nutmeg; бу́дет тебе́ на ~и!; ему́ доста́лось (попа́ло) на ~и! (*fig.*) you'll catch it!; he's caught it!; разде́лать (отде́лать) кого́-н. под о. (*coll.*) to give it someone hot. **2.** nut-tree. **3.** (*wood*) walnut; шкаф из ~а walnut cup-board.

оре́ховк|а, и, *f.* (*orn.*) nutcracker.

оре́х|овый, *adj. of* ~; ~овое де́рево nut-tree; (*wood*) walnut; ~овая скорлупа́ nutshell; ~ового цве́та nut-brown; о. шокола́д nut chocolate.

орехотво́рк|а, и, *f.* (*zool.*) gall-fly.

оре́ш|ек, ка, *m.* *dim. of* оре́х; черни́льный о. nut-gall.

оре́шник, а, *m.* **1.** (hazel) nut-tree. **2.** hazel--grove.

оригина́л, а, *m.* **1.** original. **2.** eccentric (person).

оригина́льнича|ть, ю, *impf.* (*of* с~) (*coll.*) to put on an act, try to be clever.

оригина́л|ьный (~ен, ~ьна), *adj.* (*in var. senses*) original.

ориентали́ст, а, *m.* orientalist.

ориента́льный, *adj.* oriental.

ориента́ци|я, и, *f.* **1.** (на+*a.*) orientation (toward); direction of attention (toward). **2.** (*fig.*) (в+*p.*) understanding (of), grasp (of); у него́ хоро́шая о. в ю́жно-амери-ка́нских дела́х he has a firm grasp of South American affairs; у меня́ нет ~и в торго́вом де́ле I have no head for business.

ориенти́р, а, *m.* (*mil.*) reference point; guiding line; (есте́ственный) о. landmark.

ориенти́рова|нный, *p.p.p. of* ~ть *and adj.* knowledgeable.

ориенти́р|овать, ую, *impf. and pf.* **1.** to orient, orientate; (в+*p.*) to enlighten (concerning); он не ~ова́л меня́ в экономи́ческом положе́нии he did not put me in the picture about the economic position. **2.** (на+*a.*) to direct (toward).

ориенти́р|оваться, уюсь, *impf. and pf.* **1.** to orient oneself; to find one's bearings (*also fig.*); я пло́хо ~уюсь I have a poor sense of direction; она́ ско́ро ~ова́лась в но́вой обстано́вке (*fig.*) she soon found her feet in her new surroundings. **2.** (на+*a.*) to head (for), make (for); (*fig.*) to direct one's attention (to, toward); о. на рабо́чих слу́шателей to cater for a working-class audience.

ориентиро́вк|а, и, *f.* = ориента́ция.

ориентиро́вочно, *adv.* tentatively; approximately; гру́бо о. as a rough guide.

ориентиро́воч|ный, *adj.* **1.** position-finding. **2.** (~ен, ~на) tentative; rough, approximate.

орке́стр, а, *m.* **1.** orchestra; band. **2.** orchestra-pit.

оркестра́нт, а, *m.* member of an orchestra *or* band.

оркестрио́н, а, *m.* (*obs.*) orchestrion.

оркестр|ова́ть, у́ю, *impf. and pf.* to orchestrate.

оркестро́вк|а, и, *f.* orchestration.

оркестро́вый, *adj.* **1.** *adj. of* орке́стр. **2.** orchestral.

орла́н, а, *m.* sea eagle.

орл|ёнок, ёнка, *pl.* ~я́та, ~я́т, *m.* eaglet.

орле́ц, а́, *m.* **1.** (*min.*) rhodonite. **2.** (*eccl.*) round hassock (*with woven design of eagle; placed under feet of officiating bishop*).

орли́ный, *adj. of* орёл; aquiline; о. взгляд eagle eye; о. нос aquiline nose.

орли́ц|а, ы, *f.* female eagle.

орло́вский, *adj.* (of) Oryol.

орля́нк|а, и, *f.* pitch-and-toss.

орна́мент, а, *m.* ornament; ornamental design.

орнамента́льный, *adj.* ornamental.

орнамента́ци|я, и, *f.* ornamentation.

орнаменти́р|овать, ую, *impf. and pf.* to ornament.

орнито́лог, а, *m.* ornithologist.

орнитологи́ческий, *adj.* ornithological.

орнитоло́ги|я, и, *f.* ornithology.

орнитопте́р, а, *m.* (*aeron.*) ornithopter.

оробе́лый, *adj.* timid; frightened.

оробе́|ть, ю, *pf. of* робе́ть.

ороговé|ть, ет, *pf.* to become horny.

орографи́ческий, *adj.* orographic(al).

орогра́фи|я, и, *f.* orography.

ороси́тельный, *adj.* irrigation; irrigating; о. кана́л irrigation canal.

оро|си́ть, шу́, си́шь, *pf.* (*of* ~ша́ть) to irrigate; to water; о. слеза́ми to wash with tears.

оро|ша́ть, ша́ю, *impf. of* ~си́ть.

ороше́ни|е, я, *n.* irrigation; поля́ ~я sewage-farm.

ортодо́кс, а, *m.* orthodox person, conformist.

ортодокса́л|ьный (~ен, ~ьна), *adj.* orthodox.

ортодо́кси|я, и, *f.* orthodoxy.

ортопеди́ст, а, *m.* orthopaedic specialist.

ортопеди́ческий, *adj.* orthopaedic.

ортопе́ди|я, и, *f.* orthopaedy.

ору́ди|е, я, *n.* 1. instrument; implement; tool (*also fig.*); сельскохозя́йственные ~я agricultural implements. 2. piece of ordnance; gun; зени́тное о. anti-aircraft gun; полево́е о. field-gun; самохо́дное о. self-propelled gun.

оруд|и́йный, *adj. of* ~ие 2; о. ого́нь gun-fire; о. око́п gun-entrenchment; ~и́йная пальба́ cannonade; о. расчёт gun crew.

ору́д|овать, ую, *impf.* (*coll.*; +*i.*) 1. to handle. 2. (*fig., pejor.*) to be active; он там всем ~ует he bosses the whole show.

оруже́йник, а, *m.* gunsmith, armourer.

оруж|е́йный, *adj. of* ~ие; ~е́йная пала́та armoury; о. ма́стер armourer.

оружено́с|ец, ца, *m.* armour-bearer, sword-bearer; (*fig.*) henchman.

ору́жи|е, я, *n.* arm(s); weapons; огнестре́льное о. fire-arm(s); стрелко́вое о. small arms; холо́дное о. cold steel; род ~я arm of the service; к ~ю! to arms!; бра́ться за о. to take up arms; подня́ть о. (на+*a.*) to take up arms (against); положи́ть о., сложи́ть о. to lay down one's arms; бить кого́-н. его́ же ~ем (*fig.*) to beat someone at his own game.

орфографи́ческ|ий, *adj.* orthographic(al); ~ая оши́бка spelling mistake.

орфогра́фи|я, и, *f.* orthography, spelling.

орфоэпи́ческий, *adj.* о. слова́рь pronouncing dictionary.

орфоэ́пи|я, и, *f.* (rules of) correct pronunciation.

орхиде́|я, и, *f.* (*bot.*) orchid.

оря́син|а, ы, *f.* (*coll.*) rod, pole.

ос|а́, ы́, *pl.* ~ы, *f.* wasp.

оса́д|а, ы, *f.* siege; снять ~у to raise a siege.

оса|ди́ть[1], жу́, ди́шь, *pf.* (*of* ~жда́ть) to besiege, lay siege to; to beleaguer; о. вопро́сами to ply with questions; о. про́сьбами to bombard with requests.

оса|ди́ть[2], жу́, ~ди́шь, *pf.* (*of* ~жда́ть) (*chem.*) to precipitate.

оса|ди́ть[3], жу́, ~ди́шь, *pf.* (*of* ~жи́вать) 1. to check, halt; to force back; о. ло́шадь to rein in a horse. 2. (*fig.*) о. кого́-н. to put someone in his place, take someone down a peg.

оса́дк|а, и, *f.* 1. set, settling (*of soil, etc.*). 2. (*naut.*) draught; су́дно с небольшо́й ~ой vessel of shallow draught.

оса́д|ный, *adj. of* ~а; ~ная артилле́рия siege artillery; ~ная война́ siege war(fare); ~ное положе́ние state of siege.

оса́д|ок, ка, *m.* 1. (*pl.*) precipitation. 2. sediment, deposition. 3. (*fig.*) after-taste; у меня́ от э́того разгово́ра был неприя́тный о. the conversation left an unpleasant taste in my mouth.

оса́д|очный, *adj. of* ~ок; ~очные поро́ды (*geol.*) sedimentary rocks; о. чан (*chem.*) precipitation tank; ~очная маши́на (*tech.*) upsetting machine.

осажда́|ть, ю, *impf. of* осади́ть[1, 2].

осажда́|ться, юсь, *impf.* 1. (*of atmospheric precipitations*) to fall. 2. (*chem.*) to be precipitated; to fall out.

осаждённый, *p.p.p. of* осади́ть[1, 2].

оса́женный, *p.p.p. of* осади́ть[3].

оса́жива|ть, ю, *impf. of* осади́ть[3].

оса́нист|ый (~, ~а), *adj.* portly.

оса́нк|а, и, *f.* carriage, bearing.

оса́нн|а, ы, *f.* hosanna; восклица́ть, петь ~у кому́-н. (*fig.*) to sing someone's praises.

осатане́лый, *adj.* (*coll.*) possessed; diabolical, demoniacal.

осва́ива|ть(ся), ю(сь), ю(сь), *impf. of* осво́ить(ся).

осведоми́тел|ь, я, *m.* informant.

осведоми́тельн|ый, *adj.* 1. informative. 2. (*giving, conveying*) information; ~ая рабо́та information work, publicity work.

осве́дом|ить, лю, ишь, *pf.* (*of* ~ля́ть) to inform.

осве́дом|иться, люсь, ишься, *pf.* (*of* ~ля́ться) (о+*p.*) to inquire (about).

осведомле́ни|е, я, *n.* informing, notification.

осведомлённост|ь, и, *f.* knowledge, (possession of) information; у него́ хоро́шая о. в исла́ндских са́гах he is very knowledgeable about the Icelandic sagas.

осведомлённый, *p.p.p. of* осве́домить *and adj.* (в+*p.*) well-informed (about), knowledgeable (about); versed (in), conversant (with).

осведом|ля́ть(ся), ля́ю(сь), *impf. of* ~ить(ся).

освеж|а́ть, а́ю, *impf. of* ~и́ть.

освеж|ева́ть, у́ю, *pf. of* свежева́ть.

освежи́тельный, *adj.* refreshing.

освеж|и́ть, у́, и́шь, *pf.* (*of* ~а́ть) **1.** to refresh; to freshen; о. ко́мнату to give a room an airing. **2.** (*fig.*) to refresh, revive; о. свои́ зна́ния to refresh one's knowledge; о. соста́в предприя́тия (*coll.*) to introduce fresh blood into the staff of an enterprise.

освети́тел|ь, я, *m.* **1.** person in charge of lighting effects. **2.** condenser (*of microscope*).

освети́тельн|ый, *adj.* lighting, illuminating; ~ая бо́мба candle bomb; ~ая раке́та (*aeron.*) flare; ~ая сеть lighting system; о. снаря́д star shell.

осве|ти́ть, щу́, ти́шь, *pf.* (*of* ~ща́ть) to light up; to illuminate, illumine; (*fig.*) to throw light on; to cover, report (*in the press*).

осве|ти́ться, щу́сь, ти́шься, *pf.* (*of* ~ща́ться) **1.** to light up; to brighten; её лицо́ ~ти́лось улы́бкой (*fig.*) a smile lit up her face. **2.** *pass. of* ~ти́ть.

осветли́тел|ь, я, *m.* (*chem.*) clarifying agent.

осветл|и́ть, ю́, и́шь, *pf.* (*of* ~я́ть) (*chem.*) to clarify.

осветл|я́ть, я́ю, *impf. of* ~и́ть.

освеща́|ть(ся), ю(сь), *impf. of* освети́ть(ся).

освеще́ни|е, я, *n.* light, lighting, illumination; иску́сственное о. artificial light(ing); электри́ческое о. electric light.

освещённост|ь, и, f. (*degree of, area of*) illumination.

осве|щённый, *p.p.p. of* ~ти́ть; о. звёздами star-lit; о. луно́й moonlit; о. свеча́ми candle-lit.

освиде́тельств|овать, ую, *pf. of* свиде́тельствовать 3.

освинц|ева́ть, у́ю, *pf.* to lead, lead-plate.

осви|ста́ть, щу́, ~щешь, *pf.* (*of* ~стывать) to hiss (off), catcall; о. актёра to hiss an actor off the stage.

освистыва|ть, ю, *impf. of* освиста́ть.

освободи́тел|ь, я, *m.* liberator.

освободи́тельн|ый, *adj.* liberation, emancipation; ~ая война́ war of liberation.

освобо|ди́ть, жу́, ди́шь, *pf.* (*of* ~жда́ть) **1.** to free, liberate; to release, set free; to emancipate; о. аресто́ванного to discharge a prisoner; о. от вое́нной слу́жбы to exempt from military service. **2.** to dismiss; о. от до́лжности to relieve of one's post. **3.** to vacate; to clear, empty.

освобо|ди́ться, жу́сь, ди́шься, *pf.* (*of* ~жда́ться) **1.** (от) to free oneself (of, from); to become free. **2.** *pass. of* ~ди́ть.

освобожда́|ть(ся), ю(сь), *impf. of* освободи́ть(ся).

освобожде́ни|е, я, *n.* **1.** liberation; release; emancipation; discharge. **2.** dismissal. **3.** vacation (*of premises, etc.*).

освобо|ждённый, *p.p.p. of* ~ди́ть; о. от нало́га tax-free, exempt from tax.

освое́ни|е, я, *n.* assimilation, mastery, familiarization; о. но́вой те́хники learning to handle new machinery; о. кра́йнего се́вера the opening up of the Far North.

осво́|ить, ю, ишь, *pf.* (*of* осва́ивать) **1.** to assimilate, master; to cope (with); to become familiar (with). **2.** (*bot.*) to acclimatize.

осво́|иться, юсь, ишься, *pf.* (*of* осва́иваться) **1.** (c+*i.*) to familiarize oneself (with). **2.** to feel at home; о. в но́вой среде́ to get the feel of new surroundings.

освя|ти́ть, щу́, ти́шь, *pf.* **1.** (*impf.* святи́ть) (*eccl.*) to consecrate; to bless, sanctify. **2.** (*impf.* ~ща́ть) (*fig.*) to sanctify, hallow.

освяща́|ть, ю, *impf. of* освяти́ть.

освя|щённый, *p.p.p. of* ~ти́ть; обы́чай, о. века́ми time-honoured custom.

ос|ево́й, *adj. of* ~ь; axial; о. кана́л (*electr.*) axial duct; ~ева́я ша́йба axle tree.

оседа́ни|е, я, *n.* **1.** settling, subsidence. **2.** settlement.

оседа́|ть, ю, *impf. of* осе́сть.

осёдл|анный, *p.p.p. of* ~а́ть.

оседла́|ть, ю, pf. **1.** (*impf.* седла́ть) to saddle. **2.** (*mil.; fig.*) to establish a grip (upon); о. доро́гу to get astride a road.

осе́длост|ь, и, f. settled (way of) life; черта́ ~и (*hist.*) the Pale of Settlement (*area to which Jews were confined in tsarist Russia*).

осе́длый, *adj.* settled (*as opp. to nomadic*).

осека́|ться, юсь, *impf. of* осе́чься.

ос|ёл, ла́, *m.* donkey; ass (*also fig. of a human being*).

оселе́д|ец, ца, *m.* top-knot (*hist.; long forelock left by Ukrainians on shaven head*).

осел|о́к, ка́, *m.* **1.** touchstone (*also fig.*). **2.** whetstone; oil-stone; hone.

осемене́ни|е, я, *n.* (*artificial*) insemination.

осемен|и́ть, ю́, и́шь, *pf.* (*of* ~я́ть) to inseminate (*by artificial means*).

осемен|я́ть, я́ю, *impf. of* ~и́ть.

осен|и́ть, ю́, и́шь, *pf.* (*of* ~я́ть) **1.** to overshadow; (*fig.*) to shield; о. кресто́м to make the sign of the cross (over). **2.** (*fig.*) to dawn upon, strike; его́ ~и́ла мысль it dawned upon him; меня́ внеза́пно ~и́ло (*impers.*) it suddenly occurred to me.

осен|и́ться, ю́сь, и́шься, *pf.* (*of* ~я́ться) *pass. of* ~и́ть; о. кресто́м to cross oneself.

осе́нний, *adj. of* о́сень; autumnal.

о́сен|ь, и, *f.* autumn.

о́сенью, *adv.* in autumn.

осен|я́ть(ся), я́ю(сь), *impf. of* ~и́ть(ся).

осер|ди́ться, жу́сь, ~дишься, *pf.* (на + *a.*; *coll.*) to become angry (with).

осерча́|ть, ю, *pf. of* серча́ть.

ос|е́сть, я́ду, я́дешь, *past* ~е́л, ~е́ла, *pf.* (*of* ~еда́ть) **1.** to settle, subside; to sink; to form a sediment. **2.** (*of human beings*) to settle.

осети́н, а, *g. pl.* о., *m.* Ossetian, Ossete.

осети́н|ка, ки, *f. of* ~.

осети́нский, *adj.* Ossetian.

осётр, á, *m.* sturgeon.

осетри́н|а, ы, *f.* (flesh of) sturgeon.

осетро́вый, *adj. of* осётр.

осе́чк|а, и, *f.* misfire; дать ~y to misfire (*also fig.*).

осе́|чься, ку́сь, чёшься, ку́тся, *past* ~кся, ~кла́сь, *pf.* (*of* ~ка́ться) (*coll.*) **1.** to misfire (*also fig.*). **2.** to stop short (*in speaking*).

оси́лива|ть, ю, *impf. of* оси́лить.

оси́л|ить, ю, ишь, *pf.* (*of* ~ивать) **1.** to overpower. **2.** (*coll.*) to master; to manage; о. гре́ческий алфави́т to master the Greek alphabet; я е́ле ~ил ещё оди́н стака́н I was hardly able to manage another glass.

оси́н|а, ы, *f.* asp(en).

оси́нник, а, *m.* aspen wood.

оси́н|овый, *adj. of* ~a; дрожа́ть как о. лист to tremble like an aspen leaf.

ос|и́ный, *adj. of* ~á; ~и́ное гнездо́ (*fig.*) hornets' nest; потрево́жить ~и́ное гнездо́ to bring a hornets' nest about one's ears; ~и́ная та́лия wasp waist.

оси́плый, *adj.* hoarse, husky.

оси́п|нуть, ну, нешь, *past* ~, ~ла, *pf.* to go hoarse.

осироте́лый, *adj.* orphaned.

осироте́|ть, ю, *pf.* to become an orphan, be orphaned.

оска́блива|ть, ю, *impf. of* оскобли́ть.

оска́л, а, *m.* bared teeth; grin.

оска́лива|ть(ся), ю(сь), *impf. of* оска́лить(ся).

оска́л|ить, ю, ишь, *pf.* (*of* ска́лить *and* ~ивать) о. зу́бы to bare one's teeth.

оска́л|иться, юсь, ишься, *pf.* (*of* ска́литься *and* ~иваться) to bare one's teeth.

оскальпи́р|овать, ую, *pf. of* скальпи́ровать.

осканда́л|ить(ся), ю(сь), ишь(ся), *pf. of* сканда́лить(ся).

оскверне́ни|е, я, *n.* defilement; profanation.

оскверн|и́ть, ю́, и́шь, *pf.* (*of* ~я́ть) to defile; to profane.

оскверн|и́ться, ю́сь, и́шься, *pf.* (*of* ~я́ться) **1.** to defile oneself. **2.** *pass. of* ~и́ть.

оскверн|я́ть(ся), я́ю(сь), *impf. of* ~и́ть(ся).

оскла́б|иться, люсь, ишься, *pf.* to grin.

оскобл|и́ть, ю́, ~и́шь, *pf.* (*of* оска́бливать) to scrape (off).

оско́л|ок, ка, *m.* splinter, sliver; fragment.

оско́ло|чный, *adj. of* ~к; ~чная бо́мба fragmentation bomb, anti-personnel bomb.

оско́мин|а, ы, *f.* bitter taste (in the mouth); наби́ть ~y to set the teeth on edge (*also fig.*).

оско́мист|ый (~, ~а), *adj.* (*coll.*) sour, bitter.

оскоп|и́ть, лю́, и́шь, *pf.* (*of* ~ля́ть) to castrate.

оскопля́|ть, ю, *impf. of* оскопи́ть.

оскорби́тельност|ь, и, *f.* abusiveness.

оскорби́тел|ьный (~ен, ~ьна), *adj.* insulting, abusive.

оскорб|и́ть, лю́, и́шь, *pf.* (*of* ~ля́ть) to insult, offend.

оскорб|и́ться, лю́сь, и́шься, *pf.* (*of* ~ля́ться) to take offence; to be offended, be hurt.

оскорбле́ни|е, я, *n.* insult; о. де́йствием (*leg.*) assault and battery; о. сло́вом contumely; переноси́ть ~я to bear insults.

оскорб|лённый, *p.p.p. of* ~и́ть; ~лённая неви́нность outraged innocence.

оскорбля́|ть, ю, *impf. of* оскорби́ть.

оскоро́м|иться, люсь, ишься, *pf. of* скоро́миться.

оскрёб|ки, ков, *sing.* ~ок, ~ка, *m.* (*coll.*) scrapings.

оскудева́|ть, ю, *impf. of* оскуде́ть.

оскуде́лый, *adj.* scarce, scanty.

оскуде́ни|е, я, *n.* scarcity; impoverishment.

оскуде́|ть, ю, *pf.* (*of* скуде́ть *and* ~ва́ть) to grow scarce.

ослабева́|ть, ю, *impf. of* ослабе́ть.

ослабе́лый, *adj.* weakened, enfeebled.

ослабе́|ть, ю, *pf.* (*of* слабе́ть *and* ~ва́ть) to weaken, become weak; to slacken; to abate.

ослаби́тел|ь, я, *m.* (*phot.*) clearing agent.

осла́б|ить, лю, ишь, *pf.* (*of* ~ля́ть) **1.** to weaken. **2.** to slacken, relax; to loosen; о. внима́ние to relax one's attention; о. нажи́м to slacken pressure; о. по́яс to loosen a belt.

ослабле́ни|е, я, *n.* weakening; slackening, relaxation; о. напряже́ния slackening of tension.

ослабля́|ть, ю, *impf. of* осла́бить.

осла́б|нуть, ну, нешь, *past* ~, ~ла, *pf.* = ~е́ть.

осла́в|ить, лю, ишь, *pf.* (*of* ~ля́ть) (*coll.*) to defame, decry; to give a bad name.

осла́в|иться, люсь, ишься, *pf.* (*of* ~ля́ться) (*coll.*) to get a bad name.

ославля́|ть(ся), ю(сь), *impf. of* осла́вить(ся).

осл|ёнок, ёнка, *pl.* ~я́та, *m.* foal (*of ass*).

ослепи́тел|ьный (~ен, ~ьна), *adj.* blinding, dazzling.

ослеп|и́ть, лю́, и́шь, *pf.* (*of* ~ля́ть) to blind, dazzle (*also fig.*).

ослепле́ни|е, я, *n.* 1. blinding, dazzling. 2. (*fig.*) blindness; де́йствовать в ~и to act blindly.

ослепля́|ть, ю, *impf. of* ослепи́ть.

ослеп|ну́ть, ну, нешь, *past* ~, ~ла, *pf. of* сле́пнуть.

осли́злый, *adj.* slimy.

осли́з|нуть, нет, *past* ~, ~ла, *pf.* to become slimy.

осли́ный, *adj. of* осёл ass's; (*fig.*) asinine.

осли́ц|а, ы, *f.* she-ass.

осложне́ни|е, я, *n.* complication.

осложн|и́ть, ю́, и́шь, *pf.* (*of* ~я́ть) to complicate.

осложн|и́ться, ю́сь, и́шься, *pf.* (*of* ~я́ться) to become complicated.

осложн|я́ть(ся), я́ю(сь), *impf. of* ~и́ть(ся).

ослуша́ни|е, я, *n.* disobedience.

ослу́ш|аться, аюсь, *pf.* (*of* ~иваться) to disobey.

ослу́шива|ться, юсь, *impf. of* ослу́шаться.

ослу́шник, а, *m.* (*obs.*) disobedient person.

ослы́ш|аться, усь, ишься, *pf.* to mishear, not hear aright.

ослы́шк|а, и, *f.* mishearing, mistake of hearing.

осма́н, а, *m.* Osmanli Turk, Ottoman.

осма́нский, *adj.* Osmanli, Ottoman.

осма́трива|ть(ся), ю(сь), *impf. of* осмотре́ть(ся).

осме́ива|ть, ю, *impf. of* осмея́ть.

осмеле́|ть, ю, *pf. of* смеле́ть.

осме́лива|ться, юсь, *impf. of* осме́литься.

осме́л|иться, юсь, ишься, *pf.* (*of* ~иваться) (+*inf.*) to dare; to take the liberty (of); ~юсь доложи́ть... (*obs. polite formula*) I beg to report ....

осме|я́ть, ю́, ёшь, *pf.* (*of* ~ивать) to mock, ridicule.

о́сми|й, я, *m.* (*chem.*) osmium.

осмо́л, а, *m.* tar-impregnated wood.

осмол|и́ть, ю́, и́шь, *pf. of* смоли́ть.

о́смос, а, *m.* (*phys.*) osmosis.

осмоти́ческий, *adj.* (*phys.*) osmotic.

осмо́тр, а, *m.* examination, inspection; медици́нский о. medical (examination).

осмотр|е́ть, ю́, ~ишь, *pf.* (*of* осма́тривать) to examine, inspect; to look round, look over.

осмотр|е́ться, ю́сь, ~ишься, *pf.* (*of* осма́триваться) 1. to look round. 2. (*fig.*) to take one's bearings, see how the land lies. 3. *pass. of* ~е́ть.

осмотри́тельност|ь, и, *f.* circumspection.

осмотри́тел|ьный (~ен, ~ьна), *adj.* circumspect.

осмо́трщик, а, *m.* inspector.

осмы́сл|енный, *p.p.p. of* ~ить *and adj.* intelligent, sensible.

осмы́слива|ть, ю, *impf. of* осмы́слить.

осмы́сл|ить, ю, ишь, *pf.* (*of* ~ивать *and* ~я́ть) to interpret, give a meaning to; to comprehend.

осмысл|я́ть, я́ю, *impf.* = ~ивать.

осна|сти́ть, щу́, сти́шь, *pf.* (*of* ~ща́ть) (*naut.*) to rig; (*fig.*) to fit out, equip.

осна́стк|а, и, *f.* (*naut.*) rigging.

оснаща́|ть, ю, *impf. of* оснасти́ть.

оснаще́ни|е, я, *n.* 1. rigging; fitting out. 2. equipment.

оснеж|ённый, *p.p.p. of* ~и́ть *and adj.* snow-covered.

оснеж|и́ть, у́, и́шь, *pf.* (*poet.*) to cover with snow.

осно́в|а, ы, *f.* 1. base, basis, foundation; ~ы fundamentals; лежа́ть в ~е (+*g.*) to be the basis (of). 2. (*gram.*) stem. 3. (*text.*) warp.

основа́ни|е, я, *n.* 1. founding, foundation. 2. (*chem., math., etc.*) base; foundation (*of building*); о. горы́ foot of a mountain; (*fig.*) коло́нны (*archit.*) column socle; разру́шить до ~я to raze to the ground; изучи́ть до ~я (*fig.*) to study from A to Z. 3. (*fig.*) foundation, basis; ground, reason; на како́м ~и вы э́то утвержда́ете? on what grounds do you assert this?; на ра́вных ~ях with equal reason; не без ~я not without reason; име́ть о. предполага́ть to have reason to suppose; с по́лным ~ем with good reason.

основа́тел|ь, я, *m.* founder.

основа́тел|ьный (~ен, ~ьна), *adj.* 1. well-founded; just; ~ьная жа́лоба reasonable complaint. 2. solid, sound (*also fig.*); thorough; ~ьные до́воды sound arguments. 3. (*coll.*) bulky.

осн|ова́ть, ую́, уёшь, *pf.* (*of* ~о́вывать) 1. to found. 2. (на+*p.*) to base (on).

осн|ова́ться, ую́сь, уёшься, *pf.* (*of* ~о́вываться) 1. to settle. 2. *pass. of* ~ова́ть.

основ|но́й, *adj.* fundamental, basic; principal; ~о́е значе́ние primary meaning; о. капита́л (*fin.*) fixed capital; ~а́я мысль keynote; ~ы́е цвета́ primary colours; в ~о́м on the whole.

осно́в|ный[1], *adj. of* ~а 3; ~ные ни́ти warp threads.

осно́в|ный[2], *adj. of* ~а́ние 2 (*chem.*); ~ные со́ли basic salts.

основополо́жник, а, *m.* founder, initiator.

осно́выва|ть, ю, *impf. of* основа́ть.

осно́выва|ться, юсь, *impf.* 1. *impf. of* основа́ться. 2. *impf. only* (на+*p.*) to base oneself (on); to be based, founded (on); о. на дога́дках to base oneself on conjecture.

осо́б|а, ы, *f.* person, individual, personage; ва́жная о. (*iron.*) big noise, big-wig.

осо́бенно, *adv.* especially; particularly; unusually; не о. not very, not particularly; она́ сего́дня ве́чером о. болтли́ва

she is unusually talkative this evening; вы
лю́бите соба́к? — не о. do you like dogs?
Not very much.

осо́бенност|ь, и, *f.* peculiarity; **в ~и**
especially, in particular, (more) particularly.

осо́бенн|ый, *adj.* (e)special, particular,
peculiar; **ничего́ ~ого** nothing in particular; nothing much.

особня́к, á, *m.* private residence; detached
house.

особняко́м, *adv.* by oneself; **держа́ться о.**
to keep aloof.

осо́б|ый, *adj.* special; particular; peculiar;
оста́ться при ~ом мне́нии to reserve one's
own opinion; (*leg.*) to dissent; **удели́ть ~ое**
внима́ние (+*d.*) to give special attention
(to).

осо́б|ь, и, *f.* individual.

осо́бь, *indecl. adj. only in phrase* **о. статья́** (*coll.*)
quite another matter.

осове́лый, *adj.* (*coll.*) dazed, dreamy.

осове́|ть, ю, *pf.* (*coll.*) to fall into a dazed,
dreamy state.

осовре́менива|ть, ю, *impf. of* **осовреме́нить.**

осовреме́н|ить, ю, ишь, *pf.* (*of* **~ивать**) to
bring up to date; to modernize.

осоёд, а, *m.* (*orn.*) honey-buzzard.

осозна|ва́ть, ю́, ёшь, *impf. of* **~ть.**

осозна́|ть, ю, *pf.* (*of* **~ва́ть**) to realize.

осо́к|а, и, *f.* (*bot.*) sedge.

осоко́р|ь, я, *m.* (*bot.*) black poplar.

осолове́лый, *adj.* (*coll.*) = **осове́лый.**

осолове́|ть, ю, ешь, *pf. of* **солове́ть.**

óсп|а, ы, *f.* **1.** smallpox; **ветряна́я о.**
chicken-pox; **коро́вья о.** cow-pox; **чёрная**
о. smallpox. **2.** (*coll.*) pock-marks; vac-
cination marks; **лицо́ в ~е** pock-marked
face.

оспа́рива|ть, ю, *impf.* **1.** *impf. of* **оспо́рить.**
2. *impf. only* to contend (for); **он ~ет**
зва́ние чемпио́на ми́ра he is contending
for the title of world champion.

óсп|енный, *adj. of* **~a;** variolar, variolic,
variolous; **о. знак** pock-mark.

óспин|а, ы, *f.* pock-mark.

оспоприва́ни|е, я, *n.* vaccination.

оспо́р|ить, ю, ишь, *pf.* (*of* **оспа́ривать**) to
dispute, question; **о. завеща́ние** to dispute
a will.

осрам|и́ть(ся), лю́(сь), и́шь(ся), *pf. of*
срами́ть(ся).

ост¹, а, *m.* (*naut.*) east.

ОСТ², а, *m. abbr. of* **общесою́зный станда́рт.**

оста|ва́ться, ю́сь, ёшься, *impf. of* **оста́ться.**

оста́в|ить, лю, ишь, *pf.* (*of* **~ля́ть**) **1.** to
leave; to abandon, give up; **о. в поко́е** to
leave alone, let alone; **о. на второ́й год**
(*in schools*) to keep in the same form, not
move up; **~ь(те)!** stop that!, lay off! **2.** to

reserve; to keep; **о. за собо́й пра́во** to reserve the right.

оставля́|ть, ю, *impf. of* **оста́вить; ~ет жела́ть**
мно́гого (*or* **лу́чшего**) it leaves much to be
desired.

остальн|о́й, *adj.* the rest (of); **в ~о́м** in other
respects; *as noun* **~ы́е** the others; **~о́е** the
rest; **всё ~о́е** everything else.

остана́влива|ть(ся), ю(сь), *impf. of* **остано-**
ви́ть(ся).

оста́нк|и, ов, *no sing.* remains.

остано́в, а, *m.* (*tech.*) stop, stopper, ratchet-
-gear.

останов|и́ть, лю́, ~ишь, *pf.* (*of* **остана́вли-**
вать) **1.** to stop. **2.** to stop short, restrain.
3. (**на**+*p.*) to direct (to), concentrate (on);
о. взгляд to rest one's gaze (on); **о. вни-**
ма́ние to concentrate one's attention (on).

останов|и́ться, лю́сь, ~ишься, *pf.* (*of*
остана́вливаться) **1.** to stop; to come to a
stop, come to a halt; **ни пе́ред чем не о.**
(*fig.*) to stop at nothing. **2.** to stay, put up,
(*coll.*) stop; **о. у знако́мых** to stay with
friends. **3.** (**на**+*p.*) (*fig.*) to dwell (on) (*in*
a speech, lecture, etc.); to settle (on), rest (on);
взор ма́льчика ~и́лся на но́вой игру́шке
the boy's gaze rested on the new toy.

остано́вк|а, и, *f.* **1.** stop; stoppage; **о. за**
ва́ми you are holding us up; **о. за ви́зами**
there is a hold-up over the visas. **2.** ('*bus,*
tram) stop; **коне́чная о.** terminus; **мне на́до**
прое́хать ещё одну́ ~у I have to go one
stop further.

остано́в|очный, *adj. of* **~ка; о. пункт** stop,
stopping place.

оста́т|ок, ка, *m.* **1.** (*in var. senses*) remainder;
rest; residue; remnant (*of material*); *pl.* remains; leavings, leftovers; **распрода́жа**
~ков clearance sale. **2.** (*chem.*) residuum.
3. (*fin., comm.*) rest, balance.

оста́то|чный, *adj. of* **~к;** (*chem., tech.*) re-
sidual.

оста́|ться, нусь, нешься, *pf.* (*of* **~ва́ться**)
to remain; to stay; to be left (over); **о. в**
барыша́х to gain, be up; **о. в долгу́** to be
in debt; **о. в живы́х** to survive, come
through; **о. на́ ночь** to stay the night; **о.**
при своём мне́нии to remain of the same
opinion; **о. на второ́й год в том же**
кла́ссе to remain in the same form a
second year; **за ним ~лось пять фу́нтов** he
owes five pounds; **по́сле него́ ~лись жена́**
и тро́е дете́й he left a wife and three children; **от обе́да ничего́ не ~лось** there is
nothing left over from dinner; *impers.* **~ётся,**
~лось (+*d.*) it remains (remained), it is
(was) necessary; **нам не ~лось ничего́**
друго́го, как согласи́ться we had no choice
but to consent; **~лось то́лько заплати́ть** it
remained only to pay.

остеклене|ть, ю, *pf. of* стекленеть.

остекл|и́ть, ю́, и́шь, *pf.* (*of* ~я́ть) to glaze.

остекл|я́ть, я́ю, *impf. of* ~и́ть.

остео́лог, а, *m.* osteologist.

остеологи́ческий, *adj.* osteological.

остеоло́ги|я, и, *f.* osteology.

остеомиэли́т, а, *m.* (*med.*) osteomyelitis.

остепен|и́ть, ю́, и́шь, *pf.* (*of* ~я́ть) to make staid; to calm, mellow.

остепен|и́ться, ю́сь, и́шься, *pf.* (*of* ~я́ться) to settle down; to become staid, become respectable; to mellow.

остервене́лый, *adj.* frenzied.

остервене́ни|е, я, *n.* frenzy; рабо́тать с ~ем to work like a maniac.

остервене́|ть, ю, *pf. of* стервене́ть.

остервен|и́ться, ю́сь, и́шься, *pf.* to be frenzied.

остерега́|ть, ю, *impf. of* остере́чь.

остерега́|ться, ю́сь, *impf.* (*of* остере́чься) (+*g. or inf.*) to beware (of); to be careful (of); ~йтесь соба́ки! beware of the dog!; ~йся, что́бы не упа́сть! mind you don't fall!

остере́|чь, гу́, жёшь, гу́т, *past* ~г, ~гла́, *pf.* (*of* ~га́ть) to warn, caution.

остере́|чься, гу́сь, жёшься, гу́тся, *past* ~гся, ~гла́сь, *pf. of* ~га́ться.

остери́|я, и, *f.* inn, hostelry (*in Italy*).

остзе́|ец, йца, *m.* (*obs.*) Baltic German.

остзе́йский, *adj.* (*obs.*) Baltic (German); о. баро́н (*hist.*) 'Baltic baron'.

ости́ст|ый (~, ~а), *adj.* (*bot.*) awned, bearded, aristate.

ости́т, а, *m.* (*med.*) osteitis.

о́стов, а, *m.* 1. frame, framework (*also fig.*); shell; hull. 2. (*anat.*) skeleton.

осто́йчивост|ь, и, *f.* (*naut.*) stability.

осто́йчив|ый (~, ~а), *adj.* (*naut.*) stable.

остолбене́лый, *adj.* (*coll.*) dumbfounded.

остолбене́|ть, ю, *pf. of* столбене́ть.

остоло́п, а, *m.* (*coll.*) blockhead.

осторо́жно, *adv.* carefully; cautiously; guardedly; gingerly; о.! look out! mind out!; (*on package*) with care.

осторо́жност|ь, и, *f.* care; caution.

осторо́ж|ный (~ен, ~на), *adj.* careful; cautious; бу́дьте ~ны! take care! be careful!

осточерте́|ть, ю, *pf.* (+*d.*; *coll.*) to bore; to repel; мне э́то ~ло I am fed up with it.

остраки́зм, а, *m.* ostracism; подве́ргнуть ~y to ostracize.

остра́стк|а, и, *f.* (*coll.*) warning, caution; в ~y, для ~и as a warning.

острека́в|ить, лю, ишь, *pf. of* стрека́вить.

острига́|ть(ся), ю(сь), *impf. of* остри́чь(ся).

остри́|ё, я́, *n.* 1. point; spike; о. кли́на (*mil.*) spearhead of the attack. 2. (cutting) edge; о. кри́тики (*fig.*) the edge of a criticism.

остр|и́ть[1], ю́, и́шь, *impf.* to sharpen, whet.

остр|и́ть[2], ю́, и́шь, *impf.* (*of* с~) to be witty; to make witticisms, crack jokes; о. на чужо́й счёт to be witty at others' expense, score off others.

остри́|чь, гу́, жёшь, гу́т, *past* ~г, ~гла́, *pf.* (*of* стричь and ~га́ть) to cut; to clip.

остри́|чься, гу́сь, жёшься, гу́тся, *past* ~гся, ~гла́сь, *pf.* (*of* стри́чься and ~га́ться) to cut one's hair; to have one's hair cut.

о́стров, а, *pl.* ~а́, *m.* island; isle.

островитя́н|ин, ина, *pl.* ~е, ~, *m.* islander.

островно́й, *adj.* island; insular.

остров|о́к, ка́, *m.* islet; о. безопа́сности island (*in road, for pedestrians crossing*).

остро́г, а, *m.* 1. (*obs.*) gaol. 2. (*hist.*) stockaded town. 3. (*hist.*) stockade, palisade.

острог|а́, и́, *f.* fish-spear, harpoon.

острогла́з|ый (~, ~а), *adj.* (*coll.*) sharp-sighted, keen-eyed.

острогу́бц|ы, ев (*tech.*) cutting nippers.

остро́жник, а, *m.* (*obs.*) imprisoned criminal, convict.

остро́|жный, *adj. of* ~г.

остроконе́чный, *adj.* pointed.

остроли́ст, а, *m.* (*bot.*) holly.

остроно́с|ый (~, ~а), *adj.* sharp-nosed; (*fig.*) pointed, tapered.

остросло́в, а, *m.* wit.

остро́т|а, ы, *f.* witticism, joke; зла́я о. sarcasm; пло́ская о. stupid joke; то́нкая о. subtle crack.

острот|а́, ы́, *f.* sharpness; keenness; acuteness; pungency, poignancy.

остроуго́льник, а, *m.* (*math.*) acute-angled figure.

остроуго́ль|ный (~ен, ~ьна), *adj.* (*math.*) acute-angled.

остроу́ми|е, я, *n.* 1. wit; wittiness. 2. ingenuity.

остроу́м|ный (~ен, ~на), *adj.* witty.

о́стр|ый (~ and остёр, ~а́, ~о), *adj.* sharp (*also fig.*); pointed (*also fig.*); acute; keen; ~ое воспале́ние (*med.*) acute inflammation; ~ое замеча́ние pointed remark; о. за́пах acrid smell; ~ое зре́ние keen eyesight; о. интере́с (к) keen interest (in); о. недоста́ток acute shortage; ~ое положе́ние critical situation; о. со́ус piquant sauce; о. сыр strong cheese; о. у́гол (*math.*) acute angle; он остёр на язы́к (*coll.*) he has a sharp tongue.

остря́к, а́, *m.* wit.

осту|ди́ть, жу́, ~дишь, *pf.* (*of* студи́ть and ~жа́ть) to cool.

остужа́|ть, ю, *impf. of* остуди́ть.

оступ|а́ться, а́юсь, *impf. of* ~и́ться.

оступ|и́ться, лю́сь, ~ишься, *pf.* (*of* ~а́ться) to stumble.

остыва́|ть, ю, *impf. of* остыть.

осты́|ть, ну, нешь, *pf.* (*of* ~ва́ть) to get

cold; (*fig.*) to cool (down); у вас чай ~л your tea is cold.

ост|ь, и, *pl.* ~и, ~е́й, *f.* (*bot.*) awn, beard.

осу|ди́ть, жу́, ~ди́шь, *pf.* (*of* ~жда́ть) 1. to censure, condemn. 2. (*leg.*) to condemn, sentence; to convict.

осужда́|ть, ю, *impf. of* осуди́ть.

осужде́ни|е, я, *n.* 1. censure, condemnation. 2. (*leg.*) conviction.

осуждённ|ый, *p.p.p. of* осуди́ть *and adj.* condemned; convicted; *as noun* о., ~ого, *m.* convict, convicted person.

осу́н|уться, усь, ешься, *pf.* (*coll.*) (*of the face*) to grow thin, get pinched(-looking).

осуш|а́ть, а́ю, *impf. of* ~и́ть.

осуше́ни|е, я, *n.* drainage.

осуш|и́тельный, *adj. of* ~е́ние; о. кана́л drainage canal.

осуш|и́ть, у́, ~ишь, *pf.* (*of* ~а́ть) to drain; to dry; о. глаза́ to dry one's eyes; о. луга́ to drain meadows; о. слёзы кому́-н. to console someone; о. стака́н пи́ва to drain a glass of beer.

осуществи́м|ый (~, ~а), *adj.* practicable, realizable, feasible.

осуществ|и́ть, лю́, и́шь, *pf.* (*of* ~ля́ть) to realize, bring about; to accomplish, carry out; to implement.

осуществ|и́ться, и́тся, *pf.* (*of* ~ля́ться) 1. to be fulfilled, come true; её де́тская мечта́ ~и́лась her childhood dream has come true. 2. *pass. of* ~и́ть.

осуществле́ни|е, я, *n.* realization; accomplishment; implementation.

осуществля́|ть(ся), ю(сь), *impf. of* осуществи́ть.

осцилло́граф, а, *m.* (*phys.*) oscillograph.

осцилля́тор, а, *m.* (*phys.*) oscillator.

осчастли́в|ить, лю, ишь, *pf.* (*of* ~ливать) to make happy; to grace (*iron.*).

осчастли́влива|ть, ю, *impf. of* осчастли́вить.

осы́па|нный, *p.p.p. of* ~ть; о. звёздами star-studded, star-spangled.

осы́п|ать, лю, лешь, *pf.* (*of* ~а́ть) 1. (+*a. and i.*) to strew (with); to shower (on); (*fig.*) to heap (on); о. кого́-н. бра́нью to heap abuse on someone; о. поцелу́ями to smother with kisses; о. кого́-н. уда́рами to rain blows on someone. 2. to pull down, knock down (*a heap of sand, etc.*). 3. to shed (*foliage, etc.*).

осы́п|аться, люсь, лешься, *pf.* (*of* ~а́ться) to crumble; (*of leaves, etc.*) to fall.

осы́п|ать(ся), а́ю(сь), *impf. of* ~ать(ся).

о́сып|ь, и, *f.* scree.

ос|ь, и, *pl.* ~и, ~е́й, *f.* 1. axis; земна́я о. axis of the equator; име́ющий о́бщую о. coaxial. 2. axle; (*tech.*) spindle; pin.

осьмино́г, а, *m.* (*zool.*) octopus.

осяза́ем|ый (~, ~а), *adj.* tangible; palpable.

осяза́ни|е, я, *n.* touch; чу́вство ~я sense of touch.

осяза́тел|ьный (~ен, ~ьна), *adj.* 1. tactile, tactual; ~ьные о́рганы tactile organs. 2. (*fig.*) tangible, palpable, sensible; ~ьные результа́ты tangible results.

осяза́|ть, ю, *impf.* to feel.

от (ото) *prep.* +*g.* from; of; for; 1. (*indicates initial point, point of origin of action, prior of pair of termini, source, etc.*) от це́нтра го́рода from the centre of the town; отплы́ть от бе́рега to put out from the shore; от нача́ла до конца́ from beginning to end; от Пу́шкина до Маяко́вского from Pushkin to Mayakovsky; от девяти́ (часо́в) до пяти́ (часо́в) from nine (o'clock) to five (o'clock); де́ти в во́зрасте от пяти́ до десяти́ лет children from five to ten (years); це́ны от рубля́ и вы́ше prices from a rouble upward; бли́зко от го́рода near the town; на се́вер от Ленингра́да to the north of Leningrad; вре́мя от вре́мени from time to time; день ото дня from day to day; от всей души́ with all one's heart; от и́мени (+*g.*) on behalf (of); сло́во, произведённое от лати́нского a word derived from the Latin; узна́ть от дру́га to learn from a friend; я получи́л письмо́ от до́чери I have received a letter from my daughter; сын от пре́жнего бра́ка a son by a previous marriage; жеребёнок от А. и Б. a foal by A. out of B. 2. (*indicates cause or instrumentality*) вскри́кнуть от ра́дости to cry out for joy; дрожа́ть от стра́ха to tremble with fear; умере́ть от го́лода to die of hunger; глаза́, кра́сные от слёз eyes red with weeping. 3. (*indicates date of document*) ва́ше письмо́ от пе́рвого а́вгуста your letter of the first of August. 4. (*indicates use, purpose, or assignment*) ключ от две́ри door key; пу́говица от пиджака́ coat button; цепо́чка от часо́в watch-chain; рабо́чий от станка́ machine operative. 5. for; against; сре́дство от сенно́й лихора́дки remedy for hay-fever; миксту́ра от ка́шля cough mixture; защища́ть глаза́ от со́лнца to shield one's eyes from the sun; застрахова́ть от огня́ to insure against fire.

от- (*also* ото- *and* отъ-) *verbal prefix indicating* 1. completion of action *or* task assigned. 2. action *or* motion away from given point. 3. (*verbs in form reflexive*) action of negative character.

отав|а, ы, *f.* (*agric.*) after-grass, aftermath.

ота́плива|ть, ю, *impf. of* отопи́ть.

ота́р|а, ы, *f.* large flock (*of sheep*).

отба́в|ить, лю, ишь, *pf.* (*of* ~ля́ть) to pour off.

отбавля́|ть, ю, *impf. of* **отба́вить; хоть ~й** (*coll.*) more than enough.

отбараба́н|ить, ю, ишь, *pf.* (*coll.*) to rattle off.

отбега́|ть, ю, *impf. of* **отбежа́ть.**

отбе|жа́ть, гу́, жи́шь, гу́т, *pf.* (*of* ~га́ть) to run off.

отбел|ённый, *p.p.p. of* ~и́ть; **о. чугу́н** chilled cast iron.

отбе́лива|ть, ю, *impf. of* **отбели́ть.**

отбел|и́ть, ю́, ~ишь, *pf.* (*of* ~ива́ть) to bleach; (*tech.*) to blanch; to chill, refine.

отбе́лк|а, и, *f.* bleaching; (*tech.*) blanching; chilling, refining.

отбе́льный, *adj.* (*tech.*) blanching; chilling, refining.

отбива́|ть(ся), ю(сь), *impf. of* **отби́ть(ся).**

отби́вк|а, и, *f.* 1. marking out, delineation. 2. whetting, sharpening.

отбивн|о́й, *adj.* ~а́я котле́та (*cul.*) chop.

отбира́|ть, ю, *impf. of* **отобра́ть.**

отби́ти|е, я, *n.* repulse; repelling.

отби́|ть, отобью́, отобьёшь, *pf.* (*of* ~ва́ть) 1. to beat off, repulse, repel; **о. ата́ку** to beat off an attack; **о. мяч** (*sport*) to return a ball; **о. уда́р** to parry a blow. 2. to take (*by force*); to win over; (*coll.*) **о. у кого́-н.** to take off someone, do someone out of; **о. пле́нных** to liberate prisoners; **о. покупа́телей** (*fig.*) to win customers; **он ~л у това́рища его́ де́вушку** he has taken his friend's girl. 3. to remove, dispel; **о. у кого́-н. охо́ту к чему́-н.** to discourage someone from something, take away someone's inclination for something. 4. to break off, knock off; **о. но́сик у ча́йника** to knock the spout off a tea-pot. 5. to whet, sharpen. 6. **о. такт** to beat (out) time. 7. to knock up; to damage by blows, by knocks; **о. ру́ку нело́вким уда́ром** to hurt one's hand with a clumsy blow. 8. to mark out.

отби́|ться, отобью́сь, отобьёшься, *pf.* (*of* ~ва́ться) 1. (от) to defend oneself (against); to repulse, beat off. 2. to drop behind, straggle; **о. от ста́да** to stray from the herd; **о. от рук** (*coll.*) to get out of hand. 3. to break off. 4. *pass. of* ~ть.

отбла́гове|стить, щу, стишь, *pf. of* **благове́стить.**

отблагодар|и́ть, ю́, и́шь, *pf.* to show one's gratitude (to).

о́тблеск, а, *m.* reflection.

отбо́|й, я, *m.* 1. repulse; repelling; **о. мяча́** (*sport*) return; **~ю нет** (от; *coll.*) there is no getting rid (of). 2. (*mil.*) retreat; **о. возду́шной трево́ги** all-clear signal; **бить о.** to beat a retreat (*also fig.*); **труби́ть о.** to sound off. 3. ringing off (*on telephone*); **дать о.** to ring off.

отбо́йк|а, и, *f.* (*tech.*) breaking, cutting.

отбо́й|ный, *adj.* 1. *adj. of* ~ка; **о. молото́к** miner's pick; **пневмати́ческий о. молото́к** pneumatic drill (*for coal-cutting*). 2. *adj. of* ~ 3.

отбомб|и́ться, лю́сь, и́шься, *pf.* (*coll.*) to have dropped one's load (of bombs).

отбо́р, а, *m.* selection; **есте́ственный о.** (*biol.*) natural selection.

отбо́рн|ый, *adj.* choice, select(ed); picked; **~ые войска́** crack troops; **~ые выраже́ния** refined language; **~ая ру́гань** choice swear-words.

отбо́рочн|ый, *adj.* **~ая коми́ссия** selection board; **~ое соревнова́ние** (*sport*) knock-out competition.

отбо́рщик, а, *m.* 1. grader, sorter. 2. selector.

отбоя́рива|ться, юсь, *impf.* (*of* **отбоя́риться**) (*coll.*) to try to escape, get out of.

отбоя́р|иться, юсь, ишься, *pf.* (*of* ~иваться) (*coll.*; от) to escape (from), get rid (of), give the slip (to).

отбра́сыва|ть, ю, *impf. of* **отбро́сить.**

отбрива́|ть, ю, *impf. of* **отбри́ть.**

отбр|и́ть, е́ю, е́ешь, *pf.* (*of* ~ива́ть) (*coll.*) to rebuff, rebuke.

отбро́с|ы, ов, *sing.* ~, ~а, *m.* garbage, refuse; offal; **ведро́ для ~ов** dust-bin; **о. произво́дства** industrial waste; **о. о́бщества** (*fig.*) dregs of society.

отбро́|сить, шу, сишь, *pf.* (*of* **отбра́сывать**) 1. to throw off; to cast away; **о. тень** to cast a shadow. 2. (*mil.*) to throw back, thrust back, hurl back. 3. to give up, reject, discard; **о. мысль** to give up an idea.

отбукси́р|овать, ую, *pf.* to tow off.

отбыва́ни|е, я, *n.* serving; **о. сро́ка наказа́ния** serving of a sentence.

отбыва́|ть, ю, *impf. of* **отбы́ть.**

отбы́ти|е, я, *n.* departure.

от|бы́ть[1], бу́ду, бу́дешь, *past* ~бы́л, ~была́, ~бы́ло, *pf.* (*of* ~быва́ть) to depart, leave.

от|бы́ть[2], бу́ду, бу́дешь, *past* ~бы́л, ~была́, ~бы́ло, *pf.* (*of* ~быва́ть) to serve (a period of); **о. наказа́ние** to serve one's sentence, do time (*in prison*); **о. во́инскую пови́нность** to serve one's time in the army, do (one's) military service.

отва́г|а, и, *f.* courage, bravery.

отва́|дить, жу, дишь, *pf.* (*of* ~живать) 1. (+*a.* от) to break (of), make to stop; **о. кого́-н. от пья́нства** to break someone of drunkenness. 2. to scare away, drive off.

отва́жива|ть, ю, *impf. of* **отва́дить.**

отва́ж|иться, усь, ишься, *pf.* (+*inf.*) to dare, venture; to have the courage (to).

отва́ж|ный (~ен, ~на), *adj.* courageous, brave.

отва́л[1], а, *m.* до ~а (*coll.*) to satiety; **нае́сться до ~а** to stuff oneself.

отва́л², а, *m.* **1.** mould-board (*of a plough*). **2.** (*mining*) dump; slag-heap; bank, terrace (*of open-cast mine*).

отва́л³, а, *m.* (*naut.*) putting off, pushing off, casting off.

отва́лива|ть(ся), ю(сь), *impf. of* отвали́ть(ся).

отвал|и́ть, ю́, ~ишь, *pf.* (*of* ~ивать) **1.** to heave off; to push aside. **2.** (*naut.*) to put off, push off, cast off. **3.** (*coll.*) to fork out, stump up (*a sum of money*).

отвал|и́ться, ю́сь, ~ишься, *pf.* (*of* ~иваться) **1.** to fall off, slip. **2.** *pass. of* ~и́ть.

отва́л|ьный, *adj. of* ~²,³; *as noun* ~ьная, ~ьной, *f.* (*coll., obs.*) farewell party.

отва́р, а, *m.* broth; decoction; ячме́нный о. barley-water.

отва́рива|ть, ю, *impf. of* отвари́ть.

отвар|и́ть, ю́, ~ишь, *pf.* (*of* ~ивать) **1.** to boil (*cabbage, etc.*). **2.** (*tech.*) to unweld.

отварно́й, *adj.* (*cul.*) boiled.

отве́д|ать, аю, *pf.* (*of* ~ывать) (+*a. or g.*) to taste; to try.

отве́|дённый, *p.p.p. of* ~сти́.

отве́дыва|ть, ю, *impf. of* отве́дать.

отвез|ти́, у́, ёшь, *past* ~, ~ла́, *pf.* (*of* отвози́ть) to take (away); to cart away.

отверг|а́ть, а́ю, *impf. of* ~нуть.

отве́рг|нуть, ну, нешь, *past* ~, ~ла, *pf.* (*of* ~а́ть) to reject, turn down; to repudiate; to spurn.

отвердева́|ть, ю, *impf. of* отверде́ть.

отверде́лост|ь, и, *f.* hardening, callus.

отверде́лый, *adj.* hardened.

отверде́|ть, ю, *pf.* (*of* ~ва́ть) to harden.

отве́ржен|ец, ца, *m.* outcast.

отве́р|женный, *p.p.p.* (*obs.*) *of* ~гнуть *and adj.* outcast.

отверз|а́ть, а́ю, *impf.* (*of* ~ть) (*obs., poet.*) to open.

отве́рз|ть, у, ешь, *past* ~, ~ла, *pf. of* ~а́ть.

отвер|ну́ть, ну́, нёшь, *pf.* (*of* ~тывать) **1.** (*impf. also* отвора́чивать) to turn away, turn aside; о. лицо́ to turn one's face away; о. одея́ло to turn down a blanket. **2.** to turn on (*a tap, etc.*). **3.** to unscrew. **4.** (*coll.*) to screw off, twist off; он едва́ не ~ну́л мне ру́ку he almost twisted my arm off.

отвер|ну́ться, ну́сь, нёшься, *pf.* (*of* ~тываться) **1.** (*impf. also* отвора́чиваться) to turn away, turn aside; о. от кого́-н. (*fig.*) to turn one's back upon someone; to send someone to Coventry. **2.** (*of a tap, etc.*) to come on. **3.** to come unscrewed.

отве́рсти|е, я, *n.* **1.** opening, aperture, orifice; hole; входно́е о. inlet; выходно́е о. выпускно́е о. outlet; о. для опуска́ния моне́ты slot; о. решета́, о. си́та mesh. **2.** (*zool.*) foramen; заднепрохо́дное о. (*anat.*) anus.

отве́рст|ый (~, ~а), *adj.* (*obs., poet.*) open.

отвер|те́ть, чу́, ~тишь, *pf.* (*of* ~тывать) **1.** to unscrew. **2.** to screw off, twist off.

отверт|е́ться¹, ~ится, *pf.* (*of* ~ываться) to come unscrewed.

отвер|те́ться², чу́сь, ~тишься, *pf.* (*coll.*; от) to get off; to get out (of), wriggle out (of); нам удало́сь о. we managed to get out of it.

отвёртк|а, и, *f.* screwdriver.

отвёртыва|ть(ся), ю(сь), *impf. of* отверну́ть(ся) *and* отверте́ть(ся).

отве́с, а, *m.* **1.** (*tech.*) plumb, plummet; груз ~a bob. **2.** slope; по ~у plumb, perpendicularly.

отве́|сить, шу, сишь, *pf.* (*of* ~шивать) to weigh out; о. фунт са́хару to weigh out a pound of sugar; о. покло́н (+*d.*) to make a low bow (to); о. пощёчину (+*d.*) (*fig., coll.*) to deal someone a slap in the face.

отве́сно, *adv.* plumb; sheer.

отве́с|ный (~ен, ~на), *adj.* perpendicular; steep.

отве|сти́, ду́, дёшь, *past* ~л, ~ла́, *pf.* (*of* отводи́ть) **1.** to lead, take, conduct; о. ло́шадь в коню́шню to lead a horse to the stable. **2.** to draw aside, take aside; о. от собла́зна to lead out of temptation's way. **3.** to deflect; to draw off; о. войска́ (*mil.*) to draw off one's troops; о. во́ду (из) to drain; о. ду́шу to unburden one's heart; о. обвине́ние to justify oneself; о. уда́р to parry a blow; он не мог о. глаз от неё he could not take his eyes off her; о. глаза́ кому́-н. (*fig.*) to distract someone's attention, pull the wool over someone's eyes. **4.** to reject; (*leg.*) to challenge (*jurors, etc.*). **5.** to allot, assign.

отве́т, а, *m.* **1.** answer, reply, response; держа́ть о. to answer; в о. (на+*a.*) in reply (to), in response (to). **2.** (*obs.*) responsibility; быть в ~е (за+*a.*) to be answerable (for); призва́ть к ~у to call to account.

ответв|и́ть, лю́, и́шь, *pf.* (*of* ~ля́ть)· (*tech.*) to take off, tap, shunt.

ответв|и́ться, лю́сь, и́шься, *pf.* (*of* ~ля́ться) to branch off.

ответвле́ни|е, я, *n.* branch, offshoot (*also fig.*); branch pipe; (*electr.*) tap, shunt.

ответв|лённый, *p.p.p. of* ~и́ть; ~лённая цепь (*electr.*) branch circuit, derived circuit.

ответвля́|ть(ся), ю(сь), *impf. of* ответви́ть(ся).

отве́|тить, чу, тишь, *pf.* (*of* ~ча́ть) **1.** (на+*a.*) to answer, reply (to); о. на письмо́ to answer a letter; о. уро́к to repeat one's lesson. **2.** (на+*a.* +*i.*) to answer (with), return; о. на чьё-н. чу́вство to return someone's feelings. **3.** (за+*a.*) to answer (for), pay (for); вы ~ти́те за э́ти слова́! you will pay for these words!

отве́тн|ый, *adj.* given in answer, answering о. вы́стрел reply (to shots fired); ~ое чу́вство response, reciprocation of feelings.

отве́тственност|ь, и, *f.* responsibility; (*leg.*) amenability; снять о. с кого́-н. to relieve someone of responsibility; привле́чь к ~и (за + *a.*) to call to account, bring to book.

отве́тствен|ный (~, ~на), *adj.* **1.** responsible; о. реда́ктор editor-in-chief; о. рабо́тник executive. **2.** crucial; о. моме́нт crucial point.

отве́тств|овать, ую, *impf. and pf.* (*obs.*) to answer, reply.

отве́тчик, а, *m.* **1.** (*leg.*) defendant, respondent. **2.** (*coll.*) bearer of responsibility.

отвеча́|ть, ю, *impf.* **1.** *impf. of* отве́тить. **2.** (за + *a.*) to answer (for), be answerable (for). **3.** (+ *d.*) to answer (to), meet, be up (to); о. своему́ назначе́нию to answer the purpose, be up to the mark; о. тре́бованиям to meet requirements.

отве́шива|ть, ю, *impf. of* отве́сить.

отви́лива|ть, ю, *impf. of* отвильну́ть.

отвильн|у́ть, у́, ёшь, *pf.* (*of* отви́ливать) (*coll., pejor.*; от) to dodge.

отвин|ти́ть, чу́, ти́шь, *pf.* (*of* ~чивать) to unscrew.

отвин|ти́ться, чу́сь, ти́шься, *pf.* (*of* ~чиваться) to unscrew, come unscrewed.

отви́нчива|ть(ся), ю(сь), *impf. of* отвинти́ть(ся).

отвис|а́ть, а́ю, *impf.* (*of* ~нуть) to hang down, sag.

отви|се́ться, шу́сь, си́шься, *pf.* (*coll.*) дать пла́тью о. to hang out a dress so as to remove the creases.

отви́слы|й, *adj.* loose-hanging, baggy; с ~ми уша́ми lop-eared.

отви́с|нуть, ну, нешь, *past* ~, ~ла, *pf. of* ~а́ть.

отвлека́|ть(ся), ю(сь), *impf. of* отвле́чь(ся).

отвлека́|ющий, *pres. part. act. of* ~ть; ~ющее сре́дство (*med.*) counter-attraction.

отвлече́ни|е, я, *n.* **1.** abstraction. **2.** distraction; для ~я внима́ния to distract attention. **3.** (*med.*) counter-attraction.

отвлечён|ный (~, ~на), *adj.* abstract; ~ная величина́ abstract quantity; ~ное и́мя существи́тельное abstract noun.

отвле́|чь, ку́, чёшь, ку́т, *past* ~к, ~кла́, *pf.* (*of* ~ка́ть) **1.** to distract, divert; о. чьё-н. внима́ние to divert someone's attention. **2.** to abstract.

отвле́|чься, ку́сь, чёшься, ку́тся, *past* ~кся, ~кла́сь, *pf.* (*of* ~ка́ться) **1.** to be distracted; о. от те́мы to digress; его́ мы́сли ~кли́сь далеко́ his thoughts were far away. **2.** (от) to abstract oneself (from).

отво́д, а, *m.* **1.** leading, taking, conducting. **2.** taking aside; deflection; diversion; о. воды́ draining off of water; о. войск withdrawal of troops; для ~а глаз (*coll.*) as a blind. **3.** rejection; (*leg.*) challenge; дать о. кандида́ту to reject a candidate. **4.** allotment, allocation; полоса́ ~а designated strip of land (*for building of railway, highway, etc.*) **5.** (*tech.*) pipe-bend, elbow. **6.** (*electr.*) tap, tapping; о. тепла́ heat elimination.

отво|ди́ть, жу́, ~дишь, *impf. of* отвести́.

отво́дк|а, и, *f.* (*tech.*) **1.** branch pipe. **2.** belt shifter.

отво́дн|ый, *adj.* (*tech.*) branch; drain, outlet; о. кана́л drain; о. кран drain cock; ~ая труба́ branch pipe; outlet pipe, discharge pipe.

отво́д|ок, ка, *m.* (*hort.*) cutting, layer.

отво́д|ящий, *pres. part. act. of* ~и́ть *and adj.* о. (му́скул) (*anat.*) abductor; ~ящая труба́ (*tech.*) exhaust (pipe).

отво|ева́ть¹, юю, юешь, *pf.* (*of* ~ёвывать) (у) to win back (from), reconquer (from).

отво|ева́ть², юю, юешь, *pf.* (*coll.*) **1.** to fight, spend in fighting; мы де́сять лет ~ева́ли we have fought for ten years. **2.** to finish fighting, finish the war.

отвоёвыва|ть, ю, *impf. of* отвоева́ть.

отво|зи́ть, жу́, ~зишь, *impf. of* отвезти́.

отвола́кива|ть, ю, *impf. of* отволо́чь.

отволо́|чь, ку́, чёшь, ку́т, *past* ~к, ~кла́, *pf.* (*of* отвола́кивать) to drag away, drag aside.

отвора́чива|ть(ся), ю(сь), *impf. of* отверну́ть(ся) *and* отвороти́ть(ся).

отвор|и́ть, ю́, ~ишь, *pf.* (*of* ~я́ть) to open; о. кровь (*med.*; *obs.*) to let blood.

отвор|и́ться, ю́сь, ~и́шься, *pf.* (*of* ~я́ться) to open.

отворо́т, а, *m.* lapel, flap; top (*of boot*).

отворо|ти́ть, чу́, ~тишь, *pf.* (*of* отвора́чивать) to turn away, turn aside; о. взгляд to avert one's gaze.

отворо|ти́ться, чу́сь, ~ти́шься, *pf.* (*of* отвора́чиваться) to turn away, turn aside; о. от кого́-н. to look away from someone; (*fig.*) to turn one's back on someone, cut someone.

отвор|я́ть(ся), я́ю(сь), *impf. of* ~и́ть(ся).

отврати́тел|ьный (~ен, ~ьна), *adj.* repulsive, disgusting, loathsome; abominable.

отвра|ти́ть, щу́, ти́шь, *pf.* (*of* ~ща́ть) **1.** to avert, stave off. **2.** (*obs.*) (+ *a.* от) to deter (from), stay (from); о. кого́-н. от преда́тельства to deter someone from committing an act of treachery.

отвра́т|ный (~ен, ~на), *adj.* (*coll.*) = ~и́тельный.

отвраще́ни|е, я, *n.* aversion, disgust, repugnance; loathing; внуши́ть о. (+ *d.*) to disgust, fill with disgust, repel; питáть о. (к) to have an aversion (for), be repelled (by), loathe.

отвык|áть, áю, *impf. of* ~нуть.

отвы́к|нуть, ну, нешь, *past* ~, ~ла, *pf.* (*of* ~áть) (от *or* +*inf.*) to break oneself (of the habit of), give up; to get out of the habit of; to grow out (of); о. от курéния, о. кури́ть to give up smoking; о. от дурнóй привы́чки to break oneself of a bad habit.

отвя|зáть, жу́, ~жешь, *pf.* (*of* ~зывать) to untie, unfasten; to untether; (*naut.*) to unbend.

отвя|зáться, жу́сь, ~жешься, *pf.* (*of* ~зываться) **1.** to come untied, come loose. **2.** (*fig.*, *coll.*; от) to get rid (of), shake off, get shut (of). **3.** (*fig.*, *coll.*; от) to leave alone, leave in peace; stop nagging; ~жи́сь от меня́! leave me alone!

отвя́зыва|ть(ся), ю(сь), *impf. of* отвязáть(ся).

отгад|áть, áю, *pf.* (*of* ~ывать) to guess.

отгáдк|а, и, *f.* answer (*to a riddle*).

отгáдчик, а, *m.* (*coll.*) guesser, diviner.

отгáдыва|ть, ю, *impf. of* отгадáть.

отгибá|ть(ся), ю(сь), *impf. of* отогнýть(ся).

отглагóльный, *adj.* (*gram.*) verbal.

отглá|дить, жу, дишь, *pf.* (*of* ~живать) to iron (out).

отглáжива|ть, ю, *impf. of* отглáдить.

отглодá|ть, ю, *pf.* (*coll.*) to bite off.

отговáрива|ть(ся), ю(сь), *impf. of* отговори́ть(ся).

отговор|и́ть, ю́, и́шь, *pf.* (*of* отговáривать) (от *or* +*inf.*) to dissuade (from); я ~и́л егó éхать I have talked him out of going.

отговор|и́ться, ю́сь, и́шься, *pf.* (*of* отговáриваться) (+*i.*) to excuse oneself (on the ground of); to plead; о. нездорóвьем to plead ill-health.

отговóрк|а, и, *f.* excuse; pretext; пустáя о. lame excuse, hollow pretence.

отголóс|ок, ка, *m.* echo (*also fig.*).

отгóн¹, а, *m.* **1.** driving off. **2.** pasturing (*of cattle*).

отгóн², а, *m.* (*tech.*) distillation products.

отгóнк|а¹, *f.* driving off.

отгóнк|а², и, *f.* distillation.

отгоня́|ть, ю, *impf. of* отогнáть.

отгорáжива|ть(ся), ю(сь), *impf. of* отгороди́ть(ся).

отгоро|ди́ть, жу́, ~ди́шь, *pf.* (*of* отгорáживать) to fence off, partition off; о. ши́рмой to screen off.

отгоро|ди́ться, жу́сь, ~ди́шься, *pf.* (*of* отгорáживаться) to fence oneself off; (*fig.*, *coll.*; от) to shut oneself off (from), cut oneself off (from).

отго|сти́ть, щу́, сти́шь, *pf.* (*coll.*; у) to have been a guest (of), have stayed (with).

отграни́чива|ть, ю, *impf. of* отграни́чить.

отграни́ч|ить, у, ишь, *pf.* (*of* ~ивать) to delimit.

отгребá|ть, ю, *impf. of* отгрести́.

отгре|сти́¹, бу́, бёшь, *past* ~б, ~блá, *pf.* (*of* ~бáть) to rake away.

отгре|сти́², бу́, бёшь, *past* ~б, ~блá, *pf.* (*of* ~бáть) to row off.

отгружá|ть, ю, *impf. of* отгрузи́ть.

отгру|зи́ть, жу́, ~зи́шь, *pf.* (*of* ~жáть) to ship, dispatch.

отгрýзк|а¹, и, *f.* shipment, dispatching.

отгрýзк|а², и, *f.* unloading.

отгрыз|áть, áю, *impf. of* ~ть.

отгры́з|ть, у́, ёшь, *past* ~, ~ла, *pf.* (*of* ~áть) to bite off, gnaw off.

отгýлива|ть, ю, *impf. of* отгуля́ть 2.

отгул|я́ть, я́ю, *pf.* (*coll.*) **1.** to have spent, to have finished (*holidays*, *leave*, *etc.*); мы ~я́ли óтпуск our holidays are over. **2.** (*impf.* ~ивать) to take (time) off; о. день to take a day off.

отда|вáть¹(ся), ю́(сь), ёшь(ся), *impf. of* отдáть(ся).

отда|вáть², ёт, *impf.* (*coll.*; *impers.*+*i.*) to taste (of); to smell (of); (*fig.*) to smack (of) от негó ~ёт вóдкой he reeks of vodka; э́то ~ёт суевéрием this smacks of superstition.

отдав|и́ть, лю́, ~ишь, *pf.* to crush; о. комý-н. нóгу to tread on someone's foot.

отдалéни|е, я, *n.* **1.** removal; (*fig.*) estrangement. **2.** distance; держáть в ~и to keep at a distance.

отдалённост|ь, и, *f.* remoteness.

отдалён|ный (~, ~на), *adj.* distant, remote; о. рóдственник distant relative; ~ное схóдство remote likeness.

отдал|и́ть, ю́, и́шь, *pf.* (*of* ~я́ть) **1.** to remove; (*fig.*) to estrange, alienate. **2.** to postpone, put off.

отдал|и́ться, ю́сь, и́шься, *pf.* (*of* ~я́ться) **1.** (от) to move away (from) (*also fig.*). **2.** (*fig.*) to digress; о. от тéмы to stray from the subject. **3.** *pass. of* ~и́ть.

отдал|я́ть(ся), я́ю(сь), *impf. of* ~и́ть(ся).

отдáни|е, я, *n.* **1.** giving back, returning; о. чéсти (*mil.*) saluting. **2.** (*eccl.*) keeping, observing (*of a festival*).

отдáрива|ть(ся), ю(сь), *impf. of* отдари́ть(ся).

отдар|и́ть, ю́, и́шь, *pf.* (*of* ~ивать) (*coll.*) to give in return.

отдар|и́ться, ю́сь, и́шься, *pf.* (*of* ~ивáться) (*coll.*) to make a present in return, repay a gift.

отд|áть, áм, áшь, áст, ади́м, ади́те, адýт, *past* ~áл, ~алá, ~áло, *pf.* (*of* ~авáть) **1.** to give back, return; о. дóлжное комý-н. to

render someone his due; o. после́дний долг
(+d.) to pay the last honours; o. себе́ отчёт
(в+p.) to be aware (of), realize; не o. себе́
отчёта (в+p.) to fail to realize. **2.** to give
(up), devote; o. жизнь нау́ке to devote
one's life to learning. **3.** +a. and d. or +a.
за+a.) to give in marriage (to), give away.
4. (в+a., под+a.) to give, put, place
(= hand over for certain purpose); o. кни́гу в
переплёт to have a book bound, send a
book to be bound; o. ма́льчика в шко́лу to
send (put) a small boy to school; o. под
стра́жу to give into custody; o. под суд to
prosecute. **5.** (in combination with certain
nouns) to give; to make (or not requiring
separate translation); o. покло́н (obs.) to bow,
make a bow; o. прика́з (+d.) to issue an
order, give orders (to); o. распоряже́ние to
give instructions; o. честь (+d.) to salute.
6. (coll.) to sell, let have; он мне э́то ~ал за
бесце́нок he let me have it for a song.
7. (of a fire-arm) to kick. **8.** мне ~а́ло в спи́ну
(fig.; impers.) I felt a twinge in my back.
9. (naut.) to unbend; to let go; to cast off;
o. я́корь to cast anchor, let go the anchor;
o. концы́! let go!

отд|**а́ться, а́мся, а́шься, а́стся, ади́мся,
ади́тесь, аду́тся,** past **~а́лся, ~ала́сь,** pf.
(of ~ава́ться) **1.** (+d.) to give oneself up
(to); to devote oneself (to); (of a woman) to
give oneself (to). **2.** to resound; to rever-
berate; to ring (in one's ears).

отда́ч|**а, и,** f. **1.** return; payment, reimburse-
ment. **2.** o. внаём letting. **3.** (naut.) letting
go; casting off. **4.** (tech.) efficiency, performance; output. **5.** (mil.) recoil, kick.

отдежу́р|**ить, ю, ишь,** pf. **1.** to come off
duty. **2.** to spend on duty; o. во́семь часо́в
to have had eight hours on (duty).

отде́л, а, m. **1.** department; o. ка́дров personnel department. **2.** section, part (of
book, periodical, etc.).

отде́л|**ать, аю,** pf. (of ~ывать) **1.** to finish,
put the finishing touches (to); o. пла́тье
кружева́ми to trim a dress with lace. **2.**
(coll.) to give a dressing down.

отде́л|**аться, аюсь,** pf. (of ~ываться) **1.** (от)
to get rid (of), get shut (of). **2.** (+i.) to
escape (with), get off (with); сча́стливо
o. to have a lucky escape; o. цара́пиной to
get off with a scratch.

отделе́ни|**е, я,** n. **1.** separation. **2.** depart-
ment, branch; o. мили́ции local police-
station; o. свя́зи local post office. **3.** compartment, section; part (of concert programme,
etc.); o. шка́фа pigeon-hole; маши́нное o.
(naut.) engine-room. **4.** (mil.) section.

отдел|ённый[1], p.p.p. of ~и́ть.

отделён|ный[2], adj. of ~ие 3; o. команди́р
section commander.

отделе́нческий, adj. department(al), branch.

отдели́м|ый (~, ~а), adj. separable.

отдели́тел|ь, я, m. (tech., chem.) separator.

отдел|**и́ть, ю, ~ишь,** pf. (of ~я́ть) **1.** to
separate, part; to detach. **2.** to separate
off; o. перегоро́дкой to partition off. **3.**
(obs.) to cut off (with portion of estate, property,
etc.).

отдел|**и́ться, юсь, ~ишься,** pf. (of ~я́ться)
1. to separate, part; to get detached; to
come apart; to come off. **2.** (obs.) to set up
on one's own.

отде́лк|**а, и,** f. **1.** finishing; trimming. **2.**
finish, decoration.

отде́лыва|**ть(ся), ю(сь),** impf. of отде́лать-
(ся).

отде́льно, adv. separately.

отде́льност|**ь, и,** f. в ~и taken separately,
individually.

отде́льный, adj. **1.** separate, individual.
2. (mil.) independent.

отдел|**я́ть(ся), я́ю(сь),** impf. of ~и́ть(ся).

отдёргива|**ть, ю,** impf. of отдёрнуть.

отдёр|**нуть, ну, нешь,** pf. (of ~гивать) **1.** to
draw aside, pull aside; o. занаве́ску to
draw back the curtain. **2.** to jerk back,
withdraw.

отдира́|**ть, ю,** impf. of отодра́ть.

отдохнове́ни|**е, я,** n. (obs.) repose.

отдохн|**у́ть, у́, ёшь,** pf. (of отдыха́ть) to
rest; to have (take) a rest.

отдуба́|**сить, шу, сишь,** pf. of дуба́сить.

отдува́|**ть, ю,** impf. of отду́ть.

отдува́|**ться, юсь,** impf. **1.** to pant, blow,
puff. **2.** (fig., coll.; за+a.) to be answerable
(for), take the rap (for).

отду́м|**ать, аю,** pf. (of ~ывать) (coll.) to
change one's mind; мы ~али перее́хать
we have changed our mind about
moving.

отду́мыва|**ть, ю,** impf. of отду́мать.

отду́|**ть, ю, ешь,** pf. (of ~ва́ть). (**1.** coll.)
to blow away. **2.** to thrash soundly.

отду́шин|**а, ы,** f. air-hole, (air) vent; (fig.)
safety-valve.

отду́шник, а, m. air-hole, (air) vent.

о́тдых, а, m. rest; relaxation; holiday; день
~а a day of rest, rest day.

отдыха́|**ть, ю,** impf. (of отдохну́ть) to be
resting; to be on holiday.

отдыха́|**ющий,** pres. part. of ~ть; as noun o.
~ющего, m. and ~ющая, ~ющей, f. holiday-maker.

отдыш|**а́ться, у́сь, ~ишься,** pf. to recover
one's breath.

отёк, а, m. (med.) oedema; o. лёгких emphy
sema.

отека́|**ть, ю,** impf. of оте́чь.

отёл, а, m. calving.

отел|**и́ться, юсь, ~ишься,** pf. of тели́ться

отéл|ь, я, *m.* hotel.

отéль|**ный**, *adj. of* ~.

отепл|**и́ть**, ю́, и́шь, *pf.* (*of* ~**я́ть**) to protect against cold, make (*house, room, etc.*) proof against cold.

отепл|**я́ть**, я́ю, *impf. of* ~**и́ть**.

от|**éц**, ца́, *m.* father (*also fig. in var. senses*); нáши ~цы́ (*fig.*) our (fore)fathers; О. небéсный (*rel.*) the heavenly Father; о. семéйства (*coll.*) paterfamilias; ~цы́ цéркви (*eccl., hist.*) the Fathers of the Church.

отéческий, *adj.* fatherly, paternal.

отéчеств|**енный**, *adj. of* ~о; ~енная промы́шленность home industry; ~енная война́ (*hist.*) the Patriotic War (*designation of Russian operations against Napoleon in 1812*); Вели́кая ~енная война́ the Great Patriotic War (*official Soviet designation of war of 1941–1945 against Germany and her allies*).

отéчеств|**о**, а, *n.* native land, fatherland, home (country).

отé|**чь**, ку́, чёшь, ку́т, *past* ~к, ~кла́, *pf.* (*of* ~**ка́ть**) 1. to swell, become swollen. 2. (*of a candle*) to gutter.

от|**жáть**[1], отожму́, отожмёшь, *pf.* (*of* ~**жимáть**) 1. to wring out. 2. (*coll.*) to press hard.

от|**жáть**[2], отожну́, отожнёшь, *pf.* (*of* ~**жинáть**) to finish harvesting.

от|**жéчь**, отожгу́, отожжёшь, *past* ~жёг, ~ожгла́, *pf.* (*of* ~**жигáть**) (*tech.*) to anneal.

отживá|**ть**, ю, *impf. of* отжи́ть.

отживá|**ющий**, *pres. part. act. of* ~**ть** *and adj.* moribund.

отжи́|**вший**, *past part. act. of* ~**ть** *and adj.* obsolete; outmoded.

отжи́г, а, *m.* (*tech.*) 1. annealing. 2. (glass) fritting.

отжигá|**ть**, ю, *impf. of* отжéчь.

отжимá|**ть**, ю, *impf. of* отжáть[1].

отжинá|**ть**, ю, *impf. of* отжáть[2].

от|**жи́ть**, живу́, живёшь, *past* ~жи́л, ~жила́, ~жи́ло, *pf.* (*of* ~**живáть**) to become obsolete, become outmoded; о. свой век to have had one's day; to go out of fashion.

тзáвтрака|**ть**, ю, *pf.* (*coll.*) to have had breakfast.

тзвон|**и́ть**, ю́, и́шь, *pf.* 1. to stop ringing; to stop striking (*of a clock*); ~и́л и с коло́кольни доло́й (*coll.*) finished and done with. 2. (*fig., coll.*) to rattle off.

тзвук, а, *m.* echo (*also fig.*).

тзвуч|**áть**, и́т, *pf.* to be heard no more.

тзы́в, а, *m.* 1. opinion, judgement; похвáльный о. honourable mention. 2. reference; testimonial; дать хоро́ший о. о ком-н. to give someone a good reference. 3. review. 4. (*mil.*) reply (*to password*).

тзы́в, а, *m.* recall (*of diplomatic representative*).

отзывá|**ть**, ю, *impf.* 1. *impf. of* отозвáть. 2. (+*i.*) to taste (of); о. го́речью to have a bitter taste.

отзывá|**ться**, юсь, *impf.* 1. *impf. of* отозвáться. 2. (+*i.*) = ~ть.

отзы́вн|**о́й**, *adj.* ~ые гра́моты letters of recall.

отзы́вчив|**ый** (~, ~а), *adj.* responsive.

оти́т, а, *m.* (*med.*) otitis.

откáз, а, *m.* 1. refusal; denial; repudiation; (*leg.*) rejection, nonsuit; получи́ть о. to be refused, be turned down; не принимáть ~а to take no denial; до ~а to overflowing, to satiety; по́лный до ~а cram-full, full to capacity. 2. (от) renunciation (of), giving up (of). 3. (*tech.*) failure; де́йствовать без ~а to run smoothly. 4. (*mus.*) natural.

отка|**зáть**, жу́, ~жешь, *pf.* (*of* ~**зывáть**) 1. (+*d.* в+*p.*) to refuse, deny; она́ ~зáла ему́ в про́сьбе she refused his request; ему́ нельзя́ о. в талáнте there is no denying that he has talent; не ~жи́те в любéзности… be so kind as . . . . 2. (+*d.* от) to dismiss, discharge; о. от до́ма to forbid the house. 3. (*obs.*) to leave, bequeath. 4. (*tech.*) to fail, break down; (*coll.*) to conk out.

отка|**зáться**, жу́сь, ~жешься, *pf.* (*of* ~**зывáться**) 1. (от *or* +*inf.*) to refuse, decline; to turn down; от предложéния to turn down a proposal; о. от свое́й по́дписи to deny one's signature; о. от свои́х слов to retract one's words; о. от уплáты до́лга to repudiate a debt; о. служи́ть (*fig., coll.*) to be out of order; мои́ часы́ ~зáлись служи́ть my watch would not go; не ~жу́сь (*coll.*) I don't mind if I do; не ~зáлся бы (*coll.*) I wouldn't say no. 2. to renounce, give up; to relinquish, abdicate; о. от борьбы́ to give up the struggle.

откáзыва|**ть(ся)**, ю(сь), *impf.* (*of* откaзáть(ся)) ни в чём себé не о. to deny oneself nothing.

откáлыва|**ть(ся)**, ю(сь), *impf. of* отколо́ть(ся).

откáпыва|**ть**, ю, *impf. of* откопáть.

откáрмлива|**ть**, ю, *impf. of* откорми́ть.

откáт, а, *m.* (*mil.*) recoil.

отка|**ти́ть**, чу́, ~тишь, *pf.* (*of* ~**тывать**) 1. to roll away. 2. (*in coalmines, etc.*) to haul; to tram, truck.

отка|**ти́ться**, чу́сь, ~тишься, *pf.* (*of* ~**тывáться**) 1. to roll away. 2. (*mil.; fig., coll.*) to roll back, be forced back.

откáтк|**а**, и, *f.* (*in coal-mines, etc.*) haulage; trucking.

откáтчик, а, *m.* haulage-man.

откач|**áть**, áю, *pf.* (*of* ~**ивать**) 1. to pump out. 2. to resuscitate (*a person saved from drowning*).

откáчива|**ть**, ю, *impf. of* откачáть.

откачн|у́ть, у́, ёшь, *pf.* **1.** to swing to one side. **2.** (*fig., coll.; impers.*) его́ ~у́ло от бы́вших его́ собуты́льников he has drifted away from his former boon-companions.

откачн|у́ться, у́сь, ёшься, *pf.* (*coll.*) **1.** to swing to one side. **2.** (*of a person*) to reel back; to slump back. **3.** (*fig.;* от) to swing away (from), turn away (from).

отка́шл|ивать, иваю, *impf. of* ~януть.

отка́шл|иваться, иваюсь, *impf. of* ~яться.

отка́шл|януть, яну, янешь, *pf.* (*of* ~ивать) to hawk up.

отка́шл|яться, яюсь, *pf.* (*of* ~иваться) to clear one's throat.

отквит|а́ть, а́ю, *pf.* (*of* ~ывать) (*coll.;* +*d.*) to settle accounts (with), give as good as one gets.

отквитыва|ть, ю, *impf. of* отквита́ть.

откидно́й, *adj.* folding, collapsible.

отки́дыва|ть(ся), ю(сь), *impf. of* отки́нуть(ся).

отки́|нуть, ну, нешь, *pf.* (*of* ~дывать) **1.** to throw away; to cast away (*also fig.*). **2.** to turn back, fold back.

отки́|нуться, нусь, нешься, *pf.* (*of* ~дываться) **1.** to lean back; to recline, settle back. **2.** *pass. of* ~нуть.

откла́дыва|ть, ю, *impf. of* отложи́ть.

откла́нива|ться, юсь, *impf. of* откла́няться.

откла́н|яться, яюсь, *pf.* (*of* ~иваться) (*obs.*) to take one's leave.

откле́ива|ть(ся), ю(сь), *impf. of* откле́ить(ся).

откле́|ить, ю, ишь, *pf.* (*of* ~ивать) to unstick.

откле́|иться, ится, *pf.* (*of* ~иваться) **1.** to come unstuck. **2.** *pass. of* ~ить.

о́тклик, а, *m.* **1.** response; (*fig.*) comment. **2.** (*fig.*) echo; repercussion.

отклик|а́ться, а́юсь, *impf.* (*of* ~нуться) (на+*a.*) to answer, respond (to) (*also fig.*).

отклик|нуться, нусь, нешься, *pf. of* ~а́ться.

отклоне́ни|е, я, *n.* **1.** deviation; divergence; о. от те́мы digression. **2.** declining, refusal. **3.** (*phys.*) deflection, declination; error; diffraction; вероя́тное о. probable error; магни́тное о. deflection of the needle; у́гол ~я angle of deviation.

отклон|и́ть, ю́, ~ишь, *pf.* (*of* ~я́ть) **1.** to deflect. **2.** to decline; о. попра́вку to vote down an amendment; о. предложе́ние to decline an offer.

отклон|и́ться, ю́сь, ~ишься, *pf.* (*of* ~я́ться) **1.** to deviate; to diverge; to swerve; о. от те́мы to digress. **2.** *pass. of* ~и́ть.

отключ|а́ть, а́ю, *impf. of* ~и́ть.

отключ|ённый, *p.p.p. of* ~и́ть *and adj.* (*electr.*) dead; опера́ция проводи́мая на ~ённом се́рдце open-heart operation.

отключ|и́ть, у́, и́шь, *pf.* (*of* ~а́ть) (*electr.*) to

cut off, disconnect; о. телефо́нный аппара́т to cut off a telephone.

отковы́рива|ть, ю, *impf. of* отковыря́ть.

отковыр|я́ть, я́ю, *pf.* (*of* ~ивать) to pick off.

отказыр|я́ть[1], ю, *pf.* (*coll.;* +*d.*) to salute.

отказыр|я́ть[2], ю, *pf.* (*coll.;* cards) to play a trump in reply.

отко́л, а, *m.* (*fig.; polit., etc.*) split; splitting splintering, breaking away.

отко́л|е, *adv.* = ~ь.

отколо|ти́ть, чу́, ~тишь, *pf.* **1.** to knock off **2.** to beat up.

откол|о́ть, ю́, ~ешь, *pf.* (*of* отка́лывать **1.** to break off; to chop off. **2.** to unpin **3.** (*coll., pejor.*) о. глу́пость to get up to a stupid trick; о. словцо́ to make a wise crack.

откол|о́ться, ю́сь, ~ешься, *pf.* (*of* отка́лы ваться) **1.** to break off. **2.** to come un pinned, come undone. **3.** (*fig.*) to break away, cut oneself off.

отколуп|а́ть, а́ю, *pf.* (*of* ~ывать) to pick off.

отколу́пыва|ть, ю, *impf. of* отколупа́ть.

отко́ль, *adv.* (*obs.*) whence, where from.

откомандир|ова́ть, у́ю, *pf.* (*of* ~о́вывать **1.** to detach; to post (*to new duties or establish ment*). **2.** (за+*i.*) (*coll.*) to send (*to fetch*).

откомандиро́выва|ть, ю, *impf. of* откоман дирова́ть.

откопа́|ть, ю, *pf.* (*of* отка́пывать) **1.** to dig out; to exhume, disinter. **2.** (*fig., coll.*) t dig up, unearth.

отко́рм, а, *m.* fattening (up).

откорм|и́ть, лю́, ~ишь, *pf.* (*of* отка́рмли вать) to fatten (up).

отко́рм|ленный, *p.p.p. of* ~и́ть *and adj.* fat fatted, fattened; о. скот fat stock.

отко́с, а, *m.* slope (*esp. of railway embankment*) о. холма́ hillside; пусти́ть по́езд под о. t derail a train; у́гол есте́ственного ~ (*phys.*) angle of rest.

откреп|и́ть, лю́, и́шь, *pf.* (*of* ~ля́ть) **1.** t unfasten, untie. **2.** to strike off the re gister.

откреп|и́ться, лю́сь, и́шься, *pf.* (*of* ~ля́ться **1.** to become unfastened. **2.** to remove one' name (*from a register, etc.*).

открепля́|ть(ся), ю(сь), *impf. of* откре пи́ть(ся).

открёщива|ться, юсь, *impf.* (*coll.;* от) t disown; to refuse to have anything to d (with).

открове́ни|е, я, *n.* revelation.

открове́нича|ть, ю, *impf.* (*coll.;* с+*i.*) t be candid (with), be frank (with).

открове́нност|ь, и, *f.* candour, frankness bluntness, outspokenness; *pl.* (*coll.*) candi revelations.

откровéн|ный (~ен, ~на), *adj.* **1.** candid, frank; blunt, outspoken. **2.** open, unconcealed; ~ная неприязнь unconcealed hostility. **3.** (*coll.*; *of dress*) revealing.

откру|тить, чу́, ~тишь, *pf.* (*of* ~чивать) to untwist; о. кран to turn off a tap.

откру|титься, чу́сь, ~тишься, *pf.* (*of* ~чиваться) **1.** to come untwisted. **2.** (*coll.*; от) to get out (of).

откру́чива|ть(ся), ю(сь), *impf.* of открути́ть(ся).

открыва́|ть(ся), ю(сь), *impf.* of откры́ть(ся).

открыл|óк, ка, *m.* (*aeron.*) stub-wing.

откры́ти|е, я, *n.* **1.** opening. **2.** discovery.

откры́тк|а, и, *f.* post-card; о. с ви́дом picture post-card.

откры́то, *adv.* (*in var. senses*) openly; жить о. (*obs.*) to keep open house.

откры́т|ый, *p.p.p.* of ~ь and *adj.* (*in var. senses*) open; в ~ую (*cards and fig.*) showing one's hand; на ~ом воздухе, под ~ым нéбом out of doors, in the open air; с ~ыми глаза́ми (*fig.*) with open eyes; при ~ых дверя́х open to the public; о. дом (*fig.*) open house; ~ое заседа́ние public sitting; ~ое мóре the open sea; ~ое письмó (*i*) post-card, (*ii*) open letter; ~ое пла́тье low-necked dress; ~ые гóрные рабóты open-cast mining; ~ая сце́на open-air stage.

откр|ы́ть, óю, óешь, *pf.* (*of* ~ыва́ть) **1.** (*in var. senses*) to open; о. комý-н. глаза́ на что-н. (*fig.*) to open someone's eyes to something; о. кровь (*med.*; *obs.*) to let blood; о. ми́тинг to open a meeting; о. огóнь (*mil.*) to open fire; о. па́мятник to unveil a monument; о. счёт to open an account. **2.** to uncover, reveal (*also fig.*); о. грудь to bare one's breast; о. ду́шу to lay bare one's heart; о. ка́рты (*fig.*) to show one's hand; о. секре́т to reveal a secret. **3.** to discover; о. Аме́рику (*fig.*, *iron.*) to retail stale news. **4.** to turn on (*gas, water, etc.*).

откр|ы́ться, óюсь, óешься, *pf.* (*of* ~ыва́ться) **1.** to open. **2.** to come to light, be revealed; пе́ред на́ми ~ы́лся великоле́пный вид a magnificent view unfolded before us. **3.** (+*d.*) to confide (in, to). **4.** *pass.* of ~ы́ть.

откýда, *adv.* (*interrog.*) whence, where from; (*relat.*) whence, from which; о. вы? where do you come from? where are you from?; о. вы об э́том зна́ете? how do you come to know about it?; о. ни возьми́сь (*coll.*) quite unexpectedly, suddenly.

откýда-либо, *adv.* from somewhere or other.

откýда-нибудь, *adv.* = о.-либо.

откýда-то, *adv.* from somewhere.

óткуп, а, *pl.* ~á, *m.* (*hist.*) farming (*of revenues, etc.*); взять на о. to farm; отда́ть на о. to farm out (*also fig.*).

откуп|а́ть(ся), а́ю(сь), *impf.* of ~и́ть(ся).

откуп|и́ть, лю́, ~ишь, *pf.* (*of* ~а́ть) to pay up.

откуп|и́ться, лю́сь, ~ишься, *pf.* (*of* ~а́ться) (от) to pay off.

откýпорива|ть, ю, *impf.* of откýпорить.

откýпор|ить, ю, ишь, *pf.* (*of* ~ивать) to uncork; to open (*a bottle*).

откýпорк|а, и, *f.* opening, uncorking.

откупщи́к, а́, *m.* tax-farmer.

откý|си́ть, шý, ~сишь, *pf.* (*of* ~сывать) to bite off; to snap off (*with pincers, etc.*).

откýсыва|ть, ю, *impf.* of откуси́ть.

откýша|ть, ю, *pf.* (*obs.*) **1.** to have finished eating. **2.** to eat; to try (*food*); позва́ть о. to invite to a meal.

отлага́тельств|о, а, *n.* delay; procrastination; де́ло не те́рпит ~a the matter is urgent.

отлага́|ть(ся), ю(сь), *impf.* of отложи́ть(ся).

отлакир|ова́ть, ýю, *pf.* of лакирова́ть.

отла́мыва|ть(ся), ю(сь), *impf.* of отлома́ть(ся) *and* отломи́ть(ся).

отлега́|ть, ю, *impf.* of отле́чь.

отлеж|а́ть, ý, и́шь, *pf.* (*of* ~ивать) я ~а́л нóгу my foot has gone to sleep.

отлеж|а́ться, у́сь, и́шься, *pf.* **1.** to lie up; to rest (*in bed*). **2.** to lie, be stored (*in order to season, ripen, etc.*).

отлёжива|ть(ся), ю(сь), *impf.* of отлежа́ть(ся).

отлеп|и́ть, лю́, ~ишь, *pf.* (*of* ~ля́ть) (*coll.*) to unstick, take off (*something adhesive*).

отлеп|и́ться, ~ится, *pf.* (*of* ~ля́ться) (*coll.*) to come unstuck, come off.

отлепля́|ть(ся), ю(сь), *impf.* of отлепи́ть(ся).

отлёт, а, *m.* flying away; departure (*of aircraft*); быть на ~e to be about to leave, be on the point of departure; держа́ть на ~e to hold in one's outstretched hand; держа́ться на ~e (*coll.*) to hold oneself aloof, be stand-offish; дом на ~e house standing by itself.

отлета́|ть[1], ю, *pf.* **1.** to have completed a flight. **2.** (*coll.*) to have been flying (*for a given period*); он ~л два́дцать лет he has done twenty years' flying.

отлет|а́ть[2], а́ю, *impf.* of ~е́ть.

отле|те́ть, чý, ти́шь, *pf.* (*of* ~та́ть) **1.** to fly (away, off); (*fig.*) to fly, vanish. **2.** to rebound, bounce back. **3.** (*coll.*; *of buttons, etc.*) to come off.

отл|е́чь, я́гу, я́жешь, я́гут, *past* ~ёг, ~егла́, *pf.* (*of* ~ега́ть) **1.** (*obs.*; от) to move away (from). **2.** (*coll.*; *impers.*) у неё ~егло́ от се́рдца she felt relieved, she felt as if a weight had been lifted from her.

отли́в[1], а, *m.* ebb, ebb-tide.

отли́в[2], а, *m.* tint; play of colours; с золоты́м ~ом shot with gold.

отлива́|ть¹, ю, *impf. of* отли́ть.

отлива́|ть², ет, *impf.* (+*i.*) to be shot (*with a colour*).

отли́вк|а, и, *f.* (*tech.*) **1.** casting, founding. **2.** cast, ingot, moulding.

отливн|о́й, *adj.* (*tech.*) cast, founded, moulded; ~а́я печь founding furnace.

отлип|а́ть, а́ет, *impf. of* ~нуть.

отли́п|нуть, нет, *past* ~, ~ла, *pf.* (*of* ~а́ть) to come off, come unstuck.

отли́т|ый (о́тлит, ~а́, о́тлито *and* ~, ~а́, ~о), *p.p.p. of* ~ь; в ~ом ви́де (*tech.*) as cast.

отли́ть, отолью́, отольёшь, *past* о́тлил, **отлила́, о́тлило,** *pf.* (*of* отлива́ть¹) **1.** (+*a.* or *g.*) to pour off; to pump out. **2.** (*tech.*) to cast, found. **3.** (*vulg.*) to urinate.

отлич|а́ть, а́ю, *impf. of* ~и́ть.

отлич|а́ться, а́юсь, *impf.* **1.** (*pf.* ~и́ться) to distinguish oneself, excel (*also joc., iron.*). **2.** (*impf. only*) (от) to differ (from). **3.** (*impf. only*) (+*i.*) to be notable (for).

отличи|е, я, *n.* **1.** difference, distinction; знак ~я distinguishing feature; (*mil.*) order, decoration; в о. от in contradistinction to. **2.** distinction (*as grade of merit*); distinguished services; получи́ть дипло́м с ~ем to obtain a distinction (*in university examination, etc.*).

отличи́тельный, *adj.* distinctive; distinguishing; о. при́знак distinguishing feature.

отлич|и́ть, у́, и́шь, *pf.* (*of* ~а́ть) **1.** to distinguish; о. одно́ от друго́го to tell one thing from another. **2.** to single out.

отлич|и́ться, у́сь, и́шься, *pf. of* ~а́ться.

отли́чник, а, *m.* **1.** pupil obtaining 'excellent' marks. **2.** о. произво́дства exemplary worker.

отли́чно 1. *adv.* excellently; perfectly; extremely well; о. знать to know perfectly well; он о. понима́ет по-ру́сски he understands Russian perfectly. **2.** *as indecl. noun* 'excellent' mark (*in school, etc.*).

отли́ч|ный (~ен, ~на), *adj.* **1.** (*obs.*) (от) different (from). **2.** excellent; perfect; extremely good; ~но! excellent!

отло́г|ий (~, ~а), *adj.* sloping.

отло́гост|ь, и, *f.* slope.

отло́|же, *comp. of* ~гий.

отложе́ни|е, я, *n.* **1.** secession. **2.** sediment, precipitation; (*geol.*) deposit.

отлож|и́ть, у́, и́шь, *pf.* **1.** (*impf.* откла́дывать) to put aside, set aside; to put away, put by; о. на чёрный день to put by for a rainy day. **2.** (*impf.* откла́дывать *and* отлага́ть) to put off, postpone; о. па́ртию to adjourn a game; о. реше́ние to suspend judgement; о. в до́лгий я́щик to shelve. **3.** (*impf.* откла́дывать) (*of insects*) to lay. **4.** (*impf.* откла́дывать) (*obs.*) to turn back, turn down. **5.** (*impf.* откла́дывать) to un-

harness. **6.** (*impf.* отлага́ть) (*geol.*) to deposit.

отлож|и́ться, у́сь, ~ишься, *pf.* (*of* отлага́ться) **1.** (*obs.*; от) to detach oneself (from), separate (from); (*polit.*) to secede. **2.** (*geol.*) to deposit, be deposited.

отложно́й, *adj.* о. воротни́к turn-down collar.

отлома́|ть, ю, *pf.* (*of* отла́мывать) to break off.

отлома́|ться, юсь, *pf.* (*of* отла́мываться) to break off.

отлом|и́ть(ся), лю́(сь), ~ишь(ся), *pf.* = ~а́ть(ся).

отлуп|и́ть, лю́, ~ишь, *pf. of* лупи́ть².

отлупц|ева́ть, у́ю, *pf. of* лупцева́ть.

отлуч|а́ть(ся), а́ю(сь), *impf. of* отлучи́ть(ся).

отлуче́ни|е, я, *n.* (*eccl. and fig.*) excommunication.

отлуч|и́ть, у́, и́шь, *pf.* (*of* ~а́ть) (*obs.*; от) to separate (from), remove (from); о. (от це́ркви) (*eccl.*) to excommunicate.

отлуч|и́ться, у́сь, и́шься, *pf.* (*of* ~а́ться) **1.** to absent oneself. **2.** *pass. of* ~и́ть.

отлу́чк|а, и, *f.* absence; самово́льная о. (*mil.*) absence without leave; быть в ~е to be absent, be away.

отлы́нива|ть, ю, *impf.* (*coll.*; от) to shirk.

отма́лчива|ться, юсь, *impf. of* отмолча́ться.

отма́тыва|ть, ю, *impf. of* отмота́ть.

отма́ха|ть¹, шу́, ~шешь, *pf.* (*of* ~хивать) **1.** to stop waving. **2.** о. ру́ки to tire one's arms by waving.

отмаха́|ть², ю, *pf.* (*coll.*) to cover (*a distance*); за день мы ~ли свы́ше тридцати́ миль in the day, we covered more than thirty miles.

отма́хива|ть(ся), ю(сь), *impf. of* отмаха́ть¹ *and* отмахну́ть(ся).

отмах|ну́ть, ну́, нёшь, *pf.* (*of* ~ивать) (*coll.*) to wave away, brush off (*with one's hand*).

отмах|ну́ться, ну́сь, нёшься, *pf.* (*of* ~иваться) (от) **1.** = ~ну́ть; о. от комаро́в to brush mosquitoes off. **2.** (*fig.*) to brush aside.

отма́чива|ть, ю, *impf. of* отмочи́ть.

отмеж|ева́ть, у́ю, *pf.* (*of* ~ёвывать) to mark off, draw a boundary line (between).

отмеж|ева́ться, у́юсь, *pf.* (*of* ~ёвываться) **1.** (от) to dissociate oneself (from); to refuse to acknowledge. **2.** *pass. of* ~ева́ть.

отмежёвыва|ть(ся), ю(сь), *impf. of* отмежева́ть(ся).

о́тмел|ь, и, *f.* (sand-)bar, (sand-)bank.

отме́н|а, ы, *f.* abolition; abrogation, repeal, revocation; cancellation, countermand; о. крепостно́го пра́ва abolition of serfdom; о. зако́на repeal of a law; о. спекта́кля cancellation of a show.

отмен|и́ть, ю́, ~ишь, *pf.* (*of* ~я́ть) to abolish; to abrogate, repeal, revoke, rescind; to cancel, countermand; (*leg.*) to disaffirm.

отме́н|ный (~ен, ~на), *adj.* excellent.

отмен|я́ть, я́ю, *impf. of* ~и́ть.

отмер|е́ть, отомрёт, *past* о́тмер, ~ла́, о́тмерло, *pf.* (*of* отмира́ть) to die off; (*fig.*) to die out, die away.

отмерз|а́ть, а́ет, *impf. of* ~нуть.

отмёрз|нуть, нет, *past* ~, ~ла, *pf.* (*of* ~а́ть) to freeze; ру́ки у меня́ ~ли my hands are frozen.

отмерива|ть, ю, *impf. of* отме́рить.

отме́р|ить, ю, ишь, *pf.* (*of* ~ивать *and* ~я́ть) to measure off.

отмер|я́ть, я́ю, *impf.* = ~ивать.

отме|сти́, ту́, тёшь, *past* ~л, ~ла́, *pf.* (*of* ~та́ть) to sweep aside (*also fig.*).

отмéстк|а, и, *f.* (*coll.*) revenge; в ~у in revenge.

отмета́|ть, ю, *impf. of* отмести́.

отмéтин|а, ы, *f.* mark; (*on forehead of horse, etc.*) star.

отмé|тить, чу, тишь, *pf.* (*of* ~ча́ть) 1. to mark, note; to make a note (of); о. пти́чкой to tick off. 2. to point to, mention, record; о. чьи-н. по́двиги to point to someone's feats. 3. to register (out), sign out (*departing tenant, etc.*). 4. to celebrate, mark by celebration.

отмé|титься, чусь, тишься, *pf.* (*of* ~ча́ться) 1. to sign one's name (*on a list*). 2. to register (out), sign out (*on departure*).

отмéтк|а, и, *f.* 1. note. 2. (*in school or examinations*) mark.

отмéтчик, а, *m.* marker.

отмеча́|ть(ся), ю(сь), *impf. of* отмéтить(ся).

отмира́ни|е, я, *n.* dying off; dying away, fading away, withering away.

отмобилиз|ова́ть, у́ю, *pf.* (*coll.*) to mobilize totally.

отмок|а́ть, а́ет, *impf. of* ~нуть.

отмо́к|нуть, нет, *past* ~, ~ла, *pf.* (*of* ~а́ть) 1. to grow wet. 2. to soak off.

отмолч|а́ться, у́сь, и́шься, *pf.* (*of* отма́лчиваться) (*coll.*) to keep silent, say nothing.

отмора́жива|ть, ю, *impf. of* отморо́зить.

отморо́жени|е, я, *n.* frost-bite.

отморо́|женный, *p.p.p. of* ~зить *and adj.* frost-bitten.

отморо́|зить, жу, зишь, *pf.* (*of* отмора́живать) to injure by frost-bite; я ~зил себе́ у́ши my ears are frost-bitten.

отмота́|ть, ю, *pf.* (*of* отма́тывать) to unwind.

отмоч|и́ть, у́, ~ишь, *pf.* (*of* отма́чивать) 1. to unstick by wetting. 2. to soak, steep. 3. (*coll.*) to do, say (*something ludicrous or outrageous*).

отмсти́ть = отомсти́ть.

отмщéни|е, я, *n.* (*obs.*) vengeance.

отмыва́|ть(ся), ю(сь), *impf. of* отмы́ть(ся).

отмыка́|ть(ся), ю(сь), *impf. of* отомкну́ть(ся).

отм|ы́ть, ою, о́ешь, *pf.* (*of* ~ыва́ть) 1. to wash clean. 2. to wash off, wash away.

отм|ы́ться, о́юсь, о́ешься, *pf.* (*of* ~ыва́ться) 1. to wash oneself clean. 2. (*of dirt, etc.*) to come out, come off.

отмы́чк|а, и, *f.* pass key, master key; lock-pick.

отмяк|а́ть, а́ет, *impf. of* ~нуть.

отмя́к|нуть, нет, *past* ~, ~ла, *pf.* (*of* ~а́ть) to grow soft.

отнéкива|ться, юсь, *impf.* (*coll.*) to refuse.

отнес|ти́, у́, ёшь, *past* ~, ~ла́, *pf.* (*of* относи́ть) 1. (в+*a.*, к) to take (to). 2. to carry away, carry off; (*impers.*) ло́дку ~ло́ тече́нием the boat was carried away by the current. 3. (*coll.*) to cut off. 4. (к) to ascribe (to), attribute (to), refer (to); ру́копись ~ли́ к пя́тому ве́ку the manuscript was believed to date from the fifth century; мы ~ли́ его́ раздражи́тельность на счёт глухоты́ we put his irritability down to his deafness.

отнес|ти́сь, у́сь, ёшься, *past* ~ся, ~ла́сь, *pf.* (*of* относи́ться) (к) 1. to treat; to regard; хорошо́ о. к кому́-н. to treat someone well, be nice to someone; скепти́чески о. к предположéнию to be sceptical about an hypothesis; как вы ~ли́сь к э́той лéкции? what did you think of the lecture? 2. (*obs.*) to apply (to).

отникелир|ова́ть, у́ю, *pf. of* никелирова́ть.

отнима́|ть(ся), ю(сь), *impf. of* отня́ть(ся).

относи́тельно 1. *adv.* relatively. 2. *prep.* (+*g.*) concerning, about, with regard to.

относи́тельност|ь, и, *f.* relativity; тео́рия ~и Эйнштéйна Einstein's Theory of Relativity.

относи́тел|ьный (~ен, ~ьна), *adj.* relative; ~ьное местоимéние (*gram.*) relative pronoun.

отно|си́ть, шу́, ~сишь, *impf. of* отнести́.

отно|си́ться, шу́сь, ~сишься, *impf.* 1. *impf. of* отнести́сь. 2. *impf. only* (к) to concern, have to do (with), relate (to); э́то к дéлу не ~сится that's beside the point, that is irrelevant; два ~сится к трём как шесть к девяти́ (*math.*) two is to three as six is to nine. 3. *impf. only* (к) to date (from); храм э́тот ~сится к двена́дцатому вéку this church dates from the twelfth century.

отношéни|е, я, *n.* 1. (к) attitude (to); treatment (of); внима́тельное о. к ста́рым consideration for the old; у негó стра́нное о. к же́нщинам he has a strange attitude to women. 2. relation; respect; имéть о. к чему́-н. to bear a relation to something, have a bearing on something; не име́ть ~я (к) to bear no relation (to), have nothing to do (with); в ~и (+g.), по ~ю (к) with respect (to), with regard (to); в не́которых ~ях in some respects. **3.** (*pl.*) relations; terms; дипломати́ческие ~я diplomatic relations; быть в дру́жеских ~ях (с+i.) to be on friendly terms (with). **4.** (*math.*) ratio; в прямо́м (обра́тном) ~и in direct (inverse) ratio. **5.** (*official*) letter, memorandum.

отны́не, *adv.* (*obs.*) henceforth, henceforward.
отню́дь, *adv.* by no means, not at all.
отня́ти|е, я, *n.* taking away; о. руки́ amputation of an arm; о. от гру́ди weaning.
от|ня́ть, ниму́, ни́мешь, *past* ~ня́л, ~няла́, ~ня́ло, *pf.* (*of* ~нима́ть) **1.** to take (away); о. от гру́ди to wean; о. жизнь у кого́-н. to take someone's life; от шести́ о. три to take away three from six; э́то ~ня́ло у меня́ три часа́ it took me three hours. **2.** to amputate.
от|ня́ться, ни́мется, *past* ~ня́лся, ~няла́сь, *pf.* (*of* ~нима́ться) to be paralyzed; у него́ ~няла́сь пра́вая рука́ he has lost the use of his right arm; у неё ~ня́лся язы́к she has lost the power of speech.
ото, *prep.* = от.
отобе́да|ть, ю, *pf.* **1.** to have finished dinner. **2.** (*obs.*) to dine, have dinner.
отобража́|ть, ю, *impf. of* отобрази́ть.
отображе́ни|е, я, *n.* reflection; representation.
отобра́|зи́ть, жу́, зи́шь, *pf.* (*of* ~жа́ть) to reflect; to represent.
от|обра́ть, беру́, берёшь, *past* ~обра́л, ~обра́ла, ~обра́ло, *pf.* (*of* отбира́ть) **1.** to take (away); to seize; о. биле́ты to collect tickets; о. показа́ние у свиде́теля (*leg.*) to take a deposition from a witness. **2.** to select, pick out.
отова́рива|ть, ю, *impf. of* отова́рить.
отова́р|ить, ю, ишь, *pf.* (*of* ~ивать) to pledge goods in support of; о. чек to issue goods against a sale receipt.
отовсю́ду, *adv.* from everywhere, from every quarter.
от|огна́ть¹, гоню́, го́нишь, *past* ~огна́л, ~огнала́, ~огна́ло, *pf.* (*of* ~гоня́ть) to drive off; to keep off; (*fig.*) to suppress.
от|огна́ть², гоню́, го́нишь, *past* ~огна́л, ~огнала́, ~огна́ло, *pf.* (*of* ~гоня́ть) (*chem.*) to distill (off).
отогн|у́ть, у́, ёшь, *pf.* (*of* отгиба́ть) to bend back; to flange.
отогн|у́ться, у́сь, ёшься, *pf.* (*of* отгиба́ться) to bend back.
отогрева́|ть(ся), ю(сь), *impf. of* отогре́ть(ся).
отогре́|ть, ю, *pf.* (*of* ~ва́ть) to warm.
отогре́|ться, юсь, *pf.* (*of* ~ва́ться) to warm oneself.

отодвига́|ть(ся), ю(сь), *impf. of* отодви́нуть(ся).
отодви́|нуть, ну, нешь, *pf.* (*of* ~га́ть) **1.** to move aside. **2.** (*fig.*) to put off, put back.
отодви́|нуться, нусь, нешься, *pf.* (*of* ~га́ться) **1.** to move aside. **2.** *pass. of* ~нуть.
от|одра́ть, деру́, дерёшь, *past* ~одра́л, ~одрала́, ~одра́ло, *pf.* (*of* ~дира́ть) **1.** to tear off, rip off. **2.** (*coll.*) to flog; о. кого́-н. за́ уши to pull someone's ears.
отож(д)еств|и́ть, лю́, и́шь, *pf.* (*of* ~ля́ть) to identify.
отож(д)ествля́|ть, ю, *impf. of* отож(д)естви́ть.
отожжённый, *p.p.p. of* отжечь *and adj.* (*tech.*) annealed.
от|озва́ть, зову́, зовёшь, *past* ~озва́л, ~озвала́, ~озва́ло, *pf.* (*of* ~зыва́ть) **1.** to take aside. **2.** to recall (*a diplomatic representative*).
от|озва́ться, зову́сь, зовёшься, *past* ~озва́лся, ~озвала́сь, ~озва́лось, *pf.* (*of* ~зыва́ться) **1.** (на+а.) to answer; to respond (to). **2.** (о+р.) to speak (of); реце́нзенты хорошо́ ~озва́лись о его́ второ́й кни́ге his second book was well received by (received good notices from) the reviewers. **3.** (на+ а.) to tell (on, upon); деторожде́ние ~озва́лось на её здоро́вье child-bearing has told on her health.
ото|йти́, йду́, йдёшь, *past* ~шёл, ~шла́, *pf.* (*of* отходи́ть¹) **1.** to move away; to move off; (*of trains, etc.*) to leave, depart. **2.** to withdraw; to recede; (*mil.*) to withdraw, fall back; (*fig.*; от) to move away (from); to digress (from), diverge (from); он далеко́ ~шёл от пре́жних взгля́дов he has moved a long way from his earlier views. **3.** (*of stains, etc.*) to come out; (от) to come away (from), come off; обо́и ~шли́ от стены́ the paper has come off (the wall). **4.** to recover (normal state); to come to oneself, come round; у меня́ ~шло́ от се́рдца (*impers.*; *coll.*) I felt better, I felt relieved. **5.** (к) to pass (to), go (to) (= *pass into the possession of, by inheritance, etc.*). **6.** to be lost (*in processing*). **7.** (*obs.*) to pass; ле́то ~шло́ summer was over; о. в ве́чность (*rhet.*) to pass away, pass to one's eternal rest.
отол|га́ться, гу́сь, жёшься, *past* ~га́лся, ~гала́сь, *pf.* (*coll.*) to lie one's way out (*of a difficult situation*).
отологи́ческий, *adj.* otological.
**отоло́ги|я, и, *f.* otology.
отомкн|у́ть, у́, ёшь, *pf.* (*of* отмыка́ть) to unlock, unbolt.
отомкн|у́ться, у́сь, ёшься, *pf.* (*of* отмыка́ться) **1.** to unlock. **2.** *pass. of* ~у́ть.
отом|сти́ть, щу́, сти́шь, *pf. of* мстить.
отопи́тельный, *adj.* heating; о. сезо́н cold season, season for fires.

отоп|и́ть, лю́, ~шь, *pf.* (*of* ота́пливать *and* отопля́ть) to heat.

отопле́н|ец, ца, *m.* heating appliances expert.

отопле́ни|е, я, *n.* heating.

отопля́|ть, ю, *impf. of* отопи́ть.

отора́чива|ть, ю, *impf. of* оторочи́ть.

ото́рванност|ь, и, *f.* isolation; loneliness; чу́вствовать о. от цивилиза́ции to feel cut off from civilization.

оторв|а́ть, у́, ёшь, *past* ~а́л, ~ала́, ~а́ло, *pf.* (*of* отрыва́ть[1]) to tear off; to tear away (*also* *fig.*); о. кого́-н. от рабо́ты to tear someone away from his work; с рука́ми о. (*coll.*) to seize with both hands.

оторв|а́ться, у́сь, ёшься, *past* ~а́лся, ~ала́сь, ~а́лось, *pf.* (*of* отрыва́ться) **1.** to come off, be torn off. **2.** (*aeron.*) о. от земли́ to take off. **3.** (*fig.*; от) to be cut off (from), lose touch (with); to break away (from); о. от проти́вника to lose contact with the enemy. **4.** (*fig.*; от) to tear oneself away (from); от э́той кни́ги я не мог о. I could not tear myself away from this book.

оторопе́лый, *adj.* (*coll.*) dumb-founded.

оторопе́|ть, ю, *pf.* (*coll.*) to be struck dumb.

о́тороп|ь, и, f. (*coll.*) confusion, fright; меня́ о. взяла́ I was dumb-founded.

оторо́ч|ить, у́, и́шь, *pf.* (*of* оторо́чивать) to edge, trim.

оторо́чк|а, и, f. edging, trimming.

ото|сла́ть, шлю́, шлёшь, *pf.* (*of* отсыла́ть) **1.** to send off, dispatch; о. де́ньги to send a remittance. **2.** (к) to refer (to); о. чита́теля к предыду́щему то́му to refer the reader to the preceding volume; его́ ~сла́ли к заве́дующему he was referred to the manager.

отосп|а́ться, лю́сь, и́шься, *past* ~а́лся, ~ала́сь, *pf.* (*of* отсыпа́ться[2]) to have a long sleep, have one's sleep out; о. по́сле доро́ги to sleep off a journey.

отоше́дший, *past part. of* отойти́.

ото|шёл, шла́, *see* ~йти́.

ото|шлю́, шлёшь, *see* ~сла́ть.

отоща́лый, *adj.* (*coll.*) emaciated.

отоща́|ть, ю, *pf. of* тоща́ть.

отпада́|ть, ю, *impf. of* отпа́сть.

отпаде́ни|е, я, *n.* falling away; (*fig.*; от) defection (from).

отпа́ива|ть[1], ю, *impf. of* отпая́ть.

отпа́ива|ть[2], ю, *impf. of* отпои́ть.

отпа́рива|ть, ю, *impf. of* отпа́рить.

отпари́р|овать, ую, *pf. of* пари́ровать.

отпа́р|ить, ю, ишь, *pf.* (*of* ~ивать) **1.** to steam; о. брю́ки to press trousers through a damp cloth. **2.** to steam off.

отпа́рыва|ть, ю, *impf. of* отпоро́ть[1].

отпа́|сть, ду́, дёшь, *past* ~л, *pf.* (*of* ~да́ть) **1.** to fall off, drop off; to fall away. **2.** (*fig.*;

от) to fall away (from), defect (from), drop away (from); мно́гие чле́ны ~ли от па́ртии many members have fallen away from the party. **3.** (*fig.*) to pass, fade; у него́ ~ла охо́та к путеше́ствию по Африке his desire to travel in Africa has passed; вопро́с об э́том ~л the question no longer arises.

отпа|я́ть, я́ю, *pf.* (*of* ~ивать[1]) to unsolder.

отпева́ни|е, я, *n.* burial service.

отпева́|ть, ю, *impf. of* отпе́ть.

от|пере́ть, опру́, опрёшь, *past* ~пер, ~перла́, ~перло, *pf.* (*of* ~пира́ть) to unlock; to open.

от|пере́ться[1], опрётся, *past* ~пёрся, ~перла́сь, *pf.* (*of* ~пира́ться) to open.

от|пере́ться[2], опру́сь, опрёшься, *past* ~пёрся, ~перла́сь, *pf.* (*of* ~пира́ться) (*coll.*; от) to deny; to disown.

отпе́т|ый *p.p.p. of* ~ь. *and adj.* (*coll.*) arrant, inveterate.

отп|е́ть, ою́, оёшь, *pf.* (*of* ~ева́ть) to read the burial service (for, over).

отпеча́т|ать, аю, *pf.* **1.** (*impf.* печа́тать) to print (off). **2.** (*impf.* ~ывать) to imprint; о. па́льцы на стекле́ to leave finger-prints on glass. **3.** (*impf.* ~ывать) to open (up).

отпеча́т|аться, ается, *pf.* **1.** to leave an imprint. **2.** *pass. of* ~ать.

отпечатле́|ться, ется, *pf.* (*obs.*) to leave its mark.

отпеча́т|ок, ка, *m.* imprint, impress (*also* *fig.*); о. па́льца finger-print.

отпеча́тыва|ть(ся), ю(сь), *impf. of* отпеча́тать(ся).

отпива́|ть, ю, *impf. of* отпи́ть.

отпи́лива|ть, ю, *impf. of* отпили́ть.

отпил|и́ть, ю́, ~ишь, *pf.* (*of* ~ивать) to saw off.

отпира́тельств|о, а, *n.* denial, disavowal.

отпира́|ть(ся), ю(сь), *impf. of* отпере́ть(ся).

отпи|са́ть, шу́, ~шешь, *pf.* (*of* ~сывать) **1.** (*obs.*) to bequeath, leave. **2.** (*obs.*) to confiscate. **3.** (*dial.*) to notify (in writing).

отпи|са́ться, шу́сь, ~шешься, *pf.* (*of* ~сываться) to make a (purely) formal reply.

отпи́ск|а, и, f. (*pejor.*) formal reply.

отпи́сыва|ть(ся), ю(сь), *impf. of* отписа́ть(ся).

от|пи́ть, опью́, опьёшь, *past* ~пил, ~пила́, ~пило, *pf.* (*of* ~пива́ть) (+*a. or g.*) to take a sip (of).

отпи́хива|ть(ся), ю(сь), *impf. of* отпихну́ть(ся).

отпих|ну́ть, ну́, нёшь, *pf.* (*of* ~ивать) (*coll.*) to push off; to shove aside.

отпих|ну́ться, ну́сь, нёшься, *pf.* (*of* ~иваться) (*coll.*) to push off (*esp. in a boat*).

отпла́т|а, ы, f. repayment.

отпла|ти́ть, чу́, ~тишь, *pf.* (*of* ~чивать) (+*d.*) to pay back (to), repay, requite; о, кому́-н. той же моне́той to pay someone in his own coin.

отпла́чива|ть, ю, *impf. of* отплати́ть.

отплёва|ть, ю, *impf. of* отплю́нуть.

отплёвыва|ться, юсь, *impf.* to spit (*also fig.*, *to express disgust*).

отплыва́|ть, ю, *impf. of* отплы́ть.

отплы́ти|е, я, *n.* sailing, departure.

отплы́|ть, ву́, вёшь, *past* ~л, ~ла́, ~ло, *pf.* (*of* ~ва́ть) to sail, set sail; to swim off.

отплю́н|уть, у, ешь, *pf.* (*of* отплёвывать) to spit (out), expectorate.

отпля|са́ть, шу́, ~**шешь,** *pf.* 1. to dance (*trans.*). 2. to finish dancing.

отпля́сыва|ть, ю, *impf.* (*coll.*) to dance with zest.

о́тповед|ь, и, *f.* reproof, rebuke.

отпо́|ить, ю́, и́шь, *pf.* (*of* отпа́ивать²) 1. to finish watering. 2. to fatten (on liquids). 3. (*coll.*; +*i.*) to cure by giving to drink; о. отра́вленного молоко́м to give milk to someone suffering from poisoning.

отполза́|ть, а́ю, *impf. of* ~ти́.

отполз|ти́, у́, ёшь, *past* ~, ~ла́, *pf.* (*of* ~а́ть) to crawl away.

отполир|ова́ть, у́ю, *pf. of* полирова́ть.

отпо́р, а, *m.* repulse; rebuff; дать о. (+*d.*) to repulse; встре́тить о. to be repulsed; to meet with a rebuff.

отпор|о́ть¹, ю́, ~**ешь,** *pf.* (*of* отпа́рывать) to rip off.

отпор|о́ть², ю́, ~**ешь,** *pf.* (*of* поро́ть) (*coll.*) to flog, thrash.

отпотева́|ть, ю, *impf. of* отпоте́ть.

отпоте́|ть, ю, *pf.* (*of* поте́ть *and* ~ва́ть) to moisten, be covered with moisture.

отпочк|ова́ться, у́ется, *pf.* (*of* ~о́вываться) (*biol.*) to gemmate, propagate by gemmation; (*fig.*) to detach oneself.

отпочко́выва|ться, юсь, *impf. of* отпочкова́ться.

отправи́тел|ь, я, *m.* sender.

отпра́в|ить, лю, ишь, *pf.* (*of* ~ля́ть) to send, forward, dispatch; о. на тот свет to send to kingdom come; о. есте́ственные потре́бности to relieve nature.

отпра́в|иться, люсь, ишься, *pf.* (*of* ~ля́ться) to set out, set off, start; to leave, depart; о. на боковую (*coll.*) to turn in, go to bed.

отпра́вк|а, и, *f.* sending off, forwarding, dispatch.

отправле́ни|е, я, *n.* 1. sending. 2. departure (*of trains, ships*). 3. function (*of the organism*). 4. exercise, performance; о. обя́занностей exercise of one's duties.

отправля́|ть, ю, *impf.* 1. *impf. of* отпра́вить. 2. (*impf. only*) to exercise, perform (*duties, functions*).

отправля́|ться, юсь, *impf.* 1. *impf. of* отпра́виться. 2. (*fig.*; от) to proceed (from).

отправн|о́й, adj. о. пункт, ~а́я то́чка starting-point.

отпра́здн|овать, ую, *pf. of* пра́здновать.

отпра́шива|ться, юсь, *impf.* (*of* отпроси́ться) to ask (for) leave.

отпресс|ова́ть, у́ю, *pf. of* прессова́ть.

отпро|си́ться, шу́сь, ~**сишься,** *pf.* (*of* отпра́шиваться) 1. to ask (for) leave. 2. to obtain leave.

отпры́гива|ть, ю, *impf. of* отпры́гнуть.

отпры́г|нуть, ну, нешь, *pf.* (*of* ~ивать) to jump back, spring back; to jump aside, spring aside; to bounce back.

о́тпрыск, а, *m.* (*bot. and fig.*) offshoot, scion.

отпряга́|ть, ю, *impf. of* отпря́чь.

отпря́дыва|ть, ю, *impf. of* отпря́нуть.

отпря́|нуть, ну, нешь, *pf.* (*of* ~дывать) to recoil, start back.

отпря́|чь, гу́, жёшь, гу́т, *past* ~г, ~гла́, *pf.* (*of* ~га́ть) to unharness.

отпу́гива|ть, ю, *impf. of* отпугну́ть.

отпуг|ну́ть, ну́, нёшь, *pf.* (*of* ~ивать) to frighten off, scare away.

о́тпуск, а, в ~**е** *or* **в** ~**у́,** *pl.* ~**а́,** ~**о́в,** *m.* 1. leave, holiday(s); (*mil.*) leave, furlough; в ~е, в ~у́ on leave; о. по боле́зни sick-leave. 2. issue, delivery, distribution. 3. (*tech.*) tempering, drawing.

отпуска́|ть, ю, *impf. of* отпусти́ть.

отпускни́к, а́, *m.* person on leave, holiday-maker; soldier on leave.

отпускн|о́й, adj. 1. *adj. of* о́тпуск 1; ~ы́е де́ньги holiday pay; ~о́е свиде́тельство authorization of leave (*of absence*); (*mil.*) leave pass. 2. (*econ.*) ~а́я цена́ selling price.

отпу|сти́ть, щу́, ~**стишь,** *pf.* (*of* ~ска́ть) 1. to let go, let off; to let out; to set free; to release; to give leave (of absence); ~сти́ мою́ ру́ку! let go (of) my arm!; о. на пра́здник to release for the holiday; о. комплиме́нт (*coll.*) to make a compliment; о. шу́тку (*coll.*) to crack a joke. 2. to relax, slacken; о. по́вод ло́шади to give a horse its head; боль ~сти́ло (*impers.*; *coll.*) the pain has eased. 3. to (let) grow; о. (себе́) бо́роду to grow a beard. 4. to issue, give out; (*in a shop, etc.*) to serve. 5. to assign, allot. 6. to remit; to forgive; о. кому́-н. грехи́ (*eccl.*) to give someone absolution. 7. (*tech.*) to temper, draw (the temper of).

отпуще́ни|е, я, *n.* remission; о. грехо́в (*eccl.*) absolution; козёл ~я (*coll.*) scapegoat.

отпу́щенник, а, *m.* (*hist.*) freedman.

отраба́тыва|ть, ю, *impf. of* отрабо́тать.

отрабо́та|нный, p.p.p. of ~ть *and adj.* (*tech.*) worked out; waste, spent, exhaust; о. газ waste gas, exhaust gas.

отрабо́та|ть¹, ю, *pf.* (*of* отраба́тывать) 1. to work off (*a debt, etc.*). 2. (*coll.*) to work (*a* *given length of time*). **3.** to work through, give a work-out to.

отрабо́та|ть², ю, *pf.* to finish one's work.

отрабо́тк|а, и, *f.* working off, paying by work.

отрабо́точн|ый, *adj.* ~ая систе́ма statute labour, corvée.

отра́в|а, ы, *f.* poison; (*fig.*) bane.

отрави́тел|ь, я, *m.* poisoner.

отрав|и́ть, лю́, ~ишь, *pf.* (*of* ~ля́ть) to poison (*also fig.*).

отрав|и́ться, лю́сь, ~ишься, *pf.* (*of* ~ля́ться) **1.** to poison oneself. **2.** *pass. of* ~и́ть.

отравля́|ть(ся), ю(сь), *impf. of* отрави́ться.

отра́д|а, ы, *f.* joy, delight; comfort.

отра́дный, *adj.* gratifying, pleasing; comforting.

отража́тел|ь, я, *m.* **1.** (*phys.*) reflector; (*radar*) scanner. **2.** (*in fire-arm*) ejector.

отража́тельн|ый, *adj.* (*tech.*) reflecting, deflecting; ~ая засло́нка, о. лист, ~ая плита́ deflector (plate), baffle (plate).

отража́|ть(ся), ю(сь), *impf. of* отрази́ть(ся).

отраже́ни|е, я, *n.* **1.** reflection; reverberation. **2.** repulse, parry; warding off.

отра|зи́ть, жу́, зи́шь, *pf.* (*of* ~жа́ть) **1.** to reflect (*also fig.*). **2.** to repulse, repel, parry; to ward off.

отра|зи́ться, жу́сь, зи́шься, *pf.* (*of* ~жа́ться) **1.** to be reflected; to reverberate. **2.** (*fig.*; на+*p.*) to affect; to tell (on); пое́здка в го́ры благоприя́тно ~зи́лась на его́ рабо́те the mountain trip had a beneficial effect on his work.

отрапорт|ова́ть, у́ю, *pf.* to report.

отраслев|о́й, *adj.* of о́трасль; ~о́е объедине́ние trade association of a branch of industry.

о́трасл|ь, и, *f.* (*obs. or fig.*) branch; о. дре́внего ро́да scion of an ancient line; о. промы́шленности branch of industry.

отраст|а́ть, а́ю, *impf. of* ~и́.

отраст|и́, у́, ёшь, *past* **отро́с, отросла́,** *pf.* (*of* ~а́ть) to grow.

отра|сти́ть, щу́, сти́шь, *pf.* (*of* ~щивать) to (let) grow; о. во́лосы to grow one's hair long; о. брю́хо (*coll.*) to develop a paunch.

отра́щива|ть, ю, *impf. of* отрасти́ть.

отреаги́р|овать, ую, *pf.* (*coll.*) *of* реаги́ровать 2.

отре́бь|е, я, *n.* (*collect.*) **1.** (*obs.*) waste, refuse. **2.** (*fig.*) rabble.

отрегули́р|овать, ую, *pf. of* регули́ровать.

отредакти́р|овать, ую, *pf. of* редакти́ровать.

отре́з, а, *m.* **1.** cut; ли́ния ~а line of the cut; perforated line; (*on document, ticket, etc.*) 'tear off here'. **2.** length (*of material*); о. на пла́тье dress length.

отре́занност|ь, и, *f.* (от) lack of communication (with), being cut off (from).

отрез|а́ть, а́ю, *impf. of* ~а́ть.

отре́|зать, жу, жешь, *pf.* (*of* ~за́ть) **1.** to cut off (*also fig.*); to divide, apportion (*land*); проти́вник ~зал нам отступле́ние the enemy had cut off our retreat. **2.** (*coll.*) to snap out.

отрезве́|ть, ю, *pf. of* трезве́ть.

отрезви́тельный, *adj.* sobering (*also fig.*).

отрезв|и́ть, лю́, и́шь, *pf.* (*of* ~ля́ть) to sober (*also fig.*).

отрезв|и́ться, лю́сь, и́шься, *pf.* (*of* ~ля́ться) to become sober, sober up.

отрезвле́ни|е, я, *n.* sobering (up).

отрезвля́|ть(ся), ю(сь), *impf. of* отрезви́ть(ся).

отрезно́й, *adj.* perforated; о. тало́н tear-off coupon.

отре́з|ок, ка, *m.* piece, cut; section; (*hist.*) portion (*of land*); (*math.*) segment; о. вре́мени space (*of time*).

отрека́|ться, юсь, *impf. of* отре́чься.

отрекоменд|ова́ть, у́ю, *pf.* to introduce.

отрекоменд|ова́ться, у́юсь, *pf.* to introduce oneself.

отремонти́р|овать, ую, *pf. of* ремонти́ровать.

отре́пь|е, я, (*pl.* ~я, ~ев), *n.* (*collect.*) rags; ходи́ть в о., в ~ях to be in rags.

отрече́ни|е, я, *n.* (от) renunciation (of); о. от престо́ла abdication.

отре́|чься, ку́сь, чёшься, ку́тся, *past* ~кся, ~кла́сь, *pf.* (*of* ~ка́ться) (от) to renounce, disavow, give up; о. от престо́ла to abdicate.

отреш|а́ть(ся), а́ю(сь), *impf. of* ~и́ть(ся).

отрешённост|ь, и, *f.* estrangement, aloofness.

отреш|и́ть, у́, и́шь, *pf.* (*of* ~а́ть) (от) to release (from); о. от до́лжности to dismiss, suspend.

отреш|и́ться, у́сь, и́шься, *pf.* (*of* ~а́ться) (от) to renounce, give up; я не мог о. от мы́сли I could not get rid of the idea.

отри́н|уть, у, ешь, *pf.* (*obs.*) to reject.

отрица́ни|е, я, *n.* denial; negation.

отрица́тел|ьный (~ен, ~ьна), *adj.* (*in var. senses*) negative; (*fig.*) bad, unfavourable; ~ьное электри́чество negative electricity; ~ьная сторона́ bad side, drawback.

отрица́|ть, ю, *impf.* to deny; to disclaim; о. вино́вность (*leg.*) to plead not guilty.

отро́г, а, *m.* (*geogr.*) spur.

о́троду, adv. (*coll.*) **1.** in age; ему́ пять лет о. he is five years old. **2.** не... о. never in one's life, never in one's born days; я о. не вида́л ничего́ подо́бного I have never seen the like

отро́дь|е, я, *n.* (*coll.*, *pejor.*) race, breed; Ха́мово о. (*obs.*) hoi polloi.

отродя́сь, *adv.* (*coll.*) не... о. never in one's life, never in one's born days.

о́трок, а, *m.* boy, lad; adolescent.

отрокови́ц|а, ы, *f.* (*obs.*) girl, lass, maiden.

отро́ст|ок, ка, *m.* **1.** (*bot.*) shoot, sprout. **2.** (*tech.*) branch, extension. **3.** (*anat.*) appendix.

о́трочеcкий, *adj.* adolescent.

о́трочеств|о, а, *n.* adolescence.

о́труб, а, *pl.* ~á, ~óв, *m.* (*hist.*) holding (*consolidated peasant small-holding, 1906–17*).

отру́б, а, *pl.* ~ы, ~ов, *m.* butt (*of tree*).

о́труб|и, éй, *no sing.* bran.

отруба́|ть, áю, *impf. of* ~и́ть.

отруб|и́ть, лю́, ~ишь, *pf.* (*of* ~а́ть) **1.** to chop off. **2.** (*fig., coll.*) to snap back.

отрубно́й, *adj. of* óтруб.

о́труб|ный, *adj. of* ~и.

отру́гива|ться, юсь, *impf.* (*coll.*) to return abuse.

отры́в, а, *m.* **1.** tearing off. **2.** (*fig.*) alienation, isolation; loss of contact, loss of communication; в ~e (от) out of touch (with); учи́ться без ~а от произво́дства to study while continuing (normal) work; о. от земли́ (*aeron.*) take-off; о. от проти́вника (*mil.*) disengagement.

отрыва́|ть¹, ю, *impf. of* оторва́ть.

отрыва́|ть², ю, *impf. of* отры́ть.

отрыва́|ться, юсь, *impf. of* оторва́ться.

отры́вист|ый (~, ~а), *adj.* jerky, abrupt; curt.

отрывно́й, *adj.* perforated; о. календа́рь tear-off calendar.

отры́в|ок, ка, *m.* fragment, excerpt; passage (*of book, etc.*).

отры́воч|ный (~ен, ~на), *adj.* fragmentary, scrappy.

отры́гива|ть, ю, *impf. of* отрыгну́ть.

отрыг|ну́ть, ну́, нёшь, *pf.* (*of* ~ивать) (+*a. or g.*) to belch.

отры́жк|а, и, *f.* **1.** belch; belching, eructation. **2.** (*fig.*) survival, throw-back.

отр|ы́ть, о́ю, о́ешь, *pf.* (*of* ~ыва́ть²) to dig out; to unearth (*also fig.*).

отря́д, а, *m.* **1.** detachment; передово́й о. (*fig.*) vanguard. **2.** (*biol.*) order.

отря|ди́ть, жу́, ди́шь, *pf.* (*of* ~жа́ть) to detach, detail, tell off.

отряжа́|ть, ю, *impf. of* отряди́ть.

отряса́|ть, áю, *impf. of* ~ти́.

отряс|ти́, у́, ёшь, *past* ~, ~ла́, *pf.* (*of* ~а́ть) (*obs.*) to shake off; о. прах от свои́х ног (*fig.*) to shake off the dust from one's feet.

отря́хива|ть(ся), ю(сь), *impf. of* отряхну́ть(ся).

отрях|ну́ть, ну́, нёшь, *pf.* (*of* ~ивать) to shake down, shake off; о. снег с воротника́ to shake snow off one's collar.

отрях|ну́ться, ну́сь, нёшься, *pf.* (*of* ~иваться) to shake oneself down.

отса|ди́ть, жу́, ~дишь, *pf.* (*of* ~живать) **1.** (*hort.*) to transplant, plant out. **2.** to seat apart. **3.** (*tech.*) to jig.

отса́дк|а, и, *f.* **1.** (*hort.*) transplanting, planting out. **2.** (*tech.*) jigging.

отса́жива|ть, ю, *impf. of* отсади́ть.

отса́жива|ться, юсь, *impf. of* отсе́сть.

отсалют|ова́ть, у́ю, *pf. of* салютова́ть.

отса́сывани|е, я, *n.* suction.

отса́сывател|ь, я, *m.* suction pump.

отса́сыва|ть, ю, *impf. of* отсоса́ть.

отсве́т, а, *m.* reflection; reflected light.

отсве́чива|ть, ю, *impf.* **1.** to be reflected; (+*i.*) to shine (with); в ко́мнате ~л с у́лицы фона́рь the light of the street-lamp was reflected in the room. **2.** (*coll.*) to stand (be) in the light.

отсебя́тин|а, ы, *f.* (*coll.*) words of one's own; something of one's own devising; (*theatr.*) ad-libbing.

отсе́в, а, *m.* **1.** sifting, selection. **2.** siftings, residue.

отсева́|ть, ю = отсе́ивать.

отсе́ива|ть(ся), ю(сь), *impf. of* отсе́ять(ся).

отсе́к, а, *m.* **1.** (*naut., etc.*) compartment; carrel (*in library*). **2.** (*astronautics*) module.

отсека́|ть, ю, *impf. of* отсе́чь.

отсе́ле, *adv.* (*obs.*) hence, from here.

отсел|и́ть, ю́, и́шь, *pf.* (*of* ~я́ть) to settle out, move further out.

отсел|и́ться, ю́сь, и́шься, *pf.* (*of* ~я́ться) to settle out, move further out.

отсе́л|ь = ~е.

отсел|я́ть(ся), я́ю(сь), *impf. of* ~и́ть(ся).

отс|е́сть, я́ду, я́дешь, *past* ~е́л, *pf.* (*of* ~а́живаться) to seat oneself apart; (от) to move away (from).

отсече́ни|е, я, *n.* cutting off, severance; дать го́лову на о. (*coll.*) to stake one's life.

отсе́чк|а, и, *f.* (*tech.*) cut-off.

отсе́|чь, ку́, чёшь, ку́т, *past* ~к, ~кла́; *pf.* (*of* ~ка́ть) to cut off, chop off, sever.

отсе́|ять, ю, ешь, *pf.* (*of* ~ивать) **1.** to sift, screen. **2.** (*fig.*) to eliminate.

отсе́|яться, юсь, ешься, *pf.* (*of* ~иваться) **1.** *pass. of* ~ять. **2.** (*fig.*) to fall off, fall away; бо́льшая часть слу́шателей ~ялась the greater part of the audience had fallen away.

отси|де́ть, жу́, ди́шь, *pf.* (*of* ~живать) **1.** to stay (for); to sit out; он ~де́л де́сять лет в тюрьме́ he has done ten years (in prison). **2.** to make numb by sitting; я ~де́л себе́ но́гу I have pins and needles in my leg.

отси|де́ться, жу́сь, ди́шься, *pf.* (*of* ~живаться) (*coll.*) to sit out (a siege); (*fig., pejor.*) to sit on the fence.

отси́жива|ть(ся), ю(сь), *impf. of* отсиде́ть(ся).

отска́блива|ть, ю, *impf. of* отскобли́ть.

отска|ка́ть, чу́, ~чешь, *pf.* (*coll.*) to gallop, cover by galloping.

отска́кива|ть, ю, *impf. of* отскочи́ть.

отскобл|и́ть, ю́, ~и́шь, *pf.* (*of* отска́бливать) to scrape off, scratch off.

отско́к, а, *m.* rebound.

отскоч|и́ть, у́, ~ишь, *pf.* (*of* отска́кивать) 1. to jump aside, jump away; to rebound, bounce back. 2. (*coll.*) to come off, break off.

отскреба́|ть, ю, *impf. of* отскрести́.

отскре|сти́, бу́, бёшь, *past* ~б, ~бла́, *pf.* (*of* ~ба́ть) to scrape off, scratch off.

отсла́ива|ться, ется, *impf. of* отслои́ться.

отслое́ни|е, я, *n.* (*geol.*) exfoliation.

отсло|и́ться, и́тся, *pf.* (*of* отсла́иваться) (*geol.*) to exfoliate; to scale off.

отслу́жива|ть, ю, *impf.* отслужи́ть.

отслуж|и́ть, у́, ~ишь, *pf.* (*of* ~ивать) 1. to serve; to serve one's time. 2. (*coll.*) (*of implements, etc.*) to have served its turn, be worn out. 3. (*eccl.*) to finish (*a service*).

отсове́т|овать, ую, *pf.* (+*d. and inf.*) to dissuade (from).

отсортир|ова́ть, у́ю, *pf.* (*of* ~о́вывать) to sort (out).

отсортиро́выва|ть, ю, *impf. of* отсортирова́ть.

отсос|а́ть, у́, ёшь, *pf.* (*of* отса́сывать) (+*a. or g.*) to suck off; to filter by suction.

отсо́х|нуть, нет, *past* ~, ~ла, *pf.* (*of* отсыха́ть) to dry up; to wither.

отсро́чива|ть, ю, *impf. of* отсро́чить.

отсро́ч|ить, у, ишь, *pf.* (*of* ~ивать) 1. to postpone, delay, defer; (*leg.*) to adjourn. 2. (*coll.*) to extend (*period of validity of a document*).

отсро́чк|а, и, *f.* 1. postponement, delay, deferment; (*leg.*) adjournment; о. наказа́ния respite; дать ме́сячную ~y to grant a month's grace. 2. (*coll.*) extension (*of period of validity of document*).

отстава́ни|е, я, *n.* lag.

отста|ва́ть, ю́, ёшь, *impf. of* ~ть.

отста́в|ить, лю, ишь, *pf.* (*of* ~ля́ть) 1. to set aside, put aside. 2. (*obs.*) to dismiss, discharge. 3. (*coll.*) to rescind; о.! (*mil. word of command*) as you were!

отста́вк|а, и, *f.* 1. dismissal, discharge; получи́ть ~y у кого́-н. to be dismissed by someone, get the sack from someone. 2. resignation; retirement; вы́йти в ~y to resign, retire; пода́ть в ~y to send in one's resignation; в ~e retired, in retirement. 3. (*coll.*) brush-off.

отставля́|ть, ю, *impf. of* отста́вить.

отставно́й, *adj.* retired.

отста́ива|ть, ю, *impf.* 1. *impf. of* отстоя́ть¹.

2. to fight, dispute; to try to vindicate; мы бу́дем о. на́шу то́чку зре́ния we shall dispute our point of view.

отста́ива|ться, юсь, *impf. of* отстоя́ться.

отста́лост|ь, и, *f.* (*fig.*) backwardness.

отста́лый, *adj.* (*fig.*) backward.

отста́|ть, ну, нешь, *pf.* (*of* ~ва́ть) 1. (от) to fall behind, drop behind; to lag behind; (*fig.*) to be backward, be retarded; to be behind, be behindhand; о. в рабо́те to be behind in (with) one's work; о. от кла́сса to be behind (the rest of) one's class; о. от ве́ка, о. от совреме́нности to be behind the times. 2. (от) to be left behind (by), become detached (from); о. от гру́ппы to become detached from a group; о. от по́езда to be left behind by the train (*sc. at a station en route*). 3. (от) to lose touch (with); to break (with); я ~л от всех свои́х знако́мых вое́нного вре́мени I have lost touch with all my war-time acquaintances. 4. (*coll.*; от) to give up; о. от привы́чки to break oneself of a habit. 5. (*of a clock or watch*) to be slow; о. на полчаса́ to be half an hour slow. 6. (*of plaster, wall-paper, etc.*) to come off. 7. (*coll.*; от) to leave alone; ~нь от меня́! leave me alone!

отста|ю́щий, *pres. part. of* ~ва́ть; *as noun* о., ~ю́щего backward pupil; рабо́та с ~ю́щими remedial work.

отстега́|ть, ю, *pf.* (*of* стега́ть¹) to beat, lash.

отстёгива|ть(ся), ю(сь), *impf. of* отстегну́ть(ся).

отстег|ну́ть, ну́, нёшь, *pf.* (*of* ~ивать) to unfasten, undo; to unbutton.

отстег|ну́ться, нётся, *pf.* (*of* ~иваться) to come unfastened, come undone.

отстир|а́ть, а́ю, *pf.* (*of* ~ывать) to wash off.

отстир|а́ться, а́юсь, *pf.* (*of* ~ыва́ться) to wash off, come out in the wash.

отсти́рыва|ть(ся), ю(сь), *impf. of* отстира́ть(ся).

отсто́|й, я, *m.* sediment, deposit.

отсто́йник, а, *m.* settling tank; sedimentation tank; cesspool.

отсто|я́ть¹, ю́, и́шь, *pf.* (*of* отста́ивать) to defend, save; to stand up for; о. свои́ права́ to assert one's rights.

отсто|я́ть², ю́, и́шь, *pf.* to stand through, stand out; мы ~я́ли весь спекта́кль we stood through the entire show.

отсто|я́ть³, ю́, и́шь, *impf.* (от) to be . . . distant (from); ста́нция ~и́т от це́нтра го́рода на два киломе́тра the station is two kilometres (away) from the centre of the town; э́ти дере́вни ~я́т друг от дру́га на пять вёрст these villages are five versts apart.

отсто|я́ться, и́тся, *pf.* (*of* отста́иваться) 1. (*chem.*) to settle, precipitate. 2. (*fig.*) to settle, become stabilized, become fixed.

отстра́ива|ть(ся), ю(сь), *impf. of* отстро́ить-(ся).

отстране́ни|е, я, *n.* 1. pushing aside. 2. dismissal, discharge.

отстран|и́ть, ю́, и́шь, *pf.* (*of* ~я́ть) 1. to push aside; о. от себя́ все забо́ты to lay aside all one's cares. 2. to dismiss, discharge.

отстран|и́ться, ю́сь, и́шься, *pf.* (*of* ~я́ться) 1. (от) to move away (from); (*fig.*) to keep out of the way (of), keep aloof (from); о. от уда́ра to dodge a blow; о. от до́лжности to relinquish a post. 2. *pass. of* ~и́ть.

отстран|я́ть(ся), я́ю(сь), *impf. of* ~и́ть(ся).

отстре́лива|ть[1], ю, *impf. of* отстрели́ть.

отстре́лива|ть[2], ю, *impf. of* отстреля́ть.

отстре́лива|ться, юсь, *impf. of* отстреля́ться[1].

отстрел|и́ть, ю́, ~ишь, *pf.* (*of* ~ивать[1]) to shoot off.

отстрел|я́ть, я́ю, *pf.* (*of* ~ивать[2]) to shoot (*for commercial purposes, etc.*).

отстрел|я́ться[1], я́юсь, *pf.* (*of* ~иваться) 1. to defend oneself (by shooting). 2. to return fire, fire back.

отстрел|я́ться[2], я́юсь, *pf.* to have finished firing; to have completed a practice (shoot).

отстрига́|ть, ю, *impf. of* отстри́чь.

отстри́|женный, *p.p.p. of* ~чь.

отстри́|чь, гу́, жёшь, гу́т, *past* ~г, ~гла, *pf.* (*of* ~га́ть) to cut off, clip.

отстр|о́ить[1], о́ю, о́ишь, *pf.* (*of* ~а́ивать) to complete construction (of), finish building; to build up.

отстр|о́ить[2], о́ю, о́ишь, *pf.* (*of* ~а́ивать) (*radio*) to tune out, reject (*interfering wavelength*).

отстр|о́иться[1], о́юсь, о́ишься, *pf.* (*of* ~а́иваться) (*coll.*) 1. to finish building. 2. *pass. of* ~о́ить[1].

отстр|о́иться[2], о́юсь, о́ишься, *pf.* (*of* ~а́иваться) (*radio*) to tune out (*adjust receiver so as to avoid interference*).

отстро́йк|а, и, *f.* (*radio*) tuning out.

отсту́к|ать, аю, *pf.* (*of* ~ивать) (*coll.*) to tap out; о. мело́дию to strum a tune; о. на маши́нке to bash out on a typewriter.

отсту́кива|ть, ю, *impf. of* отсту́кать.

о́тступ, а, *m.* (*typ.*) break off, indention.

отступа́тельный, *adj.* (*mil.*) retreat, withdrawal.

отступ|а́ть(ся), а́ю(сь), *impf. of* ~и́ть(ся).

отступ|и́ть, лю́, ~ишь, *pf.* (*of* ~а́ть) 1. to step back; to recede. 2. (*mil.*) to retreat, fall back. 3. (*fig.*) to back down; (от) to go back (on); to give up; о. от реше́ния to go back on a decision. 4. (*fig.*; от) to swerve (from), deviate (from); о. от обы́чая to depart from custom; о. от те́мы to digress. 5. (*typ.*) to indent.

отступ|и́ться, лю́сь, ~ишься, *pf.* (*of* ~а́ться) (*coll.*; от) to give up, renounce; о. от своего́ сло́ва to go back on one's word; они́ все ~и́лись от него́ they have all given him up.

отступле́ни|е, я, *n.* 1. (*mil. and fig.*) retreat. 2. deviation; digression.

отсту́пник, а, *m.* apostate; recreant.

отсту́пничеств|о, а, *n.* apostasy.

отступн|о́й, *adj.* ~ы́е де́ньги (*or as noun* ~о́е, ~о́го, *n.*) smart-money; indemnity, compensation.

отступ|я́, *ger. of* ~и́ть; *as adv.* (от) off, away (from); о. два-три ме́тра two or three metres off; немно́го о. от до́ма a little way away from the house.

отсу́тстви|е, я, *n.* absence; (+*g.*) lack (of); в его́ о. in his absence; за ~ем.(+*g.*) in the absence (of); for lack (of), for want (of); находи́ться в ~и to be absent; блиста́ть свои́м ~ем to be conspicuous by one's absence.

отсу́тств|овать, ую, *impf.* to be absent; (*leg.*) to default.

отсу́тств|ующий, *pres. part. of* ~овать *and adj.* absent (*also fig.*); о. вид blank expression; *as noun* о., ~ующего, *m.* absentee; ~ующие those absent; безве́стно о. missing person.

отсу́чива|ть, ю, *impf. of* отсучи́ть.

отсуч|и́ть, у́, ~ишь, *pf.* (*of* ~ивать) (*coll.*; рукава́, *etc.*) to roll down (sleeves, *etc.*).

отсчёт, а, *m.* reading (*on an instrument*).

отсчит|а́ть, а́ю, *pf.* (*of* ~ывать) 1. to count out, count off; о. пять шаго́в от до́ма to count five paces from the house; о. кому́-н. де́сять рубле́й to count out ten roubles to someone. 2. to read off, take a reading.

отсчи́тыва|ть, ю, *impf. of* отсчита́ть.

отсыла́|ть, ю, *impf. of* отосла́ть.

отсы́лк|а, и, *f.* 1. dispatch; о. де́нег remittance. 2. reference.

отсып|а́ть, лю, лешь, *pf.* (*of* ~а́ть) (+*a. or g.*) to pour off; to measure off.

отсып|а́ть, а́ю, *impf. of* ~ать.

отсы́п|аться, люсь, лешься, *pf.* (*of* ~а́ться[1]) 1. to pour out. 2. *pass. of* ~ать.

отсып|а́ться[1], а́юсь, *impf. of* ~аться.

отсып|а́ться[2], а́юсь, *impf. of* отоспа́ться.

отсыре́лый, *adj.* damp.

отсыре́|ть, ю, *pf. of* сыре́ть.

отсыха́|ть, ю, *impf. of* отсо́хнуть.

отсю́да, *adv.* from here; hence (*also fig.*); (*fig.*) from this; о. сле́дует, что... from this it follows that . . . .

отта́ива|ть, ю, *impf. of* отта́ять.

отта́лкивани|е, я, *n.* (*phys.*) repulsion.

отта́лкива|ть, ю, *impf. of* оттолкну́ть.

отта́лкива|ющий, *pres. part. act. of* ~ть *and adj.* repulsive, repellent.

отта́птыва|ть, ю, *impf. of* оттопта́ть.

оттаска́|ть, ю, *pf.* (*of* таска́ть 2.) to pull; о. кого́-н. за во́лосы to pull someone's hair.

отта́скива|ть, ю, *impf. of* оттащи́ть.

отта́чива|ть, ю, *impf. of* отточи́ть.

оттащ|и́ть, у́, ~ишь, *pf.* (*of* отта́скивать) to drag aside (away), pull aside (away).

отта́|ять, ю, ешь, *pf.* (*of* ~ивать) (*trans. and intrans.*) to thaw out.

оттен|и́ть, ю́, и́шь, *pf.* (*of* ~я́ть) 1. to shade (in). 2. (*fig.*) to set off, make more prominent.

оттён|ок, ка, *m.* shade, nuance (*also fig.*); tint, hue; о. значе́ния shade of meaning; он говори́л с ~ком иро́нии there was a note of irony in his voice.

оттен|я́ть, я́ю, *impf. of* ~и́ть.

о́ттепел|ь, и, *f.* thaw.

оттер|е́ть, ототру́, ототрёшь, *past* ~, ~ла, *pf.* (*of* оттира́ть) 1. to rub out, rub out. 2. to restore sensation (*to parts of the body*) by rubbing. 3. (*coll.*) to press back, push aside.

оттер|е́ться, ототру́сь, ототрёшься, *past* ~ся, ~лась, *pf.* (*of* оттира́ться) to rub out; to come out (*by rubbing*).

оттесн|и́ть, ю́, и́шь, *pf.* (*of* ~я́ть) to drive back, press back; to push aside, shove aside (*also fig.*); о. проти́вника (*mil.*) to force the enemy back; о. конкуре́нта (*fig.*) to edge a competitor out.

оттесн|я́ть, я́ю, *impf. of* ~и́ть.

о́ттиск, а, *m.* 1. impression. 2. off-print, separate.

отти́скива|ть, ю, *impf. of* оттиснуть.

отти́с|нуть, ну, нешь, *pf.* (*of* ~кивать) 1. (*coll.*) to push aside. 2. (*coll.*) to crush. 3. to print.

оттого́, *adv.* that is why; о. мы и не могли́ прие́хать that's why we couldn't come; о... что because; я о. опозда́л, что мото́р не заводи́лся I was late because the engine would not start.

отто́ле, *adv.* (*obs.*) thence, from there.

оттолкн|у́ть, у́, ёшь, *pf.* (*of* отта́лкивать) 1. to push away, push aside. 2. (*fig.*) to antagonize, alienate.

оттолкн|у́ться, у́сь, ёшься, *pf.* (*of* отта́лкиваться) 1. (от) to push off (from). 2. (*fig.*, от) to dispense (with), discard.

отто́л|ь = ~е.

оттома́нк|а, и, *f.* ottoman.

оттоп|та́ть, чу́, ~чешь, *pf.* (*of* отта́птывать) (*coll.*) 1. to hurt, damage (*by much walking*). 2. о. кому́-н. но́гу to tread (heavily) on someone's foot.

оттопы́р|енный, *p.p.p. of* ~ить *and adj.* protruding, sticking out.

оттопы́рива|ть(ся), ю(сь), *impf. of* оттопы́рить(ся).

оттопы́р|ить, ю, ишь, *pf.* (*of* ~ивать) (*coll.*) to stick out; о. ло́кти to stick out one's elbows.

оттопы́р|иться, ится, *pf.* (*of* ~иваться) to protrude, stick out; to bulge.

отторг|а́ть, а́ю, *impf. of* ~нуть.

отто́рг|нуть, ну, нешь, *past* ~, ~ла, *pf.* (*of* ~а́ть) to tear away, seize.

отторже́ни|е, я, *n.* tearing away; (*med.*) rejection (*of a transplanted organ*).

отточ|и́ть, у́, ~ишь, *pf.* (*of* отта́чивать) to sharpen, whet.

отту́да, *adv.* from there.

оттуш|ева́ть, у́ю, у́ешь, *pf.* (*of* ~ёвывать) to shade (off).

оттушёвыва|ть, ю, *impf. of* оттушева́ть.

оттяга́|ть, ю, *pf.* (*coll.*) to gain by a lawsuit.

оття́гива|ть, ю, *impf. of* оттяну́ть.

оття́жк|а, и, *f.* 1. delay, procrastination. 2. (*naut.*) guy(-rope); strut, brace, stay.

оття|ну́ть, ну́, ~нешь, *pf.* (*of* ~гивать) 1. to draw out, pull away. 2. (*mil.*) to draw off. 3. (*coll.*) to delay; что́бы о. вре́мя to gain time. 4. (*tech.*) to forge out.

оття́п|ать, аю, *pf.* (*of* ~ывать) (*coll.*) to chop off.

оття́пыва|ть, ю, *impf. of* оття́пать.

оту́жина|ть, ю, *pf.* 1. to have had supper. 2. (*obs.*) to have supper.

отума́нива|ть, ю, *impf. of* отума́нить.

отума́н|ить, ю, ишь, *pf.* (*of* ~ивать) 1. to blur; to dim; её глаза́ ~ило слеза́ми her eyes were dimmed with tears. 2. (*fig.*) to (be)cloud, obscure; моё созна́ние ~ило вино́м wine had clouded my reason.

отупе́лый, *adj.* (*coll.*) stupefied, dulled.

отупе́ни|е, я, *n.* stupefaction, dullness, torpor.

отупе́|ть, ю, *pf.* (*coll.*) to grow dull, sink into torpor.

отутю́жива|ть, ю, *impf. of* отутю́жить.

отутю́ж|ить, у, ишь, *pf.* (*of* ~ивать) 1. to iron (out). 2. (*fig., coll.*) to beat up.

отуч|а́ть(ся), а́ю(сь), *impf. of* ~и́ть(ся).

оту́чива|ться, юсь, *impf. of* отучи́ться².

отуч|и́ть, у́, ~ишь, *pf.* (*of* ~а́ть) (от *or* + *inf.*) to break (of); о. от груди́ to wean.

отуч|и́ться¹, у́сь, ~ишься, *pf.* (*of* ~а́ться) (от *or* + *inf.*) to break oneself (of).

отуч|и́ться², у́сь, ~ишься, *pf.* (*of* ~иваться) to have finished one's lessons; to finish learning.

отха́жива|ть, ю, *impf. of* отходи́ть², ³.

отха́рк|ать, аю, *pf.* (*of* ~ивать) to expectorate.

отха́ркива|ть, ю, *impf. of* отха́ркать.

отха́ркива|ться, юсь, *impf. of* отха́ркнуться.

отха́ркива|ющий, *pres. part. act. of* ~ть; ~ющее (сре́дство) (*med.*) expectorant.

отха́ркн|уть, у, ешь, *pf.* to hawk up.

отхáрк|нуться, нусь, нешься, *pf.* (*of* ~и-
ваться) **1.** (*coll.*) to clear one's throat. **2.** to
come up (*as result of expectoration*).

отхва|ти́ть, чу́, ~тишь, *pf.* (*of* ~тывать)
(*coll.*) **1.** to snip off; to chop off; он ~ти́л
себé пáлец топоро́м he chopped his finger
off with an axe. **2.** to perform, execute in
lively fashion.

отхвáтыва|ть, ю, *impf. of* отхвати́ть.

отхлеб|нýть, нý, нёшь, *pf.* (*of* ~ывать)
(*coll.*; +*a.* or *g.*) to take a sip (of); to take a
mouthful (of).

отхлёбыва|ть, ю, *impf. of* отхлебнýть.

отхле|стáть, щý, ~щешь, *pf.* (*coll.*) to give
a lashing.

отхлы́н|уть, у, ешь, *pf.* to rush back, flood
back (*also fig.*).

отхóд, а, *m.* **1.** departure; sailing. **2.** (*mil.*)
withdrawal, retirement, falling back. **3.**
(от) deviation (from); break (with). **4.** *see*
~ы.

отхо|ди́ть¹, жý, ~ди́шь, *impf. of* отойти́.

отхо|ди́ть², жý, ~ди́шь, *pf.* (*of* отхáживать)
(*coll.*) to cure, heal, nurse back to health.

отхо|ди́ть³, жý, ~ди́шь, *pf.* (*of* отхáживать)
(*coll.*) to tire, hurt (*by walking*).

отхóдн|ая, ой, *f.* prayer for the dying;
справля́ть ~ую комý-н. (*fig.*) to write someone off.

отхóдник, а, *m.* (*obs.*) seasonal worker (*esp.
of peasants going to cities*).

отхóдничеств|о, а, *n.* (*obs.*) seasonal work.

отхóдчив|ый (~, ~а), *adj.* not bearing
grudges.

отхóд|ы, ов (*tech.*) waste (products); siftings,
screenings; tailings.

отхó|женный, *p.p.p. of* ~ди́ть³; нóги у меня́
~жены I have been walked off my feet.

отхóж|ий, *adj.* о. прóмысел seasonal work;
~ее мéсто (*coll.*) latrine, earth closet.

отцве|сти́, тý, тёшь, *past* ~л, ~лá, *pf.* (*of*
~тáть) to finish blossoming, fade (*also fig.*);
онá ~лá she has lost her bloom.

отцве|тáть, тáю, *impf. of* ~сти́.

отце|ди́ть, жý, ~ди́шь, *pf.* (*of* ~жи́вать) to
strain off, filter.

отцéжива|ть, ю, *impf. of* отцеди́ть.

отцеп|и́ть, лю́, ~ишь, *pf.* (*of* ~ля́ть) to un-
hook; to uncouple.

отцеп|и́ться, лю́сь, ~ишься, *pf.* (*of* ~ля́ть-
ся) **1.** to come unhooked; to come uncoupled. **2.** (*fig., coll.*) to leave alone; ~и́сь
ты от меня́! leave me alone!

отцéпк|а, и, *f.* (*railways*) uncoupling.

отцепля́|ть(ся), ю(сь), *impf. of* отцепи́ть-
(ся).

отцеуби́йств|о, а, *n.* parricide, patricide
(*act*).

отцеуби́йц|а, ы, *m. and f.* parricide, patri-
cide (*agent*).

отцóв, *adj.* one's father's.

отцóвск|ий, *adj.* one's father's; paternal;
~ое наслéдие patrimony.

отцóвств|о, а, *n.* paternity.

отчáива|ться, юсь, *impf. of* отчáяться.

отчáлива|ть, ю, *impf. of* отчáлить; ~й!
(*coll.*) be off!

отчáл|ить, ю, ишь, *pf.* (*of* ~ивать) (*naut.*)
1. to cast off. **2.** (*intrans.*) to push off, cast off.

отчáсти, *adv.* partly.

отчáяни|е, я, *n.* despair.

отчáян|ный (~, ~на), *adj.* despairing; (*fig.,
coll.; in var. senses*) desperate; о. взор despair-
ing look; о. дурáк (*coll.*) awful fool; о. игрóк
desperate gambler; ~ное положéние desperate plight.

отчá|яться, юсь, ешься, *pf.* (*of* ~иваться)
(+*inf.* or в+*p.*) to despair (of).

óтче (*obs.*) *voc. of* отéц; О. наш our Father
(*the Lord's prayer*).

отчегó, *adv.* why; вот о. that's why.

отчегó-либо, *adv.* for some reason or other.

отчегó-то, *adv.* for some reason.

отчекáнива|ть, ю, *impf. of* отчекáнить.

отчекáн|ить, ю, ишь, *pf.* (*of* чекáнить *and*
~ивать) **1.** to coin, mint. **2.** (*fig.*) to execute clearly and distinctly; о. словá to rap
out (one's words).

отчёркива|ть, ю, *impf. of* отчеркнýть.

отчерк|нýть, нý, нёшь, *pf.* (*of* ~ивать) to
mark off.

отчерп|нýть, нý, нёшь, *pf.* (*of* ~ывать)
(+*a.* or *g.*) to ladle out.

отчéрпыва|ть, ю, *impf. of* отчерпнýть.

óтчеств|о, а, *n.* patronymic; как его́ по ~у?
what is his patronymic?

отчёт, а, *m.* account; дать о. (в+*p.*) to give
an account (of), report (on); взять дéньги
под о. to take money on account; отдáть
себé о. (в+*p.*) to be aware (of), realize.

отчётливост|ь, и, *f.* **1.** distinctness; preci-
sion. **2.** intelligibility, clarity.

отчётлив|ый (~, ~а), *adj.* **1.** distinct; pre-
cise. **2.** intelligible, clear.

отчётно-вы́борн|ый, *adj.* ~ое собрáние
meeting held to hear reports and elect new
officials.

отчётност|ь, и, *f.* **1.** book-keeping. **2.** ac-
counts.

отчёт|ный, *adj. of* ~; о. блáнк report card;
о. год financial year, current year; о. док-
лáд report.

отчи́зн|а, ы, *f.* (*poet.*) one's country, native
land; mother country, fatherland.

óтчий, *adj.* (*obs., poet.*) paternal.

óтчим, а, *m.* step-father.

óтчин|а, ы, *f.* = вóтчина.

отчислéни|е, я, *n.* **1.** deduction. **2.** assign-
ment. **3.** dismissal.

отчи́сл|ить, ю, ишь, *pf.* (*of* ~я́ть) **1.** to de-

duct; о. часть зарпла́ты в упла́ту подохо́д-
ного нало́га to deduct part of wages for
income-tax payment. **2.** to assign. **3.** to
dismiss; о. в запа́с (*mil.*) to transfer to the
reserve.

отчисл|Я́ть, Я́ю, *impf. of* ∼ить.

отчи́|стить, щу, стишь, *pf.* (*of* ∼ща́ть) **1.** to
clean off; to brush off. **2.** to clean up.

отчи́|ститься, щусь, стишься, *pf.* (*of*
∼ща́ться) **1.** to come off, come out. **2.** to
become clean.

отчит|а́ть, а́ю, *pf.* (*of* ∼ывать) (*coll.*) to read
a lecture (to), tell off.

отчит|а́ться, а́юсь, *pf.* (*of* ∼ываться) (в+*p.*)
to give an account (of), report (on); о.
пе́ред избира́телями to report back to the
electors.

отчи́тыва|ть(ся), ю(сь), *impf. of* отчита́ть-
(ся).

отчища́|ть(ся), ю(сь), *impf. of* отчи́стить-
(ся).

отчу|ди́ть, жу́, ди́шь, *pf.* (*of* ∼жда́ть) (*leg.*)
to alienate, estrange.

отчужда́|емый, *pres. part. pass. of* ∼ть *and*
adj. (*leg.*) alienable.

отчужда́|ть, ю, *impf. of* отчуди́ть.

отчужде́ни|е, я, *n.* **1.** (*leg.*) alienation. **2.**
estrangement.

отчуждённост|ь, и, *f.* estrangement.

отшага́|ть, ю, *pf.* (*coll.*) to walk; to tramp;
to trudge.

отшагн|у́ть, у́, ёшь, *pf.* (*coll.*) to step aside,
step back.

отшатн|у́ться, у́сь, ёшься, *pf.* (от) **1.** to
start back (from); to recoil (from). **2.** (*fig.*)
to give up; to forsake; to break (with); о.
от дру́га to give up a friend.

отшвы́рива|ть, ю, *impf. of* отшвырну́ть.

отшвыр|ну́ть, ну́, нёшь, *pf.* (*of* ∼ивать) to
fling away; to throw off.

отше́льник, а, *m.* hermit, anchorite; (*fig.*)
recluse.

отше́льни|ческий, *adj. of* ∼к.

отше́льничеств|о, а, *n.* a hermit's life, a
recluse's life (*also fig., iron.*).

отши́б, а, *m. only in phrase* на ∼е at a distance (*from a settlement*); жить на ∼е (*fig.*)
to live in seclusion, live a recluse's life.

отшиб|а́ть, а́ю, *impf. of* ∼и́ть.

отшиб|и́ть, у́, ёшь, *past* ∼, ∼ла, *pf.* (*of* ∼а́ть)
(*coll.*) **1.** to break off; to knock off; о. ру́чку
у ча́йника to knock the handle off a tea-
pot; у меня́ ∼ло па́мять my memory has
failed me. **2.** to hurt; о. себе́ ру́ку to
hurt one's arm. **3.** to throw back.

отши́|ть, отошью́, отошьёшь, *pf.* (*coll.*) to
snub, rebuff.

отшлёп|ать, аю, *pf.* (*of* ∼ывать) (*coll.*) to
spank.

отшлёпыва|ть, ю, *impf. of* отшлёпать.

отшлиф|ова́ть, у́ю, *pf.* (*of* ∼о́вывать) to
grind; to polish (*also fig.*).

отшпи́лива|ть(ся), ю(сь), *impf. of* отшпи́-
лить(ся).

отшпи́л|ить, ю, ишь, *pf.* (*of* ∼ивать) to un-
pin, unfasten.

отшпи́л|иться, юсь, ишься, *pf.* (*of* ∼ивать-
ся) to come unpinned, come unfastened.

отштукату́р|ить, ю, ишь, *pf. of* штукату́-
рить.

отшу|ти́ться, чу́сь, ∼тишься, *pf.* (*of* ∼чи-
ваться) to laugh off; to make a joke in reply.

отшу́чива|ться, юсь, *impf. of* отшути́ться.

отщелка́|ть, ю, *pf.* (*coll.*) to slang.

отщепе́н|ец, ца, *m.* renegade.

отщеп|и́ть, лю́, и́шь, *pf.* (*of* ∼ля́ть) to chip
off.

отщепля́|ть, ю, *impf. of* отщепи́ть.

отщип|а́ть, лю́, ∼лешь, *pf.* (*of* ∼ывать) to
pinch off, nip off.

отщи́пыва|ть, ю, *impf. of* отщипа́ть.

отъеда́|ть(ся), ю(сь), *impf. of* отъе́сть(ся).

отъе́зд, а, *m.* departure.

отъе́з|дить, жу, дишь, *pf.* (*coll.*) to have
driven; to have covered (*driving, riding*).

отъезжа́|ть, ю, *impf. of* отъе́хать.

отъезжа́|ющий, *pres. part. of* ∼ть; *as noun* о.,
∼ющего, *m.* departing person.

отъе́зжий, *adj.* (*obs.*) distant.

отъёмный, *adj.* removable, detachable.

отъе́|сть, м, шь, ст, ди́м, ди́те, дя́т, *past*
∼л, ∼ла, *pf.* (*of* ∼да́ть) to eat off.

**отъе́|сться, мся, шься, стся, ди́мся, ди́-
тесь, дя́тся,** *past* ∼лся, ∼лась, *pf.* (*of*
∼да́ться) to put on weight; to feed well.

отъе́|хать, ду, дешь, *pf.* (*of* ∼зжа́ть) to
depart.

отъя́вленный, *adj.* (*coll. pejor.*) thorough,
inveterate, out-and-out.

от|ъя́ть, ыму́, ы́мешь, *pf.* (*obs.*) = ∼ня́ть.

отыгр|а́ть, а́ю, *pf.* (*of* ∼ывать) to win back.

отыгр|а́ться, а́юсь, *pf.* (*of* ∼ываться) **1.** to
win back, get back what one has lost. **2.**
(*fig., coll.*) to get out (*of an awkward situation*).

оты́грыва|ть(ся), ю(сь), *impf. of* отыгра́ть-
(ся).

о́тыгрыш, а, *m.* sum won back.

отымённый, *adj.* (*ling.*) denominative.

оты|ска́ть, щу́, ∼щешь, *pf.* (*of* ∼скивать)
to find; to track down, run to earth.

оты|ска́ться, щу́сь, ∼щешься, *pf.* (*of* ∼ски-
ваться) to turn up, appear.

оты́скива|ть, ю, *impf.* **1.** *impf. of* отыска́ть.
2. (*impf. only*) to look for, try to find.

оты́скива|ться, юсь, *impf. of* отыска́ться.

отэкзамен|ова́ть, у́ю, *pf.* to finish examining.

отяго|ти́ть, щу́, ти́шь, *pf.* (*of* ∼ща́ть) to
burden.

отягоща́|ть, ю, *impf. of* отяготи́ть.

отягч|а́ть, а́ю, *impf. of* ~и́ть; ~а́ющие (вину́) обстоя́тельства aggravating circumstances.

отягч|и́ть, у́, и́шь, *pf.* (*of* ~а́ть) to aggravate.

отяжеле́лый, *adj.* heavy.

отяжеле́|ть, ю, *pf.* to become heavy.

офе́н|ский, *adj. of* ~я.

офе́н|я, и, *m.* (*hist.*) pedlar, huckster.

офи́т, а, *m.* (*min.*) ophite.

офице́р, а, *m.* officer.

офице́р|ский, *adj. of* ~; ~ское собра́ние officers' mess.

офице́рств|о, а, *n.* 1. (*collect.*) the officers. 2. commissioned rank.

официа́льн|ый, *adj.* official; ~ое лицо́ an official.

официа́нт, а, *m.* waiter.

официа́нтк|а, и, *f.* waitress.

официо́з, а, *m.* semi-official organ (*of press*).

официо́з|ный (~ен, ~на), *adj.* semi-official.

оформи́тел|ь, я, *m.* decorator, stage-painter.

офо́рм|ить, лю, ишь, *pf.* (*of* ~ля́ть) 1. to get up, mount, put into shape; о. пье́су to design the sets for a play. 2. to register officially, legalize; о. вступле́ние в брак to register a marriage; о. докуме́нт to draw up a paper. 3. to enrol, take on the staff.

офо́рм|иться, люсь, ишься, *pf.* (*of* ~ля́ться) 1. to take shape. 2. to be registered; to legalize one's position. 3. to be taken on the staff, join the staff.

оформле́ни|е, я, *n.* 1. get-up; mounting; сцени́ческое о. staging. 2. registration, legalization.

оформля́|ть(ся), ю(сь), *impf. of* офо́рмить(ся).

офо́рт, а, *m.* etching.

офранцу́|зить, жу, зишь, *pf.* to frenchify.

офранцу́|зиться, жусь, зишься, *pf.* to become frenchified.

офсе́т, а, *m.* (*typ.*) offset process.

офтальми́|я, и, *f.* (*med.*) ophthalmia.

офтальмо́лог, а, *m.* ophthalmologist.

офтальмологи́ческий, *adj.* ophthalmological.

офтальмоло́ги|я, и, *f.* ophthalmology.

ох, *interj.* oh! ah!

оха́ива|ть, ю, *impf. of* оха́ять.

оха́льник, а, *m.* (*coll.*) mischief-maker.

оха́льнича|ть, ю, *impf.* (*coll.*) to get up to mischief.

оха́льный, *adj.* mischievous.

о́ханье, я, *n.* (*coll.*) moaning, groaning.

оха́пк|а, и, *f.* armful; взять в ~у (*coll.*) to take in one's arms.

охарактериз|ова́ть, у́ю, *pf.* to characterize, describe.

о́х|ать, аю, *impf.* (*of* ~нуть) to moan, groan; to sigh.

оха́|ять, ю, *pf.* (*of* ха́ять *and* ~ивать) (*coll.*) to criticize, censure.

охва́т, а, *m.* 1. scope, range. 2. inclusion. 3. (*mil.*) outflanking, envelopment.

охва|ти́ть, чу́, ~ти́шь, *pf.* (*of* ~тывать) 1. to envelop; to enclose; дом ~ти́ло пла́менем the house was enveloped in flames; о. бо́чку обруча́ми to hoop a cask. 2. to grip, seize; их ~ти́л у́жас they were seized with panic. 3. (+*i.*) (*coll.*) to draw (in), involve (in); о. молодёжь обще́ственной рабо́той to draw young people into social work. 4. (*fig.*) to comprehend, take in. 5. (*mil.*) to outflank, envelop.

охва́тн|ый, *adj.* ~ое движе́ние (*mil.*) flanking movement, enveloping movement.

охва́тыва|ть, ю, *impf. of* охвати́ть.

охва́|ченный, *p.p.p. of* ~ти́ть; о. у́жасом terror-stricken.

охво́сть|е, я, *n.* (*collect.*) 1. chaff, husks. 2. (*fig.*) rabble.

охладева́|ть, ю, *impf. of* охладе́ть.

охладе́лый, *adj.* (*obs.*) cold; grown cold.

охладе́|ть, ю, *pf.* (*of* ~ва́ть) to grow cold; (*fig.*; к) to grow cool (towards), lose interest (in).

охлади́тел|ь, я, *m.* (*tech.*) cooler, refrigerator; condenser.

охлади́тельный, *adj.* cooling.

охла|ди́ть, жу́, ди́шь, *pf.* (*of* ~жда́ть) to cool, cool off (*also fig.*); о. чей-н. пыл to damp someone's ardour.

охла|ди́ться, жу́сь, ди́шься, *pf.* (*of* ~жда́ться) to become cool, cool down (*also fig.*).

охлажда́|ть(ся), ю(сь), *impf. of* охлади́ть(ся).

охлажда́|ющий, *pres. part. act. of* ~ть *and adj.* cooling, refrigerating; ~ющая жи́дкость coolant; ~ющее простра́нство condensation chamber.

охлажде́ни|е, я, *n.* 1. cooling (off); пове́рхность ~я cooling surface; с возду́шным ~ем air-cooled. 2. (*fig.*) coolness.

охло́п|ок, ка, *pl.* ~ки, ~ков (*and* ~ья, ~ьев), *m.* tuft; (*sing. only.*; *collect.*) waste (*of fibrous substances*).

охмеле́|ть, ю, *pf.* (*of* хмеле́ть) (*coll.*) to become tight.

охмел|и́ть, ю́, и́шь, *pf.* (*of* ~я́ть) to make intoxicated (*also fig.*).

охмел|я́ть, я́ю, *impf. of* ~и́ть.

о́х|нуть, ну, нешь, *pf. of* ~ать.

охоло|сти́ть, щу́, сти́шь, *pf.* to castrate, geld.

охора́шива|ться, юсь, *impf.* (*coll.*) to smarten oneself up.

охо́т|а¹, ы, *f.* hunt, hunting; chase; о. с ружьём shooting; пcóвая о. riding to hounds; соко́линая о. falconry.

охо́т|а², ы, *f.* 1. (к *or* +*inf.*) desire, wish,

inclination; у него́ бо́льше нет ~ы писа́ть he no longer has any desire to write; по свое́й ~e of one's own accord; что ему́ за о.! what makes him do it!; о. тебе́ спо́рить с ним! (*coll.*) what makes you argue with him! **2.** heat (*in female animals*).

охо́|титься, чусь, тишься, *impf.* (на+*a. or* за+*i.*) to hunt; (*fig.*; за+*i.*) to hunt for.

охо́тк|а, и, *f.* в ~у (*coll.*) with pleasure, eagerly.

охо́тник¹, а, *m.* hunter; sportsman.

охо́тник², а, *m.* **1.** (до *or* +*inf.*) lover (of); enthusiast (for); он большо́й о. до грибо́в he is a great mushroom lover. **2.** volunteer; есть ли ~и пойти́? are there any volunteers? will anyone volunteer to go?

охо́тнич|ий, *adj.* hunting; sporting, shooting; о. биле́т hunting permit; о. до́мик shooting-box; ~ье ружьё fowling-piece, sporting gun; ~ья соба́ка hound, gun-dog; о. расска́з (*joc.*) traveller's tale, tall story.

охо́тно, *adv.* willingly, gladly, readily.

охо́ч|ий (~, ~а), *adj.* (+*inf.*; *coll.*) inclined (to), keen (to), having an urge (to).

о́хр|а, ы, *f.* ochre; кра́сная о. raddle, ruddle.

охра́н|а, ы, *f.* **1.** guarding; protection; о. труда́ measures for protection of labour. **2.** guard; ли́чная о. body-guard; пограни́чная о. frontier guard; в сопровожде́нии ~ы under escort, in custody.

охране́ни|е, я, *n.* safeguarding; (*mil.*) protection; сторожево́е о. outposts.

охрани́тел|ь, я, *m.* **1.** (*rhet.*) protector, guardian. **2.** (*obs.*) conservative.

охрани́тельный, *adj.* **1.** (*leg.*) protective. **2.** (*obs.*) conservative.

охран|и́ть, ю́, и́шь, *pf.* (*of* ~я́ть) to guard, protect.

охра́нк|а, и, *f.* (*coll.*) Okhranka (*Secret Police Department in tsarist Russia*).

охра́нник, а, *m.* (*coll.*) **1.** guard. **2.** secret police agent; member of Okhranka.

охра́н|ный, *adj. of* ~а; ~ная гра́мота, о. лист safe-conduct, pass; ~ная зо́на (*mil.*) restricted area; ~ное отделе́ние (*hist.*) Secret Police Department (*in tsarist Russia*).

охран|я́ть, я́ю, *impf. of* ~и́ть.

охри́плый, *adj.* (*coll.*) hoarse.

охри́п|нуть, ну, нешь, *past* ~, ~ла, *pf.* (*of* хри́пнуть) to become hoarse.

о́хр|ить, ю, ишь, *impf.* to colour with ochre.

охроме́|ть, ю, *pf.* (*of* хроме́ть) (*coll.*) to go lame.

оху́лк|а, и, *only in phrases* ~и на́ руку не класть (положи́ть); он ~и на́ руку не поло́жит (*coll.*) he is no fool.

оцара́па|ть, ю, *pf.* (*of* цара́пать) to scratch.

оцара́па|ться, юсь, *pf.* to scratch oneself.

оце́жива|ть, ю, *impf.* о. комара́ (*fig.*) to

strain at a gnat.

оцело́т, а, *m.* (*zool.*) ocelot.

оце́нива|ть, ю, *impf. of* оцени́ть.

оцен|и́ть, ю́, ~ишь, *pf.* (*of* ~ивать) **1.** to estimate, evaluate; to appraise; о. в де́сять рубле́й to estimate at ten roubles. **2.** to appreciate; о. что-н. по досто́инству to appreciate something at its true value.

оце́нк|а, и, *f.* **1.** estimation, evaluation; appraisal; estimate; о. иму́щества valuation of property; о. обстано́вки (*mil.*) estimate of the situation. **2.** appreciation; дать настоя́щую ~у чему́-н. to give something a proper appreciation.

оце́н|очный, *adj. of* ~ка.

оце́нщик, а, *m.* valuer.

оцепене́лый, *adj.* torpid; benumbed.

оцепене́|ть, ю, *pf. of* цепене́ть.

оцеп|и́ть, лю́, ~ишь, *pf.* (*of* ~ля́ть) to surround; to cordon off.

оцепле́ни|е, я, *n.* **1.** surrounding; cordoning off. **2.** cordon.

оцепля́|ть, ю, *impf. of* оцепи́ть.

оцинко́в|анный, *p.p.p. of* ~а́ть *and adj.* zinc-coated, galvanized.

оцинк|ова́ть, у́ю, *pf.* (*of* ~о́вывать) to (coat with) zinc, galvanize.

оцинко́выва|ть, ю, *impf. of* оцинкова́ть.

оча́г, а́, *m.* **1.** hearth (*also fig.*); ку́хонный о. kitchen range; дома́шний о. (*fig.*) hearth, home. **2.** (*fig.*) centre, seat; nidus; о. войны́ seat of war; о. зара́зы nidus of infection; о. землетрясе́ния earthquake centre.

оча́нк|а, и, *f.* (*bot.*) euphrasy, eyebright.

очарова́ни|е, я, *n.* charm, fascination.

очарова́тел|ьный (~ен, ~ьна), *adj.* charming, fascinating.

очар|ова́ть, у́ю, *pf.* (*of* ~о́вывать) to charm, fascinate.

очаро́выва|ть, ю, *impf. of* очарова́ть.

очеви́д|ец, ца, *m.* eye-witness.

очеви́дно, *adv.* obviously, evidently; вы, о., не согла́сны you obviously do not agree.

очеви́д|ный (~ен, ~на), *adj.* obvious, evident, manifest, patent.

очелове́чива|ть(ся), ю(сь), *impf. of* очелове́чить(ся).

очелове́ч|ить, у, ишь, *pf.* (*of* ~ивать) to make human, humanize.

очелове́ч|иться, усь, ишься, *pf.* (*of* ~иваться) to become human.

о́чень, *adv.* very; very much.

очерви́ве|ть, ю, *pf. of* черви́веть.

очередн|о́й, *adj.* **1.** next; next in turn; о. вопро́с the next question; о. вы́пуск latest issue (*of a journal, etc.*); ~а́я зада́ча the immediate task; ~о́е зва́ние the next higher rank. **2.** periodic(al); recurrent; usual, regular; (*pejor.*) routine; ~ые неприя́тности the usual trouble; о. о́тпуск regular holidays; ~ая эпидéмия грúппа periodical epidemic of influenza.

очерёдност|ь, и, *f.* periodicity; regular succession; order of priority.

óчеред|ь, и, *pl.* ~**и,** ~**éй,** *f.* **1.** turn; пропустúть свою́ о. to miss one's turn; о. за вáми it is your turn; в свою́ о. in one's turn; на ~**и** next (in turn); по ~**и** in turn, in order, in rotation; в пéрвую о. in the first place, in the first instance. **2.** queue, line; стоя́ть в ~**и** (за + *i*.) to queue (for), stand in line (for). **3.** (*mil.*) (пулемётная) о. burst; батарéйная о. (battery) salvo.

очерёт, а, *m.* (*bot.*) bog-rush.

óчерк, а, *m.* essay, sketch, study; outline; ~**и** рýсской истóрии studies in Russian history.

очéркива|ть, ю, *impf. of* очеркнýть.

очеркúст, а, *m.* essayist.

очерк|нýть, нý, нёшь, *pf.* (*of* ~**ивать**) to place a circle round.

очерк|óвый, *adj. of* ~; ~**óвая** темáтика subject-matter for an essay.

очерн|úть, ю́, úшь, *pf. of* чернúть 2.

очерствéлый, *adj.* hardened, callous.

очерствé|ть, ю, *pf. of* черствéть 2.

очертáни|е, я, *n.* outline.

очер|тúть, чý, ~**тишь,** *pf.* (*of* ~**чивать**) to outline; ~**тя́** гóлову (*coll.*) without thinking, headlong.

очéрчива|ть, ю, *impf. of* очертúть.

очёс, а, *m.* (*collect.*) = ~**ки.**

оче|сáть, шý, ~**шешь,** *pf.* (*of* ~**сывать**) to comb out.

очёс|ки, ков, *sing.* ~**ок,** ~**ка,** *m.* combings; flocks; льняны́е о. flax tow.

очёсыва|ть, ю, *impf. of* очесáть.

очéчник, а, *m.* spectacle case.

óчи, *pl. of* óко.

очúнива|ть, ю, *impf. of* очинúть.

очин|úть, ю́, ~**ишь,** *pf.* (*of* ~**ивать** *and* чинúть²) to sharpen, point.

очúнк|а, и, *f.* sharpening; машúнка для ~**и** карандашéй pencil-sharpener.

очистúтельн|ый, *adj.* purifying, cleansing; о. аппарáт (*tech.*) purifier; rectifier; о. бак (sugar) clarifier, clearing pan; о. завóд refinery; ~**ое** срéдство cleanser, detergent.

очú|стить, щу, стишь, *pf.* (*of* ~**щáть**) **1.** to clean; to cleanse, purify; (*tech.*) to refine; to rectify. **2.** (от) to clear (of); to fee; о. почтóвый я́щик to clear a letter-box; о. кишéчник to open the bowels. **3.** to peel.

очú|ститься, щусь, стишься, *pf.* (*of* ~**щáть**ся) **1.** to clear oneself. **2.** (от) to become clear (of). **3.** *pass. of* ~**стить.**

очúстк|а, и, *f.* **1.** cleaning; cleansing, purification; (*tech.*) refinement; rectification; мóкрая о. гáза gas scrubbing; о. стóчных вод sewage disposal; для ~**и** сóвести (*coll.*)

for conscience' sake. **2.** clearance; freeing; (*mil.*) mopping-up; о. кишéчника evacuation of the bowels.

очúстк|и, ов, *no sing.* peelings.

очúт|ок, ка, *m.* (*bot.*) stonecrop.

очищá|ть(ся), ю(сь), *impf. of* очúстить(ся).

очищéни|е, я, *n.* cleansing; purification; мéсячное о. (*obs.*) menstruation.

очú|щенный, *p.p.p. of* ~**стить;** *as noun* ~**щенная,** ~**щенной,** *f.* (*coll.*) vodka.

очк|ú, óв, *no sing.* spectacles.

очк|ó¹, á, *pl.* ~**и,** ~**óв,** *n.* **1.** (*on cards or dice*) pip. **2.** (*in scoring*) point; дать ~**óв** вперёд to give points. **3.** hole; смотровóе о. peephole.

очк|ó², á, *n.* втерéть комý-н. ~**й** (*coll.*) to throw dust in someone's eyes.

очковтирáтельств|о, а, *n.* (*coll.*) deception.

очкó|вый¹, *adj. of* ~¹; ~**вая** систéма points system (of scoring).

очкóв|ый², *adj.* ~**ая** змея́ cobra.

очн|ýться, ýсь, ёшься, *pf.* **1.** to wake. **2.** to come to (oneself), regain consciousness.

óчн|ый, *adj.* **1.** (*as opp. to* заóчный) internal (*instruction, student, etc., as opp. to* external, extra-mural). **2.** ~**ая** стáвка (*leg.*) confrontation.

очýвств|оваться, уюсь, *pf.* **1.** to come to (oneself), regain consciousness. **2.** (*coll.*) to have a change of heart; to repent.

очумéлый, *adj.* (*coll.*) mad, off one's head; бежáть, как о. to run like a mad thing.

очумé|ть, ю, *pf.* (*coll.*) to go mad, go off one's head.

очут|úться, ~**ишься,** *pf.* to find oneself, come to be; о. в нелóвком положéнии to find oneself in an awkward position; как вы здесь ~**úлись**? how did you come to be here?

очýха|ться, юсь, *pf.* (*coll.*) to come to oneself.

ошалéлый, *adj.* (*coll.*) crazy, crazed.

ошалé|ть, ю, *pf. of* шалéть.

ошарáшива|ть, ю, *impf. of* ошарáшить.

ошарáш|ить, у, ишь, *pf.* (*of* ~**ивать**) (*coll.*) **1.** to beat, bang. **2.** (*fig.*) to strike dumb, flabbergast.

ошварт|овáть, ýю, *pf.* (*naut.*) to make fast.

ошéйник, а, *m.* (*animal's*) collar; собáчий о. dog-collar.

ошеломúтельный, *adj.* stunning.

ошелом|úть, лю́, úшь, *pf.* (*of* ~**ля́ть**) to stun.

ошеломлéни|е, я, *n.* stupefaction.

ошеломля́|ть, ю, *impf. of* ошеломúть; ~**ющий** stunning.

ошельм|овáть, ýю, *pf. of* шельмовáть.

ошиб|áться, áюсь, *impf. of* ~**úться.**

ошиб|úться, ýсь, ёшься, *past* ~**ся,** ~**лась,**

pf. (*of* ~а́ться) to be mistaken, make a mistake, make mistakes; to be wrong; to err, be at fault.

ошибк|а, и, *f.* mistake; error; blunder; по ~e by mistake.

ошибоч|ный (~ен, ~на), *adj.* erroneous, mistaken.

оши́ка|ть, ю, *pf.* (*of* ши́кать 2) (*coll.*) to hiss off the stage.

ошлак|ова́ть, у́ю, *pf.* (*no impf.*) (*tech.*) to form slack, form clinker.

ошмёт|ки, ков, *sing.* ~ок, ~ка, *m.* (*coll.*) worn out shoes; rags.

ошпа́рива|ть, ю, *impf. of* ошпа́рить.

ошпа́р|ить, ю, ишь, *pf.* (*of* ~ивать) to scald.

оштраф|ова́ть, у́ю, *pf. of* штрафова́ть.

оштукату́р|ить, ю, ишь, *pf. of* штукату́рить.

ошу́юю, *adv.* (*arch.*) to the left, on the left hand.

ощен|и́ться, и́тся, *pf. of* щени́ться.

ощёрива|ть(ся),ю(сь), *impf. of* ощёрить(ся).

ощёр|ить, ю, ишь, *pf.* (*of* ~ивать) (*coll.*) to gnash.

ощёр|иться, юсь, ишься, *pf.* (*of* ~иваться) (*coll.*) to gnash one's teeth.

ощети́нива|ться, юсь, *impf. of* ощети́ниться.

ощети́н|иться, юсь, ишься, *pf.* (*of* ~иваться and щети́ниться) to bristle up (*also fig.*).

ощи́п|анный, *p.p.p. of* ~а́ть *and adj.* (*fig., coll.*) wretched, piteous.

ощип|а́ть, лю́, ~лешь, *pf.* (*of* щипа́ть 4 *and* ~ывать) to pluck.

ощи́пыва|ть, ю, *impf. of* ощипа́ть.

ощу́п|ать, аю, *pf.* (*of* ~ывать) to feel; to grope about (in).

ощу́пыва|ть, ю, *impf. of* ощу́пать.

о́щуп|ь, и, *f.* на о. to the touch; by touch; идти́ на о. to grope one's way.

о́щупью, *adv.* 1. gropingly, fumblingly; by touch; иска́ть о. to grope for; пробра́ться о. to grope one's way. 2. (*fig.*) blindly.

ощут|и́мый (~и́м, ~и́ма), *adj.* = ~и́тельный.

ощути́тел|ьный (~ен, ~ьна), *adj.* 1. perceptible, tangible, palpable. 2. (*fig.*) appreciable.

ощу|ти́ть, щу́, ти́шь, *pf.* (*of* ~ща́ть) to feel, sense, experience; о. го́лод to feel hunger; он ~ти́л её отсу́тствие he felt her absence.

ощуща́|ть, ю, *impf. of* ощути́ть.

ощуще́ни|е, я, *n.* 1. (*physiol.*) sensation. 2. feeling, sense.

оягн|и́ться, и́тся, *pf. of* ягни́ться.

П

па, *indecl., n.* (*dance*) step.

па́в|а, ы, *f.* peahen.

павиа́н, а, *m.* baboon.

павильо́н, а, *m.* 1. pavilion. 2. film studio.

павли́н, а, *m.* peacock.

павли́н|ий, *adj. of* ~.

па́вод|ок, ка, *m.* flood (*esp. resulting from melting of snow*); freshet.

па́волок|а, и, f. (*hist.*) pavoloka (*in Kievan Russia, heavy ornamented brocade, imported as a luxury item*).

пагина́ци|я, и, f. pagination.

па́год|а, ы, f. pagoda.

па́голен|ок, ка, *m.* (*dial.*) leg (*of boot or stocking*).

па́губ|а, ы, f. ruin, destruction; bane.

па́губ|ный (~ен, ~на), *adj.* pernicious, ruinous; baneful; fatal.

па́дал|ь, и, f. (*usu. collect.*) carrion.

па́дан|ец, ца, *m.* faller (*fallen fruit*).

па́да|ть, ю, *impf.* 1. (*pf.* пасть *and* упа́сть) (*in var. senses*) to fall; to sink; to drop; to decline; баро́метр ~л the barometer was falling; ~ет снег it is snowing; це́ны ~ют prices are dropping; се́рдце у них ~ло

their spirits were sinking; п. ду́хом to lose heart, lose courage; п. в о́бморок to faint; п. от уста́лости to be ready to drop. 2. (*pf.* пасть) (*fig.*; на+*a.*) to fall (on, to); отве́тственность ~ет на вас the responsibility falls on you. 3. (*impf. only*) (*ling.*; *of stress or accent*) to fall, be; ударе́ние ~ет на пе́рвый слог the stress is on the first syllable. 4. (*impf. only*) (*of hair, teeth, etc.*) to fall out, drop out. 5. (*pf.* пасть; *of cattle*) to die.

па́да|ющий, *pres. part. of* ~ть *and adj.* (*phys.*) incident; ~ющие звёзды shooting stars.

паде́ж, а́, *m.* (*gram.*) case.

падёж, а́, *m.* murrain, cattle plague.

падёж|ный, *adj. of* ~; ~ное оконча́ние case ending.

падёж|ный, *adj. of* ~.

паде́ни|е, я, n. 1. fall; drop, sinking; мора́льное п. degradation; п. цен slump in prices. 2. (*phys.*) incidence; у́гол ~я angle of incidence. 3. (*geol.*) dip. 4. п. ударе́ния (*ling.*) incidence of stress.

падиша́х, а, *m.* padishah.

па́д|кий (~ок, ~ка), *adj.* (на+*a. or* до) having a weakness (for), having a penchant (for); susceptible (to); п. на де́ньги mercenary; он ~ок до сла́дкого he has a sweet tooth.

па́дуб, a, *m.* holly.

паду́ч|ий, *adj.* (*obs.*) falling; ~ая звезда́ shooting star; ~ая (боле́знь) falling sickness, epilepsy.

па́дчериц|а, ы, *f.* step-daughter.

паево́й, *adj.* of пай¹; п. взнос share.

па|ёк, йка́, *m.* ration.

паенакопле́ни|е, я, *n.* (*econ.*) share-accumulation.

паж, а́, *m.* (*hist.*) page.

па́ж|еский, *adj.* of ~; П. Ко́рпус Corps of Pages (*hist.*; *name of mil. school in St. Petersburg*).

па́жит|ь, и, *f.* (*obs., poet.*) pasture.

паз, а, о ~е, в ~у́, *pl.* ~ы́, ~о́в, *m.* (*tech.*) groove, slot, mortise, rabbet.

па|зи́ть, жу́, зи́шь, *impf.* (*tech.*) to groove, mortise.

па́зух|а, и, *f.* **1.** bosom; за ~ой in one's bosom; держа́ть ка́мень за ~ой (*fig.*) to nurse a grievance, harbour a grudge; жить как у Христа́ за ~ой to live in clover. **2.** (*anat.*) sinus; ло́бные ~и frontal sinuses. **3.** (*bot.*) axil.

па́ин|ька, ьки, *g. pl.* ~ек, *m.* and *f.* (*coll.*) good child; будь п.! be a good boy (girl)!; п.-ма́льчик good (little) boy.

па|й¹, я, *pl.* ~и́, ~ёв, *m.* share; вступи́тельный п. initial shares; това́рищество на ~я́х joint-stock company; на ~я́х (*fig., coll.*) on an equal footing, going shares.

пай², *indecl.*, *m.* and *f.* (*coll.*) good child; п.-ма́льчик good (little) boy.

па́йк|а, и, *f.* solder(ing).

пайко́вый, *adj.* of паёк; rationed.

па́йщик¹, a, *m.* shareholder.

па́йщик², a, *m.* solderer.

пак, а, *no pl.*, *m.* pack-ice.

пакга́уз, а, *m.* warehouse, storehouse; тамо́женный п. bonded warehouse.

паке́т, а, *m.* **1.** parcel, package; packet; индивидуа́льный п. (*mil.*) individual field dressing, first-aid packet. **2.** (official) letter. **3.** paper bag.

пакиста́н|ец, ца, *m.* Pakistani.

пакиста́нк|а, и, *f.* Pakistani (woman).

пакиста́нский, *adj.* Pakistani.

па́кл|я, и, *f.* tow; oakum.

пак|ова́ть, у́ю, *impf.* (*of* y~) to pack.

па́ко|стить, щу, стишь, *impf.* (*coll.*) **1.** (*pf.* за~ *and* на~) to soil, dirty. **2.** (*pf.* ис~) to spoil, mess up. **3.** (*pf.* на~) (+*d.*) to play dirty tricks (on).

па́костник, а, *m.* (*coll.*) **1.** dirty dog, wretch. **2.** debauchee.

па́кост|ный (~ен, ~на), *adj.* dirty, mean, foul; nasty.

па́кост|ь, и, *f.* **1.** dirty trick; де́лать ~и (+*d.*) to play dirty tricks (on). **2.** filth. **3.** obscenity, filthy word.

пакт, а, *m.* pact; п. о ненападе́нии non-aggression pact.

пал¹, а, *m.* (*naut.*) bollard; pawl.

пал², а, *m.* (*dial.*) fire.

пpalanти́н, а, *m.* fur tippet, stole.

пала́т|а, ы, *f.* **1.** (*pl. only*; *obs.*) palace. **2.** (*obs.*) chamber, hall; Оруже́йная п. Armoury Museum (*in Moscow*); у него́ ума́ п. (*coll.*) he is as wise as Solomon. **3.** (*hospital*) ward. **4.** (*polit.*) chamber, house; ве́рхняя, ни́жняя п. Upper, Lower Chamber; П. ло́рдов House of Lords; П. общин House of Commons. **5.** *as name of State institutions*; Всесою́зная кни́жная п. All-Union Book Chamber (*national bibliographical centre in Moscow*); П. мер и весо́в Weights and Measures Office; Торго́вая п. Chamber of Commerce.

палатализа́ци|я, и, *f.* (*ling.*) palatalization.

палатализ|ова́ть, у́ю, *impf. and pf.* (*ling.*) to palatalize.

палата́льный, *adj.* (*ling.*) palatal.

пала́тк|а, и, *f.* **1.** tent; marquee; в ~ах under canvas. **2.** stall, booth.

пала́т|ный, *adj.* of ~а; ~ная сестра́ ward sister.

пала́ццо, *indecl.*, *n.* palace (*esp. of Venetian doges*).

пала́ч, а́, *m.* hangman; executioner; (*fig.*) butcher.

пала́ш, а́, *m.* broadsword.

па́левый, *adj.* straw-coloured, pale yellow.

палёны|й, *adj.* singed, scorched; па́хнет ~м there is a smell of burning.

палео́граф, а, *m.* palaeographer.

палеографи́ческий, *adj.* palaeographic.

палеогра́фи|я, и, *f.* palaeography.

палеоза́вр, а, *m.* palaeosaurus.

палеозо́йский, *adj.* (*geol.*) palaeozoic.

палеоли́т, а, *m.* (*geol.*) palaeolithic period.

палеолити́ческий, *adj.* (*geol.*) palaeolithic.

палеонто́лог, а, *m.* palaeontologist.

палеонтологи́ческий, *adj.* palaeontologic(al).

палеонтоло́ги|я, и, *f.* palaeontology.

па́лехский, *adj.* (made in) Palekh (*place famed for its lacquer-work*).

па́л|ец, ьца, *m.* **1.** finger; п. ноги́ toe; большо́й п. thumb; указа́тельный п. forefinger, index (finger); сре́дний п. middle finger, third finger; безымя́нный п. fourth finger, ring-finger; предохрани́тельный п. finger-stall; (*fig.*) п. о п. не уда́рить, ~ьцем не шевельну́ть (*coll.*) not to raise a finger, not to stir oneself; ему́ ~ьца в рот не клади́ (*coll.*) he is not to be trusted, he needs to be

watched; ~ьцы лома́ть to tear one's hair;
смотре́ть сквозь ~ьцы на что-н. (*coll.*) to
shut one's eyes to something; знать что-н.,
как свои́ пять ~ьцев (*coll.*) to have something at one's finger-tips; обвести́ кого́-н.
вокру́г ~ьца (*coll.*) to twist someone round
one's (little) finger; вы́сосать из ~ьца (*coll.*)
to fabricate, concoct; он ~ьцем никого́ не
тро́нет he wouldn't hurt a fly; попа́сть
~ьцем в не́бо (*coll.*) to be wide of the mark;
как по ~ьцам рассказа́ть to recount in
detail, recount circumstantially. 2. (*tech.*)
pin, peg; cam, cog, tooth.

пале|я́, й, *f.* (*hist. lit.*) Palaea (*early Russian
lit. form, borrowed from Byzantium, comprising
exposition of Old Testament texts*).

палимпсе́ст, а, *m.* palimpsest.

палингене́з, а, *m.* (*biol.*) palingenesis.

палингене́з|ис, иса, *m.* = ~.

палиндро́м, а, *m.* palindrome.

палиса́д, а, *m.* 1. paling. 2. (*mil.*) palisade,
stockade.

палиса́дник, а, *m.* front garden.

палиса́ндр, а, *m.* rosewood.

палиса́ндр|овый, *adj. of* ~.

пали́тр|а, ы, *f.* palette.

пал|и́ть¹, ю́, и́шь, *impf.* 1. (*pf.* c~) to burn,
scorch. 2. (*pf.* o~) to singe.

пал|и́ть², ю́, и́шь, *impf.* (*coll.*) to fire (*from
gun*); ~и́! (*word of command*) fire!

па́лиц|а, ы, *f.* club, cudgel.

па́лк|а, и, *f.* stick; cane, staff; п. метлы́
broom-stick; поста́вить в ~и (*obs.*) to cane,
give a caning; вста́вить кому́-н. ~и в
колёса to put a spoke in someone's wheel;
из-под ~и under the lash; п. о двух конца́х
two-edged weapon; э́то п. о двух конца́х
it cuts both ways.

палла́ди|й, я, *m.* (*chem.*) palladium.

паллиати́в, а, *m.* palliative.

паллиати́вный, *adj.* palliative.

пало́мник, а, *m.* 1. pilgrim (*also fig.*). 2.
(*hist. lit.*) pilgrim's tale.

пало́мнича|ть, ю, *impf.* to go on (a) pil-
grimage.

пало́мничеств|о, а, *n.* pilgrimage (*also fig.*).

па́лочк|а, и, *f.* 1. *dim. of* па́лка; бараба́нная
п. drumstick; волше́бная п. magic wand;
дирижёрская п. conductor's baton; п.-
-выруча́лочка (*children's game*) 'I spy'. 2.
(*med.*) bacillus.

па́лочковый, *adj.* (*med.*) bacillary.

па́л|очный, *adj. of* ~ка; ~очные уда́ры
strokes of the cane; ~очная дисципли́на
discipline of the rod.

па́лтус, а, *m.* halibut, turbot.

па́луб|а, ы, *f.* deck; полётная п. flight deck;
жила́я п. messdeck; шлю́почная п. boat
deck.

па́луб|ный *adj. of* ~а; п. груз deck cargo.

па́лый, *adj.* (*dial.*; *of cattle*) dead.

пальб|а́, ы́, *f.* firing; пу́шечная п. cannon-
ade.

пальм|а, ы, *f.* palm(-tree); коко́совая п.
coco-nut(-tree); фи́никовая п. date(-palm);
получи́ть ~у пе́рвенства to bear the palm.

пальм|овый, *adj. of* ~а; ~овое де́рево box-
wood; *as noun* ~овые, ~овых Palmaceae.

па́льник, а, *m.* (*mil.*; *obs.*) linstock.

пал|ьну́ть, ьну́, ьнёшь, *inst. pf.* (*of* ~и́ть²)
to fire a shot; to discharge a volley.

пальте́ц|о́, а́, *n.* (*coll.*) *dim. of* пальто́.

пальти́ш|ко, ка, *pl.* ~ки, ~ек, *n.* (*coll.*,
pejor.) *dim. of* пальто́.

пальто́, *indecl.* *n.* (over)coat; topcoat.

пальто́|вый, *adj. of* ~.

пальцеви́д|ный (~ен, ~на), *adj.* finger-
-shaped.

пальцево́й, *adj. of* па́лец.

пальцеобра́з|ный (~ен, ~на), *adj.* (*bot.*)
digitate.

па́ль|чатый, *adj.* = ~цеобра́зный.

па́льчик, а, *m.* *dim. of* па́лец; *see* ма́льчик.

па́льщик, а, *m.* (*tech.*) shot-firer, blaster.

пал|я́щий, *pres. part. act. of* ~и́ть¹ *and adj.*
burning, scorching.

пампа́с|овый, *adj. of* ~ы; ~овая трава́ pam-
pas grass.

пампа́с|ы, ов, *no sing.* (*geogr.*) pampas.

пампу́шк|а, и, *f.* (*dial.*) pampushka (*kind of
fritter*).

памфле́т, а, *m.* lampoon.

памфлети́ст, а, *m.* lampoonist.

па́мятк|а, и, *f.* 1. (commemorative) booklet.
2. instruction, written rules. 3. (*coll.*, *obs.*)
memento.

па́мятлив|ый (~, ~а), *adj.* (*coll.*) having a
retentive memory, retentive.

па́мятник, а, *m.* monument; memorial;
tombstone; statue; ~и пи́сьменности
literary texts.

па́мят|ный (~ен, ~на), *adj.* 1. memorable.
2. serving to assist the memory; ~ная доска́
memorial plate, plaque; ~ная кни́жка
notebook, memorandum book.

па́мят|овать, ую, *impf.* (*obs.*; o+*p.*) to re-
member.

па́мят|ь, и, *f.* 1. memory; у него́ кури́ная
п. he has a memory like a sieve; на мое́й
~и within my memory; говори́ть на п. to
speak from memory; вдруг мне пришло́
на п., что... suddenly I remembered
that . . . ; по ~и from memory; по ста́рой
~и from force of habit. 2. memory, recollection, remembrance; ве́чная п. ему́! may
his memory live for ever!; оста́вить по
себе́ до́брую п. to leave fond memories
of oneself; в п. (+*g.*) in memory (of); по-
дари́ть на п. to give as a keepsake. 3.
mind, consciousness; быть без ~и to be

unconscious; быть от кого́-н. без ~и (coll.) to be head over heels in love with someone, be crazy about someone. **4.** (eccl.; +g.) commemoration of death (of), feast (of).

пан, а, pl. ~ы́, m. **1.** (hist.) Polish land-owner. **2.** gentleman; ли́бо п., ли́бо пропа́л (prov.) all or nothing.

панаги́|я, и, f. (eccl.) panagia (image worn round neck by Orthodox bishops).

пана́м|а, ы, f. Panama (hat).

панаце́|я, и, f. panacea; п. от всех зол (fig.) universal panacea.

панба́рхат, а, m. panne (dress material).

панда́н, а, m. (obs.) complement; в п. (к) to complement.

панда́н|ус, уса, m. (bot.) screw-pine.

па́ндус, а, m. (tech.) ramp.

панеги́рик, а, m. panegyric, eulogy.

панегири́ст, а, m. panegyrist, eulogist.

панегири́ческий, adj. panegyrical, eulogistic.

пане́л|ь, и, f. **1.** pavement, footpath. **2.** panel(ling), wainscot(ting).

пане́ль|ный, adj. of ~; ~ная обши́вка panelling, wainscotting.

па́н|и, indecl., f. of ~.

панибра́тский, adj. (coll.) familiar.

панибра́тств|о, а, n. (coll.) familiarity.

па́ник|а, и, f. panic; впасть в ~у to become panic-stricken, panic.

паникади́л|о, а, n. (eccl.) chandelier.

паникёр, а, m. panic-monger, scaremonger, alarmist.

паникёр|ский, adj. of ~.

паникёрств|о, а, n. alarmism.

паникёрств|овать, ую, impf. (no pf.) (coll.) to be panic-stricken, panic.

паник|ова́ть, у́ю, impf. (no pf.) (coll.) to panic.

панихи́д|а, ы, f. office for the dead; requiem; гражда́нская п. civil funeral.

панихи́д|ный, adj. of ~а; (fig.) funereal.

пани́ческий, adj. **1.** panic. **2.** (coll.) panicky.

панк, а, m. (also as indecl. adj.) punk.

па́нк|овский, adj. of ~.

па́нкреас, а, m. (anat.) pancreas.

панкреати́ческий, adj. (anat.) pancreatic.

па́нн|а, ы, f. (Polish) young lady.

панно́, indecl., n. panel.

панора́м|а, ы, f. **1.** (in var. senses) panorama. **2.** (mil.) panoramic sight.

панора́мный, adj. panoramic; п. фильм cinerama film.

пансио́н, а, m. **1.** boarding school. **2.** boarding-house. **3.** (full) board and lodging; ко́мната с ~ом room and board; жить на ~е to have full board and lodging, live en pension.

пансионе́р, а, m. **1.** boarder (in school). **2.** guest (in boarding-house).

па́н|ский, adj. of ~.

панслави́зм, а, m. (hist.) Pan-Slavism.

па́нств|о, а, n. (obs.) **1.** (collect.) Polish land-owners. **2.** superciliousness.

панталó́н|ы, ~, no sing. **1.** (obs.) trousers. **2.** (woman's) drawers, knickers.

пантали́к, а (у), m. (coll.) only in phrases сбить с ~у to drive demented; сби́ться с ~у to be driven demented, be at one's wit's end.

пантеи́зм, а, m. pantheism.

пантеи́ст, а, m. pantheist.

пантеисти́ческий, adj. pantheistic(al).

пантео́н, а, m. pantheon.

панте́р|а, ы, f. panther.

панто́граф, а, m. (tech.) pantograph.

пантоми́м|а, ы, f. pantomime, mime; dumb show.

пантоми́мический, adj. pantomimic.

пантоми́м|ный, adj. = ~и́ческий.

панту́ф|ли, ель, no sing. (obs.) slippers.

па́нт|овый, adj. of ~ы.

пантокри́н, а, m. Pantocrin (medicament prepared from antlers of young Siberian stag).

па́нт|ы, ов, no sing. antlers of young Siberian stag (as used in preparation of medicament).

па́нцирн|ый, adj. **1.** armour-clad, iron--clad. **2.** (zool.) testaceous; as noun ~ые, ~ых Testacea.

па́нцир|ь, я, m. **1.** (hist.) coat of mail, armour. **2.** (zool.) test. **3.** (obs.) diving suit.

па́п|а[1], ы, m. (coll.) papa, daddy.

па́п|а[2], ы, m. п. ри́мский (the) Pope.

папа́х|а, и, f. papakha (Caucasian fur cap).

папа́ш|а, и, m. (coll.) = па́па.

па́перт|ь, и, f. church-porch, parvis.

папи́зм, а, m. papism.

папильо́тк|а, и, f. curling-paper.

папироло́ги|я, и, f. papyrology.

папиро́с|а, ы, f. cigarette (of Russian type with cardboard mouthpiece).

папиро́сник, а, m. (coll.) cigarette vendor.

папиро́сниц|а[1], ы, f. cigarette girl.

папиро́сниц|а[2], ы, f. cigarette-case.

папиро́с|ный, adj. of ~а; ~ная бума́га rice--paper.

папи́рус, а, m. papyrus.

папи́рус|ный, adj. of ~.

папи́ст, а, m. papist.

па́пк|а, и, f. **1.** file; document case, paper--case. **2.** cardboard, pasteboard; переплетённый в ~у in boards.

па́поротник, а, m. fern.

па́поротник|овый, adj. of ~; ferny; as noun ~овые, ~овых (bot.) Filicinae.

па́прик|а, и, f. paprika.

па́пский, adj. papal; п. престо́л St. Peter's chair.

па́пств|о, а, n. papacy; papal authority.

папуа́с, а, m. Papuan.

папуа́сский, *adj.* Papuan.

папье́-маше́, *indecl.*, *n.* papier-mâché.

пар¹, а, о ~е, в ~у́, *pl.* ~ы́, *m.* 1. steam; быть под ~а́ми to be under steam, have steam up; на всех ~а́х (*fig.*) full steam ahead, at full speed; очи́стить ~а́ми to fumigate. 2. exhalation.

пар², а, *pl.* ~ы́, *m.* (*agric.*) fallow; находи́ться под ~ом to lie fallow.

па́р|а, ы, *f.* 1. (*in var. senses*) pair; couple; супру́жеская п. married couple; п. сил (*tech.*) couple; ходи́ть ~ами to walk in couples; е́хать на ~е to drive a pair (*of horses*); на ~у мину́т for a couple of minutes; п. пустяко́в! it's child's play! it's a mere bagatelle!; на ~у слов for a few words; под ~у to match, to make up a pair; она́ ему́ не п. she is no match for him; два сапога́ п. (*coll.*, *pejor.*) they make a pair. 2. suit (*of clothes*). 3. (*school sl.*) a 'two'.

пара́бол|а¹, ы, *f.* (*math.*) parabola.

пара́бол|а², ы, *f.* parable.

параболи́ческий¹, *adj.* (*math.*) parabolic.

параболи́ческий², *adj.* parabolical.

парава́н, а, *m.* (*naut.*) paravane.

пара́граф, а, *m.* paragraph.

пара́д, а, *m.* 1. parade; (*mil.*) review; возду́шный п. air display; морско́й п. naval review; приня́ть п. to inspect a parade. 2. (*coll.*, *joc.*) ceremonial get-up; быть в по́лном ~е to be all tricked out, be in one's best bib and tucker; что э́то за п. у вас? what's the big show?

паради́гм|а, ы, *f.* (*gram.*) paradigm.

пара́дно-выходн|о́й, *adj.* ~а́я фо́рма вне стро́я (*mil.*) ceremonial walking-out dress.

пара́дност|ь, и, *f.* magnificence; ostentation.

пара́д|ный (~ен, ~на), *adj.* 1. *adj.* of ~ ¹; п. костю́м ceremonial dress; ~ная фо́рма full dress (uniform). 2. gala; п. спекта́кль gala night. 3. main, front; ~ная дверь front door; п. подъе́зд main entrance; *as noun* ~ное, ~ного, *n.* and ~ная, ~ной, *f.* front door.

парадо́кс, а, *m.* paradox.

парадокса́л|ьный (~ен, ~ьна), *adj.* paradoxical.

парази́т, а, *m.* (*biol. and fig.*) parasite.

паразита́р|ный (~ен, ~на), *adj.* parasitic(al).

парази́ти́зм, а, *m.* (*biol. and fig.*) parasitism.

парази́ти́р|овать, ую, *impf.* to parasitize.

парази́ти́ческий, *adj.* (*biol. and fig.*) parasitic(al).

парази́тный, *adj.* (*biol.*) parasitic.

паразитоло́ги|я, и, *f.* parasitology.

парализо́ванност|ь, и, *f.* paralysis.

парализо́в|анный, *p.p.p.* of ~а́ть *and adj.* paralysed.

парализ|ова́ть, у́ю, *impf. and pf.* to paralyse (*also fig.*).

парали́тик, а, *m.* paralytic.

паралити́ческий, *adj.* paralytic.

парали́ч, а́, *m.* paralysis; palsy.

парали́чный, *adj.* paralytic; п. больно́й paralytic.

паралла́кс, а, *m.* (*astron.*) parallax.

параллелепи́пед, а, *m.* (*math.*) parallelepiped.

параллели́зм, а, *m.* parallelism.

параллелогра́мм, а, *m.* (*math.*) parallelogram.

паралле́л|ь, и, *f.* (*in var. senses*) parallel; провести́ п. (ме́жду) to draw a parallel (between).

паралле́льно, *adv.* (c+*i.*) 1. parallel (with). 2. simultaneously (with), at the same time (as).

паралле́льност|ь, и, *f.* parallelism.

паралле́л|ьный (~ен, ~ьна), *adj.* (*in var. senses*) parallel; ~ьные бру́сья (*sport*) parallel bars.

паралоги́зм, а, *m.* paralogism.

парамагнети́зм, а, *m.* (*phys.*) paramagnetism.

парамагни́тный, *adj.* (*phys.*) paramagnetic.

пара́метр, а, *m.* (*math.*) parameter.

парандж|а́, и́, *f.* yashmak.

парано́ик, а, *m.* (*med.*) paranoiac.

паранои́ческий, *adj.* (*med.*) paranoid; paranoiac.

парано́|я, и, *f.* (*med.*) paranoia.

парапе́т, а, *m.* parapet.

парати́ф, а, *m.* paratyphoid.

пара́ф, а, *m.* 1. paraph. 2. initials.

парафи́н, а, *m.* paraffin (wax).

парафи́н|овый, *adj.* of ~.

парафи́р|овать, ую, *impf. and pf.* (*dipl.*) to initial.

парафра́з, а, *m.* paraphrase.

парафра́з|а, ы, *f.* = ~.

парафрази́р|овать, ую, *impf. and pf.* to paraphrase.

пара́ш|а, и, *f.* (*prison sl.*) close-stool.

парашю́т, а, *m.* 1. parachute; на ~е by parachute; прыжо́к с ~ом parachute jump. 2. (*sport*, *coll.*) high cross.

парашюти́зм, а, *m.* parachute-jumping (*as sport*).

парашюти́ровани|е, я, *n.* (*aeron.*) pancaking.

парашюти́р|овать, ую, *impf.* (*of* с~) (*aeron.*) to pancake.

парашюти́ст, а, *m.* parachute jumper; (*mil.*) parachutist, paratrooper.

парвеню́, *indecl.*, *m.* parvenu, upstart.

пардо́н 1. *interj.* (I beg your) pardon. 2. *as noun*, *in phrase* проси́ть ~у to ask forgiveness.

паренхи́м|а, ы, *f.* (*anat.*, *bot.*) parenchyma.

па́рен|ый, *adj.* stewed; деше́вле ~ой ре́пы dirt-cheap.

па́р|ень, ня, *pl.* ~ни, ~не́й, *m.* 1. boy, lad. 2. (*coll.*) chap, fellow.

пари́, *indecl.*, *n.* bet; держа́ть п., идти́ на п. to bet, lay a bet; п. держу́, что... I bet that . . . .

парижа́н|ин, ина, *pl.* ~е, ~, *m.* Parisian.

парижа́н|ка, ки, *f.* Parisian (woman), Parisienne.

пари́жск|ий, *adj.* Parisian; ~ая лазу́рь, ~ая синь Paris blue, ferric ferrocyanide.

пари́к, а́, *m.* wig.

парикма́хер, а, *m.* barber; hairdresser.

парикма́херск|ая, ой, *f.* barber's (shop), hairdresser's; hair-dressing saloon.

пари́л|ьня, ьни, *g. pl.* ~ен, *f.* 1. sweating--room (*in baths*). 2. (*tech.*) steam-shop.

па́рильщик, а, *m.* sweating-room attendant.

пари́р|овать, ую, *impf. and pf.* (*pf. also* от~) to parry, counter.

парите́т, а, *m.* parity.

парите́т|ный, *adj. of* ~; на ~ных нача́лах (c+*i.*) on a par (with), on an equal footing (with).

па́р|ить, ю, ишь, *impf.* (*no pf.*) 1. to steam. 2. to steam out, sweat out (*in baths, to beat about the body with a heated besom to induce perspiration*). 3. (*cul.*) to stew. 4. (*impers.*) ~ит it is sultry.

пар|и́ть, ю́, и́шь, *impf.* (*no pf.*) to soar, swoop, hover; п. в облака́х (*fig.*) to live in the clouds.

па́р|иться, юсь, ишься, *impf.* 1. (*pf.* по~) to steam, sweat (*in baths*). 2. (*cul.*) to stew.

па́ри|я, и, *g. pl.* ~й, *m. and f.* pariah, outcast.

парк, а, *m.* 1. park; разби́ть п. to lay out a park. 2. yard, depot; (*mil.*) park, depot; артиллери́йский п. ordnance depot; трамва́йный п. tram depot. 3. fleet; stock; pool; автомоби́льный п. fleet of motor vehicles; ваго́нный п. rolling-stock.

па́рк|а[1], и, *f.* 1. steaming. 2. (*cul.*) stewing.

па́рк|а,[2] и, *f.* parka (*skin jacket worn by Eskimos, etc.*).

парке́т, а, *m.* parquet; parquetry; настла́ть п. to parquet, lay a parquet floor.

парке́тин|а, ы, *f.* parquet block.

парке́т|ный, *adj. of* ~; п. пол parquet floor; п. шарку́н (*fig., coll., pejor.*) socialite.

парке́тчик, а, *m.* parquet floor layer.

па́р|кий (~ок, ~ка), *adj.* (*coll.*) steamy.

па́рк|овый, *adj. of* ~; ~овые культу́ры park plants.

парла́мент, а, *m.* parliament.

парламентари́зм, а, *m.* parliamentarism.

парламента́ри|й, я, *m.* parliamentarian.

парламента́рный, *adj.* parliamentarian.

парламентёр, а, *m.* (*mil.*) envoy; bearer of a flag of truce.

парламентёр|ский, *adj. of* ~; п. флаг flag of truce.

парла́ментский, *adj.* parliamentary; п. зако́н Act of Parliament; п. запро́с interpellation.

парна́с|ец, ца, *m.* (*lit.*) Parnassian.

парна́сский, *adj.* (*lit.*) Parnassian.

парни́к, а́, *m.* hotbed, seed-bed; forcing bed; в ~е́ under glass.

парник|о́вый, *adj. of* ~; ~о́вые расте́ния hothouse plants.

парни́шк|а, и, *m.* (*coll.*) boy, lad.

парн|о́й, *adj.* 1. fresh; ~о́е молоко́ milk fresh from the cow; ~о́е мя́со fresh meat. 2. (*coll.*) steamy.

парноко́пытн|ые, ых, *sing.* ~ое, ~ого, *n.* (*zool.*) Artiodactyla.

па́рн|ый[1], *adj.* 1. pair; forming a pair; twin; п. носо́к, п. сапо́г, *etc.*, pair, fellow (*other one of pair of socks, boots, etc.*); ~ая гребля́ sculling. 2. pair-horse. 3. ~ые ли́стья (*bot.*) conjugate leaves.

па́рный[2], *adj.* (*coll.*) steamy.

парови́к, а́, *m.* 1. (*tech.*) boiler. 2. (*coll., obs.*) steam-engine. 3. local steam-train.

парово́з, а, *m.* (steam-)engine, locomotive.

парово́зник, а, *m.* loco man (*engine-driver or fireman*).

парово́з|ный, *adj. of* ~; ~ная брига́да engine crew; ~ное депо́ engine-shed.

паровозоремо́нтный, *adj.* engine-repair, locomotive-repair.

паровозострое́ни|е, я, *n.* engine building, locomotive building.

паровозостро|и́тельный, *adj. of* ~е́ние; п. заво́д engine-building works.

паров|о́й[1], *adj.* 1. *adj. of* пар[1]; ~ая маши́на steam-engine; ~ое отопле́ние steam heating; central heating; ~ая пра́чечная steam laundry. 2. (*cul.*) steamed.

парово́й[2], *adj.* lying fallow.

паровпускн|о́й, *adj.* (*tech.*) п. кла́пан inlet valve; ~а́я труба́ steam supply pipe.

паровыпускно́й, *adj.* (*tech.*) exhaust.

парогенера́тор, а, *m.* (*tech.*) steam-generator.

парод|и́йный, *adj. of* ~ия.

пароди́р|овать, ую, *impf. and pf.* to parody.

паро́ди|я, и, *f.* 1. parody. 2. skit. 3. travesty, caricature.

пароко́нный, *adj.* two-horse.

парокси́зм, а, *m.* paroxysm.

паро́л|ь, я, *m.* password, countersign.

паро́м, а, *m.* ferry(-boat); п.-самолёт flying bridge, air ferry; перепра́вить на ~е to ferry.

паро́мщик, а, *m.* ferryman.

паронепроница́емый, *adj.* steam-tight, steam-proof.

парообра́зный, *adj.* vaporous.

парообразовáни|е, я, *n.* (*phys., tech.*) steam-
-generation, vaporization.

пароотвóдн|ый, *adj.* ~ая трубá (*tech.*)
steam exhaust pipe, steam-escape pipe.

пароотсекáтел|ь, я, *m.* steam cut-off valve.

пароперегревáтел|ь, я, *m.* (*tech.*) steam
superheater.

паро-пескоструйный, *adj.* п. аппарáт
(*tech.*) steam sand blaster.

паропровóд, а, *m.* (*tech.*) steam pipe.

парораспределúтел|ь, я, *m.* (*tech.*) steam
distributor, steam header.

парораспределúтельн|ый, *adj.* ~ая короб-
ка (*tech.*) steam-box.

парораспылúтел|ь, я, *m.* (*tech.*) steam
atomizer.

паросбóрник, а, *m.* (*tech.*) steam collector;
dome (*of boiler*).

паросилов|óй, *adj.* ~áя устанóвка (*tech.*)
steam power plant.

парóсский, *adj.* Parian; п. мрáмор Parian
marble.

пароструйный, *adj.* steam-jet.

парохóд, а, *m.* steamer; steamship; бук-
сúрный п. steam tug; океáнский п. ocean
liner.

парохóдик, а, *m.* (*coll.*) **1.** *dim. of* парохóд.
2. toy boat.

парохóд|ный, *adj. of* ~; ~ное óбщество
steamship company.

парохóдств|о, а, *n.* **1.** steam-navigation.
2. steamship-line.

парт- *abbr. of* партúйный Party-.

пáрт|а, ы, *f.* (school) desk; сесть за ~y to
begin to learn.

партактúв, а, *m.* (*polit.*) Party activists.

партбилéт, а, *m.* (*polit.*) party-membership
card.

партеногенéз, а, *m.* (*zool.*) parthenogenesis.

партéр, а, *m.* (*theatr.*) the pit; the stalls.

партéсн|ый, *adj.* ~ое пéние (*eccl.*) part-
-singing.

партú|ец, йца, *m.* (*Soviet Communist*) Party-
member.

партизáн, а, *pl.* ~ы, ~, *m.* partisan; guerilla.

партизáн|ить, ю, ишь, *impf.* (*coll.*) to be a
partisan, fight with the partisans.

партизáн|ский, *adj.* **1.** *adj. of* ~; ~ская
войнá guerilla warfare; ~ское движéние
the Resistance (movement) (*e.g. against
Germany during Second World War*); п.
отрýд partisan detachment. **2.** (*fig., pejor.*)
unplanned, haphazard.

партизáнств|о, а, *n.* **1.** guerilla warfare;
resistance movement. **2.** (*collect.*) partisans,
guerillas.

партизáнщин|а, ы, *f.* **1.** guerilla warfare.
2. (*fig., pejor.*) unplanned work, haphazard
work.

пáртийк|а, и, *f.* (*coll.*) *dim. of* пáртия.

партúйк|а, и, *f. of* партúец.

партúйност|ь, и, *f.* **1.** Party spirit. **2.** party
membership.

партúйн|ый, *adj.* (*polit.*) **1.** party; (Commun-
ist) Party; п. билéт party-(Party-)member-
ship card; п. стаж length of party (Party)
membership; ~ая ячéйка Party cell.
2. Party (*in accordance with the spirit of the
Soviet Communist Party*); п. дух Party spirit.
3. *as noun* п., ~ого, *m.* (*Communist*) Party
member.

партикуляúзм, а, *m.* (*polit.*) particularism.

партикуляúр|ный (~ен, ~на), *adj.* (*obs.*)
1. private; unofficial. **2.** civil; ~ное плáтье
civilian clothes, mufti.

партитýр|а, ы, *f.* (*mus.*) score.

пáрти|я¹, и, *f.* (*polit.*) party; the Party.

пáрти|я², и, *f.* **1.** party, group. **2.** batch;
lot; consignment (*of goods*). **3.** (*sport*) game;
set. **4.** (*mus.*) part. **5.** (*obs.*) (good) match
(*marriage*); сдéлать хорóшую ~ю to make a
good match.

парткабинéт, а, *m.* Party educational
centre.

парткóм, а, *m.* (*abbr. of* партúйный комитéт) Party committee.

партнёр, а, *m.* partner.

партóрг, а, *m.* (*abbr. of* партúйный орга-
низáтор) Party organizer.

парторганизáци|я, и, *f.* Party organiza-
tion.

партсъéзд, а, *m.* Party congress.

пáруб|ок, ка, *m.* (*Ukrainian*) boy, lad, youth.

пáрус, а, *pl.* ~á, *m.* sail; идтú под ~áми to
sail, be under sail; поднýть ~á, постáвить
~á to make sail, set sail; на всех ~áx in full
sail (*also fig.*).

парусúн|а, ы, *f.* canvas, sail-cloth; duck.

пáрусник, а, *m.* sailing vessel, sailer.

пáрус|ный, *adj. of* ~; п. спорт sailing.

парфóрсн|ый, *adj.* ~ая ездá circus riding.

парфюмéр, а, *m.* perfumer.

парфюмéри|я, и, *f.* (*collect.*) perfumery.

парфюмéр|ный, *adj. of* ~ия; п. магазúн per-
fumer's shop; ~ная фáбрика perfumery.

парцéлл|а, ы, *f.* (*agric.*) parcel (of land).

парцеллú|ровать, ую, *impf. and pf.* (*agric.*)
to parcel (out).

парцеллýци|я, и, *f.* (*agric.*) parcelling (out).

парч|á, й, *g. pl.* ~éй, *f.* brocade.

парч|óвый, *adj. of* ~á.

парш|á, й, *f.* tetter .mange; scab.

паршúве|ть, ю, *impf.* (*of* за~ *and* о~) to be-
come mangy; to be covered with scabs.

паршúв|ец, ца, *m.* (*coll.*) lousy fellow.

паршúв|ый (~, ~а), *adj.* **1.** mangy, scabby;
~ая овцá (*fig.*) black sheep. **2.** (*coll.*) nasty;
rotten, lousy.

пас¹, а, *m.* (*cards*) pass; объявúть п. to pass;
as interj. я п. (I) pass; в этом дéле я п.

(*fig.*, *coll.*) I'm no good at this, this is not in my line.

пас², **а**, *m.* (*sport*) pass; *as interj.* п. сюда́! pass!

па́сек|а, **и**, *f.* apiary, bee-garden.

па́се|чный, *adj.* of ∼ка.

па́сквил|ь, **я**, *m.* libel, lampoon, pasquinade; squib.

па́сквильный, *adj.* libellous.

пасквиля́|нт, **а**, *m.* lampoonist, slanderer.

паску́д|ный (∼ен, ∼на), *adj.* (*coll.*) foul, filthy.

паслён, **а**, *m.* (*bot.*) solanum; morel; сла́дко-го́рький п. bitter-sweet; чёрный п. deadly nightshade.

паслён|овый, *adj.* of ∼; *as noun* ∼овые, ∼овых Solanaceae.

па́см|о, **а**, *n.* (*text.*) lea.

па́смур|ный (∼ен, ∼на), *adj.* 1. dull, cloudy; overcast. 2. (*fig.*) gloomy, sullen.

пас|ова́ть¹, **у́ю**, *impf.* (*of* с∼) 1. (*also pf. in past tense*) (*cards*) to pass. 2. (*fig.*, *coll.*) to give up, give in; п. пе́ред тру́дностями to give in to difficulties.

пас|ова́ть², **у́ю**, *impf. and pf.* (*sport*) to pass.

па́сок|а, **и**, *f.* (*anat.*; *obs.*) lymph.

па́сочниц|а, **ы**, *f.* (*cul.*) mould for paskha.

па́с|очный, *adj.* of ∼ха 3.

паспарту́, *indecl.*, *n.* passe-partout.

па́спорт, **а**, *pl.* ∼а́, *m.* 1. passport. 2. registration certificate (*of motor vehicle, piece of machinery, etc.*).

паспортиза́ци|я, **и**, *f.* 1. passport system. 2. (*tech.*) certification.

паспорти́ст, **а**, *m.* passport officer.

па́спорт|ный, *adj.* of ∼; п. стол passport office.

пасс, **а**, *m.* (*in hypnotism*) pass.

пасса́ж, **а**, *m.* 1. passage; arcade. 2. (*mus.*) passage. 3. (*obs.*, *coll.*) unexpected turn (of events); како́й п.! What a thing to happen!

пассажи́р, **а**, *m.* passenger.

пассажи́р|ский, *adj.* of ∼; ∼ское движе́ние passenger services.

пасса́т, **а**, *m.* (*geogr.*) trade wind.

пасса́т|ный, *adj.* of ∼; п. ве́тер trade wind.

пасси́в, **а**, *m.* 1. (*comm.*) liabilities. 2. (*gram.*) passive voice.

пасси́вност|ь, **и**, *f.* passiveness, passivity.

пасси́в|ный (∼ен, ∼на), *adj.* 1. passive; ∼ное избира́тельное пра́во (*polit.*) eligibility. 2. (*econ.*) п. бала́нс unfavourable balance.

па́сси|я, **и**, *f.* (*obs.*, *coll.*) passion; бы́вшая п. old flame.

па́ст|а, **ы**, *f.* paste; зубна́я п. toothpaste.

па́стбищ|е, **а**, *n.* pasture.

па́стбищный, *adj.* pasturable.

па́ств|а, **ы**, *f.* (*eccl.*) flock, congregation.

пасте́л|ь, **и**, *f.* 1. pastel, crayon. 2. pastel (drawing).

пасте́льный, *adj.* (drawn in) pastel.

пастериза́ци|я, **и**, *f.* pasteurization.

пастеризо́в|анный, *p.p.p. of* ∼а́ть *and adj.* pasteurized.

пастериз|ова́ть, **у́ю**, *impf. and pf.* to pasteurize.

пастерна́к, **а**, *m.* parsnip.

пас|ти́, **у́**, **ёшь**, *past* ∼, ∼ла́, *impf.* (*no pf.*) to graze, pasture; to shepherd, tend.

пастил|а́, **ы́**, *pl.* ∼ы, *f.* pastila (*sort of fruit fudge*).

пас|ти́сь, **ётся**, *past* ∼ся, ∼ла́сь, *impf.* (*no pf.*) to graze, pasture; to browse.

па́стор, **а**, *m.* (*Protestant*) minister, pastor.

пастора́л|ь, **и**, *f.* 1. (*lit.*) pastoral. 2. (*mus.*) pastorale.

пастора́льный, *adj.* pastoral, bucolic.

пасту́х, **а́**, *m.* herdsman; shepherd; cowboy.

пасту́|шеский, *adj.* of ∼х; п. по́сох shepherd's crook.

пасту́|ший, *adj.* of ∼х; ∼шья су́мка (*bot.*) shepherd's purse.

пасту́шк|а, **и**, *f.* shepherdess.

пастуш|о́к, **ка́**, *m.* 1. *affect. dim. of* пасту́х. 2. (*poet.*) swain. 3. водяно́й п. (*orn.*) water-rail.

па́стыр|ский, *adj.* of ∼ь; (*eccl.*) pastoral.

па́стыр|ь, **я**, *m.* 1. (*obs.*) shepherd. 2. (*eccl.*) pastor.

па|сть¹, **ду́**, **дёшь**, *past* ∼л, ∼ла, *pf. of* ∼да́ть.

пасть², **и**, *f.* mouth (*of animal*); jaws.

пастьб|а́, **ы́**, *f.* pasturage.

Па́сх|а, **и**, *f.* 1. Passover. 2. Easter. 3. п. (*cul.*) paskha (*sweet cream-cheese dish eaten at Easter*).

пасха́ли|я, **и**, *f.* (*eccl.*) paschal cycle, paschal tables.

пасынк|ова́ть, **у́ю**, *impf. and pf.* (*bot.*) to prune, remove side shoots.

па́сын|ок, **ка**, *m.* 1. stepson, stepchild. 2. (*fig.*) outcast. 3. (*bot.*) side shoot.

пасья́нс, **а**, *m.* (*card-game*) patience; раскла́дывать п. to play patience.

пат¹, **а**, *m.* (*in chess*) stalemate.

пат², **а**, *m.* (*cul.*) paste.

пате́нт, **а**, *m.* (на+*a.*) patent (for); licence (for); владе́лец ∼а patentee.

патенто́в|анный, *p.p.p. of* ∼а́ть *and adj.* patent; ∼анное лека́рство patent medicine.

патент|ова́ть, **у́ю**, *impf.* to patent, take out a patent (for).

па́тер, **а**, *m.* Father (*in designation of Catholic priest*).

патери́к, **а́**, *m.* (*eccl.*; *lit.*) Lives of the Fathers.

пате́тик|а, **и**, *f.* (the) pathetic element; emotionalism.

патети́ческий, *adj.* 1. enthusiastic; passionate. 2. emotional. 3. bombastic.

патети́ч|ный (~ен, ~на), *adj.* = ~еский.

патефо́н, а, *m.* (*small, portable*) gramophone.

патефо́н|ный, *adj. of* ~.

па́тин|а, ы, *f.* (*archaeol., tech.*) patina.

па́тл|ы, ~, *sing.* ~а, ~ы, *f.* (*coll.*) locks (*of hair*).

пат|ова́ть, у́ю, *impf.* (*of* за~) (*in chess*) to stalemate.

па́ток|а, и, *f.* treacle; syrup; све́тлая п. golden syrup; чёрная п. molasses.

пато́лог, а, *m.* pathologist.

патологи́ческий, *adj.* pathological.

патоло́ги|я, и, *f.* pathology.

па́то|чный, *adj. of* ~ка; treacly.

патриа́рх, а, *m.* (*ethnol. and eccl.*) patriarch.

патриарха́льност|ь, и, *f.* patriarchal character.

патриарха́л|ьный (~ен, ~ьна), *adj.* (*ethnol. and fig.*) patriarchal.

патриарха́т, а, *m.* (*ethnol.*) patriarchy.

патриа́рхи|я, и, *f.* (*eccl.*) patriarchate.

патриа́ршеств|о, а, *n.* (*eccl.*) patriarchate.

патриа́р|ший, *adj. of* ~х (*eccl.*).

патрио́т, а, *m.* patriot.

патриоти́зм, а, *m.* patriotism.

патриоти́ческий, *adj.* patriotic.

патриоти́ч|ный (~ен, ~на), *adj.* = ~еский.

патри́стик|а, и, *f.* (*eccl., lit.*) patristic studies.

па́триц|а, ы, *f.* (*typ.*) punch.

патрициа́нский, *adj. of* патри́ций.

патри́ци|й, я, *m.* (*hist.*) patrician.

патро́н[1], а, *m.* 1. (*in var. senses*) patron; (*eccl.*) patron saint. 2. boss.

патро́н[2], а, *m.* 1. cartridge. 2. (*tech.*) chuck (*of drill, lathe*), holder. 3. lamp socket, lamp holder. 4. (tailor's) pattern.

патрона́ж, а, *m.* home visiting (*by health service worker*).

патрона́ж|ный, *adj. of* ~; ~ная сестра́ district nurse, health visitor.

патрони́р|овать, ую, *impf.* to patronize.

патро́нник, а, *m.* (*mil.*) (cartridge-)chamber.

патро́н|ный, *adj. of* ~[2]; ~ная ги́льза cartridge case; п. заво́д cartridge factory; ~ная обо́йма charger; cartridge clip; ~ная су́мка cartridge pouch.

патронта́ш, а, *m.* bandolier, ammunition belt.

па́труб|ок, ка, *m.* (*tech.*) 1. nipple, nozzle. 2. socket, sleeve, connexion; branch pipe. 3. boss (*of thermometer*).

патрули́р|овать, ую, *impf.* (*no pf.*) (*mil.*) to patrol.

патру́л|ь, я́, *m.* patrol.

патру́ль|ный, *adj. of* ~; *as noun* п., ~ного, *m.* patrol.

па́уз|а, ы, *f.* pause; interval; (*mus.*) rest.

па́уз|ок, ка, *m.* (*river*) lighter.

пау́к, а́, *m.* spider.

паукообра́зн|ые, ых, *sing.* ~ое, ~ого, *n.* (*zool.*) Arachnida.

па́упер, а, *m.* pauper.

паупериза́ци|я, и, *f.* pauperization.

паупери́зм, а, *m.* pauperism.

паути́н|а, ы, *f.* cobweb, spider's web; gossamer; (*fig.*) web.

паути́н|ка, ки, *f. dim. of* ~а; чулки́-п. very fine stockings.

пау́|чий, *adj. of* ~к.

па́фос, а, *m.* 1. pathos. 2. (+*g.*) enthusiasm (for), zeal (for); п. коммунисти́ческого строи́тельства enthusiasm for the building of Communism. 3. spirit; emotional content; п. рома́на the spirit of a novel. 4. (*pejor.*) (*affected*) pathos, bombast.

пах, а, о ~е, в ~у́, *m.* (*anat.*) groin.

па́хан|ый, *adj.* ploughed (up); ~е зе́мли ploughland.

па́хар|ь, я, *m.* ploughman.

па|ха́ть, шу́, ~шешь, *impf.* to plough, till.

па́хн|уть, у, ешь, *impf.* (*no pf.*) (+*i.*) to smell (of); to reek (of); ~ет лу́ком there is a smell of onions; (*fig.*) to savour (of), smack (of); ~ет бедо́й this means trouble; ~уло ссо́рой a quarrel was in the air.

пахн|у́ть, ёт, *pf.* (*no impf.*) (+*i.*; coll.) to puff, blow; ~у́л ве́тер there was a gust of wind; ~уло хо́лодом (*impers.*) there came a cold blast.

паховой, *adj.* (*anat.*) inguinal.

па́хот|а, ы, *f.* ploughing, tillage.

па́хотный, *adj.* arable.

па́хтань|е, я, *n.* 1. churning. 2. butter-milk.

па́хта|ть, ю, *impf.* to churn.

паху́ч|ий (~, ~а), *adj.* odorous, strong-smelling.

паца́н, а, *m.* (*coll.*) boy, lad.

пацие́нт, а, *m.* patient.

пацифи́зм, а, *m.* pacifism.

пацифи́ст, а, *m.* pacifist.

па́че, *adv.* (*arch.*) more; *now only in phrases* тем п. the more so, the more reason; п. ча́яния contrary to expectation; beyond expectation.

па́чк|а, и, *f.* 1. bundle; batch; packet, pack; п. пи́сем bundle of letters; п. папиро́с packet of cigarettes; п. книг parcel of books. 2. (*mil.*) (*cartridge*) clip; стреля́ть ~ами (*obs.*) to fire bursts. 3. 'tutu' (*ballet dancer's fluffy skirt, with layers of underskirts*).

па́чка|ть, ю, *impf.* 1. (*pf.* за ~ *and* ис ~) to dirty, soil, stain, sully (*also fig.*); п. ру́ки (*fig.*) to soil one's hands; п. чьё-н. до́брое и́мя to sully someone's good name. 2. (*pf.* на~) (*coll.*) to daub.

па́чка|ться, юсь, *impf.* (*of* за~, ис~, *and* на~) 1. to make oneself dirty, soil oneself. 2. to become dirty.

пачкотн|я́, и́, *f.* (*coll.*) daub.

пачку́н, а́, *m.* (*coll.*) **1.** sloven. **2.** dauber.

паш|а́, и́, *g. pl.* ~е́й, *m.* pasha.

па́ш|ня, ни, *g. pl.* ~ен, *f.* ploughed field.

паште́т, а, *m.* pâté, pie.

па́юсн|ый, *adj.* ~ая икра́ pressed caviar(e).

пая́льник, а, *m.* soldering iron.

пая́льн|ый, *adj.* soldering; ~ая ла́мпа blow lamp; ~ая тру́бка blowpipe, blow torch.

пая́льщик, а, *m.* tinman, tinsmith.

па́яный, *adj.* soldered.

пая́снича|ть, ю, *impf.* (*no pf.*) (*coll.*) to clown, play the fool.

пая́|ть, ю, *impf.* (*no pf.*) to solder.

пая́ц, а, *m.* **1.** (*circus*) clown. **2.** (*fig., pejor.*) clown.

пеа́н¹, а, *m.* paean.

пеа́н², а, *m.* (*med.*) Pean's forceps, clamp forceps.

пев|е́ц, ца́, *m.* singer.

певи́ц|а, ы, *f.* of певе́ц.

певу́н, а́, *m.* (*coll.*) songster.

певу́ч|ий (~, ~а), *adj.* melodious.

пе́вч|ий **1.** *adj.* singing; ~ая пти́ца song-bird. **2.** *as noun* п., ~его, *m.* chorister, choirboy.

пега́нк|а, и, *f.* (*orn.*) shelduck.

пе́г|ий (~, ~а), *adj.* skewbald.

педаго́г, а, *m.* teacher; pedagogue.

педаго́гик|а, и, *f.* pedagogy, pedagogics.

педагоги́ческий, *adj.* pedagogic(al); educational; п. институ́т teachers' training college; п. факульте́т education department (*for training educationalists*).

педаго́гич|ный (~ен, ~на), *adj.* sensible, wise (*in sphere of education*).

педализа́ци|я, и, *f.* (*mus.*) pedalling.

педализи́р|овать, ую, *impf. and pf.* **1.** (*mus.*) to pedal. **2.** (*fig.*) to harp upon.

педа́л|ь, и, *f.* pedal; treadle; брать п., нажа́ть п. to pedal; рабо́тать ~ью, to treadle; нажа́ть на все ~и (*fig., coll.*) to go flat out.

педа́ль|ный, *adj.* of ~; п. нажи́м pedalling; п. автомоби́ль pedal car (*child's motor-car operated by pedal*).

педа́нт, а, *m.* pedant.

педанти́зм, а, *m.* pedantry.

педанти́ческий, *adj.* pedantic.

педанти́чност|ь, и, *f.* pedantry.

педанти́ч|ный (~ен, ~на), *adj.* = ~еский.

пе́дел|ь, я, *m.* bedel.

педера́ст, а, *m.* p(a)ederast, sodomite.

педера́сти|я, и, *f.* p(a)ederasty, sodomy.

педиа́тр, а, *m.* p(a)ediatrician.

педиатри́|я, и, *f.* p(a)ediatrics.

педикю́р, а, *m.* chiropody.

педикю́рш|а, и, *f.* chiropodist.

педо́метр, а, *m.* pedometer.

пе́жин|а, ы, *f.* **1.** skewbaldness. **2.** patch (*on skewbald horse*).

пезе́т|а, ы, *f.* (*Spanish currency unit*) peseta.

пейза́ж, а, *m.* **1.** landscape; scenery. **2.** (*art*) landscape.

пейзажи́ст, а, *m.* landscape painter.

пейза́ж|ный, *adj.* of ~; ~ная жи́вопись landscape painting.

пек, а, *m.* (*tech.*) pitch.

пёк, пекла́, *see* печь¹.

пека́рн|ый, *adj.* baking; ~ая печь bakehouse oven; ~ое ремесло́ bakery trade.

пека́р|ня, ни, *g. pl.* ~ен, *f.* bakery, bakehouse.

пе́кар|ский, *adj.* of ~ь; ~ские дро́жжи baker's yeast.

пе́кар|ь, я, *pl.* ~я́, ~е́й *and* ~и, ~ей, *m.* baker.

пеклева́нник, а, *m.* fine rye bread.

пеклева́нн|ый, *adj.* finely ground; ~ая мука́ rye flour (of the best quality); п. хлеб fine rye bread.

пекл|ева́ть, юю, ю́ешь, *impf.* to grind fine.

пе́кл|о, а, *n.* **1.** scorching heat; попа́сть в са́мое п. (*fig., coll.*) to get into the thick of it. **2.** (*coll.*) hell.

пекти́н, а, *m.* (*chem.*) pectin.

пекти́новы|й, *adj.* (*chem.*) pectic; ~е вещества́ pectins.

пеку́, пеку́т, *see* печь¹.

пелен|а́, ы́, *pl.* ~ы́, ~, ~а́м, *f.* shroud; с ~ (*obs., fig.*) from the cradle; у него́ (сло́вно) п. (с глаз) упа́ла the scales fell from his eyes.

пелена́|ть, ю, *impf.* (*of* за~ *and* с~) to swaddle.

пе́ленг, а, *m.* (*naut., aeron.*) bearing.

пеленга́тор, а, *m.* (*naut., aeron.*) direction finder.

пеленг|и́ровать, и́рую, *impf. and pf.* = ~ова́ть.

пеленг|ова́ть, у́ю, *impf. and pf.* (*naut., aeron.*) to take the bearings (of), set.

пелён|ка, ки, *f.* nappy; (*pl.*) swaddling clothes; с пелёнок (*fig.*) from the cradle.

пелери́н|а, ы, *f.* cape, pelerine.

пелика́н, а, *m.* pelican.

пельме́н|и, ей, *sing.* ~ь, ~я, *m.* (*cul.*) pelmeni (*kind of ravioli*).

пе́мз|а, ы, *f.* pumice(-stone).

пе́мз|овый, *adj.* of ~а.

пе́н|а, ы, *f.* **1.** foam, spume; scum; froth, head (*on liquids*); мы́льная п. soapsuds; говори́ть с ~ой у рта, с ~ой на уста́х (*fig.*) to foam at the mouth. **2.** lather (*on horses*).

пена́л, а, *m.* pencil-box.

пена́т|ы, ов, *no sing.* (*myth. and fig.*) penates; верну́ться к (свои́м, родны́м) ~ам to return to one's hearth and home.

пе́ни|е, я, *n.* singing; п. (птиц) (birds') song; п. петуха́ cock's crow.

пе́нист|ый (~, ~а), *adj.* foamy; frothy; ~ое вино́ sparkling wine.

пенитенциа́рный, adj. (leg.) penitentiary.

пе́н|ить, ю, ишь, impf. to froth.

пе́н|иться, ится, impf. to foam; to froth (intrans.).

пеницилли́н, а, m. penicillin.

пе́нк|а¹, и, f. (on milk, etc.) skin; снять ~и (c+g.) to skim; (fig.) to take the pickings (of).

пе́нк|а², и, f. (min.) морска́я п. meerschaum.

пе́нк|овый, adj. of ~а²; ~овая тру́бка meerschaum (pipe).

пе́нни, indecl., n. penny.

пе́н|ный, adj. (obs.) = ~истый.

пенопла́ст, а, m. foam rubber.

пенопласт|и́ческий, adj. of ~.

пеностекл|о́, а́, n. glass fibre.

пеностек|о́льный, adj. of ~ло́.

пе́ночк|а, и, f. (orn.) warbler (Phylloscopus).

пенс, а, m. penny.

пенсионе́р, а, m. pensioner.

пенсио́нн|ый, adj. of пе́нсия; ~ая кни́жка pension book.

пе́нси|я, и, f. pension.

пенсне́, indecl., n. pince-nez.

пента́метр, а, m. (lit.) pentameter.

пе́нтюх, а, m. (coll.) lout, bumpkin.

пень, пня, m. stump, stub; стоя́ть как п. (coll.) to be rooted to the ground; вали́ть че́рез п. коло́ду (coll.) to do a thing anyhow.

пеньк|а́, и́, f. hemp.

пенько́вый, adj. hempen.

пенью́ар, а, m. peignoir.

пе́н|я, и, f. fine.

пеня́|ть, ю, impf. (of по~) (+d. or на+a.; coll.) to blame, reproach; ~й на себя́! you have only yourself to blame!

пео́н¹, а, m. (lit.) paeon.

пео́н², а, m. peon.

пе́п|ел, ла, m. ash(es).

пепели́щ|е, а, n. 1. site of fire. 2. (hearth and) home; верну́ться на ста́рое п. to return to one's old home.

пе́пельниц|а, ы, f. ash-tray.

пе́пельно-се́рый, adj. ash-grey.

пе́пельн|ый, adj. ashy; ~ого цве́та ash-grey.

пепси́н, а, m. (physiol.) pepsin.

пепси́новый, adj. peptic.

пепто́н, а, m. (physiol.) peptone.

перва́ч, а́, m. (coll.) first-quality goods.

перве́йший, adj. (coll.) the first; first-class.

пе́рвен|ец, ца, m. first-born; (fig.) firstling.

пе́рвенств|о, а, n. first place; (sport) championship; завоева́ть п. ми́ра по футбо́лу to win the world championship at football.

пе́рвенств|овать, ую and ~ова́ть, ~у́ю, impf. (no pf.) to take first place; (над) to take precedence (of), take priority (over).

пе́рвенств|ующий, pres. part. act. of ~ова́ть and adj. pre-eminent; primary.

перви́нк|а, и, f. в ~у (coll.) for the first time; мне не в ~у предупрежда́ть её this is not the first time I have warned her.

перви́чность|ь, и, f. primacy; priority.

перви́чн|ый, adj. primary; initial; ~ая парторганиза́ция primary Party organization; п. пери́од боле́зни initial period of illness; ~ые поро́ды (geol.) primary rocks.

первобы́тный, adj. (ethnol. and fig.) primitive; primordial; primeval.

первого́д|ок, ка, m. (coll.) young of animal less than one year old.

пе́рв|ое, ого, n. first course (of a meal).

первозда́нный, adj. primordial; (geol.) primitive, primary; п. хао́с primordial chaos (also fig., iron.).

первоисто́чник, а, m. primary source; origin.

первокатего́рник, а, m. first-rank (first-flight) player (esp. of chess-players).

первокла́ссник, а, m. pupil of the first class, first-former.

первокла́ссный, adj. first-class, first-rate.

первоку́рсник, а, m. first-year student, freshman.

Первома́|й, я, m. (coll.) May Day.

первома́й|ский, adj. of ~.

пе́рво-на́перво, adv. (coll.) first of all.

первонача́льно, adv. originally.

первонача́льн|ый, adj. 1. original. 2. primary; initial; ~ое накопле́ние (econ.) primary accumulation; ~ая причи́на (philos.) first cause. 3. elementary. 4. ~ые чи́сла (math.) prime numbers.

первообра́з, а, m. prototype; protoplast.

первообра́зный, adj. prototypal; protoplastic.

первоосно́в|а, ы, f. (philos.) first principle.

первооткрыва́тел|ь, я, m. discoverer.

первоочередн|о́й, adj. first and foremost, immediate; ~а́я зада́ча immediate task.

первоочередн|о́й = ~о́й.

первопеча́тник, а, m. printing pioneer.

первопеча́тн|ый, adj. 1. printed early, belonging to the first years of printing; ~ые кни́ги incunabula. 2. first printed.

первопресто́льн|ый, adj. (rhet.) being the oldest (first) capital; as noun Первопресто́льна|я, ~ой, f. Moscow (by contrast with St. Petersburg).

первопричи́н|а, ы, f. (philos.) first cause.

первопрохо́д|ец, ца, m. (fig., rhet.) pioneer, pacemaker.

первопу́т|ок, ка, m. (coll.) the first sledging (of the winter); е́хать по ~ку to traverse a road after the first snowfall.

перворазря́дник, а, m. (sport) first-rank player.

перворазря́дный, adj. first-class, first-rank.

перворо́дный, *adj.* (*obs.*) **1.** first-born. **2.** primal; п. грех (*eccl.*) original sin.

первородств|о, а, *n.* **1.** (*leg.*) primogeniture. **2.** (*fig.*) primacy.

перворождённый, *adj.* first-born.

первосвяще́нник, а, *m.* high priest, chief priest; pontiff.

первосо́ртный, *adj.* **1.** of the best quality. **2.** (*coll.*) first-class, first-rate.

первостате́йный, *adj.* **1.** (*obs.*) of the first order; of consequence. **2.** (*coll.*) first-rate, first-class.

первостепе́нный, *adj.* paramount, of the first order.

первоцве́т, а, *m.* (*bot.*) primrose.

пе́рв|ый, *adj.* (*in var. senses*) first; former; earliest; ~ое (число́ ме́сяца) the first (of the month); ~ого января́ on the first of January; полови́на ~ого half past twelve; в ~ом часу́ after twelve, past twelve, between twelve and one; он п. вошёл he was the first to enter; быть ~ым, идти́ ~ым to come first, lead; ~ое вре́мя at first; п. встре́чный the first comer; ~ое де́ло, ~ым де́лом (*coll.*) first of all, first thing; не ~ой мо́лодости not in one's first youth; ~ая по́мощь first aid; п. рейс maiden voyage; не ~ой све́жести not quite fresh, stale; ~ая скри́пка first violin; (*fig.*) first fiddle; п. эта́ж ground floor; в ~ую го́лову (*coll.*) first and foremost; в ~ую о́чередь in the first place; из ~ых рук first-hand; на п. взгляд, с ~ого взгля́да at first sight; при ~ой возмо́жности at one's earliest convenience, as soon as possible; с ~ого ра́за from the first; п. блин ко́мом (*prov.*) practice makes perfect.

перг|а́, и́, *f.* bee-bread.

перга́мен, а, *m.* = ~т.

перга́мент, а, *m.* parchment.

перга́мент|ный, *adj.* of ~; ~ная бума́га oil--paper.

перд|е́ть, и́т, *impf.* (*vulg.*) to fart.

пере- *verbal prefix indicating* **1.** action across *or* through something (trans-). **2.** repetition of action (re-). **3.** superiority, excess, *etc.* (over-, out-). **4.** extension of action to encompass many *or* all objects *or* cases of a given kind. **5.** division into two *or* more parts. **6.** (*reflexives*) reciprocity of action.

переадрес|ова́ть, у́ю, *pf.* (*of* ~о́вывать) to re-address.

переадресо́выва|ть, ю, *impf. of* переадресова́ть.

перебази́р|овать, ую, *pf.* (*no impf.*) to shift.

перебаллоти́р|овать, ую, *pf.* (*of* ~о́вывать) to submit to second ballot.

перебаллотиро́вк|а, и, *f.* second ballot.

перебаллотиро́выва|ть, ю, *impf. of* перебаллоти́ровать.

перебáрщива|ть, ю, *impf. of* переборщи́ть.

перебега́|ть, ю, *impf. of* перебежа́ть.

перебе|жа́ть, гу́, жи́шь, гу́т, *pf.* (*of* ~га́ть) **1.** (че́рез) to cross (running); п. (че́рез) у́лицу to run across the street; п. кому́-н. доро́гу to cross someone's path. **2.** (*fig., coll.*; к) to go over (to), desert (to).

перебе́жк|а, и, *f.* (*mil.*) bound, rush.

перебе́жчик, а, *m.* deserter; (*fig.*) turncoat.

перебе́лива|ть, ю, *impf. of* перебели́ть.

перебел|и́ть, ю́, и́шь, *pf.* (*of* ~ива́ть) **1.** to whitewash again. **2.** to make a fair copy (of).

перебе|си́ться, шу́сь, ~си́шься, *pf.* **1.** to go mad, run mad. **2.** (*coll.*) to have sown one's wild oats.

перебива́|ть(ся), ю(сь), *impf. of* переби́ть(ся)¹,².

переби́вк|а, и, *f.* re-upholstering.

перебинт|ова́ть¹, у́ю, *pf.* (*of* ~о́вывать) to change the dressing (on), put a new dressing (on).

перебинт|ова́ть², у́ю, *pf.* (*of* ~о́вывать) to dress, bandage (*all, a quantity of*).

перебинто́выва|ть, ю, *impf. of* перебинтова́ть.

перебира́|ть¹(ся), ю(сь), *impf. of* перебра́ть(ся).

перебира́|ть², ю, *impf.* **1.** to finger; п. стру́ны to run one's fingers over the strings; п. чётки to tell one's beads. **2.** (+*i.*) to move, advance (*in turn or in a regular manner*).

переб|и́ть¹, ью́, ье́шь, *pf.* (*of* ~ива́ть) **1.** to re-upholster. **2.** to beat up again (*pillow, feather-bed, etc.*).

переб|и́ть², ью́, ье́шь, *pf.* (*of* ~ива́ть) **1.** to interrupt. **2.** to intercept; п. кому́-н. доро́гу to cross someone's path; п. поку́пку (*coll.*) to outbid for something.

переб|и́ть³, ью́, ье́шь, *pf.* **1.** to kill, slay, slaughter. **2.** to beat. **3.** to break.

переб|и́ться¹, ью́сь, ье́шься, *pf.* (*of* ~ива́ться) to break.

переб|и́ться², ью́сь, ье́шься, *pf.* (*of* ~ива́ться) (*coll.*) to make ends meet; п. с хле́ба на квас to live from hand to mouth.

перебо́|й, я, *m.* interruption, intermission; stoppage, hold-up; misfire (*of engine*); пульс с ~ями intermittent pulse.

перебо́йный, *adj.* interrupted, intermittent.

переболе́|ть¹, ю, *pf.* (+*i.*) to have had, have been down (*with an illness*); де́ти все ~ли коклю́шем the children have all been down with whooping-cough.

перебол|е́ть², и́т, *pf.* to recover, become well again.

перебо́рк|а¹, и, *f.* **1.** sorting out. **2.** (*tech.*) re-assembly.

перебо́рк|а², и, *f.* partition; (*naut.*) bulk-head.

перебор|о́ть, ю́, ~ешь, *pf.* (*no impf.*) to master.

переборщ|и́ть, у́, и́шь, *pf.* (*of* перебара́щивать) (в+*p.*; *coll.*) to go too far; to overdo it.

перебра́нива|ться, юсь, *impf.* (с+*i.*; *coll.*) to bandy angry words (with), have words (with).

перебран|и́ться, ю́сь, и́шься, *pf.* (с+*i.*; *coll.*) to quarrel (with), fall out (with).

перебра́нк|а, и, *f.* (*coll.*) wrangle, squabble.

перебра́сыва|ть(ся), ю(сь), *impf. of* перебро́сить(ся).

пере|бра́ть[1], беру́, берёшь, *past* ~бра́л, ~брала́, ~бра́ло, *pf.* (*of* ~бира́ть) 1. to sort out (*also fig.*); to look through. 2. (*fig.*) to turn over (in one's mind). 3. to take in excess; п. пять очко́в to score five extra points.

пере|бра́ть[2], беру́, берёшь, *past* ~бра́л, ~брала́, ~бра́ло, *pf.* (*of* ~бира́ть) 1. (*typ.*) to reset. 2. (*tech.*) to (dismantle and) reassemble.

пере|бра́ться, беру́сь, берёшься, *past* ~бра́лся, ~брала́сь, ~брало́сь, *pf.* (*coll.*) 1. to get over, cross. 2. to move; п. на но́вую кварти́ру to change one's lodgings.

перебр|оди́ть, о́дит, *pf.* to have fermented; to have risen.

переброса́|ть, ю, *pf.* to throw one after another.

перебро́|сить, шу, сишь, *pf.* (*of* перебра́сывать) 1. to throw over; п. мост че́рез ре́ку to throw a bridge across a river. 2. to transfer (*troops, etc.*).

перебро́|ситься, шусь, сишься, *pf.* (*of* перебра́сываться) 1. (+*i.*) to throw one to another; п. не́сколькими слова́ми (*fig.*) to exchange a few words. 2. (*of fire, disease, etc.*) to spread.

перебро́ск|а, и, *f.* transfer.

перебыва́|ть, ю, *pf.* to have called, have been; он везде́ ~л he has been all over the world.

перева́л, а, *m.* 1. passing, crossing. 2. (*geogr.*) pass.

перева́л|ец, ьца, *m.* ходи́ть с ~ьцем (*coll.*) to waddle.

перева́лива|ть, ю, *impf. of* перевали́ть.

перева́лива|ться[1], юсь, *impf. of* перевали́ться.

перева́лива|ться[2], юсь, *impf.* (*no pf.*) to waddle.

перевал|и́ть, ю́, ~ишь, *pf.* (*of* ~ивать) 1. to transfer, shift. 2. to cross; (*impers.*; *coll.*) ~и́ло за по́лночь it is past midnight; ей ~и́ло за́ сорок (лет) she has turned forty, she is past forty.

перевал|и́ться, ю́сь, ~ишься, *pf.* (*of* ~иваться[1]) to roll over; to fall over; п. на пра́вый бок to roll over on to one's right side.

перева́лк|а, и, *f.* 1. trans-shipment, conveyance. 2. trans-shipping point.

перева́л|очный, *adj. of* ~ка; п. пункт (*in var. senses*) staging post.

перева́рива|ть, ю, *impf. of* перевари́ть.

перевари́м|ый (~, ~а), *adj.* digestible.

перевар|и́ть[1], ю́, ~ишь, *pf.* (*of* ~ивать) 1. to cook again; to boil again. 2. (*in cooking*) to overdo.

перевар|и́ть[2], ю́, ~ишь, *pf.* (*of* ~ивать) 1. to digest; п. прочи́танное (*fig.*) to digest what one has read. 2. (*fig.*) to swallow; to bear, stand.

переве́д|аться, аюсь, *pf.* (*of* ~ываться) (*obs.*; с+*i.*) to demand satisfaction (from).

переве́дыва|ться, юсь, *impf. of* переве́даться.

перевез|ти́, у́, ёшь, *past* ~, ~ла́, *pf.* (*o* перевози́ть) 1. to take across, put across. 2. to transport, convey (*from A to B*); to (re)move (*furniture, etc.*).

переверн|у́ть, у́, ёшь, *pf.* (*of* переве́ртывать *and* перевора́чивать) to turn over; to invert; п. страни́цу to turn over the page; п. наизна́нку to turn inside out.

переверн|у́ться, у́сь, ёшься, *pf.* (*of* переве́ртываться *and* перевора́чиваться) to turn over; ~ётся в гробу́ (*joc.*) he would turn in his grave.

перевер|те́ть, чу́, ~тишь, *pf.* (*of* ~тывать *and* ~чивать) (*coll.*) to overwind.

переве́ртыва|ть(ся), ю(сь), *impf. of* перевернуть(ся) *and* перевертеть.

переве́рчива|ть, ю, *impf. of* переверте́ть.

переве́с, а, *m.* preponderance; advantage; чи́сленный п. numerical superiority; взять п. to gain the upper hand; п. на на́шей стороне́, в на́шу по́льзу the odds are in our favour.

переве́|сить[1], шу, сишь, *pf.* (*of* ~шивать) to hang somewhere else; п. карти́ну с одно́й стены́ на другу́ю to move a picture from one wall to another.

переве́|сить[2], шу, сишь, *pf.* (*of* ~шивать) 1. to weigh again. 2. to outweigh, outbalance (*also fig.*); (*fig.*) to tip the scales

переве́|ситься, шусь, сишься, *pf.* (*of* ~шиваться) to lean over.

переве|сти́[1], ду́, дёшь, *past* ~л, ~ла́, *pf.* (*o,* переводи́ть) 1. to take across; п. дете́й че́рез у́лицу to escort children across the road. 2. to transfer, move, switch, shift; п. на другу́ю рабо́ту to transfer to another post; п. в сле́дующий класс to move up into the next form; п. валю́ту to transfer currency; п. де́ньги по телегра́фу to wire money; п. стре́лку to shunt, switch; п. стре́лку часо́в вперёд (наза́д) to put a clock on (back). 3. (с+*g.* на+*a.*) to translate (from into); (в, на+*a*.) to convert (to), express (as, in); п. с рýсского языкá на англи́йский to translate from Russian into English; п. в метри́ческие мéры to convert to the metric system, express according to the metric system. 4. п. дух to take breath. 5. (*art*) to transfer, copy.

переве|сти́², дý, дёшь, *past* ~л, ~лá, *pf.* (*of* переводи́ть) (*coll.*) 1. to destroy, exterminate. 2. to spend, use up.

переве|сти́сь¹, дýсь, дёшься, *past* ~лся, ~лáсь, *pf.* (*of* переводи́ться) 1. to move, be transferred. 2. *pass. of* ~сти́¹,².

переве|сти́сь², дýсь, дёшься, *past* ~лся, ~лáсь, *pf.* (*of* переводи́ться) (*coll.*) to come to an end; to become extinct; к концý недéли дéньги у меня́ ~ли́сь by the end of the week I was spent up.

перевéш|ать¹, аю, *pf.* (*of* ~ивать) to weigh (*all or a quantity of*).

перевéш|ать², аю, *pf.* to hang (*a number of*).

перевéшива|ть, ю, *impf. of* перевéсить *and* перевéшать¹.

перевéшива|ться, юсь, *impf. of* перевéситься.

перевивá|ть, ю, *impf. of* переви́ть.

перевидá|ть, ю, *pf.* (*coll.*) to have seen (*also fig.* = to have experienced).

перевирá|ть, ю, *impf. of* переврáть.

перев|и́ть¹, ью, ьёшь, *past* ~и́л, ~илá, ~и́ло, *pf.* (*of* ~ивáть) to weave again.

перев|и́ть², ью, ьёшь, *past* ~и́л, ~илá, ~и́ло, *pf.* (*of* ~ивáть) (+*i.*) to interweave (with), intertwine (with).

перевóд¹, а, *m.* 1. transfer, move, switch, shift; п. дéнег remittance; почтóвый п. postal order; п. стрéлки shunting, switching; п. стрéлки часóв вперёд (назáд) putting a clock on (back). 2. translation; version; п. мер conversion of measures.

перевóд², а, *m.* (*coll.*) spending, using up; пустóй п. дéнег (деньгáм) squandering; нет ~у (+*d.*) there is no shortage (of), there is an inexhaustible supply (of).

перево|ди́ть(ся), жý(сь), ~ди́шь(ся), *impf. of* перевести́(сь).

переводн|óй, *adj. of* перевóд¹; ~áя бумáга carbon paper; transfer paper; ~áя карти́нка transfer.

перевóд|ный, *adj. of* ~¹; п. ромáн novel in translation; п. блáнк postal order form.

перевóдчик, а, *m.* translator; interpreter.

перевóз, а, *m.* 1. transportation. 2. ferry.

перево|зи́ть, жý, ~зишь, *impf. of* перевезти́.

перевóзк|а, и, *f.* conveyance, transportation.

перевóз|очный, *adj. of* ~ка; ~очные срéдства means of conveyance.

перевóзчик, а, *m.* 1. ferryman; boatman. 2. (*orn.*) common sandpiper.

переволн|овáть, ýю, *pf.* (*coll.*) to alarm.

переволн|овáться, ýюсь, *pf.* (*coll.*) to be alarmed; to suffer prolonged anxiety.

перевооруж|áть(ся), áю(сь), *impf. of* ~и́ть(ся).

перевооружéни|е, я, *n.* re-armament.

перевооруж|и́ть, ý, и́шь, *pf.* (*of* ~áть) to re-arm.

перевооруж|и́ться, ýсь, и́шься, *pf.* (*of* ~áться) to re-arm (*intrans.*).

перевопло|ти́ть, щý, ти́шь, *pf.* (*of* ~щáть) to reincarnate; to transform.

перевопло|ти́ться, щýсь, ти́шься, *pf.* (*of* ~щáться) to be reincarnated; to undergo a transformation.

перевоплощá|ть(ся), ю(сь), *impf. of* перевоплоти́ть(ся).

переворáчива|ть(ся), ю(сь), *impf. of* перевернýть(ся).

переворóт, а, *m.* 1. revolution; overturn; госудáрственный п. coup d'état. 2. (*geol.*) cataclysm.

переворош|и́ть, ý, и́шь, *pf.* (*coll.*) 1. to turn (over) (*also fig.*); п. сéно to turn hay; п. свою́ пáмять to search through one's memories. 2. (*fig.*) to turn upside down.

перевоспитáни|е, я, *n.* re-education.

перевоспит|áть, áю, *pf.* (*of* ~ывать) to re-educate.

перевоспит|áться, áюсь, *pf.* (*of* ~ываться) to re-educate oneself, be re-educated.

перевоспи́тыва|ть(ся), ю(сь), *impf. of* перевоспитáть(ся).

перевр|áть, ý, ёшь, *past* ~áл, ~алá, ~áло, *pf.* (*of* перевирáть) (*coll.*) to garble, confuse; to misinterpret; п. цитáту to misquote.

перевыбирá|ть, ю, *impf. of* перевы́брать.

перевы́бор|ы, ов, *no sing.* re-election.

перевы́б|рать, еру, ерешь, *pf.* (*of* ~ирáть) to re-elect.

перевыполнéни|е, я, *n.* over-fulfilment.

перевы́полн|ить, ю, ишь, *pf.* (*of* ~я́ть) to over-fulfil.

перевыполн|я́ть, я́ю, *impf. of* ~ить.

перевя|зáть¹, жý, ~жешь, *pf.* (*of* ~зывать) 1. to dress, bandage. 2. to tie up, cord.

перевя|зáть², жý, ~жешь, *pf.* (*of* ~зывать) to knit again.

перевя́зк|а, и, *f.* dressing, bandage.

перевя́з|очный, *adj. of* ~ка; п. материáл dressing; п. пункт dressing station.

перевя́зыва|ть, ю, *impf. of* перевязáть.

пéревя|зь, и, *f.* 1. (*mil., hist.*) cross-belt, shoulder-belt, baldric. 2. (*med.*) sling; рукá у негó былá на ~и he had his arm in a sling.

перегáр, а, *m.* (*coll.*) (*unpleasant*) residual taste of alcohol in the mouth; smell of alcohol; от него несло ~ом he reeked of alcohol.

перегиб, а, *m.* 1. bend, twist; fold. 2. (*fig.*) exaggeration; допустить п. в чём-н. to carry something too far.

перегиба|ть(ся), ю(сь), *impf. of* перегнуть(ся).

перегласовк|а, и, *f.* (*ling.*) mutation.

переглядыва|ться, юсь, *impf. of* переглянуться.

перегля|нуться, нусь, ~нешься, *pf.* (*of* ~дываться) (с+*i.*) to exchange glances (with).

перегн|ать, **перегоню**, **перегонишь**, *past* ~ал, ~ала, ~ало, *pf.* (*of* перегонять) 1. to outdistance, leave behind; (*fig.*) to overtake, surpass. 2. to drive (*somewhere else*; *from A to B*); п. самолёты to ferry planes. 3. (*chem., tech.*) to distil, sublimate.

перегнива|ть, ю, *impf. of* перегнить.

перегн|ить, иёт, *past* ~ил, ~ила, ~ило, *pf.* (*of* ~ивать) to rot through.

перегно́|й, я, *m.* humus.

перегно́й|ный, *adj. of* ~; ~ная по́чва humus.

перег|нуть, ну́, нёшь, *pf.* (*of* ~ибать) to bend; п. па́лку (*fig., coll.*) to go too far.

перег|нуться, нусь, нёшься, *pf.* (*of* ~ибаться) 1. to bend. 2. to lean over.

перегова́рива|ть, ю, *impf. of* переговорить[2].

перегова́рива|ться, юсь, *impf.* (с+*i.*) to exchange remarks (with).

переговор|и́ть, ю́, и́шь, *pf.* (о+*p.*) to talk (about); to talk over, discuss; п. по телефо́ну to speak over the telephone.

переговор|и́ть[2], ю́, и́шь, *pf.* (*of* перегова́ривать) to silence; to out-talk.

переговорн|ый, *adj.* ~ая бу́дка telephone booth; п. телефо́нный пункт trunk-call office.

переговор|ы, ов, *no sing.* negotiations; (*mil.*) parley; вести п. (с+*i.*) to negotiate (with), carry on negotiations (with); (*mil.*) to parley (with); иду́т п. negotiations are in progress.

перего́н[1], а, *m.* driving.

перего́н[2], а, *m.* stage (*between two railway stations*).

перего́нк|а, и, *f.* (*tech., chem.*) distillation; суха́я п. sublimation.

перего́н|ный, *adj. of* ~ка; п. заво́д distillery; п. куб still.

перегоня́|ть, ю, *impf. of* перегна́ть.

перегора́жива|ть, ю, *impf. of* перегороди́ть.

перегор|а́ть, а́ю, *impf. of* ~е́ть.

перегоре́лый, *adj.* (*coll.*) burnt out.

перегор|е́ть, и́т, *pf.* (*of* ~а́ть) 1. to burn out, fuse. 2. to burn through. 3. to rot through.

перегоро|ди́ть, жу́, ~ди́шь, *pf.* (*of* перегора́живать) to partition off.

перегоро́дк|а, и, *f.* 1. partition. 2. (*tech.*) baffle (plate). 3. (*fig.*) barrier.

перегоро́д|очный, *adj. of* ~ка.

перегре́в, а, *m.* overheating; (*tech.*) superheating.

перегрева́тел|ь, я, *m.* (*tech.*) superheater.

перегрева́|ть(ся), ю(сь), *impf. of* перегре́ть(ся).

перегре́|ть, ю, *pf.* (*of* ~ва́ть) 1. to overheat. 2. (*tech.*) to superheat.

перегре́|ться, юсь, *pf.* (*of* ~ва́ться) to burn (out), get burned.

перегружа́|ть, ю, *impf. of* перегрузи́ть.

перегру|зи́ть[1], жу́, ~зи́шь, *pf.* (*of* ~жа́ть) to overload, surcharge; п. рабо́той to overwork.

перегру|зи́ть[2], жу́, ~зи́шь, *pf.* (*of* ~жа́ть) to load (*somewhere else*; *from A to B*); to trans-ship; п. с по́езда на парохо́д to load from a train on to a ship.

перегру́зк|а[1], и, *f.* overload, surcharge; overloading; п. рабо́той overwork.

перегру́зк|а[2], и, *f.* reloading; shifting; transfer, trans-shipping.

перегру́з|очный, *adj. of* ~ка[2].

перегруппир|ова́ть, у́ю, *pf.* (*of* ~о́вывать) to re-group.

перегруппиро́вк|а, и, *f.* re-grouping.

перегруппир|о́вывать, о́вываю, *impf. of* ~ова́ть.

перегры́з|ть, у́, ёшь, *past* ~, ~ла, *pf.* (*of* ~а́ть) to gnaw through, bite through.

перегры́з|ться, у́сь, ёшься, *past* ~ся, ~лась, *pf.* (*no impf.*) (из-за; *coll.*; *of dogs*) to fight (over); (*fig.*) to quarrel (over), wrangle (about).

пе́ред *and* **пе́редо**, *prep.+i.* 1. (*of place; also fig.*) before; in front of; in the face of; п. дворцо́м in front of the palace; при́зрак стоя́л пе́редо мно́й the apparition stood before me; п. опа́сностью in the face of danger. 2. (*in relation to, as compared with*) to; извини́ться п. кем-н. to apologize to someone; ва́ша исто́рия ничто́ п. на́шей your story is nothing to ours. 3. (*of time*) before; п. обе́дом before dinner; п. тем, как (*conj.*) before.

пе́рёд, пе́реда, *pl.* ~а́, ~о́в, *m.* front, fore-part.

переда|ва́ть(ся), ю(сь), ёшь(ся), *impf. of* переда́ть(ся).

переда́|точный, *adj. of* ~ча; п. вал (*tech.*) countershaft; п. механи́зм driving gear, drive; ~точная на́дпись (*fin.*) endorsement; ~точное число́ (*tech.*) gear ratio.

переда́тчик, а, *m.* (*radio*) transmitter; п. тепла́ (*phys.*) heat conductor.

переда́|ть[1], м, шь, ст, ди́м, ди́те, ду́т, *past* пе́редал, ~ла́, пе́редало, *pf.* (*of* ~ва́ть) 1. to pass; to hand; to hand over; п. по наслéдству, to hand down; п. свой правá to make over one's rights; п. дéло в суд to bring a matter into court, take a matter to law, sue. 2. to tell; to communicate; to transmit, convey; п. по рáдио to broadcast; п. благодáрность to convey thanks; п. зарáзу to communicate infection; п. поручéние to deliver a message; п. приказáние to transmit an order; п. привéт to convey greetings, send one's regards; ~й(те) им (мой) привéт give them my regards, remember me to them. 3. to reproduce (*a sound, a thought, etc.*).

передá|ть², м, шь, ст, ди́м, ди́те, ду́т, *past* пéредал, ~лá, пéредало, *pf.* (*of* ~вáть) to pay too much, give too much; вы пéредали три рубля́ you have paid three roubles too many.

передá|ться, стся, ду́тся, *past* ~лся, ~лáсь, *pf.* (*of* ~вáться) 1. to pass; to be transmitted, be communicated; to be inherited; корь ~лáсь ему́ от живу́щих ря́дом детéй he picked up measles from the children next door. 2. (+*d.*; *coll.*) to go over, (to).

передáч|а, и, *f.* 1. passing; transmission; communication; п. иму́щества (*leg.*) assignation; без прáва ~и not transferable; Петрóву для ~и Ивановой (*form of address on letter*) (Mrs., Miss) Ivanova, c/o (Mr.) Petrov. 2. parcel (*delivered to person in hospital or prison*). 3. broadcast. 4. (*tech.*) drive; gear(ing); transmission; баланси́рная п. transmission by rocking lever; больша́я п. high gear ratio; зубча́тая п. train of gears, toothed gearing; конéчная п. end drive; пéрвая п. low gear; реверси́вная п. reversing gear; ремённая п. belt drive; червя́чная п. worm-gear.

передвигá|ть(ся), ю(сь), *impf. of* передви́нуть(ся).

передвижéни|е, я, *n.* movement; (*tech.*) travel; срéдства ~я means of conveyance.

передви́ж|ка, ки, *f.* 1. = ~éние. 2. *as adj.* travelling, itinerant; библиотéка-п. travelling library; теáтр-п. strolling players.

передви́жник, а, *m.* (*art*) Peredvizhnik (*member of Russian school of realist painters of second half of nineteenth century*).

передвижн|óй, *adj.* 1. movable, mobile; п. кран travelling crane. 2. travelling, itinerant; ~áя вы́ставка travelling exhibition.

передви́|нуть, ну, нешь, *pf.* (*of* ~гáть) to move, shift (*also fig.*); п. стрéлки часóв вперёд (назáд) to put the clock on (back); п. срóки экзáменов to alter the date of examinations.

передви́|нуться, нусь, нешься, *pf.* (*of* ~гáться) to move, shift; (*tech.*) to travel.

передéл, а, *m.* re-partition; re-division, re-

-distribution; п. земли́ re-allotment of land.

передéл|ать¹, аю, *pf.* (*of* ~ывать) to do anew; to alter; (*fig.*) to re-fashion, recast; п. плáтье to alter a dress.

передéл|ать², аю, *pf.* (*coll.*) to do; я ~ал все делá I have done all I had to do.

передел|и́ть, ю́, ~ишь, *pf.* (*of* ~я́ть) to re-divide.

передéлк|а, и, *f.* 1. alteration; отдáть что-н. в ~у to have something altered; попáсть в ~у (*coll.*) to get into a pretty mess. 2. adaptation (*of lit. work, etc.*).

передéлыва|ть, ю, *impf. of* передéлать¹.

передел|я́ть, я́ю, *impf. of* ~и́ть.

передёргива|ть(ся), ю(сь), *impf. of* передёрнуть(ся).

передерж|áть¹, у́, ~ишь, *pf.* (*of* ~ивать) 1. to overdo; to overcook. 2. (*phot.*) to over-expose.

передерж|áть², у́, ~ишь, *pf.* (*of* ~ивать) (*coll.*) п. экзáмен to take an examination again.

передéржива|ть, ю, *impf. of* передержáть.

передéржк|а¹, и, *f.* (*phot.*) over-exposure.

передéржк|а², и, *f.* (*coll.*) re-examination.

передéржк|а³, и, *f.* (*coll.*) cheating (*at cards*), juggling (*with facts*).

передёр|нуть, ну, нешь, *pf.* (*of* ~гивать) 1. to pull aside. 2. (*impers.*) егó ~нуло от бóли he was convulsed with pain. 3. to to cheat (*at cards*). 4. (*fig.*) to distort, mis-represent; п. фáкты to juggle with facts.

передёр|нуться, нусь, нешься, *pf.* (*of* ~гиваться) (*coll.*) to flinch, wince.

перед|кóвый, *adj. of* ~óк; *as noun* п., ~кóвого, *m.* (*mil.*) limber number.

передненёбный, *adj.* (*ling.*) front palatal.

передн|ий, *adj.* front; anterior; first; ~ие конéчности fore-legs; п. край оборóны (*mil.*) main line of resistance; ~яя крóмка (крылá) (*aeron.*) leading edge (*of wing*); ~яя лóшадь leader; п. план foreground; ~яя часть fore-part.

передник, а, *m.* apron; pinafore.

передн|яя, ей, *f.* ante-room; (entrance) hall, lobby.

пéредо = пéред.

передовéр|ить, ю, ишь, *pf.* (*of* ~я́ть) (+*d.*) to transfer trust (to); (*leg.*) to transfer power of attorney (to); п. договóр to sub-contract (to).

передовер|я́ть, я́ю, *impf. of* ~ить.

передови́к, á, *m.* 1. peredovik (*factory worker, etc., winning distinction for display of initiative and/or exemplary work*). 2. (*coll.*) leader-writer.

передови́ц|а, ы, *f.* (*coll.*) leading article, leader; editorial.

передов|óй, *adj.* forward, headmost; foremost, advanced (*also fig.*); ~ые взгля́ды advanced views; п. отря́д (*mil.*) advanced detachment; (*fig.*) vanguard; ~ая статья́ leading article, leader; editorial; *as noun* ~áя, ~óй, *f.* = ~ая статья́.

перед|óк, кá, *m.* 1. front (*of carriage, etc.*). 2. (*mil.*; *usu. pl.*) limber.

передóм, *adv.* (*coll.*) in front.

передóх|нуть, нет, *past* ~, ~ла, *pf.* (*no impf.*) to die off (*usually of animals*).

передохн|у́ть, у́, ёшь, *pf.* (*of* передыхáть) (*coll.*) to pause for breath, take a short rest.

передрáзнива|ть, ю, *impf. of* передразни́ть.

передразн|и́ть, ю́, ~ишь, *pf.* (*of* ~ивать) to take off, mimic.

пере|дрáться, деру́сь, дерёшься, *past* ~дрáлся, ~дралáсь, ~дрáлóсь, *pf.* (*no impf.*) (*coll.*) to fight, exchange blows (*of many people, etc.*).

передрóг|нуть, ну, нешь, *past* ~, ~ла, *pf.* (*no impf.*) (*coll.*) to get chilled through.

передря́г|а, и, *f.* (*coll.*) row, scrape.

передýм|ать, аю, *pf.* (*of* ~ывать) 1. to (think it over and) change one's mind; to think better of it. 2. to do a great deal of thinking.

передýмыва|ть, ю, *impf. of* передýмать.

передыхá|ть, ю, *impf. of* передохнýть.

передышк|а, и, *f.* respite, breathing-space; не давáя ни минýты ~и without a moment's respite.

переедáни|е, я, *n.* overeating; surfeit.

переедá|ть, ю, *impf. of* перее́сть.

перее́зд¹, а, *m.* (*in var. senses*) crossing.

перее́зд², а, *m.* removal.

переезжá|ть, ю, *impf. of* перее́хать.

перее́|сть¹, м, шь, ст, ди́м, ди́те, дя́т, *past* ~л, *pf.* (*of* ~дáть) 1. to overeat, surfeit. 2. (*coll.*) to out-eat, surpass in eating.

перее́|сть², м, шь, ст, ди́м, ди́те, дя́т *past* ~л, *pf.* (*of* ~дáть) to corrode, eat away.

перее́|хать¹, ду, дешь, *pf.* (*of* ~зжáть) 1. to cross. 2. to run over, knock down.

перее́|хать², ду, дешь, *pf.* (*of* ~зжáть) to move (*to a new place of residence*).

пережáрива|ть, ю, *impf. of* пережáрить¹.

пережáр|ить, ю, ишь, *pf.* (*of* ~ивать) to overdo, overroast.

пережáр|ить², ю, ишь, *pf.* to roast (*all or a number of*).

переждá|ть, ý, ёшь, *past* ~áл, ~алá, ~áло, *pf.* (*of* пережидáть) to wait through; мы ~áли грозу́ we waited till the storm was over.

переж|евáть, ую́, уёшь, *pf.* (*of* ~ёвывать) to masticate, chew.

пережёвыва|ть, ю, *impf.* 1. *impf. of* пережевáть. 2. (*fig.*) to repeat over and over again.

пережен|и́ться, ~ится, *pf.* (*coll.*) to marry; все её брáтья ~и́лись all her brothers have married.

переж|éчь, гу́, жёшь, гу́т, *past* ~ёг, ~глá, *pf.* (*of* ~игáть) 1. to burn more than one's quota (*of fuel, etc.*). 2. to burn through. 3. (*tech.*) to calcine.

переживáни|е, я, *n.* experience; feeling.

переживá|ть, ю, *impf.* 1. *impf. of* пережи́ть. 2. (*impf. only*) (*coll.*) to be upset, worry.

пережидá|ть, ю, *impf. of* переждáть.

пережи́т|ое, óго, *n.* one's past.

пережи́т|ок, ка, *m.* survival.

пережи́|ть, ву́, вёшь, *past* пережи́л, ~лá, пережи́ло, *pf.* (*of* ~вáть) 1. to live through; п. жизнь to live one's life through. 2. to experience; to go through; to endure, suffer; тяжелó п. что-н. to feel something keenly, take something hard; онá ещё не совсéм ~лá потрясéния she has still not completely got over the shock. 3. to outlive, outlast, survive.

перезаб|ы́ть, у́ду, у́дешь, *pf.* (*no impf.*) (*coll.*) to forget.

перезаклáдыва|ть, ю, *impf. of* перезаложи́ть.

перезаключ|áть, áю, *impf. of* ~и́ть.

перезаключ|и́ть, у́, и́шь, *pf.* (*of* ~áть) to renew; п. договóр to renew a contract.

перезалож|и́ть, у́, ~ишь, *pf.* (*of* перезаклáдывать) to pawn again, re-pawn; to mortgage again.

перезаря|ди́ть, жу́, ~ди́шь, *pf.* (*of* ~жáть) 1. to re-charge; to re-load. 2. (*electr.*) to overcharge.

перезаря́дк|а, и, *f.* 1. re-charging; re-loading. 2. (*electr.*) overcharging.

перезаряжá|ть, ю, *impf. of* перезаряди́ть.

перезвóн, а, *m.* ringing, chime.

перезим|овáть, у́ю, *pf.* (*of* зимовáть) to winter, pass the winter.

перезнакóм|ить, лю, ишь, *pf.* (*coll.*; с+*i.*) to acquaint (with), introduce (to).

перезнакóм|иться, люсь, ишься, *pf.* (*no impf.*) (*coll.*) to become acquainted (with).

перезревá|ть, ю, *impf. of* перезрéть.

перезрéлый, *adj.* overripe; (*fig.*) passé, past one's prime.

перезре́|ть, ю, *pf.* (*of* ~вáть) 1. to become overripe. 2. (*fig.*) to be past one's prime; to have lost the bloom of youth.

переигр|áть¹, áю, *pf.* (*of* ~ывать) to play again.

переигр|áть², áю, *pf.* (*of* ~ывать) (*theatr.*; *coll.*) to overact, overdo.

переигр|áть³, áю, *pf.* to play, act, perform (*all or a number of*).

переи́грыва|ть, ю, *impf. of* переигрáть¹, ².

переизбирá|ть, ю, *impf. of* переизбрáть.

переизбрáни|е, я, *n.* re-election.

переиз|бра́ть, беру́, берёшь, *past* ~бра́л, ~брала́, ~бра́ло, *pf.* (*of* ~бира́ть) to re--elect.

переизда|ва́ть, ю́, ёшь, *impf. of* ~ть.

переизда́ни|е, я, *n.* **1.** re-publication. **2.** new edition; reprint.

переизда́|ть, м, шь, ст, ди́м, ди́те, ду́т, *past* ~л, ~ла́, ~ло, *pf.* (*of* ~ва́ть) to re-publish, reprint.

переимен|ова́ть, у́ю, *pf.* (*of* ~о́вывать) (в+*a.*) to rename.

переименно́выва|ть, ю, *impf. of* переименова́ть.

переи́мчив|ый (~, ~а), *adj.* (*coll.*) imitative.

переина́чива|ть, ю, *impf. of* переина́чить.

переина́ч|ить, у, ишь, *pf.* (*of* ~ивать) to alter; to modify.

пере|йти́, йду́, йдёшь, *past* ~шёл, ~шла́, *pf.* (*of* ~ходи́ть) **1.** (+*a. or* че́рез) to cross; to get across, get over, go over; п. грани́цу to cross the frontier; п. че́рез мо́ст to go across a bridge. **2.** (в, на+*a. or* к) to pass (to); to turn (to); п. в наступле́ние to pass to the offensive, assume the offensive; п. в ру́ки (+*g.*) to pass into the hands (of); п. из рук в ру́ки to change hands; п. в сле́дующий класс (*in school*) to move up; п. в сосе́днюю ко́мнату to go into the next room; п. к друго́му владе́льцу to change hands; п. на другу́ю рабо́ту to change one's job; п. на произво́дство тра́кторов to go over to making tractors; п. на сто́рону проти́вника to go over to the enemy. **3.** (в+*a.*) to turn (into); их ссо́ра ~шла́ в дра́ку from words they came to blows.

перека́л, а, *m.* (*tech.*) overheating; overtempering.

перекале́чива|ть, ю, *impf. of* перекале́чить.

перекале́ч|ить, у, ишь, *pf.* (*of* ~ивать) to cripple, main, mutilate.

перека́лива|ть, ю, *impf. of* перекали́ть.

перекал|и́ть, ю́, и́шь, *pf.* (*of* ~ивать) (*tech.*) to overtemper; (*coll.*) to overheat.

перека́лыва|ть, ю, *impf. of* переколо́ть.

перека́пыва|ть, ю, *impf. of* перекопа́ть.

перека́рмлива|ть, ю, *impf. of* перекорми́ть.

перека́т¹, а, *m.* shoal.

перека́т², а, *m.* roll, peal (*of thunder*).

перекати́-по́л|е, я, *n.* **1.** (*bot.*) baby's breath (*Gypsophila paniculata*). **2.** (*fig.*; *of person*) rolling stone.

перека|ти́ть, чу́, ~тишь, *pf.* (*of* ~тывать) to roll (*somewhere else*).

перека|ти́ться, чу́сь, ~тишься, *pf.* (*of* ~тываться) to roll (*somewhere else*).

перека́тн|ый, *adj.* **1.** rolling; голь ~ая (*collect.*) the down-and-outs. **2.** (*geol.*) erratic.

перекача́|ть, а́ю, *pf.* (*of* ~ивать) to pump over, pump across.

перека́чива|ть, ю, *impf. of* перекача́ть.

перека́шива|ть(ся), ю(сь), *impf. of* перекоси́ть(ся).

переквалифика́ци|я, и, *f.* re-qualification; changing one's profession.

переквалифици́р|овать, ую, *impf. and pf.* to re-qualify.

переквалифици́р|оваться, уюсь, *impf. and pf.* to re-qualify; to change one's profession.

перекид|а́ть, а́ю, *pf.* (*of* ~ывать) to throw (one after another).

перекидно́й, *adj.* п. мо́стик footbridge.

переки́дыва|ть(ся), ю(сь), *impf. of* перекида́ть *and* переки́нуть(ся).

переки́|нуть, ну, нешь, *pf.* (*of* ~дывать) to throw (over).

переки́|нуться, нусь, нешься, *pf.* (*of* ~дываться) **1.** to leap (over). **2.** (*of fire, disease, etc.*) to spread. **3.** (+*i.*) to throw (one to another). **4.** (*obs., coll.*) (к) to go over (to), defect (to).

перекипя|ти́ть, чу́, ти́шь, *pf.* to boil again.

перекис|а́ть, а́ет, *impf. of* ~нуть.

переки́с|нуть, нет, *past* ~, ~ла, *pf.* (*of* ~а́ть) to turn sour.

пе́рекис|ь, и, *f.* (*chem.*) peroxide.

перекла́дин|а, ы, *f.* **1.** cross-beam, cross--piece, transom; joist. **2.** (*sport*) horizontal bar, crossbar.

перекладн|ы́е, ы́х, *sing.* ~а́я, ~о́й, *f.* (*hist.*) post-horses, relay-horses; е́хать на ~ы́х to travel by post-chaise.

перекла́дыва|ть, ю, *impf. of* переложи́ть.

перекле́ива|ть, ю, *impf. of* перекле́ить.

перекле́|ить¹, ю, ишь, *pf.* (*of* ~ивать) to re-stick; to glue again, paste again.

перекле́|ить², ю, ишь, *pf.* (*of* ~ивать) to stick (*a number of*).

перекле́йк|а¹, и, *f.* re-sticking.

перекле́йк|а², и, *f.* ply-wood.

переклик|а́ться, а́юсь, *impf.* (с+*i.*) **1.** (*pf.* ~нуться) to call to one another. **2.** (*fig.*) to have something in common (with); to call up, have a ring (of).

перекли́чк|а, и, *f.* **1.** roll-call, call-over. **2.** interchange, exchange (*of views, etc., on radio or in press*).

переключа́тел|ь, я, *m.* (*tech.*) switch; commutator; конта́ктный п. stud switch, tap switch; сенсо́рный п. touch-sensitive control.

переключ|а́ть(ся), а́ю(сь), *impf. of* ~и́ть(ся).

переключ|и́ть, у́, и́шь, *pf.* (*of* ~а́ть) (*tech. and fig.*; на+*a.*) to switch (over to); п. ско́рость to change gear; п. своё внима́ние на... to switch one's attention to ....

переключ|и́ться, у́сь, и́шься, *pf.* (*of* ~а́ться) (*tech. and fig.*; на+*a.*) to switch (over to); заня́вшись бы́ло дре́вними языка́ми, он ~и́лся на изуче́ние совреме́нных having started to study ancient languages, he switched (over) to studying modern; п. на бли́жний свет to dip one's headlights.

перек|ова́ть, ую́, уёшь, pf. (of ~о́вывать) 1. to re-forge; to hammer again; п. коня́ to re-shoe a horse. 2. to hammer out, beat out; п. мечи́ на ора́ла to beat swords into ploughshares (also fig.).

переко́вывa|ть, ю, impf. of перекова́ть.

переколо|ти́ть, чу́, ~тишь, pf. (coll.) to break, smash.

перекол|о́ть[1], ю́, ~ешь, pf. (of перека́лывать) 1. to pin (somewhere else). 2. to prick all over.

перекол|о́ть[2], ю́, ~ешь, pf. (of перека́лывать) to chop, hew.

перекопа́|ть, ю, pf. (of перека́пывать) 1. to dig over again. 2. to dig (all of). 3. to dig across.

перекорм|и́ть, лю́, ~ишь, pf. (of перека́рмливать) 1. to overfeed, surfeit. 2. (pf. only) to feed (all of, many).

перекóр|ы, ов, no sing. (coll.) squabble.

перекоря́|ться, юсь, impf. (no pf.) (coll.) to squabble.

переко|си́ть[1], шу́, ~сишь, pf. (of перека́шивать) to warp; (fig.) to distort; (impers.) ~си́ло око́нную ра́му the window-frame has warped; от зло́бы его́ ~си́ло his face was distorted with malice.

переко|си́ть[2], шу́, ~сишь, pf. to mow (all of, a large area of).

переко|си́ться, шу́сь, ~сишься, pf. (of перека́шиваться) to warp, be warped; (fig.) to become distorted.

перекоч|ева́ть, у́ю, pf. (of ~ёвывать) to migrate; to move on (of nomads, also coll.).

перекочёвывa|ть, ю, impf. of перекочева́ть.

переко́|шенный, p.p.p. of ~си́ть and adj. distorted, twisted.

перекра́ива|ть, ю, impf. of перекро́йть.

перекра́|сить[1], шу, сишь, pf. (of ~шивать) to re-colour, re-paint; to re-dye.

перекра́|сить[2], шу, сишь, pf. (of ~шивать) to colour, paint; to dye.

перекра́|ситься, шусь, сишься, pf. (of ~шиваться) 1. to change colour. 2. (fig.) to become a turn-coat.

перекра́шива|ть(ся), ю(сь), impf. of перекра́сить(ся).

перекре|сти́ть[1], щу́, ~стишь, pf. (of крести́ть 3) to make the sign of the cross over.

перекре|сти́ть[2], щу́, ~стишь, pf. (of ~щивать) to cross.

перекре|сти́ть[3], щу́, ~стишь, pf. (of ~щивать) to baptize (all of, a large number of).

перекре|сти́ться , щу́сь, ~стишься, pf. (of крести́ться 2) to cross oneself.

перекре|сти́ться[2], щу́сь, ~стишься, pf. (of ~щиваться) to cross, intersect.

перекрёстн|ый, adj. cross; п. допро́с cross-examination; п. ого́нь (mil.) cross-fire; ~ое опыле́ние (bot.) cross-pollination; ~ая ссы́лка cross-reference.

перекрёст|ок, ка, m. cross-roads, crossing; крича́ть на всех ~ках (coll.) to shout from the house-tops.

перекре́щива|ть(ся), ю(сь), impf. of перекрести́ть[2, 3](ся)[2].

перекри́кива|ть, ю, impf. of перекрича́ть.

перекри|ча́ть, чу́, чи́шь, pf. (of ~кивать) to out-voice, drown; to shout down.

перекро|и́ть, ю́, и́шь, pf. (of перекра́ивать) to cut out again; (fig.) to rehash; to re-shape; п. ка́рту ми́ра to re-draw the map of the world.

перекрыва́|ть, ю, impf. of перекры́ть.

перекры́ти|е, я, n. 1. (archit.) ceiling, overhead cover. 2. (tech.) overlap(ping); damming (of a river).

перекр|ы́ть[1], о́ю, о́ешь, pf. (of ~ыва́ть) to re-cover.

перекр|ы́ть[2], о́ю, о́ешь, pf. (of ~ыва́ть) 1. (coll.) to exceed; п. реко́рд to break a record. 2. (cards) to beat; to trump. 3. to close, cut off; to dam (a river).

перекувы́ркива|ть(ся), ю(сь), impf. of перекувырну́ть(ся).

перекувыр|ну́ть, ну́, нёшь, pf. (of ~кивать) (coll.) to upset, overturn.

перекувыр|ну́ться, ну́сь, нёшься, pf. (of ~киваться) (coll.) 1. to topple over. 2. to turn a somersault.

перекуп|а́ть[1], а́ю, impf. of ~и́ть.

перекупа́|ть[2], ю, pf. to bath.

перекупа́|ть[3], ю, pf. (coll.) to bathe too long.

перекупа́|ться, юсь, pf. (coll.) to bathe too long, stay in (the water) too long.

перекуп|и́ть, лю́, ~ишь, pf. (of ~а́ть) to buy up (something sought by others); to outbid for.

перекýпщик, a, m. second-hand dealer.

перекýр, a, m. (coll.) break for a smoke.

перекýрива|ть, ю, impf. of перекури́ть.

перекур|и́ть, ю́, ~ишь, pf. (of ~ивать) 1. to smoke to excess. 2. (coll.) to break for a smoke.

перекуса́|ть, ю, pf. to bite.

переку|си́ть, шу́, ~сишь, pf. (of ~сывать) 1. to bite through. 2. (coll.) to have a bite, have a snack.

перекýсыва|ть, ю, impf. of перекуси́ть.

перелага́|ть, ю, impf. of переложи́ть.

перела́мыва|ть(ся), ю(сь), impf. of переломи́ть(ся).

перележ|а́ть, ý, и́шь, pf. to lie too long.

перелез|а́ть, а́ю, impf. of ~ть.

перелéз|ть, у, ешь, past ~, ~ла, pf. (of ~а́ть) to climb over, get over.

перелéс|ок, ка, m. copse, coppice.

перелёсь|е, я, n. (dial.) glade.

перелёт, а, m. **1.** flight (of aircraft). **2.** migration (of birds). **3.** shot over the target, plus round.

перелет|а́ть, а́ю, impf. of ~е́ть.

переле|те́ть, чу́, ти́шь, pf. (of ~та́ть) **1.** (+a. or че́рез) to fly over. **2.** to fly too far; to overshoot (the mark).

перелётн|ый, adj. ~ая пти́ца bird of passage (also fig.); migratory bird.

пере|ле́чь, ля́гу, ля́жешь, ля́гут, past ~лёг, ~легла́, pf. (no impf.) to lie somewhere else; п. с одного́ бо́ка на друго́й to turn from one side to another.

перели́в, а, m. tint, tinge; play (of colours); modulation (of voice).

перелива́ни|е, я, n. **1.** decantation. **2.** (med.) transfusion.

перелива́|ть[1], ю, impf. of перели́ть; п. из пусто́го в поро́жнее (fig.) to mill the wind, beat the air.

перелива́|ть[2], ет, impf. (of colours) to play; п. все́ми цвета́ми ра́дуги to be iridescent.

перелива́|ться[1], юсь, impf. of перели́ться.

перелива́|ться[2], ется, impf. (of colours) to play; (of voices) to modulate; п. все́ми цвета́ми ра́дуги to be iridescent.

перели́вк|а, и, f. (tech.) re-casting.

перели́вчат|ый (~, ~а), adj. iridescent; (of voice) modulating; (of silk) shot.

перелист|а́ть, а́ю, pf. (of ~ывать) **1.** to turn over, leaf. **2.** to look through, glance at.

перели́стыва|ть, ю, impf. of перелиста́ть.

перел|и́ть[1], ью́, ьёшь, past ~и́л, ~ила́, ~и́ло, pf. (of ~ива́ть) **1.** to pour (somewhere else; from A into B); to decant; п. молоко́ из кастрю́ли в кувши́н to pour milk from a saucepan into a jug. **2.** (med.) to transfuse; п. кровь (+d.) to administer a blood transfusion (to). **3.** to let overflow.

перел|и́ть[2], ью́, ьёшь, past ~и́л, ~ила́, ~и́ло, pf. (of ~ива́ть) **1.** to re-cast. **2.** to melt down; п. колокола́ на пу́шки to melt down bells for guns.

перел|и́ться, ью́сь, ьёшься, past ~и́лся, ~ила́сь, ~и́лось, pf. (of ~ива́ться) **1.** to flow (somewhere else; from A to B). **2.** to overflow, run over.

перелиц|ева́ть, у́ю, pf. (of ~о́вывать) to turn (an article of clothing); to have turned.

перелицо́выва|ть, ю, impf. of перелицева́ть.

перелов|и́ть, лю́, ~ишь, pf. to catch (all or a number of).

перело́г, а, m. (agric.) fallow.

переложе́ни|е, я, n. (mus.) arrangement; transposition; п. в стихи́ versification.

перелож|и́ть, у́, ~ишь, pf. **1.** (impf. перекла́дывать and перелага́ть) to put some-

where else; to shift, move; (fig.) to shift off, transfer; п. руль (naut.) to put the helm over; п. отве́тственность на кого́-н. to shift off the responsibility on to someone. **2.** (impf. перекла́дывать) (+a. and i.) to interlay (with); п. посу́ду соло́мой to interlay crockery with straw. **3.** (impf. перекла́дывать) to re-set, re-lay. **4.** (impf. перелага́ть) (в, на+a.) to set (to), arrange (for); to transpose; to put (into); п. на му́зыку to set to music; п. в стихи́ to put into verse. **5.** (impf. перекла́дывать) (+g.) to put in too much; вы ~и́ли со́ли в суп you have put too much salt in the soup.

перело́жный, adj. of перело́г.

перело́|й, я, m. (obs.) gonorrhoea.

перело́м, а, m. **1.** break, breaking; fracture. **2.** (fig.) turning point, crisis; sudden change.

перелома́|ть, ю, pf. to break (all or a number of).

перелома́|ться, юсь, pf. (coll.) to break, be broken.

перелом|и́ть, лю́, ~ишь, pf. (of перела́мывать) **1.** to break in two; to break, fracture. **2.** (fig.) to break, master; п. себя́ to master oneself, restrain one's feelings; п. кому́-н. во́лю to break someone's will.

перелом|и́ться, ~ится, pf. (of перела́мываться) to break in two; to be fractured.

перело́м|ный, adj. of ~; п. моме́нт critical moment, crucial moment.

перема́|зать[1], жу, жешь, pf. (of ~зывать) (coll.; +i.) to soil (with), make dirty (with).

перема́|зать[2], жу, жешь, pf. (of ~зывать) to re-coat (with paint, etc.).

перема́|заться, жусь, жешься, pf. (of ~зываться) (coll.) to soil oneself, besmear oneself.

перема́зыва|ть(ся), ю(сь), impf. of перема́зать(ся).

перема́лыва|ть, ю, impf. of перемоло́ть.

перема́нива|ть, ю, impf. of перемани́ть.

переман|и́ть, ю́, ~ишь, pf. (of ~ивать) to entice; п. на свою́ сто́рону to win over.

перема́тыва|ть, ю, impf. of перемота́ть.

перема́хива|ть, ю, impf. of перемахну́ть.

перемах|ну́ть, ну́, нёшь, pf. (of ~ивать) (coll.) to jump over, leap over.

перемежа́|ть, ю, impf. (no pf.) (+a. and i. or c+i.) to alternate; он ~л угро́зы (с) ле́стью he alternated threats and blandishments.

перемежа́|ться, ется, impf. (no pf.) (c+i.) to alternate; снег ~лся с гра́дом snow alternated with hail, it snowed and hailed by turns; ~ющаяся лихора́дка (med.) intermittent fever, remittent (fever).

перемеж|ева́ть, у́ю, pf. (of ~ёвывать) to re-survey.

перемежёвыва|ть, ю, *impf. of* перемеже-
ва́ть.

перемéн|а, ы, *f.* 1. change, alteration; без
~ (there is) no change. 2. change (of
clothes). 3. (*school*) interval, break; боль-
ша́я п. long (*sc.* midday) break.

перемéн|и́ть, ю́, ~ишь, *pf.* (*of* ~я́ть) to
change; п. пози́цию to shift one's ground
(*also fig.*); п. тон (*fig.*) to change one's
tune.

перемéн|и́ться, ю́сь, ~ишься, *pf.* (*of* ~я́ть-
ся) to change; п. места́ми to change
places; п. в лицé to change countenance;
п. к кому́-н. to change (one's attitude)
towards someone.

перемéнн|ый, *adj.* variable; ~ая величина́
(*math.*) variable (quantity); ~ая пого́да
changeable weather; п. ток (*electr.*) alternating current (AC); рабо́тать от сéти ~ого
то́ка to operate from AC mains supply.

перемéнчив|ый (~, ~а), *adj.* (*coll.*) change-
able.

перемéн|я́ть(ся), я́ю(сь), *impf. of* ~и́ть(ся).

пере|мерéть, мрёт, *past* пéремер, ~мерла́,
пéремерло, *pf.* (*coll.*) to die (off).

перемерз|а́ть, а́ю, *impf. of* ~нуть.

перемёрз|нуть, ну, нешь, *pf.* (*of* ~а́ть)
(*coll.*) 1. to get chilled, freeze. 2. (*of plants*)
to be nipped by the frost.

перемéрива|ть, ю, *impf. of* перемéрить.

перемéр|ить[1], ю, ишь, *pf.* (*of* ~ивать) to
re-measure.

перемéр|ить[2], ю, ишь, *pf.* to try on.

переме|сти́ть, щу́, сти́шь, *pf.* (*of* ~ща́ть) to
move (*somewhere else*); to transfer.

переме|сти́ться, щу́сь, сти́шься, *pf.* (*of*
~ща́ться) 1. to move. 2. *pass. of* ~сти́ть.

переме́|тить[1], чу, тишь, *pf.* (*of* ~ча́ть) to
mark again.

переме́|тить[2], чу, тишь, *pf.* (*no impf.*) to
mark (*a quantity of*).

переметн|у́ться, у́сь, ёшься, *pf.* (*no impf.*)
(*coll.*) to go over, desert.

перемётн|ый, *adj.* ~ая сума́ saddle bag;
сума́ ~ая (*fig.*, *obs.*) weathercock.

перемеш|а́ть, а́ю, *pf.* (*of* ~ивать) 1. to
(inter)mix, intermingle; п. ка́рты to shuffle
cards; п. у́гли в пéчке to poke the fire.
2. (*coll.*) to mix up; (*fig.*) to confuse; он,
по-ви́димому, ~а́л на́ши фами́лии he
evidently got our names mixed up.

перемеш|а́ться, а́юсь, *pf.* (*of* ~ива́ться) 1.
to get mixed (up); всё у негó в головé
~а́лось he has got everything mixed up.
2. *pass. of* ~а́ть.

перемéшива|ть(ся), ю(сь), *impf. of* пере-
меша́ть(ся).

перемеща́|ть(ся), ю(сь), *impf. of* пере-
мести́ть(ся).

перемещéни|е, я, *n.* 1. transference, shift;
displacement. 2. (*geol.*) dislocation, displacement. 3. (*tech.*) travel.

переме|щённый, *p.p.p. of* ~сти́ть; ~щённые
ли́ца (*polit.*) displaced persons.

переми́гива|ться, юсь, *impf. of* перемиг-
ну́ться.

перемиг|ну́ться, ну́сь, нёшься, *pf.* (*of*
~иваться) (*coll.*; с+*i.*) to wink (at); п.
мéжду собо́й to wink at each other.

перемина́|ться, юсь, *impf.* (*no pf.*) п. с
ноги́ на́ ногу (*coll.*) to shift from one foot
to the other.

перемири|е, я, *n.* armistice, truce.

перемнож|а́ть, а́ю, *impf. of* ~ить.

перемнóж|ить, у, ишь, *pf.* (*of* ~а́ть) to mul-
tiply.

перемога́|ть, ю, *impf.* (*coll.*) 1. (*pf.* пере-
мо́чь) to overcome (*an illness, etc.*). 2. to try
to overcome (*an illness, etc.*).

перемога́|ться, юсь, *impf.* (*coll.*) to try to
overcome an illness; три дня он ~лся, но
наконéц емý пришло́сь позва́ть врача́ he
held out for three days, but in the end he
had to call in the doctor.

перемок|а́ть, а́ю, *impf. of* ~нуть.

перемо́к|нуть, ну, нешь, *past* ~, ~ла, *pf.* (*of*
~а́ть) (*coll.*) to get drenched.

перемо́лв|ить, лю, ишь, *pf.* (*no impf.*) п. сло́во
(с+*i.*; *coll.*) to exchange a word (with).

перемо́лв|иться, люсь, ишься, *pf.* (*no impf.*)
(+*i.*; с+*i.*; *coll.*) to exchange words (with);
п. нéсколькими слова́ми с сосéдом to exchange a few words with a neighbour.

перем|оло́ть, елю́, éлешь, *pf.* (*of* ~а́лывать)
to grind, mill; (*fig.*) to pulverize.

перем|оло́ться, éлется, *pf.* (*of* ~а́лываться)
pass. of ~оло́ть; ~éлется — мука́ бýдет
(*prov.*) it will all come right in the end, time
is a great healer.

перемота́|ть, ю, *pf.* (*of* перема́тывать) 1. to
wind; to reel. 2. to re-wind.

перемо́|чь, гу́, ~жешь, *pf. of* ~га́ть.

перемудр|и́ть, ю́, и́шь, *pf.* (*no impf.*) (*coll.*)
to be too clever by half.

перемýч|иться, усь, ишься, *pf.* (*no impf.*)
(*coll.*) to have suffered very much.

перемыва́|ть, ю, *impf. of* перемы́ть.

перем|ы́ть[1], о́ю, о́ешь, *pf.* (*of* ~ыва́ть) to
wash up again.

перем|ы́ть[2], о́ю, о́ешь, *pf.* to wash (up) (*all
or a quantity of*).

перемы́чк|а, и, *f.* (*tech.*) 1. straight arch.
2. cross piece; tie plate. 3. bulkhead; dam.

перенапряга́|ть(ся), ю(сь), *impf. of* пере-
напря́чь(ся).

перенапря́|чь, гу́, жёшь, *past* ~г, ~гла́, *pf.*
(*of* ~га́ть) to overstrain.

перенапря́|чься, гу́сь, жёшься, *past* ~гся,
~гла́сь, *pf.* (*of* ~га́ться) to overstrain oneself.

перенаселе́ни|е, я, *n.* overpopulation.

перенаселённост|ь, и, *f.* overpopulation; overcrowding (*in a dwelling*).

перенасел|ённый, *p.p.p. of* ~и́ть *and adj.* overpopulated; overcrowded.

перенасел|и́ть, ю́, и́шь, *pf.* (*of* ~я́ть) to overpopulate.

перенасел|я́ть, я́ю, *impf. of* ~и́ть.

перенасы́|тить, щу, тишь, *pf.* (*of* ~ща́ть) (*chem.*) to over-saturate.

перенасыща́|ть, ю, *impf. of* перенасы́тить.

перенасы́|щенный, *p.p.p. of* ~тить *and adj.* (*chem.*) over-saturated.

перенесе́ни|е, я, *n.* transference, transportation.

перенес|ти́¹, у́, ёшь, *past* ~, ~ла́, *pf.* (*of* переноси́ть) 1. to carry (*somewhere else*); to transport; to transfer; п. огóнь (*mil.*) to switch fire; п. де́ло в областно́й суд to take the matter to the oblast court; п. столи́цу в Москву́ to move the capital to Moscow. 2. п. сло́во (*typ.*) to carry over (*part of word*) to the next line. 3. to put off, postpone; to carry over.

перенес|ти́², у́, ёшь, *past* ~, ~ла́, *pf.* (*of* переноси́ть) to endure, bear, stand; п. боле́знь to have an illness; я э́того не мог п. I couldn't stand that.

перенес|ти́сь, у́сь, ёшься, *past* ~ся, ~ла́сь, *pf.* (*of* переноси́ться) 1. to be carried, be borne; (*fig.*) to be carried away (*in thought*). 2. *pass. of* ~ти́¹.

перенима́|ть, ю, *impf. of* переня́ть.

перено́с, а, *m.* 1. transfer; transportation. 2. (*typ.*) division of words; знак ~а hyphen.

переноси́м|ый (~, ~а), *pres. part. pass. of* переноси́ть *and adj.* bearable, endurable.

перено|си́ть(ся), шу́(сь), ~сишь(ся), *impf. of* перенести́(сь).

перено́сиц|а, ы, *f.* bridge of the nose.

перено́ск|а, и, *f.* carrying over, transporting; carriage.

перено́сный, *adj.* 1. portable. 2. (*ling.*) figurative; metaphorical.

перено́счик, а, *m.* carrier; п. слу́хов talebearer, rumour-monger.

переноч|ева́ть, у́ю, *pf.* (*of* ночева́ть) to spend the night.

перенумер|ова́ть, у́ю, *pf.* (*of* нумерова́ть) to number; п. страни́цы to page.

пере|ня́ть, йму́, ймёшь, *past* пе́ренял, ~няла́, пе́реняло, *pf.* (*of* ~нима́ть) (*coll.*) 1. to imitate, copy; п. привы́чку to acquire a habit; п. чей-н. приём to take a leaf out of someone's book. 2. to intercept, bar the way (to).

переобору́д|овать, ую, *impf. and pf.* to re-equip.

переобремен|и́ть, ю, и́шь, *pf.* (*of* ~я́ть) to overburden.

переобремен|я́ть, я́ю, *impf. of* ~и́ть.

переобува́|ть(ся), ю(сь), *impf. of* переобу́ть(ся).

переобу́|ть, ю, ешь, *pf.* (*of* ~ва́ть) to change someone's shoes; п. боти́нки to change one's shoes.

переобу́|ться, юсь, ешься, *pf.* (*of* ~ва́ться) to change one's shoes, boots, *etc.*

переодева́|ть(ся), ю(сь), *impf. of* переоде́ть(ся).

переоде́|ть, ну, нешь, *pf.* (*of* ~ва́ть) 1. to change someone's clothes; они́ ~ли де́вочку в наря́дное пла́тье they changed the little girl into a party frock; п. бельё ребёнку (*coll.*) to change a baby; п. пла́тье to change one's dress. 2. (+*i.*; в+*a.*) to dress up, disguise (as, in); п. де́вочку ма́льчиком to dress up a little girl as a boy.

переоде́|ться, нусь, нешься, *pf.* (*of* ~ва́ться) 1. to change (one's clothes). 2. (+*i.*, в+*a.*) to dress up, disguise oneself (as, in); она́ ~лась в ма́льчика she disguised herself as a boy.

переосвиде́тельств|овать, ую, *impf. and pf.* (*med.*) to re-examine.

переоце́нива|ть, ю, *impf. of* переоцени́ть.

переоцен|и́ть, ю́, ~ишь, *pf.* (*of* ~ивать) 1. to overestimate, overrate; п. свои́ си́лы to overestimate one's strength, bite off more than one can chew. 2. to revalue, reappraise.

переоце́нк|а, и, *f.* 1. overestimation. 2. revaluation, reappraisal.

перепа́д, а, *m.* (*tech.*) overfall.

перепа́да|ть, ет, *pf.* (*coll.*) to fall (*one after another*).

перепада́|ть, ю, *impf. of* перепа́сть.

перепа́ива|ть, ю, *impf. of* перепои́ть.

перепа́лк|а, и, *f.* (*coll.*) exchange of fire, skirmish (*also fig.*).

перепа́рхива|ть, ю, *impf. of* перепорхну́ть.

перепа́|сть, дёт, *past* ~л, *pf.* (*of* ~да́ть) (*coll.*) 1. to fall intermittently; дождь ~дёт there will be rain at intervals, it will be showery. 2. (*impers.*; +*d.*) to fall to one's lot.

перепа|ха́ть, шу́, ~шешь, *pf.* (*of* ~хивать) to plough (up) again; to plough over.

перепа́хива|ть, ю, *impf. of* перепаха́ть.

перепа́чка|ть, ю, *pf.* to soil, make dirty (all over).

перепа́чка|ться, юсь, ю, *pf.* to make oneself dirty (all over).

перепе́в, а, *m.* repetition, rehash.

перепека́|ть, ю, *impf. of* перепе́чь.

перепел, а, *pl.* ~á, *m.* (*orn.*) quail.

перепелен|а́ть, а́ю, *pf.* (*of* ~ывать) п. ребёнка to change a baby, change a baby's nappy.

перепелёныва|ть, ю, *impf. of* перепелена́ть.

перепели́ный, *adj. of* пе́репел.

перепёлк|а, и, *f.* female quail.

перепеля́тник, а, *m.* 1. quail-shooter. 2. (sparrow-)hawk.

переперчива|ть, ю, *impf. of* переперчить.

переперч|ить, у, ишь, *pf.* (*of* ~ивать) to put too much pepper into.

перепечат|ать, аю, *pf.* (*of* ~ывать) 1. to reprint. 2. to type (out).

перепечатк|а, и, *f.* 1. reprinting; п. воспреща́ется copyright reserved. 2. reprint.

перепеча́тыва|ть, ю, *impf. of* перепеча́тать.

перепе́|чь¹, ку́, чёшь, *pf.* (*of* ~ка́ть) to over-bake.

перепе́|чь², ку́, чёшь, *pf.* to bake (*all or a number of*).

перепива́|ть(ся), ю(сь), *impf. of* перепи́ть(ся).

перепи́лива|ть, ю, *impf. of* перепили́ть.

перепил|и́ть¹, ю́, ~ишь, *pf.* (*of* ~ивать) to saw in two.

перепил|и́ть², ю́, ~ишь, *pf.* to saw (*all or a number of*).

перепи|са́ть¹, шу́, ~шешь, *pf.* (*of* ~сывать) 1. to re-write; to re-type; п. на́бело to make a fair copy (of). 2. to re-copy.

перепи|са́ть², шу́, ~шешь, *pf.* (*of* ~сывать) to make a list (of), list; п. всех прису́тствующих to take the names of all those present.

перепи́ск|а, и, *f.* 1. copying; typing. 2. correspondence; быть в ~е (c+*i.*) to be in correspondence (with). 3. (*collect.*) correspondence, letters.

перепи́счик, а, *m.* copyist; typist.

перепи́сыва|ть, ю, *impf. of* переписа́ть.

перепи́сыва|ться, юсь, *impf.* (c+*i.*) to correspond (with).

пе́репис|ь, и, *f.* 1. census. 2. inventory.

переп|и́ть, ью́, ьёшь, *past* ~и́л, ~ила́, ~и́ло, *pf.* (*of* ~ива́ть) (*coll.*) 1. to drink excessively. 2. to out-drink; к утру́ он ~и́л всех това́рищей by morning he had drunk all his companions under the table.

переп|и́ться, ью́сь, ьёшься, *past* ~и́лся, ~ила́сь, ~и́ло́сь, *pf.* (*of* ~ива́ться) (*coll.*) to get completely drunk.

перепла́в|ить¹, лю, ишь, *pf.* (*of* ~ля́ть) to smelt.

перепла́в|ить², лю, ишь, *pf.* (*of* ~ля́ть) 1. to float; to raft. 2. (*fig., coll.*) to convey surreptitiously.

переплавля́|ть, ю, *impf. of* перепла́вить.

переплани́р|ова́ть, у́ю, у́ю, *pf.* (*of* ~о́вывать) 1. to re-plan, make new plans (for), alter plan (of). 2. to re-plan (*streets, districts, etc.*).

перепланиро́вк|а, и, *f.* re-planning (*of streets, districts, etc.*).

перепланиро́выва|ть, ю, *impf. of* переплани-ро́ва́ть.

перепла́т|а, ы, *f.* surplus payment.

перепла|ти́ть, чу́, ~тишь, *pf.* (*of* ~чивать) to overpay; to pay excessively.

перепла́чива|ть, ю, *impf. of* переплати́ть.

переплёвыва|ть, ю, *impf. of* переплю́нуть.

перепле|сти́¹, ту́, тёшь, *past* ~л, ~ла́, *pf.* (*of* ~та́ть) 1. to bind (*books*). 2. (+*i.*) to interlace (with), interknit (with).

перепле|сти́², ту́, тёшь, *past* ~л, ~ла́, *pf.* (*of* ~та́ть) to braid again, plait again.

перепле|сти́сь, тётся, *past* ~лся, ~ла́сь, *pf.* (*of* ~та́ться) 1. to interlace, interweave. 2. (*fig.*) to get mixed up.

переплёт, а, *m.* 1. binding; отда́ть кни́гу в п. to have a book bound. 2. binding, book-cover. 3. transom (*of door or window*); око́нный п. window-sash. 4. caning (*of a chair*). 5. (*coll.*) mess, scrape; попа́сть в п. to get into a mess, get into trouble.

переплета́|ть(ся), ю(сь), *impf. of* переплести́(сь).

переплётн|ая, ой, *f.* bindery, bookbinder's shop.

переплётчик, а, *m.* bookbinder.

переплыва́|ть, ю, *impf. of* переплы́ть.

переплы́|ть, ву́, вёшь, *past* ~л, ~ла́, ~ло, *pf.* (*of* ~ва́ть) to swim (across); to sail (across).

переплю́н|уть, у, ешь, *pf.* (*of* переплёвывать) (*coll.*) to spit further than; (*fig.*) to do better than, surpass.

переподгота́влива|ть, ю, *impf. of* переподгото́вить.

переподгото́в|ить, лю, ишь, *pf.* (*of* переподгота́вливать) to train anew.

переподгото́вк|а, и, *f.* further training; training anew; ку́рсы по ~е refresher courses.

перепо|и́ть, ю́, ~и́шь, *pf.* (*of* перепа́ивать) 1. to give too much to drink (*to an animal*). 2. (*coll.*) to make drunk.

перепо́|й, я, *m.* excessive drinking; у меня́ разболе́лась голова́ с ~я (с ~ю) I had a hangover.

переполз|а́ть, а́ю, *impf. of* ~ти́.

переполз|ти́, у́, ёшь, *past* ~, ~ла́, *pf.* (*of* ~а́ть) to crawl across; to creep across.

переполне́ни|е, я, *n.* overfilling; overcrowding; п. желу́дка repletion.

переполн|ить, ю, ишь, *pf.* (*of* ~я́ть) to over-fill; to overcrowd.

переполн|иться, ится, *pf.* (*of* ~я́ться) to overfill; to be overcrowded; её се́рдце ~илось ра́достью her heart overflowed with joy.

переполн|я́ть(ся), я́ю(сь), *impf. of* ~ить(ся).

переполо́х, а, *m.* alarm; commotion, rumpus.

переполош|и́ть, у́, и́шь, *pf.* (*coll.*) to alarm; to rouse.

перепо́нк|а, и, f. membrane; web (of bat or water-fowl); бараба́нная п. (anat.) ear--drum, tympanum.

перепончатокры́лы|й, adj. (zool.) hymenopterous; as noun ~e, ~x Hymenoptera.

перепо́нчатый, adj. membraneous, membranous; webbed; web-footed.

перепоруч|а́ть, а́ю, impf. of ~и́ть.

перепоруч|и́ть, у́, ~ишь, pf. (of ~а́ть) (+d.) to turn over (to), reassign (to); п. веде́ние де́ла друго́му защи́тнику to turn over one's case to another lawyer.

перепорхн|у́ть, у́, ёшь, pf. (of перепа́рхивать) to flutter, flit (somewhere else; from A to B).

перепра́в|а, ы, f. passage, crossing; ford.

перепра́в|ить¹, лю, ишь, pf. (of ~ля́ть) 1. to convey, transport to; take across. 2. to forward (mail).

перепра́в|ить², лю, ишь, pf. (of ~ля́ть) (coll.) to correct.

перепра́в|иться, люсь, ишься, pf. (of ~ля́ться) to cross, get across; to swim across; to sail across.

переправля́|ть(ся), ю(сь), impf. of перепра́вить(ся).

перепрева́|ть, ю, impf. of перепре́ть.

перепре́|ть, ю, pf. (of ~ва́ть) 1. to rot. 2. (coll.) to be overdone.

перепро́б|овать, ую, pf. to taste (all or a quantity of); (fig.) to try.

перепрода|ва́ть, ю́, ёшь, impf. of ~́ть.

перепродав|е́ц, ца́, m. re-seller.

перепрода́ж|а, и, f. re-sale.

перепрода́|ть, м, шь, ст, ди́м, ди́те, ду́т, past перепро́дал, ~ла́, перепро́дало, pf. (of ~ва́ть) to re-sell.

перепроизво́дств|о, а, n. overproduction.

перепры́гива|ть, ю, impf. of перепры́гнуть.

перепры́г|нуть, ну, нешь, pf. (of ~ивать) to jump (over).

перепря|га́ть, га́ю, impf. of ~́чь.

перепряжк|а, и, f. 1. changing of horses. 2. (hist.) stage (on post-chaise route).

перепря́|чь, гу́, жёшь, гу́т, past ~г, ~гла́, pf. (of ~га́ть) 1. to re-harness. 2. to change (horses).

перепу́г, а (у), m. (coll.) с ~у, от ~у in one's fright.

перепуга́|ть, ю, pf. (no impf.) to frighten, give a fright, give a turn.

перепуга́|ться, юсь, pf. (no impf.) to get a fright.

перепуска́|ть, ю, impf. of перепусти́ть.

перепу|сти́ть, щу́, ~стишь, pf. (of ~ска́ть) 1. to let flow (from A to B). 2. to let go; to slacken.

перепу́т|ать, аю, pf. (of ~ывать) 1. to entangle. 2. (fig.) to confuse, mix up, muddle up.

перепу́т|аться, аюсь, pf. (of ~ываться) 1. to get entangled. 2. (fig.) to get confused, get mixed up.

перепу́тыва|ть(ся), ю(сь), impf. of перепу́тать(ся).

перепу́ть|е, я, n. cross-roads; быть на п. (fig.) to be at the cross-roads.

перераба́тыва|ть(ся), ю(сь), impf. of переработать(ся).

переработа|ть¹, ю, pf. (of перераба́тывать) 1. (в, на+a.) to work (into), make (into); to convert (to); to treat; п. свёклу в са́хар to convert beet to sugar; п. пи́щу to digest food. 2. to re-make; (fig.) to re-cast, re--shape; п. статью́ to re-cast an article.

переработа|ть², ю, pf. (of перераба́тывать) (coll.) to exceed fixed hours of work, work overtime; мы вчера́ ~ли три часа́ we did three hours overtime yesterday.

переработа|ться¹, юсь, pf. (of перераба́тываться) pass. of ~ть.

переработа|ться², юсь, pf. (of перераба́тываться) (coll.) to overwork.

перерабо́тк|а¹, и, f. 1. working over, treatment. 2. re-making; (fig.) re-casting, re--shaping.

перерабо́тк|а², и, f. overtime work.

перераспределе́ни|е, я, n. re-distribution.

перераспредел|и́ть, ю́, и́шь, pf. (of ~я́ть) to re-distribute.

перераспредел|я́ть, я́ю, impf. of ~и́ть.

перераста́ни|е, я, n. 1. outgrowing. 2. (в+a.) growing (into), development (into). 3. (mil.) escalation.

перераст|а́ть, а́ю, impf. of ~и́.

перераст|и́, у́, ёшь, past переро́с, переросла́, pf. (of ~а́ть) 1. to outgrow, (over)top; to outstrip (in height, also fig.); трина́дцати лет она́ уже́ переросла́ отца́ at thirteen she had already topped her father; п. своего́ учи́теля to outstrip one's teacher. 2. (fig.; в+a.) to grow (into), develop (into), turn (into). 3. to be too old (for); для де́тского са́да он переро́с he is too old for kindergarten.

перерасхо́д, а, m. 1. over-expenditure. 2. (fin.) overdraft.

перерасхо́д|овать, ую, pf. (no impf.) 1. to spend to excess. 2. (fin.) to overdraw.

перерасчёт, а, m. re-computation.

перерв|а́ть, у́, ёшь, past ~а́л, ~ала́, ~а́ло, pf. (of перерыва́ть¹) to break, tear asunder.

перерв|а́ться, у́сь, ёшься, past ~а́лся, ~ала́сь, ~а́лось, pf. (of перерыва́ться¹) to break, come apart.

перерегистра́ци|я, и, f. re-registration.

перерегистри́р|овать, ую, pf. to re-register.

перерегистри́р|оваться, уюсь, pf. 1. to re-register. 2. pass. of ~овать.

перере́|зать¹, жу, жешь, *pf.* (*of* ~за́ть *and* ~зыва́ть) **1.** to cut. **2.** (*fig.*) to cut off; п. путь неприя́телю to bar the enemy's way. **3.** (*geogr.*) to break.

перере́|зать², жу, жешь, *pf.* to kill, slaughter (*all or a number of*).

перере́з|а́ть, а́ю, *impf. of* ~а́ть¹.

перере́зыва|ть, ю, *impf.* = перереза́ть.

перереш|а́ть¹, а́ю, *impf. of* ~и́ть.

перереш|а́ть², а́ю, *pf.* to solve (*all or a number of problems*).

перереш|и́ть, у́, и́шь, *pf.* (*of* ~а́ть¹) **1.** to re-solve; to decide, settle in a different way. **2.** to change one's mind, reconsider one's decision.

переро|ди́ть, жу́, ди́шь, *pf.* (*of* ~жда́ть) to regenerate.

переро|ди́ться, жу́сь, ди́шься, *pf.* (*of* ~жда́ться) **1.** (*coll.*) to be re-born. **2.** (*fig.*) to regenerate, be regenerated. **3.** (*biol. and fig.*) to degenerate.

перерожде́ни|е, я, *n.* **1.** regeneration. **2.** degeneration.

перерост|ок, ка, *m.* (*coll.*) backward child (*pupil older than his class-mates*).

переруб|а́ть, а́ю, *impf. of* ~и́ть.

переруб|и́ть, лю́, ~ишь, *pf.* (*of* ~а́ть) to chop in two; to hew asunder.

переруга́|ться, юсь, *pf.* (*coll.*; с+*i.*) to fall out (with), fall foul (of), break (with).

переру́гива|ться, юсь, *impf.* (*coll.*; с+*i.*) to quarrel (with), squabble (with).

переры́в, а, *m.* interruption; interval, break, intermission; обе́денный п. dinner *or* lunch break; п. на пять мину́т five minutes' interval; без ~а without a break; с ~ами off and on.

перерыва́|ть, ю, *impf. of* перервать.

перерыва́|ть, ю, *impf. of* перерыть.

перерыва́|ться, юсь, *impf. of* перерваться.

переры́|ть, о́ю, о́ешь, *pf.* (*of* ~ыва́ть²) **1.** to dig up. **2.** (*fig.*, *coll.*) to rummage (in).

переря|ди́ть, жу́, ~ди́шь, *pf.* (*of* ~жива́ть) (+*i.*; *coll.*) to disguise (as), dress up (as).

переря|ди́ться, жу́сь, ~ди́шься, *pf.* (*of* ~жива́ться) (+*i.*; *coll.*) to disguise oneself (as), dress up (as).

переряжива|ть(ся), ю(сь), *impf. of* переряди́ть(ся).

переса|ди́ть, жу́, ~дишь, *pf.* (*of* ~жива́ть) **1.** to make someone change his seat. **2.** п. кого́-н. че́рез что-н. to help someone across something. **3.** (*bot.*) to transplant. **4.** (*med.*) to graft.

переса́дк|а, и, *f.* **1.** (*bot.*) transplantation. **2.** (*med.*) grafting; опера́ция по~е се́рдца heart transplant operation. **3.** (*on railway*) change; changing; в Ленингра́д без ~и no change for Leningrad; through train to Leningrad.

переса́жива|ть, ю, *impf. of* пересади́ть.

переса́жива|ться, юсь, *impf. of* пересе́сть.

переса́лива|ть, ю, *impf. of* пересоли́ть.

пересда|ва́ть, ю́, ёшь, *impf. of* ~ть.

пересда́|ть, м, шь, ст, ди́м, ди́те, ду́т, *past* ~л, ~ла́, ~ло, *pf.* (*of* ~ва́ть) **1.** to re-let; to sub-let. **2.** (*cards*) to re-deal. **3.** (*coll.*) to re-sit (*an examination*).

пересека́|ть(ся), ю(сь), *impf. of* пересе́чь(ся).

пересе́лен|ец, ца, *m.* **1.** migrant, emigrant; immigrant. **2.** settler.

переселе́ни|е, я, *n.* **1.** migration, emigration; immigration; re-settlement. **2.** move (*to new place of residence*).

переселе́н|ческий, *adj. of* ~ец; ~ческая организа́ция emigration, re-settlement organization.

пересел|и́ть, ю́, и́шь, *pf.* (*of* ~я́ть) to move; to transplant; to resettle.

пересел|и́ться, ю́сь, и́шься, *pf.* (*of* ~я́ться) to move; to migrate.

пересел|я́ть(ся), я́ю(сь), *impf. of* ~и́ть(ся).

перес|е́сть, я́ду, я́дешь, *pf.* (*of* ~а́живаться) **1.** to change one's seat. **2.** to change (*trains, etc.*).

пересече́ни|е, я, *n.* crossing, intersection; то́чка ~я point of intersection.

перес|ечённый, *p.p.p. of* ~е́чь¹; ~ечённая ме́стность (*geogr.*) broken terrain.

пересе́|чь¹, ку́, чёшь, ку́т, *past* ~к, ~кла́, *pf.* (*of* ~ка́ть) **1.** to cross; to traverse; п. у́лицу to cross the road; п. путь неприя́телю (*fig.*) to cut the enemy off, bar the enemy's way. **2.** to cross, intersect.

пересе́|чь², ку́, чёшь, ку́т, *past* ~к, ~кла́, *pf.* (*of* ~ка́ть) (*coll.*) to flog.

пересе́|чься, чётся, ку́тся, *past* ~кся, ~кла́сь, *pf.* (*of* ~ка́ться) to cross, intersect.

переси|де́ть, жу́, ди́шь, *pf.* (*of* ~живать) **1.** (*coll.*) to out-sit; он ~де́л всех други́х госте́й he outstayed all the other guests. **2.** to sit too long.

переси́жива|ть, ю, *impf. of* пересиде́ть.

переси́лива|ть, ю, *impf. of* переси́лить.

переси́л|ить, ю, ишь, *pf.* (*of* ~ивать) to overpower; (*fig.*) to overcome, master.

переска́з, а, *m.* **1.** re-telling, narration. **2.** exposition.

переска|за́ть, жу́, ~жешь, *pf.* (*of* ~зывать) **1.** to re-tell, narrate; ~жи́(те) мне содержа́ние э́того рома́на tell me the story of this novel (in your own words). **2.** to retail, relate; п. слу́хи to retail rumours.

переска́зыва|ть, ю, *impf. of* пересказа́ть.

переска́кива|ть, ю, *impf. of* перескочи́ть.

перескоч|и́ть, у́, ~ишь, *pf.* (*of* переска́кивать) **1.** (+*a. or* че́рез) to jump (over); to vault (over); (*fig.*; *in reading*) to skip (over).

2. (*fig.*) to skip; п. с одно́й те́мы на другу́ю to skip from one topic to another.

пересла|сти́ть, щу́, сти́шь, *pf.* (*of* ~щивать) to make too sweet, put too much sugar (into).

пере|сла́ть, шлю́, шлёшь, *pf.* (*of* ~сыла́ть) to send; to remit; to forward.

пересла́щива|ть, ю, *impf. of* переласти́ть.

пересма́трива|ть, ю, *impf. of* пересмотре́ть.

пересме́ива|ть, ю, *impf.* (*coll.*) to mock, make fun of.

пересме́ива|ться, юсь, *impf.* (*coll.*; c+*i.*) to exchange smiles (with).

пересме́шк|а, и, *f.* (*coll.*) mockery, banter.

пересме́шник, а, *m.* 1. (*coll.*) mocker, banterer. 2. (*orn.*) mocking-bird.

пересмо́тр, а, *m.* 1. revision. 2. reconsideration; (*leg.*) review (*of a sentence*); re-trial.

пересмотр|е́ть[1], ю́, ~ишь, *pf.* (*of* пересма́тривать) 1. to revise; to go over again. 2. to re-consider; (*leg.*) to review. 3. to go through (*in search of something*).

пересмотр|е́ть[2], ю́, ~ишь, *pf.* to have seen (*all or a quantity of*); to have gone all through.

пересним|а́|ть, ю, *impf. of* пересня́ть.

пересн|я́ть, иму́, и́мешь, *past* ~я́л, ~яла́, ~я́ло, *pf.* (*of* ~има́ть) 1. to photograph again, take another photo (of). 2. to make a copy.

пересозда|ва́ть, ю́, ёшь, *impf. of* ~ть.

пересозда́|ть, м, шь, ст, ди́м, ди́те, ду́т, *past* ~л, ~ла́, ~ло, *pf.* (*of* ~ва́ть) to re-create.

пересо́л, а, *m.* excess of salt; недосо́л на столе́, п. на спине́ (*coll.*) better too little than too much.

пересол|и́ть, ю́, ~и́шь, *pf.* (*of* переса́ливать) 1. to put too much salt (into). 2. (*fig.*, *coll.*) to go too far.

пересо́х|нуть, нет, *past* ~, ~ла, *pf.* (*of* пересыха́ть) to dry out; to dry up, become parched.

пересп|а́ть, лю́, и́шь, *past* ~а́л, ~ала́, ~а́ло, *pf.* (*coll.*) 1. to oversleep. 2. to spend the night. 3. (c+*i.*; *euph.*) to sleep (with).

переспе́лый, *adj.* overripe.

переспо́р|ить, ю, ишь, *pf.* to out-argue, defeat in argument; его́ не ~ишь he must have the last word.

переспра́шива|ть, ю, *impf. of* переспроси́ть.

переспро|си́ть[1], шу́, ~сишь, *p.* (*of* переспра́шивать) to ask again; to ask to repeat.

переспро|си́ть[2], шу́, ~сишь, *pf.* to question (*all or a number of*).

перессо́р|ить, ю, ишь, *pf.* (*coll.*) to set at variance.

перессо́р|иться, юсь, ишься, *pf.* (*coll.*; c+*i.*) to quarrel (with), fall out (with).

переста|ва́ть, ю́, ёшь, *impf. of* ~ть.

переста́в|ить, лю, ишь, *pf.* (*of* ~ля́ть) to move, shift; п. ме́бель to re-arrange the furniture; п. слова́ во фра́зе to transpose the words in a sentence; п. часы́ вперёд (наза́д) to put the clock on (back).

переставля́|ть, ю, *impf. of* переста́вить.

переста́ива|ть, ю, *impf. of* перестоя́ть.

перестано́вк|а, и, *f.* 1. re-arrangement, transposition. 2. (*math.*) permutation.

перестара́|ться, юсь, *pf.* (*coll.*) to overdo it, put too much into it.

переста́р|ок, ка, *m.* (*coll.*) person over age (*for given purpose*); он мог бы ещё воева́ть —не п. he could still fight, he is not too old.

переста́|ть, ну, нешь, *pf.* (*of* ~ва́ть) (+*inf.*) to stop, cease.

перестел|и́ть, ю́, ~ешь, *pf.* (*coll.*) = перестла́ть.

перестила́|ть, ю, *impf. of* перестели́ть *and* перестла́ть.

перестир|а́ть[1], а́ю, *pf.* (*of* ~ывать) to wash again.

перестир|а́ть[2], а́ю, *pf.* (*no impf.*) to wash (*all or a number of*).

перести́рыва|ть, ю, *impf. of* перестира́ть[1].

перест|ла́ть, елю́, е́лешь, *pf.* (*of* ~ила́ть) to re-lay; п. пол в ко́мнате to re-floor a room; п. посте́ль to re-make a bed.

пересто|я́ть, ю́, и́шь, *pf.* (*of* переста́ивать) to stand too long.

перестрада́|ть, ю, *pf.* (*no impf.*) to have suffered, have gone through.

перестра́ива|ть(ся), ю(сь), *impf. of* перестро́ить(ся).

перестрах|ова́ть, у́ю, *pf.* (*of* ~о́вывать) to re-insure.

перестрах|ова́ться, у́юсь, *pf.* (*of* ~о́вываться) 1. to re-insure oneself. 2. (*fig.*, *pejor.*) to play safe (*by seeking to transfer or share responsibility*).

перестрахо́вк|а, и, *f.* 1. re-insurance. 2. (*pejor.*) playing safe, 'double insurance' (*esp. of editors of magazines unwilling to risk publishing controversial material*).

перестрахо́вщик, а, *m.* (*pejor.*) adherent of policy of 'playing safe'.

перестрахо́выва|ть(ся), ю(сь), *impf. of* перестрахова́ть(ся).

перестре́лива|ть, ю, *impf. of* перестреля́ть.

перестре́лива|ться, юсь, *impf.* to fire (at each other).

перестре́лк|а, и, *f.* firing; skirmish; exchange of fire; артилле́рийская п. artillery duel.

перестрел|я́ть, я́ю, *pf.* (*of* ~ивать) 1. to shoot (down). 2. to use up, expend (*in shooting*).

перестро́|ечный, *adj. of* ~йка.

перестро́|ить, ю, ишь, *pf.* (*of* перестра́ивать) 1. to rebuild, reconstruct. 2. to re-design, re-fashion, re-shape; to re-organize; п. фра́зу to reshape a sentence; п. на вое́нный лад to put on a war footing. **3.** (*mil.*) to re-form. **4.** (*mus., radio*) to re-tune.

перестро́|иться, юсь, ишься, *pf.* (*of* перестра́иваться) **1.** to re-form; to re-organize oneself; to improve one's methods of work. **2.** (*mil.*) to re-form. **3.** (*radio*) (на+*a.*) to switch over (to), tune (on to); п. на коро́ткую волну́ to switch over to short wave.

перестро́йк|а, и, *f.* **1.** rebuilding, reconstruction; (*polit., econ.*) perestroika. **2.** re-organization. **3.** (*mil.*) re-formation. **4.** (*mus., radio*) re-tuning.

перестукивани|е, я, *n.* (*in prison, etc.*) communication by tapping.

пересту́кива|ться, юсь, *impf.* (с+*i.*) (*in prison, etc.*) to communicate (with) by tapping.

переступ|а́ть, а́ю, *impf.* **1.** *impf. of* ⌐и́ть. **2.** (*impf. only*) to move slowly; он е́ле ⌐а́л (нога́ми) his feet would hardly carry him; п. с ноги́ на́ ногу to shift from one foot to the other.

переступ|и́ть, лю́, ⌐ишь, *pf.* (*of* ⌐а́ть) (+*a.* *or* че́рез) to step over; (*fig.*) to overstep; п. поро́г to cross the threshold; п. зако́н to break the law; п. грани́цы прили́чия to overstep the bounds of decency.

пересу́д, а, *m.* (*coll.*) re-trial.

пересу́д|ы, ов, *no sing.* (*coll.*) gossip.

пересу́шива|ть, ю, *impf. of* пересуши́ть[1].

пересуш|и́ть[1], у́, ⌐ишь, *pf.* (*of* ⌐ивать) to overdry.

пересуш|и́ть[2], у́, ⌐ишь, *pf.* (*no impf.*) to dry (*all or a quantity of*).

пересчит|а́ть[1], а́ю, *pf.* (*of* ⌐ывать) **1.** to re-count; п. ко́сти (рёбра) кому́-н. (*fig., coll.*) to give someone a drubbing. **2.** (на+*a.*) to convert (to), express (in terms of).

пересчит|а́ть[2], а́ю, *pf.* (*no impf.*) to count.

пересчи́тыва|ть, ю, *impf. of* пересчита́ть[1].

пересыла́|ть, ю, *impf. of* пересла́ть.

пересы́лк|а, и, *f.* sending; forwarding; п. де́нег remittance; сто́имость ⌐и postage; п. беспла́тно post free; carriage paid.

пересы́лочный, adj. of ⌐ка.

пересы́льн|ый, adj. transit; ⌐ая тюрьма́ transit prison.

пересы́п|ать[1], лю, лешь, *pf.* (*of* ⌐а́ть) to pour (*dry substance*) into another container; п. зерно́ в мешки́ to pour off grain into bags.

пересы́п|ать[2], лю, лешь, *pf.* (*of* ⌐а́ть) (+*i.*) **1.** to powder (with). **2.** (*fig.*) to intersperse (with); п. речь руга́тельствами to intersperse one's speech with swear-words.

пересып|а́ть, а́ю, *impf. of* ⌐ать.

пересыха́|ть, ет, *impf. of* пересо́хнуть.

перета́плива|ть, ю, *impf. of* перетопи́ть[1].

перетаск|а́ть, а́ю, *pf.* (*of* ⌐ивать) **1.** to carry away. **2.** (*fig., coll.*) to pinch, lift.

перета́скива|ть, ю, *impf. of* перетаска́ть *and* перетащи́ть.

перетас|ова́ть, у́ю, *pf.* (*of* ⌐о́вывать) to re-shuffle (*cards, also fig.*).

перетасо́выва|ть, ю, *impf. of* перетасова́ть.

перетащ|и́ть, у́, ⌐ишь, *pf.* (*of* перета́скивать) **1.** to drag over; to carry over; to move, shift; п. сунду́к на черда́к to move a trunk into the attic. **2.** (*fig., coll.*) to win over, gain over.

перека́|ть, ю, *impf. of* перете́чь.

пере|тере́ть, тру́, трёшь, *past* ⌐тёр, ⌐тёрла, *pf.* (*of* ⌐тира́ть) **1.** to wear out, wear down; терпе́ние и труд всё ⌐тру́т (*coll.*) it's dogged does it. **2.** (в+*a.*) to grind (into).

пере|тере́ться, трётся, *past* ⌐тёрся, ⌐тёрлась, *pf.* (*of* ⌐тира́ться) **1.** to wear out, wear through. **2.** *pass. of* ⌐тере́ть.

перетерп|е́ть, лю́, ⌐ишь, *pf.* (*coll.*) to suffer, endure.

перете́|чь, ку́, чёшь, ку́т, *past* ⌐к, ⌐кла́, *pf.* (*of* ⌐ка́ть) to overflow.

перетира́|ть(ся), ю(сь), *impf. of* перетере́ть(ся).

перето́лк|и, ов, *no sing.* (*coll.*) tittle-tattle.

перетолк|ова́ть[1], у́ю, *pf.* (*no impf.*) (*coll.*) to talk over, discuss; на́до нам с тобо́й об э́том п. we must talk it over.

перетолк|ова́ть[2], у́ю, *pf.* (*of* ⌐о́вывать) (*coll.*) to misinterpret.

перетолко́выва|ть, ю, *impf. of* перетолкова́ть[2].

перетоп|и́ть[1], лю́, ⌐ишь, *pf.* (*of* перета́пливать) to melt.

перетоп|и́ть[2], лю́, ⌐ишь, *pf.* (*coll.*) to heat; to kindle.

перето́ржк|а, и, *f.* re-auctioning.

перетрево́ж|ить, у, ишь, *pf.* (*no impf.*) (*coll.*) to disturb, alarm.

перетрево́ж|иться, усь, ишься, *pf.* (*no impf.*) (*coll.*) to be alarmed, become anxious.

пере|тру́, трёшь, тёр, тёрла, *see* ⌐тере́ть.

перетру́|сить, шу, сишь, *pf.* (*no impf.*) (*coll.*) to have a fright; to take fright.

перетряс|а́ть, а́ю, *impf. of* ⌐ти́.

перетряс|ти́, у́, ёшь, *past* ⌐, ⌐ла́, *pf.* (*of* ⌐а́ть) to shake up.

переть, пру, прёшь, *past* пёр, пёрла, *impf.* (*coll.*) **1.** to go, make one's way; п. сквозь толпу́ to barge through the crowd. **2.** to push, press. **3.** to drag. **4.** to come out; to appear, show; ре́вность так и прёт из неё his jealousy will out. **5.** (*pf.* с⌐) to steal, pinch.

перетя́гивани|е, я, *n.* п. кана́та (*sport*) tug-of-war.

перетя́гива|ть(ся), ю(сь), *impf. of* перетяну́ть(ся).

перетя|ну́ть[1], ну́, ↙нешь, *pf.* (*of* ↙гивать)
1. to pull, draw (*somewhere else*; *from A to B*);
п. ло́дку к бе́регу to pull the boat to the
shore. 2. (*fig., coll.*) to pull over, attract;
п. на свою́ сто́рону to win over, gain support of. 3. to pull in too tight. 4. to outbalance, outweigh.

перетя|ну́ть[2], ну́, ↙нешь, *pf.* (*of* ↙гивать)
to stretch again.

перетя|ну́ться, ну́сь, ↙нешься, *pf.* (*of*
↙гиваться) to lace oneself too tight.

переубе|ди́ть, ди́шь, *pf.* (*of* ↙жда́ть) to
make change one's mind, over-persuade.

переубе|ди́ться, дишься, *pf.* (*of* ↙жда́ться)
to change one's mind, be over-persuaded.

переубежда́|ть(ся), ю(сь), *impf. of* переубеди́ть(ся).

переу́л|ок, ка, *m.* lane, narrow street.

переупря́м|ить, лю, ишь, *pf.* (*no impf.*) (*coll.*)
to prove more stubborn than.

переусе́рдств|овать, ую, *pf.* (*no impf.*) (*coll.*)
to be over-diligent, show excess of zeal.

переустро́йств|о, а, *n.* reconstruction.

переутом|и́ть, лю́, и́шь, *pf.* (*of* ↙ля́ть) to
overtire, overstrain; to overwork.

переутом|и́ться, лю́сь, и́шься, *pf.* (*of*
↙ля́ться) to overtire oneself, overstrain oneself; to overwork; (*pf. only*) to be run
down.

переутомле́ни|е, я, *n.* overstrain; overwork.

переутомля́|ть(ся), ю(сь), *impf. of* переутоми́ть(ся).

переуч|е́сть, ту́, тёшь, *past* ёл, ла́, *pf.* (*of*
↙и́тывать) to take stock.

переучёт, а, *m.* stock-taking.

переу́чива|ть(ся), ю(сь), *impf. of* переучи́ть(ся).

переучи́тыва|ть, ю, *impf. of* переуче́сть.

переуч|и́ть, у́, ↙ишь, *pf.* (*of* ↙ивать) to
teach again.

переуч|и́ться, у́сь, ↙ишься, *pf.* (*of* ↙иваться) 1. to re-learn. 2.(*coll.*)to study too much.

переформир|ова́ть, у́ю, *pf.* (*of* ↙о́вывать)
(*mil.*) to re-form.

переформиро́выва|ть, ю, *impf. of* переформирова́ть.

перефрази́р|овать, ую, *impf. and pf.* to paraphrase.

перефразиро́вк|а, и, *f.* paraphrase.

перехва́лива|ть, ю, *impf. of* перехвали́ть.

перехвал|и́ть, ю́, ↙ишь, *pf.* (*of* ↙ивать) to
over-praise.

перехва́т, а, *m.* 1. interception. 2. intake,
taking in (*of article of clothing*).

перехва|ти́ть, чу́, ↙тишь, *pf.* (*of* ↙тывать)
1. to intercept, catch; я ↙ти́л его́ по
доро́ге на слу́жбу I caught him on the way
to work. 2. to take in; п. верёвкой to lash.
3. (*coll.*) to take a snack; to catch up (*some

thing to eat*). 4. (*coll.*) to borrow (*for a short
time*). 5. (*coll.*) to overshoot the mark.

перехва́тчик, а, *m.* (*aeron.*) interceptor.

перехва́тыва|ть, ю, *impf. of* перехвати́ть.

перехвора́|ть, ю, *pf.* (*no impf.*) (+*i.*) to have
had; to have been down (with) (*sc.* an illness).

перехитр|и́ть, ю́, и́шь, *pf.* to outwit, overreach.

перехо́д, а, *m.* 1. (*in var. senses*) passage,
transition; crossing. 2. (*mil.*) (day's) march.
3. (*rel.*) going over, conversion.

перехо|ди́ть[1], жу́, ↙дишь, *impf. of* перейти́.

перехо|ди́ть[2], жу́, ↙дишь, *pf.* (*no impf.*)
(*coll.*) to go all over.

перехо|ди́ть[3], жу́, ↙дишь, *pf.* (*no impf.*) (*coll.*;
at games) to have one's turn again, make
one's move again.

перехо́дный, *adj.* 1. transitional. 2. (*gram.*)
transitive. 3. (*tech.*) transient.

переход|я́щий, *pres. part. of* ↙и́ть *and adj.*
1. transient, transitory; п. ку́бок (*sport*)
challenge cup. 2. intermittent. 3. (*fin.*)
brought forward, carried over.

перехо́жий, *adj., see* кали́ка.

пер|ец, ца, *m.* pepper; стручко́вый п. capsicum; зада́ть кому́-н. ↙цу (*coll.*) to give
it someone hot.

перецара́па|ться, юсь, *pf.* 1. to scratch oneself. 2. to scratch each other.

перецел|ова́ть, у́ю, *pf.* (*no impf.*) to kiss (*all
or a number of*).

перецел|ова́ться, у́юсь, *pf.* (*no impf.*) to kiss
one another.

переце́нива|ть, ю, *impf. of* переоцени́ть.

переце́н|ить, ю́, ↙ишь, *pf.* (*of* ↙ивать) 1. to
price too high. 2. = переоцени́ть.

пе́реч|ень, ня, *m.* list; enumeration.

перечёркива|ть, ю, *impf. of* перечеркну́ть.

перечерк|ну́ть, ну́, нёшь, *pf.* (*of* ↙ивать) to
cross (out), cancel.

перечер|ти́ть, чу́, ↙тишь, *pf.* (*of* ↙чивать)
1. to draw again. 2. to copy, trace.

перече́рчива|ть, ю, *impf. of* перечерти́ть.

перече́|саться, ↙шешься, *pf.* (*no impf.*)
(*coll.*) 1. to do one's hair again. 2. to do
one's hair differently.

пере|че́сть[1], чту́, чтёшь, *past* ↙чёл, ↙чла́,
pf. = ↙счита́ть[2]; их мо́жно по па́льцам п.
you could count them on the fingers of one
hand.

пере|че́сть[2], чту́, чтёшь, *past* ↙чёл, ↙чла́,
pf. = ↙чита́ть.

перечи́нива|ть, ю, *impf. of* перечини́ть[1].

перечин|и́ть[1], ю́, ↙ишь, *pf.* (*of* ↙ивать) to
mend again, repair again; п. каранда́ш to
re-sharpen a pencil.

перечин|и́ть[2], ю́, ↙ишь, *pf.* to mend, repair
(*all or a number of*).

перечисле́ни|е, я, *n.* 1. enumeration. 2.
(*fin.*) transferring.

перечи́сл|ить, ю, ишь, *pf.* (*of* ~я́ть) 1. to enumerate. 2. to transfer; его́ ~или в запа́с he has been transferred to the reserve; п. на теку́щий счёт (*fin.*) to transfer to one's current account.

перечисл|я́ть, я́ю, *impf. of* ~ить.

перечит|а́ть¹, а́ю, *pf.* (*of* ~ывать) to re-read.

перечит|а́ть², а́ю, *pf.* to read (*all or a quantity of*); он ~а́л все кни́ги в библиоте́ке he has read all the books in the library.

перече́ч|ить, у, ишь, *impf.* (*no pf.*) (+*d.*; *coll.*) to contradict; to go against.

пе́речниц|а, ы, *f.* pepper-pot; чёртова п. (*vulg.*; *of cantankerous old woman*) old hag.

пе́ре|чный, *adj. of* ~ц.

перечу́вств|овать, ую, *pf.* (*no impf.*) to feel, experience.

переша́гива|ть, ю, *impf. of* перешагну́ть.

перешаг|ну́ть, ну́, нёшь, *pf.* (*of* ~ивать) to step over; п. (че́рез) поро́г to cross the threshold.

переше́|ек, йка, *m.* isthmus, neck (of land).

перешёптыва|ться, юсь, *impf.* to whisper to one another.

перешиб|а́ть, а́ю, *impf. of* ~и́ть.

перешиб|и́ть, у́, ёшь, *past* ~, ~ла, *pf.* (*of* ~а́ть) (*coll.*) to break, fracture.

перешива|ть, ю, *impf. of* перешить.

переши́вк|а, и, *f.* altering, alteration (*of clothes*).

переш|и́ть, ью, ьёшь, *pf.* (*of* ~ива́ть) 1. to alter; to have altered. 2. (*tech.*) to alter (*gauge of railway, etc.*).

перешто́п|ать¹, аю, *pf.* (*of* ~ывать) to darn over, darn again.

перешто́п|ать², аю, *pf.* (*no impf.*) to darn (*all or a number of*).

перешто́пыва|ть, ю, *impf. of* перешто́пать.

перещеголя́|ть, ю, *pf.* (*no impf.*) (*coll.*) to beat, outdo, surpass.

переэкзамен|ова́ть, у́ю, *pf.* (*of* ~о́вывать) to re-examine.

переэкзамен|ова́ться, у́юсь, *pf.* (*of* ~о́вываться) to take an examination again.

переэкзамено́вк|а, и, *f.* re-examination (*of those failing at first attempt*).

переэкзамено́выва|ть(ся), ю(сь), *impf. of* переэкзаменова́ть(ся).

пе́ри, *indecl., f.* (*myth.*) peri.

периге́|й, я, *m.* (*astron.*) perigee.

периге́ли|й, я, *m.* (*astron.*) perihelium.

перика́рд, а, *m.* (*anat.*) pericardium.

перика́рд|ий, *m.* = ~.

перикарди́т, а, *m.* (*med.*) pericarditis.

перил|а, ~, *no sing.* rail(ing); handrail; banisters.

пери́метр, а, *m.* (*math.*) perimeter.

пери́н|а, ы, *f.* feather-bed.

пери́од, а, *m.* (*in var. senses*) period; ледни-ко́вый п. (*geol.*) glacial period, ice age.

периодиза́ци|я, и,' *f.* division into periods.

периоди́к|а, и, *f.* (*collect.*) periodicals.

периоди́ческ|ий, *adj.* periodic(al); recurring; ~ая дробь recurring decimal; п. журна́л periodical, magazine; ~ая печа́ть the periodical press; (*collect.*) periodicals; ~ое явле́ние recurrent phenomenon.

периоди́чност|ь, и, *f.* periodicity.

периоди́ч|ный (~ен, ~на), *adj.* periodic(al).

перипате́тик, а, *m.* (*hist. philos.*) peripatetic.

перипат|ети́ческий, *adj. of* ~е́тик.

перипети́|я, и, *f.* (*lit.*) peripeteia; (*fig.*) reversal of fortune, upheaval.

периско́п, а, *m.* periscope.

перископи́ческий, *adj.* periscopic.

периста́льтик|а, и, *f.* (*physiol.*) peristalsis.

перисти́л|ь, я, *m.* (*archit.*) peristyle.

пе́ристо-кучево́й, *adj.* (*meteor.*) cirro--cumulus.

пе́ристы|й, *adj.* 1. (*zool., bot.*) pinnate. 2. feather-like, plumose; ~е облака́ fleecy clouds; cirri.

перитони́т, а, *m.* (*med.*) peritonitis.

перифери́йный, *adj.* provincial.

перифери́ческий, *adj.* peripheral.

перифери́|я, и, *f.* 1. periphery. 2. (*collect.*) the provinces; the outlying districts.

перифра́з|а, ы, *f.* periphrasis.

перифрази́р|овать, ую, *impf. and pf.* to use a periphrasis (for).

перифрасти́ческий, *adj.* periphrastic.

пёрк|а, и, *f.* (*tech.*) bit, flat bit, cutter, drill point; (flat) drill; ло́жечная п. shell auger.

перка́л|ь, и, *f.* (*and* ~я, *m.*) (*text.*) percale.

перколя́тор, а, *m.* (coffee) percolator.

перку́сси|я, и, *f.* (*med.*) percussion.

перкути́р|овать, ую, *impf. and pf.* (*med.*) to percuss.

перл, а, *m.* (*obs. in literal sense*; *fig., rhet. and typ.*) pearl.

перламу́тр, а, *m.* mother-of-pearl, nacre.

перламу́тр|овый, *adj. of* ~; ~овая пу́говица pearl button.

пе́рлин|ь, я, *m.* (*naut.*) hawser.

перло́в|ый, *adj.* ~ая крупа́ pearl barley.

перлюстра́ци|я, и, *f.* opening and inspection of correspondence.

перлюстри́р|овать, ую, *impf. and pf.* to open and inspect (*correspondence*).

пермане́нт, а, *m.* permanent wave.

пермане́нтный, *adj.* permanent.

пе́рм|ский, *adj.* Permian (*branch of Finno--Ugric ethnic and linguistic group*); ~ская систе́ма (*geol.*) Permian formation (*from Perm, a town in the Urals*).

перна́т|ый (~, ~a), *adj.* feathered, feathery; ~ое ца́рство 'feathered world' (*birds*).

пёр|нуть, нет (*inst. pf. of* ~де́ть) (*vulg.*) to give a fart.

пер|о́, а́, *pl.* ~ья, ~ьев, *n.* **1.** feather; ни пу́ха, ни ~а́! good luck! **2.** pen; ве́чное п. fountain-pen; взя́ться за п. (*fig.*) to take up the pen; владе́ть ~о́м to wield a skilful pen; про́ба ~а́ (*fig.*) first attempt at writing. **3.** leaf (*of onion or garlic*). **4.** fin. **5.** blade (*of an oar*); paddle (*of wheel*).

перочи́нный, *adj.* п. нож pen-knife.

перпендикуля́р, а, *m.* (*math.*) perpendicular; опусти́ть п. to drop a perpendicular.

перпендикуля́р|ный (~ен, ~на), *adj.* perpendicular.

перро́н, а, *m.* platform (*on railway station*).

перро́н|ный, *adj.* of ~; п. биле́т platform ticket.

перс, а, *m.* Persian.

пе́рс|и, ей, *no sing.* (*arch.* or *poet.*) breast, bosom.

перси́дский, *adj.* Persian; п. порошо́к insect-powder.

пе́рсик, а, *m.* **1.** peach. **2.** peach-tree.

пе́рсик|овый, *adj.* of ~; peachy; ~овое де́рево peach-tree.

перси|я́нин, я́нина, *pl.* я́не, я́н, *m.* (*obs.*) = перс.

персия́нк|а, и, *f.* Persian (woman).

персо́н|а, ы, *f.* person; ва́жная п. (*coll.*) big wig; со́бственная п. one's own self; яви́ться со́бственной ~ой (*obs.* or *iron.*) to appear in person; п. гра́та persona grata; обе́д на́ шесть ~ dinner for six.

персона́ж, а, *m.* (*lit.*) character; (*fig.*) personage.

персона́л, а, *m.* personnel, staff.

персона́льный, *adj.* personal; individual; п. пенсионе́р person in receipt of special pension.

персонифика́ци|я, и, *f.* personification.

персонифици́р|овать, ую, *impf. and pf.* to personify.

перспекти́в|а, ы, *f.* **1.** (*art*) perspective. **2.** vista, prospect. **3.** (*fig.*) prospect, outlook; что в ~е? what is in prospect?, what are the prospects?; име́ть ~у to have prospects, have a future (before one).

перспекти́в|ный, *adj.* **1.** (*art*) perspective. **2.** forward-looking; envisaging future development; ~ное плани́рование (*econ.*) long-term planning. **3.** (~ен, ~на) having prospects; promising; ~ная молода́я балери́на a promising young ballerina.

перст, а́, *m.* (*obs.*) finger; оди́н, как п. all alone.

пе́рст|ень, ня, *m.* (finger-)ring; (с печа́тью) signet-ring.

перстневи́дный, *adj.* п. хрящ (*anat.*) cricoid.

перст|ь, и, *f.* (*arch.* or *rhet.*) dust, earth.

перуа́н|ец, ца, *m.* Peruvian.

перуа́нк|а, и, *f.* Peruvian (woman).

перуа́нский, *adj.* Peruvian; п. бальза́м Peru balsam.

перу́н|ы, ов, *no sing.* (*obs., poet.*) thunderbolts; (*fig.*) fulminations; мета́ть п. to fulminate.

перфе́кт, а, *m.* (*gram.*) perfect (tense).

перфока́рт|а, ы, *f.* punched card (*in computer programming, etc.*).

перфоле́нт|а, ы, *f.* punched tape.

перфора́тор, а, *m.* (*tech.*) **1.** perforator; punch. **2.** drill, boring machine.

перфора́ци|я, и, *f.* (*tech.*) **1.** perforation, punching. **2.** drilling, boring.

перфори́р|овать, ую, *impf. and pf.* (*tech.*) **1.** to perforate, punch. **2.** to drill, bore.

перха́|ть, ю, *impf.* (*no pf.*) (*coll.*) to cough (*in trying to remove an irritation of the throat*).

перхлора́т, а, *m.* (*chem.*) perchlorate.

перхо́т|а, ы, *f.* (*coll.*) tickling in the throat.

перхот|ь, и, *f.* dandruff, scurf.

перце́пци|я, и, *f.* (*philos.*) perception.

перцо́вк|а, и, *f.* pepper-brandy.

перцо́вый, *adj.* of пе́рец.

перча́тк|а, и, *f.* glove; gauntlet; бро́сить ~у (*fig.*) to throw down the gauntlet.

перчи́нк|а, и, *f.* peppercorn.

пе́рч|ить, у, ишь, *impf.* (*of* на~ *and* по~) (*coll.*) to pepper.

першеро́н, а, *m.* percheron (*breed of horse*).

перш|и́ть, и́т, *impf.* (*coll.*; *impers.*) у меня́ в го́рле ~и́т I have a tickle in my throat.

пе́рыш|ко, ка, *pl.* ~ки, ~ек, ~кам, *n.* (*coll.*) *dim. of* перо́; лёгкий, как п. light as a feather.

пёс, пса, *m.* (*coll.*) dog; (*astron.*) созве́здие Большо́го Пса Canis Major; созве́здие Ма́лого Пса Canis Minor; (*coll.*) п. зна́ет the devil only knows.

пе́сельник, а, *m.* (*coll.*) singer.

пе́сенк|а, и, *f.* song; его́ п. спе́та (*coll.*) his song is ended, he has had it.

пе́сенник, а, *m.* **1.** song-book. **2.** (chorus) singer. **3.** song-writer.

пе́с|енный, *adj.* of ~ня.

песе́т|а, ы, *f.* (*Spanish currency unit*) peseta.

пес|е́ц, ца́, *m.* polar fox; бе́лый, голубо́й п. white, blue fox (fur).

пёс|ий *and* пе́сий, *adj.* of ~; пе́сья зьезда́ (*astron.*) Sirius, the Dog Star.

пёсик, а, *m.* (*coll.*) *dim. of* пёс; doggie.

песка́р|ь, я́, *m.* gudgeon (*fish*).

пескостру́йный, *adj.* (*tech.*) sand-blast.

песнопе́в|ец, ца, *m.* **1.** (*obs. rhet.*) singer; psalmist. **2.** (*poet.*) poet, bard.

песнопе́ни|е, я, *n.* **1.** (*eccl.*) psalm; canticle. **2.** (*poet.*) poetry, poesy.

песн|ь, и, *g. pl.* ~ей, *f.* **1.** (*obs.*) song; П. ~ей the Song of Songs, Song of Solomon. **2.** (*lit.*) canto, book.

пе́с|ня, ни, *g. pl.* ~ен, *f.* song; air; до́лгая п. (*fig., coll.*) a long story; э́то стара́ (стара́я) п. (*coll.*) it's the same old story; тяну́ть всё ту же ~ню (*coll.*) to harp on one string; п. спе́та = пе́сенка спе́та.

пес|о́к, ка́, *m.* 1. sand; золото́й п. gold dust; са́харный п. granulated sugar; стро́ить на ~ке́ (*fig.*) to build on sand; как п. морско́й, как ~ку́ морско́го (numerous) as the sands of the sea. 2. (*pl.*) sands; зыбу́чие ~ки́ quicksands. 3. (*med.*) gravel.

песо́чник, a, *m.* (*orn.*) sand-piper.

песо́чниц|а, ы, *f.* 1. sand-box. 2. sanding apparatus.

песо́чн|ый, *adj.* 1. *adj. of* песо́к; sandy; ~ые часы́ sand-glass, hour-glass. 2. (*cul.*) short; ~ое пече́нье shortbread, shortcake.

пессими́зм, a, *m.* pessimism.

пессими́ст, a, *m.* pessimist.

пессимисти́ческий, *adj.* pessimistic.

пессимисти́ч|ный (~ен, ~на), *adj.* = ~еский.

пест, а́, *m.* pestle; п., знай свою́ сту́пу (*prov.*) cobbler, stick to your last; как п. в ло́жках a square peg in a round hole.

пе́стик¹, a, *m.* (*bot.*) pistil.

пе́стик², a, *m. dim. of* пест.

пе́ст|овать, ую, *impf.* (*of* вы́~) 1. (*obs.*) to nurse. 2. (*fig.*) to cherish, foster.

пестр|е́ть¹, е́ет, *impf.* (*no pf.*) 1. to become many-coloured. 2. (+*i.*) to be gay (with); корабли́ ~е́ли фла́гами the ships were gay with bunting. 3. to show colourfully, make a brave show (*of objects of different colours*).

пестр|е́ть², и́т, *impf.* (*no pf.*) 1. (*of many-coloured objects*) to strike the eye (*also fig.*); его́ и́мя ~и́т в газе́тах (*coll.*) he is always getting his name in the papers. 2. (*coll.*) to be too gaudy, be flashy. 3. (+*i.*) to abound (in), be rich (in); письмо́ ~и́т оши́бками the letter bristles with mistakes.

пестр|и́ть, ю́, и́шь, *impf.* (*no pf.*) 1. to make gaudy; to make colourful. 2. (*impers.*) у меня́ ~и́ло в глаза́х I was dazzled (*sc.* by the colours).

пестрот|а́, ы́, *no pl., f.* diversity of colours; (*fig.*) mixed character.

пестру́шк|а, и, *f.* 1. speckled trout. 2. (*zool.*) lemming.

пёстр|ый (~, ~а́, ~о *and* ~о́), *adj.* 1. motley, variegated, many-coloured, parti-coloured. 2. (*fig., coll.*) mixed; п. соста́в населе́ния mixed population. 3. (*fig.*) florid; pretentious, mannered; п. слог florid style.

пестрядёвый, *adj. of* пестря́дь.

пе́стряд|ь, и, *f.* a coarse, coloured, cotton fabric.

песту́н, а́, *m.* (*obs.*) mentor.

пес|цо́вый, *adj. of* ~е́ц.

песча́ник, a, *m.* (*geol.*) sandstone.

песча́нк|а, и, *f.* (*orn.*) sanderling.

песча́н|ый, *adj.* sandy; ~ая коса́ sandbar; п. холм dune.

песчи́нк|а, и, *f.* grain of sand.

пета́рд|а, ы, *f.* 1. (*hist. mil.*) petard. 2. detonating cartridge (*as alarm signal on railways*). 3. fire-cracker.

пети́т, a, *m.* (*typ.*) brevier.

пети́ци|я, и, *f.* petition.

петли́ц|а, ы, *f.* 1. buttonhole. 2. tab (*on uniform collar*).

пе́т|ля, ли, *g. pl.* ~ель, *f.* 1. loop; мёртвая п. (*aeron.*) loop; сде́лать мёртвую ~лю to loop the loop. 2. (*fig.*) noose; он досто́ин ~ли he deserves to hang; лезть в ~лю to put one's neck into the noose, take risks needlessly; наде́ть ~лю на ше́ю to hang a millstone about one's neck. 3. buttonhole; мета́ть ~ли to work button-holes, buttonhole; (*fig., joc.*) (i) to conceal one's tracks, (ii) to confuse the issue. 4. stitch; спусти́ть ~лю to drop a stitch; to ladder one's stocking. 5. hinge; дверь соскочи́ла с ~ель the door has come off its hinges.

петля́|ть, ю, *impf.* (*coll.*) to dodge.

петрифика́ци|я, и, *f.* petrification; fossilization.

петро́граф, a, *m.* petrographer.

петрогра́фи|я, и, *f.* petrography.

петроле́йный, *adj.* (*chem.*) petroleum.

петру́шк|а¹, и, *f.* parsley.

петру́шк|а², и, *m. and f.* 1. (*m.*) Punch. 2. (*f.*) Punch-and-Judy show. 3. (*f.*) (*fig., coll.*) foolishness, absurdity; кака́я-то п. получи́лась an absurd thing happened; брось валя́ть ~y! stop being a fool!

пету́ни|я, ии, *f.* (*bot.*) petunia.

пету́н|ья, ьи, *g. pl.* ~ий, *f.* = ~ия.

пету́х, а́, *m.* 1. cock; инде́йский п. turkey-cock; фаза́н-п. cock-pheasant; до ~о́в before cock-crow; встать с ~а́ми to rise with the lark; пусти́ть ~а́ (*mus. sl.*) to let out a squeak (*on a high note*); пусти́ть кра́сного ~а́ to set fire, commit act of arson. 2. *fig., of an irascible person.*

пету́|ший, *adj. of* ~x; п. гре́бень cockscomb.

петуши́ный, *adj. of* пету́х; п. бой cock-fight(-ing); п. го́лос (*fig.*) squeaky voice.

петуш|и́ться, у́сь, и́шься, *impf.* (*of* вс~) (*coll.*) to ride the high horse; to take umbrage.

петуш|о́к, ка́, *m.* 1. cockerel; идти́ ~ко́м (*coll., joc.*) to strut. 2. (*electr.*) commutator lug, commutator riser.

пе́т|ый, *p.p.p. of* ~ь; (*coll.*) п. дура́к perfect fool.

петь, пою́, поёшь, *impf.* (*of* про~ *and* с~) to sing (*also of birds and, fig., of inanimate objects*); to chant, intone; п. ба́сом to have a bass voice; п. ве́рно, фальши́во to sing in tune, out of tune; п. вполго́лоса to hum; п. другу́ю пе́сню to sing another tune; п. Ла́заря (coll., pejor.) to bemoan one's fate, grumble, complain; п. сла́ву (+d.) to sing the praises (of).

пехо́т|а, ы, f. infantry, foot; морска́я п.(the) marines.

пехоти́н|ец, ца, m. infantryman.

пехо́тный, adj. infantry.

печа́л|ить, ю, ишь, impf. (of о~) to grieve, sadden.

печа́л|иться, юсь, ишься, impf. (of о~) to grieve, be sad.

печа́л|ь, и, f. grief, sorrow; кака́я п.! how sad!; не твоя́ п. it's no concern of yours; тебе́ что за п.? what has that to do with you?

печа́льник, а, m. (obs., now iron.) one who feels for others, sympathizer.

печа́л|ьный (~ен, ~ьна), adj. 1. sad, mournful, doleful; wistful. 2. grievous; п. коне́ц dismal end, bad end; ~ьные результа́ты unfortunate results; оста́вить по себе́ ~ьную па́мять to leave a bad reputation.

печа́тани|е, я, n. printing.

печа́та|ть, ю, impf. (of на~) to print; to type.

печа́та|ться, юсь, impf. (of на~) 1. to write (for a journal, etc.); to have (literary compositions, etc.) published; тридцати́ лет он ещё нигде́ не ~лся at thirty he had not yet had anything published. 2. to be at the printer's, be in the press.

печа́тк|а, и, f. signet.

печа́тник, а, m. printer.

печа́тн|ый, adj. 1. printing; ~ое де́ло printing; п. лист quire, printer's sheet; п. стано́к printing-press. 2. printed; in the press; ~ая кни́га printed book (as opp. to manuscript); п. о́тзыв о но́вом рома́не press comment on a new novel. 3. писа́ть по ~ому, ~ыми бу́квами to (write in) print; to write in block capitals.

печа́т|ь¹, и, f. seal, stamp (also fig.); госуда́рственная п. State Seal, Great Seal; наложи́ть п. (на+a.) to affix a seal (to); носи́ть п. (+g.) to have the seal (of), bear the stamp (of); п. го́ря the stamp of grief; на мои́х уста́х п. молча́ния my lips are sealed.

печа́т|ь², и, f. 1. print(ing); быть в ~и to be in print, be at the printer's; вы́йти из ~и to appear, come out, be published; подписа́ть к ~и to send to press; «подписа́но к ~и» 'passed for printing'. 2. print, type; ме́лкая п. small print; кру́пная п. large print; убо́ристая п. close print. 3. (the) press; свобо́да ~и freedom of the press; име́ть благоприя́тные о́тзывы в ~и to have a good press.

пече́ни|е, я, n. baking.

печёнк|а, и, f. 1. liver (of animal, as food). 2. (coll.) liver; сиде́ть (у кого́-н.) в ~ах to plague (someone).

печёночник, а, m. (bot.) liverwort.

печён|очный, adj. of ~ка and пе́чень; hepatic.

печёный, adj. (cul.) baked.

пе́чен|ь, и, f. liver; воспале́ние ~и (med.) hepatitis, inflammation of the liver.

пече́нь|е, я, n. pastry; biscuit; минда́льное п. macaroon.

пе́чк|а, и, f. stove; танцева́ть от ~и (coll., iron.) to begin again from the beginning.

печни́к, а́, m. stove-setter; stove-repairer.

печ|но́й, adj. of ~ь²; п. агрега́т furnace unit; п. газ furnace gas; п. ка́мень oven-stone; ~но́е отопле́ние stove heating; ~на́я труба́ chimney, flue.

печь¹, пеку́, печёшь, пеку́т, past пёк, пекла́, impf. (of ис~) to bake; со́лнце пекло́ there was a scorching sun.

печ|ь², и, о ~и, в ~й, pl. ~и, ~е́й, f. 1. stove; oven. 2. (tech.) furnace, kiln, oven; до́менная п. blast-furnace; кремацио́нная п. incinerator.

пе́чься¹, печётся, пеку́тся, past пёкся, пекла́сь, impf. (of ис~) to bake; to broil (in the sun).

пе́чься², пеку́сь, печёшься, пеку́тся, past пёкся, пекла́сь, impf. (no pf.) (о+p.) to take care (of), care (for), look after.

пешедра́лом, adv. (coll.) = пешко́м.

пешехо́д, а, m. pedestrian.

пешехо́дн|ый, adj. pedestrian; п. мост foot-bridge; ~ая тропа́ footpath.

пе́ш|ечный, adj. of ~ка.

пе́ш|ий, adj. 1. pedestrian; по о́бразу ~его хожде́ния on Shanks' mare. 2. (mil.) unmounted, foot.

пе́шк|а, и, f. (in chess, also fig.) pawn.

пешко́м, adv. on foot.

пеще́р|а, ы, f. cave, cavern; grotto.

пеще́рист|ый (~, ~а), adj. 1. with many caves. 2. (anat.) cavernous.

пеще́р|ный, adj. of ~а; п. челове́к (archaeol.) cave-dweller, cave-man, troglodyte.

пи, indecl., n. (math.) pi (π).

пиани́но, indecl., n. (upright) piano.

пиани́ссимо, adv. (mus.) pianissimo.

пиани́ст, а, m. pianist.

пиа́но, adv. (mus.) piano.

пиано́л|а, ы, f. (mus.) pianola.

пиа́стр, а, m. piastre.

пива́|ть, ю, impf. (coll.) freq. of пить.

пивн|а́я, о́й, f. alehouse; pub.

пивн|о́й, adj. of ~о; ~ы́е дро́жжи brewer's yeast; ~а́я кру́жка beer mug.

пи́в|о, а, n. beer; све́тлое п. pale ale; тёмное п. brown ale; ~а не сва́ришь с ним (fig., coll.) he's an awkward customer.

пивова́р, а, *m.* brewer.

пивваре́ни|е, я, *n.* brewing.

пивова́ренн|ый, *adj.* п. заво́д brewery;
~ая промы́шленность brewing.

пи́галиц|а, ы, *f.* (*orn.*) lapwing, peewit;
(*fig., coll.*) puny person.

пигме́|й, я, *m.* pygmy (*also fig.*).

пигме́нт, а, *m.* pigment.

пигмента́ци|я, и, *f.* pigmentation.

пигме́нтный, *adj.* pigmental, pigmentary.

пиджа́к, а́, *m.* jacket, coat.

пиджа́|чный, *adj. of* ~к; п. костю́м,
~чная па́ра (lounge-)suit.

пиете́т, а, *m.* respect, reverence.

пижа́м|а, ы, *f.* pyjamas.

пижо́н, а, *m.* (*coll.*) fop; (*sl., pejor.*) twit.

пизд|а́, ы́, *f.* (*vulg.*) cunt.

пии́т, а, *m.* (*arch.*) poet.

пик[1], а, *m.* (*geogr.*) peak; spire; pinnacle.

пик[2], а, *m.* peak (*of work, traffic, etc.*); п.
нагру́зки (*electr.*) peak load; (*as indecl. adj.*)
часы́ пик rush-hour.

пи́к|а[1], и, *f.* pike, lance.

пи́к|а[2], и, *f.* (*cards*) spade; да́ма ~ the queen
of spades; пойти́ ~ой to play a spade.

пи́к|а[3], и, *f. only in phrase* сде́лать что-н.
в ~у кому́-н. to do a thing to spite someone.

пика́нтност|ь, и, *f.* piquancy, savour,
zest.

пика́нт|ный (~ен, ~на), *adj.* piquant (*also
fig.*), savoury; (*fig.*) poignant; п. анекдо́т
risqué story.

пика́п, а, *m.* pick-up (van).

пике́[1], *indecl., n.* (*text.*) piqué.

пике́[2], *indecl., n.* (*aeron.*) dive; перейти́ в п.
to go into a dive.

пике́|йный, *adj. of* ~[1].

пике́т[1], а, *m.* picket (picquet, piquet).

пике́т[2], а, *m.* (*card-game*) piquet.

пикети́р|овать, ую, *impf.* to picket.

пике́тчик, а, *m.* picket.

пики́ровани|е, я, *n.* (*aeron.*) dive, diving.

пики́рованный, *adj.* (*obs.*) piqued, in pique.

пики́р|овать, ую, *impf. and pf.* (*pf. also* с~)
(*aeron.*) to dive, swoop.

пикир|ова́ть, у́ю, *impf. and pf.* (*agric.*) to
thin out.

пики́р|оваться, уюсь, *impf.* (*no pf.*) (с+*i.*)
to exchange caustic remarks, cross swords.

пирро́вк|а[1], и, *f.* (*agric.*) thinning.

пирро́вк|а[2], и, *f.* (*coll.*) altercation, slang-
ing-match.

пики́ровщик, а, *m.* dive-bomber.

пики́р|ующий, *pres. part of* ~овать *and adj.*;
п. бомбардиро́вщик dive-bomber.

пи́кколо, *indecl., n.* piccolo.

пи́кник, а, *m.* (*anthrop.*) pyknic person.

пикни́к, а́, *m.* picnic.

пи́кн|уть, у, ешь, *pf.* (*coll.*) to let out a
squeak; (*fig.*) to make a sound (of protest);

попро́буй то́лько п. (*with implied threat*) one
sound out of you!; п. не сметь not to dare
utter a word; он п. не успе́л before he
could say knife.

пи́к|овый, *adj.* 1. *adj. of* ~а[2]; ~овая да́ма
queen of spades; ~овая масть spades. 2.
(*fig., coll.*) awkward; unfavourable; по-
па́сть в ~овое положе́ние to get into a
pretty mess; оста́ться при ~овом интере́се
to get nothing for one's pains.

пикра́т, а, *m.* (*chem.*) picrate.

пикри́новый, *adj.* (*chem.*) picric.

пиксафо́н, а, *m.* liquid tar soap.

пиктографи́ческий, *adj.* pictographic.

пиктогра́фи|я, и, *f.* pictography.

пи́кул|и, ей, *no sing.* pickles.

пил|а́, ы́, *pl.* ~ы, ~, *f.* 1. saw; ле́нточная п.
band-saw; лучко́вая п. sash saw, bow saw;
механи́ческая п. frame-saw; попере́чная
п. cross-cut saw; столя́рная п. buck-saw.
2. (*fig.*) nagger.

пила́в, а, *m.* (*cul.*) pilaff (pilau, pilaw).

пила́-ры́ба, пилы́-ры́бы, *f.* saw-fish.

пилёный, *adj.* sawn; п. лес timber; п.
са́хар lump sugar.

пилигри́м, а, *m.* pilgrim.

пили́ка|ть, ю, *impf.* (*coll.*) to scrape, strum
(*on a fiddle, etc.*).

пил|и́ть, ю́, ~ишь, *impf.* 1. to saw. 2. (*fig.,
coll.*) to nag (at).

пи́лк|а, и, *f.* 1. sawing. 2. fret-saw. 3. nail-
-file.

пи́ллерс, а, *m.* (*naut.*) deck stanchion.

пиломатериа́л|ы, ов, *no sing.* saw-timber.

пило́н, а, *m.* (*archit.*) pylon.

пилообра́зный, *adj.* serrated, notched.

пилора́м|а, ы, *f.* power-saw bench.

пило́т, а, *m.* pilot.

пилота́ж, а, *m.* pilotage; вы́сший п. aerobatics.

пилоти́р|овать, ую, *impf.* to pilot.

пило́тк|а, и, *f.* (*mil.*) forage cap.

пиль, *interj.* (*command to hounds*) take!

пи́льщик, а, *m.* sawyer, wood-cutter.

пилю́л|я, и, *f.* pill (*also fig.*); проглоти́ть ~ю
(*fig.*) to swallow the pill; позолоти́ть ~ю to
gild the pill.

пиля́стр|а, ы, *f.* (*archit.*) pilaster.

пим|ы́, о́в, *sing.* ~, ~а́, *m.* pimy (1. *deer-skin
boots worn in N. regions of U.S.S.R.* 2. *dial.
name for valenki*).

пинакоте́к|а, и, *f.* picture gallery.

пина́|ть, ю, *impf. of* пнуть.

пингви́н, а, *m.* penguin.

пинг-по́нг, а, *m.* ping-pong.

пине́тк|а, и, *f.* (baby's) bootee.

пи́ни|я, и, *f.* Italian pine.

пин|о́к, ка́, *m.* (*coll.*) kick.

пи́нт|а, ы, *f.* pint.

пинце́т, а, *m.* pincers, tweezers.

пи́нчер, а, *m.* (*breed of dog*) Dandie Dinmont, pincher.

пио́н, а, *m.* (*bot.*) peony.

пионе́р, а, *m.* (*in var. senses*) pioneer; (ю́ный) пионе́р Pioneer (*member of Communist children's organization in U.S.S.R.*).

пионервожа́т|ый, ого, *m.* (*and* ~**ая,** ~**ой,** *f.*) Pioneer leader.

пионе́ри|я, и, *f.* (*collect.*; *coll.*), Pioneers.

пионе́р|ский, *adj.* of ~.

пиоре́|я, и, *f.* (*med.*) pyorrhoea.

пипе́тк|а, и, *f.* pipette; medicine dropper; reservoir (*of fountain-pen*).

пи-пи́, *indecl.* (*in children's speech*) wee-wee.

пир, а, о ~е, в ~у́, *pl.* ~**ы́,** *m.* feast, banquet; п. горо́й, п. на весь мир sumptuous feast; в чужо́м ~у́ похме́лье *see under* похме́лье.

пирами́д|а, ы, *f.* pyramid.

пирамида́льный, *adj.* pyramidal; п. то́поль Lombardy poplar.

пирамидо́н, а, *m.* (*pharm.*) pyramidon, amidopyrine; headache tablets.

пира́т, а, *m.* pirate.

пира́тский, *adj.* piratic(al).

пира́тств|о, а, *n.* piracy.

пирене́йский, *adj.* Pyrenean.

пири́т, а, *m.* (*min.*) pyrites.

пир|ова́ть, у́ю, *impf.* to feast, banquet; to celebrate with feasting.

пирови́нн|ый, *adj.* ~**ая кислота́** (*chem.*) pyrotartaric acid.

пиро́г, а́, *m.* pie; tart; п. с мя́сом meat pie; возду́шный п. soufflé; сва́дебный п. wedding cake; ешь п. с гриба́ми, держи́ язы́к за зуба́ми (*prov.*) keep your breath to cool your porridge.

пиро́г|а, и, *f.* pirogue.

пирогравю́р|а, ы, *f.* pyrogravure, poker-work.

пиро́жник, а, *m.* pastry-cook.

пиро́жн|ое, ого, *n.* **1.** (*collect.*) pastries; (fancy) cake, pastry. **2.** (*obs.*) sweet.

пирож|о́к, ка́, *m.* pasty, patty, pie.

пироксили́н, а, *m.* pyroxylin, gun-cotton.

пироксили́н|овый, *adj.* of ~; ~**овая ша́шка** slab of gun-cotton.

пиро́метр, а, *m.* (*phys.*, *tech.*) pyrometer.

пиросе́рн|ый, *adj.* ~**ая кислота́** (*chem.*) pyrosulphuric acid.

пироте́хник, а, *m.* pyrotechnics.

пиротехни́ческий, *adj.* pyrotechnic.

пирри́хи|й, я, *m.* (*lit.*) pyrrhic (foot).

пи́рров, *adj.* ~**а побе́да** Pyrrhic victory.

пиру́шк|а, и, *f.* (*coll.*) carousal; binge.

пируэ́т, а, *m.* pirouette.

пи́ршеств|о, а, *n.* feast, banquet.

пи́ршеств|овать, ую, *impf.* to feast, banquet.

писа́к|а, и, *m.* (*coll.*) scribbler, quill-driver.

писа́ни|е, я, *n.* **1.** writing. **2.** writing, screed; (свяще́нное) п. Holy Scripture, Holy Writ.

пи́сан|ый, *adj.* written, manuscript; ~**ая краса́вица** a picture (of beauty); говори́ть как по-~**ому** to speak as from the book; носи́ться с чем-н. как (дура́к) с ~**ой то́рбой** to fuss over something like a child with a new toy.

писарско́й, *adj.* of пи́сарь.

пи́сар|ь, я, *pl.* ~**я́,** *m.* (*obs.*) clerk.

писа́тел|ь, я, *m.* writer, author.

писа́тель|ский, *adj.* of ~; п. труд writing, literary work.

писа́|ть, ю, *impf.* (*vulg.*) to piss.

пи|са́ть, шу́, ~шешь, *impf.* (*of* на~) **1.** to write; п. на маши́нке to type; п. про́зой, стиха́ми to write prose, verse; п. дневни́к to keep a diary; п. под дикто́вку to take dictation; не про нас ~**сано** (*coll.*) (i) it is Greek to us, (ii) it is not (intended, meant) for us; дурака́м зако́н не ~**сан** (*coll.*) fools rush in where angels fear to tread; ~**ши́** пропа́ло it is as good as lost. **2.** (+*i.*) to paint (in); п. портре́ты ма́слом to paint portraits in oils.

пи|са́ться, шу́сь, ~шешься, *impf.* **1.** to spell, be spelled; как ~**шется э́то сло́во?** how do you spell this word? **2.** (*impers.*; +*d.*) to feel an inclination for writing; мне сего́дня не ~**шется** I don't feel like writing today. **3.** (+*i.*; *obs.*) to style oneself; to sign oneself; он ~**шется** торго́вцем he styles himself a merchant. **4.** *pass. of* ~**са́ть.**

пис|е́ц, ца́, *m.* **1.** (*obs.*) clerk. **2.** (*hist.*) scribe.

писк, а, *m.* peep; chirp; squeak; (*of chicks*) cheep.

пискли́в|ый (~, ~**а**), *adj.* squeaky.

пискля́в|ый (~, ~**а**), *adj.* (*coll.*) = пискли́вый.

пи́скн|уть, у, ешь, *inst. pf.* (*of* пища́ть) (*coll.*) to give a squeak; то́лько ~**и** у меня́! (*with implied threat*) one squeak out of you!

пискотн|я́, и́, *f.* (*coll.*) squeaking; chirruping.

писку́н, а́, *m.* (*coll.*) **1.** squeaker. **2.** whiner.

писсуа́р, а, *m.* urinal.

пистоле́т, а, *m.* pistol; п.-пулемёт sub-machine-gun.

писто́н, а, *m.* **1.** (percussion) cap. **2.** (*mus.*) piston.

писто́н|ный, *adj.* of ~; ~**ное ружьё** percussion musket.

писцо́в|ый, *adj.* of писе́ц; ~**е кни́ги** (*hist.*) cadastres.

писчебума́жны|й, *adj.* п. магази́н stationer's (shop); ~**е принадле́жности** stationery.

пи́сч|ий, *adj.* ~**ая бума́га** writing paper; п. материа́л writing materials.

письмена́, письмён, ~м, *no sing.* characters, letters; дре́вние еги́петские п. ancient Egyptian characters.

пи́сьменно, *adv.* in writing, in written form; изложи́ть п. to set down in writing, put down on paper.

пи́сьменност|ь, и, *f.* **1.** literature; (*collect.*) literary texts. **2.** the written language.

пи́сьменн|ый, *adj.* **1.** writing; п. прибо́р desk set; п. стол writing-table, bureau. **2.** written; в ~ом ви́де, в ~ой фо́рме in writing, in written form; п. знак letter; п. о́тзыв written testimonial; п. экза́мен written examination.

письм|о́, а́, *pl.* ~а, пи́сем, ~ам, *n.* **1.** letter; заказно́е п. registered letter; це́нное п. registered letter (with statement of value); поздрави́тельное п. letter of congratulation; п.-секре́тка letter-card. **2.** writing; иску́сство ~а́ art of writing. **3.** script; hand(-writing); ара́бское п. Arabic script; ме́лкое п. small hand.

письмо́вник, а, *m.* (*hist.*) manual of letter-writing (*containing specimen letters*).

письмоводи́тел|ь, я, *m.* (*obs.*) clerk.

письмоно́с|ец, ца, *m.* postman.

пита́ни|е, я, *n.* **1.** nourishment, nutrition; feeding; недоста́точное п. malnutrition; обще́ственное п. public catering; уси́ленное п. high-calorie diet, nourishing diet. **2.** (*tech.*) feed, feeding; резервуа́р ~я feed tank. **3.** (*electr.*) power supply.

пита́тел|ь, я, *m.* (*tech.*) feeder.

пита́тельност|ь, и, *f.* nutritiousness, food value.

пита́тел|ьный (~ен, ~ьна), *adj.* **1.** nourishing, nutritious; supplying nutriment; п. пункт refreshment place (*kiosk, etc.*); ~ьная среда́ (*biol.*) culture medium; (*fig.*) breeding-ground; ~ьное сре́дство nutriment. **2.** (*anat.*) alimentary. **3.** (*tech.*) feed, feeding; ~ьная труба́ feed pipe, supply pipe.

пита́|ть, ю, *impf.* (*of* на~) **1.** to feed; to nourish (*also fig.*); to sustain; п. больно́го to feed a patient; п. наде́жду to nourish the hope; п. отвраще́ние (к) to have an aversion (for); п. привя́занность (к) to be attached (to), cultivate an attachment (to). **2.** (*tech.*) to feed, supply; п. го́род электро-эне́ргией to supply a city with electricity.

пита́|ться, юсь, *impf.* (+*i.*) to feed (on), live (on); хорошо́ п. to be well fed, eat well; п. наде́ждами to live on hope.

пите́йн|ый, *adj.* (*obs.*) п. дом, ~ое заведе́ние public house.

питека́нтроп, а, *m.* (*anthrop.*) pithecanthropus.

пи́терский, *adj.* (*coll.*) of St. Petersburg.

пито́м|ец, ца, *m.* **1.** foster-child, nursling; charge. **2.** pupil; alumnus.

пито́мник, а, *m.* nursery (*for plants or animals; also fig.*); древе́сный п. arboretum.

пито́н, а, *m.* python.

пить, пью, пьёшь, *past* пил, пила́, пи́ло, *impf.* (*of* вы́~) to drink; to have, take (*liquids*); мне п. хо́чется I am thirsty; п. за (+*a.*), за здоро́вье (+*g.*) to drink to, to the health (of); п. го́рькую, п. мёртвую (*coll.*) to drink hard; как п. дать (*coll.*) for sure, as sure as eggs is eggs; как п. дать придёт he will come for sure.

пить|ё, я́, *n.* **1.** drinking. **2.** drink, beverage.

питьев|о́й, *adj.* drinkable; ~а́я вода́ drinking water; ~а́я со́да household soda.

пифагоре́|ец, йца, *m.* Pythagorean.

пифагоре́йский, *adj.* Pythagorean.

пифаго́ров, *adj.* ~а теоре́ма Pythagoras' theorem.

пифи|я, и, *f.* (*hist.*) the Pythian, Pythoness.

пих|а́ть, а́ю, *impf.* (*of* ~ну́ть) (*coll.*) **1.** to push; to elbow, jostle. **2.** to shove, cram; п. ве́щи в чемода́н to cram things into a suitcase.

пиха́|ться, юсь, *impf.* (*coll.*) to push; to elbow, shove; to jostle one another.

пих|ну́ть, ну́, нёшь, *pf. of* ~а́ть.

пи́хт|а, ы, *f.* fir(-tree) (*Abies*); европе́йская п. silver fir (*Abies alba, Abies pectinata*).

пи́хт|овый, *adj. of* ~а.

пиццика́то = пиччика́то.

пи́чка|ть, ю, *impf.* (*of* на~) (*coll.*) to stuff, cram (*also fig.*).

пичу́г|а, и, *f.* (*coll.*) bird.

пичу́жк|а, и, *f.* (*coll.*) = пичу́га.

пиччика́то, *indecl.*, *n.*, *and adv.* (*mus.*) pizzicato.

пи́шущ|ий, *pres. part. act. of* писа́ть *and adj.*; п. э́ти стро́ки the present writer; ~ая бра́тия (*coll.*) the literary fraternity; ~ая маши́нка typewriter.

пи́щ|а, и, *no pl., f.* food; п. для ума́ food for thought; mental pabulum; дава́ть ~у слу́хам to feed rumours.

пища́л|ь, и, *f.* (*hist.*) (h)arquebus.

пищ|а́ть, у́, и́шь, *impf.* (*of* пи́скнуть) **1.** to squeak; (*of chicks, etc.*) to cheep, peep. **2.** (*fig., coll.*) to whine; to sing (*of kettle, etc.*).

пищеваре́ни|е, я, *n.* digestion; расстро́й-ство ~я indigestion, dyspepsia.

пищевари́тельный, *adj.* digestive; п. кана́л alimentary canal.

пищеви́к, а́, *m.* worker in food industry.

пищево́д, а, *m.* (*anat.*) oesophagus, gullet.

пищ|ево́й, *adj. of* ~а; ~евы́е проду́кты foodstuffs; eatables; ~евая́ промы́шлен-ность food industry.

пи́щик, а, *m.* **1.** (*hunting*) pipe for luring birds. **2.** (*mus.*) reed. **3.** buzzer.

пия́вк|а, и, *f.* leech; ста́вить ~и (*med.*) to apply leeches; пристава́ть как п. (*fig., coll.*) to stick like a leech.

плав, а, *m.* на ~у́ afloat.

пла́вани|е, я, *n.* 1. swimming. 2. sailing; navigation; су́дно да́льнего ~я ocean-going ship; отпра́виться в п., пусти́ться в п. to put out to sea.

пла́вательн|ый, *adj.* swimming; natatorial, natatory; п. бассе́йн swimming pool; ~ая перепо́нка (*of birds, bats*) web; (*of tortoise*) flipper; п. пузы́рь (fish-)sound, swimming-bladder.

пла́ва|ть, ю, *impf.* 1. *indet. of* плыть; ме́лко п. (*fig., coll.*) to be a shallow person. 2. to float (*have the property of floating*).

пла́в|ень, ня, *m.* (*tech.*) flux, fusing agent.

плави́к, а́, *m.* (*min.*) fluorspar.

плавико́в|ый, *adj. of* плави́к; ~ая кислота́ (*chem.*) hydrofluoric acid; п. шпат (*min.*) fluorspar.

плави́льник, а, *m.* (*tech.*) crucible.

плави́льн|ый, *adj.* (*tech.*) melting, smelting; п. горн smelting hearth; п. жар fusion temperature; ~ая печь smelting furnace; п. ти́гель crucible, melting pot.

плави́л|ьня, ьни, *g. pl.* ~ен, *f.* foundry, smeltery.

плави́льщик, а, *m.* founder, smelter.

пла́в|ить, лю, ишь, *impf.* to melt, smelt; to fuse.

пла́в|иться, ится, *impf.* to melt; to fuse (*intrans.*).

пла́вк|а, и, *f.* fusing; fusion.

пла́в|ки, ок, *no sing.* swimming trunks.

пла́вк|ий, *adj.* fusible; п. предохрани́тель, п. штепсель, ~ая про́бка (*electr.*) fuse; ~ая про́волока fuse wire.

пла́вкост|ь, и, *f,* fusibility.

плавле́ни|е, я, *n.* melting, fusion; то́чка ~я melting point.

пла́вленый, *adj.* п. сыр processed cheese.

пла́вн|и, ей, *no sing.* (*reed-covered*) flats (*on lower reaches of rivers Dnieper, Kuban, etc.*).

плавни́к, а́, *m.* fin; flipper; брюшно́й п. abdominal fin; грудно́й п. thoracic fin; спинно́й п. dorsal fin; хвостово́й п. caudal fin.

плавн|о́й, *adj.* ~а́я сеть drift net.

пла́вност|ь, и, *f.* smoothness; facility.

пла́в|ный (~ен, ~на), *adj.* 1. smooth; ~ная речь flowing speech; п. стих rhythmical verse. 2. (*ling.*) liquid.

плаву́н, а́, *m.* (*geol.*) quick ground.

плаву́н|е́ц, ца́, *m.* жук-п. (*zool.*) water-tiger.

плаву́нчик, а, *m.* (*orn.*) phalarope.

плаву́чест|ь, и, *f.* buoyancy.

плаву́ч|ий, *adj.* 1. floating; ~ая льди́на ice-floe; п. маяк lightship, light-vessel; ~ая бурова́я устано́вка sea drilling rig. 2. buoyant.

плагиа́т, а, *m.* plagiarism.

плагиа́тор, а, *m.* plagiarist.

плаз, а, *m.* (*shipbuilding*) loft.

пла́зм|а, ы, *f.* (*biol. and phys.*) plasma.

пла́кальщик, а, *m.* (*hired*) mourner, mute.

плака́т, а, *m.* placard; poster, bill.

плакати́ст, а, *m.* poster artist.

плака́т|ный, *adj. of* ~; ~ные кра́ски poster paints.

пла́|кать, чу, чешь, *impf.* 1. to weep, cry; п. навзры́д to sob; хоть ~чь! it is enough to make you weep!; ~кали де́нежки! (*coll.*) the money has simply vanished (*sc.* has been spent)! 2. to weep (for), cry (for); to mourn.

пла́|каться, чусь, чешься, *impf.* (*of* по~) (на+*a.*) to complain (of), lament; п. на свою́ судьбу́ to bemoan one's fate.

плакир|ова́ть, у́ю, *impf. and pf.* (*tech.*) to plate.

плакиро́вк|а, и, *f.* (*tech.*) plating.

пла́кс|а, ы, *m. and f.* (*coll.*) cry-baby.

плакси́в|ый (~, ~а), *adj.* (*coll.*) whining; (*fig.*) piteous, pathetic; п. ребёнок cry-baby; п. тон pathetic tone.

плаку́н-трав|а́, ы́, *f.* (*bot.*) purple loosestrife (*Lythrum salicaria*).

плаку́ч|ий, *adj.* weeping; ~ая и́ва weeping willow.

пламегаси́тел|ь, я, *m.* (*mil.*) 1. flash eliminator, flash-hider. 2. flash extinguisher,· anti-flash charge.

пламене́|ть, ю, *impf.* (*poet.*) to flame, blaze; п. стра́стью to burn with passion.

пла́менник, а, *m.* 1. (*poet.*) torch, flambeau. 2. (*bot.*) phlox.

пла́менност|ь, и, *f.* ardour.

пла́менн|ый, *adj.* 1. flaming, fiery; (*fig.*) ardent, burning. 2. (*tech.*) ~ая труба́ flue; ~ая печь flame furnace, reverbatory furnace; п. у́голь bituminous coal.

пла́мен|ь, и, *m.* (*obs., poet.*) = пла́мя.

пла́м|я, ени, *n.* flame; fire, blaze; вспы́хнуть ~енем to burst into flame.

план, а, *m.* 1. (*in var. senses*) plan; scheme; уче́бный п. curriculum; по ~у according to plan. 2. plane (*also fig.*); пере́дний п. foreground; за́дний п. background; кру́пный п. close-up (*in filming*); вы́двинуть на пе́рвый п. (*fig.*) to bring to the forefront.

плане́р, а, *m.* (*aeron.*) glider; п. самолёта airframe.

планери́зм, а, *m.* gliding.

планери́ст, а, *m.* glider-pilot.

планёр|ный, *adj. of* ~; п. спорт gliding.

плане́т|а, ы, *f.* 1. planet; больши́е ~ы major planets; ма́лые ~ы minor planets. 2. (the) planet (= Earth). 3. (*obs., coll.*) (bad) fortune.

планета́ри|й, я, *m.* planetarium.

планéт|ный, *adj. of* ~а; planetary.
планимéтр, **а**, *m.* (*surveying*) planimeter.
планиметр|и́ческий, *adj.* **1.** *of* ~. **2.** *of* ~ия.
планимéтри|я, **и**, *f.* (*math.*) plane geometry.
плани́ровани|е[1], **я**, *n.* planning; п. городóв town-planning.
плани́ровани|е[2], **я**, *n.* (*aeron.*) gliding; glide.
плани́р|овать[1], **ую**, *impf.* (*of* за~) to plan.
плани́р|овать[2], **ую**, *impf.* (*of* с~) (*aeron.*) to glide (down).
планир|овáть, **ýю**, *impf.* (*of* рас~) to lay out (*a park, etc.*).
планирóвк|а, **и**, *f.* laying out; lay-out.
планирóвщик, **а**, *m.* workman engaged in laying out (*park, etc.*).
планисфéр|а, **ы**, *f.* (*astron.*) planisphere.
плáнк|а, **и**, *f.* lath, slat.
планктóн, **а**, *m.* (*biol.*) plankton.
планктóн|ный, *adj. of* ~.
планови́к, **á**, *m.* planner.
плáновост|ь, **и**, *f.* planned character; development according to plan.
плáнов|ый, *adj.* **1.** planned, systematic; ~ое хозя́йство planned economy. **2.** planning; ~ая коми́ссия planning commission.
планомéрност|ь, **и**, *f.* systematic character, planned character.
планомéр|ный (~ен, ~на), *adj.* systematic, planned, regular.
плантáж, **а**, *m.* deep ploughing.
плантáтор, **а**, *m.* planter.
плантáци|я, **и**, *f.* plantation.
планшáйб|а, **ы**, *f.* (*tech.*) face plate.
планшéт, **а**, *m.* **1.** (*surveying*) plane-table; огневóй п. (*mil.*) artillery board. **2.** map--case. **3.** busk (*of corset*).
планши́р, **а**, *m.* (*naut.*) gunwale, top strake.
планши́р|ь, **я**, *m.* = ~.
пласт, **á**, *m.* layer; sheet; (*archit.*) course; (*geol.*) stratum, bed; лежáть ~óм to lie motionless; to be on one's back.
пластá|ть, **ю**, *impf.* to cut in layers.
плáстик, **а**, *m.* plastic (*material*).
плáстик|а, **и**, *f.* **1.** (*collect.*) the plastic arts. **2.** eurhythmics.
пластили́н, **а**, *m.* plasticine.
пласти́н|а, **ы**, *f.* plate.
пласти́нк|а, **и**, *f.* **1.** (*in var. senses*) plate; граммофóнная п. gramophone record; чувстви́тельная п. (*phot.*) sensitive plate. **2.** (*bot.*) blade, lamina.
пласти́нчатый, *adj.* lamellar, lamellate.
пласти́ческ|ий, *adj.* plastic; ~ая мáсса plastic; ~ая хирурги́я plastic surgery.
пласти́чност|ь, **и**, *f.* plasticity.
пласти́ч|ный, *adj.* **1.** plastic; supple, pliant. **2.** (~ен, ~на) rhythmical; fluent, flowing; ~ное движéние тéла rhythmical movement of the body; п. жест flowing gesture.

пластмáсс|а, **ы**, *f.* (*abbr. of* пласти́ческая мáсса) plastic.
пластмáсс|овый, *adj. of* ~а.
пласт|овáть, **ýю**, *impf.* **1.** to lay in layers. **2.** to cut in layers.
пластýн, **á**, *m.* (*hist.*) dismounted Cossack.
пластýн|ский, *adj. of* ~; переползáние по-~ски (*mil.*) the leopard crawl.
плáстыр|ь, **я**, *m.* **1.** (*med.*) plaster; вытяжнóй п. drawing plaster; ли́пкий п. sticking plaster. **2.** (*naut.*) collision mat.
плат, **а**, *m.* (*obs.*) = ~óк.
плáт|а, **ы**, *f.* **1.** pay; salary; зáработная п. wages. **2.** payment, charge; fee; входнáя п. entrance fee; п. за проéзд fare.
платáн, **а**, *m.* plane(-tree), platan.
платá|ть, **ю**, *impf.* (*of* за~) (*coll.*) to patch.
платёж, **á**, *m.* payment; налóженным ~óм cash on delivery; прекрати́ть ~й suspend payment(s).
платёжеспосóбност|ь, **и**, *f.* solvency.
платёжеспосóб|ный (~ен, ~на), *adj.* solvent.
платёж|ный, *adj. of* ~; п. балáнс balance of payments; ~ная вéдомость pay-sheet; pay-roll; п. день pay-day.
платéльщик, **а**, *m.* payer.
плáтин|а, **ы**, *f.* (*min.*) platinum.
плáтин|овый, *adj. of* ~а.
пла|ти́ть, **чý**, ~тишь, *impf.* (*of* за~) **1.** to pay; п. дань (+*d.*) to pay tribute (to); п. нали́чными to pay in cash, pay in ready money; п. натýрой to pay in kind. **2.** (*fig.*; +*i.* за+*a.*) to pay back, return; п. комý-н. услýгой за услýгу to make it up to someone, return a favour; п. комý-н. взаи́мностью to reciprocate someone's love.
пла|ти́ться, **чýсь**, ~тишься, *impf.* (*of* по~) (+*i.* за+*a.*) to pay (with for); п. жи́знью за свои́ оши́бки to pay for one's mistakes with one's life.
плáт|ный, *adj.* **1.** paid; requiring payment, chargeable; ~ое мéсто paid seat. **2.** paying; п. посети́тель paying guest.
платó, *indecl., n.* plateau.
плат|óк, **ká**, *m.* shawl; kerchief; носовóй п. (pocket) handkerchief.
платони́зм, **а**, *m.* Platonism.
платóник, **а**, *m.* Platonist.
платони́ческий, *adj.* (*philos.*) Platonic; (*fig.*) platonic.
платфóрм|а, **ы**, *f.* **1.** platform (*of railway station*). **2.** (open) goods truck. **3.** (*fig.*, *polit.*) platform.
плáть|е, **я**, *g. pl.* ~ев, *n.* **1.** clothes, clothing; вéрхнее п. outer garments. **2.** dress, gown, frock; вечéрнее п. evening dress.
плат|янóй, *adj. of* ~ье; п. шкаф wardrobe; ~янáя щётка clothes-brush.
плаýн, **á**, *m.* (*bot.*) lycopodium, wolf's-claw, club-moss.

плафо́н, а, *m.* 1. (*archit.*) plafond. 2. shade (*for lamp suspended from ceiling*).

пла́х|а, и, *f.* block; (*hist.*) executioner's block; взойти́ на ~у to mount the scaffold.

плац, а, о ~е, на ~у́, *m.* (*mil.*) parade-ground; уче́бный п. drill square.

плацда́рм, а, *m.* 1. (*mil.*) bridgehead; beachhead. 2. (*polit.*; *fig.*) base.

плаце́нт|а, ы, *f.* (*anat.*) placenta.

плацка́рт|а, ы, *f.* reserved seat *or* berth ticket.

плацка́рт|ный, *adj.* of ~а; п. ваго́н carriage with numbered reserved seats; ~ное ме́сто reserved seat.

плац-пара́д, а, *m.* (*mil.*) parade ground.

плач, а, *m.* 1. weeping, crying. 2. (*ceremonial*) wailing; keening. 3. lament.

плачёв|ный (~ен, ~на), *adj.* 1. mournful, sad; име́ть п. вид to be a sorry sight. 2. (*fig.*) lamentable, deplorable, sorry; в ~ном состоя́нии in a sad state, in a sorry plight.

плашко́ут, а, *m.* (*naut.*) lighter.

плашко́утный, *adj.* п. мост pontoon bridge.

плашмя́, *adv.* flat; flatways; prone; упа́сть п. to fall flat; уда́рить са́блей п. to strike with the flat of the sword.

плащ, а́, *m.* 1. cloak. 2. mackintosh, raincoat; waterproof cape.

плащани́ц|а, ы, *f.* (*eccl.*) shroud of Christ.

плащ-пала́тк|а, и, *f.* ground sheet.

плебе́|й, я, *m.* (*hist.*) plebeian.

плебе́йский, *adj.* plebeian.

плебисци́т, а, *m.* plebiscite.

плебс, а, (*collect.*; *hist.*) plebs.

плев|а́, ы́, *f.* (*anat.*) membrane, film, coat; де́вственная п. hymen; лёгочная п. pleura.

плева́тельниц|а, ы, *f.* spittoon.

плева́ть, плюю́, плюёшь, *impf.* (*of* плю́нуть) 1. to spit; to expectorate; п. в потоло́к (*fig.*, *joc.*) to idle, fritter away the time. 2. (на+а.; *coll.*) to spit (upon); not to care a rap about; им п. на всё they don't give a damn about anything.

плева́ться, плюю́сь, плюёшься, *impf.* (*coll.*) to spit.

пле́вел, а, *m.* (*bot.*) darnel, cockle; weed.

плев|о́к, ка́, *m.* 1. spit(tle). 2. (*med.*) sputum.

плевр|а́, ы, *f.* (*anat.*) pleura.

плеври́т, а, *m.* (*med.*) pleurisy.

плёв|ый, *adj.* (*coll.*) 1. worthless; rubbishy; п. челове́к good-for-nothing. 2. trifling, trivial; де́ло ~ое trifling matter.

плед, а, *m.* rug; plaid.

плейстоце́н, а, *m.* (*geol.*) pleistocene.

плейстоце́новый, *adj.* of ~.

племенно́й, *adj.* 1. tribal. 2. pedigree; п. скот pedigree cattle, bloodstock.

пле́м|я, ени, *pl.* ~ена́, ~ён, ~ена́м, *n.* 1.

tribe. 2. breed; на п. for breeding. 3. (*fig.*) tribe; breed, stock; пти́чье п. (*joc.*) the feathered tribe.

племя́нник, а, *m.* nephew.

племя́нниц|а, ы, *f.* niece.

плен, а, о ~е, в ~у́, *m.* captivity; быть в ~у́ to be in captivity; взять в п. to take prisoner; попа́сть в п. (к) to be taken prisoner (by).

плена́рный, *adj.* plenary.

плене́ни|е, я, *n.* (*obs.*) capture; captivity.

плени́тельност|ь, и, *f.* fascination.

плени́тел|ьный (~ен, ~ьна), *adj.* captivating, fascinating, charming.

плен|и́ть, ю́, и́шь, *pf.* (*of* ~я́ть) 1. (*obs.*) to take prisoner, take captive. 2. (*fig.*) to captivate, fascinate, charm.

плен|и́ться, ю́сь, и́шься, *pf.* (*of* ~я́ться) (+*i.*) to be captivated (by), be fascinated (by).

плёнк|а, и, *f.* (*in var. senses*) film; pellicle.

пле́нник, а, *m.* (*obs. or fig.*) prisoner, captive.

пле́нн|ый, *adj.* captive; *as noun* п., ~ого, *m.* captive, prisoner.

плён|очный, *adj.* of ~ка; filmy.

пле́нум, а, *m.* plenum, plenary session.

плен|я́ть(ся), я́ю(сь), *impf.* of ~и́ть(ся).

плеона́зм, а, *m.* (*lit.*) pleonasm.

плеонасти́ческий, *adj.* (*lit.*) pleonastic.

плёс, а, *m.* reach (*of river*); stretch (*of river or lake*).

пле́сенный, *adj.* mouldy, musty.

пле́сен|ь, и, *f.* mould.

плеск, а, *m.* splash; п. вёсел plash of oars; п. волн lapping of waves.

пле|ска́ть, щу́, ~щешь, *impf.* (*of* ~сну́ть) to splash; to plash; to lap; п. о бе́рег to lap against the shore; п. на кого́-н. водо́й to splash someone (with water).

пле|ска́ться, щу́сь, ~щешься, *impf.* to splash; to lap.

пле́снев|еть, еет, *impf.* (*of* за~) to grow mouldy, grow musty.

плес|ну́ть, ну́, нёшь, *pf.* of ~ка́ть.

пле|сти́, ту́, тёшь, *past* ~л, ~ла́, *impf.* (*of* с~) to braid, plait; to weave, tat; п. вено́к to make a wreath; п. корзи́ну to make a basket; п. небыли́цы (*coll.*, *pejor.*) to spin yarns; п. паути́ну to spin a web; п. се́ти to net; п. вздор, п. чепуху́ (*coll.*, *pejor.*) to talk rubbish.

пле|сти́сь, ту́сь, тёшься, *past* ~лся, ~ла́сь, *impf.* (*coll.*) to drag oneself along, trudge; п. в хвосте́ (*fig.*) to lag behind.

плете́ни|е, я, *n.* 1. braiding, plaiting; п. слове́с (*iron.*) verbiage. 2. wicker-work.

плете́нк|а, и, *f.* 1. (wicker) basket. 2. hurdle.

плетён|ый, *adj.* wattled, wicker; ~ая корзи́нка wicker basket.

плет|е́нь, ня́, *m.* hurdle; wattle fencing.

плётк|а, и, *f.* lash.

плет|ь, и, *pl.* ~и, ~éй, *f.* lash.

плечев|óй, *adj.* (*anat.*) humeral; ~áя кость humerus.

плéчик|и, ов, *no sing.* (*coll.*) (coat-)hanger.

плéчик|о, а, *pl.* ~и, ~ов, *n.* 1. shoulder--strap. 2. *dim. of* плечó.

плечúст|ый (~, ~а), *adj.* broad-shouldered.

плеч|ó, á, *pl.* ~и, ~, ~áм, *n.* 1. shoulder; лéвое, прáвое п. вперёд! (*mil.*) right wheel, left wheel!; всё э́то у меня́ за ~áми (*fig.*) all that is behind me; ~óм к ~ý shoulder to shoulder; взять нá ~и to shoulder; на п.! (*mil.*) slope arms!; на ~áх проти́вника on top of, on the heels of the enemy; имéть гóлову на ~áх to have a good head on one's shoulders; вы́нести на свои́х ~áх to bear (the full brunt of); э́то емý не по ~ý he is not up to it; с ~á straight from the shoulder; (слóвно) горá с мои́х ~ свали́-лась that's a weight off my mind; с ~ долóй! that's done, thank goodness; с чужóго ~á (*of clothing*) worn, second-hand; пожáть ~áми to shrug one's shoulders. 2. (*anat.*) upper arm, humerus. 3. (*tech.*) arm.

плешúве|ть, ю, *impf.* (*of* о~) to grow bald.

плешúв|ый (~, ~а), *adj.* bald.

плешúн|а, ы, *f.* bald patch.

плеш|ь, и, *f.* bald patch; bare patch.

плея́д|ы, ~, *sing.* ~а, ~ы, *f.* 1. П. (*astron.*) Pleiades. 2. (*sing.; fig.*) Pleiad; galaxy.

пли, *interj.* (= палй) (*mil.*; *obs.*) fire!

плúнтус, а, *m.* 1. plinth. 2. skirting board.

плиоцéн, а, *m.* (*geol.*) pl(e)iocene.

плис, а, *m.* velveteen.

плúс|овый, *adj. of* ~.

плиссé, *indecl.*, *n.* pleat(s); *as adj.* pleated; юбка п. pleated skirt.

плиссир|овáть, ýю, *impf.* (*no pf.*) to pleat.

плиссирóвк|а, и, *f.* pleating.

плит|á, ы́, *pl.* ~ы, *f.* 1. plate, slab; flag-(stone); моги́льная п. gravestone, tomb-stone; мрáморная п. marble slab. 2. stove; cooker.

плúтк|а, и, *f.* 1. *dim. of* плитá; tile, (thin) slab; крáски в ~ax solid water-colours; п. шоколáда bar of chocolate. 2. stove; cooker.

плитня́к, á, *m.* flagstone.

плúт|очный, *adj. of* ~ка; п. пол tiled floor.

плúц|а, ы, *f.* 1. bailer. 2. (*obs.*) blade (*of paddle-wheel*).

плов, а, *m.* (*cul.*) = пилáв.

плов|éц, цá, *m.* swimmer.

пловýчий, *adj.* = плавýчий.

плод, á, *m.* fruit (*also fig.*); приноси́ть п. to bear fruit; запрéтный п. (*fig.*) forbidden fruit. 2. (*biol.*) foetus.

пло|ди́ть, жý, ди́шь, *impf.* (*of* рас~) to pro-duce, procreate; to engender (*also fig.*).

пло|ди́ться, жýсь, ди́шься, *impf.* (*of* рас~) to multiply; to propagate.

плóдный, *adj.* 1. (*biol.*) fertile. 2. fertilized.

плодови́тост|ь, и, *f.* fruitfulness, fertility, fecundity.

плодови́т|ый (~, ~а), *adj.* fruitful, prolific (*also fig.*); fertile, fecund; п. писáтель pro-lific writer.

плодовóдств|о, а, *n.* fruit-growing.

плодовóд|ческий, *adj. of* ~ство.

плодóв|ый, *adj. of* плод; ~ое дéрево fruit--tree; п. сад orchard.

плодоли́стик, а, *m.* (*bot.*) carpel.

плодонóжк|а, и, *f.* (*bot.*) fruit stem.

плодоно|си́ть, ~си́т, *impf.* (*no pf.*) to bear fruit.

плодонóс|ный (~ен, ~на), *adj.* fruit-bear-ing, fruitful.

плодоóвощ|и, éй, *no sing.* fruit and vegetables.

плодоовощнóй, *adj.* fruit and vegetable.

плодорóди|е, я, *n.* fertility, fecundity.

плодорóд|ный (~ен, ~на), *adj.* fertile, fecund.

плодосмéнн|ый, *adj.* ~ая систéма (*agric.*) rotation of crops.

плодотвóр|ный (~ен, ~на), *adj.* fruitful.

плоён|ый, *adj.* (*obs.*) pleated; ~ые вóлосы waved hair.

пло|и́ть, ю́, и́шь, *impf.* (*of* на~) (*obs.*) to pleat; to wave (*hair*).

плóмб|а, ы, *f.* 1. (*lead*) stamp, seal. 2. stop-ping, filling (*for tooth*); стáвить ~у в зуб to stop, fill a tooth.

пломби́р, а, *m.* 'plombières' (*ice-cream with candied fruit*).

пломбир|овáть, ýю, *impf.* 1. (*pf.* о~) to seal. 2. (*pf.* за~) to stop, fill (*a tooth*).

плóс|кий (~ок, ~кá, ~ко), *adj.* 1. flat; plane; ~кая грудь flat chest; ~кая повéрх-ность plane surface; ~кая стопá (*med.*) flat-foot. 2. (*fig.*) trivial, tame; ~кая шýтка feeble joke.

плоскогóрь|е, я, *n.* plateau; tableland.

плоскогрýд|ый (~, ~а), *adj.* flat-chested.

плоскогýбц|ы, ев, *no sing.* pliers.

плоскодóнк|а, и, *f.* flat-bottomed boat; punt.

плоскодóнный, *adj.* flat-bottomed.

плоскостнóй, *adj.* plane.

плоскостóпи|е, я, *n.* (*med.*) flat-foot, flat feet.

плóскост|ь, и, *pl.* ~и, ~éй, *f.* 1. flatness. 2. plane (*also fig.*); наклóнная п. inclined plane; кати́ться по наклóнной ~и (*fig.*) to go downhill. 3. platitude, triviality.

плот, á, *m.* raft.

плотв|á, ы́, *f.* (*fish*) roach.

плоти́н|а, ы, *f.* dam; weir; dike, dyke.

плотнé|ть, ю, *impf.* (*of* по~) to grow stout.

плóтник, а, *m.* carpenter.

плóтнича|ть, ю, *impf.* to work as a carpenter.

плóтничеств|о, а, *n.* carpentry.

плóтничный, *adj.* carpentering.

плóтно, *adv.* 1. close(ly), tightly; п. заколотить дверь to board up, nail up a door. 2. п. поéсть to have a square meal, eat heartily.

плóтност|ь, и, *f.* 1. thickness; compactness; solidity, strength; п. населéния density of population. 2. (*phys.*) density.

плóт|ный (~ен, ~нá, ~но), *adj.* 1. thick; compact; dense (*also phys.*); п. огóнь (*mil.*) heavy fire. 2. solid, strong; (*of a person*; *coll.*) thick-set, solidly built. 3. tightly-filled. 4. (*coll.*; *of a meal*) square, hearty.

плотовóд, а, *m.* rafter, raftsman (*floating timber on rafts*).

плотовщи́к, á, *m.* rafter, raftsman (*floating timber or ferrying passengers on rafts*).

плотоя́д|ный (~ен, ~на), *adj.* 1. carnivorous. 2. lustful; voluptuous.

плóтский, *adj.* (*arch.*) carnal, fleshly.

плот|ь, и, *f.* flesh; во ~й in the flesh; п. от ~и flesh of one's flesh; п. и кровь (one's) flesh and blood; облéчь в п. и кровь to embody; крáйняя п. (*anat.*) foreskin, prepuce.

плóхо, 1. *adv.* bad(ly); ill; п. вести́ себя́ to behave badly; п. обращáться (с+*i.*) to ill-treat, ill-use; чýвствовать себя́ п. to feel unwell, feel bad; п. пáхнуть to smell bad; п. кóнчить (*coll.*) to come to a bad end; п. лежáть (*coll.*) to lie in temptation's way; п.-п. (*coll.*) at (the very) least. 2. *as indecl. noun, n.* bad mark; я опя́ть получи́л п. по áлгебре I have got a bad mark in algebra again.

плоховáто, *adv.* (*coll.*) rather badly, not too well.

плоховáт|ый (~, ~а), *adj.* (*coll.*) rather bad, not too good.

плох|óй (~, ~á, ~о), *adj.* (*in var. senses*) bad; poor; ~áя погóда bad weather; ~ое настроéние bad mood, low spirits; п. рабóтник a poor workman; ~ое пищеварéние poor digestion; ~ое утешéние poor consolation; с ним шýтки ~и he is not one to be trifled with; (*as pred.*) емý óчень ~о he is very bad, he is in a very bad way.

плошá|ть, ю, *impf.* (*of* с~) (*coll.*) to make a mistake, slip up.

плóшк|а, и, *f.* 1. (*coll.*) flat dish, saucer. 2. lampion.

площáдк|а, и, *f.* 1. ground, area; дéтская п. children's playground; спорти́вная п. sports ground; строи́тельная п. building site; тéннисная п. tennis court. 2. landing (*on staircase*). 3. platform; пусковáя п. launching pad (*of rocket*).

площадн|óй, *adj.* vulgar, coarse; ~áя брань Billingsgate language.

плóщад|ь, и, *pl.* ~и, ~éй, *f.* 1. (*math.*) area. 2. area; space; жилáя п. living space, floor-space; посевнáя п. sown area, area under crops. 3. square; базáрная п. market-place.

плó|ще, *comp. of* ~ский *and* ~ско.

плуг, а, *pl.* ~й, *m.* plough.

плугáр|ь, я́, *m.* ploughman.

плуговóй, *adj. of* плуг.

плýнжер, а, *m.* (*tech.*) plunger.

плут, á, *m.* 1. cheat, swindler, knave. 2. (*joc.*) rogue.

плутá|ть, ю, *impf.* (*coll.*) to stray.

плути́шк|а, и, *m.* (*coll.*) little rogue, mischievous imp.

плýтн|и, ей, *sing.* ~я, ~и, *f.* (*coll.*) cheating, swindling; tricks.

плутовáт|ый (~, ~а), *adj.* cunning.

плут|овáть, ýю, *impf.* (*of* на~ *and* с~) (*coll.*) to cheat, swindle.

плутóвк|а, и, *f. of* плут, плути́шка.

плутовск|óй, *adj.* 1. knavish; ~ие приéмы knavish tricks. 2. (*coll.*) roguish, mischievous. 3. (*lit.*) picaresque.

плутовств|ó, á, *n.* cheating; trickery, knavery.

плутокрáт, а, *m.* plutocrat.

плутократи́ческий, *adj.* plutocratic.

плутокрáти|я, и, *f.* plutocracy.

плывýн, á, *m.* = плавýн.

плывýчий, *adj.* flowing, deliquescent.

плы|ть, вý, вёшь, *past* ~л, ~лá, ~ло, *impf.* (*det. of* плáвать) 1. to swim; to float; п. стóя to tread water; п. комý-н. в рýки (*fig.*, *coll.*) to drop into someone's lap; всё ~ло пéред мои́ми глазáми everything was swimming before my eyes. 2. to sail; п. на вéслах to row; п. под парусáми to sail, go under sail; п. по течéнию to go down stream; (*fig.*) to go with the stream; п. прóтив течéния to go up stream; (*fig.*) to go against the stream; п. по вóле волн to drift.

плювиóметр, а, *m.* pluviometer.

плюгáв|ый (~, ~а), *adj.* (*coll.*) shabby, mean; despicable.

плюмáж, а, *m.* plume (*on hat*).

плюн|уть, у, ешь, *pf. of* плевáть; п. нéкуда no room to swing a cat.

плюрали́зм, а, *m.* (*philos.*) pluralism.

плюралисти́ческий, *adj.* (*philos.*) pluralistic.

плюрáльный, *adj.* п. вóтум (*leg.*) plural vote.

плюс, а, *m.* 1. plus; *as connective in math. expressions* два п. два равнó четырём two plus two equals four. 2. (*fig.*, *coll.*) advantage; э́тот проéкт не без ~ов this scheme has some advantages.

плюс|нá, ны́, *pl.* ~ны, ~ен, ~нам, *f.* (*anat.*) metatarsus.

плюс|ова́ть, у́ю, *impf.* (*tech.*) to dip, immerse.

плюс|овый, *adj. of* ~; п. гандика́п (*sport*) plus handicap.

плюх|ать(ся), аю(сь), *impf. of* ~нуть(ся).

плюх|нуть, ну, нешь, *pf.* (*of* ~ать) (*coll.*) to flop (down), plump (down); п. в кре́сло to flop into an arm-chair.

плюх|нуться, нусь, нешься, *pf.* (*of* ~аться) = ~нуть.

плюш, а, *m.* plush.

плюш|евый, *adj. of* ~.

плюшк|а, и, *f.* (*coll.*) bun.

плющ, а́, *m.* ivy; вью́щийся п. tree ivy.

плющи́льн|ый, *adj.* (*tech.*) flattening, laminating; п. мо́лот planing hammer, flatter; п. стано́к flatting mill, rolling mill; ~ая маши́на upsetting machine.

плющ|ить, у, ишь, *impf.* (*of* с~) (*tech.*) to flatten, laminate.

пляж, а, *m.* beach.

пляс, а, *no pl.*, *m.* (*coll.*) dance; пусти́ться в п. to break into a dance.

пля́ск|а, и, *f.* dance; dancing (*esp. folk-dancing*); п. свято́го Ви́та (*med.*) St. Vitus's dance, chorea.

пля|са́ть, шу́, ~шешь, *impf.* (*of* с~) to dance.

пляс|о́й, *adj.* dancing; *as noun* ~а́я, ~о́й, *f.* dance tune.

плясу́н, а́, *m.* (*coll.*) dancer; кана́тный п. rope-dancer.

пневма́тик, а, *m.* pneumatic tire.

пневма́тик|а, и, *f.* pneumatics.

пневмати́ческий, *adj.* pneumatic.

пневмоко́кк, а, *m.* (*med.*) pneumococcus.

пневмони́|я, и, *f.* pneumonia.

пневмото́ракс, а, *m.* (*med.*) pneumothorax.

пни́ст|ый (~, ~а), *adj. of* пень.

пнуть, пну, пнёшь, *pf.* (*of* пина́ть) (*coll.*) to kick.

по, *prep.* I. +*d.* 1. on; along; идти́ по траве́ to walk on the grass; спусти́ться по верёвке to come down on a rope; е́хать по у́лице to go along the street; идти́ по следа́м (+*g.*) to follow in the tracks (of); хло́пнуть по спине́ to slap on the back; по всему́, по всей all over. 2. round, about (*or not translated*); ходи́ть по магази́нам to go round the shops; ходи́ть по ко́мнате to pace the room; размести́ть войска́ по го́роду to quarter troops about the town. 3. by, on, over (*sc. some means of communication*); по во́здуху by air; по желе́зной доро́ге by rail, by train; по по́чте by post; по ра́дио on the wireless, over the radio; по телефо́ну on, over the telephone; переда́ть по ра́дио to broadcast. 4. according to; by; in accordance with; по пра́ву by right(s); по расписа́нию according to schedule; по

статье́ зако́на according to the letter of the law; жени́ться по любви́ to marry for love; звать по и́мени to call by first name; рабо́тать по пла́ну to work according to plan; су́дя по результа́там judging by results; по мне in my opinion, in my view, as far as I am concerned; жить по сре́дствам to live within one's means; по Плато́ну according to Plato. 5. by, in (= *in respect of*); по профе́ссии by profession; по положе́нию by one's position; ex officio; по происхожде́нию он армяни́н he is an Armenian by descent, he is of Armenian origin; лу́чший по ка́честву better in quality; това́рищ по ору́жию comrade in arms; това́рищ по шко́ле school-mate; ро́дственник по ма́тери a relative on one's mother's side. 6. at, on, in (= *in the field of*); чемпио́н по ша́хматам champion at chess, chess champion; ле́кции по европе́йской исто́рии lectures on European history; специали́ст по я́дерной фи́зике specialist in (on) nuclear physics. 7. by (reason of); on account of; from; по боле́зни on account of sickness; по рассе́янности from absentmindedness; его́ прости́ли по мо́лодости лет he was pardoned by reason of his youth; по счастли́вому стече́нию обстоя́тельств by a happy conjunction of circumstances. 8. (*indicating the object of an action or feeling*) at, for (*or not translated*); стреля́ть по проти́внику to fire at the enemy; охо́та по кру́пному зве́рю big game hunting; скуча́ть по де́тям to miss one's children; тоска́ по до́му, по ро́дине homesickness; по а́дресу (+*g.*) to the address (of); э́то по его́ а́дресу (*fig.*) this is meant for him. 9. (*in temporal phrases*) on; in; по понеде́льникам on Mondays; по пра́здникам on holidays; она́ рабо́тает по утра́м she works (in the) mornings; я не вида́л её по це́лым неде́лям I did not see her for weeks at a time; он прие́дет по весне́ he will come in the spring.

II. +*d. or a. of cardinal num. forms distributive num.* (+*d.*, *but also* +*a.*, *esp. in coll. usage*) по одному́ (одно́й); по пяти́, по шести́, *etc.*; по оди́ннадцати, *etc.*; по двадцати́, *etc.*; по ста; по пятисо́т, *etc.*; по полтора́ (полторы́); (+*a.*) по́ два (две), по́ три, по четы́ре; по две́сти, по три́ста, по четы́реста; да́йте им по (*sc.* одному́) я́блоку give them an apple each; мы получи́ли по три фу́нта we received three pounds each; по рублю́ шту́ка one rouble each; по де́сять (десяти́) рубле́й шту́ка ten roubles each; по́ два, по́ двое in twos, two by two.

III. +*a.* 1. to, up to; по по́яс в воде́ up to the waist in water; за́нят по го́рло up to one's eyes in work; по́ уши в долга́х up to one's ears in debt; по́ уши влюблён head over heels in love; по сего́дня up to today; по пе́рвое ма́я up to (and including) the first of May; по сю (ту) сто́рону on this (that) side. 2. (*following verbs of motion*; *coll.*) for (= *to fetch*, *to get*); идти́ по́ воду to go for water.

IV. +*p.* 1. on, after; по истече́нии сро́ка on expiry of the term set; по оконча́нии рабо́ты after work; по прибы́тии on arrival; по рассмотре́нии on examination. 2. (*after verbs of grieving, mourning, etc.*) for; пла́кать по му́же to mourn (for) one's husband; носи́ть тра́ур по ком-н. to be in mourning for someone. 3. по нём, *etc.*, as he, *etc.*, likes, is used.

по-[1] *as verbal prefix.* 1. *forms perfective aspect.* 2. *indicates action of short duration or of incomplete character, as* порабо́тать to do a little work; поспа́ть to have a sleep. 3. (+*suffixes* -ыва-, -ива-) *indicates action repeated at intervals or of indet. duration, as* позва́нивать to keep ringing.

по-[2] +*d. of adj. or ending* -ски *forms adv. indicating* 1. *manner of action, conduct, etc., as* жить по-ста́рому to live in the old style; рабо́тать по-това́рищески to work in a comradely fashion. 2. *use of given language, as* говори́ть по-ру́сски to speak Russian. 3. *accordance with opinion or wish, as* по-мо́ему in my opinion; пусть бу́дет по-ва́шему (let it be) as you wish.

по-[3] *modifies comp. adj. or adv., as* погро́мче a little louder.

поаккордн|ый, *adj.* ~ая пла́та piece-work rate.

побагрове́|ть, ю, *pf. of* багрове́ть.

поба́ива|ться, юсь, *impf.* (+*g. or inf.*; *coll.*) to be rather afraid.

поба́лива|ть, ю, *impf.* (*coll.*) to ache a little; to ache on and off.

по-ба́рски, *adv.* like a lord.

побасёнк|а, и, *f.* (*coll.*) tale, story.

побе́г[1], а, *m.* flight; escape.

побе́г[2], а, *m.* (*bot.*) sprout, shoot; sucker; set; graft.

побе́га|ть, ю, *pf.* to run a little, have a run.

побегу́шк|и: быть у кого́-н. на ~ах (*coll.*) to run errands for someone; (*fig.*) to be at someone's beck and call.

побе́д|а, ы, *f.* victory; война́ до по́лной ~ы total war; одержа́ть ~у to gain a victory.

победи́тел|ь, я, *m.* victor, conqueror; (*sport*) winner.

побед|и́ть, и́шь, *pf.* (*of* побежда́ть) to conquer, vanquish; to defeat, win a victory (over); (*fig.*) to master, overcome.

побе́дный, *adj.* victorious, triumphant.

победоно́с|ный (~ен, ~на), *adj.* victorious, triumphant.

побежа́лост|ь, и, *f.* (*chem.*, *tech.*) iridescence; цвет ~и oxide tint.

побе|жа́ть, гу́, жи́шь, гу́т, *pf.* 1. *pf. of* бежа́ть. 2. to break into a run.

побежда́|ть, ю, *impf. of* победи́ть.

побе́жк|а, и, *f.* pace, gait.

побеле́|ть, ю, *pf. of* беле́ть.

побел|и́ть, ю́, ~и́шь, *pf. of* бели́ть 2.

побе́лк|а, и, *f.* whitewashing.

побере́жный, *adj.* coastal.

побере́жь|е, я, *n.* coast, seaboard, littoral.

побере́|чь, гу́, жёшь, гу́т, *past* ~г, ~гла́, *pf.* (*coll.*) to look after, take care (of); п. здоро́вье to take care of one's health; ~ги́ мои́ ве́щи до моего́ возвраще́ния look after my things until I come back.

побере́|чься, гу́сь, жёшься, гу́тся, *past* ~гся, ~гла́сь, *pf.* to take care of oneself; ~ги́сь! mind out!

побесе́д|овать, ую, *pf.* to have a (little) talk, have a chat.

побеспоко́|ить, ю, ишь, *pf. of* беспоко́ить 2; позво́льте вас п. may I trouble you?

побеспоко́|иться, юсь, ишься, *pf.* 1. *pf. of* беспоко́иться 2. 2. to be rather worried.

побира́|ться, юсь, *impf.* (*coll.*) to beg, live by begging.

побиру́шк|а, и, *m. and f.* (*coll.*) beggar.

поб|и́ть, ью, ьёшь, *pf.* 1. *pf. of* бить 1, 2; п. реко́рд to break a record. 2. (*of rain, hail, etc.*) to beat down; (*of frost*) to nip. 3. to break, smash (*a number of*). 4. to kill (*a number of*).

поб|и́ться, ьётся, *pf.* 1. *pf. of* би́ться. 2. to break.

поблагодар|и́ть, ю́, и́шь, *pf. of* благодари́ть.

побла́жк|а, и, *f.* indulgence; allowance(s); де́лать ~у (+*d.*) to indulge, make allowance(s) (for).

побледне́|ть, ю, *pf. of* бледне́ть.

поблёклый, *adj.* faded; withered.

поблёк|нуть, ну, нешь, *past* ~, ~ла, *pf. of* блёкнуть.

поблёскива|ть, ю, *impf.* to gleam.

побли́зости, *adv.* near at hand, hereabout(s); п. (от) near (to).

побож|и́ться, у́сь, и́шься, *pf. of* божи́ться.

побо́|и, ев, *no sing.* beating, blows; терпе́ть п. to take a beating.

побо́ищ|е, а, *n.* slaughter, carnage; bloody battle; ледо́вое п. *see* ледо́вый.

поболта́|ть, ю, *pf.* (*coll.*) to have a chat.

побо́рник, а, *m.* champion, upholder.

побор|о́ть, ю́, ~ешь, *pf.* to overcome; to fight down; to beat (*in wrestling*).

побо́р|ы, ов, *sing.* ~, ~а, *m.* requisitions; extortion.

побо́чн|ый, *adj.* side; secondary; collateral; п. эффе́кт side effect; п. насле́дник col-

lateral heir; п. проду́кт by-product; ~ая
рабо́та side-line; п. сын natural son.

побо|я́ться, ю́сь, и́шься, *pf.* (+*g. or inf.*) to
be afraid; он хоте́л возрази́ть, да ~я́лся
he wanted to raise an objection but did not
venture to.

побран|и́ть, ю́, и́шь, *pf.* to give a scolding,
tick off.

побран|и́ться, ю́сь, и́шься, *pf.* (с+*i.*; *coll.*)
to have a quarrel, have words (with).

побрата́|ться, юсь, *pf. of* брата́ться.

побрати́м, а, *m.* 1. (*obs.*) sworn brother. 2.
twin(ned) town.

побрати́мств|о, а, *n.* (*obs.*) sworn brotherhood.

по-бра́тски, *adv.* like a brother; fraternally.

по|бра́ть, беру́, берёшь, *past* ~бра́л,
~брала́, ~бра́ло, *pf.* (*coll.*) to take (*a quantity of*); чёрт тебя́ ~бери́, чёрт бы тебя́
~бра́л! the devil take you!

побре́зга|ть, ю, *pf. of* бре́згать; не ~йте!
(*coll.*; *polite form of invitation*) make yourself
free!

побре|сти́, ду́, дёшь, *past* ~л, ~ла́, *pf.* to
plod.

побр|и́ть(ся), е́ю(сь), *pf. of* бри́ть(ся).

побро|ди́ть[1], жу́, ~дишь, *pf.* to wander for
some time.

побро|ди́ть[2], жу́, ~дишь, *pf.* to ferment for
some time.

поброса́|ть, ю, *pf.* 1. to throw up; to throw
about. 2. to desert, abandon.

побря́к|ать, аю, *pf.* (*of* ~ивать) (+*i.*; *coll.*)
to rattle.

побря́кива|ть, ю, *impf. of* побря́кать.

побряку́шк|а, и, *f.* (*coll.*) trinket; rattle.

побуди́тельн|ый, *adj.* stimulating; ~ая
причи́на motive, incentive; ~ые сре́дства
stimulants.

побу|ди́ть[1], жу́, ~дишь, *pf.* 1. to try to
wake. 2. to wake, rouse.

побу|ди́ть[2], жу́, ~ди́шь, *pf.* (*of* ~жда́ть) (к
or +*inf.*) to induce (to), impel (to), prompt
(to), spur (to); что ~ди́ло вас уйти́? what
made you go?

побу́дк|а, и, *f.* (*mil.*) reveille.

побужда́|ть, ю, *impf. of* побуди́ть.

побужде́ни|е, я, *n.* motive; inducement;
incentive; по со́бственному ~ю of one's
own accord.

побуре́|ть, ю, *pf. of* буре́ть.

побыва́льщин|а, ы, *f.* (*obs.*) narration; true
story.

побыва́|ть, ю, *pf.* 1. to have been, have
visited; он ~л всю́ду he has been everywhere; в про́шлом году́ мы ~ли в Норве́гии и в Шве́ции last year we were in
Norway and Sweden. 2. (*coll.*) to look in,
visit; мне на́до п. в конто́ре I have to look
in at the office.

побы́вк|а, и, *f.* leave, furlough; прие́хать
домо́й на ~у to come home on leave.

по|бы́ть, бу́ду, бу́дешь, *past* ~был, ~была́,
~было, *pf.* to stay (*for a short time*); мы
~были в Ло́ндоне два дня we stayed in
London for two days.

пова́|дить, жу, дишь, *pf.* (*of* ~живать[1])
(*coll.*) to accustom; to train.

пова́|диться, жусь, дишься, *pf.* (+*inf.*;
coll., *pejor.*) to get into the habit (of);
to take to going (somewhere).

пова́дк|а, и, *f.* (*coll.*) habit.

пова́дливост|ь, и, *f.* (*coll.*) susceptibility;
amenableness.

пова́длив|ый (~, ~а), *adj.* (*coll.*) susceptible;
amenable.

пова́дно, *only in phrase* чтобы не́ было п.
(+*d.*) (in order) to teach not to do so
(again).

пова́жива|ть[1], ю, *impf. of* пова́дить.

пова́жива|ть[2], ю, *impf.* (*coll.*) to take from
time to time.

повал|и́ть[1], ю́, ~ишь, *pf. of* вали́ть[1].

повал|и́ть[2], ю́, ~ишь, *pf.* to begin to throng,
begin to pour; дым ~и́л из трубы́ smoke
began to belch from the chimney; снег
~и́л хло́пьями snow began to fall in
flakes.

пова́льно, *adv.* without exception.

пова́льн|ый, *adj.* general, mass; п. о́быск
general search; ~ая боле́знь epidemic.

пова́нива|ть, ет, *impf.* (*coll.*) to smell slightly.

пова́пленный, *adj. only in phrase* гроб п.
(*fig.*) whited sepulchre.

по́вар, а, *pl.* ~а́, *m.* cook.

пова́ренн|ый, *adj.* culinary; ~ая кни́га
cookery-book; ~ая соль common salt,
table salt (*sodium chloride*).

повар|ёнок, ёнка, *pl.* ~я́та, ~я́т, *m.* (*coll.*)
kitchen-boy.

поварёшк|а, и, *f.* (*coll.*) ladle, strainer.

повари́х|а, и, *f. of* по́вар.

пова́рнича|ть, ю, *impf.* (*coll.*) to cook, be a
cook.

пова́р|ня, ни, *g. pl.* ~ен, *f.* (*obs.*) kitchen.

поварско́й, *adj. of* по́вар.

по-ва́шему, *adv.* 1. in your opinion. 2. as
you wish.

пове́д|ать, аю, *pf.* (*of* ~ывать) to relate,
communicate; п. та́йну to disclose a secret.

поведе́ни|е, я, *n.* conduct, behaviour.

пове́дыва|ть, ю, *impf. of* пове́дать.

повез|ти́, у́, ёшь, *past* ~, ~ла́, *pf. of* везти́.

повелева́|ть, ю, *impf.* 1. (+*i.*; *obs.*) to command, rule. 2. (+*d.*. *and inf.*) to enjoin;
так ~ет мне со́весть thus my conscience
enjoins.

повеле́ни|е, я, *n.* (*obs.*) command, injunction.

повел|е́ть, ю́, и́шь, *pf.* to order, command.

повели́тел|ь, я, *m.* (*obs.*, *rhet.*) sovereign, master.

повели́тельниц|а, ы, *f.* (*obs.*, *rhet.*) sovereign, mistress, lady.

повели́тел|ьный (~ен, ~ьна), *adj.* imperious, peremptory; authoritative; п. жест imperious gesture; п. тон peremptory tone; ~ьное наклоне́ние (*gram.*) imperative mood.

повенча́|ть(ся), ю(сь), *pf. of* венча́ть(ся)[1].

поверг|а́ть, а́ю, *impf. of* ~нуть.

пове́рг|нуть, ну, нешь, *past* ~, ~ла, *pf.* (*of* ~а́ть) 1. (*obs.*) to throw down, lay low; боле́знь ~ла его́ в посте́ль the illness has prostrated him. 2. (в+*a.*) to plunge (into); п. в отча́яние, уны́ние to plunge into despair, depression.

пове́р|енный, *p.p.p. of* ~ить[2]; *as noun* п., ~енного, *m.* 1. (*also* ~енная, ~енной, *f.*) confidant(e). 2. attorney; прися́жный п. (*obs.*) barrister; п. в дела́х chargé d'affaires.

пове́р|ить[1], ю, ишь, *pf. of* ве́рить.

пове́р|ить[2], ю, ишь, *pf.* (*of* ~я́ть) 1. to check (up); to verify. 2. (+*d.*) to confide (to), entrust (to); п. кому́-н. та́йну to confide a secret to someone.

пове́рк|а, и, *f.* 1. check, check-up; checking up, verification; (*math.*) proof. 2. (*mil.*) roll-call; п. карау́лов turning-out of the guard.

повер|ну́ть, ну́, нёшь, *pf.* (*of* ~тывать) to turn; (*fig.*) to change; п. разгово́р to change the subject (*of a conversation*).

повер|ну́ться, ну́сь, нёшься, *pf.* (*of* ~тываться) to turn; п. круго́м to turn round, turn about; п. спино́й (к) to turn one's back (upon); п. на я́коре to swing at anchor; п. к лу́чшему to take a turn for the better.

повер|о́чный, *adj. of* ~ка; ~очные испыта́ния tests.

поверстн|ый, *adj.* (*measured*) by versts; ~ая пла́та payment by the verst.

повёртыва|ть(ся), ю(сь), *impf. of* поверну́ть(ся).

пове́рх, *prep.*+*g.* over, above; on top of; смотре́ть п. очко́в to look over the top of one's spectacles.

пове́рхностност|ь, и, *f.* superficiality.

пове́рхност|ный, *adj.* 1. surface, superficial; ~ная зака́лка (*tech.*) case hardening; ~ное натяже́ние (*tech.*) surface tension; п. разря́д (*electr.*) surface discharge; ~ная ра́на superficial injury; ~ное унаво́живание (*agric.*) top dressing. 2. (~ен, ~на) (*fig.*) superficial; shallow; perfunctory.

пове́рхност|ь, и, *f.* surface.

пове́рху, *adv.* on the surface, on top.

повер|ье, ья, *g.pl.* ~ий, *n.* popular belief, superstition.

повер|я́ть, я́ю, *impf. of* ~ить.

пове́с|а, ы, *m.* (*coll.*) rake, scapegrace.

повеселе́|ть, ю, *pf.* to cheer up, become cheerful.

повесел|и́ть(ся), ю́(сь), и́шь(ся), *pf. of* весели́ть(ся).

по-весе́ннему, *adv.* as in spring.

пове́|сить(ся), шу(сь), сишь(ся), *pf. of* ве́шать(ся)[1].

пове́снича|ть, ю, *impf.* (*coll.*) to lead a wild life.

повествова́ни|е, я, *n.* narrative, narration.

повествова́тельный, *adj.* narrative.

повеств|ова́ть, у́ю, *impf.* (о+*p.*) to narrate, recount, relate.

пове|сти́[1], ду́, дёшь, *past* ~л, ~ла́, *pf. of* вести́ 1.

пове|сти́[2], ду́, дёшь, *past* ~л, ~ла́, *pf.* (*of* поводи́ть[1]) (+*i.*) to move; п. бровя́ми to raise one's eye-brows; он и бро́вью не ~л he did not turn a hair.

пове|сти́сь, ду́сь, дёшься, *past* ~лся, ~ла́сь, *pf. of* вести́сь; уж так ~ло́сь (*coll.*) such is the custom.

пове́стк|а, и, *f.* 1. notice, notification; п. на заседа́ние notice of meeting; п. в суд summons, writ, sub-poena; п. дня agenda, order of the day; на ~е дня on the agenda (*also fig.*). 2. signal; bugle call.

по́вест|ь, и, *pl.* ~и, ~е́й, *f.* story, tale.

пове́три|е, я, *n.* (*coll.*) epidemic, infection (*also fig.*); п. на дифтери́т diphtheria epidemic.

пове́т|ь, и, *f.* (*dial.*) loft (*in peasant hut*).

пове́шени|е, я, *n.* hanging.

пове́|шенный, *p.p.p. of* ~сить; *as noun* п., ~шенного, *m.* hanged man.

пове́|ять, ет, *pf.* 1. to begin to blow; to blow softly. 2. (*impers.*, +*i.*) to breathe (of); (*fig.*) to begin to be felt; ~яло прохла́дой there came a breath of fresh air.

повздо́р|ить, ю, ишь, *pf. of* вздо́рить.

повзросле́|ть, ю, *pf.* to grow up.

повива́льн|ый, *adj.* (*obs.*) obstetric; ~ая ба́бка midwife; ~ое иску́сство midwifery.

повида́|ть, ю, *pf.* (*coll.*) to see.

повида́|ться, юсь, *pf. of* вида́ться.

по-ви́димому, *adv.* apparently, to all appearance, seemingly.

пови́дл|о, а, *n.* jam.

повили́к|а, и, *f.* (*bot.*) dodder.

повин|и́ться, ю́сь, и́шься, *pf. of* вини́ться.

пови́нн|ая, ой, *f.* confession, acknowledgement of guilt; принести́ ~ую, яви́ться с ~ой to give oneself up; to plead guilty; to acknowledge one's guilt, own up.

пови́нност|ь, и, *f.* duty, obligation; доро́жная п. compulsory road maintenance; во́инская п. compulsory military service, conscription.

пови́н|ный (~ен, ~на), *adj.* **1.** guilty. **2.** (*obs.*) obliged, bound.

повин|ова́ться, у́юсь, *impf.* (*in past tense also pf.*) (+*d.*) to obey.

повинове́ни|е, я, *n.* obedience.

пови|са́ть, а́ю, *impf. of* ~нуть.

пови|се́ть, шу́, си́шь, *pf.* to hang for a time.

пови́с|нуть, ну, нешь, *past* ~, ~ла, *pf.* (*of* ~а́ть) **1.** (на+*p.*) to hang (by). **2.** to hang down, droop; п. в во́здухе (*fig.*) to hang in mid-air, (*of a joke*) to fall flat.

повиту́х|а, и, *f.* (*coll.*) midwife.

повлажне́|ть, ю, *pf. of* влажне́ть.

повле́|чь, ку́, чёшь, ку́т, *past* ~к, ~кла́, *pf.* (за собо́й) to entail, bring in one's train; п. за собо́й неприя́тные после́дствия to have unpleasant consequences.

повлия́|ть, ю, *pf. of* влия́ть.

по́вод¹, а, *pl.* ~ы, *m.* (к) occasion, cause, ground (for, of); п. к войне́ casus belli; дать п. (+*d.*) to give occasion (to), give cause (for); дать п. к нападкам to lay oneself open; без вся́кого ~а without cause; по ~у (+*g.*) apropos (of), as regards, concerning; по како́му ~у? in what connection? why?

по́вод², а, о ~е, на ~у́, *pl.* ~а́, ~ов, *or* ~ья, ~ьев, *m.* rein; быть у кого́-н. на ~у́ (*fig.*) to be under someone's thumb.

пово|ди́ть¹, жу́, ~дишь, *impf. of* повести́².

пово|ди́ть², жу́, ~дишь, *pf.* to make go; п. ло́шадь to walk a horse.

повод|о́к, ка́, *m.* (dog's) lead.

поводы́р|ь, я́, *m.* (*coll.*) leader, guide.

пово́зк|а, и, *f.* **1.** vehicle, conveyance. **2.** (*unsprung*) carriage.

пово́йник, а, *m.* (*obs.*) povoynik (*kind of kerchief worn on the head by married Russian peasant woman*).

пово́лжский, *adj.* situated on the Volga.

повора́чива|ть(ся), ю(сь), *impf. of* повороти́ть(ся); ~йся!, ~йтесь! (*coll.*) get a move on! look sharp!

повораж|и́ть, у́, и́шь, *pf. of* ворожи́ть.

поворо́т, а, *m.* turn(ing); огни́ ~а direction indicator lamps (*of car*); (*fig.*) turning--point; п. реки́ bend; пе́рвый п. напра́во the first turning to the right; на ~е доро́ги at the turn of the road; п. к лу́чшему turn for the better.

поворо|ти́ть(ся), чу́(сь), ~тишь(ся), *pf. of* повора́чивать(ся) to turn.

поворо́тливост|ь, и, *f.* **1.** nimbleness, agility, quickness. **2.** (*tech., naut.*) manoeuvrability, handiness.

поворо́тлив|ый (~, ~а), *adj.* **1.** nimble, agile, quick. **2.** (*tech., naut.*) manoeuvrable, handy.

поворо́тн|ый, *adj.* rotary, rotating, revolving; (*fig.*) turning; п. кран slewing crane,

swing crane; п. круг turn-table; п. крюк shackle hook; п. мост swing bridge; п. резе́ц swing tool; ~ое сиде́нье swivel seat; ~ые сала́зки swivel carriage; п. моме́нт, п. пункт turning-point.

повре|ди́ть, жу́, ди́шь, *pf.* **1.** *pf. of* вреди́ть. **2.** (*pf. of* ~жда́ть) to damage; to injure, hurt; п. себе́ но́гу to hurt one's leg.

повре|ди́ться, жу́сь, ди́шься, *pf.* (*of* ~жда́ться) to be damaged; to be injured; п. в уме́ (*coll.*) to become mentally deranged.

поврежда́|ть(ся), ю(сь), *impf. of* повреди́ть(ся).

поврежде́ни|е, я, *n.* damage, injury.

повре|ждённый, *p.p.p. of* ~ди́ть; п. в уме́ (*coll.*) mentally deranged.

повремен|и́ть, ю́, и́шь, *pf.* (*coll.*) to wait a little; (с+*i.*) to delay (over).

повреме́нн|ый, *adj.* **1.** periodical. **2.** reckoned on time basis; ~ая опла́та payment by time (*by the hour, etc.*); ~ая рабо́та time-work (*work paid by the hour, etc.*).

повседне́вно, *adv.* daily, every day.

повседне́вност|ь, и, *f.* daily occurrence.

повседне́вн|ый, *adj.* daily; everyday; ~ая рабо́та daily task; п. слу́чай everyday occurrence.

повсеме́стно, *adv.* everywhere, in all parts.

повсеме́ст|ный (~ен, ~на), *adj.* universal, general.

повска|ка́ть, ~чет, *pf.* to jump up one after another.

повска́кива|ть, ет, *pf.* = повскака́ть.

повста́н|ец, ца, *m.* insurgent, rebel.

повста́нческий, *adj.* insurgent, rebel.

повстреча́|ть, ю, *pf.* (*coll.*) to meet, run into.

повстреча́|ться, юсь, *pf.* (+*d.* or с+*i.*) to meet, run into; мне ~лся знако́мый, я ~лся с знако́мым I met an acquaintance.

повсю́ду, *adv.* everywhere.

повторе́ни|е, я, *n.* **1.** repetition; reiteration; кра́ткое п. recapitulation. **2.** recurrence. **3.** revision (*of school work*).

повтори́тельный, *adj.* recapitulatory; п. курс refresher course.

повтор|и́ть, ю́, и́шь, *pf.* (*of* ~я́ть) **1.** to repeat; to reiterate. **2.** to revise (*school work*).

повтор|и́ться, ю́сь, и́шься, *pf.* (*of* ~я́ться) **1.** to repeat oneself. **2.** to recur. **3.** *pass. of* ~и́ть.

повто́рный, *adj.* repeated; recurring.

повтор|я́ть(ся), я́ю(сь), *impf. of* ~и́ть(ся).

повыси́тельный, *adj.* (*electr.*) step-up.

повы́|сить, шу, сишь, *pf.* (*of* ~ша́ть) **1.** to raise, heighten; п. вдво́е, втро́е to double, treble; п. в пять раз, *etc.*, to raise five-fold, *etc.*; п. давле́ние to increase pressure; п. го́лос to raise one's voice (*also fig., in anger*).

2. to promote, prefer, advance; п. кого́-н. по слу́жбе to give someone promotion.

повы́|ситься, шусь, сишься, *pf.* (*of* ~ша́ться) 1. to rise; to improve; п. в чьём-н. мне́нии to rise in someone's estimation; на́ши а́кции ~сились our shares have gone up; (*fig.*) our stock has risen. 2. to be promoted, receive advancement.

повыша́|ть(ся), ю(сь), *impf. of* повы́сить(ся).

повы́ше, *comp. adj. and adv.* a little higher (up); a little taller.

повыше́ни|е, я, *n.* rise, increase; п. по слу́жбе advancement, promotion, preferment.

повы́|шенный, *p.p.p. of* ~сить *and adj.* heightened; increased; ~шенное настрое́ние state of excitement; ~шенная температу́ра high temperature; ~шенная чувстви́тельность heightened sensibility.

повя|за́ть¹, жу́, ~жешь, *pf.* (*of* ~зывать) to tie; п. га́лстук to tie a tie; п. го́лову платко́м to tie a scarf on one's head.

повя|за́ть², жу́, ~жешь, *pf.* to do a little knitting, knit for a while.

повя|за́ться, жу́сь, ~жешься, *pf.* (*of* ~зываться) (+*i.*) to tie oneself (with); п. платко́м to tie a scarf on one's head.

повя́зк|а, и, f. 1. band; fillet. 2. bandage.

повя́зыва|ть(ся), ю(сь), *impf. of* повяза́ть(ся).

погада́|ть, ю, *pf. of* гада́ть.

пога́н|ец, ца, m. (*coll.*) rascal.

пога́н|ить, ю, ишь, *impf.* (*of* о~) (*coll.*) to pollute, defile.

пога́нк|а, ки, f. 1. = ~ый гриб. 2. shelldrake. 3. *f. of* ~ец.

пога́н|ый (~, ~а), adj. 1. foul, unclean; п. гриб non-edible mushroom, toadstool; ~ая пи́ща (*rel.*) unclean food; ~ое ведро́ garbage can, refuse pail. 2. (*coll.*) foul, filthy, vile; ~ое настрое́ние foul mood. 3. (*obs.*) non-Christian.

по́ган|ь, и, f. (*collect.*; *pejor.*) filth; dregs.

погаса́|ть, ю, *impf.* to go out, be extinguished.

пога|си́ть, шу́, ~сишь, *pf.* (*of* гаси́ть *and* ~ша́ть) to liquidate, cancel; п. долг to clear off a debt; п. ма́рку to cancel a stamp.

пога́с|нуть, ну, нешь, *past* ~, ~ла, *pf. of* га́снуть.

погаша́|ть, ю, *impf. of* погаси́ть.

пога́|шенный, *p.p.p. of* ~си́ть *and adj.* used (*of postage stamps, etc.*); cashed.

погиб|а́ть, а́ю, *impf. of* ~нуть.

поги́бел|ь, и, f. (*obs.*) ruin, perdition; согну́ться в три ~и to be hunched up; (*fig.*) to be reduced to submission, be cowed.

поги́бельный, adj. (*obs.*) ruinous, fatal.

поги́б|нуть, ну, нешь, *past* ~, ~ла, *pf.* (*of*

ги́бнуть *and* ~а́ть) to perish; (*naut. and fig.*) to be lost; кора́бль ~ со всей кома́ндой the ship was lost with all hands.

поги́б|ший, *past part. of* ~нуть *and adj.* (*obs.*) lost, ruined.

погла́|дить¹, жу, дишь, *pf. of* гла́дить.

погла́|дить², жу, дишь, *pf.* to do a little ironing.

погла́жива|ть, ю, *impf.* to stroke (*every so often, from time to time*).

поглазе́|ть, ю, *pf. of* глазе́ть.

погло|ти́ть, щу́, ~тишь, *pf.* (*of* ~ща́ть) to swallow up, take up, absorb (*also fig.*); п. во́ду to absorb water; п. чьё-н. внима́ние to engross someone; п. рома́н to devour a novel.

поглоща́емост|ь, и, f. absorbability.

поглоща́|ть, ю, *impf. of* поглоти́ть.

поглупе́|ть, ю, *pf. of* глупе́ть.

погля|де́ть, жу́, ди́шь, *pf.* 1. *pf. of* гляде́ть. 2. to have a look. 3. to look for a while.

погля|де́ться, жу́сь, ди́шься, *pf. of* гляде́ться.

погля́дыва|ть, ю, *impf.* 1. (на+*a.*) to cast looks, glance (at, upon); to look from time to time (at). 2. (за+*i.*; *coll.*) to keep an eye (on).

по|гна́ть, гоню́, го́нишь, *past* ~гна́л, ~гнала́, ~гна́ло, *pf.* to drive; to begin to drive.

по|гна́ться, гоню́сь, го́нишься, *past* ~гна́лся, ~гнала́сь, ~гна́ло́сь, *pf.* (за+*i.*) to run (after); to start in pursuit (of), give chase; (*fig.*) to strive (after, for); п. за эффе́ктами to strive for effect.

погни|ть, ю, ёшь, *past* ~л, ~ла́, ~ло, *pf.* to rot, decay, moulder.

погн|у́ть, у́, ёшь, *pf.* to bend.

погн|у́ться, ётся, *pf.* to bend (*intrans.*).

погнуша́|ться, юсь, *pf. of* гнуша́ться.

погова́рива|ть, ю, *impf.* (о+*p.*) to talk (of); ~ют there is talk (of), it is rumoured; ~ют о его́ жени́тьбе there is talk of his marrying, it is rumoured that he is getting married.

поговор|и́ть, ю́, и́шь, *pf.* to have a talk.

погово́рк|а, и, f. (*proverbial*) saying, by-word; войти́ в ~у to become a by-word, become proverbial.

пого́д|а, ы, f. weather; кака́я бы ни была́ п. rain or shine, wet or fine; э́то не де́лает ~ы that is not what counts, this does not affect the matter; ждать у мо́ря (*or* у мо́ря) ~ы to wait for something to turn up.

пого|ди́ть, жу́, ди́шь, *pf.* (*coll.*) to wait a little; ~ди́те! wait a moment! one moment!; немно́го ~дя́ a little later.

пого́д|ки, ков, sing. ~ок, ~ка, m. brothers *or* sisters born at a year's interval; мы с ней п. there is a year's difference between us.

пого́дный¹, adj. annual, yearly.

погóд|ный², *adj. of* ~а.

погóжий, *adj.* fine, lovely (*of weather*).

поголóвно, *adv.* one and all; (all) to a man.

поголóвн|ый, *adj.* general, universal; п. налóг poll-tax, capitation(-tax); ~ое ополчéние levy in mass; ~ая пéрепись universal census.

поголóвь|е, я, *n.* (number of) live-stock.

поголубé|ть, ю, *pf. of* голубéть.

погóн¹, а, *m.* (*mil.*) 1. shoulder-strap. 2. (rifle-)sling.

погóн², а, *m.* distillate, fraction.

погóнный, *adj.* linear.

погóнщик, а, *m.* driver, teamster; п. мýлов muleteer.

погóн|я, и, *f.* pursuit, chase.

погоня́|ть¹, ю, *impf.* to urge on, drive (*also fig.*)

пог |ть², ю, *pf.* to drive (*for a certain time*).

погор|áть, áю, *impf. of* ~éть¹.

погорéл|ец, ьца, *m.* one who has lost all his possessions in a fire.

погор|éть¹, ю, йшь, (*of* ~áть) 1. to lose all one's possessions in a fire. 2. to burn down; to be burnt out.

погор|éть², ю, йшь, *pf.* to burn for a while.

погоря́ч|иться, усь, йшься, *pf.* to get heated (*fig.*), get worked up.

погóст, а, *m.* (*obs.*) 1. country churchyard. 2. pogost (*country church together with cemetery and clergy house and adjacent buildings*).

пого|стить, щý, стишь, *pf.* (у) to stay for a while (at, with).

погран- frontier(-).

пограни́чник, а, *m.* frontier-guard.

пограни́чн|ый, *adj.* frontier; boundary; п. столб boundary post; ~ая стрáжа frontier guards.

пóгреб, а, *pl.* ~á, *m.* cellar (*also fig.*); ви́нный п. wine-cellar; пороховóй п. powder-magazine (*also fig.*).

погребáльн|ый, *adj.* funeral; п. звон knell; ~ое пéние dirge.

погребá|ть, ю, *impf. of* погрести́¹.

погребéни|е, я, *n.* burial, interment.

погреб|éц, цá, *m.* (*obs.*) provisions hamper.

погремýшк|а, и, *f.* rattle.

погре|сти́¹, бý, бёшь, *past* ~б, ~блá, *pf.* (*of* ~бáть) to bury.

погре|сти́², бý, бёшь, *past* ~б, ~блá, *pf.* to row a little.

погрé|ть, ю, *pf.* to warm.

погрé|ться, юсь, *pf.* to warm oneself.

погреш|áть, áю, *impf. of* ~и́ть.

погреш|и́ть, ý, и́шь, *pf.* (*of* ~áть) (прóтив) to sin (against); to err.

погрéшност|ь, и, *f.* error, mistake, inaccuracy; треугóльник ~и (*naut.*) cocked hat.

погро|зи́ть, жý, зи́шь, *pf. of* грози́ть 2.

погро|зи́ться, жýсь, зи́шься, *pf. of* грози́ться.

погрóм, а, *m.* pogrom, massacre.

погрóм|ный, *adj. of* ~.

погрóмщик, а, *m.* person organizing *or* taking part in a pogrom.

погромых|áть, áю, *pf.* (*of* ~ивать) (*of thunder*) to rumble intermittently.

погромы́хива|ть, ю, *impf. of* погромыхáть.

погружá|ть(ся), ю(сь), *impf. of* погрузи́ть(ся); ~емый нагревáтель immersion heater.

погружéни|е, я, *n.* sinking, submergence; immersion; (*of a submarine*) dive, diving.

погру́|женный *and* ~жённый, *p.p.p. of* ~зи́ть; п. в вóду immersed (in water); п. в размышлéния deep in thought; п. в себя́ wrapped up in oneself.

погру|зи́ть, жý, ~зи́шь, *pf.* (*of* ~жáть) 1. (в+*a.*) to dip (into), plunge (into), immerse; to submerge; to duck. 2. *pf. of* грузи́ть 2.

погру|зи́ться, жýсь, ~зи́шься, *pf.* 1. (в+*a.*) to sink (into), plunge (into); (*of a submarine*) to submerge, dive; (*fig.*) to be plunged (in); to be absorbed (in), be buried (in), be lost (in); п. в темнотý to be plunged into darkness; п. в чтéние to be absorbed in reading; п. в размышлéния to be deep in thought. 2. *pf. of* грузи́ться.

погру́зк|а, и, *f.* loading; lading, shipment.

погру́зочно-разгру́зочный, *adj.* loading-and-unloading.

погру́зочный, *adj.* loading; п. жёлоб loading chute.

погряз|áть, áю, *impf. of* ~нуть.

погря́з|нуть, ну, нешь, *past* ~, ~ла, *pf.* (*of* ~áть) (в+*p.*) to be stuck (in); to be bogged down (in); to wallow (in) (*also fig.*); п. в долгáх to be up to one's eyes in debt.

погуб|и́ть, лю, ~ишь, *pf. of* губи́ть.

погу́дк|а, и, *f.* (*coll.*) tune, melody; стáрая п. на нóвый лад (*fig.*) the same tune in a new setting, the (same) old story.

погу́лива|ть, ю, *impf.* (*coll.*) 1. to walk up and down. 2. to go on the spree from time to time.

погуля́|ть, ю, *pf. of* гуля́ть.

погустé|ть, ет, *pf. of* густéть.

под¹, а, о ~е, на ~ý, *m.* hearth(-stone); sole (*of furnace*).

под² *and* подо, *prep.* 1. (+*a. and i.*) under; постáвить п. стол to put under the table; находи́ться п. столóм to be under the table; п. арéстом under arrest; п. ви́дом (+*g.*) under, in the guise (of); п. влия́нием (+*g.*) under the influence (of); п. вопрóсом open to question; пóд гору downhill; п. замкóм under lock and key; п. землёй underground; быть п. ружьём to be under arms; взять когó-н. пóд руку to take someone's arm; п. руко́й (close) at hand, to hand; отда́ть п. суд to prosecute; п. усло́вием on condition. **2.** (+*a. and i.*) in the environs of; near; жить п. Москво́й to live in the environs of Moscow; пое́хать на да́чу п. Ленингра́д to go to a dacha near Leningrad; би́тва п. Бородино́м the battle of Borodino. **3.** (+*i.*) occupied by, used as; (+*a.*) for; (to serve) as; помеще́ние под шко́лой premises occupied by a school; отвести́ помеще́ние п. шко́лу to earmark premises for a school; ба́нка п. варе́нье jam-jar; по́ле п. пшени́цей wheat-field. **4.** (+*a.*) towards (*of time*); on the eve of; п. ве́чер towards evening; п. Но́вый год on New Year's Eve; ему́ п. пятьдеся́т (*лет*) he is getting on for fifty. **5.** (+*a.*) to (the accompaniment of); танцева́ть п. граммофо́нные пласти́нки to dance to gramophone records; писа́ть п. дикто́вку to write from dictation. **6.** (+*a.*) in imitation of; э́то сде́лано п. оре́х it is imitation walnut; он пи́шет п. Турге́нева he writes in imitation of (*the style of*) Turgenev. **7.** (+*a.*) on (= *in exchange for*); п. зало́г on security; п. распи́ску on receipt. **8.** (+*i.*) (*meant, etc.*) by; что на́до понима́ть п. э́тим выраже́нием? what is meant by this expression?; что п. подразумева́ется? what is implied by this? **9.** (+*i.*; *cul.*) in, with; ры́ба п. бешаме́лью fish cooked in white sauce; говя́дина п. хре́ном beef with horse-radish.

под- (**подо-**, **подъ-**)[1] *as verbal prefix indicates* **1.** *action from beneath or affecting lower part of something, as* подчеркну́ть *to underline.* **2.** *motion upwards, as* подня́ть *to raise.* **3.** *motion towards, as* подъе́хать *to approach.* **4.** *action carried out or event occurring in slight degree, as* подкра́сить *to touch up;* поджи́ть *to begin to heal up.* **5.** *supplementary action, as* подрабо́тать *to earn additionally.* **6.** *underhand action, as* подкупи́ть *to bribe.*

под- (**подо-**, **подъ-**)[2] *as prefix of nouns and adjs.* under-, sub-.

подава́льщик, а, *m.* **1.** waiter. **2.** supplier. **3.** (*sport; in game of lapta*) pitcher.

подава́льщиц|а, ы, *f.* waitress.

пода|ва́ть(ся), ю́(сь), ёшь(ся), *impf. of* пода́ть(ся).

подав|и́ть[1]**, лю́, ~ишь,** *pf.* (*of* ~ля́ть) **1.** to suppress, put down; to repress; п. восста́ние to put down a rising; п. стон to stifle a groan. **2.** (*fig.*) to depress; to crush, overwhelm. **3.** (*mil.*) to neutralize.

подав|и́ть[2]**, лю́, ~ишь,** *pf.* (*no impf.*) **1.** (*coll.*) to press, trample (*a quantity of*). **2.** to press, squeeze for a time.

подав|и́ться, лю́сь, ~ишься, *pf. of* дави́ться.

подавле́ни|е, я, *n.* **1.** suppression; repression. **2.** (*mil.*) neutralization.

пода́вленность|ь, и, *f.* depression; blues.

пода́в|ленный, *p.p.p. of* ~и́ть *and adj.* **1.** suppressed; п. стон muffled groan. **2.** depressed, dispirited.

пода́влива|ть, ю, *impf.* to exert slight pressure.

подавля́|ть, ю, *impf. of* подави́ть[1].

подавля́|ющий, *pres. part. act. of* ~ть *and adj.* overwhelming; overpowering; ~ющее большинство́ overwhelming majority.

пода́вно, *adv.* so much the more, all the more.

подáгр|а, ы, *f.* gout, podagra.

подáгрик, а, *m.* gouty person, sufferer from gout.

подагри́ческий, *adj.* gouty.

пода́льше, *adv.* (*coll.*) a little farther.

подар|и́ть, ю́, ~ишь, *pf. of* дари́ть.

подáр|ок, ка, *m.* present, gift; получи́ть в п. to receive as a present.

подáтел|ь, я, *m.* bearer (*of a letter, etc.*); п. проше́ния petitioner.

подáтливост|ь, и, *f.* **1.** pliancy, pliability. **2.** (*fig.*) complaisance.

подáтлив|ый (~, ~a), *adj.* **1.** pliant, pliable. **2.** (*fig.*) complaisant.

податн|о́й, *adj.* (*hist.*) tax, duty; п. инспе́ктор assessor of taxes; ~а́я систе́ма taxation; *as noun* п., ~о́го, *m.* = п. инспе́ктор.

по́дат|ь, и, *pl.* ~и, ~е́й, *f.* (*hist.*) tax, duty, assessment.

по|да́ть, да́м, да́шь, да́ст, дади́м, дади́те, даду́т, *past* ~да́л, ~дала́, ~да́ло, *pf.* (*of* ~дава́ть) **1.** (*in var. senses*) to give; to proffer; п. го́лос to vote; п. знак to give a sign; п. по́мощь to lend a hand, proffer aid; п. приме́р to set an example; п. ру́ку (+*d.*) to offer one's hand; п. сигна́л to give the signal; ~да́йте ей пальто́ help her on with her coat. **2.** to serve (*food*); п. на стол to serve up; обе́д ~дан dinner is served. **3.** to bring up (*train or other conveyance*); сле́дующий по́езд ~даду́т на э́ту платфо́рму the next train will come in at this platform. **4.** to put, move, turn; п. ло́шадь в гало́п to put a horse into a gallop. **5.** (*sport*) п. мяч to serve. **6.** to serve, forward, present, hand in (*application, complaint, etc.*); п. апелля́цию to appeal; п. жа́лобу to lodge a complaint; п. заявле́ние to hand in an application; п. телегра́мму to send a telegram; п. в отста́вку to send in one's resignation; п. в суд (на+*a.*) to bring an action (against). **7.** (*lit., theatr.*) to present, display. **8.** (*tech.*) to feed.

по|да́ться, да́мся, да́шься, да́стся, дади́мся, дади́тесь, даду́тся, *past* ~да́лся, ~дала́сь, ~дало́сь, *pf.* (*of* ~дава́ться) **1.** to move; п. наза́д to draw back; п. в сто́рону to move aside. **2.** (*coll.*) to give way, yield (*also fig.*); to cave in, collapse. **3.** (на+*a.*; *coll.*) to make (for), set out (for).

пода́ч|а, и, *f.* **1.** giving, presenting; п. го́лоса voting; п. заявле́ния sending in of application. **2.** (*sport*) service, serve. **3.** (*tech.*) feed, feeding, supply; (*chem.*) introduction; высота́ ~и lift (*of pump*); коро́бка ~и gear-box, feed unit.

пода́чк|а, и, *f.* (*coll.*) **1.** sop; crumb. **2.** (*fig.*) tip.

подая́ни|е, я, *n.* charity, alms; dole.

подба́в|ить, лю, ишь, *pf.* (*of* ~ля́ть) (+*a. or g.*) to add; п. са́хару в ко́фе to put (more) sugar in coffee; п. ро́му в чай to lace tea with rum.

подба́вк|а, и, *f.* addition.

подбавля́|ть, ю, *impf. of* подба́вить.

подба́лтыва|ть, ю, *impf. of* подболта́ть.

подбега́|ть, ю, *impf. of* подбежа́ть.

подбе|жа́ть, гу́, жи́шь, гу́т, *pf.* (*of* ~га́ть) (к) to run up (to), come running up (to).

подберёзовик, а, *m.* brown mushroom (*Boletus scaber*).

подбива́|ть, ю, *impf. of* подби́ть.

подби́вк|а, и, *f.* **1.** lining. **2.** re-soling.

подбира́|ть(ся), ю(сь), *impf. of* подобра́ть(ся).

подби́т|ый, *p.p.p. of* ~ь; п. ва́той wadded; п. ме́хом fur-lined; п. глаз black eye.

под|би́ть, обью́, обьёшь, *pf.* (*of* ~бива́ть) **1.** (+*i.*) to line (with). **2.** to re-sole. **3.** to injure; to bruise; п. кому́-н. глаз to give someone a black eye. **4.** (*mil.*) to put out of action, knock out; п. самолёт to shoot down a plane. **5.** (+*inf. or* на+*a.*; *coll.*) to incite (to), instigate (to).

подбодр|и́ть, ю́, и́шь, *pf.* (*of* ~я́ть) (*coll.*) to cheer up, encourage.

подбодр|и́ться, ю́сь, и́шься, *pf.* (*of* ~я́ться) to cheer up, take heart.

подбодр|я́ть(ся), я́ю(сь), *impf. of* ~и́ть(ся).

подбо́йк|а, и, *f.* **1.** lining. **2.** re-soling. **3.** (*tech.*) swage.

подболта́|ть, ю, *pf.* (*of* подба́лтывать) (+*a. or g.*) to mix in, stir in; п. молока́ в суп to stir milk into soup.

подбо́р, а, *m.* **1.** selection, assortment; (как) на п. choice, well-matched. **2.** в п. (*typ.*) run on.

подбо́рк|а, и, *f.* set, selection (*esp. a section of related news items under a single heading in a newspaper*).

подборо́д|ок, ка, *m.* chin.

подбоче́нива|ться, юсь, *impf. of* подбоче́ниться.

подбоче́нившись, *adv.* with one's arms akimbo, with one's hands on one's hips.

подбоче́н|иться, юсь, ишься, *pf.* (*of* ~иваться) to place one's arms akimbo.

подбра́сыва|ть, ю, *impf. of* подбро́сить.

подбро́|сить, шу, сишь, *pf.* (*of* подбра́сывать) **1.** to throw up, toss up; (под) to throw (under); п. моне́ту to toss up. **2.** (+*a. or g.*) to throw in, throw on; п. резе́рвы (*mil.*) to throw in one's reserves; п. дров в печь to throw more wood on the fire. **3.** to place surreptitiously; п. младе́нца to abandon a baby.

подбрю́шник, а, *m.* belly-band (*of horse*).

подва́л, а, *m.* **1.** cellar; basement. **2.** (*in newspaper*) feuilleton.

подва́лива|ть, ю, *impf. of* подвали́ть.

подвал|и́ть, ю́, ~ишь, *pf.* (*of* ~ивать) **1.** (*coll.*) (+*a. or g.*) to heap up. **2.** (+*a. or g.*) (*coll.*) to add; наро́ду ~и́ло (*impers.*) still more people came. **3.** (*naut.*; к) to come in (to), steam in (to).

подва́л|ьный, *adj. of* ~; п. эта́ж basement.

подва́рива|ть, ю, *impf. of* подвари́ть.

подвар|и́ть, ю́, ~ишь, *pf.* (*of* ~ивать) (*coll.*) **1.** (+*g.*) to boil in addition. **2.** to heat up again.

подва́хтенны|й, *adj.* ~е матро́сы (*naut.*) watch below.

подве́домствен|ный (~, ~на), *adj.* (+*d.*) dependent (on), within the jurisdiction (of).

подвез|ти́, у́, ёшь, *past* ~, ~ла́, *pf.* (*of* подвози́ть) **1.** to bring, take (with one); to give a lift (*on the road*). **2.** (+*a. or g.*) to bring up, transport. **3.** (*coll.*) мне, *etc.*, ~ло́ I, *etc.*, have had a stroke of luck.

подвене́чн|ый, *adj.* ~ое пла́тье wedding dress.

подверг|а́ть(ся), а́ю(сь), *impf. of* ~нуть(ся).

подве́рг|нуть, ну, нешь, *past* ~, ~ла, *pf.* (*of* ~а́ть) (+*d.*) to subject (to); to expose (to); п. испыта́нию to put to the test; п. наказа́нию to impose a penalty (upon); п. опа́сности to expose to danger, endanger; п. сомне́нию to call in question; п. штра́фу to fine.

подве́рг|нуться, нусь, нешься, *past* ~ся, ~лась, *pf.* (*of* ~а́ться) **1.** (+*d.*) to undergo. **2.** *pass. of* ~нуть.

подве́рженност|ь, и, *f.* (+*d.*) liability (to), susceptibility (to).

подве́ржен|ный (~, ~а), *adj.* (+*d.*) subject (to), liable (to); susceptible (to).

подвер|ну́ть, ну́, нёшь, *pf.* (*of* ~тывать) **1.** to screw up a little; п. винт to tighten a screw. **2.** to tuck in, tuck up; п. одея́ло to tuck in a blanket; п. брю́ки to tuck up one's trousers. **3.** to twist, sprain; п. но́гу to sprain one's ankle.

подвер|ну́ться, ну́сь, нёшься, *pf.* (*of* ~тываться) **1.** to be twisted, sprained; нога́ у

меня́ ~ну́лась I have sprained my ankle.
2. (*fig.*, *coll.*) to turn up, crop up; он кста́ти ~ну́лся he turned up just at the right moment. **3.** *pass. of* ~ну́ть.

подвёртыва|ть(ся), ю(сь), *impf. of* подверну́ть(ся).

подве́с, а, *m.* (*tech.*) suspension; hanger.

подвесе́льный, *adj.* at the oars.

подве́|сить, шу, сишь, *pf.* (*of* ~шивать) to hang up, suspend.

подве́|ситься, шусь, сишься, *pf.* (*of* ~шиваться) (на+*p.*) to hang (on to, on by), be suspended (from).

подве́ск|а, и, *f.* **1.** hanging up, suspension. **2.** pendant; серьги с ~ами drop ear-rings. **3.** (*tech.*) hanger; suspension bracket, suspension clip.

подвесно́й, *adj.* hanging, suspended, pendant; overhead; п. конве́йер overhead conveyer; п. мост suspension bridge; п. мото́р outboard motor.

подве́с|ок, ка, *m.* pendant.

подве|сти́, ду́, дёшь, *past* ~л, ~ла́, *pf.* (*of* подводи́ть) **1.** to lead up, bring up; to extend; п. резе́рвы to bring up reserves. **2.** (под+*a.*) to place (under); п. фунда́мент to under-pin; п. дом под кры́шу to roof a house; п. ми́ну под мост to mine a bridge; п. про́чную ба́зу под свои́ до́воды to place one's arguments on a sound footing; п. бро́ви to pencil one's eyebrows. **3.** to subsume; to put together; п. бала́нс (+*g.*) to balance; п. ито́ги to reckon up; to sum up (*also fig.*); он ~л ва́ши гру́бые слова́ под оскорбле́ние he took your rude words as an insult. **4.** (*coll.*) to let down; to put in a spot. **5.** (*impers.*; *coll.*) у меня́ живо́т ~ло́ I feel pinched (with hunger).

подве́тренн|ый, *adj.* leeward; п. борт (*naut.*) lee side; бе́рег с ~ой стороны́ lee shore.

подве́шива|ть(ся), ю(сь), *impf. of* подве́сить(ся).

подвздо́шный, *adj.* (*anat.*) iliac.

подвива́|ть(ся), ю(сь), *impf. of* подви́ть(ся).

по́двиг, а, *m.* exploit, feat; heroic deed; боево́й п. feat of arms; герои́ческий п. epic of heroism.

подвига́|ть, ю, *pf.* (+*i.*) to move a little.

подвига́|ть(ся), ю(сь), *impf. of* подви́нуть(ся).

подви́гн|уть, у, ешь, *pf.* (на+*a.*) (*rhet.*, *obs.*) to rouse (to).

подви́д, а, *m.* (*biol.*) subspecies.

подви́жник, а, *m.* **1.** (*rel.*) ascetic; zealot. **2.** (*fig.*) zealot, devotee; hero; п. нау́ки person utterly devoted to (*the cause of*) learning.

подви́жничеств|о, а, *n.* **1.** (*rel.*) asceticism. **2.** selfless devotion (*to a cause*); heroic conduct; endeavour.

подвижн|о́й, *adj.* **1.** (*in var. senses*) mobile; movable; (*tech.*) travelling; п. блок travelling block; п. го́спиталь mobile hospital; ~ые и́гры outdoor games; п. кран travelling crane; п. масшта́б sliding scale; п. пра́здник (*eccl.*) movable feast; ~о́е равнове́сие (*chem.*) mobile equilibrium; п. соста́в (*railway*) rolling stock. **2.** lively; agile; ~о́е лицо́ mobile features.

подви́жност|ь, и, *f.* **1.** mobility. **2.** liveliness; agility.

подви́жный, *adj.* mobile; lively; agile.

подвиза́|ться, юсь, *impf.* (*rhet. or iron.*) to work, act; to pursue an occupation; п. на юриди́ческом по́прище to follow the law; п. на сце́не to tread the boards.

подвин|ти́ть, чу́, ти́шь, *pf.* (*of* ~чивать) **1.** to screw up, tighten. **2.** (*fig.*, *coll.*) to urge, goad.

подви́|нуть, ну, нешь, *pf.* (*of* ~га́ть) **1.** to move; to push. **2.** (*fig.*) to advance, push forward.

подви́|нуться, нусь, нешься, *pf.* (*of* ~га́ться) **1.** to move. **2.** (*fig.*) to advance, progress.

подви́нчива|ть, ю, *impf. of* подвинти́ть.

под|ви́ть, овью́, овьёшь, *past* ~ви́л, ~вила́, ~ви́ло, *pf.* (*of* ~вива́ть) to curl slightly, friz(z).

под|ви́ться, овью́сь, овьёшься, *past* ~ви́лся, ~вила́сь, ~ви́лось, *pf.* (*of* ~вива́ться) to curl one's hair slightly, friz(z) one's hair.

подвла́ст|ный (~ен, ~на), *adj.* (+*d.*) subject to, dependent on.

подво́д, а, *m.* (*tech.*) supply, feed, admission; (*electr.*) lead, feeder.

подво́д|а, ы, *f.* cart.

подво|ди́ть, жу́, ~дишь, *impf. of* подвести́.

подво́дник, а, *m.* (*naut.*) submariner.

подводн|о́й, *adj.* ~а́я труба́ (*tech.*) feed pipe.

подводн|ый¹, *adj.* submarine; under-water; п. загради́тель mine-layer; п. ка́бель submarine cable; п. ка́мень reef, rock; ~ая ло́дка submarine; ~ое тече́ние undercurrent.

подво́д|ный², *adj. of* ~а; ~ная пови́нность (*hist.*) obligation to provide transport.

подво́дчик, а, *m.* carter.

подво́з, а, *m.* transport; supply.

подво|зи́ть, жу́, ~зишь, *impf. of* подвезти́.

подво́|й, я, *m.* (*bot.*) wilding.

подво́рн|ый, *adj.* household; ~ая пе́репись census of (*peasant*) households; ~ая по́дать (*hist.*) hearth-money, chimney-money; п. спи́сок list of homesteads.

подворотнич|о́к, ка́, *m.* undercollar (*of soldier's tunic*).

подворо́т|ня, ни, *g. pl.* ~ен, *f.* **1.** space between gate and ground. **2.** board attached to bottom of gate.

подво́р|ье, ья, *g. pl.* ∼ий, *n.* (*obs.*) **1.** town house (*daughter church in town, usu. with hostel attached, belonging to monastery*). **2.** town residence, town house (*belonging to person normally residing elsewhere*).

подво́х, а, *m.* (*coll.*) dirty trick; устро́ить п. кому́-н. to play someone a dirty trick.

подвы́пи|вший, *past part. of* ∼ть *and adj.* (*coll.*) slightly tight.

подвы́п|ить, ью, ьешь, *pf.* (*coll.*) to become slightly tight.

подвя|за́ть, жу́, ∼жешь, *pf.* (*of* ∼зывать) to tie up; to keep up.

подвя́зк|а, и, *f.* garter; (*stocking*) suspender.

подвя́зыва|ть, ю, *impf. of* подвяза́ть.

подга́|дить, жу, дишь, *pf.* (*coll.*) **1.** to spoil the effect (of), make a mess (of). **2.** (+*d.*) to play a dirty trick (on).

подгиба́|ть(ся), ю(сь), *impf. of* подогну́ть(ся).

подгла́зь|е, я, *n.* bag under the eyes.

подгля|де́ть, жу́, ди́шь, *pf.* (*of* ∼дывать) (в+*a.*; *coll.*) to peep (at); to spy (on), watch furtively.

подгля́дыва|ть, ю, *impf. of* подгляде́ть.

подгнива́|ть, ю, *impf. of* подгни́ть.

подгни́|ть, ю, ёшь, *past* ∼л, ∼ла́, ∼ло, *pf.* (*of* ∼ва́ть) to begin to rot, rot slightly.

подгова́рива|ть, ю, *impf. of* подговори́ть.

подговор|и́ть, ю, и́шь, *pf.* (*of* подгова́ривать) (на+*a.* or +*inf.*) to put up (to), incite (to), instigate (to).

подголо́вник, а, *m.* head-rest.

подголо́с|ок, ка, *m.* **1.** (*mus.*) second part, supporting voice. **2.** (*coll., pejor.*) yes-man.

подгоня́|ть, ю, *impf. of* подогна́ть.

подгор|а́ть, а́ю, *impf. of* ∼е́ть.

подгоре́лый, *adj.* slightly burnt.

подгор|е́ть, и́т, *pf.* (*of* ∼а́ть) to burn slightly.

подго́рный, *adj.* lowland.

подгоро́дный, *adj.* situated in the outskirts of a town.

подгота́влива|ть(ся), ю(сь), *impf. of* подгото́вить(ся).

подготови́тельн|ый, *adj.* preparatory; ∼ая рабо́та spade-work.

подгото́в|ить, лю, ишь, *pf.* (*of* подгота́вливать *and* ∼ля́ть) (для, к) to prepare (for); п. по́чву (*fig.*) to pave the way.

подгото́в|иться, люсь, ишься, *pf.* (*of* подгота́вливаться *and* ∼ля́ться) (к) to prepare (for), get ready (for).

подгото́вк|а, и, *f.* **1.** (к) preparation (for), training (for); артилле́рийская п. artillery preparation, preparatory bombardment. **2.** (в+*p.* or по+*d.*) grounding (in), schooling (in).

подгото́вленност|ь, и, *f.* preparedness.

подготовля́|ть(ся), ю(сь), *impf. of* подгото́вить(ся).

подгреба́|ть, ю, *impf. of* подгрести́.

подгре|сти́[1], бу́, бёшь, *past* ∼б, ∼бла́, *pf.* (*of* ∼ба́ть) to rake up.

подгре|сти́[2], бу́, бёшь, *past* ∼б, ∼бла́, *pf.* (*of* ∼ба́ть) (к) to row up (to).

подгру́д|ок, ка, *m.* dewlap.

подгру́пп|а, ы, *f.* sub-group.

подгу́зник, а, *m.* nappy, diaper, pilch.

подгуля́|ть, ю, *pf.* (*coll.*) **1.** to take a drop too much, be slightly under the weather. **2.** (*joc.*) to be rather bad, be rather poor, be pretty poor; обе́д немно́го ∼л the dinner was pretty poor.

подда|ва́ть(ся), ю́(сь), ёшь(ся), *impf. of* подда́ть(ся).

поддавк|и́, о́в, *no sing.* игра́ть в п. to play at give-away (*to play draughts according to convention that winner is the first player to lose all his pieces*).

подда́кива|ть, ю, *impf.* (*of* подда́кнуть) (+*d.*; *coll.*) to say yes (to), assent (to); (*also pejor.*).

подда́к|нуть, ну, нешь, *pf. of* ∼ивать.

по́дданн|ый, *p.p.p. of* подда́ть; *as noun* п., ∼ого, *m., and* ∼ая, ∼ой, *f.* subject, national.

по́дданств|о, а, *n.* citizenship, nationality.

под|да́ть, да́м, да́шь, да́ст, дади́м, дади́те, даду́т, *past* ∼да́л, ∼дала́, ∼да́ло, *pf.* (*of* ∼дава́ть) **1.** to kick. **2.** (at draughts, etc.) to give away. **3.** (+*g.*; *coll.*) to add, increase; п. жа́ру to add fuel to the fire; п. па́ру to increase steam; п. га́зу to get a move on.

под|да́ться, да́мся, да́шься, да́стся, дади́мся, дади́тесь, даду́тся, *past* ∼да́лся, ∼дала́сь, *pf.* (*of* ∼дава́ться) **1.** (+*d.*) to yield (to), give way (to), give in (to); дверь не ∼дала́сь the door would not give; п. искуше́нию to yield to temptation; не п. описа́нию to beggar description; п. отча́янию to give way to despair; п. угро́зам to give in to threats. **2.** (*coll.*) to give oneself up.

поддева́|ть, ю, *impf. of* подде́ть.

поддёвк|а, и, *f.* poddyovka (*man's light tight--fitting coat*).

подде́л|ать, аю, *pf.* (*of* ∼ывать) to counterfeit, falsify, fake; to forge; to fabricate; п. по́дпись to forge a signature.

подде́л|аться, аюсь, *pf.* (*of* ∼ываться) **1.** (под+*a.*) to imitate, put on. **2.** (к; *coll.*) to ingratiate oneself (with).

подде́лк|а, и, *f.* falsification; forgery; counterfeit; imitation, fake; п. под же́мчуг imitation pearls.

подде́лывател|ь, я, *m.* forger; counterfeiter, falsifier.

подде́лыва|ть(ся), ю(сь), *impf. of* подде́лать(ся).

подде́льн|ый, *adj.* false, counterfeit; forged;

sham, spurious; ~ые драгоце́нности arti-ficial jewelry; ~ая моне́та counterfeit coin; п. па́спорт forged passport.

поддёргива|ть, ю, *impf. of* поддёрнуть.

поддержа́ни|е, я, *n.* maintenance.

поддерж|а́ть, у́, ~ишь, *pf.* (*of* ~ива́ть) **1.** to support (*also fig.*); to back (up), second; мора́льно п. to give moral support; п. резолю́цию to second a resolution. **2.** to keep up, maintain; п. ого́нь to keep up the fire; п. разгово́р to keep up a conversation; п. регуля́рное сообще́ние to maintain a regular service; п. отноше́ния (с+*i.*) to keep in touch (with).

подде́ржива|ть, ю, *impf.* **1.** *impf. of* подержа́ть. **2.** (*impf. only*) to bear, support.

подде́ржк|а, и, *f.* **1.** (*in var. senses*) support; backing; seconding; огневая п. (*mil.*) fire support; covering fire. **2.** support, prop, stay.

поддёр|нуть, ну, нешь, *pf.* (*of* ~гивать) to pull up.

подде́|ть, ну, нешь, *pf.* (*of* ~ва́ть) **1.** (под +*a.*; *coll.*) to put on under, wear under; ~нь(те) сви́тер под ку́ртку put a sweater on under your jacket. **2.** to hook; to catch up. **3.** (*fig., coll.*) to catch out.

поддо́нник, а, *m.* saucer (*placed under flower-pot*).

поддра́знива|ть, ю, *impf. of* поддразни́ть.

поддразн|и́ть, ю́, ~ишь, *pf.* (*of* ~ивать) (*coll.*) to tease.

поддува́л|о, а, *n.* ash-pit (*of stove, furnace*).

поддува́|ть, ю, *impf.* **1.** to blow (*from under-neath*). **2.** to blow slightly.

по-де́довски, *adv.* (*coll.*) as of old.

поде́йств|овать, ую, *pf. of* де́йствовать 2.

подека́дно, *adv.* every ten days.

поде́ла|ть, ю, *pf.* (*no impf.*) (*coll.*) **1.** to do; ничего́ не ~ешь there is nothing to be done, it can't be helped; ничего́ не могу́ с ни́ми п.! I can't do anything with them. **2.** to make, build.

подел|и́ть(ся), ю(сь), ~ишь(ся), *pf. of* дели́ть(ся).

поде́лк|а, и, *f.* **1.** odd job. **2.** article; ~и из де́рева wood articles.

подело́м, *adv.*; (*coll.*) п. ему́, *etc.*, it serves him, *etc.*, right.

поде́лыва|ть, *impf.* (*coll.*) *only used in question* что ~ешь?, что ~ете? how are you getting on?

подёнк|а, и, *f.* (*insect*) ephemeron, ephe-mera.

подённо, *adv.* by the day.

подённ|ый, *adj.* by the day; ~ая опла́та pay by the day; ~ая рабо́та day-labour, time-work.

подёнщик, а, *m.* day-labourer, time--worker.

подёнщин|а, ы, *f.* work paid by the day, day-labour.

подёнщиц|а, ы, *f.* woman hired by the day.

подёрг|ать, аю, *pf. of* ~ивать.

подёргивани|е, я, *n.* twitch(ing), jerk.

подёргива|ть, ю, *impf.* **1.** (*impf. of* подёр-гать) (+*a. or* за+*a.*) to pull (at), tug (at). **2.** (*impf. only*) (+*i.*) to twitch.

подёргива|ться, юсь, *impf.* to twitch.

подержа́ни|е, я, *n.* на п. for temporary use; взять на п. to borrow; дать на п. to lend.

поде́ржанный, *adj.* second-hand.

подерж|а́ть, у́, ~ишь, *pf.* to hold for some time; to keep for some time.

подерж|а́ться, у́сь, ~ишься, *pf.* **1.** (за+*a.*) to hold (on to) for some time. **2.** to hold (out), last, stand.

подёрн|уть, ет, *pf.* to cover, coat; реку́ ~уло льдом (*impers.*) the river was coated with ice.

подёрн|уться, ется, *pf.* (+*i.*) to be covered (with).

подешеве́|ть, ет, *pf. of* дешеве́ть.

поджа́рива|ть(ся), ю(сь), *impf. of* поджа́-рить(ся).

поджа́рист|ый (~, ~а), *adj.* brown, browned; crisp.

поджа́р|ить, ю, ишь, *pf.* (*of* ~ивать) to fry, roast, grill (slightly); п. хлеб to toast bread.

поджа́р|иться, юсь, ишься, *pf.* (*of* ~ивать-ся) **1.** to fry, roast (slightly). **2.** *pass. of* ~ить.

поджа́рк|а, и, *f.* (*cul.*; *coll.*) grilled or fried piece of beef.

поджа́р|ый (~, ~а), *adj.* (*coll.*) lean, wiry, sinewy.

под|жа́ть, ожму́, ожмёшь, *pf.* (*of* ~жима́ть) to draw in; п. гу́бы to purse one's lips; п. хвост to have one's tail between one's legs (*also fig.*); сиде́ть ~жа́в но́ги to sit cross--legged.

поджелу́дочн|ый, *adj.* ~ая железа́ (*anat.*) pancreas.

под|же́чь, ожгу́, ожжёшь, ожгу́т, *past* ~жёг, ~ожгла́, *pf.* (*of* ~жига́ть) **1.** to set fire (to), set on fire (*with criminal intent or otherwise*). **2.** (*coll.*) to burn slightly.

поджива́|ть, ю, *impf. of* поджи́ть.

поджига́тел|ь, я, *m.* **1.** incendiary. **2.** (*fig.*) instigator; п. войны́ warmonger.

поджига́тельский, *adj.* inflammatory.

поджига́тельств|о, а, *n.* **1.** incendiarism. **2.** (*fig.*) instigation; п. войны́ warmongering.

поджига́|ть, ю, *impf. of* подже́чь.

поджида́|ть, ю, *impf.* to wait (for); to lie in wait (for).

поджи́л|ки, ок, *no sing.* knee tendons; у меня́ от стра́ха п. затрясли́сь (*fig., coll.*) I was shaking in my shoes, I was quaking with fear.

поджима́|ть, ю, *impf. of* поджа́ть.

подж|и́ть, ивёт, *past* ~и́л, ~ила́, ~и́ло, *pf.* (*of* ~ива́ть) to heal (up); (*of a cut*) to close (up).

поджо́г, а, *m.* arson.

подзаб|ы́ть, у́ду, у́дешь, *pf.* (*coll.*) to forget partially; я ~ы́л ру́сский язы́к my Russian is a little rusty.

подзаголо́в|ок, ка, *m.* sub-title, sub-heading.

подзадо́рива|ть, ю, *impf. of* подзадо́рить.

подзадо́р|ить, ю, ишь, *pf.* (*of* ~ивать) (*coll.*) to egg on, set on.

подзаты́льник, а, *m.* (*coll.*) clip (on the back of the head).

подзащи́тн|ый, ого, *m.* (*leg.*) client.

подземе́л|ье, ья, *g.pl.* ~ий, *n.* cave; dungeon.

**подзёмк|а, и, *f.* (*coll.*) underground (railway), tube.

подзёмн|ый, *adj.* underground, subterranean; ~ая (городска́я) желе́зная доро́га underground (railway), tube; ~ые рабо́ты underground workings; п. толчо́к earthquake shock; tremor.

подзерка́льник, а, *m.* looking-glass table, dressing-table with looking-glass.

подзо́л, а, *m.* (*agric.*) podzol (*sterile greyish--white soil, deficient in salts*).

подзо́лист|ый (~, ~а), *adj.* (*agric.*) containing podzol.

подзо́р, а, *m.* 1. cornice (*of Russian wood building*). 2. edging, trimming.

подзо́рн|ый, *adj.*; ~ая труба́ spy-glass, telescope.

подзу|ди́ть, жу́, ~дишь, *pf.* (*of* ~жива́ть) (*coll.*) to egg on, set on.

подзу́жива|ть, ю, *impf. of* подзуди́ть.

подзыва́|ть, ю, *impf. of* подозва́ть.

поди́[1] (*coll.*) = пойди́ (*imp. of* пойти́); п. сюда́! come here!

поди́[2] (*coll.*) 1. probably, I dare say, I shouldn't wonder; *or translated* must (be), is sure (to be); ты, п., уста́ла you must be tired; он, п., забы́л he has probably forgotten; они́, п., прие́дут I dare say they'll be there. 2. *particle expressing amazement, incredulity, etc.* (*also* на́ п.); п. ты, ра́зве он э́то сказа́л? go on, he never said that?; impossible! he couldn't have said that!; он на́чал так руга́ться, что на́ п. he began to swear so, you can't imagine; вот п. ж ты just imagine; well, who would have thought it possible. 3. *particle* + *imp.* just try; п. удержи́ его́ just try to stop him.

подив|и́ть, лю́, и́шь, *pf.* (*no impf.*) (*coll., obs.*) to cause to marvel, astonish.

подиви́ться, лю́сь, и́шься, *pf. of* диви́ться.

подира́|ть, ет, *impf.* моро́з по ко́же ~ет (*coll.*) it makes one's flesh creep, it gives one the creeps.

подка́лыва|ть, ю, *impf. of* подколо́ть.

подка́пыва|ть(ся), ю(сь), *impf. of* подкопа́ть(ся).

подкарау́лива|ть, ю, *impf.* (*of* подкарау́лить) 1. to catch. 2. (*impf. only*) to be on the watch (for), lie in wait (for).

подкарау́л|ить, ю, ишь, *pf. of* подкарау́ливать.

подка́рмлива|ть, ю, *impf. of* подкорми́ть.

подка|ти́ть, чу́, ~тишь, *pf.* (*of* ~тывать) 1. to roll. 2. (*coll.; of a carriage, etc.*) to roll up, drive up. 3. (*coll.*) у меня́ ком ~ти́л к го́рлу I felt a lump rise in my throat.

подка|ти́ться, чу́сь, ~тишься, *pf.* (*of* ~тываться) (под+*a.*) to roll (under).

подка́тыва|ть(ся), ю(сь), *impf. of* подкати́ть(ся).

подкач|а́ть, а́ю, *pf.* (*of* ~ивать) (*coll.*) to make a mess (of things); to let one down.

подка́чива|ть, ю, *impf. of* подкача́ть.

**подка́чк|а, и, *f.* (*phys.*) pump.

подка́шива|ть(ся), ю(сь), *impf. of* подкоси́ть(ся).

подка́шлива|ть, ю, *impf.* (*coll.*) to cough (*intentionally, to draw attention, etc.*).

подка́шлян|уть, у, ешь, *pf.* to give a cough.

подки́дыва|ть, ю, *impf. of* подки́нуть.

подки́дыш, а, *m.* foundling.

подки́|нуть, ну, нешь, *pf.* (*of* ~дывать) = подбро́сить.

подки́сл|енный, *p.p.p. of* ~и́ть *and adj.* (*chem.*) acidified, acidulous.

подкисл|и́ть, ю́, и́шь, *pf.* (*of* ~я́ть) (*chem.*) to acidify.

подкисл|я́ть, я́ю, *impf. of* ~и́ть.

**подкла́дк|а, и, *f.* 1. lining; на шёлковой ~е silk-lined. 2. (*fig., coll.*) the inside, the secret (of); мы обнару́жили ~у э́того собы́тия we have discovered what lay behind this event.

подкладно́|й, *adj.* put under; ~е су́дно bed-pan.

подкла́д|очный, *adj. of* ~ка; п. материа́л lining (material).

подкла́дыва|ть, ю, *impf. of* подложи́ть.

подкла́сс, а, *m.* (*biol.*) sub-class.

подкле́ива|ть, ю, *impf. of* подкле́ить.

подкле́|ить, ю, ишь, *pf.* (*of* ~ивать) 1. (под+*a.*) to glue (under), paste (under). 2. to glue up, paste up. 3. *pf. of* кле́ить 2.

**подкле́йк|а, и, *f.* glueing, pasting.

подключ|а́ть(ся), а́ю(сь), *impf. of* ~и́ть(ся).

подключ|и́ть, у́, и́шь, *pf.* (*of* ~а́ть) (*coll.*) 1. (*tech.*) to link up, connect up. 2. (*fig.*) to attach; его́ ~и́ли ко второ́му ку́рсу he has been attached to the second year.

подключ|и́ться, у́сь, и́шься, *pf.* (*of* ~а́ться) (*coll.*) 1. (*tech. and fig.*) pass. of ~и́ть. 2. (*fig.*) to settle down; to get the hang of things.

подключи́чный, *adj.* (*anat.*) subclavian, subclavicular.

подко́в|а, ы, *f.* (horse-)shoe.

подк|ова́ть, ую́, уёшь, *pf.* (*of* кова́ть *and* ~о́вывать) **1.** to shoe. **2.** (в+*p.*; *fig.*, *coll.*) to ground (in), give a grounding (in).

подко́выва|ть, ю, *impf. of* подкова́ть.

подковы́рива|ть, ю, *impf. of* подковырну́ть.

подковы́рк|а, и, *f.* (*coll.*) catch; attempt to catch out.

подковыр|ну́ть, ну́, нёшь, *pf.* (*of* ~ивать) **1.** to pick (*a sore, etc.*). **2.** (*fig.*, *coll.*) to catch out.

подко́жный, *adj.* subcutaneous, hypodermic.

подколе́нный, *adj.* (*anat.*) popliteal.

подколо́дн|ый, *adj.* змея́ ~ая (*fig.*, *coll.*) snake in the grass.

подкол|о́ть, ю́, ~ешь, *pf.* (*of* подка́лывать) **1.** to pin up. **2.** to chop up. **3.** to attach, append (*to a document or file*).

подкоми́сси|я, и, *f.* sub-committee.

подкомите́т, а, *m.* sub-committee.

подконтро́льный, *adj.* under control.

подко́п, а, *m.* **1.** undermining. **2.** underground passage. **3.** (*fig.*, *coll.*) intrigue(s), underhand plotting.

подкопа́|ть, ю, *pf.* (*of* подка́пывать) to undermine, sap.

подкопа́|ться, юсь, *pf.* (*of* подка́пываться) (под+*a.*) **1.** to undermine, sap; (*of animals*) to burrow (under). **2.** (*fig.*, *coll.*) to intrigue (against).

подко́рм|и́ть, лю́, ~ишь, *pf.* (*of* подка́рмливать) **1.** to feed up; to fatten (*livestock*). **2.** (*agric.*) to add fertilizer to.

подко́рмк|а, и, *f.* **1.** feeding; fattening. **2.** additional fertilization.

подко́с, а, *m.* (*tech.*) strut, brace, angle brace.

подко|си́ть, шу́, ~сишь, *pf.* (*of* подка́шивать) **1.** to cut down. **2.** to fell, lay low (*also fig.*); э́то оконча́тельно ~си́ло (меня́, его́, *etc.*) that was the last straw.

подкос|и́ться, ~ится, *pf.* (*of* подка́шиваться) to give way, fail one.

подкра́дыва|ться, юсь, *impf. of* подкра́сться.

подкра́|сить, шу, сишь, *pf.* (*of* ~шивать) to tint, colour; to touch up (*make-up*, etc.).

подкра́|ситься, шусь, сишься, *pf.* (*of* ~шиваться) to touch up one's make-up.

подкра́|сться, ду́сь, дёшься, *pf.* (*of* ~дываться) (к) to steal up (to), sneak up (to).

подкра́шива|ть(ся), ю(сь), *impf. of* подкра́сить(ся).

подкреп|и́ть, лю́, и́шь, *pf.* (*of* ~ля́ть) **1.** to support. **2.** (*fig.*) to support, back; to confirm, corroborate; п. пригово́р ссы́лкой на прецеде́нты to support a judgement by reference to precedent. **3.** to fortify, recruit (*with food and/or drink*); п. себя́ перед

дорого́й to fortify oneself for a journey. **4.** (*mil.*) to reinforce.

подкреп|и́ться, лю́сь, и́шься, *pf.* (*of* ~ля́ться) **1.** to fortify oneself (*with food and/or drink*). **2.** *pass. of* ~и́ть.

подкрепле́ни|е, я, *n.* **1.** confirmation, corroboration. **2.** sustenance. **3.** (*mil.*) reinforcement.

подкрепля́|ть(ся), ю(сь), *impf. of* подкрепи́ть(ся).

подкузьм|и́ть, лю́, и́шь, *pf.* (*coll.*) to do a bad turn; to do (down).

подкула́чник, а, *m.* (*pejor.*) kulak's henchman, kulak's man.

по́дкуп, а, *m.* bribery; graft.

подкуп|а́ть, а́ю, *impf. of* ~и́ть.

подкуп|и́ть, лю́, ~ишь, *pf.* (*of* ~а́ть) **1.** to bribe; to suborn. **2.** (*fig.*) to win over; всех нас ~и́ла её доброта́ her kindness won all our hearts.

подла́|диться, жусь, дишься, *pf.* (*of* ~живаться) (к; *coll.*) **1.** to adapt oneself (to), fit in (with). **2.** to humour; to make up (to).

подла́жива|ться, юсь, *impf. of* подла́диться.

подла́мыва|ться, ется, *impf. of* подломи́ться.

по́дле, *prep.*+*g.* by the side of, beside.

подлёдный, *adj.* under the ice.

подлеж|а́ть, у́, и́шь, *impf.* (+*d.*) to be liable (to), be subject (to); п. ве́дению кого́-н. to be within someone's competence; э́тот дом ~и́т сно́су this house is to be pulled down; п. суду́ to be indictable; «не ~и́т оглаше́нию» (*classification of document*) 'Confidential'; не ~и́т сомне́нию it is beyond doubt, it is not open to question.

подлежа́щ|ее, его, *n.* (*gram.*) subject.

подлежа́|щий, *pres. part. act. of* ~ть *and adj.* (+*d.*) liable (to), subject (to); п. обложе́нию сбо́ром dutiable; не п. обложе́нию сбо́ром exempt from duty, duty-free; не п. оглаше́нию confidential, private; off-the-record.

подлез|а́ть, а́ю, *impf. of* ~ть.

подлез|ть, у, ешь, *pf.* (*of* ~а́ть) (под+*a.*) to crawl (under), creep (under).

подле́кар|ь, я, *m.* (*obs.*) doctor's assistant.

подле́с|ок, ка, *m.* undergrowth.

подлет|а́ть, а́ю, *impf. of* ~е́ть.

подле|те́ть, чу́, ти́шь, *pf.* (*of* ~та́ть) (к) to fly up (to); (*fig.*) to run up (to), rush up (to).

подле́|ть, ю, ешь, *impf.* (*of* о~) (*coll.*) to grow mean; to become a scoundrel.

подле́ц, а́, *m.* scoundrel, villain, rascal.

подле́чива|ть(ся), ю(сь), *impf. of* подлечи́ть(ся).

подлеч|и́ть, у́, ~ишь, *pf.* (*of* ~ивать) (*coll.*) to treat.

подлеч|и́ться, у́сь, ~ишься, *pf.* (*of* ~иваться) (*coll.*) to take medical treatment.

подлива́|ть, ю, *impf. of* подли́ть.

подли́вк|а, и, *f.* sauce, dressing; gravy.

подливн|о́й, *adj.* ∼о́е колесо́ (*tech.*) under-shot wheel.

подли́з|а, ы, *m. and f.* (*coll.*) lickspittle, toady.

подли|за́ть, жу́, ∼жешь, *pf.* (*of* ∼зыва́ть) to lick up.

подли|за́ться, жу́сь, ∼жешься, *pf.* (*of* ∼зыва́ться) (к; *coll.*) to lick someone's boots; to suck up (to).

подли́зыва|ть(ся), ю(сь), *impf. of* подлиза́ть(ся).

по́длинник, а, *m.* original (*as opp. to* copy).

по́длинно, *adv.* really; genuinely; п. хоро́-ший фильм a really good film.

по́длинност|ь, и, *f.* authenticity.

по́длин|ный (∼ен, ∼на), *adj.* **1.** genuine; authentic; original; его́ ∼ные слова́ his very words, his own words; «с ∼ным ве́рно» 'certified true copy'. **2.** true, real; п. учёный a true scholar.

под|ли́ть, олью́, ольёшь, *past* ∼ли́л, ∼лила́, ∼ли́ло, *pf.* (*of* ∼лива́ть) (+*a. or g.* в+*a.*) to add (to); п. ма́сла в ого́нь (*fig.*) to add fuel to the fire.

по́длича|ть, ю, *impf.* to act meanly; to be-have like a scoundrel, cad.

подло́г, а, *m.* forgery.

подлож|и́ть, у́, ∼ишь, *pf.* (*of* подкла́ды-вать) **1.** (под+*a.*) to lay under; to line; п. ва́ту to wad. **2.** (+*a. or g.*) to add; ∼и́те дрова́ *or* дров put some more wood on. **3.** to put furtively; п. свинью́ кому́-н. to play a dirty trick on someone.

подло́ж|ный (∼ен, ∼на), *adj.* false, spurious; counterfeit, forged.

подлоко́тник, а, *m.* elbow-rest; arm (*of chair*).

подлом|и́ться, ∼ится, *pf.* (*of* подла́мы-ваться) (под+*i.*) to break (under).

по́длост|ь, и, *f.* **1.** meanness, baseness. **2.** mean trick, low-down trick.

подлу́нный, *adj.* sublunar.

по́дл|ый (∼, ∼а́, ∼о), *adj.* mean, base, ignoble.

подма́|зать, жу, жешь, *pf.* (*of* ∼зывать) to grease, oil; (*fig., coll.*) to grease someone's palm.

подма́|заться, жусь, жешься, *pf.* (*of* ∼зы-ваться) **1.** to touch up one's make-up. **2.** (к) to curry favour (with), make up (to).

подма́зыва|ть(ся), ю(сь), *impf. of* подма́-зать(ся).

подмал|ева́ть, юю, юешь, *pf.* (*of* ∼ёвывать) to tint, colour; to touch up.

подмалёвыва|ть, ю, *impf. of* подмалева́ть.

подманда́тн|ый, *adj.* (*polit.*) mandated; ∼ая террито́рия mandated territory.

подма́нива|ть, ю, *impf. of* подмани́ть.

подман|и́ть, ю́, ∼ишь, *pf.* (*of* ∼ивать) to call (to); to beckon.

подмасте́рь|е, я, *g. pl.* ∼ев, *m.* apprentice.

подма́хива|ть, ю, *impf. of* подмахну́ть.

подмах|ну́ть, ну́, нёшь, *pf.* (*of* ∼ивать) (*coll.*) to scribble a signature to; to sign (hastily and negligently).

подма́чива|ть, ю, *impf. of* подмочи́ть.

подме́н, а, *m.* substitution (*of something false for something real*).

подме́н|а, ы, *f.* = ∼.

подме́нива|ть, ю, *impf. of* подмени́ть.

подмен|и́ть, ю́, ∼ишь, *pf.* (*of* ∼ивать *and* ∼я́ть) (+*a. and i.*) to substitute (for) (*inten-tionally*); кто́-то на вечери́нке ∼и́л мне шля́пу someone at the party took my hat (and left his instead).

подмен|я́ть, я́ю, *impf. of* ∼и́ть.

подмерз|а́ть, а́ет, *impf. of* ∼нуть.

подмёрз|нуть, нет, *past* ∼, ∼ла, *pf.* (*of* ∼а́ть) to freeze slightly.

подме|си́ть, шу́, ∼сишь, *pf.* (*of* ∼шивать[1]) to add, mix in.

подме|сти́, ту́, тёшь, *past* ∼л, ∼ла́, *pf.* (*of* ∼та́ть[1]) to sweep.

подмета́|ть[1], ю, *impf. of* подмести́.

подме|та́ть[2], чу́, ∼чешь, *pf.* (*of* ∼тывать) to baste, tack.

подме́|тить, чу, тишь, *pf.* (*of* ∼ча́ть) to notice.

подмётк|а, и, *f.* sole; в ∼и кому́-н. не годи́ться (*coll.*) not to be fit to hold a candle to someone.

подмётн|ый, *adj.* ∼ое письмо́ (*obs.*) anony-mous letter.

подмётыва|ть, ю, *impf. of* подмета́ть[2].

подмеча́|ть, ю, *impf. of* подме́тить.

подмеш|а́ть, а́ю, *pf.* (*of* ∼ивать[2]) to stir in.

подме́шива|ть[1], ю, *impf. of* подмеси́ть.

подме́шива|ть[2], ю, *impf. of* подмеша́ть.

подми́гива|ть, ю, *impf. of* подмигну́ть.

подмиг|ну́ть, ну́, нёшь, *pf.* (*of* ∼ивать) (+*d.*) to wink (at).

подмина́|ть, ю, *impf. of* подмя́ть.

подмо́г|а, и, *f.* (*coll.*) help, assistance; идти́ на ∼у (+*d.*) to come to the aid (of), lend a hand.

подмок|а́ть, а́ю, *impf. of* ∼нуть.

подмо́к|нуть, ну, нешь, *past* ∼, ∼ла, *pf.* (*of* ∼а́ть) to get slightly wet.

подмора́жива|ть, ет, *impf. of* подморо́зить.

подморо́женный, *adj.* frost-bitten, frozen (slightly).

подморо́з|ить, ит, *pf.* (*of* подмора́живать) to freeze; к ве́черу ∼ило towards evening it began to freeze.

подмоско́вн|ый, *adj.* (situated) near Mos-cow; *as noun* ∼ая, ∼ой, *f.* (*obs.*) estate near Moscow.

подмо́стк|и, ов, *no sing.* 1. scaffolding, staging. 2. (*theatr.*) stage; boards.

подмо́ч|енный, *p.p.p. of* ~и́ть *and adj.* 1. slightly wet, damp. 2. damaged (*also fig.*); ~енная репута́ция tarnished reputation.

подмоч|и́ть, у́, ~ишь, *pf.* (*of* подма́чивать) 1. to wet slightly, damp. 2. to damage by exposing to damp.

подмы́в, а, *m.* washing away, undermining.

подмыва́|ть, ю, *impf.* 1. *impf. of* подмы́ть. 2. (*impers.*) to urge; меня́ так и ~ет (+*inf.*) I feel an urge (to), I can hardly keep (from).

подмы́|ть, о́ю, о́ешь, *pf.* (*of* ~ва́ть) 1. to wash. 2. to wash away, undermine.

подмы́ш|ечный, *adj. of* ~ки.

подмы́шк|а, и, *f.* arm-pit (*of article of clothing*).

подмы́ш|ки, ек, *no sing.* arm-pits (*see also* мы́шка²).

подмы́шник, а, *m.* dress protector.

под|мя́ть, омну́, омнёшь, *pf.* (*of* ~мина́ть) to crush; to trample down.

поднадзо́р|ный (~ен, ~на), *adj.* under surveillance, under supervision.

поднаж|а́ть, му́, мёшь, *pf.* (на+*a.*; *coll.*) to press, put pressure (on); to chivvy.

поднача́льный, *adj.* (*obs., now joc. only*) subordinate.

подна́чива|ть, ю, *impf. of* подна́чить.

подна́ч|ить, у, ишь, *pf.* (*of* ~ивать) (*coll.*) to egg on.

поднебе́сн|ая, ой, *f.* (*folk poet.*) the earth.

поднебе́сь|е, я, *n.* (*folk poet.*) the heavens.

поднево́ль|ный (~ен, ~ьна), *adj.* 1. dependent; subordinate. 2. forced; п. труд forced labour.

поднес|ти́, у́, ёшь, *past* ~, ~ла́, *pf.* (*of* подноси́ть) 1. (к) to take (to), bring (to). 2. (+*d. and a.*) to present (with); to take (as a present); to treat (to); п. кому́-н. буке́т цвето́в to present someone with a bouquet; ~й ему́ рю́мку коньяку́ take him, treat him to a (glass of) brandy.

подне́сь, *adv.* (*obs.*) to this day, up to now.

по́дниз|ь, и, *f.* (*obs.*) string (*of beads, etc.*).

поднима́|ть(ся), ю(сь), *impf. of* подня́ть(ся); ~й вы́ше! (*coll.*) try again!

поднов|и́ть, лю́, и́шь, *pf.* (*of* ~ля́ть) to renew, renovate.

подновля́|ть, ю, *impf. of* поднови́ть.

подногото́н|ая, ой, *f.* (*coll.*) the whole truth, all there is to know; the ins and outs, the tricks of the trade; он зна́ет про них всю ~ую he knows all (there is to know) about them.

подно́жи|е, я, *n.* 1. foot (*of an inanimate object, mountain, etc.*). 2. pedestal.

подно́жк|а¹, и, *f.* step, footboard.

подно́жк|а², и, *f.* (*in wrestling*) backheel;

дать кому́-н. ~у to trip someone up.

подно́жн|ый, *adj.* п. корм pasture, pasturage; быть на ~ом корму́ to be at grass; пусти́ть на п. корм to put to grass.

подно́с, а, *m.* tray; salver; ча́йный п. tea-tray.

подноси́тел|ь, я, *m.* giver, donor.

подно|си́ть, шу́, ~сишь, *impf. of* поднести́.

подно́ск|а, и, *f.* transporting, bringing up.

подно́счик, а, *m.* 1. carrier; п. патро́нов ammunition carrier. 2. innkeeper's assistant, drinks server.

подноше́ни|е, я, *n.* 1. presenting, giving. 2. present, gift; цвето́чные ~я floral tributes.

подня́ти|е, я, *n.* raising; rise; rising; п. за́навеса curtain-rise; голосова́ть ~ем рук to vote by show of hands.

под|ня́ть, ниму́, ни́мешь, *past* ~ня́л, ~няла́, ~ня́ло, *pf.* (*of* ~нима́ть) 1. (*in var. senses*) to raise; to lift; to hoist; п. ка́рту to colour a map; п. настрое́ние (+*g.*) to cheer up, raise the spirits (of); п. ору́жие to take up arms; п. паруса́ to raise sail, set sail; п. ру́ку (на+*a.*) to lift up one's hand (against); п. флаг to hoist a flag; (*naut.*) to make the colours; п. целину́ to open up virgin lands, break fresh ground; п. шерсть to bristle up; п. я́корь to weigh anchor; п. на во́здух to blow up; п. на́ смех to make a laughingstock (of). 2. to pick up; п. пе́тли to pick up stitches. 3. to rouse, stir up; п. восста́ние to stir up rebellion; п. ссо́ру to pick a quarrel; п. на́ ноги to rouse, get up. 4. (*fig.*) to improve; to enhance; п. де́ло (*coll.*) to cope with an affair, manage an affair successfully.

под|ня́ться, ниму́сь, ни́мешься, *past* ~ня́лся́, ~няла́сь, *pf.* (*of* ~ня́ться) 1. (*in var. senses*) to rise; to go up; to get up; н. на́ ноги to rise to one's feet; п. в ата́ку to go in to the attack; п. в гало́п to break into a gallop. 2. (на+*a.*) to climb, ascend, go up. 3. to arise; to break out, develop; ~няла́сь ссо́ра a quarrel arose; ~няла́сь дра́ка a fight started. 4. (*econ.*; *fig.*) to improve; to recover.

подо, *prep.* = под.

подоба́|ть, ет, *impf.* (*impers.*; +*d. and inf.*) to become, befit; как ~ет as befits one; не ~ет it does not do.

подоба́|ющий, *pres. part. act. of* ~ть *and adj.* proper, fitting.

подо́би|е, я, *n.* 1. likeness; по своему́ о́бразу и ~ю in one's own image. 2. (*math.*) similarity.

подо́блачный, *adj.* under the clouds.

подо́бно, *adv.* (+*d.*) like; п. верблю́ду like a camel; п. тому́, как just as.

подо́бн|ый (~ен, ~на), *adj.* like; similar;

~ное поведéние such behaviour; ~ные треугóльники (*math.*) similar triangles; я никогдá не встречáл ~ного дуракá I have never met such a fool; ничегó ~ного! (*coll.*) nothing of the kind!; и томý ~ное (*abbr.* и т. п.) and so on, and such like.

подобострáсти|е, я, *n.* servility.

подобострáст|ный (~ен, ~на), *adj.* servile.

подóбранность|ь, и, *f.* neatness, tidiness.

подóбр|анный, *p.p.p. of* ~áть *and adj.* neat, tidy.

под|обрáть, берý, берёшь, *past* ~обрáл, ~обралá, ~обрáло, *pf.* (*of* ~бирáть) 1. to pick up; п. колóсья to glean. 2. to tuck up; to take up; п. вóлосы to put up one's hair. 3. to select, pick; п. деся́тников to pick foremen; п. ключ к замкý to fit a key to a lock; п. джéмпер под цвет костю́ма to choose a jumper to match a suit.

под|обрáться, берýсь, берёшься, *past* ~обрáлся, ~обралáсь, ~обралóсь, *pf.* (*of* ~бирáться) 1. (к) to steal up (to), approach stealthily. 2. to make oneself tidy. 3. *pass. of* ~обрáть.

подобрé|ть, ю, *pf. of* добрéть[1].

подобрý-поздорóву, *adv.* (*coll.*) in good time, while the going is good.

подóвый, *adj.* baked in the hearth.

подóг, á, *m.* (*dial.*) stick.

под|огнáть, гоню́, гóнишь, *past* ~огнáл, ~огналá, ~огнáло, *pf.* (*of* ~гоня́ть) 1. (к) to drive (to). 2. (*coll.*) to drive on, urge on, hurry. 3. (к) to adjust (to), fit (to).

под|огнýть, огнý, огнёшь, *pf.* (*of* ~гибáть) to tuck in; to bend under.

под|огнýться, огнýсь, огнёшься, *pf.* (*of* ~гибáться) to bend; нóги, колéни у негó ~огнýлись he was bent, doubled up (*from fatigue, etc.*).

подогрéв, а, *m.* (*tech.*) heating; предвар*и*тельный п. pre-heating.

подогревáтел|ь, я, *m.* (*tech.*) heater.

подогревáтельный, *adj.* (*tech.*) heating.

подогревá|ть, ю, *impf. of* подогрéть.

подогрé|ть, ю, *pf.* (*of* ~вáть) to warm up, heat up; (*fig.*) to rouse.

пододвигá|ть, ю, *impf. of* пододвúнуть.

пододви|нуть, ну, нешь, *pf.* (*of* ~гáть) (к) to move up (to), push up (to).

подожд|áть, ý, ёшь, *past* ~áл, ~алá, ~áло, *pf.* (+*a. or g.*) to wait (for).

под|озвáть, зовý, зовёшь, *past* ~озвáл, ~озвалá, ~озвáло, *pf.* (*of* ~зывáть) to call up; to beckon.

подозревá|емый, *pres. part. pass. of* ~ть *and adj.* suspected; suspect.

подозревá|ть, ю, *impf.* (*no pf.*) to suspect (*someone or that something is the case*); я ~ю егó

в преступлéнии I suspect him of a crime; я ~ю, что он совершúл преступлéние I suspect that he has committed a crime.

подозрéни|е, я, *n.* suspicion; остáться вне ~й to remain above suspicion; по ~ю (в+*p.*) on suspicion (of); быть под ~ем, на ~и to be under suspicion.

подозрúтельно, *adv.* suspiciously; вестú себя́ п. to behave suspiciously; смотрéть п. (на+*a.*) to regard with suspicion.

подозрúтельност|ь, и, *f.* suspiciousness.

подозрúтел|ьный (~ен, ~ьна), *adj.* 1. suspicious; suspect; shady, fishy; ~ьного вúда suspicious-looking; п. субъéкт shady character. 2. suspicious (= mistrustful).

подо|úть, ю́, ~úшь, *pf. of* доúть.

подóйник, а, *m.* milk-pail.

подо|йтú, йдý, йдёшь, *past* ~шёл, ~шлá, *pf.* (*of* подходúть) 1. (к) to approach (*also fig.*); to come up (to), go up (to); пóезд ~шёл к стáнции the train pulled in to the station; джýнгли ~шлú к сáмому поселéнию the jungle came right up to the settlement; критúчески п. к вопрóсу to approach a question critically, adopt a critical approach to a question. 2. (+*d.*) to do (for); to suit; to fit; э́тот пиджáк óчень мне ~йдёт this coat will suit me very well; э́то слóво не ~йдёт в дáнном контéксте this word will not do in the context under consideration; вáше крéсло едвá ли ~йдёт к стúлю кóмнаты your chair will hardly go with the room.

подокóнник, а, *m.* window-sill.

подóл, а, *m.* 1. hem (*of skirt*); держáться за чей-н. п. to cling to someone's skirts. 2. (*dial.*) lower part, lower slopes; foot (*of hill*).

подóлгу, *adv.* for long; for hours, days, weeks, months, *etc.*; мы с ним п. болтáли he and I used to chat by the hour; онú п. к нам не заходúли they have not been in to see us for ages.

подоль|стúться, щýсь, стúшься, *pf.* (к; *coll.*) to worm oneself into someone's favour, into someone's good graces.

подольщá|ться, юсь, *impf. of* подольстúться.

по-домáшнему, *adv.* simply; without ceremony; одéт п. (dressed) in clothes worn about the house.

подóн|ки, ков, *sing.* ~ок, ~ка, *m.* dregs (*also fig.*); (*fig.*) scum; riff-raff.

подопéчн|ый, *adj.* under wardship; ~ая территóрия (*polit.*) trust territory.

подоплёк|а, и, *f.* (*coll.*) the real (*as opp. to the ostensible, apparent*) state of affairs; the real cause, the underlying cause; знать ~у перемéны отношéний to know the real cause of a volte-face.

подо́пытный, *adj.* experimental; п. кро́лик (*fig.*) guinea-pig.

подорв|а́ть, у́, ёшь, *past* ~а́л, ~ала́, ~а́ло, *pf.* (*of* подрыва́ть[1]) 1. to blow up; to blast. 2. (*fig.*) to undermine; to sap; to damage severely; п. чей-н. авторите́т to undermine someone's authority; п. здоро́вье to sap one's health.

подо́рлик, а, *m.* (*orn.*) spotted eagle.

подорожа́|ть, ю, *pf. of* дорожа́ть.

подоро́жн|ая, ой, *f.* (*hist.*) order for (fresh) post-horses.

подоро́жник, а, *m.* 1. (*bot.*) plantain. 2. (*coll.*) provisions taken on a journey. 3. (*obs.*) highwayman. 4. лапла́ндский п. (*orn.*) Lapland bunting.

подоро́жный, *adj.* on the road, along the road; п. столб milestone.

подоси́новик, а, *m.* orange-cap boletus (*mushroom*) (*Boletus versipellis*).

подо|сла́ть, шлю́, шлёшь, *pf.* (*of* подсыла́ть) to send, dispatch (*secretly, on a secret mission*).

подоснов|а, ы, *f.* real cause, underlying cause.

подоспева́|ть, ю, *impf. of* подоспе́ть.

подоспе́|ть, ю, *pf.* (*of* ~ва́ть) (*coll.*) to arrive, appear (*in time*).

под|остла́ть, стелю́, сте́лешь, *pf.* (*of* ~стила́ть) (под+*a.*) to lay (under), stretch (under).

подотде́л, а, *m.* section, subdivision.

подоткн|у́ть, у́, ёшь, *pf.* (*of* подтыка́ть) to tuck in, tuck up; п. простыню́ to tuck in a sheet; п. ю́бку to tuck up one's skirt.

подотря́д, а, *m.* (*biol.*) sub-order.

подотчёт|ный (~ен, ~на), *adj.* 1. (+*d.*) accountable (to). 2. (*fin.*) on account; ~ная су́мма sum paid out on account; imprest.

подо́хн|уть, у, ешь, *pf.* (*of* до́хнуть *and* подыха́ть) 1. (*of animals*) to die. 2. (*coll.; of human beings*) to peg out, kick the bucket.

подохо́дный, *adj.* п. нало́г income tax.

подо́шв|а, ы, *f.* 1. sole (*of foot or boot*). 2. foot (*of slope*). 3. (*tech.*) base.

подо́шв|енный, *adj. of* ~а.

подпада́|ть, ю, *impf. of* подпа́сть.

подпа́ива|ть, ю, *impf. of* подпои́ть.

подпа́лин|а, ы, *f.* burnt place, scorch-mark; ло́шадь с ~ой dappled horse.

подпал|и́ть, ю́, и́шь, *pf.* (*of* ~ивать) (*coll.*) 1. to singe, scorch. 2. to set on fire.

подпа́рыва|ть(ся), ю(сь), *impf. of* подпоро́ть(ся).

подпа́с|ок, ка, *m.* herdsboy.

подпа́|сть, ду́, дёшь, *past* ~л, *pf.* (*of* ~да́ть) (под+*a.*) to fall (under); п. под чьё-н. влия́ние to fall under someone's influence.

подпа́х|ать, шу́, ~шешь, *pf.* (*of* ~хивать) to plough a little.

подпа́хива|ть[1], ю, *impf. of* подпаха́ть.

подпа́хива|ть[2], ет, *impf.* (*coll.*) to stink a little.

подпева́л|а, ы, *m. and f.* (*coll.*) yes-man.

подпева́|ть, ю, *impf.* (+*d.*) to join (in singing); to take up a song; (*fig.*) to echo.

под|пере́ть, опру́, опрёшь, *past* ~пёр, ~пёрла, *pf.* (*of* ~пира́ть) to prop up.

подпи́лива|ть, ю, *impf. of* подпили́ть.

подпил|и́ть, ю́, ~ишь, *pf.* (*of* ~ивать) 1. to saw; to file. 2. to saw a little off; to file down.

подпи́л|ок, ка, *m.* file.

подпира́|ть, ю, *impf. of* подпере́ть.

подписа́вш|ий, его, *m.* signatory.

подписа́ни|е, я, *n.* signing.

подпи|са́ть, шу́, ~шешь, *pf.* (*of* ~сывать) 1. to sign. 2. to add (*to something written*); п. ещё одно́ подстро́чное примеча́ние to add another footnote. 3. to subscribe (= *include in list of subscribers*); п. кого́-н. на журна́л to take out a magazine subscription for someone.

подпи|са́ться, шу́сь, ~шешься, *pf.* (*of* ~сываться) 1. (под+*i.*) to sign, put one's name (to); (*fig.*) to subscribe (to). 2. (на+ *a.*) to subscribe (to, for); п. на журна́л to subscribe to, take out a subscription for a magazine.

подпи́ск|а, и, *f.* 1. subscription. 2. engagement; written undertaking; signed statement; дать ~у о невы́езде to give a written undertaking not to leave a place.

подписн|о́й, *adj.* subscription; п. лист subscription list; ~а́я цена́ the price of subscription.

подпи́счик, а, *m.* (на+*a.*) subscriber (to).

по́дпис|ь, и, *f.* 1. signature; поста́вить свою́ п. (под+*i.*) to put one's signature (to, beneath), affix one's signature (to); за ~ью (+*g.*) signed (by); за ~ью и печа́тью signed and sealed. 2. caption; inscription.

подплыва́|ть, ю, *impf. of* подплы́ть.

подплы́|ть, ву́, вёшь, *past* ~л, ~ла́, ~ло, *pf.* (*of* ~ва́ть) (к) to swim up (to); to sail up (to).

подпо|и́ть, ю́, ~и́шь, *pf.* (*of* подпа́ивать) (*coll.*) to make tipsy.

по́дпол, а, *m.* (*dial.*) cellar.

подполз|а́ть, а́ю, *impf. of* ~ти́.

подполз|ти́, у́, ёшь, *past* ~, ~ла́, *pf.* (*of* ~а́ть) (к) to creep up (to); (под+*a.*) to creep (under).

подполко́вник, а, *m.* lieutenant-colonel.

подпо́ль|е, я, *n.* 1. cellar. 2. (*fig.*) underground work; (the) underground (organization); уйти́ в п. to go underground.

подпо́льный, *adj.* 1. under the floor. 2. (*fig.*) underground; secret, clandestine.

подпо́льщик, а, *m.* member of an underground organization.

подпо́р, а, *m.* (*tech.*) head (*of water*).

подпо́р|а, ы, *f.* prop, support; brace, strut.

подпо́рк|а, и, *f.* = подпо́ра.

подпо́р|ный, *adj.* *of* ~а; ~ная сте́нка breast--wall; (*naut.*) bulkhead.

подпор|о́ть, ю́, ~ешь, *pf.* (*of* подпа́рывать) to rip; to unpick, unstitch.

подпор|о́ться, ~ется, *pf.* (*of* подпа́рываться) to rip; to come unpicked, come un-stitched.

подпору́чик, а, *m.* (*hist.*) second lieutenant.

подпо́чв|а, ы, *f.* subsoil, substratum.

подпо́чвенн|ый, *adj.* subsoil; subterranean; ~ая вода́ underground water; п. слой pan.

подпоя́|сать, шу, шешь, *pf.* (*of* ~сывать) to belt; to gird (on).

подпоя́|саться, шусь, шешься, *pf.* (*of* ~сываться) to belt oneself; to gird oneself; to put on a belt, girdle.

подпоя́сыва|ть(ся), ю(сь), *impf.* *of* под-поя́сать(ся).

подпра́в|ить, лю, ишь, *pf.* (*of* ~ля́ть) to rectify; to touch up, retouch.

подправля́|ть, ю, *impf.* *of* подпра́вить.

подпру́г|а, и, *f.* saddle-girth, belly-band.

подпры́гива|ть, ю, *impf.* *of* подпры́гнуть.

подпры́г|нуть, ну, нешь, *pf.* (*of* ~ивать) to leap up, jump up; to bob up and down.

подпуска́|ть, ю, *impf.* *of* подпусти́ть.

подпу́|стить, щу́, ~стишь, *pf.* (*of* ~ска́ть) 1. to allow to approach; п. на расстоя́ние вы́стрела to allow to come within range. 2. (+*a.* *or* *g.*; *coll.*) to add in. 3. (*coll.*) to get in, put in (*a sarcasm, a witticism, etc.*).

подпя́тник, а, *m.* (*tech.*) step bearing.

подраба́тыва|ть, ю, *impf.* *of* подрабо́тать.

подрабо́та|ть, ю, *pf.* (*of* подраба́тывать) (*coll.*) 1. (+*a.* *or* *g.*) to earn additionally. 2. to work up.

подра́внива|ть, ю, *impf.* *of* подровня́ть.

подра́гива|ть, ю, *impf.* (*coll.*) to shake, tremble intermittently.

подража́ни|е, я, *n.* imitation.

подража́тел|ь, я, *m.* imitator.

подража́тел|ьный (~ен, ~ьна), *adj.* imita-tive.

подража́тельств|о, а, *n.* (*pejor.*) imitative-ness.

подража́|ть, ю, *impf.* (*no pf.*) (+*d.*) to imi-tate.

подразде́л, а, *m.* subsection.

подразделе́ни|е, я, *n.* 1. subdivision. 2. (*mil.*) sub-unit, element.

подраздел|и́ть, ю́, и́шь, *pf.* (*of* ~я́ть) to sub-divide.

подраздел|я́ть, я́ю, *impf.* *of* ~и́ть.

подразумева́|ть, ю, *impf.* to imply, entail, mean.

подразумева́|ться, ется, *impf.* to be im-plied, be entailed, be meant; что ~ется

под э́тим выраже́нием? what is meant by this expression?; (само́ собо́й) ~ется it is understood, it goes without saying.

подра́мник, а, *m.* stretcher (*frame for canvas*).

подра́м|ок, ка, *m.* = ~ник.

подра́н|ок, ка, *m.* (*hunting*) wounded game; winged bird.

подраст|а́ть, а́ю, *impf.* *of* ~и́; ~а́ющее поко-ле́ние the rising generation.

подраст|и́, у́, ёшь, *past* подро́с, подросла́, *pf.* to grow (a little).

подра|сти́ть, щу́, сти́шь, *pf.* (*of* ~щивать) to grow; to breed; п. цыпля́т to keep chickens.

по|дра́ть(ся), деру́(сь), дерёшь(ся), *past* ~дра́л(ся), ~драла́(сь), ~дра́ло́(сь), *pf.* *of* дра́ть(ся).

подра́щива|ть, ю, *impf.* *of* подрасти́ть.

подрёберный, *adj.* (*anat.*) sub-costal.

подре́|зать, жу, жешь, *pf.* (*of* ~за́ть) 1. to cut; to clip, trim; to prune, lop; п. коло́ду (*cards*; *sl.*) to cut the pack; п. кому́-н. кры́лья (*fig.*) to clip someone's wings. 2. (+*g.*) to cut off in addition; п. хле́ба to cut some more bread.

подреза́|ть, ю, *impf.* *of* подре́зать.

подрем|а́ть, лю́, ~лешь, *pf.* to have a nap; to doze.

подрешётник, а, *m.* counter-lathing.

подрис|ова́ть, у́ю, *pf.* (*of* ~о́вывать) 1. to retouch, touch up. 2. to add, put in (*on a painting, photograph, etc.*).

подрисо́выва|ть, ю, *impf.* *of* подрисова́ть.

подро́бно, *adv.* minutely, in detail; at (great) length.

подро́бност|ь, и, *f.* 1. detail; вдава́ться в ~и to go into detail; рассказа́ть, не вда-ва́ясь в ~и to relate without going into detail; во всех ~ях in every detail; до мельча́йших ~ей to the minutest detail. 2. minuteness.

подро́б|ный (~ен, ~на), *adj.* detailed, minute.

подровня́|ть, ю, *pf.* (*of* подра́внивать) to level, even; to trim.

подро́ст|ок, ка, *m.* juvenile; teenager; youth; young girl.

подруб|а́ть, а́ю, *impf.* *of* ~и́ть.

подруб|и́ть[1], лю́, ~ишь, *pf.* (*of* ~а́ть) to hew.

подруб|и́ть[2], лю́, ~ишь, *pf.* (*of* ~а́ть) to hem.

подру́г|а, и, *f.* (*female*) friend; п. по шко́ле school-friend; п. жи́зни helpmate (*sc.* one's wife).

по-дру́жески, *adv.* in a friendly way; as a friend.

подруж|и́ться, у́сь, и́шься, *pf.* *of* дружи́ть-ся.

подру́жк|а, и, *f.* affect. dim. *of* подру́га.

подру́лива|ть, ю, *impf. of* подрули́ть.

подрул|и́ть, ю́, и́шь, *pf.* (*of* ～ивать) (к; *aeron.*) to taxi up (to).

подрумя́нива|ть(ся), ю(сь), *impf. of* подрумя́нить(ся).

подрумя́н|ить, ю, ишь, *pf.* (*of* ～ивать) **1.** to rouge; to touch up with rouge. **2.** to make ruddy, make rosy; моро́з ～ил им щёки the frost brought a flush to their cheeks. **3.** (*cul.*) to brown.

подрумя́н|иться, юсь, ишься, *pf.* (*of* ～иваться) **1.** to apply rouge, use rouge. **2.** to become ruddy, become rosy; to flush, become flushed. **3.** (*cul.*) to brown.

подру́чн|ый, *adj.* **1.** at hand, to hand; improvised, makeshift; ～ые сре́дства improvised means. **2.** *as noun* п., ～ого, *m.* assistant, mate; п. водопрово́дчика plumber's mate.

подры́в, а, *m.* undermining; (*fig.*) injury, detriment; п. самолю́бия a blow to one's pride; п. здоро́вья sapping of health; п. торго́вли injury to trade.

подрыва́|ть[1], ю, *impf. of* подорва́ть.

подрыва́|ть[2], ю, *impf. of* подры́ть.

подрывни́к, а́, *m.* (*mil.*) member of demolition squad.

подрывн|о́й, *adj.* blasting, demolition; (*fig.*) undermining, subversive; ～а́я рабо́та blasting, demolition work; ～а́я де́ятельность subversive activities.

подр|ы́ть, о́ю, о́ешь, *pf.* (*of* ～ыва́ть[2]) to undermine, sap.

подря́д[1], *adv.* in succession; running; on end; три го́да п. three years running; не́сколько дней п. шёл дождь it rained for days on end.

подря́д[2], а, *m.* contract; по́～у by contract; взять п. на постро́йку плоти́ны to contract for the building of a dam; сдать п. (на+*a.*), сдать с ～а to put out to contract.

подря|ди́ть, жу́, ди́шь, *pf.* (*of* ～жа́ть) (*coll.*) to hire.

подря|ди́ться, жу́сь, ди́шься, *pf.* (*of* ～жа́ться) (*coll.*) **1.** to contract, undertake. **2.** *pass. of* ～ди́ть.

подря́д|ный, *adj. of* ～[2]; ～ная рабо́та work done by contract.

подря́дчик, а, *m.* contractor.

подряжа́|ть(ся), ю(сь), *impf. of* подряди́ть(ся).

подря́сник, а, *m.* cassock.

подса́д, а, *m.* (*forestry*) plantation.

подса|ди́ть[1], жу́, ～дишь, *pf.* (*of* ～живать) **1.** to help (to) sit down; п. кого́-н. на ло́шадь to help someone mount a horse. **2.** (к) to place next (to); меня́ ～ди́ли к глухо́й да́ме I was placed next to a deaf lady. **3.** to fit in (*extra people in a compartment, etc.*).

подса|ди́ть[2], жу́, ～дишь, *pf.* (*of* ～живать) (+*a. or g.*) to plant some more.

подсадн|о́й, *adj.* ～а́я у́тка decoy duck.

подса́жива|ть, ю, *impf. of* подсади́ть.

подса́жива|ться, юсь, *impf. of* подсе́сть.

подса́лива|ть, ю, *impf. of* подсоли́ть.

подса́чива|ть, ю, *impf. of* подсочи́ть.

подсве́чник, а, *m.* candlestick.

подсви́стыва|ть, ю, *impf.* (+*d.*) to whistle as accompaniment to.

подсева́|ть, ю, *impf. of* подсе́ять.

подсе́д, а, *m.* (*disease of horses*) malanders, mallenders.

подседе́льник, а, *m.* girth, belly-band.

подсе́к|а, и, *f.* (*hist., agric.*) slash-burn clearing.

подсека́|ть, ю, *impf. of* подсе́чь.

подсе́кци|я, и, *f.* sub-section.

под|се́сть, ся́ду, ся́дешь, *past* ～се́л, *pf.* (*of* ～са́живаться) (к) to sit down (near, next to), take a seat (near, next to).

подсе́|чь, ку́, чёшь, ку́т, *past* ～к, ～кла́, *pf.* (*of* ～ка́ть) **1.** to hew; to hack (down). **2.** hook, strike (*a fish*).

подсе́|ять, ю, ешь, *pf.* (*of* ～ва́ть) (+*a. or g.*) to sow (*in addition*).

подси|де́ть, жу́, ди́шь, *pf.* (*of* ～живать) lie in wait (for). **2.** (*fig., coll.*) to scheme, intrigue (against).

подси́живани|е, я, *n.* (*coll.*) scheming, intriguing.

подси́жива|ть, ю, *impf. of* подсиде́ть.

подси́нива|ть, ю, *impf. of* подсини́ть.

подсин|и́ть, ю́, и́шь, *pf.* (*of* ～ивать) to blue, apply blueing to.

подска́блива|ть, ю, *impf. of* подскобли́ть.

подска|за́ть, жу́, ～жешь, *pf.* (*of* ～зывать) (+*d.*) to prompt (*also fig.*); to suggest.

подска́зк|а, и, *f.* prompting.

подска́зчик, а, *m.* prompter (*in verbal sense; in theatre* = суфлёр).

подска́зыва|ть, ю, *impf. of* подсказа́ть.

подска|ка́ть, чу́, ～чешь, *pf.* (*of* ～кивать[1]) (к) to come galloping up (to).

подска́кива|ть[1], ю, *impf. of* подскака́ть.

подска́кива|ть[2], ю, *impf. of* подскочи́ть.

подскобл|и́ть, ю́, ～и́шь, *pf.* (*of* подска́бливать) to scrape off.

подскоч|и́ть, у́, ～ишь, *pf.* (*of* подска́кивать[2]) **1.** (к) to run up (to), come running (to). **2.** to jump up, leap up; п. от ра́дости to jump with joy; це́ны ～и́ли prices soared.

подскреба́|ть, ю, *impf. of* подскрести́.

подскре|сти́, бу́, бёшь, *past* ～б, ～бла́, *pf.* (*of* ～ба́ть) to scrape; to scrape clean.

подсла|сти́ть, щу́, сти́шь, *pf.* (*of* ～щивать) to sweeten, sugar.

подсла́щива|ть, ю, *impf. of* подсласти́ть.

подслѣ́дственный, *adj.* (*leg.*) under investigation.

подслепова́т|ый (~, ~а), *adj.* weak-sighted.

подслу́жива|ться, юсь, *impf. of* подслужи́ться.

подслуж|и́ться, у́сь, ~ишься, *pf.* (*of* ~иваться) (к; *coll.*) to fawn (upon), cringe (before); to worm oneself into the favour (of).

подслу́ш|ать, аю, *pf.* (*of* ~ивать) to overhear; to eavesdrop (on).

подслу́шива|ть, ю, *impf. of* подслу́шать.

подсма́трива|ть, ю, *impf. of* подсмотре́ть.

подсме́ива|ться, юсь, *impf.* (над) to laugh (at), make fun (of).

подсме́н|а, ы, *f.* next shift; relief.

подсмотр|е́ть, ю́, ~ишь, *pf.* (*of* подсма́тривать) to spy.

подсне́жник, а, *m.* (*bot.*) snowdrop.

подсо́бк|а, и, *f.* (*coll.*) box-room.

подсо́бн|ый, *adj.* subsidiary, supplementary; secondary; auxiliary; ancillary; ~ое предприя́тие subsidiary enterprise; п. проду́кт by-product; п. рабо́чий ancillary worker.

подсо́выва|ть, ю, *impf. of* подсу́нуть.

подсозна́ни|е, я, *n.* the subconscious.

подсозна́тел|ьный (~ен, ~ьна), *adj.* subconscious.

подсол|и́ть, ю́, ~и́шь, *pf.* (*of* подса́ливать) to add more salt (to), put more salt (into).

подсо́лнечник, а, *m.* sunflower.

подсо́лнечн|ый[1], *adj. of* ~ик; ~ое ма́сло sunflower oil.

подсо́лнечн|ый[2], *adj.* in the sun; ~ая сторона́ the sunny side; *as noun* ~ая, ~ой, *f.* (*obs.*) the universe.

подсо́лнух, а, *m.* (*coll.*) 1. sunflower. 2. sunflower-seeds.

подсо́х|нуть, ну, нешь, *pf.* (*of* подсыха́ть) to get dry, dry out a little.

подсоч|и́ть, у́, и́шь, *pf.* (*of* подса́чивать) to tap (*trees, for resin or sap*).

подсо́чк|а, и, *f.* tapping.

подспо́рь|е, я, *n.* (*coll.*) help, support; служи́ть больши́м ~ем to be a great help.

подспу́дн|ый, *adj.* latent; unused; secret, hidden; ~ые си́лы latent strength; ~ые мы́сли secret thoughts.

подста́в|а, ы, *f.* (*obs.*) relay (*of horses*).

подста́в|ить, лю, ишь, *pf.* (*of* ~ля́ть) 1. (под+*a.*) to put (under), place (under); п. го́лову под струю́ воды́ из кра́на to put one's head under a tap; п. но́жку кому́-н. to trip someone up (*also fig.*). 2. (+*d.*) to bring up (to), put up (to); to hold up (to); п. кому́-н. стул to offer someone a seat. 3. (*fig.*) to expose, lay bare; п. ферзя́ под уда́р (*chess*) to expose one's queen. 4. (*math.*) to substitute.

подста́вк|а, и, *f.* stand; support, rest, prop.

подставля́|ть, ю, *impf. of* подста́вить.

подставн|о́й, *adj.* false; substitute; ~о́е

лицо́ dummy, figure-head, man of straw; ~ые свиде́тели suborned witnesses.

подстака́нник, а, *m.* glass-holder (*for use in drinking Russian tea*).

подстано́вк|а, и, *f.* (*math.*) substitution.

подста́нци|я, и, *f.* sub-station.

подстёгива|ть, ю, *impf. of* подстегну́ть.

подстег|ну́ть[1], ну́, нёшь, *pf.* (*of* ~ивать) to fasten underneath.

подстег|ну́ть[2], ну́, нёшь, *pf.* (*of* ~ивать) to whip up, urge forward, urge on (*also fig.*).

подстерега́|ть, ю, *impf. of* подстере́чь.

подстере́|чь, гу́, жёшь, гу́т, *past* ~г, ~гла́, *pf.* (*of* ~га́ть) to be on the watch (for), lie in wait (for); п. моме́нт to seize an opportunity.

подстила́|ть, ю, *impf. of* подостла́ть.

подсти́лк|а, и, *f.* bedding; litter.

подсторо́жива|ть, ю, *impf.* (*of* подсторожи́ть) to be on the watch for.

подсторож|и́ть, у́, и́шь, *pf. of* подсторо́живать.

подстра́ива|ть, ю, *impf. of* подстро́ить.

подстрека́тел|ь, я, *m.* instigator; firebrand.

подстрека́тельств|о, а, *n.* instigation, incitement, setting-on.

подстрек|а́ть, а́ю, *impf. of* ~ну́ть.

подстрек|ну́ть, ну́, нёшь, *pf.* (*of* ~а́ть) 1. (к) instigate (to), incite (to), set on (to). 2. to excite; п. любопы́тство to excite one's curiosity.

подстре́лива|ть, ю, *impf. of* подстрели́ть.

подстрел|и́ть, ю́, ~ишь, *pf.* (*of* ~ивать) to wound (*by a shot*); to wing.

подстрига́|ть(ся), ю(сь), *impf. of* подстри́чь(ся).

подстри́|женный, *p.p.p. of* ~чь; ко́ротко ~женные во́лосы (closely) cropped hair.

подстри́|чь, гу́, жёшь, гу́т, *past* ~г, ~гла, *pf.* (*of* ~га́ть) to cut; to clip, trim; to prune; п. бо́роду to trim one's beard; п. но́гти to cut one's nails.

подстри́|чься, гу́сь, жёшься, гу́тся, *past* ~гся, ~глась, *pf.* (*of* ~га́ться) to trim one's hair; to have a hair-trim.

подстро́|ить, ю, ишь, *pf.* (*of* подстра́ивать) 1. (к) to build on (to); п. фли́гель к до́му to build on a wing to a house. 2. to tune (up). 3. (*fig.*, *coll.*) to contrive; (*pejor.*) to arrange; п. шу́тку (+*d.*) to play a trick (on); э́то де́ло ~ено it's a put-up job.

подстро́чник, а, *m.* word for word translation.

подстро́чн|ый, *adj.* п. перево́д word for word translation; ~ое примеча́ние footnote.

по́дступ, а, *m.* (*geogr.*; *fig.*) approach; да́льние ~ы к го́роду the distant approaches to the city; к нему́ и ~а нет he is quite inaccessible.

подступ|а́ть(ся), а́ю(сь), *impf. of* ~и́ть(ся).

подступ|и́ть, лю́, ~ишь, *pf.* (*of* ~а́ть) (к) to approach, come up (to), come near; слёзы ~и́ли к её глаза́м tears came to her eyes.

подступ|и́ться, люсь, ~ишься, *pf.* (*of* ~а́ться) (к) to approach; к нему́ не ~ишься he is quite inaccessible; к э́тому мне не п. it is quite beyond my means.

подсуди́м|ый, ого, *m.* (*leg.*) defendant; the accused; prisoner at the bar; скамья́ ~ых the dock, the bar.

подсу́дност|ь, и, *f.* jurisdiction; cognizance.

подсу́д|ный (~ен, ~на), *adj.* (+*d.*) under, within the jurisdiction (of); within the competence (of); cognizable (to).

подсу́м|ок, ка, *m.* (*mil.*) cartridge pouch.

подсу́н|уть, у, ешь, *pf.* (*of* подсо́вывать) 1. (под+*a.*) to shove (under). 2. (+*d. and a.*; *coll.*) to slip (into); to palm off (on, upon); они́ мне ~ули не ту кни́гу they palmed off the wrong book on me.

подсу́шива|ть, ю, *impf. of* подсуши́ть.

подсуш|и́ть, у́, ~ишь, *pf.* (*of* ~ивать) to dry a little.

подсчёт, а, *m.* calculation; count.

подсчит|а́ть, а́ю, *pf.* (*of* ~ывать) to count up, reckon up; to calculate.

подсчи́тыва|ть, ю, *impf. of* подсчита́ть.

подсыла́|ть, ю, *impf. of* подосла́ть.

подсы́п|ать, лю, лешь, *pf.* (*of* ~а́ть) (+*a. or g.*) to add, pour in.

подсыха́|ть, ю, *impf. of* подсо́хнуть.

подта́ива|ть, ет, *impf. of* подта́ять.

подта́лкива|ть, ю, *impf. of* подтолкну́ть.

подта́плива|ть, ю, *impf. of* подтопи́ть.

подта́скива|ть, ю, *impf. of* подтащи́ть.

подтас|ова́ть, у́ю, *pf.* (*of* ~о́вывать) to shuffle unfairly; (*fig.*) to garble, juggle (with); п. фа́кты to juggle with facts.

подтасо́вк|а, и, *f.* unfair shuffling; (*fig.*) garbling, juggling.

подтасо́выва|ть, ю, *impf. of* подтасова́ть.

подта́чива|ть, ю, *impf. of* подточи́ть.

подтащ|и́ть, у́, ~ишь, *pf.* (*of* подта́скивать) (к) to drag up (to).

подта́|ять, ет, *pf.* (*of* ~ивать) to thaw a little, melt a little.

подтверди́тельн|ый, *adj.* confirmatory; посла́ть ~ое письмо́ to send a letter to confirm.

подтвер|ди́ть, жу́, ди́шь, *pf.* (*of* ~жда́ть) to confirm; to corroborate, bear out; п. получе́ние чего́-н. to acknowledge receipt of something.

подтвержда́|ть, ю, *impf. of* подтверди́ть.

подтвержде́ни|е, я, *n.* confirmation; corroboration.

подтёк, а, *m.* bruise.

подтека́|ть, ет, *impf.* 1. *impf. of* подте́чь. 2. (*impf. only*) to leak; to be leaking.

подте́кст, а, *m.* concealed meaning; угада́ть п. to read between the lines.

подтексто́вк|а, и, *f.* 1. words (*of song or other vocal music*). 2. composition of words (*for vocal music*).

под|тере́ть, отру́, отрёшь, *past* ~тёр, ~тёрла, *pf.* (*of* ~тира́ть) to wipe (up).

подте́|чь, чёт, ку́т, *past* ~к, ~кла́, *pf.* (*of* ~ка́ть) (под+*a.*) to flow (under), run (under).

подтира́|ть, ю, *impf. of* подтере́ть.

подтолкн|у́ть, у́, ёшь, *pf.* (*of* подта́лкивать) 1. to push slightly; п. ло́ктем to nudge. 2. (*fig.*) to urge on.

подтоп|и́ть, лю́, ~ишь, *pf.* (*of* подта́пливать) (*coll.*) to heat a little.

подточ|и́ть, у́, ~ишь, *pf.* (*of* подта́чивать) 1. to sharpen slightly, give an edge (to). 2. to eat away, gnaw; to undermine (*also fig.*); тюре́мное заключе́ние ~и́ло его́ здоро́вье imprisonment has undermined his health.

подтру́нива|ть, ю, *impf. of* подтруни́ть.

подтрун|и́ть, ю́, и́шь, *pf.* (*of* ~ивать) (над) to chaff, tease.

подтуш|ева́ть, у́ю, *pf.* (*of* ~ёвывать) to shade slightly.

подтушёвыва|ть, ю, *impf. of* подтушева́ть.

подтыка́|ть, ю, *impf. of* подоткну́ть.

подтя́гива|ть(ся), ю(сь), *impf. of* подтяну́ть(ся).

подтя́ж|ки, ек, *no sing.* braces, suspenders.

подтя́нутост|ь, и, *f.* smartness.

подтя́н|утый, *p.p.p. of* ~у́ть *and adj.* smart.

подтя|ну́ть, ну́, ~нешь, *pf.* (*of* ~гивать) 1. to tighten. 2. (к) to pull up (to), haul up (to); п. ло́дку к бе́регу to haul up a boat on shore. 3. (*mil.*) to bring up, move up. 4. (*fig., coll.*) to take in hand, pull up, chase up.

подтя|ну́ться, ну́сь, ~нешься, *pf.* (*of* ~гиваться) 1. to gird oneself more tightly; п. по́ясом to tighten one's belt. 2. to pull oneself up (*on gymnastic apparatus, etc.*). 3. (*mil.*) to move up, move in. 4. (*fig., coll.*) to pull oneself together, take oneself in hand.

поду́ма|ть, ю, *pf.* 1. *pf. of* ду́мать; п. (то́лько), ~й(те) (то́лько)! just think!; ~ешь (*as iron. interj.*; *coll.*) I say!; what do you know?; ~ешь, кака́я блестя́щая мысль! I say, what a brain-wave!; и не ~ю! I wouldn't think of it!, I wouldn't dream of it; мо́жно п. one might think. 2. to think a little, for a while.

поду́мыва|ть, ю, *impf.* (о+*p. or* +*inf.*; *coll.*) to think (of, about); п. об отъе́зде, п. уе́хать to think of leaving.

по-дура́цки, *adv.* (*coll.*) foolishly, like a fool.

подура́ч|иться, усь, ишься, *pf.* (*coll.*) to fool about, play the fool.

подурне́|ть, ю, *pf. of* дурне́ть.

поду́ськ|ать, аю, *pf.* (*of* ~ивать) (*coll.*) to set on; (*fig.*) to egg on; п. соба́ку на кого́-н. to set a dog on someone.

поду́ськива|ть, ю, *impf. of* поду́ськать.

поду́|ть, ю, ешь, *pf.* 1. *pf. of* дуть 1. 2. to begin to blow.

поду́чива|ть(ся), ю(сь), *impf. of* подучи́ть-(ся).

подуч|и́ть, у́, ~ишь, *pf.* (*of* ~ивать) 1. (+*a. and d.*) to teach, instruct (in); п. кого́-н. стрельбе́ to give someone a few lessons in shooting. 2. to learn. 3. (*inf.*; *coll.*) to prompt (to), egg on (to), put up (to).

подуч|и́ться, у́сь, ~ишься, *pf.* to learn (a little more, a little better).

поду́шечк|а, и, *f.* 1. *dim. of* поду́шка; п. для була́вок pincushion. 2. sweet, bon--bon.

подуш|и́ть, у́, ~ишь, *pf.* to spray with perfume.

подуш|и́ться, у́сь, ~ишься, *pf.* to spray oneself with perfume, put some perfume on.

поду́шк|а, и, *f.* 1. pillow; cushion; п. для штемпеле́й ink-pad. 2. (*tech.*) cushion; bolster.

поду́шн|ый, *adj.* ~ая по́дать (*hist.*) poll-tax, capitation.

подфа́рник, а, *m.* (*tech.*) fender lamp, side--light.

подхали́м, а, *m.* toady, lickspittle.

подхалима́ж, а, *m.* (*coll.*) toadying, boot-licking, grovelling.

подхали́мнича|ть, ю, *impf.* (*coll.*) to toady.

подхали́мств|о, а, *n.* = подхалима́ж.

подхва|ти́ть, чу́, ~тишь, *pf.* (*of* ~тывать) (*in var. senses*) to catch (up); to pick up; to take up; п. су́мку to catch up one's bag; п. мяч to catch a ball; п. на́сморк to catch, pick up a cold; п. пе́сню to catch up a melody, join in a song.

подхва́тыва|ть, ю, *impf. of* подхвати́ть.

подхлест|ну́ть, ну́, нёшь, *pf.* (*of* ~ывать) to whip up (*also fig., coll.*).

подхлёстыва|ть, ю, *impf. of* подхлестну́ть.

подхо́д, а, *m.* (*in var. senses*) approach; у него́ непра́вильный п. к де́лу he has the wrong approach to the matter.

подхо́д|ец, ца, *m.* (*coll.*) approach; говори́ть с ~цем to make reservations, speak in a roundabout way.

подхо|ди́ть, жу́, ~дишь, *impf. of* подойти́.

подход|я́щий, *pres. part. of* ~и́ть *and adj.* suitable, proper, appropriate; п. моме́нт the right moment.

подцеп|и́ть, лю́, ~ишь, *pf.* (*of* ~ля́ть) to hook on, couple on; (*fig., joc.*) to pick up; п. ваго́н-рестора́н к по́езду to attach a restaurant car to a train; п. на́сморк to pick up a cold.

подцепля́|ть, ю, *impf. of* подцепи́ть.

подча́с, *adv.* sometimes, at times.

подча́с|ок, ка, *m.* relief sentry.

подчелюстно́й, *adj.* (*anat.*) sub-maxillary.

подчёркива|ть, ю, *impf. of* подчеркну́ть.

подчерк|ну́ть, ну́, нёшь, *pf.* (*of* ~ивать) 1. to underline; to score under. 2. (*fig.*) to emphasize, stress, accentuate.

подчине́ни|е, я, *n.* 1. subordination; submission, subjection; быть в ~и (у) to be subordinate (to). 2. (*gram.*) subordination.

подчинённост|ь, и, *f.* subordination.

подчин|ённый 1. *p.p.p. of* ~и́ть; (+*d.*) under, under the command (of). 2. *adj.* subordinate; ~ённое госуда́рство tributary state; *as noun* п., ~ённого, *m.* subordinate.

подчини́тельный, *adj.* (*gram.*)subordinative.

подчин|и́ть, ю́, и́шь, *pf.* (*of* ~я́ть) (+*d.*) to subordinate (to), subject (to); to place (under), place under the command (of); п. свое́й во́ле to bend to one's will.

подчин|и́ться, ю́сь, и́шься, *pf.* (*of* ~я́ться) (+*d.*) to submit (to); п. прика́зу to obey an order.

подчин|я́ть(ся), я́ю(сь), *impf. of* ~и́ть(ся).

подчи́|стить, щу, стишь, *pf.* (*of* ~ща́ть) to rub out, erase.

подчи́стк|а, и, *f.* rubbing out, erasure.

подчисту́ю, *adv.* (*coll.*) completely, without remainder; мы съе́ли всё п. we left our plates clean.

подчи́тчик, а, *m.* (*typ.*) copy-holder.

подчища́|ть, ю, *impf. of* подчи́стить.

подшефник, а, *m.* dependent (*person or institution*).

подше́фный, *adj.* aided, assisted; (+*d.*) under the patronage (of), sponsored by, supported (by).

подшиб|а́ть, а́ю, *impf. of* ~и́ть.

подшиб|и́ть, у́, ёшь, *past* ~, ~ла, *pf.* (*o, ~а́ть*) to knock; п. кому́-н. глаз to give someone a black eye.

подшиб|ленный, *p.p.p. of* ~и́ть; п. глаз black eye.

подшива́|ть, ю, *impf. of* подши́ть.

подши́вк|а, и, *f.* 1. hemming; lining; soling. 2. hem. 3. filing (*of papers*); п. газе́ты newspaper file.

подши́пник, а, *m.* (*tech.*) bearing; bush; обыкнове́нный п. journal bearing; ро́ликовый п. roller bearing; ша́риковый п. ball bearing.

подши́пник|овый, *adj. of* ~; п. сплав babbit; п. щит bearing housing.

под|ши́ть, ошью́, ошьёшь, *pf.* (*of* ~шива́ть) 1. to sew underneath; to hem; to line; to sole. 2. to file (*papers*).

подшле́мник, а, *m.* cap comforter.

подшта́нник|и, ов, *no sing.* (*coll.*) drawers.

подштóп|ать, аю, *pf.* (*of* ~ывать) to darn.

подштóпыва|ть, ю, *impf. of* подштóпать.

подшу|ти́ть, чу́, ~тишь, *pf.* (*of* ~чивать) (над) to chaff, mock (at); to play a trick (on).

подшу́чива|ть, ю, *impf. of* подшути́ть.

подъеда́|ть, ю, *impf. of* подъе́сть.

подъе́зд, а, *m.* 1. porch, entrance, doorway. 2. approach(es).

подъезд|нóй, *adj. of* ~ 2; ~на́я алле́я drive; ~на́я доро́га access road; п. путь spur track.

подъе́зд|ный, *adj. of* ~ 1.

подъезжá|ть, ю, *impf. of* подъе́хать.

подъём, а, *m.* 1. lifting; raising; п. флáга hoisting of colours; п. затону́вшего су́дна salvaging of a sunken vessel; п. парóв ploughing up. 2. ascent. 3. (*aeron.*) climb. 4. rise, upgrade slope. 5. (*fig.*) raising, development; rise; промы́шленный п. boom, upsurge; круто́й п. произво́дства a sharp rise in production; на ~е on the up and up, on the upgrade. 6. (*fig.*) élan; enthusiasm, animation; говори́ть с бо́льшим ~ом to speak with great animation; лёгок на п. quick on one's toes, quick off the mark; тяжёл на п. sluggish, slow to start. 7. instep. 8. rising time; (*mil.*) reveille. 9. (*tech.*) lever, hand screw, jack.

подъёмник, а, *m.* lift, elevator, hoist.

подъёмн|ый, *adj.* 1. lifting; п. кран crane, jenny, derrick; ~ая маши́на lift; п. механи́зм, ~ое устрóйство lifting device, hoist; ~ое окнó sash window. 2. п. мост drawbridge, bascule bridge. 3. ~ые (де́ньги) travelling expenses (*when moving house*).

подъ|е́сть, е́м, е́шь, е́ст, еди́м, еди́те, едя́т, *past* ~е́л, *pf.* (*of* ~еда́ть) (*coll.*) 1. to eat up, finish off. 2. to eat through, eat into.

подъе́|хать, ду, дешь, *pf.* (*of* ~зжáть) (к) 1. to drive up (to), draw up (to). 2. (*coll.*) to call (on). 3. (*fig., coll.*) to get round.

подъязы́чный, *adj.* (*anat.*) sub-lingual.

подъяре́мн|ый, *adj.* yoked; ~ое живóтное beast of burden; ~ая жизнь (*fig.*) a life under the yoke, enslavement.

подыгр|а́ть, áю, *pf.* (*of* ~ывать) (+*d.*; *coll.*) 1. (*mus.*) to accompany; to vamp. 2. (*theatr.*) to play up (to). 3. (*cards*) to play into someone's hand.

подыгр|а́ться, áюсь, *pf.* (*of* ~ываться) (к; *coll.*) to get round.

поды́грыва|ть, ю, *impf. of* подыгра́ть.

поды́грыва|ться, юсь, *impf.* 1. *impf. of* подыгра́ться. 2. (*impf. only*) to try to get round.

подымá|ть(ся), ю(сь), *impf.* (*coll.*) = поднимáть(ся).

поды|скáть, щý, ~щешь, *pf.* (*of* ~скивать) to seek out, find.

поды́скива|ть, ю, *impf.* 1. *impf. of* подыскáть. 2. (*impf. only*) to seek, try to find.

подытóжива|ть, ю, *impf. of* подытóжить.

подытóж|ить, у, ишь, *pf.* (*of* ~ивать) to sum up.

подыхá|ть, ю, *impf. of* подóхнуть.

подыш|áть, ý, ~ишь, *pf.* to breathe; вы́йти п. све́жим вóздухом to go out for a breath of fresh air.

подья́ч|ий, его, *m.* (*hist.*) scrivener, clerk, government official (*in Muscovite Russia*).

поеда́|ть, ю, *impf. of* пое́сть.

поеди́н|ок, ка, *m.* duel, single combat.

поедóм, *adv.* п. есть когó-н. (*coll.*) to make someone's life a misery (by nagging).

пóезд, а, *pl.* ~á, *m.* 1. train; ~ом by train; п. да́льнего сле́дования long-distance train; п. прямóго сообще́ния through train. 2. (*obs.*) convoy, procession (*of vehicles*); сва́дебный п. wedding procession.

поéз|дить, жу, дишь, *pf.* to travel about.

поéздк|а, и, *f.* journey; trip, excursion, outing, tour.

пóездник, а, *m.* (*coll.*) commuter (*by rail*).

поезд|нóй, *adj. of* пóезд; ~на́я брига́да train crew.

поезжáй(те): *used as imp. of* éхать and поéхать.

поезжáн|ин, ина, *pl.* ~е, ~, *m.* (*obs.*) member of wedding procession.

поёмн|ый, *adj.* under water at flood times; ~ые лугá water-meadows.

поёный, *adj.* (*agric.*) udder-fed.

по|éсть, éм, éшь, éст, еди́м, еди́те, едя́т, *past* ~éл, *pf.* (*of* ~еда́ть) 1. to eat (up). 2. to eat a little; to take some food, have a bite. 3. (*of rodents, insects, etc.*) to eat, devour.

поé|хать, ду, дешь, *pf.* (*of* éхать) to go (*in or on a vehicle or on an animal*); to set off, depart; ~хали! (*coll.*) come on!, come along!, let's go!; ну, ~хал! (*coll.*) now he's off!

пожалé|ть, ю, *pf. of* жалéть.

пожáл|овать, ую, *pf. of* жáловать; добрó п.! welcome!; ~уйте *formula of polite request*; ~уйте сюдá! would you mind coming here?; this way, please!; ~уйте в столóвую! dinner (supper, *etc.*) is served!

пожáл|оваться, уюсь, *pf. of* жáловаться.

пожáлуй, *adv.* perhaps; very likely; it may be; if you like; мы, п., поéдем we shall very likely go; п., ты прав you may be right; по мне п. (*coll.*) it's all right by me.

пожáлуйста, *particle* 1. please; переда́йте мне, п., карандáш will you please pass me a pencil; сади́тесь, п. please sit down. 2. (*polite expression of consent*) certainly!, by all means!, with pleasure! (*or not translated*); мóжно посмотре́ть э́ти сни́мки? — п. may I look at these photos? Certainly; переда́йте мне, п., кни́гу. — п. would you mind passing me the book? — There you are. **3.** (*polite acknowledgement of thanks*) don't mention it; not at all.

пожа́р, а, *m.* fire; conflagration; как на п. бежа́ть (*coll.*) to run like hell; не на п.! (*coll.*) hold your horses!, there's no hurry!

пожа́рищ|е¹, а, *m.* (*coll.*) big fire.

пожа́рищ|е², а, *n.* site of a fire.

пожа́рник, а, *m,* fireman.

пожа́р|ный, *adj. of* ~; ~ная кома́нда fire--brigade; п. кран fire-cock; ~ная маши́на fire-engine; п. насо́с fire-pump; в ~ном поря́дке (*coll., joc.*) hastily, in slapdash fashion; на вся́кий п. слу́чай (*coll., joc.*) in case of dire need; *as noun* п., ~ного, *m.* fireman.

пожа́ти|е, я, *n.* п. руки́ handshake.

по|жа́ть¹, жму́, жмёшь, *pf.* (*of* ~жима́ть) press, squeeze; п. ру́ку (+*d.*) to shake hands (with); п. плеча́ми to shrug one's shoulders.

по|жа́ть², жну́, жнёшь, *pf.* (*of* ~жина́ть) to reap (*also fig.*); п. сла́ву to win renown; п. плоды́ чужо́го труда́ (*fig.*) to reap where one has not sown; что посе́ешь, то и ~жнёшь (*prov.*) one must reap as one has sown.

по|жа́ться, жму́сь, жмёшься, *pf.* (*of* ~жима́ться) to shrink up, huddle up.

пож|ева́ть, ую́, уёшь, *pf.* (*of* ~ёвывать) to chew, masticate.

пожёвыва|ть, ю, *impf. of* пожева́ть.

пожела́ни|е, я, *n.* wish, desire.

пожела́|ть, ю, *pf. of* жела́ть.

пожелте́лый, *adj.* yellowed; gone yellow.

пожелте́|ть, ю, *pf. of* желте́ть.

пожен|и́ть, ю́, ~ишь, *pf. of* жени́ть.

пожен|и́ться, ~имся, *pf.* (*pl. used only; of man and woman*) to get married.

поже́ртвовани|е, я, *n.* donation, offering.

поже́ртв|овать, ую, *pf. of* же́ртвовать.

по|же́чь, жгу́, жжёшь, жгут, *past* ~жёг, ~жгла́, *pf.* to burn up; to destroy by fire.

пожи́в|а, ы, *f.* (*coll.*) gain, profit.

пожива́|ть, ю, *impf.* to live; как (вы) ~ете? how are you (getting on)?; ста́ли они́ жить-п. да добра́ нажива́ть they lived happily ever after.

пожив|и́ться, лю́сь, и́шься, *pf.* (+*i.*; *coll.*) to live (off), profit (by); п. на счёт друго́го to make good at another's expense.

пожи́|вший, *past part. act. of* ~ть *and adj.* (*usu. pejor.*) experienced.

пожиде́|ть, ю, *pf.* (*coll.*) (*of liquids*) to become thinner, become more dilute.

пожи́зненн|ый, *adj.* life; for life; ~ое заключе́ние life imprisonment; ~ая ре́нта life annuity.

пожило́й, *adj.* middle-aged; elderly.

пожима́|ть(ся), ю(сь), *impf. of* пожа́ть¹(ся).

пожина́|ть, ю, *impf. of* пожа́ть².

пожира́|ть, ю, *impf. of* пожра́ть; п. глаза́ми to devour with one's eyes.

пожи́тк|и, ов, *no sing.* (*coll.*) belongings; (one's) things; goods and chattels; со все́ми ~ами bag and baggage.

по|жи́ть, живу́, живёшь, *past* ~жил, ~жила́, ~жило, *pf.* **1.** to live (*for a time*); to stay; мы ~жи́ли три го́да в Ки́еве we lived for three years in Kiev; я там ~живу́ неде́ли две I shall stay there about a couple of weeks. **2.** (*coll.*) to lead a gay life, live it up, live fast; п. в своё удово́льствие to lead a gay life, live for pleasure; ~живём-уви́дим we shall see what we shall see.

пожм|у́, ёшь, *see* пожа́ть¹

пожн|у́, ёшь, *see* пожа́ть².

по́ж|ня, ни, *g. pl.* ~ен, *f.* (*dial.*) stubble (-field).

пожр|а́ть, у́, ёшь, *past* ~а́л, ~ала́, ~а́ло, *pf.* (*of* пожира́ть) to devour; (*coll.*) to gobble up.

по́з|а, ы, *f.* pose, attitude, posture; (*fig.*) pose; приня́ть каку́ю-н. ~у to strike an attitude, adopt a pose; приня́ть ~у вели́кого учёного to pose as a great scholar; э́то то́лько п. it is a mere pose.

позаба́в|ить, лю, ишь, *pf.* to amuse a little.

позаба́в|иться, люсь, ишься, *pf.* to amuse oneself a little.

позабо́|титься, чусь, тишься, *pf. of* забо́титься.

позабыва́|ть, ю, *impf. of* позабы́ть.

позаб|ы́ть, у́ду, у́дешь, *pf.* (*of* ~ыва́ть) (+*a.* or о+*p.*; *coll.*) to forget (about).

позави́д|овать, ую, *pf. of* зави́довать.

поза́втрака|ть, ю, *pf. of* за́втракать.

позавчера́, *adv.* the day before yesterday.

позавчера́|шний, *adj. of* ~.

позади́¹, *adv.* (*of place*; *fig. of time*) behind; оста́вить п. to leave behind; наиху́дшие времена́ оста́лись п. the worst times are behind, are past.

позади́², *prep.*+*g.* behind.

позаи́мств|овать, ую, *pf. of* заи́мствовать.

позапро́шлый, *adj.* before last; п. год the year before last.

позар|и́ться, юсь, ишься, *pf. of* за́риться.

по|зва́ть, зову́, зовёшь, *past* ~зва́л, ~звала́, ~зва́ло, *pf. of* звать.

по-зве́рски, *adv.* brutally, like a beast.

позволе́ни|е, я, *n.* permission, leave; с ва́шего ~я with your permission, by your leave; с ~я сказа́ть if one may say so; э́тот, с ~я сказа́ть, вождь (*iron.*) this apology for a leader; this, if one may so call him, leader.

позволи́тел|ьный (~ен, ~ьна), *adj.* per-missible.

позво́л|ить, ю, ишь, *pf. (of* ~**я́ть) (**+*d. of person and inf.,* +*a. of inanimate object)* to allow, permit; е́сли доктора́ ~ят мне пое́хать, я уви́жу вас в Москве́ if the doctors allow me to travel, I shall see you in Moscow; п. себе́ (+*inf.*) to permit oneself, venture, take the liberty (of); (+*a.*) to be able to afford; п. себе́ сде́лать замеча́ние to venture a remark; п. себе́ пое́здку в Пари́ж to be able to afford a trip to Paris; п. себе́ во́льность (с+*i.*) to take liberties (with); ~ь(те) (*i*) *polite form of request* ~ьте предста́вить до́ктора X. allow me to introduce Doctor X., (*ii*) *expression of disagreement or objection* ~ьте, что э́то зна́чит? excuse me, what does that mean?

позвол|я́ть, я́ю, *impf. of* ~**и́ть.**

позвон|и́ть(ся), ю́(сь), и́шь(ся), *pf. of* зво-ни́ть(ся).

позвон|о́к, ка́, *m. (anat.)* vertebra.

позвоно́чник, а, *m. (anat.)* spine, backbone, spinal column, vertebral column.

позвоно́чн|ый, *adj. (anat.)* vertebral; п. столб spinal column, vertebral column; *as noun* ~ые, ~ых (*zool.*) vertebrates.

поздн|е́е, *comp. of* ~**ий** *and* ~**о** later; приди́ не п. пяти́ часо́в come by five o'clock at latest.

поздне́йший, *adj.* later, latest.

по́здн|ий, *adj.* late; tardy; до ~ей но́чи until late at night, late into the night; ~о it is late.

по́здно, *adv.* late.

поздоро́ва|ться, юсь, *pf. of* здоро́ваться.

поздорове́|ть, ю, *pf. of* здорове́ть.

поздоро́в|иться, ится, *pf. only in phrase (coll.)* не ~ится ему́, *etc.*, (от) much good will it do him, *etc.*

поздрави́тел|ь, я, *m.* bearer of congratulations, well-wisher.

поздрави́тельный, *adj.* congratulatory.

поздра́в|ить, лю, ишь, *pf. (of* ~**ля́ть) (**с+*i.*) to congratulate (on, upon); п. кого́-н. с днём рожде́ния to wish someone many happy returns of the day; п. кого́-н. с Но́вым го́дом to wish someone a happy New Year.

поздравле́ни|е, я, *n.* congratulation.

поздравля́|ть, ю, *impf. of* поздра́вить.

позёвыва|ть, ю, *impf. (coll.)* to yawn (from time to time).

позелене́|ть, ю, *pf. of* зелене́ть 1.

позелен|и́ть, ю́, и́шь, *pf. of* зелени́ть.

позём, а, *m. (dial.)* manure.

поземе́льный, *adj.* land; п. нало́г land-tax.

позёмк|а, и, *f.* blizzard accompanied by ground wind.

позёр, а, *m.* poseur.

по́з|же, *comp. of* ~**дний** *and* ~**дно;** later (on).

по-зи́мнему, *adv.* as in winter, as for winter; оде́т п. (dressed) in winter clothes.

пози́р|овать, ую, *impf.* (+*d.*) to sit (to), pose (for); (*fig.*) to pose.

позити́в, а, *m. (phot.)* positive.

позитиви́зм, а, *m. (philos.)* positivism.

позитиви́ст, а, *m. (philos.)* positivist.

позити́в|ный (~**ен,** ~**на),** *adj. (in var. senses)* positive.

позитро́н, а, *m. (phys.)* positron, positive electron.

позицио́нн|ый, *adj. of* пози́ция; ~ая война́ trench warfare.

пози́ци|я, и, *f. (in var. senses)* position; stand; вы́годная п. advantage-ground; выжида́тельная п. wait-and-see attitude; заня́ть ~ю (*mil.*) to take up a position; (*fig.*) to take one's stand; с ~и си́лы from (a position of) strength.

позла|ти́ть, щу́, ти́шь, *pf. (of* ~**ща́ть) (***obs. or fig.*) to gild.

позлаща́|ть, ю, *impf. of* позлати́ть.

позл|и́ть, ю́, и́шь, *pf.* to tease a little.

познава́емост|ь, и, *f. (philos.)* cognoscibility.

познава́ем|ый (~, ~**а),** *pres. part. pass. of* познава́ть *and adj.* cognizable, knowable.

познава́тельный, *adj.* cognitive; п. проце́сс cognition.

позна|ва́ть, ю́, ёшь, *impf. of* ~**ть.**

позна|ва́ться, ю́сь, ёшься, *impf. (no pf.)* to become known; друзья́ ~ю́тся в беде́ (*prov.*) a friend in need is a friend indeed.

познако́м|ить(ся), лю(сь), ишь(ся), *pf. of* знако́мить(ся).

познако́м|ленный, *p.p.p. of* ~**ить.**

позна́ни|е, я, *n.* **1.** (*philos.*) cognition; тео́рия ~я theory of knowledge, epistemology. **2.** (*pl.*) knowledge.

позна́|ть, ю, *pf. (of* ~**ва́ть)** to get to know; to become acquainted with; (*philos.*) to cognize; п. го́ре to become acquainted with grief; п. же́нщину (*euph.*) to know a woman.

позоло́т|а, ы, *f.* gilding, gilt.

позоло|ти́ть, чу́, ти́шь, *pf. of* золоти́ть.

позо́р, а, *m.* shame, disgrace; infamy, ignominy; быть ~ом (для) to be a disgrace (to); вы́ставить на п. to put to shame; покры́ть себя́ ~ом to disgrace oneself, cover oneself with ignominy.

позо́р|ить, ю, ишь, *impf. (of* о~**)** to disgrace, defame, discredit.

позо́р|иться, юсь, ишься, *impf. (of* о~**)** to disgrace oneself.

позо́рищ|е, а, *n. (coll.)* shameful event, disgrace.

позо́р|ный (~**ен,** ~**на),** *adj.* shameful, disgraceful; infamous, ignominious; п. столб pillory; поста́вить к ~ному столбу́ (*fig.*) to pillory.

позумéнт, а, *m.* galoon, braid; зо́ло́то́й п. gold braid, gold lace.

позы́в, а, *m.* (*physiological*) urge, call; п. на рво́ту urge to be sick, (feeling of) nausea.

позыва́|ть, ет, *impf.* (*impers.*) to feel an urge, feel a need; меня́ ~ет на рво́ту I feel an urge to be sick.

позы́вн|о́й, *adj.* п. сигна́л (*radio*) call sign; *as noun* ~ы́е, ~ы́х call sign; (*naut.*) ship's number; подня́ть ~ы́е to make the ship's number.

поигра́|ть, ю, *pf.* to have a game, play a little.

поигрыва|ть, ю, *impf.* (*coll.*) to play now and then.

пойл|éц, ьца, *m.* п. и корми́лец (*obs.*) bread--winner.

пойлк|а, и, *f.* 1. feeding-trough; feeding--bowl. 2. feeding-vessel (*for invalids*).

поимённо, *adv.* by name; вызыва́ть п. to call over (*the roll of*).

поимённый, *adj.* nominal; п. спи́сок list of names, nominal roll.

поимен|ова́ть, у́ю, *pf.* to name, call out by name.

поимк|а, и, *f.* catching, capture; п. на ме́сте преступле́ния catching in the act, catching red-handed.

поиму́щественный, *adj.* п. нало́г property tax.

по-ино́му, *adv.* differently, in a different way.

поинтерес|ова́ться, у́юсь, *pf.* (+*i.*) to be curious (about); to display interest (in); он ~ова́лся узна́ть, кто вы he was curious to find out who you are.

по́иск, а, *m.* 1. (*pl.*) search; в ~ах (+*g.*) in search (of), in quest (of). 2. (*mil.*) (reconnaissance) raid.

пои|ска́ть, щу́, ~щешь, *pf.* to look for, search for; ~щи́те хороше́нько have a good look.

пойстине, *adv.* indeed, in truth.

по|и́ть, ю́, ~и́шь, *impf.* (*of* на~) to give to drink; to water (*cattle*); п. ребёнка to feed a baby (*at the breast*); п. вино́м to treat to wine; п. и корми́ть семью́ to maintain the family, be the family bread-winner.

по|ищу́, и́щешь, *see* ~иска́ть.

пойду́, дёшь, *see* ~ти́.

пойл|о, а, *n.* swill, mash; п. для свине́й hog--wash, pig-swill.

пойм|а, ы, *g. pl.* ~, *f.* flood-lands; water--meadow.

пойма́|ть, ю, *pf. of* лови́ть.

пойм|у́, ёшь, *see* поня́ть.

пойнтер, а, *m.* (*dog*) pointer.

пой|ти́, ду́, дёшь, *past* пошёл, пошла́, *pf.* 1. *pf. of* идти́ *and* ходи́ть; пошёл! off you go!; пошёл вон! be off!, off with you!; уж

éсли на то пошло́ if it comes to that, for that matter; (так) не ~дёт (*coll.*) that won't work, that won't wash. 2. to begin to (be able to) walk. 3. (*coll.*) to begin. 4. (в+*a.*) to take after; он пошёл в отца́ he takes after his father.

пока́[1], *adv.* for the present, for the time being; п. что (*coll.*) in the meanwhile; п. ещё, п.-то ещё (*coll.*) not for a while yet; э́то п. всё that is all for now; э́то п. оста́вьте leave it for the time being; не беспоко́йтесь, п.-то ещё он поя́вится don't worry, he won't turn up for a while yet; ну, п.! (*coll.*) cheerio!, bye-bye!

пока́[2], *conj.* 1. while; нам на́до попроси́ть его́, п. он тут we must ask him while he is here. 2. п. не until, till, before; не на́до уходи́ть, п. она́ не придёт we must not go until she comes; п. ещё не по́здно before it's too late.

пока́з, а, *m.* showing, demonstration; (*fig.*) portrayal; п. но́вого фи́льма showing of a new film.

показа́ни|е, я, *n.* 1. testimony, evidence. 2. (*leg.*) deposition; affidavit; дава́ть п. to testify, bear witness, make a deposition. 3. reading (*on an instrument*).

пока́з|анный, *p.p.p. of* ~а́ть *and adj.* 1. (*obs. or coll.*) fixed, appointed; в ~анное вре́мя at the time appointed. 2. (*med.*) indicated.

показа́тел|ь, я, *m.* 1. (*math.*) exponent, index. 2. index; (*fig.*) showing; ка́чественные ~и qualitative indices; дать хоро́шие ~и, доби́ться хоро́ших ~ей to make a good showing.

показа́тел|ьный (~ен, ~ьна), *adj.* 1. significant; instructive, revealing; о́чень ~ьное заявле́ние a very significant pronouncement. 2. model; demonstration; п. суд show-trial; п. уро́к demonstration lesson, object-lesson; ~ьное хозя́йство model farm. 3. (*math.*) exponential.

пока|за́ть, жу́, ~жешь, *pf.* (*of* ~зывать) 1. to show; to display, reveal; п. себя́ to prove oneself, prove one's worth; он ~за́л себя́ хоро́шим ора́тором he has shown himself to be a good speaker; п. свои́ зна́ния to display one's knowledge; они́ ~за́ли де́вочку врачу́ they took the little girl to the doctor; он ~за́л вид, что се́рдится he feigned anger; п. това́р лицо́м (*fig., coll.*) to display oneself in a favourable light. 2. (*of instruments*) to show, register, read. 3. (на+*a.*) to point (at, to); п. кому́-н. на дверь (*fig., coll.*) to show someone the door. 4. (*leg.*) to testify, give evidence.

пока|за́ться, жу́сь, ~жешься, *pf.* 1. *pf. of* каза́ться. 2. (*pf. of* ~зываться) to show oneself, appear; to come in sight; из-за облако́в ~за́лась луна́ the moon appeared from behind the clouds; п. врачу́ to see a doctor. **3.** *pass. of* ~за́ть.

показно́й, *adj.* for show; ostentatious.

показу́х|а, и, *f.* (*coll.*) show; э́то сплошна́я п. it's all put on, just for show.

пока́зыва|ть(ся), ю(сь), *impf. of* показа́ть-(ся).

по-каковски, *adv.* (*coll.*) in what language?

пока́лыва|ть, ю, *impf.* to prick occasionally; у меня́ ~ет в боку́ (*impers.*) I have an occasional stitch in my side.

покаля́ка|ть, ю, *pf. of* каля́кать.

пока́мест, *adv. and conj.* (*coll.*) = пока́.

покара́|ть, ю, *pf. of* кара́ть.

поката́|ть¹, ю, *pf.* to roll.

поката́|ть², ю, *pf.* to take for a drive; п. дете́й to take children out.

поката́|ться, юсь, *pf.* to go for a drive; п. на ло́дке to go out boating.

пока|ти́ть, чу́, ~ти́шь, *pf.* **1.** *pf. of* кати́ть. **2.** to start (rolling), set rolling.

пока|ти́ться, чу́сь, ~ти́шься, *pf.* **1.** *pf. of* кати́ться; п. со́ смеху (*coll.*) to roar with laughter. **2.** to start rolling.

пока́тост|ь, и, *f.* slope, incline; declivity.

пока́т|ый (~, ~a), *adj.* sloping; slanting; п. лоб retreating forehead.

покача́|ть, ю, *pf.* to rock, swing (for a time); п. ребёнка на каче́лях to give a child a swing; п. голово́й to shake one's head.

покача́|ться, юсь, *pf.* to rock, swing (for a time); to have a swing.

пока́чива|ться, юсь, *impf.* to rock slightly; идти́ ~ясь to walk unsteadily.

покачн|у́ть, у́, ёшь, *pf.* to shake.

покачн|у́ться, у́сь, ёшься, *pf.* **1.** to sway, totter, give a lurch. **2.** (*fig., coll.*) to totter, go downhill.

пока́шлива|ть, ю, *impf.* to have a slight cough; to cough intermittently.

пока́шля|ть, ю, *pf.* to cough.

покая́ни|е, я, *n.* **1.** (*eccl.*) confession. **2.** penitence, repentance; принести́ п. (в+*p.*) to repent (of); отпусти́ть ду́шу на п. (*obs. or coll.*) to let go in peace.

покая́нный, *adj.* penitential.

пока́|яться, юсь, ешься, *pf. of* ка́яться.

поквapта́льно, *adv.* by the quarter, per quarter, every quarter.

поквита́|ться, юсь, *pf.* (с+*i.*; *coll.*) to be quits (with); to get even (with); тепе́рь мы с ва́ми ~лись now we're quits; я ещё с ним ~юсь I'll get even with him yet.

по́кер, а, *m.* (*card-game*) poker.

по́кер|ный, *adj. of* ~.

покива́|ть, ю, *pf.* to nod (*several times*).

покида́|ть, ю, *impf. of* поки́нуть.

**поки́нут|ый, *p.p.p. of* ~ь *and adj.* deserted; abandoned.

поки́|нуть, ну, нешь, *pf.* (*of* ~да́ть) to leave; to desert, abandon, forsake.

поклада́я, *only in phrase* не п. рук indefatigably.

покла́дист|ый (~, ~a), *adj.* complaisant, obliging.

покла́ж|а, и, *f.* (*coll.*) load; luggage.

поклёп, а, *m.* (*coll.*) slander, calumny; взвести́ п. (на+*a.*) to slander, cast aspersions (on).

покли́|кать, чу, чешь, *pf.* (*coll.*) to call (to).

покло́н, а, *m.* **1.** bow; сде́лать п. to bow (*in greeting*); класть ~ы to bow (*in prayer*); идти́ на п., идти́ с ~ом к кому́-н. to go cap in hand to someone. **2.** (*fig.*) greeting; посла́ть ~ы to send one's compliments, send one's kind regards.

поклоне́ни|е, я, *n.* worship.

поклон|и́ться, ю́сь, ~и́шься, *pf. of* кла́нять-ся.

покло́нник, а, *m.* admirer, worshipper.

поклоня́|ться, юсь, *impf.* (+*d.*) to worship.

покля́|сться, ну́сь, нёшься, *pf. of* кля́сться.

поко́вк|а, и, *f.* (*tech.*) forging; forged piece.

поко́ем, *adv.* (*obs.*) in the shape of the letter п.

поко́|ить, ю, ишь, *impf.* (*obs.*) to tend, cherish.

поко́|иться, юсь, ишься, *impf.* **1.** (на+*p.*) to rest (on, upon), repose (on, upon), be based (on, upon); п. на дога́дке to be based on conjecture. **2.** (*of the dead*) to lie; здесь ~ится прах (+*g.*) here lies (the body of).

поко́|й¹, я, *m.* rest, peace; ве́чный п. (*fig., poet.*) eternal rest; оста́вить в ~е to leave in peace; уйти́ на п., удали́ться на п. to retire; то́чка ~я (*phys.*) point of rest, fulcrum; у́гол ~я (*phys.*) angle of repose.

поко́|й², я, *m.* (*obs.*) room, chamber.

поко́йник, а, *m.* the deceased.

поко́йниц|ая, ой, *f.* mortuary.

поко́йницкий, *adj.* (*coll.*) corpse-like.

поко́|йный¹ (~ен, ~йна), *adj.* **1.** calm, quiet; бу́дьте ~йны don't be alarmed, don't (you) worry. **2.** comfortable; restful; ~йной но́чи! good night!

поко́йн|ый², я, *adj.* (the) late; п. коро́ль the late king; *as noun* п., ~ого, *m. and* ~ая, ~ой, *f.* the deceased.

поколеб|а́ть, ~лю, ~лешь, *pf. of* колеба́ть.

поколеб|а́ться, ~лю́сь, ~ле́шься, *pf.* **1.** *pf. of* колеба́ться. **2.** to waver for a time, hesitate for a time.

поколе́ни|е, я, *n.* generation; из ~я в п. from generation to generation.

поколо|ти́ть(ся), чу́(сь), ~ти́шь(ся), *pf. of* колоти́ть(ся).

поко́нч|ить, у, ишь, *pf.* (с+*i.*) **1.** to finish off; to finish (with), be through (with), have done (with); с э́тим ~ено that's done with. **2.** to put an end (to), do away (with); п. с собо́ю to put an end to one's life, make away with oneself; п. жизнь самоубийством to commit suicide.

покоре́ни|е, я, *n.* subjugation, subdual; п. во́здуха conquest of the air.

покори́тел|ь, я, *m.* subjugator; п. серде́ц lady-killer.

покор|и́ть, ю́, и́шь, *pf.* (*of* ~я́ть) to subjugate, subdue; п. чьё-н. се́рдце to win someone's heart.

покор|и́ться, ю́сь, и́шься, *pf.* (*of* ~я́ться) (+*d.*) to submit (to); to resign oneself (to); п. свое́й у́части to resign oneself to one's lot.

покорм|и́ть(ся), лю́(сь), ~ишь(ся), *pf. of* корми́ть(ся).

покорн|ейший, *superl. of* ~ый; ваш п. слуга́ (*polite formula in concluding letter*; *obs.*) your most humble servant; ~ейшая про́сьба most humble petition.

поко́рно, *adv.* humbly; submissively, obediently; п. благодарю́ (*coll.*) thank you; благодарю́ п. (*iron.*; *expresses refusal and/or astonishment*) thank you (very much)!; благодарю́ п., я уж лу́чше пешко́м thank you, I would rather walk.

поко́рност|ь, и, *f.* submissiveness, obedience.

поко́р|ный (~ен, ~на), *adj.* **1.** (+*d.*) submissive (to), obedient; п. судьбе́ resigned to one's fate. **2.** (*in conventional expressions of politeness*; *obs.*) humble, obedient; ваш п. слуга́ your obedient servant; слуга́ п.! (*coll.*, *iron.*) no, thank you!; I'm not having any!

покоро́б|ить(ся), лю(сь), ишь(ся), *pf. of* коро́бить(ся).

поко́рств|овать, ую, *impf.* (+*d.*; *obs.*) to submit (to); to be submissive (to), be obedient (to).

покор|я́ть(ся), я́ю(сь), *impf. of* ~и́ть(ся).

поко́с, а, *m.* **1.** mowing, haymaking; второ́й п. aftermath. **2.** meadow(-land).

покоси́|вшийся, *past part. of* ~ться *and adj.* rickety, crazy, ramshackle.

поко|си́ться, шу́сь, си́шься, *pf. of* коси́ться.

покра́ж|а, и, *f.* **1.** theft. **2.** stolen goods.

покра́п|ать, лет, *pf.* (*of rain*) to spit.

покра́пыва|ть, ет, *impf.* ~л дождь, ~ло (*impers.*) it was spitting with rain off and on.

покра́|сить, шу, сишь, *pf. of* кра́сить.

покра́ск|а, и, *f.* painting, colouring.

покрасне́|ть, ю, *pf. of* красне́ть 1.

покрив|и́ть(ся), лю́(сь), и́шь(ся), *pf. of* криви́ть(ся).

покри́кива|ть, ю, *impf.* (на+*a.*; *coll.*) to shout (at).

покро́в¹, а, *m.* **1.** cover; covering; hearse-
-cloth, pall; (*fig.*) cloak, shroud, pall; ко́жный п. (*anat.*) integument; по́чвенный п. top-soil; сне́жный п. blanket of snow; твёрдый п. (*biol.*) crust, incrustation; под ~ом но́чи under cover of night. **2.** (*obs.*) coverlet; blanket. **3.** (*fig.*, *obs.*) protection; взять под свой п. to take under one's protection.

Покро́в², а́, *m.* (*eccl.*) (Feast of) the Protection, Protective Veil (of the Virgin).

покрови́тел|ь, я, *m.* patron, protector.

покрови́тельниц|а, ы, *f.* patroness, protectress.

покрови́тельственн|ый, *adj.* **1.** (*in var. senses*) protective; ~ая систе́ма (*econ.*) protectionism; п. тари́ф (*econ.*) protective tariff; ~ая окра́ска (*zool.*) protective colouring. **2.** condescending, patronizing.

покрови́тельств|о, а, *n.* protection, patronage; О́бщество ~а живо́тным Society for the Prevention of Cruelty to Animals; под ~ом (+*g.*) under the patronage (of), under the auspices (of).

покрови́тельств|овать, ую, *impf.* (+*d.*) to protect, patronize.

покро́в|ный, *adj. of* ~; (*anat.*) integumentary; ~ные культу́ры, ~ные расте́ния (*agric.*) cover crops; ~ное стёклышко cover glass (*of microscope*).

покро́|й, я, *m.* cut (*of garment*); все на оди́н п. (*fig.*) all in the same style.

покро́мк|а, и, *f.* selvedge.

покроши́|ть, у́, ~ишь, *pf.* (+*a. or g.*) to crumble; to crumb; to mince, chop.

покругле́|ть, ю, *pf. of* кругле́ть.

покруж|и́ть, у́, ~ишь, *pf.* (*coll.*) **1.** to circle several times. **2.** to roam, wander (*for some time*).

покрупне́|ть, ю, *pf. of* крупне́ть.

покрыва́л|о, а, *n.* **1.** coverlet, bedspread, counterpane. **2.** shawl; veil. **3.** cover; нефтяно́е п. oil-slick.

покрыва́|ть(ся), ю(сь), *impf. of* покры́ть(ся).

покры́ти|е, я, *n.* **1.** covering; п. доро́ги road surfacing; п. кры́ши roofing. **2.** covering, discharge, payment; п. расхо́дов defrayment of expenses.

покр|ы́ть, о́ю, о́ешь, *pf.* (*of* крыть *and* ~ыва́ть) **1.** to cover; п. кры́шей to roof; п. кра́ской to coat with paint; п. ла́ком to varnish, lacquer; п. позо́ром to cover with shame; п. себя́ сла́вой to cover oneself with glory; п. та́йной to shroud in mystery. **2.** to meet, pay off; п. расхо́ды to cover expenses, defray expenses. **3.** to drown (*sound*). **4.** to shield, cover up (for); to hush up. **5.** to cover (*distance*). **6.** (*cards*) to cover. **7.** (*coll.*) to curse, swear (at). **8.** (*zool.*; *of stallion, bull, etc.*) to cover.

покр|ы́ться, о́юсь, о́ешься, *pf.* (*of* ~ыва́ться) to cover oneself; to get covered.

покры́шк|а, и, *f.* 1. cover(ing); ни дна ни ∼и, *see* дно. 2. tire-cover, (outer) tire.

покýда, *adv. and conj.* (*coll.*) = покá.

покум|и́ться, лю́сь, и́шься, *pf. of* куми́ться.

покупáтел|ь, я, *m.* buyer, purchaser; customer, client.

покупáтельн|ый, *adj.* purchasing; ∼ая спосóбность (*econ.*) purchasing power.

покупáтель|ский, *adj. of* ∼.

покупá|ть¹, ю, *impf. of* купи́ть.

покупá|ть², ю, *pf.* to bathe; to bath.

покупá|ться, ю́сь, *pf.* to bathe, have a bathe; to have, take a bath.

покýпк|а, и, *f.* 1. buying; purchasing, purchase. 2. (*object purchased*) purchase; вы́годная п. bargain; дéлать ∼и to go shopping.

покуп|нóй, *adj.* 1. bought, purchased (*as opp. to home-made or obtained as a gift*). 2. = ∼áтельный; ∼áя ценá purchase price.

покупщи́к, á, *m.* (*obs.*) buyer, purchaser.

покýрива|ть, ю, *impf.* (*coll.*) to smoke (a little, from time to time).

покур|и́ть, ю́, ∼ишь, *pf.* 1. *pf. of* кури́ть. 2. to have a smoke; давáй ∼им let's have a smoke.

покусá|ть, ю, *pf.* to bite; to sting.

поку|си́ться, шу́сь, си́шься, *pf.* (*of* ∼шáться) (на+*a.*) 1. to attempt, make an attempt (upon); п. на свою́ жизнь to make an attempt upon one's own life; п. на самоуби́йство to attempt suicide. 2. to encroach (on, upon); п. на чьи-н. правá to encroach on someone's rights.

покушá|ть, ю, *pf. of* кýшать.

покушá|ться, юсь, *impf. of* покуси́ться.

покушéни|е, я, *n.* attempt; п. на жизнь (+*g.*) (*or* на+*a.*) attempt upon the life (of).

пол¹, а, о ∼е, на ∼ý, *pl.* ∼ы́, *m.* floor.

пол², а, *m.* sex; обóего ∼а of both sexes.

пол- half (*as in* полчасá half an hour; полдеся́того half past nine; полдю́жины half a dozen, *etc.*).

пол|á, ы́, *pl.* ∼ы, *f.* skirt, flap, lap; из-под ∼ы́ on the sly, under cover; торговáть из--под ∼ы́ to sell under the counter.

полагá|ть¹, ю, *impf.* (*obs.*) to lay, place.

полагá|ть², ю, *impf.* to suppose, think; ∼ют, что он умирáет he is believed to be dying; нáдо п. it is to be supposed, one must suppose.

полагá|ться, юсь, *impf.* 1. *impf. of* положи́ться. 2. ∼ется (*impers.*) one is supposed (to); так ∼ется it is the custom; не ∼ется it is not done; здесь ∼ется снимáть шля́пу one is supposed to take off one's hat here. 3. ∼ется (+*d.*) to be due (to); нам э́то ∼ется it is our due, we have a right to it.

полá|дить, жу, дишь, *pf.* (с+*i.*) to come to an understanding (with); to get on (with).

полáком|ить(ся), лю(сь), ишь(ся), *pf. of* лáкомить(ся).

полáт|и, ей, *no sing.* sleeping-bench (*on high raised platform in Russian peasant hut*).

пóлб|а, ы, *f.* (*bot.*) spelt, German wheat.

полбеды́, *f.* (*coll.*) a small loss, a minor misfortune; э́то ещё п. it is not so very serious.

пóлб|енный, *adj. of* ∼а.

полвéка, полувéка, *m.* half a century.

полгóда, полугóда, *m.* half a year, six months; с п., óколо полугóда for about six months.

полгóря = полбеды́.

пóлдень, полýдня, *and* пóлдня, *m.* 1. noon, midday; за п. (*or* зá полдень) past noon; к полýдню towards noon; врéмя до полýдня forenoon; врéмя пóсле полýдня afternoon. 2. (*obs.*) south.

полднéвный, *adj. of* пóлдень.

пóлдник, а, *m.* (afternoon) snack *light meal between dinner and supper*).

пóлднича|ть, *impf.* (*coll.*) to have an (afternoon) snack.

полдорóг|и, *f.* half-way; встрéтиться на ∼е to meet half-way; остановиться на ∼е to stop half-way (*also fig.*).

пóл|е, я, *pl.* ∼я́, ∼éй, *n.* (1. (*in var. senses*) field; спорти́вное п. playing field, sports ground; п. би́твы, п. брáни (*obs.*), п. сражéния battle-field; п. дéятельности sphere of action; п. зрéния field of vision; оди́н в п. не вóин (*prov.*) the voice of one man is the voice of no one. 2. (*art*) ground; (*heraldry*) field. 3. (*pl.*) margin; замéтки на ∼я́х notes in the margin. 4. (*pl.*) brim (*of hat*).

полевéни|е, я, *n.* (*polit.*) leftward movement.

полевé|ть, ю, *pf. of* левéть.

полёвк|а, и, *f.* field-vole.

полевóдств|о, а, *n.* field-crop cultivation.

полев|óй, *adj.* (*in var. senses*) field; ∼áя артиллéрия field artillery; п. бинóкль field glasses; п. гóспиталь field hospital; ∼áя мышь field-mouse; ∼áя сýмка (*mil.*) map case; ∼ые цветы́ wild flowers; п. шпат (*min.*) feldspar.

полегáни|е, я, *n.* (*agric.*) lodging (*of crops*).

полегá|ть, ю, *impf. of* полéчь 3.

полегóньку, *adv.* (*coll.*) by easy stages.

полегчá|ть, ет, *pf. of* легчáть; больнóму ∼ло the patient is feeling better; у меня́ на душé ∼ло I feel a load off my mind.

полéгче, *comp. of* лёгкий *and* легкó 1. (*somewhat, a little*) lighter. 2. a little easier, a little less difficult; п! take it easy!, ease up a bit!, not so fast!

полеж|áть, ý, и́шь, *pf.* to lie down (*for a while*).

полёжива|ть, ю, *impf.* (*coll.*) to lie down (*off and on*).

полéз|ный (~ен, ~на), *adj.* useful; helpful; wholesome, health-giving; ~ное дéйствие efficiency, duty (*of a machine*); ~ная жилáя плóщадь actual living space; ~ная лошадиная сила effective horsepower, working horsepower; ~ная нагрýзка (*tech.*) working load, pay-load; это лекáрство óчень ~но от кáшля this medicine is very good for coughs; чем могý быть ~ен? can I help you?

полéз|ть, у, ешь, *past* ~, ~ла, *pf.* 1. *pf. of* лезть. 2. to start to climb.

полемизир|овать, ую, *impf.* (с+*i.*) to carry on polemics (with).

полéмик|а, и, *f.* polemic(s); dispute, controversy; вступить в ~y (с+*i.*) to enter into polemics (with).

полемист, а, *m.* polemicist, controversialist.

полемический, *adj.* polemic(al), controversial.

полемич|ный (~ен, ~на), *adj.* polemical.

полéнива|ться, юсь, *impf.* (*coll.*) to be rather lazy.

полен|иться, юсь, ~ишься, *pf.* (+*inf.*) to be too lazy to.

полéниц|а, ы, *m. and f.* (*folk poet.*) hero, heroine.

полéнниц|а, ы, *f.* pile (*of logs*); stack (*of firewood*).

полéн|о, а, *pl.* ~ья, ~ьев, *n.* log, billet.

полéсь|е, я, *n.* wooded locality; woodlands.

полёт, а, *m.* flight; flying; брéющий п. hedge-hopping; высóтный п. altitude flying; пикирующий п. diving; слепóй п. blind flying; фигýрный п. aerobatics; вид с птичьего ~a bird's-eye view; ~a flight of fancy; высóкого ~a (птица) (*fig.*, *often iron.*) person of exalted rank, member of the upper ten.

полетá|ть, ю, *pf.* to fly (*for a while*), do some flying.

поле|тéть, чý, тишь, *pf.* 1. *pf. of* летéть. 2. to start to fly; to fly off. 3. (*fig.*, *coll.*) to fall, go headlong.

по-лéтнему, *adv.* as in summer, as for summer; одéт п. (dressed) in summer clothes.

полеч|ить, ý, ~ишь, *pf.* to treat (*for a while*).

полеч|иться, ýсь, ~ишься, *pf.* to undergo treatment (*for a while*).

пол|éчь, ягу, яжешь, ягут, *past* ~ёг, ~еглá, *pf.* 1. to lie down (*in numbers*). 2. (*fig.*) to fall, be killed (*in numbers*). 3. (*impf.* ~егáть) (*agric.*) to be lodged (*of standing crops*).

пóлз|ать, аю, *impf.*, *indet. of* ~ти; п. в ногáх у когó-н. (*fig.*) to grovel at someone's feet.

ползкóм, *adv.* crawling, on all fours.

полз|ти, ý, ёшь, *past* ~, ~лá, *impf.* 1. to crawl, creep (along); пóезд ~ the train was

crawling. 2. to ooze (out). 3. (*fig.*, *coll.*; *of rumour*, *etc.*) to spread. 4. (*coll.*; *of fabric*) to fray, ravel out. 5. (*of soil*) to slip, collapse.

ползýн, á, *m.* (*tech.*) slide-block, slider, runner.

ползун|óк, кá, *m.* 1. (*coll.*) toddler. 2. *pl.* (*coll.*) (child's) romper suit.

ползýч|ий, *adj.* creeping; ~ие растéния (*bot.*) creepers.

поли- poly-.

полиáндри|я, и, *f.* polyandry.

полиартрит, а, *m.* (*med.*) polyarthritis.

полив|а, ы, *f.* glaze.

поливá|ть(ся), ю(сь), *impf. of* полить(ся).

поливк|а¹, и, *f.* watering.

поливк|а², и, *f.* gravy.

поливн|óй, *adj.* requiring irrigation; requiring watering; ~ые зéмли irrigation area.

полив|óчный, *adj. of* ~ка¹; ~очная жидкость cooling mixture, coolant; ~очная машина watering machine.

полигáми|я, и, *f.* polygamy.

полиглóт, а, *m.* polyglot.

полигóн, а, *m.* (*mil.*) (artillery *or* bombing) range; испытáтельный п. proving ground, testing area; учéбный п. training ground.

полиграфист, а, *m.* printing trades worker.

полиграфическ|ий, *adj.* 1. polygraphic; ~ое произвóдство printing. 2. п. отдéл non-specialist section (*of library*).

полиграфи|я, и, *f.* 1. (*tech.*) polygraphy; printing trades. 2. non-specialist section (*of library, in which books are classified by authors' names only, without regard to subject-matter*).

поликлиник|а, и, *f.* 1. polyclinic, clinic; health centre. 2. outpatients' department (*of hospital*).

полиловé|ть, ю, *pf. of* лиловéть.

полимéр, а, *m.* (*chem.*) polymer.

полимеризáци|я, и, *f.* (*chem.*) polymerization.

полиморфизм, а, *m.* polymorphism.

полиморфический, *adj.* polymorphic, polymorphous.

полимóрфный, *adj.* polymorphous.

полинези|ец, йца, *m.* Polynesian.

полинезийский, *adj.* Polynesian.

полинóм, а, *m.* (*math.*) polynomial.

полиня|лый, *adj.* faded, discoloured.

полиня|ть, ет, *pf. of* линять.

полиомиелит, а, *m.* (*med.*) poliomyelitis, infantile paralysis.

полип, а, *m.* 1. (*zool.*) polyp. 2. (*med.*) polypus.

полип|ный, *adj. of* ~.

полировáльн|ый, *adj.* polishing; ~ая бумáга sandpaper; п. станóк buffing machine.

полир|овáть, ýю, *impf.* (*of* от~) to polish.

полирóвк|а, и, *f.* polish(ing); buffing.

полирóвочный, *adj.* polishing; buffing.

полирóвщик, а, *m.* polisher.

пóлис, а, *m.* policy; страховóй п. insurance policy.

полисемантѝзм, а, *m.* (*ling.*) polysemy.

полисемантѝческий, *adj.* (*ling.*) polysemantic.

полисемѝ|я, и, *f.* (*ling.*) polysemy.

полисинтетѝческий, *adj.* (*ling.*) polysynthetic.

полисмéн, а, *m.* policeman; constable.

полиспáст, а, *m.* block and tackle; pulley block; tackle block.

полѝстный, *adj.* per sheet.

полит- *abbr., used to form compounds, of* политѝческий.

политбюрó, *indecl., n.* the Politbureau (*Political Bureau of the Central Committee of the Soviet Communist Party*).

политграмот|а, ы, *f.* elementary course of political education.

политеѝзм, а, *m.* polytheism.

политеѝст, а, *m.* polytheist.

политеистѝческий, *adj.* polytheistic.

политехнизáци|я, и, *f.* introduction of polytechnic education.

политéхник, а, *m.* student of polytechnic.

политéхникум, а, *m.* polytechnic (school).

политехнѝческий, *adj.* polytechnic(al).

политзаключённ|ый, ого, *m.* political prisoner.

полѝтик, а, *m.* 1. politician. 2. student of politics; expert on political questions. 3. (*fig., coll.*) politician, politic person.

полѝтик|а, и, *f.* 1. policy; п. на грáни войны 'brinkmanship'; провестѝ ~у to carry out a policy. 2. politics; п. сѝлы power politics; говорѝть о ~е to talk politics.

политикáн, а, *m.* (*pejor.*) politician, intriguer.

политикáнств|о, а, *n.* intrigue.

политикáнств|овать, ую, *impf.* to intrigue, be an intriguer.

политинформáтор, а, *m.* political information officer.

политипáж, а, *m.* (*typ.*) polytype.

политѝческ|ий, *adj.* political; п. дéятель political figure, politician; ~ие наýки political science; ~ая эконóмия political economy; по ~им соображéниям for political reasons.

политѝч|ный (~ен, ~на), *adj.* (*coll.*) politic.

политкаторжáн|ин, ина, *pl.* ~е, ~, *m.* political convict (*in Russia before 1917*).

политкруж|óк, кá, *m.* political study circle.

политолóги|я, и, *f.* (*coll.*) politics (= *political science*).

политпросвéт, а, *m.* (*formed from abbr. of* политѝческий *and* просветѝтельный) political education.

политрабóтник, а, *m.* political worker.

политрýк, а, *m.* (*abbr. of* политѝческий руководѝтель) political instructor (*in units of the Soviet armed forces*).

политуправлéни|е, я, *n.* Political Administration.

политýр|а, ы, *f.* polish, varnish.

политучёб|а, ы, *f.* political education; study of current affairs.

политшкóл|а, ы, *f.* political school.

пол|ѝть, ью, ьёшь, *past* ~ѝл, ~илá, ~ѝло, *pf.* (*of* ~ивáть) 1. (+*a. and i.*) to pour (on, upon); п. что-н. водóй to pour water on something; п. цветы́ to water the flowers. 2. to begin to pour.

пол|ѝться, ьюсь, ьёшься, *past* ~ѝлся, ~илáсь, ~ѝлóсь, *pf.* (*of* ~ивáться) 1. (+*i.*) to pour over oneself. 2. to begin to flow.

политэконóми|я, и, *f.* political economy.

политэмигрáнт, а, *m.* political emigrant.

полифонѝческий, *adj.* polyphonic.

полифонѝ|я, и, *f.* (*mus.*) polyphony.

полицеймéйстер, а, *m.* (*hist.*) chief of police.

полицéйск|ий, *adj.* police; п. учáсток police-station; *as noun* п., ~ого, *m.* policeman, police-officer.

полѝци|я, и, *f.* police; сыскнáя п. criminal investigation department.

полѝчн|ое, ого, *n.* поймáть с ~ым to catch red-handed.

полишинéл|ь, я, *m.* Punch(inello); секрéт ~я open secret.

полиэ́др, а, *m.* (*math.*) polyhedron.

полиэтилéн, а, *m.* polythene.

полк, á, о ~é, в ~ý, *m.* regiment; авиациóнный п. group (*in air force*); нáшего ~ý прѝбыло our numbers have grown.

пóлк|а[1], и, *f.* 1. shelf; кнѝжная п. bookshelf. 2. (*in railway sleeping-car*) berth.

пóлк|а[2], и, *f.* weeding.

полкóвник, а, *m.* colonel.

полковóд|ец, ца, *m.* (*not denoting specific mil. rank*) captain, commander; military leader.

полковóй, *adj.* regimental.

поллю́ци|я, и, *f.* (*physiol.*) spermatorrhoea, nocturnal emission.

полмиллиóна, *m.* half a million.

полминýты, *f.* half a minute.

полнéйший, *adj.* sheer, uttermost.

полнé|ть, ю, *impf.* (*of* по~) to grow stout, put on weight.

полнёхон|ький (~ек, ~ька), *adj.* (*coll.*) brim-full, crammed, packed.

полн|ѝть, ю, ѝшь, *impf.* (*coll.*) to overfill; э́то плáтье её ~ѝт this dress makes her look fat.

пóлно[1], *adv.* brim-full, full to the brim; слѝшком п. too full.

пóлно[2], *adv.* (*coll.*) 1. enough (of that)!; that

will do!; п. ворча́ть! stop grumbling! **2.** you don't mean that, you don't mean to say so.

полно́, *adv.* (+*g.*) (*coll.*) lots; в ко́мнате полно́ наро́ду the room is packed with people.

полнове́сност|ь, и, *f.* **1.** full weight. **2.** (*fig.*) soundness.

полнове́с|ный (~ен, ~на), *adj.* **1.** of full weight, full-weight. **2.** (*fig.*) sound.

полновла́сти|е, я, *n.* sovereignty.

полновла́ст|ный (~ен, ~на), *adj.* sovereign; п. хозя́ин sole master.

полново́д|ный (~ен, ~на), *adj.* deep.

полново́дь|е, я, *n.* high water.

полногла́си|е, я, *n.* (*ling.*) full vocalism, pleophony.

полнозву́ч|ный (~ен, ~на), *adj.* sonorous.

полнокро́ви|е, я, *n.* (*med.*) plethora.

полнокро́в|ный (~ен, ~на), *adj.* **1.** (*med.*) plethoric. **2.** (*fig.*) full-blooded, sanguineous.

полнолу́ни|е, я, *n.* full moon.

полнометра́жный, *adj.* п. фильм full-length film.

полномо́чи|е, я, *n.* authority, power, plenary powers; commission; (*leg.*) proxy; чрезвыча́йные ~я emergency powers; срок ~й term of office; превыше́ние ~й exceeding one's commission; дать ~я (+*d.*) to empower; име́ть ~я вы́ступить от и́мени (+*g.*) to have authority to speak (for); предъяви́ть свои́ ~я (на+*a.*) to show one's authority (to, for).

полномо́ч|ный (~ен, ~на), *adj.* plenipotentiary; п. представи́тель plenipotentiary.

полнопра́ви|е, я, *n.* full rights; competency.

полнопра́в|ный (~ен, ~на), *adj.* enjoying full rights; competent; п. член full member.

полноро́дный, *adj.* (*leg.*) full (*brother or sister, as opp. to half-brother, half-sister*).

по́лностью, *adv.* fully, in full; completely, utterly; п. верну́ть долг to pay a debt in full; п. утверди́ть ме́ру to approve a measure in its entirety.

полнот|а́, ы́, *no pl.*, *f.* **1.** fullness, completeness; plenitude; от ~ы́ се́рдца, души́ in the fullness of one's heart; п. вла́сти absolute power. **2.** stoutness, corpulence; plumpness.

по́лноте, *interj.* (*coll.*) enough! come come!

полноце́нност|ь, и, *f.* full value.

полноце́н|ный (~ен, ~на), *adj.* **1.** of full value. **2.** (*fig.*) of value; ~ная рабо́та work done in accordance with requirements.

полно́чи, *indecl.*, *f.* half the (a) night.

полно́чный, *adj.* **1.** midnight. **2.** (*obs.*) northern.

по́лночь, по́лночи, *and* **полу́ночи,** *f.* **1.** midnight; за́ п. after midnight. **2.** (*obs.*) north.

по́л|ный (~он, ~на́, ~но́), *adj.* **1.** (+*g.* or *i.*) full (of); complete, entire, total; absolute; в состоя́нии ~ного безу́мия stark mad; п. биле́т whole ticket (*as opp. to child's ticket of half fare*); ~ным го́лосом at the top of one's voice; сказа́ть ~ным го́лосом (*fig.*) to say outright; жить ~ной жи́знью to live a full life; ~ное затме́ние total eclipse; п. карма́н (+*g.*) a pocketful (of); ~ная незави́симость complete independence, full sovereignty; ~ное ничто́жество a complete nonentity; п. пансио́н full board and lodging; ~ной абсолю́тный rest; ~ное собра́ние сочине́ний complete works; п. ход вперёд! full speed ahead!; идти́ ~ным хо́дом to be in full swing; ~ная ча́ша (*fig.*) plenty; в ~ной ме́ре fully, in full measure; в ~ном расцве́те сил in one's prime; они́ пришли́ в ~ном соста́ве they came in full force; на ~ном ходу́ at full speed; он пи́шет с ~ным зна́нием де́ла he writes with a complete grasp of his subject. **2.** stout, portly; plump.

по́лным-полно́, *adv.* chock-full, chock-a-block; в авто́бусе бы́ло п.-п. наро́ду the 'bus was chock-a-block with people.

по́ло, *indecl.*, *n.* (*sport*) polo; во́дное п. water polo.

пол-оборо́та, *indecl.*, *m.* half-turn; п. нале́во, напра́во (*mil.*) left, right incline.

полов|а́, ы́, *f.* chaff.

полови́к, а́, *m.* mat, matting floor-covering; door-mat.

полови́н|а, ы, *f.* **1.** half; middle; два с ~ой two and a half; п. шесто́го half past five; в ~е девятна́дцатого ве́ка in the middle of the nineteenth century; на ~е доро́ги halfway; п. две́ри leaf of a door. **2.** (*obs.*) apartment, rooms, wing.

полови́нк|а, и, *f.* **1.** half. **2.** leaf (*of door*).

полови́нн|ый, *adj.* half; п. окла́д half-pay; заплати́ть за что-н. в ~ом разме́ре to pay half-price for something.

полови́нчатост|ь, и, *f.* half-heartedness; indeterminateness.

полови́нчат|ый (~, ~а), *adj.* **1.** halved; half-and-half; п. кирпи́ч half-brick; п. чугу́н mottled iron. **2.** (*fig.*) half-hearted; undecided; indeterminate; ~ое реше́ние compromise decision.

полови́ц|а, ы, *f.* floor board.

полбвник[1]**, а,** *m.* (*hist.*) share-cropper.

полбвник[2]**, а,** *m.* (*dial.*) ladle.

полово́дь|е, я, *n.* flood, high water (*at time of spring thaw*).

полов|о́й[1]**,** *adj.* floor; ~а́я тря́пка floor cloth; ~а́я щётка broom.

полов|о́й[2]**,** *adj.* sexual; ~о́е бесси́лие impotence; ~о́е влече́ние sexual attraction;

~а́я зре́лость puberty; ~ые о́рганы genitals, sexual organs; ~а́я связь sexual intercourse.

поло́в|о́й³, о́го, m. (obs.) waiter.

поло́вый, adj. pale yellow, sandy.

по́лог, а, m. bed-curtain; под ~ом но́чи (poet.) under cover of night.

поло́гий, adj. gently sloping.

поло́гост|ь, и, f. slope, declivity.

положе́ни|е, я, n. 1. position; whereabouts. 2. position; posture; attitude; в сидя́чем ~и in a sitting position. 3. (in var. senses) position; condition, state; situation; status, standing; circumstances; семе́йное п. marital status; социа́льное п. social status; вое́нное п. martial law; перевести́ на ми́рное п. to transfer to a peace-time footing; оса́дное п. state of siege; чрезвыча́йное п. state of emergency; п. веще́й state of affairs; при тако́м ~и дел as things stand, things being as they are; хозя́ин ~я master of the situation; быть на высоте́ ~я to be up to the mark, be on top of the situation; выходи́ть из ~я to find a way out; войти́ в чьё-н. п. to understand someone's position; челове́к с ~ем a man of high position; быть в стеснённом ~и to be in straightened, reduced circumstances; быть на неле-га́льном ~и to be in hiding; быть в (интере́сном) ~и (coll., euph.) to be in the family way, be expecting. 4. regulations, statute; по ~ю according to the regulations. 5. thesis; tenet; clause, provisions (of an agreement, etc.).

поло́ж|енный, p.p.p. of ~и́ть and adj. agreed, determined; в п. час at a time agreed.

поло́жим let us assume; он, п., всё ви́дел he saw everything, let us assume; п., что он всё ви́дел assuming that he saw everything. (Also in expressions indicating doubt or dissent.)

положи́тельно, adv. 1. positively; favourably; п. отве́тить (i) to answer in the affirmative, (ii) to give a favourable answer; to agree, consent; отнести́сь п. (к) to take a favourable view (of), look favourably (upon). 2. (coll.) positively, completely, absolutely; она́ п. ничего́ не понима́ет she understands absolutely nothing.

положи́тел|ьный (~ен, ~ьна), adj. 1. (in var. senses) positive; ~ьная сте́пень сравне́ния (gram.) positive degree; ~ьная фило-со́фия positive philosophy, positivism; п. электри́ческий заря́д positive electric charge. 2. affirmative; п. отве́т affirmative reply. 3. favourable; possessing good qualities; п. геро́й (lit.) positive hero; ~ьная оце́нка favourable reception. 4. (coll.) complete, absolute; п. дура́к complete fool.

полож|и́ть, у́, ~ишь, pf. 1. pf. of класть; п. жизнь to lay down one's life; п. ору́жие to lay down one's arms. 2. (+inf.; obs.) to decide; to agree. 3. (coll., obs.) to propose, offer; to fix; они́ ~и́ли ему́ хоро́шее жа́лованье they have offered him a good salary.

полож|и́ться, у́сь, ~ишься, pf. (of пола-га́ться) (на+a.) to rely (upon), count (upon); to pin one's hopes (upon).

по́лоз¹, а, pl. поло́зья, поло́зьев, m. (sledge) runner.

по́лоз², а, m. grass-snake.

пол|о́к¹, ка́, m. (in Russian steam bath) sweating shelf.

пол|о́к², ка́, m. dray.

поло́льник, а, m. hoe.

поло́льщик, а, m. weeder.

полома́|ть, ю, pf. to break.

полома́|ться, юсь, pf. of лома́ться.

поло́мк|а, и, f. breakage; breakdown.

поломо́йк|а, и, f. (coll.) charwoman.

поло́н, а, m. (arch.) captivity.

полоне́з, а, m. polonaise.

полониза́ци|я, и, f. polonization.

полонизи́р|овать, ую, impf. and pf. to polonize.

полони́зм, а, m. (ling.) polonism.

поло́ни|й, я, m. (chem.) polonium.

полон|и́ть, ю́, и́шь, pf. (arch.) to take captive.

полоро́ги|й, adj. horned; pl. as noun ~е, ~х horned ruminant mammals.

полос|а́, ы́, a. по́лосу, pl. по́лосы, поло́с, ~а́м, f. 1. stripe; streak; мате́рия (с) бе́лыми и голубы́ми ~а́ми material in blue and white stripes. 2. (in var. senses) strip; (of iron, etc.) band, flat bar. 3. wale, weal. 4. region; zone, belt; strip; оборони́тельная п. defence zone; песча́ная п. sandy strip; чернозёмная п. black-earth belt. 5. (agric.; obs.) patch, strip. 6. period; phase; ~о́й, ~а́ми (as adv. of time) in patches; п. хоро́шей пого́ды spell of fine weather; п. неуда́ч run of bad luck; мра́чная п. нашла́ на него́ he is going through a gloomy patch. 7. (typ.) type page.

полоса́тик, а, m. (zool.) rorqual.

полоса́т|ый (~, ~а), adj. striped, stripy.

поло́ск|а, и, f. dim. of полоса́; в ~у striped.

полоска́ни|е, я, n. 1. rinse, rinsing; gargling. 2. gargle.

полоска́тельниц|а, ы, f. slop-basin.

полоска́тельн|ый, adj. ~ая ча́шка slop--basin.

поло|ска́ть, щу́, ~щешь, impf. (of вы́~) to rinse; п. го́рло to gargle.

поло|ска́ться, щу́сь, ~щешься, impf. 1. to paddle. 2. (of a flag, sail, etc.) to flap.

полосн|у́ть, у́, ёшь, pf. (no impf.) (coll.) to slash.

поло́сный, *adj.* (*typ.*) full page.

поло́с|ова́ть, у́ю, *impf.* 1. (*pf.* рас~) (*tech.*) to make into bars. 2. (*pf.* ис~) (*coll.*) to flog, scourge, welt.

полосов|о́й, *adj.* (*tech.*) band, strip, bar; ~о́е желе́зо bar-iron.

по́лост|ь¹, и, *g. pl.* ~е́й, *f.* (*anat.*) cavity; брюшна́я п. abdominal cavity.

по́лост|ь², и, *g. pl.* ~е́й, *f.* travelling rug.

полоте́н|це, ца, *g. pl.* ~ец, *n.* towel; мохна́тое п. Turkish towel; посу́дное п. tea--towel; п. на ва́лике roller towel.

полоте́р, а, *m.* floor-polisher.

полотёрн|ый, *adj.* floor-polishing; ~ая щётка brush, broom.

полотни́щ|е, а, *n.* 1. (*of material*) width; panel; п. пала́тки tent section, ground sheet; па́рус в пять ~ sail of five panels. 2. flat (part), blade.

полот|но́, на́, *pl.* ~на, ~ен, ~нам, *n.* 1. linen; бле́дный как п. white as a sheet. 2. (*art*) canvas (*fig.* = *painting*). 3. железнодоро́жное п. permanent way. 4. (*tech.*) web; blade; п. пилы́ saw blade, saw web.

полотня́ный, *adj.* linen.

полот|о́к, ка́, *m.* (*obs.*) half of a (smoked, dried, *or* salted) bird or other game.

пол|о́ть, ю́, ~ешь, *impf.* (*of* вы́~) to weed.

полоу́ми|е, я, *n.* craziness.

полоу́м|ный (~ен, ~на), *adj.* (*coll.*) half--witted, crazy.

полпи́в|о, а, *n.* (*obs.*, *coll.*) light beer.

полпре́д, а, *m.* (*abbr. of* полномо́чный представи́тель) (ambassador) plenipotentiary.

полпути́, *indecl.*, *m.* на п. half-way; верну́ться с п. to turn back half-way; останови́ться на п. (*fig.*) to stop half-way.

полслов|а, на ~е, *n.* п. от него́ не услы́шишь you cannot get a word out of him; мо́жно вас на п.? may I have a word with you?, may I speak to you for a minute?

полти́н|а, ы, *f.* (*coll.*) = ~ник; два с ~ой two roubles fifty kopecks.

полти́нник, а, *m.* 1. fifty kopecks. 2. fifty--kopeck piece.

полтора́, полу́тора, *m. and n.* one and a half; в п. ра́за бо́льше half as much again; ни два ни п. neither one thing nor the other.

полтора́ста, полу́тораста, *num.* a hundred and fifty.

полтор|ы́, *f.* = ~а́; п. ты́сячи one and a half thousand.

полу- half-, semi-, demi-.

полуба́к, а, *m.* (*naut.*) forecastle; top-gallant forecastle.

полубессозна́тельный, *adj.* semi-unconscious.

полубо́г, а, *m.* demigod.

полуботи́н|ки, ок, *sing.* ~ок, ~ка, *m.* shoes.

полува́ттный, *adj.* (*electr.*) half-watt.

полугла́сн|ый, ого, *m.* (*ling.*) semivowel.

полуго́ди|е, я, *n.* half-year, six months.

полугоди́чны|й, *adj.* half-yearly; of six months' duration; ~е ку́рсы six-months courses.

полугодова́лый, *adj.* six-month(s)-old.

полугодово́й, *adj.* half-yearly, six-monthly; п. отчёт half-yearly report.

полугра́мотный, *adj.* semi-literate.

полу́д|а, ы, *f.* tinning; tin plate.

полу́денный, *adj.* 1. midday. 2. (*obs.*, *poet.*) southern.

полу|ди́ть, жу́, ~ди́шь, *pf. of* луди́ть.

полужёсткий, *adj.* (*tech.*) semi-rigid.

полужив|о́й (~, ~а́, ~о), *adj.* half dead; more dead than alive.

полузащи́т|а, ы, *f.* (*collect.*; *sport*) half-backs, midfield players; центр ~ы centre half.

полузащи́тник, а, *m.* (*sport*) half-back, midfield player.

полуйм|я, ени, *pl.* ~ена́, ~ён, ~ена́м, *n.* (*obs.*, *coll.*) diminutive (*of personal name*), affectionate form of name (*e.g.* Volodya *for* Vladimir, Nadya *for* Nadezhda).

полукафта́н, а, *m.* short caftan.

полуке́д|ы, ов *or* ~, *no sing.* gym shoes; sneakers.

полукро́вк|а, и, *f.* half-breed, first-hybrid.

полукру́г, а, *m.* semicircle.

полукру́глый, *adj.* semicircular.

полукру́жны|й, *adj.* ~е кана́лы (*anat.*) semicircular canals.

полулеж|а́ть, у́, ~и́шь, *impf.* to recline.

полумгл|а́, ы́, *f.* mist, half-light (*before sunrise or sunset*); gloaming.

полуме́р|а, ы, *f.* half-measure.

полуме́ртв|ый (~, ~а́), *adj.* half-dead.

полуме́сяц, а, *m.* half moon; crescent.

полуме́сячный, *adj.* fortnightly; of a fortnight's duration.

полумра́к, а, *m.* semi-darkness, shade.

полунаго́й, *adj.* half-naked.

полу́ндра, *interj.* (*naut.*) stand from under!

полуно́чник, а, *m.* (*coll.*) night-bird.

полуно́чнича|ть, ю, *impf.* (*coll.*) to burn the midnight oil.

полуно́чный, *adj.* 1. midnight. 2. (*obs.*, *poet.*) northern.

полуоборо́т, а, *m.* half-turn.

полуоде́т|ый (~, ~а), *adj.* half-dressed, half-clothed.

полуосвещённый, *adj.* half-lit.

полуо́стров, а, *m.* peninsula.

полуостровно́й, *adj.* peninsular.

полуотво́рен|ный (~, ~а), *adj.* half-open; ajar.

полуоткры́т|ый (~, ~а), *adj.* half-open; ajar.

полупальто́, *indecl.*, *n.* short coat.

полуперехо́д, а, *m.* (*mil.*) half day's march.

полуподва́льный, *adj.* п. эта́ж semi-basement.

полупокло́н, а, *m.* slight bow.

полупроводни́к, а́, *m.* (*phys.*) semi-conductor, transistor.

полупроводнико́вый, *adj.* transistor(ized).

полупья́н|ый (~, ~а́, ~о), *adj.* half tight, tipsy.

полуразру́шен|ный (~, ~а), *adj.* tumbledown, dilapidated.

полуро́т|а, ы, *f.* (*mil.*) half-company.

полусве́т¹, а, *m.* twilight.

полусве́т², а, *m.* demi-monde.

полусерьёзный, *adj.* half-serious; half in joke.

полусло́в|о, а, *n.* оборва́ть кого́-н. на ~е to cut someone short; останови́ться на ~е to stop short, stop in the middle of a sentence; поня́ть с ~а to take the hint, be quick in the uptake.

полусме́рт|ь, и, *f.* до ~и (*fig., coll.*) to death; изби́ть кого́-н. до ~и to beat someone within an inch of his life; испуга́ться до ~и to be frightened to death.

полус|о́н, на́, *m.* half sleep; somnolence, drowsiness.

полусо́нный, *adj.* half asleep; dozing.

полуспу́щенный, *adj.* п. флаг flag at half-mast.

полуста́н|ок, ка, *m.* (*railway*) halt.

полусти́ши|е, я, *n.* hemistich.

полуте́н|ь, и, о ~и, в ~й, *f.* penumbra.

полуто́н, а, *pl.* ~ы and ~а́, *m.* 1. (*mus.*) semitone. 2. (*art*) half-tint.

полуто́нк|а, и, *f.* (*coll.*) ten-hundredweight lorry.

полуторато́нк|а, и, f. (*coll.*) thirty-hundredweight lorry.

полу́торн|ый, *adj.* of one and a half; в ~ом разме́ре half as much again.

полутьм|а́, ы́, *f.* semi-darkness; twilight.

полууста́в, а, *m.* (*palaeog.*) semi-uncial.

полуфабрика́т, а, *m.* semi-finished product; prepared raw material (*esp. of foodstuffs*).

полуфина́л, а, *m.* (*sport*) semi-final.

полуфина́л|ьный, *adj.* of ~; ~ьные встре́чи semi-finals.

получасово́й, *adj.* of half an hour's duration; half-hourly.

получа́тел|ь, я, *m.* recipient.

получ|а́ть(ся), а́ю(сь), *impf. of* ~и́ть(ся).

получе́ни|е, я, *n.* receipt; распи́ска в ~и receipt; по ~и on receipt, on receiving.

получ|и́ть, у́, ~ишь, *pf.* (*of* ~а́ть) to get, receive, obtain; п. замеча́ние to receive a reprimand; п. на́сморк to catch a cold; п. обра́тно to recover, get back; п. огла́ску to become known, receive publicity; п. паёк to draw rations; п. призна́ние to ob-

tain recognition; п. прика́з to receive an order; п. примене́ние to come into use, effect; п. удово́льствие to derive pleasure.

получ|и́ться, ~ится, *pf.* (*of* ~а́ться) 1. to come, arrive, turn up; ~и́лась посы́лка a parcel has come. 2. to turn out, prove, be; результа́ты ~и́лись нева́жные the results are poor; ~и́лось, что он был прав it turned out that he was right, he proved right. 3. *pass. of* ~и́ть.

полу́чк|а, и, *f.* (*coll.*) 1. receipt. 2. pay (packet), sum paid.

полу́чше, *adv.* rather better, a little better.

полуша́ри|е, я, *n.* hemisphere; ~я головно́го мо́зга cerebral hemispheres.

полушёпот, а, *m.* говори́ть ~ом to speak in undertones.

полуше́рст|ь, и, *f.* wool mixture.

полу́шк|а, и, *f.* (*obs.*) quarter-kopeck piece; не име́ть ни ~и to be penniless.

полушто́ф, а, *m.* (*obs.*) half-shtof (*see* што́ф¹).

полушу́б|ок, ка, *m.* sheepskin coat.

полушутя́, *adv.* half in joke.

полцены́, *indecl., f.* за п. at half price; for half its value.

полчаса́, получа́са, *m.* half an hour.

по́лчищ|е, а, *n.* horde; (*fig.*) mass, flock.

полшага́, *indecl., m.* half-pace.

по́л|ый, *adj.* 1. hollow. 2. ~ая вода́ flood-water.

по́лымя, *n.* (*dial.*) flame; из огня́ да в п. (*prov.*) out of the frying-pan into the fire.

полы́н|ный, *adj.* of ~; ~ная во́дка absinth.

полы́н|ь, и, *f.* wormwood.

полы́н|ья́, ьи́, *g. pl.* ~е́й, *f.* polynia (*unfrozen patch of water in the midst of ice*).

полысе́|ть, ю, *pf. of* лысе́ть.

полыха́|ть, ет, *impf.* to blaze.

по́льз|а, ы, *f.* use; advantage, benefit, profit; кака́я от э́того п.? what good will it do?, what use is it?; что ~ы говори́ть об э́том? what's the use of talking about it?; извлека́ть из чего́-н. ~у to benefit from something, profit by something; принести́ ~у (+d.) to be of benefit (to); для ~ы (+g.) for the benefit (of); в ~у (+g.) in favour (of), on behalf (of); до́воды в ~у чего́-н. arguments in favour; э́то говори́т не в ва́шу ~у it does not speak well for you, it is not to your credit; два-ноль в ~у Дина́мо (*sport*) 2-0 to Dynamo.

по́льзовани|е, я, *n.* use; о́бщего ~я in general use; пра́во ~я (*leg.*) right of user, usufruct; находи́ться в чьём-н. ~и (*leg.*) to be in someone's use.

по́льз|овать, ую, *impf.* (*obs.*) to treat.

по́льз|оваться, уюсь, *impf.* (+*i.*) 1. to make use (of), utilize. 2. (*pf.* вос~) to profit (by); п. слу́чаем to take an opportunity. 3. to enjoy; п. дове́рием (+g.) to enjoy the confidence (of); п. креди́том to possess credit; п. права́ми to enjoy rights; п. уваже́нием to be held in respect; п. успе́хом to have success, be a success.

по́льк|а¹, и, Pole, Polish woman.

по́льк|а², и, f. polka.

по́льск|ий, adj. Polish; as noun (obs.) п., ~ого, m. polonaise.

поль|сти́ть(ся), щу́(сь), сти́шь(ся), pf. of льсти́ть(ся).

полюб|и́ть, лю́, ~ишь, pf. to come to like, grow fond (of); to fall in love (with).

полюб|и́ться, лю́сь, ~ишься, pf. (coll.) (+d.) to catch the fancy (of); to become attractive (to); она́ мне сра́зу же ~и́лась I was immediately attracted by her, I took an immediate liking to her.

полюб|ова́ться, у́юсь, pf. of любова́ться; ~у́йся, ~у́йтесь (на+a.; coll., iron.) just look; ~у́йся на э́того дурака́! just look at that fool!

полюбо́вно, adv. amicably; реши́ть, ко́нчить де́ло п. to come to an amicable agreement.

полюбо́вный, adj. amicable.

полюбопы́тств|овать, ую, pf. of любопы́тствовать.

по-лю́дски, adv. (coll.) as others do, in the accepted manner; жить п. to live as other people do; to live like a (normal) human being.

по́люс, а, m. (geogr., phys., and fig.) pole; Се́верный п. North Pole; они́ — два ~а they are poles apart.

по́люсный, adj. (phys.) polar; п. зажи́м (electr.) pole terminal.

поля́к, а, m. Pole.

поля́н|а, ы, f. glade, clearing.

поляриза́тор, а, m. (phys.) polarizer.

поляризацио́нный, adj. (phys.) polarizing.

поляриза́ци|я, и, f. (phys.) polarization.

поляриз|ова́ть, у́ю, impf. and pf. (phys.) to polarize.

поля́рник, а, m. polar explorer, member of polar expedition.

поля́рност|ь, и, f. (phys.) polarity.

поля́рн|ый, adj. 1. polar, arctic; ~ая звезда́ Pole-star, North star; се́верный п. круг arctic circle. 2. (fig.) polar, diametrically opposed.

поля́чк|а, и, f. (obs.) = по́лька¹.

пом- in compound words, abbr. of помо́щник.

помава́|ть, ю, impf. (obs.) (+i.) to wave, brandish.

пома́д|а, ы, f. pomade; губна́я п. lipstick.

пома́|дить, жу, дишь, impf. (of на~) (obs.) to pomade; п. во́лосы to grease one's hair; п. гу́бы to put lipstick on.

пома́дк|а, и, f. (collect.) fruit candy.

пома́д|ный, adj. of ~а; п. каранда́ш lipstick.

пома́зани|е, я, n. (eccl.) anointing (of monarch at coronation).

пома́занник, а, m. (eccl.) anointed sovereign.

пома́|зать, жу, жешь, pf. 1. pf. of ма́зать¹. 2. (eccl.) to anoint.

пома́|заться, жусь, жешься, pf. of ма́заться.

помаз|о́к, ка́, m. small brush (shaving brush, brush for painting throat, etc.).

помале́ньку, adv. (coll.) 1. gradually, gently; рабо́тать п. to take one's time over one's work, take things easily. 2. in a small way, modestly; жить п. to live modestly. 3. tolerably, so-so.

пома́лкива|ть, ю, impf. (coll.) to hold one's tongue, keep mum.

по-мальчи́шески, adv. in a boyish way, like a boy.

поман|и́ть, ю́, ~ишь, pf. of мани́ть.

пома́рк|а, и, f. blot; pencil mark; correction.

пома|ха́ть, шу́, ~шешь, pf. (+i.) to wave (for a while, a few times).

пома́хива|ть, ю, impf. (+i.) to wave, brandish, swing (from time to time); соба́ка ~ла хвосто́м the dog would wag his tail.

помбу́х, а, m. (abbr. of помо́щник бухга́лтера) assistant book-keeper.

поме́дл|ить, ю, ишь, pf. (c+i.; coll.) to linger (over).

помел|о́, а́, pl. ~ья, ~ьев, n. mop.

поме́ньше, comp. of ма́ленький and ма́ло somewhat smaller, a little smaller; somewhat less, a little less.

поменя́|ть(ся), ю(сь), pf. of меня́ть(ся) 2.

помера́н|ец, ца, m. bitter orange, wild orange.

помера́н|цевый, adj. of ~ец; ~цевые цветы́ orange-blossom.

по|мере́ть, мру́, мрёшь, past ~мер, ~мерла́, ~мерло, pf. (of ~мира́ть) (coll.) to die; п. со́ смеху to split one's sides (with laughing).

помере́щ|иться, усь, ишься, pf. of мере́щиться.

помёрз|нуть, ну, нешь, past ~, ~ла; pf. to be frost-bitten; (of flowers, etc.) to be killed by frost.

помер|ить(ся), ю(сь), ишь(ся), pf. of ме́рить(ся).

померк|нуть, ну, нешь, past ~, ~ла, pf. of ме́ркнуть.

помертве́лый, adj. deadly pale; (fig.) lifeless, deathly; gloomy.

помертве́|ть, ю, pf. of мертве́ть.

помести́тельност|ь, и, f. spaciousness; capaciousness.

помести́тел|ьный (~ен, ~ьна), adj. spacious, roomy; capacious.

поме|сти́ть, щу́, сти́шь, pf. (of ~ща́ть) 1. to lodge, accommodate; to put up; мы могли́ бы их п. в свобо́дную ко́мнату we could put them into the spare room. 2. to place, locate; (*fin.*) to invest; п. объявле́ние в газе́те to put an advertisement in a paper; п. на пе́рвой страни́це to carry on the front page; п. сбереже́ния в сберка́ссу to put one's savings in a savings bank.

поме|сти́ться, щу́сь, сти́шься, *pf.* (*of* ~ща́ться) 1. to find room; to put up; (*of things*) to go in; в э́тот я́щик мои́ ве́щи не ~стя́тся my things will not go into this drawer. 2. *pass. of* ~сти́ть.

поме́стн|ый¹, *adj.*; ~ое дворя́нство landed gentry; п. строй (*hist.*) estate system of land tenure.

поме́стный², *adj.* (*obs.*) local; п. собо́р (*hist.*, *eccl.*) local council.

поме́ст|ье, ья, *g. pl.* ий, *n.* (*hist.*) estate.

по́мес|ь, и, *f.* 1. cross-breed, hybrid; cross; mongrel; п. терье́ра и овча́рки, п. терье́ра с овча́ркой a cross between a terrier and a sheepdog. 2. (*fig.*) mixture, hotch-potch.

поме́сячно, *adv.* by the month; monthly, per month.

поме́сячный, *adj.* monthly.

помёт, а, *m.* 1. dung, excrement; droppings. 2. litter, brood; (*of piglets*) farrow.

поме́т|а, ы, *f.* 1. mark, note; сде́лать ~ы на поля́х to make notes in the margin. 2. style tag, usage label (*in dictionaries*).

поме́|тить, чу, тишь, *pf.* (*of* ~ча́ть) to mark; to date; п. га́лочкой to tick; я ~тил письмо́ 2-м января́ I dated my letter the 2nd of January.

поме́х|а, и, *f.* 1. hindrance; obstacle; encumbrance; быть ~ой (+*d.*) to hinder, impede, stand in the way (of). 2. (*pl. only*) (*radio*) interference.

помеча́|ть, ю, *impf. of* поме́тить.

поме́шан|ный (~, ~a), *adj.* 1. mad, crazy; insane; *as noun* п., ~ного, *m.* madman; ~ная, ~ной, *f.* madwoman. 2. (на+*p.*; *fig.*, *coll.*) mad (on, about), crazy (about); они́ ~ы на бри́дже they are mad about bridge.

помеша́тельств|о, а, *n.* 1. madness, craziness; lunacy, insanity. 2. (на+*p.*; *fig.*, *coll.*) craze (for).

помеша́|ть¹, ², ю, *pf. of* меша́ть¹, ².

помеша́|ться, юсь, *pf.* 1. to go mad, go crazy. 2. (на+*p.*; *fig.*, *coll.*) to become mad (on, about), become crazy (about).

помеща́|ть, ю, *impf. of* помести́ть.

помеща́|ться, юсь, *impf.* 1. (*impf. only*) to be; to be located, be situated; to be housed; где ~ется ваш кабине́т? where is your office? 2. (*impf. only*) в э́том стадио́не ~ется се́мьдесят ты́сяч челове́к this stadium holds seventy thousand people. 3. *impf. of* помести́ться.

помеще́ни|е, я, *n.* 1. placing, location; investment. 2. room, lodging, apartment; premises; жило́е п. housing, accommodation.

поме́щик, а, *m.* (*hist.*) landowner.

поме́щи|чий, *adj. of* ~к; п. дом manor-house.

помидо́р, а, *g. pl.* ~ов, *m.* tomato.

помидо́р|ный, *adj. of* ~.

поми́ловани|е, я, *n.* (*leg.*) pardon, forgiveness; про́сьба о ~и appeal (for pardon).

поми́л|овать, ую, *pf.* to pardon, forgive, spare; ~уй!, ~уйте! *as interj. expressing disagreement or protest* (*coll.*) pardon me!, excuse me!, for pity's sake!; Го́споди, ~уй! (*petition in liturgy*) Lord, have mercy (upon us)!

поми́мо, *prep.*+*g.* 1. apart from; besides; п. всего́ про́чего apart from anything else; п. други́х соображе́ний other considerations apart. 2. without the knowledge (of), unbeknown (to); всё э́то реши́лось п. меня́ all this was decided without my knowledge.

поми́н, а, *m.* 1. (*coll.*) mention; лёгок на ~е talk of the devil (and he is sure to appear); его́ и в ~е нет there is no trace of him; об э́том и ~у не́ было there was not so much as a mention of it. 2. (*eccl.*) prayer (*for the dead or for sick persons*).

помина́льны|й, *adj.* п. обе́д funeral repast; ~е обря́ды funeral rites, last rites.

помина́ни|е, я, *n.* (*eccl.*) 1. prayer (for the dead *or* for sick persons). 2. list of names of dead and sick persons.

помина́|ть, ю, *impf. of* помяну́ть; не ~й(те) меня́ ли́хом! remember me kindly!; а его́ ~й, как зва́ли! (*coll.*) he just vanished into thin air.

поми́н|ки, ок, *no sing.* funeral repast, funeral banquet, wake.

поминове́ни|е, я, *n.* (*eccl.*) prayer for the dead *and/or* for the sick; remembrance (of the dead *and/or* the sick) in prayer.

помину́тно, *adv.* every minute; (*fig.*, *coll.*) continually, constantly.

помину́тн|ый, *adj.* 1. occurring every minute; (*fig.*, *coll.*) continual, constant. 2. by the minute.

помира́|ть, ю, *impf. of* помере́ть.

помир|и́ть(ся), ю́(сь), и́шь(ся), *pf. of* мири́ть(ся).

по́мн|ить, ю, ишь, *impf.* (+*a. or* о+*p.*) to remember; не п. себя́ (от) to be beside oneself (with).

по́мн|иться, ится, *impf.* (*impers.*+*d.*) I, *etc.*, remember; мне ещё ~ится день пожа́ра I still remember the day of the fire; наско́лько мне ~ится as far as I can remember; ~ится, э́то произошло́ в декабре́ as I remember, it happened in December.

помно́гу, *adv.* (*coll.*) in plenty, in large quantities; in large numbers.

помнож|а́ть, а́ю, *impf. of* ~ить.

помнож|ить, у, ишь, *pf.* (*of* мно́жить *and* ~а́ть) to multiply; п. два на́ три to multiply two by three.

помога́|ть, ю, *impf. of* помо́чь.

пом|огу́, о́жешь, о́гут, *see* ~о́чь.

по-мо́ему, *adv.* 1. in my opinion; to my mind, to my way of thinking. 2. in conformity with my wishes, as I would have it.

помо́|и, ев, *no sing.* slops; обли́ть кого́-н. ~ями (*fig., coll.*) to fling mud at someone.

помо́й|ка, ки, *g. pl.* помо́ек, *f.* rubbish heap, rubbish dump; cesspit.

помо́|йный, adj. of ~и; ~йное ведро́ slop-pail; ~йная я́ма refuse pit; cesspit.

помо́л, а, *m.* grinding; мука́ кру́пного, ме́лкого ~a coarse-ground, fine-ground flour.

помо́лв|ить, лю, ишь, *pf.* (+*a.* c+*i.,* or +*a.* за+*a.*; *obs.*) to betroth (to); to announce the engagement (of); её ~или с Ива́ном *or* за Ива́на she is engaged to Ivan, her engagement to Ivan is announced.

помо́лвк|а, и, *f.* betrothal, engagement; объяви́ть ~y to announce an engagement.

помо́лв|ленный, *p.p.p. of* ~ить; быть ~ленным с кем-н. to be engaged to someone.

помол|и́ться, ю́сь, ~ишься, *pf.* 1. *pf. of* моли́ться. 2. to spend some time in prayer.

помоло́ги|я, и, *f.* pomology.

помолоде́|ть, ю, *pf. of* молоде́ть.

помолч|а́ть, у́, и́шь, *pf.* to be silent for a while.

помо́р, а, *m.* coast-dweller (*esp. of Russian inhabitants of coasts of White Sea*).

помор|и́ть, ю́, и́шь, *pf. of* мори́ть[1].

помо́р|ка, ки, *f. of* ~.

помо́рник, а, *m.* (*orn.*) skua.

поморо́|зить, жу, зишь, *pf. of* моро́зить.

помо́р|ский, adj. of ~ *and* ~ье.

помо́рщ|иться, усь, ишься, *pf. of* мо́рщиться.

помо́рь|е, я, *n.* seaboard, coastal region; балти́йское п. Pomorze, Pomerania (*S. coast of Baltic Sea*); се́верное п. White Sea Coast.

поморя́н|ин, ина, *pl.* ~е, ~, *m.* (*ethnol.*) Pomeranian (*member of W. Slav tribes inhabiting Baltic seaboard*).

помо́ст, а, *m.* dais; platform, stage, rostrum; scaffold.

помо́ч|и, ей, *no sing.* 1. leading strings; быть, ходи́ть на ~ах (*fig.*) to be in leading strings. 2. braces.

помоч|и́ться, у́сь, ~ишься, *pf. of* мочи́ться.

помо́ч|ь, и, *f.* 1. (*obs.*) = по́мощь. 2. (*obs.*) mutual aid (*afforded one another by villagers*).

помо́|чь, гу́, жешь, гут, *past* ~г, ~гла́, *pf.*

(*of* ~га́ть) 1. (+*d.*) to help, aid, assist; to succour; ~ги́(те) ей наде́ть пальто́ help her on with her coat. 2. to relieve, bring relief; инъе́кции ~гли́ от бо́ли the injections relieved the pain.

помо́щник, а, *m.* 1. help, helper; helpmate, helpmeet. 2. assistant; mate; п. дире́ктора assistant director; п. капита́на (*naut.*) mate; п. маши́ниста engine-driver's mate.

по́мощ|ь, и, *f.* help, aid, assistance; succour; relief; оказа́ть п. to help, render assistance; отказа́ть в ~и to refuse aid; пода́ть ру́ку ~и (+*d.*) to lend a hand, lend a helping hand; позва́ть на п. to call for help; прийти́ на п. (+*d.*) to come to the aid (of); на п.! help!; с ~ью (+*g.*), при ~и (+*g.*) with the help (of), by means (of); без посторо́нней ~и unaided, single-handed; ско́рая п. ambulance; каре́та ско́рой ~и (*obs.*) ambulance; п. на дому́ home visiting (*by doctors to patients*); пе́рвая п. first aid.

по́мп|а[1], ы, *f.* pomp, state.

по́мп|а[2], ы, *f.* pump.

помпе́зност|ь, и, *f.* pomposity.

помпе́зный, *adj.* pompous.

помпо́н, а, *m.* pompon.

помрач|а́ть(ся), а́ет(ся), *impf. of* ~и́ть(ся).

помраче́ни|е, я, *n.* darkening, obscuring; п. зре́ния loss of sight; уму́ п. (*of unusual event or object*) it takes one's breath away.

помрач|и́ть, и́т, *pf.* (*of* ~а́ть) (*obs.*) to darken, obscure, cloud.

помрач|и́ться, и́тся, *pf.* (*of* ~а́ться) to grow dark, become obscured, become clouded.

помрачне́|ть, ю, *pf. of* мрачне́ть.

пому|ти́ть(ся), чу́, ти́шь, ти́т(ся), *pf. of* мути́ть(ся).

пому́ч|ить, у, ишь, *pf.* to make suffer, torment.

пому́ч|иться, усь, ишься, *pf.* to suffer (*for a while*); п. с зада́чей to torment oneself over a problem.

помч|а́ть, у́, и́шь, *pf.* 1. to begin to whirl, rush. 2. (*coll.*) = ~а́ться.

помч|а́ться, у́сь, и́шься, *pf.* to begin to rush, begin to tear along.

помыка́|ть, ю, *impf.* (+*i.*; *coll.*) to order about.

по́мыс|ел, ла, *m.* thought; intention, design; благи́е ~лы good intentions.

помы́сл|ить, ю, ишь, *pf.* (*of* помышля́ть) (о+*p.*) to think (of, about), contemplate; об э́том и мы не смéли we dared not even dream of it.

пом|ы́ть(ся), о́ю(сь), о́ешь(ся), *pf. of* мы́ть(ся).

помышле́ни|е, я, *n.* (*obs.*) thought; intention, design; он оста́вил вся́кое п. о жени́тьбе he has put aside any idea of marriage.

помышля́|ть, ю, *impf. of* помы́слить.

помя́н|утый, *p.p.p. of* ~у́ть; не тем будь ~ут (~ута, ~уты) (*expression of regret at speaking ill of a person*) God forgive him (her, them)!; may it not be remembered against him (her, them)!

помян|у́ть, у́, ~ешь, *pf.* (*of* помина́ть) 1. to mention, make mention (of); п. добро́м кого́-н. to speak well of someone; ~й моё сло́во (*coll.*) mark my words. 2. to pray (for), remember in one's prayers (*pray for repose of the dead or recovery of the sick*). 3. to give a funeral banquet (for, in memory of).

помя́т|ый, *p.p.p. of* ~ь *and adj.* (*coll.*) flabby, baggy.

пом|я́ть, ну́, нёшь, *pf.* to rumple slightly; to crumple slightly.

пом|я́ться[1], ну́сь, нёшься, *pf. of* мя́ться[1].

пом|я́ться[2], ну́сь, нёшься, *pf.* (*coll.*) to vacillate, hum and ha (*for a while*).

пона- *verbal prefix indicating action performed gradually or by instalments.*

по-над, *prep.+i.* (*dial.*) along, by.

понаде́|яться, юсь, ешься, *pf.* (на+*a.*; *coll.*) to count (upon), rely (on); нельзя́ на него́ п. you cannot rely on him.

пона́доб|иться, люсь, ишься, *pf.* to be, become necessary; е́сли ~ится if necessary.

понапра́сну, *adv.* (*coll.*) in vain.

понаслы́шке, *adv.* (*coll.*) by hearsay.

по-настоя́щему, *adv.* in the right way, properly.

понача́лу, *adv.* (*coll.*) at first, in the beginning.

по-на́шему, *adv.* 1. in our opinion. 2. as we would wish.

понёв|а, ы, (*dial.*) homespun skirt (*of checked or striped pattern*).

понево́ле, *adv.* willy-nilly; against one's will.

понеде́льник, а, *m.* Monday.

понеде́льно, *adv.* by the week, per week; weekly.

понеде́льный, *adj.* weekly.

поне́же, *conj.* (*arch.*) because, since.

понемно́гу, *adv.* 1. little, a little at a time. 2. little by little.

понемно́жку, *adv.* = понемно́гу; (*in answer to question* как пожива́ете?) (doing) all right.

понес|ти́, у́, ёшь, *past* ~, ~ла́, *pf.* 1. *pf. of* нести́. 2. (*of horses*) to bolt.

понес|ти́сь, у́сь, ёшься, *past* ~ся́, ~ла́сь, *pf.* 1. *pf. of* нести́сь. 2. to rush off, tear off, dash off.

по́ни, *indecl., m.* pony.

понижа́|ть(ся), ю(сь), *impf. of* пони́зить-(ся).

пони́же, *adv.* rather lower; rather shorter.

пониже́ни|е, я, *n.* fall, drop; lowering; re-

duction; п. давле́ния drop in pressure; п. зарпла́ты wage-cut; п. цен reduction, fall in prices; п. по слу́жбе demotion; игра́ть на п. (*fin.*) to speculate for a fall, sell short, bear.

понизи́тельный, *adj.* (*electr.*) step-down.

пони́|зить, жу, зишь, *pf.* (*of* ~жа́ть) to lower; to reduce; п. го́лос to lower one's voice; п. по слу́жбе to demote.

пони́|зиться, жусь, зишься, *pf.* (*of* ~жа́ть-ся) to fall, drop, sink, go down.

понизо́вь|е, я, *n.* lower reaches.

по́низу, *adv.* low; along the ground.

поника́|ть, ю, *impf. of* пони́кнуть.

пони́к|нуть, ну, нешь, *past* ~, ~ла, *pf.* (*of* ни́кнуть *and* ~а́ть) to droop, flag, wilt; п. голово́й to hang one's head.

понима́ни|е, я, *n.* 1. understanding, comprehension; э́то вы́ше моего́ ~я it is past my comprehension, it is beyond me. 2. interpretation, conception; но́вое п. исто́рии a new interpretation of history; в моём ~и as I see it.

понима́|ть, ю, *impf.* (*of* поня́ть) 1. to understand; to comprehend; to realize; ~ю! I see! 2. to interpret; непра́вильно п. to misunderstand; как вы ~ете э́тот посту́пок? what do you make of this action? 3. (*impf. only*) (+*a. or* в+*p.*) to be a (good) judge (of), know (about); я ничего́ не ~ю в му́зыке I know nothing about music.

по-но́вому, *adv.* in a new fashion; нача́ть жить п. to start life afresh, turn over a new leaf.

поножо́вщин|а, ы, *f.* (*coll.*) knife-fight; knifing.

пономáр|ь, я́, *m.* sexton, sacristan.

поно́с, а, *m.* diarrhoea; крова́вый п. bloody flux.

поно|си́ть[1], шу́, ~сишь, *impf.* to abuse, revile.

поно|си́ть[2], шу́, ~сишь, *pf.* 1. to carry (*for a while*). 2. to wear (*for a while*).

поно́ск|а, и, *f.* 1. object carried by a dog between its teeth. 2. carrying; обучи́ть соба́ку ~е to train a dog to carry things.

поно́сный, *adj.* (*obs.*) abusive, defamatory.

поно́|шенный, *p.p.p. of* ~си́ть[2] *and adj.* worn, shabby, threadbare; п. вид (*fig.*) haggard appearance, worn look.

понра́в|иться, люсь, ишься, *pf. of* нра́вить-ся.

понтёр, а, *m.* (*cards*) punter.

понти́р|овать, ую, *impf.* (*of* с~) (*cards*) to punt.

понто́н, а, *m.* 1. pontoon. 2. pontoon bridge.

понтонёр, а, *m.* pontoneer, pontonier.

понто́н|ный, *adj. of* ~; ~ный мост pontoon bridge.

понуди́тельный, *adj.* impelling, pressing; coercive.

пону́|дить, жу, дишь, *pf.* (*of* ~жда́ть) to force, compel, coerce; to impel; его́ ~дили к реше́нию he was forced into a decision.

понужда́|ть, ю, *impf. of* понуди́ть.

понука́|ть, ю, *impf.* (*coll.*) to urge on, goad.

пону́р|ить, ю, ишь, *pf.* п. го́лову to hang one's head.

пону́р|иться, юсь, ишься, *pf.* to hang one's head.

пону́рый, *adj.* downcast, depressed.

по́нчик, а, *m.* doughnut.

поны́не, *adv.* (*obs.*) up to the present, until now.

поню́ха|ть, ю, *pf. of* ню́хать.

поню́шк|а, и, *f.* п. табаку́ pinch of snuff; ни за ~у табаку́ (*fig., coll.*) for nothing, to no purpose.

поня́ти|е, я, *n.* **1.** concept. **2.** notion, idea; у него́ о́чень сму́тное п. о геогра́фии he has very confused notions about geography; име́ть п. (о+*p.*) to have an idea (about, of); ~я не име́ю! (*coll.*) I've no idea!; где нахо́дится центр го́рода? — не име́ю ни мале́йшего ~я! where is the city centre? I haven't the faintest idea! **3.** (*usu. pl.*) notions; level (of understanding); счита́ться с ~ями слу́шателей to take into account one's audience level.

поня́тийный, *adj.* conceptual.

поня́тливост|ь, и, f. comprehension, understanding.

поня́тлив|ый (~, ~а), *adj.* quick (in the uptake).

поня́тност|ь, и, f. clearness, intelligibility; perspicuity.

поня́т|ный (~ен, ~на), *adj.* **1.** understandable; ~но, что... it is understandable that...; it is natural that...; ~но (*coll.*) of course, naturally; я, ~но, не мог согласи́ться of course, I could not consent; ~ное де́ло (*coll.*) of course, naturally. **2.** clear, intelligible; perspicuous; ~но? (*coll.*) (do you) see?; is that clear?; ~но! (*coll.*) I see!; I understand!; quite!

поня́т|ой, о́го, *m.* witness (*at an official search, etc.*).

пон|я́ть, пойму́, поймёшь, *past* ~я́л, ~яла́, ~я́ло, *pf.* (*of* ~има́ть) to understand; to comprehend; to realize; п. намёк to take a hint; дать п. to give to understand.

пообе́да|ть, ю, *pf. of* обе́дать.

пообеща́|ть, ю, *pf.* (*of* обеща́ть) to promise.

пообжи́|ться, ву́сь, вёшься, *pf.* (*coll.*) to get accustomed to one's new surroundings.

пода́ль, *adv.* at some distance, a little way away.

поодино́чке, *adv.* one at a time, one by one.

поосмотр|е́ться, ю́сь, ~ишься, *pf.* (*coll.*) to take a look round; (*fig.*) to feel one's feet.

поочерёдно, *adv.* in turn, by turns.

поочерёдный, *adj.* taken in turn, proceeding by turns.

поощре́ни|е, я, *n.* encouragement; incentive, spur.

поощри́тел|ьный (~ен, ~ьна), *adj.* encouraging.

поощр|и́ть, ю́, и́шь, *pf.* (*of* ~я́ть) to encourage; to give an incentive (to), give a spur (to).

поощр|я́ть, я́ю, *impf. of* ~и́ть.

поп¹, а́, *m.* (*coll.*) priest; како́в п., тако́в и прихо́д (*prov.*) like master, like man.

поп², а́, *m.* pin (*in game of gorodki*); поста́вить на ~а́ (*coll.*) to place upright.

попада́ни|е, я, *n.* hit (*on target*); прямо́е п. direct hit.

попада́|ть, ет, *pf.* to fall (*of a number of objects*).

попада́|ть(ся), ю(сь), *impf. of* попа́сть(ся).

попадь|я́, и́, f. (*coll.*) priest's wife.

**попа́|ло, как п., etc., see* ~сть.

попа́рно, *adv.* in pairs, two by two.

попа́|сть, ду́, дёшь, *past* ~л, *pf.* (*of* ~да́ть) **1.** (в+*a.*) to hit; п. в цель to hit the target; не п. в цель to miss; пу́ля ~ла ему́ в лоб the bullet hit him in the forehead; п. ни́ткой в ушко́ иглы́ to get a thread through a needle; п. па́льцем в не́бо (*coll.*) to be wide of the mark. **2.** (в+*a.*) to get (to), find oneself (in); (на+*a.*) to hit (upon), come (upon); п. в Ло́ндон to get to London; п. на по́езд to catch a train; п. домо́й to get home; п. в плен to be taken prisoner; п. кому́-н. в ру́ки to fall into someone's hands; п. под суд to be brought to trial; не туда́ п. to get the wrong number (*on telephone*); п. на рабо́ту to land a job; п. впроса́к to put one's foot into it; п. в беду́ to get into trouble, come to grief; п. в са́мую то́чку to hit the nail on the head; (*impers.; coll.*) ему́ ~ло he caught it (hot); ему́ ~дёт! he'll catch it! **3.** (*coll.*) ~ло *gives indefinite force to certain pronouns and adverbs*: как ~ло anyhow; helter-skelter; что ~ло any old thing; где ~ло anywhere; он э́то сде́лал чем ~ло he made it with whatever came to hand.

попа́|сться, ду́сь, дёшься, *past* ~лся *pf.* (*of* ~да́ться) **1.** to find oneself; он мне ~лся навстре́чу на у́лице I ran into him in the street; э́то письмо́ мне ~лось соверше́нно случа́йно I came across the letter quite by chance; п. кому́-н. на глаза́ to catch someone's eye; что ~дётся anything; пе́рвый ~вшийся the first comer, the first person one happens to meet. **2.** to be caught; (в+*a.*) to get (into); п. в кра́же to be caught stealing; п. с поли́чным to be taken red-handed; п. на у́дочку to swallow the bait, fall for the bait (*also fig.*); п. в беду́ to get into trouble; смотри́, бо́льше не ~ди́сь! don't let me catch you again!

попа́хива|ть, ет, *impf.* (*coll.*) (+*i.*) to smell slightly (of).

попённ|ый, *adj.* ~ая опла́та payment by number of trees cut down.

попеня́|ть, ю, *pf. of* пеня́ть.

поперёк, *adv. and prep.*+*g.* across; разре́зать п. to cut across; положи́те их п. lay them crosswise; де́рево упа́ло п. доро́ги the tree fell across the road; стоя́ть у кого́-н. п. доро́ги to be in someone's way; стать кому́-н. п. го́рла to stick in someone's throat; вдоль и п. far and wide; знать что-н. вдоль и п. to know something inside out, know all the ins and outs of something.

попереме́нно, *adv.* in turn, by turns.

попере́чин|а, ы, *f.* cross-beam, cross-piece, cross-bar; boom jib (*of crane*).

попере́чник, а, *m.* diameter; шесть ме́тров в ~е six metres in diameter, six metres across.

попере́чн|ый, *adj.* transverse, diametrical, cross; (*aeron.*) dihedral; ~ая ба́лка cross--beam, cross-tie; ~ая пила́ cross-cut saw; ~ая си́ла transverse force; п. разре́з, ~ое сече́ние cross-section; (ка́ждый) встре́чный и п. anybody and everybody, (every) Tom, Dick, and Harry.

поперхн|у́ться, у́сь, ёшься, *pf.* (+*i.*) to choke (over).

попе́рч|ить, у, ишь, *pf. of* пе́рчить.

попече́ни|е, я, *n.* care; charge; быть на ~и (+*g.*) to be in the charge (of); оста́вить дете́й на п. отца́ to leave children in care of their father; отложи́ть п. о чём-н. to cease caring about something.

попечи́тел|ь, я, *m.* 1. guardian, trustee. 2. (*hist.*) warden, administrator (*of educational or similar institution or district*).

попечи́тель|ный, *adj.* 1. (*obs.*) solicitous. 2. *adj. of* ~ство; п. сове́т board of guardians.

попечи́тельств|о, а, *n.* 1. guardianship, trusteeship. 2. (*hist.*) board of guardians.

попива́|ть, ю, *impf.* (*coll.*) to have a little drink (of); стать п. to take to drink.

попира́|ть, ю, *impf. of* попра́ть.

попи́скива|ть, ю, *impf.* to cheep, give a cheep.

попи́сыва|ть, ю, *impf.* (*coll.*) to write (*from time to time*); (*of a literary man; iron.*) to do a bit of writing.

по́пито, *p.p.p. of* попи́ть (*coll.*); нема́ло бы́ло п. a fair quantity was drunk.

по|пи́ть, пью, пьёшь, *past* ~пи́л, ~пила́, ~пи́ло, *pf.* to have a drink.

по́пк|а, и, *m.* (*coll.*) parrot; Polly.

поппла́ва|ть, ю, *pf.* to have, take a swim.

поплав|ко́вый, *adj. of* ~о́к; ~ко́вая ка́мера float chamber (*of carburettor*); п. кран ballcock.

поплав|о́к, ка́, *m.* 1. float. 2. (*coll.*) floating restaurant.

попла́|кать, чу, чешь, *pf.* to cry (*a little, for a while*); to shed a few tears.

попла|ти́ться, чу́сь, ~ти́шься, *pf. of* плати́ться.

попл|ева́ть, юю́, юёшь, *pf.* (*coll.*) to spit (a few times).

поплёвыва|ть, ю, *impf.* (*coll.*) to spit (at intervals).

попле|сти́сь, ту́сь, тёшься, *past* ~лся́, ~ла́сь, *pf.* (*coll.*) to push off; to drag oneself along; я тепе́рь ~ту́сь домо́й I shall push off home now.

попли́н, а, *m.* (*text.*) poplin.

попли́н|овый, *adj. of* ~.

поплотне́|ть, ю, *pf. of* плотне́ть.

поплы́|ть, ву́, вёшь, *past* ~л, ~ла́, ~ло, *pf.* to strike out, start swimming.

попля|са́ть, шу́, ~шешь, *pf.* (*coll.*) to have a bit of dancing; ты у меня́ ~шешь! (*coll.*) you'll pay for this!, you'll catch it!

попо́вич, а, *m.* (*coll.*) son of a priest.

попо́в|на, ны, *g. pl.* ~ен, *f.* (*coll.*) daughter of a priest.

попо́вник, а, *m.* (*bot.*) marguerite, white ox-eye.

попо́вский, *adj. of* поп[1].

попо́вщин|а, ы, *f.* 1. (*coll., pejor.*) religious superstition. 2. popovshchina (*movement in part of the Russian Old Believer sect, retaining role of priests*).

попо́йк|а, и, *f.* (*coll.*) drinking-bout.

попола́м, *adv.* in two, in half; half-and-half; раздели́ть п. to divide in two, divide in half, halve; дава́йте запла́тим п. let's go halves; ви́ски п. с водо́й whisky and water half-and-half.

по́полз|ень, ня, *m.* (*orn.*) nuthatch.

поползнове́ни|е, я, *n.* 1. feeble impulse; half-formed intention; я име́л п. вы́сказать своё мне́ние, но в конце́ концо́в сдержа́лся I had half a mind to say what I thought but in the end I restrained myself. 2. (на+*a.*) pretension(s) (to).

пополз|ти́, у́, ёшь, *past* попо́лз, ~ла́, *pf.* to begin to crawl.

пополне́ни|е, я, *n.* 1. replenishment; re--stocking; п. горю́чим re-fuelling. 2. (*mil.*) reinforcement; п. поте́рь replacement of casualties.

пополне́|ть, ю, *pf. of* полне́ть.

пополн|и́ть, ю, ишь, *pf.* (*of* ~я́ть) to replenish, supplement, fill up; to re-stock; (*mil.*) to reinforce; п. горю́чим to re-fuel; п. свои́ зна́ния to supplement one's knowledge.

пополн|и́ться, ится, *pf.* (*of* ~я́ться) 1. to increase. 2. *pass. of* ~и́ть.

пополн|я́ть(ся), я́ю, я́ет(ся), *impf. of* ~и́ть(ся).

пополу́дни, *adv.* in the afternoon, post meridiem; в два часа́ п. at 2 p.m.

пополу́ночи, *adv.* after midnight, ante meridiem; в два часа́ п. at 2 a.m.

попо́мн|ить, ю, ишь, *pf.* (*coll.*) 1. to remember; ~и (те) моё сло́во mark my words. 2. (+*d.*) to remind; я тебе́ э́то ~ю! I'll get even with you!

попо́н|а, ы, *f.* horse-cloth.

попо́тч|евать, ую, *pf. of* по́тчевать.

попра́ве|ть, ю, *pf. of* пра́веть.

поправи́м|ый (~, ~а), *adj.* reparable, remediable.

попра́в|ить, лю, ишь, *pf.* (*of* ~ля́ть) 1. to mend, repair. 2. to correct, set right, put right. 3. to adjust, set straight; п. причёску to tidy one's hair. 4. to improve, better; п. своё здоро́вье to restore one's health; де́ла п. нельзя́ the matter cannot be mended.

попра́в|иться, люсь, ишься, *pf.* (*of* ~ля́ться) 1. to correct oneself. 2. to get better, recover; я совсе́м ~ился I am completely recovered. 3. to put on weight; to look better; он о́чень ~ился he has put on a lot of weight; he looks much better. 4. to improve.

попра́вк|а, и, *f.* 1. mending, repairing. 2. correction; amendment; п. к резолю́ции amendment to a resolution; внести́ ~и в законопрое́кт to amend a bill. 3. adjustment. 4. recovery; де́ло идёт на ~у things are improving, things are on the mend.

поправле́ни|е, я, *n.* 1. correction, correcting. 2. recovery; improvement; он вы́ехал на Кавка́з для ~я здоро́вья he has gone to the Caucasus for his health.

поправля́|ть(ся), ю(сь), *impf. of* попра́вить(ся).

попра́вочный, *adj.* correction; п. коэффицие́нт (*phys.*) correction factor.

попр|а́ть, у́, ёшь, *pf.* (*of* попира́ть) to trample (upon); (*fig.*) to flout.

по-пре́жнему, *adv.* as before; as usual.

попрёк, а, *m.* reproach.

попрек|а́ть, а́ю, *impf.* (*of* ~ну́ть) (+*a. and i. or* +*a.* за+*a.*) to reproach (with); п. кого́-н. гру́бостью *or* за гру́бость to reproach someone with rudeness.

попрек|ну́ть, ну́, нёшь, *pf. of* ~а́ть.

по́прищ|е, а, *n.* field; walk of life, profession; вое́нное п. soldiering; литерату́рное п. the world of letters; вступи́ть на но́вое п. to embark on a new career.

по-прия́тельски, *adv.* as a friend; in a friendly manner.

попро́б|овать, ую, *pf. of* про́бовать.

попро|си́ть(ся), шу́(сь), ~сишь(ся), *pf. of* проси́ть(ся).

по́просту, *adv.* (*coll.*) simply; without ceremony; п. говоря́ to put it bluntly.

попроша́йк|а, и, *m. and f.* 1. (*obs.*) beggar. 2. (*coll., pejor.*) cadger.

попроша́йнича|ть, ю, *impf.* 1. (*obs.*) to beg. 2. (*coll., pejor.*) to cadge.

попроша́йничеств|о, а, *n.* 1. (*obs.*) begging. 2. (*coll., pejor.*) cadging.

попроща́|ться, юсь, *pf.* (с+*i.*) to take leave (of), say good-bye (to).

попру́¹, *see* попра́ть.

попру́², *see* попере́ть.

попры́гива|ть, ю, *impf.* (*coll.*) to hop about.

попрыгу́н (*oblique cases not used*) *m.* (*coll., joc.*) fidget.

попрыгу́н|ья, ьи, *f. of* ~.

попры́ска|ть, ю, *pf.* (+*i.*) to sprinkle (with).

попря́|тать, чу, чешь, *pf.* (*coll.*) to hide.

попря́|таться, чусь, чешься, *pf.* (*coll.*) to hide (oneself); п. от дождя́ to take cover from the rain.

попуга́|й, я, *m.* parrot.

попуга́йнича|ть, ю, *impf.* (*coll.*) to parrot.

попуга́|ть, ю, *pf.* (*coll.*) to scare, put the wind up a little.

попу́гива|ть, ю, *impf.* (*coll.*) to give a scare (*from time to time*).

попу́дно, *adv.* (*obs.*) by the pood (*see* пуд).

попу́др|ить, ю, ишь, *pf.* to powder.

попу́др|иться, юсь, ишься, *pf.* to powder one's face.

популяриза́тор, а, *m.* popularizer.

популяриза́ци|я, и, *f.* popularization.

популяризи́р|овать, ую, *impf. and pf.* to popularize.

популяриз|ова́ть, у́ю, *impf. and pf.* = ~и́ровать.

популя́рност|ь, и, *f.* popularity.

популя́р|ный (~ен, ~на), *adj.* popular.

попурри́, *indecl., n.* (*mus.*) pot-pourri.

попусти́тел|ь, я, *m.* (*pejor.*) one who tolerates (*dishonest practices, etc.*).

попусти́тельств|о, а, *n.* (*pejor.*) tolerance, toleration; permissiveness; connivance; при ~е (+*g.*) with the connivance (of).

попусти́тельств|овать, ую, *impf.* (+*d.*) (*pejor.*) to tolerate, put up (with); to connive (at); почему́ она́ ~ует его́ пья́нству? why does she put up with his drunkenness?

по-пусто́му, *adv.* (*coll.*) in vain, to no purpose.

по́пусту, *adv.* (*coll.*) = по-пусто́му.

попута́|ть, ет, *pf.* (*coll., joc.*) to beguile; чёрт ~л it's the devil's work.

попу́тно, *adv.* on one's way; at the same time; (*fig.*) in passing; incidentally; мо́жно п. заме́тить, что... it may be observed in passing that . . .

попу́тн|ый, *adj.* **1.** accompanying; following; passing; п. ве́тер fair wind, favourable wind; идти́ ~ым ве́тром (*naut.*) to sail free; ~ая струя́ back-eddy, backwash. **2.** (*fig.*) passing, incidental; п. вопро́с incidental question; ~ое замеча́ние passing remark.

попу́тчик, а, *m.* fellow-traveller (*also fig., polit.*).

попуще́ни|е, я, *n.* (*obs.*) **1.** (*pejor.*) tolerance; connivance. **2.** calamity.

попыта́|ть, ю, *pf.* (+*a. or g.*; *coll.*) to try (out); п. сча́стья to try one's luck.

попыта́|ться, юсь, *pf. of* пыта́ться.

попы́тк|а, и, *f.* attempt, endeavour; предприня́ть ~у to make an attempt; ~и сближе́ния (*polit.*) approaches.

попы́хива|ть, ю, *impf.* (*coll.*) to let out puffs; п. тру́бкой, п. из тру́бки to puff away at a pipe.

попя́|титься, чусь, тишься, *pf. of* пя́титься.

попя́тн|ый, *adj.* (*obs.*) backward; идти́ на п. *or* на ~ую (*coll.*) to go back on one's word.

пор|а́, ы, *f.* pore.

пор|а́, ы́, а. ~у, *f.* **1.** time, season; весе́нняя п. springtime; осе́нняя п. autumn; вече́рней ~о́й of an evening; в ~у opportunely, at the right time; не в ~у inopportunely, at the wrong time; вы прие́хали в са́мую ~у you came just at the right time; в ту ~у then, at that time; в ~е́ (*coll.*) in one's prime; до ~ы, до вре́мени for the time being; до каки́х ~? till when?, till what time?; до каки́х ~ вы остане́тесь здесь? how long will you be here?; до сих ~ till now, up to now, hitherto; (*obs.*) up to here, up to this point; до сей ~ы to this day; на пе́рвых ~а́х at first; с да́вних ~ long, for a long time, for ages; с каки́х ~?, с кото́рых ~? since when?; с тех ~, как... (ever) since . . .; с э́тих ~ since then, since that time. **2.** *as pred.* it is time; давно́ п. it is high time; п. спать! (it is) bedtime!

порабо́та|ть, ю, *pf.* to do some work, put in some work.

пораби́тел|ь, я, *m.* enslaver.

порабо|ти́ть, щу́, ти́шь, *pf.* (*of* ~ща́ть) to enslave; (*fig.*) to enthral(l).

порабоща́|ть, ю, *impf. of* пораби́ть.

порабоще́ни|е, я, *n.* enslavement; enthralment.

поравня́|ться, юсь, *pf.* (с+*i.*) to come up (to), come alongside.

пораде́|ть, ю, *pf. of* раде́ть.

пора́д|овать, ую, *pf.* **1.** *pf. of* ра́довать. **2.** to give pleasure for a while, make happy for a while.

пора́д|оваться, уюсь, *pf.* **1.** *pf. of* ра́доваться. **2.** to be happy for a while.

поража́|ть(ся), ю(сь), *impf. of* порази́ть(ся).

пораже́н|ец, ца, *m.* defeatist.

пораже́ни|е, я, *n.* **1.** defeat; не име́ть ~й (*sport*) to be unbeaten. **2.** (*mil.*) hitting (*the target, the objective*). **3.** (*med.*) affection; lesion. **4.** п. в права́х (*leg.*) disfranchisement.

пораже́нческий, *adj.* defeatist.

пораже́нчеств|о, а, *n.* defeatism.

порази́тел|ьный (~ен, ~ьна), *adj.* striking; staggering, startling.

пора|зи́ть, жу́, зи́шь, *pf.* (*of* ~жа́ть) **1.** to defeat; to rout. **2.** (*mil.*) to hit, strike; п. кинжа́лом to stab with a dagger. **3.** (*med.*) to affect, strike. **4.** (*fig.*) to strike; to stagger; to startle; меня́ ~зи́л её мра́чный вид I was struck by her gloomy appearance; нас ~зи́ли све́дения об их помо́лвке we were staggered by the news of their engagement.

пора|зи́ться, жу́сь, зи́шься, *pf.* (*of* ~жа́ться) **1.** to be staggered, be startled, be astounded. **2.** *pass. of* ~зи́ть.

по-ра́зному, *adv.* differently, in different ways.

порайо́нный, *adj.* (by) area.

пора́н|ить, ю, ишь, *pf.* to wound; to injure; to hurt.

пора́н|иться, юсь, ишься, *pf.* to injure oneself; to hurt oneself.

пораст|а́ть, а́ет, *impf. of* ~и́.

пораст|и́, ёт, *past* поро́с, поросла́, *pf.* (+*i.*) to become overgrown (with).

порв|а́ть, у́, ёшь, *past* ~а́л, ~ала́, ~а́ло, *pf.* **1.** to tear slightly. **2.** (*impf.* порыва́ть) (с+*i.*; *fig.*) to break (with); to break off (with); она́ давно́ ~ала́ с ним she broke with him long ago; п. дипломати́ческие сноше́ния to break off diplomatic relations.

порв|а́ться, ётся, *past* ~а́лся, ~ала́сь, ~а́лось, *pf.* **1.** to break (off), snap. **2.** to tear slightly. **3.** (*impf.* порыва́ться[1]) (*fig.*) to be broken (off).

пореде́|ть, ет, *pf. of* реде́ть.

поре́з, а, *m.* cut.

поре́|зать, жу, жешь, *pf.* **1.** to cut; п. себе́ па́лец to cut one's finger. **2.** (+*a. or g.*) to cut (*a quantity of*); п. хле́ба to cut some bread. **3.** (+*a. or g.*) to kill, slaughter (*a number of*).

поре́|заться, жусь, жешься, *pf.* to cut oneself.

поре́|й, я, *m.* leek.

порекоменд|ова́ть, у́ю, *pf. of* рекомендова́ть.

пореш|и́ть, у́, и́шь, *pf.* **1.** (*coll.*) to make up one's mind. **2.** (*obs.*) to decide, finish, settle; вот мы ~и́ли де́ло now we have settled the matter. **3.** (*fig., coll.*) to finish off, do away (with), do for.

поржаве́|ть, ет, *pf. of* ржаве́ть.

по́ристост|ь, и, *f.* porosity.

по́рист|ый (~, ~а), *adj.* porous.

порица́ни|е, я, *n.* blame, censure; reproof, reprimand; досто́йный ~я reprehensible; вы́разить п. (+*d.*) to censure, pass a vote of censure (on); вы́нести обще́ственное п. (+*d.*) to reprimand publicly, administer a public reprimand.

порица́тел|ьный (~ен, ~ьна), *adj.* disapproving, reproving.

порица́|ть, ю, *impf.* to blame; to censure.

по́рк|а¹, и, *f.* unstitching, unpicking, undoing, ripping.

по́рк|а², и, *f.* (*coll.*) flogging, thrashing; whipping, lashing.

порно́граф, а, *m.* pornographer.

порнографи́ческий, *adj.* pornographic.

порногра́фи|я, и, *f.* pornography.

по́ровну, *adv.* equally, in equal parts; разделить п. to divide equally, into equal parts.

поро́г, а, *m.* 1. threshold (*also fig.*); переступить п. to cross the threshold; обива́ть ~и у кого́-н. to haunt someone's threshold, pester someone; я их на п. не пущу́ they shall not set foot on my threshold, they shall not darken my door; стоя́ть на ~е сме́рти to be at death's door; светово́й п. (*physiol.*) visual threshold; слуховой п., п. слы́шимости (*physiol.*) threshold of audibility. 2. (*geogr.*) rapids. 3. (*tech.*) baffle (plate), dam, altar (*of furnace*).

поро́д|а, ы, *f.* 1. breed, race, strain, species; (*fig.*) kind, sort, type; они́ как раз одно́й и той же ~ы they are of exactly the same type. 2. (*obs.*) breeding. 3. (*geol.*) rock; го́рная п. rock; layer, bed, stratum; материко́вая п. bed-rock; matrix, gauge; пуста́я п. barren rock, dead rock.

поро́дистост|ь, и, *f.* (pure) breeding.

поро́дист|ый (~, ~а), *adj.* pure-breed; thoroughbred, pedigree.

поро|ди́ть, жу́, ди́шь, *pf.* (*of* ~жда́ть) (*obs.*) to give birth (to), beget; (*fig.*) to raise, generate, engender, give rise (to); его́ отсу́тствие ~ди́ло мно́го то́лков his absence produced a crop of rumours.

породнённост|ь, и, *f.* twinning (*of cities or towns*).

породн|ённый, *p.p.p.* of ~и́ть; ~ённые города́ linked cities, twinned cities.

породн|и́ть(ся), ю́(сь), и́шь(ся), *pf. of* родни́ть(ся).

поро́дный, *adj.* (*agric.*) pedigree.

порожда́|ть, ю, *impf. of* породи́ть.

порожде́ни|е, я, *n.* result, outcome; (*rhet.*) fruit, handiwork.

поро́жист|ый (~, ~а), *adj.* full of rapids.

поро́жний, *adj.* (*coll.*) empty; п. ход (*tech.*) idling.

порожня́к, а́, *m.* empties (*empty wagons on railway*).

порожняко́вый, *adj.* п. соста́в = порожня́к.

порожняко́м, *adv.* (*coll.*) empty, without a load.

по́рознь, *adv.* separately, apart.

порозове́|ть, ю, *pf. of* розове́ть.

поро́й (*and* поро́ю), *adv.* at times, now and then.

поро́к, а, *m.* 1. vice. 2. defect; flaw, blemish; ~и ре́чи defects of speech; п. се́рдца heart disease, heart trouble.

порос|ёнок, ёнка, *pl.* ~я́та, ~я́т, *m.* piglet; (*cul.*) sucking-pig.

порос|и́ться, и́тся, *impf.* (*of* о~) to farrow.

по́росл|ь, и, *f.* verdure, shoots.

поросяти́н|а, ы, *f.* sucking-pig (*meat*).

порос|я́чий, *adj. of* ~ёнок.

поро́тно, *adv.* (*mil.*) by companies.

пор|о́ть¹, ю́, ~ешь, *impf.* (*of* рас~) to unstitch, unpick, undo, rip; п. вздор, ерунду́, чушь (*coll.*) to talk nonsense; п. горя́чку (*coll.*) to be in a (tearing) hurry; не́чего п. горя́чку there's no hurry.

пор|о́ть², ю́, ~ешь, *impf.* (*of* вы́~) (*coll.*) to flog, thrash; to whip, lash; to give a flogging, thrashing, *etc.*

пор|о́ться, ~ется, *impf.* (*of* рас~) 1. to come unstitched, come undone; to rip. 2. *pass. of* ~о́ть¹.

по́рох, а (у), *pl.* ~а, ~о́в, *m.* gun-powder; powder; он как п. he is hot-blooded; ему́ ~а не хвата́ет (*coll.*) he has not it in him, he is not up to it; п. да́ром тра́тить to spend one's wits to no purpose; держа́ть п. сухи́м (*fig.*) to keep one's powder dry; ни синь ~а (*coll.*) not a trace; ~ом па́хнет (*fig.*) there's a smell of gunpowder in the air, there is trouble brewing; он ~а не вы́думает (*coll.*) he will not set the Thames on fire.

пороховни́ц|а, ы, *f.* powder-flask.

порохово́й, *adj. of* по́рох; п. заво́д powder-mill; п. по́греб powder-magazine.

поро́ч|ить, у, ишь, *impf.* (*of* о~) 1. to discredit; п. чьи-н. вы́воды to discredit someone's conclusions. 2. to cover with shame, bring into disrepute; to defame, denigrate; blacken, smear; п. чью-н. репута́цию to blacken someone's reputation.

поро́чность|ь, и, *f.* 1. viciousness, depravity. 2. fallaciousness.

по́р|очный, *adj. of* ~ка.

поро́ч|ный (~ен, ~на), *adj.* 1. vicious, depraved; wanton. 2. faulty, defective; fallacious; п. круг vicious circle.

поро́ш|а, и, *f.* newly-fallen snow.

пороши́нк|а, и, *f.* grain of powder.

пороши́ть, и́т, *impf.* (*of snow*) to fall in

powdery form; ~и́ло (*impers.*) it was snowing slightly, a light snow was falling.

порош|ко́вый, *adj. of* ~о́к.

порошкообра́з|ный (~ен, ~на), *adj.* powder-like, powdery.

порош|о́к, ка́, *m.* powder; зубно́й п. tooth-powder; стере́ть в п. to grind into dust; (*fig., coll.*) to make mincemeat (of).

поро́ю = поро́й.

по́рск|ать, аю, *impf. of* ~нуть.

порск|а́ть, а́ю, *impf.* (*of* ~ну́ть) to set on (*hounds*).

по́рск|нуть, ну, нешь, *pf.* (*of* ~ать) (*dial.*) **1.** to snort (*with laughter*). **2.** to flee, dash off.

порск|ну́ть, ну́, нёшь, *pf.* of ~а́ть.

порт¹, а, о ~е, в ~у́, *pl.* ~ы́, ~о́в, *m.* port; harbour; вое́нный п. naval port, naval dockyard; возду́шный п. airport; морско́й п. seaport.

порт², а, *m.* (*naut.*) port(hole).

По́рт|а, ы, *f.* (*hist.*) The (Sublime *or* Ottoman) Porte.

порта́л, а, *m.* **1.** (*archit.*) portal. **2.** (*tech.*) gantry (*of crane*).

порта́л|ьный, *adj. of* ~; п. кран gantry crane.

портати́вност|ь, и, *f.* portability, portableness.

портати́в|ный (~ен, ~на), *adj.* portable; ~ная радиоустано́вка, п. приёмник-переда́тчик portable radio set, walkie-talkie.

портве́йн, а, *m.* port (*wine*).

по́ртер, а, *m.* porter, stout.

по́ртерн|ая, ой, *f.* (*obs.*) pub, bar, ale-house.

по́ртик, а, *m.* portico.

по́р|тить, чу, тишь, *impf.* (*of* ис~) **1.** to spoil, mar; to damage; п. своё зре́ние to ruin one's eyesight; п. кому́-н. удово́льствие to mar someone's pleasure; п. механи́зм to damage the works; не ~тите себе́ не́рвы don't take it to heart; don't worry. **2.** to corrupt.

по́р|титься, чусь, тишься, *impf.* (*of* ис~) **1.** to deteriorate; (*of foodstuffs*) to go bad; (*of teeth*) to decay; to rot; не п. от жары́ to be heatproof; отноше́ния ста́ли п. relations have begun to deteriorate. **2.** to get out of order. **3.** to become corrupt.

порт|ки́, ко́в *or* ~о́к, *no sing.* (*coll.*) = ~ы́.

портмоне́, *indecl.*, *n.* (*obs.*) purse.

портни́х|а, и, *f.* dressmaker.

портно́вский, *adj.* tailor's, tailoring.

портн|о́й, о́го, *m.* tailor.

портня́ж|ить, у, ишь, *impf.* (*coll.*) to be a tailor.

портня́жнича|ть, ю, *impf.* (*coll.*) = портня́жить.

портня́жн|ый, *adj.* tailor's, sartorial; ~ое де́ло tailoring.

портови́к, а́, *m.* docker.

порто́вый, *adj. of* порт; п. го́род port; п. рабо́чий docker.

портомо́|йня, йни, *g. pl.* ~ен, *f.* (*obs.*) wash-house.

по́рто-фра́нко, *indecl.*, *n.* (*econ.*) free port.

портпле́д, а, *m.* hold-all.

портре́т, а, *m.* portrait; likeness; п. во весь рост full-length portrait; поясно́й п. half-length portrait; он — живо́й п. своего́ отца́ he is the image of his father.

портрети́ст, а, *m.* portrait-painter, portraitist.

портре́т|ный, *adj. of* ~; ~ная галере́я portrait gallery.

портсига́р, а, *m.* cigarette-case; cigar-case.

португа́л|ец, ьца, *m.* Portuguese.

португа́лк|а, и, *f.* Portuguese (woman).

португа́льский, *adj.* Portuguese.

портула́к, а, *m.* (*bot.*) purslane.

портупе́й-ю́нкер, а, *m.* (*mil., hist.*) **1.** senior cadet. **2.** junior ensign (*in pre-Revolutionary Russian cavalry*).

портупе́|я, и, *f.* (*mil.*) sword-belt; waist-belt; shoulder-belt.

портфе́л|ь, я, *m.* **1.** brief-case; portfolio. **2.** (*fig.*) portfolio; мини́стр без ~я Minister without Portfolio; он получи́л п. мини́стра просвеще́ния he has been made Minister of Education.

портше́з, а, *m.* sedan(-chair).

порт|ы́, ов, *no sing.* (*coll.*) trousers.

портье́, *indecl.*, *m.* (*hotel*) porter, doorman.

портье́р|а, ы, *f.* portière, door-curtain.

портя́нк|а, и, *f.* foot binding (*worn instead of sock or stocking*); puttee.

поруб|и́ть, лю́, ~ишь, *pf.* **1.** to chop down (*all or a large number of*). **2.** to do a bit of chopping.

пору́бк|а, и, *f.* tree-felling, wood-chopping.

пору́бщик, а, *m.* wood-stealer.

поруга́ни|е, я, *n.* profanation, desecration; отда́ть на п. to profane, desecrate.

пору́ганн|ый, *adj.* profaned, desecrated; ~ая честь outraged honour.

поруга́|ть, ю, *pf.* (*coll.*) to scold, swear (at).

поруга́|ться, юсь, *pf.* **1.** to swear, curse. **2.** (с+*i.*; *coll.*) to fall out (with).

пору́к|а, и, *f.* bail; guarantee; surety; круго́вая п. collective guarantee; взять на ~и (*i*) to bail (out), go bail (for), (*ii*) to take on probation; отпусти́ть на ~и to accept bail (for), release on bail, put on probation.

по-ру́сски, *adv.* (in) Russian; говори́ть п. to speak Russian.

поруч|а́ть, а́ю, *impf. of* ~и́ть.

поруче́йник, а, *m.* (*orn.*) marsh sandpiper.

поруче́н|ец, ца, *m.* special messenger.

поруче́ни|е, я, *n.* commission, errand; message; mission; дать п. to give a commission,

charge; по ~ю (+g.) on the instructions
(of); on behalf (of); per procurationem
(per pro., p.p.).

пóруч|ень, ня, *m.* handrail.

пору́чик, а, *m.* (*obs.*) lieutenant.

поручи́тел|ь, я, *m.* 1. guarantee, guarantor.
2. warrantor, bail, surety.

поручи́тельств|о, а, *n.* guarantee; bail.

поруч|и́ть, у́, ⌐ишь, *pf.* (*of* ~áть) to charge,
commission; to entrust; to instruct; он ~и́л
мне переда́ть вам де́ньги he charged me
to hand you the money; ма́льчика ~и́ли
тата́рской ня́не the little boy has been en-
trusted to the care of a Tatar nannie.

поруч|и́ться, у́сь, ⌐ишься, *pf. of* руча́ться.

порфи́р, а, *m.* (*min.*) porphyry.

порфи́р|а, ы, *f.* (the) purple (*as Roman em-
peror's or other monarch's robe*).

порфи́р|ный, *adj.* 1. *adj. of* ~. 2. (*obs.*)
purple.

порх|а́ть, а́ю, *impf.* (*of* ~ну́ть) to flutter,
flit, fly about.

порх|ну́ть, ну́, нёшь, *pf. of* ~а́ть.

порцио́н, а, *m.* ration; полево́й п. (*mil.*; *obs.*)
field ration allowance.

порцио́н|ный, *adj.* 1. à la carte. 2. *adj. of* ~;
~ные де́ньги (*mil.*; *obs.*) ration allowance.

пóрци|я, и, *f.* portion; (*of food*) helping; две
~и ды́ни two portions of melon, melon for
two, melon twice.

пóрч|а, и, *f.* 1. spoiling; damage; wear and
tear; п. отноше́ний deterioration of relations. 2. corruption. 3. (*dial.*) wasting
disease (*in popular belief caused by magic
spells*); навести́ ~у на кого́-н. to put the
evil eye on someone.

пóрченый, *adj.* (*coll.*) 1. spoiled; (*of food-
stuffs*) bad; damaged, out of order, un-
serviceable. 2. (*dial.*) bewitched, under the
evil eye.

пóрш|ень, ня, *m.* (*tech.*) piston; plunger,
sucker (*of pump*).

порш|нево́й, *adj. of* ⌐ень; ~невóе кольцó
piston ring; ~невáя маши́на reciprocating
engine; п. привóд piston drive; п. самолёт
piston aircraft (*as opp. to jet aircraft*); п.
сте́ржень piston rod.

порыв[1], а, *m.* 1. gust; rush. 2. (*fig.*) fit,
gust; uprush, upsurge; благорóдный п.
noble impulse; п. гне́ва fit of temper; под
влия́нием ~а on an impulse, on the spur of
the moment.

порыв[2], а, *m.* breaking, snapping.

порыва́|ть, ю, *impf. of* порва́ть.

порыва́|ться[1], юсь, *impf. of* порва́ться.

порыва́|ться[2], юсь, *impf.* 1. to make jerky
movements. 2. (+*inf.*) to try, endeavour.

пóрывисто, *adv.* fitfully, by fits and
starts.

пóрывистост|ь, и, *f.* impetuosity, violence.

пóры́вист|ый (~ , ~a), *adj.* 1. gusty. 2.
jerky. 3. (*fig.*) impetuous, violent; fitful.

порыжéлый, *adj.* (*coll.*) reddish-brown (*as
result of fading*).

порыжé|ть, ю, *pf. of* рыжéть.

пор|ы́ться, ою́сь, óешься, *pf.* (в+*p.*; *coll.*)
to rummage (in, among); п. в па́мяти to
give one's memory a jog.

по-ры́царски, *adv.* in a chivalrous manner.

порябé|ть, ю, *pf. of* рябéть.

поря|ди́ться, жу́сь, ди́шься, *pf. of* ряди́ть-
ся.

поря́дков|ый, *adj.* ordinal; ~ое числи́тель-
ное ordinal numeral.

поря́дком, *adv.* (*coll.*) 1. pretty, rather; мне
п. надоéл э́тот фильм I found it a rather
boring film. 2. properly, thoroughly; он не
объясни́л п., как туда́ попа́сть he did not
explain properly how to get there.

поря́длив|ый (~, ~a), *adj.* neat, orderly.

поря́д|ок, ка, *m.* (*in var. senses*) order. 1.
= *correct state or arrangement*; навести́ п.
(в+*a.*) to introduce order (in); привести́
в п. to put in order; привести́ себя́ в п. to
tidy oneself up, set oneself to rights; при-
зва́ть к ~ку to call to order; следи́ть за
~ком to keep order; всё в ~ке! everything
is all right!, it's quite all right!, all correct!,
O.K.!; э́то в ~ке веще́й it is in the order
of things, it is quite natural; не в ~ке out
of order, not right; у негó кише́чник ещё
не в ~ке his bowels are not right yet, there
is still something the matter with his bowels;
для ~ка (*i*) to maintain order, (*ii*) to preserve the conventions; к ~ку! (*at a meeting*)
order!; взять слóво к ~ку веде́ния собра́-
ния to rise to a point of order. 2. = *sequence*; алфави́тный п. alphabetical order;
после́довательный п. sequence; де́ло
идёт свои́м ~ком things are taking their
(regular, normal) course; по ~ку in order,
in succession; п. дня agenda, order of business, order of the day; стоя́ть в ~ке дня to
be on the agenda. 3. manner, way; procedure; в ~ке (+*g.*) by way (of), on the
basis (of); в администрати́вном ~ке administratively; в обяза́тельном ~ке without
fail; в спе́шном ~ке quickly; в устанóв-
ленном ~ке in accordance with established
procedure; закóнным ~ком legally; пре-
сле́довать суде́бным ~ком to prosecute;
п. вы́боров election procedure; п. голосо-
ва́ния voting procedure, method of voting.
4. (*mil.*) = *formation*; боевóй п. battle
order. 5. (*polit.*)' = *system*, *régime*; ста́рый п.
the old order; устанóвленный п. the established order. 6. (*pl.*) customs, usages, observances.

поря́дочно, *adv.* 1. decently; honestly;
respectably; они́ поступи́ли вполнé п.

they acted perfectly decently. 2. (coll.) fairly, pretty; a fair amount; она п. устала she was pretty tired; мы п. выпили we had a fair amount to drink. 3. (coll.) fairly well, quite decently; он поёт п. he sings quite decently, he has quite a decent voice.

поря́дочност|ь, и, f. decency; honesty, probity.

поря́доч|ный (~ен, ~на), adj. 1. decent; honest; respectable; ~ные люди respectable people, decent folk. 2. (coll.) fair, considerable, decent; они живут на ~ном расстоянии отсюда they live a fair distance from here; он уже накопил ~ную сумму he has already saved up a decent sum; п. доход a respectable income; он — п. плут he is pretty much of a rogue.

поса́д, а, m. 1. (hist.) trading quarter (situated outside city wall). 2. (obs.) suburb.

поса|ди́ть, жу́, ~дишь, pf. of сади́ть and сажа́ть.

поса́дк|а, и, f. 1. planting. 2. embarkation; boarding (train, bus, etc.); (mil.) entrainment; embussing. 3. (aeron.) landing; alighting (on water); вынужденная п. forced landing. 4. seat (manner of sitting in saddle).

поса́дник, а, m. (hist.) posadnik (governor of medieval Russian city-state, appointed by prince or elected by citizens).

поса́дничеств|о, а, n. (hist.) office of posadnik.

поса́дни|чий, adj. of ~к.

поса́дочн|ый, adj. 1. planting. 2. (aeron.) landing; ~ые огни flare path; ~ая площадка landing ground; п. пробег landing run; ~ая фара landing light.

поса́д|ский, adj. of ~; ~ские люди (hist.) tradespeople; as noun п., ~ского, m. (obs.) inhabitant of suburb.

посажа́|ть, ю, pf. (coll.) 1. (+a. or g.) to seat (a number of). 2. (+g.) to do a bit of planting.

поса́|женный, p.p.p. of ~ди́ть.

посажённый, adj. by the sazhen (see сажень); by the fathom.

поса́жёный, adj. proxy (for parent of bride or bridegroom at wedding ceremony), sponsor.

поса́пыва|ть, ю, impf. (coll.) to snuffle; to breathe heavily (in sleep).

поса́сыва|ть, ю, impf. (coll.) to suck (at).

поса́хар|ить, ю, ишь, pf. of са́харить.

посва́та|ть(ся), ю(сь), pf. of сва́тать(ся).

посвеже́|ть, ю, pf. of свеже́ть.

посве|ти́ть, чу́, ~тишь, pf. 1. to shine for a while. 2. (+d.) to hold a light (for); я тебе ~чу́ до угла переулка I will light you to the corner of the lane.

посветле́|ть, ю, pf. of светле́ть.

по́свист, а, m. whistle; whistling.

посви|ста́ть, щу́, ~щешь, pf. to whistle (to, up).

посви|сте́ть, щу́, сти́шь, pf. to whistle, give a whistle.

посви́стыва|ть, ю, impf. to whistle (softly, from time to time).

по-сво́ему, adv. in one's own way; де́лайте п., поступа́йте п. have it your own way.

по-сво́йски, adv. (coll.) 1. in one's own way; он всегда поступа́ет п. he always pleases himself. 2. in a familiar way, as between friends.

посвяти́тельный, adj. dedicatory.

посвя|ти́ть, щу́, ти́шь, pf. (of ~ща́ть) 1. (+a. в+a.) to let (into), initiate (into); мы вас ~ти́м в на́шу та́йну we will let you into our secret. 2. (+a. and d.) to devote (to), give up (to); to dedicate (to); п. себя́ нау́ке to devote oneself to (the cause of) learning; он ~ти́л пе́рвую кни́гу свое́й ма́тери he dedicated his first book to his mother. 3. (+a. в+n.-a.) to ordain, consecrate; п. в дья́коны to ordain deacon; п. в епи́скопы to consecrate bishop; п. в ры́цари to knight, confer a knighthood (upon).

посвяща́|ть, ю, impf. of посвяти́ть.

посвяще́ни|е, я, n. 1. initiation. 2. (in lit. work) dedication. 3. ordination; consecration; п. в ры́цари knighting.

посе́в, а, m. 1. sowing. 2. crops; площадь ~ов sown area, area under crops.

посевн|о́й, adj. sowing; ~а́я площадь sown area, area under crops; as noun ~а́я, ~о́й, f. sowing campaign.

поседе́лый, adj. grown grey, grizzled.

поседе́|ть, ю, pf. of седе́ть.

посейча́с, adv. (coll.) up to now, up to the present.

поселе́н|ец, ца, m. 1. settler. 2. deportee.

поселе́ни|е, я, n. 1. settling. 2. settlement. 3. deportation; отпра́вить на п. to deport.

посел|и́ть, ю́, и́шь, pf. (of ~я́ть) 1. to settle; to lodge. 2. to inspire, arouse, engender; п. вражду́ ме́жду друзья́ми to engender enmity between friends.

посел|и́ться, ю́сь, и́шься, pf. (of ~я́ться) to settle, take up residence, make one's home.

посел|ко́вый, adj. of ~о́к.

посёл|ок, ка, m. 1. settlement (of urban type); (new) housing estate. 2. (name of administrative unit in U.S.S.R.) settlement.

поселя́н|ин, ина, pl. ~е, ~, m. (obs.) peasant.

посел|я́ть(ся), я́ю(сь), impf. of ~и́ть(ся).

посему́, adv. (obs.) therefore.

посеребр|ённый, p.p.p. of ~и́ть and adj. silver-plated.

посеребр|и́ть, ю́, и́шь, pf. of серебри́ть.

посереди́, *adv. and prep.* +*g.* (*coll.*) = ~не.

посереди́не, *adv. and prep.* +*g.* in the middle (of), half way along.

посере́|ть, ю, *pf. of* cере́ть.

посессио́нный, *adj.* (*hist.*) possessional.

посесси́|я, и, *f.* (*hist., leg.*) leasehold landed property.

посети́тел|ь, я, *m.* visitor; caller; guest; ежедне́вный п. пивно́й habitué of a bar, regular.

посети́тель|ский, *adj. of* ~.

посе|ти́ть, щу́, ти́шь, *pf.* (*of* ~ща́ть) to visit, call on; п. ле́кции to attend lectures; п. музе́й to see a museum.

посе́т|овать, ую, *pf. of* се́товать.

посе́|чься, чётся, ку́тся, *pf. of* се́чься.

посеща́емост|ь, и, *f.* attendance; плоха́я п. poor attendance.

посеща́|ть, ю, *impf. of* посети́ть.

посеще́ни|е, я, *n.* visiting; visit.

посе́|ять, ю, *pf. of* се́ять.

посиве́|ть, ю, *pf. of* сиве́ть.

посиде́л|ки, ок, *no sing.* (*obs.*) young people's gathering (*for recreation on winter evenings*).

поси|де́ть, жу́, ди́шь, *pf.* to sit (*for a while*); п. вечеро́к в гостя́х to spend an evening at friends.

посил|ьный (~ен, ~ьна), *adj.* within one's powers, feasible; ~ьная зада́ча feasible task; оказа́ть ~ьную по́мощь to do what one can to help; э́то не была́ ~ьная для него́ рабо́та he was not up to the work.

посине́лый, *adj.* gone blue.

посине́|ть, ю, *pf. of* сине́ть.

поска|ка́ть[1], чу́, ~чешь, *pf. of* скака́ть.

поска|ка́ть[2], чу́, ~чешь, *pf.* to hop, jump.

поскользн|у́ться, у́сь, ёшься, *pf.* to slip.

поско́льку, *conj.* 1. so far as, as far as; никто́ не звони́л, п. мне изве́стно no one has rung as far as I know; мы путеше́ствуем посто́льку, п. позволя́ют сре́дства we travel (just) as much as we can afford. 2. in so far as, since; so long as; п. вы гото́вы подписа́ть, гото́в и я so long as you are ready to sign, I am too.

поско́нный, *adj.* hempen.

поско́н|ь, и, *f.* 1. (*bot.*) hemp-plant. 2. (*obs.*) home-spun hempen sacking.

поскоре́е, *adv.* somewhat quicker; ~! quick!, make haste!

поскрёбк|и, ов, *no sing.* scrapings, leftovers (*of food*).

поскуп|и́ться, лю́сь, и́шься, *pf. of* скупи́ться.

послабле́ни|е, я, *n.* indulgence.

посла́н|ец, ца, *m.* messenger, envoy.

посла́ни|е, я, *n.* 1. message. 2. (*lit.*) epistle; Посла́ния (*bibl.*) the Epistles.

посла́нник, а, *m.* envoy, minister; чрезвыча́йный п. и полномо́чный мини́стр

envoy extraordinary and minister plenipotentiary.

по́сл|анный, p.p.p. of ~а́ть; *as noun* п., ~анного, *m.* messenger, envoy.

по|сла́ть, шлю́, шлёшь, *pf.* (*of* ~сыла́ть) 1. to send, dispatch; п. за до́ктором to send for the doctor; п. по по́чте to post; п. покло́н to send one's regards; п. кого́-н. к чёрту (*fig., coll.*) to send someone to the devil. 2. (*sport, etc.*) to move (*part of the body*).

по́сле, *adv. and prep.* +*g.* after; afterwards, later (on); (*after a neg.*) since; п. войны́ after the war; мы с ним не вида́лись п. войны́ he and I have not seen one another since the war; он пришёл п. всех he came last; п. всего́ after all, when all is said and done; п. чего́ whereupon.

после- post-.

послевое́нный, *adj.* post-war.

после́д, а, *m.* (*anat.*) placenta.

после|ди́ть, жу́, ди́шь, *pf.* (за+*i.*) to look (after), see (to).

после́дк|и, ов, *no sing.* (*coll.*) remnants, leftovers.

после́дн|ий, *adj.* 1. last; final; (в) ~ее вре́мя, за ~ее вре́мя lately, of late, latterly, recently; (в) п. раз for the last time; до ~его вре́мени until very recently; до ~ей кра́йности to the very uttermost. 2. (the) latest; ~ие изве́стия the latest news; ~яя мо́да the latest fashion. 3. the latter. 4. (*coll.*) worst, lowest; ~ие времена́ (*obs.*) bad times, hard times; ~ее де́ло the end; э́то уже́ ~ее де́ло! it's the end!, it's the very limit!; ~яя ка́пля the drop to fill the cup, the last straw; руга́ться ~ими слова́ми to use foul language. 5. *as noun* ~ее, ~его, *n.* the last; the uttermost.

после́довател|ь, я, *m.* follower.

после́довательност|ь, и, *f.* 1. succession, sequence; п. времён (*gram.*) sequence of tenses; в стро́гой ~и in strict sequence. 2. consistency.

после́довател|ьный (~ен, ~ьна), *adj.* 1. successive, consecutive. 2. consistent, logical.

после́д|овать, ую, *pf. of* сле́довать.

после́дстви|е, я, *n.* consequence, sequel; after-effect; чрева́тый ~ями fraught, pregnant with consequences; оста́вить жа́лобу без ~й to take no action on a complaint.

после́дующий, *adj.* subsequent, succeeding, following, ensuing; (*math.*) consequent.

после́дыш, а, *m.* 1. (*coll.*) last-born child, youngest child (*in a family*). 2. (*fig., pejor.*) belated follower.

послеза́втра, *adv.* the day after tomorrow.

послеза́втра|шний, *adj. of* ~.

послело́г, а, *m.* (*gram.*) postposition.

послеобе́денный, *adj.* after-dinner.

послеоктя́брьский, *adj.* post-October (*occurring or having occurred since the 1917 Russian Revolution*).

послереволюцио́нный, *adj.* post-revolutionary.

послеродово́й, *adj.* post-natal.

послесло́ви|е, я, *n.* postface; concluding remarks.

послеуда́рный, *adj.* (*ling.*) post-tonic.

посло́виц|а, ы, *f.* proverb, saying; войти́ в ~у to become proverbial.

посло́вичный, *adj.* proverbial.

послуж|и́ть¹, у́, ~ишь, *pf. of* служи́ть.

послуж|и́ть², у́, ~ишь, *pf.* to serve (*for a while*).

послужно́й, *adj.* п. спи́сок service record.

послуша́ни|е, я, *n.* **1.** obedience. **2.** (*eccl.*) work of penance; назна́чить кому́-н. п. to impose a penance on someone.

послу́ша|ть(ся), ю(сь), *pf. of* слу́шать(ся).

по́слушник, а, *m.* novice, lay brother.

по́слушниц|а, ы, *f.* novice, lay sister.

послу́ш|ный (~ен, ~на), *adj.* obedient, dutiful.

послы́ш|ать, у, ишь, *pf.* (*obs.*) to hear.

послы́ш|аться, усь, ишься, *pf. of* слы́шаться.

послюн|и́ть, ю́, и́шь, *pf. of* слюни́ть.

посма́трива|ть, ю, *impf.* (на + *a.*) to look (at) from time to time; п. на часы́ to consult one's watch from time to time; to watch the clock; ~й(те)! keep an eye out!

посме́ива|ться, юсь, *impf.* to chuckle, laugh softly; п. в кула́к to laugh up one's sleeve.

посме́нно, *adv.* in turns, by turns; by shifts.

посме́нн|ый, *adj.* by turns, in shifts; ~ая рабо́та shift work.

посме́ртный, *adj.* posthumous.

посме́|ть, ю, *pf. of* сметь.

посме́шищ|е, а, *n.* laughing-stock, butt.

посмея́ни|е, я, *n.* mockery, ridicule; отда́ть кого́-н. на п. to make a laughing-stock of someone.

посмотр|е́ть(ся), ю́(сь), ~ишь(ся), *pf. of* смотре́ть(ся).

посмугле́|ть, ю, *pf. of* смугле́ть.

поснима́|ть, ю, *pf.* (*coll.*) to take off, take away (all *or* a number of); пора́ нам п. все рожде́ственские украше́ния it is time we took down all the Christmas decorations.

по-соба́чьи, *adv.* like a dog.

пособи|е, я, *n.* **1.** (*financial*) aid, help, relief, assistance, benefit; п. безрабо́тным unemployment benefit, the dole; ~я матеря́м family allowances; п. по боле́зни sick benefit, sick pay; п. по нетрудоспосо́бности disablement allowance. **2.**

textbook; (educational) aid; нагля́дные ~я visual aids; уче́бные ~я educational supplies; school text-books.

пособ|и́ть, лю́, и́шь, *pf.* (*of* ~ля́ть) (*coll.*) to aid; to relieve; п. го́рю to assuage grief.

пособля́|ть, ю, *impf. of* пособи́ть.

посо́бник, а, *m.* accomplice; abettor.

посо́бничеств|о, а, *n.* (+ *g.*) complicity (in); aiding and abetting.

посо́ве|ститься, щусь, стишься, *pf. of* со́веститься.

посове́т|овать(ся), ую(сь), *pf. of* сове́товать(ся).

посоде́йств|овать, ую, *pf. of* соде́йствовать.

пос|о́л¹, ла́, *m.* ambassador.

посо́л², **а,** *m.* salting.

посол|и́ть, ю́, ~и́шь, *pf. of* соли́ть.

посолове́лый, *adj.* bleary, bleared.

посолове́|ть, ю, *pf. of* солове́ть.

по́солонь, *adv.* (*obs.*) with the sun, clockwise.

посо́льс|кий, *adj.* **1.** ambassadorial, ambassador's. **2.** *adj. of* ~тво; п. автомоби́ль embassy car. **3.** П. прика́з (*hist.*) Embassies' Department (*in Muscovite Russia*).

посо́льств|о, а, *n.* embassy.

по-сосе́дски, *adv.* in a neighbourly way.

посо́тенно, *adv.* by the hundred, by hundreds.

по́сох, а, *m.* **1.** staff, crook. **2.** (bishop's) crozier.

посо́х|нуть, ну, нешь, *past* ~, ~ла, *pf.* to wither, become withered.

посо́ш|о́к, ка́, *m.* **1.** *dim. of* по́сох. **2.** (*coll., joc.*) one for the road (*final drink before departure*).

посп|а́ть, лю́, и́шь, *past* ~а́л, ~ала́, ~а́ло, *pf.* to have a sleep, have a nap, snooze.

поспева́|ть¹, ет, *impf. of* поспе́ть¹.

поспева́|ть², ю, *impf. of* поспе́ть².

поспекта́кльн|ый, *adj.* ~ая опла́та (*theatr.*) pay by the performance, pay per night.

поспе́|ть¹, ет, *pf.* (*of* ~ва́ть¹) (*coll.*) **1.** to ripen. **2.** (*of food in preparation*) to be done.

поспе́|ть², ю, *pf.* (*of* ~ва́ть²) (*coll.*) to have time; (к, на + *a.*) to be in time (for); (за + *i.*) to keep up (with), keep pace (with); ~ли ли вы? were you in time?, did you make it?; она́ е́ле-е́ле ~ла на по́езд she just caught the train; мы не могли́ п. за ни́ми we could not keep up with them.

поспеша́|ть, ю, *impf.* (*coll.*) to hurry.

поспеше́ств|овать, ую, *impf.* (+ *d.*; *arch.*) to help, assist.

поспеш|и́ть, у́, и́шь, *pf. of* спеши́ть; ~и́шь, люде́й насмеши́шь (*prov.*) more haste, less speed.

поспе́шно, *adv.* in a hurry, hurriedly, hastily; п. отступи́ть to beat a hasty retreat; п. уйти́ to hurry off, hurry away.

поспéшност|ь, и, *f.* haste.
поспéш|ный (~ен, ~на), *adj.* hasty, hurried.
посплéтнича|ть, ю, *pf.* to have a gossip; to tattle, talk scandal.
поспóр|ить[1], ю, ишь, *pf.* 1. *pf. of* спóрить. 2. (с+*i*.) to contend (with). 3. to bet, have a bet.
поспóр|ить[2], ю, ишь, *pf.* to argue (*for a while*).
посрам|и́ть, лю́, и́шь, *pf.* (*of* ~ля́ть) to disgrace.
посрам|и́ться, лю́сь, и́шься, *pf.* (*of* ~ля́ться) to disgrace oneself, cover oneself with shame.
посрамлéни|е, я, *n.* disgrace.
посрамля́|ть(ся), ю(сь), *impf. of* посрами́ть(ся).
посреди́, *adv. and prep.* +*g.* in the middle (of), in the midst (of); п. у́лицы in the middle of the street; п. толпы́ in the midst of the crowd.
посреди́не, *adv.* = посереди́не.
посрéдник, а, *m.* 1. mediator, intermediary; go-between. 2. (*comm.*) middle-man. 3. (*mil.*) umpire (*on manœuvres*).
посрéднича|ть, ю, *impf.* to act as a go-between, mediate, come in between.
посрéднический, *adj.* intermediary, mediatory.
посрéдничеств|о, а, *n.* mediation.
посрéдственно, *adv.* 1. so-so, not outstandingly well, not all that well; он п. игра́ет в тéннис he is not particularly good at tennis. 2. *as noun, indecl.* fair, satisfactory (*as examination mark*); я сдал экза́мен по фи́зике на п. I got a 'fair' in physics.
посрéдственност|ь, и, *f.* mediocrity (*also* = *mediocre person*).
посрéдствен|ный (~, ~на), *adj.* 1. mediocre, middling. 2. (*of school marks, etc.*) fair, satisfactory.
посрéдств|о, а, *n.* mediation; при ~е, чéрез п. (+*g.*) by means of, through the instrumentality of; thanks to.
посрéдством, *prep.*+*g.* by means of; by dint of; with the aid of.
посрéдствующий, *adj.* intermediate; connecting.
поссóр|ить(ся), ю(сь), ишь(ся), *pf. of* ссóрить(ся).
пост[1], á, о ~é, на ~у́, *pl.* ~ы́, *m.* (*in var. senses*) post; наблюда́тельный п. observation post; быть на своём ~у́ to be at one's post; стоя́ть на ~у́ to be at one's post; (*of policeman*) to be on one's beat; (*of traffic controller*) to be on point-duty; занима́ть высóкий п. to hold a high post; расста́вить ~ы́ (*mil.*) to post sentries.
пост[2], á, о ~é, в ~у́, *m.* 1. fasting; (*fig.,*

coll.) abstinence. 2. (*eccl.*) fast; вели́кий п. Lent.
постáв, а, *pl.* ~á, ~óв, *m.* 1. pair of mill-stones. 2. (*dial.*) loom; piece of canvas.
постáв|éц, ца́, *m.* (*obs. or dial.*) 1. provisions hamper. 2. sideboard, dresser.
постáв|ить[1], лю, ишь, *pf. of* ста́вить.
постáв|ить[2], лю, ишь, *pf.* (*of* ~ля́ть) to supply, purvey.
постáвк|а, и, *f.* supply; delivery; ма́ссовая п. bulk delivery.
поставщи́к, á, *m.* supplier, purveyor, provider; caterer; outfitter.
постамéнт, а, *m.* pedestal, base.
постана́влива|ть, ю, *impf.* = постановля́ть.
постанов|и́ть, лю́, ~ишь, *pf.* (*of* постана́вливать *and* ~ля́ть) to decide, resolve; to decree, enact, ordain.
постанóвк|а, и, *f.* 1. erection, raising. 2. (*in var. senses*) putting, placing, setting; arrangement, organization; п. вопрóса formulation of a question; у неё хорóшая п. головы́ she holds her head well; п. гóлоса (*mus.*) voice training; п. па́льцев (*mus.*) fingering; finger training; п. рабóты arrangement of work. 3. (*theatr.*) staging, production; вчера́ мы ви́дели «Ча́йку» Чéхова в нóвой ~е yesterday we saw a new production of Chekhov's 'Seagull'.
постановлéни|е, я, *n.* 1. decision, resolution; вы́нести п. to pass a resolution. 2. decree, enactment; изда́ть п. to issue a decree.
постанóв|очный, *adj. of* ~ка 3; ~очная пьéса play suitable for staging; play effective in stage production; ~очные эффéкты (stage) effects.
постанóвщик, а, *m.* producer (*of play*), stage-manager; director (*of film*).
постара́|ться, юсь, *pf. of* стара́ться.
постарé|ть, ю, *pf. of* старéть.
по-стáрому, *adv.* 1. as before. 2. as of old.
постатéйный, *adj.* by paragraphs, paragraph-by-paragraph, clause-by-clause.
постел|и́ть, ю, ~ишь, *pf.* (*coll.*) = постла́ть.
постéл|ь, и, *f.* 1. bed; лечь в п. to get into bed; лежа́ть в ~и to be in bed; встать с ~и to get out of bed; постла́ть п. to make up a bed; прикóванный к ~и bed-ridden. 2. (*geol., tech.*) bed; bottom.
постéль|ный, *adj. of* ~; ~ное бельё bed-clothes; ~ные принадлéжности bedding; п. режи́м confinement to bed; комéдия ~ного содержа́ния (*coll.*) bedroom comedy.
постепéнно, *adv.* gradually, little by little.
постепéнност|ь, и, *f.* gradualness; п. разви́тия gradual development.
постепéн|ный (~ен, ~на), *adj.* gradual.

постепе́новщин|а, ы, *f.* (*polit.*; *pejor.*) gradualism.

постесня́|ться, юсь, *pf. of* стесня́ться.

постиг|а́ть, а́ю, *impf. of* ∼ну́ть *and* пости́чь.

пости́гнуть, = пости́чь.

постиже́ни|е, я, *n.* comprehension, grasp.

постижи́м|ый (∼, ∼а), *adj.* comprehensible.

постила́|ть, ю, *impf. of* постла́ть.

пости́лк|а, и, *f.* 1. spreading, laying. 2. bedding; litter.

пости́л|очный, *adj. of* ∼ка; ∼очная соло́ма bed-straw.

постира́|ть, ю, *pf.* 1. (*coll.*) to wash. 2. to do some washing.

по|сти́ться, щу́сь, сти́шься, *impf.* to fast, keep the fast.

пости́|чь, гну, гнёшь, *past* ∼г *and* (*obs.*) ∼гну́л, ∼гла́, *pf.* (*of* ∼га́ть) 1. to comprehend, grasp. 2. to overtake, befall, strike; их ∼гло́ ещё одно́ несча́стье yet another misfortune has befallen them.

пост|ла́ть, елю́, е́лешь, *past* ∼ла́л, ∼лала́, ∼ла́ло, *pf.* (*of* стла́ть *and* ∼ила́ть) to spread, lay; п. ковёр to lay a carpet (down); п. посте́ль to make one's bed; как ∼е́лешь, так и поспи́шь (*prov.*) as you make your bed, so must you lie.

по́стник, а, *m.* faster, person observing fast.

по́стнича|ть, ю, *impf.* to fast.

по́стничеств|о, а, *n.* fasting.

по́ст|ный (∼ен, ∼на́, ∼но), *adj.* 1. lenten; п. день (*eccl.*) fast-day; ∼ная еда́ lenten fare; п. обе́д meatless dinner (*comprising fish and/or vegetables*); п. са́хар boiled sweets. 2. (*coll.*; *of meat*) lean. 3. (*fig.*, *coll.*, *joc.*) glum. 4. (*fig.*, *coll.*, *joc.*) pious, sanctimonious.

постов|о́й, *adj. of* пост[1]; ∼а́я бу́дка sentry-box; п. милиционе́р militia-man on point-duty; ∼а́я слу́жба sentry duty; *as noun* п., ∼о́го, *m.* = п. милиционе́р.

посто́й[1], ∼те (*coll.*) stop!, wait (a minute)!

посто́|й[2], я, *m.* billeting, quartering; поста́вить на п. to billet, quarter; свобо́ден от ∼я exempt from billeting.

посто́льку, *conj.* (*in main clause, following* поско́льку *in subordinate clause*) to that extent (*or not translated*); поли́тика п. поско́льку (*fig.*) wait-and-see policy, policy of sitting on the fence.

посторон|и́ться, ю́сь, ∼и́шься, *pf. of* сторони́ться.

посторо́нн|ий, *adj.* 1. strange; extraneous, outside; ∼ие вопро́сы side issues; без ∼ей по́мощи unassisted, single-handed; ∼ие соображе́ния extraneous considerations; ∼ее те́ло foreign body. 2. *as noun* п., ∼его, *m.* stranger; outsider; ∼им вход запрещён 'unauthorized persons not admitted'.

постоя́л|ец, ьца, *m.* (*obs.*) lodger; (*in hotel, etc.*) guest.

постоя́лый, *adj.* п. двор (*obs.*) coaching inn.

постоя́нн|ая, ой, *f.* (*math.*) constant; п. вре́мени time constant.

постоя́нно, *adv.* constantly, continually, perpetually, always.

постоя́н|ный, *adj.* 1. constant, continual; п. ка́шель continual cough; п. посети́тель constant visitor. 2. constant; permanent, invariable; п. а́дрес permanent address; ∼ная а́рмия regular army; ∼ная величина́ (*math.*) constant; п. жи́тель permanent resident; п. капита́л (*econ.*) constant capital; ∼ное напряже́ние (*electr.*) direct-current voltage; п. ого́нь (*naut.*) fixed light; п. ток (*electr.*) direct current. 3. (∼ен, ∼на) (*of personal, moral qualities, etc.*) constant, steadfast, unchanging; она́ далеко́ не ∼на во вку́сах she is far from constant in her tastes.

постоя́нств|о, а, *n.* constancy; permanency.

посто|я́ть[1], ю́, и́шь, *pf.* to stand (*for a while*).

посто|я́ть[2], ю́, и́шь, *pf.* (за+*a.*) to stand up (for).

постпаке́т, а, *m.* mail packet.

пострада́|вший, *past part. of* ∼ть; *as noun* п., ∼вшего, *m.* victim.

пострада́|ть, ю, *pf. of* страда́ть.

пострани́чный, *adj.* paginal, by the page, per page.

постра́нств|овать, ую, *pf.* to do some travelling.

постраща́|ть, ю, *pf. of* страща́ть.

постре́л, а, *m.* (*coll.*) little imp, little rascal.

постре́лива|ть, ю, *impf.* to fire intermittently, at intervals.

постреля́|ть, ю, *pf.* 1. to spend some time shooting, do some shooting. 2. (+*a. or g.*; *coll.*) to shoot, bag (*a number of*).

по́стриг, а, *m.* taking of monastic vows; (*of a woman*) taking the veil.

пострига́|ть(ся), ю(сь), *impf. of* постри́чь(ся)[2].

постри́жен|ец, ца, *m.* one who has taken monastic vows.

пострижéни|е, я, *n.* admission to monastic vows, tonsure; taking of monastic vows.

постри́женик, а, *m.* = постри́женец.

постри́жен|ка, ки, *f. of* ∼ец *and* ∼ик.

постри́|чь[1], гу́, жёшь, гу́т, *past* ∼г, ∼гла, *pf.* to clip, trim.

постри́|чь[2], гу́, жёшь, гу́т, (*pf.* (*of* ∼га́ть) to make a monk (nun), admit to monastic vows.

постри́|чься[1], гу́сь, жёшься, гу́тся, *past* ∼гся, ∼глась, *pf.* to have a (hair-)trim.

постри́|чься[2], гу́сь, жёшься, гу́тся, *past*

~гся, ~гла́сь, *pf.* (*of* ~га́ться) to take monastic vows; to take the veil (*of a woman*).

построéни|е, я, *n.* 1. (*in var. senses*) construction. 2. (*mil.*) formation.

постро́|ечный, *adj. of* ~йка.

постро́|ить(ся), ю(сь), ишь(ся), *pf. of* стро́ить(ся).

постро́йк|а, и, *f.* 1. (*action*) building, erection, construction. 2. (*edifice*) building. 3. building-site.

постро́мк|а, и, *f.* trace (*part of harness*).

постро́чный, *adj.* by the line, per line.

постскри́птум, а, *m.* postscript.

посту́ка|ть, ю, *pf.* to knock (*for a while*).

посту́кива|ть, ю, *impf.* to knock (*from time to time*), tap, patter; ходи́ть, ~я па́лочкой to walk tapping with one's stick.

постула́т, а, *m.* (*math., philos.*) postulate.

постули́р|овать, ую, *impf. and pf.* to postulate.

поступа́тельно-возвра́тный, *adj.* (*tech.*) reciprocating.

поступа́тельн|ый, *adj.* forward, advancing; ~ое движе́ние forward movement; (*tech.*) translation; п. ход step forward, onward march.

поступ|а́ть(ся), а́ю(сь), *impf. of* ~и́ть(ся).

поступ|и́ть, лю́, ~ишь, *pf.* (*of* ~а́ть) 1. to act; в да́нных обстоя́тельствах он пра́вильно ~и́л in the circumstances he acted rightly, did right; они́ с ним пло́хо ~и́ли they have treated him badly. 2. (в, на+*a.*) to enter, join; п. в шко́лу to go to school, enter school; п. в университе́т to enter the university; п. на рабо́ту to go to work; п. на вое́нную слу́жбу to join up, enlist. 3. (*of inanimate objects*) to come through, come in; to be forthcoming; to be received; ~и́ла жа́лоба a complaint has been received, has come in; ~и́ло ли его́ заявле́ние? has his application come through, been received?; де́ло ~и́ло в суд the matter was taken to court, came up before the court; ~и́ло 1/хıı (*of an article submitted to a periodical, etc.*) Received 1 December; п. в прода́жу to be on sale, come on the market; п. в произво́дство to go into production.

поступ|и́ться, лю́сь, ~ишься, *pf.* (*of* ~а́ться) (+*i.*) to waive, forgo; to give up; п. свои́ми права́ми to waive one's rights.

поступле́ни|е, я, *n.* 1. entering, joining; п. на вое́нную слу́жбу enlisting, joining up. 2. receipt; (*book-keeping*) entry; п. изве́стий receipt of news; п. дохо́дов revenue return.

посту́п|ок, ка, *m.* action; act, deed; (*pl., collect.*) conduct, behaviour.

по́ступ|ь, и, *f.* gait; step, tread; ме́рная п. measured tread.

постуч|а́ть(ся), у́(сь), и́шь(ся), *pf. of* стуча́ть(ся).

постфа́ктум, *adv.* post factum, after the event.

посты|ди́ть, жу́, ди́шь, *pf.* (*coll.*) to reprimand slightly, pull up.

посты|ди́ться, жу́сь, ди́шься, *pf. of* стыди́ться; ~ди́тесь! you ought to be ashamed (of yourself)!

посты́д|ный (~ен, ~на), *adj.* shameful.

посты́л|ый (~, ~а), *adj.* (*coll.*) hateful, repellent.

посу́д|а, ы, ̦. 1. (*collect.*) crockery; plates and dishes, service; гли́няная п., фая́нсовая п. earthenware; жестяна́я п. tinware; ку́хонная п. kitchen utensils; стекля́нная п. glassware; фарфо́ровая п. china; ча́йная п. tea-service; би́тая п. два ве́ка живёт (*prov.*) creaking doors hang the longest. 2. (*coll.*) vessel, crock.

посуда́ч|ить, у, ишь, *pf.* (*coll.*) to gossip.

посу́дин|а, ы, *f.* 1. vessel, crock. 2. (*coll.*) (*naut.*) old tub.

посу|ди́ть, жу́, ~дишь, *pf.* (*obs.*) to judge, consider; ~ди́ сам judge for yourself.

посу́дник, а, *m.* 1. dish-washer. 2. (*coll.*) dresser.

посу́д|ный, *adj. of* ~а; п. магази́н china-shop; ~ное полоте́нце dish-cloth, tea-towel; п. шкаф dresser, china cupboard.

посудомо́йк|а, и, *f.* dishwashing machine.

посу́л, а, *m.* 1. (*coll.*) promise. 2. (*obs.*) bribe.

посул|и́ть, ю́, и́шь, *pf. of* сули́ть.

посу́точно, *adv.* by the day, for every 24 hours.

посу́точн|ый, *adj.* 24-hour, round-the-clock; у них ~ое дежу́рство they have a 24-hour spell of duty, they have 24 hours on; ~ая опла́та pay by the day.

по́суху, *adv.* (*coll.*) on dry land.

посчастли́в|иться, ится, *pf.* (*impers.*+*d.*) to have the luck (to); to be lucky enough (to); ей ~илось побы́ть в Пари́же she had the luck to stay in Paris.

посчита́|ть, ю, *pf.* to count (up).

посчита́|ться, юсь, *pf.* 1. (с+*i.*; *coll.*) to get even (with). 2. *pf. of* счита́ться.

посыла́|ть, ю, *impf. of* посла́ть.

посы́лк|а¹, и, *f.* 1. sending. 2. parcel. 3. errand; быть на ~ах (у) to run errands (for).

посы́лк|а², и, *f.* (*philos.*) premise; больша́я, ма́лая п. major, minor premise.

посы́лочный, *adj.* parcel.

посы́льн|ый, *adj.* 1. dispatch; ~ое су́дно dispatch-boat. 2. *as noun* п., ~ого, *m.* messenger.

посып|а́ть, а́ю, *impf. of* ~ать.

посы́п|ать, лю, лешь, *pf.* (*of* ~а́ть) (+*i.*) to strew (with); to sprinkle (with); п. гра́вием to gravel; п. со́лью to sprinkle with salt, to salt.

посы́п|аться, лется, *pf.* to begin to fall; (*fig.*) to rain, pour down; ~ались ли́стья the leaves had begun to fall; несча́стья ~ались на них misfortunes came upon them thick and fast.

посяга́тельств|о, a, *n.* (на+*a.*) encroachment (on, upon), infringement (of); п. на свобо́ду infringement of liberty.

посяг|а́ть, а́ю, *impf. of* ~ну́ть.

посяг|ну́ть, ну́, нёшь, *pf.* (*of* ~а́ть) (на+*a.*) to encroach (on, upon), infringe (on, upon); п. на чью-н. жизнь to make an attempt on someone's life.

пот, a, о ~е, в ~у́, *pl.* ~ы́, ~о́в, *m.* sweat, perspiration; весь в ~у́ all of a sweat, bathed in sweat; облива́ясь ~ом dripping with sweat; в ~е лица́ by the sweat of one's brow; ~ом и кро́вью with blood and sweat; труди́ться до седьмо́го (четвёртого) ~a (*coll.*) to sweat one's guts out; вогна́ть кого́-н. в п., согна́ть семь ~о́в с кого́-н. (*coll.*) to work someone to the bone, make someone sweat blood.

потаённый, *adj.* = потайно́й.

потайно́й, *adj.* secret; (*tech.*) countersunk, flush; п. ход secret passage.

потака́|ть, ю, *impf.* (*no pf.*) (+*d.*; *coll.*) to indulge; п. же́нщине в капри́зах, п. капри́зам же́нщины to indulge a woman's whims.

потал|ь, и, *f.* Dutch gold, brass leaf.

пота́ль|ный, *adj. of* ~.

потанц|ева́ть, у́ю, *pf.* to dance (*for a while*), do some dancing.

потаска́|ть, ю, *pf.* (*coll.*) to pinch, filch (*all or a number of*).

потаску́н, a, *m.* (*coll.*) lecher, rake.

потаску́х|а, и, *f.* (*coll.*) strumpet, trollop.

потаску́шк|а, и, *f.* = потаску́ха.

потасо́вк|а, и, *f.* (*coll.*) 1. brawl, fight. 2. beating, hiding; зада́ть кому́-н. ~y to give someone a hiding. 3. *pl.* (*fig.*) tight spot(s).

пота́тчик, a, *m.* (*coll.*) indulger.

пота́чк|а, и, *f.* indulgence.

пота́ш, а́, *m.* potash.

потащ|и́ть, у́, ~ишь, *pf.* to begin to drag.

потащ|и́ться, у́сь, ~ишься, *pf.* to begin to drag oneself, begin slowly to make one's way.

по-тво́ему, *adv.* 1. in your opinion. 2. as you wish; as you advise; пусть бу́дет п. have it your own way; just as you think.

потво́рств|о, a, *n.* indulgence, pandering.

потво́рств|овать, ую, *impf.* (+*d.*) to show indulgence (towards), pander (to).

потво́рщик, a, *m.* panderer.

потёк, a, *m.* stain; damp patch.

потём|ки, ок, *no sing.* darkness.

потемне́ни|е, я, *n.* darkening; dimness.

потемне́|ть, ю, *pf. of* темне́ть.

потѐни|е, я, *n.* sweating, perspiration.

потенциа́л, a, *m.* (*phys. and fig.*) potential; ра́зность ~ов potential difference; вое́нный п. war potential.

потенциа́л|ьный (~ен, ~ьна), *adj.* potential.

потенцио́метр, a, *m.* (*electr.*) potentiometer.

потѐнци|я, и, *f.* potentiality.

потеплѐни|е, я, *n.* getting warmer; наступи́ло п. a warm spell set in.

потепле́|ть, ет, *pf. of* тепле́ть.

по|тере́ть, тру́, трёшь, *past* ~тёр, ~тёрла, *pf.* to rub.

по|тере́ться, тру́сь, трёшься, *past* ~тёрся, ~тёрлась, *pf. of* тере́ться.

потерпе́|вший, *past part. act. of* ~ть; *as noun* п., ~вшего, *m.* victim; survivor; п. от пожа́ра fire victim; п. кораблекруше́ние ship-wrecked person, shipwreck survivor.

потерп|е́ть, лю́, ~ишь, *pf.* 1. to be patient (*for a while*). 2. to suffer, tolerate, stand (for); я не ~лю́ никако́й на́глости I won't stand for any cheek. 3. to suffer, undergo; п. кораблекруше́ние to be shipwrecked; п. пораже́ние to sustain a defeat, be defeated; п. убы́тки to suffer losses.

потёртост|ь, и, *f.* place sore from rubbing.

потёр|тый, *p.p.p. of* ~е́ть *and adj.* (*coll.*) 1. shabby, threadbare. 2. (*fig.*) washed-out.

потѐр|я, и, *f.* loss; waste; *pl.*; (*mil.*) losses; п. вре́мени waste of time; спи́сок ~ь (*mil.*) casualty list; ~и уби́тыми и ра́неными losses in killed and wounded.

потѐр|янный, *p.p.p. of* ~я́ть *and adj.* (*fig.*) lost; у неё был п. вид she had a lost expression; он — челове́к п. he is done for.

потѐря|ть(ся), ю(сь), *pf. of* теря́ть(ся).

потесн|и́ть, ю́, и́шь, *pf. of* тесни́ть.

потесн|и́ться, ю́сь, и́шься, *pf.* to make room; to sit closer, stand closer, move up (*so as to make room for others*).

потѐ|ть, ю, *impf.* 1. (*pf.* вс~) to sweat, perspire. 2. (*pf.* за~ *and* от~) to mist over, become covered with steam. 3. (*impf. only*) (над; *fig.*) to sweat (over), toil (over).

потѐха, и, *f.* (*coll.*) fun, amusement; устро́ить что-н. для ~и to do something for fun; вот п.! what fun!; и пошла́ п.! now the fun has begun!

потѐ|чь, ку́, чёшь, ку́т, *past* ~к, ~кла́, *pf.* to begin to flow.

потеша́|ть, ю, *impf.* to amuse.

потеша́|ться, юсь, *impf.* 1. to amuse oneself. 2. (над) to laugh (at), mock (at), make fun (of).

потѐш|ить, у, ишь, *pf.* 1. *pf. of* те́шить. 2. to amuse (for a while).

потѐш|иться, усь, ишься, *pf.* 1. *pf. of* тѐшиться. **2.** to amuse oneself (*for a while*), have a bit of fun.

потѐш|ный, *adj.* **1.** (~ен, ~на) (*coll.*) funny, amusing. **2.** (*obs.*) (done, contrived) for fun, for amusement; п. полк (*hist.*) 'poteshny' regiment, 'toy-soldiers' (*regiment of boy-soldiers formed by Peter the Great*). **3.** *as noun* (*pl.*) ~ные, ~ных = п. полк.

потѝр, а, *m.* (*eccl.*) chalice.

потирѐ|ть, ю, *impf.* to rub (*from time to time*); п. рѝки от рѐдости to rub one's hands with joy.

потихѐньку, *adv.* (*coll.*) **1.** slowly. **2.** softly, noiselessly. **3.** on the sly, secretly.

потлѝвост|ь, и, *f.* disposition to sweat, perspire.

потлѝв|ый (~, ~а), *adj.* sweaty; subject to sweating.

потнѝк, ѐ, *m.* sweat-cloth, saddle-cloth.

пѐт|ный (~ен, ~нѐ, ~но), *adj.* **1.** sweaty, damp with perspiration; ~ные рѝки clammy hands. **2.** (*of glass, etc.*) misty, covered with steam.

потов|ѐй, *adj.* of пот; ~ые жѐлезы sweat glands; п. жир wool yolk, suint.

потогѐнн|ый, *adj.*; ~ое (срѐдство) (*med.*) sudorific, diaphoretic; ~ая систѐма трудѐ sweated labour system.

потѐк, а, *m.* **1.** (*in var. senses*) stream; flow; гѐрный п. mountain stream; людскѐй п. stream of people; проходѝть нескончѐемым ~ом to file past in an endless stream; п. слов flow of words; скос ~а (*aeron.*) downwash; лить ~и слѐз to weep in floods; отдѐть на п. и разграблѐние (*hist.*) to give over to wholesale pillage. **2.** production line. **3.** (*in education*) stream, group.

потолкѐ|ться, юсь, *pf.* (*coll.*) to knock about.

потолк|овѐть, ѝю, (с+*i.*; *coll.*) to have a talk (with).

потол|ѐк, кѐ, *m.* ceiling (*also aeron.*); взять что-н. с ~кѐ (*joc.*) to make something up.

потолѐ|чный, *adj.* of ~к; (*fig., joc.*) chance, random; ~чные доказѐтельства unfounded arguments.

потолстѐ|ть, ю, *pf.* of толстѐть.

потѐм, *adv.* afterwards; later (on); then, after that; мы п. придѐм we shall come later; ну, что вы сдѐлали п.? well, what did you do then?

потѐм|ок, ка, *m.* descendant; scion; *pl.* offspring, progeny.

потѐмственный, *adj.* hereditary; он п. серѐбряных дел мѐстер he comes of a family of silversmiths.

потѐмств|о, а, *n.* (*collect.*) posterity, descendants.

потомѝ **1.** *adv.* that is why; я был в отпускѝ, п. я и не знал об ѐтом I was on leave,

that is why I did not know about it. **2.** *conj.* п. что; п. ... что because, as; я не знал об ѐтом, п. что был в отпускѝ I did not know about it because I was on leave; я п. не знал об ѐтом, что был в отпускѝ (*division of conj. alters emphasis*) the reason I did not know about it was that I was on leave.

потон|ѝть, ѝ, ~ешь, *pf.* of тонѝть.

потѐп, а, *m.* flood, deluge; всемѝрный п. (*bibl.*) the Flood, the Deluge; до ~а (*fig., joc.*) before the Flood.

потопѐ|ть, ю, *impf.* = тонѝть.

потоп|ѝть[1], лю, ~ишь, *pf.* to heat (*for a while*).

потоп|ѝть[2], лю, ~ишь, *pf.* (*of* ~лѝть) to sink.

потоплѐни|е, я, *n.* sinking.

потоп|тѐть, чѝ, ~чешь, *pf.* of топтѐть.

поторѐплива|ть, ю, *impf.* (*coll.*) to hurry up, urge on.

поторѐплива|ться, юсь, *impf.* (*coll.*) to hurry, make haste; ~йтесь! get a move on!

поторг|овѐться, ѝюсь, *pf.* (*coll.*) to bargain (*for a while*), haggle.

потороп|ѝть(ся), лю(сь), ~ишь(ся), *pf.* of торопѝть(ся).

потѐ|чный, *adj.* of ~к; ~чная ѝ ния production line; мѐссовое ~чное произвѐдство mass production.

потрѐв|а, ы, *f.* damage (*caused to crops by cattle*).

потрав|ѝть, лю, ~ишь, *pf.* of травѝть[1] 4.

потрѐ|тить(ся), чу(сь), тишь(ся), *pf.* of трѐтить(ся).

потрѐф|ить, лю, ишь, *pf.* (*of* ~лѝть) (+*d.* or на+*a.*; *coll.*) to please, satisfy; им не ~ишь there's no pleasing them.

потрафлѝ|ть, ю, *impf.* of потрѐфить.

потрѐб|а, ы, *f.* (*obs.*) need, want.

потребѝтел|ь, я, *m.* consumer, user.

потребѝтельн|ый, *adj.* consumption; ~ая стѐимость (*econ.*) use value.

потребѝтель|ский, *adj.* of ~; ~ская коoperѐция (*collect.*) consumers' co-operatives.

потреб|ѝть, лю, ѝшь, *pf.* of ~лѝть.

потреблѐни|е, я, *n.* consumption, use; товѐры широкого ~я consumer goods.

потреблѝ|ть, ю, *impf.* (*of* потребѝть) to consume, use.

потрѐбност|ь, и, *f.* need, want, necessity, requirement; жѝзненные ~и the necessities of life; физѝческая п. physical need; испѝтывать п. в чѐм-н. to feel a need for something; какѐя у вас п. в кнѝгах? what are your requirements for books?

потрѐб|ный (~ен, ~на), *adj.* necessary, required, requisite.

потрѐб|овать(ся), ѝю(сь), *pf.* of трѐбовать(ся).

потревѐж|ить(ся), у(сь), ишь(ся), *pf.* of тревѐжить(ся).

потрёп|анный, *p.p.p. of* ~а́ть *and adj.* **1.** shabby; ragged, tattered; ~анные брю́ки frayed trousers; ~анная кни́га a tattered book. **2.** battered. **3.** (*fig.*) worn, seedy.

потреп|а́ть(ся), лю́, ~лет(ся), *pf. of* трепа́ть(ся).

потре́ска|ться, ется, *pf. of* тре́скаться.

потре́скива|ть, ю, *impf.* to crackle.

потро́га|ть, ю, *pf.* to touch, run one's hand over (*to get the feel of something*); п. па́льцем to finger.

потрох|а́, о́в, *no sing.* pluck (*animal viscera*); жа́реные п. haslet(s); гуси́ные п. goose giblets; свины́е п. pig's fry; со все́ми ~а́ми (*fig., joc.*) lock, stock, and barrel.

потрош|и́ть, у́, и́шь, *impf.* (*of* вы~) to disembowel, clean; to draw (*fowl*).

потру|ди́ться, жу́сь, ~ди́шься, *pf.* **1.** to take some pains; to do some work. **2.** ~ди́сь, ~ди́тесь (+*inf.*) (*official or joc. injunction*) be so kind as (to); ~ди́тесь зайти́ ко мне за́втра be so kind as to call on me tomorrow; ~ди́сь, ~ди́тесь вы́йти! kindly leave the room!

потряса́|ющий, *pres. part. act. of* ~ть *and adj.* (*coll.*) staggering, stupendous, tremendous.

потряс|а́ть, а́ю, *impf. of* ~ти́.

потрясе́ни|е, я, *n.* shock.

потряс|ти́[1], у́, ёшь, *past* ~, ~ла́, *pf.* (*of* ~а́ть) **1.** to shake; to rock; п. во́здух кри́ками to rend the air with shouts; п. до основа́ния to rock to its foundations. **2.** (+*i.*) to brandish, shake; п. кулако́м to shake one's fist. **3.** (*fig.*) to shake; to stagger, stun.

потряс|ти́[2], у́, ёшь, *past* ~, ~ла́, *pf.* to shake (*a little, a few times*).

потря́хива|ть, ю, *impf.* (+*i.*) to shake (*a little, from time to time*); to jolt.

поту́г|а, и, *f.* **1.** muscular contraction; родовы́е ~и birth-pangs. **2.** (*fig.*) (*vain, unsuccessful*) attempt; ~и на остроу́мие attempts to be funny.

поту́п|ить, лю, ишь, *pf.* (*of* ~ля́ть) to lower, cast down; ~я взор with downcast eyes.

поту́п|и́ть, лю́, ~ишь, *pf.* to blunt.

поту́п|иться, люсь, ишься, *pf.* (*of* ~ля́ться) to look down, cast down one's eyes.

потупля́|ть(ся), ю(сь), *impf. of* поту́пить(ся).

по-туре́цки, *adv.* in Turkish; in the Turkish fashion; сиде́ть п. to sit cross-legged.

потускне́лый, *adj.* tarnished; (*fig.*) lacklustre.

потускне́|ть, ю, *pf. of* тускне́ть.

потусторо́нний, *adj.*; п. мир the other world.

потуха́ни|е, я, *n.* extinction.

потух|а́ть, а́ю, *impf. of* ~нуть.

поту́х|нуть, ну, нешь, *past* ~, ~ла, *pf.* (*of* ту́хнуть[1] *and* ~а́ть) to go out; (*fig.*) to die out.

поту́х|ший, *past part. act. of* ~нуть *and adj.* extinct; (*fig.*) lifeless, lack-lustre; п. вулка́н extinct volcano.

потучне́|ть, ю, *pf. of* тучне́ть.

потуш|и́ть[1], у́, ~ишь, *pf. of* туши́ть.

потуш|и́ть[2], у́, ~ишь, *pf.* to stew (*for a while*); to leave to stew.

по́тч|евать, ую, *impf.* (*of* по~) (+*i.*; *coll.*) to regale (with), treat (to), entertain (to).

потяга́|ться, юсь, *pf. of* тяга́ться.

потя́гивани|е, я, *n.* stretching oneself.

потя́гива|ть, ю, *impf.* (*coll.*) **1.** to pull (*a little*); to tug (at), give a tug; п. папиро́су to draw at a cigarette. **2.** to sip; to have a swig (of).

потя́гива|ться, юсь, *impf. of* потяну́ться.

потяго́т|а, ы, *f.* (*coll.*) = потя́гивание.

потя́н|уть, у́, ~ешь, *pf.* to begin to pull.

потя́н|у́ться, у́сь, ~ешься, *pf.* (*of* тяну́ться *and* потя́гиваться) to stretch oneself.

поу́жина|ть, ю, *pf. of* у́жинать.

поумне́|ть, ю, *pf. of* умне́ть.

поуро́чно, *adv.* **1.** by the piece. **2.** by the lesson.

поуро́чн|ый, *adj.* **1.** by the piece; ~ая опла́та piece-work payment. **2.** by the lesson.

поутру́, *adv.* (*coll.*) in the morning.

поуча́|ть, ю, *impf.* **1.** (*obs.*) to teach, instruct. **2.** (*coll., iron.*) to preach (at), lecture.

поуче́ни|е, я, *n.* (*lit.*) exhortation, homily; (*coll., iron.*) preaching; sermon, sermonizing.

поучи́тел|ьный (~ен, ~ьна), *adj.* instructive.

поуч|и́ть, у́, ~ишь, *pf.* **1.** to do a bit of teaching. **2.** (+*a. and d.*) to give a bit of instruction (in); to give a few tips (on).

поуч|и́ться, у́сь, ~ишься, *pf.* to study (*for a while*); to do a bit of studying.

пофа́рт|ить, и́т, *pf.* (*of* фарти́ть) (*impers.* +*d.*; *sl.*) to be lucky, be in luck; нам ~и́ло we were in luck.

пофор|си́ть, шу́, си́шь, *pf.* (+*i.*; *coll.*) to show off, parade.

поха́бник, а, *m.* (*coll.*) foul-mouthed person.

поха́бнича|ть, ю, *impf.* (*of* с~) (*coll.*) to use foul language, use obscenities.

поха́б|ный (~ен, ~на), *adj.* (*coll.*) obscene, bawdy, smutty.

поха́бщин|а, ы, *f.* (*coll.*) obscenity, bawdiness, smuttiness.

поха́жива|ть, ю, *impf.* (*coll.*) **1.** to pace; to stroll. **2.** to come, go (*from time to time*).

похвал|а́, ы́, *f.* praise; отозва́ться с ~о́й (о+*p.*) to praise, speak favourably (of).

похва́лива|ть, ю, *impf.* (*coll.*) to praise; to pay repeated tributes to.

похвал|и́ть(ся), ю́(сь), ~ишь(ся), *pf. of* хвали́ть(ся).

похвальб|а́, ы́, f. (coll.) bragging, boasting.

похва́л|ьный (~ен, ~ьна), adj. 1. praiseworthy, laudable, commendable. 2. laudatory; ~ьная гра́мота, п. лист (obs.) certificate of merit; (school) certificate of good conduct and progress; ~ьное сло́во eulogy, encomium, panegyric.

похваля́|ться, юсь, impf. (+i.; coll.) to boast (of, about), brag (about).

похва́рыва|ть, ю, impf. (coll.) to be frequently unwell, be subject to indisposition.

похва́ста|ть(ся), ю(сь), pf. of хва́стать(ся).

похе́р|ить, ю, ишь, pf. (coll.) to cross out, cancel.

похити́тел|ь, я, m. thief; kidnapper; abductor; hijacker.

похи́|тить, щу, тишь, pf. (of ~ща́ть) to steal; to kidnap; to abduct, carry off; to hijack.

похища́|ть, ю, impf. of похи́тить.

похище́ни|е, я, n. theft; kidnapping; abduction; hijacking.

похлёбк|а, и, f. soup, broth, skilly.

похло́па|ть, ю, pf. to slap, clap (a few times).

похлопо|та́ть, чу́, ~чешь, pf. of хлопота́ть.

похме́ль|е, я, n. hangover; 'the morning after the night before'; быть с ~я to have a hangover; в чужо́м пиру́ п. unpleasantness suffered through no fault of one's own.

похо́д¹, а, m. 1. march; (naut.) cruise; вы́ступить в п. to take the field, get on the march; в ~е (naut.) cruising, on cruise; на ~е on the march. 2. (mil.; fig.) campaign; кресто́вый п. crusade. 3. walking tour, hike.

похо́д², а, m. (coll.) overweight.

похода́тайств|овать, ую, pf. of хода́тайствовать.

похо|ди́ть¹, жу́, ~дишь, impf. (на+a.) to resemble, bear a resemblance (to), be like.

похо|ди́ть², жу́, ~дишь, pf. to walk (for a while).

похо́дк|а, и, f. gait, walk, step.

похо́д|ный, adj. of ~¹; п. го́спиталь field hospital; ~ное движе́ние march; ~ная жизнь camp life; ~ная коло́нна column of route; ~ная крова́ть camp-bed; ~ная ку́хня mobile kitchen, field kitchen; ~ная пе́сня marching song; п. поря́док marching order; ~ная ра́ция walkie-talkie set; ~ное снаряже́ние field kit; п. строй march formation; ~ная фо́рма marching order, field dress.

по́ходя, adv. (coll.) 1. as one goes along; on the march; мы е́ли п. we ate as we went along. 2. (fig.) in passing; in an offhand manner.

похожде́ни|е, я, n. adventure, escapade.

похо́ж|ий (~, ~а), adj. resembling, alike; (на+a.) like; он ~ на де́да he is like his grandfather; они́ о́чень ~и друг на дру́га they are very much alike; э́то на неё не ~e (fig.) that's not like her; э́то на Пе́тю ~e! just like Petya!, that's Petya all over!; он не ~ на самого́ себя́ he is not himself; э́то ни на что́ не ~e (fig., pejor.) it's like nothing on earth; it is unheard of. 2. (coll.) ~e it appears, it would appear; ~e на то, что... it looks as if . . .; он, ~e, бо́лен it would appear he is ill.

по-хозя́йски, adv. thriftily; израсхо́довать насле́дство п. to spend a legacy wisely.

похолода́ни|е, я, n. fall of temperature, cold spell, cold snap.

похолода́|ть, ет, pf. of холода́ть.

похолоде́|ть, ю, pf. of холоде́ть.

похолодне́|ть, ю, pf. of холодне́ть.

похорон|и́ть, ю́, ~ишь, pf. of хорони́ть.

похоро́нн|ый, adj. 1. funeral; ~ое бюро́ undertaker's, funeral parlour; п. звон (funeral) knell; п. марш dead march. 2. (fig., coll.) funereal.

по́хор|оны, о́н, она́м, no sing. funeral; burial.

по-хоро́шему, adv. in an amicable way.

похороше́|ть, ю, pf. of хороше́ть.

похотли́вост|ь, и, f. lustfulness, lewdness, lasciviousness.

похотли́в|ый (~, ~а), adj. lustful, lewd, lascivious.

похотни́к, а́, m. (anat.) clitoris.

по́хот|ь, и, f. lust.

похохо|та́ть, чу́, ~чешь, pf. to laugh (a little, for a while); to have a laugh.

похрабре́|ть, ю, pf. of храбре́ть.

похра́пыва|ть, ю, impf. (coll.) to snore (softly, gently).

похристо́с|оваться, уюсь, pf. of христо́соваться.

похуде́|ть, ю, pf. of худе́ть.

похул|и́ть, ю́, и́шь, pf. (obs.) to curse, abuse.

поцара́па|ть, ю, pf. to scratch slightly.

поцара́па|ться, юсь, pf. to get slightly scratched.

поца́рств|овать, ую, pf. to reign (for some time).

поцел|ова́ть(ся), у́ю(сь), pf. of целова́ть(ся).

поцелу́|й, я, m. kiss.

поцеремо́н|иться, юсь, ишься, pf. of церемо́ниться.

почасово́й, adj. by the hour.

поча́т|ок, ка, m. 1. (bot.) ear; spadix; п. кукуру́зы corn-cob. 2. (text.) cop.

поч|а́ть, ну́, нёшь, past ~а́л, ~ала́, ~а́ло, pf. (of ~ина́ть) (obs. or dial.) to begin.

по́чв|а, ы, f. 1. soil, ground, earth. 2. (fig.) ground, basis, footing; на ~е (+g.) owing (to), because (of); вы́бить ~у из-под чьих-н. ног to cut the ground from under someone's feet, take the wind out of someone's sails; зонди́ровать ~у to explore the ground; подгото́вить ~у to prepare the ground, pave the way; стоя́ть на твёрдой ~е, не теря́ть ~ы под нога́ми to be on firm ground; его́ утвержде́ния не име́ют под собо́й никако́й ~ы his assertions have no foundation.

пóчвенник, а, *m.* (*hist.*) member of 'back-to-the-soil' movement.

пóчвенничеств|о, а, *n.* (*hist.*) 'back-to-the-soil' movement.

пóчв|енный, *adj. of* ~a.

почвове́д, а, *m.* soil scientist.

почвове́дени|е, я, *n.* soil science.

почвоутомле́ни|е, я, *n.* (*agric.*) exhaustion of soil, soil depletion.

почём[1], *interrog. and relat. adv.* (*coll.*) how much; п. сего́дня я́блоки? how much are apples today?; узна́ть, п. фунт ли́ха (*coll.*) to fall upon hard times, plumb the depths of misfortune.

почём[2], *interrog. adv.* (*only used with parts of verb* знать; *coll.*) how?; п. знать? who knows?, who can tell?, how is one to know?; п. я зна́ю, кто ей э́то рассказа́л? how should I know who told her about it?

почему́ 1. *interrog. and relat. adv.* why; п. вы так ду́маете? why do you think that?; я зна́ю и́стинную причи́ну, п. он так ду́мает I know the real reason why he thinks that. **2.** *as conj.* (and) so; (and) that's why; она́ простуди́лась, п. и оста́лась до́ма she has caught a cold, (and) so she has stayed at home.

почему́-либо = почему́-нибудь.

почему́-нибудь, *adv.* for some reason or other.

почему́-то, *adv.* for some reason.

пóчерк, а, *m.* hand(writing).

почерне́лый, *adj.* darkened.

почерне́|ть, ю, *pf. of* черне́ть.

почерп|а́ть, а́ю, *impf. of* ~нуть.

почерп|ну́ть, ну́, нёшь, *pf.* (*of* ~а́ть) **1.** (+*a. or g.*) to draw. **2.** (*fig.*) to get; п. све́дения to glean, pick up information.

почерстве́|ть, ю, *pf. of* черстве́ть.

поче|са́ть(ся), шу́(сь), ~шешь(ся), *pf. of* чеса́ть(ся).

пóчест|ь, и, *f.* honour; возда́ть ~и, оказа́ть ~и (+*d.*) to do honour (to), render homage (to).

по|че́сть, чту́, чтёшь, *past* ~чёл, ~чла́, *pf.* (*of* ~чита́ть[1]) (*obs.*) to consider, think; он ~чёл свои́м до́лгом вы́ступить he considered it his duty to speak.

почёсыва|ть, ю, *impf.* (*coll.*) to scratch (*from time to time*).

почёт, а, *m.* honour; respect, esteem; быть в ~е у кого́-н., по́льзоваться ~ом у кого́-н.

to stand high in someone's esteem; to be highly thought of by someone; п. и уваже́ние! (*coll.*) my compliments!

почёт|ный, *adj.* **1.** honoured, respected, esteemed; п. гость guest of honour. **2.** honorary; ~ное зва́ние honorary title; п. член honorary member. **3.** (~ен, ~на) honourable; doing honour; п. карау́л guard of honour; ~ное ме́сто place of honour; п. мир honourable peace.

пóч|ечный[1], *adj. of* ~ка[1].

пóчечн|ый[2], *adj.* (*anat., med.*) nephritic; renal; ~ые ка́мни gall-stones; ~ая лоха́нка calix (of kidney).

почечу́|й, я, *m.* (*obs.*) piles.

почива́л|ьня, ьни, *g. pl.* ~ен, *f.* (*obs.*) bed-chamber.

почива́|ть, ю, *impf.* (*obs.*) **1.** to sleep. **2.** *impf. of* почи́ть.

почи́|вший, *past part. of* ~ть; *as noun* п., ~вшего, *m. and* ~вшая, ~вшей, *f.* the deceased.

почи́н, а, *m.* **1.** initiative; взять на себя́ п. to take the initiative; по со́бственному ~у on one's own initiative. **2.** beginning, start; (*comm.*) first sale of day.

почин|и́ть, ю́, ~ишь, *pf.* (*of* чини́ть[1] *and* ~я́ть) to repair, mend.

почи́нк|а, и, *f.* repairing, mending; отда́ть что́-н. в ~у to have something repaired, mended.

почи́н|ок, ка, *m.* (*dial.*) **1.** forest clearing. **2.** small *or* new settlement.

почин|я́ть, я́ю, *impf. of* ~и́ть.

почи́|стить(ся), щу(сь), стишь(ся), *pf. of* чи́стить(ся).

почита́й, *adv.* (*dial.*) **1.** almost; nigh on. **2.** it seems; very likely.

почита́ни|е, я, *n.* **1.** honouring; (+*g.*) respect (for). **2.** reverence, worship.

почита́тел|ь, я, *m.* admirer; worshipper.

почита́|ть[1], ю, *impf. of* поче́сть.

почита́|ть[2], ю, *impf.* **1.** to honour, respect, esteem. **2.** to revere.

почита́|ть[3], ю, *pf.* **1.** to read (a little, for a while). **2.** (*coll.*) to read.

почи́тыва|ть, ю, *impf.* (*coll.*) to read (now and then).

почи́|ть, ю, ешь, *pf.* (*of* ~ва́ть (*rhet.*) to rest, take one's rest; (*fig.*) to pass away, pass to one's rest; п. на ла́врах to rest on one's laurels.

почи́ще, *adv.* **1.** cleaner. **2.** (*fig., coll.*) better; stronger, more vividly; он вы́разился п. остальны́х he expressed himself more vividly than the others.

пóчк|а[1], и, *f.* **1.** (*bot.*) bud. **2.** (*bot., zool.*) gemma.

пóч|ка[2], ки, *f.* **1.** (*anat.*) kidney; воспале́ние ~ек nephritis. **2.** (*pl.*; *cul.*) kidneys.

почкова́ни|е, я, *n.* (*biol.*) budding; gemmation.

почк|ова́ться, у́ется, *impf.* (*biol.*) to bud; to gemmate.

по́чк|овый, *adj. of* ~а¹.

по́чт|а, ы, *f.* 1. post; возду́шная п. air mail; спе́шная п. special delivery, express delivery; посла́ть по ~е, ~ой to send by post, post; с у́тренней (с вече́рней) ~ой by the morning (evening) post; с обра́тной ~ой by return (of post). 2. (the) post, (the) mail; пришла́ ли п.? has the post come? 3. post office; рабо́тники ~ы postal workers.

почтальо́н, а, *m.* postman.

почта́мт, а, *m.* head post office (*of city or town*); гла́вный п. General Post Office.

почте́ни|е, я, *n.* respect, esteem; deference; относи́ться с ~ем (к) to treat with respect; с соверше́нным ~ем (*epistolary formula*) respectfully yours; моё п.! (*coll.*) my compliments!

почте́н|ный (~ен, ~на), *adj.* 1. honourable; respectable, estimable; venerable; ~ная рабо́та estimable work; п. во́зраст venerable age. 2. (*fig., coll.*) considerable, respectable; труд ~ных разме́ров a work of respectable dimensions.

почти́, *adv.* almost, nearly; п. ничего́ next to nothing; п. что = п.

почти́тельност|ь, и, *f.* respect, deference.

почти́тел|ьный (~ен, ~ьна), *adj.* 1. respectful, deferential. 2. (*fig., coll.*) considerable, respectable.

по|чти́ть, чту́, чти́шь, *pf.* to honour; п. чью-н. па́мять встава́нием to stand in someone's memory.

почтме́йстер, а, *m.* (*obs.*) postmaster.

почто́, *adv.* (*obs.*) why: what for.

почтови́к, а́, *m.* postal worker.

почто́во-телегра́фн|ый, *adj.* post and telegraph; ~ое учрежде́ние postal and telecommunications establishment.

почт|о́вый, *adj. of* ~а; ~о́вая бума́га note-paper; п. ваго́н mail-van; п. го́лубь carrier-pigeon, homing pigeon; п. и́ндекс post-code, Zip code; ~о́вая ка́рточка postcard; ~о́вая ма́рка (postage) stamp; ~о́вое отделе́ние post-office; п. перево́д postal order; п. по́езд mail train; ~о́вые расхо́ды postage; п. я́щик letter-box, pillar-box; е́хать на ~о́вых (*hist.*) to travel by post-chaise.

поч|ту́¹, тёшь, *see* ~е́сть.

поч|ту́², ти́шь, *see* ~ти́ть.

почу́вств|овать, ую, *pf. of* чу́вствовать.

почу́д|иться, ится, *pf. of* чу́диться.

почу́|ять, ю, *pf. of* чу́ять.

пошаба́ш|ить, у, ишь, *pf. of* шаба́шить.

поша́лива|ть, ю, *impf.* (*coll.*) 1. to be

naughty; to play up (*from time to time*) (*also fig.*); се́рдце у меня́ ~ет my heart plays me up, I have trouble with my heart (*from time to time*). 2. (*fig.*) to engage in robbery; в э́том райо́не ~ют your wallet isn't safe in these parts.

пошал|и́ть, ю́, и́шь, *pf.* to play pranks, get up to mischief (*for a while*).

поша́р|ить, ю, ишь, *pf. of* ша́рить.

пошатн|у́ть, у́, ёшь, *pf.* to shake (*also fig.*); п. чью-н. ве́ру to shake someone's faith; меня́ ~у́ло (*impers.*) I was shaken.

пошатн|у́ться, у́сь, ёшься, *pf.* 1. to shake; to totter, reel, stagger; он ~у́лся и упа́л he staggered and fell. 2. (*fig.*) to be shaken; её здоро́вье ~у́лось her health has cracked.

поша́тыва|ться, юсь, *impf.* to totter, reel, stagger.

пошеве́лива|ть, ю, *impf.* (*coll.*) to stir (*from time to time*).

пошеве́лива|ться, юсь, *impf.* (*coll.*) to stir, budge (*from time to time*); ну, ~йся! come on!, get a move on!

пошевел|и́ть(ся), ю́(сь), ~и́шь(ся), *pf. of* шевели́ть(ся).

пошевельн|у́ть(ся), у́(сь), ёшь(ся), *pf.* = пошевели́ть(ся).

по́шевн|и, ей, *no sing.* (*dial.*) (wide) sledge.

пош|ёл, ла́, *see* пойти́.

пошеп|та́ть, чу́, ~чешь, *pf.* to say in a whisper; to talk in whispers (*for a while*).

пошеп|та́ться, чу́сь, ~чешься, *pf.* (*coll.*) to converse in whispers.

пошехо́н|ец, ца, *m.* Gothamite; bumpkin (*from* Пошехо́нье, *place popularized by* Saltykov-Shchedrin *as symbol of backwardness*).

поши́б, а, *m.* (*coll.*) manners; ways.

поши́вк|а, и, *f.* sewing.

поши́вочн|ый, *adj.* sewing; ~ая мастерска́я (sewing) workshop.

пошле́|ть, ю, *impf.* (*of* о~) (*coll.*) to become commonplace, become vulgar.

по́шлин|а, ы, *f.* duty; customs; ввозна́я п., и́мпортная п. import duty; э́кспортная п. export duty; ге́рбовая п. stamp-duty; суде́бная п. costs, legal expenses; тамо́женная п. customs; обложи́ть ~ой to impose duty (on).

по́шлин|ный, *adj. of* ~а.

по́шлост|ь, и, *f.* 1. vulgarity, commonness. 2. triviality; triteness, banality; говори́ть ~и to utter banalities, talk commonplaces.

по́шл|ый (~, ~а́, ~о), *adj.* 1. vulgar, common; у него́ о́чень ~ые вку́сы he has very vulgar tastes. 2. commonplace, trivial; trite, banal; ~ая по́весть banal story.

пошля́к, а́, *m.* (*coll.*) vulgar person, common person.

пошля́тин|а, ы, *f.* (*coll.*) 1. vulgarity; vulgar action. 2. triviality; triteness, banality.

пошту́чно, *adv.* by the piece.

пошту́чн|ый, *adj.* by the piece; ~ая опла́та piecework payment.

пошум|е́ть, лю́, и́шь, *pf.* to make a bit of a noise.

пошу|ти́ть, чу́, ~ти́шь, *pf. of* шути́ть.

пощад|а, ы, *f.* mercy; без ~ы without mercy; не дать ~ы to give no quarter; проси́ть ~ы to ask for mercy, cry quarter.

поща|ди́ть, жу́, ди́шь, *pf. of* щади́ть.

пощеко|та́ть, чу́, ~чешь, *pf. of* щекота́ть.

пощёлкивани|е, я, *n.* clicking.

пощёлкива|ть, ю, *impf.* (+*i.*) to click; п. па́льцами to snap one's fingers.

пощёчин|а, ы, *f.* box on the ear; slap in the face (*also fig.*); дать ~у (+*d.*) to slap in the face.

пощип|а́ть, лю́, ~лешь, *pf.* 1. (+*a. or g.*) to nibble. 2. (*coll.*) to pull out, pull up. 3. (*fig., joc.*) to pinch (from), rob. 4. (*fig., joc.*) to pick holes in; to tear a strip off.

пощи́пыва|ть, ю, *impf.* (*coll.*) to pinch (*from time to time*).

пощу́па|ть, ю, *pf. of* щу́пать.

поэ́зи|я, и, *f.* poetry.

поэ́м|а, ы, *f.* poem (*usu. of large proportions, as opp. to* стихотворе́ние).

поэ́т, а, *m.* poet.

поэте́сс|а, ы, *f.* poetess.

поэтизи́р|овать, ую, *impf. and pf.* to poeticize, wax poetic (about).

поэ́тик|а, и, *f.* 1. poetics; theory of poetry. 2. poetic manner, poetic style; п. Пу́шкина Pushkin's (poetic) manner.

поэти́ческ|ий, *adj.* (*in var. senses*) poetic(al); ~ая во́льность poetic licence.

поэти́ч|ный (~ен, ~на), *adj.* (*fig.*) poetic(al).

поэ́тому, *adv.* therefore, and so.

по|ю́¹, ёшь, *see* петь.

по|ю́², и́шь, *see* пои́ть.

появ|и́ться, лю́сь, ~ишься, *pf.* (*of* ~ля́ться) to appear, make one's appearance; to show up; to heave in sight; луна́ ~и́лась из-за облако́в the moon emerged from behind the clouds.

появле́ни|е, я, *n.* appearance.

появля́|ться, юсь, *impf. of* появи́ться.

поя́рковый, *adj.* felt.

поя́р|ок, ка, *no pl.*, *m.* lamb's wool.

по́яс, а, *pl.* ~а́, ~о́в, *m.* 1. belt, girdle; waistband; спаса́тельный п. lifebelt; заткну́ть за́ п. (*coll.*) to outdo. 2. (*fig.*) waist; кла́няться в п. to bow from the waist; по п. up to the waist, waist-deep, waist-high. 3. (*pl.* ~ы́) (*geogr., econ.*) zone, belt; поля́рный п. frigid zone; тропи́ческий п. torrid zone.

поясне́ни|е, я, *n.* explanation, elucidation.

поясни́тельный, *adj.* explanatory, elucidatory.

поясн|и́ть, ю́, и́шь, *pf.* (*of* ~я́ть) to explain, elucidate.

поясни́ц|а, ы, *f.* waist, loins; small of the back; боль, простре́л в ~е lumbago.

поясни́чный, *adj.* (*anat.*) lumbar.

поясн|о́й, *adj.* 1. *adj. of* по́яс 1; п. реме́нь (waist-)belt. 2. to the waist, waist-high; ~а́я ва́нна hip-bath; п. покло́н bow from the waist; п. портре́т half-length portrait. 3. (*geogr., econ.*) zonal; ~о́е вре́мя zone time; п. тари́ф zonal tariff; ~о́е распреде́ление zoning.

поясн|я́ть, я́ю, *impf. of* ~и́ть.

прабаб|ка, ки, *f.* = ~ушка.

прабабушк|а, и, *f.* great-grandmother.

правд|а, ы, *f.* 1. truth; the truth; э́то и́стинная п. (*coll.*) it's the simple truth; су́щая п. the honest truth; э́то п. it is true, it is the truth; по ~е сказа́ть, ~у говоря́ to tell the truth, truth to tell; ва́ша п. you are right; что п., то п. there's no denying the truth; все́ми ~ами и непра́вдами by fair means or foul; п. глаза́ ко́лет (*prov.*) home truths are hard to swallow. 2. justice; иска́ть ~ы to seek justice. 3. (*hist.*) law, code of laws; Сали́ческая п. the Salic Law. 4. п.? is that so?, indeed?, really?; п. (ли)? is it so?, is it true?; п. ли, что он умира́ет? is it true that he is dying?; не п. ли? *in interrog. sentences indicates that affirmative answer is expected*; вы погаси́ли свет, не п. ли? you (did) put out the light, didn't you? 5. (*as concessive conj.*) true; п., я ему́ не написа́л, но я вот-во́т собира́лся позвони́ть true I had not written to him, but I was on the point of ringing.

правди́вост|ь, и, *f.* 1. truth; veracity. 2. truthfulness; uprightness.

правди́в|ый (~, ~а), *adj.* 1. true; veracious; п. расска́з true story. 2. truthful; upright; п. отве́т honest answer.

правди́ст, а, *m.* (*coll.*) person employed on production of newspaper 'Pravda'.

правдоподо́би|е, я, *n.* verisimilitude; probability, likelihood; plausibility.

правдоподо́б|ный (~ен, ~на), *adj.* probable, likely; plausible.

пра́ведник, а, *m.* righteous man; upright person, moral person; спать сном ~а to sleep the sleep of the just.

пра́ведн|ица, ицы, *f. of* ~ик.

пра́ведн|ый (~ен, ~на), *adj.* 1. righteous; upright. 2. just.

правёж, а́, *m.* (*hist.*) flogging (*of insolvent debtor*); поста́вить кого́-н. на п. to have someone flogged.

правѐ|ть, ю, *impf.* (*of* по~) (*polit.*) to become more conservative, swing to the right.

пра́вил|о, а, *n.* **1.** rule; regulation; грамматѝческие ~a grammatical rules; тройно́е п. (*math.*) the rule of three; ~a внутреннего распоря́дка the regulations (*of an establishment*); ~a у́личного движе́ния traffic regulations, highway code; как п. as a rule; по всем ~ам according to all the rules. **2.** rule, principle; взять за п. to make it a rule; взять себе́ за п. (+*inf.*) to make a point (of).

прави́л|о, а, *n.* **1.** (*tech.*) reversing rod, guide-bar; (*mil.*) traversing handspike. **2.** boot-tree. **3.** (*hunting*) tail, brush. **4.** (*obs.*) helm, rudder.

пра́вильно, *adv.* **1.** rightly; correctly; п. ли иду́т ва́ши часы́? is your watch right? **2.** regularly.

пра́вильност|ь, и, *f.* **1.** rightness; correctness. **2.** regularity.

пра́вил|ьный (~ен, ~ьна), *adj.* **1.** right, correct; п. отве́т the right answer; ~ьное реше́ние sound decision; ~ьная дробь proper fraction; ~ьно (*as pred.*) it is correct; ~ьно! that's right!, exactly!, just so! **2.** (*in var. senses*) regular; ~ьное движе́ние поездо́в regular train service(s); ~ьное соотноше́ние just proportion; ~ьное спряже́ние (*gram.*) regular conjugation; ~ьные черты́ лица́ regular features. **3.** (*math.*) rectilineal, rectilinear.

прави́л|ьный, *adj.* **1.** adj. of ~o. **2.** (*tech.*) correcting, levelling, straightening; ~ьная маши́на levelling machine.

прави́тел|ь, я, *m.* **1.** ruler. **2.** (*obs.*) manager, head; п. дел head clerk, first secretary.

прави́тельственн|ый, *adj.* governmental; government; ~ое реше́ние governmental decision; ~ое учрежде́ние government establishment.

прави́тельств|о, а, *n.* government.

пра́в|ить¹, лю, ишь, *impf.* (*no pf.*) (+*i.*) **1.** to rule (over), govern. **2.** to drive; п. маши́ной to drive a car; п. рулём to steer.

пра́в|ить², лю, ишь, *impf.* (*no pf.*) **1.** to correct; п. корректу́ру to read, correct proofs. **2.** to set (*metal tools*).

пра́вк|а, и, *f.* **1.** correcting; п. корректу́ры proof correcting, proof-reading. **2.** setting (*of metal tools*).

правле́н|ец, ца, *m.* (*coll.*) board member.

правле́ни|е, я, n. **1.** governing, government; о́браз ~я form of government. **2.** board (*of directors, of management, etc.*), governing body; быть чле́ном ~я to be on the board.

пра́вленый, *adj.* corrected; п. экземпля́р fair copy.

пра́внук, а, *m.* great-grandson.

пра́внучк|а, и, f. great-granddaughter.

пра́в|о¹, а, *pl.* ~á, *n.* **1.** law; гражда́нское п. civil law; обы́чное п. common law, customary law; уголо́вное п. criminal law; изучи́ть п. to study law, read for the law. **2.** right; (води́тельские) ~á driving licence; п. ве́то (right of) veto; п. го́лоса, избира́тельное п. the vote, suffrage; лиши́ть ~a го́лоса to disfranchise; ~á гражда́нства civic rights; п. да́вности (*leg.*) prescriptive right; п. убе́жища asylum, right of sanctuary; п. на насле́дство right of inheritance; по ~у by rights; с по́лным ~ом rightfully; быть в ~е (+*inf.*) to have the right (to), be entitled (to); воспо́льзоваться свои́м ~ом (на+a.) to exercise one's right (to); восстанови́ться в ~áх to be rehabilitated; вступи́ть в свои́ ~á to come into one's own; име́ть п. (на+a.) to have the right (to), be entitled (to).

пра́во², *adv.* (*coll.*) really, truly, indeed; я, п., не зна́ю, куда́ де́лась I really do not know where she has got to.

правобере́жный, *adj.* situated on the right bank, right-bank.

правове́д, а, *m.* **1.** lawyer, jurist. **2.** (*obs.*) student, graduate of law school.

правове́дени|е, я, n. (*obs.*) jurisprudence, science of law.

правове́рност|ь, и, f. orthodoxy.

правове́р|ный (~ен, ~на), *adj.* (*rel.*) **1.** orthodox. **2.** *as noun* п., ~ного, *m.* true believer (*esp. of Moslems*); ~ные the faithful.

правови́к, á, *m.* (*coll.*) jurist.

правов|о́й, *adj.* **1.** legal, of the law; п. контра́кт legal contract. **2.** lawful, rightful; ~ о́е госуда́рство (*polit.*) state functioning in accordance with (constitutional) law, *Rechtsstaat.*

правоме́р|ный (~ен, ~на), *adj.* lawful, rightful.

правомо́чи|е, я, n. competence.

правомо́ч|ный (~ен, ~на), *adj.* competent.

правонаруше́ни|е, я, n. infringement of the law, offence.

правонаруши́тел|ь, я, m. infringer of the law, offender, delinquent; ю́ный п. juvenile delinquent.

правописа́ни|е, я, n. spelling, orthography.

правопоря́д|ок, ка, m. law and order.

правосла́ви|е, я, n. (*rel.*) Orthodoxy.

правосла́вн|ый, *adj.* (*rel.*) orthodox; ~ая це́рковь Orthodox Church; *as noun* п., ~ого, *m. and* ~ая, ~ой, *f.* member of the Orthodox Church.

правоспосо́бност|ь, и, f. (*leg.*) (legal) capacity.

правоспосо́б|ный (~ен, ~на), *adj.* (*leg.*) capable.

правосу́ди|е, я, n. justice; отправля́ть п. to administer the law.

правот|а́, ы́, *f.* rightness; (*leg.*) innocence; доказа́ть свою́ ~у́ to prove one's case.

правофланго́вый, *adj.* right-flank, right--wing.

пра́в|ый¹, *adj.* **1.** right; right-hand; (*naut.*) starboard; п. борт starboard side; ~ая ло́шадь off(-side) horse; ~ая рука́ (*fig.*) right hand, right-hand man; ~ая сторона́ right side, off side. **2.** (*polit.*) right-wing, right; ~ая па́ртия party of the right.

пра́в|ый² (~, ~а́, ~о), *adj.* **1.** right, correct; вы не совсе́м ~ы you are not quite right. **2.** righteous, just; ~ое де́ло a just cause. **3.** (*leg.*) innocent, not guilty.

пра́в|ящий, *pres. part. act. of* ~ить *and adj.* ruling; ~ящая верху́шка ruling clique; ~ящие кла́ссы the ruling classes.

прагмати́зм, а, *m.* (*philos.*) pragmatism.

прагма́тик, а, *m.* (*philos.*) pragmatist.

прагмати́ческ|ий, *adj.* pragmatic; ~ая са́нкция (*hist.*) pragmatic sanction.

пра́дед, а, *m.* **1.** great-grandfather. **2.** (*pl.*) ancestors, forefathers.

прадéдовск|ий, *adj. of* пра́дед; ~ие времена́ ancestral times.

прадéдушк|а, и, *m. dim. of* пра́дед.

пра́зднеств|о, а, *n.* festival, solemnity; festivities.

пра́здник, а, *m.* **1.** (public) holiday; (religious) feast, festival; по ~ам on high days and holidays; с ~ом! compliments of the season; бу́дет и на на́шей у́лице п. (*fig.*) our day will come. **2.** festive occasion, occasion for celebration; по слу́чаю ~а to celebrate the occasion.

пра́здничн|ый, *adj.* holiday; festive; п. день red-letter day, holiday; п. наря́д holiday attire; ~ое настрое́ние festive mood.

празднова́ни|е, я, *n.* celebration.

пра́здн|овать, ую, *impf.* (*of* от~) to celebrate.

празднословие, я, *n.* idle talk, empty talk.

пра́здност|ь, и, *f.* **1.** idleness, inactivity. **2.** emptiness.

праздношата́ни|е, я, *n.* (*coll.*) idling, lounging.

пра́здн|ый (~ен, ~на), *adj.* **1.** idle, inactive; ~ная жизнь a life of idleness. **2.** idle, empty; ~ное любопы́тство idle curiosity; п. разгово́р empty talk. **3.** idle, vain, useless; ~ные попы́тки idle attempts.

пра́ктик, а, *m.* **1.** practical worker; он хоро́ший п., но слаб в теорети́ческих зна́ниях he is a good practical worker but his theoretical knowledge is weak. **2.** practical person.

пра́ктик|а, и, *f.* **1.** (*in var. senses*) practice; на ~е in practice; вам нужна́ ещё разгово́рная п. you need more conversational practice; у на́шего врача́ больша́я п. our doctor has a large practice. **2.** practical work.

практика́нт, а, *m.* probationer; student engaged in practical work.

практик|ова́ть, у́ю, *impf.* **1.** to practise, apply in practice. **2.** (*intrans.; of a doctor or lawyer*) to practise.

практик|ова́ться, у́юсь, *impf.* **1.** (*pf.* на~) (в+*p.*) to practise, have practice (in); п. в игре́ на скри́пке to practise the violin; п. в ру́сском языке́ to practise speaking Russian. **2.** *pass. of* ~ова́ть; э́тот приём бо́льше не ~у́ется this method is no longer used.

пра́ктикум, а, *m.* practical work.

практици́зм, а, *m.* **1.** practicalness; (*slightly pejor.*) savoir-faire. **2.** (*in polit. philosophy of Lenin, etc.*) over-emphasis of practice (*as opp. to theory*).

практи́ческ|ий, *adj.* (*in var. senses*) practical; ~ие заня́тия practical training; ~ая медици́на applied medicine; ~ая рабо́та practical work.

практи́чност|ь, и, *f.* practicalness; efficiency.

практи́ч|ный (~ен, ~на), *adj.* practical; efficient; п. челове́к practical person; п. спо́соб efficient method.

прама́тер|ь, и, *f.* (*rhet.*) the first mother; mother of the human race.

пра́от|ец, ца, *m.* forefather; отпра́виться к ~ца́м (*joc.*) to be gathered to one's forefathers.

пра́порщик, а, *m.* (*in tsarist army*) ensign.

прароди́тел|ь, я, *m.* primogenitor.

праславя́нский, *adj.* (*ling.*) Common Slavonic.

пра́сол, а, *m.* (*obs.*) cattle-dealer; fish- and meat-wholesaler.

прах, а, *no pl., m.* **1.** (*obs. or rhet.*) dust, earth; обрати́ть в п., пове́ргнуть в п. to reduce to dust, to ashes; отрясти́ п. с ног (*fig.*) to shake the dust from one's feet; пойти́ ~ом, рассы́паться ~ом to go to rack and ruin; п. и суета́ a hollow sham; разби́ть, разнести́ в пух и п., *see* пух. **2.** ashes, remains; здесь поко́ится п. (+*g.*) here lies; мир ~у его́ may he rest in peace. **3.** п. его́ возьми́! may he rot!

пра́чечн|ая, ой, *f.* laundry; wash-house.

пра́чк|а, и, *f.* laundress.

пращ|а́, и́, *g. pl.* ~е́й, *f.* sling (*weapon*).

пра́щур, а, *m.* ancestor, forefather.

праязы́к, а́, *m.* (*ling.*) parent language.

пре-¹ *adjectival prefix indicating superlative degree* very, most, exceedingly.

пре-² *verbal prefix indicating action in extreme degree or superior measure* sur-, over-, out- (*cf.* пере-).

преа́мбул|а, ы, *f.* preamble.

пребыва́ни|е, я, *n.* stay, sojourn; ме́сто постоя́нного ~я permanent residence, permanent address; п. в до́лжности, п. на посту́ tenure of office, period of office.

пребыва́|ть, ю, *impf.* **1.** to be; to abide, reside; п. в отсу́тствии to be absent. **2.** to be (*in a state of*); п. в неве́дении to be in the dark; п. в уны́нии to be in the dumps; п. у вла́сти to be in power.

превали́р|овать, ую, *impf.* to prevail.

превенти́вн|ый, *adj.* preventive; ~ая война́ preventive war.

превзо|йти́, йду́, йдёшь, *past* ~шёл, ~шла́, *pf.* (*of* превосходи́ть) (в+*p.* or +*i.*) to surpass (in); to excel (in); п. всех в мета́нии ди́ска to excel in discus-throwing; п. все ожида́ния to exceed expectations; п. самого́ себя́ to surpass oneself; п. чи́сленностью to outnumber.

превозмога́|ть, ю, *impf. of* превозмо́чь.

превозмо́|чь, гу́, ~жешь, ~гут, *past* ~г, ~гла́, *pf.* (*of* ~га́ть) to overcome, surmount.

превознес|ти́, у́, ёшь, *past* ~, ~ла́, *pf.* (*of* превозноси́ть) to extol.

превозно|си́ть, шу́, ~сишь, *impf. of* превознести́.

превозно|си́ться, шу́сь, ~сишься, *impf.* to put on airs, have a high opinion of oneself.

превосходи́тельный, *adj.* having the title of excellency.

превосходи́тельств|о а, *n.* (*as title*) Excellency.

превосхо|ди́ть, жу́, ~дишь, *impf. of* превзойти́.

превосхо́д|ный (~ен, ~на), *adj.* **1.** superlative; superb, outstanding. **2.** (*obs.*) superior; ~ные си́лы superior forces. **3.** ~ная сте́пень (*gram.*) superlative degree.

превосхо́дств|о, а, *n.* superiority; чи́сленное п. numerical superiority; я́вное п. marked superiority; п. в во́здухе (*mil.*) air superiority.

превосхо́д|ящий, *pres. part. of* ~йть and *adj.* superior.

превра|ти́ть, щу́, ти́шь, *pf.* (*of* ~ща́ть) (в+*a.*) to convert (into), turn (to, into), reduce (to); to transmute; п. я́рды в ме́тры to convert yards into metres; п. в ка́мень to turn to stone; п. в у́голь to carbonize; п. в шу́тку to turn into a joke.

превра|ти́ться, щу́сь, ти́шься, *pf.* (*of* ~ща́ться) (в+*a.*) to turn (into), change (into); п. в слух to be all ears.

превра́тно, *adv.* wrongly; п. истолкова́ть to misinterpret.

превра́тност|ь, и, *f.* **1.** wrongness, falsity. **2.** vicissitude; ~и судьбы́ vicissitudes of fate, reverses of fortune.

превра́т|ный (~ен, ~на), *adj.* **1.** wrong, false; у него́ бы́ло ~ное поня́тие о том, что произошло́ he had a false impression of what happened. **2.** changeful, incon-

stant, perverse; ~ная судьба́ perverse fate.

превраща́|ть(ся), ю(сь), *impf. of* преврати́ть(ся).

превраще́ни|е, я, *n.* transformation, conversion; transmutation; metamorphosis.

превы́|сить, шу, сишь, *pf.* (*of* ~ша́ть) to exceed; п. власть, п. полномо́чия to exceed one's authority; п. свой креди́т в ба́нке to overdraw (one's account).

превыша́|ть, ю, *impf. of* превы́сить.

превы́ше, *adv.* (*obs.*) far above; п. всего́ above all.

превыше́ни|е, я, *n.* exceeding, excess; п. вла́сти exceeding one's authority; п. своего́ креди́та в ба́нке overdrawing; зада́ние бы́ло вы́полнено с ~ем the task was accomplished and to spare.

прегра́д|а, ы, *f.* bar, barrier; obstacle.

прегра|ди́ть, жу́, ди́шь, *pf.* (*of* ~жда́ть) to bar, obstruct, block; п. путь кому́-н. to bar someone's way.

прегражда́|ть, ю, *impf. of* прегради́ть.

прегреш|а́ть, а́ю, *impf. of* ~и́ть.

прегреше́ни|е, я, *n.* sin, transgression.

прегреш|и́ть, у́, и́шь, *pf.* (*of* ~а́ть) (*obs.*) to sin, transgress.

пред, *prep.* = пе́ред.

пред-¹ *prefix* pre-, fore-, ante-.

пред-² *abbr., in compound formations, of* председа́тель.

преда|ва́ть(ся), ю(сь), ёшь(ся), *impf. of* преда́ть(ся).

преда́ни|е¹, я, *n.* legend; tradition.

преда́ни|е², я, n. handing over, committing; п. забве́нию burying in oblivion; п. земле́ committing to the earth; п. сме́рти putting to death; п. суду́ bringing to trial.

пре́данност|ь, и, *f.* devotion.

пре́дан|ный (~, ~на), *p.p.p. of* преда́ть and *adj.* (+*d.*) devoted (to); п. друг staunch friend, faithful friend; п. Вам (*epistolary formula*) yours faithfully, yours truly.

преда́тел|ь, я, *m.* traitor, betrayer; оказа́ться ~ем to turn traitor.

преда́тельниц|а, ы, *f.* traitress.

преда́тельск|ий, *adj.* traitorous, perfidious; treacherous (*also fig.*); ~ая пого́да treacherous weather; п. румя́нец telltale blush.

преда́тельств|о, а, *n.* treachery, betrayal, perfidy.

пре|да́ть, да́м, да́шь, да́ст, дади́м, дади́те, даду́т, *past* ~да́л, ~дала́, ~да́ло, *pf.* (*of* ~дава́ть) **1.** (+*d.*) to hand over (to), commit (to); п. гла́сности to make known, make public; п. забве́нию to bury in oblivion; п. земле́ to commit to the earth; п. огню́ to commit to the flames; п. огню́ и мечу́ to give over to fire and sword; п. суду́ to bring to trial. **2.** to betray.

пре|да́ться, да́мся, да́шься, да́стся, да-
ди́мся, дади́тесь, даду́тся, *past* ~да́лся,
~дала́сь, *pf.* (*of* ~дава́ться) (+*d.*) **1.** to
give oneself up (to); п. мечта́м to fall into
a reverie, lapse into day-dreams; п. отча́я-
нию to give way to despair; п. поро́кам
to indulge in vices; п. страстя́м to abandon
oneself to one's passions. **2.** (*obs.*) to entrust
oneself (to), put oneself in the hands (of);
п. врагу́ to go over to the enemy.

предба́нник, а, *m.* dressing-room (*in a bath-
-house*).

предваре́ни|е, я, *n.* **1.** (*obs.*) forewarning,
telling beforehand. **2.** forestalling; п. рав-
ноде́нствия (*astron.*) precession (of the
equinox); п. впу́ска па́ра (*tech.*) pre-admis-
sion of steam. **3.** (*tech.*) lead.

предвари́лк|а, и, *f.* (*coll.*) lock-up (*place of
detention before trial*).

предвари́тельно, *adv.* beforehand; as a preliminary; п. нагре́ть to pre-heat.

предвари́тельн|ый, *adj.* preliminary; prior;
~ое заключе́ние (*leg.*) imprisonment before trial; ~ая кома́нда (*mil.*) preparatory
command; п. нагре́в (*tech.*) pre-heating;
~ые перегово́ры preliminary talks, pour-
parlers; ~ая прода́жа биле́тов advance
sale of tickets, advance booking; ~ое
сле́дствие (*leg.*) preliminary investigation,
inquest; по ~ому соглаше́нию by prior
arrangement; ~ое усло́вие prior condition,
pre-requisite; п. экза́мен preliminary examination.

предвар|и́ть, ю́, и́шь, *pf.* (*of* ~я́ть) **1.** (*obs.*)
to forewarn, tell beforehand. **2.** to fore-
stall, anticipate.

предвар|я́ть, я́ю, *impf. of* ~и́ть.

предве́сти|е, я, *n.* presage, portent.

предве́стник, а, *m.* forerunner, precursor;
herald, harbinger; presage, portent.

предве́ч|ный (~ен), *adj.* (*theol.*; *epithet of
God*) everlasting; existing from before time.

предвеща́|ть, ю, *impf.* (*no pf.*) to betoken,
foretoken, foreshadow, herald, presage,
portend; ту́чи ~ли грозу́ the clouds be-
tokened a storm; э́то ~ет хоро́шее this
bodes well, this augurs well.

предвзя́тост|ь, и, *f.* preconception; preju-
dice, bias.

предвзя́т|ый (~, ~а), *adj.* preconceived;
prejudiced, biassed.

предви́дени|е, я, *n.* foresight, prevision;
foreseeing; foreknowledge.

предви́|деть, жу, дишь, *impf.* (*no pf.*) to
foresee.

предви́д|еться, ится, *impf.* (*no pf.*) to be
foreseen; to be expected.

предвку|си́ть, шу́, ~си́шь, *pf.* (*of* ~ша́ть)
to look forward (to), anticipate (with pleasure).

предвкуша́|ть, ю, *impf. of* предвкуси́ть.

предвкуше́ни|е, я, *n.* (pleasurable) antici-
pation.

предводи́тел|ь, я, *m.* leader; п. дворя́нства
(*hist.*) marshal of the nobility (*in tsarist
Russia: representative of nobility of province or
district, elected to manage their affairs and represent their interests in local government organs*).

предводи́тельств|о, а, *n.* **1.** leadership; под
~ом (+*g.*) under the leadership (of), under
the command (of). **2.** (*hist.*) office of marshal of the nobility.

предводи́тельств|овать, ую, *impf.* (+*i.*) to
lead, be the leader (of).

предводи́тельш|а, и, *f.* (*hist.*; *coll.*) wife of
marshal of the nobility.

предвое́нный, *adj.* **1.** preceding the out-
break of war. **2.** pre-war.

предвозве|сти́ть, щу́, сти́шь, *pf.* (*of* ~ща́ть)
to foretell.

предвозве́стник, а, *m.* herald; harbinger,
precursor.

предвозвеща́|ть, ю, *impf. of* предвозве-
сти́ть.

предвосхи́|тить, щу, тишь, *pf.* (*of* ~ща́ть)
to anticipate; п. пригово́р to anticipate the
verdict.

предвосхища́|ть, ю, *impf. of* предвосхи́тить.

предвосхище́ни|е, я, *n.* anticipation.

предвы́борн|ый, *adj.* (pre-)election; ~ая
кампа́ния election campaign; ~ое собра́-
ние (pre-)election meeting.

предго́р|ье, ья, *g. pl.* ~ий, *n.* foothills.

предгрозов|о́й, *adj.*; ~а́я мо́лния light-
ning before a storm.

предгро́зь|е, я, *n.* time before a storm (*also
fig.*).

преддве́ри|е, я, *n.* threshold (*also fig.*); в ~и
(+*g.*) on the threshold (of).

преде́л, а, *m.* (*in var. senses*) limit; bound,
boundary; end; (*pl.*) range; в ~ах (+*g.*)
within, within the limits (of), within the
bounds (of); за ~ами (+*g.*) outside, beyond
the bounds (of); в ~ах го́рода, городско́й
черты́ within the city, within the bounds of
the city; в ~ах досяга́емости within striking distance; в ~ах го́да within the year;
за ~ами страны́ outside the country;
вы́йти за ~ы го́рода to go outside the city
boundary; вы́йти за ~ы (+*g.*) to overstep
the limits (of), exceed the bounds (of); э́то
за ~ами мои́х сил it is beyond my power;
родны́е ~ы (*arch. or poet.*) one's native
borders; п. жела́ний summit, pinnacle ᴑ
(one's) desires; ~ы колеба́ния темпера-
ту́ры temperature range; п. насыще́ния
saturation point; п. про́чности (*tech.*)
breaking point; положи́ть п. (+*d.*) to put
an end (to), terminate.

преде́л|ьный, *adj.* **1.** *adj. of* ~; п. во́зраст

age-limit; ~ьная ли́ния boundary line; п. срок time-limit, deadline; п. у́гол critical angle. **2.** maximum; utmost; ~ное напряже́ние (*tech.*) breaking point, pressure limit; ~ьная ско́рость maximum speed; с ~ьной я́сностью with the utmost clarity. **3.** (*chem.*) saturated.

предержа́щ|ий, *only in phrase* вла́сти ~ие (*obs. or iron.*) the powers that be.

предзака́тный, *adj.* before sunset.

предзнаменова́ни|е, я, *n.* omen, augury.

предзнамен|ова́ть, у́ю, *impf.* to bode, augur, portend.

предика́т, а, *m.* (*philos. and gram.*) predicate.

предикати́вный, *adj.* (*gram.*) predicative; п. член predicate.

предика́ци|я, и, *f.* (*philos. and gram.*) predication.

предисло́ви|е, я, *n.* preface, foreword; без ~й without more ado; про́сим без ~й! don't beat about the bush!

предкры́л|ок, ка, *m.* (*aeron.*) stat.

предлага́|ть, ю, *impf. of* предложи́ть.

предло́г¹, а, *m.* pretext; под ~ом (+*g.*) on the pretext (of), on a plea (of); под разли́чными ~ами on various pretexts; п. для ссо́ры an excuse for a quarrel.

предло́г², а, *m.* (*gram.*) preposition.

предложе́ни|е¹, я, *n.* **1.** offer; proposition; proposal (of marriage); п. по́мощи offer of assistance; сде́лать п. кому́-н. to propose (marriage) to someone; приня́ть п. to accept an offer; to accept a proposal (of marriage). **2.** (*at meeting, etc.*) proposal, motion; suggestion; внести́ п. to introduce a motion; отклони́ть п. to turn down a proposal. **3.** (*econ.*) supply; зако́н спро́са и ~я law of supply and demand.

предложе́ни|е², я, *n.* **1.** (*gram.*) sentence; гла́вное п. main clause; прида́точное п. subordinate clause; усло́вное п. conditional sentence; вво́дное п. parenthesis, parenthetic clause. **2.** (*philos.*) proposition.

предлож|и́ть, у́, ~ишь, *pf.* (*of* предлага́ть) **1.** to offer; п. свои́ услу́ги to offer one's services, come forward; п. ру́ку (и се́рдце) кому́-н. (*obs.*) to make a proposal of marriage to someone. **2.** to propose; to suggest; п. резолю́цию to move a resolution; п. тост to propose a toast; п. чью-н. кандидату́ру to propose someone for election; п. кого́-н. в председа́тели to propose someone for chairman; п. внима́нию to call attention (to); мы ~или ей обрати́ться к врачу́ we suggested that she should see a doctor; они́ ~или нам вме́сте с ни́ми пое́хать на бе́рег мо́ря they have invited us to go with them to the sea-side *or* they have suggested that we might go with them to the sea-side. **3.** to put, set, propound; п. вопро́с to put

a question; п. зада́чу to set a problem; п. но́вую тео́рию to propound a new theory. **4.** to order, require; им ~и́ли освободи́ть кварти́ру they have been ordered to vacate their apartment.

предло́жный, *adj.* (*gram.*) prepositional; п. паде́ж prepositional case.

предма́йский, *adj.* pre-May Day (*taking place in the period immediately preceding May Day*).

предме́ст|ье, ья, *g. pl.* ~ий, *n.* suburb.

предме́т, а, *m.* **1.** object; article, item; (*pl.*) goods; ~ы дома́шнего обихо́да household goods, domestic utensils; ~ы пе́рвой необходи́мости necessities; ~ы широ́кого потребле́ния consumer goods. **2.** subject, topic, theme; (+*g.*) object (of); п. насме́шек object of ridicule, butt; п. спо́ра point at issue; п. (любви́) (*obs.*) object of one's affections; како́й п. ва́шего иссле́дования? what is the subject of your research? **3.** (*school*) subject; она́ сдала́ экза́мен по пяти́ ~ам she passed the examination in five subjects. **4.** ме́стный п. (*mil.*) (ground) feature. **5.** object (= *purpose*); на п. (+*g.*) with the object (of); на сей п. (*official or joc.*) to this end, with this object; име́ть в ~е (*obs.*) to have in view.

предме́тник, а, *m.* (*teachers' sl.*) specialist.

предме́т|ный, *adj. of* ~; п. уро́к object-lesson; п. катало́г subject catalogue; п. указа́тель subject index; п. сто́лик stage (*of microscope*).

предмо́стн|ый, *adj.*; п. плацда́рм, ~ое укрепле́ние bridge-head.

предназнача́|ть, а́ю, *impf. of* ~ить.

предназначе́ни|е, я, *n.* **1.** earmarking. **2.** (*obs.*) destiny.

предназна́ч|ить, у, ишь, *pf.* (*of* ~а́ть) (для, *or* на+*a.*) to destine (for), intend (for), mean (for); to earmark (for), set aside (for); бо́мбу ~или для импера́тора the bomb was intended for the emperor; мы ~или э́ти де́ньги на поку́пку автомоби́ля we set aside this money to buy a car.

преднаме́ренно, *adv.* by design, deliberately.

преднаме́ренност|ь, и, *f.* premeditation.

преднаме́рен|ный (~, ~на), *adj.* premeditated; aforethought; deliberate.

предначерта́ни|е, я, *n.* outline, plan, design; п. судьбы́ predestination.

предначе́рт|анный, p.p.p. of ~а́ть; п. судьбо́й predestined.

предначерта́|ть, ю, *pf.* to plan beforehand; to foreordain.

предо = пред.

предобе́денный, *adj.* before-dinner, preprandial.

пре́д|ок, ка, *m.* forefather, ancestor; (*pl.*) forbears.

предоктя́брьский, *adj.* pre-October (*taking place during the period immediately preceding the Russian Revolution of October 1917 or its anniversary*).

предоперацио́нный, *adj.* (*med.*) pre-operative.

предопределе́ни|е, я, *n.* 1. pre-determining. 2. predestination.

предопредел|и́ть, ю́, и́шь, *pf.* (*of* ~я́ть) to pre-determine; to predestine, foreordain.

предопредел|я́ть, я́ю, *impf. of* ~и́ть.

предоста́в|ить, лю, ишь, *pf.* (*of* ~ля́ть) 1. to let; to leave; нам ~или сами́м реши́ть де́ло the decision was left to us, we were left to decide the matter for ourselves; п. кого́-н. самому́ себе́ to leave someone to his own devices, to his own resources. 2. to give, grant; п. креди́т to give credit; п. пра́во to concede a right; п. возмо́жность to afford an opportunity, give a chance; п. кому́-н. сло́во to let someone have the floor, call upon someone to speak; они́ ~или ко́мнату в на́ше распоряже́ние they have put a room at our disposal.

предоставля́|ть, ю, *impf. of* предоста́вить; ~ю сло́во това́рищу X (*formula of chairman introducing speaker at meeting*) I call upon Comrade X to speak.

предостерега́|ть, ю, *impf. of* предостере́чь.

предостереже́ни|е, я, *n.* warning, caution.

предостере́|чь, гу́, жёшь, гу́т, *past* ~г, ~гла́, *pf.* (*of* ~га́ть) (от) to warn (against), caution (against), put on one's guard (against).

предосторо́жност|ь, и, *f.* 1. (*no pl.*) caution; ме́ры ~и precautionary measures, precautions. 2. precaution.

предосуди́тельност|ь, и, *f.* reprehensibility, blameworthiness.

предосуди́тел|ьный (~ен, ~ьна), *adj.* wrong, reprehensible, blameworthy.

предотвра|ти́ть, щу́, ти́шь, *pf.* (*of* ~ща́ть) to prevent, avert; to stave off; п. войну́ to avert a war; п. опа́сность to stave off danger.

предотвраща́|ть, ю, *impf. of* предотврати́ть.

предотвраще́ни|е, я, *n.* prevention, averting; staving off.

предохране́ни|е, я, *n.* (от) protection (against), preservation (from).

предохрани́тел|ь, я, *m.* guard, safety device; safety catch; (пла́вкий) п. (*electr.*) safety fuse, cut-out; п. от обледене́ния (*aeron.*) de-icer.

предохрани́тельн|ый, *adj.* 1. preservative; preventive; ~ые ме́ры precautionary measures, precautions; ~ая приви́вка preventive inoculation. 2. (*tech.*) safety; protective; п. кла́пан safety-valve; ~ая коро́бка fuse box; ~ые очки́ safety goggles; ~ая

плита́ (*radio*) baffle plate; п. штепсель fuse; п. щит guard shield, fender.

предохран|и́ть, ю́, и́шь, *pf.* (*of* ~я́ть) (от) to preserve, protect (from, against).

предохран|я́ть, я́ю, *impf. of* ~и́ть.

предписа́ни|е, я, *n.* order, injunction; (*pl.*) directions, instructions; (*med., etc.*) prescription; п. суда́ court order; согла́сно ~ю by order.

предпи|са́ть, шу́, ~шешь, *pf.* (*of* ~сывать) 1. (+*inf.*) to order, direct, instruct (to). 2. to prescribe (*a cure, a diet, etc.*); врач ~са́л ей курс инъе́кций the doctor prescribed for her, put her on a course of injections.

предпи́сыва|ть, ю, *impf. of* предписа́ть.

предпле́ч|ье, ья, *g. pl.* ~ий, *n.* (*anat.*) forearm.

предплу́жник, а, *m.* (*agric.*) coulter.

предплюс|на́, ны́, *pl.* ~ны, ~ен, *f.* (*anat.*) tarsus.

предполага́емый, *pres. part. pass. of* предполага́ть *and adj.* proposed.

предполага́|ть, ю, *impf.* 1. *impf. of* предположи́ть. 2. (*impf. only*) to intend, propose; to contemplate; мы ~ем оста́вить дете́й у ба́бушки we propose to leave the children at their grandmother's; он как бу́дто ~ет жени́ться apparently he is contemplating marrying. 3. (*impf. only*) to presuppose; успе́х в э́том де́ле ~ет хоро́шую пого́ду the success of this business presupposes good weather.

предполага́|ться, ется, *impf.* 1. *pass. of* ~ть. 2. ~ется (*impers.*) it is proposed, it is intended; ~ется проложи́ть отсю́да автостра́ду it is proposed to build a motorway from here.

предположе́ни|е, я, *n.* 1. supposition, assumption. 2. intention; у меня́ п. жени́ться I am thinking of marrying.

предположи́тельно, *adv.* 1. supposedly, presumably. 2. (*in parenthesis*) probably; мы прие́дем в Ло́ндон, п., к десяти́ часа́м we shall be in London probably by ten o'clock.

предположи́тельн|ый, *adj.* conjectural; hypothetical; estimated; э́то ещё лишь ~о this is still only hypothetical.

предполож|и́ть, у́, ~ишь, *pf.* (*of* предполага́ть) to suppose, assume; to conjecture, surmise; ~им, что он опозда́л на по́езд (let us) suppose he missed the train.

предпо́л|ье, я, *n.* (*mil.*) forward defensive positions.

предполя́рный, *adj.* sub-arctic.

предпо|сла́ть, шлю́, шлёшь, *pf.* (*of* ~сыла́ть) (+*d. and a.*) to preface (with); дире́ктор шко́лы ~сла́л вы́говору не́скольк общих замеча́ний the headmaster prefaced the ticking-off with a few general remarks

предпоследн|ий, *adj.* penultimate, last but one, next to last; one from the bottom (*on list*); Ваше ~ее письмо your last letter but one; п. слог penultimate syllable.

предпосыла|ть, ю, *impf. of* предпослать.

предпосы́лк|а, и, *f.* 1. pre-requisite, pre--condition. 2. (*philos.*) premise.

предпоч|есть, ту́, тёшь, *past* ~ёл, ~ла́, *pf.* (*of* ~ита́ть) to prefer; п. говя́дину бара́нине to prefer beef to mutton; я ~ёл бы идти́ пешко́м I would rather walk, go on foot.

предпочита́|ть, ю, *impf. of* предпоче́сть.

предпочте́ни|е, я, *n.* preference; predilection; оказа́ть п., отда́ть п. (+*d.*) to show a preference (for), give preference.

предпочти́тельно, *adv.* 1. rather, preferably. 2. (пе́ред; *obs.*) in preference (to).

предпочти́тел|ьный (~ен, ~ьна), *adj.* preferable.

предпра́здничн|ый, *adj.* holiday (*taking place in the period immediately preceding a holiday*); ~ое настрое́ние holiday mood; ~ая суета́ holiday rush.

предприи́мчивост|ь, и, *f.* enterprise.

предприи́мчив|ый (~, ~а), *adj.* enterprising.

предпринима́тел|ь, я, *m.* owner (of a firm *or* business); employer; entrepreneur.

предпринима́тель|ский, *adj. of* ~.

предпринима́тельств|о, а, *no pl.*, *n.* (private) business undertakings; свобо́дное п. free enterprise.

предпринима́|ть, ю, *impf. of* предприня́ть.

предпри|ня́ть, му́, ~мешь, *past* ~ня́л, ~няла́, ~ня́ло, *pf.* (*of* ~нима́ть) to undertake; (*mil.*, *etc.*) to launch; п. ата́ку to launch an attack; п. шаги́ to take steps.

предприя́ти|е, я, *n.* 1. undertaking, enterprise; business; риско́ванное п. risky undertaking, venture. 2. (*econ.*) enterprise, concern, business; works; ме́лкое п. small business; фабри́чно-заводско́е п. (industrial) works.

предрасполага́|ть, ю, *impf. of* предрасположи́ть.

предрасположе́ни|е, я, *n.* (к) predisposition (to); (*med.*) diathesis.

предрасполо́ж|енный, *p.p.p. of* ~и́ть; (к) predisposed (to).

предрасполож|и́ть, у́, ~ишь, *pf.* (*of* предрасполага́ть) (к) to predispose (to).

предрассве́тн|ый, *adj.* occurring before dawn; ~ая мгла early morning mist; ~ые су́мерки false dawn; п. хо́лод the chill of approaching dawn.

предрассу́д|ок, ка, *m.* prejudice; закосне́лый в ~ках steeped in prejudice.

предрека́|ть, ю, *impf. of* предре́чь.

предре́|чь, ку́, чёшь, ку́т, *past* ~к, ~кла́, *pf.* (*of* ~ка́ть) (*obs.*) to foretell.

предреш|а́ть, а́ю, *impf. of* ~и́ть.

предреш|и́ть, у́, и́шь, *pf.* (*of* ~а́ть) 1. to decide beforehand. 2. to pre-determine.

председа́тел|ь, я, *m.* chairman; president.

председа́тель|ский, *adj. of* ~; ~ское ме́сто the chair (*at a meeting*); заня́ть ~ское ме́сто to take the chair.

председа́тельств|о, а, *n.* chairmanship; presidency.

председа́тельств|овать, ую, *impf.* to be in the chair, preside.

председа́тельств|ующий, *pres. part. act. of* ~овать; *as noun* п., ~ующего, *m.* chairman.

предсе́рди|е, я, *n.* (*anat.*) auricle.

предсказа́ни|е, я, *n.* prediction; forecast, prophecy; prognostication.

предсказа́тел|ь, я, *m.* foreteller, forecaster; soothsayer.

предска|за́ть, жу́, ~жешь, *pf.* (*of* ~зывать) to foretell, predict; to forecast, prophesy; to prognosticate.

предска́зыва|ть, ю, *impf. of* предсказа́ть.

предсме́ртн|ый, *adj.* occurring before death; ~ое жела́ние dying wish; ~ые страда́ния death-agony; п. час one's last hour.

предста|ва́ть, ю́, ёшь, *impf. of* ~ть.

представи́тел|ь, я, *m.* 1. representative; (+*g.*) spokesman (for); полномо́чный п. plenipotentiary. 2. (*bot.*, *etc.*) specimen.

представи́тельност|ь, и, *f.* imposingness; imposing appearance, presence.

представи́тельный¹, *adj.* (*polit.*, *leg.*) representative.

представи́тел|ьный² (~ен, ~ьна), *adj.* imposing.

представи́тельств|о, а, *n.* 1. representation, representing. 2. (*collect.*) representation, representatives; дипломати́ческое п. diplomatic representatives; торго́вое п. trade delegates. 3. (*polit.*, *leg.*) election of, sending of representatives (*to organs of government*).

предста́в|ить, лю, ишь, *pf.* (*of* ~ля́ть) 1. to present; п. тру́дности to offer difficulty; п. интере́с to be of interest, have interest. 2. to produce, submit; п. доказа́тельства to produce evidence; п. спи́сок чле́нов ассоциа́ции to submit a list of members of an association. 3. (+*a. and d.*) to introduce (to), present (to). 4. (к) to recommend (for), put forward (for); п. кого́-н. к о́рдену to recommend someone for a decoration. 5. п. себе́ to imagine, fancy, picture, conceive; ~ь(те) себе́, кака́я э́то была́ доса́да! (just) imagine what a nuisance that was! 6. to represent, display; п. что́-то в смешно́м ви́де to hold something up to ridicule. 7. (*theatr.*) to perform; to play.

предста́в|иться, люсь, ишься, *pf.* (*of* ~ля́ться) 1. to present itself, occur, arise; на́шим глаза́м ~ила́сь мра́чная карти́на a gloomy picture rose before our eyes; ~и́лся слу́чай пое́хать в Москву́ a chance arose to go to Moscow; я им сообщу́, как то́лько ~и́тся возмо́жность I will inform them as soon as an opportunity arises. **2.** (*impers.* +*d.*) to seem (to); э́то тебе́ то́лько ~и́лось you only imagined it, it was just your imagination. **3.** (+*d.*) to introduce oneself (to). **4.** (+*i.*) to pretend (to be), pass oneself off (as); п. больны́м to feign sickness.

представле́ни|**е, я,** *n.* **1.** presentation; п. но́вого сотру́дника introduction of a new colleague; п. про́пуска presentation of a permit. **2.** (written) declaration, statement; representation; ~я бы́ли сде́ланы всем прави́тельствам representations have been made to all the governments. **3.** (*theatr.*) performance. **4.** (*psych.*) representation. **5.** idea, notion, conception; дать п. (о+*p.*) to give an idea (of); я не име́ю ни мале́йшего ~я I have not the faintest idea, remotest conception.

представля́|**ть, ю,** *impf.* **1.** *impf. of* предста́вить. **2.** (*impf. only*) to represent; он ~ет США в ООН he represents the U.S.A. in UNO. **3.** п. собо́й to represent, be; to constitute; э́то ~ет собо́й исключе́ние this constitutes an exception.

представля́|**ться, юсь,** *impf. of* предста́виться.

представа́тел|**ь, я,** *m.* (*obs.*) protector; champion.

представа́тельн|**ый,** *adj.* ~ая железа́ (*anat.*) prostate (gland).

предста́|**ть, ну, нешь,** *pf.* (*of* ~ва́ть) (пе́ред) to appear (before); п. пе́ред судо́м to appear in court.

предсто|**я́ть, и́т,** *impf.* to be in prospect, lie ahead, be at hand; to be in store; ~я́ла суро́вая зима́ a hard winter lay ahead; нам ~и́т мно́го неприя́тностей we are in for a lot of trouble, there is a lot of trouble in store for us; ему́ ~и́т предста́вить диссерта́цию к пе́рвому ию́ня he has to submit his dissertation by the first of June.

предстоя́|**щий,** *pres. part. of* ~ть *and adj.* coming, forthcoming; impending, imminent; ~щие вы́боры the forthcoming elections; она́ страши́лась ~щего меди́цинского осмо́тра she was dreading the impending medical (examination).

предте́ч|**а, и,** *m. and f.* forerunner, precursor; Иоа́нн п. John the Baptist.

предубе|**ди́ть, ди́шь,** *pf.* (*of* ~жда́ть) (*obs.*) to prejudice, bias.

предубежда́|**ть, ю,** *impf. of* предубеди́ть.

предубежде́ни|**е, я,** *n.* prejudice, bias.

предубе|**жде́нный,** *p.p.p. of* ~ди́ть (*obs.*) *and adj.* prejudiced, biased.

предуведо́м|**ить, лю, ишь,** *pf.* (*of* ~ля́ть) to inform beforehand, give advance notice; to warn, forewarn; вам сле́довало п. их о ва́шем прие́зде you should have warned them that you were coming.

предуведомле́ни|**е, я,** *n.* warning, forewarning; notice in advance.

предуведомля́|**ть, ю,** *impf. of* предуведо́мить.

предугад|**а́ть, а́ю,** *pf.* (*of* ~ывать) to guess (in advance).

предуга́дыва|**ть, ю,** *impf. of* предугада́ть.

предуда́рный, *adj.* (*ling.*) pre-tonic.

предумы́шленность|**ь, и,** *f.* premeditation.

предумы́шленный, *adj.* premeditated, aforethought.

предупреди́тельность|**ь, и,** *f.* courtesy; attentiveness.

предупреди́тел|**ьный,** *adj.* **1.** preventive, precautionary. **2.** (~ен, ~ьна) courteous; attentive; obliging.

предупре|**ди́ть, жу́, ди́шь,** *pf.* (*of* ~жда́ть) **1.** (о+*p.*) to let know beforehand (about), notify in advance (about), warn (about); to give notice (of, about); надлежи́т п. экскурсово́да о жела́нии посети́ть за́мок notice is to be given to the guide if it is wished to visit the castle; п. за неде́лю об увольне́нии to give a week's notice (*of dismissal*). **2.** to prevent, avert; п. ава́рию to prevent an accident. **3.** to anticipate; to forestall; п. замеча́ние to anticipate a remark; я как раз э́то хоте́л сказа́ть, но вы ~ди́ли меня́ that is just what I was about to say, but you took the words out of my mouth.

предупрежда́|**ть, ю,** *impf. of* предупреди́ть.

предупрежде́ни|**е, я,** *n.* **1.** notice; notification. **2.** prevention. **3.** anticipating; forestalling. **4.** warning; получи́ть вы́говор с ~ем (*leg.*) to be dismissed with a caution.

предусма́трива|**ть, ю,** *impf. of* предусмотре́ть.

предусмотр|**е́ть, ю́, ~ишь,** *pf.* (*of* предусма́тривать) to envisage, foresee; to stipulate (for), provide (for), make provision (for); п. все возмо́жности to provide for every eventuality.

предусмотри́тельность|**ь, и,** *f.* foresight, prudence.

предусмотри́тел|**ьный** (~ен, ~ьна), *adj.* prudent; provident; far-sighted; ~ьная поли́тика far-sighted policy.

предустано́вленный, *adj.* (*obs.*) pre-established, pre-determined.

преду́тренний, *adj.* occurring immediately before morning; п. час the hour before dawn.

предчу́встви|**е, я,** *n.* presentiment; foreboding, misgiving, premonition.

предчу́вств|овать, ую, *impf.* to have a presentiment (of, about), have a premonition (of, about); я ~овал, что вы сего́дня поя́витесь I had a feeling that you would turn up today.

предше́ственник, а, *m.* predecessor; forerunner, precursor.

предше́ств|овать, ую, *impf.* (+*d.*) to go in front (of); to precede; её сме́рти ~овала дли́тельная боле́знь her death was preceded by a long illness.

предше́ств|ующий, *pres. part. act. of* ~овать *and adj.* previous; foregoing; *as noun* ~ующее, ~ующего, *n.* the foregoing.

предъяви́тел|ь, я, *m.* bearer; п. и́ска plaintiff, claimant; чек на ~я cheque payable to bearer.

предъяв|и́ть, лю́, ~ишь, *pf.* (*of* ~ля́ть) **1.** to show, produce, present; п. биле́т to show one's ticket; п. доказа́тельства to produce evidence, present proofs. **2.** (*leg., etc.*) to bring (forward); п. иск (к) to bring a suit (against); п. обвине́ние (+*d.* в+*p.*) to charge (with), bring an accusation (against of); ему́ ~и́ли обвине́ние в поджо́ге he is charged with arson; п. пра́во (на+*a.*) to lay claim (to), raise a claim (to); п. тре́бование (к) to lay claim (to); п. высо́кие тре́бования (к) to make big demands (of, on).

предъявле́ни|е, я, n. **1.** showing, producing, presentation; вход разреша́ется по ~и удостовере́ния ли́чности entry is permitted on presentation of identity card. **2.** (*leg., etc.*) bringing; п. и́ска bringing of a suit; п. обвине́ния (в+*p.*) accusation (of), charge (of); п. пра́ва assertion of a claim.

предъявля́|ть, ю, *impf. of* предъяви́ть.

предыду́щ|ий, *adj.* previous, preceding; *as noun* ~ее, ~его, *n.* the foregoing; из ~его сле́дует from the foregoing it follows.

предыстори́ческий, *adj.* prehistoric.

предысто́ри|я, и, f. prehistory.

прее́мник, а, *m.* successor.

прее́мственност|ь, и, f. succession; continuity.

прее́мствен|ный (~, ~на), *adj.* successive.

прее́мств|о, а, n. succession.

пре́жде **1.** *adv.* (*opp. to* пото́м) before; first; п. чем *as conj.* before; на́до бы́ло ду́мать об э́том п. you should have thought about it before; ты до́лжен дое́сть ка́шу, п. чем взять ды́ню you must eat up your kasha before you have any melon. **2.** *adv.* (*opp. to* тепе́рь) formerly, in former times; before; п. он учи́л в интерна́те he taught in a boarding-school before. **3.** *prep.*+*g.* before; они́ пришли́ п. нас they arrived before us; п. всего́ first of all, to begin with; first and foremost.

преждевре́менно, *adv.* prematurely; before one's time.

преждевре́менност|ь, и, f. prematurity, untimeliness.

преждевре́мен|ный (~ен, ~на), *adj.* premature, untimely; ~ные ро́ды (*med.*) premature birth.

пре́жн|ий, *adj.* previous, former; в ~ее вре́мя in the old days, in former times.

презе́нт, а, *m.* (*obs. or joc.*) present.

презента́бел|ьный (~ен, ~ьна), *adj.* presentable.

презент|ова́ть, у́ю, *impf. and pf.* (*obs. or joc.*) to present.

презервати́в, а, *m.* **1.** contraceptive. **2.** (*med.; obs.*) prophylactic.

презервати́вный, *adj.* (*med.*) prophylactic, preventive.

презерва́ци|я, и, f. preservation.

президе́нт, а, *m.* president.

президе́нт|ский, *adj. of* ~; ~ские вы́боры presidential elections.

президе́нтств|о, а, n. presidency.

прези́диум, а, *m.* presidium.

презира́|ть, ю, *impf.* **1.** (*impf. only*) to despise, hold in contempt. **2.** (*pf.* презре́ть) to disdain; п. опа́сность to scorn danger.

презре́ни|е, я, n. disdain, contempt, scorn.

презре́н|ный (~, ~на), *adj.* contemptible, despicable; п. мета́лл (*coll.*) filthy lucre.

презр|е́ть, ю́, и́шь, *pf. of* презира́ть.

презри́тел|ьный (~ен, ~ьна), *adj.* contemptuous, scornful, disdainful.

презу́мпци|я, и, f. (*philos., leg.*) presumption.

преиму́щественно, *adv.* mainly, chiefly, principally.

преиму́щественн|ый, *adj.* **1.** primary, prime, principal. **2.** preferential, priority. **3.** (*leg.*) preferential; ~ое пра́во preference; ~ое пра́во на поку́пку pre-emption.

преиму́ществ|о, а, n. **1.** advantage; име́ть п. (пе́ред) to possess, have an advantage (over); получи́ть п. (пе́ред) to gain an advantage (over); они́ име́ют то п., что у них телефо́н they have the advantage of being on the telephone. **2.** preference; по ~у for the most part, chiefly. **3.** (*leg.*) privilege.

преиспо́дн|яя, ей, f. (*obs.*) the nether regions, the underworld, inferno.

преиспо́лн|енный, p.p.p. of ~ить *and adj.* (+*g. or i.*) filled (with), full (of); п. опа́сности fraught with danger; п. реши́мости firmly resolved.

преиспо́лн|ить, ю, ишь, *pf.* (*of* ~я́ть) (+*g. or i.*) to fill (with).

преиспо́лн|иться, юсь, ишься, *pf.* (*of* ~я́ться) (+*g. or i.*) to be filled (with), become full (of).

преисполн|я́ть(ся), я́ю(сь), *impf. of* ~ить-(ся).

прейскура́нт, а, *m.* price-list; bill of fare.

пре|йти́, йду́, йдёшь, *past* ~шёл, ~шла́, *pf.* (*of* ~ходи́ть) (*obs.*) **1.** to cross. **2.** to pass, have passed.

преклоне́ни|е, я, *n.* (пе́ред) admiration (for), worship (for).

преклон|и́ть, ю́, и́шь, *pf.* (*of* ~я́ть) to incline, bend; to lower; п. го́лову to bow (one's head) (*in token of respect or worship*); п. коле́на to genuflect.

преклон|и́ться, ю́сь, и́шься, *pf.* (*of* ~я́ться) (пе́ред) **1.** to bow down (before), bend down (before). **2.** (*fig.*) to admire, worship.

прекло́нный, *adj.* п. во́зраст old age, declining years.

преклон|я́ть(ся), я́ю(сь), *impf. of* ~и́ть(ся).

прекосло́ви|е, я, *n.* (*obs.*) contradiction; без вся́кого ~я without contradiction.

прекосло́в|ить, лю, ишь, *impf.* (+*d.*) to contradict.

прекра́сно, *adv.* **1.** excellently; perfectly well; они́ п. зна́ют, что э́то воспрещено́ they know perfectly well that it is forbidden. **2.** *as interj.* excellent!, splendid!

прекраснодуши|е, я, *n.* (*iron.*) starry-eyed idealism.

прекраснодуш|ный (~ен, ~на), *adj.* (*iron.*) starry-eyed.

прекра́с|ный (~ен, ~на), *adj.* **1.** beautiful, fine; п. пол the fair sex; ра́ди ~ных глаз pour les beaux yeux; в оди́н п. день one fine day, once upon a time; *as noun* ~ное, ~ного, *n.* (*philos.*) the beautiful. **2.** excellent, capital, first-rate.

прекра|ти́ть, щу́, ти́шь, *pf.* (*of* ~ща́ть) to stop, cease, discontinue; to put a stop (to), put an end (to); to break off, sever, cut off; п. войну́ to end the war; п. вое́нные де́йствия to cease hostilities; п. знако́мство (с+*i.*) to break (it off) (with), give up; п. обсужде́ние вопро́са to drop the subject; п. ого́нь (*mil.*) to cease fire; п. платежи́ to suspend, stop payments; п. подпи́ску to discontinue a subscription, stop subscribing; п. пода́чу га́за to cut off the gas (supply); п. пре́ния to close a debate; п. рабо́ту to leave off work, down tools; п. рабо́ту to stop work(ing); п. сноше́ния (с+*i.*) to sever relations (with).

прекра|ти́ться, ти́тся, *pf.* (*of* ~ща́ться) **1.** to cease, end. **2.** *pass. of* ~ти́ть.

прекраща́|ть(ся), ю, ет(ся), *impf. of* прекрати́ть(ся).

прекраще́ни|е, я, *n.* stopping, ceasing, cessation, discontinuance; п. вое́нных де́йствий cessation of hostilities; п. огня́ cease-fire; п. платеже́й suspension of payments; п. пре́ний closure of a debate.

прела́т, а, *m.* prelate.

преле́ст|ный (~ен, ~на), *adj.* charming, delightful, lovely.

пре́лест|ь, и, *f.* charm, fascination; кака́я п.! how lovely!; ~и жи́зни в дере́вне the delights of living in the country; езда́ в автомоби́ле уже́ потеря́ла п. новизны́ the novelty of driving had already worn off.

прелимина́ри|и, ев, *no sing.* (*dipl.*) preliminaries.

прелимина́рный, *adj.* (*dipl.*) preliminary.

прелом|и́ть, лю́, ~ишь, *pf.* (*of* ~ля́ть) **1.** (*phys.*) to refract. **2.** (*fig.*) to interpret, put a construction (upon).

прелом|и́ться, ~ится, *pf.* (*of* ~ля́ться) **1.** (*phys.*) to be refracted. **2.** (*fig.*) to be interpreted; to take on a different aspect; в све́те но́вых све́дений исто́рия ~и́лась по-ино́му in the light of new information a different construction was put upon the affair.

преломле́ни|е, я, *n.* **1.** (*phys.*) refraction. **2.** (*fig.*) interpretation, construction.

преломля́емост|ь, и, *f.* (*phys.*) refrangibility.

преломля́|емый, *pres. part. pass. of* ~ть *and adj.* (*phys.*) refractable, refrangible.

преломля́|ть(ся), ю, ет(ся) *impf. of* преломи́ть(ся).

преломля́|ющий, *pres. part. act. of* ~ть *and adj.* (*phys.*) refractive, refracting.

пре́л|ый (~, ~а), *adj.* rotten, fusty.

прел|ь, и, *f.* rot, mouldiness, mould.

прель|сти́ть, щу́, сти́шь, *pf.* (*of* ~ща́ть) **1.** to attract; его́ ~сти́ла перспекти́ва повы́шенной зарпла́ты he was attracted by the prospect of higher wages. **2.** to lure, entice; п. обеща́ниями to lure with promises.

прель|сти́ться, щу́сь, сти́шься, *pf.* (*of* ~ща́ться) (+*i.*) to be attracted (by); to be tempted (by), fall (for); мы ~сти́лись предложе́нием со́бственной кварти́ры we fell for the offer of having accommodation of our own.

прельща́|ть(ся), ю(сь), *impf. of* прельсти́ть(ся).

прелюбоде́|й, я, *m.* (*obs.*) adulterer.

прелюбоде́йств|овать, ую, *impf.* (*obs.*) to commit adultery.

прелюбодея́ни|е, я, *n.* (*obs.*) adultery.

прелю́ди|я, и, *f.* (*mus. and fig.*) prelude.

премиа́льн|ый, *adj. of* пре́мия; ~ая систе́ма bonus system; п. фонд bonus funds; *as noun (pl.)* ~ые, ~ых bonus.

премин|у́ть, у, ешь, *pf. only with neg.* (+*inf.*) not to fail (to); я не ~у зайти́ к вам I shall not fail to call in to see you.

премирова́ни|е, я, *n.* awarding of a prize; awarding of a bonus.

премиро́в|анный, *p.p.p. of* ~а́ть *and adj.*

prize-winning, prize; п. прое́кт па́мятника prize-winning design for a monument; п. бык prize bull; *as noun* п., ~анного, *m.* prize-winner.

премир|ова́ть, у́ю, *impf. and pf.* to award a prize (to); to give a bonus (to).

пре́ми|я, и, *f.* **1.** prize; bonus; bounty, gratuity; Нобелевская п. Nobel Prize. **2.** (*fin.*) premium; страхова́я п. premium, insurance.

премно́го, *adv.* (*obs.*) very much, extremely.

прему́дрост|ь, и, *f.* wisdom; ~и (*iron.*) subtleties.

прему́др|ый (~, ~а), *adj.* (very) wise, sage.

премье́р, а, *m.* **1.** prime minister, premier. **2.** (*theatr.*) leading actor, lead.

премье́р|а, ы, *f.* (*theatr.*) première, first night, opening night.

премье́р-мини́стр, а, *m.* prime minister, premier.

премье́рш|а, и, *f.* (*theatr.*) leading lady, lead.

пренебрега́|ть, ю, *impf. of* пренебре́чь.

пренебреже́ни|е, я, *n.* 1. scorn, contempt, disdain; обнару́жить, вы́казать своё п. (к) to show one's contempt (for); говори́ть с ~ем (о+*p.*) to disparage, speak slightingly (of). **2.** neglect, disregard; п. свои́ми обя́занностями neglect of one's duties, dereliction of duty.

пренебрежи́тельност|ь, и, *f.* scorn.

пренебрежи́тел|ьный (~ен, ~ьна), *adj.* scornful, slighting, disdainful.

пренебре́|чь, гу́, жёшь, гу́т, *past* ~г, ~гла́, *pf.* (*of* ~га́ть) (+*i.*) **1.** to scorn, despise; п. опа́сностью to scorn danger; п. сове́том to scorn advice. **2.** to neglect, disregard.

пре́ни|е, я, *n.* rotting.

пре́ни|я, й, *no sing.* debate; discussion; суде́бные п. pleadings; откры́ть, прекрати́ть п. to open, close a debate.

преоблада́ни|е, я, *n.* predominance.

преоблада́|ть, ет, *impf.* to predominate; to prevail.

преоблада́|ющий, *pres. part. act. of* ~ть *and adj.* predominant; prevalent.

преобража́|ть, ю, *impf. of* преобрази́ть.

преображе́ни|е, я, *n.* 1. transformation. **2.** (*rel.*) the Transfiguration.

преобра|зи́ть, жу́, зи́шь, *pf.* (*of* ~жа́ть) to transform, transfigure.

преобразова́ни|е, я, *n.* 1. transformation. **2.** reform; re-organization.

преобразова́тел|ь, я, *m.* **1.** reformer; re-organizer. **2.** (*phys., tech.*) transformer.

преобраз|ова́ть, у́ю, *pf.* (*of* ~о́вывать) **1.** to transform (*also phys., tech.*). **2.** to reform, re-organize.

преобразо́выва|ть, ю, *impf. of* преобразова́ть.

преодолева́|ть, ю, *impf. of* преодоле́ть.

преодоле́|ть, ю, *pf.* (*of* ~ва́ть) to overcome, get over; п. препя́тствия to surmount obstacles; п. тру́дности to get over difficulties; п. отстава́ние to make up lee-way.

преодоли́м|ый (~, ~а), *adj.* surmountable; э́то затрудне́ние ~о this difficulty is not insuperable.

преосвяще́нн|ый, *adj.* **1.** (*title of bishop*) Right Reverend. **2.** (*eccl.*) pre-consecrated; ~ые дары́ reserved sacrament.

**преосвяще́нств|о, а, *n.* его́ п. (*title of bishop*) his Grace.

препара́т, а, *m.* (*chem., pharm.*) preparation.

препара́тор, а, *m.* laboratory assistant.

препари́р|овать, ую, *impf. and pf.* (*chem., pharm.*) to prepare, make a preparation (of).

**препина́ни|е, я, *n.*; зна́ки ~я (*gram.*) stops, punctuation marks.

**препира́тельств|о, а, *n.* altercation, wrangling, squabbling.

препира́|ться, юсь, *impf.* (с+*i.*; *coll.*) to wrangle (with), squabble (with).

**преподава́ни|е, я, *n.* teaching, tuition, instruction.

преподава́тел|ь, я, *m.* teacher; (*in university or other higher education institution*) lecturer, instructor; п.-предме́тник subject teacher.

преподава́тель|ский, *adj. of* ~; п. соста́в teaching staff.

препода|ва́ть, ю́, ёшь, *impf.* to teach; п. хи́мию to teach, be a lecturer in chemistry.

препода́|ть, м, шь, ст, ди́м, ди́те, ду́т, *past* препо́дал, ~ла́, препо́дало, *pf.* (*obs.*) to give (*advice, a lesson, etc.*).

**преподнесе́ни|е, я, *n.* presentation.

преподнес|ти́, у́, ёшь, *past* ~, ~ла́, *pf.* (*of* преподноси́ть) (+*a. and d.*) to present (with), make a present (of to); он ~ нам неприя́тную но́вость he brought us a piece of bad news; п. что-н. кому́-н. в гото́вом ви́де (*fig.*) to hand something to someone on a plate.

преподно|си́ть, шу́, ~сишь, *impf. of* преподнести́.

**преподо́би|е, я, *n.* его́ п. (*title of priest*) his Reverence, the Reverend.

преподо́бный, *adj.* (*title of canonized monks*) Saint; Venerable.

препо́н|а, ы, *f.* (*obs.*) obstacle, impediment.

препоруч|а́ть, а́ю, *impf. of* ~и́ть.

препоруч|и́ть, у́, ~ишь, *pf.* (*of* ~а́ть) (*obs.*) to entrust, commit.

препоя́|сать, шу, шешь, *pf.* (*obs.*) to gird; п. свои́ чре́сла (*fig., rhet.*) to gird up one's loins.

препроводи́тельный, *adj.* accompanying (*document, etc.*).

препрово|ди́ть, жу́, ди́шь, *pf.* (*of* ~жда́ть) to send, forward, dispatch.

препровожда|ть, ю, *impf. of* препроводи́ть.

препровожде́ни|е¹, я, *n.* forwarding, dispatching.

препровожде́ни|е², я, *n.* passing; для ~я вре́мени to pass the time.

препя́тстви|е, я, *n.* **1.** obstacle, impediment, hindrance; чини́ть кому́-н. ~я to put obstacles in someone's way. **2.** (*sport*) obstacle; бег с ~ями, ска́чки с ~ями steeple-chase; взять п. to clear an obstacle; (*fig.*) to clear a hurdle; сбить п. to bring down an obstacle.

препя́тств|овать, ую, *impf.* (*of* вос~) (+*d.*) to hinder, impede, hamper; to stand in the way (of); непого́да ~овала их свида́ниям bad weather interfered with their rendezvous.

прерв|а́ть, у́, ёшь, *past* ~а́л, ~ала́, ~а́ло, *pf.* (*of* прерыва́ть) to break off, sever; to interrupt; to cut short; п. заня́тия to interrupt one's studies; п. молча́ние to break a silence; п. ора́тора to interrupt a speaker; п. дипломати́ческие отноше́ния to break off, sever diplomatic relations; п. перегово́ры to break off negotiations, suspend talks; п. рабо́ту to take a break; п. рабо́ту на кани́кулы (*of parliament, etc.*) to go into recess; п. разгово́р to interrupt a conversation; нас ~а́ли (*of telephone conversation*) we have been cut off.

прерв|а́ться, ётся, *past* ~а́лся, ~ала́сь, ~а́ло́сь, *pf.* (*of* прерыва́ться) **1.** to be interrupted; перегово́ры ~а́лись conversations have been broken off, have broken down. **2.** (*of a voice, from emotion*) to break.

пререка́ни|е, я, *n.* altercation, wrangle, argument; вступи́ть в п. с кем-н. to start an argument with someone.

пререка́|ться, юсь, *impf.* (c+*i.*) to argue (with).

прери|я, и, *f.* prairie.

прерогати́в|а, ы, *f.* prerogative.

прерыва́тел|ь, я, *m.* (*radio*) interrupter; (*electr.*) (circuit) breaker, cut-out.

прерыва́|ть(ся), ю(сь), *impf. of* прерва́ть(ся).

прерыва́|ющийся, *pres. part. of* ~ться; ~ющимся го́лосом with a catch in one's voice.

преры́висто, *adv.* in a broken way; говори́ть п. to speak in a staccato way; дыша́ть п. to gasp.

преры́вист|ый (~, ~а), *adj.* broken, interrupted, intermittent; п. ток (*tech.*) intermittent current.

пресви́тер, а, *m.* (*eccl.*) **1.** presbyter. **2.** (*in Presbyterian Church*) elder.

пресвитериа́нский, *adj.* (*rel.*) Presbyterian.

пресвитериа́нств|о, а, *n.* (*rel.*) Presbyterianism.

пресека́|ть(ся), ю, ет(ся), *impf. of* пресе́чь(ся).

пресече́ни|е, я, *n.* **1.** interruption, cutting off. **2.** (*lit.*; *obs.*) caesura.

пресе́|чь, ку́, чёшь, ку́т, *past* ~к, ~кла́, *pf.* (*of* ~ка́ть) to cut short, stop; п. в ко́рне to nip in the bud.

пресе́|чься, чётся, ку́тся, *past* ~кся, ~кла́сь, *pf.* (*of* ~ка́ться) **1.** to stop. **2.** (*of a voice, from emotion*) to break. **3.** *pass. of* ~чь.

пресле́довани|е, я, *n.* **1.** pursuit, chase. **2.** persecution, victimization; ма́ния ~я persecution complex. **3.** (*leg.*) суде́бное п. prosecution.

пресле́довател|ь, я, *m.* persecutor.

пресле́д|овать, ую, *impf.* **1.** to pursue, chase, be after; (*fig.*) to haunt; подозре́ние ~ует меня́ a suspicion haunts me. **2.** (*fig.*) to strive (for, after); pursue; п. цель to pursue an end. **3.** to persecute, torment; to victimize. **4.** (*leg.*) to prosecute.

пресловутый, *adj.* notorious; (*iron.*) famous, celebrated.

пресмыка́тельств|о, а, *n.* grovelling, crawling.

пресмыка́|ться, юсь, *impf.* **1.** (*obs.*) to creep, crawl. **2.** (пе́ред; *fig.*) to grovel (before), cringe (before), lick the boots (of).

пресмыка́ющ|ееся, егося, *n.* reptile.

пресново́дный, *adj.* freshwater.

пре́с|ный (~ен, ~на́, ~но), *adj.* **1.** (*of water*) fresh, sweet. **2.** unsalted; п. хлеб unleavened bread. **3.** (*of food*) flavourless, tasteless; (*fig.*) insipid, vapid, flat; ~ные остро́ты feeble jokes.

преспоко́йно, *adv.* (*coll.*) **1.** very quietly. **2.** calmly, coolly.

преспоко́|йный (~ен, ~йна), *adj.* (*coll.*) very quiet; very peaceful.

пресс, а, *m.* press; punch.

пре́сс|а, ы, *f.* (*collect.*) the press.

пресс-атташе́, *indecl., m.* press attaché.

пресс-бюро́, *indecl., n.* press department.

пресс-конфере́нци|я, и, *f.* press conference.

пресс|ова́ть, у́ю, *impf.* (*of* с~) to press, compress.

прессо́вк|а, и, *f.* pressing, compressing.

прессовщи́к, а́, *m.* presser, press operator.

пресс-папье́, *indecl., n.* **1.** paper-weight. **2.** blotter.

преста́в|иться, люсь, ишься, *pf.* (*obs.*) to pass away.

представле́ни|е, я, *n.* (*obs.*) passing (away).

престаре́лый, *adj.* aged; advanced in years.

престидижита́тор, а, *m.* juggler, prestidigitator.

прести́ж, а, *m.* prestige; поте́ря ~а loss of face; охраня́ть свой п. to save one's face.

престо́л, а, *m.* **1.** throne; вступи́ть на п. to

come to the throne, mount the throne; отре́чься от ~а to abdicate; све́ргнуть с ~а to dethrone. **2.** (*eccl.*) altar, communion table.

престолонасле́ди|е, я, *n.* succession to the throne.

престолонасле́дник, а, *m.* successor to the throne.

престо́л|ьный, *adj. of* ~; п. го́род capital (city); п. пра́здник patron saint's day, patronal festival.

преступ|а́ть, а́ю, *impf. of* ~и́ть.

преступ|и́ть, лю, ~ишь, *pf.* (*of* ~а́ть) to transgress, trespass (against); п. зако́н to violate the law.

преступле́ни|е, я, *n.* crime, offence; (*leg.*) felony; transgression; госуда́рственное п. treason; уголо́вное п. criminal offence; п. по до́лжности (*leg.*) malfeasance; соста́в ~я (*leg.*) corpus delicti.

престу́пник, а, *m.* criminal, offender; (*leg.*) felon; вое́нный п. war criminal.

престу́пност|ь, и, *f.* **1.** criminality. **2.** (*collect.*) crime; рост ~и increase in crime.

престу́п|ный (~ен, ~на), *adj.* criminal; (*leg.*) felonious.

пресуществле́ни|е, я, *n.* (*rel.*) transubstantiation.

пресы́|тить, щу, тишь, *pf.* (*of* ~ща́ть) (*obs.*) (+*i.*) to satiate (with); to surfeit (on), sate (with).

пресы́|титься, щусь, тишься, *pf.* (*of* ~ща́ться) (+*i.*) to be satiated (with); be surfeited (with), have had a surfeit (of).

пресыща́|ть(ся), ю(сь), *impf. of* пресы́тить(ся).

пресыще́ни|е, я, *n.* satiety; surfeit; до ~я to satiety.

пресы́щенност|ь, и, *f.* satiety; surfeit.

пресы́|щенный, *p.p.p. of* ~тить *and adj.* satiated; surfeited, sated, replete.

претворе́ни|е, я, *n.* conversion; transubstantiation (*esp. rel.*); п. в жизнь realization, putting into practice.

претвор|и́ть, ю́, и́шь, *pf.* (*of* ~я́ть) **1.** (в+*a.*). to turn (into), change (into), convert (into); to transubstantiate (*esp. rel.*). **2.** п. в жизнь, п. в де́ло to realize, carry out, put into practice.

претвор|и́ться, и́тся, *pf.* (*of* ~я́ться) **1.** (в+*a.*) to turn (into), become; вода́ ~и́лась в вино́ the water was turned into wine. **2.** п. в жизнь to be realized, come true; моя́ мечта́ ~и́лась в жизнь my dream has come true.

претвор|я́ть(ся), я́ю, я́ет(ся), *impf. of* ~и́ть(ся).

претенде́нт, а, *m.* (на+*a.*) **1.** claimant (to, upon), aspirant (to); candidate (for); он п. на ру́ку принце́ссы he aspires to the hand of the princess. **2.** pretender (to); п. на престо́л pretender to the throne.

претенд|ова́ть, у́ю, *impf.* (на+*a.*) to pretend (to), have pretensions (to); to aspire (to); to lay claim (to); он ~у́ет на до́лжность мини́стра иностра́нных дел he aspires to the position of Minister of Foreign Affairs.

прете́нзи|я, и, *f.* **1.** claim; име́ть ~ю (на+*a.*) to claim, lay claim (to), make claims (on); заяви́ть ~ю to lodge a claim; отклони́ть ~ю to reject a claim. **2.** pretension; челове́к с ~ями, без ~й a pretentious, an unpretentious person; у него́ нет никаки́х ~й на остроу́мие he has no pretensions to wit; быть в ~и на кого́-н. to have a grudge, grievance against someone.

претенцио́зност|ь, и, *f.* pretentiousness, affectation.

претенцио́з|ный (~ен, ~на), *adj.* pretentious, affected.

претерпева́|ть, ю, *impf. of* претерпе́ть.

претерп|е́ть, лю́, ~ишь, *pf.* (*of* ~ева́ть) to undergo; to suffer, endure; план ~е́л изме́нения the plan has undergone changes; п. лише́ния to endure privations.

прет|и́ть, и́т, *impf.* (+*d.*) to sicken; от э́той пи́щи мне ~и́т I am nauseated by this food.

преткнове́ни|е, я, *n.* ка́мень ~я stumbling-block.

пре́тор, а, *m.* (*hist.*) praetor.

претория́н|ец, ца, *m.* (*hist.*) praetorian (guard).

претория́нский, *adj.* (*hist.*) praetorian.

пре|ть, ю, *impf.* **1.** (*pf.* со~) to rot. **2.** (*impf. only*) to become damp (*of ground, in spring, from warmth of atmosphere*). **3.** (*pf* у~) to stew. **4.** (*pf.* взо~) (*coll.*) to sweat, perspire.

преувеличе́ни|е, я, *n.* exaggeration; overstatement.

преувели́чива|ть, ю, *impf. of* преувели́чить.

преувели́ч|ить, у, ишь, *pf.* (*of* ~ивать) to exaggerate; to overstate.

преуменьш|а́ть, а́ю, *impf. of* ~и́ть.

преуменьше́ни|е, я, *n.* underestimation; understatement.

преуме́ньш|ить, ~у́, ~и́шь, *pf.* (*of* ~а́ть) to underestimate, minimize; to belittle; to understate; п. опа́сность to underestimate the danger; п. чью-н. по́мощь to belittle someone's assistance.

преуспева́|ть, ю, *impf.* **1.** *impf. of* преуспе́ть. **2.** (*impf. only*) to thrive, prosper, flourish.

преуспева́|ющий, *pres. part. act. of* ~ть *and adj.* successful, prosperous.

преуспе́|ть, ю, *pf.* (*of* ~ва́ть) (в+*p.*) to succeed (in), be successful (in); п. в жи́зни to get on in life.

преуспе́яни|е, я, *n.* (*obs. or iron.*) success.

префе́кт, а, *m.* prefect.

префекту́р|а, ы, *f.* prefecture.

преферáнс, а, *m.* preference (*card-game*).

préфикс, а, *m.* (*gram.*) prefix.

префи́кс, *indecl., adj.*; платёж п. (*comm.*) payment made before term appointed, prior payment.

префиксáльный, *adj.* (*gram.*) with a prefix.

префиксáци|я, и, *f.* (*gram.*) addition of prefix (*to a verb, etc.*).

прехо|ди́ть, жу́, ~дишь, *impf. of* прейти́.

преходя́щий, *adj.* transient.

прецеде́нт, а, *m.* precedent; установи́ть п. to establish a precedent.

прецéсси|я, и, *f.* (*astron.*) precession.

прецизио́нный, *adj.* (*tech.*) precision; п. прибо́р precision instrument.

при, *prep.+p.* **1.** (*of local proximity*) by, at; in the presence of; при доро́ге by the road(-side); би́тва при Бородине́ the battle of Borodino; письмо́ бы́ло подпи́сано при мне the letter was signed in my presence; не на́до так выражáться при дéтях you should not use such language in front of the children. **2.** attached to, affiliated to, under the auspices of (*usu. not translated*); он рабóтает при университе́те he is attached to the university; военврáч при батальóне battalion medical officer. **3.** (*indicating possession, presence of object(s) mentioned*) by, with; about, on; у негó нé было при себé дéнег he had no money on him; есть ли у вас при себé перочи́нный нож? do you have a pen-knife about you?; быть при ору́жии to have arms about one, be armed. **4.** with (= *taking into account the attribute, etc., referred to*); for, notwithstanding; при таки́х талáнтах он должнó быть далекó пойдёт with such talent he ought to go far; при желáнии всегó мóжно доби́ться where there's a will there's a way; при всех егó достóинствах, он мне не нрáвится for all his virtues, I do not like him; при всём том (*i*) with it all, moreover, (*ii*) for all that. **5.** in the time of, in the days of; under (*sc. the rule of*); during; при Ивáне Грóзном during the reign of, in the time of Ivan the Terrible; при Ромáновых under the Romanovs; при мне бы́ло не так in my day it was not like this. **6.** (*indicating accompanying circumstances*) by; при дневнóм свéте by daylight; при свéте лáмпы by lamplight. **7.** (*referring to action on occasion unspecified*) when; on; in case of; при перехóде чéрез у́лицу when crossing the street; при слу́чае when the occasion arises, at convenience; при анáлизе on analysis; при маляри́и in case of malaria; при услóвии under the condition (that). **8.** with (= *by means of, thanks to*); при пóмощи рыбакóв нам удалóсь оттолкну́ть

лóдку with the aid of the fishermen we succeeded in pushing the boat off.

при-[1] *verbal prefix indicating* **1.** *completion of action or motion up to given terminal point, as* приéхать *to arrive.* **2.** *action of attaching, as* пристрóить *to build on.* **3.** *direction of action towards speaker, as* пригласи́ть *to invite.* **4.** *direction of action from above downward, as* придави́ть *to press down.* **5.** *incompleteness or tentativeness of action, as* приоткры́ть *to open slightly.* **6.** *exhaustiveness of action, as* приучи́ть *to train.* **7.** (+*suffixes* -ыва-, -ива-) *accompaniment, as* приплáсывать *to dance (to a tune).*

при-[2] *as prefix of nouns and adjs.* (*esp. geogr.*) *indicates juxtaposition or proximity, as* приозéрье *lake-side;* прибрéжный, примóрский *coastal.*

прибáв|ить, лю, ишь, *pf.* (*of* ~ля́ть) **1.** (+*a. or g.*) to add; п. (в вéсе) to put on (weight); за три мéсяца онá ~ила дéсять фу́нтов she put on ten pounds in three months. **2.** (+*g.*) to increase, augment; п. жáлованья to increase a salary, give a rise; п. шáгу to quicken, hasten one's steps; п. хóду (*coll.*) to put on speed. **3.** (в+*p.*) to lengthen, widen (*part of an item of clothing*); нáдо п. в рукавáх the sleeves need to be lengthened. **4.** (*fig., coll.*) to lay it on (= *exaggerate*).

прибáв|иться, ится, *pf.* (*of* ~ля́ться) **1.** to increase; (*of water*) to rise; (*of the moon*) to wax; п. в вéсе to put on weight; воды́ ~илось (*impers.*) the water has risen; нарóду ~илось (*impers.*) the crowd has grown; день ~и́лся the days are getting longer. **2.** *pass. of* ~ить.

прибáвк|а, и, *f.* **1.** addition, augmentation, **2.** increase, supplement; получи́ть ~у to get a rise.

прибавлéни|е, я, *n.* **1.** addition, augmentation; п. семéйства addition to the family; сказáть в п. to say in addition, add. **2.** supplement, appendix. **3.** (*fig., coll.*) embroidery (= *exaggeration*).

прибавля́|ть(ся), ю, ~ет(ся), *impf. of* прибáвить(ся).

прибáвочн|ый, *adj.* **1.** additional. **2.** (*econ.*) surplus; ~ая стóимость surplus value.

прибалти́йский, *adj.* Baltic (= *adjacent to the Baltic Sea*).

прибау́тк|а, и, *f.* humorous catchphrase, facetious saying.

прибегá|ть[1]**, ю,** *impf. of* прибéгнуть.

прибегá|ть[2]**, ю,** *impf. of* прибежáть.

прибéг|нуть, ну, нешь, *past* ~, ~ла, *pf.* (*o ~áть*[1]) (к) to resort (to), have resort (to); to fall back (on); п. к си́ле to resort to force.

прибедн|и́ться, ю́сь, и́шься, *pf.* (*of* ~я́ться)

(*coll.*) **1.** to pretend to be poorer than one is, feign poverty. **2.** to show false modesty.

прибедн|я́ться, я́юсь, *impf. of* ~и́ться.

прибе|жа́ть, гу́, жи́шь, гу́т, *pf.* (*of* ~га́ть²) to come running.

прибе́жищ|е, а, *n.* refuge; после́днее п. (*fig.*) last resort; найти́ п. (в+*p.*) to take refuge (in).

прибега́|ть, ю, *impf. of* прибере́чь.

прибере́|чь, гу́, жёшь, гу́т, *past* ~г, ~гла́, *pf.* (*of* ~га́ть) to save up.

прибива́|ть, ю, *impf. of* прибить¹.

прибира́|ть(ся), ю(сь), *impf. of* прибра́ть(ся).

приб|и́ть¹, ью́, ьёшь, *pf.* (*of* ~ива́ть) **1.** to nail, affix with nails; п. флаг к дре́вку to nail a flag to a pole. **2.** to lay, flatten; град ~и́л посе́вы the hail has laid the corn. **3.** (*usu. impers.*) to throw up; труп ~и́ло к бе́регу a body was washed ashore.

приб|и́ть², ью́, ьёшь, *pf. of* бить 1.

приближа́|ть, ю, *impf. of* прибли́зить.

приближа́|ться, юсь, *impf.* **1.** *impf. of* прибли́зиться. **2.** (*impf. only*) to approximate; п. к и́стине to approximate to the truth.

приближе́ни|е, я, n. **1.** approach; approaching, drawing near. **2.** (*math.*) approximation.

приближённост|ь, и, f. proximity.

приближённый¹, *adj.* approximate, rough; п. ме́тод (*math.*) method of approximation.

приближённ|ый², ого, m. (*obs.*) retainer, person in attendance; (*pl.*) retinue.

приблизи́тельно, *adv.* approximately, roughly.

приблизи́тельност|ь, и, f. approximateness.

приблизи́тел|ьный (~ен, ~ьна), *adj.* approximate, rough.

прибли́|зить, жу, зишь, *pf.* (*of* ~жа́ть) **1.** to bring nearer, move nearer; п. кни́гу к глаза́м to bring a book nearer one's eyes. **2.** to hasten, advance; я наме́рен п. мой отъе́зд I intend to hasten my departure; ~зили его́ призы́в в а́рмию the date of his call-up has been advanced.

прибли́|зиться, жусь, зишься, *pf.* (*of* ~жа́ться) (к) to approach, draw near; to draw nearer (to), come nearer (to).

приблу́дный, *adj.* (*coll.*; *of animals*) stray.

прибо́|й, я, m. surf, breakers.

прибо́р, а, m. **1.** instrument, device, apparatus, appliance, gadget. **2.** set; бри́твенный п. shaving things; ками́нный п. set of fire-irons; пи́сьменный п. desk-set; столо́вый п. cover; накры́ть стол на шесть ~ов to lay (places) for six; туале́тный п. toilet set, washing things; ча́йный п. tea-service. **3.** fittings; печно́й п. stove fittings.

прибо́р|ный, *adj. of* ~; ~ная доска́ dashboard; (*aeron.*) instrument panel.

приборострое́ни|е, я, n. instrument-making.

при|бра́ть, беру́, берёшь, *past* ~бра́л, ~брала́, ~бра́ло, *pf.* (*of* ~бира́ть) **1.** to clear up, clean up, tidy (up); п. посте́ль to make a bed; п. ко́мнату, п. в ко́мнате to do a room; п. на столе́ to clear the table; п. кого́-н. к рука́м to take someone in hand; п. что-н. к рука́м to lay one's hands on something. **2.** to put away; ~бери́ игру́шки — пора́ спать! put your toys away, it's time for bed!

при|бра́ться, беру́сь, берёшься, *past* ~бра́лся, ~брала́сь, ~бра́лось, *pf.* (*of* ~бира́ться) to tidy oneself up; to have a clear-up of one's things.

прибре́жн|ый, *adj.* **1.** coastal, littoral; ~ые острова́ off-shore islands; ~ая полоса́ coastal strip. **2.** riverside; riverain, riparian.

прибре́жь|е, я, n. littoral; coastal strip.

прибре|сти́, ду́, дёшь, *past* ~л, ~ла́, *pf.* (*coll.*) to come trudging (along); п. домо́й to crawl home.

прибыва́|ть, ю, *impf. of* прибы́ть.

при́был|ь, и, f. **1.** profit, gain (*also fig.*); return; валова́я п. gross profit; чи́стая п. net profit; кака́я мне в э́том п.? (*coll.*) what do I get out of it? **2.** increase, rise; п. населе́ния increase of population; вода́ идёт на п. the water is rising. **3.** (*tech.*) riser; п. отли́вки head of casting, lost head.

при́быльност|ь, и, f. profitability, lucrativeness.

при́быль|ный, *adj.* **1.** profitable, lucrative. **2.** *adj. of* ~ 3; п. коне́ц deadhead.

прибы́ти|е, я, n. arrival.

при|бы́ть¹, бу́ду, бу́дешь, *past* ~был, ~была́, ~было, *pf.* (*of* ~быва́ть) to arrive; (*of a train, etc.*) to get in; по́езд ~был the train is in; по́чта ~была́ the post has come.

при|бы́ть², бу́дет, *past* ~был, ~была́, ~было, *pf.* (*of* ~быва́ть) (*coll.*) to increase, grow; (*of water*) to rise, swell; (*of the moon*) to wax; вода́ ~была́ the water has risen; на́шего полку́ ~было our numbers have grown.

прива́д|а, ы, f. lure, bait (*put out to catch birds or fish*).

прива́|дить, жу, дишь, *pf.* (*of* ~живать). **1.** to train (*a bird, etc., by putting out food*). **2.** (к) to attract (to), predispose (towards).

прива́жива|ть, ю, *impf. of* прива́дить.

прива́л, а, m. **1.** halt, stop. **2.** stopping-place.

прива́лива|ть, ю, *impf. of* привали́ть.

привал|и́ть, ю́, ~ишь, *pf.* (*of* ~ивать) **1.** to lean, rest; п. дрова́ к забо́ру to pile logs against the fence. **2.** (*of a vessel*) to come alongside. **3.** (*fig., coll.*) to turn up; на матч ~и́ло мно́го наро́ду people flocked to the match; сча́стье нам ~и́ло fortune smiled on us.

прива́рива|ть, ю, *impf. of* привари́ть.

привар|и́ть, ю́, ~ишь, *pf.* (*of* ~ивать) **1.** (к) to weld on (to). **2.** (+a. or g.) to boil some more, cook some more.

прива́рк|а, и, *f.* welding.

прива́р|ок, ка, *m.* (*mil. and coll.*) **1.** (*collect.*) victuals, rations. **2.** cooked food, hot meal.

прива́т-доце́нт, а, *m.* privat-docent (*unestablished university lecturer*).

прива́т-доценту́р|а, ы, *f.* **1.** post of privat-docent. **2.** (*collect.*) the privat-docents.

прива́тный, *adj.* (*obs.*) private.

приведе́ни|е, я, *n.* **1.** bringing; п. к прися́ге administration of oath, swearing in. **2.** putting; п. в движе́ние setting in motion; п. в исполне́ние carrying out, putting into effect; п. в поря́док putting in order. **3.** (*math.*) reduction; п. к о́бщему знамена́телю reduction to a common denominator. **4.** adduction, adducing; п. приме́ров adducing of instances.

привез|ти́, у́, ёшь, *past* ~, ~ла́, *pf.* (*of* привози́ть) to bring (*not on foot*).

привере́длив|ый (~, ~a), *adj.* fastidious, pernickety; squeamish.

привере́дник, а, *m.* fastidious person; squeamish person.

привере́днича|ть, ю, *impf.* to be hard to please; to be fastidious; to be squeamish.

приве́ржен|ец, ца, *m.* adherent; follower.

приве́рженност|ь, и, *f.* adherence; attachment, devotion.

приве́ржен|ный (~, ~a), *adj.* (к) attached (to), devoted (to).

приверн|у́ть, у́, ёшь, *pf.* (*of* приве́ртывать) **1.** to screw tight, tighten, clamp. **2.** to turn down; п. фити́ль to turn a wick down.

привер|те́ть, чу́, ~тишь, *pf.* (*of* ~тывать) to screw tight, tighten, clamp.

приве́ртыва|ть, ю, *impf. of* привернуть *and* привертеть.

приве́с, а, *m.* additional weight.

приве́|сить, шу, сишь, *pf.* (*of* ~шивать) to hang up, suspend.

приве́с|ок, ка, *m.* (*coll.*) **1.** makeweight. **2.** (*fig.*) appendage.

приве|сти́, ду́, дёшь, *past* ~л, ~ла́, *pf.* (*of* приводи́ть) **1.** to bring; to lead, take; он ~л с собо́й неве́сту he has brought his fiancée (with him); п. кого́-н. к прися́ге to administer the oath to someone, swear someone in; ~л Бог сви́деться! (*obs.*) we were meant to meet again! **2.** (к; *fig.*) to lead (to), bring (to), conduce (to), result (in); э́то к добру́ не ~дёт no good will

come of it; её поведе́ние ~ло́ меня́ к заключе́нию, что она́ душе́вно расстро́ена her behaviour led me to the conclusion that she is out of her mind. **3.** (в+a.) to put, set (*or translated by verb corresponding to noun governed by* в); п. в бе́шенство to throw into a rage, drive mad; п. в движе́ние, в де́йствие to set in motion, set going; п. в затрудне́ние to cause difficulties, put in a difficult position; п. в изумле́ние to astonish, astound; п. в исполне́ние to carry out, carry into effect, put into effect; п. пригово́р в исполне́ние to execute a sentence; п. в хоро́шее настрое́ние to put in a good mood; п. в него́дность to put out of commission; п. в отча́яние to reduce to despair; п. в поря́док to put in order, tidy (up); to arrange, fix; п. в у́жас to horrify; п. в чу́вство to bring to, bring round. **4.** (к; *math.*) to reduce (to). **5.** to adduce, cite; п. доказа́тельства to adduce proofs; п. приме́р to give an example, cite an instance; п. цита́ту (из) to make a quotation (from), quote.

приве|сти́сь, дётся, *past* ~ло́сь, *pf.* (*of* приводи́ться) (*impers.*+d.; *coll.*) to happen, chance; to be one's lot; мне ~ло́сь там быть тогда́, когда́ они́ проезжа́ли I happened to be there when they drove past; ему́ ~ло́сь быть свиде́телем преступле́ния it was his lot to be a witness of the crime.

приве́т, а, *m.* greeting(s); regards; горя́чий п. (one's) warmest regards; переда́ть п., слать п. to send one's regards; моя́ жена́ шлёт вам п. my wife sends her regards, asks to be remembered to you; переда́йте п. ва́шим колле́гам remember me to your colleagues, my regards to your colleagues; с серде́чным ~ом (*epistolary formula*) yours sincerely; п. из Москвы́! greetings from Moscow!

приве́тливост|ь, и, *f.* affability; cordiality.

приве́тлив|ый (~, ~a), *adj.* affable; cordial.

приве́тственн|ый, *adj.* salutatory; welcoming; ~ая речь speech of welcome.

приве́тстви|е, я, *n.* **1.** greeting, salutation. **2.** speech of welcome.

приве́тств|овать, ую, *impf.* **1.** (*in past tense also pf.*) to greet, salute, hail; to welcome. **2.** (*fig.*) to welcome; п. предложе́ние to welcome a suggestion. **3.** (*also pf.*) (*mil.*) to salute.

приве́|шенный, p.p.p. of ~сить; у него́ язы́к хорошо́ ~шен (*coll.*) he has a ready tongue.

приве́шива|ть, ю, *impf. of* приве́сить.

привива́|ть(ся), ю, ет(ся), *impf. of* приви́ть(ся).

приви́вк|а, и, *f.* **1.** (от, про́тив; *med.*) inoculation (against); vaccination. **2.** (*bot.*) inoculation, grafting, engrafting.

приви́в|очный, *adj. of* ~ка.

привиде́ни|е, я, *n.* ghost, spectre; apparition.

приви́|деться, дится, *pf. of* ви́деться 2.

привилегиро́ванност|ь, и, *f.* privilege(s).

привилегиро́ванн|ый, *adj.* privileged; ~ое положе́ние privileged position.

привиле́ги|я, и, *f.* privilege.

привин|ти́ть, чу́, ти́шь, *pf.* (*of* ~чивать) to screw on.

приви́нчива|ть, ю, *impf. of* привинти́ть.

привира́|ть, ю, *impf. of* привра́ть.

приви́ти|е, я, *n.* inculcation.

прив|и́ть, ью́, ьёшь, *past* ~и́л, ~ила́, ~и́ло, *pf.* (*of* ~ива́ть) (+*a. and d.*) **1.** (*med.*) to inoculate (with); п. кому́-н. о́спу to vaccinate someone against smallpox. **2.** (*bot.*) to graft, engraft (upon); to inoculate (with); (*fig.*) to implant (in). **3.** (*fig.*) to inculcate (in); to cultivate (in), foster (in); п. кому́-н. вкус к стиха́м to inculcate in someone a taste for poetry; п. но́вую мо́ду to set a new fashion.

прив|и́ться, ьётся, *past* ~и́лся, ~ила́сь, *pf.* (*of* ~ива́ться) **1.** (*of an inoculation or graft*) to take. **2.** (*fig.*) to become established, find acceptance, catch on; э́ти взгля́ды ~или́сь не всю́ду these views did not find universal acceptance; мо́да носи́ть цветны́е чулки́ не ~ила́сь у нас the fashion for coloured stockings did not catch on here.

при́вкус, а, *m.* after-taste; smack (*also fig.*); его́ слова́ име́ли п. на́глости his words smacked of insolence.

привлека́тельност|ь, и, *f.* attractiveness.

привлека́тел|ьный (~ен, ~на), *adj.* attractive; fetching; ~ьная улы́бка smile.

привлека́|ть, ю, *impf. of* привле́чь.

привлече́ни|е, я, *n.* attraction.

привле́|чь, ку́, чёшь, ку́т, *past* ~к, ~кла́, *pf.* (*of* ~ка́ть) **1.** to draw, attract; п. внима́ние to attract attention; кри́ки ~кли́ нас к ра́неному cries drew us to the wounded man. **2.** to draw in; п. на свою́ сто́рону to win over (*to one's side*); п. к рабо́те to recruit, enlist the services (of). **3.** (*leg.*) to have up; п. к суду́ to sue (in court), take to court; to bring to trial, put on trial; п. к отве́тственности (за+*a.*) to make answer (for), make answerable (for), call to account (for); п. к уголо́вной отве́тственности to institute criminal proceedings (against).

привнес|ти́, у́, ёшь, *past* ~, ~ла́, *pf.* (*of* привноси́ть) to introduce, insert; п. эле́мент коми́зма в де́ло to introduce an element of comedy into proceedings.

привно|си́ть, шу́, ~сишь, *impf. of* привнести́.

приво́д[1], а, *m.* (*leg.*) bringing to court (*of accused or witness for questioning*); taking into custody; постановле́ние о ~е warrant for arrest.

приво́д[2], а, *m.* (*tech.*) drive, driving gear; кулачко́вый п. cam drive; ремённый п. belt drive; ручно́й п. hand gear; червя́чный п. worm gear.

приво́|дить(ся), жу́(сь), ~дишь(ся), *impf. of* привести́(сь).

приво́дк|а, и, *f.* (*typ.*) registration.

приводне́ни|е, я, *n.* splash-down.

приводн|и́ться, ю́сь, и́шься, *pf.* (*of* ~я́ться) to land, come down on water.

приводн|о́й, *adj.* (*tech.*) driving; п. вал driving shaft; п. механи́зм driving gear; ~а́я радиоста́нция homing wireless set; ~а́я цепь sprocket chain, chain drive.

приводн|я́ться, я́юсь, *impf. of* ~и́ться.

приво|жу́[1], ~дишь, *see* ~ди́ть.

приво|жу́[2], ~зишь, *see* ~зи́ть.

приво́з, а, *m.* **1.** bringing, supply; import, importation. **2.** (*coll.*) load.

приво|зи́ть, жу́, ~зишь, *impf. of* привезти́.

привозно́й, *adj.* imported.

привозн|ый = ~о́й.

приво́|й, я, *m.* (*agric.*) graft.

привола́кива|ть, ю, *impf. of* приволочи́ть *and* приволо́чь.

привола́кива|ться, юсь, *impf. of* **1.** приволочи́ться *and* приволо́чься. **2.** приволокну́ться.

приволокн|у́ться, у́сь, ёшься, *pf.* (*of* привола́киваться) (за+*i.*; *coll.*) to flirt (with).

приволоч|и́ть(ся), у́(сь), и́шь(ся), *pf.* = ~ь(ся).

приволо́|чь, ку́, чёшь, ку́т, *past* ~к, ~кла́, *pf.* (*of* привола́кивать) (*coll.*) to drag (over).

приволо́|чься, ку́сь, чёшься, ку́тся, *past* ~кся, ~кла́сь, *pf.* (*of* привола́киваться) (*coll.*) to drag oneself.

приво́ль|е, я, *n.* **1.** free space; степны́е ~я 'wide open spaces' of the steppe. **2.** freedom.

приво́льн|ый, *adj.* free; ~ая жизнь free and easy life.

привора́жива|ть, ю, *impf. of* приворожи́ть.

приворож|и́ть, у́, и́шь, *pf.* (*of* привора́живать) (*obs. or fig.*) to bewitch, charm.

приворо́тн|ый, *adj.*; ~ое зе́лье (*folk poet.*) love-philtre.

приврат́ник, а, *m.* **1.** door-keeper, porter, janitor. **2.** (*anat.*) pylorus.

приври́|ть, у́, ёшь, *past* ~а́л, ~ала́, ~а́ло, *pf.* (*of* привира́ть) (*coll.*) to make up; to exaggerate.

привска́кива|ть, ю, *impf. of* привскочи́ть.

привскоч|и́ть, у́, ~ишь, *pf.* (*of* привска́кивать) to start, jump up.

привста|ва́ть, ю́, ёшь, *impf. of* ~ть.

привста́|ть, ну, нешь, *pf. (of* ~ва́ть) to rise, stand up (*for a moment*); to half-rise; когда́ судья́ вошёл, все ~ли when the judge entered everyone stood up.

привходя́щ|ий, *adj.* ~ие обстоя́тельства attendant circumstances.

привык|а́ть, а́ю, *impf. of* ~нуть.

привы́к|нуть, ну, нешь, *past* ~, ~ла, *pf. (of* ~а́ть) (к *or*+*inf.*) 1. to get accustomed (to), get used (to); она́ ско́ро ~ла к его́ храпе́нию she soon got used to his snoring. 2. to get into the habit (of), get into the way (of); он ~ руга́ться he has got into the habit of swearing.

привы́чк|а, и, *f.* habit; войти́ в ~у to become a habit; вы́работать в себе́ ~у to form a habit; име́ть ~у (к) to be accustomed (to); to be in the habit (of), be given (to); приобрести́ ~у (+*inf.*) to get into the habit (of), fall into the habit (of); э́то не в на́ших ~ах it is not our habit, not our practice.

привы́чност|ь, и, *f.* habitualness.

привы́ч|ный (~ен, ~на), *adj.* 1. habitual, usual, customary. 2. (к) accustomed (to), used (to); он челове́к п. he is a man of habit, of set habits.

привя́занност|ь, и, *f.* 1. (к) attachment (to); affection (for, towards). 2. (*fig.*) (object of) attachment, object of affection; ста́рая п. old flame.

привя́з|анный, *p.p.p. of* ~а́ть *and adj.* (к) attached (to).

привя|за́ть, жу́, ~жешь, *pf. (of* ~зывать) (к) 1. to tie (to), bind (to), fasten (to), attach (to), secure (to); п. козу́ to tether a goat. 2. (к себе́; *fig.*) to attach (to oneself), get a hold (over the affections of).

привя|за́ться, жу́сь, ~жешься, *pf. (of* ~зыва́ться) (к) 1. to become attached (to); она́ о́чень к вам ~за́лась she has become very attached to you. 2. to attach oneself (to); на доро́ге како́й-то ни́щий ~за́лся к нам a beggar attached himself to us on the road. 3. (*coll.*) to pester, bother.

привязно́й, *adj.* fastened, secured; п. аэроста́т captive balloon, balloon on bearings; п. реме́нь seat-belt (*in cars, etc.*).

привя́зчивост|ь, и, *f.* 1. capacity for giving affection; susceptibility to affection. 2. disposition to annoy, pester, bother.

привя́зчив|ый (~, ~а), *adj.* 1. affectionate; susceptible (*to affection*), given to forming attachments easily. 2. importunate, annoying; given to pestering.

привя́з|ь, и, *f.* tie; lead, leash; tether; на ~и on a leash; посади́ть соба́ку на п. to put a dog on a leash.

прига́р, а, *m.* (*coll.*) burnt place, burnt part (*of cooked food*).

при́гар|ь, и, *f.* taste of burning; молоко́ с ~ью milk tasting burned.

пригвожда́|ть, ю, *impf. of* пригвозди́ть.

пригвоз|ди́ть, жу́, ди́шь, *pf. (of* пригвожда́ть) (к) to nail (to); (*fig.*) to pin (down); п. к ме́сту to root to the spot; п. к позо́рному столбу́ to pillory; п. взгля́дом to fix with a look.

пригиба́|ть(ся), ю(сь), *impf. of* пригну́ть(ся).

пригла́|дить, жу, дишь, *pf. (of* ~живать) to smooth.

пригла́|диться, жусь, дишься, *pf. (of* ~живаться) to smooth one's hair

пригла́жива|ть(ся), ю(сь), *impf. of* пригла́-дить(ся).

пригласи́тельный, *adj.* conveying an invitation; п. биле́т invitation card.

пригла|си́ть, шу́, си́шь, *pf. (of* ~ша́ть) 1. to invite, ask; п. на обе́д to invite, ask to dinner; п. на та́нцы to ask to a dance; п. кого́-нибудь. на та́нец to ask someone to dance, ask someone for a dance; п. в го́сти to invite, ask round. 2. to call (*a doctor, etc.*). 3. to offer; его́ ~си́ли на рабо́ту в но́вой шко́ле he has been offered a job in a new school.

приглаша́|ть, ю, *impf. of* пригласи́ть.

приглаше́ни|е, я, *n.* 1. invitation; по ~ю by invitation; разосла́ть ~я to send out invitations. 2. offer (*of employment*).

приглуш|а́ть, а́ю, *impf. of* ~и́ть.

приглуш|и́ть, у́, и́шь, *pf. (of* ~а́ть) to damp down; to muffle, deaden (*sound*); to choke, damp (*a fire*).

пригля|де́ть, жу́, ди́шь, *pf. (of* ~дывать) (*coll.*) 1. to choose; to find, look out; п. себе́ удо́бную кварти́ру to look oneself out convenient lodgings. 2. (за+*i.*) to look after; п. за детьми́ to look after children.

пригля|де́ться, жу́сь, ди́шься, *pf. (of* ~дываться) (*coll.*) 1. (к) to look closely (at), scrutinize. 2. (к) to get accustomed (to), get used (to); п. к темноте́ to get accustomed to darkness. 3. (+*d.*) to tire, bore; мне ~де́лись кинофи́льмы о вое́нных де́йствиях I am tired of war-films.

пригля́дыва|ть(ся), ю(сь), *impf. of* пригля-де́ть(ся).

пригля́н|уться, у́сь, ~ешься, *pf.* (+*d.*; *coll.*) to take one's fancy, attract; она́ сра́зу ~у́лась ему́ he was attracted by her instantly.

при|гна́ть[1], гоню́, го́нишь, *past* ~гна́л, ~гнала́, ~гна́ло, *pf. (of* ~гоня́ть) to drive home, bring in (*cattle*).

при|гна́ть[2], гоню́, го́нишь, *past* ~гна́л, ~гнала́, ~гна́ло, *pf. (of* ~гоня́ть) to fit, adjust, joint.

пригн|у́ть, у́, ёшь, *pf. (of* пригиба́ть) to bend down, bow.

пригн|у́ться, у́сь, ёшься, *pf.* (*of* пригиба́ться) to bend down, bow.

пригова́рива|ть¹, ю, *impf.* (*coll.*) to keep saying, keep repeating (*as accompaniment to given action*).

пригова́рива|ть², ю, *impf. of* приговори́ть.

пригово́р, а, *m.* sentence; verdict; вы́нести п. to pass sentence; to bring in a verdict.

приговор|и́ть, ю́, и́шь, *pf.* (*of* пригова́ривать²) (к) to sentence (to), condemn (to); п. к пожи́зненному заключе́нию to sentence to imprisonment for life.

приго|ди́ться, жу́сь, ди́шься, *pf.* (+*d.*) to prove useful (to); to come in useful, come in handy; to stand in good stead.

приго́дность|ь, и, *f.* fitness, suitableness.

приго́д|ный (~ен, ~на), *adj.* (к) fit (for), suitable (for), good (for); useful; ни к чему́ не п. good-for-nothing, worthless.

приго́ж|ий (~, ~а), *adj.* (*folk poet.*) **1.** comely. **2.** (*of weather*) fine.

приголу́б|ить, лю, ишь, *pf.* (*of* голу́бить *and* ~ливать) (*folk poet.*) to caress, fondle.

приголу́блива|ть, ю, *impf. of* приголу́бить.

приго́н, а, *m.* **1.** driving home, bringing in. **2.** drove, herd.

пригонк|а, и, *f.* fitting, adjusting, jointing; п. часте́й (*tech.*) assembling.

пригоня́|ть, ю, *impf. of* пригна́ть.

пригор|а́ть, а́ет, *impf. of* ~е́ть.

пригоре́лый, *adj.* burnt.

пригор|е́ть, и́т, *pf.* (*of* ~а́ть) to be burnt; молоко́ ~е́ло the milk is burnt.

при́город, а, *m.* **1.** suburb. **2.** (*hist.*) subject town; small town.

при́городн|ый, *adj.* suburban; ~ое движе́ние (*railways*) local service(s); п. по́езд local train.

пригор|ок, ка, *m.* hillock, knoll.

при́горш|ня, ни, *g. pl.* ~ен *and* ~ней, *f.* handful; пить во́ду ~нями to drink water from cupped hands; ме́рить по́лными ~нями to give good measure; хвата́ть по́лными ~нями to seize with both hands.

пригорю́нива|ться, юсь, *impf. of* пригорю́ниться.

пригорю́н|иться, юсь, ишься, *pf.* (*of* ~иваться) (*folk poet.*) to become sad.

пригота́влива|ть(ся), ю(сь), *impf.* = приготовля́ть(ся).

приготови́тельный, *adj.* preparatory.

пригото́в|ить, лю, ишь, *pf.* (*of* пригота́вливать *and* ~ля́ть) to prepare; п. обе́д to cook, prepare a dinner; п. роль to learn (up) a part; п. ру́копись к набо́ру to prepare a manuscript for setting-up; п. кому́-н. сюрпри́з to prepare a surprise for someone.

пригото́в|иться, люсь, ишься, *pf.* (*of* пригота́вливаться *and* ~ля́ться) (+*inf.*) to prepare (to); (к) to prepare (oneself) (for).

приготовле́ни|е, я, *n.* preparation; без ~я off-hand, extempore.

приготовля́|ть(ся), ю(сь), *impf. of* пригото́вить(ся).

пригреба́|ть(ся), ю(сь), *impf. of* пригрести́(сь).

пригрева́|ть, ю, *impf. of* пригре́ть.

пригре́|зиться, жусь, зишься, *pf. of* гре́зиться.

пригре|сти́, бу́, бёшь, *past* ~б, ~бла́, *pf.* (*of* ~ба́ть) (*coll.*) **1.** to rake up. **2.** (к) to row (towards).

пригре|сти́сь, бу́сь, бёшься, *past* ~бся, ~бла́сь, *pf.* (*of* ~ба́ться) (*coll.*) = ~сти́ 2.

пригре́|ть, ю, *pf.* (*of* ~ва́ть) **1.** to warm. **2.** (*fig.*) to cherish; to give shelter (to), take to one's care; п. змею́ на груди́ to cherish a snake in one's bosom.

пригро|зи́ть, жу́, зи́шь, *pf. of* грози́ть 1.

пригу́б|ить, лю, ишь, *pf.* to take a sip (of), taste.

прида|ва́ть, ю́, ёшь, *impf. of* прида́ть.

придав|и́ть, лю́, ~ишь, *pf.* (*of* ~ливать) to press; to press down, weigh down (*also fig.*); to squeeze.

прида́влива|ть, ю, *impf. of* придави́ть.

прида́ни|е, я, *n.* adding, giving, imparting; для ~я хра́брости to give courage; для ~я зако́нной си́лы (+*d.*; *leg.*) for the enforcing (of).

прида́н|ое, ого, *n.* **1.** dowry; trousseau. **2.** layette.

прида́т|ок, ка, *m.* appendage, adjunct.

прида́точн|ый, *adj.* **1.** additional, supplementary. **2.** (*gram.*) subordinate; ~ое предложе́ние subordinate clause. **3.** (*bot.*) adventitious.

прида́|ть, м, шь, ст, ди́м, ди́те, ду́т, *past* при́дал, ~ла́, при́дало, *pf.* (*of* ~ва́ть) **1.** to add; (*mil.*) to attach. **2.** to increase, strengthen; п. бо́дрости (+*d.*) to hearten, put heart (into); п. ду́ху (+*d.*) to inspire, encourage. **3.** (+*a. and d.*) to give (to), impart (to); (*fig.*) attach (to); п. вкус to impart relish (to), give piquancy (to); п. лоск to give a polish, impart lustre (to); п. водонепроница́емость to waterproof; п. значе́ние to attach importance (to).

прида́ч|а, и, *f.* **1.** adding; (*mil.*) attaching. **2.** addition, supplement; в ~у into the bargain, in addition.

придвига́|ть(ся), ю(сь), *impf. of* придви́нуть(ся).

придви́|нуть, ну, нешь, *pf.* (*of* ~га́ть) to move (up), draw (up); ~нь(те) кре́сло к пе́чке draw your chair up to the stove.

придви́|нуться, нусь, нешься, *pf.* (*of* ~га́ться) to move up, draw near.

придво́рн|ый, *adj.* court; п. врач court physician; п. поэ́т poet laureate; п. шут court jester; *as noun* п., ~ого, *m.* courtier.

приде́л, а, *m.* (*eccl.*) side-altar; side-chapel.

приде́л|ать, аю, *pf.* (*of* ~ывать) (к) to fix (to), attach (to).

приде́лыва|ть, ю, *impf. of* приде́лать.

придерж|а́ть, у́, ~ишь, *pf.* (*of* ~ивать) to hold back (*also fig.*); п. това́р to hold back goods; п. язы́к to hold one's tongue.

приде́ржива|ть, ю, *impf. of* придержа́ть.

приде́ржива|ться, юсь, *impf.* 1. (за+*a.*) to hold on (to); п. за по́ручень to hold on to the rail. 2. (+*g.*) to hold (to), keep (to) (*also fig.*); (*fig.*) to stick (to), adhere (to); п. пра́вой стороны́ to keep to the right; п. догово́ра to adhere to an agreement; п. мне́ния to hold the opinion, be of the opinion; п. те́мы to stick to the subject; он ~ется рю́мочки (*coll.*) he is fond of the bottle.

приди́р|а, ы, *m. and f.* (*coll.*) caviller, captious fellow, fault-finder.

придира́|ться, юсь, *impf. of* придра́ться.

приди́рк|а, и, *f.* (*coll.*) cavil, captious objection; (*pl.*) fault-finding, nagging, carping.

приди́рчивост|ь, и, *f.* captiousness.

приди́рчив|ый (~, ~а), *adj.* captious, fault-finding, carping, nagging.

придоро́жный, *adj.* roadside, wayside.

при|дра́ться, деру́сь, дерёшься, *past* ~дра́лся, ~драла́сь, ~драло́сь, *pf.* (*of* ~дира́ться) (к) 1. to find fault (with), cavil (at), carp (at); to nag (at), pick (on); п. к кому́-н. из-за пустяко́в to find fault with someone over trifles. 2. (*coll.*) to seize (on, upon); п. к слу́чаю to seize (upon) an opportunity.

приду́м|ать, аю, *pf.* (*of* ~ывать) to think (of), think up, devise, invent; п. отгово́рку to think up an excuse; п. развлече́ние to devise an entertainment.

приду́мыва|ть, ю, *impf. of* приду́мать.

придуркова́тост|ь, и, *f.* (*coll.*) silliness, daftness, imbecility.

придуркова́т|ый (~, ~а), *adj.* (*coll.*) silly, daft, imbecile, half-baked.

при́дур|ь, и, *f.*; с ~ью (*coll.*) a bit crazy, a bit daft.

придуш|и́ть, у́, ~ишь, *pf.* (*coll.*) to strangle, smother.

придыха́ни|е, я, *n.* (*ling.*) aspiration.

придыха́тельн|ый, *adj.* (*ling.*) aspirate; *as noun* п., ~ого, *m.* aspirate.

при|ду́, *see* ~йти́.

приеда́|ться, юсь, *impf. of* прие́сться.

прие́зд, а, *m.* arrival, coming; с ~ом! welcome!

приезжа́|ть, ю, *impf. of* прие́хать.

приезжа́ющ|ий, *pres. part. of* приезжа́ть; *as noun* п., ~его, *m. and* ~ая, ~ей, *f.* newcomer, (new) arrival; гости́ница для ~их hotel.

прие́зж|ий, *adj.* newly arrived; passing through; ~ая тру́ппа troupe on tour; *as noun* п., ~его, *m.*; ~ая, ~ей, *f.* newcomer; (*in hotel, etc.*) visitor; ~ие лю́ди strangers (*as opp. to local inhabitants*).

прие́м, а, *m.* 1. receiving; reception; часы́ ~а (reception) hours, calling hours; (*of a doctor*) surgery (hours). 2. reception, welcome; оказа́ть кому́-н. раду́шный п. to accord someone a hearty welcome. 3. admittance (*to membership of association, party, etc.*). 4. reception (= *formal party*). 5. dose. 6. go; motion, movement; в оди́н п. at one go; вы́пить стака́н в два ~а to drain a glass in two draughts; испо́лнить кома́нду в три ~а to execute a command in three movements. 7. method, way, mode; device, trick (*also pejor.*); (*sport*) hold, grip; лече́бный п. method of treatment; жу́льнический п. a rogue's trick, a cad's trick. 8. (*mil.*) position; (*pl.; collect.*) manual; п. «в ру́ку» 'trail arms' position; руже́йные ~ы manual of the rifle; ~ы с ору́жием manual of arms.

приёмк|а, и, *f.* 1. formal acceptance (*of building, etc., on completion of construction*). 2. quality control (*procedure or organization*).

прие́млемост|ь, и, *f.* acceptability; admissibility.

прие́млем|ый (~, ~а), *adj.* acceptable; admissible.

приёмн|ая, ой, *f.* 1. waiting-room. 2. drawing-room; reception room.

приёмник[1], а, *m.* wireless (set), radio (set), receiver.

приёмник[2], а, *m.* reception centre (*for orphaned children, etc.*).

приёмн|ый, *adj.* 1. receiving; reception; п. день visiting day; 'at home' day; ~ые часы́ (reception) hours, calling hours; (*of a doctor*) surgery (hours); п. поко́й casualty ward; п. жёлоб hopper; ~ое отве́рстие intake, inlet. 2. relating to admittance, entrance; ~ая коми́ссия selection committee, selection board; п. экза́мен entrance examination. 3. foster, adoptive; п. оте́ц foster-father; ~ая мать foster-mother; п. сын adopted son, foster-son.

приёмо-переда́точный, *adj.* (*radio*) two-way.

приёмочн|ый, *adj.* reception; acceptance; п. пункт reception centre; п. акт acceptance certificate, inspection certificate; ~ое испыта́ние acceptance test, official test.

приёмщик, а, *m.* examiner, inspector (*of goods at a factory*).

приёмыш, а, *m.* adopted child, foster-child.

при|е́сться, е́стся, едя́тся, *past* ~е́лся, ~е́лась, *pf.* (*of* ~еда́ться) (+*d.*; *coll.*) to pall (on), tire, bore; мне ~е́лась э́та рабо́та I am fed up with this work.

прие́|хать, ду, дешь, *pf.* (*of* ~зжа́ть) to arrive, come (*not on foot*).

прижа́т|ый, *p.p.p. of* ~ь; быть ~ым к стене́ (*fig.*) to have one's back to the wall.

приж|а́ть, му́, мёшь, *pf.* (*of* ~има́ть) **1.** (к) to press (to), clasp (to); п. к земле́ (*mil.*) to pin down; п. к груди́ to clasp to one's bosom; п. к стене́ (*fig.*) to drive into a corner; п. у́ши (*of a horse*) to lay back its ears. **2.** (*fig.*) to press, bring pressure to bear (upon); п. до́лжников to press one's debtors.

приж|а́ться, му́сь, мёшься, *pf.* (*of* ~има́ться) **1.** (к) to press oneself (to, against); to cuddle up (to), snuggle up (to), nestle up (to); п. к стене́ to flatten oneself against the wall. **2.** *pass. of* ~а́ть.

при|же́чь, жгу́, жжёшь, жгут, *past* ~жёг, ~жгла́, *pf.* (*of* ~жига́ть) to cauterize, sear.

прижива́л|ка, ки, *f. of* ~ьщик.

прижива́льщик, а, *m.* (**1.** (*hist.*) dependant. **2.** (*fig.*) hanger-on, sponger, parasite.

прижива́|ть(ся), ю(сь), *impf. of* прижи́ть(ся).

прижига́ни|е, я, *n.* (*med.*) cauterization, searing.

прижига́|ть, ю, *impf. of* приже́чь.

прижи́зненный, *adj.* occurring during one's lifetime.

прижима́|ть(ся), ю(сь), *impf. of* прижа́ть(ся).

прижи́мист|ый (~, ~а), *adj.* (*coll.*) close-fisted, tight-fisted, stingy.

прижи́мк|а, и, *f.* (*fig., coll.*) pressure; clamping down.

прижи́|ть, иву́, ивёшь, *past* ~и́л, ~ила́, ~и́ло, *pf.* (*of* ~ива́ть) (*coll.*) to beget (*usu. of extra-marital unions*).

прижи́|ться, иву́сь, ивёшься, *past* ~и́лся, ~ила́сь, *pf.* (*of* ~ива́ться) **1.** to settle down, get acclimatized. **2.** (*of plants*) to take root, strike root.

приз¹, а, *pl.* ~ы́, *m.* prize; переходя́щий п. challenge prize; получи́ть п. to win a prize; присуди́ть п. (+*d.*) to award a prize (to).

приз², а, *m.* (*naut., leg.*) prize.

призаду́м|аться, аюсь, *pf.* (*of* ~ываться) to become thoughtful, become pensive.

призаду́мыва|ться, юсь, *impf. of* призаду́маться.

приза|ня́ть, йму́, ймёшь, *past* ~ня́л, ~няла́, ~ня́ло, *pf.* (*coll.*) to borrow.

призва́ни|е, я, *n.* vocation, calling; сле́довать своему́ ~ю to follow one's vocation; чу́вствовать п. к духо́вному са́ну to have a vocation to go into the church; хиру́рг по ~ю a surgeon by vocation.

при|зва́ть, зову́, зовёшь, *past* ~зва́л, ~звала́, ~зва́ло, *pf.* (*of* ~зыва́ть) to call, summon; to call upon, appeal; п. на по́-

мощь to call for help; п. на вое́нную слу́жбу to call up (*for military service*), call to the colours; п. к поря́дку to call to order; п. прокля́тия на чью-н. го́лову to call down curses on someone's head.

при|зва́ться, зову́сь, зовёшься, *past* ~зва́лся, ~звала́сь, ~звало́сь, *pf.* (*of* ~зыва́ться) **1.** to be called up. **2.** *pass. of* ~зва́ть.

при́звук, а, *m.* additional sound.

призе́мист|ый (~, ~а), *adj.* stocky, squat; thickset.

приземле́ни|е, я, *n.* (*aeron.*) landing, touch-down.

приземл|и́ть, ю́, и́шь, *pf.* (*of* ~я́ть) (*aeron.*) to land, bring in to land.

приземл|и́ться, ю́сь, и́шься, *pf.* (*of* ~я́ться) (*aeron.*) to land, touch down.

приземля́|ть(ся), ю(сь), *impf. of* приземли́ть(ся).

призёр, а, *m.* prize-winner, prizeman.

при́зм|а, ы, *f.* prism; сквозь ~у (+*g.*; *fig.*) in the light (of).

призмати́ческий, *adj.* prismatic.

призна|ва́ть(ся), ю́(сь), ёшь(ся), *impf. of* призна́ть(ся).

при́знак, а, *m.* sign; indications; п. боле́зни symptom; служи́ть ~ом (+*g.*) to be a sign (of); обнару́живать ~и (+*g.*) to show signs (of); име́ются все ~и того́, что there is every indication that; не подава́ть ~ов жи́зни to show no sign of life; по ~у (+*g.*) on the basis (of).

призна́ни|е, я, *n.* **1.** confession, declaration; admission, acknowledgement; нево́льное п. involuntary admission; п. вины́ avowal of guilt; п. в любви́ declaration of love; по о́бщему ~ю by general admission. **2.** recognition; п. де-фа́кто (*leg., polit.*) de facto recognition; получи́ть п. to obtain, win recognition; получи́ть всео́бщее п. to be generally recognized.

при́зн|анный, *p.p.p. of* ~а́ть *and adj.* acknowledged, recognized.

призна́тельност|ь, и, *f.* gratitude.

призна́тел|ьный (~ен, ~ьна), *adj.* grateful.

призна́|ть, ю, *pf.* (*of* ~ва́ть) **1.** to recognize; to spot, identify; вы меня́ не ~ли? did you not recognize me?; я ~л в нём иностра́нца по оде́жде I spotted him as a foreigner by his dress. **2.** (*leg., polit.*) to recognize; п. прави́тельство to recognize a government. **3.** to admit, own, acknowledge; п. вину́, п. себя́ вино́вным (*leg.*) to plead guilty; п. свою́ оши́бку to admit one's mistake; п. себя́ побеждённым to acknowledge defeat. **4.** to deem, vote; п. ну́жным to deem (it) necessary; п. недействи́тельным to declare invalid, nullify; п. (не)вино́вным to find (not) guilty; п. неуда́чным to vote a failure.

призна|ться, юсь, *pf.* (*of* ~**ваться**) (в+*p.*) to confess (to), own (to); п. в любви́ to make a declaration of love; п. в преступле́нии to confess to a crime; на́до п., что it must be admitted that, the truth is that; п. (сказа́ть) to tell the truth; п., и фами́лии его́ не зна́ю to tell the truth I don't even know his name.

призов|о́й, *adj. of* приз; ~**ые де́ньги** prize-money; ~**о́е су́дно** (*naut., leg.*) prize.

призо́р, а, *m.* **без** ~**а** (*coll.*) untended, neglected.

при́зрак, а, *m.* spectre, ghost, phantom, apparition; гоня́ться за ~**ами** to catch at shadows.

призрачност|ь, и, *f.* illusoriness.

при́зрач|ный (~**ен,** ~**на**), *adj.* **1.** spectral, ghostly, phantasmal. **2.** (*fig.*) illusory, imagined; ~**ная опа́сность** imagined danger.

призрева́|ть, ю, *impf. of* призре́ть.

призре́ни|е, я, *n.* care, charity; **дом** ~**я бе́дных** alms-house, poor people's home.

призр|е́ть, ю, ~**и́шь,** *pf.* (*of* ~**ева́ть**) to support by charity.

призы́в, а, *m.* **1.** call, appeal; **откли́кнуться на чей-н. п.** to respond to someone's call. **2.** slogan; **первома́йские** ~**ы** May-day slogans; **3.** (*mil.*) call-up, conscription. **4.** (*collect.; mil.*) levy; (group of) conscripts, draft; **ле́нинский п.** (*hist.*) the Lenin Enrolment (*large entry into Soviet Communist Party after death of Lenin*).

призыва́|ть(ся), ю(сь), *impf. of* призва́ть(ся).

призывни́к, а́, *m.* man called up for military service; man due for call-up.

призывно́й, *adj.* call-up; п. **во́зраст** call-up age; п. **уча́сток** reception unit.

призы́вный, *adj.* invocatory; inviting; п. **клич** call.

при́иск, а, *m.* mine (*for precious metals*); **золоты́е** ~**и** gold-field(s).

прииска́ни|е, я, *n.* finding.

прииска́тел|ь, я, *m.* miner, mine worker.

при|иска́ть, ищу́, и́щешь, *pf.* (*of* ~**и́скивать**) to find.

прии́скива|ть, ю, *impf.* (*coll.*) **1.** *impf. of* прииска́ть. **2.** (*impf. only*) to look for, hunt for; мы ~**ем кварти́ру без ме́бели** we are looking for unfurnished accommodation.

прии́сковый, *adj. of* при́иск.

при|йти́, ду́, дёшь, *past* ~**шёл,** ~**шла́,** *pf.* (*of* ~**ходи́ть**) (*in var. senses*) to come; to arrive; п. **пе́рвым** to come in first; п. **в восто́рг (от)** to go into raptures (over); п. **в плохо́е настрое́ние** to get into a bad mood; п. **в у́жас** to be horrified; п. **в я́рость** to fly into a rage; п. **в го́лову кому́-н., на ум кому́-н.** to occur to someone, strike someone, cross

one's mind; мысль ~**шла́ мне в го́лову** the idea occurred to me; п. **в себя́,** п. **в чу́вство** to come round, regain consciousness; (*fig.*) to come to one's senses; п. **к концу́** to come to an end; п. **к заключе́нию,** п. **к убежде́нию** to come to the conclusion, arrive at a conclusion; п. **к соглаше́нию** to come to an agreement.

при|йти́сь, ду́сь, дёшься, *past* ~**шёлся,** ~**шла́сь,** *pf.* (*of* ~**ходи́ться**) **1.** (по+*d.*) to fit; **ковёр** ~**шёлся как раз по разме́рам спа́льни** the carpet fitted the bedroom floor just right; п. **кому́-н. по вку́су, по нра́ву** to be to someone's taste, liking; **га́лстук** ~**шёлся мне по вку́су** the tie was just what I wanted. **2.** (на+*a.; of dates, days or occasions*) to fall (on); **Па́сха** ~**шла́сь на 28-ое ма́рта** Easter fell on the 28th of March. **3.** (*impers.+d.*) to have (to); **нам** ~**шло́сь подожда́ть ещё два часа́** we had to wait another two hours; **ей** ~**дётся неме́дленно верну́ться в Москву́** she will have to return to Moscow immediately. **4.** (*impers.+d.*) to happen (to), fall to the lot (of); мне ~**шло́сь быть ря́дом в тот моме́нт, когда́ он упа́л в о́бморок** I happened to be standing by when he fainted; им **ту́го** ~**шло́сь** they had a rough time; как ~**дётся** (*coll.*) anyhow, at haphazard. **5.** (*impers.;* на+*a. or* с+*g.; coll.*) to be owing (to, from); **на ка́ждого** ~**шло́сь по фу́нту** they got a pound each; **с вас** ~**дётся де́сять рубле́й** there is ten roubles to come from you.

прика́з, а, *m.* **1.** order, command; по ~**у** by order; п. **по войска́м** order of the day; п. **о выступле́нии** (*mil.*) marching orders; **отда́ть п.** to give an order, issue an order. **2.** (*hist.*) office, department.

приказа́ни|е, я, *n.* order, command, injunction.

прика|за́ть, жу́, ~**жешь,** *pf.* (*of* ~**зывать**) (+*d.*) to order, command; to give orders; to direct; п. **до́лго жить** (*coll.*) to pass on, depart this life; **что** ~**жете?** what do you wish?, what can I do for you?; **как** ~**жете** as you please, as you wish; **как** ~**жете понима́ть э́то?** how am I supposed to take this?; what do you mean by this?

прика́з|ный, *adj.* **1.** *adj. of* ~ **1;** в ~**ном поря́дке** in the form of an order. **2.** (*hist.*) departmental; п. **язы́к** chancery language (*as opp. to literary language*); *as noun* **п.,** ~**ного,** *m.* clerk, scribe. **3.** *as noun* (*obs.*) petty official.

прика́зчик, а, *m.* (*obs.*) **1.** shop-assistant, salesman. **2.** steward, bailiff.

прика́зыва|ть, ю, *impf. of* приказа́ть.

прика́лыва|ть, ю, *impf. of* приколо́ть.

прика́нчива|ть, ю, *impf. of* прикончить.

прикарма́нива|ть, ю, *impf. of* прикарма́-
нить.

прикарма́н|ить, ю, ишь, *pf. (of ~ивать)*
(*coll.*) to pocket.

прика́рмлива|ть, ю, *impf.* 1. *impf. of* при-
корми́ть. 2. (*impf. only*) to give additional
food (*during the weaning period*).

прикаса́|ться, юсь, *impf. of* прикосну́ться.

прика|ти́ть, чу́, ~тишь, *pf. (of ~тывать)*
1. (к) to roll up (to). 2. (*coll.*) to roll up,
turn up.

прика́тыва|ть, ю, *impf. of* прикати́ть.

прики́дыва|ть(ся), ю(сь), *impf. of* прики́-
нуть(ся).

прики́|нуть, ну, нешь, *pf. (of ~дывать)*
1. to throw in, add. 2. to estimate (approximately); п. на веса́х to weigh; п. в
уме́ (*fig.*) to weigh (up), ponder.

прики́|нуться, нусь, нешься, *pf. (of ~ды-
ваться)* (+*i.*; *coll.*) to pretend (to be), feign;
п. больны́м to pretend to be ill, feign illness;
п. лисо́й to fawn, toady; п. раска́явшимся
to feign repentance; он ~нулся, что не
ви́дит меня́ he pretended that he could not
see me.

прикла́д¹, а, *m.* butt, butt-stock (*of firearm*).

прикла́д², а, *m.* trimmings (*used by tailor or
boot-maker*).

прикла́дк|а, и, *f.* levelling (*of rifle*); posi-
tion; п. лёжа, п. с коле́на, п. сто́я lying,
kneeling, standing position (*with rifle in
hand*).

прикладн|о́й, *adj.* applied; ~о́е иску́сство
applied art(s); ~а́я фи́зика applied physics.

прикла́дыва|ть(ся), ю(сь), *impf. of* прило-
жи́ть(ся).

прикле́ива|ть(ся), ю(сь), *impf. of* при-
кле́ить(ся).

прикле́|ить, ю, ишь, *pf. (of ~ивать)* to
stick; to glue; to paste; to affix; п. ма́рку to
stick on a stamp; п. афи́шу к стене́ to stick
(up) a bill on a wall.

прикле́|иться, ится, *pf. (of ~иваться)* (к)
to stick (to), adhere (to).

приклеп|а́ть, а́ю, *pf. (of ~ывать)* to rivet.

прикле́пыва|ть, ю, *impf. of* приклепа́ть.

приклёпыва|ть, ю, *impf. of* приклепа́ть.

приклон|и́ть, ю́, ~ишь, *pf.*; п. го́лову to lay
one's head; у него́ не́где п. го́лову he has
nowhere to lay his head; п. слух, п. у́хо
(*obs.*) to listen intently.

приключ|а́ть(ся), а́ю, а́ет(ся), *impf. of*
~и́ть(ся).

приключе́ни|е, я, *n.* adventure.

приключе́нческий, *adj.* adventure; п. рома́н
adventure story.

приключе́нчеств|о, а, *n.* adventure litera-
ture.

приключ|и́ть, у́, и́шь, *pf. (of ~а́ть)* (*tech.*) to
connect up.

приключ|и́ться, и́тся, *pf. (of ~а́ться)* (*coll.*)
to happen, occur.

прикноп|и́ть, лю́, ~ишь, *pf.* to pin up (*with
a drawing pin*).

прико́в|анный, *p.p.p. of* ~а́ть; п. к посте́ли
bed-ridden, confined to one's bed.

прик|ова́ть, ую́, уёшь, *pf. (of ~о́вывать)*
1. (к) to chain (to). 2. (*fig.*) to chain; to
rivet; на́ше внима́ние ~ова́ла к себе́ их
блестя́щая фо́рма our attention was riveted
on their gorgeous uniforms; страх ~ова́л
нас к ме́сту fear rooted us to the spot.

прико́выва|ть, ю, *impf. of* прикова́ть.

прико́л, а, *m.* stake; пала́точный п. tent-
-peg; стоя́ть на ~е (*naut.*) to be laid up, be
idle.

прикола́чива|ть, ю, *impf. of* приколоти́ть.

приколо|ти́ть, чу́, ~тишь, *pf. (of* прикола́-
чивать*)* to nail, fasten with nails.

прикол|о́ть, ю́, ~ешь, *pf. (of* прика́лывать*)*
1. to pin, fasten with a pin. 2. (*coll.*) to stab,
transfix; п. штыко́м to bayonet.

прикомандир|ова́ть, у́ю, *pf. (of ~о́вывать)*
(к) to attach (to), second (to).

прикомандиро́выва|ть, ю, *impf. of* прико-
мандирова́ть.

прико́нч|ить, у, ишь, *pf. (of* прика́нчивать*)*
(*coll.*) 1. to use up. 2. (*fig.*) to finish off.

прикоп|и́ть, лю́, ~ишь, *pf.* (+*a. or g.*; *coll.*)
to save (up), put by.

прико́рм, а, *m.* 1. lure, bait (*for birds or fish*).
2. additional food.

прикорм|и́ть, лю́, ~ишь, *pf. (of* прика́рмли-
вать*)* to lure (*by putting out food*).

прико́рм|ка, ки, *f.* = ~.

прикорн|у́ть, у́, ёшь, *pf.* (*coll.*) (к) to lean
up (against), prop oneself up (against) (*with
a view to taking a nap*); п. на дива́не to curl
up on the sofa.

прикоснове́ни|е, я, *n.* 1. touch; то́чка ~я
point of contact. 2. (*sing. only*) concern; я не
име́ю никако́го ~я к э́тому де́лу this affair
is no concern of mine, is nothing to do with
me.

прикоснове́нност|ь, и, *f.* (к) concern (in),
involvement (in).

прикоснове́н|ный (~, ~на), *adj.* (к) con-
cerned (in), involved (in), implicated (in);
он был ~ к уби́йству he was implicated in
a murder.

прикосн|у́ться, у́сь, ёшься, *pf. (of* прика-
са́ться*)* (к) to touch (lightly).

прикра́с|а, ы, *f.* (*coll.*) embellishment; без
~ unvarnished, unadorned; рассказа́ть
без ~ to give a straightforward account.

прикра́|сить, шу, сишь, *pf. (of ~шивать)*
to embellish, embroider (*in speech*).

прикра́шива|ть, ю, *impf. of* прикра́сить.

прикрепи́тельный, *adj.* п. тало́н registration card (*document certifying that customer is*

registered with stated retailer for supply of provisions, etc.).

прикреп|и́ть, лю́, и́шь, pf. (of ~ля́ть) (к) 1. to fasten (to). 2. (fig.) to attach (to); п. де́тский сад к больни́це to attach a kindergarten to a hospital.

прикреп|и́ться, лю́сь, и́шься, pf. (of ~ля́ться) (к) 1. to register (at, with). 2. pass. of ~и́ть.

прикрепле́ни|е, я, n. 1. fastening. 2. (fig.) attachment; п. к земле́ (hist.) attaching to the soil (as serf). 3. registration.

прикрепля́|ть(ся), ю(сь), impf. of прикрепи́ть(ся).

прикри́кива|ть, ю, impf. of прикри́кнуть.

прикри́к|нуть, ну, нешь, pf. (of ~ивать) (на+a.) to shout (at), raise one's voice (at).

прикру|ти́ть, чу́, ~тишь, pf. (of ~чивать) 1. (к) to tie (to), bind (to), fasten (to). 2. (coll.) to turn down (a wick).

прикру́чива|ть, ю, impf. of прикрути́ть.

прикрыва́|ть(ся), ю(сь), impf. of прикры́ть(ся).

прикры́ти|е, я, n. cover; escort; (fig.) screen, cloak; под ~ем (+g.) under cover (of), screened (by); артиллери́йское п. artillery cover; п. истреби́телями fighter cover, fighter escort.

прикр|ы́ть, о́ю, о́ешь, pf. (of ~ыва́ть) 1. (+i.) to cover (with); to screen; п. кастрю́лю кры́шкой to put the lid on a saucepan. 2. to protect, shelter, shield; п. глаза́ руко́й to shade, shield one's eyes (with one's hand); п. наступле́ние артилле́рией to cover an attack with an artillery barrage. 3. (fig.) to cover (up), conceal, screen; п. своё неве́жество to conceal one's ignorance. 4. (coll.) to close down, wind up.

прикр|ы́ться, о́юсь, о́ешься, pf. (of ~ыва́ться) 1. (+i.) to cover oneself (with); (fig.) to use as a cover, take refuge (in), shelter (behind); он ~ы́лся положе́нием иностра́нца he took refuge in the fact of being a foreigner. 2. (coll.) to close down, go out of business. 3. pass. of ~ы́ть.

прикуп|а́ть, а́ю, impf. of ~и́ть.

прикуп|и́ть, лю́, ~ишь, pf. (of ~а́ть) (+a. or g.) to buy (some more).

прику́пк|а, и, f. additional purchase.

прику́рива|ть, ю, impf. of прикури́ть.

прикур|и́ть, ю́, ~ишь, pf. (of ~ивать) (у кого́-н.) to get a light (from someone's cigarette).

прику́с, а, m. bite.

прику|си́ть, шу́, ~сишь, pf. (of ~сывать) to bite; п. (себе́) язы́к to bite one's tongue; (fig., coll.) to hold one's tongue, keep one's mouth shut.

прику́сыва|ть, ю, impf. of прикуси́ть.

прила́в|ок, ка, m. counter; рабо́тник ~ка counter hand, salesman, (shop) assistant.

прилага́|емый, pres. part. pass. of ~ть and adj. accompanying; enclosed; subjoined; п. почто́вый перево́д the enclosed postal order.

прилага́тельн|ый, adj. и́мя ~ое (or as noun ~ое, ~ого, n.) adjective.

прилага́|ть, ю, impf. of приложи́ть.

прила́|дить, жу, дишь, pf. (of ~живать) (к) to fit (to), adjust (to).

прила́жива|ть, ю, impf. of прила́дить.

приласка́|ть, ю, pf. to caress, fondle, pet.

приласка́|ться, юсь, pf. (к) to snuggle up (to).

прилгн|у́ть, у́, ёшь, pf. (coll.) to insert fabrications (into a narrative).

прилега́|ть, ет, impf. (к) 1. (pf. приле́чь[1]) to fit. 2. (no pf.) to adjoin, be adjacent (to), border (upon); сад ~ет к те́ннисному ко́рту the garden adjoins the tennis court.

прилега́|ющий, pres. part. of ~ть and adj. 1. close-fitting, tight-fitting. 2. (к) adjoining, adjacent (to), contiguous (to).

прилежа́ни|е, я, n. diligence, industry, assiduousness; application.

прилежа́щий, adj. (math.) adjacent, adjoining, contiguous.

приле́ж|ный (~ен, ~на), adj. diligent, industrious, assiduous.

прилеп|и́ть, лю́, ~ишь, pf. (of ~ля́ть) (к) to stick (to, on).

прилеп|и́ться, лю́сь, ~ишься, pf. (of ~ля́ться) 1. (к) to stick (to, on). 2. pass. of ~и́ть.

прилепля́|ть(ся), ю(сь), impf. of прилепи́ть(ся).

прилёт, а, m. arrival (by air).

прилет|а́ть, а́ю, impf. of ~е́ть.

приле|те́ть, чу́, ти́шь, pf. (of ~та́ть) 1. to arrive (by air), fly in. 2. (fig., coll.) to fly, come flying.

при|ле́чь[1], ля́жет, ля́гут, past ~лёг, ~легла́, pf. of ~лега́ть.

при|ле́чь[2], ля́гу, ля́жешь, ля́гут, past ~лёг, ~легла́, pf. 1. to lie down (for a short while). 2. (of standing crops) to be laid flat.

прили́в, а, m. 1. flow, flood (of tide); rising tide; (fig.) surge, influx; волна́ ~a tidal wave; п. и отли́в ebb and flow; п. негодова́ния (up)surge of indignation. 2. (med.) congestion; п. кро́ви rush of blood; (fig.) п. эне́ргии burst of energy. 3. (tech.) boss, lug; (naut.) cleat.

прилива́|ть, ет, impf. of прили́ть.

прили́вный, adj. tidal.

прили́з|анный, p.p.p. of ~а́ть; ~анные во́лосы smarmed-down hair.

прили|зáть, жу́, ~жешь, *pf.* (*of* ~зывать) to lick smooth.

прилúзыва|ть, ю, *impf. of* прилизáть.

прилип|áть, áет, *impf. of* ~нуть.

прилúп|нуть, нет, *past* ~, ~ла, *pf.* (*of* ~áть) (к) to stick (to), adhere (to).

прилúпчив|ый (~, ~a), *adj.* (*coll.*) 1. sticking, adhesive. 2. (*fig.*) boring, tiresome. 3. (*of diseases*) catching.

прилúстник, а, *m.* (*bot.*) stipule.

при|лúть, льёт, *past* ~лúл, ~лилá, ~лúло, *pf.* (*of* ~ливáть) (к) to flow (to); (*of blood*) to rush (to); кровь ~лилá к её щекáм blood rushed to her cheeks.

прилúчеств|овать, ует, *impf.* (+*d.*; *obs.*) to befit, become.

прилúчи|е, я, *n.* decency, propriety; decorum; соблюдáть ~я to observe the decencies, the proprieties.

прилúч|ный (~ен, ~на), *adj.* 1. decent, proper; decorous, seemly; a clean story. 2. (+*d.*; *obs.*) fitting; appropriate (to). 3. (*coll.*) decent, tolerable, fair; ~ная зарплáта a decent wage.

приложéни|е, я, *n.* 1. application; п. я́дерной фи́зики к констру́кции подво́дных ло́док the application of nuclear physics to the design of submarines. 2. affixing; apposition; п. печáти affixing of a seal. 3. enclosure (*of document, etc., with letter*). 4. supplement (*to newspaper, periodical, etc.*). 5. appendix (*to a book*). 6. (*gram.*) apposition.

прилож|úть, ý, ~ишь, *pf.* 1. (*impf.* прикла́дывать) (к) to put (to), hold (to); п. ру́ку ко лбу to put one's hand to one's head; п. ру́ку to put one's hand (to), take a hand (in); to add one's signature (to). 2. (*impf.* прикла́дывать *and* прилагáть) to add, join; to enclose; to affix; п. к заявлéнию характери́стику to enclose a testimonial with an application; п. печáть to affix a seal. 3. (*impf.* прилагáть) to apply; п. си́лу to apply force; п. все уси́лия to strain every effort; п. всё старáние to do one's best, try one's hardest.

прилож|úться, у́сь, ~ишься, *pf.* (*of* прикла́дываться) 1. (+*i.*, к) to put (*one's ear, eye, or mouth*) (to); п. глáзом к замо́чной сквáжине to put one's eye to the keyhole; п. (губáми) to kiss. 2. to take aim. 3. *pass. of* ~úть; остальнóе ~ится the rest will come.

прилунéни|е, я, *n.* landing on the Moon.

прилун|úться, ю́сь, и́шься, *pf.* to land on the Moon.

прильн|ýть, ý, ёшь, *pf. of* льнуть.

при́м|а, ы, *f.* (*mus.*) 1. tonic. 2. first string, top string. 3. first violin.

при́ма-балери́на, при́мы-балери́ны, *f.* prima ballerina.

примадо́нн|а, ы, *f.* prima donna.

примá|заться, жусь, жешься, *pf.* (*of* ~зываться) (к; *coll.*, *pejor.*) to attach oneself (to), get in (with).

примáзыва|ться, юсь, *impf. of* примáзаться.

примáнива|ть, ю, *impf. of* приманúть.

приман|úть, ю́, ~ишь, *pf.* (*of* ~ивать) (*coll.*) to lure; to decoy; to entice, allure.

примáнк|а, и, *f.* bait, lure; (*fig.*) enticement, allurement.

примáс, а, *m.* (*eccl.*) primate.

примáт¹, а, *m.* (*philos.*) primacy; pre-eminence.

примáт², а, *m.* (*zool.*) primate.

примáчива|ть, ю, *impf. of* примочúть.

примелькá|ться, юсь, *pf.* (*coll.*) to become familiar; её лицó мне óчень ~лось her face is very familiar to me.

применéни|е, я, *n.* application; use; п. к мéстности (*mil.*) use of ground, adaptation to terrain; нáши мéтоды получи́ли широ́кое п. our methods have been widely adopted; в ~и (к) in application (to).

применúмост|ь, и, *f.* applicability.

применúм|ый (~, ~a), *adj.* applicable, suitable.

применúтельно, *adv.* (к) conformably (to), in conformity (with); as applied (to).

примен|úть, ю́, ~ишь, *pf.* (*of* ~я́ть) to apply; to employ, use; п. свои́ знáния to apply one's knowledge; п. на прáктике to put into practice.

примен|úться, ю́сь, ~ишься, *pf.* (*of* ~я́ться) (к) to adapt oneself (to), conform (to).

примéр, а, *m.* 1. example, instance; привести́ п. to give an example; привести́ в п. to cite as an example; поясни́ть ~ом to illustrate by means of an example; к ~у (*coll.*) by way of illustration, for example. 2. example; model; брать п. с когó-н., слéдовать чьему́-н. ~у to follow someone's example; подавáть п. to set an example; показáть п. to give an example, give the lead; для ~а as an example; по ~у (+*g.*) after the example (of), on the pattern (of); не в п. (+*d.*; *coll.*) unlike; (+*comp.*) far more, by far; не в п. прóчим unlike the others; онá сегóдня игрáет не в п. лу́чше, чем игрáла на той недéле her playing today is better by far than it was last week.

примерз|áть, áю, *impf. of* ~нуть.

примёрз|нуть, ну, нешь, *past* ~, ~ла, *pf.* (*of* ~áть) (к) to freeze (to).

примéр|ить, ю, ишь, *pf.* (*of* мéрить 2 *and* ~я́ть) to try on; to fit.

примéр|иться, юсь, ишься, *pf.* (*of* ~я́ться) (*coll.*) to contrive.

примéрк|а, и, *f.* trying on; fitting.

примéрно, *adv.* 1. in exemplary fashion;

п. вести́ себя́ to be an example. 2. approximately, roughly.

приме́р|ный (~ен, ~на), *adj*. 1. exemplary, model; п. перево́д a model version. 2. approximate, rough.

пример|я́ть(ся), я́ю(сь), *impf. of* ~ить(ся).

при́мес|ь, и, *f*. admixture; dash; (*fig.*) touch; без ~ей unadulterated; молоко́ с ~ью ко́фе milk with a dash of coffee.

приме́т|а, ы, *f*. sign, token; mark; име́ть на ~е to have one's eye (on); быть на ~е to be before the eye, be the centre of attention.

примет|а́ть, а́ю, *pf*. (*of* ~ывать) to tack (on), stitch (on).

приме́|тить, чу, тишь, *pf*. (*of* ~ча́ть) to notice, perceive.

приме́тливост|ь, и, *f*. power(s) of observation.

приме́тлив|ый (~, ~а), *adj*. (*coll.*) observant.

приме́тно, *adv*. perceptibly, visibly, noticeably; он п. похуде́л he has grown perceptibly thinner.

приме́т|ный (~ен, ~на), *adj*. 1. perceptible, visible, noticeable. 2. conspicuous, prominent.

примётыва|ть, ю, *impf. of* примета́ть.

примеча́ни|е, я, *n*. note, footnote; снабди́ть ~ями to annotate. 2. (*pl.*) comment(s), commentary.

примеча́тельност|ь, и, *f*. noteworthiness.

примеча́тел|ьный (~ен, ~ьна), *adj*. noteworthy, notable, remarkable.

примеча́|ть, ю, *impf*. 1. *impf. of* приме́тить. 2. (*impf. only*) (за+*i*.) (*coll.*) to keep an eye (on), keep a watch out (on); ~й за ним, а то он дое́ст все конфе́ты keep a watch out on him, or else he'll finish off all the sweets.

примеш|а́ть, а́ю, *pf*. (*of* ~ивать) (+*a. or g.*) to add, admix; (*tech.*) to alloy.

приме́шива|ть, ю, *impf. of* примеша́ть.

примина́|ть, ю, *impf. of* примя́ть.

примире́н|ец, ца, *m*. (*pejor.*) conciliator, compromiser.

примире́ни|е, я, *n*. reconciliation.

примире́нческий, *adj*. (*pejor.*) compromising.

примире́нчеств|о, а, *n*. (*pejor.*) conciliatoriness, spirit of compromise, appeasement.

примир|и́мый (~и́м, ~и́ма), *pres. part. pass. of* ~и́ть *and adj*. reconcilable.

примири́тел|ь, я, *m*. reconciler, conciliator, peace-maker.

примири́тел|ьный (~ен, ~ьна), *adj*. conciliatory.

примир|и́ть, ю́, и́шь, *pf*. (*of* ~я́ть) to reconcile; to conciliate; п. супру́гов to reconcile a husband and wife; п. кого́-н. с необхо-

ди́мостью больши́х жертв to reconcile someone to the necessity for great sacrifices.

примир|и́ться, ю́сь, и́шься, *pf*. (*of* ~я́ться) (с+*i*.) 1. to be reconciled (to), make it up (with). 2. to reconcile oneself (to); п. с неудо́бствами to reconcile oneself to, accept discomforts.

примир|я́ть(ся), я́ю(сь), *impf. of* ~и́ть(ся).

примити́в, а, *m*. 1. (*art*) primitive. 2. primitive artefact; specimen, *etc.*, in rude, undeveloped state. 3. (*coll.*) primitive person.

примитиви́зм, а, *m*. (*art*) primitivism.

примити́в|ный (~ен, ~на), *adj*. primitive; rude, crude.

примкн|у́ть, у́, ёшь, *pf*. (*of* примыка́ть) (к) 1. to fix (to), attach (to); п. штыки́! fix bayonets! 2. (*fig.*) to join, attach oneself (to); to side (with).

примо́лкн|уть, у, ешь, *pf*. (*coll.*) to fall silent.

примо́рский, *adj*. seaside; maritime; п. куро́рт seaside resort.

примо́рь|е, я, *n*. littoral, seaside.

примо|сти́ть, щу́, сти́шь, *pf*. (*coll.*) to find room (for), stick (*in a crowded place or inconvenient surroundings*).

примо|сти́ться, щу́сь, сти́шься, *pf*. (*coll.*) to find room for oneself, perch oneself (*in a crowded place or inconvenient surroundings*).

примоч|и́ть, у́, ~ишь, *pf*. (*of* прима́чивать) to bathe, moisten; п. себе́ глаз to bathe one's eye.

примо́чк|а, и, *f*. wash, lotion; свинцо́вая п. Goulard (water); п. для глаз eye-lotion.

при́мул|а, ы, *f*. primula, primrose.

при́мус, а, *m*. primus(-stove).

при́мус|ный, *adj*. *of* ~; ~ная иго́лка primus pricker.

примч|а́ть, у́, и́шь, *pf*. (*coll.*) 1. to bring in a hurry, hurry along with. 2. = ~а́ться.

примч|а́ться, у́сь, и́шься, *pf*. to come tearing along.

примыка́ни|е, я, *n*. 1. contiguity. 2. (*gram.*) agglutination.

примыка́|ть, ю, *impf*. 1. *impf. of* примкну́ть. 2. (*impf. only*) (к) to adjoin, border (upon), abut (upon).

примыка́|ющий, *pres. part. act. of* ~ть *and adj*. affiliated.

при|мя́ть, мну́, мнёшь, *pf*. (*of* ~мина́ть) to crush, flatten; to trample down, tread down.

принадлеж|а́ть, у́, и́шь, *impf*. 1. (+*d.*) to belong (to); to appertain (to); п. по пра́ву to belong by right, belong rightfully; ему́ ~и́т честь э́того откры́тия to him belongs the credit for this discovery. 2. (к) to belong (to), be a member (of); п. к аэроклу́бу to belong to a flying club.

принадле́жност|ь, и, *f.* **1.** (к) belonging (to), membership (of); п. к ассоциа́ции membership of an association. **2.** (*obs.*) property. **3.** по ~и to the proper quarter, through the proper channels. **4.** (*pl.*) accessories, appurtenances; equipment; outfit, tackle; бри́твенные ~и shaving tackle; канцеля́рские ~и office equipment; ~и костю́ма accessories (*gloves, handbag, etc.*).

принa|ле́чь, ля́гу, ля́жешь, ля́гут, *past* ~лёг, ~легла́, *pf.* (на+*a.*; *coll.*) **1.** to rest lightly (upon). **2.** to apply oneself (to), go (at, to) with a will; п. на вёсла to ply one's oars vigorously, pull vigorously.

принаря|ди́ть, жу́, ~ди́шь, *pf.* (*of* ~жа́ть) (*coll.*) to dress up, deck out.

принаря|ди́ться, жу́сь, ~ди́шься, *pf.* (*of* ~жа́ться) (*coll.*) to get oneself up, doll oneself up.

принаряжа́|ть(ся), ю(сь), *impf. of* принаряди́ть(ся).

принево́лива|ть, ю, *impf. of* принево́лить.

принево́л|ить, ю, ишь, *pf.* (*of* ~ивать) (+ *inf.*; *coll.*) to force (to), make; они́ ~или его́ жени́ться they made him marry.

принес|ти́, у́, ёшь, *past* ~, ~ла́, *pf.* (*of* приноси́ть) **1.** to bring (*also fig.*); to fetch; п. обра́тно to bring back; ~ла́ тебя́, *etc.*, нелёгкая! why the devil did you, *etc.*, have to turn up?; п. благода́рность to express gratitude, tender thanks; п. жа́лобу (на+ *a.*) to bring, lodge a complaint (against); п. сча́стье to bring luck; п. в же́ртву to sacrifice. **2.** to bear, yield; to bring in; п. плоды́ to bear fruit, yield fruit; на́ша ко́шка ~ла́ шесть котя́т our cat had six kittens; п. большо́й дохо́д to bring in big revenue, show a large return; п. по́льзу to be of use, be of benefit.

принес|ти́сь, у́сь, ёшься, *past* ~ся, ~ла́сь, *pf.* (*of* приноси́ться) (*coll.*) **1.** to come tearing along. **2.** *pass. of* ~ти́; (*of sounds, etc.*) to be borne along.

принижа́|ть, ю, *impf. of* прини́зить.

приниже́ни|е, я, *n.* disparagement, belittling, depreciation.

прини́|женный, *p.p.p. of* ~зить *and adj.* humbled, submissive.

прини́|зить, жу, зишь, *pf.* (*of* ~жа́ть) **1.** to humble, humiliate. **2.** to disparage, belittle, depreciate; п. значе́ние морско́го фло́та to belittle the importance of the Navy.

приник|а́ть, а́ю, *impf. of* ~нуть.

прини́к|нуть, ну, нешь, *past* ~, ~ла, *pf.* (*of* ~а́ть) (к) to press oneself (against), press oneself close (to); to nestle up (against); п. у́хом к замо́чной сква́жине to put one's ear to the keyhole.

принима́|ть, ю, *impf.* **1.** *impf. of* приня́ть.

2. (*impf. only*) to be 'at home', entertain; to receive (*guests, visitors, patients*); они́ ~ют по четверга́м they are 'at home' on Thursdays; она́ ча́сто ~ет she does a lot of entertaining; до́ктор Петро́в сего́дня не ~ет Doctor Petrov does not see patients today. **3.** to deliver (*at birth of child*).

принима́|ться, юсь, *impf. of* приня́ться.

приноравлива́|ть(ся), ю(сь), *impf. of* приноро́вить(ся).

приноро́в|ить, лю, и́шь, *pf.* (*of* принора́вливать) (*coll.*) to fit, adapt, adjust; п. перее́зд на но́вую кварти́ру к ле́тним кани́кулам to arrange a move to new lodgings to fit in with the summer holidays.

приноро́в|иться, лю́сь, и́шься, *pf.* (*of* принора́вливаться) (к; *coll.*) to adapt oneself (to), accommodate oneself (to).

прино|си́ть(ся), шу́(сь), ~сишь(ся), *impf. of* принести́(сь).

приноше́ни|е, я, *n.* gift, offering.

принуди́тел|ьный (~ен, ~ьна), *adj.* **1.** compulsory, forced, coercive; ~ьные рабо́ты forced labour, hard labour; п. сбор levy. **2.** (*tech.*) forced; positive; ~ьное движе́ние positive motion; ~ьная переме́на хо́да positive reversing; ~ьная пода́ча forced feed; positive feed.

прину́|дить, жу, дишь, *pf.* (*of* ~жда́ть) to force, compel, coerce, constrain.

принужда́|ть, ю, *impf. of* прину́дить.

принужде́ни|е, я, *n.* compulsion, coercion, constraint; по ~ю under compulsion, under duress.

принуждённост|ь, и, *f.* constraint; stiffness.

принуждённый, *p.p.p. of* прину́дить *and adj.* constrained, forced; п. смех forced laughter.

принц, а, *m.* prince (*other than a Russian* князь).

принце́сс|а, ы, *f.* princess.

при́нцип, а, *m.* principle; в ~е in principle, theoretically; из ~а on principle.

принципа́л, а, *m.* (*obs.*) principal, head.

принципа́т, а, *m.* (*hist.*) principate.

принципиа́льно, *adv.* **1.** on principle; on a question of principle. **2.** in principle.

принципиа́льност|ь, и, *f.* adherence to principle(s).

принципиа́л|ьный (~ен, ~ьна), *adj.* **1.** of principle; based on, guided by principle; п. вопро́с question of principle; п. челове́к man of principle; ~ьное разногла́сие disagreement on a question of principle; име́ть ~ьное значе́ние to be a matter of principle; подня́ть вопро́с на ~ьную высоту́ to make a question a matter of principle. **2.** in principle; general; они́ да́ли ~ьное согла́сие they consented in principle.

приню́х|аться, аюсь, *pf.* (*of* ~иваться) (к; *coll.*) to get used to the smell (of).

приню́хива|ться, юсь, *impf. of* приню́хаться.

приня́ти|е, я, *n.* **1.** taking; taking up, assumption; п. пи́щи taking of food; п. прися́ги taking of the oath; п. поста́ taking up a post. **2.** acceptance. **3.** admission, admittance; п. гражда́нства naturalization.

при́нят|ый, *p.p.p. of* приня́ть; ~о it is accepted, it is usual; не ~о it is not done.

при|ня́ть, му́, ~**мешь,** *past* ~**ня́л,** ~**няла́,** ~**ня́ло,** *pf.* (*of* ~има́ть) **1.** (*in var. senses*) to take; to accept; п. ва́нну to take, have a bath; п. гражда́нство to be naturalized; п. брита́нское гражда́нство to take British citizenship, become a British citizen; п. креще́ние to be baptized; п. лека́рство to take medicine; п. ме́ры to take measures; п. ме́ры предосторо́жности to take precautions; п. мона́шество to take monastic vows, become a monk; to take the veil; п. наме́рение to form the intention; п. пода́рок to accept a present; п. прися́гу to take the oath; п. реше́ние to take, reach, come to a decision; п. това́ры to take receipt of goods; ~ми́те моё сочу́вствие accept my condolences; п. уча́стие (в+*p.*) to take part (in); participate (in), partake (in, of); п. христиа́нство to adopt, embrace Christianity; п. во внима́ние, п. в расчёт, п. к све́дению to take into consideration, take into account, take cognizance (of); не п. во внима́ние, не п. к све́дению to disregard; не п. в расчёт to discount, fail to take account of; п. в шу́тку to take as a joke; п. всерьёз to take seriously; п. за пра́вило to make it a rule; п. (бли́зко) к се́рдцу to take, lay to heart; п. что-н. на свой счёт to take something as referring to oneself; п. на себя́ to take upon oneself; п. на себя́ обяза́тельство to assume an obligation, take on a commitment; п. на себя́ труд (+*inf.*) to undertake the labour (of); п. под распи́ску to sign for. **2.** to take up (*a post, a command, etc.*); to take over; п. но́вое назначе́ние to take up a new appointment; п. кома́ндование (+*i.*) to take command (of), assume command (of, over); п. диви́зию to take up command of a division; п. духо́вный сан to take holy orders; п. дела́ (от) to take over duties (from). **3.** to accept; п. бой to accept battle; п. зако́н to pass a law; п. законопрое́кт to approve a bill; п. оправда́ния to accept excuses; п. предложе́ние to accept an offer; to accept a proposal; п. резолю́цию to pass, adopt, carry a resolution; п. сове́т to take advice; п. как до́лжное to

accept as one's due, take as a matter of course. **4.** (в, на+*a.*) to admit (to); to accept (for); п. в па́ртию to admit to a party; п. в шко́лу to admit to, accept for a school; п. на слу́жбу to accept for a job; п. в гражда́нство to grant citizenship. **5.** (*see also* ~има́ть) to receive; п. больны́х, госте́й, делега́цию to receive patients, guests, a delegation; они́ ~ня́ли нас раду́шно they gave us a warm welcome, a cordial reception; п. в штыки́ (*coll.*) to meet with the point of the bayonet. **6.** to assume, take (on); п. весёлый вид to assume an air of gaiety; боле́знь ~няла́ серьёзный хара́ктер the illness assumed a grave character; перегово́ры ~ня́ли благоприя́тный оборо́т the talks took a favourable turn. **7.** (+*a.* за+*a.*) to take (for); по акце́нту я ~нял вас за шотла́ндца I took you for a Scotsman by your accent. **8.** to move; п. в сто́рону (*mil.*) to execute a side step; ~ми́ к стороне́! stand aside!, make way! **9.** (*coll.*) to remove, take away; ~ми́те ру́ки прочь! take your hands off!

при|ня́ться, му́сь, ~**мешься,** *past* ~**ня́лся,** ~**няла́сь,** *pf.* (*of* ~има́ться) **1.** (+*inf.*) to begin; to start. **2.** (за+*a.*) to set (to), get down (to); п. за рабо́ту to set to work; п. за чте́ние to get down to reading. **3.** (за+*a.*; *coll.*) to take in hand. **4.** (*of plants*) to strike root, take root; (*of injections*) to take.

приободр|и́ть, ю́, и́шь, *pf.* (*of* ~я́ть) to cheer up, encourage, hearten.

приободр|и́ться, ю́сь, и́шься, *pf.* (*of* ~я́ться) to cheer up, feel more cheerful, feel happier.

приободр|я́ть(ся), я́ю(сь), *impf. of* ~и́ть(ся).

приобре|сти́, ту́, тёшь, *past* ~л, ~ла́, *pf.* (*of* ~та́ть) to acquire, gain; п. о́пыт to gain experience; п. меланхоли́ческий вид to acquire a melancholy look; п. но́вое значе́ние to acquire a new significance.

приобрета́|ть, ю, *impf. of* приобрести́.

приобрете́ни|е, я, *n.* **1.** acquisition, acquiring. **2.** acquisition, gain; (*fig., coll.*) bargain; 'a find'.

приобщ|а́ть(ся), а́ю(сь), *impf. of* ~и́ть(ся).

приобщ|и́ть, у́, и́шь, *pf.* (*of* ~а́ть) **1.** (к) to introduce (to), associate (with); п. приёмного сы́на к семе́йной жи́зни to introduce an adopted son to family life. **2.** to join, attach; п. к де́лу to file. **3.** (*eccl.*) to administer the sacrament (to), communicate.

приобщ|и́ться, у́сь, и́шься, *pf.* (*of* ~а́ться) **1.** (к) to join (in); п. к обще́ственной жи́зни to join in social life. **2.** (*eccl.*) to communicate (*intrans.*).

приоде́|ть, ну, нешь, *pf.* (*coll.*) to dress up, deck out.

приодé|ться, нусь, нешься, *pf.* (*coll.*) to dress up, get oneself up.

приозёрный, *adj.* lakeside, lakeland.

прио́р, а, *m.* (*eccl.*) prior.

приоритéт, а, *m.* priority.

приоса́нива|ться, юсь, *impf. of* приоса́нить- ся.

приоса́н|иться, юсь, ишься, *pf.* (*coll.*) to assume a dignified air.

приостанá́влива|ть(ся), ю(сь), *impf. of* приостанови́ть(ся).

приостанов|и́ть, лю́, ~ишь, *pf.* (*of* приостанá́вливать) to call a halt (to), suspend, check; п. исполнéние пригово́ра to suspend sentence.

приостанов|и́ться, лю́сь, ~ишься, *pf.* (*of* приостанá́вливаться) to halt, come to a halt; выступа́я с рéчью, п. to pause in making a speech.

приостано́вк|а, и, *f.* halt, suspension; п. исполнéния пригово́ра suspension of sentence; п. рабо́т stoppage (*of work*).

приотвор|и́ть, ю́, ~ишь, *pf.* (*of* ~я́ть) to open slightly, half-open; п. дверь to set a door ajar.

приотвор|и́ться, ~ится, *pf.* (*of* ~я́ться) to open slightly, half-open.

приотвор|я́ть(ся), я́ю(сь), *impf. of* ~и́ть- (ся).

приоткрывá|ть(ся), ю(сь), *impf. of* приоткры́ть(ся).

приоткр|ы́ть(ся), о́ю(сь), о́ешь(ся), *pf.* = приотвори́ть(ся).

приохо́|тить, чу, тишь, *pf.* (к; *coll.*) to give a taste (for).

приохо́|титься, чусь, тишься, *pf.* (к; *coll.*) to acquire a taste (for), take (to).

припадá|ть, ю, *impf.* 1. *impf. of* припáсть[1]. 2. (*impf. only*) to be slightly lame; п. на лéвую но́гу to be lame in the left leg.

припáд|ок, ка, *m.* fit; attack; paroxysm; нéрвный п. attack of nerves; сердéчный п. heart attack; эпилепти́ческий п. epileptic fit; п. бéшенства paroxysm of rage.

припáдочн|ый, *adj.* subject to fits; ~ые явлéния fits; *as noun* п., ~ого, *m.* epileptic.

припáива|ть, ю, *impf. of* припая́ть.

припáйк|а, и, *f.* soldering; brazing.

припáрк|а, и, *f.* (*med.*) poultice; fomentation; приложи́ть ~у (+d.) to poultice, foment.

припас|áть, áю, *impf. of* ~ти́.

припас|ти́, у́, ёшь, *past* ~, ~лá, *pf.* (*of* ~áть) (+a. or g.; *coll.*) to store, lay in, lay up; п. консéрвов to lay in tinned food.

припá|сть[1], ду́, дёшь, *past* ~л, *pf.* (*of* ~дáть) (к) to press oneself (to), fall down (before); п. к чьим-н. ногáм to prostrate oneself before someone; п. у́хом to press one's ear (to).

припá|сть[2], дёт, *past* ~л, *pf.* (*coll., obs.*) to appear, show itself.

припáс|ы, ов, *no sing.* stores, supplies; боевы́е п. ammunition; воéнные п. munitions; съестны́е п. provisions, victuals.

припáхива|ть, ет, *impf.* (*coll.*) to stink.

припая́|ть, ю, *pf.* (*of* припáивать) (к) to solder (to); to braze (to); (*fig., coll.*) ему́ ~ли пять лет he was sentenced to five years.

припéв, а, *m.* refrain, burden.

припевá|ть, ю, *impf.* to hum; жить ~ючи (*coll.*) to live in clover.

припёк[1], а, *m.* surplus (*excess in weight of loaf when baked over that of flour used*).

припёк[2], а, *m.*; на ~e (*coll.*) right in the sun, exposed to the full heat of the sun.

припёк|а, и, *f.* сбо́ку п. (*coll.*) for no reason at all.

припекá|ть, ет, *impf.* (*coll.*) (*of the sun*) to be very hot.

при|перéть, пру́, прёшь, *past* ~пёр, ~пёрла, *pf.* (*of* ~пирáть) 1. (к) to press (against); п. стул к двéри, п. дверь сту́лом to put a chair against the door; п. кого́-н. к стéнке (*fig., coll.*) to drive someone into a corner, put someone in a spot. 2. (*coll.*) to set ajar. 3. (*sl.*) to barge in, roll up.

припечáт|ать, аю, *pf.* (*of* ~ывать) (*coll.*) to seal; п. сургучо́м to apply sealing-wax (to).

припечáтыва|ть, ю, *impf. of* припечáтать.

припирá|ть, ю, *impf. of* припере́ть.

припи|сáть, шу́, ~шешь, *pf.* (*of* ~сывать) 1. to add (*to something written*). 2. (к) to attach (to), register (at). 3. (+d.) to attribute (to); to ascribe (to); to put down (to), impute (to); п. стихотворéние Эсхи́лу to attribute a poem to Aeschylus; п. неудá́чу лéности to put a failure down to laziness.

припи́ск|а, и, *f.* 1. addition; postscript; п. к завещáнию (*leg.*) codicil. 2. attaching, registration; порт ~и (*naut.*) port of registration.

приписно́й, *adj.* attached; on the establishment.

припи́сыва|ть, ю, *impf. of* приписáть.

приплáт|а, ы, *f.* additional payment.

приплá|ти́ть, чу́, ~тишь, *pf.* (*of* ~чивать) to pay in addition.

приплáчива|ть, ю, *impf. of* приплати́ть.

приплe|сти́, ту́, тёшь, *past* ~л, ~лá, *pf.* (*of* ~тáть) 1. to plait in. 2. (*fig., coll.*) to drag in; рáзве бы́ло необходи́мо п. моё и́мя? was it really necessary to drag my name in?

приплe|сти́сь, ту́сь, тёшься, *past* ~лся, ~лáсь *pf.* to drag oneself along.

приплетá|ть, ю, *impf. of* приплести́.

приплóд, а, *m.* issue, increase (*of animals*).

приплывá|ть, ю, *impf. of* приплы́ть.

приплы|ть, ву́, вёшь, past ~л, ~ла́, ~ло, pf. (of ~ва́ть) to swim up; to sail up; п. к бе́регу to reach the shore.

приплю́снут|ый, p.p.p. of ~ь and adj. п. нос flat nose.

приплю́сн|уть, у, ешь, pf. (of приплю́щивать) to flatten.

приплюс|ова́ть, у́ю, pf. (of ~о́вывать) (coll.) to add on.

приплюсо́выва|ть, ю, impf. of приплюсова́ть.

приплю́щива|ть, ю, impf. of приплю́снуть.

припля́сыва|ть, ю, impf. to dance, hop, trip, skip; идти́ ~я по тротуа́ру to trip along the pavement.

приподнима́|ть(ся), ю(сь), impf. of приподня́ть(ся).

припо́днятост|ь, и, f. elation; animation.

припо́дн|ятый, p.p.p. of ~я́ть and adj. elated; animated; uplifted.

приподн|я́ть, иму́, и́мешь, past ~я́л, ~яла́, ~я́ло, pf. (of ~има́ть) to raise slightly; to lift slightly.

приподн|я́ться, иму́сь, и́мешься, past ~я́лся, ~яла́сь, pf. (of ~има́ться) to raise oneself a little); п. на ло́кте to raise oneself on one's elbow; п. на цы́почках to stand on tiptoe; п. на носки́ to rise on one's toes.

припо́|й, я, m. solder; кре́пкий п. brazing solder.

приполз|а́ть, а́ю, impf. of ~ти́.

приполз|ти́, у́, ёшь, past ~, ~ла́, pf. (of ~а́ть) to creep up, crawl up.

приполя́рный, adj. polar.

припомина́|ть, ю, impf. of припо́мнить.

припо́м|нить, ню, нишь, pf. (of ~ина́ть) 1. to remember, recollect, recall; сму́тно п. to have a hazy recollection (of). 2. (+d.) to remind; я э́то тебе́ ~ню! (coll.) you won't forget this!; I'll get even with you for this!

приправ|а, ы, f. relish, condiment, flavouring, seasoning, dressing; п. к сала́ту salad dressing.

приправ|ить[1], лю, ишь, pf. (of ~ля́ть) (+i.) to season (with), flavour (with), dress (with).

приправ|ить[2], лю, ишь, pf. (of ~ля́ть) (typ.) to make ready.

припра́вк|а, и, f. (typ.) making ready.

приправля́|ть, ю, impf. of приправить.

припры́гива|ть, ю, impf. (coll.) to hop, skip.

припря́|тать, чу, чешь, pf. (of ~тывать) (coll.) to secrete, put by (for further use).

припря́тыва|ть, ю, impf. of припря́тать.

припу́гива|ть, ю, impf. of припугну́ть.

припуг|ну́ть, ну́, нёшь, pf. (of ~ивать) (coll.) to intimidate, scare.

припу́дрива|ть(ся), ю(сь), impf. of припу́дрить(ся).

припу́др|ить, ю, ишь, pf. (of ~ивать) 1. to powder. 2. (tech.) to dust.

припу́др|иться, юсь, ишься, pf. (of ~иваться) to powder oneself.

при́пуск, а, m. (tech.) allowance, margin; п. на уса́дку shrinkage allowance; оста́вить п. (на+a.) to allow (for).

припуска́|ть, ю, impf. of припусти́ть.

припу|сти́ть, щу́, ~стишь, pf. (of ~ска́ть) 1. (к) to put (to) (for coupling or feeding); п. телёнка к коро́ве to put a calf to the cow. 2. (tailoring) to let out. 3. (coll.) to urge on. 4. (coll.) to quicken one's pace. 5. (coll.; of rain) to come down harder.

припу́т|ать, аю, pf. (of ~ывать) 1. to tie on, fasten. 2. (к; fig., coll.) to drag in (to), implicate (in).

припу́тыва|ть, ю, impf. of припу́тать.

припух|а́ть, а́ет, impf. of ~нуть.

припу́хлост|ь, и, f. (slight) swelling.

припу́хлый, adj. (slightly) swollen.

припу́х|нуть, нет, past ~, ~ла, pf. (of ~а́ть) to swell up a little.

прирабо́тыва|ть, ю, impf. of прирабо́тать.

прирабо́т|ать, ю, pf. (of прираба́тывать) to earn extra, earn in addition.

при́работ|ок, ка, m. extra earnings, additional earnings.

прира́внива|ть, ю, impf. of приравня́ть.

приравн|я́ть, я́ю, pf. (of ~ивать) (к) to equate (with); to place on the same footing (as).

прираст|а́ть, а́ю, impf. of ~и́.

прираст|и́, у́, ёшь, past приро́с, приросла́, pf. (of ~а́ть) 1. (к) to adhere (to); (of a graft) to take; п. к ме́сту, п. к земле́ (fig.) to become rooted to the spot, to the ground. 2. to increase; to accrue.

прираще́ни|е, я, n. 1. increase, increment. 2. (ling.) augment.

приревн|ова́ть, у́ю, pf. (к) to be jealous (of); она́ ~ова́ла му́жа к свое́й прия́тельнице she was jealous of her husband's interest in her friend.

прирез|а́ть, а́ю, impf. of ~ать[2].

прире́|зать[1], жу, жешь, pf. (of ~зывать) (coll.) to kill; to cut the throat (of).

прире́|зать[2], жу, жешь, pf. (of ~за́ть and ~зывать) to add on; п. уча́сток к огоро́ду to add on a piece to a garden.

прире́з|ок, ка, m. additional piece.

прире́зыва|ть, ю, impf. of прире́зать.

прире́льсовый, adj. adjoining the (railway) line.

прире́чный, adj. riverside, riverain.

приро́д|а, ы, f. 1. nature; мёртвая п. the inorganic world; зако́н ~ы law of nature; отда́ть долг ~е (i) (rhet.) to pay the debt to nature, (ii) (coll., euph.) to answer a call of nature. 2. nature, character; от ~ы by nature, congenitally; по ~e by nature, naturally; э́то в ~e веще́й it is in the nature of things.

приро́дн|ый, *adj.* **1.** natural; ~ые бога́тства natural resources; п. газ natural gas. **2.** born; п. англича́нин an Englishman by birth. **3.** inborn, innate; п. ум native wit.

природове́д, а, *m.* natural historian, naturalist.

природове́дени|е, я, *n.* natural history.

прирождённый, *adj.* **1.** inborn, innate. **2.** a born; п. лгун a born liar.

приро́ст, а, *m.* increase, growth.

приро́ст|ок, ка, *m.* (*bot.*; *coll.*) growth, excrescence.

прирубе́жный, *adj.* situated near the frontier, near the border.

прируч|а́ть, а́ю, *impf. of* ~и́ть.

прируче́ни|е, я, *n.* taming, domestication.

прируч|и́ть, у́, и́шь, *pf.* (*of* ~а́ть) to tame (*also fig.*); to domesticate.

приса́жива|ться, юсь, *impf. of* присе́сть.

приса́лива|ть, ю, *impf. of* присоли́ть.

приса́сыва|ться, юсь, *impf. of* присоса́ться.

присва́ива|ть, ю, *impf. of* присво́ить.

при́свист, а, *m.* **1.** whistle. **2.** sibilance, hissing in one's speech.

присви́стыва|ть, ю, *impf.* **1.** to whistle. **2.** to sibilate.

присвое́ни|е, я, *n.* **1.** appropriation; незако́нное п. misappropriation. **2.** awarding, conferment.

присво́|ить, ю, ишь, *pf.* (*of* присва́ивать) **1.** to appropriate; незако́нно п. сре́дства to misappropriate funds. **2.** (+*a. and d.*) to give, award, confer; п. и́мя (+*d. and g.*) to name (after); ему́ ~или сте́пень до́ктора he has been given the degree of Doctor, a doctorate has been conferred upon him; моско́вскому метро́ ~ено и́мя Ле́нина the Moscow Underground (*railway*) was named after Lenin.

приседа́ни|е, я, *n.* **1.** squatting. **2.** (*obs.*) curts(e)y.

приседа́|ть, ю, *impf. of* присе́сть.

присе́ст, а, *m.* в оди́н п., за оди́н п. (*coll.*) at one sitting, at a stretch.

при|се́сть, ся́ду, ся́дешь, *past* ~се́л, *pf.* **1.** (*impf.* ~са́живаться) to sit down, take a seat. **2.** (*impf.* ~седа́ть) to squat; (*in fright*) to cower. **3.** (*impf.* ~седа́ть) to curts(e)y, drop curts(e)ys.

при́сказк|а, и, *f.* (*story-teller's*) introduction; flourish, embellishment (*of a story*).

приска|ка́ть, чу́, ~чешь, *pf.* **1.** to come galloping, arrive at a gallop; (*fig., coll.*) to rush, tear. **2.** to hop, come hopping.

приско́рби|е, я, *n.* sorrow, regret; к моему́ ~ю to my regret; мы с глубо́ким ~ем извеща́ем о сме́рти (+*g.*) (*formula of*

obituary notices) we announce with deep regret the death (of).

приско́рб|ный (~ен, ~на), *adj.* regrettable, lamentable, deplorable.

приску́ч|ить, у, ишь, *pf.* (+*d.*; *coll.*) to bore, tire, weary.

при|сла́ть, шлю́, шлёшь, *pf.* (*of* ~сыла́ть) to send, dispatch.

присло́вь|е, я, *n.* **1.** (*coll.*) saying (*introduced into a speech, etc.*). **2.** (*gram.*; *obs.*) inseparable particle (*e.g.* -то, -ка).

прислон|и́ть, ю́, ~и́шь, *pf.* (*of* ~я́ть) (к) to lean (against), rest (against).

прислон|и́ться, ю́сь, ~и́шься, *pf.* (*of* ~я́ться) (к) to lean (against), rest (against).

прислон|я́ть(ся), я́ю(сь), *impf. of* ~и́ть(ся).

прислу́г|а, и, *f.* **1.** maid, servant. **2.** (*collect.*; *obs.*) servants, domestics. **3.** (*mil.*) crew; оруди́йная п. gun crew.

прислу́жива|ть, ю, *impf.* (+*d.*; *obs.*) to wait (upon), attend.

прислу́жива|ться, юсь, *impf. of* прислу-жи́ться.

прислуж|и́ться, у́сь, ~ишься, *pf.* (*of* ~и-ваться) (к; *obs.*) to worm oneself into the favour (of), fawn (upon), cringe (to).

прислу́жник, а, *m.* **1.** (*obs.*) servant. **2.** (*coll.*) lickspittle; underling.

прислу́жничеств|о, а, *n.* subservience, servility.

прислу́ш|аться, аюсь, *pf.* (*of* ~иваться) (к) **1.** to listen (to). **2.** (*fig.*) to listen (to), lend an ear (to); to heed, pay attention (to); п. к чьему́-н. сове́ту to listen to someone's advice. **3.** (*coll.*) to accustom one's ear (to), become accustomed to the sound (of); мы уже́ ~ались к ночно́му у́личному движе́нию we are now accustomed to the (noise of) traffic at night.

прислу́шива|ться, юсь, *impf. of* прислу́-шаться.

присма́трива|ть(ся), ю(сь), *impf. of* при-смотре́ть(ся).

присмире́|ть, ю, *pf.* to grow quiet.

присмо́тр, а, *m.* care, looking after, tending; supervision, surveillance.

присмотр|е́ть, ю́, ~ишь, *pf.* (*of* присма́три-вать) **1.** (за+*i.*) to look after, keep an eye (on); to supervise, superintend; п. за ребён-ком to mind the baby. **2.** (*coll.*) to look for; п. себе́ рабо́ту to look for a job.. **3.** *pf. only* to find.

присмотр|е́ться, ю́сь, ~ишься, *pf.* (*of* при-сма́триваться) (к) **1.** to look closely (at); п. к кому́-н. to size someone up, take some-one's measure. **2.** to get accustomed (to), get used (to).

присн|и́ться, ю́сь, и́шься, *pf. of* сни́ться.

приснопа́мятный, *adj.* (*rhet.*) memorable, unforgettable.

при́сн|ый, *adj*. **1.** (*obs.*) eternal, everlasting. **2.** *as noun* ые, ~ых (*coll.*) associates; ты и твои́ ~ые you and your gang, you and your mates.

присове́т|овать, ую, *pf.* = посове́товать.

присовокуп|и́ть, лю́, и́шь, *pf.* (*of* ~ля́ть) to add; to say in addition; п. бума́гу к де́лу to file a paper.

присовокупля́|ть, ю, *impf. of* присовокупи́ть.

присоедине́ни|е, я, *n.* **1.** addition. **2.** (*polit.*) annexation, joining. **3.** (к) joining, associating oneself (with), adhesion (to). **4.** (*electr.*) connexion.

присоедини́тельный, *adj.* (*gram.*) connective.

присоедин|и́ть, ю́, и́шь, *pf.* (*of* ~я́ть) **1.** to add; to join. **2.** (*polit.*) to annex, join. **3.** (*electr.*) to connect.

присоедин|и́ться, ю́сь, и́шься, *pf.* (*of* ~я́ться) (к) **1.** to join; пора́ нам п. к остальны́м it is time we joined the others. **2.** (*fig.*) to join, associate oneself (with); п. к мне́нию to subscribe to an opinion.

присоедин|я́ть(ся), я́ю(сь), *impf. of* ~и́ть-(ся).

присол|и́ть, ю́, ~и́шь, *pf.* (*of* приса́ливать) (*coll.*) to salt, add a pinch of salt (to).

присос|а́ться, у́сь, ёшься, *pf.* (*of* приса́сываться) (к) to stick (to), attach oneself (to) by suction; (*fig., pejor.*) to fasten on (to).

присосе́|диться, жусь, дишься, *pf.* (к; *coll.*) to sit down next (to).

присо́ск|а, и, *f.* (*biol., zool.*) sucker.

присо́х|нуть, нет, *past* ~, ~ла, *pf.* (*of* присыха́ть) (к) to adhere (in drying) (to); to stick (to), dry (on).

приспева́|ть, ю, *impf. of* приспе́ть.

приспе́|ть, ю, *pf.* (*of* ~ва́ть) (*coll.; of time*) to come, draw nigh, be ripe.

приспе́шник, а, *m.* stooge, myrmidon.

приспич|ить, ит, *pf.* (*impers.+d. and inf.*; *coll.*) to feel, have an urge (to); to be impatient (to); им ~ило уходи́ть they were impatient to be off.

приспоса́блива|ть(ся), ю(сь), *impf.* = приспособля́ть(ся).

приспосо́б|ить, лю, ишь, *pf.* (*of* ~ля́ть) to fit, adjust, adapt, accommodate; п. шко́лу под больни́цу to adapt a school as a hospital.

приспосо́б|иться, люсь, ишься, *pf.* (*of* ~ля́ться) **1.** (к) to adapt oneself (to), accommodate oneself (to). **2.** *pass. of* ~ить.

приспособле́н|ец, ца, *m.* time-server.

приспособле́ни|е, я, *n.* **1.** adaptation, accommodation; п. к кли́мату acclimatization. **2.** device, contrivance, contraption; appliance, gadget.

приспосо́бленност|ь, и, *f.* fitness, suitability.

приспособле́нческий, *adj.* time-serving.

приспособле́нчеств|о, а, *n.* time-serving.

приспособля́емост|ь, и, *f.* adaptability.

приспособля́|ть(ся), ю(сь), *impf. of* приспосо́бить(ся).

приспуска́|ть, ю, *impf. of* приспусти́ть.

приспу|сти́ть, щу́, ~стишь, *pf.* (*of* ~ска́ть) to lower a little; п. флаг to lower a flag to half-mast; (*naut.*) to half-mast the colours.

приспу́|щенный, *p.p.p. of* ~сти́ть; ~щенные фла́ги flags at half-mast.

при́став, а, *pl.* ~а́, *m.* (*hist.*) police-officer; станово́й п. district superintendent of police; суде́бный п. bailiff.

пристава́ни|е, я, *n.* pestering, bothering.

приста|ва́ть, ю́, ёшь, *impf. of* приста́ть.

приста́в|ить, лю, ишь, *pf.* (*of* ~ля́ть) **1.** (к) to put (to, against), place (to, against), set (to, against), lean (against); п. ле́стницу к стене́ to put a ladder against the wall. **2.** to add (*a piece of material, etc.*). **3.** (к) to appoint to look after; п. проводника́ к иностра́нным тури́стам to appoint a guide to look after foreign tourists.

приста́вк|а, и, *f.* (*gram.*) prefix.

приставля́|ть, ю, *impf. of* приста́вить.

пристав|но́й, *adj.* added, attached; ~а́я ле́стница step ladder.

приста́вочный, *adj.* (*gram.*) **1.** of a prefix. **2.** having a prefix.

при́стально, *adv.* fixedly, intently; п. смотре́ть (на+*a.*) to look fixedly, intently (at); to stare (at), gaze (at).

при́стал|ьный (~ен, ~ьна), *adj.* fixed, intent; п. взгляд fixed, intent look; stare, gaze; с ~ьным внима́нием intently.

приста́нищ|е, а, *n.* refuge, shelter, asylum.

пристанцио́нный, *adj.* station.

при́стан|ь, и, *pl.* ~и, ~е́й, *f.* **1.** landing-stage, jetty; pier; wharf. **2.** (*obs.*) refuge, asylum. **3.** (*fig., poet.*) haven.

приста́|ть, ну, нешь, *pf.* (*of* ~ва́ть) **1.** (к) to stick (to), adhere (to). **2.** (к) to join, attach oneself (to); п. к гру́ппе экскурса́н-тов to join a party of excursionists; ко мне ~ла чужа́я соба́ка someone's dog attached itself to me. **3.** (к; *fig., coll.; of infectious disease*) to be passed on (to); к де́тям ~ла ветря́ная о́спа the children have picked up chickenpox. **4.** (к) to pester, bother, badger; п. с предложе́ниями to pester with suggestions. **5.** (к; *naut.*) to put in (to), come alongside. **6.** *pf. only* (*impers.+d.*; *coll.*) to befit; не ~ло тебе́ так говори́ть you ought not to speak like that. **7.** *pf. only* (+*d.*; *coll.*) to become, suit.

пристёгива|ть, ю, *impf. of* пристегну́ть.

пристег|ну́ть, ну́, нёшь, *pf.* (*of* ~ивать) **1.** to fasten; to button up. **2.** (*fig., coll.*) to drag in.

пристежн|óй, *adj.* fastening (*as opp. to sewn on*); рубáшка с ～ым воротничкóм shirt with separate collar.

пристóйност|ь, и, *f.* decency, propriety, decorum.

пристó|йный (～ен, ～йна), *adj.* decent, proper, decorous, becoming, seemly.

пристрáива|ть(ся), ю(сь), *impf. of* пристрóить(ся).

пристрáсти|е[1], я, *n.* (к) 1. weakness (for), predilection (for), passion (for); у неё п. к верховóй ездé she has a passion for riding. 2. partiality (for, towards), bias (towards); вы́казать п. to show partiality.

пристрáсти|е[2], я, *n.* допрóс с ～ем (*hist. and fig., joc.*) interrogation under torture.

пристра|сти́ть, щý, сти́шь, *pf.* (к; *coll.*) to give one an impulse (to), make keen (on); егó доклáд ～сти́л меня́ к заня́тиям по истóрии Индии his talk made me keen on studying the history of India.

пристра|сти́ться, щýсь, сти́шься, *pf.* (к) to take (to); to conceive a liking (for).

пристрáстност|ь, и, *f.* partiality, bias.

пристрáст|ный (～ен, ～на), *adj.* partial, biassed.

пристрáчива|ть, ю, *impf. of* пристрочи́ть.

пристращ|áть, áю, *pf.* (*of* ～ивать) (*coll.*) to intimidate.

пристрáщива|ть, ю, *impf. of* пристращáть.

пристрéлива|ть, ю, *impf. of* пристрели́ть *and* пристреля́ть.

пристрéлива|ться, юсь, *impf. of* пристреля́ться.

пристрел|и́ть, ю́, ～ишь, *pf.* (*of* ～ивать) to shoot (down).

пристрéлк|а, и, *f.* (*mil.*) adjustment (of fire), ranging; fire for adjustment; п. ви́лки bracketing for range; п. репéра registration; вести́ ～у to find the range.

пристрéлочн|ый, *adj.* (*mil.*) ranging; registering; п. ориенти́р registration point; ～ое орýдие registration gun; п. снаря́д projectile with spotting charge.

пристрéльный, *adj.* (*mil.*) п. огóнь straddling fire.

пристрéл|янный, *p.p.p. of* ～я́ть *and adj.* (*mil.*) adjusted.

пристрел|я́ть, я́ю, *pf.* (*of* ～ивать) (*mil.*) to adjust.

пристрел|я́ться, я́юсь, *pf.* (*of* ～иваться) (*mil.*) to adjust fire; to find the range.

пристрó|ить, ю, ишь, *pf.* (*of* пристрáивать) 1. (к) to add (*to a building*), build on (to). 2. (*coll.*) to place, settle, fix up; п. когó-н. на слýжбу to settle someone in a job. 3. (к; *mil.*) to join up (with), form up (with).

пристрó|иться, юсь, ишься, *pf.* (*of* пристрáиваться) 1. (*coll.*) to be placed, be settled, be fixed up, get a place; он ～и́лся

в контóру he has got a place in an office. 2. (к; *mil.*) to join up (with), form up (with); (*aeron.*) to take up formation (with).

пристрóйк|а, и, *f.* annexe, extension; outhouse; lean-to.

пристроч|и́ть, ý, ～и́шь, *pf.* (*of* пристрáчивать) (к) to sew on (to).

пристрýнива|ть, ю, *impf. of* пристрýнить.

пристрýн|ить, ю, ишь, *pf.* (*of* ～ивать) (*coll.*) to take in hand.

пристýкива|ть, ю, *impf. of* пристýкнуть.

пристýк|нуть[1], ну, нешь, *pf.* (*of* ～ивать) (+*i.*; *coll.*) to tap; п. каблукáми to tap one's heels.

пристýк|нуть[2], ну, нешь, *pf.* (*of* ～ивать) (*coll.*) to club to death; to kill (*with a blow*).

при́ступ, а, *m.* 1. (*mil.*) assault, storm; пойти́ на п. to go in to the assault; взять ～ом to take by storm. 2. fit, attack; bout, touch; п. бóли pang; paroxysm; п. гнéва fit of temper; п. гри́ппа bout of influenza; п. кáшля fit, bout of coughing. 3. (*fig., coll.*) access; к немý ～у нет he is inaccessible, unapproachable; к э́той матéрии ～у нет this material is out of the question (= *is too expensive*).

приступ|áть(ся), áю(сь), *impf. of* ～и́ть(ся).

приступ|и́ть, лю́, ～ишь, *pf.* (*of* ～áть) (к) 1. (*obs.*) to approach; (*fig.*) to importune, pester. 2. to set about, get down (to), start; п. к дéлу to set to work, get down to business.

приступ|и́ться, лю́сь, ～ишься, *pf.* (*of* ～áть-ся) (к; *coll.*) to approach, accost, go up (to); к немý не ～ишься, нельзя́ п. he is inaccessible, unapproachable.

приступ|óк, кá, *m.* (*coll.*) step.

присты|ди́ть, жý, ди́шь, *pf. of* стыди́ть.

пристя́жк|а, и, *f.* 1. в ～е (*of a horse*) in traces. 2. trace-horse, outrunner.

пристяжн|áя, óй, *f.* trace-horse, outrunner.

прису|ди́ть, жý, ～дишь, *pf.* (*of* ～ждáть) 1. (+*a.* к *or* +*a. and d.*) to sentence (to), condemn (to); п. когó-н. к заключéнию, п. заключéние комý-н. to sentence someone to imprisonment; п. к штрáфу, п. штраф (+*d.*) to fine, impose a fine (on). 2. (*leg.; coll.*) to award. 3. (+*d.*) to award, adjudge (to); to confer (on); емý ～ди́ли стéпень дóктора a doctorate has been conferred on him.

присуждá|ть, ю, *impf. of* присуди́ть.

присуждéни|е, я, *n.* awarding, adjudication; conferment.

присýтственн|ый, *adj.* (*obs.*) п. день working-day; ～ое мéсто office, work-place; ～ые часы́ office hours, business hours.

присýтстви|е, я, *n.* 1. presence; в ～и детéй in the presence of the children, in front of the children; п. дýха presence of mind.

2. (*obs.*) business (of the day). 3. (*obs.*) office.

присутств|овать, ую, *impf.* (на+*p.*) to be present (at), attend, assist (at).

присутств|ующий, *pres. part. act. of* ~овать *and adj.* present; *as noun* ~ующие, ~ующих those present; о ~ующих не говоря́т present company (always) excepted.

прису́щ|ий (~, ~а), *adj.* (+*d.*) inherent (in); characteristic, distinctive; ~ая ей ще́дрость the generosity characteristic of her; неприя́тные ~ие положе́нию после́дствия the disagreeable consequences inherent in the situation.

присчит|а́ть, а́ю, *pf.* (*of* ~ывать) to add on.

присчи́тыва|ть, ю, *impf. of* присчита́ть.

присы́п|ать, лю, лешь, *pf.* (*of* ~а́ть) 1. (+*a.* or *g.*) to add some more, pour some more. 2. (+*a. and i.*) to sprinkle (with), dust (with).

присып|а́ть, а́ю, *impf. of* ~ать.

присы́пк|а, и, *f.* 1. sprinkling, dusting. 2. powder.

присыха́|ть, ю, *impf. of* присо́хнуть.

прися́г|а, и, *f.* oath; oath of allegiance; ло́жная п. perjury; дать ~у to swear; приня́ть ~у to take the oath; привести́ к ~е to swear in, administer the oath (to); под ~ой on oath, under oath.

присяг|а́ть, а́ю, *impf.* (*of* ~ну́ть) (в+*p.*) to swear (to); to take one's oath, swear an oath; п. в ве́рности (+*d.*) to swear allegiance (to).

присяг|ну́ть, ну́, нёшь, *pf. of* ~а́ть.

прися́жн|ый, *adj.* 1. (*leg.*; *obs.*) sworn; п. пове́ренный barrister; п. заседа́тель juror, juryman; *as noun* п., ~ого, *m.* = п. заседа́тель; суд ~ых jury. 2. (*coll.*) born, inveterate; п. ворчу́н born grumbler.

прита́|и́ться, ю́сь, и́шься, *pf.* to hide, conceal oneself.

прита́птыва|ть, ю, *impf.* 1. *impf. of* притопта́ть. 2. *impf. only* (*coll.*) to tap (with) one's heels.

прита́скива|ть, ю, *impf. of* притащи́ть.

притач|а́ть, а́ю, *pf.* (*of* ~ивать) (к) to stitch (to), sew on (to).

прита́чива|ть, ю, *impf. of* притача́ть.

притащ|и́ть, у́, ~ишь, *pf.* (*of* прита́скивать) to bring, drag, haul.

притащ|и́ться, у́сь, ~ишься, *pf.* (*coll.*) to drag oneself.

притвор|и́ть, ю́, ~ишь, *pf.* (*of* ~я́ть) to set ajar; to leave not quite shut.

притвор|и́ться¹, ~ится, *pf.* (*of* ~я́ться) to be ajar; to be not quite shut.

притвор|и́ться², ю́сь, и́шься, *pf.* (*of* ~я́ться) (+*i.*) to pretend (to be); to feign, simulate; to sham; п. больны́м to pretend to be ill,

feign illness; п. безразли́чным to feign indifference.

притво́р|ный (~ен, ~на), *adj.* pretended, feigned, affected, sham; ~ное неве́жество feigned ignorance; ~ные слёзы crocodile tears.

притво́рств|о, а, *n.* pretence; sham; dissembling.

притво́рщик, а, *m.* 1. pretender, sham. 2. dissembler, hypocrite.

притвор|я́ть(ся), я́ю(сь), *impf. of* ~и́ть(ся).

притека́|ть, ю, *impf. of* прите́чь.

при|тере́ть, тру́, трёшь, *past* ~тёр, ~тёрла, *pf.* (*of* ~тира́ть) 1. to rub in lightly. 2. (*tech.*) to grind in, lap.

притерп|е́ться, лю́сь, ~ишься, *pf.* (к; *coll.*) to get accustomed (to), get used (to).

притёр|тый, *p.p.p. of* ~е́ть *and adj.*; ~тая про́бка ground-in stopper (*of bottle*); ~тое стекло́ ground glass.

притесне́ни|е, я, *n.* oppression.

притесни́тел|ь, я, *m.* oppressor.

притесни́тел|ьный (~ен, ~ьна), *adj.* oppressive.

притесн|и́ть, ю́, и́шь, *pf.* (*of* ~я́ть) to oppress, keep down.

притесн|я́ть, я́ю, *impf. of* ~и́ть.

прите́|чь, чёт, ку́т, *past* ~к, ~кла́, *pf.* (*of* ~ка́ть) to flow in, pour in (*also fig.*); выраже́ния соболезнова́ния ~кли́ со всех сторо́н messages of sympathy poured in from all sides.

притира́|ть, ю, *impf. of* притере́ть.

прити́скива|ть, ю, *impf. of* прити́снуть.

прити́с|нуть, ну, нешь, *pf.* (*of* ~кивать) (*coll.*) to press, squeeze; п. па́лец две́рью to pinch one's finger in the door.

притих|а́ть, а́ю, *impf. of* ~нуть.

прити́х|нуть, ну, нешь, *past* ~, ~ла, *pf.* (*of* ~ать) to quiet down, grow quiet, hush; (*fig.*) to pipe down, sing small.

приткн|у́ть, у́, ёшь, *pf.* (*of* притыка́ть) (*coll.*) to stick; ~и́ свои́ ве́щи куда́ хо́чешь stick your things anywhere you like.

приткн|у́ться, у́сь, ёшься, *pf.* (*coll.*) to perch oneself, find room for oneself; мне бы́ло не́где п. I could not find a spare inch.

прито́к, а, *m.* 1. (*geogr.*) tributary. 2. inflow, influx (*also fig.*); intake; п. све́жего во́здуха supply of fresh air; п. но́вых ка́дров (*fig.*) intake of fresh blood.

при́толок|а, и, *f.* lintel.

прито́м, *conj.* (and) besides; он был там не раз и п. прекра́сно зна́ет язы́к he has been there several times, (and) besides he knows the language extremely well.

притом|и́ть, лю́, и́шь, *pf.* (*coll.*) to tire.

притом|и́ться, лю́сь, и́шься, *pf.* (*coll.*) to get tired.

прито́н, а, *m.* den, haunt; воровско́й п. den

of thieves; игóрный п. gambling-den, gambling-hell.

притóп|нуть, ну, нешь, *pf.* (*of* ~ывать) to stamp one's foot; п. каблукáми to tap one's heels.

притоп|тáть, чý, ~чешь, *pf.* (*of* притáптывать) to tread down.

притóпыва|ть, ю, *impf. of* притóпнуть.

приторáчива|ть, ю, *impf. of* приторочить.

притóрност|ь, и, *f.* sickly sweetness, excessive sweetness.

притóр|ный (~ен, ~на), *adj.* sickly sweet, luscious, cloying (*also fig.*); ~ная улыбка unctuous smile.

приторóч|ить, ý, ишь, *pf.* (*of* приторáчивать) to strap.

притрáгива|ться, юсь, *impf. of* притрóнуться.

притрóн|уться, усь, ешься, *pf.* (*of* притрáгиваться) (к) to touch; они не ~улись к ýжину they have not touched their supper.

притул|иться, юсь, ишься, *pf.* (*coll.*) to find room for oneself; to find shelter.

притуп|ить, лю, ~ишь, *pf.* (*of* ~лять) to blunt, dull, take the edge of; (*fig.*) to dull, deaden.

притуп|иться, люсь, ~ишься, *pf.* (*of* ~ляться) to become blunt; (*fig.*) to become dull.

притупля|ть(ся), ю(сь), *impf. of* притупить(ся).

притуш|ить, ý, ~ишь, *pf.* (*coll.*) to damp (*a fire*); п. фáры to dip lights.

притч|а, и, *f.* parable; что за п.? (*coll.*) what is the meaning of all this?; what an extraordinary thing!; п. во языцех (*joc.*) the talk of the town.

притыкá|ть, ю, *impf. of* приткнýть.

притягáтельност|ь, и, *f.* attractiveness.

притягáтел|ьный (~ен, ~ьна), *adj.* attractive, magnetic.

притя́гива|ть, ю, *impf. of* притянýть.

притяжáтельный, *adj.* (*gram.*) possessive.

притяжéни|е, я, *n.* (*phys.*) attraction; закóн земнóго ~я law of gravity.

притязáни|е, я, *n.* claim, pretension; имéть ~я (на+*a.*) to have claims (to, on).

притязáтел|ьный (~ен, ~ьна), *adj.* demanding, exacting.

притязá|ть, ю, *impf.* (на+*a.*) to lay claim (to).

притя́н|утый, *p.p.p. of* ~ýть; п. зá уши, п. зá волосы (*fig.*) far-fetched.

притя́|нуть, нý, ~нешь, *pf.* (*of* ~гивать) 1. to drag (up), pull (up); п. зá уши, зá волосы доказáтельства to adduce far-fetched arguments. 2. (*fig.*) to draw, attract; п. как магнит to attract like a magnet. 3. (*coll.*) to summon; п. к отвéту to call to account; п. к судý to have up, sue.

приуготóв|ить, лю, ишь, *pf.* (*of* ~лять) (*obs.*) to prepare, have in store (*usu. fig.*).

приуготовля́|ть, ю, *impf. of* приуготóвить.

приудáр|ить, ю, ишь, *pf.* (*of* ~я́ть) 1. to deal a light blow. 2. (*fig., coll.*) to get cracking. 3. (за+*i.*; *fig., coll.*) to go (after), pursue (= *begin courting*).

приудар|я́ть, я́ю, *impf. of* ~ить.

приукрá|сить, шу, сишь, *pf.* (*of* ~шивать) (*coll.*) to adorn; (*fig.*) to embellish, embroider.

приукрáшива|ть, ю, *impf. of* приукрáсить.

приуменьш|áть, áю, *impf. of* ~ить.

приумéньш|ить, ~ý, ~ишь, *pf.* (*of* ~áть) to diminish, lessen, reduce.

приумнож|áть(ся), áю(сь), *impf. of* ~ить(ся).

приумножéни|е, я, *n.* increase, augmentation.

приумнóж|ить, у, ишь, *pf.* (*of* ~áть) to increase, augment, multiply.

приумнóж|иться, ится, *pf.* (*of* ~áться) to increase, multiply.

приумóлк|нуть, ну, нешь, *past* ~, ~ла, *pf.* (*coll.*) to fall silent (*for a while*).

приун|ы́ть, óю, óешь, *pf.* (*coll.*) to become depressed, become gloomy.

приурóчива|ть, ю, *impf. of* приурóчить.

приурóч|ить, у, ишь, *pf.* (*of* ~ивать) (к) to time (for, to coincide with); ~или издáние книги к прибытию áвтора publication of the book was timed to coincide with the author's arrival.

приусáдебный, *adj.* adjoining the farm (-house); п. учáсток (колхóзника) personal plot (belonging to collective farmer).

приути́х|нуть, ну, нешь, *past* ~, ~ла, *pf.* to quiet down; (*of a storm*) to abate; (*of wind*) to fall, drop.

приуч|áть(ся), áю(сь), *impf. of* ~ить(ся).

приуч|и́ть, ý, ~ишь, *pf.* (*of* ~áть) (к *or* +*inf.*) to train (to), school (to, in); to inure, accustom; п. когó-н. к дисциплине to inculcate discipline in someone; п. когó-н. купáться в холóдной водé to school someone to taking cold baths.

приуч|и́ться, ýсь, ~ишься, *pf.* (*of* ~áться) (+*inf.*) to train oneself (to), school oneself (to), discipline oneself (to); to become inured (to), accustom oneself (to).

прифран|ти́ться, чýсь, ти́шься, *pf.* (*coll.*) to dress up, put on one's best bib and tucker.

прифронтовóй, *adj.* (*mil.*) front, front-line.

прихвáрыва|ть, ю, *impf.* (*coll.*) to be unwell off and on.

прихвастн|ýть, ý, ёшь, *pf.* (*coll.*) to boast a little, brag a little.

прихва|ти́ть, чý, ~тишь, *pf.* (*of* ~тывать) (*coll.*) 1. to catch up, seize up (= to take;

to get). 2. to tie up, fasten. 3. (*of frost*) to touch, nip.

прихва́тыва|ть, ю, *impf. of* прихвати́ть.

прихворн|у́ть, у́, ёшь, *pf.* (*coll.*) to be indisposed, be unwell.

при́хвост|ень, ня, *m.* (*coll.*) hanger-on, stooge.

прихлеба́тел|ь, я, *m.* (*coll.*) sponger.

прихлеба́тельств|о, а, *n.* (*coll.*) sponging.

прихлебн|у́ть, у́, ёшь, *pf.* to take a sip.

прихлёбыва|ть, ю, *impf.* (*coll.*) to sip.

прихло́п|нуть, ну, нешь, *pf.* (*of* ~ывать) (*coll.*) 1. to slam. 2. to squeeze, pinch; п. па́лец две́рью to pinch one's finger in the door. 3. (*sl.*) to kill.

прихло́пыва|ть, ю, *impf.* 1. *impf. of* прихло́пнуть. 2. *impf. only* to clap.

прихлы́н|уть, у, ешь, *pf.* (к) to rush (towards), surge (towards).

прихо́д¹, а, *m.* coming, arrival; advent.

прихо́д², а, *m.* receipts; п. и расхо́д credit and debit.

прихо́д³, а, *m.* (*eccl.*) parish; како́в поп, тако́в и п. (*prov.*) like master, like man.

прихо|ди́ть, жу́, ~дишь, *impf. of* прийти́.

прихо|ди́ться, жу́сь, ~дишься, *impf.* 1. *impf. of* прийти́сь. 2. *impf. only* (+*d. and i.*) to be (*in a given degree of relationship to*); я ей ~жу́сь дя́дей I am her uncle; они́ нам ~дятся ро́дственниками they are related to us.

прихо́д|ный, *adj. of* ~²; ~ная кни́га receipt-book.

прихо́д|овать, ую, *impf.* (*of* за~) (*book-keeping*) to enter (*of person receiving sum from client, customer, etc.*).

прихо́до-расхо́дн|ый, *adj.* credit and debit; ~ая кни́га account-book.

прихо́дский, *adj.* parochial; parish; п. свяще́нник parish priest; parson, vicar, rector.

прихо́д|я́щий, *pres. part. act. of* ~и́ть *and adj.* non-resident; п. больно́й outpatient; ~я́щая домрабо́тница daily maid, charwoman; п. учени́к day-boy.

прихожа́н|ин, ина, *pl.* ~е, ~, *m.* parishioner.

прихо́ж|ая, ей, *f.* (entrance) hall, lobby; antechamber.

прихора́шива|ться, юсь, *impf.* (*coll.*) to doll oneself up, smarten oneself up.

прихотли́вост|ь, и, *f.* capriciousness, fastidiousness, whimsicality.

прихотли́в|ый (~, ~а), *adj.* 1. capricious, fastidious, whimsical. 2. fanciful, intricate (*of pattern, etc.*).

при́хот|ь, и, *f.* whim, caprice, whimsy, fancy.

прихра́мыва|ть, ю, *impf.* to limp, hobble.

прице́л, а, *m.* 1. back-sight; опти́ческий п. telegraphic sight; п. для бомбомета́ния

bomb sight; взять на п. to take aim (at), aim (at), point (at). 2. aiming.

прице́лива|ться, юсь, *impf. of* прице́литься.

прице́л|иться, юсь, ишься, *pf.* (*of* ~иваться) to take aim, take sight.

прице́л|ьный, *adj. of* ~; ~ьная бомбарди́ровка precision bombing; ~ьная коло́дка back-sight bed; ~ьная ли́ния line of sight; п. ого́нь aimed fire; ~ьная пла́нка back-sight leaf; ~ьные приспособле́ния sighting device; back-sight; п. хому́тик back-sight slide.

прице́нива|ться, юсь, *impf. of* прицени́ться.

прицен|и́ться, ю́сь, ~ишься, *pf.* (*of* ~иваться) (к; *coll.*) to ask the price (of).

прице́п, а, *m.* trailer.

прицеп|и́ть, лю́, ~ишь, *pf.* (*of* ~ля́ть) (к) 1. to hitch (to), hook on (to); to couple (to); п. ваго́ны к парово́зу to couple trucks to a locomotive. 2. (*coll.*) to pin on (to), fasten (to), tack (to), tag on (to).

прицеп|и́ться, лю́сь, ~ишься, *pf.* (*of* ~ля́ться) (к) 1. to stick (to), cling (to). 2. (*fig., coll.*) to pester; to nag (at).

прице́пк|а, и, *f.* 1. hitching, hooking on; coupling. 2. (*coll.*) pestering; nagging. 3. (*coll.*) chaser.

прицепля́|ть(ся), ю(сь), *impf. of* прицепи́ть(ся).

прицепно́й, *adj.;* п. ваго́н trailer; п. инвента́рь (*agric.*) tractor-drawn implements.

прича́л, а, *m.* 1. mooring, making fast. 2. mooring line. 3. berth, moorage; у ~ов at its, her moorings.

прича́лива|ть, ю, *impf. of* прича́лить.

прича́л|ить, ю, ишь, *pf.* (*of* ~ивать) 1. (к) to moor (to). 2. (*intrans.*) to moor.

прича́л|ьный, *adj. of* ~; п. кана́т mooring line.

прича́сти|е¹, я, *n.* (*gram.*) participle.

прича́сти|е², я, *n.* (*eccl.*) 1. communion; the eucharist. 2. making one's communion, communicating.

прича|сти́ть, щу́, сти́шь, *pf.* (*of* ~ща́ть) (*eccl.*) to give communion.

прича|сти́ться, щу́сь, сти́шься, *pf.* (*of* ~ща́ться) (*eccl.*) to receive communion, make one's communion, communicate.

прича́ст|ный¹ (~ен, ~на), *adj.* (к) participating (in), concerned (in), connected (with), involved (in); privy (to); быть ~ным (к) to participate (in), be concerned (in), connected (with), be involved (in); to be privy (to); быть ~ным к теа́тру to be connected with the theatre; быть ~ным к покуше́нию на жизнь короля́ to be privy to an attempt on the life of the king.

прича́стный², *adj.* (*gram.*) participial.

прича́ст|ный³, *adj. of* ~ие²; ~ное вино́ communion wine.

причаща́|ть(ся), ю(сь), *impf.* of прича-сти́ть(ся).

причаще́ни|е, я, *n.* (*eccl.*) receiving communion, making one's communion, communicating.

причём, *conj.* **1.** moreover, and (*or translated by means of participial clause*); бы́ло о́чень темно́, п. я пло́хо ориенти́руюсь в э́той ме́стности it was very dark and I don't know this area well. **2.** while (+*participial clause*); despite the fact that; он реши́л пое́хать, п. отдава́л себе́ отчёт в опа́сности he decided to go, while recognizing the danger.

приче|са́ть, шу́, ~шешь, *pf.* (*of* ~сыва́ть) to comb; п. кого́-н. to do someone's hair; to brush, comb someone's hair.

приче|са́ться, шу́сь, ~шешься, *pf.* (*of* ~сыва́ться) to do one's hair; to brush, comb one's hair; to have one's hair done.

причёск|а, и, *f.* haircut; hair style, hair-do, coiffure.

при|че́сть, чту́, чтёшь, *past* ~чёл, ~чла́, *pf.* (*of* ~чи́тывать) **1.** (*coll.*) to add on. **2.** (*obs.*) to number, reckon.

причё́сыва|ть(ся), ю(сь), *impf.* of приче-са́ть(ся).

причётник, а, *m.* (*eccl.*) junior deacon.

причи́н|а, ы, *f.* cause; reason; уважи́тельная п. good cause, good reason; по той и́ли ино́й ~е for some reason or other, for one reason or another; по той просто́й ~е, что for the simple reason that; по ~е (+*g.*) by reason (of), on account (of), owing (to) because (of).

причи́н|ить, ю, и́шь, *pf.* (*of* ~я́ть) to cause; to occasion.

причи́нност|ь, и, *f.* causality.

причи́нн|ый, *adj.* causal, causative; ~ая связь causation; ~ое ме́сто (*coll.*) privy parts.

причин|я́ть, я́ю, *impf.* of ~и́ть.

причи́сл|ить, ю, ишь, *pf.* (*of* ~я́ть) (к) **1.** to add on (to). **2.** to reckon (among), number (among), rank (among); его́ ~или к са́мым выдаю́щимся матема́тикам he was ranked among the foremost mathematicians. **3.** to attach (to).

причисл|я́ть, я́ю, *impf.* of ~ить.

причита́ни|е, я, *n.* (ritual) lamentation; похоро́нные ~я keen, keening.

причита́|ть, ю, *impf.* (по+*p.*) to lament (for), keen (over); to bewail.

причита́|ться, ется, *impf.* (+*d.*; c+*g.*) to be due (to; from); вам ~ется два рубля́ there is two roubles due to you, you have two roubles to come; с вас ~ется два рубля́ you have two roubles to pay.

причи́тыва|ть, ю, *impf.* of приче́сть.

причмо́кива|ть, ю, *impf. of* причмо́кнуть.

причмо́к|нуть, ну, нешь, *pf.* (*of* ~ивать) to smack one's lips.

причт, а, *m.* (*collect.*) the clergy of a parish.

причу́д|а, ы, *f.* caprice, whim, whimsy, fancy; oddity, vagary; челове́к с ~ами crank, odd person, queer person.

причу́д|иться, ится, *pf.* of чу́диться.

причу́дливост|ь, и, f. **1.** oddity, queerness; quaintness, fantasticality. **2.** (*coll.*) capriciousness, whimsicality.

причу́длив|ый (~, ~а), adj. 1. odd, queer; quaint, fantastical. **2.** (*coll.*) capricious, whimsical.

причу́дник, а, *m.* (*coll.*) crank, odd person, queer person.

пришварт|ова́ть, у́ю, *pf.* (*of* ~о́вывать) (к) to moor (to), make fast (to).

пришварт|ова́ться, у́юсь, *pf.* (*of* ~о́вывать-ся) (к) to moor (to), tie up (at).

пришварто́выва|ть(ся), ю(сь), *impf.* of пришвартова́ть(ся).

пришле́|ец, ьца, *m.* newcomer, stranger.

пришепётыва|ть, ю, *impf.* (*coll.*) to lisp slightly.

прише́стви|е, я, *n.* (*obs.*) advent, coming; до второ́го ~я (*joc.*) till doomsday.

пришиб|и́ть, у́, ёшь, *past* ~, ~ла, *pf.* (*coll.*) **1.** to strike dead. **2.** (*fig.*) to knock out, break (= *to dispirit*).

пришиб|ленный, *p.p.p.* of ~и́ть *and adj.* (*coll.*) broken; crest-fallen.

пришива́|ть, ю, *impf.* of приши́ть.

пришивно́й, *adj.* sewn on; п. воротничо́к attached collar.

приш|и́ть, ью́, ьёшь, *pf.* (*of* ~ива́ть) **1.** to sew on. **2.** to nail on. **3.** (+*a.* к *or* +*a. and d.*; *fig.*, *coll.*) to pin (on), pin an accusation (of on).

пришко́льный, *adj.* (adjoining a) school.

при́шлый, *adj.* newly come, arrived; strange, alien.

пришпи́лива|ть, ю, *impf.* of пришпи́лить.

пришпи́л|ить, ю, ишь, *pf.* (*of* ~ивать) to pin.

пришпо́рива|ть, ю, *impf.* of пришпо́рить.

пришпо́р|ить, ю, ишь, *pf.* (*of* ~ивать) to spur; to put, set spurs (to).

прищёлкива|ть, ю, *impf.* of прищёлкнуть.

прищёлк|нуть, ну, нешь, *pf.* (*of* ~ивать) п. кнуто́м to crack the whip; п. па́льцами to snap one's fingers.

прищем|и́ть, лю́, и́шь, *pf.* (*of* ~ля́ть) to pinch, squeeze; п. себе́ па́лец две́рью to pinch one's finger in the door.

прищемля́|ть, ю, *impf.* of прищеми́ть.

прищеп|и́ть, лю́, и́шь, *pf.* (*of* ~ля́ть) (*bot.*) to graft.

прищепля́|ть, ю, *impf.* of прищепи́ть.

прище́пк|а, и, *f.* (clothes-) peg.

прище́п|ок, ка, *m.* = ~ка.

прищу́рива|ть(ся), ю(сь), *impf.* of при-щу́рить(ся).

прищу́р|ить, ю, ишь, *pf.* (*of* ~ивать); п. глаза́ = ~иться.

прищу́р|иться, юсь, ишься, *pf.* (*of* ~ивать-ся) to screw up one's eyes.

прию́т, а, *m.* 1. shelter, refuge. 2. (*obs.*) asylum; де́тский п. orphanage, orphan--asylum; роди́льный п. maternity home, lying-in hospital.

прию́|ти́ть, чу́, ти́шь, *pf.* to shelter, give refuge.

прию́|ти́ться, чу́сь, ти́шься, *pf.* to take shelter.

прия́знен|ный (~, ~на), *adj.* (*obs.*) friendly, amicable.

прия́зн|ь, и, *f.* (*obs.*) friendliness, good-will.

прия́тел|ь, я, *m.* friend.

прия́тельниц|а, ы, *f.* 1. (female) friend. 2. girl-friend, lady-friend.

прия́тельский, *adj.* friendly, amicable.

прия́т|ный (~ен, ~на), *adj.* nice, pleasant, agreeable, pleasing; п. на вид nice-looking, gratifying to the eye; п. на вкус palatable, tasty; ~но (*impers., pred.*) it is pleasant, it is nice.

при|я́ть, му́, ⊾мешь, *pf.* (*obs.*) = ~ня́ть.

про, *prep.*+*a.* 1. about; мы говори́ли про вас we were talking about you. 2. (*coll.*) for; э́то не про нас this is not for us. 3. про себя́ to oneself; я поду́мал про себя́ I thought to myself; прочти́ письмо́ вслух, а не про себя́! read the letter aloud, not to yourself!

про-¹ *verbal prefix indicating* 1. *action through, across or past object, as* прострели́ть to shoot through; прое́хать to pass (by). 2. *overall or exhaustive action, as* прогре́ть to warm thoroughly. 3. *duration of action throughout given period of time, as* просиде́ть всю ночь to sit up all night. 4. *loss or failure, as* проигра́ть to lose (*a game*).

про-² *as prefix of nouns and adjs.* pro-.

проанализи́р|овать, ую, *pf. of* анализи́ровать.

про́б|а, ы, *f.* 1. trial, test; try-out; assay; п. го́лоса voice test; п. сил trial of strength; взять на ~у to take on trial. 2. sample. 3. standard (*measure of purity of gold*); зо́лото 56-ой ~ы 14 carat gold; зо́лото 96-ой ~ы pure gold, 24 carat gold. 4. hallmark.

пробавля́|ться, юсь, *impf.* (*coll.*) to subsist (on), make do (on).

проба́лтыва|ть(ся), ю(сь), *impf. of* пробол-та́ть(ся).

проба|си́ть, шу́, си́шь, *pf.* (*coll.*) to speak in a bass, deep voice.

пробе́г, а, *m.* 1. (*sport*) run, race; лы́жный п. ski-run. 2. run, mileage, distance covered; су́точный п. парово́за 24 hours' run for a locomotive; находи́ться в ~е to be working, be operating.

пробе́га|ть, ю, *pf.* (*coll.*) to run about (*for a certain time*).

пробега́|ть, ю, *impf. of* пробежа́ть.

пробе́|жа́ть, гу́, жи́шь, гу́т, *pf.* (*of* ~га́ть) 1. to pass (running), run past, run by; to run through; to run along; п. па́льцами по клавиату́ре to run one's fingers over the keyboard. 2. to run; to cover; по́езд ~жа́л шестьдеся́т миль ро́вно в час the train covered sixty miles in exactly one hour. 3. (*fig.*) to run, flit (over, down, across); хо́лод ~жа́л по её спине́ a chill ran down her spine. 4. (*fig., coll.*) to run through, look through, skim.

пробе́|жа́ться, гу́сь, жи́шься, гу́тся, *pf.* to run, take a run.

пробе́л, а, *m.* 1. blank, gap; hiatus; lacuna; запо́лнить ~ы to fill in the blanks. 2. (*fig.*) deficiency, gap; ~ы в зна́ниях gaps in one's knowledge.

пробива́|ть(ся), ю(сь), *impf. of* проби́ть(ся).

проби́вк|а, и, *f.* 1. holing, piercing; punching. 2. caulking.

пробивн|о́й, *adj.* 1. piercing, punching; ~а́я си́ла penetrating power (*of missile*); п. ста-но́к (*tech.*) punch. 2. (*electr.*) disruptive. 3. (*coll.*) go-ahead, go-getting.

пробира́|ть(ся), ю(сь), *impf. of* пробра́ть(ся).

проби́рк|а, и, *f.* test-tube.

проби́рн|ый, *adj.* testing; assaying; п. ка́мень touchstone; ~ое клеймо́ hallmark; п. мета́лл test metal; ~ая пала́та assay office; ~ая скля́нка test-tube.

проби́р|овать, ую, *impf.* to test, assay.

проби́рщик, а, *m.* assayer, assay-master.

про|би́ть¹, бью, бьёшь, *past* ⊾би́л, ~би́ла, ⊾би́ло, *pf. of* бить 9.

про|би́ть², бью, бьёшь, *past* ⊾би́л, ~би́ла, *pf.* (*of* ~бива́ть) to make a hole (in); to hole, pierce; to punch; п. кора́бль to hole a ship; п. сте́ну to breach a wall; п. ши́ну to puncture a tyre; п. путь, доро́гу to open the way (*also fig.*); п. себе́ доро́гу (·*fig.*) to carve one's own way.

про|би́ться¹, бью́сь, бьёшься, *pf.* (*of* ~би-ва́ться) 1. to fight, force, make one's way through; to break, strike through; п. трудо́м to struggle along; п. сквозь толпу́ to fight one's way through the crowd. 2. (*of plants*) to shoot, show, push up.

про|би́ться², бью́сь, бьёшься, *pf.* (над) to struggle (with) (*for a certain time*).

про́бк|а, и, *f.* 1. cork (*substance*). 2. cork; stopper; plug; глуп как п. daft as a brush. 3. (*electr.*) fuse. 4. (*fig.*) traffic jam; conges-tion.

про́бков|ый, *adj.* cork; subereous, suberic; п. дуб cork-oak; ~ая кислота́ suberic acid; п. по́яс cork jacket, life-jacket.

проблéм|а, ы, *f.* problem.

проблемáтик|а, и, *f.* (*collect.*) problems.

проблемати́ческий, *adj.* problematic(al).

проблемати́чност|ь, и, *f.* problematical character.

проблемати́ч|ный (~ен, ~на), *adj.* = ~еский.

прóблеск, а, *m.* flash; ray, gleam (*also fig.*); п. надéжды ray of hope.

проблéскива|ть, ю, *impf. of* проблеснýть.

проблес|нýть, нý, нёшь, *pf.* (*of* ~кивать) to flash, gleam.

проблуждá|ть, ю, *pf.* to wander, rove, roam (*for a certain time*).

прóбный, *adj.* 1. trial, test, experimental; п. кáмень touchstone; п. ковш assay spoon; п. полёт test flight; п. спирт proof spirit; п. шар ballon d'essai; п. экземпля́р specimen copy. 2. hallmarked.

прóб|овать, ую, *impf.* (*of* по~) 1. to test; п. пи́щу to taste, try food. 2. (+*inf.*) to try (to), attempt (to), endeavour (to).

прободá|ть¹, ет, *pf.* to gore.

прободá|ть², ет, *impf.* (*med.*) to perforate, puncture.

прободéни|е, я, *n.* (*med.*) perforation.

пробóин|а, ы, *f.* hole (*esp. caused by missile*); получи́ть ~у to be holed.

пробó|й, я, *m.* 1. clamp, hasp, holdfast. 2. (*electr.*) spark-over.

пробóйник, а, *m.* (*tech.*) punch.

проболé|ть¹, ю, *pf.* to be ill (*for a certain time*).

пробол|éть², и́т, *pf.* to hurt (*for a certain time*).

проболтá|ть, ю, *pf.* (*of* пробáлтывать) (*coll.*) 1. to play for time by talking. 2. to blab (out).

проболтá|ться¹, юсь, *pf.* (*of* пробáлтываться) (*coll.*) to blab, blurt out a secret, let the cat out of the bag.

проболтá|ться², юсь, *pf.* (*coll.*) to idle, loaf.

пробóр, а, *m.* parting (*of the hair*); прямóй п. parting in the middle; косóй п. parting at one side; дéлать (себé) п. to part one's hair.

пробормо|тáть, чý, ~чешь, *pf. of* бормотáть.

прóбочник, а, *m.* (*coll.*) corkscrew.

пробрáсыва|ть, ю, *impf. of* пробрóсить.

про|брáть, берý, берёшь, *past* ~брáл, ~бралá, ~брáло, *pf.* (*of* ~бирáть) 1. to penetrate; морóз ~брáл меня́ до костéй I was chilled to the marrow; их ~брáл страх fear had struck them; егó ничéм не ~берёшь he cannot be got at. 2. (*coll.*) to scold, rate. 3. (*agric.*) to clear, weed.

про|брáться, берýсь, берёшься, *past* ~брáлся, ~бралáсь, ~брáлóсь, *pf.* (*of* ~бирáться). 1. to fight, force one's way. 2. to steal

(through, past); п. óщупью to feel one's way; п. на цы́почках to tiptoe (through).

пробро|ди́ть, жý, ~дишь, *pf.* to wander (*for a certain time*).

пробрó|сить, шу, сишь, *pf.* (*of* пробрáсывать) (*coll.*) 1. to count up (*on an abacus*). 2. to overcount (by).

пробст, а, *m.* (*eccl.*) provost (*in Lutheran Church, clergyman in charge of principal church in town*).

пробу|ди́ть, жý, ~дишь, *pf.* (*of* буди́ть *and* ~ждáть) to wake; to awaken, rouse, arouse (*also fig.*).

пробу|ди́ться, жýсь, ~дишься, *pf.* (*of* ~ждáться) to wake up, awake (*also fig.*).

пробуждá|ть(ся), ю(сь), *impf. of* пробуди́ть(ся).

пробуждéни|е, я, *n.* waking up, awakening.

пробурáв|ить, лю, ишь, *pf.* (*of* ~ливать) to bore, drill, perforate.

пробурáвлива|ть, ю, *impf. of* пробурáвить.

пробурч|áть, ý, и́шь, *pf. of* бурчáть.

проб|ы́ть, ýду, ýдешь, *past* ~ы́л, ~ылá, *pf.* to stay, remain; to be (*for a certain time*); он ~ы́л у нас три недéли he stayed with us for three weeks.

провáл, а, *m.* 1. downfall. 2. (*geogr.*) gap; funnel. 3. failure; п. пáмяти failure of memory; какóй п.! what a flop!

провáлива|ть, ю, *impf.* 1. *impf. of* провали́ть. 2. ~й! (*coll.*) off with you!, get moving!, beat it!, hop it!

провáлива|ться, юсь, *impf. of* провали́ться.

провал|и́ть, ю, ~ишь, *pf.* (*of* ~ивать) 1. to cause to collapse, knock down. 2. (*fig., coll.*) to ruin, make a mess (of); п. рóль (*theatr.*) to ruin a part. 3. (*fig.*) to reject; п. кандидáта на экзáмене to fail a candidate in an examination; п. законопроéкт to kill a bill.

провал|и́ться, юсь, ~ишься, *pf.* (*of* ~иваться) 1. to collapse, come down, fall through; потолóк ~и́лся the ceiling has come down. 2. (*fig., coll.*) to fail, miscarry; (*in an examination*) to fail, be ploughed; пóлностью п. to be a complete, utter failure. 3. (*coll.*) to disappear, vanish; он как сквозь зéмлю ~и́лся he vanished into thin air; я готóв был сквозь зéмлю ~и́ться I wished the earth could swallow me up; п. мне на э́том мéсте, éсли... I'll be damned if....

провансáл|ь, я, *m.* mayonnaise, salad dressing.

провансáльский, *adj.* Provençal.

провáнск|ий, *adj.* ~ое мáсло olive oil, salad-oil.

провáрива|ть, ю, *impf. of* провари́ть.

провар|и́ть, ю́, ~ишь, *pf.* (*of* ~ивать) to boil thoroughly.

провéд|ать, аю, *pf.* (*of* ~ывать) (*coll.*) 1. to

come to see, call on. **2.** (o+*p*.) to find out (about), learn (of, about).

проведе́ни|е, я, *n*. **1.** leading, taking; piloting. **2.** building; installation. **3.** carrying out, through; conducting; п. кампа́нии (*mil. and fig.*) conduct of a campaign; п. в жизнь putting into effect.

проведыва|ть, ю, *impf. of* прове́дать.

провез|ти́, у́, ёшь, *past* ~, ~ла́, *pf.* (*of* провози́ть) **1.** to convey, transport; п. контраба́ндой to smuggle. **2.** to bring (with one).

провентили́р|овать, ую, *pf. of* вентили́ровать.

прове́р|енный, *p.p.p. of* ~ить *and adj.* proved, of proved worth.

прове́р|ить, ю, ишь, *pf.* (*of* ~я́ть) **1.** to check (up on); to verify; to audit; п. биле́ты to examine tickets; п. ка́ссу to check the till; п. чью-н. рабо́ту to check up on someone's work; п. тетра́ди to correct exercise-books. **2.** to test; п. свои́ си́лы to try one's strength.

прове́рк|а, и, *f*. **1.** checking; examination; verification; check-up; п. исполне́ния work check-up; п. нали́чия stock-taking, inventory-making; п. счето́в audit(ing); п. боя́ ору́жия (*mil.*) checking the zero of a weapon; п. управле́ния огнём (*mil.*) verification of fire. **2.** testing.

провер|ну́ть, ну́, нёшь, *pf.* (*of* ~тывать) (*coll.*) **1.** to bore, perforate, pierce. **2.** to crank (*a motor*). **3.** (*fig.*) to rush through (*discussion of a question, etc.*).

прове́рочн|ый, *adj*. checking, verifying; ~ая рабо́та test paper.

провер|те́ть, чу́, ~тишь, *pf.* (*of* ~тывать) (*coll.*) to bore, perforate, pierce.

провёртыва|ть, ю, *impf. of* проверну́ть *and* проверте́ть.

прове́рщик, а, *m*. checker, inspector.

провер|я́ть, я́ю, *impf. of* ~ить.

провѐс¹, а, *m*. short weight.

провѐс², а, *m*. sag; dip (*of wire*).

прове́|сить¹, шу, сишь, *pf.* (*of* ~шивать) to give short weight.

прове́|сить², шу, сишь, *pf.* (*of* ~шивать) to dry in the open, air.

прове́|сить³, шу, сишь, *pf.* (*of* ~шивать) (*tech.*) to plumb.

прове|сти́, ду́, дёшь, *past* ~л, ~ла́, *pf.* (*of* проводи́ть¹) **1.** to lead, take; п. су́дно (*naut.*) to pilot a vessel. **2.** to build; to install; п. железнодоро́жную ве́тку to build a branch line; п. водопрово́д to lay on water; п. электри́чество to install electricity. **3.** to carry out, carry on; to conduct, hold; п. о́пыты to carry out tests; п. заседа́ние to conduct a meeting; п. рефо́рмы to carry out reforms; п. бесе́ду to give a talk. **4.** to carry through; to carry, pass,

get through (*a resolution, a bill, etc.*); to implement (*a decision, etc.*); им не удало́сь п. законопрое́кт че́рез Пала́ту ло́рдов they did not succeed in getting the bill through the House of Lords; п. иде́ю в жизнь to put an idea into effect, implement an idea. **5.** to advance, put forward (*an idea, etc.*). **6.** (*book-keeping*) to register; п. по кни́гам to book; п. по ка́ссе to register, ring up on the till. **7.** to draw (*a line, etc.*); п. грани́цу to draw a boundary-line. **8.** (+*i*.) to pass over, run over; она́ ~ла́ руко́й по лбу she passed her hand over her forehead. **9.** to spend, pass (*time*); чтобы п. вре́мя to pass the time; как вы ~ли вре́мя? (*addressed to person on return from holiday, etc.*) did you have a good time?, what sort of time did you have? **10.** (*coll.*) to take in, trick, fool; меня́ не ~дёшь you can't fool me.

прове́трива|ть(ся), ю(сь), *impf. of* прове́трить(ся).

прове́тр|ить, ю, ишь, *pf.* (*of* ~ивать) to air; to ventilate.

прове́тр|иться, юсь, ишься, *pf.* (*of* ~иваться) **1.** to have an airing; (*fig., coll.*) to have a change of scene. **2.** *pass. of* ~ить.

прове́шива|ть, ю, *impf. of* прове́сить.

провиа́нт, а, *m*. provisions, victuals.

прови́дени|е, я, *n*. foresight, forecast.

провиде́ни|е, я, *n*. (*rel.*) Providence.

прови́|деть, жу, дишь, *impf*. to foresee.

прови́д|ец, ца, *m*. (*obs., rhet.*) seer, prophet.

провизи|о́нный, *adj*. *of* ~я; п. магази́н provision shop.

прови́зи|я, и, *no pl., f*. provisions; снабди́ть ~ей to cater (for); to provision, victual.

прови́зор, а, *m*. (*qualified*) pharmaceutical chemist.

провизо́р|ный (~ен, ~на), *adj*. provisional; temporary.

провин|и́ться, ю́сь, и́шься, *pf*. (в+*p*.) to be guilty (of); to commit an offence; п. пе́ред кем-н. to wrong someone, do someone an injury; в чём мы ~и́лись? what have we done wrong?

прови́нност|ь, и, *f*. (*coll.*) fault; offence.

провинциа́л, а, *m*. provincial (*person*).

провинциали́зм, а, *m*. provincialism.

провинциа́льност|ь, и, *f*. provinciality.

провинциа́л|ьный (~ен, ~ьна), *adj*. provincial (*also fig.*).

прови́нци|я, и, *f*. **1.** province. **2.** the provinces (*as opp. to capital or other centre*); жить в глухо́й ~и to live in the depths of the country.

провира́|ться, юсь, *impf. of* провра́ться.

прови́с|ать, а́ет, *impf. of* ~нуть.

прови́с|нуть, нет, *pf.* (*of* ~а́ть) to sag.

про́вод, а, *pl.* ~а́, *m*. wire, lead, conductor; возду́шный п. aerial conductor; заземля́ющий п. earth(-wire); п. с пу́щенным то́ком live wire.

проводи́мост|ь, и, *f.* (*electr.*) conductivity, conduction; акти́вная п., ва́ттная п. conductance; уде́льная п. specific conductivity.

прово|ди́ть¹, жу́, ~ди́шь, *impf.* 1. *impf. of* провести́. 2. *impf. only* (*phys., electr.*) to conduct, be a conductor.

прово|ди́ть², жу́, ~ди́шь, *pf.* (*of* ~жа́ть) to accompany; to see off; п. на по́езд to see off (on the train); п. кого́-н. домо́й to take, see someone home; п. кого́-н. до двере́й to see someone to the door; п. поко́йника to attend a funeral; п. глаза́ми to follow with one's eyes.

прово́дк|а, и, *f.* 1. leading, taking. 2. building; installation. 3. (*collect.; electr.*) wiring, wires.

проводни́к¹, а́, *m.* 1. guide. 2. (*of train*) conductor; guard.

проводни́к², а́, *m.* 1. (*phys., electr.*) conductor. 2. (*fig.*) bearer; transmitter.

проводни́|ца, цы, *f. of* ~к¹.

проводн|о́й, *adj. of* про́вод; ~а́я связь telegraphic communication (*as opp. to radio*).

про́вод|ы, ов, *no sing.* seeing-off; send-off.

провожа́т|ый, ого, *m.* guide, escort.

провожа́|ть, ю, *impf. of* проводи́ть².

прово́з, а, *m.* carriage, conveyance, transport; пла́та за п. payment for carriage.

провозве|сти́ть, щу́, сти́шь, *pf.* (*of* ~ща́ть) (*obs.*) 1. to prophesy. 2. to proclaim.

провозвеща́|ть, ю, *impf. of* провозвести́ть.

провозгла|си́ть, шу́, си́шь, *pf.* (*of* ~ша́ть) to proclaim; п. ло́зунг to advance a slogan; п. тост to propose a toast; п. тост за кого́-н. to propose someone's health; его́ ~си́ли королём he was proclaimed king.

провозглаша́|ть, ю, *impf. of* провозгласи́ть.

провозглаше́ни|е, я, *n.* proclamation; declaration.

прово|зи́ть, жу́, ~зи́шь, *impf. of* провезти́.

прово|зи́ться¹, жу́сь, ~зи́шься, *pf.* 1. (*coll.*) to play about (*for a certain time*). 2. (*c+i.*) to spend (*a certain time*) (over, in seeing to); я~зи́лся це́лый ме́сяц с получе́нием ви́зы I spent a whole month over obtaining the visa.

прово|зи́ться², жу́сь, ~зи́шься, *impf. pass., of* ~зи́ть.

провозоспосо́бност|ь, и, *f.* carrying capacity (*of railways*).

провока́тор, а, *m.* 1. agent provocateur. 2. (*fig.*) instigator, provoker.

провокацио́нный, *adj.* provocative.

провока́ци|я, и, *f.* provocation.

про́волок|а, и, *f.* wire; колю́чая п. barbed wire.

про́волочк|а, и, *f. dim. of* про́волока; short wire, fine wire.

проволо́чк|а, и, *f.* (*coll.*) delay, procrastination.

про́воло|чный, *adj. of* ~ка; ~чное загражде́ние wire entanglement; ~чная сеть wire netting.

провоня́|ть, ет, *pf.* (+*i.; coll.*) to stink (of).

прово́рност|ь, и, *f.* = прово́рство.

прово́р|ный (~ен, ~на), *adj.* 1. quick, swift, expeditious. 2. agile, nimble, adroit, dexterous.

провор|ова́ться, у́юсь, *pf.* (*coll.*) to be caught stealing, embezzling.

проворо́н|ить, ю, ишь, *pf.* (*coll.*) to miss, let slip, lose; п. свою́ о́чередь to miss one's turn; п. ме́сто to lose one's place.

прово́рств|о, а, *n.* 1. quickness, swiftness. 2. agility, nimbleness, adroitness, dexterity.

проворч|а́ть, у́, и́шь, *pf.* to mutter.

провоци́р|овать, ую, *impf. and pf.* (*pf. also* с~) to provoke.

провр|а́ться, у́сь, ёшься, *past* ~а́лся, ~ала́сь, ~ало́сь, *pf.* (*of* провира́ться) (*coll.*) to give oneself away, slip up (*in lying*).

провя́л|ить, ю, ишь, *pf. of* вя́лить.

прогад|а́ть, а́ю, *pf.* (*of* ~ывать) (*coll.*) to miscalculate.

прога́дыва|ть, ю, *impf. of* прогада́ть.

прогаз|ова́ть, у́ю, *pf.* (*coll.*) to run up (*an engine*).

прога́лин|а, ы, *f.* glade.

проги́б, а, *m.* (*tech.*) caving in, sagging, flexure, deflection; camber; стрела́ ~а sag, sagging; depth of camber.

прогиба́|ть(ся), ю(сь), *impf. of* прогну́ть(ся).

прогла́|дить¹, жу, дишь, *pf.* (*of* ~живать) to iron (out).

прогла́|дить², жу, дишь, *pf.* to iron (*for a certain time*).

прогла́жива|ть, ю, *impf. of* прогла́дить¹.

прогла́тыва|ть, ю, *impf. of* проглоти́ть; ~я слова́ to swallow one's words.

прогло|ти́ть, чу́, ~тишь, *pf.* (*of* прогла́тывать) to swallow (*also fig.*); п. оскорбле́ние to swallow, pocket an insult; п. язы́к to lose one's tongue; п. кни́гу to devour a book; язы́к ~тишь it makes your mouth water.

прогля|де́ть¹, жу́, ди́шь, *pf.* (*of* ~дывать) to look through, glance through; п. глаза́ (*coll.*) to wear one's eyes out.

прогля|де́ть², жу́, ди́шь, *pf.* to overlook.

прогля́дыва|ть, ю, *impf. of* прогляде́ть *and* проглянуть.

прогля|ну́ть, ~нет, *pf.* (*of* ~дывать) to show (up, through), peep (out, through); to be perceptible; со́лнце ~ну́ло из-за облако́в the sun peeped out from behind the clouds; в её взгля́де ~ну́ла тоска́ there was a touch of wistfulness in her look.

про|гна́ть, гоню́, го́нишь, *past* ~гна́л, ~гнала́, ~гна́ло, *pf.* (*of* ~гоня́ть) **1.** to drive away (*also fig.*); (*fig.*) to banish; п. с глаз доло́й to banish from one's sight; п. забо́ты to banish care. **2.** to drive (through); п. коро́в в по́ле to drive the cows into the field; п. кого́-н. сквозь строй (*hist.*) to make someone run the gauntlet. **3.** (*coll.*) to sack, fire.

прогне́ва|ть, ю, *pf.* (*obs.*) to anger, incense.

прогне́ва|ться, юсь, *pf.* (*obs.*) (на+*a.*) to become angry (with).

прогнев|и́ть, лю́, и́шь, *pf. of* гневи́ть.

прогнива́|ть, ю, *impf. of* прогни́ть.

прогн|и́ть, ию́, иёшь, *past* ~и́л, ~ила́, ~и́ло, *pf.* (*of* ~ива́ть) to rot through.

прогно́з, а, *m.* prognosis; forecast; п. пого́ды weather forecast.

прогн|у́ть, у́, ёшь, *pf.* (*of* прогиба́ть) to cause to cave in, cause to sag.

прогн|у́ться, у́сь, ёшься, *pf.* (*of* прогиба́ться) to cave in, sag.

проговáрива|ть(ся), ю(сь), *impf. of* проговори́ть(ся).

проговор|и́ть, ю́, и́шь, *pf.* (*of* проговáривать) **1.** to say, pronounce, utter; п. сквозь зу́бы to mutter; он ни сло́ва не ~и́л he did not utter a word. **2.** to speak, talk (*for a certain time*); они́ ~и́ли три часа́ подря́д they talked for three hours on end.

проговор|и́ться, ю́сь, и́шься, *pf.* (*of* проговáриваться) to blab (out), talk; to let the cat out of the bag.

проголода́|ть, ю, *pf.* to starve, go hungry.

проголода́|ться, юсь, *pf.* to get hungry, grow hungry.

проголос|ова́ть, у́ю, *pf. of* голосова́ть.

прого́н[1], а, *m.* **1.** (*archit.*) purlin; (*of a bridge*) bearer, baulk. **2.** (*archit.*) well, well-shaft (*for a staircase*).

прого́н[2], а, *m.* (*dial.*) cattle track.

прого́н[3], а, *m.* (*theatr. sl.*) run-through(= *first full rehearsal of play in order of scenes*).

прого́н|ный, *adj. of* ~ы; ~ные (де́ньги) (*obs.*) travelling allowance.

прого́н|ы, ов, *no sing.* (*obs.*) fare (*for journey by post-chaise*).

прогоня́|ть, ю, *impf. of* прогна́ть.

прогор|а́ть, а́ю, *impf. of* ~е́ть[1].

прогор|е́ть[1], ю́, и́шь, *pf.* (*of* ~а́ть) **1.** to burn through; to burn to a cinder. **2.** (*coll.*) to go bankrupt, go bust.

прогор|е́ть[2], ю́, и́шь, *pf.* to burn (*for a certain time*).

прого́рклост|ь, и, *f.* rancidity, rankness.

прого́рклый, *adj.* rancid, rank.

прого́рк|нуть, ну, нешь, *past* ~, ~ла, *pf. of* го́ркнуть.

прого|сти́ть, щу́, сти́шь, *pf.* to stay.

програ́мм|а, ы, *f.* programme; schedule; театра́льная п. play-bill; уче́бная п. syllabus; curriculum; п. ска́чек race-card; п. спорти́вных состяза́ний fixture list.

программи́р|овать, ую, *impf.* (*of* за~) to programme.

программи́ст, а, *m.* (computer) programmer.

програ́мм|ный, *adj.* **1.** *adj. of* ~а; ~ная му́зыка programme music; ~ное обеспе́чение (computer) software. **2.** (*tech.*) programmed, automatically operated.

прогрева́|ть(ся), ю(сь), *impf. of* прогре́ть(ся).

прогре́сс, а, *m.* progress.

прогресси́вк|а, и, f. (*abbr. of* прогресси́вная опла́та; *coll.*) payment on sliding scale (*for completion of piece-work in excess of plan*).

прогресси́в|ный (~ен, ~на), *adj.* (*in var. senses*) progressive.

прогресси́р|овать, ую, *impf.* to progress, make progress; (*of an illness*) to grow progressively worse.

прогре́сси|я, и, f. (*math.*) progression.

прогре́|ть, ю, *pf.* (*of* ~ва́ть) to heat, warm thoroughly; п. мото́р to warm up an engine.

прогре́|ться, юсь, *pf.* (*of* ~ва́ться) to get thoroughly warmed; (*of an engine, etc.*) to warm up.

прогрохо|ти́ть, чу́, ти́шь, *pf. of* грохоти́ть.

прогу́л, а, *m.* absence (from work); absenteeism; truancy.

прогу́лива|ть, ю, *impf.* **1.** *impf. of* прогуля́ть[1]. **2.** *impf. only* to walk; п. ло́шадь to walk a horse.

прогу́лива|ться, юсь, *impf.* **1.** *impf. of* прогуля́ться. **2.** *impf. only* to stroll, saunter.

прогу́лк|а, и, f. **1.** walk; stroll; ramble; п. для моцио́на constitutional. **2.** outing; п. в экипа́же, п. в автомоби́ле drive; п. в ло́дке row; п. под паруса́ми sail; п. верхо́м ride.

прогу́л|очный, *adj. of* ~ка; ~очная зо́на pedestrian precinct; ~очная . ло́дка pleasure-boat (*as opp. to racing-craft*).

прогу́л|ьный, *adj. of* ~; ~ьное вре́мя time off work (*without good cause*).

прогу́льщик, а, *m.* absentee; truant.

прогуля́|ть[1], ю, *pf.* (*of* прогу́ливать) **1.** to be absent from work (*without good cause*); to play truant. **2.** to miss; п. обе́д to miss one's dinner (*as result of failing to appear at right time*); п. уро́ки to play truant.

прогуля́|ть[2], ю, *pf.* to walk; to stroll.

прогуля́|ться, юсь, *pf.* (*of* прогу́ливаться) to take a walk, stroll.

прода|ва́ть, ю́, ёшь, *impf. of* ~́ть.

прода|ва́ться, ю́сь, ёшься, *impf.* **1.** (*impf. only*) to be on sale, be for sale; дом ~ётся the house is for sale; ~ётся мотоци́кл (*for-*

mula of advertisement of sale) 'motor-cycle for sale'. **2.** (*impf. only*) to sell; дёшево п. to sell cheap, go cheap; его́ но́вый рома́н хорошо́ ~ётся his new novel is selling well, is having good sales. **3.** *impf. of* ~ться.

продав|е́ц, ца́, *m.* **1.** seller; vendor. **2.** salesman, shop-assistant.

продав|и́ть, лю́, ~ишь, *pf.* (*of* ~ливать) to break (through); to crush.

прода́влива|ть, ю, *impf. of* продави́ть.

продавщи́ц|а, ы, *f.* **1.** seller; vendor. **2.** saleswoman, shop-assistant, shop-girl.

прода́ж|а, и, *f.* sale, selling; опто́вая п. wholesale; п. в ро́зницу retail; п. с торго́в auction sale, public sale; пусти́ть в ~у to put on sale; пойти́ в ~у to be offered for sale, be on the market, be up for sale; поступи́ть в ~у to go on sale, be on the market; нет в ~е is not on sale, is not obtainable; (*of a book*) is out of print.

прода́жност|ь, и, *f.* mercenariness, venality.

прода́ж|ный, *adj.* **1.** to be sold, for sale; ~ная цена́ sale price. **2.** (~ен, ~на) (*fig.*) mercenary, venal; ~ная душа́ mercenary creature; ~ная же́нщина streetwalker.

прода́лблива|ть, ю, *impf. of* продолби́ть.

прода́|ть, м, шь, ст, ди́м, ди́те, ду́т, *past* про́дал, ~ла́, про́дало, *pf.* (*of* ~ва́ть) **1.** to sell; п. о́птом to sell wholesale; п. в ро́зницу to sell retail; п. с торго́в to auction; п. в креди́т to sell on credit, on tick; п. себя́ в убы́ток to sell at a loss. **2.** (*fig., pejor.*) to sell, sell out.

прода́|ться, мся, шься, стся, ди́мся, ди́тесь, ду́тся, *past* ~лся, ~ла́сь, *pf.* (*of* ~ва́ться) to sell oneself.

продвига́|ть(ся), ю(сь), *impf. of* продви́нуть(ся).

продвиже́ни|е, я, *n.* **1.** advancement. **2.** (*mil.; fig.*) progress, advance.

продви́|нуть, ну, нешь, *pf.* (*of* ~га́ть) **1.** to move forward, push forward. **2.** (*fig.*) to promote, further, advance; п. по слу́жбе to promote, give promotion; п. де́ло to expedite a matter.

продви́|нуться, нусь, нешься, *pf.* (*of* ~га́ться) **1.** to advance (*also fig.*); to move on, move forward; to push on, push forward; to forge ahead; п. вперёд (*mil. and fig.*) to gain ground, make headway, make an advance. **2.** to be promoted, receive promotion, receive advancement. **3.** *pass. of* ~нуть.

продева́|ть, ю, *impf. of* проде́ть.

продежу́р|ить, ю, ишь, *pf.* to be on duty (*for a certain time*).

продеклами́р|овать, ую, *pf. of* деклами́ровать.

проде́л|ать, аю, *pf.* (*of* ~ывать) **1.** to make (*an aperture, a way through, etc.*). **2.** to do,

perform, accomplish; п. большу́ю рабо́ту to accomplish a great work.

проде́лк|а, и, *f.* trick; prank, escapade; моше́нническая п. dirty trick, swindle, fraud.

проде́лыва|ть, ю, *impf. of* проде́лать.

продемонстри́р|овать, ую, *pf. of* демонстри́ровать.

продёрг|ать, аю, *pf.* (*of* ~ивать) (*agric.*) to thin (out), weed (out).

продёргива|ть, ю, *impf. of* продёргать *and* продёрнуть.

продерж|а́ть, у́, ~ишь, *pf.* to hold (*for a certain time*); to keep (*for a certain time*); его́ ~а́ли два ме́сяца в больни́це he was kept in hospital for two months.

продерж|а́ться, у́сь, ~ишься, *pf.* to hold out.

продёр|нуть, ну, нешь, *pf.* (*of* ~гивать) (*coll.*) **1.** to pass, run; п. ни́тку в иго́лку to thread a needle. **2.** (*fig.*) to tear to shreds, pull to pieces (= *to criticize severely*).

проде́|ть, ну, нешь, *pf.* (*of* ~ва́ть) to pass, run; п. ни́тку в иго́лку to thread a needle.

продефили́р|овать, ую, *pf. of* дефили́ровать.

продешев|и́ть, лю́, и́шь, *pf.* (*coll.*) to sell too cheap.

продикт|ова́ть, у́ю, *pf. of* диктова́ть.

продира́|ть(ся), ю(сь), *impf. of* продра́ть(ся).

продлева́|ть, ю, *impf. of* продли́ть.

продле́ни|е, я, *n.* extension, prolongation.

продлённый, p.p.p. of ~и́ть; шко́ла с ~ённым днём extended-day school.

продл|и́ть, ю́, и́шь, *pf.* (*of* ~ева́ть) to extend, prolong; п. о́тпуск to extend leave; п. срок де́йствия ви́зы to extend a visa.

продл|и́ться, ю́сь, и́шься, *pf. of* дли́ться.

проднало́г, а, *m.* (*abbr. of* продово́льственный нало́г) (*hist.*) tax in kind.

продово́льств|енный, *adj. of* ~ие; ~енная ка́рточка ration book, ration card, food-card; п. магази́н grocery (store), provision store; ~енные райо́ны food-producing areas; п. склад food store; (*mil.*) ration store, ration dump; ~енное снабже́ние food supply; ~енные това́ры food-stuffs.

продово́льстви|е, я, n. food-stuffs, provisions; (*mil.*) rations; но́рма ~я ration scale.

продолб|и́ть, лю́, и́шь, *pf.* (*of* прода́лбливать) to make a hole (in), chisel through.

продолгова́тост|ь, и, f. oblong form.

продолгова́т|ый (~, ~а), *adj.* oblong; п. мозг (*anat.*) medulla oblongata.

продолжа́тел|ь, я, m. continuer, successor.

продолж|а́ть, а́ю, *impf.* **1.** to continue, go on, proceed; п. свою́ рабо́ту to continue, go on with one's work; п. рабо́тать to continue to work, go on working. **2.** *impf.* *of* ~ить.

продолж|а́ться, а́ется, *impf.* (*of* ~и́ться) to continue, last, go on, be in progress; восста́ние ~а́ется уже́ второ́й год the insurrection is now in its second year.

продолже́ни|е, я, *n.* **1.** continuation; sequel; п. сле́дует to be continued. **2.** extension, prolongation; continuation; п. ли́нии extension of a line; забо́р слу́жит ~ем стены́ the fence serves as a continuation of the wall. **3.** в п. (+*g.*) in the course (of), during, for, throughout; в п. го́да throughout the year; в п. почти́ двух лет я ни ра́зу её не вида́л during almost two years I did not see her once.

продолжи́тельность|ь, и, *f.* duration, length.

продолжи́тел|ьный (~ен, ~ьна), *adj.* long; prolonged, protracted.

продо́лж|ить, у, ишь, *pf.* (*of* ~а́ть) to extend, prolong.

продо́лж|иться, усь, ишься, *pf.* *of* ~а́ться.

продо́льн|ый, *adj.* longitudinal, lengthwise, linear; (*naut.*) fore-and-aft; ~ая ось longitudinal axis; ~ая перебо́рка (*naut.*) fore-and-aft bulkhead; ~ая пила́ rip-saw; п. разре́з longitudinal section.

продохн|у́ть, у́, ёшь, *pf.* (*coll.*) to breathe freely.

продразвёрстк|а, и, *f.* (*abbr. of* продово́льственная развёрстка) (*hist.*) requisitioning of farm produce.

про|дра́ть, деру́, дерёшь, *past* ~дра́л, ~драла́, ~дра́ло, *pf.* (*of* ~дира́ть) (*coll.*) to tear; to wear holes (in); п. глаза́ to open one's eyes.

про|дра́ться, деру́сь, дерёшься, *past* ~дра́лся, ~драла́сь, ~дра́лось, *pf.* (*of* ~дира́ться) (*coll.*) **1.** to tear; to wear into holes; у меня́ ло́кти ~дра́лись my coat is out at the elbows. **2.** to squeeze through, force one's way through.

продрем|а́ть, лю́, ~лешь, *pf.* to doze (*for a certain time*).

продро́г|нуть, ну, нешь, *past* ~, ~ла, *pf.* to be chilled to the marrow.

продува́ни|е, я, *n.* = продувка.

продува́тельный, *adj.* = продувочный.

продува́|ть, ю, *impf.* **1.** *impf. of* проду́ть. **2.** (*impf. only*) to blow (*from all sides*); прия́тно ~л ветеро́к there was a pleasant breeze.

продува́|ться, юсь, *impf. of* проду́ться.

проду́вк|а, и, *f.* (*tech.*) blowing through, blowing off; scavenging.

проду́в|но́й[1], *adj.* (*tech.*) = ~о́чный.

продувн|о́й[2], *adj.* (*coll.*) crafty, sly, roguish; ~а́я бе́стия rogue.

проду́в|очный, *adj. of* ~ка; п. во́здух scavenging air; п. кла́пан blow valve,

blow-off valve; п. насо́с scavenging pump; ~очная труба́ blow-off pipe, blast pipe.

проду́кт, а, *m.* **1.** product; побо́чный п. by-product; ~ы сгора́ния (*chem.*) products of combustion. **2.** *pl.* produce; provisions, food-stuffs; моло́чные ~ы dairy produce; ~ы се́льского хозя́йства farm produce.

продукти́вно, *adv.* productively; with a good result, to good effect.

продукти́вность|ь, и, *f.* productivity.

продукти́в|ный (~ен, ~на), *adj.* (*in var. senses*) productive; (*fig.*) fruitful; п. скот productive livestock; п. су́ффикс (*ling.*) productive suffix.

продукто́вый, *adj.* food, provision; п. магази́н grocery (store), provision store.

проду́кци|я, и, *f.* production, output.

проду́ма|нный, *p.p.p. of* ~ть *and adj.* well thought-out, considered; ~нное реше́ние a considered decision.

проду́м|ать, аю, *pf.* (*of* ~ывать) to think over; to think out.

проду́мыва|ть, ю, *impf. of* проду́мать.

проду́|ть, ю, ешь, *pf.* (*of* ~ва́ть) **1.** to blow through; (*tech.*) to blow through, blow off, blow out; to scavenge. **2.** (*impers.*+*a.*) to be in a draught; придви́ньте стул, а то вас ~ет bring your chair up, or else you will be in a draught. **3.** (*coll.*) to lose (*at games*).

проду́|ться, юсь, ешься, *pf.* (*of* ~ва́ться) (*coll.*) to lose (*at games*).

проду́шин|а, ы, *f.* air-hole, vent.

продыря́в|ить, лю, ишь, *pf.* (*of* ~ливать) to make a hole (in), pierce.

продыря́в|иться, люсь, ишься, *pf.* (*of* ~ливаться) to become full of holes.

продыря́влива|ть(ся), ю(сь), *impf. of* продыря́вить(ся).

проеда́|ть(ся), ю(сь), *impf. of* прое́сть(ся).

прое́зд, а, *m.* **1.** passage, thoroughfare; ~а нет! no thoroughfare! **2.** journey.

прое́з|дить[1], жу, дишь, *pf.* (*of* ~жа́ть) **1.** to exercise (*a horse, etc.*). **2.** (*coll.*) to spend on a journey, in travelling; мы ~дили сто рубле́й we got through a hundred roubles on the journey.

прое́з|дить[2], жу, дишь, *pf.* to spend (*a certain time*) driving, riding, travelling; они́ ~дили тро́е су́ток they had travelled for three days and nights.

прое́з|диться, жусь, дишься, *pf.* (*coll.*) to have spent all one's money on a journey, in travelling.

проездн|о́й, *adj.* travelling; п. биле́т ticket; ~а́я пла́та fare; *as noun* ~ы́е, ~ы́х travelling expenses.

прое́здом, *adv.* en route, in transit, while passing through.

проезжа́|ть, ю, *impf. of* прое́здить *and* прое́хать.

проéзж|ий, *adj.*; ~ая дорóга thoroughfare, public road; ~ие лю́ди passers-by; *as noun* п., ~его, *m.* passer-by.

проéкт, а, *m.* 1. project, scheme, design. 2. draft; п. договóра draft treaty.

проекти́вн|ый, *adj.* ~ая геомéтрия descriptive geometry, projecting geometry.

проекти́ровани|е, я, *n.* projecting, planning, designing.

проекти́р|овать[1], ую, *impf.* 1. (*pf.* за~ *and* с~) to project, plan, design; п. нóвый теáтр to design a new theatre. 2. *impf. only* (*fig.*) to plan; мы ~уем уéхать веснóй we plan to go away in the spring.

проекти́р|овать[2], ую, *impf.* (*math.*) to project.

проекти́рóвк|а, и, *f.* = проекти́рование.

проекти́рóвщик, а, *m.* planner, designer.

проéктн|ый, *adj.* 1. planning, designing; ~ое бюрó planning office. 2. designed; ~ая мóщность (*tech.*) rated capacity; ~ая скóрость designed speed.

проекцио́нный, *adj.* п. фонáрь projector, magic lantern.

проéкци|я, и,*f.* 1. (*math.*) projection; вертикáльная п. vertical projection, front view; elevation; горизонтáльная п. horizontal projection, plan view. 2. projection (*on to a screen*).

проём, а, *m.* (*archit.*) aperture; embrasure; двернóй п. doorway.

проé|сть, м, шь, ст, ди́м, ди́те, дя́т, *past* ~л, *pf.* (*of* ~дáть) 1. to eat through; to corrode. 2. (*coll.*) to spend on food.

проé|сться, мся, шься, стся, ди́мся, ди́тесь, дя́тся, *past* ~лся, *pf.* (*of* ~дáться) (*coll.*) to spend all one's money on food.

проé|хать, ду, дешь, *pf.* (*of* ~зжáть) 1. to pass (by, through); to drive (by, through), ride (by, through). 2. to pass, go past (*inadvertently or by mistake*). 3. to go, do, make, cover (*a certain distance*).

проé|хаться, дусь, дешься, *pf.* (*coll.*) to go for an outing; п. на чей-н. счёт, п. по чьему́-н. áдресу (*joc.*) to take it out of someone, have a laugh at someone's expense.

прожáр|енный, *p.p.p. of* ~ить *and adj.* (*cul.*) well-done.

прожáрива|ть(ся), ю(сь), *impf. of* прожáрить(ся).

прожáр|ить, ю, ишь, *pf.* (*of* ~ивать) to fry, roast thoroughly.

прожáр|иться, юсь, ишься, *pf.* (*of* ~иваться) 1. to fry, roast thoroughly. 2. *pass. of* ~ить.

прожд|áть, у́, ёшь, *past* ~áл, ~алá, ~áло, *pf.* (+*a. or g.*) to wait (for), spend (*a certain time*) waiting (for).

прож|евáть, ую́, уёшь, *pf.* (*of* ~ёвывать) to chew well, masticate well.

прожёвыва|ть, ю, *impf. of* прожевáть.

прожéкт, а, *m.* 1. (*obs.*) = проéкт. 2. (*coll., iron.*) (hare-brained, impracticable) project, scheme.

прожектёр, а, *m.* deviser of impracticable schemes.

прожектёрств|о, а, *n.* penchant for, indulging in, hare-brained schemes.

прожектёрств|овать, ую, *impf.* to devote oneself to devising hare-brained schemes.

прожéктор, а, *pl.* ~ы *and* ~á, *m.* searchlight; п. залива́ющего свéта floodlight projector.

прожекторúст, а, *m.* searchlight operator.

прожéктор|ный, *adj. of* ~.

прóжелт|ь, и,*f.* yellow tint.

про|жéчь, жгу, жжёшь, жгут, *past* ~жёг, ~жглá *pf.* (*of* ~жигáть) 1. to burn thorough; п. дыру́ в чём-н. to burn a hole in something. 2. to burn, leave alight (*for a certain time*).

про|жжённый, *p.p.p. of* ~жéчь. *and adj.* (*coll.*) arch, double-dyed; п. плут arch--scoundrel.

прожива́|ть, ю, *impf.* 1. to live, reside. 2. *impf. of* прожи́ть.

прожива́|ться, юсь, *impf. of* прожи́ться.

прожига́тел|ь, я, *m.* п. жи́зни fast liver.

прожига́|ть[1], ю, *impf. of* прожéчь.

прожига́|ть[2], ю, *impf.* п. жизнь to lead a fast life, live fast.

прожи́лк|а, и,*f.* (*in var. senses*) vein.

прожи́ти|е, я, *n.* living, livelihood; хвата́ет ли у них дéнег на п.? have they enough to live on?

прожи́точный, *adj.* necessary, sufficient to live on; п. ми́нимум living wage, subsistence wage.

про|жи́ть, живу́, живёшь, *past* ~жил, ~жилá, ~жило, *pf.* (*of* ~жива́ть) 1. to live; он ~жил сто лет he lived to be a hundred (*years of age*). 2. to spend; мы ~жили мéсяц áвгуст на берегу́ мóря we spent the month of August at the seaside. 3. to spend, run through (*money*); в оди́н год я ~жил наслéдство in a year I had run through the legacy.

про|жи́ться, живу́сь, живёшься, *past* ~жи́лся, ~жила́сь, *pf.* (*of* ~жива́ться) (*coll.*) to have spent all one's money, be spent up.

прожóрливост|ь, и,*f.* voracity, voraciousness, gluttony.

прожóрлив|ый (~, ~а), *adj.* voracious, gluttonous.

прожужж|áть, у́, и́шь, *pf.* to buzz, drone, hum; п. у́ши кому́-н. (*coll.*) to keep dinning something into someone's ears, drone on at someone.

про́**з**|**а, ы,** *f.* prose; п. жи́зни the prosaic side of life.

прозаи́**зм, а,** *m.* prosaic expression (*in poetry*).

прозаи́**ик, а,** *m.* prose-writer, prosaist.

прозаи́**ческий,** *adj.* **1.** prose; п. перево́д prose translation. **2.** prosaic; matter-of-fact; prosy.

прозаи́**чност**|**ь, и,** *f.* **1.** matter-of-factness; prosiness. **2.** (*fig.*) dullness, flatness.

прозаи́**ч**|**ный** (~**ен,** ~**на**)**,** *adj.* **1.** prosaic; matter-of-fact; prosy. **2.** (*fig.*) commonplace, humdrum.

прозакла́дыва|**ть, ю,** *impf. and pf.* (*coll.*) **1.** to stake, wager. **2.** (*obs.*) to lose (*in betting*).

прозва́ни|**е, я,** *n.* nickname, sobriquet; по ~ю nicknamed, otherwise known as.

про|**зва́ть, зову́, зове́шь,** *past* ~**зва́л,** ~**звала́,** ~**зва́ло,** *pf.* (*of* ~**зыва́ть**) to nickname, name.

про́**звищ**|**е, а,** *n.* nickname, sobriquet.

прозвони́**ть, ю́, и́шь,** *pf.* **1.** to ring out, peal. **2.** to ring for, announce by ringing; ~и́ли обе́д, ~и́ли обе́дать the bell (gong, *etc.*) went for dinner.

прозвуча́**ть, и́т,** *pf. of* звуча́ть.

прозева́|**ть¹, ю,** *pf. of* зева́ть 3; (*coll.*) to miss.

прозева́|**ть², ю,** *pf.* to yawn (*for a certain time*).

прозе́**ктор, а,** *m.* prosector, dissector.

прозе́**кторск**|**ая, ой,** *f.* dissecting-room.

прозели́т, а, *m.* proselyte.

прозим|**ова́ть, у́ю,** *pf. of* зимова́ть.

прозна́|**ть, ю,** *pf.* (+*a. or* о+*p.*; *coll.*) to find out (about), hear (about).

прозоде́**жд**|**а, ы,** *f.* (*abbr. of* производственная оде́жда) working clothes; overalls.

прозорли́вост|**ь, и,** *f.* sagacity, perspicacity, intuition.

прозорли́в|**ый** (~**,** ~**а**)**,** *adj.* sagacious, perspicacious.

прозра́чност|**ь, и,** *f.* transparence, transparency.

прозра́ч|**ный** (~**ен,** ~**на**)**,** *adj.* transparent (*also fig.*); limpid, pellucid; п. намёк transparent hint.

прозрева́|**ть, ю,** *impf. of* прозре́ть.

прозре́ни|**е, я,** *n.* **1.** recovery of sight. **2.** (*fig.*) insight.

прозр|**е́ть, ю, и́шь,** *pf.* (*of* ~**ева́ть**) **1.** to recover one's sight. **2.** (*fig.*) to begin to see clearly; ту́т-то я и ~е́л my eyes were opened, I saw the light.

прозыва́|**ть, ю,** *impf. of* прозва́ть.

прозыва́|**ться, юсь,** *impf.* to be nicknamed, have a nickname.

прозяба́ни|**е, я,** *n.* vegetation (*also fig.*).

прозяба́|**ть, ю,** *impf.* to vegetate (*also fig.*).

прозя́б|**нуть, ну, нешь,** *past* ~**,** ~**ла,** *pf.* (*coll.*) to be chilled.

проигр|**а́ть¹, а́ю,** *pf.* (*of* ~**ывать**) to lose (= *to be defeated, etc.*); п. фигу́ру to lose a piece (*at chess*); п. суде́бный проце́сс to lose a case; мы ничего́ не ~а́ли, прие́хав авто́бусом we lost nothing in coming by 'bus; п. в чьём-н. мне́нии to sink in someone's estimation.

проигр|**а́ть², а́ю,** *pf.* (*of* ~**ывать**) to play (through, over); п. конце́рт на патефо́нных пласти́нках to play through a concerto on gramophone records; п. магнитофо́нную ле́нту to play over a tape (*on a tape recorder*).

проигр|**а́ть³, а́ю,** *pf.* to play (*for a certain time*).

проигр|**а́ться, а́юсь,** *pf.* (*of* ~**ываться**) to lose all one's money (*at gambling*).

проигрыватель, я, *m.* record-player.

проигрыва|**ть(ся), ю(сь),** *impf. of* проигра́ть(ся).

про́**игрыш, а,** *m.* loss; оста́ться в ~е to be the loser, come off loser.

произведе́ни|**е, я,** *n.* **1.** work, production; и́збранные ~я Л. Н. Толсто́го selected works of L. N. Tolstoy; ме́лкие ~я minor works. **2.** (*math.*) product.

произве|**сти́, ду́, де́шь,** *past* ~**л,** ~**ла́,** *pf.* (*of* производи́ть) **1.** to make; to carry out; to execute; п. вы́стрел to fire a shot; п. о́пыты to carry out experiments; п. плате́ж to effect payment; п. сле́дствие to hold an inquest; п. смотр (+*d.*) to hold a review (of), review; п. съёмку кинофи́льма to shoot a film; п. уче́ние (*mil.*) to drill, train. **2.** to give birth (to); п. на свет to bring into the world. **3.** (*fig.*) to cause, produce; п. впечатле́ние (на+*a.*) to make, create an impression (on, upon); п. сенса́цию to cause, make a sensation. **4.** (в+ *n.-a.*) to promote (to, to the rank of); его́ ~ли в подполко́вники he has been promoted (to the rank of) lieutenant-colonel.

производи́тел|**ь¹, я,** *m.* **1.** producer; ме́лкие ~и small producers. **2.** sire; жеребе́ц-п. stud-horse.

производи́тел|**ь², я,** *m.* п. рабо́т clerk of the works.

производи́тельност|**ь, и,** *f.* productivity, output; productiveness.

производи́тел|**ьный** (~**ен,** ~**ьна**)**,** *adj.* productive; efficient.

произво|**ди́ть, жу́,** ~**дишь,** *impf.* **1.** *impf. of* произвести́. **2.** *impf. only* to produce. **3.** *impf. only* (*ling.*) to derive.

произво́дн|**ый,** *adj.* derivative, derived; ~ое сло́во derivative; *as noun* ~**ая,** ~**ой,** *f.* (*math.*) derivative.

произво́дственник, а, *m.* one (directly) engaged in production.

произво́дств|енный, *adj. of* ~о; ~енное зада́ние production target, production quota; ~енное обуче́ние industrial training; ~енная пра́ктика practical training; ~енное совеща́ние production conference; п. стаж industrial work record, industrial experience.

произво́дств|о, а, *n.* 1. production, manufacture; изде́ржки ~а production costs; сре́дства ~а means of production; изде́лия куста́рного, фабри́чного ~а hand-made, factory-made goods; сове́тского ~а Soviet-made, Soviet-produced; рабо́тать на ~е to work on production. 2. factory, works; пойти́ на п. to go to work at a factory. 3. carrying-out, execution. 4. (в+*n.-a.*) promotion (to, to the rank of).

производ|я́щий, *pres. part. act. of* ~и́ть *and adj.* (*econ.*) producing, producer.

произво́л, а, *m.* 1. arbitrariness; оста́вить на п. судьбы́ to leave to the mercy of fate. 2. arbitrary rule.

произво́льно, *adv.* 1. arbitrarily. 2. at will.

произво́льност|ь, и, *f.* arbitrariness.

произво́л|ьный (~ен, ~ьна), *adj.* arbitrary.

произнесе́ни|е, я, *n.* pronouncing; utterance, delivery.

произнес|ти́, у́, ёшь, *past* ~, ~ла́, *pf.* (*of* произноси́ть) 1. to pronounce; to articulate. 2. to pronounce, say, utter; п. пригово́р to pronounce sentence; п. речь to deliver a speech; он не ~ ни сло́ва he did not utter a word.

произноси́тельн|ый, *adj.* (*ling.*) articulatory; п. аппара́т articulatory apparatus; ~ые тру́дности англи́йского языка́ the difficulties of English pronunciation.

произно|си́ть, шу́, ~сишь, *impf. of* произнести́.

произноше́ни|е, я, *n.* pronunciation; articulation.

произо|йти́, йду́, йдёшь, *past* ~шёл, ~шла́, *pf.* (*of* происходи́ть) 1. to happen, occur, take place. 2. (от, из-за) to spring (from), arise (from), result (from); ава́рия ~шла́ от небре́жности the crash resulted from carelessness. 3. (из, от) to come (from, of), descend (from), be descended (from).

произраста́ни|е, я, *n.* growth, growing, sprouting.

произраст|а́ть, а́ет, *impf. of* ~и́.

произраст|и́, ёт, *past* произро́с, произросла́, *pf.* (*of* ~а́ть) to grow, sprout, spring up.

проиллюстри́р|овать, ую, *pf.* (*of* иллюстри́ровать) to illustrate.

проинструкти́р|овать, ую, *pf.* (*of* инструкти́ровать) to instruct, give instructions (to).

проинтервью́и́р|овать, ую, *pf.* (*of* интервью́и́ровать) to interview.

проинформи́р|овать, ую, *pf.* (*of* информи́ровать) to inform.

прои|ска́ть, щу́, ~щешь, *pf.* to look (for), search (for), spend (*a certain time*) in search (of).

про́иск|и, ов, *no sing.* intrigues; machinations, underhand plotting.

проистека́|ть, ю, *impf. of* происте́чь.

происте́|чь, ку́, чёшь, ку́т, *past* ~к, ~кла́, *pf.* (*of* ~ка́ть) (из, от) to spring (from), result (from).

происхо|ди́ть, жу́, ~дишь, *impf.* 1. *impf. of* произойти́. 2. *impf. only* to go on, be going on; что тут ~дит? what is going on here?

происхожде́ни|е, я, *n.* (*in var. senses*) origin; provenance; parentage, descent, extraction, birth; п. ви́дов (*biol.*) origin of species; он по ~ю армяни́н he is an Armenian by birth, he is of Armenian extraction.

происше́стви|е, я, *n.* event, incident, happening, occurrence; accident; отде́л ~й (*in newspaper*) local news.

пройдо́х|а, и, *m. and f.* (*coll.*) creeper; scoundrel, rascal.

про́йм|а, ы, *f.* armhole.

про|йти́, йду́, йдёшь, *past* ~шёл, ~шла́, *pf.* (*of* ~ходи́ть[1]) 1. to pass (by, through); to go (by, through); п. ми́мо to pass by, go by, go past; (+*g.*; *fig.*) to overlook, disregard; п. по́лем to go by, through the field(s); п. торже́ственным ма́ршем to march past; п. молча́нием to pass over in silence; п. по мосту́ to cross a bridge; п. в жизнь to be put into effect. 2. to pass, go past (*inadvertently or by mistake*). 3. to go, do, make, cover (*a certain distance*); п. две ты́сячи миль за неде́лю to do two thousand miles in a week. 4. (*of news, rumours, etc.*) to travel, spread. 5. (*of rain, etc.*) to fall. 6. (*of time*) to pass, elapse, go, go by; ~шёл це́лый год a whole year had passed; не ~шло́ шести́ ме́сяцев, как он верну́лся not six months had passed before he returned. 7. to be over; to pass (off), abate, let up; ~шло́ ле́то summer was over; боль ~шла́ the pain passed (off); дождь ~шёл the rain abated. 8. (+*a. or* че́рез) to pass, go through, get through; де́ло ~шло́ мно́го инста́нций the case went through many instances; его́ пье́са снача́ла не ~шла́ че́рез цензу́ру his play at first did not pass the censorship; э́то не ~йдёт (*coll.*) it won't work. 9. to go, go off; как ~шёл ваш докла́д? how did your lecture go?; заседа́ние ~шло́ уда́чно the meeting went off successfully. 10. (в+*n.-a.*) to become, be made; to be placed (on), be taken (on); он ~шёл в доце́нты he has been made a reader, he has received a readership; она́

~шла́ в штат she has been taken on the staff. **11.** (*coll.*) to do, take; п. хи́мию to do chemistry; мы уже́ ~шли́ вое́нную слу́жбу we have already done military service; п. курс лече́ния to take a course of treatment.

про|йти́сь, йду́сь, йдёшься, *past* ~шёлся, ~шла́сь, *pf.* (*of* ~ха́живаться) **1.** to walk up and down, stroll; to take a stroll; п. по ко́мнате to pace up and down the room. **2.** (*coll.*) to dance. **3.** (по+*d.*; *coll.*) to run (over), go (over); п. по кла́вишам to run one's fingers over the keys. **4.** п. на чей-н. счёт, п. по чьему́-н. а́дресу (*coll.*) to have a fling at someone, give someone a bad write-up.

прок, а (у), *m.* (*coll.*) use, benefit; что в э́том ~у? what is the good of it?; из э́того не бу́дет ~у no good will come of this.

прокаже́нн|ый, *adj.* leprous; *as noun* п., ~ого, *m. and* ~ая, ~ой, *f.* leper.

прока́з|а¹, ы, *f.* leprosy.

прока́з|а², ы, *f.* mischief, prank, trick.

прока́|зить, жу, зишь, *impf.* (*of* на~) (*coll.*) to be up to mischief, play pranks.

прока́злив|ый (~, ~а), *adj.* mischievous.

прока́зник, а, *m.* mischievous person; mischievous child, bundle of mischief.

прока́знича|ть, ю, *impf.* (*of* на~) = прока́зить.

прока́лива|ть, ю, *impf. of* прокали́ть.

прокал|и́ть, ю́, и́шь, *pf.* (*of* ~ива́ть) (*tech.*) to temper, anneal; to calcine, fire.

прока́лк|а, и, *f.* (*tech.*) tempering.

прока́лыва|ть, ю, *impf. of* проколо́ть.

проканите́л|ить(ся), ю(сь), ишь(ся), *pf. of* каните́лить(ся).

прока́пчива|ть, ю, *impf. of* прокопти́ть.

прока́пыва|ть, ю, *impf. of* прокопа́ть.

прокарау́л|ить¹, ю, ишь, *pf.* (*coll.*) to let slip, let go (*by carelessness, inattention*) while on guard; он ~ил аресто́ванного he let the prisoner escape.

прокарау́л|ить², ю, ишь, *pf.* to be on guard (*for a certain time*); to guard, watch (*for a certain time*).

прока́т¹, а, *m.* (*tech.*) **1.** rolling. **2.** rolled iron.

прока́т², а, *m.* hire.

прока́т|а́ть¹, а́ю, *pf.* (*of* ~ывать) **1.** to spread flat with a roller. **2.** (*tech.*) to roll, laminate.

прока́т|а́ть², а́ю, *pf.* to take out (for a drive, *etc.*) (*for a certain time*).

прока́т|а́ться¹, а́юсь, *pf.* (*of* ~ываться) (*tech.*) to roll out.

прока́т|а́ться², а́юсь, *pf.* to go out (for a drive, *etc.*) (*for a certain time*).

прока|ти́ть, чу́, ~тишь, *pf.* (*of* ~тывать) **1.** to take out; to take for a drive, ride. **2.** to roll. **3.** to roll by, past. **4.** (*coll.*) to

slate. **5.** п., (*obs.*) п. на вороны́х to blackball.

прока|ти́ться, чу́сь, ~тишься, *pf.* (*of* ~тываться) **1.** to roll (*also fig., of thunder, etc.*). **2.** to go for a drive, go for a spin.

прока́тк|а, и, *f.* (*tech.*) rolling, lamination.

прока́тн|ый¹, *adj.* (*tech.*) rolling; ~ое желе́зо rolled iron; п. стан rolling mill.

прока́тный², *adj.* hired, let out on hire.

прока́тчик, а, *m.* rolling mill operative.

прока́тыва|ть(ся), ю(сь), *impf. of* прока́та́ть(ся)¹ *and* прокати́ть(ся).

прока́шлива|ть(ся), ю(сь), *impf. of* прока́шлять(ся).

прока́шл|ять, яю, *pf.* **1.** to cough. **2.** (*impf.* ~ивать) to cough up.

прока́шл|яться, яюсь, *pf.* (*of* ~иваться) to clear one's throat.

прокип|е́ть, и́т, *pf.* to boil thoroughly, sufficiently.

прокипя|ти́ть, чу́, ти́шь, *pf.* to boil thoroughly, sufficiently.

прокис|а́ть, а́ет, *impf. of* ~нуть.

проки́с|нуть, нет, *pf.* (*of* ~а́ть) to turn (sour).

прокла́дк|а, и, *f.* **1.** laying; building, construction; п. доро́ги road building; breaking a road; п. трубопрово́да pipe laying. **2.** (*tech.*) washer, gasket; packing, padding.

прокладн|о́й, *adj.* packing; кни́га с ~ыми листа́ми book with blank sheets (*for notes*).

прокла́дыва|ть, ю, *impf. of* проложи́ть.

проклама́ци|я, и, *f.* (political) leaflet.

проклами́р|овать, ую, *impf. and pf.* to proclaim.

прокле́ива|ть, ю, *impf. of* прокле́ить.

прокле́|ить, ю, ишь, *pf.* (*of* ~ивать) to paste, glue; to size.

проклина́|ть, ю, *impf.* **1.** *impf. of* прокля́сть. **2.** (*coll.*) to curse, swear at.

прокл|я́сть, яну́, янёшь, *past* ~я́л, ~яла́, ~я́ло, *pf.* (*of* ~ина́ть) to curse, damn.

прокля́ти|е, я, *n.* **1.** damnation; преда́ть ~ю to consign to perdition. **2.** curse; imprecation. **3.** *as interj.* п.! curse it!, damn it!, damnation!

**про́кл|ятый, *p.p.p.* of ~я́сть; будь я ~ят, е́сли... I'm damned if, I'll be damned if...; будь он ~ят! damn him!, curse him!

прокля́тый, *adj.* accursed, damned; (*coll.*) damnable, confounded.

прокови́рива|ть, ю, *impf. of* проковыря́ть.

проковыр|я́ть, я́ю, *pf.* (*of* ~ивать) to pick a hole (in).

проко́л, а, *m.* **1.** puncture. **2.** pricking, piercing. **3.** (*coll.*) endorsement (*on driving licence*).

проко́л|о́ть, ю́, ~ешь, *pf.* (*of* прока́лывать) **1.** to prick, pierce; to perforate; п. нары́в to lance a boil; п. ши́ну to puncture a tyre. **2.** to run through (*with a bayonet, etc.*).

прокомменти́р|овать, ую, *pf.* to comment (upon).

прокомпости́р|овать, ую, *pf. of* компости́ровать.

проконопа́|тить, чу, тишь, *pf. of* конопа́тить.

проконспекти́р|овать, ую, *pf. of* конспекти́ровать.

проко́нсул, а, *m.* (*hist.*) proconsul.

проконсульти́р|овать(ся), ую(сь), *pf. of* консульти́ровать(ся).

проконтроли́р|овать, ую, *pf. of* контроли́ровать.

прокопа́|ть, ю, *pf.* (*of* прока́пывать) 1. to dig. 2. to dig through.

прокопа́|ться, юсь, *pf.* (*coll., pejor.*) to dawdle, mess about (*for a certain time*).

прокопте́л|ый, *adj.* (*coll.*) sooty, soot-caked.

прокоп|ти́ть, чу́, ти́шь, *pf.* (*of* прока́пчивать) 1. to smoke, cure in smoke. 2. (*coll.*) to foul with smoke, soot.

проко́рм, а, *m.* nourishment, sustenance.

прокорм|и́ть(ся), лю́(сь), ∠ишь(ся), *pf. of* корми́ть(ся).

прокорректи́р|овать, ую, *pf. of* корректи́ровать.

проко́с, а, *m.* swath.

прокра́дыва|ться, юсь, *impf. of* прокра́сться.

прокра́|сить, шу, сишь, *pf.* (*of* ∠шивать) to paint over, cover with paint.

прокра́|сться, ду́сь, дёшься, *pf.* (*of* ∠дываться) to steal; п. ми́мо to steal by, past.

прокра́шива|ть, ю, *impf. of* прокра́сить.

прокрич|а́ть, у́, и́шь, *pf.* 1. to shout, cry; to give a shout, raise a cry. 2. (о+*p.*; *coll.*) to trumpet; п. у́ши кому́-н. о чём-н. to din something into someone's ears.

прокру́стов, *adj.* ∠о ло́же (*myth. and fig.*) bed of Procrustes.

прокурату́р|а, ы, *f.* office of public prosecutor.

проку́рива|ть, ю, *impf. of* прокури́ть.

прокур|и́ть, ю́, ∠ишь, *pf.* (*of* ∠ивать) (*coll.*) 1. to spend on smoking. 2. to fill with tobacco smoke.

прокуро́р, а, *m.* public prosecutor; procurator; investigating magistrate; counsel for the prosecution (*in criminal cases*); речь ∠а speech for the prosecution.

прокуро́р|ский, *adj. of* ∼; п. надзо́р powers of procurator; довести́ до све́дения ∼ского надзо́ра to inform the procurator's office.

проку́с, а, *m.* bite.

проку|си́ть, шу́, ∠сишь, *pf.* (*of* ∠сывать) to bite through.

проку́сыва|ть, ю, *impf. of* прокуси́ть.

проку|ти́ть, чу́, ∠тишь, *pf.* (*of* ∠чивать) (*coll.*) 1. to squander, dissipate. 2. to go on the spree, go on the binge.

проку|ти́ться, чу́сь, ∠тишься, *pf.* (*of* ∠чиваться) (*coll.*) to dissipate one's money.

проку́чива|ть(ся), ю(сь), *impf. of* прокути́ть(ся).

прола́га|ть, ю, *impf. of* проложи́ть.

прола́з|а, ы, *m. and f.* (*coll.*) creeper; scoundrel, rascal.

прола́мыва|ть(ся), ю(сь), *impf. of* проломать(ся) *and* проломи́ть(ся).

пролега́|ть, ет, *impf.* to lie, run; доро́га ∼ла вдоль бе́рега кана́ла the path lay by the canal.

пролеж|а́ть, у́, и́шь, *pf.* (*of* ∠ивать) to lie; to spend (*a certain time*) lying; она́ всю зи́му ∼а́ла в посте́ли she spent the whole winter in bed; посы́лка неде́лю ∼а́ла на по́чте the parcel lay for a week in the post office.

про́леж|ень, ня, *m.* (*med.*) bedsore.

пролёжива|ть, ю, *impf. of* пролежа́ть.

пролеза́|ть, а́ю, *impf. of* ∼ть.

проле́з|ть, у, ешь, *past* ∼, ∼ла, *pf.* (*of* ∼а́ть) 1. to get through, climb through. 2. (в+*a.*; *fig., coll., pejor.*) to worm oneself (into, on to); он ∼ в чле́ны комите́та he has wormed his way on to the committee.

пролёт[1], а, *m.* flight.

пролёт[2], а, *m.* 1. (*archit.*) bay; п. мо́ста span. 2. stair-well. 3. (*coll.*) stage (*distance between stations on railway*).

пролетариа́т, а, *m.* proletariat.

пролетариза́ци|я, и, *f.* proletarianization.

пролетаризи́р|овать, ую, *impf. and pf.* to proletarianize.

пролета́ри|й, я, *m.* proletarian; ∼и всех стран, соединя́йтесь! workers of the world, unite!

пролета́рский, *adj.* proletarian.

пролет|а́ть[1], а́ю, *impf. of* ∼е́ть.

пролет|а́ть[2], а́ю, *pf.* to fly (*for a certain time*).

проле|те́ть, чу́, ти́шь, *pf.* (*of* ∼та́ть[1]) 1. to fly, cover (*a certain distance*). 2. to fly (by, through, past) (*also fig.*); кани́кулы ∼те́ли the holidays flew (by). 3. (*fig.*) to flash, flit; у неё в голове́ ∼те́ла мысль a thought flashed through her mind.

пролётк|а, и, *f.* droshky, (horse-)cab.

пролётн|ый, *adj.* ∼ая пти́ца bird of passage.

проли́в, а, *m.* (*geogr.*) strait, sound.

пролива́|ть, ю, *impf. of* проли́ть.

проливно́й, *adj.* п. дождь pouring rain, pelting rain; шёл п. дождь it was pouring.

проли́ти|е, я, *n.* shedding; п. кро́ви bloodshed.

прол|и́ть, ью́, ьёшь, *past* ∼и́л, ∼ила́, ∼и́ло, *pf.* (*of* ∼ива́ть) to spill, shed; п. чью-н. кровь to shed someone's blood; п. слёзы (по+*d. or p.*, о+*p.*) to shed tears (over); п. свет (на+*a.*; *fig.*) to shed light (on).

про́лог, а, *m.* (*lit.*) calendar (*collection of*

saints' lives, homilies, etc., arranged in order of the calendar).

проло́г, а, *m.* prologue.

проло́ж|и́ть, у́, ~ишь, *pf.* (*of* прокла́дывать) **1.** (*impf. also* пролага́ть) to lay; to build, construct; п. доро́гу to build, break a road; (*fig.*) to pave the way; п. себе́ доро́гу че́рез толпу́ to hack one's way through the crowd; п. курс (*naut., aeron.*) to lay a course; п. путь (*fig.*) to pave the way; п. но́вые пути́ (*fig.*) to pioneer, blaze new trails. **2.** (ме́жду *or* +*a. and* i.) to interlay; to insert (between); п. кни́гу бе́лыми листа́ми to interleave a book; п. соло́му ме́жду стекля́нными изде́лиями, п. стекля́нные изде́лия соло́мой to insert straw between items of glass-ware.

проло́м, а, *m.* **1.** breach, break; gap. **2.** (*med.*) fracture.

пролома́|ть, ю, *pf.* (*of* прола́мывать) to break (through); п. лёд to break the ice.

пролома́|ться, ется, *pf.* (*of* прола́мываться) to break.

пролом|и́ть, лю́, ~ишь, *pf.* (*of* прола́мывать) to break (through); п. дыру́ to make a hole; п. себе́ че́реп to fracture one's skull.

пролом|и́ться, ~ится, *pf.* (*of* прола́мываться) to break (down), give way; береги́тесь! по́ручень ~и́лся look out! the handrail has given way.

пролонга́ци|я, и, *f.* (*leg., fin.*) prolongation.

пролонги́р|овать, ую, *impf. and pf.* (*leg., fin.*) to prolong.

пром- *abbr. of* промы́шленный.

прома́|зать[1], жу, жешь, *pf.* (*of* ~зывать) to smear thoroughly; to oil thoroughly.

прома́|зать[2], жу, жешь, *pf. of* ма́зать 5.

прома́ргива|ть, ю, *impf. of* проморга́ть.

промарин|ова́ть, у́ю, *pf.* (*of* маринова́ть (*coll.*) to delay (intentionally), hold up, shelve (*for a certain time*).

прома́сл|енный, p.p.p. of ~ить *and adj.* oiled, greased; oily, greasy; ~енная бума́га oil-paper.

прома́слива|ть, ю, *impf. of* прома́слить.

прома́сл|ить, ю, ишь, *pf.* (*of* ~ивать) to oil, treat with oil, grease.

прома́тыва|ть(ся), ю(сь), *impf. of* промота́ть(ся).

про́мах, а, *m.* miss; (*fig.*) slip, blunder; дать п. to be unlucky; он ма́лый не п. (*coll.*) he's nobody's fool.

прома́хива|ться, юсь, *impf. of* промахну́ться.

промах|ну́ться, ну́сь, нёшься, *pf.* (*of* ~иваться) to miss, miss the mark; (*at billiards*) to miscue; (*fig., coll.*) to miss the mark, be wide of the mark; to make a mistake; to miss an opportunity.

прома́чива|ть, ю, *impf. of* промочи́ть.

промедле́ни|е, я, *n.* delay; procrastination.

промедл|ить, ю, ишь, *pf.* to delay, dally; to procrastinate.

проме́ж, *prep.* (+*g. or* i.) (*coll.*) between; among; п. нас between ourselves.

проме́жность|ь, и, *f.* (*anat.*) perineum.

промежу́т|ок, ка, *m.* interval; space; п. вре́мени period, space, stretch of time; interim.

промежу́точный, *adj.* intermediate (*also fig.*); intervening; interim.

промелькн|у́ть, у́, ёшь, *pf.* **1.** to flash; (*of time*) to fly by; п. в голове́ to flash through one's mind. **2.** to be faintly perceptible; в его́ слова́х ~у́ло разочарова́ние there was a shade of disappointment in his words.

проме́нива|ть, ю, *impf. of* променя́ть.

промен|я́ть, я́ю, *pf.* (*of* ~ивать) (на+*a.*). **1.** to exchange (for), trade (for), barter (for). **2.** to change (for).

проме́р, а, *m.* **1.** measurement; survey; sounding. **2.** error in measurement.

промерз|а́ть, а́ю, *impf. of* ~нуть.

промёрзлый, *adj.* frozen.

промёрз|нуть, ну, нешь, *past* ~, ~ла, *pf.* (*of* ~а́ть) to freeze through.

проме́рива|ть, ю, *impf. of* проме́рить.

проме́р|ить, ю, ишь, *pf.* (*of* ~ивать *and* ~ять) **1.** to measure; to survey; to sound. **2.** (*pf. only*) to make an error in measurement.

проме́р|ять, я́ю, *impf.* = ~ивать.

проме|си́ть, шу́, ~сишь, *pf.* (*of* ~шивать) to stir well, thoroughly; to knead well, thoroughly.

проме́шива|ть, ю, *impf. of* промеси́ть.

проме́шка|ть, ю, *pf.* (*coll.*) to linger, dawdle.

промина́|ть(ся), ю(сь), *impf. of* промя́ть(ся).

промо́зглый, *adj.* dank.

промо́ин|а, ы, *f.* pool, gully (*formed by flood, rain, etc.*).

промока́тельн|ый, *adj.*; ~ая бума́га blotting-paper.

промок|а́ть[1], а́ю, *impf.* **1.** *impf. of* ~нуть. **2.** *impf. only* to let water through, not be waterproof; э́ти боти́нки ~а́ют these boots are not waterproof. **3.** *impf. only* to absorb ink.

промок|а́ть[2], а́ю, *impf. of* ~ну́ть.

промока́шк|а, и, *f.* (*coll.*) blotting-paper.

промо́к|нуть, ну, нешь, *pf.* (*of* ~а́ть[1]) to get soaked, get drenched; п. до косте́й to get soaked to the skin.

промок|ну́ть, ну́, нёшь, *pf.* (*of* ~а́ть[2]) (*coll.*) to blot.

промо́лв|ить, лю, ишь, *pf.* to say, utter.

промолч|а́ть, у́, и́шь, *pf.* to keep silent, say nothing, hold one's peace.

проморга́|ть, ю, *pf.* (*of* прома́ргивать)

(*coll.*) to miss, overlook; п. удо́бный слу́чай to miss an opportunity, let a chance slip.

промор|и́ть, ю́, и́шь, *pf.* (*coll.*) 1. (го́лодом) to starve (*for a certain time*). 2. to impose privations (upon) (*for a certain time*).

промота́|ть, ю, *pf.* (*of* мота́ть² *and* прома́тывать) to squander.

промота́|ться, ю́сь, *pf.* (*of* прома́тываться) (*coll.*) to squander one's money, dissipate one's substance.

промоч|и́ть, у́, ~ишь, *pf.* (*of* прома́чивать) to get wet (through); to soak, drench; п. но́ги to get one's feet wet; п. го́рло, п. гло́тку (*coll.*) to wet one's whistle.

промтова́р|ный, *adj. of* ~ы; п. магази́н manufactured goods shop.

промтова́р|ы, ов, *no sing.* (*abbr. of* промы́шленные това́ры) manufactured goods (*collect. name of manufactured consumer goods other than foodstuffs*).

промфинпла́н, а, *m.* (*abbr. of* промы́шленно-фина́нсовый план) industrial and financial plan.

промч|а́ться, у́сь, и́шься, *pf.* 1. to tear (by, past, through); п. стрело́й to dart (by, past), flash (by, past). 2. (*fig.*; *of time*) to fly (by).

промыва́ни|е, я, *n.* washing (out); (*med.*) bathing, irrigation; (*tech.*) scrubbing.

промыва́|ть, ю, *impf. of* промы́ть.

промы́вк|а, и, f. washing, flushing.

про́мыс|ел, ла, m. 1. hunting, catching; охо́тничий п. hunting; game-shooting; пушно́й п. trapping; ры́бный п. fishing. 2. trade, business; го́рный п. mining; куста́рный п. handicraft industry, cottage industry; отхо́жий п. seasonal work; пушно́й п. fur trade. 3. *pl.* works; го́рные ~лы mines; золоты́е ~лы gold-fields, gold-mines; нефтяны́е ~лы oil-fields; соляны́е ~лы salt-mines, salt-works.

про́мысл, а, m. (*rel.*) Providence.

промы́сл|ить, ю, ишь, *pf.* (*of* промышля́ть) (*coll.*) to get, come by.

промыслови́к, а́, m. 1. hunter. 2. miner.

промысло́в|ый, *adj.* 1. *adj. of* про́мысел 1; ~ая избу́шка shooting-box, hunter's (trapper's, *etc.*) hut; ~ые пти́цы game-birds; ~ое свиде́тельство licence. 2. *adj. of* про́мысел 2, 3; ~ая коопера́ция traders' co-operative (*organization*), producers' co-operative; п. нало́г business tax; ~ая ры́ба marketable fish.

пром|ы́ть, о́ю, о́ешь, *pf.* (*of* ~ыва́ть) 1. to wash well, thoroughly; п. мозги́ (+*d.*) to brain-wash. 2. (*med.*) to bathe; п. желу́док to irrigate the stomach. 3. (*tech.*) to wash; to scrub (*gas*); п. зо́лото to pan out gold; п. руду́ to jig ore.

промы́шленник, а, m. manufacturer, industrialist.

промы́шленност|ь, и, f. industry.

промы́шленный, *adj.* industrial.

промышля́|ть, ю, *impf.* 1. *impf. of* промы́слить. 2. (+*i.*) to earn one's living (by). 3. to hunt; to trade (in).

промя́мл|ить, ю, ишь, *pf. of* мя́млить 1.

про|мя́ть, мну́, мнёшь, *pf.* (*of* ~мина́ть) 1. to break (through), crush. 2. (*coll.*) to give a shaking-up; п. но́ги to stretch one's legs.

про|мя́ться, мну́сь, мнёшься, *pf.* (*of* ~мина́ться) (*coll.*) to stretch one's legs.

прона́шива|ть(ся), ю(сь), *impf. of* проноси́ть(ся)¹.

пронес|ти́, у́, ёшь, *past* ~, ~ла́, *pf.* (*of* проноси́ть³) 1. to carry (by, past, through). 2. (*impers.*; *coll.*) to have a motion; to open one's bowels. 3. ~ло́! the danger is over!

пронес|ти́сь, у́сь, ёшься, *past* ~ся́, ~ла́сь, *pf.* (*of* проноси́ться²) 1. to rush (by, past, through); (*of clouds*) to scud (past). 2. (*fig.*) to fly by. 3. (*of rumours, etc.*) to spread.

пронз|а́ть, а́ю, *impf. of* ~и́ть.

пронзи́тел|ьный (~ен, ~ьна), *adj.* penetrating; piercing; (*of sounds*) shrill, strident; п. взгляд penetrating glance; ~ьным го́лосом in a shrill voice; п. крик piercing shriek.

прон|зи́ть, жу́, зи́шь, *pf.* (*of* ~за́ть) to pierce, run through, transfix; п. взгля́дом to pierce with a glance.

прони|за́ть, жу́, ~жешь, *pf.* (*of* ~зыва́ть) to pierce; to permeate, penetrate; (*fig.*) to run through; свет ~за́л темноту́ the light pierced the darkness; одна́ иде́я ~за́ла все его́ произведе́ния one idea ran through all his works.

прони́зыва|ть, ю, *impf. of* прониза́ть.

прони́зыва|ющий, *pres. part. act. of* ~ть *and adj.* piercing, penetrating.

проник|а́ть, а́ю, *impf. of* ~нуть.

проникнове́ни|е, я, n. 1. penetration. 2. = проникнове́нность.

проникнове́нност|ь, и, f. feeling; heartfelt conviction; говори́ть с ~ью to speak with feeling.

проникнове́н|ный (~ен, ~на), *adj.* full of feeling; heartfelt.

прони́кнут|ый (~, ~а), adj. (+*i.*) imbued (with), instinct (with), full (of).

прони́к|нуть, ну, нешь, *past* ~, ~ла, *pf.* (*of* ~а́ть) (в+*a.*) to penetrate (*also fig.*); (че́рез) to percolate (through); п. в чьи-н. наме́рения to fathom someone's designs; п. в суть де́ла to get to the bottom of the matter.

пронима́|ть, ю, *impf. of* проня́ть.

проница́емост|ь, и, f. penetrability, permeability, perviousness.

проница́ем|ый (~, ~а), *adj.* permeable, pervious; п. для све́та pellucid.

проница́тельност|ь, и, *f.* penetration; perspicacity; insight, acumen, shrewdness.

проница́тел|ьный (~ен, ~ьна), *adj.* perspicacious; acute, shrewd; penetrating; п. взор penetrating gaze.

проница́|ть, ю, *impf.* (*obs.*) to penetrate.

проно|си́ть¹, шу́, ~сишь, *pf.* (*of* прона́шивать) to wear out, wear to shreds.

проно|си́ть², шу́, ~сишь, *pf.* to wear (*for a certain time*).

проно|си́ть³, шу́, ~сишь, *impf. of* пронести́.

проно|си́ться¹, ~сится, *pf.* (*of* прона́шиваться) to wear through, wear to shreds.

проно|си́ться², шу́сь, ~сишься, *impf. of* пронести́сь.

проны́р|а, ы, *m. and f.* (*coll.*) pushful person; sly-boots; intriguer.

проны́рлив|ый (~, ~а), *adj.* pushful, pushing.

проню́х|ать, аю, *pf.* (*of* ~ивать) (*coll.*) to smell out, nose out, get wind (of).

проню́хива|ть, ю, *impf. of* проню́хать.

про|ня́ть, йму́, ймёшь, *past* ~ня́л, ~няла́, ~ня́ло, *pf.* (*of* ~нима́ть) (*coll.*) **1.** to penetrate, strike through. **2.** (*fig.*) to get at; его́ ниче́м не ~ймёшь you can't get through to him.

прообраз, а, *m.* prototype.

пропага́нд|а, ы, *f.* propaganda; propagation.

пропаганди́р|овать, ую, *impf.* to engage in propaganda (for); to propagandize.

пропаганди́ст, а, *m.* propagandist.

пропаганди́ст|ский, *adj. of* ~.

пропада́|ть, ю, *impf. of* пропа́сть.

пропа́ж|а, и, *f.* **1.** loss. **2.** lost object, missing object.

пропа́лыва|ть, ю, *impf. of* прополо́ть.

про́паст|ь, и, *f.* **1.** precipice (*also fig.*); abyss; на краю́ ~и (*fig.*) on the brink of a precipice. **2.** (*coll.*) a mass (of), masses (of); у него́ п. де́нег he has masses of money; наро́ду бы́ло п. there were swarms of people; бы́ло их до ~и there were scores of them.

пропа́|сть, ду́, дёшь, *past* ~л, *pf.* (*of* ~да́ть) **1.** to be missing; to be lost; п. без вести (*mil.*) to be missing; пиши́ ~ло (*coll.*) it is as good as lost. **2.** to disappear, vanish; куда́ вы ~ли? where did you vanish to?; очарова́ние ~ло the glamour faded away. **3.** to be lost, be done for; (*of flowers, etc.*) to die; тепе́рь мы ~ли! now we're done for!; ~ди́ про́падом! (*coll.*) the devil take it! **4.** to be wasted; п. да́ром to go for naught, go to waste; всё у́тро и без того́ ~ло the whole morning was wasted as it was.

пропа|ха́ть¹, шу́, ~шешь, *pf.* (*of* ~хивать) to plough thoroughly.

пропа|ха́ть², шу́, ~шешь, *pf.* to plough (*for a certain time*).

пропа́хива|ть, ю, *impf. of* пропаха́ть¹.

пропа́х|нуть, ну, нешь, *past* ~, ~ла, *pf.* to become permeated with the smell (of).

пропа́шк|а, и, *f.* (*agric.*) tilling between rows.

пропа́шник, а, *m.* (*agric.*) cultivator, furrow plough.

пропашн|о́й, *adj.*; ~ы́е культу́ры crops requiring tilling between rows; п. тра́ктор tractor-cultivator.

пропа́щ|ий, *adj.* (*coll.*) hopeless; good-for-nothing; он п. челове́к he's a hopeless case; э́то ~ее де́ло it's a bad job.

пропеде́втик|а, и, *f.* propaedeutics; preliminary study.

пропедевти́ческий, *adj.* propaedeutic; п. курс introductory course.

пропека́|ть(ся), ю(сь), *impf. of* пропе́чь(ся).

пропе́ллер, а, *m.* propeller.

проп|е́ть¹, ою́, оёшь, *pf.* **1.** *pf. of* петь. **2.** п. го́лос (*coll.*) to lose one's voice (*from singing*); to sing oneself hoarse.

проп|е́ть², ою́, оёшь, *pf.* to sing (*for a certain time*).

пропеча́т|ать, аю, *pf.* (*of* ~ывать) (*coll.*) to expose (*in the press*).

пропеча́тыва|ть, ю, *impf. of* пропеча́тать.

пропе́|чь, ку́, чёшь, ку́т, *past* ~к, ~кла́, *pf.* (*of* ~ка́ть) to bake well, thoroughly.

пропе́|чься, ку́сь, чёшься, ку́тся, *past* ~кся, ~кла́сь, *pf.* (*of* ~ка́ться) to bake well, get baked through.

пропива́|ть(ся), ю(сь), *impf. of* пропи́ть(ся).

пропи́л, а, *m.* (saw-)kerf, slit, notch.

пропи́лива|ть, ю, *impf. of* пропили́ть.

пропил|и́ть, ю́, ~ишь, *pf.* (*of* ~ивать) to saw through.

пропи|са́ть, шу́, ~шешь, *pf.* (*of* ~сывать) **1.** to prescribe. **2.** to register; п. па́спорт to stamp a passport. **3.** (+*d.*; *coll.*) to give it hot, tear off a strip.

пропи|са́ться, шу́сь, ~шешься, *pf.* (*of* ~сываться) to register (*intrans.*).

пропи́ск|а, и, *f.* **1.** registration; п. па́спорта stamping of a passport. **2.** residence permit.

прописн|о́й, *adj.* **1.** (*of letters of the alphabet*) capital; писа́ться с п. бу́квы to be written with a capital letter. **2.** commonplace, trivial; ~а́я и́стина truism; ~а́я мора́ль copy-book ethics.

пропи́сыва|ть(ся), ю(сь), *impf. of* прописа́ть(ся).

про́пис|ь, и, *f.* **1.** *usu. pl.* sample(s) of writing. **2.** (*fig., pejor.*) copy-book maxim; жить по ~ям to live according to the copy-book.

про́писью, *adv.* in words, in full; написа́ть число́ п. to write out a number in words, in full.

пропита́ни|е, я, *n.* subsistence, sustenance; зарабо́тать себе́ на п. to earn one's living.

пропит|а́ть, а́ю, *pf.* (*of* ~ывать) 1. to keep, provide (for). 2. (+*i.*) to impregnate (with), saturate (with), soak (in), steep (in); п. ма́слом to oil.

пропит|а́ться, а́юсь, *pf.* (*of* ~ываться) 1. (+*i.*) to become saturated (with), become steeped (in). 2. *pass. of* ~а́ть.

пропи́тк|а, и, *f.* (*tech.*) impregnation.

пропи́тыва|ть(ся), ю(сь), *impf. of* пропита́ть(ся).

про|пи́ть, пью, пьёшь, *past* ~пи́л, ~пила́, ~пи́ло, *pf.* (*of* ~пива́ть) 1. to spend on drink, squander on drink. 2. (*coll.*) to ruin (*through excessive drinking*).

про|пи́ться, пью́сь, пьёшься, *past* ~пи́лся, ~пила́сь, ~пи́лось, *pf.* (*of* ~пива́ться) (*coll.*) to ruin oneself (*through excessive drinking*).

пропих|а́ться, а́юсь, *pf.* = ~ну́ться.

пропи́хива|ть(ся), ю(сь), *impf. of* пропихну́ть(ся).

пропих|ну́ть, ну́, нёшь, *pf.* (*of* ~ивать) (*coll.*) to shove through, force through.

пропих|ну́ться, ну́сь, нёшься, *pf.* (*of* ~иваться) (*coll.*) to shove, force one's way through.

проплáва|ть, ю, *pf.* to swim (*for a certain time*); to sail (*for a certain time*).

пропла́|кать, чу, чешь, *pf.* to cry, weep (*for a certain time*); п. глаза́ (*coll.*) to cry one's eyes out.

проплéсневе|ть, ет, *pf.* to go mouldy all through.

проплы́в, а, *m.* (*swimming*) race, heat.

проплыва́|ть, ю, *impf. of* проплы́ть.

проплы́|ть, ву́, вёшь, *past* ~л, ~ла́, ~ло, *pf.* (*of* ~ва́ть) 1. to swim (by, past, through); to sail (by, past, through); to float, drift (by, past, through); (*fig., joc.*) to sail (by, past). 2. to cover (*a certain distance*).

проповéдник, а, *m.* 1. preacher. 2. (+*g.*; *fig.*) advocate (of).

проповéд|овать, ую, *impf.* 1. to preach. 2. (*fig.*) to advocate, propagate.

про́повед|ь, и, *f.* 1. sermon; homily. 2. (+*g.*; *fig.*) advocacy (of), propagation (of).

пропо́йный, *adj.* (*coll.*) drunken, besotted.

пропо́йц|а, ы, *m.* (*coll.*) drunkard.

прополáскива|ть, ю, *impf. of* прополоскáть.

прополз|а́ть, а́ю, *impf. of* ~ти́.

прополз|ти́, у́, ёшь, *past* ~, ~ла́, *pf.* (*of* ~а́ть) to creep, crawl (by, past, through).

прополк|а, и, *f.* weeding.

прополо|скáть, щу́, ~щешь, *pf.* (*of* про-

полáскивать) to rinse, swill; п. го́рло to gargle.

прополо|о́ть, ю́, ~ешь, *pf.* (*of* пропáлывать) to weed.

пропорциона́льност|ь, и, *f.* proportionality; proportion; обра́тная п. inverse proportion.

пропорциона́л|ьный (~ен, ~ьна), *adj.* 1. proportional; proportionate; ~ьное представи́тельство proportional representation; сре́днее ~ьное (*math.*) the mean proportional. 2. well-proportioned.

пропо́рци|я, и, *f.* proportion; ratio.

пропоте́лый, *adj.* sweat-soaked.

пропоте́|ть, ю, *pf.* 1. to sweat thoroughly. 2. to be soaked in sweat.

про́пуск, а, *m.* 1. *no pl.* admission. 2. (*pl.* ~и *and* ~á) pass, permit. 3. (*pl.* ~á) (*mil.*) password. 4. (*pl.* ~и) (+*g.*) non-attendance (at), absence (from). 5. (*pl.* ~и) blank, gap.

пропускá|ть, ю, *impf.* 1. *impf. of* пропусти́ть. 2. *impf. only* to let pass; п. во́ду to leak; не п. воды́ to be waterproof; э́та бума́га ~ет черни́ла this paper absorbs ink.

пропускн|о́й, *adj.* ~а́я бума́га blotting-paper; ~а́я спосо́бность capacity.

пропу|сти́ть, щу́, ~стишь, *pf.* (*of* ~скáть) 1. to let pass, let through; to make way (for); to let in, admit; to take, have a capacity (of); п. на перро́н to let on to the platform; вы́ставка ~сти́ла пять миллио́нов посети́телей the exhibition had five million visitors; п. ми́мо уше́й to give no ear (to), pay no heed (to). 2. (че́рез) to run (through), pass (through); п. че́рез фильтр to filter. 3. to omit, leave out; (*in reading*) to skip. 4. to miss; to let slip; п. ле́кцию to miss a lecture, cut a lecture; п. удо́бный слу́чай to miss an opportunity. 5. (*coll.*) to drink.

пропылесо́с|ить, ю, ишь, *pf. of* пылесо́сить.

пропых|те́ть, чу́, ти́шь, *pf. of* пыхте́ть.

прораб, а, *m.* (*abbr. of* производи́тель рабо́т) clerk of the works.

прорабáтыва|ть, ю, *impf. of* прорабóтать¹.

прорабóта|ть¹, ю, *pf.* (*of* прорабáтывать) (*coll.*) 1. to work (at), study; to get up, mug up. 2. to slate, pick holes (in).

прорабóта|ть², ю, *pf.* to work (*for a certain time*).

прорабóтк|а, и, *f.* 1. study, studying, getting up. 2. slating.

прора́н, а, *m.* (*tech.*) passage (*through dam while under construction*).

прораста́ни|е, я, *n.* germination; sprouting.

прораст|а́ть, а́ет, *impf. of* ~и́.

прораст|и́, ёт, *past* проро́с, проросла́, *pf.* (*of* ~а́ть) to germinate, sprout, shoot (*of plant*).

про́рв|а, ы, *f.* (*coll.*) 1. (+*g.*) a mass (of); masses (of), heaps (of). 2. glutton.

прорв|а́ть, у́, ёшь, *past* ~а́л, ~ала́, ~а́ло, *pf.* (*of* прорыва́ть) 1. to break through; to tear, make a rent (in), make a hole (in); п. блока́ду to run the blockade; п. ли́нию оборо́ны проти́вника to break through the enemy's defence line; ~а́ло плоти́ну (*impers.*) the dam has burst; я ~а́л носо́к I have a hole in my sock. 2. (*impers.; coll.*) to lose patience.

прорв|а́ться, у́сь, ёшься, *past* ~а́лся, ~ала́сь, ~а́лось, *pf.* (*of* прорыва́ться) 1. to break, burst (open). 2. to tear. 3. to break (out, through); to force one's way (through).

проре|ди́ть, жу́, ди́шь, *pf.* (*of* ~жива́ть) (*agric.*) to thin out.

проре́жива|ть, ю, *impf. of* прореди́ть.

проре́з, а, m. cut; slit, notch, nick.

проре́|зать, жу, жешь, *pf.* (*of* ~зыва́ть *and* ~за́ть) to cut through (*also fig.*)

проре́|заться, жется, *pf.* (*of* ре́заться, ~зыва́ться *and* ~за́ться) (*of teeth*) to cut, come through; у неё уже́ ~зались зу́бы she has already cut her teeth.

прорез|а́ть(ся), а́ю(сь), *impf. of* ~а́ть(ся).

прорези́нива|ть, ю, *impf. of* прорези́нить.

прорези́н|ить, ю, ишь, *pf.* (*of* ~ивать) to rubberize.

проре́зывани|е, я, n. п. зубо́в teething, dentition.

проре́зыва|ть(ся), ю(сь), *impf. of* проре́зать(ся).

про́рез|ь, и, f. opening, aperture.

проре́ктор, а, m. pro-rector.

прорепети́р|овать, ую, *pf. of* репети́ровать.

проре́х|а, и, f. 1. rent, tear. 2. (*in garment*) slit; застегну́ть ~у (брюк) to do up one's flies. 3. (*fig., coll.*) gap, deficiency.

прорецензи́р|овать, ую, *pf. of* рецензи́ровать.

проржа́ве|ть, ет, *pf.* to rust through.

прорис|ова́ть, у́ю, *pf.* (*of* ~о́вывать) to trace clearly.

прорисо́выва|ть, ю, *impf. of* прорисова́ть.

прорица́ни|е, я, n. (*obs.*) soothsaying, prophecy.

прорица́тел|ь, я, m. (*obs.*) soothsayer, prophet.

прорица́|ть, ю, *impf.* (*obs.*) to prophesy.

проро́к, а, m. prophet.

пророн|и́ть, ю́, ~ишь, *pf.* to utter, breathe, drop (*a word, a sound, etc.*); он не ~и́л ни зву́ка he did not utter a sound.

проро́ческий, *adj.* prophetic, oracular.

проро́честв|о, а, n. prophecy, oracle.

проро́честв|овать, ую, *impf.* (о+*p.*) to prophesy.

проро́ч|ить, у, ишь, *impf.* (*of* на~) to prophesy, predict.

проруб|а́ть, а́ю, *impf. of* ~и́ть.

проруб|и́ть, лю́, ~ишь, *pf.* (*of* ~а́ть) to hack through, cut through, hew through.

про́руб|ь, и, f. ice-hole.

прору́х|а, и, f. (*coll.*) blunder, mistake.

проры́в, а, m. 1. break; (*mil.*) break-through, breach. 2. (*fig.*) hitch, hold-up; по́лный п. breakdown.

прорыва́|ть¹, ю, *impf. of* прорва́ть.

прорыва́|ть², ю, *impf. of* проры́ть.

прорыва́|ться¹, юсь, *impf. of* прорва́ться.

прорыва́|ться², юсь, *impf. of* проры́ться.

прор|ы́ть, о́ю, о́ешь, *pf.* (*of* ~ыва́ть²) to dig through.

прор|ы́ться, о́юсь, о́ешься, *pf.* (*of* ~ыва́ться²) to dig one's way through, burrow through.

проса|ди́ть¹, жу́, ~ди́шь, *pf.* (*of* ~жива́ть) (+*i.; coll.*) to stick (into); п. но́гу гвоздём to get a nail into one's foot.

проса|ди́ть², жу́, ~ди́шь, *pf.* (*of* ~жива́ть) (*coll.*) to squander, lose.

проса́жива|ть, ю, *impf. of* просади́ть.

проса́лива|ть¹, ю, *impf. of* проса́лить.

проса́лива|ть², ю, *impf. of* просоли́ть.

проса́л|ить, ю, ишь, *pf.* (*of* ~ивать¹) to grease.

проса́чивани|е, я, n. 1. percolation; oozing, exudation. 2. (*fig.*) leakage; infiltration.

проса́чива|ться, юсь, *impf. of* просочи́ться.

просва́та|ть, ю, *pf.* (*of bride-to-be's parents*) to promise in marriage.

просве́рлива|ть, ю, *impf. of* просверли́ть.

просверл|и́ть, ю́, и́шь, *pf.* (*of* ~ивать) to drill, bore; to perforate, pierce.

просве́т, а, m. 1. shaft of light; (*fig.*) ray of hope. 2. (*archit.*) light; aperture, opening.

просвети́тел|ь, я, m. 1. educator, teacher. 2. (*hist.*) representative of the Enlightenment.

просвети́тельн|ый, *adj.* educational; ~ая филосо́фия (*hist.*) philosophy of the Enlightenment.

просвети́тель|ский, *adj. of* ~.

просвети́тельств|о, а, n. educational activities, cultural activities.

просве|ти́ть¹, щу́, ти́шь, *pf.* (*of* ~ща́ть) to educate; to enlighten.

просве|ти́ть², чу́, ~ти́шь, *pf.* (*of* ~чива́ть¹) (*med.*) to X-ray.

просветле́ни|е, я, n. 1. (*of weather*) clearing up, brightening up. 2. (*fig.*) lucid interval.

просветл|ённый, *p.p.p. of* ~и́ть *and adj.* (*fig.*) clear, lucid.

просветле́|ть, ю, *pf.* 1. (*of weather*) to clear up, brighten up. 2. (*fig.*) to brighten; п. от ра́дости to light up with joy. 3. (*fig.; of consciousness, etc.*) to become lucid.

просветл|и́ть, ю́, и́шь, *pf.* (*of* ~я́ть) to clarify.

просветл|я́ть, я́ю, *impf. of* ~и́ть.

просвечива|ть¹, ю, *impf. of* просветить².

просвечива|ть², ю, *impf.* **1.** to be translucent. **2.** (через, сквозь) to be visible (through), show (through), appear (through); to shine (through); шрам ∼л через её чулок the scar showed through her stocking.

просвеща|ть, ю, *impf. of* просветить¹.

просвещён|ец, ца, *m.* educationalist.

просвещени|е, я, *n.* **1.** education, instruction; народное п. public education. **2.** enlightenment; эпоха П∼я (*hist.*) the Age of the Enlightenment.

просвещённост|ь, и, *f.* enlightenment, culture.

просве|щённый, *p.p.p. of* ∼тить¹ *and adj.* enlightened; educated, cultured; ∼щённое мнение expert opinion; п. человек educated person.

просвир|а, ы, *pl.* **просвиры, просвир, просвирам,** *f.* (*eccl.*) (communion) bread; host.

просвир|ня, ни, *g. pl.* ∼ен, *f.* woman making communion bread.

просвирняк, а, *m.* (*bot.*) marsh mallow.

просви|стеть, щу, стишь, *pf.* **1.** to whistle; п. мелодию to whistle a tune. **2.** to give a whistle; to whistle (by, past); ∼стела над головой пуля a bullet whistled overhead.

просед|ь, и, *f.* streak(s) of grey; волосы с ∼ью greying hair, hair touched with grey.

просеива|ть, ю, *impf. of* просеять.

просек|а, и, *f.* cutting (*in a forest*).

просёл|ок, ка, *m.* country road, cart-track.

просеминар, а, *m.* (*in higher educational institutions*) beginners' class, beginners' seminar.

просеминари|й, я, *m.* (*obs.*) = просеминар.

просе|ять, ю, ешь, *pf.* (*of* ∼ивать) to sift, riddle, screen; ∼янный игрок (*sport*) seed.

просигнализир|овать, ую, *pf. of* сигнализировать.

проси|деть¹, жу, дишь, *pf.* (*of* ∼живать) to sit (*for a certain time*); п. ночь у постели больного to sit up all night with a patient.

проси|деть², жу, дишь, *pf.* (*of* ∼живать) to wear out the seat (of); to wear into holes (*by sitting*).

проси|жива|ть, ю, *impf. of* просидеть.

просин|ь, и, *f.* (*coll.*) bluish tint.

просител|ь, я, *m.* applicant; suppliant; petitioner.

просительный, *adj.* pleading.

про|сить, шу, ∼сишь, *impf.* (*of* по∼) **1.** (+*a.* of person asked; +*a.* or *g.* of thing sought, or о+*p.*) to ask (for), beg; ∼шу (вас) please; п. кого-н. о помощи to ask someone for help, ask someone's assistance; п. времени на размышление to ask for time to think (something) over; п. разрешения to ask

permission; п. совета to ask (for) advice; п. извинения у кого-н. to beg someone's pardon, apologize to someone; п. милостыню to beg, go begging; ∼шу покорнейше (*coll., obs.*; *as expression of surprise*) if you please. **2.** (за+*a.*) to intercede (for). **3.** to invite; вас ∼сят к столу please to take your places at the table; ∼сят не курить no smoking.

про|ситься, шусь, ∼сишься, *impf.* (*of* по∼) **1.** (+*inf.* or в+*a.*, на+*a.*) to ask (for); to apply (for); п. в отпуск to apply for leave. **2.** (*of children and household pets*) to want to go (*sc.* to relieve oneself). **3.** (*fig., coll.*) to ask (for); п. с языка to be on the tip of one's tongue; закат так и ∼сился на картину the sunset was just asking to be painted.

просия|ть, ю, *pf.* **1.** (*of the sun*) to begin to shine. **2.** (от) to beam (with), light up (with); она ∼ла от счастья she beamed with joy; лицо у него ∼ло his face lit up.

проска|кать, чу, ∼чешь, *pf.* to gallop (by, past, through).

проскакива|ть, ю, *impf. of* проскочить.

проскальзыва|ть, ю, *impf. of* проскользнуть.

просквоз|ить, ит, *pf.* (*impers.*; *coll.*) меня, *etc.*, ∼ило I, *etc.*, have caught cold from being in a draught.

проскложня|ть, ю, *pf. of* склонять².

проскользн|уть, у, ёшь, *pf.* (*of* проскальзывать) (*coll.*) to slip in, creep in (*also fig.*); ∼уло много ошибок many errors have crept in.

проскоч|ить, у, ∼ишь, *pf.* (*of* проскакивать) **1.** to rush by, tear by. **2.** (через) to slip (through). **3.** (сквозь, между) to fall (through, between); п. между пальцами to fall through one's fingers. **4.** (*fig., coll.*) to slip in, creep in; ∼ило несколько ошибок a few errors crept in.

проскрип|еть, лю, ишь, *pf.* **1.** *pf. of* скрипеть. **2.** (*coll.*) to creak along.

проскрипционный, *adj.* п. список (*hist.*) proscription list; black list.

проскрипци|я, и, *f.* (*hist.*) proscription.

проскурняк, а, *m.* (*bot.*) marsh mallow.

проскуча|ть, ю, *pf.* to have a dull, boring time; мы ∼ли всю неделю we had a dull week.

прослаб|ить, ит, *pf. of* слабить.

прослав|ить, лю, ишь, *pf.* (*of* ∼лять) to glorify; to bring glory (to), bring fame (to); to make famous, make illustrious.

прослав|иться, люсь, ишься, *pf.* (*of* ∼ляться) (+*i.*) to become famous (for), become renowned (for); он ∼ился остротами he became famous for his witticisms.

прославлени|е, я, *n.* glorification; apotheosis.

прослáв|ленный, *p.p.p. of* ~ить *and adj.* famous, renowned, celebrated, illustrious.

прославля|ть(ся), ю(сь), *impf. of* прослá-вить(ся).

прослáива|ть, ю, *impf. of* прослóить.

просле|дить, жý, дишь, *pf.* (*of* ~живать) 1. to track (down). 2. to trace (through); to trace back, retrace; п. развитие пáпства to trace the development of the papacy.

прослéд|овать, ую, *pf.* to proceed, go in state.

прослéжива|ть, ю, *impf. of* проследить.

просле|зиться, жýсь, зишься, *pf.* to shed a few tears.

просло|ить, ю, ишь, *pf.* (*of* прослáивать) (+*i.*) to interlay (with), sandwich (with).

прослóйк|а, и, *f.* 1. layer, stratum (*also fig.*). 2. (*geol.*) seam, streak.

прослуж|ить, ý, ~ишь, *pf.* 1. to work, serve (*for a certain time*); он ~ил три гóда на Дáльнем Востóке he served for three years in the Far East. 2. to be in use, serve; это пальтó ~ит мне ещё один год this coat will last me another year.

прослýш|ать, аю, *pf.* 1. (*impf.* слýшать) to hear (through); п. курс лéкций to attend a course of lectures. 2. (*impf.* ~ивать) (*med.*) to listen to; п. чьё-н. сéрдце to listen to someone's heart. 3. (*impf.* ~ивать) (*coll.*) to miss, not to catch; простите, я ~ал, что вы сказáли I am sorry, I did not catch what you said.

прослýшива|ть, ю, *impf. of* прослýшать.

прослы|ть, вý, вёшь, *past* ~л, ~лá, ~ло, *pf.* (+*i.*) to pass (for), be reputed.

прослыш|ать, у, ишь, *pf.* (*coll.*) to find out, hear; я тóлько что ~ал о вáшем несчáст-ном слýчае I have only just heard about your accident.

просмáлива|ть, ю, *impf. of* просмолить.

просмáтрива|ть, ю, *impf. of* просмотрéть.

просмол|ить, ю, ишь, *pf.* (*of* просмáливать) to tar; to coat, impregnate with tar; (*naut.*) to pay.

просмóтр, а, *m.* survey; view, viewing; п. докумéнтов examination of papers; закры-тый п. private view; предварительный п. preview.

просмотр|éть, ю, ~ишь, *pf.* (*of* просмáтри-вать) 1. to survey; to view. 2. to look over, look through; to glance over, glance through; to run over; п. рýкопись to glance through a manuscript; п. партитýру to run over the score. 3. to overlook, miss.

прос|нýться, нýсь, нёшься, *pf.* (*of* ~ыпáть-ся[1]) to wake up, awake.

прóс|о, а, *n.* millet.

просóвыва|ть(ся), ю(сь), *impf. of* просý-нуть(ся).

просодический, *adj.* (*lit.*) prosodic, proso-dial.

просóди|я, и, *f.* (*lit.*) prosody.

просол|ить, ю, ~ишь, *pf.* (*of* просáливать[2]) to salt; п. мясо to corn meat.

просóх|нуть, ну, нешь, *past* ~, ~ла, *pf.* (*of* просыхáть) to get dry, dry out.

просоч|иться, ится, *pf.* (*of* просáчиваться) 1. to percolate; to filter; to leak, ooze; to seep out. 2. (*fig.*) to filter through; to leak out; ~ились свéдения о пораже́нии news of the defeat filtered through.

просп|áть[1], лю, ишь, *past* ~áл, ~алá, ~áло, *pf.* (*of* просыпáть[2]) 1. to oversleep. 2. to miss, pass (*due to being asleep*).

просп|áть[2], лю, ишь, *past* ~áл, ~алá, ~áло, *pf.* to sleep (*for a certain time*).

просп|áться, люсь, ишься, *past* ~áлся, ~алáсь, ~áлось, *pf.* (*coll.*) to sleep one-self sober, sleep off one's drunkenness.

проспéкт[1], а, *m.* avenue.

проспéкт[2], а, *m.* 1. prospectus. 2. summary, résumé.

проспирт|овáть, ýю, *pf.* (*of* ~óвывать) to alcoholize.

проспиртóвыва|ть, ю, *impf. of* проспирто-вáть.

проспóрива|ть, ю, *impf. of* проспóрить[1].

проспóр|ить[1], ю, ишь, *pf.* (*of* ~ивать) to lose (*in a wager*).

проспóр|ить[2], ю, ишь, *pf.* to argue (*for a certain time*).

проспряга|ть, ю, *pf. of* спрягáть.

просрóч|енный, *p.p.p. of* ~ить *and adj.* over-due.

просрóчива|ть, ю, *impf. of* просрóчить.

просрóч|ить, у, ишь, *pf.* (*of* ~ивать) to exceed the time limit; п. óтпуск to over-stay one's leave; п. платёж to fail to pay in time.

просрóчк|а, и, *f.* delay; expiration of a time limit; п. в предъявлéнии иска (*leg.*) non--claim.

простáв|ить, лю, ишь, *pf.* (*of* ~лять) 1. to put down (in writing), state, fill in; п. дáту (в, на+*p.*) to date. 2. (*coll.*) to stake and lose (*at cards, etc.*).

простáвля|ть, ю, *impf. of* простáвить.

простáива|ть, ю, *impf. of* простоять.

простáк, á, *m.* simpleton.

простáт|а, ы, *f.* (*anat.*) prostate, prostatic gland.

простег|áть, áю, *pf.* (*of* ~ивать) to quilt.

простёгива|ть, ю, *impf. of* простегáть.

простéйш|ий, *superl. of* простóй; *pl. as noun* ~ие, ~их (*zool.*) protozoa.

простéн|ок, ка, *m.* (*archit.*) pier.

прóстенький, *adj.* (*coll.*) quite simple; plain, unpretentious.

прос|терéть, трý, трёшь, *past* ~тёр, ~тёрла,

pf. (*of* ～тира́ть¹). **1.** to extend, hold out, reach out; п. ру́ку to hold out one's hand. **2.** (*fig.*) to raise, stretch; они́ сли́шком далеко́～тёрли свои́ тре́бования they raised their demands too high.

прос|тере́ться, трётся, *past* ～тёрся, ～тёрлась, *pf.* (*of*～тира́ться¹) to stretch, extend; п. на со́тни миль to stretch for hundreds of miles.

простира́|ть¹, ю, *impf. of* простере́ть.

простира́|ть², ю, *pf.* to wash (*for a certain time*).

простир|а́ть³, а́ю, *pf.* (*of* ～ывать) (*coll.*) to wash well, thoroughly.

простира́|ться, юсь, *impf. of* простере́ться.

простирн|у́ть, у́, ёшь, *pf.* (*coll.*) to give a wash.

прости́рыва|ть, ю, *impf. of* простира́ть³.

прости́тел|ьный (～ен, ～ьна), *adj.* pardonable, excusable, justifiable.

проститу́ир|овать, ую, *impf. and pf.* to prostitute.

проститу́тк|а, и, *f.* prostitute.

проститу́ци|я, и, *f.* prostitution.

про|сти́ть, щу́, сти́шь, *pf.* (*of* ～ща́ть) **1.** to forgive, pardon; п. грехи́ to forgive sins; ～сти́те (меня́)! excuse me!, I beg your pardon! **2.** to remit; п. долг кому́-н. to remit someone's debt. **3.** ～сти́(те)! (*obs.*) good-bye!, farewell!; сказа́ть после́днее ～сти́ to say the last farewell.

про|сти́ться, щу́сь, сти́шься, *pf.* (*of*～ща́ться) (c+*i.*) to say good-bye (to), take one's leave (of), bid farewell.

про́сто, *adv.* simply; п. по привы́чке from mere habit, purely out of habit; п. так for no particular reason; э́то п. невероя́тно it is simply incredible; я п. не зна́ю I really don't know.

простова́тост|ь, и, *f.* simplicity, simplemindedness.

простова́т|ый (～, ～а), *adj.* simple, simpleminded.

простоволо́с|ый (～, ～а), *adj.* bare-headed, with head uncovered.

простоду́ши|е, я, *n.* open-heartedness; simple-heartedness, simple-mindedness; ingenuousness, artlessness.

простоду́ш|ный (～ен, ～на), *adj.* open-hearted; simple-hearted, simple-minded; ingenuous, artless.

прост|о́й¹ (～, ～а́, ～о,) *adj.* **1.** simple; easy; вам ～о кри́тикова́ть it is easy for you, all very well for you to criticize. **2.** simple (= *unitary*); ～о́е предложе́ние (*gram.*) simple sentence; ～о́е те́ло (*chem.*) simple substance, element; ～о́е число́ (*math.*) prime number. **3.** simple; ordinary; ～ы́м гла́зом with the naked eye; п. наро́д the common people; ～о́е письмо́ non-regis-

tered letter. **4.** simple, plain; unaffected, unpretentious; ～ы́е лю́ди ordinary people; homely people; ～ы́е мане́ры unaffected manners; п. о́браз жи́зни plain living. **5.** mere; ～о́е любопы́тство mere curiosity; п. сме́ртный a mere mortal; по той ～о́й причи́не, что for the simple reason that.

просто́|й², я, *m.* standing idle, enforced idleness; stoppage; пла́та за п. demurrage.

простоква́ш|а, и, *f.* sour milk, yoghurt.

простолюди́н, а, *m.* man of the common people.

про́сто-на́просто, *adv.* (*coll.*) simply.

простонаро́д|ный (～ен, ～на), *adj.* of the common people.

простонаро́дь|е, я, *n.* the common people.

простон|а́ть, у́, ～ешь, *pf.* **1.** to utter a groan, moan. **2.** to groan, moan (*for a certain time*).

просто́р, а, *m.* **1.** spaciousness; space, expanse; степны́е ～ы the expanses of the steppe(s). **2.** freedom, scope; elbow-room; дать п. (+*d.*) to give scope, give free range, give full play.

просторе́чи|е, я, *n.* popular speech; в ～и in common parlance.

просторе́ч|ный (～ен, ～на), *adj. of* ～ие.

просто́р|ный (～ен, ～на), *adj.* spacious, roomy; (*of clothing*) ample; здесь ～но there is plenty of room here, there is ample space here.

простосерде́чи|е, я, *n.* simple-heartedness; frankness; openness.

простосерде́ч|ный (～ен, ～на), *adj.* simple-hearted; frank; open.

простот|а́, ы́, *f.* (*in var. senses*) simplicity; по ～е́ серде́чной in one's innocence.

простофи́л|я, и, *m. and f.* (*coll.*) duffer, ninny.

просто|я́ть, ю́, и́шь, *pf.* (*of* простаивать) **1.** to stay, stand (*for a certain time*); по́езд ～я́л на запасно́м пути́ всю ночь the train stood in a siding all night. **2.** to stand idle, lie idle. **3.** to stand, last.

простра́нност|ь, и, *f.* **1.** extensiveness, extent. **2.** diffuseness, prolixity; verbosity.

простра́н|ный (～ен, ～на), *adj.* **1.** extensive, vast. **2.** diffuse, prolix; verbose.

простра́нственный, *adj.* spatial.

простра́нств|о, а, *n.* space; expanse; возду́шное п. air space; безвозду́шное п. (*phys.*) vacuum; вре́дное п. (*tech.*) clearance; мёртвое п. (*mil.*) dead ground; пусто́е п. void; боя́знь ～а (*med.*) agoraphobia.

простра́ци|я, и, *f.* prostration (*mental and physical exhaustion*).

простра́чива|ть, ю, *impf. of* прострочи́ть.

простре́л, а, *m.* (*coll.*) lumbago.

простре́лива|ть, ю, *impf.* **1.** *impf. of* простре-ли́ть. **2.** *impf. only* (*mil.*) to rake, sweep with fire. **3.** *impf. only* (*mil.*) to cover, have covered.

простре́лива|ться, юсь, *impf.* (*mil.*) **1.** to be exposed to fire. **2.** *pass. of* ~ть.

прострел|и́ть, ю́, ~ишь, *pf.* (*of* ~ивать) to shoot through.

простроч|и́ть, у́, ~ишь, *pf.* (*of* простра́чивать) to stitch; to back-stitch.

просту́д|а, ы, *f.* cold; chill; схвати́ть ~у (*coll.*) to catch (a) cold, catch a chill.

просту|ди́ть, жу́, ~дишь, *pf.* (*of* ~жа́ть) to let catch cold.

просту|ди́ться, жу́сь, ~дишься, *pf.* (*of* ~жа́ться) to catch (a) cold; to catch, take a chill.

просту́дный, *adj.* catarrhal.

простужа́|ть(ся), ю(сь), *impf. of* просту-ди́ть(ся).

просту́|женный, *p.p.p. of* ~ди́ть *and adj.*; я вновь ~жен I have caught another cold.

просту́к|ать, аю, *pf.* (*of* ~ивать) (*med.*) to tap.

просту́кива|ть, ю, *impf. of* просту́кать.

проступ|а́ть, а́ет, *impf. of* ~и́ть.

проступ|и́ть, ~ит, *pf.* (*of* ~а́ть) to appear, show through, come through; сыры́е пя́тна ~и́ли на стена́х damp patches have appeared on the walls; пот ~и́л у него́ на лбу perspiration stood out on his forehead.

просту́п|ок, ка, *m.* fault; breach of manners; (*leg.*) misdemeanour.

простыва́|ть, ю, *impf. of* просты́ть.

просты́н|ный, *adj. of* ~я́; ~ное полотно́ sheeting.

простын|я́, и́, *pl.* про́стыни, ~ь, ~я́м, *f.* sheet.

просты́|ть, ну, нешь, *pf.* (*of* ~ва́ть) **1.** to get cold; to cool; и след ~л (+*g.*; *coll.*) not a trace (of). **2.** (*coll.*) to catch cold.

просу́н|уть, у, ешь, *pf.* (*of* просо́вывать) (в+*a.*) to push (through, in), shove (through, in), thrust (through, in).

просу́н|уться, усь, ешься, *pf.* (*of* просо́вываться) to push through, force one's way through.

просу́шива|ть(ся), ю(сь), *impf. of* просу-ши́ть(ся).

просуш|и́ть, у́, ~ишь, *pf.* (*of* ~ивать) to dry thoroughly, properly.

просуш|и́ться, у́сь, ~ишься, *pf.* (*of* ~ивать-ся) to (get) dry.

просу́шк|а, и, *f.* drying.

просуществ|ова́ть, у́ю, *pf.* to exist (*for a certain time*); to last, endure.

просфор|а́, ы́, *f.* (*eccl.*) (communion) bread; host.

просце́ниум, а, *m.* (*theatr.*) proscenium.

просчёт, а, *m.* **1.** counting (up), reckoning (up). **2.** error (*in counting, reckoning*).

просчит|а́ть, а́ю, *pf.* (*of* ~ывать) **1.** to count (up), reckon (up). **2.** to count out, give in error; вы ~а́ли пятьдеся́т рубле́й you have given fifty roubles too much.

просчит|а́ться, а́юсь, *pf.* (*of* ~ывать) **1.** to make an error in counting; to be out in counting; to go wrong; мы ~а́лись на два́дцать рубле́й we are out by twenty roubles. **2.** (*fig.*) to miscalculate.

просчи́тыва|ть(ся), ю(сь), *impf. of* просчи-та́ть(ся).

про́сып, а, *m.*; без ~у (*coll.*) without waking, without stirring.

просы́п|ать, лю, лешь, *pf.* (*of* ~а́ть[1]) to spill.

просып|а́ть[1], а́ю, *impf. of* ~ать.

просып|а́ть[2], а́ю, *impf. of* проспа́ть.

просы́п|аться, лется, *pf.* (*of* ~а́ться[2]) to spill, get spilled.

просып|а́ться[1], а́юсь, *impf. of* проснуться.

просып|а́ться[2], а́юсь, *impf. of* ~аться.

просыха́|ть, ю, *impf. of* просо́хнуть.

про́сьб|а, ы, *f.* **1.** request; обраща́ться с ~ой to make a request; удовлетвори́ть ~у to comply with a request; у меня́ к вам п. I have a favour to ask you; по мое́й ~е at my request; п. не кури́ть! no smoking, please! **2.** (*obs.*) application, petition; пода́ть ~у об отста́вке to send in one's resignation.

прося́нк|а, и, *f.* овся́нка-п. (*orn.*) corn-bunting.

просяно́й, *adj.* millet.

прота́лин|а, ы, *f.* thawed patch (*of earth*).

прота́лкива|ть, ю, *impf. of* протолкну́ть.

прота́лкива|ться, юсь, *impf. of* протол-ка́ться *and* протолкну́ться.

протанц|ева́ть, у́ю, *pf.* **1.** to dance; п. вальс to dance a waltz, do a waltz. **2.** to dance (*for a certain time*).

прота́плива|ть, ю, *impf. of* протопи́ть.

прота́птыва|ть, ю, *impf. of* протопта́ть.

протара́н|ить, ю, ишь, *pf.* (*of* тара́нить) **1.** (*mil.*) to ram. **2.** (*fig.*) to break through, smash.

прота́скива|ть, ю, *impf. of* протащи́ть.

прота́чива|ть, ю, *impf. of* проточи́ть.

протащ|и́ть, у́, ~ишь, *pf.* (*of* прота́скивать) **1.** to pull (through, along), drag (through, along), trail. **2.** (*coll., pejor.*) to insinuate, work in.

прота́|ять, ю, ешь, *pf.* to thaw through.

протеже́, *indecl.*, *m. and f.* protégé(e).

протежи́р|овать, ую, *impf.* (+*d.*) to favour; to pull strings (for).

проте́з, а, *m.* prosthetic appliance; artificial limb; зубно́й п. false tooth, denture.

протези́р|овать, ую, *impf. and pf.* to equip with a prosthetic appliance; to make a prosthetic appliance.

протéзн|ый, *adj.* prosthetic; ~ая мастер-скáя orthopaedic workshop.
протеи́н, а, *m.* (*chem.*) protein.
протекá|ть, ю, *impf.* 1. *impf. of* протéчь. 2. *impf. only* (*of a river or stream*) to flow, run. 3. *impf. only* to leak, be leaky.
протéктор, а, *m.* 1. (*polit.*) power exercising protectorate. 2. (*obs.*) protector, patron. 3. (*tech.*) protector, protective device; двойнóй п. double tread (*of pneumatic tire*).
протекторáт, а, *m.* protectorate.
протекциони́зм, а, *m.* 1. (*polit., econ.*) protectionism. 2. (*coll.*) favouritism.
протекциони́ст, а, *m.* protectionist.
протéкци|я, и, *f.* patronage, influence; оказáть комý-н. ~ю to use one's influence on someone's behalf, pull strings for someone.
протé|кший, *past part. act. of* ~чь *and adj.* past, last.
про|терéть, трý, трёшь, *past* ~тёр, ~тёрла, *pf.* (*of* ~тирáть) 1. to rub a hole (in); to wear into holes. 2. to rub through, grate; п. чéрез си́то to rub through a sieve. 3. to rub over, wipe over. 4. п. глазá (*coll.*) to rub one's eyes.
про|терéться, трётся, *past* ~тёрся, ~тёрлась, *pf.* (*of* ~тирáться) to wear through, wear into holes.
протерп|éть, лю́, ~ишь, *pf.* to wait, last out; to endure, stand.
протесн|и́ться, ю́сь, и́шься, *pf.* to push one's way (through), elbow one's way (through), barge (through).
протéст, а, *m.* 1. protest; remonstrance; заяви́ть п. to make a protest; подáть п. to enter, register a protest. 2. п. вéкселя (*fin., comm.*) protest of a promissory note. 3. (*leg.*) objection; принести́ п. to bring an objection.
протестáнт[1], а, *m.* protester, objector.
протестáнт[2], а, *m.* (*rel.*) Protestant.
протестанти́зм, а, *m.* = протестáнтство.
протестáнтский, *adj.* (*rel.*) Protestant.
протестáнтств|о, а, *n.* (*rel.*) Protestantism.
протест|овáть, ýю, *impf.* (про́тив) to protest (against), object (to).
протé|чь, чёт, кýт, *past* ~к, ~клá, *pf.* (*of* ~кáть) 1. to ooze, seep. 2. (*of time*) to elapse, pass; кани́кулы бы́стро ~кли́ the holidays flew by. 3. (*of an illness, etc.*) to take its course.
про́тив, *prep.+g.* 1. (*in var. senses*) against; п. течéния against the current; не найдётся ли у вас что-н. п. головнóй бóли? do you happen to have anything for a headache?; за и п. for and against, pro and con; имéть что-н. п. to have something against; to mind, object; вы ничегó не имéете п. того, что я курю́? do you mind my smok-

ing?; вы ничегó не бýдете имéть п., éсли я закурю́? will you mind if I smoke? 2. opposite; facing; друг п. дрýга facing one another; останови́тесь, пожáлуйста, п. цéркви please stop opposite the church. 3. contrary to; п. нáших ожидáний contrary to our expectations. 4. (*coll.*) as against; in proportion to; according to; в э́том годý п. прóшлого this year as against last (year); дéсять шáнсов п. одногó ten to one; кáждому п. потрéбностей егó to each according to his needs.
про́тив|ень, ня, *m.* griddle.
противи́тельный, *adj.* (*gram.*) adversative.
проти́в|иться, люсь, ишься, *impf.* (*of* вос~) (+*d.*) to oppose; to resist, stand up (against).
проти́вник, а, *m.* 1. opponent, adversary, antagonist. 2. (*collect.; mil.*) the enemy.
проти́вно[1], *adv.* in a disgusting way.
проти́вно[2], *prep.+d.* against; contrary to; поступáть п. своéй сóвести to go against one's conscience.
проти́вн|ый[1], *adj.* 1. opposite; contrary; п. вéтер contrary wind, head wind; ~ое мнéние a contrary opinion; в ~ом слýчае otherwise; доказáтельство от ~ого the rule of contraries. 2. opposing, opposed; ~ые стóроны opposing sides.
проти́в|ный[2] (~ен, ~на), *adj.* nasty, offensive, disgusting; unpleasant, disagreeable; п. зáпах nasty smell; он мне ~ен I find him offensive; мне ~но припоминáть э́то происшéствие I find it disagreeable to recollect the event.
противо- anti-, contra-, counter-.
противоалкогóльный, *adj.* temperance; п. закóн prohibition.
противобóрств|о, а, *n.* struggle; (*polit.*) confrontation.
противобóрств|овать, ую, *impf.* (+*d.*; *obs.*) to oppose; to fight (against).
противовéс, а, *m.* (*tech. and fig.*) counterbalance, counterpoise.
противовоздýшн|ый, *adj.* anti-aircraft; ~ая оборóна air defence.
противогáз, а, *m.* gas-mask, respirator.
противогáзов|ый, *adj.* anti-gas; ~ая сýмка gas-mask case.
противодéйстви|е, я, *n.* opposition, counteraction.
противодéйств|овать, ую, *impf.* (+*d.*) to oppose, counteract.
противодетони́рующий, *adj.* п. материáл (*tech.*) anti-knock compound.
противоестéствен|ный (~, ~на), *adj.* unnatural.
противозакóнност|ь, и, *f.* illegality.
противозакóн|ный (~ен, ~на), *adj.* unlawful; (*leg.*) illegal.

противозача́точн|ый, *adj.* contraceptive; ~ые сре́дства contraceptives.

противозени́тны|й, *adj.* п. манёвр (*aeron.*) evasive action.

противоипри́тный, *adj.* anti-mustard-gas.

противокисло́тный, *adj.* acid-proof.

противолежа́щий, *adj.* (*math.*) opposite; п. у́гол alternate angle.

противолихора́дочн|ый, *adj.* (*med.*) anti--febrile; ~ое сре́дство febrifuge.

противоло́дочный, *adj.* (*naut.*) anti-submarine.

противоми́нн|ый, *adj.* (*naut.*) anti-mine-and--torpedo; ~ая артилле́рия secondary armament.

противообще́ственный, *adj.* antisocial.

противоотка́тн|ый, *adj.* (*mil.*) anti-recoil; ~ые устро́йства recoil mechanism.

противоподло́дочный, *adj.* (*naut.*) anti--submarine.

противопожа́рн|ый, *adj.* anti-fire; ~ые ме́ры fire-prevention measures.

противопоказа́ни|е, я, n. 1. (*leg.*) contra-dictory evidence. 2. (*med.*) contra-indica-tion.

противопока́занный, *adj.* (*med.*) contra--indicated.

противополага́|ть, ю, *impf. of* противополо-жи́ть.

противоположе́ни|е, я, n. opposition.

противополож|и́ть, у́, ~ишь, *pf.* (*of* противо-полага́ть) (+*d.*) to oppose (to).

противополо́жность|ь, и, f. 1. opposition; contrast; в п. (+*d.*) as opposed (to), by contrast (with). 2. opposite, antipode, antithesis; по́лная п. complete antithesis; пряма́я п. exact opposite.

противополо́ж|ный (~ен, ~на), *adj.* 1. op-posite. 2. opposed, contrary; диаметра́ль-но п. diametrically opposed.

противопоста́в|ить, лю, ишь, *pf.* (*of* ~ля́ть) (+*d.*) 1. to oppose (to). 2. to contrast (with), set off (against).

противопоставле́ни|е, я, n. (+*d.*) 1. oppos-ing (to), opposition (to). 2. contrasting (with), setting off (against).

противопоставля́|ть, ю, *impf. of* противо-поста́вить.

противоправи́тельственный, *adj.* anti--government(al).

противораке́тн|ый, *adj.* (*mil.*) anti-missile; ~ая раке́та anti-missile missile.

противоречи́вост|ь, и, f. contradictori-ness; discrepancy.

противоречи́в|ый (~, ~а), *adj.* contra-dictory; discrepant, conflicting; ~ые со-обще́ния conflicting reports.

противоре́чи|е, я, n. 1. contradiction; in-consistency; ~я в показа́ниях contradic-tions in evidence. 2. contrariness; defiance;

дух ~я spirit of defiance, contrariness; вы э́то де́лаете про́сто из ду́ха ~я you are doing it simply out of contrariness. 3. con-flict, clash; кла́ссовые ~я conflicts of class interests; находи́ться в ~и (c+*i.*) to be at variance (with), conflict (with).

противоре́ч|ить, у, ишь, *impf.* (+*d.*) 1. to contradict; п. самому́ себе́ to contradict oneself; он всё ~ил ма́тери he was always contradicting his mother. 2. to be at variance (with), conflict (with), run counter (to), be contrary (to); э́то ~ит действи́-тельности it is contrary to the facts; их показа́ния ~ат одно́ друго́му their evi-dence is conflicting.

противосамолётный, *adj.* (*mil.*) anti-aircraft.

противоснаря́дный, *adj.* (*mil.*) shell-proof.

противостолбня́чный, *adj.* (*med.*) anti--tetanus.

противостоя́ни|е, я, n. 1. (*astron.*) opposi-tion. 2. (*polit.*) confrontation.

противосто|я́ть, ю́, и́шь, *impf.* (+*d.*) 1. to resist, withstand. 2. to countervail. 3. (*astron.*) to be in opposition.

противота́нков|ый, *adj.* anti-tank; anti--mechanized; ~ая лову́шка tank trap; ~ое ружьё anti-tank rifle.

противото́к, а, m. (*tech.*) counter-current, counterflow.

противохими́ческий, *adj.* (*mil.*) anti-gas.

противоцинго́тный, *adj.* (*med.*) anti-scorbutic.

противочу́мный, *adj.* (*med.*) anti-plague.

противоя́ди|е, я, n. antidote.

протира́|ть(ся), ю(сь), *impf. of* протере́ть-(ся).

проти́рк|а, и, f. cleaning rag.

проти́ск|аться, аюсь, *pf.* (*of* ~иваться) to push one's way through, elbow one's way through.

проти́скива|ть, ю, *impf. of* проти́снуть.

проти́скива|ться, юсь, *impf. of* проти́скаться.

проти́с|нуть, ну, нешь, *pf.* (*of* ~кивать) to push through, shove through.

проти́с|нуться, нусь, нешься, *pf.* = ~кать-ся.

проткн|у́ть, у́, ёшь, *pf.* (*of* протыка́ть) to pierce; to transfix; to spit, skewer.

протодья́кон, а, m. (*eccl.*) archdeacon.

протозо́а, *indecl. pl.* (*zool.*) protozoa.

протоиере́|й, я, m. (*eccl.*) archpriest.

протоисто́ри|я, и, f. pre-history.

прото́к, а, m. 1. channel. 2. (*anat.*) duct.

протоко́л, а, m. 1. minutes, record of pro-ceedings; report; вести́ п. to take the minutes, record the minutes; занести́ в п. to enter in the minutes. 2. (*leg.*) statement; charge-sheet; п. дозна́ния, п. допро́са examination record; соста́вить п. to draw up a report. 3. (*diplomatic*) protocol.

протоколи́зм, а, *m.* dry, factual exposition.

протоколи́р|овать, ую, *impf. and pf. (pf. also* за~) to minute; to record.

протоко́л|ьный, *adj. of* ~; п. отде́л protocol department; п. стиль (*fig.*) officialese (= *dry, factual style of exposition,* not *long--winded jargon*).

протолка́|ться, юсь, *pf. (of* прота́лкиваться) (*coll.*) 1. to force, jostle one's way (through). 2. to lounge about.

протолкн|у́ть, у́, ёшь, *pf. (of* прота́лкивать) to push through, press through; (*fig.*) п. де́ло to push a matter forward.

протолкн|у́ться, у́сь, ёшься, *pf.* = протол-ка́ться.

прото́н, а, *m.* (*phys.*) proton.

прото́н|ный, *adj. of* ~.

протоп|и́ть, лю́, ~ишь, *pf. (of* прота́пли-вать) to heat thoroughly.

протопла́зм|а, ы, *f.* (*biol.*) protoplasm.

протопо́п, а, *m.* (*obs.*) archpriest.

протоп|та́ть, чу́, ~чешь, *pf. (of* прота́пты-вать) 1. to beat, make (*by walking*); п. тропи́нку to make a path. 2. to wear out (*footwear*).

проторг|ова́ть, у́ю, *pf.* (*coll.*) to lose (*in trading*).

проторг|ова́ться, у́юсь, *pf.* (*coll.*) to have losses (*in trading*); to be ruined (*in trade, in business*).

протор|ённый, *p.p.p. of* ~и́ть *and adj.* beaten, well-trodden; ~ённая доро́жка beaten track.

про́тор|и, ей, *no sing.* (*obs.*) expenses.

протор|и́ть, ю́, и́шь, *pf. (of* ~я́ть) to beat; п. путь to blaze a trail.

протор|я́ть, я́ю, *impf. of* ~и́ть.

прототи́п, а, *m.* prototype.

проточ|енный, *p.p.p. of* ~и́ть; п. червя́ми worm-eaten.

проточ|и́ть, у́, ~ишь, *pf. (of* прота́чивать) 1. to gnaw through, eat through. 2. (*of running water*) to wash. 3. to turn (*on a lathe*).

прото́чн|ый, *adj.* flowing, running; ~ая вода́ running water; п. пруд pond fed by springs.

протра́в|а, ы, *f.* (*chem.*) mordant; pickle; dip.

протрави́тел|ь, я, *m.* 1. (*tech.*) mordanting machine, pickling machine. 2. (*chem.*) mor-dant.

протрав|и́ть¹, лю́, ~ишь, *pf. (of* ~ливать *and* ~ля́ть) (*tech.*) 1. to treat with a mor-dant; to pickle, dip. 2. to etch.

протрав|и́ть², лю́, ~ишь, *pf.* (*in hunting*) to fail to catch, let go.

протра́влива|ть, ю, *impf. of* протрави́ть¹.

протравл|я́ть, я́ю, *impf.* = ~ивать.

протра́л|ить, ю, ишь, *pf. of* тра́лить.

протрезв|и́ть, лю́, и́шь, *pf. (of* ~ля́ть) to sober.

протрезв|и́ться, лю́сь, и́шься, *pf. (of* ~ля́ться) to sober up, get sober.

протрезвля́|ть(ся), ю(сь), *impf. of* протрез-ви́ть(ся).

протубера́н|ец, ца, *m.* (*astron.*) solar pro-minence; solar flare.

протур|и́ть, ю́, ~и́шь, *pf.* (*coll.*) to drive away, chuck out.

протух|а́ть, а́ю, *impf. of* ~нуть.

проту́х|нуть, ну, нешь, *past* ~, ~ла, *pf. (of* ~а́ть) to become foul, rotten; to go bad.

проту́х|ший, *past part. act. of* ~нуть *and adj.* foul, rotten; (*of food*) bad, tainted.

протыка́|ть, ю, *impf. of* проткну́ть.

протя́гива|ть(ся), ю(сь), *impf. of* протя-ну́ть(ся).

протяже́ни|е, я, *n.* 1. extent, stretch; dis-tance, expanse, area; на большо́м ~и over a wide area; на всём ~и (+*g.*) along the whole length (of), all along. 2. space (*of time*); на ~и (+*g.*) during, for the space (of).

протяжённост|ь, и, *f.* extent, length.

протяжён|ный (~, ~на), *adj.* extensive.

протя́жност|ь, и, *f.* slowness; п. ре́чи drawl.

протя́ж|ный (~ен, ~на), *adj.* long drawn--out; ~ное произноше́ние drawl.

протя|ну́ть, ну́, ~нешь, *pf. (of* ~гивать) 1. to stretch; to extend. 2. to stretch out, extend, hold out, reach out; п. ру́ку to hold out one's hand; п. ру́ку по́мощи to extend a helping hand; п. табаке́рку to proffer a snuff-box; п. но́ги (*fig., coll.*) to turn up one's toes. 3. to protract. 4. to drawl out. 5. (*pf. only*) to last; больно́й недо́лго ~нет the patient won't last long. 6. (*hunting*) to fly over (*of birds*).

протя|ну́ться, ну́сь, ~нешься, *pf. (of* ~ги-ваться) 1. to stretch out; to reach out; п. на дива́не to stretch out on the sofa. 2. to extend, stretch, reach. 3. *pf. only* to last, go on.

проу́л|ок, ка, *m.* (*coll.*) lane.

проу́чива|ть, ю, *impf. of* проучи́ть¹.

проуч|и́ть¹, у́, ~ишь, *pf. (of* ~ивать) (*coll.*) to teach, give a good lesson; я его́ ~у́! I'll teach him!

проуч|и́ть², у́, ~ишь, *pf.* to study, learn up (*for a certain time*).

проуч|и́ться, у́сь, ~ишься, *pf.* to spend (*a certain time*) in study.

проу́шин|а, ы, *f.* lug; staple.

проф- *abbr. of* 1. профессиона́льный. 2. профсою́зный.

профа́н, а, *m.* 1. (*in relation to a given field of knowledge*) layman. 2. ignoramus.

профана́ци|я, и, *f.* profanation.

профани́р|овать, ую, *impf. and pf.* to profane.

профбиле́т, а, *m.* (*abbr. of* профсою́зный биле́т) trade-union card.

профершпи́л|иться, юсь, ишься, *pf.* (*coll.*) to lose all one's money, be ruined.

профессиона́л, а, *m.* professional.

профессионали́зм, а, *m.* **1.** professionalism. **2.** (*ling.*) specialist term.

профессиона́льн|ый, *adj.* **1.** professional, occupational; ~ое заболева́ние occupational disease; ~ое образова́ние vocational training; п. сою́з trade union. **2.** professional (*as opp. to* amateur).

профе́сси|я, и, *f.* profession, occupation, trade; по ~и by profession, by trade.

профе́ссор, а, *pl.* ~а́, *m.* professor.

профе́ссорск|ий, *adj.* **1.** professorial. **2.** *as noun* ~ая, ~ой, *f.* staff common room.

профе́ссорств|о, а, *n.* professorship, (university) chair.

профе́ссорств|овать, ую, *impf.* to be a professor, have a (university) chair.

профессу́р|а, ы, *f.* **1.** professorship, (university) chair. **2.** (*collect.*) the professors.

профила́ктик|а, и, *f.* **1.** (*med.*) prophylaxis. **2.** (*collect.*) preventive measures, precautions.

профилакти́ческий, *adj.* **1.** (*med.*) prophylactic. **2.** preventive, precautionary.

профилакто́ри|й, я, *m.* dispensary.

про́фил|ь, я, *m.* **1.** profile; side-view; (*fig.*) outline; в п. in profile, half-faced. **2.** section; попере́чный п. cross-section; п. крыла́ (*aeron.*) airfoil. **3.** type; шко́лы ра́зного ~я schools of various types.

про́филь|ный, *adj. of* ~; ~ное желе́зо section iron; п. резе́ц, п. фре́зер (*tech.*) profile cutter, forming tool.

профильтр|ова́ть, у́ю, *pf. of* фильтрова́ть.

профин|ти́ть, чу́, ти́шь, *pf.* (*coll.*) to squander.

профко́м, а, *m.* (*abbr. of* профсою́зный комите́т) trade-union committee.

профконсульта́нт, а, *m.* careers adviser.

профо́рг, а, *m.* (*abbr. of* профсою́зный организа́тор) trade-union organizer.

профо́рм|а, ы, *f.* form, formality; чи́стая п. pure, mere formality; для ~ы, ра́ди ~ы for form's sake, as a matter of form.

профрабо́т|а, ы, *f.* (*abbr. of* профсою́зная рабо́та) trade-union work.

профрабо́тник, а, *m.* (*abbr. of* профсою́зный рабо́тник) trade-union official.

профсою́з, а, *m.* (*abbr. of* профессиона́льный сою́з) trade union.

профсою́зный, *adj.* trade-union.

профтехшко́л|а, ы, *f.* (*abbr. of* профессиона́льно-техни́ческая шко́ла) trade school.

профшко́л|а, ы, *f.* (*abbr. of* профсою́зная

шко́ла) trade-union school.

проха́жива|ться, юсь, *impf. of* пройти́сь.

прохва|ти́ть, чу́, ~тишь, *pf.* (*of* ~тывать) (*coll.*) **1.** (*of cold, draught, etc.*) to penetrate; меня́ ~ти́ло на сквозняке́ I caught a chill from being in a draught. **2.** to bite through. **3.** (*fig.*) to tear to pieces.

прохва́тыва|ть, ю, *impf. of* прохвати́ть.

прохвора́|ть, ю, *pf.* (*coll.*) to be ill (*for a certain time*); to be laid up (*for a certain time*).

прохво́ст, а, *m.* (*coll.*) scoundrel.

прохла́д|а, ы, *f.* coolness.

прохла́д|ец, ца, *m.* с ~цем (*coll.*) without making much effort; listlessly.

прохлади́тельн|ый, *adj.* refreshing, cooling; ~ые напи́тки soft drinks.

прохла|ди́ться, жу́сь, ди́шься, *pf.* (*coll.*) to cool off.

прохла́д|ный (~ен, ~на), *adj.* **1.** cool; fresh; ~но (*impers., pred.*) it is cool, it is fresh. **2.** (*fig.*) cool; отноше́ния у них ста́ли ~ными there has been a cooling-off between them.

прохла́д|ца, цы, *f.* = ~ец.

прохлажда́|ться, юсь, *impf.* (*coll.*) to take it easy.

прохо́д, а, *m.* **1.** (*in var. senses*) passage; пра́во ~а right of way; не дава́ть ~а (+*d.*) to give no peace, pester; мне от него́ ~а нет I cannot get rid of him, shake him off. **2.** passageway; gangway, aisle; кры́тый п. covered way. **3.** (*anat.*) duct; за́дний п. anus; слухово́й п. acoustic duct.

проходи́м|ец, ца, *m.* rogue, rascal.

проходи́мост|ь, и, *f.* **1.** (*of roads, etc.*) passability. **2.** (*anat.*) permeability. **3.** (*of motor, etc., transport*) cross-country ability.

проходи́м|ый (~, ~а), *adj.* passable.

прохо|ди́ть[1], жу́, ~дишь, *impf.* **1.** *impf. of* пройти́. **2.** *impf. only* (че́рез) to lie (through), go (through), pass (through); кана́л ~дит че́рез джу́нгли the canal passes through jungle.

прохо|ди́ть[2], жу́, ~дишь, *pf.* to walk (*for a certain time*); мы ~ди́ли весь день we have spent the whole day walking.

прохо́дк|а, и, *f.* (*mining*) working; sinking (*of shaft*); drift.

проходн|о́й, *adj.* of passage; ~а́я бу́дка entrance check-point, entrance lodge; ~а́я ко́мната inter-communicating room, room giving access into another; ~а́я конто́ра entrance-gate office; ~о́е свиде́тельство (*hist.*) travel permit, travel document (*issued by police to deportees*).

прохо́дчик, а, *m.* (*mining*) shaft sinker; drifter.

прохожде́ни|е, я, *n.* passing, passage; п. торже́ственным ма́ршем (*mil.*) march past.

прохо́ж|ий, *adj.* passing, in transit; *as noun* **п.**, **~его**, *m. and* **~ая**, **~ей**, *f.* passer-by.

процвета́ни|е, **я**, *n.* prosperity, well-being; flourishing, thriving.

процвета́|ть, **ю**, *impf.* to prosper, flourish, thrive.

проце|ди́ть, **жу́**, **~дишь**, *pf.* (*of* **~живать**) to filter, strain.

процеду́р|а, **ы**, *f.* 1. procedure. 2. (*usu. pl.*) treatment.

процежива|ть, **ю**, *impf. of* **процеди́ть**.

проце́нт, **а**, *m.* 1. percentage; rate (per cent); сто **~ов** one hundred per cent; ба́нковский учётный п. bank rate; просты́е, сло́жные **~ы** (*math.*) simple, compound interest; рабо́тать на **~ах** to work on a percentage basis. 2. interest; разме́р **~а** rate of interest.

проце́нт|ный, *adj. of* **~** interest-bearing; **~ное** отноше́ние percentage; **~ные** бума́ги interest-bearing securities; **~ные** облига́ции interest-bearing bonds.

проце́сс, **а**, *m.* 1. process. 2. (*leg.*) trial; legal action, legal proceedings; lawsuit; cause, case; вести́ п. (c+*i*.) to be at law (with). 3. (*med.*) active condition; п. в лёгких active pulmonary tuberculosis.

процесси|я, **и**, *f.* procession.

процессуа́льн|ый, *adj. of* **проце́сс** 2; **~ые** но́рмы legal procedure.

процити́р|овать, **ую**, *pf. of* **цити́ровать**.

прочёркива|ть, **ю**, *impf. of* **прочеркну́ть**.

прочерк|ну́ть, **ну́**, **нёшь**, *pf.* (*of* **~ивать**) to strike through, draw a line through.

прочер|ти́ть, **чу́**, **~тишь**, *pf.* (*of* **~чивать**) to draw.

прочёрчива|ть, **ю**, *impf. of* **прочерти́ть**.

проче|са́ть, **шу́**, **~шешь**, *pf.* (*of* **~сывать**) 1. to comb out thoroughly. 2. (*mil.*; *fig.*) to comb.

прочёск|а, **и**, *f.* screening (*as a security measure*).

про|че́сть, **чту́**, **чтёшь**, *past* **~чёл**, **~чла́**, *pf.* = **~чита́ть**.

прочёсыва|ть, **ю**, *impf. of* **прочеса́ть**.

прочёт, **а**, *m.* (*coll.*) error (*in counting*).

про́ч|ий, *adj.* other; и **~ее** (*abbr.* и пр., и проч.) etcetera, and so on; **~ие** (the) others; ме́жду **~им** by the way; поми́мо всего́ **~его** in addition.

прочи|стить, **щу**, **стишь**, *pf.* (*of* **~ща́ть**) to clean; to cleanse thoroughly; п. тру́бку to clean a pipe.

прочита́|ть¹, **ю**, *pf. of* чита́ть.

прочита́|ть², **ю**, *pf.* to read (*for a certain time*).

прочи́тыва|ть, **ю**, *impf.* (*coll.*) to read through, peruse.

проч|ить, **у**, **ишь**, *impf.* (в+*a*.) to intend

(for), destine (for); его́ **~или** в свяще́нники he was intended for the church.

прочища́|ть, **ю**, *impf. of* **прочи́стить**.

про́чно, *adv.* firmly, soundly, solidly, well.

про́чност|ь, **и**, *f.* firmness, soundness, stability, solidity; durability; endurance; п. на изги́б (*tech.*) bending strength; п. на изно́с (*tech.*) resistance to wear; п. на разры́в (*tech.*) tensile strength; п. на уда́р (*tech.*) resistance to shock, impact value; запа́с **~и**, коэффицие́нт **~и** safety factor, safety margin.

про́ч|ный (**~ен**, **~на́**, **~но**), *adj.* firm, sound, stable, solid; durable, lasting; **~ные** зна́ния sound knowledge; **~ная** кра́ска fast dye; **~ное** сча́стье lasting happiness; **~ная** ткань durable fabric.

прочте́ни|е, **я**, *n.* reading; perusal; по **~и** (+*g*.) on reading.

прочу́вствова|нный, *p.p.p. of* **~ть** *and adj.* full of emotion; heart-felt.

прочу́вств|овать, **ую**, *pf.* 1. to feel deeply, acutely, keenly. 2. to experience, go through. 3. to feel, get the feel (of); п. свою́ роль to get the feel of one's part.

прочь, *adv.* 1. away, off; (поди́) п.! go away!, be off!; (пошёл) п. отсю́да! get out of here!; п. с глаз мои́х! get out of my sight!; п. с доро́ги! (get) out of the way!, make way!; ру́ки п.! hands off! 2. (*pred.*) averse (to); не п. (+ *inf.*; *coll.*) to have no objection (to), not to be averse (to); я не п. пойти́ туда́ I have no objection to going there, I am quite willing to go there; он не п. вы́пить стака́нчик he is not averse to taking a drop.

проше́дш|ий, *past part. act. of* пройти́ *and adj.* past; last; **~им** ле́том last summer; **~ее** вре́мя (*gram.*) past tense; *as noun* **~ее**, **~его**, *n.* the past.

проше́ни|е, **я**, *n.* application, petition; пода́ть п. to submit an application, forward a petition.

прошеп|та́ть, **чу́**, **~чешь**, *pf. of* шепта́ть.

проше́стви|е, **я**, *n.* по **~и** (+*g*.) after the lapse (of), after the expiration (of); по **~и** сро́ка after the expiration of the term.

прошиб|а́ть, **а́ю**, *impf. of* **~и́ть**.

прошиб|и́ть, **у́**, **ёшь**, *past* **~**, **~ла**, *pf.* (*of* **~а́ть**) (*coll.*) 1. to break through. 2. его́ **~** пот he broke into a sweat; её **~ла** слеза́ she shed a tear.

прошива́|ть, **ю**, *impf. of* **проши́ть**.

проши́вк|а, **и**, *f.* 1. insertion (*on linen, etc.*). 2. (*tech.*) broach, broaching bit.

прош|и́ть, **ью́**, **ьёшь**, *pf.* (*of* **~ива́ть**) 1. to sew, stitch. 2. (*tech.*) to broach.

прошлого́дний, *adj.* last year's; of last year.

про́шл|ый, *adj.* 1. past; bygone, former; э́то де́ло **~ое** it's a thing of the past; *as noun*

~ое, ~ого, *n.* the past; далёкое ~ое the distant past; отойти́ в ~ое to become a thing of the past. 2. last; в ~ом году́ last year; на ~ой неде́ле last week.

прошля́п|ить, лю, ишь, *pf.* (*coll.*) to blunder, slip up.

прошмы́гива|ть, ю, *impf. of* прошмыгну́ть.

прошмыг|ну́ть, ну́, нёшь, *pf.* (*of* ~ивать) (*coll.*) to slip (by, past, through).

прошнур|ова́ть, у́ю, *pf. of* шнурова́ть 2.

прошпакл|ева́ть, юю, юешь, *pf.* (*of* ~ёвывать) to putty; (*naut.*) to caulk.

прошпаклёвыва|ть, ю, *impf. of* прошпаклева́ть.

проштра́ф|иться, люсь, ишься, *pf.* (*coll.*) to be at fault.

проштуди́р|овать, ую, *pf. of* штуди́ровать.

прошум|е́ть, лю, и́шь, *pf.* 1. to roar past. 2. (*fig.*) to become famous.

проща́й(те) good-bye!; farewell!, adieu!

проща́льн|ый, *adj.* farewell, parting; valedictory; ~ая пиру́шка farewell party; ~ые слова́ parting words.

проща́ни|е, я, *n.* farewell; parting, leave-taking; на п. at parting.

проща́|ть(ся), ю(сь), *impf. of* прости́ть(ся).

про́ще, *comp. of* просто́й *and* про́сто; simpler; plainer; easier.

прощелы́г|а, и, *m. and f.* (*coll.*) knave, rogue.

проще́ни|е, я, *n.* forgiveness, pardon; absolution; проси́ть ~я у кого́-н. to ask someone's pardon; прошу́ ~я! I beg your pardon!, (I am) sorry!

прощу́п|ать, аю, *pf.* (*of* ~ывать) 1. to feel; to detect (*by feeling*). 2. (*fig., coll.*) to sound (out).

прощу́пыва|ть, ю, *impf. of* прощу́пать.

проэкзамен|ова́ть(ся), у́ю(сь), *pf. of* экзаменова́ть(ся).

прояви́тел|ь, я, *m.* (*phot.*) developer.

прояв|и́ть, лю́, ~ишь, *pf.* (*of* ~ля́ть) 1. to show, display, manifest, reveal; п. забо́ту (о+*p.*) to show concern (for, about), take trouble (about); п. интере́с (к) to show interest (in); п. себя́ to show one's worth; п. себя́ (+*i.*) to show oneself, prove (to be); он ~и́л себя́ пре́данным колле́гой he proved to be a loyal colleague. 2. (*phot.*) to develop.

прояв|и́ться, ~ится, *pf.* (*of* ~ля́ться) 1. to show (itself), reveal itself, manifest itself. 2. *pass. of* ~и́ть.

проявле́ни|е, я, *n.* display, manifestation; при пе́рвом ~и (+*g.*) at the first sign(s) of.

проявля́|ть(ся), ю(сь), *impf. of* прояви́ть(ся).

прояс́не|ть, ет, *pf.* (*of the sky*) to clear; ~ло (*impers.*) it cleared up.

прояснé|ть, ет, *pf.* to brighten (up); лицо́ ма́льчика вдруг ~ло the boy's face sud-

denly brightened up.

проясн|и́ться, и́тся, *pf.* (*of* ~я́ться) (*of weather and fig.*) to clear (up); днём ~и́лось in the afternoon it cleared up.

проясн|я́ться, я́ется, *impf. of* ~и́ться.

пруд, а́, в ~у́, *pl.* ~ы́, *m.* pond.

пру|ди́ть, жу́, ~ди́шь, *impf.* (*of* за~) to dam (up); хоть пруд ~ди́ (*coll.*) in abundance; де́нег у них — хоть пруд ~ди́ they are rolling in money.

прудово́й, *adj. of* пруд.

пружи́н|а, ы, *f.* spring; гла́вная п. mainspring (*also fig.*); боева́я п. (*mil.*) mainspring, firing pin spring; п.-волосо́к hairspring.

пружи́нистост|ь, и, *f.* springiness, elasticity.

пружи́нист|ый (~, ~а), *adj.* springy, elastic.

пружи́н|ить, ю, ишь, *impf.* 1. (*trans.*) to tense. 2. (*intrans.*) to be elastic, possess spring; хорошо́ п. to be well sprung.

пружи́нк|а, и, *f.* 1. (*of watch or clock*) mainspring; hairspring. 2. loop, coil (*contraceptive device*).

пружи́н|ный, *adj. of* ~а; ~ные весы́ spring scales, spring balance; п. матра́ц spring mattress; ~ная рессо́ра coil spring.

пруса́к, а́, *m.* (*coll.*) cockroach.

прусса́к, а́, *m.* Prussian.

пру́сск|ий, *adj.* Prussian; ~ая си́няя (кра́ска) Prussian blue.

прут, а–а́, *m.* 1. (*pl.* ~ья, ~ьев) twig; switch; и́вовый п. withe, withy. 2. (*pl.* ~ы́, ~о́в) (*tech.*) bar.

пру́тик, а, *m. dim. of* прут.

прутко́в|ый, *adj.* rod-shaped; ~ое желе́зо (*tech.*) rod iron, wire rod.

пры́галк|а, и, *f.* (*coll.*) skipping-rope.

пры́гани|е, я, *n.* jumping, leaping; skipping.

пры́г|ать, аю, *impf.* (*of* ~нуть) 1. to jump, leap, spring; to bound; п. на одно́й ноге́ to hop on one leg; п. со скака́лкой to skip; п. с упо́ром to vault; п. с шесто́м (*sport*) to pole-vault; п. от ра́дости to jump with, for joy. 2. to bounce.

пры́г|нуть, ну, нешь, *pf. of* ~ать.

прыгу́н, а́, *m.* 1. (*sport*) jumper. 2. (*coll.*) fidget, restless person.

прыж|о́к, ка́, *m.* 1. jump, leap, spring; caper; де́лать ~ки́ to caper, cut capers. 2. (*sport*) jump; ~ки́ jumping; ~ки́ в во́ду diving; ~ки́ с парашю́том parachute jumping; п. в высоту́ high jump; п. в длину́ long jump; п. с упо́ром vault(ing); п. с шесто́м pole-vault; п. с ме́ста standing jump; п. с разбе́га running jump.

пры́ска|ть, ю, *impf. of* пры́снуть.

пры́ска|ться, юсь, *impf.* (*of* по~) (+*i.*; *coll.*) to (be)sprinkle oneself (with), spray oneself (with).

пры́с|нуть, ну, нешь, *pf.* (*of* ∼кать) (*coll.*) 1. (+*i.*) to (be)sprinkle (with); to spray (with). 2. to spurt, gush; (со́ сме́ху) (*fig.*) to burst out laughing.

пры́т|кий (∼ок, ∼ка́, ∼ко), *adj.* quick, lively, sharp.

пры́т|ь, и, *f.* (*coll.*) 1. speed; во всю п. at full speed, as fast as one's legs can carry one. 2. quickness, liveliness, go; отку́да у него́ така́я п.? where does he get his energy from?

прыщ, а́, *m.* pimple; (*med.*) pustule; лицо́ в ∼а́х pimply face.

прыща́ве|ть, ю, *impf.* (*of* о∼) to become covered in pimples.

прыща́в|ый (∼, ∼а), *adj.* pimply, pimpled.

прыщева́т|ый (∼, ∼а), *adj.* somewhat pimply.

прюне́л|евый, *adj. of* ∼ь.

прюне́л|ь, и, *f.* (*text.*) prunella.

пря́да|ть, ю, *impf.* (*obs. or dial.*) п. уша́ми (*of, or in the manner of, a horse*) to move its ears.

пряде́ни|е, я, *n.* spinning.

пря́деный, *adj.* spun.

пряди́льн|ый, *adj.* spinning; п. стано́к spinning loom; ∼ая фа́брика spinning mill.

пряди́л|ьня, ьни, *g. pl.* ∼ен, *f.* (*obs.*) spinning mill.

пряди́льщик, а, *m.* spinner.

пряд|ь, и, *f.* 1. lock (*of hair*). 2. strand.

пря́ж|а, и, *no pl., f.* yarn, thread; шерстяна́я п. woollen yarn, worsted.

пря́жк|а, и, *f.* buckle, clasp.

пря́лк|а, и, *f.* distaff; spinning-wheel.

прям|а́я, о́й, *f.* straight line; провести́ ∼у́ю to draw a straight line; расстоя́ние по ∼о́й distance as the crow flies.

прямёхонько, *adv.* (*coll.*) straight, directly.

прямизн|а́, ы́, *f.* straightness.

прямико́м, *adv.* (*coll.*) straight; across country.

пря́мо, *adv.* 1. straight (on); п.! (*mil. word of command*) forward!; иди́те п.! (go) straight on!; держа́ться п. to hold oneself straight, erect. 2. straight, directly; п. к де́лу to the point; попа́сть п. в цель to hit the bull's eye (*also fig.*); смотре́ть п. в глаза́ кому́-н. to look someone straight in the face; п. со шко́льной скамьи́ (*fig.*) straight from school. 3. (*fig.*) straight; frankly, openly, bluntly; сказа́ть что-н. кому́-н. п. в лицо́ to say something to someone's face; мы ему́ п. сказа́ли, что э́то ему́ не уда́стся we told him straight that he would not succeed. 4. (*coll.*) real; really; он п. идио́т he is a real idiot; я п. не зна́ю, что с ней ста́ло I really don't know what has become of her.

прямоду́ши|е, я, *n.* directness, straightforwardness.

прямоду́ш|ный (∼ен, ∼на), *adj.* direct, straightforward.

прямое́зжий, *adj.* (*folk poet.*) straight.

прям|о́й (∼, ∼а́, ∼о), *adj.* 1. straight; upright, erect; ∼а́я кишка́ (*anat.*) rectum; п. пробо́р parting in the middle; п. у́гол (*math.*) right angle; п. у́зел reef knot; п. ход forward stroke (*of engine*). 2. (*of means of communication, etc.*) through; direct; по́езд ∼о́го сообще́ния through train; п. про́вод direct (*telephone*) line. 3. (*in var. senses*) direct; ∼ые вы́боры direct elections; ∼ое дополне́ние (*gram.*) direct object; ∼а́я наво́дка (*mil.*) direct laying; ∼о́й наво́дкой over open sights; п. нало́г direct tax; п. насле́дник heir in a direct line, direct heir; п. нача́льник immediate superior; ∼ое попада́ние (*mil.*) direct hit; ∼а́я противоположность direct opposite, exact opposite; ∼а́я речь (*gram.*) direct speech, oratio recta; п. смысл сло́ва the literal sense of a word. 4. (*of character*) straightforward. 5. (*coll.*) real; п. убы́ток sheer loss; п. расчёт пойти́ самому́ it is really worth while going oneself.

прямокры́л|ые, ых, *pl.* (*zool.*) orthoptera.

прямолине́йност|ь, и, *f.* straightforwardness.

прямолине́|йный (∼ен, ∼йна), *adj.* 1. rectilinear. 2. (*fig.*) straightforward; direct.

прямот|а́, ы́, *f.* straightforwardness; plain dealing.

прямото́чный, *adj.* (*tech.*) uniflow, direct-flow; п. котёл continuously operating boiler; п. дви́гатель (*aeron.*) ram jet engine.

прямоуго́льник, а, *m.* (*math.*) rectangle.

прямоуго́льный, *adj.* right-angled; rectangular; п. треуго́льник right-angled triangle.

пря́ник, а, *m.* spice cake; gingerbread; медо́вый п. honey-cake; (*fig., see* хлыст¹).

пря́ни|чный, *adj. of* ∼к.

пря́ност|ь, и, *f.* spice.

пря́|нуть, ну, нешь, *pf.* (*obs.*) to jump aside.

пря́ный, *adj.* spicy (*also fig.*; *of smells*) heady.

пря|сть¹, ду́, дёшь, *past* ∼л, ∼ла́, ∼ло, *impf.* (*of* с∼) to spin.

пря|сть², ду́, дёшь, *impf.* = ∼дать.

пря́|тать, чу, чешь, *impf.* (*of* с∼) to hide, conceal; to put away.

пря́|таться, чусь, чешься, *impf.* (*of* с∼) to hide, conceal oneself; to take refuge.

пря́т|ки, ок, *no sing.* hide-and-seek; игра́ть в п. to play hide-and-seek.

пря́х|а, и, *f.* spinner.

псал|о́м, ма́, *m.* psalm.

псало́мщик, а, *m.* (*eccl.*) (psalm-)reader; sexton.

псалты́р|ь, и, *f.* and (*coll.*) п., ~я, *m.* (*eccl.*) Psalter.

псар|ня, ни, *g. pl.* ~ен, *f.* kennel.

псар|ь, я́, *m.* huntsman (*person in charge of hounds*).

псе́вдо- pseudo-.

псевдогеро́ический, *adj.* (*lit.*) mock-heroic.

псевдони́м, а, *m.* pseudonym; pen-name; alias.

пси́н|а, ы, *f.* (*coll.*) 1. dog's flesh. 2. dog's smell, doggy smell. 3. dog.

пси́ный, *adj.* dog's; doggy.

псих, а, *m.* (*abbr. of* психопа́т) (*coll.*) madman, lunatic, crank, nut(-case).

психасте́ник, а, *m.* (*med.*) psychasthenic.

психастени́ческий, *adj.* (*med.*) psychasthenic.

психастени́|я, и, *f.* (*med.*) psychasthenia.

психиа́тр, а, *m.* psychiatrist.

психиатри́ческ|ий, *adj.* psychiatric(al); ~ая лече́бница mental hospital.

психиатри́|я, и, *f.* psychiatry.

пси́хик|а, и, *f.* state of mind; psyche; psychology; нездоро́вая п. unhealthy state of mind; вре́дно де́йствовать на ~у to have a harmful effect on the psyche; п. лётчиков-истреби́телей the psychology of fighter-pilots.

психи́чески, *adv.* mentally, psychically, psychologically; п. больно́й mentally diseased; *as noun* п. больно́й, п. больно́го, *m.* mental patient, mental case.

психи́ческ|ий, *adj.* mental, psychical; ~ая боле́знь mental illness, mental disease; ~ая ата́ка (*mil.*) psychological attack.

психоана́лиз, а, *m.* psychoanalysis.

психоаналити́ческий, *adj.* psychoanalytic(al).

псих|ова́ть, у́ю, *impf.* (*coll.*) 1. to behave like a madman; to feign insanity. 2. to be upset, hysterical; to have a (nervous) breakdown.

психо́з, а, *m.* mental illness; (*med.*) psychosis; вое́нный п. war hysteria.

психо́лог, а, *m.* psychologist.

психологи́зм, а, *m.* (*philos.*) psychologism.

психологи́ческий, *adj.* psychological.

психоло́ги|я, и, *f.* psychology.

психоневро́з, а, *m.* (*med.*) psychoneurosis.

психопа́т, а, *m.* psychopath; (*coll.*) lunatic.

психопатологи́ческий, *adj.* psychopathological.

психопатоло́ги|я, и, *f.* psychopathology.

психотерапе́вт, а, *m.* psychotherapist.

психотерапи́|я, и, *f.* psychotherapy.

психоте́хник|а, и, *f.* vocational psychology.

психофи́зик|а, и, *f.* psychophysics.

психофизиоло́ги|я, и, *f.* psychophysiology.

психофизи́ческий, *adj.* psychophysical.

псо́в|ый, *adj.* ~ая охо́та the chase, hunting (*with hounds*).

пта́шк|а, и, *f.* little bird; birdie; ра́нняя п. (*fig.*) early bird.

птен|е́ц, ца́, *m.* nestling; fledg(e)ling (*also fig.*).

птерода́ктил|ь, я, *m.* pterodactyl.

пти́ц|а, ы, *f.* bird; боло́тная п. wader; водопла́вающие ~ы waterfowl; дома́шняя п. (*collect.*) poultry; перелётная п. bird of passage; хи́щные ~ы birds of prey; ва́жная п. (*fig., coll.*) big noise; обстре́лянная п., стре́ляная п. (*fig.; coll.*) old hand.

птицево́д, а, *m.* poultry farmer, poultry breeder.

птицево́дств|о, а, *n.* poultry farming, poultry-keeping.

птицево́дческий, *adj.* poultry-farming, poultry-keeping.

птицело́в, а, *m.* fowler.

птицело́вств|о, а, *n.* fowling.

птицефе́рм|а, ы, *f.* poultry farm.

пти́ч|ий, *adj. of* пти́ца; п. двор poultry-yard; ~ье молоко́ (*coll., joc.*) pigeon's milk; вид с ~ьего полёта bird's-eye view; жить на ~ьих права́х to live from hand to mouth.

пти́чк|а[1], и, *f. dim. of* пти́ца.

пти́чк|а[2], и, *f.* tick; ста́вить ~у to tick.

пти́чник[1], а, *m.* poultry-yard, hen-run; hen-house.

пти́чник[2], а, *m.* poultryman.

птома́йн, а, *m.* (*chem.*) ptomaine.

пуа́нт, а, *m.*; на ~ах (*theatr.*) on the tips of the toes (*also fig.*).

пу́блик|а, и, *f.* (*collect.*) (the) public; (*in theatres, etc.*) (the) audience.

публика́ци|я, и, *f.* 1. publication. 2. advertisement, notice; помести́ть ~ю в газе́те to place an advertisement in a newspaper; п. о сме́рти obituary notice.

публик|ова́ть, у́ю, *impf.* (*of* о~) to publish.

публици́ст, а, *m.* publicist; commentator on current affairs.

публици́стик|а, и, *f.* social and political journalism; writing on current affairs.

публицисти́ческий, *adj.* publicistic.

публи́чно, *adv.* publicly; in public; openly.

публи́чность|ь, и, *f.* publicity.

публи́чн|ый, *adj.* public; ~ая библиоте́ка public library; п. дом brothel; ~ая же́нщина prostitute; ~ое пра́во public law; ~ые торги́ auction, public sale.

пу́гал|о, а, *n.* scarecrow.

пу́ган|ый, *adj.* (*coll.*) scared; ~ая воро́на (и) куста́ бои́тся (*prov.*) the burnt child dreads the fire; once bitten twice shy.

пуга́|ть, ю, *impf.* (*of* ис~) 1. to frighten, scare. 2. to intimidate; (+*i.*) to threaten (with).

пуга́|ться, юсь, *impf.* (*of* ис~) (+*g.*) to be frightened (of), be scared (of); to take fright (at); (*of a horse*) to shy (at).

пугáч, á, *m.* 1. toy-pistol. 2. (*orn.*) screech owl.

пуглѝвост|ь, и, *f.* fearfulness, timorousness, timidity.

пуглѝв|ый (~, ~a), *adj.* fearful, timorous; timid.

пугн|ýть, ý, ёшь, *pf.* to give a fright, give a scare.

пýговиц|а, ы, *f.* button; застегнýться на все ~ы to have all one's buttons done up; держáть за ~y (*coll.*) to buttonhole.

пýгови|чный, *adj.* of ~ца; ~чное произвóдство button-making.

пýговк|а, и, *f.* (*small*) button.

пуд, а, *pl.* ~ы, ~óв, *m.* pood (*Russian measure of weight* = 16·38 *kg or approx. 36 lb. avoirdupois*).

пýдел|ь, я, *pl.* ~и, ~ей *or* ~я, ~ей, *m.* poodle.

пýдинг, а, *m.* pudding.

пудлингóвани|е, я, *n.* (*tech.*) puddling.

пудлинг|овáть, ýю, *impf. and pf.* (*tech.*) to puddle.

пýдлингов|ый, *adj.* (*tech.*) puddling, puddled; ~ое желéзо puddle iron; ~ая печь puddling furnace.

пудовѝк, á, *m.* 1. one-pood bag. 2. one--pood weight.

пудовóй, *adj.* one pood in weight.

пýдр|а, ы, *f.* powder; сáхарная п. castor sugar.

пýдрениц|а, ы, *f.* powder-case, powder--compact.

пýдреный, *adj.* powdered.

пýдр|ить, ю, ишь, *impf.* (*of* на~) to powder.

пýдр|иться, юсь, ишься, *impf.* (*of* на~) to use powder, powder one's face.

пузáн, á, *m.* (*coll.*) person with a paunch.

пузáт|ый (~, ~a), *adj.* (*coll.*) big-bellied, pot-bellied.

пýз|о, a, *n.* (*coll.*) belly, paunch.

пузыр|ёк, ькá, *m.* 1. phial, vial. 2. bubble; bleb.

пузы́р|иться, ится, *impf.* 1. (*coll.*) to bubble; to effervesce. 2. (*coll.*) to pout, sulk.

пузы́рник, а, *m.* (*bot.*) senna-pod.

пузы́рчат|ый (~, ~a), *adj.* (*coll.*) covered with bubbles; blebby.

пузы́р|ь, я́, *m.* 1. bubble; мы́льный п. soap--bubble; пускáть мы́льные ~и́ to blow bubbles. 2. blister. 3. (*anat.*) bladder; жёлчный п. gall-bladder; мочевóй п. (urinary) bladder; плáвательный п. (fish-)sound, swimming-bladder. 4. air-bladder; п. со льдом ice-bag. 5. (*coll.*) kid, kiddy.

пук, а, *pl.* ~и́, *m.* bunch, bundle; tuft; п. цветóв bunch of flowers; п. солóмы wisp of straw.

пул|евóй, *adj.* of ~я.

пулемёт, а, *m.* machine-gun; ручнóй п.

light machine-gun; станкóвый п. heavy machine-gun.

пулемёт|ный, *adj.* of ~; ~ная лéнта (machine-gun) cartridge belt; ~ная огневáя тóчка machine-gun emplacement.

пулемётчик, а, *m.* machine-gunner.

пулестóйкий, *adj.* bullet-proof.

пулóвер, а, *m.* pullover.

пульверизáтор, а, *m.* pulverizer, atomizer, sprayer.

пульверизáци|я, и, *f.* pulverization, spraying.

пульверизѝр|овать, ую, *impf. and pf.* to pulverize, spray.

пýльк|а¹, и, *f.* dim. of пýля.

пýльк|а², и, *f.* (*cards*) pool.

пýльп|а, ы, *f.* (*anat.*) pulp.

пульс, а, *m.* pulse; pulse rate; биéние ~a pulsation, beating of the pulse; считáть п. to take the pulse; щýпать п. to feel the pulse.

пульсáци|я, и, *f.* pulsation, pulse.

пульсѝр|овать, ую, *impf.* 1. to pulse, pulsate; to beat, throb. 2. (*tech.*) to pulse, pulsate.

пульсóметр, а, *m.* (*tech.*) pulsometer, vacuum pump.

пульт, а, *m.* 1. desk, stand; дирижёрский п. conductor's stand. 2. (*in power station, etc.*) control panel; (*on aerodrome, etc.*) (traffic) control panel.

пýл|я, и, *f.* bullet; лить, отливáть ~и (*fig., coll.*) to tell lies.

пуля́рк|а, и, *f.* fatted fowl.

пýм|а, ы, *f.* puma, cougar.

пунѝческий, *adj.* (*hist.*) Punic.

пункт, а, *m.* 1. point; spot; наблюдáтельный п. observation post; населённый п. inhabited locality; built-up area; опóрный п. (*mil.*) strong point; исхóдный п., начáльный п. starting point; конéчный п. terminus, terminal; кульминациóнный п. culmination, climax. 2. (*centre operating special services*) point; centre; медицѝнский п. (*mil.*) dressing-station, aid post; переговóрный п. (*collect.*) public (telephone) call-boxes; призывнóй п. recruiting centre; ссыпнóй п. grain-collecting centre. 3. point; paragraph, item; plank (*of polit. programme*); по ~ам point by point; соглашéние из трёх ~ов a three-point agreement. 4. (*typ.*) full point.

пýнктик, а, *m.* (*coll.*) 1. dim. of пункт. 2. (*fig.*) eccentricity, peculiarity; он — человéк с ~ом he is a bit odd.

пунктѝр, а, *m.* dotted line.

пунктѝрн|ый, *adj.* ~ая лѝния dotted line.

пунктуáльност|ь, и, *f.* punctuality.

пунктуáл|ьный (~ен, ~ьна), *adj.* punctual.

пунктуáци|я, и, *f.* punctuation.

пу́нкци|я, и, *f.* (*med.*) puncture.

пу́ночк|а, и, *f.* (*orn.*) snow-bunting.

пунсо́н, а, *m.* (*tech.*) punch, die, stamp.

пунцо́вый, *adj.* crimson.

пунш, а, *m.* punch (*drink*).

пу́нш|евый, *adj.* of ~.

пуп, а́, *m.* navel; (*anat.*) umbilicus; п. земли́ the hub of the universe.

пупови́н|а, ы, *f.* (*anat.*) umbilical cord; navel-string.

пуп|о́к, ка́, *m.* 1. navel. 2. (*of birds*) gizzard.

пупо́чн|ый, *adj.* (*anat.*) umbilical; ~ая гры́жа umbilical hernia.

пупы́рыш|ек, ка, *m.* (*coll.*) pimple.

пург|а́, и́, *no pl., f.* snow-storm, blizzard.

пури́зм, а, *m.* purism.

пури́ст, а, *m.* purist.

пурита́н|ин, ина, *pl.* ~е, ~, *m.* Puritan.

пурита́нский, *adj.* Puritan; (*fig.*) puritanical.

пурита́нств|о, а, *n.* Puritanism.

пу́рпур, а, *m.* purple.

пурпу́рный, *adj.* purple.

пурпу́р|овый, *adj.* = ~ный; ~овая кислота́ (*chem.*) purpuric acid.

пуск, а, *m.* starting (up); setting in motion.

пуска́й, *particle and conj.* (*coll.*) = пусть.

пуска́|ть(ся), ю(сь), *impf. of* пусти́ть(ся).

пуско́в|о́й, *adj.* starting; п. пери́од starting period, initial phase (*of working of factory, etc.*); ~а́я руко́ятка starting crank; ~о́е устро́йство starter; ~а́я площа́дка (rocket) launching platform.

пустельг|а́, и́, *f.* 1. (*orn.*) kestrel; staniel, windhover. 2. *m. and f.* (*coll.*) worthless fellow.

пусте́|ть, ет, *impf.* (*of* о~) to (become) empty; to become deserted.

пу|сти́ть, щу́, ~стишь, *pf.* (*of* ~ска́ть) 1. to let go; п. на во́лю to set free; п. кровь кому́-н. to bleed someone. 2. to let; to allow, permit; п. кого́-н. в о́тпуск to let someone go on leave; нас не ~сти́ли в пала́ту they would not let us into the ward; ~сти́те соба́ку на двор let the dog go out. 3. to let in, allow to enter; не п. to keep out; п. по предъявле́нии биле́та to allow to enter on showing a ticket; п. жильцо́в to take in lodgers; п. козла́ в огоро́д (*prov.*) to set a cat among the pigeons. 4. to start, set in motion, set going; to set working; п. во́ду to turn on water; п. волчо́к to spin a top; п. заво́д to start up a factory; п. змея́ to fly a kite; п. слух to start a rumour; п. фейерве́рк to let off fireworks; п. фонта́н to set a fountain playing; п. часы́ to start a clock. 5. to set, put; to send; п. себе́ пу́лю в лоб to blow out one's brains, put a bullet through one's head; п. в обраще́ние to put in circulation; п. ло́шадь во

весь опо́р to give a horse his head; п. прода́жу to offer, put up for sale; п. в произво́дство to put in production; п. в ход to start, launch, set going, set in train; п. в ход все сре́дства to move heaven and earth; п. кора́бль ко дну to send a ship to the bottom; п. по́ миру to ruin utterly; п. по́езд под отко́с to derail a train; п. по́ле под пар to put a field to lie fallow. 6. (+*a. or i.*) to throw, shy; п. ка́мнем в окно́ to throw a stone at a window; п. пыль в глаза́ to cut a dash, show off. 7. (*bot.*) to put forth, put out; п. ко́рни to take root (*also fig.*); п. ростки́ to shoot, sprout. 8. (*coll.*; *in painting*) to put on; to touch up; п. каёмку лило́вым to put violet on the border.

пу|сти́ться, щу́сь, ~стишься, *pf.* (*of* ~ска́ться) (в+*a. or* +*inf.*; *coll.*) 1. to set out, start; п. в путь to set out, get on the way. 2. to begin, start; to set to; п. в оправда́ния to start making excuses; п. в пляс to break into a dance.

пустобрёх, а, *m.* (*coll.*) chatterbox, windbag.

пустова́т|ый (~, ~а), *adj.* 1. rather empty. 2. fatuous.

пуст|ова́ть, у́ю, *impf.* to be empty, stand empty; to be tenantless, be uninhabited; (*of land*) to lie fallow.

пустоголо́в|ый (~, ~а), *adj.* empty-headed.

пустозво́н, а, *m.* (*coll.*) idle talker, windbag.

пустозво́н|ить, ю, ишь, *impf.* (*coll.*) to engage in idle talk.

пустозво́нств|о, а, *n.* (*coll.*) idle talk.

пуст|о́й (~, ~а́, ~о), *adj.* 1. empty; void; hollow; tenantless, uninhabited; deserted; ~о́е ме́сто blank space; ~а́я поро́да (*geol.*) barren rock, waste rock, dead rock; на п. желу́док on an empty stomach; с ~ыми рука́ми empty-handed; чтоб тебе́ ~о бы́ло! (*coll.*) I wish you at the bottom of the sea!, the devil take you! 2. (*fig.*) idle; shallow; futile, frivolous; ~а́я болтовня́ idle talk; п. челове́к shallow person. 3. (*fig.*) vain, ungrounded; ~а́я зате́я vain enterprise; ~ые мечты́ castles in the air; ~а́я отгово́рка lame excuse; ~ые слова́ mere words; ~ые угро́зы empty threats, bluster.

пустоме́л|я, и, *m. and f.* (*coll.*) idle talker, windbag.

пустопоро́жний, *adj.* (*coll.*) empty, vacant.

пустосло́в, а, *m.* (*coll.*) idle talker, windbag.

пустосло́ви|е, я, *n.* (*coll.*) idle talk, verbiage.

пустосло́в|ить, лю, ишь, *impf.* (*coll.*) to engage in idle talk.

пустот|а́, ы́, *pl.* ~ы, *f.* 1. emptiness; void; (*phys.*) vacuum. 2. (*fig.*) shallowness; futility, frivolousness.

пустоте́лый, *adj.* hollow.

пустоцве́т, а, *m.* barren flower (*also fig.*).

пу́стош|ь, и, *f.* waste (plot of) land, waste ground.

пусты́нник, а, *m.* hermit, anchorite.

пусты́н|ный (~ен, ~на), *adj.* 1. uninhabited; п. о́стров desert island. 2. deserted.

пу́стын|ь, и, *f.* hermitage, monastery.

пусты́н|я, и, *f.* desert, wilderness.

пусты́р|ь, я́, *m.* waste land, vacant plot (of land).

пусты́шк|а, и, *f.* (*coll.*) 1. baby's dummy. 2. hollow object; (*fig.*) shallow person, hollow man.

пусть 1. *particle* let; п. бу́дет так! so be it!; п. она́ сама́ реши́т let her decide herself; п. *x* ра́вен 3 (*math.*) let *x* = 3. 2. *as conj.* though, even if: п. им бу́дет проти́вно, но я до́лжен вы́сказать своё мне́ние even if they don't like it, I must express my opinion. 3. *particle* (*coll.*) all right, very well.

пустя́к, а́, *m.* trifle; bagatelle; су́щий п. a mere bagatelle; спо́рить из-за ~о́в to split hairs; па́ра ~о́в! (*coll.*) child's play!; ~и́! (*i*) it's nothing!, never mind!, (*ii*) nonsense!, rubbish!

пустяко́вый, *adj.* trifling, trivial.

пустя́чный, *adj.* = пустяко́вый.

пу́таник, а, *m.* muddle-headed person.

пу́таниц|а, ы, *f.* muddle, confusion; mess, tangle.

пу́таный, *adj.* 1. muddle, confused; confusing. 2. (*coll.*) muddle-headed.

пу́та|ть, ю, *impf.* (*of* с~) 1. to tangle (*a thread, etc.*). 2. to confuse, muddle; он все́ ~л слу́шателей примене́нием анало́гий he always muddled his audience by his use of analogy. 3. to confuse, mix up; ты ещё ~ешь на́ши имена́ you are still mixing our names up. 4. (*pf.* в~) (в+*a.*; *coll.*) to implicate (in), mix up (in).

пу́та|ться, юсь, *impf.* (*of* с~) 1. to get tangled. 2. (*of thoughts*) to get confused. 3. to get mixed up, get muddled; п. в расска́зе to give a muddled account; п. в показа́ниях to contradict oneself in one's evidence. 4. (*pf.* в~) (в+*a.*; *coll.*) to get mixed up (in); п. в тёмные дели́шки to get mixed up in shady business. 5. *impf. only* (*coll.*) to mooch about. 6. (с+*i.*; *coll.*) to get mixed up (with), get entangled (with); to carry on (with) (*a person of the opposite sex*).

путёвк|а, и, *f.* 1. pass, authorization; сде́лать зая́вку на ~у в санато́рий to apply for a place in a sanatorium; п. в жизнь a start in life. 2. place in a tourist group; я купи́л ~у в Чехослова́кию I have booked a place on a tour of Czechoslovakia. 3. schedule of duties (*of public transport workers*).

путеводи́тел|ь, я, *m.* guide, guide-book.

путево́дн|ый, *adj.* guiding; ~ая звезда́ guiding star; (*fig.*) lodestar.

путев|о́й, *adj.* travelling, itinerary; ~ы́е заме́тки travel notes; ~а́я ка́рта road-map; п. ко́мпас (*naut.*) steering compass; п. обхо́дчик, п. сто́рож (*railways*) permanent way man; ~а́я ско́рость (*aeron.*) absolute speed, ground speed.

путе́|ец, йца, *m.* (*coll.*) 1. railway engineer. 2. permanent way man.

путём[1], *prep.* (+*g.*) by means of, by dint of.

путём[2], *adv.* (*coll.*) properly; coherently; он ничего́ п. не уме́ет объясни́ть he cannot explain anything coherently.

путеме́р, а, *m.* pedometer.

путеобхо́дчик, а, *m.* (*railways*) permanent way man.

путепрово́д, а, *m.* 1. (*on roads*) overpass, flyover; underpass. 2. (*railway*) overbridge.

путеше́ственник, а, *m.* traveller.

путеше́стви|е, я, *n.* 1. journey; trip; (*on the sea*) voyage; cruise. 2. *pl.* (*lit.*) travels.

путеше́ств|овать, ую, *impf.* to travel, go on travels; (*on the sea*) to voyage.

пути́н|а, ы, *f.* fishing season.

пу́тлищ|е, а, *n.* stirrup strap.

пу́тник, а, *m.* traveller, wayfarer.

пу́тн|ый, *adj.* (*coll.*) sensible; из него́ ничего́ ~ого не вы́йдет you'll never make a man of him.

путч, а, *m.* (*polit.*) putsch.

пу́ты, пут, *no sing.* 1. hobble. 2. (*fig.*) fetters, chains, trammels.

пут|ь, и́, *i.* ём, о ~и́, *pl.* ~и́, ~е́й, ~я́м, *m.* 1. way, track, path; (*aeron.*) track; (*astron.*) race; (*fig.*) road, course; во́дный п. water-way; морски́е ~и́ shipping-routes, sea-lanes; са́нный п. sledge-track; тылово́й п. (*mil.*) line of retreat; ~и́ сообще́ния communications; жи́зненный п. (*fig.*) life; на пра́вильном ~и́ on the right track; друго́го, ино́го ~и́ нет there are no two ways about it; сби́ться с (ве́рного) ~и́ to lose one's way; (*fig.*) to go astray; стоя́ть поперёк ~и́ кому́-н. (*fig.*) to stand in someone's path. 2. (railway) track; запа́сный п. siding. 3. journey; voyage; в ~и́ on one's way, en route; в четырёх днях ~и́ (от) four days' journey (from); на обра́тном ~и́ on the way back; по ~и́ on the way; нам с ва́ми по ~и́ we are going the same way; держа́ть п. (на+*a.*) to head (for), make (for); счастли́вого ~и́! bon voyage! 4. *pl.* (*anat.*) passage, duct; дыха́тельные ~и́ respiratory tract. 5. (*fig.*) way, means; каки́м ~ём? how?, in what way?; ми́рным ~ём amicably, peaceably; око́льным ~ём, око́льными ~я́ми in, by a roundabout way; найти́ ~и́ и сре́дства to find ways and means; пойти́ по ~и́ (+*g.*) to take the path (of). **6.** (*coll.*) use, benefit; без ~й in vain, uselessly.

пуф, а, *m.* **1.** pouf(fe). **2.** canard, hoax.

пух, а, о ~е, в ~у́, *m.* down; fluff; в п. и прах (*coll.*) completely, utterly; разряди́ться в п. и прах[1] to put on all one's finery; разби́ть в п. и прах to put to complete rout; ни ~а, ни пера́! (*coll.*) good luck!

пухл|ый (~, ~а́, ~о), *adj.* chubby, plump.

пухля́к, а́, *m.* (*orn.*) willow tit.

пу́х|нуть, ну, нешь, *past* ~, ~ла, *impf.* to swell.

пухови́к, а́, *m.* feather-bed.

пухо́вк|а, и, *f.* powder-puff.

пухо́вый, *adj.* downy.

пучегла́зи|е, я, *n.* (*med.*) exophthalmus.

пучегла́з|ый (~, ~а), *adj.* goggle-eyed, lobster-eyed.

пучи́н|а, ы, *f.* gulf, abyss (*also fig.*); the deep.

пу́ч|ить, у, ишь, *impf.* (*coll.*) **1.** (*pf.* вс~) to become swollen; у него́ живо́т ~ит (*impers.*) he is troubled with wind. **2.** (*pf.* вы́~) п. глаза́ to goggle.

пу́чност|ь, и, *f.* (*radio*) antinode, loop.

пуч|о́к, ка́, *m.* **1.** bunch, bundle; (*bot.*) fascicle; п. луче́й (*phys.*) pencil (of rays); п. се́на wisp of hay; п. цвето́в bunch of flowers. **2.** (*coll.*) bun (*hair-do*).

пу́ш|ечный, *adj.* of ~ка[1]; п. ого́нь gunfire, cannon fire; ~ечное мя́со cannon-fodder.

пуши́нк|а, и, *f.* bit of fluff; п. сне́га snow-flake.

пуши́ст|ый (~, ~а), *adj.* fluffy, downy.

пуш|и́ть, у́, и́шь, *impf.* (*of* рас~) **1.** to fluff up. **2.** (*coll.*) to swear at.

пу́шк|а[1], и, *f.* gun, cannon; стреля́ть из пу́шек по воробья́м (*prov.*) to swat a fly with a sledgehammer.

пу́шк|а[2], и, *f.* (*coll.*) lying, lies; на ~у взять кого́-н. to trick someone; получи́ть на ~у (*i*) to obtain by a trick, (*ii*) to get for nothing.

пушка́р|ь, я́, *m.* **1.** (*hist.*) cannon-founder. **2.** (*obs., coll.*) gunner.

пушкини́ст, а, *m.* Pushkin scholar.

пушкинове́дени|е, я, *n.* Pushkin studies.

пушни́н|а, ы, *f.* (*collect.*) furs, fur-skins, pelts.

пушно́й, *adj.* **1.** fur-bearing; п. зверь (*collect.*) fur-bearing animals. **2.** fur; п. про́мысел fur trade; п. това́р furs.

пуш|о́к, ка́, *m.* **1.** fluff. **2.** (*on fruit*) bloom.

пу́щ|а, и, *f.* dense forest, virgin forest.

пу́ще, *adv.* (*coll.*) more; п. всего́ most of all.

пу́щий, *adj.*, *only in phrase* для ~ей ва́жности for greater show.

пчел|а́, ы́, *pl.* ~ы, *f.* bee; рабо́чая п. worker bee.

пчел|и́ный, *adj. of* ~а́; п. воск beeswax; ~и́ная ма́тка queen bee; п. рой swarm of bees; п. у́лей beehive.

пчелово́д, а, *m.* bee-keeper, bee-master, apiarist.

пчелово́дств|о, а, *n.* bee-keeping, apiculture.

пчелово́дческий, *adj.* bee-keeping.

пче́льник, а, *m.* bee-garden, apiary.

пшени́ц|а, ы, *f.* wheat; ярова́я п. spring wheat; ози́мая п. winter wheat.

пшени́чный, *adj.* wheaten.

пшённик, а, *m.* millet-pudding.

пшён|ный, *adj. of* ~о́.

пшен|о́, а́, *n.* millet.

пшик, а, *m.* (*coll.*) nothing; око́нчиться ~ом (*fig.*) to fizzle out, come to nought; оста́лся оди́н п. nothing was left.

пыж, а́, *m.* wad (*used in loading fire-arm from muzzle*).

пы́жик, а, *m.* young deer; fur of young deer.

пы́жиковый, *adj.* deerskin.

пы́ж|иться, усь, ишься, *impf.* (*of* на~) (*coll.*) **1.** to be puffed up, strut. **2.** to go all out.

пыл, а, о ~е, в ~у́, *m.* **1.** (*dial.*) heat; пирожки́ с ~у hot pasties. **2.** (*fig.*) heat, ardour; ю́ный п. youthful ardour; в ~у́ сраже́ния in the heat of the battle.

пыла́|ть, ю, *impf.* **1.** to blaze, flame. **2.** (*fig.; of the face*) to glow. **3.** (+*i.; fig.*) burn (with); п. стра́стью to be afire with passion.

пылесо́с, а, *m.* vacuum cleaner, Hoover.

пылесо́с|ить, ю, ишь, *impf.* (*of* про~) to vacuum-clean, Hoover.

пыли́нк|а, и, *f.* speck of dust.

пыл|и́ть, ю́, и́шь, *impf.* **1.** (*pf.* на~) to raise dust. **2.** (*pf.* за~) to cover with dust, make dusty.

пыл|и́ться, ю́сь, и́шься, *impf.* (*of* за~) to get dusty, get covered with dust.

пы́л|кий (~ок, ~ка́, ~ко), *adj.* ardent, passionate; fervent; fervid; ~кое воображе́ние fervid imagination; ~кая речь impassioned speech.

пы́лкост|ь, и, *f.* ardour, passion; fervency.

пыл|ь, и, о ~и, в ~й, *f.* dust; водяна́я п. spray; у́гольная п. coal-dust; slack; смести́ п. (с+*g.*) to dust.

пы́льник[1], а, *m.* (*bot.*) anther.

пы́льник[2], а, *m.* dust-coat.

пы́л|ьный (~ен, ~ьна́, ~ьно), *adj.* **1.** dusty; ~ная тря́пка (*coll.*) duster. **2.** п. котёл (*agric.*) dust bowl.

пыльц|а́, ы́, *f.* (*bot.*) pollen.

пыре́|й, я, *m.* (*bot.*) couch-grass.

пырн|у́ть, у́, ёшь, *pf.* (*coll.*) to jab; п. ножо́м to thrust a knife (into); п. рога́ми to butt.

пыта́|ть, ю, *impf.* **1.** to torture (*also fig.*);

(*fig.*) to torment. **2.** (*coll.*) to try (for);
п. сча́стье to try one's luck.

пыта́|ться, юсь, *impf.* (*of* по~) to try,
attempt, endeavour.

пы́тк|а, и, *f.* torture, torment (*also fig.*);
ору́дие ~и instrument of torture.

пытли́вост|ь, и, *f.* inquisitiveness.

пытли́в|ый (~, ~a), *adj.* inquisitive; п.
взгляд a searching look.

пы́|хать, шу, шешь, *impf.* **1.** (жа́ром) to
blaze. **2.** (*fig.*) п. гне́вом to blaze with
anger; п. здоро́вьем to be a picture of
health.

пых|те́ть, чу, ти́шь, *impf.* to puff, pant.

пы́шк|а, и, *f.* **1.** bun; doughnut. **2.** (*fig.*,
coll.) chubby child; plump woman.

пы́шност|ь, и, *f.* splendour, magnificence.

пы́ш|ный (~ен, ~на́, ~но), *adj.* **1.** splen-
did, magnificent. **2.** fluffy; light; luxuriant;
~ные во́лосы fluffy hair; п. пиро́г light
pie; ~ные рукава́ puffed sleeves.

пьедеста́л, а, *m.* pedestal (*also fig.*); вознес-
ти́ на п. (*fig.*) to place on a pedestal.

пьезо́метр, а, *m.* (*tech.*) piezometer.

пье́ксы, пьекс, *no sing.* ski boots.

пье́с|а, ы, *f.* **1.** (*theatr.*) play. **2.** (*mus.*) piece.

пьяне́|ть, ю, ешь, *impf.* (*of* о~) to get
drunk, get intoxicated.

пьян|и́ть, ю, и́шь, *impf.* (*of* о~) to make
drunk, intoxicate (*also fig.*); (*fig.*) to go to
one's head.

пья́ниц|а, ы, *m. and f.* drunkard; tippler,
toper; го́рький п. hard drinker, sot.

пья́нк|а, и, *f.* (*coll.*) drinking-bout, binge,
booze-up.

пья́нств|о, а, *n.* drunkenness; hard drink-
ing.

пья́нств|овать, ую, *impf.* to drink hard,
drink heavily.

пья́н|ый (~, ~а́, ~о), *adj.* **1.** drunk;
drunken; tipsy, tight; intoxicated; по ~ой
ла́вочке, с ~ых глаз (*coll.*) one over the
eight; *as noun* п., ~ого, *m.* (a) drunk.
2. heady, intoxicating.

пэр, а, *m.* peer.

пюпи́тр, а, *m.* desk, reading-desk; но́тный
п. music-stand.

пюре́, *indecl.,* *n.* (*cul.*) purée; карто́фельное
п. mashed potatoes.

пяд|ь, и, *pl.* ~и, ~е́й, *f.* span; ни ~и не
уступи́ть (*fig.*) not to yield an inch; будь
он семи́ ~е́й во лбу (*fig.*) be he a Solomon.

пя́л|ить, ю, ишь, *impf.* п. глаза́ (на+*a.*;
coll.) to stare (at).

пя́л|ьцы, ец, *no sing.* tambour; lace-frame.

пяст|ь, и, *f.* (*anat.*) metacarpus.

пят|а́, ы́, *pl.* ~ы, ~, ~а́м, *f.* **1.** heel; ахил-
ле́сова п. Achilles' heel; ходи́ть за кем-н.
по ~а́м to follow on someone's heels, tread
on someone's heels; под ~ой (+*g.*; *fig.*)

under the heel (of); с, от головы́ до ~
from top to toe, all over, altogether. **2.**
(*tech.*) abutment; п. сво́да skewback.

пята́к, а́, *m.* (*coll.*) five-copeck piece.

пятач|о́к¹, ка́, *m.* (*coll.*) = пята́к; аэро-
дро́м с п. pocket handkerchief aerodrome.

пятач|о́к², ка́, *m.* (*coll.*) snout.

пятери́чный, *adj.* fivefold, quintuple.

пятёрк|а, и, *f.* **1.** (*number*) five. **2.** five (*top
mark in Russian school marking system*). **3.** (*coll.*)
five-rouble note. **4.** (*cards*) five; козырна́я
п. five of trumps.

пятерн|я́, и́, *g. pl.* ~е́й, *f.* (*coll.*) five fingers;
palm with fingers extended.

пя́тер|о, ы́х, *num.* five.

пятиалты́нн|ый, ого, *m.* (*coll.*) fifteen-
-kopeck piece.

пятибо́рь|е, я, *n.* (*sport*) pentathlon; со-
време́нное п. modern pentathlon.

пятигра́нник, а, *m.* (*math.*) pentahedron.

пятигра́нный, *adj.* (*math.*) pentahedral.

пятидесятиле́ти|е, я, *n.* **1.** fifty years. **2.**
fiftieth anniversary; fiftieth birthday.

пятидесятиле́тний, *adj.* **1.** fifty-year, of
fifty years. **2.** fifty-year-old.

пятидеся́тник, а, *m.* **1.** (*hist.*) man of the
'Fifties (*member of group of Russian intelli-
gentsia active during the 1850s*). **2.** (*rel.*)
Pentecostalist.

Пятидеся́тниц|а, ы, *f.* (*eccl.*) Pentecost.

пятидеся́т|ый, *adj.* fiftieth; ~ые го́ды the
fifties; п. но́мер number fifty; ~ая страни́-
ца page fifty.

пятидне́вк|а, и, *f.* five-day period; five-day
week.

пятикла́ссник, а, *m.* fifth-form pupil, fifth-
-former.

Пятикни́жи|е, я, *n.* (*eccl., lit.*) Pentateuch.

пятиконе́чн|ый, *adj.*; ~ая звезда́ five-
-pointed star.

пятикра́тный, *adj.* fivefold, quintuple.

пятиле́ти|е, я, *n.* **1.** five years. **2.** fifth anni-
versary.

пятиле́тк|а, и, *f.* **1.** five years. **2.** (*econ.*) five-
year plan. **3.** five-year-old; де́вочка-п.
five-year-old girl.

пятиле́тний, *adj.* **1.** five-year; п. план
(*econ.*) five-year plan. **2.** five-year-old.

пятиме́сячный, *adj.* **1.** five-month. **2.** five-
-months-old.

пятинеде́льный, *adj.* **1.** five-week. **2.** five-
-week-old.

пятио́кис|ь, и, *f.* (*chem.*) pentoxide.

пятипо́ль|е, я, *n.* (*agric.*) five-field crop ro-
tation.

пятисло́жный, *adj.* pentasyllabic.

пятисло́йный, *adj.* five-ply.

пятисо́тенный, *adj.* five-hundred-rouble.

пятисотле́ти|е, я, *n.* **1.** five centuries. **2.**
quincentenary.

пятисóтый, *adj.* five-hundredth.

пятистóпный, *adj.* (*lit.*) pentameter; п. ямб iambic pentameter.

пятитóнк|а, и, *f.* (*coll.*) five-ton lorry.

пятитысячный, *adj.* five-thousandth.

пя́|тить, чу, тишь, *impf.* (*of* по~) to back, move back.

пя́|титься, чусь, тишься, *impf.* (*of* по~) to back, move backward(s); (*of a horse*) to jib.

пятиугóльник, а, *m.* (*math.*) pentagon.

пятиугóльный, *adj.* pentagonal.

пятиэтáжный, *adj.* five-storied.

пя́тк|а, и, *f.* heel (*also of sock or stocking*); лизáть комý-н. ~и to lick someone's boots; показáть ~и to show a clean pair of heels; удирáть так, что тóлько ~и сверкáют to take to one's heels, show a clean pair of heels; у меня́ душá в ~и ушлá my heart sank to my boots.

пятнадцатилéтний, *adj.* **1.** fifteen-year. **2.** fifteen-year-old.

пятнáдцатый, *adj.* fifteenth.

пятнáдцат|ь, и, *num.* fifteen.

пятна́|ть, ю, *impf.* (*of* за~) **1.** to spot, stain, smirch (*also fig.*). **2.** (*coll.*) to catch (*at tag*).

пятнáш|ки, ек, *no sing.* (*coll.*) (*children's game*) tag.

пятни́ст|ый (~, ~а), *adj.* spotted, dappled; п. олéнь spotted deer.

пя́тниц|а, ы, *f.* Friday; по ~ам on Fridays, every Friday; у негó семь ~ на недéле he keeps changing his mind.

пят|нó, нá, *pl.* ~на, ~ен, ~нам, *n.* **1.** (*in var. senses*) spot; patch; blot; stain; родúмое п. birth-mark; сóлнечные ~на (*astron.*) sun-spots; тёмное п. (*astron.*) nebula; выводúть ~на to remove stains. **2.** (*fig.*) blot, stain; stigma, blemish.

пя́тныш|ко, ка, *pl.* ~ки, ~ек, ~кам, *n.* speck.

пят|óк, кá, *m.* (+*g.*; *coll.*) five (*similar objects*).

пя́т|ый, *adj.* fifth; главá ~ая chapter five; ~ая колóнна fifth column; п. нóмер number five; size five; ~ое числó (мéсяца) the fifth (*day of the month*); в ~ом часý after four (o'clock), past four; рассказáть из ~ого в деся́тое to tell a story in snatches.

пят|ь, и́, ью́, *num.* five.

пятьдеся́т, пятúдесяти, пятью́десятью, *num.* fifty.

пятьсóт, пятисóт, пятистáм, *num.* five hundred.

пя́тью, *adv.* five times.

р

раб, á, *m.* slave (*also fig.*); bondsman.

раб- *abbr. of* рабóчий.

раб|á, ы́, *f.* slave; bondwoman, bondmaid.

рабкóр, а, *m.* (*abbr. of* рабóчий корреспондéнт) worker correspondent.

рабовладéл|ец, ьца, *m.* slave-owner.

рабовладéльческий, *adj.* slave-holding, slave-owning.

раболéпи|е, я, *n.* servility.

раболéп|ный (~ен, ~на), *adj.* servile.

раболéпств|о, а, *n.* servility.

раболéпств|овать, ую, *impf.* (пéред) to fawn (on), cringe (to).

рабóт|а, ы, *f.* **1.** work, working; functioning, running; лёгкая, тяжёлая р. (*tech.*) light, heavy duty; единúца ~ы (*phys.*) unit of work; режúм ~ы, услóвия ~ы (*tech.*) operating conditions, working conditions; обеспéчить нормáльную ~у (+*g.*) to ensure normal functioning (of). **2.** (*in var. senses*) work; labour; домáшняя р. homework; кáторжные ~ы (*obs.*) penal servitude; лепнáя р. stucco work, plaster work; mouldings; принудúтельные ~ы forced labour; сельскохозя́йственные ~ы agricultural work; совмéстная р. collaboration; ýмственная р. mental work, brain-work; взять в ~у (*coll.*) to take to task. **3.** work, job; постоя́нная р. regular work; случáйная р. casual work, odd job(s); искáть ~у to look for a job; поступúть на ~у to go to work; снять с ~ы to lay off, dismiss; быть без ~ы, не имéть ~ы to be out of work. **4.** work, workmanship.

рабóта|ть, ю, *impf.* **1.** (на+*a.*; над) to work (for; on); р. сверхурóчно to work overtime; р. сдéльно to do piece-work; врéмя ~ет на нас time is on our side; он ~ет над нóвым ромáном he is working on a new novel. **2.** to work, run, function; не р. not to work, be out of order; р. на нéфти to run on oil. **3.** (*of an institution, etc.*) to be open; галерéя не ~ет по воскресéньям the gallery is not open on Sundays. **4.** (+*i.*) to work, operate; р. вёслами to ply the oars; р. локтя́ми (*coll.*) to elbow; р. рычагóм to operate a lever.

рабóта|ться, ется, *impf.* (*impers.*; *coll.*) сегóдня хорошó ~ется work is going well today; вчерá мне не ~лось I didn't feel like working yesterday; I couldn't get on with my work yesterday.

рабóтник, а, *m.* worker; workman; hand, labourer; наýчный р. member of staff of scientific *and/or* learned institution; р. искусства person working in the arts, in the artistic world; р. народного образования educationalist; р. умственного труда brain worker; р. физического труда manual worker.

работниц|а, ы, *f.* (woman-)worker; домашняя р. domestic servant, (house)maid; home help.

работн|ый, *adj.* р. дом (*obs.*) workhouse; ~ые люди (*hist.*) workers, working men.

работодател|ь, я, *m.* employer.

работоргов|ец, ца, *m.* slave-trader, slaver.

работоргов|я, и, *f.* slave-trade.

работоспособност|ь, и, *f.* capacity for work, efficiency.

работоспособ|ный (~ен, ~на), *adj.* **1.** able-bodied. **2.** hardworking.

работяг|а, и, *m. and f.* (*coll.*) hard worker; slogger.

работящий, *adj.* (*coll.*) hard-working, industrious.

рабоч|ий¹, его, *m.* worker; working man; workman; hand, labourer; ~ие (*collect.; as social class*) the workers; подённый р. day-labourer; сезонный р. seasonal worker; сельскохозяйственный р. farm labourer, agricultural worker; р. от станка factory worker, bench-worker.

рабоч|ий², *adj.* **1.** worker's, working-class; ~ее движение working-class movement; р. класс the working class; ~ая молодёжь young workers; р. поезд workmen's train. **2.** work, working; ~ая команда (*mil.*) fatigue party, work party; ~ая лошадь draught-horse; р. муравей worker ant; ~ая пчела worker bee; ~ие руки hands; ~ая сила (*i*) (*collect.*) manpower, labour force, (*ii*) labour; р. скот draught animals. **3.** working; ~ее время working time, working hours; р. день working day; р. костюм, ~ее платье working clothes; ~ее место operator's position; ~ая характеристика (*tech.*) performance, performance curve. **4.** (*tech.*) working, driving; ~ее давление working pressure, effective pressure; ~ее колесо driving wheel; rotor wheel (*of turbine*); р. ход working stroke; р. чертёж working drawing.

рабселькор, а, *m.* (*abbr. of* рабоче-сельский корреспондент) worker-peasant correspondent.

раб|ский, *adj.* **1.** *adj. of* ~; р. труд slave labour. **2.** (*fig.*) servile.

рабств|о, а, *n.* slavery, servitude; отмена ~а abolition of slavery.

рабфак, а, *m.* (*hist.*) (*abbr. of* рабочий факультет) 'rabfak'; workers' school (*educational establishment in existence during the first years after the Russian Revolution, set up to pre-*

pare workers and peasants for higher education).

рабфаков|ец, ца, *m.* 'rabfak' student.

рабфак|овский, *adj. of* ~.

рабын|я, и, *g. pl.* ~ь, *f.* slave, bondwoman, bondmaid.

раввин, а, *m.* rabbi.

равелин, а, *m.* (*mil., hist.*) ravelin.

равендук, а, *m.* (*text.*) duck.

равенств|о, а, *n.* equality; знак ~а (*math.*) sign of equality, equals sign.

равнени|е, я, *n.* **1.** dressing, alignment; р. налево, р. направо! (*mil. words of command*) left dress!, right dress! **2.** (на+*a.*) emulation (of).

равнин|а, ы, *f.* plain.

равнин|ный, *adj. of* ~а; р. житель plainsman; ~ная местность flat country.

равно¹, *adv.* **1.** alike, in like manner. **2.** (*as conj.*) р. как (и), а р. и as well as; and also, as also; (*after neg.*) nor; золотой браслет, р. как и другие её драгоценности, пропал a gold bracelet, as well as other jewellery of hers, had disappeared.

равно², *n. pred. form of* равный **1.** (*math.*) make(s), equals, is; три плюс три р. шести three plus three equals six. **2.** всё р. it is all the same, it makes no difference; *as adv.* all the same; всё р., что it is just the same as, it is equivalent to; мне всё р. I don't mind; it's all the same, all one to me; я всё р. вам позвоню I will ring you all the same; не всё ли р.? what difference does it make?, what's the difference?; what does it matter?

равно- equi-, iso-.

равнобедренный, *adj.* (*math.*) isosceles.

равновелик|ий (~, ~а), *adj.* (*math.*) equivalent; (*phys.*) isometric, equigraphic; ~ие треугольники equivalent triangles.

равновеси|е, я, *n.* equilibrium (*also fig.*); balance, equipoise; душевное р. mental equilibrium; политическое р. balance of power; вывести из ~я to disturb the equilibrium (of), upset the balance (of); привести в р. to balance; сохранять р. to keep one's balance.

равнодействующ|ая, ей, *f.* (*math., phys.*) resultant (force).

равноденственный, *adj.* equinoctial, equidiurnal.

равноденстви|е, я, *n.* equinox; весеннее, осеннее р. vernal, autumnal equinox; точка ~я equinoctial point.

равнодуши|е, я, *n.* indifference.

равнодуш|ный (~ен, ~на), *adj.* (к) indifferent (to).

равнозначащий, *adj.* equivalent, equipollent.

равнознач|ный (~ен, ~на), *adj.* = ~ащий.

равномерност|ь, и, *f.* evenness; uniformity.

равномéр|ный (~ен, ~на), *adj.* even; (*phys.*, *tech.*) uniform; ~ное распределéние even distribution.

равноóсный, *adj.* (*math.*, *phys.*) equiaxial.

равноотстоя́щий, *adj.* (*math.*) equidistant.

равнопра́ви|е, я, *n.* equality (of rights), possession of equal rights.

равнопра́в|ный (~ен, ~на), *adj.* possessing, enjoying equal rights.

равноси́л|ьный (~ен, ~ьна), *adj.* 1. of equal strength; equally matched. 2. (+*d.*) equal (to), equivalent (to), tantamount (to); э́то ~ьно измéне it is tantamount to treachery, it amounts to treachery.

равносторóнний, *adj.* (*math.*) equilateral.

равноуго́льный, *adj.* (*math.*) equiangular.

равноускóренный, *adj.* (*phys.*, *tech.*) uniformly accelerated.

равноцéн|ный (~ен, ~на), *adj.* of equal value, of equal worth; equivalent.

ра́в|ный (~ен, ~на́, ~нó), *adj.* equal; ~ным óбразом equally, likewise; при прóчих ~ных услóвиях other things being equal; емý нет ~ного he has no equal, there is no match for him.

равня́|ть, ю, *impf.* (*of с~*) 1. to make even; to treat equally; р. счёт (*sport*) to equalize. 2. (с+*i.*; *coll.*) to compare (with), treat as equal (to).

равня́|ться, юсь, *impf.* (*of с~*) 1. (по+*d.*) (*mil.*) to dress; ~йсь! (*word of command*) right dress!; р. в заты́лок to cover off. 2. (с+*i.*; *coll.*) to compete (with), compare (with), match; по подáче никтó не мог р. с ним (*sport*) in serving no one could compete with him. 3. *impf. only* (+*d.*) to equal, be equal (to); (*fig.*) to be equivalent (to), be tantamount (to), amount (to); два́жды пять ~ется десяти́ twice five is ten.

рагý, *indecl.*, *n.* (*cul.*) ragout.

рад (~а, ~о), *pred. adj.* (+*d.*; +*inf.*; что) glad (of; to; that); я был óчень р. слýчаю поговори́ть с ни́ми I was very glad of the opportunity to talk to them; óчень р. (познакóмиться с ва́ми)! (*acknowledgement of introduction*) very pleased to meet you!; р. стара́ться! (*i*) (*coll.*) gladly!, with pleasure!; (*ii*) (*obs.*; *soldiers' acknowledgement of commendation*) very good, sir!; и не р., сам не р. (*coll.*) I, etc., regret it; I, etc., am sorry; и не р., что пошёл I'm sorry I went; р. не р. (*coll.*) willy-nilly, like it or not; р.-радёшенек (*coll.*) pleased as Punch, chuffed.

ра́д|а, ы, *f.* council, soviet (*in Ukraine and Byelorussia*).

рада́р, а, *m.* radar.

рада́р|ный, *adj.* of ~.

радéни|е, я, *n.* (*obs.*) 1. zeal. 2. (*rel.*) rites (*of some Russian sects*).

радé|ть, ю, ешь, *impf.* (*obs.*) 1. (*pf.* по~) (+*d.*) to oblige; (о+*p.*) to be concerned (about). 2. *impf. only* (*rel.*; *of some Russian sects*) to carry out rites.

ра́дж|а, и, *m.* rajah.

ра́ди, *prep.*+*g.* for the sake of; чегó р.? what for?; шýтки р. for fun; р. Бóга, р. всегó свято́го (*coll.*) for God's sake, for goodness' sake.

радиа́льный, *adj.* (*math.*, *tech.*) radial.

радиа́тор, а, *m.* radiator.

радиацио́нный, *adj.* radiation.

радиа́ци|я, и, *f.* radiation.

ра́диев|ый, *adj.* radium; ~ая ка́псула radium seed.

ра́ди|й, я, *m.* (*chem.*) radium.

радика́л¹, а, *m.* (*math.*, *chem.*) radical.

радика́л², а, *m.* (*polit.*) radical.

радикали́зм, а, *m.* (*polit.*) radicalism.

радика́льност|ь, и, *f.* 1. (*polit.*) radicalism. 2. radical nature, drastic nature, sweeping character.

радика́л|ьный (~ен, ~ьна), *adj.* 1. (*polit.*) radical. 2. radical, drastic, sweeping; ~ьные измене́ния sweeping changes; ~ьные ме́ры drastic measures; ~ьное сре́дство drastic remedy.

ра́дио, *indecl.*, *n.* 1. radio, wireless; по р. by radio, over the air; переда́ть по р. to broadcast; слýшать р. to listen in. 2. radio set, wireless; провести́ р. to install a radio set, wireless. 3. (*coll.*) public address system, tannoy (system).

радиоакти́вност|ь, и, *f.* (*chem.*, *phys.*) radio-activity.

радиоакти́в|ный (~ен, ~на), *adj.* (*chem.*, *phys.*) radio-active; ~ное загрязне́ние, ~ное зараже́ние radio-active contamination; р. изото́п radio-active isotope, radio-isotope; ~ные оса́дки radio-active fall-out; р. ряд radio-active family, radio-active series, disintegration series, decay chain; р. яд radio-active poison, radiation poison.

радиоаппара́т, а, *m.* radio set.

радиобиологи́ческий, *adj.* radio-biological.

радиобиоло́ги|я, и, *f.* radio-biology.

радиовеща́ни|е, я, *n.* broadcasting.

радиовеща́тельн|ый, *adj.* broadcasting; ~ая ста́нция broadcasting station, transmitter.

радиоволн|а́, ы́, *f.* radio-wave.

радиогра́мм|а, ы, *f.* radio-telegram, wireless message.

радио́граф, а, *m.* radiographer.

радиографи́ческий, *adj.* radiographic.

радиогра́фи|я, и, *f.* radiography.

радиозо́нд, а, *m.* radio-sounding apparatus.

радио́л|а, ы, *f.* radiogram.

радио́лог, а, *m.* radiologist.

радиологи́ческ|ий, *adj.* radiological; ~ая устано́вка radiological unit.

радиоло́ги|я, и, *f.* radiology.

радиолока́тор, а, *m.* radio-location set; radar set.

радиолок|ацио́нный, *adj. of* ~а́ция.

радиолока́ци|я, и, *f.* radio-location, radar.

радиолюби́тел|ь, я, *m.* radio amateur, 'ham'; wireless enthusiast.

радиома́чт|а, ы, *f.* radio-mast, wireless mast.

радиома́|як, а́, *m.* radio-beacon.

радиопе́ленг, а, *m.* radio directional bearing.

радиопеленга́тор, а, *m.* radio direction finder.

радиопеленга́ци|я, и, *f.* radio homing.

радиопереда́тчик, а, *m.* (wireless) transmitter.

радиопереда́ча, и, *f.* transmission, broadcast.

радиоперекли́чк|а, и, *f.* radio link-up.

радиоперехва́т, а, *m.* radio interception; radio intercept.

радиополуко́мпас, а, *m.* radio compass.

радиопостано́вк|а, и, *f.* radio show.

радиоприбо́р, а, *m.* wireless (set), radio (set).

радиоприёмник, а, *m.* (wireless) receiver; wireless (set), radio (set).

радиору́бк|а, и, *f.* (*naut., aeron.*) radio room, radio cabin.

радиосвя́з|ь, и, *f.* wireless communication.

радиосе́т|ь, и, *f.* radio network.

радиослу́шател|ь, я, *m.* (radio) listener.

радиоста́нци|я, и, *f.* radio station, broadcasting station.

радиотелегра́ф, а, *m.* radio telegraph.

радиотелеграфи́|я, и, *f.* radio-telegraphy, wireless telegraphy.

радиотелефо́н, а, *m.* radio-telephone.

радиотерапи́|я, и, *f.* radio-therapy.

радиоте́хник, а, *m.* radio mechanic.

радиоте́хник|а, и, *f.* radio engineering.

радио|техни́ческий, *adj. of* ~те́хника.

радиотрансляцио́нный, *adj.* broadcasting.

радиоу́з|ел, ла́, *m.* radio relay centre.

радиофика́ци|я, и, *f.* installation of radio.

радиофици́р|овать, ую, *impf. and pf.* to instal radio (in), equip with radio.

радиохими́ческий, *adj.* radiochemical.

радиохи́ми|я, и, *f.* radiochemistry.

ради́р|овать, ую, *impf. and pf.* to radio.

ради́ст, а, *m.* wireless operator, radio operator; (*naut.*) telegraphist.

ра́диус, а, *m.* radius.

ра́д|овать, ую, *impf.* (*of* об~) to gladden, make glad, make happy; р. се́рдце to rejoice the heart.

ра́д|оваться, уюсь, *impf.* (*of* об~) (+*d.*) to be glad (at), be happy (at), rejoice (in).

ра́дост|ный (~ен, ~на), *adj.* glad, joyous, joyful; ~ное изве́стие glad tidings, good news.

ра́дост|ь, и, *f.* gladness, joy; р. жи́зни joie de vivre; не чу́вствовать себя́ от ~и to be beside oneself with joy; на ~ях (+*g.*; *coll.*) in celebration (of), to celebrate; с ~ью with pleasure, gladly; моя́ р., р. моя́ my darling.

ра́дуг|а, и, *f.* rainbow.

ра́дужно, *adv.* cheerfully; р. смотре́ть (на+*a.*) to look on the bright side (of).

ра́дужн|ый, *adj.* 1. iridescent, opalescent; ~ая оболо́чка (гла́за) (*anat.*) iris. 2. cheerful; optimistic; ~ые наде́жды high hopes; ~ое настрое́ние high spirits.

раду́ши|е, я, *n.* cordiality.

раду́ш|ный (~ен, ~на), *adj.* cordial; р. приём hearty welcome; р. хозя́ин kind host.

ра|ёк, йка́, *m.* (*theatr.*; *obs.*) gallery; the gods.

раж, а, *m.* (*coll.*) rage, passion; войти́ в р., прийти́ в р. to fly into a rage.

раз[1], а, *pl.* ~ы́, ~, *m.* 1. time; occasion; оди́н р., ка́к-то р. once; два ~а twice; мно́го р. many times; ещё р. once again, once more; не р. more than once; time and again; ни ~у not once, never; р. навсегда́ once (and) for all; р. в день once a day; вся́кий р. every time, each time; вся́кий р., когда́ whenever; ино́й р. sometimes, now and again; во второ́й р. for the second time; в друго́й р. another time, some other time; в са́мый р. (*coll.*) at the right moment; just right; до друго́го ~а till another time; р. за ~ом time after time; на э́тот р. this time, on this occasion, for (this) once; с пе́рвого ~а from the very first; вот тебе́ (и) р.! (*coll.*) well, I never!; как р. just, exactly; как р. то the very thing. 2. (*num.*) one.

раз[2], *adv.* once, one day.

раз[3], *conj.* if; since; р. вы бу́дете во Фра́нции, не смо́жете ли вы прие́хать и сюда́? if you are going to be in France, can't you come here, too?

раз- (разо-, разъ-, рас-) *verbal prefix indicating* 1. division into parts (dis-, un-). 2. distribution; direction of action in different directions; (dis-). 3. action in reverse (un-). 4. termination of action *or* state. 5. intensification of action.

разба́в|ить, лю, ишь, *pf.* (*of* ~ля́ть) to dilute.

разбавля́|ть, ю, *impf. of* разба́вить.

разбаза́ривани|е, я, *n.* (*coll.*) squandering.

разбаза́рива|ть, ю, *impf. of* разбаза́рить.

разбаза́р|ить, ю, ишь, *pf.* (*of* ~ивать) (*coll.*) to squander.

разба́лива|ться, юсь, *impf. of* разболе́ться.

разба́лтыва|ть(ся), ю(сь), *impf. of* разбол-та́ть(ся).

разбе́г, а, *m.* run, running start; пры́гнуть с ~у to take a running jump; нырну́ть с ~у to take a running dive; прыжо́к с ~у

running jump; р. при взлёте (*aeron.*) take-
-off run.

разбегá|ться, юсь, *impf. of* разбежáться.

разбе|жáться, гýсь, жúшься, гýтся, *pf.* (*of*
~**гáться**) **1.** to take a run, run up. **2.** to
scatter, disperse; р. по местáм to run to
one's places, (*mil.*) to one's stations, posts.
3. (*of thoughts, etc.*) to be scattered; глазá у
меня ~жáлись I was dazzled.

разбере|дúть, жý, дúшь, *pf. of* бередúть.

разбивá|ть(ся), ю(сь), *impf. of* разбúть(ся).

разбúвк|а, и, *f.* **1.** laying out (*of a garden,
etc.*). **2.** (*typ.*) spacing (out).

разбинт|овáть, ýю, *pf.* (*of* ~**óвывать**) to
remove a bandage (from).

разбинт|овáться, ýюсь, *pf.* (*of* ~**óвываться**)
1. to remove one's bandage(s). **2.** (*of a
bandage*) to come off, come undone. **3.** to
come unbandaged; ногá у меня ~овáлась
the bandage has come off my leg.

разбинтóвыва|ть(ся), ю(сь), *impf. of* раз-
бинтовáть(ся).

разбирáтельств|о, а, *n.* (*leg.*) examination,
investigation; судéбное р. court examination.

разбирá|ть, ю, *impf.* **1.** *impf. of* разобрáть.
2. (*impf. only*) to be fastidious; не ~я indis-
criminately.

разбирá|ться, юсь, *impf. of* разобрáться.

разбитнóй, *adj.* (*coll.*) bright, sprightly; sharp.

разбúт|ый, *p.p.p. of* ~**ь** *and adj.* (*coll.*) jaded,
down.

раз|бúть, обью, обьёшь, *pf.* (*of* ~**бивáть**)
1. (*impf. also* бить) to break, smash; р.
вдрéбезги to smash to smithereens. **2.** to
divide (up); to break up, break down; р.
на грýппы to divide up into groups; р.
комплéкт to break a set. **3.** to lay out,
mark out; р. кóлышками to peg out; р.
лáгерь to pitch a camp. **4.** to damage
severely, hurt badly; to fracture; р. комý-н.
нос в кровь to make someone's nose bleed.
5. to beat, defeat, smash (*also fig.*); р. чьи-н.
дóводы to destroy someone's arguments.
6. (*typ.*) to space (out).

раз|бúться, обьюсь, обьёшься, *pf.* (*of*
~**бивáться**) **1.** to break, get broken, get
smashed. **2.** to divide, break up. **3.** to hurt
oneself badly; to smash oneself up.

разблагове|стить, щу, стишь, *pf. of* блáго-
вестить.

разблокúр|овать, ую, *pf.* (*mil.*) to lift the
blockade (of).

разбогатé|ть, ю, ешь, *pf. of* богатéть.

разбó|й, я, *m.* robbery, brigandage; мор-
скóй р. piracy.

разбóйник, а, *m.* **1.** robber, brigand; морскóй р. pirate; р. с большóй дорóги highwayman. **2.** (*joc.; affect. form of address to
child, etc.*) scamp!, scallywag!

разбóйнича|ть, ю, *impf.* to rob, plunder.

разбóйни|чий, *adj. of* ~**к**; р. притóн den of
thieves.

разболé|ться[1], юсь, ешься, *pf.* (*of* разбáли-
ваться) (*coll.*) to become ill; он совсéм ~лся
his health has completely cracked.

разбол|éться[2], ится, *pf.* (*of* разбáливаться)
to begin to ache badly.

разбóлт|анный, *p.p.p. of* ~**áть[1]** *and adj.* (*fig.*)
disorderly.

разболтá|ть[1], ю, *pf.* (*of* разбáлтывать) **1.** to
shake up, stir up. **2.** to loosen.

разболтá|ть[2], ю, *pf.* (*of* разбáлтывать) (*coll.*)
to blab out, give away.

разболтá|ться, юсь, *pf.* (*of* разбáлтываться)
1. to mix (*as result of stirring*). **2.** to come
loose, work loose. **3.** (*fig.*) to get out of
hand; to come unstuck.

разбомб|úть, лю, úшь, *pf.* (*no impf.*) to
destroy by bombing.

разбóр, а, *m.* **1.** stripping, dismantling.
2. buying up. **3.** sorting out. **4.** investigation; р. дéла (*leg.*) trial, hearing (*of a case*).
5. (*gram.*) parsing; analysis. **6.** critique.
7. selectiveness; без ~у indiscriminately,
promiscuously; с ~ом discriminatingly,
fastidiously. **8.** sort, quality; пéрвого, вто-
рóго ~a first, second quality.

разбóрк|а, и, *f.* **1.** sorting out. **2.** stripping,
dismantling, taking to pieces.

разбóрный, *adj.* collapsible.

разбóрчивост|ь, и, *f.* **1.** fastidiousness;
scrupulousness. **2.** legibility.

разбóрчив|ый (~, ~а), *adj.* **1.** fastidious,
exacting; discriminating; scrupulous. **2.**
legible.

разбран|úть, ю, úшь, *pf.* (*coll.*) to berate;
to blow up.

разбран|úться, юсь, úшься, *pf.* (с+*i.; coll.*)
to fall out (with); to quarrel (with),
squabble (with).

разбрáсыватель|ь, я, *m.* (*agric.*) spreader.

разбрáсыва|ть, ю, *impf. of* разбросáть.

разбрáсыва|ться, юсь, *impf.* **1.** *impf. of*
разбросáться. **2.** (*fig.*) to dissipate one's
energies; to try to do too much at once.

разбредá|ться, юсь, *impf. of* разбрестúсь.

разбре|стúсь, дýсь, дёшься, *past* ~**лся,**
~**лáсь,** *pf.* (*of* ~**дáться**) to disperse; to
straggle; р. по домáм to disperse and go
home.

разбрóд, а, *m.* disorder.

разбронúр|овать, ую, *pf.* to cancel reser-
vation (of), de-reserve.

разбрóсанност|ь, и, *f.* **1.** sparseness; scat-
tered nature. **2.** (*fig.*) disconnectedness, in-
coherence.

разбрóс|анный, *p.p.p. of* ~**áть** *and adj.*
1. sparse, scattered; straggling. **2.** (*fig.*) dis-
connected, incoherent.

разброса́|ть, ю, *pf.* (*of* разбра́сывать) to throw about; to scatter, spread, strew; р. наво́з to spread manure; р. де́ньги на ве́тер to squander one's money.

разброса́|ться, юсь, *pf.* (*of* разбра́сываться) to throw oneself *or* one's things about.

разбры́з|гать, жу, жешь, *pf.* (*of* ~гивать) to splash; to spray.

разбры́згива|ть, ю, *impf. of* разбры́згать.

разбу|ди́ть, жу́, ~дишь, *pf. of* буди́ть.

разбух|а́ть, а́ет, *impf. of* ~нуть.

разбу́х|нуть, нет, *past* ~, ~ла, *pf.* (*of* ~а́ть) to swell (*also fig.*).

разбуш|ева́ться, у́юсь, *pf.* 1. (*of a storm*) to rage; to blow up; (*of the sea*) to run high. 2. (*coll.*) to fly into a rage.

разбуя́н|иться, юсь, ишься, *pf.* (*coll.*) to fly into a rage.

развя́жнича|ться, юсь, *pf.* (*coll.*) to put on airs.

разва́л, а, *m.* breakdown, disintegration, disruption; disorganization.

развал|ец, ьца, *m.* (*coll.*) ходи́ть с ~ьцем to shamble; рабо́тать с ~ьцем to go slow.

разва́лива|ть(ся), ю(сь), *impf. of* развали́ть(ся).

разва́лин|а, ы, *f.* 1. *pl.* ruins; гру́да ~ a heap of débris; лежа́ть в ~ах to be in ruins; преврати́ть в ~ы to reduce to ruins. 2. (*fig., coll.*; *of a person*) wreck, ruin.

развал|и́ть, ю, ~ишь, *pf.* (*of* ~ивать) 1. to pull down (*a building, etc.*). 2. (*fig.*) to mess up.

развал|и́ться, ю́сь, ~ишься, *pf.* (*of* ~иваться) 1. to fall down, tumble down, collapse. 2. (*fig.*) to go to pieces, fall to pieces, break down. 3. (*coll.*) to lounge, sprawl.

разва́л|ьца, ьцы, *f.* = ~ец.

разва́рива|ть(ся), ю(сь), *impf. of* развари́ть(ся).

развар|и́ть, ю, ~ишь, *pf.* (*of* ~ивать) to boil soft.

развар|и́ться, ю́сь, ~ишься, *pf.* (*of* ~иваться) to be boiled soft; р. в ка́шу to be boiled to a pulp.

разварно́й, *adj.* boiled.

ра́зве 1. *interrog. particle, neutral or indicating that neg. answer is expected*; +*neg.* indicates *that affirmative answer is expected* р. они́ все вместя́тся в э́ту маши́ну? will they (really) all get in this car?; р. ты не знал, что он ру́сский? didn't you know that he is Russian?, surely you knew that he is Russian? 2. *interrog. particle, expressing hesitation about course of action to be followed* (+*inf.*; *coll.*) р. отложи́ть нам пое́здку? perhaps we had better postpone the trip?; р. поговори́ть вам с её отцо́м? perhaps you should have, mightn't it be a good thing to have a talk with her father? 3. р. (что), р. (то́лько) *as*

adv. only; perhaps; *as conj.* except that, only; кро́ме р. (+*g.*) except perhaps, with the possible exception (of); он вы́глядит так же как всегда́, р. что похуде́л he looks the same as ever, except that he has lost weight. 4. *conj.* (*obs.*) unless.

развева́|ть, ю, *impf.* 1. *impf. of* разве́ять. 2. *impf. only* to blow about; ве́тер ~л зна́мя the banner was flapping, streaming in the wind.

развева́|ться, юсь, *impf.* 1. *impf. of* разве́яться. 2. *impf. only* to fly, flutter; с ~ющимися знамёнами with banners flying.

развед- *abbr. of* разве́дывательный.

разве́д|ать, аю, *pf.* (*of* ~ывать) 1. (о+р.; *coll.*) to find out (about), ascertain. 2. (*mil.*) to reconnoitre. 3. (на+а.; *geol.*) to prospect (for); *pf. only* to locate; р. на нефть to prospect for oil.

разведе́ни|е[1], я, *n.* breeding, rearing; cultivation.

разведе́ни|е[2], я, *n.* opening, swinging open (*of a bascule bridge or draw-bridge*).

разведённ|ый, *p.p.p. of* развести́ *and adj.* divorced; *as noun* р., ~ого, *m. and* ~ая, ~ой, *f.* divorcee.

разве́дк|а, и, *f.* 1. (*geol., etc.*) prospecting. 2. (*mil.*) reconnaissance; звукова́я р. sound ranging; опти́ческая р. flash ranging; р. бо́ем reconnaissance in force; р. в глубину́ reconnaissance in depth. 3. (*mil.*) reconnaissance party. 4. secret service, intelligence service.

разве́дочн|ый, *adj.* (*geol.*) prospecting, exploratory; ~ая сква́жина test well.

разве́дчик[1], а, *m.* 1. (*mil.*) scout. 2. secret service man; intelligence officer. 3. (*geol.*) prospector.

разве́дчик[2], а, *m.* reconnaissance aircraft.

разве́дывательн|ый, *adj.* (*mil.*) 1. reconnaissance; р. бой probing attack; reconnaissance in force; р. дозо́р reconnaissance patrol; р. отря́д reconnaissance detachment. 2. intelligence; р. отде́л intelligence section; ~ая рабо́та intelligence work, secret-service work; ~ая слу́жба Intelligence Service (*corresponding to Intelligence Corps in British Army*); Гла́вное ~ое управле́ние Main Intelligence Directorate (*in U.S.S.R. Ministry of Defence*).

разве́дыва|ть, ю, *impf. of* разве́дать.

развез|ти́[1], у́, ёшь, *past* ~, ~ла́, *pf.* (*of* развози́ть) to convey, deliver.

развез|ти́[2], у́, ёшь, *past* ~, ~ла́, *pf.* (*of* развози́ть) (*coll.*) 1. to exhaust, wear out; от жары́ нас ~ло́ (*impers.*) we were exhausted from the heat. 2. to make impassable, make unfit for traffic; доро́гу ~ло́ от дожде́й (*impers.*) the road was made impassable by rain.

развéива|ть(ся), ю(сь), *impf. of* развéять-(ся).

развенч|áть, áю, *pf.* (*of* ~ивать) **1.** to dethrone. **2.** (*fig.*) to debunk.

развéнчива|ть, ю, *impf. of* развенчáть.

разверз|áть(ся), áю(сь), *impf. of* ~нуть(ся).

разве́рз|нуть, ну, нешь, *past* ~, ~ла, *pf.* (*of* ~áть) (*obs., poet.*) to open wide.

разве́рз|нуться, нусь, нешься, *past* ~ся, ~лась, *pf.* (*of* ~áться) (*obs., poet.*) to open wide, yawn, gape.

развёрн|утый, *p.p.p. of* ~у́ть *and adj.* **1.** extensive, large-scale, all-out. **2.** detailed; ~утая програ́мма detailed programme, comprehensive programme. **3.** (*mil.*) deployed; р. строй extended line formation.

развер|ну́ть, ну́, нёшь, *pf.* (*of* ~тывать *and* развора́чивать) **1.** to unfold; to unroll; to unwrap; to unfurl; р. ковёр to unroll a carpet; р. зна́мя to unfurl a banner. **2.** (*mil.*) to deploy. **3.** (в+*a.; mil.*) to expand (into); р. батальо́н в полк to expand a battalion into a regiment. **4.** (*fig.*) to show, display. **5.** (*fig.*) to develop; to expand; р. аргумента́цию to develop a line of argument; р. торго́влю to expand trade. **6.** to turn; to swing (about, around). **7.** (*tech.*) to ream, broach. **8.** (*radar*) to scan.

развер|ну́ться, ну́сь, нёшься, *pf.* (*of* ~тываться *and* развора́чиваться) **1.** to unfold; to unroll; to come unwrapped. **2.** (*mil.*) to deploy. **3.** (в+*a.; mil.*) to expand (into), be expanded (into). **4.** (*fig.*) to show oneself, display oneself. **5.** (*fig.*) to develop; to spread; to expand. **6.** to turn, swing (about, around); (*naut.*) to slew (about).

разверст|áть, áю, *pf.* (*of* ~ывать) to distribute, allot, apportion.

развёрстк|а, и, *f.* allotment, apportionment.

разверстыва|ть, ю, *impf. of* разверстáть.

развёр|стый, *p.p.p. of* ~знуть *and adj.* (*obs., poet.*) open, yawning, gaping; ~стая пасть gaping maw.

развер|тéть, чу́, ~тишь, *pf.* (*of* ~чивать) **1.** to unscrew. **2.** (*tech.*) to ream.

развёртк|а¹, и, *f.* **1.** (*math.*) development, evolvement. **2.** (*tech.*) reaming. **3.** (*radar*) scanning.

развёртк|а², и, *f.* (*tech.*) reamer, broach bit.

развёртывани|е, я, *n.* **1.** unfolding; unrolling; unwrapping. **2.** (*mil.*) deployment. **3.** (*fig.*) development; expansion.

развёртыва|ть(ся), ю(сь), *impf. of* развернýть(ся).

разве́рчива|ть, ю, *impf. of* развертéть.

развéс, а, *m.* weighing out.

развесел|и́ть, ю́, и́шь, *pf.* to cheer up, amuse.

развесел|и́ться, ю́сь, и́шься, *pf.* to cheer up.

развесёлый, *adj.* (*coll.*) merry, gay.

развéсист|ый (~, ~a), *adj.* branchy; р. кашта́н spreading chestnut; ~ая клю́ква myth, fable (*of credulous travellers' tales*).

разве́|сить¹, шу, сишь, *pf.* (*of* ~шивать) to weigh out.

разве́|сить², шу, сишь, *pf.* (*of* ~шивать) **1.** to hang. **2.** to spread (*branches*); р. у́ши (*fig., coll.*) to listen open-mouthed.

разве́|сить³, шу, сишь, *pf.* (*of* ~шивать) to hang.

развесно́й, *adj.* sold by weight.

разве|сти́¹, ду́, дёшь, *past* ~л, ~ла́, *pf.* (*of* разводи́ть) **1.** to take, conduct; р. детéй по дома́м to take the children to their homes; р. войска́ по кварти́рам to disperse troops to their billets; р. часовы́х to post sentries. **2.** (*in var. senses*) to part, separate; р. мост to raise a bridge, swing a bridge open; р. пилу́ to set a saw; р. рука́ми to spread one's hands (*in a gesture of helplessness*). **3.** to divorce. **4.** to dilute; to dissolve; р. порошо́к водо́ю, в воде́ to dissolve powder in water.

разве|сти́², ду́, дёшь, *past* ~л, ~ла́, *pf.* (*of* разводи́ть) **1.** to breed, rear; to cultivate; р. сад to plant a garden; р. парк to lay out a park. **2.** to start (*a source of heat or power*); р. костёр to make a camp fire; р. ого́нь to light a fire, kindle a fire; р. пары́ to raise steam, get up steam. **3.** (*fig., coll.; pejor.*) to start; р. чепуху́ to start talking nonsense.

разве|сти́сь¹, ду́сь, дёшься, *past* ~лся, ~ла́сь, *pf.* (*of* разводи́ться) (с+*i.*) to divorce, be divorced (from).

разве|сти́сь², ду́сь, дёшься, *past* ~лся, ~ла́сь, *pf.* (*of* разводи́ться) to breed, multiply.

разветв|и́ться, и́тся, *pf.* (*of* ~ля́ться) to branch; to fork; to ramify.

разветвлéни|е, я, *n.* **1.** branching; ramification; forking. **2.** branch; fork (*of road, etc.*); р. нéрва (*anat.*) radicle.

разветвля́|ться, юсь, *impf. of* разветви́ться.

развéш|ать, аю, *pf.* (*of* ~ивать) to hang.

развéшива|ть, ю, *impf. of* развéсить *and* развéшать.

разве́|ять, ю, ешь, *pf.* **1.** (*impf.* ~ивать) to scatter, disperse; (*fig.*) to dispel; р. миф to shatter a myth. **2.** (*impf.* ~ва́ть) to cause to flutter.

разве́|яться, юсь, ешься, *pf.* (*of* ~иваться *and* ~ва́ться) to disperse; (*fig.*) to be dispelled.

развива́|ть(ся), ю(сь), *impf. of* разви́ть(ся).

разви́лин|а, ы, *f.* fork, bifurcation.

разви́лист|ый (~, ~a), *adj.* forked.

развин|ти́ть, чу́, ти́шь, *pf.* (*of* ⌐чивать) to unscrew.

развин|ти́ться, чу́сь, ти́шься, *pf.* (*of* ⌐чиваться) 1. to come unscrewed. 2. (*fig.*) to come unstuck.

разви́нченност|ь, и, *f.* (*coll.*) unbalance.

разви́н|ченный, *p.p.p. of* ⌐ти́ть *and adj.* (*coll.*) 1. unstrung, unstuck. 2. (*of gait*) unsteady, lurching.

разви́нчива|ть(ся), ю(сь), *impf. of* развинти́ть(ся).

разви́ти|е, я, *n.* 1. (*in var. senses*) development; evolution; р. бо́я (*mil.*) progress of battle. 2. (*intellectual*) maturity.

развит|о́й (ра́звит, ⌐а́, ра́звито), *adj.* 1. developed. 2. (intellectually) mature; adult.

разви́т|ый (⌐, ⌐а́, ⌐о), *p.p.p. of* ⌐ь.

раз|ви́ть[1], овью́, овьёшь, *past* ⌐ви́л, ⌐вила́, ⌐ви́ло, *pf.* (*of* ⌐вива́ть) to unwind, untwist.

раз|ви́ть[2], овью́, овьёшь, *past* ⌐ви́л, ⌐вила́, ⌐ви́ло, *pf.* (*of* ⌐вива́ть) (*in var. senses*) to develop; р. мускулату́ру to develop one's muscles; р. мысль to develop an idea; р. ско́рость to gather, pick up speed.

раз|ви́ться[1], овью́сь, овьёшься, *past* ⌐ви́лся, ⌐вила́сь, *pf.* (*of* ⌐вива́ться) to untwist; (*of hair*) to come uncurled, lose its curl.

раз|ви́ться[2], овью́сь, овьёшься, *past* ⌐ви́лся, ⌐вила́сь, *pf.* (*of* ⌐вива́ться) (*in var. senses*) to develop.

развлека́тел|ьный (⌐ен, ⌐ьна), *adj.* entertaining; ⌐ьное чте́ние light reading.

развлека́|ться, ю́сь, *impf. of* развле́чь(ся).

развлече́ни|е, я, *n.* entertainment; amusement; diversion.

развле́|чь, ку́, чёшь, ку́т, *past* ⌐к, ⌐кла́, *pf.* (*of* ⌐ка́ть) to entertain, amuse; to divert.

развле́|чься, ку́сь, чёшься, ку́тся, *past* ⌐кся, ⌐кла́сь, *pf.* (*of* ⌐ка́ться) 1. to have a good time; to amuse oneself. 2. to be diverted, be distracted.

разво́д[1], а, *m.* divorce; дать р. кому́-н. to give someone a divorce, agree to a divorce; проце́сс о ⌐е divorce suit, divorce proceedings; они́ в ⌐е they are divorced.

разво́д[2], а, *m.* (*mil.*) р. карау́лов guard mounting; р. часовы́х posting of sentries.

разво́д[3], а, *m.* breeding; оста́вить на р. to keep for breeding.

разво|ди́ть(ся), жу́(сь), ⌐дишь(ся), *impf. of* развести́(сь).

разво́дк|а[1], и, *f.* separation; р. мо́ста raising of a bridge, swinging a bridge open; р. пилы́ saw setting.

разво́дк|а[2], и, *f.* (*tech.*) saw set.

разводно́й, *adj.* р. ключ adjustable spanner, monkey wrench; р. мост drawbridge.

разво́д|ы, ов, *no sing.* 1. design, pattern.

2. stains; черни́льные р. ink-stains.

разво́дь|е, я, *g. pl.* ⌐ев, *n.* 1. (*dial.*) spring floods. 2. patch of ice-free water.

разводя́щ|ий, его, *m.* (*mil.*) corporal of the guard; guard commander.

разво|ева́ться, ю́юсь, ю́ешься, *pf.* (*coll.*) to bluster.

разво́з, а, *m.* conveyance.

разво|зи́ть, жу́, ⌐зишь, *impf. of* развезти́.

разво|зи́ться, жу́сь, ⌐зишься, *pf.* (*coll.*) (*of children*) to kick up a din.

развозк|а, и, *f.* 1. conveying; delivery. 2. (*coll.*) delivery cart.

разволн|ова́ть, у́ю, *pf.* to excite, agitate.

разволн|ова́ться, у́юсь, *pf.* to get excited, get agitated.

развора́чива|ть, ю, *impf. of* разверну́ть *and* развороти́ть.

развора́чива|ться, юсь, *impf. of* разверну́ться.

развор|ова́ть, у́ю, *pf.* (*of* ⌐о́вывать) to loot, clean out.

разворо́выва|ть, ю, *impf. of* разворова́ть.

разворо́т, а, *m.* 1. (*aeron., etc.*) turn; (*of motor transport*) U-turn. 2. (*coll.*) development; р. торго́вли growth of trade.

разворо|ти́ть, чу́, ⌐тишь, *pf.* (*of* развора́чивать) 1. to make havoc (of); to knock to pieces. 2. to smash up, break up.

разворош|и́ть, у́, и́шь, *pf.* to turn upside down, scatter.

развра́т, а, *m.* debauchery, depravity, dissipation.

разврати́тел|ь, я, *m.* debaucher, seducer, corrupter.

разврa|ти́ть, щу́, ти́шь, *pf.* (*of* ⌐ща́ть) 1. to debauch, corrupt. 2. (*fig.*) to deprave.

разврa|ти́ться, щу́сь, ти́шься, *pf.* (*of* ⌐ща́ться) to become corrupted, become depraved; to go to the bad.

развра́тник, а, *m.* debauchee, profligate, libertine.

развра́тнича|ть, ю, *impf.* to indulge in debauchery, lead a depraved life.

развра́тност|ь, и, *f.* depravity, profligacy; corruptness.

развра́т|ный (⌐ен, ⌐на), *adj.* debauched, depraved, profligate; corrupt.

разврaщá|ть(ся), ю(сь), *impf. of* разврати́ть(ся).

развращённост|ь, и, *f.* corruptness.

разврa|щённый, *p.p.p. of* ⌐ти́ть *and adj.* corrupt.

разв|ы́ться, о́юсь, о́ешься, *pf.* (*coll.*) to begin to howl, set up a howl.

развью́чива|ть, ю, *impf. of* развью́чить.

развью́ч|ить, у, ишь, *pf.* (*of* ⌐ивать) to unload, unburden.

развя|за́ть, жу́, ⌐жешь, *pf.* (*of* ⌐зывать) to untie, unbind, undo; to unleash; р.

кому́-н. ру́ки to untie someone's hands (*also fig.*); p. войну́ to unleash war.

развя|за́ться, жу́сь, ~жешься, *pf.* (*of* ~зываться) **1.** to come untied, come undone; у него́ ~за́лся язы́к (*fig.*) his tongue has been loosened. **2.** (c+*i.*; *fig.*) to have done (with), be through (with).

развя́зк|а, и, *f.* **1.** (*lit.*) dénouement. **2.** outcome, issue, upshot; счастли́вая p. happy ending; де́ло идёт к ~e things are coming to a head. **3.** p. движе́ния, кольцева́я (тра́нспортная) p. (traffic) roundabout.

развя́з|ный (~ен, ~на), *adj.* (unduly) familiar; free-and-easy.

развя́зыва|ть(ся), ю(сь), *impf. of* развяза́ть(ся).

разгад|а́ть, а́ю, *pf.* (*of* ~ывать) **1.** to guess the meaning (of); p. зага́дку to solve a riddle; p. сны to interpret dreams; p. шифр to break a cipher. **2.** to guess, divine; p. челове́ка to size a person up, get to the bottom of a person.

разга́дк|а, и, *f.* solution (*of a riddle, etc.*).

разга́дыва|ть, ю, *impf. of* разгада́ть.

разга́р¹, а, *m.* в ~e (+*g.*) at the height (of); в по́лном ~e in full swing; в ~e бо́я in the heat of the battle.

разга́р², а, *m.* erosion (*of firearm barrel*).

разгиба́|ть(ся), ю(сь), *impf. of* разогну́ть-(ся); не ~я спины́ without a let-up; ~ющий му́скул (*anat.*) extensor.

разгильдя́|й, я, *m.* (*coll.*) sloven; sloppy individual.

разгильдя́йнича|ть, ю, *impf.* (*coll.*) to be slovenly, be sloppy; to be slipshod.

разглаго́льствовани|е, я, *n.* (*coll.*) big talk, lofty phrases.

разглаго́льств|овать, ую, *impf.* (*coll.*) to hold forth, expatiate; to talk big, use lofty phrases.

разгла́|дить, жу, дишь, *pf.* (*of* ~живать) to smooth out; to iron out, press; (*tech.*) to planish.

разгла́|диться, дится, *pf.* (*of* ~живаться) **1.** to become smoothed out. **2.** *pass. of* ~дить.

разгла́жива|ть(ся), ет(ся), *impf. of* разгла́дить(ся).

разгла|си́ть, шу́, си́шь, *pf.* (*of* ~ша́ть) **1.** to divulge, give away, let out. **2.** (o+*p.*; *coll.*) to trumpet, broadcast.

разглаша́|ть, ю, *impf. of* разгласи́ть.

разглаше́ни|е, я, *n.* divulging, (unauthorized) disclosure; p. вое́нной та́йны divulging of military secrets.

разгля|де́ть, жу́, ди́шь, *pf.* to make out, discern, descry.

разгля́дыва|ть, ю, *impf.* to examine closely, scrutinize.

разгне́ва|ть, ю, *pf.* to anger, incense.

разгне́ва|ться, юсь, *pf. of* гне́ваться.

разгова́рива|ть, ю, *impf.* (c+*i.*) to talk (to, with), speak (to, with), converse (with); переста́ньте p.! stop talking!; они́ друг с дру́гом не ~ют they are not on speaking terms.

разгов|е́ться, е́юсь, е́ешься, *pf.* (*of* ~ля́ться) to break a (period of) fast.

разговля́|ться, юсь, *impf. of* разгове́ться.

разгово́р, а (у), *m.* talk, conversation; кру́пный p. high words; перемени́ть p. to change the subject; об э́том и ~у быть не мо́жет there can be no question about it; об э́том бы́ло мно́го ~ов there was a great deal of talk about it; без ~ов! and no argument!

разгово́р|ить, ю́, и́шь, *pf.* (*coll.*) to dissuade.

разговор|и́ться, ю́сь, и́шься, *pf.* **1.** (c+*i.*) to get into conversation (with). **2.** to warm to one's theme; заста́вить кого́-н. p. to get someone talking.

разгово́рник, а, *m.* phrase-book.

разгово́р|ный, *adj.* **1.** colloquial; p. язы́к spoken language. **2.** ~ная бу́дка telephone booth; p. уро́к conversation class.

разгово́рчивост|ь, и, *f.* talkativeness, loquacity.

разгово́рчив|ый (~, ~a), *adj.* talkative, loquacious.

разго́н, а, *m.* **1.** dispersal; dissolution; p. собра́ния breaking up of a meeting. **2.** быть в ~e (*coll.*) to be out. **3.** (*sport*) run, running start; прыжо́к с ~a running jump. **4.** distance (*between similar objects*). **5.** (*typ.*) space.

разго́нист|ый (~, ~a), *adj.* (*coll.*; *of handwriting or type*) spaced-out.

разгоня́|ть(ся), ю(сь), *impf. of* разогна́ть-(ся).

разгора́жива|ть, ю, *impf. of* разгороди́ть.

разгор|а́ться, а́ется, *impf. of* ~е́ться.

разгор|е́ться, и́тся, *pf.* (*of* ~а́ться) **1.** to flame up, flare up. **2.** (*fig.*) to flare up; ~е́лся спор a heated argument developed; стра́сти ~е́лись feeling ran high, passions rose; глаза́ у неё ~е́лись на бриллиа́нтовое кольцо́ (*coll.*) she hankered after, she set her heart on a diamond ring. **3.** (*fig.*) flush.

разгоро|ди́ть, жу́, ~ди́шь, *pf.* (*of* разгора́-живать) to partition off.

разгоряч|и́ть, у́, и́шь, *pf. of* горячи́ть.

разгоряч|и́ться, у́сь, и́шься, *pf.* (*of* горячи́ться) (от) to be flushed (with); p. от вина́ to be flushed with wine.

разгра́б|ить, лю, ишь, *pf.* to plunder, pillage, loot.

разграбле́ни|е, я, *n.* plunder, pillage.

разгра|ди́ть, жу́, ди́шь, *pf.* (*of* ~жда́ть)

(*mil.*) to remove obstacles (from); to clear (*of mines*).

разгражда́|ть, ю, *impf. of* разгради́ть.

разгражде́ни|е, я, *n.* (*mil.*) removal of obstacles.

разграниче́ни|е, я, *n.* 1. demarcation, delimitation. 2. differentiation.

разграни́чива|ть, ю, *impf. of* разграни́чить.

разграничи́тельн|ый, *adj.* ~ая ли́ния line of demarcation, dividing line.

разграни́ч|ить, у, ишь, *pf.* (*of* ~ивать) 1. to delimit, demarcate. 2. to differentiate, distinguish.

разграф|и́ть, лю́, и́шь, *pf.* (*of* графи́ть *and* ~ля́ть) to rule (*in squares, columns, etc.*).

разграфле́ни|е, я, *n.* ruling.

разграфля́|ть, ю, *impf. of* разграфи́ть.

разгреба́|ть, ю, *impf. of* разгрести́.

разгре|сти́, бу́, бёшь, *past* ~б, ~бла́, *pf.* (*of* ~ба́ть) to rake (aside, away); to shovel (aside, away).

разгро́м, а, *m.* 1. crushing defeat, utter defeat, rout; knock-out blow. 2. (*coll.*) havoc, devastation; карти́на ~а scene of devastation; в кварти́ре был по́лный р. there was complete chaos in the flat.

разгром|и́ть, лю́, и́шь, *pf. of* громи́ть.

разгружа́|ть(ся), ю(сь), *impf. of* разгрузи́ть(ся).

разгру|зи́ть, жу́, ~зи́шь, *pf.* (*of* ~жа́ть) 1. to unload. 2. (от; *fig., coll.*) to relieve (of); р. от доба́вочных обя́занностей to relieve of extra commitments.

разгру|зи́ться, жу́сь, ~зи́шься, *pf.* (*of* ~жа́ться) 1. to unload. 2. (от; *fig., coll.*) to be relieved (of).

разгру́зк|а, и, *f.* 1. unloading. 2. (*fig., coll.*) relieving, affording relief.

разгрузн|о́й, *adj.* ~о́е су́дно (*naut.*) lighter.

разгру́зочн|ый, *adj.* unloading; ~ые рабо́ты unloading operations; ~ое су́дно (*naut.*) lighter.

разгруппир|ова́ть, у́ю, *pf.* (*of* ~о́вывать) to divide into groups, group.

разгруппиро́выва|ть, ю, *impf. of* разгруппирова́ть.

разгрыза́|ть, ю, *impf. of* разгры́зть.

разгры́з|ть, у́, ёшь, *past* ~, ~ла, *pf.* (*of* ~а́ть) to crack (*with one's teeth*); р. оре́х to crack a nut.

разгу́л, а, *m.* 1. revelry, debauch. 2. (+g.; *fig.*) raging (of); wild outburst (of); р. антисемити́зма a wild outburst of anti-semitism.

разгу́лива|ть, ю, *impf.* 1. to stroll about, walk about. 2. *impf. of* разгуля́ть.

разгу́лива|ться, юсь, *impf. of* разгуля́ться.

разгу́ль|е, я, *n.* (*coll.*) merry-making.

разгу́л|ьный (~ен, ~ьна), *adj.* (*coll.*) loose,

wild, rakish; вести́ ~ьную жизнь to lead a wild life.

разгул|я́ть, я́ю, *pf.* (*of* ~ивать) (*coll.*) 1. to amuse so as to keep awake. 2. to dispel; р. чью-н. хандру́ to dispel someone's gloom.

разгул|я́ться, я́юсь, *pf.* (*of* ~ивать́ся) (*coll.*) 1. to spread oneself; to have free scope. 2. (*of children*) to wake up, stop feeling sleepy. 3. (*of weather*) to clear up, improve; день ~я́лся it has turned out a fine day.

разда|ва́ть(ся), ю́(сь), ёшь(ся), *impf. of* разда́ть(ся).

раздав|и́ть, лю́, ~ишь, *pf.* (*of* ~ливать) 1. to crush; to squash. 2. (*fig.*) to crush, overwhelm. 3. (*coll.*) to down, sink (*alcoholic beverages*).

разда́влива|ть, ю, *impf. of* раздави́ть.

разда́рива|ть, ю, *impf. of* раздари́ть.

раздар|и́ть, ю́, ~ишь, *pf.* (*of* ~ивать) (+d.) to give away (to), make a present of.

разда́точн|ый, *adj.* distributing, distribution; ~ая ве́домость list of those due to receive (*gifts, money, etc.*); р. пункт distribution centre.

разда́тчик, а, *m.* distributor, dispenser.

разда́|ть[1], м, шь, ст, ди́м, ди́те, ду́т, *past* ро́здал, ~ла́, ро́здало, *pf.* (*of* ~ва́ть) to distribute, give out, serve out, dispense; р. ми́лостыню to dispense charity; р. кни́ги to give out books.

разда́|ть[2], м, шь, ст, ди́м, ди́те, ду́т, *past* ро́здал, ~ла́, ро́здало, *pf.* (*of* ~ва́ть) (*coll.*) to stretch (*footwear*); to enlarge, widen, let out (*clothing*).

разда́|ться[1], мся, шься, стся, ди́мся, ди́тесь, ду́тся, *past* ~лся, ~ла́сь, ~ло́сь, *pf.* (*of* ~ва́ться) to be heard; to resound; to ring (out); ~лся вы́стрел a shot rang out; ~лся стук (в дверь) a knock at the door was heard.

разда́|ться[2], мся, шься, стся, ди́мся, ди́тесь, ду́тся, *past* ~лся, ~ла́сь, ~ло́сь, *pf.* (*of* ~ва́ться) (*coll.*) 1. to make way. 2. to stretch, expand. 3. to put on weight.

разда́ч|а, и, *f.* distribution.

раздва́ива|ть(ся), ю(сь), *impf. of* раздвои́ть(ся).

раздвига́|ть(ся), ю(сь), *impf. of* раздви́нуть(ся).

раздвижно́й, *adj.* expanding; sliding; р. за́навес (*theatr.*) draw curtain; р. стол leaf table, expanding table.

раздви́|нуть, ну, нешь, *pf.* (*of* ~га́ть) to move apart, slide apart; р. занаве́ски to draw back the curtains; р. стол to extend a table, insert a leaf into a table.

раздви́|нуться, нется, *pf.* (*of* ~га́ться) to move apart, slide apart; за́навес ~нулся the curtain was drawn back; (*in theatre*) the curtain rose; толпа́ ~нула́сь the crowd made way.

раздвое́ни|е, я, *n.* division into two; bifurcation; р. ли́чности (*med.*) split personality.

раздво́|енный (*and* **раздвоённый**), *p.p.p. of* ~и́ть *and adj.* **1.** forked; bifurcated; ~енное копы́то cloven hoof; ~енное созна́ние split mind. **2.** (*bot.*) dichotomous, furcate.

раздво|и́ть, ю́, и́шь, *pf.* (*of* раздва́ивать) to divide into two; to bisect.

раздво|и́ться, ю́сь, и́шься, *pf.* (*of* раздва́иваться) to bifurcate, fork, split, become double.

раздева́лк|а, и, *f.* (*coll.*) cloak-room.

раздева́льный, *adj.* (for) undressing.

раздева́л|ьня, ьни, *g. pl.* ~ен, *f.* =~ка.

раздева́ни|е, я, *n.* undressing.

раздева́|ть(ся), ю(сь), *impf. of* разде́ть(ся).

разде́л, а, *m.* **1.** division; partition; allotment. **2.** section, part (*of book, etc.*).

разде́л|ать, аю, *pf.* (*of* ~ывать) to dress, prepare; р. гря́дки to prepare (flower-)beds (*for sowing*); р. под дуб to grain in imitation of oak; р. кого́-н. под оре́х (*coll.*) to give it someone hot.

разде́л|аться, аюсь, *pf.* (*of* ~ываться) (с+*i.*) **1.** to be through (with); to settle (accounts) (with); р. с долга́ми to pay off debts. **2.** (*fig.*) to settle accounts (with), get even (with).

разделе́ни|е, я, *n.* division; р. труда́ division of labour.

раздели́м|ый (~, ~а), *adj.* divisible.

раздели́тельн|ый, *adj.* **1.** dividing, separating; ~ая черта́ dividing line. **2.** (*philos.*, *gram.*) disjunctive; (*gram.*) distributive; р. сою́з disjunctive conjunction; ~ое место-име́ние distributive pronoun.

раздел|и́ть, ю́, ~ишь, *pf.* (*of* ~я́ть) **1.** to divide. **2.** to separate, part. **3.** to share.

раздел|и́ться, ю́сь, ~ишься, *pf.* (*of* ~я́ться) **1.** (на+*a.*) to divide (into); to be divided; нам придётся р. на две гру́ппы we shall have to divide into two groups; мне́ния ~и́лись opinions were divided. **2.** to separate, part company. **3.** *pf. only* (на+*a.*) to be divisible (by); число́ со́рок де́вять ~ится на семь forty-nine is divisible by seven.

разде́льн|ый, *adj.* **1.** separate; ~ое обуче́ние separate education for boys and girls. **2.** (*of pronunciation*) clear, distinct.

раздел|я́ть, я́ю, *impf. of* ~и́ть; р. чьи-н. взгля́ды to share someone's views.

раздел|я́ться, я́юсь, *impf. of* ~и́ться.

разде́рг|ать, аю, *pf.* (*of* ~ивать) (*coll.*) to tear up.

разде́ргива|ть, ю, *impf. of* разде́ргать *and* раздёрнуть.

раздёр|нуть, ну, нешь, *pf.* (*of* ~гивать) to draw apart, pull apart; р. занаве́ски to draw back the curtains.

разде́т|ый, *p.p.p. of* ~ь *and adj.* **1.** unclothed. **2.** poorly clothed, ill-clad.

разде́|ть, ну, нешь, *pf.* (*of* ~ва́ть) to undress.

разде́|ться, нусь, нешься, *pf.* (*of* ~ва́ться) to undress, strip; to take off one's things.

раздира́|ть, ю, *impf.* **1.** *impf. of* разодра́ть. **2.** *impf. only* (*fig.*) to rend, tear, lacerate, harrow.

раздира́|ться, ю, ет(ся), *impf. of* разо-дра́ться.

раздира́|ющий, *pres. part. act. of* ~ть *and adj.*; р. (ду́шу) heart-rending, heart-breaking, harrowing.

раздобре́|ть, ю, *pf. of* добре́ть².

раздо́бр|иться, юсь, ишься, *pf.* (*coll.*) to become generous, become kind.

раздобыва́|ть, ю, *impf. of* раздобы́ть.

раздо|бы́ть, бу́ду, бу́дешь, *past* ~бы́л, *pf.* (*of* ~быва́ть) (*coll.*) get, procure, come by, get hold of; р. де́нег to raise money, come by some money.

раздо́ль|е, я, *n.* **1.** expanse. **2.** (*fig.*) freedom, liberty; им р. they are quite free to do as they please.

раздо́ль|ный (~ен, ~ьна), *adj.* free.

раздо́р, а, *m.* discord, dissension; я́блоко ~а apple of discord, bone of contention; се́ять р. to breed strife.

раздоса́д|овать, ую, *pf.* to vex.

раздраж|а́ть(ся), а́ю(сь), *impf. of* ~и́ть(ся).

раздража́|ющий, *pres. part. act. of* ~ть *and adj.* irritating, annoying, exasperating; *as noun* ~ющее, ~ющего, *n.* irritant.

раздраже́ни|е, я, *n.* irritation.

раздражи́тел|ь, я, *m.* (*med.*) irritant.

раздражи́тельност|ь, и, *f.* irritability; shortness of temper.

раздражи́тельн|ый (~ен, ~ьна), *adj.* irritable; short of temper, short-tempered.

раздраж|и́ть, у́, и́шь, *pf.* (*of* ~а́ть) **1.** to irritate, annoy, exasperate, put out. **2.** (*med.*) to irritate.

раздраж|и́ться, у́сь, и́шься, *pf.* (*of* ~а́ться) **1.** to get irritated, get annoyed. **2.** (*med.*) to become inflamed.

раздразн|и́ть, ю́, ~ишь, *pf.* **1.** to tease. **2.** to stimulate; р. чей-н. аппети́т to whet someone's appetite.

раздроб|и́ть, лю́, и́шь, *pf.* **1.** *pf. of* дроби́ть. **2.** (*impf.* ~ля́ть) (в+*a.*; *math.*) to turn (into), reduce (to); р. гра́ммы в сантигра́ммы to turn grams into centigrams.

раздроб|и́ться, и́тся, *pf. of* дроби́ться.

раздробле́ни|е, я, *n.* **1.** breaking, smashing to pieces. **2.** (*math.*) reduction.

раздро́б|ленный (*and* **раздроблённый**), *p.p.p. of* ~и́ть *and adj.* **1.** (*of a bone*) shattered. **2.** (*fig.*) small-scale; fragmented,

раздробля́|ть, ю, *impf. of* раздроби́ть.

раздруж|и́ться, у́сь, и́шься, *pf.* (*coll.*) to break it off (with); to break off friendly relations (with).

раздува́льный, *adj.* р. мех (*tech.*) bellows.

раздува́|ть(ся), ю(сь), *impf. of* раздуть(ся).

разду́м|ать, аю, *pf.* (*of* ∼ывать) to change one's mind; (+*inf.*) to decide not (to); я ∼ал подава́ть заявле́ние на э́то ме́сто I decided not to apply for that job, I changed my mind about applying for that job.

разду́м|аться, аюсь, *pf.* (о+*р.*; *coll.*) to be absorbed in thinking (about).

разду́мыва|ть, ю, **1.** *impf. of* разду́мать. **2.** *impf. only* (о+*р.*) to ponder (on, over), consider; я давно́ ∼ю, купи́ть ли маши́ну и́ли нет for a long time I have been considering whether or not to buy a car; не ∼я without a moment's thought.

разду́мь|е, я, *n.* **1.** meditation; thought, thoughtful mood; в глубо́ком р. deep in thought. **2.** hesitation; меня́ взяло́ р. I can't make up my mind.

разду́т|ый, *p.p.p. of* ∼ь *and adj.* (*fig., coll.*) exaggerated; inflated; ∼ые шта́ты inflated staffs.

разду́|ть, ю, ешь, *pf.* (*of* ∼ва́ть) **1.** to blow; to fan; р. пла́мя (*fig.*) to fan the flames. **2.** to blow (out); р. щёки to blow out one's cheeks; у него́ ∼ло щёку (*impers.*) his cheek is swollen. **3.** (*fig., coll.*) to exaggerate; to inflate, swell; р. поте́ри to exaggerate losses. **4.** to blow about; ∼ло бума́ги по́ полу (*impers.*) the papers had blown all over the floor.

разду́|ться, юсь, ешься, *pf.* (*of* ∼ва́ться) to swell.

раздуш|и́ть, у́, ∼ишь, *pf.* (*coll.*) to drench in perfume.

разева́|ть, ю, *impf. of* рази́нуть.

разжа́лоб|ить, лю, ишь, *pf.* to move (to pity).

разжа́лоб|иться, люсь, ишься, *pf.* to be moved to pity.

разжа́ловани|е, я, *n.* demotion, degrading.

разжа́лова|нный, *p.p.p. of* ∼ть; *as noun* р., ∼нного, *m.* (*mil.*) demoted, degraded officer.

разжа́л|овать, ую, *pf.* (*mil.*) to demote, degrade; р. в солда́ты to reduce to the ranks.

раз|жа́ть, ожму́, ожмёшь, *pf.* (*of* ∼жима́ть) to unclasp; to release, unfasten, undo; р. кула́к to unclench one's fist; р. ру́ки to unclasp one's hands.

раз|жа́ться, ожмётся, *pf.* (*of* ∼жима́ться) to come loose; to relax.

разж|ева́ть, ую́, уёшь, *pf.* (*of* ∼ёвывать) **1.** to chew, masticate; (*fig., coll.*) to chew over. **2.** (*fig.*) to spell out.

разжёвыва|ть, ю, *impf. of* разжева́ть.

раз|же́чь, ожгу́, ожжёшь, ожгу́т, *past* ∼жёг, ∼ожгла́, *pf.* (*of* ∼жига́ть) **1.** to kindle. **2.** (*fig.*) to kindle, rouse, stir up; р. стра́сти to arouse passion.

разжи́в|а, ы, *f.* (*coll.*) gain, profit.

разжива́|ться, юсь, *impf. of* разжи́ться.

разжига́ни|е, я, *n.* kindling (*also fig.*).

разжига́|ть, ю, *impf. of* разже́чь.

разжи|ди́ть, жу́, ди́шь, *pf.* (*of* ∼жа́ть) to dilute, thin.

разжижа́|ть, ю, *impf. of* разжиди́ть.

разжиже́ни|е, я, *n.* dilution, thinning; rarefaction.

разжима́|ть(ся), ет(ся), *impf. of* разжа́ть(ся).

разжире́|ть, ю, *pf. of* жире́ть.

разж|и́ться, иву́сь, ивёшься, *past* ∼и́лся, ∼ила́сь, *pf.* (*of* ∼ива́ться) (*coll.*) **1.** to get rich, make a pile. **2.** (+*i.*) to come by, get hold of.

раззаво́д, а, *m.* на р. (*coll.*) for breeding.

раззадо́рива|ть(ся), ю(сь), *impf. of* раззадо́рить(ся).

раззадо́р|ить, ю, ишь, *pf.* (*of* ∼ивать) (*coll.*) to stir up, excite.

раззадо́р|иться, юсь, ишься, *pf.* (*of* ∼иваться) (*coll.*) to get excited, get worked up.

раззва́нива|ть, ю, *impf. of* раззвони́ть.

раззвон|и́ть, ю́, и́шь, *pf.* (*of* раззва́нивать) (о+*р.*; *coll.*) to trumpet, proclaim (from the housetops).

раззнако́м|ить, лю, ишь, *pf.* to alienate.

раззнако́м|иться, люсь, ишься, *pf.* (с+*i.*) to break off one's acquaintance (with), break (with).

раззуд|е́ться, и́тся, *pf.* (*coll.*) to begin to itch (*also fig.*).

раззя́в|а, ы, *m. and f.* = рази́ня.

рази́н|уть, у, ешь, *pf.* (*of* разева́ть) (*coll.*) to open wide (*the mouth*); to gape; слу́шать, ∼ув рот to listen open-mouthed.

рази́н|я, и, *m. and f.* (*coll.*) scatter-brained person.

рази́тел|ьный (∼ен, ∼ьна), *adj.* striking; р. приме́р striking example.

ра|зи́ть[1], жу́, зи́шь, *impf.* to strike, smite, hit.

раз|и́ть[2], и́т, *impf.* (*impers.* +*i.*; *coll.*) to reek (of), stink (of); из ко́мнаты ∼и́ло чесно-ко́м the room reeked of garlic.

разлага́|ть(ся), ю(сь), *impf. of* разложи́ть(ся).

разла́д, а, *m.* **1.** disorder. **2.** discord, dissension.

разла́|дить, жу, дишь, *pf.* (*of* ∼живать) to derange; (*coll.*) to mess up.

разла́|диться, дится, *pf.* (*of* ∼живаться) to get out of order; (*coll.*) to go wrong.

разла́ком|ить, лю, ишь, *pf.* (+*i*.; *coll.*) to give someone a taste (for).

разла́ком|иться, люсь, ишься, *pf.* (+*i*.; *coll.*) to get a taste (for).

разла́мыва|ть(ся), ю, ет(ся), *impf. of* разло-ма́ть(ся) *and* разломи́ть(ся).

разлёжива|ться, юсь, *impf.* (*coll.*, *pejor.*) to lie about.

разлеза́|ться, а́ется, *impf. of* ~ться.

разле́з|ться, ется, *past* ~ся, ~лась, *pf.* (*of* ~а́ться) (*coll.*) to come to pieces; to come apart at the seams; to fall apart.

разле́нива|ться, юсь, *impf. of* разлени́ться.

разлен|и́ться, ю́сь, ~ишься, *pf.* (*of* ~ива́ть-ся) (*coll.*) to become sunk in sloth.

разлеп|и́ть, лю́, ~ишь, *pf.* (*of* ~ля́ть) to unstick.

разлеп|и́ться, ~ится, *pf.* (*of* ~ля́ться) to come unstuck.

разлепля́|ть(ся), ю(сь), ет(ся), *impf. of* разлепи́ть(ся).

разлёт, а, *m.* (*of birds*) flying away, departure.

разлета́|ться, а́юсь, *impf. of* ~е́ться.

разле|те́ться, чу́сь, ти́шься, *pf.* (*of* ~та́ться) **1.** to fly away; to scatter (*in the air*). **2.** (*coll.*) to smash, shatter; ста́туя ~те́лась вдре́-безги the statue smashed to smithereens. **3.** (*fig., coll.*) to vanish, be shattered; её мечта́ ~те́лась her dream was shattered; все на́ши наде́жды ~те́лись all our hopes were dashed. **4.** (*coll.*) to rush.

разл|е́чься, я́гусь, я́жешься, *past* ~ёгся, ~егла́сь, *pf.* (*coll.*) to sprawl, stretch oneself out.

разли́в, а, *m.* **1.** bottling. **2.** flood; overflow.

разлива́ни|е, я, *n.* pouring out.

разлива́нн|ый, *adj. only used in phrase* ~ое мо́ре (*joc.*) oceans, lashings (*usu. of alcoholic beverages*).

разлива́тельн|ый, *adj.*; ~ая ло́жка ladle.

разлива́|ть(ся), ю, ет(ся), *impf. of* разли́ть-(ся).

разли́вк|а, и, *f.* **1.** bottling. **2.** (*tech.*) teeming, casting.

разливн|о́й, *adj.* on tap, on draught; ~о́е вино́ wine from the wood.

разли́вочн|ый, *adj.* (*tech.*) teeming, casting; ~ая маши́на casting machine, liquid filling machine.

разлин|ова́ть, у́ю, *pf.* (*of* ~о́вывать) to rule (*paper, etc.*).

разлино́выва|ть, ю, *impf. of* разлинова́ть.

разли́ти|е, я, *n.* overflow; р. жёлчи (*med.*) bilious attack.

раз|ли́ть, олью́, ольёшь, *past* ~ли́л, ~лила́, ~ли́ло, *pf.* (*of* ~лива́ть) **1.** to pour out; р. по буты́лкам to bottle; р. чай to pour out tea. **2.** to spill; р. водо́й to pour

water (over), douse, drench; их водо́й не ~ольёшь (*coll.*) they are thick as thieves. **3.** (*fig.*) to pour out, spread, broadcast.

раз|ли́ться, ольётся, *past* ~ли́лся, ~лила́сь, *pf.* (*of* ~лива́ться) **1.** to spill; суп ~ли́лся по ска́терти the soup has spilled over the table-cloth. **2.** to overflow; река́ ~лила́сь the river has overflowed, has burst its banks. **3.** (*med.*) у него́ ~лила́сь жёлчь he had a bilious attack. **4.** (*fig.*) to spread; по её лицу́ ~лила́сь улы́бка a smile spread across her face.

различа́|ть, а́ю, *impf. of* ~и́ть.

различа́|ться, юсь, *impf.* to differ.

разли́чи|е, я, *n.* distinction; difference; де́лать р. (ме́жду) to make distinctions (between); без ~я without distinction; зна́ки ~я (*mil.*) badges of rank.

различи́тельный, *adj.* distinctive; р. при́-знак distinctive, distinguishing feature.

различ|и́ть, у́, и́шь, *pf.* (*of* ~а́ть) **1.** to distinguish; to tell the difference (between). **2.** to discern, make out.

разли́ч|ный (~ен, ~на), *adj.* **1.** different; у нас бы́ли ~ные мне́ния our opinions differed. **2.** various, diverse; ~ные лю́ди all manner of people; по ~ным соображе́ниям for various reasons.

разложе́ни|е, я, *n.* **1.** breaking down; (*chem.*) decomposition; (*math.*) expansion; (*phys.*) resolution. **2.** decomposition, decay; putrefaction. **3.** (*fig.*) demoralization; disintegration.

разлож|и́вшийся, *past part. act. of* ~и́ться *and adj.* **1.** decomposed, decayed. **2.** (*fig.*) demoralized.

разлож|и́ть¹, у́, ~ишь, *pf.* (*of* раскла́ды-вать) **1.** to put away; р. свои́ ве́щи по я́щикам to put away one's things in their respective drawers. **2.** to lay out; to spread (out); to (lay and) make (*a fire*); р. ого́нь to make a fire; р. ска́терть to spread a table-cloth; р. складну́ю крова́ть to put up a camp bed. **3.** to distribute, apportion; р. при́быль to distribute, share out profits.

разлож|и́ть², у́, ~ишь, *pf.* (*of* разлага́ть) **1.** to break down; (*chem.*) to decompose; (*math.*) to expand; (*phys.*) to resolve; р. вещество́ на составны́е ча́сти to break a substance down into its component parts; р. число́ на мно́жители to factorize a number. **2.** (*fig.*) to break down, demoralize.

разлож|и́ться¹, у́сь, ~ишься, *pf.* (*of* раскла́дываться) (*coll.*) to arrange one's things, put one's things out.

разлож|и́ться², у́сь, ~ишься, *pf.* (*of* разлага́ться) **1.** (*chem.*) to decompose; (*math.*) to expand. **2.** to decompose, rot, decay; труп уже́ ~и́лся the body has already

decomposed. **3.** (*fig.*) to become demoral-
ized; to disintegrate, crack up, go to pieces.
разлóм, а, *m.* **1.** breaking. **2.** break.
разломá|ть, ю, *pf.* (*of* разлáмывать) to
break (in pieces); р. дом to pull down a
house.
разломá|ться, ется, *pf.* (*of* разлáмываться)
to break (in pieces); to break up.
разлом|и́ть, лю́, ~ишь, *pf.* (*of* разлáмы-
вать) **1.** to break (in pieces). **2.** (*impers.*;
coll.) меня́ всего́ ~и́ло every bone in my
body aches.
разлом|и́ться, ~ится, *pf.* (*of* разлáмы-
ваться) to break in pieces.
разлу́к|а, и, *f.* **1.** separation; жить в ~е
(c+*i.*) to live apart (from), be separated
(from). **2.** parting; час ~и hour of parting.
разлуч|áть(ся), áю(сь), *impf. of* ~и́ть(ся).
разлуч|и́ть, у́, и́шь, *pf.* (*of* ~áть) (+*a.* c+*i.*)
to separate (from), part (from), sever (from).
разлуч|и́ться, у́сь, и́шься, *pf.* (*of* ~áться)
(c+*i.*) to separate, part (from).
разлюб|и́ть, лю́, ~ишь, *pf.* to cease to love,
stop loving; to cease to like, like no longer.
размагни́|тить, чу, тишь, *pf.* (*of* ~чивать)
(*tech.*) to demagnetize.
размагни́|титься, чусь, тишься, *pf.* (*of*
~чиваться) **1.** (*tech.*) to become demagne-
tized. **2.** (*fig.*, *coll.*) to lose grip; to become
unbalanced.
размагни́чива|ть(ся), ю(сь), *impf. of* раз-
магни́тить(ся).
разма́|зать, жу, жешь, *pf.* (*of* ~зывать)
1. to spread, smear; р. варéнье по всему́
лицу́ to get jam all over one's face. **2.** (*coll.*)
to pad out, amplify (*a narration*).
разма́|заться, жется, *pf.* (*of* ~зываться) to
spread; to get smeared.
размазн|я́, и́, *g. pl.* ~éй, *f.* (*coll.*) **1.** thin
gruel, thin porridge; (*fig.*) slush. **2.** *m. and f.*
(*fig.*) ninny, wishy-washy person.
разма́зыва|ть(ся), ю, ет(ся), *impf. of* раз-
ма́зать(ся).
разма́ива|ть(ся), ю(сь), *impf. of* размáять-
(ся).
размал|евáть, ю́ю, ю́ешь, *pf.* (*of* ~ёвывать)
(*coll.*) to daub.
размалёвыва|ть, ю, *impf. of* размалевáть.
разма́лыва|ть, ю, *impf. of* размолóть.
разма́рива|ть(ся), ю(сь), *impf. of* размо-
ри́ть(ся).
разма́тыва|ть(ся), ю, ет(ся), *impf. of* раз-
мотáть(ся).
разма́х, а, *m.* **1.** sweep; со всегó ~у with all
one's might; уда́рить с ~у to strike with
all one's might. **2.** span; р. кры́льев (*aeron.*)
wing-span, wing-spread. **3.** (*tech.*) swing,
amplitude (*of pendulum*). **4.** (*fig.*) scope,
range, sweep, scale; широ́кий р. wide
range, grand scale; у них широ́кий р.

жи́зни they live in style, they do things in
a big way.
разма́хива|ть, ю, *impf.* (+*i.*) to swing; to
brandish; р. рука́ми to gesticulate.
разма́хива|ться, юсь, *impf. of* размах-
ну́ться.
размах|ну́ться, ну́сь, нёшься, *pf.* (*of*
~иваться) **1.** to swing one's arm (*to strike
or as if to strike*). **2.** (*fig.*, *coll.*) to do things
in a big way; (*pejor.*) to bite off more than
one can chew.
разма́чива|ть, ю, *impf. of* размочи́ть.
разма́шисто, *adv.* sweepingly, boldly;
писа́ть р. to write a bold hand; р. грести́ to
row with vigorous strokes.
разма́шист|ый (~, ~a), *adj.* sweeping; р.
жест sweeping gesture; р. по́черк bold
hand; р. стиль (*fig.*) happy-go-lucky style.
разма́|ять, ю, ешь, *pf.* (*of* ~ивать) (*coll.*) to
keep awake, prevent from sleeping.
разма́|яться, юсь, ешься, *pf.* (*of* ~иваться)
(*coll.*) to become wakeful, cease to feel
sleepy.
размежевáни|е, я, *n.* demarcation, delimi-
tation.
размеж|евáть, ю́ю, ю́ешь, *pf.* (*of* ~ёвывать)
to divide out, delimit (*also fig.*); р. сфéры
влия́ния to delimit spheres of influence.
размеж|евáться, ю́юсь, ю́ешься, *pf.* (*of*
~ёвываться) **1.** to fix the boundaries; (*fig.*)
to delimit the functions, spheres of action.
2. (*fig.*) to break off relations.
размежёвыва|ть(ся), ю(сь), *impf. of* раз-
межевáть(ся).
размельч|áть, áю, *impf. of* ~и́ть.
размельч|и́ть, у́, и́шь, *pf.* (*of* ~áть) to
divide into particles; to pulverize.
размéн, а, *m.* exchange; р. дéнег changing
of money.
размéнива|ть(ся), ю(сь), *impf. of* раз-
меня́ть(ся).
размéнн|ый, *adj.* ~ая монéта small change.
размен|я́ть, я́ю, *pf.* (*of* ~ивать) to change;
р. сторублёвку to change a hundred-
-rouble note.
размен|я́ться, я́юсь, *pf.* (*of* ~иваться) (*coll.*)
1. (+*i.*) to exchange; р. пéшками (*in chess*)
to exchange pawns. **2.** (*fig.*) to dissipate
one's talents.
размéр, а, *m.* **1.** dimensions; воро́нка ~ом
в дéсять квадра́тных мéтров a crater
measuring ten square metres. **2.** size; (*pl.*)
measurements; како́й ваш р.? what size
do you take? **3.** rate, amount; получа́ть
зарпла́ту в ~е дéсяти рублéй в день to be
paid at the rate of ten roubles per day.
4. scale, extent; (*pl.*) proportions; в широ́-
ких ~ах on a large scale; увели́читься до
огро́мных ~ов to assume enormous proportions. **5.** metre (*of verse*); (*mus.*) measure.

размер|енный, *p.p.p. of* ~ить *and adj.* measured; ~енная походка measured tread.

размер|ить, ю, ишь, *pf.* (*of* ~ять) to measure off; p. свои силы (*fig.*) to measure one's strength.

размер|ять, яю, *impf. of* ~ить.

разме|сить, шу, ~сишь, *pf.* (*of* ~шивать) to knead.

разме|сти, ту, тёшь, *past* ~л, ~ла, *pf.* (*of* ~тать¹) 1. to sweep clear; p. дорожку to clear a path. 2. to shovel, sweep away.

разме|стить, щу, стишь, *pf.* (*of* ~щать) 1. to place, accommodate; to stow; p. делегатов по гостиницам to accommodate the delegates in hotels; p. войска по квартирам to quarter troops. 2. to distribute; p. заём to float a loan.

разме|ститься, щусь, стишься, *pf.* (*of* ~щаться) 1. to take one's seat. 2. *pass. of* ~стить.

размета́|ть¹, ю, *impf. of* размести́.

разме|тать², чу, ~чешь, *pf.* (*of* ~тывать) to scatter, disperse.

разме|таться, чусь, ~чешься, *pf.* 1. (*coll.*) to toss (*in sleep or delirium*). 2. to sprawl.

разме́|тить, чу, тишь, *pf.* (*of* ~чать) to mark; p. курсивный шрифт to mark italics.

разме́точн|ый, *adj.* (*tech.*) ~ая плита layout block; ~о-сверлильный станок jig borer.

разме́тчик, а, *m.* marker.

разме́тыва|ть, ю, *impf. of* размета́ть².

размеча́|ть, ю, *impf. of* разме́тить.

размеш|а́ть, а́ю, *pf.* (*of* ~ивать) to stir.

разме́шива|ть, ю, *impf. of* размеси́ть *and* размеша́ть.

размеща́|ть(ся), ю(сь), *impf. of* размести́ть(ся).

размеще́ни|е, я, *n.* 1. placing, accommodation; distribution, disposal, allocation; siting; p. груза stowage; p. войск по квартирам quartering, billeting of troops; p. вооружённых сил stationing of armed forces; p. промышленности location of industry. 2. (*fin.*) placing, investment; p. займа floating a loan.

размина́|ть(ся), ю(сь), *impf. of* размя́ть(ся).

размини́́́́рова́ни|е, я, *n.* (*mil.*) mine clearing.

размини́р|овать, ую, *pf.* to clear of mines.

размин|ка, и, *f.* (*sport*) limbering-up; knock-up, knocking-up.

размин|у́ться, у́сь, ёшься, *pf.* (*coll.*) 1. (c+i.) to pass (*without meeting*); to miss; когда я вошёл, никого не было; мы должно-быть ~у́лись с ним на дороге when I went in there was no one there; we must have passed one another on the road. 2. (*of letters*) to cross. 3. to (be able to) pass; на этом участке дороги машинам нельзя p. it is impossible for cars to pass on this part of the road.

размнож|а́ть(ся), а́ю, ает(ся), *impf. of* ~ить(ся).

размноже́ни|е, я, *n.* 1. reproduction in quantity; duplicating; mimeographing. 2. (*biol.*) reproduction, propagation.

размнож|ить, у, ишь, *pf.* (*of* ~а́ть) 1. to multiply (copies of), manifold, duplicate; to mimeograph. 2. to breed, rear.

размнож|иться, ится, *pf.* (*of* ~а́ться) 1. (*biol.*) to propagate itself; to breed; to spawn. 2. *pass. of* ~ить.

размозж|и́ть, у́, и́шь, *pf.* to smash.

размок|а́ть, а́ет, *impf. of* ~нуть.

размо́к|нуть, нет, *past* ~, ~ла, *pf.* (*of* ~а́ть) to get soaked; to get sodden.

размо́л, а, *m.* 1. grinding. 2. quality (*of ground grain*); мука крупного, мелкого ~а coarse, coarse-ground flour; fine, finely ground flour.

размо́лвк|а, и, *f.* tiff, disagreement.

раз|моло́ть, мелю́, ме́лешь, *pf.* (*of* разма́лывать) to grind.

размора́жива|ть(ся), ю(сь), *impf. of* разморо́зить(ся).

размор|и́ть, и́т, *pf.* (*of* разма́ривать) (*coll.*) to exhaust; её ~и́ло на солнце (*impers.*) the sun was too much for her.

размор|и́ться, ю́сь, и́шься, *pf.* (*of* разма́риваться) (*coll.*) to be worn out.

разморо́|зить, жу, зишь, *pf.* (*of* размора́живать) to unfreeze, de-freeze (*frozen foods*); to de-frost (*a refrigerator*).

разморо́|зиться, жусь, зишься, *pf.* (*of* размора́живаться) to become unfrozen, de-frozen; to become de-frosted.

размота́|ть, ю, *pf.* (*of* разма́тывать) to unwind, uncoil, unreel.

размота́|ться, ется, *pf.* (*of* разма́тываться) to unwind, uncoil, unreel; to come unwound.

размоч|и́ть, у́, ~ишь, *pf.* (*of* разма́чивать) to soak, steep.

размусо́лива|ть, ю, *impf. of* размусо́лить.

размусо́л|ить, ю, ишь, *pf.* (*of* ~ивать) (*coll.*) 1. to slobber all over. 2. (*fig.*) to relate in a drivelling fashion.

размы́в, а, *m.* wash-out, erosion.

размыва́|ть, ю, *impf. of* размы́ть.

размыка́ни|е, я, *n.* (*electr.*) breaking, break, disconnection.

размы́ка|ть, ю, *pf.* (*coll.*) to shake off; p. го́ре (*poet.*) to shake off one's grief.

размыка́|ть, ю, *impf. of* разомкну́ть.

размы́сл|ить, ю, ишь, *pf.* (*of* размышля́ть) (o+p.) to reflect (on, upon), meditate (on, upon), ponder (over), muse (on, upon), turn over in one's mind.

размы́|ть, ́ю, ́ешь, *pf.* (*of* ~ва́ть) to wash away; (*geol.*) to erode.

размышле́ни|е, я, *n.* reflection, meditation, thought; тяжёлые ~я brooding; по зре́лом ~и on second thoughts, on reflection; быть погружённым в ~я to be lost in thought.

размышля́|ть, ю, *impf. of* размы́слить.

размягч|а́ть(ся), а́ю(сь), *impf. of* ~и́ть(ся).

размягче́ни|е, я, *n.* softening; р. мо́зга (*med.*) softening of the brain.

размягч|и́ть, у́, и́шь, *pf.* (*of* ~а́ть) to soften.

размягч|и́ться, у́сь, и́шься, *pf.* (*of* ~а́ться) to soften, grow soft.

размя́|к|нуть, ну, нешь, *past* ~, ~ла, *pf. of* мя́кнуть.

раз|мя́ть, омну́, омнёшь, *pf.* (*of* мять *and* ~мина́ть) 1. to knead; to mash (*potatoes, etc.*). 2. р. но́ги (*coll.*) to stretch one's legs.

раз|мя́ться, омну́сь, омнёшься, *pf.* (*of* ~мина́ться) 1. to grow soft (*as result of kneading*). 2. (*coll.*) to stretch one's legs; (*sport*) to limber up, loosen up.

разна́шива|ть(ся), ю, ет(ся), *impf. of* разноси́ть(ся)¹.

разнёжива|ть(ся), ю(сь), *impf. of* разнё-жить(ся).

разнёж|ить, у, ишь, *pf.* (*of* ~ивать) (*coll.*) to appeal to the tender feelings (of).

разнёж|иться, усь, ишься, *pf.* (*of* ~иваться) (*coll., pejor.*) to grow soft, become too soft.

разнемо́|чься, гу́сь, ~жешься, ~гутся, *past* ~гся, ~гла́сь, *pf.* (*coll.*) to become ill, be taken ill.

разнес|ти́, у́, ёшь, *past* ~, ~ла́, *pf.* (*of* разноси́ть²) 1. to carry, convey; to take round; р. газе́ты to deliver newspapers; р. слух to spread a rumour. 2. to enter, note down; р. цита́ты на ка́рточки to note down quotations on cards. 3. to smash, break up. 4. to scatter, disperse. 5. (*coll.*) to cause to swell; его́ щёку ~ло́ (*impers.*) his cheek is swollen. 6. (*fig., coll.*) to blow up.

разнес|ти́сь, ётся, *past* ~ся, ~ла́сь, *pf.* (*of* разноси́ться²) 1. to spread. 2. to resound.

разнима́|ть, ю, *impf. of* разня́ть.

ра́зн|иться, юсь, ишься, *impf.* to differ.

ра́зниц|а, ы, *f.* difference; disparity; кака́я р.? (*coll.*) what difference does it make?

разнобо́|й, я, *m.* lack of co-ordination; difference, disagreement.

разнове́с, а, *m.* (*collect.*) set of weights.

разнови́дност|ь, и, *f.* variety.

разновре́менный, *adj.* taking place at different times.

разногла́си|е, я, *n.* 1. difference, disagreement; р. во взгля́дах difference of opinion. 2. discrepancy; р. в показа́ниях conflicting evidence.

разноголо́сиц|а, ы, *f.* discordance, dissonance (*also fig., coll.*); р. во мне́ниях dissent.

разноголо́сый, *adj.* discordant.

разнокали́берный, *adj.* 1. (*mil.*) of different calibres. 2. (*fig., coll.*) mixed, heterogeneous.

разнома́стный, *adj.* 1. of different colours. 2. (*cards*) of different suits.

разномы́сли|е, я, *n.* difference of opinion(s).

разнообра́зи|е, я, *n.* variety, diversity; для ~я for a change.

разнообра́|зить, жу, зишь, *impf.* to vary, diversify.

разнообра́зност|ь, и, *f.* = разнообра́зие.

разнообра́з|ный (~ен, ~на), *adj.* various, varied, diverse.

разноплемённый, *adj.* of different races, tribes.

разнорабо́ч|ий, его, *m.* unskilled labourer.

разноречи́в|ый (~, ~а), *adj.* contradictory, conflicting.

разноре́чи|е, я, *n.* (*obs.*) contradiction.

разноро́дност|ь, и, *f.* heterogeneity.

разноро́д|ный (~ен, ~на), *adj.* heterogeneous.

разно́с, а, *m.* 1. carrying; delivery (*of mail, etc.*). 2. (*fig., coll.*) blowing-up.

разно|си́ть¹, шу́, ~сишь, *pf.* (*of* разна́шивать) to wear in (*footwear*).

разно|си́ть², шу́, ~сишь, *impf. of* разнести́.

разно|си́ться¹, ~сится, *pf.* (*of* разна́шиваться) (*of footwear*) to become comfortable.

разно|си́ться², ~сится, *impf. of* разнести́-(сь).

разно́ск|а, и, *f.* delivery.

разносклоня́емый, *adj.* (*gram.*) irregularly declined.

разно́сн|ый¹, *adj.* ~ая кни́га delivery book; ~ая торго́вля street-trading, street-hawking.

разно́сн|ый², *adj.* (*coll.*) abusive; ~ая реце́нзия slashing review; ~ые слова́ swear-words.

разносо́л, а, *m.* (*cul.*) 1. (*obs.*) pickle(s). 2. (*pl. only*) (*coll.*) dainties, delicacies.

разноспряга́емый, *adj.* (*gram.*) irregularly conjugated.

разносторо́н|ний, *adj.* 1. (*math.*) scalene. 2. (~ен, ~ня) (*fig.*) many-sided; versatile; ~нее образова́ние all-round education.

разносторо́нност|ь, и, *f.* versatility.

ра́зност|ь, и, *f.* 1. (*math.*) difference. 2. difference, diversity; ра́зные ~и (*coll.*) this and that.

разно́счик, а, *m.* pedlar, hawker; barrow boy.

разнохара́ктер|ный (~ен, ~на), *adj.* diverse, varied.

разноцве́тный, *adj.* of different colours; many-coloured, variegated, motley.

разночи́н|ец, ца, *m.* (*hist.*) raznochinets (*in 19th century, Russian intellectual not of gentle birth*).

разночи́н|ный, *adj. of* ~ец.

разночте́ни|е, я, *n.* (*philol.*) variant reading.

разношёрст|ный (~ен, ~на), *adj.* **1.** (*of animals*) with coats of different colour. **2.** (*fig., coll.*) mixed; ill-assorted.

разошёрст|ый, *adj.* = ~ный.

разноязы́чный, *adj.* polyglot.

разну́зд|анный, *p.p.p. of* ~а́ть *and adj.* unbridled, unruly.

разнузд|а́ть, а́ю, *pf.* (*of* ~ывать) to unbridle.

разну́здыва|ть, ю, *impf. of* разнузда́ть.

ра́зн|ый, *adj.* **1.** different, differing. **2.** various, diverse; ~ого ро́да of various kinds; *as noun* ~ое, ~ого, *n.* (*on agenda of meeting, etc.*) any other business.

разню́х|ать, аю, *pf.* (*of* ~ивать) (*coll.*) to smell out (*also fig.*); (*fig.*) to nose out, ferret out.

разню́хива|ть, ю, *impf. of* разню́хать.

раз|ня́ть, ниму́, ни́мешь, *past* ~ня́л (*and* ро́знял), ~няла́, ~ня́ло (*and* ро́зняло), *pf.* (*of* ~нима́ть) **1.** to take to pieces, dismantle, disjoint. **2.** to part, separate (*persons fighting*).

разоби́|деть, жу, дишь, *pf.* (*coll.*) to offend greatly; to put someone's back up properly.

разоби́|деться, жусь, дишься, *pf.* (*coll.*) to take offence.

разоблач|а́ть(ся), а́ю(сь), *impf. of* ~и́ть(ся).

разоблаче́ни|е, я, *n.* exposure, unmasking.

разоблачи́тел|ь, я, *m.* unmasker.

разоблач|и́ть, у́, и́шь, *pf.* (*of* ~а́ть) **1.** (*eccl. or joc.*) to disrobe, divest. **2.** (*fig.*) to expose, unmask.

разоблач|и́ться, у́сь, и́шься, *pf.* (*of* ~а́ться) **1.** (*eccl. or joc.*) to disrobe. **2.** (*fig.*) to be exposed, be unmasked.

раз|обра́ть, беру́, берёшь, *past* ~обра́л, ~обрала́, ~обра́ло, *pf.* (*of* ~бира́ть) **1.** to take to pieces, strip, dismantle; р. дом to pull down a house. **2.** to buy up, take. **3.** to sort out. **4.** to investigate, look into; р. де́ло (*leg.*) to hear a case. **5.** (*gram.*) to parse; to analyse. **6.** to make out, understand; я не могу́ р. его́ по́черк I cannot make out his handwriting; мы не мо́жем р., в чём де́ло we cannot understand what it is all about. **7.** (*fig., coll.*) to fill (with), seize (with); её ~обрала́ ре́вность she was filled with jealousy.

раз|обра́ться, беру́сь, берёшься, *past* ~обра́лся, ~обрала́сь, ~обра́лось, *pf.* (*of* ~бира́ться) **1.** (*coll.*) to unpack. **2.** (*в+p.*) to investigate, look into; to understand; р. в пчелово́дстве to know about bee-keeping; я в нём не ~обра́лся I could not make him out.

разобщ|а́ть(ся), а́ю(сь), *impf. of* ~и́ть(ся).

разобще́ни|е, я, *n.* disconnection, uncoupling.

разобщённо, *adv.* apart, separately; де́йствовать р. to act independently.

разобщи́тел|ь, я, *m.* (*tech.*) disconnector.

разобщ|и́ть, у́, и́шь, *pf.* (*of* ~а́ть) **1.** to separate; (*fig.*) to estrange, alienate. **2.** (*tech.*) to disconnect, uncouple, disengage.

разобщ|и́ться, у́сь, и́шься, *pf.* (*of* ~а́ться) **1.** (*tech.*) to become disconnected. **2.** *pass. of* ~и́ть.

ра́зовый, *adj.* valid for one occasion (only).

раз|огна́ть, гоню́, го́нишь, *past* ~огна́л, ~огнала́, ~огна́ло, *pf.* (*of* ~гоня́ть) **1.** to drive away; to disperse; (*fig.*) to dispel; р. демонстра́цию to break up a demonstration; р. го́ре to dispel grief. **2.** (*coll.*) to drive at high speed, race. **3.** (*typ.*) to space.

раз|огна́ться, гоню́сь, го́нишься, *past* ~огна́лся, ~огнала́сь, ~огна́лось, *pf.* (*of* ~гоня́ться) to gather speed; to gather momentum.

разогн|у́ть, у́, ёшь, *pf.* (*of* разгиба́ть) to unbend, straighten; р. спи́ну to straighten one's back.

разогн|у́ться, у́сь, ёшься, *pf.* (*of* разгиба́ться) to straighten oneself up.

разогре́в, а, *m.* (*tech.*) initial heating; firing (*of furnace*).

разогрева́ни|е, я, *n.* warming-up.

разогрева́|ть(ся), ю(сь), *impf. of* разогре́ть(ся).

разогре́|ть, ю, *pf.* (*of* ~ва́ть) to warm up.

разогре́|ться, юсь, *pf.* (*of* ~ва́ться) to warm up, grow warm.

разоде́т|ый, *p.p.p. of* ~ь *and adj.* dressed up; весь р. all dressed up, in one's best bib and tucker.

разоде́|ть, ну, нешь, *pf.* (*coll.*) to dress up.

разоде́|ться, нусь, нешься, *pf.* (*coll.*) to dress up; р. в пух и прах to be dressed to kill.

разодолж|а́ть, а́ю, *impf. of* ~и́ть.

разодолж|и́ть, у́, и́шь, *pf.* (*of* ~а́ть) (*coll.*) to give a nasty surprise.

раз|одра́ть, деру́, дерёшь, *past* ~одра́л, ~одрала́, ~одра́ло, *pf.* (*of* ~дира́ть) to tear up.

раз|одра́ться, дерётся, *past* ~одра́лся, ~одрала́сь, ~одра́лось, *pf.* (*of* ~дира́ться) (*coll.*) to tear.

разозл|и́ть, ю́, и́шь, *pf.* (*of* зли́ть) to make angry, enrage.

разозл|и́ться, ю́сь, и́шься, *pf.* (*of* зли́ться) to get angry, get in a rage.

раз|ойти́сь, ойду́сь, ойдёшься, *past* ~ошёлся, ~ошла́сь, *pf.* (*of* расходи́ться) **1.** to go away; to disperse; толпа́ ~ошла́сь the crowd broke up; ту́чи ~ошли́сь the clouds dispersed. **2.** (*с+i.*) to part (from), separate (from), to get divorced (from); мы ~ошли́сь друзья́ми we parted friends; он ~ошёлся с жено́й he has separated from his wife. **3.** to branch off, diverge; to radiate. **4.** to pass (*without meeting*). **5.** (c+*i*.) to be at variance (with), conflict (with); р. во мне́нии с кем-н. to disagree with someone. **6.** to dissolve; to melt. **7.** to be sold out; to be spent; (*of a book*) to be out of print; все де́ньги ~ошли́сь all the money has been spent. **8.** (*coll.*) to gather speed. **9.** (*coll.*) to let oneself go, fly off the handle; бу́ря ~ошла́сь the storm raged.

разо́к, ка́, *m.* (*coll.*) *dim. of* ~; ещё р. once more; р. друго́й once or twice.

ра́зом, *adv.* (*coll.*) at once, at one go.

разо́мкн|утый, *p.p.p. of* ~у́ть *and adj.*; р. строй (*mil.*) open order.

разомкн|у́ть, у́, ёшь, *pf.* (*of* размыка́ть) to open, unfasten; (*tech.*) to break, disconnect.

разомле́|ть, ю, *pf.* (*coll.*) to languish, grow languid.

разонра́в|иться, люсь, ишься, *pf.* (*coll.*; +*d.*) to cease to please, lose its attraction (for).

разопрева́|ть, ю, *impf. of* разопре́ть.

разопре́|ть, ю, *pf.* (*of* ~ва́ть) **1.** to become soft (*in cooking*). **2.** (*coll.*) to be worn out, done in (*from heat*).

разо́р, а, *m.* (*coll.*) ruin, destruction.

разор|а́ться, у́сь, ёшься, *pf.* (*coll.*) to become uproarious, raise a hullabaloo.

разорв|а́ть, у́, ёшь, *past* ~а́л, ~ала́, ~а́ло, *pf.* (*of* разрыва́ть¹) **1.** to tear (to pieces); р. кого́-н. на ча́сти (*fig.*, *coll.*) to wear someone out (*with requests, entreaties, etc.*). **2.** (*impers.*) to blow up, burst; котёл ~а́ло the boiler has burst. **3.** (*fig.*) to break (off), sever; р. дипломати́ческие сноше́ния to break off diplomatic relations.

разорв|а́ться, ётся, *past* ~а́лся, ~ала́сь, ~а́лось, *pf.* (*of* разрыва́ться) **1.** to break, snap; to tear, become torn. **2.** to blow up, burst; to explode, go off. **3.** (*coll.*; *usu.*+*neg.*) to be everywhere at once; я не могу́ р. I can't be everywhere at once, I can't do half a dozen things at once; хоть ~и́сь! hold hard!, give us a chance!

разоре́ни|е, я, *n.* destruction, ravage; ruin.

разори́тел|ьный (~ен, ~ьна), *adj.* ruinous; wasteful.

разор|и́ть, ю́, и́шь, *pf.* (*of* ~я́ть) **1.** to destroy, ravage. **2.** to ruin, bring to ruin.

разор|и́ться, ю́сь, и́шься, *pf.* (*of* ~я́ться) to ruin oneself; to be ruined.

разоруж|а́ть(ся), а́ю(сь), *impf. of* ~и́ть(ся).

разоруже́ни|е, я, *n.* disarmament.

разоруж|и́ть, у́, и́шь, *pf.* (*of* ~а́ть) to disarm; (*naut.*) to dismantle, unrig.

разоруж|и́ться, у́сь, и́шься, *pf.* (*of* ~а́ться) to disarm.

разор|я́ть(ся), я́ю(сь), *impf. of* ~и́ть(ся).

разо|сла́ть, шлю, шлёшь, *pf.* (*of* рассыла́ть) **1.** to send round, circulate; р. листо́вки to distribute leaflets. **2.** to send out, despatch.

разосп|а́ться, лю́сь, и́шься, *past* ~а́лся, ~ала́сь, ~а́лось, *pf.* (*coll.*) to be fast asleep; to oversleep.

разостла́ть (*and* **расстели́ть**), расстелю́, рассте́лешь, *pf.* (*of* расстила́ть) to spread (out), lay.

разостла́|ться (*and* **расстели́ться**), рассте́лется, *pf.* (*of* расстила́ться) to spread; тума́н ~лся по всей сте́пи fog spread over the whole steppe.

разохо́|тить, чу, тишь, *pf.* (к, на+*a.*; *coll.*) to stimulate (to), arouse an inclination (to, for).

разохо́|титься, чусь, тишься, *pf.* (+*inf.*; *coll.*) to take a liking (to), feel an inclination (for); сперва́ он не хоте́л танцева́ть, а тепе́рь ~тился he did not want to go to the dance at first, but now he is keen to go.

разочарова́ни|е, я, *n.* disappointment.

разочаро́в|анный, *p.p.p. of* ~а́ть *and adj.* disappointed, disillusioned.

разочар|ова́ть, у́ю, *pf.* (*of* ~о́вывать) to disappoint.

разочар|ова́ться, у́юсь, *pf.* (*of* ~о́вываться) (в ком-н., в чём-н.) to be disappointed (in someone, with something).

разочаро́выва|ть(ся), ю(сь), *impf. of* разочарова́ть(ся).

разраба́тыва|ть, ю, *impf. of* разрабо́тать.

разрабо́та|ть, ю, *pf.* (*of* разраба́тывать) **1.** (*agric.*) to cultivate. **2.** (*mining*) to work, exploit. **3.** to work out, work up; to develop; to elaborate; р. вопро́с to work up a subject; р. го́лос to develop a voice; р. ме́тоды to devise methods; р. пла́ны to work out plans.

разрабо́тк|а, и, *f.* **1.** (*agric.*) cultivation. **2.** (*mining*) working, exploitation; откры́тая р. open-cast mining. **3.** field; pit, working; р. сла́нца slate quarry. **4.** working out, working up; elaboration.

разра́внива|ть, ю, *impf. of* разровня́ть.

разража́|ться, юсь, *impf. of* разрази́ться.

разра|зи́ться, жу́сь, зи́шься, *pf.* (*of* ~жа́ться) (*of a storm, etc.*) to break out, burst out; р. слеза́ми to burst into tears; р. сме́хом to burst out laughing.

разраст|а́ться, а́ется, *impf. of* ~и́сь.

разраст|и́сь, ётся, *past* разро́сся, разросла́сь, *pf.* (*of* ~а́ться) to grow (up) (*also fig.*); to spread; to grow thickly; де́ло разросло́сь the business has grown; но́вый посёлок разро́сся a new estate has grown up.

разрев|е́ться, у́сь, ёшься, *pf.* (*coll.*) to raise a howl, start howling.

разре|ди́ть, жу́, ди́шь, *pf.* (*of* ~жа́ть) **1.** to thin out, weed out. **2.** to rarefy.

разрежа́|ть, ю, *impf. of* разреди́ть.

разре|жённый, *p.p.p. of* ~ди́ть *and adj.* (*phys.*) rarefied, rare; ~жённый во́здух rarefied air.

разре́з, а, *m.* **1.** cut; slit. **2.** section; попере́чный р. cross-section; продо́льный р. longitudinal section; р. глаз shape of one's eyes. **3.** (*fig., coll.*) point of view; в ~е (+*g.*) from the point of view (of), in the context (of).

разре́|зать, жу, жешь, *pf.* (*of* ~за́ть) to cut; to slit.

разреза́|ть, а́ю, *impf. of* ~ать.

разрезн|о́й, *adj.* **1.** cutting; р. нож paper--knife; ~а́я пила́ rip saw. **2.** slit, with slits; ~а́я ю́бка slit skirt.

разреш|а́ть, а́ю, *impf. of* ~и́ть.

разреш|а́ться, а́юсь, *impf.* **1.** *impf. of* ~и́ться. **2.** *impf. only* to be allowed; здесь кури́ть не ~а́ется no smoking (is allowed here).

разреше́ни|е, я, *n.* **1.** permission; с ва́шего ~я with your permission, by your leave. **2.** permit, authorization; р. на въезд entry permit. **3.** solution (*of a problem*). **4.** settlement (*of a dispute*). **5.** (*med.*) resolution; р. от бре́мени (*obs.*) delivery.

разреши́м|ый (~, ~а), *adj.* solvable.

разреш|и́ть, у́, и́шь, *pf.* (*of* ~а́ть) **1.** (+*d.*) to allow, permit; ~и́те пройти́ allow me to pass; do you mind letting me pass? **2.** to authorize; р. кни́гу к печа́ти to authorize the printing of a book. **3.** (от; *obs.*) to release (from); (*eccl.*) to absolve (from), give dispensation (from); р. кого́-н. от обяза́тельства to release someone from an obligation; р. от поста́ to give dispensation from a fast. **4.** to solve (*a problem*). **5.** to settle; р. сомне́ния to resolve doubts.

разреш|и́ться, у́сь, и́шься, *pf.* (*of* ~а́ться) **1.** to be solved. **2.** to be settled. **3.** (от бре́мени) (+*i.*; *obs.*) to be delivered (of); она́ ~и́лась де́вочкой she was delivered of a girl.

разрис|ова́ть, у́ю, *pf.* (*of* ~о́вывать) **1.** to cover with drawings. **2.** (*fig.*) to paint a picture (of).

разрисо́выва|ть, ю, *impf. of* разрисова́ть.

разровня́|ть, ю, *pf.* (*of* разра́внивать) to level.

разро́зн|енный, *p.p.p. of* ~ить *and adj.* **1.** unco-ordinated. **2.** odd; р. компле́кт broken set, set made up of odd parts; ~енные тома́ odd volumes.

разро́знива|ть, ю, *impf. of* разрознить.

разро́зн|ить, ю, ишь, *pf.* (*of* ~ивать) to break a set (of).

разруб|а́ть, а́ю, *impf. of* ~и́ть.

разруб|и́ть, лю́, ~ишь, *pf.* (*of* ~а́ть) to cut, cleave; р. го́рдиев у́зел to cut the Gordian knot.

разруга́|ть, ю, *pf.* (*coll.*) to berate; to blow up.

разруга́|ться, юсь, *pf.* (с+*i.*; *coll.*) to quarrel (with).

разрумя́нива|ть(ся), ю(сь), *impf. of* разрумя́нить(ся).

разрумя́н|ить, ю, ишь, *pf.* (*of* ~ивать) **1.** to rouge. **2.** to flush, redden; моро́з ~ил её щёки the frost brought a flush to her cheeks.

разрумя́н|иться, юсь, ишься, *pf.* (*of* ~иваться) **1.** to put rouge on. **2.** to blush; to be flushed.

разру́х|а, и, *f.* ruin, collapse; привести́ хозя́йство к ~е to dislocate the economy.

разруш|а́ть(ся), а́ю, а́ет(ся), *impf. of* ~ить(ся).

разруше́ни|е, я, *n.* destruction; (*pl.*) havoc.

разруши́тел|ьный (~ен, ~ьна), *adj.* destructive.

разру́ш|ить, у, ишь, *pf.* (*of* ~а́ть) **1.** to destroy; to demolish, wreck; to ruin (*also fig.*). **2.** (*fig.*) to frustrate, blast, blight; р. чьи-н. наде́жды to blight someone's hopes.

разру́ш|иться, ится, *pf.* (*of* ~а́ться) **1.** to go to ruin, collapse; все их пла́ны ~ились all their plans have fallen to the ground. **2.** *pass. of* ~ить.

разры́в, а, *m.* **1.** (*in var. senses*) break; gap; rupture, severance; breach; р. ли́нии фро́нта (*mil.*) breach in the front line; р. дипломати́ческих отноше́ний rupture, severance of diplomatic relations; ме́жду ни́ми произошёл р. they have broken it off. **2.** (*shell*) burst, explosion.

разрыва́|ть[1], ю, *impf. of* разорва́ть.

разрыва́|ть[2], ю, *impf. of* разрыть.

разрыва́|ться, юсь, *impf. of* разорва́ться.

разрывно́й, *adj.* explosive, bursting.

разр|ы́ть, о́ю, о́ешь, *pf.* (*of* ~ыва́ть[2]) **1.** to dig up. **2.** (*fig., coll.*) to turn upside-down, rummage through.

разрыхле́ни|е, я, *n.* loosening.

разрыхл|и́ть, ю́, и́шь, *pf.* (*of* ~я́ть) to loosen; to hoe.

разрыхл|я́ть, я́ю, *impf. of* ~и́ть.

разря́д[1], а, *m.* discharge.

разря́д[2], а, *m.* category, rank; sort; (*sport*) class, rating; пе́рвого ~а first-class.

разря|ди́ть[1], жу́, ~ди́шь, *pf.* (*of* ~жа́ть) (*coll.*) to dress up.

разря|ди́ть[2], жу́, ди́шь, *pf.* (*of* ~жа́ть) **1.** (*electr.*) to discharge; р. атмосфе́ру (*fig.*) to relieve tension, clear the air. **2.** to unload (*a fire-arm*). **3.** (*typ.*) to space out.

разря|ди́ться[1], жу́сь, ~ди́шься, *pf.* (*of* ~жа́ться) to dress up, doll oneself up.

разря|ди́ться², ди́тся, *pf.* (*of* ~жа́ться) **1.** (*electr.*) to run down; (*fig.*) to clear, ease; атмосфе́ра ~ди́лась the atmosphere has become less tense. **2.** *pass. of* ~ди́ть².

разря́дк|а, и, *f.* **1.** discharging; unloading; р. напряжённости (*polit.*) lessening of tension, détente. **2.** (*typ.*) spacing (out).

разря́дник¹, а, *m.* (*electr.*) discharger; spark--gap.

разря́дник², а, *m.* (*sport*) player with official rating.

разря́д|ный, *adj. of* ~¹; ~ная ёмкость, ~ная мо́щность discharge capacity.

разряжа́|ть(ся), ю(сь), *impf. of* разряди́ть-(ся).

разубе|ди́ть, жу́, ди́шь, *pf.* (*of* ~жда́ть) (в+*p.*) to dissuade (from), argue (out of); мы их ~ди́ли we have made them change their mind.

разубе|ди́ться, жу́сь, ди́шься, *pf.* (*of* ~жда́ться) (в+*p.*) to change one's mind (about), change one's opinion (about).

разубежда́|ть(ся), ю(сь), *impf. of* разубе-ди́ть(ся).

разува́|ть(ся), ю(сь), *impf. of* разу́ть(ся).

разуве́рени|е, я, *n.* dissuasion.

разуве́р|ить, ю, ишь, *pf.* (*of* ~я́ть) (в+*p.*) to undermine faith (in); to argue (out of).

разуве́р|иться, юсь, ишься, *pf.* (*of* ~я́ться) (в+*p.*) to lose faith (in).

разузна|ва́ть, ю́, ёшь, *impf.* **1.** *impf. of* разузна́ть, **2.** *impf. only* to make inquiries (about).

разузна́|ть, ю, *pf.* (*of* ~ва́ть) to find out.

разукра́|сить, шу, сишь, *pf.* (*of* ~шивать) to adorn, decorate, embellish.

разукра́|ситься, шусь, сишься, *pf.* (*of* ~шиваться) to adorn oneself, decorate oneself.

разукра́шива|ть(ся), ю|сь/, *impf. of* разу-кра́сить(ся).

разукрупн|и́ть, ю, и́шь, *pf.* (*of* ~я́ть) to break up into smaller units.

разукрупн|и́ться, и́тся, *pf.* (*of* ~я́ться) to break up into smaller units.

разукрупн|я́ть(ся), я́ю, я́ет(ся), *impf. of* ~и́ть(ся).

ра́зум, а, *m.* reason; mind, intellect; у него́ ум за р. зашёл (*coll.*) he is, was at his wit's end.

разуме́ни|е, я, *n.* **1.** (*obs.*) understanding. **2.** opinion, viewpoint; по моему́ ~ю to my mind, as I see it.

разуме́|ть, ю, *impf.* **1.** (*obs.*) to understand. **2.** (под) to understand (by), mean (by).

разуме́|ться, ется, *impf.* to be understood, be meant; под э́тим ~ется... by this is meant . . . ; (са́мо собо́й) ~ется it stands to reason; it goes without saying, of course; он, ~ется, не знал, что вы уже́ пришли́ he,

of course, did not know that you were already here.

разу́мник, а, *m.* (*coll.*) clever chap, clever boy.

разу́м|ный (~ен, ~на), *adj.* **1.** possessing reason. **2.** judicious, intelligent. **3.** reasonable; э́то (вполне́) ~но it is (perfectly) reasonable, that makes (good) sense.

разу́|ть, ю, ешь, *pf.* (*of* ~ва́ть); р. кого́-н. to take someone's shoes off.

разу́|ться, юсь, ешься, *pf.* (*of* ~ва́ться) to take one's shoes off.

разуха́бист|ый (~, ~а), *adj.* (*coll.*) **1.** rollick-ing. **2.** (*pejor.*) free-and-easy.

разучива|ть(ся), ю(сь), *impf. of* разучи́ть-(ся).

разуч|и́ть, у́, ~ишь, *pf.* (*of* ~ивать) to learn (up); р. роль to learn, study one's part.

разуч|и́ться, у́сь, ~ишься, *pf.* (*of* ~иваться) (+*inf.*) to forget (how to), lose the art (of); я ~и́лся ходи́ть на лы́жах I have forgotten how to ski.

разъеда́|ть(ся), ю(сь), *impf. of* разъе́сть(ся).

разъедине́ни|е, я, *n.* **1.** separation. **2.** (*electr.*) disconnection, breaking.

разъедини́тел|ь, я, *m.* (*electr.*) disconnecting switch, cut-out switch.

разъедин|и́ть, ю́, и́шь, *pf.* (*of* ~я́ть) **1.** to separate. **2.** (*electr.*) to disconnect, break; нас ~и́ли we were cut off (*on telephone*).

разъедин|и́ться, ю́сь, и́шься, *pf.* (*of* ~я́ться) **1.** to separate, part. **2.** *pass. of* ~и́ть.

разъедин|я́ть(ся), я́ю(сь), *impf. of* ~и́ть-(ся).

разъе́зд, а, *m.* **1.** departure; dispersal. **2.** (*pl.*) travel, journeyings. **3.** (*mil.*) mounted patrol. **4.** section of double track (*on single-line railway*); station, halt (*on single--line railway*).

разъездн|о́й, *adj.* р. аге́нт (*obs.*) traveller, travelling representative; ~ы́е де́ньги travelling expenses; р. путь (*railway*) siding.

разъезжа́|ть, ю, *impf.* to drive (about, around), ride (about, around); to travel; р. по дела́м слу́жбы to travel about on business.

разъезжа́|ться, юсь, *impf. of* разъе́хаться.

разъе́|сть, ст, дя́т, *past* ~л, *pf.* (*of* ~да́ть) to eat away; to corrode (*also fig.*); его́ ~ли сомне́ния he was consumed with doubts.

разъе́|сться, мся, шься, стся, ди́мся, ди́тесь, дя́тся, *past* ~лся, *pf.* (*of* ~да́ться) (*coll.*) to get fat (*from good living*).

разъе́|хаться, дусь, дешься, *pf.* (*of* ~зжа́ть-ся) **1.** to depart; to disperse; прие́хавшие на по́хороны ~хались the mourners have departed. **2.** to separate, cease living together. **3.** to (be able to) pass; тут грузовика́м нельзя́ р. it is impossible for lorries to pass here. **4.** to pass one another (*without meeting*), miss one another. **5.** (*coll.*) to slide apart. **6.** (*coll.*) to fall to pieces, fall apart.

разъяр|и́ть, ю́, и́шь, *pf.* (*of* ~я́ть) to infuriate, rouse to fury.

разъяр|и́ться, ю́сь, и́шься, *pf.* (*of* ~я́ться) to become furious, get into a fury.

разъяр|я́ть(ся), я́ю(сь), *impf. of* ~и́ть(ся).

разъясне́ни|е, я, *n.* explanation, elucidation; interpretation.

разъясни́тельный, *adj.* explanatory, elucidatory.

разъясн|и́ть, и́т, *pf.* (*coll.*) (*impers.*) to clear up (*of the weather*).

разъясн|и́ть, ю́, и́шь, *pf.* (*of* ~я́ть) to explain, elucidate; to interpret.

разъясн|и́ться, и́тся, *pf.* = ~и́ть.

разъясн|и́ться, и́тся, *pf.* (*of* ~я́ться) to become clear, be cleared up.

разъясн|я́ть(ся), я́ю, я́ет(ся), *impf. of* ~и́ть(ся).

разыгр|а́ть, а́ю, *pf.* (*of* ~ывать) **1.** to play (through); to perform; р. дурака́ to play the fool. **2.** to draw (*a lottery, etc.*); to raffle. **3.** (*coll.*) to play a trick (on), play a practical joke (on).

разыгр|а́ться, а́юсь, *pf.* (*of* ~ываться) **1.** to be carried away by a game, by play. **2.** (*of a pianist, an actor, etc.*) to warm up. **3.** (*of wind or sea*) to rise; to get up; (*of a storm*) to break; (*fig.*; *of feelings*) to run high.

разы́грыва|ть(ся), ю(сь), *impf. of* разыгра́ть(ся) 2, 3.

разыска́ни|е, я, *n.* **1.** hunting down, searching out. **2.** (piece of) research.

разы|ска́ть, щу́, ~щешь, *pf.* to find (after searching).

разы|ска́ться, щу́сь, ~щешься, *pf.* **1.** (*impf.* ~скиваться) to be sought for. **2.** to turn up, be found.

разы́скива|ть, ю, *impf.* to hunt, search for.

разы́скива|ться, юсь, *impf. of* разыска́ться; р. поли́цией to be wanted by the police.

ра|й, я, о ~е, в ~ю́, *m.* (*bibl.*) paradise; (Garden of) Eden; земно́й р., р. земно́й (*fig.*) earthly paradise.

рай- *abbr. of* райо́нный.

райко́м, а, *m.* (*abbr. of* райо́нный комите́т) raion committee, district committee.

райо́н, а, *m.* **1.** region; area; zone. **2.** (*designation of administrative division of U.S.S.R.*) raion, district.

райони́ровани|е, я, *n.* **1.** division into districts. **2.** earmarking for a given area; zoning.

райони́р|овать, ую, *impf. and pf.* **1.** to divide into districts. **2.** to earmark for a given area; to zone.

райо́н|ный, *adj. of* ~.

ра́й|ский, *adj. of* ~; (*fig.*) heavenly; ~ская пти́ца bird of paradise.

райсове́т, а, *m.* (*abbr. of* райо́нный сове́т) raion soviet, district soviet.

рак, а, *m.* **1.** (*zool.*) crawfish, crayfish; кра́сный как р. red as a lobster; показа́ть, где ~и зиму́ют (*coll.*) to give it someone hot; знать, где ~и зиму́ют (*coll.*) to know a thing or two, know what's what. **2.** (*med.*) cancer; (*bot.*) canker. **3.** P. (*astron.*) Crab, Cancer; тро́пик ~а (*geogr.*) Tropic of Cancer.

ра́к|а, и, *f.* (*eccl.*) shrine (*of a saint*).

раке́т|а¹, ы, *f.* **1.** (air-)rocket; flare; пусти́ть ~у to let off a rocket. **2.** (*mil.*) rocket, ballistic missile; межконтинента́льная р. inter-continental ballistic missile (ICBM). **3.** (*outer-space*) rocket. **4.** (*coll.*) hydrofoil (vessel).

раке́т|а², ы, *f.* = ~ка.

раке́т|ка, ки, *f.* (*sport*) racket.

раке́тниц|а, ы, *f.* rocket projector; Very pistol, signal pistol.

раке́тный¹, *adj.* rocket(-powered), jet; р. дви́гатель rocket engine, jet engine.

**раке́т|ный², ** *adj. of* ~а².

раке́тчик, а, *m.* **1.** rocket signaller. **2.** missile specialist.

раки́т|а, ы, *f.* (*bot.*) brittle willow.

раки́тник, а, *m.* broom (*bush*); broom plantation.

ра́ковин|а, ы, *f.* **1.** shell; ушна́я р. (*anat.*) aural cavity. **2.** sink; wash-basin. **3.** (*in metal*) blister, bubble; уса́дочная р. air hole, blow hole.

ра́к|овый, *adj. of* ~; (*med.*) cancerous; ~овая о́пухоль cancerous tumour.

ракообра́зн|ые, ых, *sing.* ~ое, ~ого, *n.* (*zool.*) Crustacea.

ракообра́зный, *adj.* (*zool.*) cancroid.

раку́рс, а, *m.* (*art*) foreshortening; в ~е foreshortened.

**раку́шечник, а, ** *m.* (*geol.*) coquina, shell rock.

раку́шк|а, и, *f.* cockle-shell; mussel.

ра́м|а, ы, *f.* **1.** frame; око́нная р. window-frame, sash; вста́вить в ~у to frame. **2.** chassis, carriage.

рам|ена́, е́н, ена́м, *no sing.* (*arch. or poet.*) shoulders.

ра́мен|ь, и, *f.* (*dial.*) coniferous forest.

ра́мен|ье, ья, *n.* = ~ь.

ра́мк|а, и, *f.* frame; в ~е framed; без ~и unframed; объявле́ние о сме́рти в тра́урной ~е black-bordered obituary announcement.

ра́м|ки, ок, (*pl. only*) framework; limits; в ~ках (+*g.*) within the framework (of), within the limits (of); вы́йти за р. (+*g.*) to exceed the limits (of).

ра́м|ный, *adj. of* ~а.

ра́м|очный, *adj. of* ~ка; ~очная анте́нна loop aerial, frame aerial.

ра́мп|а, ы, *f.* (*theatr.*) footlights.

ра́н|а, ы, *f.* wound.

ранг, а, *m.* class, rank.

рангоу́т, а, *m.* (*naut.*) masts and spars.

рангоу́т|ный, *adj. of* ~; ~ное де́рево (*naut.*) spar.

ранево́й, *adj. of* ра́на.

ра́нее, *adv.* = ра́ньше.

ране́ни|е, я, *n.* 1. wounding. 2. wound; injury.

ра́нен|ый, *adj.* wounded; injured; *as noun* р., ~ого, *m.* wounded man; injured man.

ране́т, а, *m.* rennet (*kind of apple*).

ра́н|ец, ца, *m.* knapsack, haversack; satchel; (*mil.*) pack.

ранжи́р, а, *m.* по ~у (*coll.*) in order of size.

ра́н|ить, ю, ишь, *impf. and pf.* to wound; to injure.

ра́нн|ий, *adj.* early; ~им у́тром early in the morning; ~яя пти́чка (*fig.*) early bird; с ~его де́тства from early childhood; с ~их лет from (one's) earliest years.

ра́но¹, *pred.* it is early; ещё р. ложи́ться спать it is too early for bed.

ра́но², *adv.* early; р. и́ли по́здно sooner or later.

рант, а, о ~е, на ~у́, *m.* welt; сапоги́ на ~у́ welted boots.

рантье́, *indecl., m.* rentier.

ран|ь, и, *f.* (*coll.*) early hour; куда́ ты направля́ешься в таку́ю р.? where are you bound for at this ungodly hour?

ра́ньше, *adv.* 1. earlier; как мо́жно р. as early as possible; as soon as possible. 2. before; до Ло́ндона он не дое́дет р. ве́чера he will not reach London before evening. 3. first (of all). 4. before, formerly; р. мы жи́ли в дере́вне we used to live in the country.

папи́р|а, ы, *f.* foil.

ра́порт, а, *m.* report.

рапорт|ова́ть, у́ю, *impf. and pf.* to report.

рапс, а, *m.* (*bot.*) rape.

рапсо́ди|я, и, *f.* (*mus.*) rhapsody.

рарите́т, а, *m.* rarity, curiosity.

ра́с|а, ы, *f.* race.

раси́зм, а, *m.* racialism.

раси́ст, а, *m.* racialist.

раска́ива|ться, юсь, *impf. of* раска́яться.

раскал|ённый, *p.p.p. of* ~и́ть *and adj.* scorching, burning hot; р. добела́ white-hot; р. докрасна́ red-hot.

раскал|и́ть, ю́, и́шь, *pf.* (*of* ~я́ть) to bring to a great heat; р. добела́ to make white-hot; р. докрасна́ to make red-hot.

раскал|и́ться, ю́сь, и́шься, *pf.* (*of* ~я́ться) to glow, become hot; р. добела́ to become

white-hot; р. докрасна́ to become red-hot.

раска́лыва|ть(ся), ю(сь), *impf. of* расколо́ть(ся).

раскал|я́ть(ся), я́ю(сь), *impf. of* ~и́ть(ся).

раска́пыва|ть, ю, *impf. of* раскопа́ть.

раска́рмлива|ть, ю, *impf. of* раскорми́ть.

раскасси́р|овать, ую, *pf.* (*mil.*) to disband; (*fig.*) to wind up, liquidate.

раска́т, а, *m.* roll, peal; р. гро́ма peal of thunder.

раскат|а́ть, а́ю, *pf.* (*of* ~ывать) 1. to unroll. 2. to roll (out); to smooth out; to level; р. те́сто to roll out dough.

раскат|а́ться, а́юсь, *pf.* (*of* ~ываться) 1. to unroll. 2. to roll out.

раска́тист|ый (~, ~а), *adj.* rolling, booming; р. смех peal(s) of laughter.

раска|ти́ть, чу́, ~тишь, *pf.* (*of* ~тывать) 1. to set rolling. 2. to roll away.

раска|ти́ться, чу́сь, ~тишься, *pf.* (*of* ~тываться) 1. to gather momentum. 2. to roll away.

раска́тыва|ть, ю, *impf.* 1. *impf. of* раската́ть *and* раскати́ть. 2. (*coll.*) to drive (about, around), ride (about, around).

раска́тыва|ться, юсь, *impf. of* раската́ть(ся) *and* раскати́ть(ся).

раскач|а́ть, а́ю, *pf.* (*of* ~ивать) 1. to swing; to rock. 2. to loosen, shake loose. 3. (*fig., coll.*) to shake up, stir up.

раскач|а́ться, а́юсь, *pf.* (*of* ~иваться) 1. to swing (oneself); to rock (oneself). 2. to shake loose. 3. (*fig., coll.*) to bestir oneself, get into the swing of.

раска́шля|ться, юсь, *pf.* to have a fit of coughing.

раска́яни|е, я, *n.* repentance.

раска́|яться, юсь, *pf.* (*of* ка́яться *and* ~иваться) (в+*p.*) to repent (of).

расквартирова́ни|е, я, *n.* quartering, billeting.

расквартир|ова́ть, у́ю, *pf.* (*of* ~о́вывать) to quarter, billet.

расквартиро́выва|ть, ю, *impf. of* расквартирова́ть.

расква́|сить, шу, сишь, *pf.* (*of* ~шивать) (*coll.*) to punch (*and draw blood from*); р. кому́-н. нос to give someone a bloody nose.

расква́шива|ть, ю, *impf. of* расква́сить.

расквита́|ться, юсь, *pf.* (с+*i.; coll.*) to settle accounts (with) (*also fig.*); (*fig.*) to get even (with).

раскида́|ть, а́ю, *pf.* (*of* ~ывать) to scatter; to throw about.

раски́дист|ый (~, ~а), *adj.* branchy, spreading.

раскидно́й, *adj.* folding.

раски́дыва|ть, ю, *impf. of* раскида́ть *and* раски́нуть.

раски́дыва|ться, юсь, *impf. of* раски́нуться.

раски́|нуть, ну, нешь, *pf.* (*of* ~дывать) 1. to stretch (out); р. ру́ки to stretch one's arms. 2. to spread (out); to set up; р. шатёр to pitch a tent. 3. р. умо́м to consider, think over.

раски́|нуться, нусь, нешься, *pf.* (*of* ~дываться) 1. to spread out, stretch out; по всему́ скло́ну холма́ ~нулось вое́нное кла́дбище the entire side of the hill was occupied by a military cemetery. 2. (*coll.*) to sprawl.

раскис|а́ть, а́ю, *impf. of* ~нуть.

раскисле́ни|е, я, *n.* (*chem.*) deoxidization.

раскисл|и́ть, ю́, и́шь, *pf.* (*of* ~я́ть) (*chem.*) to deoxidize, reduce.

раскисл|я́ть, я́ю, *impf. of* ~и́ть.

раски́с|нуть, ну, нешь, *past* ~, ~ла, *pf.* (*of* ~а́ть) 1. to rise (*from fermentation*). 2. (*fig., coll.*) to become limp.

раскла́дк|а, и, *f.* apportionment; going shares.

раскладу́шк|а, и, *f.* (*coll.*) folding bed, divan bed.

раскладн|о́й, *adj.* folding; ~а́я крова́ть camp-bed.

раскла́дыва|ть(ся), ю(сь), *impf. of* разложи́ть(ся)[1].

раскла́нива|ться, юсь, *impf. of* раскла́няться.

раскла́н|яться, яюсь, *pf.* (*of* ~иваться) 1. to exchange bows (*on meeting or leave-taking*). 2. to take leave (of).

раскле́ива|ть(ся), ю(сь), *impf. of* раскле́ить(ся).

раскле́|ить, ю, ишь, *pf.* (*of* ~ивать) 1. to unstick. 2. to stick, paste (*in various places*).

раскле́|иться, юсь, ишься, *pf.* (*of* ~иваться) 1. to come unstuck. 2. (*fig., coll.*) to fall through, fail to come off; сде́лка ~илась the deal fell through. 3. (*fig., coll.*) to feel seedy, be off colour; он совсе́м ~ился he has gone to pieces.

раскле́йк|а, и, *f.* sticking, pasting.

раскле́йщик, а, *m.* bill-sticker.

расклеп|а́ть, а́ю, *pf.* (*of* ~ывать) to unrivet, unclench.

расклёпыва|ть, ю, *impf. of* расклепа́ть.

раск|ова́ть, ую́, уёшь, *pf.* (*of* ~о́вывать) 1. to unchain, unfetter; to unshoe (*a horse*). 2. to hammer out, flatten; (*tech.*) to upset, jump (up).

раск|ова́ться, ую́сь, уёшься, *pf.* (*of* ~о́вываться) 1. (*of a horse*) to cast a shoe. 2. to free oneself (*from fetters*).

раско́выва|ть(ся), ю(сь), *impf. of* расковáть(ся).

расковы́р|ять, я́ю, *pf.* (*of* ~ивать) to pick open; to scratch raw.

раско́ка|ть, ю, *pf.* (*coll.*) to drop and break.

раско́л, а, *m.* 1. (*rel., hist.*) schism, dissent. 2. (*polit., etc.*) split, division.

раскола́чива|ть, ю, *impf. of* расколоти́ть.

расколо|ти́ть, чу́, ~ти́шь, *pf.* (*of* расколáчивать) 1. to unnail; to prise open. 2. to stretch (*footwear*). 3. (*coll.*) to break; to smash (*crockery, etc.; fig., the enemy*).

раскол|о́ть, ю́, ~ешь, *pf.* 1. *pf. of* коло́ть[1]. 2. (*impf.* раскáлывать) (*fig.*) to disrupt, break up.

раскол|о́ться, ю́сь, ~ешься, *pf.* (*of* раскáлываться) to split (*also fig.*).

раско́льник, а, *m.* 1. (*rel., hist.*) schismatic, dissenter. 2. (*polit.; fig.*) splitter.

раско́льническ|ий, *adj.* 1. (*rel., hist.*) schismatic, dissenting. 2. ~ая та́ктика (*polit.*) splitting tactics.

раскопа́|ть, ю, *pf.* (*of* раскáпывать) to dig up, unearth (*also fig.*); (*archaeol.*) to excavate.

раско́пк|а, и, *f.* digging up; *pl.* (*archaeol.*) excavations.

раскорм|и́ть, лю́, ~ишь, *pf.* (*of* раскáрмливать) to fatten.

раскоря́к|а, и, *m. and f.* (*coll.*) bow-legged person; ходи́ть ~ой to walk bow-legged.

раско́с, а, *m.* (*tech.*) cross stay, diagonal strut, angle brace.

раско́сый, *adj.* (*of eyes*) slanting.

раскоше́лива|ться, юсь, *impf. of* раскоше́литься.

раскоше́л|иться, юсь, ишься, *pf.* (*of* ~иваться) (*coll.*) to loosen one's purse-strings; to fork out.

раскра́дыва|ть, ю, *impf. of* раскра́сть.

раскра́ива|ть, ю, *impf. of* раскрои́ть.

раскра́|сить, шу, сишь, *pf.* (*of* ~шивать) to paint, colour.

раскра́ск|а, и, *f.* 1. painting, colouring. 2. colours, colour scheme.

раскрасне́|ться, юсь, *pf.* to flush, go red (in the face).

раскра́|сть, ду́, дёшь, *past* ~л, *pf.* (*of* ~дывать) to loot, clean out.

раскрепо|сти́ть, щу́, сти́шь, *pf.* (*of* ~ща́ть) to set free, liberate, emancipate.

раскрепо|сти́ться, щу́сь, сти́шься, *pf.* (*of* ~ща́ться) 1. to free oneself, liberate oneself. 2. *pass. of* ~сти́ть.

раскрепоща́|ть(ся), ю(сь), *impf. of* раскрепости́ть(ся).

раскрепоще́ни|е, я, *n.* liberation, emancipation; р. же́нщины emancipation of women.

раскритик|ова́ть, у́ю, *pf.* to criticize severely, slate.

раскрич|а́ться, у́сь, и́шься, *pf.* 1. to start shouting, start crying. 2. (на+*a.*) to shout (at), bellow (at).

раскро|и́ть, ю́, и́шь, *pf.* (*of* раскрáивать)

1. to cut out (*material*). **2.** (*fig.*, *coll.*) to cut open; р. кому́-н. че́реп to split someone's skull.

раскрош|и́ть(ся), **у́(сь)**, **⌣ишь(ся)**, *pf. of* кроши́ть(ся).

раскру|ти́ть, **чу́**, **⌣тишь**, *pf.* (*of* ⌣чива́ть) to untwist, untwine, undo.

раскру|ти́ться, **ти́тся**, *pf.* (*of* ⌣чива́ться) to come untwisted, come undone.

раскру́чива|ть(ся), **ю**, **ет(ся)**, *impf. of* раскрути́ть(ся).

раскрыва́|ть(ся), **ю(сь)**, *impf. of* раскры́ть-(ся).

раскры́ти|е, **я**, *n.* **1.** opening. **2.** exposure, disclosing.

раскр|ы́ть, **о́ю**, **о́ешь**, *pf.* (*of* ⌣ыва́ть) **1.** to open (wide); р. зо́нтик to put up an umbrella; р. кни́гу to open a book; р. ско́бки to open brackets. **2.** to expose, bare. **3.** to reveal, disclose, lay bare; to discover; р. секре́т to disclose a secret; р. свои́ ка́рты (*fig.*) to show one's cards, show one's hand.

раскр|ы́ться, **о́юсь**, **о́ешься**, *pf.* (*of* ⌣ыва́ть-ся) **1.** to open; лепестки́ то́лько что ⌣ы́лись the petals have only just opened. **2.** to uncover oneself. **3.** to come out, come to light.

раскуда́х|таться, **чусь**, **чешься**, *pf.* (*coll.*) to set up a cackling.

раскула́чивани|е, **я**, *n.* dispossession of the kulaks, de-kulakization.

раскула́чива|ть, **ю**, *impf. of* раскула́чить.

раскула́ч|ить, **у**, **ишь**, *pf.* (*of* ⌣ивать) to dispossess the kulaks, de-kulakize.

раскуме́ка|ть, **ю**, *pf.* (*coll.*) to learn, find out.

раскуп|а́ть, **а́ю**, *impf. of* ⌣и́ть.

раскуп|и́ть, **лю́**, **⌣ишь**, *pf.* (*of* ⌣а́ть) to buy up.

раску́порива|ть(ся), **ю**, **ет(ся)**, *impf. of* раску́порить(ся).

раску́пор|ить, **ю**, **ишь**, *pf.* (*of* ⌣ивать) to uncork, open.

раску́пор|иться, **ится**, *pf.* (*of* ⌣иваться) to open, come uncorked.

раску́порк|а, **и**, *f.* uncorking, opening.

раску́рива|ть(ся), **ю**, **ет(ся)**, *impf. of* раскури́ть(ся).

раскур|и́ть, **ю́**, **⌣ишь**, *pf.* (*of* ⌣ивать) **1.** to puff at (*a pipe or cigarette*). **2.** to light up.

раскур|и́ться, **⌣ится**, *pf.* (*of* ⌣иваться) (*of a pipe or cigarette*) to draw.

раску|си́ть, **шу́**, **⌣сишь**, *pf.* (*of* ⌣сывать) **1.** to bite through. **2.** (*pf. only*) to get to the core, heart (of); р. кого́-н. to see through someone, rumble someone.

раскусыва|ть, **ю**, *impf. of* раскуси́ть.

раску́т|ать, **аю**, *pf.* (*of* ⌣ывать) to unwrap.

раску́т|аться, **аюсь**, *pf.* (*of* ⌣ываться) to unwrap oneself.

раску|ти́ться, **чу́сь**, **⌣тишься**, *pf.* (*coll.*) to take to going on drinking-bouts.

раску́тыва|ть(ся), **ю(сь)**, *impf. of* раску́тать(ся).

ра́совый, *adj.* racial.

распа́д, **а**, *m.* **1.** disintegration, break-up; (*fig.*) collapse. **2.** (*chem.*) decomposition, dissociation.

распада́|ться, **ю**, **ет(ся)**, *impf. of* распа́сться.

распа́ива|ть(ся), **ю(сь)**, **ет(ся)**, *impf. of* распая́ть(ся).

распак|ова́ть, **у́ю**, *pf.* (*of* ⌣о́вывать) to unpack.

распак|ова́ться, **у́юсь**, *pf.* (*of* ⌣о́вываться) **1.** (*of a parcel, etc.*) to come undone. **2.** (*coll.*) to unpack (one's things).

распако́выва|ть(ся), **ю(сь)**, *impf. of* распакова́ть(ся).

распал|и́ть, **ю́**, **и́шь**, *pf.* (*of* ⌣я́ть) **1.** to make burning hot. **2.** (*fig.*) to inflame; р. гне́вом to incense.

распал|и́ться, **ю́сь**, **и́шься**, *pf.* (*of* ⌣я́ться) **1.** to get burning hot. **2.** (+*i.*; *fig.*) to burn (with); р. гне́вом to be incensed.

распал|я́ть(ся), **я́ю(сь)**, *impf. of* ⌣и́ть(ся).

распа́р, **а**, *m.* (*tech.*) bosh, body (*of blast furnace*).

распа́рива|ть(ся), **ю(сь)**, *impf. of* распа́-рить(ся).

распа́р|ить, **ю**, **ишь**, *pf.* (*of* ⌣ивать) **1.** to steam out; to stew well. **2.** to cause to sweat.

распа́р|иться, **юсь**, **ишься**, *pf.* (*of* ⌣ивать-ся) **1.** to steam out; to be well stewed. **2.** to break into a sweat.

распа́рыва|ть(ся), **ю**, **ет(ся)**, *impf. of* распоро́ть(ся).

распа́|сться, **дётся**, *past* ⌣лся, *pf.* (*of* ⌣да́ться) **1.** to disintegrate, fall to pieces; (*fig.*) to break up; to collapse; коали́ция ⌣лась the coalition broke up. **2.** (*chem.*) to decompose, dissociate.

распа|ха́ть, **шу́**, **⌣шешь**, *pf.* (*of* ⌣хивать) to plough up.

распа́хива|ть, **ю**, *impf. of* распаха́ть *and* распахну́ть.

распа́хива|ться, **юсь**, *impf. of* распахну́ться.

распах|ну́ть, **ну́**, **нёшь**, *pf.* (*of* ⌣ивать) to open wide; to fling open, throw open; широко́ р. две́ри (+*d.*) to open wide the doors (to) (*also fig.*).

распах|ну́ться, **ну́сь**, **нёшься**, *pf.* (*of* ⌣иваться) **1.** to open wide; to fly open, swing open. **2.** to throw open one's coat.

распа́шк|а, **и**, *f.* ploughing up.

распашно́й¹, *adj.* (*obs.*; *of clothing*) worn open, unfastened.

распашн|о́й², *adj.* ⌣о́е весло́ paddle; ⌣а́я гре́бля paddling.

распашн|о́й³, *adj.* (*dial.*) for ploughing up; ~а́я земля́ ploughland.

распашо́нк|а, и, *f.* baby's loose jacket.

распа|я́ть, я́ю, *pf.* (*of* ~ивать) to unsolder.

распа|я́ться, я́ется, *pf.* (*of* ~иваться) to come unsoldered.

распева́|ть, ю, *impf.* **1.** *impf. of* распе́ть. **2.** to sing for a certain time.

распека́|ть, ю, *impf. of* распе́чь.

распелен|а́ть, а́ю, *pf.* (*of* ~ывать) to unswaddle.

распере́ть, разопру́, разопрёшь, *past* распёр, распёрла, *pf.* (*of* распира́ть) (*coll.*) to burst open, cause to burst.

распетуш|и́ться, у́сь, и́шься, *pf.* (*coll.*) to get into a paddy; to have one's hackles up.

расп|е́ть, ою́, оёшь, *pf.* (*of* ~ева́ть) **1.** to sing through. **2.** to practise (*one's voice*).

расп|е́ться, ою́сь, оёшься, *pf.* (*coll.*) **1.** (*of a singer*) to warm up. **2.** to sing away.

распеча́т|ать, аю, *pf.* (*of* ~ывать) to unseal; р. письмо́ to open a letter.

распеча́т|аться, ается, *pf.* (*of* ~ываться) to come unsealed; to come open.

распеча́тыва|ть(ся), ю, ет(ся), *impf. of* распеча́тать(ся).

распе́|чь, ку́, чёшь, *past* ~к, ~кла́, *pf.* (*of* ~ка́ть) (*coll.*) to blow up.

распива́|ть, ю, *impf. of* распи́ть.

распи́вочно, *adv.* прода́жа пите́й р. sale of liquor for consumption on the premises.

распи́вочн|ый, *adj.* (*obs.*) for consumption on the premises; *as noun* ~ая, ~ой, *f.* (*obs.*) tavern, bar.

распи́л, а, *m.* saw cut.

распи́лива|ть, ю, *impf. of* распили́ть.

распил|и́ть, ю́, ~ишь, *pf.* (*of* ~ивать) to saw up.

распи́лк|а, и, *f.* sawing.

распило́вк|а, и, *f.* = распи́лка.

распина́|ть, ю, *impf. of* распя́ть.

распина́|ться, юсь, *impf.* (за кого́-н.; *coll.*) to put oneself out (on someone's behalf).

распира́|ть, ю, *impf. of* распере́ть.

расписа́ни|е, я, *n.* time-table, schedule; боево́е р. (*mil.*) order of battle; (*naut.*) battle stations; по ~ю according to time-table, according to schedule.

распи|са́ть, шу́, ~шешь, *pf.* (*of* ~сывать) **1.** to enter; to note down; р. счета́ по кни́гам to enter bills in the account-book. **2.** to assign, allot. **3.** to paint. **4.** (*fig., coll.*) to paint a picture (of).

распи|са́ться, шу́сь, ~шешься, *pf.* (*of* ~сываться) **1.** to sign (one's name); (в+*p.*) to sign (for); прочти́те э́ту бума́гу и ~ши́тесь read this paper and sign your name; р. в получе́нии заказно́го паке́та to sign for a registered letter. **2.** (*coll.*) to register

one's marriage. **3.** (в+*p.*; *fig.*) to acknowledge, testify (to); р. в со́бственном неве́жестве to acknowledge one's own ignorance.

распи́ск|а¹, и, *f.* painting.

распи́ск|а², и, *f.* receipt; р. в получе́нии (+*g.*) receipt (for); письмо́ с обра́тной ~ой letter with advice of delivery; сда́ть письмо́ под ~у to make someone sign for a letter.

расписно́й, *adj.* painted, decorated.

распи́сыва|ть(ся), ю(сь), *impf. of* расписа́ть(ся).

рас|пи́ть, разопью́, разопьёшь, *past* ~пи́л (*and* ро́спил), ~пила́, ~пи́ло (*and* ро́спило), *pf.* (*of* ~пива́ть) (*coll.*) to drink up; р. буты́лку (с кем-н.) to split a bottle (with someone).

распих|а́ть, а́ю, *pf.* (*of* ~ивать) (*coll.*) **1.** to push aside. **2.** to shove; р. я́блоки по карма́нам to stuff apples into one's pockets.

распи́хива|ть, ю, *impf. of* распиха́ть.

распла́в|ить, лю, ишь, *pf.* (*of* ~ля́ть) to melt, fuse.

распла́в|иться, ится, *pf.* (*of* ~ля́ться) to melt, fuse (*intrans.*).

расплавле́ни|е, я, *n.* melting, fusion.

расплавля́|ть(ся), ю, ет(ся), *impf. of* распла́вить(ся).

распла|ка́ться, чусь, чешься, *pf.* to burst into tears.

распланир|ова́ть, у́ю, *pf. of* плани́рова́ть.

распласт|а́ть, а́ю, *pf.* (*of* ~ывать) **1.** to split, divide into layers. **2.** to spread; р. кры́лья to spread one's wings.

распласт|а́ться, а́юсь, *pf.* (*of* ~ываться) to sprawl.

распла́стыва|ть(ся), ю(сь), *impf. of* распласта́ть(ся).

распла́т|а, ы, *f.* payment; (*fig.*) retribution; час ~ы day of reckoning.

распла|ти́ться, чу́сь, ~тишься, *pf.* (*of* ~чиваться) **1.** (с+*i.*) to pay off; to settle accounts (with), get even (with) (*also fig.*); р. с долга́ми to pay off one's debts; р. по ста́рым счета́м to pay off old scores. **2.** (за+*a.*; *fig.*) to pay (for).

распла́чива|ться, юсь, *impf. of* расплати́ться.

распле|ска́ть, щу́, ~щешь, *pf.* (*of* ~ски-вать) to spill.

распле|ска́ться, щу́сь, ~щешься, *pf.* (*of* ~скиваться) **1.** to spill. **2.** *pass. of* ~ска́ть.

расплёскива|ть(ся), ю(сь), *impf. of* расплеска́ть(ся).

распле|сти́, ту́, тёшь, *past* ~л, ~ла́, *pf.* (*of* ~та́ть) to untwine, untwist, unweave, undo; to unplait.

распле|сти́сь, тётся, *past* ~лся, ~ла́сь, *pf.*

(*of* ~та́ться) to untwine, untwist; to come undone; to come unplaited.

расплета́|ть(ся), ю, ет(ся), *impf. of* расплести́(сь).

распло|ди́ть(ся), жу́(сь), ди́шь(ся), *pf. of* плоди́ть(ся).

расплыва́|ться, ется, *impf. of* расплы́ться.

расплы́вчат|ый (~, ~а), *adj.* dim, indistinct; diffuse, vague; ~ые очерта́ния dim outlines; р. стиль woolly style.

расплы́|ться, вётся, *past* ~лся, ~ла́сь, *pf.* (*of* ~ва́ться) **1.** to run; черни́ла ~лись the ink has run. **2.** (*coll.*) to spread; to run to fat; р. в улы́бку to break into a smile.

расплю́щива|ть(ся), ю, ет(ся), *impf. of* расплю́щить(ся).

расплю́щ|ить, у, ишь, *pf.* (*of* ~ивать) to flatten out, hammer out.

расплю́щ|иться, ится, *pf.* (*of* ~иваться) to become flat.

распознава́|емый, *pres. part. pass. of* ~ть *and adj.* recognizable, identifiable.

распознава́ни|е, я, *n.* recognition, identification.

распозна|ва́ть, ю́, ёшь, *impf. of* ~ть.

распозна́|ть, ю, ешь, *pf.* (*of* ~ва́ть) to recognize, identify; р. боле́знь to diagnose an illness.

располага́|ть¹, ю, *impf.* **1.** (+*i.*) to dispose (of), have at one's disposal, have available; р. вре́менем to have time available; р. больши́ми сре́дствами to dispose of ample means. **2.** (+*inf.*; *obs.*) to intend, propose.

располага́|ть², ю, *impf. of* расположи́ть.

располага́|ться, юсь, *impf. of* расположи́ться¹.

располага́|ющий, *pres. part. act. of* ~ть *and adj.* prepossessing.

располз|а́ться, а́юсь, *impf. of* ~ти́сь.

располз|ти́сь, у́сь, ёшься, *past* ~ся, ~ла́сь, *pf.* (*of* ~а́ться) **1.** to crawl (away). **2.** (*of clothing, etc.*; *coll.*) to come unravelled; to tear, give at the seams.

расположе́ни|е, я, *n.* **1.** disposition, arrangement; р. по кварти́рам (*mil.*) billeting; р. не́рвов (*bot.*) nervation; р. слов word-order. **2.** situation, location; р. на ме́стности (*mil.*) location on the ground. **3.** favour, liking; sympathies; по́льзоваться чьим-н. ~ем to enjoy someone's favour, be liked by someone, be in someone's good books; чу́вствовать к кому́-н. р. to be favourably disposed towards someone. **4.** (к) disposition, inclination (to, for); tendency (to), propensity (to); bias (towards), penchant (for); у неё р. к бронхи́ту she has a tendency to bronchitis, she is inclined to be bronchial. **5.** р. (ду́ха) disposition, mood, humour; быть в плохо́м ~и ду́ха to be in a bad

mood; у меня́ нет ~я танцева́ть I am not in the mood for dancing.

располо́жен|ный (~, ~а), *p.p.p. of* расположи́ть *and pred. adj.* **1.** (к) well disposed (to, towards). **2.** (к or +*inf.*) disposed (to), inclined (to); in the mood (for); я не ~ к отвлечённому размышле́нию I am not disposed to, am not in the mood for abstract speculation; я не о́чень ~ сего́дня рабо́тать I don't feel much like working today.

располож|и́ть, у́, ~ишь, *pf.* (*of* располага́ть²) **1.** to dispose, arrange, set out; р. свои́ войска́ to dispose, station one's troops. **2.** to win over, gain; р. кого́-н. к себе́, в свою́ по́льзу to gain someone's favour.

располож|и́ться¹, у́сь, ~ишься, *pf.* (*of* располага́ться) to take up position; to settle oneself, compose oneself, make oneself comfortable; р. спать to settle oneself to sleep.

располож|и́ться², у́сь, ~ишься, *pf.* (+*inf.*; *obs.*) to resolve, make up one's mind.

распо́р, а, *m.* (*tech.*) thrust.

распо́рк|а, и, *f.* (*tech.*) cross-bar, strut, tie-beam, tie-rod, spreader bar.

распор|о́ть, ю́, ~ешь, *pf.* (*of* поро́ть¹ *and* распа́рывать) to unstitch, unpick, undo, rip.

распор|о́ться, ~ется, *pf.* (*of* поро́ться *and* распа́рываться) to come unstitched, come undone, rip.

распоряди́тел|ь, я, *m.* manager; master of ceremonies.

распоряди́тельност|ь, и, *f.* good management; efficiency; отсу́тствие ~и mismanagement.

распоряди́тел|ьный (~ен, ~ьна), *adj.* capable; efficient; р. челове́к a good organizer.

распоря|ди́ться, жу́сь, ди́шься, *pf.* (*of* ~жа́ться) **1.** (о+*p. or* +*inf.*) to order; to see (that); мы ~ди́мся о проведе́нии э́того реше́ния we will see that this decision is implemented; я ~жу́сь возмести́ть вам расхо́ды I will see that you are reimbursed for the expenses. **2.** (+*i.*) to manage; to deal (with); разреши́ть кому́-н. р. по своему́ усмотре́нию to give someone a free hand; как р. э́тими деньга́ми? what is to be done with this money?, how should this money be used?

распоря́д|ок, ка, *m.* order; routine; пра́вила вну́треннего ~ка (в учрежде́нии, на фа́брике, *etc.*) (office, factory, *etc.*) regulations; р. дня the daily routine.

распоряжа́|ться, юсь, *impf.* **1.** *impf. of* распоряди́ться. **2.** *impf. only* to give orders, be in charge; to be the boss; р. как у себя́ до́ма to behave as though the place belongs to one.

распоряже́ни|е, я, *n.* **1.** order; instruction,

direction; до осо́бого ~я until further notice. 2. disposal, command; быть в ~и кого́-н. to be at someone's disposal; име́ть в своём ~и to have at one's disposal, command.

распоя́|сать, шу, шешь, *pf.* (*of* ~сывать) to ungird.

распоя́|саться, шусь, шешься, *pf.* (*of* ~сываться) 1. to take off one's belt, ungird oneself. 2. (*fig., coll., pejor.*) to throw aside all restraint, let oneself go.

распоя́сыва|ть(ся), ю(сь), *impf. of* распоя́сать(ся).

распра́в|а, ы, *f.* 1. (*hist.*) punishment, execution; твори́ть суд и ~у to administer justice and mete out punishment. 2. violence; reprisal; крова́вая р. massacre; кула́чная р. fist-law; коро́ткая р. short shrift; у нас с ни́ми р. коротка́ we'll give them short shrift, we'll make short work of them.

распра́в|ить, лю, ишь, *pf.* (*of* ~ля́ть) 1. to straighten; to smooth out; р. морщи́ны to smooth out wrinkles. 2. to spread, stretch; р. кры́лья to spread one's wings (*also fig.*).

распра́в|иться¹, ится, *pf.* (*of* ~ля́ться) to get smoothed out.

распра́в|иться², люсь, ишься, *pf.* (*of* ~ля́ться) (c+*i.*) to deal (with), make short work (of), give short shrift; р. без суда́ to take the law into one's own hands.

расправля́|ть(ся), ю(сь), *impf. of* распра́вить(ся).

распределе́ни|е, я, *n.* distribution; allocation, assignment; р. нало́гов assessment of taxes; р. войск (*mil.*) order of battle.

распредели́тел|ь, я, *m.* 1. distributor; retailer; закры́тый р. retail establishment closed to persons not registered. 2. (*electr.*) distributor; spreader.

распредели́тельн|ый, *adj.* distributive, distributing; ~ая доска́, р. щит (*tech.*) switchboard; р. вал (*tech.*) cam shaft; р. кла́пан (*tech.*) regulating valve; ~ая коро́бка (*electr.*) switch box, junction box, panel box.

распредел|и́ть, ю́, и́шь, *pf.* (*of* ~я́ть) to distribute; to allocate, allot, assign; р. своё вре́мя to allocate one's time.

распредел|и́ться, и́тся, *pf.* (*of* ~я́ться) 1. to divide up, split up. 2. *pass. of* ~и́ть.

распредел|я́ть(ся), я́ю(сь), *impf. of* ~и́ть(ся).

распрекра́с|ный (~ен, ~на), *adj.* (*coll.*) beautiful, fine, splendid.

распрода|ва́ть, ю́, ёшь, *impf. of* ~ть.

распрода́ж|а, и, *f.* sale; clearance sale, bargain sale.

распрода́|ть, м, шь, ст, ди́м, ди́те, ду́т, *past* **распро́дал, ~ла́, распро́дало,** *pf.* (*of* ~ва́ть)

to sell off; to sell out; биле́ты распро́даны all the tickets are sold.

распростер|е́ть, *fut. tense not used, past* ~, ~ла, *pf.* (*of* распростира́ть) to stretch out, extend.

распростер|е́ться, *fut. tense not used, past* ~ся, ~лась, *pf.* (*of* распростира́ться) 1. to stretch oneself out, prostrate oneself. 2. (*fig.*) to spread.

распростёр|тый, *p.p.p. of* ~е́ть *and adj.* 1. outstretched; встре́тить с ~тыми объя́тиями to receive with outstretched arms. 2. prostrate, prone.

распростира́|ть(ся), ю(сь), *impf. of* распростере́ть(ся).

распро|сти́ться, щу́сь, сти́шься, *pf.* (c+*i.*) to take final leave (of); р. с мечто́й to bid farewell to one's dream(s).

распростране́ни|е, я, *n.* spreading, diffusion; dissemination; р. зара́зы spreading of infection; име́ть большо́е р. to be widely practised.

распространённост|ь, и, *f.* prevalence; diffusion.

распростран|ённый, *p.p.p. of* ~и́ть *and adj.* 1. widespread, prevalent; широко́ р. widely-distributed. 2. ~ённое предложе́ние (*gram.*) extended sentence.

распространи́тел|ь, я, *m.* spreader.

распространи́тельн|ый, *adj.* extended; (excessively) wide; ~ое толкова́ние прика́за a wide interpretation of an injunction.

распростран|и́ть, ю́, и́шь, *pf.* (*of* ~я́ть) 1. to spread, diffuse; to disseminate, propagate; to popularize; р. слух to spread a rumour; р. но́вое уче́ние to disseminate a new doctrine. 2. to extend; р. де́йствие зако́на на всех to extend the application of a law to all. 3. to give off, give out (*a smell*).

распростран|и́ться, ю́сь, и́шься, *pf.* (*of* ~я́ться) 1. to spread; to extend; (*of a law, etc.*) to apply. 2. (o+*p.*; *coll.*) to enlarge (on), expatiate (on), dilate (on).

распростран|я́ть(ся), я́ю(сь), *impf. of* ~и́ть(ся).

распроща́|ться, юсь, *pf.* (c+*i.*; *coll.*) = распрости́ться.

распры́ска|ть, ю, *pf.* (*coll.*) to spray about; to use up (in spraying).

ра́спр|я, и, *g. pl.* ~ей, *f.* quarrel, feud.

распряга́|ть(ся), ю(сь), *impf. of* распря́чь(ся).

распрям|и́ть, лю́, и́шь, *pf.* (*of* ~ля́ть) to straighten, unbend.

распрям|и́ться, лю́сь, и́шься, *pf.* (*of* ~ля́ться) to straighten oneself up.

распрямля́|ть(ся), ю(сь), *impf. of* распрями́ть(ся).

распря́|чь, гу́, жёшь, гу́т, *past* ~г, ~гла́, *pf.* (*of* ~га́ть) to unharness.

распря́|чься, жётся, гу́тся, *past* **~гся, ~гла́сь,** *pf.* (*of* ~га́ться) to get unharnessed.

распу́блик|ова́ть, у́ю, *pf.* (*of* ~о́вывать) to publish; to promulgate.

распублико́выва|ть, ю, *impf. of* распубликова́ть.

распуг|а́ть, а́ю, *pf.* (*of* ~ивать) to scare away, frighten away.

распуска́|ть(ся), ю(сь), *impf. of* распусти́ть(ся).

распу|сти́ть, щу́, ~стишь, *pf.* (*of* ~ска́ть) 1. to dismiss; to disband; р. парла́мент to dissolve parliament; р. кома́нду (*naut.*) to pay off a crew; р. на кани́кулы to dismiss for the holidays. 2. to let out; to relax; р. во́лосы to let one's hair down; р. знамёна to unfurl banners; р. паруса́ to set sail. 3. (*fig.*) to allow to become undisciplined, allow to get out of hand; to spoil. 4. to dissolve; to melt. 5. (*coll.*) to spread, put out (*rumours, etc.*).

распу|сти́ться, щу́сь, ~стишься, *pf.* (*of* ~ска́ться) 1. (*bot.*) to open, blossom out, come out. 2. to come loose; чуло́к у неё ~сти́лся her stocking had come down. 3. (*fig.*) to become undisciplined, get out of hand, let oneself go. 4. to dissolve; to melt.

распу́т|ать, аю, *pf.* (*of* ~ывать) 1. to untangle, disentangle; to unravel. 2. to untie, loose (*an animal*). 3. (*fig.*) to disentangle, unravel; to puzzle out.

распу́т|аться, аюсь, *pf.* (*of* ~ываться) 1. to get disentangled, come undone. 2. (*fig., coll.*) to get disentangled, be cleared up. 3. (с+*i.*; *coll.*) to rid oneself (of), shake off.

распу́тиц|а, ы, *f.* time (*during spring and autumn*) of bad roads.

распу́тник, а, *m.* profligate, libertine.

распу́тнича|ть, ю, *impf.* to lead a dissolute life.

распу́т|ный (~ен, ~на), *adj.* dissolute, dissipated, debauched.

распу́тств|о, а, *n.* dissipation, debauchery, profligacy, libertinism.

распу́тыва|ть(ся), ю(сь), *impf. of* распу́тать(ся).

распу́ть|е, я, *n.* crossroads; быть на р. (*fig.*) to be at the crossroads, be at the parting of the ways.

распух|а́ть, а́ю, *impf. of* ~нуть.

распу́х|нуть, ну, нешь, *past* ~, ~ла, *pf.* (*of* ~а́ть) 1. to swell up. 2. (*fig., coll.*) to swell, become inflated.

распуш|и́ть, у́, и́шь, *pf. of* пуши́ть.

распу́щенност|ь, и, *f.* 1. lack of discipline. 2. dissoluteness, dissipation.

распу́|щенный, *p.p.p. of* ~сти́ть *and adj.* 1. undisciplined; р. ребёнок spoiled child. 2. dissolute, dissipated.

распылéни|е, я, *n.* 1. spraying; atomiza-

tion. 2. dispersion, scattering; р. средств dissipation of resources.

распыли́тел|ь, я, *m.* spray(er), atomizer, pulverizer.

распыл|и́ть, ю́, и́шь, *pf.* (*of* ~я́ть) 1. to spray; to atomize; to pulverize. 2. (*fig.*) to disperse, scatter; р. си́лы to scatter one's forces.

распыл|и́ться, и́тся, *pf.* (*of* ~я́ться) 1. to disperse; to get scattered. 2. *pass. of* ~и́ть.

распыл|я́ть(ся), я́ю(сь), *impf. of* ~и́ть(ся).

распя́лива|ть, ю, *impf. of* распя́лить.

распя́л|ить, ю, ишь, *pf.* (*of* ~ивать) to stretch (*on a frame*).

распя́ти|е, я, *n.* 1. crucifixion. 2. cross, crucifix.

расп|я́ть, ну́, нёшь, *pf.* (*of* ~ина́ть) to crucify.

расса́д|а, ы, *no pl., f.* seedlings.

расса|ди́ть, жу́, ~дишь, *pf.* (*of* ~жива́ть) 1. to seat, offer seats. 2. to separate, seat separately. 3. to transplant, plant out.

расса́дк|а, и, *f.* transplanting, planting out.

расса́дник, а, *m.* 1. seed-plot. 2. (*fig.*) hot-bed, breeding-ground.

расса́жива|ть, ю, *impf. of* рассади́ть.

расса́жива|ться, юсь, *impf. of* рассе́сться[1].

расса́сывани|е, я, *n.* (*med.*) resolution, re-sorption.

расса́сыва|ться, юсь, *impf. of* рассоса́ться.

рассве|сти́, тёт, *past* ~ло́, *pf.* (*of* ~та́ть) to dawn; уже́ ~ло́ it was already light; соверше́нно ~ло́ it was broad daylight.

рассве́т, а, *m.* dawn, daybreak.

рассвета́|ть, ет, *impf. of* рассвести́; ~ет day is breaking.

рассвирепé|ть, ю, *pf.* (*of* свирепе́ть) to become savage; to turn nasty.

рассе́да|ться, юсь, *impf. of* рассе́сться[2].

рассе́дл|ать, а́ю, *pf.* (*of* ~ывать) to un-saddle.

рассе́ивани|е, я, *n.* dispersion; dispersal, scattering, dissipation.

рассе́ива|ть(ся), ю(сь), *impf. of* рассе́ять(ся).

рассека́|ть, ю, *impf. of* рассе́чь.

рассекрé|тить, чу, тишь, *pf.* (*of* ~чивать) 1. to declassify, remove from secret list. 2. to deny access to secret documents; to take off secret work.

рассекре́чива|ть, ю, *impf. of* рассекрети́ть.

рассело́ни|е, я, *n.* 1. settling (*in a new place*). 2. separation; settling apart.

рассе́лин|а, ы, *f.* cleft, fissure.

рассел|и́ть, ю́, и́шь, *pf.* (*of* ~я́ть) 1. to settle (*in a new place*). 2. to separate; to settle apart.

рассел|и́ться, ю́сь, и́шься, *pf.* (*of* ~я́ться) 1. to settle (*in a new place*). 2. to separate, settle separately.

рассел|я́ть(ся), я́ю(сь), *impf. of* ~и́ть(ся).

рассер|ди́ть, жу́, ~дишь, *pf.* to anger, make angry.

рассер|ди́ться, жу́сь, ~дишься, *pf.* (на+*a.*) to get, become angry (with).

рассе́р|женный, *p.p.p. of* ~ди́ть *and adj.* angry.

рассерча́|ть, ю, *pf.* (*coll.*) to get angry.

рас|се́сться¹, ся́дусь, ся́дешься, *past* ~се́л-ся, *pf.* (*of* ~са́живаться) 1. to take one's seat. 2. (*coll.*) to sprawl.

рас|се́сться², ся́дется, *past* ~се́лся, *pf.* (*of* ~седа́ться) to crack.

рассе́|чь, ку́, чёшь, ку́т, *past* ~к, ~кла́, *pf.* (*of* ~ка́ть) 1. to cut through; to cleave (*also fig.*). 2. to cut (badly); я ~к себе́ па́лец I have cut my finger badly.

рассе́яни|е, я, *n.* diffusion; dispersion; р. тепла́ (*phys.*) dissipation of heat, thermal dispersion; р. све́та (*phys.*) diffusion of light.

рассе́янност|ь, и, *f.* 1. diffusion; disper-sion; dissipation. 2. absent-mindedness, distraction.

рассе́я|нный, *p.p.p. of* ~ть *and adj.* 1. dif-fused; dissipated; р. свет (*phys.*) diffused light. 2. scattered, dispersed; ~нное насе-ле́ние scattered population. 3. absent--minded; р. взгляд vacant look. 4. (*fig.*) dissipated.

рассе́|ять, ю, ешь, *pf.* (*of* ~ивать) 1. to sow broadcast, scatter. 2. (*fig.*) to place (about), establish (about), dot (about). 3. to dis-perse, scatter; (*fig.*) to dispel; р. чьи-н. сомне́ния to dispel someone's doubts.

рассе́|яться, юсь, ешься, *pf.* (*of* ~иваться) 1. to disperse, scatter; толпа́ ~я́лась the crowd dispersed; неприя́тельский отря́д ~я́лся the enemy detachment scattered; тума́н ~я́лся the fog cleared; её го́ре ~я́лось her grief passed; р. как дым to vanish into thin air, into smoke. 2. to divert oneself, distract oneself; ему́ на́до р. he needs a break.

расси|де́ться, жу́сь, ди́шься, *pf.* (*of* ~жи-ваться) (*coll.*) to sit for a long time.

расси́жива|ться, юсь, *impf. of* расси-де́ться.

расска́з, а, *m.* 1. account, narrative. 2. story, tale.

расска|за́ть, жу́, ~жешь, *pf.* (*of* ~зывать) to tell, narrate, recount.

расска́зчик, а, *m.* story-teller, narrator.

расска́зыва|ть, ю, *impf. of* рассказа́ть.

расслабева́|ть, ю, *impf. of* расслабе́ть.

расслабе́|ть, ю, *pf.* (*of* ~ва́ть) to weaken, grow weak; to tire; to grow limp.

расслаб|ить, лю, ишь, *pf.* (*of* ~ля́ть) to weaken, enfeeble; to enervate.

расслаб|ленный, *p.p.p. of* ~ить *and adj.* weak; limp.

расслабля́|ть, ю, *impf. of* рассла́бить.

расслаб|нуть, ну, нешь, *past* ~, ~ла, *pf.* (*coll.*) = ~е́ть.

рассла́в|ить, лю, ишь, *pf.* (*of* ~ля́ть) (*coll.*) 1. to praise to the skies. 2. to shout from the house-tops.

расславля́|ть, ю, *impf. of* рассла́вить.

рассла́ива|ть(ся), ю, ет(ся), *impf. of* рас-сло́ить(ся).

рассле́довани|е, я, *n.* investigation, exa-mination; (*leg.*) inquiry; назна́чить р. (+*g.*) to order an inquiry (into); произ-вести́ р. (+*g.*) to hold an inquiry (into).

рассле́д|овать, ую, *impf. and pf.* to investi-gate, look into, hold an inquiry (into).

рассло́ени|е, я, *n.* stratification (*also fig.*); exfoliation.

рассло|и́ть, ю́, и́шь, *pf.* (*of* рассла́ивать) to divide into layers, stratify (*also fig.*).

рассло|и́ться, и́тся, *pf.* (*of* рассла́иваться) to become stratified (*also fig.*); to exfoliate, flake off.

рассло́йк|а, и, *f.* 1. stratification. 2. (*geol.*) stratum.

расслу́ша|ть, ю, *pf.* (*obs.*) to listen properly (to).

расслы́ш|ать, у, ишь, *pf.* to catch; я не ~ал вас I didn't catch what you said.

рассма́трива|ть, ю, *impf.* 1. *impf. of* рас-смотре́ть. 2. *impf. only* to regard (as), con-sider; мы ~ем э́то как обма́н we regard it as a fraud. 3. *impf. only* to scrutinize, examine.

рассмеш|и́ть, у́, и́шь, *pf.* to make laugh, set laughing.

рассме́|яться, ю́сь, ёшься, *pf.* to burst out laughing.

рассмотре́ни|е, я, *n.* examination, scrutiny; consideration; предста́вить на р. to sub-mit for consideration; быть на ~и to be under consideration; оста́вить жа́лобу без ~я to reject a complaint; переда́ть де́ло на но́вое р. to submit a case for re-con-sideration.

рассмотр|е́ть, ю́, ~ишь, *pf.* (*of* рассма́три-вать) 1. to descry, discern, make out; мы с трудо́м ~е́ли на́дпись на па́мятнике we had difficulty in making out the inscription on the monument. 2. to examine, consider; р. заявле́ние to consider an application.

расс|ова́ть, ую́, уёшь, *pf.* (*of* ~о́вывать) (*coll.*) to shove (about), stuff (about); р. свои́ ве́щи по чемода́нам to stuff one's things into suitcases.

рассо́выва|ть, ю, *impf. of* рассова́ть.

рассо́л, а, *m.* 1. brine. 2. (*cul.*) pickle.

рассо́льник, а, *m.* rassolnik (*meat or fish soup with pickled cucumbers*).

рассо́р|ить, ю, ишь, *pf.* to set at variance, set at loggerheads.

рассо́р|и́ть, ю́, и́шь, *pf.* (*coll.*) to drop (over); р. оку́рки по́ полу to litter the floor with cigarette-butts.

рассо́р|иться, ю́сь, и́шься, *pf.* (с+*i.*) to fall out (with), fall foul (of).

рассортир|ова́ть, у́ю, *pf.* (*of* ~о́вывать) to sort out.

рассортиро́вк|а, и, *f.* sorting out.

рассортиро́выва|ть, ю, *impf. of* рассортирова́ть.

рассос|а́ться, ётся, *pf.* (*of* расса́сываться) (*med.*) to resolve.

рассо́х|нуться, нется, *past* ~ся, ~лась, *pf.* (*of* рассыха́ться) to crack.

расспра́шива|ть, ю, *impf. of* расспроси́ть.

расспро́с, а, *m.* question, questioning; надо́есть ~ами to pester with questions.

расспро|си́ть, шу́, ~сишь, *pf.* (*of* расспра́шивать) to question; р. кого́-н. о доро́ге to ask someone the way.

рассредото́чени|е, я, *n.* (*mil.*) dispersion, dispersal.

рассредото́чива|ть, ю, *impf. of* рассредото́чить.

рассредото́ч|ить, у, ишь, *pf.* (*of* ~ивать) (*mil.*) to disperse.

рассро́чива|ть, ю, *impf. of* рассро́чить.

рассро́ч|ить, у, ишь, *pf.* (*of* ~ивать) to spread (*over a period*); р. вы́плату до́лга to allow payment of a debt by instalments; р. изда́ние энциклопе́дии на де́сять лет to spread the publication of an encyclopaedia over (a period of) ten years.

рассро́чк|а, и, *f.* instalment system; в ~у by, in instalments; купи́ть с ~ой платежа́ to purchase by instalments, on the hire--purchase system; предоста́вить ~у to grant the right to pay by instalments.

расстава́ни|е, я, *n.* parting; при ~и on parting.

расста|ва́ться, ю́сь, ёшься, *impf. of* расста́ться.

расста́в|ить, лю, ишь, *pf.* (*of* ~ля́ть) 1. (*impf. also* расстана́вливать) to place, arrange; р. часовы́х to post sentries; р. ша́хматы to set out chess-men. 2. to move apart; р. но́ги to stand with one's legs apart. 3. (*tailoring*) to let out.

расста́вк|а, и, *f.* (*tailoring*) letting out.

расставля́|ть, ю, *impf. of* расста́вить.

расстана́влива|ть, ю, *impf. of* расста́вить.

расстано́вк|а, и, *f.* 1. placing, arrangement; р. зна́ков препина́ния punctuation. 2. pause; spacing; говори́ть с ~ой to speak without haste, speak slowly and deliberately.

расста́|ться, нусь, нешься, *pf.* (*of* ~ва́ться) (с+*i.*) 1. to part (with); to leave; ~немся друзья́ми let us part friends. 2. to give up;

р. с мы́слью to put the thought out of one's head.

расстега́|й, я, *m.* open-topped pasty.

расстёгива|ть(ся), ю(сь), *impf. of* расстег-ну́ть(ся).

расстег|ну́ть, ну́, нёшь, *pf.* (*of* ~ивать) to undo, unfasten; to unbutton; to unhook, unclasp, unbuckle.

расстег|ну́ться, ну́сь, нёшься, *pf.* (*of* ~иваться) 1. to come undone, become unfastened; to become unbuttoned; to become unhooked. 2. to undo one's coat, unbutton one's coat; to undo one's buttons.

расстел|и́ть(ся), ю́(сь), ~ишь(ся), *pf.* = разостла́ть(ся).

расстила́|ть, ю, *impf. of* разостла́ть.

расстила́|ться, юсь, *impf.* 1. *impf. of* разостла́ться. 2. *impf. only* to extend, unfold; пе́ред на́шими глаза́ми ~лась вели́чественная панора́ма гор before our eyes unfolded a magnificent mountain panorama.

расстоя́ни|е, я, *n.* distance, space, interval; на бли́зком ~и (от) at a short distance (from), a short way away (from); на далё-ком ~и in the far distance, a great way off; на ~и пу́шечного вы́стрела within gunshot; на ~и челове́ческого го́лоса within hail; они́ живу́т на ~и двух миль от ближа́йшего сосе́да they live two miles from their nearest neighbour; держа́ть кого́-н. на ~и to keep someone at arm's length; держа́ться на ~и to keep one's distance, hold aloof.

расстра́ива|ть(ся), ю(сь), *impf. of* расстро́ить(ся).

расстре́л, а, *m.* 1. (military) execution; приговори́ть к ~у to sentence to be shot. 2. shooting up.

расстре́лива|ть, ю, *impf. of* расстреля́ть.

расстрел|я́ть, я́ю, *pf.* (*of* ~ивать) 1. to shoot, execute by shooting. 2. to shoot up; to fire upon at close range. 3. to use up (*in firing*).

расстри́г|а, и, *m.* unfrocked priest, unfrocked monk.

расстрига́|ть, ю, *impf. of* расстри́чь.

расстри́|чь, гу́, жёшь, гу́т, *past* ~г, ~гла, *pf.* (*of* ~га́ть) (*eccl.*) to unfrock.

расстро́|енный, *p.p.p. of* ~ить *and adj.* disordered, deranged; р. вид downcast appearance.

расстро́|ить, ю, ишь, *pf.* (*of* расстра́ивать) 1. to disorder, derange; to throw into confusion; to unsettle; to upset; р. желу́док to cause indigestion; р. за́мыслы to thwart schemes; р. своё здоро́вье to ruin one's health; р. чьи-н. пла́ны to upset someone's plans; р. ряды́ проти́вника to break the enemy's ranks; р. сва́дьбу to break an engagement; р. хозя́йство to shatter the economy. 2. to upset, put out. 3. (*mus.*) to put out of tune, untune.

расстро́|иться, юсь, ишься, *pf.* (*of* расстра́иваться) 1. to fall into confusion, fall apart; (*fig.*) to fall to the ground, fall through; все на́ши пла́ны ∼и́лись all our plans have fallen through. 2. (от) to be upset (over, about), be put out (about). 3. (*mus.*) to become out of tune.

расстро́йств|о, а, *n.* 1. disorder; derangement; confusion; р. желу́дка stomach disorder, stomach upset; (*coll.*) diarrhoea; р. пищеваре́ния indigestion; р. ре́чи speech defect; внести́ р. (в+*a.*), привести́ в р. to throw into confusion, derange, disorganize; дела́ пришли́ в р. things are in a sad state. 2. (*coll.*) upset; привести́ в р. to upset, put out; быть в ∼е to be upset, be put out.

расступ|а́ться, а́ется, *impf. of* ∼и́ться.

расступ|и́ться, ∼и́тся, *pf.* (*of* ∼а́ться) to part, make way; толпа́ ∼и́лась the crowd parted; земля́ ∼и́лась (*poet.*) the earth opened.

расстыко́вк|а, и, *f.* (*of space vehicles*) un-docking.

рассуди́тельност|ь, и, *f.* reasonableness; good sense.

рассуди́тел|ьный (∼ен, ∼ьна), *adj.* reasonable; sober-minded; sensible.

рассу|ди́ть, жу́, ∼дишь, *pf.* 1. to judge (between), arbitrate (between); ∼ди́те нас settle our dispute, be an arbiter between us; р. спор to settle a dispute. 2. to think, consider; to decide; нам на́до р., как сообщи́ть ей э́ти но́вости we have to think how to break this news to her; мы ∼ди́ли, что пришло́ вре́мя верну́ться домо́й we decided that the time had come to return home.

рассу́д|ок, ка, *m.* 1. reason; intellect; го́лос ∼ка the voice of reason; в по́лном ∼ке in full possession of one's faculties; лиши́ться ∼ка to lose one's reason, go out of one's mind. 2. common sense, good sense.

рассу́доч|ный (∼ен, ∼на), *adj.* 1. rational, of the reason. 2. governed by the reason (*to exclusion of feelings*); ∼ная любо́вь intellectual love.

рассужда́|ть, ю, *impf.* 1. to reason. 2. (о+*p.*) to discuss, debate; to argue (about); to discourse (on); р. на каку́ю-н. те́му to discuss a topic.

рассужде́ни|е, я, *n.* 1. reasoning. 2. (*usu. pl.*) discussion, debate; argument; discourse; без ∼й without argument, without arguing. 3. (*obs.*) dissertation. 4. в ∼и (+*g.*; *obs.*) with regard to, as regards.

рассу́чива|ться, ю, ет(ся), *impf. of* рассучи́ть(ся).

рассуч|и́ть, у́, ∼ишь, *pf.* (*of* ∼ивать) to untwist; to undo; р. рукава́ to roll one's sleeves down.

рассуч|и́ться, ∼ится, *pf.* (*of* ∼иваться) to untwist; to come undone.

рассчи́т|анный, *p.p.p. of* ∼а́ть *and adj.* 1. calculated, deliberate; ∼анная гру́бость calculated rudeness. 2. (на+*a.*) intended (for), meant (for), designed (for); кни́га, ∼анная на широ́кого чита́теля a book intended for the general public; автостра́да, ∼анная на бы́строе движе́ние motorway designed for fast traffic.

рассчит|а́ть, а́ю, *pf.* (*of* ∼ывать) 1. to calculate, compute; (*tech.*) to rate; не р. свои́х сил to overrate one's strength. 2. to dismiss, sack. 3. (*mil.*) to number off, order to number.

рассчит|а́ться, а́юсь, *pf.* (*of* ∼ываться) 1. (с+*i.*) to settle accounts (with), reckon (with). 2. (*mil.*) to number; по поря́дку номеро́в ∼а́йсь! (*word of command*) number!

рассчи́тыва|ть, ю, *impf.* 1. *impf. of* рассчита́ть *and* рассче́сть. 2. *impf. only* (на+*a.*) to calculate (on, upon), count (on, upon), reckon (on, upon); (+*inf.*) to expect (to), hope (to); р. на многочи́сленную пу́блику to count on a large attendance; мы ∼ли ко́нчить рабо́ту в э́том году́ we were hoping to finish the work this year. 3. *impf. only* (на+*a.*) to count (on, upon), rely (on, upon), depend (upon).

рассчи́тыва|ться, юсь, *impf. of* рассчита́ться *and* рассче́сться.

рассыла́|ть, ю, *impf. of* разосла́ть.

рассы́лк|а, и, *f.* distribution, delivery.

рассы́льн|ый, *adj.* ∼ая кни́га delivery book; *as noun* р., ∼ого, *m.* delivery man, errand-boy.

рассы́п|ать, лю, лешь, *pf.* (*of* ∼а́ть) to spill; to strew, scatter; р. в цепь (*mil.*) to draw up in extended line.

рассы́п|аться, люсь, лешься, *pf.* (*of* ∼а́ться) 1. to spill, scatter. 2. to spread out, deploy; р. в цепь (*mil.*) to extend. 3. to crumble; to go to pieces, disintegrate (*also fig.*). 4. (в+*p.*) to be profuse (in); р. в благода́рностях to be profuse in the expression of thanks; р. в похвала́х (+*d.*) to shower praises (upon).

рассып|а́ть(ся), а́ю(сь), *impf. of* ∼ать(ся).

рассыпн|о́й, *adj.* 1. (sold) loose, (sold) by the piece; ∼ы́е папиро́сы cigarettes sold loose. 2. р. строй (*mil.*) extended order.

рассы́пчат|ый (∼, ∼а), *adj.* friable; (*cul.*) short, crumbly; ∼ое пече́нье shortbread.

рассыха́|ться, юсь, *impf. of* рассо́хнуться.

раста́лкива|ть, ю, *impf. of* растолка́ть.

раста́плива|ть(ся), ю, ет(ся), *impf. of* растопи́ть(ся).

раста́птыва|ть, ю, *impf. of* растопта́ть.

растаск|а́ть, а́ю, *pf.* (*of* ～ивать) **1.** to take away, remove (*little by little, bit by bit*). **2.** to pilfer, filch.

растаска|ть, ю, *impf. of* растаска́ть *and* растащи́ть.

растас|ова́ть, у́ю, *pf.* (*of* ～о́вывать) (*coll.*) to shuffle (*cards*).

растасо́выва|ть, ю, *impf. of* растасова́ть.

раста́чива|ть, ю, *impf. of* расточи́ть².

растащ|и́ть, у́, ～ишь, *pf.* (*of* раста́скивать) **1.** to part, separate, drag asunder. **2.** = растаска́ть.

раста́|ять, ю, ешь, *pf. of* та́ять.

раство́р¹, а, *m.* (extent of) opening, span; р. две́ри doorway; р. окна́ extent to which a window is opened; р. ци́ркуля spread of a pair of compasses.

раство́р², а, *m.* **1.** (*chem.*) solution. **2.** (*tech.*) mortar; строи́тельный р. grout.

растворе́ни|е, я, *n.* solution, dissolution.

раствори́мост|ь, и, *f.* (*chem.*) solubility.

раствори́м|ый (～, ～а), *adj.* (*chem.*) soluble; р. в воде́ water-soluble.

раствори́тел|ь, я, *m.* (*chem.*) solvent.

раствор|и́ть¹, ю́, ～ишь, *pf.* (*of* ～я́ть) to open.

раствор|и́ть², ю́, и́шь, *pf.* (*of* ～я́ть) to dissolve.

раствор|и́ться¹, ～ится, *pf.* (*of* ～я́ться) to open.

раствор|и́ться², и́тся, *pf.* (*of* ～я́ться) to dissolve.

раствор|я́ть(ся), я́ю(сь), *impf. of* ～и́ть(ся).

растека́|ться, юсь, *impf. of* расте́чься.

расте́ни|е, я, *n.* plant; одноле́тнее р. annual; многоле́тнее р. perennial; ползу́чее р. creeper.

растениево́д, а, *m.* plant-grower.

растениево́дств|о, а, *n.* plant-growing.

растере́ть, разотру́, разотрёшь, *past* растёр, **растёрла,** *pf.* (*of* растира́ть) **1.** to grind; р. в порошо́к to grind to powder; (*chem.*) to triturate. **2.** (по+*d.*) to rub (over), spread (over). **3.** to rub, massage.

растере́ться, разотру́сь, разотрёшься, *past* **растёрся, растёрлась,** *pf.* (*of* растира́ться) **1.** to become powdered, turn into powder; (*chem.*) to become triturated. **2.** (+*i.*) to rub oneself briskly (with).

растерз|а́ть, а́ю, *pf.* (*of* ～ывать) **1.** to tear to pieces. **2.** (*fig., poet.*) to lacerate; to harrow.

расте́рзыва|ть, ю, *impf. of* растерза́ть.

расте́рива|ть(ся), ю(сь), *impf. of* растеря́ть(ся).

расте́рянност|ь, и, *f.* confusion, perplexity, dismay.

расте́р|янный, *p.p.p. of* ～я́ть *and adj.* confused, perplexed, dismayed; р. взгляд look of dismay.

растер|я́ть, я́ю, *pf.* (*of* ～ивать) to lose (little by little).

растер|я́ться, я́юсь, *pf.* (*of* ～иваться) **1.** to get lost. **2.** to lose one's head.

расте́|чься, чётся, ку́тся, *past* ～кся, ～кла́сь,** *pf.* (*of* ～ка́ться) **1.** to spill; to run. **2.** (*fig.*) to spread; по её лицу́ ～кла́сь улы́бка a smile spread over her face.

раст|и́, у́, ёшь, *past* **рос, росла́,** *impf.* **1.** (*biol., bot.*) to grow; (*of children*) to grow up; он рос на Украи́не he grew up in the Ukraine. **2.** (*fig.*) to grow, increase. **3.** (*fig.*) to advance, develop; to grow in stature.

растира́ни|е, я, *n.* **1.** grinding. **2.** (*med.*) massage.

растира́|ть(ся), ю(сь), *impf. of* растере́ть(ся).

расти́ск|ать, аю, *pf.* (*of* ～ивать) (*coll.*) to shove (in).

расти́скива|ть, ю, *impf. of* расти́скать *and* расти́снуть.

расти́с|нуть, ну, нешь, *pf.* (*of* ～кивать) (*coll.*) to unclench.

расти́тельност|ь, и, *f.* **1.** vegetation; verdure; лишённый ～и barren. **2.** hair (*on face or body*).

расти́тельн|ый, *adj.* vegetable; ～ое ма́сло vegetable oil; р. мир, ～ое ца́рство the vegetable kingdom; ～ая пи́ща vegetable diet; жить ～ой жи́знью (*fig., iron.*) to vegetate.

ра|сти́ть, щу́, сти́шь, *impf.* **1.** to raise, bring up; to train; р. дете́й to raise children. **2.** to grow, cultivate; р. бо́роду to grow a beard.

растлева́|ть, ю, *impf. of* растли́ть.

растле́ни|е, я, *n.* **1.** seduction (*of minors*). **2.** (*fig.*) corruption; decay, decadence.

растле́нный, *adj.* corrupt; decadent.

растл|и́ть, ю́, и́шь, *pf.* (*of* ～ева́ть) **1.** to seduce (*minors*). **2.** (*fig.*) to corrupt.

растолка́|ть, ю, *pf.* (*of* раста́лкивать) **1.** to push asunder, apart. **2.** to shake (*in order to awaken*).

растолкн|у́ть, у́, ёшь, *pf.* (*coll.*) to push asunder, part forcibly.

растолк|ова́ть, у́ю, *pf.* (*of* ～о́вывать) to explain.

растолко́выва|ть, ю, *impf. of* растолкова́ть.

растол|о́чь, ку́, чёшь, ку́т, *past* ～о́к, ～окла́,** *pf. of* толо́чь.

растолсте́|ть, ю, *pf.* to grow stout, put on weight.

растоп|и́ть¹, лю́, ～ишь, *pf.* (*of* раста́пливать) to light, kindle.

растоп|и́ть², лю́, ～ишь, *pf.* (*of* раста́пливать) to melt; to (cause to) thaw.

растоп|и́ться¹, ～ится, *pf.* (*of* раста́пливаться) to begin to burn.

растоп|и́ться², **∼ится**, *pf.* (*of* раста́пливаться) to melt.

расто́пк|а, **и**, *f.* 1. lighting, kindling. 2. (*collect.*) kindling (wood).

растоп|та́ть, **чу́**, **∼чешь**, *pf.* (*of* раста́птывать) to trample, stamp (on), crush.

растопы́рива|ть, **ю**, *impf. of* растопы́рить.

растопы́р|ить, **ю**, **ишь**, *pf.* (*of* ∼ивать) to spread wide, open wide.

расторг|а́ть, **а́ю**, *impf. of* ∼ну́ть.

расто́рг|нуть, **ну**, **нешь**, *past* ∼, **∼ла**, *pf.* (*of* ∼а́ть) to cancel, dissolve, annul, abrogate (*a contract or agreement*); р. брак to dissolve a marriage.

расторг|ова́ть, **у́ю**, *pf.* (*of* ∼о́вывать) (*coll.*) to sell out.

расторг|ова́ться, **у́юсь**, *pf.* (*of* ∼о́вываться) (*coll.*) 1. to begin to do a brisk trade. 2. to have sold out.

расторже́ни|е, **я**, *n.* cancellation, dissolution, annulment, abrogation.

растормош|и́ть, **у́**, **и́шь**, *pf.* (*coll.*) 1. to tug (*in order to awaken*). 2. (*fig.*) to stir up, spur to activity.

растаро́п|ный (**∼ен**, **∼на**), *adj.* (*coll.*) quick, prompt, smart; efficient.

расточ|а́ть, **а́ю**, *impf.* (*of* ∼и́ть¹) 1. to waste, squander, dissipate. 2. (*fig.*) to lavish, shower; р. похвалы́ (+*d.*) to lavish praises (on, upon).

расточи́тел|ь, **я**, *m.* squanderer, waster, spendthrift.

расточи́тел|ьный (**∼ен**, **∼ьна**), *adj.* extravagant, wasteful.

расточ|и́ть¹, **у́**, **и́шь**, *pf. of* ∼а́ть.

расточ|и́ть², **у́**, **∼ишь**, *pf.* (*of* раста́чивать) (*tech.*) to bore (out).

расто́чк|а, **и**, *f.* (*tech.*) boring.

растрав|и́ть, **лю́**, **∼ишь**, *pf.* (*of* ∼ля́ть) to irritate; р. ра́ну (*fig.*) to rub salt in a wound; р. ста́рое го́ре (*fig.*) to re-open an old wound.

растравля́|ть, **ю**, *impf. of* растрави́ть.

растранжи́р|ить, **ю**, **ишь**, *pf. of* транжи́рить.

растра́т|а, **ы**, *f.* 1. spending; waste, squandering. 2. embezzlement, peculation.

растра́|тить, **чу**, **тишь**, *pf.* (*of* ∼чивать) 1. to spend; to waste, squander, dissipate; р. си́лы to dissipate one's energies; р. своё вре́мя to fritter away one's time. 2. to embezzle, peculate.

растра́тчик, **а**, *m.* embezzler, peculator.

растра́чива|ть, **ю**, *impf. of* растра́тить.

растрево́ж|ить, **у**, **ишь**, *pf.* (*coll.*) to alarm, agitate; to put the wind up; р. муравей́ник to stir up an ant-hill.

растрево́ж|иться, **усь**, **ишься**, *pf.* (*coll.*) to get the wind up.

растрезво́н|ить, **ю**, **ишь**, *pf. of* трезво́нить.

растрёп|а, **ы**, *m. and f.* (*coll.*) sloven; tousle-head.

растрёп|анный, *p.p.p. of* ∼а́ть *and adj.* tousled, dishevelled; tattered; быть в ∼анных чу́вствах (*coll.*) to be confused, be mixed up.

растреп|а́ть, **лю́**, **∼лешь**, *pf.* 1. to disarrange; р. во́лосы кому́-н. to tousle someone's hair. 2. to tatter, tear (*a book, etc.*).

растреп|а́ться, **∼лется**, *pf.* 1. to get disarranged, get dishevelled. 2. to get tattered, get torn.

растре́ск|аться, **ается**, *pf.* (*of* ∼иваться) to crack; (*of skin*) to chap.

растре́скива|ться, **ется**, *impf. of* растре́скаться.

растро́га|ть, **ю**, *pf.* to move, touch; р. кого́-н. до слёз to move someone to tears.

растро́га|ться, **юсь**, *pf.* to be (deeply) moved, touched.

растру́б, **а**, *m.* funnel-shaped opening; bell, bell-mouth; socket (*of pipe*); с ∼ом bell-shaped, bell-mouthed; брю́ки с ∼ами bell-bottomed trousers; соедине́ние ∼ом bell-and-spigot joint.

растру́б|ить, **лю́**, **и́шь**, *pf.* (+*a. or* о+*p.*; *coll.*) to trumpet.

растряс|ти́, **у́**, **ёшь**, *past* ∼, **∼ла́**, *pf.* 1. to strew (*hay, etc.*). 2. (*coll.*) to shake (*in order to awaken*). 3. (*impers.*) to jolt about. 4. (*coll.*) to squander.

растуш|ева́ть, **у́ю**, **у́ешь**, *pf.* (*of* ∼ёвывать) to shade.

растушёвк|а, **и**, *f.* 1. shading. 2. stump (*for softening pencil-marks, etc., in drawing*).

растушёвыва|ть, **ю**, *impf. of* растушева́ть.

растя́гива|ть(ся), **ю(сь)**, *impf. of* растяну́ть(ся); ∼ющиеся носки́ stretch socks.

растяже́ни|е, **я**, *n.* tension; stretch, stretching; (*med.*) strain, sprain.

растяжи́мост|ь, **и**, *f.* tensility, tensile strength; extensibility; expansibility.

растяжи́м|ый (**∼**, **∼а**), *adj.* tensile; extensible; expansible; ∼ое поня́тие loose concept.

растя́жк|а, **и**, *f.* 1. stretching, extension, lengthening out. 2. (*aeron.*) bracing wire, anti-drag wire.

растя́нутост|ь, **и**, *f.* 1. long-windedness, prolixity. 2. (*mil.*) extension, stretching out.

растя́н|утый, *p.p.p. of* ∼у́ть *and adj.* 1. long-winded, prolix. 2. stretched; р. фронт (*mil.*) extended front.

растя|ну́ть, **ну́**, **∼нешь**, *pf.* (*of* ∼ги́вать) 1. to stretch (out). 2. (*med.*) to strain, sprain; р. себе́ му́скул to pull a muscle; р. себе́ связ́ку to strain a ligament. 3. to stretch too far; (*fig.*) to prolong, drag out; р. расска́з to drag out, spin out a story; р. слова́ to drawl.

расстя|ну́ться, ну́сь, ~не́шься, *pf.* (*of* ~ги-
ваться) **1.** to stretch (out), lengthen out.
2. to stretch too far; (*fig.*) to be prolonged,
drag out; обсужде́ние его́ докла́да ~ну́-
лось на полтора́ часа́ discussion of his lecture dragged out for an hour and a half.
3. to stretch oneself out, sprawl. **4.** *pf. only*
(*coll.*) to measure one's length, go headlong.

растя́п|а, ы, *m. and f.* (*coll.*) muddler,
bungler.

расфас|ова́ть, у́ю, *pf.* (*of* ~о́вывать) to
pack up, parcel up.

расфасо́вк|а, и, *f.* packing, parcelling.

расфасо́выва|ть, ю, *impf. of* расфасо-
ва́ть.

расформирова́ни|е, я, *n.* breaking up;
(*mil.*) disbandment.

расформир|ова́ть, у́ю, *pf.* (*of* ~о́вывать) to
break up; (*mil.*) to disband.

расформиро́выва|ть, ю, *impf. of* расфор-
мирова́ть.

расфран|ти́ться, чу́сь, ти́шься, *pf.* (*coll.*)
to dress up.

расфранчённый, *adj.* (*coll.*) dressed up to
the nines; overdressed.

расфуфы́р|иться, юсь, ишься, *pf.* (*coll.*,
pejor.) to dress flashily.

расха́жива|ть, ю, *impf.* to walk, pace; ~ро.
ко́мнате to pace up and down a room.

расхва́лива|ть, ю, *impf. of* расхвали́ть.

расхвал|и́ть, ю́, ~ишь, *pf.* (*of* ~ивать) to
lavish, shower praise (on, upon).

расхва́рыва|ться, юсь, *impf. of* расхво-
ра́ться.

расхва́ста|ться, юсь, *pf.* (о+*p.*; *coll.*) to
boast extravagantly (of, about); to shoot
a line (about).

расхват|а́ть, а́ю, *pf.* (*of* ~ывать) to snatch,
seize (*with the object of purchasing, etc.*).

расхва́тыва|ть, ю, *impf. of* расхвата́ть.

расхвора́|ться, юсь, *pf.* (*of* расхва́рываться)
to fall ill; она́ не на шу́тку ~лась she is
seriously ill.

расхити́тел|ь, я, *m.* plunderer.

расхи́|тить, щу, тишь, *pf.* (*of* ~ща́ть) to
plunder, misappropriate.

расхища́|ть, ю, *impf. of* расхи́тить.

расхище́ни|е, я, *n.* plunder, plundering,
misappropriation.

расхлеб|а́ть, а́ю, *pf.* (*of* ~ывать) **1.** to eat
up (*without leaving anything*). **2.** (*fig.*) to
disentangle.

расхлёбыва|ть, ю, *impf. of* расхлеба́ть;
завари́л ка́шу, тепе́рь сам и ~й (*coll.*) you
got yourself into this mess, now get yourself
out of it.

расхля́банност|ь, и, *f.* **1.** looseness; insta-
bility. **2.** (*fig.*) slackness; laxity, lack of
discipline.

расхля́банн|ый, *adj.* (*coll.*) **1.** loose; un-
stable; ~ое здоро́вье tottering health; ~ая
похо́дка unstable gait, slouching. **2.** (*fig.*)
lax, undisciplined.

расхля́ба|ться, юсь, *pf.* (*coll.*) **1.** to come
loose, work loose. **2.** (*fig.*) to go to pieces.

расхо́д, а, *m.* **1.** expense; (*pl.*) expenses, outlay, cost; накладны́е ~ы overhead ex-
penses, overheads; де́ньги на карма́нные
~ы pocket-money; ввести́ в ~ы to put to
expense; взять на себя́ ~ы to bear the
expenses. **2.** (*in var. senses*) expenditure,
consumption; р. горю́чего fuel consumption. **3.** (*book-keeping*) expenditure, outlay;
прихо́д и р. income and expenditure; спи-
са́ть в р. to write off; (*fig.*, *coll.*) to liquidate;
быть в ~е (*fig.*, *coll.*) to be absent, be
missing. **4.** вы́вести в р. (*coll.*) to shoot.

расхо|ди́ться, жу́сь, ~ди́шься, *impf. of*
разойти́сь.

расхо́д|ный, *adj. of* ~; ~ная кни́га expenses
book, housekeeping book.

расхо́довани|е, я, *n.* expense, expenditure.

расхо́д|овать, ую, *impf.* (*of* из~) **1.** to spend,
expend. **2.** to use up, consume.

расхо́д|оваться, уюсь, *impf.* (*of* из~) **1.**
(*coll.*) to spend; to lay out money. **2.** *pass.*
of ~овать.

расхожде́ни|е, я, *n.* divergence; р. во
мне́ниях difference of opinion.

расхола́жива|ть, ю, *impf. of* расхолоди́ть.

расхоло|ди́ть, жу́, ди́шь, *pf.* (*of* расхола́жи-
вать) to damp the ardour (of).

расхо|те́ть, чу́, ~чешь, ти́м, ти́те, тя́т, *pf.*
(+*inf.*; *coll.*) to cease to want.

расхо|те́ться, ~чется, *pf.* (*impers.*+*d.*; *coll.*)
to cease to want; мне ~те́лось есть I no
longer want to eat.

расхохо|та́ться, чу́сь, ~че́шься, *pf.* to
burst out laughing; to start roaring with
laughter.

расхрабр|и́ться, ю́сь, и́шься, *pf.* (*coll.*) to
screw up one's courage, pluck up courage.

расцара́п|ать, аю, *pf.* (*of* ~ывать) to scratch
(all over).

расцара́п|аться, аюсь, *pf.* (*of* ~ываться) to
scratch oneself.

расцара́пыва|ть(ся), ю(сь), *impf. of* рас-
цара́пать(ся).

расцве|сти́, ту́, тёшь, *past* ~л, ~ла́, *pf.* (*of*
~та́ть) to bloom; to blossom (out) (*also*
fig.); (*fig.*) to flourish; не дать чему́-н. р.
(*fig.*) to nip something in the bud; его́ лицо́
~ло́ улы́бкой his face was wreathed in
smiles.

расцве́т, а, *m.* bloom, blossoming (out);
(*fig.*) flourishing; flowering, heyday; в ~е
сил in the prime of life, in one's prime, in
one's heyday.

расцвета́|ть, ю, *impf. of* расцвести́.

расцве|ти́ть, чу́, ти́шь, *pf.* (*of* ⌣чивать)
1. to paint in bright colours. **2.** to deck,
adorn; р. фла́гами (*naut.*) to dress.

расцве́тк|а, и, *f.* colours; coloration,
colouring; нас порази́ла я́ркая р. обста-
но́вки в их кварти́ре we were struck by the
bright colours of the furnishings in their flat.

расцве́чивани|е, я, *n.* (*naut.*) dressing.

расцве́чива|ть, ю, *impf. of* расцвети́ть.

расцел|ова́ть, у́ю, *pf.* to kiss, smother with
kisses.

расцел|ова́ться, у́юсь, *pf.* to exchange kisses.

расце́нива|ть, ю, *impf. of* расцени́ть.

расцен|и́ть, ю́, ⌣ишь, *pf.* (*of* ⌣ивать) **1.** to
estimate, assess, value. **2.** (*fig.*) to rate,
assess; to regard, consider; как вы ⌣и́ли
его́ игру́? what did you think of his acting?

расце́нк|а, и, *f.* **1.** valuation. **2.** price.
3. (wage-)rate.

расце́н|очный, *adj. of* ⌣ка; ⌣очно-кон-
фли́ктная коми́ссия rates and disputes tribunal.

расцеп|и́ть, лю́, ⌣ишь, *pf.* (*of* ⌣ля́ть) to
uncouple, unhook; to disengage, release.

расцеп|и́ться, ⌣ится, *pf.* (*of* ⌣ля́ться) to
come uncoupled, come unhooked.

расцепле́ни|е, я, *n.* uncoupling, unhook-
ing; disengaging, release; механи́зм ⌣я
release gear.

расцепля́|ть(ся), ю, ет(ся), *impf. of* рас-
цепи́ть(ся).

расча́лк|а, и, *f.* (*tech.*, *aeron.*) brace, bracing
wire.

расчер|ти́ть, чу́, ⌣тишь, *pf.* (*of* ⌣чивать)
to rule, line.

расче́рчива|ть, ю, *impf. of* расчерти́ть.

расче|са́ть, шу́, ⌣шешь, *pf.* (*of* ⌣сывать)
1. to comb; to card. **2.** to scratch.

расче|са́ться, шу́сь, ⌣шешься, *pf.* (*of*
⌣сываться) (*coll.*) **1.** to comb one's hair.
2. to scratch oneself.

расчёск|а, и, *f.* **1.** combing. **2.** comb.

расче́сть, разочту́, разочтёшь, *past* расчёл,
разочла́, *pf.* (*of* рассчи́тывать) **1.** to cal-
culate, compute. **2.** to dismiss, sack.

расче́сться, разочту́сь, разочтёшься, *past*
расчёлся, разочла́сь, *pf.* (*of* рассчи́ты-
вать(ся) (c+*i.*) to settle accounts (with).

расчёсыва|ть(ся), ю(сь), *impf. of* рас-
чеса́ть(ся).

расчёт¹, а, *m.* **1.** calculation (*also tech.*);
computation; estimate, reckoning; из ⌣а
(+*g.*) on the basis (of), at a rate (of);
распредели́ть тантье́му из ⌣а чи́стой
при́были to distribute a bonus on the basis
of net profits; из ⌣а трёх проце́нтов
годовы́х at three per cent per annum;
приня́ть в р. to take into account, consideration; не принима́ть в р. to leave out
of account; не принима́емый в р. negli-

gible; по мои́м ⌣ам by my reckoning; э́то
не входи́ло в мои́ ⌣ы I had not reckoned
with that, I had not bargained for that;
ошиби́ться в свои́х ⌣ах to be out in one's
reckoning, miscalculate. **2.** (*coll.*) gain,
advantage; нет ⌣а (+*inf.*) it is not worth
while, there is nothing to be gained. **3.**
(c+*i.*) settling (with); нали́чный р. cash
payment; безнали́чный р. payment by
written order, by cheque; быть в ⌣е (c+*i.*)
to be quits (with), be even (with). **4.** dismissal, discharge; дать р. (+*d.*) to dismiss,
sack; получи́ть р. to be dismissed, get the
sack; взять р. to leave one's work, hand in
notice.

расчёт², а, *m.* (*mil.*) crew, team, detachment; оруди́йный р. gun crew.

расчётливост|ь, и, *f.* economy, thrift.

расчётлив|ый (⌣, ⌣а), *adj.* economical,
thrifty; careful.

расчётн|ый, *adj.* **1.** calculation, computa-
tion; ⌣ое ме́сто (*navigation*) dead reckoning
position; ⌣ая оши́бка error in computation; ⌣ая табли́ца calculation table. **2.**
pay, accounts; р. бала́нс balance of pay-
ments; ⌣ая ве́домость pay-roll, pay-sheet;
р. день pay-day; ⌣ая кни́жка pay-book;
р. отде́л accounts department. **3.** (*tech.*)
rated, calculated, designed; ⌣ая величина́
rating; ⌣ая мо́щность rated capacity; ⌣ая
ско́рость rated speed.

расчётчик, а, *m.* estimator, designer.

расчи́сл|ить, ю, ишь, *pf.* (*of* ⌣я́ть) to cal-
culate, compute, reckon.

расчисл|я́ть, я́ю, *impf. of* ⌣ить.

расчи́|стить, щу, стишь, *pf.* (*of* ⌣ща́ть) to
clear.

расчи́|ститься, стится, *pf.* (*of* ⌣ща́ться)
1. (*of the sky*) to clear. **2.** *pass. of* ⌣стить.

расчи́стк|а, и, *f.* clearing.

расчиха́|ться, юсь, *pf.* to sneeze repeatedly.

расчища́|ть(ся), ю, ет(ся), *impf. of* рас-
чи́стить(ся).

расчлене́ни|е, я, *n.* **1.** dismemberment; par-
tition. **2.** (*mil.*) development; dispersal;
deployment; extension.

расчлен|ённый, *p.p.p. of* ⌣и́ть *and adj.*; р.
поря́док (*mil.*) dispersed formation; р.
строй (*mil.*) extended order, open order
formation.

расчлен|и́ть, ю́, и́шь, *pf.* (*of* ⌣я́ть) **1.** to dis-
member; to partition; to break up, divide.
2. (*mil.*) to develop; to disperse; to deploy;
to extend.

расчлен|я́ть, я́ю, *impf. of* ⌣и́ть.

расчу́вств|оваться, уюсь, *pf.* (*coll.*) to be
deeply moved.

расчу́ха|ть, ю, *pf.* (*coll.*) to nose out; (*fig.*)
to scent, sense; он ⌣л, в чём де́ло he sensed
what was the matter.

расшал|и́ться, ю́сь, и́шься, *pf.* to get up to mischief, start playing about.

расша́рк|аться, аюсь, *pf.* (*of* ∼иваться) (*obs.*) to bow, scraping one's feet; (*fig.*) to bow and scrape.

расша́ркива|ться, юсь, *impf. of* расша́ркаться.

расша́танност|ь, и, *f.* shakiness; shattered condition.

расша́т|анный, p.p.p. of ∼а́ть *and adj.* shaky; rickety; tottering; ∼анные не́рвы shattered nerves.

расшат|а́ть, а́ю, *pf.* (*of* ∼ывать) 1. to shake loose; to make rickety. 2. (*fig.*) to shatter; to impair; э́тот уда́р ∼а́л её здоро́вье the blow shattered her health; р. дисципли́ну to impair discipline.

расшат|а́ться, а́юсь, *pf.* (*of* ∼ываться) 1. to get loose; to become rickety. 2. (*fig.*) to go to pieces, crack up.

расша́тыва|ть(ся), ю(сь), *impf. of* расшата́ть(ся).

расшвы́рива|ть, ю, *impf. of* расшвыря́ть.

расшвыр|я́ть, я́ю, *pf.* (*of* ∼ивать) to throw about, throw left and right, send flying.

расшеве́лива|ть, ю, *impf. of* расшевели́ть.

расшевел|и́ть, ю́, и́шь, *pf.* (*of* ∼ивать) to stir, shake; (*fig.*) to stir, rouse.

расшевел|и́ться, ю́сь, и́шься, *pf.* to begin to stir; (*fig.*) to rouse oneself.

расшиб|а́ть(ся), а́ю(сь), *impf. of* расшиби́ть(ся).

расшиб|и́ть, у́, ёшь, *past* ∼, ∼ла, *pf.* (*of* ∼а́ть) (*coll.*) 1. to hurt; to knock, stub; р. па́лец ноги́ об ка́мень to stub one's toe on a rock. 2. to break up, smash to pieces.

расшиб|и́ться, у́сь, ёшься, *past* ∼ся, ∼лась, *pf.* (*of* ∼а́ться) (*coll.*) to hurt oneself, knock oneself.

расши́в|а, ы, *f.* rasshiva (*large flat-bottomed sailing-boat in use on Volga and Caspian Sea*).

расшива́|ть, ю, *impf. of* расши́ть.

расшивно́й, *adj.* embroidered.

расшире́ни|е, я, *n.* 1. broadening, widening, expansion, extension. 2. (*phys.*) expansion. 3. (*med.*) dilation, dilatation; distension; р. се́рдца dilation of the heart; р. вен varicose veins.

расши́р|енный, p.p.p. of ∼ить *and adj.* broadened, expanded; enlarged; dilated; more extensive, more comprehensive; ∼енная програ́мма more extensive programme; ∼енные зрачки́ dilated pupils; с ∼енными глаза́ми wide-eyed; ∼енное воспроизво́дство (*phys.*) breeding.

расшири́тел|ь, я, *m.* (*tech.*) dilator; reamer.

расшири́тельн|ый, *adj.* broad, extended; ∼ое толкова́ние broad interpretation.

расши́р|ить, ю, ишь, *pf.* (*of* ∼я́ть) to broaden, widen; to enlarge; to expand; to

extend; р. чей-н. кругозо́р to broaden someone's outlook, mind; р. сфе́ру влия́ния to extend a sphere of influence.

расши́р|иться, юсь, ишься, *pf.* (*of* ∼я́ться) 1. to broaden, widen, gain in breadth; to extend. 2. (*phys.*) to expand, dilate.

расшир|я́ть(ся), я́ю(сь), *impf. of* ∼ить(ся).

расши́ть¹, разошью́, разошьёшь, *pf.* (*of* расшива́ть) to embroider.

расши́ть², разошью́, разошьёшь, *pf.* (*of* расшива́ть) to undo, unpick.

расшифр|ова́ть, у́ю, *pf.* (*of* ∼о́вывать) to decipher, decode; (*fig.*) to interpret.

расшифро́вк|а, и, *f.* deciphering, decoding; р. аэрофотосни́мков (*mil.*) interpretation of aerial photographs.

расшифро́вщик, а, *m.* decoder.

расшифро́выва|ть, ю, *impf. of* расшифрова́ть.

расшнур|ова́ть, у́ю, *pf.* (*of* ∼о́вывать) to unlace.

расшнур|ова́ться, у́юсь, *pf.* (*of* ∼о́вываться) 1. to come unlaced, come undone. 2. to unlace oneself (*from a corset, etc.*).

расшнуро́выва|ть(ся), ю(сь), *impf. of* расшнурова́ть(ся).

расшум|е́ться, лю́сь, и́шься, *pf.* (*coll.*) to get noisy, kick up a din.

расще́др|иться, юсь, ишься, *pf.* (*coll., also iron.*) to have a fit of generosity.

расще́лин|а, ы, *f.* cleft, crevice.

расще́лкива|ть, ю, *impf. of* расще́лкнуть.

расще́лк|нуть, ну, нешь, *pf.* (*of* ∼ивать) to crack open.

расще́п, а, *m.* split.

расщеп|и́ть, лю́, и́шь, *pf.* (*of* ∼ля́ть) 1. to split, splinter. 2. (*phys.*) to split; (*chem.*) to break up.

расщеп|и́ться, и́тся, *pf.* (*of* ∼ля́ться) to split, splinter.

расщепле́ни|е, я, *n.* 1. splitting, splintering. 2. (*phys.*) splitting, fission; (*chem.*) break-up, disintegration; р. ядра́ nuclear fission.

расщепля́|ть(ся), ю, ет(ся), *impf. of* расщепи́ть(ся).

расщепля́|ющийся, pres. part. of ∼ться *and adj.* (*phys.*) fissile, fissionable.

ра́та|й, я, *m.* (*folk poet.*) ploughman.

ратификацио́нн|ый, *adj.* ∼ые гра́моты (*dipl.*) instruments of ratification.

ратифика́ци|я, и, *f.* (*dipl.*) ratification.

ратифици́р|овать, ую, *impf. and pf.* (*dipl.*) to ratify.

ра́тник, а, *m.* 1. (*arch.*) warrior. 2. (*obs.*) militiaman.

ра́тный, adj. (*obs. or poet.*) martial, warlike; р. по́двиг feat of arms.

ра́т|овать, ую, *impf.* (*obs.*) (за + *a.*) to fight (for), stand up (for); (про́тив) to declaim (against), inveigh (against).

ра́туш|а, и, *f.* **1.** (*esp. in Poland and the Baltic States*) town hall. **2.** (*hist.*) town council.

рат|ь, и, *f.* (*arch. or poet.*) **1.** host, army. **2.** war; battle; идти́ на р. to go into battle.

ра́унд, а, *m.* (*sport*) round.

ра́ут, а, *m.* (*obs.*) rout; reception.

рафина́д, а, *m.* lump sugar.

рафина́д|ный, *adj. of* ~; р. заво́д sugar refinery.

рафинёр, а, *m.* (*tech.*; *of paper*) refiner.

рафини́рованност|ь, и, *f.* refinement.

рафини́рова|нный, *p.p.p. of* ~ть *and adj.* (*fig.*) refined.

рафини́р|овать, ую, *impf. and pf.* to refine.

раха́т-луку́м, а, *m.* Turkish delight.

рахи́т, а, *m.* (*med.*) rachitis, rickets.

рахи́тик, а, *m.* sufferer from rachitis, rickets.

рахити́чный, *adj.* (*med.*) rachitic, rickety.

раце́|я, и, *f.* (*coll., iron.*) sermon, lecture; чита́ть кому́-н. ~ю to read someone a lecture.

рацио́н, а, *m.* ration, food allowance.

рационализа́тор, а, *m.* rationalizer.

рационализа́тор|ский, *adj. of* ~; ~ское предложе́ние rationalization proposal, proposal for improving production methods.

рационализа́ци|я, и, *f.* rationalization, improvement.

рационализи́р|овать, ую, *impf. and pf.* to rationalize, improve.

рационали́зм, а, *m.* (*philos.*) rationalism.

рационали́ст, а, *m.* rationalist.

рационалисти́ческий, *adj.* rationalistic.

рационалисти́ч|ный (~ен, ~на), *adj.* rational.

рациона́льно, *adv.* rationally; efficiently; р. испо́льзовать to make efficient use (of), make good use (of).

рациона́л|ьный (~ен, ~ьна), *adj.* **1.** rational; efficient. **2.** (*math.*) rational.

ра́ци|я, и, *f.* portable radio transmitter, walkie-talkie set.

ра́чий, *adj. of* рак; ра́чьи глаза́ goggle eyes.

рачи́тельност|ь, и, *f.* (*obs.*) zealousness; assiduity.

рачи́тел|ьный (~ен, ~ьна), *adj.* (*obs.*) zealous; assiduous.

ра́шкул|ь, я, *m.* (*art*) charcoal-pencil.

ра́шпил|ь, я, *m.* (*tech.*) rasp, rasp file; grater.

рван|у́ть, у́, ёшь, *pf.* **1.** to jerk; to tug (at); р. кого́-н. за рука́в to tug someone by the sleeve. **2.** to start with a jerk, get off with a jerk; вдруг ~у́л ве́тер suddenly a wind got up.

рван|у́ться, у́сь, ёшься, *pf.* to rush, dash, dart.

рва́н|ый, *adj.* torn; lacerated; ~ые башмаки́ broken shoes; ~ая ра́на (*med.*)

lacerated wound, laceration.

рван|ь, и, *no pl., f.* **1.** rags; broken footwear. **2.** (*coll.*) scoundrel, scamp; (*collect.*) riff-raff.

рвать¹, рву, рвёшь, *past* **рвал, рвала́, рва́ло,** *impf.* **1.** to tear; to rend; to rip; р. в клочки́ to tear to pieces; р. на себе́ во́лосы to tear one's hair; р. и мета́ть to rant and rave. **2.** to pull out, tear out; р. зу́бы to pull out teeth; р. из рук у кого́-н. to snatch out of someone's hands; р. с ко́рнем to uproot. **3.** to pick, pluck; р. цветы́ to pick flowers. **4.** to blow up. **5.** (*fig.*) to break off, sever; р. отноше́ния с кем-н. to break off relations with someone.

рвать², рвёт, *past* **рва́ло,** *impf.* (*of* **вы́рвать²**) (*impers.*; *coll.*) to vomit, throw up, be sick.

рва́|ться¹, рвётся, *past* ~лся, ~ла́сь, ~ло́сь, *impf.* **1.** to break; to tear. **2.** to burst, explode.

рва́|ться², рвусь, рвёшься, *past* ~лся, ~ла́сь, ~ло́сь, *impf.* to strain (to, at); to be bursting (to); р. в бой to be bursting to go into action; р. в дра́ку to be spoiling for a fight; р. на свобо́ду to be dying to be free; р. с при́вязи to strain at the leash.

рвач, а́, *m.* (*coll.*) self-seeker, grabber.

рва́ческий, *adj.* (*coll.*) self-seeking, grabbing.

рва́честв|о, а, *n.* (*coll.*) self-seeking, grabbing.

рве́ни|е, я, *n.* zeal, fervour, ardour.

рво́т|а, ы, *f.* **1.** vomiting, retching. **2.** vomit.

рво́тн|ый, *adj.* vomitive, emetic; р. ка́мень nux vomica; р. ко́рень ipecacuanha; ~ое сре́дство, *also as noun* ~ое, ~ого, *n.* emetic.

рде|ть, ю, *impf.* (*of something red*) to glow.

реабилита́ци|я, и, *f.* rehabilitation.

реабилити́р|овать, ую, *impf. and pf.* to rehabilitate.

реабилити́р|оваться, у́юсь, *impf. and pf.* **1.** to vindicate oneself. **2.** *pass. of* ~овать.

реаге́нт, а, *m.* (*chem.*) reagent.

реаги́р|овать, ую, *impf.* (на+*a.*) **1.** to react (to). **2.** (*pf.* от~) to react (to), (*fig.*) respond (to).

реакти́в, а, *m.* (*chem.*) reagent.

реакти́вност|ь, и, *f.* (*physiol.*) reactivity.

реакти́вн|ый, *adj.* **1.** (*chem., phys.*) reactive; ~ая бума́га (*chem.*) reagent paper, test-paper; ~ая кату́шка (*electr.*) reactive coil, choke coil, inductance coil. **2.** (*tech., aeron.*) jet propulsion; jet(-propelled); р. дви́гатель jet engine; р. самолёт jet-propelled aircraft.

реа́ктор, а, *m.* (*phys., tech.*) reactor, pile; р. для дви́гателей propulsion reactor; р. на бы́стрых нейтро́нах fast (neutron) reactor; р.-размножи́тель, р. с расши́ренным воспроизво́дством я́дерного горю́чего breeder reactor, breeder plant.

реакционе́р, а, *m.* (*polit.*) reactionary.

реакцио́н|ный (~ен, ~на), *adj.* (*polit.*) reactionary.

реа́кци|я, и, *f.* (*chem., phys., polit.*; *fig.*) reaction; (*polit., collect.*) reactionaries.

реа́л¹, а, *m.* (*hist.*) real (*Spanish coin*).

реа́л², а, *m.* (*typ.*) composing frame.

реализа́ци|я, и, *f.* realization (= (i) implementation. (ii) sale).

реали́зм, а, *m.* (*in var. senses*) realism.

реализ|ова́ть, у́ю, *impf. and pf.* to realize (= (i) to implement. (ii) to sell); р. це́нные бума́ги to realize securities.

реали́ст, а, *m.* (*in var. senses*) realist.

реалисти́ческий, *adj.* **1.** (*art, lit., etc.*) realist. **2.** realistic.

реалисти́ч|ный (~ен, ~на), *adj.* = ~еский 2.

реа́льност|ь, и, *f.* **1.** reality. **2.** practicability.

реа́л|ьный (~ен, ~ьна), *adj.* **1.** real. **2.** realizable, practicable, workable; р. план workable plan. **3.** realistic; practical; вести́ ~ьную поли́тику to pursue a realistic policy; ~ьная за́работная пла́та real wages; ~ьное учи́лище (*obs.*) modern school (*non-classical secondary school*).

ребён|ок, ка (*as pl.* **ребя́та, ребя́т** *and* **де́ти, дете́й**), *m.* child, infant; грудно́й р. child in arms.

рёберный, *adj.* (*anat.*) costal.

ребо́рд|а, ы, *f.* flange.

реби́ст|ый (~, ~а), *adj.* **1.** having prominent ribs. **2.** (*tech.*) ribbed; costate; finned.

ребр|о́, а́, *pl.* ~а, рёбер, ~ам, *n.* **1.** (*anat., tech.*) rib; (*tech.*) fin; ни́жние ~а short ribs; пересчита́ть кому́-н. ~а (*coll.*) to give someone a drubbing. **2.** edge, verge; поста́вить ~о́м to place edgewise, place on its side; поста́вить вопро́с ~о́м to put a question point-blank.

ре́бус, а, *m.* rebus.

ребя́та, ребя́т (*coll.*) **1.** (*sing.* ребёнок) children. **2.** (*of adults*) boys, lads.

ребяти́ш|ки, ек, кам, *no sing.* (*coll.*) children, kids.

ребя́ческий, *adj.* **1.** of a child, childish. **2.** (*fig.*) childish, infantile, puerile.

ребя́честв|о, а, *n.* childishness, puerility.

ребя́чий, *adj.* (*coll.*) childish.

ребя́ч|иться, усь, ишься, *impf.* (*coll.*) to behave like a child, behave childishly.

рев- *abbr. of* революцио́нный.

рёв, а, *m.* **1.** roar; bellow, howl; р. ве́тра the howling of the wind. **2.** (*coll.*) howl (*of a child, etc.*); подня́ть р. to raise a howl.

рева́нш, а, *m.* revenge; (*sport*) return match.

реванши́зм, а, *m.* (*polit.*) revanchism.

реванши́ст, а, *m.* (*polit.*) revanchist, revenge-seeker.

реве́н|ный, *adj. of* ~ь; р. порошо́к gregory-powder.

реве́н|ь, я́, *m.* rhubarb.

реве́ранс, а, *m.* (*obs.*) curts(e)y; сде́лать р. to curts(e)y, drop a curts(e)y.

ревербера́ци|я, и, *f.* (*tech.*) reverberation.

ре́верс, а, *m.* **1.** reverse (*of coin, etc.*). **2.** (*tech.*) reversing gear. **3.** (*obs.*) caution-money (*deposit required to be paid by young officers on marrying*).

реверси́вный, *adj.* (*tech.*) reversing, reversible.

реве́рси|я, и, *f.* **1.** (*leg.*) reversion. **2.** (*biol.*) reversion (to type). **3.** (*tech.*) reversing.

рев|е́ть, у́, ёшь, *impf.* **1.** to roar; to bellow, howl. **2.** (*coll.*) to howl; ревмя́ р. to set up a fearful howl.

ревизиони́зм, а, *m.* (*polit.*) revisionism.

ревизиони́ст, а, *m.* (*polit.*) revisionist.

ревизио́нн|ый, *adj.* ~ая коми́ссия inspection commission; auditing commission.

реви́зи|я, и, *f.* **1.** inspection; audit. **2.** revision. **3.** (*hist.*) census.

ревиз|ова́ть, у́ю, *impf. and pf.* **1.** (*pf. also* об~) to inspect. **2.** to revise.

ревизо́р, а, *m.* inspector.

ревко́м, а, *m.* (*abbr. of* революцио́нный комите́т) revolutionary committee.

ревмати́зм, а, *m.* rheumatism; rheumatics; суставно́й р. rheumatic fever.

ревма́тик, а, *m.* rheumatic.

ревмати́ческий, *adj.* rheumatic.

рев|мя́, *see* ~е́ть.

ревни́в|ец, ца, *m.* jealous man.

ревни́в|ый (~, ~а), *adj.* jealous.

ревни́тел|ь, я, m. (+*g.*; *obs.*) adherent (of), enthusiastic supporter (of).

ревн|ова́ть, у́ю, *impf.* to be jealous; р. кого́-н. (к) to be jealous because of someone's attachment (to), begrudge someone's attachment (to); она́ ~ова́ла му́жа к его́ рабо́те she was jealous of her husband's work.

ре́вност|ный (~ен, ~на), *adj.* zealous, earnest, fervent.

ре́вност|ь, и, *f.* **1.** jealousy. **2.** (*obs.*) zeal, earnestness, fervour.

револьве́р, а, *m.* revolver, pistol; шести́-заря́дный р. six-shooter.

револьве́р|ный, *adj.* **1.** *adj. of* ~. **2.** (*tech.*) ~ная голо́вка capstan head; р. стано́к capstan lathe, turret lathe.

револьве́рщик, а, *m.* capstan, turret lathe operator.

революционе́р, а, *m.* revolutionary.

революциони́зи́р|овать, ую, *impf. and pf.* **1.** to spread revolutionary ideas (among, in). **2.** to revolutionize.

революционизи́р|оваться, уюсь, *impf. and pf.* **1.** to become permeated with revolutionary ideas. **2.** to be revolutionized.

револЮцио́н|ный (~ен, ~на), *adj.* revolutionary.

револЮци|я, и, *f.* (*polit. and fig.*) revolution.

реву́н, а́, *m.* (*zool.*; *coll.*) howler.

ревю́, *indecl.*, *n.* revue.

рега́ли|я, и, *f.* (*hist.*) state monopoly.

рега́ли|и, й, *pl.* (*sing.* ~я, ~и), *f.* regalia.

ре́гби, *indecl.*, *n.* Rugby (football), rugger.

регенерати́вный, *adj.* (*tech.*) regenerative.

регенера́ци|я, и, *f.* (*tech.*) regeneration.

ре́гент, а, *m.* 1. regent. 2. (*mus.*) precentor.

ре́гентств|о, а, *n.* regency.

регио́н, а, *m.* region, area.

региона́льный, *adj.* regional.

реги́стр, а, *m.* (*in var. senses*) register.

регистра́тор, а, *m.* registrar.

регистрату́р|а, ы, *f.* registry.

регистра́ци|я, и, *f.* registration.

регистри́р|овать, ую, *impf. and pf.* (*pf. also* за~) to register, record.

регистри́р|оваться, уюсь, *impf. and pf.* (*pf. also* за~) 1. to register (oneself). 2. to register one's marriage. 3. *pass. of* ~овать.

регла́мент, а, *m.* 1. regulations; standing orders. 2. (*at a meeting*) time-limit; установи́ть р. to fix a time-limit.

регламента́ци|я, и, *f.* regulation.

регламенти́р|овать, ую, *impf. and pf.* to regulate.

регла́н, а, *m.* raglan (*coat*).

регресси́в|ный (~ен, ~на), *adj.* regressive.

регресси́р|овать, ую, *impf.* to regress.

регули́ровани|е, я, *n.* 1. regulation, control. 2. adjustment.

регули́р|овать, ую, *impf.* 1. (*pf.* у~) to regulate; to control; р. у́личное движе́ние to control traffic. 2. (*pf.* от~) to adjust; р. мото́р to tune an engine.

регулиро́вщик, а, *m.* traffic-controller.

ре́гул|ы, ~, *no sing.* (*obs.*) menses, menstruation.

регуля́рност|ь, и, *f.* regularity.

регуля́р|ный (~ен, ~на), *adj.* regular; ~ные войска́ regular troops, regulars.

регуля́тор, а, *m.* (*tech.*) regulator; governor.

редакти́ровани|е, я, *n.* editing.

редакти́р|овать, ую, *impf.* 1. (*pf.* от~) to edit (*a manuscript, etc.*). 2. (*impf. only*) to be editor of (*a journal, etc.*). 3. (*pf.* с~) to word.

реда́ктор, а, *m.* editor; гла́вный р., отве́тственный р. editor-in-chief.

реда́кторский, *adj.* editorial.

реда́кторств|о, а, *n.* editorship.

реда́кторств|овать, ую, *impf.* (*coll.*) to be (an) editor.

редакцио́нн|ый, *adj.* editorial, editing; ~ая коми́ссия drafting committee.

реда́кци|я, и, *f.* 1. editorial staff. 2. edi-

torial office. 3. editing; под ~ей (+*g.*) edited (by). 4. wording.

реде́|ть, ю, *impf.* (*of* по~) to thin, thin out; ~ющие во́лосы thinning hair.

реди́с, а, *no pl.*, *m.* radish(es).

реди́ск|а, и, *f.* radish.

ре́д|кий (~ок, ~ка́, ~ко), *adj.* 1. thin, sparse; ~кие во́лосы thin hair; ~кие зу́бы widely spaced teeth; р. лес sparse wood; ~кая ткань flimsy fabric. 2. rare; uncommon; ~кая кни́га rare book; ~кая красота́ rare beauty; он — р. подража́тель he is a rare mimic.

ре́дко, *adv.* 1. sparsely; far apart. 2. rarely, seldom.

редколе́сь|е, я, *n.* sparse growth of trees.

редколле́ги|я, и, *f.* (*abbr. of* редакцио́нная колле́гия) editorial board.

ре́дкост|ный (~ен, ~на), *adj.* rare; uncommon.

ре́дкост|ь, и, *f.* 1. thinness, sparseness. 2. rarity; на р. uncommonly; на р. прони́ца́тельный челове́к a person of rare discernment; не р., что not uncommonly; не р., что он проси́живает ночь за кни́гой it is not unusual for him to sit up all night reading. 3. rarity, curiosity, curio.

реду́ктор, а, *m.* 1. (*tech.*) reducing gear. 2. (*chem.*) reducing agent.

реду́кци|я, и, *f.* (*in var. senses*) reduction.

реду́т, а, *m.* (*mil.*, *hist.*) redoubt.

редуци́рова|нный, *p.p.p. of* ~ть *and adj.* (*ling.*) reduced.

редуци́р|овать, ую, *impf. and pf.* (*in var. senses*) to reduce.

ре́дьк|а, и, *f.* radish; надое́ло э́то мне ху́же го́рькой ~и I am sick and tired of it.

редю́йт, а, *m.* (*mil.*) reduit.

рее́стр, а, *m.* list, roll, register.

ре́|же, *comp. of* ~дкий *and* ~дко.

режи́м, а, *m.* 1. (*polit.*) régime. 2. routine; procedure; (*med.*) regimen; (*tech.*) mode of operation; шко́льный р. school routine; р. пита́ния diet; р. безопа́сности safety measures; р. эконо́мии policy of economy. 3. conditions; (*tech.*) working conditions, operating conditions; р. реки́ habits of a river. 4. (*tech.*) rate; р. набо́ра высоты́ (*aeron.*) rate of climb.

режи́мный, *adj.* secret, classified.

режиссёр, а, *m.* (*theatr.*) producer; (*cinema*) director.

режиссёр|ский, *adj. of* ~.

режисси́р|овать, ую, *impf.* (*theatr.*) to produce, stage; (*cinema*) to direct.

режиссу́р|а, ы, *f.* (*theatr.*) 1. producing; profession of producer. 2. production. 3. (*collect.*) producers.

ре́жущ|ий, *pres. part. act. of* ре́зать *and adj.* cutting, sharp; ~ая кро́мка cutting edge, blade; р. уда́р slash.

реза́к, а́, *m.* **1.** chopping-knife, chopper; pole-axe. **2.** slaughterhouse worker.

ре́зан|ый, *adj.* **1.** cut; р. хлеб cut loaf. **2.** (*sport*) slice, sliced; ~ая пода́ча (*tennis*) slice service; р. уда́р slice.

ре́|зать, жу, жешь, *impf.* **1.** *impf. only* to cut; to slice. **2.** *impf. only* (*med.*) to operate, open; (*coll., joc.*) to carve. **3.** *impf. only* to cut (= *to have the power of cutting*); э́ти но́жницы бо́льше не ~жут these scissors do not cut any longer. **4.** (*pf.* за~) to kill; to slaughter; to knife. **5.** *impf. only* (по+*d.*) to carve (on), engrave (on). **6.** *impf. only* to cut (into); to cause sharp pain; реме́нь ~зал его́ плечо́ the strap was cutting into his shoulder; у меня́ ~зало в желу́дке I had griping pains in the stomach; р. глаза́ to irritate the eyes; р. слух to pain the ear, grate upon the ears. **7.** (*coll.*) to speak bluntly; р. пра́вду в глаза́ to speak the truth boldly. **8** . *impf. only* to pass close (to), shave; р. корму́ (*naut.*) to pass close astern. **9.** (*pf.* с~) (*sport*) to slice, cut, chop.

ре́|заться, жусь, жешься, *impf.* **1.** (*pf.* про~) (*of teeth*) to cut, come through; у него́ уже́ ~жутся зу́бы he is already teething, cutting teeth. **2.** *impf. only* to play furiously.

резв|и́ться, лю́сь, и́шься, *impf.* to sport, gambol, caper, romp.

ре́звост|ь, и, *f.* **1.** sportiveness, playfulness, friskiness. **2.** (*sport; of a horse*) speed; показа́ть хоро́шую р. to show a good time.

ре́зв|ый (~, ~а́, ~о), *adj.* **1.** sportive, playful, frisky. **2.** (*sport; of a horse*) fast.

резед|а́, ы́, *f.* (*bot.*) mignonette.

резе́кци|я, и, *f.* (*med.*) resection.

резе́рв, а, *m.* (*mil., etc.*) reserve(s); име́ть в ~е to have in reserve; перевести́ в р. (*mil.*) to transfer to the reserve.

резерва́ци|я, и, *f.* reservation.

резерви́р|овать, ую, *impf. and pf.* to reserve.

резерви́ст, а, *m.* (*mil.*) reservist.

резе́рвный, *adj.* (*mil. and fin.*) reserve.

резервуа́р, а, *m.* reservoir, vessel, tank.

рез|е́ц, ца́, *m.* **1.** (*tech.*) cutter; cutting tool; chisel. **2.** (*tooth*) incisor.

резиде́нт, а, *m.* (*dipl., etc.*) resident (*esp. of member of Intelligence Service operating in foreign country*).

резиде́нци|я, и, *f.* residence.

рези́н|а, ы, *f.* (india-)rubber.

рези́нк|а, и, *f.* **1.** (india-)rubber, eraser. **2.** (piece of) elastic. **3.** rubber band. **4.** chewing-gum.

рези́нов|ый, *adj.* **1.** rubber; ~ая промы́шленность rubber industry; ~ые сапоги́ gum boots; ~ая тесьма́, ле́нта rubber

band. **2.** elastic.

рези́нщик, а, *m.* worker in rubber industry.

ре́зк|а, и, *f.* cutting.

ре́з|кий (~ок, ~ка́, ~ко), *adj.* sharp; harsh; abrupt; р. ве́тер sharp wind, cutting wind; р. го́лос shrill voice; р. за́пах strong smell; ~кое измене́ние abrupt change, sudden switch; ~кие мане́ры abrupt manners; р. свет strong, harsh light; ~кие слова́ sharp words; ~кое увеличе́ние dramatic increase; ~кие черты́ лица́ sharp features.

ре́зкост|ь, и, *f.* **1.** sharpness; harshness; abruptness. **2.** sharp words, harsh words; наговори́ть ~ей to use harsh words.

резн|о́й, *adj.* carved, fretted; ~а́я рабо́та (*archit.*) carving, fretwork.

резн|я́, и́, *f.* slaughter, butchery, carnage.

резолюти́вн|ый, *adj.* containing conclusions, containing a resolution; в ~ой фо́рме in the form of a resolution.

резолю́ци|я, и, *f.* **1.** resolution; вы́нести, приня́ть ~ю to pass, adopt, approve, carry a resolution. **2.** instructions (*on a document*); наложи́ть ~ю to append instructions.

резо́н, а, *m.* (*coll.*) **1.** reason, basis; в э́том есть свой р. there is a reason for this. **2.** reasoning, argument; они́ не хоте́ли слу́шать никаки́х ~ов they would not listen to any argument.

резона́нс, а, *m.* **1.** (*phys.*) resonance. **2.** (*fig.*) echo, response; дать, име́ть р. to have repercussions.

резонёр, а, *m.* arguer, moralizer.

резонёрств|овать, ую, *impf.* to argue, moralize.

резони́р|овать, ую, *impf.* to resound.

резо́н|ный (~ен, ~на), *adj.* reasonable.

результа́т, а, *m.* result; outcome; ~ы обсле́дования findings; дать ~ы to yield results; в ~е (+*g.*) as a result (of).

результати́вный, *adj.* successful.

ре́з|че, *comp. of* ~кий *and* ~ко.

ре́зчик, а, *m.* engraver, carver.

рез|ь, и, *f.* colic; gripe.

резьб|а́, ы́, *f.* **1.** carving, fretwork. **2.** (*tech.*) thread(ing).

резюме́, *indecl., n.* summary, résumé.

резюми́р|овать, ую, *impf. and pf.* to sum up, summarize, recapitulate.

рейд¹, а, *m.* (*naut.*) road(s), roadstead.

рейд², а, *m.* **1.** (*mil.*) raid. **2.** 'swoop' (*by group of journalists, to investigate alleged malpractice, grievance, etc.*); special (*journalistic*) assignment.

ре́йдер, а, *m.* (*naut.*) (commerce) raider.

ре́йк|а, и, *f.* **1.** lath. **2.** зубча́тая р. (*tech.*) rack; переда́ча зубча́той ~ой rack and pinion gear. **3.** (*surveyor's*) rod, pole.

рейнве́йн, а, *m.* hock.

рейнск|ий, *adj.* Rhine, Rhenish; ~ое (вино) Rhine wine, hock.

рейс¹, а, *m.* trip, run (*of public transport vehicle*); voyage, passage; пéрвый р. maiden voyage, maiden trip.

рейс², а, *m.* reis (*Portuguese or Brazilian coin*).

рейсфéдер, а, *m.* 1. drawing-pen, mapping pen. 2. pencil-holder.

рейсши́н|а, ы, *f.* T-square.

рейту́з|ы, ~, *no sing.* 1. (riding-)breeches. 2. (*women's or children's*) pantaloons, knickers. 3. tights.

рекá, реку́, реки́, *pl.* **рéки, рек, рéкам, рéками, рéках,** *f.* river; ли́ться, *etc.*, рекóй (*fig.*) to pour, flood.

рéквием, а, *m.* (*eccl. and mus.*) requiem.

реквизи́р|овать, ую, *impf. and pf.* to requisition, commandeer.

реквизи́т, а, *m.* (*theatr.*) properties, props.

реквизи́тор, а, *m.* (*theatr.*) property-man.

реквизи́ци|я, и, *f.* requisition, commandeering.

реклáм|а, ы, *f.* 1. advertising, publicity. 2. advertisement.

рекламáци|я, и, *f.* claim for replacement (*of defective goods, etc.*).

реклами́р|овать, ую, *impf. and pf.* to advertise, publicize; to boost, push.

реклами́ст, а, *m.* 1. composer of advertisements. 2. (*coll., pejor.*) one given to self--advertisement.

реклáмный, *adj.* publicity.

рекламодáтел|ь, я, *m.* advertiser.

рекогносци́р|овать, ую, *impf. and pf.* (*mil.*) to reconnoitre.

рекогносциро́вк|а, и, *f.* (*mil.*) reconnaissance; reconnoitring.

рекогносциро́вочный, *adj.* reconnaissance.

рекомендáтельн|ый, *adj.* р. óтзыв recommendation, testimonial; ~ое письмó letter of recommendation; р. спи́сок книг list of recommended books.

рекомендáци|я, и, *f.* recommendation.

рекоменд|овáть, у́ю, *impf. and pf.* 1. (*pf. also* по~ *and* от~) to recommend; to speak well for; э́то егó не óчень ~ýет this does not speak too well for him. 2. (*pf. also* по~) (+*inf.*) to recommend, advise; я вам ~у́ю посовéтоваться с дóктором I recommend you to see a doctor.

рекоменд|овáться, у́юсь, *impf. and pf.* 1. (*pf. also* от~) to introduce oneself. 2. *pass. of* ~овáть; не ~ýется it is not recommended, it is not advisable.

реконструи́р|овать, ую, *impf. and pf.* to reconstruct.

реконструкти́вный, *adj.* р. перíод period of reconstruction.

реконстру́кци|я, и, *f.* reconstruction.

рекóрд, а, *m.* record; поби́ть р. to break a record; установи́ть р. to set up, establish a record.

рекорди́ст, а, *m.* (*agric.*) champion.

рекóрдный, *adj.* record, record-breaking.

рекордсмéн, а, *m.* record-holder; record--breaker.

рекордсмéн|ка, ки, *f. of* ~.

рéкрут, а, *m.* (*hist.*) recruit.

рекрути́р|овать, ую, *impf. and pf.* to recruit.

рекру́т|ский, *adj. of* ~; р. набóр recruiting, recruitment.

ректификáт, а, *m.* rectified spirit.

ректификáци|я, и, *f.* (*tech.*) rectification.

ректифици́р|овать, ую, *impf. and pf.* (*tech.*) to rectify.

рéктор, а, *m.* rector, vice-chancellor, principal (*head of a university*).

релé, *indecl., n.* (*tech.*) relay.

релé|йный, *adj. of* ~.

религиóзность|ь, и, *f.* religiosity; piety, piousness.

религиóз|ный, *adj.* 1. of religion, religious; ~ные вóйны (*hist.*) Wars of Religion; р. обря́д religious ceremony. 2. (~ен, ~на) religious; pious.

рели́ги|я, и, *f.* religion.

рели́кви|я, и, *f.* relic.

рели́кт, а, *m.* relic; survival.

рели́кт|овый, *adj. of* ~; surviving.

рельéф, а, *m.* (*art and geol.*) relief.

рельéфно, *adv.* in relief, boldly; р.-тóчечный шрифт braille (script).

рельéф|ный (~ен, ~на), *adj.* relief, raised, bold; ~ная рабóта embossed work; ~ная кáрта relief map.

рельс, а, *g. pl.* ~ов, *m.* rail; сойти́ с ~ов to be derailed, go off the rails; постáвить на ~ы (*fig.*) to get going, launch.

рéльс|овый, *adj. of* ~; р. путь railway, track.

релятиви́зм, а, *m.* (*philos.*) relativity.

реля́ци|я, и, *f.* (*mil.*; *obs.*) communiqué, report.

ремáрк|а, и, *f.* (*theatr.*) stage direction.

ремённ|ый, *adj.* belt; ~ая передáча (*tech.*) belt-drive.

рем|éнь, ня́, *m.* strap; belt; thong; пояснóй р. (*mil.*) (waist-)belt; привязнóй р. seat--belt; ружéйный р. rifle sling; р. для прáвки бритв (razor) strop.

ремéсленник, а, *m.* 1. artisan, craftsman. 2. (*fig., pejor.*) hack. 3. pupil of trade school.

ремéсленнический, *adj.* (*pejor.*) hack-working, mechanical.

ремéсленничеств|о, а, *n.* 1. workmanship, craftsmanship. 2. (*pejor.*) hack-work.

ремéсленн|ый, *adj.* 1. handicraft; trade; ~ое учи́лище trade school, industrial school. 2. (*fig., pejor.*) mechanical; stereotyped.

ремес|лó, лá, *pl.* ~лá, ~ел, *n.* 1. handicraft; trade. 2. profession.

ремеш|óк, кá, *m.* small strap; wristlet.

реми́з, а, *m.* (*cards*) fine; постáвить р. to pay a fine.

ремилитаризáци|я, и, *f.* remilitarization.

ремилитаризи́р|овать, ую, *impf. and pf.* to remilitarize.

ремилитариз|овáть, у́ю, *impf. and pf.* to remilitarize.

реминисцéнци|я, и, *f.* reminiscence.

ремóнт, а, *m.* 1. repair(s); maintenance; капитáльный р. overhaul, refit, major repairs; текýщий р. maintenance, routine repairs; закры́т на р. closed for repairs; в ~е under repair. 2. (*mil.*) remount (service).

ремонтёр, а, *m.* (*mil.; obs.*) remount officer.

ремонти́р|овать, ую, *impf. and pf.* 1. (*pf. also* от~) to repair; to refit, recondition, overhaul. 2. (*mil.*) to remount.

ремóнт|ный, *adj. of* ~; ~ная летýчка mobile repair shop; ~ная мастерскáя repair shop; ~ная лóшадь (*mil.*) remount.

ренегáт, а, *m.* renegade.

ренегáтств|о, а, *n.* desertion; apostasy.

ренéт, а, *m.* rennet (*apple*).

ренклóд, а, *m.* greengage.

реномé, *indecl., n.* reputation.

ренóнс, а, *m.* (*cards*) revoke.

рéнт|а, ы, *f.* 1. rent; земéльная р. ground-rent. 2. income (*from investments, etc.*); ежегóдная р. annuity; госудáрственная р. (income from) government securities.

рентáбел|ьный (~ен, ~ьна), *adj.* paying, profitable.

рентгéн, а, *m.* X-ray treatment, X-rays.

рентгенизáци|я, и, *f.* X-raying.

рентгенизи́р|овать, ую, *impf. and pf.* to X-ray.

рентгéнов, *adj.* ~ы лучи́ X-rays.

рентгéновск|ий, *adj.* X-ray; р. кабинéт X-ray room; ~ие лучи́ X-rays; р. сни́мок X-ray photograph.

рентгеногрáмм|а, ы, *f.* X-ray photograph, radiograph, röntgenogram.

рентгеногрáфи|я, и, *f.* radiography.

рентгенóлог, а, *m.* radiologist.

рентгенолóги|я, и, *f.* radiology, röntgenology.

рентгенотерапи́|я, и, *f.* X-ray therapy.

Реомю́р, а, *m.* Réaumur; 10° по ~у 10° Réaumur.

реорганизáци|я, и, *f.* reorganization.

реорганиз|овáть, у́ю, *impf. and pf.* to reorganize.

реостáт, а, *m.* (*electr.*) rheostat.

рéп|а, ы, *f.* turnip; дешéвле пáреной ~ы (*coll.*) dirt-cheap.

репар|ациóнный, *adj. of* ~áция.

репарáци|я, и, *f.* reparation.

репатриáнт, а, *m.* repatriate.

репатриáци|я, и, *f.* repatriation.

репатрии́р|овать, ую, *impf. and pf.* to repatriate.

репатрии́р|оваться, уюсь, *impf. and pf.* to repatriate oneself.

репéйник, а, *m.* 1. (*bot.*) burdock. 2. Velcro.

репéр, а, *m.* 1. (*surveying*) bench-mark, datum mark. 2. (*mil.*) registration mark, registration point.

репертуáр, а, *m.* (*theatr. and fig.*) repertoire.

репети́р|овать, ую, *impf.* 1. (*pf.* про~ *and* с~) (*theatr.*) to rehearse. 2. *impf. only* to coach.

репети́тор, а, *m.* coach (*tutor*).

репетициóнный, *adj.* rehearsal.

репети́ци|я, и, f. 1. rehearsal; генерáльная р. dress rehearsal. 2. repeater mechanism (*in watch*); часы́ с ~ей repeater.

рéплик|а, и, f. 1. rejoinder, retort; heckling comment; подавáть ~и орáтору to heckle a speaker. 2. (*theatr.*) cue; подáть ~у to give the cue.

реполóв, а, *m.* (*orn.*) linnet.

репортáж, а, *m.* reporting; account, piece of reporting.

репортёр, а, *m.* reporter.

репортёрств|овать, ую, *impf.* to report, be a reporter.

репрессáл|ии, ий, *pl.* (*sing.* ~ия, ~ии *rare*) *f.* (*polit.*) reprisals.

репресси́в|ный (~ен, ~на), *adj.* repressive.

репресси́р|овать, ую, *impf. and pf.* to subject to repression.

репрéсси|я, и, *f.* punitive measure.

репрогрáфи|я, и, *f.* reprographics.

репродýктор, а, *m.* loud-speaker.

репродýкци|я, и, *f.* reproduction (*of a picture, etc.*).

репс, а, *m.* (*text.*) rep(p), reps.

репти́ли|я, и, f. 1. reptile. 2. (*pejor.*) mercenary person, mercenary newspaper, *etc.*

репти́л|ьный (~ен, ~ьна), *adj.* (*pejor.*) mercenary, venal.

репутáци|я, и, f. reputation, name; пóльзоваться хорóшей ~ей to have a good reputation, name; пóльзоваться ~ей (+*g.*) to have a reputation, name (for); спасти́ свою́ ~ю to save one's face.

рéпчатый, *adj.* turnip-shaped; р. лук large onion.

ресни́ц|а, ы, f. eyelash.

ресни́чк|а, и, f. 1. *dim. of* ресни́ца. 2. *pl.* (*biol.*) cilia.

ресни́чный, *adj.* (*biol.*) ciliary.

респектáбельност|ь, и, *f.* respectability.

респектáбел|ьный (ен, ~ьна), *adj.* respectable.

респирáтор, а, *m.* respirator.

респýблик|а, и, *f.* republic.

республикáн|ец, ца, *m.* republican.

республика́нский, *adj.* **1.** republican. **2.** of (situated in, *etc.*) a constituent republic of the U.S.S.R.

рессо́р|а, ы, *f.* spring (*of vehicle*).

рессо́рный, *adj.* spring; sprung.

реставра́тор, а, *m.* restorer.

реставра́ци|я, и, *f.* restoration.

реставри́р|овать, ую, *impf. and pf.* to restore.

рестора́н, а, *m.* restaurant.

рестора́тор, а, *m.* (*obs.*) restaurateur, restaurant-keeper.

ресу́рс, а, *m.* resource; де́нежные ~ы у них ничто́жны their financial resources are negligible; после́дний р. the last resort.

рети́в|ое, о́го, *n.* (*folk poet.*) heart.

рети́вост|ь, и, *f.* zeal, ardour.

рети́в|ый (~, ~а), *adj.* (*coll.*) zealous, ardent.

рети́н|а, ы, *f.* (*anat.*) retina.

ретир|ова́ться, у́юсь, *impf. and pf.* **1.** (*obs.*) to retire, withdraw. **2.** (*iron.*) to make off.

рето́рси|я, и, *f.* (*polit.*) retortion.

рето́рт|а, ы, *f.* (*chem.*) retort.

ретрогра́д, а, *m.* retrograde person, reactionary.

ретрогра́д|ный (~ен, ~на), *adj.* retrograde, backward, reactionary.

ретрораке́т|а, ы, *f.* retro-rocket (*on space craft*).

ретроспекти́в|ный (~ен, ~на), *adj.* retrospective; р. взгляд backward glance.

ретушёр, а, *m.* retoucher.

ретуши́р|овать, ую, *impf. and pf.* (*pf. also* от~) to retouch.

ре́туш|ь, и, *f.* retouching.

рефера́т, а, *m.* **1.** synopsis, abstract (*of a book, dissertation, etc.*). **2.** paper, essay.

рефере́ндум, а, *m.* referendum.

рефере́нт, а, *m.* reader of a paper; seminar leader, colloquium leader. **2.** assessor (*of thesis, book, etc.*).

рефери́р|овать, ую, *impf. and pf.* to abstract, make a synopsis of.

рефле́кс, а, *m.* reflex; усло́вный р., безусло́вный р. conditioned, unconditioned reflex.

рефле́кси|я, и, *f.* reflection; introspection.

рефлексоло́ги|я, и, *f.* (*physiol.*) study of reflexes.

рефлекти́в|ный (~ен, ~на), *adj.* (*physiol.*) reflex.

рефле́ктор, а, *m.* reflector.

рефлекто́рный, *adj.* (*physiol., astron.*) reflex.

рефо́рм|а, ы, *f.* reform.

реформа́тор, а, *m.* reformer.

реформа́торский, *adj.* reformative, reformatory.

реформа́|тский, *adj.* of ~ция; ~тская це́рковь Reformed Church.

реформа́ци|я, и, *f.* (*hist.*) Reformation.

реформи́зм, а, *m.* (*polit.*) reformism.

реформи́р|овать, ую, *impf. and pf.* to reform.

реформи́ст, а, *m.* (*polit.*) reformist.

рефра́ктор, а, *m.* (*phys., astron.*) refractor.

рефра́кци|я, и, *f.* (*phys., astron.*) refraction.

рефре́н, а, *m.* (*lit.*) refrain, burden.

рефрижера́тор, а, *m.* **1.** (*tech.*) refrigerator; condenser, cooler. **2.** refrigerator van, ship.

рехн|у́ться, у́сь, ёшься, *pf.* (*coll.*) to go mad, go off one's head.

рецензе́нт, а, *m.* reviewer.

рецензи́р|овать, ую, *impf.* (*of* про~) to review, criticize.

рецензи|я, и, *f.* **1.** review; (*theatr.*) notice; р. на кни́гу, р. о кни́ге book review; дать на ~ю to send for review. **2.** (*philol.*) recension.

реце́пт, а, *m.* **1.** (*med.*) prescription. **2.** (*cul.*) recipe; (*fig.*) method, way, practice; поступи́ть по ста́рому ~у to follow the old practice.

рецепту́р|а, ы, *f.* (*med.*) principles of prescription-writing.

рециди́в, а, *m.* **1.** (*med., etc.*) recurrence; relapse. **2.** (*leg.*) repeated commission (*of offence*).

рецидиви́зм, а, *m.* (*leg.*) recidivism.

рецидиви́ст, а, *m.* (*leg.*) recidivist.

рециркули́р|овать, ую, *impf. and pf.* to recycle.

речев|о́й, *adj.* speech; vocal; р. аппара́т organs of speech, vocal organs; ~ы́е на́выки speech habits.

рече́ни|е, я, *n.* (*obs.*) set phrase; saying; (*ling.*) locution.

речи́ст|ый (~, ~а), voluble, garrulous.

речитати́в, а, *m.* (*mus.*) recitative.

ре́чк|а, и, *f.* small river; rivulet.

речн|о́й, *adj.* river; riverine, fluvial; р. вокза́л river (steamer and 'bus) station; ~о́е сообще́ние river communication; ~ы́е пути́ сообще́ния inland waterways; ~о́е судохо́дство river navigation; р. трамва́й river 'bus, water 'bus.

реч|ь, и, *f.* **1.** speech; дар ~и faculty of speech, gift of speech. **2.** enunciation, speech, way of speaking; горта́нная р. guttural speech; отчётливая р. distinct enunciation. **3.** style of speaking, language; делова́я р. business language. **4.** discourse; о чём была́ р.? what was the topic of discussion?, what was it all about?; р. идёт о том, где сле́дует назна́чить ме́сто встре́чи the question is where to fix the meeting-place; е́сли р. идёт о сре́дствах if it is a question of funds, with regard to funds; не об э́том р. that is not the point; о пое́здке за грани́цу не мо́жет быть в э́том году́ и ~и a trip abroad is out of the question this year; завести́ р. (о+*p.*) to lead, turn the conversation (towards); р. несомне́нно зайдёт о вопро́сах рели́гии the conversation will undoubtedly turn to religion. **5.** speech; oration; address; вступи́тельная р. opening address; засто́льная р. after-dinner speech; защити́тельная р. speech for the defence; торже́ственная р. oration; вы́ступить с ~ью to make a speech. **6.** (*gram.*) speech; пряма́я р. direct speech, oratio recta; ко́свенная р. indirect speech, oratio obliqua; ча́сти ~и parts of speech.

реш|а́ть(ся), а́ю(сь), *impf. of* ~и́ть(ся).

реша́|ющий, *pres. part. act. of* ~ть *and adj.* decisive, deciding; key, conclusive; р. го́лос deciding vote, casting vote; р. фа́ктор decisive factor; (*tech.*) determinant.

реше́ни|е, я, *n.* **1.** decision; приня́ть р. to take a decision, make up one's mind. **2.** decree, judg(e)ment; decision, verdict; зао́чное р. judg(e)ment by default; вы́нести р. to deliver a judg(e)ment; to pass a resolution; отмени́ть р. to revoke a decision; (*leg.*) to quash a sentence. **3.** solution; answer (*to a problem*).

реше́тин|а, ы, *f.* lath.

решётк|а, и, *f.* grating; grille, railing; lattice; trellis; fender, fireguard; за ~ой (*fig., coll.*) behind bars (= *in prison*); посади́ть за ~у to put behind bars. **2.** (fire-)grate. **3.** (*coll.*) tail (*of coin*).

решётчат|ый (*and* **решётчатый**), *adj.* lattice, latticed; trellised; ~ая ба́лка, ~ая фе́рма lattice girder; ~ая констру́кция lattice-work; р. люк grating.

реши́мост|ь, и, *f.* resolution, resoluteness.

реши́тельно, *adv.* **1.** resolutely. **2.** decidedly, definitely; р. отказа́ться to refuse flatly; я р. про́тив э́того прое́кта I am definitely opposed to this scheme. **3.** absolutely; э́то мне р. всё равно́ it makes absolutely no difference to me; мы р. не зна́ли, куда́ мы попа́ли we had absolutely no idea where we had got to; его́ жда́ли на вокза́ле р. все practically everyone was at the station to meet him.

реши́тельност|ь, и, *f.* resolution, resoluteness, determination.

реши́тел|ьный (~ен, ~ьна), *adj.* **1.** resolute, determined; decided; firm; р. вид resolute air; ~ьные ме́ры strong measures, drastic measures; р. тон firm tone. **2.** definite; р. отве́т definite reply. **3.** decisive; crucial; р. моме́нт crucial point; ~ьная побе́да sweeping victory. **4.** (*coll.*) absolute, blatant; р. дура́к absolute fool.

реш|и́ть, у́, и́шь, *pf.* (*of* ~а́ть) **1.** (+*inf. or* +*a.*) to decide, determine; to make up

one's mind; р. де́ло в чью-н. по́льзу to decide a case in someone's favour; р. чью-н. уча́сть to decide someone's fate. **2.** to solve; to settle; р. зада́чу to solve a problem; to accomplish a task.

реш|и́ться, у́сь, и́шься, *pf.* (*of* ~а́ться) **1.** (на+*a. or* +*inf.*) to make up one's mind (to), decide (to), determine (to), resolve (to); to bring oneself (to). **2.** (+*g.*; *coll.*) to lose, be deprived (of).

ре́шк|а, и, *f.* (*coll.*) tail (*of coin*); орёл и́ли р.? heads or tails?

реэвакуа́ци|я, и, *f.* re-evacuation.

реэвакуи́р|овать, ую, *impf. and pf.* to re-evacuate.

ре́|ять, ю, ешь, *impf.* **1.** to soar, hover. **2.** to flutter.

рж|а, и, *f.* (*obs.*) = ржа́вчина.

ржа́ве|ть, ет, *impf.* (*of* за~ *and* по~) to rust.

ржа́вост|ь, и, *f.* rustiness.

ржа́вчин|а, ы, *f.* **1.** rust. **2.** (*bot.*) mildew.

ржа́вый, *adj.* rusty.

ржа́ни|е, я, *n.* neighing.

ржа́нк|а, и, *f.* (*orn.*) plover; р. глу́пая dotterel; золоти́стая р. golden plover.

ржано́й, *adj.* rye.

рж|ать, у, ёшь, *impf.* to neigh; (*coll.*) laugh loudly.

ри́г|а, и, *f.* threshing barn.

ри́гел|ь, я, *m.* (*tech.*) cross-bar, collar-beam.

ригори́зм, а, *m.* rigorism.

ригористи́ческий, *adj.* rigorist.

ри́дер, а, *m.* (microfiche) reader.

ридикю́л|ь, я, *m.* (*obs.*) handbag.

ри́жский, *adj.* (of) Riga.

ри́з|а, ы, *f.* **1.** (*eccl.*) chasuble. **2.** (*on icons*) riza. **3.** (*obs., poet.*) raiment, garments; напи́ться до положе́ния ~ to drink oneself insensible.

ри́зниц|а, ы, *f.* (*eccl.*) vestry, sacristy.

рикоше́т, а, *m.* ricochet, rebound; ~ом at the rebound (*also fig.*).

рикошети́р|овать, ую, *impf.* to ricochet.

ри́кш|а, и, *f.* rickshaw, jinricksha.

ри́млян|ин, ина, *pl.* ~е, ~, *m.* Roman.

ри́мск|ий, *adj.* Roman; па́па р. the Pope; р. нос roman nose; ~ое пра́во Roman law; ~ая свеча́ roman candle; ~ие ци́фры roman numerals.

ринг, а, *m.* (*sport*) ring.

ри́н|уться, усь, ешься, *pf.* to dash, dart.

рис, а, *m.* rice; paddy.

риск, а, *m.* risk; на свой (страх и) р. at one's own risk, at one's peril; с ~ом (для) at the risk (of); пойти́ на р. to run risks, take chances; р. — благоро́дное де́ло (*prov.*) nothing venture, nothing gain.

рискн|у́ть, у́, ёшь, *pf.* (+*inf.*) to take the risk (of), venture (to).

риско́ванност|ь, и, *f.* riskiness.

рискóван|ный (~, ~на), *adj.* **1.** risky; ~ная игрá gamble; ~ное предприя́тие risky business, venture. **2.** risqué.

риск|овáть, ýю, *impf.* **1.** to run risks, take chances. **2.** (+*i.*) to risk; (+*inf.*) to risk, take the risk (of); р. головóй to risk one's neck; ничéм не р. to run no risk; не хотéть ничéм р. to take no chances; р. опоздáть на пóезд to risk missing the train.

рисовáльн|ый, *adj.* drawing; ~ое перó lettering pen.

рисовáльщик, а, *m.* graphic artist; draughtsman; я óчень плохóй р. I am no good at drawing, no draughtsman.

рисовáни|е, я, *n.* drawing.

рис|овáть, ýю, *impf.* (*of* на~) **1.** to draw; р. акварéлью to paint in water-colours; р. с натýры to draw, paint from life. **2.** (*fig.*) to depict, paint, portray.

рис|овáться, ýюсь, *impf.* **1.** to be silhouetted; to appear, present oneself; воéнная жизнь ~овáлась емý чи́стым кошмáром he saw life in the army as a pure nightmare. **2.** (*pejor.*) to pose, act. **3.** *pass. of* ~овáть.

рисóвк|а, и, *f.* (*pejor.*) posing, acting.

рисовóдств|о, а, *n.* rice-growing.

рисóв|ый, *adj.* rice; ~ая кáша rice pudding; ~ое пóле rice-field, paddy-field.

ристáлищ|е, а, *n.* (*obs.*) stadium; hippodrome.

рисýн|ок, ка, *m.* **1.** drawing; illustration; (*in scientific work, article, etc.*) figure; pattern, design; outline; акварéльный р. water-colour painting. **2.** drawing, draughtsmanship (*as opp. to use of colour*).

рисýнчатый, *adj.* patterned, ornamented.

ритм, а, *m.* rhythm.

ри́тмик|а, и, *f.* **1.** (*lit.*) rhythm system. **2.** eurhythmics.

ритми́ческий, *adj.* rhythmic(al).

ритми́чност|ь, и, *f.* rhythm.

ритми́ч|ный (~ен, ~на), *adj.* rhythmic(al); ~ная рабóта smooth functioning.

ри́тор, а, *m.* **1.** (*hist.*) teacher of rhetoric. **2.** (*obs.*) rhetorician, orator.

ритóрик|а, и, *f.* rhetoric.

риторический, *adj.* rhetorical; р. вопрóс rhetorical question.

ритуáл, а, *m.* ritual; ceremonial.

ритуáльный, *adj.* ritual.

риф¹, а, *m.* reef; корáлловый р. coral reef.

риф², а, *m.* (*naut.*) reef; брать ~ы to reef.

рифлéни|е, я, *n.* (*tech.*) channelling, grooving, fluting, corrugating.

рифлён|ый, *adj.* (*tech.*) chequered, channelled, grooved, fluted, corrugated; ~ое желéзо corrugated iron.

рифм|а, ы, *f.* rhyme.

рифм|овáть, ýю, *impf.* (*of* с~) **1.** to rhyme. **2.** to select in order to make rhyme.

рифм|овáться, ýюсь, *impf.* to rhyme.

рифмóвк|а, и, *f.* rhyming, rhyme system.

рифмоплёт, а, *m.* (*pejor.*) rhymer, rhymester.

рици́н, а, *m.* **1.** (*bot.*) castor plant. **2.** (*med.*) castor oil.

рици́н|овый, *adj. of* ~; ~овое мáсло castor oil.

рóббер, а, *m.* (*cards*) rubber.

робé|ть, ю, *impf.* (*of* о~) to be timid; to quail; не ~й(те)! don't be afraid!

рóб|кий (~ок, ~кá, ~ко), *adj.* timid, shy.

рóбост|ь, и, *f.* timidity, shyness.

рóбот, а, *m.* robot.

робототéхник|а, и, *f.* robot technology.

рóбче, *comp. of* рóбкий.

ров, рва, о рве, во рву, *m.* ditch; крепостнóй р. moat, fosse; противотáнковый р. anti-tank ditch.

ровéсник, а, *m.* person of the same age; мы с ним ~и we are of the same age.

рóвно, *adv.* **1.** regularly, evenly. **2.** exactly; (*of time*) sharp; р. пять рублéй five roubles exactly; р. в час at one o'clock sharp, on the stroke of one. **3.** (*coll.*) absolutely; онá р. ничегó не знáет she knows absolutely nothing. **4.** (*coll.*) exactly like, just like.

рóвност|ь, и, *f.* regularity, evenness.

рóв|ный (~ен, ~нá, ~но), *adj.* **1.** flat, even, level; ~ная повéрхность plane surface. **2.** regular, even; equable; р. пульс regular pulse; р. харáктер even temper, equable temperament. **3.** exact, even; equal; р. счёт even account, exact money; для ~ного счёта to make it even; to bring to a round figure; ~ным счётом ничегó (*coll.*) precisely nothing; не ~ен час *see* нерóвный.

рóвн|я, рóвни, *m. and f.* equal, match; он ей не р. he is not her equal, he is no match for her.

ровня́|ть, ю, *impf.* (*of* с~) to even, level; р. с землёй to raze to the ground.

ровня́|ться, юсь, *impf.* (*of* с~) **1.** to become even, become level. **2.** (по~+*d.*) to attain to the level (of).

рог, а, *pl.* ~á, ~óв, *m.* **1.** horn; antler; р. изоби́лия horn of plenty, cornucopia; брать быкá за ~á (*coll.*) to take the bull by the horns; настáвить ~á (+*d.; coll.*) to cuckold; согнýть в барáний р. (*coll.*) to make knuckle under; сломáть ~á (+*d.; coll.*) to bring to one's knees. **2.** bugle, horn; охóтничий р. hunting-horn.

рогáст|ый (~, ~а), *adj.* (*coll.*) large-horned.

рогáтин|а, ы, *f.* bear-spear.

рогáтк|а, и, *f.* **1.** turnpike; *pl.* chevaux-de-frise. **2.** (*boy's*) catapult.

рогáт|ый (~, ~а), *adj.* **1.** horned; крýпный р. скот cattle; мéлкий р. скот small cattle, sheep and goats. **2.** (*coll.*) cuckolded.

рогáч, á, *m.* **1.** stag. **2.** stag-beetle.

рогови́ц|а, ы, *f.* (*anat.*) cornea.
рогов|о́й, *adj.* horn; horny; corneous; ~ы́е очки́ horn-rimmed spectacles; ~а́я оболо́чка гла́за (*anat.*) cornea; ~а́я му́зыка music for horn; ~а́я обма́нка (*min.*) hornblende.
рого́ж|а, и, *f.* bast mat, matting.
рого́з, а, *m.* (*bot.*) reed mace.
рогоно́с|ец, ца, *m.* (*coll., joc.*) cuckold.
рогу́льк|а, и, *f.* (*cul.*) croissant.
род, а, о ~е, в ~у́, *pl.* **~ы́, ~о́в,** *m.* **1.** family, kin, clan; челове́ческий р. mankind, human race; без ~у, без пле́мени without kith or kin. **2.** birth, origin, stock; generation; он ~ом из Ирла́ндии he is an Irishman by birth, a native of Ireland; из ~а в р. from generation to generation; ему́ на ~у́ напи́сано (+*inf.*) he was pre-ordained (to); ей де́сять лет о́т ~у she is ten years of age. **3.** (*biol.*) genus. **4.** sort, kind; литерату́рный р. literary genre; р. войск arm of the service; вся́кого ~а of all kinds, all kind of; тако́го ~а of such a kind, such; в э́том ~е of this sort; что-то в э́том ~е something of the kind, something to that effect; в не́котором ~е in some sort, to some extent; в своём ~е in one's own way; своего́ ~а a kind of; in one's own way; он своего́ ~а ге́ний he is a genius in his own way. **5.** (*gram.*) gender.
рода́нист|ый, *adj.* (*chem.*) thiocyanate (of), sulphocyanate (of); ~ая кислота́ thiocyanic acid, sulphocyanic acid.
роддо́м, а, *m.* (*abbr. of* роди́льный дом) maternity home.
ро́ди|й, я, *m.* (*chem.*) rhodium.
роди́льниц|а, ы, *f.* woman recently confined.
роди́льн|ый, *adj.* р. дом maternity home, lying-in hospital; ~ая горя́чка puerperal fever; ~ое отделе́ние delivery room.
роди́мчик, а, *m.* (*coll.*) convulsions (*of mother or child about time of birth*).
роди́м|ый, *adj.* **1.** own; native. **2.** ~ое пятно́ birth-mark. **3.** (*as form of address*) (my) dear.
ро́дин|а, ы, *f.* native land, mother country; home, homeland; верну́ться на ~у to return home; тоска́ по ~е home-sickness, nostalgia.
ро́динк|а, и, *f.* birth-mark.
роди́н|ы, ~, *no sing.* (*obs.*) celebration of birth of child.
роди́тел|и, ей, *no sing.* parents.
роди́тел|ь, я, *m.* (*obs.*) father.
роди́тельниц|а, ы, *f.* (*obs.*) mother.
роди́тельский, *adj.* (*gram.*) genitive.
роди́тельский, *adj.* parental, parents'; paternal; р. комите́т parents' committee.
ро|ди́ть, жу́, ди́шь, *past* ~ди́л, ~дила́, ~ди́ло, *impf. and pf.* **1.** (*impf. also* рожа́ть) to bear, give birth (to); в чём мать ~дила́

(*joc.*) in one's birthday suit. **2.** (*impf. also* рожда́ть) (*fig.*) to give birth, rise (to).
ро|ди́ться, жу́сь, ди́шься, *past* ~ди́лся, ~дила́сь, ~дило́сь, *impf. and pf.* **1.** (*impf. also* рожда́ться) to be born; р. преподaва́телем to be a born teacher. **2.** (*impf. also* рожда́ться) (*fig.*) to arise, come into being. **3.** to spring up, thrive; кукуру́за у нас ~дила́сь хорошо́ we had a good maize-crop.
ро́дич, а, *m.* (*coll.*) relation, relative.
родни́к, а́, *m.* spring.
родников́|ый, *adj.* of родни́к; ~ая вода́ spring water.
родн|и́ть, ю, и́шь, *impf.* to make related, link.
родн|и́ться, ю́сь, и́шься, *impf.* (*of* по~) (с+*i.*) to become related (with).
роднич|о́к¹, ка́, *m. dim. of* родни́к.
роднич|о́к², ка́, *m.* (*anat.*) fontanel(le).
родн|о́й, *adj.* **1.** own (*by blood relationship in direct line*); р. брат one's brother (*as opp. to cousin, etc.*); *as noun* ~ы́е, ~ы́х relations, relatives, one's people; в кругу́ ~ы́х in the family circle, with one's people. **2.** native; home; intimate, familiar; ~а́я страна́, ~а́я земля́ native land; р. го́род home town; р. язы́к mother tongue. **3.** (*as form of address*) (my) dear.
родн|я́, и́, *f.* **1.** (*collect.*) relations, relatives, kinsfolk. **2.** relation, relative.
родови́тост|ь, и, *f.* blood; high birth, good birth.
родови́т|ый (~, ~a), *adj.* high-born, well-born, of the blood.
родов|о́й¹, *adj.* **1.** (*ethnol.*) clan. **2.** ancestral, patrimonial; ~о́е име́ние, ~о́е иму́щество patrimony. **3.** (*biol.*) generic. **4.** (*gram.*) gender.
родов|о́й², *adj.* birth, labour; ~ы́е схва́тки birth throes, labour.
родовспомога́тельн|ый, *adj.* ~ое учрежде́ние maternity home.
рододе́ндрон, а, *m.* (*bot.*) rhododendron.
родонача́льник, а, *m.* ancestor, forefather; (*fig.*) father.
родосло́вн|ая, ой, *f.* genealogy, pedigree.
родосло́вн|ый, *adj.* genealogical; ~ое де́рево family tree; ~ая кни́га family register; stud-book; ~ая табли́ца genealogical table.
ро́дственник, а, *m.* relation, relative; ближа́йший р. next of kin.
ро́дственност|ь, и, *f.* **1.** connection, tie. **2.** familiarity, intimacy.
ро́дствен|ный (~, ~на), *adj.* **1.** kindred, related; ~ные отноше́ния blood relations; ~ные свя́зи kinship ties. **2.** kindred, related, allied; ~ные наро́ды related peoples; ~ные языки́ cognate languages. **3.** familiar, intimate.

ро́дств|о, а́, *n.* **1.** relationship, kinship (*also fig.*); кро́вное р. blood relationship, blood tie, consanguinity; быть в ∼é (c+*i.*) to be related (to); не по́мнящий ∼а́ (*in official documents; obs.*) ancestry unknown. **2.** (*collect., coll.*) relations, relatives.

ро́д|ы, ов, *no sing.* birth; childbirth, delivery, lying-in; в ∼ах in labour; стимуля́ция ∼ов induction (of labour).

рое́ни|е, я, *n.* swarming (*of bees, etc.*).

рож|а¹, и, *f.* (*coll.*) mug (= *face*).

рож|а², и, *f.* (*med.*) erysipelas.

рожа́|ть, ю, *impf. of* роди́ть.

рожда́емост|ь, и, *f.* birth-rate.

рожда́|ть(ся), ю(сь), *impf. of* роди́ть(ся).

рожде́ни|е, я, *n.* **1.** birth; день ∼я birthday; ме́сто ∼я birth-place; глухо́й от ∼я deaf from birth. **2.** birthday.

рождённый, *p.p.p. of* роди́ть; (+*inf.*) born (to), destined (to).

рожде́ственск|ий, *adj.* Christmas; р. дед Father Christmas, Santa Claus; ∼ая ёлка Christmas-tree; р. пост Advent; р. соче́льник Christmas Eve.

Рождеств|о́, а́, *n.* Christmas; the Nativity; на Р. at Christmas(-time).

роже́ниц|а, ы, *f.* woman in childbirth.

роже́чник, а, *m.* horn-player; bugler.

ро́жист|ый, *adj.* (*med.*) erysipelatous; ∼ое воспале́ние erysipelas.

рож|о́к, ка́, *m.* **1.** small horn. **2.** (*mus.*) horn, clarion; bugle; францу́зский р. French horn. **3.** ear-trumpet. **4.** feeding-bottle; корми́ть с ∼ка́ to bottle-feed. **5.** (га́зовый) (gas-)burner, (gas-)jet. **6.** shoe-horn.

рож|о́н, на́, *m.* лезть, идти́ на р. (*coll.*) to kick against the pricks; про́тив ∼на́ пере́ть (*coll.*) to swim against the tide; како́го ещё ∼на́ на́до? (*coll.*) what the hell more do you need?

рожь, ржи, *f.* rye.

ро́з|а, ы, *f.* **1.** rose; rose-tree, rose-bush. **2.** (*archit.*) rose-window, rosace.

роза́ри|й, я, *m.* rosarium, rose-garden.

ро́звальн|и, ей, *no sing.* rozvalni (*low, wide sledge*).

ро́з|га, ги, g. pl. ∼ог, *f.* **1.** birch (rod); наказа́ть ∼гой to birch. **2.** *pl.* blows of the birch; дать ∼ог to give the birch.

ро́зговень|е, я, *n.* (*eccl.*) first meal after fast.

ро́здых, а, *m.* (*coll.*) pause (*from work*), breather.

розео́л|а, ы, *f.* (*med.*) roseola.

розе́тк|а, и, *f.* **1.** rosette. **2.** (*electr.*) socket; wall-plug. **3.** jam-dish. **4.** candle-ring (*glass, metal, or china ring on candlestick to collect wax*). **5.** (*archit.*) rose-window.

розмари́н, а, *m.* (*bot.*) rosemary.

ро́зниц|а, ы, *f.* retail; торгова́ть в ∼у to engage in retail trade.

ро́зничный, *adj.* retail; р. торго́вец retailer.

ро́зно, *adv.* (*coll.*) apart, separately.

ро́зн|ь, и, *f.* **1.** difference; челове́к челове́ку р. there are no two people alike, there are people and people. **2.** disagreement, dissension.

розова́т|ый (∼, ∼а), *adj.* pinkish.

розове́|ть, ю, *impf.* (*of* по∼) to turn pink.

розовощёкий, *adj.* pink-cheeked, rosy-cheeked.

ро́зов|ый (∼, ∼а), *adj.* **1.** *adj. of* ро́за; ∼ое де́рево rosewood; р. куст rose-bush; ∼ое ма́сло attar of roses. **2.** pink, rose-coloured. **3.** (*fig.*) rosy; смотре́ть сквозь ∼ые очки́ to view through rose-coloured spectacles.

ро́зыгрыш, а, *m.* **1.** drawing (*of a lottery, etc.*). **2.** (*sport*) playing off (*of a cup-tie, etc.*). **3.** (*sport*) draw, drawn game. **4.** practical joke.

ро́зыск, а, *m.* **1.** search. **2.** (*leg.*) inquiry; Уголо́вный р. Criminal Investigation Department.

ро|и́ться, и́тся, *impf.* (*of bees, etc.*) to swarm; (*fig.; of thoughts*) to crowd.

рой, ро́я, pl. рои́, *m.* swarm (*of bees, etc.*).

рок, а, *m.* fate.

рока́д|а, ы, *f.* (*mil.*) belt road, lateral road.

рока́дный, *adj.* (*mil.*) belt, lateral.

рокир|ова́ть(ся), у́ю(сь), *impf. and pf.* (*chess*) to castle.

рокиро́вк|а, и, *f.* (*chess*) castling; (*mil.; fig.*) lateral troop movement.

роков|о́й, *adj.* **1.** fateful; fated; ∼а́я краса́вица femme fatale. **2.** fatal.

рококо́, *indecl., n.* rococo.

ро́кот, а, *m.* roar, rumble.

роко|та́ть, чу́, ∼чешь, *impf.* to roar, rumble.

ро́лик, а, *m.* **1.** roller, castor. **2.** (*electr.*) (porcelain) cleat. **3.** *pl.* roller skates.

ро́лик|овый, *adj. of* ∼; р. подши́пник roller bearing.

ро́ллер, а, *m.* (*child's*) scooter.

ро́л|ь, и, pl. ∼и, ∼е́й, *f.* (*theatr.*) role (*also fig.*); part; в ∼и (+*g.*) in the role (of); игра́ть р. (+*g.*) to take the part (of), play, act; (*fig.*) to matter, count, be of importance; э́то не игра́ет ∼и it is of no importance, it does not count; вы́держать свою́ р. (*fig.*) to keep up one's part.

ром, а, *m.* rum.

рома́н, а, *m.* **1.** novel; romance. **2.** (*coll.*) love affair; romance.

романи́ст¹, а, *m.* novelist.

романи́ст², а, *m.* Romance philologist.

романи́ческий, *adj.* romantic.

рома́нс, а, *m.* (*mus.*) romance.

рома́нск|ий, *adj.* Romance, Romanic; р. стиль (*archit.*) Romanesque; ∼ие языки́ Romance languages.

романти́зм, а, *m.* romanticism.

романтик, а, *m.* (*in var. senses*) romantic; romanticist.

романтик|а, и, *f.* romance; р. медицинских исследований the romance of medical research.

романтический, *adj.* romantic.

романтичность|ь, и, *f.* romantic quality.

романтич|ный (~ен, ~на), *adj.* = ~еский.

ромашк|а, и, *f.* (*bot. and pharm.*) camomile.

ромашк|овый, *adj. of* ~а; р. чай camomile tea.

ромб, а, *m.* (*math.*) rhomb(us); (*mil.*) diamond formation; (*aeron.*) box of four.

ромбический, *adj.* (*math.*) rhombic.

ромейский, *adj.* (*hist.*) Romaic, of East Rome.

ро́мовый, *adj. of* ром.

рóндо, *indecl., n.* (*mus.*) rondo.

рондо́, *indecl., n.* (*lit.*) rondeau, rondel.

роня́|ть, ю, *impf.* (*of* уронить) 1. to drop, let fall; р. слёзы to shed tears; р. слово to let fall a word. 2. *impf. only* to shed; р. листья to shed its leaves; р. оперение to moult. 3. (*fig.*) to injure, discredit; р. себя в общественном мнении to drop in public estimation.

рóпот, а, *m.* murmur, grumble.

роп|тáть, щу, ~щешь, *impf.* to murmur, grumble.

рос, ла, *see* расти.

рос|á, ы́, *pl.* ~ы, *f.* dew; точка ~ы dew-point; медовая р. (*bot.*) honey dew; до ~ы first thing (in the morning); по ~é while the dew is still on the ground.

росинк|а, и, *f.* dewdrop; (ни) маковой ~и во рту не было neither food nor drink has passed (my) lips.

росист|ый (~, ~а), *adj.* dewy.

роскошеств|о, а, *n.* 1. extravagant taste, exotic taste. 2. extravagance.

роскошеств|овать, ую, *impf.* to luxuriate, live in luxury.

роскош|ный (~ен, ~на), *adj.* 1. luxurious, sumptuous. 2. (*coll.*) luxuriant; splendid.

рóскош|ь, и, *f.* 1. luxury. 2. luxuriance; splendour.

рóслый, *adj.* tall, strapping.

рóсный¹, *adj.* р. ладан benzoin, benjamin.

рóс|ный², *adj.* (*dial.*) *of* ~á.

росомáх|а, и, *f.* (*zool.*) wolverene, glutton.

рóспис|ь, и, *f.* 1. list, inventory. 2. painting; р. стен wall-painting(s), mural(s).

рóспуск, а, *m.* dismissal; (*mil.*) disbandment; р. парламента dissolution of Parliament; р. на каникулы breaking up for the holidays.

российский, *adj.* Russian.

рóсказн|и, ей, *no sing.* (*coll.*) old wive's tale, cock-and-bull story.

рóссып|ь, и, *f.* 1. scattering; грузить зерно ~ью to load grain loose. 2. (*pl.; min.*) deposit, placer.

рост, а, *m.* 1. growth (*also fig.*); (*fig.*) increase, rise. 2. height, stature; ~ом in height; он ~ом с вас he is (of) your height; высокого ~а tall; во весь р. full length; (*fig.*) in all its magnitude; встать во весь р. to stand upright, stand up straight. 3. (*obs.*) interest; дать деньги в р. to lend money on interest.

рóстбиф, а, *m.* roast beef.

ростовщик, á, *m.* usurer, money-lender.

ростовщический, *adj.* usurious.

ростовщичеств|о, а, *n.* usury, money-lending.

рост|óк, ká, *m.* sprout, shoot; пустить ~ки to sprout, put out shoots.

рóстр, а, *m.* (*hist.*) beak (*of war-galley*), rostrum.

рóстр|а, ы, *f.* (*hist.*) rostrum.

рострáльный, *adj.* (*archit.*) rostral.

рóстр|ы, ~, *no sing.* (*naut.*) booms.

рóсчерк, а, *m.* flourish; одним ~ом пера with a stroke of the pen.

росянк|а, и, *f.* (*bot.*) sundew.

рот, ртá, о рте́, во рту́, *m.* mouth; дышать ртом to breathe through one's mouth; у меня пять ртов в семье I have five mouths to feed in my family; не брать в р. (+*g.*) not to touch; она мяса в р. не брала she would never touch meat; разинуть р. to stand agape, be open-mouthed; не сметь рта раскрыть not to dare to open one's mouth; зажать, заткнуть р. кому-н. to stop someone's mouth, shut someone up; смотреть в р. кому-н. to hang on someone's words; хлопот полон р. (*coll.*) to have one's hands full.

рóт|а, ы, *f.* (*mil.*) company.

ротáтор, а, *m.* duplicator, duplicating machine.

ротаци́зм, а, *m.* (*ling.*) rhotacism.

ротацио́нн|ый, *adj.* ~ая машина (*typ.*) rotary press.

ротáци|я, и, *f.* 1. = ~онная машина. 2. (*agric.*) rotation.

рóтмистр, а, *m.* (*mil.*) captain (*of cavalry in tsarist Russian army*).

рóт|ный, *adj. of* ~а; *as noun* р., ~ного, *m.* company commander.

ротозé|й, я, *m.* (*coll.*) scatter-brain, gaper.

ротозéйнича|ть, ю, *impf.* (*coll.*) to be scatter-brained.

ротозéйств|о, а, *n.* (*coll.*) scatter-brainedness.

ротóнд|а, ы, *f.* 1. (*archit.*) rotunda. 2. (*lady's*) cloak.

ротоно́г|ие, их (*sing.* ~ое, ~ого), *n.* (*zool.*) Stomatopoda.

рóтор, а, *m.* (*tech.*) rotor.

ро́хл|я, и, g. pl. ~ей, m. and f. (coll.) dawdler.

ро́щ|а, и, f. small wood, grove.

ро́щиц|а, ы, f. dim. of ро́ща.

рояли́ст, а, m. royalist.

рояли́стский, adj. royalist.

роя́л|ь, я, m. piano; grand piano; игра́ть на ~е to play the piano; у ~я at the piano.

рту́тн|ый, adj. mercury, mercurial; р. выпрями́тель (electr.) mercury arc rectifier, mercury vapour rectifier; ~ая ла́мпа (electr.) mercury vapour lamp, mercury arc lamp; ~ая мазь (pharm.) mercury ointment; ~ое отравле́ние (med.) mercurialism, mercury poisoning; р. столб mercury (column).

ртут|ь, и, f. mercury, quicksilver.

руба́к|а, и, m. (coll.) fine swordsman.

руба́н|ок, ка, m. (tech.) plane.

руба́х|а, и, f. shirt; р.-па́рень (coll.) straightforward fellow.

руба́шк|а, и, f. 1. shirt; ни́жняя р., нате́льная р. petticoat, vest, singlet; ночна́я р. night-shirt, night-dress; роди́ться в ~е to be born with a silver spoon in one's mouth; своя́ р. бли́же к те́лу (prov.) charity begins at home. 2. colour (of animal's coat). 3. back (of playing cards). 4. (tech.) jacket, casing, lining.

рубе́ж, а́, m. 1. boundary, border(line); за ~о́м abroad. 2. (mil.) line; р. ата́ки assault position.

руб|е́ц¹, ца́, m. 1. scar, cicatrice; weal. 2. hem, seam.

руб|е́ц², ца́, m. 1. (zool.) paunch (ruminant's first stomach). 2. (cul.) tripe.

руби́ди|й, я, m. (chem.) rubidium.

руби́льник, а, m. (electr.) knife-switch.

руби́н, а, m. ruby.

руби́новый, adj. ruby; ruby(-coloured).

руб|и́ть, лю́, ~ишь, impf. 1. to fell (trees). 2. to hew, chop, hack. 3. (cul.) to mince, chop up. 4. to put up, erect (of logs).

руб|и́ться, лю́сь, ~ишься, impf. to fight (with cold steel).

ру́бищ|е, а, no pl., n. rags, tatters.

ру́бк|а¹, и, f. 1. felling. 2. hewing, chopping, hacking. 3. mincing, chopping up.

ру́бк|а², и, f. (naut.) deck house, deck cabin; боева́я р. conning tower; кормова́я р. roundhouse; рулева́я р. wheel-house; штурма́нская р. chart house.

рубле́вк|а, и, f. (coll.) one-rouble note.

рубл|ёвый, adj. 1. adj. of ~ь. 2. one rouble (in price).

ру́блен|ый, adj. 1. minced, chopped; ~ая капу́ста chopped cabbage; ~ое мя́со minced meat, hash; ~ые котле́ты rissoles. 2. of logs; ~ая изба́ log hut, log cabin.

рубл|ь, я́, m. rouble.

ру́брик|а, и, f. 1. rubric, heading. 2. column (of figures).

рубц|ева́ться, у́ется, impf. (of за~) to cicatrize.

ру́бчатый, adj. ribbed.

ру́бчик, а, m. 1. dim. of рубе́ц¹. 2. rib (on material).

ру́ган|ь, и, f. abuse, bad language, swearing.

руга́тел|ь, я, m. habitual user of bad language.

руга́тельн|ый, adj. abusive; ~ые слова́ bad language, swear-words.

руга́тельств|о, а, n. oath, swear-word.

руга́|ть, ю, impf. (of вы́~ and из~) 1. to curse, swear (at), abuse. 2. to tear to pieces, lash (= criticize severely).

руга́|ться, юсь, impf. 1. to curse, swear, use bad language; р. как изво́зчик to swear like a trooper. 2. to swear at one another, abuse one another.

ругн|у́ть(ся), у́(сь), ёшь(ся), pf. to swear.

руд|а́, ы́, pl. ~ы, f. ore; желе́зная р. iron-ore, iron-stone.

рудиме́нт, а, m. rudiment.

рудимента́рный, adj. rudimentary.

рудни́к, а́, m. mine, pit.

руднико́вый, adj. of рудни́к.

рудни́|чный, adj. of ~к; р. газ fire-damp; ~чная сто́йка pit prop; ~чная ла́мпа miner's lamp, Davy lamp.

ру́д|ный, adj. of ~а́; ~ная жи́ла vein; ~ное месторожде́ние ore deposit.

рудоко́п, а, m. miner.

рудоно́с|ный (~ен, ~на), adj. ore-bearing.

рудоподъёмник, а, m. ore lift.

рудопромы́вочный, adj. ore-washing.

руже́йник, а, m. gunsmith.

руже́йн|ый, adj. of ружьё; р. вы́стрел rifle-shot; р. ма́стер armourer, gunsmith; ~ые приёмы manual of the rifle.

руж|ьё, ья́, pl. ~ья, ~ей, ~ьям, n. (hand-)gun, rifle; дробово́е р. shot-gun; охо́тничье р. fowling-piece, sporting gun; противота́нковое р. anti-tank rifle; стать в р. to fall in; в р.! (mil. command) to arms!; быть под ~ьём to be under arms; призва́ть под р. to call to arms, call to the colours.

руи́н|а, ы, f. ruin (usu. pl.).

рук|а́, и́, a. ~у, pl. ~и, ~, ~а́м, f.

I. 1. hand; arm; пода́ть ~у (+d.) to offer one's hand; пожа́ть ~у (+d.), здоро́ваться за́ ~у (c+i.) to shake hands (with); ~и вверх! hands up!; ~а́ми не тро́гать! please, do not touch!; вести́ за́ ~у to lead by the hand; взя́ться за́ ~у to join hands, link arms; из ~ в ~и from hand to hand; взять на́ ~у to take in one's arms; держа́ть на ~а́х to hold in one's arms; р. о́б ~у hand in hand; написа́ть от ~и́ to write out by hand; взять кого́-н. по́д ~у to take someone's arm; идти́ с кем-н. по́д ~у to walk arm in arm

with someone, walk with someone on one's arm. **2.** hand, handwriting; signature; приложи́ть ~у to append one's signature. **3.** side, hand; на ле́вой ~е́ on the left; по пра́вую ~у at the right hand. **4.** *pl.* hands (*fig.* = power, possession); взять в свои́ ~и to take into one's own hands; взять (себя́) в ~и to take (oneself) in hand; держа́ть в свои́х ~а́х to have in one's clutches, have under one's thumb; попа́сться в ~и кому́-н. to fall into someone's hands; прибра́ть к ~а́м to appropriate; быть в хоро́ших ~а́х to be in good hands; ско́лько у вас на ~а́х сове́тской валю́ты? how much Soviet currency have you on you?; свобо́да ~ a free hand; в со́бственные ~и (*on cover of letter, etc.*) 'personal'. **5.** (*fig.*) hand (*of person giving or receiving proposal of marriage*); проси́ть ~и́ у кого́-н. to ask someone's hand in marriage. **6.** (*fig.*) hand; source, authority; из пе́рвых, вторы́х ~ at first, second hand; узна́ть из ве́рных ~ to have on good authority. **7.** (*g. sing.*; *coll.*, *obs.*) sort, kind, quality; сре́дней ~и́ of medium quality; большо́й ~и́ негодя́й a scoundrel of the first order.
II. (*fig.*; *in var. senses*) hand; отда́ть в ~и кому́-н. to hand over to someone in person; игра́ть (на роя́ле) в четы́ре ~и́ to play duets (on the piano); переда́ть де́ло в чьи-н. ~и to put a matter in someone's hands; перейти́ в други́е ~и, из ~ в ~и to change hands; сон в ~у the dream has come true; вали́ться из ~ *see* вали́ться; из ~ вон (пло́хо) (*coll.*) thoroughly bad, quite useless; вы́дать на ~и to hand out; име́ть на ~а́х to have on one's hands; умере́ть на чьих-н. ~а́х to die in someone's arms; ма́стер на все ~и Jack of all trades; э́то бу́дет им на ~у that will serve their purpose; it will be playing into their hands; на ~у нечи́ст (*coll.*) dishonest, underhand; на ско́рую ~у off-hand; быть свя́занным по ~а́м и нога́м to be bound hand and foot; дать кому́-н. по ~а́м (*coll.*) to give rap over the knuckles; уда́рить по ~а́м to strike a bargain; по ~а́м! it's a bargain!, done!; говори́ть кому́-н. под ~у to distract someone by talking; под ~ой at hand, to hand; под пья́ную ~у under the influence (of drink); с ~ доло́й off one's hands; сбыть с ~ to get off one's hands; э́то тебе́ не сойдёт с ~ (*coll.*) you won't get away with it; греть ~и (на+*p.*) to make a good thing (out of); дать во́лю ~а́м (*coll.*) to bring one's fists into play; дать ~у на отсече́ние to swear; э́то де́ло чужи́х ~ this is someone else's doing; живо́й ~о́й rapidly; как ~о́й сня́ло it has vanished as if by magic; ло-

ма́ть ~и to wring one's hands; махну́ть ~о́й (на+*a.*) to give up as lost; наби́ть ~у to get one's hand in; наложи́ть на себя́ ~и to lay hands on oneself; не поднима́ется р. (+*inf.*) one cannot bring oneself (to); мне не р. (+*inf.*) I have no call (to), it does not suit me (to); приложи́ть ~у (к) to put one's hand (to), take a hand (in) (*see also* I. 2); развяза́ть ~и (+*d.*) to give a free hand; р. у него́ не дро́гнет (+*inf.*) he will not scruple (to); ~и у меня́ не дохо́дят до э́того it is beyond me, I've no time to do it; ~и прочь! hands off!; ~о́й пода́ть a stone's throw away, but a step; умы́ть ~и (в+*p.*) to wash one's hands (of); у меня́ ~и че́шутся (+*inf.*) my fingers are itching (to), I itch (to).

рука́в, а́, *pl.* **~а́,** *m.* **1.** sleeve; спустя́ ~а́ (*coll.*) in a slipshod manner. **2.** branch, arm (*of river*). **3.** (*tech.*) hose; пожа́рный р. fire-hose.

рукави́ц|а, ы, *f.* mitten; gauntlet; держа́ть в ежо́вых ~ах to rule with a rod of iron.

рука́вчик, а, *m.* **1.** *dim. of* рука́в. **2.** cuff.

рукоби́ть|е, я, *n.* (*obs.*) shaking hands on a bargain.

рукоблу́ди|е, я, *n.* masturbation.

рукоблу́дник, а, *m.* masturbator.

рукоблу́днича|ть, ю, *impf.* to indulge in masturbation.

руководи́тел|ь, я, *m.* **1.** leader; manager; кла́ссный р. (*in school*) form monitor. **2.** instructor; guide; нау́чный руководи́тель supervisor of studies.

руково|ди́ть, жу́, ди́шь, *impf.* (+*i.*) to lead; to guide; to direct, manage.

руково|ди́ться, жу́сь, ди́шься, *impf.* (+*i.*) to follow; to be guided (by).

руково́дств|о, а, *n.* **1.** leadership; guidance; direction. **2.** guiding principle, guide; р. к де́йствию guide to action. **3.** handbook, guide, manual; р. по эксплуата́ции instructions for use. **4.** (*collect.*) (the) leadership, leaders; governing body.

руково́дств|оваться, уюсь, *impf.* (+*i.*) to follow; to be guided (by).

руково|дя́щий, *pres. part. act. of* ~ди́ть *and adj.* leading; guiding; ~дя́щая статья́ editorial, leader; р. комите́т steering committee.

рукоде́ли|е, я, *n.* **1.** needlework. **2.** (*pl.*) hand-made wares.

рукоде́льниц|а, ы, *f.* needlewoman.

рукоде́льнича|ть, ю, *impf.* to do needle-work.

рукокры́л|ые, ых (*sing.* **~ое, ~ого**), *n.* (*zool.*) Cheiroptera.

рукомо́йник, а, *m.* wash-stand, wash-hand-stand.

рукопа́шн|ая, ой, *f.* hand-to-hand fight(-ing).

рукопа́шный, *adj.* hand-to-hand.

рукопи́сный, *adj.* manuscript; p. шрифт cursive, italics.

ру́копис|ь, и, *f.* manuscript.

рукоплеска́ни|е, я, *n.* applause, clapping.

рукопле|ска́ть, щу́, ~щешь, *impf.* (+*d.*) to applaud, clap.

рукопожа́ти|е, я, *n.* handshake; обменя́ться ~ями (с+*i.*) to shake hands (with).

рукоя́тк|а, и, *f.* 1. handle; hilt; haft, helve; shaft; по ~у up to the hilt. 2. crank, crank handle.

рула́д|а, ы, *f.* (*mus.*) roulade, run.

рулев|о́й, *adj.* of руль; ~о́е колесо́ steering wheel; ~а́я коло́нка steering column; p. механи́зм, ~о́е устро́йство steering gear; *as noun* p., ~о́го, *m.* helmsman, man at the wheel.

рулёжк|а, и, *f.* (*aeron.*) taxiing.

руле́т, а, *m.* (*cul.*) 1. roll; мясно́й p. meat loaf. 2. boned gammon.

руле́тк|а, и, *f.* 1. tape-measure. 2. roulette. игра́ть в ~у to play roulette.

рул|и́ть, ю́, и́шь, *impf.* (*aeron.*) to taxi.

руло́н, а, *m.* roll.

рул|ь, я́, *m.* rudder; helm (*also fig.*); (steering-)wheel; handle-bars; p. высоты́ (*aeron.*) elevator; p. поворо́та (*aeron.*) rudder; пра́вить ~ём, сиде́ть за ~ём, быть на ~é, стоя́ть на ~é to steer; стать за p. to take the helm; ле́во руля́ port the helm; стоя́ть на ~é (*fig.*) to be at the helm; без ~я́ и без ветри́л (*fig.*) without any sense of purpose.

румб, а, *m.* (*naut.*) (compass) point.

ру́мпел|ь, я, *m.* (*naut.*) tiller.

румы́н, а, *m.* Romanian.

румы́нк|а, и, *f.* Romanian (woman).

румы́нский, *adj.* Romanian.

румя́н|а, ~, *no sing.* rouge.

румя́н|ец, ца, *m.* (high) colour; flush; blush.

румя́н|ить, ю, ишь, *impf.* 1. (*pf.* за~) to redden (*also fig.*); to cause to glow. 2. (*pf.* на~) to rouge.

румя́н|иться, юсь, ишься, *impf.* 1.(*pf.* за~) to redden; to glow; to flush. 2.(*pf.* на~) to use rouge.

румя́н|ый (~, ~а), *adj.* rosy, ruddy, rubicund.

ру́н|а, ы, *f.* (*philol.*) rune.

рунду́к, а́, *m.* (*obs.*) locker, bin.

руни́ст|ый (~, ~а), *adj.* (*obs.*) fleecy.

руни́ческий, *adj.* (*philol.*) runic.

рун|о́¹, а́, *pl.* ~а, *n.* (*obs. or poet.*) fleece; золото́е p. (*myth.*) the Golden Fleece.

рун|о́², а́, *pl.* ~а and ~ья, *n.* (*dial.*) school (*of fish*).

ру́пи|я, и, *f.* rupee.

ру́пор, а, *m.* megaphone, speaking-trumpet; loud hailer; (*fig.*) mouthpiece.

руса́к¹, а́, *m.* (grey) hare.

руса́к², а́, *m.* (*coll.*) Russian.

руса́лк|а, и, *f.* mermaid.

руса́л|очий, *adj.* of ~ка.

руси́зм, а, *m.* (*ling.*) Russicism, borrowing from Russian.

руси́н, а, *m.* Ruthenian.

руси́нский, *adj.* Ruthenian.

руси́ст, а, *m.* specialist in Russian philology.

руси́стик|а, и, *f.* Russian philology.

русифика́тор, а, *m.* russifier, russianizer.

русифика́ци|я, и, *f.* russification, russianization.

русифици́р|овать, ую, *impf. and pf.* to russify, russianize.

ру́сл|о, а, *g. pl.* ~, *n.* 1. (river-)bed, channel; измени́ть p. реки́ to change the course of a river. 2. (*fig.*) channel, course; мои́ дела́ пошли́ по но́вому ~у my affairs have taken a new turn.

русоволо́с|ый (~, ~а), *adj.* having light-brown hair.

ру́сск|ая, ой, *f.* 1. Russian (woman). 2. russkaya (*Russian folk-dance*).

ру́сск|ий, *adj.* Russian (*also as noun* p., ~ого, *m.*).

ру́с|ый (~, ~а), *adj.* light brown.

руте́ни|й, я, *m.* (*chem.*) ruthenium.

рути́л, а, *m.* (*min.*) rutile.

рути́н|а, ы, *f.* (*pejor.*) routine; rut, groove.

рутинёр, а, *m.* slave to routine, person in a rut, in a groove.

рутинёр|ский, *adj.* of ~; ~ские взгля́ды rigid views.

рутинёрств|о, а, *n.* slavery to routine.

рути́н|ный, *adj.* of ~а.

ру́хляд|ь, и, *f.* (*collect.*; *coll.*) junk, lumber.

ру́хн|уть, у, ешь, *pf.* to crash down, tumble down, collapse; (*fig.*) to crash, fall to the ground.

руча́тельств|о, а, *n.* guaranty, warrant; guarantee; с ~ом guaranteed.

руча́|ться, юсь, *impf.* (*of* поручи́ться) (за+*a.*) to warrant, guarantee, certify; to answer (for), vouch (for); p. голово́й (за+*a.*) to stake one's life (on); я не могу́ за него́ p. I cannot vouch for him.

руче|ёк, йка́, *m.* ˙*dim. of* ручей.

руч|е́й, ья́, *m.* 1. brook, stream; ~ьи́ слёз floods of tears. 2. (*tech.*) groove, calibre, pass (*of roller*).

ру́чк|а, и, *f.* 1. *dim. of* рука́. 2. handle; arm (*of chair*); p. две́ри door-handle, door-knob; дойти́ до ~и (*fig.*, *coll.*) to reach the end of one's tether. 3. penholder; pen; автомати́ческая p. fountain-pen.

ручни́к, а́, *m.* (*tech.*) bench hammer.

ручн|о́й, *adj.* 1. hand; arm; manual; ~а́я

гранáта hand grenade; ~ая кладь hand luggage; ~ая пилá hand-saw; ~ое полотéнце hand towel; ~ая продáжа counter sale; ~ая продáжа лекáрств sale of medicines without prescription; р. пулемёт light machine-gun; ~ая рабóта handwork; ~ая телéжка hand-cart; р. труд manual labour; ~ые часы́ wrist watch. 2. tame.

рýш|ить¹, у, ишь, *impf.* to pull down.

рýш|ить², у, ишь, *impf.* to husk.

рýш|иться, усь, ишься, *impf. and pf.* to fall in, collapse; (*fig.*) to fall to the ground.

рыб|а, ы, *f.* fish; (*pl., astron.*) Pisces; ни р., ни мя́со neither fish, flesh nor fowl; чýвствовать себя́ как р. в водé to feel in one's element; би́ться как р. об лёд to struggle desperately.

рыбáк, á, *m.* fisherman.

рыбáлк|а, и, *f.* 1. (*coll.*) fishing; fishing trip; идти́ на ~у to go fishing. 2. (*dial.*) fishing spot. 3. (*dial.*) seagull.

рыбáр|ь, я (~я́), *m.* (*obs.*) = рыбáк.

рыбáцкий, *adj. of* ~к; р. посёлок fishing village.

рыбáчий, *adj. of* ~к; ~чья лóдка fishing-boat.

рыбáч|ить, у, ишь, *impf.* to fish.

рыбáчк|а, и, *f.* 1. fisherwoman. 2. fisherman's wife.

рыбёшк|а, и, *f.* (*coll.*) small fry.

ры́бий, *adj.* 1. fish; piscine; р. жир cod-liver oil; р. клей isinglass, fish-glue. 2. fish-like, fishy.

ры́бник, а, *m.* 1. fishmonger, fish vendor. 2. fish marketer.

ры́бн|ый, *adj.* fish; ~ые консéрвы tinned fish; ~ая лóвля fishing; р. магази́н fish-shop, fishmonger's; р. прóмысел fishery; р. ры́нок fish market; р. садóк fish-pond.

рыбовóд, а, *m.* fish-breeder.

рыбовóдств|о, а, *n.* fish-breeding.

рыбозавóд, а, *m.* fish-factory; плавýчий р. fish-factory ship.

рыбоконсéрвный, *adj.*; р. завóд fish cannery.

рыболóв, а, *m.* fisherman; angler.

рыболовéцкий, *adj.* fishing.

рыболóвн|ый, *adj.* fishing; ~ые принадлéжности, ~ая снасть fishing tackle; р. райóн fishing-ground, fishery.

рыболóвств|о, а, *n.* fishing, fishery (*as branch of economy*).

рыбопромы́шленност|ь, и, *f.* fishing industry.

рыботоргóв|ец, ца, *m.* fishmonger.

рыботоргóвк|а, и, *f.* fishwife.

рыбохóд, а, *m.* fish-run (*in dam*).

рыв|óк, ка, *m.* 1. jerk. 2. (*sport*) dash, burst, spurt.

рыг|áть, áю, *impf.* (*of* ~нýть) to belch.

рыг|нýть, нý, нёшь, *pf. of* ~áть.

рыдá|ть, ю, *impf.* to sob.

рыдвáн, а, *m.* (*hist.*) large coach.

рыжевáт|ый (~, ~а), *adj.* reddish; rust-coloured.

рыжеволóс|ый (~, ~а), *adj.* red-haired.

рыжé|ть, ю, *impf.* (*of* по~) to turn reddish.

ры́ж|ий (~, ~á, ~е), *adj.* 1. red, red-haired, ginger; (*of a horse*) chestnut. 2. of faded red-brown colour. 3. *as noun* р., ~его, *m.* circus clown; я что, р.? (*coll.*) why leave me out?

ры́жик¹, а, *m.* saffron milk-cap (*mushroom*).

ры́жик², а, *m.* (*coll.*) 'Ginger', 'Sandy' (*pet name for red-haired child, or for dog, etc., with red coat*).

рыкá|ть, ю, *impf.* to roar.

ры́л|о, а, *n.* 1. snout (*of pig, etc.*). 2. (*coll.*) snout, mug.

ры́л|ьце, ьца, *g. pl.* ~ец, *n.* 1. *dim. of* ~о; (*dial.*) spout; у негó р. в пухý he has been at the jam-pot. 2. (*bot.*) stigma.

рым, а, *m.* (*naut.*) (mooring-)ring, eyebolt.

ры́нд|а¹, ы, *f.* (*hist.*) rynda (*bodyguard of tsars in Muscovite period*).

ры́нд|а², ы, *f.* ship's bell.

ры́н|ок, ка, *m.* 1. market(-place). 2. (*econ.*) market.

ры́но|чный, *adj. of* ~к; р. день market-day; ~чная торгóвля marketing; по~чной ценé at the market price.

рысáк, á, *m.* trotter.

ры́с|ий, *adj.* lynx; ~ьи глазá (*fig.*) lynx eyes.

рыси́ст|ый, *adj.* ~ые испытáния trotting races; ~ая лóшадь trotter.

рыс|и́ть, и́шь, *impf.* to trot.

ры́|скать, щу, щешь, *impf.* 1. to rove, roam. 2. (по+*d.*) to scour, ransack (*in search of something*); р. по скáлам to scour the cliffs; р. по кармáнам to ransack one's pockets. 3. (*naut.*) to gripe, yaw.

рысц|á, ы́, *f.* jog-trot; éхать ~óй to go at a jog-trot.

рыс|ь¹, и, о ~и, на ~и́, *f.* trot; крýпная р. round trot; на ~я́х at a trot.

рыс|ь², и, *f.* lynx.

ры́сью, *adv.* at a trot.

ры́твин|а, ы, *f.* rut, groove.

рыть, рóю, рóешь, *impf.* to dig; to burrow; to root up; р. окóпы to dig trenches; р. зéмлю копы́том to paw the ground (*also fig.*).

рыть|ё, я́, *n.* digging.

ры́ться, рóюсь, рóешься, *impf.* (в+*p.*) to dig (in); (*fig.*) to rummage (in), ransack, burrow (in).

рыхлé|ть, ю, *impf.* (*of* по~) to become friable.

рыхл|и́ть, ю́, и́шь, *impf.* to loosen; to make friable.

ры́хл|ый (~, ~á, ~о), *adj.* 1. friable; mellow (*of soil*); loose; porous. 2. (*fig.*) podgy.

рыцар|ский, *adj.* **1.** *adj. of* ~ь; р. поедѝнок joust; р. ромáн tale of chivalry. **2.** (*fig.*) chivalrous.

рыцарств|о, a, *n.* **1.** (*collect.*; *hist.*) knights. **2.** knighthood; получѝть р. to receive a knighthood. **3.** (*fig.*) chivalry.

рыцар|ь, я, *m.* knight; стрáнствующий р. knight errant.

рычáг, á, *m.* lever; (*fig.*) key factor, linch-pin; переводнóй р. switch lever; р. управлéния control lever; дéйствие ~á leverage.

рычá|жный, *adj. of* ~г; ~жные весы́ beam balance; р. мóлот sledge hammer.

рычáни|е, я, *n.* growl, snarl.

рыч|áть, ý, ѝшь, *impf.* to growl, snarl.

рьяност|ь, и, *f.* zeal.

рья́н|ый (~, ~a), *adj.* zealous.

рюкзáк, á, *m.* rucksack, knapsack.

рюмк|а, и, *f.* wine-glass.

рюмочк|а, и, *f.* *dim. of* рюмка; тáлия ~ой, в ~y (*coll.*) wasp waist.

рябѝн|а¹, ы, *f.* **1.** rowan-tree, mountain ash, service-tree. **2.** rowan-berry, ashberry.

рябѝн|а², ы, *f.* (*coll.*) pit, pock; лицó с ~ами pocked-marked face.

рябѝнник, a, *m.* (*orn.*) fieldfare.

рябѝновк|а, и, *f.* rowanberry vodka.

рябѝн|овый, *adj. of* ~a.

ряб|ѝть, ѝт, *impf.* **1.** to ripple. **2.** (*impers.*) у меня ~ѝт в глазáх I am dazzled.

ряб|óй (~, ~á, ~o), *adj.* **1.** pitted, pock-marked. **2.** speckled.

ряб|óк, кá, *m.* (*orn.*) sandgrouse.

рябчик, a, *m.* (*orn.*) hazel-grouse, hazel-hen.

ряб|ь, и, *f.* **1.** ripple(s). **2.** dazzle.

ря́вк|ать, аю, *impf.* (*of* ~нуть) (на+*a.*; *coll.*) to bellow (at), roar (at).

ря́вк|нуть, ну, нешь, *pf. of* ~ать.

ряд, a, в ~e *and* в ~ý, *pl.* ~ы́, ~óв, *m.* **1.** (*in var. senses*) row; line; пéрвый р., послéдний р. (*theatr.*) front row, back row; р. зa ~ом row upon row; из ~a вон выходя́щий out-standing, extraordinary, out of the common (run); стоя́ть в однóм ~ý (c+*i.*) to rank (with). **2.** (*mil.*) file, rank; непóлный р. blank file; ~ы́ вздвóй! (*command*) form fours!; в ~áх áрмии in the ranks of the army; в пéрвых ~áx in the first ranks; (*fig.*) in the forefront. **3.** series (*also math.*); number; в цéлом ~e слýчаев in a number of cases.

ря|дѝть¹, жý, ~дишь, *impf.* (+*i.*) to dress up (as), get up (as).

ря|дѝть², жý, ~дишь, *impf.* (*obs.*) **1.** to ordain, lay down the law. **2.** to contract.

ря|дѝться¹, жýсь, ~дишься, *impf.* **1.** (*coll.*) to dress up. **2.** (+*i.*) to dress up (as), disguise oneself (as).

ря|дѝться², жýсь, ~дишься, *impf.* (*of* по~) (*obs.*) **1.** (c+*i.*) to bargain (with). **2.** (+*inf.*) to undertake (to), contract (to).

рядкóм, *adv.* = ря́дом.

рядов|óй¹, *adj.* **1.** ordinary, common. **2.** (*mil.*) р. состáв rank and file; men, other ranks; *as noun* р., ~óго, *m.* private (soldier).

рядов|óй², *adj.* (*agric.*) ~áя сéялка seed drill; р. посéв sowing in drills.

ря́дом, *adv.* **1.** alongside, side by side; (c+*i.*) next to; он сидѝт р. с премьéр--минѝстром he is sitting next to the Prime Minister. **2.** near, close by, just by, next door; э́то совсéм р. it is a stone's throw away; он жил р. с бóйней he lived next door to the slaughter-house. **3.** сплошь и р. more often than not; pretty often.

ря́дышком, *adv.* (*coll.*) = ря́дом.

ряж, a, *m.* (*tech.*) crib(-work).

ряжев|óй, *adj. of* ряж; ~áя плотѝна crib--dam.

ря́жен|ый, *adj.* dressed up, disguised; *as noun* р., ~ого, *m.*; ~ая, ~ой, *f.* mummer.

ря́с|а, ы, *f.* cassock.

ря́ск|а, и, *f.* (*bot.*) duckweed.

ря́шк|а, и, *f.* (*coll.*) mug (= face).

С

c, *prep.*

  I. +*g.* **1.** (*in var. senses*) from; off; c ю́го-востóка from the South-East; c Вóлги from the Volga; c Кавкáза from the Caucasus; c ты́ла from the rear; c головы́ до ног from head to foot; co снa half awake; c пéрвого взгля́да at first sight; шум co спортѝвной площáдки the noise from the playing-field; пóшлина c табакá duty on tobacco; перевóд c рýсского translation from Russian; сдáча c рубля́ change of a rouble; вернýться c рабóты to return from work; убрáть посýду co столá to clear the things from the table; упáсть c камѝнной пóлки to fall off the mantelpiece; устáть c дорóги to be tired after a journey; ходѝть c тузá to lead with the ace; снять c когó-н. фотогрáфию to take someone's photo-graph; взять примéр c когó-н. to follow someone's example; довóльно c тебя́! that's enough for you!; скóлько c меня́! how much do I owe? **2.** for, from, with;

с ра́дости for joy; со стыда́ for shame, with shame. **3.** (*of position*) on, from; с ле́вой стороны́ от желе́зной доро́ги on the left--hand side of the railway; с одно́й, с друго́й стороны́ on the one, on the other hand; с како́й то́чки зре́ния? from what point of view? **4.** with (= *on the basis of*); с разреше́ния дире́ктора шко́лы with the headmaster's permission; с ва́шего согла́сия with your consent. **5.** by, with (= *by means of*); взять с бо́ю to take by storm; писа́ть с большо́й бу́квы to write with a capital letter. **6.** (*of time*) from; since; as from; с девяти́ (часо́в) до пяти́ from nine (o'clock) till five; с де́тства from childhood; с утра́ since morning; мы с ней не ви́делись с января́ I have not seen her since January; они́ бу́дут в Москве́ с двадца́того числа́ they will be in Moscow from the twentieth; с 1850 по 1900 from 1850 to 1900.

.II. +*a.* **1.** about; я бу́ду там с год I shall be there about a year; мы прошли́ с ми́лю we walked about a mile. **2.** the size of; с дом the size of a house; на́ша до́чка ро́стом с ва́шу our daughter is about the same height as yours; ма́льчик с па́льчик Tom Thumb.

III. +*i.* **1.** (*in var. senses*) with; and; с удово́льствием with pleasure; мы с ва́ми you and I; он с сестро́й he and his sister. **2.** (*indicates possession*) хлеб с ма́слом bread and butter; челове́к со стра́нностями queer, peculiar person. **3.** by, on (= *by means of*); получи́ть с пе́рвой по́чтой to receive by first post; я прие́хал с экспре́ссом I came on the express. **4.** with (= *with the passage of*); с года́ми with the years; с ка́ждым днём every day. **5.** with (*or not translated*) (= *in regard to, as regards*); как обстои́т у вас с рабо́той? how is the work going?; что с ва́ми? what is the matter with you?, what's up?; у неё пло́хо с се́рдцем her heart is bad; как у вас с деньга́ми? how are you off for money?

с- (со-, съ-) *verbal prefix indicating* **1.** *unification, movement from various sides to a point, as* свари́ть to weld. **2.** *movement or action made in a downward direction, as* спусти́ться to descend. **3.** *removal of something from somewhere, as* сорва́ть to tear off.

саа́м, а, *m.* Lapp, Laplander.
саа́мк|а, и, *f.* Lapp (woman).
саа́мский, *adj.* Lappish.
са́бельный, *adj.* sabre.
са́б|ля, ли, *g. pl.* ∼ель, *f.* sabre.
сабота́ж, а, *m.* sabotage.
сабота́жник, а, *m.* saboteur.
сабота́жнича|ть, ю, *impf.* (*coll.*) to engage in sabotage.

саботи́р|овать, ую, *impf. and pf.* to sabotage.
сабу́р, а, *m.* (*pharm.*) juice of aloe leaves.
са́ван, а, *m.* shroud, cerement; сне́жный с. blanket of snow.
сава́нн|а, ы, *f.* (*geogr.*) savannah.
савра́сый, *adj.* (*of horses*) light brown with black mane and tail.
са́г|а, и, *f.* saga.
сагити́р|овать, ую, *pf.* **1.** *pf. of* агити́ровать. **2.** (*pf. only*) to win over.
са́го, *indecl., n.* (*bot.*) sago.
са́го|вый, *adj. of* ∼; ∼вая ка́ша sago pudding.
сад, а, о ∼е, в ∼у́, *pl.* ∼ы́, *m.* garden; фрукто́вый с. orchard; зоологи́ческий с. zoological gardens, zoo; де́тский с. kindergarten.
сади́зм, а, *m.* sadism.
сади́ст, а, *m.* sadist.
сади́стский, *adj.* sadistic.
са|ди́ть¹, жу́, ∼дишь, *impf.* (*of* по∼) to plant.
са|ди́ть², жу́, ∼дишь, *impf.* (*coll.*) **1.** to slap. **2.** (*fig.*) to hurtle; to dash; to stream.
са|ди́ться, жу́сь, ди́шься, *impf.* (*of* сесть); ∼ди́(те)сь! (*polite request*) sit down!, take a seat!
са́дн|ить, ит, *impf.* (*impers.; coll.*) to smart, burn.
садо́вник, а, *m.* gardener.
садово́д, а, *m.* gardener; horticulturist.
садово́дств|о, а, *n.* **1.** gardening; horticulture. **2.** horticultural establishment.
садово́дческий, *adj.* horticultural.
сад|о́вый, *adj.* **1.** *adj. of* ∼. **2.** garden, cultivated (*as opp. to wild*).
сад|о́к, ка́, *m.* place for keeping live creatures; кро́личий с. rabbit-hutch; ры́бный с. fish-pond; живоры́бный с. fish-well (*in river vessel or barge*); с. для птиц bird--cage.
са́ж|а, и, *f.* soot, lamp-black.
сажа́|ть, ю, *impf.* (*of* посади́ть) **1.** to plant. **2.** to seat; to set, put; to offer a seat; с. пти́цу в кле́тку to cage a bird; с. хлеб в печь to put bread into the oven; с. в тюрьму́ to put into prison, imprison, jail; с. ку́рицу на я́йца to set a hen on eggs; с. на хлеб и на во́ду to put on bread and water; с. под аре́ст to put under arrest.
са́жен|ец, ца, *m.* seedling; sapling.
са́жён|ки, ок, *no sing.* overarm stroke (*in swimming*).
саже́нный (and са́женный), *adj.* (*coll.*) huge, enormous.
са́женый, *adj.* planted.
саже́н|ь, и, *pl.* ∼и, са́жен *and* саже́ней, *f.* sazhen (*Russian measure of length, equivalent to* 2·13 *metres*); морска́я с. Russian fathom (1·83 *metres*).

сазáн, а, *m.* wild carp (*Cyprinus carpo*).

сайг|á, и́, *f.* (*zool.*) saiga.

сáйк|а, и, *f.* (bread) roll.

сак, а, *m.* (*obs.*) 1. bag. 2. (*woman's*) sack-coat.

саквоя́ж, а, *m.* travelling-bag, grip.

сáкл|я, и, *g. pl.* ~ей, *f.* saklya (*Caucasian mountain hut*).

сакрамента́л|ьный (~ен, ~ьна), *adj.* sacramental; sacred.

саксау́л, а, *m.* (*bot.*) haloxylon.

саксо́н|ец, ца, *m.* Saxon.

саксо́нский, *adj.* Saxon; с. фарфо́р Dresden (or Meissen) china.

саксофо́н, а, *m.* saxophone.

сала́з|ки, ок, *no sing.* 1. hand sled, toboggan. 2. (*tech.*) slide, slide rails; с. станка́ sliding carriage.

салама́ндр|а, ы, *f.* salamander.

салама́т|а, ы, *f.* (*obs. or dial.*) (*cul.*) salamata (*kind of porridge*).

сала́т, а, *m.* 1. lettuce. 2. salad.

сала́тник, а, *m.* salad-dish, salad-bowl.

сала́тниц|а, ы, *f.* = сала́тник.

сала́т|ный, *adj. of* ~; ~ного цве́та light green.

са́линг, а, *m.* (*naut.*) cross-trees.

са́л|ить, ю, ишь, *impf.* to grease.

салици́л, а, *m.* (*chem.*) salicylate.

салици́лк|а, и, *f.* (*coll.*) salicylic acid.

салици́ловый, *adj.* (*chem.*) salicylic.

са́л|ки, ок, *sing.* ~ка, ~ки, *f.* 1. (*children's game*) tag, 'he'. 2. (*sing.*) 'he' (*in this game*); кто у нас ~ка? who is 'he'?

са́л|о, а, *n.* 1. fat, lard; suet. 2. tallow. 3. thin broken ice (*on surface of water*); slush.

сало́н, а, *m.* 1. salon. 2. saloon.

сало́н-ваго́н, а, *m.* saloon car, saloon carriage.

сало́н|ный, *adj. of* ~; ~ные бесе́ды small talk; ~ное воспита́ние high society upbringing.

сало́п, а, *m.* (*obs.*) (*woman's*) coat.

салопи́йский, *adj.* (*geol.*) Salopian.

сало́пниц|а, ы, *f.* (*coll., obs.*) 1. slut. 2. scandalmonger.

салото́пенный, *adj.* tallow-melting.

салты́к, *only in phrase* (*coll., obs.*) на свой с. in one's own fashion, in one's own way.

салфе́тк|а, и, *f.* serviette, (table-)napkin.

салфе́т|очный, *adj. of* ~ка; ~очное полотно́ diaper-cloth, damask.

са́льдо, *indecl., n.* (*book-keeping*) balance.

са́льник, а, *m.* 1. (*anat.*) epiploon. 2. (*tech.*) stuffing box, (packing) gland.

са́льность|, и, *f.* obscenity, bawdiness.

са́льн|ый, *adj.* 1. tallow; ~ая свеча́ tallow candle. 2. (*anat.*) sebaceous; ~ая железа́ sebaceous gland. 3. greasy. 4. obscene, bawdy; с. анекдо́т bawdy story, dirty joke.

са́льто-морта́ле, *indecl., n.* somersault.

салю́т, а, *m.* (*mil., naut.*) salute.

салют|ова́ть, у́ю, *impf. and pf.* (*pf. also* от~) (+*d.*) to salute.

сам¹, самого́; *f.* сама́, само́й, *a.* само́е (*and* саму́); *n.* ~о́; *pl.* са́ми, сами́х, *reflexive pron.* myself, yourself, himself, *etc.*; с. по себе́ in itself, per se; by oneself, unassisted; с. собо́й of itself, of its own accord; он с. не свой he is not himself; с. себе́ хозя́ин one's own master; она́ — сама́ доброта́ she is kindness itself.

сам², самого́, *m.* (*coll.*) boss, chief.

сама́н, а, *m.* adobe.

сама́н|ный, *adj. of* ~; с. кирпи́ч adobe (brick).

самаря́н|ин, ина, *pl.* ~е, ~, *m.* (*bibl., hist.*) Samaritan.

са́мбо, *indecl., n.* (*abbr. of* самооборо́на без ору́жия) unarmed combat.

самбу́к, а, *m.* (*cul.*) fruit purée.

сам- (*see* сам-дру́г, *etc.*) 1. (*of harvest yield*) x fold. 2. (*not alone but*) accompanied by x other persons (*reckoning the speaker as one*).

сам-дру́г, *indecl. adj.* 1. with one other, accompanied by one other person. 2. (*of harvest*) double, twice as much.

сам|е́ц, ца́, *m.* male (*of species*).

самизда́т, а, *m.* (*coll.*) samizdat (*unofficial reproduction of unpublished MSS.*).

са́мк|а, и, *f.* female (*of species*).

само- *prefix* self-, auto-.

самоана́лиз, а, *m.* self-examination, introspection.

самобичева́ни|е, я, *n.* 1. self-flagellation. 2. (*fig.*) self-reproach.

самобы́тность|, и, *f.* originality.

самобы́т|ный (~ен, ~на), *adj.* original.

самова́р, а, *m.* samovar.

самовла́сти|е, я, *n.* absolute power, despotism.

самовла́ст|ный (~ен, ~на), *adj.* 1. absolute. 2. (*fig.*) despotic, autocratic.

самовлюблённость|, и, *f.* narcissism.

самовлюблённый, *adj.* narcissistic; (*fig.*) vain, conceited.

самовнуше́ни|е, я, *n.* auto-suggestion.

самовозгора́ни|е, я, *n.* spontaneous combustion, spontaneous ignition.

самовозгора́|ться, ется, *impf.* to ignite spontaneously.

самово́ли|е, я, *n.* licence.

самово́л|ьный (~ен, ~ьна), *adj.* 1. wilful, self-willed. 2. unauthorized; ~ьная отлу́чка (*mil.*) absence without leave.

самовоспламене́ни|е, я, *n.* spontaneous ignition.

самовосхвале́ни|е, я, *n.* self-praise, self-glorification.

самовя́з, а, *m.* tying (*as opp. to made-up*) tie.

самого́н, а, *m.* home-distilled vodka, hooch.
самого́н|ка, ки, *f.* = ~.
самодви́жущийся, *adj.* self-propelled.
самоде́йствующий, *adj.* self-acting, automatic.
самоде́лк|а, и, *f.* (*coll.*) home-made product.
самоде́л|ьный (~ен, ~ьна), *adj.* 1. home-made. 2. self-made.
самодержа́ви|е, я, *n.* autocracy.
самодержа́в|ный (~ен, ~на), *adj.* autocratic.
самоде́рж|ец, ца, *m.* autocrat.
самоде́ятельност|ь, и, *f.* 1. initiative, spontaneous action. 2. amateur performance, amateur talent activities (*theatricals, music, etc.*); ве́чер ~и amateurs' night.
самоде́ятельный, *adj.* 1. amateur. 2. (*econ.*) self-employed.
самодисципли́н|а, ы, *f.* self-discipline.
самодовле́ющий, *adj.* self-sufficing, self-sufficient.
самодово́л|ьный (~ен, ~ьна), *adj.* self-satisfied, smug, complacent.
самодово́льств|о, а, *n.* self-satisfaction, smugness, complacency.
самоду́р, а, *m.* petty tyrant, wilful person.
самоду́рств|о, а, *n.* petty tyranny, wilfulness.
самое́д, а, *m.* (*ethnol., obs.*) Samoyed.
самозабве́ни|е, я, *n.* selflessness.
самозабве́нный, *adj.* selfless.
самозаводя́щийся, *adj.* self-winding.
самозагото́вк|а, и, *f.* laying-in of one's own supplies.
самозажига́ющийся, *adj.* self-igniting.
самозака́лк|а, и, *f.* (*tech.*) air-hardened steel.
самозарожде́ни|е, я, *n.* (*biol.*) spontaneous generation.
самозаря́дный, *adj.* self-loading.
самозащи́т|а, ы, *f.* self-defence; я уби́л его́ в ~е I killed him in self-defence.
самозва́н|ец, ца, *m.* impostor, pretender.
самозва́нный, *adj.* false, self-styled.
самозва́нств|о, а, *n.* imposture.
самоинду́кци|я, и, *f.* (*phys.*) self-induction.
самока́т, а, *m.* 1. (*mil., obs.*) bicycle. 2. (*child's*) scooter.
самока́тчик, а, *m.* (*mil., obs.*) bicyclist.
самокри́тик|а, и, *f.* self-criticism.
самокрити́ч|ный (~ен, ~на), *adj.* containing self-criticism.
самокру́тк|а¹, и, *f.* (*coll.*) home-made cigarette, cigarette rolled by smoker.
самокру́тк|а², и, *f.* (*obs., coll.*) secret marriage, elopement.
самолёт, а, *m.* aeroplane, aircraft.
самолёт|ный, *adj.* of ~; ~ная радиоста́нция airborne radio set.
самолётовожде́ни|е, я, *n.* air navigation.
самолётовы́лет, а, *m.* sortie (*of aircraft*).

самолётостро́ени|е, я, *n.* aircraft construction.
самолёт-снаря́д, самолёта-снаря́да, *m.* flying bomb.
самоли́чно, *adv.* (*coll.*) oneself; сде́лать что-н. с. to do something by oneself; я с. ви́дел э́то I saw it with my own eyes.
самоли́чн|ый, *adj.* (*coll.*) personal; ~ое прису́тствие attendance in person.
самолюби́в|ый (~, ~а), *adj.* proud; touchy.
самолюби|е, я, *n.* pride, self-esteem; ло́жное с. false pride; щади́ть чьё-н. с. to spare, respect someone's pride.
самомне́ни|е, я, *n.* conceit, self-importance; он с больши́м ~ем he has a high opinion of himself.
самонаблюде́ни|е, я, *n.* (*psych.*) introspection.
самонадея́нност|ь, и, *f.* (*pejor.*) conceit, arrogance.
самонадея́н|ный (~, ~на), *adj.* (*pejor.*) conceited, arrogant.
самоназва́ни|е, я, *n.* native name, own name; ро́мэни — с. цыга́н 'Romany' is the gypsies' own name for themselves.
самообвине́ни|е, я, *n.* self-accusation.
самооблада́ни|е, я, *n.* self-control, self-possession; composure.
самообложе́ни|е, я, *n.* voluntary rate-paying.
самообма́н, а, *m.* self-deception.
самообольще́ни|е, я, *n.* self-deception; пребыва́ть в ~и to live in a fool's paradise.
самооборо́н|а, ы, *f.* self-defence.
самообразова́ни|е, я, *n.* self-education.
самообслу́живани|е, я, *n.* self-service.
самооку́паемост|ь, и, *f.* ability to pay its way (*without subsidy*).
самооку́пающийся, *adj.* paying its way.
самооплодотворе́ни|е, я, *n.* (*biol.*) self-fertilization.
самоопределе́ни|е, я, *n.* (*polit.*) self-determination.
самоопредел|и́ться, ю́сь, и́шься, *pf.* (*of* ~я́ться) (*polit.*) to define one's position.
самоопредел|я́ться, я́юсь, *impf. of* ~и́ться.
самооки́дывающийся, *adj.* self-tipping; с. грузови́к tip-up lorry.
самоопыле́ни|е, я, *n.* (*bot.*) self-fertilization.
самоотверже́ни|е, я, *n.* = самоотве́рженность.
самоотве́рженност|ь, и, *f.* selflessness.
самоотве́ржен|ный (~, ~на), *adj.* selfless, self-sacrificing.
самоотво́д, а, *m.* withdrawal (*of candidature*), refusal to accept (*nomination for an office, etc.*).
самоотрече́ни|е, я, *n.* self-denial, (self-)abnegation, renunciation.
самооце́нк|а, и, *f.* self-appraisal.

самоочевидный, *adj.* self-evident.

самопи́шущ|ий, *adj.* (self-)recording, (self-) registering; с. прибóр recording instrument; ~ее перó fountain-pen.

самопожéртвовани|е, я, *n.* self-sacrifice.

самопознáни|е, я, *n.* (*philos.*) self-knowledge.

самопóмощ|ь, и, *f.* self-help, mutual aid.

самопроизвóльность|ь, и, *f.* spontaneity.

самопроизвóл|ьный (~ен, ~ьна), *adj.* spontaneous.

самопря́лк|а, и, *f.* (treadle) spinning-wheel.

самопýск, а, *m.* (*tech.*) self-starter.

саморазгружáющ|ийся, *adj.* self-unloading; ~аяся бáржа hopper(-barge).

саморазоблачéни|е, я, *n.* self-exposure.

саморегули́рующий, *adj.* self-regulating.

саморекла́м|а, ы, *f.* self-advertisement.

саморóдный, *adj.* (*min.*) native, virgin.

саморóд|ок, ка, *m.* (*min.*) native metal, native ore; nugget; (*fig.*) person without education but possessing natural talents; композитор-с. born composer, natural composer.

самосáд, а, *m.* home-grown tobacco.

самосáдочн|ый, *adj.* ~ая соль lake-salt; ~ое óзеро salt lake.

самосвáл, а, *m.* tip-up (lorry), dump truck.

самосмáзк|а, и, *f.* (*tech.*) self-lubrication, automatic lubrication.

самосожжéни|е, я, *n.* self-immolation.

самосознáни|е, я, *n.* (self-)consciousness.

самосохранéни|е, я, *n.* self-preservation.

самости́йник, а, *m.* Ukrainian separatist.

самостоя́тельно, *adv.* independently; on one's own.

самостоя́тельност|ь, и, *f.* independence.

самостоя́тел|ьный (~ен, ~ьна), *adj.* (*in var. senses*) independent; ~ьное госудáрство independent state; с. учёный труд work of original scholarship.

самострéл[1], а, *m.* (*hist.*) arbalest, cross-bow.

самострéл[2], а, *m.* person with self-inflicted wound (*designed to escape onerous military duty, etc.*).

самострéльный, *adj.* self-firing, automatic.

самосýд, а, *m.* lynch law, mob law.

самотёк, а, *m.* drift (*also fig.*); (*tech.*) gravity feed; пустить дéло на с. to let things slide.

самотёком, *adv.* **1.** (*tech.*) by gravity. **2.** (*fig.*) haphazard; of its own accord; идти́ с. to drift.

самотё|чный, *adj.* of ~к; ~чное орошéние natural irrigation.

самоторможéни|е, я, *n.* self-braking.

самоуби́йственный, *adj.* suicidal (*also fig.*).

самоуби́йств|о, а, *n.* suicide; кончáть ~ом, покóнчить жизнь ~ом to commit suicide.

самоуби́йц|а, ы, *m. and f.* suicide (*agent*).

самоуважéни|е, я, *n.* self-esteem.

самоувéренность|ь, и, *f.* self-confidence, self-assurance.

самоувéрен|ный (~, ~на), *adj.* self-confident, self-assured.

самоунижéни|е, я, *n.* self-abasement, self--disparagement.

самоуничижéни|е, я, *n.* = самоунижéние.

самоуплотнéни|е, я, *n.* **1.** voluntary giving up of part of one's dwelling space. **2.** (*tech.*) self-packing.

самоуплотн|и́ться, ю́сь, и́шься, *pf.* (*of* ~я́ться) to give up voluntarily part of one's dwelling space.

самоуплотн|я́ться, я́юсь, *impf. of* ~и́ться.

самоуправлéни|е, я, *n.* self-government; мéстное с. local government.

самоуправля́ющийся, *adj.* self-governing.

самоупрáвно, *adv.* arbitrarily; поступáть с. to take the law into one's own hands.

самоупрáвный, *adj.* arbitrary.

самоупрáвств|о, а, *n.* arbitrariness.

самоуспокоéни|е, я, *n.* complacency.

самоуспокóенность|ь, и, *f.* = самоуспокоéние.

самоустанáвливающийся, *adj.* (*tech.*) self--adjusting, self-aligning.

самоустран|и́ться, ю́сь, и́шься, *pf.* (*of* ~я́ться) (от) to get out (of), dodge.

самоустран|я́ться, я́юсь, *impf.* **1.** *impf. of* ~и́ться. **2.** *impf. only* (от) to try to get out (of), try to dodge.

самоучи́тел|ь, я, *m.* self-instructor, manual for self-tuition; с. англи́йского языкá English self-taught.

самоучк|а, и, *m. and f.* self-taught person.

самохвáльств|о, а, *n.* self-advertisement.

самохóд, а, *m.* (*tech.*) self-feed, self-act travel.

самохóдк|а, и, *f.* (*mil.*) self-propelled gun.

самохóдный, *adj.* self-propelled.

самоцвéт, а, *m.* semi-precious stone, gem.

самоцвéт|ный, *adj.* с. кáмень = ~.

самоцéл|ь, и, *f.* end in itself.

самочи́нный, *adj.* arbitrary, unauthorized.

самочýвстви|е, я, *n.* general state; у негó плохóе с. he feels bad, he is in a bad way; как вáше с.? how do you feel?; (*in general, not restricted to sick persons*) how are you?

сам-пя́т, *indecl.*, *adj.* **1.** with four others. **2.** (*of harvest*) fivefold.

сам-сём, *indecl.*, *adj.* **1.** with six others. **2.** (*of harvest*) sevenfold.

сам-трéтéй, *indecl.*, *adj.* **1.** with two others. **2.** (*of harvest*) threefold.

самýм, а, *m.* simoom.

самурá|й, я, *m.* samurai.

сам-четвéрт, *indecl.*, *adj.* **1.** with three others. **2.** (*of harvest*) fourfold.

самши́т, а, *m.* box(-tree).

сам-шóст, *indecl.*, *adj.* **1.** with five others. **2.** (*of harvest*) sixfold.

са́м|ый, *pron.* **1.** (*in conjunction with nouns, esp. denoting points of time or place, and with* тот *and* э́тот) the very, right; в ~ое вре́мя at the right time; с ~ого нача́ла from the very outset, right from the start; с ~ого утра́ ever since the morning, since first thing; в ~ом углу́ right in the corner; до ~ого ве́рха to the very top, right to the top; до ~ого Владивосто́ка right to, all the way to Vladivostok; в с. раз (*coll.*) just right; в ~ом де́ле indeed; в ~ом де́ле? indeed?, really?; на ~ом де́ле actually, in (actual) fact; тот с. челове́к, кото́рый... the very man who . . .; на э́том ~ом ме́сте on this very spot (*but* э́тот с. *is often purely pleonastic, being roughly equivalent to coll. Eng.* this here). **2.** тот же с. (кото́рый, что); тако́й же с. (как) the same (as); э́тот же с. the same. **3.** *forms superl. of adjs.; also expresses superl. in conjunction with certain nouns denoting degree of quantity or quality;* с. глу́пый the stupidest, the most stupid; ~ые пустяки́ the merest trifles; погоди́те ~ую ма́лость! wait just one moment, just a fraction of a second!

сан, **а**, *m.* dignity, office; высо́кий с. high office; духо́вный с. holy orders, the cloth; быть посвящённым в духо́вный с. to be ordained; из уваже́ния к ва́шему ~у out of respect for your cloth.

сан- *abbr. of* санита́рный.

санато́ри|й, **я**, *m.* sanatorium.

санато́р|ный, *adj. of* ~ий; с. режи́м sanatorium regimen.

санато́р|ский, *adj. of* ~ий; с. слу́жащий sanatorium attendant.

сангви́н, **а**, *m.* (*art*) sanguine.

сангви́н|а, **ы**, *f.* = ~.

сангви́ник, **а**, *m.* sanguine person.

сангвини́ческий, *adj.* sanguine.

санда́л, **а**, *m.* sandal-wood tree.

сандале́т|ы, ~, *no sing.* (*woman's*) sandals.

сандали|я, **и**, *f.* sandal.

санда́ловый, *adj.* sandal-wood.

са́н|и, **е́й**, *no sing.* sledge, sleigh; е́хать в, на ~ях to drive in a sledge.

санита́р, **а**, *m.* hospital attendant, hospital orderly; (*mil.*) medical orderly.

санитари́|я, **и**, *f.* sanitation.

санита́рн|ый, *adj.* **1.** medical; hospital; ~ое дово́льствие medical supplies; ~ая каре́та, ~ая маши́на ambulance; ~ая кни́жка (*mil.*) health record; с. по́езд hospital train; ~ая полева́я су́мка (*mil.*) first-aid kit; с. самолёт ambulance plane, aerial ambulance; ~ая слу́жба health service, medical service; ~ое су́дно hospital ship; ~ая часть (*mil.*) medical unit; с. я́щик first-aid box. **2.** sanitary; sanitation; с. врач sanitary inspector; с. день

(room-)cleaning day (*in university hostels, etc.*); ~ые пра́вила sanitary regulations; с. у́зел lavatory; sanitary arrangements.

са́н|ки, **ок**, *no sing.* **1.** = ~и. **2.** toboggan.

санкциони́р|овать, **ую**, *impf. and pf.* to sanction.

са́нкци|я, **и**, *f.* **1.** sanction, approval. **2.** *pl.* (*polit., econ.*) sanctions.

са́н|ный, *adj. of* ~и; с. путь sleigh-road.

санови́т|ый (~, ~а), *adj.* **1.** of exalted rank. **2.** (*fig.*) imposing.

сано́вник, **а**, *m.* dignitary, high official.

сано́вный, *adj.* of exalted rank.

са́ноч|ки, **ек**, *no sing. affect. dim. of* са́нки; лю́бишь ката́ться, люби́ и с. вози́ть (*prov.*) you must take the rough with the smooth.

санскри́т, **а**, *m.* Sanscrit.

санскрито́лог, **а**, *m.* Sanscrit scholar.

санскри́тский, *adj.* Sanscrit.

сантигра́мм, **а**, *m.* centigramme.

санти́м, **а**, *m.* centime.

сантиме́нт|ы, **ов**, *no sing.* (*coll.*) sentimentality; развести́ с. to sentimentalize.

сантиме́тр, **а**, *m.* **1.** centimetre. **2.** tape-measure.

сантони́н, **а**, *m.* (*pharm.*) santonin.

сану́з|ел, **ла́**, *m. see* санита́рный.

сап¹, **а**, *m.* (*med.*) glanders.

сап², **а**, *m.* (*coll.*) stertorous breathing.

са́п|а, **ы**, *f.* (*mil.*) sap; ти́хой ~ой on the sly, on the quiet.

сапёр, **а**, *m.* (*mil.*) sapper; pioneer.

сапёр|ный, *adj. of* ~; ~ные рабо́ты field engineering; ~ная ро́та engineer company; pioneer company.

сапно́й, *adj.* (*med.*) glanderous.

сапо́г, **а́**, *g. pl.* сапо́г, *m.* (high) boot; top-boot, jackboot; два ~а́ па́ра they make a pair.

сапо́жник, **а**, *m.* shoemaker, bootmaker, cobbler.

сапо́жнича|ть, **ю**, *impf.* to be a shoemaker.

сапо́жн|ый, *adj.* boot, shoe; ~ая ва́кса, с. крем blacking, shoe-polish; ~ое ремесло́ shoemaking; ~ая щётка shoe-brush.

сапфи́р, **а**, *m.* sapphire.

сапфи́ческий, *adj.* (*lit.*) sapphic.

сараба́нд|а, **ы**, *f.* (*mus.*) saraband.

сара́|й, **я**, *m.* shed; (*fig.; of uncomfortable room or dwelling*) barn; каре́тный с. coach-house; сенно́й с. hay-loft; с. для дров wood-shed.

саранч|а́, **и́**, *no pl., f.* locust(s).

сарафа́н, **а**, *m.* sarafan (*Russian peasant women's dress, without sleeves and buttoning in front*); tunic dress.

сараци́н, **а**, *m.* (*hist.*) Saracen.

сарде́льк|а, **и**, *f.* polony, saveloy.

сарди́н|а, **ы**, *f.* sardine, pilchard; ~ы в ма́сле (tinned) sardines.

сарди́н|ка, ки, *f.* = ~а.

сардони́ческий, *adj.* sardonic.

са́рж|а, и, *f.* (*text.*) serge.

сарка́зм, а, *m.* sarcasm.

саркасти́ческий, *adj.* sarcastic.

саркофа́г, а, *m.* sarcophagus.

сарма́тский, *adj.* (*hist.*) Sarmatian.

сарпи́нк|а, и, *f.* (*text.*) printed calico.

сары́ч, а́, *m.* (*orn.*) buzzard.

сатан|а́, ы́, *m.* Satan.

сатани́нский, *adj.* satanic.

сателли́т, а, *m.* **1.** (*astron.*; *fig.*) satellite. **2.** (*tech.*) planet pinion (*of gear*), planet wheel.

сати́н, а, *m.* (*text.*) sateen.

сатине́т, а, *m.* (*text.*) satinet(te).

сатини́р|овать, ую, *impf. and pf.* to satin.

сати́н|овый, *adj. of* ~.

сати́р, а, *m.* (*myth.*) satyr.

сати́р|а, ы, *f.* satire.

сати́рик, а, *m.* satirist.

сатири́ческий, *adj.* satiric(al).

сатра́п, а, *m.* satrap.

сатра́пи|я, и, *f.* satrapy.

сатура́тор, а, *m.* soda-fountain.

сатурна́л|ии, ий, *no sing.* (*hist.*) saturnalia.

сафья́н, а, *m.* morocco (*leather*).

сафья́новый, *adj.* morocco.

са́хар, а (у), *m.* sugar; свеклови́чный с. beet sugar; тростнико́вый с. cane-sugar; моло́чный с. (*chem.*) milk sugar, lactose.

сахари́н, а, *m.* saccharin(e).

са́харист|ый (~, ~а), *adj.* sugary; saccharine.

са́хар|ить, ю, ишь, *impf.* (*of* по~) to sugar, sweeten.

са́харниц|а, ы, *f.* sugar-basin.

са́хар|ный, *adj. of* ~; (*fig.*) sugary; ~ная боле́знь (*med.*) diabetes; ~ная глазу́рь icing; ~ная голова́ sugar-loaf; с. заво́д sugar-refinery; ~ная кислота́ (*chem.*) saccharic acid; с. песо́к granulated sugar; ~ная пу́дра icing sugar; ~ная свёкла sugar-beet; с. тростни́к sugar-cane.

сахароваре́ни|е, я, *n.* sugar refining.

сахарозаво́дчик, а, *m.* (*obs.*) sugar manufacturer, owner of a sugar-refinery.

сахаро́з|а, ы, *f.* (*chem.*) saccharose, sucrose.

сачк|ова́ть, у́ю, *impf.* (*coll.*) to skive, loaf.

сач|о́к¹, ка́, *m.* net; с. для ры́бы landing--net; с. для ба́бочек butterfly-net.

сач|о́к², ка́, *m.* (*coll.*) skiver, loafer.

сба́в|ить, лю, ишь, *pf.* (*of* ~ля́ть) (с+g.) to take off (from), deduct (from); с. с цены́ to reduce the price; с. в ве́се to lose weight; с. газ (*tech.*) to throttle back; с. спе́си кому́-н. (*coll.*) to take someone down a peg; с. тон (*fig.*) to change one's tune.

сбавля́|ть, ю, *impf. of* сба́вить.

сбаланси́р|овать, ую, *pf. of* баланси́ровать.

сба́лтыва|ть, ю, *impf. of* сболта́ть.

сбе́га|ть, ю, *pf.* (за+i.; *coll.*) to run (for), run to fetch; ~й за до́ктором! run for a doctor!

сбега́|ть(ся), ю(сь), *impf. of* сбежа́ть(ся).

сбе|жа́ть, гу́, жи́шь, гу́т, *pf.* (*of* ~га́ть) **1.** (с+g.) to run down (from); с. с ле́стницы to run downstairs. **2.** to run away. **3.** (с+g.; *fig.*) to disappear, vanish; хму́рое выраже́ние ~жа́ло с его́ лица́ the frown vanished from his face.

сбе|жа́ться, жи́тся, гу́тся, *pf.* (*of* ~га́ться) to come running; to gather, collect.

сберега́тельн|ый, *adj.* ~ая ка́сса savings bank; ~ая кни́жка savings-bank book.

сберега́|ть, ю, *impf. of* сбере́чь.

сбереже́ни|е, я, *n.* **1.** economy; с. сил (*mil.*) economy of force. **2.** (*pl.*) savings.

сбере́|чь, гу́, жёшь, гу́т, *past* ~г, ~гла́, *pf.* (*of* ~га́ть) **1.** to save, preserve; to protect; с. шу́бу от мо́ли to protect a fur coat from moth. **2.** to save, save up, put aside.

сберка́сс|а, ы, *f.* (*abbr. of* сберега́тельная ка́сса) savings bank.

сбива́лк|а, и, *f.* (*cul.*) (egg-)whisk.

сбива́|ть, ю, *impf. of* сбить.

сбива́|ться, юсь, *impf.* **1.** *impf. of* сби́ться. **2.** *impf. only* (на+a.) to resemble; to remind one (of).

сби́вчивост|ь, и, *f.* inconsistency, contradictoriness.

сби́вчив|ый (~, ~а), *adj.* inconsistent, contradictory.

сби́т|ень, ня, *m.* (*hist.*) sbiten (*hot drink made with honey and spices*).

сби́т|ый, *p.p.p. of* ~ь *and adj.*; ~ые сли́вки whipped cream.

сбить, собью́, собьёшь, *pf.* (*of* сбива́ть) **1.** to bring down, knock down; to knock off, dislodge; с. самолёт to bring down, shoot down an aircraft; с. проти́вника с пози́ций to dislodge the enemy from his positions; с. це́ну to beat down the price; с. спесь с кого́-н. to bring someone down a peg. **2.** to put out; to distract; to deflect; с. с та́кта to throw out of time; с. кого́-н. с то́лку to muddle someone, confuse someone; с. кого́-н. с доро́ги to misdirect someone; с. кого́-н. с пути́ и́стинного (*fig.*) to lead astray. **3.** to wear down, tread down; с. каблуки́ to wear one's shoes down at the heels. **4.** to knock together; с. я́щик из досо́к to knock together a box out of planks. **5.** (*impf. also* бить) to churn; to beat up, whip, whisk.

сби́ться, собью́сь, собьёшься, *pf.* (*of* сбива́ться) **1.** to be dislodged; to slip; твоя́ шля́па сби́лась на́бок your hat is crooked, skew-whiff; с. с ног (*coll.*) to be run off one's legs, off one's feet. **2.** to be deflected;

to go wrong; с. в вычисле́ниях to be out in one's calculations; с. в показа́ниях to be inconsistent in one's testimony, contradict oneself in one's evidence; с. с доро́ги, с. с пути́ to lose one's way; to go astray (*also fig.*); с. с ноги́ to lose the step; с. со счёта to lose count; с. с та́кта to get out of time. **3.** to become worn down; to become blunt. **4.** с. в ку́чу, с. толпо́й to bunch, huddle.

сближа́|ть(ся), ю(сь), *impf. of* сбли́зить(ся).

сближе́ни|е, я, *n.* **1.** rapprochement. **2.** (*mil.*) approach, closing in. **3.** intimacy.

сбли́|зить, жу, зишь, *pf.* (*of* ~жа́ть) to bring together, draw together.

сбли́|зиться, жусь, зишься, *pf.* (*of* ~жа́ться) **1.** to draw together, converge. **2.** (с+*i.*) to become good friends (with). **3.** (*mil.*) to approach, close in.

сбо|й¹, я, *m.* (*collect.*) head, legs, and entrails (of animal; *as meat*).

сбо|й², я, *m.* failure, shortcoming.

сбо́ку, *adv.* from one side; on one side; вид с. side-view; смотре́ть на кого́-н. с. to look sideways at someone.

сболта́|ть, ю, *pf.* (*of* сба́лтывать) to stir up, shake up, mix up; с. лека́рство to shake (a bottle of) medicine.

сбор, а, *m.* **1.** collection; с. урожа́я harvest (-carrying); с. нало́гов tax collection; с. по́дписей collection of signatures. **2.** dues; duty; takings, returns; ге́рбовый с. stamp-duty; порто́вый с. harbour dues; тамо́женный с. customs duty; по́лный с. (*theatr.*) full house; де́лать хоро́шие ~ы (*theatr.*) to play to full houses, get good box-office returns. **3.** assemblage, gathering; быть в ~е to be assembled, be in session. **4.** (*mil.*) assembly (= *signal to assemble*). **5.** (*mil.*) (periodical) training; ла́герный с. camp; уче́бный с. refresher course. **6.** (*pl.*) preparations.

сбо́рищ|е, а, *n.* assemblage, mob.

сбо́рк|а, и, f. **1.** (*tech.*) assembling, assembly, erection. **2.** (*in dress, etc.*) gather; в ~ах, со ~ами with gathers.

сбо́рник¹, а, *m.* **1.** collection (*of stories, articles, etc.*). **2.** (*tech.*) storage tank, receptacle.

сбо́рник², а, *m.* (*sport, coll.*) member of representative team.

сбо́рн|ый, *adj.* **1.** that can be taken to pieces, detachable; с. дом pre-fabricated house. **2.** mixed, combined; ~ая кома́нда (*sport*) combined team, representative team. **3.** (*mil.*) assembly; с. пункт assembly point, rallying point. **4.** с. лист (*typ.*) preliminary sheets ('prelims').

сбо́рочный, *adj.* (*tech.*) assembly; с. конве́йер assembly belt; с. цех assembly shop.

сбо́рчатый, *adj.* gathered, with gathers.

сбо́рщик, а, *m.* **1.** collector; с. нало́гов tax-collector. **2.** (*tech.*) assembler, fitter, mounter.

сбра́сыва|ть(ся), ю(сь), *impf. of* сбро́сить-(ся).

сбрива́|ть, ю, *impf. of* сбрить.

сбрить, сбре́ю, сбре́ешь, *pf.* (*of* сбрива́ть) to shave off.

сброд, а, *no pl., m.* (*collect.*) riff-raff, rabble.

сбро́дн|ый, *adj.* (*coll.*) assembled by chance; ~ая компа́ния motley assembly, chance collection of people.

сброс, а, *m.* **1.** (*tech.*) overflow disposal (system). **2.** (*geol.*) fault, break. **3.** dropping, shedding. **4.** (*cards*) discard.

сбро́|сить, шу, сишь, *pf.* (*of* сбра́сывать) **1.** to throw down; to drop; с. бо́мбы to drop bombs; с. на парашю́те to drop by parachute. **2.** to throw off (*also fig.*); to cast off, shed; с. с себя́ одея́ло to throw off a blanket; с. и́го to throw off the yoke. **3.** (*cards*) to throw away, discard.

сбро́|ситься, шусь, сишься, *pf.* (*of* сбра́сываться) (с+*g.*) to leap (off, from).

сброшюр|ова́ть, у́ю, *pf. of* брошюрова́ть.

сбру́|я, и, f. (*collect.*) harness.

сбыва́|ть(ся), ю(сь), *impf. of* сбыть(ся).

сбыт, а, *no pl., m.* (*econ., comm.*) sale; ры́нок ~a (*seller's*) market; хоро́ший с. good sales; найти́ себе́ хоро́ший с. to sell well.

сбытово́й, *adj.* (*econ., comm.*) selling, marketing.

сбы́точный, *adj.* (*obs.*) possible, feasible.

сбыть¹, сбу́ду, сбу́дешь, *past* сбыл, сбыла́, сбы́ло, *pf.* (*of* сбыва́ть) **1.** to sell, market. **2.** (*coll.*) to get rid (of), rid oneself (of); (*comm.*) to dump, push off; с. с рук to get off one's hands.

сбыть², сбу́дет, *past* сбыл, сбыла́, сбы́ло, *pf.* (*of* сбыва́ть) (*of level of water*) to fall.

сбыться, сбу́дется, *past* сбы́лся, сбыла́сь, *pf.* (*of* сбыва́ться) **1.** to come true, be realized. **2.** (*obs.*) to happen; что сбу́дется с ней? what will become of her?

сва́дебный, *adj.* wedding; nuptial; с. пода́рок wedding present.

сва́д|ьба, ьбы, g. pl. ~eб, *f.* wedding; справля́ть ~ьбу to celebrate a wedding.

свайнобо́йный, *adj.* pile-driving.

сва́йн|ый, *adj.* pile; ~ые постро́йки pile-dwellings.

сва́лива|ть(ся), ю(сь), *impf. of* свали́ться.

свал|и́ть¹, ю, ~ишь, *pf.* (*of* вали́ть¹ *and* ~ивать) **1.** to throw down, bring down; to overthrow; to lay low. **2.** to heap up, pile up; с. вину́ (на+*a.*) to lump the blame (on).

свал|и́ть², ~ит, *pf.* (*coll.*) to sink, drop, fall, abate.

свал|и́ться, ю́сь, ~ишься, *pf.* (*of* вали́ться *and* ~иваться) to fall (down), collapse; с. как снег на́ го́лову to come like a bolt from the blue.

сва́лк|а, и, *f.* **1.** dump; scrap heap. **2.** (*coll.*) scuffle, fight; о́бщая с. free-for-all, mêlée.

сва́лочн|ый, *adj. of* сва́лка; ~ое ме́сто dump, scrap heap (*also fig.*).

сваля́|ть, ю, *pf. of* валя́ть 3, 4.

сваля́|ться, ется, *pf.* to get tangled.

сва́рива|ть(ся), ю(сь), *impf. of* свари́ть(ся).

свар|и́ть, ю́, ~ишь, *pf.* **1.** *pf. of* вари́ть. **2.** (*impf.* ~ивать) (*tech.*) to weld.

свар|и́ться, ю́сь, ~ишься, *pf.* **1.** *pf. of* вари́ться. **2.** (*impf.* ~иваться) (*tech.*) to weld (together).

сва́рк|а, и, *f.* (*tech.*) welding; с. в прить́к butt welding; с. в цепь chain welding; с. по шву, с. со швом seam welding; с. с то́чками spot welding.

сварли́в|ый (~, ~а), *adj.* peevish, shrewish; ~ая же́нщина shrew.

сварно́й, *adj.* (*tech.*) welded; с. шов welded joint.

сва́рочн|ый, *adj.* (*tech.*) welding; ~ая горе́лка welding torch, burner; ~ое желе́зо weld iron, wrought iron; ~ая сталь weld steel, puddled steel.

сва́рщик, а, *m.* welder.

сва́стик|а, и, *f.* swastika.

сват, а, *m.* **1.** matchmaker. **2.** son-in-law's father; daughter-in-law's father.

сва́та|ть, ю, *impf.* (*of* по~) **1.** (*pf. also* со~) (+*a. and d.*) to propose as husband; (*also* +*a.* за+*a.*) to propose as wife; to (try to) marry off (to); to (try to) arrange a match (between); ему́, за него́ ~ют каку́ю-то неме́цкую ба́рышню they are trying to arrange a match for him with a German girl, they are trying to marry him off to a German girl. **2.** to ask in marriage.

сва́та|ться, юсь, *impf.* (*of* по~) (к; за+*a.*) to woo, court; to ask, seek in marriage.

сва́ть|я, и, *f.* son-in-law's mother; daughter-in-law's mother.

сва́х|а, и, *f.* matchmaker.

сва́|я, и, *f.* pile.

сведе́ни|е, я, *n.* **1.** piece of information; (*pl.*) information, intelligence; по полу́ченным ~ям according to information received. **2.** knowledge; attention, consideration, notice; дойти́ до чьего́-н. ~я to come to someone's notice; довести́ до чьего́-н. ~я to bring to someone's notice, inform someone; приня́ть к ~ю to take into consideration, take cognizance (of). **3.** (*pl.*) knowledge; у него́ больши́е ~я по исто́рии Росси́и he is very knowledgeable about the history of Russia. **4.** report, minute; отчётные ~я returns; предста́вить с. to

present a report.

сведе́ни|е, я, *n.* **1.** reduction; с. счётов settling of accounts. **2.** (*med.*) contraction, cramp.

све́дущ|ий (~, ~а), *adj.* (в+*p.*) knowledgeable (about); versed (in), experienced (in); ~ие ли́ца experts, persons in the know.

свеж|ева́ть, у́ю, *impf.* (*of* о~) to skin, dress.

свежезаморо́женный, *adj.* fresh-frozen, chilled.

свежеиспечённый, *adj.* newly-baked; (*fig.*, *coll.*) raw, newly-fledged.

свежепросо́льный, *adj.* fresh-salted.

све́жест|ь, и, *f.* freshness; coolness; не пе́рвой ~и (*coll.*) past its (*fig.*, *joc.*; one's) best.

свеже́|ть, ю, *impf.* (*of* по~) **1.** to become cooler; (*of the wind*) to freshen (up), blow up. **2.** to freshen up, acquire a glow of health.

све́ж|ий (~, ~а́, ~о́, ~и́), *adj.* (*in var. senses*) fresh; ~ее бельё clean underclothes; с. ве́тер fresh wind, fresh breeze; на ~ем во́здухе in the fresh air; ~ие но́вости recent news; ~ая ры́ба fresh fish; со ~ими си́лами with renewed strength; с. цвет лица́ fresh complexion; ~о́ в па́мяти fresh in one's memory; (*as pred.*) ~о́ (*impers.*) it is fresh, it is blowing up.

свез|ти́, у́, ёшь, *past* ~, ~ла́, *pf.* (*of* свози́ть[1]) **1.** to take, convey; его́ ~ли́ в больни́цу he has been taken to hospital. **2.** to take down. **3.** to take away, clear away.

свёкл|а, ы, *f.* beet, beetroot; кормова́я с. mangel-wurzel; са́харная с. sugar-beet, white beet; столо́вая с. red beet.

свекло́ви́ц|а, ы, *f.* sugar-beet.

свекло́ви́|чный, *adj. of* ~ца; с. са́хар beet-sugar.

свекло́во́дств|о, а, *n.* (sugar-)beet raising.

свекло́са́харный, *adj.* sugar-beet; beet-sugar.

свекло́совхо́з, а, *m.* State (sugar-)beet farm.

свеко́льник, а, *m.* **1.** beetroot soup. **2.** beetroot leaves.

свеко́льный, *adj. of* свёкла.

свёк|ор, ра, *m.* father-in-law (*husband's father*).

свекро́в|ь, и, *f.* mother-in-law (*husband's mother*).

свербёж, а́, *m.* (*coll.*) itch, irritation.

сверб|е́ть, и́т, *impf.* (*coll.*) to itch, irritate.

сверг|а́ть, а́ю, *impf. of* ~нуть.

сверг|нуть, ну, нешь, *past* ~, ~ла, *pf.* (*of* ~а́ть) to throw down, overthrow; с. с престо́ла to dethrone.

свержё́ни|е, я, *n.* overthrow; с. с престо́ла dethronement.

свёр|зиться, жусь, зишься, *pf.* (с+*g.*; *coll.*) to tumble (off, from).

свéр|ить, ю, ишь, *pf.* (*of* ~я́ть) (+*a.* c+*i.*) to collate (with); to check (against); c. часы́ to check one's watch; c. корректу́ру с ру́кописью to check proofs against a manuscript.

свéр|иться, юсь, ишься, *pf.* (*of* ~я́ться) (c+*i.*) to check (with).

свéрк|а, и, *f.* collation.

сверкáни|е, я, *n.* sparkling, twinkling; glitter; glare.

сверкá|ть, ю, *impf.* to sparkle, twinkle; to glitter; to gleam.

сверкн|у́ть, у́, ёшь, *pf.* to flash (*also fig.*); у меня́ в головé ~у́ла мысль a thought flashed through my mind.

сверли́льный, *adj.* (*tech.*) boring, drilling; c. станóк boring machine, drilling machine, drill.

сверл|и́ть, ю́, и́шь, *impf.* 1. (*tech.*) to bore, drill; c. зуб to drill a tooth. 2. to bore through. 3. (*fig.*; *of mental or physical pain*) to nag (at), gnaw (at); егó ~и́ла мысль об уби́том the image of the murdered man nagged at him; у меня́ ~и́т в у́хе I have a nagging ear-ache.

сверл|ó, á, *pl.* ~á, *n.* (*tech.*) borer, drill, auger.

сверлóвщик, а, *m.* borer, driller.

сверл|я́щий, *pres. part. act. of* ~и́ть *and adj.*; ~я́щая боль nagging, gnawing pain.

сверн|у́ть, у́, ёшь, *pf.* (*of* свёртывать *and* свора́чивать) 1. to roll (up); c. ковёр to roll up the carpet; c. папиро́су to roll a cigarette; c. паруса́ to furl sails; c. шéю комý-н. to wring someone's neck. 2. (*fig.*) to reduce, contract, curtail, cut down; c. шта́ты to axe the establishment. 3. to turn; с налéво to turn to the left; c. с доро́ги to turn off the road; c. на прéжнее (*fig.*) to revert (*to former topic of conversation, etc.*).

сверн|у́ться, у́сь, ёшься, *pf.* (*of* свёртываться *and* свора́чиваться) 1. to roll up, curl up; to coil up; (*of petals or leaves*) to fold; c. клубкóм to roll oneself up into a ball. 2. to curdle, coagulate, turn. 3. (*fig.*) to contract. 4. *pass. of* ~у́ть.

верстá|ть, ю, *pf. of* верстáть¹.

свéрстник, а, *m.* person of the same age; мы с ним ~и he and I are the same age.

свёрт|ок, ка, *m.* package, parcel, bundle.

свёртывани|е, я, *n.* 1. rolling (up). 2. curdling, turning; coagulation. 3. (*fig.*) reduction, curtailment, cutting down; c. произвóдства production cutting, cuts.

свёртыва|ть(ся), ю(сь), *impf. of* свернýть(ся).

сверх, *prep.*+*g.* 1. over, above, on top of. 2. (*fig.*) above, beyond; over and above; in excess of; c. плáна in excess of the plan, over and above the plan; c. сил beyond one's strength; c. (вся́кого) ожида́ния beyond (all) expectation; c. всегó to crown all, on top of everything; c. тогó moreover, besides.

сверх- super-, supra-, extra-, over-, preter-.

сверхзвуковóй, *adj.* (*phys., aeron.*) supersonic.

сверхкомплéктный, *adj.* supernumerary.

сверхмóщный, *adj.* (*tech.*) super-power, extra-high-power.

сверхнациона́льный, *adj.* supranational.

сверхнóв|ый, *adj.* ~ая (звездá) (*astron.*) super-nova.

сверхпла́новый, *adj.* over and above the plan.

сверхпри́был|ь, и, *f.* excess profit.

сверхпроводи́мост|ь, и, *f.* (*electr.*) super--conductivity.

сверхскоростнóй, *adj.* super-high-speed.

сверхсмéтный, *adj.* in excess of estimates, not budgeted for.

сверхсрочнослýжащ|ий, его, *m.* (*mil.*) man re-engaging after completion of statutory military service.

сверхсрóчн|ый, *adj.* (*mil.*); ~ая слýжба additional service (*voluntarily undertaken after completion of statutory period*); c. военно-слýжащий = ~ослýжащий.

свéрху, *adv.* 1. from above (*also fig.*); from the top; c. до́низу from top to bottom; директи́ва c. a directive from above; смотрéть на когó-н. c. вниз (*fig.*) to look down on someone. 2. on the surface.

сверхурóчн|ый, *adj.* overtime; ~ая рабóта overtime; *as noun* ~ые, ~ых (*payment for*) overtime.

сверхчеловéк, а, *m.* superman, overman.

сверхчеловéческий, *adj.* superhuman.

сверхчувстви́тельный, *adj.* supersensitive.

сверхшта́тный, *adj.* supernumerary.

сверхъестéственный, *adj.* supernatural, preternatural.

сверч|óк, кá, *m.* (*zool.*) cricket; всяк c. знай свой шестóк (*prov.*) the cobbler should stick to his last.

сверша́|ть(ся), ю(сь), *impf.* = совершáть-(ся).

сверш|и́ть(ся), ý(сь), и́шь(ся), *pf.* = со-вершáть(ся); ~и́лось! it has come to pass! it has come off!

свéрщик, а, *m.* collator.

свер|я́ть(ся), я́ю(сь), *impf. of* ~ить(ся).

свес, а, *m.* overhang.

свé|сить, шу, сишь, *pf.* (*of* ~шивать) 1. to let down, lower; сидéть, ~сив нóги to sit with one's legs dangling. 2. to weigh.

свé|ситься, шусь, сишься, *pf.* (*of* ~ши-ваться) to lean over; to hang over, over-hang; c. чéрез пери́ла to lean over the banisters.

све|сти́, ду́, дёшь, *past* ~л, ~ла́, *pf.* (*of* своди́ть¹) **1.** to take; с. дете́й в шко́лу to take the children to school; с. в моги́лу to send to the grave, be the death (of). **2.** (c+*g*.) to take down (from, off); с. кого́-н. с пьедеста́ла to take someone off his pedestal; с. с ума́ to drive mad. **3.** to take away; to lead off; с. коро́ву с доро́ги to take a cow off the road; с. разгово́р на другу́ю те́му to lead the conversation onto a different subject. **4.** to remove; с. пятно́ to remove, get out a stain. **5.** to bring together; to put together; to unite; с. ста́рых друзе́й to bring old friends together; судьба́ ~ла́ их fate threw them together; с. да́нные в табли́цу to tabulate data; с. концы́ с конца́ми to make (both) ends meet. **6.** с. дру́жбу (c+*i*.), с. знако́мство (c+*i*.) to make friends (with). **7.** (к, на+*a*.) to reduce (to), bring (to); с. на нет to bring to naught; с. к са́мому необходи́мому to reduce to barest essentials; с. расска́з к немно́гим слова́м to condense a story to a few words. **8.** to trace, transfer. **9.** to cramp, convulse; у меня́ ~ло́ но́гу I have cramp in my foot.

све|сти́сь, дётся, *past* ~лся, ~ла́сь, *pf.* (*of* своди́ться) **1.** (к, на+*a*.) to come (to), reduce (to); с. на нет to come to naught. **2.** (*of a transfer*) to come off.

свет¹, а, *m.* **1.** light (*also fig.*); лу́нный с. moonlight; заже́чь с. to put, turn the light on; в два ~а with two rows of windows; в ~е (+*g*.) in the light (of); предста́вить в невы́годном ~е to represent in an unfavourable light; на ~у́ in the light; при ~е (+*g*.) by the light (of); при ~е свечи́ by candlelight; стоя́ть про́тив ~а to stand in the light. **2.** daybreak; чем с. first thing (in the morning); чуть с. at daybreak, at first light; ни с., ни заря́ before dawn; (*iron.*) at the crack of dawn. **3.** (*pl. only* ~á; *art*) lights; ~á и те́ни lights and shades.

свет², а, *m.* **1.** world (*also fig.*); Ста́рый, Но́вый с. the Old, the New World; тот с. the next, the other world; коне́ц ~а doomsday, the end of the world; стра́ны ~а the cardinal points (*of the compass*); произвести́ на с. to bring into the world; (по)яви́ться на с. to come into the world; вы́пустить в с. to bring out (= to publish); его́ нет на ~е he has departed this life; ни за что на ~е not for the world; на чём с. стои́т like nothing on earth, like hell; for all one is, was worth. **2.** society, beau monde; вы́сший с. the upper ten; мо́дный с. the fashionable set, the smart set.

света́|ть, ет, *impf.*; ~ет (*impers.*) it is dawning, it is getting light, day is breaking.

светёлк|а, и, *f.* (*obs.*) attic.

свети́л|о, а, *n.* luminary (*also fig.*); небе́сные ~а heavenly bodies.

свети́льник, а, *m.* **1.** lamp. **2.** (*obs.*) lampion.

свети́льный, *adj.* illuminating.

свети́л|ьня, ьни, *g. pl.* ~ен, *f.* wick.

све|ти́ть, чу́, ~тишь, *impf.* **1.** to shine. **2.** (+*d*.) to give light; to shine a light (for); он ~ти́л нам в тунне́ле he lit us through the tunnel.

све|ти́ться, чу́сь, ~тишься, *impf.* to shine, gleam; в окне́ ~тится огонёк there is a light in the window; в его́ глаза́х ~ти́лась безжа́лостность there was a hard glint in his eye(s).

светле́йший, *adj.* (*obs.*) (his, her) Highness (*as title of princes, etc.*).

светле́|ть, ю, *impf.* (*of* по~)· to brighten (*also fig.*); (*of weather*) to clear up, brighten up.

светли́ц|а, ы, *f.* (*obs.*) front room.

све́тло- light.

све́тлост|ь, и, *f.* **1.** brightness (*also fig.*); lightness. **2.** его́, *etc.*, с. (*title of dukes and archbishops*) his, *etc.*, Gráce.

свет|лый (~ел, ~ла́, ~ло), *adj.* **1.** (*in var. senses*) light; bright; light-coloured; ~лые во́лосы light hair; с. день bright day; с. шрифт (*typ.*) light-face; на дворе́ ~ло́ it is daylight; ~ло́ вам, и́ли хоти́те, что́бы я зажёг свет? can you see, or do you want me to put the light on? **2.** (*fig.*) bright, radiant, joyous; pure, unclouded; ~лое бу́дущее radiant future; ~лая ли́чность good person, good soul; ~лой па́мяти of blessed memory. **3.** (*fig.*) lucid, clear; он ~лая голова́ he has a lucid mind, a good head; ~лые мину́ты lucid intervals. **4.** (*eccl.*) Easter; ~лая неде́ля Easter week.

светлынь, и, *f.* brightness (*of moonlight and/or starlight*).

светля́к, á, *m.* glow-worm; fire-fly.

светобоя́зн|ь, и, *f.* (*med.*) photophobia.

светов|о́й, *adj. of* свет¹; с. ба́кан light buoy; ~а́я волна́ light wave; ~а́я рекла́ма illuminated signs; с. сигна́л light signal, flare; с. эффе́кт (*theatr.*) lighting effect; ~о́е явле́ние luminous phenomenon.

светоза́р|ный (~ен, ~на), *adj.* (*poet.*) shining, flashing; radiant.

светозвукоспекта́кл|ь, я, *m.* son et lumière.

светокопирова́льный, *adj.* photostating; blueprinting.

светоко́пи|я, и, *f.* photostat; blueprint.

светолече́ни|е, я, *n.* (*med.*) phototherapy.

светомаскиро́вк|а, и, *f.* black-out.

светонепроница́емый, *adj.* light-proof.

светопреставле́ни|е, я, *n.* **1.** the end of the world, doomsday. **2.** (*fig., coll.*) chaos.

светосигнализа́ци|я, и, *f.* (*mil.*) lamp signalling.

светосигна́льн|ый, *adj.* (*mil.*) signal-lamp; ~ая связь lamp communication.

светоси́л|а, ы, *f.* (*phys.*) illumination; candlepower.

светосто́|йкий (~ек, ~йка), *adj.* (*chem.*) stable in light; fast to light.

светоте́н|ь, и, *f.* (*art*) chiaroscuro.

светоте́хник|а, и, *f.* lighting engineering.

светофи́льтр, а, *m.* light filter.

светофо́р, а, *m.* traffic lights; light signal.

све́точ, а, *m.* 1. (*obs.*) torch, lamp. 2. (*fig.*) light, luminary; torch-bearer.

светочувстви́тельност|ь, и, *f.* photo-sensitivity; speed (*of film*).

светочувстви́тел|ьный (~ен, ~ьна), *adj.* sensitive to light.

све́тск|ий, *adj.* 1. society, fashionable; ~ая жизнь high life; с. челове́к man of the world, man about town. 2. (*obs.*) genteel, refined; ~ие мане́ры genteel manners. 3. temporal, lay, secular; worldly; ~ая власть temporal power.

све́тскост|ь. и, *f.* good manners, good breeding.

свет|я́щийся, *pres. part. of* ~и́ться *and adj.* luminous, luminescent, fluorescent, phosphorescent.

свеч|а́, и́, *i.* ~о́й, *pl.* ~и, ~ *and* ~е́й, ~а́м, *f.* 1. candle; taper; жечь ~у́ с двух концо́в to burn the candle at both ends. 2. зажига́тельная с., запа́льная с. sparking-plug. 3. lamp candle-power; ла́мпочка в пятьдеся́т ~е́й lamp of fifty candle-power. 4. (*sport*) lob.

свече́ни|е, я, *n.* luminescence, fluorescence; phosphorescence.

све́чк|а, и, *f.* 1. candle. 2. (*med.*) suppository.

свеч|но́й, *adj. of* ~а́; с. ога́рок candle-end.

све́ша|ть, ю, *pf.* to weigh.

све́шива|ть(ся), ю(сь), *impf. of* све́сить(ся).

свива́льник, а, *m.* swaddling-bands, swaddling-clothes.

свива́|ть, ю, *impf.* 1. *impf. of* свить. 2. *impf. only* to swaddle.

свида́ни|е, я, *n.* meeting; appointment; rendezvous; date; назна́чить с. (на+*a.*) to make an appointment (for), make a date (for); до ~я! good-bye!; до ско́рого ~я! see you soon!

свиде́тел|ь, я, *m.* witness; с. обвине́ния, защи́ты witness for the prosecution, for the defence; призва́ть кого́-н. в ~и to call someone to witness; вы́звать кого́-н. ~ем, в ка́честве ~я (*leg.*) to subpoena as a witness.

свиде́тель|ский, *adj. of* ~ь.

свиде́тельств|о, а, *n.* 1. evidence; testimony. 2. certificate; метри́ческое с. birth certificate; с. о бра́ке certificate of marriage, marriage lines; с. о прода́же bill of sale.

свиде́тельств|овать, ую, *impf.* 1. (о+*p.*, +*a.* *or* +что) (*leg.*) to give evidence (concerning); to testify (to) (*also fig.*); (*fig.*) to show, attest, be evidence (of); письмо́ э́то ~ует о его́ беста́ктности this letter is evidence of his tactlessness. 2. (*pf.* за~) to witness; to attest, certify; с. ко́пию to certify a copy; с. по́дпись to witness a signature; с. почте́ние (+*d.*) to pay one's respects (to), present one's compliments (to). 3. (*pf.* о~) to examine, inspect; с. больно́го to examine a patient.

свиде́тельств|оваться, уюсь, *impf.* 1. *pass. of* ~овать. 2. (+*i. or d.*) (*obs.*) to call to witness.

сви́|деться, жусь, дишься, *pf.* (с+*i.*; *coll.*) to meet; to see one another.

свилева́т|ый (~, ~а), *adj.* knotty, gnarled.

свил|ь, и, *f.* 1. knot (*in wood*). 2. waviness (*flaw in glass*).

свина́рк|а, и, *f.* pig-tender.

свина́рник, а, *m.* pigsty.

свина́р|ня, ни, *g. pl.* ~ен, *f.* = ~ник.

свин|е́ц, ца́, *m.* lead (*also fig.* = bullet); о́кись ~ца́ lead oxide.

свини́н|а, ы, *f.* pork.

свин|ка́[1], ки, *f.* *dim. of* ~ья́; морска́я с. guinea-pig.

сви́нк|а[2], и, *f.* (*med.*) mumps.

сви́нк|а[3], и, *f.* (*tech.*) pig, ingot, bar; чугу́н в ~ах pig iron.

свиново́д, а, *m.* pig-breeder.

свиново́дств|о, а, *n.* pig-breeding.

свиново́д|ческий, *adj. of* ~ство.

свин|о́й, *adj. of* ~ья́; ~а́я ко́жа pigskin; ~о́е ры́ло snout; ~а́я котле́та pork chop; ~о́е мя́со pork; ~о́е са́ло lard.

свинома́тк|а, и, *f.* sow.

свинопа́с, а, *m.* swineherd.

свинофе́рм|а, ы, *f.* pig-farm.

сви́нский, *adj.* (*coll.*) swinish; с. посту́пок swinish trick.

сви́нств|о, а, *n.* (*coll.*) swinishness; swinish trick.

свин|ти́ть, чу́, ти́шь, *pf.* (*of* ~чивать) 1. to screw together. 2. to unscrew.

сви́нтус, а, *m.* (*coll., joc.*) swine, rogue.

свинц|ева́ть, у́ю, *impf.* (*tech.*) to plate with lead.

свинцо́в|ый, *adj.* lead; leaden; leaden-coloured; ~ые бели́ла white lead; с. блеск (*min.*) galena; ~ая дробь lead shot; ~ая кислота́ plumbic acid; ~ое отравле́ние lead-poisoning; ~ая примо́чка Goulard water; ~ая руда́ lead-ore; с. су́рик red lead, minium; с. у́ксус vinegar of lead; с. шлак lead dross, lead scoria.

сви́нчива|ть, ю, *impf. of* свинти́ть.

свин|ья́, ьи́, *pl.* ~ьи, ~е́й, *f.* 1. pig, swine; hog; sow; морска́я с. porpoise. 2. (*fig.*)

swine; cad; вести́ себя́ ~ьёй to behave caddishly; подложи́ть ~ью (+d.; coll.) to play a dirty trick (on).

свире́л|ь, и, f. (reed-)pipe.

свирепе́|ть, ю, impf. to grow fierce, grow savage.

свире́пост|ь, и, f. fierceness, ferocity, savageness; truculence.

свире́пств|овать, ую, impf. to rage.

свире́п|ый, adj. fierce, ferocious, savage; truculent; ~ая эпиде́мия violent epidemic.

свиристе́л|ь, я, m. (orn.) waxwing.

свис|а́ть, а́ю, impf. (of ~нуть) to hang down, droop, dangle; to trail.

свис|нуть, ну, нешь, pf. of ~а́ть.

свист, а, m. whistle; whistling; (of birds) singing, piping, warbling; hiss, hissing; с. в карма́не (coll., joc.) empty pockets.

сви|ста́ть, щу́, ~щешь, impf. to whistle; (of birds) to sing, pipe, warble; с. в свисто́к to blow a whistle; с. всех наве́рх (naut.) to pipe all hands on deck.

сви|сте́ть, щу́, сти́шь, impf. to whistle; to hiss; ищи́ ~щи́ (coll.) you can whistle for it; с. в кула́к to whistle for it.

свистн|у́ть, у, ешь, pf. 1. to give a whistle. 2. (coll.) to slap, smack; с. по́ уху to clip on the ear. 3. (coll.) to sneak (off with).

свист|о́к, ка́, m. whistle.

свистопля́ск|а, и, f. (coll.) pandemonium, bedlam; подня́ть ~y to let all hell loose.

свисту́льк|а, и, f. penny whistle, tin whistle.

свисту́н, а́, m. whistler.

сви́т|а, ы, f. 1. suite, retinue. 2. (geol.) suit, series, set.

сви́тер, а, m. sweater.

сви́т|ок, ка, m. roll, scroll.

свить, совью́, совьёшь, past свил, свила́, сви́ло, pf. (of вить and свива́ть) to twist, wind.

сви́ться, совью́сь, совьёшься, past сви́лся, свила́сь, pf. (of ви́ться) to roll up, curl up, coil.

свихн|у́ть, у́, ёшь, pf. to dislocate, sprain; с. себе́ ше́ю (fig., coll.) to come a cropper; с. с ума́ to go off one's head.

свихн|у́ться, у́сь, ёшься, pf. (coll.) 1. to go off one's head. 2. to go astray, go off the rails.

свищ, а́, m. 1. (tech.) flaw; (in metals) honeycomb. 2. (in wood) knot hole. 3. (med.) fistula.

свия́з|ь, и, f. (orn.) wigeon.

свобо́д|а, ы, f. freedom, liberty; с. во́ли free will; с. рук a free hand; с. сло́ва freedom of speech; с. собра́ний freedom of assembly; с. со́вести liberty of conscience; с. торго́вли free trade; вы́пустить на ~y

to set free, set at liberty; предоста́вить по́лную ~y де́йствий (+d.) to give a free hand, give carte blanche; на ~e (i) at leisure, (ii) at large.

свобо́дно, adv. 1. freely; easily, with ease; fluently; дыша́ть с. to breathe freely; она́ с. говори́т на пяти́ языка́х she speaks five languages fluently. 2. (of clothing) loose, loosely.

свобо́д|ный (~ен, ~на), adj. 1. free (= at liberty). 2. free (= unhampered, unrestrained); easy; с. до́ступ easy access; с. уда́р (sport) free kick; с. от недоста́тков free from defects; челове́к ~ной профе́ссии professional man. 3. free (= disengaged); vacant; spare; ~ное вре́мя free time, time off; spare time; ~ное ме́сто vacant place, vacant seat; вы ~ны сего́дня ве́чером? will you be free this evening? 4. free(-and-easy). 5. (of clothing) loose, loose-fitting; flowing. 6. (chem.) free, uncombined.

свободолюби́в|ый (~, ~а), adj. freedom-loving.

свободолю́би|е, я, n. love of freedom.

свободомы́сли|е, я, n. free-thinking.

свободомы́слящ|ий, adj. free-thinking; as noun с., ~его, m. free-thinker.

свод¹, а, m. code; collection (of documents, manuscripts, etc.); с. зако́нов code of laws.

свод², а, m. arch, vault; небе́сный с. the firmament, the vault of heaven.

сво|ди́ть¹, жу́, ~дишь, impf. of свести́.

сво|ди́ть², жу́, ~дишь, pf. to take (and bring back); вчера́ мы ~ди́ли дете́й в кино́ we took the children to the cinema yesterday.

сво|ди́ться, жу́сь, ~дишься, impf. of свести́сь.

сво́дк|а, и, f. summary, resumé; report; операти́вная с. (mil.) summary of operations; с. пого́ды weather forecast, weather report.

сво́дник, а, m. procurer, pander, pimp.

сво́днича|ть, ю, impf. to procure, pander.

сво́дничеств|о, а, n. procuring, pandering, pimping.

сво́дн|ый, adj. 1. composite, combined; collated; ~ая афи́ша теа́тров theatre guide (bill listing all current productions); с. отря́д (mil.) combined force; ~ая табли́ца summary table, index. 2. step-; с. брат step-brother.

сво́дн|я, и, f. (coll.) procuress.

сво́дчатый, adj. arched, vaulted.

своевла́ст|ный (~ен, ~на), adj. despotic.

своево́ли|е, я, n. self-will, wilfulness.

своево́льнича|ть, ю, impf. to be self-willed, be wilful.

своево́л|ьный (~ен, ~ьна), adj. self-willed, wilful.

своевре́менно, *adv.* in good time; opportunely.

своевре́мен|ный (~ен, ~на), *adj.* timely, opportune; well-timed.

своекоры́сти|е, я, *n.* self-interest.

своекоры́ст|ный (~ен, ~на), *adj.* self-interested, self-seeking.

своеко́штный, *adj.* (*obs.*) (fee-)paying.

своенра́ви|е, я, *n.* wilfulness, waywardness, capriciousness.

своенра́в|ный (~ен, ~на), *adj.* wilful, wayward, capricious.

своеобра́зи|е, я, *n.* originality; peculiarity.

своеобра́з|ный (~ен, ~на), *adj.* original; peculiar, distinctive.

сво|зи́ть¹, жу́, ~зишь, *impf. of* свезти́.

сво|зи́ть², жу́, ~зишь, *pf.* to take (*and bring back*); мы ~зи́ли дете́й в цирк we took the children to the circus.

свой, *possessive adj.* one's (my, your, his, *etc.*, *in accordance with subject of sentence or clause*), one's own; у них с. дом they have a house of their own; своё варе́нье one's own, home-made jam; свои́ войска́ friendly troops; кри́кнуть не свои́м го́лосом to give a frenzied scream; умере́ть свое́й сме́ртью to die a natural death; в своё вре́мя (*i*) at one time; in my, his, *etc.*, time, (*ii*) in due time, in due course; в своём ро́де in one's own way; он не в своём уме́ he is not right in the head; на свои́х на двои́х on Shanks' mare, pony; она́ сама́ не своя́ she is not herself; он у нас с. челове́к he's one of us, he's quite at home here; *as noun* свой one's (own) people; своё one's own; доби́ться своего́ to get one's own way; to hold one's own; получи́ть своё to get one's own back.

сво́йственник, а, *m.* relation, relative by marriage; он мне с. he is related to me by marriage.

сво́йствен|ный (~ *and* ~ен, ~на), *adj.* (+*d.*) characteristic (of).

сво́йств|о, а, *n.* property, quality, attribute, characteristic.

свойств|о́, а́, *n.* relationship by marriage, affinity; быть в ~е́ с кем-н. to be related to someone by marriage.

свола́кива|ть, ю, *impf. of* сволочь.

сволочно́й, *adj.* (*coll.*) worthless, rubbishy.

сво́лоч|ь, и, *g. pl.* ~е́й, *f.* (*coll.*) 1. (*as term of abuse*) scum, swine. 2. (*collect.*) riff-raff, dregs.

своло́|чь, ку́, чёшь, ку́т, *past* ~к, ~кла́, *pf.* (*of* своло́кивать) (*coll.*) 1. to drag off. 2. (*fig.*) to knock off.

свор|а, ы, *f.* 1. leash; (*fig.*) pair (*of greyhounds*). 2. (*collect.*) pack (*of hounds*); (*fig.*) gang.

свора́чива|ть, ю, *impf. of* сверну́ть *and* свороти́ть.

свор|ова́ть, у́ю, *pf. of* ворова́ть.

своро|ти́ть, чу́, ~тишь, *pf.* (*of* свора́чивать) (*coll.*) 1. to dislodge, displace, shift. 2. to turn, swing (*also trans.*); с. с доро́ги to turn off the road; с. с ума́ to go off one's head. 3. to twist, dislocate; to break.

своя́к, а́, *m.* brother-in-law (*husband of wife's sister*).

своя́чениц|а, ы, *f.* sister-in-law (*wife's sister*).

свык|а́ться, а́юсь, *impf. of* ~нуться.

свы́к|нуться, нусь, нешься, *past* ~ся, ~лась, *pf.* (*of* ~а́ться) (с+*i.*) to get used (to), accustom oneself (to).

высока́, *adv.* (*pejor.*) in a haughty manner, condescendingly; обраща́ться с кем-н. с. to condescend to, patronize someone.

свы́ше 1. *adv.* from above; (*rel.*) from on high. 2. *prep.*+*g.* over, more than; beyond; с. ты́сячи самолётов уча́ствовало в налёте over a thousand planes took part in the raid; э́то с. мои́х сил it is beyond me.

свя́з|анный, *p.p.p. of* ~а́ть *and adj.* 1. constrained; ~анная речь halting utterance. 2. (*chem.*) combined, bound.

свя|за́ть, жу́, ~жешь, *pf.* (*of* вяза́ть *and* ~зывать) 1. to tie; to bind (*also fig.*); с. в у́зел to bundle (up); с. по рука́м и нога́м to tie, bind hand and foot (*also fig.*); с. обеща́нием to bind by promise; с. свою́ судьбу́ (с+*i.*) to throw in one's lot (with). 2. (*fig.*) to connect, link; быть (те́сно) ~занным, ~зано (с+*i.*) to be (closely) connected (with), be bound up (with), be tied up (with). 3. (быть) ~зано (с+*i.*; *fig.*) to involve, entail; э́то предприя́тие бу́дет ~зано с огро́мными расхо́дами this undertaking will involve huge expense. 4. to connect, associate; не́которые ~за́ли эпиде́мию с плохи́м водоснабже́нием some connected the epidemic with the bad water-supply.

свя|за́ться, жу́сь, ~жешься, *pf.* (*of* ~зываться) (с+*i.*) 1. to get in touch (with), communicate (with); с. по ра́дио to establish a radio link. 2. (*coll.*, *pejor.*) to get involved (with), get mixed up (with).

связи́ст, а, *m.* 1. (*mil.*) signaller; member of Signal Corps. 2. postal *and/or* telecommunications worker.

свя́зк|а, и, *f.* 1. sheaf, bunch; с. бума́г sheaf of papers; с. ключе́й bunch of keys. 2. (*anat.*) chord; ligament; copula; голосовы́е ~и vocal chords. 3. (*gram.*) copula.

связн|о́й, *adj.* (*mil.*) liaison, communication; с. самолёт liaison aircraft; ~а́я соба́ка messenger dog; *as noun* с., ~о́го, *m.* messenger, runner, orderly.

свя́зный, *adj.* connected, coherent.

свя́зочный, *adj.* (*anat.*) ligamentous.

связу́ющий, *adj.* connecting, linking.

свя́зыва|ть, ю, *impf. of* связа́ть.

свя́зыва|ться, юсь, *impf.* **1.** *impf. of* связа́ть-ся. **2.** *impf. only* (c+*i.*) to have to do (with); не ~йся с ни́ми don't have anything to do with them.

связ|ь, и, о ~и, в ~й, *f.* **1.** connexion; причи́нная с. (*philos.*) causation; в ~й с э́тим in this connexion. **2.** link, tie, bond; дру́жеские ~и friendly relations, ties of friendship; с. Великобрита́нии с содру́-жеством на́ций the link between Great Britain and the Commonwealth; потеря́ть с. (c+*i.*) to lose touch (with). **3.** (*sexual*) liaison, association; вступи́ть в с. (c+*i.*) to form an association (with). **4.** (*pl.*) con-nexions, contacts; у него́ мно́го влия́тель-ных ~ей в Москве́ he has many influential connexions in Moscow. **5.** communica-tion; (*mil.*) intercommunication; signals; liaison; возду́шная с. aerial communica-tion; с. по ра́дио radio communication; с. с во́здухом (*mil.*) ground–air communi-cation; с. с землёй (*mil.*) air–ground com-munication. **6.** (*sing. only*) (postal and tele-)communications; Министе́рство ~и Ministry of Communications; отделе́ние ~и (branch) post office; рабо́тник ~и post office worker. **7.** (*tech.*) tie, stay, brace, strut; (*electr.*) coupling.

святе́йшеств|о, а, *n.* его́ с. (*title of Patriarchs and of the Pope*) His Holiness.

святе́йший, *adj.* most holy (*pertaining to the Patriarchs and synod of the Orthodox Church, also to the Pope*); с. патриа́рх His Holiness the Patriarch; с. престо́л the papal throne.

святи́лищ|е, а, *n.* sanctuary.

святи́тел|ь, я, *m.* prelate.

свя|ти́ть, чу́, ти́шь, *impf.* (*of* о~) to conse-crate; to bless, sanctify.

свя́т|ки, ок, *no sing.* Christmas-tide.

свя́то, *adv.* piously; religiously; с. бере́чь to treasure; с. чтить to hold sacred.

свят|о́й (~, ~а́, ~о), *adj.* **1.** holy; sacred (*also fig.*); ~а́я вода́ holy water; с. долг sacred duty; с. дух the Holy Ghost, the Holy Spirit; ~а́я (неде́ля) Holy Week; ~а́я ~ы́х holy of holies, sanctum. **2.** saintly. **3.** (*fig.*) pious. **4.** *preceding name, or as noun* с., ~о́го, *m.*; ~а́я, ~о́й, *f.* saint; причи́слить к ли́ку ~ы́х (*eccl.*) to canonize.

свя́тост|ь, и, *f.* holiness; sanctity.

святота́т|ец, ца, *m.* person committing sacrilege.

святота́тственный, *adj.* sacrilegious.

святота́тств|о, а, *n.* sacrilege.

святота́тств|овать, ую, *impf.* to commit sacrilege.

свят|о́чный, *adj. of* ~ки; с. расска́з Christ-mas tale.

свято́ш|а, и, *m. and f.* sanctimonious person.

свя́тц|ы, ев, *no sing.* (church) calendar.

святы́н|я, и, f.* **1. (*eccl.*) object of worship; sacred place. **2.** (*fig.*) sacred object.

свяще́нник, а, *m.* priest (*of Orthodox Church*); clergyman.

свяще́ннический, *adj.* priestly; sacerdotal.

священноде́йстви|е, я, *n.* **1.** religious rite. **2.** (*fig.*) solemn performance (of ceremony, duties, *etc.*).

священноде́йств|овать, ую, *impf.* **1.** to per-form a religious rite. **2.** (*fig.*) to do some-thing with solemnity, with pomp.

священнослужи́тел|ь, я, *m.* clergyman (*priest or deacon*).

свяще́н|ный (~ен, ~на), *adj.* holy; sacred (*also fig.*); ~ное писа́ние Holy Writ, Scrip-ture; С. сою́з (*hist.*) the Holy Alliance.

свяще́нств|о, а, *n.* priesthood (*also collect.*).

сгиб, а, *m.* **1.** bend. **2.** (*anat.*) flexion.

сгиба́ем|ый (~, ~а), *adj.* flexible, pliable.

сгиба́|ть(ся), ю(сь), *impf. of* согну́ть(ся).

сги́н|уть, у, ешь, *pf.* (*coll.*) to disappear, vanish; ~ь с глаз мои́х! out of my sight!

сгла́|дить, жу, дишь, *pf.* (*of* ~живать) **1.** to smooth out. **2.** (*fig.*) to smooth over, soften.

сгла́|диться, дится, *pf.* (*of* ~живаться) **1.** to become smooth. **2.** (*fig.*) to be smoothed over, be softened; to diminish, abate.

сгла́жива|ть(ся), ю(сь), *impf. of* сгла́дить-(ся).

сглаз, а (у), *m.* (*coll.*) the evil eye.

сгла́|зить, жу, зишь, *pf.* to put the evil eye (on, upon); (*fig., coll.*) to endanger the suc-cess (of) (*an undertaking, etc., by forecasting the outcome*); чтобы не с.! touch wood!

сглуп|и́ть, лю́, и́шь, *pf. of* глупи́ть.

сгнива́|ть, ю, *impf. of* сгнить.

сгни|ть, ю, ёшь, *pf.* (*of* гнить *and* ~ва́ть) to rot, decay.

сгно|и́ть, ю, и́шь, *pf. of* гнои́ть.

сгова́рива|ть(ся), ю(сь), *impf. of* сгово-ри́ть(ся).

сго́вор, а, *m.* **1.** (*obs.*) betrothal. **2.** (*usu. pejor.*) agreement, compact, deal.

сговор|и́ть, ю́, и́шь, *pf.* (*of* сгова́ривать) (*obs.*) to give consent to the marriage (of); to betroth.

сговор|и́ться, ю́сь, и́шься, *pf.* (*of* сгова́ри-ваться) (c+*i.*) **1.** to arrange (with), make an appointment (with); мы ~и́лись встре́-титься с ни́ми при вхо́де в парк we ar-ranged to meet them at the entrance to the park. **2.** to come to an arrangement (with), reach an understanding (with).

**сгово́рчивост|ь, и, f.* compliancy, tracta-bility.

сгово́рчив|ый (~, ~а), *adj.* compliant, complaisant, tractable.

сгон, а, *m.* driving; herding, rounding-up.

**сго́нк|а, и, f.* rafting, floating.

сго́нн|ый, *adj.* 1. rounding up; rounded up; ~ая рабо́та rounding up, herding. 2. rafting, floating.

сго́нщик, а, *m.* 1. herdsman, drover. 2. (lumber-)rafter.

сгоня́|ть, ю, *impf. of* согна́ть.

сгора́ни|е, я, *n.* combustion; дви́гатель вну́треннего ~я internal-combustion engine.

сгор|а́ть, а́ю, *impf.* 1. *impf. of* ~е́ть. 2. (от; *fig.*) to burn (with); с. от стыда́, любопы́тства to burn with shame, curiosity.

сго́рб|ить(ся), лю(сь), ишь(ся), *pf. of* го́рбить(ся).

сго́рб|ленный, *p.p.p. of* ~ить *and adj.* crooked, bent; hunchbacked.

сгор|е́ть, ю́, и́шь, *pf.* (*of* ~а́ть) 1. to burn down; to be burnt out, down; наш до́м ~е́л our house was burnt down. 2. (*of fuel*) to be consumed, be used up; за го́д у нас ~е́ло три це́нтнера угля́ in the year we burned three hundredweight of coal. 3. (*fig., coll.*) to burn oneself out.

сгоряча́, *adv.* in the heat of the moment; in a fit of temper.

сгреба́|ть, ю, *impf. of* сгрести́.

сгре|сти́, бу́, бёшь, *past* ~б, ~бла́, *pf.* (*of* ~ба́ть) 1. to rake up, rake together. 2. (с+*g.*) to shovel (off, from); с. снег с кры́ши to shovel snow off the roof.

сгруд|и́ться, и́тся, *pf.* (*coll.*) to crowd, mill, bunch.

сгружа́|ть, ю, *impf. of* сгрузи́ть.

сгру|зи́ть, жу́, ~зи́шь, *pf.* (*of* ~жа́ть) to unload.

сгруппир|ова́ть(ся), у́ю(сь), *pf. of* группирова́ть(ся).

сгрыза́|ть, ю, *impf. of* сгрызть.

сгрыз|ть, у́, ёшь, *past* ~, ~ла, *pf.* (*of* ~а́ть) to chew (up).

сгуб|и́ть, лю́, ~ишь, *pf.* (*coll.*) to ruin.

сгу|сти́ть, щу́, сти́шь, *pf.* (*of* ~ща́ть) to thicken; to condense; с. кра́ски (*fig.*) to lay it on thick.

сгу|сти́ться, сти́тся, *pf.* (*of* ~ща́ться) to thicken; to condense; to clot.

сгу́ст|ок, ка, *m.* clot; с. кро́ви clot of blood.

сгуща́|ть(ся), ю, ет(ся), *impf. of* сгусти́ть(ся).

сгуще́ни|е, я, *n.* thickening, condensation; clotting.

сгу|щённый, *p.p.p. of* ~сти́ть *and adj.*; ~щённое молоко́ condensed milk, evaporated milk.

сда́брива|ть, ю, *impf. of* сдо́брить.

сда|ва́ть, ю́, ёшь, *impf. of* сдать; с. экза́мен to take, sit an examination.

сда|ва́ться¹, ю́сь, ёшься, *impf. of* ~ться¹.

сда|ва́ться², ётся, *impf.* (*impers., coll.*) it seems; мне ~ётся it seems to me, I think.

сдав|и́ть, лю́, ~ишь, *pf.* (*of* ~ливать) to squeeze.

сда́влива|ть, ю, *impf. of* сдави́ть.

сда́точн|ый, *adj.* delivery; ~ая квита́нция receipt; с. пункт delivery point.

сда́тчик, а, *m.* deliverer.

сдать¹, сдам, сдашь, сдаст, сдади́м, сдади́те, сдаду́т, *past* сдал, сдала́, сда́ло, *pf.* (*of* сдава́ть) 1. to hand over, pass; с. дела́ прее́мнику to hand over to one's successor; с. бага́ж на хране́ние to deposit, leave one's luggage; с. в архи́в (*fig., coll.*) to give up as a bad job, write off. 2. to let, let out, hire out; с. в аре́нду to lease. 3. to give change; с. пятьдеся́т копе́ек to give fifty kopecks change. 4. to surrender, yield, give up; с. пе́рвенство (*sport*) to yield first place. 5. to pass (*an examination, examination subject, etc.*); он сдал то́лько латы́нь he only passed in Latin. 6. to deal (*cards*).

сдать², сдам, сдашь, сдаст, сдади́м, сдади́те, сдаду́т, *pf.* (*of* сдава́ть) 1. to give out, give way; мото́р сдал the engine gave out. 2. to be weakened, be in a reduced state.

сда́|ться¹, мся, шься, стся, ди́мся, ди́тесь, ду́тся, *past* ~лся, ~ла́сь, *pf.* (*of* ~ва́ться¹) to surrender, yield; (*chess*) to resign; с. на про́сьбы to yield to entreaties.

сда́|ться², *not used in fut.*, ~лся, ~ла́сь, *pf.* (*coll.*) to be necessary; на что нам ~ли́сь их сове́ты? what need had we of advice from them?

сда́ч|а, и, *f.* 1. handing over. 2. letting out, hiring out; с. в аре́нду leasing. 3. surrender. 4. change; три рубля́ ~и three roubles change; с. с рубля́ change from one rouble; дать ~и (+*d.*; *fig., coll.*) to give as good as one got. 5. (*cards*) deal; ва́ша с. it is your deal.

сдва́ива|ть, ю, *impf. of* сдвои́ть(ся).

сдвиг, а, *m.* 1. displacement; (*geol.*) fault, dislocation; (*tech.*) shear; с. фа́з (*electr.*) phase shift. 2. (*fig.*) change (for the better), improvement.

сдвига́|ть(ся), ю(сь), *impf. of* сдви́нуть(ся).

сдвижн|о́й, *adj.* movable; ~а́я ма́чта (*naut.*) telescopic mast.

сдви́нут|ый, *p.p.p. of* ~ь *and adj.*; с. по фа́зе (*electr.*) out of phase.

сдви́|нуть, ну, нешь, *pf.* (*of* ~га́ть) 1. to shift, move, displace; его́ с ме́ста не ~нешь he won't budge; с. с ме́ста (*fig.*) to get moving, set in motion. 2. to move together, bring together; с. бро́ви to knit one's brows.

сдви́|нуться, нусь, нешься, *pf.* (*of* ~га́ться) 1. to move, budge; с. с ме́ста (*fig.*) to progress; де́ло не ~нулось с ме́ста no headway has been made. 2. to come together.

сдво|и́ть, ю́, и́шь, *pf.* (*of* сдва́ивать) to double.

сде́ла|ть(ся), ю(сь), *pf. of* де́лать(ся).

сде́лк|а, и, *f.* transaction, deal, bargain; войти́ в ~у (c+*i.*) to strike a bargain (with); заключи́ть ~у to conclude a bargain, do a deal.

сде́льно, *adv.* by the job.

сде́льн|ый, *adj.* piecework; ~ая опла́та payment by the piece, by the job; ~ая рабо́та piecework.

сде́льщик, а, *m.* piece-worker.

сде́льщин|а, ы, *f.* piece-work.

сдёргива|ть, ю, *impf. of* сдёрнуть.

сде́ржанно, *adv.* with restraint, with reserve.

сде́ржанност|ь, и, *f.* restraint, reserve.

сде́ржан|ный, *p.p.p. of* сдержа́ть *and* (~, ~на) *adj.* restrained, reserved.

сдерж|а́ть[1], у́, ~ишь, *pf.* (*of* ~ивать) 1. to hold (back); to hold in check, contain; с. проти́вника to hold the enemy in check. 2. (*fig.*) to keep back, restrain; с. слёзы to suppress tears.

сдерж|а́ть[2], у́, ~ишь, *pf.* (*of* ~ивать) to keep (*a promise, etc.*); с. сло́во to keep one's word.

сдерж|а́ться, у́сь, ~ишься, *pf.* (*of* ~иваться) to control oneself; to restrain oneself; contain oneself; to check oneself.

сде́ржива|ть(ся), ю(сь), *impf. of* сдержа́ть(ся).

сдёр|нуть, ну, нешь, *pf.* (*of* ~гивать) to pull off.

сдира́|ть, ю, *impf. of* содра́ть.

сдо́б|а, ы, *f.* 1. (*cul.*) shortening. 2. (fancy) cake, bun (*also collect*).

сдо́бн|ый, *adj.* (*cul.*) rich, short; ~ая бу́лка bun; ~ое те́сто fancy pastry.

сдо́бр|ить, ю, ишь, *pf.* (*of* сда́бривать) (+*i.*) to flavour (with), spice (with); to add to taste.

сдоброва́ть, *only in phrase* ему́, *etc.*, не с. (*coll.*) it will be a bad look out for him, *etc.*

сдо́хн|уть, у, ешь, *pf.* (*of* сдыха́ть) (*of cattle, also coll. of people*) to die.

сдре́йф|ить, лю, ишь, *pf. of* дре́йфить.

сдруж|и́ть, у́, и́шь, *pf.* to bring together, unite in friendship.

сдруж|и́ться, у́сь, и́шься, *pf.* (с+*i.*) to become friends (with).

сдува́|ть, ю, *impf. of* сдуть.

сду́ру, *adv.* (*coll.*) stupidly, not thinking what one was doing; он с. забы́л ключ до́ма he stupidly left his key at home.

сду|ть, ~ю, ~ешь, *pf.* (*of* ~ва́ть) 1. to blow away, blow off. 2. (с+*g.*, у; *school sl.*) to crib (from).

сдыха́|ть, ю, *impf. of* сдо́хнуть.

се, *particle* (*arch.*) lo, behold.

сё, сего́, *pron.* this (*arch. except in certain set phrases*; *see* тот).

сеа́нс, а, *m.* 1. (*in cinema, etc.*) performance, showing, house; после́дний с. the last showing, the last house. 2. sitting; написа́ть чей-н. портре́т в двена́дцать ~ов to paint someone's portrait in twelve sittings.

себе́[1], *see* себя́.

себе́[2], *particle* (*coll.*) *modifying verb or pron. and usu. containing hint of reproach*; он с. идёт вперёд he just goes ahead; а они́ с. молча́ли and they just kept their mouths shut; он о́чень с. на уме́ he is very crafty, wily; ничего́ с. not bad; так с. so-so.

себесто́имост|ь, и, *f.* (*econ.*) cost (*of manufacture*); cost price; прода́ть по ~и to sell at cost price.

себя́, себе́, собо́й (собо́ю), о себе́, *reflexive pron.* oneself; myself, yourself, himself, *etc.*; собо́ю in appearance; хоро́ш собо́ю nicelooking; прийти́ в с. (от) to get over; to come to one's senses; не в себе́ not oneself; от с. (*i*) away from oneself, outwards, (*ii*) for oneself, on one's own behalf; рабо́та не по себе́ work that is beyond one; ка́к-то не по себе́ not quite oneself; чита́ть про с. to read to oneself; у с. at home, at one's (own) place.

себялю́б|ец, ца, *m.* egoist.

себялюби́в|ый (~, ~а), *adj.* egoistical, selfish.

себялюби́|е, я, *n.* self-love, egoism.

сев, а, *m.* sowing.

се́вер, а, *m.* north.

се́вернее, *adv.* (+*g.*) to the north (of).

се́верн|ый, *adj.* north, northern; northerly; с. оле́нь reindeer; ~ое сия́ние northern lights, Aurora Borealis.

се́веро-восто́к, а, *m.* north-east.

се́веро-восто́чный, *adj.* north-east, north-eastern.

се́веро-за́пад, а, *m.* north-west.

се́веро-за́падный, *adj.* north-west, north-western.

северя́н|ин, ина, *pl.* ~е, ~, *m.* northerner.

севооборо́т, а, *m.* rotation of crops.

севр, а, *m.* Sèvres (*porcelain*).

се́вр|ский, *adj. of* ~.

севрю́г|а, и, *f.* stellate sturgeon (*Acipenser stellatus*).

сегме́нт, а, *m.* segment.

сегмента́ци|я, и, *f.* segmentation.

сего́дня, *adv.* today; с. ве́чером this evening, tonight; не с.-за́втра any day now.

сего́дня|шний, *adj. of* ~; с. день today; ~шняя газе́та today's paper.

седа́лищ|е, а, *n.* (*anat.*) seat, buttocks.

седа́лищн|ый, *adj.* (*anat.*) sciatic; воспале́ние ~ого не́рва (*med.*) sciatica.

седе́льник, а, *m.* saddler.

седе́льн|ый, *adj. of* седло́; ~ая лука́ saddle-bow.

седе́|ть, ю, *impf.* (*of* по~) to go grey, turn grey.

седе́|ющий, *pres. part. act. of* ~ть *and adj.* grizzled, greying.

седин|а́, ы́, *pl.* ~ы, ~, *f.* **1.** grey hair(s). **2.** grey streak (*in fur*).

седла́|ть, ю, *impf.* (*of* о~) to saddle.

сед|ло́, ла́, *pl.* ~ла, ~ел, *n.* saddle.

седловин|а, ы, *f.* **1.** arch, saddle (*of back of animal*). **2.** (*geogr.*) col, saddle.

седоборо́д|ый (~), *adj.* grey-bearded.

седовла́с|ый (~, ~а), *adj.* grey-haired.

седоволо́с|ый (~, ~а), *adj.* = седовла́сый.

сед|о́й (~, ~а́, ~о), *adj.* (*of hair*) grey, gray; hoary; grey-haired; flecked with white; ~а́я старина́ hoary antiquity.

седо́к, а́, *m.* **1.** fare (*passenger*). **2.** rider, horseman.

седьм|о́й, *adj.* seventh; быть на ~о́м не́бе to be in the seventh heaven; одна́ ~а́я one seventh.

сеза́м, а, *m.* (*bot.*) sesame; с., откро́йся! open sesame!

сезо́н, а, *m.* season.

сезо́нник, а, *m.* seasonal worker.

сезо́нн|ый, *adj.* seasonal; с. биле́т season ticket; ~ые рабо́ты seasonal work.

сей, f. сия́, n. сие́, *pl.* **сий,** *pron.* this; сию́ мину́ту this (very) minute; at once, instantly; сего́ го́да of this year; сего́ ме́сяца (*abbr.* с. м.) of this month; ва́ше письмо́ от 16-го с. м. (*formula of official correspondence*) your letter of the 16th inst.; до сих пор up to now, till now, hitherto; (*obs.*) up to here, up to this point; на с. раз this time, for this once; о сю по́ру (*obs.*) at the present time; по сю по́ру (*obs.*) up to now, up to the present; под сим ка́мнем поко́ится here lies; при сём прилага́ется (there is) enclosed herewith, herewith please find.

сейм, а, *m.* *m.* (*hist., representative assembly*) diet; (*in Poland*) the Sejm.

се́йн|а, ы, *f.* seine.

се́йнер, а, *m.* seiner.

сейсми́ческий, *adj.* seismic.

сейсмо́граф, а, *m.* seismograph.

сейсмогра́фи|я, и, *f.* seismography.

сейсмологи́ческий, *adj.* seismological.

сейсмоло́ги|я, и, *f.* seismology.

сейсмо́метр, а, *m.* seismometer.

сейф, а, *m.* safe.

сейча́с, *adv.* **1.** now, at present, at the (present) moment; они́ с. в Аме́рике they are in America at present. **2.** just, just now (= *in the immediate past*); она́ с. вы́шла she has just gone out. **3.** presently, soon; с. же at once, immediately; с.! in a minute!, half a minute! **4.** (*coll.*) straight away, immediately; с. бы́ло ви́дно, что ему́ э́то не

нра́вилось it was immediately apparent that he did not like it.

се́канс, а, *m.* (*math.*) secant.

сека́тор, а, *m.* secateurs.

секве́стр, а, *m.* **1.** (*leg.*) sequestration; наложи́ть с. (на+а.) to sequestrate. **2.** (*med.*) sequestrum.

секвестр|ова́ть, у́ю, *impf. and pf.* (*leg.*) to sequestrate.

секи́р|а, ы, *f.* pole-axe; hatchet, axe.

секре́т[1], а, *m.* **1.** secret; по ~у secretly, confidentially, in confidence; под больши́м ~ом in strict confidence; с. полишине́ля open secret. **2.** hidden mechanism. **3.** (*mil.*) listening post.

секре́т[2], а, *m.* (*physiol.*) secretion.

секретариа́т, а, *m.* secretariat.

секрета́рский, *adj.* secretarial; secretary's.

секрета́рств|о, а, *n.* secretaryship; secretarial duties.

секрета́рств|овать, ую, *impf.* to be a secretary, act as secretary.

секрета́рш|а, и, *f.* (woman) secretary.

секрета́р|ь, я́, *m.* secretary; генера́льный с. secretary-general; ли́чный с. private secretary, personal secretary; непреме́нный с. permanent secretary.

секре́тнича|ть, ю, *impf.* (*coll.*) **1.** to be secretive; to keep things secret, keep things dark. **2.** to converse in confidential tones.

секре́тно, *adv.* secretly, in secret; сообщи́ть с. to tell in confidence; (*on documents, etc.*) 'secret', 'confidential'; соверше́нно с. 'top secret'.

секре́тност|ь, и, *f.* secrecy.

секре́т|ный (~ен, ~на), *adj.* secret; confidential; с. замо́к combination lock; с. прика́з secret order; с. сотру́дник secret agent, undercover agent.

секрето́рный, *adj.* (*physiol.*) secretory.

секре́ци|я, и, *f.* (*physiol.*) secretion.

секс, а, *m.* sex.

сексо́т, а, *m.* (*abbr. of* секре́тный сотру́дник) secret agent, undercover agent.

се́кст|а, ы, *f.* (*mus.*) sixth.

секста́нт, а, *m.* sextant.

сексте́т, а, *m.* (*mus.*) sextet.

сексуа́льност|ь, и, *f.* sexuality.

сексуа́л|ьный (~ен, ~ьна), *adj.* sexual.

се́кт|а, ы, *f.* sect.

секта́нт, а, *m.* sectarian; member of a sect.

секта́нтский, *adj.* sectarian.

секта́нтств|о, а, *n.* sectarianism.

се́ктор, а, *m.* **1.** (*math., mil.*) sector; с. обстре́ла (*mil.*) sector of fire, zone of fire. **2.** (*fig.*) section, part, zone, sphere; (*econ.*) sector; с. ка́дров personnel section; госуда́рственный с. хозя́йства State(-owned) sector of economy.

секуляриза́ци|я, и, *f.* secularization.

секуляриз|ова́ть, у́ю, *impf. and pf.* to secularize.

секу́нд|а, ы, *f.* (*of time*) second; сию́ ~у! just a moment!

секунда́нт, а, *m.* (*in a duel or in boxing*) second.

секу́нд|ный, *adj. of* ~а; ~ная стре́лка second hand.

секундоме́р, а, *m.* stop-watch.

секу́щ|ая, ей, *f.* (*math.*) secant.

секцио́нный, *adj.* sectional.

се́кци|я, и, *f.* 1. section. 2. unit (*of furniture*).

селадо́н, а, *m.* (*obs.*) ladies' man, womanizer.

сел|ево́й, *adj. of* ~ь.

селёдк|а, и, *f.* herring.

селёдочниц|а, ы, *f.* herring-dish.

селёд|очный, *adj. of* ~ка.

селезёнк|а, и, *f.* (*physiol.*) spleen; воспале́ние ~и (*med.*) splenitis.

селез|ень, ня, *m.* drake.

селекти́вность|ь, и, *f.* (*radio*) selectivity.

селекцио́нный, *adj.* (*agric.*) selection.

селекци|я, и, *f.* (*agric.*) selection, breeding.

селе́ни|е, я, *n.* settlement.

селени́стый, *adj.* (*chem.*) selenious; selenide (of).

селени́т[1], а, *m.* (*min.*) selenite.

селени́т[2], а, *m.* Moon-man (*in science fiction*).

селе́новый, *adj.* (*chem.*) selenium, selenic.

сели́тебный, *adj.* built-up; (allocated for) building, development.

сели́тр|а, ы, *f.* (*chem.*) saltpetre, nitre; ка́лийная с. potassium nitrate.

сели́тр|яный, *adj. of* ~а; ~яная кислота́ nitric acid.

сел|и́ть, ю́, и́шь, *impf.* (*of* по~) to settle.

сели́тьб|а, ы, *f.* 1. developed land. 2. settlement.

сел|и́ться, ю́сь, и́шься, *impf.* (*of* по~) to settle.

сел|о́, а́, *pl.* ~а, *n.* village; на ~е́ (*collect.*) in the country; ни к ~у́, ни к го́роду (*coll.*) for no reason at all; neither here nor there.

сел|ь, я, *m.* (seasonal) mountain torrent.

сель- *abbr. of* се́льский.

сельдере́|й, я, *m.* celery.

сельд|ь, и, *pl.* ~и, ~е́й, *f.* herring; как ~и в бо́чке (*coll.*) like sardines (*of a crowd*).

сельд|яно́й, *adj. of* ~ь.

селько́р, а, *m.* (*abbr. of* се́льский корреспонде́нт) rural correspondent.

сельпо́, *indecl.*, *n.* (*abbr. of* се́льское потреби́тельское о́бщество) village general stores.

се́льск|ий, *adj.* 1. country, rural; ~ая ме́стность rural area; countryside; ~ое хозя́йство agriculture, farming. 2. village.

сельскохозя́йственный, *adj.* agricultural, farming.

сельсове́т, а, *m.* (*abbr. of* се́льский сове́т) village soviet, rural area soviet.

се́льтерск|ий, *adj.* ~ая вода́ seltzer water.

селян|и́н, и́на, *pl.* ~е, ~, *m.* (*obs.*) peasant, villager.

селя́н|ка[1], ки, *f. of* ~и́н.

селя́нк|а[2], и, *f.* (*cul.*) hot-pot; сбо́рная с. (*fig.*) hotchpotch, hodge-podge.

сема́нтик|а, и, *f.* 1. semantics. 2. meanings (*of a particular word*).

семанти́ческий, *adj.* semantic.

семасиологи́ческий, *adj.* semasiological.

семасиоло́ги|я, и, *f.* semasiology.

семафо́р, а, *m.* (*railways and naut.*) semaphore, signal-post; с. откры́т the signal is down.

семафо́р|ить, ю, *impf.* to semaphore.

сёмг|а, и, *f.* salmon.

семе́йн|ый, *adj.* 1. family; domestic; с. ве́чер family party; с. круг family circle; по ~ым обстоя́тельствам for domestic reasons; о́тпуск по ~ым обстоя́тельствам (*mil.*) compassionate leave. 2. having a family; с. челове́к family man.

семе́йственност|ь, и, *f.* 1. attachment to family life. 2. (*pejor.*) nepotism; use of 'influence'.

семе́йственн|ый, *adj.* 1. attached to family life. 2. (*fig., pejor.*) conducted by 'arrangement', by 'influence'; ~ые отноше́ния 'old boy system'.

семе́йств|о, а, *n.* family.

семена́, *see* се́мя.

семен|и́ть, ю́, и́шь, *impf.* to mince (*of gait*).

семен|и́ться, и́тся, *impf.* (*agric.*) to seed.

семенни́к, а́, *m.* 1. (*biol.*) testicle. 2. (*bot.*) pericarp; ~и́ трав grass seeds.

семенн|о́й, *adj.* 1. seed; с. карто́фель seed potato. 2. (*biol.*) seminal, spermatic; ~а́я нить spermatozoon.

семеново́дств|о, а, *n.* seed-growing.

семеново́д|ческий, *adj. of* ~ство.

семери́чный, *adj.* septenary.

семёрк|а, и, *f.* 1. seven; number seven ('*bus, tram, etc.*). 2. с. треф, *etc.* (*cards*) the seven of clubs, *etc.* 3. group of seven persons.

семерно́й, *adj.* sevenfold, septuple.

се́мер|о, ы́х, *num.* (*collect.*) seven.

семе́стр, а, *m.* term, semester.

се́меч|ко, ка, *pl.* ~ки, ~ек, *n.* 1. *dim. of* се́мя. 2. (*pl.*) sunflower seeds.

сёмжин|а, ы, *f.* salmon (*flesh*).

семивёрстн|ый, *adj.* of seven versts; ~ые сапоги́ seven-league boots.

семидесятиле́ти|е, я, *n.* 1. seventy years. 2. seventieth anniversary; seventieth birthday.

семидесятиле́тний, *adj.* 1. seventy-year, of seventy years. 2. seventy-year-old.

семидеся́т|ый, *adj.* seventieth; ~ые го́ды the seventies; с. но́мер number seventy; страни́ца ~ая page seventy.

семи́к, а́, *m.* (*eccl.*) feast of seventh Thursday after Easter.

семикла́ссник, а, *m.* seventh form pupil.

семикра́тный, *adj.* sevenfold, septuple.

семиле́ти|е, я, *n.* 1. seven years; seven-year period. 2. seventh anniversary.

семиле́тк|а, и, *f.* 1. seven-year school. 2. (*econ.*) seven-year plan. 3. (*coll.*) child of seven.

семиле́тний, *adj.* 1. seven-year; septennial. 2. seven-year-old.

семиме́сячный, *adj.* 1. seven-month. 2. seven-month-old.

семими́льн|ый, *adj.* of seven miles, seven-mile; идти́ ~ыми шага́ми (*fig.*) to make gigantic strides.

семина́р, а, *m.* seminar.

семина́ри|й, я, *m.* seminar.

семинари́ст, а, *m.* seminarist.

семина́ри|я, и, *f.* seminary, training college; духо́вная с. theological college; учи́тельская с. (*obs.*) teachers' training college.

семина́р|ский, *adj.* of ~ and ~ия.

семинеде́льный, *adj.* 1. seven-week. 2. seven-week-old.

семисо́тый, *adj.* seven-hundredth.

семисто́пный, *adj.* с. ямб (*lit.*) iambic heptameter.

семи́т, а, *m.* Semite.

семити́ческий, *adj.* Semitic.

семи́т|ский = ~и́ческий.

семито́лог, а, *m.* Semitologist.

семитоло́ги|я, и, *f.* Semitology.

семиты́сячный, *adj.* seven-thousandth.

семиуго́льник, а, *m.* (*math.*) heptagon.

семиуго́льный, *adj.* heptagonal.

семичасово́й, *adj.* 1. seven-hour, of seven hours' duration. 2. seven o'clock.

семнадцатиле́тний, *adj.* 1. seventeen-year. 2. seventeen-year-old.

семна́дцатый, *adj.* seventeenth.

семна́дцат|ь, и, *f.*, *num.* seventeen.

сёмужий, *adj.* salmon.

сем|ь, и́, *i.* ~ью́, *num.* seven.

се́мьдесят, семи́десяти, семью́десятью, *num.* seventy.

семьсо́т, семисо́т, семиста́м, семьюста́ми, о семиста́х, *num.* seven hundred.

се́мью, *adv.* seven times.

сем|ья́, ьи́, *pl.* ~ьи, ~е́й, ~ьям, *f.* family.

семьяни́н, а, *pl.* ~ы, *m.* family man.

се́м|я, ени, *pl.* ~ена́, ~я́н, ~ена́м, *n.* 1. (*bot.* and *fig.*) seed; пойти́ в ~ена́ to go to seed, run to seed; ~ена́ раздо́ра seeds of discord. 2. semen, sperm.

семядо́л|я, и, *g. pl.* ~ей, *f.* (*bot.*) seed-lobe, cotyledon.

семяизлия́ни|е, я, *n.* (*physiol.*) ejaculation.

семяпо́чк|а, и, *f.* (*bot.*) seed-bud.

сена́т, а, *m.* senate.

сена́тор, а, *m.* senator.

сена́торский, *adj.* senatorial.

сена́т|ский, *adj.* of ~.

сенберна́р, а, *m.* St. Bernard (*dog*).

се́н|и, е́й, *no sing.* (entrance-)hall, vestibule.

сенни́к, а́, *m.* 1. hay-mattress. 2. (*dial.*) hay-loft.

сенн|о́й[1], *adj.* hay; ~а́я лихора́дка hay fever.

сен|но́й[2], *adj.* of ~и́; ~на́я де́вушка (*obs.*) maid.

се́н|о, а, *n.* hay.

сенова́л, а, *m.* hay-loft, mow.

сенозагото́в|ки, ок, *sing.* ~ка, ~ки, *f.* State hay purchases.

сеноко́с, а, *m.* 1. hay-mowing, haymaking. 2. haymaking (*time*). 3. hayfield.

сенокоси́лк|а, и, *f.* (hay-)mowing machine.

сеноко́сный, *adj.* haymaking.

сеноубо́рк|а, и, *f.* hay harvesting, haymaking.

сенсацио́н|ный (~ен, ~на), *adj.* sensational.

сенса́ци|я, и, *f.* sensation.

сенсибилиза́тор, а, *m.* (*phot.*) sensitizer.

сенсибилиза́ци|я, и, *f.* (*phot.*) sensitization.

сенсо́рный, *adj.* (*physiol.*) sensory.

сенсуали́зм, а, *m.* (*philos.*) sensationalism.

сенсуали́ст, а, *m.* (*philos.*) sensationalist.

сенсуа́льный, *adj.* (*philos.*) sensational.

сентенцио́зный, *adj.* sententious.

сенте́нци|я, и, *f.* maxim.

сентиментали́зм, а, *m.* sentimentalism (*also hist., lit.*).

сентиментали́ст, а, *m.* sentimentalist.

сентимента́льнича|ть, ю, *impf.* 1. to be sentimental, sentimentalize. 2. (с+*i.*) to be soft (with).

сентимента́льност|ь, и, *f.* sentimentality.

сентимента́л|ьный (~ен, ~ьна), *adj.* sentimental.

сентя́бр|ь, я́, *m.* September; смотре́ть ~ём (*coll.*) to look glum.

сентя́брь|ский, *adj.* of ~.

се́н|цы, цев, *no sing.*, *dim.* of ~и.

сен|ь, и, о ~и, в ~й, *f.* (*obs.* or *poet.*) canopy; под ~ью (+*g.*) under the protection (of).

сеньо́р, а, *m.* 1. (*hist.*) seigneur, seignior. 2. señor, senhor.

сепарати́вный, *adj.* (*polit.*) separatist.

сепарати́зм, а, *m.* (*polit.*) separatism.

сепарати́ст, а, *m.* (*polit.*) separatist.

сепара́тный, *adj.* (*polit.*) separate; с. ми́рный догово́р separate peace treaty.

сепара́тор, а, *m.* (*agric.*) separator.

се́пи|я, и, *f.* 1. sepia. 2. sepia drawing; sepia photograph.

сéпсис, а, *m.* (*med.*) sepsis, septicaemia.

септéт, а, *m.* (*mus.*) septet(te).

септи́ческий, *adj.* (*med.*) septic.

сéр|а, ы, *f.* **1.** (*chem.*) sulphur, brimstone; двуо́кись ~ы sulphur dioxide. **2.** ear-wax.

серáл|ь, я, *m.* seraglio.

серб, а, *m.* Serb, Serbian.

сербия́нк|а, и, *f.* (*obs.*) = сéрбка.

сéрб|ка, ки, *f. of* ~.

сербохорвáтский, *adj.* Serbo-Croatian; с. язы́к Serbo-Croat.

сéрбский, *adj.* Serbian.

сервáнт, а, *m.* sideboard; dumb-waiter.

серви́з, а, *m.* service, set; столо́вый с. dinner service.

сервир|овáть, у́ю, *impf. and pf.* **1.** с. стол to lay a table. **2.** to serve; с. зáвтрак to serve breakfast.

сервиро́вк|а, и, *f.* **1.** laying. **2.** (*collect.*) table appointments (*crockery and table linen*).

сéрвис, а, *m.* (consumer) service.

сервомото́р, а, *m.* (*tech.*) servo-motor.

сердéчник¹, а, *m.* (*tech.*) core; strand (*of cable*).

сердéчник², а, *m.* (*coll.*) **1.** heart specialist. **2.** sufferer from heart disease.

сердéчник³, а, *m.* (*bot.*) cuckoo-flower, ladies' smock (*Cardamine*).

сердéчност|ь, и, *f.* cordiality; warmth.

сердéч|ный (~ен, ~на), *adj.* **1.** of the heart (*also fig.*); (*anat.*) cardiac; ~ная болéзнь heart disease; с. припáдок heart attack; ~ное срéдство, ~ное лекáрство cardiac; ~ные делá love affairs. **2.** cordial, hearty; heartfelt, sincere; ~ная благодáрность heartfelt gratitude, hearty thanks; оказáть с. приём (+*d.*) to extend a cordial welcome (to); ~ное соглáсие (*hist.*) Entente cordiale. **3.** warm, warm-hearted.

серди́т|ый, *adj.* **1.** (на+*a.*) angry (with, at, about), cross (with, about); irate. **2.** (*fig.*, *coll.*; *of tobacco, mustard, etc.*) strong. **3.** дёшево и ~о (*coll.*) cheap but good; a good bargain.

сер|ди́ть, жу́, ~дишь, *impf.* (*of* рас~) to anger, make angry.

сер|ди́ться, жу́сь, ~дишься, *impf.* (*of* рас~) (на+*a.*) to be angry (with, at, about), be cross (with, about).

сердобóли|е, я, *n.* soft-heartedness.

сердобóльнича|ть, ю, *impf.* (*coll., iron.*) to be (too) soft-hearted.

сердобóл|ьный (~ен, ~ьна), *adj.* (*coll.*) soft-hearted.

сердоли́к, а, *m.* (*min.*) cornelian, sard.

сердоли́к|овый, *adj. of* ~.

сéрд|це, ца, *pl.* ~цá, ~éц, *n.* (*in var. senses*) heart; золото́е с. heart of gold; в ~цáх in (a fit of) temper; с глаз доло́й, из ~ца вон (*prov.*) out of sight, out of mind; приня́ть

(бли́зко) к ~цу to take to heart; от всего́ ~ца from the bottom of one's heart, whole-heartedly; у меня́ отлегло́ от ~ца I felt relieved; по ~цу (*coll.*) to one's liking; с ~цем testily, crossly; с замирáнием ~ца with a sinking heart; имéть с. (на+*a.*; *coll.*) to be cross (with); с. боли́т (+*inf.*) it pains one, one's heart bleeds; у него́ не лежи́т с. (к) he has no inclination (to, for).

сердцебиéни|е, я, *n.* palpitation; (*med.*) tachycardia.

сердцевéд, а, *m.* student of human nature, reader of the human heart.

сердцеви́д|ный (~ен, ~на), *adj.* heart-shaped; (*bot.*) cordate.

сердцеви́н|а, ы, *f.* core, pith, heart (*also fig.*).

сердцеéд, а, *m.* (*coll.*) lady-killer.

серéбреник, а, *m.* = срéбреник.

серебрёный, *adj.* silver-plated.

серебри́ст|ый (~, ~а), *adj.* silvery; с. то́поль silver poplar.

серебр|и́ть, ю́, и́шь, *impf.* (*of* по~) to silver, silver-plate.

серебр|и́ться, и́тся, *impf.* **1.** to silver, become silvery. **2.** *pass. of* ~и́ть.

серебр|о́, á, *n.* **1.** silver. **2.** (*collect.*) silver; столо́вое с. silver, plate; сдáча ~о́м change in silver.

сереброно́с|ный (~ен, ~на), *adj.* argentiferous.

серéбряник, а, *m.* silversmith.

серéбрян|ый, *adj.* silver; с. блеск (*min.*) silver glance; ~ая свáдьба silver wedding.

среди́н|а, ы, *f.* middle, midst; золотáя с. the golden mean; держáться ~ы, знать ~у (*fig.*) to observe the mean.

среди́нный, *adj.* middle, mean, intermediate.

серёдк|а, и, *f.* (*coll.*) middle, centre; с. на полови́нку neither one thing nor another.

середня́к, á, *m.* **1.** peasant of average means (*classified as intermediate between* кулáк *and* бедня́к). **2.** (*fig., coll.*) middling person, undistinguished person.

серёжк|а, и, *f.* **1.** ear-ring. **2.** (*bot.*) catkin, amentum.

серенáд|а, ы, *f.* serenade.

сéренький, *adj.* grey (*also fig.*); (*fig.*) dull, drab.

серé|ть, ю, *impf.* **1.** (*pf.* по~) to turn grey, go grey. **2.** (*impf. only*) to show grey.

сержáнт, а, *m.* sergeant.

сери́йный, *adj.* (*tech., econ.*) serial.

сéристый, *adj.* (*chem.*) sulphureous.

сéри|я, и, *f.* series; (*of film*) part; кинофи́льм в нéскольких ~ях film in several parts; с. бомб (*mil.*) bomb train.

сермя́г|а, и, *f.* sermyaga (*coarse, undyed cloth or caftan of this material*).

сéрн|а, ы, *f.* (*zool.*) chamois.

серни́ст|ый, *adj.* (*chem.*) sulphureous; sulphide (of); с. аммо́ний ammonium sulphide; ~ое желе́зо ferrous sulphide.

серноки́сл|ый, *adj.* (*chem.*) sulphate (of); ~ая соль sulphate.

се́рн|ый, *adj.* sulphuric; ~ая кислота́ sulphuric acid; с. цвет flowers of sulphur.

серова́т|ый, *adj.* greyish.

сероводоро́д, а, *m.* (*chem.*) hydrogen sulphide, sulphuretted hydrogen.

серогла́з|ый (~, ~а), *adj.* grey-eyed.

серозём, а, *m.* (*agric.*) grey earth.

серо́зный, *adj.* (*physiol.*) serous.

сероуглеро́д, а, *m.* (*chem.*) carbon bisulphide.

серп, а́, *m.* sickle, reaping-hook; с. луны́ crescent moon.

серпанти́н, а, *m.* 1. paper streamer. 2. hairpin-bend road (*in mountainous terrain*).

серпенти́н, а, *m.* (*min.*) serpentine.

серпови́дный, *adj.* crescent(-shaped).

серсо́, *indecl.*, *n.* hoopla.

сертифика́т, а, *m.* certificate.

се́рум, а, *m.* (*med.*) serum.

серча́|ть, ю, *impf.* (*of* о~) (*coll.*) to be angry, be cross.

се́р|ый (~, ~а́, ~о), *adj.* 1. grey; с. в я́блоках dappled. 2. (*fig.*) grey, dull; drab; с. день grey day. 3. (*fig.*) dull, dim (= *uneducated*).

серьг|а́, и́, *pl.* ~и, серёг, ~а́м, *f.* 1. ear-ring. 2. (*tech.*) link. 3. (*naut.*) slip rope.

серьёзно, *adv.* seriously; earnestly; in earnest; с.? seriously?, really?

серьёзност|ь, и, *f.* seriousness; earnestness; gravity.

серьёз|ный (~ен, ~на, ~но), *adj.* serious; earnest; grave.

сессио́нный, *adj.* sessional.

се́сси|я, и, *f.* session, sitting; (*leg.*) term.

сестр|а́, ы́, *pl.* ~ы, сестёр, ~а́м, *f.* 1. sister; двою́родная с. (first) cousin. 2. медици́нская с., с. милосе́рдия (*obs.*) nurse; ста́ршая с. (*nursing*) sister; с.-хозя́йка (*hospital*) matron.

сестрёнк|а, и, *f.* little sister.

се́стрин, *adj.* sister's.

се́стринский, *adj.* nurse's; nursing.

сестри́ц|а, ы, *f.* affect. dim. of сестра́.

сесть¹, ся́ду, ся́дешь, *past* сел, се́ла, *pf.* (*of* сади́ться) 1. to sit down; с. за стол to sit down to table; с. обе́дать to sit down to dinner; с. в ва́нну to get into the bath; с. рабо́тать to get down to work; с. в кало́шу, с. в лу́жу (*coll.*) to get into a mess, into a fix. 2. (в, на+а.) to board, take; с. на по́езд to board a train; с. на ло́шадь to mount a horse. 3. to alight, settle, perch; (*of an aircraft*) to land. 4. (*of the heavenly bodies*) to set. 5. с. в тюрьму́ to go to prison, jail.

сесть², ся́дет, *past* сел, *pf.* (*of* сади́ться) to shrink.

сет, а, *m.* (*sport*) set.

сетево́й, *adj.* net, netting, mesh.

се́тк|а, и, *f.* 1. net, netting; (luggage) rack; с. для головы́ hair-net; игра́ть у ~и (*tennis*) to play at net. 2. (*coll.*) string-bag. 3. (*geogr.*) grid; (*collect.*) co-ordinates. 4. (*radio*) grid. 5. scale (*of charges, etc.*).

се́т|овать, ую, *impf.* (*of* по~) 1. (на+а.) to complain (of), cry out (upon). 2. (о+*p.*) to lament, mourn.

се́точный, *adj.* 1. net. 2. (*radio*) grid.

се́ттер, а, *m.* setter (*dog*).

сетча́тк|а, и, *f.* (*anat.*) retina.

сетчатокры́л|ые, ых, *sing.* ~ое, ~ого, *n.* (*zool.*) Neuroptera.

се́тчат|ый, *adj.* netted, network; reticular; ~ая оболо́чка гла́за (*anat.*) retina.

сет|ь, и, о ~и, в ~и *and* в ~й, *pl.* ~и, ~е́й, *f.* 1. net (*also fig.*); расста́вить ~и кому́-н. to set a trap for someone. 2. network; circuit, system.

се́ч|а, и, *f.* (*obs.*) battle.

сече́ни|е, я, *n.* 1. cutting; ке́сарево с. Caesarean birth, operation. 2. section; живо́е с. cross section.

се́чк|а, и, *f.* 1. chopper, vegetable-cutting knife. 2. chopped straw, chaff.

сечь¹, секу́, сечёшь, секу́т, *past* сек, секла́, *impf.* 1. (*impf. only*) to cut to pieces. 2. (*pf.* вы́~, *past* сек, се́кла) to beat, flog.

Сеч|ь², и, *f.* (*hist.*) (Cossack) host.

се́|чься, чётся, ку́тся, *past* ~кся, ~кла́сь, *impf.* (*of* по~) (*of hairs*) to split; (*of fabric*) to cut.

се́ялк|а, и, *f.* (*agric.*) sowing-machine, seed drill.

се́яльщик, а, *m.* sower.

се́ян|ец, ца, *m.* seedling.

се́ятел|ь, я, *m.* sower (*also fig., rhet.*); disseminator.

се́|ять, ю, ешь, *impf.* (*of* по~) 1. to sow (*also fig.*); с. раздо́р to sow the seeds of dissension. 2. (*fig., coll.*) to throw about; с. де́ньги to throw one's money about.

сжа́л|иться, юсь, ишься, *pf.* (над) to take pity (on).

сжа́ти|е, я, *n.* 1. pressing, pressure; grasp, grip. 2. compression, condensation; ка́мера ~я compression chamber.

сжа́тост|ь, и, *f.* 1. compression. 2. conciseness.

сжа́т|ый, *p.p.p. of* ~ь¹ *and* ~ь² *and adj.* 1. compressed (*air, gas*). 2. (*fig.*) condensed, compact; concise; ~ое изложе́ние exposition in condensed form.

сжать¹, сожму́, сожмёшь, *pf.* (*of* сжима́ть) to squeeze; to compress (*also fig.*); to grip; с. гу́бы to compress one's lips; с. зу́бы to grit one's teeth; с. кулаки́ to clench one's fists; с. в объя́тиях to hug; с. изложе́ние to compress an exposition.

сжать², сожну́, сожнёшь, *pf. of* жать².

сжа́|ться, сожму́сь, сожмёшься, *pf.* (*of* сжима́ться) **1.** to tighten, clench. **2.** to shrink, contract; её душа́ ∼ла́сь her heart sank.

сж|ева́ть, ую́, уёшь, *pf.* to chew up.

сжечь, сожгу́, сожжёшь, сожгу́т, *past* сжёг, сожгла́, *pf.* (*of* жечь *and* сжига́ть) to burn (up, down); to cremate; с. свои́ корабли́ (*fig.*) to burn one's boats.

сжива́|ть(ся), ю(сь), *impf. of* сжи́ть(ся).

сжига́|ть, ю, *impf. of* сжечь.

сжи|ди́ть, жу́, ди́шь, *pf.* (*of* ∼жа́ть) (*chem.*) to liquefy.

сжижа́|ть, ю, *impf. of* сжиди́ть.

сжиже́ни|е, я, *n.* (*chem.*) liquation, liquefaction.

сжи́женный, *adj.* (*chem.*) liquefied.

сжим, а, *m.* clip, grip, clamp.

сжима́емост|ь, и, *f.* compressibility, condensability.

сжима́|ть(ся), ю(сь), *impf. of* сжа́ть¹(ся).

сжи|ть, ву́, вёшь, *past* ∼л, ∼ла́, ∼ло, *pf.* (*of* ∼ва́ть) (*coll.*) to force out, edge out; с. со све́ту to be the death (of).

сжи́|ться, ву́сь, вёшься, *past* ∼лся, ∼ла́сь, *pf.* (*of* ∼ва́ться) (с+*i.*) to get used (to), get accustomed (to); с. с ро́лью (*theatr.*) to identify oneself with a part.

сжу́льнича|ть, ю, *pf. of* жу́льничать.

сза́ди, *adv. and prep.* +*g.* **1.** *adv.* from behind; behind; from the rear; from the rear; вид с. rear view; тре́тий ваго́н с. the third coach from the rear. **2.** *prep.*+*g.* behind.

сзыва́|ть, ю, *impf. of* созва́ть.

сиа́мский, *adj.* Siamese.

сибари́т, а, *m.* sybarite.

сибари́тский, *adj.* sybaritic.

сибари́тств|о, а, *n.* sybaritism.

сибари́тств|овать, ую, *impf.* to lead the life of a sybarite.

сибиля́нт, а, *m.* (*ling.*) sibilant.

сибиреи́звенный, *adj.* (*med.*) anthrax.

сиби́рк|а, и, *f.* **1.** (*obs.*) sibirka (*waist-length caftan*). **2.** (*coll., obs.*) clink (= *prison*). **3.** (*hist.*) sibirka (*paper money issued in Siberia during the Civil War, 1918–20*). **4.** (*coll.*) = сиби́рская я́зва.

сиби́рный, *adj.* (*coll., obs.*) hard, severe.

сиби́рск|ий, *adj.* Siberian; ∼ая ко́шка Persian cat; ∼ая я́зва (*med.*) anthrax.

сибиря́к, а́, *m.* Siberian.

сибиря́чк|а, и, *f.* Siberian (woman).

сиве́|ть, ю, *impf.* (*of* по∼) to turn grey.

си́вк|а, и, *f.* dark grey (horse).

сивк|о́, а́, *m.* = ∼а.

сивола́пый, *adj.* (*coll.*) rough, clumsy.

сиву́х|а, и, *f.* raw vodka.

сиву́шн|ый, *adj.*; ∼ое ма́сло fusel oil.

си́в|ый (∼, ∼а́, ∼о), *adj.* **1.** (*of horses*) grey; бред ∼ой кобы́лы (*coll.*) raving nonsense. **2.** (*of hair*) grey, greying.

сиг, а́, *m.* white fish (*freshwater fish of salmon family*).

сиган|у́ть, у́, ёшь, *pf.* (*coll.*) to leap.

сига́р|а, ы, *f.* cigar.

сигаре́т|а, ы, *f.* **1.** cigarette (*without mouthpiece*). **2.** small cigar.

сигаре́т|ный, *adj. of* ∼а.

сигарк|а, и, *f.* (*coll.*) (home-made) cigarette (*of shag rolled in newspaper*).

сига́р|ный, *adj. of* ∼а.

сига́рочниц|а, ы, *f.* cigar box.

сигна́л, а, *m.* signal; вызывно́й с. call signal; пожа́рный с. fire-alarm; с. бе́дствия distress signal; с. возду́шной трево́ги air-raid alarm; с. на трубе́ trumpet-call; с. на рожке́, с. на го́рне bugle-call.

сигнализа́тор, а, *m.* (*tech.*) signalling apparatus.

сигнализа́ци|я, и, *f.* signalling.

сигнализи́р|овать, ую, *impf. and pf.* **1.** (*pf. also* про∼) to signal. **2.** (+*a. or* о+*p.*; *fig.*) to give warning (of).

сигна́л|ьный, *adj. of* ∼; ∼ьная бу́дка signal--box; ∼ьная ла́мпа signal lamp; с. пистоле́т Very pistol, signal pistol, flare gun; ∼ьное полотни́ще signal panel, marking panel; ∼ьная тормозна́я верёвка communication cord.

сигна́льщик, а, *m.* signaller, signal-man.

сигнату́р|а, ы, *f.* **1.** (*pharm.*) label. **2.** (*typ.*) signature.

сиде́л|ец, ьца, *m.* **1.** (*obs.*) salesman; shop--walker.

сиде́лк|а, и, *f.* (sick-)nurse.

сиде́ни|е, я, *n.* sitting.

сид|ень, ня, *m.* (*coll.*) stay-at-home; сиде́ть ∼нем to be a stay-at-home.

сиде́нь|е, я, *n.* seat.

сидери́т, а, *m.* (*min.*) siderite.

си|де́ть, жу́, ди́шь, *impf.* **1.** to sit; с., поджа́в но́ги to sit cross-legged; с. верхо́м to be on horseback; с. на ко́рточках to squat; с. на насе́сте to roost, perch; с. на я́йцах to sit (on eggs), brood; с. у мо́ря, ждать пого́ды (*coll.*) to wait for something to turn up; вот где ∼ди́т кто-н., что-н. (*coll.*) that's where all the trouble lies, that's the source of all the trouble. **2.** to be; с. (в тюрьме́) to be in prison, serve a term of imprisonment; с. под аре́стом to be under arrest; с. без де́ла to have nothing to do; с. за кни́гой to be (engaged in) reading. **3.** (*of a vessel*) to draw (*water*); с. глубоко́ to be deep in the water, draw much water. **4.** (на+*p.*; *of clothing*) to fit, sit (on).

сид|е́ться, и́тся, *impf.* (*impers.*+*d.*) ему́, *etc.*, не ~и́тся до́ма he, *etc.*, can't bear staying at home; ей не ~и́тся на ме́сте she can't keep still.

сидр, а, *m.* cider.

сидя́ч|ий, *adj.* 1. sitting; в ~ей по́зе in a sitting posture. 2. (*fig.*) sedentary; с. о́браз жи́зни sedentary life. 3. (*zool.*) sessile.

сие́, *see* сей.

сие́н|а, ы, *f.* sienna; жжёная с. burnt sienna.

сиени́т, а, *m.* (*min.*) syenite.

сизиги́йный, *adj.* с. прили́в spring tide.

сизиги́|я, и, *f.* (*astron.*) syzygy.

сизи́фов, *adj.*; ~ труд labour of Sisyphus.

сизоворо́нк|а, и, *f.* (*orn.*) roller.

си́з|ый (~, ~á, ~о), *adj.* blue-grey, dove--coloured.

сиккати́в, а, *m.* (*tech.*) siccative.

сикомо́р, а, *m.* (*bot.*) sycamore.

си́л|а, ы, *f.* 1. strength, force; в ~у (+*g.*) on the strength (of), by virtue (of), because (of); быть в ~ах (+*inf.*) to have the strength (to), have the power (to); изо всех ~, что есть ~ы with all one's might; крича́ть изо всех ~ to shout at the top of one's voice; от ~ы (*coll.*) at most; сверх ~, свы́ше ~, не по ~ам beyond one's power(s); outside one's competence; че́рез ~у beyond one's powers; рабо́тать че́рез ~у to overwork; ~ой by force; с по́мощью гру́бой ~ы by brute force; свои́ми ~ами unaided; ~ою веще́й through force of circumstances; ~ою (+*g. or* в+*a.*) to the strength (of); с. во́ли will-power; с. ду́ха strength of mind; с. привы́чки force of habit; в ~у привы́чки by force of habit. 2. (*phys., tech.*) force, power; жива́я с. kinetic energy; лошади́ная с. horse-power; подъёмная с. (*aeron.*) lift; с. све́та в свеча́х candle-power; с. тя́ги tractive force; с. тя́жести, с. притяже́ния force of gravity. 3. (*leg. and fig.*) force; име́ющий ~у valid; в ~е in force, valid; войти́, вступи́ть в ~у to come into force; take effect; оста́ться в ~е to remain valid; (*fig.*) to hold good. 4. (*pl., mil.*) forces; вооружённые ~ы armed forces; вое́нно-возду́шные ~ы air force(s); сухопу́тные ~ы land forces, ground forces. 5. (*coll.*) point, essence; с. в том, что the crux of the matter is that. 6. (*coll.*) quantity, multitude.

сила́ч, á, *m.* strong man.

силика́т, а, *m.* (*min.*) silicate.

си́л|иться, юсь, ишься, *impf.* to try, make efforts.

силици|й, я, *m.* (*chem.*) silicium.

силко́м, *adv.* (*coll.*) by (main) force.

силлаби́ческий, *adj.* (*lit.*) syllabic.

силлоги́зм, а, *m.* (*philos.*) syllogism.

силови́к, á, *m.* power-plant worker.

силов|о́й, *adj.* power; ~а́я ли́ния (*phys.*) line of force; ~о́е по́ле (*phys.*) field of force; с. про́вод (*electr.*) power-line; ~а́я ста́нция power-station, power-house; ~а́я устано́вка power-plant.

си́лой, *adv.* (*coll.*) by (main) force.

сил|о́к, ка́, *m.* noose, snare.

силоме́р, а, *m.* dynamometer.

си́лос, а, *m.* (*agric.*) 1. silo. 2. silage.

силосова́ни|е, я, *n.* siloing.

силос|ова́ть, у́ю, *impf. and pf.* to silo, ensile.

силосоре́зк|а, и, *f.* silage cutter.

силури́йский, *adj.* (*geol.*) Silurian.

силуэ́т, а, *m.* silhouette.

си́льно, *adv.* 1. strongly; violently; с. ска́зано that's going too far, that's putting it too strongly. 2. very much, greatly; badly; с. нужда́ться в чём-н. to want something badly.

сильноде́йствующий, *adj.* virulent; drastic.

си́л|ьный (~ен *and* **~ён, ~ьна́, ~ьно, ~ьны́)**, *adj.* (*in var. senses*) strong; powerful; ~ьная во́ля strong will; с. до́вод powerful argument; ~ьное жела́ние intense desire; с. за́пах strong smell; с. моро́з hard frost; ~ьная речь impressive speech; он не ~ён в языка́х he is not good at languages, languages are not his strong suit.

сильф, а, *m.* (*myth.*) sylph.

сильфи́д|а, ы, *f.* (*myth. and fig.*) sylph.

симбио́з, а, *m.* (*biol.*) symbiosis.

си́мвол, а, *m.* symbol; emblem; с. ве́ры (*rel.*) creed.

символиза́ци|я, и, *f.* symbolization.

символизи́р|овать, ую, *impf.* to symbolize.

символи́зм, а, *m.* symbolism.

симво́лик|а, и, *f.* symbolism.

символи́ст, а, *m.* symbolist.

символи́ст|ский, *adj.* of ~.

символи́ческий, *adj.* symbolic(al).

символи́чность|ь, и, *f.* symbolical character.

символи́ч|ный (~ен, ~на), *adj.* = ~еский.

симметри́ческий, *adj.* symmetrical.

симметри́чность|ь, и, *f.* symmetry.

симметри́ч|ный (~ен, ~на), *adj.* = ~еский.

симметри́|я, и, *f.* symmetry.

симони́|я, и, *f.* (*hist.*) simony.

симпатизи́р|овать, ую, *impf.* 1. (+*d.*) be in sympathy (with), sympathize (with). 2. (с+*i.*) (*obs.*) to accord (with).

симпати́ческ|ий, *adj.* (*physiol.*, *etc.*) sympathetic; ~ая не́рвная систе́ма sympathetic nervous system; ~ие черни́ла invisible ink.

симпати́ч|ный (~ен, ~на), *adj.* likeable, attractive, nice.

симпа́ти|я, и, *f.* 1. (к) liking (for); чу́вствовать ~ю к кому́-н. to take a liking to someone, be drawn to someone. 2. (*fig., coll.*) loved one, object of one's affections.

симпто́м, а, *m.* symptom.

симптома́тик|а, и, *f.* (*med.*) study of symptoms.

симптомати́ческий, *adj.* 1. symptomatic. 2. (*med.*) eliminating symptoms, palliative.

симптомати́ч|ный (∼ен, ∼на), *adj.* = ∼еский.

симули́р|овать, ую, *impf. and pf.* to simulate, feign, sham.

симуля́нт, а, *m.* simulator; malingerer.

симуля́ци|я, и, *f.* simulation.

симфони́ческий, *adj.* symphonic; с. орке́стр symphony orchestra.

симфо́ни|я, и, *f.* 1. symphony. 2. (*eccl.*, *lit.*) concordance.

синаго́г|а, и, *f.* synagogue.

синдетико́н, а, *m.* seccotine.

синдикали́зм, а, *m.* (*polit.*) syndicalism.

синдикали́ст, а, *m.* (*polit.*) syndicalist.

синдикали́стский, *adj.* (*polit.*) syndicalist, syndicalistic.

синдика́т, а, *m.* (*econ.*) syndicate.

синдици́р|овать, ую, *impf. and pf.* (*econ.*) to syndicate.

синев|а́, ы́, *f.* blue colour; с. небе́с the blue of the sky; с. под глаза́ми dark patches under the eyes.

синева́т|ый (∼, ∼а), *adj.* bluish.

синегла́з|ый (∼, ∼а), *adj.* blue-eyed.

синедрио́н, а, *m.* (*hist.*) sanhedrin; (*joc.*) meeting.

сине́кдох|а, и, *f.* (*lit.*) synecdoche.

синеку́р|а, ы, *f.* sinecure.

сине́л|ь, и, *f.* chenille.

синеро́д, а, *m.* (*chem.*) cyanogen.

синеро́дист|ый, *adj.* (*chem.*) cyanous; cyanide (of); ∼ая кислота́ cyanic acid.

синеро́дный, *adj.* (*chem.*) cyanic; cyanide (of).

сине́|ть, ю, *impf.* 1. (*pf.* по∼) to turn blue, become blue. 2. (*impf. only*) to show blue.

си́н|ий (∼ь, ∼я, ∼е), *adj.* (dark) blue; с. чуло́к (*fig.*) blue-stocking.

сини́льн|ый, *adj.* ∼ая кислота́ (*chem.*) prussic acid, hydrocyanic acid.

сини́|ть, ю, и́шь, *impf.* (*of* по∼) 1. to paint blue. 2. to rinse in blue, blue.

сини́ц|а, ы, *f.* tit, titmouse, tomtit.

синкли́т, а, *m.* (*joc.*) council, synod.

синко́п|а, ы, *f.* (*mus. and ling.*) syncope.

синкрети́зм, а, *m.* syncretism.

сино́д, а, *m.* synod.

синода́льный, *adj.* synodal.

синоди́ческий, *adj.* (*astron.*) synodic(al).

сино́д|ский, *adj.* = ∼а́льный.

сино́лог, а, *m.* sinologist.

синоло́ги|я, и, *f.* sinology.

сино́ним, а, *m.* synonym.

синони́мик|а, и, *f.* 1. study of synonyms. 2. (*collect.*) synonyms.

синони́ми|я, и, *f.* synonymy, synonymity.

сино́птик, а, *m.* weather forecaster, weather-chart maker.

сино́птик|а, и, *f.* weather forecasting.

синопти́ческ|ий, *adj.* synoptical; ∼ая ка́рта weather-chart.

си́нтаксис, а, *m.* syntax.

синтакси́ческий, *adj.* syntactical.

си́нтез, а, *m.* synthesis.

синтези́р|овать, ую, *impf. and pf.* to synthesize.

синтети́ческий, *adj.* synthetic.

си́нус[1], а, *m.* (*math.*) sine.

си́нус[2], а, *m.* (*anat.*) sinus.

синусо́ид|а, ы, *f.* (*math.*) sinusoid.

синхрониза́тор, а, *m.* (*tech.*) synchronizer.

синхрониза́ци|я, и, *f.* synchronization.

синхронизи́р|овать, ую, *impf. and pf.* to synchronize.

синхрони́зм, а, *m.* synchronism.

синхрони́ст, а, *m.* simultaneous interpreter.

синхрони́ческий, *adj.* synchronic.

синхрони́|я, и, *f.* synchronism.

синхро́нный, *adj.* synchronous.

син|ь, и, *f.* blue colour.

синьг|а́, и́, *f.* (*orn.*) common scoter.

си́ньк|а, и, *f.* 1. blue, blueing. 2. blueprint.

синьо́р, а, *m.* signor.

синьо́р|а, ы, *f.* signora.

синьори́н|а, ы, *f.* signorina.

синю́х|а, и, *f.* (*med.*) cyanosis.

синя́к, а́, *m.* bruise; с. под гла́зом black eye; ∼и́ под глаза́ми shadows, dark patches under the eyes; изби́ть до ∼о́в to beat black and blue.

сиони́зм, а, *m.* Zionism.

сиони́ст, а, *m.* Zionist.

сиони́стский, *adj.* Zionist.

сипа́|й, я, *m.* sepoy.

сип|е́ть, лю́, и́шь, *impf.* 1. to make hoarse sounds; to speak hoarsely. 2. (*impers.*) to be hoarse; у него́ в го́рле ∼и́т he is hoarse.

си́плый, *adj.* hoarse, husky.

си́пн|уть, у, ешь, *impf.* (*coll.*) to become hoarse, become husky.

сипу́х|а, и, *f.* (*orn.*) barn owl.

сире́н|а, ы, *f.* (*in var. senses*) siren.

сире́невый, *adj.* lilac; lilac-coloured.

сире́н|ь, и, *f.* lilac.

си́речь, *particle* (*arch.*) that is to say.

сири́|ец, йца, *m.* Syrian.

сири́|йка, йки, *f. of* ∼ец.

сири́йский, *adj.* Syrian.

сиро́кко, *indecl.*, *m.* sirocco.

сиро́п, а, *m.* syrup.

сирот|а́, ы́, *pl.* ∼ы, *m. and f.* orphan; каза́нская с. (*fig.*, *coll.*) person with 'hard luck story'.

сироте́|ть, ю, *impf.* to be orphaned.

сиротли́в|ый (∼, ∼а), *adj.* lonely; (*fig.*) lost, stray.

сиро́т|ский, adj._of ~á; с. дом orphanage; ~ская зима́ mild winter.

сиро́тств|о, а, n. orphanhood.

си́р|ый (~, ~á, ~о), adj. (obs.) 1. orphaned. 2. (fig.) lonely.

систе́м|а, ы, f. 1. (in var. senses) system; стать ~ой, войти́ в ~y to become the rule. 2. type; пулемёт но́вой ~ы machine-gun of a new type.

систематиза́ци|я, и, f. systematization.

систематизи́р|овать, ую, impf. and pf. to systematize.

система́тик|а, и, f. 1. systematization. 2. (biol.) taxonomy.

систематический, adj. systematic; methodical.

систематичность|ь, и, f. systematic character; system.

систематич|ный (~ен, ~на), adj. systematic; methodical.

си́стол|а, ы, f. (med.) systole.

си́с|ька, ьки, g. pl. ~ек, f. (coll.) nipple; tit.

си́т|ец, ца, m. cotton (print); calico (print); chintz.

си́теч|ко, ка, pl. ~ки, ~ек, n. dim. of си́то; ча́йное с. tea-strainer.

си́тник[1], а, m. = си́тный хлеб.

си́тник[2], а, m. (bot.) rush.

си́тн|ый, adj. (obs.) sifted; с. хлеб loaf made of sifted flour; as noun с., ~ого, m. = с. хлеб.

си́т|о, а, n. sieve; bolter.

ситро́, indecl. n. fruit-flavoured mineral water.

ситуа́ци|я, и, f. situation.

си́т|цевый, adj. of ~ец.

ситценабивно́й, adj. (text.) printing.

ситцепеча́тани|е, я, n. (text.) printing.

сифилис, а, m. (med.) syphilis.

сифили́тик, а, m. syphilitic.

сифилити́ческий, adj. syphilitic.

сифо́н, а, m. siphon.

сиюмину́т|ный (~ен, ~на), adj. present, current.

сия́ни|е, я, n. radiance; се́верное с. northern lights, Aurora Borealis.

сия́тельств|о, а, n. его́, etc., с. (title of princes and counts) his, etc., Highness.

сия́|ть, ю, impf. to shine, beam; to be radiant.

скабрёзность|ь, и, f. scabrousness; говори́ть ~и to use scabrous language.

скабрёз|ный (~ен, ~на), adj. scabrous.

сказ, а, m. 1. tale; вот тебе́ и весь с. (coll.) that's the long and the short of it. 2. narration in first person.

сказа́ни|е, я, n. story, tale, legend.

сказан|у́ть, у́, ёшь, pf. (coll.) to blurt (out); ну и ~у́л словцо́! that's a fine thing to say!

ска|за́ть, жу́, ~жешь, pf. 1. pf. of говори́ть;

~жи́(те)! (coll., iron.) I say!; как с. how shall I put it?; лу́чше с., верне́е с., точне́е с. or rather; не́чего с.! well, to be sure!; ~зано — сде́лано (coll.) no sooner said than done. 2. to interpose, object; ничего́ не ~жешь, он прав there is no gainsaying it, he is right.

ска|за́ться[1], жу́сь, ~жешься, pf. (of ~зываться) (coll.) 1. (+d.) to inform; to give notice, give warning; они́ уе́хали не ~за́вшись they went away without (giving) warning. 2. (+i.) to proclaim oneself; с. больны́м to report sick.

ска|за́ться[2], жу́сь, ~жешься, pf. (of ~зываться) (на+p., в+p.) to tell (on); бомбёжка ~за́лась на её не́рвах the bombing told on her nerves; в э́том посту́пке я́вно ~за́лась его́ некульту́рность this act just showed his lack of manners.

сказ́итель|ь, я, m. folk-tale narrator, story-teller.

ска́зк|а, и, f. 1. tale, story; волше́бная с. fairy-tale; с. про бе́лого бычка́ (coll.) the same old story. 2. (coll.) (tall) story, fib.

ска́зочник, а, m. story-teller.

ска́зочн|ый, adj. fairytale; fabulous, fantastic; ~ая страна́ fairyland; ~ое бога́тство fabulous wealth.

сказу́ем|ое, ого, n. (gram.) predicate.

ска́зыва|ться, юсь, impf. of сказа́ться.

скак, m. only found in p. sing.; на всём ~у́ at full tilt.

скака́лк|а, и, f. skipping-rope.

ска|ка́ть, чу́, ~чешь, impf. 1. to skip, jump; с. на одно́й ноге́ to hop. 2. to gallop.

скаков́|о́й, adj. race, racing; ~ая доро́жка racecourse; ~ая ло́шадь racehorse.

скаку́н, á, m. fast horse, racer.

ска́л|а, ы, f. (obs.) scale.

скал|á, ы́, pl. ~ы, f. rock face, crag; (отве́сная) с. cliff; подво́дная с. reef.

скаламбу́р|ить, ю, ишь, pf. of каламбу́рить.

скали́ст|ый (~, ~а), adj. rocky.

скал|ить, ю, ишь, impf. (of o~) с. зу́бы to show one's teeth, bare one's teeth; (impf. only) (fig. pejor.) to grin, laugh.

ска́лк|а, и, f. (cul.) rolling-pin; beater.

скалола́з, а, m. rock-climber.

ска́лыва|ть, ю, impf. of сколо́ть.

скальд, а, m. (hist., lit.) scald, skald.

скальки́р|овать, ую, pf. of кальки́ровать.

скалькули́р|овать, ую, pf. of калькули́ровать.

ска́льн|ый, adj. (geol.) rock, rocky; ~ые рабо́ты rock excavations.

ска́льпел|ь, я, m. scalpel.

скальпи́р|овать, ую, impf. and pf. (pf. also о~) to scalp.

скаме́ечк|а, и, f. small bench; с. для ног footstool.

скаме́йк|а, и, *f.* bench.

скам|ья́, ьи́, *pl.* **~ьи́, ~е́й,** *f.* bench; с. подсуди́мых (*leg.*) the dock; на шко́льной ~ье́ during one's schooldays; со шко́льной ~ьи́ straight from school.

сканда́л, а, *m.* 1. scandal; disgrace; како́й с.! what a scandal!, how scandalous! 2. brawl; rowdy scene.

скандализи́р|овать, ую, *impf. and pf.* to scandalize.

скандали́ст, а, *m.* brawler; trouble-maker; rowdy.

сканда́л|ить, ю, ишь, *impf.* 1. (*pf.* на~) (*coll.*) to brawl; to start a row. 2. (*pf.* о~) to scandalize.

сканда́л|иться, юсь, ишься, *impf.* (*of* о~) to disgrace oneself.

сканда́л|ьный (~ен, ~ьна), *adj.* 1. scandalous. 2. (*coll.*) rowdy; с. челове́к = ~и́ст. 3. scandal; ~ьная хро́ника scandal column, page (*of newspaper*).

ска́нди|й, я, *m.* (*chem.*) scandium.

скандина́в, а, *m.* Scandinavian.

скандина́в|ка, ки, *f. of* ~.

скандина́вский, *adj.* Scandinavian.

сканди́ровани|е, я, *n.* (*lit.*) scansion.

сканди́р|овать, ую, *impf. and pf.* to declaim, recite (*stressing individual syllables of words*).

скан|ь, и, *f.* (*art*) filigree.

ска́плива|ть(ся), ю(сь), *impf. of* скопи́ть(ся).

скапу́|ститься, щусь, стишься, *pf.* (*sl.*) to fold up, pack up; to peg out.

ска́пыва|ть, ю, *impf.* (*of* скопа́ть) to shovel away, level with a spade.

скарабе́|й, я, *m.* scarab.

скарб, а, *m.* (*coll.*) goods and chattels; со всем ~ом bag and baggage.

ска́ред, а, *m.* (*coll.*) stingy person, miser.

ска́реднича|ть, ю, *impf.* (*coll.*) to be stingy.

ска́ред|ный (~ен, ~на), *adj.* (*coll.*) stingy, miserly, niggardly.

скарифика́тор, а, *m.* 1. (*agric.*) scarifier. 2. (*med.*) scarificator.

скарифици́р|овать, ую, *impf.* (*agric.*) to scarify.

скарлати́н|а, ы, *f.* (*med.*) scarlet fever, scarlatina.

скарлати́н|ный, *adj. of* ~а.

ска́рмлива|ть, ю, *impf. of* скорми́ть.

скат[1], а, *m.* slope, incline; pitch (*of a roof*).

скат[2], а, *m.* (*tech.*) wheelbase.

скат[3], а, *m.* (*zool.*) ray, skate; электри́ческий с. electric ray.

скат|а́ть, а́ю, *pf.* (*of* ~ывать) 1. to roll (up); с. па́рус to furl a sail. 2. (за+*i.*; *coll.*) to run to fetch. 3. (*school sl.*) to crib.

ска́терт|ь, и, *pl.* **~и, ~е́й,** *f.* table-cloth; ~ью доро́га! (*coll.*) good riddance!

ска|ти́ть, чу́, ~тишь, *pf.* (*of* ~тывать) to roll down.

ска|ти́ться, чу́сь, ~тишься, *pf.* (*of* ~тываться) to roll down; (*fig., pejor.*) to slip, slide.

ска́тк|а, и, *f.* 1. (*mil.*) greatcoat roll. 2. rolling.

ска́тный, *adj.* (*folk poet., of a pearl*) large, round, and even.

ска́тыва|ть, ю, *impf. of*ската́ть *and* скати́ть.

ска́тыва|ться, юсь, *impf. of* скати́ться.

ска́ут, а, *m.* (boy) scout.

скафа́ндр, а, *m.* protective suit (*of divers, astronauts, etc.*).

ска́чк|а, и, *f.* 1. gallop, galloping. 2. (*pl.*) horse-race; race meeting, the races; с. с препя́тствиями steeplechase.

скачкообра́з|ный (~ен, ~на), *adj.* spasmodic; uneven.

скач|о́к, ка́, *m.* 1. jump, leap, bound; ~ка́ми by leaps. 2. (*fig.*) a great advance, leap forward.

ска́шива|ть, ю, *impf. of* скоси́ть.

ска́щива|ть, ю, *impf. of* скости́ть.

сква́жин|а, ы, *f.* slit, chink; бурова́я с. (*tech.*) bore-hole; замо́чная с. key-hole.

сква́жистый, *adj.* porous.

сквалы́г|а, и, *m. and f.* (*coll.*) stingy person, miser.

сквер, а, *m.* public garden.

скверн|а, ы, *no pl.* (*collect.*; *obs.*) pollution; filth.

скве́рно, *adv.* badly; с. чу́вствовать себя́ to feel bad, feel poorly; с. поступи́ть с кем-н. to treat someone badly.

скверносло́в, а, *m.* foul-mouthed person.

скверносло́ви|е, я, *n.* foul language.

скверносло́в|ить, лю, ишь, *impf.* to use foul language.

скве́р|ный (~ен, ~на́, ~но), *adj.* nasty, foul; bad; ~ная пого́да foul weather; мне ~но (*impers.*) I feel bad.

сквита́|ться, юсь, *pf.* (с+*i.*; *coll.*) to be quits (with), be even (with).

сквоз|и́ть, и́т, *impf.* 1. (*impers.*) ~и́т there is a draught. 2. (*obs.*) to be transparent, show light through. 3. to show through, be seen through (*also fig.*); синева́ не́бес ~и́ла меж ветвя́ми the blue of the sky could be seen through the branches; в его́ слова́х ~и́ла жа́лость к себе́ there was a hint of self-pity in his words.

сквозн|о́й, *adj.* 1. through; с. ве́тер draught; ~о́е движе́ние through traffic; с. по́езд through train. 2. all-round. 3. transparent.

сквозня́к, а́, *m.* draught.

сквозь, *prep.*+*a.* through.

скворе́ц, ца́, *m.* starling.

скворе́чник, а, *m.* starling-house (*wooden box affixed to pole or on tree adjoining house*).

скворе́ч|ница, ницы, *f.* = ~ник.

скворе́ч|ня, ни, *g. pl.* **~ен,** *f.* = ~ник.

скелет, а, *m.* skeleton,

скепсис, а, *m.* scepticism.

скептик, а, *m.* sceptic.

скептицизм, а, *m.* scepticism.

скептический, *adj.* sceptic.

скептич|ный (~ен, ~на), *adj.* sceptical.

скерцо, *indecl., n.* (*mus.*) scherzo.

скетинг-ринг, а, *m.* roller-skating rink.

скетч, а, *m.* (*theatr.*) sketch.

скид|ать¹, аю, *impf.* (*coll.*) to throw off.

скид|ать², аю, *pf.* (*of* ~ывать²) (*coll.*) to throw off.

скидк|а, и, *f.* 1. rebate, reduction, discount; со ~ой (в+*a.*) with a reduction (of), at a discount (of). 2. (на+*a.*; *fig.*) allowance(s) (for); сделать ~у на возраст to make allowances for age.

скидыва|ть¹, ю, *impf. of* скинуть.

скидыва|ть², ю, *impf. of* скидать².

скин|уть, ну, нешь, *pf.* (*of* ~дывать¹) 1. (*coll.*) to throw off, down; с. с себя одежду to throw off one's clothes. 2. (*coll.*) to knock off (*from price*).

скип, а, *m.* (*tech.*) skip.

скипетр, а, *m.* sceptre.

скипидар, а, *m.* turpentine.

скипидар|ный, *adj. of* ~.

скирд, á, *pl.* ~ы́, *m.* stack, rick.

скирд|á, ы́, *pl.* ~ы, ~, ~áм, *f.* = ~.

скирд|овать, ýю, *impf.* (*of* за~) to stack.

скис|ать, аю, *impf. of* ~нуть.

скис|нуть, ну, нешь, *past* ~, ~ла, *pf.* (*of* ~ать) to go sour, turn sour.

скит, á, о ~é, в ~ý, *m.* (small and secluded) monastery.

скитал|ец, ьца, *m.* wanderer.

скитальческий, *adj.* wandering.

скитальчеств|о, а, *n.* wandering.

скита|ться, юсь, *impf.* to wander; с. по свету to be a globe-trotter.

скиф¹, а, *m.* (*hist.*) Scythian.

скиф², а, *m.* skiff.

скифский, *adj.* (*hist.*) Scythian.

склад¹, а, *m.* 1. storehouse; (*mil.*) depot; таможенный с. bonded warehouse; товарный с. warehouse. 2. store; с. боеприпасов (*mil.*) ammunition dump.

склад², а, *m.* 1. stamp, mould; с. ума cast of mind, mentality. 2. (*coll.*) logical connexion; ни ~у, ни ладу neither rhyme nor reason.

склад³, а, *pl.* ~ы́, *m.* syllable; читать по ~ам to read haltingly, spell out.

склад|ень, ня, *m.* 1. hinged icon. 2. (*obs.*) folding object.

складир|овать, ую, *impf. and pf.* to store.

складк|а, и, *f.* 1. fold; pleat, tuck; crease; юбка в ~у pleated skirt; с. на брюках trouser crease. 2. wrinkle. 3. (*geol.*) fold; с. местности natural feature, accident of terrain.

складно, *adv.* smoothly, coherently.

складн|ой, *adj.* folding, collapsible; ~áя кровать camp bed.

склад|ный (~ен, ~на́, ~но), *adj.* 1. (*coll.*; *of human beings or animals*) well-knit, well-built. 2. (*coll.*) well-made. 3. (*of speech*) well-rounded, smooth, coherent; с. рассказ well-put-together story.

складочн|ый, *adj.* storage, warehousing; ~ое место store-room, lumber-room.

склад|ской, *adj.* = ~очный.

складчатый, *adj.* (*geol.*) plicated, folded.

складчин|а, ы, *f.* clubbing, pooling; устроить ~y to club together, pool one's resources; купить автомобиль в ~у to club together to buy a car.

складыва|ть(ся), ю(сь), *impf. of* сложить(ся).

склеива|ть(ся), ю(сь), ет(ся), *impf. of* склеить(ся).

скле|ить, ю, ишь, *pf.* (*of* ~ивать) to stick together; to glue together, paste together.

скле|иться, ится, *pf.* (*of* ~иваться) to stick together (*intrans.*)

склейк|а, и, *f.* glueing together, pasting together.

склеп, а, *m.* burial vault, crypt.

склеп|ать, аю, *pf.* (*of* ~ывать) to rivet.

склёпк|а, и, *f.* riveting.

склёпыва|ть, ю, *impf. of* склепать.

склероз, а, *m.* (*med.*) sclerosis.

склеротический, *adj.* (*med.*) sclerotic, sclerous.

склик|ать, чу, чешь, *pf. of* ~кать.

склик|ать, аю, *impf.* (*of* ~ать) (*coll.*) to call together.

склок|а, и, *f.* squabble; row.

склон, а, *m.* slope; на ~е лет in one's declining years.

склонени|е, я, *n.* 1. (*math.*) inclination; (*astron.*) declination; с. компаса variation of the compass; угол ~я angle of declination; круг ~я светила hour-circle of a celestial body. 2. (*gram.*) declension.

склон|ить, ю, ~ишь, *pf.* (*of* ~ять¹) 1. to incline, bend, bow; с. голову (перед) (*fig.*) to bow one's head (to, before). 2. (*fig.*) to incline; to win over, gain over.

склон|иться, юсь, ~ишься, *pf.* (*of* ~яться¹) 1. to bend, bow. 2. (к; *fig.*) to give in (to), yield (to).

склонность, и, *f.* (к) inclination (to, for); disposition (to); susceptibility (to); bent (for); penchant (for).

склон|ный (~ен, ~на́, ~но), *adj.* (к) inclined (to), disposed (to), susceptible (to), given (to), prone (to).

склоня|емый, *pres. part. pass. of* ~ть² *and adj.* (*gram.*) declinable.

склон|ять¹, я́ю, *impf. of* ~ить.

склон|я́ть², я́ю, *impf.* (*of* про~) (*gram.*) to decline.

склон|я́ться¹, я́юсь, *impf. of* ~и́ться.

склон|я́ться², я́ется, *impf.* (*gram.*) to be declined.

склóчник, а, *m.* (*coll.*) squabbler, trouble-maker.

склóчнича|ть, ю, *impf.* (*coll.*) to squabble; to cause rows.

склóч|ный (~ен, ~на), *adj.* (*coll.*) troublesome, trouble-making.

склянк|а, и, *f.* 1. phial; bottle. 2. (*naut.*; *obs.*) hour-glass. 3. (*naut.*) bell (= *one half-hour*); шесть склянок six bells.

скоб|á, ы́, *pl.* ~ы, ~áм, *f.* cramp(-iron), clamp; staple; catch, fastening; (*naut.*) shackle.

скóбел|ь, я, *m.* adze, scraper(-knife), drawing-knife.

скóбк|а¹, и, *f.* 1. *dim. of* скобá. 2. (*mark of punctuation, also math.*) bracket; *pl. also* parentheses; фигу́рные ~и braces; заключи́ть в ~и to parenthesize; в ~ах in brackets; (*fig.*) in parenthesis, by the way, incidentally.

скóбк|а², и, *f.* стри́чься в ~у to have one's hair cut in a fringe.

скобл|и́ть, ю́, ~ишь, *impf.* to scrape, plane.

скóбочн|ый, *adj. of* скобá *and* скóбка; ~ая маши́на stapler, stapling machine.

скобян|óй, *adj.* с. товáр, ~ые издéлия hardware.

скóв|анный 1. *p.p.p. of* ~áть; с. льдáми ice-bound. 2. *adj.* constrained.

сковá|ть, скую́, скуёшь, *pf.* (*of* скóвывать) 1. to forge, hammer out. 2. to forge together. 3. to chain; to fetter, bind (*also fig.*). 4. (*mil.; fig.*) to pin down, hold, contain. 5. (*of frost or ice*) to lock; морóз ~л рéку the river was frozen over.

сковород|á, ы́, *pl.* скóвороды, сковорóд, ~áм, *f.* 1. frying-pan. 2. (*tech.*) pan.

сковорóд|ень, ня, *m.* (*tech.*) dovetail (joint); вя́зка ~нем, соединéние ~нем dove-tailing.

сковорóдк|а, и, *f.* (*coll.*) frying-pan.

скóвыва|ть, ю, *impf. of* сковáть.

сковы́рива|ть, ю, *impf. of* сковырну́ть.

сковыр|ну́ть, ну́, нёшь, *pf.* (*of* ~ивать) 1. to pick off, scratch off. 2. (*coll.*) to knock over, push over.

скок, а, *m.* galloping; во весь с. at full gallop, at full tilt.

скола́чива|ть, ю, *impf. of* сколоти́ть.

скóл|ок, ка, *m.* 1. chip. 2. pricked pattern. 3. (*fig.*) copy.

сколо|ти́ть, чу́, ~тишь, *pf.* (*of* скола́чивать) 1. to knock together, knock up. 2. (*fig., coll.*) to put together, knock up; с. состоя́ние to knock up a fortune.

скол|óть¹, ю́, ~ешь, *pf.* (*of* скáлывать) to split off, chop off.

скол|óть², ю́, ~ешь, *pf.* (*of* скáлывать) to pin together.

сколь, *adv.* how.

скольжéни|е, я, *n.* sliding, slipping; с. зву́ка (*mus., ling.*) glide; с. на крылó (*aeron.*) side-slip.

сколь|зи́ть, жу́, зи́шь, *impf.* to slide, slip; to glide; с. глаза́ми (по+*d.*) to cast one's eye (over).

скóльз|кий (~ок, ~кá, ~ко), *adj.* slippery (*also fig.*); ~кое положéние tricky position; говори́ть на ~кую тéму to be on slippery ground.

скользн|у́ть, у́, ёшь, *pf.* to slide, slip; с. в дверь to slip through the door.

скольз|я́щий, *pres. part. act. of* ~и́ть *and adj.* sliding; с. гра́фик рабóты flexi-time; ~я́щая шкалá sliding scale; с. у́зел slip-knot.

скóлько, *interrog. and relat. adv.* 1. how much; how many; с. стóит? how much does it cost?; с. вам лет? how old are you?; с. врéмени? what time is it?; с. душé угóдно to one's heart's content; с. раз я тебé об э́том напомина́л! how many times have I reminded you about it!; с. лет, с. зим! (*coll.*) what ages it has been (since we met)! 2. = наскóлько.

скóлько-нибудь, *adv.* any; есть у вас при себé с.-н. дéнег? have you any money on you?

скоманд|овать, ую, *pf. of* комáндовать.

скомбини́р|овать, ую, *pf. of* комбини́ровать.

скóмка|ть, ю, *pf. of* кóмкать.

скоморóх, а, *m.* 1. (*hist.*) skomorokh (*wandering minstrel-cum-clown*). 2. (*fig.*) buffoon, clown.

скоморóшеств|о, а, *n.* buffoonery.

скоморóшнича|ть, ю, *impf.* to play the buffoon.

скомпили́р|овать, ую, *pf. of* компили́ровать.

скомпон|овáть, у́ю, *pf. of* компоновáть.

скомпромети́р|овать, ую, *pf. of* компромети́ровать.

сконструи́р|овать, ую, *pf. of* конструи́ровать.

сконфу́|женный, *p.p.p. of* ~зить *and adj.* confused, abashed, disconcerted.

сконфу́|зить(ся), жу(сь), зишь(ся), *pf. of* конфу́зить(ся).

сконцентри́р|овать, ую, *pf. of* концентри́ровать.

скончáни|е, я, *n.* 1. (*obs.*) end, termination. 2. end, decease, passing.

скончá|ться, юсь, *pf.* to pass away (= to die).

скоп|á, ы́, *f.* (*orn.*) osprey.

скопá|ть, ю, *pf. of* скáпывать.

скоп|е́ц, ца́, m. eunuch.

скопидо́м, а, m. (coll.) hoarder, miser.

скопидо́мнича|ть, ю, impf. (coll.) to be a hoarder, miser.

скопидо́мств|о, а, n. (coll.) hoarding; miserliness.

скопи́р|овать, ую, pf. of копи́ровать.

скоп|и́ть¹, лю́, ∼ишь, pf. (of ска́пливать) (+a. or g.) to save (up); to amass, pile up.

скоп|и́ть², лю́, и́шь, impf. to castrate.

скоп|и́ться, ∼ится, pf. (of ска́пливаться) 1. to accumulate, pile up. 2. (of people) to gather, collect.

ско́пищ|е, а, n. (pejor.) crowd, assemblage, throng.

скопле́ни|е, я, n. 1. accumulation. 2. crowd; concentration, conglomeration.

скопн|и́ть, ю́, и́шь, pf. of копни́ть.

ско́пом, adv. (coll.) in a crowd, in a bunch, en masse.

ско́пческий, adj. of a eunuch.

скорб|е́ть, лю́, и́шь, impf. (о+p.) to grieve (for, over), mourn (for, over), lament.

скорб|ный (∼ен, ∼на), adj. sorrowful, mournful, doleful.

скорбу́т, а, m. (med.) scurvy.

скорбу́тный, adj. (med.) scorbutic.

скорб|ь, и, pl. ∼и, ∼е́й, f. sorrow, grief.

скор|е́е (and ∼е́й) 1. comp. of ∼ый and ∼о; как мо́жно с. as soon as possible. 2. adv. rather, sooner; с. всего́ most likely, most probably.

скорлуп|а́, ы́, pl. ∼ы, f. shell; с. оре́ха nutshell; замкну́ться в свою́ ∼у́ to retire into one's shell.

скорм|и́ть, лю́, ∼ишь, pf. (of ска́рмливать) (+d.) to feed (to).

скорня́жн|ый, adj. ∼ое де́ло furriery; с. това́р furs.

скорня́к, а́, m. furrier, fur-dresser.

ско́ро, adv. 1. quickly, fast. 2. soon; с. весна́! spring will soon be here!; как с., коль с. (conj.) as soon as.

скороб|и́ться, лю́сь, ишься, pf. of коро́биться.

скороговрк|а, и, f. 1. patter. 2. tongue-twister.

скором|и́ться, лю́сь, ишься, impf. (of о∼) to break a fast, eat meat during a fast.

скоро́мник, а, m. (coll.) 1. person failing to observe fast. 2. lewd person.

скоро́м|ный (∼ен, ∼на), adj. 1. (of food) forbidden to be consumed during fast (viz. meat dishes or dishes containing milk products); ∼ные дни meat days; ∼ное ма́сло animal (as opp. to vegetable) fat; as noun ∼ное, ∼ного, n. dishes containing meat and/or milk products. 2. (obs.) lewd.

скоропали́тель|ный (∼ен, ∼ьна), adj. (coll.) hasty, rash.

скоропеча́тный, adj. с. стано́к (typ.) engine press.

скоропи́сный, adj. cursive.

ско́ропис|ь, и, f. 1. cursive (hand). 2. (obs.) shorthand.

скороподъёмност|ь, и, f. (aeron.) rate of climb.

скоропо́ртящийся, adj. perishable.

скоропости́жн|ый, adj. ∼ая смерть sudden death.

скоропреходя́щий, adj. transient, transitory.

скороспе́л|ый (∼, ∼а), adj. 1. early; fast-ripening. 2. (fig., coll.) premature; hasty; с. вы́вод hasty conclusion.

скоростни́к, а́, m. high-speed worker; high-speed performer.

скоростно́й, adj. high-speed; с. авто́бус express bus.

скоростре́льный, adj. rapid-firing, quick-firing.

ско́рост|ь, и, pl. ∼и, ∼е́й, f. 1. speed; velocity; rate; дозво́ленная с. (езды́) speed-limit; со ∼ью тридцати́ миль в час at thirty miles per hour; с. подъёма (aeron.) rate of climb; с. све́та velocity of light. 2. коро́бка ∼е́й (tech.) gear-box; перейти́ на другу́ю с. to change gear. 3. (on railways) category of transit; ма́лой ∼ью by (slow) goods train; большо́й ∼ью by fast goods train; отпра́вить груз пассажи́рской ∼ью to send a consignment by passenger train. 4. в ∼и (coll.) soon; in the near future.

скоросшива́тел|ь, я, m. loose-leaf binder.

скорота́|ть, ю, pf. of корота́ть.

скороте́ч|ный (∼ен, ∼на), adj. 1. (obs.) transient, short-lived. 2. (med.) fulminant; ∼ная чахо́тка galloping consumption.

скорохо́д, а, m. 1. (obs.) footman. 2. fast runner; конькобе́жец-с. high-speed skater.

скорпио́н, а, m. scorpion; С. Scorpio (sign of zodiac).

ско́рч|ить, у, ишь, pf. of ко́рчить.

ско́р|ый (∼, ∼а́, ∼о), adj. 1. quick, fast; rapid; с. по́езд fast train; ∼ая по́мощь ambulance (service); на ∼ую ру́ку offhand, in rough-and-ready fashion. 2. near, forthcoming, impending; в ∼ом бу́дущем in the near future; в ∼ом вре́мени shortly, before long; до ∼ого (свида́ния)! see you soon!

скос¹, а, m. (agric.) mowing.

скос², а, m. slant, splay, chamfer, taper; у́гол ∼а angle of taper.

ско|си́ть¹, шу́, ∼сишь, pf. (of коси́ть¹ and ска́шивать) to mow.

ско|си́ть², шу́, си́шь, pf. (of коси́ть² and ска́шивать) to squint.

ско|сти́ть, щу́, сти́шь, pf. (of ска́щивать) (coll.) to strike off, knock off; с. три рубля́ с цены́ to knock three roubles off the price.

скот, á, *m.* **1.** (*collect.*) cattle; livestock. **2.** (*fig.*, *coll.*) swine, beast.

скотин|а, ы, *f.* **1.** (*collect.*) cattle; livestock. **2.** (*also m.*) (*fig.*, *coll.*) swine, beast.

скотинк|а, и, *f.* *dim.* of скотина; серая с. (*coll.*) simple soldiery.

скóтник, а, *m.* herd, herdsman; cowman.

скóт|ный, *adj.* of ~; с. двор cattle-yard.

скотобó|ец, йца, *m.* slaughterer.

скотобó|йня, йни, *g. pl.* ~ен, *f.* slaughter-house.

скотовóд, а, *m.* cattle-breeder.

скотовóдств|о, а, *n.* cattle-breeding, cattle-raising.

скотовóдческий, *adj.* cattle-breeding.

скотокрáдств|о, а, *n.* cattle-stealing.

скотолóжств|о, а, *n.* bestiality.

скотопригóнный, *adj.* с. двор stock-yard.

скотопромы́шленник, а, *m.* cattle-dealer.

скотопромы́шленност|ь, и, *f.* cattle-dealing, cattle-trade.

скотопромы́шленн|ый, *adj.* of ~ость.

скóтский, *adj.* brutal, brutish, bestial.

скотств|ó, á, *n.* brutality, brutishness, bestiality.

скрáдыва|ть, ю, *impf.* to conceal, make less evident.

скрá|сить, шу, сишь, *pf.* (*of* ~шивать) (*fig.*) to smooth over; to relieve, take the edge off; он мнóго читáл, чтóбы с. своё одинóчество he read a lot to relieve his loneliness.

скрáшива|ть, ю, *impf.* of скрáсить.

скребкóвый, *adj.* (*tech.*) scraping, scraper.

скребни́ц|а, ы, *f.* curry-comb, horse-comb.

скреб|óк, кá, *m.* scraper.

скрéжет, а, *m.* gnashing, gritting (*of teeth*).

скреже|тáть, щý, ~щешь, *impf.* (зубáми) to gnash, grit one's teeth.

скрéп|а, ы, *f.* **1.** (*tech.*) tie, clamp, brace. **2.** counter-signature, authentication; кóпия за ~ой секретаря́ copy countersigned by the secretary.

скрéпер, а, *m.* (*tech.*) earth-moving machine.

скреп|и́ть, лю́, и́шь, *pf.* (*of* ~ля́ть) **1.** to fasten (together), make fast; to pin (together); to clamp, brace; ~я́ сéрдце reluctantly, grudgingly. **2.** to countersign, authenticate, ratify.

скрéпк|а, и, *f.* paper-clip.

скреплéни|е, я, *n.* **1.** fastening; clamping. **2.** (*tech.*) tie, clamp.

скрепля́|ть, ю, *impf.* of скрепи́ть.

скре|сти́, бý, бёшь, *past* ~б, ~блá, *impf.* **1.** to scrape; to scratch, claw. **2.** (*impers.*) (*fig.*, *coll.*) to nag, goad; у неё ~блó на сéрдце she felt a nagging anxiety.

скре|сти́сь, бýсь, бёшься, *past* ~бся, ~блáсь, *impf.* to scratch, make a scratching noise.

скре|сти́ть, щý, сти́шь, *pf.* (*of* ~щивать) **1.** to cross; с. мечи́, с. шпáги (с+*i.*) to cross swords (with) (*also fig.*). **2.** (*biol.*) to cross, interbreed.

скрест|и́ться, и́тся, *pf.* (*of* скрéщиваться) **1.** to cross; (*fig.*) to clash. **2.** (*biol.*) to cross, interbreed.

скрещéни|е, я, *n.* crossing; intersection.

скрéщивани|е, я, *n.* **1.** crossing. **2.** (*biol.*) crossing, interbreeding.

скрéщива|ть(ся), ю, ет(ся), *impf.* of скрести́ть(ся).

скрив|и́ть(ся), лю́(сь), и́шь(ся), *pf.* of криви́ть(ся).

скрижáл|ь, и, *f.* tablet, table (*with sacred text inscribed upon* it); ~и (*fig.*, *arch.*) annals, memorials, records.

скрип, а, *m.* squeak, creak; crunch.

скрипáч, á, *m.* violinist.

скрип|éть, лю́, и́шь, *impf.* **1.** to squeak, creak; to crunch. **2.** (*coll.*, *joc.*) to be just alive, just keep going.

скрипи́чный, *adj.* violin; с. мáстер violin-maker; с. ключ treble clef, G clef; с. концéрт violin concerto.

скри́пк|а, и, *f.* violin; пéрвая с. first violin; (*fig.*, *coll.*) first fiddle.

скри́пн|уть, у, ешь, *pf.* to squeak, creak.

скрипу́чий, *adj.* (*coll.*) squeaky, creaking; с. гóлос rasping voice; с. снег crunching snow.

скро|и́ть, ю́, и́шь, *pf.* of крои́ть.

скрóмник, а, *m.* modest man.

скрóмнича|ть, ю, *impf.* to be overmodest.

скрóмност|ь, и, *f.* modesty.

скрóм|ный (~ен, ~нá, ~но), *adj.* (*in var. senses*) modest; по моему́ ~ному мнéнию in my humble opinion.

скру́пул, а, *m.* (*measure of weight*) scruple.

скрупулёзност|ь, и, *f.* scrupulousness, scrupulosity.

скрупулёз|ный (~ен, ~на), *adj.* scrupulous.

скру|ти́ть, чý, ~тишь, *pf.* (*of* крути́ть *and* ~чивать) **1.** to twist; to roll. **2.** to bind, tie up.

скру́чива|ть, ю, *impf.* of скрути́ть.

скрыва́|ть, ю, *impf.* of скрыть.

скрыва́|ться, юсь, *impf.* **1.** *impf.* of скры́ться. **2.** *impf. only* to lie in hiding; to lie low.

скры́тнича|ть, ю, *impf.* (*coll.*) to be secretive, be reticent.

скры́т|ный (~ен, ~на), *adj.* reticent, secretive.

скры́т|ый, *p.p.p.* of ~ь *and adj.* secret, concealed; latent (*also phys.*); с. смысл hidden meaning; ~ая теплотá (*phys.*) latent heat.

скр|ы́ть, óю, óешь, *pf.* (*of* ~ыва́ть) (от) to hide (from), conceal (from); не с. того́, что to make no secret of the fact that; с. от кого́-н. неприя́тные изве́стия to keep bad news from someone.

скр|**ы́ться, о́юсь, о́ешься,** *pf.* (*of* ~ыва́ться) (от) **1.** to hide (oneself) (from); to go into hiding. **2.** to steal away (from), escape, give the slip. **3.** to disappear, vanish.

скрюч|**ить, у, ишь,** *pf. of* крючить.

скрюч|**иться, усь, ишься,** *pf.* to bend (*intrans.*); to hunch oneself up.

скря́г|**а, и,** *m. and f.* miser, skinflint.

скря́жнича|**ть, ю,** *impf.* (*coll.*) to be a miser, be a skinflint.

скуде́л|**ь, и,** *f.* (*arch.*) **1.** potter's clay. **2.** pot, vessel.

скуде́ль|**ный,** *adj.* **1.** *adj. of* ~. **2.** (*fig.*) frail, fragile; сосу́д с. (*eccl. or rhet.*) weak vessel.

скуде́|**ть, ю,** *impf.* (*of* о~) to grow scanty, run short; (+*i.*) to be short (of).

скуд|**ный** (~ен, ~на́, ~но), *adj.* **1.** scanty, poor; slender, meagre; scant; с. обе́д meagre repast; ~ные све́дения scant information; ~ные сре́дства slender means. **2.** (+*i.*) poor (in), short (of).

скудост|**ь, и,** *f.* scarcity; poverty.

скудоу́ми|**е, я,** *n.* feeble-mindedness.

скудоу́м|**ный** (~ен, ~на), *adj.* feeble--minded.

ску́к|**а, и,** *f.* boredom, tedium; кака́я с.! what a bore!

скул|**а́, ы́,** *pl.* ~ы, *f.* cheek-bone.

скула́ст|**ый** (~, ~а), *adj.* with high cheek--bones, with prominent cheek-bones.

скул|**и́ть, ю́, ишь,** *impf.* (*of a dog*) to whine, whimper (*also fig.*).

скулово́й, *adj.* (*anat.*) malar.

ску́льптор, а, *m.* sculptor.

скульпту́р|**а, ы,** *f.* sculpture.

скульпту́рный, *adj.* sculptural; (*fig.*) statuesque.

ску́мбри|**я, и,** *f.* mackerel; scomber.

скунс, а, *m.* skunk.

скуп|**а́ть, а́ю,** *impf. of* ~и́ть.

скуперд|**я́й, я,** *m.* (*coll.*) miser, skinflint.

скуп|**е́ц, ца́,** *m.* miser, skinflint.

скуп|**и́ть, лю́, ~ишь,** *pf.* (*of* ~а́ть) to buy up; to corner.

скуп|**и́ться, лю́сь, и́шься,** *impf.* (*of* по~) (+*inf. or* на+*a.*) to stint, grudge, skimp; to be sparing (of); с. на де́ньги to be close--fisted; не с. на похвалы́ not to stint one's praise.

ску́пк|**а, и,** *f.* buying up; cornering.

скуп|**но́й,** *adj. of* ~ка.

ску́по, *adv.* sparingly.

скуп|**о́й** (~, ~а́, ~о), *adj.* **1.** stingy, miserly, niggardly; с. на похвалы́ chary of praise; с. на слова́ sparing of words. **2.** (*fig.*) inadequate; с. свет inadequate illumination.

ску́пост|**ь, и,** *f.* stinginess, miserliness, niggardliness.

скуп|**очный,** *adj. of* ~ка.

ску́пщик, а, *m.* buyer-up; с. кра́деного fence.

ску́тер, а, *m.* outboard-motor boat.

скуфе́йк|**а, и,** *f. dim. of* скуфья́.

скуфь|**я́, и́,** *f.* (*clerical*) skull-cap, calotte.

скуча́|**ть, ю,** *impf.* **1.** to be bored. **2.** (по+*d. or p.*) to miss, yearn (for).

ску́ченност|**ь, и,** *f.* density, congestion; с. населе́ния overcrowding.

ску́ченный, *adj.* dense, congested.

ску́чива|**ть(ся), ю(сь),** *impf. of* ску́чить(ся).

ску́ч|**ить, у, ишь,** *pf.* (*of* ~ивать) to crowd (together).

ску́ч|**иться, усь, ишься,** *pf.* (*of* ~иваться) to flock, cluster; to crowd together, huddle together.

ску́ч|**ный** (~ен, ~на́, ~но), *adj.* **1.** boring, depressing, tedious, dull. **2.** bored; с. взгляд look of boredom; *as pred.* мне, *etc.*, ~но I, *etc.*, am bored, depressed.

ску́ша|**ть, ю,** *pf. of* ку́шать.

слабе́|**ть, ю,** *impf.* (*of* о~) to weaken, grow weak(er); (*of wind, etc.*) to slacken, drop.

слабин|**а́, ы́,** *no pl., f.* **1.** (*in a rope, etc.*) slack; вы́брать ~у́ (*naut.*) to haul in the slack. **2.** (*coll.*) weak spot, weak point.

слаби́тельн|**ый,** *adj.* (*med.*) laxative, purgative; *as noun* ~ое, ~ого, *n.* laxative, purgative.

слаб|**и́ть, ит,** *impf.* (*of* про~) **1.** (*impers.*) его́ ~ит he has diarrhoea. **2.** to purge, act as a laxative.

слаб|**нуть, ну, нешь,** *past* ~, ~ла, *impf.* (*of* о~) (*coll.*) **1.** to weaken, grow weak(er). **2.** to become slack.

слабово́ли|**е, я,** *n.* weak will.

слабово́л|**ьный** (~ен, ~ьна), *adj.* weak--willed.

слабогру́д|**ый** (~, ~а), *adj.* weak-chested.

слабоду́ши|**е, я,** *n.* faint-heartedness.

слабоду́ш|**ный** (~ен, ~на), *adj.* faint--hearted.

слабора́звитый, *adj.* (*econ.*) under-developed.

слабоси́ли|**е, я,** *n.* weakness, feebleness, debility.

слабоси́л|**ьный** (~ен, ~ьна), *adj.* **1.** weak, feeble. **2.** (*tech.*) low-powered.

сла́бост|**ь, и,** *f.* **1.** weakness, feebleness; debility. **2.** (к) weakness (for); foible; чу́вствовать с. (к) to have a weakness (for).

слабото́чный, *adj.* (*tech.*) low-current.

слабоу́ми|**е, я,** *n.* feeble-mindedness, imbecility.

слабоу́м|**ный** (~ен, ~на), *adj.* feeble--minded, imbecile.

слабохара́ктер|**ный** (~ен, ~на), *adj.* characterless, of weak character.

сла́б|**ый** (~, ~а́, ~о), *adj.* (*in var. senses*)

weak; feeble; slack, loose; (*fig.*) poor;
~ое здоро́вье delicate health; ~ое ме́сто,
~ая сторона́ weak point, weak place; ~ая
наде́жда faint hope, slender hope; ~ое
оправда́ние lame excuse; с. пол the weaker
sex; с. результа́т poor result.

сла́в|а, ы, *f.* **1.** glory; fame; во ~у (+*g.*) to
the glory (of); на ~у (*coll.*) wonderfully
well, excellently; (*as interj.*, +*d.*) hurrah
(for)!, с. Бо́гу thank God, thank goodness.
2. fame, name, repute, reputation; до́брая
с. good name; дурна́я с. ill fame. **3.** (*coll.*)
rumour.

сла́вильщик, а, *m.* (*obs.*) wait, carol-singer.

слави́ст, а, *m.* Slavist; Slavonic scholar.

слави́стик|а, и, *f.* Slavonic studies; Slavonic
philology.

сла́в|ить, лю, ишь, *impf.* **1.** to celebrate,
hymn, sing the praises (of); с. Христа́ to go
carol-singing. **2.** (*coll.*) to give a bad name.

сла́в|иться, люсь, ишься, *impf.* (+*i.*) to be
famous (for), be famed (for), be renowned
(for); to have a reputation (for).

сла́вк|а, и, *f.* (*orn.*) warbler.

сла́в|ный (~ен, ~на́, ~но), *adj.* **1.** glorious;
famous, renowned. **2.** (*coll.*) nice, splendid;
с. ма́лый good chap, nice chap.

славосло́ви|е, я, *n.* **1.** (*eccl.*) doxology; gloria.
2. glorification, eulogy.

славосло́в|ить, лю, ишь, *impf.* to eulogize,
extol, overpraise.

славяни́зм, а, *m.* (*ling.*) **1.** Slavism (*in a
non-Slavonic language*). **2.** Slavonicism (*in
Russian*).

славя́н|ин, и́на, *pl.* ~е, ~, *m.* Slav.

славянове́д, а, *m.* Slavist; Slavonic scholar.

славянове́дени|е, я, *n.* Slavonic studies.

славянофи́л, а, *m.* Slavophil.

славянофи́л|ьский, *adj.* of ~ *and* ~ьство.

славянофи́льств|о, а, *n.* Slavophilism.

славя́нский, *adj.* Slavonic.

славя́нств|о, а, *n.* (*collect.*) the Slavonic
peoples.

слага́ем|ое, ого, *n.* **1.** (*math.*) item. **2.** (*fig.*)
component.

слага́|ть(ся), ю(сь), *impf.* of сложи́ть(ся).

слад, а (у), *m.*, *now only in phrase* с ним, *etc.*,
~у нет (*coll.*) he, *etc.*, is unmanageable, is
out of hand.

сла́ден|ький (~ек, ~ька), *adj.* (*coll.*) sweet-
ish; (*fig.*) sugary, honeyed; ~ькая улы́бка
sugary smile.

сла́|дить, жу, дишь, *pf.* (*of* ~живать) **1.**
(*coll.*) to arrange. **2.** (с+*i.*) to cope (with),
manage, handle; он про́сто не уме́л с. с
подчинёнными he simply did not know
how to handle his subordinates.

сла́д|кий (~ок, ~ка́, ~ко), *adj.* **1.** sweet
(*also fig.*); ~кое мя́со (*cul.*) sweetbread;
для меня́ э́то не ~ко (*of food*) it is not sweet

enough for me; *as noun* ~кое, ~кого, *n.*
sweet (course), dessert. **2.** (*fig.*, *pejor.*)
sugary, sugared, honeyed.

сладкое́жк|а, и, *m. and f.* (*coll.*) (person with)
sweet tooth.

сладкозву́ч|ный (~ен, ~на), *adj.* (*obs.*)
mellifluous.

сладкоречи́в|ый (~, ~а), *adj.* smooth-
-spoken, smooth-tongued.

сла́дост|ный (~ен, ~на), *adj.* (*obs.*) sweet,
delightful.

сладостра́сти|е, я, *n.* voluptuousness.

сладостра́стник, а, *m.* voluptuary.

сладостра́ст|ный (~ен, ~на), *adj.* volup-
tuous.

сла́дост|ь, и, *f.* **1.** sweetness. **2.** (*coll.*)
sweetening. **3.** (*pl.*) sweets, sweetmeats.

сла́женност|ь, и, *f.* co-ordination, harmony,
order.

сла́|женный, *p.p.p.* of ~дить *and adj.* (well)
co-ordinated, harmonious, orderly.

сла́жива|ть, ю, *impf.* of сла́дить.

сла́|зить, жу, зишь, *pf.* (*coll.*) to go; с. в
подва́л за дрова́ми to go down to the cellar
for logs.

слайд, а, *m.* slide, transparency.

слайдопрое́ктор, а, *m.* slide projector.

сла́лом, а, *m.* (*sport*) slalom.

сла́н|ец, ца, *m.* (*min.*) shale, schist; slate;
гли́нистый с. argillaceous schist; горю́чий
с., нефтено́сный с. oil shale, bituminous
shale.

сла́нцев|ый, *adj.* schistose, schistous; slate,
slaty; shale; ~ое ма́сло shale oil; с. пласт
schist.

сла|сти́ть, щу́, сти́шь, *impf.* (*of* по~) to
sweeten.

сластолю́б|ец, ца, *m.* voluptuary.

сластолюби́в|ый (~, ~а), *adj.* volup-
tuous.

сластолюби|е, я, *n.* voluptuousness.

сласт|ь, и, *pl.* ~и, ~е́й, *f.* **1.** (*pl.*) sweets,
sweetmeats. **2.** (*fig.*) delight, pleasure; что
за с. гуля́ть одному́? what fun is there in
going out alone?

слать, шлю, шлёшь, *impf.* to send; с.
приве́т to send greetings.

слаща́в|ый (~, ~а), *adj.* (*lit. and fig.*) sugary,
sickly-sweet.

сла́ще, *comp.* of сла́дкий.

сле́ва, *adv.* (от) on the left (of), to the left
(of); с. напра́во from left to right.

слег|а́, и́, *pl.* ~и, ~, ~а́м, *f.* beam.

слегка́, *adv.* lightly, gently; slightly, somewhat; с. суту́литься to stoop slightly; с.
гла́дить to stroke gently.

след[1], а(у), *pl.* ~ы́, ~о́в, *m.* **1.** track; trail,
footprint, footstep; верну́ться по свои́м
~а́м to retrace one's steps; замести́ свои́
~ы́ to cover up one's tracks; идти́ по

чьим-н. ~áм (*fig.*) to follow in someone's footsteps. **2.** (*fig.*) trace, sign, vestige; ~а нет егó there is no trace of it; ~ы óспы pockmarks. **3.** sole (*of the foot*).

след²: не с. (*coll.*) = не ~ует.

сле|ди́ть¹, жу́, ди́шь, *impf.* (за+*i.*) **1.** to watch; to track; to shadow; с. глазáми за полётом мячá to follow (with one's eyes) the flight of a ball. **2.** (*fig.*) to follow; to keep up (with); с. за междунарóдными собы́тиями to keep up with international affairs. **3.** to look after; to keep an eye (on); с. за детьми́ to look after children; с. за порядком to keep order; с. за тем, чтóбы to see to it that.

сле|ди́ть², жу́, ди́шь, *impf.* (*of* на~) (на+*p.*) to mark; to leave traces (on), leave footmarks, footprints (on).

следовани|е, я, *n.* movement, proceeding; пóезд дáльнего ~я long-distance train; во врéмя ~я пóезда while the train is moving; на всём пути́ ~я all along the line, throughout the entire journey; по пути́ ~я войск (*mil.*) along the line of march.

следовател|ь, я, *m.* investigator.

следовательно, *conj.* consequently, therefore, hence.

след|овать¹, ую, *impf.* (*of* по~) **1.** (за+*i.*) to follow, go after; с. за кем-н. по пятáм to follow hard on someone's heels. **2.** (+*d.*) to follow; с. отцу́ to follow in one's father's footsteps. **3.** (+*d.*) to follow; to comply (with); с. прáвилам to conform to the rules; с. при́хоти to follow a whim. **4.** (*impf. only*) (до, в+*a.*) to be bound (for); этот пóезд ~ует в Варшáву this train is (bound) for Warsaw. **5.** (*impf. only*) to follow; to result; из э́того ~ует, что мы оши́блись it follows from this that we were mistaken.

след|овать², ует, *impf.* (*impers.*) **1.** (+*d. and inf.*) ought, should; вам ~ует обрати́ться к рéктору you should approach the rector; не ~ует забывáть it should not be forgotten; кудá ~ует to the proper quarter; как и ~овало ожидáть as was to be expected; как ~ует as it should be, properly, well and truly, good and proper. **2.** (+*d.* and с+*g.*) to be owed, be owing; скóлько вам ~ует с меня́? how much do I owe you?; с вас ~ует дéсять рублéй you have ten roubles to pay.

слéдом, *adv.* (за+*i.*) immediately (after, behind); идти́ с. за кем-н. to follow someone close(ly).

следопыт, а, *m.* pathfinder, tracker.

слéдств|енный, *adj. of* ~ие; ~енная коми́ссия committee of inquiry; с. материáл evidence; ~енные óрганы investigation agencies.

слéдстви|е¹, я, *n.* consequence, result; причи́на и с. cause and effect.

слéдстви|е², я, *n.* (*leg.*) investigation; судéбное с. inquest.

слéдуем|ый, *adj.* (+*d.*) due (to); отдáть кáждому ~ое to give each his due.

слéд|ующий, *pres. part. act. of* ~овать *and adj.* following, next; на с. день next day; на ~ующей недéле next week; постановлено ~ующее it has been resolved as follows.

слеж|áться, и́тся, *pf.* (*of* ~ивáться) to become caked; to deteriorate in storage.

слёжива|ться, ется, *impf. of* слежáться.

слёжк|а, и, *f.* shadowing; установи́ть ~у за кем-н. to have someone shadowed.

слез|á, ы́, *pl.* ~ы, ~, ~áм, *f.* tear; крокоди́ловы ~ы crocodile tears; довести́ до ~ to reduce to tears; э́то до ~ оби́дно it is enough to make one weep.

слезá|ть, ю, *impf. of* слезть.

слез|и́ться, и́тся, *impf.* to water; её глазá ~и́лись her eyes were watering.

слезли́в|ый (~, ~а), *adj.* **1.** given to crying. **2.** tearful, lachrymose.

слёзно, *adv.* (*coll.*) tearfully, with tears in one's eyes; (*fig.*) humbly, plaintively.

слёзн|ый, *adj.* **1.** (*anat.*) lachrymal; ~ая железá lachrymal gland; с. протóк lachrymal duct, tear duct. **2.** (*fig., coll.*) humble, plaintive; ~ая прóсьба humble petition.

слезоотделéни|е, я, *n.* tear-shedding; (*med.*) epiphora.

слезотечéни|е, я, *n.* = слезоотделéние.

слезоточи́в|ый (~, ~а), *adj.* **1.** ~ые глазá running eyes. **2.** lachrymatory; с. газ tear-gas.

слез|ть, у, ешь, *past* ~, ~ла, *pf.* (*of* ~áть) (с+*g.*) **1.** to come down (from), get down (from); to dismount (from). **2.** to alight (from), get off; с. с трамвáя to get off a tram. **3.** (*of paint or skin*) to come off, peel.

слеп|éнь, ня́, *m.* gadfly, horse-fly.

слеп|éц, ца́, *m.* blind man.

слеп|и́ть¹, лю́, и́шь, *impf.* to blind; to dazzle.

слеп|и́ть², лю́, ~ишь, *pf. of* лепи́ть.

слеп|и́ть³, лю́, ~ишь, *pf.* (*of* ~ля́ть) **1.** to stick together. **2.** to make by sticking together.

слеп|и́ться, ~ится, *pf.* (*of* ~ля́ться) to stick together.

слепля́|ть(ся), ю(сь), *impf. of* слепи́ть³(ся).

слéп|нуть, ну, нешь, *past* ~, ~ла *and* ~нул, ~нула, *impf.* to become blind, go blind.

слéпо, *adv.* **1.** (*fig.*) blindly; с. повиновáться to obey blindly. **2.** indistinctly.

слеп|óй (~, ~á, ~о), *adj.* **1.** blind (*also fig.*); с. на оди́н глаз blind in one eye; ~áя кишкá blind gut, caecum; с. мéтод маши́нописи touch-typing; с. полёт blind flying; ~ое пятнó (*anat.*) blind spot; *as noun* с., ~óго, *m.* blind person; (*pl., collect.*) the blind. 2. indistinct.

слéп|ок, ка, *m.* mould, copy.

слепорождённый, *adj.* blind from birth.

слепот|á, ы́, *f.* blindness (*also fig.*).

слепы́ш, á, *m.* mole-rat.

слесáрн|ый, *adj.* metal-work, metal worker's; ~ое дéло metal work; ~ая (мастерскáя) metal workshop.

слесáр|ня, ни, *g. pl.* ~ен, *f.* metal workshop.

слéсар|ь, я, *pl.* ~и, ~ей and ~я́, ~éй, *m.* metal worker; locksmith.

слёт, а, *m.* 1. flying together. 2. gathering, meeting; rally.

слётанност|ь, и, *f.* (*of aircrews*) co-ordination.

слетá|ть¹, ю, *pf.* 1. to fly (there and back). 2. (*fig., coll.*) to fly, dash, nip.

слет|áть², áю, *impf. of* ~éть.

слетá|ться¹, юсь, *pf.* to achieve co-ordination in flying.

слет|áться², áюсь, *impf. of* ~éться.

сле|тéть, чу́, ти́шь, *pf.* (*of* ~тáть²) (с+g.). 1. to fly down (from). 2. (*coll.*) to fall down, fall off; с. с лóшади to fall from a horse. 3. to fly away.

слет|éться, и́тся, *pf.* (*of* ~áться²) to fly together; (*of birds*) to congregate.

слечь, сля́гу, сля́жешь, *past* слёг, слеглá, *pf.* to take to one's bed.

слив, а, *m.* 1. pouring away; discharge. 2. sink, drain.

сли́в|а, ы, *f.* 1. plum. 2. plum-tree.

сливá|ть(ся), ю(сь), *impf. of* сли́ть(ся).

сли́в|ки, ок, *no sing.* cream (*also fig.*); снимáть с. (с+g.) to skim the cream (off); с. óбщества the cream of society.

сливн|óй, *adj.* 1. poured together. 2. overflow, waste; ~áя трубá overflow pipe. 3. collection (*of milk and other fluid products*); сдать молокó на с. пункт to deliver milk to the collection point.

сли́в|овый, *adj. of* ~а; с. джем plum jam.

сли́вочник, а, *m.* cream-jug.

сли́вочн|ый, *adj.* cream; creamy; ~ое мáсло butter; ~ое морóженое ice-cream.

сливя́нк|а, и, *f.* plum brandy, slivovitz; sloe-gin.

сли|зáть, жу́, ~жешь, *pf.* (*of* ~зывáть) 1. to lick off. 2. (*fig., coll.*) to copy; он э́то с меня́ слизáл he got that idea from me.

сли́зист|ый (~, ~а), *adj.* mucous; mucilaginous, slimy; ~ая оболóчка (*anat.*) mucous membrane.

слизня́к, á, *m.* 1. slug. 2. (*pejor., coll.*) pathetic, worthless, helpless person.

сли́зыва|ть, ю, *impf. of* слизáть.

слиз|ь, и, *f.* mucus; mucilage, slime.

слимóн|ить, ю, ишь, *pf. of* лимóнить.

слиня́|ть, ет, *pf.* 1. to moult; to slough (off). 2. (*coll.*) to fade (*of colours*).

слип|áться, áется, *impf. of* ~нуться.

сли́п|нуться, нется, *past* ~ся, ~лась, *pf.* (*of* ~áться) to stick together.

сли́тно, *adv.* together.

сли́тн|ый, *adj.* joint, united, continuous; ~ое написáние слов omission of hyphen from words.

сли́т|ок, ка, *m.* ingot, bar; зóлото в ~ках gold bullion.

слить, солью́, сольёшь, *past* слил, слилá, сли́ло, *pf.* (*of* сливáть) 1. to pour out, pour off. 2. to pour together; (*fig.*) to fuse, merge, amalgamate; с. два концéрна to amalgamate two concerns.

сли́ться, солью́сь, сольёшься, *past* сли́лся, слилáсь, *pf.* (*of* сливáться) 1. to flow together. 2. (*fig.*) to blend, mingle; to merge, amalgamate.

слич|áть, áю, *impf. of* ~и́ть.

сличéни|е, я, *n.* collation, checking.

сличи́тельн|ый, *adj.* checking; ~ая вéдомость check-list.

слич|и́ть, у́, и́шь, *pf.* (*of* ~áть) (с+i.) to collate (with), check (with, against).

сли́шком, *adv.* too; too much; э́то с.! this is too much!

слия́ни|е, я, *n.* 1. confluence. 2. (*fig.*) blending, merging, amalgamation; merger.

слобод|á, ы́, *pl.* слóбоды, слобóд, ~áм, *f.* 1. (*hist.*) sloboda (*settlement exempted from normal State obligations*). 2. (*obs.*) suburb.

слобожáн|ин, ина, *pl.* ~е, ~, *m.* (*hist.*) inhabitant of sloboda.

словáк, а, *m.* Slovak.

словáрный, *adj.* 1. lexical; с. состáв языкá vocabulary; с. фонд word stock. 2. lexicographic, dictionary.

словáр|ь, я́, *m.* 1. dictionary; glossary, vocabulary (*to particular text*). 2. (*collect.*) vocabulary.

словáцкий, *adj.* Slovak, Slovakian.

словáчк|а, и, *f.* Slovak (woman.)

словéн|е, ~, *no sing.* (*obs.*) the Slavs.

словéн|ец, ца, *m.* Slovene.

словéнк|а, и, *f.* Slovene (woman).

словéнский, *adj.* Slovene, Slovenian.

словéсник, а, *m.* 1. philologist; student of philology. 2. language and literature teacher.

словéсност|ь, и, *f.* 1. literature. 2. (*obs.*) philology.

словéсн|ый, *adj.* 1. verbal, oral; с. прикáз verbal order. 2. literary. 3. (*obs.*) philological; ~ые науки philology.

словéч|ко, ка, *pl.* ~ки, ~ек, *n., dim. of* слóво (*coll.*); замóлвить с. за когó-н. to put in a word for someone.

словник, а, *m.* glossary; word-list, selection of words (*for inclusion in a dictionary*).

словно, *conj.* **1.** as if. **2.** like, as.

слов|о, а, *pl.* ~**á,** *n.* **1.** (*in var. senses*) word; другими ~áми in other words; одним ~ом in a word; с. в с. word for word; с. зá с. little by little; к ~у (пришлóсь, сказáть) by the way, by the by; на ~áх (*i*) by word of mouth, (*ii*) in word; вéрить нá с. кому-н. в чём-н. to take someone's word for something; человéк ~а a man of his word; игрá ~ play on words; ~ нет (*coll.*) it goes without saying; ~ нет, как тут дýрно пáхнет there is an indescribably nasty smell. **2.** speech, speaking; дар ~а a talent for speaking; свобóда ~а freedom of speech. **3.** speech, address; заключительное с. concluding remarks; надгрóбное с. funeral oration; дать, предостáвить с. (+*d.*) to give the floor; to ask, call upon to speak; пéрвое с. принадлежит товáрищу X I call upon Comrade X to open the discussion; вам принадлежит решáющее с. (*fig.*) the final say rests with you. **4.** (*lit.; hist.*) lay, tale.

словоблýди|е, я, *n.* (mere) verbiage, phrase-mongering.

словоизвержéни|е, я, *n.* (*iron.*) spate of words.

словоизменéни|е, я, *n.* (*ling.*) inflection, accidence.

словолитный, *adj.* type-founding.

словолит|ня, ни, *g. pl.* ~**ен,** *f.* type foundry.

слóвом, *adv.* in a word, in short.

словообразовáни|е, я, *n.* (*ling.*) word-formation.

словообразовáтельный, *adj.* word-forming.

словоохóтливост|ь, и, *f.* talkativeness, loquacity.

словоохóтлив|ый (~, ~а), *adj.* talkative, loquacious.

словопрéни|е, я, *n.* (*obs.*) logomachy.

словопроизвóдный, *adj.* (*ling.*) productive.

словопроизвóдств|о, а, *n.* (*ling.*) derivation.

словосочетáни|е, я, *n.* combination of words; устóйчивое с. set phrase.

словотвóрчеств|о, а, *n.* creation of words.

словоупотреблéни|е, я, *n.* use of words, usage.

словц|ó, á, *n.* (*coll.*) word; для крáсного ~á for effect, in order to be witty.

слог¹, а, *pl.* ~**и, ~óв,** *m.* syllable.

слог², а, *m.* style.

слогов|óй, *adj.* **1.** syllabic; ~**áя** áзбука syllabary. **2.** syllable-forming.

слогообразýющий, *adj.* syllable-forming.

слоéни|е, я, *n.* stratification.

слоёный, *adj.* с. пирóг puff-pastry pie; с. детéктор (*phys.*) sandwich detector.

сложéни|е, я, *n.* **1.** adding; composition; (*math.*) addition; с. сил (*phys.*) composition of forces. **2.** build, constitution; крéпкого ~я of strong build, sturdily-built.

слóж|енный, *p.p.p. of* ~**ить.**

сложён|ный (~, ~á), *adj.* formed, built; хорошó с. well built, of fine physique.

сложи|вшийся, *past part. of* ~**ться;** вполнé с. fully developed, fully formed.

слож|ить¹, ý, ~ишь, *pf.* **1.** (*impf.* склáдывать) to put (together), lay (together); to pile, heap, stack; с. свои вéщи в сундýк to pack one's things in a trunk. **2.** (*impf.* склáдывать) to add (up). **3.** (*impf.* склáдывать) to fold (up); с. вдвóе to fold in two; с. рýки to give up the struggle; ~á рýки with arms folded; (*fig.*) idle. **4.** (*impf.* слагáть) to make up, compose; с. пéсню to compose a song.

слож|ить², ý, ~ишь, *pf.* **1.** (*impf.* склáдывать) to take off, put down, set down; с. груз to set down a load. **2.** (*impf.* слагáть) (с+*g.*; *fig.*) to lay down; to relieve (of); с. гóлову (*rhet.*) to lay down one's life; с. орýжие to lay down one's arms; с. с себя обязанности to resign; с. наказáние to remit a punishment.

слож|иться¹, ýсь, ~ишься, *pf.* (*of* склáдываться) (с+*i.*) to club together (with); to pool one's resources.

слож|иться², ýсь, ~ишься, *pf.* (*of* склáдываться) to form, turn out; to take shape; to arise; обстоятельства ~ились не осóбенно благоприятно circumstances did not turn out particularly favourably; у меня ~илось убеждéние the conviction has grown up in me.

сложноподчинённ|ый, *adj.* ~**ое** предложéние *gram.*) complex sentence.

сложносокращённ|ый, *adj.* compounded of abbreviations; ~**ое** слóво acronym.

сложносочинённ|ый, *adj.* ~**ое** предложéние (*gram.*) compound sentence.

слóжност|ь, и, *f.* complication; complexity; в óбщей ~и all in all, in sum.

сложноцвéтн|ые, ых, *sing.* ~**ое, ~ого,** *n.* (*bot.*) Compositae.

слóж|ный (~ен, ~нá, ~но), *adj.* **1.** compound; complex, multiple; ~**ное** предложéние (*gram.*) compound or complex sentence; ~**ные** процéнты compound interest; ~**ное** слóво compound (word); ~**ное** числó complex number; с. эфир (*phys.*) ester. **2.** complicated, complex, intricate.

слоист|ый (~, ~а), *adj.* stratified; lamellar; flaky, foliated; (*min.*) schistose, schistous; ~**ые** облакá strati.

сло|ить, ю, ишь, *impf.* to stratify; to make in layers.

сло|й, я, *pl.* **~й,** *m.* layer; stratum (*also fig.*); coat(ing) (*of paint*), film; все ~й населéния all sections of the population.

слóйк|а, и, *f.* puff-pastry.

слом, а, *m.* pulling down, demolition, breaking up; пойти на с. to be scrapped.

сломá|ть(ся), ю(сь), *pf. of* ломáть(ся).

слом|и́ть, лю, ~ишь, *pf.* to break, smash; (*fig.*) to overcome; ~и́ гóлову (*coll.*) like mad, at breakneck speed.

слом|и́ться, лю́сь, ~ишься, *pf.* to break.

слон, á, *m.* 1. elephant; дéлать из мýхи ~á to make mountains out of mole-hills; ~á не примéтить to miss the point. 2. (*chess*) bishop.

слон|ёнок, ёнка, *pl.* **~я́та, ~я́т,** *m.* elephant calf.

слони́х|а, и, *f.* she-elephant, cow-elephant.

слонóвост|ь, и, *f.* (*med.*) elephantiasis.

слонóв|ый, *adj. of* слон; elephantine; ~ая болéзнь = ~ость; ~ая бумáга ivory paper; ~ая кость ivory.

слоня́|ться, юсь, *impf.* (*coll.*) to loiter about, mooch about.

слуг|á, и́, *pl.* **~и, ~,** *m.* 1. servant. 2. man, manservant.

служáк|а, и, *m.* (*coll.*) campaigner; old hand, veteran.

служáнк|а, и, *f.* maid, maidservant, housemaid.

служáщ|ий, его, *m.* employee; white--collar worker, office worker.

слýжб|а, ы, *f.* 1. (*in var. senses*) service; work; employment; действи́тельная с. (*mil.*) active service, service with the colours; идти на ~у to go to work; быть на ~е у когó-н. to be in someone's employ, work for someone; по делáм ~ы on official business; сослужи́ть комý-н. ~у to do someone a good turn, stand someone in good stead; не в ~у, а в дрýжбу (*coll.*) as a favour. 2. (special) service; с. движéния (*railways*) traffic management; с. пути́ (*railways*) track maintenance; с. свя́зи (*mil.*) signals service; ~ы ты́ла (*mil.*) supply services. 3. *pl.* (*obs.*) outbuildings.

служби́ст, а, *m.* (*coll.*) red-tape-monger; martinet.

служéбн|ый, *adj.* 1. *adj. of* слýжба; office; official; work; ~ое врéмя office hours, working hours; ~ое дéло official business; с. наря́д duty roster; ~ая поéздка business trip; в ~ом поря́дке in the line of duty; ~ое прави́тельство (*polit.*) caretaker government; с. простýпок dereliction of duty; с. путь official channels; с. стаж seniority; ~ая характери́стика service record. 2. auxiliary; secondary; ~ ое слóво (*gram.*) connective word.

служéни|е, я, *n.* service, serving.

служи́в|ый, ого, *m.* (*coll., obs.*) soldier.

служи́л|ый, *adj.* (*hist.*) service; ~ые лю́ди, ~ое сослóвие service class (*persons bound by obligations of service, esp. military service, to the Muscovite Russian state*).

служи́тел|ь, я, *m.* 1. (*obs.*) servant, attendant. 2. votary, devotee; с. кýльта priest, minister.

служ|и́ть, ý, ~ишь, *impf.* (*of* по~) 1. (+*d.*) to serve, devote oneself (to). 2. (+*i.*) to serve (as); to work (as), be employed (as), be; с. в áрмии to serve in the Army; он ~ит дипломати́ческим курьéром he is (employed as) a diplomatic courier; с. доказáтельством (+*g.*) to serve as evidence (of). 3. *impf. only* (+*i. or* для) to serve (for), do (for), be used (for); гости́ная ~ит нам и спáльней our sitting-room serves also for a bedroom. 4. to be in use, do duty, serve; мой стáрый пластмáссовый плащ ещё ~ит my old plastic mac(k)intosh is still in use. 5. (*eccl.*) to celebrate; to conduct, officiate (at); с. обéдню to celebrate mass. 6. *impf. only* (*of a dog*) to (sit up and) beg.

слýжк|а, и, *m.* (*eccl.*) lay brother.

слукáв|ить, лю, ишь, *pf. of* лукáвить.

слуп|и́ть, лю́, ~ишь, *pf. of* лупи́ть.

слух, а, *m.* 1. hearing, ear; абсолю́тный с. absolute pitch; игрáть по ~у, на с. to play by ear; онá вся обрати́лась в с. she was all ears. 2. rumour; hearsay; есть с., что it is rumoured that; ни ~у ни дýху (о+*p.*) (*coll.*) not a word has been heard (of).

слухáч, á, *m.* monitor.

слухов́|óй, *adj.* acoustic, auditory, aural; с. аппарáт hearing aid; с. нерв (*anat.*) auditory nerve; ~óе окнó dormer(-window); с. рожóк, ~áя трýбка ear-trumpet.

случá|й, я, *m.* 1. case; во вся́ком ~е in any case, anyhow, anyway; ни в кóем ~е in no circumstances; в лýчшем, хýдшем ~е at best, at worst; в проти́вном ~е otherwise; в такóм ~е in that case; в ~е чегó (*coll.*) if anything crops up; на вся́кий с. to be on the safe side, just in case; на крáйний с. in case of special emergency; по ~ю (+*g.*) by reason (of), on account (of), on the occasion (of); купи́ть по ~ю (*coll.*) to buy secondhand. 2. event, incident, occurrence; несчáстный с. accident. 3. opportunity, occasion, chance; упусти́ть удóбный с. to miss an opportunity; при ~е when an opportunity offers; при ~е я емý сообщý I will inform him when I have the chance; стихи́ на с. occasional verse; от ~я к ~ю occasionally. 4. chance.

случáйно, *adv.* 1. by chance, by accident, accidentally; не с. он приéхал как раз вчерá it was no accident that he came yesterday; я с. подслýшал их разговóр

I happened to overhear their conversation.
2. by any chance; вы, с., не ви́дели моего́
зо́нтика? have you by any chance seen my
umbrella?

случа́йност|ь, и, *f.* chance; по счастли́вой
~и by a lucky chance, by sheer luck.

случа́|йный (~ен, ~йна), *adj.* **1.** accidental,
fortuitous; ~йная встре́ча chance meeting;
~йное уби́йство (*leg.*) homicide by misad-
venture. **2.** chance, casual, incidental; с.
за́работок casual earnings.

случ|а́ть, а́ю, *impf. of* ~и́ть.

случ|а́ться, а́ется, *impf. of* ~и́ться.

случ|и́ть, у́, и́шь, *pf.* (*of* ~а́ть) (с+*i.*) (*of
animals*) to couple (with), pair (with), mate
(with).

случ|и́ться¹, и́тся, *pf.* (*of* ~а́ться) (*of
animals*) to couple, pair, mate.

случ|и́ться², и́тся, *pf.* (*of* ~а́ться) **1.** to
happen, come about, come to pass, befall;
что бы ни ~и́лось whatever happens, come
what may. **2.** (*impers.*; +*d. and inf.*) to
happen; мне ~и́лось попа́сть в Москву́
I happened to land up in Moscow. **3.** (*coll.*)
to turn up, show up; ~и́лось у меня́ как
раз пять рубле́й I happened to have just
five roubles on me.

случк|а, и, *f.* coupling, pairing, mating.

слу́шани|е, я, *n.* **1.** audition; hearing; с.
ле́кции attendance at a lecture. **2.** (*leg.*)
hearing.

слу́шател|ь, я, *m.* **1.** hearer, listener; (*pl.*;
collect.) audience. **2.** student.

слу́ша|ть, ю, *impf.* (*of* по~) **1.** to listen (to),
hear; с. ле́кцию to attend a lecture; ~й(те)!
(*coll.*) listen!, look here!; ~ю! at your service!, very good!; (*on telephone*) hullo! **2.** to
attend lectures (on), go to lectures (on).
3. to listen (to), obey. **4.** (*leg.*) to hear.

слу́ша|ться, юсь, *impf.* (*of* по~) ((*obs.*)+*g.*)
1. to listen (to), obey; с. руля́ (*naut.*) to
answer the helm; ~юсь! (*mil.*) yes, sir!
(*indicating readiness to carry out order*). **2.** *pass.
of* ~ть.

слуш|о́к, ка́, *m.* (*coll.*) rumour.

слы|ть, ву́, вёшь, *past* ~л, ~ла́, ~ло, *impf.*
(*of* про~) (+*i. or* за+*a.*) to have a reputation (for), be said (to); to pass (for); он
~вёт безде́льником, за безде́льника he
has a reputation for being an idler.

слыха́ть, *no pres., impf.* **1.** to hear; что у вас
с.? (*coll.*) what news have you of yourself?,
tell us what you have been up to!; ничего́
не с. nothing can be heard. **2.** *as adv.* (*coll.*)
apparently, it seems; ты, с., пи́шешь
но́вый рома́н we hear you are writing a
new novel.

слы́ш|ать, у, ишь, *impf.* (*of* у~) **1.** to hear;
~ишь, ~ите (*coll.*) do you hear? (*emphasizing command or direction*). **2.** (*impf. only*) to

have the sense of hearing; не с. to be hard
of hearing. **3.** to notice; to feel, sense. **4.**
(*coll.*) to smell.

слы́ш|аться, ится, *impf.* (*of* по~) to be
heard; to be audible.

слы́шимост|ь, и, *f.* audibility.

слы́шим|ый (~, ~а), *adj.* audible.

слы́шно¹, *adv.* audibly.

слы́шно², *as pred., impers.* **1.** one can hear;
бы́ло с., как она́ рыда́ла one could hear
her sobbing; нам никого́ не́ было с. we
could not hear anyone. **2.** (*coll.*); что с.?
what news?, any news?; о них ничего́ не
с. nothing has been heard of them. **3.** (*coll.*)
it is said, they say, it is rumoured; она́,
с., бере́менна they say she is pregnant.

слы́ш|ный (~ен, ~на́, ~но) *adj.* audible.

слю́бится, *see* стерпе́ться.

слюд|а́, ы́, *f.* mica.

слюдяно́й, *adj.* mica, micaceous.

слюн|а́, ы́, *f.* saliva.

слюн|и, е́й, *no sing.* (*coll.*) slobber, spittle;
пусти́ть с. to slobber, drivel; распусти́ть
с. (*coll.*) to dither, become a ditherer.

слюн|и́ть, ю́, и́шь, *impf.* **1.** (*pf.* по~) to wet
with saliva. **2.** (*pf.* за~) to slobber over.

слюн|ки, ок, *no sing., dim. of* ~и; от э́того с.
теку́т it makes one's mouth water.

слюноотделе́ни|е, я, *n.* salivation.

слюнотече́ни|е, я, *n.* (*med.*) excessive saliva-
tion; (*fig., pejor.*) sentimentalism.

слюнтя́|й, я, *m.* (*coll.*) ditherer.

слюня́в|ить, лю, ишь, *impf.* (*coll.*) to slobber
over.

слюня́вый, *adj.* (*coll.*) dribbling, drivelling.

сля́котный, *adj.* slushy.

сля́кот|ь, и, *f.* slush.

сля́мз|ить, ю, ишь, *pf. of* ля́мзить.

сма́|зать, жу, жешь, *pf.* (*of* ~зывать) **1.** to
oil, lubricate; to grease; с. йо́дом to paint
with iodine. **2.** (*fig., coll.*) to grease the
palm (of), grease the wheels (of). **3.** to
smudge; to rub off. **4.** (*fig., coll.*) to slur
(over). **5.** (*fig., coll.*) to bash, dot.

сма́|заться, жусь, жешься, *pf.* (*of* ~зывать-
ся) **1.** to grease oneself. **2.** (*of paint, etc.*) to
become smudged; to come off.

сма́зк|а, и, *f.* **1.** oiling, lubrication; greas-
ing. **2.** oil, lubricant; grease.

смазли́в|ый (~, ~а), *adj.* (*coll.*) pretty.

смазн|о́й, *adj.* ~ы́е сапоги́ blacked boots.

сма́зочн|ый, *adj. of* сма́зка; ~ая кана́вка
(*tech.*) lubricating groove, oil groove; ~ая
коро́бка oil can; ~ое ма́сло lubricating
oil; с. материа́л, ~ое сре́дство lubricant.

сма́зчик, а, *m.* greaser.

сма́зывани|е, я, *n.* **1.** oiling, lubrication;
greasing. **2.** (*fig.*) slurring over.

сма́зыва|ть(ся), ю(сь), *impf. of* сма́зать(ся).

смак, а, *m.* (*coll.*) relish, savour (*also fig.*); со ᴗ́ом with relish, with gusto.

смак|овáть, ýю, *impf.* (*coll.*) to savour; to eat, drink with relish; to relish (*also fig.*).

смáл|ец, ьца, *m.* lard.

смáльт|а, ы, *f.* smalt.

смáнива|ть, ю, *impf. of* сманúть.

сман|úть, ю, ᴗ́ишь, *pf.* (*of* ᴗ́ивать) to entice, lure.

смарáгд, а, *m.* (*obs.*) emerald.

смарáгд|овый, *adj. of* ᴗ.

смастер|úть, ю, úшь, *pf. of* мастерúть.

смáтыва|ть, ю, *impf. of* смотáть.

смáтыва|ться, юсь, *impf. of* смотáться.

смáхива|ть¹, ю, *impf. of* смахнýть.

смáхива|ть², ю, *impf.* (на + *a.*; *coll.*) to look like, resemble.

смах|нýть, нý, нёшь, *pf.* (*of* ᴗ́ивать¹) to brush (away, off), flick (away, off), whisk (away, off), flap (away, off); с. пыль (с + *g.*) to dust.

смáчива|ть, ю, *impf. of* смочúть.

смáч|ный (ᴗен, ᴗнá, ᴗно), *adj.* (*coll.*) **1.** savoury, tasty. **2.** (*fig., pejor.*) fruity; ᴗная рýгань colourful language.

смеж|áть, áю, *impf. of* ᴗ́ть.

смеж|úть, ý, úшь, *pf.* (*of* ᴗ́ть) (*obs. or poet.*); с. глазá to close one's eyes.

смéжник, а, *m.* factory producing parts for use by another.

смéжность|ь, и, *f.* contiguity.

смéж|ный (ᴗен, ᴗна), *adj.* adjacent, contiguous, adjoining, neighbouring; ᴗные понятия closely-related concepts; с. ýгол (*math.*) adjacent angle.

смекáлист|ый (ᴗ, ᴗа), *adj.* (*coll.*) sharp, keen-witted.

смекáлк|а, и, *f.* (*coll.*) native wit, mother wit; nous; sharpness.

смек|áть, áю, *impf.* (*of* ᴗнýть) (*coll.*) to see the point (of), grasp; ᴗаешь, в чём дéло? do you get it?, do you see the point?

смек|нýть, нý, нёшь, *pf. of* ᴗáть.

смеле́|ть, ю, *impf.* (*of* о ᴗ) to grow bold(er).

смéло, *adv.* **1.** boldly; я могý с. сказáть I can safely say; с.! don't be afraid!, have a try! **2.** easily, with ease; в этом зáле с. поместятся пятьсóт человéк this hall will hold five hundred with ease.

смéлост|ь, и, *f.* boldness, audacity, courage; взять на себя с. (+ *inf.*) to take the liberty (of), make bold (to).

смéл|ый (ᴗ, ᴗá, ᴗо), *adj.* bold, audacious, courageous, daring.

смельчáк, á, *m.* (*coll.*) bold spirit; dare-devil.

смéн|а, ы, *f.* **1.** changing, change; replacement; с. караýла changing of the guard; идти на ᴗу (+ *d.*) to come to take the place (of), come to relieve. **2.** (*collect.*) replacements; successors; (*mil.*) relief; готóвить себé ᴗу to prepare successors (*to take one's place, to take over*). **3.** shift; ýтренняя, дневнáя, вечéрняя с. morning, day, night shift; рабóтать в три ᴗы to work in three shifts, work a three-shift system. **4.** change (*of linen, etc.*).

смен|úть, ю, ᴗ́ишь, *pf.* (*of* ᴗ́ять¹) **1.** to change; to replace; (*mil.*) to relieve; с. бельё to change linen; с. завéдующего to replace the manager; с. караýл to relieve the guard; с. шúны to change tyres; с. гнев на мúлость to temper justice with mercy. **2.** to replace, relieve, succeed (someone).

смен|úться, юсь, ᴗ́ишься, *pf.* (*of* ᴗ́яться) **1.** to hand over; (*mil.*) to be relieved; с. с дежýрства to go off duty. **2.** (+ *i.*) to give place (to); дневнóй зной ᴗ́ился прохлáдой вéчера the day's heat gave way to the coolness of evening.

смéнность|ь, и, *f.* shift system, shiftwork.

смéнн|ый, *adj.* **1.** shift; с. мáстер shift foreman; ᴗая рабóта shift work. **2.** (*tech.*) changeable; ᴗое колесó spare wheel.

смéнщик, а, *m.* relief (worker); *pl.* (*collect.*) new shift.

сменя|емый, *pres. part. pass. of* ᴗть¹ *and adj.* removable, interchangeable.

смен|ять¹, яю, *impf. of* ᴗ́ть.

смен|ять², яю, *pf.* (на + *a.*; *coll.*) to exchange (for).

смен|яться, яюсь, *impf. of* сменúться.

смерд, а, *m.* (*hist.*) peasant farmer.

смер|дéть, жý, дúшь, *impf.* (*obs.*) to stink.

смерз|áться, áется, *impf. of* ᴗнуться.

смёрз|нуться, нется, *past* ᴗся, ᴗлась, *pf.* (*of* ᴗáться) to freeze together.

смéр|ить, ю, ишь, *pf.* (*coll.*) to measure; с. взглядом to look (someone) up and down, measure at a glance.

смерк|áться, áется, *impf.* (*of* ᴗнуться) to get dark; ᴗáлось it was getting dark, twilight was falling.

смéрк|нуться, нется, *pf. of* ᴗáться.

смертéльно, *adv.* **1.** mortally; с. рáненный mortally wounded. **2.** (*coll.*) extremely, terribly; с. устáть to be dead tired, be dead-beat.

смертéл|ьный (ᴗен, ᴗьна), *adj.* **1.** mortal, deadly enemy; с. удáр mortal blow. **2.** (*coll.*) extreme, terrible.

смéртник, а, *m.* prisoner sentenced to death.

смéртност|ь, и, *f.* mortality, death-rate.

смéрт|ный (ᴗен, ᴗна), *adj.* **1.** mortal; *as noun* с., ᴗного, *m.* mortal; простóй с. ordinary mortal. **2.** death; с. бой fight to the death; с. грех (*eccl.*) mortal sin; семь ᴗных грехóв (*lit.*) the Seven Deadly Sins; ᴗная казнь capital punishment, death

penalty; ~ное ло́же deathbed; на ~ном
одре́ on one's deathbed; с. пригово́р death
sentence; (*fig.*) death-warrant; с. час last
hour(s). **3.** (*fig.*) deadly, extreme.

смертоно́с|ный (~ен, ~на), *adj.* death-
-dealing, mortal, fatal, lethal; с. уда́р
mortal blow.

смертоуби́йств|о, а, *n.* (*obs.*) murder.

смерт|ь, и, *pl.* ~и, ~е́й, *f.* **1.** death, decease;
ве́рная с. certain death; умере́ть голо́дной
~ью to starve to death; умере́ть свое́й
~ью to die a natural death; до́ ~и (*fig.*,
coll.) to death; я уста́л до́ смерти I'm dead
tired; боро́ться не на жизнь, а на с. to
fight to the death; разби́ть на́ с. (*coll.*) to
smash to bits; свиде́тельство о ~и death
certificate; быть при ~и to be dying; двум
~ям не быва́ть, одно́й не минова́ть you
only die once. **2.** с. как *as adv.* (*coll.*)
awfully, terribly; ему́, *etc.*, с. как хо́чется
(+*inf.*) he, *etc.*, is dying (for); мне с. как
хо́чется купа́ться I'm dying for a bathe.

смерч, а, *m.* **1.** waterspout. **2.** sand-storm,
tornado.

смеси́тельный, *adj.* (*tech.*) mixing.

сме|си́ть, шу́, ~сишь, *pf. of* меси́ть.

сме|сти́, ту́, тёшь, *past* ~л, ~ла́, *pf.* (*of*
~та́ть²) **1.** to sweep off, sweep away; с.
кро́шки со стола́ to sweep crumbs off the
table; с. с лица́ земли́ to wipe off the face
of the earth. **2.** to sweep into, together.

сме|сти́ть, щу́, сти́шь, *pf.* (*of* ~ща́ть) **1.** to
displace, remove, move. **2.** (*fig.*) to remove,
dismiss (*from one's post*).

сме|сти́ться, щу́сь, сти́шься, *pf.* (*of* ~ща́ть-
ся) to change position, become displaced.

смес|ь, и, *f.* (*in var. senses*) mixture; blend,
miscellany, medley.

смет|а, ы, *f.* (*fin.*) estimate.

смета́н|а, ы, *f.* soured (cultured) cream.

смет|а́ть¹, а́ю, *pf.* (*of* мета́ть² *and* ~ывать) to
tack (together).

смета́|ть², ю, *pf. of* смести́.

сметк|а, и, *f.* (*coll.*) quickness (in the up-
take); gumption.

сме́тлив|ый (~, ~а), *adj.* quick (in the
uptake).

смет|ный, *adj. of* ~а; ~ные ассигно́вки
budget allowances.

сме́тыва|ть, ю, *impf. of* смета́ть¹.

сме|ть, ю, *impf.* (*of* по~) to dare; to make
bold; не ~й(те)! don't you dare!

смех, а (у), *m.* laughter; laugh; разрази́ть-
ся ~ом to burst out laughing; меня́ раз-
бира́л с. I couldn't help laughing; без ~у
joking apart, in earnest; в с., на́ с., ~а
ра́ди for a joke, for fun, in jest, jokingly;
нам не до ~у we are in no mood for
laughter; с. да и то́лько (*coll.*) one can't
but laugh.

смехот|а́, ы́, *f.* (*coll.*) matter for laughter;
э́то пря́мо с.! this is simply ludicrous!

смехотво́р|ный (~ен, ~на), *adj.* laughable,
ludicrous, ridiculous.

смеш|анный, *p.p.p. of* ~а́ть *and adj.* mixed;
combined; ~анное акционе́рное о́бщест-
во joint-stock company; ~анная опера́ция
(*mil.*) combined operation; телефо́н ~ан-
ного по́льзования party-line; ~анная
поро́да crossbreed; ~анное число́ (*math.*)
mixed number.

смеш|а́ть, а́ю, *pf.* (*of* меша́ть² *and* ~ивать)
1. (c+*i.*) to mix (with), blend (with). **2.** to
lump together. **3.** to confuse, mix up.

смеш|а́ться, а́юсь, *pf.* (*of* ~ива́ться) **1.** to
mix; to (inter)blend, blend in; to mingle;
с. с толпо́й to mingle in the crowd. **2.** to
become confused, get mixed up.

смеше́ни|е, я, *n.* **1.** mixture, blending,
merging. **2.** confusion, mixing up; с.
поня́тий confusion of ideas.

сме́шива|ть(ся), ю(сь), *impf. of* смеша́ть-
(ся).

смеш|и́ть, у́, и́шь, *impf.* to make laugh.

смешли́вост|ь, и, *f.* risibility.

смешли́в|ый (~, ~а), *adj.* risible; easily
amused.

смеш|но́й (~о́н, ~на́), *adj.* **1.** funny, droll;
as pred. ~но́ it is funny, it makes one laugh;
вам ~но́? do you find it funny? **2.** absurd,
ridiculous, ludicrous; э́то — ~но́е пред-
ложе́ние this is an absurd suggestion; до
~но́го to the point of absurdity.

смеш|о́к, ка́, *m.* (*coll.*) chuckle; giggle.

смеща́|ть(ся), ю(сь), *impf. of* смести́ть(ся).

смеще́ни|е, я, *n.* displacement, removal.
2. (*geol.*) slip, heave, upheaval, dislocation.
3. (*radio*) bias.

сме|я́ться, ю́сь, ёшься, *impf.* **1.** to laugh;
с. шу́тке to laugh at a joke. **2.** (над) to
laugh (at), mock (at), make fun (of). **3.** to
joke, say in jest.

сми́л|оваться, уюсь, *pf.* to have mercy,
take pity.

смире́ни|е, я, *n.* humbleness, humility,
meekness.

смире́нник, а, *m.* humble person, meek
person.

смире́нност|ь, и, *f.* humility.

смире́н|ный (~, ~на), *adj.* humble, meek.

смири́тельн|ый, *adj.* ~ая руба́шка strait-
-jacket.

смир|и́ть, ю́, и́шь, *pf.* (*of* ~я́ть) to restrain,
subdue.

смир|и́ться, ю́сь, и́шься, *pf.* (*of* ~я́ться) to
submit; to resign oneself.

сми́рно, *adv.* quietly; с.! (*mil. word of command*) attention!

сми́р|ный (~ен, ~на́, ~но), *adj.* quiet; sub-
missive.

смир|Я́ть(ся), Я́ю(сь), *impf. of* ~и́ть(ся).

смодели́р|овать, ую, *pf. of* модели́ровать.

смо́кв|а, ы, *f.* fig.

смо́кинг, а, *m.* dinner-jacket.

смоко́вниц|а, ы, *f.* fig-tree.

смол|а́, ы́, *pl.* ~ы, *f.* resin; pitch, tar; rosin; иску́сственная c. synthetic resin.

смолёный, *adj.* resined; tarred, pitched.

смоли́ст|ый (~, ~а), *adj.* resinous.

смол|и́ть, ю́, и́шь, *impf. (of* вы~ *and* o~) to resin; to tar, pitch.

смолк|а́ть, а́ю, *impf. of* ~нуть.

смо́лк|нуть, ну, нешь, *past* ~, ~ла, *pf. (of* ~а́ть) to fall silent; *(of sound)* to cease.

смо́лоду, *adv.* from, in one's youth.

смолоку́р, а, *m.* tar-extractor.

смолоку́рени|е, я, *n.* extraction of tar.

смолоку́р|ня, ни, *g. pl.* ~ен, *f.* tar-works.

смоло|ти́ть, чу́, ~ти́шь, *pf. of* молоти́ть.

смоло́ть, смелю́, сме́лешь, *pf. of* моло́ть.

смолч|а́ть, у́, и́шь, *pf.* to hold one's tongue.

смоль, *only in phrase* чёрный как c. jet-black.

смол|яно́й, *adj. of* ~а́; ~яна́я бо́чка tar barrel; c. ка́мень pitchstone; ~яна́я кислота́ resin acid; c. клей resin sizing; ~яно́е ма́сло resin oil; c. соста́в resinous compound.

смонти́р|овать, ую, *pf. of* монти́ровать.

сморгн|у́ть, у́, ёшь, *pf. (coll.)* гла́зом не c. not to turn a hair, not to bat an eyelid.

сморка́|ть, ю, *impf. (of* вы~) c. нос to blow one's nose.

сморка́|ться, юсь, *impf. (of* вы~) to blow one's nose.

сморо́дин|а, ы, *no pl., f.* 1. currant; currant bush. 2. *(collect.)* currants; кра́сная, чёрная c. red currants, black currants.

сморо́дин|ный, *adj. of* ~а.

сморч|о́к, ка́, *m.* 1. morel *(mushroom).* 2. *(fig., coll.; of person)* shrimp.

сморщ|енный, *p.p.p. of* ~ить *and adj.* wrinkled.

смо́рщ|ить(ся), у(сь), ишь(ся), *pf. of* мо́рщить(ся).

смота́|ть, ю, *pf. (of* сма́тывать) to wind, reel; *(coll.)* c. у́дочки to take to one's heels, make off, clear out.

смота́|ться, юсь, *pf. (of* сма́тываться) *(coll.)* 1. to dash (there and back). 2. to take to one's heels, make off.

смотр, а, *m.* 1. (на ~у́, *pl.* ~ы́) review, inspection; произвести́ c. (+*d.*) to review, inspect. 2. (на ~е, *pl.* ~ы) public showing; c. худо́жественной самоде́ятельности amateur arts' festival.

смотр|е́ть, ю́, ~ишь, *impf. (of* по~) 1. (на+ *a.,* в+*a.*) to look (at); c. в окно́ to look out of the window; c. в глаза́, в лицо́ (+*d.*) to look in the face; c. в о́ба *(coll.)* to keep one's eyes open, be on one's guard; c. сквозь па́льцы

(на+*a.; coll.*) to make light (of), wink (at). 2. to see; to watch; to look through; c. чемпиона́т по те́ннису to see a tennis championship; c. телеви́дение to watch television. 3. to examine; to review, inspect; c. больно́го to inspect a patient. 4. (за+*i.*) to look (after); to be in charge (of), supervise; c. за поря́дком to keep order. 5. (на+*a.; coll.*) to follow the example (of). 6. *impf. only* (в+*a.,* на+*a.*) to look (on to, over); о́кна в мое́й ко́мнате ~ят в сад my windows look on to the garden. 7. *impf. only* (+*i.; coll.*) to look (like); он ~ит простако́м he looks a simple fellow. 8. ~й(те)! mind!, take care!; ~йте не опозда́йте! mind you are not late!; ~йте, чтобы на́шим гостя́м бы́ло удо́бно see that our guests are comfortable. 9. ~я́ (где, как, *etc.*) it depends (where, how, *etc.*); ~я́ (по+*d.*) depending (on), in accordance (with).

смотр|е́ться, ю́сь, ~ишься, *impf. (of* по~) 1. to look at oneself; c. в зе́ркало to look at oneself in the looking-glass. 2. *pass. of* ~е́ть.

смотри́н|ы, ~, *no sing. (hist.)* smotriny *(Russian folk-rite of inspection of prospective bride).*

смотри́тел|ь, я, *m.* supervisor; *(in museum, etc.)* keeper, custodian.

смотров|о́й, *adj.* 1. *(mil.)* review. 2. ~о́е окно́ inspection window; ~о́е отве́рстие sighting aperture *(of gun sight);* ~а́я щель vision slit *(in tank).*

смоч|и́ть, у́, ~ишь, *pf. (of* сма́чивать) to damp, wet, moisten.

смо́|чь, гу́, ~жешь, *past* ~г, ~гла́, *pf. of* мочь.¹

смоше́нни|ча|ть, ю, *pf. of* моше́нничать.

смрад, а, *m.* stink, stench.

смра́д|ный (~ен, ~на), *adj.* stinking.

смугле́|ть, ю, *impf.* to become dark-complexioned.

смуглоли́ц|ый (~, ~а), *adj.* dark-complexioned.

сму́гл|ый (~, ~а́, ~о), *adj.* dark-complexioned.

смугля́нк|а, и, *f.* dark-complexioned woman, girl.

сму́т|а, ы, *f. (obs.)* disturbance, sedition; се́ять ~у to sow discord.

сму|ти́ть, щу́, ти́шь, *pf. (of* ~ща́ть) 1. to embarrass, confuse. 2. to disturb, trouble; c. чей-н. поко́й to disturb someone's peace and quiet.

сму|ти́ться, щу́сь, ти́шься, *pf. (of* ~ща́ться) to be embarrassed, be confused.

сму́т|ный (~ен, ~на́, ~но), *adj.* 1. vague; confused; dim; muffled; ~ные воспомина́ния dim recollections. 2. disturbed; troubled; ~ное вре́мя *(hist.)* Time of Troubles *(1605–13).*

смутья́н, а, *m.* (*coll.*) trouble-maker.

сму́шк|а, и, *f.* astrakhan.

сму́шковый, *adj.* astrakhan.

смуща́|ть(ся), ю(сь), *impf. of* смути́ть(ся).

смуще́ни|е, я, *n.* embarrassment, confusion.

сму|щённый, *p.p.p. of* ~ти́ть *and adj.* embarrassed, confused.

смыв, а, *m.* (*geol.*) wash-out.

смыва́|ть(ся), ю(сь), *impf. of* смы́ть(ся).

смыка́|ть(ся), ю(сь), *impf. of* сомкну́ть(ся).

смысл, а, *m.* 1. sense, meaning; purport; прямо́й, перено́сный с. literal, metaphorical sense; в изве́стном ~е in a sense; в по́лном ~е сло́ва in the true sense of the word; в ~е (+*g.*) as regards. 2. sense, point; име́ть с. to make sense; нет никако́го ~а (+*inf.*) there is no sense (in), there is no point (in). 3. (good) sense; здра́вый с. common sense.

смы́сл|ить, ю, ишь, *impf.* (в+*p.*; *coll.*) to understand.

смыслов|о́й, *adj. of* смысл; ~ы́е отте́нки shades of meaning.

смыть, смо́ю, смо́ешь, *pf.* (*of* смыва́ть) 1. to wash off; (*fig.*) to clear, wipe away; (*mil.*) to wipe out. 2. to wash away; с. волно́й с су́дна to wash overboard.

смы́ться, смо́юсь, смо́ешься, *pf.* (*of* смыва́ться) 1. to wash off, come off. 2. (*fig.*, *coll.*) to slip away.

смычк|а, и, *f.* union; linking.

смыч|ко́вый, *adj. of* ~о́к.

смы́чный, *adj.* (*ling.*) occlusive; stop.

смыч|о́к, ка́, *m.* (*mus.*) bow.

смышлён|ый (~, ~а), *adj.*(*coll.*) clever, bright.

смягч|а́ть(ся), а́ю(сь), *impf. of* ~и́ть(ся).

смягча́|ющий 1. *pres. part. act. of* ~ть; ~ющие вину́ обстоя́тельства extenuating circumstances. 2. *adj.* (*med.*) emollient.

смягче́ни|е, я, *n.* 1. softening. 2. mollification; mitigation; extenuation. 3. (*ling.*) palatalization.

смягч|и́ть, у́, и́шь, *pf.* (*of* ~а́ть) 1. (*impf. also* мягчи́ть) to soften. 2. to mollify; to ease, alleviate; to assuage; с. боль to alleviate pain; с. гнев to assuage anger; с. наказа́ние to mitigate a punishment; с. напряже́ние to ease tension. 3. (*ling.*) to palatalize.

смягч|и́ться, у́сь, и́шься, *pf.* (*of* ~а́ться) 1. to soften, become soft, grow softer. 2. to be mollified; to relent, relax; to grow mild; to ease (off). 3. *pass. of* ~и́ть.

смяте́ни|е, я, *n.* confusion, disarray; commotion.

смяте́н|ный (~, ~на), *adj.* (*obs.*) troubled, perturbed.

смять, сомну́, сомнёшь, *pf.* (*of* мять) 1. to crumple; to rumple; с. пла́тье to crush a dress. 2. (*mil.*) to crush.

смя́ться, сомнётся, *pf.* (*of* мя́ться[1]) to get creased; to get crumpled.

снаб|ди́ть, жу́, ди́шь, *pf.* (*of* ~жа́ть) (+*i.*) to supply (with), furnish (with), provide (with).

снабжа́|ть, ю, *impf. of* снабди́ть.

снабжё́н|ец, ца, *m.* supplier, provider.

снабже́ни|е, я, *n.* supply, supplying, provision.

снабже́н|ческий, *adj. of* ~ие.

сна́доб|ье, ья, *g. pl.* ~ий, *n.* (*coll.*) drug.

сна́йпер, а, *m.* sniper; sharp-shooter.

снару́жи, *adv.* on the outside; from (the) outside.

снаря́д, а, *m.* 1. projectile, missile; shell; управля́емый с. guided missile. 2. contrivance, machine, gadget; гимнасти́ческие ~ы gymnastic apparatus. 3. (*collect.*) tackle, gear; рыболо́вный с. fishing tackle.

снаря|ди́ть, жу́, ди́шь, *pf.* (*of* ~жа́ть) to equip, fit out.

снаря|ди́ться, жу́сь, ди́шься, *pf.* (*of* ~жа́ться) to equip oneself, get ready.

снаря́дн|ый, *adj.* 1. shell, projectile; ammunition; с. по́греб shell-room, (ammunition) magazine. 2. ~ая гимна́стика (*sport*) apparatus work.

снаряжа́|ть(ся), ю(сь), *impf. of* снаряди́ть(ся).

снаряже́ни|е, я, *n.* equipment, outfit; ко́нское с. harness.

снаст|ь, и, *pl.* ~и, ~е́й, *f.* 1. (*collect.*) tackle, gear. 2. (*usu. pl.*) rigging.

снача́ла, *adv.* 1. at first, at the beginning. 2. all over again.

сна́шива|ть, ю, *impf. of* сноси́ть.

снег, а, *pl.* ~а́, *m.* snow; как с. на́ голову like a bolt from the blue.

снеги́р|ь, я́, *m.* bullfinch; пусти́ть ~я́ (*coll.*) to make someone's nose bleed.

снегов|о́й, *adj.* snow; ~а́я ли́ния snow-line.

снегозадержа́ни|е, я, *n.* (*agric.*) retention of snow on fields (*as protection against drought and frost*).

снегозащи́тн|ый, *adj.* ~ое огражде́ние, с. щит snow-fence.

снегоочисти́тел|ь, я, *m.* snow-plough.

снегопа́д, а, *m.* snow-fall.

снегосту́пы, ов, *m.* (*sport*) snow-shoes.

снегота́ялк|а, и, *f.* snow-melter.

снегоубо́рочн|ый, *adj.* snow-removal; ~ая маши́на snow-plough.

снегохо́д, а, *m.* snow-tractor (*tracked vehicle used by Antarctic expeditions*).

Снегу́рочк|а, и, *f.* (*folklore*) Snow-Maiden.

снеда́|ть, ю, *impf.* to consume, gnaw; ~емый за́вистью consumed with envy.

снед|ь, и, *f.* (*obs. or dial.*) food, eatables.

снежи́нк|а, и, *f.* snow-flake.

снѣ́жн|ый, *adj.* snow; snowy; ~ая ба́ба snow man; с. зано́с, с. сугро́б snow-drift; ~ая зима́ snowy winter; снѣ́жная бѣлизна́ snow-whiteness.

снеж|о́к, ка́, *m.* 1. light snow. 2. snowball; игра́ть в ~ки́ to play snowballs, have a snowball fight.

снес|ти́², у́, ёшь, *past* ~, ~ла́, *pf.* (*of* сноси́ть) 1. to take; с. письмо́ на по́чту to take a letter to the post. 2. to fetch down, bring down; с. сунду́к с чердака́ to fetch down a trunk from the attic. 3. (*usu. impers.*) to carry away; to blow off, take off; урага́ном ~ло́ кры́шу a hurricane took the roof off. 4. to demolish, take down, pull down. 5. to cut off, chop off; с. го́лову кому́-н. to chop someone's head off. 6. (*cards*) to throw away.

снес|ти́², у́, ёшь, *pf.* (*of* сноси́ть) to bring together, pile up.

снес|ти́³, у́, ёшь, *pf.* (*of* сноси́ть) to bear, endure, suffer, stand, put up (with).

снес|ти́⁴, у́, ёшь, *pf.* (*of* нести́²) to lay (*eggs*).

снес|ти́сь¹, у́сь, ёшься, *past* ~ся, ~ла́сь, *pf.* (*of* сноси́ться) (с+*i.*) to communicate (with).

снес|ти́сь², ётся, *pf. of* нести́сь².

снет|о́к, ка́, *m.* (*fish*) smelt, sparling.

снижа́|ть(ся), ю(сь), *impf. of* сни́зить(ся).

сниже́ни|е, я, *n.* 1. lowering, reduction; с. зарпла́ты wage cut. 2. (*aeron.*) loss of height; идти́ на с. to reduce height.

сни́|зить, жу, зишь, *pf.* (*of* ~жа́ть) 1. to bring down, lower. 2. (*fig.*) to bring down, lower, reduce; с. себесто́имость to cut production costs; с. стиль (*lit.*) to deflate one's style; с. тон to sing small; с. по до́лжности to reduce, demote.

сни́|зиться, жусь, зишься, *pf.* (*of* ~жа́ться) 1. to descend, come down; (*of an aircraft*) to lose height. 2. (*fig.*) to fall, sink, come down; це́ны ~зились prices have come down.

снизо|йти́, йду́, йдёшь, *past* ~шёл, ~шла́, *pf.* (*of* снисходи́ть) (к) to condescend (to); с. к чьей-н. про́сьбе to deign to grant someone's request.

сни́зу, *adv.* from below (*polit.*; *also fig.*); from the bottom; с. вверх upwards; с. до́верху from top to bottom.

сни́к|нуть, ну, нешь, *pf. of* ни́кнуть.

снима́|ть(ся), ю(сь), *impf. of* снять(ся).

сни́м|ок, ка, *m.* photograph, photo, print.

сни|ска́ть, щу́, ~щешь, *pf.* (*of* сни́скивать) (*obs.*) to gain, get, win; с. чьё-н. расположе́ние to win someone's approval.

сни́скива|ть, ю, *impf. of* сниска́ть.

снисходи́тельност|ь, и, *f.* 1. condescension. 2. indulgence, tolerance, leniency.

снисходи́тель|ный (~ен, ~ьна), *adj.* 1. condescending. 2. indulgent, tolerant, lenient, forbearing.

снисхо|ди́ть, жу́, ~дишь, *impf. of* снизойти́.

снисхожде́ни|е, я, *n.* indulgence, leniency; име́ть с. (к) to be lenient (towards); заслу́живает ~я (*leg. formula*) recommended for mercy.

сни́|ться, снюсь, сни́шься, *impf.* (*of* при~) (+*d.*) to dream; ей ~лось, что she dreamed that; мне ~ся лев I dreamed about a lion.

сноб, а, *m.* snob.

сноби́зм, а, *m.* snobbery.

сно́ва, *adv.* again, anew, afresh.

снова́льный, *adj.* (*text.*) warping.

снова́льщик, а, *m.* (*text.*) warper.

снова́ть¹, сную́, снуёшь, *impf.* to scurry about, dash about.

снова́ть², сную́, снуёшь, *impf.* (*text.*) to warp.

сновиде́ни|е, я, *n.* dream.

сногсшиба́тел|ьный (~ен, ~ьна), *adj.* (*coll., joc.*) stunning.

сноп, а́, *m.* sheaf; с. луче́й shaft of light; с. траекто́рий (*mil.*) cone of fire.

снопвяза́лк|а, и, *f.* (*agric.*) binder.

снопвяза́льн|ый, *adj.* ~ая маши́на = снопвяза́лка.

снорови́ст|ый (~, ~а), *adj.* (*coll.*) quick, smart, clever.

снорови́к|а, и, *f.* skill, knack.

снос¹, а, *m.* 1. demolition, pulling down; дом назна́чен на с. the house is to be pulled down. 2. drift; у́гол ~а (*aeron.*) angle of drift.

снос², а (у), *m.* wear; тако́й мате́рии ~у нет this material won't wear out; не знать ~у to wear well, be very hard-wearing.

снос³: быть на ~ях (*coll.*; *of a pregnant woman*) to be near her time.

сно|си́ть¹, шу́, ~сишь, *pf.* (*of* сна́шивать) to wear out.

сно|си́ть², шу́, ~сишь, *pf.* (*coll.*) to take (*and bring back*); ему́ не с. головы́ it will cost him dear, he will pay for it.

сно|си́ть³, шу́, ~сишь, *impf. of* снести́¹, ², ³.

сно|си́ться, шу́сь, ~сишься, *impf. of* снести́сь¹.

сно́ск|а, и, *f.* footnote.

сно́сно, *adv.* (*coll.*) tolerably, so-so.

сно́с|ный (~ен, ~на), *adj.* (*coll.*) tolerable; fair, reasonable.

снотво́р|ный (~ен, ~на), *adj.* soporific (*also fig.*); ~ное сре́дство soporific, sleeping draught, tablet.

снох|а́, и́, *pl.* ~и, *f.* (father's) daughter-in-law.

сноше́ни|е, я, *n.* (*usu. pl.*) intercourse; relations, dealings; дипломати́ческие ~я diplomatic relations; име́ть ~я (с+*i.*) to have dealings (with); to have (sexual) intercourse (with).

сну|ю́, ёшь, *see* снова́ть.

снюха|ться, юсь, *pf.* (*coll.*) **1.** to get to know one another by scent. **2.** (*pejor.*) to come to terms, come to an understanding.

сня́ти|е, я, *n.* **1.** taking down; с. урожа́я gathering in the harvest. **2.** removal; с. запре́та lifting of a ban; с. с рабо́ты dismissal, the sack. **3.** taking, making; с. ко́пии copying.

снят|о́й, *adj.* ~о́е молоко́ skimmed milk.

сня|ть, сниму́, сни́мешь, *past* ~л, ~ла́, ~ло, *pf.* (*of* снима́ть) **1.** to take off; to take down; с. шля́пу to take one's hat off; с. карти́ну to take down a picture; с. кора́бль с ме́ли to refloat a ship; с. сли́вки с молока́ to skim milk, take the cream off milk; с. пье́су to take a play off; с. урожа́й to gather in the harvest; с. оса́ду to raise a siege; с. с себя́ to divest oneself (of); с. с себя́ отве́тственность to decline responsibility. **2.** (*fig.*) to remove; to withdraw, cancel; с. взыска́ние to remit a punishment; с. запре́т to lift a ban; с. предложе́ние to withdraw a motion; с. с рабо́ты to discharge, sack; с. с учёта to strike off the register; с. с фро́нта to withdraw from the front. **3.** (*mil.*) to pick off. **4.** to take, make; to photograph, make a photograph (of); с. ко́пию (с+g.) to copy, make a copy (of); с. ме́рку с кого́-н. to take someone's measurements; с. план to make a plan; с. показа́ния to take (down) evidence; с. показа́ния га́зового счётчика to read a gas--meter; с. фильм to shoot a film. **5.** to take, rent (*a house, etc.*); с. в аре́нду to take on lease. **6.** (*cards*) to cut.

сня́|ться, сниму́сь, сни́мешься, *past* ~лся, ~ла́сь, *pf.* (*of* снима́ться) **1.** to come off. **2.** to move off; с. с я́коря to weigh anchor; to get under way (*also fig.*). **3.** to have one's photograph taken.

со = с.

соа́втор, а, *m.* co-author.

соа́вторств|о, а, *n.* co-authorship.

соба́к|а, и, *f.* dog; дворо́вая с. watchdog; морска́я с. dogfish; охо́тничья с. gun dog, hound; служе́бная с. guard dog, patrol dog; с.-ище́йка bloodhound; с. на се́не (*coll.*) dog in the manger; уста́ть как с. to be dog-tired; ве́шать ~ (на+а.; *coll.*) to call names, pull to pieces; вот где с. зары́та! so that's the crux of the matter!; so that's what's at the bottom of it!; как ~ нере́занных (+g.; *coll.*) any amount (of); ~у съесть (на+p.; *coll.*) to have at one's fingertips, know inside out.

собаково́д, а, *m.* dog-breeder.

собаково́дств|о, а, *n.* dog-breeding.

соба́|чий, *adj. of* ~ка; canine; ~чья жизнь dog's life; с. хо́лод intense cold.

соба́чк|а¹, и, f. little dog, doggie.

соба́чк|а², и, f. **1.** trigger. **2.** (*tech.*) catch, trip, arresting device; pawl (*of ratchet*).

соба́чник, а, *m.* (*coll.*) dog-lover.

собезья́нни|ть, ю, *pf. of* обезья́нничать.

собе́с, а, *m.* (*abbr. of* социа́льное обеспе́чение) social security department (*of local soviet*).

собесе́дник, а, *m.* collocutor, interlocutor; он — заба́вный с. he is amusing company.

собесе́довани|е, я, *n.* conversation, discussion, interlocution.

собира́тел|ь, я, *m.* collector.

собира́тельный, *adj.* (*gram.*) collective.

собира́тельств|о, а, *n.* collecting.

собира́|ть, ю, *impf. of* собра́ть.

собира́|ться, юсь, *impf.* **1.** (*impf. of* собра́ться) **2.** (+*inf.*) to intend (to), be about (to), be going (to); я ~лся позвони́ть вам I was going to ring you up.

соблаговол|и́ть, ю, и́шь, *pf.* (+*inf.; obs.*) to deign (to), condescend (to); наконе́ц она́ ~и́ла отве́тить finally she deigned to reply.

собла́зн, а, *m.* temptation.

соблазни́тел|ь, я, m.* **1. tempter. **2.** seducer.

**соблазни́тел|ьниц|а, ы. f.* temptress.

соблазни́тел|ьный (~ен, ~ьна), *adj.* **1.** tempting; alluring; seductive. **2.** suggestive, corrupting.

соблазн|и́ть, ю, и́шь, *pf.* (*of* ~я́ть) **1.** to tempt. **2.** to seduce, entice.

соблазн|я́ть, я́ю, *impf. of* ~и́ть.

соблюда́|ть, ю, *impf. of* соблюсти́.

соблюде́ни|е, я, *n.* observance; maintenance; с. обы́чая observance of a custom; с. поря́дка maintenance of order.

соблю|сти́, ду́, дёшь, *past* ~л, ~ла́, *pf.* (*of* ~да́ть) to keep (to), stick to; to observe; с. зако́н to observe a law; с. сро́ки to keep to schedule.

соболе́знова́ни|е, я, *n.* sympathy, condolence.

соболе́зн|овать, ую, *impf.* (+*d.*) to sympathize (with), condole (with).

собо́л|ий, ья, ье, *adj. of* со́боль; с. мех sable.

собо|ли́ный, *adj.* sable; ~ли́ные бро́ви (*poet.*) sable brows.

со́бол|ь, я, *pl.* ~я́, ~е́й *and* ~и, ~ей, *m.* **1.** sable. **2.** (*pl.* ~я́, ~е́й) sable (fur).

собо́р, а, *m.* **1.** (*hist.*) council, synod, assembly; вселе́нский с. ecumenical council; зе́мский с. Assembly of the Land (*in Muscovite Russia*). **2.** cathedral.

собо́рност|ь, и, *f.* (*eccl., philos.*) conciliarism.

собо́р|ный, *adj. of* ~.

собо́ровани|е, я, *n.* (*eccl.*) extreme unction.

собо́р|овать, у́ю, *impf. and pf.* (*eccl.*) to administer extreme unction (to), anoint.

собо́р|оваться, у́юсь, *impf. and pf.* (*eccl.*) to receive extreme unction.

собо́ю = собо́й, *see* себя́.

собра́ни|е, я, *n.* **1.** meeting, gathering; о́бщее с. general meeting; с. правле́ния board meeting. **2.** assembly; учреди́тельное с. constituent assembly. **3.** collection; с. зако́нов code (of laws); с. сочине́ний collected works; по́лное с. сочине́ний complete works.

со́бр|анный, *p.p.p. of* ~а́ть *and adj.*; с. челове́к precise, accurate, self-disciplined person.

собра́т, а, *pl.* ~ья, ~ьев, *m.* colleague; с. по ору́жию brother-in-arms; с. по ремеслу́ fellow-worker, colleague.

собр|а́ть, соберу́, соберёшь, *past* ~а́л, ~ала́, ~а́ло, *pf.* (*of* собира́ть) **1.** to gather, collect, pick; с. цветы́ to pick flowers; с. све́дения to collect information. **2.** to assemble, muster; to convoke, convene; с. войска́ to muster troops; с. всё своё му́жество to muster up one's courage; с. после́дние си́лы to make a last effort. **3.** (*tech.*) to assemble, mount. **4.** to obtain, poll (*stated number or percentage of votes*). **5.** to prepare, make ready, equip; с. кого́-н. в доро́гу to equip someone for a journey; с. на́ стол to lay the table. **6.** (*dressmaking*) to gather, make gathers (in), take in.

собр|а́ться, соберу́сь, соберёшься, *past* ~а́лся, ~ала́сь, ~а́ло́сь, *pf.* (*of* собира́ться) **1.** to gather, assemble, muster; to be amassed. **2.** (в+*a.*) to prepare (for), make ready (for); с. в го́сти to get ready to go away (*to visit someone*). **3.** (+*inf.*) to intend (to), be about (to), be going (to). **4.** (с+*i.*; *fig.*) to collect; с. с ду́хом (*i*) to get one's breath, (*ii*) to pluck up one's courage; to pull oneself together; с. с мы́слями to collect one's thoughts; с. с си́лами to summon up one's strength, brace oneself, nerve oneself. **5.** с. в комо́к to hunch up.

со́бственник, а, *m.* owner, proprietor; земе́льный с. landowner.

со́бственнический, *adj.* possessive, proprietary.

со́бственно 1. *adv.* strictly; с. говоря́ strictly speaking, properly speaking, as a matter of fact; он, с. (говоря́), был прав strictly speaking he was right. **2.** *particle* proper; его́ не интересу́ет с. медици́на he is not interested in medicine proper.

собственнору́чно, *adv.* with one's own hand.

собственнору́чн|ый, *adj.* done, made, written with one's own hand(s); ~ая по́дпись autograph.

со́бственност|ь, и, *f.* **1.** property. **2.** possession, ownership; приобрести́ в с. to become the owner (of).

со́бственн|ый, *adj.* **1.** (one's) own; proper; ~ыми глаза́ми with one's own eyes; в ~ые ру́ки (*inscription on envelope, etc.*) 'personal'; чу́вство ~ого досто́инства proper pride, self-respect; ~ой персо́ной in person; и́мя ~ое (*gram.*) proper name. **2.** true, proper; в ~ом смы́сле in the true sense. **3.** (*tech.*) natural; internal; ~ое сопротивле́ние internal resistance; ~ая ско́рость actual speed; ~ая частота́ (*radio*) natural frequency.

собуты́льник, а, *m.* (*coll.*) drinking companion, boon companion.

собы́ти|е, я, *n.* event; теку́щие ~я current affairs.

сов-, *abbr. of* сове́тский.

сов|а́, ы́, *pl.* ~ы, *f.* owl.

сов|а́ть, сую́, суёшь, *impf.* (*of* су́нуть) to shove, thrust, poke; с. ру́ки в карма́ны to stick one's hands in one's pockets; с. моне́ту кому́-н. в ру́ку to slip a coin into someone's hand; с. нос, с. ры́ло (в+*a.*) (*coll.*) to poke one's nose (into), pry (into).

сов|а́ться, сую́сь, суёшься, *impf.* (*of* су́нуться) (*coll.*) **1.** to push, strain; не зна́вши бро́ду, не су́йся в во́ду (*prov.*) look before you leap. **2.** (в+*a.*; *fig.*) to butt (in), poke one's nose (into).

сов|ёнок, ёнка, *pl.* ~я́та, ~я́т, *m.* owlet.

соверш|а́ть(ся), а́ю, а́ет(ся), *impf. of* ~и́ть(ся).

соверше́ни|е, я, *n.* accomplishment, fulfilment; perpetration.

соверше́нно, *adv.* **1.** perfectly. **2.** absolutely, utterly, completely, totally, perfectly; с. ве́рно! quite right!, perfectly true!, quite so!

совершенноле́ти|е, я, *n.* majority; дости́гнуть ~я to come of age, attain one's majority.

совершенноле́тний, *adj.* of age.

соверше́н|ный[1] (~ен, ~на), *adj.* **1.** perfect. **2.** (*coll.*) absolute, utter, complete, total, perfect; с. идио́т absolute idiot.

соверше́нный[2], *adj.* (*gram.*) perfective.

соверше́нств|о, а, *n.* perfection; в ~е perfectly, to perfection.

соверше́нств|овать, у́ю, *impf.* (*of* у~) to perfect; to develop, improve.

соверше́нств|оваться, у́юсь, *impf.* (*of* у~) (в+*p.*) to perfect oneself (in), to improve.

соверш|и́ть, у́, и́шь, *pf.* (*of* ~а́ть) **1.** to accomplish, carry out; to perform; to commit, perpetrate; с. оши́бку to make a mistake; с. преступле́ние to commit a crime. **2.** to complete, conclude; с. сде́лку to complete a transaction, make a deal.

соверш|и́ться, и́тся, *pf.* (*of* ~а́ться) (*lit.*) 1. to happen. 2. to be accomplished, be completed.

со́ве|стить, щу, сти́шь, *impf.* to shame, put to shame.

со́ве|ститься, щусь, сти́шься, *impf.* (*of* по~) (+*g. or inf.*; *obs.*) to be ashamed (of).

со́вестлив|ый (~, ~а), *adj.* conscientious.

со́вестно, *as pred.*+*d. and inf. or* что to be ashamed; ему́ бы́ло с. проси́ть де́нег he was ashamed to ask for money; как вам не с.! you ought to be ashamed of yourself!

со́вест|ь, и, *f.* conscience; чи́стая, нечи́стая с. clear, guilty conscience; со споко́йной ~ью with a clear conscience; для очи́стки ~и to clear one's conscience; по ~и (говоря́) to be honest; свобо́да ~и freedom of worship; угрызе́ния ~и pangs of conscience; рабо́тать на ~ to work conscientiously.

сове́т¹, а, *m.* advice, counsel; (*leg.*) opinion.

сове́т², а, *m.* 1. Soviet, soviet. 2. council. С. Безопа́сности Security Council. 3. council, conference; вое́нный с. council of war.

сове́т³, а, *m.* (*arch.*) concord, harmony.

сове́тник, а, *m.* 1. adviser. 2. (*title of office*) councillor.

сове́т|овать, ую, *impf.* (*of* по~) (+*d.*) to advise.

сове́т|оваться, уюсь, *impf.* (*of* по~) (с+*i.*) to consult, ask advice (of), seek advice (from).

сове́то́лог, а, *m.* Sovietologist.

сове́тологи|я, и, *f.* Sovietology.

сове́тск|ий, *adj.* 1. Soviet, of the Soviet Union; ~ая власть Soviet power, the Soviet régime; с. наро́д the Soviet people; С. Сою́з the Soviet Union. 2. soviet (= *of local soviets*); ~ие рабо́тники officials of the soviets; ~ое строи́тельство development of the soviets.

сове́тчик, а, *m.* adviser, counsellor.

совеща́ни|е, n. conference, meeting; с. на верха́х summit conference.

совеща́тельный, *adj.* consultative, deliberative.

совеща́|ться, юсь, *impf.* 1. (o+*p.*) to deliberate (on, about), consult (on, about). 2. (с+*i.*) to confer (with), consult.

сов|и́ный, *adj. of* ~а́; owlish.

совлада́|ть, ю, *pf.* (с+*i.*; *coll.*) to control; с. с собо́й to control oneself.

совладе́л|ец, ьца, *m.* joint owner, joint proprietor.

совладе́ни|е, я, n. joint ownership.

совмести́мост|ь, и, *f.* compatibility.

совмести́м|ый (~, ~а), *adj.* compatible.

совмести́тел|ь, я, m. person holding more than one office, combining jobs; pluralist.

совмести́тельств|о, а, n. holding of more than one office; pluralism; рабо́тать по ~у to hold more than one office, combine jobs.

совмести́тельств|овать, ую, *impf.* to hold more than one office, combine jobs.

совме|сти́ть, щу́, сти́шь, *pf.* (*of* ~ща́ть²) to combine.

совме|сти́ться, сти́тся, *pf.* (*of* ~ща́ться) 1. to coincide. 2. to be combined, combine.

совме́стно, *adv.* in common, jointly.

совме́стн|ый, *adj.* joint, combined; ~ые де́йствия concerted action; (*mil.*) combined operations; ~ое заседа́ние joint sitting; ~ое обуче́ние co-education; ~ая рабо́та team-work.

совмеща́|ть¹, ю, *impf.* to hold more than one office, combine jobs.

совмеща́|ть²(ся), ю(сь), *impf. of* совмести́ть(ся).

совми́н, а, m. (*abbr. of* Сове́т Мини́стров) Council of Ministers.

совнарко́м, а, m. (*abbr. of* Сове́т Наро́дных Комисса́ров; *re-named, in 1946,* Сове́т Мини́стров) Council of People's Commissars.

совнархо́з, а, m. (*abbr. of* Сове́т наро́дного хозя́йства) (*hist.*) Council of National Economy (*central or regional economic management board in U.S.S.R.*).

сов|о́к, ка́, m. shovel, scoop; садо́вый с. trowel; с. для му́сора dustpan.

совокуп|и́ть, лю́, и́шь, *pf.* (*of* ~ля́ть) to combine, unite.

совокуп|и́ться, лю́сь, и́шься, *pf.* (*of* ~ля́ться) (с+*i.*) to copulate (with).

совокупле́ни|е, я, n. copulation.

совокупля́|ть(ся), ю(сь), *impf. of* совокупи́ть(ся).

совоку́пно, *adv.* in common, jointly.

совоку́пност|ь, и, f. aggregate, sum total; totality; в ~и in the aggregate; по ~и (+*g.*) on the basis (of), on the strength (of).

совоку́пн|ый, *adj.* joint, combined, aggregate; ~ые уси́лия combined efforts.

совою́ющий, *adj.* co-belligerent.

совпада́|ть, ю, *impf. of* совпа́сть.

совпаде́ни|е, я, n. coincidence.

совпа́|сть, ду́, дёшь, *past* ~л, *pf.* (*of* ~да́ть) 1. (с+*i.*) to coincide (with); части́чно с. to overlap. 2. to agree, concur, tally; их показа́ния не ~ли their evidence did not agree.

соврати́тел|ь, я, m. perverter, seducer.

совра|ти́ть, щу́, ти́шь, *pf.* (*of* ~ща́ть) to pervert, seduce; с. с пути́ и́стинного to lead astray.

совра|ти́ться, щу́сь, ти́шься, *pf.* (*of* ~ща́ться) to go astray.

совр|а́ть, у́, ёшь, *past* ~а́л, ~ала́, ~а́ло, *pf. of* врать.

соврашá|ть(ся), ю(сь), *impf. of* совратúть-(ся).

соврашéни|е, я, *n.* perverting, seducing, seduction.

совремéнник, а, *m.* contemporary.

совремéнност|ь, и, *f.* 1. contemporaneity. 2. the present (time).

совремéн|ный (~ен, ~на), *adj.* 1. (+*d.*) contemporaneous (with), of the time (of); ~ные Ивáну Грóзному понятия ideas of the time of Ivan the Terrible. 2. contemporary, present-day; modern; up-to-date; ~ная англúйская литератýра modern English literature.

совсéм, *adv.* quite, entirely, completely, altogether; с. не not at all, not in the least; с. не то nothing of the kind.

совхóз, а, *m.* sovkhoz, State farm.

совхóз|ный, *adj. of* ~.

согбéн|ый (~, ~на), *adj.* (*obs.*) bent, stooping.

соглáси|е, я, *n.* 1. consent; assent; с вáшего ~я with your consent; с óбщего ~я by common consent; дать своё с. to give one's consent. 2. agreement; в ~и (с+*i.*) in accordance (with). 3. accord; concord, harmony.

согласúтельн|ый, *adj.* conciliatory; ~ая комúссия conciliation commission.

согла|сúть, шý, сúшь, *pf.* (*of* ~шáть) to reconcile.

согла|сúться, шýсь, сúшься, *pf.* (*of* ~шáть-ся) 1. (на+*a.* or +*inf.*) to consent (to), agree (to). 2. (с+*i.*) to agree (with), concur (with).

соглáсно, *adv.* 1. in accord, in harmony, in concord; петь с. to sing in harmony. 2. *as prep.* (+*d.* or с+*i.*) in accordance (with); according (to); с. договóру in accordance with the treaty, under the treaty.

соглáсност|ь, и, *f.* harmony, harmoniousness.

соглáс|ный¹ (~ен, ~на), *adj.* 1. (на+*a.*) agreeable (to); онú нé были ~ны на нáши услóвия they would not agree to our conditions. 2. (с+*i.*) in agreement (with), concordant (with); быть ~ным to agree (with); ~ен, ~на, ~ны? do you agree? 3. harmonious, concordant.

соглáсн|ый², *adj.* (*gram.*) consonant(al); *as noun* с., ~ого, *m.* consonant.

согласовáни|е, я, *n.* 1. co-ordination; concordance, agreement. 2. (*gram.*) concord, agreement; с. времён sequence of tenses.

согласóванност|ь, и, *f.* co-ordination; с. во врéмени synchronization.

согласóв|анный, *p.p.p. of* ~áть *and adj.* co-ordinated; ~анные дéйствия concerted action; с. текст agreed text.

соглас|овáть, ýю, *pf.* (*of* ~óвывать) (с+*i.*)

1. to co-ordinate (with). 2. с. что-н. с кем-н. to submit something to someone's approval; to come to an agreement with someone about something. 3. (*gram.*) to make agree (with).

соглас|овáться, ýется, *impf. and pf.* (с+*i.*) 1. to accord (with); to conform (to). 2. (*gram.*) to agree (with).

согласóвыва|ть, ю, *impf. of* согласовáть.

соглашáтел|ь, я, *m.* (*polit.*; *pejor.*) compromiser; appeaser.

соглашáтель|ский, *adj. of* ~; ~ская полúтика policy of compromise, appeasement policy.

соглашáтельств|о, а, *n.* (*polit.*; *pejor.*) compromise, appeasement.

соглашá|ть(ся), ю(сь), *impf. of* согласúть-(ся).

соглашéни|е, я, *n.* 1. agreement, understanding. 2. agreement, covenant; заключúть с. to conclude an agreement.

соглядáта|й, я, *m.* (*obs.*) spy.

согнá|ть¹, сгоню, сгóнишь, *past* ~л, ~лá, ~ло, *pf.* (*of* сгонять) to drive away.

согнá|ть², сгоню, сгóнишь, *past* ~л, ~лá, ~ло, *pf.* (*of* сгонять) to drive together, round up.

согн|ýть, ý, ёшь, *pf.* (*of* гнуть *and* сгибáть) to bend, curve, crook.

согн|ýться, ýсь, ёшься, *pf.* (*of* гнýться *and* сгибáться) to bend, bow (down); to stoop.

согражданúн, а, *m.* fellow-citizen.

согревáтельный, *adj.* с. компрéсс (*med.*) hot compress.

согревá|ть(ся), ю(сь), *impf. of* согрéть(ся).

согрé|ть, ю, *pf.* (*of* ~вáть) to warm, heat.

согрé|ться, юсь, *pf.* (*of* ~вáться) to get warm; to warm oneself.

согреш|áть, áю, *impf. of* ~úть.

согрешéни|е, я, *n.* sin, trespass.

согреш|úть, ý, úшь, *pf.* (*of* ~áть) (прóтив) to sin (against), trespass (against).

сóд|а, ы, *f.* soda, sodium carbonate; питьевáя с. household soda.

содéйстви|е, я, *n.* assistance, help; good offices.

содéйств|овать, ую, *impf. and pf.* (*pf. also* по~) (+*d.*) to assist, help; to further, promote; to make (for), contribute (to); с. успéху предприятия to contribute to the success of an undertaking.

содержáни|е, я, *n.* 1. maintenance, upkeep, keeping; allowance; дéнежное с. money allowance, financial support; с. под арéстом custody; быть на ~и у когó-н. to be kept, supported by someone. 2. pay; оклáд ~я rate of pay; óтпуск с сохранé-нием ~я holiday(s) with pay. 3. content; кубúческое с. volume; с большúм ~ем (+*g.*) rich (in). 4. matter, substance; content; фо́рма и с. form and content. **5.** content(s); plot (*of a novel, etc.*). **6.** table of contents.

содержа́нк|а, и, *f.* (*obs.*) kept woman.

содержа́тел|ь, я, *m.* (*obs.*) landlord (*of an inn, etc.*).

содержа́тел|ьный (~ен, ~ьна), *adj.* rich in content; ~ьное письмо́ interesting letter.

содерж|а́ть, у́, ~ишь, *impf.* **1.** to keep, maintain, support; с. семью́ to keep a family. **2.** to keep, have (*a business, enterprise, etc.*); с. магази́н to keep a shop. **3.** (в+*p.*) to keep (*in a given state*); с. в испра́вности to keep going, in working order; с. в поря́дке to keep in order; с. в та́йне to keep (as a) secret; с. под аре́стом to keep under arrest. **4.** to contain; его́ перево́д ~ит мно́го оши́бок his translation contains many mistakes.

содерж|а́ться, у́сь, ~ишься, *impf.* **1.** to be kept, be maintained. **2.** to be kept, be; с. под аре́стом to be under arrest. **3.** (в+*p.*) to be contained (by); в э́той руде́ ~ится ура́н this ore contains uranium.

содержи́м|ое, ого, *n.* contents.

соде́|ять, ю, ешь, *pf.* (*obs. or rhet.*) to commit, carry out.

соде́|яться, ется, *pf.* (*obs. or joc.*) to happen.

со́дов|ый, *adj.* soda; ~ая вода́ soda (water).

содокла́д, а, *m.* supplementary report, supplementary paper.

содокла́дчик, а, *m.* reader of supplementary report *or* paper.

содо́м, а, *m.* (*coll.*) uproar, row; подня́ть с. to raise hell.

содра́|ть, сдеру́, сдерёшь, *past* ~л, ~ла́, ~ло, *pf.* (*of* сдира́ть) **1.** to tear off, strip off; с. ко́жу (с+*g.*) to skin, flay; с. кору́ (с+*g.*) to bark. **2.** *pf. only* (*fig., coll.*) to fleece; с. с кого́-н. втри́дорога to make someone pay through the nose.

содрога́ни|е, я, *n.* shudder.

содрог|а́ться, а́юсь, *impf. of* ~ну́ться.

содрог|ну́ться, ну́сь, нёшься, *pf.* (*oj* ~а́ться) to shudder, shake, quake.

содру́жеств|о, а, *n.* **1.** concord; рабо́тать в те́сном ~е (с+*i.*) to work in close co-operation (with). **2.** community, commonwealth; Брита́нское с. на́ций the British Commonwealth.

со́евый, *adj.* soya.

соедине́ни|е, я, *n.* **1.** joining, conjunction, combination. **2.** (*tech.*) joint, join, junction. **3.** (*chem.*) compound. **4.** (*mil.*) formation.

соедин|ённый, *p.p.p. of* ~и́ть *and adj.* united, joint; Соединённое Короле́вство the United Kingdom (*of Great Britain and Northern Ireland*).

соедини́тельн|ый, *adj.* connective, con-

necting; с. брус draw bar; ~ое звено́ connecting link; ~ая коро́бка (*electr.*) junction box; ~ые ско́бки (*typ.*) brace; с. сою́з (*gram.*) copulative conjunction; ~ая ткань (*biol.*) connective tissue; ~ая тя́га coupling rod.

соедин|и́ть, ю́, и́шь, *pf.* (*of* ~я́ть) **1.** to join, unite. **2.** to connect, link; с. по телефо́ну to put through. **3.** (*chem.*) to combine.

соедин|и́ться, ю́сь, и́шься, *pf.* (*of* ~я́ться) **1.** to join, unite. **2.** (*chem.*) to combine. **3.** *pass. of* ~и́ть.

соедин|я́ть(ся), я́ю(сь), *impf. of* ~и́ть(ся).

сожале́ни|е, я, *n.* **1.** regret (for); к на́шему ~ю to our sorrow, regrettably; к ~ю unfortunately. **2.** (к) pity (for).

сожале́|ть, ю, *impf.* (о+*p.* or +что) to regret, deplore.

сожже́ни|е, я, *n.* burning; cremation; с. на костре́ burning at the stake; преда́ть ~ю to commit to the flames.

сожи́тел|ь, я, *m.* **1.** room-mate. **2.** lover.

сожи́тельниц|а, ы, *f.* **1.** room-mate. **2.** mistress.

сожи́тельств|о, а, *n.* **1.** living together, lodging together. **2.** (*fig.*) living together, cohabitation.

сожи́тельств|овать, ую, *impf.* (с+*i.*) **1.** to live (with), lodge (with); to live together. **2.** (*fig.*) to live (with); to live together, cohabit.

сожр|а́ть, у́, ёшь, *past* ~а́л, ~ала́, ~а́ло, *pf. of* жрать.

созва́нива|ться, юсь, *impf. of* созвони́ться.

созва́|ть, созову́, созовёшь, *past* ~л, ~ла́, ~ло, *pf.* **1.** (*impf.* сзыва́ть) to gather; to invite. **2.** (*impf.* созыва́ть) to call (together), summon; to convoke, convene; с. ми́тинг to call a meeting.

созве́зди|е, я, *n.* constellation.

созвон|и́ться, ю́сь, и́шься, *pf.* (*of* созва́ниваться) **1.** (с+*i.*; *coll.*) to speak on the telephone (to). **2.** (о+*p.*; *coll.*) to arrange (*something*) on the phone; мы с тобо́й созвони́мся об э́том we'll arrange that over the telephone.

созву́чи|е, я, *n.* **1.** (*mus.*) accord, consonance. **2.** (*lit.*) assonance.

созву́ч|ный (~ен, ~на), *adj.* **1.** harmonious. **2.** (+*d.*) consonant (with), in keeping (with); произведе́ние, созву́чное эпо́хе a work in keeping with the times.

созда|ва́ть(ся), ю́, ёт(ся), *impf. of* ~ть(ся).

созда́ни|е, я, *n.* **1.** creation, making. **2.** creation, work. **3.** creature.

созда́тел|ь, я, *m.* **1.** creator; founder, originator. **2.** the Creator.

созда́|ть, м, шь, ст, ди́м, ди́те, ду́т, *past* со́здал, ~ла́, со́здало, *pf.* (*of* ~ва́ть) (*in var. senses*) to create; to found, originate; to set up, establish; с. впечатлéние to create the impression, give the impression; с. иллю́зию to create an illusion.

создá|ться, стся, ду́тся, *past* ~лся, ~лáсь, *pf.* (*of* ~вáться) to be created; to arise, spring up; ~лóсь неприя́тное положéние a disagreeable situation arose; у нас ~лóсь впечатлéние, что we gained the impression that.

созерцáни|е, я, *n.* contemplation.

созерцáтел|ь, я, *m.* contemplative person; passive observer.

созерцáтел|ьный (~ен, ~ьна), *adj.* contemplative, meditative.

созерцá|ть, ю, *impf.* to contemplate.

созидáни|е, я, *n.* creation.

созидáтел|ь, я, *m.* creator.

созидáтел|ьный (~ен, ~ьна), *adj.* creative, constructive.

созидá|ть, ю, *impf.* (*no pf.*) to build up.

созна|вáть, ю́, ёшь, *impf.* **1.** *impf. of* ~ть. **2.** to be conscious (of), realize; я́сно с. to be alive (to); он ещё не ~ёт, что он сдéлал he still does not realize what he has done.

созна|вáться, ю́сь, ёшься, *impf. of* ~ться.

сознáни|е, я, *n.* **1.** (*in var. senses*) consciousness; клáссовое с. class-consciousness; потеря́ть с. to lose consciousness; прийти́ в с. to regain, recover consciousness. **2.** recognition, acknowledgement; с. дóлга sense of duty. **3.** confession.

сознáтельност|ь, и, f. **1.** awareness; intelligence, acumen; полити́ческая с. political awareness, political sense. **2.** deliberateness.

сознáтел|ьный (~ен, ~ьна), *adj.* **1.** conscious; politically conscious. **2.** intelligent; у негó ~ьное отношéние к собы́тиям he has an intelligent attitude to events. **3.** deliberate.

сознá|ть, ю, *pf.* (*of* ~вáть) to recognize, acknowledge; с. свою́ оши́бку to recognize one's mistake.

сознá|ться, ю́сь, *pf.* (*of* ~вáться) (в+*p.*) to confess (to); (*leg.*) to plead guilty; нельзя́ не с. it must be confessed.

созорничá|ть, ю, *pf. of* озорничáть.

созревá|ть, ю, *impf. of* созрéть.

созрé|ть, ю, *pf.* (*of* ~вáть) to ripen, mature.

созы́в, а, *m.* calling, summoning; convocation; с. заседáния calling of a meeting; Верхóвный Совéт СССР девя́того ~а ninth U.S.S.R. Supreme Soviet (*i.e. ninth four-year term since adoption of new Soviet Constitution in 1936*).

созывá|ть, ю, *impf. of* созвáть.

соизвóл|ить, ю, ишь, *pf.* (*of* ~я́ть) (+*inf.*; *obs.*) to deign (to), be pleased (to).

соизвол|я́ть, я́ю, *impf. of* ~ить.

соизмери́мост|ь, и, f. commensurability.

соизмери́м|ый (~, ~а), *adj.* commensurable.

соискáни|е, я, *n.* competition; диссертáция на с. дóкторской стéпени doctoral dissertation.

соискáтел|ь, я, m. (+*g.*) competitor (for).

сóйк|а, и, g, pl.* сóек, f. (*orn.*) jay.

со|йти́[1], йду́, йдёшь, *past* ~шёл, ~шлá, *pf.* (*of* сходи́ть) **1.** to go down, come down; to descend, get off, alight; с. с лéстницы to go downstairs; с. с лóшади to dismount; с. на нéт to come to naught. **2.** to leave; с. с дорóги to get out of the way, step aside; с. с рéльсов to be derailed, come off the rails; снег ~шёл the snow has melted; с. со сцéны to leave the stage; (*fig.*) to quit the stage; с. с умá to go mad, go off one's head. **3.** (*of paint, skin, etc.*) to come off.

со|йти́[2], йду́, йдёшь, *pf.* (*of* сходи́ть) **1.** (за+*a.*) to pass (for), be taken (for). **2.** (*coll.*) to pass, go off; ~шлó благополу́чно it went off all right; ~йдёт и так it will do as it is; э́то ~шлó ему́ с рук he got away with it.

со|йти́сь, йду́сь, йдёшься, *past* ~шёлся, ~шлáсь, *pf.* (*of* сходи́ться) **1.** to meet; to come together, gather. **2.** (с+*i.*) to meet, take up (with), become friends (with); to become (*sexually*) intimate (with). **3.** (+*i.*, в+*p. or* на+*p.*) to agree (about); с. в ценé to agree about a price; с. харáктером to get on, hit it off; они́ не ~шли́сь харáктерами they could not get on. **4.** (*fig.*) to agree, tally; счетá не ~шли́сь the figures did not tally.

сок, а (у), *o* ~*e,* в *and* на ~у́, *m.* juice; sap; желу́дочный с. (*physiol.*) gastric juice; (*coll.*) в (пóлном) ~у́ in the prime of life; вари́ться в сóбственном ~у́ to keep oneself to oneself.

соквартирáнт, а, m. flat-sharer, lodgings-sharer.

сóкол[1], а, m. falcon (*also fig., rhet.; of Soviet air aces*); гол как сóкол (*coll.*) as poor as a church mouse.

сóкол[2], а, m. **1.** = ~óк. **2.** (*tech.*) poker, slice bar. **3.** (*dial.*) battering-ram.

соколи́н|ый, *adj. of* сóкол[1]; ~ая охóта falconry; ~ые óчи (*poet.*) hawk eyes.

соколóк, кá, m. (*builder's*) trowel.

сокóльник, а, m. (*hist.*) falconer.

сокóльнич|ий, его, m. (*hist.*) falconer (*boyar in charge of falconry*).

сократи́м|ый (~, ~а), *adj.* **1.** (*math.*) able to be cancelled. **2.** (*physiol.*) contractile.

сокра|ти́ть, щу́, ти́шь, *pf.* (*of* ~щáть) **1.** to shorten; to curtail; to abbreviate; to abridge. **2.** to reduce, cut down; с. расхóды to cut down expenses, retrench; с. штáты to reduce the establishment, cut down the staff. **3.** to dismiss, discharge, lay off. **4.** (*math.*) to cancel.

сокра|ти́ться, ти́тся, *pf.* (*of* ~ща́ться) **1.** grow shorter. **2.** to decrease, decline. **3.** (*coll.*) to cut down (*on expenses*). **4.** (на+ *a.*; *math.*) to be cancelled (by). **5.** (*physiol.*) to contract.

сокраща́|ть(ся), ю(сь), *impf. of* сократи́ть-(ся).

сокраще́ни|е, я, *n.* **1.** shortening. **2.** abridgement; с ~ями abridged, in abridged form. **3.** abbreviation. **4.** reduction, cutting down; curtailment; с. шта́тов staff reduction; уво́лить по ~ю шта́тов to dismiss on grounds of redundancy. **5.** (*math.*) cancellation. **6.** (*physiol.*) contraction; с. се́рд-ца systole.

сокращённо, *adv.* briefly; in abbreviated form.

сокра|щённый, *p.p.p. of* ~ти́ть *and adj.* brief; ~щённое сло́во abbreviation, contraction.

сокрове́нность|ь, и, *f.* secrecy.

сокрове́н|ный (~, ~на), *adj.* secret, concealed; ~ные мы́сли innermost thoughts.

сокро́вищ|е, а, *n.* treasure; ни за каки́е ~а not for the world.

сокро́вищниц|а, ы, *f.* treasure-house, treasury, storehouse, depository (*also fig.*); с. иску́сства treasure-house of art.

сокруш|а́ть, а́ю, *impf. of* ~и́ть.

сокруша́|ться, юсь, *impf.* (о+*p.*) to grieve (for, over); to be distressed (about).

сокруше́ни|е, я, *n.* **1.** smashing, shattering. **2.** (*obs.*) grief, distress.

сокруш|ённый, *p.p.p. of* ~и́ть *and adj.* grief--stricken.

сокруши́тел|ьный (~ен, ~ьна), *adj.* shattering; нанести́ с. уда́р (+*d.*) to deal, strike a crippling blow.

сокруш|и́ть, у́, и́шь, *pf.* (*of* ~а́ть) **1.** to shatter, smash. **2.** (*fig.*) to shatter; to distress.

сокры́ти|е, я, *n.* concealment; с. кра́деного receiving of stolen goods.

сокр|ы́ть, о́ю, о́ешь, *pf.* (*obs.*) to hide, conceal, cover up.

сокр|ы́ться, о́юсь, о́ешься, *pf.* (*obs.*) to hide, conceal oneself.

со|лга́ть, лгу́, лжёшь, лгут, *past* ~лга́л, ~лгала́, ~лга́ло, *pf. of* лгать.

солда́т, а, *g. pl.* ~, *m.* soldier; служи́ть в ~ах (*obs.*) to soldier, be a soldier.

солда́тик, а, *m.* **1.** *dim. of* солда́т. **2.** toy soldier; игра́ть в ~и to play soldiers.

солда́тк|а, и, *f.* soldier's wife.

солдатн|я́, и́, f. (*collect.*; *pejor.*) soldiery.

солда́т|ский, *adj. of* ~; ~ская кни́жка soldier's pay book; ~ская ла́вка canteen.

солда́тчин|а, ы, *f.* **1.** (*hist.*) levy. **2.** military service; soldiering.

солдафо́н, а, *m.* (*coll.*) crude, loud-mouthed soldier.

солева́р, а, *m.* salt-worker.

солеваре́ни|е, я, *n.* salt production.

солева́р|енный (*and* ~ный), *adj. of* ~е́ние; с. заво́д salt-works.

солева́р|ня, ни, *g. pl.* ~ен, *f.* salt-works, saltern.

соле́ни|е, я, *n.* salting; pickling.

солено́ид, а, *m.* (*electr.*) solenoid.

солён|ый, *adj.* **1.** salt; ~ое о́зеро salt lake. **2.** (со́лон, солона́, со́лоно) salty; у меня́ во рту со́лоно I have a salt taste in my mouth. **3.** salted; pickled; с. огуре́ц pickled cucumber; *as noun* ~ое, ~ого, *n.* pickles. **4.** (*fig.*, *coll.*) salty, spicy; с. анекдо́т spicy story. **5.** (*short forms only*) (*fig.*) hot; ему́ со́лоно пришло́сь he got it hot; в Пари́же им со́лоно доста́лось Paris was their undoing; Paris became too hot for them; верну́ться не со́лоно хлеба́вши to come home empty-handed.

соле́нь|е, я, *n.* salted food(s); pickles.

солеци́зм, а, *m.* solecism.

соле́|й, и́, f. (*eccl.*) solium.

солидариза́ци|я, и, f. making common cause.

солидаризи́р|оваться, уюсь, *impf. and pf.* (с+*i.*) to express one's solidarity (with), make common cause (with), identify oneself (with); с. с чьим-н. мне́нием to express one's agreement with someone's opinion.

солида́рно, *adv.* (*leg.*) collectively, jointly.

солида́рност|ь, и, f. **1.** solidarity; из ~и (с+*i.*) in sympathy (with); ста́чка ~и sympathetic strike. **2.** (*leg.*) collective, joint responsibility.

солида́р|ный, *adj.* **1.** (~ен, ~на) (с+*i.*) at one (with), in sympathy (with). **2.** (*leg.*) solidary.

соли́д|ный (~ен, ~на), *adj.* **1.** solid, strong, sound; ~ные зна́ния sound knowledge. **2.** (*fig.*) solid, sound; reliable, respectable; с. челове́к a solid man; с. журна́л respectable magazine. **3.** (*coll.*) respectable, sizable; ~ная су́мма tidy sum. **4.** middle-aged; челове́к ~ных лет a middle-aged man.

соли́ст, а, *m.* soloist.

солите́р, а, *m.* (*min.*) solitaire (diamond).

солитёр, а, *m.* tapeworm.

сол|и́ть, ю́, ~и́шь, *impf.* (*of* по~) **1.** to salt. **2.** to pickle; с. мя́со to corn meat.

со́лк|а, и, f. salting; pickling.

со́лнечн|ый, *adj.* **1.** sun; solar; ~ая ва́нна sun-bath; ~ая вспы́шка (*astron.*) solar flare; ~ое затме́ние solar eclipse; с. луч sunbeam; ~ая пане́ль solar panel; ~ые пя́тна (*astron.*) sun-spots; с. свет sunlight, sunshine; ~ая систе́ма solar system; ~ое

~ое сплете́ние (*anat.*) solar plexus; с. уда́р (*med.*) sunstroke; ~ые часы́ sun-dial. **2.** sunny.

со́лнц|е, а, *n.* sun; го́рное с. artificial sunlight, sun-lamp; ло́жное с. (*astron.*) parhelion; на с. in the sun; гре́ться на с. to sun oneself, bask in the sun; по ~y by the sun; with the sun, clockwise; про́тив ~a against the sun, anti-clockwise.

солнцепёк, а, *m.* на ~е right in the sun, in the full blaze of the sun.

солнцестоя́ни|е, я, *n.* solstice.

со́ло, *indecl.,* *n.* solo (*also as adv.*).

солов|е́й, ья́, *m.* nightingale; восто́чный с. thrush-nightingale.

солове́|ть, ю, ешь, *impf.* (*of* о~) (*coll.*) to become drowsy.

соло́вый, *adj.* light bay.

солов|ьи́ный, *adj. of* ~е́й.

со́лод, а, *m.* malt.

солоди́л|ьня, ьни, *g. pl.* ~ен, *f.* malt-house.

соло|ди́ть, жу́, ди́шь, *impf.* (*of* на~) to malt.

соло́дк|а, и, *f.* liquorice.

соло́дковый, *adj. of* соло́дка; с. ко́рень (*pharm.*) liquorice.

солодо́венный, *adj.* с. заво́д malt-house.

соложе́ни|е, я, *n.* malting.

соло́м|а, ы, *f.* straw; thatch; крыть ~ой to thatch.

соло́менн|ый, *adj.* **1.** straw; ~ая вдова́ grass widow; ~ая кры́ша thatch, thatched roof; ~ая шля́па straw hat. **2.** straw-coloured; ~ые во́лосы straw-coloured hair.

соло́минк|а, и, *f.* straw; хвата́ться за ~y to catch, clutch at a straw.

соло́мк|а, и, *f.* **1.** *dim. of* соло́ма. **2.** match-stick; спи́чечная с. (*collect.*) matchwood. **3.** (*collect.*) straw packing. **4.** stick (of toffee). **5.** (*collect.*) stick-like biscuits.

соломоре́зк|а, и, *f.* (*agric.*) chaff-cutter.

солони́н|а, ы, *f.* salted beef, corned beef.

соло́нк|а, и, *f.* salt-cellar.

со́лоно, *see* солёный.

солонча́к, а́, *m* **1.** saline soil. **2.** salt-marsh.

сол|ь¹, и, *pl.* ~и, ~е́й, *f.* **1.** salt; ка́менная с. rock-salt; ню́хательная с. smelling salts; пова́ренная с. common salt, sodium chloride; столо́вая с. table-salt. **2.** (*fig.*) salt, spice; point; с. земли́ the salt of the earth; вот в чём вся с. that's the whole point; мно́го ~и съесть (с кем-н.) to spend a long time together (with someone).

соль², *indecl.,* *n.* (*mus.*) sol, G; с.-дие́з G sharp; с.-бемо́ль G flat; ключ с. treble clef, G clef.

со́л|ьный 1. *adj. of* ~o; с. но́мер solo; ~ьная па́ртия solo part. **2.** *adj. of* ~ь²; с. ключ treble clef.

сольфе́джио, *indecl.,* *n.* (*mus.*) solfeggio, sol-fa, solmization; петь с. to sol-fa, solmizate.

соля́нк|а, ~и, *f.* solyanka (*a sharp-tasting Russian soup of vegetables and meat or fish*).

соля́н|о́й, *adj.* salt, saline; ~а́я кислота́ (*chem.*) hydrochloric acid; ~ые ко́пи salt-mines; с. раство́р saline solution, brine.

солянокислый, *adj.* (*chem.*) hydrochloric.

соля́ри|й, я, *m.* solarium.

сом, а́, *m.* sheat-fish.

сомати́ческий, *adj.* somatic.

со́мкн|утый, *p.p.p. of* ~у́ть *and adj.*; с. строй (*mil.*) close order.

сомкн|у́ть, у́, ёшь, *pf.* (*of* смыка́ть) to close; с. глаза́ to close one's eyes; с. ряды́ (*mil.*) to close the ranks; ~и́сь! (*mil. word of command*) close order, march!

сомкн|у́ться, ётся, *pf.* (*of* смыка́ться) to close (up).

сомна́мбул|а, ы, *m. and f.* sleep-walker, somnambulist.

сомнамбули́зм, а, *m.* sleep-walking, somnambulism.

сомнева́|ться, юсь, *impf.* **1.** (в+*p.*) to doubt; to question; я не ~юсь в его́ че́стности I do not question his integrity. **2.** to worry; мо́жете не с., всё бу́дет в поря́дке you need not worry, everything will be all right.

сомне́ни|е, я, *n.* doubt; uncertainty; без (вся́кого) ~я, вне ~я without (any) doubt, beyond doubt; не подлежи́т ни мале́йшему ~ю, что there cannot be the slightest doubt that.

сомни́тел|ьный (~ен, ~ьна), *adj.* **1.** doubtful, questionable; ~ьно it is doubtful, it is open to question. **2.** dubious; equivocal; с. комплиме́нт dubious compliment; ~ьные дела́ shady dealings.

сомно́житель|ь, я, *m.* (*math.*) factor.

сон, сна, *m.* **1.** sleep; ве́чный с. (*fig.*) eternal rest; во сне, сквозь с. in one's sleep; на с. гряду́щий at bedtime, the last thing; со сна half awake; у меня́ сна ни в одно́м глазу́ нет (*coll.*) I am not in the least sleepy. **2.** dream; ви́деть во сне to dream, have a dream (about).

сонасле́дник, а, *m.* co-heir.

сона́т|а, ы, *f.* (*mus.*) sonata.

сонати́н|а, ы, *f.* (*mus.*) sonatina.

соне́т, а, *m.* sonnet.

сонли́в|ец, ца, *m.* (*obs., coll.*) sleepyhead.

сонли́вост|ь, и, *f.* sleepiness, drowsiness; somnolence.

сонли́в|ый (~, ~a), *adj.* sleepy, drowsy; somnolent.

сонм, а, *m.* (*arch. or joc.*) assembly, throng; (*fig.*) swarm.

со́нмищ|е, а, *n.* = сонм.

сóнник, а, *m.* book of dream interpretations.

сóнн|ый, *adj.* 1. sleepy, drowsy (*also fig.*); somnolent; slumberous; ~ая артéрия (*anat.*) carotid artery; ~ая болéзнь (*med.*) (*i*) sleeping sickness (*morbus dormitivus*), (*ii*) sleepy sickness (*encephalitis lethargica*); ~ое цáрство the land of Nod; у них сейчáс ~ое цáрство they are all asleep. 2. sleeping, soporific; ~ые кáпли sleeping-draught.

сонóрный, *adj.* (*ling.*) sonorous; sonant.

сóн|я, и, *f.* 1. dormouse. 2. *m. and f.* (*coll.*) sleepy person, sleepyhead.

соображá|ть, ю, *impf.* 1. *impf. of* сообразúть. 2. *impf. only* хорошó, плóхо с. to be quick, slow in the uptake.

соображéни|е, я, *n.* 1. consideration, thought; принять в с. to take into consideration; поступáть без ~я to act without thinking. 2. understanding, grasp. 3. consideration, reason; notion, idea; по финáнсовым ~ям for financial reasons; вы́сказать свои́ ~я to express one's views.

сообразúтельност|ь, и, *f.* quickness, quick-wittedness.

сообразúтел|ьный (~ен, ~ьна), *adj.* quick-witted, quick, sharp, bright.

сообра|зúть, жу́, зи́шь, *pf.* (*of* ~жáть) 1. to consider, ponder, think out; to weigh (the pros and cons of). 2. to understand, grasp. 3. (*coll.*) to think up, arrange.

сообрáзно, *adv.* (с+*i.*) in conformity (with).

сообрáзност|ь, и, *f.* conformity.

сообрáз|ный (~ен, ~на), *adj.* (с+*i.*) conformable (to), in conformity (with); э́то ни с чем не ~но it makes no sense at all.

сообраз|овáть, у́ю, *impf. and pf.* (с+*i.*) to conform (to), make conformable (to), adapt (to); с. расхóды с дохóдами to adapt expenditure to income.

сообраз|овáться, у́юсь, *impf. and pf.* (с+*i.*) to conform (to), adapt oneself (to).

сообщá, *adv.* together, jointly.

сообщ|áть, áю, *impf. of* ~и́ть.

сообщ|áться, áюсь, *impf.* 1. *impf. of* ~и́ться. 2. *impf. only* (с+*i.*) to communicate (with), be in communication (with).

сообщéни|е, я, *n.* 1. communication, report; по послéдним ~ям according to latest reports; прочéсть с., сдéлать с. to read a communication (*at a meeting of a learned society, etc.*). 2. communication; воздýшное с. aerial communication; прямóе с. through connexion; пути́ ~я communications (*rail, road, canal, etc.*).

сообществ|о, а, *n.* association, fellowship; в ~е (с+*i.*) in association (with), together (with).

сообщ|и́ть, у́, и́шь, *pf.* (*of* ~áть) 1. (+*a.* or

о+*p.*) to communicate, report, inform, announce; с. послéдние извéстия to communicate the latest news; по рáдио ~и́ли о заключéнии ми́рного договóра the conclusion of a peace treaty has been announced on the radio; нам ~и́ли, что вас призвáли на воéнную слýжбу we were told that you had been called up. 2. to impart; с. материáлу огнеупóрность to make a material fireproof.

сообщ|и́ться, и́тся, *pf.* (*of* ~áться) to be communicated, communicate itself.

сообщник, а, *m.* accomplice, confederate; partner (*in crime*); (*leg.*) accessory.

сообщничеств|о, а, *n.* complicity.

сору|ди́ть, жу́, ди́шь, *pf.* (*of* ~жáть) to build, erect.

сооружéни|е, я, *n.* 1. building, erection. 2. building, structure; воéнные ~я military installations; оборони́тельные ~я (*mil.*) defensive works, defences.

соотвéтственно, *adv.* 1. accordingly, correspondingly. 2. (+*d.*) according (to), in accordance (with), in conformity (with), in compliance (with).

соотвéтствен|ный (~, ~на), *adj.* (+*d.*) corresponding (to).

соотвéтстви|е, я, *n.* accordance, conformity, correspondence; в ~и (с+*i.*) in accordance (with); привести́ в с. (с+*i.*) to bring into line (with).

соотвéтств|овать, ую, *impf.* (+*d.*) to correspond (to, with), conform (to), be in keeping (with); с. действи́тельности to correspond to the facts; с. трéбованиям to meet the requirements; с. цéли to answer the purpose.

соотвéтств|ующий, *pres. part. act. of* ~овать *and adj.* 1. (+*d.*) corresponding (to). 2. proper, appropriate, suitable; поступáть ~ующим óбразом to act accordingly.

соотéчественник, а, *m.* compatriot, fellow-countryman.

соотнес|ти́, у́, ёшь, *past* ~, ~лá, *pf.* (*of* соотноси́ть) to correlate.

соотноси́тел|ьный (~ен, ~ьна), *adj.* correlative.

соотно|си́ть, шу́, ~си́шь, *impf. of* соотнести́.

соотно|си́ться, ~си́тся, *impf.* to correspond.

соотношéни|е, я, *n.* correlation; ratio; с. сил correlation of forces, alignment of forces.

сопéрник, а, *m.* rival.

сопéрнича|ть, ю, *impf.* to be rivals; (с+*i.*) to compete (with), vie (with).

сопéрничеств|о, а, *n.* rivalry.

соп|éть, лю́, и́шь, *impf.* to breathe heavily and noisily through the nose.

сóпк|а, и, *f.* 1. knoll, hill, mound. 2. (*in Far East*) volcano.

соплеменник, а, *m.* fellow-tribesman.

соплеменный, *adj.* related, of the same tribe.

соплив|ый (~, ~а), *adj.* (*coll.*) snotty.

сопл|о, а, *pl.* **~ла, ~ел,** *n.* (*tech.*) nozzle.

сопл|я, и, *pl.* **~и, ~ей,** *f.* **1.** (nose-)drip; (*pl.*) snivel, snot. **2.** (*coll., pejor.*) = **сопляк.**

сопляк, а, *m.* (*coll., pejor.*) **1.** whimperer, sniveller. **2.** spineless creature; milksop.

соподчинени|е, я, *n.* co-ordination.

соподчинён|ный (~, ~а), *adj.* (*gram.*) co-ordinative.

сопостави́м|ый (~, ~а), *adj.* comparable.

сопостав|ить, лю, ишь, *pf.* (*of* **~лять**) (c+*i.*) to compare (with), confront (with).

сопоставлени|е, я, *n.* comparison, confrontation.

сопоставля|ть, ю, *impf. of* **сопоставить.**

сопрано, *indecl.* (*mus.*) **1.** *n.* soprano (*voice*). **2.** *f.* soprano (*singer*).

сопредел|ьный (~ен, ~ьна), *adj.* contiguous; (*fig.*) kindred, related.

сопре|ть, ю, *pf. of* **преть.**

соприкаса́|ться, юсь, *impf.* (*of* **соприкоснуться**) (c+*i.*) **1.** to adjoin, be contiguous (to). **2.** (*fig.*) to come into contact (with).

соприкосновени|е, я, *n.* contiguity; (*mil. and fig.*) contact; иметь с. (c+*i.*) to come into contact (with).

соприкосн|у́ться, у́сь, ёшься, *pf. of* **соприкаса́ться.**

сопричастност|ь, и, *f.* complicity, participation.

сопричаст|ный (~ен, ~на), *adj.* быть с. (к) to be implicated (in), be a participant (in).

сопроводи́тел|ь, я, *m.* escort.

сопроводи́тельн|ый, *adj.* accompanying; ~ое письмо covering letter.

сопрово|ди́ть, жу́, ди́шь, *pf. of* **~жда́ть.**

сопровожда́|ть, ю, *impf.* (*of* **сопроводи́ть**) (*in var. senses*) to accompany; to escort; to convey.

сопровождени|е, я, *n.* accompaniment; escort, convoy; в ~и (+*g.*) accompanied (by); escorted (by).

сопротивлени|е, я, *n.* resistance, opposition; (*phys., tech.*) strength; (*electr.*) resistance, impedance; оказа́ть с. to offer, put up resistance; с. материа́лов (study of) strength of materials; с. разры́ву tensile strength; идти́ по ли́нии наиме́ньшего ~я to take the line of least resistance.

сопротивля́емост|ь, и, *f.* capacity to resist; (*electr.*) resistivity.

сопротивля́|ться, юсь, *impf.* (+*d.*) to resist, oppose.

сопряжён|ный (~, ~а́), *adj.* **1.** (c+*i.*) linked (with), attended (by), entailing; ваш прое́кт ~ с больши́м ри́ском your scheme

entails great risk. **2.** (*math., chem., tech.*) conjugate; bilateral.

сопу́тств|овать, ую, *impf.* (+*d.*) to accompany; ~ующие обстоя́тельства attendant circumstances, concomitants.

сор, а, *m.* litter, dust; не выноси́ть ~а из избы́ not to wash one's dirty linen in public.

соразме́р|ить, ю, ишь, *pf.* (*of* **~я́ть**) (c+*i.*) to make commensurate (with), balance (with), match (with).

соразме́рност|ь, и, *f.* proportionality.

соразме́р|ный (~ен, ~на), *adj.* proportionate, commensurate; balanced; of the same order.

соразмер|я́ть, я́ю, *impf. of* **~ить.**

сора́тник, а, *m.* companion-in-arms, comrade-in-arms.

сорван|е́ц, ца́, *m.* (*coll.*; *of a child*) a terror; (*of a girl*) tomboy.

сорв|а́ть, у́, ёшь, *past* **~а́л, ~ала́, ~а́ло,** *pf.* (*of* **срыва́ть**) **1.** to tear off, break off, tear away, tear down; to pick, pluck; с. ве́тку to break off a branch; ве́тер ~а́л с меня́ шля́пу the wind took my hat off; с. ма́ску с кого́-н. to unmask someone. **2.** (*coll.*) to get, extract; с. с кого́-н. де́сять рубле́й to get ten roubles out of someone. **3.** (на+*p.*) to vent (upon); с. гнев на ком-н. to vent one's anger upon someone. **4.** to smash, wreck, ruin, spoil; с. вра́жеские пла́ны to foil, frustrate the enemy's plans; с. рабо́ту to upset work; с. забасто́вку to break a strike; с. банк (*cards*) to break the bank.

сорв|а́ться, у́сь, ёшься, *past* **~а́лся, ~ала́сь, ~ало́сь,** *pf.* (*of* **срыва́ться**) **1.** to break away, break loose; с. с пе́тель to come off its hinges, come unhinged; с. с ме́ста (*coll.*) to dart off; с. с це́пи (*fig., coll.*) to break out, break loose; с. с языка́ to escape one's lips. **2.** to fall, come down; с. с колоко́льни to fall from the belfry. **3.** (*coll.*) to fall through, fall to the ground, miscarry.

сорвиголов|а́, ы́, *pl.* **сорвиголо́вы, сорвиголо́в, сорвиголова́м,** *m. and f.* (*coll.*) daredevil; desperate character.

сorganиз|ова́ть, у́ю, *pf. of* **организова́ть.**

со́рго, *indecl., n.* (*bot.*) sorghum.

соревнова́ни|е, я, *n.* **1.** (*sport*) competition, contest; event; кома́ндное с. team event; отбо́рочные ~я elimination contests; с. на пе́рвенство ми́ра world championship. **2.** competition, emulation; социалисти́ческое с. socialist emulation.

соревн|ова́ться, у́юсь, *impf.* (c+*i.*) to compete (with, against), contend (with); to engage in competition.

соревн|у́ющийся, *pres. part. of* **~ова́ться;** *as noun* **с., ~у́ющегося,** *m.* competitor, contender.

соригина́льнича|ть, ю, *pf. of* оригина́льничать.

сори́нк|а, и, *f.* mote; speck of dust.

сор|и́ть, ю́, и́шь, *impf.* (*of* на∼) (+*a. or i.*) to litter; to throw about (*also fig.*); to make a mess; с. в ко́мнате оку́рками to litter a room with cigarette butts; с. деньга́ми to throw one's money about.

со́рн|ый, *adj.* 1. *adj. of* сор; ∼ое ведро́ refuse pail; с. я́щик dustbin. 2. ∼ое расте́ние, ∼ая трава́ weed; ∼ая трава́ (*collect.*) weeds.

сорня́к, а́, *m.* weed.

соро́дич|а, *m.* 1. relative, kinsman. 2. fellow--countryman; person from same part of country.

со́рок, *all other cases* а́, *num.* forty; с. ∼о́в (*obs.*) a multitude, a great number.

соро́к|а, и, *f.* magpie; с. на хвосте́ принесла́ (*joc.; of something learned from an unrevealed source*) a little bird told me, us, etc.

сорокале́ти|е, я, *n.* 1. forty years. 2. fortieth anniversary, fortieth birthday.

сорокале́тний, *adj.* 1. forty-year, of forty years. 2. forty-year-old.

сороков|о́й, *adj.* fortieth; ∼ы́е го́ды the forties; с. но́мер number forty; ∼а́я страни́ца page forty.

сороконо́жк|а, и, *f.* centipede.

сорокопу́т, а, *m.* (*orn.*) shrike.

сорокоу́ст, а, *m.* (forty days') prayers for the dead.

соро́чк|а, и, *f.* 1. shirt; blouse; camisole; ночна́я с. night-shirt, night-dress. 2. reverse (*of playing-card*). 3. (*med.*) caul; роди́ться в ∼е to be born with a silver spoon in one's mouth 4. jacket, cover.

сорт, а, *pl.* ∼а́, *m.* 1. grade, quality; brand; вы́сший с. best quality; пе́рвого ∼а first grade, first quality; first-rate. 2. sort, kind, variety.

сорта́мент, а, *m.* = сортиме́нт.

сортиме́нт, а, *m.* (*tech.*) assortment.

сорти́р, а, *m.* (*coll.*) loo.

сортир|ова́ть, у́ю, *impf.* to sort, assort, grade; с. по разме́рам to size.

сортиро́вк|а, и, *f.* 1. sorting, grading, sizing. 2. (*agric.*) separator.

сортиро́вочн|ая, ой, *f.* marshalling yard.

сортиро́вочный, *adj.* sorting.

сортиро́вщик, а, *m.* sorter.

со́ртност|ь, и, *f.* grade, quality.

со́ртный, *adj.* of high quality.

сортов|о́й, *adj.* high-grade, of high quality; ∼о́е желе́зо section iron, profile iron, shaped iron; с. стан jobbing mill, shape mill.

соса́ни|е, я, *n.* sucking, suction.

соса́тельный, *adj.* sucking.

сос|а́ть, у́, ёшь, *impf.* to suck.

сосва́та|ть, ю, *pf. of* сва́тать.

сосе́д, а, *pl.* ∼и, ∼ей, *m.* neighbour.

сосе́д|ить, ишь, *impf.* (с+*i.*) to neighbour.

сосе́дн|ий, *adj.* neighbouring; adjacent, next; с. дом the house next door; ∼яя ко́мната the next room.

сосе́д|ский, *adj. of* ∼; ∼ские де́ти the neighbours' children, the children next door.

сосе́дств|о, а, *n.* neighbourhood, vicinity; по ∼у (+*g.*) in the neighbourhood (of), in the vicinity (of); мы с ни́ми живём по ∼у we (and they) are neighbours.

соси́ск|а, и, *f.* sausage; frankfurter.

со́ск|а, и, *f.* baby's dummy.

соска́блива|ть, ю, *impf. of* соскобли́ть.

соска́кива|ть, ю, *impf. of* соскочи́ть.

соска́льзыва|ть, ю, *impf. of* соскользну́ть.

соскобл|и́ть, ю́, ∼и́шь, *pf.* (*of* соска́бливать) to scrape off.

соскользн|у́ть, у́, ёшь, *pf.* (*of* соска́льзывать) to slip off, slide off; to slide down, glide down.

соскоч|и́ть, у́, ∼ишь, *pf.* (*of* соска́кивать) 1. to jump off, leap off; to jump down, leap down; с. с крова́ти to jump out of bed; с. с трамва́я to jump off a tram. 2. to come off; с. с пе́тель to come off its hinges. 3. (с+*g.*; *coll.*) to disappear (from), leave; хмель ∼и́л с него́ he sobered up.

соскреба́|ть, ю, *impf. of* соскрести́.

соскре|сти́, бу́, бёшь, *past* ∼б, ∼бла́, *pf.* (*of* ∼ба́ть) to scrape away, off.

соску́ч|иться, усь, ишься, *pf.* 1. to become bored. 2. (по+*p., preceding sing. nouns*; по+*d., preceding pl. nouns*) to miss; с. по дере́вне to miss the country; с. по друзья́м to miss one's friends.

сослага́тельный, *adj.* (*gram.*) subjunctive.

со|сла́ть, шлю́, шлёшь, *pf.* (*of* ссыла́ть) to exile, banish, deport.

со|сла́ться[1], шлю́сь, шлёшься, *pf.* (*of* ссыла́ться) (на+*a.*) 1. to refer (to), allude (to), cite, quote. 2. to plead, allege; с. на недомога́ние to plead indisposition.

со|сла́ться[2], шлю́сь, шлёшься, *pf.* (*of* ссыла́ться) *pass. of* ∼сла́ть.

со́слепа, *adv.* (*coll.*) due to poor sight.

со́слепу, *adv.* = ∼а.

сосло́ви|е, я, *n.* 1. estate; дворя́нское с. the nobility; the gentry; духо́вное с. the clergy; купе́ческое с. the merchants. 2. corporation, professional association.

сосло́в|ный, *adj. of* ∼ие; ∼ная мона́рхия limited monarchy; ∼ное представи́тельство (*hist.*) representation of the estates; с. предрассу́док class prejudice.

сослужи́в|ец, ца, *m.* colleague, fellow-employee.

сослуж|и́ть, у́, ∼ишь, *pf.* с. кому́-н. слу́жбу

to do someone a good turn, stand someone in good stead.

сосн|а́, ы́, *pl.* **~ы, со́сен**, *f.* pine(-tree); заблуди́ться в трёх **~ах**, *see* заблуди́ться.

сосно́в|ый, *adj.* pine; pinewood; deal; с. бор pine forest; **~ая** ме́бель deal furniture; **~ая** смола́ pine tar.

сосн|у́ть, у́, ёшь, *pf.* (*coll.*) to have, take a nap.

сосня́к, а́, *m.* pine forest.

сос|о́к, ка́, *m.* nipple, teat.

сосо́ч|ек, ка, *m.* 1. *dim. of* сосо́к. 2. (*anat.*) papilla.

сосредото́чени|е, я, *n.* (*mil., etc.*) concentration.

сосредото́ченность, и, *f.* (degree of) concentration.

сосредото́ч|енный, *p.p.p. of* **~ить** *and adj.* concentrated; (*tech.*) lumped, centred; с. взгляд fixed stare; **~енное** внима́ние rapt attention; **~енная** нагру́зка (*tech.*) point load; с. ого́нь (*mil.*) concentrated fire, convergent fire.

сосредото́чива|ть(ся), ю(сь), *impf. of* сосредото́чить(ся).

сосредото́ч|ить, у, ишь, *pf.* (*of* **~ивать**) to concentrate; to focus; с. внима́ние (на + *p.*) to concentrate one's attention (on, upon).

сосредото́ч|иться, усь, ишься, *pf.* (*of* **~иваться**) 1. (на + *p.*) to concentrate (on, upon). 2. *pass. of* **~ить**.

соста́в, а, *m.* 1. composition, make-up; structure; социа́льный с. social structure; хими́ческий с. (*i*) chemical composition, (*ii*) chemical compound; входи́ть в с. (+ *g.*) to form part (of); с. преступле́ния (*leg.*) corpus delicti. 2. staff; membership, composition; strength; ли́чный с. personnel; нали́чный с. available personnel; (*mil.*) effectives; офице́рский с. the officers; в по́лном **~е** with its full complement; in, at full strength; в **~е** (+ *g.*) numbering, consisting (of), amounting (to); делега́ция в **~е** тридцати́ челове́к a delegation of thirty (persons); входи́ть в с. (+ *g.*) to become a member (of). 3. train; подвижно́й с. rolling-stock.

состави́тел|ь, я, *m.* compiler, author; с. поездо́в train maker-up.

соста́в|ить¹, лю, ишь, *pf.* (*of* **~ля́ть**) 1. to put together, make up; с. винто́вки в ко́злы (*mil.*) to pile arms, stack arms; с. по́езд to make up a train; с. посу́ду to stack crockery. 2. to compose, make up, draw up; to compile; to form, construct; с. библиоте́ку to form a library; с. мне́ние to form an opinion; с. предложе́ние to construct a sentence; с. прое́кт to draw up a draft; с. слова́рь to compile a dictionary; с. спи́сок to make a list. 3. to be, consti-

tute, make; э́то не **~ит** исключе́ния из пра́вила this will not constitute an exception to the rule; с. чье-н. сча́стье to make someone's happiness. 4. to form, make, amount to, total; с. в сре́днем to average; расхо́ды **~или** пятьсо́т фу́нтов expenditure amounted to five hundred pounds. 5. с. себе́ to make (for oneself); с. себе́ и́мя to make a name for oneself.

соста́в|ить², лю, ишь, *pf.* (*of* **~ля́ть**) to take down, put down; с. я́щик на пол to put a drawer down on the floor.

соста́в|иться, ится, *pf.* (*of* **~ля́ться**) to form, be formed, come into being.

составля́|ть(ся), ю(сь), *impf. of* соста́вить(ся).

составн|о́й, *adj.* 1. compound, composite; **~ая** кни́жная по́лка sectional book-shelf. 2. component; **~ая** часть component, constituent.

соста́р|ить(ся), ю(сь), ишь(ся), *pf. of* ста́рить(ся).

состоя́ни|е, я, *n.* 1. state, condition; position; в хоро́шем, плохо́м **~и** in good, bad condition; прийти́ в него́дное с. to be past repair; с. войны́ state of war; быть в **~и** войны́ (с + *i.*) to be at war (with); с. пого́ды state of the weather, weather conditions; быть в **~и** (+ *inf.*) to be able (to), be in a position (to). 2. (*obs.*) status, condition; гражда́нское с. civil status. 3. fortune; нажи́ть с. to make a fortune.

состоя́тельност|ь¹, и, *f.* 1. solvency. 2. wealth.

состоя́тельност|ь², и, *f.* justifiability, strength (*of an argument, etc.*).

состоя́тел|ьный¹ (~ен, ~ьна), *adj.* 1. solvent. 2. well-off, well-to-do.

состоя́тел|ьный² (~ен, ~ьна), *adj.* well-grounded; не вполне́ с. до́вод lame argument.

состо|я́ть, ю́, и́шь, *impf.* 1. (из) to consist (of), comprise, be made up (of); кварти́ра **~и́т** из трёх ко́мнат the flat consists of three rooms; име́ние **~и́т** преиму́щественно из торфяно́го боло́та the estate is largely made up of a peatbog. 2. (в + *p.*) to consist (in), lie (in), be; ра́зница **~и́т** в том, что the difference is that; в чём **~и́т** на́ши обя́занности? what are our duties? 3. to be; с. чле́ном о́бщества to be a member of a society; с. в до́лжности заве́дующего to occupy the post of director; с. на вооруже́нии (*mil.*) to be part of standard equipment; с. на своём иждиве́нии to keep oneself; с. под судо́м to be awaiting trial; с. при посо́льстве to be attached to the embassy.

состо|я́ться, и́тся, *pf.* to take place; визи́т не **~я́лся** the visit did not take place;

изда́ние не ~я́лось the edition was never printed.

состра́гива|ть, ю, *impf. of* сострога́ть.

сострада́ни|е, я, *n.* compassion, sympathy.

сострада́тел|ьный (~ен, ~ьна), *adj.* compassionate, sympathetic.

сострада́|ть, ю, *impf.* (+*d.*; *obs.*) to feel pity (for).

сострига́|ть, ю, *impf. of* состри́чь.

состр|и́ть, ю́, и́шь, *pf. of* остри́ть.

состри́|чь, гу́, жёшь, гу́т, *past* ~г, ~гла, *pf.* (*of* ~га́ть) to shear, clip off.

сострога́|ть, ю, *pf.* (*of* состра́гивать) to plane off.

состро́|ить, ю, ишь, *pf. of* стро́ить з.; с. грима́су, с. ро́жу (*coll.*) to make a face.

состру́га|ть, ю, *pf.* = сострога́ть.

состря́па|ть, ю, *pf. of* стря́пать.

состы́к|овать(ся), у́ю(сь), *pf. of* стыкова́ть(ся).

состяза́ни|е, я, *n.* **1.** competition, contest; match; с. в пла́вании swimming contest; с. по фехтова́нию fencing match; с. в остроу́мии battle of wits. **2.** (*leg.*) controversy.

состяза́тельный, *adj.* (*leg.*) controversial.

состяза́|ться, юсь, *impf.* (с+*i.*) to compete (with), contend (with).

сосу́д, а, *m.* (*in var. senses*) vessel; кровено́сные ~ы blood vessels.

сосу́дистый, *adj.* (*anat., biol.*) vascular.

сосу́льк|а, и, *f.* icicle.

сосуществова́ни|е, я, *n.* co-existence; ми́рное с. (*polit.*) peaceful co-existence.

сосуществ|ова́ть, у́ю, *impf.* to co-exist.

сос|у́щий, *pres. part. act. of* ~а́ть *and adj.* (*zool.*) suctorial.

сосцеви́д|ный (~ен, ~на), *adj.* mammiform, mammilliform.

сосчита́|ть, ю, *pf. of* счита́ть.

сосчита́|ться, юсь, *pf.* (с+*i.*) to settle accounts (with), get even (with) (*also fig.*).

сотворе́ни|е, я, *n.* creation, making; с. ми́ра the creation of the world.

сотвор|и́ть, ю́, и́шь, *pf. of* твори́ть.

со́тенн|ая, ой, *f.* (*coll.*) hundred-rouble note.

со́тенный, *adj.* (*coll.*) worth a hundred roubles.

со́тк|а, и, *f.* hundredth part.

сотк|а́ть, у́, ёшь, *past* ~а́л, ~ала́, ~а́ло, *pf. of* ткать.

со́тник, а, *m.* (*hist.*) sotnik (*lieutenant of Cossack troops*).

сот|ня, ни, *g. pl.* ~ен, *f.* **1.** a hundred (*esp. a hundred roubles*). **2.** (*hist.*) sotnya, company (*mil. unit, originally of a hundred men*); каза́чья с. Cossack squadron.

сотова́рищ, а, *m.* associate, partner.

сотови́д|ный (~ен, ~на), *adj.* honeycomb.

со́т|овый, *adj.* **1.** *adj. of* ~ы; с. мёд comb-honey. **2.** (*tech.*; *fig.*) honeycomb; ~овая кату́шка honeycomb coil.

сотрапе́зник, а, *m.* (*obs.*) table-companion.

сотру́дник, а, *m.* **1.** collaborator. **2.** employee, official; нау́чный с. research officer, research fellow, research assistant (*of a learned body or scientific institution*); с. посо́льства embassy official. **3.** contributor (*to a newspaper, journal, etc.*).

сотру́днича|ть, ю, *impf.* **1.** (с+*i.*) to collaborate (with). **2.** (в+*p.*) to contribute (to); с. в газе́те to contribute to a newspaper; to work on a newspaper.

сотру́дничеств|о, а, *n.* collaboration, co-operation.

сотряс|а́ть(ся), а́ю(сь), *impf. of* ~ти́(сь).

сотрясе́ни|е, я, *n.* shaking; с. мо́зга (*med.*) concussion.

сотряс|ти́, у́, ёшь, *past* ~, ~ла́, *pf.* (*of* ~а́ть) to shake.

сотряс|ти́сь, у́сь, ёшься, *past* ~ся, ~ла́сь, *pf.* (*of* ~а́ться) to shake, tremble.

со́т|ы, ов, *no sing.* honeycombs; мёд в ~ах honey in combs.

со́т|ый, *adj.* hundredth; с. год the year one hundred; с. но́мер number one hundred; *as noun* ~ая, ~ой, *f.* (a) hundredth.

соу́мышленник, а, *m.* accomplice.

со́ус, а, *m.* sauce; gravy; dressing.

со́усник, а, *m.* sauce-boat, gravy-boat.

соуча́ств|овать, ую, *impf.* (в+*p.*) to participate (in), take part (in).

соуча́сти|е, я, *n.* participation; complicity.

соуча́стник, а, *m.* participator; accomplice; с. преступле́ния, с. в преступле́нии (*leg.*) accessory to a crime.

соучени́к, а́, *m.* schoolmate, schoolfellow.

соф|а́, ы́, *pl.* ~ы, *f.* sofa.

софи́зм, а, *m.* sophism, sophistry.

софи́ст, а, *m.* sophist.

софи́стик|а, и, *f.* sophistry.

софисти́ческий, *adj.* sophistic(al).

сох|а́, и́, *pl.* ~и, *f.* (*wooden*) plough (*also old land measure*).

соха́т|ый (~, ~а), *adj.* (*dial.*) with branching antlers; *as noun* с., ~ого, *m.* elk.

со́х|нуть, ну, нешь, *past* ~, ~ла, *impf.* **1.** to dry, get dry; to become parched. **2.** to wither; (*fig.*) to pine.

сохране́ни|е, я, *n.* **1.** preservation; conservation; care, custody, charge; зако́н ~я эне́ргии law of conservation of energy; отда́ть кому́-н. на с. to give into someone's charge. **2.** retention; о́тпуск с ~ем содержа́ния holiday(s) with pay.

сохран|и́ть, ю́, и́шь, *pf.* (*of* ~я́ть) **1.** to preserve, keep; to keep safe; с. ве́рность (+*d.*) to remain faithful, loyal (to), keep, stand by; с. на па́мять to keep as a souvenir.

2. to keep, retain, reserve; с. хладнокро́вие to keep cool, keep one's head; с. за собо́й пра́во to reserve the right.

сохран|**и́ться, юсь, и́шься,** *pf.* (*of* ~**я́ться**) **1.** to remain (intact); to last out, hold out; здоро́вье у неё ~и́лось до девяно́ста лет her health lasted out right up to her ninetieth year; он хорошо́ ~и́лся he is well preserved. **2.** *pass. of* ~и́ть.

сохра́нно, *adv.* safely, intact.

сохра́нность|**ь, и,** *f.* **1.** safety, undamaged state; радиоприёмник пришёл в по́лной ~и the radio arrived quite intact. **2.** safe keeping.

сохра́н|**ный** (~**ен,** ~**на**), *adj.* safe; undamaged.

сохран|**я́ть(ся), я́ю(сь),** *impf. of* ~**и́ть(ся).**

соц- *abbr. of* **1.** социа́льный. **2.** социалисти́ческий.

соцве́ти|**е, я,** *n.* (*bot.*) inflorescence.

соцдо́говор, а, *m.* socialist emulation agreement.

социа́л-демокра́т, а, *m.* social democrat.

социа́л-демократи́ческий, *adj.* social democratic.

социа́л-демокра́ти|**я, и,** *f.* social democracy.

социализа́ци|**я, и,** *f.* socialization.

социализи́р|**овать, ую,** *impf. and pf.* to socialize.

социали́зм, а, *m.* socialism.

социали́ст, а, *m.* socialist.

социалисти́ческий, *adj.* socialist.

социали́ст-революционе́р, а, *m.* (*hist.*) socialist revolutionary.

социа́л-революцио́нный, *adj.* (*hist.*) socialist-revolutionary.

социа́льно-бытово́й, *adj.* social, welfare.

социа́льн|**ый,** *adj.* (*in var. senses*) social; ~ое обеспе́чение social security; ~ое положе́ние social status; ~ая психоло́гия social psychology.

социогра́фи|**я, и,** *f.* descriptive sociology.

социо́лог, а, *m.* sociologist.

социологи́ческий, *adj.* sociological.

социоло́ги|**я, и,** *f.* sociology.

соцреали́зм, а, *m.* (*abbr. of* социалисти́ческий реали́зм) socialist realism.

соцсоревнова́ни|**е, я,** *n.* (*abbr. of* социалисти́ческое соревнова́ние) socialist emulation.

соцстра́х, а, *m.* (*abbr. of* социа́льное страхова́ние) social insurance.

соче́льник, а, *m.* (*eccl.*) рожде́ственский с. Christmas Eve; креще́нский с. Twelfth-night, eve of the Epiphany.

сочета́ни|**е, я,** *n.* combination.

сочета́|**ть, ю,** *impf. and pf.* (с+*i.*) to combine (with); с. бра́ком (*obs.*) to marry (to), wed (to).

сочета́|**ться, юсь,** *impf. and pf.* **1.** to combine; в ней ~лся ум с красото́й she combined intelligence and good looks. **2.** (с+*i.*) to harmonize (with), go (with); to match. **3.** с. бра́ком (с+*i.*; *obs.*) to contract matrimony (with).

сочине́ни|**е, я,** *n.* **1.** composing. **2.** (*literary*) work; и́збранные ~я Го́голя selected works of Gogol. **3.** (*school*) composition, essay. **4.** (*gram.*) co-ordination.

сочини́тел|**ь, я,** *m.* **1.** (*obs.*) writer, author. **2.** (*coll.*) story-teller, fabricator.

сочини́тельный, *adj.* (*gram.*) co-ordinative.

сочини́тельств|**о, а,** *n.* **1.** (*obs.*) writing. **2.** (*pejor.*) scribbling, hack-writing. **3.** (*coll.*) fabrication.

сочин|**и́ть, ю́, и́шь,** *pf.* (*of* ~**я́ть**) **1.** to compose (*a lit. or mus. work*); to write. **2.** to make up, fabricate.

сочин|**я́ть, я́ю,** *impf.* **1.** *impf. of* ~**и́ть. 2.** (*obs.*) to write, be a writer.

соч|**и́ть, у́, и́шь,** *impf.* to ooze (out), exude.

соч|**и́ться, и́тся,** *impf.* to ooze (out), exude, trickle; с. кро́вью to bleed.

сочле́н, а, *m.* fellow member.

сочлене́ни|**е, я,** *n.* (*anat. and tech.*) articulation, joint, coupling.

сочлен|**и́ть, ю́, и́шь,** *pf.* (*of* ~**я́ть**) to join.

сочлен|**я́ть, я́ю,** *impf. of* ~**и́ть.**

со́чност|**ь, и,** *f.* juiciness, succulence.

со́ч|**ный** (~**ен,** ~**на́,** ~**но**), *adj.* **1.** juicy (*also fig.*); succulent. **2.** (*fig.*) rich; lush; с. го́лос fruity voice; ~ная расти́тельность lush vegetation.

сочу́вственност|**ь, и,** *f.* sympathy.

сочу́вствен|**ный** (~, ~**на**), *adj.* sympathetic.

сочу́встви|**е, я,** *n.* sympathy; вы́звать с. to gain sympathy.

сочу́вств|**овать, ую,** *impf.* (+*d.*) to sympathize (with), feel (for).

сочу́вств|**ующий,** *pres. part. act. of* ~**овать** *and adj.* sympathetic; *as noun* с., ~**ующего,** *m.* sympathizer.

со́шк|**а, и,** *f.* **1.** *dim. of* соха́; ме́лкая с. (*coll.*) small fry. **2.** (*mil.*) bipod.

сошни́к, а́, *m.* **1.** ploughshare. **2.** (*mil.*) trail spade (*of gun carriage*).

со́|шный, *adj. of* ~**ха́.**

сощу́рива|**ть(ся), ю(сь),** *impf. of* сощу́рить(ся).

сощу́р|**ить, ю, ишь,** *pf.* (*of* щу́рить *and* ~**ивать**) с. глаза́ to screw up one's eyes.

сощу́р|**иться, юсь, ишься,** *pf.* (*of* щу́риться *and* ~**иваться**) to screw up one's eyes.

сою́з¹, а, *m.* **1.** alliance, union; agreement; заключи́ть с. (с+*i.*) to conclude an alliance (with). **2.** union; league; профессиона́льный с. trade union; Сове́тский С. the Soviet Union.

сою́з², а, *m.* (*gram.*) conjunction.

союзк|а, и, *f.* vamp (*of footwear*).

союзник, а, *m.* ally.

союзнический, *adj.* ally's.

союзно-республикáнский, *adj.* Union-Re-public (*in administration of U.S.S.R.*).

союз|ный[1], *adj.* 1. allied; ~ые держáвы allied powers; (*hist.*) the Allies. 2. (*of the U.S.S.R.*) Union; ~ое граждáнство citizen-ship of the (Soviet) Union.

союз|ный[2], *adj.* of ~[2].

со́|я, и, *f.* soya bean.

спад, а, *m.* 1. (*econ.*) slump, recession. 2. abatement.

спадá|ть, ю, *impf.* of спасть.

спазм, а, *m.* spasm.

спáзм|а, ы, *f.* = ~.

спáива|ть[1], ю, *impf.* of спойть.

спáива|ть[2], ю, *impf.* of спаять.

спа́|й, я, *m.* (*tech.*) (soldered) joint.

спáйк|а, и, *f.* 1. soldering; soldered joint. 2. (*anat.*) commissure. 3. (*fig.*) cohesion; union.

спал|и́ть, ю, йшь, *pf.* of пали́ть[1].

спáльник, а, *m.* (*coll.*) sleeping-bag.

спáльн|ый, *adj.* sleeping; с. вагóн sleeping--car; ~ое мéсто berth, bunk; с. мешóк sleeping-bag; ~ые принадлéжности bed-ding.

спáл|ьня, ьни, *g. pl.* ~ен, *f.* 1. bedroom. 2. bedroom suite.

спань|ё, я́, *n.* sleep(ing).

спарашютúр|овать, ую, *pf.* of парашютú-ровать.

спáр|енный, *p.p.p.* of ~ить *and adj.* paired, coupled; ~енная ездá (*railways*) double--manning; с. пулемёт coaxial machine--gun; ~енная устанóвка (*mil.*) combination gun mount.

спáрж|а, и, *f.* asparagus.

спáрива|ть(ся), ю(сь), *impf.* of спáрить(ся).

спáр|ить, ю, ишь, *pf.* (*of* ~ивать) 1. to couple, pair, mate (*animals*). 2. to pair off (*to work together*).

спáр|иться, юсь, ишься, *pf.* (*of* ~иваться) 1. (*of animals*) to couple, pair, mate. 2. to pair off (*to work together*).

спартакиáд|а, ы, *f.* sports and/or athletics meeting; sports day.

спартáн|ец, ца, *m.* Spartan.

спартáнский, *adj.* Spartan.

спáрхива|ть, ю, *impf.* of спорхнýть.

спáрыва|ть, ю, *impf.* of спорóть.

Спас, а, *m.* (*rel.*) the Saviour.

спасáни|е, я, *n.* rescuing, life-saving.

спасáтельн|ый, *adj.* rescue, life-saving; с. круг, с. пóяс lifebelt; ~ая лóдка lifeboat; ~ая экспедúция rescue party.

спасá|ть(ся), ю(сь), *impf.* of спастú(сь).

спасéни|е, я, *n.* 1. rescuing, saving. 2. rescue, escape; salvation.

спасúбо, *particle* thanks; thank you; с. и на том that's something at least, we must be thankful for small mercies; *as noun* thanks; большóе вам с. thank you very much, many thanks; сдéлать что-н. за (однó) с. (*coll.*) to do something for love.

спасúтел|ь, я, *m.* 1. rescuer, saver. 2. (*rel.*) the Saviour.

спасúтел|ьный (~ен, ~ьна), *adj.* saving; salutary; с. вы́ход, ~ьное срéдство means of escape.

спас|овáть, у́ю, *pf.* of пасовáть[1].

спас|тú, у́, ёшь, *past* ~, ~лá, *pf.* (*of* ~áть) to save; to rescue; с. положéние to save the situation.

спас|тúсь, у́сь, ёшься, *past* ~ся, ~лáсь, *pf.* (*of* ~áться) 1. to save oneself, escape. 2. (*rel.*) to be saved, save one's soul.

спа|сть, дý, дёшь, *past* ~л, *pf.* (*of* ~дáть) 1. (с+*g.*) to fall down (from); с. с гóлоса (*coll.*) to lose one's voice; с. с лицá (*coll.*) to become thin in the face; с. с тéла (*coll.*) to lose weight. 2. to abate; (*of water*) to fall.

спа|ть, сплю, спишь, *past* ~л, ~лá, ~ло, *impf.* to sleep, be asleep; с. мёртвым сном to be fast asleep; лечь с. to go to bed; порá с. it is bedtime; с. и ви́деть (*fig.*) to dream (of); с. с(+*i.*) to sleep with (*euph.*).

спá|ться, спится, *past* ~лось, *impf.* (*impers. +d.*) мне не спи́тся (*i*) I cannot sleep, I cannot get to sleep, (*ii*) I am not sleepy; ей плóхо ~лóсь she did not sleep well.

спáянност|ь, и, *f.* cohesion, unity.

спа|я́ть, я́ю, *pf.* (*of* ~ивать[2]) 1. to solder together, weld. 2. (*fig.*) to weld together.

спевá|ться, юсь, *impf.* of спéться.

спéвк|а, и, *f.* (choir) practice, rehearsal.

спекá|ться, юсь, *impf.* of спéчься.

спектáкл|ь, я, *m.* (*theatr.*) performance; show.

спектр, а, *m.* (*phys.*) spectrum.

спектрáльный, *adj.* (*phys.*) spectral, spectrum.

спектроскóп, а, *m.* (*phys.*) spectroscope.

спектроскопú|я, и, *f.* (*phys.*) spectroscopy.

спекулú́р|овать, ую, *impf.* 1. (+*i. or* на+*p.*) to speculate (in); to profiteer (in); to gamble (on). 2. (на+*p.*; *fig.*) to gamble (on), reckon (on); to profit (by).

спекуля́нт, а, *m.* speculator, profiteer.

спекуляти́вн|ый, *adj.* speculative; по ~ым цéнам at speculative prices.

спекуля́ци|я[1], и, *f.* 1. (+*i.*, с+*i.*, *or* на+*p.*) speculation (in); profiteering; с. на иност-ра́нной валю́те speculation in foreign cur-rency. 2. (на+*p.*; *fig.*) gamble (on).

спекуля́ци|я[2], и, *f.* (*philos.*) speculation.

спелена́|ть, ю, *pf.* of пелена́ть.

спéл|ый (~, ~á, ~о), *adj.* ripe.

спéнсер, а, *m.* (*obs.*) spencer (*short woollen jacket*).

сперва́, *adv.* (*coll.*) at first; first.

спе́реди, *adv. and prep.*+*g.* in front (of); at the front, from the front.

спер|е́ть[1], **сопрёт**, *past* ~, ~ла, *pf.* (*of* спира́ть) (*coll.*) to press; у меня́ дыха́нье ~ло it took my breath away.

спер|е́ть[2], **сопру́, сопрёшь**, *past* ~, ~ла, *pf.* (*of* переть 5) (*coll.*) to filch, pinch.

спе́рм|а, ы, *f.* sperm.

сперматозо́ид, а, *m.* (*biol.*) spermatozoon.

спермаце́т, а, *m.* (*pharm.*) spermaceti.

спёр|тый, *p.p.p.* of ~е́ть[1] *and adj.* close, stuffy.

спеси́в|ец, ца, *m.* arrogant, conceited person.

спеси́вост|ь, и, *f.* arrogance, conceit, haughtiness, loftiness.

спеси́в|ый (~, ~а), *adj.* arrogant, conceited, haughty, lofty, stuck-up.

спес|ь, и, *f.* arrogance, conceit, haughtiness, loftiness; сбить с. с кого́-н. to take someone down a peg.

спе|ть[1]**, ет,** *impf.* to ripen.

спеть[2]**, спою́, споёшь,** *pf.* of петь.

спе́ться, спою́сь, споёшься, *pf.* 1. (*impf.* спева́ться) (*of a choir*) to practise, rehearse. 2. *pf. only* (*coll.*) to get on, agree, see eye to eye.

спех, а (у), *m.* (*coll.*) hurry; что за с.? what's the hurry?; мне не к ~у I'm in no hurry.

спец, а, *m.* = специали́ст.

специализа́ци|я, и, *f.* specialization.

специализи́рова|нный, *p.p.p.* of ~ть *and adj.* specialized.

специализи́р|овать, ую, *impf. and pf.* to assign a specialization (to); to earmark for a special role.

специализи́р|оваться, уюсь, *impf. and pf.* (в+*p. or* по+*d.*) to specialize (in).

специали́ст, а, *m.* (в+*p. or* по+*d.*) specialist (in), expert (in).

специа́льно, *adv.* specially, especially.

специа́льност|ь, и, *f.* 1. speciality, special interest. 2. profession; trade.

специа́льный, *adj.* 1. special, especial; с. корреспонде́нт special correspondent; по́езд ~ьного назначе́ния special (train); со ~ьной це́лью with the express purpose. 2. (~ен, ~ьна) specialist; ~ьное образова́ние specialist education; с. те́рмин technical term.

специ́фик|а, и, *f.* specific character.

спецификаци|я, и, *f.* specification.

специфици́р|овать, ую, *impf. and pf.* to specify.

специфи́ческий, *adj.* specific.

спе́ци|я, и, *f.* spice.

спецко́р, а, *m.* (*abbr. of* специа́льный корреспонде́нт) special correspondent.

спецо́вк|а, и, *f.* (*coll.*) = спецоде́жда.

спецоде́жд|а, ы, *f.* working clothes, overalls.

спе́|чься, чётся, кутся, *past* ~кся, ~кла́сь, *pf.* (*of* ~ка́ться) 1. (*of blood*) to coagulate, curdle. 2. (*of coal*) to cake, clinker.

спе́шива|ть(ся), ю(сь), *impf. of* спе́шить(ся).

спе́ш|ить, у, ишь, *pf.* (*of* ~ивать) to dismount.

спеш|и́ть, у́, и́шь, *impf.* (*of* по~) 1. to hurry, be in a hurry; to make haste, hasten; (с+*i.*) to hurry up (with), get a move on (with); с. домо́й to be in a hurry to get home; де́лать не ~á to do in leisurely style, take one's time over. 2. (*of a timepiece*) to be fast; ва́ши часы́ ~а́т на че́тверть часа́ your watch is a quarter of an hour fast.

спеш|и́ться, у́сь, и́шься, *pf.* (*of* ~иваться) to dismount.

спе́шк|а, и, *f.* hurry, haste, rush.

спе́шност|ь, и, *f.* hurry, haste.

спе́ш|ный (~ен, ~на), *adj.* urgent, pressing; с. зака́з rush order; ~ное письмо́ express letter; ~ная по́чта express delivery; в ~ном поря́дке quickly.

спиба́|ться, юсь, *impf. of* спи́ться.

спид, *see* Appendix I.

спидве́|й, я, *m.* speedway (racing).

спидо́метр, а, *m.* speedometer.

спики́р|овать, ую, *pf. of* пики́ровать.

спи́лива|ть, ю, *impf. of* спили́ть.

спил|и́ть, ю́, ~ишь, *pf.* (*of* ~ивать) to saw down; to saw off.

спин|а́, ы́, а. ~у, *pl.* ~ы, *f.* back; за ~о́й у кого́-н. (*fig.*) behind someone's back; гнуть ~у (пе́ред) to cringe (to), kowtow (to); нож в ~у, уда́р в ~у (*fig.*) stab in the back; узна́ть на со́бственной ~е́ to learn from (one's own) bitter experience.

спи́нк|а, и, *f.* 1. *dim.* of спина́. 2. back (*of article of furniture or clothing*).

спи́ннинг, а, *m.* (*sport*) 1. spinning (*fishing technique*). 2. spoon-bait.

спиннинги́ст, а, *m.* fisherman employing spinning technique.

спинно́й, *adj.* spinal; с. мозг spinal cord; с. хребе́т spinal column.

спинномозгов|о́й, *adj.* ~а́я жи́дкость (*anat.*) spinal fluid.

спира́л|ь, и, *f.* spiral.

спира́льный, *adj.* spiral, helical.

спира́|ть, ет, *impf. of* спере́ть[1].

спири́т, а, *m.* spiritualist, spiritist.

спирити́зм, а, *m.* spiritualism, spiritism.

спирити́ческий, *adj.* spiritualistic, spiritistic; с. сеа́нс (spiritualistic) seance.

спиритуали́зм, а, *m.* (*philos.*) spiritualism.

спиритуали́ст, а, *m.* (*philos.*) spiritualist.

спирохе́т|а, ы, *f.* (*biol.*) spirochaete.

спирт, а, *m.* alcohol, spirit(s); безво́дный с.

absolute alcohol; дре́весный с. wood alcohol.

спирт|о́й, *adj.* alcoholic, spirituous; ~ые напи́тки alcoholic drinks, spirits; *as noun* ~бе, ~бго, *n.* = ~ые напи́тки.

спирто́вк|а, и, *f.* spirit-lamp.

спиртов|о́й, *adj.* alcoholic, spirituous; ~ые кра́ски *(text.)* spirit colours.

спиртоме́р, а, *m.* alcoholometer.

спи|са́ть, шу́, ~шешь, *pf. (of* ~сывать*)* **1.** (c+g.) to copy from. **2.** (y) to copy (off), crib (off). **3.** to write off. **4.** с. с корабля́ *(naut.)* to transfer, post (from a ship).

спи|са́ться, шу́сь, ~шешься, *pf. (of* ~сываться) (c+i.) **1.** to settle by letter, arrange by letter. **2.** to exchange letters. **3.** с. с корабля́ *(naut.)* to leave ship.

спи́с|ок, ка, *m.* **1.** manuscript copy. **2.** list; roll; именно́й с. nominal roll; с. избира́телей voters' list, electoral roll; с. опеча́ток errata; с. уби́тых и ра́неных casualty list; с. ли́чного соста́ва *(mil.)* muster-roll. **3.** record; послужно́й с., трудово́й с. service record.

спи́сыва|ть(ся), ю(сь), *impf. of* списа́ть(ся).

спито́й, *adj.* *(coll.; of hot beverages)* weak, watered down to excess; с. чай weak tea.

спи́|ться, сопью́сь, сопьёшься, *past* ~лся, ~ла́сь, ~ло́сь, *pf. (of* ~ва́ться) to become a drunkard, take to drink; с. с кру́гу *(coll.)* to go to seed through drink.

спи́хива|ть, ю, *impf. of* спихну́ть.

спих|ну́ть, ну́, нёшь, *pf. (of* ~ивать*)* to push aside, shove aside; to push down.

спи́ц|а, ы, *f.* **1.** knitting needle. **2.** spoke; после́дняя с. в колесни́це mere cog in the machine; пя́тая с. в колесни́це minor character.

спич, а, *m.* speech, address.

спи́чечниц|а, ы, *f.* **1.** match-box. **2.** match-box stand.

спи́ч|ечный, *adj. of* ~ка; ~ечная коро́бка match-box.

спи́чк|а, и, *f.* match.

сплав[1], а, *m.* *(tech.)* alloy; fusion.

сплав[2], а, *m.* (timber) floating.

спла́в|ить[1], лю, ишь, *pf. (of* ~ля́ть*)* *(tech.)* to alloy, melt, fuse.

спла́в|ить[2], лю, ишь, *pf. (of* ~ля́ть*)* **1.** to float (timber); to raft. **2.** *(coll.)* to send packing, shake off.

спла́в|иться, ится, *pf. (of* ~ля́ться) to fuse together, coalesce.

сплавля́|ть(ся), ю, ет(ся), *impf. of* спла́вить(ся).

спла́вщик[1], а, *m.* *(tech.)* melter.

спла́вщик[2], а, *m.* (timber-)floater, rafter.

сплани́р|овать, ую, *pf. of* плани́ровать[2].

спла́чива|ть(ся), ю(сь), *impf. of* сплоти́ть-(ся).

сплёвыва|ть, ю, *impf. of* сплю́нуть.

сплёскива|ть, ю, *impf. of* сплесну́ть.

сплес|ну́ть, ну́, нёшь, *pf. (of* ~кивать*)* to splash (down).

спле|сти́, ту́, тёшь, *past* ~л, ~ла́, *pf. (of* плести́ *and* ~та́ть*)* to weave, plait, interlace.

сплета́|ть, ю, *impf. of* сплести́.

сплете́ни|е, я, *n.* **1.** interlacing; с. лжи tissue of lies; с. обстоя́тельств combination of circumstances. **2.** *(anat.)* plexus.

спле́тник, а, *m.* gossip, scandalmonger.

спле́тниц|а, ы, *f. of* спле́тник.

сплетнича|ть, ю, *impf. (of* на~*)* to gossip, tittle-tattle; to talk scandal.

спле́т|ня, ни, g. pl.* ~ен, *f.* gossip, tittle-tattle; piece of scandal.

сплеча́, *adv.* **1.** straight from the shoulder *(also fig.)*. **2.** *(fig., coll.)* on the spot, on the spur of the moment.

спло|ти́ть, чу́, ти́шь, *pf. (of* спла́чивать*)* **1.** to join. **2.** *(fig.)* to unite, rally; с. ряды́ to close the ranks.

спло|ти́ться, чу́сь, ти́шься, *pf. (of* спла́-чиваться) to unite, rally; to close the ranks.

сплох|ова́ть, у́ю, *pf. (coll.)* to make a blunder, slip up.

сплочённост|ь, и, *f.* cohesion, unity.

спло|чённый, *p.p.p. of* ~ти́ть *and adj.* **1. unbroken. **2.** united, firm; ~чённые ряды́ serried ranks.

сплоша́|ть, ю, *pf. of* плоша́ть.

сплошн|о́й, *adj.* **1.** unbroken, continuous; с. лёд solid mass of ice, ice-field; с. лес dense forest; ~а́я ма́сса solid mass. **2.** all-round, complete; ~а́я гра́мотность universal literacy. **3.** *(fig., coll.)* sheer, solid, complete and utter, unreserved; с. восто́рг sheer joy; ~а́я чепуха́ utter rubbish.

сплошь, *adv.* **1.** all over, throughout; without a break; её но́ги бы́ли с. покры́ты комари́ными уку́сами her legs were covered all over with gnat bites; с. и (да) ря́дом *(coll.)* nearly always; pretty often. **2.** *(coll.)* completely, utterly; without exception.

сплут|ова́ть, у́ю, *pf. of* плутова́ть.

сплыва́|ть(ся), ет(ся), *impf. of* сплы́ть(ся).

сплы́|ть, вёт, *past* ~л, ~ла́, ~ло, *pf. (of* ~ва́ть*)* *(coll.)* **1.** to be carried away *(by a current of water, by a flood)*; бы́ло да ~ло it was a short-lived joy; it's all over. **2.** to overflow, run over.

сплы́|ться, вётся, *past* ~лся, ~ла́сь, *pf. (of* ~ва́ться) *(coll.)* to run (together), merge, blend.

сплю́н|уть, у, ешь, *pf. (of* сплёвывать) **1.** to spit. **2.** *(coll.)* to spit out.

сплюсн|уть, у, ешь, *pf. =* сплю́щить.

сплю́шк|а, и, *f.* *(orn.)* scops owl.

сплю́щива|ть(ся), ю(сь), *impf. of* сплю́щить(ся).

сплю́щ|ить, у, ишь, *pf. (of* плю́щить *and* ~ивать) to flatten, laminate.

сплю́щ|иться, ится, *pf. (of* ~иваться) to become flat.

спля|са́ть, шу́, ~шешь, *pf.* to dance.

сподви́жник, а, *m. (rhet.)* associate; comrade-in-arms.

сподо́б|ить, ит, *pf. (impers.+inf.; obs. or joc.)* to manage (to), come (to), contrive (to); как э́то тебя́ ~ило упа́сть в ре́ку? how did you manage to fall in the river?

сподо́б|иться, люсь, ишься, *pf.* (+*g. or* +*inf.; obs. or joc.)* to be honoured (with), have the honour (of).

сподру́чник, а, *m.* 1. *(obs.)* assistant, right-hand man. 2. *(pejor.)* myrmidon.

сподру́чн|ый¹ (~ен, ~на), *adj. (coll.)* easy; convenient, handy.

сподру́чн|ый², ого, *m.* = ~ик.

спозара́нку, *adv. (coll.)* very early (in the morning).

спо|и́ть, ю́, и́шь, *pf. (of* спа́ивать¹) 1. to give to drink. 2. to accustom to drinking; to make a drunkard (of).

споко́|йный (~ен, ~йна), *adj.* 1. quiet; calm, tranquil; placid, serene; ~йное мо́ре calm sea; с. о́браз жи́зни quiet life; ~йная со́весть clear conscience; ~йная улы́бка serene smile; бу́дьте ~йны! don't worry!, rest assured!; ~йной но́чи! good night! 2. quiet, composed. 3. comfortable; ~йное кре́сло easy chair.

споко́йстви|е, я, *n.* 1. quiet, tranquillity; calm, calmness. 2. order; наруше́ние обще́ственного ~я breach of the peace, breach of public order. 3. composure, serenity; с. ду́ха peace of mind.

споко́н: с. ве́ку, с. веко́в *(coll.)* from time immemorial.

спола́скива|ть, ю, *impf. of* сполосну́ть.

сполз|а́ть, а́ю, *impf. of* ~ти́.

сполз|ти́, у́, ёшь, *past* ~, ~ла́, *pf. (of* ~а́ть) 1. (с+*g.*) to climb down (from). 2. (в+ *a.*, к; *fig., coll.*) to slip (into), fall away (into).

сполна́, *adv.* completely, in full; де́ньги полу́чены с. 'received in full'.

сполосн|у́ть, у́, ёшь, *pf. (of* спола́скивать) to rinse (out).

споло́х|и, ов, *no sing. (dial.)* 1. northern lights. 2. lightning.

спонде́и́ческий, *adj. (lit.)* spondaic.

спонде́|й, я, *m. (lit.)* spondee.

спонта́нност|ь, и, *f.* spontaneity.

спонта́нный, *adj.* spontaneous.

спонти́р|овать, ую, *pf. of* понти́ровать.

спор, а, *m.* 1. argument; controversy; debate; зате́ять с. to start an argument; ~у

нет indisputably, undoubtedly; there's no denying. 2. *(leg.)* dispute.

спо́р|а, ы, *f. (biol.)* spore.

спора́ди́ческий, *adj.* sporadic.

спора́нги|й, я, *m. (biol.)* sporangium, spore-case.

спо́р|ить, ю, ишь, *impf. (of* по~) (о+*p.*) 1. to argue (about); to dispute (about), debate; с. о слова́х to quibble over words; о вку́сах не ~ят tastes differ. 2. to dispute; с. о насле́дстве to dispute a legacy. 3. to bet (on), have a bet (on).

спо́р|иться, ится, *impf. (coll.)* to succeed, go well; у него́ всё ~ится he never puts a foot wrong.

спо́р|ный (~ен, ~на), *adj.* disputable, debatable, questionable; disputed, at issue; с. вопро́с moot point, vexed question; с. мяч *(in basketball)* jump ball, held ball; ~ное насле́дство disputed legacy.

спор|о́ть, ю́, ~ешь, *pf. (of* спа́рывать) to unstitch, take off *(by cutting stitches)*.

спорт, а, *m.* sport.

спорти́вн|ый, *adj.* sports, sporting; с. зал gymnasium; с. инвента́рь sports goods, sports kit; ~ая площа́дка sports ground, playing-field; ~ые состяза́ния sports, sporting competitions.

спортсме́н, а, *m.* sportsman.

спортсме́нк|а, и, *f.* 1. sportswoman. 2. *(coll.)* gym-shoe.

спортсме́нский, *adj.* sportsmanlike.

спорхн|у́ть, у́, ёшь, *pf. (of* спа́рхивать) to flutter off; to flutter away.

спо́рщик, а, *m.* debater, wrangler.

спо́р|ый (~, ~а́, ~о), *adj. (coll.)* successful, profitable; ~ая рабо́та good work.

спорынь|я́, и́, *f. (bot.)* ergot, spur.

спо́соб, а, *m.* way, mode, method; means; таки́м ~ом in this way; сле́дующим ~ом as follows; с. употребле́ния лека́рства 'directions for use' of a medicine.

спосо́бност|ь, и, *f.* 1. *(usu. pl.; к)* ability (for), talent (for), aptitude (for), flair (for); челове́к с больши́ми ~ями person of great abilities; с. к языка́м facility for languages, linguistic ability. 2. capacity; покупа́тельная с. purchasing power; purchasing capacity; пропускна́я с. capacity.

спосо́б|ный (~ен, ~на), *adj.* 1. able, talented, gifted, clever; с. к матема́тике good at mathematics, with a gift for mathematics. 2. *(*на+*a. or* +*inf.)* capable (of), able (to); они́ ~ны на всё they are capable of anything.

спосо́бств|овать, ую, *impf. (of* по~) (+*d.*) 1. to assist. 2. to be conducive (to), further, promote, make (for); с. успе́ху бра́ка to make for the success of a marriage.

споткн|у́ться, у́сь, ёшься, *pf. (of* спотыка́ться) **1.** (o + *a.*) to stumble (against, over). **2.** (на + *p.* or o + *a.*; *fig., coll.*) to get stuck (on); в перево́де я ~у́лся на сло́ве „наро́дность" in my translation I got stuck on the word наро́дность.

спотыка́|ться, юсь, *impf. of* споткну́ться.

спохва|ти́ться, чу́сь, ~**ти́шься,** *pf. (of* ~**тываться)** *(coll.)* to remember suddenly, think suddenly; я написа́л бы́ло вам на ста́рый а́дрес, но ~ти́лся во́ время I was on the point of writing to you at your old address but remembered just in time *(sc.* that you had moved).

спра́ва, *adv.* (от) to the right (of).

справедли́вост|ь, и, *f.* **1.** justice; equity, fairness; по ~и (говоря́) in (all) fairness, by rights; отда́ть с. (+ *d.*) to do justice (to). **2.** truth, correctness.

справедли́в|ый (~, ~**a**), *adj.* **1.** (*in var. senses*) just; equitable, fair; с. судья́ impartial judge; ~ая война́ just war. **2.** justified, true, correct; на́ши подозре́ния оказа́лись ~ыми our suspicions proved to be justified.

справ|ить¹, лю, ишь, *pf. (of* ~**ля́ть)** *(coll.)* to celebrate; с. сва́дьбу to celebrate one's wedding.

справ|ить², лю, ишь, *pf. (of* ~**ля́ть)** (себе́; *coll.*) to get, procure, acquire.

справ|иться¹, люсь, ишься, *pf. (of* ~**ля́ться)** (c + *i.*) **1.** to cope (with), manage; с. с зада́чей to cope with a task, be equal to a task. **2.** to manage, deal (with), get the better (of); я с ним ~люсь! I'll deal with him!

справ|иться², люсь, ишься, *pf. (of* ~**ля́ться)** (o + *p.*) to ask (about), inquire (about); об э́том вам сле́дует с. в бухгалте́рии you must inquire about this in the accounts department; с. в словаре́ to look up (*a word*) in the dictionary, consult a dictionary.

спра́вк|а, и, *f.* **1.** information; навести́ ~у (o + *p.*) to inquire (about); обрати́ться за ~ой (в + *a.*, к) to apply for information (to). **2.** certificate; с. с ме́ста рабо́ты reference.

справля́|ть(ся), ю(сь), *impf. of* спра́вить(ся).

спра́вочник, а, *m.* reference book, handbook, vade-mecum, guide; телефо́нный с. telephone directory.

спра́вочн|ый, *adj.* inquiry, information; ~ое бюро́, с. стол inquiries office, information bureau; ~ая кни́га = ~ик.

спра́шива|ть, ю, *impf. of* спроси́ть.

спра́шива|ться, юсь, *impf.* **1.** *impf. of* спроси́ться. **2.** *impf. only* ~ется the question is, arises.

спресс|ова́ть, у́ю, *pf. of* прессова́ть.

спринт, а, *m. (sport)* sprint.

спри́нтер, а, *m. (sport)* sprinter.

спринц|ева́ть, у́ю, *impf.* to syringe.

спринцо́вк|а, и, *f.* **1.** syringing. **2.** syringe.

спрова́|дить, жу, дишь, *pf. (of* ~**живать)** *(coll.)* to show out, show the door, send on his way.

спрова́жива|ть, ю, *impf. of* спрова́дить.

спровоци́р|овать, ую, *pf. of* провоци́ровать.

спроекти́р|овать, ую, *pf. of* проекти́ровать¹.

спрос, а, *m.* **1.** *(econ.)* demand; (на + *a.*) demand (for), run (on); с. и предложе́ние supply and demand; по́льзоваться больши́м ~ом to be much in demand. **2.** без ~а (~у) *(coll.)* without permission, without asking leave.

спро|си́ть, шу́, ~**сишь,** *pf. (of* спра́шивать) **1.** (o + *p.*) to ask (about), inquire (about). **2.** (+ *a.* or *g.*) to ask (for); to ask to see, desire to speak (to); с. резинку to ask for a rubber; с. сове́та to ask (for) advice; ~си́те хозя́йку ask to see the landlady. **3.** (c + *g.*) to make answer (for), make responsible (for).

спро|си́ться, шу́сь, ~**сишься,** *pf. (of* спра́шиваться) **1.** (+ *g.* or у) to ask permission (of). **2.** (*impers.*) ~сится с него́, *etc.*, he, *etc.*, will be answerable.

спросо́нок, *adv. (coll.)* being only half-awake.

спрост|а́, *adv. (coll.)* without reflection; off the reel.

спрут, а, *m.* octopus.

спры́гива|ть, ю, *impf. of* спры́гнуть.

спры́г|нуть, ну, нешь, *pf. (of* ~**ивать)** (c + *g.*) to jump off (from), leap off (from); to jump down (from), leap down (from).

спры́скива|ть, ю, *impf. of* спры́ск[нуть].

спры́с|нуть, ну, нешь, *pf. (of* ~**кивать) 1.** to sprinkle. **2.** *(coll.)* to celebrate, drink (to); с. сде́лку to wet a bargain.

спряга́|ть¹, ю, *impf. (of* про~) *(gram.)* to conjugate.

спряга́|ть², ю, *impf. of* спрячь.

спряга́|ться, ется, *impf. (gram.)* to conjugate, be conjugated.

спряже́ни|е, я, *n. (gram.)* conjugation.

спря|сть, ду́, дёшь, *past* ~л, ~ла́, ~ло, *pf. of* прясть.

спря́та|ть(ся), ю(сь), *pf. of* пря́тать(ся).

спря́|чь, гу́, жёшь, гу́т, *past* ~г, ~гла́, *pf. (of* ~га́ть) to harness together.

спу́гива|ть, ю, *impf. of* спугну́ть.

спуг|ну́ть, ну́, нёшь, *pf. (of* ~**ивать)** to frighten off, scare off.

спуд, а, *m. (arch.)* bushel; *now only used in phrases* (i) под ~ом under a bushel; держа́ть под ~ом (*fig.*) to hide under a bushel, keep back, (ii) из-под ~а from hiding; вы́тащить, извле́чь из-под ~а to bring into the light of day, put to use.

спуск, а, *m.* **1.** lowering, hauling down; с.

корабля́ launch(ing). **2.** descent, descending. **3.** release; draining. **4.** slope, descent. **5.** (*in fire-arms*) trigger. **6.** (*typ.*) imposition. **7.** (*coll.*) quarter; не дава́ть ~у (+*d.*) to give no quarter, not to let off.

спуска́|ть, ю, *impf. of* спусти́ть; не с. глаз (с+*g.*) not to take one's eyes (off), keep one's eyes glued (on); not to let out of one's sight.

спуска́|ться, юсь, *impf. of* спусти́ться.

спускн|о́й, *adj.* drain; с. кран drain-cock; ~а́я труба́ drain-pipe.

спусков|о́й, *adj.* trigger; с. крючо́к trigger; с. механи́зм trigger mechanism, trigger guard group; ~а́я скоба́ trigger guard.

спу|сти́ть, щу́, ~стишь, *pf.* (*of* ~ска́ть) **1.** to let down, lower; to haul down; с. кора́бль (на во́ду) to launch a ship; с. флаг to lower a flag; (*naut.*) to haul down the ensign; (*fig.*) to strike the colours; ~стя́ рукава́ (*coll.*) in a slipshod fashion, carelessly; с. с ле́стницы (*fig., coll.*) to kick downstairs. **2.** to let go, let loose, release; с. куро́к to pull, release the trigger; с. затво́р (*phot.*) to release the shutter; с. пе́тлю to drop a stitch; с. соба́ку с при́вязи to unleash a dog. **3.** to let out, drain; с. во́ду из бассе́йна для пла́вания to drain a swimming-bath; с. во́ду в убо́рной to flush a water closet. **4.** to send down, send out; с. директи́ву в райсове́ты to send down a directive to the district soviets. **5.** (*of objects inflated with air*) to go down; одна́ из за́дних шин ~сти́ла one of the back tyres has gone down. **6.** (*coll.*) to pardon, let off, let go, let pass. **7.** (*coll.*) to lose (*weight*). **8.** (*coll.*) to lose, throw away, squander; за оди́н ве́чер он ~сти́л в ка́рты всю полу́чку he lost the whole of his pay-packet at cards in an evening.

спу|сти́ться, щу́сь, ~стишься, *pf.* (*of* ~ска́ться) **1.** to descend; to come down, go down; to go downstream; (*of darkness*) to fall; с. с ле́стницы to come downstairs; ~сти́лась мгла a mist came down; на её чулке́ ~сти́лась пе́тля she has laddered her stocking. **2.** *pass. of* ~сти́ть.

спустя́, *prep.*+*a.* after; later; с. дней де́сять after about ten days; с. год a year later.

спу́та|ть(ся), ю(сь), *pf. of* пу́тать(ся).

спу́тник, а, *m.* **1.** (travelling) companion; fellow-traveller. **2.** concomitant. **3.** (*astron.*) satellite; иску́сственный с. земли́ artificial earth satellite, sputnik.

спу́щенный, *p.p.p. of* спусти́ть *and adj.* (*of a flag*) at half-mast.

спьяна́, *adv.* in a state of drunkenness, in one's cups.

спья́н|у, *adv.* = ~а.

спя́|тить, чу, тишь, *pf.*; с. с ума́ (*coll.*) to go barmy, go off one's rocker.

спя́чк|а, и, *f.* **1.** (*of animals*) hibernation. **2.** (*coll.*) sleepiness, lethargy.

сраба́тыва|ться, юсь, *impf. of* сработаться.

сраб́отанност|ь¹, и, *f.* harmony in work, harmonious team-work.

сраб́отанност|ь², и, *f.* wear.

сраб́отанный, *adj.* worn (out).

сраб́ота|ть, ю, *pf.* (*coll.*) **1.** to make. **2.** (+*i.*) to work, operate.

сраб́ота|ться¹, юсь, *pf.* to achieve harmony in work, work well together.

сраб́ота|ться², ется, *pf.* to wear out.

сравне́ни|е, я, *n.* **1.** comparison; по ~ю (с+*i.*) by comparison (with), as compared (with), as against; вне ~я beyond comparison; не идёт в с. (с+*i.*) it cannot be compared (with). **2.** (*lit.*) simile.

сра́внива|ть, ю, *impf. of* сравни́ть *and* сравня́ть.

сравни́тельно, *adv.* **1.** (с+*i.*) by comparison (with). **2.** comparatively.

сравни́тельн|ый, *adj.* comparative; ~ая сте́пень (*gram.*) comparative (degree).

сравн|и́ть, ю́, и́шь, *pf.* (*of* ~ивать) (с+*i.*) to compare (to, with).

сравн|и́ться, ю́сь, и́шься, *pf.* (с+*i.*) to compare (with), come up (to), touch; в зна́нии Арктики никто́ не мо́жет с ним с. for a knowledge of the Arctic no one can touch him.

сравн|я́ть, я́ю, *pf.* (*of* равня́ть *and* ~ивать) to make even; с. счёт (*sport*) to equalize, bring the score level.

сравня́|ться, юсь, *pf. of* равня́ться.

сража́|ть, ю, *impf. of* срази́ть.

сража́|ться, юсь, *impf.* (*of* срази́ться) (с+*i.*) to fight; to join battle (with).

сраже́ни|е, я, *n.* battle, engagement; дать с. to give battle.

сра|зи́ть, жу́, зи́шь, *pf.* (*of* ~жа́ть) **1.** (*obs.*) to slay, strike down, fell. **2.** (*fig.*) to overwhelm, crush; её ~зи́ла весть о катаст-ро́фе в ша́хте she was crushed by the news of the pit disaster.

сра|зи́ться, жу́сь, зи́шься, *pf. of* ~жа́ться.

сра́зу, *adv.* **1.** at once. **2.** straight away, right away; straight off.

срам, а, *m.* **1.** shame; како́й с.! for shame! **2.** (*coll.*) privy parts.

срам|и́ть, лю́, и́шь, *impf.* (*of* о~) to shame, put to shame.

срам|и́ться, лю́сь, и́шься, *impf.* (*of* о~) to cover oneself with shame.

срамни́к, а́, *m.* (*coll.*) shameless person.

срамн|о́й, *adj.* **1.** (*coll.*) shameless. **2.** ~ые гу́бы (*anat.*) labia; ~а́я часть (*obs.*) privy parts.

срамот|а́, ы́, *f.* (*coll.*) shame.

срастани|е, я, n. (physiol., med.) growing together, inosculation; (of bones) knitting.

сраст|аться, ается, impf. of ~ись.

сраст|ись, ётся, past сросся, срослась, pf. (of ~аться) (physiol., med.) to grow together, inosculate; (of bones) to knit.

сра|стить, щу, стишь, pf. (of ~щивать) 1. to join, joint. 2. to splice.

сращени|е, я, n. union.

сращивани|е, я, n. 1. joining; splicing. 2. (fig.) fusion, merging.

сращива|ть, ю, impf. of срастить.

сребреник, а, m. silver coin, piece of silver; продать за тридцать ~ов to sell for thirty pieces of silver.

сребролюб|ец, ца, m. (obs.) money-grubber.

сребролюбив|ый (~, ~а), adj. (obs.) money-grubbing.

сребролюби|е, я, n. (obs.) greed for money.

среброносный (~ен, ~на), adj. argentiferous.

сред|а¹, ы, a. ~у, pl. ~ы, f. 1. environment, surroundings; milieu; (biol.) habitat; в нашей ~é in our midst, among us. 2. (phys.) medium.

сред|а², ы, a. ~у, pl. ~ы, ~ам, f. Wednesday; по ~ам on Wednesdays, every Wednesday.

средактир|овать, ую, pf. of редактировать.

среди, prep.+g. 1. among, amongst; amidst; с. них among them, in their midst. 2. in the middle (of); с. бела дня in broad daylight.

средиземноморский, adj. Mediterranean.

средин|а, ы, f. (obs.) middle.

срединн|ый, adj. middle; ~ое отклонение (mil.) probable error (in artillery firing).

средне, adv. (coll.) middling, so-so.

среднеазиатский, adj. Central Asian (of Soviet Central Asia).

среднеанглийский, adj. с. язык Middle English.

средневековый, adj. medieval.

средневековь|е, я, n. the Middle Ages.

среднегодовой, adj. average annual.

среднекалиберный, adj. (mil.) medium (-calibre).

среднемесячный, adj. average monthly.

среднесуточный, adj. average daily.

среднеязычный, adj. (ling.) medio-lingual.

средн|ий, adj. 1. middle; medium; с. бомбардировщик medium bomber; ~ие века the Middle Ages; ~яя история history of the Middle Ages; с. залог (gram.) middle voice; ~их лет middle-aged; ~его роста of medium height; ~ee ухо (anat.) middle ear. 2. mean, average; ~ee время mean time; с. заработок average earnings; ~яя ошибка mean error, standard deviation; ~ee пропорциональное (math.) the mean

proportional; as noun ~ee, ~его, n. mean, average; в ~ем on average; выше ~его above (the) average. 3. (coll.) middling, average; ~ие способности average abilities. 4. (in education) secondary; ~яя школа secondary school. 5. с. род (gram.) neuter (gender). 6. (aeron.) waist, belly; с. стрелок waist gunner.

средостени|е, я, n. 1. (anat.) mediastinum. 2. (fig.) partition, barrier.

средоточи|е, я, n. focus, centre point.

средств|о, а, n. 1. means; facilities; ~а передвижения means of conveyance; ~а сообщения means of communication; ~а к существованию means of subsistence; пустить в ход все ~а to move heaven and earth. 2. (от) remedy (for); с. от кашля cough medicine, something for a cough; с. от насекомых insecticide. 3. (pl.) resources; credits. 4. (pl.) means; человек со ~ами man of means; жить не по ~ам to live beyond one's means.

средь, prep.+g. = среди.

срез, а, m. 1. cut; microscopic section. 2. (tech.) shear, shearing; плоскость ~а shear plane. 3. (sport) slice, slicing.

сре|зать, жу, жешь, pf. 1. (impf. ~зать) to cut off; с. угол (fig.) to cut off a corner; с. на экзамене (school sl.) to plough. 2. (impf. резать) (sport) to slice, cut, chop.

среза|ть, ю, impf. of срезать.

сре|заться, жусь, жешься, pf. (of ~заться) (school sl.) to fail, be ploughed.

среза|ться, юсь, impf. of срезаться.

срепетир|овать, ую, pf. of репетировать.

сретени|е, я, n. 1. (arch. or poet.) meeting. 2. С. (eccl.) Candlemas Day; Feast of the Purification.

срис|овать, ую, pf. (of ~овывать) to copy.

срисовыва|ть, ю, impf. of срисовать.

сровня|ть, ю, pf. of ровнять.

сродни, adv. akin; быть, приходиться с. (+d.) to be related (to).

сродн|ить, ю, ишь, pf. (с+i.) to link (with).

сродн|иться, юсь, ишься, pf. (с+i.) to become closely linked (with); to get used (to); с. с работой to get the hang of a job.

срод|ный (~ен, ~на), adj. (+d. or с+i.) related (to).

сродств|о, а, n. relationship, affinity; химическое с. chemical affinity.

сроду, adv. (coll.) in one's life; с. я не видал такой огромной кошки I have never seen such a huge cat (in all my life).

срок, а (у), m. 1. time, period; term; месячный с. a period of one month; в кратчайший с. in the shortest possible time; с. военной службы call-up period; с. действия period of validity; с. полномочий term of office; с. работы life (of *machine, etc.*); по истечéнии ⌣а when the time is up, when the time expires; продлить с. визы to extend a visa; ⌣ом до трёх мéсяцев within three months; дáй(те) с. (*coll.*) wait a minute!, give us time!; ни óтдыху, ни ⌣у не давáть (+*d.*) to give no peace. 2. date, term; крáйний с. closing date; с. арéнды term of lease; с. дáвности (*leg.*) prescription; с. платежá date of payment; пропустить с. платежá to fail to pay by the date fixed; в укáзанный с., к устанóвленному ⌣у by the date fixed, by a specified date; в с., к ⌣у in time, to time.

срóст|ок, ка, *m.* joint, splice.

срóчно, *adv.* urgently; quickly.

срóчност|ь, и, *f.* urgency; hurry; что за с.? what's the hurry?

срóч|ный (~ен, ~нá, ~но), *adj.* 1. urgent, pressing; с. закáз rush order. 2. at a fixed date; for a fixed period; ~ная слýжба (*mil.*) service for a fixed period. 3. periodic, routine; ~ное донесéние (*mil.*) routine report.

сруб, а, *m.* 1. felling; на с. for timber. 2. frame(work), shell (*of an izba, well, etc.*). 3. (*hist.*) framework.

сруб|áть, áю, *impf. of* ~úть.

сруб|úть, лю, ~ишь, *pf.* (*of* ~áть) 1. to fell, cut down. 2. to build (*of logs*).

срыв, а, *m.* disruption; derangement, frustration; с. переговóров break-down of talks; с. рабóты derangement of work, stoppage.

срывá|ть¹, ю, *impf. of* сорвáть.

срывá|ть², ю, *impf. of* срыть.

срывá|ться, юсь, *impf. of* сорвáться.

срыть, срóю, срóешь, *pf.* (*of* срывáть²) to raze, level to the ground.

сряду, *adv.* (*coll.*) running; два рáза с. twice running.

ссáдин|а, ы, *f.* scratch, abrasion.

сса|дúть¹, жý, ~дишь, *pf.* (*of* ~живать) (*coll.*) to scratch.

сса|дúть², жý, ~дишь, *pf.* (*of* ~живать) 1. to help down, help to alight; с. когó-н. с лóшади to help someone down from a horse. 2. to put off, make get off (*from public transport*).

ссáжива|ть, ю, *impf. of* ссадúть.

сседá|ться, ется, *impf. of* ссéсться.

ссел|úть, ю, úшь, *pf.* (*of* ~ять) to settle collectively.

ссел|ять, яю, *impf. of* ~úть.

ссé|сться, ссядется, *past* ~лся, ~лась, *pf.* (*of* ~дáться) (*coll.*) 1. (*of materials*) to shrink. 2. (*of milk*) to turn.

ссóр|а, ы, *f.* 1. quarrel; falling-out; они в ~е друг с дрýгом they have fallen out. 2. slanging-match.

ссóр|ить, ю, ишь, *impf.* (*of* по~) to cause to quarrel, cause to fall out.

ссóр|иться, юсь, ишься, *impf.* (*of* по~) (с+*i.*) to quarrel (with), fall out (with).

ссóх|нуться, нется, *past* ~ся, ~лась, *pf.* (*of* ссыхáться) 1. to shrink, shrivel, warp. 2. to harden out, dry out.

ссýд|а, ы, *f.* loan, grant.

ссу|дúть, жý, ~дишь, *pf.* (*of* ~жáть) (+*a.* and *i.* or +*d.* and *a.*) to lend, loan.

ссýд|ный, *adj. of* ~а; с. процéнт interest on a loan.

ссýдо-сберегáтельн|ый, *adj.* ~ая кáсса savings bank.

ссужá|ть, ю, *impf. of* ссудúть.

ссутýл|ить(ся), ю(сь), ишь(ся), *pf. of* сутýлить(ся).

ссуч|úть, ý, ~ишь, *pf. of* сучúть.

ссылá|ть(ся), ю(сь), *impf. of* сослáть(ся).

ссы́лк|а¹, и, *f.* exile, banishment; deportation.

ссы́лк|а², и, *f.* reference.

ссы́л|очный, *adj. of* ~ка²; ~очное примечáние reference note.

ссыльнопоселéн|ец, ца, *m.* (*hist.*) deportee, convict settler (*ex-convict obliged by court order to settle in remote area after completing prison sentence*).

ссы́льн|ый, ого, *m.* exile.

ссып|áть, áю, *impf. of* ~áть.

ссы́п|ать, лю, лешь, *pf.* (*of* ~áть) to pour.

ссыпнóй, *adj.* с. пункт grain-collecting station.

ссыхá|ться, ется, *impf. of* ссóхнуться.

стабилизáтор, а, *m.* (*tech.*) stabilizer; (*aeron.*) tail-plane.

стабилизáци|я, и, *f.* stabilization.

стабилизúр|овать, ую, *impf. and pf.* to stabilize.

стабилизúр|оваться, уюсь, *impf. and pf.* to become stable.

стабилиз|овáть(ся), ýю(сь), *impf. and pf.* = ~úровать(ся).

стабúльност|ь, и, *f.* stability.

стабúл|ьный (~ен, ~ьна), *adj.* stable, firm; с. учéбник standard text-book.

стáв|ень, ня, *g. pl.* ~ней, *m.* shutter (*on window*).

стáв|ить, лю, ишь, *impf.* (*of* по~) 1. to put, place, set; to stand; to station; с. цветы́ в вáзу to put flowers in a vase; с. бутылки в ряд to stand bottles in a row; с. гóлос комý-н. to train someone's voice; с. диáгноз to diagnose; с. рекóрд to set up, create a record; с. тóчку to put a full stop; с. тóчки на „и" to dot one's 'i's' (and cross one's 't's'); с. часы́ to set a clock; с. самовáр to put a samovar on; с. в винý что-н. комý-н. to accuse someone of something; с. в извéстность to let know, inform; с. когó-н. в нелóвкое положéние to put someone in an awkward position; с. в тупи́к to nonplus; с. в у́гол to stand in the corner; с. что-н. в упрёк кому́-н. to reproach someone with something; ни во что не с. to hold of no account; с. за пра́вило to make it a rule; с. кого́-н. на коле́ни to force someone to his knees; с. кого́-н. на ме́сто to put someone in his place; с. пе́ред совершившимся фа́ктом to present with a fait accompli. 2. to put up, erect; to install; с. па́мятник to erect a monument; с. телефо́н to install the telephone. 3. (coll.) to put in, install; с. но́вого гла́вного инжене́ра to put in a new chief engineer; с. кого́-н. в архиере́и to make someone a bishop. 4. to apply, put on; с. горчи́чник to apply a mustard plaster; с. кому́-н. термо́метр to take someone's temperature. 5. to put, present; to put on, stage; с. резо́люцию to put a resolution; с. мелодра́му to stage a melodrama. 6. (на+a.) to place, stake (money on); с. на ло́шадь to back a horse.

ста́вк|а¹, и, f. 1. rate; с. зарпла́ты wage rate; ~и нало́га tax rates. 2. stake; де́лать ~у (на+a.) to stake (on); (fig.) to count (on), gamble (on).

ста́вк|а², и, f. (mil.) headquarters; с. главнокома́ндующего General Headquarters.

ста́вк|а³, и, f. о́чная с. (leg.) confrontation.

ста́вленник, а, m. protégé.

ста́влен|ый, adj. ~ая гра́мота (eccl.) certificate of ordination.

ста́вн|я, и, f. = ста́вень.

стадиа́льный, adj. taking place by stages.

стадио́н, а, m. stadium.

ста́ди|я, и, f. stage.

ста́дност|ь, и, f. herd instinct, gregariousness.

ста́дный, adj. gregarious; с. инсти́нкт herd instinct.

ста́д|о, а, pl. ~а, n. herd; flock.

стаж, а, m. 1. length of service; record. 2. (испыта́тельный) с. probation; проходи́ть с. to work on probation.

стажёр, а, m. 1. probationer. 2. stazher (student on special course not leading to degree).

стажи́р|овать, ую, impf. to work on probation.

ста́ива|ть, ю, impf. of ста́ять.

ста́йер, а, m. (sport) long-distance runner.

стака́н, а, m. 1. glass, tumbler, beaker. 2. (mil.) body (of projectile).

стакка́то, adv. or indecl., n. (mus.) staccato.

сталагми́т, а, m. stalagmite.

сталакти́т, а, m. stalactite.

сталева́р, а, m. steel founder.

сталели́те́йный, adj. с. заво́д steel mill, steel works.

сталели́те́йщик, а, m. steel founder.

сталепрока́тный, adj. с. заво́д, с. стан steel-rolling mill.

ста́линск|ий, adj. Stalin's, of Stalin; ~ая пре́мия (hist.) Stalin Prize.

ста́лкива|ть(ся), ю(сь), impf. of столкну́ть(ся).

ста́ло быть, conj. (coll.) consequently, therefore, accordingly.

стал|ь, и, f. steel; нержаве́ющая с. stainless steel.

стальн|о́й, adj. steel; ~о́го цве́та steel-blue; ~ые во́лосы iron-grey hair; ~а́я во́ля iron will; ~ые не́рвы nerves of steel.

стаме́ск|а, и, f. (tech.) chisel.

стан¹, а, m. figure, torso.

стан², а, m. 1. camp (also fig.); в ~е врага́ in the enemy's camp. 2. (hist.) (police) district (from 1837).

стан³, а, m. (tech.) mill.

станда́рт, а, m. (in var. senses) standard.

стандартиза́ци|я, и, f. standardization.

стандартиз|ова́ть, у́ю, impf. and pf. to standardize.

станда́рт|ный (~ен, ~на), adj. standard.

стани́н|а, ы, f. (tech.) mounting, bed (plate); боковая с. side plate, cheek; с. лафе́та cheek, side plate of gun-carriage.

станио́л|ь, я, m. tin foil.

стани́ц|а¹, ы, f. stanitsa (large Cossack village).

стани́ц|а², ы, f. (obs.) flock.

стани́чник, а, m. (Cossack) inhabitant of stanitsa.

стани́|чный, adj. of ~ца¹.

станко́в|ый, adj. 1. adj. of стано́к; с. пулемёт (mil.) heavy machine-gun. 2. ~ая жи́вопись easel (as opp. to mural) painting.

станкострое́ни|е, я, n. machine-tool construction.

станов|и́ться, лю́сь, ~ишься, impf. of стать.

становле́ни|е, я, n. (philos.) coming-to-be, coming into being; в проце́ссе ~я in the making.

станово́й¹, adj. main, chief, basic; с. хребе́т (fig.) backbone.

станов|о́й², adj. of стан²; с. при́став (hist.) district police-officer; as noun с., ~о́го, m. = с. при́став.

стан|о́к¹, ка́, m. 1. (tech.) machine-tool, machine; bench; печа́тный с. printing-press; столя́рный с. joiner's bench; тка́цкий с. loom; тока́рный с. lathe; рабо́чий от ~ка́ bench worker. 2. (mil.) mount, mounting.

стан|о́к², ка́, m. stall (for one horse).

стано́чник, а, m. machine operator, machine minder.

станс, а, m. (lit.) stanza.

станцио́нный, adj. of ста́нция; с. зал

waiting-room; с. смотри́тель (*obs.*) post-master.

ста́нци|я, и, *f.* (*in var. senses*) station; гидро-электри́ческая с. hydro-electric power station; межплане́тная с. inter-planetary station; телефо́нная с. telephone exchange; с. снабже́ния (*mil.*) railhead.

ста́пел|ь, я, *m.* (*naut.*) building slip(s), stocks; на ∼е, на ∼ях on the stocks.

ста́плива|ть, ю, *impf. of* стопи́ть.

ста́птыва|ть(ся), ю(сь), *impf. of* стопта́ть-(ся).

стара́ни|е, я, *n.* effort, endeavour; diligence; приложи́ть с. to make an effort; приложи́ть все ∼я to do one's utmost, do one's best.

стара́тел|ь, я, *m.* gold prospector, gold-digger.

стара́тельност|ь, и, *f.* application, assiduity, diligence, painstakingness.

стара́тел|ьный (∼ен, ∼ьна), *adj.* assiduous, diligent, painstaking.

стара́|ться, юсь, *impf.* (*of* по∼) to try, endeavour, seek; to make an effort; с. изо всех сил to do one's utmost, try one's hardest.

стар|е́е (*and* (*obs.*) ста́ре), *comp. of* ∼ый.

старе́йшин|а, ы, *m.* 1. (*hist., ethnol.*) elder. 2. Сове́т ∼ Council of Elders (*of U.S.S.R. Supreme Soviet*).

старе́|ть, ю, *impf.* (*of* по∼) to grow old, age.

ста́р|ец, ца, *m.* 1. elder, (venerable) old man. 2. elderly monk. 3. spiritual adviser.

стари́к, а́, *m.* old man.

старика́н, а, *m.* (*coll.*) old boy, old chap.

старика́шк|а, и, *m.* (*coll., pejor.*) old man, old chap.

старико́вский, *adj. of* стари́к; senile.

ста́рин|а, ы, *f.* (*lit.*) bylina.

старин|а́[1], ы́, *f.* 1. antiquity, olden times; в ∼у́ in olden times, in days of old. 2. (*collect.*) antiques.

старин|а́[2], ы́, *m.* (*coll.*) old fellow, old chap.

стари́нк|а, и, *f.* (*coll.*) old fashion, old custom(s); держа́ться ∼и to keep up the old customs; по ∼е in the old fashion, in the old way.

стари́нный, *adj.* 1. ancient, old; antique; с. обы́чай time-honoured custom. 2. old, of long standing; с. друг old friend.

ста́р|ить, ю, ишь, *impf.* (*of* со∼) to age; to make look old(er).

ста́р|иться, юсь, ишься, *impf.* (*of* со∼) to grow old, age.

ста́риц|а, ы, *f.* 1. elderly nun. 2. old bed (*of river*).

старич|о́к, ка́, *m.* 1. little old man. 2. (*sport*) 'veteran' (*competitor in contest for age-group 35 and over*).

старове́р, а, *m.* 1. (*rel.*) Old Believer. 2. (*fig., joc.*) conservative, laudator temporis acti.

старода́вний, *adj.* ancient.

старода́вност|ь, и, *f.* antiquity.

старожи́л, а, *m.* old inhabitant, old resident.

старозаве́т|ный (∼ен, ∼на), *adj.* 1. (*of persons*) old-fashioned, conservative. 2. (*pejor.*) old, antiquated; ∼ные взгля́ды antiquated views.

старомо́д|ный (∼ен, ∼на), *adj.* old-fashioned, outmoded; out-of-date.

старообра́з|ный (∼ен, ∼на), *adj.* old-looking.

старообря́д|ец, ца, *m.* (*rel.*) Old Believer.

старообря́д|ческий, *adj. of* ∼ец *and* ∼чество.

старообря́дчеств|о, а, *n.* (*rel.*) Old Belief.

старопеча́т|ный, *adj.* ∼ые кни́ги early printed books (*books published in Russia before the 18th century*).

старору́сский, *adj.* old Russian.

старосве́тский, *adj.* old-world; old-fashioned.

старославя́нский, *adj.* (*ling.*) Old Church Slavonic.

ста́рост|а, ы, *m.* (*elected*) head; senior (man); се́льский с. (*hist.*) village headman, elder; церко́вный с. churchwarden; с. кла́сса (*in school*) form prefect, monitor; с. ку́рса (*in college, etc.*) senior student of year.

ста́рост|ь, и, *f.* old age; на ∼и лет, под с. in one's old age.

старт, а, *m.* 1. (*sport*) start; дать с. to start; на с.! on your marks! 2. (*aeron.*) take-off point; взять с. to take off.

ста́ртер *and* (*coll.*) **стартёр**, а, (*sport and tech.*) starter.

ста́ртов|ый, *adj.* starting.

стару́х|а, и, *f.* old woman, old lady.

стару́|шечий, *adj. of* ∼ха; old-womanish.

стару́шк|а, и, *f.* (little) old lady, old woman.

ста́рческий, *adj.* old man's; senile.

старшекла́ссник, а, *m.* senior (pupil).

старшеку́рсник, а, *m.* senior student.

ста́рше, *comp. of* ста́рый; она́ с. меня́ на три го́да she is three years older than me.

ста́рш|ий, *adj.* 1. elder; *as noun* ∼ие, ∼их (one's) elders. 2. oldest, eldest. 3. senior, superior; chief, head; с. врач head physician; ∼ая медсестра́ sister; *as noun* с., ∼его, *m.* chief; (*mil.*) man in charge, senior man. 4. senior, upper, higher; ∼ая ка́рта higher card; с. класс (*in school*) higher form.

старшин|а́, ы́, *m.* 1. (*mil.*) sergeant-major; (*naut.*) petty officer. 2. войсково́й с. (*hist.*) lieutenant-colonel (*of Cossack troops*). 3. leader, senior representative (*of social group,*

professional organization, etc.); с. дипломати́-
ческого ко́рпуса doyen of the diplomatic
corps; с. прися́жных заседа́телей foreman
of the jury.

старшинств|**о́, á,** *n.* seniority; по ~ý by
seniority.

ста́р|**ый (~, ~á, ~о́),** *adj.* (*in var. senses*) old;
с. стиль the Old Style (*of the Julian calen-
dar*); ~ая де́ва old maid, spinster; по ~ой
па́мяти for old times' sake; from force of
habit; *as noun* ~ые, ~ых the old, old people;
~ое, ~ого, *n.* the old, the past; кто ~ое
помя́нет, тому́ глаз вон (*prov.*) let bygones
be bygones.

старь|**ё, я́,** *n.* (*collect.; coll.*) old things, old
clothes.

старьёвщик, а, *m.* old-clothes dealer; junk
dealer.

ста́скива|**ть, ю,** *impf. of* стащи́ть.

стас|**ова́ть, у́ю,** *pf. of* тасова́ть.

ста́тик|**а, и,** *f.* statics.

стати́ст, а, *m.* (*theatr.*) super, extra, mute.

стати́стик, а, *m.* statistician.

стати́стик|**а, и,** *f.* statistics.

статисти́ческий, *adj.* statistical.

стати́ческий, *adj.* static.

ста́т|**ный (~ен, ~на),** *adj.* stately.

ста́тор, а, *m.* (*tech.*) stator.

ста́точн|**ый,** *adj.* ~ое ли де́ло? (*coll., obs.*)
is it possible?, can it be?

статс-да́м|**а, ы,** *f.* lady-in-waiting.

ста́тский, *adj.* **1.** (*obs.*) = шта́тский. **2.**
(*hist.; as part of titles of ranks in tsarist
Russian civil service*) State; с. сове́тник Councillor of State.

статс-секрета́р|**ь, я́,** *m.* Secretary of State.

ста́тус-кво́, *indecl., m.* status quo.

стату́т, а, *m.* statute.

статуэ́тк|**а, и,** *f.* statuette, figurine.

ста́ту|**я, и,** *f.* statue.

стать¹, ста́ну, ста́нешь, *pf.* (*of* станови́ться)
1. to stand; с. на коле́ни to kneel; с. в
о́чередь to queue (up); с. в по́зу to strike
an attitude; с. на цы́почки to stand on
tip-toe; с. на чью-н. сто́рону to take someone's side, stand up for someone; с. на
защи́ту угнетённых to stand up for the
oppressed. **2.** to take up position; с. ла́герем
to camp, encamp; с. в карау́л to mount
guard; с. на рабо́ту to start work; с. на
я́корь to anchor, come to anchor. **3.** to
stop, come to a halt; мои́ часы́ ста́ли my
watch has stopped; река́ ста́ла the river
has frozen over; за чем де́ло ста́ло? (*coll.*)
what's holding things up?, what's the
hitch? **4.** (в+а.; *coll.*) to cost; во что бы
то ни ста́ло at any price, at all costs. **5.**
(*impers.; coll.*) to suffice; с него́ э́то ста́нет
it is what one might expect of him.

стать², ста́ну, ста́нешь, *pf.* (*of* станови́ться)
1. (+*inf.*) to begin (to), start; она́ ста́ла
говори́ть во сне she began talking in her
sleep; он, слов нет, ста́нет ворча́ть he will
start grousing, it goes without saying. **2.**
(+*i.*) to become, get, grow; он стал маши-
ни́стом he became an engine-driver; ста́ло
темно́ it got dark; ей ста́ло лу́чше she was
better, she had got better. **3.** (с+*i.*) to become (of), happen (to); что с ни́ми ста́ло?
what has become of them? **4.** не с. (*impers.*+*g.*) to cease to be; to disappear, be
gone; её отца́ давно́ не ста́ло her father
passed away long ago.

стат|**ь³, и,** *pl.* ~и, ~е́й, *f.* **1.** figure, build;
(*pl.*) points (*of a horse*). **2.** character, type;
быть под с. (+*d.*) to be (well) matched
(with).

стат|**ь⁴, и,** *f.* (*coll., obs.*) need, necessity; к
э́той ме́стности нам не привыка́ть с. this
area is familiar ground to us; с какой ~и?
(*coll.*) why?, what for?

ста́|**ться, нется,** *pf.* (*coll.*) to happen, be-
come; что с ни́ми ~нется? what will be-
come of us?; мо́жет с. perhaps, it may be;
вполне́ мо́жет с. it is quite possible.

стат|**ья́, ьи́, g. pl.** ~е́й, *f.* **1.** article; передо-
ва́я с. leading article, leader, editorial. **2.**
clause; item; (dictionary) entry; с. дого-
во́ра clause of a treaty; расхо́дная с.
debit item; э́то осо́бая с. that is another
matter. **3.** (*coll.*) matter, job; э́то не бу́дет
хи́трая с. that will not be difficult. **4.**
(*naut.*) class, rating; матро́с пе́рвой ~ьи
able seaman; старшина́ пе́рвой ~ьи chief
petty officer. **5.** (*pl.*) points (*of a horse*).

стафилоко́кк, а, *m.* (*med., biol.*) staphylo-
coccus.

стаха́нов|**ец, ца,** *m.* (*hist.*) Stakhanovite.

стаха́новский, *adj.* (*hist.*) Stakhanovite.

стациона́р, а, *m.* permanent establishment;
(лече́бный) с. hospital.

стациона́рн|**ый,** *adj.* **1.** stationary; с.
объ́ект (*mil.*) stationary target. **2.** permanent, fixed; ~ая библиоте́ка permanent
library; ~ая устано́вка (*mil.*) fixed mount.
3. с. больно́й in-patient; ~ое лече́ние hos-
pitalization.

стационе́р, а, *m.* (*naut.*) station ship, guard
ship.

ста́чечник, а, *m.* striker.

ста́ч|**ечный,** *adj. of* ~ка¹.

ста́чива|**ть, ю,** *impf. of* сточи́ть.

ста́чк|**а¹, и,** *f.* strike; свобо́да ста́чек free-
dom to strike.

ста́чк|**а², и, f.;** войти́ в ~у (с+*i.; coll., pejor.*)
to come to terms (with), make a compact
(with).

стащ|**и́ть, у́, ~ишь,** *pf.* (*of* ста́скивать) **1.** to
drag off, pull off; to drag down. **2.** (*coll.*)
to pinch, swipe, whip.

ста́|я, и, *f.* (*of birds*) flock, flight; (*of fish*) school, shoal; (*of dogs or wolves*) pack.

ста́|ять, ет, *pf.* (*of* ~ивать) to melt.

ствол, а́, *m.* 1. (*of tree*) trunk; stem; bole. 2. (*of firearm*) barrel. 3. (*anat.*) tube, pipe. 4. (*mining*) shaft.

стволов|о́й, о́го, *m.* (*in mine*) hanger-on; cager.

стволо́вый, *adj.* of ствол.

стволь́н|ый, *adj.* barrel; ~ая гру́ппа barrel assembly; с. кожу́х barrel housing.

створ, а, *m.* 1. = ~ка. 2. range, alignment.

ство́рк|а, и, *f.* leaf, fold; door, gate, shutter (*one of a pair*).

створо́ж|иться, ится, *pf.* to curdle.

ство́рчатый, *adj.* folding; valved.

стеари́н, а, *m.* stearin.

стеари́н|овый, *adj.* of ~; ~овая свеча́ stearin candle.

стеб́|ель, ля, *pl.* ~ли, ~ле́й, *m.* stem, stalk.

стебе́льчатый, *adj.* с. шов feather stitch.

стёганк|а, и, *f.* (*coll.*) quilted jacket.

стёган|ый, *adj.* quilted; ~ое одея́ло quilt.

стега́|ть¹, ю, *impf.* (*of* от~ *and* стегну́ть) to whip, lash.

стега́|ть², ю, *impf.* (*of* вы́~) to quilt.

стег|ну́ть, ну́, нёшь, *pf.* of ~а́ть¹.

стёжк|а¹, и, *f.* quilting.

стёжк|а², и, *f.* (*dial.*) path.

стеж|о́к, ка́, *m.* stitch.

стез|я́, и́, *g. pl.* ~е́й, *f.* (*rhet.*) path, way.

стек, а, *m.* riding-crop.

стека́|ть(ся), ю(сь), *impf. of* сте́чь(ся).

стеклене́|ть, ет, *impf.* (*of* о~) to become glassy.

стек|ло́, ла́, *pl.* ~ла, ~о́л, *n.* glass; ~ла lenses (*for spectacles*); ла́мповое с. lamp--chimney; око́нное с. window-pane; пере́днее с. wind-screen.

стеклова́т|а, ы, *f.* fibreglass.

стеклови́д|ный (~ен, ~на), *adj.* 1. glassy. 2. (*anat.*) hyaline, hyaloid; ~ное те́ло hyaloid (membrane).

стекловолокн|о́, а́, *n.* fibreglass.

стеклоду́в, а, *m.* glass-blower.

стеклоду́вный, *adj.* glass-blowing.

стёклыш|ко, ка, *pl.* ~ки, ~ек, ~кам, *n.* 1. *dim.* of стекло́. 2. piece of glass.

стекля́нн|ый, *adj.* 1. glass; ~ая бума́га glass-paper; ~ые изде́лия glassware. 2. (*fig.*) glassy.

стекля́рус, а, *m.* (*collect.*) bugles (*tube-shaped glass beads*).

стеко́льный, *adj.* glass; vitreous; с. заво́д glass-works, glass-factory.

стеко́льщик, а, *m.* glazier.

стел|и́ть(ся), ю́(сь), ~ишь(ся), *impf.* = стлать(ся).

стелла́ж, а́, *m.* 1. shelves. 2. rack, stand.

сте́льк|а, и, *f.* insole, sock; пьян как с. (*coll.*) drunk as a lord.

сте́льная, *adj.* с. коро́ва cow with calf.

стемне́|ть, ю, *pf.* of темне́ть.

стен|а́, ы́, *a.* ~у, *pl.* ~ы, ~а́м, *f.* wall (*also fig.*); обнести́ ~о́й to wall in; жить с. в ~у (c+i.) to live right on top (of); в ~а́х (+g.) within the precincts (of); в четырёх ~а́х within four walls; лезть на́ ~у (*coll.*) to climb up the wall; как об ~у горо́х (*coll.*) pointless, useless.

стена́|ть, ю, *impf.* (*obs.*) to groan, moan.

стенгазе́т|а, ы, *f.* (*abbr. of* стенна́я газе́та) wall newspaper.

стенд, а, *m.* 1. stand (*at exhibition, etc.*). 2. testing ground.

сте́ндер, а, *m.* stand-pipe.

сте́нк|а, и, *f.* 1. wall; гимнасти́ческая с. wall-bars. 2. (*anat., etc.*) side, wall.

стенн|о́й, *adj.* wall; mural; ~а́я жи́вопись mural painting.

стеноби́тный, *adj.* с. тара́н battering-ram.

стеногра́мм|а, ы, *f.* shorthand report.

стено́граф, а, *m.* stenographer.

стенографи́р|овать, ую, *impf. and pf.* to take down in shorthand.

стенографи́ст, а, *m.* = стено́граф.

стенографи́ст|ка, ки, *f. of* ~.

стенографи́ческий, *adj.* stenographic, shorthand.

стеногра́фи|я, и, *f.* stenography, shorthand.

сте́нопис|ь, и, *f.* mural (painting).

сте́ньг|а, и, *f.* (*naut.*) topmast.

степе́н|ный (~ен, ~на), *adj.* 1. staid, steady. 2. middle-aged.

сте́пен|ь, и, *g. pl.* ~е́й, *f.* 1. degree, extent; в вы́сшей ~и in the highest degree; до изве́стной ~и, до не́которой ~и to some degree, to some extent, to a certain extent; ~и сравне́ния (*gram.*) degrees of comparison. 2. (*math.*) power; возвести́ в тре́тью с. to raise to the third power. 3. (учёная) с. (academic) degree.

степ|но́й, *adj.* of ~ь.

степня́к, а́, *m.* 1. inhabitant of steppe. 2. steppe horse.

степ|ь, и, о ~и, в ~й, *pl.* ~и, ~е́й, *f.* steppe.

сте́рв|а, ы, *f.* 1. (*obs.*) dead animal, carrion. 2. (*vulg.*; *as term of abuse*) shit, stinker.

стервене́|ть, ю, *impf.* (*of* о~) (*coll.*) to become furious, get mad.

стерв|е́ц, еца́, *m.* = ~а 2.

стервя́тник, а, *m.* carrion-crow (*also fig., of enemy aircraft in Second World War*).

стерео- stereo-.

стереодальноме́р, а, *m.* (*mil.*) stereoscopic range-finder.

стереокино́, *indecl., n.* stereoscopic cinema.

стереоме́три|я, и, *f.* stereometry, solid geometry.

стереоско́п, а, *m.* stereoscope.

стереоскопи́ческий, *adj.* stereoscopic.

стереоти́п, а, *m.* stereotype.

стереоти́пн|ый, *adj.* 1. stereotype. 2. (*fig.*) stereotyped; ~ая фра́за stock phrase.

стереотруб|а́, ы́, *f.* stereoscopic telescope; (*mil.*) battery commander's telescope.

стереофони́ческий, *adj.* stereophonic.

стереохи́ми|я, и, *f.* stereochemistry.

стер|е́ть, сотру́, сотрёшь, *past* ~, ~ла, *pf.* (*of* стира́ть¹) 1. to rub out, erase; to wipe off; с. с лица́ земли́ to wipe off the face of the earth. 2. to rub sore. 3. to grind (down).

стер|е́ться, сотрётся, *past* ~ся, ~лась, *pf.* (*of* стира́ться¹) 1. to rub off; (*fig.*) to fade; с. в па́мяти to sink into oblivion. 2. to become worn down.

стере́|чь, гу́, жёшь, гу́т, *past* ~г, ~гла́, *impf.* 1. to guard, watch (over). 2. to watch (for).

сте́рж|ень, ня, *m.* 1. (*tech.*) pivot; shank, rod; поршнево́й с. piston rod. 2. (*fig.*) core.

стержнев|о́й, *adj.* pivoted; ~а́я анте́нна rod aerial; с. вопро́с key question.

стерилиза́тор, а, *m.* sterilizer.

стерилиза́ци|я, и, *f.* sterilization.

стерилиз|ова́ть, у́ю, *impf. and pf.* to sterilize.

стери́льност|ь, и, *f.* sterility.

стери́л|ьный (~ен, ~ьна), *adj.* sterile.

сте́рлинг, а, *m.* (*fin.*) sterling; фунт ~ов pound sterling.

сте́рлинг|овый, *adj. of* ~; ~овая зо́на sterling area.

сте́рляд|ь, и, *f.* sterlet.

стерн|ь, и, *f.* 1. harvest-field. 2. (*collect.*) stubble.

стерн|я́, и́, *f.* = ~ь.

стерп|е́ть, лю́, ~ишь, *pf.* to bear, suffer, endure.

стерп|е́ться, ~ишься, *pf.* (с+*i.*; *coll.*) to get used (to), accept; ~ится — слюбится you will like it when you get used to it.

стёр|тый, *p.p.p. of* ~е́ть *and adj.* worn, effaced.

стесне́ни|е, я, *n.* constraint; без вся́ких ~й quite uninhibitedly.

стесн|ённый, *p.p.p. of* ~и́ть *and adj.*; ~ённые обстоя́тельства straitened circumstances.

стесни́тельност|ь, и, *f.* 1. shyness; inhibition(s). 2. difficulty, inconvenience.

стесни́тел|ьный (~ен, ~ьна), *adj.* 1. shy; inhibited. 2. difficult, inconvenient.

стесн|и́ть, ю́, и́шь, *pf.* (*of* ~я́ть) to constrain; to hamper; to inhibit.

стесн|и́ться, ю́сь, и́шься, *pf.* (*of* тесни́ться) to crowd together.

стесн|я́ть, я́ю, *impf. of* ~и́ть.

стесня́|ться, ю́сь, *impf.* (*of* по~) (+*inf.*) to feel too shy (to), be ashamed (to); (+*g.*) to feel shy (before, of); не ~йтесь! don't be shy!

стетоско́п, а, *m.* (*med.*) stethoscope.

стече́ни|е, я, *n.* confluence; с. наро́да concourse; с. обстоя́тельств coincidence.

сте|чь, чёт, ку́т, *past* ~к, ~кла́, *pf.* (*of* ~ка́ть) to flow down.

сте́|чься, чётся, ку́тся, *past* ~кся, ~кла́сь, *pf.* (*of* ~ка́ться) to flow together; to gather, throng.

сти́бр|ить, ю, ишь, *pf. of* ти́брить.

стивидо́р, а, *m.* stevedore.

стил|ево́й, *adj. of* ~ь; ~евы́е катего́рии stylistic categories.

стиле́т, а, *m.* stiletto.

стилиза́ци|я, и, *f.* stylization.

стилиз|ова́ть, у́ю, *impf. and pf.* to stylize.

стили́ст, а, *m.* stylist.

стили́стик|а, и, *f.* (study of) style, stylistics.

стилисти́ческий, *adj.* stylistic.

стил|ь, я, *m.* (*in var. senses*) style; но́вый с. New Style (*Gregorian calendar*); ста́рый с. Old Style (*Julian calendar*).

сти́л|ьный (~ен, ~ьна), *adj.* stylish; ~ьная ме́бель period furniture.

стиля́г|а, и, *m. and f.* stilyaga (*young person given to uncritical display of extravagant fashions in dress and manners*).

сти́мул, а, *m.* stimulus, incentive.

стимули́р|овать, ую, *impf. and pf.* to stimulate.

стипендиа́т, а, *m.* grant-aided student, scholarship holder.

стипе́нди|я, и, *f.* grant, scholarship.

стира́льн|ый, *adj.* washing; ~ая маши́на washing machine.

стира́|ть¹, ю, *impf. of* стере́ть.

стира́|ть², ю, *impf.* (*of* вы́~) to wash, launder.

стира́|ться¹, юсь, *impf. of* стере́ться.

стира́|ться², ется, *impf.* to wash; хорошо́ с. to wash well.

сти́рк|а, и, *f.* washing, laundering; отда́ть в ~у to send to the wash, send to the laundry.

сти́скива|ть, ю, *impf. of* сти́снуть.

сти́с|нуть, ну, нешь, *pf.* (*of* ~кивать) to squeeze; с. зу́бы to clench one's teeth; с. в объя́тиях to hug.

стих¹, а́, *m.* 1. verse; line (*of poetry*); бе́лый с. blank verse; во́льный с. free verse; разме́р ~а́ metre. 2. (*pl.*) verses; poetry.

стих², *indecl.*, *m.* (*coll.*) mood; на него́ угрю́мый с. нашёл he was in a gloomy mood.

стих³, *see* ~ну́ть.

стиха́р|ь, я́, *m.* (*eccl.*) surplice, alb.

стих|а́ть, а́ю, *impf. of* ~ну́ть.

стихи́йност|ь, и, *f.* spontaneity.

стихи́|йный (~ен, ~йна), *adj.* 1. elemental; ~йное бе́дствие natural calamity. 2. (*fig.*) spontaneous, uncontrolled.

стихи́р|а, ы, *f.* hymn, canticle.

стихи́|я, и, *f.* element; борьба́ со ~ями struggle with the elements; быть в свое́й ~и to be in one's element.

стих|нуть, ну, нешь, *past* ~, ~ла, *pf.* (*of* ~а́ть) to abate, subside; to die down; to calm down.

стихове́дени|е, я, *n.* (study of) prosody.

стихоплёт, а, *m.* (*coll.*) rhymester, versifier.

стихосложе́ни|е, я, *n.* versification; prosody.

стихотворе́ни|е, я, *n.* poem.

стихотво́р|ец, ца, *m.* (*obs.*) poet.

стихотво́рн|ый, *adj.* in verse form; с. разме́р metre; ~ая речь poetic diction.

стихотво́рчеств|о, а, *n.* poetry-writing.

стиш|о́к, ка́, *m.* (*coll.*) verse, rhyme.

стлать, стелю́, сте́лешь, *impf.* (*of* по~) to spread; с. посте́ль to make a bed; с. ска́терть to lay a table-cloth.

стла́ться, сте́лется, *impf.* to spread; с. по земле́ (*of mist, smoke, etc.*) to creep; to hang about.

сто¹, ста, *pl.* **ста, сот, стам, ста́ми, стах,** *num.* hundred; не́сколько сот рубле́й several hundred roubles; на все сто (*coll.*) in first-rate fashion.

сто², *indecl., n.* (*hist.*) merchant guild.

стог, а, *pl.* ~а́, *m.* (*agric.*) stack, rick.

стогова́ни|е, я, *n.* (*agric.*) stacking.

стогра́дусный, *adj.* centigrade.

стоеро́сов|ый, *adj. only in phrases* (*coll.*) дуби́на ~ая!, дура́к (болва́н) с.! damned fool!

сто́ик, а, *m.* (*philos. and fig.*) stoic.

сто́имост|ь, и, *f.* 1. cost; с. перево́зки carriage. 2. (*econ.*) value; менова́я с. exchange value; приба́вочная с. surplus value.

сто́|ить, ю, ишь, *impf.* 1. to cost (*also fig.*); ско́лько ~ит э́то пла́тье? how much is this dress?; отсю́да до грани́цы ~ит сто рубле́й from here to the frontier costs one hundred roubles; до́рого с. to cost dear; э́то ему́ ничего́ не ~ило it cost him nothing. 2. (+*g.*) to be worth; to deserve; ~ит (*impers.*) it is worth while; ~ит посмотре́ть э́тот фильм this film is worth seeing; ~ит ли он её? is he worthy of her?, does he deserve her?; не ~ит того́ (*coll.*) it is not worth while; не ~ит (благода́рности) don't mention it. 3. ~ит то́лько (*impers.*+*inf.*) one has only (to); ~ит то́лько упомяну́ть её и́мя, (как) он вы́йдет из себя́ you have only to mention her name for him to fly off the handle.

стоици́зм, а, *m.* (*philos. and fig.*) stoicism.

стои́ческий, *adj.* (*philos.*) stoic; (*fig.*) stoical.

сто́йбищ|е, а, *n.* nomad camp.

сто́йк|а, и, *f.* 1. (*sport*) stand, stance; с. на кистя́х hand-stand. 2. (*hunting*) set;

сде́лать ~у to point. 3. (*tech.*) support, prop; stanchion, upright; (*aeron.*) strut. 4. bar, counter.

сто́|йкий (~ек, ~йка́, ~йко), *adj.* 1. firm, stable; (*phys., chem.*) stable; (*of poisonous substances*) persistent. 2. (*fig.*) stable; steadfast, staunch, steady.

сто́йкост|ь, и, *f.* 1. firmness, stability. 2. (*fig.*) steadfastness, staunchness; determination.

сто́йл|о, а, *n.* stall.

сто́йло|вый, *adj. of* ~; ~вое содержа́ние скота́ keeping cattle stalled.

стоймя́, *adv.* upright.

сток, а, *m.* 1. flow; drainage, outflow. 2. drain, gutter; sewer.

сто́кер, а, *m.* (*tech.*) (mechanical) stoker.

стокра́т, *adv.* (*obs.*) a hundred times, an hundredfold.

стокра́тный, *adj.* hundredfold, centuple.

стол, а́, *m.* 1. table; пи́сьменный с. writing-table, desk; сесть за с. to sit down to table; за ~о́м at table. 2. board; cooking, cuisine; диети́ческий с. invalid dietary; ры́бный с. fish diet; держа́ть с. (*obs.*) to provide board; с. и кварти́ра board and lodging. 3. department; office, bureau; с. ли́чного соста́ва personnel department; с. нахо́док lost property office. 4. (*hist.*) throne.

столб, а́, *m.* post, pole, pillar, column; телегра́фный с. telegraph pole; пыль ~о́м а cloud of dust; стоя́ть ~о́м (*coll.*) to stand rooted to the ground.

столбене́|ть, ю, *impf.* (*of* о~) (*coll.*) to be rooted to the ground.

столб|е́ц, ца́, *m.* 1. column (*in dictionary, newspaper, etc.*). 2. (*pl.*) parchment roll.

сто́лбик, а, *m.* 1. *dim. of* столб; с. рту́ти mercury (column). 2. (*bot.*) style.

столбня́к, а́, *m.* 1. (*med.*) tetanus. 2. (*coll.*) stupor; на неё нашёл с. she was stunned.

столбов|о́й, *adj. of* столб; (*fig., coll.*) main, chief; с. дворяни́н (*hist.*) member of long-established family of (Russian) gentry; ~а́я доро́га high road, highway (*also fig.*).

столе́ти|е, я, *n.* 1. century. 2. centenary.

столе́тн|ий, *adj.* 1. of a hundred years' duration; ~яя война́ the Hundred Years' War. 2. a hundred years old; centennial; ~яя годовщи́на centenary; с. стари́к centenarian.

столе́тник, а, *m.* (*bot.*) agave.

столи́ц|а, ы, *f.* capital; metropolis.

столи́|чный, *adj. of* ~ца; с. го́род capital (city).

столкнове́ни|е, я, *n.* collision; (*mil. and fig.*) clash; вооружённое с. armed conflict, hostilities; с. интере́сов clash of interests.

столкн|у́ть, у́, ёшь, *pf.* (*of* ста́лкивать) 1. to push off, push away; с. ло́дку в во́ду to push a boat off (into the water). **2.** to cause to collide; to knock together. **3.** (*coll.*) to bring together.

столкн|у́ться, у́сь, ёшься, *pf.* (*of* ста́лкиваться) **1.** (c+*i.*) to collide (with), come into collision (with) (*also fig.*); (*fig.*) to clash (with), conflict (with); здесь на́ши интере́сы ~у́лись our interests clashed at this point. **2.** (c+*i.*; *fig., coll.*) to run (into), bump (into); с. со ста́рым ученико́м to bump into an old pupil.

столк|ова́ться, у́юсь, *pf.* (*of* ~о́вываться) (c+*i.*; *coll.*) to come to an agreement (with).

столко́выва|ться, юсь, *impf. of* столкова́ться.

стол|ова́ться, у́юсь, *impf.* to have meals, receive board; to mess; он ~у́ется у друзе́й he has meals with friends.

столо́в|ая, ой, *f.* **1.** dining-room; dining-hall; mess. **2.** dining-room(s); canteen.

столоверче́ни|е, я, *n.* (*coll., iron.*) table-turning.

столо́в|ый, *adj.* **1.** table; ~ое вино́ table wine; ~ая ло́жка table-spoon; с. прибо́р cover; ~ое серебро́ (*collect.*) silver, plate; ~ая соль table-salt. **2.** feeding, catering, messing; ~ые де́ньги dinner money; (*mil.*) ration allowance, messing allowance; ~ые расхо́ды catering expenses; (*mil.*) messing expenses. **3.** ~ые го́ры (*geogr.*) mesa, tableland.

столонача́льник, а, *m.* (*obs.*) head of a 'desk' (*in civil service*).

стол|о́чь, чу́, чёшь, чу́т, *past* ~о́к, ~кла́, *pf.* (*of* толо́чь) to pound, grind.

столп, а́, *m.* (*arch. or fig.*) pillar, column; ~ы́ о́бщества pillars of society.

столп|и́ться, и́тся, *pf.* to crowd.

столпотворе́ни|е, я, *n.* вавило́нское с. babel.

столь, *adv.* so; э́то не с. ва́жно it is of no particular importance.

сто́лько, *adv.* so much; so many; ещё с. же as much again, as many again; не с. ...ско́лько not so much . . . as; где ты был с. вре́мени? where have you been all this time?; сто́лько-то so much, some.

сто́льник, а, *m.* (*hist.*) stolnik (*Russian courtier inferior in rank to boyar*).

сто́льный, *adj.* с. го́род, с. град (*hist.*) capital (city).

столя́р, а́, *m.* joiner.

столя́рнича|ть, ю, *impf.* to be a joiner.

столя́рн|ый, *adj.* joiner's; ~ое де́ло joinery; с. клей carpenter's glue.

стоматоло́ги|я, и, *f.* stomatology.

стон, а, *m.* moan, groan.

стон|а́ть, у́, ~ешь *and* ~а́ю, ~а́ешь, *impf.* to moan, groan (*also fig.*).

стоп, *interj.* stop!; сигна́л с. stop signal.

стоп|а́¹, ы́, *f.* **1.** (*pl.* ~ы́) foot (*also fig.*); напра́вить свои́ ~ы́ to direct, bend one's steps; идти́ по чьим-н. ~а́м to follow in someone's footsteps. **2.** (*pl.* ~ы) (*lit.*) foot.

стоп|а́², ы́, *pl.* ~ы, *f.* **1.** ream. **2.** pile, heap.

стоп|а́³, ы́, *pl.* ~ы, *f.* (*obs.*) winebowl.

стоп|и́ть, лю́, ~ишь, *pf.* (*of* ста́пливать) **1.** to fuse, melt. **2.** (*of* топи́ть) (*coll.*) to heat.

сто́пк|а¹, и, *f.* pile, heap.

сто́пк|а², и, *f.* small drinking vessel.

сто́пор, а, *m.* **1.** (*tech.*) stop, catch, locking device. **2.** (*naut.*) stopper.

сто́пор|ить, ю, ишь, *impf.* (*tech.*) to stop, lock; (*fig., coll.*) to bring to a standstill.

сто́пор|иться, ится, *impf.* (*coll.*) to come to a standstill.

сто́пор|ный, *adj. of* ~; с. кла́пан stop-valve; с. кран stopcock; с. механи́зм stop gear, locking device; ~ное приспособле́ние, ~ное устро́йство lock, catch; с. у́зел (*naut.*) stopper-knot.

стопоходя́щий, *adj.* (*zool.*) plantigrade.

стопроце́нтный, *adj.* hundred per cent.

стоп-сигна́л, а, *m.* brake-light (*on car*).

стоп|та́ть, чу́, ~чешь, *pf.* (*of* ста́птывать) **1.** to wear down (*footwear*). **2.** (*coll.*) to trample.

стоп|та́ться, ~чется, *pf.* (*of* ста́птываться) to wear down, be worn down (*of footwear*).

сторг|ова́ть(ся), у́ю(сь), *pf. of* торгова́ть(ся).

стори́цею, *adv.* (*obs.*) a hundredfold; возда́ть с. (+*d.*) to return a hundredfold, repay with interest.

сто́рож, а, *pl.* ~а́, ~е́й, *m.* watchman, guard; ночно́й с. night-watchman.

сторожеви́к, а́, *m.* patrol-boat.

сторожев|о́й, *adj.* watch; ~а́я бу́дка sentry-box; ~а́я вы́шка watch-tower; с. кора́бль escort vessel; с. пёс watch-dog; с. пост sentry post; ~ы́е огни́ (*naut.*) warning lights.

сторож|и́ть, у́, и́шь, *impf.* **1.** to guard, watch, keep watch (over). **2.** to lie in wait (for).

сторожи́х|а, и, *f.* **1.** female watchman. **2.** watchman's wife.

сторо́жк|а, и, *f.* lodge.

сторо́ж|кий (~ек, ~ка), *adj.* (*coll.*) watchful (*of animals and fig.*).

сторож|о́к, ка́, *m.* (*tech.*) **1.** catch. **2.** tongue, cock (*of scales*).

сторон|а́, ы́, *a.* сто́рону, *pl.* сто́роны, сторо́н, ~а́м, *f.* **1.** (*in var. senses*) side; quarter; hand (*also fig.*); feature, aspect; в сто́рону (*theatr.*) aside; шу́тки в сто́рону (*coll.*) joking aside; в ~е́ aside; держа́ться в ~е́ to keep aloof; на ~е́ (*coll.*) elsewhere, not on the spot; он рабо́тает на ~е́ he does not work on the spot; продава́ть на́ сторону sell on the black market; по ту сто́рону

(+*g.*) across, on the other side (of), on the far side (of); с пра́вой, с ле́вой ~ы on the right, left side; с како́й ~ы ве́тер? from what quarter is the wind blowing?; с мое́й ~ы for my part; э́то о́чень любе́зно с ва́шей ~ы it is very kind of you; со ~ы (+*g.*) (*indicating line of descent*) on the side (of); дед со ~ы ма́тери maternal grand-father; с одно́й ~ы..., с друго́й ~ы on the one hand . . ., on the other hand; узна́ть ~о́й to find out indirectly. **2.** side, party; вы на чьей ~é? whose side are you on?; взять чью-н. сто́рону to take someone's part, side with someone; Высо́кие Догова́ривающиеся Сто́роны (*dipl.*) the High Contracting Parties. **3.** land, place; parts; на чужо́й ~é in foreign parts.

сторон|и́ться, ю́сь, ~и́шься, *impf.* (*of* по~) **1.** to stand aside, make way. **2.** (+*g.*) to shun, avoid.

сторо́нний, *adj.* **1.** strange, foreign; с. наблюда́тель detached observer. **2.** indirect.

сторо́нник, a, *m.* supporter, adherent, advocate.

стоск|ова́ться, у́юсь, *pf.* (по+*p.*, о+*p.*) pine (for), yearn (for).

сточ|и́ть, у́, ~ишь, *pf.* (*of* ста́чивать) to grind off.

сто́чн|ый, *adj.* sewage, drainage; ~ые во́ды sewage; ~ая труба́ sewer pipe.

стошн|и́ть, и́т, *pf.* (*impers.*) to be sick, vomit; меня́ ~и́ло I was sick.

сто́я, *adv.* upright.

стоя́к, á, *m.* **1.** post, stanchion, upright. **2.** stand-pipe, rising pipe. **3.** chimney.

стоя́лый, *adj.* stagnant; stale, old.

стоя́ни|е, я, *n.* standing.

стоя́нк|а, и, f. **1.** stop; parking; с. запрещена́! 'no parking!'; во вре́мя ~и (по́езда) на ста́нции while the train is standing at a station. **2.** stopping place, halting place; parking space; moorage; с. такси́ taxi-rank. **3.** (*archaeol.*) site.

сто|я́ть, ю́, и́шь, *impf.* **1.** to stand; с. в о́череди to stand in a queue; с. на коле́нях to kneel; с. на четвере́ньках to be on all fours. **2.** to be, be situated, lie; село́ ~и́т на возвы́шенности the village is situated on rising ground; стака́ны ~я́т в шкафу́ the glasses are in the cupboard; с. во главе́ (+*g.*) to be at the head (of), head; с. на часа́х to stand guard; с. на я́коре to be at anchor; с. над душо́й у кого́-н. (*coll.*) to plague someone, worry the life out of someone; с. у вла́сти to be in power, be in office; с. у прича́ла (*naut.*) to lie alongside, be moored; с. у руля́ to be at the helm. **3.** (*of weather conditions, etc.*) to be; to continue; ~и́т моро́з there is a frost; ~я́ла

хоро́шая пого́да the weather continued fine; а́кции ~я́т высоко́ shares continue high. **4.** to stay, put up; (*mil.*) to be stationed; с. на кварти́рах, по кварти́рам (*mil.*) to be billeted; с. ла́герем to be encamped, be under canvas. **5.** (за+*a.*) to stand up (for); (на+*p.*) to stand (on), insist (on); с. горо́й за кого́-н. (*coll.*) to stand up for someone with all one's might, be whole-heartedly behind someone; с. на чьей-н. то́чке зре́ния to share someone's point of view. **6.** to stop; to come to a halt, come to a standstill; мои́ часы́ ~я́т my watch has stopped; рабо́та ~и́т work has come to a standstill; ~й(те)! stop!, halt!

стоя́ч|ий, *adj.* **1.** standing; upright, vertical; с. воротничо́к stand-up collar; ~ая ла́мпа standard lamp; ~ая труба́ stand-pipe. **2.** stagnant.

сто́|ящий, *pres. part. act. of* ~ить *and adj.* deserving; worth-while.

страв|и́ть, лю́, ~ишь, *pf.* (*of* ~ливать *and* ~ля́ть) **1.** to set on (*to fight*); с. одного́ с други́м to play off one against another. **2.** to use up in feeding (*cattle*). **3.** (*of cattle*) to spoil (*by eating and trampling*). **4.** to remove by chemical means. **5.** (*naut.*) to let steam. **6.** (*naut.*) to veer, pay out (rope).

стра́влива|ть, ю, *impf. of* страви́ть.

стравля́|ть, ю, *impf. =* стра́вливать.

стра́гива|ть(ся), ю(сь), *impf. of* стро́нуть-(ся).

стра́гива|ть, ю, *impf. of* стро́нуть.

страд|а́, ы́, *pl.* ~ы, *f.* hard work at harvest--time; period of hard work; (*fig.*) toil, drudgery.

страда́л|ец, ьца, *m.* sufferer.

страда́льческ|ий, *adj.* full of suffering; с. вид an air of suffering, a martyr's air; ~ая жизнь life of suffering.

страда́ни|е, я, *n.* suffering.

страда́тельн|ый[1], *adj.* suffering; ~ое лицо́ sufferer.

страда́тельный[2], *adj.* (*gram.*) passive.

страда|́ть, ю, *and* (*arch.*) **стра́жду, стра́ждешь,** *impf.* **1.** *impf. only* (+*i.*) to suffer (from); to be subject (to); с. бессо́нницей to suffer from insomnia. **2.** *impf. only* (от) to suffer (from), be in pain (with); с. от зубно́й бо́ли to have (a) toothache; с. от любви́ to be in love. **3.** *impf. only* с. за кого́-н. to feel for someone. **4.** *impf. only* (по+*d.* or *p.*; *coll.*) to miss; to long (for), pine (for). **5.** (*pf.* по~) to suffer; с. за ве́ру to suffer for one's faith; с. от за́сухи to suffer from the drought; с. от бомбёжки to be a victim of bombing; с. по свое́й вине́ to suffer through one's own fault. **6.** *impf. only* (*coll.*) to be weak, be poor; to be at a low ebb; у неё па́мять ~ет she has a poor memory.

стра́д|ный 1. *adj. of* ~á; ~ная пора́ busy period. 2. (*obs.*) suffering.

страж, а, *m.* (*obs., now only rhet.*) guard, custodian.

стра́ж|а, и, *f.* guard, watch; пограни́чная с. (*obs.*) frontier guard(s); быть, стоя́ть на ~е (+*g.*) to guard; под ~ей under arrest, in custody; взять, заключи́ть под ~у to take into custody.

стра́ждущ|ий, *pres. part. act.* (*obs.*) *of* страда́ть; ~ее челове́чество suffering humanity.

стра́жник, а, *m.* (*obs.*) 1. police constable (*in rural areas*). 2. берегово́й с. coastguard; лесно́й с. forest warden.

страз, а, *m.* paste (jewel); strass.

стран|á, ы́, *pl.* ~ы, *f.* 1. country; land. 2. с. све́та cardinal point (*of compass*).

страни́ц|а, ы, *f.* page (*also fig., rhet.*).

стра́нник, а, *m.* wanderer (*esp. religious* pilgrim).

стра́нниц|а, ы, *f. of* стра́нник.

стра́нно, *adv.* 1. strangely, in a strange way. 2. *as pred.* it is strange, funny, odd, queer.

странноприи́мный, *adj.* (*obs.*) hospitable to strangers; с. дом almshouse, old people's home.

стра́нност|ь, и, *f.* 1. strangeness. 2. oddity, eccentricity; за ним води́лись ~и he was an odd person, he had his quirks.

стра́н|ный (~ен, ~на́, ~но), *adj.* strange; funny, odd, queer.

странове́дени|е, я, *n.* 1. regional geography. 2. study of a country's customs and institutions.

стра́нстви|е, я, *n.* (*obs.*) wandering, journeying, travelling.

стра́нствовани|е, я, *n.* wandering, journeying, travelling.

стра́нств|овать, ую, *impf.* to wander, travel.

стра́нств|ующий, *pres. part. act. of* ~овать *and adj.*; с. актёр strolling player; с. ры́царь knight-errant.

страстн|о́й, *adj.* of Holy Week; ~а́я неде́ля Holy Week; ~а́я пя́тница Good Friday; С. четве́рг Maundy Thursday.

стра́стност|ь, и, *f.* passion.

стра́ст|ный (~ен, ~на́, ~но), *adj.* passionate; impassioned; ardent; он—с. авиамоде́лист he is mad about making model aircraft.

страстоцве́т, а, *m.* passion flower.

страст|ь[1], и, *g. pl.* ~éй, *f.* 1. (к) passion (for); до ~и (*coll.*) passionately; люби́ть до ~и to be passionately fond (of); со ~ью with fervour; у неё с. к о́перам Мо́царта she is mad about Mozart's operas. 2. ~и Христо́вы (*rel.*) the Passion; Стра́сти по

Матфе́ю (*title of oratorio*) St. Matthew Passion. 3. (*coll.*) horror; расска́зывать (про) вся́кие ~и to recount all manner of horrors.

страсть[2], *adv.* (*coll.*) 1. (как, како́й) frightfully; мне с. как хо́чется ви́деть э́тот фильм I want awfully to see this film; она́ с. кака́я на́глая she is frightfully brazen. 2. an awful lot, a terrific number.

стратаге́м|а, ы, *f.* stratagem.

страте́г, а, *m.* strategist.

стратеги́|я, и, *f.* strategy; с. измо́ра проти́вника strategy of attrition.

стратеги́ческий, *adj.* strategic.

стратифика́ци|я, и, *f.* stratification.

стратона́вт, а, *m.* stratosphere flier.

стратоста́т, а, *m.* stratosphere balloon.

стратосфе́р|а, ы, *f.* stratosphere.

стратосфе́рный, *adj.* stratospheric.

стра́ус, а, *m.* ostrich.

стра́ус|овый, *adj. of* ~; ~овое перо́ ostrich feather.

страх[1], а, *m.* 1. fear; terror; с. Бо́жий, с. Госпо́день the fear of God; с. пе́ред неизве́стностью fear of the unknown; держа́ть в ~е to keep in awe; под ~ом сме́рти on pain of death; ~а ра́ди for fear, from fear; со ~ом и тре́петом with fear and trembling; у ~а глаза́ вели́ки fear hath a hundred eyes. 2. (*pl.*) terrors. 3. risk, responsibility; на свой с. at one's own risk.

страх[2], *adv.* (*coll.*) (как) terribly; им с. хо́чется побыва́ть во Фра́нции they want terribly to go to France.

страхка́сс|а, ы, *f.* (*abbr. of* страхова́я ка́сса) insurance office.

страхова́ни|е, я, *n.* insurance; с. жи́зни life insurance; с. от несча́стных слу́чаев insurance against accidents; с. от огня́ fire insurance.

страхова́тел|ь, я, *m.* insurant.

страх|ова́ть, у́ю, *impf.* 1. (*pf.* за~) (от) to insure (against); с. себя́ (от; *fig.*) to insure (against), safeguard oneself (against). 2. (*sport*) to stand by (*in case of accident*).

страх|ова́ться, у́юсь, *impf.* (*of* за~) (от) to insure oneself (against) (*also fig.*).

страхови́к, á, *m.* (*coll.*) insurance man.

страхо́вк|а, и, *f.* 1. insurance. 2. (*fig., coll.*) insurance, guarantee.

страхо́вщик, а, *m.* insurer.

страше́нный, *adj.* (*coll.*) terrible.

страши́лищ|е, а, *m. and n.* fright (*object inspiring fear*); (*coll.*) monster; scarecrow.

страш|и́ть, у́, и́шь, *impf.* to frighten, scare.

страш|и́ться, у́сь, и́шься, *impf.* (+*g.*) to be afraid (of), fear.

стра́шно, *adv.* 1. terribly, awfully. 2. *as pred.* it is terrible; it is terrifying; нам бы́ло с. we were terrified.

стра́ш|ный (~ен, ~на́, ~но), *adj.* terrible,

awful, dreadful, frightful, fearful; terrifying, frightening; с. расскáз terrifying story; с. сон bad dream; с. шум (coll.) awful din; С. суд the Day of Judgement, Doomsday.

стращá|ть, ю, impf. (of по~) (coll.) to frighten, scare.

стрѐж|ень, ня, m. channel, main stream (of river).

стреж|невóй, adj. of ~ень; ~невы́е вóды channel, navigable waters (of a river).

стрекáв|ить, лю, ишь, impf. (of о~) (dial.) to sting (with a nettle).

стрекá|ть, ю, impf. (dial.) 1. (pf. об~) = ~вить. 2. (coll.) to take to one's heels, run for it.

стрекáч, á, m. now only in phrase (за)дáть ~á (coll.) to take to one's heels, run for it.

стрекозá|á, ы́, pl. ~ы, f. dragon-fly (also of a fidgety or lively girl).

стрекóт, а, m. chirr (of grasshoppers); (fig.) rattle, chatter (of machine-gun fire, etc.).

стрекотáни|е, я, n. chirring; (fig.) rattle, chatter.

стреко|тáть, чý, ~чешь, impf. to chirr (of grasshoppers); (fig.) to rattle, chatter (of machine-guns, etc.).

стрел|á, ы́, pl. ~ы, f. 1. arrow (also fig.); (fig.) shaft, dart; пустѝть ~ý to shoot an arrow; мчáться ~óй to fly like an arrow from the bow. 2. (bot.) shaft. 3. (archit.) rise; с. (подъёма) свóда rise of vault. 4. (tech.) arm (of crane), boom, jib; (pl.; naut.) sheer-legs. 5. с. мóста cantilever. 6. с. прогѝба (tech.) sag.

стрел|éц, ьцá, m. 1. (hist.) strelets (in Muscovite Russia in the 16th and 17th centuries; member of military corps instituted by Ivan the Terrible and enjoying special privileges). 2. С. (astron.) Sagittarius (constellation).

стрелéц|кий, adj. of ~ 1.

стрéлк|а, и, f. 1. pointer, indicator; hand (of clock or watch); needle (of compass, etc.). 2. arrow (on diagram, etc.). 3. (railways) point(s), switch; перевестѝ ~y to change the points. 4. (geogr.) spit. 5. shoot, blade (of grass, etc.).

стрелкóв|ый, adj. 1. rifle, shooting; small arms; ~ое мастерствó marksmanship; ~ое орýжие small arms; с. спорт shooting; с. тир rifle range. 2. (mil.) rifle, infantry; с. батальóн rifle battalion, infantry battalion; ~ые войскá infantry; с. окóп fire trench; ~ая цепь riflemen in extended fire positions.

стреловѝдност|ь, и, f. (aeron.) angle (of wing); самолёт с изменя́емой ~ью крылá variable geometry aircraft.

стреловѝд|ный (~ен, ~на), adj. arrow--shaped; (bot., zool.) sagittate; ~ное крылó (aeron.) swept-back wing; с. шов чéрепа (med.) sagittate suture of skull.

стрел|óк, кá, m. 1. shot; искýсный с., отлѝчный с. good shot, marksman. 2. (mil.) rifleman; (aeron.) gunner.

стрéлочник, а, m. (railways) pointsman, switchman; с. виновáт (iron.) the little man is always blamed, muggins!

стрéлочниц|а, ы, f. of стрéлочник.

стрéл|очный, adj. of ~ка 3.

стрельб|á, ы́, pl. ~ы, f. shooting, firing; shoot; ружéйная с. rifle fire, small arms fire; учéбная с. practice shoot; с. на поражéние fire for effect; с. по кáрте predicted shoot, shooting by the map; с. по плóщади area shoot, zone fire.

стрéльбищ|е, а, n. shooting range, target range.

стрельн|ýть, ý, ёшь, pf. (coll.) 1. to fire a shot. 2. у меня́ ~ýло в ýхе (impers.) I had a stab of pain in my ear. 3. to rush away. 4. (sl.) to cadge.

стрéльчат|ый, adj. 1. (archit.) lancet. 2. arched, pointed; ~ые брóви arched eyebrows.

стрéлян|ый, adj. (coll.) 1. shot; ~ая дичь shot game (as opp. to killed by strangling). 2. that has been under fire; он — солдáт с. he has had his baptism of fire; с. воробéй old hand. 3. used, fired, spent; ~ая гѝльза used cartridge, empty case.

стреля́|ть, ю, impf. 1. (в+a., по+d.) to shoot (at), fire (at); хорошó с. to be a good shot; с. из револьвéра, из ружья́ to fire a revolver, a gun; с. в цель to shoot at a target; с. по самолёту to fire at an aeroplane; с. из пýшек по воробья́м (coll.) to use a sledgehammer to smash walnuts. 2. to shoot (= to hunt, kill by shooting); с. куропáток to go partridge-shooting. 3. с. глазáми (coll.) to dart glances (at); to make eyes (at). 4. (sl.) to cadge. 5. (impers.) to have a shooting pain. 6. to produce a sharp sound; стреля́ть кнутóм crack a whip.

стреля́|ться, юсь, impf. 1. (coll.) to shoot oneself. 2. to fight a duel (with firearms). 3. pass. of ~ть 2.

стремглáв, adv. headlong.

стрем|еннóй, adj. = ~я́нный.

стремѝтел|ьный (~ен, ~ьна), adj. swift, headlong; impetuous.

стрем|ѝть, лю, ѝшь, impf. to urge.

стрем|ѝться, люсь, ѝшься, impf. 1. (obs.) to rush, speed, charge. 2. (к) to strive (for), seek, aspire (to); (+inf.) to strive (to), try (to); с. к совершéнству to strive for perfection.

стремлéни|е, я, n. (к) striving (for), aspiration (to).

стремнѝн|а, ы, f. 1. rapid (in a river). 2. (obs.) precipice.

стремнѝн|ный, adj. of ~а (obs.).

стремнист|ый (~, ~a), adj. (obs.) steep, precipitous.
стрём|я, g., d., and p. ~ени, i. ~енем, pl. ~ена́, ~я́н, ~ена́м, n. 1. stirrup; е́хать стре́мя в стре́мя ride side by side (on horseback). 2. (anat.) stirrup-bone, stapedial bone, stapes.
стремя́нк|а, и, f. step-ladder, steps.
стремя́нн|ый, adj. of стре́мя; as noun (hist.) с., ~ого, m. groom.
стренг|а, и, f. (naut., tech.) strand (of cable).
стрено́ж|ить, у, ишь, pf. of трено́жить.
стре́пет, а, m. (orn.) little bustard.
стрептоко́кк, а, m. (biol., med.) streptococcus.
стрептоко́кк|овый, adj. of ~.
стрептомици́н, а, m. (med.) streptomycin.
стресс, а, m. (psych.) stress.
стрех|а́, и́, pl. ~и, f. eaves.
стреч|о́к, ка́, m. now only in phrase (за)да́ть ~ка́ (coll.) to take to one's heels, run for it.
стрига́льн|ый, adj. ~ая маши́на (text.) cloth-shearing machine.
стрига́льщик, а, m. (text. and agric.) shearer.
стрига́льщиц|а, ы, f. of стрига́льщик.
стригу́н, а́, m. yearling (foal).
стригун|о́к, ка́, m. = стригу́н.
стригу́щий, pres. part. act. of стричь; с. лиша́й (med.) ring-worm.
стриж, а́, m. (orn.) martin, swift; берегово́й с. sand-martin; ка́менный с. stone-martin.
стри́женый, adj. 1. short-haired, close-cropped. 2. (of hair) short; (of sheep) sheared; (of tree) clipped.
стри́жк|а, и, f. 1. hair-cutting; shearing; clipping. 2. cut, hair-style, hair-do.
стри́нгер, а, m. (naut., aeron.) stringer.
стрихни́н, а, m. (med.) strychnine.
стри|чь, гу́, жёшь, гу́т, past ~г, ~гла́, impf. (of o~) 1. to cut, clip (hair or nails). 2. с. кого́-н. to cut someone's hair; с. ове́ц to shear sheep; с. пу́деля to clip a poodle; с. всех под одну́ гребёнку to treat all alike, reduce all to the same level. 3. (coll.) to cut into pieces, into strips.
стри|чься, гу́сь, жёшься, гу́тся, past ~гся, ~гла́сь, impf. (of o~) 1. to cut one's hair; to have one's hair cut. 2. to have one's hair cut short, wear one's hair short. 3. pass. of ~чь.
стробоско́п, а, m. (phys.) stroboscope.
строга́л|ь, я́, m. (coll.) = ~ьщик.
строга́льный, adj. (tech.) с. стано́к planing machine, planer; с. резе́ц planer cutter.
строга́льщик, а, m. plane operator, planer.
строга́|ть, ю, impf. (of вы́~) (tech.) to plane, shave.
строг|ий (~, ~а́, ~о), adj. (in var. senses) strict; severe; ~ая дие́та strict diet; ~ие ме́ры strong measures; с. пригово́р severe

sentence; под ~им секре́том in strict confidence; в ~ом смы́сле сло́ва in the strict sense of the word; с. стиль severe, austere style; ~ие черты́ лица́ regular features.
стро́го, adv. strictly; severely; с. говоря́ strictly speaking; с. воспреща́ется 'strictly forbidden'.
стро́го-на́строго, adv. (coll.) very strictly.
стро́гост|ь, и, f. 1. (in var. senses) strictness; severity. 2. (pl.) (coll.) strong measures.
строеви́к, а́, m. combatant soldier.
строево́й¹, adj. building; с. лес timber.
строев|о́й², adj. (mil.) 1. combatant, line; с. офице́р officer serving in line; ~ая слу́жба (front-)line service, combatant service; ~ая часть line unit. 2. drill; ~ая подгото́вка drill; с. уста́в drill regulations, drill manual; с. шаг ceremonial step.
строе́ни|е, я, n. 1. building, structure. 2. (fig.; in var. senses) structure, composition; (biol.) texture; с. земно́й коры́ (geol.) structure of the earth's crust.
строжа́йший, superl. of стро́гий.
стро́же, comp. of стро́гий and стро́го.
строи́тел|ь, я, m. 1. builder (also fig.). 2. (eccl.) Father Superior (in some monasteries).
строи́тельн|ый, adj. building, construction; ~ая брига́да construction gang; ~ое иску́сство civil engineering; architecture; с. лес building timber; ~ая площа́дка building site; с. раство́р lime mortar.
строи́тельств|о, а, n. 1. building, construction (also fig.); доро́жное с. road-building, road-making; жили́щное с. house-building; зелёное с. laying out of parks, etc.; хозя́йственное с. building-up of the economy. 2. building site, construction project. 3. (fig.) organization, structuring.
стро́|ить, ю, ишь, impf. 1. (pf. по~) to build, construct; с. плоти́ну to build a dam; с. но́вую жизнь to make a new life; с. возду́шные за́мки to build castles in the air. 2. (pf. по~) (math., etc.) to construct; to formulate; to express; с. многоуго́льник to construct a polygon; с. у́гол to plot an angle; с. фра́зу to construct a sentence; с. мысль to express a thought. 3. (pf. co~) (in phrases denoting facial expressions, etc.) to make; с. гла́зки to make eyes; с. грима́сы, с. ро́жу to make, pull faces; с. из себя́ дурака́ to make a fool of oneself. 4. (на+p.) to base (on). 5. (impf. only) с. пла́ны to make plans, plan; с. себе́ иллю́зии to create illusions for oneself. 6. (pf. по~) (mil.) to draw up, form (up).
стро́|иться, юсь, ишься, impf. (of по~) 1. to build (a house, etc.) for oneself. 2. (mil.) to draw up, form up; стро́йся! (mil.) fall in! 3. pass. of ~ить.

стро|й, я, о ～е, в ～ю, *pl.* ～и, ～ев, *m.* **1.** system, order, régime; обще́ственный с. social system, social order; феода́льный с. feudal system. **2.** (*ling.*) system, structure. **3.** (*mus.*) pitch. **3.** (*pl.* ～й, ～ёв) (*mil.*, *naut.*, *aeron.*) formation; развёрнутый с. (extended) line; разо́мкнутый с. extended order; со́мкнутый с. close order; расчленённый с. deployed formation; с. пе́ленга (*naut.*) line of bearing; с. фро́нта (*naut.*) line abreast; в ко́нном ～ю mounted; в пе́шем ～ю dismounted. **4.** (*mil.*) unit in formation; пе́ред ～ем in front of the ranks. **5.** (*mil. and fig.*) service, commission; ввести́ в с. to put into commission; вы́вести из ～я to disable; to put out of action; вступи́ть в с. to come into service, come into operation; вы́йти из ～я to be disabled; to become unserviceable; оста́ться в ～ю (*mil.*) to remain in the ranks; (*fig.*) to remain at one's post.

стро́йк|а, и, *f.* **1.** building, construction. **2.** building-site.

стро́йность|ь, и, *f.* **1.** proportion. **2.** (*mus.*, *etc.*) harmony; balance; order.

стро́|йный (～ен, ～йна́, ～йно), *adj.* **1.** (*of the human figure*) well-proportioned; (*of a woman*) shapely, having a good figure; svelte. **2.** (*mus.*, *etc.*) harmonious; well-balanced; orderly; well put together.

строк|а́, и́, *pl.* ～и, ～, ～а́м, *f.* line; кра́сная с., абза́цная с. (*typ.*) break line; с. в ～у́ line by line; нача́ть с но́вой ～и́ to begin a new paragraph; чита́ть ме́жду ～ to read between the lines.

строн|уть, у, ешь, *pf.* (*of* стра́гивать) (*coll.*) to move out, shift.

строн|уться, усь, ешься, *pf.* (*of* стра́гиваться) (*intrans.*; *coll.*) to move (out).

стронци|й, я, *m.* (*chem.*) strontium.

строп, а, *m.* sling (rope); shroud line (*of parachute*).

стропи́л|о, а, *n.* rafter, truss, beam.

стропти́в|ец, ца, *m.* obstinate person.

стропти́вость|ь, и, *f.* obstinacy, refractoriness.

стропти́в|ый (～, ～а), *adj.* obstinate, refractory; shrewish.

строф|а́, ы́, *pl.* ～ы, ～, ～а́м, *f.* (*lit.*) stanza, strophe.

строфа́нт, а, *m.* (*bot. and pharm.*) strophanthus.

строфи́ческий, *adj.* (*lit.*) strophic.

строчёный, *adj.* stitched.

строч|и́ть, у́, ～и́шь, *impf.* (*of* на～¹) **1.** to stitch. **2.** (*coll.*) to scribble, dash off. **3.** (*coll.*) to bang away (*with automatic weapons*).

строчк|а¹, и, *f.* stitch.

стро́чк|а², и, *f.* = строка́; списа́ть с. в ～у to copy out verbatim.

строчн|о́й, *adj.* ～а́я бу́ква small letter, lower-case letter; писа́ть с ～о́й бу́квы to write with a small letter.

струбци́н|а, ы, *f.* (*tech.*) (screw) clamp, cramp.

струг¹, а, *m.* (*tech.*) plane.

струг², а, *m.* (*obs.*) boat.

стру́жк|а, и, *f.* shaving, filing; снять ～у с кого́-н. (*sl.*) to tear someone off a strip.

стру|и́ть, и́т, *impf.* to pour, shed.

стру|и́ться, и́тся, *impf.* to stream, flow.

структу́р|а, ы, *f.* structure.

структурали́зм, а, *m.* (*ling.*) structuralism.

структурали́ст, а, *m.* (*ling.*) structuralist.

структу́рный, *adj.* structural; structured.

струн|а́, ы́, *pl.* ～ы, *f.* string (*of mus. instrument, tennis racket, etc.*); сла́бая с. weak point.

стру́н|ка, ки, *f.* dim. of ～а́; вы́тянуться в ～ку, стать в ～ку to stand at attention; ходи́ть по ～ке (у, пе́ред) to be at the beck and call (of), dance attendance (on).

стру́нник, а, *m.* player on stringed instrument.

стру́нный, *adj.* (*mus.*); с. инструме́нт stringed instrument; с. орке́стр string orchestra.

струп, а, *pl.* ～ья, ～ьев, *m.* scab.

стру́|сить, шу, сишь, *pf. of* тру́сить.

стручко́вый, *adj.* leguminous; с. пе́рец capsicum; с. горо́шек peas in the pod.

струч|о́к, ка́, *m.* pod.

стру|я́, и́, *pl.* ～и́, *f.* **1.** jet, spurt, stream; current (*of air*); бить ～ёй to spurt. **2.** (*fig.*) spirit; impetus; внести́ све́жую ～ю (в+*a.*) to infuse a fresh spirit (into). **3.** (*obs.*, *poet.*) water.

стря́па|ть, ю, *impf.* (*of* со～) (*coll.*) to cook; (*fig.*) to cook up, concoct.

стряпн|я́, и́, *f.* (*coll.*) cooking; (*fig.*, *pejor.*) concoction.

стряпу́х|а, и, *f.* (*coll.*) cook.

стря́пч|ий, его, *m.* **1.** (*hist.*) officer of tsar's household (*in Muscovite Russia*). **2.** (*hist.*) scrivener, attorney. **3.** (*obs.*) solicitor.

стряс|а́ть, а́ю, *impf. of* ～ти́.

стряс|ти́, у́, ёшь, *past* ～, ～ла́, *pf.* (*of* ～а́ть) to shake off, shake down.

стряс|ти́сь, ётся, *past* ～ся, ～ла́сь, *pf.* (*над*, *с*+*i.*; *coll.*) to befall; беда́ ～ла́сь с на́ми a disaster befell us.

стря́хива|ть, ю, *impf. of* стряхну́ть.

стрях|ну́ть, ну́, нёшь, *pf.* (*of* ～ивать) to shake off.

студене́|ть, ет, *impf.* (*coll.*) to thicken, acquire the consistency of jelly.

студени́ст|ый (～, ～а), *adj.* jelly-like.

студе́нт, а, *m.* student, undergraduate; с.-ме́дик medical student; с.-юри́ст law student.

студе́нт|ка, ки, *f. of* ～.

студе́нческ|ий, *adj. of* студе́нт; с. коллекти́в

the student body; ~ое общежи́тие student hostel, hall of residence.

студе́нчеств|о, а, *n.* **1.** (*collect.*) students. **2.** student days.

студён|ый (~, ~а), *adj.* (*coll.*) very cold, bitter, freezing; *as pred.* ~о it is freezing.

сту́д|ень, ня, *m.* galantine; aspic; (meat- *or* fish-)jelly.

студи́|ец, йца, *m.* (*coll.*) student (*of art school, drama school, music school, etc.*).

студи́|йка, йки, *f.* *of* ~ец.

студи́йн|ый, *adj.* *of* сту́дия; ~ая радиопереда́ча studio broadcast.

сту|ди́ть, жу́, ~дишь, *impf.* (*of* о~) to cool.

сту́ди|я, и, *f.* **1.** (*artist's or broadcasting*) studio, workshop. **2.** (*art, drama, music, etc.*) school.

сту́ж|а, и, *f.* severe cold, hard frost.

стук[1], а, *m.* knock; tap; thump; с. в дверь knock at the door; с. колёс rumble of wheels; с. копы́т clatter of hooves; с.! с.! (*onomat.*) knock!, knock!

стук[2] (*coll.*) *as pred.* = ~нул.

сту́к|ать(ся), аю(сь), *impf. of* ~нуть(ся).

стука́ч, á, *m.* (*sl.*) knocker (= informer).

сту́к|нуть, ну, нешь, *pf.* (*of* ~ать) **1.** to knock; to bang; to tap; to rap; с. в дверь to knock, bang, tap, rap at (on) the door; с. кулако́м по́ столу to bang one's fist on the table. **2.** to bang, hit, strike; с. кого́-н. по спине́ to bang someone on the back. **3.** (*sl.*) to bash (= to kill). **4.** (*sl.*) to knock back (= to drink). **5.** *pf. only* (*impers.+d.; coll.*) ему́ пятьдеся́т ско́ро ~нет he will soon be fifty. **6.** (*coll.*) ему́ вдруг ~нуло в го́лову he suddenly had a bright idea.

сту́к|нуться, нусь, нешься, *pf.* (*of* ~аться) (о, обо+а.) to knock oneself (against), bang oneself (against), bump oneself (against).

стукотн|я́, и́, *f.* (*coll.*) knocking, banging, tapping, rapping.

стул, а, *pl.* ~ья, ~ьев, *m.* **1.** chair; сиде́ть ме́жду двух ~ьев to fall between two stools. **2.** (*med.*) stool.

сту́лик, а, *m.* small chair.

стульча́к, á, *m.* (lavatory) seat.

сту́льчик, а, *m.* stool.

сту́п|а, ы, *f.* mortar.

ступ|а́ть, а́ю, *impf. of* ~и́ть; ~а́й(те) сюда́! come here!; ~а́й(те)! be off!, clear out!

ступе́нчатый, *adj.* stepped, graduated, graded.

ступ|е́нь, е́ни, *f.* **1.** (*g. pl.* ~е́ней) step (*of stairs*); rung (*of ladder*). **2.** (*g. pl.* ~ене́й) stage, grade, level, phase.

ступе́нь|ка, ки, *f.* = ~ 1.

ступ|и́ть, лю́, ~ишь, *pf.* (*of* ~а́ть) to step, take a step; to tread; тяжело́ с. to tread heavily; с. че́рез поро́г to cross the threshold

ступи́ц|а, ы, *f.* nave, hub (*of a wheel*).

ступн|я́, и́, *pl.* ~и́, ~е́й, *f.* **1.** foot. **2.** sole (*of foot*).

стуч|а́ть, у́, и́шь, *impf.* **1.** (*pf.* по~) to knock; to bang; to tap; to rap; (*of teeth*) to chatter. **2.** *impf.* (*3rd person only*) to hammer, pulse, thump, pound; ~и́т в виска́х blood hammers in the temples; се́рдце у неё ~а́ло her heart was pounding.

стуч|а́ться, у́сь, и́шься, *impf.* (*of* по~) (в+а.) to knock (at); с. в дверь to knock at the door (*also fig.*).

стуш|ева́ть, у́ю, *pf.* (*of* ~ёвывать) **1.** (*art*) to shade off. **2.** (*fig., coll.*) to smooth over, efface.

стуш|ева́ться, у́юсь, *pf.* (*of* ~ёвываться) **1.** (*art*) to shade off. **2.** (*coll.*) to retire to the background, efface oneself. **3.** to be covered with confusion.

стушёвыва|ть(ся), ю(сь), *impf. of* стушева́ть(ся).

стыд, á, *m.* shame; к на́шему ~у́ to our shame; сгоре́ть со ~á to burn with shame; с. и срам! for shame!, it's a sin and a shame!

сты|ди́ть, жу́, ди́шь, *impf.* (*of* при~) to shame, put to shame.

сты|ди́ться, жу́сь, ди́шься, *impf.* (*of* по~) (+g.) to be ashamed (of).

стыдли́в|ый (~, ~а), *adj.* bashful.

сты́дно, *as pred.* it is a shame; ему́, *etc.,* с. he, *etc.,* is ashamed; как тебе́ не с.! you ought to be ashamed of yourself!

сты́дный, *adj.* shameful.

стык, а, *m.* **1.** (*tech.*) joint, junction, butt. **2.** (*mil.*) meeting-point of flanks of adjacent units. **3.** (*fig.*) junction, meeting-point; с. доро́г road junction; на ~е двух веко́в at the turn of the century.

стык|ова́ть, у́ю, *impf.* (*of* со~) (*tech.*) to join.

стык|ова́ться, у́юсь, *impf.* (*of* со~) (*tech.*) to join (*intrans.*); (*of space vehicles*) to dock, rendezvous.

стыко́вк|а, и, *f.* (*of space vehicles*) docking, rendezvous.

стыков|о́й, *adj.* *of* стык 1; (*railways*) ~а́я накла́дка fish-plate; ~о́е соедине́ние, с. шов butt-weld, butt-joint.

сты́н|уть, у, ешь, *past* стыл, сты́ла, *impf.* **1.** to cool, get cool. **2.** to become frozen over. **3.** (*fig.*) кровь ~ет в жи́лах one's blood freezes.

стыть = сты́нуть.

сты́чк|а, и, *f.* **1.** skirmish, clash. **2.** (*coll.*) squabble.

стюарде́сс|а, ы, *f.* stewardess; (*on aeroplane*) air hostess.

стяг, а, *m.* (*rhet.*) banner.

стя́гива|ть(ся), ю(сь), *impf. of* стяну́ть(ся).

стяжа́тел|ь, я, *m.* grasping person, person on the make; money-grubber.

стяжа́тел|ьный (~ен, ~ьна), adj. greedy, grasping, on the make.

стяжа́|ть, ю, impf. and pf. 1. to gain, win. 2. (impf. only) to seek, court; с. сла́ву to court fame.

стя|ну́ть[1], ну́, ~нешь, pf. (of ~гивать) 1. to tighten; to pull together; с. на себе́ по́яс to tighten one's belt; с. шине́ль ремнём to strap in a greatcoat. 2. (mil.) to gather, assemble (trans.) 3. (impers.; coll.) to have cramp; но́гу у меня́ ~ну́ло I have cramp in my leg.

стя|ну́ть[2], ну́, ~нешь, pf. (of ~гивать) 1. to pull off. 2. (coll.) to pinch, steal.

стя|ну́ться, ну́сь, ~нешься, pf. (of ~ги-ваться) 1. to tighten (intrans.). 2. to gird oneself tightly. 3. (mil.) to gather, assemble (intrans.).

су, indecl., n. sou (French coin).

субалте́рн-офице́р, a, m. (obs.) subaltern.

субаре́нд|а, ы, f. sub-lease.

субарендáтор, a, m. sub-tenant.

суббо́т|а, ы, f. Saturday; Вели́кая с. Holy Saturday.

суббо́т|ний, adj. of ~a.

суббо́тник, a, m. subbotnik (in U.S.S.R. voluntary unpaid work on days off, originally esp. on Saturdays).

субве́нци|я, и, f. grant, subsidy, subvention.

сублима́т, a, m. (chem.) sublimate.

сублима́ци|я, и, f. (chem.) sublimation.

сублими́р|овать, ую, impf. and pf. (chem.) to sublimate, sublime.

субмари́н|а, ы, f. (naut.; obs.) submarine.

субордина́ци|я, и, f. (system of) seniority.

субре́тк|а, и, f. soubrette.

субсиди́р|овать, ую, impf. and pf. to subsidize.

субси́ди|я, и, f. subsidy, grant(-in-aid).

субстантиви́р|овать, ую, impf. and pf. (ling.) to substantivize.

субста́нци|я, и, f. (philos.) substance.

субстра́т, a, m. 1. (philos.) substance. 2. (biol., geol., and ling.) substratum.

субти́льност|ь, и, f. tenuousness; delicateness; frailty.

субти́л|ьный (~ен, ~ьна), adj. (coll.) tenuous; delicate; frail; (obs.) subtle, delicate.

субти́тр, a, m. subtitle (in film).

субтро́пик|и, ов, no sing. subtropics.

субтропи́ческий, adj. subtropical.

субъе́кт, a, m. 1. (philos., gram.) subject; (philos.) the self, the ego. 2. (med., leg.) subject; истери́чный с. hysterical subject. 3. (coll.) fellow, character, type; подозри́тельный с. suspicious character.

субъективи́зм, a, m. 1. (philos.) subjectivism. 2. subjectivity.

субъективи́ст, a, m. (philos.) subjectivist.

субъективисти́ческий, adj. (philos.) subjectivist.

субъекти́вност|ь, и, f. subjectivity.

субъекти́в|ный (~ен, ~на), adj. subjective.

субъе́кт|ный, adj. of ~.

сувени́р, а, m. souvenir.

суваре́н, а, m. (polit., leg.) sovereign.

суверените́т, a, m. (polit., leg.) sovereignty.

суваре́нный, adj. (polit., leg.) sovereign.

суво́ров|ец, ца, m. pupil of Suvorov military school.

суглини́стый, adj. loamy; argillaceous.

суглин|ок, ка, m. loam, loamy soil.

сугро́б, a, m. snow-drift.

сугу́бо, adv. especially, particularly; exclusively.

сугу́б|ый (~, ~а), adj. 1. (obs.) double, twofold. 2. especial, particular; exclusive.

суд, á, m. 1. court, law-court; с. Бо́жий (hist.) trial by single combat or by ordeal; с. че́сти court of honour; зал ~á court-room; заседа́ние ~á sitting of the court; се́ссия ~á court session; на ~е́ in court. 2. (fig.) court; trial, legal proceedings; с. да де́ло (coll.) hearing (of a case); (fig.) long-drawn-out proceedings; вы́звать в с. to summons, subpoena; пода́ть в с. на кого́-н. to bring an action against someone; отда́ть под с., преда́ть ~ý to prosecute; быть под ~ом to be on trial; на тебя́ и ~á нет no one can blame you. 3. (collect.) the judges; the bench. 4. judgement, verdict; отда́ть на с. пото́мства to submit to the verdict of posterity.

суда́к, á, m. pike-perch (fish).

суда́н|ец, ца, m. Sudanese.

суда́н|ка, ки, f. 1. Sudanese (woman). 2. = ~ская трава́.

суда́нск|ий, adj. Sudanese; ~ая трава́ Sudan grass (Sorghum halepense).

суда́рын|я, и, f. (obs.; mode of address) madam, ma'am.

су́дар|ь, я, m. (obs.; mode of address) sir.

суда́ч|ить, у, ишь, impf. (coll.) to gossip, tittle-tattle.

суде́бник, a, m. (hist.) code of laws.

суде́бн|ый, adj. judicial; legal; forensic; ~ые изде́ржки costs; с. исполни́тель officer of the court; ~ая медици́на forensic medicine; ~ая оши́бка miscarriage of justice; ~ая пала́та (hist.) (regional) appellate court; ~ым поря́дком, в ~ом поря́дке in legal form; с. при́став (obs.) bailiff; ~ое разбира́тельство legal proceedings, hearing of a case; ~ое реше́ние court decision, court order; с. сле́дователь investigator; ~ое сле́дствие investigation in court, inquest.

суде́йск|ая, ой, f. 1. judge's room; judge's quarters. 2. referees' room.

суде́йск|ий, adj. 1. judge's; as noun (obs.) с., ~ого, m. officer of the court. 2. (sport) referee's, umpire's; с. свисток referee's whistle.

судейств|о, а, *n.* (*sport*) refereeing, umpiring; judging.

судёныш|ко, ка, *pl.* ~ки, ~ек, *n.* (*coll.*) tub (*vessel, ship*).

судилищ|е, а, *n.* (*obs. or joc.*) court of law.

судимост|ь, и, *f.* (*leg.*) conviction(s); снять с кого-н. с. to expunge someone's previous convictions.

су|дить, жу́, ~дишь, *impf.* **1.** to judge; to form an opinion; насколько мы могли с. as far as we could judge; ~дите сами judge for yourself; ~дя (по+*d.*) judging (by), to judge (from); ~дя по всему to all appearances; с. да (и) рядить (*coll.*) to lay down the law, expatiate. **2.** (*leg.*) to try. **3.** to judge, pass judgement (upon); не ~дите их строго don't be hard on them. **4.** (*sport*) to referee, umpire. **5.** (*also pf.*) to predestine, preordain; но Бог ~дил иное but God decreed a different fate.

су|диться, жу́сь, ~дишься, *impf.* (с+*i.*) to be at law (with).

суд|но¹, на, *pl.* ~á, ~óв, *n.* vessel, craft; с. на воздушной подушке hovercraft; с. на подводных крыльях hydrofoil.

суд|но², на, *pl.* ~на, ~ен, *n.* chamber-pot; подкладное с. bed-pan.

судный, *adj.* (*obs.*) **1.** court; judicial. **2.** С. день (*rel.*) Day of Judgement.

судоверф|ь, и, *f.* shipyard.

судовладел|ец, ьца, *m.* shipowner.

судоводи́тел|ь, я, *m.* navigator.

судовожде́ни|е, я, *n.* navigation.

судов|ой, *adj.* ship's; marine; ~ая команда ship's crew; ~ое свидетельство ship's certificate of registry.

судоговоре́ни|е, я, *n.* (*leg.*) pleading(s).

суд|óк, ка́, *m.* **1.** sauce-boat, gravy-boat. **2.** cruet(-stand). **3.** (*usually pl.*) set of dishes with covers (*for carrying food*).

судомо́йк|а, и, *f.* kitchen-maid, scullery maid, washer-up.

судопроизво́дств|о, а, *n.* legal proceedings.

судоремо́нт, а, *m.* ship repair.

судоремо́нт|ный, *adj. of* ~.

су́дорог|а, и, *f.* cramp, convulsion, spasm.

су́дорож|ный (~ен, ~на), *adj.* convulsive, spasmodic (*also fig.*).

судостро́ени|е, я, *n.* shipbuilding.

судостро́ител|ь, я, *m.* shipbuilder, shipwright.

судострои́тельный, *adj.* shipbuilding.

судоустро́йств|о, а, *n.* judicial system.

судохо́д|ный (~ен, ~на), *adj.* **1.** navigable; с. кана́л shipping canal. **2.** ~ная компа́ния shipping company.

судохо́дств|о, а, *n.* navigation, shipping.

суд|ьба́, ьбы́, *pl.* ~ьбы, ~еб, ~ьбам, *f.* fate,

fortune, destiny, lot; ~ьбы страны́ the fortunes of the country; благодари́ть ~ьбу́ to thank one's lucky stars; искуша́ть ~ьбу́ to tempt fate, tempt providence; каки́ми ~ьба́ми? (*coll.*) fancy meeting you here!, how did you get here?; не с. нам (+*inf.*) we are not fated (to).

судьби́н|а, ы, *f.* (*folk poet.*) fate, lot.

суд|ья́, ьи́, *pl.* ~ьи, ~éй, ~ьям, *m.* **1.** judge; мирово́й с. (*obs.*) Justice of the Peace; трете́йский с. arbitrator; я вам не с. who am I to judge you? **2.** (*sport*) referee, umpire.

су́д|я, *see* ~и́ть.

суд|я́, *pres. gerund of* ~и́ть.

суеве́р, а, *m.* superstitious person.

суеве́ри|е, я, *n.* superstition.

суеве́р|ный (~ен, ~на), *adj.* superstitious.

суесло́ви|е, я, *n.* (*obs.*) idle talk.

сует|á, ы́, *f.* **1.** vanity; с. сует vanity of vanities. **2.** bustle, fuss.

суе|ти́ться, чу́сь, ти́шься, *impf.* to bustle, fuss.

суетли́в|ый (~, ~а), *adj.* fussy, bustling.

су́етност|ь, и, *f.* vanity.

су́ет|ный (~ен, ~на), *adj.* vain, empty.

суетн|я́, и́, *f.* fuss, bustle.

сужде́ни|е, я, *n.* opinion; judgement (*in logic*).

сужде́н|ный (~, ~á), *p.p.p. of* суди́ть; нам бы́ло ~ó встре́титься we were fated to meet.

су́жен|ая, ой, *f.* (*folk poet.*) intended (*bride*).

су́жен|ый, ого, *m.* (*folk poet.*) intended (*bridegroom*).

су́жива|ть(ся), ю, ет(ся), *impf. of* су́зить-(ся).

су́|зить, жу, зишь, *pf.* (*of* ~живать) to narrow (*trans.*).

су́|зиться, зится, *pf.* (*of* ~живаться) to narrow (*intrans.*), get narrow; to taper.

сук, á, о ~é, на ~у́, *pl.* ~й, ~óв *and* **су́чья, су́чьев,** *m.* **1.** bough. **2.** knot (*in wood*).

су́к|а, и, *f.* bitch (*also as term of abuse*).

су́к|ин, *adj. of* ~а; с. сын (*as term of abuse*) son of a bitch.

сук|но́, на́, *pl.* ~на, ~он, *n.* (heavy, coarse) cloth; положи́ть под с. (*fig.*) to shelve.

сукнова́л, а, *m.* fuller.

сукнова́льн|ый, *adj.* fulling; ~ая гли́на fuller's earth.

сукнова́льн|я, и, *f.* fullery, fulling mill.

сукова́т|ый (~, ~а), *adj.* with many twigs; (*of planks*) knotty.

суко́нк|а, и, *f.* piece of cloth, rag.

суко́н|ный, adj. **1.** cloth; ~ая фа́брика cloth mill. **2.** (*fig.*) rough, clumsy, crude; с. язы́к rough tongue, clumsy way of speaking; ~ое ры́ло (*obs.*) merchant.

су́кровиц|а, ы, *f.* **1.** (*physiol.*) lymph, serum. **2.** (*med.*) ichor, pus.

сулем|а́, ы́, f. (chem., med.) corrosive sublimate, mercuric chloride.

сулем|о́вый, adj. of ~а́.

суле́|я, й, f. (obs.) flask.

сул|и́ть, ю́, и́шь, impf. (of по~) to promise; с. золоты́е го́ры to promise the earth; э́то не ~и́т ничего́ хоро́шего this does not bode well.

султа́н¹, а, m. sultan.

султа́н², а, m. plume (on headdress, etc.).

султана́т, а, m. sultanate.

султа́н|ский, adj. of ~¹.

султа́нш|а, и, f. sultana (sultan's wife).

сульфа́т, а, m. (chem.) sulphate.

сульфи́д, а, m. (chem.) sulphide.

сульфо- (chem.) sulpho-.

сум|а́, ы́, f. bag, pouch; с. переме́тная (fig.) weathercock; пусти́ть с ~о́й to ruin, reduce to beggary; ходи́ть с ~о́й to beg, go a-begging.

сумасбро́д, а, m. madcap.

сумасбро́д|ка, ки, f. of ~.

сумасбро́|дить, жу, дишь, impf. (coll.) to behave wildly, extravagantly.

сумасбро́днича|ть, ю, impf. (coll.) = сумасбро́дить.

сумасбро́д|ный (~ен, ~на), adj. wild, extravagant.

сумасбро́дств|о, а, n. wild, extravagant behaviour.

сумасше́дш|ий, adj. 1. mad; as noun с., ~его, m. madman, lunatic; ~ая, ~ей, f. madwoman; бу́йный с. raving, violent lunatic; объяви́ть кого́-н. ~им to certify someone. 2. с. дом (coll.) lunatic asylum, madhouse. 3. (fig.) mad, lunatic; ~ая ско́рость lunatic speed; э́то бу́дет сто́ить ~их де́нег it will cost the earth.

сумасше́стви|е, я, n. madness, lunacy.

сумасше́ств|овать, ую, impf. (coll.) to act like a madman.

сумато́х|а, и, f. confusion, chaos, turmoil, hurly-burly.

сумато́шлив|ый (~, ~а), adj. (coll.) given to fussing.

сумато́ш|ный (~ен, ~на), adj. = ~ливый.

сумбу́р, а, m. confusion, chaos.

сумбу́р|ный (~ен, ~на), adj. confused, chaotic.

су́меречник, а, m. crepuscular animal.

су́мереч|ный (~ен, ~на), adj. 1. twilight, dusk. 2. (zool.) crepuscular.

су́мер|ки, ек, no sing. twilight, dusk.

су́мерница|ть, ю, impf. (coll.) to sit in the twilight.

суме́|ть, ю, pf. (of уме́ть) (+inf.) to be able (to), manage (to).

су́мк|а, и, f. 1. bag, handbag; satchel; с.-паке́т paper bag. 2. (biol.) pouch.

су́мм|а, ы, f. sum; вся с., о́бщая с. sum total; в ~е in sum, all in all.

сумма́р|ный (~ен, ~на), adj. 1. total. 2. summary.

сумми́р|овать, ую, impf. 1. to sum up. 2. to summarize.

су́мнича|ть, ю, pf. of у́мничать.

сумня́ся, only in phrase (obs. or joc.) ничто́же с., ничто́же сумня́шеся without a second's hesitation, not batting an eyelid.

су́мрак, а, m. dusk, twilight.

су́мрач|ный (~ен, ~на), adj. gloomy (also fig.); murky.

су́мчат|ый, adj. 1. (zool.) marsupial. 2. ~ые грибы́ (bot.) Ascomycetes.

сумя́тиц|а, ы, f. confusion, chaos.

сунду́к, а́, m. trunk, box, chest.

су́н|уть(ся), у(сь), ешь(ся), pf. of сова́ть(ся).

суп, а, pl. ~ы́, m. soup.

суперарби́тр, а, m. chief arbitrator.

суперобло́жк|а, и, f. dust-cover, jacket (of book).

суперфосфа́т, а, m. (chem.) superphosphate.

су́пес|ный, adj. of ~ь.

су́пес|ок, ка, m. = ~ь.

супесча́ный, adj. = су́песный.

су́пес|ь, и, f. sandy soil, sandy loam.

супи́н, а, m. (ling.) supine.

су́п|ить, лю, ишь, impf. (of на~) с. бро́ви to knit one's brows, frown.

су́п|иться, люсь, ишься, impf. (of на~) = су́пить бро́ви.

супов|о́й, adj. of суп; ~а́я ло́жка soup ladle; ~а́я ми́ска soup tureen.

супо́н|ь, и, f. hame-strap.

супоро́с(н)ая, adj. с. свинья́ sow in farrow.

супоста́т, а, m. (arch. or rhet.) adversary, foe; satan.

супроти́в (coll.) 1. prep.+g. against. 2. adv. and prep.+g. opposite.

супру́г, а, m. 1. husband, spouse. 2. (pl.) husband and wife, married couple.

супру́г|а, и, f. wife, spouse.

супру́жеский, adj. conjugal, matrimonial.

супру́жеств|о, а, n. conjugal state, matrimony, wedlock.

супря́г|а, и, f. (dial.) 1. yoke (of draught cattle). 2. joint tilling of land. 3. в ~е (с+i.) together (with).

сургу́ч, а́, m. sealing-wax.

сургу́ч|ный, adj. of ~.

сурди́нк|а, и, f. (mus.) mute, sordine; под ~у (coll.) on the quiet.

сурепиц|а, ы, f. (bot.) 1. cole-seed, rape. 2. charlock.

суре́п|ный, adj. of ~ица; ~ное ма́сло rape-oil, colza oil.

су́рик, а, m. (chem.) minium, red lead.

су́рик|овый, adj. of ~.

суро́вост|ь, и, f. severity, sternness.

суро́в|ый (~, ~а), *adj.* **1.** (*in var. senses*) severe, stern; rigorous; bleak. **2.** (*text.*) unbleached, brown; ~ое полотно́ crash; brown Holland.

сур|о́к, ка́, *m.* marmot; спать как с. to sleep like a log.

суррога́т, а, *m.* substitute.

суррога́тный, *adj.* substitute, ersatz.

сурьм|а́, ы́, *f.* **1.** (*chem.*) antimony. **2.** hair-dye (*containing antimony*), kohl.

сурьм|и́ть, лю́, и́шь, *impf.* (*of* на~) (*obs.*) to dye, darken (*hair, eye-brows, etc.*).

сурьм|и́ться, лю́сь, и́шься, *impf.* (*of* на~) (*obs.*) to dye, darken one's hair, eye-brows, etc.

сурьмяно́й, *adj.* antimony.

сурьмя́н|ый, *adj.* = ~о́й.

суса́л|ить, ю, ишь, *impf.* (*obs.*) to tinsel.

суса́л|ь, и, *f.* (*obs.*) tinsel.

суса́льн|ый, *adj.* **1.** tinsel; ~ое зо́лото gold leaf. **2.** (*fig., coll.*) sugary.

су́слик, а, *m.* (*zool.*) gopher.

сусл|и́ть, ю, ишь, *impf.* (*of* за~) (*coll.*) to beslobber; to spatter.

су́сл|о, а, *n.* **1.** виногра́дное с. must; пивно́е c. wort. **2.** grape-juice.

сусо́л|ить, ю, ишь, *impf.* (*of* за~) (*coll.*) = сусли́ть.

суспензо́ри|й, я, *m.* (*sport*) jock-strap.

суста́в, а, *m.* (*anat.*) joint, articulation; неподви́жность ~ов (*med.*) anchylosis.

суставно́й, *adj.* of суста́в.

сута́н|а, ы, *f.* soutane.

сутенёр, а, *m.* souteneur, ponce.

су́т|ки, ок, *no sing.* twenty-four hours; twenty-four-hour period; це́лые с. for days and nights.

су́толок|а, и, *f.* commotion, hubbub, hurly-burly; предпра́здничная с. pre-holiday rush.

су́точн|ый, *adj.* **1.** twenty-four-hour; daily; round-the-clock; ~ые де́ньги per diem subsistence allowance; *as noun* ~ые, ~ых = ~ые де́ньги. **2.** с. цыплёнок day-old chick.

сутул|ить, ю, ишь, *impf.* (*of* с~) с. спи́ну to stoop.

сутул|иться, юсь, ишься, *impf.* (*of* с~) to stoop.

сутулост|ь, и, *f.* с. фигу́ры round shoulders, stoop.

суту́л|ый (~, ~а), *adj.* round-shouldered, stooping.

сут|ь[1], и, *f.* essence; с. де́ла the heart, crux of the matter; по ~и де́ла as a matter of fact, in point of fact.

суть[2], (*arch.*) *3rd pl. pres. of* быть; э́то не с. ва́жно (*coll.*) this is not so important.

сутя́г|а, и, *m. and f.* (*coll., obs.*) litigious person.

сутя́жнича|ть, ю, *impf.* (*obs.*) to engage in (malicious) litigation.

сутя́жн|ый, *adj.* (*obs.*) litigious; ~ое де́ло malicious litigation.

суфле́, *indecl., n.* (*cul.*) soufflé.

суфлёр, а, *m.* (*theatr.*) prompter.

суфлёр|ский, *adj. of* ~; ~ская бу́дка prompt-box.

суфли́р|овать, ую, *impf.* (+*d.*) (*theatr.*) to prompt.

суфражи́зм, а, *m.* suffragette movement.

суфражи́стк|а, и, *f.* suffragette.

су́ффикс, а, *m.* (*gram.*) suffix.

суффикса́льный, *adj. of* су́ффикс.

суха́рниц|а, ы, *f.* biscuit dish; biscuit barrel.

суха́р|ь, я́, *m.* **1.** rusk. **2.** (*fig., coll.*) dried-up person.

сух|а́я, о́й, *f.* (*sport*) whitewash (*game in which loser fails to score a single point*); сде́лать ~у́ю кому́-н. to whitewash someone.

сухме́н|ь, и, *f.* (*dial.*) **1.** dry weather, drought. **2.** dry soil.

су́хо, *adv.* **1.** drily; coldly; нас при́няли с. we were received coldly. **2.** *as pred.* it is dry; на у́лице с. it is dry out of doors; у меня́ в го́рле с. my throat is parched.

сухова́т|ый (~, ~а), *adj.* dryish.

сухове́|й, я, *m.* hot dry wind.

сухове́й|ный, *adj. of* ~.

суходо́л, а, *m.* waterless valley.

сухожи́ли|е, я, *n.* (*anat.*) tendon, sinew.

сухожи́л|ьный, *adj. of* ~ие.

сух|о́й (~, ~а́, ~о), *adj.* **1.** dry; dried-up; arid; ~и́е дрова́ dry firewood; ~о́е ру́сло реки́ dried-up river-bed; ~и́м путём by land, overland; вы́йти ~и́м из воды́ to come out unscathed. **2.** (*of foodstuffs, etc.*) dry, dried; ~о́е молоко́ dried milk. **3.** (*of part of body*) dried-up, withered (*also fig.; of persons*). **4.** (*in var. senses*) dry (= unconnected with, opp. to liquid); с. док dry-dock; с. зако́н (*hist.*) 'dry law' (*e.g. in U.S.A.*); с. ка́шель dry cough; ~а́я мо́лния summer lightning; ~а́я перего́нка dry, destructive distillation; с. тума́н fog of dust, smoke, etc.; с. элеме́нт (*electr.*) dry pile. **5.** (*fig.*) dry (= dull, boring). **6.** (*fig.*) chilly, cold; с. приём chilly reception.

сухолюби́в|ый (~, ~а), *adj.* (*bot.*) xerophilous.

сухомя́тк|а, и, *f.* (*coll.*) dry food (*without any beverage*).

сухопа́рник, а, *m.* (*tech.*) steam dome.

сухопа́р|ый (~, ~а), *adj.* (*coll.*) lean, skinny.

сухопу́тн|ый, *adj.* land (*as opp. to marine, air*); ~ые си́лы (*mil.*) ground forces.

сухору́к|ий (~, ~а), *adj.* without the use of one arm; having a withered arm.

сухосто́|й[1], я, *m.* (*collect.*) dead wood, dead standing trees.

сухостó|й², я, *m.* period before calving (*when cow ceases to give milk*).

сухост|ь, и, *f.* **1.** (*in var. senses*) dryness; aridity. **2.** (*fig.*) chilliness, coldness.

сухот|á, ы́, *f.* **1.** dryness; у меня́ в го́рле с. my throat is parched. **2.** dry spell (*of weather*). **3.** (*folk poet.*; *dial.*) longing, yearning.

сухóтк|а, и, *f.* **1.** (*dial.*) wasting, emaciation. **2.** с. спинно́го мо́зга (*med.*) dorsal tabes, locomotor ataxia.

сухóточный, *adj.* (*med.*) tabetic.

сухофру́кт|ы, ов, *no sing.* dried fruits.

сухоща́в|ый (~, ~а), *adj.* lean, skinny.

сухояде́ни|е, я, *n.* dry food.

сучёный, *adj.* twisted.

суч|и́ть, у́, ~ишь, *impf.* (*of с~*) **1.** to twist, spin; to throw (*silk*). **2.** (*cul.*) to roll out (*dough*).

сучкова́т|ый (~, ~а), *adj.* knotty; gnarled.

суч|óк, ка́, *m.* **1.** twig. **2.** knot (*in wood*); без ~ка́, без задо́ринки (*coll.*) without a hitch.

су́ш|а, и, *f.* (dry) land (*as opp. to sea*).

су́ше, *comp. of* сухо́й *and* су́хо.

суше́ни|е, я, *n.* **1.** drying. **2.** (*coll.*) dried fruit.

сушёный, *adj.* dried.

суши́лк|а, и, *f.* **1.** drying apparatus, dryer. **2.** drying-room. **3.** (*cul.*) drying rack.

суши́льный, *adj.* (*tech.*) drying; с. бараба́н desiccator.

суши́л|ьня, ьни, *g. pl.* ~ен, *f.* drying-room.

суш|и́ть, у́, ~ишь, *impf.* to dry (out, up); с. вёсла (*naut.*; *not fig.*) to rest on one's oars.

суш|и́ться, у́сь, ~ишься, *impf.* to dry (*intrans.*), get dry.

су́шк|а, и, *f.* **1.** drying. **2.** (*cul.*) dry (ring-shaped) cracker.

суш|ь, и, *f.* **1.** dry spell (*of weather*). **2.** dry place. **3.** dry object.

суще́ствен|ный (~, ~на), *adj.* essential, vital; material; important; ~ное замеча́ние remark of material significance; ~ная попра́вка important amendment; игра́ть ~ную роль to play a vital part.

существи́тельн|ое, *adj.*, *only in phrase* и́мя с. *or as noun* **с.**, ~ого, *n.* noun, substantive.

существ|ó, á, *n.* **1.** essence; по ~у́ in essence, essentially; говори́ть по ~у́ to speak to the point; не по ~у́ off the point, beside the point. **2.** being, creature; люби́мое с. loved one; нигде́ не́ было ви́дно ни одного́ живо́го ~á there was nowhere a living creature in sight.

существова́ни|е, я, *n.* existence; сре́дства к ~ю livelihood; отрави́ть кому́-н. (всё) с. to make someone's life a misery.

существ|ова́ть, у́ю, *impf.* to exist (= (*i*) to be, be in existence, (*ii*) to live, subsist).

су́щ|ий, *adj.* **1.** (*obs.*) existing. **2.** (*coll.*) real; absolute, utter, downright; с. ад absolute hell; ~ие пустяки́ utter rubbish.

су́щност|ь, и, *f.* essence; с. де́ла the point; в ~и in essence, at bottom; в ~и говоря́ really and truly.

суя́гная, *adj.* с. овца́ ewe in yean.

сфабрик|ова́ть, у́ю, *pf. of* фабрикова́ть.

сфа́гновый, *adj.* sphagnum.

сфа́гнум, а, *m.* (*bot.*) sphagnum, bog-moss.

сфальц|ева́ть, у́ю, *pf. of* фальцева́ть.

сфальши́в|ить, лю, ишь, *pf. of* фальши́вить.

сфантази́р|овать, ую, *pf. of* фантази́ровать.

сфе́р|а, ы, *f.* **1.** (*in var. senses*) sphere; realm; с. влия́ния (*polit.*) sphere of influence; вы́сшие ~ы the upper crust, influential circles; быть в свое́й ~е to be on one's own ground. **2.** (*mil.*) zone, area; с. огня́ zone of fire.

сфери́ческий, *adj.* spherical.

сферо́ид, а, *m.* (*math.*) spheroid.

сфероида́льный, *adj.* (*math.*) spheroidal.

сфинкс, а, *m.* sphinx.

сфи́нктер, а, *m.* (*anat.*) sphincter.

сформир|ова́ть(ся), у́ю(сь), *pf. of* формирова́ть(ся).

сформ|ова́ть, у́ю, *pf. of* формова́ть.

сформули́р|овать, ую, *pf. of* формули́ровать.

сфотографи́р|овать(ся), ую(сь), *pf. of* фотографи́ровать(ся).

схва|ти́ть, чу́, ~тишь, *pf.* **1.** *pf. of* хвата́ть¹. **2.** (*impf.* ~тывать) (*coll.*) to catch (*a cold, etc.*). **3.** (*impf.* ~тывать) (*coll.*) to grasp, comprehend; с. смысл to grasp the meaning, catch on. **4.** (*impf.* ~тывать) (*tech.*) to clamp together.

схва|ти́ться, чу́сь, ~тишься, *pf.* **1.** *pf. of* хвата́ться. **2.** (*impf.* ~тываться) (с+*i.*) to grapple (with), come to grips (with) (*also fig.*). **3.** (*impf.* ~тываться) (с+*g.*; *coll.*) to leap (out of, from).

схва́тк|а, и, *f.* **1.** skirmish, fight, encounter. **2.** (*coll.*) squabble.

схва́т|ки, ок, *no sing.* contractions (*of muscles*); fit, spasm; родовы́е с. labour, birth pangs.

схва́тыва|ть(ся), ю(сь), *impf. of* схвати́ть(ся).

схе́м|а, ы, *f.* **1.** diagram, chart; с. обстано́вки situation map; с. ориенти́ров range card. **2.** sketch, outline, plan; с. рома́на plan of a novel. **3.** (*electr., radio*) circuit.

схематизи́р|овать, ую, *impf. and pf.* to present in sketchy form, over-simplify.

схемати́зм, а, *m.* sketchiness, over-simplification; employment of ready-made categories.

схемати́ческий, *adj.* 1. diagrammatic, schematic. 2. sketchy, over-simplified.

схемати́ч|ный (~ен, ~на), *adj.* sketchy, over-simplified.

схи́зм|а, ы, *f.* (*eccl.*) schism.

схизма́тик, а, *m.* (*eccl.*) schismatic.

схизмати́ческий, *adj.* (*eccl.*) schismatic.

схи́м|а, ы, *f.* (*eccl.*) schema (*strictest monastic rule in Orthodox Church*).

схи́мник, а, *m.* (*eccl.*) monk having taken vows of schema.

схи́мниц|а, ы, *f.* (*eccl.*) nun having taken vows of schema.

схи́мничес|кий, *adj. of* ~тво.

схи́мничеств|о, а, *n.* (*eccl.*) profession and practice of schema.

схитр|и́ть, ю́, и́шь, *pf. of* хитри́ть.

схлы́н|уть, у, ешь, *pf.* 1. (*of waves*) to break and flow back. 2. (*of a crowd*) to break up; to dwindle. 3. (*of emotions*) to subside.

сход[1], а, *m.* 1. coming off, alighting. 2. descent.

сход[2], а, *m.* (*obs.*) gathering, assembly.

схо|ди́ть[1], жу́, ~дишь, *impf. of* сойти́.

схо|ди́ть[2], жу́, ~дишь, *pf.* 1. to go (*and come back*); (за+*i.*) to go to fetch; с. посмотре́ть to go to see; ~ди́ за до́ктором! go and fetch a doctor! 2. *pf. of* ходи́ть 11.

схо|ди́ться, жу́сь, ~дишься, *impf. of* сойти́сь.

схо́дк|а, и, *f.* (*obs.*) gathering, assembly.

схо́дн|и, ей, *sing.* ~я, ~и, *f.* gangway, gang-plank.

схо́д|ный (~ен, ~на́, ~но), *adj.* 1. similar. 2. (*coll.*) reasonable, fair (*of prices, etc.*).

схо́дств|о, а, *n.* likeness, similarity, resemblance.

схо́дств|овать, ую, *impf.* (с+*i.*; *obs.*) to resemble.

схо́жест|ь, и, *f.* likeness, similarity.

схо́ж|ий (~, ~а), *adj.* like, similar.

схола́ст, а, *m.* scholastic.

схола́стик, а, *m.* = схола́ст.

схола́стик|а, и, *f.* scholasticism.

схоласти́ческий, *adj.* scholastic (*of scholasticism*).

схорон|и́ть(ся), ю́(сь), ~ишь(ся), *pf. of* хорони́ть(ся).

сца́па|ть, ю, *pf.* (*coll.*) to catch hold (of), lay hold (of).

сцара́п|ать, аю, *pf.* (*of* ~ывать) to scratch off.

сцара́пыва|ть, ю, *impf. of* сцара́пать.

сце|ди́ть, жу́, ~дишь, *pf.* (*of* ~жива́ть) to pour off, strain off, decant.

сце́жива|ть, ю, *impf. of* сцеди́ть.

сце́н|а, ы, *f.* 1. (*theatr.*) stage, boards (*also fig.*); ста́вить на ~е to stage, put on the stage; сойти́ со ~ы to go off the scene, make one's exit (*also fig.*). 2. (*theatr., lit.*)

scene. 3. (*coll.*) scene; устра́ивать ~ы to make scenes.

сцена́ри|й, я, *m.* 1. scenario. 2. film script; (по+*d.*) screen version (of).

сцена́рист, а, *m.* scenario writer; script writer.

сцена́риус, а, *m.* (*theatr.*; *obs.*) producer's assistant.

сцени́ческ|ий, *adj.* stage; ~ая рема́рка stage direction; с. шёпот stage whisper.

сцени́ч|ный (~ен, ~на), *adj.* suitable for the theatre, effective on the stage; э́та пье́са не ~на this play is not good theatre.

сцеп, а, *m.* 1. coupling; drawbar. 2. couple (*two goods trucks, agric. implements, etc., coupled together*).

сцеп|и́ть, лю́, ~ишь, *pf.* (*of* ~ля́ть) to couple.

сцеп|и́ться, лю́сь, ~ишься, *pf.* (*of* ~ля́ться) 1. to be coupled. 2. (с+*i.*; *coll.*) to grapple (with), come to grips (with).

сце́пк|а, и, *f.* coupling.

сцепле́ни|е, я, *n.* 1. coupling. 2. (*phys.*) adhesion; cohesion. 3. (*tech.*) clutch; выключе́ние ~я clutch release. 4. (*fig.*) accumulation; с. обстоя́тельств chain of events.

сцепля́|ть(ся), ю(сь), *impf. of* сцепи́ть(ся).

сцепн|о́й, *adj.* (*tech.*) coupling; ~о́е ды́шло, с. шату́н coupling rod; с. крюк, ~а́я тя́га drawbar.

сце́пщик, а, *m.* (*railways*) coupler.

сча́лива|ть, ю, *impf. of* сча́лить.

сча́л|ить, ю, ишь, *pf.* (*of* ~ивать) to lash together.

счастли́в|ец, ца, *m.* lucky man.

счастли́виц|а, ы, *f.* lucky woman.

счастли́вчик, а, *m.* (*coll.*) = счастли́вец.

сча́стливо, *adv.* happily; with luck; с. отде́латься (от) to have a lucky escape (from); счастли́во (остава́ться)! good luck!

счастли́в|ый (сча́стлив, ~а), *adj.* 1. happy. 2. lucky, fortunate. 3. successful; ~ого пути́!, ~ого пла́вания! bon voyage!

сча́сть|е, я, *n.* 1. happiness. 2. luck, good fortune; к ~ю, на с., по ~ю luckily, fortunately; на на́ше с. luckily for us; попыта́ть ~я to try one's luck.

счерп|а́ть, а́ю, *pf.* (*of* ~ывать) to skim (off).

счерпыва|ть, ю, *impf. of* счерпа́ть.

счер|ти́ть, чу́, ~тишь, *pf.* (*of* ~чивать) (*coll.*) to copy, run off.

счерчива|ть, ю, *impf. of* счерти́ть.

счесть(ся), сочту́(сь), сочтёшь(ся), *past* счёл(ся), сочла́(сь), *pf. of* счита́ть(ся)[1].

счёт, а (у), *pl.* ~ы and ~а́, *m.* 1. *sing. only* counting, calculation, reckoning; вести́ с. (+*d.*) to keep count (of); потеря́ть с. (+*d.*) to lose count (of); он не в с. he does not count; в два ~а in a jiffy, in a trice; без

~y, ~y нет countless, without number.
2. *sing. only* (*sport*) score. 3. (*pl.* ~á) bill,
account; подáть с. to present a bill. 4. (*pl.*
~á) (*book-keeping*) account; откры́ть с. to
open an account; за с. (+*g.*) at the expense
(of); на с. on account; на с. (+*g.*) on the
account (of), to the account (of). 5. (*fig.*)
account, expense; в с. (+*g.*) on the strength
(of); в конéчном ~е, в послéднем ~е in
the end; за с. (+*g.*) at the expense (of);
owing (to); на свой с. on one's own
account; на чужóй с. at others' expense;
на э́тот с. (*i*) on this score, (*ii*) in this
respect, в э́том department; предъяви́ть с.
to present a claim; приня́ть на свой с. to
take as referring to oneself; быть на хорó-
шем, дурнóм ~ý to be in good, bad (repute); to stand well, badly; имéть на
своём ~ý to have to one's credit; сбрóсить
со ~ов to dismiss, rule out. 6. ~ы (*no sing.*;
fig.) accounts, score(s); стáрые ~ы old
scores; свести́ ~ы (с+*i.*) to settle a score
(with), get even (with). 7. *see* ~ы.
счётн|ый, *adj.* 1. counting, calculating,
computing; ~ая линéйка slide-rule; ~ая
маши́на calculator, calculating machine.
2. accounts, accounting; с. рабóтник
accounts clerk; ~ая часть accounts department.
счетовóд, a, *m.* accountant; accounts clerk,
ledger clerk.
счетовóдн|ый, *adj.* accounting; ~ая кни́га
account book.
счетовóдств|о, a, *n.* accounting.
счётчик¹, a, *m.* teller; counter (*person*).
счётчик², a, *m.* meter; counter (*instrument*);
гáзовый с. gas meter; с. магни́тной лéнты
tape counter.
счётчиц|а, ы, *f. of* счётчик¹.
счёт|ы¹, ов, *no sing.* abacus, counting frame.
счёт|ы², *see* ~ 6.
счислéни|е, я, *n.* 1. numeration, counting;
систéма ~я (*math.*) scale of notation. 2. с.
пути́ (*naut.*) dead reckoning.
счи́|стить, щу, стишь, *pf.* (*of* ~щáть) to
clean off; to clear away.
счи́|ститься, стится, *pf.* (*of* ~щáться) (*of*
dirt, etc.) to come off.
счи́тан|ный (~, ~а), *p.p.p. of* счита́ть;
остаю́тся ~ные дни (до) one can count
the days (until).
счита́|ть¹, ю, *impf.* (*of* счесть) 1. (*pf. also*
со~) to count; to compute, reckon; с.
до ста to count up to a hundred; не ~я
not counting; с. звёзды, с. мух (*coll.*) to be
dreaming. 2. (+*i. or* за+*a.*) to count, consider, think; to regard (as); я ~ю егó
надёжным наблюдáтелем, я ~ю егó за
надёжного наблюдáтеля I consider him
a reliable observer; с. ну́жным, с. за ну́ж-

ное to consider it necessary; с. за счáстье
to count it one's good fortune. 3. (что) to
consider (that), hold (that); они́ ~ют, что
я не в состоя́нии об э́том суди́ть they consider that I am not in a position to be a
judge of this.
счит|áть², áю, *pf.* (*of* ~ывать) (с+*i.*) to
compare (with), check (against).
счита́|ться¹, юсь, *impf.* (*of* счéсться) (с+*i.*)
to settle accounts (with) (*also fig.*).
счита́|ться², юсь, *impf.* (*no pf.*) 1. (+*i.*) to
be considered, be thought, be reputed; to be
regarded (as); он ~ется первокла́ссным
собесéдником he is considered a first-rate
conversationalist. 2. (с+*i.*) to consider,
take into consideration, to take into account, reckon (with); с шéфом ещё нáдо с.
the boss has still to be reckoned with.
счи́тк|а, и, *f.* 1. comparison, checking; с.
грáнок с ру́кописью comparison of proofs
with manuscript. 2. (*theatr.*) reading (*of a
part in a play*).
счища́|ть(ся), ю(сь), *impf. of* счи́стить(ся).
сшиб|áть(ся), áю(сь), *impf. of* ~и́ть(ся).
сшиб|и́ть, у́, ёшь, *past* ~, ~ла, *pf.* (*of* ~áть)
(*coll.*) to knock off; с. с ног to knock down,
knock over; с. с когó-н. спесь to take someone down a peg.
сшиб|и́ться, у́сь, ёшься, *past* ~ся, ~лась,
pf. (*of* ~áться) (*coll.*) 1. to collide; to come
to blows. 2. *pass. of* ~и́ть.
сшива́|ть, ю, *impf. of* сшить.
сшить, сошью́, сошьёшь, *pf.* 1. *pf. of*
шить. 2. (*impf.* сшивáть) to sew together;
(*med.*) to suture.
съеда́|ть, ю, *impf.* to eat (up).
съедéни|е, я, *n., only in phrase* отдáть на с.
(+*d.*) to put at the mercy (of).
съедóбн|ый (~ен, ~на), *adj.* 1. edible; с.
гриб edible mushroom. 2. eatable, nice.
съёжива|ться, юсь, *impf. of* съёжиться.
съёж|иться, усь, ишься, *pf.* (*of* ёжиться *and*
~иваться) to huddle up; to shrivel, shrink.
съезд¹, a, *m.* 1. congress; conference, convention. 2. arrival, gathering.
съезд², a, *m.* descent.
съéз|дить, жу, дишь, *pf.* 1. to go (*and come
back*); с. в Ри́гу (*vulg.*) to spew (*when drunk*).
2. (*coll.*) to bash.
съéздовский, *adj.* congress.
съезжá|ть(ся), ю(сь), *impf. of* съéхать(ся).
съéзж|ая, ей, *f.* (*obs.*) cell (*in police station*).
съéзж|ий, *adj.* (*obs.*) 1. of assembly; ~ая из-
бá assembly house. 2. с. нарóд assembled
multitude.
съел, *see* съесть.
съём, a, *m.* removal.
съёмк|а, и, *f.* 1. removal. 2. survey, survey-
ing; plotting. 3. (*phot.*) exposure; shooting.

съёмный. *adj.* detachable, removable.

съём|очный, *adj. of* ∼ка; ∼очная гру́ппа film-crew; с. люк camera hatch (*in aircraft*); ∼очная площа́дка film-set; ∼очные рабо́ты surveying.

съёмщик, а, *m.* 1. tenant, lessee. 2. surveyor.

съёмщиц|а, ы, *f. of* съёмщик.

съестн|о́й, *adj.* food; ∼ы́е припа́сы food supplies, provisions; ∼ы́е проду́кты foodstuffs, victuals; *as noun* ∼о́е, ∼о́го, *n.* = ∼ы́е припа́сы.

съе|сть, м, шь, ст, ди́м, ди́те, дя́т, *past* ∼л, ∼ла, *pf. of* есть¹; с. соба́ку (на+*p.*; *coll.*) to have at one's finger-tips, know inside out.

съе́|хать, ду, дешь, *pf.* (*of* ∼зжа́ть) 1. to go down, come down. 2. с. на́ берег (*naut.*) to go ashore. 3. to move (*house*). 4. (*fig., coll.*) to come down, slip; га́лстук у тебя́ ∼хал на́бок your tie is on one side. 5. (*fig., coll.*) to come down (= to lower one's price).

съе́|хаться, дусь, дешься, *pf.* (*of* ∼зжа́ться) 1. to meet. 2. to arrive, gather, assemble.

съехи́днича|ть, ю, *pf. of* ехи́дничать.

съязв|и́ть, лю́, и́шь, *pf. of* язви́ть.

сы́воротк|а, и, *f.* 1. whey. 2. (*biol., med.*) serum.

сы́ворот|очный, *adj. of* ∼ка; serous.

сы́граннос|ть, и, *f.* team-work.

сыгра́|ть, ю, *pf. of* игра́ть; с. шу́тку (с+*i.*) to play a practical joke (on).

сыгра́|ться, юсь, *pf.* to achieve team-work; to play well together.

сы́змала, *adv.* (*coll.*) from a child, ever since one was a child.

сы́знова, *adv.* (*coll.*) anew, afresh; нача́ть с. to make a fresh start, begin all over again.

сымпровизи́р|овать, ую, *pf. of* импровизи́ровать.

сын, а, *pl.* ∼овья́, ∼ове́й *and* ∼ы́, ∼о́в, *m.* 1. (*pl.* ∼овья́) son. 2. (*pl.* ∼ы́) (*fig., rhet.*) son, child; с. своего́ вре́мени child, product of one's time.

сыни́шк|а, и, *m.* (*coll.*) dim. of сын.

сыно́вний, *adj.* filial.

сын|о́к, ка́, *m.* dim. of ∼; (*as mode of address*) sonny.

сы́п|ать, лю, лешь, *impf.* 1. to pour, strew. 2. (+*a. or i.*; *fig., coll.*) to pour forth; с. жа́лобами to pour forth complaints; с. деньга́ми to squander money.

сы́п|аться, лется, *impf.* 1. to fall; to pour out, run out; to scatter; мука́ ∼алась из мешка́ flour poured out of the bag. 2. (*of sounds, etc.*; *coll.*) to pour forth (*intrans.*), rain down; уда́ры ∼ались гра́дом blows were raining down, falling thick and fast. 3. (*of plaster, etc.*) to flake off. 4. (*of fabrics*) to fray out.

сыпно́й, *adj.* с. тиф (*med.*) typhus, spotted fever.

сыпнотифо́зный, *adj.* с. больно́й typhus patient.

сыпня́к, а́, *m.* (*coll.*) = сыпно́й тиф.

сыпу́ч|ий (∼, ∼а), *adj.* friable, free-flowing; с. грунт shifting ground; с. песо́к quicksand; ∼ие тела́ dry substances; ме́ры ∼их тел dry measures.

сып|ь, и, *f.* (*med.*) rash, eruption.

сыр, а, *pl.* ∼ы́, *m.* cheese; как с. в ма́сле ката́ться (*coll.*) to live on the fat of the land.

сыр-бор, *now only in phrase* вот отку́да с. загоре́лся (*coll.*) that was the spark that set the forest on fire.

сыре́|ть, ю, *impf.* (*of* от∼) to become damp.

сыр|е́ц, ца́, *m.* product in raw state; кирпи́ч-с. adobe; шёлк-с. raw silk.

сы́рник, а, *m.* curd fritter.

сы́р|ный, *adj. of* ∼; caseous; ∼ная неде́ля Shrovetide.

сы́ро, *as pred.* it is damp.

сырова́р, а, *m.* cheese-maker.

сырова́рени|е, я, *n.* cheese-making.

сырова́р|ня, ни, *g. pl.* ∼ен, *f.* cheese dairy, creamery.

сырова́т|ый (∼, ∼а), *adj.* 1. dampish. 2. not quite ripe. 3. (*cul.*) underdone, undercooked.

сыроде́льный, *adj.* cheese-processing.

сырое́жк|а, и, *f.* Russula (*mushroom*).

сыр|о́й (∼, ∼а́, ∼о), *adj.* 1. damp. 2. raw, uncooked; ∼а́я вода́ unboiled water; ∼о́е мя́со raw meat. 3. green; unripe. 4. raw; unfinished; ∼ые материа́лы raw materials. 5. (*coll.*) fat, podgy.

сыр|о́к, ка́, *m.* cheese curds.

сыромя́тн|ый, *adj.* dressed, tawed; ∼ая ко́жа rawhide.

сы́ромят|ь, и, *f.* tawed leather.

сы́рост|ь, и, *f.* dampness, humidity.

сыр|цо́вый, *adj. of* ∼е́ц; ∼цо́вая сталь natural steel.

сырь|ё, я́, *no pl.*, *n.* raw material(s).

сырьев|о́й, *adj. of* сырьё; ∼а́я ба́за raw material supply.

сырьём, *adv.* (*coll.*) raw; есть морко́вь с. to eat carrots raw.

сыск, а, *m.* (*obs.*) investigation, detection (*of criminals*).

сы|ска́ть, щу́, ∼щешь, *pf.* (*coll.*) to find.

сы|ска́ться, щу́сь, ∼щешься, *pf.* (*coll.*) to be found, come to light.

сыск|но́й, *adj. of* ∼; ∼на́я поли́ция (*obs.*) criminal investigation department.

сыте́|ть, ю, *impf.* (*coll.*) to become fuller.

сы́тно, *adv.* well; с. поза́втракать to have a good breakfast.

сы́т|ный (∼ен, ∼на́, ∼но), *adj.* (*of a meal*)

substantial, copious; ~ное ме́сто) *fig., joc., obs.*) fat job.

сы́тост|ь, и, *f.* satiety, repletion.

сы́т|ый (~, ~а́, ~о), *adj.* **1.** satisfied, replete, full; я ~ по го́рло I have eaten my fill, I am full up. **2.** fat; с. скот fat stock.

сыч, а́, *m.* little owl (*Athene noctua*); ~о́м сиде́ть (*coll.*) to look glum.

сычу́г, а́, *m.* (*anat.*) abomasum, rennet bag.

сычу́жин|а, ы, *f.* rennet.

сы́щик, а, *m.* detective.

сы́щиц|а, ы, *f. of* сы́щик.

сэконо́м|ить, лю, ишь, *pf. of* эконо́мить.

сэр, а, *m.* sir.

сюда́, *adv.* here, hither.

сюже́т, а, *m.* subject; topic.

сюже́т|ный, *adj. of* ~.

сюзере́н, а, *m.* (*hist.*) suzerain.

сюзере́н|ный, *adj. of* ~.

сюи́т|а, ы, *f.* (*mus.*) suite.

сюрпри́з, а, *m.* surprise.

сюрреали́зм, а, *m.* surrealism.

сюрреали́ст, а, *m.* surrealist.

сюрту́к, а́, *m.* frock-coat.

сюсю́ка|ть, ю, *impf.* to lisp.

сяк, *adv.*; (*coll.*) и так и с., *see* так.

сям, *adv.*; и там и с., ни там ни с., *see* там.

Т

таба́к, а́ (у́), *m.* **1.** tobacco-plant. **2.** tobacco; ню́хательный т. snuff; де́ло — т.! (*coll.*) things are in a bad way.

табака́, *indecl., only in phrase* (*cul.*) цыплёнок т. chicken tabak (*chicken flattened and grilled on charcoal*).

табаке́рк|а, и, *f.* snuff-box.

табаково́д, а, *m.* tobacco-grower.

табаково́дств|о, а, *n.* tobacco-growing.

табаково́д|ческий, *adj. of* ~ство.

табан|ить, ю, ишь, *impf.* to back water (*in rowing*).

таба́чник, а, *m.* **1.** tobacco-worker. **2.** (*obs.*) tobacco-user.

таба́чниц|а, ы, *f. of* таба́чник.

таба́чный, *adj.* **1.** tobacco; т. кисе́т tobacco-pouch; т. лист tobacco leaf. **2.** т. цвет snuff colour.

та́бел|ь, я, *m. also* т., ~и, *f.* **1.** (*m. and f.*) table; т. о ра́нгах (*hist.*) Table of Ranks (*introduced by Peter the Great*). **2.** (*m.*) time-board (*in factory, etc.*). **3.** (*m.*) number (*removed on arrival at work and replaced on leaving*).

та́бель|ный, *adj. of* ~; ~ная доска́ time-board; ~ные часы́ time-clock.

та́бельщик, а, *m.* timekeeper.

та́бельщиц|а, ы, *f. of* та́бельщик.

та́бес, а, *m.* (*med.*) tabes.

табле́тк|а, и, *f.* tablet, pill.

табли́ц|а, ы, *f.* table; plate (*with illustrations or diagrams*); т. умноже́ния multiplication table; ~ы логари́фмов logarithm tables; т. Менделе́ева (*chem.*) periodic table; т. прили́вов tide table; т. стрельбы́ (*mil.*) firing tables; т. вы́игрышей prize-list; т. (ро́зыгрыша) пе́рвенства (*sport*) (score-)table; пе́рвый, после́дний в ~е top, bottom of the table; внести́ в ~у to tabulate.

табли́чный, *adj.* **1.** tabular. **2.** standard, as per the tables.

табло́, *indecl., n.* indicator board, scoreboard (*with neon-lit figures*).

табльдо́т, а, *m.* table d'hôte.

та́бор, а, *m.* **1.** camp. **2.** gipsy encampment.

та́бор|ный, *adj.* **1.** *adj. of* ~. **2.** gipsy.

табу́, *indecl., n.* taboo.

табу́н, а́, *m.* herd (*usu. of horses, also of reindeer and some other animals*).

табу́н|ный, *adj. of* ~.

табу́нщик, а, *m.* horse-herd.

табуре́т, а, *m.* = ~ка.

табуре́т|ка, ки, *f.* stool.

таве́рн|а, ы, *f.* tavern, inn.

та́волг|а, и, *f.* (*bot.*) meadow-sweet.

таво́т, а, *m.* (*tech.*) axle grease, lubricating grease.

таво́тниц|а, ы, *f.* (*tech.*) grease gun, grease cup.

таврёный, *adj.* branded.

тавр#|и́ть, ю, и́шь, *impf.* (*of* за~) to brand.

тавр|о́, а́, *pl.* ~а, ~, ~а́м, *n.* brand (*on cattle, etc.*).

тавро́|вый, *adj.* **1.** *adj. of* ~. **2.** (*tech.*) T-shaped; ~вая ба́лка T-beam.

тавтологи́ческий, *adj.* tautological.

тавтоло́ги|я, и, *f.* tautology.

тага́н, а́, *m.* trivet.

таджи́к, а, *m.* Tadzhik.

таджи́кский, *adj.* Tadzhik.

таджи́чк|а, и, *f.* Tadzhik (woman).

таёжник, а, *m.* taiga dweller.

таёжный, *adj. of* тайга́.

таз¹, а, в ~у́, *pl.* ~ы́, *m.* basin; wash-basin; washing-up bowl.

таз², а, в ~е *and* в ~у́, *pl.* ~ы́, *m.* (*anat.*) pelvis.

тазобе́дренный, *adj.* (*anat.*) hip, coxal; т. суста́в hip joint.

та́зовый, *adj.* (*anat.*) pelvic.

тайнственность|ь, и, *f.* mystery.

тайнствен|ный (~, ~на), *adj.* 1. mysterious; enigmatic. 2. secret. 3. secretive; т. вид secretive look.

та́инств|о, а, *n.* 1. (*rel.*) sacrament. 2. (*obs.*) mystery, secret.

та|и́ть, ю́, и́шь, *impf.* to hide, conceal (*emotions, etc.*); `to harbour; т. в себе́ to be fraught (with); т. зло́бу (про́тив) to harbour a grudge (against); не́чего греха́ т. it must be owned.

та|и́ться, ю́сь, и́шься, *impf.* 1. (*coll.*) to be (in) hiding, lurk. 2. (*fig.*) to lurk, be lurking; что за э́тим ~и́тся? what lies behind this? 3. (*coll.*) to hold back (= to decline to reveal).

тайг|а́, и́, *f.* (*geogr.*) taiga.

тайко́м, *adv.* in secret, surreptitiously, by stealth; on the quiet, on the sly; behind someone's back.

тайм, а, *m.* (*sport*) half, period (*of game*).

таймен|ь, я, *m.* salmon-trout.

та́йн|а, ы, *f.* 1. mystery. 2. secret; держа́ть в ~е to keep secret, keep dark; храни́ть ~у to keep a secret; не т., что it is no secret that.

тайни́к, а́, *m.* hiding-place; cache; в ~а́х души́ in the inmost recesses of the heart.

тайнобра́чн|ый, *adj.* (*bot.*) cryptogamous, cryptogamic; *as noun* ~ые, ~ых Cryptogamia.

тайнопи́сный, *adj.* cryptographic.

тайнопис|ь, и, *f.* cryptographic writing.

та́йн|ый, *adj.* secret; clandestine; ~ое голосова́ние secret ballot; т. сове́т (*hist.*) Privy Council.

тайфу́н, а, *m.* typhoon.

так 1. *adv.* so; thus, in this way, like this; in such a way; т. мно́го so many; мы сде́лали т. this is what we did, we did as follows; т. бы (и)... (*expressing strong desire to do something; coll.*) how I, *etc.*, should like...; т. вот (*in proceeding with narration after digression*) and so, so then; т. же in the same way; т. и быть (*coll.*) all right, right you are, right-ho; т. и есть (*coll.*) so it is; т. и зна́й(те) (*expressing warning; coll.*) get this clear; т. ему́, *etc.*, и на́до serves him, *etc.*, right; т. и́ли ина́че (*i*) in any event, whatever happens, (*ii*) one way or another; т. называ́емый so-called; т. себе́ so-so, middling, not too good; т. сказа́ть so to speak; за т. (*coll.*) for nothing; и т. even so; as it is, as it stands; и т. да́лее and so on, and so forth; и т. и сяк this way and that; когда́ т. (*coll.*) if so; (не) т. ли? isn't it so? 2. *adv.* as it should be; не т. amiss, wrong;

т. ли я говорю́? am I right?; что́-то бы́ло не совсе́м т. something was amiss, something was not quite right. 3. *adv.* just like that (= without further action or consequences); боле́знь не пройдёт т. the illness will not pass just like that; т. ему́ э́то не пройдёт he won't get away with it like that. 4. *adv.*; т. (то́лько), про́сто т. for no special reason, for no reason in particular; just for fun, for the sake of it; т. како́й-то, т. како́й-н. (*coll., pejor.*) some sort of. 5. *particle* (*in answer to a question*) nothing in particular, nothing special; что тебе́ не понра́вилось там? — т., о́бщее положе́ние what did you not like there? — Nothing in particular, just the set-up in general. 6. т. и (*as emphatic particle*) simply, just; её глаза́ т. и сверка́ли гне́вом her eyes were simply blazing with anger; я т. и забы́л принести́ кни́гу I clean forgot, I have gone and forgotten to bring the book. 7. *conj.* then (*or not translated*); ты не спро́сишь его́, т. я спрошу́ if you won't ask him, then I will; е́хать, т. е́хать if we are going, let's go; не сего́дня, т. за́втра if not today, then tomorrow. 8. *conj.* so; т. вы зна́ете друг дру́га? so you know one another? 9. т. как *conj.* as, since. 10. *affirmative or emphatic particle* yes; т. то́чно (*in mil. parlance*) yes.

та́ка|ть, ю, *impf.* (*coll.*) to rattle, chatter (*o machine-gun fire, etc.*).

такела́ж, а, *m.* (*naut.*) rigging.

такела́жник, а, *m.* rigger, scaffolder.

такела́жн|ый, *adj.* 1. (*naut.*) rigging. 2. scaffolding; ~ые рабо́ты erection of scaffolding.

та́кже, *adv.* also, too, as well; (*after neg.*) or, nor.

-таки however, though; всё-т. nevertheless; опя́ть-т. again.

тако́в, f. ~а́, *n.* ~о́, *pl.* ~ы́, *pron.* such; все они́ ~ы́ they are all the same; ~ы́ на́ши све́дения so we are informed; и был т. (*coll.*) and that was the last we saw of him.

таков|о́й, *adj.* 1. (*obs.*) such; е́сли ~ы́е име́ются if any. 2. как т. as such.

тако́вский, *adj.* (*coll.*) of such a kind.

так|о́й, *pron.* 1. such; so; т. же the same; он т. до́брый! he is such a kind man; ~о́е пальто́ мне ну́жно I need a coat like that; ~и́м о́бразом thus, in this way; в ~о́м слу́чае in that case; до ~о́й сте́пени to such an extent. 2. (*coll.*) a kind of; бли́нчик т. a kind of pancake. 3. кто он т.? who is he?; что э́то ~о́е? what is this?; что ~о́е „кисе́ль"? what is 'kissel'?; что~о́е? what's that?, what did you say?; что ж тут ~о́го? what is there so wonderful about that?; куда́ ~о́е он пошёл? (*coll.*) wherever has he gone?

тако́й-ся́кой, *pron.* (*coll.*) (a) so-and-so.

тако́й-то, *pron.* so-and-so; such-and-such.

та́кс|а¹, ы, *f.* statutory price; tariff; по чёрной ~e at the black-market rate.

та́кс|а², ы, *f.* dachshund.

такса́тор, а, *m.* **1.** price-fixer; valuer. **2.** afforestation inspector.

такса́ци|я, и, *f.* **1.** price-fixing; valuation. **2.** afforestation inspection.

такси́, *indecl.*, *n.* taxi.

та́ксик, а, *m. dim. of* та́кса².

такси́р|овать, ую, *impf. and pf.* to fix the price (of), price.

такси́ст, а, *m.* taxi-driver.

таксо́метр, а, *m.* (taxi)meter; 'clock'.

таксомото́р, а, *m.* taxi.

таксомото́р|ный, *adj. of* ~; т. парк fleet of taxis.

таксомото́рщик, а, *m.* taxi-driver.

таксофо́н, а, *m.* automatic telephone.

так-ся́к, *adv. as pred.* ´ (*coll.*) it is tolerable, it is passable.

такт¹, а, *m.* **1.** (*mus., etc.*) time; measure; bar; отбива́ть т. to beat time; в т. in time. **2.** (*tech.*) stroke (*of engine*).

такт², а, *m.* tact.

та́к-таки, *particle* (*coll.*) after all; really.

та́ктик, а, *m.* tactician.

та́ктик|а, и, *f.* tactics.

такти́ческий, *adj.* tactical.

такти́чност|ь, и, *f.* tact.

такти́ч|ный (~ен, ~на), *adj.* tactful.

та́к-то, *adv.* (*coll.*) so; он не т. скро́мен he's not all that humble; т. так that's as it may be.

та́кт|овый, *adj. of* ~¹; ~овая черта́ bar.

тала́н, а, *m.* (*folklore*) luck, good fortune.

тала́нт, а, *m.* **1.** talent, gift(s). **2.** man of talent, gifted person. **3.** (*hist.*) talent (*ancient coin and measure*).

тала́нтливост|ь, и, *f.* talent, gifts.

тала́нтлив|ый (~, ~а), *adj.* talented, gifted.

та́лер, а, *m.* thaler (*coin*).

та́л|и, ей, *no sing.* block and tackle.

талисма́н, а, *m.* talisman, charm, mascot.

та́ли|я¹, и, *f.* waist; пла́тье в ~ю dress fitting at the waist; обня́ть кого́-н. за ~ю to put one's arm round someone's waist.

та́ли|я², и, *f.* two packs of playing cards.

та́лли|й, я, *m.* (*chem.*) thallium.

талму́д, а, *m.* (*rel.*) Talmud.

талмуди́ст, а, *m.* Talmudist; (*fig.*) pedant, doctrinaire.

талмуди́стский, *adj.* Talmudistic; (*fig.*) pedantic, doctrinaire.

талмуди́ческий, *adj.* = талмуди́стский.

тало́н, а, *m.* coupon; stub (*of cheque, etc.*).

тало́нчик, а, *m. dim. of* тало́н.

та́лреп, а, *m.* (*naut.*) lanyard; винтово́й т. turn-buckle.

та́л|ый, *adj.* thawed, melted; ~ая вода́ water from melted snow.

тальк, а, *m.* talc; talcum powder.

та́льк|овый, *adj. of* ~; т. сла́нец (*min.*) talc schist.

тальни́к, а́, *m.* willow.

там, *adv.* **1.** there; т. же in the same place; (*in footnotes, etc.*) ibidem; и т. и сям here, there and everywhere. **2.** (*coll.*) later, by and by. **3.** *as particle* (*coll.*) expresses disregard, indifference, *etc.*, вся́кие т. глу́пости говори́т he talks all kinds of nonsense; како́е т.! nothing of the kind!; not a bit of good!; чего́ т.! go on!, go ahead!

тамад|а́, ы́, *m.* master of ceremonies, toast-master.

та́мбур¹, а, *m.* **1.** (*archit.*) tambour. **2.** lobby. **3.** platform (*of railway carriage*).

та́мбур², а, *m.* chain-stitch.

тамбу́р, а, *m.* (*mus.*) **1.** tambourine. **2.** (*obs.*) tambour (= drum).

тамбури́н, а, *m.* **1.** tambourine. **2.** tambourin.

тамбурмажо́р, а, *m.* (*mil.; obs.*) drum major.

та́мбур|ный, *adj. of* ~²; т. шов chain-stitch.

тамизда́т, а, *m.* 'tamizdat' (*publication abroad*).

тамо́женник, а, *m.* customs official.

тамо́женн|ый, *adj.* customs; ~ые по́шлины, ~ые сбо́ры customs (*duties*).

тамо́жн|я, и, *f.* custom-house.

та́мошн|ий, *adj.* (*coll.*) of that place; ~ие жи́тели the local inhabitants.

тампо́н, а, *m.* (*med.*) tampon, plug.

тампона́ж, а, *m.* (*tech.*) tamping.

тампона́ци|я, и, *f.* (*med.*) tamponade.

тампони́р|овать, ую, *impf. and pf.* (*med.*) to tampon, plug.

тамта́м, а, *m.* tom-tom.

та́нгенс, а, *m.* (*math.*) tangent.

тангенциа́льный, *adj.* (*math.*) tangential.

та́нго, *indecl.*, *n.* tango.

та́н|ец, ца, *m.* **1.** dance; dancing; уро́ки ~цев dancing lessons. **2.** (*pl.*) a dance, dancing; пойти́ на ~цы to go to a dance, go dancing.

тани́н, а, *m.* tannin.

танк¹, а, *m.* (*mil.*) tank.

танк², а, *m.* container (*for transportation of liquids*).

та́нкер, а, *m.* (*naut.*) tanker.

танке́тк|а¹, и, *f.* tankette, small tank.

танке́тк|а², и, *f.* (*coll.*) (*ladies'*) wedge-heeled shoe, slipper.

танки́ст, а, *m.* member of tank crew.

та́нковый, *adj.* tank, armoured.

танкодро́м, а, *m.* tank training area.

танкострое́ни|е, я, *n.* tank-building, tank construction.

танк-парово́з, а, *m.* (*railways*) tank (engine).

танта́л, а, *m.* (*chem.*) tantalum.

тантьéм|а, ы, f. bonus.

танцевáльный, adj. dancing; т. вéчер a dance, party with dancing.

танц|евáть, ýю, impf. to dance.

танцклáсс, а, m. (obs.) school of dancing; dancing-classes.

танцмéйстер, а, m. (obs.) dancing-master.

танцóвщик, а, m. (ballet) dancer.

танцóвщиц|а, ы, f. of танцóвщик.

танцóр, а, m. dancer.

танцóрк|а, и, f. of танцóр.

танцýльк|а, и, f. (coll.) dance, hop.

тапёр, а, m. ballroom pianist.

тапёрш|а, и, f. of тапёр.

тапиóк|а, и, f. tapioca.

тапи́р, а, m. tapir.

тáпочк|а, и, f. (coll.) slipper; спорти́вная т. sports shoe, gym shoe, plimsoll.

тáр|а, ы, f. 1. packing, packaging. 2. (comm.) tare.

тарабáн|ить, ю, ишь, impf. (coll.) to clatter.

тарабáрск|ий, adj. 1. (obs.) cryptographic. 2. ~ая грáмота (coll.) double Dutch.

тарабáрщин|а, ы, f. (coll.) double Dutch, gibberish.

таракáн, а, m. cockroach.

таракáн|ий, adj. of ~.

тарáн, а, m. 1. (hist.) battering ram. 2. (mil.) ram; ramming.

тарáн|ить, ю, ишь, impf. (of про~) to ram.

тарáн|ный, adj. 1. adj. of ~. 2. ~ная кость (anat.) astragalus.

тарантáс, а, m. tarantass (springless carriage).

тарантéлл|а, ы, f. tarantella.

таран|ти́ть, чý, ти́шь, impf. (coll.) to jabber, natter.

тарáнтул, а, m. tarantula.

тарáн|ь, и, f. sea-roach (Rutilus rutilus Heckeli).

тарарáм, а, m. (coll.) row, racket, hullaba-loo.

тарарáх|ать, аю, impf. of ~нуть.

тарарáх|нуть, ну, нешь, pf. (of ~ать) (coll.) to bang; to crash.

таратáйк|а, и, f. cabriolet, gig.

таратóр|а, ы, m. and f. (coll.) chatterbox, gabbler.

таратóр|ить, ю, ишь, impf. (coll.) to jabber, natter; to gabble.

тарах|тéть, чý, ти́шь, impf. (coll.) to rattle, rumble.

тарáщ|ить, у, ишь, impf. т. глазá (на + a.) to goggle (at).

тарбагáн, а, m. Siberian marmot.

тарéлк|а, и, f. 1. plate; глубóкая т. soup-plate; быть не в своéй ~е to be not quite oneself. 2. (tech.) plate, disc. 3. (pl.) cymbals.

тарéл|очный, adj. of ~ка; т. бýфер plate buffer; ~очная ми́на (mil.) flat anti-tank mine; ~очная печь (tech.) revolving hearth.

тарéльчат|ый, adj. (tech.) plate, disc; т. клáпан disc valve; ~ая мýфта plate coupling; т. тóрмоз disc brake.

тари́ф, а, m. tariff, rate.

тарификáци|я, и, f. tariffing.

тарифици́р|овать, ую, impf. and pf. to tariff.

тари́ф|ный, adj. of ~.

тартáни|е, я, n. (tech.) (oil-)bailing.

тартарары́: провали́ться в т. (coll.) I'll be damned.

тарти́нк|а, и, f. slice of bread and butter.

тархáн, а, m. (hist.) landowner enjoying special privileges.

тархáн|ный, adj. of ~.

тáры-бáры, indecl. (coll.) tittle-tattle.

таскá|ть, ю, impf. (indet. of тащи́ть) 1. see тащи́ть. 2. (pf. от~) (coll.) to pull (as punishment); т. когó-н. зá волосы to pull someone's hair. 2. (coll.) to wear.

таскá|ться, юсь, impf. (indet. of тащи́ться) 1. see тащи́ться. 2. (coll., pejor.) to roam about; to hang about.

тас|овáть, ýю, impf. (of с~) to shuffle (cards in a pack).

тасóвк|а, и, f. shuffle, shuffling (of playing cards).

татарв|á, ы́, f. (collect., obs., pejor.) the Tatars.

татáр|ин, ина, pl. ~ы, ~, m. Tatar.

татáрк|а¹, и, f. Tatar (woman).

татáрк|а², и, f. spring onion.

татáрник, а, m. thistle.

татáрский, adj. Tatar.

татуи́р|овать, ую, impf. and pf. to tattoo.

татуи́р|оваться, уюсь, impf. and pf. to tattoo oneself; to have oneself tattooed.

татуирóвк|а, и, f. tattooing.

тат|ь, я, m. (arch.) thief, robber.

тафт|á, ы́, f. taffeta.

тахикарди́|я, и, f. (med.) tachycardia.

тахóметр, а, m. tachometer.

тахт|á, ы́, f. ottoman.

тачáнк|а, и, f. cart (used in Ukraine and Caucasus).

тачá|ть, ю, impf. (of вы́~) to stitch.

тáчк|а, и, f. wheelbarrow.

тащ|и́ть, ý, ~ишь, impf. (det. of таскáть) 1. to pull; to drag, lug; to carry. 2. (coll.) to take; (fig.) to drag off; т. когó-н. в кинó to drag someone off to the cinema. 3. to pull out. 4. (coll.) to pinch, swipe.

тащ|и́ться, ýсь, ~ишься, impf. (det. of таскáться) 1. to drag oneself along. 2. to drag, trail.

тáяни|е, я, n. thaw, thawing.

тá|ять, ю, ешь, impf. (of рас~) 1. to melt; to thaw; ~ет it is thawing. 2. (fig.) to melt away, dwindle, wane; нáши запáсы ~ют our stocks are dwindling; егó си́лы ~яли his strength was ebbing. **3.** (от; *fig.*) to melt (with), languish (with). **4.** (*impf. only*) to waste away.

тва́р|ь, и, *f.* creature; (*collect.*) creatures; all creation (*also pejor.*); вся́кой ~и по па́ре (*coll.*) all sorts and kinds of people.

тверде́ни|е, я, *n.* hardening.

тверде́|ть, ю, *impf.* to harden, become hard.

твер|ди́ть, жу́, ди́шь, *impf.* **1.** (+*a.* or о+*p.*) to repeat, say over and over again. **2.** to memorize, learn by rote.

твёрдо, *adv.* hard; firmly, firm.

твердока́менный, *adj.* (*rhet.*) steadfast, staunch.

твердоло́б|ый (~, ~а), *adj.* **1.** thick-skulled. **2.** (*polit.*) diehard.

твёрдост|ь, и, *f.* hardness; (*fig.*) firmness.

твёрд|ый (~, ~а́, ~о), *adj.* **1.** hard. **2.** firm; solid; т. грунт firm soil; т. переплёт stiff binding; ~ое те́ло (*phys., chem.*) solid; фи́зика ~ого те́ла solid state physics. **3.** (*fig. in var. senses*) firm; stable; steadfast; ~ое зада́ние specified task; ~ые зна́ния sound knowledge; ~ое реше́ние firm decision; т. срок fixed time-limit; ~ые це́ны stable, fixed prices. **4.** (*ling.*) hard; т. знак hard sign (*name of Russian letter 'ъ'*).

тверды́н|я, и, *f.* (*obs.*) stronghold (*also fig.*).

твердь, и, *f.* (*arch.*) т. земна́я the earth; т. небе́сная the firmament, the heavens.

тво|й, его́, *f.* ~я́, ~е́й, *n.* ~ё, ~его́, *pl.* ~й, ~и́х, *possessive pron.* your, yours (thy, thine); ~его́ (*after comp. adv.*; *coll.*) than you; я зна́ю лу́чше ~его́ I know better than you; что т. (*coll.*) just like; гора́ — что т. Эльбру́с the mountain is just like Mt. Elbruz; *as noun* ~й, ~и́х your people.

творе́ни|е, я, *n.* **1.** creation; work. **2.** creature, being.

твор|е́ц, ца́, *m.* creator.

твори́л|о¹, а, *n.* hatch; aperture; water-gate (*in dam*).

твори́л|о², а, *n.* lime-pit.

твори́тельный, *adj.* т. паде́ж (*gram.*) instrumental case.

твор|и́ть¹, ю́, и́шь, *impf.* (*of* со~) **1.** to create. **2.** to do; to make; т. добро́ to do good; т. суд и распра́ву (*obs.*) to deal out justice; т. чудеса́ to work wonders.

твор|и́ть², ю, и́шь, *impf.* (*obs.*) to knead; т. и́звесть to slake lime.

твор|и́ться¹, и́тся, *impf.* (*coll.*) to happen, go on; что тут ~и́тся? what is going on here?

твор|и́ться², и́тся, *impf.*, *pass. of* ~и́ть².

творо́г, а́ and **тво́рог, а,** *m.* curds, cottage cheese.

творо́жист|ый (~, ~а), *adj.* curdled, clotted.

творо́жник, а, *m.* curd pancake.

творо́жн|ый, *adj.* curd; ~ая ма́сса curds; т. сыро́к cottage cheese.

тво́рческ|ий, *adj.* creative; ~ая си́ла creative power, creativeness; т. путь Толсто́го Tolstoy's career as a writer.

тво́рчеств|о, а, *n.* **1.** creation; creative work. **2.** (*collect.*) works.

теа́тр, а, *m.* **1.** (*in var. senses*) theatre; т. вое́нных де́йствий (*mil.*) theatre of operations; анатоми́ческий т. dissecting-room. **2.** (*fig.*) the stage; т. ма́лых форм variety theatre. **3.** (*collect.*) (the) plays; т. Шекспи́ра the plays of Shakespeare.

театра́л, а, *m.* theatre-goer, playgoer; drama-lover.

театрализа́ци|я, и, *f.* adaptation for the stage.

театрализ|ова́ть, у́ю, *impf. and pf.* to adapt for the stage.

театра́л|ьный (~ен, ~ьна), *adj.* **1.** theatre; theatrical; т. зал auditorium; ~ьная ка́сса box-office; ~ьная шко́ла drama school. **2.** (*fig.*) theatrical, stagy.

театрове́дени|е, я, *n.* drama study.

тевто́н, а, *m.* Teuton.

тевто́нский, *adj.* Teutonic.

тéз|а, ы, *f.* = ~ис I.

тéзис, а, *m.* **1.** thesis, proposition, point; вы́двинуть т. to advance a thesis. **2.** thesis (*in Hegelian philosophy*).

тёзк|а, и, *m. and f.* namesake; мы с ва́ми ~и you and I share the same name.

тезоимени́тств|о, а, *n.* (*obs.*) name-day (*esp. of member of Tsar's family*).

тейзм, а, *m.* theism.

тейст, а, *m.* theist.

теисти́ческий, *adj.* theistic.

теки́н|ец, ца, *m.* Turkmen.

теки́нк|а, и, *f.* Turkmen (woman).

теки́нский, *adj.* Turkmen; т. ковёр Turkoman carpet.

текст, а, *m.* **1.** text. **2.** words, libretto.

тексти́л|ь, я, no *pl.*, *m.* (*collect.*) textiles.

тексти́льный, *adj.* textile.

тексти́льщик, а, *m.* textile worker.

тексти́льщи|ца, цы, *f. of* ~к.

текстови́к, á, *m.* librettist.

тексто́лог, а, *m.* textual critic.

текстоло́ги|я, и, *f.* textual study, textual criticism.

текстуа́л|ьный (~ен, ~ьна), *adj.* **1.** verbatim, word-for-word. **2.** (*philol.*) textual.

текто́ник|а, и, *f.* (*geol.*) tectonics.

тектони́ческий, *adj.* (*geol.*) tectonic.

теку́чест|ь, и, *f.* **1.** (*phys.*) fluidity. **2.** fluctuation, instability; т. рабо́чей си́лы fluctuation of manpower, labour fluidity.

теку́ч|ий (~, ~а), *adj.* **1.** (*phys.*) fluid. **2.** fluctuating, unstable.

теку́щ|ий, *pres. part. act. of* течь *and adj.* **1.**

current; of the present moment; в ~ем
годý in the current year; 2-го числá ~его
мéсяца the second instant; ~ие собы́тия
current events, current affairs; т. счёт current áccount. 2. routine, ordinary; ~ие
делá routine business; т. ремóнт routine
repairs.

теле- tele-.

телевещáни|е, я, *n.* television broadcasting.

телеви́дени|е, я, *n.* television.

телевизиóнный, *adj.* television.

телеви́зи|я, и, *f.* = телеви́дение.

телеви́зор, а, *m.* television set; т. цветнóго,
чёрно-бéлого изображéния colour, black-
-and-white television set.

телеви́зор|ный, *adj. of* ~.

телéг|а, и, *f.* cart, waggon.

телегрáмм|а, ы, *f.* telegram.

телегрáф, а, *m.* 1. telegraph. 2. telegraph
office.

телеграфи́р|овать, ую, *impf. and pf.* to tele-
graph, wire.

телеграфи́ст, а, *m.* telegraphist.

телеграфи́ст|ка, ки, *f. of* ~.

телеграфи́|я, и, *f.* telegraphy.

телегрáфн|ый, *adj.* telegraph; telegraphic;
т. áдрес telegraphic address; ~ая лéнта
ticker-tape; т. стиль telegraphic style,
telegraphese; т. столб telegraph-pole.

телéжк|а, и, *f.* 1. small cart, hand-cart.
2. bogie, trolley. 3. (*hist.*) post-chaise.

телé|жный, *adj. of* ~га; ~жное колесó cart-
wheel.

телезри́тел|ь, я, *m.* (television) viewer.

тéлекс, а, *m.* telex.

телеметри́ческий, *adj.* telemetric.

телеметри́|я, и, *f.* telemetry.

телеизмерéни|е, я, *n.* telemetry.

телемехáник|а, и, *f.* telemechanics, remote
control.

тел|ёнок, ёнка, *pl.* ~я́та, ~я́т, *m.* calf.

телеобъекти́в, а, *m.* (*phot.*) telescopic lens,
telephoto lens.

телеологи́ческий, *adj.* teleological.

телеолóги|я, и, *f.* teleology.

телепати́ческий, *adj.* telepathic.

телепáти|я, и, *f.* telepathy.

телепередáч|а, и, *f.* television transmission;
прямáя т. live television coverage.

телес|á, телéс, ~áм, *no sing.* (*coll., joc.*)
frame (*of a stout person*).

телескóп, а, *m.* telescope.

телескопи́ческий, *adj.* telescopic; т. прицéл
telescopic sight (*of firearm*).

телескопи́|я, и, *f.* telescopy.

телескóп|ный, *adj. of* ~.

телéсн|ый, *adj.* 1. bodily; corporal; soma-
tic; physical; ~ое наказáние corporal
punishment; ~ого цвéта flesh-coloured.
2. corporeal.

телестýди|я, и, *f.* television studio.

телеуправлéни|е, я, *n.* remote control.

телефикáци|я, и, *f.* equipping with television.

телефóн, а, *m.* 1. telephone; позвони́ть
по ~у (+*d.*) to telephone, phone, ring up;
вы́зов по ~у telephone call; т. довéрия confidential telephone; т.-автомáт public telephone, public call-box. 2. (*coll.*) telephone
number.

телефони́р|овать, ую, *impf. and pf.* to tele-
phone.

телефони́ст, а, *m.* telephone operator, tele-
phonist.

телефони́ст|ка, ки, *f. of* ~.

телефóн|ный, *adj. of* ~.

телефоногрáмм|а, ы, *f.* telephoned tele-
gram.

телефотогрáфи|я, и, *f.* telephotography.

тел|éц, ьцá, *m.* 1. (*obs.*) calf; золотóй т. the
golden calf. 2. Т. (*astron.*) Taurus.

телецéнтр, а, *m.* television centre.

телешпаргáлк|а, и, *f.* autocue, 'idiot
board'.

тел|и́ться, ~ится, *impf.* (*of* о~) to calve.

тёлк|а, и, *f.* heifer.

теллýр, а, *m.* (*chem.*) tellurium.

тéл|о, а, *pl.* ~á, ~, ~áм, *n.* (*in var. senses*)
body; (*coll.*) быть в ~е to be stout; войти́ в
т. to put on weight; спасть с ~а to grow
thin; держáть в чёрном ~е to ill-treat,
maltreat.

телогрéйк|а, и, *f.* (*woman's*) padded jacket
(*usu. sleeveless*).

телодвижéни|е, я, *n.* movement, motion.

тел|óк, кá, *m.* (*coll.*) calf.

телослóжени|е, я, *n.* build, frame.

телохрани́тел|ь, я, *m.* bodyguard.

тéльник, а, *m.* (knitted) vest.

тéл|ьный, *adj.* (*coll.*) *of* ~о; ~ьного цвéта
flesh-coloured.

тельня́шк|а, и, *f.* (*coll.*) (*sailor's*) striped vest.

теля́тин|а, ы, *f.* veal.

теля́тник¹, а, *m.* calf-house.

теля́тник², а, *m.* calf-herd.

теля́ч|ий, *adj.* 1. *adj. of* телёнок; ~ья кóжа
calf(skin). 2. (*cul.*) veal. 3. т. востóрг (*coll.*)
foolish raptures; ~ьи нéжности (*coll.*)
sloppy sentimentality.

тем 1. *i. sing. m. and n., d. pl. of* тот. 2. *conj.*
(so much) the; чем вы́ше, т. лýчше the
taller, the better; т. лýчше so much the
better; т. бóлее, что the more so as,
especially as; т. не мéнее none the less,
nevertheless.

тéм|а, ы, *f.* 1. subject, topic, theme; перейти́
к другóй ~е to change the subject;
сочинéние на ~у Наполеóновских войн
a work on the subject of the Napoleonic
Wars. 2. (*mus.*) theme; т. с вариáциями
theme and variations.

темáтик|а, и, *f.* (*collect.*) subject-matter, themes, subjects.

тематический, *adj.* **1.** *adj. of* темáтика; т. плáн plan of subjects, plan of subject-matter (*e.g. of forthcoming publications*). **2.** (*mus.*) thematic.

тембр, а, *m.* timbre.

тéмбр|овый, *adj. of* ~.

теменн|óй, *adj.* (*anat.*) sincipital; ~áя кость parietal bone.

тéмен|ь, и, *f.* (*coll.*) darkness.

тéми, *i. pl. of* тот.

темля́к, á, *m.* (*mil.*) sword-knot.

тёмн|ая, ой, *f.* (*obs.*) (*police*) cell.

темнé|ть, ю, *impf.* **1.** (*pf.* по~) to grow dark, become dark; to darken. **2.** (*pf.* с~) ~ет (*impers.*) it gets dark, it is getting dark. **3.** (*impf. only*) to show up darkly.

темнé|ться, ется, *impf.* to show up darkly.

темни́|ть, ю, и́шь, *impf.* to darken; to make darker.

темни́ц|а, ы, *f.* (*obs.*) dungeon.

темнó, *as pred.* it is dark; у меня́ в глазáх стáло т. everything went dark before my eyes.

темно- dark-.

темнокóжий, *adj.* dark-skinned, swarthy.

темноси́ний, *adj.* dark blue; navy blue.

темнот|á, ы́, *f.* **1.** dark, darkness; в ~é in the dark; до ~ы́ before dark, before it gets dark; с ~óй under cover of dark(ness). **2.** (*coll.*) ignorance; backwardness.

тём|ный (~ен, ~нá, ~нó), *adj.* **1.** dark; ~ное пятнó (*fig.*) dark stain, blemish; ~ная водá (*med.*) amaurosis; ~нá водá во óблацех the matter is wrapped in mystery. **2.** obscure, vague; ~ное мéсто (*philol.*) obscure passage; ~ное пятнó obscure place. **3.** sombre. **4.** shady, fishy, suspicious; ~ное дéло shady business. **5.** ignorant, benighted.

темп, а, *m.* **1.** (*mus.*) tempo. **2.** (*fig.*) tempo, rate, speed, pace; замéдлить т. to slacken one's pace; ускóрить т. to accelerate.

тéмпер|а, ы, *f.* **1.** distemper (*paint*). **2.** tempera (*painting*).

темперáмент, а, *m.* temperament; человéк с ~ом energetic person, spirited person.

темперáмент|ный (~ен, ~на), *adj.* energetic; spirited, vigorous.

температýр|а, ы, *f.* **1.** temperature; т. кипéния boiling-point; т. замерзáния freezing-point; кривáя ~ы temperature curve; мéрить комý-н. ~у to take someone's temperature. **2.** (*coll.*) (heightened) temperature; ходи́ть с ~ой to go about with a temperature.

температýр|ить, ю, ишь, *impf.* (*coll.*) to have a temperature.

температýр|ный, *adj. of* ~а; ~ная кривáя temperature curve; т. шов (*tech.*) heat crack, expansion joint.

темперáци|я, и, *f.* (*mus.*) temperament.

темпери́р|овать, ую, *impf. and pf.* (*mus.*) to temper.

тем|ь, и, *f.* (*coll.*) dark, darkness.

тéм|я, ени, *no pl., n.* (*anat.*) sinciput; crown, top of the head.

тенденциóз|ный (~ен, ~на), *adj.* (*pejor.*) tendentious, biased.

тендéнци|я, и, *f.* **1.** (к) tendency (to, towards); у негó т. (к) he has a tendency (to), he tends (to). **2.** (*pejor.*) bias; с ~ей tendentious, biased.

тéндер, а, *m.* **1.** (*railways*) tender. **2.** (*naut.*) cutter.

тéндер|ный, *adj. of* ~.

тенев|óй, *adj.* shady (*also fig.*); ~áя сторонá shady side; (*fig.*) bad side, seamy side.

тенелюби́в|ый (~, ~а), *adj.* (*bot.*) requiring shade.

тенёт|а, ~, *no sing.* snare.

тени́ст|ый (~, ~а), *adj.* shady.

тéннис, а, *m.* tennis.

тенниси́ст, а, *m.* tennis-player.

тенниси́ст|ка, ки, *f. of* ~.

тéнниск|а, и, *f.* (*coll.*) tennis shirt, short-sleeved shirt.

тéннисн|ый, *adj.* tennis; т. корт, ~ая площáдка tennis-court.

тéнор, а, *pl.* ~á, ~óв, *m.* (*mus.*) tenor.

тенорóвый, *adj. of* тéнор.

тент, а, *m.* awning.

тен|ь, и, в ~и́, pl. ~и, ~éй, *f.* **1.** shade; сидéть в ~и́ to sit in the shade; держáться в ~и́ (*fig.*) to keep in the background. **2.** shadow; давáть т. to cast a shadow; от негó остáлась однá т. he is but a shadow of his former self; навести́ т. (*coll.*) to confuse the issue. **3.** shadow, phantom, ghost; блéден, как т. pale as a ghost. **4.** (*fig.*) shadow, particle, vestige, atom; нет ни ~и сомнéния there is not a shadow of doubt; в егó расскáзе нет ни ~и прáвды there is not a particle of truth in his story. **5.** suspicion; брóсить т. на когó-н. to cast suspicion on someone.

теогóни|я, и, *f.* theogony.

теодицé|я, и, *f.* theodicy.

теодоли́т, а, *m.* theodolite.

теократи́ческий, *adj.* theocratic.

теокрáти|я, и, *f.* theocracy.

теологи́ческий, *adj.* theological.

теолóги|я, и, *f.* theology.

теорéм|а, ы, *f.* theorem.

теоретизи́р|овать, ую, *impf.* to theorize.

теорéтик, а, *m.* theorist.

теорети́ческий, *adj.* theoretical.

теорети́ч|ный (~ен, ~на), *adj.* (*pejor.*) theoretical, abstract, abstruse.

тео́ри|я, и, *f.* theory.

теософи́ческий, *adj.* theosophical.

теосо́фи|я, и, *f.* theosophy.

тепе́решн|ий, *adj.* (*coll.*) present; ~ие лю́ди people (of) today; в ~ее вре́мя at the present time, nowadays.

тепе́рь, *adv.* now; nowadays, today.

тёпленьк|ий, *adj.* (*coll.*) (nice and) warm; ~ое месте́чко cushy job.

тепле́|ть, ет, *impf.* (*of* по~) to get warm.

те́пл|иться, ится, *impf.* to flicker, glimmer (*also fig.*); ~ится наде́жда there is still a glimmer of hope, a ray of hope.

тепли́ц|а, ы, *f.* greenhouse, hothouse, conservatory.

тепли́|чный, *adj. of* ~ца; ~чное расте́ние hothouse plant (*also fig.*).

тепло́[1], *adv.* 1. warmly. 2. *as pred.* it is warm.

тепл|о́[2], а́, *n.* heat; warmth; де́сять гра́дусов ~а́ ten degrees above zero (*centigrade*); держа́ть в ~е́ to keep (in the) warm.

теплово́з, а, *m.* diesel locomotive.

теплово́зный, *adj.* diesel.

теплов|о́й, *adj.* heat; thermal; т. дви́гатель heat-engine; ~а́я едини́ца heat unit, thermal unit; т. ожо́г flashburn; т. уда́р (*med.*) heat stroke; ~а́я электроста́нция thermal electric power station; ~а́я эне́ргия heat energy, thermal energy.

теплоёмкост|ь, и, *f.* (*phys.*) heat capacity, thermal capacity; уде́льная т. specific heat.

теплокро́вный, *adj.* (*zool.*) warm-blooded.

теплолюби́в|ый (~, ~а), *adj.* (*bot.*) heat-loving.

тепломе́р, а, *m.* (*phys.*) calorimeter.

теплообме́н, а, *m.* (*phys.*) heat exchange.

теплопрово́д, а, *m.* hot-water system.

теплопрово́дност|ь, и, *f.* heat conductivity.

теплопрово́дный, *adj.* heat-conducting.

теплопрозра́чный, *adj.* (*phys.*) diathermic.

теплосто́йкий, *adj.* heat-proof, heat-resistant.

теплот|а́, ы́, *f.* 1. (*phys.*) heat; едини́ца ~ы́ thermal unit. 2. warmth (*also fig.*); душе́вная т. warm-heartedness.

теплотво́рност|ь, и, *f.* (*phys.*) heating value, calorific value.

теплотво́рн|ый, *adj.* (*phys.*) calorific; ~ая спосо́бность = ~ость.

теплоте́хник, а, *m.* heating engineer.

теплоте́хник|а, и, *f.* heating engineering.

теплофика́ци|я, и, *f.* introduction of a heating system.

теплофици́р|овать, ую, *impf. and pf.* to introduce a heating system (in).

теплохо́д, а, *m.* motor ship.

теплоцентра́л|ь, и, *f.* heating plant.

теплу́шк|а, и, *f.* (*coll.*) heated goods van (*for transportation of human beings*).

тёп|лый (~ел, ~ла́, ~ло́, ~лы), *adj.* 1. (*in var. senses*) warm; ~лая оде́жда warm clothing; ~лые кра́ски warm colours; ~лое месте́чко (*coll.*) cushy job. 2. warmed, heated. 3. (*fig.*) warm, cordial; kindly, affectionate; т. приём warm welcome. 4. heartfelt. 5. (*coll.*) roguish; ~лая компа́ния bunch of rogues.

теплы́н|ь, и, *f.* (*coll.*) warm weather.

тепля́к, а́, *m.* temporary covered and heated enclosure on building site.

терапе́вт, а, *m.* therapeutist.

терапевти́ческий, *adj.* therapeutic.

терапи́|я, и, *f.* therapy.

тератоло́ги|я, и, *f.* (*biol.*) teratology.

те́рби|й, я, *m.* (*chem.*) terbium.

тереби́льщик, а, *m.* flax-puller.

тереб|и́ть, лю́, и́шь, *impf.* 1. to pull (at), pick (at). 2. т. лён to pull flax. 3. (*fig., coll.*) to pester, bother.

те́рем, а, *pl.* ~а́, *m.* (*hist.*) (tower-)chamber; tower.

тере́ть, тру, трёшь, *past* тёр, тёрла, *impf.* 1. to rub. 2. to grate, grind. 3. to rub, chafe.

тере́ться, трусь, трёшься, *past* тёрся, тёрлась, *impf.* 1. to rub oneself; (о, обо + *a.*) to rub (against). 2. (о́коло; *fig., coll.*) to hang (about, round). 3. (среди́; *fig., coll.*) to mix (with), hobnob (with).

терза́|ть, ю, *impf.* 1. to tear to pieces; to pull about. 2. to torment, torture; меня́ ~ли сомне́ния I was a prey to doubts.

терза́|ться, юсь, *impf.* (+ *i.*) to suffer; to be a prey (to).

тёрк|а, и, *f.* (*cul.*) grater.

те́рмин, а, *m.* term.

терминологи́ческий, *adj.* terminological.

терминоло́ги|я, и, *f.* terminology.

терми́т[1], а, *m.* (*chem.*) thermite.

терми́т[2], а, *m.* (*zool.*) termite.

терми́т|ный, *adj. of* ~[1].

терми́ческ|ий, *adj.* (*phys., tech.*) thermic, thermal; ~ая обрабо́тка thermal treatment.

термодина́мик|а, и, *f.* thermodynamics.

термодинами́ческий, *adj.* thermodynamic.

термо́метр, а, *m.* thermometer; т. Це́льсия centigrade thermometer; поста́вить т. кому́-н. to take someone's temperature.

термообрабо́тк|а, и, *f.* (*tech.*) heat treatment, thermal treatment.

термопа́р|а, ы, *f.* (*phys.*) thermocouple.

те́рмос, а, *m.* thermos (flask).

термоста́т, а, *m.* thermostat.

термоэлектри́ческий, *adj.* thermo-electrical; т. столб thermopile.

термоэлектро́нный, *adj.* thermionic.

термоя́дерный, *adj.* thermonuclear.

те́рм|ы, ~, *no sing.* (*hist.*) thermae, (hot) baths.

тёрн, а, *m.* (*bot.*) **1.** blackthorn. **2.** sloe(s).

те́рни|е, я, *n.* (*obs.*) **1.** prickly plant. **2.** prickle, thorn.

терно́вник, а, *m.* (*bot.*) blackthorn.

терно́в|ый, *adj.* **1.** *adj. of* тёрн *and* ~ник. **2.** thorny, prickly; т. вене́ц crown of thorns.

терпели́вост|ь, и, *f.* patience.

терпели́в|ый (~, ~a), *adj.* patient.

терпе́ни|е, я, *n.* patience; endurance, perseverance; вы́вести из ~я to exasperate; вы́йти из ~я to lose patience; запасти́сь, вооружи́ться ~ем to summon up patience, have patience.

терпенти́н, а, *m.* turpentine.

терпенти́н|ный, *adj. of* ~.

терпенти́н|овый, *adj.* = ~ный.

терп|е́ть, лю́, ~ишь, *impf.* **1.** (*pf.* по~) to suffer, undergo; т. пораже́ние to suffer a defeat, be defeated. **2.** to bear, endure, stand; мы не могли́ бо́льше т. тако́го хо́лода we could bear the cold no longer. **3.** to have patience. **4.** to tolerate, suffer, put up (with); не (мочь) т. to be unable to bear, endure, stand, support; т. не могу́ I can't stand it, I hate it; вре́мя ~ит there is plenty of time; вре́мя не ~ит there is no time to be lost, time is getting short; де́ло не ~ит the matter is urgent; де́ло не ~ит отлага́тельства the matter brooks no delay.

терп|е́ться, ~ится, *impf.* (*impers.*) ему́, *etc.*, не ~ится (+*inf.*) he, *etc.*, is impatient (to).

терпи́мост|ь, и, *f.* tolerance; indulgence; дом ~и (*obs., euph.*) brothel.

терпи́м|ый (~, ~a), *adj.* **1.** tolerant; indulgent, forbearing. **2.** tolerable, bearable, supportable.

тёрп|кий (~ок, ~ка́), *adj.* astringent; tart, sharp.

тёрпкост|ь, и, *f.* astringency; tartness, sharpness, acerbity.

тёрпн|уть, ет, *impf.* (*of* за~) (*coll.*) to grow numb.

терпу́г, а́, *m.* (*tech.*) rasp.

террако́т|а, ы, *f.* terracotta.

террако́т|овый, *adj. of* ~a.

терра́ри|й, я, *m.* animal case (*for keeping small animals, esp. reptiles and amphibians*).

терра́риум, а, *m.* = терра́рий.

терра́с|а, ы, *f.* (*in var. senses*) terrace.

терраси́р|овать, ую, *impf. and pf.* to terrace.

территориа́льн|ый, *adj.* territorial; ~ая а́рмия territorial army; ~ые во́ды territorial waters.

террито́ри|я, и, *f.* territory, confines; area.

терро́р, а, *m.* terror.

террризи́р|овать, ую, *impf. and pf.* to terrorize.

террори́зм, а, *m.* terrorism.

террориз|ова́ть, у́ю, *impf. and pf.* = ~и́ровать.

террори́ст, а, *m.* terrorist.

террористи́ческий, *adj.* terrorist.

террори́ст|ка, ки, *f. of* ~.

тёрт|ый (~, ~a), *p.p.p. of* тере́ть *and adj.* (*full form only*) **1.** ground; grated. **2.** (*fig., coll.*) hardened, experienced; т. кала́ч old stager, old hand.

терце́т, а, *m.* **1.** (*mus.*) terzetto. **2.** (*lit.*) tercet, triplet.

терци́н|а, ы, *f.* (*lit.*) terza rima.

те́рци|я, и, *f.* **1.** (*mus.*) mediant; third; бо́льшая т. major third; ма́лая т. minor third. **2.** (*math.*) third (= *one sixtieth of a second*). **3.** (*typ.*) 16-point type.

терье́р, а, *m.* terrier (*dog*).

теря́|ть, ю, *impf.* (*of* по~) (*in var. senses*) to lose; т. наде́жду to lose hope; не т. головы́ to keep one's head; т. си́лу to become invalid; т. си́лу за да́вностью (*leg.*) to be lost by limitation; т. по́чву под нога́ми to feel the ground slipping away from under one's feet; т. вре́мя на что-н. to waste time on something; т. в ве́се to lose weight; т. в чьём-н. мне́нии to sink in someone's estimation; не т. и́з виду to keep in sight; (*fig.*) to remember, bear in mind; нам не́чего т. we have nothing to lose.

теря́|ться, юсь, *impf.* (*of* по~) **1.** to get lost; to disappear, vanish. **2.** to fail, decline, decrease, weaken; па́мять у него́ ~ется his memory is failing, is going. **3.** to pass unnoticed; to fail to attract notice; ре́плика не ~лась the retort did not pass unnoticed. **4.** to lose one's self-possession; to become flustered; ~юсь, ума́ не приложу́ I am at my wits' end. **5.** т. в дога́дках, т. в предположе́ниях to be lost in conjecture.

тёс, а (у), *m.* (*collect.*) boards, planks.

теса́к, а́, *m.* **1.** broadsword; cutlass. **2.** chopper, hatchet.

те|са́ть, шу́, ~шешь, *impf.* **1.** to cut, hew. **2.** to trim, square.

тесёмк|а, и, *f.* tape, ribbon, lace, braid.

тесём|очный, *adj. of* ~ка.

тесёмчатый, *adj.* tape-like; т. глист tape-worm.

тесн|а, ы, *f.* board, plank.

тес|ло́, ла́, *pl.* ~ла, ~ел, *n.* adze.

тесни́н|а, ы, *f.* gorge, ravine.

тесн|и́ть, ю, и́шь, *impf.* **1.** (*pf.* по~) to press, crowd. **2.** to squeeze, constrict; (*of clothing*) to be too tight; мне грудь ~и́т I have a tightness in my chest.

тесн|и́ться, ю́сь, и́шься, *impf.* **1.** (*pf.* по~) to press through, push a way through. **2.** (*pf.* с~) to crowd, cluster, jostle one another (*also fig.; of thoughts, etc.*).

те́сно, *adv.* **1.** closely (*also fig.*); tightly; narrowly; идти́ т. в ряд to march shoulder to shoulder; быть т. свя́зано (c+*i.*) to be closely linked (with). **2.** *as pred.* it is crowded, it is cramped; it is (too) tight; в трамва́е бы́ло о́чень т. the tram was very crowded; мне т. под мы́шками it feels tight in the arm-pits.

теснот|а́, ы́, *f.* **1.** crowded state; narrowness, narrow dimensions; tightness; closeness. **2.** crush, squash; жить в ~е́ to live cooped up; в ~е́, да не в оби́де the more the merrier.

те́с|ный (~ен, ~на́, ~но), *adj.* **1.** crowded, cramped; мир ~ен! it's a small world. **2.** narrow; т. прохо́д narrow passage. **3.** (too) tight. **4.** close, compact; ~ные ряды́ close ranks. **5.** (*fig.*) close, tight; ~ная дру́жба close friendship. **6.** (*fig., obs.*) hard, difficult; ~ные обстоя́тельства straitened circumstances. **7.** в ~ном смы́сле сло́ва in the narrow sense of the word.

тесо́вый, *adj.* board, plank.

те́ст|о, а, *n.* **1.** dough; pastry; т. для блино́в batter. **2.** paste; viscous mass.

тестообра́з|ный (~ен, ~на), *adj.* doughy, dough-like, paste-like.

тест|ь, я, *m.* father-in-law (*wife's father*).

тесьм|а́, ы́, *f.* tape, ribbon, lace, braid (*as adornment or for tying something*).

тётеньк|а, и, *f.* (*affect. form of* тётя, also used by children in addressing an unknown woman) aunty.

те́терев, а, *pl.* **~а́, ~о́в,** *m.* (*orn.*) black grouse (blackcock); глухо́й т. (*i*) capercailzie, (*ii*) (*coll.*) deaf person.

тетёрк|а, и, *f.* grey-hen (*f. of black grouse*).

тетёр|я, и, *f.* **1.** (*dial.*) = те́терев. **2.** (*coll., joc.*) chap, fellow; глуха́я т. deaf fellow; лени́вая т. lazybones; со́нная т. sleepy-head.

тетив|а́, ы́, *f.* **1.** bowstring. **2.** taut rope. **3.** (*tech.*) string-board, stringer.

тётк|а, и, *f.* **1.** aunt. **2.** (*as term of address to any elderly woman; coll.*) ma, lady.

тетра́д|ка, ки, *f.* = ~ь.

тетра́д|ь, и, *f.* **1.** exercise book; copy-book; т. для рисова́ния drawing-book; sketch-book. **2.** т. пи́счей бума́ги packet of note-paper. **3.** part, fascicule (*of publication*). **4.** quire (*of manuscript*).

тетрало́ги|я, и, *f.* tetralogy.

тетра́эдр, а, *m.* (*math.*) tetrahedron.

тётушк|а, и, *f.* (*affect. form of* тётка) aunty.

тёт|я, и, *g. pl.* **~ей,** *f.* **1.** aunt. **2.** (*used by children to any unknown woman*) lady. **3.** (*joc.*) woman.

тёфтел|и, ей, *no sing.* (*cul.*) meat-balls.

тех, *g., a., p. pl. of* тот.

тех- *abbr. of* техни́ческий.

техми́нимум, а, *m.* (*abbr. of* техни́ческий ми́нимум) required minimum of technical knowledge.

те́хник, а, *m.* **1.** technician; зубно́й т. dental mechanic. **2.** technically qualified person.

те́хник|а, и, *f.* **1.** engineering; technics, technology. **2.** technique, art; э́то — де́ло ~и it is a matter of technique; т. стихосложе́ния the technique of versification; овладе́ть ~ой to master the art. **3.** (*collect.*) technical devices; т. безопа́сности safety devices. **4.** (*collect.*) technical equipment, machinery; (*mil.*) матérial.

те́хникум, а, *m.* technical college, training college.

техници́зм, а, *m.* preoccupation with technical aspect of something.

техни́чески, *adv.* technically.

техни́ческ|ий, *adj.* **1.** (*in var. senses*) technical; engineering; ~ие нау́ки engineering sciences; т. персона́л technical staff; т. реда́ктор *see* техре́д; т. те́рмин technical term; ~ие усло́вия specifications. **2.** (*mil.*) maintenance; ~ое обслу́живание maintenance. **3.** ~ие культу́ры (*agric.*) industrial crops. **4.** ~ая ско́рость (*tech.*) maximum speed. **5.** assistant, subordinate (= not having powers of decision); т. сотру́дник junior member of staff.

технокра́т, а, *m.* technocrat.

технократи́ческий, *adj.* technocratic.

техно́лог, а, *m.* technologist.

технологи́ческий, *adj.* technological.

техноло́ги|я, и, *f.* technology.

технору́к, а, *m.* (*abbr. of* техни́ческий руководи́тель) technical director.

техре́д, а, *m.* (*abbr. of* техни́ческий реда́ктор) technical editor, copy editor.

тече́ни|е, я, *n.* **1.** flow. **2.** (*fig.*) course; с. ~ем вре́мени in the course of time, in time. **3.** current, stream (*also fig.*); по ~ю, про́тив ~я with the stream, against the stream (*also fig.*). **4.** (*fig.*) trend, tendency. **5.** в т. (+*g.*) during, in the course (of).

те́чк|а, и, *f.* heat (*in animals*).

теч|ь¹, и, *f.* leak; дать т. to spring a leak; заде́лать т. to stop a leak.

течь², теку́, течёшь, теку́т, *past* **тёк, текла́,** *impf.* **1.** to flow (*also fig.*); to stream; (*fig.; of time*) to pass; у тебя́ кровь течёт из носу your nose is bleeding; у него́ из носу течёт his nose is running; у меня́ слю́нки текли́ my mouth was watering. **2.** to leak, be leaky.

те́ш|ить, у, ишь, *impf.* (*of* по~) **1.** to amuse, entertain. **2.** to gratify, please.

те́ш|иться, усь, ишься, *impf.* (*of* по~) **1.** (+*i.*) to amuse oneself (with), play (with); чем бы дитя́ ни ~илось, лишь бы не пла́кало anything for a quiet life. **2.** (над) to make fun (of).

тёшк|а, и, *f.* tyoshka (*abdomen of fish as food-stuff*).

тёщ|а, и, *f.* mother-in-law (*wife's mother*).

тиа́р|а, ы, *f.* tiara.

тибе́т|ец, ца, *m.* Tibetan.

тибе́тк|а, и, *f.* Tibetan (woman).

тибе́тский, *adj.* Tibetan.

ти́бр|ить, ю, ишь, *impf.* (*of* с~) (*coll.*) to pinch, snaffle.

ти́г|ель, ля, *m.* (*tech.*) crucible.

ти́гель|ный, *adj. of* ~.

тигр, а, *m.* tiger.

тигр|ёнок, ёнка, *pl.* ~**я́та,** ~**я́т,** *m.* tiger cub.

тигри́ц|а, ы, *f.* tigress.

тигро́в|ый, *adj. of* тигр; ~**ая шку́ра** tiger-skin.

тик[1], а, *m.* (*med.*) tic.

тик[2], а, *m.* tick, ticking (*material*).

тик[3], а, *m.* (*bot.*) teak.

ти́кани|е, я, *n.* tick, ticking (*of a clock*).

ти́ка|ть, ю, *impf.* (*coll.*) to tick.

ти́ккер, а, *m.* (*radio*) ticker.

ти́ковый[1], *adj. of* тик[2].

ти́ков|ый[2], *adj. of* тик[3]; ~**ое де́рево** teak tree, teak wood.

тик-та́к, *onomat.* tick-tock.

ти́льд|а, ы, *f.* (*typ.*) tilde, swung dash.

ти́мберс, а, *m.* (*naut.*) beam, timber.

тимиа́н, а, *m.* = тимья́н.

тимо́л, а, *m.* (*chem.*) thymol.

тимофе́евк|а, и, *f.* (*bot.*) timothy-grass.

тимпа́н, а, *m.* **1.** (*mus.*) timbrel. **2.** (*archit.*) tympanum.

тимья́н, а. *m.* (*bot.*) thyme.

ти́н|а, ы, *no pl.,* *f.* slime, mud; mire (*also fig.*).

ти́нистый, *adj.* slimy, muddy.

тинкту́р|а, ы, *f.* tincture.

тип, а, *m.* **1.** (*in var. senses*) type; model. **2.** (*coll.*) type (= person); chap; strange character.

типа́ж, а, *m.* (*lit., art*) type.

типиза́ци|я, и, *f.* typification.

типизи́р|овать, ую, *impf. and pf.* to typify.

ти́пик[1], а, *m.* (*eccl.*) typicon (*manual of Orthodox Church containing order of services*).

ти́пик[2], а, *m.* (*coll., pejor.*) = тип 2.

типи́ческий, *adj.* **1.** typical (= constituting a type). **2.** model, standard.

типи́чност|ь, и, *f.* typicalness, typical nature.

типи́ч|ный (~**ен,** ~**на**), *adj.* typical (= characteristic).

типов|о́й, *adj.* model; standard; ~**а́я моде́ль** standard model; ~**о́е изде́лие** standard product.

типо́граф, а, *m.* **1.** printer. **2.** printing-house owner. **3.** printing machine.

типогра́фи|я, и, *f.* printing-house, printing-office, press.

типогра́фск|ий, *adj.* typographical; ~**ое иску́сство** typography.

типогра́фщик, а, *m.* (*obs.*) printer.

типолитогра́фи|я, и, *f.* typolithography.

типолитогра́фский, *adj.* typolithographical.

типологи́ческий, *adj.* typological.

типоло́ги|я, и, *f.* typology.

типу́н, а́, *m.* pip (*disease of birds*); т. **тебе́ на язы́к!** keep your trap shut!

тир[1], а, *m.* shooting-range; shooting-gallery.

тир[2], а, *m.* (*naut.*) pitch, tar.

тира́д|а, ы, *f.* tirade; sally.

тира́ж, а́, *m.* **1.** drawing (*of loan or lottery*); вы́йти в т. to be drawn; (*fig.*) to retire from the scene, take a back seat. **2.** circulation; edition; т. **э́той газе́ты полтора́ миллио́на** this newspaper has a circulation of a million and a half; т. в сто ты́сяч экземпля́ров an edition of a hundred thousand copies.

тира́н, а, *m.* tyrant.

тира́н|ить, ю, ишь, *impf.* to tyrannize (over), torment.

тирани́ческий, *adj.* tyrannical.

тирани́|я, и, *f.* (*hist. and fig.*) tyranny.

тира́нств|о, а, *n.* tyranny.

тира́нств|овать, ую, *impf.* (над) to tyrannize (over).

тире́, *indecl.,* *n.* dash.

тир|ова́ть, у́ю, *impf.* (*naut.*) to pitch, tar.

тиро́льский, *adj.* Tyrolese, Tyrolean.

тис, а, *m.* yew(-tree).

ти́ска|ть, ю, *impf.* (*of* ти́снуть) **1.** to press, squeeze. **2.** (*typ.*) to pull.

тиск|и́, о́в, *no sing.* (*tech.*) vice; зажа́ть в т. to grip in a vice; в ~**а́х** (+*g.*) in the grip (of), in the clutches (of).

тисне́ни|е, я, *n.* **1.** stamping, printing. **2.** imprint; design.

тиснёный, *adj.* stamped, printed; т. **шрифт** raised (Braille) type.

ти́с|нуть, ну, нешь, *pf. of* ~**кать.**

ти́с|овый, *adj. of* ~.

тита́н[1], а, *m.* (*myth. and fig.*) titan.

тита́н[2], а, *m.* (*chem.*) titanium.

тита́н[3], а, *m.* boiler.

титани́ческий, *adj.* titanic.

тита́н|овый, *adj. of* ~[2]; titanic.

ти́тл|о, а, *n.* **1.** (*obs.*) title; под ~**ом** entitled. **2.** (*philol.*) titlo, tilde (*mark above letter in medieval texts indicating abbreviation of word*).

ти́тло|вый, *adj. of* ~; т. **знак** titlo.

титр[1], а, *m.* (*cinema*) caption, credit.

титр[2], а, *m.* (*chem.*) titre.

титрова́ни|е, я, *n.* (*chem.*) titration.

титр|ова́ть, у́ю, *impf. and pf.* (*chem.*) to titrate.

ти́тул, а, *m.* **1.** (*in var. senses*) title. **2.** title-page.

титуло́в|анный, *p.p.p. of* ~а́ть *and adj.* titled.

титул|ова́ть, у́ю, *impf. and pf.* to style, call by one's title.

ти́тул|ьный, *adj.* 1. *of* ~; т. лист title-page. 2. ~ьные спи́ски itemised lists (*of approved building projects*).

титуля́рный, *adj.* т. сове́тник (*hist.*) titular counsellor (*civil servant of 9th grade in tsarist Russia*).

тиу́н, а, *m.* (*hist.*) tiun (*title of various officials in mediaeval Russia*).

тиф, а, *m.* typhus; брюшно́й т. typhoid (fever); сыпно́й т. typhus, spotted fever.

ти́фдрук, а, *m.* (*typ.*) mezzotint.

тифлопедаго́гик|а, и, *f.* methods of teaching the blind.

тифо́зн|ый, *adj.* typhus; typhoid; ~ая лихора́дка typhoid fever; *as noun* т., ~ого, *m.* typhus patient.

ти́х|ий (~, ~а́, ~о), *adj.* 1. quiet; (*of sounds*) low, soft, gentle, faint; т. го́лос low voice. 2. silent, noiseless; still; ~ая ночь still night. 3. (*fig.*) quiet, calm; gentle; still; ~ая жизнь quiet life; т. нрав gentle disposition; ~ая пого́да calm weather; в ~ом о́муте че́рти во́дятся (*prov.*) still waters run deep. 4. slow, slow-moving; т. ход slow speed, slow pace; ~ая торго́вля slack trade.

ти́хо¹, *adv.* 1. quietly; softly, gently; т. постуча́ть to knock gently. 2. silently, noiselessly. 3. (*fig.*) quietly, calmly; still; сиде́ть т. to sit still; т.! gently!, careful! 4. slowly; дела́ иду́т т. things are slack.

ти́хо², *as pred.* 1. it is quiet, there is not a sound; ста́ло т. it became quiet, the noise died away. 2. (*fig.*) it is quiet; it is calm; на душе́ у меня́ ста́ло т. my mind is at rest. 3. (*comm.*) it is slack; с хло́пком т. cotton is slack.

тихомо́лком, *adv.* (*coll.*) quietly, without a sound.

тихо́нько, *adv.* (*coll.*) quietly; softly, gently.

тихо́н|я, и, *g. pl.* ~ей, *m. and f.* demure person; prig; прики́дываться ~ей, смотре́ть ~ей to look as if butter would not melt in one's mouth.

тихоокеа́н|ец, ца, *m.* sailor of Pacific fleet.

тихоокеа́нский, *adj.* Pacific.

тихохо́д, а, *m.* (*zool.*) sloth.

тихохо́д|ный (~ен, ~на), *adj.* slow.

ти́ше 1. *comp. of* ти́хий *and* ти́хо. 2. т.! (*i*) (be) quiet!, silence! (*ii*) gently!, careful!

тишин|а́, ы́, *f.* quiet, silence; stillness; нару́шить ~у́ to break the silence; соблюда́ть ~у́ to keep quiet.

тишко́м, *adv.* (*coll.*) quietly; imperceptibly.

тиш|ь, и, в ~и́, *f.* quiet, silence; stillness; т. да гладь peace and quiet.

тка́н|евый, *adj. of* ~ь 1, 2.

тка́ный, *adj.* woven.

ткан|ь, и, *f.* 1. fabric, cloth; льняны́е ~и linen(s); шёлковые ~и silks. 2. (*anat.*) tissue. 3. (*fig.*) substance, essence; т. расска́за gist of a story.

тканьё|ё, я́, *n.* 1. weaving. 2. woven fabrics, cloth.

тка́нье́вый, *adj.* woven.

ткать, тку, ткёшь, *past* ткал, ткала́, тка́ло, *impf.* (*of* со~) to weave; т. паути́ну to spin a web.

тка́цк|ий, *adj.* weaver's, weaving; ~ое де́ло weaving; т. стано́к loom; т. челно́к shuttle.

ткач, а́, *m.* weaver.

тка́честв|о, а, *n.* weaving.

ткачи́х|а, и, *f. of* ткач.

ткн|у́ть(ся), у́(сь), ёшь(ся), *pf. of* ты́кать(ся).

тлен, а, *m.* (*obs.*) decay.

тле́ни|е, я, *n.* 1. decay, decomposition, putrefaction. 2. smouldering.

тле́н|ный (~ен, ~на), *adj.* (*obs.*) liable to decay.

тлетво́р|ный (~ен, ~на), *adj.* 1. putrefactive; putrid. 2. (*fig.*) pernicious, noxious.

тле|ть, ет, *impf.* 1. to rot, decay, decompose, putrefy; to moulder. 2. to smoulder (*also fig.*); ещё ~ет наде́жда there is still a glimmer of hope.

тле|ться, ется, *impf.* to smoulder.

тл|я, и, *g. pl.* ~ей, *f.* 1. plant-louse, aphis. 2. (*fig., pejor.*) louse.

тмин, а, *m.* 1. caraway. 2. (*collect.*) caraway-seeds.

тми́н|ный, *adj. of* ~; ~ная во́дка kümmel.

то¹, *pron.* (*nom. and a. sing. n. of* тот) that; то, что... the fact that...; то, что́ that which; то был, была́, бы́ло that was; то бы́ли those were; то́ есть that is (to say); то бишь that is to say; то ли де́ло (*coll.*) what a difference, how different (= how much better); а то, *see* а; (да) и то and that, at that; там лишь оди́н мужчи́на, и то восьмидесятиле́тний стари́к there is only one man there, and that an old man of eighty.

то², *conj.* 1. (*in apodosis of conditional sentence*) then (*or not translated*); е́сли вас там не бу́дет, то и я не пойду́ if you won't be there, (then) I shan't go either. 2. то..., то now..., now; то тут, то там now here, now there. 3. не то..., не то either... or; whether... or; half..., half; не то по глу́пости, не то по зло́бе either through stupidity or through malice; не то удивле́ние, не то доса́да half surprise, half annoyance. 4. не то, что́бы..., но it is not, it was not that... (but); не то, что́бы я не хоте́л слу́шать радиопереда́чу, но я про́сто забы́л о ней it was not that I did not want to hear the broadcast: I simply forgot about it. **5.** то и де́ло, то и знай (*coll.*) time and again; incessantly, perpetually.

-то¹, *emphatic particle* (*in coll. Russian often merely adds familiar tone*) just, precisely, exactly (*or not translated*); в то́м-то и де́ло that's just it; чего́ же ва́м-то боя́ться? what have *you* to be afraid of?; вот ведь беда́-то где! that's where the whole trouble lies.

-то², *particle forming indef. pronouns and advs.* (кто́-то, како́й-то, когда́-то, *etc.*).

тобо́ю, *i. of* ты.

това́р, а, *m.* goods; wares; article; commodity; ~ы широ́кого потребле́ния consumer goods; показа́ть т. лицо́м (*coll.*) to show something to good effect.

това́рищ, а, *m.* **1.** comrade; friend; companion; colleague; т. де́тства childhood friend; т. по несча́стью fellow-sufferer, companion in distress; т. по ору́жию comrade-in-arms; т. по рабо́те colleague; mate; т. по шко́ле school-friend. **2.** (*as style and as term of address in U.S.S.R.*) Comrade. **3.** person; э́тот т. прие́хал из Москвы́ this man has come from Moscow; вот т. из Министе́рства here is the man from the Ministry. **4.** (*obs.*) assistant, deputy, vice-; т. председа́теля vice-president.

това́рищеск|ий, *adj.* **1.** comradely; friendly; с ~им приве́том (*epistolary formula*) with fraternal greetings. **2.** of equals; т. суд Comrades' Court (*tribunal of fellow-citizens or fellow-workers—before 1917, of fellow-members of a profession— empowered to pass censure in cases of misconduct*). **3.** (*sport*) friendly, unofficial; ~ое состяза́ние, ~ая встре́ча friendly (match).

това́риществ|о, а, *n.* **1.** comradeship, fellowship; чу́вство ~а a feeling of solidarity. **2.** company; association, society; т. на пая́х joint-stock company. **3.** companionship, partnership.

това́рк|а, и, *f.* (*coll., obs.*) friend.

това́рност|ь, и, *f.* (*econ.*) marketability.

това́рн|ый, *adj.* **1.** goods; т. знак trade mark; т. склад warehouse. **2.** (*railways*) goods, freight; т. ваго́н goods truck; т. парк goods yard; т. соста́в goods train. **3.** (*econ.*) commodity; ~ая проду́кция commodity output; ~ое хозя́йство commodity economy. **4.** (*econ.*) marketable; ~ое зерно́ marketable grain.

товарове́д, а, *m.* commodity researcher.

товарове́дени|е, я, *n.* commodity research.

товарообме́н, а, *m.* (*econ.*) barter.

товарооборо́т, а, *m.* commodity circulation.

товароотправи́тел|ь, я, *m.* consignor, forwarder of goods.

това́ро-пассажи́рский, *adj.* т.-п. по́езд mixed train.

товарополуча́тел|ь, я, *m.* consignee.

товаропроводя́щ|ий, *adj.* ~ая сеть commodity distribution network.

тóг|а, и, *f.* (*hist.*) toga; ряди́ться в ~у (+*g.*) (*rhet.*) to don the garb (of), array oneself (as).

тогда́ 1. *adv.* then (= (*i*) at that time, (*ii*) in that case). **2.** когда́..., т. (*conj.*) when; когда́ решу́сь, т. тебе́ напишу́ I will write to you when I have decided. **3.** т. как (*conj.*) whereas, while.

тогда́шний, *adj.* (*coll.*) of that time, of those days; the then.

тогó¹, *interj.* (*filling pause in utterance*) er . . ., um . . . .

тогó², *as pred.* you know (*coll., euph.* = (*i*) abnormal, simple, (*ii*) drunk, (*iii*) mediocre); к десяти́ часа́м он был совсе́м т. by ten o'clock he was completely—you know.

тогó³, *g. sing. m. and n. of* тот.

тожде́ственност|ь, и, *f.* identity.

тожде́ствен|ный (~, ~на), *adj.* identical, one and the same.

тóждеств|о, а, *n.* identity.

тóже¹, *adv.* also, as well, too.

тóже², *particle* (*coll., iron.*) *expressing disapproval of someone's conduct or scepticism with regard to someone's pretensions to knowledge, etc.*: ты т. хоро́ш! you're a fine one, I must say; т. знато́к нашёлся! since when is he an expert!, as if he were an expert!

тожéственност|ь, и, *f.* = тожде́ственность.

тожéственный, *adj.* = тожде́ственный.

тожéств|о, а, *n.* = тóждество.

ток¹, а, *m.* (*in var. senses*) current; т. высо́кого напряже́ния (*electr.*) high-tension current; т. подогре́ва (*radio*) heater current; т. уте́чки leakage current; переме́нный т. alternating current; постоя́нный т. direct current.

ток², а, о ~е, на ~у́, *pl.* ~á, ~óв, *m.* (*birds'*) mating-place.

ток³, а, о ~é, на ~у́, *pl.* ~á *and* ~и, ~óв, *m.* threshing-floor.

ток⁴, а, *m.* toque.

тока́|й, я, *m.* Tokay (wine).

тока́йск|ое, ого, *n.* = тока́й.

тока́рн|ый, *adj.* (*tech.*) turning; ~ая мастерска́я turnery; т. резе́ц lathe tool; т. стано́к lathe; автомати́ческий т. стано́к engine lathe; т. цех turning shop; *as noun* ~ая, ~ой, *f.* = ~ая мастерска́я.

тóкар|ь, я, *pl.* ~и *and* ~я́, *m.* turner, lathe operator.

токка́т|а, ы, *f.* (*mus.*) toccata.

тóкмо, *adv.* (*arch. or coll.*) only.

ток|ова́ть, у́ет, *impf.* (*of birds*) to utter the mating-call.

токоприёмник, а, *m.* (*electr.*) current collector, trolley (*of electr. locomotive, trolley-bus, etc.*).

токсикологи́ческий, *adj.* toxicological.

токсиколо́ги|я, и, *f.* toxicology.

токси́н, а, *m.* (*med.*) toxin.

токси́ческий, *adj.* toxic.

тол, а, *m.* (*chem.*) tolite.

то́л|евый, *adj. of* ~ь.

толи́к|а, и, *f.* (*coll.*) ма́лая т., не́которая т. a little, a small quantity; a few.

толк¹, а (у), *m.* **1.** sense; understanding; без ~у senselessly, wildly; с ~ом sensibly, intelligently; сбить с ~у to confuse, muddle; взять в т. (*coll.*) to understand, grasp, get, see; от него́ ~у не добьёшься you'll get no sense out of him. **2.** (*coll.*) use, profit; из э́того не вы́йдет ~у nothing will come of it; понима́ть, знать т. (в+*p.*) to know what one is talking about (in), know one's onions (in). **3.** (*obs.*) persuasion (= sect, grouping).

толк², *as pred.* (*coll.*) = ~ну́л.

толка́тел|ь, я, *m.* (*tech.*) pusher, push rod, tappet.

толк|а́ть, а́ю, *impf.* (*of* ~ну́ть) **1.** to push, shove; to jog; т. ло́ктем to nudge. **2.** (*sport*) т. шта́нгу to weight-lift; т. ядро́ to put the shot. **3.** (на+*a.*) to push (into), incite (to), instigate (to).

толк|а́ться, а́юсь, *impf.* **1.** (*impf. only*) to push (one another). **2.** (*pf.* ~ну́ться) т. в дверь to knock on the door. **3.** (*pf.* ~ну́ться) (к) to try to get access (to). **4.** (*impf. only*) (*coll.*) to knock about.

толка́ч, а́, *m.* **1.** (*railways*) pusher. **2.** pestle, pounder. **3.** (*fig., coll.*) pusher, go-getter, fixer (*in Soviet industrial enterprises*).

то́лк|и, ов talk; rumours, gossip; иду́т т. о том, что it is said that, it is rumoured that.

толк|ну́ть, ну́, нёшь, *pf. of* ~а́ть.

толк|ну́ться, ну́сь, нёшься, *pf. of* ~а́ться 2, 3.

толкова́ни|е, я, *n.* **1.** interpretation; exegesis. **2.** (*pl.*) commentary.

толкова́тел|ь, я, *m.* interpreter, commentator, expounder.

толк|ова́ть, у́ю, *impf.* **1.** to interpret; ло́жно т. чьи-н. слова́ to misinterpret, misconstrue someone's words. **2.** (+*d.; coll.*) to explain (to); ско́лько ему́ ни ~у́й, он ничего́ не понима́ет it's a waste of time trying to explain things to him. **3.** (*coll.*) to talk; to say; т. де́ло to talk sense; он всё своё ~у́ет he keeps on about the same thing; ~у́ют, бу́дто people say that, they say that.

толко́в|ый (~, ~a), *adj.* **1.** intelligent, sensible. **2.** intelligible, clear. **3.** (*full form only*) т. слова́рь explanatory dictionary.

то́лком, *adv.* (*coll.*) **1.** plainly, clearly; поговори́ть т. to talk straight. **2.** seriously, in all seriousness.

толкотн|я́, и́, *f.* (*coll.*) crush, scrum, squash; crowding.

тол|ку́, ку́т, *see* ~о́чь.

толку́чий, *adj.* т. ры́нок (*coll.*) second-hand goods market.

толку́ч|ка, ки, *f.* (*coll.*) **1.** crush, scrum, squash; crowded place. **2.** = ~ий ры́нок.

толма́ч, а́, *m.* (*obs.*) interpreter.

то́л|овый, *adj. of* ~.

толокн|о́, а́, *n.* oat flour.

толокня́нк|а, и, *f.* (*bot.*) bearberry (*Arctostaphylos*).

толоко́|нный, *adj. of* ~но́; т. лоб blockhead.

тол|о́чь, ку́, чёшь, ку́т, *past* ~о́к, ~кла́, *impf.* (*of* рас~ *and* с~) to pound, crush; т. во́ду в сту́пе to beat the air, mill the wind.

тол|о́чься, ку́сь, чёшься, ку́тся, *past* ~о́кся, ~кла́сь, *impf.* (*coll.*) to knock about; to gad about.

толп|а́, ы́, *pl.* ~ы, *f.* crowd; throng; multitude.

толп|и́ться, и́тся, *impf.* to crowd; to throng; to cluster.

толсте́нный, *adj.* (*coll.*) very fat.

толсте́|ть, ю, *impf.* (*of* по~) to grow fat, grow stout; to put on weight.

толст|и́ть, и́т, *impf.* (*coll.*) to make (look) fat; хлеб о́чень ~и́т bread is very fattening; шу́ба её о́чень ~и́ла the fur coat made her look very fat.

толстобрю́х|ий (~, ~а), *adj.* (*coll.*) fat-bellied.

толсто́в|ец, ца, *m.* Tolstoyan.

толсто́вк|а¹, и, *f. of* толсто́вец.

толсто́вк|а², и, *f.* tolstovka (*long belted blouse*).

толсто́вств|о, а, *n.* Tolstoyism.

толстогу́б|ый (~, ~а), *adj.* thick-lipped.

толстоко́ж|ий (~, ~а), *adj.* **1.** thick-skinned (*also fig.*). **2.** (*zool.*) pachydermatous; ~ee живо́тное pachyderm.

толстомо́рдый, *adj.* (*coll.*) fat-faced.

толстопу́з|ый (~, ~а), *adj.* pot-bellied (*hist., esp. as term of abuse applied to merchants*).

толстосте́нный, *adj.* (*tech.*) thick-walled.

толстосу́м, а, *m.* (*obs., coll.*) money-bags.

толсту́х|а, и, *f.* (*coll.*) fat woman; fat girl.

толсту́шк|а, и, *f. affect. form of* толсту́ха.

то́лст|ый (~, ~а́, ~о), *adj.* **1.** fat; stout, corpulent; т. нос big nose. **2.** thick; heavy; stout; т. слой thick layer; ~ая бума́га thick paper; т. про́вод heavy-gauge wire; т. журна́л 'fat magazine' (= literary monthly, *etc.*); ~ая кишка́ (*anat.*) large intestine.

толстя́к, а́, *m.* fat man; fat boy.

толуо́л, а, *m.* (*chem.*) toluene.

толчéни|е, я, *n.* pounding, crushing.

толчёный, *adj.* pounded, crushed; ground.

тол|чёт, *see* ~о́чь.

толче|я́[1]**, и́,** *f.* (*coll.*) crush, scrum, squash.

толче|я́[2]**, и́,** *f.* (*tech.*) mill.

толч|о́к[1]**, ка́,** *m.* **1.** push, shove; (*sport*) put. **2.** jolt, bump; (earthquake) shock, tremor. **3.** (*fig.*) push, shove; incitement, stimulus; послужи́ть мо́щным ~ко́м (к) to serve as a powerful spur (to).

толч|о́к[2] = толку́чий ры́нок.

то́лщ|а, и, *f.* **1.** thickness; т. сне́га depth of snow. **2.** в ~е наро́да in the (thick of the) people.

то́лще, *comp. of* то́лстый.

толщин|а́, ы́, *f.* **1.** fatness, stoutness, corpulence. **2.** thickness.

тол|ь, я, *m.* (tarred) roofing paper.

то́лько 1. *adv.* only, merely; solely; alone; just; не т. ..., но и not only . . ., but also; поду́май(те) т.! just think!; т. и всего́, да и т. (*coll.*) that's all; (and) that's that; т. что не (*coll.*) the only thing lacking (is, was); она́ и бога́та и краси́ва, т. что не благоразу́мна she has money and looks, the only thing she lacks is sense; не т. что (*coll.*) not to mention, let alone; т. за после́дние пять лет... in the last five years alone . . . **2.** т. что (*adv. and conj.*) just, only just; он т. что позвони́л he has just rung up; т. что мы дое́хали до ста́нции, про́било шесть we had just reached the station when it struck six. **3.** *conj.* (+как, лишь) as soon as; one has only to . . . ; т. ска́жешь, я уйду́ you have only to say (the word) and I will go. **4.** *conj.* only, but; с удово́льствием, т. не сего́дня with pleasure, only not today. **5.** т. бы (+*inf.*) (*particle*) if only; т. бы получи́ть о нём ве́сточку if only we could hear news of him. **6.** *particle intensifying interrog. pronouns and advs.*: заче́м т.? why on earth?, whatever for?; кого́ т. он не зна́ет? whom does he *not* know?; где т. они́ не быва́ли? where have they *not* been?

то́лько-то́лько, *adv.* (*coll.*) only just.

том, а, *pl.* ~а́, ~о́в, *m.* volume.

томага́вк, а, *m.* tomahawk.

тома́т, а, *m.* **1.** tomato. **2.** tomato purée.

тома́тный, *adj.* tomato; т. сок tomato juice.

то́мик, а, *m.* *dim. of* том.

томи́льн|ый, *adj.* (*tech.*) т. коло́дец soaking pit; ~ая печь soaking furnace.

томи́тел|ьный (~ен, ~ьна), *adj.* wearisome, tedious, wearing; tiresome, trying; agonizing; т. зной trying heat; ~ьное ожида́ние agonizing suspense; tedious wait; ~ьная ску́ка deadly boredom.

том|и́ть, лю́, и́шь, *impf.* (*of* ис~) **1.** to tire, wear, weary; to torment; to wear down; т. в тюрьме́ to leave to languish in prison;

меня́ ~и́т жа́жда I am parched. **2.** (*cul.*) to stew; to braise. **3.** (*tech.*) to render malleable.

том|и́ться, лю́сь, и́шься, *impf.* **1.** to pine; to languish; т. жа́ждой to be parched with thirst; т. ожида́нием to be in an agony of suspense; т. в плену́, в тюрьме́ to languish in captivity. **2.** *pass. of* ~и́ть.

томле́ни|е, я, *n.* **1.** languor. **2.** (*tech.*) malleablizing, cementation.

томлён|ый, *adj.* **1.** (*cul.*) stewed; braised. **2.** (*tech.*) malleablized; ~ая сталь converted steel, cement steel.

то́мност|ь, и, *f.* languor.

то́м|ный (~ен, ~на́), *adj.* languid, languorous.

томпа́к, а́, *m.* tombac (*copper and zinc alloy*).

тон, а, *pl.* ~ы and ~а́, *m.* **1.** (*pl.* ~ы) (*mus. and fig.*) tone; ~ом вы́ше, ни́же a tone higher, lower; хоро́ший, дурно́й т. good, bad form; зада́ть т. to set the tone; переме́нить т. to change one's tone; попа́сть в т. to hit the right note. **2.** (*pl.* ~а́) (*colour*) tone, tint.

тона́льност|ь, и, *f.* (*mus.*) key.

то́ненький, *adj.* thin; slender, slim.

тонзу́р|а, ы, *f.* tonsure.

тонизи́р|овать, ую, *impf. and pf.* (*physiol.*) to tone up.

то́ник|а, и, *f.* (*mus.*) tonic, keynote.

тонин|а́, ы́, *f.* fineness.

тони́ческий[1]**,** *adj.* (*mus., lit.*) tonic.

тони́ческий[2]**,** *adj.* (*physiol., med.*) tonic.

то́н|кий (~ок, ~ка́, ~ко), *adj.* **1.** thin; slender, slim; т. ло́мтик thin slice; ~кая кишка́ (*anat.*) small intestine. **2.** fine; delicate; refined; dainty; ~кое бельё fine linen; т. за́пах delicate perfume; ~кая рабо́та fine workmanship; т. у́жин dainty supper; ~кие черты́ лица́ refined features. **3.** т. го́лос thin voice. **4.** (*fig.*) subtle, delicate; fine, nice; т. вопро́с nice point; т. знато́к connoisseur; т. кри́тик shrewd critic; ~кая лесть subtle flattery; т. намёк gentle hint; ~кое разли́чие subtle, fine, nice distinction; т. ум subtle intellect. **5.** (*of the senses*) keen. **6.** т. сон light sleep. **7.** (*coll., pejor.*) sharp; crafty, sly.

то́нко, *adv.* **1.** thinly. **2.** subtly, delicately, finely, nicely.

тонковолокни́ст|ый (~, ~а), *adj.* fine-fibred.

тонкозерни́ст|ый (~, ~а), *adj.* fine-grained.

тонкоко́ж|ий (~, ~а), *adj.* thin-skinned.

тонколисто́в|ой, *adj.* (*tech.*) sheet; ~ое желе́зо sheet iron; т. стан sheet rolling mill.

тонконтро́л|ь, я, *m.* (*radio*) tone control.

тонкопряди́льн|ый, *adj.*; ~ая маши́на fine-spinning frame.

тонкору́нный, *adj.* fine-fleeced.

тонкосте́нный, *adj.* (*tech.*) thin-walled.

то́нкост|ь, и, *f.* **1.** thinness; slenderness, slimness. **2.** fineness. **3.** subtlety. **4.** nice point, nicety, subtle point; до ~ей to a nicety; вдава́ться в ~и to split hairs.

тонкосуко́нный, *adj.* (*text.*) fine-cloth.

тонкошёрстный, *adj.* fine-wool, fine woollen.

тонкошёрст|ый = ~ный.

тонмейстер, а, *m.* (*radio*) sound director.

то́нн|а, ы, *f.* (metric) ton, tonne.

тонна́ж, а, *m.* tonnage.

тонне́л|ь, я, *m.* = тунне́ль.

то́нн|ый (~а, ~о), *adj.* (*coll., iron.*) (*obs.*) grand; comme il faut.

то́нус, а, *m.* (*physiol., med.*) tone.

тон|у́ть, у́, ~ешь, *impf.* **1.** (*pf.* по~) to sink, go down. **2.** (*pf.* у~) to drown. **3.** (*pf.* у~) (в+*p.*) to sink (in); to be lost (in); to be hidden (in, by), be covered (in, by); т. в поду́шках to sink in the pillows; т. в дела́х to be up to one's eyes in work; надгро́бный па́мятник ~ет в высо́кой траве́ the tomb-stone is hidden from view by the long grass.

тонфи́льм, а, *m.* sound film; (*radio*) recording.

то́ньше, *comp.* of то́нкий and то́нко.

то́н|я, и, *f.* **1.** fishery, fishing-ground. **2.** haul (*of fish*).

топ, *as pred.* (*coll.*) = ~нул.

топа́з, а, *m.* (*min.*) topaz.

топа́з|овый, *adj.* of ~.

то́п|ать, аю, *impf.* **1.** (*pf.* ~нуть) to stamp; т. нога́ми to stamp one's feet. **2.** (*impf. only*) (*coll.*) to go, walk.

топинамбу́р, а, *m.* Jerusalem artichoke.

топ|и́ть[1], лю́, ~ишь, *impf.* **1.** to stoke (*a boiler, a stove, etc.*). **2.** to heat.

топ|и́ть[2], лю́, ~ишь, *impf.* **1.** to melt (down), render. **2.** т. молоко́ to bake milk.

топ|и́ть[3], лю́, ~ишь, *impf.* **1.** (*pf.* по~) to sink. **2.** (*pf.* у~) to drown; (*fig., coll.*) to wreck, ruin; т. го́ре в вине́ to drown one's sorrows in drink.

топ|и́ться[1], ~ится, *impf.* (*of a stove, etc.*) to burn, be alight.

топ|и́ться[2], ~ится, *impf.* **1.** to melt. **2.** *pass.* of ~и́ть[2].

топ|и́ться[3], лю́сь, ~ишься, *impf.* (*of* у~) to drown oneself.

то́пк|а[1], и, *f.* **1.** stoking. **2.** heating. **3.** furnace; (*on locomotive*) fire-box.

то́пк|а[2], и, *f.* melting (down).

то́п|кий (~ок, ~ка́, ~ко), *adj.* boggy, marshy, swampy.

топлён|ый, *adj.* melted; ~ое молоко́ baked milk.

то́плив|ный, *adj.* of ~о; ~ная нефть fuel oil.

то́плив|о, а, *n.* fuel; жи́дкое т. fuel oil; твёрдое т. solid fuel.

топ|нуть, ну, нешь, *pf.* of ~ать.

топо́граф, а, *m.* topographer.

топографи́ческий, *adj.* topographical.

топогра́фи|я, и, *f.* topography.

то́пол|ь, *adj.* of ~ь.

то́пол|ь, я, *pl.* ~и and ~я́, *m.* poplar; пирами-да́льный т. Lombardy poplar.

топони́ми|ка, ки, *f.* (*collect.*) place-names (*of a region*).

топони́ми|я, и, *f.* toponymy.

топо́р, а́, *m.* axe; хоть т. ве́шай (*of close atmosphere*; *coll.*) you could cut it with a knife.

топо́рик, а, *m.* hatchet.

топори́щ|е[1], а, *n.* axe-handle, axe helve.

топори́щ|е[2], а, *n.* large axe.

топо́р|ный (~ен, ~на), *adj.* clumsy, crude; uncouth.

топо́рщ|ить, ит, *impf.* (*coll.*) to bristle.

топо́рщ|иться, ится, *impf.* (*coll.*) **1.** to bristle (*intrans.*). **2.** to puff up.

то́пот, а, *m.* tread; tramp; ко́нский т. clatter of horses' hoofs.

топо|та́ть, чу́, ~чешь, *impf.* (*coll.*) to stamp; (*of horses*) to clatter.

то́почн|ый, *adj.* furnace; ~ая коро́бка fire-box; ~ое простра́нство combustion chamber; ~ая труба́ furnace flue.

то́псел|ь, я, *m.* (*naut.*) topsail.

топ|та́ть, чу́, ~чешь, *impf.* **1.** to trample (down). **2.** to make dirty (*with one's feet*). **3.** to trample out (*grapes, etc.*); т. гли́ну to knead clay.

топ|та́ться, чу́сь, ~чешься, *impf.* to stamp; т. на ме́сте to mark time (*also fig.*).

Топты́гин, а, *m.* (*joc.*) Bruin.

топча́к, а́, *m.* treadmill.

топча́н, а́, *m.* trestle-bed.

топы́р|ить, ю, ишь, *impf.* (*coll.*) to bristle; to spread wide.

топы́р|иться, ится, *impf.* (*coll.*) to bristle (*intrans.*).

топ|ь, и, *f.* bog, marsh, swamp.

то́р|а, ы, *f.* (*rel.*) Torah, Pentateuch.

то́рб|а, ы, *f.* bag; носи́ться (с+*i.*) как (дура́к) с пи́саной ~ой (*coll.*) to make a great song and dance (about).

торг[1], а, о ~е, на ~у́, *pl.* ~и́, *m.* **1.** trading; bargaining, haggling. **2.** (*obs.*) market. **3.** (*pl.*) auction; прода́ть с ~о́в to sell by auction. **4.** (*pl.*) competition for a contract.

торг[2], а, *m.* (*abbr. of* торго́вое учрежде́ние, торго́вая организа́ция) trading organization.

торга́ш, а́, *m.* (*pejor.*) **1.** (small) tradesman. **2.** mercenary-minded person.

торга́ш|еский, *adj.* of ~.

торга́шеств|о, а, *n.* 1. small trading. 2. mercenary-mindedness.

торг|ова́ть, у́ю, *impf.* 1. (*impf. only*) (+*i.*) to trade (in), deal (in), sell. 2. (*impf. only*) (*of a shop or business*) to be open. 3. (*pf.* с~) (*coll.*) to bargain (for).

торг|ова́ться, у́юсь, *impf.* 1. (*pf.* с~) (с+*i.*) to bargain (with), haggle (with). 2. (*impf. only*) (*coll.*) to argue.

торго́в|ец, ца, *m.* merchant; trader, dealer; tradesman.

торго́вк|а, и, *f.* market-woman, stall--holder; woman street-trader.

торго́вл|я, и, *f.* trade, commerce.

торго́в|ый, *adj.* trade, commercial; mercantile; т. бала́нс balance of trade; т. дом business house, firm; ~ая пала́та chamber of commerce; т. представи́тель trade representative; ~ая сеть (*collect.*) shops; ~ая то́чка shop; ~ое су́дно merchant ship; т. флот merchant navy, mercantile marine.

торгпре́д, а, *m.* (*abbr. of* торго́вый представи́тель) trade representative.

торгпре́дств|о, а, *n.* (*abbr. of* торго́вое представи́тельство) trade delegation.

тореадо́р, а, *m.* toreador.

тор|е́ц, ца́, *m.* 1. butt-end, face (*of beam, plank*). 2. wooden paving-block. 3. pavement of wooden blocks.

торже́ственност|ь, и, *f.* solemnity.

торже́ствен|ный (~, ~на), *adj.* 1. ceremonial; festive; gala; т. въезд ceremonial entry; т. день red-letter day; ~ная оде́жда ceremonial attire. 2. solemn; ~ная кля́тва solemn vow; т. слу́чай solemn occasion.

торжеств|о́, а́, *n.* 1. celebration; (*pl.*) festivities, rejoicings. 2. triumph (= victory). 3. triumph, exultation; сказа́ть с ~о́м to say triumphantly; to say gloatingly.

торжеств|ова́ть, у́ю, *impf.* 1. to celebrate; т. побе́ду to celebrate a victory; (*fig.*) to be victorious. 2. (над) to triumph (over); to exult (over).

торжеств|у́ющий, *pres. part. act. of* ~ова́ть *and adj.* triumphant, exultant.

то́ржищ|е, а, *n.* (*obs.*) market, bazaar.

то́ри, *indecl.*, *m.* (*polit.*) tory.

то́ри|й, я, *m.* (*chem.*) thorium.

торкре́т, а, *m.* т.(-бето́н) (*tech.*) gunite.

торма́шк|и: вверх т., вверх ~ами (*coll.*) head over heels, upside down, topsy-turvy.

торможе́ни|е, я, *n.* 1. (*tech.*) braking. 2. (*psych.*) inhibition.

то́рмоз, а, *m.* 1. (*pl.* ~а́) brake; т. отка́та (*mil.*) recoil brake; т. нака́та (*mil.*) counter--recoil brake. 2. (*pl.* ~ы) (*fig.*) brake; drag, hindrance, obstacle.

тормо|зи́ть, жу́, зи́шь, *impf.* (*of* за~) 1. (*tech.*) to brake, apply the brake (to). 2. (*fig.*) to hamper, impede, be a drag (on),

be an obstacle in the way (of). 3. (*psych.*) to inhibit.

тормозн|о́й, *adj.* (*tech.*) brake, braking; т. башма́к brake-shoe; ~а́я площа́дка (*railways*) brake-platform.

тормош|и́ть, у́, и́шь, *impf.* (*coll.*) 1. to pull about. 2. (*fig.*) to pester, plague.

то́рн|ый, *adj.* smooth, even; пойти́ по ~ой доро́ге (*fig.*) to stick to the beaten track.

торова́т|ый (~, ~а), *adj.* (*coll.*) liberal, generous.

торо́к|а́, о́в, *no sing.* saddle-bow straps.

тороп|и́ть, лю́, ~ишь, *impf.* (*of* по~) 1. to hurry, hasten; to press; меня́ ~ят с оконча́нием рабо́ты I am being pressed to finish my work. 2. to precipitate.

тороп|и́ться, лю́сь, ~ишься, *impf.* (*of* по~) to hurry, be in a hurry, hasten.

торопли́во, *adv.* hurriedly, hastily; in a hurry, in haste.

торопли́вост|ь, и, *f.* hurry, haste.

торопли́в|ый (~, ~а), *adj.* hurried, hasty.

торопы́г|а, и, *m. and f.* (*coll.*) person always in a hurry.

торо́с, а, *m.* ice-hummock.

торо́сист|ый (~, ~а), *adj.* hummocky; т. лёд pack ice.

торпе́д|а, ы, *f.* torpedo.

торпеди́р|овать, ую, *impf. and pf.* to torpedo.

торпеди́ст, а, *m.* (*mil., naut.*) torpedo artificer.

торпе́дник, а, *m.* (*mil., naut.*) member of MTB crew.

торпе́д|ный, *adj. of* ~а; т. аппара́т torpedo--tube; т. ка́тер motor torpedo boat (MTB).

торпедоно́с|ец, ца, *m.* 1. torpedo bomber. 2. torpedo bomber pilot.

торпедоно́сный, *adj.* (*naut., aeron.*) torpedo--carrying.

торс, а, *m.* trunk; torso.

торт, а, *m.* cake.

торф, а, *m.* peat.

торфобрике́т, а, *m.* (a) peat, peat briquette.

торфодобы́ч|а, и, *f.* peat-extraction, peat--cutting.

торфоразрабо́т|ки, ок, *no sing.* peatbog.

торфяни́к, а́, *m.* 1. peatbog. 2. peat-cutter.

торфяни́ст|ый (~, ~а), *adj.* peaty.

торфян|о́й, *adj.* peat; ~о́е боло́то peatbog; т. мох (*bot.*) peatmoss.

торц|ева́ть, у́ю, *impf.* to pave with wood blocks.

торцо́в|ый, *adj. of* торе́ц; ~ая мостова́я wood pavement.

торч|а́ть, у́, и́шь, *impf.* 1. to stick up, stick out; to stand on end. 2. (*coll.*) to hang about, stick around; т. пе́ред чьи́ми-н. глаза́ми to be under someone's feet; он ~и́т це́лый день при бассе́йне для

пла́вания he hangs about at the swimming-
-pool the entire day.

торчко́м, *adv.* (*coll.*) on end, sticking up.

торч|мя́ = ~ко́м.

торше́р, а, *m.* standard lamp.

тоск|а́, и́, *f.* 1. melancholy; anguish; pangs;
у неё т. на се́рдце she is sick at heart; т.
любви́ pangs of love. **2.** depression; ennui,
boredom; одна́ т., сплошна́я т. a frightful
bore; навести́ ~у́ (на+*a.*) to depress, bore;
т. берёт (*coll.*) it makes one sick, it is sickening. **3.** (по+*d.* or *p.*) longing (for), yearning
(for), nostalgia (for); т. по ро́дине home-
-sickness.

тоскли́в|ый (~, ~а), *adj.* **1.** melancholy;
depressed, miserable. **2.** dull, dreary, depressing; ~ая пого́да depressing weather.

тоск|ова́ть, у́ю, *impf.* **1.** to be melancholy,
be depressed, be miserable. **2.** (по+*d.* or
p.) to long (for), yearn (for), pine (for),
miss.

тост, а, *m.* toast; провозгласи́ть, предло-
жи́ть т. (за+*a.*) to toast, drink (to); to
propose a toast (to).

тот, *f.* та, *n.* то, *pl.* те, *pron.* **1.** (*as opp. to*
э́тот) that; (*pl.*) those; мне бо́льше нра́-
вится та карти́на I like that picture better;
в тот раз on that occasion; в то вре́мя then,
at that time, in those days; в том слу́чае in
that case. **2.** (*as opp. to* э́тот) the former;
(*replacing 3rd sing. pron.*) he; she; it; я пере-
да́л корректу́ру профе́ссору, тот до́лжен
был вам верну́ть её I passed the proofs on
to the professor, he was supposed to return
them to you. **3.** (*as opp. to* э́тот) the other;
the opposite; на той стороне́ on the other
side; по ту сто́рону (+*g.*) beyond, on the
other side (of); с того́ бе́рега from the other
shore. **4.** (*as opp. to* сей *in certain set phrases*)
that, the other; то да сё one thing and
another; ни то ни сё neither one thing nor
another; поговори́ть о том, о сём to talk
about this and that, about one thing and
another; ни с того́ ни с чего́ for no reason
at all; without rhyme or reason. **5.** (*as opp.
to* друго́й, ино́й) the one; и тот и друго́й
both; ни тот ни друго́й neither; не тот,
так друго́й if not one, then the other. **6.**
тот..., (кото́рый) the ... (which); тот,
(кто) the one (who), the person (who); тот
фильм, кото́рый вы ви́дели вчера́ the film
(which) you saw yesterday; та, кто но́сит
ту́фли на высо́ких каблука́х the one wearing high-heeled shoes; тот факт, что the
fact that (*see also* то[1]). **7.** тот (же), тот (же)
са́мый the same; одно́ и то же one and the
same thing, the same thing over again; в
то же са́мое вре́мя at the same time, on the
other hand; он тепе́рь не тот he is not the
man he was. **8.** the right; не тот the wrong;

э́то не та дверь that's the wrong door; э́то
тот но́мер? is this the (right) room?; э́то
Федо́т, да не тот that's a horse of another
colour. **9.** +*preps. forms the following conjs.*:
для того́, что́бы in order that, in order to;
до того́, что (*i*) until, (*ii*) to such an extent
that; ме́жду тем, как whereas; несмотря́
на то, что in spite of the fact that; пе́ред
тем, как before; по́сле того́, как after; по
ме́ре того́, как in proportion as; с тем,
что́бы (*i*) in order to, with a view to, (*ii*) on
condition that, provided that. **10.** *forms
part of various adverbial phrases and particles*
(*see also* то[1]): вме́сте с тем at the same time;
к тому́ же moreover; кро́ме того́ besides;
ме́жду тем, тем вре́менем meanwhile; со
всем тем notwithstanding all this; тем
са́мым hereby; тому́ наза́д ago; и тому́
подо́бное (и т. п.) and so forth; того́ и
гляди́ any minute now; before you know
where you are; и без того́ as it is; (да) и
то сказа́ть and indeed; не без того́ that's
about it; it can't altogether be denied.

тоталитари́зм, а, *m.* (*polit.*) totalitarianism.

тоталита́рный, *adj.* (*polit.*) totalitarian.

тота́льный, *adj.* total.

тоте́м, а, *m.* totem.

тотеми́зм, а, *m.* totemism.

то́-то, *particle* (*coll.*) **1.** *emphasizes point of
utterance*: (вот) то́-то, (вот) то́-то и оно́,
(вот) то́-то и есть that's just it; precisely,
exactly. **2.** *in exclamations, expressing emotion
or emotional judgement*: то́-то прекра́сно!
there, isn't that lovely! **3.** *expresses reproach,
or recalls warning or threat conveyed in previous
utterance*: ну, то́-то же! there you are, you
see!; well, what did I tell you!

то́тчас, *adv.* at once; immediately (*also of
spatial relations*).

тоха́рский, *adj.* (*ling.*) Tokharian.

точёный, *adj.* **1.** sharpened. **2.** (*tech.*)
turned. **3.** (*fig.*; *of bodily features*) finely-
-moulded, chiselled.

то́чечн|ый, *adj.* **1.** consisting of points. **2.**
~ая сва́рка (*tech.*) spot welding.

точи́лк|а, и, *f.* (*coll.*) steel, knife-sharpener;
pencil-sharpener.

точи́л|о, а, *n.* whetstone, grindstone.

точи́льный, *adj.* grinding, sharpening; т.
ка́мень whetstone, grindstone; т. материа́л
abrasive; т. реме́нь strop; т. стано́к grinding lathe.

точи́льщик, а, *m.* grinder.

точ|и́ть[1], у́, ~ишь, *impf.* **1.** (*pf.* на~) to
sharpen; to grind; to whet, hone; т. зу́бы
на кого́-н. to have a grudge against someone. **2.** (*impf. only*) to turn (*on a lathe*).

точ|и́ть[2], у́, ~ишь, *impf.* to eat away, gnaw
away; to corrode; (*fig.*) to gnaw (at), prey
(upon).

точ|и́ть³, у́, ~и́шь, *impf.* (*obs.*) to secrete; т. слёзы to shed tears.

точ|и́ться¹, ~и́тся, *impf.*, *pass. of* ~и́ть¹,².

точ|и́ться², ~и́тся, *impf.* (*obs.*) to ooze.

то́чк|а¹, и, *f.* **1.** spot, dot; бе́лое пла́тье в ро́зовых ~ах white dress with pink spots; „i" с ~ой *name of letter* 'i' *in old Russian orthography;* ста́вить ~и на „и" to dot one's 'i's' (and cross one's 't's'). **2.** (*gram.*) full stop; т. с запято́й semicolon; поста́вить ~у to place a full stop; (*fig.*) to finish, come to the end. **3.** (*mus.*) dot. **4.** (*math., phys., tech.*) point; т. опо́ры fulcrum, point of support; (*fig.*) rallying-point; мёртвая т. dead point, dead centre; (*fig.*) dead stop, standstill; дойти́ до мёртвой ~и to come to a standstill, to a full stop. **5.** (*mil.*) point; т. встре́чи, т. попада́ния point of impact; т. наво́дки aiming point; т. прице́ливания point of aim. **6.** т. замерза́ния, кипе́ния, плавле́ния freezing, boiling, melting point; т. росы́ dew-point. **7.** (*fig.*) point; т. зре́ния point of view; т. соприкоснове́ния point of contact, meeting-ground; т. в ~у (*coll.*) exactly; to the letter, word for word; попа́сть в (са́мую) ~у (*coll.*) to hit the nail on the head; до ~и (*coll.*) to the limit, to the extreme point; дойти́ до ~и (*coll.*) to come to the end of one's tether.

то́чк|а², и, *f.* **1.** sharpening; grinding; whetting; stropping. **2.** (*tech.*) turning (*on a lathe*).

то́чно¹, *adv.* **1.** exactly, precisely; punctually; т. переписа́ть to make an exact copy; приходи́те, пожа́луйста, т. в час please, come at one o'clock sharp, punctually at one. **2.** т. так just so, exactly, precisely; т. тако́й (же) just the same. **3.** indeed.

то́чно², *particle* (*coll.*) yes; true; так т. (*in mil. parlance*) yes.

то́чно³, *conj.* as though, as if; like; он та́м стоя́л т. окамене́лый he stood there as if turned to stone.

то́чност|ь, и, *f.* exactness; precision; accuracy; punctuality; в ~и exactly, precisely; accurately; to the letter; вы́числить с ~ью до... to calculate to within . . .; с приближённой ~ью approximately; с ~ью часово́го механи́зма like clockwork.

то́ч|ный (~ен, ~на́, ~но), *adj.* exact, precise; accurate; punctual; ~ная бомбарди́ро́вка precision bombing; ~ные нау́ки exact sciences; т. перево́д accurate translation; т. прибо́р precision instrument; ~ная устано́вка sensitive adjustment; т. челове́к punctual person.

то́чь-в-то́чь, *adv.* (*coll.*) exactly; to the letter; word for word; он — т.-в-т. оте́ц he is the spit and image of his father.

тошн|и́ть, и́т, *impf.* (*impers.*) меня́, *etc.*, ~и́т

I, *etc.*, feel sick; меня́ от э́того ~и́т (*fig.*) it makes me sick, it sickens me.

то́шно, *as pred.* (*coll.*) **1.** мне, *etc.*, т. I. *etc.*, feel sick; (*fig.*) I, *etc.*, feel wretched, awful. **2.** (+*inf.*) it is sickening, it makes one sick, it is nauseating.

тошнот|а́, ы́, *f.* sickness, nausea (*also fig.*); испы́тывать ~у́ to feel sick; мне э́то надое́ло до ~ы́ I am sick to death of it.

тошнотво́р|ный (~ен, ~на), *adj.* sickening, sick-making, nauseating (*also fig.*).

то́ш|ный (~ен, ~на́, ~но), *adj.* (*coll.*) **1.** tiresome, tedious. **2.** sickening, nauseating.

тоща́|ть, ю, *impf.* (*of* о~) (*coll.*) to become thin.

то́щ|ий (~, ~а́, ~е), *adj.* **1.** gaunt, emaciated; scraggy, skinny. **2.** empty; на ~ желу́док on an empty stomach; т. карма́н (*fig.*) empty pocket. **3.** poor (= with low content of some substance); ~ее мя́со lean meat; ~ая по́чва poor soil; т. сыр skim-milk cheese; т. у́голь hard coal.

тпру, *interj.* (*to horses*) wo!, whoa!; ни т., ни ну (*fig., coll.*) he, *etc.*, won't budge.

трав|а́, ы́, *pl.* ~ы, *f.* grass; (a) grass, herb; лека́рственные ~ы medicinal herbs; морска́я т. sea-weed; со́рная т. weed; т. ~о́й, как т. (*coll.*) it has no taste at all; хоть т. не расти́ (*coll.*) (everything else) can go to hell.

травене́|ть, ет, *impf.* (*of* за~) to become overgrown (with grass).

тра́верз, а, *m.* (*naut.*) beam; на ~е on the beam, abeam.

тра́верс, а, *m.* **1.** (*mil.*) traverse; ты́льный т. parados. **2.** (*tech.*) traverse, cross-beam, cross-arm; cross member, transverse member; cross head.

тра́верс|а, ы, *f.* = ~ 2.

травести́, *indecl.*, *n.* travesty.

трави́нк|а, и, *f.* blade of grass.

трав|и́ть¹, лю́, ~ишь, *impf.* **1.** (*pf.* вы́~) to exterminate, destroy (*by poisoning*). **2.** (*coll.*) to poison. **3.** (*pf.* вы́~) to etch. **4.** (*pf.* по~) (*of cattle, etc.*) to trample down; to damage (*crops, etc.*). **5.** (*pf.* за~) to hunt; (*fig.*) to persecute, torment; to badger; to worry the life out of.

трав|и́ть², лю́, ~ишь, *impf.* (*naut.*) to pay out, ease out, slacken out; (*of anchor chain*) to veer.

трав|и́ться¹, лю́сь, ~ишься, *impf.* (*coll.*) to poison oneself.

трав|и́ться², лю́сь, ~ишься, *impf.*, *pass. of* ~и́ть¹,².

тра́в|ка¹, ки, *f.* dim of ~а́.

тра́вк|а², и, *f.* (*naut.*) paying out.

травле́ни|е, я, *n.* **1.** extermination, destruction. **2.** etching.

тра́вленый¹, *adj.* etched.

тра́вленый², *adj.* hunted; т. зверь (*fig.*, *coll.*) old hand.

тра́вл|я, и, *f.* hunting; (*fig.*) persecution, tormenting; badgering.

тра́вм|а, ы, *f.* (*med.*) trauma, injury; психи́ческая т. (*psych.*) shock, trauma.

травмати́зм, а, *m.* (*med.*) traumatism; (*collect.*) injuries; произво́дственный т. industrial injuries.

травмати́ческий, *adj.* (*med., psych.*) traumatic.

тра́вник¹, **а,** *m.* **1.** (*obs.*) herb-tea, herb--water. **2.** (*hist., lit.*) herbal. **3.** (*obs.*) herbarium.

тра́вник², **а,** *m.* (*orn.*) redshank.

травопо́ль|е, я, *n.* grassland agriculture, ley farming.

травопо́ль|ный, *adj. of* ~е; т. севооборо́т grassland crop rotation.

травосе́яни|е, я, *n.* fodder-grass cultivation.

травосто́|й, я, *m.* (*collect.*; *agric.*) grass, herbage.

травоя́дный, *adj.* herbivorous.

травяни́ст|ый (~, ~а), *adj.* **1.** grass; herbaceous. **2.** grassy. **3.** (*coll.*) tasteless, insipid.

травян|о́й, *adj.* **1.** grass; herbaceous; т. покро́в grass, herbage; ~ы́е расте́ния grasses, herbs; ~ы́е уго́дья grasslands. **2.** grassy; т. за́пах grassy smell; т. цвет grass-green. **3.** ~а́я насто́йка herb-tea, herb-water.

трагеди́йный, *adj.* (*theatr.*) tragic.

траге́ди|я, и, *f.* tragedy.

траги́зм, а, *m.* tragic element.

тра́гик, а, *m.* **1.** tragic actor. **2.** tragedian.

трагикоме́ди|я, и, *f.* tragicomedy.

трагикоми́ческий, *adj.* tragicomic.

траги́ческ|ий, *adj.* (*in var. senses*) tragic; т. актёр tragic actor; ~ое зре́лище tragic sight; приня́ть т. оборо́т to take a tragic turn.

траги́чност|ь, и, *f.* tragedy, tragic nature, tragic character.

траги́ч|ный (~ен, ~на), *adj.* tragic (= sad, terrible; *not in theatr. sense*).

традицио́нност|ь, и, *f.* traditional character.

традицио́н|ный (~ен, ~на), *adj.* traditional.

тради́ци|я, и, *f.* tradition.

траекто́ри|я, и, *f.* trajectory.

трак, а, *m.* track (*of caterpillar tractor*).

тракт, а, *m.* **1.** high road, highway; почто́вый т. (*obs.*) post road; желу́дочно--кише́чный т. (*anat.*) alimentary canal. **2.** route.

тракта́т, а, *m.* **1.** treatise. **2.** treaty.

тракти́р, а, *m.* (*obs.*) inn, eating-house.

тракти́р|ный, *adj. of* ~.

тракти́рщик, а, *m.* (*obs.*) innkeeper.

тракти́рщиц|а, ы, *f. of* тракти́рщик.

тракт|ова́ть, у́ю, *impf.* **1.** (о+*p.*) to treat (of), discuss. **2.** to interpret (*a part in a play, etc.*).

тракт|ова́ться, у́ется, *impf.* to be treated, be discussed; о чём ~у́ется в э́том рома́не? what is the subject of this novel.

тракто́вк|а, и, *f.* **1.** treatment; interpretation; э́то любопы́тная т. вопро́са this is a curious treatment of the subject.

тра́ктор, а, *m.* tractor; т. на колёсном ходу́, колёсный т. wheeler tractor; т. на гу́сеничном ходу́, гу́сеничный т. caterpillar tractor.

тракториза́ци|я, и, *f.* introduction of tractors.

тракто́рист, а, *m.* tractor driver.

тракто́рист|ка, ки, *f. of* ~.

тра́ктор|ный, *adj. of* ~; т. парк fleet of tractors; на ~ной тя́ге tractor-drawn.

тракторостро́ени|е, я, *n.* tractor-making.

тракторострои́тельный, *adj.*; т. заво́д tractor works.

трал, а, *m.* **1.** trawl. **2.** (*mil.*) mine-sweep.

тра́лени|е, я, *n.* **1.** trawling. **2.** mine-sweeping.

тра́лер, а, *m.* (*obs.*) trawler.

тра́л|ить, ю, ишь, *impf.* **1.** to trawl. **2.** (*mil.*) to sweep.

тра́ловый, *adj.* **1.** trawling; т. лов trawling. **2.** (*mil.*) mine-sweeping.

тра́л|ьный = ~овый.

тра́льщик, а, *m.* **1.** trawler. **2.** (*mil.*) mine--sweeper.

трамб|ова́ть, у́ю, *impf.* to ram.

трамбо́вк|а, и, *f.* **1.** ramming. **2.** rammer, beetle.

трамва́|й, я, *m.* **1.** tramway, tram-line. **2.** tram(-car); речно́й т. river bus.

трамва́й|ный, *adj. of* ~; т. ваго́н tram-car; ~ные ре́льсы tram-lines.

трамва́йщик, а, *m.* tram worker.

трампли́н, а, *m.* (*sport and fig.*) spring-board; jumping-off place, ski-jump.

транжи́р, а, *m.* (*coll.*) spendthrift, squander-bug.

транжи́р|а, ы, *m. and f.* = ~.

транжи́р|ить, ю, ишь, *impf.* (*of* рас~) (*coll.*) to blow, squander.

транзи́т, а, *m.* transit; пойти́ ~ом to go as transit goods.

транзи́т|ный, *adj. of* ~; ~ная ви́за transit visa; ~ная та́кса transit dues.

транквилиза́тор, а, *m.* tranquillizer.

транс, а, *m.* trance.

транс- trans-.

трансатланти́ческий, *adj.* transatlantic.

трансгре́сси|я, и, *f.* (*geol.*) transgression.

транскриби́р|овать, ую, *impf. and pf.* to transcribe.

транскри́пци|я, и, *f.* transcription.

трансли́р|овать, ую, *impf. and pf.* to broadcast, transmit (*by radio*); to relay.

транслитера́ци|я, и, *f.* transliteration.

трансляцио́нн|ый, *adj.* (*radio*) relaying; ~ая сеть relaying system, relay network; т. у́зел relaying station.

трансля́ци|я, и, *f.* broadcast, transmission; relay.

трансмисс|ио́нный, *adj. of* ~ия.

трансми́сси|я, и, *f.* (*tech.*) transmission.

транспара́нт, а, *m.* 1. black-lined paper (*placed under unruled writing-paper*). 2. transparency; banner.

трансплантаци|я, и, *f.* (*med.*) transplantation.

транспози́ци|я, и, *f.* transposition.

транспони́р|овать, ую, *impf. and pf.* (*mus.*) to transpose.

транспониро́вк|а, и, *f.* (*mus.*) transposition.

тра́нспорт, а, *m.* 1. transport. 2. transportation, conveyance. 3. consignment. 4. (*mil.*) train, transport. 5. (*naut.*) transport, supply ship; troopship.

транспо́рт, а, *m.* (*book-keeping*) carrying forward.

транспорта́бел|ьный (~ен, ~ьна), *adj.* transportable, mobile.

транспортёр, а, *m.* 1. (*tech.*) conveyer. 2. (*mil.*) carrier.

транспорти́р, а, *m.* protractor.

транспорти́ровать¹, ую, *impf. and pf.* to transport.

транспорти́р|овать², ую, *impf. and pf.* (*book-keeping*) to carry forward.

транспортиро́вк|а, и, *f.* transport, transportation.

тра́нспортник, а, *m.* 1. transport worker. 2. transport plane.

тра́нспорт|ный, *adj. of* ~; ~ная ве́домость (*mil.*) table of movements; т. парк transport pool; т. самолёт transport plane; (*mil.*) troop-carrier; ~ное су́дно = ~ 5.

транссиби́рский, *adj.* Trans-Siberian; т. магистра́ль the Trans-Siberian railway.

трансформа́тор¹, а, *m.* (*electr.*) transformer.

трансформа́тор², а, *m.* 1. quick-change actor. 2. conjurer, illusionist.

трансформа́ци|я, и, *f.* transformation.

трансформи́р|овать, ую, *impf. and pf.* to transform.

трансцендента́льный, *adj.* (*philos.*) transcendental.

трансценде́нт|ный (~ен, ~на), *adj.* (*philos., math.*) transcendental.

транше́|йный, *adj. of* ~я.

транше́|я, и, *f.* (*mil.*) trench.

трап, а, *m.* (*naut.*) ladder; (*aeron.*) gangway.

тра́пез|а, ы, *f.* 1. dining-table (*esp. in a monastery*). 2. meal; дели́ть ~у (с+*i.*) to share a meal (with). 3. refectory.

тра́пез|ный, *adj. of* ~а; *as noun* ~ная, ~ной, *f.* refectory.

трапециеви́д|ный (~ен, ~на), *adj.* 1. trapeziform, trapezoid. 2. tapered; ~ное крыло́ (*aeron.*) tapered wing.

трапе́ци|я, и, *f.* 1. (*math.*) trapezium. 2. trapeze.

тра́сс|а, ы, *f.* 1. line, course; direction; возду́шная т. airway. 2. route. 3. plan, draft, sketch.

трасса́нт, а, *m.* (*fin.*) drawer.

трасса́т, а, *m.* (*fin.*) drawee.

трасси́р|овать, ую, *impf. and pf.* to mark out, trace.

трасси́р|ующий, *pres. part. act. of* ~овать *and adj.* (*mil.*) tracer; ~ующая пу́ля tracer bullet.

тра́т|а, ы, *f.* expenditure; пуста́я т. вре́мени waste of time.

тра́|тить, чу, тишь, *impf.* (*of* ис~ *and* по~) to spend, expend, use up; to waste.

тра́|титься, чусь, тишься, *impf.* (*of* ис~ *and* по~) (на+*a.*; *coll.*) to spend one's money (on), spend up (on).

тра́тт|а, ы, *f.* (*fin.*) bill of exchange.

тра́улер, а, *m.* trawler; т. с кормовы́м тра́лением stern-trawler.

тра́ур, а, *m.* mourning; обле́чься в т. to go into mourning.

тра́урн|ый, *adj.* 1. mourning; funeral; т. марш funeral march, dead march; ~ая повя́зка (mourning) crape band; ~ое ше́ствие funeral procession. 2. mournful, sorrowful; funeral.

трафаре́т, а, *m.* 1. stencil; раскра́сить, расписа́ть по ~у to stencil. 2. engraved inscription. 3. (*fig.*) conventional, stereotyped pattern; cliché; мы́слить по ~у to think along conventional lines.

трафаре́тност|ь, и, *f.* conventionality; stereotyped character.

трафаре́т|ный, *adj.* 1. stencilled; т. рису́нок stencil drawing. 2. (~ен, ~на) (*fig.*) conventional, stereotyped; trite, hackneyed.

тра́ф|ить, лю, ишь, *impf.* (*coll.*) to please, oblige.

трах, *interj.* bang! (*also as pred.* = ~нул).

тра́х|ать, аю, *impf. of* ~нуть.

трахеи́т, а, *m.* (*med.*) tracheitis.

трахе́йный, *adj.* (*anat.*) tracheal.

трахеотоми́|я, и, *f.* (*med.*) tracheotomy.

трахе́|я, и, *f.* (*anat.*) trachea, windpipe.

тра́х|нуть, ну, нешь, *pf.* (*of* ~ать) (*coll.*) to bang, crash; т. кого́-н. по спине́ to bang someone on the back; т. из ружья́ to loose off with a gun.

трахо́м|а, ы, *f.* (*med.*) trachoma.
тре́б|а¹, ы, *f.* occasional religious rite (*christening, marriage, funeral, etc.*).
тре́ба², as *pred.* (*dial.*) it is necessary.
тре́бник, а, *m.* prayer-book (*containing order of service of all ceremonies and rites except the Eucharist and the ordination of priests*).
тре́бовани|е, я, *n.* 1. demand, request; по ~ю on demand, by request; остано́вка по ~ю request stop; по ~ю (+*g.*) at the request (of), at the instance (of); по ~ю суда́ by order of the court. 2. demand, claim; согласи́ться на чьи-н. ~я to agree to someone's demands; вы́двинуть т. to put in a claim. 3. requirement, condition; отвеча́ть ~ям to meet requirements. 4. (*pl.*) aspirations; needs. 5. requisition, order; т. на то́пливо fuel requisition.
тре́бовател|ьный (~ен, ~ьна), *adj.* 1. demanding, exacting; particular. 2. ~ьная ве́домость requisition sheet, order form.
тре́б|овать, ую, *impf.* (*of* по~) 1. (+*g. or* +чтобы) to demand, request, require; т. извине́ния у кого́-н. to demand an apology from someone; они́ ~уют, чтобы мы извини́лись they demand that we apologize. 2. (*impf. only*) (+*g.* от) to expect (from), ask (of); вы ~уете сли́шком мно́го от ва́ших ученико́в you expect too much from your pupils. 3. (*pf.* по~) (+*g.*) to require, need, call (for); т. неме́дленного реше́ния to require an immediate decision. 4. to send for, call, summon; её ~уют к умира́ющему де́ду she is being sent for to her grandfather's bedside.
тре́б|оваться, уется, *impf.* (*of* по~) 1. to be needed, be required; на э́то ~уется мно́го вре́мени it takes a lot of time; ~уется приходя́щая домрабо́тница 'daily woman required'; что и ~овалось доказа́ть (*math.*) Q.E.D. 2. *pass. of* ~овать.
требух|а́, и́, *no pl.*, *f.* 1. entrails; (*cul.*) offal, tripe. 2. (*fig., coll.*) tripe, rubbish.
трево́г|а, и, *f.* 1. alarm, anxiety; uneasiness, disquiet. 2. alarm, alert; возду́шная т. air-raid warning, alert; пожа́рная т. fire-alarm; бить ~у to sound the alarm (*also fig.*).
трево́ж|ить, у, ишь, *impf.* 1. (*of* вс~) to alarm; to disturb; worry, trouble. 2. (*pf.* по~) to disturb, interrupt; нас всё вре́мя ~ат посети́тели we are continually disturbed by callers. 3. to annoy, bait; не т. to leave alone. 4. т. ра́ну to re-open a wound.
трево́ж|иться, усь, ишься, *impf.* 1. to worry, be anxious, be alarmed, be uneasy. 2. (*pf.* по~) to worry oneself, trouble oneself, put oneself out; не ~ьтесь! don't bother (yourself)!

трево́ж|ный (~ен, ~на), *adj.* 1. worried, anxious, uneasy, troubled. 2. alarming, disturbing, disquieting; ~ные слу́хи alarming reports. 3. alarm; т. звоно́к alarm (bell).
треволне́ни|е, я, *n.* (*now coll., joc.*) agitation, disquiet.
трегла́вый, *adj.* 1. with three cupolas. 2. (*poet.*) three-headed.
тред-юнио́н, а, *m.* trade union.
тред-юниони́зм, а, *m.* trade-unionism.
тред-юниони́ст, а, *m.* trade unionist.
тре́звенник, а, *m.* teetotaller, abstainer.
трезве́|ть, ю, *impf.* (*of* о~) to sober (up), become sober.
трезво́н, а, *m.* 1. peal (of bells). 2. (*coll., joc.*) rumours, gossip. 3. (*coll., pejor.*) row, shindy; подня́ть т., зада́ть ~y to kick up a row.
трезво́н|ить, ю, ишь, *impf.* 1. to ring (a peal). 2. (о+*p.*; *coll.*) to noise abroad; т. по всему́ го́роду to proclaim from the housetops.
тре́звост|ь, и, *f.* 1. soberness, sobriety (*also fig.*). 2. abstinence; temperance.
трезву́чи|е, я, *n.* (*mus.*) triad.
тре́зв|ый (~, ~а́, ~о), *adj.* 1. sober (*also fig.*); име́ть т. взгляд на собы́тия to take a sober view of events. 2. teetotal, abstinent.
трезу́б|ец, ца, *m.* trident.
трек, а, *m.* (*sport*) track.
трекля́тый, *adj.* (*coll.*) accursed.
трел|ь, и, *f.* (*mus.*) trill, shake; warble.
трелья́ж, а, *m.* 1. trellis. 2. three-leaved mirror.
тре́моло, *indecl.*, *n.* (*mus.*) tremolo.
трен, а, *m.* (*obs.*) train (of dress).
тре́нер, а, *m.* (*sport*) trainer, coach.
тре́нер|ский, *adj. of* ~.
тре́нзел|ь, я, *pl.* ~и and ~я́, *m.* snaffle.
тре́ни|е, я, *n.* 1. friction, rubbing. 2. (*pl.*) (*fig.*) friction.
трени́р|ова́ть, у́ю, *impf.* (*of* на~) to train, coach.
трени́р|ова́ться, у́юсь, *impf.* (*of* на~) to train oneself, coach oneself; to be in training.
трениро́вк|а, и, *f.* training, coaching.
трениро́вочный, *adj.* training; practice.
трено́г|а, и, *f.* tripod.
трено́гий, *adj.* three-legged.
трено́ж|ить, у, ишь, *impf.* (*of* с~) to hobble.
трено́жник, а, *m.* tripod.
тре́нька|ть, ю, *impf.* (*coll.*) to strum.
трепа́к, а́, *m.* trepak (*Russian folk-dance*).
трепа́л|о, а, *n.* (*tech.*) swingle, scutcher.
трепа́льный, *adj.* scutching.
трепа́льщик, а, *m.* scutcher.

трепа́н, а, *m.* (*med.*) trepan.

трепана́ци|я, и, *f.* (*med.*) trepanation.

трепа́нг, а, *m.* (*zool.*) ̄trepang.

трепа́ни|е, я, *n.* scutching.

трепани́р|овать, ую, *impf. and pf.* (*med.*) to trepan.

трёпаный, *adj.* **1.** (*of flax, etc.*) scutched. **2.** torn, tattered. **3.** dishevelled.

треп|а́ть, лю, ⌣лешь, *impf.* **1.** (*impf. only*) to scutch, swingle (*flax, hemp, etc.*). **2.** (*pf.* по⌣) to pull about; (*of the wind*) to blow about; to dishevel, tousle; т. кого́-н. за во́лосы to pull someone's hair; т. чьи-н. во́лосы to tousle someone's hair; т. язы-ко́м (*coll.*) to prattle, blather; т. чьи-н. не́рвы to get on someone's nerves; его́ ⌣лет лихора́дка he is feverish; т. чьё-н. и́мя to bandy someone's name about. **3.** (*pf.* по⌣) (*coll.*) to tear; to wear out. **4.** (*pf.* по⌣) to pat.

треп|а́ться, лю́сь, ⌣лешься, *impf.* **1.** (*pf.* по⌣) to tear, fray; to wear out. **2.** (*impf. only*) to flutter, blow about. **3.** (*impf. only*) т. по земле́ to trail along the ground. **4.** (*impf. only*) (*coll., pejor.*) to go round; to hang out. **5.** (*impf. only*) (c+*i.*; *fig., coll.*) to go (with) (*someone of the opposite sex*). **6.** (*impf. only*) (*coll.*) to blather, talk rubbish; to play the fool.

трепа́ч, а́, *m.* (*coll.*) blatherskite, bletherer.

тре́пет, а, *m.* trembling, quivering (*from fear, etc., or from pleasurable sensation*); быть в ⌣е to be a-tremble, be in a dither.

трепе|та́ть, щу́, ⌣щешь, *impf.* **1.** to tremble, quiver; to flicker; to palpitate. **2.** (*fig.*) to tremble; to thrill, palpitate; т. за челове́-чество to tremble for humanity; т. от восто́рга to thrill with joy; т. при мы́сли (o+*p.*) to tremble at the thought (of). **3.** (пе́ред *or* (*obs.*) +*a.*; *fig.*) to tremble (before).

тре́петный, *adj.* **1.** trembling; flickering; palpitating. **2.** anxious. **3.** timid.

трёпк|а, и, *f.* **1.** scutching. **2.** (*coll.*) dressing--down, scolding. **3.** т. не́рвов nervous strain.

трепыха́|ться, юсь, *impf.* (*coll.*) to flutter, quiver.

треск, а, *m.* **1.** crack, crash; crackle, crack-ling; т. руже́йных вы́стрелов crackle of gun-fire; т. огня́ crackling of a fire; т. лома́ющихся су́чьев snapping of twigs; т. мото́ра popping of an engine; с ⌣ом про-вали́ться (*fig., coll.*) to come a crasher, flop. **2.** (*fig., coll.*) noise, fuss.

треск|а́, и́, *f.* cod.

тре́ска|ть, ю, *impf.* (*coll.*) to guzzle.

тре́ска|ться¹, ется, *impf.* (*of* по⌣) to crack; to chap.

тре́ска|ться², юсь, *impf. of* тре́снуться.

треск|о́вый, *adj. of* ⌣а́; т. жир cod-liver oil.

трескотн|я́, и́, *f.* (*coll.*) **1.** crackle, crackling; chirring (*of grasshoppers*). **2.** (*fig.*) chatter, blather.

треску́ч|ий (⌣, ⌣а), *adj.* **1.** (*pejor.*) high--faulting, high-flown. **2.** т. моро́з hard frost, ringing frost.

тре́сн|уть, у, ешь, *pf.* **1.** to snap, crackle, pop. **2.** to crack; to chap; (*fig., coll.*) to crash, flop; хоть ⌣и (*coll.*) for the life of me. **3.** (+*i.* по+*d. or* +*a.* по+*d.*; *coll.*) to bring down with a crash (on); to hit, bang; т. кулако́м по столу́ to bang one's fist on the table; т. кого́-н. по заты́лку to bang someone on the back of the head.

тре́с|нуться, нусь, нешься, *pf.* (*of* ⌣кать-ся²) (+*i.* о+*a.*; *coll.*) to bang (against); т. голово́й о две́рцу шка́фа to bang one's head against the door of a cupboard.

трест, а, *m.* (*econ.*) trust (*in U.S.S.R., a group of industrial or commercial enterprises with centralized direction*).

трест|а́, ы́, *f.* flax *or* hemp straw.

трести́р|овать, ую, *impf. and pf.* to combine into a trust.

тре́ст|овский, *adj. of* ⌣.

трете́йск|ий, *adj.* arbitration; ⌣ое реше́ние конфли́кта arbitration; т. суд arbitration tribunal; т. судья́ arbitrator.

тре́т|ий, ья, ье, *adj.* **1.** third; глава́ ⌣ья chapter three; т. но́мер number three; полови́на ⌣ьего half past two; в ⌣ьем часу́ between two and three; ⌣ьего дня the day before yesterday; до ⌣ьих петухо́в until dawn; ⌣ье лицо́ (*gram.*) third person; Т⌣ье отделе́ние (*hist.*) Third Section (*of the Imperial Chancellery, responsible for political police, 1826–1904*); ⌣ье сосло́вие (*hist.*) third estate; ⌣ья сторона́ third party; т. такт (*tech.*) power stroke; из ⌣ьих рук indirectly; увольне́ние по ⌣ьему пу́нкту (*hist.*) summary dismissal. **2.** *as noun* ⌣ье, ⌣ьего, *n.* sweet, dessert.

трети́р|овать, ую, *impf.* to slight.

трети́чный, *adj.* (*geol., chem., etc.*) tertiary, ternary.

трет|ь, и, *pl.* ⌣и, ⌣е́й, *f.* third.

тре́тьево́дни, *adv.* (*dial.*) the day before yesterday.

третьекла́ссник, а, *m.* third-former.

третьекла́ссный, *adj.* third-class (*also fig.*).

третьеочередно́й, *adj.* of third-rate impor-tance.

третьесо́ртный, *adj.* third-rate.

третьестепе́нный, *adj.* **1.** insignificant, minor. **2.** mediocre, third-rate.

треуго́лк|а, и, *f.* cocked hat.

треуго́льник, а, *m.* triangle.

треугóльный, *adj.* three-cornered, triangular.

треýх, **а**, *m.* (*obs.*) 'three-eared' cap (*cap with ear-flaps and back flap*).

треф, **а**, *m.* food forbidden by the Jewish faith.

треф|á, **ы**, *f.* (*cards*) 1. *see* ~ы. 2. (*coll.*) a club.

трефнóй, *adj.* (*of food*) forbidden by the Jewish faith.

трéфовый, *adj.* (*cards*) of clubs.

треф|ы́, **~**, *sing.* ~**а**, ~**ы́**, *f.* (*cards*) clubs; дáма ~ queen of clubs.

трёх- three-, tri-.

трёхвалéнтный, *adj.* (*chem.*) trivalent.

трёхвёрст|ка, **ки**, *f.* = ~ная кáрта.

трёхвёрстн|ый, *adj.* 1. three versts in length. 2. ~ая кáрта map on scale of three versts to an inch.

трёхгодúчный, *adj.* three-year.

трёхгодовáлый, *adj.* three-year-old.

трёхгóлос(н)ый, *adj.* (*mus.*) three-part.

трёхгрáнный, *adj.* three-edged; (*math.*) trihedral.

трёхднéвн|ый, *adj.* three-day; ~ая лихорáдка tertian ague.

трёхдюймóвк|а, **и**, *f.* 1. (*obs.*) three-inch field-gun. 2. three-inch board.

трёхдюймóвый, *adj.* three-inch.

трёхзнáчный, *adj.* three-digit, three-figure.

трёхколёсный, *adj.* three-wheeled; т. велосипéд tricycle.

трёхлéти|е, **я**, *n.* 1. period of three years. 2. third anniversary.

трёхлéтний, *adj.* 1. three-year. 2. three-year-old. 3. (*bot.*) triennial.

трёхлéт|ок, **ка**, *m.* three-year-old (*animal*).

трёхлинéй|ка, **ки**, *f.* = ~ная винтóвка.

трёхлинéйн|ый, *adj.* of three eighths of an inch calibre; ~ая винтóвка .375 rifle.

трёхлúстный, *adj.* (*bot.*) trifoliate.

трёхмéрный, *adj.* three-dimensional.

трёхмéстный, *adj.* three-seater.

трёхмéсячный, *adj.* 1. three-month; quarterly. 2. three-month-old.

трёхнедéльный, *adj.* 1. three-week. 2. three-week-old.

трёхóсный, *adj.* triaxial.

трёхпáл|ый, *adj.* (*zool.*) tridactylous; ~ая чáйка (*orn.*) kittiwake.

трёхпóль|е, **я**, *n.* (*agric.*) three-field system.

трёхпóль|ный, *adj.* of ~е.

трёхпроцéнтный, *adj.* three per cent.

трёхрублёвк|а, **и**, *f.* (*coll.*) three-rouble note.

трёхслóжный, *adj.* trisyllabic.

трёхслóйный, *adj.* three-layered; three-ply.

трёхсотлéти|е, **я**, *n.* 1. three hundred years. 2. tercentenary.

трёхсотлéтний, *adj.* 1. of three hundred years. 2. tercentennial.

трёхсóтый, *adj.* three-hundredth.

трёхствóльный, *adj.* three-barrelled.

трёхствóрчатый, *adj.* three-leaved.

трёхсторóнний, *adj.* 1. three-sided; (*math.*) trilateral. 2. tripartite.

трёхтóнк|а, **и**, *f.* (*coll.*) three-ton lorry.

трёхфáзный, *adj.* (*electr.*) three-phase.

трёххóдов|óй, *adj.* 1. (*tech.*) three-way, three-pass. 2. ~ая задáча (*chess*) three-move problem.

трёхцвéтный, *adj.* three-coloured; tricolour(ed); (*phot.*) trichromatic.

трёхчасовóй, *adj.* 1. three-hour. 2. three o'clock.

трёхчлéн, **а**, *m.* (*math.*) trinomial.

трёхчлéн|ный, *adj.* of ~.

трёхъязы́чный, *adj.* trilingual.

трёхэтáжный, *adj.* three-storeyed.

трёшк|а, **и**, *f.* (*coll.*) three-rouble note.

трёшниц|а, **ы**, *f.* = трёшка.

трещ|áть, **ý**, **úшь**, *impf.* 1. to crack; (*fig.*) to crack up; у меня головá ~úт I have a splitting headache; т. по всем швам (*fig.*) to go to pieces. 2. to crackle; (*of furniture*) to creak; (*of grasshoppers*) to chirr; ~áт морóзы there is a ringing frost. 3. (*coll.*) to jabber, chatter.

трéщин|а, **ы**, *f.* crack, split (*also fig.*); cleft, fissure; chap (*of skin*); дать ~y to crack, split; (*fig.*) to show signs of cracking.

трещóтк|а, **и**, *f.* 1. rattle. 2. *m. and f.* (*fig.*, *coll.*) chatterbox. 3. (*tech.*) ratchet-drill.

три, **трёх**, **трём**, **тремя́**, о **трёх**, *num.* three.

триáд|а, **ы**, *f.* triad.

триангуля́ци|я, **и**, *f.* (*math.*, *geod.*) triangulation.

триáсовый, *adj.* (*geol.*) triassic.

трибрáхи|й, **я**, *m.* (*lit.*) tribrach.

трибýн, **а**, *m.* (*hist. or rhet.*) tribune.

трибýн|а, **ы**, *f.* 1. platform, rostrum; tribune. 2. stand (*at sports stadiums*).

трибунáл, **а**, *m.* tribunal.

тривиáльност|ь, **и**, *f.* triviality, banality; triteness.

тривиáл|ьный (~**ен**, ~**ьна**), *adj.* trivial, banal; trite, hackneyed.

триглúф, **а**, *m.* (*archit.*) triglyph.

тригонометрúческий, *adj.* trigonometric(al).

тригономéтри|я, **и**, *f.* trigonometry.

тридевя́т|ый, *adj.* в ~ом цáрстве = за трúдевять земéль.

трúдевять: за т. земéль (*in legends and fig.*, *coll.*) at the other end of the world.

тридцатилéти|е, **я**, *n.* 1. thirty years. 2. thirtieth anniversary.

тридцатилéтний, *adj.* 1. thirty-year. 2. thirty-year-old.

тридцáт|ый, *adj.* thirtieth; ~ые гóды the thirties.

три́дцат|ь, и́, *i.* ью, *num.* thirty.

три́дцатью, *adv.* thirty times.

триеди́ный, *adj.* (*theol. and fig.*) triune.

три́ер, а, *m.* (*agric.*) separator, grader, sifter; grain cleaner.

три́жды, *adv.* three times, thrice.

три́зн|а, ы, *f.* (*hist.*) funeral feast.

трико́, *indecl., n.* **1.** tricot (*woollen fabric*). **2.** tights. **3.** (*women's stockinet*) knickers, pants.

трико́вый, *adj.* tricot.

трикота́ж, а, *m.* **1.** stockinet, jersey. **2.** (*collect.*) knitted wear, knitted garments.

трикота́жн|ый, *adj.* stockinet, jersey; knitted; ~ые изде́лия knitted wear; ~ая фа́брика knitted-goods factory.

триктра́к, а, *m.* backgammon.

трили́стник, а, *m.* (*bot.*) trefoil.

триллио́н, а, *m.* trillion.

трило́ги|я, и, *f.* trilogy.

триме́стр, а, *m.* term (*at educational establishment*).

триме́тр, а, *m.* (*lit.*) trimeter.

три́ммер, а, *m.* (*aeron. and electr.*) trimmer.

тринадцатиле́тний, *adj.* **1.** thirteen-year. **2.** thirteen-year-old.

трина́дцатый, *adj.* thirteenth.

трина́дцат|ь, и, *num.* thirteen.

трино́м, а, *m.* (*math.*) trinomial.

три́о, *indecl., n.* (*mus.*) trio.

трио́д, а, *m.* (*radio*) triode.

трио́д|ь, и, *f.* (*eccl.*) service-book; по́стная т. book containing liturgy from Septuagesima to Easter; цветна́я т. book containing liturgy from Easter to All Saints' week.

триоле́т, а, *m.* (*lit.*) triolet.

трио́л|ь, и, *f.* (*mus.*) triplet.

трип, а, *m.* velveteen.

трипла́н, а, *m.* triplane.

три́плекс, а, *m.* triplex (*safety glass*).

три́ппер, а, *m.* (*med.*) gonorrhoea.

трипси́н, а, *m.* (*biol.*) trypsin.

трире́м|а, ы, *f.* trireme.

три́сел|ь, я, *m.* (*naut.*) trysail.

три́ста, трёхсо́т, трёмста́м, тремяста́ми, трёхста́х, *num.* three hundred.

трито́н, а, *m.* (*zool.*) triton.

триумвира́т, а, *m.* triumvirate.

триу́мф, а, *m.* triumph; с ~ом triumphantly, in triumph.

триумфа́льный, *adj.* triumphal.

триумфа́тор, а, *m.* triumpher; victor.

трифто́нг, а, *m.* triphthong.

трихи́н|а, ы, *f.* trichina (*parasitical worm*).

трихино́з, а, *m.* (*med.*) trichinosis.

троака́р, а, *m.* (*med.*) trocar.

тро́гател|ьный (~ен, ~ьна), *adj.* touching; moving, affecting.

тро́га|ть[1], ю, *impf.* (*of* тро́нуть) **1.** to touch. **2.** to disturb, trouble; не ~й его́! don't

disturb him!, leave him be! **3.** to touch, move, affect; т. до слёз to move to tears.

тро́га|ть[2], ю, *impf.* (*of* тро́нуть) (*coll.*) to start; ну ~й! go ahead!, get going!

тро́га|ться[1], юсь, *impf.* (*of* тро́нуться[1]) *pass. of* ~ть[1]; to be touched, be moved, be affected.

тро́га|ться[2], юсь, *impf. of* тро́нуться[2].

троглоди́т, а, *m.* troglodyte (*also fig. of a person*).

тро́е, трои́х, *num.* (*preceding m. nouns denoting living beings and pluralia tantum*) three; т. су́ток seventy-two hours.

троебо́рь|е, я, *n.* (*sport*) triathlon.

троекра́тный, *adj.* thrice-repeated.

троепе́рсти|е, я, *n.* (*eccl.*) making the sign of the cross with three fingers.

тро|и́ть, ю́, и́шь, *impf.* **1.** (*obs.*) to treble. **2.** to divide into three.

тро|и́ться, и́тся, *impf.* **1.** to be trebled. **2.** to appear treble.

Тро́иц|а, ы, *f.* **1.** (*theol.*) Trinity. **2.** (*eccl.*) Trinity; Whitsun(day). **3.** (*coll.*) trio.

Тро́ицын, *adj.* Т. день Trinity; Whitsun(day).

тро́йк|а, и, *f.* **1.** three. **2.** (*school mark*) three (*out of five*). **3.** (*cards*) the three (*of a suit*). **4.** troika. **5.** (*coll.*) three-piece suit. **6.** No. 3 'bus, tram, *etc.* **7.** three-man commission.

тройни́к, а́, *m.* **1.** object *or* measure containing three units. **2.** (*tech.*) tee; T-joint, T-pipe, T-bend. **3.** (*electr.*) branch box, T-junction box.

тройни́чный, *adj.* **1.** triple. **2.** (*anat.*) trigeminal, trifacial.

тройн|о́й, *adj.* triple, threefold, treble; т. кана́т three-ply rope; ~о́е пра́вило (*math.*) the rule of three; в ~о́м разме́ре threefold, treble.

тройн|я́, и, *f.* triplets.

тро́йственн|ый, *adj.* triple; ~ое согла́сие (*hist.*) Triple Entente (*of England, France and Russia, concluded in 1907*).

трок, а, *m.* surcingle.

тролле́|й, я, *m.* (*tech.*) trolley.

тролле́йбус, а, *m.* trolley-bus.

тролле́йбус|ный, *adj. of* ~.

тромб, а, *m.* (*med.*) clot of blood.

тромбо́з, а, *m.* (*med.*) thrombosis.

тромбо́н, а, *m.* trombone.

тромбони́ст, а, *m.* trombonist.

тромбофлеби́т, а, *m.* (*med.*) thrombo-phlebitis.

трон, а, *m.* throne.

тро́нк|а, и, *f.* (*dial.*) sheep-bell.

тро́н|ный, *adj. of* ~; т. зал throne-room; ~ная речь king's speech.

тро́|нуть, ну, нешь, *pf. of* ~гать.

тро́|нуться[1], нусь, нешься, *pf.* **1.** *pf. of*

~гаться¹. 2. (*pf. only*) (*fig., coll.*) to be touched (= to lose one's mind); он немно́го ~ну́лся he is a bit touched, he is a bit cracked.

тро́|нуться², нусь, нешься, *pf.* (*of* ~гаться²) 1. to start, set out; т. с ме́ста to make a move, get going; по́езд ~ну́лся the train started; лёд ~ну́лся the ice has begun to break (*also fig.*). 2. (*coll.*) to go bad.

троп, а, *m.* (*lit.*) trope.

троп|а́, ы́, *f.* path.

тропа́р|ь, я́, *m.* (*eccl.*) anthem (*for festival or saint's day*); troparion.

тро́пик, а, *m.* (*geogr.*) 1. tropic; т. Ра́ка tropic of Cancer; т. Козеро́га tropic of Capricorn. 2. (*pl.*) the tropics.

тропи́нк|а, и, *f.* path.

тропи́ческ|ий, *adj.* tropical; ~ая лихора́дка jungle fever; т. по́яс torrid zone.

тропосфе́р|а, ы, *f.* (*meteor.*) troposphere.

трос, а, *m.* rope, cable, hawser.

трости́нк|а, и, *f.* thin reed.

трости́к, а́, *m.* reed; rush; са́харный т. sugar-cane.

тростнико́вый, *adj.* reed; т. са́хар cane-sugar.

тро́сточк|а, и, *f.* = трость.

трост|ь, и, *pl.* ~и́, ~е́й, *f.* cane, walking-stick.

троти́л, а, *m.* (*chem., mil.*) trotyl, trinitrotoluol (T.N.T.).

тротуа́р, а, *m.* pavement.

трофе́|й, я, *m.* trophy (*also fig.*); (*pl.*) spoils of war, booty; captured material.

трофе́йн|ый, *adj.* (*mil.*) captured; ~ая пу́шка captured gun; ~ое отделе́ние captured (enemy) материel section.

трохеи́ческий, *adj.* (*lit.*) trochaic.

трохе́|й, я, *m.* (*lit.*) trochee.

троцки́зм, а, *m.* Trotskyism.

троцки́ст, а, *m.* Trotskyist, Trotskyite.

троцки́стский, *adj.* Trotskyist, Trotskyite.

трою́родн|ый, *adj.* т. брат, ~ая сестра́ second cousin; т. племя́нник second cousin once removed (*son of second cousin*).

троя́кий, *adj.* threefold, triple.

троя́ко, *adv.* in three (different) ways.

труб|а́, ы́, *pl.* ~ы, *f.* 1. (*in var. senses*) pipe; conduit; tube; т. орга́на organ-pipe; подзо́рная т. telescope. 2. chimney, flue; funnel, smoke-stack. 3. (*mus.*) trumpet; игра́ть на ~е́ to play the trumpet. 4. (*anat.*) tube; duct. 5. *as symbol of failure or ruin*: де́ло т. (*coll.*) things are in a bad way; it's a wash-out; вы́лететь в ~у́ (*coll.*) to go bust, go smash; пусти́ть в ~у́ (*coll.*) to blow, squander.

трубаду́р, а, *m.* troubadour.

труба́ч, а́, *m.* trumpeter; trumpet-player.

труб|и́ть, лю́, и́шь, *impf.* 1. (в+*a.*; *mus.*) to

blow. 2. (*of trumpets, etc.*) to sound; to blare. 3. to sound (*by blast of trumpet, etc.*); т. сбор (*mil.*) to sound assembly. 4. (о+*p.*; *coll.*) to trumpet, proclaim from the house-tops.

тру́бк|а, и, *f.* 1. tube; pipe; сверну́ть ~ой to roll up. 2. (tobacco-)pipe; наби́ть ~у to fill a pipe. 3. (*mil., etc.*) fuse; т. уда́рного де́йствия instantaneous fuse; т. с замедли́телем delayed action fuse. 4. (*telephone*) receiver.

тру́бный, *adj.* trumpet; т. сигна́л trumpet-call; т. глас (*rel., lit.*) the last trump.

тру́боли́те́йный, *adj.* pipe-casting, tube-casting.

трубопрово́д, а, *m.* pipe-line; piping, tubing; manifold.

трубопрока́тный, *adj.* (*tech.*) tube-rolling.

трубочи́ст, а, *m.* chimney-sweep.

тру́бочн|ый, *adj. of* тру́бка; т. таба́к pipe tobacco; ~ая гли́на pipeclay.

тру́бчатый, *adj.* tubular.

трувер, а, *m.* (*hist. lit.*) trouvère.

труд, а́, *m.* 1. labour, work; лю́ди ~а́ the workers. 2. difficulty, trouble; взять на себя́ т., дать себе́ т. (+*inf.*) to take the trouble (to); не сто́ит ~а́ it is not worth the trouble; с ~о́м with difficulty, hardly. 3. (scholarly) work; (*pl., in titles of scholarly periodicals, etc.*) transactions.

тру|ди́ться, жу́сь, ~дишься, *impf.* to toil, labour, work; не ~ди́тесь! (please) don't trouble.

тру́дно, *as pred.* it is hard, it is difficult; т. сказа́ть it is hard to say; т. мне суди́ть it is hard for me to tell.

трудновоспиту́ем|ый (~, ~а), *adj.* т. ребёнок difficult child.

труднодосту́п|ный (~ен, ~на), *adj.* difficult of access.

труднопроходи́мый, *adj.* difficult (to traverse).

тру́дност|ь, и, *f.* difficulty; obstacle.

тру́д|ный (~ен, ~на́, ~но), *adj.* 1. (in var. senses) difficult, hard; arduous. 2. difficult, awkward. 3. (*coll.*; *of illness*) serious, grave; т. больно́й patient seriously ill.

трудови́к, а́, *m.* (*hist.*) Trudovik (*member of Labour group in Russian Duma, 1906–17*).

трудов|о́й, *adj.* 1. labour, work; т. день day's work; ~а́я кни́жка work-book, work record; т. ко́декс Labour Code; ~а́я пови́нность labour conscription; ~о́е уве́чье industrial disablement. 2. working; living on one's own earnings; т. наро́д working people. 3. earned; hard-earned.

трудод|е́нь, ня́, *m.* (*hist.*) work-day (*unit of payment on collective farms*).

трудоёмк|ий (~ок, ~ка), *adj.* labour-consuming; labour-intensive.

трудолюби́в|ый (~, ~а), *adj.* hard-working, industrious.

трудолюби|е, я, *n.* industry; liking for hard work.

трудоспособност|ь, и, *f.* ability to work, capacity for work.

трудоспосо́б|ный (~ен, ~на), *adj.* able-bodied; capable of working.

трудотерапи|я, и, *f.* occupational therapy.

трудоустро́йств|о, а, *n.* placing in a job; resettlement (*of demobilized servicemen in civilian occupations*).

труд|я́щийся, *pres. part. of* ~и́ться *and adj.* working; *as noun* ~я́щиеся, ~я́щихся the working people, the workers.

тру́женик, а, *m.* toiler.

тру́жени|ческий, *adj. of* ~к; ~ческая жизнь life of toil.

трун|и́ть, ю́, и́шь, *impf.* (над; *coll.*) to make fun (of), mock.

труп, а, *m.* dead body, corpse; carcass.

тру́п|ный, *adj. of* ~; т. за́пах putrid smell; ~ное разложе́ние putrefaction; т. яд ptomaine; отравле́ние ~ным я́дом ptomaine poisoning.

тру́пп|а, ы, *f.* troupe, company.

трус¹, а, *m.* coward; ~а пра́здновать (*coll.*) to show the white feather.

трус², а, *m.* (*arch.*) earthquake.

тру́сик|и, ов, *no sing.* shorts; swimming trunks.

тру́|сить, шу, сишь, *impf.* (*of* с~) **1.** to be a coward; to funk; to have cold feet. **2.** (пе́ред *or* +*a.*) to be afraid (of), be frightened (of).

тру|си́ть¹, шу́, си́шь, *impf.* (*of* на~) to shake out, scatter.

тру|си́ть², шу́, си́шь, *impf.* to trot, jog.

трусих|а, и, *f. of* трус.

трусли́в|ый (~, ~а), *adj.* **1.** cowardly. **2.** faint-hearted, timorous; apprehensive.

тру́сост|ь, и, *f.* cowardice.

трусц|а́, ы́, *f.* (*coll.*) jog-trot; бег ~о́й (*sport*) jogging.

трус|ы́, о́в, *no sing.* = ~и́ки.

трут, а, *m.* tinder; amadou.

тру́т|ень, ня, *m.* drone (*also fig.*).

тру́тник, а, *m.* tinder-fungus, punk.

трутови́к, а́, *m.* (*bot.*) polyporus, tree-fungus.

трух|а́, и́, *f.* dust (*of rotted wood*); hay-dust; (*fig.*) trash.

трухля́ве|ть, ет, *impf.* to moulder.

трухля́в|ый (~, ~а), *adj.* mouldering; rotten.

трущо́б|а, ы, *f.* **1.** overgrown place (*in forest, etc.*). **2.** (*fig.*) hole, out-of-the-way place. **3.** slum. **4.** (*coll.*) thieves' den.

трын-трава́, *as pred.* (+*d.*; *coll.*) it makes no odds, it's all the same.

трюк, а, *m.* **1.** feat, stunt. **2.** (*fig., pejor.*) trick.

трюка́ч, а́, *m.* crafty, wily person.

трюка́чес|кий, *adj. of* ~тво; т. приём crafty trick, stunt.

трюка́честв|о, а, *n.* (*pejor.*) craft, wiliness.

трюк|о́вый, *adj. of* ~ 1; т. но́мер turn.

трюм, а, *m.* (*naut.*) hold.

трюм|ный, *adj. of* ~.

трюмо́, *indecl., n.* **1.** cheval-glass, pier-glass. **2.** (*archit.*) pier.

трюфел|ь, я, *pl.* ~и, ~е́й, *m.* truffle.

тряпи́ц|а, ы, *f.* (*coll.*) rag.

тряпи́чник, а, *m.* rag (-and-bone) merchant.

тряпи́чный, *adj.* **1.** rag. **2.** (*coll., pejor.*) soft, spineless.

тря́пк|а, и, *f.* **1.** rag; duster. **2.** (*pl., coll.*) finery, glad rags. **3.** (*coll., pejor.*) milksop, spineless creature.

тряпь|ё, я́, *n.* (*collect.*) rags; (*coll.*) clothes, things.

тряси́н|а, ы, *f.* quagmire.

тря́ск|а, и, *f.* shaking, jolting.

тря́с|кий (~ок, ~ка), *adj.* **1.** shaky, jolty. **2.** bumpy.

трясогу́зк|а, и, *f.* (*orn.*) wagtail.

тряс|ти́, у́, ёшь, *past* ~, ~ла́, *impf.* **1.** to shake; т. кому́-н. ру́ку to shake someone's hand. **2.** to shake out. **3.** to cause to shake, cause to shiver (*usu. impers.*); его́ ~ла́ лихора́дка he was in the grip of a fever; её ~ло́ от стра́ха she was trembling with fear. **4.** (+*i.*) to swing; to shake; т. гри́вой (*of an animal*) to toss its mane. **5.** (*coll.*) to jolt, be jolty.

тряс|ти́сь, у́сь, ёшься, *past* ~ся, ~ла́сь, *impf.* **1.** to shake; to tremble, shiver; т. от сме́ха to shake with laughter; т. от хо́лода to shiver with cold. **2.** (*coll.*) to bump along, jog along; to be jolted. **3.** (над; *coll.*) to watch (over) (= to fear to lose); они́ ~у́тся над ка́ждой копе́йкой they watch every penny.

тряхн|у́ть, у́, ёшь, *pf.* **1.** to shake. **2.** т. старино́й (*coll.*) to hark back to days of yore, revive the customs of the (good) old days; т. мо́лодостью (*coll.*) to hark back to (the days of) one's youth. **3.** (+*i.*; *coll.*) to make free (with); т. мошно́й, карма́ном to throw one's money about, open one's purse-strings.

тсс, *interj.* ssh!, hush!

туале́т, а, *m.* **1.** dress; toilet. **2.** toilet, dressing; соверша́ть т. (*obs.*) to make one's toilet, dress. **3.** dressing-table. **4.** lavatory, toilet; public convenience.

туале́т|ный, *adj. of* ~; ~ная бума́га toilet-paper; ~ное мы́ло toilet-soap; ~ные принадле́жности toilet articles; т. сто́лик dressing-table.

туалéтчик, а, *m.* lavatory attendant.
туалéтчиц|а, ы, *f. of* туалéтчик.
тýб|а¹, ы, *f.* (*mus.*) tuba.
тýб|а², ы, *f.* tube.
туберкулёз, а, *m.* tuberculosis; т. лёгких pulmonary tuberculosis, consumption.
туберкулёзник, а, *m.* (*coll.*) 1. tuberculosis specialist. 2. tubercular patient; consumptive.
туберкулёз|ный, *adj. of* ~; т. больнóй tubercular patient; consumptive; ~ная пáлочка tuberculosis bacillus; *as noun* т., ~ного, *m.*; ~ная, ~ной, *f.* = т. больнóй; ~ная больнáя.
туберóз|а, ы, *f.* (*bot.*) tuberose.
тувúн|ец, ца, *m.* Tuvinian.
тувúн|ка, ки, *f.* Tuvinian (woman).
тувúнский, *adj.* Tuvinian.
тýго, *adv.* 1. tight(ly), taut; т. набúть чемодáн to pack a suitcase tight; т. натянýть to stretch tight, taut. 2. with difficulty; т. продвигáться вперёд to make slow progress. 3. *as pred.* т. приходúться (+*d.*; *coll.*) to have difficulties, be in straits, be in a spot; с деньгáми у нас т. we are in a tight spot financially.
тугодýм, а, *m.* (*coll.*) slow-witted person.
туг|óй (~, ~á, ~о), *adj.* 1. tight; taut; т. ýзел tight knot; т. воротничóк tight collar. 2. tightly-filled; т. кошелёк tightly-stuffed purse. 3. т. нá ухо hard of hearing. 4. (*fig.*, *coll.*) tight, close (*with money*); т. на расплáту close-fisted. 5. (*fig.*, *coll.*) difficult; делá у них ~úе they are in a (tight) spot.
тугоплáв|кий (~ок, ~ка), *adj.* (*tech.*) refractory.
тугоýздый, *adj.* (*of a horse*) hard-mouthed.
тýгрик, а, *m.* tugrik (*unit of currency of Mongolian People's Republic*).
тудá, *adv.* there, thither; that way; to the right place; т. и обрáтно there and back; билéт т. и обрáтно return ticket; не т.! not that way!; ни т. ни сюдá neither one way nor the other; вы не т. попáли (*on tele-phone*) you have got the wrong number; т. емý и дорóга (*coll.*) it serves him right; т. же (*coll.*) the same, likewise, following suit (*of someone attempting something of which he is not capable or to which he has not the right; also as interj.*).
тудá-сюдá, *adv.* (*coll.*) 1. hither and thither. 2. *as pred.* it will do, it will pass muster.
тý|евый, *adj. of* ~я.
тýер, а, *m.* (*naut.*) chain-tug.
тýже, *comp. of* тугóй *and* тýго.
туж|úть, ý, ~úшь, *impf.* (о, по+*p.*; *coll.*) to grieve (for).
тýж|иться, усь, ишься, *impf.* (*coll.*) to make an effort.

тужýрк|а, и, *f.* (*man's*) double-breasted jacket.
туз¹, á, *m.* 1. (*cards*) ace; пойтú с ~á to lead an ace; т. к мáсти (*coll.*) just the job. 2. (*coll.*) bigwig, big pot; big shot.
туз², а, *m.* two-oar dinghy.
тузéм|ец, ца, *m.* native.
тузéм|ка, ки, *f. of* ~ец.
тузéмный, *adj.* native, indigenous.
ту|зúть, жý, зúшь, *impf.* (*of* от~) (*coll.*) to punch; to pummel.
тук¹, а, *m.* 1. (*obs.*) fat. 2. (*pl.*) mineral fertilizers.
тук², *as pred.* = ~нул.
тýк|ать, аю, *impf.* (*of* ~нуть) (*coll.*) to bash, bonk.
тýк|нуть, ну, нешь, *pf. of* ~ать.
тýк|нуться, нусь, нешься, *pf.* (о+*a.*; *coll.*) to bang oneself (against, on).
тýковый, *adj.* fertilizer.
тук-тýк, *interj.* (*coll.*) rat-tat (*also as pred.*).
тýлли|й, я, *m.* (*chem.*) thulium.
тýловищ|е, а, *n.* trunk; torso.
тулумбáс, а, *m.* 1. big drum, bass drum. 2. (*coll.*, *joc.*) punch; дать комý-н. ~а to punch someone.
тулýп, а, *m.* sheepskin (*or hareskin*) coat.
тул|ья́, ьи́, *g. pl.* ~éй, *f.* crown (*of headgear*).
туляремú|я, и, *f.* (*med.*) tularaemia.
тумáк¹, á, *m.* (*coll.*) cuff, punch.
тумáк², á, *m.* tunny(-fish).
тумáн, а, *m.* fog; mist, haze; у негó был т. в глазáх there was a mist before his eyes; у меня́ т. в головé (*fig.*) I see no light, I am groping in the dark; напустúть ~у (*coll.*) to obscure the issue.
тумáн|ить, ит, *impf.* to dim, cloud, obscure (*also fig.*).
тумáн|иться, ится, *impf.* 1. to grow misty, grow hazy; to become enveloped in mist. 2. (*fig.*, *coll.*) to be in a fog, be befogged.
тумáнно, *as pred.* it is foggy, it is misty.
тумáнност|ь, и, *f.* 1. fog, mist. 2. (*astron.*) nebula. 3. haziness, obscurity.
тумáн|ный (~ен, ~на), *adj.* 1. foggy; misty; hazy; ~ная полосá fog patch. 2. (*fig.*) dull, lacklustre. 3. (*fig.*) hazy, obscure, vague. 4. (*obs.*) ~ные картúны (magic) lantern slides.
тýмб|а, ы, *f.* 1. curbstone; post; причáльная т. (*naut.*) bollard. 2. pedestal. 3. advertisement hoarding (*of cylindrical shape*). 4. (*fig.*, *joc.*; *of a person*) lump.
тýмбочк|а, и, *f.* 1. bedside table. 2. *dim. of* тýмба.
тунг, а, *m.* tung-tree.
тýнг|овый, *adj. of* ~; ~овое мáсло tung-oil.
тýндр|а, ы, *f.* (*geogr.*) tundra.
тýндр|еный, *adj.* = ~овый.
тýндр|овый, *adj. of* ~а.

тун|е́ц, ца́, *m.* tunny(-fish).

туне́йд|ец, ца, *m.* parasite, sponger.

туне́йдств|о, а, *n.* parasitism, sponging.

туне́йдств|овать, ую, *impf.* to be a parasite; to sponge.

туннέл|ь, я, *m.* tunnel; subway.

туннέль|ный, *adj. of* ∼.

тупе́|й, я, *m.* (*obs.*) tuft of hair.

тупе́|ть, ю, *impf.* (*of* о∼) to become blunt; to grow dull.

ту́пик, а, *m.* (*orn.*) puffin.

тупи́к, á, *m.* **1.** blind alley, cul-de-sac. **2.** (*railways*) siding. **3.** (*fig.*) impasse, deadlock; зайти́ в т. to reach a deadlock. **4.** поста́вить в т. to stump, nonplus; стать в т. to be stumped, be nonplussed, be at a loss.

туп|и́ть, лю́, ∼ишь, *impf.* to blunt.

туп|и́ться, ∼ится, *impf.* to become blunt.

тупи́ц|а, ы, *m. and f.* (*coll.*) dolt, blockhead, dimwit.

тупоголо́в|ый (∼, ∼а), *adj.* (*coll.*) dim-witted.

туп|о́й (∼, ∼á, ∼о), *adj.* **1.** blunt. **2.** т. у́гол (*math.*) obtuse angle. **3.** (*fig.*) dull (*pain, sensation, etc.*). **4.** (*fig.*) vacant, stupid, meaningless; ∼áя улы́бка vacant smile. **5.** (*fig.*) dull, obtuse; slow; dim; т. ум dull wits. **6.** (*fig.*) blind, unquestioning; ∼áя поко́рность blind submission.

тупоконе́чн|ый, *adj.* blunt-pointed; ∼ая пу́ля blunt-nosed bullet.

туполо́б|ый (∼, ∼а), *adj.* (*coll.*) dull, dim-witted.

тупоно́с|ый (∼, ∼а), *adj.* blunt-nosed (*also fig.*).

ту́пост|ь, и, f. **1.** bluntness. **2.** (*fig.*) vacancy. **3.** (*fig.*) dullnesss, slowness.

тупоу́ми|е, я, *n.* dullness, obtuseness.

тупоу́м|ный (∼ен, ∼на), *adj.* dull, obtuse.

тур¹, а, *m.* **1.** turn (*in a dance*). **2.** (*at sports and games; also fig.*) round.

тур², а, *m.* (*obs.*) gabion.

тур³, а, *m.* (*zool.*) **1.** aurochs. **2.** Caucasian goat (*Capra caucasica*).

тур|á, ы́, f. (*chess*) castle, rook.

турба́з|а, ы, f. tourist centre.

турби́н|а, ы, f. (*tech.*) turbine.

турби́нный, *adj.* turbine.

турбовинтово́й, *adj.* (*tech., aeron.*) turbo-prop.

турбово́з, а, *m.* turbine locomotive.

турбогенера́тор, а, *m.* (*tech.*) turbo-alternator.

турбореакти́вный, *adj.* (*tech., aeron.*) turbo-jet.

туре́л|ь, и, f. (*mil.*) (gun-)turret; ring mount(ing).

туре́цк|ий, *adj.* Turkish; т. бараба́н big drum, bass drum; ∼ие бобы́ haricot beans;

т. горо́х chick pea; ∼ая му́зыка (*mus.*; *obs.*) percussion instruments; ∼ая пшени́ца (*obs.*) maize; гол, как т. свято́й (*coll.*) poor as a church mouse; ∼ое седло́ (*anat.*) sella turcica.

тури́зм, а, *m.* tourism; outdoor pursuits; во́дный т. boating; го́рный т. mountaineering.

ту́рий, *adj. of* тур³.

тури́ст, а, *m.* tourist, hiker.

туристи́ческ|ий, *adj.* tourist; т. похо́д walking tour; ∼ие путеше́ствия travels.

тури́стск|ий, *adj.* tourist; ∼ая ба́за tourist centre.

тур|и́ть, ю́, и́шь, *impf.* (*coll.*) to throw out, chuck out.

туркме́н, а, g. pl. т., *m.* Turkmen.

туркме́нк|а, и, f. Turkmen (woman).

туркме́нский, *adj.* Turkmen.

ту́рман, а, *m.* tumbler-pigeon; полете́ть ∼ом (*coll.*) to fall down head over heels.

турне́, *indecl., n.* tour (*esp. of troupe of artistes or of sportsmen*).

турне́пс, а, *m.* swede.

турни́к, á, *m.* (*sport*) horizontal bar.

турнике́т, а, *m.* **1.** turnstile. **2.** (*med.*) tourniquet.

турни́р, а, *m.* tournament (*at chess, etc., also hist.*).

турн|у́ть, у́, ёшь, pf. (*coll.*) to chuck out.

турню́р, а, *m.* bustle.

ту́р|ок, ка, g. pl. т., m. Turk.

турпа́н, а, *m.* (*orn.*) scoter.

туру́с|ы, ов, *no sing.* (*coll.*) idle gossip; т. на колёсах nonsense, rubbish, twaddle.

турухта́н, а, *m.* (*orn.*) ruff (*Philomachus pugnax*).

турча́нк|а, и, f. Turkish woman.

ту́скл|ый (∼, ∼á, ∼о), *adj.* **1.** dim, dull; matt; tarnished. **2.** wan; lacklustre. **3.** (*fig.*) dim, dull; colourless; tame; т. го́лос flat voice; т. стиль colourless style.

тускне́|ть, ет, *impf.* (*of* по∼) **1.** to grow dim, grow dull; to tarnish; to grow wan, lose its lustre. **2.** (пе́ред; *fig.*) to pale (before, by the side of).

тут, adv. **1.** here; кто т.? who's there?; и всё т. (*coll.*) and that's it, and that was that; т. как т. (*coll.*) there he is, there they are. **2.** now; т. же there and then.

ту́товник, а, *m.* **1.** mulberry (tree). **2.** mulberry grove.

ту́тов|ый, *adj.* mulberry; ∼ое де́рево mulberry (tree); т. шелкопря́д silkworm.

ту́т-то, adv. (*coll.*) **1.** right here. **2.** there and then. **3.** не т.-то бы́ло! nothing of the sort!, far from it!

туф, а, *m.* (*geol., min.*) tufa; tuff.

ту́фл|я, и, f. shoe; slipper.

ту́ф|овый, *adj. of* ∼.

тухли́нк|а, и, *f.* (*coll.*) bad smell.

ту́хл|ый (∼, ∼á, ∼о), *adj.* rotten, bad; ∼ое мя́со tainted meat.

тухля́тин|а, ы, *f.* (*coll.*) bad food; tainted meat.

ту́х|нуть¹, нет, *past* ∼, ∼ла, *impf.* (*of* по∼) (*of source of light or heat*) to go out.

ту́х|нуть², нет, *past* ∼, ∼ла, *impf.* to go bad, become rotten.

ту́ч|а, и, *f.* 1. (rain) cloud; storm-cloud (*also fig.*); не из ∼и гром a bolt from the blue; ∼и собрали́сь, нави́сли (над) (*fig.*) the clouds are gathering (over). 2. *as symbol of sombre appearance or gloomy mood*: смотре́ть ∼ей to look black, scowl, lour; сиде́ть т.-∼ей to be in a black mood. 3. cloud, swarm, host; т.-∼ей in a swarm.

туч|ево́й, *adj. of* ∼а.

ту́чк|а, и, *f. dim. of* ту́ча.

тучне́|ть, ю, *impf.* (*of* по∼) 1. to grow stout, grow fat. 2. (*of soil*) to become fertile.

ту́чност|ь, и, *f.* 1. fatness, stoutness, obesity, corpulence. 2. (*of soil*) richness, fertility.

ту́ч|ный (∼ен, ∼на́, ∼но), *adj.* 1. fat, stout, obese, corpulent. 2. (*of soil*) rich, fertile. 3. (*of grass*) succulent.

туш, а, *m.* (*mus.*) flourish.

ту́ш|а, и, *f.* carcass. 2. (*fig.*; *of a fat man*) hulk.

туше́, *indecl.*; *n.* 1. (*mus.*) touch. 2. (*fencing*) touché.

туш|ева́ть, у́ю, *impf.* (*of* за∼) to shade.

тушёвк|а, и, *f.* shading.

тушёный, *adj.* (*cul.*) braised, stewed.

туш|и́ть¹, у́, ∼ишь, *impf.* (*of* по∼) 1. to extinguish, put out. 2. (*fig.*) to suppress, stifle, quell.

туш|и́ть², у́, ∼ишь, *impf.* (*cul.*) to braise, stew.

тушка́нчик, а, *m.* jerboa.

туш|ь, и, *f.* Indian ink.

ту́|я, и, *f.* (*bot.*) thuya.

тща́ни|е, я, *n.* (*obs.*) zeal, assiduity.

тща́тельност|ь, и, *f.* thoroughness, carefulness; care.

тща́тел|ьный (∼ен, ∼ьна), *adj.* thorough, careful; painstaking.

тщеду́ши|е, я, *n.* feebleness, frailty; debility.

тщеду́ш|ный (∼ен, ∼на), *adj.* feeble, frail, weak; puny.

тщесла́ви|е, я, *n.* vanity, vainglory.

тщесла́в|ный (∼ен, ∼на), *adj.* vain, vainglorious.

тщет|а́, ы́, *f.* vanity.

тще́тно, *adv.* vainly, in vain.

тще́тност|ь, и, *f.* futility, vainness.

тще́т|ный (∼ен, ∼на), *adj.* vain, futile; unavailing.

тщ|и́ться, усь, и́шься, *impf.* (+*inf.*; *obs.*) to try (to), endeavour (to).

ты, тебя́, тебе́, тобо́й (*and* тобо́ю), о тебе́, *2nd sing. personal pron.* you; thou; быть „на ты“ (с+*i.*), говори́ть „ты“ (+*d.*) to be on familiar terms (with).

ты́|кать¹, чу, чешь, *impf.* (*of* ткнуть) 1. (+*i.* в+*a.* or +*a.* в+*a.*) to stick (into) (*also fig.*); to poke (into); to prod; to jab (into); т. була́вкой во что-н. to stick a pin into something; т. па́лкой to prod with a stick; т. ко́лья в зе́млю to stick stakes into the ground; т. (свой) нос (в+*a.*; *fig.*, *pejor.*) to stick, poke one's nose (into); т. в нос кому́-н. чем-н. (*fig.*, *coll.*) to cast something in someone's teeth; т. кого́-н. но́сом во что-н. (*fig.*, *coll.*) to rub someone's nose in something. 2. т. па́льцем (на+*a.*; *coll.*) to point (at), poke one's finger (at).

ты́ка|ть², ю, *impf.* (*coll.*) to address as „ты“; to be on familiar terms (with).

ты́|каться, чусь, чешься, *impf.* (*of* ткну́ться) (*coll.*) 1. (в+*a.*) to knock (against, into). 2. to rush about, fuss about.

ты́кв|а, ы, *f.* pumpkin; gourd.

ты́кв|енный, *adj. of* ∼а; *as noun* ∼енные, ∼енных (*bot.*) gourd family, Cucurbitaceae.

тыл, а, о ∼е, в ∼у́, *pl.* ∼ы́, *m.* 1. back, rear. 2. (*mil.*) rear; home front; напа́сть с ∼а to attack in the rear. 3. (*pl.*; *mil.*) rear services, rear organizations. 4. the (whole) country (*as opp. to front or frontier areas*), the interior.

тылови́к, á, *m.* (*mil.*) man serving in rear.

тылов|о́й, *adj.* (*mil.*) rear; ∼а́я часть service element (*of unit.*); т. го́спиталь base hospital.

ты́льн|ый, *adj.* 1. back, rear; ∼ая пове́рхность руки́ back of the hand. 2. (*mil.*) rear; ∼ая заста́ва, ∼ая часть rear party; т. тра́верс parados.

тын, а, *m.* paling; palisade, stockade.

ты́сяцк|ий, ого, *m.* 1. (*hist.*) captain, leader. 2. (*obs. or dial.*) master of ceremonies (*at peasant wedding ceremony*).

ты́сяч|а, и, *i.* ∼ей *and* ∼ью, *num. and noun,f.* thousand; в ∼у раз a thousand times (*also fig.*).

тысячеле́ти|е, я, *n.* 1. a thousand years; millennium. 2. thousandth anniversary.

тысячеле́тний, *adj.* thousand-year; millennial.

ты́сячник, а, *m.* (*coll.*) 1. record-breaking worker (*with production figures of so many thousand units*). 2. person with capital amounting to thousands.

ты́сячн|ый, *adj.* 1. thousandth; *as noun* ∼ая, ∼ой, *f.* thousandth. 2. of many thousands. 3. worth a thousand, many thousand roubles.

тычи́нк|а, и, *f.* (*bot.*) stamen.

тыч|о́к, ка́, *m.* 1. sharp object sticking up; быть, сиде́ть на ∼ке́ (*i*) to be in an

uncomfortable position, (*ii*) (*fig.*) to be con-
spicuously perched. **2.** (*tech.*) bond-stone;
header. **3.** hit, prod, jab.

тьм|а́¹, ы, *no pl., f.* darkness (*also fig. = ig-
norance*); т. еги́петская, т. кроме́шная outer
darkness (*bibl.*), pitch darkness.

тьм|а́², ы, *g. pl.* **тем,** *f.* **1.** (*arch.*) ten thou-
sand. **2.** (*coll.*) host, swarm, multitude;
т.-тьму́щая countless multitudes.

тьфу, *interj.* (*coll.*) pah!; т., про́пасть! con-
found it!

тюбете́йк|а, и, tyubeteyka (*embroidered
skull-cap worn in Central Asia*).

тю́бик, а, *m.* tube (*of tooth-paste, etc.*).

тюк, а́, *m.* bale, package.

тю́к|ать, аю, *impf.* (*of* ~нуть) (*coll.*) to chop,
hack.

тю́к|нуть, ну, нешь, *pf. of* ~ать.

тю́левый, *adj.* (*text.*) tulle.

тюле́невый, *adj.* sealskin.

тюле́н|ий, *adj. of* ~ь; т. про́мысел sealing,
seal-fishery.

тюле́н|ь, я, *m.* **1.** (*zool.*) seal, **2.** (*fig., coll.*)
clumsy clot.

тюл|ь, я, *m.* (*text.*) tulle.

тюльпа́н, а, *m.* **1.** tulip. **2.** (*obs.*) (glass)
lamp-shade.

тюльпа́н|ный, *adj. of* ~; ~ное де́рево tulip-
-tree.

тюни́к|а, и, f. **1.** (*obs.*) over-skirt. **2.** bal-
lerina's dress.

тюрба́н, а, *m.* turban.

тюр|е́мный, *adj. of* ~ьма́; ~е́мное заклю-
че́ние imprisonment; т. смотри́тель prison
governor.

тюрк, а, *m.* (*ethnol.*) Turki (*member of ethnic
group having Turkic language*).

тю́ркский, *adj.* (*ethnol., ling.*) Turkic.

тюр|ьма́, ьмы́, *pl.* ~ьмы, ~ем, *f.* **1.** prison;
jail, gaol; заключи́ть в ~ьму́ to put into
prison, imprison, jail; сиде́ть в ~ьме́ to be
in prison. **2.** imprisonment.

тюр|я, и, f. (*cul.*) tyurya (*a pulp of bread and
milk, water, or kvass*).

тю́тельк|а, и, f. т. в ~у (*coll.*) to a T.

тю́тька|ться, юсь, *impf.* (с+*i.*; *coll., pejor.*)
to nursemaid.

тю-тю́, *as pred.* (*coll., joc.*) it's all gone;
we've (you've, they've) had it.

тютю́н, а́, *m.* (*dial.*) shag (tobacco).

тюфя́к, а́, *m.* **1.** mattress (*filled with straw,
hay, etc.*). **2.** (*fig., coll.*) flabby fellow.

тюфя́|чный, *adj. of* ~к.

тя́вк|ать, аю, *impf.* (*of* ~нуть) to yap,
yelp.

тя́вк|нуть, ну, нешь, *pf. of* ~ать.

тяг, у, *m.*; дать ~у (*coll.*) to take to one's
heels, show a clean pair of heels.

тяг|а́¹, и, f. **1.** traction; locomotion; си́ла
~и tractive force; на ко́нной ~е horse-

-drawn. **2.** (*collect.*) locomotives. **3.** (*aeron.*)
thrust. **4.** (*in boiler chimney, etc.*) draught;
регуля́тор ~и damper. **5.** (к, на+*a*; *fig.*)
pull (towards), attraction (towards), thirst
(for), craving (for), taste (for); bent (for), inclination (to, for); т. к зна́нию thirst for
knowledge; он испы́тывает си́льную ~у
к Восто́ку he is strongly drawn towards
the East.

тя́г|а², и, f. flight (*esp. of woodcock*) at
mating-season, *etc.*

тяга́|ть, ю, *impf.* (*coll.*) to pull (up, out); т.
лён to pull flax.

тяга́|ться, юсь, *impf.* (*of* по~) (с+*i.*) **1.** (*obs.*)
to be at law (with). **2.** to have a tug-of-war
(with). **3.** (*coll.*) to contend (with), vie (with),
measure one's strength (with).

тяга́ч, а́, *m.* tractor (*for pulling train of
trailers*).

тя́гл|о¹, а, n. (*collect.*) draught animals.

тя́гл|о², а, *g. pl.* **тя́гол, n.** (*hist.*) **1.** tax, im-
post. **2.** household (*as unit for tax assessment*).
3. dues (*corvée, quit-rent, etc.*). **4.** strip of
land (*worked by one household*).

тя́гловый¹, *adj.* = тя́глый.

тя́гловый², *adj.* (*hist.*) taxed, liable to tax.

тя́глый, *adj.* draught (*of cattle*).

тя́гов|ый, *adj.* traction, tractive; т. кана́т
hauling rope; т. крюк trace hook, towing
hook, drawbar hook; т. сте́ржень drawbar; ~ая си́ла tractive force.

тягоме́р, а, *m.* (*tech.*) draught gauge; suction gauge; blast meter.

тя́гост|ный (~ен, ~на), *adj.* **1.** burden-
some, onerous. **2.** painful, distressing;
~ное зре́лище painful spectacle.

тя́гост|ь, и, f. **1.** weight, burden; быть
кому́-н. в т. to be a burden to someone,
weigh on someone. **2.** fatigue.

тягот|а́, ы́, *pl.* **тя́готы, f.** weight, burden.

тяготе́ни|е, я, n. **1.** (*phys.*) gravity, gravita-
tion; зако́н (всеми́рного) ~я law of gravity.
2. (к) attraction (towards), taste (for);
bent (for), inclination (to, for); т. к детек-
ти́вным рома́нам taste for detective stories.

тяготе́|ть, ю, *impf.* **1.** (к) (*phys.*) to gravitate
(towards). **2.** (к) (*fig.*) to gravitate (towards), be drawn (by, towards), be
attracted (by, towards). **3.** (над) to hang
(over), threaten; стра́шный рок ~ет над
на́ми a terrible fate hangs over us.

тяго|ти́ть, щу́, ти́шь, *impf.* to burden, be
a burden (on, to); to lie heavy (on), oppress.

тяго|ти́ться, щу́сь, ти́шься, *impf.* to be
weighed down, oppressed.

тягу́чест|ь, и, f. **1.** malleability, ductility.
2. viscosity.

тягу́ч|ий (~, ~а), *adj.* **1.** malleable, ductile.
2. viscous. **3.** (*fig.*) slow, leisurely, unhur-
ried.

тягча́йш|ий, *superl. of* тя́жкий; ~ее пре-
ступле́ние very serious crime.

тяж, а́, *m.* **1.** (*tech.*) drawing rod; т. тормоз-
ного ва́ла brake rod. **2.** shaft brace.

тя́жб|а, ы, *f.* **1.** (*obs.*) (civil) suit, lawsuit;
litigation. **2.** (*fig., coll.*) competition,
rivalry.

тя́ж|ебный, *adj. of* ~ба 1.

тяжел|е́е, *comp. of* ~ый *and* ~о́.

тяжеле́|ть, ю, *impf.* **1.** to become heavier;
to put on weight. **2.** to become heavy with
sleep (*of eyes*).

тяжело́[1], *adv.* **1.** heavily. **2.** seriously,
gravely; т. бо́лен seriously ill. **3.** with
difficulty.

тяжело́[2], *as pred.* **1.** it is hard; it is painful,
it is distressing. **2.** ему́, *etc.*, т. he, *etc.*, feels
miserable, wretched.

тяжелоатле́т, а, *m.* weight-lifter; athlete
competing in weight-lifting and/or wrestling.

тяжелоатлети́ческ|ий, *adj.* ~ое состяза́ние
meeting, competition comprising weight-
-lifting and/or wrestling.

тяжелове́с[1], а, *m.* (*sport*) heavyweight.

тяжелове́с[2], а, *m.* (*min.*) Siberian topaz.

тяжелове́с|ный (~ен, ~на), *adj.* **1.** heavily-
-loaded; т. соста́в heavy goods train. **2.**
(*fig., pejor.*) heavy, ponderous; clumsy, unwieldy; heavy-handed; ~ная остро́та ponderous witticism.

тяжелово́з, а, *m.* **1.** heavy draught-horse.
2. heavy lorry.

тяжелоду́м, а, *m.* (*coll.*) slow-witted person.

тяжёл|ый (~, ~á), *adj.* **1.** (*in var. senses*)
heavy; т. чемода́н heavy suitcase; ~ая
артилле́рия heavy artillery; ~ая атле́тика
(*sport*) weight-lifting and/or wrestling; ~ая
вода́ (*chem.*) heavy water; ~ое дыха́ние
heavy breathing; ~ая промы́шленность
heavy industry; ~ое то́пливо heavy fuel
(*oil, petrol*); т. шаг heavy step, tread. **2.**
expresses idea of excessive, disagreeable heaviness:
т. во́здух close air; т. за́пах oppressive,
strong smell; ~ая пи́ща heavy, indigestible
food. **3.** hard, difficult; ~ая зада́ча hard
task; ~ые ро́ды difficult confinement. **4.**
slow; т. ум slow brain, wits; т. на подъём
hard to move, sluggish. **5.** heavy, severe;
~ые поте́ри heavy casualties; т. нака-
за́ние severe punishment; т. уда́р severe
blow. **6.** (*of illness, etc.*) serious, grave, bad;
seriously| ill; ~ое ране́ние serious injury,
wound. **7.** heavy, hard, painful; ~ое
чу́вство heavy heart; misgivings; ~ые вре-
мена́ hard times; ~ая обя́занность painful
duty; т. день bad, hard day. **8.** (*of
character*) difficult. **9.** (*of lit. style, etc.*)
heavy, ponderous, unwieldy.

тя́жест|ь, и, *f.* **1.** (*phys.*) gravity; центр ~и

centre of gravity (*also fig.*); (*fig.*) gravamen.
2. weight, heavy object; подня́тие ~ей
(*sport*) weight-lifting. **3.** weight, heaviness;
вся т. чего́-н. (*fig.*) the whole weight, the
brunt of something; т. ули́к weight of evidence. **4.** difficulty. **5.** heaviness, severity.

тя́ж|кий (~ек, ~ка́, ~ко), *adj.* **1.** (*fig.*)
heavy, hard. **2.** severe; serious, grave;
~кая боле́знь dangerous illness; ~кое
преступле́ние grave crime; т. уда́р severe
blow. **3.** пусти́ться во все ~кие (*coll.*) to
plunge into dissipation.

тяжкоду́м, а, *m.* (*coll.*) slow-witted person.

тя́жущийся, *adj.* litigant.

тяну́льный, *adj.* ·(*tech.*) stretching.

тян|у́ть, у́, ~ешь, *impf.* **1.** to pull, draw; to
haul; to drag; т. на букси́ре to tow; т.
кого́-н. за рука́в to pull someone by the
sleeve, tug at someone's sleeve; т. кого́-н.
за́ душу to torment someone; т. ля́мку
(*coll.*) to drudge, toil. **2.** (*tech.*) to draw
(*wire*). **3.** to lay; to put up (*wire, cable, etc.*);
т. телефо́нную ли́нию to lay a telephone
cable. **4.** т. жре́бий to draw lots. **5.** (*fig.*)
to draw, attract; меня́, *etc.*, ~ет I long, I
want; его́ ~ет домо́й he wants to go home;
меня́ ~ет ко сну I feel sleepy; нас ~ет на
Юг we are drawn towards, attracted by the
South; меня́ ~ет купа́ться I'm dying for
a swim. **6.** to drawl, drag out; т. слова́ to
drawl; т. но́ту to sustain a note. **7.** to drag
out, protract, delay; т. с отве́том to delay
one's answer, delay over answering. **8.** to
weigh (*intrans.*). **9.** to draw up; to take in,
suck in; т. в себя́ во́здух to inhale deeply;
т. че́рез соло́минку to suck through a
straw. **10.** (из, с) to extract (from); to
extort (from), squeeze (out of); т. все
си́лы из кого́-н. to exhaust all the strength
from someone. **11.** (*of a chimney, etc.*) to
draw; печь пло́хо ~ет the stove is not
drawing well. **12.** *impers.* +*i.*; *of a stream
of air, of a smell*: ~ет хо́лодом из-под две́ри
there is a draught coming from beneath the
door; от поле́й ~у́ло за́пахом се́на a smell
of hay was wafted from the fields. **13.** (*usu.*)
impers.) to press, be tight; ~ет в плеча́х it
feels tight in the shoulders.

тян|у́ться, у́сь, ~ешься, *impf.* **1.** (*of rubber,
etc.*) to stretch. **2.** (*pf.* по~) to stretch out,
stretch oneself. **3.** (*of landscape features, etc.*)
to stretch, extend; по ту сто́рону на со́тни
киломе́тров ~ется тайга́ on that side for
hundreds of kilometres stretches the taiga.
4. (*of time*) to drag on; to crawl, hang
heavy. **5.** (*coll.*) to last out, hold out; за-
па́сы ещё ~нутся supplies are still holding
out. **6.** (к) to reach (for), reach out (for); to
strive (after); т. к сла́ве to strive after fame.
7. (за +*i.*; *fig., coll.*) to try to keep up (with),

try to equal. **8.** to move one after the other. **9.** (*of clouds, smoke, etc.*) to drift.

тяну́чк|а, и, *f.* toffee, caramel.

тя́н|ущий, *pres. part. act. of* ∼у́ть *and adj.*; ∼ущая боль nagging, persistent pain.

тя́п|ать, аю, *impf.* (*of* ∼нуть) (*coll.*) **1.** to hit; to chop (at), hack (at). **2.** to grab,

snatch; (*fig.*) to pinch. **3.** to knock back (= to drink off).

тя́пк|а, и, *f.* chopper.

тяп-ля́п, *adv. or as pred.* (*coll.*) anyhow (*o careless, slipshod work*).

тя́п|нуть, ну, нешь, *pf. of* ∼ать.

тя́т|я, и, *m.* (*dial.*) dad, daddy.

У

у¹, *interj.* (*expressing reproach or fear*) oh.

у², *prep.+g.* **1.** by; at; у окна́ by the window; у воро́т at the gate; у мо́ря by the sea; у роя́ля at the piano; у руля́ at the helm (*also fig.*); у вла́сти in power. **2.** at; with (*often* = *French* chez); у нас (*i*) at our place, with us, (*ii*) in our country; у себя́ at one's (own) place, at home; я был у парикма́хера I was at the hairdresser's; она́ учи́лась у знамени́того испа́нского скрипача́ she was taught by a celebrated Spanish violinist; он шьёт костю́м у хоро́шего портно́го he is having a suit made by a good tailor; ты у меня́ смотри́! (you) watch out! **3.** *expresses relationship of possession, of part to whole, etc.*: зуб у меня́ боли́т my tooth aches; ши́на у пере́днего колеса́ ло́пнула there is a puncture in (the tyre of) the front wheel; мать у неё больна́ her mother is ill. **4.** (*indicating source, place of origin, etc., of something obtained*) from, of; я за́нял де́сять рубле́й у сосе́да I borrowed ten roubles from a neighbour; спроси́те у него́ о́ттиск ask him to let you have an offprint; он вы́играл у меня́ три па́ртии в ша́хматы he won three games of chess from me. **5.** у меня́, *etc.*, I, *etc.*, have; у них великоле́пный дог they have a magnificent Great Dane; есть у вас радиоприёмник? have you a wireless?; у меня́ к вам ма́ленькая про́сьба I have a small favour to ask of you.

у- *verbal prefix indicating* **1.** *movement away from a place, as* улете́ть to fly away. **2.** *insertion in something, as* умести́ть to put in. **3.** *covering of something all over, as* усе́ять to strew. **4.** *reduction, curtailment, etc., as* уба́вить to reduce. **5.** *achievement of aim sought, as* уговори́ть to persuade; *with adjectival roots forms verbs expressing comparative degree, as* ускори́ть to accelerate.

уба́в|ить, лю, ишь, *pf.* (*of* ∼ля́ть) **1.** (+*a. or g.*) to reduce, lessen, diminish; у. ход to reduce speed; у. рука́в to shorten a sleeve. **2.** у. в ве́се to lose weight.

уба́в|иться, ится, *pf.* (*of* ∼ля́ться) to diminish, decrease; дни ∼ились the days

are shorter; воды́ ∼илось the water(-level) has fallen.

убавля́|ть(ся), ю(сь), *impf. of* уба́вить(ся).

убаю́к|ать, аю, *pf.* (*of* ∼ивать) to lull (*also fig.*).

убаю́кива|ть, ю, *impf. of* убаю́кать.

убега́|ть, ю, *impf. of* убежа́ть.

убеди́тельност|ь, и, *f.* persuasiveness, cogency.

убеди́тел|ьный (∼ен, ∼ьна), *adj.* **1.** convincing, persuasive, cogent; быть ∼ьным to carry conviction. **2.** pressing; earnest; ∼ьная про́сьба pressing request, earnest entreaty.

убе|ди́ть, *1st person sing. not used,* **ди́шь,** *pf.* (*of* ∼жда́ть) **1.** (в+*p.*) to convince (of). **2.** (+*inf.*) to persuade (to), prevail on (to).

убе|ди́ться, *1st person sing. not used,* **ди́шься,** *pf.* (*of* ∼жда́ться) **1.** (в+*p.*) to make certain (of), satisfy oneself (of). **2.** *pass. of* ∼жда́ть.

убе|жа́ть, гу́, жи́шь, гу́т, *pf.* (*of* ∼га́ть) **1.** to run away, run off, make off. **2.** to escape. **3.** (*coll.*) to boil over.

убежда́|ть(ся), ю(сь), *impf. of* убеди́ть(ся).

убежде́ни|е, я, *n.* **1.** persuasion, attempt to persuade; путём ∼я by means of persuasion. **2.** conviction, belief.

убеждённо, *adv.* with conviction.

убеждённост|ь, и, *f.* conviction.

убеждён|ный, *p.p.p. of* убеди́ть *and adj.* **1.** (∼, ∼á) (в+*p.*) convinced (of), persuaded (of); я в э́том соверше́нно ∼ I am absolutely convinced of this. **2.** convinced, confirmed; staunch, stalwart; у. пацифи́ст convinced pacifist; у. сторо́нник staunch supporter.

убе́жищ|е, а, *n.* **1.** refuge, asylum; sanctuary; иска́ть ∼а to seek refuge, asylum; пра́во ∼а right of asylum. **2.** (air-raid, *etc.*) shelter; (*mil.*) dug-out.

убел|ённый, *p.p.p. of* ∼и́ть; у. седино́й, седи́нами hoary with age.

убел|и́ть, ю, и́шь, *pf.* to whiten.

уберега́|ть(ся), ю(сь), *impf. of* убере́чь(ся).

убере́|чь, гу́, жёшь, гу́т, *past* ∼г, ∼гла́, *pf.*

(*of* ~гать) (от) to protect (against), guard (against), keep safe (from), preserve (from); у. шубу от моли to protect a fur coat against moth.

убере|чься, гусь, жёшься, гутся, *past* ~гся, ~глась, *pf.* (*of* ~гаться) (от) to protect oneself (against), guard (*intrans.*) (against).

убива|ть, ю, *impf. of* убить.

убива|ться, юсь, *impf.* 1. (*impf. only*) (o+*p.*; *coll.*) to grieve (over). 2. *impf. of* убиться.

убийствен|ный (~, ~на), *adj.* 1. (*obs.*) death-dealing; ~ная стрела deadly arrow. 2. (*fig., coll.*) killing, murderous; у. климат killing climate; у. взгляд murderous look.

убийств|о, а, *n.* murder; assassination.

убийц|а, ы, *m. and f.* murderer; assassin; killer.

убира|ть(ся), ю(сь), *impf. of* убрать(ся); ~йся! clear off!, beat it!, hop it!

убира|ющийся, *pres. part. of* ~ться; ~ющееся шасси (*aeron.*) retractable undercarriage.

убит|ый (~, ~а) 1. *p.p.p. of* ~ь; неприятель потерял две тысячи ~ыми the enemy lost two thousand killed; *as noun* у., ~ого, *m.* dead man; спать, как у. to sleep like a log; молчать, как у. to be silent as the grave; ходить, как у. to be dazed (with grief, *etc.*). 2. у. Богом (*coll.*) simple, dumb. 3. *adj.* (*fig.*) crushed, broken.

уб|ить, ью, ьёшь, *pf.* (*of* ~ивать) 1. to kill; to murder; to assassinate; хоть ~ей (*coll.*) for the life of me, to save my life; у. бобра *see* бобр. 2. (*fig.*) to kill, finish; to break, smash; её отказ ~ил его her refusal finished him; у. чьи-н. надежды to smash someone's hopes. 3. (*coll.*) to expend; to waste; у. время to kill time; у. молодость to waste one's youth. 4. (*cards; coll.*) to cover.

уб|иться, ьюсь, ьёшься, *pf.* (*of* ~иваться) 1. (*coll.*) to hurt oneself, bruise oneself. 2. *pass. of* ~ить.

ублаготвор|ить, ю, ишь, *pf.* (*of* ~ять) (*obs. or coll., joc.*) to satisfy.

ублаготвор|ять, яю, *impf. of* ~ить.

ублаж|ать, аю, *impf. of* ~ить.

ублаж|ить, у, ишь, *pf.* (*of* ~ать) (*coll.*) to indulge; to gratify.

ублюд|ок, ка, *m.* mongrel (*also fig.*).

ублюдочный, *adj.* 1. mongrel, cross-bred. 2. (*fig., pejor.*) compromise; half-hearted.

убог|ий (~, ~а), *adj.* 1. poverty-stricken, beggarly (*also fig.*); wretched, squalid; ~ое воображение poverty-stricken imagination; ~ое жилище wretched habitation; *as noun* у., ~ого, *m.* pauper, beggar. 2. (*obs.*) crippled; *as noun* у., ~ого, *m.*; ~ая, ~ой, *f.* cripple.

убогост|ь, и, *f.* poverty, penury (*also fig.*); wretchedness, squalor.

убожеств|о, а, *n.* 1. (*obs.*) physical disability; infirmity. 2. (*fig.*) poverty; lack ⌣ distinction; mediocrity; у. идей poverty of ideas.

убо|й, я, *m.* slaughter (*of livestock*); кормить на у. to fatten (*livestock*); (*fig.*) to feed up, stuff with food.

убойност|ь, и, *f.* (*mil.*) effectiveness, destructive power (*of missile, weapon*).

убойн|ый, *adj.* 1. у. скот livestock for slaughter. 2. (*mil.*) killing, destructive, lethal; ~ая дистанция killing range; ~ая мощность destructive power.

убор, а, *m.* 1. (*obs.*) dress, attire. 2. головной у. headgear, head-dress.

уборист|ый (~, ~а), *adj.* close, small (*of handwriting, etc.*).

уборк|а, и, *f.* 1. harvesting, reaping, gathering in; picking. 2. (*mil.*) collection, removal (*of casualties from field of battle*). 3. clearing up, tidying up.

уборн|ая, ой, *f.* 1. (*theatr.*) dressing-room. 2. lavatory; public convenience.

уборочн|ый, *adj.* harvest(ing); ~ая машина harvester.

уборщик, а, *m.* cleaner.

уборщиц|а, ы, *f.* cleaner (*in offices, etc.*); charwoman, charlady.

убранств|о, а, *n.* furniture, appointments; (*poet.*) attire.

убра|ть, уберу, уберёшь, *past* ~л, ~ла, ~ло, *pf.* (*of* убирать) 1. to remove, take away; у. с дороги to put out of the way (*also fig.*); у. со стола to clear the table. 2. (*fig., coll.*) to kick out, chuck out; to sack; у. кого-н. из комнаты to chuck someone out of the room. 3. to put away; to store; у. якорь to stow the anchor. 4. to harvest, reap, gather in. 5. to clear up, tidy up; у. комнату to do a room; у. постель to make the bed. 6. to decorate, adorn.

убра|ться, уберусь, уберёшься, *past* ~лся, ~лась, ~лось, *pf.* (*of* убираться) 1. (*coll.*) to clear up, tidy up, clean up. 2. (*obs. or poet.*) to attire oneself. 3. (*coll.*) to clear off, beat it.

убыва|ть, ю, *impf. of* убыть.

убыл|ь, и, *f.* 1. diminution, decrease; subsidence (*of water*); идти на у. to decrease; to subside, fall, go down, recede. 2. (*mil.*) losses, casualties.

убыстр|ить, ю, ишь, *pf.* (*of* ~ять) to speed up; to hasten.

убыстр|ять, яю, *impf. of* ~ить.

убыт|ок, ка, *m.* 1. loss; терпеть, нести ~ки to incur losses; в у., с ~ком at a loss; быть в ~ке to lose, be down. 2. (*pl.*) damages;

взыска́ть ～ки to claim damages; компен-
си́ровать ～ки to pay damages; определи́ть
～ки to assess damages.

убы́точно, *adv.* at a loss.

убы́точ|ный (～ен, ～на), *adj.* unprofitable;
～ная торго́вля trading at a loss.

убы́ть, убу́ду, убу́дешь, *past* у́был, убыла́,
у́было, *pf.* (*of* убыва́ть) **1.** to decrease,
diminish; (*of water*) to subside, fall, go
down; (*of the moon*) to wane, be on the wane
(*also fig.*). **2.** тебя́, *etc.*, не убу́дет (от; *coll.*)
you, *etc.*, won't be any the worse (for);
nothing will happen to you, *etc.* (as a result
of). **3.** to go away, leave; y. в командиро́в-
ку to go away on business; y. в о́тпуск to go
on leave; y. по боле́зни to go sick.

уважа́|емый, *pres. part. pass. of* ～ть *and adj.*
respected; (*in opening formal letter*) dear.

уважа́|ть, ю, *impf.* to respect, esteem.

уваже́ни|е, я, *n.* respect, esteem; внуша́ть
y. to command respect; пита́ть глубо́кое
y. к кому́-н. to have a profound respect for
someone; из ～я (к) out of respect (for), in
deference (to); с уваже́нием (*in letters*)
yours sincerely.

уважи́тельност|ь, и, *f.* **1.** validity. **2.**
respectfulness.

уважи́тел|ьный (～ен, ～ьна), *adj.* **1.** valid;
～ьная причи́на valid cause, good reason.
2. respectful, deferential.

ува́ж|ить, у, ишь, *pf.* **1.** to comply (with).
2. (*coll.*) to humour.

ува́л, а, *m.* steep slope.

у́вал|ень, ьня, *m.* (*coll.*) bumpkin, clod-
hopper.

ува́лист|ый (～, ～а), *adj.* steeply-sloping.

ува́рива|ться, ется, *impf. of* увари́ться.

увар|и́ться, ～ится, *pf.* (*of* ～ива́ться) (*coll.*)
1. to be thoroughly cooked. **2.** to boil away.

уведоми́тельн|ый, *adj.* ～ое письмо́ letter
of advice, notice.

уве́дом|ить, лю, ишь, *pf.* (*of* ～ля́ть) to
inform, notify.

уведомле́ни|е, я, *n.* information, notifica-
tion.

уведомля́|ть, ю, *impf. of* уве́домить.

увез|ти́, у́, ёшь, *past* ～, ～ла́, *pf.* (*of* увози́ть)
1. to take (away); to take with one. **2.** to
abduct, kidnap.

увекове́чива|ть, ю, *impf. of* увекове́чить.

увекове́ч|ить, у, ишь, *pf.* (*of* ～ивать) **1.** to
immortalize. **2.** to perpetuate.

увеличе́ни|е, я, *n.* **1.** increase; augmenta-
tion; extension. **2.** magnification (*by means
of an optical instrument*); (*phot.*) enlargement.

увели́чива|ть(ся), ю(сь), *impf. of* увели́-
чить(ся).

увеличи́тельн|ый, *adj.* **1.** magnifying; ～ое
стекло́ magnifying glass; y. аппара́т (*phot.*)
enlarger. **2.** (*gram.*) augmentative.

увели́ч|ить, у, ишь, *pf.* (*of* ～ивать) **1.** t
increase; to augment; to extend; to en
hance. **2.** to magnify; (*phot.*) to en
large.

увели́ч|иться, ится, *pf.* (*of* ～иваться) t
increase, grow, rise.

увенч|а́ть, а́ю, *pf.* (*of* венча́ть 1, 2, *an*
～ивать) to crown.

увенч|а́ться, а́ется, *pf.* (*of* ～ива́ться) (+*i.*
fig., rhet.) to be crowned (with); y. успе́хо*
to be crowned with success.

уве́нчива|ть(ся), ю(сь), *impf. of* увенча́ть
(ся).

увере́ни|е, я, *n.* assurance; protestation.

уве́ренност|ь, и, *f.* **1.** confidence; y. в себ
self-confidence. **2.** confidence, certitude
certainty; мо́жно с ～ью сказа́ть one ca
say with confidence, it is safe to say; я бы
в по́лной ～и, что пойдёт дождь I wa
quite certain that it would rain.

уве́рен|ный (～, ～на), *adj.* **1.** confiden
sure; ～ная рука́ sure hand. **2.** *as prea*
(～, ～а) confident, sure, certain; быт
～ным to be sure, be certain; бу́дь(те
～(ы)! you may be sure, you may rely on i

уве́р|ить, ю, ишь, *pf.* (*of* ～я́ть) to assure
to convince, persuade.

уве́р|иться, юсь, ишься, *pf.* (*of* ～я́ться) t
assure oneself, satisfy oneself; to becom
convinced.

увер|ну́ться, ну́сь, нёшься, *pf.* (*of* ～ты
ваться) (от) to dodge; to evade (*also fig.*)
y. от прямо́го отве́та to avoid giving
direct answer.

уве́р|овать, ую, *pf.* (в+*a.*) to come to be
lieve (in).

уве́ртк|а, и, *f.* dodge, evasion; subterfuge
(*pl.*) wiles.

увертли́в|ый (～, ～а), *adj.* evasive, shifty.

уверты́ва|ться, юсь, *impf. of* уверну́ться.

увертю́р|а, ы, *f.* (*mus.*) overture.

увер|я́ть(ся), я́ю(сь), *impf. of* ～и́ть(ся).

увеселе́ни|е, я, *n.* entertainment, amuse
ment.

увесели́тельн|ый, *adj.* pleasure, entertai
ment, amusement; ～ая пое́здка pleasure
-trip, jaunt.

увесел|и́ть, ю, и́шь, *pf.* (*of* ～я́ть) to enter
tain, amuse.

увесел|я́ть, я́ю, *impf. of* ～и́ть.

увеси́ст|ый (～, ～а), *adj.* (*coll.*) weighty; y
уда́р heavy blow (*also fig.*).

уве|сти́, ду́, дёшь, *past* ～л, ～ла́, *pf.* (*of* уво
ди́ть) **1.** to take (away); to take with on
2. (*coll.*) to carry off, lift, walk off wit
(= to steal).

уве́т, а, *m.* (*obs.*) = увеща́ние.

уве́ч|ить, у, ишь, *impf.* to maim, mutilat
cripple.

уве́чн|ый, *adj.* maimed, mutilated

crippled; *as noun* **у**, **~ого**, *m.*; **~ая, ~ой**,
f. cripple.

увечь|е, я, *n.* maiming, mutilation.

увеш|ать, аю, *pf.* (*of* **~ивать**) to cover (*with
objects suspended*); **у.** стéну картúнами to
cover a wall with pictures.

увешива|ть, ю, *impf. of* увéшать.

увещáни|е, я, *n.* exhortation, admonition.

увещá|ть, ю, *impf.* (*obs.*) = увещевáть.

увещевá|ть, ю, *impf.* to exhort, admonish.

увивá|ть, ю, *impf. of* увúть.

увивá|ться, юсь, *impf.* (за+*i.*; *coll., pejor.*)
to hang round; to try to get round.

увидá|ть, ю, *pf.* (*of* видáть) (*coll.*) to see.

увидá|ться, юсь, *pf.* (*coll.*) to see one an-
other.

уви|деть, жу, дишь, *pf.* **1.** *pf. of* вúдеть.
2. to catch sight of.

уви|деться, жусь, дишься, *pf. of* вúдеться.

увилива|ть, ю, *impf.* (от) **1.** *impf. of* увиль-
нýть. **1.** (*impf. only*) to try to get out
(of).

увильн|ýть, ý, ёшь, *pf.* (*of* увúливать) (от;
coll.) **1.** to dodge. **2.** (*fig.*) to evade, shirk;
to get out (of); **у.** от отвéта to get out of
replying.

ув|úть, ью, ьёшь, *past* **~úл, ~илá, ~úло,**
pf. (*of* **~ивáть**) to twine all over.

увлажн|úть, ю́, úшь, *pf.* (*of* **~я́ть**) to
moisten, damp, wet.

увлажн|я́ть, я́ю, *impf. of* **~úть**.

увлекáтел|ьный (~ен, ~ьна), *adj.* fascinat-
ing; absorbing.

увлекá|ть(ся), ю(сь), *impf. of* увлéчь(ся).

увлечéни|е, я, *n.* **1.** animation. **2.** (+*i.*)
passion (for); enthusiasm (for), keenness
(on); crush (on). **3.** (object of) passion;
планерúзм — егó **у.** gliding is his passion,
he is mad about gliding; стáрое **у.** old
flame.

увлé|чь, кý, чёшь, кýт, *past* **~к, ~клá,** *pf.*
(*of* **~кáть**) **1.** to carry along. **2.** (*fig.*) to
carry away, distract. **3.** to captivate, fascin-
ate. **4.** to entice, allure.

увлé|чься, кýсь, чёшься, кýтся, *past* **~кся,
~клáсь,** *pf.* (*of* **~кáться**) (+*i.*) **1.** to be
carried away (by); to become keen (on),
become mad (about); орáтор **~кся** the
speaker got carried away; онá **~клáсь** ез-
дóй верхóм she is mad about riding. **2.** to
become enamoured (of), become keen (on),
fall (for).

увóд, а, *m.* **1.** taking away; **у.** войск withdrawal of troops. **2.** (*coll.*) carrying off;
lifting (= stealing); женúтьба **~ом** (*obs.*)
elopement.

уво|дúть, жý, ~дишь, *impf. of* увестú.

увóз, а, *m.* (*coll.*) abduction; carrying off,
lifting; женúтьба **~ом** (*obs.*) elopement.

уво|зúть, жý, ~зишь, *pf. of* увезтú.

уволáкива|ть, ю, *impf. of* уволóчь.

увóл|ить, ю, ишь, *pf.* (*of* **~ня́ть**) **1.** to dis-
charge, dismiss; to sack, fire; **у.** в отстáвку
to retire, pension off; **у.** в запáс (*mil.*) to
transfer to the reserve; **у.** в óтпуск to give
a holiday, grant leave (of absence). **2.** (*pf.
only*) (от; *obs.*) to spare; **~ьте** нас от под-
рóбного расскáза spare us the details.

увóл|иться, юсь, ишься, *pf.* (*of* **~ня́ться**)
1. to retire; (*mil.*) to leave the service, get
one's discharge; **у.** в отстáвку to retire, go
into retirement. **2.** *pass. of* **~ить**.

увол|óчь, окý, очёшь, окýт, *past* **~óк, ~оклá,**
pf. (*of* **~áкивать**) (*coll.*) **1.** to drag away;
éле нóги **у.** to have a narrow escape. **2.** to
carry off, make off with.

увольнéни|е, я, *n.* discharge, dismissal; re-
tiring, pensioning off; **у.** в запáс (*mil.*)
transfer to the reserve; предупреждéние
об **~и** notice (of dismissal).

увольнúтельн|ый, *adj.* discharge, dis-
missal; **у.** билéт, **~ая** запúска (*mil.*) leave-
-pass.

увольня́|ть(ся), ю(сь), *impf. of* увóлить(ся).

увор|овáть, ýю, *pf.* (*coll.*) to pinch, swipe.

уврач|евáть, ýю, *pf. of* врачевáть.

увуля́рный, *adj.* (*ling.*) uvular.

увы́, *interj.* alas!

увядá|ть, ю, *impf. of* увя́нуть.

увя|зáть¹, жý, ~жешь, *pf.* (*of* **~зывать**)
1. to tie up; to pack up. **2.** to co-ordinate.

увя|зáть², áю, *impf. of* **~нуть**.

увя|зáться, жýсь, ~жешься, *pf.* (*of* **~зы-
ваться**) (*coll.*) **1.** to pack. **2.** (за кем-н.) to
dog (someone's footsteps).

увя́зк|а, и, *f.* **1.** tying up, roping, strapping.
2. co-ordination. **3.** (*polit.*) linkage.

увя́з|нуть, ну, нешь, *past* **~, ~ла,** *pf.* (*of*
~áть²) (в+*p.*) to get stuck (in); to get
bogged down (in) (*also fig.*).

увя́зыва|ть, ю, *impf. of* увязáть¹.

увя́зыва|ться, юсь, *impf. of* увязáться.

увя́|нуть, ну, нешь, *pf.* (*of* **~дáть**) to fade,
wither, wilt, droop (*also fig.*).

угад|áть¹, áю, *pf.* (*of* **~ывать**) to guess
(right), divine.

угад|áть², áю, *pf.* (в+*a.*; *coll.*) to get (into),
fall (into).

угáдыва|ть, ю, *impf. of* угадáть¹.

угáр¹, а, *m.* **1.** carbon monoxide fumes,
charcoal fumes. **2.** carbon monoxide
poisoning; у них **у.** they are suffering from
carbon monoxide poisoning. **3.** (*fig.*)
ecstasy, intoxication; в **~е** (+*g.*) carried
away (by), blinded (by); в **~е** страстéй in
the heat of passion.

угáр², а, *m.* (*tech., text.*) waste (*from metal
smelting, etc., or from cotton spinning*).

угáрно, *as pred.*; здесь **у.** there is a smell of
fumes here.

уга́рный[1], *adj.* full of (monoxide) fumes; (*tech.*) у. газ coal-gas, carbon monoxide.

уга́рный[2], *adj.* (*tech., text.*) waste.

угаса́|ть, ́ет, *impf.* 1. *impf. of* ~нуть. 2. (*impf. only*) to die down (*of a fire and fig.*); си́лы у него́ ~а́ли his strength was failing.

уга́с|нуть, нет, *pf.* (*of* ~а́ть) to go out.

углево́д, а, *m.* (*chem.*) carbohydrate.

углеводоро́д, а, *m.* (*chem.*) hydrocarbon.

углевыжига́тельн|ый, *adj.* ~ая печь charcoal kiln.

угледобы́ч|а, и, *f.* coal extraction.

углежже́ни|е, я, *n.* charcoal burning.

углежо́г, а, *m.* charcoal-burner.

углекислот|а́, ы́, *f.* (*chem.*) carbonic acid, carbon dioxide.

углеки́слый, *adj.* (*chem.*) carbonate (of); у. газ carbonic acid gas; у. аммо́ний ammonium carbonate.

углеко́п, а, *m.* (*obs.*) coal-miner, collier.

углепромы́шленност|ь, и, *f.* coal-mining, coal industry.

углеро́д, а, *m.* (*chem.*) carbon.

углеро́дист|ый, *adj.* (*chem.*) carbonaceous; carbide (of); ~ое желе́зо iron carbide.

углова́т|ый (~, ~а), *adj.* 1. angular. 2. (*fig., coll.*) awkward.

углов|о́й, *adj.* 1. (*math., phys., tech.*) angle; angular; ~а́я ско́рость angular velocity; ~а́я частота́ angular frequency. 2. angle; corner; у. дом corner house, house on the corner; *as noun* у., ~о́го, *m.* (*sport*) corner; пода́ть у. to take a corner.

угломе́р, а, *m.* 1. (*tech.*) goniometer, azimuth instrument, protractor, clinometer. 2. (*mil.*) deflection.

углуб|и́ть, лю́, и́шь, *pf.* (*of* ~ля́ть) 1. to deepen, make deeper. 2. to drive in deeper, sink deeper. 3. (*fig.*) to extend; у. свои́ зна́ния to extend one's knowledge.

углуб|и́ться, лю́сь, и́шься, *pf.* (*of* ~ля́ться) 1. to deepen, become deeper. 2. (*fig.*) to become intensified. 3. (в+*a.*) to go deep (into); to delve deeply (into) (*also fig.*); у. в ко́рень веще́й to go to the root of the matter. 4. (в+*a.; fig.*) to become absorbed (in); у. в кни́гу to become absorbed in a book; у. в себя́ to become introspective.

углубле́ни|е, я, *n.* 1. deepening. 2. (*fig.*) extending; intensification; для ~я свои́х зна́ний in order to extend one's knowledge. 3. (*geogr.*) hollow, depression, dip. 4. (*naut.*) draught (*of a vessel*).

углубля́|ть(ся), ю(сь), *impf. of* углуби́ть(ся).

угль, угля́, *m.* (*arch. or poet.*) = у́голь.

угля|де́ть, жу́, ди́шь, *pf.* (*coll.*) 1. to espy, spot. 2. (за+*i.*) to look after; не у. (за+*i.*) to fail to take proper care (of).

угна́|ть, угоню́, уго́нишь, *past* ~л, ~ла́, ~ло, *pf.* (*of* угоня́ть) 1. to drive away.

2. (*coll.*) to send off, despatch. 3. (*coll.*) to steal, lift.

угна́|ться, угоню́сь, уго́нишься, *past* ~лся, ~ла́сь, ~ло́сь, *pf.* (за+*i.*) to keep pace (with); to keep up (with) (*also fig., coll.*).

угнезд|и́ться, и́шься, *pf.* (*coll.*) to nestle, settle down (*in a confined space*).

угнета́тел|ь, я, *m.* oppressor.

угнета́тельский, *adj.* oppressive.

угнета́|ть, ю, *impf.* 1. to oppress. 2. to depress, dispirit.

угнете́ни|е, я, *n.* 1. oppression. 2. depression; быть в ~и to be depressed.

угнетённост|ь, и, *f.* depression, low spirits.

угнетённ|ый, *adj.* 1. oppressed. 2. depressed; быть в ~ом состоя́нии to be depressed, be in low spirits.

угова́рива|ть, ю, *impf.* 1. *impf. of* уговори́ть. 2. (*impf. only*) to try to persuade, urge.

угова́рива|ться, юсь, *impf. of* уговори́ться.

угово́р, а, *m.* 1. persuasion. 2. agreement, compact; с ~ом... on condition . . ., with the proviso . . . .

уговор|и́ть, ю́, и́шь, *pf.* (*of* угова́ривать) (+*inf.*) to persuade (to), induce (to); to talk (into).

уговор|и́ться, ю́сь, и́шься, *pf.* (*of* угова́риваться) (+*inf.*) to arrange (to), agree (to).

уго́д|а, ы, *f.* в ~у (+*d.*) to please.

уго|ди́ть[1]**, жу́, ди́шь,** *pf.* (*of* ~жда́ть) (+*d. or* на+*a.*) to please, oblige.

уго|ди́ть[2]**, жу́, ди́шь,** *pf.* (*coll.*) 1. (в+*a.*) to fall (into), get (into); to bang (against); у. в за́падню to fall into a trap; у. в тюрьму́ to land up in prison. 2. (+*d.* в+*a.*) to hit (in, on), get (in, on); у. кому́-н. в глаз ка́мнем to hit someone in the eye with a stone.

уго́длив|ый (~, ~а), *adj.* obsequious.

уго́дник, а, *m.* 1. (*coll.*) person anxious to please. 2. свято́й у. saint.

уго́днича|ть, ю, *impf.* (пе́ред; *coll.*) to cringe (to).

уго́дничеств|о, а, *n.* subservience, servility.

уго́дно 1. *as pred.* (+*d.*) что вам у.? what would you like?, what can I do for you; как вам у. as you please; please yourself; ско́лько душе́ у. to one's heart's content; не у. ли вам? (i) (*as polite invitation*) would you like?, (ii) (*iron.; expressing request*) would you be good enough, would you mind; не у. ли (*iron.*) if you please. 2. *forms indef. pronouns and adverbs:* кто у. anyone (you like), whoever you like; что у. anything (you like), whatever you like; ско́лько у. as much as you like; any amount.

уго́д|ный (~ен, ~на), *adj.* pleasing, welcome.

угóд|ье, ья, *g. pl.* **~ий,** *n.* **1.** object *or* area of economic significance; лесны́е ~ья forests; полевы́е ~ья arable land; ры́бные ~ья fishing-ground. **2.** (*obs.*) advantage, favourable side, good point.

угождá|ть, ю, *impf. of* угоди́ть[1].

ýг|ол, лá, об ~лé, в ~лý, *m.* **1.** (в ~лé) (*math., phys.*) angle; у. встре́чи angle of impact; angle of incidence; у. засе́чки angle of intersection; у. зре́ния visual angle; (*fig.*) point of view; у. пока́тости angle of slope, gradient; под ~ло́м (в+*a.*) at an angle (of); под прямы́м ~ло́м at right angles. **2.** corner; в ~лý in the corner; на ~лý at the corner; за ~ло́м round the corner; поста́вить в у. to put in the corner, make stand in the corner; из-за ~лá (from) round the corner; (*fig.*) on the sly, behind someone's back; загнáть в у. to drive into a corner; сре́зать у. to cut off a corner. **3.** part of a room. **4.** place; име́ть свой у. to have a place of one's own; глухо́й у., медве́жий у. remote part, God-forsaken spot.

угол|ёк, ькá, *m.* small piece of coal.

уголóвник, а, *m.* (*coll.*) criminal.

уголóвн|ый, *adj.* criminal; ~ое де́ло criminal case; у. ко́декс criminal code; ~ое пра́во criminal law; у. престу́пник criminal; у. ро́зыск Criminal Investigation Department.

угол|óк, кá, *m.* *dim. of* ýгол; corner; у. приро́ды nature study corner; живо́й у. pets' corner; кра́сный у. recreation and reading room.

ýг|оль, угля́, *m.* **1.** (*pl.* ýгли, угле́й) coal; ка́менный у. coal; бу́рый у. lignite; древе́сный у. charcoal. **2.** (*pl.* ýгли, угле́й *and* ~я́, ~ев) a coal; piece of coal; сиде́ть как на ~ях to be on thorns. **3.** (*art*) charcoal.

угóльник, а, *m.* **1.** set square. **2.** (*tech.*) corner iron; стыково́й у. angle bracket.

ýгольн|ый, *adj.* **1.** coal; у. бассе́йн coal-field; у. райо́н coal-mining area. **2.** carbon; ~ая дугова́я ла́мпа carbon arc lamp. **3.** (*chem.*) carbonic; ~ая кислотá carbonic acid.

угóльный, *adj.* (*coll.*) corner.

ýгольщик[1], а, *m.* **1.** coal-miner, collier. **2.** charcoal-burner.

ýгольщик[2], а, *m.* collier (*ship*).

угомóн, а (у), *m.* (*coll.*) peace (and quiet); на них ~у нет they give one no peace; не знать ~у to have no peace.

угомон|и́ть, ю́, и́шь, *pf.* (*coll.*) to calm.

угомон|и́ться, ю́сь, и́шься, *pf.* (*coll.*) to calm down.

угóн, а, *m.* **1.** driving away. **2.** (*coll.*) lifting, stealing; hi-jacking. **3.** (*railways*) creep (*of lines*).

угóнщик, а, *m.* hijacker.

угоня́|ть, ю, *impf. of* угнáть.

угорáзд|ить, ит, *pf.* (+*inf.*, *usu. impers.*; *coll.*) to urge, make; как э́то его́ ~ило жени́ться на ней? what on earth made him marry her?

угор|áть, áю, *impf. of* ~е́ть.

угоре́лый, *adj.* **1.** (*obs.*) poisoned by charcoal fumes. **2.** как у. like a madman, like one possessed.

угор|е́ть[1], ю́, и́шь, *pf.* (*of* ~áть) **1.** to be poisoned by charcoal fumes, get carbon monoxide poisoning. **2.** (*coll.*) to be mad, be crazy; что ты, ~е́л? are you out of your mind?

угор|е́ть[2], ю́, и́шь, *pf.* (*of* ~áть) to burn away, burn down.

угóрский, *adj.* (*ethnol., ling.*) Ugrian.

ýг|орь[1], ря́, *m.* eel; живо́й как у. as lively as a cricket.

ýг|орь[2], ря́, *m.* blackhead.

уго|сти́ть, щу́, сти́шь, *pf.* (*of* ~щáть) (+*i.*) to entertain (to), treat (to); у. кого́-н. обе́дом to have someone to dinner.

уготóван|ный, *p.p.p. as pred. adj.* (*obs.*) prepared, in store; им ~о све́тлое бу́дущее a splendid future is in store for them.

уготóв|ить, лю, ишь, *pf.* (*obs.*) to prepare.

угощá|ть, ю, *impf. of* угости́ть.

угощéни|е, я, *n.* **1.** (+*i.*) entertaining (to, with), treating (to). **2.** refreshments; fare.

угр, а, *m.* (*ethnol.*) Ugrian (*member of ethnic group comprising Hungarians, Ostyaks and Voguls*).

угревáт|ый (~, ~а), *adj.* covered with blackheads; pimply.

угрóб|ить, лю, ишь, *pf.* (*sl.*) **1.** to do in. **2.** (*fig.*) to ruin, wreck; у. чью-н. репутáцию to ruin someone's reputation.

угрожá|ть, ю, *impf.* to threaten.

угрожá|ющий, *pres. part. act. of* ~ть *and adj.* threatening, menacing; ~ющая катастро́фа impending disaster.

угрóз|а, ы, *f.* threat, menace; под ~ой (+*g.*) under threat (of); поста́вить под ~у to threaten, endanger, imperil, jeopardize.

угрóзыск, а, *m.* (*abbr. of* уголо́вный ро́зыск) Criminal Investigation Department.

ýгро-фи́нский, *adj.* Finno-Ugrian.

угрызéни|е, я, *n.* pangs; ~я со́вести remorse; чу́вствовать ~я со́вести to feel pangs of conscience.

угрю́м|ый (~, ~а), *adj.* sullen, morose, gloomy.

удáв, а, *m.* (*zool.*) boa, boa constrictor.

удá|вáться, ётся, *impf. of* ~ться.

удав|и́ть, лю́, ~ишь, *pf.* to strangle.

удав|и́ться, лю́сь, ~ишься, *pf.* (*of* дави́ться 2) to hang oneself.

удáвк|а, и, *f.* running knot, half hitch, timber hitch.

удавле́ни|е, я, *n.* strangling, strangulation.

уда́вленник, а, *m.* (*coll.*) person who has hanged himself; victim of strangling.

удале́ни|е, я, *n.* 1. removal; у. зу́ба extraction of a tooth. 2. sending away; у. с по́ля (*sport*) sending off the field. 3. moving off.

удалённост|ь, и, *f.* remoteness, distance.

удал|ённый, *p.p.p. of* ∼и́ть *and adj.* remote.

удал|е́ц, ьца́, *m.* daring person.

удал|и́ть, ю́, и́шь, *pf.* (*of* ∼я́ть) 1. to remove; у. зуб to extract a tooth. 2. to remove, send away; у. с рабо́ты to dismiss, sack; у. с по́ля (*sport*) to send off (the field). 3. to move away.

удал|и́ться, ю́сь, и́шься, *pf.* (*of* ∼я́ться) 1. to move off, move away; поспе́шно у. to beat a hasty retreat. 2. to leave, withdraw, retire; у. на поко́й to retire to a quiet life; у. от о́бщества to withdraw from society.

удал|о́й (уда́л, ∼а́, уда́ло), *adj.* daring, bold.

у́дал|ь, и, *f.* daring, boldness.

удальств|о́, а́, *n.* (*coll.*) = у́даль.

удал|я́ть(ся), я́ю(сь), *impf. of* ∼и́ть(ся).

уда́р, а, *m.* 1. (*in var. senses*) blow; stroke; одни́м ∼ом at one stroke; нанести́ у. to strike a blow; у. в спи́ну (*fig.*) stab in the back; у. гро́ма thunder-clap; у. гро́ма средь я́сного не́ба bolt from the blue. 2. stroke (*sound*); ∼ы пу́льса stroke of the pulse. 3. (*mil.*) blow; attack; thrust; у. в штыки́ bayonet charge; у. с во́здуха air strike; под ∼ом exposed (to attack). 4. быть в ∼е (*coll.*) to be in good form; не быть в ∼е to be off one's stroke. 5. (*med.*) stroke, seizure; со́лнечный у. sun-stroke.

ударе́ни|е, я, *n.* 1. (*ling.*) stress, accent; (*fig.*) stress, emphasis; поста́вить у. to stress, accent; сде́лать у. (на+*p. or* на+*a.*) to stress, emphasize. 2. stress(-mark).

уда́р|енный, *p.p.p. of* ∼ить *and adj.* (*ling.*) stressed, accented.

уда́р|ить, ю, ишь, *pf.* (*of* ∼я́ть *and, in some senses, of* бить) 1. (+*a.* по+*d. or* в+*a.*) to strike; to hit; у. кого́-н. по лицу́ to slap someone's face; у. кулако́м по столу́ to bang on the table with one's fist; мо́лния ∼ила в де́рево the tree was struck by lightning. 2. (в+*a. or* +*a.*) to strike; to sound; to beat; у. в бараба́н to beat a drum; у. в наба́т, у. трево́гу to sound the alarm; часы́ ∼или по́лночь the clock struck midnight; у. в смычки́ (*mus.*) to strike up. 3. у. в го́лову (*of blood*) to rush to one's head; (*of wine, etc.*) to go to one's head. 4. (на+*a. or* по+*d.*) (*mil.*) to strike (against), attack. 5. (по+*d.*) to strike (at), hit (at); to combat; у. по кумовству́ to combat nepotism; у. по карма́ну (*coll.*) to hit one's pocket, set one back. 6. (*of weather conditions, etc.*; *coll.*)

to strike; to set in; ну и моро́зец ∼ил the frosts have really set in. 7. у. по рука́м to strike a bargain. 8. па́лец о па́лец не у. (*coll.*) not to raise, lift a finger.

уда́р|иться, ю́сь, ишься, *pf.* (*of* ∼я́ться) 1. (о+*a. or* в+*a.*) to strike (against), hit; у. о подво́дный ка́мень to strike a reef. 2. (в+*a. or* +*inf.*) to break (into); у. в бе́гство, у. бежа́ть to break into a run; у. в слёзы to burst into tears. 3. (в+*a.*) to become addicted (to), become keen (on). 4. у. в кра́йность to run to an extreme; у. из одно́й кра́йности в другу́ю to run from one extreme to another.

уда́рник[1], а, *m.* 1. shock-worker, udarnik. 2. (*mil.*) member of striking force.

уда́рник[2], а, *m.* (*in fire-arm*) striker, firing pin; (*in detonator*) plunger.

уда́рниц|а, ы, *f. of* уда́рник[1].

уда́рн|ый, *adj.* 1. (*tech. and mil.*) percussive; percussion; ∼ая возду́шная волна́ blast wave; у. ка́псюль percussion cap; ∼ая ми́на (*naut.*) contact mine; ∼ая сва́рка percussive welding; ∼ая си́ла striking power, force of impact; ∼ая тру́бка percussion tube, percussion primer. 2. (*mus.*) percussion. 3. (*mil.*) striking, shock; ∼ая гру́ппа striking force, main attack force; ∼ые ча́сти shock troops. 4. shock(-working); ∼ая рабо́та shock work; ∼ые те́мпы accelerated tempo (*of work*). 5. urgent; ∼ое зада́ние urgent task, rush job; в ∼ом поря́дке with great despatch.

удар|я́ть(ся), я́ю(сь), *impf. of* ∼ить(ся).

уда́|ться, стся, ду́тся, *past* ∼лся, ∼ла́сь, *pf.* (*of* ∼ва́ться) 1. to succeed, be a success, be successful, work (well); опера́ция ∼ла́сь the operation was a success. 2. (*impers.*+*d. and inf.*) to succeed, manage; мне не ∼ло́сь присутствовать на их сва́дьбе I did not manage to attend their wedding.

уда́ч|а, и, *f.* success; good luck, good fortune; жела́ть ∼и to wish good luck; им всегда́ у. they are always lucky.

уда́чливост|ь, и, *f.* success, luck.

уда́члив|ый (∼, ∼а), *adj.* successful, lucky.

уда́чник, а, *m.* (*coll.*) lucky person.

уда́ч|ный (∼ен, ∼на), *adj.* 1. successful. 2. felicitous, apt, good; у. перево́д felicitous translation; у. оборо́т apt turn of phrase; у. вы́бор happy choice.

удва́ива|ть, ю, *impf. of* удво́ить.

удвое́ни|е, я, *n.* doubling, redoubling; (*ling.*) reduplication.

удво́|енный, *p.p.p. of* ∼ить *and adj.* doubled, redoubled; (*ling.*) reduplicated; (*of letter of the alphabet*) double.

удво́|ить, ю, ишь, *pf.* (*of* удва́ивать) to double, redouble; (*ling.*) to reduplicate; у. свои́ уси́лия to redouble one's efforts.

уде́л, а, *m.* **1.** lot, destiny; доста́ться в у. кому́-н. to fall to one's lot. **2.** (*hist.*) apanage principality (*in Kievan Russia*). **3.** (*hist.*) crown domain, crown landed property.

уде́л|и́ть, ю́, и́шь, *pf.* (*of* ~я́ть) to give, spare, devote; у. часть из полу́чки на что-н. to give up part of one's wage--packet for something; у. вре́мя чему́-н. to spare the time for something; нам на́до у. внима́ние э́тому вопро́су we must give the matter thought.

уде́льн|ый¹, *adj.* (*phys.*) specific; у. вес specific gravity; (*fig.*) proportion, share; ~ая мо́щность horse power per pound of weight.

уде́льн|ый², *adj.* (*hist.*) **1.** apanage; у. князь apanage prince (*in Kievan Russia*); у. пери́од period of apanage principalities. **2.** crown; ~ые зе́мли crown lands, crown domains.

уде́л|я́ть, я́ю, *impf. of* ~и́ть.

у́держ, у, *m.* без ~у (*coll.*) uncontrollably, unrestrainedly, without restraint; пла́кать без ~у to weep uncontrollably; ~у нет ему́, на него́ (*coll.*) there's no holding him; ~у не знать (*coll.*) to be immoderate, know no bounds.

удержа́ни|е, я, *n.* **1.** keeping, holding, reretention. **2.** deduction; у. из зарпла́ты money stopped from wages.

удерж|а́ть, у́, ~ишь, *pf.* (*of* ~ивать) **1.** to hold, hold on to, not let go. **2.** to keep, retain; у. своё ме́сто в чемпиона́те to retain one's place in a championship competition; у. в па́мяти to retain in one's memory. **3.** to hold back, keep back, restrain; у. лошаде́й to hold horses back; у. кого́-н. от опроме́тчивого посту́пка to restrain some from a headstrong action. **4.** to keep down, suppress; у. слёзы to stifle one's tears. **5.** to deduct, keep back; у. из зарпла́ты to stop from wages.

удерж|а́ться, у́сь, ~ишься, *pf.* (*of* ~иваться) **1.** to hold one's ground, hold on, hold out; to stand firm; у. на нога́х to remain on one's feet. **2.** (от) to keep (from), refrain (from); у. от собла́зна to resist a temptation; не могли́ у. от сме́ха we couldn't help laughing.

уде́ржива|ть(ся), ю(сь), *impf. of* удержа́ть(ся).

удеся́тер|и́ть, ю́, и́шь, *pf.* (*of* ~я́ть) to increase tenfold.

удеся́тер|и́ться, и́тся, *pf.* (*of* ~я́ться) to increase (*intrans.*) tenfold.

удеся́тер|я́ть(ся), я́ю, я́ет(ся), *impf. of* ~и́ть(ся).

удешев|и́ть, лю́, и́шь, *pf.* (*of* ~ля́ть) to reduce the price (of).

удешев|и́ться, и́тся, *pf.* (*of* ~ля́ться) to become cheaper.

удешевле́ни|е, я, *n.* reduction of prices.

удешевля́|ть(ся), ю, ет(ся), *impf. of* удешеви́ть(ся).

удиви́тельно, *adv.* **1.** astonishingly, surprisingly. **2.** wonderfully, marvellously. **3.** very, extremely.

удиви́тел|ьный (~ен, ~ьна), *adj.* **1.** astonishing, surprising, amazing; ~ьно (*as pred.*) it is astonishing, it is surprising, it is amazing; it is funny; не ~ьно, что no wonder that. **2.** wonderful, marvellous.

удив|и́ть, лю́, и́шь, *pf.* (*of* ~ля́ть) to astonish, surprise, amaze.

удив|и́ться, лю́сь, и́шься, *pf.* (*of* ~ля́ться) (+*d.*) to be astonished (at), be surprised (at), be amazed (at); to marvel (at).

удивле́ни|е, я, *n.* astonishment, surprise, amazement; к моему́ вели́кому ~ю to my great surprise; на у. (*as pred.; coll.*) excellent(ly), splendid(ly), marvellous(ly); приём вы́шел на у. the reception went off splendidly.

удивля́|ть(ся), ю(сь), *impf. of* удиви́ть(ся).

удил|а́, уди́л, ~а́м, *no sing.* bit; закуси́ть у. to take the bit between one's teeth (*also fig.*).

уди́лищ|е, а, *n.* fishing-rod.

уди́льн|ый, *adj.* ~ые принадле́жности fishing tackle.

уди́льщик, а, *m.* angler.

уди́льщиц|а, ы, *f. of* уди́льщик.

удира́|ть, ю, *impf. of* удра́ть.

уди́ть, ужу́, у́дишь, *impf.* у. ры́бу to fish, angle.

уди́ться, у́дится, *impf.* (*of fish*) to bite.

удлине́ни|е, я, *n.* lengthening; у. сро́ка extension (of time).

удлин|и́ть, ю́, и́шь, *pf.* (*of* ~я́ть) to lengthen; to extend, prolong.

удлин|и́ться, и́тся, *pf.* (*of* ~я́ться) to become longer; to be extended, be prolonged.

удлин|я́ть(ся), я́ю(сь), *impf. of* ~и́ть(ся).

удму́рт, а, *m.* Udmurt.

удму́ртк|а, и, *f.* Udmurt (woman).

удму́ртский, *adj.* Udmurt.

удо́бно¹, *adv.* **1.** comfortably. **2.** conveniently.

удо́бно², *as pred.* **1.** (+*d.*) to feel, be comfortable; to be at one's ease; нам здесь вполне́ у. we are very comfortable here. **2.** (+*d.*) it is convenient (for), it suits; у. ли вам сра́зу же прие́хать? is it convenient for you to come at once? **3.** it is proper, it is in order; у. ли зада́ть тако́й вопро́с? is it proper to ask such a question?

удо́б|ный (~ен, ~на), *adj.* **1.** comfortable; cosy. **2.** convenient, suitable, opportune; по́льзоваться ~ным слу́чаем to take an opportunity. **3.** proper, in order.

удобовари́м|ый (~, ~а), *adj.* digestible.

удобоисполни́м|ый (~, ~а), *adj.* easy to carry out; ~ая про́сьба simple request.

удобообтека́емый, *adj.* streamlined.

удобопоня́т|ный (~ен, ~на), *adj.* comprehensible, intelligible.

удобопроизноси́м|ый (~, ~а), *adj.* easy to pronounce.

удобочита́ем|ый (~, ~а), *adj.* easy to read; legible.

удобре́ни|е, я, *n.* (*agric.*) **1.** fertilization, manuring. **2.** fertilizer.

удобр|и́ть, ю, ишь, *pf.* (*of* ~я́ть) to fertilize, manure.

удобр|я́ть, я́ю, *impf. of* ~и́ть.

удо́бств|о, а, *n.* comfort. **2.** convenience; кварти́ра со все́ми ~ами flat with all conveniences.

удовлетворе́ни|е, я, *n.* satisfaction, gratification; тре́бовать ~я у кого́-н. to demand satisfaction from someone; отмеча́ть с ~ем to note with satisfaction.

удовлетворённост|ь, и, *f.* satisfaction, contentment.

удовлетвор|ённый, *p.p.p. of* ~и́ть *and adj.* satisfied, contented.

удовлетвори́тельно, *adv.* **1.** satisfactorily. **2.** *as noun, indecl.* 'satisfactory', 'fair' (*as school mark*).

удовлетвори́тел|ьный (~ен, ~ьна), *adj.* satisfactory.

удовлетвор|и́ть, ю́, и́шь, *pf.* (*of* ~я́ть) **1.** to satisfy; to give satisfaction (to); to comply (with); у. запро́сы to satisfy requirements; у. про́сьбу to comply with a request. **2.** (+*d.*) to answer, meet; у. тре́бованиям to answer requirements. **3.** (+*i.*) to supply (with), furnish (with); у. провиа́нтом to victual.

удовлетвор|и́ться, ю́сь, и́шься, *pf.* (*of* ~я́ться) **1.** (+*i.*) to content oneself (with), be satisfied (with). **2.** *pass. of* ~и́ть.

удовлетвор|я́ть(ся), я́ю(сь), *impf. of* ~и́ть(ся).

удово́льстви|е, я, *n.* **1.** (*sing. only*) pleasure; доста́вить у. (+*d.*) to give pleasure. **2.** amusement; мно́го ~й a lot of fun.

удово́льств|оваться, уюсь, *pf. of* дово́льствоваться.

удо́д, а, *m.* (*orn.*) hoopoe.

удо́|й, я, *m.* **1.** yield of milk. **2.** milking.

удо́йлив|ый (~, ~а), *adj.* yielding much milk; ~ая коро́ва good milker.

удо́йност|ь, и, *f.* yield of milk; milking capacity.

удо́й|ный, *adj.* **1.** *adj. of* ~. **2.** = ~ливый.

удорожа́ни|е, я, *n.* rise in price(s).

удорож|а́ть, а́ю, *impf. of* ~и́ть.

удорож|и́ть, у́, и́шь, *pf.* (*of* ~а́ть) to raise the price (of).

удоста́ива|ть(ся), ю(сь), *impf. of* удосто́ить(ся).

удостовере́ни|е, я, *n.* **1.** certification, attestation; в у. (+*g.*) in witness (of). **2.** certificate; у. ли́чности identity card; у. пра́ва вожде́ния автомоби́ля driving licence; у. о сме́рти death certificate.

удостове́р|ить, ю, ишь, *pf.* (*of* ~я́ть) to certify, attest, witness; у. по́дпись to witness a signature; у. ли́чность кого́-н. to identify someone.

удостове́р|иться, юсь, ишься, *pf.* (*of* ~я́ться) (в+*p.*) to make sure (of), assure oneself (of); у. в по́длинности докуме́нта to assure oneself of the genuineness of a document.

удостовер|я́ть(ся), я́ю(сь), *impf. of* ~и́ть(ся).

удосто́|ить, ю, ишь, *pf.* (*of* удоста́ивать) **1.** (+*a. and g.*) to award (to), confer (on); у. кого́-н. ле́нинской пре́мии to award someone a Lenin prize. **2.** (+*i.*; *usu. iron.*) to favour (with), vouchsafe; у. улы́бкой to favour with a smile.

удосто́|иться, юсь, ишься, *pf.* (*of* удоста́иваться) (+*g.*) **1.** to receive, be awarded (*an honour, a prize, etc.*). **2.** (*usu. iron.*) to be favoured (with), be vouchsafed.

удосу́жива|ться, юсь, *impf. of* удосу́житься.

удосу́ж|иться, усь, ишься, *pf.* (*of* ~иваться) (+*inf.*; *coll.*) to find time (to), to manage.

удочер|и́ть, ю́, и́шь, *pf.* (*of* ~я́ть) to adopt (*as a daughter*).

удочер|я́ть, я́ю, *impf. of* ~и́ть.

у́дочк|а, и, *f.* (fishing-)rod (*also in fig., coll. phrases*); заки́нуть ~у to cast a line; to put a line out (= to try to discover something); пойма́ть, подде́ть на ~у to catch out; попа́сться на ~у to swallow the bait.

удра́|ть, удеру́, удерёшь, *past* ~л, ~ла́, ~ло, *pf.* (*of* удира́ть) (*coll.*) to make off; to do a bunk, flit.

удруж|и́ть, у́, и́шь, *pf.* (+*d.*; *coll.*) to do a good turn (*also iron.,* = to do a bad turn).

удруч|а́ть, а́ю, *impf. of* ~и́ть.

удручённост|ь, и, *f.* depression, despondency.

удруч|и́ть, у́, и́шь, *pf.* (*of* ~а́ть) to depress, dispirit.

уду́м|ать, аю, *pf.* (*of* ~ывать) (*coll.*) to think up.

уду́мыва|ть, ю, *impf. of* уду́мать.

удуш|а́ть, а́ю, *impf. of* ~и́ть.

удуше́ни|е, я, *n.* smothering, suffocation; asphyxiation.

удуш|и́ть, у́, ~ишь, *pf.* (*of* ~а́ть) to smother, stifle, suffocate; to asphyxiate.

уду́шлив|ый (~, ~а), *adj.* stifling, suffocating; asphyxiating; ~ая жара́ stifling heat; у. газ asphyxiating gas.

удушь|е, я, *n.* asthma; asphyxia.

уединéни|е, я, *n.* solitude; seclusion.

уединённост|ь, и, *f.* solitariness, seclusion.

уединён|ный (~, ~на), *p.p.p.* of уединить *and adj.* solitary, secluded; lonely.

уедин|и́ть, ю́, и́шь, *pf.* (*of* ~я́ть) to seclude, set apart.

уедин|и́ться, ю́сь, и́шься, *pf.* (*of* ~я́ться) (от) to retire (from), withdraw (from); to go off (by oneself); у. в свою́ ко́мнату to retire to one's room.

уедин|я́ть(ся), я́ю(сь), *impf.* of ~и́ть(ся).

уéзд, а, *m.* (*hist.*) uyezd (*lowest administrative division, now* райóн).

уéзд|ный, *adj.* of ~; у. гóрод chief town of uyezd.

уéть, уебу́, уебёшь, *past* уёб, уебли́, *pf.* (*of* еть *and* ебáть) (*vulg.*) to fuck.

уéхать, уéду, уéдешь, *imp.* уезжáй(те), *pf.* (*of* уезжáть) to go away, leave, depart.

уж¹, á, *m.* grass-snake.

уж² 1. *adv.* = ужé. 2. *emphatic particle* (*coll.*) to be sure, indeed, certainly; уж он узнáет he is sure to find out; уж мы искáли, искáли we searched all over the place. 3. *particle emphasizing certain pronouns and adverbs* very; э́то не так уж слóжно it's not so very complicated, it's not all that complicated.

ужáл|ить, ю, ишь, *pf.* of жáлить.

ужáрива|ться, ется, *impf.* of ужáриться.

ужáр|иться, ится, *pf.* (*of* ~иваться) (*coll.*) 1. to be thoroughly roasted, fried. 2. to roast away, be roasted up, shrink.

у́жас, а, *m.* 1. horror, terror; внуши́ть у. (+*d.*) to inspire with horror, horrify; навести́ у. (на+*a.*) to instil terror (into); объя́тый ~ом horror-struck, terror-stricken; к моему́ ~у to my horror. 2. (*usu. pl.*) horror; ~ы осáды the horrors of a siege. 3. *as pred.* (*coll.*) it is awful, it is terrible. 4. у. (как) *as adv.* (*coll.*) awfully, terribly; у. как грóмко awfully loud.

ужас|áть(ся), áю(сь), *impf.* of ~ну́ть(ся).

ужáсно¹, *adv.* 1. horribly, terribly; у. себя́ чу́вствовать to feel awful. 2. (*coll.*) awfully, terribly, frightfully; он у. плóхо игрáет he plays terribly badly.

ужáсно², *as pred.* (*coll.*) it is awful, it is terrible, it is ghastly.

ужас|ну́ть, ну́, нёшь, *pf.* (*of* ~áть) to horrify, terrify.

ужас|ну́ться, ну́сь, нёшься, *pf.* (*of* ~áться) to be horrified, be terrified.

ужáс|ный (~ен, ~на), *adj.* (*in var. senses*) awful, terrible, ghastly, frightful; у. вид awful sight; у. нáсморк awful cold.

у́же, *comp.* of у́зкий *and* у́зко.

ужé 1. *adv.* already; now; by now; у. не no longer; они́ у. при́были they are here

already; он, должнó-быть, у. уéхал he must have gone by now; онá у. не ребёнок she is no longer a child. 2. *emphatic particle* = уж; э́то у. другóе дéло that's quite a different matter.

ужéли, ужéль, *adv.* (*obs.*) = неужéли.

ужéни|е, я, *n.* fishing, angling.

ужива́|ться, юсь, *impf.* of ужи́ться.

ужи́вчив|ый (~, ~а), *adj.* easy to get on with.

ужи́мк|а, и, *f.* grimace.

у́жин, а, *m.* supper.

у́жина|ть, ю, *impf.* (*of* по~) to have supper.

ужи́|ться, ву́сь, вёшься, *past* ~лся, ~лáсь, *pf.* (*of* ~вáться) (с+*i.*) to get on (with); мы с ней так и не ~ли́сь she and I simply couldn't get on.

ужó, *adv.* (*coll.*) 1. later, by and by. 2. *as threat:* у. тебé! just you wait!; я тебя́ у. проучу́! just you wait—I'll show you!

ужóвый, *adj.* of уж¹.

узаконéни|е, я, *n.* 1. legalization, legitimization. 2. statute.

узакóнива|ть, ю, *impf.* of узакóнить.

узакóн|ить, ю, ишь, *pf.* (*of* ~ивать *and* ~я́ть) to legalize, legitimize.

узакон|я́ть, я́ю, *impf.* = ~ивать.

узбéк, а, *m.* Uzbek.

узбéкский, *adj.* Uzbek.

узбéчк|а, и, *f.* Uzbek (woman).

узд|á, ы́, *pl.* ~ы, *f.* bridle (*also fig.*); держáть в ~é to keep in check, restrain.

уздéчк|а, и, *f.* 1. bridle. 2. (*anat.*) fraenum.

уздцы́: под у. by the bridle.

у́з|ел, лá, *m.* 1. knot (*also fig. and naut. measurement of speed*); bend, hitch; завязáть у. to tie a knot; завязáть ~лóм to knot; у. противорéчий knot of contradictions. 2. junction; centre; у. дорóг road junction; промы́шленный у. industrial centre; у. сопротивлéния (*mil.*) centre of resistance. 3. нéрвный у. (*anat.*) nerve-centre, ganglion. 4. (*bot.*) node. 5. (*tech.*) group, assembly. 6. bundle, pack.

узел|óк, кá, *m.* 1. small knot. 2. (*bot.*) nodule. 3. small bundle.

у́з|кий (~ок, ~кá, ~ко), *adj.* 1. narrow; ~кая колея́ (*railways*) narrow gauge; ~кое мéсто (*fig.*) bottleneck. 2. tight. 3. (*fig.*) narrow, limited; в ~ком смы́сле слóва in the narrow sense of the word. 4. (*fig.*) narrow, narrow-minded; у. человéк narrow-minded person.

узковáт|ый (~, ~а), *adj.* rather narrow, rather tight.

узкогóрлый, *adj.* (*of a vessel*) narrow-necked.

узкоколéйный, *adj.* narrow-gauge.

узколóб|ый (~, ~а), *adj.* 1. having a narrow forehead. 2. (*fig.*) narrow-minded.

узли́ст|ый (~, ~а), *adj.* knotty; nodose.

узлова́т|ый (~, ~а), *adj.* knotty; nodose; gnarled.

узлов|о́й, *adj.* 1. junction; ~а́я ста́нция (*railways*) junction. 2. main, principal, central, key; у. вопро́с central question. 3. (*bot.*) nodal.

узна|ва́ть, ю́, ёшь, *impf. of* ~ть.

узна́|ть, ю, *pf.* (*of* ~ва́ть) 1. to recognize. 2. to get to know, become familiar with. 3. to learn, find out.

у́зник, а, *m.* (*obs. or rhet.*) prisoner.

у́зниц|а, ы, *f. of* у́зник.

узо́р, а, *m.* pattern, design.

узо́р|ный, *adj.* 1. *adj. of* ~. 2. decorated with a pattern, design.

узо́рчат|ый (~, ~а), *adj.* decorated with a pattern, design.

у́зост|ь, и, *f.* narrowness (*also fig.*); tightness.

узр|е́ть, ю́, ~ишь, *pf.* 1. *pf. of* зреть². 2. (*fig.*) to see; to take (as); она́ ~е́ла в моём замеча́нии оби́ду she took my remark as an insult.

узурпа́тор, а, *m.* usurper.

узурпа́ци|я, и, *f.* usurpation.

узурпи́р|овать, ую, *impf. and pf.* to usurp.

у́зус, а, *m.* (*leg.*) usage.

у́з|ы, ~, *no sing.* (*fig.*) bonds, ties.

уйгу́р, а, *m.* Uighur.

уйгу́рк|а, и, *f.* Uighur (woman).

уйгу́рский, *adj.* Uighur.

уй|ду́, дёшь, *see* ~ти́.

у́йм|а, ы, *no pl.*, *f.* (*coll.*) lots (of), masses (of), heaps (of).

уйм|у́, ёшь, *see* уня́ть.

уй|ти́, ду́, дёшь, *past* ушёл, ушла́, *pf.* (*of* уходи́ть) 1. to go away, go off, leave; у. из ко́мнаты to leave the room; у. ни с чем to go away empty-handed; у. в монасты́рь to go into a monastery. 2. (от, из) to escape (from), get away (from); to evade. 3. (от, из, с) to retire (from), give up; у. от поли́тики to retire from politics; у. от жи́зни to retire from life; у. из жи́зни to pass away (= to die); у. со сце́ны to quit the stage. 4. (в+а.) to sink (into); (*fig.*) to bury oneself (in); у. в себя́ to retire into one's shell. 5. to be used up, be spent. 6. (*of time, youth, etc.*) to pass away, slip away. 7. (*coll.*) to boil over; to spill. 8. (*obs.*) to pass, outdistance. 9. (вперёд) (*of a timepiece*) to gain, be fast.

ука́з, а, *m.* 1. decree; edict, ukase. 2. (*as pred.*+*neg.*) (it is) not an order, not obligatory; ты мне не у. I'm not obliged to do as *you* say.

указа́ни|е, я, *n.* 1. indication, pointing out. 2. instruction, direction; дать ~я to give instructions.

ука́з|анный, *p.p.p. of* ~а́ть *and adj.* fixed,

appointed, stated; на ~анном ме́сте at the place appointed.

указа́тел|ь, я, *m.* 1. indicator; marker; у. направле́ния road sign; у. (возду́шной) ско́рости airspeed indicator; у. оборо́тов (*tech.*) revolution counter; у. кольца́ угло́ме́ра azimuth scale index; у. у́ровня воды́ water gauge. 2. index; у. со́бственных имён index of proper names. 3. guide, directory.

указа́тельн|ый, *adj.* 1. indicating; ~ая пласти́нка dial; ~ая стре́лка pointer; у. па́лец, у. перст forefinger, index finger; у. столб road sign. 2. ~ое местоиме́ние (*gram.*) demonstrative pronoun.

ука|за́ть, жу́, ~жешь, *pf.* (*of* ~зывать) 1. to show, indicate. 2. (на+*a.*) to point (at, to); (*fig.*) to point out; у. на оши́бку to point out a mistake. 3. to explain; to give directions. 4. (*obs. or coll.*) to give orders.

указк|а, и, *f.* 1. pointer, fescue. 2. (*coll., pejor.*) orders; по чужо́й ~е at someone else's bidding.

ука́з|ный, *adj.* (*obs.*) 1. *adj. of* ~. 2. established by decree.

указу́ющий, *adj.* у. перст (*obs.*) forefinger, index finger.

ука́зчик, а, *m.* (*coll.*) person who gives orders; ты нам не у. you can't give us orders.

ука́зыва|ть, ю, *impf. of* указа́ть.

ука́лыва|ть, ю, *impf. of* уколо́ть.

укарау́л|ить, ю, ишь, *pf.* (*coll.*) to guard, watch.

ука́т|а́ть, а́ю, *pf.* (*of* ~ывать¹) 1. to roll (out); у. доро́гу to roll, make smooth a road. 2. (*coll.*) to wear out, tire out.

ука́т|а́ться, а́ется, *pf.* (*of* ~ываться¹) (*of a road surface, etc.*) to become smooth.

ука|ти́ть, чу́, ~тишь, *pf.* (*of* ~тывать²) 1. to roll away. 2. (*coll.*) to drive off.

ука|ти́ться, чу́сь, ~тишься, *pf.* (*of* ~тываться²) to roll away (*intrans.*).

ука́тыва|ть(ся)¹, ю, ет(ся), *impf. of* укатать(ся).

ука́тыва|ть(ся)², ю(сь), *impf. of* укати́ть(ся).

укач|а́ть, а́ю, *pf.* (*of* ~ивать) 1. to rock to sleep. 2. (*of motion of sea or of means of transport*) to make sick; меня́ ~а́ло (*impers.*) на парохо́де the motion of the boat made me sick, I was (sea-)sick on the boat.

ука́чива|ть, ю, *impf. of* укача́ть.

укип|а́ть, а́ю, *impf. of* ~е́ть.

укип|е́ть, лю́, и́шь, *pf.* (*of* ~а́ть) (*coll.*) to boil away.

укла́д, а, *m.* structure; у. жи́зни style of life; обще́ственно-экономи́ческий у. social and economic structure.

укла́дк|а, и, *f.* 1. packing; stacking, piling

stowing. **2.** laying (*of rails, sleepers, pipes, etc.*).

уклáдчик, а, *m.* **1.** packer. **2.** layer (*of rails, sleepers, etc.*).

уклáдыва|ть, ю, *impf. of* уложи́ть.

уклáдыва|ться[1], юсь, *impf. of* уложи́ться.

уклáдыва|ться[2], юсь, *impf. of* улéчься.

уклéйк|а, и, *f.* (*fish*) bleak (*Alburnus alburnus*).

уклóн, а, *m.* **1.** slope, declivity; inclination; gradient. **2.** (*fig.*) bias, tendency. **3.** (*polit.*) deviation.

уклонéни|е, я, *n.* deviation; у. от тéмы digression; у. от воéнной слýжбы evasion of military service.

уклони́зм, а, *m.* (*polit.*) deviationism.

уклони́ст, а, *m.* (*polit.*) deviationist.

уклон|и́ть, ю́, ∼и́шь, *pf.* (*of* ∼я́ть) to turn, fend off.

уклон|и́ться, ю́сь, ∼и́шься, *pf.* (*of* ∼я́ться) **1.** (от) to avoid; to evade; у. от удáра to dodge a blow; у. от прямóго отвéта to avoid giving a direct answer. **2.** to turn off, turn aside.

уклóнчив|ый (∼, ∼а), *adj.* **1.** evasive. **2.** (*obs.*) meek; compliant.

уклон|я́ть(ся), я́ю(сь), *impf. of* ∼и́ть(ся).

уключин|а, ы, *f.* rowlock.

укокóш|ить, у, ишь, *pf.* (*sl.*) to bump off.

укóл, а, *m.* **1.** prick; jab. **2.** (*mil.*) thrust. **3.** injection, 'jab'.

укол|óть, ю́, ∼ешь, *pf.* (*of* укáлывать) **1.** to prick. **2.** (*fig.*) to sting, wound; у. чьё-н. самолю́бие to touch someone's pride.

укомплектовáни|е, я, *n.* bringing up to strength.

укомплектóв|анный, *p.p.p. of* ∼áть *and adj.* complete, at full strength.

укомплект|овáть, ýю, *pf.* (*of* комплектовáть *and* ∼óвывать) **1.** to complete; to bring up to (full) strength; to man. **2.** (+*i.*) to equip (with), furnish (with).

укомплектóвыва|ть, ю, *impf. of* укомплектовáть.

укóр, а, *m.* reproach; ∼ы сóвести pangs of conscience.

укорáчива|ть, ю, *impf. of* укороти́ть.

укоренéни|е, я, *n.* **1.** implanting, inculcation. **2.** taking root, striking root.

укорен|и́ть, ю́, и́шь, *pf.* (*of* ∼я́ть) to implant, inculcate.

укорен|и́ться, ю́сь, и́шься, *pf.* (*of* ∼я́ться) to take, strike root (*also fig.*).

укорен|я́ть(ся), я́ю(сь), *impf. of* ∼и́ть(ся).

укори́зн|а, ы, *f.* reproach.

укори́зненный, *adj.* reproachful.

укор|и́ть, ю́, и́шь, *pf.* (*of* ∼я́ть) (+*a.* в+*p.*) to reproach (with).

укоро|ти́ть, чý, ти́шь, *pf.* (*of* укорáчивать) to shorten.

укор|я́ть, я́ю, *impf. of* ∼и́ть.

укóс[1], а, *m.* hay-harvest, hay crop.

укóс[2], а, *m.* = ∼и́на.

укóсин|а, ы, *f.* (*tech.*) strut, brace; cantilever; (crane) jib.

украдкóй, *adv.* stealthily, furtively, by stealth.

украи́н|ец, ца, *m.* Ukrainian.

украи́нк|а[1], и, *f.* Ukrainian (woman).

украи́нк|а[2], и, *f.* Ukrainka (*variety of winter wheat*).

украи́нский, *adj.* Ukrainian.

укрá|сить, шу, сишь, *pf.* (*of* ∼шáть) to adorn, decorate, ornament (*also fig.*).

укрá|ситься, шусь, сишься, *pf.* (*of* ∼шáться) **1.** *pass. of* ∼сить. **2.** to adorn oneself.

укрá|сть, дý, дёшь, *past* ∼л, *pf.* (*of* крáсть) to steal.

украшá|ть(ся), ю(сь), *impf. of* украси́ть(ся).

украшéни|е, я, *n.* **1.** adorning, decoration. **2.** adornment, decoration, ornament.

укреп|и́ть, лю́, и́шь, *pf.* (*of* ∼ля́ть) **1.** to strengthen; to reinforce; to make fast. **2.** (*mil.*) to fortify. **3.** (*fig.*) to fortify, brace. **4.** (*fig.*) to strengthen; to enhance; у. дисципли́ну to tighten up discipline.

укреп|и́ться, лю́сь, и́шься, *pf.* (*of* ∼ля́ться) **1.** to become stronger. **2.** (*mil.*) to fortify one's position. **3.** (*fig.*) to become firmly established.

укреплéни|е, я, *n.* **1.** strengthening, reinforcing. **2.** (*mil.*) fortification; work.

укреп|лённый, *p.p.p. of* ∼и́ть *and adj.* (*mil.*) fortified.

укрепля́|ть(ся), ю(сь), *impf. of* укрепи́ть(ся).

укрепля́ющ|ее, его, *n.* tonic, restorative.

укрóм|ный (∼ен, ∼на), *adj.* secluded; sheltered; cosy.

укрóп, а, *m.* (*bot.*) dill (*Anethum graveolens*); волóшский у. fennel (*Foeniculum vulgare*); морскóй у. samphire (*Crithmum maritimum*).

укрóп|ный, *adj. of* ∼; ∼ное мáсло dill oil.

укроти́тел|ь, я, *m.* (animal-)tamer.

укро|ти́ть, щý, ти́шь, *pf.* (*of* ∼щáть) **1.** to tame. **2.** to curb, subdue, check; у. свои́ стрáсти to curb one's passions.

укро|ти́ться, щýсь, ти́шься, *pf.* (*of* ∼щáться) **1.** to become tame. **2.** to calm down, die down.

укрощá|ть(ся), ю(сь), *impf. of* укроти́ть(ся).

укрупнéни|е, я, *n.* enlargement, extension; amalgamation (*of collective farms, etc.*).

укрупн|и́ть, ю́, и́шь, *pf.* (*of* ∼я́ть) to enlarge, extend; to amalgamate.

укрупн|я́ть, я́ю, *impf. of* ∼и́ть.

укрывáтел|ь, я, *m.* (*leg.*) concealer, harbourer; у. крáденого receiver (of stolen goods).

укрыва́тельств|о, а, *n.* (*leg.*) concealment, harbouring; у. кра́деного receiving (of stolen goods).

укрыва́|ть(ся), ю(сь), *impf. of* укры́ть(ся).

укры́ти|е, я, *n.* (*mil., etc.*) cover, concealment; shelter; у. от огня́ cover (from fire); у. от взо́ров concealment; стреля́ть из ∼й to fire from covered positions.

укры́т|ый, *p.p.p. of* ∼ь *and adj.* (*mil.*) concealed, covered.

укр|ы́ть, о́ю, о́ешь, *pf.* (*of* ∼ыва́ть) 1. to cover (up). 2. to conceal, harbour; to give shelter; to receive (*stolen goods*); у. уби́йцу to harbour a murderer; у. от дождя́ to give shelter from the rain.

укр|ы́ться, о́юсь, о́ешься, *pf.* (*of* ∼ыва́ться) 1. to cover oneself (up). 2. to take cover; to seek shelter. 3. to escape notice; от меня́ не ∼ы́лось it has not escaped my notice.

у́ксус, а (у), *m.* vinegar.

у́ксусник, а, *m.* vinegar-cruet.

у́ксусниц|а, ы, *f.* = у́ксусник.

уксусноки́сл|ый, *adj.* (*chem.*) acetate (of); ∼ая соль acetate.

у́ксусн|ый, *adj.* 1. *adj. of* у́ксус. 2. acetic; ∼ая кислота́ acetic acid; ∼ая плёнка flower of vinegar; ∼ая эссе́нция vinegar essence.

уку́порива|ть, ю, *impf. of* уку́порить.

уку́пор|ить, ю, ишь, *pf.* (*of* ∼ивать) 1. to cork (up). 2. (*coll.*) to pack (up), crate.

уку́порк|а, и, *f.* 1. corking. 2. packing, crating.

уку́с, а, *m.* bite; sting.

уку|си́ть, шу́, ∼сишь, *pf.* to bite; to sting; кака́я му́ха его́ ∼си́ла? (*coll.*) what's bitten him?, what's got into him?

уку́т|ать, аю, *pf.* (*of* ∼ывать) (в+*a.*) to wrap up (in).

уку́т|аться, аюсь, *pf.* (*of* ∼ываться) to wrap oneself up.

уку́тыва|ть(ся), ю(сь), *impf. of* уку́тать(ся).

ула́влива|ть, ю, *impf. of* улови́ть.

ула́|дить, жу, дишь, *pf.* (*of* ∼живать) 1. to settle, arrange. 2. (*obs.*) to reconcile.

ула́жива|ть, ю, *impf. of* ула́дить.

ула́мыва|ть, ю, *impf. of* улом́ать.

ула́н, а, *g. pl.* ∼ов *and* (*in collect. sense*) ула́н, *m.* (*mil.*) uhlan.

ула́н|ский, *adj. of* ∼.

улеж|а́ть, у́, и́шь, *pf.* (*coll.*) to lie down.

у́л|ей, ья, *m.* (bee)hive.

улепет|ну́ть, ну́, нёшь, *pf. of* ∼ывать.

улепётыва|ть, ю, *impf.* (*of* улепетну́ть) (*coll.*) to make off, bolt; ∼й! hop it!

уле|сти́ть, щу́, сти́шь, *pf.* (*of* ∼ща́ть) (*coll.*) to butter up, chat up.

улет|а́ть, а́ю, *impf. of* ∼е́ть.

уле|те́ть, чу́ ти́шь, *pf.* (*of* ∼та́ть) 1. to fly

(away). 2. (*fig.*) to fly; to vanish; вре́мя ∼те́ло the time had flown by.

улету́чива|ться, юсь, *impf. of* улету́читься.

улету́ч|иться, усь, ишься, *pf.* (*of* ∼иваться) 1. to evaporate, volatilize. 2. (*coll.*) to vanish, disappear.

ул|е́чься, я́гусь, я́жешься, я́гутся, *past* ∼ёгся, ∼егла́сь, *pf.* 1. (*impf.* укла́дываться²) to lie down. 2. (*impf.* укла́дываться²) to find room (*lying down*). 3. (*of dust, etc.*) to settle. 4. (*fig.*) to subside; to calm down; ве́тер ∼ёгся the wind dropped.

улеща́|ть, ю, *impf. of* улести́ть.

улизн|у́ть, у́, ёшь, *pf.* (*coll.*) to slip away, steal away.

ули́к|а, и, *f.* (piece of) evidence.

ули́тк|а, и, *f.* 1. (*zool.*) snail; (*pl.*) Gastropoda. 2. (*anat.*) cochlea.

у́лиц|а, ы, *f.* street; (*fig.*; *pejor.*) 'the streets' на ∼е (*i*) in the street, (*ii*) out of doors, outside; оказа́ться на ∼е (*fig.*) to find onesel in the street; бу́дет и на на́шей ∼е пра́зд ник our day will come; с ∼ы from out o doors; челове́к с ∼ы anyone (who happen to be about).

улич|а́ть, а́ю, *impf. of* ∼и́ть.

улич|и́ть, у́, и́шь, *pf.* (*of* ∼а́ть) (в+*p.*) to establish the guilt (of).

ули́чн|ый, *adj.* street (*also fig.*, *pejor.*); у. бо street fighting; ∼ая де́вка (*coll.*) street walker; ∼ая пре́сса gutter press.

уло́в, а, *m.* catch (*of fish*).

улов|и́мый, *pres. part. pass. of* ∼и́ть *and ad* perceptible; audible.

улови́тел|ь, я, *m.* (*tech.*) detector, locator.

улов|и́ть, лю́, ∼ишь, *pf.* (*of* ула́вливат 1. (*tech.*) to catch, pick up, locate (*a soun wave, etc.*). 2. to detect, perceive; у. но́тк нетерпе́ния в чьём-н. го́лосе to detect note of impatience in someone's voic 3. (*coll.*) to seize (*an opportunity, etc.*).

уло́вк|а, и, *f.* trick, ruse, subterfuge.

уложе́ни|е, я, *n.* (*leg.*) code (*esp.*, *hist.*) the Russian Law Code of 1649).

улож|и́ть, у́, ∼ишь, *pf.* (*of* укла́дыват 1. to lay; у. в посте́ль, у. спать to put bed; у. в гроб (*fig.*) to be the death (o 2. to pack; to stow; to pile, stack. 3. (+ to cover (with), lay (with). 4. to lay (*rai sleepers, etc.*). 5. (*pf. only*) (*coll.*) to lay o (= to kill).

улож|и́ться, у́сь, ∼ишься, *pf.* (*of* укла́д ваться¹) 1. to pack (up). 2. (в+*a.*) to (in), fit (in); шу́ба не ∼ится в э́тот чемод a fur coat won't go into that case 3. (в+ *coll.*) to keep (within), confine oneself у. в стипе́ндию to keep within the bour of, manage on a scholarship; у. в полча to confine oneself to half an hour. 4. у голове́, в созна́нии to sink in, go in.

уломá|ть, ю, *pf.* (*of* улáмывать) (*coll.*) to talk round; (+*inf.*) to talk into, prevail upon (to).

у́лочк|а, и, *f. dim. of* у́лица.

улу́с, а, *m.* ulus (= (i) *settlement or nomad camp in some parts of Siberia,* (ii) *former administrative division in Yakut A.S.S.R., etc.*).

улуч|áть, áю, *impf. of* ~и́ть.

улуч|и́ть, у́, и́шь, *pf.* (*of* ~áть) (*coll.*) to find, seize, catch; у. момéнт для разговóра to find a moment for a talk; у. удóбный слу́чай to seize an opportunity.

улучш|áть(ся), áю(сь), *impf. of* ~и́ть(ся).

улучшéни|е, я, *n.* improvement, amelioration.

улу́чш|ить, у, ишь, *pf.* (*of* ~áть) to improve; to ameliorate, make better; to better.

улу́чш|иться, усь, ишься, *pf.* (*of* ~áться) to improve; to get better.

улыб|áться, áюсь, *impf.* (*of* ~ну́ться) **1.** to smile. **2.** (+*d.*; *fig.*) to smile (upon). **3.** (*impf. only*) (+*d.*; *coll.*) to please; задáча э́та мне вóвсе не ~áется I don't like the idea of this task at all.

улы́бк|а, и, *f.* smile.

улыб|ну́ться, ну́сь, нёшься, *pf.* **1.** *pf. of* ~áться. **2.** (*coll.*) to fail to materialize; to fall through; to vanish, disappear; нáша нóвая квартира ~ну́лась our new flat failed to materialize, our hopes of a new flat were dashed.

улы́бчив|ый (~, ~а), *adj.* (*coll.*) smiling; happy.

ультимати́в|ный (~ен, ~на), *adj.* categorical, having the nature of an ultimatum.

ультимáтум, а, *m.* ultimatum

ультра- ultra-.

ультразвуковóй, *adj.* (*phys., aeron.*) supersonic.

ультракорóтк|ий, *adj.* (*radio*) ultra-short; ~ие вóлны VHF waveband.

ультрамари́н, а, *m.* ultramarine.

ультрафиолéтовый, *adj.* ultra-violet.

улюлю́ка|ть, ю, *impf.* **1.** (*hunting*) to halloo. **2.** (*coll., pejor.*) to whoop (*in mockery*).

ум, á, *m.* mind, intellect; wits; склад ~á mentality; ~á не приложу́ (*coll.*) it's beyond me, I give up; у меня́ ум за рáзум захóдит (*coll.*) I am at my wits' end; быть без ~á (от) to be out of one's mind (about), be mad, crazy (about); (считáть, *etc.*) в ~é (to count, *etc.*) in one's head; в умé ли ты? (*coll.*) are you in your right mind?; и в ~é у меня́ нé было (*coll.*) the thought never even entered my head; взя́ться за ум (*coll.*) to come to one's senses; э́то у меня́ из ~á нейдёт (*coll.*) I can't get it out of my head; прийти́ на ум (+*d.*) (*coll.*) to occur to one, cross one's mind; быть на ~é (*coll.*)

to be on one's mind; от большóго ~á (*coll., iron.*) in one's infinite wisdom; свести́ с ~á (*coll.*) to drive mad; (*fig.*) to make wild (*with delight, admiration*), send; сойти́ с ~á to go mad; (по+*d. or p.*; *fig.*) to go crazy (about); с ~óм (*coll.*) sensibly, intelligently; с умá сойти́! (*coll.*) incredible!

умалéни|е, я, *n.* belittling, disparagement.

умал|и́ть, ю́, и́шь, *pf.* (*of* ~я́ть) **1.** (*obs.*) to decrease, lessen. **2.** to belittle, disparage.

умалишéнн|ый, *adj.* mad, lunatic; *as noun* у., ~ого, *m.*; ~ая, ~ой, *f.* madman, madwoman; lunatic; дом ~ых lunatic asylum.

умáлчива|ть, ю, *impf. of* умолчáть.

умал|я́ть, я́ю, *impf. of* ~и́ть.

умáслива|ть, ю, *impf. of* умáслить.

умáсл|ивать, ю, ишь, *pf.* (*of* ~ивать) (*coll.*) to butter up.

ума|сти́ть, щу́, сти́шь, *pf.* (*of* ~щáть) (*obs.*) to anoint.

умащá|ть, ю, *impf. of* умасти́ть.

умá|ять, ю, *pf.* (*coll.*) to tire out.

у́мбр|а, ы, *f.* umbre.

умéл|ец, ьца, *m.* skilled craftsman.

умéл|ый, *adj.* able, skilful; capable; у. рабóтник able workman; ~ая поли́тика astute policy.

умéни|е, я, *n.* ability, skill; know-how.

уменьшáем|ое, ого, *n.* (*math.*) minuend.

уменьш|áть(ся), áю(сь), *impf. of* ~и́ть(ся).

уменьшéни|е, я, *n.* reduction, diminution, decrease, lessening, abatement; у. скóрости deceleration.

уменьши́тельн|ый, *adj.* **1.** diminishing. **2.** (*gram.*) diminutive. **3.** ~ое и́мя familiar variant of first name (*as* Kolya *for* Nikolai).

умéньш|ить, ~у, ~ишь, *pf.* (*of* ~áть) to reduce, diminish, decrease, lessen; у. ход to reduce speed; у. цéны to reduce prices; у. расхóды to cut down expenditure.

умéньш|иться, ~усь, ~ишься, *pf.* (*of* ~áться) **1.** to diminish, decrease, drop, dwindle; to abate. **2.** *pass. of* ~ить.

умéренност|ь, и, *f.* moderation, moderateness; temperance.

умéр|енный, *p.p.p. of* ~ить *and adj.* **1.** (~ен, ~енна) moderate (*polit.*; *also fig.*); у. аппети́т moderate appetite; ~енная поли́тика moderate policy. **2.** (*geogr., meteor.*) temperate; moderate; у. пóяс temperate zone; у. вéтер moderate breeze (*on Beaufort scale*).

умер|éть, умру́, умрёшь, *past* у́мер, ~лá, у́мерло, *pf.* (*of* умирáть) to die; у. естéственной, наси́льственной смéртью to die a natural, a violent death; у. от, со ску́ки to be bored to death.

умéр|ить, ю, ишь, *pf.* (*of* ~я́ть) to moderate; to restrain.

умéр|иться, юсь, ишься, *pf.* (*of* ~я́ться)

1. to become more moderate; to abate, die down. **2.** *pass. of* ~ить.

умер|твить, щвлю, твишь, *pf.* (*of* ~щвлять) to kill, destroy (*also fig.*); to mortify; у. все свои творческие побуждения to stifle all one's creative impulses.

умерщвлени|е, я, *n.* killing, destruction (*also fig.*); mortification.

умерщвля|ть, ю, *impf. of* умертвить.

умер|ять(ся), яю(сь), *impf. of* ~ить(ся).

уме|стить (ся), щу, стишь, *pf.* (*of* ~щать) to get in, fit in, find room (for); она не могла у. все покупки в сумку she could not get all her purchases into her bag.

уме|ститься, щусь, стишься, *pf.* (*of* ~щаться) to go in, fit in, find room.

уместно¹, *adv.* appropriately; opportunely.

уместно², *as pred.* it is appropriate; it is in order, it is proper, it is not out of place; у. было бы сделать намёк it would not be out of place to drop a hint.

умест|ный (~ен, ~на), *adj.* appropriate; pertinent, to the point; opportune, timely; у. вопрос pertinent question; ваше предложение вполне ~но your suggestion is quite in order.

уме|ть, ю, *impf.* (*of* с~) (+ *inf.*) to be able (to), know how (to).

умеща|ть(ся), ю(сь), *impf. of* уместить(ся).

умеючи, *adv.* (*coll.*) skilfully.

умилени|е, я, *n.* emotion; tenderness; прийти в у. to be moved; лить слёзы ~я to shed tears of emotion, weep with emotion.

умилител|ьный (~ен, ~ьна), *adj.* moving, touching, affecting.

умил|ить, ю, ишь, *pf.* (*of* ~ять) to move, touch.

умил|иться, юсь, ишься, *pf.* (*of* ~яться) to be moved, be touched.

умилосерд|ить, ишь, *pf.* to propitiate, mollify.

умилостив|ить, лю, ишь, *pf.* = умилосердить.

умил|ьный (~ен, ~ьна), *adj.* **1.** touching, affecting; ~ьное личико nice face. **2.** (*pejor.*) ingratiating, smarmy.

умил|ять(ся), яю(сь), *impf. of* ~ить(ся).

умина|ть, ю, *impf. of* умять.

умирани|е, я, *n.* dying.

умира|ть, ю, *impf. of* умереть.

умир|ить, ю, ишь, *pf.* (*of* ~ять) (*obs.*) to calm.

умиротворени|е, я, *n.* pacification; conciliation; appeasement.

умиротворён|ный (~, ~на), *adj.* tranquil; contented.

умиротвор|ить, ю, ишь, *pf.* (*of* ~ять) to pacify; to appease.

умиротвор|ять, яю, *impf. of* ~ить.

умир|ять, яю, *impf. of* ~ить.

умлаут, а, *m.* (*ling.*) umlaut.

умн|ее, *comp. of* ~ый *and* ~о.

умне|ть, ю, *impf.* (*of* по~) to grow wiser.

умник, а, *m.* **1.** good boy; (*coll.*) clever person. **2.** (*iron.*) know-all, smart Alec.

умниц|а, ы, (*coll.*) **1.** (*f.*) good girl. **2.** (*m. and f.*) clever person.

умнича|ть, ю, *impf.* (*of* с~) (*coll.*) **1.** (*iron.*) to show off one's intelligence. **2.** (*pejor.*) to try to be clever.

умнож|ать, аю(сь), *impf. of* ~ить(ся).

умножени|е, я, *n.* **1.** increase, rise. **2.** (*math.*) multiplication.

умнож|итель, я, *m.* у. частоты (*radio*) frequency multiplier.

умнож|ить, у, ишь, *pf.* (*of* множить *and* ~ать) **1.** to increase, augment. **2.** (*math.*) to multiply.

умнож|иться, усь, ишься, *pf.* (*of* множиться *and* ~аться) **1.** to increase, multiply (*intrans.*). **2.** *pass. of* ~ить.

умно¹, *adv.* cleverly, wisely; sensibly.

умно², *as pred.* it is wise; it is sensible.

ум|ный (~ён, ~на, ~но), *adj.* clever, wise, intelligent; sensible.

умозаключ|ать, аю, *impf. of* ~ить.

умозаключени|е, я, *n.* deduction; conclusion, inference.

умозаключ|ить, у, ишь, *pf.* (*of* ~ать) to deduce; to conclude, infer.

умозрени|е, я, *n.* (*philos.*) speculation.

умозрител|ьный (~ен, ~ьна), *adj.* (*philos.*) speculative.

умоисступлени|е, я, *n.* delirium; действовать в ~и to act while the balance of one's mind is disturbed.

умол|ить, ю, ишь, *pf.* (*of* ~ять) to move by entreaties.

умолк: без ~у (*to talk, etc.*) unceasingly, incessantly.

умолк|ать, аю, *impf. of* ~нуть.

умолк|нуть, ну, нешь, *past* ~, ~ла, *pf.* (*of* ~ать) to fall silent, lapse into silence; (*of noises*) to cease, stop.

умолот, а, *m.* (*agric.*) yield (*of threshed grain*).

умолчани|е, я, *n.* **1.** passing over in silence, failure to mention, suppression. **2.** (*lit.*) aposiopesis.

умолча|ть, ю, *pf.* (*of* умалчивать) (о+*p.*) to pass over in silence, fail to mention, suppress, hush up.

умол|ять, яю, *impf.* **1.** *impf. of* ~ить. **2.** to entreat, implore.

умоля|ющий, *pres. part. act. of* ~ть *and adj.* imploring, pleading, suppliant.

умонастроени|е, я, *n.* frame of mind.

умопомешательств|о, а, *n.* derangement of mind.

умопомрачени|е, я, *n.* (*obs.*) derangement

of mind; fit of insanity; до ~я (*coll.*) stupendously, tremendously.

умопомрачи́тел|ьный (~ен, ~ьна), *adj.* (*coll.*) stupendous, tremendous, terrific.

умо́р|а, ы, *f.* **1.** (*dial.*) exhaustion. **2.** (*as pred.*) (*coll.*) it's killing, it's incredibly funny.

умори́тельн|о¹, *adv. of* ~ый.

умори́тельно², *as pred.* = умо́ра 2.

умори́тел|ьный (~ен, ~ьна), *adj.* (*coll.*) killing, incredibly funny.

умор|и́ть, ю́, и́шь, *pf.* (*of* мори́ть¹) (*coll.*) **1.** to kill; (*fig.*) to be the death (of); у. кого́-н. со́ смеху to make someone die of laughing. **2.** to tire out, exhaust.

у́мственн|о, *adv. of* ~ый; у. отста́лый retarded, backward.

у́мственн|ый, *adj.* mental, intellectual; у. бага́ж mental equipment, store of knowledge; у. труд brainwork; рабо́тник ~ого труда́ brainworker.

у́мствовани|е, я, *n.* (*pejor.*) theorizing, philosophizing.

у́мств|овать, ую, *impf.* (*pejor.*) to theorize, philosophize.

умудр|и́ть, ю́, и́шь, *pf.* (*of* ~я́ть) to teach, make wiser.

умудр|и́ться, ю́сь, и́шься, *pf.* (*of* ~я́ться) (*coll.*) to contrive, manage (*also, iron., to do something which might easily have been avoided*).

умудр|я́ть(ся), я́ю(сь), *impf. of* ~и́ть(ся).

умфо́рмер, а, *m.* (*electr.*) transformer.

умч|а́ть, у́, и́шь, *pf.* to whirl, hurtle away.

умч|а́ться, у́сь, и́шься, *pf.* **1.** to whirl, hurtle away (*intrans.*). **2.** (*fig.*) to fly away.

умыва́льн|ая, ой, *f.* wash-room.

умыва́льник, а, *m.* wash-(hand-)stand; wash-basin.

умыва́льн|ый, *adj.* wash, washing; ~ая ко́мната wash-room; у. таз wash-basin.

умыва́|ть(ся), ю(сь), *impf. of* умы́ть(ся).

умыка́ни|е, я, *n.* (*ethnol.*) abduction (*of bride from her parents*).

у́мыс|ел, ла, *m.* design, intention; со злым ~лом with malicious intent; (*leg.*) of malice prepense.

умы́сл|ить, ю, ишь, *pf.* (*of* умышля́ть) (+*inf.*) to intend, design; (+*a.*) to plan, plot.

ум|ы́ть, о́ю, о́ешь, *pf.* (*of* ~ыва́ть) to wash; у. ру́ки to wash one's hands (*also fig.*).

ум|ы́ться, о́юсь, о́ешься, *pf.* (*of* ~ыва́ться) to wash (oneself).

умы́шленно, *adv.* purposely, intentionally.

умы́|шленный, *p.p.p. of* ~слить *and adj.* intentional, deliberate, premeditated.

умышля́|ть, ю, *impf. of* умы́слить.

умягч|а́ть, а́ю, *impf. of* ~и́ть.

умягч|и́ть, у́, и́шь, *pf.* (*of* ~а́ть) to soften; to mollify.

умя́ть, умну́, умнёшь, *pf.* (*of* умина́ть) **1.** to knead well. **2.** (*coll.*) to press down; to tread down. **3.** (*sl.*) to stuff down (= to eat).

унава́живать = унаво́живать.

унаво́жива|ть, ю, *impf. of* унаво́зить.

унаво́|зить, жу, зишь, *pf.* (*of* навози́ть *and* ~живать) to manure.

унасле́д|овать, ую, *pf. of* насле́довать 1.

унди́н|а, ы, *f.* undine, water-sprite.

унес|ти́, у́, ёшь, *past* ~, ~ла́, *pf.* (*of* уноси́ть) **1.** to take away. **2.** (*coll.*) to carry off, make off with. **3.** to carry away, remove; ло́дку ~ло́ (*impers.*) тече́нием the boat was carried away by the current; ~и́ ты моё го́ре! (*interj. expressing disapproval*) heaven help us! **4.** (*fig.*) to carry (*in thought*).

унес|ти́сь, у́сь, ёшься, *past* ~ся, ~ла́сь, *pf.* (*of* уноси́ться) **1.** to whirl away (*intrans.*). **2.** (*fig.*) to fly away, fly by; го́ды ~ли́сь the years flew by. **3.** (*fig.*) to travel (*in thought*).

униа́т, а, *m.* (*rel.*) member of Uniat(e) Church.

униа́тский, *adj.* (*rel.*) Uniat(e).

универма́г, а, *m.* (*abbr. of* универса́льный магази́н) department store.

универса́л, а, *m.* **1.** all-round craftsman. **2.** (*geod.*) theodolite.

универса́л|ьный (~ен, ~ьна), *adj.* **1.** universal; all-round; ~ьное сре́дство panacea; у. магази́н department store; ~ьные зна́ния encyclopaedic knowledge. **2.** many-sided; versatile; ~ьное образова́ние many-sided education; у. челове́к versatile person. **3.** (*tech.*) multi-purpose, all-purpose; у. инструме́нт (*astron. and geod.*) theodolite; у. ключ universal wrench; ~ьное пита́ние (*electr.*) mains-or-battery power supply.

универса́м, а, *m.* supermarket.

университе́т, а, *m.* university; у. культу́ры 'university of culture' (*institution providing lecture courses, etc., on general and political topics for adults*); поступи́ть в у. to enter, go up to university; око́нчить у. to graduate (*from a university*).

университе́т|ский, *adj. of* ~.

унижа́|ть(ся), ю(сь), *impf. of* уни́зить(ся).

униже́ни|е, я, *n.* humiliation, degradation, abasement.

уни́жен|ный, *p.p.p. of* уни́зить *and adj.* (~, ~на) humble.

унижён|ный (~, ~на), *adj.* oppressed, degraded.

уни|за́ть, жу́, ~жешь, *pf.* (*of* ~зыва́ть) (+*i.*) to cover (with), stud (with).

унизи́тел|ьный (~ен, ~ьна), *adj.* humiliating, degrading.

уни|зить, жу, зишь, *pf.* (*of* ~жа́ть) to humble, humiliate; to lower, degrade.

уни|зиться, жусь, зишься, *pf.* (*of* ~жáться) to debase oneself, demean oneself; у. до шантажá to stoop to blackmail.

унизывá|ть, ю, *impf. of* унизáть.

уникáл|ьный (~ен, ~ьна), *adj.* unique.

ýникум, а, *m.* unique object (*of its kind*).

унимá|ть(ся), ю(сь), *impf. of* унять(ся).

унисóн, а, *m.* (*mus. and phys.*) unison; в у. in unison; (*fig.*) in unison, in concert.

унитáз, а, *m.* lavatory pan.

унитáрный, *adj.* unitary; у. патрóн (*mil.*) fixed round.

унификáци|я, и, *f.* unification; standardization.

унифицúр|овать, ую, *impf. and pf.* to unify; to standardize.

унифóрм|а, ы, *f.* 1. (*obs.*) uniform. 2. (*collect.*) circus staff (*in the ring*).

униформúст, а, *m.* circus hand (*in the ring*).

уничижá|ть, ю, *impf.* (*obs.*) to disparage.

уничижéни|е, я, *n.* disparaging, disparagement.

уничижúтел|ьный (~ен, ~ьна), *adj.* 1. (*obs.*) disparaging. 2. (*gram.*) pejorative.

уничтож|áть, áю, *impf. of* ~ить.

уничтожá|ющий, *pres. part. act. of* ~ть *and adj.* destructive; у. взгляд murderous look; ~ющее замечáние scathing comment.

уничтожéни|е, я, *n.* 1. destruction, annihilation; extermination, obliteration. 2. abolition, elimination.

уничтóж|ить, у, ишь, *pf.* (*of* ~áть) 1. to destroy, annihilate; to wipe out; to exterminate, obliterate; у. силы протúвника to wipe out the enemy's forces. 2. to abolish; to do away with, eliminate; to cancel (out); у. крепостнóе прáво to abolish serfdom. 3. (*fig.*) to crush, make mincemeat (of), tear to shreds (*with an argument, etc.*).

ýни|я, и, *f.* (*hist., eccl.*) union (*esp. of the act of 1596 by which the Uniat(e) Church was set up*).

унóс, а, *m.* 1. taking away, carrying away. 2. (*obs.*) pair (*of a team of horses*).

уно|сúть(ся), шý(сь), ~сишь(ся), *impf. of* унестú(сь).

ýнтер, а, *m.* = ~-офицéр.

ýнтер-офицéр, а, *m.* non-commissioned officer.

унт|ы́, óв, *sing.* ~, ~á, *m.* (*and* ýнт|ы, ~, *sing.* ~а, ~ы, *f.*) high boots (*of inverted pelt or goatskin*).

ýнци|я, и, *f.* ounce (*measure*).

унывá|ть, ю, *impf.* to be depressed, be dejected.

уны́л|ый (~, ~а), *adj.* 1. (*of persons*) depressed, dejected, despondent, downcast. 2. (*of thoughts, looks, etc.*) melancholy, doleful, cheerless.

уны́ни|е, я, *n.* depression, dejection, despon-

dency; впасть в у. to become depresse[d] навестú у. to depress.

уня́|ть, уймý, уймёшь, *past* ~л, ~лá, ~[л] *pf.* (*of* унимáть) 1. to calm, soothe, paci[fy] у. дерýщихся to stop a fight. 2. (*coll.*) stop, check; у. пожáр to stop a fire. 3. suppress (*feelings*).

уня́|ться, уймýсь, уймёшься, *past* ~л[ся] ~лáсь, *pf.* (*of* унимáться) 1. to calm dow[n] 2. (*coll.*) to stop, abate, die down; кро[вь] течéние ~лóсь the bleeding has stoppe[d]

упá|вший, *past part. act. of* ~сть *and adj.* falle[n] (*of voice or tone*) weak (*from emotion or fear*)

упáд: до ~у to the point of exhaustion, [till] one drops.

упадá|ть, ю, *impf.* (*obs.*) to fall.

упáд|ок, ка, *m.* 1. decline (*of polit. syste[m]* *culture, etc.*); в состоя́нии ~ка on the d[e]cline. 2. decline, decay, collapse (*of ph[ysi]cal or spiritual faculties*); у. дýха depressio[n] у. сил breakdown.

упáдочнический, *adj.* decadent.

упáдочничеств|о, а, *n.* decadence.

упáдоч|ный (~ен, ~на), *adj.* 1. *adj.* упáдок 1; decadent. 2. depressive; ~н[ое] настроéние depression.

упак|овáть, ýю, *pf.* (*of* паковáть *and* ~óв[ы]вать) to pack (up), wrap (up), bale.

упакóвк|а, и, *f.* 1. packing (*action*), wra[p]ping, baling. 2. packing (*material*), pa[ck]age.

упакóвочн|ый, *adj.* packing; ~ая кл[еть] packing crate; у. материáл packi[ng] material; *as noun* ~ая, ~ой, *f.* packi[ng] -house.

упакóвщик, а, *m.* packer.

упакóвыва|ть, ю, *impf. of* упаковáть.

упáрива|ть, ю, *impf. of* упáрить.

упáр|ить, ю, ишь, *pf.* (*of* ~ивать) to b[oil] down, concentrate.

упас|тú, ý, ёшь, *past* ~, ~лá, *pf.* (*coll.*) save, preserve; ~й Бог, Бóже ~й (i) (*expre[ss]ing warning not to do something*) God prese[rve] you!, heaven help you!, (ii) (*expressing vi[gor]ous denial*) good God, no!; God forbid!

упá|сть, дý, дёшь, *past* ~л, *pf.* (*of* пáдать) (*in var. senses*) to fall.

упёк[1], а, *m.* loss of weight in baking.

упёк[2], *see* упéчь.

упер|éть, упрý, упрёшь, *past* ~, ~ла, *pf.* упирáть) 1. (*a.* в+*a.*) to rest (agains[t]) prop (against), lean (against); у. лéстни[цу] в стéну to rest a ladder against the wall; глазá в когó-н. (*coll.*) to fasten one's g[aze] upon someone. 2. (*sl.*) to pinch, filch.

упер|éться, упрýсь, упрёшься, *past* ~[ся] ~лáсь, *pf.* (*of* упирáться) 1. (+*i.* в+*a.*) rest (against), prop (against), lean (agains[t]) у. лóктем в стол to rest one's elbow on [a] table; у. ногáми в зéмлю to dig one's h[eels] in the ground. **2.** (в+*a.*; *coll.*) to come up (against), bump (into) (*an obstacle*). **3.** (*coll.*) to jib; (*fig.*) to dig one's heels in.

упе́|чь, ку́, чёшь, ку́т, *past* ~к, ~кла́, *pf.* (*of* ~ка́ть) **1.** to bake thoroughly. **2.** (*coll.*) to drag off (*against one's will*); у. под суд to drag into court, through the courts.

упива́|ться, юсь, *impf. of* упи́ться.

упира́|ть, ю, *impf.* **1.** *impf. of* упере́ть. **2.** (*impf. only*) (на+*a.*; *coll.*) to stress, insist (on).

упира́|ться, юсь, *impf.* **1.** *impf. of* упере́ться. **2.** (*impf. only*) (в+*a.*; *coll.*) to come up (against), be held up (by), be stuck (on account of); прое́кт экспеди́ции ~ется в недоста́ток де́нег the plan for an expedition is held up for want of funds.

упи|са́ть[1], шу́, ~шешь, *pf.* (*of* ~сывать) to get in, fit in (*something written*); у. всё письмо́ на одно́м листе́ to get the whole letter on one sheet (*of paper*).

упи|са́ть[2], шу́, ~шешь, *pf.* (*of* ~сывать) (*coll.*) to get through, consume (= to eat up).

упи|са́ться, ~шется, *pf.* (*of* ~сываться) (*of something written*) to go in, fit in.

упи́сыва|ть(ся), ю(сь), *impf. of* уписа́ть(ся).

упи́танност|ь, и, *f.* nutritional state.

упи́тан|ный, *p.p.p. of* упита́ть *and adj.* (~, ~на) well-fed; fattened, fatted; plump.

упит|а́ть, а́ю, *pf.* (*of* ~ывать) to fatten (up).

упи́тыва|ть, ю, *impf. of* упита́ть.

упи́|ться, упью́сь, упьёшься, *past* ~лся, ~ла́сь, *pf.* (*of* ~ва́ться) (+*i.*) **1.** (*coll.*) to get drunk (on). **2.** (*fig.*) to revel (in), be intoxicated (by) (*sights, sounds, etc.*).

упла́т|а, ы, *f.* payment, paying; в ~у on account, in payment; подлежа́щий ~е payable.

упла|ти́ть, чу́, ~тишь,.*pf.* (*of* ~чивать) to pay; у. чле́нский взнос to pay a (membership) subscription; у. по счёту to pay a bill, settle an account.

упла́тный, *adj.* relating to payment.

упле|сти́, ту́, тёшь, *past* ~л, ~ла́, *pf.* (*of* ~та́ть) (*coll.*) to tuck in (to).

уплета́|ть, ю, *impf. of* уплести́.

уплотне́ни|е, я, n.* **1. consolidation, concentration, compression; packing (in); у. кварти́ры reduction of space per person in living accommodation; у. рабо́чего дня tightening up time-schedules to increase amount of work done. **2.** (*tech.*) sealing, luting. **3.** (*med.*) hardening (*of skin*).

уплотн|и́ть, ю́, и́шь, *pf.* (*of* ~я́ть) **1.** to consolidate, concentrate, compress; to pack (in); у. кварти́ру to reduce space per person in living accommodation, increase number of occupants per flat; у. рабо́чий день to plan the working day to increase

amount of work done. **2.** (*tech.*) to seal, lute.

уплотн|и́ться, юсь, и́шься, *pf.* (*of* ~я́ться) **1.** (*med.*) to harden. **2.** (+*i.*) to take in, give up part of one's accommodation (to). **3.** to condense, thicken; (*of fuel in combustion*) to sinter, clinker.

уплотн|я́ть(ся), я́ю(сь), *impf. of* ~и́ть(ся).

уплыва́|ть, ю, *impf. of* уплы́ть.

уплы́|ть, ву́, вёшь, *past* ~л, ~ла́, ~ло, *pf.* (*of* ~ва́ть) **1.** to swim away; to sail, steam away. **2.** to be lost to sight. **3.** (*fig., coll.*) to fly away, pass, elapse; нема́ло вре́мени ~ло much water has flowed beneath the bridges. **4.** (*fig., coll.*) to vanish, ebb; наде́жда ~ла́ hope faded.

**упова́ни|е, я, n.* (*obs.*) hope; возлага́ть все ~я (на+*a.*) to set all one's hopes (upon).

упова́|ть, ю, *impf.* (на+*a.*) to put one's trust (in); (+*inf.*) to hope to.

уподо́б|ить, лю, ишь, *pf.* (*of* ~ля́ть) to liken.

уподо́б|иться, люсь, ишься, *pf.* (*of* ~ля́ться) (+*d.*) **1.** to become like. **2.** (*ling.*) to become assimilated (to).

уподобле́ни|е, я, n.* **1. likening, comparison. **2.** (*ling.*) assimilation.

уподобля́|ть(ся), ю(сь), *impf. of* уподо́бить(ся).

**упое́ни|е, я, n.* ecstasy, rapture, thrill; с ~ем ecstatically.

упоён|ный, *part. as adj.* (+*i.*) intoxicated (with), thrilled (by), in raptures (about, over).

упои́тел|ьный (~ен, ~ьна), *adj.* intoxicating, ravishing.

**упокое́ни|е, я, n.* rest, repose; ме́сто ~я resting-place (= grave).

упоко́|ить, ю, ишь, *pf.* (*obs.*) to lay to rest (= to bury).

упоко́|иться, юсь, ишься, *pf.* (*obs.*) to find repose; to find one's resting-place (= to be buried).

уполз|а́ть, а́ю, *impf. of* ~ти́.

уполз|ти́, у́, ёшь, *past* ~, ~ла́, *pf.* (*of* ~а́ть) to creep, crawl away.

уполномо́ч|енный, *p.p.p. of* ~ить; *as noun* у., ~енного, *m.* plenipotentiary, representative, person authorized.

уполномо́чива|ть, ю, *impf. of* уполномо́чить.

**уполномо́чи|е, я, n.* authorization; подписа́ть докуме́нт по ~ю кого́-н. to sign a document on someone's authority.

уполномо́ч|ить, у, ишь, *pf.* (*of* ~ивать) to authorize, empower.

**уполо́вник, а, m.* (*dial.*) ladle.

**упомина́ни|е, я, n.* mentioning; (о+*p.*) mention (of), reference (to).

упомина́|ть, ю, *impf. of* упомяну́ть.

упомн|ить, ю, ишь, *pf.* (*coll.*) to remember.

упомян|у́ть, у́, ~ешь, *pf.* (*of* упомина́ть) (+*a. or* о+*p.*) to mention, refer (to).

упо́р, а, *m.* **1.** rest, prop, support; (*tech.*) stay, brace. **2.** (*tech.*) stop, lug; arresting device. **3.** в у. (*mil.*) point-blank (*also fig.*); сказа́ть кому́-н. в у. to tell someone point-blank, flat(ly); смотре́ть на кого́-н. в у. to stare straight at someone. **4.** сде́лать у. (на+*a. or p.*) to lay special stress (on).

упо́р|ный (~ен, ~на), *adj.* **1.** stubborn, unyielding, obstinate; dogged, persistent; sustained; у. челове́к stubborn person; у. ка́шель persistent cough; ~ная оборо́на sustained defence. **2.** (*tech.*) supporting; у. като́к bogie wheel; у. подши́пник thrust bearing. **3.** (*tech.*) stop; у. болт stop; у. рыча́г stop lever.

упо́рств|о, а, *n.* stubbornness, obstinacy; doggedness, persistence.

упо́рств|овать, ую, *impf.* to be stubborn, unyielding; (в+*p.*) to persist (in).

упорхн|у́ть, у́, ёшь, *pf.* to fly, flit away.

упоря́дочива|ть(ся), ю(сь), *impf. of* упоря́дочить(ся).

упоря́доч|ить, у, ишь, *pf.* (*of* ~ивать) to regulate, put in (good) order, set to rights.

упоря́доч|иться, ится, *pf.* (*of* ~иваться) to come right.

употреби́тельност|ь, и, *f.* (frequency of) use.

употреби́тел|ьный (~ен, ~ьна), *adj.* (widely-)used; common, generally accepted, usual; у. эвфеми́зм widely-used euphemism.

употреб|и́ть, лю́, и́шь, *pf.* (*of* ~ля́ть) (*in var. senses*) to use; to make use (of); to take (*drink, medicine, etc.*); у. все уси́лия to make every effort, do one's utmost; у. чьё-н. дове́рие во зло to abuse someone's confidence.

употребле́ни|е, я, *n.* use; application; спо́соб ~я direction for use (*of medicine, etc.*); для вну́треннего ~я to be taken internally; не для вну́треннего ~я not to be taken; вы́йти из ~я to go out of use, fall into disuse; вы́шедший из ~я out of use, obsolete.

употребля́|ть, ю, *impf. of* употреби́ть.

упра́в|а, ы, *f.* **1.** (*coll.*) control. **2.** (*coll.*) justice, satisfaction; иска́ть ~ы to seek justice; найти́ на кого́-н. ~у to obtain satisfaction from someone. **3.** (*hist.*) office, board, authority; у. благочи́ния police headquarters.

управде́л, а, *m.* (*abbr. of* управля́ющий дела́ми) office manager, business manager.

управдо́м, а, *m.* (*abbr. of* управля́ющий до́мом) manager of block of flats, house manager.

управи́тел|ь, я, *m.* (*obs.*) manager; bailiff, steward.

упра́в|иться, люсь, ишься, *pf.* (*of* ~ля́ться) (с+*i.*; *coll.*) **1.** to cope (with), manage. **2.** to deal (with) (= to get the better of).

управле́н|ец, ца, *m.* (*coll.*) manager, executive.

управле́ни|е, я, *n.* **1.** management, administration; direction; у. госуда́рством government; орке́стр под ~ем Мрави́нского orchestra conducted by Mravinsky. **2.** (*tech.*) control; driving; piloting; steering; у. на расстоя́нии remote control; у. по ра́дио radio control; у. автомоби́лем driving (a car); теря́ть у. to get out of control. **3.** government; о́рганы ме́стного ~я local government organs. **4.** (*governmental organ*) administration, authority, directorate, board; гла́вное у. ры́бного хозя́йства chief administration of fisheries. **5.** (*tech.*) controls; steering; щит ~я control panel. **6.** (*gram.*) government.

управле́н|ческий, *adj. of* ~ие 3, 4; у. аппара́т government apparatus.

управл|я́емый, *pres. part. pass. of* ~я́ть *and adj.*; у. снаря́д guided missile.

управля́|ть, ю, *impf.* (+*i.*) **1.** to manage, administer, direct, run; to govern; to be in charge (of); у. канцеля́рией to manage an office. **2.** (*tech.*) to control, operate (a machine); to drive (a car, etc.); to pilot; to steer; у. су́дном (*naut.*) to navigate a vessel; у. весло́м to row. **3.** (*gram.*) to govern.

управл|я́ющий, *pres. part. act. of* ~я́ть *and adj.* control, controlling; у. вал (*tech.*) camshaft; *as noun* у., ~я́ющего, *m.* manager; bailiff, steward; у. по́ртом harbour master.

упражне́ни|е, я, *n.* exercise.

упражня́|ть, ю, *impf.* to exercise, train; у. му́скулы to exercise one's muscles; у. па́мять to train one's memory.

упражня́|ться, юсь, *impf.* (в+*p.*, на+*p.*, с+*i.*) to practise, train (at); у. в стрельбе́ в цель to practise marksmanship.

упраздне́ни|е, я, *n.* abolition; cancellation, annulment.

упраздн|и́ть, ю́, и́шь, *pf.* (*of* ~я́ть) to abolish; to cancel, annul.

упраздн|я́ть, я́ю, *impf. of* ~и́ть.

упра́шива|ть, ю, *impf. of* упроси́ть.

упрева́|ть, ю, *impf. of* упре́ть.

упре|ди́ть, жу́, ди́шь, *pf.* (*of* ~жда́ть) (*obs.*) **1.** to warn. **2.** to forestall, anticipate.

упрежда́|ть, ю, *impf. of* упреди́ть.

упрежде́ни|е, я, *n.* **1.** (*obs.*) warning. **2.** (*obs.*) forestalling, anticipation. **3.** (*mil.*) range correction, lead (*for firing at moving target*).

упрёк, а, *m.* reproach, reproof; бро́сить кому́-н. to reproach, reprove someone; ста́вить кому́-н. что-н. в у. to hold something against someone.

упрек|а́ть, а́ю, *impf.* (*of* ~ну́ть) to reproach, reprove; (в+*p.*) to accuse (of), charge (with).

упрек|ну́ть, ну́, нёшь, *pf. of* ~а́ть.

упре́|ть, ю, *pf.* (*of* ~ва́ть) (*coll.*) 1. to be well stewed. 2. to be covered with sweat.

упро|си́ть, шу́, ~сишь, *pf.* (*of* упра́шивать) 1. to beg, entreat. 2. (*pf. only*) to prevail upon.

упро|сти́ть, щу́, сти́шь, *pf.* (*of* ~ща́ть) 1. to simplify; (до) to reduce (to). 2. (*pejor.*) to oversimplify.

упро|сти́ться, сти́тся, *pf.* (*of* ~ща́ться) to become simpler, be simplified.

упроче́ни|е, я, *n.* strengthening, consolidation; fixing, securing.

упро́чива|ть(ся), ю(сь), *impf. of* упро́чить-(ся).

упро́ч|ить, у, ишь, *pf.* (*of* ~ивать) 1. to strengthen, consolidate; to fix, secure; to establish firmly, place on firm foundations. 2. (за+*i.*) to grant permanent possession (to), leave (to); у. за кем-н. всё своё состоя́ние to leave one's entire estate to someone. 3. (за+*i.*) to ensure; его́ Пе́рвая симфо́ния ~ила за ним репута́цию выдаю́щегося компози́тора his First Symphony ensured his reputation as an outstanding composer.

упро́ч|иться, усь, ишься, *pf.* (*of* ~иваться) 1. to be strengthened, consolidated; to become firmer; to be firmly established; на́ше положе́ние ~илось our position is firmly established. 2. to establish oneself (firmly), settle oneself. 3. (за+*i.*) (*of property, etc.*) to be settled (upon). 4. (за+*i.*) to be ensured; to become firmly attached (to); за ним ~ила́сь сла́ва ко́мика his name as a comic actor was made; про́з-вище ~ило́сь за ней the nickname stuck to her.

упроща́|ть(ся), ю(сь), *impf. of* упрости́ть-(ся).

упроще́н|ец, ца, *m.* (*coll.*) oversimplifier.

упроще́ни|е, я, *n.* simplification.

упрощённост|ь, и, *f.* 1. simplified character. 2. oversimplification.

упро|щённый, *p.p.p. of* ~сти́ть *and adj.* 1. simplified. 2. oversimplified.

упроще́нческий, *adj.* (*pejor.*) oversimplified.

упроще́нчеств|о, а, *n.* (*pejor.*) oversimplification.

упру́г|ий (~, ~а), *adj.* 1. elastic, resilient; ~ая похо́дка springy gait. 2. (*phys.*) expansible, extensible (*of gases*).

упру́гост|ь, и, *f.* 1. elasticity, resilience; spring, bound; преде́л ~и (*phys.*) elastic limit. 2. (*phys.*) expansibility, extensibility.

упру́|же, *comp. of* ~гий.

упряжк|а, и, *f.* 1. team, relay (*of horses, dogs,* *etc.*). 2. harness, gear. 3. (*obs., coll.*) shift, stint.

упряжн|о́й, *adj.* draught; ~а́я ло́шадь draught-horse, carriage-horse; ~а́я тя́га draw-bar.

у́пряж|ь, и, *f.* harness, gear.

упря́м|ец, ца, *m.* (*coll.*) obstinate person.

упря́м|иться, люсь, ишься, *impf.* to be obstinate; (в+*p.*) to persist (in).

упря́миц|а, ы, *f. of* упря́мец.

упря́мств|о, а, *n.* obstinacy, stubbornness.

упря́мств|овать, ую, *impf.* = упря́миться.

упря́м|ый (~, ~а), *adj.* 1. obstinate, stubborn. 2. persistent.

упря́|тать, чу, чешь, *pf.* (*of* ~тывать) 1. to hide, conceal. 2. (*fig., coll.*) to put away, banish.

упря́|таться, чусь, чешься, *pf.* (*of* ~тываться) (*coll.*) to hide (*intrans.*).

упря́тыва|ть(ся), ю(сь), *impf. of* упря́тать-(ся).

упуска́|ть, ю, *impf. of* упусти́ть.

упу|сти́ть, щу́, ~стишь, *pf.* (*of* ~ска́ть) 1. to let go, let slip, let fall; у. пово́дья to let the reins go. 2. (*fig.*) to let go, let slip; to miss; to lose; у. возмо́жность to miss an opportunity; у. и́з виду to overlook, fail to take account (of). 3. (*coll.*) to neglect.

упуще́ни|е, я, *n.* 1. omission. 2. (careless) slip; negligence; у. по слу́жбе neglect of duty, dereliction of duty.

упы́р|ь, я́, *m.* (*coll.*) vampire.

упятер|и́ть, ю́, и́шь, *pf.* (*of* ~я́ть) to increase fivefold.

упятер|я́ть, я́ю, *impf. of* ~и́ть.

ура́, *interj.* hurrah!, hurray! (*exclamation* (*i*) *expressing exultation or approbation,* (*ii*) *of troops going in to attack*); на у. (*i*) (*mil.*) by storm, (*ii*) (*iron.*) by luck (= without due preparation).

ура́- blind, unthinking (*e.g.* ура́-патрио-ти́зм, а, *m.* jingoism).

уравне́ни|е, я, *n.* 1. equalization. 2. (*math.*) equation; у. пе́рвой сте́пени simple equation.

ура́внива|ть[1], ю, *impf. of* уравня́ть.

ура́внива|ть[2], ю, *impf. of* уровня́ть.

уравни́ловк|а, и, *f.* (*coll.*) (*pejor. in Soviet usage*) egalitarianism; у. в опла́те труда́ wage-levelling.

уравни́тел|ь, я, *m.* 1. (*tech.*) equalizer, leveller; regulator; у. хо́да governor. 2. (*polit.*) egalitarian.

уравни́тельн|ый, *adj.* (*in var. senses*) equalizing, levelling; ~ая переда́ча (*tech.*) differential gear.

уравнове́|сить, шу, сишь, *pf.* (*of* ~шивать) 1. to balance; (*tech.*) to equilibrate. 2. (*fig.*) to counterbalance; to neutralize.

уравнове́шенност|ь, и, *f.* (*fig.*) balance, steadiness, composure.

уравнове|шенный, *p.p.p. of* ~сить *and adj.* (*fig.*) balanced, steady, composed.

уравновешивани|е, я, *n.* balancing; (*tech.*) equilibration.

уравновешива|ть, ю, *impf. of* уравновесить.

уравня|ть, ю, *pf.* (*of* ура́внивать[1]) to equalize, make equal, make level.

урага́н, а, *m.* hurricane; (*fig.*) storm.

урага́н|ный, *adj. of* ~; у. ого́нь (*mil.*) drum-fire.

уразумева́|ть, ю, *impf. of* уразуме́ть.

уразуме́|ть, ю, *pf.* (*of* ~ва́ть) to comprehend.

ура́льский, *adj.* (*geogr.*) Ural(s).

ура́н, а, *m.* 1. У. (*astron.*) Uranus. 2. (*chem.*) uranium.

уранини́т, а, *m.* (*min.*) uraninite, pitchblende.

ура́новый, *adj.* uranium, uranic.

урв|а́ть, у́, ёшь, *past* ~а́л, ~ала́, ~а́ло, *pf.* (*of* урыва́ть) (*coll.*) to snatch (*also fig.*), grab; у. мину́ту-две для бесе́ды to snatch a minute or two for a chat.

урв|а́ться, у́сь, ёшься, *past* ~а́лся, ~ала́сь, ~а́лось, *pf.* (*of* урыва́ться) (*coll.*) to break loose; (*fig.*) to get away, snatch a free minute.

урду́, *indecl., m.* Urdu (*language*).

урегули́ровани|е, я, *n.* regulation; settlement, adjustment.

урегули́р|овать, ую, *pf.* (*of* регули́ровать) to regulate; to settle, adjust; у. спо́рную пробле́му to settle a dispute.

уре́з, а, *m.* (*coll.*) reduction, cut.

уре́|зать, жу, жешь, *pf.* (*of* ~зать *and* ~зывать) 1. (*coll.*) to cut off; to shorten. 2. to cut down, reduce; to axe; у. шта́ты to cut down the staff.

уреза́|ть, а́ю, *impf. of* ~ать.

урезо́нива|ть, ю, *impf. of* урезо́нить.

урезо́н|ить, ю, ишь, *pf.* (*of* ~ивать) (*coll.*) to make to see reason, bring to reason.

уре́зыва|ть, ю, *impf.* = уреза́ть.

урем|а́, ы́ (*and* урём|а, ы), *f.* (*dial.*) woods along a river.

уреми́ческий, *adj.* (*med.*) uraemic.

уреми́|я, и, *f.* (*med.*) uraemia.

уре́тр|а, ы, *f.* (*anat.*) urethra.

уретри́т, а, *m.* (*med.*) urethritis.

уретроско́п, а, *m.* (*med.*) urethroscope.

ури́льник, а, *m.* (*obs.*) chamber-pot.

ури́н|а, ы, *f.* (*med.*) urine.

у́рк|а, и, *m. and f.* (*prison sl.*) 'urka' (*criminal serving time as opp. to political prisoner*).

у́рн|а, ы, *f.* 1. urn. 2. избира́тельная у. ballot-box. 3. refuse bin, litter receptacle.

у́ров|ень, ня, *m.* 1. (*in var. senses*) level, plane; standard; у. мо́ря sea level; высота́ над ~нем мо́ря altitude above sea level; в у. (c+*i.*) (*i*) level (with), at the height (of); flush (with), (*ii*) (*fig.*) abreast (of), in pace

(with); на ~не земли́ at ground level; быть на ~не to satisfy requirements; совеща́ние на высо́ком ~не (*polit.*) high-level conference. 2. (*tech.*) level, gauge.

уровнеме́р, а, *m.* (*tech.*) water-level.

уровня́|ть, ю, *pf.* (*of* ура́внивать[2]) to level, make even.

уро́д, а, *m.* 1. freak, monster; deformed person. 2. ugly person; (*morally*) depraved person.

уро́дин|а, ы, *m. and f.* (*coll.*) = уро́д.

уро|ди́ть, жу́, ди́шь, *pf.* (*coll.*) to bear, bring forth.

уро|ди́ться, жу́сь, ди́шься, *pf.* 1. (*of crops, etc.*) to ripen; (*of a human being*) to be born. 2. (в+*a.*; *coll.*) to take after.

уро́дливост|ь, и, *f.* 1. deformity. 2. ugliness.

уро́длив|ый (~, ~а), *adj.* 1. deformed, misshapen. 2. ugly. 3. (*fig.*) ugly, bad; abnormal; faulty; distorting, distorted; ~ое воспита́ние bad upbringing; у. перево́д faulty translation.

уро́д|овать, ую, *impf.* (*of* из~) 1. to deform, disfigure, mutilate. 2. to make ugly. 3. (*fig.*) to distort.

уро́д|ский, *adj.* (*coll.*) 1. *adj. of* ~. 2. distorted.

уро́дств|о, а, *n.* 1. deformity; disfigurement. 2. ugliness. 3. (*fig.*) abnormality.

урожа́|й, я, *m.* 1. harvest; crop, yield; собра́ть у. to gather in the harvest. 2. bumper crop, abundance (*also fig., coll.*); в э́том году́ был урожа́й на детекти́вные рома́ны this year there has been a bumper crop of detective stories.

урожа́йност|ь, и, *f.* productivity (*of crops*), (level of) yield.

урожа́|йный (~ен, ~йна), *adj.* 1. *adj. of* ~й. 2. producing high yield, productive; у. год good year (*for a crop*).

урожде́нн|ый, *p.p.p. of* уроди́ть *and adj.* 1. ~ая (*before maiden name*) née. 2. (*obs.*) inborn, born.

урожё́н|ец, ца, *m.* (+*g.*) native (of).

урожё́н|ка, ки, *f. of* ~ец.

уро́к, а, *m.* 1. lesson (*also fig.*); брать ~и (+*g.*) to have, take lessons, tuition (in); дава́ть ~и (+*g.*) to teach, give lessons, give tuition (in); дать кому́-н. у. (*fig.*) to teach someone a lesson; жить на ~е (*obs.*) to be, earn one's living as a (private) tutor. 2. homework; lesson, task; зада́ть у. to set homework; отвеча́ть у. to repeat one's lesson. 3. (*obs.*) task, work.

уро́лог, а, *m.* (*med.*) urologist.

урологи́ческий, *adj.* (*med.*) urological.

уроло́ги|я, и, *f.* (*med.*) urology.

уро́н, а, *no pl., m.* losses, casualties; нанести́ у. to inflict casualties.

урон|ить, ю, ~ишь, *pf.* **1.** *pf.* of **ронять. 2.** (*obs., coll.*) to ruin, cause to collapse.

урочищ|е, а, *n.* (*geogr.*) **1.** natural boundary. **2.** isolated terrain feature (*e.g. wood in swamp country*).

урочн|ый, *adj.* **1.** (*obs.*) fixed, agreed; ~ая работа piece-work; ~ая цена fixed price. **2.** usual, established.

уругва|ец, йца, *m.* Uruguayan.

уругвайк|а, и, *f.* Uruguayan (woman).

уругвайский, *adj.* Uruguayan.

урчáни|е, я, *n.* rumbling; у. в желудке (*coll.*) tummy-rumbling.

урч|áть, ý, úшь, *impf.* to rumble.

урывá|ть(ся), ю(сь), *impf. of* **урвáть(ся).**

уры́вками, *adv.* (*coll.*) in snatches, by fits and starts; at odd moments.

уры́воч|ный (~ен, ~на), *adj.* (*coll.*) fitful; occasional.

урю́к, а (у), *no pl., m.* (*collect.*) dried apricots.

урю́к|овый, *adj. of* ~.

уря́д, а, *m.* (*obs.*) **1.** rule; customs, observances. **2.** rank.

уря|ди́ть, жý, ~ди́шь, *pf.* (*of* ~жáть) (*obs.*) to arrange, put in order.

уря́дник, а, *m.* (*hist.*) **1.** Cossack N.C.O. (*in tsarist Russian army*). **2.** village constable.

уряжá|ть, ю, *impf. of* **уряди́ть.**

ус, а, *m.* **1.** (*see also* ~ы́) moustache hair; и в ус (себе́) не дуть (*coll.*) not to give a damn; мотáть (себе́) на ус (*coll.*) to take good note (of). **2.** whisker (*of an animal*). **3.** antenna, feeler (*of an insect*). **4.** (*bot.*) tendril; awn. **5.** китóвый ус whalebone, baleen.

усáд|ебный, *adj. of* ~ьба; у. быт life of country gentry.

уса|ди́ть, жý, ~дишь, *pf.* (*of* ~живать) **1.** to seat, help sit down; to make sit down; у. в тюрьмý (*coll.*) to throw into jail; у. в печь (*coll.*) to put into the oven. **2.** (за+*a. or* +*inf.*) to set (to, at); у. когó-н. за роя́ль to set someone to (play at) the piano. **3.** (+*i.*) to plant (with). **4.** (+*i.*) to cover (with); стенá, ~женная пя́тнами a wall covered with stains.

усáдк|а, и, *f.* shrinking; shrinkage; contraction.

усáдьб|а, ы, *g. pl.* ~ *and* **усáдеб,** *f.* **1.** (*hist.*) country estate; country-seat. **2.** farmstead; farm centre (*of collective or State farm*).

усáжива|ть, ю, *impf. of* **усади́ть.**

усáжива|ться, юсь, *impf. of* **усéсться.**

усáст|ый (~), *adj.* (*coll.*) with a big moustache.

усáт|ый (~, ~а), *adj.* **1.** moustached; with a big moustache. **2.** (*of animals*) whiskered.

усáхар|ить, ю, ишь, *pf.* (*coll.*) **1.** to sugar plentifully. **2.** to win over by flattery. **3.** (*obs.*) to beat to death.

усáч, á, *m.* **1.** (*coll.*) man with a (big) moustache. **2.** barbel (*fish*). **3.** capricorn beetle (*Agapanthia dahli*).

усвáива|ть, ю, *impf. of* **усвóить.**

усвоéни|е, я, *n.* mastering; assimilation.

усвó|ить, ю, ишь, *pf.* (*of* усвáивать) **1.** to adopt, acquire (*a habit, etc.*); to imitate; у. чужóй вы́говор to pick up someone else's accent. **2.** to master (= to learn); to assimilate; у. прáвила ýличного движéния to master the traffic regulations. **3.** (+*d.*; *obs.*) to inculcate (in). **4.** to assimilate (*food, medicine, etc.*).

усвоя́емост|ь, и, *f.* **1.** comprehensibility; хорóшая у. ease of comprehension, easiness. **2.** (*chem.*) assimilability.

усéива|ть, ю, *impf. of* **усéять.**

усекá|ть, ю, *impf. of* **усéчь.**

усекновéни|е, я, *n.* (*rel.*) у. главы́ beheading (*of St. John Baptist*).

усéрди|е, я, *n.* zeal; diligence, painstakingness.

усéрд|ный (~ен, ~на), *adj.* zealous; diligent, painstaking.

усéрдств|овать, ую, *impf.* to be zealous; to take pains.

усé|сться, уся́дусь, уся́дешься, *past* ~лся, ~лась, *pf.* (*of* усáживаться) **1.** to take a seat; to settle (down). **2.** (за+*a. or* +*inf.*) to set (to), settle down (to); у. за кáрты to settle down to (a game of) cards.

усеч|ённый, *p.p.p. of* ~ь *and adj.* (*math.*) truncated.

усé|чь, кý, чёшь, кýт, *past* ~к, ~клá, *pf.* (*of* ~кáть) to cut off, truncate.

усé|ять, ю, ешь, *pf.* (*of* ~ивать) (+*i.*) **1.** to sow (with). **2.** to cover (with), dot (with), stud (with), litter (with), strew (with); лицó, ~янное весну́шками face covered with freckles; бéрег мóря, ~янный меду́зами sea-shore littered with jelly-fish.

уси|дéть, жý, ди́шь, *pf.* **1.** to keep one's place, remain sitting; он так волновáлся, что éле мог у. he was so excited that he could hardly sit still. **2.** (*coll.*) to hold down a job, keep a job. **3.** (*sl.*) to guzzle; to knock back (*drink*).

уси́дчивост|ь, и, *f.* assiduity.

уси́дчив|ый (~, ~а), *adj.* assiduous; painstaking.

ýсик, а, *m.* **1.** (*pl.*) small moustache. **2.** (*bot.*) tendril; awn; runner (*of strawberry, etc.*). **3.** (*zool.*) antenna, feeler.

усилéни|е, я, *n.* **1.** strengthening; reinforcement. **2.** intensification; aggravation; (*radio*) amplification.

уси́л|енный, *p.p.p. of* ~ить *and adj.* **1.** reinforced; ~енное питáние high-caloric diet. **2.** intensified, increased; ~енная рабóта high pressure of work. **3.** earnest, urgent, importunate; ~енные про́сьбы earnest entreaties.

усилива|ть, ю, *impf. of* уси́лить.

усилива|ться, юсь, *impf.* **1.** *impf. of* уси́литься. **2.** (+*inf.*; *obs.*) to try (to), make an effort (to).

уси́ли|е, я, *n.* effort; exertion; приложи́ть все ~я to make every effort, spare no effort.

усили́тел|ь, я, *m.* **1.** (*tech.*) amplifier. **2.** (*radio*) booster. **3.** (*chem.*) active filler (*of rubber*).

усили́тельный, *adj.* **1.** (*tech.*) booster. **2.** (*radio*) amplifying.

уси́л|ить, ю, ишь, *pf.* (*of* ~ивать) **1.** to strengthen, reinforce. **2.** to intensify, increase, heighten; to aggravate; (*radio*) to amplify.

уси́л|иться, ится, *pf.* (*of* ~иваться) to become stronger; to intensify, increase (*intrans.*); to become aggravated; (*of sound*) to swell, grow louder.

уси́льный, *adj.* (*obs.*) earnest, urgent, importunate.

уска|ка́ть, чу́, ~чешь, *pf.* **1.** to bound away; (*coll.*) to skip off, slip off. **2.** to gallop off.

ускольз|а́ть, а́ю, *impf. of* ~ну́ть.

ускольз|ну́ть, ну́, нёшь, *pf.* (*of* ~а́ть) **1.** to slip off. **2.** (*coll.*; *of a person*) to slip off, steal away; to get away. **3.** (*fig.*) to disappear; to escape; у. от внима́ния to escape one's notice. **4.** (от; *coll.*) to evade, avoid; у. от прямо́го отве́та to avoid giving a direct answer.

ускоре́ни|е, я, *n.* acceleration; speeding-up.

уско́р|енный, *p.p.p. of* ~ить *and adj.* accelerated; rapid; hasty; у. аллю́р increased gait.

ускори́тел|ь, я, *m.* (*tech.*) accelerator.

уско́р|ить, ю, ишь, *pf.* (*of* ~я́ть) **1.** to quicken; to speed up, accelerate; у. шаг to quicken one's pace. **2.** to hasten; to precipitate.

уско́р|иться, ится, *pf.* (*of* ~я́ться) **1.** to quicken; to accelerate. **2.** *pass. of* ~ить.

ускор|я́ть, я́ю, *impf. of* ~ить.

ускор|я́ться, я́ется, *impf. of* ~иться.

усла́вливаться = усло́вливаться.

усла́д|а, ы, *f.* (*obs.*) joy, delight; enjoyment.

услади́тел|ьный (~ен, ~ьна), *adj.* (*obs.*) pleasing, delightful.

усла|ди́ть, жу́, ди́шь, *pf.* (*of* ~жда́ть) (*obs. or poet.*) **1.** to delight, charm. **2.** to soften, mitigate.

усла|ди́ться, жу́сь, ди́шься, *pf.* (*of* ~жда́ться) (+*i.*; *obs. or poet.*) to delight (in).

услажда́|ть(ся), ю(сь), *impf. of* услади́ть(ся).

усла|сти́ть, щу́, сти́шь, *pf.* (*of* ~ща́ть) to sweeten.

усла́|ть, ушлю́, ушлёшь, *pf.* (*of* усыла́ть) to

send away, despatch; у. на ка́торгу (*coll.*) to send away to (do) hard labour.

услаща́|ть, ю, *impf. of* усласти́ть.

усле|ди́ть, жу́, ди́шь, *pf.* (за+*i.*) **1.** to keep an eye (on), mind. **2.** to follow; у. за хо́дом расска́за to follow a story.

усло́ви|е, я, *n.* **1.** condition; clause, term; stipulation, proviso; поста́вить ~ем to make it a condition, stipulate; под ~ем, что; при ~и, что; с ~ем, что on condition that, provided that, providing. **2.** (*obs.*) agreement; заключи́ть у. to conclude an agreement. **3.** (*pl.*) conditions; ~я пого́ды weather conditions; ~я приёма (*radio*) reception; при про́чих ра́вных ~ях other things being equal.

усло́в|иться, люсь, ишься, *pf.* (*of* ~ливаться) to agree, settle; to arrange, make arrangements; мы ~ились о ме́сте свида́ния we agreed on a meeting-place.

усло́вленный, *adj.* agreed, fixed, stipulated; в у. час at the hour agreed.

усло́влива|ться, юсь, *impf. of* усло́виться.

усло́вност|ь, и, *f.* **1.** conditional character. **2.** convention, conventionality.

усло́в|ный, *adj.* **1.** conventional; agreed, pre-arranged; у. знак conventional sign; ~ное назва́ние code name; у. жест conventional gesture. **2.** (~ен, ~на) conditional; у. пригово́р (*leg.*) suspended sentence; ~ное согла́сие conditional consent. **3.** (~ен, ~на) relative. **4.** theoretical; ~ное то́пливо ideal fuel, comparison fuel. **5.** (*gram.*) conditional. **6.** у. рефле́кс (*physiol.*) conditioned reflex.

усложне́ни|е, я, *n.* complication.

усложн|ённый, *p.p.p. of* ~и́ть *and adj.* complicated.

усложн|и́ть, ю́, и́шь, *pf.* (*of* ~я́ть) to complicate.

усложн|и́ться, и́тся, *pf.* (*of* ~я́ться) to become complicated.

усложн|я́ть, я́ю, *impf. of* ~и́ть.

усложн|я́ться, я́ется, *impf. of* ~и́ться.

услу́г|а, и, *f.* **1.** service; good turn; до́брые ~и (*dipl.*) good offices; оказа́ть ~у to do a service; предложи́ть свои́ ~и to offer one's services; к ва́шим ~ам at your service. **2.** (*pl.*) service(s); ко́мната со все́ми ~ами room with service; коммуна́льные ~и public utilities. **3.** (*collect.*; *obs.*) servants, domestics.

услуже́ни|е, я, *n.* (*obs.*) service; быть в ~и (у) to be in service (with); (*fig., iron.*) to be a lackey (of).

услу́жива|ть, ю, *impf.* (*obs.*) **1.** *impf. of* услужи́ть. **2.** to serve, act as a servant.

услуж|и́ть, у́, ~ишь, *pf.* (*of* ~ивать) (+*d.*) to do a service, good turn.

услу́жлив|ый (~, ~а), *adj.* obliging.

услыха́ть = услы́шать.

услы́ш|ать, у, ишь, *pf.* (*of* слы́шать) **1.** to hear. **2.** (*coll.*) to perceive, sense; (*of animals*) to scent.

усма́трива|ть, ю, *impf. of* усмотре́ть.

усмех|а́ться, а́юсь, *impf. of* ~ну́ться.

усмех|ну́ться, ну́сь, нёшься, *pf.* (*of* ~а́ться) to smile; to grin.

усме́шк|а, и, *f.* smile; grin.

усмире́ни|е, я, *n.* suppression, putting down; pacification.

усмир|и́ть, ю́, и́шь, *pf.* (*of* ~я́ть) **1.** to pacify; to calm, quieten; (*fig.*) to tame. **2.** to suppress, put down (*a mutiny, etc.*).

усмир|я́ть, я́ю, *impf. of* ~и́ть.

усмотре́ни|е, я, *n.* discretion, judgement; предоста́вить чьему́-н. ~ю, на чье́-н. у. to leave to someone's discretion; поступи́ть по своему́ ~ю to use one's own discretion, act as one thinks best.

усмотр|е́ть, ю́, ~ишь, *pf.* (*of* усма́тривать) **1.** (за+*i.*) to keep an eye (on). **2.** (*coll.*) to perceive, observe. **3.** (в+*p.*) to see (in); to regard (as), interpret (as); у. угро́зу в заявле́нии to interpret the statement as a threat.

усна|сти́ть, щу́, сти́шь, *pf.* (*of* ~ща́ть) (+*i.*; *coll.*) **1.** to rig (*a boat*). **2.** (*fig.*) to adorn (with); to stuff (with), lard (with); у. речь ци́фрами to stuff a speech with figures.

уснаща́|ть, ю, *impf. of* уснасти́ть.

усн|у́ть, у́, ёшь, *pf.* **1.** to go to sleep, fall asleep (*also fig.*); у. ве́чным сном, наве́ки (*rhet.*) to pass to one's eternal rest. **2.** (*of fish*) to die.

усо́биц|а, ы, *f.* (*hist.*) intestine strife.

усоверше́нствовани|е, я, *n.* **1.** finishing, qualifying; ку́рсы ~я finals course(s). **2.** improvement, development, refinement.

усоверше́нствов|анный, *p.p.p. of* ~ать *and adj.* **1.** finished, complete (*education, etc.*). **2.** improved (*model of machine, etc.*).

усоверше́нств|овать(ся), ую(сь), *pf. of* соверше́нствовать(ся).

усове|сти́ть, щу, сти́шь, *pf.* (*of* ~щивать) to appeal to the conscience (of); to make ashamed.

усове|сти́ться, щусь, сти́шься, *pf.* (*of* ~щиваться) to be sorry, be conscience-stricken.

усове́щива|ть(ся), ю(сь), *impf. of* усове́стить(ся).

усомн|и́ться, ю́сь, и́шься, *pf.* (в+*p.*) to doubt.

усо́пш|ий, *adj.* (*obs.*) deceased; *as noun* у., ~его, *m.*; ~ая, ~ей, *f.* the deceased.

усо́х|нуть, ну, нешь, *past* ~, ~ла, *pf.* (*of* усыха́ть) to dry up, dry out.

успева́емост|ь, и, *f.* progress (*in studies*).

успева́|ть, ю, *impf.* **1.** *impf. of* успе́ть. **2.**

(*impf. only*) (в+*p. or* по+*d.*) to make progress (in), get on well (in, at) (*of studies*).

успе́ется, *impers., pf.* (*coll.*) there is still time, there is no need to hurry.

успе́ни|е, я, *n.* (*eccl.*) **1.** death, passing. **2.** У. (Feast of) the Dormition, Assumption (of the Virgin).

успе́н|ский, *adj. of* ~ие 2.

успе́|ть, ю, *pf.* (*of* ~ва́ть) **1.** to have time; to manage; у. написа́ть to have time to write; у. на заседа́ние to be in time for the meeting; у. к по́езду to manage to catch the train; не у. сде́лать что-н., как... not to have time to do something before . . . **2.** (в+*p.*) to succeed (in), be successful (in).

успе́х, а, *m.* **1.** success; име́ть большо́й у. to be a great success; по́льзоваться ~ом to be a success; с тем же ~ом equally well, with the same result. **2.** (*pl.*) success, progress; как ва́ши ~и? how are you getting on?; де́лать ~и (в+*p.*) to make progress (in), get on (at).

успе́шност|ь, и, *f.* success; progress.

успе́ш|ный (~ен, ~на), *adj.* successful.

успока́ива|ть(ся), ю(сь), *impf. of* успоко́ить(ся).

успока́ива|ющий, *pres. part. act. of* ~ть *and adj.* sedative; ~ающее сре́дство sedative.

успокое́ни|е, я, *n.* **1.** calming, quieting, soothing; (*med.*) sedation. **2.** calm; peace, tranquillity.

успоко́енност|ь, и, *f.* calmness; tranquillity.

успокои́тел|ьный (~ен, ~ьна), *adj.* calming, soothing; reassuring; *as noun* ~ьное, ~ьного, *n.* sedative.

успоко́|ить, ю, ишь, *pf.* (*of* успока́ивать) **1.** to calm, quiet, soothe; to reassure, set at rest, set one's mind at rest. **2.** to assuage, deaden (*pain, etc.*); у. чьи-н. подозре́ния to still someone's suspicions. **2.** (*coll.*) to reduce to order, control; у. дете́й to make children be quiet.

успоко́|иться, юсь, ишься, *pf.* (*of* успока́иваться) **1.** to calm down; to compose oneself. **2.** (на дости́гнутом) to rest content (with what has been achieved). **3.** (*of pain, etc.*) to abate; (*of the sea*) to become still; (*of the wind*) to drop. **4.** *pass. of* ~ить.

уст|а́, ~, ~а́м, *no sing.* (*obs. or poet.*) mouth, lips; вложи́ть в чьи-н. у. (*fig.*) to put into someone's mouth; из ~ в у. by word of mouth; узна́ть из пе́рвых, вторы́х ~ to learn at first, second hand; на ~а́х все́х на ~а́х everyone's talking about it; твои́ми бы ~а́ми мёд пить if only you were right.

уста́в¹, а, *m.* regulations, rules, statutes; (*mil.*) service regulations; (*monastic*) rule; у. ·университе́та university statutes; У. КПСС Rules of the C.P.S.U.; У. ООН U.N.O Charter.

уста́в², а, *m.* (*palaeog.*) uncial (writing).

уста|ва́ть, ю́, ёшь, *impf. of* ~ть; не ~ва́я (*as adv.*) incessantly, uninterruptedly.

уста́в|ить, лю, ишь, *pf.* (*of* ~ля́ть) (*coll.*) 1. to set, arrange, dispose; у. ме́бель в ко́мнате to arrange furniture about the room. 2. (+*i*.) to cover (with), fill (with), pile (with); у. стол буты́лками to cover a table with bottles. 3. (глаза́, *etc.*, на+*a*.) to direct, fix (one's gaze, *etc.*, upon).

уста́в|иться, люсь, ишься, *pf.* (*of* ~ля́ться) (*coll.*) 1. to find room, go in. 2. (на+*a*.) to fix one's gaze (upon), stare (at). 3. (*obs.*) to become fixed, become steady.

уставля́|ть(ся), ю(сь), *impf. of* уста́вить-(ся).

уста́вный¹, *adj.* regulation, statutory, prescribed.

уста́в|ный², *adj. of* ~².

уста́лост|ь, и, *f.* fatigue, tiredness, weariness; у. мета́лла (*tech.*) metal fatigue; испыта́ние на у. fatigue test.

уста́лый, *adj.* tired, weary, fatigued.

у́стал|ь, и, *f.* (*obs. or coll.*) = ~ость; без ~и tirelessly, untiringly, unceasingly.

устана́влива|ть(ся), ю(сь), *impf. of* установи́ть(ся).

установ|и́ть, лю́, ~ишь, *pf.* (*of* устана́вливать) 1. to place, put, set up; (*tech.*) to install, mount, rig up. 2. (на+*a*.; по+*d*.) to adjust, regulate, set (to; by); у. часы́ по ра́дио to set one's watch by the radio. 3. to establish, institute; у. связь (с+*i*.; *mil.*) to establish communication (with). 4. to fix, prescribe, establish; у. сро́ки о́тдыха to fix holidays. 5. to secure, obtain; у. тишину́ to secure quiet. 6. to establish, determine; to ascertain; у. причи́ну ава́рии to establish the cause of a crash.

установ|и́ться, люсь, ~ишься, *pf.* (*of* устана́вливаться) 1. (*coll.*) to take position, dispose oneself. 2. to be settled, be established; to set in; ~и́лся обы́чай it has become a custom; пого́да ~и́лась the weather has become settled. 3. (*of character, etc.*) to be formed, be fixed.

устано́вк|а, и, *f.* 1. placing, putting, setting up, arrangement; (*tech.*) installation, mounting, rigging. 2. adjustment, regulation, setting; у. взрыва́теля fuse setting. 3. (*tech.*) plant, unit, installation. 4. aim, purpose; име́ть ~у (на+*a*.) to aim (at). 5. directions, directive.

установле́ни|е, я, *n.* 1. (*in var. senses*) establishment. 2. (*obs.*) statute; institution.

установ|ленный, *p.p.p. of* ~и́ть *and adj.* established, fixed, prescribed, regulation; в ~ленном поря́дке in prescribed manner; по ~ленной фо́рме in due form, in accordance with set form.

установ|очный, *adj.* 1. (*tech.*) *adj. of* ~ка 2; у. винт adjusting screw; у. кронште́й mounting bracket. 2. *adj. of* ~ка 5; вопро́с fundamental question.

устано́вщик, а, *m.* fitter, mounter; (*mi* (instrument) setter.

устарева́|ть, ю, *impf. of* устаре́ть.

устаре́|вший, *past part. act. of* ~ть *and a* obsolete.

устаре́лый, *adj.* obsolete; antiquated, o of date.

устаре́|ть, ю, *pf.* (*of* ~ва́ть) 1. (*obs.*) to gro old. 2. to become obsolete; to becon antiquated, out of date.

уста́|ть, ну, нешь, *pf.* (*of* ~ва́ть) to becon tired; я ~л I am tired.

устерега́|ть, ю, *impf. of* устере́чь.

устере́|чь, гу́, жёшь, гу́т, *past* ~г, ~гла́, (*of* ~га́ть) (от; *coll.*) to guard (against); keep watch over.

устила́|ть, ю, *impf. of* устла́ть.

устла́ть, устелю́, усте́лешь, *pf.* (*of* уст ла́ть) (+*i*.) to cover (with); to pave (with

у́стно, *adv.* orally, by word of mouth.

у́стн|ый, *adj.* oral, verbal; ~ая речь spok language; ~ая слове́сность oral literatu folk poetry (*orally transmitted*); у. экза́м oral (examination).

усто́|й¹, я, *m.* 1. (*tech.*) abutment, buttre pier (*of bridge*). 2. foundation, suppo 3. (*pl.*; *fig.*) foundations, bases.

усто́|й², я, *m.* (*coll.*) thickened layer on su face of liquid; у. молока́ cream.

усто́йчивост|ь, и, *f.* stability, steadine firmness.

усто́йчив|ый (~, ~а), *adj.* stable, stead firm (*also fig.*); ~ая валю́та stable currenc ~ая пого́да settled weather; ~ое соед не́ние (*chem.*) stable compound.

усто|я́ть, ю́, и́шь, *pf.* 1. to keep on balance, remain standing. 2. (*fig.*) to sta one's ground. 3. to resist, hold out; пе́ред собла́зном to resist a temptation.

усто|я́ться, и́тся, *pf.* 1. (*esp. of liquids*) settle. 2. (*coll.*; *of beer, etc.*) to have sto (*sufficient time*). 3. (*coll.*) to become fixe become permanent.

устра́ива|ть(ся), ю(сь), *impf. of* устро́и (ся).

устране́ни|е, я, *n.* removal, eliminatic clearing.

устран|и́ть, ю́, и́шь, *pf.* (*of* ~я́ть) 1. to move, eliminate, clear; у. прегра́ды to move obstacles. 2. to remove (*from offic* dismiss.

устран|и́ться, ю́сь, и́шься, *pf.* (*of* ~я́тьс 1. to resign, retire, withdraw. 2. *pass.* ~и́ть.

устран|я́ть(ся), я́ю(сь), *impf. of* ~и́ть(с)

устраш|а́ть(ся), а́ю(сь), *impf. of* ~и́ть(с)

устраша́|ющий, *pres. part. act. of* ~ть *and adj.* frightening, appalling.

устраше́ни|е, я, *n.* **1.** frightening; сре́дство ~я (*mil., polit.*) deterrent. **2.** fright, fear.

устраш|и́ть, у́, и́шь, *pf.* (*of* ~а́ть) to frighten, scare, inspire fear (in).

устраш|и́ться, у́сь, и́шься, *pf.* (*of* ~а́ться) to be afraid, take fright, be scared.

устрем|и́ть, лю́, и́шь, *pf.* (*of* ~ля́ть) (на+*a.*) **1.** (*obs.*) to throw (*troops, etc.*) (against). **2.** to direct (to, at); у. глаза́ на что-н. to fasten one's gaze upon something.

устрем|и́ться, лю́сь, и́шься, *pf.* (*of* ~ля́ться) **1.** (на+*a.*) to rush (upon, at); to head (for). **2.** (на+*a.*; к) to be directed (at, towards), be fixed (upon), be concentrated (on); (*of a person*) to concentrate (on).

устремле́ни|е, я, *n.* **1.** rush. **2.** striving, aspiration.

устремлённост|ь, и, *f.* tendency.

устремля́|ть(ся), ю(сь), *impf. of* устреми́ть(ся).

у́стриц|а, ы, *f.* oyster.

у́стри|чный, *adj. of* ~ца; ~чная ра́ковина oyster shell; у. заво́д oyster farm.

устрое́ни|е, я, *n.* **1.** arranging, organization. **2.** (*obs.*) apparatus, mechanism.

устро́итель|ь, я, *m.* organizer.

устро́|ить, ю, ишь, *pf.* (*of* устра́ивать) **1.** to make, construct. **2.** to arrange, organize; to establish; у. конце́рт to arrange a concert. **3.** (*fig., coll.*) to make, cause, create; у. сканда́л to make a scene. **4.** to settle, order, put in (good) order; у. свои́ дела́ to put one's affairs in order. **5.** to place, fix up; to get, secure; у. кого́-н. на рабо́ту to fix someone up with work, find someone a job; у. кому́-н. ко́мнату (*coll.*) to get someone a room. **6.** (*impers.; coll.*) to suit, be convenient (to, for).

устро́|иться, юсь, ишься, *pf.* (*of* устра́иваться) **1.** to work out (well); to come right. **2.** to manage, make arrangements. **3.** to settle down, get settled. **4.** to get fixed up (*in a job*); он ~и́лся на желе́зную доро́гу кочега́ром he has got a job on the railway as a fireman.

устро́йств|о, а, *n.* **1.** arrangement, organization. **2.** (mode of) construction; layout; (*tech.*) working principle(s). **3.** apparatus, mechanism, device. **4.** structure, system; обще́ственное у. social structure.

усту́п, а, *m.* **1.** shelf, ledge (*of wall or cliff*); spur (*of hill*); terrace; (*geol.*) bench; располо́женный ~ами terraced. **2.** (*mil.*) echelon formation (*of artillery*).

уступ|а́ть, а́ю, *impf. of* ~и́ть.

уступи́тельный, *adj.* (*gram.*) concessive.

уступ|и́ть, лю́, ~ишь, *pf.* (*of* ~а́ть) **1.** (+*d.*) to let have, give up (to); to cede (to); to concede (to); у. кому́-н. ме́сто to give up one's place to someone; у. доро́гу (+*d.*) to make way (for), let pass. **2.** (+*d.*) to yield (to), give in (to). **3.** (+*d.*) to be inferior (to); как заба́вник, он никому́ не ~ит as an entertainer he is second to none. **4.** (*coll.*) to let have (= to sell). **5.** (*coll.*) to take off, knock off (= to reduce the price by).

усту́пк|а, и, *f.* **1.** concession, compromise; сде́лать ~и to make concessions, compromise. **2.** reduction (*of price*).

усту́пчат|ый (~, ~а), *adj.* ledged, stepped, terraced.

усту́пчивост|ь, и, *f.* pliancy; compliance, tractability.

усту́пчив|ый (~, ~а), pliant, pliable; compliant, tractable.

усты|ди́ть, жу́, ди́шь, *pf.* to shame, put to shame.

усты|ди́ться, жу́сь, ди́шься, *pf.* (+*g.*) to be ashamed (of); to feel embarrassed (for).

у́сть|е, я, *g. pl.* ~ев, *n.* **1.** mouth, estuary (*of a river*). **2.** mouth, orifice (*of furnace, pipe, etc.*).

у́стье|вый (and устьево́й), *adj. of* ~.

у́стьиц|е, а, *n.* **1.** *dim. of* у́стье. **2.** (*bot.*) stoma.

усугуб|и́ть, ~лю́, ~и́шь, *pf.* (*of* ~ля́ть) to increase; to intensify; to aggravate.

усугубля́|ть, ю, *impf. of* усугуби́ть.

усуш|а́ться, а́ется, *impf. of* ~и́ться.

усуш|и́ться, ~ится, *pf.* (*of* ~а́ться) **1.** (*coll.*) to shrink (*in drying*). **2.** to lose weight (*in drying*).

усу́шк|а, и, f.* **1. (*coll.*) shrinkage (*in drying*). **2.** (*comm.*) wastage, loss of weight (*through drying*).

ус|ы́, о́в, *sing.* **ус, а,** *m.* moustache (*see also* ус); мы, *etc.,* са́ми с ~а́ми (*coll.*) we, *etc.,* weren't born yesterday.

усыла́|ть, ю, *impf. of* усла́ть.

усынов|и́ть, лю́, и́шь, *pf.* (*of* ~ля́ть) to adopt.

усыновле́ни|е, я, *n.* adoption.

усыновля́|ть, ю, *impf. of* усынови́ть.

**усыпа́льниц|а, ы, f.* burial-vault.

усы́п|ать, лю, лешь, *pf.* (*of* ~а́ть) (+*i.*) to strew (with), scatter (with); (*fig.*) to cover (with).

усып|а́ть, а́ю, *impf. of* ~ать.

усыпи́тел|ьный (~ен, ~на), *adj.* soporific (*also fig.*); ~ьное сре́дство sleeping-draught.

усып|и́ть, лю́, и́шь, *pf.* (*of* ~ля́ть) **1.** to put to sleep (*by means of narcotics, etc.*); to lull to sleep. **2.** (*fig.*) to lull; to weaken, undermine, neutralize; у. со́весть to lull one's conscience; у. боль to deaden pain. **3.** to put (*an animal*) to sleep.

усыпле́ни|е, я, *n.* **1.** putting to sleep; lulling (to sleep). **2.** (*obs.*) sleep.

усыпля́|ть, ю, *impf. of* усыпи́ть.

усыха́|ть, ю, *impf. of* усо́хнуть.

у́ська|ть, ю, *impf.* (*hunting and fig.*; *coll.*) to set on.

ута́ива|ть, ю, *impf. of* утаи́ть.

ута|и́ть, ю́, и́шь, *pf.* (*of* ~ивать) **1.** to conceal; to keep to oneself, keep secret. **2.** to appropriate.

ута́йк|а, и, *f.* (*coll.*) **1.** concealment; без ~и frankly, openly. **2.** appropriation.

ута́птыва|ть, ю, *impf. of* утопта́ть.

ута́скива|ть, ю, *impf. of* утащи́ть.

утащ|и́ть, у́, ~ишь, *pf.* (*of* ута́скивать) **1.** to drag away, off (*also fig.*); у. кого́-н. в кино́ (*coll.*) to drag someone off to the cinema. **2.** (*coll.*) to make off with (= to steal).

у́твар|ь, и, *no pl., f.* (*collect.*) utensils, equipment.

утверди́тел|ьный (~ен, ~ьна), *adj.* affirmative.

утвер|ди́ть, жу́, ди́шь, *pf.* (*of* ~жда́ть) **1.** (*obs.*) to fix, secure. **2.** to establish (*securely, firmly*); у. диктату́ру to establish a dictatorship; у. за кем-н. пра́во на име́ние to establish someone's right to an estate. **3.** (в+*p.*) to confirm (in) (*intention, opinion, etc.*). **4.** to approve; to confirm; to sanction, ratify; у. пове́стку дня to approve an agenda; у. завеща́ние to prove a will; у. кого́-н. в до́лжности to confirm someone's tenure of an office.

утвер|ди́ться, жу́сь, ди́шься, *pf.* (*of* ~жда́ться) **1.** to gain a foothold, gain a firm hold (*also fig.*); to become firmly established. **2.** (в+*p.*) to be confirmed (in) (*one's resolve, etc.*); у. в мы́сли to become firmly convinced.

утвержда́|ть, ю, *impf.* **1.** *impf. of* утверди́ть. **2.** (*impf. only*) to assert, affirm, hold, maintain, claim, allege.

утвержда́|ться, юсь, *impf. of* утверди́ться.

утвержде́ни|е, я, n. **1.** assertion, affirmation, claim, allegation. **2.** approval; confirmation; ratification; (*leg.*) probate. **3.** establishment.

утека́|ть, ю, *impf. of* утечь.

ут|ёнок, ёнка, *pl.* ~я́та, ~я́т, *m.* duckling.

утепле́ни|е, я, n. warming, heating.

утепл|ённый, *p.p.p. of* ~и́ть *and adj.* heated; insulated.

утепли́тел|ь, я, m. (*tech.*) **1.** heater. **2.** insulator (*building material*).

утепл|и́ть, ю́, и́шь, *pf.* (*of* ~я́ть) to warm, heat.

утепл|я́ть, я́ю, *impf. of* ~и́ть.

утер|е́ть, утру́, утрёшь, *past* ~, ~ла, *pf.* (*of* утира́ть) to wipe (off); to wipe dry; у. пот со лба to wipe the sweat off one's brow; у. кому́-н. нос (*coll.*) to score off someone.

утер|е́ться, утру́сь, утрёшься, *past* ~ся, ~лась, *pf.* (*of* утира́ться) to wipe oneself, dry oneself.

утерп|е́ть, лю́, ~ишь, *pf.* to restrain oneself.

утер́|я, и, f. loss.

утеря́|ть, ю, *pf.* to lose, mislay; to forfeit.

утёс, а, m. cliff, crag.

утёсист|ый (~, ~а), *adj.* steep, precipitous.

утесне́ни|е, я, n. oppression.

утесн|и́ть, ю́, и́шь, *pf.* (*of* ~я́ть) **1.** (в+*a.*; *coll.*) to stuff (into), squeeze (into). **2.** (*obs.*) to oppress, persecute.

утесн|я́ть, я́ю, *impf. of* ~и́ть.

уте́х|а, и, f. (*coll.*) **1.** pleasure; delight; для ~и for fun. **2.** comfort, consolation.

уте́чк|а, и, f. leak, leakage (*also fig.*); loss, wastage, dissipation; у. га́за gas escape.

уте́|чь, ку́, чёшь, ку́т, *past* ~к, ~кла́, *pf.* (*of* ~ка́ть) **1.** to flow away; to leak; (*of gas, etc.*) to escape; мно́го воды́~кло́ (*fig.*) much water has flowed (under the bridges). **2.** (*of time*) to pass, go by. **3.** (*coll.*) to run away.

утеш|а́ть(ся), а́ю(сь), *impf. of* ~и́ть(ся).

утеше́ни|е, я, n. comfort, consolation.

утеши́тел|ь, я, m. comforter.

утеши́тел|ьный (~ен, ~ьна), *adj.* comforting, consoling.

уте́ш|ить, у, ишь, *pf.* (*of* ~а́ть) to comfort, console.

уте́ш|иться, усь, ишься, *pf.* (*of* ~а́ться) **1.** to console oneself. **2.** (+*i.*) to take comfort (in).

утилизацио́нный, *adj.* у. заво́д salvage factory, by-products factory; у. цех salvage department.

утилиза́ци|я, и, f. **1.** utilization. **2.** salvaging; melting-down (*of scrap, etc., for re-use*).

утилизи́р|овать, ую, *impf. and pf.* to utilize.

утилитари́зм, а, m. utilitarianism.

утилитари́ст, а, m. utilitarian.

утилита́рност|ь, и, f. utilitarian attitude.

утилита́рный, *adj.* utilitarian.

ути́л|ь, я, *no pl., m.* (*collect.*) salvage, utility waste (*metal scrap, waste paper, etc.*).

ути́ль|ный, *adj. of* ~; ~ное желе́зо scrap iron.

утильсырь|ё, я́, *no pl., n.* (*collect.*) = ути́ль; сбо́рщик ~я́ salvage collector.

ути́льщик, а, m. salvage collector.

ути́ный, *adj. of* у́тка I.

утира́льник, а, m. (*coll.*) hand-towel.

утира́|ть(ся), ю(сь), *impf. of* утере́ть(ся).

ути́рк|а, и, f. **1.** (*coll.*) wiping (off). **2.** (*dial.*) handkerchief; hand-towel.

утих|а́ть, а́ю, *impf. of* ~нуть.

утих|нуть, ну, нешь, *past* ~, ~ла, *pf.* (*of* ~а́ть) **1.** to become quiet, still; (*of sounds*) to cease, die away. **2.** to abate, subside, slacken; (*of wind*) to drop. **3.** to become calm, calm down.

утихоми́рива|ть(ся), ю(сь), *impf. of* утихо-
ми́рить(ся).

утихоми́р|ить, ю, ишь, *pf.* (*of* ~ивать)
(*coll.*) to calm down; to pacify, placate.

утихоми́р|иться, юсь, ишься, *pf.* (*of*
~иваться) (*coll.*) to calm down; to abate,
subside.

у́тк|а, и, *f.* 1. duck. 2. canard, false report;
пусти́ть ~y to start a canard. 3. bed-
-pan.

уткн|у́ть, у́, ёшь, *pf.* (*coll.*) to bury; to fix;
у. нос в кни́гу to bury oneself in a book;
у. глаза́ (в+a.) to fix one's gaze (upon),
stare steadily (at).

уткн|у́ться, у́сь, ёшься, *pf.* (в+a.; *coll.*)
1. to bury oneself (in), one's head (in); у. в
па́пку to bury one's head in a file. 2. to
bump (into), come to rest (upon), come up
(against); ло́дка ~у́лась в бе́рег the boat
bumped into the bank.

утконо́с, а, *m.* (*zool.*) duck-billed platypus.

утлега́р|ь, я, *m.* (*naut.*) jib-boom.

у́тлый, *adj.* 1. frail; unsound, unseaworthy.
2. poor, wretched.

ут|о́к, ка́, *m.* (*text.*) woof, weft.

утоли́|ть, ю́, и́шь, *pf.* (*of* ~я́ть) 1. to quench,
slake (*thirst*); to satisfy (*hunger*). 2. to relieve,
alleviate, soothe.

утол|сти́ть, щу́, сти́шь, *pf.* (*of* ~ща́ть) to
thicken, make thicker.

утол|сти́ться, щу́сь, сти́шься, *pf.* (*of*
~ща́ться) to become thicker.

утолща́|ть(ся), ю(сь), *impf. of* утолсти́ть-
(ся).

утолще́ни|е, я, *n.* 1. thickening. 2. thick-
ened part, bulge; (*tech.*) reinforcement, rib,
boss.

утол|щённый, *p.p.p. of* ~сти́ть *and adj.* rein-
forced.

утол|я́ть, я́ю, *impf. of* ~и́ть.

утоми́тел|ьный (~ен, ~ьна), *adj.* 1. weari-
some, tiring, fatiguing. 2. tiresome;
tedious.

утом|и́ть, лю́, и́шь, *pf.* (*of* ~ля́ть) to tire,
weary, fatigue.

утом|и́ться, лю́сь, и́шься, *pf.* (*of* ~ля́ться)
to get tired.

утомле́ни|е, я, *n.* tiredness, weariness,
fatigue.

утом|лённый, *p.p.p. of* ~и́ть *and adj.* tired,
weary, fatigued.

утомля́|ть(ся), ю(сь), *impf. of* утоми́ть(ся).

утон|у́ть, у́, ~ешь, *pf.* (*of* тону́ть *and* уто-
па́ть) 1. to drown, be drowned, sink. 2.
(в+p.; *fig.*) to be lost (in).

утонч|а́ть(ся), а́ю(сь), *impf. of* ~и́ть(ся).

утончённост|ь, и, *f.* refinement.

утонч|ённый, *p.p.p of* ~и́ть *and adj.* refined;
exquisite, subtle.

утонч|и́ть, у́, и́шь, *pf.* (*of* ~а́ть) 1. to make

thinner; to taper. 2. (*fig.*) to refine, make
refined.

утонч|и́ться, у́сь, и́шься, *pf.* (*of* ~а́ться)
1. to become thinner; to taper (*intrans.*).
2. (*fig.*) to become refined.

утопа́|ть, ю, *impf.* 1. *impf. of* утону́ть. 2.
(*impf. only*) (в+p.; *fig.*) to roll (in), wallow
(in).

утопи́зм, а, *m.* Utopianism.

утопи́ст, а, *m.* Utopian.

утоп|и́ть, лю́, ~ишь, *pf.* (*of* топи́ть) 1. to
drown. 2. (*fig., coll.*) to ruin. 3. to bury,
embed, countersink.

утоп|и́ться, лю́сь, ~ишься, *pf.* (*of* топи́ть-
ся) to drown oneself.

утопи́ческий, *adj.* Utopian.

уто́пи|я, и, *f.* Utopia.

уто́пленник, а, *m.* drowned man.

уто́пленниц|а, ы, *f. of* уто́пленник.

уто́п|ленный, *p.p.p. of* ~и́ть *and adj.* (*tech.*)
built-in; ~ленная голо́вка countersink.

утоп|та́ть, чу́, ~чешь, *pf.* (*of* ута́птывать)
to trample down, pound.

у́точк|а, и, *f. dim. of* у́тка; ходи́ть ~ой to
waddle along.

уточне́ни|е, я, *n.* more precise definition,
amplification, elaboration.

уточн|и́ть, ю́, и́шь, *pf.* (*of* ~я́ть) to make
more precise, define more precisely; to
amplify, elaborate.

уто́чный, *adj. of* уто́к.

уточн|я́ть, я́ю, *impf. of* ~и́ть.

утра́ива|ть, ю, *impf. of* утро́ить.

утрамб|ова́ть, у́ю, *pf.* (*of* ~о́вывать) to
ram, tamp (*road material, etc.*).

утрамб|ова́ться, у́ется, *pf.* (*of* ~о́вываться)
1. to become flat, level (*also fig.*). 2. *pass. of*
~ова́ть.

утрамбо́выва|ть(ся), ю(сь), *impf. of* утрам-
бова́ть(ся).

утра́т|а, ы, *f.* (*in var. senses*) loss; у. трудо-
спосо́бности disablement.

утра́|тить, чу, тишь, *pf.* (*of* ~чивать) to
lose.

утра́чива|ть, ю, *impf. of* утра́тить.

у́тренн|ий, *adj.* morning, early; ~ие за́мо-
розки morning frost; ~яя заря́ dawn, daybreak; (*mil.*) reveille.

у́тренник, а, *m.* 1. morning frost. 2. morning performance, matinée.

у́трен|я, и, *f.* (*eccl.*) matins.

у́тречком, *adv.* (*coll.*) in the morning.

утри́р|овать, ую, *impf. and pf.* to exaggerate;
to overplay.

утриро́вк|а, и, *f.* exaggeration.

у́тр|о, а (до ~á, с ~á), *d.* у (к ~ý), *pl.* ~а, ~,
~ам (по ~áм), *n.* 1. morning; в семь
часо́в ~á at 7 a.m.; с ~á early in the
morning; с ~á до ве́чера from morn till
night; до́брое у.!, с до́брым ~ом! good

morning! 2. *(obs.)* morning performance, matinée.

утрóб|а, ы, *f.* **1.** womb. **2.** *(coll.)* belly; напихáть свою́ ~у to stuff one's belly. **3.** ~ой *(coll.)* by instinct.

утрóбист|ый (~, ~а), *adj.* *(coll.)* big-bellied.

утрóбный, *adj.* **1.** uterine, foetal; у. плод foetus; у. пери́од разви́тия period of gestation. **2.** internal; *(of sounds)* deep, hollow; у. смех belly-laugh.

утрó|ить, ю, ишь, *pf.* *(of* утрáивать*)* to treble.

у́тром, *adv.* in the morning; сегóдня у. this morning.

утру|ди́ть, жу́, ди́шь, *pf.* *(of ~жда́ть)* to trouble, to tire.

утру|ди́ться, жу́сь, ди́шься, *pf.* *(of ~жда́ть-ся)* *(coll.)* to trouble oneself, take trouble.

утружда́|ть(ся), ю(сь), *impf. of* утруди́ть-(ся).

утру́ск|а, и, *f.* *(comm.)* spillage.

утряс|а́ть, а́ю, *impf. of* ~ти́.

утряс|ти́, у́, ёшь, *pf.* *(of ~а́ть)* *(coll.)* **1.** to shake down. **2.** to shake up, give a shaking. **3.** to settle; у. вопрóс to have a matter out.

утучн|и́ть, ю́, и́шь, *pf.* *(of ~я́ть)* **1.** to fatten. **2.** to enrich, manure *(soil).*

утучн|я́ть, я́ю, *impf. of* ~и́ть.

утуш|а́ть, а́ю, *impf. of* ~и́ть.

утуш|и́ть, у́, ~ишь, *pf.* *(of ~а́ть)* *(coll.)* **1.** to put out, extinguish. **2.** *(fig.)* to suppress.

уты́к|ать, аю, *pf.* *(of ~а́ть and ~ивать)* *(coll.)* **1.** to stick (in) all over. **2.** to stop up, caulk.

утык|а́ть, а́ю, *impf. of* ~а́ть.

уты́кива|ть, ю, *impf.* = утыка́ть.

утю́г, á, *m.* (flat) iron.

утю́ж|ить, у, ишь, *impf.* *(of вы́~)* **1.** to iron, press. **2.** *(coll.)* to smooth. **3.** *(coll.)* to beat; to lambast *(also fig.).*

утю́жк|а, и, *f.* ironing, pressing.

утя́гива|ть, ю, *impf. of* утяну́ть.

утяжели́тел|ь, я, *m.* *(tech.)* weighting compound.

утяжел|и́ть, ю́, и́шь, *pf.* *(of ~я́ть)* to make heavier, increase the weight (of).

утяжел|и́ться, и́тся, *pf.* *(of ~я́ться)* to become heavier.

утяжел|я́ть(ся), я́ю, я́ет(ся), *impf. of* ~и́ть(ся).

утян|у́ть, у́, ~ешь, *pf.* *(of* утя́гивать*)* to drag away, off.

утя́тин|а, ы, *f.* *(cul.)* duck.

уф, *interj.* *(expressing (i) relief, (ii) fatigue, physical discomfort, etc.)* ooh!, ee!, gosh!

ух, *interj.* **1.** *(expresses various strong feelings)* ooh!, gosh! **2.** bang!

ух|á, и́, *f.* ukha *(fish-soup).*

ухáб, а, *m.* pot-hole, pit *(in road).*

ухáбист|ый (~, ~а), *adj.* full of pot-holes; bumpy.

ухажёр, а, *m.* *(coll.)* ladies' man; admirer.

ухáжива|ть, ю, *impf.* (за+*i.*) **1.** to nurse, tend; to look after. **2.** to court *(a woman)*; to pay court (to), make advances (to). **3.** to make up (to), try to get round.

у́харский, *adj.* *(coll.)* smart, 'fancy'; dashing; rakish.

у́харств|о, а, *n.* *(coll.)* bravado.

у́хар|ь, я, *m.* *(coll.)* 'lad', smart fellow; dashing fellow.

у́ха|ть(ся), ю(сь), *impf. of* у́хнуть(ся).

ухвáт, а, *m.* **1.** oven fork. **2.** *(tech.)* clip.

ухвáтист|ый (~, ~а), *adj.* *(coll.)* adroit, sure, strong.

ухва|ти́ть, чу́, ~тишь, *pf.* **1.** to lay hold (of); *(fig.)* to seize. **2.** *(fig., coll.)* to grasp.

ухва|ти́ться, чу́сь, ~тишься, *pf.* (за+*a.* **1.** to grasp, lay hold (of); у. за ве́тку to grasp a branch. **2.** *(coll.)* to set (to, about) у. за нóвую рабóту to get stuck in to a new job. **3.** *(fig., coll.)* to seize; to jump (at); to take up; у. за предложéние to jump at an offer.

ухвáтк|а, и, *f.* *(coll.)* **1.** grip. **2.** *(fig.)* grasp (a) skill; trick. **3.** manner.

ухитр|и́ться, ю́сь, и́шься, *pf.* *(of ~я́ться* (+*inf.*; *coll.)* to manage (to), contrive (to)

ухитр|я́ться, я́юсь, *impf. of* ~и́ться.

ухищрéни|е, я, *n.* contrivance, shift, device, trick, dodge.

ухищрённый, *adj.* cunning, artful.

ухищря́|ться, ю́сь, *impf.* to contrive; to resort to contrivance.

ухлóп|ать, аю, *pf.* *(of ~ывать)* *(coll.)* **1.** to kill, do for. **2.** to squander.

ухлóпыва|ть, ю, *impf. of* ухлóпать.

ухмы́лк|а, и, *f.* *(coll.)* smirk, grin.

ухмыльн|у́ться, у́сь, ёшься, *pf.* *(of* ухмыля́ться) *(coll.)* to smirk, grin.

ухмыл|я́ться, я́юсь, *impf. of* ~ьну́ться.

у́хн|уть, у, ешь, *pf.* *(of* у́хать*)* *(coll.)* **1.** to cry out *(from surprise, pleasure, pain, fatigue etc.)*; *(of owls)* to hoot. **2.** to crash, bang, rumble; to ring out with a bang; вдруг ~ул гром there was a sudden crash of thunder; слы́шно бы́ло, как ~ула бóмба the thud of a bomb (exploding) could be heard. **3.** to slip, fall; to come a cropper *(also fig.).* **4.** *(fig.)* to come to grief; to go for a Burton. **5.** to drop. **6.** to lose, squander, spend up. **7.** to bang, slap; кулакóм по столу́ to bang one's fist on the table.

у́хн|уться, усь, ешься, *pf.* *(of* у́хаться*)* *(coll.)* to fall with a bang.

у́х|о, а, *pl.* у́ши, ушéй, *n.* **1.** ear; нару́жное у. auricle; срéднее у. middle ear; воспалéние ~а *(med.)* otitis; у́ши вя́нут (от) *(co* it makes one sick to hear; и ~ом не вести not to listen (= to pay no heed); краем ~а слушать to listen with half an ear; прожужжать, прокричать кому-н. уши to talk someone's head off; у. в у. (c+i.) level (with), alongside; дать, заехать, съездить кому-н. в у. (coll.) to box someone's ears; дуть, петь в уши кому-н. to whisper (= to pass on scandal) to someone; во все уши слушать to be all ears; за уши тащить кого-н. (fig.) to give someone a leg-up; пропустить мимо ушей (coll.) to turn a deaf ear (to), pay no heed (to); говорить кому-н. на у. to have a word in someone's ear, have a private word with someone; по уши up to one's eyes (in work, etc.), over head and ears, head over heels (in love, etc.). 2. ear-flap, ear-piece (of cap, etc.). 3. (tech.) ear, lug, hanger.

уховёртк|а, и, f. (zool.) earwig.

уход¹, a, m. going away, leaving, departure; withdrawal; выйти ~ом (замуж), взять ~ом (женý) (obs.) to marry in secret, elope with.

уход², a, m. (за+i.) nursing, tending, looking after; care (of); maintenance.

ухо|дить¹, жу, ~дишь, impf. 1. impf. of уйти. **2.** impf. only to stretch, extend.

ухо|дить², жу, ~дишь, pf. (coll.) **1.** to wear out, tire out. **2.** to remove, rid oneself (of); to do in.

ухо|диться, жусь, ~дишься, pf. (coll.) **1.** to be worn out, be tired out. **2.** to calm down; to be rested.

ухорéз, a, m. (coll.) desperate fellow.

ухудш|ать(ся), áю, áет(ся), impf. of ~ить(ся).

ухудшéни|е, я, n. worsening, deterioration.

ухýдш|енный, p.p.p. of ~ить and adj. inferior.

ухýдш|ить, у, ишь, pf. (of ~áть) to make worse, worsen, deteriorate.

ухýдш|иться, ится, pf. (of ~áться) to become worse, worsen, deteriorate (intrans.).

уцелé|ть, ю, pf. to remain intact, escape destruction; to remain alive, survive; to remain at liberty, escape.

уцен|ённый, p.p.p. of ~ить and adj. reduced (-price).

уцéнива|ть, ю, impf. of уценить.

уцен|ить, ю, ~ишь, pf. (of ~ивать) to reduce the price (of).

уцеп|ить, лю, ~ишь, pf. (coll.) to catch hold (of), grasp, seize.

уцеп|иться, люсь, ~ишься, pf. (за+a.) **1.** to catch hold (of), grasp, seize. **2.** (fig., coll.) to jump (at).

учáств|овать, ую, impf. 1. (в+p.) to take part (in), participate (in). **2.** (в+p.) to have a share (in), have shares (in); у. в ак-

ционéрном обществе to have shares in a (joint-stock) company. **3.** (+d.; obs.) to sympathize (with), extend sympathy (to).

учáств|ующий, pres. part. act. of ~овать; as noun у., ~ующего, m. participant.

учáсти|е, я, n. 1. taking part, participation; при ~и, с ~ем (+g.) with the participation (of), with the assistance (of), including, featuring; принимáть у. (в+p.) to take part (in), participate (in), take a hand (in). **2.** share, sharing. **3.** sympathy, concern; принимáть у. в ком-н. to extend sympathy to someone, display concern for someone.

уча|стить, щý, стишь, pf. (of ~щáть) to make more frequent.

участ|иться, ится, pf. (of учащáться) to become more frequent; (of pulse) to quicken.

участкóв|ый, adj. of учáсток; у. уполномóченный divisional inspector (of police); у. пристáв (hist.) = у. уполномóченный (in tsarist Russia); as noun у., ~ого, m. = у. уполномóченный, у. пристáв.

учáстлив|ый (~, ~a), adj. sympathetic.

учáстник, a, m. (+g.) participant (in), member (of); у. состязáния participant in a competition, competitor; у. литерату́рного кружкá member of a literary society.

учáст|ок, ка, m. 1. (of land) plot, strip; lot, parcel. **2.** part, section, portion; length (of road, etc.); (railways) division. **3.** (mil.) sector (area occupied by one regiment of Army); area, zone; у. глáвного удáра area of main strike; у. проры́ва breakthrough area. **4.** district, area, zone (as administrative unit); избирáтельный у. (i) electoral district, ward, (ii) polling station. **5.** (fig.) field, sphere (of activity). **6.** (hist.) (i) police division, district; (ii) police-station.

ýчаст|ь, и, f. lot, fate, portion.

учá|ть, учнý, учнёшь, past ~л, ~лá, ~ло, pf. (coll.) to begin.

учащá|ть(ся), ю, ет(ся), impf. of участить(ся).

уча|щённый, p.p.p. of ~стить and adj. quickened; faster; у. пульс quickened pulse.

учáщ|ийся, pres. part. of учиться; as noun у., ~егося, m. student; pupil.

учéб|а, ы, f. 1. studies; studying, learning; за ~ой at one's studies. **2.** drill, training.

учéбник, a, m. text-book; manual; primer.

учéбно- educational-.

учéбн|ый, adj. 1. educational; school; ~ое врéмя school-hours, instruction, term-time; у. год academic year, school year; ~ое заведéние educational institution; у. план curriculum; у. предмéт subject; ~ая часть instructional side (of school); завéдующий ~ой чáстью director of studies. **2.** (mil.) training, practice; у. патрóн dummy cartridge (*used in training*); ~ое пóле training ground; у. самолёт training aircraft, trainer; у. сбор reserve training period; ~ая стрельбá practice shoot; ~ое сýдно training ship.

учéни|е, я, *n.* 1. learning; studies; apprenticeship; отдáть в у. (+*d.*) to apprentice (to). 2. teaching, instruction. 3. (*mil.*) exercise; (*pl.*) training. 4. teaching, doctrine.

ученúк, á, *m.* 1. pupil; у.-лётчик student pilot. 2. apprentice. 3. disciple, follower.

ученúц|а, ы, *f. of* ученúк.

ученú|ческий, *adj.* 1. *adj. of* ~к. 2. raw, crude, immature.

ученúчеств|о, а, *n.* 1. period spent as a pupil, student. 2. apprenticeship. 3. rawness, immaturity.

учёност|ь, и, *f.* learning, erudition (*also iron.*).

учён|ый (~, ~а), *adj.* 1. learned, erudite; (*coll.*) educated. 2. scholarly; academic; ~ая статья́ scholarly article; ~ая стéпень (university) degree. 3. *forms part of title of certain academic posts and institutions in U.S.S.R.:* у. секретáрь academic secretary; у. совéт academic council. 4. (*of animals*) trained, performing. 5. *as noun* у., ~ого, *m.* scholar; scientist.

уч|éсть, учтý, учтёшь, *past* ~ёл, ~лá, *pf.* (*of* ~ú́тывать) 1. to take into account, consideration; to allow (for); to bear in mind. 2. to take stock (of), make an inventory (of). 3. (*fin.*) to discount.

учёт, а, *m.* 1. stock-taking, inventory-making; reckoning, calculation; вестú у. (+*g.*) to take stock (of). 2. taking into account; без ~а (+*g.*) disregarding. 3. registration; взять на у. to register; встать, стать на у. to be registered; состоя́ть на ~е to be on the books; снять с ~а to strike off the register, take off the books. 4. (*fin.*) discount, discounting.

учетвер|ú́ть, ю́, ú́шь, *pf.* (*of* ~я́ть) to quadruple.

учетвер|я́ть, я́ю, *impf. of* ~ú́ть.

учётно-во́инский, *adj.* у.-в. докумéнт (*mil.*) discharge papers (*also* document indicating military service-liability status).

учётно-медицúнск|ий, *adj.*; ~ая кáрточка medical record, medical card.

учётн|ый, *adj.* 1. registration; ~ая кáрточка registration form; ~ое отделéние records section. 2. (*fin.*) discount; у. процéнт, ~ая стáвка бáнковского процéнта rate of discount; bank rate.

учётчик, а, *m.* tally clerk.

училищ|е, а, *n.* school, college (*now = institution providing specialist instruction at secondary level*); воéнное у. military school; ремéсленное у. trade school.

учúлищ|ный, *adj. of* ~е.

учин|ú́ть, ю́, ú́шь, *pf.* (*of* ~я́ть) to make, commit; у. скандáл (*coll.*) to make a scene.

учин|я́ть, я́ю, *impf. of* ~ú́ть.

учúтел|ь, я, *m.* 1. (*pl.* ~я́) teacher. 2. (*pl.* ~и) (*fig.*) teacher, master (= *authority*).

учúтельниц|а, ы, *f. of* учúтель.

учúтельный, *adj.* (*obs.*) 1. skilled in teaching. 2. edifying, instructive.

учúтель|ский, *adj. of* ~; *as noun* ~ская, ~ской, *f.* teachers' common room, staff (common) room.

учúтыва|ть, ю, *impf. of* учéсть.

уч|ú́ть, ý, ~ишь, *impf.* 1. (*pf.* вы́~, на~, and об~) (+*a.* and *d.* or +*inf.*) to teach; у. кого́-н. немéцкому языкý to teach someone German; у. игрáть на скрúпке to teach to play the violin. 2. to be a teacher. 3. (что) (*of a theory, etc.*) to teach (that), say (that). 4. (*pf.* вы́~) (+*a.*) to learn; to memorize.

уч|ú́ться, ýсь, ~ишься, *impf.* 1. (*pf.* вы́~, на~, and об~) (+*d.* or +*inf.*) to learn, study. 2. to be a student; у. в шко́ле to go to, be at school. 3. (на кого́-н.; *coll.*) to study (to be, to become), learn (to be); он ~ится на перево́дчика he is studying to be an interpreter.

учредúтел|ь, я, *m.* founder.

учредúтельн|ый, *adj.* constituent; ~ое собрáние (*polit.*) constituent assembly.

учре|дú́ть, жý, дú́шь, *pf.* (*of* ~ждáть) to found, establish, set up; to introduce, institute.

учрежда́|ть, ю, *impf. of* учредú́ть.

учреждéни|е, я, *n.* 1. founding, establishment (*action*), setting up; introduction. 2. establishment, institution (*object*).

учреждéн|ческий, *adj. of* ~ие 2.

учтúвост|ь, и, *f.* civility, courtesy.

учтúв|ый (~, ~а), *adj.* civil, courteous.

учý|ять, ю, ешь, *pf.* (*coll.*) to smell, nose out; (*fig.*) to sense.

ушáнк|а, и, *f.* (*coll.*) cap with ear-flaps.

ушáст|ый (~, ~а), *adj.* (*coll.*) big-eared.

ушáт, а, *m.* tub (*carried on pole slung through handles*).

ýши, *see* ýхо.

ушúб, а, *m.* 1. injury; knock; bruise; (*med.*) contusion. 2. injured place.

ушиб|áть(ся), áю(сь), *impf. of* ~ú́ть(ся).

ушиб|ú́ть, ý, ёшь, *past* ~, ~ла, *pf.* (*of* ~áть) 1. to injure (*by knocking*); to bruise. 2. (*fig., coll.*) to hurt, shock.

ушиб|ú́ться, ýсь, ёшься, *past* ~ся, ~лась, *pf.* (*of* ~áться) to hurt oneself, give oneself a knock; to bruise oneself.

ушивá|ть, ю, *impf. of* ушúть.

уш|ú́ть, ью́, ьёшь, *pf.* (*of* ~ивáть) (*dressmaking*) to take in.

ушка́н, а, *m.* (*dial.*) hare.

у́шк|о, а, *pl.* ~и, у́шек, *n. dim. of* у́хо; у него́ ~и на маку́шке he is on the qui-vive.

ушк|о́, а́, *pl.* ~и́, ~о́в, *n.* 1. (*tech.*) eye, lug. 2. tab, tag (*of boot*). 3. eye (*of needle*). 4. (*pl.*) (*cul.*) noodles.

ушку́|й, я, *m.* (*hist.*) flat-bottomed boat (*propelled by sail or oars*).

ушку́йник, а, *m.* (*hist.*) river-pirate.

ушни́к, а́, *m.* (*coll.*) ear-specialist.

ушн|о́й, *adj.* ear, aural; ~а́я боль ear-ache; у. врач ear-specialist; ~а́я ра́ковина (*anat.*) auricle; ~а́я се́ра ear-wax.

ущели́ст|ый (~, ~а), *adj.* abounding in ravines.

ущел|ье, ья, *g. pl.* ~ий, *n.* ravine, gorge, canyon.

ущем|и́ть, лю́, и́шь, *pf.* (*of* ~ля́ть) 1. to pinch, jam, nip; у. себе́ па́лец две́рью to pinch one's finger in the door. 2. (*fig.*) to limit; to encroach (upon). 3. (*fig.*) to wound, hurt; у. чье́-н. самолю́бие to hurt someone's pride.

ущемле́ни|е, я, *n.* 1. pinching, jamming, nipping; у. гры́жи (*med.*) strangulation of hernia. 2. (*fig.*) limitation. 3. (*fig.*) wounding, hurting; frustration.

ущемля́|ть, ю, *impf. of* ущеми́ть.

ущем|лённый, *p.p.p. of* ~и́ть *and adj.* (*fig.*) wounded, hurt; frustrated.

ущёрб, а, *m.* 1. detriment; loss; damage, injury; без ~а (для) without prejudice (to); в у. (+*d.*) to the detriment (of), to the prejudice (of). 2. weakening, decline. 3. на ~е (*of the moon*) on the wane; (*fig.*) on the decline.

ущерб|и́ть, лю́, и́шь, *pf.* 1. to injure, damage. 2. (*fig.*) to limit.

ущёрбный, *adj.* (*of the moon*) waning; (*fig.*) on the decline.

ущипн|у́ть, у́, ёшь, *pf.* to pinch, tweak.

уэ́льс|ец, ца, *m.* Welshman.

уэ́льский, *adj.* Welsh.

ую́т, а, *m.* comfort, cosiness.

ую́т|ный (~ен, ~на), *adj.* comfortable, cosy.

уязви́м|ый (~, ~а), *adj.* vulnerable (*also fig.*); ~ое ме́сто (*fig.*) weak spot, sensitive spot.

уязв|и́ть, лю́, и́шь, *pf.* (*of* ~ля́ть) to wound, hurt.

уязвля́|ть, ю, *impf. of* уязви́ть.

уясне́ни|е, я, *n.* explanation, elucidation.

уясн|и́ть, ю́, и́шь, *pf.* (*of* ~я́ть) 1. (себе́) to understand, make out. 2. (*obs.*) to explain.

уясн|я́ть, я́ю, *impf. of* ~и́ть.

Ф

фа, *indecl.*, *n.* (*mus.*) fa.

фаб- *abbr. of* фабри́чный.

фабза́вуч, а, *m.* (*abbr. of* фабри́чно-заво́дское учи́лище) factory workshop-school.

фа́брик|а, и, *f.* factory, mill.

фа́брика-ку́хня, фа́брики-ку́хни, *f.* (*large--scale*) canteen, municipal restaurant.

фабрика́нт, а, *m.* (*obs.*) manufacturer, factory-owner, mill-owner.

фабрика́т, а, *m.* finished product.

фабрика́ци|я, и, *f.* fabrication (*also fig.*).

фабрик|ова́ть, у́ю, *impf.* 1. (*obs.*) to manufacture, make. 2. (*pf.* с~) (*fig.*, *coll.*) to fabricate, forge.

фабр|ить, ю, ишь, *impf.* (*of* на~) (*obs.*) to dye (*moustache or beard*).

фабри́чно-заводско́й (*and* ф.-заво́дский), *adj.* factory, works, industrial.

фабри́чн|ый, *adj.* 1. factory; industrial, manufacturing; ф. го́род manufacturing town; ~ая ма́рка trade mark; ~ое произво́дство manufacturing; *as noun* ф., ~ого, *m.*; ~ая, ~ой, *f.* factory worker. 2. factory--made.

фа́бул|а, ы, *f.* (*lit.*) plot, story.

фавн, а, *m.* (*myth.*) faun.

фаво́р, а, *m.* (*obs.*) быть в ~е (у), по́льзо-

ваться ~ом (у) to be in favour (with); быть не в ~е у кого́-н. to be in someone's bad books.

фавори́т, а, *m.* favourite (*also sport*).

фавори́тизм, а, *m.* favouritism.

фаго́т, а, *m.* (*mus.*) bassoon.

фаготи́ст, а, *m.* bassoon-player.

фагоци́т, а, *m.* (*biol.*) phagocyte.

фа́з|а, ы, *f.* (*in var. senses*) phase; stage.

фаза́н, а, *m.* pheasant.

фаза́н|ий, *adj. of* ~.

фаза́них|а, и, *f.* hen pheasant.

фа́зис, а, *m.* phase.

фа́зн|ый, *adj.* (*tech.*) phase; ~ая обмо́тка phase winding.

фа́з|овый, *adj.* = ~ный; (*phys.*, *tech.*) ф. сдвиг phase shift; ~овая ско́рость phase velocity; ф. у́гол phase angle.

фазотро́н, а, *m.* (*phys.*) synchro-cyclotron.

фай, фа́я, *m.* (*text.*) faille.

файдеши́н, а, *m.* (*text.*) faille de Chine.

фа́кел, а, *m.* torch, flare; ф.-ло́цман pilot flame.

фа́кел|ьный, *adj. of* ~; ~ьное ше́ствие torch-light procession.

фа́кельщик, а, *m.* 1. torch-bearer. 2. (*fig.*, *pejor.*) incendiary, fire-bug.

факи́р, а, *m.* fakir.

факси́миле, *indecl., n.* (*also as indecl. adj.*) facsimile.

факт, а, *m.* **1.** fact; соверши́вшийся ф. fait accompli; показа́ть на ~ах to show proof; факт, что (*coll.*) it is a fact that; ф. остаётся ~ом the fact remains.

факти́чески, *adv.* in fact, actually; practically, virtually, to all intents and purposes.

факти́ческ|ий, *adj.* actual; real; virtual; ~ие да́нные the facts.

факти́ч|ный (~ен, ~на), *adj.* factual, authentic.

фактографи́ч|ный (~ен, ~на), *adj.* factual, based on fact, authentic.

фактогра́фи|я, и, *f.* factual account.

фа́ктор, а, *m.* factor.

факто́ри|я, и, *f.* trading station.

факту́р|а, ы, *f.* **1.** (*arts and lit.*) style; manner of execution; texture. **2.** (*comm.*) invoice, bill.

факту́р|ный, *adj of* ~a.

факультати́в|ный (~ен, ~на), *adj.* optional.

факульте́т, а, *m.* faculty, department (*of higher education institution*).

факульте́т|ский, *adj. of* ~.

фал, а, *m.* (*naut.*) halyard.

фала́нг|а, и, *f.* **1.** (*hist.; fig.*) phalanx. **2.** (*polit.*) Falange. **3.** (*anat.*) phalanx, phalange.

фалангист, а, *m.* (*polit.*) Falangist.

фаланстéр, а, *m.* (*polit. philos.*) phalanstery.

фа́лд|а, ы, *f.* tail, skirt (*of coat*).

фа́лин|ь, я, *m.* (*naut.*) painter.

фалли́ческий, *adj.* phallic.

фалло́пиев, *adj.* ~а труба́ (*med.*) Fallopian tube.

фа́ллос, а, *m.* phallus.

фалре́п, а, *m.* (*naut.*) side-rope, side-boy.

фальсифика́тор, а, *m.* falsifier; forger.

фальсифика́ци|я, и, *f.* **1.** falsification; forging. **2.** adulteration. **3.** forgery, fake, counterfeit.

фальсифици́р|овать, ую, *impf. and pf.* **1.** to falsify; to forge. **2.** to adulterate.

фальц, а, *m.* **1.** (*tech.*) rabbet; groove. **2.** (*typ.*) fold (*of printed sheet*).

фальцго́бел|ь, я, *m.* (*tech.*) fillister, rabbeting plane.

фальц|ева́ть, у́ю, *impf.* (*of* с~) **1.** (*tech.*) to rabbet, groove. **2.** to fold, crease.

фальце́т, а, *m.* (*mus.*) falsetto.

фальцо́вочный, *adj.* (*tech.*) rabbeting, grooving; ф. стано́к rabʋeting machine.

фальшбо́рт, а, *m.* (*naut.*) bulwark, rails.

фальши́в|ить, лю, ишь, *impf.* **1.** to be a hypocrite; to act insincerely. **2.** (*pf.* с~) (*mus.*) to sing, play out of tune.

фальши́вк|а, и, *f.* (*coll.*) forged docume

фальшивомонéтчик, а, *m.* counterfeit coiner (*of false money*).

фальши́в|ый (~, ~a), *adj.* **1.** false; spurio forged, fake; artificial, imitation; ф. до мéнт forged document; ~ые зу́бы fa teeth; ф. жéмчуг imitation pearl. **2.** fal hypocritical, insincere; ф. комплимéнт sincere compliment; попа́сть в ~ое по жéние to put oneself into a false positic **3.** (*mus.*) false (= *out of tune*). **4.** (*nau* temporary, jury-; ~ая ма́чта jury-mast.

фальшки́л|ь, я, *m.* (*naut.*) false keel.

фальш|ь, и, *f.* **1.** deception, trickery. falsity; hypocrisy, insincerity. **3.** (*mu* singing, playing out of tune.

фами́ли|я, и, *f.* **1.** surname. **2.** family, k

фами́льный, *adj.* family.

фамилья́рнича|ть, ю, *impf.* (*coll.*) to (too) familiar.

фамилья́рност|ь, и, *f.* (excessive) far liarity; unceremoniousness.

фамилья́р|ный (~ен, ~на), *adj.* (exc sively) familiar; unceremonious, off-har

фанабéри|я, и, *f.* (*coll.*) arrogance, bum tiousness.

фанати́зм, а, *m.* fanaticism.

фана́тик, а, *m.* fanatic.

фанати́ческий, *adj.* fanatical.

фанати́ч|ный (~ен, ~на), *adj.* fanatic(a

фанéр|а, ы, *f.* **1.** veneer. **2.** plywood.

фанéр|ный, *adj. of* ~a; ф. лист plywo sheet; ~ная рабо́та veneering.

фанз|а́, ы-ы́, *f.* fanza (*peasant domicile China or Korea*).

фанз|а́, ы́, *f.* (*text.*) foulard.

фа́нов|ый, *adj.* waste, sewage; ~ая тру waste pipe.

фант, а, *m.* forfeit (*in game 'forfeits'*); игра́ в ~ы to play forfeits.

фантазёр, а, *m.* dreamer, visionary.

фантази́р|овать, ую, *impf.* **1.** (*impf. only*) dream, indulge in fantasies. **2.** (*pf.* с~) make up, dream up. **3.** (*impf. only*) to i provise (*on piano, etc.*).

фанта́зи|я, и, *f.* **1.** fantasy; imaginatic бога́тая ф. fertile imagination. **2.** fanta fancy; предава́ться ~ям to indulge in fa tasies. **3.** fabrication. **4.** (*coll.*) fan whim. **5.** (*mus.*) fantasia.

фантасмаго́ри|я, и, *f.* phantasmagoria.

фанта́ст, а, *m.* **1.** fantasy-monger; pers with powerful imagination; dream visionary. **2.** writer, artist treating fantastic.

фанта́стик|а, и, *f.* **1.** the fantastic; (*colle lit.*) fantastic tales. **2.** fantasy, fiction opp. to reality); нау́чная ф. science fictior

фантасти́ческий, *adj.* **1.** fantastical. **2.** var. senses*) fantastic; fabulous; imaginar

фантастич|ный (~ен, ~на), *adj.* = ~еский.

фантóм, а, *m.* phantom.

фантóмный, *adj.* **1.** (*physiol.*) imaginary, false. **2.** (*electr.*) phantom.

фанфáр|а, ы, *f.* (*mus.*) **1.** bugle. **2.** fanfare.

фанфарóн, а, *m.* (*coll.*) braggart.

фанфарóн|ить, ю, ишь, *impf.* (*coll.*) to brag.

фанфарóнств|о, а, *n.* (*coll.*) bragging.

фáр|а, ы, *f.* headlight (*on motor vehicle, locomotive, etc.*); посáдочные ~ы landing lights (*on aircraft*).

фарáд|а, ы, *f.* (*electr.*) farad.

фараóн, а, *m.* **1.** (*hist.*) pharaoh (*also nickname for policeman*). **2.** faro (*card-game*).

фарабнов, *adj.* pharaoh's; ~а мышь (*zool.*) ichneumon.

фарвáтер, а, *m.* (*naut.*) fairway, channel; плыть, быть в чём-н. ~е (*fig.*) to follow someone's lead, side with someone.

Фаренгéйт, а, *m.* Fahrenheit (thermometer); 80° по ~у 80° Fahrenheit.

фарингúт, а, *m.* (*med.*) pharyngitis.

фарисé|й, я, *m.* Pharisee (*also fig.*).

фарисéйский, *adj.* pharisaical (*also fig.*).

фарисéйств|о, а, *n.* pharisaism.

фарисéйств|овать, ую, *impf.* to act pharisaically.

фармазóн, а, *m.* (*coll., obs.*) freemason.

фармакóлог, а, *m.* pharmacologist.

фармакологúческий, *adj.* pharmacological.

фармакóлоги|я, и, *f.* pharmacology.

фармакопé|я, и, *f.* pharmacopoeia.

фармацéвт, а, *m.* pharmaceutical chemist.

фармацéвтик|а, и, *f.* pharmaceutics.

фармацевтúческий, *adj.* pharmaceutical.

фармацú|я, и, *f.* pharmacy.

фарс, а, *m.* (*theatr.*) farce (*also fig.*).

фарт, а, *m.* (*sl.*) luck.

фарт|úть, úт, *impf.* (*of* по~) (*impers.+d.*; *sl.*) to be in luck.

фартóвый, *adj.* (*sl.*) **1.** lucky. **2.** fine, smashing.

фáртук, а, *m.* **1.** apron. **2.** carriage-rug.

фарфóр, а, *m.* **1.** porcelain, china. **2.** (*collect.*) china.

фарфóр|овый, *adj. of* ~; ~овая глúна china clay, kaolin; ~овая посýда china(-ware).

фарцóвщик, а, *m.* (*sl.*) dealer, trafficker (*in goods or currency illegally bought from foreigners*).

фарш, а, *m.* (*cul.*) force-meat; sausage-meat; stuffing.

фарширóв|анный, *p.p.p. of* ~áть *and adj.* (*cul.*) stuffed, farci.

фаршир|овáть, ýю, *impf* (*of* за~) (*cul.*) to stuff.

фас, а, m. **1.** front, façade; в ф. en face. **2.** (*mil.*) face (*of salient*); ф. прóволочного заграждéния straight leg of barbed-wire entanglement.

фасáд, а, *m.* façade, front.

фасéт, а, *m.* facet.

фасéт|очный, *adj. of* ~; ~очные глазá (*zool.*) compound eyes.

фáск|а, и, *f.* (*tech.*) face, facet; (bevel) edge.

фас|овáть, ýю, *impf.* (*comm.*) to pre-pack (*in measured quantities*).

фасóвк|а, и, *f.* (*comm.*) pre-packing.

фасóвочн|ый, *adj.* (*comm.*) (pre-)packing, packaging; *as noun* ~ая, ~ой, *f.* packing department.

фасóл|евый, *adj. of* ~ь.

фасóл|ь, и, *f.* haricot bean, French bean.

фасóн, а, *m.* **1.** cut (*of dress, etc.*); fashion, style; не ф. (*coll.*) it's not done. **2.** (*coll.*) style, manner, way. **3.** (*coll.*) swank, showing off; держáть ф. to swank, show off.

фасóнист|ый (~, ~а), *adj.* (*coll.*) fashionable, stylish.

фасóнн|ый, *adj.* (*tech.*) **1.** fashioned, shaped; ~ое желéзо shaped iron, profile iron, section iron. **2.** form(ing), shape, shaping; ~ая наковáльня die block; ~ая обрабóтка profiling; ф. резéц form tool, shaper tool; ~ая фрезерóвка form milling.

фат, а, *m.* fop.

фат|á, ы́, *f.* (*bridal*) veil.

фаталúзм, а, *m.* fatalism.

фаталúст, а, *m.* fatalist.

фаталистúческий, *adj.* **1.** fatalistic. **2.** fatal.

фатáльност|ь, и, *f.* fatality, fate.

фатáл|ьный (~ен, ~ьна), *adj.* **1.** fatal, fated. **2.** resigned (to one's fate); ф. вид resigned appearance.

фатовáт|ый (~, ~а), *adj.* foppish.

фáтум, а, *m.* fate.

фáун|а, ы, *f.* fauna.

фаустпатрóн, а, *m.* (*mil.*) 'panzer-faust' (*bazooka-type weapon*).

фахвéрк, а, *m.* frame building.

фахвéрковый, *adj.* frame-built.

фашизúр|овать, ую, *impf. and pf.* to run on Fascist lines; to impose Fascism (upon).

фашизúр|оваться, уюсь, *impf. and pf.* **1.** to become Fascist. **2.** *pass. of* ~овать.

фашúзм, а, *m.* Fascism.

фашúн|а, ы, *f.* fascine, faggot.

фашúн|ный, *adj. of* ~а; ф. нож fascine-cutting knife.

фашúст, а, *m.* Fascist.

фашúстский, *adj.* Fascist.

фаэтóн, а, *m.* phaeton.

фая́нс, а, *m.* faience, pottery, glazed earthenware.

фая́нс|овый, *adj. of* ~.

феврáл|ь, я́, *m.* February.

феврáль|ский, *adj. of* ~.

федералúзм, а, *m.* federalism.

федералúст, а, *m.* federalist.

федерáльный, *adj.* federal.

федератúвный, *adj.* federative, federal.

федера́ци|я, и, *f.* federation.

феери́ческий, *adj.* **1.** (*theatr.*) (based on a) fairytale. **2.** fairy-like; magical.

фее́ри|я, и, *f.* **1.** play, ballet, *etc.*, based on a fairytale. **2.** magical sight.

фейерве́рк, а, *m.* firework(s).

фейерве́ркер, а, *m.* (*hist.*) bombardier (*artillery N.C.O. in tsarist Russian army*).

фека́л|ии, ий, *sing.* ~ия, ~ии, *f.* faeces.

фека́льный, *adj.* faecal.

фелла́х, а, *m.* fellah.

фельдма́ршал, а, *m.* field-marshal.

фельдфе́бел|ь, я, *m.* (*hist.*) sergeant-major.

фе́льдшер, а, *pl.* ~а́, *m.* doctor's assistant, medical attendant (*medical practitioner lacking graduate qualification*).

фельдшери́ц|а, ы, *f.* of фе́льдшер.

фе́льдшер|ский, *adj.* of ~.

фельдъе́гер|ский, *adj.* of ~ь; ~ская связь communication by courier.

фельдъе́гер|ь, я, *m.* (*hist.*) courier, special messenger.

фельето́н, а, *m.* feuilleton; satirical article.

фельетони́ст, а, *m.* feuilletonist; composer of satirical articles.

фельето́н|ный, *adj.* of ~.

фелю́г|а, и, *f.* (*naut.*) felucca.

femини́зм, а, *m.* feminism.

femини́ст, а, *m.* feminist.

femини́ст|ка, ки, *f.* of ~.

фен, а, *m.* (hair-)drier.

фён, а, *m.* föhn (*wind*).

фе́никс, а, *m.* **1.** (*mythol.*) phoenix. **2.** (*obs.*) marvel, prodigy.

фено́л, а, *m.* (*chem.*) phenol, carbolic acid.

феноло́ги|я, и, *f.* (*biol.*) phenology.

фено́мен, а, *m.* phenomenon; phenomenal occurrence, person.

феноменали́зм, а, *m.* (*philos.*) phenomenalism.

феномена́л|ьный (~ен, ~ьна), *adj.* phenomenal.

феноменоло́ги|я, и, *f.* (*philos.*) phenomenology.

фе́нхел|ь, я, *m.* (*bot.*) fennel.

феод, а, *m.* (*hist.*) feud, fief.

феода́л, а, *m.* (*hist.*) feudal lord.

феодали́зм, а, *m.* feudalism.

феода́льный, *adj.* feudal.

ферз|евый, *adj.* of ~ь.

ферз|ь, я́, *pl.* ~и́, ~е́й, *m.* (*chess*) queen.

фе́рм|а¹, ы, *f.* farm.

фе́рм|а², ы, *f.* (*tech.*) girder.

ферма́т|а, ы, *f.* (*mus.*) fermata.

фе́рм|енный, *adj.* of ~а²; lattice.

ферме́нт, а, *m.* (*biol., chem.*) ferment.

ферменти́р|овать, ую, *impf.* to ferment.

фе́рмер, а, *m.* farmer.

фе́рмер|ский, *adj.* of ~; ф. дом farm-house.

фе́рмерств|о, а, *n.* **1.** (*private*) farming. **2.** (*collect.*) farmers.

фе́рмер|ша, ши, *f.* (*coll.*) **1.** *f.* of ~. **2.** farmer's wife.

фе́рм|овый, *adj.* of ~а².

фермуа́р, а, *m.* (*obs.*) **1.** clasp (*on necklace, purse, etc.*). **2.** necklace.

фернамбу́к, а, *m.* (*bot.*) Brazil wood (*Caesalpinia brasiliensis*).

феронье́рк|а, и, *f.* (*obs.*) frontlet, coronet.

ферроспла́в, а, *m.* ferro-alloy.

ферт, а, *m.* **1.** old name of letter 'ф'; ~ом стоя́ть to stand with arms akimbo. **2.** (*coll.*) fop; smug person; ~ом гляде́ть to look smug; ~ом ходи́ть to strut about.

феру́л|а, ы, *f.* **1.** (*obs.*) ruler, ferula (*as instrument of punishment in school*). **2.** surveillance.

фе́ряз|ь, и, *f.* (*hist.*) feryaz (*loose tunic formerly worn by Russians*).

фес, а, *m.* (and фе́ск|а, и, *f.*) fez.

фестива́л|ь, я, *m.* festival.

фесто́н, а, *m.* (*dressmaking*) scallops (*decoration on fabrics*).

фети́ш, а, *m.* fetish.

фетишизи́р|овать, ую, *impf.* to make a fetish (of).

фетиши́зм, а, *m.* fetishism.

фетиши́ст, а, *m.* fetishist.

фетр, а, *m.* felt.

фе́тр|овый, *adj.* of ~.

фефёл|а, ы, *f.* (*coll.*) slattern.

фе́фер, а(у), *m.* only in phrases (*coll.*) зада́ть, показа́ть ~у (+*d.*) to give it hot (to).

фехтова́льный, *adj.* fencing.

фехтова́льщик, а, *m.* fencer; ф. рапи́рой foil fencer; ф. шпа́гой épée fencer.

фехтова́ни|е, я, *n.* fencing.

фехт|ова́ть, у́ю, *impf.* to fence.

фешене́бел|ьный (~ен, ~ьна), *adj.* (*obs.*) fashionable.

фе́|я, и, *f.* fairy.

фи, *interj.* fie!, pah!

фиа́л, а, *m.* phial; (*poet.*) goblet, beaker.

фиа́лк|а, и, *f.* violet.

фиа́лк|овый, *adj.* of ~а; ф. ко́рень orrisroot; *as noun* ~овые, ~овых (*bot.*) Violaceae.

фиа́ско, *indecl., n.* failure; потерпе́ть ф. to be a flop.

фи́бр|а, ы, *f.* **1.** (*anat., bot.*) fibre (*also fig.*); все́ми ~ами души́ in every fibre (of one's being). **2.** fibre (*leather-substitute material*).

фи́бр|овый, *adj.* of ~а 2.

фибро́зный, *adj.* (*anat., bot.*) fibrous.

фибро́м|а, ы, *f.* (*med.*) fibroma.

фи́г|а, и, *f.* **1.** fig(-tree). **2.** (*coll.*) = ку́киш.

фигаро́, *indecl., n.* bolero (*short jacket*).

фи́гли-ми́гли, фи́глей-ми́глей, *no sing.* (*coll.*) tricks.

фигля́р, а, *m*. 1. (*obs.*) (circus) acrobat; clown. 2. poseur; (*pejor.*) actor.

фигля́р|ить, ю, ишь, *impf*. (*coll.*) to put on an act.

фигля́рнича|ть, ю, *impf*. = **фигля́рить.**

фи́г|овый, *adj*. of ~а; ~овое де́рево fig-tree; ф. листо́к fig-leaf (*also fig*. = pretence).

фигу́р|а, ы, *f*. 1. (*in var. senses*) figure. 2. (*cards*) court-card, picture-card. 3. chess-man (*excluding pawns*).

фигура́л|ьный (~ен, ~ьна), *adj*. 1. figurative, metaphorical. 2. (*of lit. style*) ornate, involved.

фигура́нт, а, *m*. (*theatr*.) 1. figurant (*in ballet*). 2. super, extra.

фигури́р|овать, ую, *impf*. to figure, appear.

фигури́ст, а, *m*. figure skater.

фигури́ст|ка, ки, *f*. of ~.

фигу́р|ка, ки, *f*. 1. *dim*. of ~а. 2. figurine, statuette.

фигу́рн|ый, *adj*. 1. figured; ornamented; irregularly shaped. 2. ф. резе́ц (*tech*.) form tool. 3. ~ое ката́ние на конька́х figure skating; ф. пило́та́ж aerobatics.

фидеи́зм, а, *m*. (*philos*.) fideism.

фи́жм|ы, ~, *no sing*. farthingale.

физ- physical.

фи́зик, а, *m*. physicist.

фи́зик|а, и, *f*. physics.

физио́лог, а, *m*. physiologist.

физиологи́ческий, *adj*. physiological.

физиоло́ги|я, и, *f*. physiology.

физионо́ми|я, и, *f*. physiognomy (*also joc*.).

физиотерапе́вт, а, *m*. physiotherapist.

физиотерапи́|я, и, *f*. physiotherapy.

физи́ческ|ий, *adj*. 1. physical; ~ая культу́ра physical training, gymnastics; ф. труд manual labour. 2. *adj*. of фи́зика; ф. кабине́т physics laboratory.

физкульту́р|а, ы, *f*. (*abbr. of* физи́ческая культу́ра) physical training, gymnastics.

физкульту́рник, а, *m*. gymnast, athlete.

физкульту́рни|ца, цы, *f*. of ~к.

физкульту́рн|ый, *adj*. gymnastic; athletic, sports; ф. зал gymnasium; ~ая подгото́вка physical training.

фикс¹, а, *m*. 1. fixed price. 2. fixed sum.

фикс², а, *m*. (*coll*.) false gold tooth-capping.

фикса́ж, а, *m*. (*phot*.) fixing solution, fixer.

фиксати́в, а, *m*. (*art*) fixative.

фикса́тор, а, *m*. (*tech*.) 1. stop; index pin. 2. fixing solution.

фиксатуа́р, а, *m*. fixative, hair-grease.

фикси́р|овать, ую, *impf. and pf*. (*pf. also* за~) 1. to record (*in writing, etc.*). 2. (*in var. senses*) to fix; ф. день свида́ния to fix a date to meet, make a date.

фикти́в|ный (~ен, ~на), *adj*. fictitious.

фи́кус, а, *m*. (*bot*.) ficus.

фи́кци|я, и, *f*. fiction.

филантро́п, а, *m*. philanthropist.

филантропи́ческий, *adj*. philanthropic.

филантро́пи|я, и, *f*. philanthropy.

филармо́ни|я, и, *f*. philharmonic society.

филатели́ст, а, *m*. philatelist, stamp collector.

филатели́|я, и, *f*. philately.

филе́¹, *indecl.*, *n*. (*cul*.) 1. sirloin. 2. fillet (*of meat or fish*).

филе́², *indecl.*, *n*. (*dressmaking*) drawn-thread work.

филе́|й, я, *m*. = ~¹.

филе́йный, *adj*. of ~¹, ².

филёнк|а, и, *f*. panel, slat.

филёр, а, *m*. detective, sleuth.

филиа́л, а, *m*. branch (*of an institution*).

филиа́л|ьный, *adj*. of ~; ~ьное отделе́ние branch (office).

филигра́нный, *adj*. 1. filigree. 2. (*fig*.) meticulous.

филигра́н|ь, и, *f*. 1. filigree. 2. water-mark.

фи́лин, а, *m*. eagle owl (*Bubo bubo*).

фили́ппик|а, и, *f*. philippic.

филиппи́нский, *adj*. Philippine.

фили́стер, а, *m*. philistine.

фили́стер|ский, *adj*. of ~.

фили́стерств|о, а, *n*. philistinism.

филогене́з, а, *m*. (*biol*.) phylogenesis.

фило́лог, а, *m*. philologist, student of language and literature.

филологи́ческий, *adj*. philological; ф. факульте́т faculty of languages and literature.

фило́логи|я, и, *f*. philology; study of language and literature.

филомени́ст, а, *m*. phillumenist (*collector of matchbox labels*).

филосо́ф, а, *m*. philosopher.

филосо́фи|я, и, *f*. philosophy.

филосо́фский, *adj*. philosophic(al).

филосо́фств|овать, ую, *impf*. to philosophize.

фильдеко́с, а, *m*. Lisle thread.

фильер|а, ы, *f*. (*tech*.) draw plate; die; spinneret.

фи́лькин, *adj*. ~а гра́мота invalid, crudely-written, obscure document.

фильм, а, *m*. (*cinema*) film.

фи́льм|а, ы, *f*. (*obs*.) = ~.

фильмоте́к|а, и, *f*. film library.

фильтр, а, *m*. filter.

фильтра́т, а, *m*. filtrate.

фильтра́ци|я, и, *f*. filtration.

фильтрова́льный, *adj*. ф. насо́с filter pump; ф. слой filter-bed.

фильтр|ова́ть, у́ю, *impf*. (*of* про~) 1. to filter. 2. (*fig., coll*.) to screen, check.

фимиа́м, а, *m*. incense; кури́ть ф. (+*d*.) to praise to the skies, sing the praises (of).

фин- *abbr. of* фина́нсовый.

финáл, а, *m.* **1.** finale. **2.** (*sport*) final.

финáльный, *adj.* final; ф. аккóрд (*mus.*) final chord; ф. матч (*sport*) final.

финанси́р|овать, ую, *impf. and pf.* to finance.

финанси́ст, а, *m.* **1.** financier. **2.** financial expert.

финáнсовый, *adj.* financial; ф. год fiscal year; ф. отдéл finance department.

финáнс|ы, ов, *no sing.* **1.** finance(s). **2.** (*coll.*) money.

фи́ник, а, *m.* date (*fruit*).

фи́ник|овый, *adj. of* ∼; ∼овая пáльма date-palm.

фини́фтевый, *adj.* (*obs.*) enamelled.

фининспéктор, а, *m.* (*abbr. of* финáнсовый инспéктор) inspector of finance(s).

фини́фт|ь, и, *f.* (*obs.*) enamel.

фини́фт|яный = ∼евый.

фи́ниш, а, *m.* (*sport*) **1.** finish; finishing post. **2.** final lap.

фи́нишер, а, *m.* (*naut.*) batsman (*on aircraft carrier*).

финиши́р|овать, ую, *impf. and pf.* (*sport*) to finish, come in.

фи́ниш|ный, *adj. of* ∼; ∼ная лéнточка finishing tape.

фи́нк|а¹, и, *f. of* финн.

фи́нк|а², и, *f.* **1.** Finnish knife. **2.** Finnish cap (*round, flat cap with fur band*). **3.** Finnish pony. **4.** = фи́нна.

финля́ндский, *adj.* Finnish.

финн, а, *m.* Finn.

фи́нн|а, ы, *f.* (*zool.*) pork tapeworm.

финнóз, а, *m.* measles (*disease of swine*).

фи́нно-угóрский, *adj.* (*ling.*) Finno-Ugric.

финотдéл, а, *m.* (*abbr. of* финáнсовый отдéл) finance department.

фи́нский, *adj.* Finnish, Finnic; Ф. зали́в Gulf of Finland; ф. нож Finnish knife.

финт, а, *m.* (*sport*) feint.

фин|ти́ть, чу́, ти́шь, *impf.* (*coll.*) to be crafty, resort to ruses.

финтифáнт|ы, ов, *no sing.* (*coll., obs.*) **1.** вы-дéлывать, выки́дывать ф. to display finesse. **2.** trifles.

финтифлю́шк|а, и, *f.* (*coll.*) **1.** bagatelle. **2.** (*pl.*) trifles. **3.** flibbertigibbet.

фиолéтовый, *adj.* violet.

фиóрд, а, *m.* (*geogr.*) fiord, fjord.

фиориту́р|а, ы, *f.* (*mus.*) grace(-note).

фи́рм|а, ы, *f.* **1.** (*econ.*) firm. **2.** (*obs.*) sign, mark, signature; под ∼ой (+*g.*) under the sign (of). **3.** (*coll.*) appearance, pretext. **4.** (*sl.*) foreigner; foreign goods.

фи́рм|енный, *adj. of* ∼а 1; ∼енная этикéт-ка proprietary label; ф. бланк letterhead.

фирн, а, *m.* (*geogr.*) névé, glacier snow.

фисгармóни|я, и, *f.* (*mus.*) harmonium.

фиск, а, *m.* fisc.

фискáл, а, *m.* (*hist.*) fiscal, finance inspector; (*coll.*) sneak, tale-bearer.

фискáл|ить, ю, ишь, *impf.* (*coll.*) to (be a) sneak.

фискáльный, *adj.* (*leg.*) fiscal.

фистáшк|а, и, *f.* pistachio(-tree).

фистáшков|ый, *adj.* **1.** pistachio; ф. лак mastic varnish; ∼ая смолá mastic. **2.** pistachio-green.

фи́стул|а¹, ы-ы́, *f.* (*med.*) fistula.

фистул|á², ы́, *f.* **1.** (*mus.*) pipe, flute. **2.** falsetto.

фити́л|ь, я́, *m.* **1.** wick; fuse. **2.** (*naut. sl.*) rocket (= reprimand).

фито- (*biol.*) phyto-.

фитю́льк|а, и, *f.* (*coll.*) little thing; (*of a person*) midget.

фиф|а, ы́, *f.* (*coll.*) flibbertigibbet.

фи́шк|а, и, *f.* **1.** counter, chip (*for scoring, recording stake, etc., in games*). **2.** (*sl.*) face.

флаг, а, *m.* flag; вы́кинуть ф. to put out a flag; держáть (свой) ф. (на+*p.*; *naut.*) to sail (in), be (in); спусти́ть ф. to lower a flag; остáться за ∼ом (*sport*; *fig.*) to fail to make the distance; под ∼ом (+*g.*) (*i*) flying the flag (of), (*ii*) (*fig.*) under the guise (of).

флáгдук, а, *m.* (*naut.*) bunting.

флáгман, а, *m.* (*naut.*) **1.** flag-officer. **2.** flag-ship; (*aeron.*) leader's plane of bomber squadron. **3.** (*fig.*) leader.

флáгман|ский, *adj. of* ∼; ф. корáбль = ∼ 2.

флаг-офицéр, а, *m.* flag-officer.

флагштóк, а, *m.* flagstaff.

флажкóв|ый, *adj. of* флажóк; ∼ая сигнали-зáция flag signalling.

флáжный, *adj.* flag.

флаж|óк, кá, *m.* (*small*) flag; signal flag.

флажолéт, а, *m.* (*mus.*) flageolet.

флакóн, а, *m.* (scent-)bottle, flask.

фламáнд|ец, ца, *m.* Fleming.

фламáнд|ка, ки, *f. of* ∼ец.

фламáндский, *adj.* Flemish.

флами́нго, *indecl., m.* flamingo.

фланг, а, *m.* (*mil.*) flank; wing.

флангóв|ый, *adj.* (*mil.*) flank; ф. охвáт flanking movement, envelopment; *as noun* ф., ∼ого, *m.* flank man.

фланéлевк|а, и, *f.* (*coll.*) flannel (*sailor's blouse*).

фланéлевый, *adj.* flannel.

фланéл|ь, и, *f.* flannel.

фланёр, а, *m.* flâneur, idler.

флáн|ец, ца, *m.* (*tech.*) flange.

флани́р|овать, ую, *impf.* (*coll.*) to idle; to mooch.

фланки́р|овать, ую, *impf. and pf.* (*mil.*) to flank.

флáн|цевый, *adj. of* ∼ец.

флáтов|ый, *adj.* ∼ая бумáга (*typ.*) flat paper.

флеби́т, а, *m.* (*med.*) phlebitis.

флёгм|а, ы, *f.* **1.** (*fig.*) phlegm. **2.** (*coll.*) phlegmatic person.

флегма́тик, а, *m.* phlegmatic person.

флегмати́ч|ный (~ен, ~на), *adj.* phlegmatic.

фле́йт|а, ы, *f.* flute.

флейти́ст, а, *m.* flautist.

флéйт|овый, *adj. of* ~а.

флéкси|я, и, *f.* (*ling.*) inflexion.

флекти́вный, *adj.* (*ling.*) inflected.

флёр, а, *m.* crêpe; наки́нуть ф. (на+*a.*; *fig.*) to draw a veil (over).

флёрдора́нж, а, *m.* orange blossom.

флибустьéр, а, *m.* filibuster.

фли́гел|ь, я, *pl.* ~я́, ~éй, *m.* **1.** wing (*of building*). **2.** outhouse, outbuilding.

фли́гель-адъюта́нт, а, *m.* (*hist.*) aide-de-camp.

флирт, а, *m.* flirtation.

флирт|ова́ть, у́ю, *impf.* (c+*i.*) to flirt (with).

флóр|а, ы, *f.* flora.

флори́ст, а, *m.* specialist in study of flora.

флори́стик|а, и, *f.* (study of) flora.

флот, а, *m.* **1.** fleet; вое́нно-морско́й ф. navy. **2.** возду́шный ф. air force.

флота́ци|я, и, *f.* (*min.*) flotation.

флоти́ли|я, и, *f.* flotilla.

флотовóд|ец, ца, *m.* naval commander.

флóтск|ий, *adj.* naval; *as noun* ф., ~ого., *m.* sailor.

флуоресцéнци|я, и, *f.* fluorescence.

флуоресци́р|овать, ует, *impf.* (*phys.*) to fluoresce; ~ующий fluorescent.

флюга́рк|а, и, *f.* **1.** (*naut.*) pennant; distinguishing plate (*of boat*). **2.** (*chimney*) cowl. **3.** weather-vane.

флю́гер, а, *pl.* ~а́, *m.* **1.** weather-vane; weathercock (*also of a person*). **2.** (*mil.*; *obs.*) pennant.

флюи́д|ы, ов, *sing.* ~, ~а, *m.* ectoplasm; (*fig.*) emanations.

флюс¹, а, *pl.* ~ы, *m.* dental abscess, gumboil.

флюс², а, *pl.* ~ы, *m.* (*tech.*) flux.

фля́г|а, и, *f.* **1.** flask; (*mil.*) water bottle. **2.** churn.

фля́жк|а, и, *f.* dim. of фля́га.

фойé, *indecl.*, *n.* foyer.

фок, а, *m.* (*naut.*) foresail.

фок- (*naut.*) fore-.

фока́льный, *adj.* (*phys.*) focal.

фокстерьéр, а, *m.* fox-terrier.

фокстрóт, а, *m.* foxtrot.

фóкус¹, а, *m.* (*math., phys., med., and fig.*) focus.

фóкус², а, *m.* **1.** (conjuring) trick; пока́зывать ~ы to do conjuring tricks. **2.** trick, secret (*of mechanism, etc.*); в тóм-то и ф. that's the whole point, that's just it. **3.** (*coll.*) whim, caprice.

фокуси́р|овать, ую, *impf.* (*phys., phot.*) to focus.

фóкусник, а, *m.* ∙**1.** conjurer, juggler. **2.** (*coll.*) rogue, tricky customer.

фокуснича|ть, ю, *impf.* **1.** (*obs.*) to do conjuring tricks. **2.** (*coll.*) to play tricks.

фóкусный, *adj.* (*phys., phot.*) focal.

фолиа́нт, а, *m.* folio.

фолли́кул, а, *m.* (*anat.*) follicle.

фольва́рк, а, *m.* farm (*in West Russia, Poland, and Lithuania*).

фольг|а́, и́, *f.* foil.

фольклóр, а, *m.* folklore.

фольклори́ст, а, *m.* student of folklore.

фóмк|а, и, *f.* (*coll.*) jemmy.

фон, а, *m.* background (*also fig.*).

фона́рик, а, *m.* small lamp; torch, flash-light.

фона́р|ный, *adj. of* ~ь; ф. столб lamppost.

фона́рщик, а, *m.* (*obs.*) **1.** lamplighter. **2.** torch-bearer.

фона́р|ь, я́, *m.* **1.** lantern; lamp; light. **2.** (*archit.*) light; skylight; ф. каби́ны (*aeron.*) cockpit canopy. **3.** (*coll.*) black eye.

фонд, а, *m.* **1.** (*fin.*) fund; stock, reserves, resources; валю́тный ф. currency reserves; земéльный ф. available land; золотóй ф. gold reserves. **2.** (*pl.*) (*fin.*) stocks; (*fig.*) stock; ~ы егó повы́сились his stock has risen. **3.** fund, foundation (*in U.S.S.R., organization serving as channel for State subsidies to writers, artists, etc.*). **4.** archive.

фóнд|овый, *adj. of* ~; ~овая би́ржа stock exchange.

фонéм|а, ы, *f.* (*ling.*) phoneme.

фонендоскóп, а, *m.* (*med.*) phonendoscope.

фонéтик|а, и, *f.* phonetics.

фонети́ст, а, *m.* phonetician.

фонети́ческий, *adj.* phonetic.

фони́р|овать, ую, *impf. and pf.* (*sl.*) to 'bug'.

фони́ческий, *adj.* **1.** phonic. **2.** ф. аппара́т (*mil.*) telephone with voice frequency signalling.

фонóграф, а, *m.* phonograph.

фонолóги|я, и, *f.* phonemics.

фонотéк|а, и, *f.* gramophone record library, sound recording library.

фонта́н, а, *m.* fountain; (*fig.*) stream; нефтянóй ф. oil gusher; бить ~ом to gush forth.

фонтани́р|овать, ует, *impf.* to gush forth.

фóр|а, ы, *f.* дать ~у (+*d.*) to give odds, give a start (*in a game*).

фóрвард, а, *m.* (*sport.*; *obs.*) forward.

фордеви́нд, а, *m.* (*naut.*) following wind; идти́ на ф. to run before the wind.

форéйтор, а, *m.* (*obs.*) postilion.

форéл|ь, и, *f.* trout.

фóрзац, а, *m.* fly-leaf (*of a book*).

фóринт, а, *m.* forint (*Hungarian currency unit*).

фóрм|а, ы, *f.* **1.** (*in var. senses*) form; по ~е,

...по содержа́нию in form, ... in content; по (всей) ~e in due form, properly. 2. shape; (*pl.*) contours (*of human body*). 3. (*tech.*) mould, cast; отли́ть в ~y to mould, cast. 4. uniform. 5. быть в ~e (*coll.*) to be in (good) form.

формали́зм, а, *m.* formalism (*pejor. in Marxist criticism of bourgeois art, etc.*).

формали́н, а, *m.* formalin.

формали́ст, а, *m.* formalist.

формали́стик|а, и, *f.* 1. formalism. 2. formalities.

формальдеги́д, а, *m.* (*chem.*) formaldehyde.

форма́льност|ь, и, *f.* formality.

форма́л|ьный (~ен, ~ьна), *adj.* (*in var. senses*) formal; ~ьное доказа́тельство formal proof; ~ьная ло́гика formal logic.

фор-ма́рс, а, *m.* (*naut.*) foretop.

форма́т, а, *m.* size, format.

форма́ци|я, и, *f.* 1. structure; stage (of development). 2. stamp, mentality. 3. (*geol.*) formation.

фо́рменк|а, и, *f.* (*coll.*) (*sailor's*) duck blouse.

фо́рменный, *adj.* 1. uniform. 2. (*obs.*) formal. 3. (*coll.*) proper, regular, positive.

формирова́ни|е, я, *n.* 1. forming; organizing. 2. (*mil.*) unit, formation.

формир|ова́ть, у́ю, *impf.* (*of c~*) to form; to organize; ф. хара́ктер to form character; ф. батальо́н to raise a battalion; ф. по́езд to make up a train.

формир|ова́ться, у́юсь, *impf.* (*of c~*) 1. to form, shape, develop (*intrans.*). 2. *pass. of* ~ова́ть.

форм|ова́ть, у́ю, *impf.* (*of c~*) to form, shape; to model; (*tech.*) to mould, cast.

формо́вк|а, и, *f.* forming, shaping; (*tech.*) moulding, casting.

формо́вочн|ый, *adj.* (*tech.*) moulding, casting; ~ая гли́на foundry loam; ~ые черни́ла (foundry) blacking.

формо́вщик, а, *m.* moulder.

фо́рмул|а, ы, *f.* formula; formulation.

формули́р|овать, ую, *impf. and pf.* (*pf. also* c~) to formulate.

формулиро́вк|а, и, *f.* 1. formulation. 2. formula.

формуля́р, а, *m.* 1. (*obs.*) record of service. 2. (*tech.*) logbook (*of installation, machine, etc.*). 3. library card (*card inserted in book recording details thereof*); reader's record card (*card kept by library for each reader, recording details of books loaned*).

форпо́ст, а, *m.* (*mil.*) advanced post; outpost (*also fig.*).

форс, а (у), *m.* (*coll.*) swank; для ~a to show off; сбить кому́-н. ф. to take someone down a peg.

форси́ров|анный, *p.p.p. of* ~а́ть *and adj.* forced; accelerated; ф. марш forced march.

форси́р|овать, ую, *impf. and pf.* 1. to force; to speed up. 2. (*mil.*) to force (*a crossing of*).

фор|си́ть, шу́, си́шь, *impf.* (*coll.*) to swank, show off.

форс-мажо́р, а, *m.* force majeur.

форсу́нк|а, и, *f.* (*tech.*) sprayer, atomizer, jet; fuel injector.

форт, а, о ~e, в ~у́, *pl.* ~ы́, *m.* (*mil.*) fort.

фо́ртел|ь, я, *m.* (*coll.*) trick, stunt.

фортепья́нист, а, *m.* (*obs.*) pianist.

фортепья́нный, *adj.* piano; ф. конце́рт piano concerto.

фортепья́но, indecl., n. piano.

фортификацио́нный, *adj.* fortification.

фортифика́ци|я, и, *f.* fortification.

фо́рточк|а, и, *f.* fortochka (*small hinged pane for ventilation in window of Russian houses*).

фо́рум, а, *m.* forum.

форшла́г, а, *m.* (*mus.*) grace-note.

форшма́к, а́, *m.* (*cul.*) forshmak (*baked hashed meat or herring with sliced potatoes and onions*).

форштев|ень, ня, *m.* (*naut.*) stem.

фосге́н, а, *m.* (*chem.*) phosgene.

фосфа́т, а, *m.* (*chem.*) phosphate.

фо́сфор, а, *m.* (*chem.*) phosphorus.

фосфоресце́нци|я, и, *f.* phosphorescence.

фосфоресци́р|овать, ую, *impf.* to phosphoresce; ~ующая кра́ска luminous paint.

фо́сфорист|ый, *adj.* (*chem.*) phosphorous; ~ая бро́нза phosphor bronze.

фосфори́ческий, *adj.* phosphoric.

фосфорноки́смый, *adj.* (*chem.*) phosphate (*of*).

фо́сфорный, *adj.* (*chem.*) phosphorous, phosphoric.

фота́ри|й, я, *m.* (*med.*) radiation therapy room.

фо́то, indecl., n. (*coll.*) photo.

фото- photo-.

фотоальбо́м, а, *m.* photograph album.

фотоаппара́т, а, *m.* camera.

фотобума́г|а, и, *f.* photographic paper.

фотогени́ч|ный (~ен, ~на), *adj.* photogenic.

фотограмметри́ческий, *adj.* photogrammetric.

фотограмме́три|я, и, *f.* photogrammetry, photographic survey.

фото́граф, а, *m.* photographer.

фотографи́р|овать, ую, *impf.* (*of c~*) to photograph.

фотографи́р|оваться, уюсь, *impf.* (*of c~*) to be photographed, have one's photo taken.

фотографи́ческ|ий, *adj.* photographic; ~ая плёнка photographic film.

фотогра́фи|я, и, *f.* 1. photography. 2. photograph. 3. photographer's studio.

фотодешифро́вщик, а, *m.* aerial photograph interpreter.

фотодонесéни|е, я, *n.* (*mil.*) intelligence photograph.

фотокáрточк|а, и, *f.* photograph.

фотокóпи|я, и, *f.* photostat (copy).

фотолáмп|а, ы, *f.* 1. dark room lamp. 2. (*electr.*) photoelectric cell.

фотолюбúтел|ь, я, *m.* amateur photographer.

фотóн, а, *m.* (*phys.*) photon.

фотообъектúв, а, *m.* (camera) lens.

фоторепортáж, а, *m.* picture story.

фоторепортёр, а, *m.* press photographer.

фото-рóбот, а, *m.* identikit (picture).

фотосúнтез, а, *m.* (*bot.*) photosynthesis.

фотостáт, а, *m.* photostat (apparatus).

фототéк|а, и, *f.* photograph library, photograph collection.

фотоувеличúтел|ь, я, *m.* photographic enlarger.

фотохрóник|а, и, *f.* news in pictures.

фотоэлемéнт, а, *m.* (*electr.*) photoelectric cell.

фóфан, а, *m.* (*coll.*) dim-wit.

фрагмéнт, а, *m.* fragment.

фрагментáр|ный (~ен, ~на), *adj.* fragmentary.

фрáер, а, *m.* (*sl.*) 1. trendy chap, guy. 2. boy-friend.

фрáз|а, ы, *f.* 1. sentence. 2. phrase.

фразеологúческий, *adj.* phraseological.

фразеолóги|я, и, *f.* 1. phraseology. 2. mere verbiage.

фразёр, а, *m.* phrase-monger.

фразúр|овать, ую, *impf.* 1. to use empty phrases. 2. (*mus.*) to observe the phrasing (of).

фрак, а, *m.* tail-coat, tails.

фракúйский, *adj.* Thracian.

фрактýр|а, ы, *f.* (*typ.*) Gothic type, black letter.

фракционúр|овать, ую, *impf. and pf.* (*chem.*) to fractionate.

фракцióнност|ь, и, *f.* (*polit.*) fractionalism.

фракцióнный¹, *adj.* (*polit.*) fractional; factional.

фракцióнный², *adj.* (*chem.*) fractional.

фрáкци|я¹, и, *f.* (*polit.*) fraction; faction, group.

фрáкци|я², и, *f.* (*chem.*) fraction.

фрамýг|а, и, *f.* upper part of window *or* door; casement.

франк¹, а, *m.* (*hist.*) Frank.

франк², а, *m.* franc.

франкúр|овать, ую, *impf. and pf.* to prepay, pay the postage (of).

франкирóвк|а, и, *f.* prepayment.

франкмасóн, а, *m.* freemason.

франкмасóн|ский, *adj.* of ~.

фрáнко- (*comm.*) free, prepaid; ф.-борт, ф.-сýдно free on board.

фрáнковый, *adj.* costing, worth a franc.

фрáнкский, *adj.* (*hist.*) Frankish.

франт, а, *m.* dandy.

фран|тúть, чý, тúшь, *impf.* (*coll.*) to play the dandy, dress foppishly.

франтúх|а, и, *f.* of франт.

франтовáт|ый (~, ~а), *adj.* (*coll.*) 1. dandyish. 2. fussy, pernickety.

франтовскóй, *adj.* dandyish, dandyfied.

франтовств|ó, á, *n.* dandyism.

францýженк|а, и, *f.* Frenchwoman.

францýз, а, *m.* Frenchman.

францýзский, *adj.* French; ф. ключ (*tech.*) monkey wrench.

фраппúр|овать, ую, *impf. and pf.* (*obs.*) to shock.

фрахт, а, *m.* freight.

фрахт|овáть, ýю, *impf.* (of за~) to charter.

фрáчн|ый, *adj.* of фрак; *as noun* ф., ~ого, *m.* (*obs.*) person not wearing uniform (*i.e. not in Government service*).

фрегáт, а, *m.* 1. (*naut.*) frigate. 2. frigate-bird.

фрéз|а, ы, *f.* (*tech.*) mill, milling cutter, cutter; ф.-барабáн drum shredder (*for cutting peat*).

фрéзер, а, *m.* = фрéза.

фрéзерный, *adj.* (*tech.*) milling; ф. станóк milling machine; ф. торф peat cut with drum shredder.

фрезер|овáть, ýю, *impf. and pf.* (*tech.*) to mill, cut.

фрезерóвк|а, и, *f.* (*tech.*) milling, cutting.

фрезерóвщик, а, *m.* milling-machine operator.

фрéйлин|а, ы, *f.* (*hist.*) maid of honour.

френóлог, а, *m.* phrenologist.

френологúческий, *adj.* phrenological.

френолóги|я, и, *f.* phrenology.

френч, а, *m.* service jacket.

фрéск|а, и, *f.* fresco.

фривóльност|ь, и, *f.* frivolity.

фривóл|ьный (~ен, ~ьна), *adj.* frivolous.

фриз, а, *m.* (*archit.*) frieze.

фрикадéльк|а, и, *f.* meat-ball, fish-ball (*in soup*).

фрикассé, *indecl., n.* fricassé.

фрикатúвный, *adj.* (*ling.*) fricative.

фрикцióн, а, *m.* (*tech.*) friction clutch.

фрикцióнн|ый, *adj.* (*tech.*) friction; ~ое колесó friction wheel, adhesion wheel.

фрóнд|а, ы, *f.* (*hist.*) Fronde (*also fig.*).

фрондёр, а, *m.* (*hist.*) Frondeur (*also fig.*).

фрондúр|овать, ую, *impf.* to express discontent.

фронт, а, *pl.* ~ы́, ~óв, *m.* (*mil.; fig.*) front; на два ~а on two fronts; стать во ф. to stand to attention.

фронтáльн|ый, *adj.* frontal; ~ая атáка frontal attack.

фронтиспи́с, а, *m.* (*archit.*, *typ.*) frontispiece.

фронтови́к, а́, *m.* front-line soldier.

фронтов|о́й, *adj.* (*mil.*) front(-line); ~а́я полоса́ zone of action of a front; ~ы́е пи́сьма letters from the front.

фронто́н, а, *m.* (*archit.*) pediment.

фрукт, а, *m.* 1. fruit. 2. (*coll.*, *pejor.*) fellow, type.

фрукто́вый, *adj.* fruit; ф. нож fruit knife; ф. сад orchard; ф. са́хар fruit sugar, fructose.

фр|я, и, *f.* (*coll.*) personage.

фря́жский, *adj.* (*obs.*) western European, foreign.

фтор, а, *m.* (*chem.*) fluorine.

фтори́́ровани|е, я, *n.* (*med.*) fluoridation.

фто́ристый, *adj.* fluorine; fluoride (of).

фу, *interj.* 1. (*expressing contempt, revulsion, etc.*) ugh! 2. (*expressing fatigue, etc.*) oh!, ooh! 3. фу́ ты (*expressing surprise or annoyance*) my word!, my goodness!

фу́г|а, и, *f.* (*mus.*) fugue.

фуга́н|ок, ка, *m.* (*tech.*) smoothing-plane.

фуга́с, а, *m.* (*mil.*) landmine, fougasse.

фуга́ск|а, и, *f.* (*coll.*) 1. landmine. 2. high--explosive bomb.

фуга́с|ный, *adj.* 1. *adj. of* ~. 2. high-explosive; ~ная бо́мба high-explosive bomb.

фуг|ова́ть, у́ю, *impf.* (*tech.*) to joint, mortise.

фуже́р, а, *m.* tall wine glass.

фузе́|я, и, *f.* (*hist.*) flint-lock rifle.

фу́к|ать, аю, *impf. of* ~нуть.

фу́к|нуть, ну, нешь, *pf.* (*of* ~ать) (*coll.*) 1. to blow; to blow out. 2. to snort. 3. (*at draughts*) to huff. 4. (*sl.*) to chuck out.

фу́кси|я, и, *f.* fuchsia.

фуля́р, а, *m.* (*text.*) foulard.

фунда́мент, а, *m.* foundation, base (*also fig.*); substructure; seating (*of boiler, etc.*).

фундамента́л|ьный (~ен, ~ьна), *adj.* 1. solid, sound; (*fig.*) thorough(-going). 2. main, basic; ~ьная библиоте́ка main library.

фунди́рованный, *adj.* (*fin.*) funded, consolidated.

фуникулёр, а, *m.* funicular (railway), cable railway.

функциона́льный, *adj.* functional.

функциони́р|овать, ую, *impf.* to function.

фу́нкци|я, и, *f.* (*in var. senses*) function.

фунт, а, *m.* 1. pound (*measure of weight*). 2. (стерлингов) pound (sterling).

фу́нтик, а, *m.* (*cone-shaped*) paper bag.

фу́ра, ы, *f.* (baggage-)waggon.

фура́ж, а́, *m.* forage, fodder.

фуражи́р, а, *m.* 1. fodder storeman. 2. (*mil.*) forager.

фуражи́р|овать, ую, *impf.* (*mil.*) to forage.

фуражиро́вк|а, и, *f.* (*mil.*) foraging.

фура́жк|а, и, *f.* peak-cap; (*mil.*) service cap.

фура́ж|ный, *adj. of* ~; ~ное зерно́ fodder grain; ~ная да́ча forage ration.

фурго́н, а, *m.* 1. van; estate car. 2. caravan.

фу́ри|я, и, *f.* 1. (*myth.*) Fury. 2. (*fig.*) fury, termagant, virago.

фу́рман, а, *m.* (*obs.*) driver.

фу́рм|енный, *adj. of* ~а; ~енная коро́бка tuyère box, blast box (*in cupola furnace*).

фурниту́р|а, ы, *f.* accessories.

фуру́нкул, а, *m.* (*med.*) furuncle.

фурункулёз, а, *m.* (*med.*) furunculosis.

фурьери́зм, а, *m.* (*polit.*, *philos.*) Fourierism.

фут, а, *m.* 1. foot (*measure of length*). 2. foot rule.

футбо́л, а, *m.* football, soccer.

футболи́ст, а, *m.* football-player, footballer.

футбо́лк|а, и, *f.* (*coll.*) football jersey, sports shirt.

футбо́л|ьный, *adj. of* ~; ~ьные бу́тсы football boots; ф. мяч football.

футер|ова́ть, у́ю, *impf.* (*tech.*) to line, fettle.

футеро́вк|а, и, *f.* (*tech.*) (brick-)lining, fettling.

футля́р, а, *m.* case; container; (*tech.*) casing, housing; ф. для очко́в spectacle--case; ф. телеви́зора TV cabinet.

фу́товый, *adj.* one-foot.

футури́зм, а, *m.* futurism.

футури́ст, а, *m.* futurist.

футуристи́ческий, *adj.* futuristic.

футшто́к, а, *m.* (*naut.*) tide-gauge; sounding rod.

фуфа́йк|а, и, *f.* jersey.

фуфу́; на ф. (*coll.*) anyhow, carelessly.

фьорд, а, *m.* = фио́рд.

фы́рк|ать, аю, *impf.* (*of* ~нуть) 1. to snort (*also fig.*, *of a machine*). 2. (*coll.*) to chuckle. 3. (*coll.*) to grouse.

фы́рк|нуть, ну, нешь, *pf. of* ~ать.

фюзеля́ж, а, *m.* (*aeron.*) fuselage.

X

хаба́р, а, *m.* (*and* ~а́, ~ы́, *f.*) (*coll.*, *obs.*) bribe.

ха́вбек, а, *m.* (*sport*; *obs.*) half(-back).

хавро́нь|я, и, *f.* (*coll.*) sow.

хаджи́, *indecl.*, *m.* Hadji (*title of Mohammedan pilgrim who has been to Mecca*).

ха́живать, *pres. tense not used*, *impf.* (*coll.*) *freq. of* ходи́ть.

хайл|о́, а́, *pl.* ~а, *n.* **1.** (*coll.*) aperture. **2.** (*sl.*) gob.

хака́с, а, *m.* Khakas (*indigenous inhabitant of Khakas Autonomous Oblast in Siberia*).

хака́с|ка, ки, *f. of* ~.

хака́сский, *adj.* Khakas.

ха́ки, *indecl. adj. and noun, n.* khaki.

хала́т, а, *m.* **1.** dressing-gown. **2.** overall; до́кторский х. doctor's smock. **3.** (*oriental*) robe.

хала́тност|ь, и, *f.* carelessness, negligence.

хала́т|ный, *adj.* **1.** *adj. of* ~. **2.** (~ен, ~на) careless, negligent.

халв|а́, ы́, *f.* (*cul.*) halva (*Eastern sweet made from ground nuts and caramel*).

халде́|й, я, *m.* Chaldean.

халде́й|ский, *adj. of* ~.

хали́ф, а, *m.* (*hist.*) caliph.

халифа́т, а, *m.* (*hist.*) caliphate.

халту́р|а, ы, *f.* (*coll.*) **1.** pot-boiler; (*collect.*) hack-work. **2.** extra work; money made on the side.

халту́р|ить, ю, ишь, *impf.* (*coll.*) **1.** to turn out pot-boilers; to do hack-work. **2.** to make money on the side (*by doing extra work*).

халту́р|ный, *adj. of* ~а.

халту́рщик, а, *m.* (*coll.*) **1.** person turning out pot-boilers; hack(-worker). **2.** person making money on the side (*by extra work*).

халу́п|а, ы, *f.* peasant house (*in Ukraine and Byelorussia*).

халцедо́н, а, *m.* (*min.*) chalcedony.

хам, а, *m.* (*coll.*) boor, lout.

хамеле́он, а, *m.* chameleon (*also fig.*).

хам|и́ть, лю́, и́шь, *impf.* (+*d.*) to be rude (to).

хамс|а́, ы́, *f.* khamsa (*small fish of anchovy family*).

ха́мский, *adj.* (*coll.*) boorish, loutish.

ха́мств|о, а, *n.* (*coll.*) boorishness, loutishness.

хан, а, *m.* khan.

хандр|а́, ы́, *f.* depression.

хандр|и́ть, ю́, и́шь, *impf.* to be depressed.

ханж|а́, и́, *g. pl.* ~е́й, *m. and f.* sanctimonious person; canting hypocrite.

ха́нжеск|ий (*and* ~о́й), *adj.* sanctimonious; hypocritical.

ханжеств|о́, а́, *n.* sanctimoniousness; hypocrisy.

ханж|и́ть, у́, и́шь, *impf.* (*coll.*) to display sanctimoniousness; to play the hypocrite.

ха́н|ский, *adj. of* ~.

ха́нств|о, а, *n.* khanate.

ханты́, *indecl., m. and f.* Khanty (*formerly Ostyak(s), inhabitant(s) of Khanty-Mansi National Region*).

ханты́йский, *adj.* Khanty.

ха́ос, а, *m.* (*myth.*) Chaos.

хао́с, а, *m.* chaos (*disorder*).

хаоти́ческий, *adj.* chaotic.

хаоти́чност|ь, и, *f.* chaotic character; state of chaos.

хаоти́ч|ный (~ен, ~на), *adj.* = ~еский.

ха́п|ать, аю, *impf. of* ~нуть.

ха́п|нуть, ну, нешь, *pf.* (*of* ~ать) (*coll.*) **1.** to seize, grab. **2.** (*fig.*) to nab, pinch, scrounge.

хапу́г|а, и, *m. and f.* (*coll.*) thief, scrounger.

хара́ктер, а, *m.* character, personality, nature, disposition (*of a human being*); они́ не сошли́сь ~ами they could not get on (together); э́то не в его́ ~е it's not like him. **2.** (strong) character; челове́к с ~ом determined person, strong character. **3.** character, nature, type; х. рабо́ты type of work.

характериз|ова́ть, у́ю, *impf. and pf.* **1.** to describe. **2.** to characterize, be characteristic (*of*).

характериз|ова́ться, у́юсь, *impf.* (+*i.*) to be characterized (by), feature.

характери́стик|а, и, *f.* **1.** description. **2.** reference; х. с ме́ста пре́жней слу́жбы reference from former place of work. **3.** (*math.*) characteristic (*of logarithm*). **4.** (*tech.*) characteristic curve; performance graph.

хара́ктерно, *as pred.* it is characteristic, it is typical.

хара́ктерный, *adj.* (*obs. or coll.*) having a strong character; strong-willed; temperamental.

характе́р|ный (~ен, ~на), *adj.* **1.** characteristic; typical; э́то для него́ ~но it is typical of him. **2.** distinctive. **3.** (*theatr.*) character; х. актёр character actor.

ха́риус, а, *m.* (*fish*) grayling, umber.

ха́ркань|е, я, *n.* (*coll.*) expectoration.

ха́рк|ать, аю, *impf.* (*of* ~нуть) (*coll.*) to spit, expectorate; х. кро́вью to spit blood.

ха́рк|нуть, ну, нешь, *pf. of* ~ать.

ха́рти|я, и, *f.* charter.

харче́вн|я, и, *f.* (*obs.*) eating-house.

харч|и́, е́й, *sing.* ~, ~а́, *m.* (*coll.*) grub.

харчо́, *indecl., n.* kharcho (*Caucasian mutton soup*).

ха́р|я, и, *f.* (*sl.*) mug (= face).

ха́т|а, ы, *f.* **1.** peasant house (*in S. Russia, Ukraine, and Byelorussia*); моя́ х. с кра́ю it's no concern of mine; that's your, their, *etc.*, funeral. **2.** (*sl.*) 'pad'.

ха́хал|ь, я, *m.* (*sl.*) fancy man.

ха́|ять, ю, ешь, *impf.* (*of* о~) (*coll.*) to play down, run down, knock (*fig.*).

хвал|а́, ы́, *f.* praise; х. Бо́гу! thank God!

хвале́б|ный (~ен, ~на), *adj.* laudatory, eulogistic, complimentary.

хвалёный, *adj.* (*iron.*) much-vaunted, celebrated.

хвал|и́ть, ю́, ~ишь, *impf.* (*of* по~) to praise, compliment.

хвал|и́ться, ю́сь, ~ишься, *impf.* (*of* по~) (+*i.*) to boast (of).

хва́стать = ~ся.

хва́ста|ться, юсь, *impf.* (*of* по~) (+*i.*) to boast (of).

хвастли́в|ый (~, ~а), *adj.* boastful.

хвастовств|о́, а́, *n.* boasting, bragging.

хвасту́н, а́, *m.* (*coll.*) boaster, braggart.

хват, а, *m.* (*coll.*) dashing blade.

хват|а́ть¹, а́ю, *impf.* (*of* ~и́ть¹ *and* схвати́ть) **1.** to snatch, seize, catch hold (of); to grab, grasp; х. что попа́ло to seize up whatever comes to hand. **2.** (*impf. only*) (*coll.*) to bite (*of fish*). **3.** (*impf. only*) (*coll.*) to pick up (= to detain).

хват|а́ть², а́ет, *impf.* (*of* ~и́ть²) *impers.* **1.** (+*g.*) to suffice, be sufficient, enough; to last out; у меня́, *etc.*, не ~а́ет I, *etc.*, am short (of); вре́мени не ~а́ло there was not long enough; у нас не ~а́ет де́нег we have not enough money; э́того ещё не ~а́ло! that's the last straw! **2.** (+*g.* на+*a.*) to be up to, be capable (of); его́ не ~а́ет на тако́й посту́пок he is not up to such an act.

хват|а́ться, а́юсь, *impf.* (*of* ~и́ться *and* схвати́ться) (за+*a.*) **1.** to snatch (at), catch (at), pluck (at); х. за соло́минку to reach for a straw; х. за́ ум to come to one's senses. **2.** to take up, try out.

хва|ти́ть¹, чу́, ~тишь, *pf.* (*coll.*) **1.** *pf. of* ~та́ть¹. **2.** to drink up, knock back; х. ли́шнего to have one too many. **3.** to suffer, endure. **4.** to stick one's neck out; to blurt out; х. че́рез край to go too far. **5.** (*in var. senses*) to strike; to hit; to smash; его́ ~ти́л уда́р he has had a stroke; моро́зом ~ти́ло посе́в (*impers.*) the frost hit the crops. **6.** to strike up, start up; х. плясову́ю to strike up a tune for dancing.

хват|и́ть², ~ит, *pf.* (*of* ~а́ть²); ~ит that will do!, that's enough!; с меня́ ~ит! I've had enough!; ~ит тебе́ хны́кать! that's enough of your whining!

хва|ти́ться, чу́сь, ~тишься, *pf.* **1.** *pf. of* ~та́ться. **2.** (+*g.*; *coll.*) to notice the absence (*of*), remember (*that one has left behind*); по́здно ~ти́лись! you thought of it too late! **3.** (о+*a.*; *coll.*) to hit, bump (into).

хва́тк|а, и, *f.* **1.** grasp, grip, clutch. **2.** (*coll.*) method, technique. **3.** skill.

хва́т|кий (~ок, ~ка́, ~ко), *adj.* (*coll.*) **1.** strong (*of hands, grip, etc.*); tenacious. **2.** skilful, crafty.

хвать (*coll.*) *used in place of various forms of* хвати́ть¹ *and* хвати́ться 2 (*also as interj.*); я х. его́ за воротни́к I grabbed him by the collar; я чуть бы́ло не сел на по́езд, а — х.! — биле́та нет I was just about to board the train when suddenly I found I had no got my ticket.

хво́йн|ый, *adj.* **1.** *adj. of* хвоя́; х. покро́ covering of (pine) needles; х. дёготь pine -tar. **2.** coniferous; *as noun* ~ые, ~ых (*bot.* conifers.

хвора́|ть, ю, *impf.* (*coll.*) to be ill, sick.

хво́рост, а (у), *m.* (*collect.*) **1.** brushwood **2.** (*cul.*) (pastry) straws, twiglets.

хворости́н|а, ы, *f.* stick, switch (*for drivin cattle, etc.*).

хво́рост|ь, и, *f.* (*coll.*) illness, ailment.

хворостяно́й, *adj. of* хво́рост 1.

хво́р|ый (~, ~а́, ~о), *adj.* (*coll.*) ill, sick.

хвор|ь, и, *f.* (*coll.*) illness, ailment.

хвост, а́, *m.* **1.** tail (*also fig.*; *of aircraf comet, etc.*); tail-feathers; маха́ть ~о́м т wag one's tail; задра́ть х. to get on one' high horse; поджа́ть х. to draw in one' horns; показа́ть х. (*coll.*) to show a clea pair of heels; (и) в х. и в гри́ву (*coll.*) nec and crop. **2.** (*fig.*) tail, rear, end, tail-end х. по́езда rear (coaches) of train; быть плести́сь в ~é to get behind, lag behind **3.** (*coll.*) train (*of dress*); наступи́ть на х кому́-н. (*coll.*) to tread on someone's toes corns. **4.** (*coll.*) throng, following. **5.** (*coll.* queue, line; х. за хле́бом bread queue. **6** (*coll.*) unfinished portion (*of work, etc.*) **7.** (*tech.*) shank, shaft (*of tool*). **8.** (*pl.*) (*min.* tails, tailings.

хвоста́т|ый (~, ~а), *adj.* **1.** having a tail caudate. **2.** having a large tail.

хвости́зм, а, m. (*polit.*) 'tailism' (*limitatio of revolutionary aims to those intelligible to back ward masses*).

хво́стик, а, m. *dim. of* хвост; с ~ом and little more; сто с ~ом a hundred odd.

хвости́ст, а, m. 1. (*polit.*) 'tailist' (*see* хво сти́зм). **2.** (*coll.*) student failing to obtai required number of passes in examina tion.

хвостов|о́й, *adj. of* хвост; ~а́я ве́на (*anat.* caudal vein; х. ого́нь (*aeron.*) tail light ~о́е опере́ние (*aeron.*) tail unit; х. патро́ (*mil.*) ignition charge, cartridge.

хвощ, а́, m. (*bot.*) horse-tail, mare's ta (*Equisetum*).

хво́|я, и, f. 1. needle(s) (*of conifer*). **2.** (*col lect.*) branches (*of conifer*).

хе́рес, а (у), m. sherry.

хер|и́ть, ю, ишь, *impf.* (*coll., obs.*) to cros out.

херуви́м, а, m. cherub.

херуви́м|ский, *adj.* **1.** *adj. of* ~. **2.** (*coll.* cherubic.

хе́ттский, *adj.* (*hist. and ling.*) Hittite.

хиба́р|а, ы, f. (*coll.*) shack, hovel.

хиба́р|ка, ки, f. *dim. of* ~a.

хи́жин|а, ы, f. shack, hut.

хиле́|ть, ю, *impf.* (*of* за~) (*coll.*) to become weak, sickly.

хи́л|ый (~, ~а́, ~о), *adj.* weak, sickly; puny; decrepit.

хим- *abbr. of* хими́ческий.

химе́р|а, ы, *f.* 1. chimera. 2. (*archit.*) gargoyle.

химери́ческий, *adj.* chimerical.

химиза́ци|я, и, *f.* 'chemicalisation' (*intensified development of chemical industry and utilization of its products*).

хими́зм, а, *m.* chemistry (= chemical composition).

хи́мик, а, *m.* 1. chemist. 2. chemical industry worker.

химика́л|ии, ий, *no sing.* chemicals.

химика́т|ы, ов, *sing.* ~, ~а, = химика́лии.

хими́ческ|ий, *adj.* 1. chemical; х. каранда́ш indelible pencil; ~ие препара́ты chemicals; ~ая чи́стка (оде́жды) dry-cleaning; х. элеме́нт chemical element. 2. chemistry; х. кабине́т chemistry laboratory. 3. (*mil.*) chemical warfare, gas; ~ая бо́мба gas bomb; ~ая война́ chemical warfare; ~ое подразделе́ние chemical warfare unit.

хи́ми|я, и, *f.* chemistry.

химчи́стк|а, и, *f.* dry-cleaning.

хи́нди, *indecl.*, *m.* Hindi (*language*).

хини́н, а, *m.* cinchona, quinine.

хи́нн|ый, *adj.* cinchona; ~ое де́рево cinchona (tree); ~ая ко́рка Peruvian bark.

хин|ь, и, *f.*; идёт ~ью (*coll., obs.*) it is in vain, to no purpose.

хире́|ть, ю, *impf.* (*of* за~) to grow sickly; (*of plants*) to wither; (*fig.*) to decay.

хирома́нт, а, *m.* chiromancer, palmist.

хирома́нти|я, и, *f.* chiromancy, palmistry.

хирото́ни|я, и, *f.* (*eccl.*) consecration, ordination (*to bishopric, priesthood, diaconate*).

хиру́рг, а, *m.* surgeon.

хирурги́ческ|ий, *adj.* surgical; ~ие но́жницы forceps; ~ая сестра́ theatre nurse.

хирурги́|я, и, *f.* surgery.

хити́н, а, *m.* (*biol.*) chitin.

хити́новый, *adj.* (*biol.*) chitinous.

хито́н, а, *m.* tunic.

хитре́ц, а́, *m.* sly, cunning person.

хитрец|а́, ы́, *f.* (*coll.*) cunning, guile; говори́ть с ~о́й to speak disingenuously.

хитри́нк|а, и, *f.* = хитреца́.

хитр|и́ть, ю́, и́шь, *impf.* (*of* с~) to use cunning, guile; to dissemble.

хитросплете́ни|е, я, *n.* 1. cunning trick, stratagem. 2. (*pl.*) fanciful construction; hair-splitting.

хитросплетённый, *adj.* intricate, contrived.

хи́трост|ь, и, *f.* 1. cunning, guile, craft, wiles. 2. ruse, stratagem. 3. (*coll.*) skill, resource. 4. (*coll.*) intricacy, subtlety.

хитроу́ми|е, я, *n.* cunning; resourcefulness.

хитроу́м|ный (~ен, ~на), *adj.* 1. cunning; resourceful. 2. intricate, complicated.

хи́т|рый (~ёр, ~ра́, ~ро), *adj.* 1. cunning, sly, crafty, wily. 2. (*coll.*) skilful, resourceful. 3. (*coll.*) intricate, subtle; complicated.

хихи́к|ать, аю, *impf.* (*of* ~нуть) to giggle, titter, snigger.

хихи́к|нуть, ну, нешь, *pf. of* ~ать.

хище́ни|е, я, *n.* theft; embezzlement, misappropriation.

хи́щник, а, *m.* 1. beast, bird of prey. 2.(*fig.*) plunderer, despoiler.

хи́щнический, *adj.* 1. *adj. of* хи́щник. 2. predatory, rapacious. 3. destructive; injurious (*to the economy*).

хи́щничеств|о, а, *n.* 1. preying. 2. predatoriness. 3. injurious exploitation of natural resources. 4. embezzlement, misappropriation.

хи́щ|ный (~ен, ~на), *adj.* 1. predatory; ~ные зве́ри, пти́цы beasts, birds of prey. 2. rapacious, grasping, greedy.

хлад, а, *m.* (*obs. or poet.*) cold.

хладнокро́ви|е, я, *n.* coolness, composure, presence of mind, sang-froid.

хладнокро́в|ный (~ен, ~на), *adj.* cool, composed.

хладноло́мкий, *adj.* (*tech.*) cold-short, brittle at atmospheric temperature.

хла́д|ный (~ен, ~на), *adj.* (*obs. or poet.*) cold.

хладосто́|йкий, (~ек, ~йка), *adj.* (*tech.*) cold-resistant; х. соста́в anti-freeze.

хлам, а, *m.* (*collect.*) rubbish, trash.

хлами́д|а, ы, *f.* 1. (*hist.*) chlamys. 2. (*coll.*) long, loose-fitting garment.

хлеб, а, *pl.* ~ы and ~а́, *m.* 1. (*sing. only*) bread (*also fig.*); х. насу́щный daily bread; добыва́ть х. (*fig.*) to win one's bread; отби́ть у кого́-н. х. to take the bread out of someone's mouth; перебива́ться с ~а на квас to live from hand to mouth. 2. (*pl.* ~ы) loaf. 3.(*pl.* ~а́) bread-grain;(*pl.*) corn, crops; cereals. 4. (*pl.* ~а́) (*coll.*) food; жить на ~а́х у кого́-н. (*i*) to board with someone, (*ii*) to be dependent on someone, live off someone; идти́ на ~а́ к кому́-н. to become dependent on someone.

хлеба́|ть, ю, *impf.* 1. to gulp (down). 2. (*coll.*) to eat, drink (*liquids*) with a spoon.

хле́б|ец, ца, *m.* small loaf.

хле́бин|а, ы, *f.* bee-bread.

хле́бник, а, *m.*˙ (*obs.*) baker.

хле́бниц|а, ы, *f.* bread-plate; bread-basket.

хлебн|у́ть, у́, ёшь, *pf.* (*coll.*) 1. to drink down. 2. (+*g.*) to go through, endure, experience.

хле́бн|ый, *adj.* 1. *adj. of* хлеб 1; ~ые дро́жжи baker's yeast; ~ые запа́сы bread supplies; x. магази́н baker's shop; ~ое де́рево bread-fruit tree. **2.** *adj. of* хлеб 3; x. амба́р granary; ~ое вино́ (*obs.*) vodka; ~ые зла́ки bread-grains, cereals; x. спирт grain alcohol, ethyl alcohol. **3.** rich (*in grain*), abundant; grain-producing. **4.** (*coll.*) lucrative, profitable.

хлёбов|о, a, *n.* (*coll.*) gruel.

хлебозаво́д, a, *m.* bread-baking plant, bakery.

хлебо|заготови́тельный, *adj. of* ~заготовка.

хлебозаготовк|а, и, *f.* (State) grain procurement.

хлебозаку́пк|а, и, *f.* (State) grain-purchase.

хлеб|о́к, ка́, *m.* (*coll.*) mouthful (*of liquid food*).

хлебопа́шеств|о, a, *n.* (*obs.*) tillage, cultivation, arable farming.

хлебопа́ш|ец, ца, *m.* (*obs.*) tiller of the soil.

хлебопа́шный, *adj.* ploughing; arable.

хлебопёк, a, *m.* baker.

хлебопека́рный, *adj.* baking.

хлебопека́рн|я, и, *f.* bakery, bake-house.

хлебопоста́вк|а, и, *f.* grain delivery (*to State*).

хлеборо́б, a, *m.* peasant (engaged in arable farming); (*rhet.*) corn-producer.

хлеборо́д|ный (~ен, ~на), *adj.* rich (in grain crops), abundant; x. год good year (for grain crops).

хлебосо́л, a, *m.* hospitable person.

хлебосо́л|ьный (~ен, ~ьна), *adj.* hospitable.

хлебосо́льств|о, a, *n.* hospitality.

хлеботорго́в|ец, ца, *m.* corn-merchant, grain-merchant.

хлеботорго́вл|я, и, *f.* corn-trade.

хлебоубо́рк|а, и, *f.* (corn-)harvest.

хлебоубо́рочный, *adj.* harvest(ing); x. комба́йн combine harvester.

хлеб-со́ль, хле́ба-со́ли bread and salt (*offered to guest as symbol of hospitality*); hospitality.

хлев, a, в ~е *or* **в ~у́,** *pl.* **~á,** *m.* cow-house, cattle-shed, byre; (*fig., coll.*) pig-sty.

хлестако́вщин|а, ы, *f.* shameless bragging (*in the manner of Khlestakov, hero of Gogol's comedy 'The Government Inspector'*).

хле|ста́ть, щу́, ~щешь, *impf.* (*of* ~стну́ть) **1.** (+*a. or* по+*d.*) to lash; to whip. **2.** (*of rain, etc.*) to lash (down), beat (down), pour; to stream, gush. **3.** (*coll.*) to swill (= to drink in large quantities).

хлёст|кий (~ок, ~ка́, ~ко), *adj.* **1.** biting. **2.** (*fig.*) biting, scathing; trenchant. **3.** (*of sounds, etc.*) sharp. **4.** (*coll.*) lively, gay.

хлест|ну́ть, ну́, нёшь, *pf. of* ~а́ть.

хлёст|че, *comp. of* ~кий.

хле́ще, *comp. of* хлёсткий.

хли́па|ть, ю, *impf.* (*coll.*) to sob.

хли́п|кий (~ок, ~ка́, ~ко), *adj.* (*coll.*) rickety, shaky. **2.** (*fig.*) weak, fragile. watery, slushy.

хлобы|ста́ть, щу́, ~щешь, *impf.* (*of* ~стну́т (*coll.*) to lash.

хлобыст|ну́ть, ну, нёшь, *inst. pf. of* ~а́ть.

хлоп[1]**,** *interj.* bang! (*as pred.; stands for pre and past tenses of* ~ать, ~нуть, *and* ~аться

хлоп[2]**, a,** *m.* (*coll.*) bang, clatter.

хло́па|ть, ю, *impf.* (*of* хло́пнуть) **1.** (+*i.* по+*d.*) to bang; to slap; x. кали́ткой bang the gate; x. кого́-н. по спине́ to sla someone on the back; x. глаза́ми (*i*) t look blank, (*ii*) to be at a loss what to sa (*in answer to a question*); x. уша́ми (*coll.* to look dumb. **2.** (в ладо́ши) (+*d.*) to clap applaud. **3.** (*coll.*) to shoot. **4.** (*coll.*) t knock back (= to drink).

хло́па|ться, юсь, *impf.* (*of* хло́пнуться) (*coll* to flop down.

хло́п|ец, ца, *m.* (*coll. or dial.*) lad.

хлопково́д, a, *m.* cotton-grower.

хлопково́дств|о, a, *n.* cotton-growing.

хлопково́дческий, *adj.* cotton-growing.

хло́пков|ый, *adj.* cotton; ~ое ма́сло cotton -seed oil; ~ые очёски cotton waste; ~a пря́жа cotton yarn.

хлопкопряди́льный, *adj.* cotton-spinning.

хлопкоро́б, a, *m.* cotton-grower.

хлопкоубо́рочный, *adj.* cotton-picking.

хлоп|нуть(ся), ну(сь), нешь(ся), *pf.* ~ать(ся).

хлоп|о́к, ка, *m.* cotton; x.-сыре́ц cotton wool.

хлоп|о́к, ка́, *m.* **1.** clap. **2.** bang.

хлопо|та́ть, чу́, ~чешь, *impf.* (*of* по~) (*impf. only*) to busy oneself; to bustle abou toil. **2.** (о+*p. or* + чтобы) to make efforts to take trouble, go to pains; to solicit, pet tion (for); x., что́бы привести́ кого́-н. чу́вство to endeavour to bring someon round. **3.** (за+*a. or* о+*p.*) to plead (for make efforts on behalf (of).

хлопотли́в|ый (~, ~a), *adj.* **1.** troublesome bothersome; involving (much) trouble, r quiring (great) pains, exacting. **2.** bus bustling, restless.

хлопот|ный (~ен, ~на), *adj.* (*coll.*) involv ing (much) trouble, exacting.

хлопотн|я́, и́, *f.* (*coll.*) efforts, labour, toil.

хлопоту́н, á, *m.* (*coll.*) busy, restless person

хлопо́т|ы, хлопо́т, ~ам, *no sing.* **1.** troubl **2.** (о+*p.*) efforts (on behalf of, for); pain

хлопу́шк|а, и, *f.* **1.** fly-swatter. **2.** (Chris mas) cracker. **3.** (*bot.*) catchfly (*Sile venosa*). **4.** (*tech.*) gate valve.

хлопча́тк|а, и, *f.* (*coll.*) cotton (*fabric*).

хлопча́тник, a, *m.* cotton(-plant).

хлопчатобума́жный, *adj.* cotton; x. по́ро gun-cotton.

хлопча́т|ый[1], *adj.* ~ая бума́га (*obs.*) (*i*) cotton-plant, (*ii*) cotton (*fabric, thread*).

хлопча́тый[2], *adj.* flaky.

хло́пчик, а, *m.* (*coll. or dial.*) boy.

хлопьеви́д|ный (~ен, ~на), *adj.* flaky, flocculent.

хлопь|я, ев, *no sing.* flakes (*of snow, etc., or as component of name of certain cereal foods*); кукуру́зные х., пшени́чные х. corn flakes.

хлор, а, *m.* (*chem.*) chlorine.

хлори́р|овать, ую, *impf. and pf.* to chlorinate.

хлористоводоро́дный, *adj.* (*chem.*) hydrochloride (of).

хло́ристый, *adj.* (*chem.*) chlorine; chloride (of); х. водоро́д hydrogen chloride.

хлори́т, а, *m.* (*min.*) chlorite.

хло́рк|а, и, *f.* (*coll.*) bleaching powder (*of calcium hypochlorite*).

хло́р|ный, *adj.* of ~.

хлоро́з, а, *m.* (*bot. and med.*) chlorosis.

хлорофи́лл, а, *m.* (*bot.*) chlorophyll.

хлорофо́рм, а, *m.* chlorophorm.

хлороформи́р|овать, ую, *impf. and pf.* (*pf. also* за~) to chloroform.

хлорпикри́н, а, *m.* (*chem. and agric.*) chloropicrin.

хлы́н|уть, у, ешь, *pf.* 1. (*of blood, rain, etc.*) to gush, pour. 2. (*fig.*) to pour, rush, surge; на пло́щадь ~ула толпа́ наро́ду a crowd poured into the square.

хлыст[1], **á,** *m.* 1. whip, switch; х. и пря́ник (*fig., coll.*) stick and carrot. 2. trunk (*of felled tree*).

хлыст[2], **á,** *m.* Khlyst (*member of sect*).

хлыстовств|о, а, *n.* Khlysts (*Russian religious sect*).

хлыщ, á, *m.* (*coll.*) fop.

хлюпа|ть, ю, *impf.* (*coll.*) 1. to squelch. 2. to flounder (*through mud, etc.*). 3. to snivel; х. но́сом to sniff.

хлю́пик, а, *m.* (*coll.*) sniveller, milksop.

хлю́п|кий (~ок, ~ка́, ~ко), *adj.* (*coll.*) 1. soggy. 2. rickety. 3. (*fig.*) frail, feeble.

хлюст[1], **á,** *m.* (*coll.*) smart Alec.

хлюст[2], **á,** *m.* (*coll.*) suit (*in a hand at cards*).

хляб|ь, и, *f.* 1. (*obs. or poet.*) abyss; ~и небе́сные разве́рзлись (*joc.*) the heavens opened (*of heavy rain*). 2. (*coll.*) mud, muddy ground.

хля́стик, а, *m.* half-belt (*sewn or buttoned on to back of coat*).

хмелево́д, а, *m.* hop-grower.

хмелево́дств|о, а, *n.* hop-growing.

хмел|ево́й, *adj.* of ~ь.

хмел|ёк, ька́, *m. dim. of* ~ь; под ~ько́м tipsy, tight.

хмеле́|ть, ю, *impf.* (*of* за ~ *and* о ~) to become tipsy, get tight.

хмел|ь, я, *m.* 1. (*bot.*) hop(s); hop-plant. 2. (о ~е, во ~ю́) drunkenness, tipsiness;

под ~ем, во ~ю́, tipsy, tight.

хмел|ьно́й (~ён, ~ьна́), *adj.* 1. drunken, tipsy. 2. intoxicating; *as noun* ~ьно́е, ~ьно́го, *n.* intoxicating liquor, alcohol.

хму́р|ить, ю, ишь, *impf.* (*of* на~) х. лицо́ to frown; х. бро́ви to knit one's brows.

хму́р|иться, юсь, ишься, *impf.* (*of* на~) 1. to frown. 2. to become gloomy. 3. to be overcast, cloudy.

хму́рост|ь, и, *f.* 1. gloom. 2. cloudiness.

хму́р|ый (~, ~а́, ~о), *adj.* 1. gloomy, sullen. 2. overcast, cloudy; lowering; х. день dull day; ~ое не́бо lowering sky.

хмы́ка|ть, ю, *impf.* (*coll.*) to hem (*expressing surprise, annoyance, doubt, etc.*).

хн|а, ы, *f.* henna.

хны́ка|ть, ю (*and* хны́ч|у, ешь), *impf.* (*coll.*) to whimper, (*fig.*) to whine.

хо́бби, *indecl., n.* hobby.

хо́бот, а, *m.* 1. (*zool.*) trunk, proboscis. 2. (*tech.*) tool-holder. 3. х. лафе́та (*mil.*) trail of gun-carriage.

хоботно́й, *adj. of* хо́бот 1.

хо́бот|овый, *adj. of* ~ 2, 3.

хобот|о́к, ка́, *m.* proboscis (*of insects*).

ход, а (у), о ~е, в (на) ~е *and* ~ý, *m.* 1. (в ~е, на ~ý) motion, movement, travel, going; speed, pace; три часа́ ~у three hours' going; за́дний х. backing, reversing; ма́лый х., ти́хий х. slow speed; по́лный х. full speed; по́лный х.! full speed ahead!; по́лным ~ом (*fig.*) in full swing; свобо́дный х. free-wheeling, coasting; сре́дний х. half-speed; дать х. (+*d.*) to set in motion, set going; д. ~у (*i*) (*coll.*) to increase pace, go faster, (*ii*) (*coll.*) to take to one's heels; не дать ~у кому́-н. not to give someone a chance, hold someone back; идти́ свои́м ~ом (*i*) to travel under one's own steam, (*ii*) to take its course; пойти́ в х. to come to be widely used, acquire a vogue; пусти́ть в х. to start, set in motion, set going (*also fig.*), put into operation, put into service; быть в ~ý to be in demand, be in vogue; на ~ý (*i*) in transit, on the move, without halting, (*ii*) in motion, in operation; на по́лном ~ý at full speed, full blast; с ~у (*coll.*) without a pause, straight off. 2. (*eccl.*) procession. 3. (в, на ~е) (*fig.*) course, progress; х. мы́слей train of thought; х. собы́тий course of events. 4. (в ~е, на ~е *and* ~ý) (*tech.*) work, operation, running; на холосто́м ~ý idling. 5. (в, на ~е; *pl.* ~ы, ~о́в) (*tech.*) stroke (*of piston*), blow (*of press*); cycle; travel; х. вверх, х. вниз, х. сжа́тия (*of piston*) upstroke, downstroke, compression stroke. 6. (на ~е; *pl.* ~ы́) (*chess, draughts*) move; (*cards*) lead; х. бе́лых white's move. 7. (в ~е; *pl.* ~ы) (*fig.*) move, gambit, manœuvre;

лóвкий x. shrewd move. **8.** (в ~е *and* ~ý; *pl.* ~ы́) entrance (*to building*); знать все ~ы́ и вы́ходы to know all the ins and outs. **9.** (в, на ~е *and* ~ý; *pl.* ~ы́, ~óв) passage, covered way, thoroughfare; ~ы́ сообщéния (*mil.*) communication trench. **10.** (в, на ~ý; *pl.* ~ы́ *and* ~á, ~óв) (*tech.*) wheel-base; runners (*of sledge*); гýсеничный x. caterpillar tracks.

ходáта|й, я, *m.* **1.** intercessor, mediator. **2.** (*obs.*) (по делáм) solicitor.

ходáтайств|о, a, *n.* **1.** petitioning; entreaty, pleading. **2.** petition; application.

ходáтайств|овать, ую, *impf.* (*of* по~) **1.** (о+*p.* *or* за+*a.*) to petition (for); to apply (for). **2.** (за+*a.*) to defend, intercede (for), plead (for).

ходéбщик, a, *m.* (*obs.*) hawker, pedlar.

хóдик|и, ов, *no sing.* (*coll.*) grandfather clock (*worked by weights*).

хо|ди́ть, жý, ~ди́шь, *impf.* **1.** to (be able to) walk. **2.** (*indet. of* идти́) to go (*on foot*); х. в гóсти to be invited out, visit (friends); х. в кинó to go to the cinema; х. в атáку to go into the attack; х. на парусáх to go sailing; х. пó миру to be a beggar. **3.** (*of trains, etc.*) to run. **4.** to pass, go round; х. из рук в рýки, по рукáм to pass from hand to hand; недóбрые вéсти ~дят bad news is going round. **5.** (*cards*) to lead, play; (*chess, etc.*) to move; х. с пик to lead a spade; х. ферзём to move one's queen. **6.** (*indet. only*) (за+*i.*) to look after, take care of, tend. **7.** to sway, shake, wobble. **8.** (*coll., obs.*) to cost; to pass, be current. **9.** (в+*p.*; *coll.*) to be (= to occupy the post of, work as). **10.** (в+*p.*) to wear. **11.** (*pf.* с~) (*coll.*) to go (= to excrete).

хóд|кий (~ок, ~кá, ~ко), *adj.* (*coll.*) **1.** fast, fleet. **2.** saleable, marketable; popular, in great demand, much sought after; х. товáр popular line; ~кое выражéние popular phrase.

ходов|óй, *adj.* **1.** (*tech.*) running, working; ~óe врéмя working time; х. золотник throttle valve; ~ы́е испытáния running tests; х. механи́зм running gear; х. рóлик traveller. **2.** in (good) working order. **3.** (*tech., naut.*) free, running (= not secured). **4.** (*coll.*) popular; current; х. анекдóт (currently) popular story. **5.** (*coll.*) smart, clever.

ходóк, á, *m.* **1.** walker. **2.** быть ~óм (кудá-н.) (*coll.*) to make regular visits (to). **3.** envoy, petition-bearer. **4.** (на+*a.*, по+*d.*) (*coll.*) person clever (at). **5.** (*tech.*) passage (*in mine*).

ходýл|и, ей, *sing.* ~я, ~и, *f.* stilts.

ходýл|ьный (~ен, ~ьна), *adj.* stilted; pompous.

ходýн, á, *m.* now only in phrase ~óм ходи́ть (*coll.*) to shake, rock; (*fig.*) to rush about.

ходьб|á, ы́, *f.* walking; цéрковь нахóдится в пяти́ минýтах ~ы́ отсю́да the church is five minutes' walk from here.

ходя́ч|ий, *adj.* **1.** walking; able to walk. **2.** (*fig., coll., iron.*) the personification (of); ~ая добродéтель virtue personified. **3.** popular; current; ~ее выражéние current phrase.

хождéни|е, я, *n.* **1.** walking; going; х. по мýкам (*fig.*) (going through) purgatory. **2.** имéть x. to be in circulation, pass current.

хозрасчёт, a, *m.* (*abbr. of* хозя́йственный расчёт) (*econ.*) self-supporting running, self-financing (*system whereby an industrial undertaking, etc., in the U.S.S.R. finances itself without the aid of central State funds*).

хозрасчёт|ный, *adj. of* ~.

хозя́|ин, ина, *pl.* ~ева, ~ев, *m.* **1.** owner, proprietor. **2.** master; boss. **3.** landlord (*in relation to tenant*). **4.** host; ~ева пóля (*sport*) the home team. **5.** хорóший, плохóй x. good, bad manager. **6.** (*coll.*) husband. **7.** (*biol.*) host.

хозя́йк|a, и, *g. pl.* **хозя́ек,** *f.* **1.** owner, proprietress. **2.** mistress. **3.** landlady. **4.** (*coll.*) wife.

хозя́йнича|ть, ю, *impf.* **1.** to manage, carry on management. **2.** to keep house. **3.** (*fig., pejor.*) to lord it; to throw one's weight about.

хозя́йский, *adj.* **1.** *adj. of* хозя́ин. **2.** solicitous, careful. **3.** (*pejor.*) proprietary; imperious.

хозя́йственник, a, *m.* economic planner.

хозя́йствен|ный (~, ~на), *adj.* **1.** economic, of the economy; ~ная жизнь страны́ the country's economy. **2.** x. расчёт see хозрасчёт. **3.** household; home management; х. инвентáрь household equipment. **4.** economical, thrifty. **5.** commanding; confident.

хозя́йств|о, a, *n.* **1.** economy; сéльское x. agriculture; домáшнее x. housekeeping; вести́ x. to manage, carry on management. **2.** equipment. **3.** (*agric.*) farm, holding. **4.** housekeeping; хлопотáть по ~у to be busy about the house.

хозя́йств|овать, ую, *impf.* to manage, carry on management.

хозя́йчик, a, *m.* (*coll.*) small proprietor.

хоккéист, a, *m.* hockey-player.

хоккé|й, я, *m.* hockey; х. с шáйбой ice hockey.

хоккéй|ный, *adj. of* ~; ~ная клю́шка hockey-stick.

хóленый, *adj.* well-groomed, carefully tended; sleek.

холéр|a, ы, *f.* (*med.*) cholera (*also as expletive*)

холе́рик, а, *m.* **1.** choleric person. **2.** (*coll.*) person suffering from cholera.

холери́ческий, *adj.* choleric.

холе́р|ный, *adj. of* ~а; х. вибрио́н cholera bacillus.

хо́л|ить, ю, ишь, *impf.* to tend, care for.

хо́лк|а, и, *f.* withers; намы́лить ~у кому́-н. (*coll.*) to give someone a dressing-down.

холл, а, *m.* hall, vestibule, foyer.

холм, а́, *m.* hill.

холми́ст|ый (~, ~а), *adj.* hilly.

хо́лод, а (у), *pl.* ~а́, ~о́в, *m.* **1.** cold; coldness (*also fig.*). **2.** cold (spell of) weather.

холода́|ть, ю, *impf.* **1.** (*pf.* по~; *impers.*) to become cold, turn cold. **2.** (*coll.*) to endure cold.

холоде́|ть, ю, *impf.* (*of* по~) to grow cold; (*impers.*) to turn cold.

хо́лод|е́ц, ца́, *m.* (*coll.*) meat *or* fish in jelly.

холоди́льник, а, *m.* **1.** refrigerator; ваго́н-х. refrigerator van. **2.** (*tech.*) condenser.

холоди́льн|ый, *adj.* refrigeration, refrigeratory; ~ая те́хника refrigeration engineering; ~ая устано́вка cold storage plant.

холо|ди́ть, жу́, ди́шь, *impf.* **1.** (*pf.* на~) (*coll.*) to cool. **2.** to cause a cold sensation (*also impers.*).

хо́лодно¹, *adv.* (*fig.*) coldly.

хо́лодно², *as pred.* it is cold; мне, *etc.*, х. I, *etc.*, am cold, feel cold.

холоднова́т|ый (~, ~а), *adj.* rather cold, chilly.

холоднока́таный, *adj.* (*tech.*) cold-rolled.

холоднокро́вный, *adj.* (*zool.*) cold-blooded.

холодноло́мкий, *adj.* (*tech.*) cold-short.

хо́лодность, и, *f.* coldness.

холо́д|ный (хо́лоден, ~на́, хо́лодно), *adj.* **1.** (*in var. senses*) cold; х. ве́тер cold wind; х. отве́т cold reply; х. по́яс (*geogr.*) frigid zone; ~ная война́ cold war; ~ное ору́жие side-arms, cold steel; *as noun* ~ная, ~ной, *f.* (*obs.*, *coll.*) 'the cooler' (= place of detention); ~ное, ~ного, *n.* meat *or* fish in jelly. **2.** inadequate (*of clothing, etc.*; = not affording protection against cold).

холод|о́к, ка́, *m.* **1.** coolness, chill (*also fig.*). **2.** cool breeze. **3.** cool place. **4.** cool of the day.

холодосто́й|кий (~ек, ~йка), *adj.* (*agric.*) cold-resistant.

холо́п, а, *m.* **1.** (*hist.*) villein, bond slave. **2.** serf. **3.** (*fig., pejor.*) lackey.

холо́п|ий, *adj. of* ~ 1.

холо́п|ский, *adj.* **1.** *adj. of* ~. **2.** servile.

холо́пств|о, а, *n.* **1.** (*hist.*) villeinage, bond slavery. **2.** servility.

холо́пств|овать, ую, *impf.* to display servility.

холостёж|ь, и, *f.* (*collect.*) (*coll.*) bachelors.

холо|сти́ть, щу́, сти́шь, *impf.* to castrate, geld (*an animal*).

холост|о́й (хо́лост, ~а́), *adj.* **1.** unmarried, single; bachelor. **2.** (*tech.*) idle, free-running; на ~о́м ходу́ idling. **3.** (*mil.*) blank, dummy; х. патро́н blank cartridge.

холостя́к, а́, *m.* bachelor.

холостя́|цкий, *adj. of* ~к.

холоще́ни|е, я, *n.* castration, gelding.

холощёный, *adj.* castrated, gelded.

холст, а́, *m.* **1.** canvas; sackcloth. **2.** (*art*) canvas.

холсти́н|а, ы, *f.* **1.** = холст. **2.** piece of canvas.

холсти́нк|а, и, *f.* (*text.*) gingham.

холу́|й, я́, *m.* (*obs. and fig.*) lackey.

холщо́вый, *adj. of* холст 1.

хо́л|я, и, *f.* (*coll.*) care, attention; жить в ~е to be well cared for.

хому́т, а́, *m.* **1.** (horse's) collar; (*fig.*) burden. **2.** (*tech.*) clamp, ring.

хомя́к, а́, *m.* hamster.

хонинг|ова́ть, у́ю, *impf.* (*tech.*) to hone.

хор, а, *pl.* ~ы́ (*and* ~ы), *m.* **1.** choir. **2.** (*mus. and fig.*) chorus; ~ом all together.

хора́л, а, *m.* chorale.

хорва́т, а, *m.* Croat.

хорва́т|ка, ки, *f. of* ~.

хорва́тский, *adj.* Croatian.

хо́рд|а, ы, *f.* **1.** (*math.*) chord. **2.** (*biol.*) notochord.

хо́рд|овый, *adj. of* ~а 2; *as noun* ~овые, ~овых (*zool.*) chordata.

хор|ёвый, *adj. of* ~ь.

хоре́ический, *adj.* (*lit.*) trochaic.

хоре́|й, я, *m.* (*lit.*) trochee.

хор|ёк, ька́, *m.* polecat, ferret.

хореографи́ческий, *adj.* choreographic.

хореогра́фи|я, и, *f.* choreography.

хоре́|я, и, *f.* (*med.*) chorea, St. Vitus' dance.

хори́ст, а, *m.* **1.** member of a choir, chorister. **2.** member of a chorus.

хорме́йстер, а, *m.* **1.** choir master. **2.** chorus master.

хорово́д, а, *m.* round dance (*traditional Slavonic folk dance*).

хорово́|диться, жусь, дишься, *impf.* (с+*i.*) (*coll.*) **1.** to be occupied (with), take up one's time (with). **2.** to carry on (with) (= to have a sexual liaison).

хорово́й, *adj.* **1.** choral. **2.** (*obs.*) joint, collective.

хоро́м|ы, ~, *no sing.* (*obs.*) mansion.

хорон|и́ть, ю́, ~ишь, *impf.* (*of* по~) **1.** (*pf. also* за~ *and* с~) to bury (*also fig.*); to inter. **2.** (*obs. or coll.*) to hide, conceal; х. концы́ to cover up one's tracks.

хорон|и́ться, ю́сь, ~ишься, *impf.* (*of* с~) **1.** (*coll.*) to hide, conceal oneself. **2.** *pass. of* ~и́ть 1.

хорохо́р|иться, юсь, ишься, *impf.* (*coll.*) to swagger; to boast.

хоро́шенький, *adj.* pretty, nice (*also iron.*).

хороше́нько, *adv.* (*coll.*) properly, thoroughly, well and truly.

хороше́|ть, ю, *impf.* (*of* по~) to grow prettier.

хоро́ш|ий (~, ~а́, ~о́), *adj.* **1.** (*in var. senses*) good. **2.** nice (*often iron.*). **3.** (*short forms*) pretty, good looking.

хорошо́¹, *adv.* **1.** well; nicely. **2.** (*as particle expressing agreement, acceptance*) all right!, very well! **3.** *as noun* (*indecl.*) good (*mark*).

хорошо́², *as pred.* it is good; it is nice, pleasant; х., что вы успе́ли прие́хать it is good that you managed to come; им х. — ведь у них своя́ маши́на it is all right for them, they have a car of their own.

хорт, а, *m.* (*hunting*) greyhound.

хо́ртый, *adj.* smooth-haired (*of a dog*).

хору́гв|ь, и, f.* **1. (*mil.; obs.*) ensign, standard. **2.** (*eccl.*) banner.

хору́нж|ий, его, *m.* (*hist.*) **1.** (*mil.*) standard-bearer. **2.** cornet (*junior commissioned rank in Cossack cavalry*).

хо́р|ы, ~ and ~ов (musicians') gallery.

хор|ь, я́, *m.* polecat.

хор|ько́вый, *adj. of* ~ёк.

хоте́ни|е, я, *n.* desire, wish.

хоте́|ть, хочу́, хо́чешь, хо́чет, хоти́м, хоти́те, хотя́т, *impf.* (*of* за~) (+*g.,* inf. or чтобы) to want, desire; я ~л бы I should like; х. пить to be thirsty; х. сказа́ть to mean; е́сли хоти́те if you like (*also =* perhaps).

хоте́|ться, хо́чется, *impf.* (*of* за~) (*impers.* +*d.*) to want; мне хо́чется I want; мне ~лось бы I should like.

хоть, *conj. and particle* **1.** *conj.* although. **2.** *conj.* even if (*esp. in set phrases*); у него́ де́нег х. отбавля́й he has money enough and to spare; х. убе́й, не скажу́ I couldn't tell you to save my life; х. бы и так (*coll.*) even so, even at that. **3.** *particle* (*also* х. бы) at least, if only; ты бы посмотре́л х. на мину́точку you should take a look, if only for a minute. **4.** *particle* (*coll.*) for example, to take only, even; вот, х. его́ семиле́тняя сестрёнка, ведь, догада́лась why, even his little seven-year-old sister had guessed it. **5.** х. бы if only. **6.** + *relat. pron. forms indefinite pron.*: х. кто anyone; х. где anywhere, everywhere; х. куда́ (*as pred.; coll.*) first-rate, terrific. **7.** х. бы что (+*d.; coll.*) it does not affect, does not bother.

хотя́, *conj.* **1.** although, though. **2.** х. бы even if. **3.** *as particle* х. бы if only; э́то я́вствует х. бы из заключи́тельной фра́зы его́ ре́чи this is evident if only from the final sentence of his speech.

хохла́т|ый (~, ~a), *adj.* crested, tufted; cristate.

хо́хл|иться, юсь, ишься, *impf. of* на ~.

**хо́хм|а, ы, f.* joke, quip, gag.

хох|о́л, ла́, *m.* **1.** crest; topknot, tuft of hair. **2.** (*joc.*) Ukrainian (*from custom of shaving head except for single tuft of hair*).

хо́хот, а, *m.* guffaw, loud laugh.

хохо|та́ть, чу́, ~чешь, *impf.* to guffaw, laugh loudly.

хохоту́н, а́, *m.* (*coll.*) laughter, joker.

храбре́ц, а́, *m.* brave person.

храбр|и́ться, ю́сь, и́шься, *impf.* (*coll.*) to try not to appear afraid; to make a show of bravery.

**хра́брост|ь, и, f.* bravery, courage, valour.

хра́бр|ый (~, ~а́, ~о), *adj.* brave, courageous, valiant.

храм, а, *m.* temple, church, place of worship.

храмо́вник, а, *m.* (*hist.*) knight Templar.

храм|ово́й, *adj. of* ~; х. пра́здник patronal festival.

хране́ни|е, я, *n.* keeping, custody; storage, conservation; ка́мера ~я cloakroom, left luggage office; сдать на х. to store, deposit, leave in a cloakroom.

храни́лищ|е, я, *n.* storehouse, depository.

храни́тел|ь, я, *m.* **1.** keeper, custodian; (*fig.*) repository. **2.** curator.

хран|и́ть, ю́, и́шь, *impf.* (*in var. senses*) to keep; to preserve, maintain; to store; х. молча́ние to keep silence; х. в та́йне to keep secret.

храни́т|ься, ~ся, *impf.* **1.** to be, be kept. **2.** to be preserved.

храп, а, *m.* snore; snoring.

храпан|у́ть, у, ёшь, *pf.* (*coll.*) to have a good kip.

храп|е́ть, лю́, и́шь, *impf.* **1.** to snore. **2.** (*of an animal*) to snort.

храпови́к, а́, *m.* (*tech.*) ratchet.

храпови́цк|ий: *only in phrase* зада́ть ~ого (*coll.*) to fall fast asleep (and snore).

храпово́й, *adj.* (*tech.*) ratchet; х. механи́зм ratchet gear.

хреб|е́т, та́, *m.* **1.** (*anat.*) spine, spinal column; (*fig., coll.*) back. **2.** (mountain) range; ridge; (*fig.*) crest, peak.

хреб|то́вый, *adj. of* ~е́т.

хрен, а(у), *m.* horseradish; говя́дина под ~ом roast beef with horseradish sauce; х. ре́дьки не сла́ще (*fig.*) it's six of one to half a dozen of the other; ста́рый х. (*fig., coll.*) old fogey, old sod; х. с (+*i.*) to hell (with).

хрен|о́вый, *adj. of* ~; (*sl.*) rotten, lousy.

хрестома́т|ийный, *adj. of* ~ия.

**хрестома́ти|я, и, f.* reader (= selections of literature, etc. for study); х. по дре́вней

ру́сской литерату́ре medieval Russian literature reader.

хризантем|а, ы, *f.* chrysanthemum.

хризоли́т, а, *m.* (*min.*) chrysolite.

хрип, а, *m.* wheeze, wheezing sound.

хрип|е́ть, лю́, и́шь, *impf.* to wheeze.

хрипли́в|ый (~, ~a), *adj.* (rather) hoarse; wheezy.

хрипл|ый (~, ~á, ~o), *adj.* hoarse; wheezy.

хри́п|нуть, ну, нешь, *past* ~, ~ла, *impf.* (*of* o~) to become hoarse, lose one's voice.

хрипот|á, ы́, *f.* hoarseness.

христара́дник, а, *m.* (*obs.*) beggar, mendicant.

христара́днича|ть, ю, *impf.* (*obs.*) to beg; to be a beggar, mendicant.

христианиза́ци|я, и, *f.* 1. conversion to Christianity. 2. adaptation to Christianity.

христианизи́р|овать, ую, *impf. and pf.* to convert to Christianity.

христианизи́р|оваться, уюсь, *impf. and pf.* become Christian; to adopt Christianity.

христи|ани́н, ани́на, *pl.* ~а́не, ~а́н, *m.* Christian.

христиа́нк|а, и, *f.* Christian (woman).

христиа́нский, *adj.* Christian; провести́ в х. вид, прида́ть (+*d.*) х. вид (*joc.*) to give an air of respectability.

христиа́нств|о, а, *n.* 1. Christianity. 2. (*collect.*) Christendom.

христ|о́в, *adj. of* ~о́с; Х. день (*obs. or eccl.*) Easter day; жить ~о́вым и́менем (*obs.*) to live by begging, on alms.

Христо́с, Христа́, *m.* Christ; жить Христа́ ра́ди (*obs., coll.*) (*i*) to live on alms, (*ii*) (у кого́-н.) to live on (someone's) charity; вот тебе́ (те) Х. (*obs., coll.*) it's the very truth.

христосла́в|ы, ов, *no sing.* carol singers, waits.

христо́с|оваться, уюсь, *impf.* (*of* по~) to exchange a triple kiss (*as Easter salutation*).

хром[1], а, *m.* (*chem.*) chromium; chrome.

хром[2], а, *m.* box-calf.

хромати́зм, а, *m.* 1. (*phys.*) chromatism. 2. (*mus.*) chromatic scale.

хромат|и́ческий, *adj. of* ~и́зм; ~и́ческая га́мма (*mus.*) chromatic scale.

хрома́|ть, ю, *impf.* 1. to limp, be lame; х. на о́бе ноги́ (*fig., coll.*) to be in a poor way. 2. (*fig., coll.*) to be weak, unsatisfactory; арифме́тика у тебя́ ~ет your arithmetic is very shaky.

хроме́|ть, ю, *impf.* (*of* o~) to go lame.

хроми́р|овать, ую, *impf. and pf.* to chromium-plate.

хро́м|истый, *adj. of* ~[1].

хро́мовый[1], *adj.* (*chem.*) chromium, chromic.

хро́м|овый[2], *adj. of* ~[2].

хром|о́й (~, ~á, ~o), *adj.* 1. lame, limping; х. на ле́вую но́гу lame in the left leg; *as noun* х., ~о́го, *m.*; ~а́я, ~о́й, *f.* lame man, woman. 2. (*of leg; coll.*) lame. 3. (*of article of furniture; coll.*) shaky (*having one leg broken or shorter than others*).

хромоно́г|ий (~, ~а), *adj.* lame, limping.

хромоно́жк|а, и, *f.* (*coll.*) lame woman.

хромосо́м|а, ы, *f.* (*biol.*) chromosome.

хромот|á, ы́, *f.* lameness.

хро́ник, а, *m.* (*coll.*) chronic invalid.

хро́ник|а, и, *f.* 1. (*hist. and lit.*) chronicle. 2. (*section of newspaper or radio news service*) chronicle (of events), news items. 3. (*cinema*) (*i*) newsreel, (*ii*) historical film.

хроника́льный, *adj. of* хро́ника 2, 3; х. фильм = хро́ника 3.

хроникёр, а, *m.* news-snippets man (*reporter supplying material for chronicle section of newspaper*).

хрони́ческ|ий, *adj.* (*med. and fig.*) chronic; х. больно́й chronic invalid; ~ая безрабо́тица chronic unemployment.

хроно́граф[1], а, *m.* (*hist.*) chronicle.

хроно́граф[2], а, *m.* stopwatch.

хронологи́ческий, *adj.* chronological.

хроноло́ги|я, и, *f.* chronology.

хроно́метр, а, *m.* chronometer.

хронометра́ж, а, *m.* time study, time-keeping.

хронометражи́ст, а, *m.* time study specialist, timekeeper.

хру́п|кий (~ок, ~ка́, ~ко), *adj.* 1. fragile, brittle. 2. (*fig.*) fragile, frail; delicate.

хру́пкост|ь, и, *f.* 1. fragility, brittleness. 2. (*fig.*) fragility, frailness.

хруст, а, *m.* crunch; crackle.

хруста́лик, а, *m.* (*anat.*) crystalline lens.

хруста́л|ь, я́, *m.* cut glass, crystal; го́рный х. rock crystal.

хруста́льный, *adj.* 1. cut-glass, crystal. 2. (*fig.*) crystal-clear.

хру|сте́ть, щу́, сти́шь, *impf.* (*of* ~стнуть) to crunch (*of snow, etc.*); to crackle.

хру́ст|нуть, ну, нешь, *pf. of* ~е́ть.

хруст|я́щий, *pres. part. of* ~е́ть *and adj.*; х. карто́фель potato crisps.

хрущ, á, *m.* cockchafer, may bug.

хрыч, á, *m.* ста́рый х. (*coll.*) old fogey, old sod.

хрычо́вк|а, и, *f.* ста́рая х. (*coll.*) old hag, old bag.

хрю́кань|е, я, *n.* grunting (*of a pig*).

хрю́к|ать, аю, *impf.* (*of* ~нуть) to grunt (*of a pig*).

хрю́к|нуть, ну, нешь, *pf.* (*of* ~ать) to give a grunt (*of a pig*).

хряк, á, *m.* (*dial.*) hog.

хря́стн|уть, у, ешь, *pf.* (*coll.*) 1. (*dial.*) to snap (off). 2. to bash.

хрящ¹, á, *m.* (*anat.*) cartilage, gristle.

хрящ², á, *m.* gravel, grit.

хрящевáт|ый¹ (~, ~а), *adj.* cartilaginous, gristly.

хрящевáт|ый² (~, ~а), *adj. of* хрящ².

хрящ|евóй¹, ², adj. of ~¹, ².

худ|ée, *comp. of* ~óй¹, ³.

худé|ть, ю, *impf.* (*of* по~) to grow thin.

хýд|о¹, а, *n.* harm, ill, evil; нет ~а без добрá every cloud has a silver lining.

хýдо², *adv.* ill, badly.

хýдо³, *as pred.* (*impers.+d.*) емý, etc., х. (*i*) he, *etc.*, feels poorly, unwell, (*ii*) he, *etc.*, is in a bad way, is having a bad time.

худоб|á, ы́, *f.* thinness, leanness.

худóжественност|ь, и, *f.* artistry, artistic merit.

худóжествен|ный (~, ~на), *adj.* 1. of art, of the arts; ~ная литератýра belles-lettres, fiction; ~ная самодéятельность amateur art (and dramatic) activities, amateur theatricals; Х. теáтр Arts Theatre (*in Moscow*); х. фильм feature film; ~ная шкóла art school. 2. artistic; tasteful; aesthetically satisfying.

худóжеств|о, а, *n.* 1. art; *pl.* (*obs.*) the arts; Акадéмия ~ Academy of Arts. 2. (*obs.*) artistry. 3. (*coll.*) trick, escapade.

худóжник, а, *m.* artist (*practitioner of fine arts; also fig., of writers, craftsmen, etc.*).

худ|óй¹ (~, ~á, ~о), *adj.* thin, lean.

худ|óй² (~, ~á, ~о), *adj.* bad; на х. конéц if the worst comes to the worst; не говоря́ ~óго слóва (*coll.*) without a word, without warning.

худ|óй³ (~, ~á, ~о), *adj.* (*coll.*) in holes, full of holes; worn; tumbledown.

худорóд|ный (~ен, ~на), *adj.* (*obs.*) of humble birth.

худорóдств|о, а, *n.* (*obs.*) humble birth.

худощáвост|ь, и, *f.* thinness, leanness.

худощáв|ый (~, ~а), *adj.* thin, lean.

хýд|ший, *superl. of* ~óй² *and* плохóй, (the) worst.

ху|ёвый, *adj. of* ~й; (*vulg.*) rotten, lousy.

хý|же, *comp. of* ~дóй² *and* ~до², плохóй *and* плóхо; worse.

хуй, хýя, *m.* (*vulg.*) prick, tool (= penis); ни хуя́ (*vulg.*) not a bloody thing.

хул|á, ы́, *f.* abuse, (hostile) criticism.

хулигáн, а, *m.* hooligan.

хулигáн|ить, ю, ишь, *impf.* to engage in hooliganism; to behave like a hooligan.

хулигáн|ский, *adj. of* ~.

хулигáнств|о, а, *n.* hooliganism.

хули́тел|ьный (ен, ~ьна), *adj.* abusive.

хул|и́ть, ю́, и́шь, *impf.* to abuse, criticize (*from a hostile position*).

хýнт|а, ы, *f.* (*polit.*) junta.

хурáл, а, *m.* hural (*name of national and local organs of government in Mongolian People's Republic*).

хурм|á, ы́, *f.* (*bot.*) persimmon (*Diospyros*).

хýтор, а, *pl.* ~á, *m.* 1. farm; farmstead. 2. small village (*in the Ukraine and areas of Cossack settlement in S. Russia*).

хуторск|óй, *adj. of* хýтор; ~и́е казаки́ Cossack farmers; ~óе хозя́йство individual (*as opp. to collective or State*) farm.

хуторя́н|ин, ина, *pl.* ~е, ~, *m.* farmer.

Ц

цáнг|и, ~, *no sing.* (*tech.*) pliers, tongs.

цáнг|овый, *adj. of* ~и; ц. патрóн draw-in attachment.

цап *as pred.* (*coll.*) = ~нул.

цáп|ать, аю, *impf.* (*of* ~нуть) 1. to seize, snatch, grab. 2. to scratch. 3. (за+*a.*) to snatch, grab.

цáп|аться, аюсь, *impf* (*of* ~нуться) (*coll.*) 1. to scratch one another. 2. (*pf. also* по~) (*fig.*) to bicker, squabble.

цáпк|а, и, *f.* hoe.

цáп|ля, ли, *g. pl.* ~ель, *f.* heron.

цáп|нуть(ся), ну(сь), нешь(ся), *pf. of* ~ать(ся).

цáпф|а, ы, *f.* 1. (*tech.*) pin, pivot, journal (*of shaft*). 2. (*mil.*) trunnion.

цап-царáп, *as pred.* (*coll.*) he, *etc.*, grabbed, made a grab.

царáп|ать, аю, *impf.* 1. (*pf.* о~ *and* ~нуть) to scratch. 2. (*coll.*) to scribble.

царáпа|ться, юсь, *impf.* 1. to scratch (*intrans.*); to scratch one another. 2. to scramble (along).

царáпин|а, ы, *f.* scratch; abrasion.

царáп|нуть, ну, нешь, *pf. of* ~ать.

царéвич, а, *m.* tsarevich, czarevitch (*son of a tsar*).

царéв|на, ны, *g. pl.* ~ен, *f.* tsarevna, czarevna (*daughter of a tsar*).

царедвóр|ец, ца, *m.* (*obs.*) courtier.

цар|ёк, ька́, *m.* princeling, ruler.

цареуби́йств|о, а, *n.* regicide (*action*).

цареуби́йц|а, ы, *m. and f.* regicide (*agent*).

цари́зм, а, *m.* tsarism, czarism.

цари́стский, *adj.* tsarist, czarist.

цар|и́ть, ю́, и́шь, *impf.* 1. (*obs.*) to be tsar

2. to hold sway. **3.** (*fig.*) to reign, prevail; ~йла тишина silence reigned.

цари́ц|а, ы, f. 1. tsarina, czarina (*empress in own right or wife of tsar*). **2.** (*fig.*) queen.

ца́рск|ий, adj. 1. tsar's, of the tsar; royal; ц. двор tsar's court; ~ая во́дка aqua regia; ~ие врата́ (*eccl.*) royal gates (*central doors in iconostasis in Orthodox churches*); ц. ко́рень (*bot.*) masterwort. **2.** tsarist, czarist. **3.** (*fig.*) regal, kingly; ~ая ро́скошь regal splendour.

ца́рствен|ный (~, ~на), adj. 1. (*obs.*) of the tsar. **2.** (*fig.*) regal, kingly.

ца́рств|о, а, n. 1. kingdom, realm. **2.** reign. **3.** (*fig.*) realm, domain; живо́тное ц. animal kingdom; со́нное ц. land of Nod.

ца́рствовани|е, я, n. reign; в ц. (+g.) during the reign (of).

ца́рств|овать, ую, impf. to reign (*also fig.*).

цар|ь, я́, m. 1. tsar, czar; он с ~ём (без ~я́) в голове́ (*coll.*) he is wise (stupid). **2.** (*fig.*) king, ruler.

ца́ц|а, ы, f. (*coll.*) big-head.

ца́цка|ться, юсь, impf. (с кем-н.; *coll.*) to make a fuss (of someone).

цвель, и, f. (*dial.*) mould (*on foodstuffs or on walls, rocks, pond surfaces, etc.*).

цве|сти́, ту́, тёшь, past ~л, ~ла́, ~ло́, impf. 1. to flower, bloom, blossom (*also fig.*); ц. здоро́вьем to be radiant with health. **2.** (*fig.*) to prosper, flourish. **3.** to be covered with mould. **4.** (*dial.*) to be covered with spots.

цвет¹, а, pl. ~а́, m. colour; ц. лица́ complexion.

цвет², а, m. 1. (*pl.* ~ы́) (*coll.*) flower. **2.** (*fig.*) flower, cream, pick (*best part*). **3.** blossom-time; (*fig.*) prime; в цвету́ in blossom; дать ц. to blossom, flower; во ~е сил in one's prime, at the height of one's powers. **4.** blossom.

цвета́ст|ый (~, ~а), adj. (*coll.*) gaudy, garish.

цвете́ни|е, я, n. (*bot.*) flowering, florescence, blossoming.

цве́т|ень, ня, m. (*coll.*) pollen.

цвети́ст|ый (~, ~а), adj. 1. multi-coloured, variegated. **2.** (*fig.*) flowery, florid.

цветко́в|ый, adj. ~ые расте́ния (*bot.*) flowering plants, phanerogams.

цветни́к¹, а́, m. 1. flower-bed. **2.** (*fig.*) array, galaxy.

цветни́к², а́, m. (*coll.*) worker in non-ferrous metals industry.

цветн|о́й, adj. 1. coloured; colour; ~о́е стекло́ stained glass; ~а́я литогра́фия chromolithography; ~а́я капу́ста cauliflower; *as noun* ц., ~о́го, m. coloured person. **2.** (*tech.*) non-ferrous; ~ы́е мета́ллы non-ferrous metals.

цветово́д, а, m. flower-grower.

цветово́дств|о, а, n. flower-growing, floriculture.

цветов|о́й, adj. of цвет¹; ~а́я га́мма colour spectrum; ~а́я слепота́ colour-blindness.

цвет|о́к, ка́, pl. ~ы́, ~о́в, m. flower; (*pl. also* ~ки́, ~ко́в) flower (*as opp. to other parts of plant*).

цветоло́ж|е, а, n. (*bot.*) receptacle.

цветоно́жк|а, и, f. (*bot.*) peduncle.

цветоно́сный, adj. flower-bearing.

цвето́ч|ек, ка, m. dim. of цвето́к.

цвето́чник, а, m. florist; flower-seller.

цвето́чн|ый, adj. of цвето́к; ~ая клу́мба flower-bed; ц. магази́н flower-shop, florist's; ц. чай flower tea.

цвету́щий, pres. part. act. of цвести́ *and adj.* **1.** flowering, blossoming, blooming (*also fig.*). **2.** (*fig.*) prosperous, flourishing.

це́вк|а, и, f. (*tech.*) bobbin, spool.

цевни́ц|а, ы, f. (*obs.*) pipe (*musical instrument*).

цевь|ё, я́, n. 1. fore-end (*of rifle stock*). **2.** pivot.

цеди́лк|а, и, f. (*coll.*) strainer (*cul.*), filter.

цеди́льн|ый, adj. filter, filtering; ~ая бума́га filter paper; ~ая поду́шка filter pad.

це|ди́ть, жу́, ~дишь, impf. 1. to strain, filter; to percolate. **2.** to decant (*liquids*). **3.** (*coll.*) to say (speaking through set teeth); to mutter (*often of a person barely containing anger*).

це́др|а, ы, f. (dried) lemon *or* orange peel.

цежёный, adj. (*coll.*) strained.

це́зи|й, я, m. (*chem.*) caesium.

цезу́р|а, ы, f. (*lit.*) caesura.

цейло́н|ец, ца, m. Ceylonese.

цейло́нк|а, и, f. Ceylonese (woman).

цейло́нский, adj. of Ceylon, Cingalese, Sinhalese.

цейтно́т, а, m. находи́ться в ~е to be in time-trouble (*at chess*).

цейхга́уз, а, m. (*mil.; obs.*) armoury, stores.

целе́бность, и, f. curative, healing properties.

целе́б|ный (~ен, ~на), adj. curative, healing, medicinal.

цел|ево́й, adj. 1. adj. of ~ь. **2.** having a special purpose; ~евы́е сбо́ры funds earmarked for a special purpose.

целена́правленность, и, f. purposefulness, single-mindedness.

целена́правлен|ный (~, ~на), adj. purposeful, single-minded.

целесообра́зность, и, f. expediency.

целесообра́з|ный (~ен, ~на), adj. expedient.

целеустремлённость, и, f. purposefulness.

целеустремлён|ный (~, ~а́), adj. purposeful.

це́лик, а, m. (*mil.*) sight (*on fire-arm*).

цели́к, а́, m. 1. (*coll.*) virgin land, forest, *etc.* **2.** (*min.*) pillar, block (*of untouched ore*).

целико́м, *adv.* **1.** whole; проглоти́ть ц. to swallow whole. **2.** wholly, entirely; ц. и по́лностью utterly and completely.

целин|а́, ы́, *f.* virgin lands, virgin soil (*esp. of the steppe lands of Kazakhstan and Western Siberia, extensively cultivated since 1954*).

цели́нник, а, *m.* worker in the virgin lands (*of Kazakhstan and W. Siberia*).

цели́н|ный, *adj. of* ~а́; ~ные зе́мли virgin lands.

цели́тел|ьный (~ен, ~ьна), *adj.* curative, healing, medicinal.

це́л|ить, ю, ишь, *impf.* (*of* на~) **1.** to take aim; (в+*a.*) to aim (at). **2.** (*obs.*) to mean, intend. **3.** (+*inf.*; *coll.*) to aim (to).

цел|и́ть, ю́, и́шь, *impf.* (*obs.*) to heal, cure.

це́л|иться, юсь, ишься, *impf.* (*of* на~) = ~ить.

целко́в|ый, ого, *m.* (*coll.*) one rouble (*obs., silver coin*).

целлофа́н, а, *m.* cellophane.

целлуло́ид, а, *m.* celluloid.

целлюло́з|а, ы, *f.* cellulose.

целова́льник, а, *m.* **1.** (*hist.*) tax-collector. **2.** (*obs.*) inn-keeper, publican.

цел|ова́ть, у́ю, *impf.* (*of* по~) to kiss.

цел|ова́ться, у́юсь, *impf.* (*of* по~) to kiss (one another).

це́л|ое, ого, *n.* **1.** whole. **2.** (*math.*) integer.

целому́дрен|ный (~, ~на), *adj.* chaste.

целому́дри|е, я, *n.* chastity.

це́лостност|ь, и, *f.* integrity.

це́лост|ный (~ен, ~на), *adj.* integral; entire, complete.

це́лост|ь, и, *f.* **1.** safety; в ~и и сохра́нности intact. **2.** unity.

це́л|ый, *adj.* **1.** whole, entire; ~ое число́ whole number, integer; в ~ом as a whole; по ~ым неде́лям for weeks on end. **2.** (~, ~а́, ~о) safe, intact; ~ и невреди́м safe and sound.

цел|ь, и, *f.* **1.** target; бить в ц., попа́сть в ц. to hit the target; бить ми́мо ~и to miss. **2.** aim, object, goal, end, purpose; с ~ью (+*inf.*) with the object (of), in order (to); отвеча́ть ~и to answer the purpose; пресле́довать ц. to pursue an object; ста́вить себе́ ~ью (+*inf.*) to set oneself (to).

цельнометалли́ческий, *adj.* all-metal.

це́л|ьный, *adj.* **1.** of one piece, solid. **2.** (~ен, ~ьна́, ~ьно) entire, integral; single. **3.** undiluted. **4.** (*coll.*) = ~ый.

це́льност|ь, и, *f.* wholeness, entirety, integrity.

Це́льси|й, я, *m.* Celsius, centigrade (thermometer); 10° по ~ю 10° centigrade.

цеме́нт, а, *m.* cement.

цемента́ци|я, и, *f.* (*tech.*) **1.** cementation. **2.** carbonization (*of wrought iron*), case-hardening.

цементи́р|овать, ую, *impf. and pf.* **1.** (*tech.*) to cement; to case-harden. **2.** (*fig.*) to cement.

цеме́нт|ный, *adj. of* ~.

цен|а́, ы́, *a.* ~у, *pl.* ~ы, *f.* **1.** price, cost; ~о́ю (+*g.*) at the price (of), at the cost (of); любо́й ~о́й at any price; э́тому ~ы́ нет it is invaluable; э́то в ~е́ it is very costly. **2.** worth, value; знать ~у (+*d.*) to know the worth (of); знать себе́ ~у to be self-assured, self-possessed.

ценз, а, *m.* qualification (*for enjoyment of political rights, etc.*).

це́нз|овый, *adj. of* ~.

це́нзор, а, *m.* censor.

цензу́р|а, ы, *f.* censorship.

цензу́р|ный, *adj.* **1.** *adj. of* ~a. **2.** (~ен, ~на) decent (*of words or phrases*).

цензур|ова́ть, у́ю, *impf.* (*obs.*) to censor.

цени́тел|ь, я, *m.* judge, connoisseur, expert.

цен|и́ть, ю́, ~ишь, *impf.* **1.** (*coll.*) to fix a price for; (*fig.*) to assess, evaluate. **2.** to value, appreciate; высоко́ ц. to rate highly.

це́нник, а, *m.* price-list.

це́нност|ь, и, *f.* **1.** price, value. **2.** (*fig.*) value, importance. **3.** (*pl.*) valuables; values.

це́н|ный (~ен, ~на), *adj.* **1.** containing valuables; representing a stated value; ~ная бандеро́ль registered postal packet (*with statement of value of contents*); ~ные бума́ги (*fin.*) securities. **2.** valuable, costly; ц. пода́рок costly present. **3.** (*fig.*) valuable; precious; important; ц. докуме́нт important document.

цент, а, *m.* cent (*unit of currency*).

це́нтнер, а, *m.* centner (= 100 kg).

центр, а, *m.* (*in var. senses*) centre; ц. тя́жести centre of gravity.

центра́л, а, *m.* (*hist.*) central prison.

централиза́ци|я, и, *f.* centralization.

централи́зм, а, *m.* (*polit.*) centralism.

централиз|ова́ть, у́ю, *impf. and pf.* to centralize.

централ|ь, и, *f.* (*tech.*) main (*in electricit transmission network, etc.*).

центра́льн|ый, *adj.* (*in var. senses*) central ~ые газе́ты national newspapers (*news papers published in the capital*); ц. напада́ю щий (*sport*) centre forward; ~ая не́рвна систе́ма central nervous system; ~ое ото пле́ние central heating.

центри́р|овать, ую, *impf. and pf.* (*tech.*) t centre.

центрифу́г|а, и, *f.* **1.** (*tech.*) centrifuge. **2** spin drier.

центробе́жный, *adj.* centrifugal; ц. насо́ rotary pump.

центрово́й, *adj.* (*tech.*) central, centre.

центростреми́тельный, *adj.* centripetal.

цеп, á, *m.* (*agric.*) flail.

цепене́|ть, ю, *impf.* (*of* о~) to become rigid, freeze (up), be rooted to the spot (*from cold or from strong emotion*).

цéп|кий (~ок, ~ка́, ~ко), *adj.* **1.** tenacious, strong (*also fig.*); prehensile. **2.** (*of soil, mud, etc.*) sticky, tacky, loamy. **3.** (*coll.*) obstinate, persistent, strong-willed.

цéпкост|ь, и, *f.* **1.** tenacity, strength. **2.** (*coll.*) obstinacy, persistence, strength of will.

цепля́|ть, ю, *impf.* (*coll.*) **1.** (за+а.) = ~ть- ся. **2.** to clutch (at), try to grasp.

цепля́|ться, юсь, *impf.* **1.** (за+а.) to clutch (at), try to grasp. **2.** (за+а.; *coll.*) to cling (to); to stick (to). **3.** (к, за+а.; *coll.*) to pick (on) (= *to carp at, complain of*).

цеп|ной, *adj. of* ~ь; ~на́я собáка watchdog, house-dog; ~нóе колесó sprocket wheel; ~на́я ли́ния (*math.*) catenary; ц. мост chain bridge, suspension bridge; ~на́я реáкция (*chem., phys.; fig.*) chain reaction; ~на́я тя́га (*tech.*) chain traction.

цепóчк|а, и, *f.* **1.** (small) chain. **2.** file, series; идти́ ~ой to walk in file.

цеп|ь, и, о ~и, на ~й, *pl.* **~и, ~éй,** *f.* **1.** chain; (*pl.*) chains (= *fetters; also fig.*); посади́ть нá ц. (*or* на цéпь) to chain (up), shackle. **2.** row, series; range (*of mountains*). **3.** (*mil.*) line, file. **4.** (*fig.*) series, succession; ц. катастрóф succession of disasters. **5.** (*electr.*) circuit; ввести́ в ц. to connect.

Цéрбер, а, *m.* (*myth.; fig.*) Cerberus.

церемониáл, а, *m.* **1.** ceremonial, ritual; order, procedure. **2.** пройти́ ~ом (*mil.; obs.*) to march past.

церемониáл|ьный, *adj.* **1.** *adj. of* ~. **2.** solemn, ceremonial; ц. марш (*mil.*) march-past.

церемониймéйстер, а, *m.* (*obs.*) master of ceremonies.

церемóн|иться, юсь, *impf.* (*of* по~) **1.** to stand upon ceremony. **2.** (с кем-н.) to treat excessively considerately.

церемóни|я, и, *f.* **1.** ceremony. **2.** (*pl.*) ceremony (*pejor.*), exaggerated observation of convention, etiquette.

церемóн|ный (~ен, ~на), *adj.* **1.** ceremonious. **2.** (*pejor.*) excessively strict in observing etiquette, protocolaire.

цéри|й, я, *m.* (*chem.*) cerium; зáкись ~я cerous oxide; óкись ~я ceric oxide.

церкóвник, а, *m.* **1.** churchman, church- -goer. **2.** clergyman, minister of reli- gion.

церковноприхóдский, *adj.* (*eccl.*) parish.

церковнославя́нский, *adj.* (*ling.*) Church Slavonic.

церковнослужи́тел|ь, я, *m.* church officer (*sexton, etc.*).

церкóвн|ый, *adj.* church; ~ое прáво eccle- siastical law, canon law; ц. стáроста churchwarden; ц. стóрож sexton.

цéрк|овь, ви, *i.* **~овью,** *pl.* **~ви, ~вéй, вáм,** *f.* church (*building and organization*).

цесарéвич, а, *m.* cesarevitch (*heir to throne in tsarist Russia*).

цесáрк|а, и, *f.* guinea-fowl.

цех, а, в ~е *and* (*coll.*) **в ~у́,** *pl.* **~и** *and* (*coll.*) **~á,** *m.* **1.** shop, section (*in factory*). **2.** (*hist.*) guild, corporation.

цех|овóй, *adj.* **1.** *adj. of* ~. **2.** (*pejor.*) limited, parochial.

цеховщи́н|а, ы, *f.* (*pejor.*) narrow profes- sionalism.

цецé, *indecl., f.* tsetse (fly).

циáн, а, *m.* (*chem.*) cyanogen.

циáнистый, *adj.* (*chem.*) cyanogen; cyanide (of); ц. кáлий potassium cyanide.

циáнов|ый, *adj.* (*chem.*) cyanic; ~ая кислотá cyanic acid; ~ая ртуть mercuric cyanide.

цианóз, а, *m.* (*med.*) cyanosis.

цй́бик, а, *m.* (*obs.*) tea-chest.

цивилизáтор, а, *m.* (*usu. iron.*) civilizer.

цивилизáци|я, и, *f.* civilization.

цивилизóв|анный, *p.p.p. of* ~áть *and adj.* civilized.

цивилиз|овáть, у́ю, *impf. and pf.* to civilize.

цивили́ст, а, *m.* (*leg.*) specialist in civil law.

циви́льный, *adj.* (*obs.*) civil, civilian; ц. лист civil list.

цигáрк|а, и, *f.* (*coll.*) home-rolled cigarette.

цигéйк|а, и, *f.* beaver lamb.

цигéйковый, *adj.* beaver-lamb.

цидýлк|а, и, *f.* (*coll., obs.*) note; billet-doux.

цикáд|а, ы, *f.* cicada.

цикл, а, *m.* (*in var. senses*) cycle.

циклáмéн, а, *m.* cyclamen.

цикли́ческий, *adj.* cyclic(al).

цикли́ч|ный (~ен, ~на), *adj.* = ~еский.

циклóид|а, ы, *f.* (*math.*) cycloid.

циклóн, а, *m.* (*meteor.*) cyclone.

циклони́ческий, *adj.* (*meteor.*) cyclonic.

циклопи́ческий, *adj.* (*archit.*) cyclopean.

циклотрóн, а, *m.* (*phys.*) cyclotron.

цй́кл|я, и, *f.* (*tech.*) scraper.

цикóри|й, я, *m.* chicory.

цикóр|ный, *adj. of* ~ий.

цикýт|а, ы, *f.* (*bot.*) water hemlock (*Cicuta virosa*).

цили́ндр, а, *m.* **1.** (*math.*) cylinder. **2.** (*tech.*) cylinder, drum. **3.** top hat.

цилиндри́ческий, *adj.* cylindrical.

цили́ндр|овый, *adj. of* ~ 2.

цимбали́ст, а, *m.* cymbalist.

цимбáл|ы, ~, *no sing.* (*mus.*) cymbals.

цинг|á, й, *f.* (*med.*) scurvy.

цинг|óтный, *adj. of* ~á; scorbutic.

цини́зм, а, *m.* cynicism.
ци́ник, а, *m.* cynic.
цини́ческий, *adj.* cynical.
цини́ч|ный (~ен, ~на), *adj.* cynical.
цинк, а, *m.* (*chem.*) zinc.
цинк|ова́ть, у́ю, *impf.* (*tech.*) to zinc-plate.
ци́нковый, *adj.* zinc.
цино́вк|а, и, *f.* mat.
цино́в|очный, *adj. of* ~ка.
цирк, а, *m.* circus.
цирка́ч, а́, *m.* (*coll.*) circus artiste.
цирка́чес|кий, *adj. of* ~тво.
цирка́честв|о, а, *n.* (*fig., pejor.*) playing to the gallery, exhibitionism.
цирк|ово́й, *adj. of* ~.
цирко́н, а, *m.* (*min.*) zircon.
цирко́ни|й, я, *m.* (*chem.*) zirconium.
циркора́м|а, ы, *f.* (*cinema*) circorama.
циркули́р|овать, ую, *impf.* **1.** to circulate (*of liquids, etc.*; *also fig.*); ~ова́ли слу́хи rumours were circulating. **2.** (*coll.*) to pass, go to and fro.
ци́ркул|ь, я, *m.* (pair of) compasses; dividers.
ци́ркуль|ный, *adj. of* ~.
циркуля́р, а, *m.* (*official*) instruction.
циркуля́рн|ый¹, *adj.* circulated; ~ое письмо́ circular (letter).
циркуля́рный², *adj.* circular; circulating; ц. нож knife with circular action.
циркуляцио́нный, *adj.* (*tech.*) circulating, circulation; ц. насо́с circulation pump.
циркуля́ци|я, и, *f.* (*in var. senses*) circulation; (*naut.*) gyration.
цирро́з, а, *m.* (*med.*) cirrhosis.
цирю́льник, а, *m.* (*obs.*) barber.
цирю́ль|ня, ьни, *g. pl.* ~ен, *f.* (*obs.*) barber's shop.
цисте́рн|а, ы, *f.* cistern, tank; ваго́н-ц. tank-truck (*rail or road transport*).
цитаде́л|ь, и, *f.* citadel; (*fig.*) bulwark, stronghold.
цита́т|а, ы, *f.* quotation.
цита́тничеств|о, а, *n.* (*pejor.*) quotation-mongering (*in political argumentation*).
цитва́рн|ый, *adj.* (*bot.*) santonic, wormseed; ~ая полы́нь santonin; ~ое се́мя santonin, wormseed (*med.*; *used as anthelmintic*).
цити́р|овать, ую, *impf.* (*of* про~) to quote.
цитоло́ги|я, и, *f.* (*biol.*) cytology.

ци́тр|а, ы, *f.* (*mus.*) zither.
ци́трус, а, *m.* citrus.
цитрусово́дств|о, а, *n.* citrus-growing.
ци́трус|овый, *adj. of* ~; *as noun* ~овые, ~овых citrus plants.
цифербла́т, а, *m.* dial, face (*of clocks, watches, and measuring instruments*).
цифи́р|ь, и, *f.* (*obs.*) **1.** (*collect.*) figures. **2.** counting, calculation; arithmetic.
цифр|а, ы, *f.* **1.** figure; number, numeral. **2.** (*pl.*) figures (= *statistical data*).
цифр|ова́ть, у́ю, *impf.* to number.
цифр|ово́й, *adj.* **1.** numerical. **2.** digital.
ци́церо, *indecl.*, *n.* (*typ.*) pica.
цо́к|ать¹, аю, *impf.* (*of* ~нуть) to clatter (*of the sound of metal against stone*).
цо́к|ать², аю, *impf.* to pronounce 'ч' as 'ц' (*as in some North Russian dialects*).
цо́к|нуть, ну, *pf. of* ~ать¹.
цо́кол|ь, я, *m.* **1.** (*archit.*) socle, plinth, pedestal. **2.** (*electr.*) cap (*metal extremity of light bulb which is fitted into socket*).
цо́коль|ный, *adj. of* ~; ц. эта́ж ground floor.
цо́кот, а, *m.* clatter (*as of horses' hoofs on paving-stones*).
цоко|та́ть, чу́, ~чешь, *impf.* (*coll.*) to clatter.
цуг, а, *m.* team (*of horses harnessed tandem or in pairs*).
цу́гом, *adv.* **1.** (*of horses in harness*) tandem. **2.** (*coll.*) in file.
цука́т, а, *m.* candied peel.
цыга́н, а, *pl.* ~е, ~ (*obs.* ~ы, ~ов), *m.* Gipsy.
цыга́н|ка, ки, *f. of* ~.
цыга́нский, *adj.* gipsy.
цы́к|ать, аю, *impf.* (*of* ~нуть) (на кого́-н.) *coll.*) to shut up.
цы́к|нуть, ну, *pf. of* ~ать.
цы́пк|а, и, *f.* (*coll.*) chicken, chick (*also used as affectionate mode of address to women*).
цы́п|ки, ок, *sing.* ~ка, ~ки, *f.* (*coll.*) red spots (*on hands, etc.*).
цыпл|ёнок, ёнка, *pl.* ~я́та, ~я́т, *m.* chick(en).
цыпля́тник, а, *m.* chicken-house.
цыпл|я́чий, *adj. of* ~ёнок.
цы́почк|и; на ц., на ~ах on tiptoe.
цып-цы́п, *interj.*, cry made in calling chicken.
цыц, *interj.* (*coll.*) cry indicating prohibition or enjoining silence.

Ч

чаба́н, а́, *m.* shepherd.
чаба́н|ский, *adj. of* ~.
чаб|ёр, ра́, *m.* (*bot.*) savory (*Satureia*).
чабре́ц, а́, *m.* (*bot., cul.*) thyme (*Satureia hortensis*).
ча́вк|ать, аю, *impf.* (*of* ~нуть) **1.** to champ, smack one's lips (*whilst eating*); to munch noisily. **2.** to tramp, tread noisily; to make a crunching, squelching noise.
ча́вк|нуть, ну, нешь, *pf. of* ~ать.
чад, а (у), о ~е, в~у́, *m.* **1.** fumes. **2.** (*fig.*) intoxication.

ча|ди́ть, жу́, ди́шь, *impf.* (*of* на~) to smoke, emit fumes.

ча́д|ный (~ен, ~на, ~но), *adj.* 1. smoky, smoke-laden; ~но (*as pred.*) it is smoky, full of smoke. 2. (*fig.*) doped, drugged, stupefied; stupefying.

ча́д|о, а, *n.* 1. (*obs. or joc.*) child, offspring, progeny. 2. (*fig.*) child, product, creature; ч. двадца́того ве́ка product of the twentieth century.

чадолюби́в|ый (~, ~а), *adj.* (*obs. or joc.*) fond of one's child(ren).

чадр|а́, ы́, *f.* veil, yashmak (*worn by Moslem women*).

чаёвник, а, *m.* (*coll.*) tea-drinker (*person partial to tea-drinking*).

чаёвнича|ть, ю, *impf.* (*coll.*) to drink tea, indulge in tea-drinking.

чаево́д, а, *m.* tea-grower.

чаево́дств|о, а, *n.* tea-growing.

чаево́д|ческий, *adj. of* ~ство.

чаев|ы́е, ы́х, *no sing.* tip, gratuity.

ча|ёк, ~йка́ (у́), *m.* = чай.

чаепи́ти|е, я, *n.* tea-drinking.

чайнк|а, и, *f.* tea-leaf.

ча|й¹, я (ю), *pl.* ~й, ~ёв, *m.* 1. tea. 2. tea (-drinking); за ~ем, за ча́шкой ~я over (a cup of) tea; пригласи́ть на ч., на ча́шку ~я to invite to tea. 3. дать (+*d.*) на ч. to tip.

чай², *as adv.* (*coll.*) 1. probably, maybe; no doubt; вам тут, ч., ску́чно you must find it dull here. 2. (= ведь) after all, for.

ча́йк|а, и, *g. pl.* ча́ек, *f.* (sea-)gull.

ча́йн|ая, ой, *f.* tea-room, tea-shop.

ча́йник, а, *m.* teapot; kettle.

ча́йниц|а, ы, *f.* tea-caddy.

ча́йнича|ть, ю, *impf.* (*coll.*) to drink tea, have tea.

ча́йн|ый, *adj.* (*in var. senses*) tea; ~ая колбаса́ bologna sausage; ч. куст tea-plant; ~ая ло́жка tea-spoon; ~ая ро́за tea-rose; ~ая ча́шка teacup.

чайхан|а́, ы́, *f.* chaikhana (*tea-drinking establishment in Central Asia*).

чалдо́н, а, *m.* native of Siberia (*of Russian extraction*).

чалдо́н|ский, *adj. of* ~.

ча́л|ить, ю, ишь, *impf.* (*naut.*) to tie up, moor.

ча́лк|а, и, *f.* (*naut.*) 1. tieing up, mooring. 2. tie-rope, mooring rope.

чалм|а́, ы́, *f.* turban.

ча́лый, *adj.* (*of colour of horse's coat*) roan.

чан, а, в ~е *or* в ~у́, *pl.* ~ы́, *m.* vat, tub, tank.

чапы́г|а, и, *f.* (*dial.*) plough-handle.

ча́р|а, ы, *f.* (*arch. or folk poet.*) cup, goblet.

ча́р|ка, ки, *f.* = ~а.

чар|ова́ть, у́ю, *impf.* 1. (*obs.*) to bewitch. 2. (*fig.*) to charm, captivate, enchant.

чароде́|й, я, *m.* magician, enchanter, wizard (*also fig.*).

чароде́йств|о, а, *n.* magic, charms.

ча́ртерный, *adj.* ч. рейс (*aeron.*) charter flight.

ча́р|ы, ~, *no sing.* magic, charms (*also fig.*).

час, а, о ~е, **в** ~у́ *and* в ~е, *pl.* ~ы́, *m.* 1. hour (*also fig.*); че́тверть ~а́ a quarter of an hour; ч. проби́л the hour has struck, has come; ч. в ч. at the time appointed, on the dot; ч. от ~у with every passing hour; с ~у на ч. (*i*) hourly, with every passing hour, (*ii*) any moment; че́рез ч. (*i*) in an hour, (*ii*) at hourly intervals; в до́брый ч.! good luck! 2. (*in time measurement: g. sing.* ~а́ *after numerals* 2, 3, 4) o'clock; час one o'clock; два ~а́ two o'clock; во второ́м ~у́ between one and two (o'clock); кото́рый ч.? what is the time? 3. (*usually pl.*) hours, time, period; ч. пик, ~ы́ пик rush hour; ~ы́ заня́тий working hours; ч. рисова́ния (*in school, etc.*) drawing period. 4. ~ы́ (*mil.*) guard-duty; стоя́ть на ~а́х to stand guard. 5. ~ы́ (*eccl.*) (canonical) hours.

часа́ми, *adv.* for hours.

часо́в|ня, ни, *g. pl.* ~ен, *f.* chapel.

часов|о́й¹, о́го, *m.* sentry, sentinel, guard.

часов|о́й², *adj.* (*of* час) 1. of one hour's duration; ч. переры́в one hour's interval. 2. (measured) by the hour; ~а́я опла́та payment by the hour; ч. по́яс time zone. 3. one o'clock; ч. по́езд one o'clock train.

часов|о́й³, *adj. of* часы́; ч. замыка́тель clockwork fuse; ч. магази́н watch shop, watchmaker's, watch repair shop; ~ы́х дел ма́стер watchmaker; ч. механи́зм clockwork; ~а́я стре́лка clock hand, hour hand; по ~о́й стре́лке clockwise.

часовщи́к, а́, *m.* watchmaker.

ча́сом, *adv.* (*coll.*) 1. sometimes, at times. 2. by chance, by the way.

часосло́в, а, *m.* (*eccl.*) Book of Hours.

часте́нько, *adv.* (*coll.*) quite often, fairly often.

части́к, а́, *m.* 1. thick net. 2. fish caught in such a net.

ча|сти́ть, щу́, сти́шь, *impf.* (*coll.*) 1. to do something *or* speak rapidly, hurriedly. 2. (к) to visit frequently, see much (of).

части́ц|а, ы, *f.* 1. small part, element. 2. (*phys.*) particle. 3. (*gram.*) particle.

части́чно, *adv.* partly, partially.

части́ч|ный (~ен, ~на), *adj.* partial.

ча́стник, а, *m.* (*coll.*) private trader; private medical practitioner.

частновладе́льческий, *adj.* privately--owned.

ча́стн|ое, ого, *n.* (*math.*) quotient.

частнособственнический, *adj.* private-
-ownership.

ча́стност|ь, и, *f.* detail; в ~и in particular.

ча́стн|ый, *adj.* 1. private, personal; ~ым
о́бразом privately; ~ая пра́ктика private
(*medical*) practice. 2. (*econ.*) private, privately-owned; ~ая со́бственность private
property. 3. particular, individual; *as noun*
~ое, ~ого, *n.* the particular. 4. (*mil.*) local;
ч. успе́х local gain. 5. (*hist.*) district; ч.
дом district police station.

ча́сто, *adv.* often, frequently.

частоко́л, а, *m.* fence, paling; palisade.

частот|а́, ы́, *pl.* ~ы, *f.* (*in var. senses*) fre-
quency.

частот|ный, *adj.* (*tech.*) of ~а́.

частýшк|а, и, *f.* chastushka (*two-line or
four-line rhymed poem or ditty on some topical or
humorous theme*).

част|ый (~, ~á, ~о), *adj.* 1. frequent; он у
нас ч. гость he is a frequent visitor at our
house. 2. close (together); dense, thick;
close-woven; ч. гре́бень fine-tooth comb;
~ые дере́вни villages close together; ч.
дождь steady rain; ~ая и́згородь thick
hedge; ~ое си́то fine sieve. 3. quick,
rapid; ч. ого́нь (*mil.*) rapid fire.

част|ь, и, *pl.* ~и, ~е́й, *f.* 1. part; portion; ~и
ре́чи (*gram.*) parts of speech; разобра́ть на
~и to take to pieces, dismantle; бо́льшей
~ью, по бо́льшей ~и for the most part,
mostly; рвать кого́-н. на ~и to give someone no peace. 2. section, department, side;
уче́бная (*as opp. to administrative*) side (*in
educational institution*). 3. sphere,
field; э́то не по мое́й ~и this is not my province; по ~и (+*g.*) in connexion (with).
4. (*coll.*) share; войти́, вступи́ть в ч. с кем-н.
to join forces with someone (*usually in commerce*). 5. (*mil.*) unit. 6. (в ~й) (*hist.*) administrative region (*of city*); police station
(*responsible for such region*); fire brigade. 7.
(*obs.*) fate.

ча́стью, *adv.* partly, in part.

час|ы́¹, о́в, *no sing.* clock, watch.

часы́², *see* час 4, 5.

ча́хл|ый (~, ~а), *adj.* 1. (*of vegetation*)
stunted; poor, sorry. 2. weakly, sickly, puny.

ча́х|нуть, ну, нешь, *past* ~, ~ла, *impf.* (*of
за~*) 1. (*of vegetation*) to wither away. 2. to
become weak, (go into a) decline; (*fig.*) to
tire oneself out, become exhausted.

чахо́тк|а, и, *f.* (*coll.*) consumption; кар-
ма́нная ч. (*joc.*) an empty pocket.

чахо́точный, *adj.* (*coll.*) 1. consumptive.
2. poor, sorry, feeble.

ча́ш|а, и, *f.* cup, bowl (*also fig.*); (*eccl.*)
chalice; ч. весо́в scale, pan; ч. на́шего
терпе́ния перепо́лнилась our patience was
exhausted; сия́ ч. минова́ла его́ he has

survived the ordeal.

чашели́стик, а, *m.* (*bot.*) sepal.

ча́шечк|а, и, *f.* 1. *dim. of* ча́шка. 2. (*bot.*)
calyx.

ча́ш|ечный, *adj.* 1. *adj. of* ~ка. 2. cup-
-shaped.

ча́шк|а, и, *f.* 1. cup; bowl, pan. 2. ч. весо́в
pan (*of scales*). 3. (коле́нная) knee-cap.
4. (*tech.*) housing.

ча́шник, а, *m.* (*hist.*) cellarer.

ча́щ|а, и, *f.* thicket.

ча́ще, *comp. of* ча́стый *and* ча́сто more often,
more frequently; ч. всего́ most often, mostly.

ча́яни|е, я, *n.* expectation; aspiration;
па́че ~я, сверх ~я unexpectedly, contrary
to expectation.

ча́|ять, ю, ешь, *impf.* (*obs. or coll.*) 1. to
think, suppose. 2. (+*g. or inf.*) to hope (for),
expect.

чва́н|иться, юсь, ишься, *impf.* to boast.

чванли́вост|ь, и, *f.* boastfulness, arrogance.

чванли́в|ый (~, ~а), *adj.* boastful, arro-
gant, conceited.

чва́нный, *adj.* conceited, arrogant, proud
(*pejor.*).

чва́нств|о, а, *n.* conceit, arrogance, pride
(*pejor.*).

чебота́р|ь, я́, *m.* (*dial.*) cobbler, shoemaker.

чёбот|ы, ов, *sing.* ~, ~а, *m.* (*dial.*) boots,
shoes.

чебура́хн|уть, у, ешь, *pf.* (*coll.*) to crash
down (*trans.*).

чебура́хн|уться, усь, ешься, *pf.* (*coll.*) to
crash down (*intrans.*).

чебуре́к, а, *m.* cheburek (*kind of meat pasty
eaten in the Crimea and the Caucasus*).

чебуре́чн|ая, ой, *f.* stall selling chebureki.

чего́¹ *interrog. adv.* (*coll.*) why? what for?

чего́², *g. of* что.

чей, чья, чьё, *interrog. and relat. pron.* whose.

чей-либо, *pron.* anyone's.

чей-нибудь, *pron.* anyone's.

чей-то, *pron.* someone's.

чек, а, *m.* 1. cheque; вы́писать ч. to draw a
cheque. 2. (*in shops, etc.*) bill, chit (*indicating
amount to be paid*); receipt (*for payment, to be
presented at counter when claiming purchase*).

чек|а́¹, и́, *f.* pin, linchpin, cotter-pin.

Чек|а́², *indecl. or* (*coll.*) *g.* ~и́, *f.* (*coll.*) Cheka
(*abbr. of* Чрезвыча́йная Коми́ссия по
борьбе́ с контрреволю́цией, сабота́жем
и спекуля́цией the Soviet security organ, 1918–
1922).

чека́н, а, *m.* 1. stamp, die. 2. caulking
iron. 3. (*orn.*) chat; лугово́й ч. whinchat;
черного́рлый ч. stonechat.

чека́н|ить, ю, ишь, *impf.* 1. (*pf.* вы́~, от~)
to mint, coin; to stamp, engrave, emboss,
chase. 2. (*pf.* от~) to do, make with precision; ч. слова́ to enunciate one's words

clearly, speak abruptly; ч. шаг to measure out one's pace, step out. **3.** (*pf.* рас~) (*tech.*) to caulk. **4.** (*agric., hort.*) to prune.

чека́нк|а, и, *f.* **1.** coinage, coining, minting; stamping, engraving, embossing, chasing. **2.** (*tech.*) caulking. **3.** (*agric., hort.*) pruning. **4.** stamp, engraving, relief work.

чека́нн|ый, *adj.* **1.** stamping, engraving, embossing; ~ая рабо́та = чека́нка 4. **2.** stamped, engraved, embossed, chased. **3.** (*fig.*) precise, expressive, sharp.

чека́н|очный, *adj.* = ~ный 1; ч. пресс stamping press; ч. штамп die.

чека́нщик, а, *m.* coiner; stamper, engraver; caulker.

чеки́ст, а, *m.* official of Cheka (*hist.*); official of Soviet security service, security officer.

чекма́р|ь, я́, *m.* (*dial.*) rammer, beetle.

чекме́н|ь, я́, *m.* (cloth) jacket.

че́к|овый, *adj.* of ~; ~овая кни́жка cheque book.

челе́ст|а, ы, *f.* (*mus.*) glockenspiel.

чёлк|а, и, *f.* fringe (*of hair or as name of hair-style*); forelock.

чёлн, á, *pl.* ~ы́ or ~ы́, *m.* **1.** dug-out (canoe). **2.** (*obs. or poet.*) boat.

челно́к, á, *m.* **1.** = чёлн. **2.** shuttle.

челно́|чный, *adj.* of ~к 2; ч. полёт (*aeron.*) shuttle flight; ~чная дипломатия shuttle diplomacy.

чел|о́[1], á, *n.* forehead, brow; бить ~о́м кому́-н. (*hist. or iron.*) (*i*) to bow to someone (*in greeting*), (*ii*) to petition someone, (*iii*) to offer someone humble thanks.

чел|о́[2], á, *pl.* ~a, *n.* (*tech.*) stoking hole (*in furnace*).

челоби́тн|ая, ой, *f.* (*hist.*) petition.

челоби́тчик, а, *m.* (*hist.*) petitioner.

челоби́ть|е, я, *n.* (*hist.*) **1.** low bow. **2.** petition.

челове́к, а, *pl.* лю́ди (*g. pl., etc.,* **челове́к**, ~**ам**, ~**ами**, о ~**ах** *only in combination with numerals*) *m.* **1.** man, person, human being. **2.** (*obs.*) servant, man; waiter.

челове́ко-де́нь, ч. -дня́, *m.* (*econ.*) man-day.

человеколюби́в|ый (~, ~а), *adj.* philanthropic.

человеколю́би|е, я, *n.* philanthropy, love of fellow-men.

человеконенави́стник, а, *m.* misanthrope.

человеконенави́стнический, *adj.* misanthropic.

человеконенави́стничеств|о, а, *n.* misanthropy.

человекообра́з|ный (~ен, ~на), *adj.* anthropomorphous; (*zool.*) anthropoid.

человекоподо́б|ный (~ен, ~на), *adj.* resembling a human being.

челове́ко-ча́с, а, *m.* (*econ.*) man-hour.

челове́ч|ек, ка, *m.* little man.

челове́ческий, *adj.* **1.** human. **2.** humane.

челове́честв|о, а, *n.* humanity, mankind.

челове́|чий, *adj.* of ~к.

челове́чин|а, ы, (*coll.*) **1.** (*m. and f.*) human being, man. **2.** (*f.*) human flesh (*as meat*).

челове́чност|ь, и, *f.* humaneness, humanity.

челове́ч|ный (~ен, ~на), *adj.* humane.

челюстно́й, *adj.* jaw; (*anat.*) maxillary.

че́люст|ь, и, *f.* **1.** jaw, jaw-bone; (*anat.*) maxilla. **2.** dental plate, set of false teeth.

че́ляд|ь, и, *f.* (*collect.*; *hist.*) servants, retainers, men.

чем, *conj.* **1.** than. **2.** (+*comp.*) ч. ..., тем... the more ..., the more ...; ч. скоре́е, тем лу́чше the sooner, the better. **3.** (+*inf.*) rather than, instead of; чем писа́ть, ты бы лу́чше позвони́л you'd do better to ring up rather than write. **4.** ч. свет at daybreak.

чембу́р, а, *m.* halter.

чемода́н, а, *m.* suitcase.

чемпио́н, а, *m.* champion.

чемпиона́т, а, *m.* championship.

чемпио́н|ка, ки, *f.* of ~.

чемпио́нств|о, а, *n.* champion's title.

чеп|е́ц, ца́, *m.* (*woman's*) cap.

чепра́к, á, *m.* saddle-cloth.

чепух|а́, и́, *f.* (*coll.*) **1.** nonsense, rubbish. **2.** a trifle, trifling matter; trivialities.

чепухо́вый, *adj.* (*coll.*) **1.** nonsensical. **2.** trifling; trivial; insignificant.

че́пчик, а, *m.* **1.** = чепе́ц. **2.** (*child's*) bonnet.

че́рв|а, ы, *f.* (*collect.*) larvae (*of bees*).

червеобра́зный, *adj.* vermiform, vermicular; ч. отро́сток (*anat.*) appendix.

че́рв|и[1], е́й *and* ~**ы,** ~ *sing.* ~**а,** ~**ы,** hearts (*card suit*); коро́ль ~е́й king of hearts.

че́рв|и[2], *pl.* of ~ь.

черви́ве|ть, ет, *impf.* (*of* о~) to become worm-eaten.

черви́в|ый (~, ~а), *adj.* worm-eaten.

червлёный, *adj.* (*obs.*) dark red.

черв|о́вый, *adj.* of ~и[1].

черво́н|ец, ца, *m.* **1.** (*hist.*) chervonets (*gold coin of 3, 5, or 10 roubles' denomination; or 10-rouble bank-note in circulation 1922–47*). **2.** (*pl.*) (*coll., obs.*) money.

черво́нн|ый[1], *adj.* **1.** (*obs. or dial.*) red, dark red; ~ое зо́лото pure gold (*as having a reddish tint*). **2.** *adj.* of черво́нец 1.

черв|о́нный[2], *adj.* of ~и[1]; ч. туз ace of hearts.

червото́чин|а, ы, *f.* **1.** worm-hole, maggot hole. **2.** (*fig.*) rottenness.

черв|ь, я́, *pl.* ~**и,** ~**е́й,** *m.* **1.** worm; maggot. **2.** (*fig.*) bug, virus, germ; его́ то́чит ч. сомне́ния he is nagged by doubts.

червя́к, á, *m.* **1.** = червь. **2.** (*tech.*) worm.

червя́чн|ый, *adj.* of червя́к 2; ~ое колесо́, ~ая шестерня́ worm wheel; ~ая переда́ча worm gearing.

червяч|о́к, ка́, m. dim. of червя́к 1; замо-
ри́ть ~ка́ (coll.) to have a bite to eat.

черда́к, а́, m. attic, loft.

черда́|чный, adj. of ~к.

черевик|и, ов, (sing. ~, ~а), m. chereviki
(high-heeled leather boots worn by women in the
Ukraine).

черёд, а́, о ~е́, в ~у́, m. 1. turn; идти́
свои́м ~о́м to take its course. 2. (coll.)
queue.

черед|а́¹, ы́, f. 1. (obs.) = черёд 1. 2.
sequence. 3. file (of people).

черед|а́², ы́, f. (bot.) bur-marigold (Bidens).

чередова́ни|е, я, n. alternation, inter-
change, rotation; ч. гла́сных (ling.) vowel
interchange.

черед|ова́ть, у́ю, impf. (c+i.) to alternate
(with).

черед|ова́ться, у́юсь, impf. to alternate; to
take turns.

чередо́м, adv. (coll.) properly.

че́рез, prep.+a. 1. (of place) across; over;
through. 2. via. 3. through (=by means of,
with the aid of); ч. печа́ть through the press;
ч. перево́дчика through an interpreter.
4. (coll.) through (= due to, in consequence of);
ч. боле́знь through illness. 5. (of time) in; ч.
полчаса́ in half an hour's time; я верну́сь
ч. год I shall be back in a year's time. 6. (of
space) after; (further) on; ч. три киломе́тра
three kilometres (further) on. 7. (i) indicates repetition at stated unit of time or space:
принима́ть ч. час по столо́вой ло́жке
to take one tablespoonful every hour; ч.
ка́ждые три страни́цы every three pages,
(ii) indicates repetition alternating at stated unit
of time or space: дежу́рить ч. день to be on
duty every other day, on alternate days;
печа́тать ч. строку́ to double-space.

череми́с, а, m. (hist.) Cheremis (former name
of Mari).

черёмух|а, и, f. bird cherry (Padus).

черёмух|овый, adj. of ~а.

черемш|а́, и́, f. (bot.) ramson.

черенк|ова́ть, у́ю, impf. (of от~) (hort.) 1.
to graft. 2. to take a cutting (of).

черен|о́к, ка́, m. 1. handle, haft (of imple-
ment). 2. (hort.) graft, cutting, slip.

че́реп, а, pl. ~а́, m. skull, cranium.

черепа́х|а, и, f. 1. tortoise; turtle; идти́ ~ой
to go at a snail's pace. 2. tortoise-shell.

черепа́ховый, adj. tortoise, turtle; tortoise-
-shell.

черепа́|ший, adj. 1. adj. of ~ха 1. 2. (fig.)
very slow.

черепи́ц|а, ы, f. tile.

черепи́чный, adj. tile; tiled.

черепн|о́й, adj. of че́реп; ~а́я коро́бка
cranium.

череп|о́к, ка́, m. broken piece of pottery.

чересполо́сиц|а, ы, f. strip farming.

черессе́дельник, а, m. back-band.

чересчу́р, adv. too; too much.

чере́шн|евый, adj. of ~я.

чере́шн|я, и, f. cherry(-tree) (Cerasus avium).

черка́|ть, ю, (and чёрка|ть, ю), impf. (coll.)
to cross out, cross through.

черке́с, а, m. Circassian.

черке́ск|а, и, f. Circassian coat (long, narrow,
collar-less coat worn by Caucasian highlanders).

черке́сский, adj. Circassian.

черке́шенк|а, и, f. of черке́с.

черкн|у́ть, у́, ёшь, pf. (coll.) 1. to make,
leave a line on. 2. to dash off, scribble.

черне́т|ь, и, f. (orn.) морска́я ч. scaup;
хохла́тая ч. tufted duck.

черне́|ть, ю, impf. 1.(pf. по~) to turn black,
grow black. 2. to show up black.

чернец, а́, m. (hist.) monk.

черни́к|а, и, f. bilberry, blaeberry, whortle-
berry (Vaccinium myrtillus).

черни́л|а, ~, no sing. ink.

черни́льниц|а, ы, f. ink-pot, ink-well.

черни́л|ьный, adj. 1. adj. of ~а; ч. каран-
да́ш indelible pencil; ч. оре́шек oak-gall,
nut-gall. 2. (iron.) paper, verbal.

черн|и́ть, ю́, и́шь, impf. 1.(pf. за~ and на~)
to blacken, paint black. 2. (pf. о~) (fig.) to
blacken, slander. 3. to burnish.

черни́ц|а, ы, f. (hist.) nun.

черни́|чный, adj. of ~ка.

чернобу́рк|а, и, f. (coll.) silver fox (fur).

черновик, а́, m. rough copy, draft.

чернов|о́й, adj. 1. rough, draft; preparatory.
2. ~а́я рабо́та (coll.) heavy, rough, dirty
work. 3. (tech.; of metals) crude.

черноволо́с|ый (~, ~а), adj. black-haired,

черногла́з|ый (~, ~а), adj. black-eyed.

черного́р|ец, ца, m. Montenegrin.

черного́р|ка, ки, f. of ~ец.

черного́рский, adj. Montenegrin.

чернозём, а, m. (agric., geol.) chernozem,
black earth.

чернозём|ный, adj. of ~.

чернозо́бик, а, m. (orn.) dunlin.

чернокни́жи|е, я, n. (obs.) black magic.

чернокни́жник, а, m. (obs.) practitioner of
black magic.

черноко́ж|ий (~, ~а), adj. black, coloured;
as noun ч., ~его, m. negro, black (man).

чернолесь|е, я, n. deciduous forest.

черномаз|ый (~, ~а), adj. (coll.) swarthy.

черномо́р|ец, ца, m. sailor of Black Sea
fleet.

черномо́рский, adj. Black Sea.

чернорабо́ч|ий, его, m. unskilled labourer.

чернори́з|ец, ца, m. (hist.) monk.

черносли́в, а (у), m. (collect.) prunes.

черносмороди́нный, adj. blackcurrant.

черносо́тен|ец, ца, m. (hist. or iron.) member

of 'Black Hundred' (*name of armed anti-*
-revolutionary groups in Russia, active 1905–7).
черносо́тен|ный, *adj. of* ~ец.
чернот|а́, ы́, *f.* blackness (*also fig.*); dark-
ness.
чернота́л, а, *m.* (*bot.*) bay-leaf willow (*Salix
pentandra*).
черну́шк|а, и, *f.* **1.** (*bot.*) nutmeg flower
(*Nigella sativa*). **2.** (*coll.*) swarthy, dark-
-haired *or* dark-eyed woman.
чёр|ный (~ен, ~на́, ~но́), *adj.* **1.** (*in var.
senses*) black; ~ная би́ржа, ч. ры́нок black
market; ч. глаз (*coll.*) evil eye; (отложи́ть
на) ч. день (to put by for) a rainy day; ~ное
де́рево ebony; ~ное духове́нство regular
clergy, monks; ~ное зо́лото 'black gold'
(= oil); ч. лес deciduous forest; ч. наро́д
(*hist.*) common people; ~ное сло́во (*dial.*)
bad language; держа́ть в ~ном те́ле to
ill-treat; ~ным по бе́лому in black and
white; *as noun* ч., ~ного, *m.* negro, black
(man). **2.** (*as opp. to* пара́дный) back; ч.
ход back entrance, back door. **3.** (*of work*)
heavy; unskilled. **4.** (*hist.*) State (*as opp. to
privately-owned*). **5.** (*tech.*) ferrous (*as opp.
to* цветно́й). **6.** (*fig.*) gloomy, melancholy.
черн|ь¹, и, *f.* mob, common people.
черн|ь², и, *f.* niello; black enamel.
черпа́к, а́, *m.* scoop; bucket; grab.
черпа́лк|а, и, *f.* scoop; ladle.
че́рп|ать, аю, *impf.* (*of* ~ну́ть) **1.** to draw
(up); to scoop; to ladle. **2.** (*fig.*) to extract,
derive, draw.
черп|ну́ть, ну́, нёшь. *pf. of* ~ать.
черстве́|ть, ю, *impf.* **1.** (*pf.* за~) to become
stale. **2.** (*pf.* о~) to grow hardened, become
hard (*fig.*).
чёрств|ый (~, ~а́, ~о), *adj.* **1.** stale. **2.** (*fig.*)
hard, callous.
чёрт, а, *pl.* **че́рти, ~е́й,** *m.* devil; ч. (его́)
возьми́! the devil take it!; ч. его́ зна́ет! the
devil only knows!; до ~а̀ devilishly, hell-
ishly; на кой ч.? why the hell?; ~а с два
like hell!; у ~а на рога́х, на кули́чках at
the back of beyond.
черт|а́, ы́, *f.* **1.** line; провести́ ~у́ to draw
a line; подвести́ ~у́ (под) (*fig.*) to draw a
line (under), put an end (to), dispose (of). **2.**
boundary; ч. осе́длости (*hist.*) the (Jewish)
Pale. **3.** trait, characteristic; ~ы́ лица́
features; в о́бщих ~а́х in general outline.
чертёж, а́, *m.* draught, drawing, sketch;
blueprint, plan, scheme; ч. на ка́льке trac-
ing.
чертёжн|ая, ой, *f.* drawing office.
чертёжник, а, *m.* draughtsman.
чертёжн|ый, *adj.* drawing; ~ая доска́ draw-
ing board; ~ая мастерска́я drawing office;
~ое перо́ lettering pen.
чертён|ок, ка, *pl.* ~я́та, ~я́т, *m.* (*coll.*) imp.

чер|ти́ть¹, чу́, ~тишь, *impf.* (*of* на~) to
draw; to draw up.
чер|ти́ть², чу́, ти́шь, *impf.* (*coll.*) to go on
a binge, on the booze.
чёртов, *adj.* **1.** devil's; ~а дю́жина baker's
dozen. **2.** (*coll.*) devilish, hellish.
черто́вк|а, и, *f.* she-devil; (*as term of abuse*)
bitch.
черто́вский, *adj.* (*coll.*) devilish, damnable.
чертовщи́н|а, ы, *f.* **1.** (*collect.*) devils,
demons. **2.** (*fig., coll.*) devilry; idiocy.
черто́г, а, *m.* (*obs.*) hall, mansion.
чертополо́х, а, *m.* thistle.
черто́чк|а, и, *f.* **1.** *dim. of* черта́ I. **2.**
hyphen.
чертых|а́ться, а́юсь, *impf.* (*of* ~ну́ться)
(*coll.*) to swear.
чертых|ну́ться, ну́сь, нёшься, *pf. of* ~а́ться.
черче́ни|е, я, *n.* drawing; sketching.
чёс, а, *m.* (*coll.*) itch(ing); зада́ть ~у (*i*)
кому́-н. to tick someone off, (*ii*) to make off.
чеса́лк|а, и, *f.* (*text.*) comb, combing
machine.
чеса́льный, *adj.* (*text.*) combing, carding.
чеса́льщик, а, *m.* (*text.*) comber, carder.
чёсаный, *adj.* (*text.*) combed, carded.
че|са́ть, шу́, ~шешь, *impf.* (*of* по~) **1.** to
scratch; ч. заты́лок, в заты́лке to scratch
one's head (*also fig.*); ч. язы́к to wag one's
tongue. **2.** (*coll.*) to comb (*hair*). **3.** (*text.*) to
comb, card. **4.** (*coll.*) *expresses rapid or vigorous action* (*translated in accordance with context*).
че|са́ться, шу́сь, ~шешься, *impf.* (*of* по~)
1. to scratch oneself. **2.** (*impf. only*) to itch;
ру́ки у него́, *etc.*, ~шутся (+*inf.*) he is, *etc.*,
itching to . . . **3.** (*coll.*) to comb one's hair.
чесно́к, а́ (у́), *m.* garlic.
чесно́|чный, *adj. of* ~к.
чесо́тк|а, и, *f.* **1.** (*med.*) scab; rash; mange.
2. itch.
чесо́т|очный, *adj. of* ~ка; ч. клещ itch-mite.
че́ствовани|е, я, *n.* (кого́-н.) celebration (in
honour of someone).
че́ств|овать, ую, *impf.* to celebrate (*an
occasion, etc.*); to honour, arrange a celebration in honour of (*someone*).
че|сти́ть, щу́, сти́шь, *impf.* **1.** (*coll.*) to
abuse. **2.** (*obs.*) to honour.
честн|о́й, *adj.* (*obs.*) **1.** (*eccl.*) sanctified,
sainted; saintly; мать ~а́я! (*coll.*) my
sainted aunt! **2.** worthy, honoured; ~а́я
компа́ния (*iron.*) gang, network.
че́стност|ь, и, *f.* honesty, integrity.
че́ст|ный (~ен, ~на́, ~но), *adj.* honest, up-
right; ~ное сло́во! honestly!, upon my
honour!
честолю́б|ец, ца, *m.* ambitious person.
честолюби́в|ый (~, ~а), *adj.* ambitious.
честолюби|е, я, *n.* ambition.

чест|ь¹, и, *f.* **1.** honour; в ч. (+*g.*) in honour (of); по ~и сказа́ть to say in all honesty; счита́ть за ч. to consider (it) an honour; отда́ть ч. (+*d.*) (*i*) to salute, (*ii*) (*joc.*) to do honour (to); проси́ть ~ью to urge; пора́ и ч. знать (*coll.*) it is time to go (*joc. formula used on taking leave of host, etc.*); ч. ~ью (*coll.*) fittingly, properly; ч. и ме́сто! (*coll., obs.*) please be seated! **2.** regard, respect; быть в ~й to be in favour.

честь², чту, чтёшь, *impf.* (*obs.*) **1.** to consider. **2.** to read.

чесуч|а́, и́, *f.* tussore.

чесуч|о́вый, *adj. of* ~á.

чёт, а, *m.* even number.

чет|а́, ы́, *f.* pair, couple; счастли́вая ч. (the) happy couple; не ч. кому́-н. no match for someone (*as being, by implication, either worse or better*).

четве́рг, а́, *m.* Thursday.

четве́ро́ньк|и (*coll.*) на ч., на ~ах on all fours, on one's hands and knees; стать на ч. to go down on all fours.

четвери́к, а́, *m.* chetverik (*old Russian dry measure, equivalent to* 26·239 *litres*).

четвёрк|а, и, *f.* (*coll.*) **1.** number '4'; No. 4 (*bus, tram, etc.*). **2.** 'four' (*as school mark—out of five, hence* = 'good'). **3.** four (*at cards*; *team of horses*; *rowing-boat, etc.*).

четверно́й, *adj.* fourfold, quadruple.

четверн|я́, и́, *f.* **1.** team of four horses. **2.** quadruplets.

четвер|о, ы́х, *num.* four; нас бы́ло ч. there were four of us.

четвероно́г|ий, *adj.* four-legged; *as noun* ~ое, ~о́го, *n.* quadruped.

четверости́ши|е, я, *n.* (*lit.*) quatrain.

четверта́к, а́, *m.* (*obs*). 25 kopecks.

четверти́нк|а, и, *f.* (*coll.*) quarter-litre bottle (*of vodka or wine*).

четверти́чный, *adj.* (*geol.*) quaternary.

четвертно́й, *adj.* **1.** quarter. **2.** (*obs.*) costing, worth 25 roubles.

четверт|ова́ть, у́ю, *impf. and pf.* to quarter (*as means of execution; hist.*).

четвёртый, *adj.* fourth.

че́тверт|ь, и, *g. pl.* ~е́й, *f.* **1.** (*in var. senses*) quarter (*as liquid measure, approx. equivalent to 3 litres; as dry measure—to 210 litres*). **2.** quarter (of an hour); без ~и час a quarter to one; ч. деся́того a quarter past nine. **3.** (*mus.*) fourth. **4.** term.

четвертьфина́л, а, *m.* (*sport*) quarter-final.

чёт|ки, ок, *no sing.* (*eccl.*) rosary.

чёт|кий (~ок, ~ка́, ~ко), *adj.* **1.** precise; clear-cut; ~кое движе́ние precise movement. **2.** clear, well-defined; (*of handwriting*) legible; (*of sound*) plain, distinct; (*of speech*) articulate.

чёткост|ь, и, *f.* **1.** precision, preciseness.

2. clarity, clearness, definition; legibility; distinctness.

чётный, *adj.* even (*of numbers*).

четы́р|е, ёх, ём, ьмя́, о ~ёх, *num.* four.

четы́режды, *adv.* four times.

четы́р|еста, ёхсо́т, ёмста́м, ьмяста́ми, о ~ёхста́х, *num.* four hundred.

четырёх- four-, quadri-, tetra-.

четырёхгоди́чный, *adj.* four-year.

четырёхголо́сный, *adj.* (*mus.*) four-part.

четырёхгра́нник, а, *m.* (*math.*) tetrahedron.

четырёхгра́нный, *adj.* (*math.*) tetrahedral.

четырёхдоро́жечный, *adj.* four-track (*of tape recorder*).

четырёхкра́тный, *adj.* fourfold.

четырёхле́ти|е, я, *n.* **1.** four-year period. **2.** fourth anniversary.

четырёхле́тний, *adj.* **1.** four years', of four years' duration. **2.** four-year-old.

четырёхме́стный, *adj.* four-seater.

четырёхме́сячный, *adj.* **1.** four-month, four months', of four months' duration. **2.** four-month-old.

четырёхмото́рный, *adj.* four-engined.

четырёхсотле́ти|е, я, *n.* **1.** four hundred years. **2.** quatercentenary.

четырёхсотле́тний, *adj.* **1.** four hundred years', of four hundred years' duration. **2.** quatercentenary.

четырёхсо́тый, *adj.* fourhundredth.

черырёхсто́пный, *adj.* (*lit.*) tetrameter.

черырёхсторо́нний, *adj.* **1.** quadrilateral. **2.** (*polit., etc.*) quadripartite.

четырёхта́ктный, *adj.* **1.** (*tech.*) four-stroke. **2.** (*mus.*) four-beat.

четырёхуго́льник, *adj.* quadrangle.

четырёхуго́льный, *adj.* quadrangular.

четырёхчасово́й, *adj.* **1.** four hours', of four hours' duration. **2.** four o'clock.

четы́рнадцатый, *adj.* fourteenth.

четы́рнадцат|ь, и, *num.* fourteen.

чех, а, *m.* Czech.

чехард|а́, ы́, *f.* leap-frog (*also fig.*; *of rapid changes in governmental appointments, etc.*).

чехл|и́ть, ю́, и́шь, *impf.* (*of* за~) to cover.

чех|о́л, ла́, *m.* **1.** cover, case; ч. для кре́сла chair-cover. **2.** underdress.

чехослова́к, а, *m.* Czechoslovak.

чехослова́цкий, *adj.* Czechoslovak.

чехослова́чк|а, и, *f.* Czechoslovak (woman).

чечеви́ц|а¹, ы, *f.* lentil.

чечеви́ц|а², ы, *f.* (*obs.*) lens.

чечеви́|чный, *adj. of* ~ца¹; прода́ть за ~чную похлёбку to sell for a mess of pottage.

чече́н|ец, ца, *m.* Chechen.

чечётк|а, и, *f.* **1.** (*orn.*) redpoll. **2.** chechotka (*kind of tap-dance*).

чёшк|а, и, *f. of* чех.

чёшский, *adj.* Czech.

чешуйк|а, и, *f.* scale (*of fish*).

чешуйчат|ый, *adj.* scaly; squamose, lamellar; **~ые, ~ых** (*zool.*) Squamata.

чешу|я, й, *no pl., f.* (*zool.*) scales.

чибис, а, *m.* (*orn.*) lapwing.

чиж, á, *m.* (*orn.*) siskin.

чижик, а, *m.* **1.** = чиж. **2. ~и** tip-cat (*children's game*).

чик|ать, аю, *impf.* (*of* **~нуть**) to tick, click.

чик|нуть, ну, нешь, *pf. of* **~ать.**

чилибух|а, и, *f.* (*bot.*) Nux vomica.

чили|ец, йца, *m.* Chilean.

чили|йка, йки, *f. of* **~ец.**

чилийск|ий, *adj.* Chilean; **~ая селитра** (*chem.*) Chile saltpetre, sodium nitrate.

чилим, а, *m.* (*bot.*) water chestnut (*Trapa natans*).

чин, а, *pl.* **~ы́,** *m.* **1.** rank; **быть в ~áх** to hold, be of high rank. **2.** official. **3.** rite, ceremony, order; **ч. ~ом** properly, fittingly; **без ~óв** without ceremony; **держáть ч.** (*obs.*) to conduct a ceremony.

чинáр, а, *m.* plane (tree).

чинáр|а, ы, *f.* = **~.**

чинёный, *adj.* (*coll.*) old, patched (*of clothing, etc.*).

чин|и́ть¹, ю́, ~ишь, *impf.* (*of* по**~**) to repair, mend.

чин|и́ть², ю́, ~ишь, *impf.* (*of* о**~**) to sharpen.

чин|и́ть³, ю́, йшь, *impf.* to carry out, execute; to cause; **ч. препятствия** (+*d.*) to impede; **ч. распрáву** to carry out reprisals.

чин|и́ться, ю́сь, йшься, *impf.* (*obs.*) to stand on ceremony, hold back, be shy.

чи́нност|ь, и, *f.* decorum, propriety, orderliness.

чи́н|ный (~ен, ~нá, ~но), *adj.* decorous, proper, orderly; well-ordered.

чинóвник, а, *m.* **1.** (*hist.*) official, functionary. **2.** (*pejor.*) bureaucrat.

чинóвни|ческий, *adj.* **1.** *adj. of* **~к. 2.** (*pejor.*) bureaucratic.

чинóвничеств|о, а, *n.* **1.** (*collect.*) officials, officialdom. **2.** (*pejor.*) red tape.

чинóвнич|ий, *adj.* = **~еский.**

чинóвный, *adj.* (*obs.*) **1.** official, holding an official post. **2.** of high rank.

чину́ш|а, и, *m.* (*pejor.*) bureaucrat.

чи́пс|ы, ов, *no sing.* (potato) crisps.

чи́р|ей, ья, *m.* (*coll.*) boil.

чири́ка|ть, ю, *impf.* to chirp, twitter.

чири́к|и, ов *or* **чирик|и́, óв,** (*dial.*) shoes.

чири́кн|уть, у, ешь, *pf.* to give a chirp.

чи́рк|ать, аю, *impf.* (*of* **~нуть**) (о+*a.,* по+*d.*) to strike sharply (against, on); **ч. спи́чкой** to strike a match.

чи́рк|нуть, ну, нешь, *pf. of* **~ать.**

чир|óк, кá, *m.* (*orn.*) teal.

чи́сленност|ь, и, *f.* numbers; (*mil.*) strength.

чи́сленный, *adj.* numerical.

числи́тел|ь, я, *m.* (*math.*) numerator.

числи́тельн|ое, ого, *n.* (*gram.*) numeral.

числи́тельн|ый, *adj.* **и́мя ~ое** (*gram.*) numeral.

числ|ить, ю, ишь, *impf.* to count, reckon.

числ|иться, юсь, ишься, *impf.* **1.** to be (*in context of calculation or official records*); **в нáшей деревне ~ится триста жи́телей** there are three hundred inhabitants in our village; **ч. в отпуску** to be (recorded) as on leave; **он ~ится в ко́нкурсе** his name is down for the competition. **2.** (+*i.*) to be reckoned, be on paper; **он ещё ~ился заведующим отделом, а все обязанности исполняли его заместители** he was still head of the department on paper, but all the duties were being performed by his deputies. **3.** (за+*i.*) to be attributed (to), have; **за ним ~ится много недостáтков** he has many failings.

чис|ло́, лá, *pl.* **~ла, ~ел,** *n.* **1.** number; **теория ~ел** theory of number; **~ло́м in** number; **нет им ~лá** they are innumerable; **без ~лá** without number, in great numbers; **в ~ле́** (+*g.*) among; **в том ~ле́** including. **2.** date, day (*of month*); **какое сего́дня ч.?** what is the date today?; **какого ~лá вы уезжáете?** what is the date of your departure, which day are you leaving?; **без ~лá** undated; **поме́тить** (за́дним) **~лом** to date (antedate). **3.** (*gram.*) number; **единственное, мно́жественное ч.** singular, plural.

числово́й, *adj.* numerical.

чисти́лищ|е, а, *n.* (*rel.*) purgatory.

чи́стильщик, а, *m.* cleaner; **ч. сапо́г** shoeblack, bootblack.

чи́|стить, щу, стишь, *impf.* **1.** (*pf.* по**~**, вы**~**) to clean; (щёткой) to brush; to scour; **ч. посу́ду** to wash dishes, wash up; **ч. трубу́** to sweep a chimney. **2.** (*pf.* по**~**, вы**~**) to clear; to dredge. **3.** (*pf.* о**~**) to peel (*vegetables, fruit*); to shell (*nuts*); to clean (*fish*). **4.** (*pf.* по**~**) (*polit.*) to purge. **5.** (*coll.*) to clean out (= to rob). **6.** (*coll.*) to swear at; to beat up.

чи́|ститься, щусь, стишься, *impf.* **1.** (*pf.* по**~**, вы**~**) to clean oneself (up). **2.** *pass. of* **~стить.**

чи́стк|а, и, *f.* **1.** cleaning; **отдáть в ~у** to have cleaned, send to be cleaned. **2.** (*polit.*) purge.

чи́сто¹, *as pred.* it is clean.

чи́ст|о², *adv.* **1.** *adv. of* **~ый;** **ч.-нáчисто** spotlessly clean. **2.** purely, merely; completely; **я ч. случáйно его́ нашёл** it was by mere chance that I found it. **3.** *as conj.* (*coll.*) just like, just as if.

чистови́к, á, *m.* (*coll.*) fair copy.

чистово́й, *adj.* **1.** fair, clean; ч. экземпля́р fair copy. **2.** (*tech.*) finishing, planishing.

чистога́н, а, *m.* (*coll.*) cash, ready money.

чистокро́вный, *adj.* thorough-bred, pure-blooded.

чистописа́ни|е, я, *n.* calligraphy.

чистопло́т|ный (~ен, ~на), *adj.* **1.** clean, cleanly; neat, tidy. **2.** (*fig.*) clean, decent, upright.

чистоплю́|й, я, *m.* (*coll.*) cissy; fastidious person.

чистопо́ль|е, я, *n.* (*coll.*) open country.

чистопоро́д|ный (~ен, ~на), *adj.* thorough-bred.

чистопро́бный, *adj.* pure (*of gold or silver*).

чистосерде́ч|ие, ия, *n.* = ~ность.

чистосерде́чность|ь, и, *f.* frankness, sincerity, candour.

чистосерде́ч|ный (~ен, ~на), *adj.* frank, sincere, candid.

чистот|а́, ы́, *f.* **1.** cleanness, cleanliness; neatness, tidiness. **2.** (*in var. senses*) purity.

чистоте́л, а, *m.* (*bot.*) celandine.

чи́ст|ый (~, ~а́, ~о), *adj.* **1.** clean; neat, tidy; (*of speech, voice, etc.*) pure. **2.** (*fig.*) pure, upright, unsullied; ч. понеде́льник (*eccl.*) first Monday in Lent; от ~ого се́рдца, с ~ой со́вестью with a clear conscience. **3.** pure; undiluted, neat; ~ое зо́лото, ~ая шерсть pure gold, wool; ~ое иску́сство art for art's sake; ч. спирт pure, neat alcohol; ~ой воды́ (*min.*) of the first water; (*fig.*) pure, first-class; вы́вести на ~ую во́ду to expose, unmask; за ~ые де́ньги for cash; приня́ть что-н. за ~ую моне́ту to take something at its face value. **4.** clear, open; ~ое не́бо clear sky; на ~ом во́здухе in the open air; ч. лист blank sheet; ~ое по́ле open field. **5.** (*fin., etc.*) net, clear; ~ая при́быль clear profit. **6.** (*obs.*) main; special, ceremonial, show; ч. вход front entrance. **7.** (*of work or product of work*) skilled; finished; ~ая рабо́та craftsmanship. **8.** (*obs.; as social criterion*) better-class, 'best'. **9.** (*coll.*) pure, utter; mere, sheer; complete, absolute; ч. вздор utter nonsense; ~ая беста́ктность sheer tactlessness; ~ая случа́йность pure chance; ~ая отста́вка (*obs.*) final retirement; по ~ой (*coll.*) finally, once and for all.

чистю́л|я, и, *m. and f.* (*coll.*) person with passion for cleanliness *or* tidiness.

чита́емост|ь, и, *f.* popularity, wide circulation (*of literature*).

чита́|емый 1. *pres. part. pass. of* ~ть *and adj.* widely-read, popular.

чита́льн|ый, *adj.* ч. зал = ~я.

чита́л|ьня, ьни, *g. pl.* ~ен, *f.* reading-room.

чита́тел|ь, я, *m.* reader.

чита́тель|ский, *adj. of* ~.

чита́|ть, ю, *impf.* (*of* про~, проч́сть) **1.** to read. **2.** ч. ле́кции to lecture, give lectures; ч. стихи́ to recite poetry; ч. кому́-н. наставле́ния, нравоуче́ния to lecture someone.

чита́|ться, ется, *impf.* **1.** *pass. of* ~ть. **2.** to be legible. **3.** (*fig.*) to be visible, be discernible. **4.** (*impers.*) мне, *etc.*, не ~ется I, *etc.*, don't feel like reading.

чи́тк|а, и, *f.* **1.** reading (*usually of documents, etc., by a group*). **2.** (*theatr.*) (first) reading, reading through.

чи́тывать, *pres. tense not used, impf., freq. of* чита́ть.

чих, а, *m.* (*coll.*) sneeze; *as interj., onomat. of sound of sneezing.*

чиха́нь|е, я, *n.* sneezing; на вся́кое ч. не наздра́вствуешься you can't please everyone.

чиха́тельный, *adj.* causing sneezing, sternutatory; ч. газ sneezing gas.

чих|а́ть, а́ю, *impf.* (*of* ~ну́ть) **1.** to sneeze. **2.** (на+*a.*; *coll.*) to scorn; ч. мне на него́! I don't give a damn for him!

чих|ну́ть, ну́, нёшь, *pf. of* ~а́ть.

чихо́т|а, ы, *f.* (*coll.*) sneezing (fit).

чи́ще, *comp. of* чи́стый, чи́сто.

член, а, *m.* **1.** (*in var. senses*) member; ч.-корреспонде́нт corresponding member (*of an Academy*). **2.** (*math.*) term; (*gram.*) part (*of sentence*). **3.** limb, member. **4.** (*gram.*) article.

члене́ни|е, я, *n.* articulation.

чле́ник, а, *m.* (*zool.*) segment.

членисто́ног|ие, их (*zool.*) arthropoda.

чле́нистый, *adj.* (*zool.*) articulated, segmented.

член|и́ть, ю́, и́шь, *impf.* (*of* рас~) to divide into parts, articulate.

членовреди́тельств|о, а, *n.* maiming, mutilation; self-mutilation.

членоразде́л|ьный (~ен, ~ьна), *adj.* articulate.

чле́н|ский, *adj. of* ~; ~ские взно́сы membership fee, dues.

членств|о, а, *n.* membership.

чмо́к|ать, аю, *impf.* (*of* ~нуть) **1.** to make a smacking sound with one's lips. **2.** (*coll.*) to give a smacking kiss. **3.** to squelch, make a squelching sound.

чмо́к|нуть, ну, нешь, *pf. of* ~ать.

чо́глок, а, *m.* hobby (*bird of falcon family*).

чо́кань|е, я, *n.* clinking of glasses.

чо́к|аться, аюсь, *impf.* (*of* ~нуться) to clink glasses (*when drinking toasts*).

чо́кнутый, *adj.* odd, rum.

чо́к|нуться, нусь, нешься, *pf. of* ~аться.

чо́порност|ь, и, f. primness; standoffishness, stiffness.

чо́пор|ный (~ен, ~на), *adj.* prim; stuck-up; standoffish, stiff.

чо́хом, *adv.* (*coll.*) wholesale.

чрева́т|ый (~, ~а), *adj.* **1.** (+*i.*) fraught (with). **2.** ~ая (*obs.*) pregnant.

чре́в|о, а, *n.* (*obs. or rhet., fig.*) belly; womb.

чревовеща́ни|е, я, *n.* ventriloquy.

чревовеща́тел|ь, я, *m.* ventriloquist.

чревоуго́ди|е, я, *n.* gluttony.

чревоуго́дник, а, *m.* glutton, gourmand.

чред|а́, ы́, *f.* (*obs.*) **1.** (*poet.*) turn, succession. **2.** sphere (*of activity*).

чрез = че́рез.

чрезвыча́йно, *adv.* extremely, extraordinarily, exceedingly.

чрезвыча́|йный (~ен, ~йна), *adj.* **1.** extraordinary (= exceptional, unusual). **2.** special, extreme, extraordinary; ~йные ме́ры emergency measures; ~йное положе́ние state of emergency; ч. и полномо́чный посо́л ambassador extraordinary and plenipotentiary.

чрезме́рно, *adv.* excessively, to excess.

чрезме́р|ный (~ен, ~на), *adj.* excessive, inordinate, extreme.

чре́сл|а, ~, *no sing.* (*arch. or poet.*) hips, loins.

чте́ни|е, я, *n.* **1.** reading; ч. карт map-reading; ч. ле́кций lecturing. **2.** reading-matter.

чтец, а́, *m.* reader; (*professional*) reciter.

чти́в|о, а, *n.* (*coll., pejor.*) reading-matter.

чтить, чту, чтишь, чтят (*and* чтут), *impf.* to honour.

чти́ц|а, ы, *f. of* чтец.

что¹, чего́, чему́, о чём, *interrog. pron.* **1.** what?; что с тобо́й? what's the matter (with you)?; что де́лать, что поде́лаешь? it can't be helped; для чего́? why?, what . . . for?; к чему́? why?; с чего́? whence?, on what grounds?; что ты (вы)! (*expressing surprise, fear, etc.*) you don't mean to say so!; что ему́, *etc.*, до...? what does it matter to him, *etc.*? **2.** how?; что сего́дня На́дя? how is Nadya today? **3.** why?; что вы не пьёте? why aren't you drinking? **4.** (*coll.*) how much?; что сто́ит? how much does it cost?; что то́лку? what is the sense?

что² (*sometimes printed* что), *relat. pron.* which, that; (*coll.*) who; я зна́ю, что вы име́ете в виду́ I know what you mean; па́рень, что стоя́л ря́дом со мной the fellow (who was) standing next to me; он всё молча́л, что для него́ не характе́рно he said nothing the whole time, which is unlike him.

что³, (*coll.*) = что́-нибудь; е́сли что слу́чится if anything happens.

что⁴, as far as; что есть мо́чи with all one's might; что до, что каса́ется (+*g.*) as far, with regard (to), as far as . . . is concerned.

что⁵, *conj.* that; то, что... the fact that . . .

чтоб = чтобы.

чтобы, *conj.* **1.** (*expressing purpose*) in order to, in order that; ч. ...не lest. **2.** (*after neg.*) (that); я никогда́ не вида́л, ч. он яви́лся пья́ным на рабо́ту I have never seen him turn up drunk for work; сомнева́юсь, ч. вам э́то понра́вилось I doubt whether you will like it. **3.** (*as particle*) expresses wish: ч. я тебя́ бо́льше не ви́дел! may I never see your face again!

что ж (*coll.*) expresses admission, acceptance of argument: yes; all right, right you are.

что за (*coll.*) **1.** (*interrog.*) what? what sort of . . .?; что э́то за пти́ца? what sort of bird is that? **2.** (*interj.*) что за день! what a (marvellous) day!; что за ерунда́! what (utter) nonsense!

что ли (*coll.*) expresses uncertainty or hesitation: пора́ нам идти́, что ли? perhaps we should be going?; позвони́ть тебе́, что ли? do you want me to ring you, then?

что́-либо, чего́-либо, *indef. pron.* anything.

что ни, *indef. pron.*; что ни день every day, not a day that passes but . . .; что ни говори́ no matter what you may say, say what you like; во что бы то ни ста́ло at whatever cost.

что́-нибудь, чего́-нибудь, *indef. pron.* anything.

что́-то¹, чего́-то, *indef. pron.* something.

что́-то², *adv.* (*coll.*) **1.** somewhat, slightly; на слу́шателей его́ выступле́ние произвело́ что́-то не о́чень прия́тное впечатле́ние his speech made a somewhat disagreeable impression on the audience. **2.** somehow, for no obvious reason; что́-то мне не хо́чется идти́ I don't feel like going for some reason.

чу, *interj.* hark!

чуб, а, *pl.* ~ы́, *m.* forelock (*hist.; single lock on otherwise shaven head, as worn formerly by Ukrainian Cossacks*).

чуба́рый, *adj.* (*of a horse's coat*) dappled.

чубу́к, а́, *m.* **1.** stem (*of smoking pipe*); chibouk. **2.** grape stalk.

чува́л, а, *m.* (*dial.*) pannier, basket.

чува́ш, а (*and* а́), *pl.* ~и, ~ей (*and* ~й, ~е́й), *m.* Chuvash.

чува́шк|а, и, *f.* Chuvash (woman).

чува́шский, *adj.* Chuvash.

чуви́х|а, и, *f.* (*sl.*) bird (= girl).

чу́вственност|ь, и, *f.* sensuality.

чу́вствен|ный, *adj.* **1.** (~, ~на) sensual. **2.** (*philos.*) perceptible, sensible; ~ное восприя́тие perception.

чувстви́тельност|ь, и, *f.* **1.** (*in var. senses*) sensitivity, sensitiveness; (*of phot. film*) speed. **2.** perceptibility, sensibility. **3.** sentimentality. **4.** tenderness; (deep) feeling.

чувстви́тел|ьный (~ен, ~ьна), *adj.* 1. (*in var. senses*) sensitive. 2. perceptible, sensible. 3. sentimental. 4. tender; (*of feelings*) deep.

чу́вств|о, а, *n.* 1. (*physiol.*) sense; ч. вку́са sense of taste; о́рганы ~ senses, organs of sense; обма́н ~ delusion. 2. (*sing. or pl.*) senses (= consciousness); без ~ unconscious; лиши́ться ~, упа́сть без ~ to faint, lose consciousness; привести́ в ч. to bring round; прийти́ в ч. to come round, regain consciousness, come to one's senses. 3. (*in var. senses*) feeling; sense; ч. ло́ктя feeling of comradeship, of solidarity; ч. ю́мора sense of humour; пита́ть к кому́-н. не́жные ~а to have a soft spot for someone.

чу́вств|овать, ую, *impf.* (*of* по~) 1. to feel, sense; ч. себя́ to feel (*intrans.*); ч. го́лод to feel hungry; дава́ть себя́ ч. to make itself felt; как вы себя́ ~уете? how do you feel? 2. to appreciate, have a feeling (for) (*music, etc.*).

чу́вств|оваться, уется, *impf.* 1. to be perceptible; to make itself felt. 2. *pass. of* ~овать.

чувя́к|и, ов, *sing.* ~, ~а, *m.* slippers (*worn mainly in the Caucasus and Crimea*).

чугу́н, а́, *m.* 1. cast iron; ч. в болва́нках pig-iron. 2. cast-iron pot, vessel.

чугу́нк|а, и, *f.* (*coll.*) 1. (cast-iron) stove. 2. (*obs.*) railway.

чугу́нный, *adj.* cast-iron (*also fig.*).

чугунолите́йный, *adj.* ч. заво́д iron foundry.

чуда́к, а́, *m.* eccentric, crank.

чуда́ческий, *adj.* eccentric.

чуда́честв|о, а, *n.* eccentricity, crankiness.

чуда́ч|ить, у, ишь, *impf.* (*coll.*) = чуди́ть.

чуда́чк|а, и, *f. of* чуда́к.

чуде́с|ный (~ен, ~на), *adj.* 1. miraculous; ~ное исцеле́ние miraculous healing. 2. marvellous, wonderful.

чуд|и́ть, *1st person not used*, и́шь, *impf.* (*coll.*) 1. to behave eccentrically, oddly. 2. to clown, act the fool.

чу́д|иться, ится, *impf.* (*of* по~ *and* при~) (*coll.*) to seem.

чудн|о́й (~ён, ~а́, ~о́), *adj.* strange, odd; ~о́ *as pred.* it is strange, it is odd.

чу́д|ный (~ен, ~на), *adj.* 1. magic. 2. (*fig.*) magical; marvellous, wonderful; lovely; ~но *as pred.* it is marvellous, wonderful, lovely.

чу́д|о, а, *pl.* ~еса́, ~е́с, *n.* 1. miracle. 2. wonder, marvel; ~еса́ те́хники wonders of engineering; ч. как *as adv.* marvellously; ч., что... *as pred.* it is a marvel that . . .

чу́до-богаты́р|ь, я́, *m.* hero.

чудо́вищ|е, а, *n.* monster.

чудо́вищ|ный (~ен, ~на), *aaj.* 1. monstrous (*also fig., pejor.*). 2. enormous.

чудоде́|й, я, *m.* 1. (*obs.*) miracle-worker. 2. (*coll.*) crank.

чудоде́йствен|ный (~, ~на), *adj.* miracle--working; miraculous.

чу́дом, *adv.* miraculously; ч. спасти́сь to be saved by a miracle.

чудотво́р|ец, ца, *m.* miracle-worker.

чудотво́рный, *adj.* miracle-working; (*fig.*) marvellous.

чу́до-ю́до, *indecl., n.* (*folk poet.*) monster.

чужа́к, а́, *m.* (*coll.*) stranger; (*pejor.*) alien, interloper.

чужан|и́н, и́на, *pl.* ~е, ~, *m.* (*folk poet. or coll.*) stranger.

чужби́н|а, ы, *f.* foreign land, country.

чужда́|ться, юсь, *impf.* (+*g.*) to shun, avoid; to stand aloof (from), remain unaffected (by).

чу́жд|ый (~, ~а́, ~о), *adj.* 1. (+*d.*) alien (to); extraneous. 2. (+*g.*) free (from), devoid (of); он ~ зло́бы he is devoid of malice.

чужезе́м|ец, ца, *m.* (*obs.*) foreigner, stranger.

чужезе́мный, *adj.* (*obs.*) foreign.

чужеро́д|ный, (~ен, ~на), *adj.* alien, foreign.

чужестра́н|ец, ца, *m.* (*obs.*) = чужезе́мец.

чужестра́нный, *adj.* (*obs.*) = чужезе́мный.

чужея́дный, *adj.* (*bot.*) parasitic.

чуж|о́й, *adj.* 1. someone else's, another's, others'; на ч. счёт at someone else's expense; с ~и́х слов at second-hand; *as noun* ~о́е, ~о́го, *n.* someone else's belongings, what belongs to others. 2. strange, alien; foreign; ~и́е края́ = ~би́на; попа́сть в ~и́е ру́ки to fall into strange hands; *as noun* ч., ~о́го, *m.* stranger.

чу́йк|а, и, *f.* (*obs.*) 1. chuyka (*knee-length cloth jacket formerly worn by men as outer garment*). 2. (*coll.*) nouveau-riche person.

чуко́тский, *adj.* Chukchi.

чу́кч|а, и, *m.* Chukchi (man).

чукча́нк|а, и, *f.* Chukchi (woman).

чула́н, а, *m.* 1. store-room, lumber-room. 2. larder.

чул|о́к, ка́, *g. pl.* ч., *m.* stocking.

чуло́чник, а, *m.* stocking-maker.

чуло́чно-носо́чн|ый, *adj.* ~ые изде́лия hosiery.

чуло́чный, *adj. of* чуло́к.

чум|а́, ы́, *f.* plague (*also as form of abuse*).

чума́з|ый (~, ~а), *adj.* (*coll.*) grubby, dirty; *as noun* (*obs., pejor.*) ч., ~ого, *m.* upstart, parvenu, kulak.

чума́к, а́, *m.* (*obs.*) chumak (*in Ukraine, ox--cart driver transporting fish, salt, and grain*).

чума́|цкий, *adj. of* ~к.

чуми́чк|а, и, *f.* 1. (*dial.*) ladle. 2. (*coll., obs.*) servant-girl. 3. (*coll.*) slut, slattern.

чум|но́й, *adj. of* ~а́; plague-stricken; ~на́я па́лочка plague bacillus.

чумово́й, *adj.* (*sl.*) crazy, half-witted.

чу́н|и, ей, *sing.* ~я, ~и, *f.* (*dial.*) **1.** rope shoes. **2.** galoshes.

чуприн|а, ы, *f.* (*dial.*) = чуб.

чур, *interj.* (*coll.*) keep away!; mind!; ч. меня́ (*in children's games, etc.*) keep away from me!

чура́|ться, юсь, *impf.* (+*g.*; *coll.*) to shun, avoid, steer clear (of).

чурба́н, а, *m.* **1.** block, log. **2.** (*coll.*) blockhead.

чу́рк|а, и, *f.* block, lump, chock.

чу́т|кий (~ок, ~ка́, ~ко), *adj.* **1.** (*of senses of hearing and smell*) keen, sharp, quick; ч. нюх keen sense of smell; ~кая соба́ка keen-nosed dog; ч. сон light sleep. **2.** (*fig.*) sensitive; sympathetic; tactful.

чу́ткост|ь, и, *f.* **1.** keenness, sharpness, quickness. **2.** sensitivity; sympathetic attitude; tactfulness.

чуто́к, *adv.* (*coll.*) a little.

чу́точк|а, и, *f.* ни ~и (*coll.*) not in the least.

чу́точку, *adv.* (*coll.*) a little, a wee bit.

чу́точный, *adj.* (*coll.*) tiny, wee.

чу́т|че, *comp. of* ~кий.

чуть (*coll.*) **1.** *adv.* hardly, scarcely; just; ч. (бы́ло) не, ч. ли не almost, nearly, all but. **2.** *adv.* (just) a little, very slightly. **3.** *conj.* as soon as; ч. свет at daybreak, at first light; ч. что at the slightest provocation.

чуть|ё, я́, *n.* **1.** (*of animals*) scent. **2.** (*fig.*) flair, feeling (for).

чуть-чу́ть, *adv.* (*coll.*) a tiny bit; ч.-ч. не= чуть не.

чухо́н|ец, ца, *m.* (*obs., pejor.*) Finn.

чухо́н|ка, ки, *f. of* ~ец.

чухо́нск|ий, *adj.* (*obs., pejor.*) Finnish; ~ое ма́сло butter.

чу́чел|о, а, *n.* **1.** stuffed animal. **2.** scarecrow (*also fig.*).

чу́шк|а, и, *f.* **1.** (*coll.*) piglet. **2.** (*tech.*) pig, ingot, bar.

чуш|ь, и, *f.* (*coll.*) nonsense, rubbish.

чу́|ять, ю, ешь, *impf.* to scent, smell; (*fig.*) to sense, feel.

чу́|яться, ется, *impf.* (*impers.*) to make itself felt.

Ш

ша́баш, а, *m.* (*rel.*) sabbath; ш. ведьм witches' sabbath; (*fig.*) orgy.

шаба́ш, а, *m.* **1.** (*obs., coll.*) end of work, knocking-off time. **2.** *as pred.* that's enough!, that'll do!; (*naut.*) ship oars!

шаба́ш|ить, у, ишь, *impf.* (*coll.*) (*trans. and intrans.*) to stop (work); to knock off, down tools.

ша́бер, а, *m.* (*tech.*) scraper.

шаб|ёр, ра́, *m.* (*dial.*) neighbour; жить в ~ра́х to live next door.

шабло́н, а, *m.* **1.** (*tech.*) template, pattern; mould, form; stencil. **2.** (*fig., pejor.*) cliché; (fixed) pattern; routine; рабо́тать по ~у to work by rote, work mechanically.

шабло́нност|ь, и, *f.* triteness, banality.

шабло́н|ный, *adj.* **1.** *adj. of* ~. **2.** (~ен, ~на) trite, banal; stereotyped; routine.

ша́вк|а, и, *f.* (*coll.*) (small) dog.

шаг, а (у) (*after numerals* 2, 3, 4 ~а́), о ~е, в (на) ~у́, *pl.* ~и́, ~о́в, *m.* **1.** step (*also fig.*); pace; stride; ш. на ме́сте marking time; ни ~у да́льше! not a step further!, stay where you are!; идти́ бы́стрыми ~а́ми to make rapid strides; ~у ступи́ть нельзя́ (не даю́т) one can't do anything; заме́длить ш. to slow down; приба́вить ~у to quicken one's pace; ши́ре ш.! (*i*) step out, take bigger strides!, (*ii*) (*fig.*) get a move on!; в двух ~а́х, в не́скольких ~а́х a stone's throw away; у́зки в ~у́ (*of cut of trousers*)

tight in the seat; на ка́ждом ~у́ everywhere, at every turn, continually; с пе́рвого ~у (*obs.*) from the outset. **2.** (*tech.*) pitch, spacing.

шаг|а́ть, а́ю, *impf.* (*of* ~ну́ть) **1.** to step; to walk, stride; to pace. **2.** (*coll.*) to go, come.

шага́|ющий, *pres. part. act. of* ~ть; ш. экскава́тор self-propelled excavator.

шаги́стик|а, и, *f.* (*pejor.*) square-bashing (*as part of military training*).

шаг|ну́ть, ну́, нёшь, *pf.* (*of* ~а́ть) to take a step; (*fig.*) to make progress; ш. нельзя́ (не даю́т) one can't do anything, there's no scope for action.

ша́гом, *adv.* at a walk, at walking pace; slowly; ш. марш! (*mil. word of command*) quick march!

шагоме́р, а, *m.* pedometer.

шагре́н|евый, *adj. of* ~ь.

шагре́н|ь, и, *f.* shagreen leather.

шажко́м, *adv.* (*coll.*) taking short steps.

шаж|о́к, ка́, *m., dim. of* шаг.

ша́йб|а, ы, *f.* **1.** (*tech.*) washer. **2.** (*sport*) puck; хокке́й с ~ой ice hockey.

ша́йк|а¹, и, *g. pl.* ша́ек, *f.* tub (*two-handled, of wood or metal*).

ша́йк|а², и, *g. pl.* ша́ек, *f.* gang, band.

шайта́н, а, *m.* (*in Moslem theology*) evil spirit; (*coll.; as term of abuse*) devil.

шака́л, а, *m.* jackal.

шала́нд|а, ы, *f.* (*flat-bottomed*) barge, lighter.

шала́ш, а́, *m.* (*hunter's or fisherman's*) cabin (*made of branches and straw, etc.*).

шале́|ть, ю, *impf.* (*of o~*) (*coll.*) to go crazy.

шал|и́ть, ю, и́шь, *impf.* **1.** to be naughty (*of children*); to play up, play tricks (*also of inanimate objects*); ~и́шь! (*as rebuke*) don't try that on me!, don't come that with me! **2.** (*obs., coll.*) to carry out robberies.

шаловли́в|ый (~, ~а), *adj.* **1.** (*of children*) naughty, apt to get into mischief. **2.** mischievous; flirtatious.

шалопа́|й, я, *m.* (*coll.*) good-for-nothing, idler, skiver.

ша́лост|ь, и, *f.* (*childish*) prank, game; (*pl.*) mischief, naughtiness. **2.** (*obs., coll.*) robbery.

шалу́н, а́, *m.* naughty child.

шалу́н|ья, ьи, *f. of ~.*

шалфе́|й, я, *m.* (*bot.*) sage.

ша́лый, *adj.* (*coll.*) mad, crazy.

шал|ь, и, *f.* shawl.

шальн|о́й, *adj.* mad, crazy; wild; ~ые де́ньги easy money; ~а́я пу́ля stray bullet.

шама́н, а, *m.* (*rel.*) shaman.

шама́н|ский, *adj. of ~.*

шама́нств|о, а, *n.* (*rel.*) shamanism.

ша́ма|ть, ю, *impf.* (*sl.*) to eat.

ша́мка|ть, ю, *impf.* to mumble.

шамо́вк|а, и, *f.* (*sl.*) grub (*food*).

шамо́т, а, *m.* (*tech.*) fire-clay.

шамо́т|ный, *adj. of ~*; ш. кирпи́ч fire-brick, refractory brick.

шампа́нск|ое, ого, *n.* champagne.

шампиньо́н, а, *m.* field mushroom (*Agaricus campestris* or *Psalliota campestris*).

шампу́н|ь, я, *m.* shampoo.

шанда́л, а, *m.* (*obs.*) candlestick.

ша́н|ец, ца, *m.* (*hist.*) field-work; entrenchment.

шанкр, а, *m.* (*med.*) chancre.

шанс, а, *m.* chance; име́ть мно́го ~ов, больши́е ~ы (на+*a.*) to have a good chance (of).

шансоне́тк|а, и, *f.* **1.** (music-hall) song. **2.** singer (*in music-hall or café chantant*).

шанта́ж, а́, *m.* blackmail.

шантажи́р|овать, ую, *impf.* to blackmail.

шантажи́ст, а, *m.* blackmailer.

шантрап|а́, ы́, *m. and f.* (*coll.*) worthless individual; scum, riff-raff.

ша́н|цевый, *adj. of ~ец*; ш. инструме́нт entrenching tool.

ша́пк|а, и, *f.* **1.** cap; заломи́ть ~у to wear one's cap at a rakish angle; лома́ть ~у (пе́ред; *obs., coll.*) to touch one's forelock (to); дать по~е (+*d.*; *coll.*) (*i*) to hit, strike, (*ii*) to sack, fire (= dismiss); получи́ть по ~е (*coll.*) (*i*) to receive a blow, (*ii*) to be sacked, fired; ~ами закида́ем it's in the bag (= we expect to win without diffi-

culty); на во́ре ш. гори́т he's given the game away; по Се́ньке ш. he's got his deserts. **2.** banner headline(s). **3.** (*fig.*; *something covering or crowning other objects*) cap, crown, head, cupola; ш. ды́ма wreath of smoke, smoke-haze.

шапова́л, а, *m.* (*obs.*) fuller.

шапокля́к, а, *m.* opera-hat.

ша́почк|а, и, *f.*, *dim. of* ша́пка.

ша́почн|ый, *adj. of* ша́пка; ~ое знако́мство nodding acquaintance; прийти́ к ~ому разбо́ру (*fig., coll.*) to miss the bus.

шар, а (*after numerals* 2, 3, 4 ~а́), *pl.* ~ы́, *m.* **1.** (*math.*) sphere; земно́й ш. the Earth, globe. **2.** spherical object; ball; возду́шный ш. balloon; хоть ~о́м покати́ completely empty. **3.** (*obs.*) ballot; vote. **4.** (*pl.*) (*sl.*) eyes.

шара́х|ать, аю, *impf.* (*of* ~нуть) (*coll.*) to strike; to hit, shoot.

шара́х|аться, аюсь, *impf.* (*of* ~нуться) (*coll.*) **1.** to shy (*of a horse*); to start (up); to rush, dash. **2.** (о+*a.*) to hit, strike.

шара́х|нуть(ся), ну(сь), нешь(ся), *pf. of* ~ать(ся).

шарж, а, *m.* caricature, cartoon; дру́жеский ш. harmless, well-meant caricature.

шаржи́р|овать, ую, *impf.* to caricature.

ша́рик, а, *m. dim. of* шар; (кровяно́й) ш. (blood) corpuscle.

ша́рик|овый, *adj. of ~*; ~овая (авто)ру́чка ball-point pen; ш. подши́пник (*tech.*) ball--bearing.

шарикоподши́пник, а, *m.* (*tech.*) ball--bearing.

шарикоподши́пник|овый, *adj. of ~.*

ша́р|ить, ю, ишь, *impf.* (в+*p.*, по+*d.*) to grope about, feel, fumble (in, through); (*of machine-gun fire, searchlight beams, etc.*) to sweep (*in order to locate a target*).

ша́рканье, я, *n.* shuffling (*of the feet or footwear*).

ша́рк|ать, аю, *impf.* (*of* ~нуть) **1.** (+*i.*) to shuffle. **2.** (ного́й; *obs.*) to click one's heels. **3.** (*coll.*) to hit, strike.

ша́рк|нуть, ну, нешь, *pf. of* ~ать.

шарлата́н, а, *m.* charlatan, fraud; quack.

шарлата́н|ить, ю, ишь, *impf.* to be a charlatan.

шарлата́н|ский, *adj. of ~.*

шарлата́нств|о, а, *n.* charlatanism.

шарло́тк|а, и, *f.* (*cul.*) charlotte.

шарма́нк|а, и, *f.* barrel-organ, street organ.

шарма́нщик, а, *m.* organ-grinder.

шарни́р, а, *m.* (*tech.*) hinge, joint; на ~ах hinged; быть как на ~ах (*fig.*) to be on edge, be restless, fidget.

шарни́р|ный, *adj. of ~*; ш. болт link bolt; ш. кла́пан flap valve; ~ная опо́ра rocker bearing, tip bearing; ~ное соедине́ние hinge joint, ball and socket joint, toggle joint.

шаровáр|ы, ~, *no sing.*, wide trousers (*as worn by certain Eastern peoples, or for certain sports*).

шаровúд|ный (~ен, ~на), *adj.* spherical, globe-shaped.

шар|овóй, *adj. of* ~; globular; ш. клáпан ball-cock; ш. шарнúр, ~овóе шарнúрное соединéние ball and socket joint.

шаромы́г|а, и, *m. and f.* (*coll.*) parasite; rogue, scoundrel.

шаромы́жник, а, *m.* = шаромы́га.

шарообрáз|ный (~ен, ~на), *adj.* spherical, ball-shaped.

шартрёз, а, *m.* Chartreuse (*liqueur*).

шарф, а, *m.* scarf.

шассú, *indecl., n.* 1. chassis. 2. (*aeron.*) under-carriage.

шáста|ть, ю, *impf.* (*coll.*) to roam, hang about.

шатáни|е, я, *n.* 1. swaying, reeling. 2. roaming, wandering. 3. (*fig.*) vacillation; instability.

шатá|ть, ю, *impf.* to rock, shake, cause to reel.

шатá|ться, юсь, *impf.* 1. (*intrans.*) to rock, sway, reel. 2. to be, come loose; to be unsteady. 3. (*coll.*) to roam; to loaf, lounge about.

шатá|ющийся, *pres. part. of* ~ться *and adj.* loose (*of a screw, tooth, etc.*).

шатéн, а, *m.* person with auburn, brown hair.

шатéн|ка, ки, *f. of* ~.

шат|ёр, рá, *m.* 1. tent, marquee. 2. (*archit.*) hipped roof.

шáти|я, и, *f.* (*coll., pejor.*) gang, crowd, 'mob'.

шáт|кий (~ок, ~ка), *adj.* 1. unsteady; shaky; loose. 2. (*fig.*) unstable, insecure, shaky; unreliable; vacillating; ш. в убеж-дéниях lacking the courage of one's con-victions.

шáткост|ь, и, *f.* 1. unsteadiness; shakiness. 2. (*fig.*) instability; vacillation.

шатрóв|ый, *adj. of* шатёр; ~ая крыша hipped roof.

шатýн¹, á, *m.* (*tech.*) connecting rod.

шатýн², á, *m.* (*coll.*) loafer, idler.

шáфер, а, *pl.* ~á, *m.* best man (*at wedding*).

шафрáн, а, *m.* (*bot.*) saffron.

шафрáн|ный, *adj. of* ~.

шах¹, а, *m.* Shah.

шах², а, *m.* (*chess*) check; ш. и мат check-mate; объявúть ш. (+*d.*) to put in check; под ~ом in check.

шáхер-мáхер, а, *m.* (*coll.*) shady deal.

шахматúст, а, *m.* chess-player.

шáхматн|ый, *adj.* 1. chess; ш. дебют chess

opening, opening gambit; ~ая доскá chess--board; ~ая пáртия game of chess. 2. chess--board, checkered; staggered; ~ая скáтерть check table-cloth; в ~ом порядке stag-gered.

шáхмат|ы, ~, *no sing.* 1. chess. 2. chessmen.

шáхт|а, ы, *f.* 1. mine, pit. 2. (*tech.*) shaft.

шахтёр, а, *m.* miner.

шахтёр|ский, *adj. of* ~.

шáхт|ный, *adj. of* ~а; ш. ствол pit-shaft.

шáхт|овый, *adj. of* ~а.

шáшечниц|а, ы, *f.* draught-board, chess--board.

шáшк|а¹, и, f. 1. block (*of stone or wood plank, for paving*). 2. charge (*of explosive*).

шáшк|а², и, f. 1. draught, draughtsman (*piece in game of draughts*). 2. (*pl.*) draughts (*game*).

шáшк|а³, и, f. sabre, cavalry sword.

шашлы́к, á, *m.* (*cul.*) shashlik, kebab.

шашлы́чн|ая, ой, f. shashlik-house.

шáшн|и, ей, *no sing.* (*coll., pejor.*) 1. tricks. 2. amorous intrigues; affair; завестú ш. с(+*i.*) to take up with.

шва, *g. sing. of* шов.

швáбр|а, ы, f. mop, swab.

швал|ь, и, f. (*coll.*) 1. (*collect.*) rubbish, worthless stuff. 2. good-for-nothing.

швáльн|я, и, f. (*obs.*) tailor's shop.

швáркн|уть, у, ешь, *pf.* (*coll.*) to hurl.

швартóв, а, *m.* (*naut.*) hawser, mooring line; отдáть ~ы to cast off.

шварт|овáть, ýю, *impf.* (*of* при~) (*naut.*) to moor.

шварт|овáться, ýюсь, *impf.* (*of* при~) (*naut.*) to moor, make fast.

швах, *as pred.* (*coll.*) poor, bad; in a bad way.

швед, а, *m.* Swede.

швéд|ка, ки, f. of ~.

швéдский, *adj.* Swedish.

швéйник, а, *m.* sewer, sewing industry worker.

швéйн|ый, *adj.* sewing; ~ые изделия ready--made garments; ~ая машúна sewing--machine; ~ая фáбрика garment factory.

швейцáр, а, *m.* porter, door-keeper, com-missionaire.

швейцáр|ец, ца, *m.* Swiss.

швейцáр|ка, ки, f. of ~ец.

швейцáрск|ая, ой, f. porter's lodge.

швейцáрский¹, *adj.* Swiss.

швейцáр|ский², *adj. of* ~.

швéрмер, а, *m.* squib (*firework*).

швец, á, *m.* 1. (*obs.*) tailor; и ш., и жнец, и в дýду игрéц (*fig..*) jack of all trades. 2. (*dial.*) cobbler.

шве|я́, й, f. seamstress; ш.-моторúстка electric sewing-machine operator; ш.-рýч-ница (*coll.*) hand finisher.

шво́р|ень, ня, *m.* = шкво́рень.

швырко́в|ый, *adj.* ~ые дрова́ logs, fire-wood.

швыр|ну́ть, ну́, нёшь, *pf. of* ~я́ть.

швыр|о́к, ка́, *m.* **1.** throw. **2.** (*collect.*) logs, firewood. **3.** (*moving*) practice target.

швыр|я́ть, я́ю, *impf.* (*of* ~ну́ть) (+*a. or i.*; *coll.*) to throw, fling, chuck, hurl; ш. де́ньги (деньга́ми) to fling one's money about.

швыря́|ться, юсь, *impf.* (*coll.*) (+*i.*) **1.** to throw, fling, hurl (at one another). **2.** to make light (of), trifle (with).

шевел|и́ть, ю́, и́шь, *impf.* (*of* ~ьну́ть *and* по~) **1.** to turn over. **2.** (+*i.*) to move, stir, budge; ш. мозга́ми (*coll., joc.*) to use one's wits, use one's loaf.

шевел|и́ться, ю́сь, и́шься, *impf.* (*of* ~ьну́ть-ся *and* по~) **1.** to move, stir, budge; у него́ ~я́тся де́ньги (*coll.*) he has a tidy bank balance. **2.** (*fig.*) to stir (*of hopes, fears, etc.*). **3.** ~и́сь, ~и́тесь! (*coll.*) get a move on!, get cracking!

шевел|ьну́ть, ьну́, ьнёшь, *pf.* (*of* ~и́ть); бро́вью не ш. not to bat an eyelid; па́льцем не ш. not to lift a finger.

шевел|ьну́ться, ьну́сь, ьнёшься, *pf. of* ~и́ться.

шевелю́р|а, ы, *f.* (head of) hair.

шевио́т, а, *m.* (*text.*) cheviot (*cloth*).

шевио́т|овый, *adj. of* ~.

шевро́, *indecl., n.* kid (*leather*).

шевро́|вый, *adj. of* ~.

шевро́н, а, *m.* (*mil.*) long-service stripe.

шеде́вр, а, *m.* masterpiece, chef d'œuvre.

ше́йк|а, и, *g. pl.* ше́ек, *f.* **1.** *dim. of* ше́я. **2.** (*narrow part of various objects*) neck; (*tech.*) pin, journal; ш. ги́льзы cartridge neck; ш. ре́льса web (*of rail*). **3.** (*anat.*) cervix.

ше́йный, *adj. of* ше́я; (*anat.*) jugular, cervical.

шейх, а, *m.* sheikh.

шёл, *see* идти́.

ше́лест, а, *m.* rustle, rustling.

шелест|е́ть, *1st person not used*, и́шь, *impf.* to rustle.

шёлк, а (у), о ~е, на (в) ~у́, *pl.* ~а́, *m.* silk (*also fig. of an object resembling silk in softness, etc., or of a gentle-natured person*); ш.-сыре́ц raw silk; ходи́ть в ~а́х to wear silks; в долгу́ как в ~у́ up to the eyes in debt.

шелкови́нк|а, и, *f.* silk thread.

шелкови́ст|ый (~, ~а), *adj.* silky.

шелкови́ц|а, ы, *f.* mulberry (tree).

шелкови́|чный, *adj. of* ~ца; ш. червь silk-worm.

шелково́д, а, *m.* silkworm breeder.

шелково́дств|о, а, *n.* silkworm breeding, seri(ci)culture.

шелково́д|ческий, *adj. of* ~ство.

шёлковый, *adj.* **1.** silk. **2.** (*fig., coll.*) meek, good (= tractable).

шелкопря́д, а, *m.* silkworm.

шелкопряде́ни|е, я, *n.* silk-spinning.

шелкопряд|и́льный, *adj. of* ~е́ние.

шёлкотка́цкий, *adj.* silk-weaving.

шело́м, а, *m.* (*arch. or poet.*) = шлем.

шелохн|у́ть, у́, ёшь, *pf.* to stir, agitate.

шелохн|у́ться, у́сь, ёшься, *pf.* to stir, move.

шелуди́в|ый (~, ~а), *adj.* (*coll.*) mangy.

шелух|а́, и́, *f.* skin (*of vegetables or fruit*); peel; pod; scale (*of fish*).

шелуше́ни|е, я, *n.* **1.** peeling, shelling (*action*). **2.** peeling (*of human skin*).

шелуш|и́ть, у́, и́шь, *impf.* to peel; to shell.

шелуш|и́ться, и́тся, *impf.* (*of skin*) to peel. **2.** (*of paint, etc.*) to come off, peel off.

ше́льм|а, ы, *m. and f.* (*coll.*) rascal, scoundrel.

шельмова́т|ый (~, ~а), *adj.* (*coll.*) rascally, sly, wily.

шельм|ова́ть, у́ю, *impf.* (*of* о~) **1.** (*hist.*) to punish publicly. **2.** (*coll.*) to blacken (*fig.*); to defame.

шельф, а, *m.* (*geogr.*) shelf.

шемя́кин, *adj., only in phrase* ш. суд unjust trial.

ше́нкел|ь, я, *pl.* ~я́, ~е́й, *m.* (*horsemanship*) leg (*of rider*).

шепеля́в|ить, лю, ишь, *impf.* to lisp, hiss (*pronounce 's', 'z' as 'sh', 'zh'*).

шепеля́в|ый (~, ~а), *adj.* lisping, hissing.

шеп|ну́ть, ну́, нёшь, *pf. of* ~та́ть.

шёпот, а, *m.* whisper (*also fig.* = rumour).

шёпотом, *adv.* in a whisper.

шептал|а́, ы́, *f.* (*collect.*) dried apricots *or* peaches.

шеп|та́ть, чу́, ~чешь, *impf.* (*of* ~ну́ть) to whisper.

шеп|та́ться, чу́сь, ~чешься, *impf.* to whisper, converse in whispers.

шептун|; а́, *m.* (*coll.*) **1.** one who speaks in a whisper. **2.** (*fig.*) whisperer, tell-tale, informer.

шербе́т, а, *m.* sherbet.

шере́нг|а, и, *f.* rank (= row); file, column.

шери́ф, а, *m.* sheriff.

шерохова́тост|ь, и, *f.* roughness (*also fig.*); unevenness.

шерохова́т|ый (~, ~а), *adj.* rough (*also fig.*); uneven; rugged.

шерсте- wool-.

шерсти́нк|а, и, *f.* strand of wool.

шерсти́ст|ый (~, ~а), *adj.* woolly, fleecy.

шерст|и́ть, и́т, *impf.* **1.** to irritate, tickle (*of a woollen garment*). **2.** (*fig., coll.*) to blow up, tear a strip off.

шерсто- wool-.

шерстоби́т, а, *m.* wool-beater.

шерстобо́йн|я, и, *f.* wool-beating mill.

шерстопрядéни|е, я, *n.* wool-spinning.

шерстопряд|и́льный, *adj. of* ~éние.

шерсточеса́льный, *adj.* wool-carding.

шерст|ь, и, *pl.* ~и, ~éй, *f.* **1.** hair (*of animals*); гла́дить кого́-н. про́тив ~и (*fig.*) to rub someone up the wrong way. **2.** wool. **3.** woollen material; worsted.

шерстян|о́й, *adj.* wool, woollen; ш. пот suint; ~а́я пря́жа wool yarn.

шерхе́бел|ь, я, *m.* (*tech.*) rough plane.

шерша́ве|ть, ет, *impf.* to become rough.

шерша́в|ый (~, ~а), *adj.* rough; ~ые ру́ки horny hands.

ше́рш|ень, ня, *m.* hornet.

шест, а́, *m.* pole; staff.

ше́стви|е, я, *n.* procession.

ше́ств|овать, ую, *impf.* to walk (*as in procession*).

шестерёнк|а, и, *f. dim. of* шестерня́².

шестерён|очный, *adj. of* ~ка; ~очная коробка gear-box.

шестёрк|а, и, *f.* **1.** figure '6'; six, group of six. **2.** (*cards*) six. **3.** six-in-hand. **4.** six--oar (boat).

шестерно́й, *adj.* sixfold, sextuple.

шестерн|я́¹, й, *g. pl.* ~éй, *f.* (*obs.*) six-in-hand.

шестер|ня́², ни́, *g. pl.* ~ён, *f.* (*tech.*) gear (wheel), cogwheel, pinion.

ше́стер|о, ы́х, *collect. num.* six.

шести- six-.

шестигра́нник, а, *m.* (*math.*) hexahedron.

шестидесятиле́ти|е, я, *n.* **1.** sixty years, sixty-year period. **2.** sixtieth anniversary.

шестидесятиле́тний, *adj.* **1.** of sixty years, sixty-year. **2.** sixty-year-old.

шестидеся́тник, а, *m.* (*hist.*) 'man of the sixties' (*of Russian public figures and social thinkers who flourished in the 1860's—e.g., Chernyshevsky and Dobrolyubov*).

шестидеся́тый, *adj.* sixtieth.

шестикла́ссник, а, *m.* sixth-former.

шестисотле́ти|е, я, *n.* **1.** six hundred years. **2.** six-hundredth anniversary, sexcentenary.

шестисо́тый, *adj.* six-hundredth.

шестисто́пный, *adj.* ш. ямб (*lit.*) alexandrine.

шестиуго́льник, а, *m.* (*math.*) hexagon.

шестиуго́льный, *adj.* hexagonal.

шестичасово́й, *adj.* **1.** lasting six hours. **2.** (*coll.*) occurring at, timed for six o'clock.

шестнадцати- sixteen-.

шестнадцатиле́тний, *adj.* **1.** of sixteen years, sixteen-year. **2.** sixteen-year-old.

шестна́дцатый, *adj.* sixteenth.

шестна́дцат|ь, и, *num.* sixteen.

шест|о́й, *adj.* sixth; одна́ ~а́я one sixth.

шест|о́к, ка́, *m.* **1.** hearth (*in Russian stove*). **2.** roost.

шест|ь, и, ью́, *num.* six.

шестьдеся́т, шести́десяти, шестью́десятью, о шести́десяти, *num.* sixty.

шест|ьсо́т, ~исо́т, ~иста́м, ~ьюста́ми, о ~иста́х, *num.* six hundred.

ше́стью, *adv.* six times.

шеф, а, *m.* **1.** (*coll.*) boss, chief. **2.** (*of an organization*) patron, sponsor.

шеф-по́вар, а, *pl.* ~а́, ~о́в, *m.* chef.

шеф|ский, *adj. of* ~ство.

шеф́ств|о, а, *n.* patronage, sponsorship (*in the U.S.S.R., relationship between two organizations—e.g. a factory and a collective farm—in which one 'adopts' the other, or arrangement by which an organization takes a special interest in a priority construction project*); взять ш. (над) to take under one's patronage.

шеф́ств|овать, ую, *impf.* (над) to act as patron, sponsor (to).

ше́|я, и, *f.* neck; броса́ться на ~ю кому́-н. to throw one's arms around someone's neck; на свою́ ~ю (*coll.*) to one's own detriment; бить по ~ям (*coll.*) to beat up, knock the daylight out of; ве́шаться на ~ю кому́-н. (*fig., coll.*) to hang round someone's neck; прогна́ть, вы́толкать кого́-н. в ~ю, в три ~и (*coll.*) to throw someone out on his ear; сиде́ть на ~е у кого́-н. (*coll.*) to live off someone; слома́ть, сверну́ть (себе́) ~ю на чём-н. (*coll.*) to come a cropper over something.

шиба́|ть, ю, *impf.* (*coll.*) **1.** (+*a. or i.*) to throw, chuck. **2.** to hit (*also, impers., of smells, etc.*).

ши́бер, а, *m.* (*tech.*) damper; gate (valve), slide (valve).

ши́б|кий (~ок, ~ка́, ~ко), *adj.* (*coll.*) fast, quick.

ши́бк|о, *adv.* (*coll.*) **1.** *adv. of* ~ий. **2.** hard; much, very; ш. испуга́ться to be scared stiff.

ши́б|че, *comp. of* ~кий *and* ~ко.

ши́ворот, а, *m.* (*coll.*) за ш. by the collar, by the scruff of the neck; ш.-навы́ворот (*adv.*) topsy-turvy, upside down, haywire.

ши́зик, а, *m.* (*sl.*) crackpot, freak.

шизофре́ник, а, *m.* (*med.*) schizophrenic.

шизофрени|я, и, *f.* (*med.*) schizophrenia.

шик, а (у), *m.* ostentatious smartness, stylishness; style.

шика́рно, *as pred.* it is splendid, magnificent.

шика́р|ный (~ен, ~на), *adj.* **1.** chic, smart, stylish. **2.** ostentatious, done for effect. **3.** (*coll.*) splendid, magnificent.

ши́к|ать, аю, *impf.* (*of* ~нуть) (*coll.*) **1.** (на+*a.*) to hush (*by crying 'sh'*). **2.** (+*d.*) to hiss (at), boo, catcall.

ши́к|нуть, ну, нешь, *pf. of* ~ать.

ши́к|нуть, ну, нёшь, *pf. of* ~ова́ть.

шик|ова́ть, у́ю, *impf.* (*of* ~ну́ть) (+*i. or intrans.*; *coll.*) to parade; to show off.

ши́л|о, а, *pl.* ~ья, ~ьев, *n.* awl.

шилохво́ст|ь, и, *f.* (*orn.*) pintail.

шимпанзе́, *indecl., m.* chimpanzee.

ши́н|а, ы, *f.* **1.** tyre. **2.** (*med.*) splint. **3.** (*electr.*) bus-bar.

шине́л|ь, и, *f.* (*mil. or uniform*) greatcoat.

шине́ль|ный, *adj. of* ~.

шинка́р|ка, ки, *f. of* ~ь.

шинка́рств|о, а, *n.* (*obs.*) bootlegging.

шинка́р|ь, я́, *m.* (*obs.*) **1.** tavern-keeper, publican. **2.** bootlegger.

шинко́в|анный, *p.p.p. of* ~а́ть *and adj.* (*cul.*) shredded, chopped.

шинк|ова́ть, у́ю, *impf.* (*cul.*) to shred, chop.

ши́н|ный, *adj. of* ~а; ~ное желе́зо band iron, hoop-iron; ш. заво́д tyre factory.

шин|о́к, ка́, *m.* (*obs.*) **1.** tavern. **2.** (*coll.*) bootlegging establishment.

шиншилл|а, ы, *f.* chinchilla.

шип¹, а́, m. **1.** (*bot.*) thorn, spine. **2.** spike, crampon, nail (*on running shoes, mountaineering boots, etc., to prevent slipping*). **3.** (*tech.*) pin, tenon; lug; ш. и гнездо́ mortise and tenon.

шип², а, m. (*coll.*) hissing (sound).

шипе́ни|е, я, *n.* hissing; sizzling; sputtering.

шип|е́ть, лю́, и́шь, *impf.* **1.** to hiss; to sizzle; to fizz; to sputter. **2.** to make the sound 'sh' (*to comfort a child, etc., or to enjoin silence*).

шипо́вник, а, m. (*bot.*) dogrose.

шипу́чий, *adj.* (*of drinks*) sparkling; fizzy.

шипу́чк|а, и, *f.* (*coll.*) fizzy drink.

шип|я́щий, *pres. part. act. of* ~е́ть *and adj.* (*ling.*) hushing.

шир|е, comp. of ~о́кий *and* ~око́; ш. шаг, *see* шаг.

ширин|а́, ы́, *f.* width, breadth; gauge (*of railway track*); ш. фро́нта (*mil.*) frontage.

шири́нк|а, и, *f.* **1.** (*coll.*) fly (*of trousers*). **2.** (*dial.*) (piece of) cloth.

ши́р|ить, ю, ишь, *impf.* to extend, expand.

ши́р|иться, ится, *impf.* to spread, expand (*intrans.*).

ши́рм|а, ы, *f.* screen (*also fig.*).

широ́к|ий (~, ~а́, ~о́, pl. ~й), adj. **1.** wide, broad (*also fig.*); ~ая колея́ (*railways*) broad gauge; ш. экра́н (*cinema*) wide screen; в ~ом смы́сле in a broad sense. **2.** (*fig.*) big, extensive, large-scale, general; ~ие пла́ны big plans; ~ие ма́ссы the general public; ш. чита́тель the average reader, the general reading public; това́ры ~ого потребле́ния (*econ.*) consumer goods; жить на ~ую но́гу to live in grand style; у него́ ~ая нату́ра he likes to do things in a big way (*not pejor.*).

широко́, *adv.* **1.** wide, widely, broadly (*also fig.*); ш. раскры́ть глаза́ to open one's eyes

wide; ш. толкова́ть to interpret loosely. **2.** extensively, on a large scale.

широко- wide-, broad-.

широковеща́ни|е, я, *n.* (*radio*) broadcasting.

широковеща́тельный, *adj.* **1.** broadcasting. **2.** (*pejor.*) loud, loud-mouthed; containing large promises.

ширококоле́йный, *adj.* (*railways*) broad--gauge.

ширококо́стный, *adj.* big-boned.

широкопле́ч|ий (~, ~а), adj. broad-shouldered.

широкопо́лый, *adj.* wide-brimmed (*of hats*); full-skirted (*of clothes*).

широкоэкра́нный, *adj.* wide-screen.

широт|а́, ы́, *pl.* ~ы, ~, *f.* **1.** width, breadth. **2.** (*geogr.*) latitude.

широ́тный, *adj.* (*geogr.*) latitudinal, of latitude.

широча́йший, *superl. of* широ́кий.

широче́нный, *adj.* (*coll.*) very wide, broad.

ширпотре́б, а, m. (*econ.; coll.*) consumption; (*collect.*) consumer goods.

шир|ь, и, *f.* (wide) expanse; во всю ш. to full width; (*fig.*) to the full extent.

ши́то-кры́то, *adv.* (*coll.*) всё ш.-к. it's all being kept dark.

ши́т|ый, *p.p.p. of* ~ь *and adj.* embroidered.

шить, шью, шьёшь, *impf.* (*of* с~) **1.** to sew. **2.** make (*by sewing*); ш. себе́ что-н. to have something made. **3.** (*impf. only*) to embroider.

шить|ё, я́, *n.* **1.** sewing, needlework. **2.** embroidery.

ши́фер, а, m. slate.

ши́фер|ный, *adj. of* ~; ~ное ма́сло shale oil.

шифо́н, а, m. (*text.*) chiffon.

шифонье́рк|а, и, *f.* chest of drawers.

шифр, а, m. **1.** cypher, cipher; code. **2.** pressmark. **3.** (*obs.*) monogram.

шифрова́льщик, а, m. cypher clerk.

шифро́в|анный, *p.p.p. of* ~а́ть *and adj.* (in) cypher.

шифр|ова́ть, у́ю, *impf.* (*of* за~) to encipher.

шифро́вк|а, и, *f.* **1.** enciphering. **2.** (*coll.*) cipher communication.

ши́хт|а, ы, *f.* (*tech.*) (*furnace*) charge, batch, burden.

шиш, а́, m. (*coll.*) **1.** (*vulg.*) fig; показа́ть ш. to pull a long nose. **2.** nothing; ни ~а́ damn all. **3.** (*hist.*) ruffian, brigand.

шиша́к, а́, m. (*hist.*) spiked helmet.

ши́шк|а, и, *f.* **1.** (*bot.*) cone. **2.** bump; lump. **3.** (*tech.*) (mould) core. **4.** (*coll., joc.*) big--wig, big wheel.

шишкова́т|ый (~, ~а), adj. knobby, knobbly; bumpy.

шишкови́д|ный (~ен, ~на), adj. cone--shaped.

шишконо́сный, *adj.* (*bot.*) coniferous.

шкал|а́, ы́, *pl.* ~ы, *f.* scale; dial.

шка́лик, а, *m.* (*obs.*) 1. shkalik (*old Russian unit of liquid volume, equivalent to 0·06 litres*). 2. bottle *or* glass (*containing above measure*).

шка́н|ечный, *adj. of* ~цы; ш. журна́л log (book).

шка́нц|ы, ев, *no sing.* (*naut.*) quarterdeck.

шкап, а, *m.* (*arch. or dial.*) = шкаф.

шкату́лк|а, и, *f.* box, casket, case.

шкаф, а, о ~е, в ~ý, *pl.* ~ы́, *m.* cupboard, wardrobe; dresser; духово́й ш. oven; кни́жный ш. bookcase (*with doors*); несгора́емый ш. safe.

шкафу́т, а, *m.* (*naut.*) waist (*of ship*).

шка́фчик, а, *m.* closet, locker.

шквал, а, *m.* squall (*also, fig., of artillery fire*); ш. вопро́сов barrage of questions.

шква́листый, *adj.* squally.

шква́льный, *adj.* ш. ого́нь (*mil.*) heavy fire, mass barrage.

шква́р|ки, ок, *sing.* ~ка, ~ки, *f.* (*cul.*) crackling.

шквор|ень, ня, *m.* (*tech.*) pintle, kingpin, kingbolt, draw-bolt.

шкет, а, *m.* (*sl.*) boy, lad.

шкив, а, *pl.* ~ы́, *m.* (*tech.*) pulley; sheave.

шки́пер, а, *pl.* ~ы *and* ~а́, *m.* (*naut.*) skipper, master.

шко́д|а, ы, *f.* (*coll.*) 1. harm, damage. 2. trick, mischief.

шкодли́в|ый (~, ~а), *adj.* (*coll.*) 1. harmful. 2. mischievous.

шко́л|а, ы, *f.* 1. (*in var. senses*) school; ходи́ть в ~у to go to school; око́нчить ~у to leave school; ш.-интерна́т boarding school; вы́сшая ш. university, college; (*in abstract sense*) higher education. 2. schooling, training.

шко́л|ить, ю, ишь, *impf.* (*of* вы́~) (*coll.*) to train, discipline.

шко́льник, а, *m.* schoolboy.

шко́льниц|а, ы, *f.* schoolgirl.

шко́льнический, *adj.* schoolboy(ish).

шко́льничеств|о, а, *n.* schoolboyish behaviour, schoolboy tricks.

шко́льн|ый, *adj.* school; ш. во́зраст school age; со ~ой скамьи́ since one's schooldays; ш. учи́тель school-teacher, schoolmaster.

школя́р, а́, *m.* (*obs.*) schoolboy.

школя́рств|о, а, *n.* scholasticism, pedantry.

шкот, а, *m.* (*naut.*) sheet.

шко́т|овый, *adj. of* ~; ш. у́зел sheet bend.

шку́р|а, ы, *f.* 1. skin (*also fig.*), hide, pelt; волк в ове́чьей ~е wolf in sheep's clothing; быть в чьей-н. ~е to be in someone's shoes; драть ~у (с кого́-н.) to fleece someone; дрожа́ть за свою́ ~у to be concerned for one's own skin; чу́вствовать что-н. на свое́й ~е to know what something feels like. 2. (*coll., pejor.*) = ~ник.

шку́рк|а, и, *f.* 1. skin. 2. (*coll.*) rind. 3. emery paper, sandpaper.

шку́рник, а, *m.* (*coll., pejor.*) person concerned only with self-advantage.

шку́рный, *adj.* (*pejor.*) selfish, self-seeking.

шла, *see* идти́.

шлагба́ум, а, *m.* barrier (*of swing-beam type, at road or rail crossing*).

шлак, а, *m.* slag; dross; cinder; clinker.

шлакобето́н, а, *m.* slag concrete (*made of slag, cement, and sand*).

шлакобло́к, а, *m.* breeze block (*building material made of cinder with addition of cement*).

шла́к|овый, *adj. of* ~.

шланг, а, *m.* hose.

шла́ф|ор, а, *m.* = ~ро́к.

шлафро́к, а, *m.* (*obs.*) housecoat, dressing-gown.

шлейф, а, *m.* train (*of dress*).

шлем¹, а, *m.* helmet.

шлем², а, *m.* (*cards*) slam; большо́й, ма́лый ш. grand, little slam.

шлемофо́н, а, *m.* (*mil.*) helmet with earphones, intercom head-set.

шлёпан|цы, цев, *sing.* ~ец, ~ца, *m.* bedroom slippers.

шлёп|ать, аю, *impf.* (*of* ~нуть) 1. to smack, spank. 2. (*coll.*) to shuffle; to tramp.

шлёп|аться, аюсь, *impf.* (*of* ~нуться) (*coll.*) to fall with a plop, thud.

шлёп|нуть(ся), ну(сь), нешь(ся), *pf. of* ~ать(ся).

шлеп|о́к, ка́, *m.* smack, slap.

шле|я́, и́, *f.* breech-band, breast-band (*part of harness*).

шли, *see* идти́.

шлифова́льный, *adj.* (*tech.*) polishing, burnishing; grinding; ш. материа́л abrasive(s); ш. стано́к grinding-machine.

шлифова́ни|е, я, *n.* (*tech.*) polishing, burnishing; grinding.

шлиф|ова́ть, у́ю, *impf.* (*of* от~) 1. (*tech.*) to polish, burnish; to grind. 2. (*fig.*) to polish, perfect.

шлифо́вк|а, и, *f.* (*tech.*) 1. polishing, burnishing; grinding. 2. polish (*result of action*).

шли́хт|а, ы, *f.* (*tech.*) size.

шлихт|ова́ть, у́ю, *impf.* (*tech.*) to smooth, finish; to size, dress.

шло, *see* идти́.

шлюз, а, *m.* lock, sluice, floodgate.

шлюз|ова́ть, у́ю, *impf. and pf.* 1. to construct locks (on). 2. to lock through, convey through a lock.

шлюз|ово́й, *adj. of* ~; ~ова́я ка́мера lock chamber.

шлюпба́лк|а, и, *f.* (*naut.*) davit.

шлю́пк|а, и, *f.* launch, boat; спаса́тельная ш. lifeboat.

шлю́х|а, и, *f.* (*vulg.*) streetwalker, tart.

шля́п|а, ы, *f.* **1.** hat; де́ло в ~е (*coll.*) it's in the bag, all is well. **2.** *coll., pejor.*; *of a feeble, helpless person.*

шля́пк|а, и, *f.* **1.** (*woman's*) hat. **2.** head (*of nail, etc.*); cap (*of mushroom*).

шля́пник, а, *m.* milliner, hatter.

шля́п|ный, *adj.* of ~a.

шля́|ться, юсь, *impf.* (*coll.*) to loaf about.

шлях, а, о ~е, на ~у́, *m.* highway, high road (*in the Ukraine and S. Russia*).

шляхе́т|ский, *adj.* of ~ство *and* шля́хта.

шляхе́тств|о, а, *n.* **1.** = шля́хта. **2.** (*hist.*) (Russian) nobility, gentry (*designation used in early 18th century*, = дворя́нство).

шля́хт|а, ы, *f.* (*hist.*) szlachta (*Polish gentry*).

шляхта́нк|а, и, *f.* of шля́хтич.

шля́хтич, а, *m.* (*hist.*) member of szlachta.

шмат|о́к, ка́, *m.* (*coll.*) bit, piece.

шмел|ь, я́, *m.* bumble-bee.

шмоня́|ть, ю, *impf.* (*sl.*) to frisk.

шмуцти́тул, а, *m.* (*typ.*) bastard-title.

шмы́г|ать, аю, *impf.* (*of* ~ну́ть) (*coll.*) **1.** (+*i.*) to rub, brush; ш. но́сом to sniff. **2.** to rush up and down.

шмыг|ну́ть, ну́, нёшь, *pf.* (*coll.*) **1.** *inst. pf. of* ~ать. **2.** to dart, nip, sneak (= to move rapidly, in order to escape notice).

шмя́к|ать, аю, *impf.* (*of* ~нуть) (*coll.*) to drop with a thud.

шмя́к|нуть, ну, нешь, *pf. of* ~ать.

шни́цел|ь, я, *m.* (*cul.*) schnitzel.

шнур, á, *m.* **1.** cord; lace. **2.** (*electr.*) flex, cable.

шнур|ова́ть, у́ю, *impf.* **1.** (*pf.* за~) to lace up. **2.** (*pf.* про~) to tie (*leaves of a document, etc.*).

шнур|ова́ться, у́юсь, *impf.* (*of* за~) **1.** to lace oneself up. **2.** *pass. of* ~ова́ть.

шнуро́вк|а, и, *f.* **1.** lacing, tying. **2.** (*obs.*) corset.

шнур|ово́й, *adj.* of ~.

шнур|о́к, ка́, *m.* lace.

шныр|ну́ть, ну́, нёшь, *pf. of* ~я́ть.

шныр|я́ть, я́ю, *impf.* (*of* ~ну́ть) (*coll.*) to dart about, dart in and out.

шов, шва, *m.* **1.** seam; без шва seamless; держа́ть ру́ки по швам to stand to attention; треща́ть по всем швам (*fig.*) to burst at the seams, fall to pieces, crack up, collapse. **2.** stitch (*in embroidery*). **3.** (*med.*) stitch, suture; наложи́ть, снять швы to put in, remove stitches. **4.** (*tech.*) joint, junction.

шовини́зм, а, *m.* chauvinism.

шовини́ст, а, *m.* chauvinist.

шовинисти́ческий, *adj.* chauvinistic.

шок, а, *m.* (*med.*) shock.

шоки́р|овать, ую, *impf.* to shock.

шокола́д, а, *m.* chocolate.

шокола́дк|а, и, *f.* (*coll.*) bar of chocolate, a chocolate (*sweet*).

шокола́д|ный, *adj.* **1.** *adj.* of ~. **2.** chocolate-coloured.

шо́мпол, а, *pl.* ~á, *m.* (*mil.*) **1.** cleaning rod. **2.** (*obs.*) ramrod.

шо́мпол|ьный, *adj.* of ~; ~ьное ружьё muzzle-loading gun.

шо́рник, а, *m.* saddler, harness-maker.

шо́рн|ый, *adj.* harness; ~ая мастерска́я = ~я.

шо́рн|я, и, *f.* saddler's shop, saddle-maker's, harness-maker's.

шо́рох, а, *m.* rustle.

шо́рт|ы, ~, *no sing.* shorts.

шо́р|ы, ~, *no sing.* **1.** blinkers (*also fig.*); держа́ть кого́-н. в ~ах (*fig.*) to keep someone in blinkers. **2.** harness (*with breech-band, but without collar*).

шоссе́, *indecl., n.* highway; surfaced road.

шоссе́|йный, *adj.* of ~; ~йная доро́га = ~.

шосси́р|овать, ую, *impf. and pf.* to metal, surface (*a road*).

шотла́нд|ец, ца, *m.* Scotsman, Scot.

шотла́нд|ка[1], ки, *f.* of ~ец.

шотла́нд|ка[2], ки, *f.* (*text.*) tartan, plaid.

шотла́ндский, *adj.* Scottish, Scots.

шофёр, а, *m.* driver (*of a motor vehicle*), chauffeur.

шофёр|ский, *adj.* of ~; ~ское свиде́тельство, ~ские права́ driver's, driving licence.

шпа́г|а, и, *f.* sword; обнажи́ть ~y to draw one's sword; скрести́ть ~и to cross swords (*also fig.*); взять на ~y (*obs.*) to gain by the sword; отда́ть ~y (*obs.*) to surrender.

шпага́т, а, *m.* **1.** string, cord; (*agric.*) binder twine. **2.** (*gymnastics*) the splits.

шпагоглота́тел|ь, я, *m.* sword-swallower.

шпа́жник, а, *m.* (*bot.*) gladiolus.

шпак, а, *m.* (*obs., pejor.*) civilian.

шпакл|ева́ть, ю́ю, ю́ешь, *impf.* (*of* за~) to fill, putty, stop (*holes*); (*naut.*) to caulk.

шпаклёвк|а, и, *f.* **1.** filling, puttying, stopping up. **2.** putty.

шпа́л|а, ы, *f.* (*railways*) sleeper.

шпале́р|а, ы, *f.* **1.** trellis, lattice-work. **2.** hedge, line of trees (*lining road*). **3.** (*mil.*) line (*of soldiers along ceremonial route*); стоя́ть ~ами to line the route. **4.** *pl.* (*obs.*) wall-paper.

шпан|а́, ы́, *f.* (*coll.*) hooligan, ruffian; (*also collect.*) rabble.

шпангóут, а, *m.* (*tech.*) frame (*of aircraft*); ribs (*of ship*).

шпа́н|ка, ки, *f.* **1.** black cherry. **2.** = ~ская му́шка.

шпа́нск|ий, *adj.* ~ая ви́шня black cherry; ~ая му́шка (*zool., med.*) Spanish fly, cantharides.

шпарга́лк|а, и, *f.* (*coll.*) crib (*in school*).

шпа́р|ить, ю, ишь, *impf.* (*of* о~) (*coll.*)
1. to scald, pour boiling water on. 2. to
go, speak, read, *etc.*, in a rush.

шпат, а, *m.* (*min.*) spar; полевой ш. feld-
spar.

шпа́тел|ь, я, *m.* 1: (*tech.*, *art*) palette-knife.
2. (*med.*) spatula.

шпа́ци|я, и, *f.* (*typ.*) space.

шпен|ёк, ька́, *m.* pin, peg, prong.

шпига́т, а, *m.* (*naut.*) scupper.

шпиг|ова́ть, у́ю, *impf.* (*of* на~) 1. (*cul.*) to
lard. 2. (*coll.*) ш. кого́-н. to suggest to
someone, work upon someone, put it into
someone's head.

шпик¹, а (у), *m.* (*cul.*) lard.

шпик², а́, *m.* (*coll.*) secret agent; plain-
-clothes detective.

шпил|ь, я, *m.* 1. spire, steeple. 2. (*naut.*)
capstan, windlass.

шпи́льк|а, и, *f.* 1. hairpin; hat-pin. 2. (*tech.*)
peg, dowel, cotter pin; tack, brad. 3. (*fig.*)
caustic remark; подпусти́ть ~и (кому́-н.)
to get at, have a dig at (someone).

шпина́т, а, *m.* spinach.

шпингале́т, а, *m.* 1. catch, latch (*of door or
window*). 2. (*coll.*) urchin, boy.

шпио́н, а, *m.* spy.

шпиона́ж, а, *m.* espionage.

шпио́н|ить, ю, ишь, *impf.* (за + *i.*) to spy
(on), engage in espionage.

шпио́н|ский, *adj. of* ~.

шпиц¹, а, *m.* (*obs.*) spire, steeple.

шпиц², а, *m.* Pomeranian (*dog*).

шплинт, а, *m.* (*tech.*) split pin, cotter-pin.

шпон, а, *m.* 1. (*typ.*) lead. 2. veneer sheet
(*of wood*).

шпо́н|а, ы, *f.* = ~.

шпо́нк|а, и, *f.* (*tech.*) bushing key, dowel.

шпо́р|а, ы, *f.* spur; дать ~ы (+ *d.*) to spur
on.

шприц, а, *m.* (*med.*) syringe.

шпро́т|ы, ~, *sing.* ~а, ~ы, *f. and* ~, ~а, *m.*
sprats.

шпу́льк|а, и, *f.* spool, bobbin.

шпунт, а́, *m.* (*tech.*) groove, tongue, rabbet.

шпур, а, *m.* (*min.*) blast-hole, bore-hole.

шпыня́|ть, ю, *impf.* (*coll.*) to needle, nag.

шрам, а, *m.* scar.

шрапне́л|ь, и, *f.* shrapnel.

шрифт, а, *pl.* ~ы́, *m.* 1. type, type face;
курси́вный ш. cursive; прямо́й ш. upright.
2. script.

шрифт|ово́й, *adj. of* ~.

штаб, а, *pl.* ~ы́, *m.* (*mil.*) staff; headquarters.

шта́бел|ь, я, *pl.* ~я́, ~е́й, *m.* stack, pile.

штаби́ст, а, *m.* (*coll.*) staff officer.

штаб-кварти́р|а, ы, *f.* (*mil.*) headquarters.

штабни́к, а́, *m.* (*coll.*) staff officer.

штаб|но́й, *adj. of* ~; ~на́я рабо́та staff work;
~но́е подразделе́ние headquarters unit.

штаб-офице́р, а, *m.* (*mil.*, *hist.*) officer of
field rank.

штабс-капита́н, а, *m.* (*hist.*; *in tsarist
army*) staff-captain (*officer of rank intermediate between lieutenant and captain*).

штаг, а, *m.* (*naut.*) stay.

штаке́тник, а, *m.* fence, fencing.

шталме́йстер, а, *m.* (*hist.*) equerry.

штамб, а, *m.* (*bot.*) stem, trunk (*of tree*).

штамм, а, *m.* (*biol.*) strain, breed.

штамп, а, *m.* 1. (*tech.*) die, punch. 2. stamp,
impress; letter-head. 3. (*fig.*, *pejor.*) cliché,
stock phrase.

штампова́льный, *adj.* (*tech.*) punching,
stamping, pressing.

штампо́в|анный, *p.p.p. of* ~а́ть *and adj.*
1. (*tech.*) punched, stamped, pressed. 2.
(*fig.*) trite, hackneyed; stock, standard.

штамп|ова́ть, у́ю, *impf.* 1. (*tech.*) to punch,
press. 2. to stamp, die. 3. (*fig.*) to carry
out, go through mechanically; to rubber-
-stamp.

штампо́вк|а, и, *f.* 1. (*tech.*) punching, press-
ing; горя́чая ш. drop forging. 2. (die-)
stamping.

штампо́|щик, а, *m.* puncher; stamp opera-
tor.

штамп-час|ы́, о́в, *no sing.* time-clock.

шта́нг|а, и, *f.* 1. (*tech.*) bar, rod, beam. 2.
(*sport*) weight. 3. (*sport*) post (*of goal*).

штангенци́ркул|ь, я, *m.* (*tech.*) sliding
calipers, slide gauge.

штанги́ст, а, *m.* (*sport*) weight-lifter.

штанда́рт, а, *m.* (*obs.*) standard.

штани́н|а, ы, *f.* (*coll.*) trouser-leg.

штани́ш|ки, ек, *no sing.*, *dim. of* штаны́.

штан|ы́, о́в, *no sing.* trousers, breeches.

шта́пел|ь, я, *m.* (*text.*) staple.

шта́пельный, *adj.* (*text.*) staple.

штат¹, а, *m.* state (*administrative unit*);
Соединённые ~ы Аме́рики United States
of America.

штат², а, *m.* (*sing or pl.*) staff, establishment;
~ы ми́рного вре́мени peace-time establishment; сокраще́ние ~ов reduction of staff;
зачи́слить в ш. to take on the staff, establish; оста́ться за ~ом (*i*) (*obs.*) to be dis-
established, declared supernumerary, (*ii*)
(*fig.*) to be superfluous.

штати́в, а, *m.* tripod, base, support, stand.

шта́т|ный, *adj. of* ~²; ~ная до́лжность
established post; ш. рабо́тник permanent
member of staff; ~ное расписа́ние list of
members of staff.

штатск|ий, *adj.* civilian; ~ое (пла́тье)
civilian clothes, civvies, mufti; *as noun* ш.,
~ого, *m.* civilian.

штафи́рк|а, и, *m.* (*coll.*, *pejor.*) civilian.

штев|ень, ня, *m.* (*naut.*) stem- *or* stern-post.

штéйгер, а, *m.* foreman miner.

штемпел|ева́ть, ю́ю, ю́ешь, *impf.* (*of* за~) to stamp; to frank, postmark.

ште́мпел|ь, я, *pl.* ~я́, *m.* stamp; почто́вый ш. postmark.

ште́мпель|ный, *adj. of* ~.

ште́псел|ь, я, *pl.* ~я́, *m.* (*electr.*) plug, socket.

ште́псель|ный, *adj. of* ~; ~ная ви́лка plug; ~ная розе́тка socket.

штибле́т|ы, ~, *sing.* ~а, ~ы, *f.* 1. (*lace-up*) boots, shoes. 2. (*obs.*) gaiters.

штил|ево́й, *adj. of* ~ь.

штил|ь, я, *m.* (*naut.*) calm.

штифт, а́, *m.* (*tech.*) (joint-)pin, dowel, sprig.

шток, а, *m.* 1. (*tech.*) (coupling) rod; ш. по́ршня piston rod. 2. (*geol.*) stock, shoot.

штокро́з|а, ы, *f.* (*bot.*) hollyhock.

штольн|я, и, *g. pl.* што́лен, *f.* (*mining*) gallery.

што́пальный, *adj.* darning.

што́па|ть, ю, *impf.* (*of* за~) to darn.

што́пк|а, и, *f.* 1. darning; худо́жественная ш. invisible mending. 2. darning thread, wool. 3. (*coll.*) darn (*darned place*).

што́пор, а, *m.* 1. corkscrew. 2. (*aeron.*) spin; ~ом (*as adv.*) in a spin.

што́пор|ить, ю, ишь, *impf.* (*aeron.*) to descend in a spin.

штор|а, ы, *f.* blind.

шторм, а, *m.* (*naut.*) strong gale; си́льный ш. whole gale (*wind force 9*); жесто́кий ш. storm (*wind force 11*).

шторм|ова́ть, у́ет, *impf.* (*naut.*) to ride out a storm.

шторм|ово́й, *adj. of* ~; ве́тер ~ово́й си́лы wind of gale force; ш. костю́м weatherproof clothing.

штормтра́п, а, *m.* (*naut.*) jacob's ladder.

штор|ный, *adj. of* ~а.

штоф¹, а, *m.* shtof (*old Russian unit of liquid measure* (= *1·23 litres*) *or bottle of this measure*).

штоф², а, *m.* (*text.*) damask, brocade.

што́ф|ный¹, *adj. of* ~¹; ~ная ла́вка drinking-shop.

што́ф|ный², *adj. of* ~².

штраф, а, *m.* fine; взима́ть ш. (с+*g.*) to fine; наложи́ть ш. to impose a fine.

штрафни́к, а́, *m.* (*coll.*) soldier in the 'glass-house'.

штраф|но́й, *adj.* 1. *adj. of* ~. 2. penal, penalty; ш. батальо́н (*mil.*) penal battalion; ш. журна́л (*obs.*) penalties book; ~на́я площа́дка (*sport*) penalty area; ш. уда́р (*sport*) penalty kick.

штраф|ова́ть, у́ю, *impf.* (*of* о~) to fine.

штрейкбре́хер, а, *m.* strike-breaker, blackleg.

штрейкбре́херств|о, а, *n.* strike-breaking, blacklegging.

штрек, а, *m.* (*mining*) drift.

штрих, а́, *m.* 1. stroke (*in drawing*); hachure (*on map*). 2. (*fig.*) feature, trait.

штрих|ова́ть, у́ю, *impf.* (*of* за~) to shade, hatch.

штрих|ово́й, *adj. of* ~; ш. рису́нок line drawing; ш. пункти́р dash line.

штуди́р|овать, ую, *impf.* (*of* про~) to study.

шту́к|а, и, *f.* 1. item, one of a kind (*often not translated*); по рублю́ ш. one rouble each; пять ~ яи́ц five eggs; я возьму́ шесть ~ I'll have six (*of item in question*). 2. piece (*of cloth, fabric*). 3. (*coll.*) thing; вот так ш.! well I'll be damned! 4. (*coll.*) trick; сыгра́ть ~у to play a trick; не ш. it's not too hard, it doesn't take much.

штука́р|ь, я́, *m.* (*coll.*) joker; rogue.

штукату́р, а, *m.* plasterer.

штукату́р|ить, ю, ишь, *impf.* (*of* о~ and от~) to plaster.

штукату́рк|а, и, *f.* 1. plastering. 2. plaster. 3. stucco.

штукату́р|ный, *adj. of* ~ка.

штук|ова́ть, у́ю, *impf.* 1. to mend invisibly. 2. (*sl.*) to chain-smoke.

штурва́л, а, *m.* steering-wheel; controls; стоя́ть за ~ом to be at the wheel, helm, controls.

штурва́л|ьный, *adj. of* ~; *as noun* ш., ~ьного, *m.* helmsman, pilot.

штурм, а, *m.* (*mil.*) storm, assault.

штурман, а, *pl.* ~ы and ~а́, *m.* (*naut., aeron.*) navigator.

штурман|ский, *adj. of* ~; ~ская ру́бка (*naut.*) chart house.

штурм|ова́ть, у́ю, *impf.* to storm, assault.

штурмови́к, а́, *m.* low-flying attack air--craft.

штурмо́вк|а, и, *f.* low-flying air attack.

штурм|ово́й, *adj. of* ~ and ~о́вка; ~ова́я авиа́ция ground support aircraft; ~овы́е де́йствия ground support action; ~ова́я ле́стница (*hist.*) scaling ladder; ~ова́я ло́дка assault craft; ~ова́я полоса́ assault course; ш. самолёт = ~ови́к.

штурмовщи́н|а, ы, *f.* (*pejor.*) rushed work, production spurt, sporadic effort.

штуф, а, *m.* (*min.*) piece of ore.

шту́цер, а, *pl.* ~а́, *m.* 1. carbine. 2. (*tech.*) connecting pipe.

шту́чн|ый, *adj.* (by the) piece; ш. пол parquet floor; ~ая рабо́та piece-work; ш. това́р goods sold by the piece (*and not by weight*); ш. хлеб bread rolls.

штык, а́, *m.* 1. bayonet; идти́ в ~й to fight at bayonet point; встре́тить, приня́ть в ~й (*fig.*) to give a hostile reception (to), oppose adamantly. 2. (*mil.*) = man, soldier. 3. (*naut.*) bend. 4. spade's depth. 5. (*min.*) bar, ingot.

штык|ово́й, *adj. of* ~; ш. уда́р bayonet thrust.

штыр|ь, я́, *m.* (*tech.*) pin, dowel, pintle.

шу́б|а, ы, *f.* fur coat.

шу́б|ный, *adj.* 1. *adj. of* ~a. 2. fur-bearing. 3. ш. клей (*obs.*) carpenter's glue.

шуг|а́, и́, *f.* sludge ice.

шуг|а́ть, а́ю, *impf.* (*of* ~ну́ть) (*coll.*) to scare off.

шуг|ну́ть, ну́, нёшь, *pf. of* ~а́ть.

шу́йц|а, ы, *f.* (*arch.*) left hand.

шу́лер, а, *pl.* ~а́, *m.* card-sharper, cheat.

шу́лер|ский, *adj. of* ~.

шу́лерств|о, а, *n.* card-sharping, sharp practice.

шум, а (у), *m.* 1. noise. 2. din, uproar, racket; подня́ть ш. to kick up a racket. 3. (*fig.*) sensation, stir.

шум|е́ть, лю́, и́шь, *impf.* 1. to make a noise. 2. (*coll.*) to row, wrangle. 3. (*coll.*) to make a stir, fuss; to cause a sensation, stir.

шуми́х|а, и, *f.* (*coll.*) sensation, stir.

шумли́в|ый (~, ~a), *adj.* noisy.

шу́м|ный (~ен, ~на́, ~но), *adj.* 1. noisy; loud. 2. sensational.

шумови́к, а́, *m.* (*theatr.*) sound effects man.

шумо́вк|а, и, *f.* (*cul.*) perforated spoon, straining ladle.

шум|ово́й, *adj. of* ~; ш. орке́стр percussion band; ш. фон (*radio*) background noise; ~о́вые эффе́кты sound effects.

шум|о́к, ка́, *m.* (*coll.*) noise; под ш. on the quiet.

шу́р|ин, ина, *pl.* ~ья́, ~ьёв *m.* brother-in-law (*wife's brother*).

шур|ова́ть, у́ю, *impf.* to stoke, poke (*a furnace*).

шуру́п, а, *m.* (*tech.*) screw.

шурф, а, *m.* (*mining*) prospecting shaft.

шурф|ова́ть, у́ю, *impf.* (*mining*) to excavate, make a prospecting dig.

шурш|а́ть, у́, и́шь, *impf.* to rustle (*also* +*i.*, *trans.*), crackle.

шу́ры-му́ры, *indecl. pl.* (*coll.*) love affair(s).

шу́ст|рый (~ёр, ~ра́, ~ро), *adj.* (*coll.*) smart, bright, sharp.

шут, а́, *m.* 1. (*hist.*) fool, jester. 2. fool, buffoon, clown; разыгра́ть ~а́ to play the fool. 3. (*coll.*) *in certain phrases* devil; на кой ш.?, како́го ~a? why the devil?

шу|ти́ть, чу́, ~тишь, *impf.* (*of* по~) 1. to joke, jest; я же не ~чу́ but I'm not joking; чем чёрт не ~тит! (*coll.*) we can but see (what will happen)! 2. (c+*i.*) to play with), trifle (with); ш. с огнём to play with fire. 3. (над) to laugh (at), make fun (of).

шути́х|а, и, *f.* 1. *f. of* шут. 2. firecracker, rocket.

шу́тк|а, и, *f.* 1. joke, jest; не ш. it's no joke; ш. (ли) +*inf.* it's not so easy, it's no laughing matter (to); с ней ~и пло́хи she is not to be trifled with; ~и в сто́рону, ~и прочь let's get down to business; без шу́ток joking apart; сказа́ть в ~у to say as a joke; не на ~у in earnest. 2. trick; сыгра́ть ~у (c+*i.*) to play a trick (on). 3. (*theatr.*) farce.

шутли́в|ый (~, ~a), *adj.* 1. humorous. 2. joking, light-hearted.

шутни́к, а́, *m.* joker, wag.

шут|овско́й, *adj. of* шут; ш. колпа́к fool's сар; ~овски́е вы́ходки clowning, buffoonery.

шутовств|о́, а́, *n.* buffoonery.

шу́точ|ный (~ен, ~на), *adj.* comic; joking; де́ло не ~ное it's no joke, no laughing matter.

шут|я́, *pres. gerund of* ~и́ть *and adv.* 1. easily, lightly; ш. отде́латься to get off lightly. 2. for fun, in jest; не ш. in earnest.

шу́шер|а, ы, *f.* (*coll.*) rubbish; riff-raff.

шушу́ка|ться, юсь, *impf.* (*coll.*) to whisper; (*fig.*) to gossip.

шхе́р|ный, *adj. of* ~ы.

шхе́р|ы, ~, *no sing.* (*geogr.*) skerries.

шху́н|а, ы, *f.* schooner.

Щ

щаве́л|евый, *adj.* 1. *adj. of* ~ь. 2. (*chem.*) oxalic; соль ~евой кислоты́ oxalate.

щаве́л|ь, я́, *m.* (*bot.*) sorrel (*Rumex*).

щаве́льник, а, *m.* (*coll.*) sorrel soup.

ща|ди́ть, жу́, ди́шь, *impf.* (*of* по~) to spare; to have mercy (on); щ. чьи-н. чу́вства to spare someone's feelings; не щ. враго́в to give one's enemies no quarter.

щебёнк|а, и, *f.* = щебень.

ще́б|ень, ня, *m.* 1. crushed stone, ballast (*as road surfacing*). 2. (*geol.*) detritus.

щебет, а, *m.* twitter, chirp.

щебета́ни|е, я, *n.* twittering, chirping.

щебе|та́ть, чу́, ~чешь, *impf.* to twitter, chirp.

щегл|ёнок, ёнка, *pl.* ~я́та, *m.* 1. young goldfinch. 2. = щего́л.

щег|о́л, ла́, *m.* goldfinch.

щеголева́т|ый (~, ~a), *adj.* foppish, dandified.

щёгол|ь, я, *m.* fop, dandy.

щегол|ьну́ть, ьну́, ьнёшь, *pf. of* ~я́ть 2.

щегольско́й, *adj.* foppish, dandified.

щегольств|о́, а́, *n.* foppishness, dandyism.

щегол|я́ть, я́ю, *impf.* **1.** to dress ultra-fashionably, foppishly; to strut around. **2.** (*pf.* ~ьну́ть) (+*i.*; *coll.*) to show off, parade, flaunt.

щедрост|ь, и, *f.* generosity.

щедро́т|ы, ~, *sing.* ~а, ~ы, *f.* (*obs.*) munificence; подари́ть от свои́х ~ (*iron.*) to donate generously.

ще́др|ый (~, ~а́, ~о), *adj.* **1.** generous. **2.** lavish, liberal; щ. на похвалы́ lavish in praises.

щек|а́, и́, *a.* ~у, *pl.* ~и, ~, ~а́м, *f.* **1.** cheek; уда́рить кого́-н. по ~е́ to slap someone's face; упи́сывать, уплета́ть за о́бе ~й (*coll.*) to eat ravenously, guzzle. **2.** (*tech.*) side, sidepiece, stock.

щеко́лд|а, ы, *f.* latch; catch, pawl.

щеко|та́ть, чу́, ~чешь, *impf.* (*of* по~) **1.** to tickle (*also fig.*). **2.** (*impers.*) у меня́ в го́рле, *etc.,* ~чет I have a tickle in my throat, *etc.*

щеко́тк|а, и, *f.* tickling; боя́ться ~и to be ticklish.

щекотли́в|ый (~, ~а), *adj.* **1.** ticklish, delicate; ~ая те́ма delicate topic. **2.** (*obs.*) = щепети́льный.

щеко́тно, *as pred.* (*impers.*; +*i.*) it tickles.

щел|ево́й, *adj.* **1.** *adj. of* ~ь. **2.** = ~и́нный.

щели́нный, *adj.* (*ling.*) fricative.

щели́ст|ый (~, ~а), *adj.* (*coll.*) full of chinks.

щёлк, а, *m.* snap, crack.

щёлк|а, и, *f.* chink.

щёлканье, я, *n.* **1.** flicking. **2.** clicking, snapping, cracking, popping. **3.** trilling (*of some birds*).

щёлк|ать, аю, *impf.* (*of* ~нуть) **1.** to flick. **2.** (+*i.*) to click, snap, crack, pop; щ. затво́ром to click the shutter (*of a camera*); щ. па́льцами to snap one's fingers; щ. кнуто́м to crack a whip. **3.** (*impf. only*) to crack (*nuts*). **4.** (*impf. only*) to trill (*of some birds*).

щёлк|нуть, ну, нешь, *pf. of* ~ать.

щелкопёр, а, *m.* (*obs., pejor.*) scribbler, hack.

щелку́нчик, а, *m.* nutcracker.

щёлок, а, *m.* alkaline solution, lye.

щелочно́й, *adj.* (*chem.*) alkaline.

щёлочность|ь, и, *f.* (*chem.*) alkalinity.

щёлоч|ь, и, *pl.* ~и, ~е́й, *f.* (*chem.*) alkali.

щелч|о́к, ка́, *m.* **1.** flick (of the fingers). **2.** (*fig., coll.*) insult, slight, blow.

щел|ь, и, *pl.* ~и, ~е́й, *f.* **1.** crack; chink; slit; fissure, crevice. **2.** (*mil.*) slit trench. **3.** голосова́я щ. (*anat.*) glottis.

щем|и́ть, и́т, *impf.* **1.** (*coll.*) to press, pinch. **2.** to oppress, grieve (*also impers.*).

щем|я́щий, *pres. part. act. of* ~и́ть *and adj.* **1.** aching, nagging; ~я́щая боль ache. **2.** (*fig.*) painful, melancholy, oppressive.

щен|и́ться, и́тся, *impf.* (*of* о~) to whelp cub.

щен|о́к, ка́, *pl.* ~ки́, ~ко́в *and* ~я́та, ~я́т, *m.* puppy, pup (*also fig.*); whelp, cub.

щеп|а́, ы́, *pl.* ~ы, ~, ~а́м, *f.* (*wood*) splinter, chip; (*collect.*) kindling.

щеп|а́ть, лю́, ~ле́шь, *impf.* to chip, chop (*wood*).

щепети́л|ьный (~ен, ~ьна), *adj.* punctilious, correct; (over-)scrupulous, fussy, finicky.

щепк|а, и, *f.* = щепа́; худо́й как щ. thin as a rake; лес ру́бят — ~и летя́т (*prov.*) you can't make omelettes without breaking eggs.

щепо́т|ка, ки, *f.* = щепо́ть.

щепо́т|ь, и, *f.* pinch (*of salt, snuff, etc.*).

щерба́т|ый (~, ~а), *adj.* **1.** dented; chipped. **2.** (*coll.*) pock-marked. **3.** (*coll.*) gap-toothed.

щерби́н|а, ы, *f.* **1.** indentation; gap, hole. **2.** pock-mark.

щети́н|а, ы, *f.* bristle; (*coll.*) stubble (*of beard*).

щети́нист|ый (~, ~а), *adj.* bristly, bristling; (*coll.*) stubble-covered.

щети́н|иться, ится, *impf.* (*of* о~) to bristle (*also fig.*).

щётк|а, и, *f.* **1.** brush (*also electr.*); зубна́я щ. toothbrush; щ. для воло́с hairbrush. **2.** fetlock.

щёт|очный, *adj. of* ~ка; щ. па́лец (*electr.*) brush-holder arm.

щёчный, *adj. of* щека́.

щи, щей (*coll.* щец), щам, ща́ми, о ща́х, *no sing.* shchi (*cabbage soup*); попа́сть как кур во́ щи to get into hot water.

щи́колотк|а, и, *f.* ankle.

щип|а́ть, лю́, ~ле́шь, *impf.* **1.** (*pf.* ~ну́ть) to pinch, nip, tweak. **2.** (*impf. only*) to sting, bite (*of frost, etc.*); to burn (*of condiments, hot liquids, etc.*). **3.** (*impf. only*) to nibble, munch, browse (on). **4.** (*pf.* об~ *and* о~) to pluck.

щип|а́ться, лю́сь, ~ле́шься, *impf.* (*coll.*) **1.** to pinch (each other). **2.** *pass. of* ~а́ть.

щип|е́ц, ца́, *m.* **1.** (*archit.*) gable. **2.** (*hunting*) muzzle (*of dog*).

щипко́в|ый, *adj.* ~ые музыка́льные инстру́менты (*mus.*) stringed instruments played by plucking.

щипко́м, *adv.* (*mus.*) pizzicato.

щип|ну́ть, ну́, нёшь, *pf. of* ~а́ть 1.

щип|о́к, ка́, *m.* pinch, nip, tweak.

щипц|ы́, о́в, *no sing.* tongs, pincers, pliers; forceps; щ. для зави́вки воло́с curling-irons; щ. для са́хара sugar-tongs.

щи́пчик|и, ов, *no sing.* tweezers.

щит, а́, *m.* **1.** (*in var. senses*) shield; подня́ть на щ. to extol, eulogize, boost; верну́ться на ~е́ to suffer defeat; верну́ться со ~о́м to be triumphant, victorious. **2.** (*tech.*) shield, screen. **3.** sluice-gate. **4.** (*zool.*) (tortoise-)shell; scutum. **5.** (display) board.

6. (*tech.*) panel; распредели́тельный щ. switchboard.

щитови́дный, *adj.* (*anat.*) thyroid.

щит|о́к, ка́, *m.* **1.** *dim. of* ~ 2–6; dashboard (*of motor vehicle*). **2.** (*zool.*) thorax. **3.** (*bot.*) cyme, corymb. **4.** (*sport*) shin-pad.

щу́к|а, и, *f.* pike (*fish*).

щуп, а, *m.* (*tech.*) **1.** probe, sounding borer. **2.** (*mil.*) probing rod (*in mine detection*). **3.** clearance gauge. **4.** (*coll.*) dipstick.

щу́пальц|е, а, *g. pl.* **щу́палец**, *n.* (*zool.*) tentacle; antenna.

щу́па|ть, ю, *impf.* (*of* по~) to feel (for),

touch; to probe; щ. глаза́ми to scan; щ. пульс (*med.*) to feel the pulse.

щу́пл|ый (~, ~а́, ~о), *adj.* weak, puny, frail.

щур¹, а, *m.* (*ethnol.*) ancestor.

щур², а́, *m.* (*orn.*) pine grosbeak.

щу́р|ить, ю, ишь, *impf.* (*of* со~); щ. глаза́ = ~иться.

щу́р|иться, юсь, ишься, *impf.* (*of* со~) **1.** to screw up one's eyes. **2.** (*of the eyes*) to narrow.

щу́рк|а, и, *f.* (*orn.*) bee-eater.

щу́|чий, *adj. of* ~ка; как по ~чьему веле́нью as if of its own volition, as if by magic.

Э

эбе́новый, *adj.* ebony.

э́ва¹, *particle* (*coll. or dial.*) there is, here is.

э́ва², *interj.* (*coll.*) **1.** (*expressing surprise, incredulity, etc.*) what's that!; you don't mean to say so! **2.** (*expressing disagreement*) nonsense!

эвако- = эвакуацио́нный.

эвакуацио́нный, *adj. of* эвакуа́ция; э. пункт evacuation centre; э. райо́н evacuation area.

эвакуа́ци|я, и, *f.* evacuation.

эвакуи́ров|анный, *p.p.p. of* ~ать; *as noun* э., ~анного, *m.* and ~анная, ~анной, *f.* evacuee.

эвакуи́р|овать, ую, *impf. and pf.* to evacuate (*trans.*).

эвакуи́р|оваться, уюсь, *impf. and pf.* **1.** to evacuate (*intrans.*). **2.** *pass. of* ~овать.

эвентуа́л|ьный (~ен, ~ьна), *adj.* possible.

эвкали́пт, а, *m.* (*bot.*) eucalyptus.

эвкали́пт|овый, *adj. of* ~; ~овое ма́сло eucalyptus oil.

эволюциони́р|овать, ую, *impf. and pf.* to evolve.

эволюциони́ст, а, *m.* evolutionist.

эволюцио́нн|ый, *adj.* evolutionary; ~ое уче́ние (*biol.*) doctrine of evolution.

эволю́ци|я, и, *f.* **1.** evolution. **2.** (*mil.*) manœuvre.

эвфеми́зм, а, *m.* euphemism.

эвфемисти́ческий, *adj.* euphemistic.

эвфони́ческий, *adj.* euphonious.

эвфони́|я, и, *f.* euphony.

эги́д|а, ы, *f.* aegis; под ~ой (+*g.*) under the aegis (of).

эгои́зм, а, *m.* egoism, selfishness.

эгои́ст, а, *m.* egoist.

эгоисти́ческий, *adj.* egoistic, selfish.

эгоисти́ч|ный (~ен, ~на), *adj.* = ~еский.

эготи́зм, а, *m.* egotism.

эгре́т, а, *m.* egret-plume.

э́дак(ий) = э́так(ий).

эдельве́йс, а, *m.* (*bot.*) edelweiss.

эди́пов, *adj.* э. ко́мплекс (*psych.*) Oedipus complex.

эзо́пов = ~ский.

эзо́повский, *adj.* Aesopian; э. язы́к 'Aesopian language' (*especially of allegorical language used by Russian non-conformist publicists to conceal anti-régime sentiments*).

эй, *interj.* heigh!, hi!

эк (*and* э́ко, э́ка), *particle* (*coll.*) *expressing surprise, indignation, etc.* my goodness!

эквадо́р|ец, ца, *m.* Ecuadorian.

эквадо́р|ка, ки, *f. of* ~ец.

эквадо́рский, *adj.* Ecuadorian.

эква́тор, а, *m.* equator.

экваториа́льный, *adj.* equatorial.

эквивале́нт, а, *m.* equivalent.

эквивале́нт|ный (~ен, ~на), *adj.* equivalent.

эквилибри́ст, а, *m.* tightrope-walker.

эквилибри́стик|а, и, *f.* tightrope-walking (*also fig.*).

экзальта́ци|я, и, *f.* exaltation; excitement.

экзальти́рован|ный (~, ~на), *adj.* in a state of exaltation, exalté, excited.

экза́мен, а, *m.* examination; держа́ть, сдава́ть э. to take, sit an examination; вы́держать, сдать э. to pass an examination; провали́ться на ~е to fail an examination.

экзамена́тор, а, *m.* examiner.

экзамен|ацио́нный, *adj. of* экза́мен; э. биле́т examination question(-paper); ~ацио́нная се́ссия examination period, exams.

экзамен|ова́ть, у́ю, *impf.* (*of* про~) to examine.

экзамен|ова́ться, у́юсь, *impf.* (*of* про~) **1.** to go in for an examination. **2.** *pass. of* ~ова́ть.

экзамен|у́ющийся, *pres. part. of* ~ова́ться; *as noun* э., ~у́ющегося, *m.* examinee.

экза́рх, а, *m.* (*eccl.*) exarch.

экзарха́т, а, *m.* (*eccl.*) exarchate.

экзеку́тор, а, *m.* (*obs.*) administrator.

экзеку́ци|я, и, *f.* (*obs.*) 1. corporal punishment. 2. (*leg.*) execution.

экзе́м|а, ы, *f.* (*med.*) eczema.

экземпля́р, а, *m.* 1. copy; в двух, трёх ~ах in duplicate, in triplicate; переписа́ть в двух ~ах to make two copies. 2. specimen, example.

экзистенциали́зм, а, *m.* existentialism.

экзистенциали́ст, а, *m.* existentialist.

экзо- exo-.

экзо́тик|а, и, *f.* exotica, exotic objects.

экзоти́ческий, *adj.* exotic.

экивок|и, ов, *sing.* ~, ~а, *m.* 1. double entendre. 2. quibbling, evasion, hedging; говори́ть без ~ов to call a spade a spade. 3. subtleties, intricacies.

э́кий, *pron.* (*coll.*) what (a).

экипа́ж[1], а, *m.* carriage.

экипа́ж[2], а, *m.* crew (*of ship, aircraft, tank*); ship's company.

экипир|ова́ть, у́ю, *impf. and pf.* to equip.

экипиро́вк|а, и, *f.* 1. equipping. 2. equipment.

э́ккер, а, *m.* (*geod.*) cross-staff (*instrument for erecting a perpendicular*).

эклекти́зм, а, *m.* eclecticism.

экле́ктик, а, *m.* eclectic.

эклекти́ч|ный (~ен, ~на), *adj.* eclectic.

экли́птик|а, и, *f.* (*astron.*) ecliptic.

экло́г|а, и, *f.* (*lit.*) eclogue.

э́ко, *see* эк[2].

экологи́ческий, *adj.* ecological.

экологи|я, и, *f.* ecology.

эконо́м, а, *m.* (*obs.*) 1. steward, housekeeper. 2. economist.

экономайзер, а, *m.* (*tech.*) economiser, waste gas heater.

экономи́зм, а, *m.* (*hist., polit.*) economism.

эконо́мик|а, и, *f.* 1. economics 2. economy (*of a country, etc.*).

эконо́мист, а, *m.* economist.

эконо́м|ить, лю, ишь, *impf.* (*of* с~) 1. to use sparingly, husband; to save. 2. (на+*p.*) to economise (on), save (on).

экономи́ческ|ий, *adj.* economic; э. райо́н economic region; э. журна́л economics journal; ~ая горе́лка pilot burner; ~ая ско́рость cruising speed.

экономи́ч|ный (~ен, ~на), *adj.* economical.

эконо́ми|я, и, *f.* 1. economy, saving; режи́м ~и economy effort; соблюда́ть ~ю to economize. 2. полити́ческая э. political economy. 3. (*obs.*) estate.

эконо́мк|а, и, *f.* housekeeper.

эконо́мнича|ть, ю, *impf.* (*coll.*) to be (excessively) economical.

эконо́м|ный (~ен, ~на), *adj.* economical; careful, thrifty.

экра́н, а, *m.* 1. (*cinema*) screen. 2. (*fig.*) screen (= *cinema industry, cinema art*). 3. (*phys., tech.*) screen, shield, shade.

экраниза́ци|я, и, *f.* (*cinema*) filming, screening; film version (*of novel, etc.*).

экранизи́р|овать, ую, *impf. and pf.* (*cinema*) to film, screen.

экрани́р|овать, ую, *impf. and pf.* (*tech.*) to screen, shield.

экс-, ex-.

экскава́тор, а, *m.* (*tech.*) excavator, earth-moving machine.

экскава́торщик, а, *m.* excavator operator.

экскреме́нт|ы, ов, *no sing.* excrement.

э́кскурс, а, *m.* excursus, digression.

экскурса́нт, а, *m.* tourist; participant in (conducted) tour *or* excursion.

экскурс|ио́нный, *adj. of* ~ия.

экску́рси|я, и, *f.* 1. excursion, (conducted) tour, trip; outing. 2. tourist group, excursion party.

экскурсово́д, а, *m.* guide.

экскли́брис, а, *m.* book-plate.

экспанси́в|ный (~ен, ~на), *adj.* effusive.

экспансиони́зм, а, *m.* (*polit.*) expansionism.

экспа́нси|я, и, *f.* (*polit.*) expansion.

экспеди́р|овать, ую, *impf. and pf.* to despatch.

экспеди́тор, а, *m.* 1. forwarding agent, shipping clerk. 2. (*obs.*) head clerk (*head of a section in a large office*).

экспедицио́нный, *adj.* 1. despatch, forwarding. 2. expeditionary.

экспеди́ци|я, и, *f.* 1. despatch, forwarding. 2. despatch office. 3. (*obs.*) section, department (*of an office*). 4. expedition.

экспериме́нт, а, *m.* experiment.

эксперимента́льный, *adj.* experimental.

эксперимента́тор, а, *m.* experimenter.

эксперименти́р|овать, ую, *impf.* (над, с+*i.*) to experiment (on, with).

экспе́рт, а, *m.* expert.

эксперти́з|а, ы, *f.* (*leg., med.*) 1. (expert) examination, expert opinion; произвести́ ~y to make an examination. 2. commission of experts.

экспе́рт|ный, *adj. of* ~; ~ная коми́ссия commission of experts.

эксплози́вный, *adj.* (*ling.*) plosive.

эксплуата́тор, а, *m.* exploiter.

эксплуатац|ио́нный, *adj. of* ~ия 2; ~ио́нные ка́чества operating characteristics; ~ио́нные расхо́ды running costs; ~ио́нные усло́вия working conditions.

эксплуата́ци|я, и, *f.* 1. (*polit.; pejor.*) exploitation. 2. exploitation (*econ.*); utilization; operation, running; сдать в ~ю to commission, put into operation.

эксплуати́р|овать, ую, *impf.* **1.** (*polit.*; *pejor.*) to exploit. **2.** to exploit (*econ.*); to operate, run, work.

экспози́ци|я, и, *f.* **1.** layout (*of an exhibition, etc.*). **2.** (*lit.*) exposition. **3.** (*phot.*) exposure.

экспона́т, а, *m.* exhibit.

экспоне́нт, а, *m.* **1.** exhibitor. **2.** (*math.*) exponent, index.

экспони́р|овать, ую, *impf. and pf.* **1.** to exhibit. **2.** (*phot.*) to expose.

экспоно́метр, а, *m.* (*phot.*) exposure meter.

э́кспорт, а, *m.* export.

экспортёр, а, *m.* exporter.

экспорти́р|овать, ую, *impf. and pf.* to export.

э́кспорт|ный, *adj.* of ~.

экспре́сс, а, *m.* express (*train, motor coach, etc.*).

экспресси́в|ный (~ен, ~на), *adj.* expressive.

экспрессиони́зм, а, *m.* (*art*) expressionism.

экспре́сси|я, и, *f.* expression.

экспре́сс|ный, *adj.* of ~.

экспро́мт, а, *m.* impromptu, improvisation, extemporisation.

экспро́мтом, *adv.* **1.** impromptu; петь, игра́ть, *etc.*, э. to extemporise, improvise. **2.** suddenly, without warning.

экспроприа́тор, а, *m.* expropriator.

экспроприа́ци|я, и, *f.* expropriation.

экспроприи́р|овать, ую, *impf. and pf.* to expropriate, dispossess.

экста́з, а, *m.* ecstasy.

экстенси́в|ный (~ен, ~на), *adj.* extensive.

эксте́рн, а, *m.* **1.** external student; око́нчить университе́т ~ом to take an external degree. **2.** (*obs.*) externe (*unpaid hospital doctor*).

экстерна́т, а, *m.* external studies.

экстерриториа́льност|ь, и, *f.* extraterritoriality, exterritoriality.

экстерриториа́л|ьный (~ен, ~ьна), *adj.* extraterritorial, exterritorial.

экстерье́р, а, *m.* form, figure (*of an animal*).

экстравага́нт|ный (~ен, ~на), *adj.* eccentric, bizarre, preposterous.

экстраги́р|овать, ую, *impf. and pf.* (*chem., med.*) to extract.

экстради́ци|я, и, *f.* (*leg.*) extradition.

экстра́кт, а, *m.* **1.** (*cul.*) extract. **2.** resumé, précis.

экстра́кци|я, и, *f.* (*chem., med.*) extraction.

экстраордина́р|ный (~ен, ~на), *adj.* extraordinary; э. профе́ссор (*obs.*) professor extraordinary.

э́кстрен|ный (~, ~на), *adj.* **1.** urgent; emergency; э. вы́зов urgent summons; в ~ном слу́чае in case of emergency. **2.** extra, special; ~ное заседа́ние extraordinary session; ~ное изда́ние special edition.

эксце́нтрик¹, а, *m.* **1.** clown. **2.** (*obs.*) eccentric (person).

эксце́нтрик², а, *m.* (*tech.*) cam, eccentric.

эксце́нтрик|а, и, *f.* clowning.

эксцентрицитет, а, *m.* (*tech.*) eccentricity, off-centre.

эксцентри́ческий, *adj.* (*tech.*) eccentric.

эксцентри́чност|ь, и, *f.* eccentricity.

эксцентри́ч|ный (~ен, ~на), *adj.* eccentric.

эксце́сс, а, *m.* excess.

экумени́ческий, *adj.* ecumenical, oecumenical.

эласти́ч|ный (~ен, ~на), *adj.* **1.** elastic (*also fig.*). **2.** (*fig.*) springy, resilient.

элева́тор, а, *m.* **1.** (*agric.*) elevator. **2.** (*tech.*) hoist.

элега́нтност|ь, и, *f.* elegance.

элега́нт|ный (~ен, ~на), *adj.* elegant, smart.

элеги́ческий, *adj.* (*lit., mus.*) elegiac.

элеги́ч|ный (~ен, ~на), *adj.* melancholy.

эле́ги|я, и, *f.* (*lit., mus.*) elegy.

электриза́ци|я, и, *f.* (*phys., med.*) electrification; treatment by electric charge(s).

электриз|ова́ть, у́ю, *impf.* **1.** (*phys., med.*) to electrify, subject to electric charge(s). **2.** (*fig.*) to electrify.

эле́ктрик, а, *m.* electrician.

электри́к, *adj., indecl.* electric blue.

электрифика́ци|я, и, *f.* electrification.

электрифици́р|овать, ую, *impf. and pf.* (*tech.*) to electrify.

электри́ческий, *adj.* electric(al).

электри́честв|о, а, *n.* **1.** electricity. **2.** electric light; заже́чь э. to turn on the light.

электри́чк|а, и, *f.* (*coll.*) (suburban) electric train.

электро- electro-, electric.

электробытов|о́й, *adj.* electrical; ~ые прибо́ры electrical appliances (*irons, cleaners, etc.*).

электрово́з, а, *m.* electric locomotive.

электро́д, а, *m.* (*phys.*) electrode.

электродви́гател|ь, я, *m.* electric motor.

электродви́жущий, *adj.* (*phys.*) electromotive.

электродина́мик|а, и, *f.* electrodynamics.

электродои́льный, *adj.* electric milking.

электродо́йк|а, и, *f.* **1.** electric milking. **2.** electric milking machine.

электродугов|о́й, *adj.* ~а́я сва́рка electric arc welding.

электроёмкост|ь, и, *f.* (*phys.*) capacity.

электрока́р, а, *m.* electric trolley, float.

электрола́мп|а, ы, *f.* electric light bulb.

электролече́ни|е, я, *n.* (*med.*) electrical treatment.

электро́лиз, а, *m.* (*phys.*) electrolysis.

электромагни́т, а, *m.* electromagnet.

электромагни́тный, *adj.* electromagnetic.

электромеха́ник|а, и, *f.* electromechanics.
электромонтёр, а, *m.* electrician.
электро́н, а, *m.* (*phys.*) electron.
электро́ник|а, и, *f.* electronics.
электро́нно- electronic-.
электро́н|ный, *adj.* 1. *adj. of* ~; ~ная ла́мпа electron tube, thermionic valve; э. микроско́п electron microscope. 2. electronic; ~ная вычисли́тельная маши́на electronic computer.
электропереда́ч|а, и, *f.* electricity transmission.
электропе́ч|ь, и, *f.* electric furnace.
электроплит́к|а, и, *f.* (electric) hotplate.
электропо́езд, а, *m.* electric train.
электроприбо́р, а, *m.* electrical appliance.
электропро́вод, а, *m.* electricity cable.
электропрово́дк|а, и, *f.* electric wiring.
электропромы́шленност|ь, и, *f.* electrical industry.
электросва́рк|а, и, *f.* electric welding.
электросилово́й, *adj.* electric power.
электроста́л|ь, и, *f.* electric steel.
электроста́нци|я, и, *f.* electric power station.
электроте́хник, а, *m.* electrical engineer.
электроте́хник|а, и, *f.* electrical engineering.
электротех|ни́ческий, *adj. of* ~ника.
электротя́г|а, и, *f.* electric traction.
электрохими́ческий, *adj.* electrochemical.
электрохи́ми|я, и, *f.* electro-chemistry.
электроцентра́л|ь, и, *f.* electric power plant.
электроча́йник, а, *m.* electric kettle.
электроэне́рги|я, и, *f.* electric power.
элеме́нт, а, *m.* 1. (*in var. senses*) element. 2. (*coll.*) type, character; подозри́тельный э. suspicious type. 3. (*electr.*) cell, battery; сухо́й э. dry cell; рабо́тать от ~ов to be battery-operated.
элемента́р|ный (~ен, ~на), *adj.* (*in var. senses*) elementary.
элеро́н, а, *m.* (*aeron.*) aileron.
эли́т|а, ы, *f.* 1. (*collect.*; *agric.*) best specimens; э. карто́феля highest-quality potatoes. 2. élite.
эли́т|ный, *adj. of* ~а.
э́ллин, а, *m.* ancient Greek, Hellene.
э́ллинг, а, *m.* 1. (*naut.*) slipway. 2. (*aeron.*) shed, hangar (*for airships or balloons*).
эллини́зм, а, *m.* 1. Hellenism. 2. (*hist.*) the Hellenistic period.
эллини́ст, а, *m.* Hellenist.
эллинисти́ческий, *adj.* (*hist.*) Hellenistic.
э́ллин|ка, ки, *f. of* ~.
э́ллинский, *adj.* ancient Greek, Hellenic.
э́ллипс, а, *m.* (*math.*, *lit.*) ellipse.
э́ллипс|ис, а, *m.* = ~.
эллипти́ческий, *adj.* elliptic(al).

эл|ь, я, *m.* ale.
эльф, а, *m.* elf.
элю́ви|й, я, *m.* (*geol.*) eluvium.
эма́левый, *adj.* enamel.
эмалиро́в|анный, *p.p.p. of* ~а́ть *and adj.* enamelled; ~анная посу́да enamel ware.
эмалир|ова́ть, у́ю, *impf.* to enamel.
эмалиро́вк|а, и, *f.* 1. enamelling. 2. enamel.
эма́л|ь, и, *f.* enamel.
эмана́ци|я, и, *f.* emanation.
эмансипа́ци|я, и, *f.* emancipation.
эмансипи́р|овать, ую, *impf. and pf.* to emancipate.
эмба́рго, *indecl.*, *n.* (*econ.*) embargo; наложи́ть э. (на+*a.*) to embargo, place an embargo (on).
эмбле́м|а, ы, *f.* 1. emblem. 2. (*mil.*) insignia.
эмболи́|я, и, *f.* (*med.*) embolism.
эмбриоло́ги|я, и, *f.* embryology.
эмбрио́н, а, *m.* (*biol.*) embryo.
эмерита́льн|ый, *adj.* ~ая ка́сса old age insurance scheme.
эмериту́р|а, ы, *f.* (*obs.*) old age benefit (*secured by voluntary contributions*).
эмигра́нт, а, *m.* emigré, emigrant.
эмигра́нт|ский, *adj. of* ~.
эмигра|цио́нный, *adj. of* ~ция.
эмигра́ци|я, и, *f.* 1. emigration. 2. (*collect.*) emigration, emigrés.
эмигри́р|овать, ую, *impf. and pf.* to emigrate.
эмисса́р, а, *m.* emissary.
эмисс|ио́нный, *adj. of* ~ия.
эми́сси|я, и, *f.* (*fin.*, *phys.*) emission.
эмоциона́л|ьный (~ен, ~ьна), *adj.* emotional.
эмо́ци|я, и, *f.* emotion.
эмпире́|й, я, *m.* empyrean; вита́ть в ~ях to have one's head in the clouds.
эмпири́зм, а, *m.* empiricism.
эмпи́рик, а, *m.* empiricist.
эмпириокритици́зм, а, *m.* (*philos.*) empirio-criticism.
эмпири́ческий, *adj.* 1. (*philos.*) empiricist. 2. empirical.
эмпири́ч|ный (~ен, ~на), *adj.* = ~еский 2.
э́му, *indecl.*, *m.* emu.
эму́льси|я, и, *f.* emulsion.
эмфа́з|а, ы, *f.* (*ling.*) emphasis.
эмфати́ческий, *adj.* (*ling.*) emphatic.
эндокри́нн|ый, *adj.* (*physiol.*) endocrine; ~ые же́лезы endocrine glands, ductless glands.
эндокриноло́ги|я, и, *f.* endocrinology.
э́ндшпил|ь, я, *m.* (*chess*) end-game.
энерге́тик, а, *m.* power engineering specialist.
энерге́тик|а, и, *f.* power engineering.
энергет|и́ческий, *adj. of* ~ика; ~и́ческая ба́за (*econ.*) power supply sources, power base.

энерги́ч|ный (~ен, ~на), adj. energetic, vigorous, forceful.

эне́рги|я, и, f. 1. (phys.) energy; затра́та ~и energy consumption; растра́та ~и energy loss. 2. (fig.) energy; vigour, effort.

энерго-, power-.

энергоёмкий, adj. power-consuming.

энергосисте́м|а, ы, f. power (supply) system.

энкли́тик|а, и, f. (ling.) enclitic.

энклити́ческий, adj. (ling.) enclitic.

э́нн|ый, adj. (expressing indefinite quantity, size, duration of time, etc.) 'N', 'X'; any, unspecified; в ~ой сте́пени to the nth degree; ~ое коли́чество вре́мени n hours, an inordinate length of time.

э́нск|ий, adj. (denoting a military unit, establishment, etc., which cannot be identified for reasons of security) 'N', an unspecified; ~ая заста́ва погранво́йск frontier guards' post 'N'.

энтомо́лог, а, m. entomologist.

энтомологи́ческий, adj. entomological.

энтомоло́ги|я, и, f. entomology.

энтропи́|я, и, f. (phys.) entropy.

энтузиа́зм, а, m. enthusiasm.

энтузиа́ст, а, m. (+g.) enthusiast (about, for), devotee (of); э. футбо́ла football enthusiast.

энцефали́т, а, m. (med.) encephalitis.

энци́клик|а, и, f. (eccl.) encyclical.

энциклопеди́зм, а, m. encyclopaedic learning.

энциклопеди́ст, а, m. 1. (hist.) Encyclopaedist. 2. person of encyclopaedic learning.

энциклопеди́ческий, adj. encyclopaedic; э. слова́рь encyclopaedia; э. ум encyclopaedic brain.

энциклопе́ди|я, и, f. encyclopaedia; ходя́чая э. (joc.) walking encyclopaedia.

эоли́т, а, m. (archaeol.) eolithic period.

эо́лов, adj. ~а а́рфа Aeolian harp.

эоце́н, а, m. (geol.) eocene period.

эпати́р|овать, ую, impf. and pf. to shock.

эпиго́н, а, m. (pejor.) imitator, unoriginal follower.

эпиго́н|ский, adj. of ~.

эпиго́нств|о, а, n. (pejor.) imitation, unoriginal following (of another's work).

эпигра́мм|а, ы, f. epigram.

эпи́граф, а, m. epigraph.

эпигра́фик|а, и, f. epigraphy.

эпиде́ми|я, и, f. epidemic.

эпиде́рм|а, ы, f. (obs.) = ~ис.

эпиде́рмис, а, m. (biol.) epidermis.

эпизо́д, а, m. episode.

эпизоди́ческий, adj. episodic; occasional, sporadic.

эпизооти́|я, и, f. epizootic (of cattle diseases).

э́пик, а, m. epic poet.

э́пик|а, и, f. epic poetry.

эпикуре́|ец, йца, m. epicurean.

эпикуре́йский, adj. epicurean.

эпикуре́йств|о, а, n. epicureanism.

эпиле́пси|я, и, f. (med.) epilepsy.

эпиле́птик, а, m. epileptic (person).

эпилепти́ческий, adj. epileptic.

эпило́г, а, m. epilogue.

эпистоля́рный, adj. epistolary.

эпита́фи|я, и, f. epitaph.

эпи́тет, а, m. epithet.

эпице́нтр, а, m. (geol.) epicentre.

эпици́кл, а, m. (math.) epicycle.

эпи́ческий, adj. epic.

эполе́т|ы, ~, sing. ~а, ~ы, f. epaulettes.

эпопе́|я, и, f. (lit. or fig.) epic.

э́пос, а, m. epos, epic literature.

эпо́х|а, и, f. epoch, age, era.

эпоха́льный, adj. epoch-making.

эпю́р, а, m. diagram, drawing.

э́р|а, ы, f. era; до на́шей ~ы в.с.; на́шей ~ы A.D.

эрг, а, m. erg (unit of work).

э́ре, indecl., n. öre, øre (Scandinavian unit of currency).

эре́кци|я, и, f. (physiol.) erection.

эрза́ц, а, m. ersatz.

эритроци́т, а, m. (physiol.) red corpuscle.

э́ркер, а, m. (archit.) oriel (window).

эроди́р|овать, ую, impf. to erode.

эро́зи|я, и, f. erosion.

эроти́зм, а, m. eroticism.

эро́тик|а, и, f. sensuality.

эроти́ческий, adj. erotic, sensual.

эроти́ч|ный (~ен, ~на), adj. = ~еский.

эротома́н, а, m. erotomaniac, sexual maniac.

эротома́ни|я, и, f. erotomania.

эрсте́д, а, m. oersted (unit of magnetism).

эруди́рован|ный (~, ~на), adj. erudite.

эруди́т, а, m. erudite person.

эруди́ци|я, и, f. erudition.

эрцге́рцог, а, m. archduke.

эрцгерцоги́н|я, и, f. archduchess.

эрцге́рцогств|о, а, n. archduchy, archdukedom.

эсде́к, а, m. (hist.) S.D. (member of Social Democratic Party).

эсе́р, а, m. (hist.) S.R. (member of Socialist Revolutionary Party).

эсе́ровский, adj. (hist.) S.R. (Socialist Revolutionary).

эска́др|а, ы, f. (naut.) squadron.

эска́др|енный, adj. of ~а; э. броненосец (obs.) battleship; э. миноносец destroyer.

эскадри́л|ьный, adj. of ~ья.

эскадри́л|ья, ьи, g. pl. ~ий, f. (aeron.) squadron.

эскадро́н, а, *m.* (*mil.*) (*cavalry*) squadron, troop.

эскадро́н|ный, *adj. of* ~.

эскала́тор, а, *m.* escalator.

эскала́ци|я, и, *f.* (*mil.*) escalation.

эскало́п, а, *m.* (*cul.*) cutlet(s).

эска́рп, а, *m.* (*mil.*) scarp, escarpment.

эски́з, а, *m.* sketch, study; draft, outline.

эски́з|ный, *adj. of* ~; э. чертёж draft, outline sketch.

эскимо́, *indecl., n.* choc(olate) ice.

эскимо́с, а, *m.* Eskimo.

эскимо́с|ка, ки, *f. of* ~.

эскимо́сский, *adj.* Eskimo.

эско́рт, а, *m.* (*mil.*) escort.

эскорти́р|овать, ую, *impf. and pf.* (*mil.*) to escort.

эсми́н|ец, ца, *m.* (*abbr. of* эска́дренный миноно́сец) (*naut.*) destroyer.

эспадро́н, а, *m.* (*fencing*) cutting-sword, back-sword.

эспаньо́лк|а, и, *f.* imperial (*beard*).

эспарце́т, а, *m.* (*bot.*) sainfoin.

эссе́, *indecl., n.* essay.

эссе́нци|я, и, *f.* (*in var. senses*) essence.

эстака́д|а, ы, *f.* 1. viaduct, platform (*carrying elevated railway*); gantry. 2. flyover. 3. (*naut.*) pier. 4. (*naut.*) boom (*of harbour*).

эстака́д|ный, *adj. of* ~а; ~ная желе́зная доро́га elevated railway; э. кран gantry crane.

эста́мп, а, *m.* (*art*) print, engraving, plate.

эстафе́т|а, ы, *f.* 1. (*sport*) relay race. 2. baton (*in relay race*); приня́ть у кого́-н. ~у (*fig.*) to carry on someone's work, maintain someone's tradition. 3. (*obs.*) mail (*carried by relays of horsemen*).

эсте́т, а, *m.* aesthete.

эстети́зм, а, *m.* aestheticism.

эсте́тик|а, и, *f.* 1. aesthetics. 2. design; промы́шленная э. industrial design.

эстети́ческий, *adj.* aesthetic.

эсте́т|ский, *adj. of* ~.

эсте́тств|о, а, *n.* aestheticism.

эсто́н|ец, ца, *m.* Estonian.

эсто́н|ка, ки, *f. of* ~ец.

эсто́нский, *adj.* Estonian.

эстраго́н, а, *m.* (*bot.*) tarragon.

эстра́д|а, ы, *f.* 1. stage, platform; вы́йти на ~у to come on stage. 2. variety (*art*); арти́ст ~ы variety performer, artiste.

эстра́д|ный, *adj. of* ~а; э. конце́рт variety show.

эстуа́ри|й, я, *m.* estuary.

эсэ́сов|ец, ца, *m.* (*hist.*) SS man.

эсэ́совский, *adj.* (*hist.*) SS.

эта́ж, а́, *m.* storey, floor; пе́рвый, второ́й, *etc.*, э. ground floor, first floor, *etc.*

этаже́рк|а, и, *f.* bookcase, shelves.

эта́жност|ь, и, *f.* number of storeys.

э́так, *adv.* (*coll.*) 1. so, thus; мо́жно э́то сде́лать и так и э. you can do it like this or like that. 2. about, approximately.

э́такий, *pron.* (*coll.*) such (a), what (a).

этало́н, а, *m.* standard (*of weights and measures*).

эта́н, а, *m.* (*chem.*) ethane.

эта́п, а, *m.* 1. stage, phase. 2. (*sport*) lap. 3. halting-place, stage (*for troops; formerly, for groups of deported convicts in transit*); отпра́вить по ~у, ~ом to transport, deport (*under guard*).

эта́пник, а, *m.* (*hist.*) convict in transit.

эта́п|ный, *adj. of* ~; ~ное собы́тие (*fig.*) landmark, turning-point; отпра́вить ~ным поря́дком (*hist.*) to transport, deport (*under guard*).

э́тик|а, и, *f.* ethics.

этике́т, а, *m.* etiquette.

этике́тк|а, и, *f.* label.

эти́л, а, *m.* (*chem.*) ethyl.

этиле́н, а, *m.* (*chem.*) ethylene.

эти́л|овый, *adj. of* ~; э. спирт ethyl alcohol.

этимо́лог, а, *m.* etymologist.

этимологи́ческий, *adj.* etymological.

этимоло́ги|я, и, *f.* etymology; наро́дная э. popular etymology.

эти́ческий, *adj. of* э́тика.

эти́ч|ный (~ен, ~на), *adj.* ethical.

этни́ческий, *adj.* ethnic.

этно́граф, а, *m.* ethnographer, social anthropologist.

этнографи́ческий, *adj.* ethnographic(al).

этногра́фи|я, и, *f.* ethnography, social anthropology.

э́то[1], *see* э́тот.

э́то[2], *emphatic particle* (*coll.*); куда́ э. он де́лся? wherever has he got to?; что э. ты не гото́в? why on earth aren't you ready?; э. вы спра́шивали? was it *you* who was asking?

э́то[3], *pron.* (*as noun*) this (is), that (is); э. наш дом this is our house; э. вам помо́жет this will help you; э. ве́рно that is true; не в э́том де́ло that's not the point; об э́том я вам пото́м расскажу́ I will tell you about it later; э. я ви́жу so I can see.

э́тот, э́та, э́то, *pl.* э́ти, *pron.* this (these); *as noun* (*i*) this one, (*ii*) the latter.

этру́ск, а, *m.* Etruscan.

этру́сский, *adj.* Etruscan.

этю́д, а, *m.* 1. (*art, lit.*) study, sketch. 2. (*mus.*) étude. 3. (*mus.*) exercise; (*chess*) problem.

эфемери́д|ы, ~, *sing.* ~а, ~ы, *f.* 1. (*zool.*) ephemeridae. 2. (*astron.*) ephemerides.

эфеме́р|ный (~ен, ~на), *adj.* ephemeral.

эфе́с, а, *m.* hilt, handle (*of sword, sabre, etc.*).

эфио́п, а, *m.* Ethiopian.

эфио́п|ка, ки, *f. of* ~.

эфиопский, *adj.* Ethiopian.

эфи́р, а, *m.* **1.** ether; (*fig.*) air; передава́ть в э. to put on the air, broadcast. **2.** (*chem.*) ether; просто́й э. ether; сло́жный э. ester.

эфи́р|ный (~ен, ~на), *adj.* **1.** ethereal. **2.** (*chem.*) ether, ester; ~ное ма́сло essential oil, volatile oil.

эфироно́с, а, *m.* volatile-oil-bearing plant.

эфироно́сный, *adj.* volatile-oil-bearing.

эффе́кт, а, *m.* **1.** effect, impact; произвести́ э. (на + *a.*) to have an effect (on), make an impression (on). **2.** (*econ.*) result, consequences. **3.** (*pl.*) (*theatr.*) effects; шумовы́е ~ы sound effects.

эффекти́в|ный (~ен, ~на), *adj.* effective, efficacious.

эффе́кт|ный (~ен, ~на), *adj.* **1.** effective (= *making an impact*), striking. **2.** done for effect.

эх, *interj.* *expressing regret, reproval, amazement, etc.*; eh!, oh!

эхма́, *interj.* = эх.

э́х|о, а, *n.* echo.

эхоло́т, а, *m.* (*naut.*) sonic depth finder, echo sounder.

эшафо́т, а, *m.* scaffold; взойти́ на э. to mount the scaffold.

эшело́н, а, *m.* **1.** (*mil.*) échelon. **2.** special train.

эшелони́р|овать, ую, *impf. and pf.* (*mil.*) to échelon; э. оборо́ну to dispose defence in depth.

Ю

юа́н|ь, я, *m.* yuan (*Chinese currency unit*).

юбиле́|й, я, *m.* **1.** anniversary; jubilee. **2.** anniversary celebrations.

юбиле́й|ный, *adj.* of ~.

юбиля́р, а, *m.* person (or institution) whose anniversary is celebrated.

ю́бк|а, и, *f.* skirt; держа́ться за чью-н. ~у to cling to someone's apron-strings.

ю́бочк|а, и, *f.* short skirt.

ю́бочник, а, *m.* (*coll.*) womanizer.

ю́б|очный, *adj.* of ~ка.

ювели́р, а, *m.* jeweller.

ювели́р|ный, *adj.* **1.** *adj. of* ~; ~ные изде́лия gold and silver ware, jewelry; ю. магази́н jeweller's. **2.** (*fig.*) fine, intricate.

юг, а, *m.* south; the South (*of Russia, etc.*); на ю́ге in the south; к ю́гу от to the south of.

юго-восто́к, а, *m.* south-east.

юго-восто́чный, *adj.* south-east(ern).

юго-за́пад, а, *m.* south-west.

юго-за́падный, *adj.* south-west(ern).

югосла́в, а, *m.* Yugoslav.

югосла́в|ка, ки, *f.* of ~.

югосла́вский, *adj.* Yugoslav.

юдо́л|ь, и, *f.* (*arch.*) valley; ю. пла́ча, ю. печа́ли, земна́я ю. 'vale of tears'.

юдофо́б, а, *m.* anti-Semite.

юдофо́бств|о, а, *n.* anti-Semitism.

южа́н|ин, ина, *pl.* ~е, ~, *m.* southerner.

южн|е́е, comp. *of* ~ый; ю. Ло́ндона to the south of London.

ю́жный, *adj.* south, southern; Ю. по́люс South Pole; Ю. поля́рный круг antarctic circle; ю. темпера́мент (*fig.*) southern temperament.

ю́зом, *adv.* skidding, in a skid.

ю́кк|а, и, *f.* (*bot.*) yucca.

юл|а́, ы́, *f.* **1.** top (*child's toy*). **2.** (*coll.*) fidget. **3.** (*orn.*) wood lark.

юл|и́ть, ю́, и́шь, *impf.* (*coll.*) **1.** to fuss, fidget. **2.** (пе́ред) to play up (to).

ю́мор, а, *m.* humour; чу́вство ~а a sense of humour.

юморе́ск|а, и, *f.* (*mus., lit.*) humoresque.

юмори́ст, а, *m.* humourist.

юмори́стик|а, и, f. **1.** (*collect.*) humour. **2.** (*coll.*) something funny.

юмористи́ческий, *adj.* humorous, comic, funny.

юнг|а, и, *m.* ship's boy; sea cadet.

юн|е́ц, ца́, *m.* (*coll.*) youth.

ю́нкер, а, *m.* (*hist.*) **1.** (*pl.* ~а́, ~о́в) cadet. **2.** (*pl.* ~ы, ~ов) Junker (*Prussian landowner*).

ю́нкер|ский, *adj.* of ~.

юнна́т, а, *m.* abbr. of ю́ный натурали́ст.

ю́ност|ь, и, *f.* youth (*age*).

ю́нош|а, и, *m.* youth (*person*).

ю́ношеский, *adj.* youthful.

ю́ношеств|о, а, *n.* **1.** youth (*age*). **2.** (*collect.*) youth, young people.

ю́н|ый (~, ~а́, ~о), *adj.* **1.** young; теа́тр ~ого зри́теля young people's theatre; ю. натурали́ст member of junior natural history study group. **2.** youthful.

юпи́тер, а, *m.* floodlight.

юр, а, *m.* only in phrase на ~у́ (*i*) in a high, exposed place, (*ii*) (*fig.*) in the limelight, in the forefront.

ю́р|а, ы, *f.* (*geol.*) Jurassic period.

юр|а́, ы́, *f.* (*dial.*) large shoal (*of fish*); school (*of marine animals*).

юриди́ческ|ий, *adj.* legal, juridical; ~ая консульта́ция legal advice office; ~ое лицо́ juridical person; ~ие нау́ки jurisprudence, law; ю. факульте́т faculty of law.

юрисди́кци|я, и, *f.* jurisdiction.

юрисконсу́льт, а, *m.* legal adviser.

юриспруде́нци|я, и, *f.* jurisprudence, law (*as an academic discipline*).

юри́ст, а, *m.* legal expert, lawyer.

юр|кий (~о́к, ~ка́, ~ко), *adj.* 1. quick-moving, brisk. 2. (*fig., coll.*) clever, sharp, smart.

юркн|у́ть, у́, ёшь, *pf.* to scamper away, dart away, plunge.

юро́див|ый, *adj.* 1. crazy, simple, touched. 2. *as noun* **ю., ~ого,** *m.* 'God's fool' (*idiot believed to possess divine gift of prophecy*).

юро́дств|о, а, *n.* 1. craziness, idiocy. 2. idiotic action.

юро́дств|овать, ую, *impf.* to behave like an idiot.

ю́рский, *adj.* (*geol.*) Jurassic.

юрт|а, ы, *f.* yurt, yurta (*nomad's tent in Central Asia*).

ю́рьев, *adj.* Ю. день St. George's Day; вот тебе́ и Ю. день! here's a fine how d'ye do!

юс, а, *pl.* **~ы́,** *m.* (*ling.*) yus (*name of two letters originally representing nasal vowels in Old Church Slavonic*); юс большо́й large 'yus' (Ж); юс ма́лый little 'yus' (Ѧ).

юстир|ова́ть, у́ю, *impf. and pf.* to adjust, regulate (*instruments*).

юсти́ци|я, и, *f.* justice.

ют, а, *m.* (*naut.*) quarter-deck.

ю|ти́ться, чу́сь, ти́шься, *impf.* to huddle (together); to take shelter.

юфт|евый, *adj. of* ~ь.

юфт|ь, и, *f.* yuft, Russia leather.

юфт|яно́й = ~евый.

Я

я, меня́, мне, мной (мно́ю), обо мне, *personal pron.* I (me); я не я (*coll.*) it's nothing to do with me; (я) не я бу́ду, е́сли не добью́сь от него́ извине́ния I'll damn well see that I get an apology from him; *as noun, n., indecl.* the self, the ego; второ́е я alter ego.

я́бед|а, ы, *f.* 1. (*obs.*) information, slander. 2. (*m. and f.*) = ~ник.

я́бедник, а, *m.* (*coll.*) informer, sneak.

я́беднича|ть, ю, *impf.* (*of* на~) (на+*a.*; *coll.*) to inform (on), tell tales (about).

я́блок|о, а, *pl.* **~и, ~,** *n.* apple; глазно́е я. eyeball; в ~ах (*of a horse's coat*) dappled; я. раздо́ра bone of contention; ~у не́где упа́сть there's not room to swing a cat.

я́блон|евый, *adj. of* ~я.

я́блон|ный = ~евый.

я́блон|я, и, *f.* apple-tree.

я́блочк|о, а, *n. dim. of* я́блоко.

я́бло|чный, *adj. of* ~ко.

яв|и́ть, лю́, ~ишь, *pf.* (*of* ~ля́ть) to show, display; я. (собо́й) приме́р (+*g.*) to give an example (of), display.

яв|и́ться, лю́сь, ~ишься, *pf.* (*of* ~ля́ться) 1. to appear, present oneself; to report; я. в суд to appear before the court; я. на слу́жбу to report for duty; я. с пови́нной to give oneself up. 2. to turn up, arrive, show up. 3. to arise, occur; у меня́ ~и́лась блестя́щая мысль I had a brilliant idea; ~и́лся удо́бный слу́чай a suitable opportunity presented itself.

я́вк|а, и, *f.* 1. appearance, attendance; я. в суд appearance in court. 2. secret rendezvous; signal for secret rendezvous. 3. (*obs.*) information.

явле́ни|е, я, *n.* 1. phenomenon; occurrence, happening. 2. (*theatr.*) scene.

явле́нный, *adj.* (*rel.*) appearing miraculously (*esp. of icons*).

явля́|ть, ю, *impf. of* яви́ть.

явля́|ться, юсь, *impf.* 1. *impf. of* яви́ться. 2. (*impf. only*) (+*i.*) to be; to serve (as); э́то ~ется кощу́нством this is blasphemy.

я́вно¹, *adv.* manifestly, patently; obviously.

я́вно², *as pred.* it is manifest, patent; it is obvious.

я́в|ный (~ен, ~на), *adj.* 1. manifest, patent; overt, explicit. 2. obvious.

я́вор, а, *m.* sycamore (*tree*).

я́вор|овый, *adj. of* ~.

я́вочн|ый, *adj.* 1. *adj. of* я́вка 2; ~ая кварти́ра secret rendezvous. 2. (*mil.*) reporting; recruiting; я. пункт reporting point (*for conscripts*); я. уча́сток recruiting office. 3. ~ым поря́дком on the spur of the moment, without prior arrangement.

я́вствен|ный (~, ~на), *adj.* clear, distinct.

я́вств|овать, ует, *impf.* to appear; to be clear, apparent, obvious; to follow (*logically*).

яв|ь, и, *f.* reality.

ягдта́ш, а, *m.* game-bag.

я́гел|ь, я, *m.* (*bot.*) Iceland moss, reindeer moss.

ягн|ёнок, ёнка, *pl.* **~я́та, ~я́т,** *m.* lamb.

ягн|и́ться, и́тся, *impf.* (*of* о~) to lamb.

ягня́тник, а, *m.* lammergeier (*vulture*).

я́год|а, ы, *f.* berry; (*collect.*) soft fruit (*strawberries, blackcurrants, etc.*); ви́нная я. dried fig; пойти́ по ~ы to go berry-picking; одного́ по́ля я. a soul-mate.

я́годиц|а, ы, *f.* buttock(s).
я́годи|чный, *adj. of* ~ца.
я́годник, а, *m.* 1. berry plantation. 2. berry bush. 3. (*coll.*) berry-picker.
я́год|ный, *adj. of* ~a.
ягуа́р, а, *m.* jaguar.
яд, а (у), *m.* poison; venom (*also fig.*).
я́дерн|ый, *adj.* 1. (*phys.*) nuclear; ~ое расщепле́ние nuclear fission; я. реа́ктор nuclear reactor; ~ая фи́зика nuclear physics. 2. *adj. of* ядро́.
ядови́т|ый (~, ~а), *adj.* 1. poisonous; toxic; я. газ poison gas; ~ая змея́ poisonous snake. 2. (*fig.*) venomous, malicious.
ядохимика́т, а, *m.* (*agric.*) chemical weed- and/or pest-killer.
ядрён|ый (~, ~а), *adj.* (*coll.*) 1. having a large kernel (*of nuts*); juicy (*of fruit*); hearty (*of cabbages*). 2. (*fig.*) healthy, vigorous. 3. (*fig.*) fresh, bracing.
ядр|о́, á, *pl.* ~a, **я́дер,** ~ам, *n.* 1. kernel; core. 2. (*phys.*) nucleus. 3. (*mil., etc.*) main body (*of a unit, group*). 4. (*hist., mil.*) ball, shot. 5. (*sport*) shot; толка́ние ~á putting the shot.
ядро́|вый, *adj. of* ~ I; ~вое мы́ло high--grade soap.
я́дрышк|о, а, *pl.* ~и, *n.* 1. *dim. of* ядро́. 2. (*biol.*) nucleolus.
я́зв|а, ы, *f.* 1. ulcer, sore; я. желу́дка stomach ulcer; морова́я я. plague; сиби́р-ская я. malignant anthrax. 2. (*fig.*) harm; plague, curse. 3. (*fig., coll.*) malicious per-son; (*as term of abuse*) scum.
я́звенн|ый, *adj.* ulcerous; ~ая боле́знь stomach ulcer.
я́звин|а, ы, *f.* 1. indentation, pit. 2. (*coll.*) large ulcer.
язви́тел|ьный (~ен, ~ьна), *adj.* caustic, biting, sarcastic.
язв|и́ть, лю́, и́шь, *impf.* (*of* съ~) 1. (*obs.*) to wound; to sting. 2. to say sarcastically; to mock; я. на чей-н. счёт to be sarcastic at someone's expense.
язы́к¹, á, *pl.* ~и́, *m.* 1. tongue; у него́ я. без косте́й he is too fond of talking; у него́ что на уме́, то и на ~é (*coll.*) he cannot keep his thoughts to himself; держа́ть я. за зуба́ми, придержа́ть я. to hold one's tongue; прикуси́ть я. (*coll.*) to shut up; я. у него́ хорошо́ подве́шен (*coll.*) he has a glib tongue; распусти́ть я. (*coll.*) to talk too glibly; дёргать, тяну́ть кого́-н. за я. (*coll.*) to make someone talk; сорвало́сь с ~á (*fig.*) it slipped out; лиши́ться ~á (*fig.*) to lose one's tongue; я. у меня́ не поверну́лся э́то сказа́ть (*coll.*) I could not bring myself to say it; чеса́ть, болта́ть ~óм (*coll.*) to natter, blather; я. у меня́ чеса́лся (*coll.*) I was itching to speak; я. прогло́тишь (*coll.*)

it makes one's mouth water. 2. (*cul.*) tongue; копчёный я. smoked tongue. 3. clapper (*of a bell*). 4. (*mil.; coll.*) prisoner who will talk (*will provide information when interrogated*).
язы́к², á, *pl.* ~и́, *m.* 1. language (*also fig.*); владе́ть мно́гими ~а́ми to know many languages; говори́ть на ло́маном ру́сском ~é to talk in broken Russian; найти́ о́бщий я. (*fig.*) to find a common language. 2. (*pl.* ~и) (*obs.*) people, nationality, nation.
языка́ст|ый (~, ~а), *adj.* (*coll.*) sharp--tongued.
языкове́д, а, *m.* linguist, specialist on lin-guistics.
языкове́дени|е, я, *n.* linguistics.
языкове́д|ческий, *adj. of* ~ение.
языково́й, *adj.* linguistic.
языко́вый, *adj.* 1. (*anat.*) tongue, lingual. 2. (*cul.*) tongue.
языкозна́ни|е, я, *n.* linguistics, science of language.
язы́ческий, *adj.* heathen, pagan.
язы́честв|о, а, *n.* heathenism, paganism.
язы́ч|ковый, *adj. of* ~о́к; я. инструме́нт (*mus.*) reed instrument.
язы́чник, а, *m.* heathen, pagan.
язы́|чный, *adj. of* ~к¹ I.
язы́ч|о́к, ка́, *m.* 1. (*anat.*) uvula. 2. (*mus.*) reed. 3. (*tech.*) catch, lug. 4. *dim. of* язы́к.
язь|, я́, *m.* ide (*fish of carp family*).
яи́чк|о, а, *pl.* ~и, *n.* 1. (*anat.*) testicle. 2. *dim. of* яйцо́.
яи́чник, а, *m.* (*anat.*) ovary.
яи́чниц|а, ы, *f.* (*cul.*) fried eggs (*also* я.-глазу́нья); я.-болту́нья scrambled eggs.
яи́чн|ый, *adj. of* яйцо́; я. бело́к white of egg; я. желто́к yolk of egg; я. порошо́к dried egg(s); ~ая скорлупа́ egg-shell.
яйл|á, ы́, *f.* (*dial.*) mountain pasture (*in Crimea*).
яйцеви́д|ный (~ен, ~на), *adj.* egg-shaped, oval, oviform, ovoid.
яйцево́д, а, *m.* (*anat.*) oviduct.
яйцекла́д, а, *m.* (*zool.*) ovipositor.
яйцекле́тк|а, и, *f.* (*biol.*) ovule.
яйцено́ск|ий, *adj.* (*agric.*) ~ие ку́ры good laying hens.
яйцено́скост|ь, и, *f.* (*agric.*) egg-laying qualities.
яйцеро́дный, *adj.* (*zool.*) oviparous.
яйц|о́, á, *pl.* ~a, **яи́ц,** ~ам, *n.* egg; (*biol.*) ovum; нести́ ~a to lay eggs; я. всмя́тку lightly-boiled egg; я. вкруту́ю hard-boiled egg; я. в мешо́чек medium-boiled egg.
як, а, *m.* yak.
якоби́н|ец, ца, *m.* (*hist., polit.*) Jacobin.
якоби́н|ский, *adj. of* ~ец.
я́кобы 1. *conj.* (*expressing doubt about validity of another's statement*) that; говоря́т, я. он

у́мер they say (= they claim) that he has died. 2. *conj.* as if, as though; он вообрази́л, я. его́ произвели́ в генера́лы he imagined he had been made a general. 3. *particle* supposedly, ostensibly, allegedly, purportedly; мы посмотре́ли э́ту я. стра́шную карти́ну we have seen this supposedly dreadful film.

я́кор|ный, *adj. of* ~ь; ~ная лебёдка capstan; ~ное ме́сто, ~ная стоя́нка anchorage.

я́кор|ь, я, *pl.* ~я́, ~е́й, *m.* 1. (*naut.*) anchor; я. спасе́ния (*fig.*) sheet-anchor; стать на я. to anchor; бро́сить я. to cast, drop anchor; стоя́ть на ~е to ride at anchor; сня́ться с ~я to weigh anchor. 2. (*electr.*) armature; rotor.

яку́т, а, *m.* Yakut.

яку́т|ка, ки, *f. of* ~.

яку́тский, *adj.* Yakut.

якша́|ться, юсь, *impf.* (с+*i.*; *coll.*) to consort (with), hob-nob (with).

ял, а, *m.* whaler, pinnace; yawl.

я́лик, а, *m.* skiff, dinghy; yawl.

я́личник, а, *m.* ferryman.

я́ли|чный, *adj. of* ~к.

я́лове|ть, ет, *impf.* to be barren, dry (*of cows*).

я́ловк|а, и, *f.* barren cow, dry cow.

я́ловость|ь, и, *f.* barrenness, dryness (*in cows*).

я́ловый, *adj.* barren, dry (*of cows*).

ям, а, *m.* (*hist.*) mail staging-post.

я́м|а, ы, *f.* 1. pit, hole; возду́шная я. air pocket; выгребна́я я. cesspit; у́гольная я. coal bunker; рыть кому́-н. ~у (*fig.*) to lay a trap for someone. 2. (*geogr.*; *coll.*) depression, hollow. 3. (*obs.*) prison.

яма́йский, *adj.* Jamaican.

ямб, а, *m.* (*lit.*) iambus, iambic verse.

ямби́ческий, *adj.* iambic.

я́мк|а, и, *f. dim. of* я́ма; я. на щека́х dimple.

ямщи́к, а́, *m.* coachman.

янва́р|ский, *adj. of* ~ь.

янва́р|ь, я́, *m.* January.

я́нки, *indecl.*, *m.* Yankee.

янта́рн|ый, *adj.* 1. amber; ~ая кислота́ succinic acid. 2. amber-coloured.

янта́р|ь, я́, *m.* amber.

яныча́р, а, *m.* (*hist.*) janissary.

япо́н|ец, ца, *m.* Japanese.

япо́н|ка, ки, *f. of* ~ец.

япо́нский, *adj.* Japanese; я. лак Japan lacquer, japan.

яр¹, а, о ~е, на ~у́, *m.* 1. steep bank (*of river, lake, etc.*); slope (*of ravine*). 2. ravine.

яр², а, *m.* (*physiol.*) heat.

ярд, а, *m.* yard (*measure*).

яре́мн|ый, *adj. of* ярмо́; ~ая ве́на (*anat.*) jugular vein.

яр|и́ться, ю́сь, и́шься, *impf.* 1. (*obs.*) to

rage, be in a fury. 2. (*physiol.*) to be in heat.

я́рк|а, и, *f.* young ewe (*up to first lambing*).

я́р|кий (~ок, ~ка́, ~ко), *adj.* 1. bright (*of light, colours, etc.*). 2. (*fig.*) colourful, striking; vivid, graphic; ~кая карти́на graphic picture; я. приме́р striking, glaring example. 3. (*fig.*) brilliant, outstanding; impressive; ~кая речь brilliant speech; я. тала́нт outstanding gifts.

я́ркост|ь, и, *f.* 1. brightness. 2. (*fig.*) brilliance.

ярлы́к, а́, *m.* 1. (*hist.*) yarlyk, edict (*of khans of Golden Horde*). 2. label, tag. 3. (*fig.*) label; прикле́ить я. кому́-н. to pin a label on someone.

я́рмарк|а, и, *f.* (trade) fair.

я́рмар|очный, *adj. of* ~ка.

ярм|о́, а́, *pl.* ~а, *n.* yoke (*also fig.*); сбро́сить с себя́ я. (*fig.*) to cast off the yoke.

яровиза́ци|я, и, *f.* (*agric.*) vernalization.

яровизи́р|овать, ую, *impf. and pf.* (*agric.*) to vernalize.

яров|о́й, *adj.* (*agric.*) spring; ~а́я пшени́ца spring wheat; *as noun* ~о́е, ~о́го, *n.* spring crop.

я́рост|ный (~ен, ~на), *adj.* furious, fierce, savage, frenzied.

я́рост|ь, и, *f.* fury, rage, frenzy.

я́рус, а, *m.* 1. (*theatr.*) circle. 2. tier. 3. (*geol.*) stage, layer.

я́рус|ный, *adj.* 1. *adj. of* ~. 2. tiered; stepped; graduated.

ярча́йший, *superl. of* я́ркий.

я́р|че, *comp. of* ~кий *and* ~ко.

яры́г|а, и, *m.* 1. (*hist.*) constable. 2. (*obs.*) drunkard.

я́р|ый¹ (~, ~а), *adj.* 1. furious, raging; violent. 2. vehement, fervent.

я́рый², *adj.* (*obs.*) light; bright.

я́рь-медя́нка, я́ри-медя́нки, *f.* (*chem.*) verdigris.

я́с|ельный, *adj. of* ~ли.

я́сен|евый, *adj. of* ~ь.

я́сен|ь, я, *m.* ash-tree.

я́сл|и, ей, *no sing.* 1. manger, crib (*for cattle*). 2. crèche, day nursery.

ясне́|ть, ет, *impf.* to become clear(er).

я́сн|о¹, *adv. of* ~ый.

я́сно², *as pred.* 1. (*of weather*) it is fine. 2. (*fig.*) it is clear. 3. (*as affirmative particle*) yes, of course.

яснови́дени|е, я, *n.* clairvoyance.

яснови́д|ец, ца, *m.* clairvoyant.

яснови́дящий, *adj.* (*also as noun*) clairvoyant.

я́сност|ь, и, *f.* clearness, clarity; lucidity; внести́ я. во что-н. to clarify something.

я́с|ный (~ен, ~на́, ~но), *adj.* 1. clear; bright; (*of weather*) fine; ~ное не́бо clear sky; гром средь ~ного не́ба a bolt from the blue. **2.** distinct. **3.** serene. **4.** (*fig.*) clear, plain; сде́лать ~ным to make it clear; ~ное де́ло of course. **5.** lucid; precise, logical; я. ум precise mind.

я́ств|а, ~, *sing.* ~**о**, ~**а**, *n.* viands, victuals.

я́стреб, а, *pl.* ~**а́** *and* ~**ы**, *m.* hawk.

ястреби́н|ый, *adj.* of я́стреб; ~ая охо́та falconry; с ~ым взгля́дом hawk-eyed; я. нос hawk nose.

ястреб|о́к, ка́, m. **1.** *dim. of* я́стреб. **2.** (*coll.*) fighter (*plane*).

ятага́н, а, *m.* yataghan.

ятры́шник, а, *m.* (*bot.*) orchis.

ят|ь, я, *m.* yat′ (*name of old Russian letter* 'ѣ' *replaced by* 'e' *in 1918*); на я. (*coll.*) first--class; splendid(ly).

яфети́ческий, *adj.* (*ling.*) Japhetic.

я́хонт, а, *m.* (кра́сный) ruby; (си́ний) sapphire.

я́хонт|овый, *adj. of* ~.

я́хт|а, ы, *f.* yacht.

я́хт-клу́б, а, *m.* yacht club.

яхтсме́н, а, *m.* yachtsman.

яче́ист|ый (~, ~**а**), *adj.* cellular, porous.

ячéйк|а, и, *g. pl.* ячéек, *f.* **1.** (*biol., polit.*) cell. **2.** (*mil.*) foxhole; slit trench.

ячéйк|овый, *adj. of* ~а.

я́честв|о, а, *n.* (*pejor.*) individualism, egocentrism.

яче|я́, и́, *f.* (*biol.*) cell.

я́чий, *adj. of* як.

ячмéн|ный, *adj. of* ~ь¹; ~ное зерно́ barley--corn; я. отва́р barley-water; я. са́хар barley-sugar, malt-sugar.

ячмéн|ь¹, я́, *m.* barley.

ячмéн|ь², я́, *m.* sty (*in the eye*).

я́чневый, *adj.* of crushed, coarse barley.

я́шм|а, ы, *f.* (*min.*) jasper.

я́шм|овый, *adj. of* ~а.

я́щериц|а, ы, *f.* lizard.

я́щик, а, *m.* **1.** box, chest, case; cabinet; му́сорный я. dustbin; почто́вый я. letter--box, pillar-box; откла́дывать в до́лгий я. (*fig.*) to shelve, put off. **2.** drawer. **3.** (*fig.*) hush-hush institution (*designated by post--office box number*).

я́щи|чный, *adj. of* ~к.

я́щур, а, *m.* foot-and-mouth disease.

я́щур|ный, *adj.* **1.** *adj. of* ~. **2.** infected with foot-and-mouth disease.

APPENDIX I

PRINCIPAL ABBREVIATIONS

(a) Official abbreviations

Note. This select list comprises only abbreviations made up of initial letters of words. A very much larger group is that of words formed by compounding entire syllables: the most important of these are found in the body of the Dictionary (*see* исполко́м, колхо́з, etc.), while the meaning of many others may be deduced from prefixes (e.g. авиа-, гос-) and entries for the relevant component words.

АМН	Акаде́мия медици́нских нау́к Academy of Medical Sciences
АН	Акаде́мия нау́к Academy of Sciences
АН-	Анто́нов- (*make of aircraft*)
АО	автоно́мная о́бласть autonomous oblast
АПН	Аге́нтство печа́ти «Но́вости» Novosti news agency
АССР	Автоно́мная Сове́тская Социалисти́ческая Респу́блика Autonomous Soviet Socialist Republic
АТС	автомати́ческая телефо́нная ста́нция automatic telephone exchange
АЭС	а́томная электроста́нция atomic electric power-station.
БАМ	Байка́ло-Аму́рская (железнодоро́жная) магистра́ль Baykal–Amur railway
БССР	Белору́сская Сове́тская Социалисти́ческая Респу́блика Byelorussian Soviet Socialist Republic
БСЭ	Больша́я Сове́тская Энциклопе́дия the Large Soviet Encyclopedia
ВАО	Всесою́зное акционе́рное о́бщество All-Union joint-stock company
ВАСХНИЛ	Всесою́зная Акаде́мия сельскохозя́йственных нау́к и́мени Ле́нина All-Union Lenin Academy of Agricultural Sciences
ВВС	Вое́нно-Возду́шные Си́лы Air Force
ВГИК	Всесою́зный госуда́рственный институ́т кинематогра́фии All-Union State Cinematography Institute
ВДНХ	Вы́ставка достиже́ний наро́дного хозя́йства Exhibition of Economic Achievements (*in Moscow*)
ВИНИТИ	Всесою́зный институ́т нау́чной и техни́ческой информа́ции All-Union Scientific and Technical Information Institute
ВКП(б)	Всесою́зная Коммунисти́ческая па́ртия (большевико́в) (*hist.*) All-Union Communist Party (Bolsheviks)
ВЛКСМ	Всесою́зный Ле́нинский Коммунисти́ческий Сою́з Молодёжи All-Union Leninist Communist Youth League
ВМФ	Вое́нно-Морско́й Флот Navy
ВНИИ	всесою́зный нау́чно-иссле́довательский институ́т All-Union scientific research institute
ВНР	Венге́рская Наро́дная Респу́блика Hungarian People's Republic
ВО	вое́нный о́круг military district
ВОКС	Всесою́зное о́бщество культу́рных свя́зей с заграни́цей (*hist.*) All-Union Society for Cultural Relations with Foreign Countries
ВПШ	Вы́сшая парти́йная шко́ла Higher Party School
ВСМ	Всеми́рный Сове́т Ми́ра World Peace Council
ВЦИК	Всеросси́йский Центра́льный Исполни́тельный Комите́т (*hist.*) All-Russian Central Executive Committee

ВЦСПС	Всесоюзный Центральный Совет Профессиональных Союзов All-Union Central Trade Union Council
ВЧК	Всероссийская чрезвычайная комиссия по борьбе с контрреволюцией, саботажем и спекуляцией (*hist.*) All-Russian Special Commission for Combatting Counter-revolution, Sabotage, and Speculation ('Cheka')
ГАБТ	Государственный академический большой театр (State Academic) Bolshoi Theatre
ГАЗ	Горьковский автомобильный завод (vehicle produced by) Gorky motor-vehicle factory
ГАИ	Государственная автомобильная инспекция State motor-vehicle inspectorate
ГДР	Германская Демократическая Республика German Democratic Republic
ГИТИС	Государственный институт театрального искусства State Institute of Dramatic Art
ГК	Гражданский кодекс Civil Law Code
ГКО	Государственный Комитет Обороны (*hist.*) State Defence Committee
ГОСТ	государственный общесоюзный стандарт State All-Union standard
ГОЭЛРО	Государственная комиссия по электрификации России (*hist.*) State Commission for Electrification of Russia
ГПК	Гражданско-процессуальный кодекс Civil Law Procedure Code
ГПУ	Государственное политическое управление (*hist.*) State Political Directorate ('GPU')
ГРУ	Главное разведывательное управление (*mil.*) Main Intelligence Directorate
ГРЭС	государственная районная электростанция State regional electric power-station
ГТО	Готов к труду и обороне! Ready for labour and defence! (*inscription on physical efficiency badge*)
ГУМ	Государственный универсальный магазин State department store
ГЭС	гидроэлектростанция hydro-electric power-station
ДОСААФ	Добровольное общество содействия армии, авиации и флоту Voluntary Society for Collaboration with the Army, Air Force, and Navy
ДРВ	Демократическая Республика Вьетнам Democratic Republic of Vietnam
ЖАКТ	жилищно-арендное кооперативное общество housing lease cooperative society
ЖЭК	жилищно-эксплуатационная контора housing office
ЗАГС	(отдел) записи актов гражданского состояния register office.
ЗИЛ	Завод имени Лихачёва (vehicle produced by) Likhachev motor-vehicle factory
ЗИМ	Завод имени Молотова (*hist.*) (vehicle produced by) Molotov motor-vehicle factory
ЗИС	Завод имени Сталина (*hist.*) (vehicle produced by) Stalin motor-vehicle factory
ИККИ	Исполнительный комитет Коммунистического Интернационала (*hist.*) Executive Committee of the Communist International
ИЛ-	Ильюшин- Ilyushin- (*make of aircraft*)
ИМЛ	Институт марксизма-ленинизма Institute of Marxism-Leninism
ИМЭЛС	Институт Маркса, Энгельса, Ленина и Сталина (*hist.*) Institute (for study) of Marx, Engels, Lenin, and Stalin
КГБ	Комитет государственной безопасности State Security Committee.
КЗоБиС	Кодекс законов о браке и семье Marriage and Family Law Code
КЗоТ	Кодекс законов о труде Labour Law Code
КМО	Комитет молодёжных организаций Youth Organisations' Committee

КНДР	Коре́йская Наро́дно-Демократи́ческая Респу́блика Korean People's Democratic Republic
КНР	Кита́йская Наро́дная Респу́блика Chinese People's Republic
КП	Коммунисти́ческая па́ртия Communist Party
КПСС	Коммунисти́ческая па́ртия Сове́тского Сою́за Communist Party of the Soviet Union
КУТВ	Коммунисти́ческий университе́т трудя́щихся Восто́ка (*hist.*) Communist University of the Toilers of the East
ЛГУ	Ленингра́дский госуда́рственный университе́т Leningrad State University
МАЗ	Ми́нский автомоби́льный заво́д (vehicle produced by) Minsk motor-vehicle factory
МАИ	Моско́вский авиацио́нный институ́т Moscow Aeronautical Institute
МВТ	Министе́рство вне́шней торго́вли Ministry of Foreign Trade
МВТУ	Моско́вское вы́сшее техни́ческое учи́лище Moscow Technical High School
МВД	Министе́рство вну́тренних дел Ministry of Internal Affairs
МГК	Моско́вский городско́й комите́т Moscow City Committee (*of Communist Party, etc.*)
МГУ	Моско́вский госуда́рственный университе́т Moscow State University
МИГ	Микоя́н и Гуре́вич Mikoyan and Gurevich ('Mig') (*make of aircraft*)
МИД	Министе́рство иностра́нных дел Ministry of Foreign Affairs
МК	Моско́вский комите́т Moscow (Oblast) Committee (*of Communist Party, etc.*)
МНР	Монго́льская Наро́дная Респу́блика Mongolian People's Republic
МТС	маши́нно-тра́кторная ста́нция (*hist.*) machinery and tractor station
МХАТ	Моско́вский худо́жественный академи́ческий теа́тр Moscow Arts Theatre
МЭИ	Моско́вский энергети́ческий институ́т Moscow Power Engineering Institute
НИИ-	нау́чно-иссле́довательский институ́т scientific research institute
НКВД	Наро́дный комиссариа́т вну́тренних дел (*hist.*) People's Commissariat for Internal Affairs
НО	Национа́льный о́круг National Area.
НОТ	нау́чная организа́ция труда́ scientific organization of work, work study
НРБ	Наро́дная Респу́блика Болга́рии People's Republic of Bulgaria
НЭП	Но́вая экономи́ческая поли́тика (*hist.*) New Economic Policy ('Nep')
ОВиР	отде́л виз и регистра́ции visa and registration department
ОГИЗ	Объедине́ние госуда́рственных изда́тельств Central State Publishing House
ОГПУ	Объединённое госуда́рственное полити́ческое управле́ние (*hist.*) Unified State Political Directorate ('Ogpu')
ОЗЕТ	О́бщество землеустро́йства евре́ев трудя́щихся (*hist.*) Society for Settlement of Working Jews on the Land
ОИЯИ	Объединённый институ́т я́дерных иссле́дований Joint Nuclear Research Institute
ОНО	отде́л наро́дного образова́ния education department (*of local authority*)
ООН	Организа́ция Объединённых На́ций United Nations Organisation
ОРС	отде́л рабо́чего снабже́ния workers' supply department
ОРУД	отде́л регули́рования у́личного движе́ния street traffic control department (*traffic police*)
ОТК	отде́л техни́ческого контро́ля technical inspection department (*of factories, etc.*)
ПВО	противовозду́шная оборо́на (*mil.*) anti-aircraft defences

ПНР	Польская Народная Республика Polish People's Republic
ПСЗ	Полное собрание законов complete collection of laws
РАПП	Российская ассоциация пролетарских писателей (*hist.*) Russian Proletarian Writers' Association
РВС	революционно-военный совет (*hist.*) Revolutionary Military Council
РЖ	реферативный журнал Journal of Abstracts
РКИ	Рабоче-крестьянская инспекция (Рабкрин) (*hist.*) Workers' and Peasants' Inspectorate
РККА	Рабоче-Крестьянская Красная Армия (*hist.*) Workers' and Peasants' Red Army
РОСТА	Российское телеграфное агентство (*hist.*) Russian Telegraph Agency
РСДРП	Российская социал-демократическая рабочая партия (*hist.*) Russian Social Democratic Workers' Party
РСФСР	Российская Советская Федеративная Социалистическая Республика Russian Soviet Federal Socialist Republic
РТС	ремонтно-техническая станция (*agric.*) repairs and engineering station
СЗ	сборник законов collection of laws
СМУ	строительно-монтажное управление building and erection directorate
СНК	Совет Народных Комиссаров (*hist.*) Council of People's Commissars
СНХ	совет народного хозяйства Council of National Economy
СОБЕС	(отдел) социального обеспечения social security department (*of local authority*)
СП	сборник постановлений collection of decrees
СП-	Северный полюс- North Pole- (No. 1, 2, 3, etc.) (*designation of Soviet Arctic research stations*)
СПБ, СПб	Санкт-Петербург St. Petersburg
СПИД	синдром приобретённого иммунного дефицита (*med.*) AIDS
СРР	Социалистическая Республика Румынии Socialist Republic of Rumania
ССР	Советская Социалистическая Республика Soviet Socialist Republic
СССР	Союз Советских Социалистических Республик Union of Soviet Socialist Republics (USSR)
СУ	(*i*) сборник указов collection of decrees (*ii*) строительное управление building directorate
СФРЮ	Социалистическая Федеративная Республика Югославии Socialist Federal Republic of Yugoslavia
США	Соединённые Штаты Америки United States of America
СЭВ	Совет Экономической Взаимопомощи Council for Mutual Economic Aid ('Comecon')
ТАСС	Телеграфное агентство Советского Союза Telegraph Agency of the Soviet Union
ТОЗ	товарищество по обработке земли (*hist.*) association for tilling the soil
ТУ-	Туполев- Tupolev (*make of aircraft*)
ТЭЦ	тепловая электроцентраль thermal electric power-station
УК	Уголовный кодекс Criminal Law Code
УПК	Уголовно-процессуальный кодекс Criminal Law Procedure Code
ФРГ	Федеративная Республика Германии Federal Republic of Germany
ЦАГИ	Центральный аэрогидродинамический институт Central Aero- and Hydro-dynamics Institute (*in Moscow*)
ЦГАДА	Центральный государственный архив древних актов Central State Archive of Ancient Documents
ЦДСА	Центральный дом Советской Армии Central Club of the Soviet Army
ЦИК	Центральный Исполнительный Комитет (*hist.*) Central Executive Committee
ЦК	Центральный Комитет Central Committee

ЦКК	Центра́льная контро́льная коми́ссия (*hist.*) Central Control Commission
ЦРУ	Центра́льное разве́дывательное управле́ние Central Intelligence Agency (*U.S.A.*)
ЦСКА	Центра́льный спорти́вный клуб А́рмии Central Army Sports Club
ЦСУ	Центра́льное статисти́ческое управле́ние Central Statistical Board
ЦУМ	Центра́льный универса́льный магази́н Central department store
ЧССР	Чехослова́цкая Социалисти́ческая Респу́блика Czechoslovak Socialist Republic
ЭВМ	электро́нно-вычисли́тельная маши́на electronic computer

(*b*) *Common abbreviations*

в.	век century	оз.	о́зеро lake
г.	(*i*) год year, (*ii*) го́род city, town, (*iii*) гора́ mountain, (*iv*) господи́н Mr.	пл.	пло́щадь square.
		п. о.	почто́вое отделе́ние post office
га	гекта́р hectare	р.	(*i*) река́ river, (*ii*) рубль rouble
г-жа	госпожа́ Mrs., Miss	р-н	райо́н raion
г-н	господи́н Mr.	с.	(*i*) село́ village, (*ii*) страни́ца page
гр.	граждани́н, гражда́нка citizen		
д.	дом house	с. г.	сего́ го́да of this year
до н. э.	до на́шей э́ры в.с.	см.	смотри́ see, *vide*
ж. д.	желе́зная доро́га railway	соч.	сочине́ния works (*of an author*)
и др.	и други́е & со.; *et al.*	ср.	сравни́ compare, cf.
и пр.	и про́чее etc.	ст.	(*i*) статья́ article.(*of law, etc.*), (*ii*) столе́тие century
и т. д.	и так да́лее etc., and so on		
и т. п.	и тому́ подо́бное etc., and so on	ст. ст.	ста́рый стиль Old Style (*of calendar*)
им.	и́мени named after		
к.	копе́йка kopeck	стр.	страни́ца page
кв.	кварти́ра flat, apartment	с.-х.	сельскохозя́йственный agricultural
м.	(*i*) мину́та minute, (*ii*) мыс (*geogr.*) cape		
		т.	(*i*) това́рищ Comrade, (*ii*) том volume (*of printed work*)
напр.	наприме́р for example		
н. ст.	но́вый стиль New Style (*of calendar*)	т. е.	то есть that is, *i.e.*
		т. к.	так как as, since
н. э.	на́шей э́ры A.D.	тов.	това́рищ Comrade
о.	о́стров island, isle	тт.	(*i*) това́рищи Comrades, (*ii*) тома́ volumes (*of printed work*)
обл.	о́бласть oblast		
о-во	о́бщество society	ул.	у́лица street, road
		ч.	час hour; ~á, ~óв o'clock

APPENDIX II

RUSSIAN GEOGRAPHICAL NAMES

Note. The principle criterion for selection is the importance of the country, city, etc.; but important place-names may be excluded if the English equivalent of a Russian name (e.g. Kiev) or the Russian version of a foreign name (e.g. Бонн) is an exact transcription.

The list includes some names selected for historical interest.

Абисси́ния	Abyssinia
Австра́лия	Australia
А́встрия	Austria
Адди́с-Абе́ба	Addis-Ababa
Адриати́ческое мо́ре	Adriatic Sea
Азербайджа́н	Azerbaijan/Azerbaydzhan
А́зия	Asia
Азо́вское мо́ре	Sea of Azov
Азо́рские о-ва́	Azores (*islands*)
Алба́ния	Albania
Алжи́р	(1) Algeria, (2) Algiers
А́лма-Ата́	Alma-Ata (to 1921—Vernyy)
А́льпы	(the) Alps
Аля́ска	Alaska
Амазо́нка	Amazon (*river*)
Аме́рика	America
А́нглия	(1) England, (2) Britain
Анго́ла	Angola
А́нды	(the) Andes
Антаркти́да	Antarctica (*continent*)
Анта́рктика	the Antarctic (*region*)
Антве́рпен	Antwerp
Ара́вия	Arabia
Ара́льское мо́ре	Aral Sea
Аргенти́на	Argentina
А́рктика	the Arctic
Арме́ния	Armenia
Арха́нгельск	Archangel, Arkhangel'sk
Атланти́ческий океа́н	Atlantic Ocean
Афганиста́н	Afghanistan
Афи́ны	Athens
Афо́н	(Mt.) Athos
А́фрика	Africa
Бава́рия	Bavaria
Бага́мские о-ва́	Bahamas (*islands*)
Багда́д	Baghdad
Балеа́рские о-ва́	Balearic Islands
Балка́ны	the Balkans
Бангладе́ш	Bangladesh
Ба́ренцево (*formerly* Ба́ренцово) мо́ре	Barents Sea

Бахре́йн	Bahrein
Бейру́т	Beirut
Белгра́д	Belgrade
Бели́з	Belize
Белору́ссия	Byelorussia, (obs.) White Russia
Бе́лфаст	Belfast
Бе́льгия	Belgium
Бенга́льский зали́в	Bay of Bengal
Бени́н	Benin
Бе́рингов проли́в	Bering Strait
Берли́н	Berlin
Берму́дские о-ва́	Bermudas (islands), Bermuda
Бессара́бия	Bessarabia
Би́рма	Burma
Би́рмингем	Birmingham
Боге́мия	Bohemia
Болга́рия	Bulgaria
Боли́вия	Bolivia
Босфо́р	(the) Bosporus
Ботни́ческий зали́в	Gulf of Bothnia
Ботсва́на	Botswana
Брази́лия	(1) Brazil, (2) Brasilia
Брета́нь	Brittany
Бристо́ль	Bristol
Брюссе́ль	Brussels
Будапе́шт	Budapest
Бухаре́ст	Bucharest
Буэ́нос-А́йрес	Buenos Aires
Варша́ва	Warsaw
Вашингто́н	Washington
Везу́вий	(Mt.) Vesuvius
Великобрита́ния	Great Britain
Ве́на	Vienna
Ве́нгрия	Hungary
Венесуэ́ла	Venezuela
Вене́ция	Venice
Ве́рный see А́лма-Ата́	
Верса́ль	Versailles
Ве́рхнее о́зеро	Lake Superior
Вест-И́ндия	West Indies
Византи́я	(hist.) Byzantium
Ви́льно/Ви́льна see Ви́льнюс	
Ви́льнюс	Vilnius (Wilno/Vilna)
Ви́сла	Vistula (river)
Владивосто́к	Vladivostok
Владикавка́з see Орджоники́дзе	
Во́лга	Volga (river)
Вологра́д	Volgograd (to 1925—Tsaritsyn; 1925-61— Stalingrad)
Ворошиловгра́д	Voroshilovgrad (to 1935 and 1958-70— Lugansk)
Вро́цлав	Wrocław (1742-1945—Breslau)
Вьетна́м	Vietnam

Гаа́га	The Hague
Гава́йи	Hawaii
Гава́на	Havana
Гавр	Le Havre
Гаи́ти	Haiti
Гали́сия	Galicia (*Spain*)
Гали́ция	Galicia (*Eastern Europe*)
Га́мбия	Gambia
Га́мбург	Hamburg
Га́на	Ghana
Ганг	Ganges (*river*)
Ганно́вер	Hanover
Гватема́ла	Guatemala
Гвине́я	Guinea
Гданьск	Gdańsk (to 1945—Danzig)
Ге́нуя	Genoa
Герма́ния	Germany
Гибралта́р	Gibraltar
Гимала́и	(the) Himalayas
Гла́зго	Glasgow
Голла́ндия	Holland
Гондура́с	Honduras
Гонко́нг	Hong Kong
Го́рький	Gor'kiy (to 1935—Nizhniy Novgorod)
Гренла́ндия	Greenland
Гре́ция	Greece
Гру́зия	Georgia
Дама́ск	Damascus
Да́ния	Denmark
Да́нциг *see* Гданьск	
Де́ли	Delhi
Дерпт *see* Та́рту	
Джака́рта	Djakarta
Днепр	Dnieper (*river*)
Днепропетро́вск	Dnepropetrovsk (to 1926—Yekaterinoslav)
Днестр	Dniester (*river*)
Домини́ка	Dominica
Доминика́нская Респу́блика	Dominican Republic
Доне́цк	Donetsk (to 1924—Yuzovka; 1924–*c.*1935 —Stalin; *c.*1935–61—Stalino)
Ду́блин	Dublin
Дувр	Dover
Дуна́й	Danube (*river*)
Душанбе́	Dushanbe (to 1929—Dyushambe; 1929–61 —Stalinabad)
Дюшамбе́ *see* Душанбе́	
Евро́па	Europe
Евфра́т	Euphrates (*river*)
Еги́пет	Egypt
Екатеринбу́рг *see* Свердло́вск	
Екатериносла́в *see* Днепропетро́вск	
Елизаветгра́д *see* Кировогра́д	

Енисе́й	Yenisey (*river*)
Ерева́н	Yerevan
Жда́нов	Zhdanov (to 1948—Mariupol')
Жене́ва	Geneva
Заи́р	Zaire
Замбе́зи	Zambezi (*river*)
За́мбия	Zambia
Зимба́бве	Zimbabwe
Ива́но-Франко́вск	Ivano-Frankovsk (to 1945—Stanisławów; 1945–62—Stanislav)
Иерусали́м	Jerusalem
Изра́иль	Israel
Инд	Indus (*river*)
Инди́йский океа́н	Indian Ocean
И́ндия	India
Индокита́й	Indo-China
Индоне́зия	Indonesia
Иога́ннесбург	Johannesburg
Иорда́н	Jordan (*river*)
Иорда́ния	Jordan (*state*)
Ира́к	Iraq
Ира́н	Iran
Ирла́ндия	Ireland
Исла́ндия	Iceland
Испа́ния	Spain
Ита́лия	Italy
Йе́мен	Yemen
Йорк	York
Кабу́л	Kabul
Кавка́з	Caucasus
Каза́нь	Kazan'
Казахста́н	Kazakhstan
Каи́р	Cairo
Калинингра́д	Kaliningrad (to 1946—Königsberg)
Кальку́тта	Calcutta
Камбо́джа	Cambodia
Кана́да	Canada
Ка́нберра	Canberra
Ка́рдифф	Cardiff
Карпа́ты	(the) Carpathians
Каспи́йское мо́ре	Caspian Sea
Ка́фа	(*hist.*) Caffa (from 1783—Feodosiya)
Кве́бек	Quebec
Кёльн	Cologne
Ке́мбридж	Cambridge
Кёнигсберг	(*hist.*) Königsberg (from 1946—Kaliningrad)
Ке́ния	Kenya
Ки́ль(ский кана́л)	Kiel (Canal)
Кипр	Cyprus
Кирги́зия	Kirghizia

Кировогра́д	Kirovograd (to 1924—Yelizavetgrad; 1924–36—Zinovievsk; 1936–9—Kirovo)
Кита́й	China
Кишинёв	Kishinyov (to 1940—Chişinău)
Кла́йпеда	Klaypeda (1918–23, 1941–4—Memel)
Колу́мбия	Colombia
Ко́нго	Congo (*river and state*)
Константино́поль	(*hist.*) Constantinople
Копенга́ген	Copenhagen
Коре́я	Korea
Ко́ста-Ри́ка	Costa Rica
Кра́ков	Kraków/Cracow
Крит	Crete
Крым	Crimea
Ку́ба	Cuba
Куве́йт	Kuwait
Ку́йбышев	Kuybyshev (to 1935—Samara)
Ла́дожское о́зеро	Lake Ladoga
Ла-Ма́нш	the English Channel
Лао́с	Laos
Ла́твия	Latvia
Ленингра́д	Leningrad (1703–1914—St. Petersburg; 1914–24—Petrograd)
Лива́н	Lebanon
Ливерпу́ль	Liverpool
Ли́вия	Libya
Лиссабо́н	Lisbon
Литва́	Lithuania
Ли́хтенштейн	Liechtenstein
Ло́ндон	London
Лос-А́нджелес	Los Angeles
Лотари́нгия	(*hist.*) Lorraine
Луга́нск *see* Ворошиловгра́д	
Львов	L'vov/Lwów
Лю́ксембу́рг	Luxemburg
Маври́кий	Mauritius
Маврита́ния	Mauritania
Мадагаска́р	Madagascar
Мадри́д	Madrid
Македо́ния	Macedonia
Мала́ви	Malawi
Малагаси́йская Респу́блика	Malagasy Republic
Мала́йзия	Malaysia
Мала́йя	Malaya
Мали́	Mali
Мальди́вские о-ва́	Maldive Islands
Ма́льта	Malta
Ма́нчестер	Manchester
Маньчжу́рия	Manchuria
Марафо́н	(*hist.*) Marathon
Маро́кко	Morocco
Марсе́ль	Marseille

Мексика	Mexico
Мельбурн	Melbourne
Мемель *see* Клайпеда	
Мехико	Mexico City
Микены	(*hist.*) Mycenae
Мозамбик	Mozambique
Молдавия	Moldavia
Монблан	Mont Blanc
Монголия	Mongolia
Монреаль	Montreal
Москва	(1) Moscow (*city*), (2) Moskva (*river*)
Мраморное море	Sea of Marmara
Мэн	(Isle of) Man
Мюнхен	Munich
Наветренные о-ва	Windward Islands
Неаполь	Naples
Неман	Niemen (*river*)
Нигер	Niger (*river and state*)
Нигерия	Nigeria
Нидерланды	Netherlands
Нижний Новгород *see* Горький	
Никарагуа	Nicaragua
Нил	Nile (*river*)
Ницца	Nice
Новая Гвинея	New Guinea
Новая Зеландия	New Zealand
Новая Земля	Novaya Zemlya
Новая Шотландия	Nova Scotia
Новониколаевск *see* Новосибирск	
Новосибирск	Novosibirsk (to 1925—Novonikolaevsk)
Новый Южный Уэльс	New South Wales
Норвегия	Norway
Нормандия	Normandy
Нормандские о-ва	Channel Islands
Нью-Йорк	New York
Ньюфаундленд	Newfoundland
Нюрнберг	Nuremberg
Огненная Земля	Tierra del Fuego
Океания	Oceania
Окс	(*hist.*) Oxus (*river*) (now Amu-Dar′ya)
Олимп	(*geogr. and myth.*) (Mt.) Olympus
Ольстер	Ulster
Орджоникидзе	Ordzhonikidze (to 1939—Vladikavkaz)
Оренбург	Orenburg (1938–57—Chkalov)
Оркнейские о-ва	Orkney Islands
Осло	Oslo
Оттава	Ottawa
Па-де-Кале	Pas de Calais/Straits of Dover
Пакистан	Pakistan
Палестина	Palestine
Панама	Panama

Папуа	Papua
Парагвай	Paraguay
Париж	Paris
Парнас	(*geogr.*, *myth.*, and *lit.*) (Mt.) Parnassus
Пекин	Peking
Пенджаб	Punjab
Персидский залив	Persian Gulf
Перу	Peru
Петроград *see* Ленинград	
Пирей	Piraeus
Пиренеи	(the) Pyrenees
Плимут	Plymouth
Польша	Poland
Портсмут	Portsmouth
Португалия	Portugal
Прага	Prague
Пуэрто-Рико	Puerto Rico
Пхеньян	Pyongyang
Рангун	Rangoon
Ревель *see* Таллин	
Рейкьявик	Reykjavik
Рейн	Rhine (*river*)
Рига	Riga
Рим	Rome
Рио-де-Жанейро	Rio de Janeiro
Родос	Rhodes
Россия	Russia
Румыния	Romania
Русь	(*hist.*) Russia, Rus'
Саксония	Saxony
Сальвадор	El Salvador
Самара *see* Куйбышев	
Санкт-Петербург *see* Ленинград	
Сан-Франциско	San Francisco
Саудовская Аравия	Saudi Arabia
Сауггемптон	Southampton
Сахара	Sahara (*desert*)
Свердловск	Sverdlovsk (to 1924—Yekaterinburg)
Севастополь	Sevastopol
Северный Ледовитый океан	Arctic Ocean
Сейшельские о-ва	Seychelles (*islands*)
Сена	Seine (*river*)
Сенегал	Senegal
Сеул	Seoul
Сибирь	Siberia
Сидней	Sydney
Симбирск *see* Ульяновск	
Сингапур	Singapore
Сирия	Syria
Сицилия	Sicily
Скалистые горы	Rocky Mountains
Словакия	Slovakia

Слове́ния	Slovenia
Сове́тск	Sovetsk (to 1946—Tilsit)
Сомали́	Somalia
Софи́я	Sofia
Средизе́мное мо́ре	Mediterranean Sea
Сталинаба́д *see* Душанбе́	
Сталингра́д *see* Волгогра́д	
Ста́лино *see* Доне́цк	
Стамбу́л	Istanbul
Стокго́льм	Stockholm
Суда́н	(the) Sudan
Суэ́ц(кий кана́л)	Suez (Canal)
Таджикиста́н	Tadzhikistan
Таила́нд	Thailand
Тайва́нь	Taiwan (Formosa)
Та́ллин	Tallin(n) (to 1917—Revel/Reval)
Танза́ния	Tanzania
Та́рту	Tartu (1030–1224 and 1893–1918—Yur′ev; 1224–1893—Derpt/Dorpat)
Та́хо/Те́жу	Tagus (*river*)
Ташке́нт	Tashkent
Тбили́си	Tbilisi (to 1935—Tiflis)
Тегера́н	Teh(e)ran
Тель-Ави́в	Tel-Aviv
Те́мза	Thames (*river*)
Теха́с	Texas
Тибе́т	Tibet
Тибр	Tiber (*river*)
Тигр	Tigris (*river*)
Тильзи́т *see* Сове́тск	
Тиро́ль	Tyrol
Ти́флис *see* Тбили́си	
Ти́хий океа́н	Pacific Ocean
То́кио	Tokyo
Туни́с	(1) Tunisia, (2) Tunis
Туркме́ния	Turkmenia
Ту́рция	Turkey
Уа́йт	(Isle of) Wight
Уга́нда	Uganda
Узбекиста́н	Uzbekistan
Украи́на	(the) Ukraine
Ула́н-Ба́тор	Ulan-Bator
Улья́новск	Ul′yanovsk (to 1924—Simbirsk)
Уругва́й	Uruguay
Уэ́льс	Wales
Фаре́рские о-ва́	Faeroe Islands
Феодо́сия	Feodosiya (to 1783—Caffa)
Фермопи́лы	(*hist.*) Thermopylae
Фи́вы	(*hist.*) Thebes
Филиппи́ны	(the) Philippines
Финля́ндия	Finland

Фи́нский зали́в	Gulf of Finland
Фолкле́ндские о-ва́	Falkland Islands
Фра́нция	France
Хано́й	Hanoi
Харту́м	Khart(o)um
Хе́льсинки	Helsinki
Хироси́ма	Hiroshima
Хорва́тия	Croatia
Хошими́н	Ho Chi Minh City (formerly Saigon)
Цари́цын *see* Волгогра́д	
Царьгра́д	(*hist.*) Constantinople
Цейло́н	Ceylon
Цю́рих	Zurich
Ченстохо́ва	Częstochowa
Черного́рия	Montenegro
Чехослова́кия	Czechoslovakia
Чи́ли	Chile
Чудско́е о́зеро	(*hist.*) Chudskoe Lake (now L. Peipus)
Шанха́й	Shanghai
Шва́рцвальд	Black Forest
Швейца́рия	Switzerland
Шве́ция	Sweden
Шетла́ндские о-ва́	Shetland Islands
Шотла́ндия	Scotland
Шпицбе́рген	Spitsbergen
Шри-Ла́нка́	Sri Lanka
Ще́цин	Szczecin (to 1945—Stettin)
Эвере́ст	(Mt.) Everest
Эге́йское мо́ре	Aegean Sea
Э́динбург	Edinburgh
Эквадо́р	Ecuador
Э́льба	(1) Elbe (*river*), (2) Elba (*island*)
Эльза́с	Alsace
Эритре́я	Eritrea
Эр-Рия́д	Riyadh
Эсто́ния	Estonia
Эфио́пия	Ethiopia
Югосла́вия	Yugoslavia
Ю́зовка *see* Доне́цк	
Ю́рьев *see* Та́рту	
Я́ва	Java
Я́лта	Yalta
Яма́йка	Jamaica
Янцзы́	Yangtse (*river*)
Япо́ния	Japan
Я́ссы	Iaşi

INDEX OF SUPPLEMENTARY MATERIAL
IN SECOND EDITION

(a) Additional Entries

(b) *Additional Meanings Recorded*